BAXANDALL · LUCIANO · HUTCHI
· ROODENKO · HO CHI MINH · COLE · TOLSTOY
LAMPE · HERBER · GOODMAN · RADER · LYND
BOULDING · WILLIAMS · GARSON · KOPKIND
ROTHSTEIN · BELL · JEZER · HENTOFF · SARTRE
SHERO · AYRES · SINCLAIR · DAY · JOYE · WOLF
KEMPTON · NEWFIELD · ROSSMAN · HAYDEN
CONK · CHOMSKY · BARDACKE · MCDERMOTT
DARLINGTON · DENNISON · GITLIN · MARCUSE
· SIMON · DI PRIMA · LEVERTOV · RIDGEWAY
HARRIS · FERRY · GINSBERG · JACOBS · LAHR
FRIEDENBERG · OGLESBY · LESTER · LAUGHLIN
MULHERIN · THOREAU · GENET · SNYDER · HOLT
CLEAVER · DELLINGER · SEALE · KING · GANDHI
MARIN · CHAVEZ · CALVERT · GELBER · KNIGHT
DEMING · VANZETTI · HERSEY · JOYCE · CLEAGE
BALDWIN · HARDING · COWAN · DOUGLASS
HEINS · MALCOLM X · SCHWARTZ · NEWTON
PECK · CANNON · MAJOR · COLLIER · RANSOM
FEIFFER · HOFFMAN · DAVIS · BROWN · MUSTE
BUHLE · COFFIN · DORR · MULLOY · CHEVIGNY
ROSZAK · JOHNSON · BERRIGAN · MCGINNIS ·
SMITH · YOUNG · HOLDEN · PIERCY · CANNON
NICOLAUS AND ASSORTED OTHER FREAKS
· STUDENTS · SOLDIERS · REVOLUTIONARIES ·
LIBERATED WOMEN · RADICALS AND FOILS

Inside front cover: *Rosa Parks, who began Montgomery bus boycott by refusing to sit in back of a bus, sat up front after Supreme Court overthrew racist law.*

THE MOVEMENT
TOWARD
A NEW AMERICA
THE BEGINNINGS
OF A
LONG REVOLUTION

(A COLLAGE)
A WHAT?

1. A COMPREHENSION 2. A COMPENDIUM
3. A HANDBOOK 4. A GUIDE
5. A HISTORY 6. A REVOLUTION KIT
7. A WORK-IN-PROGRESS

ASSEMBLED BY MITCHELL GOODMAN

A Charter Member of the Great Conspiracy, in behalf of The Movement

PILGRIM PRESS, PHILADELPHIA/ALFRED A. KNOPF, NEW YORK/1970

<u>EDITOR'S ACCOMPLICE</u>
KATHY MULHERIN

<u>DESIGNER, PROJECT DIRECTOR</u>
ROBBIE KAHN PFEUFER

<u>PROJECT ASSISTANTS</u>
SUE CUSTANCE
MAGGIE STEWART

<u>PROJECT STAFF</u>
CAROL GEORGE
JANE MARTELL
THE OLD MOLE COLLECTIVE
ERIC PFEUFER

<u>HEADLINE FIGURES BY</u>
SUSAN R. PHELPS

Published in the United States by Alfred A. Knopf, Inc., New
York, and Pilgrim Press, Philadelphia. Published simultan-
eously in Canada by Random House of Canada Limited,
Toronto. Distributed by Random House, Inc., New York.

Library of Congress Catalog Card Number: 72-130454
Manufactured in the United States of America
SBN 394-70944-6

WHAT IT IS

This is not a book of the mind alone. There are minds here — some of the best in America. The Movement is not mindless. It is a book of bodies, souls, minds — inseparable.

It is a book of the Movement experience; ideas, theories, analysis are set in the experiential context. It is a book of acts, of voices, plans, hopes — of how to live, what to do.

Roughly it is made up of two elements: 1) the body of the cumulative experience, and 2) reflections and speculations on that experience. The first element makes up the great bulk of the book. It comprises the Movement as it plans, organizes, acts from day to day. It tells of certain crucial events and shows the lives of certain people (who are meant to be representative examples of the great range of men and women who make their lives in the Movement). The second is a smaller element, a group of a dozen or so items that might be seen as the central nervous system of the book. These are scattered through it in such a way as, to relate, more or less directly, to the material around them (as well as to the whole). They are analyses, reflections, cogitations, overviews. Each is called a Comprehension *and is labelled that way.*

You don't have to start at the beginning and read to the end. But certain sequences and juxtapositions are built into the book to help make the connections. They are true to the process of cross-fertilization by which the Movement builds and renews itself.

Some people might want to read the Comprehensions *first. Others will want to start where they are — with that material (models, alternatives) that will reinforce them in their Movement work, or suggest what they might be doing in the Movement. If you want history, it's there. Or biography, or conversation. Or if you want to begin with a specific model of what to do and how to do it, it's there.*

The strong actuality of The Movement is most substantially embodied for me in the figures of a few people who have shown me new ways to go, to move. Among them are A.J. Muste, Dave Dellinger, Frank Bardacke and Kathy Mulherin. For five months of the two years I have worked to put this book together, Kathy has worked with me. It has been a struggle. Without her energy and intelligence we might not have made it. At a later stage I found still another collaborator strong enough to deal with the density, weight and sheer mass of the material, Robbie Pfeufer, the designer. Their struggle, like mine, has been to make a book that would serve the Movement.

Now comes an Introduction, *so called — to say something about who put this thing together, and why. Beyond that, it is the book of the Movement and it speaks for itself.*

M.G.

WHAT'S HAPPENING

How many men ever know what is happening in their own time – can experience, bear to experience, its conflicts and contradictions? The essential experience of the Movement is a willingness to live under the burden of change, to carry it and to articulate it as they who speak in this book do, from moment to moment. Painfully, with their bodies, their feelings, as well as their minds.

We live in confusion verging on chaos, in the midst of a process of change we barely understand. Only the young (and those who grow with them) begin to understand: they are native to a world in which there is no predictable future, in which governments offer control and terror in place of the "pursuit of happiness." A world in which war criminals are called leaders. They lie, day after day. Masses of men driven by greed and fear swallow the lies of those leaders and hate themselves for it, and turn on one another, seeking the "enemy" on whom they can vent their rage. There is no sense of shared interest, of shared belief. There is no center. The country falls apart. Men who prepare to commit the crimes of nuclear and germ war try to impose "law and order." They fail. The law is suspect and disorder is built into the system. The courts are revealed as agents of control, not justice. Capitalism shows itself as engaged in never-ending social and economic warfare. Profit is a form of theft. War profit is a form of murder. Land, air, water and peoples' minds are polluted for profit. Police take the law into their own hands, using terror to crush out spirit that offends their own mechanical lives. They will fail, here as in Vietnam.

Something is happening. It goes deep, deeper than we know. Some call it revolution. Too easily, at times. Too simply. Often without knowing what they mean, until the word is thinned out. Yet it persists. And we are no longer afraid of the word. We begin to see what it means, in peculiarly American terms. There *is* a revolution. No other word for it. It has only begun. It lives in the minds of a handful of men and in the hearts of many more. It shows itself in our most intimate lives, and on the streets. It will take a long time – a long revolution. If it succeeds, there will be no end to it.

Millions know that something has happened. What exactly? For myself I have tried to find out with this book.

What I know now is that no one man knows what it is. One man sees this, another sees that, among the many facets. And yet it is only the top of the iceberg they see. The iceberg is the Movement – but how and why does it move, and where?

It pervades every corner of our lives. It reaches from San Francisco and New York into the isolated farming towns of Maine and Kansas and Indiana. It penetrates the churches, the army, the theater, the high schools – even the elementary schools. The corporations begin to feel it. It is sexual, political, cultural. It works to break down the artificial categories into which we "box" our lives: we find out that sex is politics, politics is culture, culture is land and politics and sex. We begin to see – and make – the connections. We begin to break through the inhibitions, stereotyped ways of looking at our world: Voting does not make democracy. War does not make peace. Authority does not make wisdom.

Has it begun? Who does it? How is it done? When the idea for this book *came to me* in the late summer of 1968 I had been declared a criminal and a traitor in the U.S. Federal Court in Boston. At the Justice Department with the draft resisters, on the steps of the Pentagon, trying to block the Whitehall St. Induction Center – in those actions that led to this Court – I had learned something. I wanted to tell others what I had learned – about the people who were resisting, and who wanted to go beyond resistance to make a revolution. An American revolution. I thought I knew something about it. I didn't – not much at any rate. I learned from this book, from the making of it. It has given me my first concrete sense of what this country – liberated – might be.

In a sense this is not a book at all. It is people making their own history – not letting it just happen to them. It is not "explanation" or "description." It is making – an action. It is representation. Re-presentation. An acting out. The energy in this book comes straight from the kinetics of the Movement: an interaction of scenes, voices, statements, stories, faces, meetings, demonstrations, reflections, visions, comprehensions, confrontations. It is people fighting for their lives.

Underlying the visible change is something so profound – so integral to human potential – that it can be called a biological change, a biological response in the sense that when a species is threatened with extinction or suffocation of its energies it responds – for survival – by throwing up a mutation. In a sense, what we see happening to the young today is such a process of mutation: they are becoming a new strain – the new Americans.

The making of the book began for me as a search for the Movement. I thought it would be simple, I thought I knew what to look for. I found much more than I was

looking for. I was surprised, then overwhelmed. It was so much deeper and broader than I knew. It kept moving. Not a quantity, not a program – but a process, a multi-dimensional struggle to rediscover America (and one's self in America), to go down to its (our) roots, to scatter seeds, to start new growth.

As I worked, the Movement grew. I was in it, changed by it. Could hardly keep up with it, all its aspects, forms, actions. It's much more than a question of size and scope. The Movement has a life of its own – a complex, dynamic way of speaking and thinking and acting that makes it like nothing else that has happened in America. It began in racism and war. It is an ongoing revelation. Acting in it, acted upon by it, we learn. America is the unknown country; it does not cohere; no one yet knows what it is. The Movement is the act of *getting ourselves together.* Clarity. Coherence. Community. It is also a vision.

Example: As I write, Berkeley is under military-police occupation. Reagan has suspended the Bill of Rights; there is a curfew. It doesn't work. The people of Berkeley assemble, speak, march in defiance of the "state of emergency." They do it as a community. For the sake of the People's Park: physical locus for a community of those who are intent on making, with their own hands, the conditions of their own lives. One stage in a long struggle to make a community of radical change, and to give it a place, turf, ground to stand on, to grow on. On the first day of this effort, 110 people were shot in the streets. Guns, clubs, tear gas sprayed from helicopters have not stopped them. Students, non-students, street people, young mothers – getting themselves together, discovering one another, continuing.

The young have the right to power because they are numerous and are directly affected by what goes on, but especially because their new point of view is indispensable to cope with changing conditions, they themselves being part of the changing conditions. This is why Jefferson urged us to adopt a new constitution every generation. (Paul Goodman)

What's Happening
The Open Truth and Fiery Vehemence of Youth – a "sort of soliloquy," written by a man called Peter Marin. It comes first in this book. It reappears, in flashes. Whatever else you do with this book, I ask you to read *it* first. It is in a sense the ground, the matrix. It is the bass-note, the sounding board. If the book is a play of voices, then this is the opening voice. If it is a tapestry,

then this is the strong sombre red thread that establishes the design. It brings one back to one's senses. That's crucial: he who does not come to this movement with his senses — seeing, hearing, touching — will miss it.

Peter Marin is a man of the Movement. I've never met him. If it had not been for a mutual friend, John Holt, I might never have heard of him. In February 1969, when I told John Holt of this book, he said: "Read Peter Marin." So it is that the book has grown (like the Movement) man to man. Hand to hand.

When I heard Peter Marin it was as if I heard a voice speaking out of myself. (If I were a black man, i.e., if the term were more natural to me, I would not hesitate to call him *brother*.*) We look at the world from the same angle. We depend on the same sources. We have very much the same hopes. When he speaks of his intention and his way of working, he confirms my sense of what this book should say and do:

...I have chosen an eccentric method of composition, one that may seem fragmentary, jumpy, and broken. This article will be more like a letter, and the letter itself is an accumulation of impressions and ideas, a sampling of thoughts at once disconnected but related. There is a method to it that may disappear in its mild madness, but I do not know at this juncture how else to proceed. Shuffling through my notes I feel like an archeologist with a mass of uncatalogued shards. There is a pattern to all this, a coherence of thought, but all I can do here is assemble the bits and pieces and lay them out for you and hope that you can sense how I get from one place to another.

An entire system is hiding behind this, just beginning to take form, and these notes are like a drawing, a preliminary sketch. I feel comfortable with that notion, more comfortable than with the idea of forcing them together, cutting and pasting, to make a more conventional essay. I can perceive in myself at this moment what I also see in the young: I am reluctant to deal in sequence with my ideas and experience, I am impatient with transition, the habitual ways of getting "from here to there." I think restlessly; my mind, like the minds of my students, works in flashes, in sudden perceptions and brief extended clusters of intuition and abstraction — and I have stuck stubbornly to that method of composition. There is still in me the ghost of an apocalyptic adolescent, and I am trying to move it a few steps toward the future.

Until I found "the open truth" of Peter Marin, I had no real clarity about what is happening in our time. I had only intimations of some massive force — a natural force — working its way up from the depths. I said to myself that it was coming out of the unconscious — what Jung calls the collective unconscious. And now as I write this I see that for "unconscious" I might have said *soul* — a

word I first learned to take seriously from D. H. Lawrence years ago, a word that now comes back to me, that stays with me. It is my one sure clue to that other world of the blacks, whose brotherhood of *soul* we so badly need. Having said that much, I must go on to say that I am driven by a religious impulse. I am drawn to the Movement by its spirit. A spirit that inter-plays in many bodies, that come together as they move and touch, and give one another warmth, hope. Let me explain.

I'm not an intellectual; I'm a writer. I live — when I live — by my senses and through the immediacy of feeling. When I see what is happening, when I hear it, when I begin to imagine in my flesh and blood what is happening to the black man and the Vietnamese, compassion comes into me. And courage, from their example. I am moved — one step further. I act. In action, energized, I learn. "My mind, like the minds of my students, works in flashes, in sudden perceptions and brief extended clusters of intuition and abstraction..." And always I return to the concrete through the senses. (*No ideas but in things,* William Carlos Williams said, who was another of my teachers.) And through the concrete, the life forces (what Marin, and D. H. Lawrence, call *the gods*) play. Ideas find embodiment; and act themselves out. The imagination sees alternatives: other ways to live. As far as I can tell, that is my process. It is also the process of this book, which in turn corresponds organically to the process of the Movement. Experiment. Interaction. Embodiment. Consolidation. Movement. Moving on.

The Movement as Primitive (Counter) Culture
For me, that process is the life of the Movement. Its essential spirit. Without it, no movement and no revolution. (We are not yet in revolution; we are in movement toward it, trying to get ready for it.) With it, nothing can stop us: we may fail — but we will not be stopped.

But one more word, to be clear: When I think of "spirit" I think too of the American Indians who knew how to live in community on this land without destroying its nature or their own.

Blacks, Vietnamese, Indians. From them the young in America have something to learn — and they know it. The young in America are a *class,* in the neo-Marxian sense, — abused, processed, exploited — and they have come to see their common interest. But more important, they are a tribe, a primitive tribe held together by their remarkable peer-group solidarity. (Their elders have failed them. Most of their learning is from one another. They make mistakes, but learn from them. They *want* to learn. They are willing to start from scratch.)

From Paul Radin: *Primitive Man as Philosopher* (as quoted by Peter Marin):
It is conceivably demanding too much of a man to whom the pleasures of life are largely bound up with the life of contemplation and to whom analysis and

introspection are the self-understood pre-requisites for a proper understanding of the world, that he appreciate...expressions which are largely non-intellectual — where life seems, predominatingly, a discharge of physical vitality, a simple and naive release of emotions or an enjoyment of sensations for their own sake. Yet...it is just such an absorption in a life of sensations that is the outward characteristic of primitive peoples.

From C. M. Bowra: *Primitive Song:*
"*...primitive man seems to be less conscious than civilized man of himself as a separate individual or of his own inner thoughts. Of course he has his own feelings and his own ideas, but he is not acutely aware of his severance from his fellows. Indeed, in most societies he feels that he is inextricably tied to them. ... It is natural for him to express this feeling through communal song, which enhances and increases it and makes it more real. Though he does not belong to a class of being different from ourselves, he is more aware of his closeness to others, and of this awareness song is an expression. If he feels that something calls for celebration, he assumes that it must be shared with them, if only because it will give pleasure and create confidence all round. There is no question of song being confined to a clique or a class; for such do not exist and the performers and the audience represent both more and less than themselves — more, because they speak confidently for their social unit; less because they merge their private, individual feelings into a general mood which they share with others.*

From Gary Snyder: *Earth House Hold:We use the term Tribe because it suggests the type of new society now emerging within the industrial nations. In America of course the word has associations with the American Indians, which we like. This new sub-culture is in fact more similar to that ancient and successful tribe, the European Gypsies — a group without nation or territory which maintains its own values, its language and religion, no matter what country it may be in. ... We all know what primitive cultures don't have. What they do have is this knowledge of connection and responsibility which amounts to a spiritual ascesis for the whole community. ... Class-structured civilized society is a kind of mass ego. To transcend the ego is to go beyond society as well. "Beyond" there lies, inwardly, the unconscious. Outwardly, the equivalent of the unconscious is the wilderness: both of these terms meet, one step even further on, as* one."

I see the Movement, then, as primitive culture. Perhaps I should say this is an analogy and no more — but I'm not so sure. I don't want to press it: it is at the least a suggestive analogy, a useful speculation: a way to define, roughly, a still-emerging organism. The Movement-as-primitive-culture may even — as the leviathan state collapses under stress and breaks up into human-scale political entities — become the model for the new decentralized society. The Movement is anarchist in its deepest impulses: it is decentralization that leads back to community and wholeness and away from the atomized non-community of men helpless in the machinery of the centralized state. It is primitive at least in the sense that it involves a return to sensation, to the living body and its senses, its capacity for feeling and imagining the life in others — that state in which a man knows again "at first hand, through his own energies, the possibilities of life."

Primitive, then. But in what sense a "culture"? I see the people of the Movement as New Americans, who recognize that the old America is destroying itself, and that in its paroxysms of fear, greed and hate it may destroy the whole earth. They see the necessity, then, to make a new culture: "Forming the new society within the shell of the old" — the Wobbly slogan of 50 years ago. To *make it new* because what we now have is not a culture at all but a mechanism for commerce and war, embellished with certain "refinements" like museums and symphony orchestras, energized by money. A culture is a live organism: a body of thought, of things, of forms that sustain life, nurture it. A field of creative energy: improvising, imagining, inventing. One look

at our schools, our cities, our television, our chemicalized agribusiness, our destruction of earth, air, water, tells us that we have no such culture. Yes, we have our "ideas," our "laws," our "rituals." But they are static, thin, debased. The American Way of Life. What ever happened to *that*? It became a machine, a car, a skyscraper, a helicopter, napalm. It took us for a ride; and disappeared into the cesspools of Vietnam and Chicago. End of the ballgame.

Yet something remains: remnants of a religious tradition, some feeling for brotherhood and equality, resourcefulness, expansiveness, generosity, and a stubborn determination not to be *ruled*. Usable pieces of the technology: airplane, telephone, the electronic tools for making music. Printing, photo-offset, mimeograph. Black culture. Street culture. A language that William Carlos Williams called the American idiom — full of energy, still a language of experiment, of discovery.

(The first wave of a new vitality in the sub-culture came with the new poetry of the 50's and 60's. One of its crucial sources was in the work of William Carlos Williams, who pioneered the re-exploration of America and its language as early as the 1920's. [See *In The American Grain* and *Paterson*.] I see him as a prophetic precursor of the Movement.)

sending out springs of fresh cold water? Or an iceberg (but hot!) — one with several peaks, a small continent — the great bulk of it invisible? How does it act? Like an earthquake? A volcano? Nothing will do but to mix the metaphors: the nature of the Movement is mixed, multi-dimensional, multi-functional. But now as I think about it, this new image comes to me — and it is the one I like best, because it includes man as a maker, a learner, with a tool: Try looking at the Movement as if it were the bit of a wood-drill moving in a downward-turning spiral, digging into the body of a huge tree: with each spiralling turn something is revealed, is learned; with each turn the bit bites deeper (into the substance of the society) and the wood thrown up and out by the drill shows us clear samples of the rot (and the good wood) inside the body. Digging in, we learn more about the grain, as well—the nature of the wood.

Seen in yet another light the Movement, as men take hold of it, is a human (and humanizing) activity — and its internal dynamic process is human, as opposed to narrowly "political." How does it work? Basically, it teaches as it learns, and learns as it teaches. It begins with action (protest, demonstration, confrontation, etc.), moves through reflection to interpretation and invention, and returns to action. It is impelled by immediacy of feeling: in the beginning we had the energy of outrage and the hope of reform; now it is the energy of anguish and the hope is for transformation, for revolution; a hope that has come to us (and often fails us) on the other side of despair. It goes from action to immediate analysis, then to reflection; to "rapping" and writing: what happened, why, with what effect? More reflection; then planning, then action again. Yet it is never that simple or linear: most of the time we are improvising, moving in several directions at once, *inter-playing;* we are, as Peter Marin says, "reluctant to deal in sequence with my (our) ideas and experience. . .impatient with transition, the habitual ways of getting 'from here to there.' (We) think restlessly. . .(our minds) work in flashes, in sudden perceptions . . .trying to move. . .a few steps toward the future." So it is that we learn, and teach. Teach and learn. We follow Emerson: "Do the thing and you have the power. He who does not do the thing has not the power." Immediacy of feeling. Immediacy of experience. Impelled by conscience, by conviction, by a vision of what life might be. *Love* the young have called it. And have heard the sneers of those who "have no options, no sense of alternative or growth" (Marin). What do they mean by *love*? I think they mean a quality of attention to each other, to all that is around them. Through the senses — an appetite, a reverence. Love of life, of living things, of what's held in common. A sharing, a communion, a community. Members one of another.

THE NATURE AND DYNAMICS OF THE MOVEMENT

Kinesis. *Kinetic:* from the Greek — moving, producing or causing motion; of or relating to motion; due to or resulting from motion. *Kinetic energy:* the power of doing work possessed by a moving body by virtue of its motion.

Moved by its conflicts and contradictions, the inert mass of the American colossus is turning upside down. Is that a revolution? How do you measure it? How many revolutions per minute does the turning have to take before it becomes a revolution?

It is too deep and too fast to be called evolution. The events have a momentum of their own. The energy is kinetic.

Kinetics is that branch of dynamics which investigates the relations between the motions of bodies and the forces acting upon them; opposite to statics, which treats of bodies in equilibrium.

The statics of 20th-century American history ends with the equilibrium of the devitalized Eisenhower regime. We've moved a long way since Rosa Parks refused to go to the back of the bus in Montgomery in 1956. Non-cooperation: end of the old social contract, which said: If you do what you're told you'll get the goods. End of acquiesence. Today there is no equilibrium. The furor in the static

society comes from the fear of motion, the disturbance of the stand-still condition. Especially the fear is of the young and the blacks: their energy, spontaneity and mobility (rooted in solidarity) is deeply threatening to the eating and shitting routines of the fixed society, the society of every-man-for-himself. The automatic control mechanisms — school, draft, police, corporations — are breaking down: their authority is denied. The old envy, fear and hatred of the blacks is now paralleled by envy, fear and hatred of the young — the surest sign of a "disturbed" death-oriented society.

A Movement: like an event in nature. No not *like* — it *is* an event in nature. A force, coming up out of the unconscious, from the gods,". . .divinities whose honor we have neglected. Those marvelous and threatening energies." (Marin) A biological response to the threat of extinction, emasculation, suffocation, nuclear destruction. A natural force, emerging out of ourselves, which we are learning to use. Natural, opposed to the unnatural rigidity, the *clutching*, in fear, of a society bent on its own destruction.

The Movement: how is it to be seen? Is it a glacier, scouring down to the roots, cracking the earth, preparing new ground,

Where's your program? they taunt, the critics - those who do nothing, who play it safe. Where's your theory? They don't see what's happening; it's beyond their horizon. We don't have a road map because there are no road maps. There are no roads until we make them. We're in the wilderness, exploring the unknown. We're in the early stages of creating a new society; we have migrated; we are what Camus called "strangers," aliens (in our own country). A new culture that contains a new politics.

So we are primitives – looking for a way to say what we feel. We are not against "reason"; we are for *feeling intelligence*, thought that is inseparable from emotion. And at every step we are asked to explain ourselves "rationally." That is, we are asked to think in a language – a vocabulary – of rationality that denies feeling – a language eroded and deformed by misuse, and which was formulated by a non-culture that has never undergone our experience. Barzun, Hook, Kennan, Commager, Bettelheim, et al. – the "reasonable" men who today wonder and complain about the young; the faculties so concerned with an "academic freedom" that turns out to be freedom to go on doing what they have always done – authoritarian teaching, when the students no longer believe in their "authority": These men are themselves outworn institutions. They take no risks; they "think" and by "thinking" protect themselves from the experience of their own time. They act as if nothing had happened. Wait, they kept telling us, in the Johnson era – wait for the elections of 1968; then you can get "orderly change."

The Movement is trying to create a language with which it can define itself, its hopes, its objectives. It has repudiated the most basic assumptions of this society – e.g., the belief that human welfare depends on an ever-expanding economy. (Among the things we have learned is that such an economy leads to imperialism and war; that we are 6% of the world's population and control about 65% of its resources; and that our economy, in turn, is controlled by a relative handful of corporations, operated by, and returning huge profits to, a group of oligarchs that is no more than 1% of the U.S. population. A dog-eat-dog society.)

No one today can afford to be innocent, or indulge himself in ignorance of contemporary governments, politics and social orders. The national polities of the modern world maintain their existence by deliberately fostered craving and fear: monstrous protection rackets. The "free world" has become economically dependent on a fantastic system of stimulation of greed which cannot be fulfilled, sexual desire which cannot be satiated and hatred which has no outlet except against oneself, the persons one is supposed to love, or the revolutionary aspirations of pitiful, poverty-stricken marginal societies like Cuba or Vietnam. The conditions of the Cold War have turned all modern societies – Communist included – *into vicious distorters of man's true potential. They create populations of "preta" – hungry ghosts, with giant appetites and throats no bigger than needles.* (Gary Snyder)

No amount of *reason* alone will tell us what is happening, or where we are headed, or the nature of the change. Only an act of the imagination, inventing the language for what it discovers, *as* it discovers, can do that.

"It is characteristic of revolutionary change, as distinct from simple reform, that its ultimate aim is not describable in the available language. . . . A revolutionary is not merely one who tries to make political changes; he is out to change the meaning of the word politics. (He is) concerned with the transcendant. . .. He points toward an unimaginable future. He is there to tell us that the future *is* unimaginable." (Herbert McCabe)

The documents that make up this book, this *collage*, are, then, fragments or fiery particles of Kinesis; not conclusions, but elements of process: a work in progress.

Motion. Momentum, Movement. The Movement.

MITCHELL GOODMAN Berkeley, May 1969; Boston, May 1970.
*Reading this again in May 1970, I find that the word brother comes more easily to me. And there are many others now whom I call "brother" and "sister."

COLLABORATOR'S NOTE

If you think of the movement as a kind of emerging personality whose various facets are coming into focus, you will see that this book reflects that process. Some sections of the book are clearer, stronger than others – the material on black community is more fully developed than the section on Chicanos or the one on women. Nor is the process one in which each group merely passes through stages already mastered by those preceding it. The younger movements within the movement promise to transform it, push it in new and unique directions.

So it should be understood when reading the section on women for example, that it is little more than a skeletal framework, that it only raises basic questions and offers a brief glimpse of the emerging organizational forms of the women's liberation movement. Even as this book goes to press extraordinary things are happening which we cannot point to, mainly because the activity and the debates within the movement are only now coming to the surface and appearing in women's journals and newspapers which are themselves no more than a few months old. For example over the last year there has been a heated discussion about whether the women's liberation movement should remain independent and follow its own course, choosing its own issues, defining its own ultimate goals, or whether it should stay intimately tied to the radical-revolutionary movement as a whole, defining itself in the anti-capitalist and anti-imperialist terms that movement uses. While all this talk is going on the question is being resolved – on some level anyway – by a whole series of recent events: lately, a number of movement institutions, especially newspapers, have been taken over by women.

The same points might be made about the section on G.I.s – it isn't much more than a display case. By the time the book appears in stores the G.I. movement may well be the most important and revolutionary group in America, next to the Panthers.

In general the movement is rapidly being transformed as people of color and working class white groups move into the leadership. The national media persist in presenting the movement as strictly a phenomenon of the white student middle class and a few angry blacks. It isn't true.

The movement changes and grows every day. This book, like all others, has to stop at some point and allow itself to be fixed in black ink and enclosed in book covers.

KATHY MULHERIN May 1970

*Note to the Underground:
We're not advocating you rip off the pictures in this book, but if you do they might as well look good. The half tone screen is 120.*

ONE THING LEADS TO ANOTHER
A QUICK CHRONOLOGY OF THE MOVEMENT

1956 | Rosa Parks refuses to go to the back of the bus in Montgomery, Ala. Martin Luther King leads blacks in 381-day boycott.

1958 | Left students contest student government elections at Berkeley, Chicago, Oberlin, Columbia.

1959 | Cuban Revolution.
Student Peace Union formed in Chicago.

1960 | First sit-in by black students, Greensboro, N.C. Others follow throughout the South.
March in San Francisco against execution of Caryl Chessman.
SNCC organized.
Students demonstrate against HUAC in San Francisco.
SDS gets organized.
Thousands of students visit Cuba.

1961 | Bay of Pigs, organized by CIA.
Assassination of Patrice Lamumba.
CORE & SNCC on Freedom Rides in the South. SNCC begins voter registration.
Widespread civil disobedience against bomb shelter edicts.
Robert Williams in N.C. calls for armed self-defense by blacks; is framed and forced into exile.

1962 | Port Huron Statement (the testament of the New Left) approved by SDS convention.
Cuban missile crisis.

1963 | SNCC activists intensify voter registration campaign in South.
Timothy Leary & Richard Alpert fired from Harvard faculty for LSD experiments with students.
Civil Rights march on Washington.
Kennedy assassinated.
SDS moves into community organizing.

1964 | Malcolm X breaks from Muslims.
Mississippi Summer
Harlem riots
Mississippi Freedom Democratic Party defrauded at Democratic Convention.
Political activity prohibited on Berkeley campus; students revolt in the Free Speech Movement; they win by paralyzing the university; the student movement is on.

1965 | Malcolm X assassinated
Systematic bombing of N. Vietnam begins.
Selma to Montgomery march
Watts rebellion
First anti-war Teach-in at U. of Michigan. Hundreds more follow.
American invasion of Dominican Republic
First anti-war march on Washington; SDS grows to 100 chapters.
First all-black party, Lowndes County Freedom Org., formed in Alabama.
First Free University (New York)

1966

Sit-ins against war and draft at many universities
Ramparts editor Scheer runs as radical for Congress in Bay Area, gets 45% of the vote.
SDS formulates student-power strategy
Stokeley Carmichael, new president of SNCC, articulates Black Power
Many individual students pledge to refuse draft; SDS pledges to build anti-draft unions.
Ft. Hood Three refuse army order to go to Vietnam
Black rebellions in Cleveland and Chicago

1967

CIA infiltration of NSA exposed
Black rebellion in Newark, Detroit and other cities
First Be-in, Golden Gate Park; Haight Ashbury Community flourishing.
The Resistance formed in California; spreads across the country; many draft cards burned on Sheep Meadow in N.Y., Vietnam summer: 30,000 students working against the war in over 700 cities.
Demonstrations at Justice Dept and Pentagon, following first national turn-in of draft cards.
Stop-the-Draft Week demonstrations, Oakland and New York.
Huey Newton shot by police, jailed for murder of cop.

1968

Boston 5 and Oakland 7 indicted for conspiracy
Stanford and Berkeley ROTC buildings burned down
3 Black students murdered by state troopers during rebellion at Orangeburg, S.C.
Kerner Commission says pervasive American racism and exploitation cause blacks to rebel.
Martin Luther King assassinated in Memphis. Ghettos rise up.
Columbia U. rebellion and strike.
Worker-student uprising in Paris. ✓
Battle of Chicago Convention. The Police State surfaces.
San Francisco State: the first great strike in a non-elite American Univ., led by blacks and chicanos.
Black students fight for autonomy at Brandeis, Colgate, Northwestern, Cornell, Howard, etc.

1969

Third World Strike at Berkeley
Harvard Strike
The fight for the Peoples Park, Berkeley
Women's Liberation Movement moves, builds its base. ✓
Woodstock
More than a million draft files burned by revolutionary priests and others.
Dow Chemical and General Electric HQ raided.
G.I. resistance develops at many army bases.
Over half a million demonstrate in Washington in November. ✓
U.S. Government and its local allies begin open warfare against the Black Panthers.
The Conspiracy on trial in Chicago.
Civil war skirmishing in Santa Barbara, Wisconsin and elsewhere. Bombing of corporation HQ's and ROTC buildings.

1970

Nixon-Agnew-Mitchell declare war on bums, radicals and other criminal elements. Reagan calls for a "bloodbath" to settle the student "problem."
The Movement gathers in New Haven to support the Panthers.
Kent State and Cambodia. Nationwide student strikes.
Murder of black students and other young blacks by state troopers in Georgia and Mississippi.
Draft Resistance regenerated: Union for National Draft Opposition organized at Princeton.

SECTIONS

SUB-SECTIONS

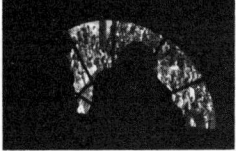    

   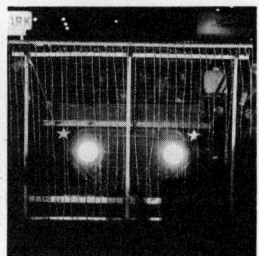

COMPREHENSIONS

Socialist papers have often a tendency to become mere annals of complaints about existing conditions. The oppression of the laborers in the mine, the factory, the field is related; the misery and sufferings of the workers during strikes are told in vivid pictures; their helplessness in the struggle against employers is insisted upon; and this succession of hopeless efforts exercises a most depressing influence on the reader. . .I thought, on the contrary, that a revolutionary paper must be, above all, a record of these symptoms which everywhere announce the coming of a new era, the germination of new forms of social life, the growing revolt against antiquated institutions. Those symptoms should be watched, brought together in their intimate connection, and so grouped as to show to the hesitating minds of the greater number the invisible and often unconscious support which advanced ideas find everywhere when a revival of thought takes place in society. . .It is hope, not despair, which makes successful revolutions.

Socialist literature has never been rich in books. It is written for workers, for whom one penny is money, and its main force lies in its small pamphlets and its newspapers. Moreover, he who seeks for information about socialism finds in books little of what he requires most. They contain the theories or the scientific arguments in favor of socialist aspirations, but they give no idea how the workers accept socialist ideals, and how the latter could be put into practice. There remains nothing but to take collections of papers and read them all through — the news as well as the leading articles, and the former perhaps even more than the latter. Quite a new world of social relations and methods of thought and action is revealed by this reading, which gives an insight into what cannot be found anywhere else, — namely, the depth and the moral force of the movement, the degree to which men are imbued with the new theories, their readiness to carry them out in their daily life and to suffer for them. All discussions about the impracticability of socialism and the necessary slowness of evolution are of little value, because the speed of evolution can only be judged from a close knowledge of the human being of whose evolution we are speaking. What estimate of a sum can be made without knowing its components?

Kropotkin — writing about the 1870's

THE OPEN TRUTH
AND FIERY VEHEMENCE OF YOUTH
A SORT OF SOLILOQUY

It is midnight and I am sitting here with my notes, enough of them to make two books and a half and a volume of posthumous fragments, trying to make some smaller sense of them than the grand maniacal design I have in my mind. I don't know where to begin. Once, traveling in summer across the country with a friend from Hollywood and my young son in a battered green Porsche, I stopped for lunch somewhere in Kansas on a Sunday morning. As we walked into the restaurant, bearded, wearing dark glasses and strange hats, and followed by my long-haired boy, one Kansas matron bent toward another and whispered: "I bet those two men have kidnapped that little girl." I took a deep breath and started to speak, but I did not know where to begin or how to explain just how many ways she was mistaken. Now, trying to write clearly about education and adolescence, I feel the same way.

For that reason I have chosen an eccentric method of composition, one that may seem fragmentary, jumpy, and broken. This article will be more like a letter, and the letter itself is an accumulation of impressions and ideas, a sampling of thoughts at once disconnected but related. There is a method to it that may disappear in its mild madness, but I do not know at this juncture how else to proceed. Shuffling through my notes I feel like an archeologist with a mass of uncatalogued shards. There is a pattern to all this, a coherence of thought, but all I can do here is assemble the bits and pieces and lay them out for you and hope that you can sense how I get from one place to another.

An entire system is hiding behind this, just beginning to take form, and these notes are like a drawing, a preliminary sketch. I feel comfortable with that notion, more comfortable than with the idea of forcing them together, cutting and pasting, to make a more conventional essay. I can perceive in myself at this moment what I also see in the young: I am reluctant to deal in sequence with my ideas and experience, I am impatient with transition, the habitual ways of getting "from here to there." I think restlessly; my mind, like the minds of my students, works in flashes, in sudden perceptions and brief extended clusters of intuition and abstraction—and I have stuck stubbornly to that method of composition. There is still in me the ghost of an apocalyptic adolescent, and I am trying to move it a few steps toward the future.

One theme, as you will see, runs through what I have written or thought: we must rethink our ideas of childhood and schooling. We must dismantle them and start again from scratch. Nothing else will do. Our visions of adolescence and education confine us to habit, rule perception out. We make do at the moment with a set of ideas inherited from the nineteenth century, from an industrial, relatively puritanical, repressive, and "localized" culture; we try to gum them like labels to new kinds of experience. But

that won't do. Everything has changed. The notions with which I began my job as a high-school director have been discarded one by one. They make no sense. What emerges through these children as the psyche of this culture is post-industrial, relatively unrepressed, less literate and local: a new combination of elements, almost a new strain. Adolescents are, each one of them, an arena in which the culture transforms itself or is torn between contrary impulses; they are the victims of a culture raging within itself like man and wife, a schizoid culture—and these children are the unfinished and grotesque products of that schism.

They are grotesque because we give them no help. They are forced to make among themselves adjustments to a tension that must be unbearable. They do the best they can, trying, in increasingly eccentric fashions, to make sense of things. But we adults seem to have withdrawn in defeat from that same struggle, to have given up. We are enamored, fascinated, and deluded by adolescence precisely because it is the last life left to us; only the young rebel with any real passion against media, machines, the press of circumstance itself. Their elders seem to have no options, no sense of alternative or growth. Adult existence is bled of life and we turn in that vacuum toward children with the mixed repulsion and desire of wanton Puritans toward life itself.

As for me, an adult, I think of myself as I write as an observer at a tribal war—an anthropologist, a combination of Gulliver and a correspondent sending home news by mule and boat. By the time you hear of it, things will have changed. And that isn't enough, not enough at all. Somebody must step past the children, must move into his own psyche or two steps past his own limits into the absolute landscape of fear and potential these children inhabit. That is where I am headed. So these ideas, in effect, are something like a last message tacked to a tree in a thicket or tucked under a stone. I mean: we cannot *follow* the children any longer, we have to step ahead of them. Somebody has to mark a trail.

Adolescence: a few preliminary fragments . . .

(FROM MY STUDENT, V): *yr whole body moves in a trained way & you know that youve moved this way before & it contains all youve been taught its all rusty & slow something is pushing under that rusted mesh but STILL YOU CANNOT MOVE you are caught between 2 doors & the old one is much closer & you can grab it all the time but the other door it disappears that door you cant even scratch & kick (like the early settlers were stung by the new land) but this new land doesnt even touch you & you wonder if youre doing the right thing to get in*

(FROM FRANZ KAFKA): *He feels imprisoned on this earth, he feels constricted; the melancholy, the impotence, the sicknesses, the feverish fancies of the captive afflict him; no comfort can comfort him, since it is merely comfort, gentle headsplitting comfort glazing the brutal fact of imprisonment. But if he is asked what he wants he cannot reply. . . . He has no conception of freedom.*

(FROM TAPES RECORDED IN PACIFIC PALISADES, 1966, SEVERAL BOYS AND GIRLS AGED 12-14):—*Things are getting younger and younger. Girls twelve will do it now. One guy said I fuck a girl every Friday night. What sexual pleasure do you get out of this (he's very immature you know) and he would say, I don't know I'm just going to fuck.*

or

—How old are you? —*Twelve.* —Will you tell us your first experience with drugs, how you got into it? —*Well, the people I hung around with were big acidheads. So one day my friend asked me if I wanted to get stoned and I said yes. That was about five months ago and I've been getting on it every since. Started taking LSD about one month ago. Took it eleven times in one month. I consider it a good thing. For getting high, smoking grass is better, or hashish—it's about six times stronger than marijuana.*

(FROM PAUL RADIN: Primitive Man As Philosopher): *It is conceivably demanding too much of a man to whom the pleasures of life are largely bound up with the life of contemplation and to whom analysis and introspection are the self-understood prerequisites for a proper understanding of the world, that he appreciate . . . expressions which are largely non-intellectual —where life seems, predominatingly, a discharge of physical vitality, a simple and naive release of emotions or an enjoyment of sensations for their own sake. Yet . . . it is just such an absorption in a life of sensations that is the outward characteristic of primitive peoples.*

Can you see where my thought leads? It is precisely at this point, adolescence, when the rush of energies, that sea-sex, gravitation, the thrust of the ego up through layers of childhood, makes itself felt, that the person is once more like an infant, is swept once more by energies that are tidal, unfamiliar, and unyielding. He is in a sense born again, a fresh identity beset inside and out by the rush of new experience. It is at this point, too—when we seem compelled by a persistent lunacy to isolate him—that what is growing within the adolescent demands expression, requires it, and must, in addition, be received by the world and given form—or it will wither or turn to rage. Adolescence is a second infancy. It is then that a man desires solitude and at the same time contact with the vivid world; must test within social reality the new power within himself; needs above all to discover himself for the first time as a bridge between inner and outer, a maker of value, a vehicle through which culture perceives and transforms itself. It is now, ideally, that he begins to understand the complex and delicate nature of the ego itself as a thin skin between living worlds, a synaptic jump, the self-conscious point at which nature and culture combine.

In this condition, with these needs, the adolescent is like a primitive man, an apocalyptic primitive; he exists for the moment in that stage of single vision in which myth is still the raw stuff of being, he knows at first hand through his own energies the possibilities of life—but he knows these in muddled, sporadic, contradictory ways. The rush of his pubescent and raw energy seems at odds with public behavior, the *order* of things, the tenor of life around him, especially in a culture just emerging—as is ours—from a tradition of evasion, repression, and fear.

The contradictions within the culture itself intensify his individual confusion. We are at the moment torn between future and past: in the midst of a process of transformation we barely understand. The development of adolescent energy and ego—difficult at any time—is complicated in our own by the increase in early sexuality, the complicated messages of the media, and the effects of strong and unfamiliar drugs. These three elements are, in themselves, the salient features of a culture that is growing more permissive, less repressive. They are profound, complex, and strong: heavy doses of experience demanding changes in attitude, changes in behavior. The direction and depth of feeling responds accordingly; the adolescent tries—even as a form of self-defense against the pressure of his own energies—to move more freely, to change his styles of life, to "grow." But it is then that he finds he is locked into culture, trapped in a web of ideas, law, and rituals that keep him a child, deprive him of a chance to test and assimilate his newer self. It is now that the culture turns suddenly repressive. His gestures are evaded or denied; at best he is "tolerated," but even then his gestures, lacking the social support of acknowledgment and reward, must seem to him lacking in authenticity—more like forms of neurosis or selfishness than the natural stages in growth.

He is thrust back upon himself. The insistent natural press within him toward becoming whole is met perpetually by unbudging resistance. Schools, rooted as they are in a Victorian century and seemingly suspicious of life itself, are his natural enemies. They don't help, as they might, to make that bridge between his private and the social worlds; they insist, instead, upon their separation. Indeed, family, community, and school all combine—especially in the suburbs—to isolate and "protect" him from the adventure, risk, and participation he needs; the same energies that relate him at this crucial point to nature result in a kind of exile from the social environment.

Thus the young, in that vivid confrontation with the thrust of nature unfolding in themselves, are denied adult assistance. I once wrote that education through its limits denied the gods, and that they would return in the young in one form or another to haunt us. That is happening now. You can sense it as the students gather, with their simplistic moral certainty, at the gates of the universities. It is almost as if the young were once more possessed by Bacchanalian gods, were once again inhabited by divinities whose honor we have neglected. Those marvelous and threatening energies! What disturbs me most about them is that we lack rituals for their use and balance, and the young—and perhaps we ourselves—now seem at their mercy. The young have moved, bag and baggage, into areas where adults cannot help them, and it is a scary landscape they face, it is crowded with strange forms and faces, and if they return from it raddled, without balance and pitched toward excess, who can pretend to be surprised—or blameless?

At times they seem almost shell-shocked, survivors of a holocaust in which the past has been destroyed and all the bridges to it bombed. I cannot describe with any certainty what occurs in their minds, but I do know that most adults must seem to the young like shrill critics speaking to them in an alien language about a Greek tragedy in which they may lose their lives. The words we use, our dress, our tones of voice, the styles of adult lives—all of these are so foreign to that dramatic crisis that as we approach them we seem to increase the distance we are trying to cross. Even our attention drives them further away, as if adolescents perceived that adults, coming closer, diminish in sense and size.

The inner events in an adolescent demand from what surrounds him life on a large scale, in a grand style. This is the impulse to apocalypse in the young, as if they were in exile from a nation that does not exist—and yet they can sense it, they know it is there —if only because their belief itself demands its presence. Their demand is absolute and unanswerable, but it exists and we seem unable at this point in time to suppress or evade it. For one reason or another, massive shifts in cultural balances, the lessening of repression for whatever reasons—economic, technological, evolutionary—those energies, like gods, have appeared among us again. But what can we make of them? The simple problem is that our institutions are geared to another century, another set of social necessities, and cannot change quickly enough to contain, receive, or direct them—and as we suppress or refuse them they turn to rage.

Primitive cultures dealt with this problem, I think, through their initiation rites, the rites of passage; they legitimized and accepted these energies and turned them toward collective aims; they were merged with the life of the tribe and in this way acknowledged, honored, and domesticated—but not destroyed. In most initiation rites the participant is led through the mythical or sacred world (or a symbolic version) and is then returned, transformed, to the secular one as a new person, with a new role. He is introduced through the rites to a dramatic reality coexistent with the visible or social one and at its root; he is put in direct touch with the sources of energy, the divinities of the tribe. In many cultures the symbolic figures in the rites are unmasked at the end, as if to reveal to the initiate the interpenetration of the secular and sacred worlds. Occasionally the initiate is asked at some point to don the ritual mask himself—joining, as he does, one world with another and assuming the responsibility for their connection. This shift in status, in *relation,* is the heart of the rite; a liturgized merging of the individual with shared sources of power.

Do you see what I am driving at? The rites are in a sense a social contract, a binding up; one occurring specifically, profoundly, on a deep psychic level. The individual is redefined in the culture by his new relation to its mysteries, its gods, to one form or another of nature. His experience of that hidden and omnipotent mythical world is the basis for his relation to the culture and his fellows, each of whom has a similar bond—deep, personal, and unique, but somehow shared, invisibly but deeply. These ritualized relationships of each man to the shared gods bind

the group together; they form the substance of culture: an invisible landscape that is real and felt, commonly held, a landscape which resides in each man and in which, in turn, each man resides.

I hope that makes sense. That is the structure of the kaleidoscopic turning of culture that Blake makes in "The Crystal Cabinet," and it makes sense too, in America, in relation to adolescents. What fascinates me is that our public schools, designed for adolescents —who seem, as apocalyptic men, to demand this kind of drama, release, and support—educate and "socialize" their students by depriving them of everything the rites bestow. They manipulate them through the repression of energies; they isolate them and close off most parts of the community; they categorically refuse to make use of the individual's private experience. The direction of all these tendencies is toward a cultural schizophrenia in which the student is forced to choose between his own relation to reality or the one demanded by the institution. The schools are organized to weaken the student so that he is forced, in the absence of his own energies, to accept the values and demands of the institution. To this end we deprive the student of mobility and experience; through law and custom we make the only legal place for him the school, and then, to make sure he remains dependent, manipulable, we empty the school of all vivid life.

We appear to have forgotten in our schools what every primitive tribe with its functional psychology knows: allegiance to the tribe can be forged only at the deepest levels of the psyche and in extreme circumstance demanding endurance, daring, and awe; that the participant must be given *direct* access to the sources of cultural continuity—by and in himself; and that only a place in a coherent community can be exchanged for a man's allegiance.

I believe that it is precisely this world that drugs replace; adolescents provide for themselves what we deny them: a confrontation with some kind of power within an unfamiliar landscape involving sensation and risk. It is there, I suppose, that they hope to find, by some hurried magic, a new way of seeing, a new relation to things, to discard one identity and assume another. They mean to find through their adventures the *ground* of reality, the resonance of life we deny them, as if they might come upon their golden city and return still inside it: at home. You can see the real veterans sometimes on the street in strange costumes they have stolen from dreams: American versions of the Tupi of Brazil, who traveled thousands of miles each year in search of the land where death and evil do not exist. Theirs is a world totally alien to the one we discuss in schools; it is dramatic, it enchants them; its existence forms a strange brotherhood among them and they cling to it—as though they alone had been to a fierce land and back. It is that which draws them together and makes of them a loose tribe. It is, after all, some sort of shared experience, some kind of foray into the risky dark; it is the best that they can do.

When you begin to think about adolescence in this way, what sense can you make of our schools? None of the proposed changes makes sense to me: revision

of curriculum, teaching machines, smaller classes, encounter groups, redistributions of power—all of these are stopgap measures, desperate attempts to keep the young in schools that are hopelessly outdated. The changes suggested and debated don't go deeply enough; they don't question or change enough. For what needs changing are not the methods of the school system but its aims, and what is troubling the young and forcing upon their teachers an intolerable burden is the *idea* of childhood itself; the ways we think about adolescents, their place in the culture itself. More and more one comes to see that changes in the schools won't be enough; the crisis of the young cuts across the culture in all its areas and includes the family and the community. The young are displaced; there seems no other word for it. They are trapped in a prolonged childhood almost unique.

In few other cultures have persons of fifteen or eighteen been so uselessly isolated from participation in the community, or been deemed so unnecessary (in their elders' eyes), or so limited by law. Our ideas of responsibility, our parental feelings of anxiety, blame, and guilt, all of these follow from our curious vision of the young; in turn, they concretize it, legitimize it so that we are no longer even conscious of the ways we see childhood or the strain that our vision puts upon us. That is what needs changing: the definitions we make socially and legally of the role of the young. They are trapped in the ways we see them, and the school is simply one function, one aspect, of the whole problem. What makes real change so difficult in the schools is only in part their natural unwieldness; it is more often the difficulty we have in escaping our preconceptions about things.

In general the school system we have inherited seems to me based upon three particular things:

☐ What Paul Goodman calls the idea of "natural depravity": our puritanical vision of human nature in which children are perceived as sinners or "savages" and in which human impulse or desire is not to be trusted and must therefore be constrained or "trained."

☐ The necessity during the mid-nineteenth century of "Americanizing" great masses of immigrant children from diverse backgrounds and creating, through the schools, a common experience and character.

☐ The need in an industrialized state for energy and labor to run the machines: the state, needing workers, educates persons to be technically capable but relatively dependent and responsive to authority so that their energies will be available when needed.

These elements combine with others—the labor laws that make childhood a "legal" state, and a population explosion that makes it necessary now to keep adolescents off both the labor market and the idle street—to "freeze" into a school system that resists change even as the culture itself and its needs shift radically. But teachers can't usually see that, for they themselves have been educated in this system and are committed to ideas that they have never clearly understood. Time and again, speaking to them, one hears the same questions and anguish:

"But what will happen to the students if they don't go to school?" "How will they learn?" "What will they do without adults?"

What never comes clear, of course, is that such questions are, at bottom, statement. Even while asking them teachers reveal their unconscious and contaminating attitudes. They can no longer imagine what children will do "outside" schools. They regard them as young monsters who will, if released from adult authority or help, disrupt the order of things. What is more, adults no longer are capable of imagining learning or child-adult relationships outside the schools. But mass schooling is a recent innovation. Most learning—especially the process of socialization or acculturation—has gone on outside schools, more naturally, in the fabric of the culture. In most cultures the passage from childhood to maturity occurs because of social necessity, the need for responsible adults, and is marked by clear changes in role. Children in the past seem to have learned the ways of the community or tribe through constant contact and interchange with adults, and it was taken for granted that the young learned continually through their place close to the heart of the community.

We seem to have lost all sense of that. The school is expected to do what the community cannot do and that is impossible. In the end, we will have to change far more than the schools if we expect to create a new coherence between the experiences of the child and the needs of the community. We will have to rethink the meaning of childhood; we will begin to grant greater freedom *and* responsibility to the young; we will drop the compulsory-schooling age to fourteen, perhaps less; we will take for granted the "independence" of adolescents and provide them with the chance to live alone, away from parents and with peers; we will discover jobs they can or want to do in the community—anything from mail delivery to the teaching of smaller children and the counseling of other adolescents. At some point, perhaps, we will even find that the community itself—in return for a minimum of work or continued schooling—will provide a minimal income to young people that will allow them to assume the responsibility for their own lives at an earlier age, and learn the ways of the community outside the school; finally, having lowered the level of compulsory schooling, we will find it necessary to provide different *kinds* of schools, a wider choice, so that students will be willing voluntarily to continue the schooling that suits their needs and aims.

All these changes, of course, are aimed at two things: the restoration of the child's "natural" place in the community and lowering the age at which a person is considered an independent member of the community. Some of them, to be sure, can be made in the schools, but my sense of things, after having talked to teachers and visited the schools, is that trying to make the changes in schools *alone* will be impossible.

One problem, put simply, is that in every school I have visited, public or private, traditional or "innovational," the students have only these two choices: to drop out (either physically or mentally) or to make themselves smaller and smaller until they can act in ways their elders expect. One of my students

picked up a phrase I once used, "the larger and smaller worlds." The schools we visit together, he says, are always the smaller world: smaller at least than his imagination, smaller than the potential of the young. The students are asked to put aside the best things about themselves—their own desires, impulses, and ideas—in order to "adjust" to an environment constructed for children who existed one hundred years ago, if at all. I wonder sometimes if this condition is simply the result of poor schooling; I am more inclined to believe that it is the inevitable result of mass compulsory schooling and the fabrication of artificial environments by adults for children. Is it possible at all for adults to understand what children need and to change their institutions fast enough to keep up with changes in culture and experience? Is it possible for children to grow to their full size, to feel their full strength, if they are deprived of individual volition all along the line and forced to school? I don't know. I know only that during the Middle Ages they sometimes "created" jesters by putting young children in boxes and force-feeding them so that, as they grew, their bones would warp in unusual shapes. That is often how the schools seem to me. Students are trapped in the boxes of pedagogic ideas, and I am tempted to say to teachers again and again: more, much more, you must go further, create more space in the schools, you must go deeper in thought, create more resonance, a different feeling, a different and more human, more daring style.

Even the best teachers, with the best intentions, seem to diminish their students as they work through the public-school system. For that system is, at bottom, designed to produce what we sometimes call good citizens but what more often than not turn out to be good soldiers; it is through the schools of the state, after all, that we produce our armies. I remember how struck I was while teaching at a state college by the number of boys who wanted to oppose the draft but lacked the courage or strength to simply say no. They were trapped; they had always been taught, had always tried, to be "good." Now that they wanted to refuse to go, they could not, for they weren't sure they could bear the consequences they had been taught would follow such refusal: jail, social disgrace, loss of jobs, parental despair. They could not believe in institutions, but they could not trust themselves and their impulse and they were caught in their own impotence: depressed and resentful, filled with self-hatred and a sense of shame.

That is a condition bred in the schools. In one way or another our methods produce in the young a condition of pain that seems very close to a mass neurosis: a lack of faith in oneself, a vacuum of spirit into which authority or institutions can move, a dependency they feed on. Students are encouraged to relinquish their own wills, their freedom of volition; they are taught that value and culture reside outside oneself and must be acquired from the institution, and almost everything in their education is designed to discourage them from activity, from the wedding of idea and act. It is almost as if we hoped to discourage them from thought itself by making ideas so lifeless, so hopeless, that their despair would be enough to make them manipulable and obedient.

The system breeds obedience, frustration, dependence, and fear: a kind of gentle violence that is usually turned against oneself, one that is sorrowful and full of guilt, but a violence nonetheless, and one realizes that what is done in the schools to persons is deeply connected to what we did to the blacks or are doing now in Vietnam. That is: we don't teach hate in the schools, or murder, but we do isolate the individual; we empty him of life by ignoring or suppressing his impulse toward life; we breed in him a lack of respect for it, a loss of love—and thus we produce gently "good" but threatened men, men who will kill without passion, out of duty and obedience, men who have in themselves little sense of the vivid life being lost nor the moral strength to refuse.

From first to twelfth grade we acclimatize students to a fundamental deadness and teach them to restrain themselves for the sake of "order." The net result is a kind of pervasive cultural inversion in which they are asked to separate at the most profound levels their own experience from institutional reality, self from society, objective from subjective, energy from order —though these various polarities are precisely those which must be made coherent during adolescence.

I remember a talk I had with a college student.

"You know what I love to do," he said. "I love to go into the woods and run among the trees."

"Very nice," I said.

"But it worries me. We shouldn't do it."

"Why not?" I asked.

"Because we get excited. It isn't *orderly*."

"Not orderly?"

"Not orderly."

"Do you run into the trees?" I asked.

"Of course not."

"Then it's orderly," I said.

In a small way this exchange indicates the kind of thinking we encourage in the schools: the mistaking of rigidity and stillness for order, of order as the absence of life. We try to create and preserve an order which depends upon the destruction of life both inside and out and which all life, when expressed, must necessarily threaten or weaken.

The natural process of learning seems to move naturally from experience through perception to abstraction in a fluid continuous process that cannot be clearly divided into stages. It is in that process that energy is somehow articulated in coherent and meaningful form as an act or thought or a made object. The end of learning is wisdom and wisdom to me, falling back as I do on a Jewish tradition, is, in its simplest sense, "intelligent activity" or, more completely, the suffusion of activity with knowledge, a wedding of the two. For the Hassidic Jews every gesture was potentially holy, a form of prayer, when it was made with a reverence for God. In the same way a gesture is always a form of wisdom—an act is wisdom—when it is suffused with knowledge, made with a reverence for the truth.

Does that sound rhetorical? I suppose it does. But I mean it. The end of education is intelligent activity, *wisdom,* and that demands a merging of opposites, a sense of process. Instead we produce the opposite: immobility, insecurity, an inability to act without institutional blessing or direction, or, at the

opposite pole, a headlong rush toward motion without balance or thought. We cut into the natural movement of learning and try to force upon the students the end product, abstraction, while eliminating experience and ignoring their perception. The beginning of thought is in the experience through one's self of a particular environment—school, community, culture. When this is ignored, as it is in schools, the natural relation of self and knowledge is broken, the parts of the process become polar opposites, antitheses, and the young are forced to choose between them: objectivity, order, and obedience as against subjectivity, chaos, and energy. It doesn't really matter which they choose; as long as the two sets seem irreconcilable their learning remains incomplete. Caught between the two, they suffer our intellectual schizophrenia until it occupies them, too. They wait. They sit. They listen. They learn to "behave" at the expense of themselves. Or else—and you can see it happening now—they turn against it with a vengeance and may shout, as they did at Columbia, "Kill all adults," for they have allied themselves with raw energy against reason and balance—our delicate, hard-won virtues—and we should not be surprised. We set up the choices ourselves, and it is simply that they have chosen what we hold to be the Devil's side. If this is the case, what are the alternatives? I thought at one time that changes in schooling could be made, that the school itself could become at least a microcosm of the community outside, a kind of halfway house, a preparatory arena in which students, in semi-protective surroundings, would develop not only the skill but the character that would be needed in the world. But more and more, as I have said, it seems to me impossible to do that job in a setting as isolated and restrictive as our schools. Students don't need the artificiality of schools; they respond more fully and more intelligently when they make direct contact with the community and are allowed to choose roles that have some utility for the community and themselves. What is at stake here, I suppose, is the freedom of volition, for this is the basic condition with which people must learn to deal, and the sooner they achieve within that condition wit, daring, and responsibility the stronger they will be. It seems absurd to postpone the assumption of that condition as long as we do. In most other cultures, and even in our own past, young people have taken upon themselves the responsibility of adults and have dealt with it as successfully as most adults do now. The students I have seen can do that, too, when given the chance. What a strain it must be to have that capacity, to sense in one's self a talent for adventure or growth or meaning, and have that sense continually stifled or undercut by the role one is supposed to play.

Thus, it seems inescapably clear that our first obligation to the young is to create a place in the community for them to act with volition and freedom. They are ready for it, certainly, even if we aren't. Adolescents seem to need at least some sense of risk and gain "out there" in the world: an existential sense of themselves that is vivid to the extent that the dangers faced are "real." The students I have worked with seem strongest and most alive when they are in the mountains of Mexico or the Oakland ghetto or out in the desert or simply hitchhiking or riding freights to see what's happening. They thrive on distance and motion—and the right to solitude when they want it. Many of them want jobs; they themselves arrange to be teachers in day-care centers, political canvassers, tutors, poolroom attendants, actors, governesses, gardeners. They returned from these experiences immeasurably brightened and more sure of themselves, more willing, in that new assurance, to learn many of the abstract ideas we had been straining to teach them. It was not simply the experience in itself that brought this about. It was also the feeling of freedom they had, the sense that they could come and go at will and make any choice they wanted—no matter how absurd—if they were willing to suffer what real consequences followed. Many wanted to work and travel and others did not; they wanted to sit and think or read or live alone or swim or, as one student scrawled on my office wall, "ball and goof." What they finally came to understand, of course, was that the school made no pretense at either limiting or judging their activities; we considered them free agents and limited our own activities to advice, to what "teaching" they requested, and to support when they needed it in facing community, parents, or law.

What we were after was a *feeling* to the place: a sense of intensity and space. We discarded the idea of the microcosm and replaced it with an increased openness and access to the larger community. The campus itself became a place to come back to for rest or discussion or thought; but we turned things inside out to the extent that we came to accept that learning took place more naturally elsewhere, in any of the activities that our students chose, and that the school was in actuality wherever they were, whatever they did. What students learned at the school was simply the feel of things; the sense of themselves as makers of value; the realization that the environment is at best an extension of men and that it can be transformed by them into what they vitally need.

What we tried to create was a flexible environment, what a designer I know has called permissive space. It was meant to be in a sense a model for the condition in which men find themselves, in which the responsibility of a man was to make connections, value, and sense. We eliminated from the school all preconceptions about what was proper, best, or useful; we gave up rules and penalties; we refused at all levels to resort to coercive force and students were free to come and go at will, to do anything. What we were after was a "guilt-free" environment, one in which the students might become or discover what they were without having to worry about preconceived ideas of what they had to be.

What we found was that our students seemed to need, most of all, relief from their own "childhood"—what was expected of them. Some of them needed merely to rest, to withdraw from the strange grid of adult expectation and demand for lengthy periods of introspection in which they appeared to grow mysteriously, almost like plants. But an even greater number seemed to need independent commerce with the world outside the school: new sorts of social existence. Nothing could replace that. The simple fact seemed to be that our students grew when they were allowed to move freely into and around the adult community; when they were not, they languished.

We came to see that learning is natural, yes, but it results naturally from most things adolescents do. By associating learning with one particular form of intellection and insisting upon that in school we make a grave error. When students shy away from that kind of intellection it doesn't mean they are turning away forever from learning or abstractions; it means simply that they are seeking another kind of learning momentarily more natural to themselves. That may be anything from physical adventure or experimental community work to withdrawn introspection and an exploration of their fantasies and dreams.

Indeed, it is hard for them to do anything without some kind of learning, but that may be what we secretly fear—that those other forms of learning will make them less manageable or less like ourselves. That, after all, may be one reason we use all those books. Levi-Strauss insists on the relation of increased literacy and the power of the state over the individual. It may well be that dependence on print and abstraction is one of the devices we use to make students manipulable, as if we meant to teach them that ideas exist in talk or on the page but rarely in activity. We tried to avoid that. When we permitted students the freedom of choice and gave them easy access to the community, we found that ideas acquired weight and value to the extent that students were allowed to try them out in action. It was in practical and social situations that their own strength increased, and the merging of the two—strengthened self and tested knowledge—moved them more quickly toward manhood than anything else I have seen.

One might make a formula of it: to the extent that students had freedom of volition and access to experience knowledge became important. But volition and access were of absolute value; they took precedence over books or parental anxiety; without them, nothing worked. So we had to trust the students to make their own choices, no matter what we thought of them. We learned to take their risks with them—and to survive. In that sense we became equals, and that equality may in the end be more educational for students than anything else. That, in fact, may be the most important thing we learned. New ways in seeing them were more effective than changes in curriculum, and without them nothing made much difference. But we must understand too that the old way of seeing things—the traditional idea of childhood—is in some way baked into the whole public-school system at almost every level and also hidden in most pedagogy.

In some ways it is compulsory schooling itself which is the problem, for without real choice students will remain locked in childhood and schools, away from whatever is vivid in life. But real choice, as we know, includes dominion over one's own time and energies, and the right to come and go on the basis of what has actual importance. And I wonder if we will ever get round, given all our fears, to granting that privilege to students.

One thing alone of all I have read has made recent sense to me concerning adolescents. That is the im-

plicit suggestion in Erik Erikson's *Young Man Luther* that every sensitive man experiences in himself the conflicts and contradictions of his age. The great man, he suggests, is the man who articulates and resolves these conflicts in a way that has meaning for his time; that is, he is himself, as was Luther, a victim of his time and its vehicle and, finally, a kind of resolution. But all men, not only the great, have in some measure the capacity to experience in themselves what is happening in the culture around them. I am talking here about what is really shared among the members of a particular culture is a condition, a kind of internal "landscape," the psychic shape that a particular time and place assumes within a man as the extent and limit of his perceptions, dreams, and pleasure and pain.

If there is such a shared condition it seems to me a crucial point, for it means that there is never any real distance between a man and his culture, no real isolation or alienation from society. It means that adolescents are not in their untutored state cut off from culture nor outside it. It means instead that each adolescent is an arena in which the contradictions and currents sweeping through the culture must somehow be resolved, must be resolved by the person himself, and that those individual resolutions are, ideally, the means by which the culture advances itself.

Do you see where this leads? I am straining here to get past the idea of the adolescent as an isolate and deviant creature who must be joined—as if glued and clamped—to the culture. For we ordinarily think of schools, though not quite consciously, as the "culture" itself, little models of society. We try to fit the student into the model, believing that if he will adjust to it he will in some way have been "civilized." That approach is connected to the needs of the early century, when the schools were the means by which the children of immigrant parents were acculturated and moved from the European values of their parents toward more prevalent American ones. But all of that has changed now. The children in our schools, all of them, are little fragments of *this* culture; they no longer need to be "socialized" in the same ways. The specific experiences of every adolescent—his fears, his family crises, his dreams and hallucinations, his

habits, his sexuality—all these are points at which the general culture reveals itself in some way. There is no longer any real question of getting the adolescent to "adjust" to things.

The problem is a different one: What kind of setting will enable him to discover and accept what is already within him; to articulate it and perceive the extent to which it is shared with others; and, finally, to learn to change it within and outside himself? For that is what I mean when I call the adolescent a "maker of value." He is a trustee, a trustee of a world that already exists in some form within himself—and we must both learn, the adolescent and his teachers, to respect it.

In a sense, then, I am calling for a reversal of most educational thought. The individual is central; the individual, in the deepest sense, *is* the culture, not the institution. His culture resides in him, in experience and memory, and what is needed is an education that has at its base the sanctity of the individual's experience and leaves it intact.

What keeps running through my mind is a line I read twelve years ago in a friend's first published story: *The Idea in that idea is: there is no one over you.* I like that line: *There is no one over you.* Perhaps that signifies the gap between these children and their parents. For the children it is true, they sense it: there is no one over them; believable authority has disappeared; it has been replaced by experience. As Thomas Altizer says, God is dead; he is experienced now not as someone above or omnipotent or omniscient or "outside," but inwardly, as conscience or vision or even the unconscious or Tillich's "ground of being." This is all too familiar to bother with here, but this particular generation is a collective dividing point. The parents of these children, the fathers, still believe in "someone" over them, insist upon it; in fact, demand it for and from their children. The children themselves cannot believe it; the idea means nothing to them. It is almost as if they are the first real Americans—suddenly free of Europe and somehow fatherless, confused, forced back on their own experience, their own sense of things, even though, at the same time, they are forced to defy their families and schools in order to keep it.

This is, then, a kind of Reformation. Arnold was wrong when he said that art would replace religion; education replaced it. Church became School, the principal vehicle for value, for "culture," and just as men once rebelled against the established Church as the mediator between God and man, students now rebel against the *public* school (and its version of things) as the intermediary between themselves and experience, between themselves and experience and the making of value. Students are expected to reach "reality" (whether of knowledge or society) through their teachers and school. No one, it is said, can participate in the culture effectively without having at one time passed through their hands, proven his allegiance to them, and been blessed. This is the authority exercised by priests or the Church. Just as men once moved to shorten the approach to God, they are moved now to do the same thing in relation to learning and to the community. For just as God was argued to appear within a man—unique, private, and yet shared—so culture is, in some way, grounded in the individual; it inhabits him. The schools, like the Church, must be the expression of that habitation, not its exclusive medium. This is the same reformative shift that occurred in religion, a shift from the institutional (the external) to the individual (the internal), and it demands, when it occurs, an agony, an apocalyptic frenzy, a destruction of the past itself. I believe it is happening now. One sees and feels it everywhere: a violent fissure, a kind of quake.

I remember one moment in the streets of Oakland during the draft demonstrations. The students had sealed off the street with overturned cars and there were no police; the gutters were empty and the students moved into them from the sidewalks, first walking, then running, and finally almost dancing in the street. You could almost see the idea coalesce on their faces: The street is ours! It was as if a weight had been lifted from them, a fog; there was not at that moment any fury in them, any vengefulness or even politics; rather, a lightness, delight, an exhilaration at the sudden inexplicable sense of being free. George Orwell describes something similar in *Homage to Catalonia*: that brief period in Barcelona when the anarchists had apparently succeeded and men shared what power there was. I don't know how to describe it, except to say that one's inexplicable sense of invisible authority had vanished: the oppressive father, who is not really there, was gone.

That sudden feeling is familiar to us all. We have all had it from time to time in our own lives, that sense of "being at home," that ease, that feeling of a Paradise which is neither behind us nor deferred but is around us, a natural household. It is the hint and beginning of Manhood: a promise, a clue. One's attention turns to the immediate landscape and to one's fellows: toward what is there, toward what can be felt as a part of oneself. I have seen the same thing as I watched Stokely Carmichael speaking to a black audience and telling them that they must stop begging the white man, like children, for their rights. They were, he said, neither children nor slaves, no, they were—and here they chanted, almost cried, in unison —a beautiful people: *yes our noses are broad and our lips are thick and our hair is kinky . . . but we are beautiful, we are beautiful, we are black and beautiful*. Watching, you could sense in that released joy an emergence, a surfacing of pride, a refusal to accept shame or the white man's dominance—and a turning to one another, to their own inherent value.

But there is a kind of pain in being white and watching that, for there is no one to say the same things to white children; no "fathers" or brothers to give them that sense of manhood or pride. The adolescents I have seen—white, middle-class—are a long way from those words *we are beautiful, we are beautiful*. I cannot imagine how they will reach them, deprived as they are of all individual strength. For the schools exist to deprive one of strength. That is why one's own worth must be proven again and again by the satisfaction of external requirements with no inherent value or importance; it is why one must satisfy a set of inexplicable demands; it is why there is a continual separation of self and worth and the

intrusion of a kind of institutional guilt: failure not of God but of *the system*, the nameless "others," the authority that one can never quite see; and it explains the oppressive sense of some nameless transgression, almost a shame at Being itself.

It is this feeling that pervades both high schools and college, this Kafkaesque sense of faceless authority that drives one to rebellion or withdrawal, and we are all, for that reason, enchanted by the idea of the Trial, that ancient Socratic dream of confrontation and vindication or martyrdom. It is then, of course, that Authority shows its face. In the mid-fifties I once watched Jack Kerouac on a television show and when the interviewer asked him what he wanted he said: to see the face of God. How arrogant and childish and direct! And yet, I suppose, it is what we all want as children: to have the masks of authority, all its disguises, removed and to see it plain. That is what lies in large part behind the riots in the schools. Their specific grievances are incidental; their real purpose is to make God show his face, to have whatever pervasive and oppressive force makes us perpetual children reveal itself, declare itself, commit itself at last. It is Biblical; it is Freudian; it reminds me in some way of the initiation rites: the need to unmask the gods and assume their power, to become an equal— and to find in that the manhood one has been denied.

The schools seem to enforce the idea that there *is* someone over you; and the methods by which they do it are ritualized, pervasive. The intrusion of guilt, shame, alienation from oneself, dependence, insecurity—all these feelings are not the accidental results of schools; they are intentional, and they are used in an attempt to make children manipulable, obedient, "good citizens" we call it, and useful to the state. The schools are the means by which we deprive the young of manhood—that is what I mean to say— and we must not be surprised when they seek that manhood in ways that must of necessity be childish and violent.

But I must admit this troubles me, for there is little choice between mindless violence and mindless authority, and I am just enough of an academic, an intellectual, to want to preserve much of what will be lost in the kind of rebellion or apocalypse that is approaching. And yet, and yet . . . the rapidity of events

leaves me with no clear idea, no solution, no sense of what will be an adequate change. It may be that all of this chaos is a way of breaking with the old world and that from it some kind of native American will emerge. There is no way of knowing, there no longer seems any way of estimating what is necessary or what will work. I know only that the problem now seems to be that our response to crisis is to move away or back rather than forward, and that we will surely, for the sake of some imagined order, increase in number and pressure the very approaches that have brought us to this confusion. I don't know. I believe that the young must have values, of course, be responsible, care, but I know too that most of the violence I have seen done to the young has been done in the name of value, and that the well-meaning people who have been so dead set on making things right have had a hand in bringing us to where we are now. The paradox is a deep and troubling one for me. I no longer know if change can be accomplished—for the young, for any of us, without the apocalyptic fury that seems almost upon us. The crisis of youth and education is symptomatic of some larger, deeper fault in our cities and minds, and perhaps nothing can be done consciously in those areas until the air itself is violently cleared one way or another.

So I have no easy conclusions, no startling synthesis with which to close. I have only a change in mood, a softening, a kind of sadness. It may be, given that, that the best thing is simply to close with an unfinished fragment in which I catch for myself the hint of an alternative:

. . . I am trying to surround you, I see that, I am trying to make with these words a kind of city so natural, so familiar, that the other world, the one that appears to be, will look by comparison absurd and flat, limited, unnecessary. What I am after is liberation, not my own, which comes often enough these days in solitude or sex, but yours, and that is arrogant, isn't it, that is presumptuous, and yet that is the function of art: to set you free. It is that too which is the end of education: a liberation from childhood and what holds us there, a kind of midwifery, as if the nation itself were in labor and one wanted to save both the future and the past—for we are both, we are, we are the thin bridge swaying between them, and to tear one from the other means a tearing of ourselves, a partial death.

And yet it may be that death is inevitable, useful. It may be. Perhaps, as in the myth, Aphrodite can rise only where Cronos' testicles have fallen into the sea. It may be that way with us. The death of the Father who is in us, the death of the old authority which is part of us, the death of the past which is also our death; it may all be necessary: a rending and purgation. And yet one still seeks another way, somethings less (or is it more) apocalyptic, a way in which the past becomes the future in ourselves, in which we become the bridges between: makers of culture.

Unless from us the future takes place, we are Death only, said Lawrence, meaning what the Chassids do: that the world and time reside within, not outside, men; that there is no distance, no "alienation," only a perpetual wedding to the world. It is that—the presence in oneself of Time—that makes things interesting, is more gravid and interesting than guilt. I don't want to lose it, don't want to relinquish that sense in the body of another dimension, a distance, the depth of the body as it extends backward into the past and forward, as it contains and extends and transforms.

What I am after is an alternative to separation and rage, some kind of connection to things to replace the system of dependence and submission—the loss of the self—that now holds sway, slanted toward violence. I am trying to articulate a way of seeing, of feeling, that will restore to the young a sense of manhood and potency without at the same time destroying the past. That same theme runs through whatever I write: the necessity for each man to experience himself as an extension and maker of culture, and to feel the whole force of the world within himself, not as an enemy—but as himself:

. . . An act of learning is a meeting, and every meeting is simply the discovery in the world of a part of oneself that had previously been unacknowledged by the self. It is the recovery of the extent of one's being. It is the embrace of an eternal but elusive companion, the shadowy "other" in which one truly resides and which blazes, when embraced, like the sun.

Peter Marin, now a Visiting Fellow of the Center, was, in 1967-68, the Director of Pacific High School, an experimental private day school in the Santa Cruz mountains outside Palo Alto, California.

THE CENTER MAGAZINE Jan 1969

THE NEW AMERICANS

What keeps running through mind is a line I read twelve years ago in a friend's first published story: *The idea in that idea is: there is no one over you.* I like that line: *There is no one over you.* Perhaps that signifies the gap between these children and their parents. For the children it is true, they sense it: there is no one over them; believable authority has disappeared; it has been replaced by experience. As Thomas Altizer says, God is dead; he is experienced now not as someone above or omnipotent or omniscient or "outside," but inwardly, as conscience or vision or even the unconscious or Tillich's "ground of being." This is all too familiar to bother with here, but this particular generation is a collective dividing point. The parents of these children, the fathers, still believe in "someone" over them, insist upon it; in fact, demand it for and from their children. The children themselves cannot believe it; the idea means nothing to them. It is almost as if they are the first real Americans — suddenly free of Europe and somehow fatherless, confused, forced back on their own experience, their own sense of things, even though, at the same time, they are forced to defy their families and schools in order to keep it.

PETER MARIN

The only possible adjustment which we can give to the child under existing conditions is that which arises through putting him in complete possession of all his powers. With the advent of democracy and modern industrial conditions, it is impossible to foretell definitely just what civilization will be twenty years from now. Hence it is impossible to prepare the child for any precise set of conditions.

JOHN DEWEY, *"My Pedagogic Creed"*, 1897

Today, nowhere in the world are there elders who know what the children know, no matter how remote and simple the societies are in which the children live. In the past there were always some elders who knew more than any children in terms of their experience of having grown up within a cultural system. Today there are none. It is not only that parents are no longer guides, but that there are no guides, whether one seeks them in one's own country or abroad. There are no elders who know what those who have been reared within the last twenty years know about the world into which they were born.

MARGARET MEAD, *Youth Revolt: The Future Is Now*

There is in America today a generation of white youth that is truly worthy of a black man's respect, and this is a rare event in the foul annals of American history. From the beginning of the contact between blacks and whites, there has been very little reason for a black man to respect a white, with such exceptions as John Brown and others lesser known. But respect commands itself and it can neither be given nor withheld when it is due. If a man like Malcom X could change and repudiate racism, if I myself and other former Muslims can change, if young whites can change, then there is hope for America. . . The sins of the fathers are visited upon the heads of the children — but only if the children continue in the evil deeds of the fathers.

ELDRIDGE CLEAVER, *Soul On Ice*

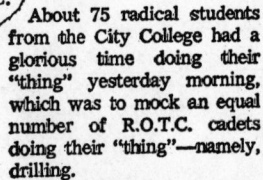

THE DESCENDANTS OF THE MARX BROTHERS JOIN THE R.O.T.C.

Radicals 'Take on' Cadets

About 75 radical students from the City College had a glorious time doing their "thing" yesterday morning, which was to mock an equal number of R.O.T.C. cadets doing their "thing"—namely, drilling.

For two hours the students skipped, danced, scampered and tumbled around the cadets, like a swarm of gnats. Half the cadets, with ever-straight faces, practiced marching drills and the others ran obstacle courses and races.

Since it was the first field practice for the students enrolled in the Army's Reserve Officer Training Corps, many were without uniforms, dressed in suits and ties or jeans and shirts.

The radicals' demonstrations started somewhat hesitantly at first, at 8 A.M. on the dust-covered field at Lewisohn Stadium.

"Brothers!" called a long-haired youth over a portable public address box. "Frisbee classes are now beginning in Lewisohn Stadium. You people in R.O.T.C., we're getting some orange juice. You're welcome to have some and join us."

Red, white and blue frisbees began to soar on one half of the field while a group of cadets stood at attention on the other. As the cadets began to drill—"Attention! Right face! Forward march!" yelped the student lieutenants — some of the demonstrators shouted: "Let's have a snake dance."

"What's a snake dance?" a student asked.

"Gather round, children," said Ronald McGuire, a 20-year-old student from the Bronx. "I'll show you."

Snake Dance Falters

A six-foot pole was produced and Mr. McGuire stood on one side of it, holding it in front of him at waist level. Twenty-one students, in rows of three, aligned themselves on the other side, the first rank of three holding the pole and the ranks behind holding the belts of the lines in front.

"The idea of a snake dance," he said, "is to set up a beat." He lifted his left foot high, then his right. "One, two, three, four."

"Hut, two, three, four," echoed the student soldiers across the field.

The snake group caught on —almost. They began to prance, chanting "Hell No Don't Go," for 10 feet, when their feet got tangled and they tripped to a halt.

The cadets went on drilling to commands of "About Face! Forward, march!"

The dancers, representing the C.C.N.Y. commune, Students for a Democratic Society and the Youth International Party (Yippies), tried again, unsuccessfully.

"No, no, you're doing it all wrong," said the leader, who was marching backwards facing his squad. "Lift your feet high. There's a tendency for people to speed up the cadence."

"Now," he continued, "let's try Washoi. Washoi."

"What's Washoi?" someone called.

"Down with imperialism. Up the Establishment," came some answers.

"Washoi," Mr. McGuire said, "is Japanese and means whatever you want it to mean. It's the thing of the future, so let's learn now how to use it."

Washoi is a Japanese word that has no literal meaning but is used in religious festivals when heavy, portable shrines are carried through the streets. Japanese leftist students borrowed the term for their "dragon marches"

when huge crowds of students trot along briskly together. The word produces rhythm and spirit, just as the English term "rah" generates fervor at football games.

But Washoi didn't help the snake dance, and people began to fall off the line. "Well, that's enough discipline for me," said a girl dressed in a bright pink sari and sandals, as she stalked away.

It was 8:30 as a second group of about 25 cadets ran across the field, dressed in fatigues, to an area laid out with hurdles and taped lines.

"It's all yours," shouted a student leader. "Let's march in in our nonmilitary way and take it." They followed the cadets in fatigues and from then on, had a field day. They somersaulted over each other, played leap frog, waved their arms in amorphous dances, and raced with the cadets who were crawling, running and jumping obstacle courses.

The radicals excelled in this phase of their antiwar demonstration, which they called "A Celebration of Life."

They joined in a drill where the cadets raced carrying other cadets on their backs, in fireman fashion.

The civilian students came in first, second, third and fifth among four other teams made up of cadets.

They lampooned the cadets continuously, marching behind them, running in front of them, shouting slogans.

The black flag of anarchy appeared and was used to lead cadets running around the field track.

Polite, Lively Dialogue

Then, resting intermittently from the strenuous exercise, the civilian students began to engage the military students in political conversations. The dialogue was lively, intelligent and polite.

"You have a free will and it is your right to exercise it," a radical student said to a uniformed cadet. "It is morally impossible to to support this war."

"I have that free will," the other countered, "and I choose to support the war."

Mr. McGuire explained why the students were demonstrating. "We think R.O.T.C. is a destructive thing on campus," he said. "The university should not teach people how to kill. We want a society dedicated to life."

Until they left at 10 o'clock, the students celebrating life did not interfere physically with the cadets. No police appeared.

"We are just ignoring them," explained Lt. Col. Arthur Lucia of the R.O.T.C. program But he added he hoped "maybe we can attract some of them to come join the R.O.T.C. program" to which one student replied, "He's got to be kidding!"

The New York Times
9/28/68

Q: What do you see happening?

PETER: What's happening is the question of the generation. What's happening is exactly the question of the generation.

Q: What is that question?

PETER: What's happening?

Q: Tell me what you think is happening.

PETER: People are beginning to tell it. The foundation of a civilization is growing here . . . built on people who are really very wishful. . . . Hope is the shot. Walking around with empty baskets. Hope . . . people with empty flour bins . . . hope. Hope [is the] handle. That's the foundation of it. Then the forms it takes are the wishful forms that are either overdue or are the best that can be made.

Something is coming that is going to make the most of what we are doing. . . . Y'know, the mark of history on a thing dates it, makes it anachronistic. . . . Talkin' about the French Revolution, about changing the names of the months, well, any historian would write, "In the flush of revolutionary fervor, they even felt [that] they must change the names of the months." That isn't what the people felt. I don't think the people felt they had to change the names of the months. I think that they had a distinctly different vision of the universe. They started there — popped open. Freedom, revolution, liberation pops the cork of imagination, just lets it out. And they were full out. In the flush of liberation spring those roots. Take things up in the Haight-Ashbury. There are forms of a civilization to come, after this deal goes down.

Q: What is this deal that's going to go down?

PETER: Roughly the same position as the Soviet Union in 1917. It was the only country which hadn't had a democracy — 1848 settled the hash for all the European countries, and there was Russia, sitting there with every accommodating gesture suddenly being made. . . . And what the serfs were doing was roaming in bands of thirty to three hundred going from mansion to mansion burning down aristocrats' estates, raping the women, cutting up the cats and quartering 'em, killing the animals and roasting 'em, pulling out the booze and drinking it, tearing down the drapes, dancing on the pianos, using them for firewood, waking up in the morning with a hangover with the smell of burning flesh and ruins around them, and going on to the next town to do it again. They did that from 1915 to 1917 — they were doing it all over Russia. Finely tuned, precise intellectual abstractions about revolution didn't make any difference. And this is what the people were actually doing — they were doing it to accommodate their desire. The desire was to kill the aristocrats, break down the drapes, eat the food, and get on someplace quick.

Q: You think we're in a situation like that in this country?

PETER: It's exactly what it's like.

Q: What do you suppose produced this particular kind of moment? What happened to make all these kids suddenly appear on this scene? Why 1965?

PETER: I don't think it happened in '65. Notice most of the people that are involved are from before '65. They say it's the failures of the fifties . . . what sometimes has been called the ideology of failure was developed in the fifties. It became the basis of life for people thereafter. When I read *Howl*, I knew I didn't have anything to lose. That's what did it. That's what sent people out in search of experience. Ex-per-i-ence. Expedient experience. 'Cause it kept 'em busy durin' Korea — Korea was something nobody wanted to think about too much. During that time, people sought out the junkies, con-men, hard-living jailbirds, down-and-outers, and gave them credence. . . . When the people followed this — followed the line of failure in the fifties — and gave credence to where it would go, credence to junkies, the hardest-hit junkies, mainlining people, hop-heads. In love with something a hustler could tell you more about than you'd be able to pick up from Mom or Tab Hunter — Mom and Tab Hunter almost the same thing. They are the same thing.

Q: Where were you born, Peter?

PETER: New York.

Q: When?

PETER: '37.

Q: Quick, how old does that make you?

PETER: Twenty-nine.

Q: Did you grow up in New York?

PETER: Till I was about seven.

Q: Then where?

PETER: Florida, northern Florida is southern Georgia. Call the rednecks there "Florida crackers." And that gets outcast. [I was] cast out of that society — nigger-lovin', motherfuckin', New York Yankee Jew.

Q: Is that what you are?

PETER: Well, I wasn't, but I became all those things.

Q: Where did you have your adolescence? In Florida?

PETER: Dade County — Miami. I was a car-hiker in Miami Beach. When I was sixteen, worked a club called the Beachcomber, and that's where I learned to drive. Used to drag-race Cadillacs . . . put a nice little Lincoln in the seawall. . . . It's a bizarre kinda world. It's like . . . Nathanael West kind of reality going down. It's a place like Biscayne Bay and "Lots for Sale" signs. Imperial Sunshine Parkway Village signs floating at low tide with rubber tires and condoms with sailor's choice, come in and get hit by the barracuda in moonlight. This tide is a netherworld. It's a spaced-out kind of reality. Hillbilly kids that went to war with shotguns, bicycle chains, brass knucks. . . . I was with the hillbilly kids.

Q: How'd you get in with them if you were from New York?

PETER: Protection, adventure, beauty, sex —

Q: How old were you?

PETER: The girls fucked a lot. I was fifteen. When you're fifteen you want to fuck a lot, there were girls that fucked a lot at fifteen. No, I'm just sayin' that like crying over somebody's virginal bedroom fantasy is not where those chicks were at. . . . All this nostalgia may fit like some strange image of yours. It seems to me that it flatters an illusion of adolescence that you may have concerning me or someone else.

Q: No. I had an adolescence too.

PETER: That's very good of you. . . . I grew up bein' called "boy." You know, really, I feel very strong about that shit. Don't you know to what degree people are kept impotent in this society? . . . There're only certain roles that you can play, saying certain kinds of things. You can be queer, you can be a character, you can be an entertainer or an artist, you can be an adolescent, you can be a woman — you can't be a man. I don't think you can be a man in the power sense of the society. . . . I grew up in the South.

The South is full of naked power. The power's made very obvious. When I wasn't a nigger-lover — or when I *was* a nigger-lover — the society I grew up in checked me one way or the other. "How'd you like one to go to bed with your sister?" was a mystique. It kept your urinal cigar-straight.

Q: When you were growing up, you didn't know any Negroes?

PETER: There was no access, there was no access for me. I mean, there were several things that kept me from it, one was my mind.

Q: You were . . . ?

PETER: I mean, my mind was a white mind.

Q: When did you really get to know black people?

PETER: As soon as I got out of the South. I made it a point to —

Q: I want to get back to the college scene, because —

PETER: Ain't no black people in the college I went to. I was brought to the dean for putting up signs that said "Integrate in '58."

Q: When was that?

PETER: In '57. . . . We were all called into the dean's office. . . .

Q: Did you pick up a political orientation in college?

PETER: I picked up a political orientation as a child, man! . . . My father was — through frustration or anguish or an image of his own intellect, I don't know which, because I only saw him right before he died . . . — he was a politically conscious man, described as everything from a paranoid alcoholic to a street teacher.

. . . Steinbeck, when I was eleven-twelve years old, *Grapes of Wrath* turned me on. The kinds of books that were in the house were *Grapes of Wrath*, books by Defoe, Dickens . . . and the Russians were good people. . . . [Also] no matter how middle-class or suburban a high school might be, there's gonna be some contact with poor people. If there's contact with poor people, then credence has to be given to the gangs that are in the school, because if you don't give 'em credence, they're gonna beat the shit out of you. High-school politicos are the kinds of guys who've had their neckties grabbed a couple a times and been shoved up against the lockers once or twice, kneed in the nuts on the football field — that kinda thing. And so credence is taken of that, and gangs — you should know that gangs in the United States, urban gangs even in Miami, Florida, are politically conscious and are political power. It's fourteen- or fifteen-year-old black kids that are gonna lead their revolutions — they're leading it now. . . . It would be utterly square to assume that gangs aren't politically conscious. . . .

Q: But you didn't join a group like the Young People's Socialist League?

PETER: There wasn't any of it around.

Q: What was your major?

PETER: I was seventeen, hadn't straightened it out. The last year they wanted some information so that they could sort the credits out. So I told 'em. They said which one would be best for you, and I said psychology. [They said,] "But the degree you'll get in psychology'll be worthless." And I said great, yeah. So I started going more for literature, took a course in modern drama; a senior-level course with the drama department and tore it apart. I was the only one that got an A at the end of the thing. I guess that was enough of an education, y'know; that's what I was interested in, and what I was interested in I would do. . . . That's what happened, I drifted, drifted, and the drift was toward myself.

Q: But you did graduate?

PETER: Yeah, I was in San Francisco in 1958. I decided to drop out of college. I went to San Francisco to meet Allen Ginsberg,

who had just written *Howl*, which I read in a bar and I read on peyote and understood very clearly. I wanted to come meet these wondrous old men, Henry Miller and Kenneth Rexroth. . . . So I came out to meet them and hung around and got lost and wasn't ready —

Q: Did you run with Ginsberg at all?

PETER: No. . . . I wasn't a part of any of the establishment cabals, y'know. I belonged to a cabal. The fifties were cabalistic times, man, that's when people belonged to cabals. I can tell you a great deal about Dick and Marvin — I can't tell you that much about Jack and Gary. I want you to understand . . . that the thing the beat people established was the reality of small groups of kindred turned-on people. So it doesn't matter to me whether Kerouac was writing about Gary Snyder. It could be me writing about Marvin, or Marvin writing about me. Because that's what they were doing. They were celebrating their cabal. I say cabal because it was the only form — life-affirming form — that was available at the time. Ginsberg is a veteran of several million cabals, I suppose. Universal cabals. And now he's gotten into the biggest cabal of all — the man cabal.

Q: Had you any sense that you were joining the Beat Generation?

PETER: I don't think anybody joined. That's what I was tryin' to tell you. I took peyote when I was seventeen years old, the first thing I ever took in my life —

Q: Where?

PETER: University of Florida. Sent away to Texas for peyote buttons, five dollars for fifty in a crate. I didn't even know what to do —

Q: You mean you could do it by mail?

PETER: Sure you could do it by mail. Texas Cactus Company in some small Texas town. . . . Don't you know that all this is drugs? All this is the revolution, did you know that? Drug consciousness is the key to it. Drugs . . . because of their properties invited the distance that was necessary for us to find out who we really were. That to undertake the sexual explorations that were paraded in front of our consciousness by the "daddies" of the thirties and the bent-up twisted beauties; we had to get that kind of separation to be able to do it and survive. We had to sever feedback, status-gains off the culture we were born into. Severing it . . . and in that was our beauty. . . .

In Rock Creek Park in Washington, D.C., in a graveyard with a bottle of Pernod, smoking reefers, balling a beautiful girl named Sandy . . . We got into a crypt . . . and erosion was carrying those graves into a creek. We walked through the high grass and saw that shit . . . mausoleum with sprung door; we looked inside, where the casket had been canted at an angle, and we just had to go make it in there. We made it and came out with mold and cobwebs all over our clothes and smelling of this musty stuff. We ran down to the creek and waded up to our waists, then read Chinese poetry, Li Po, squatting on the rock near that creek.

Q: Did she like it?

PETER: She liked everything. Blonde hair, blue-eyed Jewish girl from Virginia who didn't know what *schmaltz* meant. Her father was a Socialist candidate for governor of Virginia. He got a thousand votes, all from Norfolk. . . . Kicks. Hard kicks. Hard kicks became the way out, became the way. My parents, man, I came from what you call a "broken home" — in television tragedy language. . . . And it was like: "Broken-home-booby-baby-you-never-had-a-break." It sounds like a song, a song from the fifties. But that's where it really is and how those people fucked themselves up so bad. . . . People in [their] forties were wreckage, nothing but wreckage, complete syndromic wreckage. . . . Don't you know that thing when you're walking on the surface of the world, you're walking on the surface of the world, and you bring your broken mind, broken spirit, into a linoleum hospital, a hospital for linoleum, a linoleum hospital for people, for linoleum people, a hospital, broken hospital for linoleum people, linoleum hospital, where it's more important to keep the linoleum clean than to keep the people, to keep the linoleum clean, linoleum hospital people, linoleum hospital people . . . well, that's where it was.

It was walking on the surface and linoleum, on aluminum, on a cellophane surface of the world. It's not advertising, it's to walk that way as though, if you can just keep your linoleum straight, you'd be all right, just keep up your linoleum, baby, just wrap it up in linoleum, man, eat that linoleum, I used to eat that linoleum, linoleum pie, linoleum soul and that's what it was about. And the fact is that gods didn't make it through . . . nobody ever made it through there. . . . [And] what I was tryin' to tell you, is that hard kicks is the only impetus to reality. . . .

These hard-livers paid dues. [You can't] have the beauty of being a hard-liver without payin' those dues. You're not gonna do it. You try it, you're not gonna do it.

Why are hard-livers beautiful? It's what they said, y'know. To have a pair of balls! For a man to stand up and scream, "There's nothing but anguish." Allen Ginsberg really incorporated the dead man of the thirties — he really got the dead man of the thirties in the strong homosexual of the fifties that he was. He captured the dead man of the thirties soul and stood up with a pair of balls and started bellowing and saying, "Oh, what! Say who! Fuck what, man!" That was the thing. . . .

Before I was talkin' about black people actually being picked up as slaves [and] that's why they are the black mirror. We see our dark image in black people. We'll always stand for the hypocrisy of this civilization, in the same way the white Southerners were sold an illusion of freedom so complete that it effectively castrated them all. Had to, because, baby, when the governor of Florida comes into Palatka, he comes in with fifty black-and-white highway patrol cars, ten motorcycle escorts, there's a lotta heat on the street that day. A tremendous amount. There's a lot of flexin' and rubbin' legs against motorcycles, there's an awful lot of masturbating billy-clubs goes down that day; and the cats crouch and mouth and make that platform secure for their Good Governor, their Good Old Boy, their Good Old Mistah-Governah-Man. Now that little sweet piece of castration happened a long time ago, and you just say about the governor that he's a good old boy. You say about that sheriff, "He's a good old boy," and he'll say back, he'll say, "These niggers, they just good old boys, we just good old boys. Boy, we're just good old boys." I'm trying to tell you, it's a mystique, it's a fascism of the United States, it's explicit. Then you'd be able to see that General Motors is a Nazi symbol.

What keeps you from seeing General Motors as a Nazi symbol, if anything keeps you, is the "good old boys." We're all good old boys, good old white boys. All of us are good old boys, sure, old Rockefeller he just hit it rich, anybody can hit it rich. Just a good old boy. And if it turns out that we can't hit it rich without hitting somebody else in the head from 50,000 feet with a 500-pound bomb, well then we'll do it that way. We're all supposed to hit it rich because we're all supposed to be good old boys, a democratic country club there, boy. Good old boy. You're all gonna get in that good old country club, boy. . . .

Q: Did you go to New York after Florida?
PETER: Yeah, sure.
Q: How long did you stay in New York?
PETER: Long enough to get awful blue there.
Q: What are the blues like?
PETER: The blues life is a mystique. When I was over the blues-life mystique, I left New York. . . . And the blues-life mystique

is that if you want to do anything, you have to lose your left arm. You have to pay a lot of dues . . . to live full out — full out, not far out — as you can, if the cost is in dues. The only people that can do it are oppressed . . . the hard-kick seekers who laid down the patterns of extreme beauty for this civilization . . . like the blues singers and John Dillinger, Willie Sutton and Billie Holiday. . . . They're all people who got burned for what they did . . . being repressed beyond recourse. . . . Don't you know what that means? . . . People who lived it were essentially oppressed beyond action, oppressed beyond action. To be oppressed without recourse is blues life. . . .

Q: Oppressed beyond recourse?
PETER: The beauty of being oppressed beyond recourse — don't you know what that means?
Q: I'm trying to understand.
PETER: Nobody wants to be ugly, nobody wants to be plastic except Andy Asshole, who *wants* to be a plastic man. . . . One wants to be real, to feel that one's being is actually there. . . . The thing about hard kicks. Hard kicks is a way of acquiring life, y'know, breaking into life, so the masters of hard kicks became the wizards of a few years ago. Now hard kicks is available to anyone because LSD is really, y'know, like the hardest kick that was ever discovered. Now maybe STP gonna be harder. It's going to be the mind-cracking motherfucking drugs that gonna be the hard kicks. Hard kicks is a way of looking at your existence, not like mistreating your body or throwing your mind to the crows. It's a way of extending yourself [so that] something spectacular and beautiful can be available to you. But you gotta reach through linoleum to get it — that's the thing. You gotta push past the crap of recognition. You know: "Yes-sir-no-sir-thank-you." . . . There's an edge of non-living, non-being that is pushed on you fuckin' hard, man. . . . We live in the most manipulated society ever created by man. It's an economic, psychological, cultural, manipulation of such a high order and such a degree — because of this thing about individualist pigs that the thing becomes rapacious. Hard kicks and then drugs, drugs, distance, then hard kicks is the extension of the spine, is the extension of individual spirit, to be able to comprehend a large shot that's going down. This is history. This is time. This is moment. This is grand. It is mean. . . .

The common reaction of people who get high the first time is, "Wow! is that real! Is that really what's happening? Wow! did you see it? It's real!" Not a specimen world anymore. It's not consumer-conveyor, consumer-conveyor-sit-in-a-slot-boom-boom-boom-boom-boom-boom-boom-boom-boom-boom-FEED-boom-boom-boom-SHIT-boom-boom-boom-SLEEP-boom-boom-boom . . . it's not that. It's like sentences don't have so many periods, it's like getting more dashes and colons and commas and involutions.

Q: How is a hard kick more real than a soft kick?
PETER: I'm not saying it's *more* real. I'm saying hard kicks are the perimeters of existence. A being.
Q: Is there a special value in being at the perimeter instead of, say, at the center?
PETER: It's called Life. I'd rather shiver when it rains than not. Pure lightning, mental or otherwise. Fantastic sky-break —
Q: Being struck by it really blows your mind.
PETER: The Hopi have a struck-by-lightning fraternity. You can only get in if you've been struck by lightning. People that have survived lightning bolts belong to it. They're considered special seers.
Q: People in the community talk about acid as being the key to insight. Is this of any interest to you?
PETER: Insight, sight-in what? In what sight?
Q: They look inside, they claim to see their hangups.

PETER: And then what?

Q: That's what I'm asking. . . .

PETER: That's where we start, man. Now, do it. Now, do it, shit, now, go ahead, drop out now. What, now what, what now, now, what, whatever you want, go ahead, do it, do it. . . . You doin' what you want to? Uh-huh? *Sure* it's what you want to do? Do what you want to do, right? Can't do what you want to do? Uh-oh. Now things get very real. . . . Go do what you want to do. You tell me you're free, you tell me you're free, man. Tell me you're free, man, you do whatever you want to do, you tell me that. Now what. What happens now? Got busted? Did what? Free store, free food, wow, beautiful! Free theater, free poems, like that, we got busted! Yeah. You assume freedom? *Assume* freedom. Now what? It's pure intuition, man. Come on, we're talking about freedom. . . . You sit on the floor. You tell me what you can do tomorrow. You tell me what you can do, what you can get away with. . . . And then we find it's necessary to bail each other out.

There are internal contradictions in the society that have been heightened to such a degree that the country has become the equivalent of fascist. It's General Motors fascism. That's out front. Our lives are in fact revolutionary within the context of General Motors fascism. We expect to live our lives and to defend them. We have been cultural outsiders in this civilization. We will become the political dynamic of the new society because we are *living* a new civilization. My life is now political, it's ultimately political. . . .

The internal contradictions in this country are creating a void that one would have to be blind not to see. The void is rushing at us so fast now that Zen is breakfast. Within a short time, the general cultural movement will become more social. The issue is being forced by the black people. . . . We are in the middle, we people, and we find our vanity can no longer be a shield. So we have to adopt the state of mind that's proper to the world that's opening for us. Our life style is the mode of existence for free men, a new vision of freedom that is bought at the price that freedom has always been bought. Our people are in jails. What we do now will be called treason. . . . It is necessary to take the responsibility for being. . . . There is no escape; there can only be confrontation. . . . And there's every chance that we won't be allowed the opportunity to carry it out without an interim period where there's going to be a great deal of death. We've passed the meridian. . . . We're passing now into a time of death, and we have to confront death with the vision of life.

Q: What do you foresee?

PETER: Civil war. Civil war with some attendant trips.

Q: Like what?

PETER: Well, psychedelic celebration . . . hand-holding, candle-watching, high-on-acid-trust-and-hope routine. That's attendant. LSD hand-holding is not the end. Civil war with these things: the life-affirming banners. We're going to view what we're doing as the best we could come up with. It's only the best, scratch it. Scratch sixty-seven. Summer in San Francisco has been the first be-together. Summer in San Francisco '67 First Be-Together for Escapees and Refugees. . . . Our part now coming up is to communicate in direct spinal language. Nothing said that can't be done. . . . To push as hard as we can . . . to move past the Civil War in the United States to our planetary concerns, the forms and modes of which we are developing now . . . to get those models out and to prepare ourselves to carry them out. . . . The U.S. goes down. . . . The world *has* to get past. . . . The species on the planet has to get past the non-living of the last century, that most barren sterile time. The time when men died for wages, when lives were counted against profit-sharing coupons . . . when coupons and clip-outs became days and nights, when sunup was time to go to work and sundown was exhausted relief, or an alcoholic night out. . . . When grass was lunch outside the office, when flowers were passed on the way to work or grown on the weekend . . . ol' lady lawn, ol' lady lawn. . . .

It's the moment . . . and the thing moves, and the moment moves. . . .

Y'know, when people are high, man, they're talking music — and music was to Plato the highest form of art, because music imitates the harmony of the spheres. And we're trying to move our minds as sensuous instruments . . . to bring the species and ourselves . . . to move the school of fish we swim in. . . . To move onto the next place that we've got to go because if we don't move from where we are now, the barracuda are going to hit us. And they do. Every time the tide turns, the barracuda turns. Everybody turns when the tide turns.

Ed. Note: Leonard Wolf says of Berg: "A radical activist, a former member of The Mime Troupe, and a founder of the Digger Movement, Peter is a feverishly brilliant leader, a shrewd strategist, and creator of street theater."

From *Voices from the Love Generation* by Leonard Wolf, Little Brown

---

So there's a very interesting and a very key connection between insurrection and acts carried out by oneself, a private, personal civil war. We define a civil war as when a society splits down the middle and you have two opposing sides. Does that have to be the definition? Can 5000 people launch a civil war? Can 4000, 3000, two or one? Or one-half of 1000? Or half of that? Can one person? Can one person engage in civil war? I'm not a lawyer. I'm definitely not a judge, but I would say that one person acting alone could in fact be engaged in a civil war against an oppressive system.

ELDRIDGE CLEAVER

The tradition of all the dead generations weighs like a nightmare on the brain of the living.

KARL MARX, *The Eighteenth Brumaire of Louis Bonaparte*

Above and beyond everything else is the moral matter. The most fundamental right of man is the right to his life. The use of force against that right — as in the draft law — is clearly wrong.

BARRY GOLDWATER

For the first time in my life I enjoyed working. I think lots of people had that experience. Ever since I was 18 I hated every job and either quit or was fired. But this was something different. With aching back and sweat on my brow, there was no boss. What we were creating was our own desires, so we worked like madmen and loved it.

ONE WHO HELPED TO MAKE THE PEOPLE'S PARK in Berkeley, Spring 1969

I can understand the anguish of the younger generation. They lack models, they have no heroes, they see no great purpose in the world. But conscientious objection is destructive of a society. The imperatives of the individual are always in conflict with the organization of society. Conscientious objection must be reserved for only the greatest moral issues, and Vietnam is not of this magnitude.

HENRY A. KISSINGER, speaking to an editor of *Look.* Kissinger is Nixon's "security advisor."

We do not feel like a cool, swinging generation — we are eaten up inside by an intensity that we cannot name.

STUDENT SPEAKER at Radcliffe graduation ceremonies — June 1968

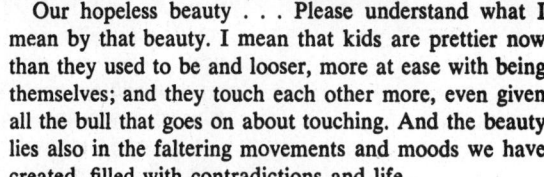

OUR HOPELESS BEAUTY . . .

LOOK, MA: NO HOPE

A multiple memoir of the New Left

MICHAEL ROSSMAN

That man in Chicago or wherever, the one they were doing the operation on and his heart stopped unexpectedly, and they iced his head and all while they finally got it started again, but by every test known to medical science he was dead for five full minutes. And it changed him; and after, he wrote a book about what it was like beyond, and about coming back. But didn't he touch the ground differently, though! and feel the way his shirt rubbed his neck, and use his eyes with a different style, after he'd been genuinely certifiably dead, even if his heart was frail and might go at any moment.

We're somewhat like that, our motion has the grace of coming after Impossible. I mean the set of changes in my generation, and in the younger kids, which is all we know of social health and social hope, and of community. The changes started showing up first in our public behavior, color them The New Activism, and then in our fairly private behavior, color them Hippyism. I happen to think a strong case can be made for the deep interrelation of these "movements," two faces of a coherent cultural transition; and that we already can begin a useful description of the sources of this transition, in terms of the sharply-new social and cultural technologies that define our time.

But there's a different way in which I think about where our change came from—which I do a lot, trying to figure out where it's going and what it's heading into, these days whose surfaces glitter with paranoid flashes of fear. Aside from the whole Black thing, and aside from the distant mythic Cain/Abel brother-rending thing—looming beyond and deeper than the real generational clash which the present trivial hippy-pogrom portends—there's the War, the War. It presses upon our lives. My kid brother, scholarship freshman, is on the Dean's reprimand list for the Dow sit-in; where will he be when they try to close the Boston Induction Center? My sister, her sad and daredevil lover 1-AO near Pleiku, is gone with a nest of others to begin a grave and impossible building-peace project in a hostile town. Jan comes onto me about jail in the supermarket, I balance near the napkins, paralyzed by her voice's shadows. "But you were only in for nine weeks," she says, almost accusingly, "look how long it took you to come back. What about five years?" I tried to close my self off with statistics, what could I say? Two thousand burnt draftcards now. So many like her Marty, who won't flee to Canada and won't go in: he waits in the graduate lottery. They live it over and over again in advance, to make it hurt less when it comes. "I'm going to learn typing," she says, "so I can get a job in Kentucky or wherever they send him." Last week, friends who helped organize the October anti-draft protests were indicted for criminal conspiracy, 1-to-3. Karen looks up, the fear she would mask betrayed for an instant when I tell her, be back later, going to a meeting. "What kind?" "Planning." An incomplete gesture of her right hand: "I wish you w . . . ," unwillingly, signing the Complicity Statement with her left hand. (Karen is left-handed.) No, brothers and sisters and comrades, the horizon is heavy with darkness; I think and hope it is not hope that drives and sustains us in our difference.

HAPPY AV

Our hopeless beauty . . . Please understand what I mean by that beauty. I mean that kids are prettier now than they used to be and looser, more at ease with being themselves; and they touch each other more, even given all the bull that goes on about touching. And the beauty lies also in the faltering movements and moods we have created, filled with contradictions and life.

Our hopeless beauty, then, flowered from a barren landscape of Impossible. Granted: our motion once begun, the Monday-morning political historian can sort through the newsclips and our letters, and trick out a real pattern of contagion and causality: we grew in a describable way: in that sense and in retrospect, it wasn't impossible. But I no longer believe things work in that neat and sensible fashion: I don't think a description of seeds and forces sufficiently accounts for our change and its character, for the manner of its birth. For there is a sense of Impossible intimately connected with this birth, which will never be displayed in the social equations we build with our data.

Summer, 1964, some months before the Free Speech Movement illuminated our lives. During six years in Berkeley, I had watched new left politics begin with us, crest with the 1960 HUAC and Chessman demonstrations, and fill out its first phase that Spring, with successful waves of mass sit-ins at hotels and auto showrooms in San Francisco. Something real was in motion, with a puzzling newness which touched and promised my life. That was what struck me, that summer: the newness I sensed, and how so much of what we had we'd made ourselves, because there was no other way to get it. And I tried to remember where it'd been at when we started moving, what the landscape of possibility had seemed:

When the long season of fear settled in,
they felt the icebergs of loneliness grow:
friends froze and fell away,
informed, ate shit.
         The rocks of insult
hardening children
          the arrows of letters
bearing divorces, betrayals, flights from
and to
        the emptinesses of lost jobs,
feared chances
        the tangible moments
of voiceless despair at the imagined awaited
knock at the door, brought
by strayed sound in the early darkness
all chipped away at the heart,
crumbled the granite of hope and belief,
and not content then ground them
in the ground: doors were fear,
they wrote lies and spoke words
carefully whitewashed, friends
were strangers, confidence closed,
and they waited for word of the trials
eight years, till the heart was gone,
leaving a bleak moraine scored
by the irresistible gravel of pain
and disbelief, amputation and closure:
hard, compacted, smooth, nothing left
to be torn away.
        And the heart
was gone, that's all, not
handed on: gone good
and simple and forever. They'll never measure
how those draining years bled the color
from a landscape, left us empty outline.

That was how it was when we began, I thought four

years ago and think still. No one really believed anyone could do anything much about anything. In America those years, before the black people spoke up, with protest crushed and an empty glossy monolithic politics, a man who wanted change—and believed we would die without it—could throw his empty coffeecup on the ground and make it break; but not much else. It was against this background that we began to move: not out of hope, but because we had to, because that context of Impossible granted us a weird sort of freedom.

It's hard to get a handle on that freedom, for we're still just beginning to explore its implications. May I call it the Freedom of the Children of the Bomb? For that is the larger, or louder, background. Remember ten years ago, when to be Thoughtful about Television was the fashion: "All that watching, what is it doing to the children?" The question was never answered and people stopped wondering—until McLuhan suggested that those 15,000-hours-per-18-year-old might all along have been pressing heads in a rather odd fashion which is only now showing up. (Pardon me ma if I act funny.) Likewise, everyone used to make a big thing about how we were the first kids to grow up with the Bomb. As we were: though there may be many of my generation who can't remember waking up with those nightmares, there's enough who can so that they're probably our most common property. But nobody ever said what all that *meant*.

What did it do to us, to learn as children to imagine the death of the world with a sound-shaped BOMB? At some deep and irrevocable level, I submit, we imagine—hence believe, hence accept—absolute annihilation, from the Latin *nihil*, nothing. It's all over, baby blue: pfffft, gone, done, that's it. *It has already happened.* Just as your lover's death and your own stalk, believed and living, in the jungles of the unexplored source of the Nile of your motions—which is part of what it is, to be a man—so the death of the race lives newly within us. With the reality of the possible, *it has already happened.* That shapes us, that spreads an indelible stain through our doing, that grants us the freedom to be what we are, for we are all there is. (Pardon me ma if I act free.)

With that deep knowledge—which would be a presence even without the Cuban crisis, *On The Beach,* the Greenland H-bombs as constant reminder—kids are learning to touch what is, each other, and themselves. For this is the constant broad direction of the vehicles we choose for our motion: the kinds of educational reform we push, how we use pot and acid, the group-games we investigate, the way we try to style our political/social action, and so on: towards Touch. There are other descriptions; I put it this way because of that man from Chicago or wherever, and how he must have touched the ground differently after (while his heart stood watching like an unpredictable bomb; but I don't think that part really matters).

Mario Savio during the Free Speech Movement.

Well there ain't no time to wonder why
Whoopee!
        (sing Country Joe and the Fish,
        in "Vietnam Rag")
                we're all gonna die!

What strikes me is the genuineness of that raucous cry's humor and cheer, so distinctively ours. Call it Absurd Affirmation if you must, though that name doesn't ring true to me. All I know is that it comes from accepting Impossible and going on from there, free; and it has nothing to do with hope. I can't explain this. I can only tell you about the event that led me to see it this way—the way I now see our response to the McCarthy Winter

and the Bomb, as I sit watching our time advance with headline wings on a dark horizon, and think about going down to the Induction Center in April.

It was Oct. 2, 1964, and we were sitting around a car, waiting. We'd been sitting there for 30 hours, a thousand kids, trapping a police car in Sproul Plaza. The car was there to haul away a kid arrested for sitting at an "illegal" CORE table, collecting money and members. The table was "illegal" because the Administration had up and changed the rules governing campus political activity on us—by some coincidence, just when Civil Rights work seemed to be having a real impact, with the successful hotel and Auto Row sit-ins. And so, for the first time, because it was something a lot of people had learned to care about, we fought back actively, to defend what had grown to be our own as we'd grown. And what happened after that, we called the Free Speech Movement.

Much was memorable about the FSM, which remains not only the longest and most energetic campus movement of our decade of rising protest, but also the one in which the characteristic traits of our political style (and its existential roots) appear most clearly. But that's a long story, I'm writing a book. More to the point are the images that remain with me from that vigil around the car. A night of huddled community, showered by eggs and cigarettes from a minor mob of drunken fraternity kids. Minstrels in the morning, playing while shared sleepingbags were rolled and the Plaza swept clean. Strong Fall sun, sandwiches and lemonade and salt-tablets circulating among a weary sweating crowd, as if we had just invented cooperation, or on a warm and desperate picnic seen into each other's eyes. The sockfooted solemn file at the microphone atop the car, in the first real public dialogue I had ever heard, speaking of ideas as though they had real substance and meaning, as though they might somehow be made relevant to the lives clustered there.

The news of 600 police, late in the second afternoon, massed on the other side of Sproul Hall, about to repossess their car; and no word at all from our negotiators, let alone from the faculty. (It is only now, with the first murders on campuses and troops guarding the Pentagon, that the number 600 and the danger seem ordinary.) "Take off your pierced earrings, remove your ties," advised the microphone, "if we link arms it is likely they will club us apart." Someone standing by the car in those closing minutes, with a big box of green pippin apples, tossing them out to faces without appetite but lit by sudden beams, as we sang "We are not afraid" in voices shaking with fear, and waited, free.

"That event," remarks Mario, in response to my notion that the whole of the FSM was rooted and pre-performed in those galvanizing and transforming hours, "has always seemed to me to have the archaic, primitive quality of a childhood dream." And it was such a thing of our beginnings, that I despair of ever being able to describe it usefully. For that, one would have to invent a form having somewhat of the slow, violent multiplex beauty of *Ulysses in Nighttown.*

But what I remember most clearly is this. I was standing by the car itself during the last hour: watching the faces and motions of those with whom I shared this complex action that was somehow of value; thinking in last-minute flash detail of the incident history of our seven years of politics: of how it had left us, changed, and given us nothing but our selves. Around our waiting touching disc of seated bodies, 3,000 ringed, a sizable number crying for our blood. Literally: chanting, "We want blood, blood, blood." And it was clear that if the cops came in, as we expected, someone would be badly hurt, likely someone killed. A lot of people, even not-so-liberal faculty, have said so since, and I believed it at the time. I mean, we had this car, which was the only tangible thing we'd ever gotten (save for the sit-in successes; but this was their incarnation), and we just weren't about to move.

A corny background chorus is singing "We shall not be moved," and images of irresistible forces gather in the dark air, in the failing light. I stood by the car, thinking of how by the car was the most dangerous place to be and of going back out towards the edge where I'd been, and I stood by the car, running it all over in my head with a lucidity that clarified only complexity, and I stood by the car, munching on the live green of a pippin apple, and I stood by the car. There was nothing brave about this, nor grim, nor even in any sense dramatic, despite the spectacular setting: I was simply there, and accepted being there. Above all, my presence was not out of hope, nor accompanied by her. For I remember with perfect clarity thinking then: no matter what happens, whether or not the cops charge us, whatever we do or build or become: those jars for money and lists for names will never be back on the tables. And, hope given up, I was free to be there as I was, and I was.

———

We won that round: we got the tables back, for the time being, and in the process sparked a community whose life has persisted and grown. Now, 40 months later, we again are advocating actions that turn out to be illegal; the tables are recruiting people for another try at closing down the Induction Centers. That we will be left free to speak on seems unlikely; to close the Centers is clearly impossible. But then, we do not act from hope. I keep coming back to this, these days when the heart stops for a moment, trying to scan ahead into the chill mad currents of history. These threatening days, when our newness still stands on colt-unsteady legs, like an unauthorized fragile card-table on the edge of our campus generations: bearing a message only our own kind can or care to read, in glad amateur posters of care and despair: there is much to love and no reason to hope, be free.

commonweal 4/12/69

★ ★ ★ ★ AND WE DO A LOT OF STRANGE THINGS ★

BILLY T. & KIDS FOR EARTH

On 10 May 1966 Billy Tieckelmann was interviewed in San Francisco by W. Bruce Allbin, Special Agent, INTC of the United States Army. Here are excerpts from this interview as transcribed by Special Agent Allbin and furnished to Billy.

Q. Mr. Tieckelmann, it is the policy of the Department of the Army to provide any individual who registers for Selective Service, and who qualifies in any way his Statement of Personal History, DD Form 398, or his Armed Forces Security Questionnaire, DD Form 98, an opportunity to fully explain these qualifications, and to furnish any additional information that might be useful in making a determination of his case. This interview is also being conducted to ascertain your political ideologies, your willingness to serve in the Armed Forces of the United States, and your organizational affiliations. Your qualification of the previously mentioned forms has become a matter of concern to Department of Army in that it has made questionable your acceptability for military service. Upon a resolution of your case, you may be considered acceptable for military service, not acceptable for military service, or acceptable with the stipulation that you are not eligible for a security clearance. I have read and explained to you the Fifth Amendment to the Constitution of the United States. Do you understand your rights under the Fifth Amendment and the purpose of this interview?

A. Yes...Can I read this over to myself? "I fully recognize the fact that multitudes of young men (both American and foreign) are being driven to their death by power structures that are able to instill fear and hate as powerful personal preoccupations." Yes, well that's true. I can't say anything else about that, it's true. "I recognize and feel compassion for their piteous state and shall not therefore, at any cost, submit my person nor my intellect to any organization (in this case the United States Armed Forces) which deals in the subversion of love and life and which teaches death and hate above understanding." Yeah, the thing about the Army is, you see, I have ideas about personal relationships and people that definitely extend—like large organs, nations and countries and things like that. I feel that all these people are kind of misguided, somehow. The things I feel about war, mainly is that it's some kind of manifestation of, like sado/masochistic tendencies in people. I mean there's people who're really crazy and screwed up and they're that way—like you, you got a place where you can rid yourself of these sado/masochistic things. You don't have to, you know, like go out and get somebody in the street and that's like wars and things. Well, countries do that. That's what's happening. "My contention is that the United States Army is guilty of murdering every man that dies in its service." That's because I don't think anybody has to die.

Q. In what respect do you mean this?

A. I mean that, like you can find better outlets for these things—you don't have to be making it with some man in the street. It doesn't have to be going to war. Like me, I paint. I paint hateful things. The more hateful I get, the more beautiful I paint. "Furthermore, it is presently a militant aggressor in a South Vietnamese struggle for self-determination and national independence." Yes, well they're trying to come around to the same thing. I mean they're just way back. I don't understand them at all.

Q. Who is that?

A. The Vietnamese and our place in it. I just don't understand how people can do that.

Q. Have war?

A. Yes, I don't understand what people could do that stuff for. It's just beyond me. Figure, they're doing it there. We shouldn't get into it, you know? We should know more about what's happening with ourselves and the way we act with other people. I just don't know why we should help them out. When a kid acts bad, you don't act like a kid. You spank them or something or you pinch them sometimes. You don't go to war with them. "I advocate the overthrow of the government of the United States as well as the other militant governments of the world through understanding..." You see what I mean by understanding, you tell them something...

Q. What would be the means you would utizile to overthrow the U.S. government?

A. By being smarter than they are.

Q. Would you use violent or unconstitutional means?

A. I'd protest a whole hell of a lot and try to get a lot of kids on my side because there's more kids than anything else. Over half the population, I think, is under 21 now. I've got this organization. I'm pretty serious about it. It's called "Kids for Earth" and it seems to be funny to a lot of people but we advocate not listening. You know, listen to rock and roll or something else. If you haven't got anything to say and you don't want to listen, you shouldn't have to. Kids will do it, I guess...

Q. What will be the nature of your overthrow? Violent or nonviolent?

A. Just by not listening enough until the whole country rots. The whole thing—if they—the kids—didn't listen or try to listen and they're pretty much like me and most of the people younger than me—there're a lot of crazy kids around who might listen. If all the kids just paid no attention to armies, you know, just didn't pay any attention at all... Oh, another thing that we advocate is taking away the age of our government officers. That's a political thing. They're just old people who don't understand except what was happening back when wars were going on. You know, World War People, and I belong to a generation that came after the war, war babies, they call us. We're different. We're rock and roll, we're friendly and we do a lot of strange things.

Q. What steps have you taken toward

your desire to effect the overthrow of the government "through understanding" and by persuading the youth of these countries not to participate in any form of military service?

A. What steps? Well, I suppose the first thing to do is to have buttons made. Right? Those guys over in Berkeley have the right idea—make a lot of buttons. They just don't have the right organizations. I suppose once you have buttons you have a good organization.

Q. Have you had any buttons made?

A. No, we don't have any. We don't have any money but this is the first step because we're looking for buttons and we're got people who are going to give us money for buttons. Mostly there's only about 75 or 80 very interested people. This thing is just being organized and we should be doing something that someone might hear about by the summer.

Q. What types of things are you going to do besides the buttons?

A. Rock and roll dances. That's where you can go and not listen.

Q. How do you intend to have them understand your point of view if they're not listening?

A. Oh, well they don't have to listen if they don't want to...

Q. Well, you indicated "Yes" that you have associated with groups, individuals, and organizations.

A. That was the kids back there.

Q. Which groups or organizations were these?

A. Kids. "Kids for Earth." Just kids, you know. They don't like government. They're my friends. None of my friends do.

Q. With what people would you have associated with?

A. Schoolmates and people that I met out of school after I quit school. Friends. Just people who didn't like that stuff.

Q. This was not organized?

A. No, just persons. I'm not a member—

Q. Would you care to mention their names?

A. No, they don't advocate any more than I do...

Q. Do you feel that communism as it exists in the world today presents any form of threat against the security of the United States?

A. I think the communist government presents as much threat to the people as the United States government does.

Q. How?

A. Just in that it's an un-understanding, thick-headed, slow-moving form of government with backward thinking.

Q. How do you feel it's un-understanding, thick-headed and slow-moving?

A. Do you have a photographic memory or something? You remember an awful lot good.

Q. On what do you base this philosophy of "Kids for Earth"?

A. My philosophy? I thought I was telling it to you all the time.

Q. What do you base your objection to war, etc. on?

A. Because, I don't know. I see a big war as a bunch of people getting a charge and there's people who come back and say, "How great it is." Particularly like in Vietnam now. That Sargent Barry what's his name who wrote that song. He says that, you know, some guy got killed and he wants his son to get killed too. That is—I want my son to be a Green Beret. I'm sure he wouldn't say that after he's dead. But somebody who would say that, ask for his kid to die, must be crazy. He must hope for some-

thing more for his kid than bleeding to death and being maimed and torn apart in some desolate country.

Q. Do you feel that individuals or nations have the right for self-defense?

A. Yes, I suppose. I can't think of any reason why not. But, I've been able to defend myself without hitting anybody. Except once I almost killed a guy and that was the last time.

Q. Do you feel that a nation has the right to protect itself or to assist its friends in danger who ask for protection?

A. They don't know who their friends are, first of all. Second, not in Vietnam. That is no friend at all.

Q. Refer to your DD Form 98, Armed Forces Security Questionaire, where you indicated you have subscribed to publications or organizations or groups listed, what publications were these?...

A. When I was in prep school, I just thought that maybe I'd like to do something political and tried to find out what's happening in politics on both sides...I don't know any Russians, so I went down to the Russian Embassy and got a whole bunch of their books and read them and they seemed as screwed up as our books so I gave it up...

Q. How did you get in touch with the Russian Embassy? Did anybody suggest it to you?

A. I walked in. We went to Washington on a political trip to the government and I did not like it at all so I thought Id just walk over to the Russian Embassy.

Q. What kind of a political trip was this?

A. Oh, I guess we were supposed to talk to Vice President Johnson and he had a "What, me worry?"—in his office—you know, that little kid from Mad magazine. There's some crazy people.

Q. Were you part of an organization that went to see—?

A. Yes, my political science class...

Q. Do you believe in the right of an individual to choose what form of governmental body he'll have governing him?

A. Yes, or none.

Q. None?

A. None, you can choose none.

Q. You believe you do not necessarily have to have a body above you?

A. Not authoritarian but you have to have a body that can organize things. But they don't have to make rules. I'm against rules.

Q. In other words they don't have to have any—no justice at all?

A. There isn't any justice now...

Q. Are you willing to serve in the Armed Forces of the United States?

A. No. I'm hoping that—some people like to get killed, too—as well as kill. They'll help out the Army, I think. Anyway, what is the question again?

Q. Are you willing to serve in the Armed Forces of the United States?

A. Oh, no. Oh, I was going to say —I wish to make a request at this time. I'm a conscientious objector, I think; but not in the same sense of a conscientious objector as read to me. I object entirely and wholly to it—not that I'll do it if I don't have to fight. I object to the whole and entire idea. The thing is that I'm asking politely and nicely, at first, to be allowed not to go. I suppose you can ask me to go, then see what you get. That's all.

Q. Would you be willing to serve a jail sentence in lieu of going in the service?

A. No, I'd go into the service. I'd go in the service before...I don't think they'd want me. I've been known to be extremely crazy. It's like—a lot of

people call it "childish."

Q. Have you taken steps toward having yourself officially classified a conscientious objector?

A. No, the guy—the last person I talked to said that—read it to me and asked me if I'd fit under conscientious objector. I said, "Well, not like that. Not the way you read conscientious objector to me." Not the way—I mean, I don't believe in God or anything like that. I don't believe in anything except me and my girl friend...

Q. Do you support the advocacy for the violent and unconstitutional overthrow of the government?

A. No, but I don't object to it.

Q. Do you believe that such a violent or unconstitutional overthrow is inevitable?

A. Overthrow is a funny word, you know. Tends to mean, "violently", just like that. But as far as overthrow means changing quickly, expedience, or something like that—have to change that word. But as far as changing it, I think it should be changed as quickly as possible.

Q. Would you do this violently?

A. Myself, I wouldn't.

Q. What will you do if you are drafted?

A. I can't say. I haven't been. I won't say.

Q. Are you willing to serve in the Armed Forces of the United States against all enemies, to obey the orders of the Commander in Chief and of your superiors and to uphold and defend the Constitution of the United States?

A. No.

Q. Do you support the advocacy for the violent and unconstitutional overthrow of the United States Government or have you associated with any organizations, groups, or individuals that do so advocate?

A. Yes, as revised by my statement.

Q. Do you believe in the inevitability of such an overthrow or revolution?

A. Yes, with the same qualifications.

Q. Would you support such an overthrow or revolution?

A. No, I wouldn't support anything. I won't support the government and I won't support anti-government.

Q. Is there anything you'd like to add to your statement?

A. No.

"Kids for Earth" is flourishing. Billy has split the country into four sections, with a coordinator for each. Jeff Freidland is in New Orleans and Randy Kosek in San Francisco, Strawberries at Antioch (to contact, leaflet for a few days asking WHATEVER HAPPENED TO STRAWBERRIES?—they will contact you) and the Boston coordinator is Jim Hayes at 110 Arlington Street.

On December 24, snow or no snow, "Kids for Earth" plans to build "the world's largest snowman" on Boston Commons, "to assure the world that we love them."

win

Fall 1966

DEAD VISIONS
DEAD PURPOSES
DEAD POLITICS

In The Nation: The Trouble With the Campaign By TOM WICKER

Assumptions of the Past

Nor is the campaign irrelevant entirely because Mr. Humphrey's speeches so often lapse into the rhetoric and assumptions of the past that old-timers half-expect him to denounce economic royalists or the do-nothing Eightieth Congress; or because the mechanistic Mr. Nixon, punching his points home with the aid of his extensive repertoire of emphatic gestures, insists that just as soon as he puts in a good Republican Attorney General the streets will be safe for decent folk.

It is not merely these noises blaring from a thousand hired P.A. systems, but the political system itself that seems so little germane to modern America—as if actors continue to play their parts along after the audience has left and the theater has been demolished.

In a brilliant speech to the International City Managers Association, Horace Busby—the former special assistant to President Johnson — recently pictured the incredible growth and change wrought in recent decades by a "high-velocity, high-intensity, turned-on society" as the true "anarchist in our midst."

The result, he said, was that for the actuality of modern American life "we are short of talent, short of people, thin on experience, thinner on patience.

"This new American life is strangely hard. . . . Yet the American pace is unrelenting. Knowledge is our great industry, but the knowledge we are capable of utilizing is falling farther and farther behind the sum of knowledge we possess. Increasingly, ours is a society slipping out of phase. In sector after sector—from the delivery of medical services to the de-livery of daily mail — we are barely able to do what we are doing, with no assurance how long we can continue."

In such times, Mr. Busby said, "our kinship is not so much with the year 2000 as with the year 1776. We are back to the basics of organizing a new society and providing for its governance.

But nobody is talking like this in the campaign. Which candidate, for instance is advocating basic structural changes in the governmental system, or urging new thought and new concepts about such things as "the roles and rewards of both labor and business" or "the values and ends of education"? Is either able or willing to say, as Mr. Busby did, that "we are back to basic questions about how our society and system are to function—and, indeed, whether either can continue to function as now organized"?

'Dead Politics'

No such thing is being said. Nor is there any evidence that either candidate or party remotely grasps the point—that in a time of profound and shattering change, reaching into every institution and process of national life, the accumulated weight of political, administrative, judicial and private decisions and customs has produced rote thinking and ritual action — "dead visions, dead purposes and dead politics"—in a time that demands dynamic adjustment to new realities.

That is why there is so much turgidity and so little relevance in the 1968 campaign. What else could be expected of a political process geared to other times, other needs?

𝕿𝖍𝖊 𝕹𝖊𝖜 𝖄𝖔𝖗𝖐 𝕿𝖎𝖒𝖊𝖘 10/24/68

The Wily Old Men

Despite the change in administrations, little will be new about the House of Representatives; in that continuity lies the possibility of real crisis. The standing committee chairmen, whose massive powers repeatedly blocked Executive requests during the 90th Congress, were overwhelmingly returned to "lead" in the 91st Congress.

The House assigns all proposed legislation to its twenty standing committees. No less than nineteen of the twenty chairmen in the 90th Congress stood for re-election and all nineteen won, most of them by crushing margins. In seven Southern districts, so disorganized and demoralized was the opposition that no challenger bothered to file. Included among the seven Representatives who thus had no need to conduct even a token campaign are the chairmen of the most important committees of the House: Appropriations, Rules, and Ways and Means.

Rep. George Mahon (D., Tex.) was, by Southern standards, sympathetic to the Great Society. Though chairman of Appropriations, his stature in the House was often inadequate to the task of stopping economy drives at the expense of the politically weak and powerless. Rep. Wilbur Mills (D., Ark.) used his formidable powers as head of Ways and Means to advance his conviction of the necessity for full examination of national priorities. What he had in mind became clearer in the anti-welfare amendments he pressed through. Rep. William Colmer (D., Miss.), of the Rules Committee, learned most of the tricks of obstruction from wily Judge Smith, with whom he was allied through the last three Presidencies.

L. Mendel Rivers (D., S.C.), the super-hawk chairman of Armed Services, also had no competition. Apparently the extensive military construction assigned to his Charleston, S.C., seigniory dissuaded both Wallaceites and Republicans from contending.

Even the twelve chairmen who were opposed needed for the most part to make but token campaigns; in only one case was there what might be called a serious challenge. Wayne Aspinall (D., Colo.), head of Interior and Insular Affairs, won by "only" 54.9 per cent of the popular vote. In every other instance the chairmen's vote exceeded 60 per cent and some reached pluralities above 80 per cent. Mayor Daley's machine could not muster enough votes to carry Illinois for his national ticket, but the Mayor's one standing committee chairman, William Dawson of Government Operations, won by near acclamation in his South Chicago district.

Winds of change and rebellion may have blown through Chicago, Miami and even Birmingham, but the quiet of Pascagoula, Miss., and College Station, Tex., were undisturbed by 1968.

As the country grows younger, the men whose voices are heaviest in Congress grow older. The remarkable fact is that more than a third of the new House chairmen were born in the 19th century. Two of the nineteen returning chairmen entered the House before Franklin Roosevelt entered the White House; ten more took the oath of office while Roosevelt served as Chief Executive. Just two chairmen are younger than 60 years of age; the rest range up to 80 years.

Many rank-and-file members of the House believe something more sensible than seniority should be used to determine the leadership of vital committees. But if there is no break with the seniority system, control over the events of the last third of the 20th century will in large measure be in the hands of men born in the last third of the 19th century.

JOHN E. CROW

NATION 12/30/68

Academia in Rebellion

By Allen Young

"We're engaged in counter-guerrilla warfare on our campuses," said University of California President Charles J. Hitch to an audience of lawmakers in Hawaii recently.

"This is not just the hijinks of overenthusiastic students. This is insurrection. Organized society cannot back down without giving up our rights," said California Governor Ronald Reagan.

"There has had to be an escalation on this campus," said San Francisco State College President S.I. Hayakawa.

The Californians in effect were speaking for establishment political and educational leaders from Coast to Coast. America's campuses are in full-scale rebellion. And no wonder the terms are military! As students reject the orderly picketlines and neat mass arrests vaguely reminiscent of sheep farms and concentration camps, and as administrators rely on the use of police repression, so the terms of rebellion change.

L.N.S. Dec. 1968

THANK YOU FOR YOUR INATTENTION

It is often asked what is wrong with the half of the country under twenty-eight years old. Let us answer:

America is a great country with great ideals, but we are not living up to them. We are turning from a democracy to a hypocrisy.

No one is for air and water pollution, and yet they surround us. The Thirteenth Amendment to the United States Constitution specifically prohibits involuntary servitude, and the government is supposed to be the servant of the people. And yet young men who cannot even vote are drafted to kill and die in a war that is never explained.

We are taught, Thou shall not kill, do unto others as you would have others do unto you, and love thy neighbor. And yet 10 percent of our gross national product is spent on war every year while hunger, poverty, and overpopulation abound both at home and abroad.

The fault lies not in the black man aspiring for what is rightfully his, or in Communist stars, but in ourselves. For the true tragedy is we are not even trying to reach our ideals.

And those few who do put principle above personal ambition are threatened with prison, such as Dr. Spock, the twentieth-century Sir Thomas More. Or ridiculed as Governor Stassen, the modern Don Quixote.

As Sancho Panza told Don Quixote, Don't die, Don Quixote, don't die. For the greatest guilt in this life is to die without good reason.

Thank you for your inattention. Paul Walters
In seconding the nomination of Harold Stassen
1968 Republican National Convention

Action is shaping already on the national level. The National Institute of Mental Health (NIMH) granted the American Council of Education (ACE) $300,000 to do research on the nature and causes of student unrest. The council's Director of Research, Alexander Astin, speculates—according to the February 10 issue of the influential *Chronicle of Higher Education*—that with the research "admissions officers could virtually assure that there would or would not be demonstrations on their campuses by systematically admitting or rejecting students with 'protest-prone' characteristics."

Now, isn't that a piece of paranoid news?

At first the matter was quite embarrassing to the august American Council of Education. Though the research director was hot for the grant, the Council's president was terrified of the possible bad publicity. They considered funding the research in the same way that the CIA funded the National Student Association (NSA): through a secondary or "conduit" private institution. But details of the grant were already too public for secrecy.

So the American Council on Education accepted the grant openly and quietly. Anxious to have it appear legitimate, they are trying to get NSA itself to take a piece of the action. NSA has been offered the chance to run a sub-study aimed at finding out what distinguishes peaceful campuses from campuses prone to disruption. At the moment, NSA is deciding whether to be greedy for money and a chance to keep the study "honest and relevant," or to be noble and denounce the study—and perhaps win back in the eyes of the student movement a fraction of the legitimacy lost during the CIA scandal.

What the matter amounts to is that the government is subsidizing initial counter-insurgency research against its domestic (youth) rebellion. The universities have already performed the service of research to be used against foreign liberation movements in Vietnam, the Philippines and elsewhere; and against the domestic black liberation (mostly in the form of studies of urban and riot management, and of the black family). Why should they not be used again, against their own inhabitants?

Why not, indeed? And who will understand our violent bitterness then, or now, or our growing fear, save we who feel them too strongly for words, indelibly staining our hope?

From *Rolling Stone*, a special supplement by Michael Rossman 4/5/69

Margaret Mead says, truly, that young people are in modern times like native sons, whereas we others use the technology gingerly and talk like foreign born. . .

PAUL GOODMAN

Up against the wall, motherfucker

POLICE DEPT. FOLK SAYING adopted by strikers at Columbia

THE WORD

"... will bring us back to objective reality, however crude."

fuck (fŭk) *v.* **fucked, fucking, fucks.** —*tr.* **1.** *Vulgar.* To have sexual intercourse with. **2.** *Vulgar Slang.* To deal with in an aggressive, unjust, or spiteful manner. **3.** *Vulgar Slang.* To mishandle; bungle. Usually used with *up.* —*intr.* **1.** *Vulgar.* To engage in sexual intercourse. **2.** *Vulgar Slang.* To meddle; interfere. Used with *with.* —*n.* **1.** *Vulgar.* An act or instance of sexual intercourse. **2.** *Vulgar Slang.* A partner in sexual intercourse. [Middle English *fucken*; a Germanic verb originally meaning "to strike, move quickly, penetrate" (akin to or perhaps borrowed from Middle Dutch *fokken,* to strike, copulate with); details uncertain owing to lack of early attestations. See **peig-** in Appendix.*]

The American Heritage Dictionary of the English Language, Houghton Mifflin, 1969

Obscenity Fight Splits City of Wellesley After LeRoi Jones Play Is Given at High School

By J. ANTHONY LUKAS
Special to The New York Times

WELLESLEY, Mass.— It is nearly fall again, and soon the girls from the college will be wheeling their bikes through the crisp fallen leaves.

But unlike other college towns, where the students' return signals more demonstrations, Wellesley has not had time to worry about the college girls. It has been too busy worrying about what is going on at the high school.

For this leafy, well-groomed Boston suburb, best known for the college that bears its name, has been divided this summer by a dispute stemming from an allegedly "obscene" play presented at the high school last spring.

The angry dispute has brought to the surface some of the community's deepest anxieties about the country's race and youth rebellions, which many Wellesley residents fear threaten their way of life.

The culmination of the dispute will come today when two Wellesley High School teachers and a town resident are scheduled to appear for a preliminary hearing in Norfolk County District Court on a complaint by the town police that they introduced obscene matter into the school.

Penalty Is Defined

If convicted, they could be imprisoned for five years, fined up to $5,000, or both.

At issue is a 10-minute segment of LeRoi Jones's "The Slave," which was presented in the school gymnasium on May 31 as part of a "Program on Poverty and Racial Crisis in America."

The program was developed by several of the school's teachers and a community group called the Committee on Racism in response to a state directive that high schools study the implications of the report of the National Advisory Commission on Civil Disorders.

It included speeches by representatives of the Congress of Racial Equality, the Urban League and other groups; panel discussions, films contrasting suburban and slum life and a 50-minute program by the Boston Theater Company.

The racially mixed acting company presented, among other things, scenes from Richard Wright's "Native Son," Jean Genet's "The Blacks" and Bertolt Brecht's "The Exception and the Rule." But it was the 10-minute segment from "The Slave" that outraged several members of the audience.

The play, which Mr. Jones calls "a fable," is set at some future time when Negroes and whites are openly at war in America's streets. It describes the verbal and sometimes physical conflict between a black poet-guerrilla fighter, his former wife, who is a white woman, and her new husband, a white college professor.

Like most of Mr. Jones's plays, it is studded with four-letter words.

The 10 - minute segment chosen by the Boston Theater Company included only a few of the blunt words. But when they sounded through the gymnasium that night in May, several teachers walked out and tried to persuade the school principal, Samuel Graves, to stop the play. He refused to do so.

A few days later, saying they were acting on complaints by parents, the Wellesley police served notices for the hearing to Mrs. Kay Cottle, an English teacher; Thomas Fitzsimmons, a speech and drama teacher, and Pemberton F. Minster, an officer of the Wellesley Committee on Racism.

The hearing was delayed until today because Mrs. Cottle had a baby this summer.

Meanwhile, the community uproar was building up. On June 10 the School Committee held a public hearing in the high school auditorium, and 1,-200 persons showed up for what became one of the most tumultuous meetings in the town's long history.

According to persons who attended the hearing, the front rows were filled with several hundred students who demonstrated their support for the accused teachers and for the concepts behind the school program.

However, the students were outnumbered by angry adults. State Representative David Locke said that he had long been concerned by the trend in the area's schools, and the play confirmed his fears.

Sal Simone, a teacher at the school, said, "I am damned sick of what is going on here and shocked at the decline in moral strength."

Then the chairman recognized Edward Bryant Jr., a former model student who had just graduated. In a quiet voice, Mr. Bryant read a line from the play containing one of the four-letter words. He repeated the word for emphasis and then said, "I first heard that word right here in Wellesley when I was five years old."

As he calmly discussed the history of the word and its use, the adults in the audience began murmuring angrily. The murmurs grew to a roar, interspersed with shouts of "Kill him!" "Get him out of here!" and "Get him!"

Mr. Bryant was taken from the hall by a policeman, placed in handcuffs and charged with disorderly conduct. The case was later suspended after he agreed to apologize to the School Committee and publish an apology in a Wellesley newspaper.

Mrs. Pat Griffith, a leader of the Committee on Racism, contends that the furor over the play reflects a strong residue of bitterness among many residents over Wellesley's decision to participate in a program to bus black children into local schools.

The area-wide program, called the Metropolitan Council for Educational Opportunities, was opposed vigorously two years ago by Wellesley members of Americans for Constitutional Action and the John Birch Society.

A community of 26,000 persons with the highest median income in the state (close to $12,000 a year), Wellesley has only 13 Negro families, and the busing has clearly stirred fears among some people that the community will be inundated by Negroes.

The New York Times

In addition to simply uncovering the contradictions within the given usage, linguistic therapy requires a reversal of the present administered meaning of values and concepts, and the re-direction of these *against* the given social order.

The category of obscenity provides a case in point:

Obscene is not the picture of a naked woman who exposes her pubic hair but that of fully clad general who exposes his medals rewarded in a war of aggression; obscene is not the ritual of the Hippies but the declaration of high dignitary of the Church that war is necessary for peace.

In the language of radical politics, obscenities thus become part of the standard vocabulary—partly because obscenities form about the only area that has *not* been utilized in the publicity of domination.

The methodical use of "obscenities" in the political language of the radicals is the elemental act of giving a new name to men and things, obliterating the false and hypocritical name which the renamed figures proudly bear in and for the system.

Hence the following quote from *The Seed:* "Fighting for peace is like fucking for chastity." Unlike its usage in "ordinary language," the slogan "fighting for peace" is here grasped *as a contradiction,* and is immediately placed in the category where it belongs: obscenity. Again, "a systematic linguistic rebellion" is occuring in the language of the black militants: "Homosexuality is a sickness, just as are baby-rape or wanting to become the head of General Motors." Here Eldridge Cleaver states what would certainly be a contradiction in the administered hygiene of the language of advertising; yet is *not* a contradiction, and Cleaver deliberately places the ambition of the Rising Young Executive in the exact category where it belongs: sickness, obscenity. The politics of the pig thus emerge as part of a continuing effort at linguistic therapy, at calling things by their proper names. No longer are the Congressman, mayor, policeman, et. al., unanimously accorded the respect they may never have deserved; rather, they are called—"Pig."

Linguistic therapy thus acts as an essential element in the process of critical thinking. For through shattering the congealed whole of administered language, the irrationality of that whole—and of the society which it serves—is brought into the light of day. The mystification of rhetoric (political and otherwise), of "news" and of advertizing is thus broken. Critical thinking thus acts as a process of demystification, for

Today, the mystifying elements are mastered and employed in productive publicity, propaganda, and politics. Magic, witchcraft, and ecstatic surrender are practiced in the daily routine of the home, the shop, and the office, and the rational accomplishments conceal the irrationality of the whole. For example, the scientific approach to the vexing problem of mutual annihilation—the mathematics and calculations of kill and over-kill, the measurement of spreading and not-quite-so-spreading fallout, the experiments of endurance in abnormal situations is mystifying to the extent to which it promotes (and even demands) behavior which accepts insanity. It thus counteracts a truly rational behavior—namely, the refusal to go along, and the effort to do away with the conditions which produce insanity.

From "Herbert Marcuse and Happy Consciousness" by Donald Duclow,

LIBERATION Oct 1969

COLUMBIA: A WATERSHED

... I must help myself out from twilight and sleep... exert myself to arouse and shape half grown and halfdead faculties in myself, if I am not in the end to escape into a sad resignation, where one consoles oneself with other unripe and powerless beings, and, when a crisis comes, confronts the demand of humanity with one's negative virtue. Better the grave than such a state. HOLDERIN, 1794

Government is a monopoly on violence.

BAKUNIN

Wherever you want to go everything revolves around profit and private property. Those are the premises, and you can't question the logic. The logic is consistent. . .But there's a passion for religious meaning, for spirituality that's just been squelched for so long: people are dying for spirituality. *Me. I'm* dying.

PETER COHON, a member of the San Francisco Mime Troupe, a founder of the Diggers.

To enter history, each generation of youth must find an identity consonant with its own childhood and consonant with an ideological promise in the perceptible historical process. But in youth the tables of childhood dependence begin slowly to turn; no longer is it merely for the old to teach the young the meaning of life, whether individual or collective. It is the young who, by their responses and actions, tell the old whether life as represented by the old and as presented to the young has meaning; and it is the young who carry in them the power to confirm those who confirm them and joining the issues, to

renew and to regenerate, or to reform and to rebel.

ERIK H. ERIKSON, *Youth Change and Challenge* Basic Books, 1963.

Students are approaching the Establishment, trying to discover if they can chart their own destiny, if they can have greater control over it. One of the themes on our campus might be termed "impotent outrage." We want so badly to have an impact on the society in which we live.

KIRK HANSON, Stanford University, *Look* Magazine

It is almost as if they are the first real Americans — suddenly free of Europe and somehow fatherless, confused, forced back on their own experience, their own sense of things.

PETER MARIN

I know now that I'm not afraid to die.

TED GOLD, Vice Chairman of Columbia SDS during the Columbia Strike. Later a weatherman Died in 1970, in a bomb factory explosion.

Big Bust on Morningside Heights

MARVIN HARRIS

Mr. Harris is professor of anthropology at Columbia University and former chairman of the department. He is the author of The Nature of Cultural Things *(Random House) and the recently published* The Rise of Anthropological Theory *(Thomas Y. Crowell).*

At 2:30 A.M., Tuesday, April 30, a thousand New York City policemen attacked an approximately equal number of students barricaded inside five Columbia University buildings. The action lasted three hours and injured at least 148 persons in varying degrees. Many students were thrown or dragged down stairways. Girls were pulled out by the hair; their arms were twisted; they were punched in the face. Faculty members were kicked in the groin, tossed through hedges, punched in the eye. Noses and cheekbones were broken. A diabetic student fell into a coma. One faculty member suffered a nervous collapse. Many students bled profusely from head wounds opened by handcuffs wielded as weapons. Dozens of moaning people lay about the grass unattended. At one point an estimated 2,000 spectators were set upon by the police and pinned against the gates. Outside the campus, mounted police chased screaming knots of people, young and old, up and down Broadway in a scene from *Planet of the Apes*. It took a line of paddy wagons stretching along Amsterdam Avenue from 118th to 110th Street to carry off the 720 persons who were arrested. They were driven away, unrepentant, beating on the bars, cursing the police, President Grayson Kirk and Vice President David Truman.

It would seem self-evident that an event so contrary to the routine and purpose of a great university compels all who were its victims and participants to speak out concerning what happened, to establish the sequence of events, and to contribute to the analysis of both remote and immediate causes. Yet there are many members of the administration and faculty who feel that the well-being of Columbia requires rapid termination of all such inquiries, and the development of an attitude of studied indifference to the questions of who and what were responsible for the disaster. There is much talk about the need for "binding up the wounds" and for forgetting in a spirit of constructive reconciliation acts and statements produced under stressful circumstances.

I do not impugn the motives of the majority of these hushers and forgetters, but I do challenge their assumptions about what it will take to secure the university's future. The attempt to discover and disseminate truth is at all times the proper function of professors and students, but we all know that the truth seldom proclaims itself in a simple blinding image, jointly experienced by all observers. Establishing the truth in human affairs is in part a political process in which theories and anti-theories are the symbols of conflicting wills and countervailing interests. The search for the truth at Columbia is thus an aspect of an unfolding political struggle. Under these circumstances, to remain quiet in the name of academic dignity is to take a highly defined political position.

The number of Columbia faculty who are perfectly aware that political acts manifest themselves in not doing or saying as well as in doing and saying is probably as great as at any university in the world. Columbia's faculty are linked by personal and commercial bonds to New York's intellectual establishment, and many enjoy in their own right the privilege of being literary or sociological muezzins. Yet in the present crisis this enlightened faculty

has given little evidence that it comprehends how loudly dignified silence speaks for the *status quo*.

Most astonishing is the failure of the liberal Columbia establishment, hitherto identifiable by vanguard efforts in civil rights and the peace movement, collectively to take a principled and unambiguous position on a single important issue in the current dispute. While the buildings were occupied, the segment of the faculty from which an independent critique of the situation might have been expected consumed its energies in a futile attempt to mediate between the enraged students and the equally enraged administration. These mediation efforts were conducted by the steering committee of an informal, self-constituted group of concerned instructors and professors, who called themselves the Ad Hoc Faculty Committee. The good will and dedication of the majority of this group and of its steering committee are beyond dispute. Their analysis of what was happening, however, was inadequate. The actions and in-actions which they undertook, in conformity with certain false assumptions, resulted in a series of unintended disasters, culminating in the great bust.

By playing the role of mediator, this group actually prevented the beginning of negotiations between the administration and the students. The Columbia administration has repeatedly asserted that "we ignored no opportunity for negotiations," and the news media have stressed the assertion that student intransigence during negotiations between the administration and the strikers left the administration with no alternative but to call in the police. Contrary to popular impression, there were few sessions during which members of the students' strike steering committee and members of the administration actually met to talk with each other. To communicate with the students in Hamilton Hall—"liberated" by black students and converted to Malcolm X University—the administration relied on a number of high-level mediators supplied by the Mayor's office and the black community. As far as the students in the other four buildings were concerned, however, there appears to have been only one instance of what might be called a negotiating session. This took place early in the morning of Friday, April 26. Thereafter, for almost four days preceding the police action, there were no negotiations with the main body of the strikers. Instead, numerous delegated or self-appointed members of the Ad Hoc Faculty Committee rushed back and forth between the students and the administration, sounding out both sides with a series of proposals intended to serve as the basis for a start of negotiations. Some of these suggestions —as, for example, the so-called Galanter-Trilling-Hovde proposal for the creation of a tripartite disciplinary body —were actually voted on by the Ad Hoc Faculty Committee. But many other proposals that were dangled before the students were purely the result of the momentary fancy of the faculty mediators.

Even when a proposal had been voted on by the Ad Hoc Committee, the students were correct to view it with skepticism, since if they agreed to a particular point, there was no way for the Ad Hoc Committee to guarantee that the administration would endorse its side of the bargain. Several faculty mediators actually tried to split the strikers by deliberately proposing solutions which they knew would appeal to students in some of the buildings but not in others. It was common for faculty mediators to tell students that they had already won two of their main objectives—termination of the gymnasium project

Joining the president's office sit-in, Apr. 28

and severance of all ties with the Institute of Defense Analysis—and on this basis to appeal for the withdrawal of their other demands, especially the demand that the strikers not be punished. Yet the faculty mediators could not guarantee the ultimate decision of the administration on either of these issues and, by the existing charter of the university, were completely at the mercy of the Board of Trustees in all such matters. The faculty mediators asked the strikers to trust them, pledging their professional integrity and moral influence, but the students became increasingly distrustful of the divisive solicitation carried out by representatives of a faculty group whose legitimacy from the point of view of the administration was as dubious as that of the strikers themselves, and who in the actual situation seemed even more powerless.

Contrary to official pronouncements and to the misrepresentations of the mass media, there is no evidence that the Columbia administration ever seriously intended to clear the occupied buildings (with the exception of Hamilton Hall) by means of negotiation. The chronology of events at Columbia has been so complex and rapid that even many participants have forgotten that the police were first officially asked to intervene on the second day of the strike—12:30 A.M., Friday, April 26—four days before the actual bust. The circumstances of this call and the reasons why it did not result in an attempt to clear the buildings must be given due consideration. On Wednesday, the 24th, at an official meeting of the faculty of Columbia College (presided over by President Kirk and Vice President Truman) a motion had been passed asking for the peaceful settlement of the dispute and trusting that police action would not be used. The sentiment against police action was further confirmed on Thursday when more than 200 members of the Ad Hoc Committee affixed their signatures to a document, point 4 of which stated: "Until this crisis is settled, we will stand before the occupied buildings to prevent forcible entry by police or others." In conformity with this resolution, shifts of faculty volunteers had been maintaining a twenty-four-hour-a-day vigil at the entrances to the struck buildings. By late Thursday evening, however, there were many rumors indicating that the police were about to be used. At midnight, a high-ranking member of the administration appeared before the Ad Hoc Faculty Committee to insist that the rumors were baseless and that the administration did not contemplate any such action. One half-hour later a hush fell over the group as Vice President Truman—in his final appearance before the Ad Hoc Committee—entered the room. "I know you are not going to like what I have to tell you, gentlemen, but five minutes ago President Kirk was on the phone asking the Mayor for permission to use the police to preserve peace and order."

This announcement, coming so close on the denial, elicited voluminous hissing and booing and an almost unanimous cry of "shame!" Most of the faculty rushed from the room to take up positions in front of the buildings; a handful remained to phone the Mayor's office to ask that the police be stopped. Some contingents of police actually did go into action. At about 1:15 A.M. twenty-five plain-clothes men charged the entrance to Low Memorial Library and injured several faculty members who stood in their way. But the crowd around the building had grown to dangerous proportions. It included large numbers of faculty and students, some of them opposed to the strikers' demands but united in their opposition to the use of the police. The administration wavered and called off the action (which it had probably intended as a means of clearing only Low Memorial Library, leaving the other buildings to be dealt with on a separate basis).

To the faculty who had interfered it was made clear that the administration was determined to pursue a hard line and that under no circumstances would it consider amnesty for the strikers. Influential representatives of the faculty accepted the rejection of amnesty as an ultimate and unmodifiable condition. They merely argued that it

was too soon to resort to the police since there was still a possibility that some students could be split off and made to come out of the buildings by offering leniency rather than amnesty. The administration replied, in effect, that it would give the faculty a few more days to talk some sense into the strikers, and the sleepless faculty mediators hurried back to their task with a renewed sense of urgency.

But in accepting the administration's intransigence on the amnesty question, the faculty mediators ceased to be mediators and became instead the more or less unwitting accomplices of the administration's plans to use physical force to crush the strike and then to jail and expel the strike's leaders. When it gradually became clear to the students that the faculty mediators regarded the no-amnesty position as a requisite for negotiations, the strikers became increasingly hostile to and suspicious of the Ad Hoc Committee, and in some instances refused to speak further with its representatives.

The response of the faculty to the administration's threat to seek a bloody solution to its long-festering problems with radical students was either spineless or masochistic. This was an administration which could ill afford to give ultimatums to its professors. It was an administration which had foolishly risked the physical survival of the Morningside Heights campus by clinging to a disputed construction site in a public park overlooking what is perhaps the world's most volatile ghetto. Obviously, there are other ways to provide adequate gymnasium facilities. The university recently built a twelve-story school of business on top of the old gymnasium—Uris Hall, named after the family of one of the trustees—right in the center of the campus. A simple matter of dollars and cents prevented the remodeling of the old gymnasium under Uris or the construction of a new one in place of Uris. The park site, at $3,000 a year for 2.1 acres, seemed a tempting deal. But a university is not a construction firm or a discount department store; it is a semi-public corporation whose budget must include social costs and social benefits.

As officers of the corporation, the faculty could well appreciate the efforts made by the administration to hold the line on expenses and to manage the endowment funds with proper sobriety. The benefits of such policies could at least be passed on in the form of lower tuition and higher salaries. The paradox here is that tuition at Columbia has risen faster than the cost of living, while faculty salaries have barely kept pace with the rate of inflation. The only reason why there has not been a mass faculty exodus to schools which offer $4,000 to $5,000 per annum above Columbia's salaries at the associate professor level is that the artistic, intellectual and commercial fringe benefits of New York City subsidize the cost of keeping the faculty in place. On the other hand, the reason why the trustees have not been able to pay the faculty at the going market rate—according to a recent analysis of the fiscal condition of private universities carried out by the Ford Foundation—is that they have been unduly conservative in their investment policies. There has been too much concern with mortgages, not enough with common stocks. (The only institution with greater real estate holdings in Manhattan is the Catholic Church.) In other words they have been acquiring real estate—and thus making a mess of community relations—in the name of an investment policy which crippled the university's finances.

The trustees' capacity to subordinate social values to a false sense of economy is well illustrated in the case of the Strickman cigarette filter. In that instance the president of the university proposed to link increments in faculty salaries to the sale of carcinogens. On the basis of wholly inadequate research and testing, Dr. Kirk himself gave what amounted to a TV commercial in which the university urged the public to buy its filter because it produced less tar per puff. Kirk was later obliged to withdraw this claim under questioning by the U.S. Senate Commerce Committee, and subsequent tests carried out by qualified members of the university prompted the administration to

Blacks in occupied Hamilton Hall, Apr. 24.

After the bust. . . the beginning.

abandon its plans for cashing in on the cancer business.

There are further indignities for which the faculty might have been expected to hold the administration accountable. Not the least of these consists of a series of misrepresentations concerning the extent of university involvement with CIA cold-war research, especially through Columbia's Regional Institutes and the School of International Affairs. More immediate to the present crisis, however, was the assurance given by the dean of the Graduate Faculties to several hundred people in Low Memorial Library on March 23, 1967, that "Columbia has no institutional connection with IDA" (the Institute for Defense Analysis). Subsequently, student activists forced the administration to acknowledge that its graduate dean had been mistaken and that Columbia had been an institutional member of IDA since 1960. On March 30, 1967, IDA's vice president, Norman L. Christeller, informed the student newspaper: "We consider Columbia to be one of the three or four primary university sponsors of the IDA."

The most remarkable aspect of this confrontation between suspicious students and a less than candid or ill-informed dean, is that Columbia's connection with IDA was a public arrangement, the conditions of which were available to anyone who was curious enough to ask for IDA's unclassified reports. With one or two exceptions, however, Columbia's large contingent of pro-McCarthy, anti-Vietnamese War liberals (not to mention the politically apathetic center that makes up the majority of the faculty) remained ignorant of the university's tie with IDA or failed to grasp its significance. In this instance at least, the student activists carried out a genuine educational task on a matter of paramount importance to the entire university community. They did indeed educate their professors, however unorthodox their teaching methods.

Columbia's affiliation with IDA was institutionalized through a contract which named Grayson Kirk as a member of IDA's Board of Trustees. The chairman of the Board of Trustees of IDA is William A. M. Burden who, in addition to serving as a director of the Allied Chemical Corporation, American Metal Climax Corporation, Columbia Broadcasting System, Inc., Lockheed Aircraft Co., and the Manufacturers Hanover Trust Co., is also one of the trustees of Columbia University. In a brilliant example of the intellectual triviality of micro-focused political theory, Columbia's David Truman recently argued that Burden's additional affiliation with Columbia was a mere "accident." Other members of the administration have attempted to pooh-pooh the IDA tie on the ground that no substantial contracts have been established between IDA and Columbia for specific research purposes. (Kirk called IDA "a phony issue" on the C.B.S. program, *Face the Nation* May 5). Although it is true that direct contracts between IDA and Columbia have been negligible (one for $18,950 is known), IDA's influence on campus has been substantial indeed.

Through Lawrence O'Neil, former associate dean of Columbia's School of Engineering, the university has been deeply involved in projects coordinated by IDA. One of IDA's most important divisions is known as Jason. It is to the Jason Division that the Pentagon's Advanced Research Projects Agency assigned the task of coordinating work on the theoretical analysis of "ballistic missile defense and exoatmospheric nuclear detonations" (*Science*, 17 May 1968, Vol. 160, p. 746). O'Neil has been a steady consultant to IDA. O'Neil is also the director of what used to be Columbia's Electronic Research Laboratory, now called the Riverside Research Institute. Under O'Neil, the Electronic Research Laboratory enjoyed a budget of $5.5 million a year, much of it derived from classified research concerned with the development of radar systems for ballistic missile defense under contract with the above mentioned Advanced Research Projects Agency. No doubt this is another one of Dr. Truman's "accidents." Recently IDA has turned to research more directly associated with the Vietnamese War, concentrating on such projects as: Small Arms for Counter-Guerrilla Operations, Tactical Nuclear

Mark Rudd at gymsite, Apr. 23

Tearing down fence surrounding gym site, Apr. 23

Weapons, Chemical Control of Vegetation, Night Vision for Counter-Insurgents, Interdiction of Trucks from the Air at Night, and Helicopter Aural Detection of Tactical Situations. The extent of the university's involvement in these projects is suggested by the fact that when adjunct professor of physics, Richard Garwin, a member of IDA's Jason Division, took a trip to the Far East early this year, he touched off a world-wide rumor that tactical nuclear weapons were to be used in Vietnam [see "The Secret Thinkers," by Michael Klare; *The Nation*, April 15].

In 1965 IDA noted that it "was proud to grace the pages of our report with scenes of the campuses of our Twelve Member Universities" (see *Science*, 17 May, 1968, p. 748). I invite my colleagues who have husbanded the political independence of their university, and who have scrupulously refrained from using Columbia's name in their off-campus activities, except for identification purposes, to reflect on the audacity of a unilateral administrative decision which committed the entire university to the support of developing weaponry systems for a military clique.

It was the students who pressed for the exposure of Columbia's contribution to IDA. Having collected 1,800 signatures on a petition requesting the end of the university's connection with IDA, 200 students entered Low Memorial Library to confront Grayson Kirk with their findings. They were told that they were in violation of a ban on indoor demonstrations, and five of their leaders were placed on disciplinary probation. To protest this action, the students called a rally. Attended by more than 500 sympathizers, the rally ended in an abortive attempt to enter Low Memorial Library. The students were deflected by the campus guards, veered off toward Morningside Park, and pulled down the fence surrounding the gymnasium construction site. When one of the demonstrators was arrested by the police, the group returned to the campus. After some hesitation, they decided to invade Hamilton Hall, and to take a dean hostage in return, they said, for the student they had lost to the police. Thus the IDA issue met and fused with the gymnasium issue, leading directly to the strike and the big bust.

I share a feeling of repugnance with my liberal colleagues over the vulgarity and brashness of some of the actions of some of the students. A professor's sense of style is inevitably jarred by the crude slogans and tactics being used. From the students' point of view, however, there is, in turn, something seriously lacking in the faculty's style. From teaching too long, they apparently have forgotten how to be taught. They take their lessons very ungraciously and seem to want to make the students suffer for having achieved a superior understanding of the true nature of their university.

The failure of the administration to act quickly and seriously in response to various student charges concerning the university's complicity in the detested Vietnamese War contributed heavily to the breakdown of trust and communication between the student activists and their administrative counterparts. Columbia's destiny up to now has been under the control of a Board of Trustees consisting almost entirely of top-ranking businessmen—directors of more than sixty banks, insurance companies, utilities and manufacturing corporations including IBM, C.B.S., Con Ed, Ford, Equitable Life, Shell Oil, AT&T, Metropolitan Life, Irving Trust Co. and the Chase Manhattan Bank. Insofar as these men are leaders of bureaucratic empires which our best students associate with massive acts of social irresponsibility, evasion, hypocrisy and exploitation, their image is unsuited to attempts to establish cross-generational dialogues under the present circumstances. Nothing which the trustees of Columbia University have done during the past two years has indicated that the negative impression which they create on young minds thirsting for principled commitments to life and humanity is incorrect.

The disparity in class identity, and hence in social

values, between the trustees and the majority of students, is clearly one of the fundamental causes of the strike and of the catastrophic bust. Contempt for the "establishment" has reached crisis proportions throughout wide segments of the youth of the developed nations. Too many people in the older generation have tended to ignore or dismiss these manifestations of distrust and disillusionment as mere youthful aberration. Thus, the final indignity suffered by the faculty was that the administration had let its relations with the student body deteriorate to the point where five of the university's buildings were under siege, with the rest of the university virtually paralyzed. And then to solve the problem, the administration declared itself irrevocably determined to precipitate an even larger catastrophe by inviting the police to attack its own students and professors.

Why didn't the faculty step in and demand that the administration grant amnesty or, at the very least, indicate that it held the administration to be as much in need of amnesty as the students? Why didn't the faculty indicate its own unalterable determination to oppose a solution through force? Evidently, most of the faculty refused to accept the students' arguments on behalf of amnesty. These arguments rested on the following principle: The seizure of the buildings had been carried out in order to awaken the university community to the ethical blunders of the IDA affiliation and of the gymnasium site. Due to the authoritarian structure of the university, there were available no adequate democratic means of redress. Hence, amnesty rather than punishment was required, since people should not be punished for bringing about changes which, as among the faculty, were widely regarded as necessary and just. It should be noted, furthermore, that most of the faculty were convinced, even before the police action, that student interests were inadequately represented at the university. Indeed, after the bust, dozens of committees were formed at the departmental level to begin the work of making the university more democratic, thereby confirming the strikers' contention that the normal avenues of protest and communication had previously been inadequate.

Nevertheless, most of the faculty apparently accepted the administration's view. According to Kirk and Truman, the strikers had been duped by a small band of fanatical agitators who were bent upon achieving a confrontation with authority. If amnesty were granted, these agitators would be back in the buildings every other week, and the university would be incapable of discharging its educational responsibilities. Although the administration admitted that the claims about the lack of democratic representation were in part true, it held that the students had violated the rule of law. According to Truman, law and morality are identical. Hence, the transgressors must be punished. In accepting these arguments, it must be supposed that the faculty were especially concerned about the rifling of Grayson Kirk's files by strikers who occupied the president's office in Low Memorial Library.

I believe that there is a connection between the mentality expressed in the Columbia administration's viewpoint and that which was responsible for driving this country deeper and deeper into the Vietnamese War. It is the domino theory, all over again. If we don't punish the revolutionaries for taking over the president's office, how are we going to stop them from taking over the entire university? The answer, as we have almost learned in Vietnam, is that if there are well-formed structural reasons for mass resentments against existing laws and authority, the dominoes have a good chance of falling no matter how many policemen are brought in to shore them up. The threat of radical political change cannot be met by strategies which are temporarily successful in the prevention of muggings or shop lifting. On Tuesday, April 23, there were only about 150 hard-core members of Students for a Democratic Society (and most of these were opposed to a confrontation). A week later, at the height

of the strike, more than 6,000 students were actively expressing their hostility to the Columbia administration. Was this the work of a handful of superstudents whose demagogic skills proved too much for the honest defenders of the university's good name? The proposition is as absurd as trying to blame the Third World's hostility toward America on agitators like Che Guevara or General Giap. On Thursday, April 25, a referendum at Columbia, carried out under independent student auspices, showed that students were in favor, 4,093 to 1,433, of ending construction of the gymnasium. The vote for ending ties with IDA was carried, 3,572 to 1,855. (In large part the strikers in the buildings did not vote.)

It is clear that the original handful of protesters had been able to convince 1,000 of their fellow students to join them in the occupation of the buildings at great personal risk because the issues involved in the strike were relevant to the deeply felt social needs of additional thousands of students. To propose that amnesty would have meant recurrent invasions of Low Memorial Library at the whim of irresponsible anarchists is to insult the intelligence and to demean the social conscience of many of the university's brightest and most responsible students. They were not in those buildings to protest a ban on panty raids, or to demand higher grades or better food in the dorms. The issues involved were of supreme importance: racial prejudice and *de facto* discrimination; complicity of the educational establishment in the slaughter of an innocent peasantry. As long as the university's policies remain ambiguous on these issues, it can expect periodic visitations from larger and more militant striking bodies. Calling in the police at Columbia or elsewhere will only make such confrontations bigger.

I regard it as regrettable that the strikers broke into President Kirk's files and copied documents out of his private correspondence. But breaking into official files (the strikers refused to acknowledge Kirk's right to have secrets about Columbia) was not the worst offense. The most serious act was the overnight detention of the acting dean of Columbia College and two of his assistants in Hamilton Hall. This was the only instance in which the strikers could be said to have committed crimes against persons as opposed to crimes against property. After 5:00 A.M., Thursday, April 25, all of the white strikers left Hamilton Hall and the hostages were held until 3:00 P.M. by black students. In addition to holding hostages, some of the blacks (allegedly nonstudents) were said to have been in possession of firearms. These same students threatened the administration with the specter of mobs summoned up from Harlem who would burn the campus to the ground. When Rap Brown and Stokely Carmichael broke through the police barriers on Friday, April 26, to confer with the blacks inside Hamilton Hall, the very survival of the university hung in the balance.

Despite the violent nature of the threats which the blacks in Hamilton posed, the administration's strategy from the outset was to deal with the white students in the four other buildings on a separate and harsher basis. Mediators sent by the Mayor's office—William Booth, Theodore Kheel and Sid Davidoff—conferred with the blacks in Hamilton, but not with the whites in the other buildings. According to David Truman (as quoted in *Newsweek*, May 13), the blacks were immediately made "an offer of nothing more than disciplinary warning" (virtual amnesty). The reason for this special treatment, said Truman, was that the blacks were "a totally different cut as far as performance is concerned," as compared with the whites. "I must say I admire the way they conducted themselves." This novel form of racism appealed to others as well. At the Ad Hoc Committee, distinguished professors arose to plead for separate treatment of the blacks on the ground that they had behaved like gentlemen, while the whites in the other buildings were like wild beasts. Finally, late in the afternoon preceding the bust, when many members of the faculty knew that the police action was

On ledge outside President Kirk's office, Apr. 19.

The march to Harlem May 1, following police raid.

imminent, Prof. Lionel Trilling openly argued that the time had come for granting amnesty to the blacks and only to the blacks!

One of the consequences of this indulgent attitude toward black strikers was that none of the black students in Hamilton Hall was injured during the bust. They exited through underground tunnels under the watchful eyes of William Booth and Kenneth Clark. While Clark and Booth complimented the police on their exemplary handling of the black students, pandemonium reigned in front of and inside the other buildings. (Clark, however, later condemned the police action in the rest of the campus.) What was said to the black students in order to get them to walk quietly into the paddy wagons is a source of continuing speculation. The point here, however, is that many faculty members, who found the notion of amnesty abhorrent when applied to the white students, found themselves ready to forgive and forget when it came to the blacks—even though the blacks took hostages and constituted the gravest physical threat to the university.

It is clear that the harsher punishment recommended for the white students (and already received by them at the hands of the police) has nothing to do with principles of law and equity. There are plenty of precedents in the labor movement and in the civil rights movement in this country for granting amnesty to demonstrators who have committed trespass. Recently the Uniformed Sanitationmen's Association staged a strike in defiance of the laws of the state of New York. Their action resulted in the accumulation of refuse in the streets to the point of menacing the health of 8 million people. When Mayor Lindsay put their leader in jail, the Governor of New York, Nelson Rockefeller himself, granted him a pardon!

Local kids climb on Alma Mater, May

In the light of the recent history of Columbia's administration, it is difficult to accept Kirk and Truman's assurance that they took a hard line only because it slowly dawned on them that they were up against a completely cynical band of opportunists and demagogues. Everyone seems to have forgotten that an unprecedented shake-up in administrative personnel took place less than a year ago in which the provost and dean of faculties, the vice president and the dean of the graduate faculties, among others, abruptly resigned en masse. Truman, who was then dean of Columbia College, moved up to the specially created post of provost and vice president, leaving only an ineffectual acting dean behind him in the college. At the same time, the post of dean of graduate faculties was left unfilled. Thus during the month immediately preceding his fatal confrontation with the students, Truman was in virtually unqualified control of the statutory or *de facto* powers formerly possessed by two deans, the provost and the vice president!

Nor was this an "accident." The massive shake-up in question occurred shortly after the launching of Columbia's $200 million fund drive, the largest ever undertaken by a "private" university. To explain the sudden departure of almost every top-ranking administrator except Kirk, the university issued a statement in which the success of fund-raising activities was said to depend upon the greater centralization of administrative authority. The significance of this explanation was lost upon the majority of the faculty and students. The main problem in reaching the $200 million goal was not, as it then seemed, a question of lack of coordination and organizational diffuseness. Rather, the problem was that pressure from the neighborhood community and from the "radical" anti-draft and anti-war students threatened to blow the whole university sky-high. It is known, for example, that the former provost, Jacques Barzun, was unable or unwilling to control his contempt in the presence of neighborhood protesters. It was known also that former Vice President Lawrence Chamberlain was far too concerned about the disagreeable side effects which occur when unruly students are squashed down to size. His departure for a prolonged fishing trip in Colorado marked the end of ideology at Columbia. Truman took power precisely because he thought he knew how to

keep the lid on, at least until the fund drive was completed: it was the hard line.

Almost exactly one year before the big bust, the pattern for disaster had been laid down in conformity with Truman's understanding of the science of campus politics. The SDS, in familiar possession of the university's jugular, was about to administer the *coup de grâce* to $200 million. They were seeking to prevent the United States Marine Corps from recruiting on campus. There had already been an ugly brawl when a group of college athletes attempted to clear out several hundred protesters who were baiting the Marines about Vietnam. The Marines left the campus, but they were scheduled to return the next day. What to do? The crowds would be bigger and both sides would be more eager for violence. Yet how could a needy American campus refuse to play host to those widely traveled, clean-cut patriots? The Marines came back, largely on Truman's assurance that he could maintain order. Two groups of opposing students, numbering perhaps 1,000 on each side, threatened each other throughout the day; but aside from a few minor fist fights, Truman's decision seemed to have been vindicated. Asked why he had chosen to risk the physical welfare of so many of his students on behalf of an organization which had nothing to contribute to campus life, and which did not lack for opportunities to get its message across to the nation's youth, Truman replied: "If we had given in, there would have been no end to their demands. We had to stand firm or they would eventually try to take over Low Library."

The students, outraged by the moral ambiguities of the administration's response to their substantive demands, escalated their own tactics to meet the challenge of Truman's campus *Realpolitik*. When the administration placed a ban on indoor demonstrations, they collected their 1,800 signatures and held a demonstration inside Low. Truman played the hard line again and tried to pick off the five most important leaders of SDS with disciplinary probations. Meanwhile, the fund drive was lagging and the pressures to keep the campus quiet were greater than ever. At some unknown point, well before the bust, it became clear to Truman that his career as an administrator was now wholly dependent on his ability to rid the campus of the band of agitators who refused to knuckle under to his textbook show of force. Similarly, the idea at some point got across to the students that only the most radical of measures stood a chance of deflecting Kirk and Truman from their determination to sanitize the campus and to ignore the justice of the students' substantive claims. I do not condone the student take-over of the university buildings, but I regard it as wholly undemonstrable that the administration was interested in providing the students with genuine alternatives.

After the bust, when Truman was asked at a press conference if he had any advice to give other college administrators, he replied without hesitation: "Don't wait. Call in the police." Apparently, he still believes that the only thing wrong with his hard line was that it wasn't hard enough (especially when he hesitated because a few faculty members had gotten in the way).

Four weeks after the bust the students were back in Hamilton Hall. In the "second battle of Columbia," another 170 students were arrested and an even more vicious and uncontrolled display of police brutality was unleashed across the campus. Flailing out on their own, with a premeditated disregard of constitutionally guaranteed rights of due process, the administration is moving toward the suspension or expulsion of perhaps as many as 500 of its students whom it has charged with criminal trespass. In this grim fashion political identities will be acquired by the various segments of the university. Members of the faculty, who have been so troubled to decide if they approve or disapprove of meeting the complaints of their students by wounding and expelling them, will have plenty of additional opportunities to make up their minds.

Radicals try to evict non-strikers from Fayerweather Hall using fire hose and clubs, May.

COLUMBIA:

TO STRIKE
IS ONLY A
BEGINNING

Strike leadership included Mark Rudd (2nd left) and Ted Gold (extreme left). Gold died in an accidental Weatherman bomb explosion in a N.Y. City townhouse, early 1970.

ROAR lion ROAR ?

The scene was the same, as was the action; the result, however, was quite different. One year to a day after a thousand cops marched onto the Columbia campus and dragged students out of buildings, 200 students—mostly members of Columbia SDS—occupied two buildings on the Columbia campus. A day later they left, not as conquering heros this time, but almost as young Mafiosi, hiding their faces from the cameras. For the "nth" time this year SDS (this time it was *only* SDS) had failed to mobilize the campus.

The situation at Columbia—this year as well as last—may best be defined by what happened outside of the buildings. There was some establishment justice in the unselective police clubbings of students outside of the buildings last year, for students in and out of the buildings were spiritual complicitors in the same movement (Spock's judge may have been a bad constitutionalist but he was a good sociologist). They all belonged to a growing moral community last year; those in the buildings were only part of it, catalyzing, defining and symbolizing it by their actions.

This situation was different this year; those outside the buildings just watched. Significantly, many, if not most, of those outside of the buildings this year had been in the buildings last year. A good number met for the first time in a year. This time, however, they watched, rather than participated and asked each other, "Why aren't you in the buildings?" Last year's participants were this year's observers. Last years observers were not even sufficiently interested to come and watch; they stayed home, or in the libraries, or went to class.

Columbia SDS's plight this year was ironic. Rebellion died with a whimper at The American College which precipitated and set the model for this year's widespread campus rebellions. This failure took place in spite of a much greater and more conscious attempt to organize the campus—SDS even tried to reach athletes and fraternity members—and in the presence of a situation which seemed ripe for another rebellion. There was no McCarthy to "co-opt" students this year; there was almost no one to argue that disruption was not sometimes necessary or legitimate. There was a student body which defined itself as "radical" and a student newspaper which was much more consciously activist and intolerant of the administration and faculty than in past years. Yet from registration day SDS almost never attracted more than a few hundred students to its rallies.

Many explanations have and can be offered to deal with the present situation at Columbia. Most are elitist insofar as they deal with individuals or groups—the administration, the faculty, SDS—rather than with the student body which is more important. Some merely deal with symptoms, e.g., the effect of the use of injunctions, rather than causes, e.g., why the injunction was effective. All (including this one) are highly ideological, for in a polarized academic community and nation we all have intellectual and emotional needs to explain away or to define into controllable terms the conflict in which we all in one way or another participate. Yet what happened at Columbia must be understood, for this year's events, like last year's, may be symptomatic of the general state of student radicalism.

Two things must first be noted for those who know Columbia only through the *New York Times* and similar apologists for the university. The administration, faculty and trustees have not changed, in spite of better public relations (Columbia hired a new PR firm to handle its image) and a few general statements regarding restructuring which most students understand to be nothing more than talk. Cordier may be smarter than Kirk, but he still makes mistakes. For example, when two weeks before the "big events" a few hundred students occupied Philosophy Hall, the administration got a restraining order and sent university policemen to serve it in spite of the decision of students inside the building to leave in a few hours. The administration's action precipitated some violence and again showed the administration to be paranoid, stupid, and inflexible. The faculty too, once "normalcy" was restored, showed itself hard to reach and unwilling to share significant power or responsibility with students. The famous Columbia Senate—which grossly underrepresents students—was imposed from above and legitimated in an all-or-nothing plebiscite. As one candid senior faculty member said regarding the restructuring of the history department, if you want power you are going to have to take it, for we do not consider your demands legitimate or just. The trustees also have continued in the ways of the past. They, too, made it clear that they would not give up any real power and delayed deciding about ROTC for about two months.

There was no lack of "issues" this year either. Instead of the Strickmann filter there was the Rockland land controversy. Instead of Grayson Kirk, there was the gift to Grayson Kirk of an estate in Riverdale ("to raise money") which could have been applied to much better academic use. Instead of IDA (although secret research continues) there was ROTC. Instead of the gym (we still do not know where it is going to be built) there were more evictions and a continuing elitist admissions policy (there may be as many as one black student in the History Department). The list could go on and on, but the point is that if Columbia deserved to get it last year, it deserved it this year too. If anything, it deserved it more, for students knew a great deal more about the intransigence of those who wield power. (To again paraphrase a senior member of the history faculty, students come to Columbia for one reason: to be graded; hence they cannot grade the graders.)

But issues and attitudes do not tell the whole story. They tend to be symbolic and their expression ritualistic. The major functions of issues may be to delegitimize the authority of those who have power and to rationalize actions which may be participated in for more subjective and less articulatable reasons. Student mood, and subjective reality, play a very important role.

When students returned to Columbia last fall it was clear that many were emotionally spent. The preceding spring had been a truly creative period and a great catharsis. That and Chicago had drained a great deal of political energy out of many (one must remember that they spent a good deal of the summer explaining and rationalizing over and over again the spring's events to friends, parents and strangers). While the more politically oriented were drained, many of the less political students who had suffered from a great deal of anomie in the spring when normal social processes had broken down, needed some sort of authority to identify with. Neither tired radicals nor isolated SDS leaders nor the clearly impotent moderate leaders were able to provide persuasive leadership. In this situation many students returned to their traditionally atomized life hoping for stability.

The process of restructuring and the "temporary" nature of the Cordier administration further drained the remaining energy and diffused, sublimated, and postponed anger. Restructuring committees proliferated around the campus, most groups not knowing what the others were doing, and held forth the promise of some change. While students exerted a great deal of effort running from committee to committee, students found that the problem of changing a vast institution in which areas of authority and action

Opposition to building occupations.

tend to overlap was depressingly complex. Restructuring was an exclusive rather than inclusive process as it necessitated small committees. Many activists were effectually coopted by the process of restructuring for as student representatives they had more access to faculty members and gained a separate status in their relations with the faculty. At the same time Cordier's presence was less obnoxious than Kirk's. He was new and temporary, and while clearly insincere, he proved to be much less obnoxious and dislikable than Kirk. His license plate was not ACI and while he was as invisible as Kirk, he did not shiver when he saw students. Such mundane and irrelevant factors tend to inhibit rebellions.

There were problems but it is not clear that they could not have been overcome. Restructuring, for example, could and did in many cases expose the nature of power at Columbia. One should not be confused by the SDS-administration-*NY Times* definition of radicalism and alienation which tends to only identify certain manifest expressions of radicalism. One can be radical and not be in SDS. One can be radical and not want to disrupt daily. One can even be angry and not show it. One of the major causes of student anger and frustration is atomization and that atomization in many cases precludes demonstrable expression of alienation—until tapped.

Due to the heterogeneous and unorganized nature of radicalism at Columbia only one group could tap that

alienation this year: SDS. It could be because it was organized, because it received most of the media attention, because it had some continuity in leadership, because it was the only real institutionalized expression of campus-focused radicalism which at all extended beyond departments and schools, and because no matter what they did, non-SDS radicals were identified with SDS by those who they were trying to reach. (Distrust of SDS, for example, hindered organization of the non-SDS Graduate Students Union.) SDS could not take advantage of this opportunity.

SDS failed for a large number of reasons. As noted in a *WIN* article last year, SDS isolated itself by *appearing* to be manipulative* and by not dealing with the issue which primarily concerned students: restructuring. By the fall, many students, including a large number of radicals were both distrusting of and antipathetic toward SDS. When SDS acted in the fall it *appeared* to be disrupting for disruption's sake. It continued to opt away from dealing with those issues which directly affected students' lives such as restructuring and the draft. (Restructuring may be a misleading issue and students may be naive; but at times in order to lead and expose it may be necessary to particpate in what one finds stupid. SDS was unable to do this, I fear, because many of its members were more concerned with appearing to be radical than with succeeding as radicals.) SDS members continued to talk in a rhetoric which

many students saw as cant, irrelevant, and intellectually embarrassing. And as one member of SDS warned the day before the two-building occupation, you have to talk to people, not at or down to them, if you are going to reach them. On top of everything else, SDS tended to be boring. It seemed to be repeating itself and was very predictable. Not only did this help the administration to cope with it, but it made the group even more unattractive to those who had to be convinced; a revolution may have to be interesting in order to succeed.

SDS's main problem is shared by most of the New Left: a lack of long term strategy. This leads to an unattractive form of goal displacement in which disruption (the means) becomes an end in itself. It also limits the ability to attract others to what appears to be an irrelevant action by explaining the long term purpose of that action—for example, how does one justify a demand directed at the Columbia administration to free the Panther 21? When one cannot justify demands which appear to be irrelevant to the needs of potential supporters, one can only depend on mood. The right mood was absent this spring, given that fact it might have been advisable to wait.

But SDS did not wait. It didn't because it felt compelled to act in some way and disruption seemed to be the only course; it didn't because it exaggerated its role in last year's uprisings. But even here it might not have been lost: (1) if its choice of Black demands and the decision to make them non-negotiable did not seem to be opportunistic and at times contradictory, (2) if it did not effectively announce its intentions in advance and inform the left liberals that SDS knew—even if they didn't—that the liberals would ultimately join, (3) if it realized that when there is little potential for action, catalysts have nothing to catalyze. On top of all this the target was wrong. Low Library or the Business School or the Riverside Research Labs or the ROTC office or some other places would have been more attractive targets to many students.

I do not like to dump on SDS, especially since many non-SDS radicals have not done much to help it. In addition, SDS-baiting tends to be the great rationalization for a cop out by both students who do not want to act and by those in power who do not want to move. Yet SDS's failures like its successes affect much more than its own organization since its adversaries, and the media have made SDS the personification of radicalism. Thus when Columbia SDS blew it this spring, it may have blown it for others also.

The mistakes are understandable. If SDS members listened to the *Times* the administration, or many of Columbia's erudite social analysts, they

would tend to overestimate their role. It is also very hard to know what to do now. Political frustration is historically and socially structured and student radicals are now feeling the crux of it. Yet such frustration may lead to counterproductive actions, and I fear that all of last year's actions were counterproductive. It seems to me that there are two basic political requirements for campus actions. If these are not met, the campus may merely become a lightning rod for political activity which might better be expended off the campus. Actions must lead to concrete goals or strengthen the movement. At this time the movement can be strengthened by expanding its size and scope—the radicalization of others or the expanding of their political consciousness. Ritualistic actions, such as the current disruptions, may also reinforce existent political attitudes or function as rites of passage. The achievement of these goals depends on inclusiveness, not exclusiveness, on reaching people, not turning them off.

Not only were people turned off this year, but many of those who were turned away were previously susceptive to being moved because of the nature of least year's events. It is hard to overestimate the psychic importance of last year's actions to many moderate and left-liberal students. Their actions became for them a statement of commitment and of community with their fellow students and generation. In Durkheim's terminology, last year was a sacred period, while this one was profane—a return to the mundane. SDS did not have to be contained; it contained itself. Buildings may have been occupied, but the normal processes of the university went on. As last year's events demonstrated, if power is in the people and you have the people, you can shut down an institution with very little force. The time for criticism is now, not after the next mistake—a time for all radicals to think about the effects of their own actions or inactions.

—David Osher

* *I would like to point out for those individuals who have used my article to condemn student radicalism that to point to manipulation is to both condemn and to state a fact of political life. The faculty and administration also manipulate. Unfortunately the name of the game is not to get court.*

 June 1969

GUIDED MISSILE FROM THE GHETTO

. . .then, as if a signal had been given, as if the Mind had shouted to the Body, "I'm ready!"—the Twist, superseding the Hula Hoop, burst upon the scene like a nuclear explosion, sending its fallout rhythms into the Minds and Bodies of the people. The fallout: the Hully Gully, the Mashed Potato, the Dog, the Smashed Banana, the Watusi, the Frug, the Swim. The Twist was a guided missile, launched from the ghetto to the very heart of suburbia. The Twist was a form of therapy for a convalescing nation. . .(which) responded so dramatically. . .to the Twist precisely because it afforded them the possibility of reclaiming their Bodies again after generations of alienated and disembodied existence. . . They came from every level of society. . . feeling. . .release from some unknown prison in which their Bodies had been encased, a sense of freedom they had never known before, a feeling of communion with some mystical root-source of life and vigor, from which sprang a new awareness and enjoyment of the flesh, a new appreciation of the possibilities of their Bodies. . .

This spectacle truly startled many Negroes, because they perceived it as an intrusion by the Mind into the province of the Body, and this intimated chaos;. . . These Negroes knew something fundamental had changed.

"Man, what done got into them ofays?" one asked.

"They trying to get back," said another.

"Shit," said a young Negro who made his living by shoplifting. "If you ask me, I think it must be the end of the world."

"Oooo-weee!" said a Negro musician who had been playing at a dance and was now standing back checking the dancers. "Baby, I don't dig this action at all! Look here, baby, pull my coat to what's going down! I mean, have I missed it somewhere? Where've I been? Baby, I been blowing all my life and I ain't never dug no happenings like this. You know what, man, I'm gon' cut that fucking weed alcose. Oooo-weee! Check tha little bitch right there! What the fuck she trying to do? Is she trying to shake it or break it? Oooo-weee!"

A Negro girl said: "Take me home, I'm sick!"

Another one said: "No, let's stay! This is too much!"

And a bearded Negro cat,. . .he said, sitting at the table with a tinsel-minded female: "It ain't nothing. They just trying to get back, that's all."

"Get back?" said the girl, arching her brows quizzically, "Get back from where?"

"From wherever they've been," said the cat, "where else?"

From *Soul On Ice* by Eldridge Cleaver

(From my student, V): yr whole body moves in a trained way & you know that youve moved this way before & it contains all youve been taught its all rusty & slow something is pushing under that rusted mesh but STILL YOU CANNOT MOVE you are caught between 2 doors & the old one is much closer & you can grab it all the time but the other door it disappears that door you cant even scratch & kick (like the early settlers were stung by the new land) but this new land doesnt even touch you & you wonder if youre doing the right thing to get in

• • • • • • •

(From Paul Radin: *Primitive Man as Philosopher*):
It is conceivably demanding too much of a man to whom the pleasures of life are largely bound up with the life of contemplation and to whom analysis and introspection are the self-understood prerequisites for a proper understanding of the world, that he appreciate. . .expressions which are largely non-intellectual—where life seems, predominatingly, a discharge of physical vitality, a simple and naive release of emotions or an enjoyment of sensations for their own sake. Yet. . .it is just such an absorption in a life of sensations that is the outward characteristic of primitive peoples.

PETER MARIN

step on his head
James Laughlin

Let's step on daddy's head shout
the children my dear children as
we walk in the country on a sunny

summer day my shadow bobs dark on
the road as we walk and they jump
on its head and my love of them

fills me all full of soft feelings
now I duck with my head so they'll
miss when they jump & they screech

with delight and I moan oh you're
hurting you're hurting me stop and
they jump all the harder and love

fills the whole road but I see it run
on through the years and I know
how some day they must jump when

it won't be this shadow but really
my head (as I stepped on my own
father's head) it will hurt really

hurt and I wonder if then I will
have love enough will I have love

Catch a Nigger by the Toe If He Hollers Let Him Go
sandy darlington

Well hello, it's little modern America! You woke up in the middle of the night and found yourself alone and it's upset you. Now you come toddling into my head in your Doctor Dentons looking for comfort. But instead of greeting me with sleepy hellos, you've got a shrieky Halloween mask on, and you're banging a drum and throwing up all over me.

What did you do to deserve this? You ate a nigger by the toe, didn't you, and now it's got you a tummy-ache, so you have these nightmares about slant-eyed Charley Chan Chinese laundry boys, and it's tearing you apart.

You're such a young country to be having such bad dreams. It wasn't long ago that you were all forests and free animals. The people who lived here then didn't know they were the First Americans, they were just people. And they lived accordingly. And to give riches to the people, the beautiful cactus held up their fingers and showers of diamonds sparkled from them in the clear light of dawn. Long before there was a Tiffanys. Long before there was a jewelry store

But you, little America, have become Modern and Responsible, and you've forgotten all that, and now you're in a hurry to die because you can't figure out how to live. Betty told Dupree, Daddy, I want a diamond ring. And Dupree told Betty, you can have most anything. Then the fool went out and did his version of a 9 to 5, which was to knock off a jewelry store. Of course he got killed in the end, in the good old American clean-living, clean-dying electric chair.

woman? No, he was led astray by himself, because although he wanted her so bad, he didn't know how to just come out and say: I want you so bad. So he did it on a rabbit and carrot stick basis: If I get you that diamond, can I have you, huh? A swap. Cash on the line for goods received. Whereas if he was really ready to love her, he would have said: It's just me and you, baby. And then they would have lived together.

But because your whole melodrama is your inability to come right out and do anything affectionate, you flip over Bonnie and Clyde. It's not because they are beautiful heroes and lovers, it's because he is a stupid hick who can't get a hard-on, and she is strung out on diet pills but from a good family, and they yearn for each other but they are on such entirely different wave lengths that the only thing they can think to do together is rob banks.

That's the same way with you, little America. You can't figure out how to groove in your own land, so you go out and burn down a whole continent of little yellow people. Or you buy a gun and rant about law and order.

And to show where you are really at, you come up with a slogan like Stand Up For America. What kind of bad phallic symbol joke is that? We thought vaudeville was dead, and here it is running for President. And it's all because although you're a young and strong and rich and beautiful country, you just can't seem to let yourself go, to just let it happen.

So you play with your juvenile political conventions and you use your cops and robbers against us and black people. In the name of freedom, you want to make the rules tighter. You want us to be Standardized Americans. It seems to make good sense to your modern way of thinking, but it's really hopeless, and it's a crime against the real law and order, against nature, against all the eternity you are ignoring. You are trying to regain your own lost youth and innocence by destroying your children. It can't be done.

You come to me (and here I flash on all the hordes of news analysts, educators, Senators, social workers, cops, and in-depth on-the-spot reporters who come flocking to Youth with their faces full of ??????) and you look up to me like I was Cary Grant and you were a ten-year-old kid, and you say, "What's the answer?"

And I say, "Be yourself, just live, let it start from there."

Then you look at me, with that Archie-incredulous look on your face: Aw gee, coach, there must be more to the game than that. But that's it: there is no game. Then, instead of the Gala Epic you were waiting for, I tell you a simple tale about meeting a girl on the street and getting laid, and how we have a lot of friends we like to hang out with.

And then you stop me short and say, "No, no, I don't want to hear that, I want to hear the real story."

That's such a bring down until I realize that the reason you do it is because you don't know any better. You're such a young country. You'll learn some day. Then you'll forget all the horseshit about merit badges and wedding nights and fraternities and patriotism and being In.

You'll find out that it's all a story about some people who got together and dug each other. Then, maybe, little America, you'll be able to groove on my story, which will be yours too, and it will settle your stomach ache, and maybe you'll cheer up and relax a little and quit pointing that shotgun at me and my friends.

San Francisco
Express Times

Joan McWilliams is having what she calls "marriage try-outs" with boys, protecting herself against pregnancy with a bootlegged supply of birth-control pills that she bought with her piggy-bank savings last June.

The girl, who asked that her name be disguised, is 16 and a junior in a Manhattan private high school. She talked over many cups of coffee, and with many nervous tugs at her shoulder-length hair, in the Starks restaurant at Madison Avenue and 78th Street, a meeting place for many East Side young people.

Offers Two Reasons

Of the three affairs she has had since June she said: "My parents don't know anything about what I'm doing. Why should they? It's my business. And besides, I know what they would say, that a girl should stay a virgin until she gets married. They don't really believe that any more than I do, but they think they have to say it.

"Well, I won't be getting married for a long time. Not until I go to college for a couple of years at least. So what am I supposed to do until then, live like a nun? I don't know anyone else who does."

Joan offered two reasons for what she was doing: It was helping her to grow up and it was helping her to prepare for marriage.

But then she added: "I don't kid myself, and since you aren't going to use my name I won't kid you either. One, I just don't want to wait until I'm 21 or 22. Life's too short to wait for anything as important as sex. The other is the pill. If I couldn't use the pill or something just as sure, I'd be scared to try it, to go with any boy. There's too much to lose."

WHAT IS THERE TO WORRY ABOUT?

Marijuana Users Are Sociable, Michigan Student Survey Finds

LANSING, Mich., Dec. 16 (UPI) — Researchers said today that the results of a questionnaire administered to Michigan high school seniors did not show that young people who use marijuana seek to withdraw from society.

They said marijuana smokers appeared to be more likely than nonsmokers to participate in political activities and become involved in social change.

"Marijuana users, judging from our data, do not seem to be 'copping out' or withdrawing from society," the researchers said in a 48-page report.

The survey was conducted by Dr. Roy G. Smith of the University of Hawaii School of Public Health, Richard A. Bogg of the University of Michigan School of Public Health and Susan D. Russell of Michigan State University.

It was coordinated by the Michigan Health Department under the direction of a legislative subcommittee on alcoholism and drug use.

The researchers said the eight-month study involved 1,379 seniors from 11 high schools of varying sizes in rural and urban areas.

The students were given questionnaires in classrooms and study halls and were assured that their names would not be used.

"Our data appeared to support the thesis that drug use by young people, particularly use of marijuana, represents a social form of recreation far removed in nature from the traditional problem of narcotics addiction or alcoholism," the researchers said.

State Representative Dale Warner, the subcommittee chairman, said the survey underscored the need for a "total re-evaluation and reform of our drug control laws" to combat the use of drugs among young people through education and rehabilitation.

Danger Is Doubted

"The medical evidence on marijuana is less than convincing, and students may be aware of this fact," the report said. "Overstatement of the dangers of marijuana use may serve to discredit the spokesman."

The "typical" high school marijuana user, according to the study, drinks alcoholic beverages and smokes cigarettes regularly.

He is male, though many females reported using the drug, and he does as well in school as the nonuser. He dates earlier and is more socially minded.

The user tends to be activist and to be critical of adults and the war in Vietnam. He is not alienated from his surroundings, the report said.

The New York Times

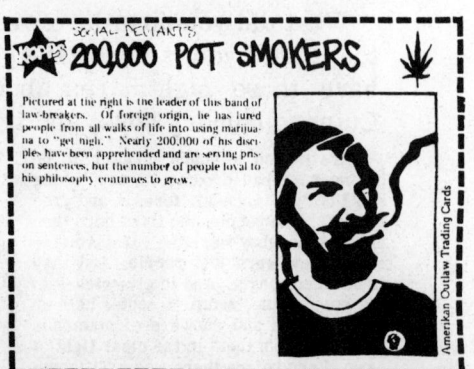

MAYBE THIS IS A VERY GOOD THING

War is war perverted. The problem is not the war but the perversion. And the perversion is a repression; war is sex perverted. 'War is energy enslav'd.'

N.O. BROWN, *Love's Body*

And then there is Wayne of Berkeley: "We started expressing ourselves and it was accurate because we could feel it. Through our conversations we really got to like each other [several months after they were already living together]. It was not a physical thing at first at all. I sat down and I just watched her. And I had lots of really very good thoughts as I watched her. I could see the integrity of her independence. So I said to myself, maybe this is a very good thing."

"We're not just eating and sleeping together," says a Detroit student, "we're protesting the war together."

"We like what we are doing," he says. "We're quite happy the way we are. Living together we can screw all the time."

One advantage of the arrangement, of course, is that it is so easily entered into—no blood tests, no papers, no waiting. In fact, there is often so little to be said about so unset and undetermined an undertaking that, most often, nothing is said at all. "People fall into it," says Linda LeClair. "It's a nonverbal thing."

Take DeeDee and Mike at Columbia. "We began studying together," she says. "Then I made his dinner before we studied. Then we came back and I made him coffee. At first, I let him out. Then he let himself out, then he stayed and I made him coffee in the morning. Then he went shopping for groceries and in a week he was here all the time."

"Do you consider yourselves engaged or going steady or . . .?" a couple at Florida State University in Tallahassee was asked. "We don't consider ourselves anything," the nonmate said. "We've never tried to pin it down." In Iowa City, Iowa, a girl says, "I guess he came and never left." At L.S.U., Dale says brightly that her arrangement with Tom "is the first time I've gone steady."

"It's not exactly the new morality that everyone used to talk about a few years ago," a Harvard senior says. "It's a fundamental new consciousness that is much bigger than morality."

May 1968

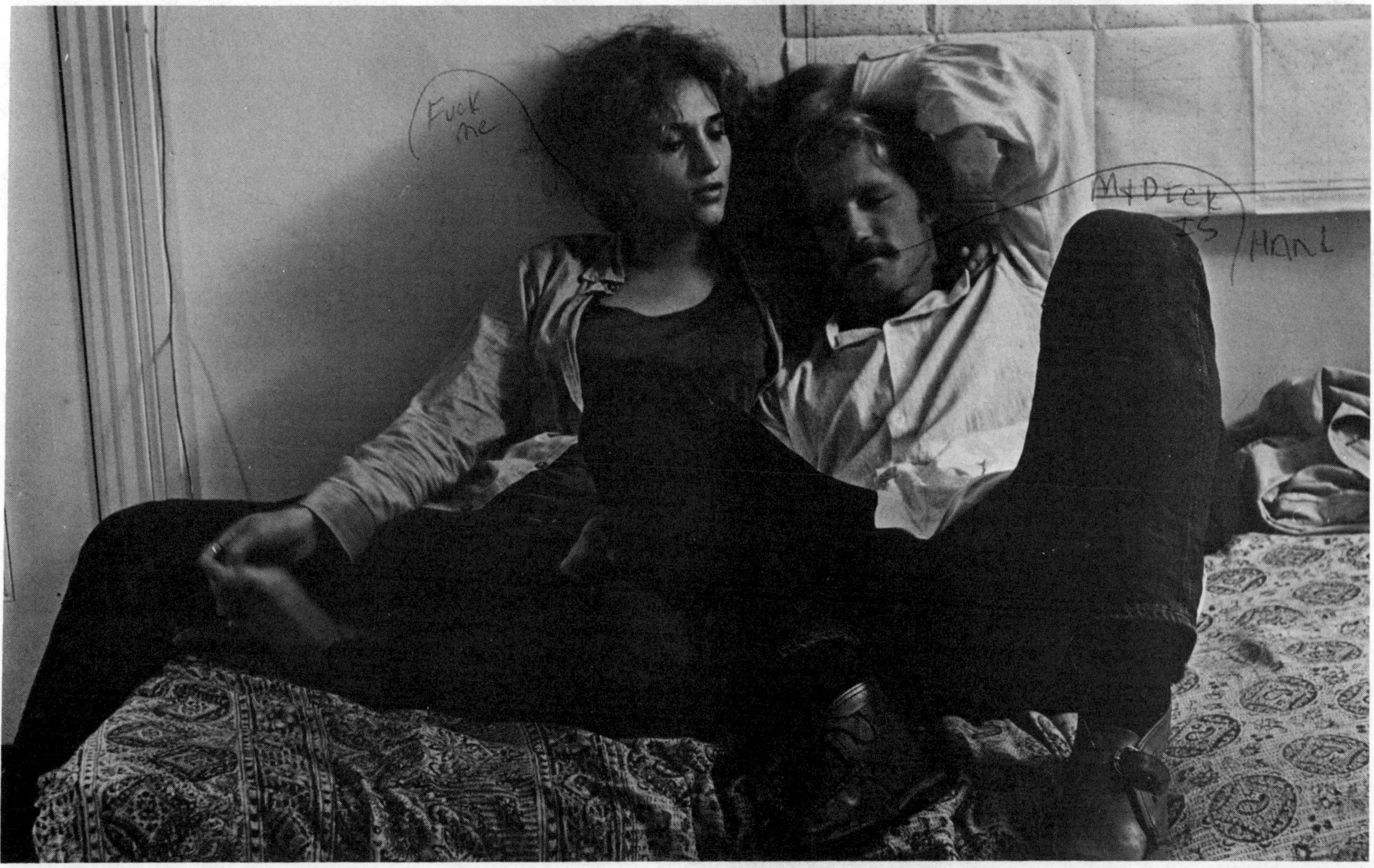

WOMEN'S LIBERATION

Understanding Orgasm

TIRESIAS, WHO HAD BEEN both man and woman, was asked, as Ovid's legend goes, to mediate in a dispute between Jove and Juno as to which sex got more pleasure from lovemaking. Tiresias unhesitatingly answered that women did. Yet in the intervening 2000 years between Ovid's time and our own, a mythology has been built up which not only holds the opposite to be true, but has made this belief an unswerving ideology dictating the quality of relations between the sexes. Women's sexuality, defined by men to benefit men, has been downgraded and perverted, repressed and channeled, denied and abused until women themselves, thoroughly convinced of their sexual inferiority to men, would probably be dumbfounded to learn that there is scientific proof that Tiresias was indeed right.

The myth was codified by Freud as much as anyone else. In *Three Essays on the Theory of Sexuality,* Freud formulated his basic ideas concerning feminine sexuality: for little girls, the leading erogenous zone in their bodies is the clitoris; in order for the transition to womanhood to be successful, the clitoris must abandon its sexual primacy to the vagina; women in whom this transition has not been complete remain clitorally-oriented, or "sexually anaesthetic," and "psychosexually immature." In the context of Freud's total psychoanalytic view of women—that they are not whole human beings but mutilated males who long all their lives for a penis and must struggle to reconcile themselves to its lack—the requirement of a transfer of erotic sensation from clitoris to vagina became a prima facie case for their inevitable sexual inferiority. In Freud's logic, those who struggle to become what they are not must be inferior to that to which they aspire.

Freud himself admitted near the end of his life that his knowledge of women was inadequate. "If you want to know more about femininity, you must interrogate your own experience, or turn to the poets, or wait until science can give you more profound and more coherent information," he said; he also hoped the female psychoanalysts who followed him would be able to find out more. But the post-Freudians adhered rigidly to the doctrine of the master, and, as with most of his work, what Freud hoped would be taken as a thesis for future study became instead a kind of canon law.

While the neo-Freudians haggled over the correct reading of the Freudian bible, watered-down Freudianism was wending its way into the cultural mythology via Broadway plays, novels, popular magazines, social scientists, marriage counselors and experts of various kinds who found it useful in projecting desired images of woman. The superiority of the vaginal over the clitoral orgasm was particularly useful as a theory, since it provided a convenient basis for categorization: clitoral women were deemed immature, neurotic, bitchy and masculine; women who had vaginal orgasms were maternal, feminine, mature and normal. Though frigidity should technically be defined as total inability to achieve orgasm, the orthodox Freudians (and pseudo-Freudians) preferred to define it as inability to achieve vaginal orgasm, by which definition, in 1944, Edmond Bergler adjudged between 70 and 80 per cent of all women frigid. The clitoral vs. vaginal debate raged hot and heavy among the sexologists— Kinsey's writings stressed the importance of the clitoris to female orgasm and contradicted Bergler's statistics — but it became clear that there was something indispensable to society in the Freudian view which allowed it to remain unchalleged in the public consciousness.

In 1966, Dr. William H. Masters and Mrs. Virginia E. Johnson published *Human Sexual Response,* a massive clinical study of the physiology of sex. Briefly and simply, the Masters and Johnson conclusions about the female orgasm, based on observation of and interviews with 487 women, were these:

1) That the dichotomy of vaginal and clitoral orgasms is entirely false. Anatomically, all orgasms are centered in the clitoris, whether they result from direct manual pressure applied to the clitoris, indirect pressure resulting from the thrusting of penis during intercourse, or generalized sexual stimulation of other erogenous zones like the breasts.

2) That women are naturally multiorgasmic; that is, if a woman is immediately stimulated following orgasm, she is likely to experience several orgasms in rapid succession. This is not an exceptional occurrence, but one of which most women are capable.

3) That while women's orgasms do not vary in kind, they vary in intensity. The most intense orgasms experienced by the research subjects were by masturbatory manual stimulation, followed in intensity by manual stimulation by the partner; the least intense orgasms were experienced during intercourse.

4) That there is an "infinite variety in female sexual response" as regards intensity and duration of orgasms.

To anyone acquainted with the body of existing knowledge of feminine sexuality, the Masters and Johnson findings were truly revolutionary and liberating in the extent to which they demolished the established myths. Yet two years after the study was published, it seems hardly to have made any impact at all. Certainly it is not for lack of information that the myths persist; *Human Sexual Response,* despite its weighty scientific language, was an immediate best seller, and popular paperbacks explicated it to millions of people in simpler language and at a cheaper price. The myths remain because a male-dominated American culture has a vested interest in their continuance.

Before Masters and Johnson, men defined feminine sexuality in a way as favorable to themselves as possible. If woman's pleasure was obtained through the vagina, then she was totally dependent on the man's erect penis to achieve orgasm; she would receive her satisfaction only as a concomitant of man's seeking his. With the clitoral orgasm, woman's sexual pleasure was independent of the male's, and she could seek her satisfaction as aggressively as the man sought his, a prospect which didn't appeal to too many men. The definition of feminine sexuality as normally vaginal, in other words, was a part of keeping women down, of making them sexually as well as economically, socially and politically subservient.

In retrospect, particularly with the additional perspective of our own times, Freud's theory of feminine sexuality appears an historical rationalization for the realities of Victorian society. A prisoner of the Victorian ethos, Freud had to play the paterfamilias. Freud's analysis implied that woman's low status had not been conferred upon her by men, but by God, who created her without a penis.

The superiority of the vaginal orgasm seems almost a demoniac determination on Freud's part to complete the Victorians' repression of feminine eroticism, to stigmatize the remaining vestiges of pleasure felt by women and thus make them unacceptable to the women themselves. For there were still women whose sexuality hadn't been completely destroyed, as evidenced by one Dr. Isaac Brown Baker, a surgeon who performed numerous clitoridectomies on women to prevent the sexual excitement which, he was convinced, caused "insanities," "catalepsy," "hysteria," "epilepsy" and other diseases. The Victorians needed to repress sexuality for the success of Western industrialized society; in particular, the total repression of woman's sexuality was crucial to ensure her subjugation. So the Victorians honored only that aspect of sexuality which was necessary to the survival of the species—the male ejaculation; made women submissive to sex by creating a mystique of the sanctity of motherhood; and, supported by Freud, passed on to us the heritage of the double standard.

When Kinsey laid to rest the part of the double standard that maintained women got no pleasure at all from sex, everyone cried out that there was a sexual revolution afoot. But such talk, as usual, was deceptive. Morality, outside the marriage bed, remained the same, and children were socialized as though Kinsey had never described what they would be like when they grew up. Boys were taught that they should get their sex where they could find it, "go as far" as they could. On the old assumption that women were asexual creatures, girls were taught that since they needed sex less than boys did, it was up to them to impose sexual restraints. In whatever sex education adolescents did manage to receive, they were told that men had penises and women vaginas; the existence of the clitoris was not mentioned, and *pleasure* in sex was never discussed at all.

Adolescent boys growing up begging for sexual crumbs from girls frightened for their "reputations"—a situation that remains unchanged to this day—hardly constitutes the vanguard of a sexual revolution. However, the marriage manual craze that followed Kinsey assumed that a lifetime of psychological destruction could, with the aid of a little booklet, be abandoned after marriage, and that husband and wife should be able to make sure that the wife was not robbed of her sexual birthright to orgasm, just so long as it was *vaginal* (though the marriage manuals did rather reluctantly admit that since the clitoris was the most sexually sensitive organ in the female body, a little clitoral stimulation was in order), and so long as their orgasms were *simultaneous*.

The effect of the marriage manuals of course ran counter to their ostensible purpose. Under the guise of frankness and sexual liberation, they dictated prudery and restraint. Sex was made so mechanized, detached and intellectual that it was robbed of its sensuality. Man became a spectator of his own sexual experience. And the marriage manuals put new pressure on women. The swing was from repression to preoccupation with the orgasm. Men took the marriage manuals to mean that their sexuality would be enhanced by bringing women to orgasm and, again coopting feminine sexuality for their own ends, they put pressure on women to perform. The marriage manuals' endorse-

ment of the desirability of vaginal orgasm insured that women would be asked not only, "Did you come?" but also, "Did you conform to Freud's conception of a psychosexually mature woman, and thereby validate my masculinity?"

Appearances notwithstanding, the age-old taboos against conversation about personal sexual experience haven't yet been broken down. This reticence has allowed the mind-manipulators of the media to create myths of sexual supermen and superwomen. So the bed becomes a competitive arena, where men and women measure themselves against these mythical rivals, while simultaneously trying to live up to the ecstasies promised them by the marriage manuals and the fantasies of the media ("If the earth doesn't move for me, I must be missing something"). Our society has made sex a sport, with its record-breakers, its judges, its rules and its spectators.

As anthropologists have shown, woman's sexual response is culturally conditioned; historically, women defer to whatever model of their sexuality is offered them by men. So the sad thing for women is that they have participated in the destruction of their own eroticism. Women have helped make the vaginal orgasm into a status symbol in a male-dictated system of values. A woman would now perceive her preference for clitoral orgasm as a "secret shame," ignominious in the eyes of other women as well as those of men. This internalization can be seen in literature: Mary McCarthy and Doris Lessing's writings on orgasm do not differ substantially from Ernest Hemingway's, and Simone de Beauvoir, in *The Second Sex,* refers to vaginal orgasm as the only "normal satisfaction."

One factor that has made this possible is that female sexuality is subtle and delicate, conditioned as much by the emotions as by physiology and sociology. Masters and Johnson proved that the orgasm experienced during intercourse, the misnamed vaginal orgasm, did not differ *anatomically* from the clitoral orgasm. But this should not be seen as their most significant contribu-

tion to the s e x u a l emancipation of women. A difference remains in the *subjective* experience of orgasm during intercourse and orgasm apart from intercourse. In the complex of emotional factors affecting feminine sexuality, there is a whole panoply of pleasures: the pleasure of being penetrated and filled by a man, the pleasure of sexual communication, the pleasure of affording a man his orgasm, the erotic pleasure that exists even when sex is not terminated by orgasmic release. Masters and Johnson's real contribution was to show this "infinite variety in female sexual response"; that one experience is not better than another, but merely different.

There is no doubt that Masters and Johnson were fully aware of the implications of their study to the sexual liberation of women. As they wrote, "With orgasmic physiology established, the human female now has an undeniable opportunity to develop realistically her own sexual response levels." Two years later this statement seems naive and entirely too optimistic. Certainly the sexual problems of our society will never be solved until there is real and unfeigned equality between men and women. This idea is usually misconstrued: sexual liberation for women is wrongly understood to mean that women will adopt all the forms of masculine sexuality. As in the whole issue of women's liberation, that's really not the point. Women don't aspire to imitate the mistakes of men in sexual matters, to view sexual experiences as conquest and ego-enhancement, to use other people to serve their own ends. But if the Masters and Johnson material is allowed to filter into the public consciousness, hopefully to replace the enshrined Freudian myths, then woman at long last will be allowed to take the first step toward her emancipation: to define and enjoy the forms of her own sexuality.
—SUSAN LYDON

Ramparts
12/14/68

Women's Demonstration, Panther support rally, May Day 1970.

DISCOVERY OF TRUTH IN SEX

PLEASE BELIEVE ME IN THIS

(Ed. Note: The following letter was submitted to us anonymously by a Carleton woman. We are printing it not because it is sensational, or even well-written, but because the author has the courage and honesty to speak her piece on a subject which all students confront, but nearly all keep to themselves.

We think something that involves students as deeply as their sexual emotions deserves newspaper space as much as any committee. We hope readers take this statement seriously and in context, as the writer intends.)

I have come in my own way and as a woman to cherish my sexual experiences, to thrill at the feelings my body can have and to realize the fantastic potential of my sexual person coupled with a man. I want to tell you that I am lacking confidence in a lot of my casual relations with people, although one always hopes to go beyond this. I dress pretty thoughtfully, I think, I have really studied hard, although this year I have discovered a completely different attitude towards books, they are now more like reading. I think I am thoughtful of others — anyway I am more selfless than I have been in the past. In other words, I am not way out — I am regular, with kind of regular feelings.

I want to say this to you, that knowing yourself as a woman can be one of the most important discoveries at this time. Only until I realized that part of myself could I begin to see what was basic to life and what emotions I cared about. It allowed me to envision a much greater variety of relationships with other males. Really, when I talked to some men on campus it was so dry because I hadn't recognized myself as a woman and so I couldn't see that "man" as a man. And what it means to recognize yourself as a woman is to know that intensity and completeness of the emotions that can grip, overcome and then release you.

It is a total feeling, and I am telling you that until you know this feeling you can't imagine it or conceive of yourself as having this potential. Please believe me in this.

I am writing now to myself about winter term of my freshman year. I admit this. And what may seem to you as over enthusiasm — a preaching kind of thing — is my agonized feeling of all that I wasn't then — of all the misplaced action and ignorance then.

You must know that you can masturbate yourself — that is, that you can bring yourself to a sexual climax which is an experience of the entire body and mind. Until you discover yourself capable of this I wonder how you can know that part of yourself which is woman.

Maybe you don't feel your sexual identity is in question. I am maybe only talking to a few. I don't care about all the others, there must be some like me and like I was as a freshman. Unless you see sex in the total context of stimulation ultimately leading to intercourse, I think you are encountering sex in a perverted way. For each of my sentences I could write more and more. Each sentence is so abrupt.

I must say this — that my relationship with men has been unusual, for most of my life here at Carleton I have dated only one boy. Please don't let that make you feel apart from my experience. It just happened, for good or for bad. I never dated in high school. I don't think most of the dating here at Carleton does an awful lot for one's sexual identity. Of course, it takes an awfully self-confident person to really enjoy a date and feel richer in a meaningful way upon ending the date. It is just a plain, hard thing to carry off. Nobody much has experience before they come here, but this is a hard thing for both people to accept, I think. It is not as if I have "arrived" or anything — this is still something I am looking for with people.

Here is an example of my feeling that you must know the reasons for stimulation to understand yourself. I think if we were not inhibited by society's dictates, we would feel the natural urge to have our breasts fondled. It is a climax — a very specific feeling. When my guy first wanted to undo my bra I was completely stymied. I felt so guilty and embarrassed. This is not the way to feel. Human responses are all normal. There are reasons. The thing is to understand these reasons and you can do this only understanding yourself. My guy really thinks breasts are beautiful things.

I think women have been so perverted by society's "accepted role for women" that they have had to deny almost all of their most human, warm and giving feelings. There is nothing that a man and woman can do together which is in any sense wrong as long as there is the ability on the part of each person to have openness to the needs of the other person. You can be honest — impossible — impossible to be honest with oneself in a thousand different ways but maybe this statement will permit somebody to recognize themselves sexually in a more truthful and honest way.

I am saying something very specific. Listen to yourself carefully — your body, your mind. Learn to masturbate yourself. If the chance to develop a relationship with a man comes your way, be sensitive to yourself, to him and develop your potentials together.

The next thing I have to say must be the most important in its way. And maybe it should have been the first thing. Don't get pregnant, simply because you don't need to be pregnant unless you want to be. There are clinics up in the Cities that do not hesitate to give prescriptions to women who are not married. There is nothing devious about this. If I felt I could, I would give you the name of my doctor where many Carleton women have gone.

I really couldn't love myself in my own situation until I had escaped from all the misunderstanding of how my body was meant to be loved by myself and at times by another.

The Carletonian (Carleton College, Minn.)
10/10/68

Southern Women Talk Freedom

WE DON'T WANT EQUALITY
WITH MEN IN THE SOCIETY
AS IT IS NOW, WE WANT AN
ENTIRELY NEW SOCIETY
BASED ON NEW VALUES

By ANNE BRADEN

Recently I attended a weekend conference of Southern women in Atlanta. There were over 100 women there, from 11 states. They were talking about freedom for women and the new women's liberation movement.

The conference was called by the Southern Student Organizing Committee (SSOC), which stimulates radical organizing among Southern white students, so most of the women were young—students or recent students—and all of them were white.

They came because they were rejecting the traditional roles that Southern society has assigned to white women. They were saying they did not intend to have their lives defined for them—to be simply "somebody's daughter, somebody's date, somebody's wife, somebody's mother and somebody's widow"—but were determined to find their own identity and their own lives and, if necessary, build a new society to do it.

At 44, I was one of the few representatives of an "older generation" present. The thing that struck me was how similar the discussion was to the things my own contemporaries talked about when I was in college 25 years ago. We too thought we were a part of a "New South" and did not intend to be forced into the traditional roles of Southern white women.

Is it really true, I thought, that the more things change, the more they stay the same? People in my generation were these girls' mothers. What happened to them — that their daughters now had to fight the same battles over again?

The question answers itself. Most of them, after a period of youthful rebellion, faded back into the scenery of Southern life. If they were affluent, maybe they exchanged an old-fashioned Southern mansion for a home in the suburbs and lady-bountiful charity work for modern so-called "civic" activity. But the content—an empty, meaningless, subservient role—remained the same.

Will the young women of 1969 fade back into the scenery too? Some will—but I think they have a much better chance.

For one thing, they have today a growing organized movement to relate to. My own generation ran smack into the period of reaction after World War II, when along with a general atmosphere of repression women were deluged with "back-to-the-kitchen" propaganda.

Today, there are women's liberation groups in at least 50 cities over the country; organized groups from four Southern communities reported at the Atlanta meeting; there will be more as a result of this conference.

Another important difference is that they are examining the total society much more carefully than my generation did. Many of the women in Atlanta stressed that the causes of oppression of women are social and economic and cannot be solved on a personal basis by one woman alone.

"Just taking women out of the home and into the labor force is not what we want at all," said one young woman, speaking from the floor. "There is a whole hierarchy of work that degrades some people in this society; we want to change that."

Or, as one of the speakers, Marilyn Webb of Washington, put it: "We don't want equality with men in the society as it is now; we want an entirely new society, based on new values."

This echoes what the black movement is saying today, and indeed the similarity is more than coincidence. Many of the women who started today's women's movement came out of, or were influenced by, the black movement.

I think this is because the questions the black movement has raised about our society are so basic that they have caused many other groups and people to examine their own condition—and to realize that they too are not free. The new women's movement is only part of the resulting ferment.

The women who met in Atlanta looked into their own Southern past for historic perspective. One conference session, tied together by SSOC organizer Lyn Wells, was devoted to reports on women who were rebels in the past—in the Abolitionist, Populist, and early labor movements, and more recently in the civil rights movement.

They were interested too in what women are doing in other parts of the world, especially in socialist countries. One entire workshop dealt with women in the Soviet Union, China, Sweden, North Vietnam, and Cuba.

Two women present had recently visited Cuba. By popular demand a special session was scheduled so that people attending other workshops could hear their report. About 75 per cent of the conference came.

The general consensus seemed to be that while socialist societies provide no magic answers for women, there is much that can be learned from them.

And even as they talked about what they could do to change their society, the women wrestled with the problem of what they could do right now in their own lives.

There was much talk about "new life styles" and experiments with different living arrangements such as communes; how to work things out with the individual men in their lives, etc.

"You can either shuffle to get by—like women and black people have traditionally done," said one young woman, "or you can break up with your man—or you can try to teach him."

"The myths about women keep men in a boxed-in place too," said another workshop participant. "The man who becomes sensitized to our struggle begins to realize the boxes he's been put in too."

There seemed to be agreement that the woman who tries to find her own role as an individual and as a part of social struggle may have a harder life—on the surface.

"But the psychological rewards of struggle for freedom are so great that it's worth it," said one workshop leader. The few of us present from an older generation could say amen to that.

The weakness of the conference was that it was almost entirely middle-class and all white. The women were aware of the danger of isolation from working class women. They watched the film "Salt of the Earth" and talked about their identity with all women—and how to bridge class differences.

There was less talk about their whiteness, although everyone was aware of it. SSOC had considered trying to make the conference interracial. They decided against it after talking with some radical black women. The feeling was that radical black women would not come—and that the experiences and situation of black and white women are, at this point, very different.

That may be true for now. But I have always found that the experiences black and white women share as women are more powerful than the ones that divide them. I doubt we'll ever build a movement strong enough to free us all until this truth is recognized—on both sides of the barrier.

March 1969

the southern PATRiOT

NEITHER SHE NOR MR. BEHR BELIEVE IN MARRIAGE OR THE DRAFT OR THE SOCIETY

Co-ed Disciplined by College Becomes a Dropout at Barnard

By DEIRDRE CARMODY

Linda LeClair, the Barnard College sophomore who broke housing regulations last spring to live off-campus with her boy friend, said yesterday that she would not return to Barnard this semester or at any other time.

She said her grades were incomplete, but made it clear that she would not return to the college under any circumstances.

The 20-year-old Miss LeClair had her campus privileges curtailed by a disciplinary committee last May because she had lied to the college about her address.

She became an object of national controversy, however, because she said that many other students at Barnard—which is an all-girl college that is part of Columbia University and across the street from the Columbia campus—were living in apartments with men and that the college had no right to prevent them from doing so.

In an interview yesterday Miss LeClair talked about her "bewilderment" during the controversy, about her thoughts now and about her future.

"At the time when it was happening I was reacting against the authorities," she said. "I felt very bitter that they felt they could control me and other people like me. It's a very strange feeling not to have control over something as basic as where you can live."

However, Miss LeClair expressed sympathy with Martha Peterson, president of Barnard.

"President Peterson is in a very difficult position," she said. "She is aware of the needs of the students, aware that lots of people have become pregnant, that lots of people have abortions, aware that recognizing sexual intercourse would cause embarrassment to the ladies that give money to the college."

Miss LeClair said that new housing regulations announced last month by Barnard, which permit any student to live off campus if she has her parent's permission, were an improvement over the old rules, but that the underlying assumption

was still that students were unable to handle their own affairs.

Miss LeClair spent the month of July at a "communal farm" in Southern Vermont with her boyfriend, Peter Behr, and several other couples. But after a disagreement with the others about how the farm should be operated, Miss LeClair and Mr. Behr left and hitchhiked to the West Coast.

Neither she nor Mr. Behr believe in marriage.

They are now living in a communal apartment with other couples on the Upper West Side, and they say they do not know where they will go next. They would like to go to another communal farm, but Mr. Behr has not decided whether he will return for his senior year at Columbia. He faces induction into the Armed Forces, which he intends to refuse, on Thursday.

"We want to get out of the city," Miss LeClair said. "The city is a dying thing. We're killing ourselves off slowly here with smoke, noise, anger, guns, everything."

"We want eventually to have children, when we're settled," she said.

"We want to try another method of education," she said. "Schools today teach kids two things—obedience and competition. Both are important in a society like this one. But we don't like the society and we wouldn't like to perpetuate it, especially at the expense of our own children."

"The only way you can learn to do stuff is by attempting to do it yourself," she said. "I don't think that parents can transfer experience verbally. The child has to learn for himself.

"I'd like to be able to remember what happened to me this year," she said. "I'd like to be able to remember my need to be trusted and understood."

The New York Times 9/4/68

Ed. Note: Peter Behr is a draft resister. Both Peter and Linda participated in the Columbia strike.

LIVE NOW — 1963

They react "live now." They react "how dare you tell me what to do—you who made the world what it is." They react "I won't think about it." "I woke up one night and I thought, 'I am going to die a virgin,' " a Stanford coed recalled. "I decided it was time to do something about it." "During the Cuban crisis my best friend got on the phone with the boy she'd been dating," a Berkeley junior said. "She told him, 'Listen, I'm ready to get laid.' "

"We were sitting around," a Barnard senior said, "and we were telling each other how if this is really the end of the world coming, what would we do. It was the morning when no one knew what Russia would do about the Cuban blockade. We decided we'd run to the nearest frat house and grab the first available man." "We had just seen 'On the Beach' again," a Hollins senior said, "and I was thinking 'If I'm not married by the time I'm 21, I will have an affair.' " "I don't expect to live out the second half of my life," a City College of New York sophomore said.

From *Even Nice Girls* by Gail Greene 1963

heather dean

I was waiting for the

light to change at Bloor and St. George when I saw the first whore waiting across from me. She was slumped, smile drooping, foot-sore from cruising Fraternity Row peddling counterfeit sex to the sons of the bourgeoisie who know no better.

I felt a decent pity. (Declension: I am pitying, you are condescending, she is insufferably arrogant.) It was easy to pity her — her legs were dumpy, her lipstick faded, her clothes too tight, and she was wearing her hair in one of those lacquered stacks that you expect to find little moths trapped in.

As we passed one another she met my eyes with the flat, frozen stare of a queen cat challenged in her alley. I accepted it serenely. Noblesse oblige.

And swung on down Bloor with The Walk, accentuated by 3 inch heels — a walk that flashed my shapely calves and kept my hair brushing gracefully against my shoulders. I was feeling very full of myself indeed.

Until I saw the second whore.

No world-wary slattern, this whore was the Eternal Eve — the tawny skin of Orleans Quadroon Balls, heavy black curls, lids languorous under tangled lashes.

Truly he was beautiful.

And knew it. No more than 15 but knew it with the arrogance of the oft-pursued. No passers-by dismissed him in easy contempt; they stared at him with guilty fascination. And he met their look with imploring, violet-shadowed eyes. No quick professional assessments in the second whore's glance — rather, a limpid pleading — little boy lost, seeking not a mark but a protector.

He was dressed with studied self-awareness in a gold silk shirt open to the waist over his gold silk skin, a black suede sash, straw-colored jeans shrunk to cling to his long graceful thighs and taut buttocks, black sandals. The world ended three feet from his skin. His consciousness floated about him like a bubble, extending amoeba-like to engulf responses to himself.

As I came abreast of the little sybarite I was aware of his eyes sweeping over me in quick assessment. But I was confident. My face was on, my hair was clean and silky, and I knew that in my turquoise sarong I looked nicely leggy and bosomy, with large expanses of smooth tanned skin.

"You're wearing too much eye make-up for 5 o'clock." He catted unexpectedly and giggled.

But it was a sulky, rear-guard action and my instinctive response was to smile faintly and fleetingly as I passed to signal that I recognized its weakness.

My next response was a mental double-take whose force is still with me. Just what in the hell was the name of the game? When was I dealt in? And how did I get out?

Caricature is not debatable.

What woman can watch a transvestite swing down a staircase, self-absorbed in his her bits of theatre, and ever "make an entrance" again? We cannot watch the queen's burlesque of woman's self-conscious dramatics and know not what we do.

Suddenly I was self-aware in a new way. I tried to iron the body-consciousness sway out of my walk. Then — too much — I saw the nun.

I went through a kaleidoscope of reactions.

First amusement. What would she think when she saw the baby whore?

And the perennial wonder. "What happens to the tensions of that body, Sister? Do they spill over into dreams formless for lack of knowing the body of a man: the mouth, the hands, the smell and taste and weight of a man? Do you wander in a dreamland garden strewn with the sexual symbols your church abounds in? And do you cry 'Sweet Jesus' in your dreams?"

But she was walking. She was walking graceful as a free animal in the "sensible" shoes that emerged with each unencumbered stride from the folds of her habit. Not mincing like a prancing queen but walking.

It has been my practice as I trot awkwardly along the sidewalk trying to keep up with a freestriding male to drop back five paces, fold my hands, bow my head, and tilt along in the pigeon-toed toddle of the bound-foot peasant woman of Old China. Very funny.

I struck the mocking quotation marks from that word "sensible."

She saw the little whore. Behind her glasses her glance remained calm and rational as it rested on him. No psychic shock for her, as I had foolishly expected. She wasn't in the game. She was liberated from the game.

So, doubt. To pay a nun's price for liberation? Surely too dear.

But can you choose the price, or avoid the price? When you have seen, it is too late to look away. Once the slave has said his private "No!", he can never turn back. The walls of his cabin become a trap, not a bulwark, and he will never go in gratitude to pay his blood-rent in hand-grown cotton.

To pay the nun's price for liberation? The black man risks it daily from the red-neck's blade.

An extreme analogy? Only think... BLACK LIKE ME.

Once the slogan of the civil rights movement was "FREEDOM NOW!" As the movement was forced to add an analysis and programme to the mystic cry of freedom it was amended to "JOBS AND FREEDOM NOW!" For no poor man is free.

The black man knows in his school that one or two members of his over-flowing ranks will make it into the prestige college and the prestige jobs, while the upper 20% of the white class across town will "make it." He finds himself the last hired and first fired. Even unions discriminate against him. He earns a lower salary than a white man in the identical job. His function in the labour market is to depress wages; he provides a reserve pool of cheap labour to break strikes and to make it possible to lay off or fire workers without risking a labour shortage later on.

The black man works at the scut jobs of society — those with no security no challenge... and less pay. It is his biblical place to be a hewer of wood and a drawer of water. It is his natural place. It is his place in the scheme of evolution. Thus Darwin, God, and Nature concur in their opinion of his talents. And sometimes even he concurs.

The black man who concurs is genuinely rewarded. The liberal makes a cynical joke of the "Some of my best friends..." gambit, but he is wrong. The affection the Southerner feels for the "good nigra" is quite as real as his fear and hatred of the rebel. Why doubt it? Have men not risked their lives to rescue faithful hounds that have fallen down the shafts of abandoned mines?

The Southerner believes his ideology. The black man is contented in a life of servitude, for his nature suits him for it. His intelligence is not the logic of the white man, but a shifting intuitiveness that makes him more sensitive to, for instance, religion, than the white. But he lacks the purposive, disciplined intelligence required to command those social roles reserved for his betters.

Reformers who lack the Southerner's sympathetic understanding of his impulsive, childlike mind can mislead the black man into seeking lifeways alien to his basic nature. They hurt rather than help him. His high-pitched giggle, symbol to the Southerner of his joy, not his repressed despair, sounds no more.

Therefore, reluctantly but with love, they assume the burden of preserving him from the temptations of responsibility, and the trials of making his own political and economic choices.

Read "woman" for "black man." Read "real woman" for "good nigra." Read "male chauvinist" for "Southerner." For the Southerner's ideology, read Freud.

The black man grows up in a world where human history was made by whites. He goes to school and learns the names and faces of great generals, law-makers, conquerors, and kings, philosophers, poets, scientists and visionaries, revolutionaries, reformers, and saints. They are all white men.

Women do not exist in history, except as shadow figures "standing behind every good man." Their reality is a function of their relationship to men as mistress or Mrs.

(Strophe: Eleanor Rigby died and was buried in the church with her name today.)

Those black men who succeed in the white man's world do it because they have white blood, or at the expense of their true nature.

Those women who succeed in the white man's world are no true women: they are lesbians, go the rumours, or frigid — desexed and unlovely creatures more to be pitied than emulated. Unless they "keep their femininity" by playing Doris Day's child-idiot.

The trap of the black American is identical economically, socially, and psychologically to ours, my sisters.

But I overplay the case, you may correctly protest. Not all whites and not all men are drunk on mastery. There are white liberals and liberal men.

Truly.

There are white reformers and they have been dealt with elsewhere. And there are liberal men. There are men who want their wives to be intelligent — almost as intelligent as themselves. They want their wives to develop themselves as individuals — to read while the diapers are in the machine and the baby in the playpen. There are men who feel only slightly the prickings of social pressure when they are considered less manly for democratically consulting their wives on decisions that will disrupt their lives. They want to send their girl children to college — if they can afford it after the boys have gone. They even help with the dishes. They try.

But the seeds of arrogance are sown subtly and well within the fabric of male consciousness, just as the seeds of racism exist in the consciousness of the white liberal. A woman knows this, as a black man knows this, because the liberal is taken off guard by anyone who plays the game and confirms his prejudices.

Ask any flirt. It works. All the little Teen Magazine, Readers' Digest, Ladies Home Journal formulae for reducing the male to quivering jelly work. Ask him about himself, laugh at his unfunniest jokes, ask his advice, defer to his opinions, lean on him, flatter him subtly with wide-eyed absorption, submerge yourself in him, NEED him and he will say, "There's a REAL woman!"

No, friend. There's an unreal woman who will find a thousand subtle ways to avenge herself for the murder of her self.

They have a grievance, but they're going too far!

Whenever the oppressed find their voice, whether in unions, in "Black Power," or in the movement for female humanness, the liberal reaction wraps itself in this banner.

And behind this rationalization there lurks the fear of sexual attack. In Europe, the Jew was traditionally the subject of the mythology of sexual insecurity of which the black man and the Indian have become the North American inheritors — he had larger genitals, insatiable sexual appetites, no moral restraints. Similarly, North American women who are taking tentative and inadequate steps toward equality are accused, no less, of destroying the manhood of the North

WOMAN

American male.

The scenario runs something like this:

At seven in the morning man sallies forth from his humble castle to bring home the bacon. All day he contends with the forces of the Real World, which weary and batter him. He's under the pressure of Important, Ulcer-making Decisions. Or he sells his personality to clients. Or he smothers his resistance to the arrogance of his boss. All for her.

His ego is submerged. He is a cog in the corporate machine of technological society. He is one more sardine in the subway; one more ant on the freeway; one more rat in the race.

At five he staggers home, a beaten and belittled man. And there is Woman. She's got 16 hours to get him on his feet again. To make him feel important, necessary, competent, and resourceful.

No matter how Your day went, sermons the Readers' Digest, greet him at the door with fresh lipstick, a cheery smile, and a "how did it go?" Listen to his troubles; fetch him a beer or martini; shoo the kids out so that he can relax.

Don't encumber him with all the petty irritations of running the house; he's had enough of those at the office. But do ask his advice. Make him feel that he is still the Captain of his little ship.

Build him up.

"George, can you get the top off the peanut butter? I've been struggling with it all day!"

Be smart enough so that he can be proud of you; stupid enough that he can feel smart by comparison. Make sure he knows you would be lost without him — confer on him the glow of paternalism, and on yourself the dwarf-life of eternal childhood. Convince yourself that propping up a collapsing male ego is a true vocation and, if he's not too tired, Vaginal Orgasm shall be yours. (We have obviously moved beyond the Readers' Digest, and about time.)

If woman will not play this role of recreating man by being his recreation, is it she who is destroying him? Any man who is so readily castrated must have his balls suspended by a very slender thread.

Most of this advice is profered not by men but by women. We too have our Uncle Toms. We also have our Whitney Youngs and Martin Luther Kings. (For those of you unfamiliar with the internal politics of the black man's struggle, that's a Bad Thing.)

The most prominent of this breed in recent years has been Betty Friedan, author of The Feminine Mystique. Like some Negro "leaders," she muddles an honest analysis of the problem with weak solutions.

Friedan does a fairly good job of describing the frustration and helplessness of a woman caught between the conflicting role demands of service and self-development, of being simultaneously a tower of strength and a clinging vine. She presents an exciting history of our freedom struggle. She details with sympathy the conflicts entailed for men in the self-denying female role. And she documents at least one sinister origin for the phenomenon. The "New Woman" who was developing in the early part of the century was, to be blunt, a lousy market. She was busy and involved outside of her home. Women's magazines said explicitly to advertisers "Give us your business and we will deliver to you, through our columns, our articles, and our fiction, a woman whose main function in life will be to buy your products for her home."

But when it comes to solutions, Friedan can only suggest that women get jobs.

It just won't do.

Let us return to George, coming home after a hard day at the office, manhood shriveled. Stepping off the train he meets Martha, coming home after a hard day at her office. Do they stagger home to wrestle the top off the peanut butter jar together? Is all bliss?

The trouble is, the scenario is true. Corporate society does frustrate George; the mass media has killed his aesthetic sense, the schools have smothered his intellectual capacity. Let's face it — George is a mess!

It is a false and cruel solution to the stunting of his potential that his wife should commit psychological suicide to compensate for it. But it is no solution to suggest that his wife should trade this kind of suicide for a plunge into the lifestyle that is destroying him as a man.

Freud tended to interpret man's nature as a series of antagonistic forces — intellect vs. instinct; sex vs. culture. Man is not intrinsically an explorer, a creator, a doer. He is these things only as a function of the social restraints on his instincts. Man satisfied either his erotic or his esoteric curiosity, was either an aesthete or a sensualist. He was a closed energy system and energy expended in one direction. Freud's dualism is most marked in his understanding of masculinity and femininity. Man is in his essence a protuberance, woman an orifice, man is active, woman passive, man logical, woman intuitive, (echoes) man aggressive, woman submissive.

When a woman wants to undertake "male" activities such as voting (pushing a ballot through a slot) she is flying in the face of what God and Nature (echoes) had created for her. Why?

Well, at the age of 3 or 4, a little girl discovers the Difference. She deduces that she has been castrated. This can be particularly traumatic if her brothers are favoured, a common Victorian family pattern. In the normal course of her development, per Freud, she resolves the resulting turmoil by accepting her punishment, her mutilation, with total resignation, and adopts the passive feminine role as designated by male society.

But some little girls do not. They strive for physical and intellectual competence, but not because these are a good in themselves. They resent discrimination in education, the arts and employment and are frustrated rather than fulfilled by male domination but not for the reasons the black man in America reacts this way, not because of an essential human drive to activity and self-realization; rather, because she perceives these male activities as a symbolic substitution for the penis of which she was robbed in infancy. (You'd think they were hard to come by.)

It might seem more plausible to explain a neurotic desire for the freedom entailed in the male role than to explain a desire for "male" freedom as a symbolic repossession of a hypothetical lost penis. But it is observable in the sociology of knowledge that the "free and unbiased" pursuit of scientific truth seems to lead inexorably in every era to a rationalization of the power relations of that era.

Let us honour Freud's undisputable genius in some areas by dedicating the first solution to him. Any woman who, in her infancy, misinterpreted the differences between the sexes must say lovingly but firmly to the child that still exists in her mental accoulation, "Little girls are like little boys turned inside out, so they can fit together."

But with that behind her, she is still far from ready to consider what it means, not to be a woman, but to be a free human being. A woman must climb out of the social and psychicological box of the role definitions which she has accepted without examination all her life. Until this conditioning is seen and understood consciously, we are not able to evaluate the female role and choose to accept or reject the dictates of its components. It must be intellectualized before we attempt the freedom to choose.

The columns of girls' and women's magazines are relatively easy to counteract compared to those forms of indoctrination which infiltrate our personalities on a less conscious level — the animal instinct to imitate the mother, jokes, cartoons, movies, comics, fiction, and above all, advertising, where some of our culture's better intellects are assigned the task of identifying certain patterns of behaviour involving profits for their clients with grace, beauty, sexual felicity, power and love.

Women should undergo this process of self-examination with each other, but away from men. American Negro organizers have decided that the development of "black consciousness," liberation from white society's definition of the Negro, can only be inhibited by the assistance of even the best white organizers. Only after the Negro has confirmed his own identity will he have the assurance to form equal alliances with those whites who share his struggle for political democracy and social justice.

Similarly, women must fortify themselves against the punishment of the male chauvinist and the paternalism of the male liberal.

Once women have shared the process of self-discovery and the experience of independent decision-making, they are ready for the real struggle.

This is not a struggle against men. The phrase "Battle of the Sexes" was not coined to describe the female liberation movement. It applies to the underhanded sometimes terrible revenge women exact from men for their frustrations. Jiggs and Dagwood are not victims of free women, but of women who are playing the game.

Listen to the jokes at a pre-nuptial stag; play Ritual Murder (contract bridge) with suburbanites; read statistics on divorce, frigidity, impotence, child-beating, psychosomatic illness and nervous breakdown; watch your parents' friends. And be assured that men will not suffer from an initiative by women to change their relationship to men and society.

Frequent intellectual flirtations with lesbianism mark the writing of feminists who pursue very deeply the implications of their own thinking — e.g., "The Second Sex", by Simone de Beauvoir. The poverty of the solution mustn't distract from the size of the problem.

Who does a free woman sleep with? Not George. It would bore her and unhinge him.

Women cannot be free until men are free. A less facetious look at George is no less discouraging. He still needs to feel resourceful, competent and useful in a world which denies him a social context for his work that will fulfill these needs. He needs work that is honorable, significant and challenging. He needs schools that do not smother his brain. He needs training and opportunity for his creative talents.

Or else he needs Martha; and we can be Marthas no more.

How are the young cared for in a society that offers no alternative to female indentureship? Where do women work in an economy with 5-10% unemployment and frequent recessions?

The problems of women are problems of the whole society; the solutions for women lie in solving far-ranging social problems. But this involves nothing short of a revolutionary restructuring of the most basic institutions in society—the tax structures that can give us parks and nursery schools, the economy that can give us jobs, the schools and the arts. The task is almost too great to be contemplated. One shrinks from it.

Except for this. There is freedom in the striving.

San Francisco Express Times

Washington Free Press, (as reprinted 2/4/69)

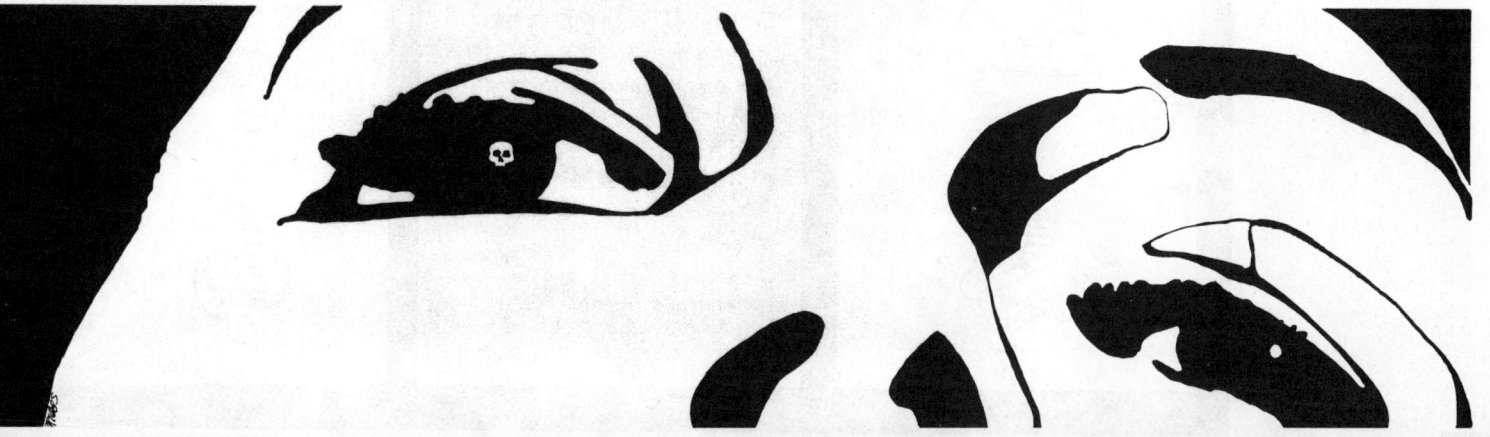

MEN + WOMEN LIVING TOGETHER

Diagrams of some women's liberation discussions

by a Bread + Roses member

When we were little, this is how we thought about marriage:

him me — little, inside safe, final

and divorce:

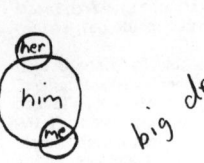

knives. power outside **(1)** cut, hammered exposed

later we had a period of free sex:

me Sue Val Nancy

then we tried: yoga, shrinks, clothes, politics, poetry, diets, bitterness, drinking, money, revenge **(2)**

When people talked about "smashing monogamy" we remembered the period of "free sex" and got scared. When we tried to put it into practice, things often worked out like this:

big deal

(6)

A man described what it would be like after monogamy was smashed:

just floatin around

I thought that was scary but I was afraid to say so because I didn't want to sound like the clinging type **(7)**

At some point we all brought whatever we had to a woman's collective. The first meeting was like this:

We had a hard time and a lot of things happened **(8)**

It made us afraid of this:

m/e

or this:

or this:

(12)

(but the whole point of it all is to achieve this:

me

and every once in a while we felt like this:

(13)

It was scary for the men. We began to see that a lot of them felt like this:

work her   him?

where?

(14)

It could work like this:

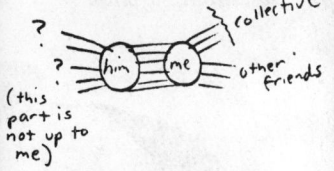

? collective
? other friends
(this part is not up to me)

or maybe even this:

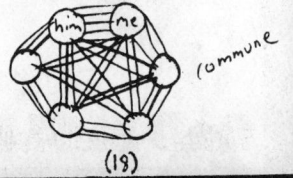

commune

(18)

But nobody can figure out all that in theory. It has to be worked out according to how we feel. It doesn't have much to do with rules about who sleeps with who, or how many people, or what sex they are.

That also depends on what we want, and what feels right

(19)

But remember we started out like this:

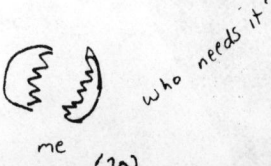

him

me   who needs it?

(20)

By the time we settled down with one man we had learned that a woman has to do her own thing as well. Our ideas and lives varied, but in general it felt like this:

(3)

sometimes we noticed this happening:

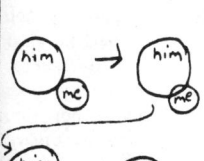

working to put him through school, his friends, housework, intellectual proof a good SLAP honey baby

(4)

Sometimes we had babies to reassert ourselves:

but really:

(5)

While I was tripping once I thought about being together and separate sort of like this:

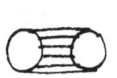

(but the picture is too static because really the image was vibrating back + forth)

thoughts
looks
experiences
memories
work
sex
laughs
climbing mountains
trips
etc
etc

(9)

I feel like we're moving toward this:

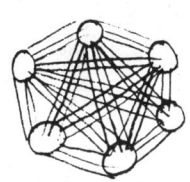

I mean not there yet

(10)

Many of us felt this beginning to happen:

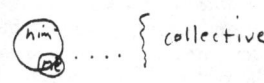
collective

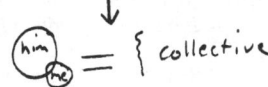
collective

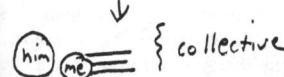
collective

Even some of us who were not with men felt this. Because it was happening to us, our heads

(11)

Some men seemed to want to do this:

but we are too small. and that would make us an awfully wierd shape

(15)

But the men seemed mainly afraid of this:

millions of women

"castrating, rejecting, cold, bitter"

"taking it all out on me"

(16)

Those of us who are with men are trying to do something like this:

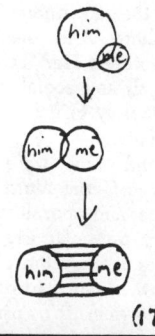

(17)

There's alot of pain and risk and fear in the changes we want. If you think there's not, you don't understand yet.
The best hope for our relationships with men is that we keep this in our minds:

That means love ourselves and each other from choice this time

(21)

many relationships will not survive these changes — often men's fears will make them fight against us, often women will decide the whole thing is too painful, or impossible, or not worth it.

more and more women will choose not to relate to men at all.

many will continue to live with men and try to work through it

(22)

But for all of us the most important thing is that for the first time, we are beginning to feel like this:

OLD MOLE

(23)

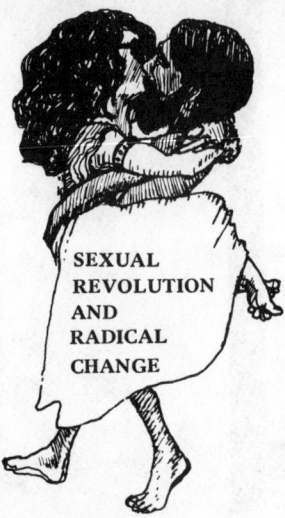

SEXUAL REVOLUTION AND RADICAL CHANGE

The Balcony is Genet's theory of revolution and counterrevolution. The play is set in a brothel and concerns a revolution which ends in failure, preempted by the patrons and staff of the Balcony who assume the roles of the former government. Having studied human relationships in the world of pimp and faggot, Genet has come to understand how sexual caste supersedes all other forms of inegalitarianism: racial, political, or economic. *The Balcony* demonstrates the futility of all forms of revolution which preserve intact the basic unit of exploitation and oppression, that between the sexes, male and female, *or* any of the substitutes for them. Taking the fundamental human connection, that of sexuality, to be the nuclear model of all the more elaborate social constructs growing out of it, Genet perceives that it is in itself not only hopelessly tainted but the very prototype of institutionalized inequality. He is convinced that by dividing humanity into two groups and appointing one to rule over the other by virtue of birthright, the social order has already established and ratified a system of oppression which will underlie and corrupt all other human relationships as well as every area of thought and experience.

The first scene, which takes place between a prostitute and a bishop, epitomizes the play much as it does the society it describes. The cleric holds power only through the myth of religion, itself dependent on the fallacy of sin, in turn conditional on the lie that the female is sexuality itself and therefore an evil worthy of the bishop's condign punishment. By such devious routes does power circle round and round the hopeless mess we have made of sexuality. And money: for it is with money that the woman is purchased, and economic dependency is but another sign of her bondage to a system whose coercive agents are not only mythical but actual. Delusions about sex foster delusions of power, and both depend on the reification of woman.

That the Bishop is actually a gasman visiting the bordello's "chambers of illusions" so that he can vicariously share in the power of the church only clarifies this satire on the sexual class system. Those males relegated to reading gas meters may still participate in the joys of mastery through the one human being any male can buy—a female as whore. And the whore, one wonders, what profits her? Nothing. Her "role" in the ritual theater where sexual, political, and social institutions are so felicitously combined is merely to accommodate the ruling passion of each of her rentiers.

In the second scene, the whore is a thief and a criminal (versions of Genet himself) so that a bank clerk may play at justice and morality. Her judge may order her whipped by a muscular executioner or grant her mercy in a transcendent imitation of the powers-that-be, powers reserved to other more fortunate males. The General of Scene III, following his own notions of masculine majesty, converts his whore into his mount and plays at hero while her mouth bleeds from the bit. No matter with which of the three leading roles of sinner, malefactor, or animal the male client may choose to mime his delusions of grandeur, the presence of the woman is utterly essential. To each masquerading male the female is a mirror in which he beholds himself. And the penultimate moment in his illusory but purchasable power fantasy is the moment when whether as Bishop, Judge, or General, he "fucks" her as woman, as subject, as chattel.

THE POLITICAL WISDOM implicit in Genet's statement in the play is that unless the ideology of real or fantasized virility is abandoned, unless the clinging to male supremacy as a birthright is finally foregone, all systems of oppression will continue to function simply by virtue of their logical and emotional mandate in the primary human situation. But what of the madame herself? Irma, the Balcony's able and dedicated administrator, makes money by selling other women, wherein it may be observed how no institution holds sway without collaborators and overseers. Chosen as queen under the counterrevolution Irma does nothing at all, for queens do not rule. In fact, they do not even exist in themselves; they die as persons once they assume their function, as the Envoy graciously explains. Their function is to serve as figureheads and abstractions to males, just as Chantal, a talented former whore who moves for a moment toward human realization by means of her hope in the revolution, wavers and then is sold anew and converted into the sexual figurehead for the uprising when it becomes corrupt and betrays its radical ideals under the usual excuse of expediency. "In order to win" it adopts the demented consciousness of its opponent and establishes a rotten new version of all it had once stood against. In no time it turns the rebellion into a suicidal carnival, an orgy of blood connected to the old phallic fantasy of "shoot and screw." Its totem is the ritual scapegoat provided by every army's beauty queen since Troy. Once Chantal enters upon the mythical territory of a primitive standard and prize over whom males will tear each other apart, the revolution passes irrevocably into counterrevolution.

Throughout *The Balcony* Genet explores the pathology of virility, the chimera of sexual congress as a paradigm of power over other human beings. He appears to be the only living male writer of first-class literary gifts to have transcended the sexual myths of our era. His critique of the heterosexual politic points the way toward a true sexual revolution, a path which must be explored if any radical social change is to come about. In Genet's analysis, it is fundamentally impossible to change society without changing personality, and sexual personality as it has generally existed must undergo the most drastic overhaul.

If we are to be free at last, Genet proposes in the last scenes of the play, we must first break those chains of our own making through our blind acceptance of common ideas. The three great cages in which we are immured must be dismantled. The first is the potential power of the "Great Figures"—the cleric, the judge and the warrior—elements of myth which have enslaved consciousness in a coil of self-imposed absurdity. The second is the omnipotence of the police state, the only virtual power in a corrupt society, all other forms of coercion being largely psychological. Last, and most insidious of all, is the cage of sex, the cage in which all others are enclosed: for is not the totem of Police Chief George a six-foot, rubber phallus, a "prick of great stature"? And the old myth of sin and virtue, the myth of guilt and innocence, the myth of heroism and cowardice on which the Great Figures repose, old pillars of an old and decadent structure, are also built on the sexual fallacy. (Or as one is tempted to pun, phallacy.) By attempting to replace this corrupt and tottering edifice while preserving its foundations, the revolution's own bid for social transformation inevitably fails and turns into the counterrevolution where the Grand Balcony, a first-class whorehouse, furnishes both costumes and actors for the new pseudo-government.

Genet's play ends as it had begun. Irma turning out the lights informs us we may go home, where all is falser than the theater's rites. The brothel will open again tomorrow for an identical ritual. The sounds of revolution begin again offstage, but unless the Police Chief is permanently imprisoned in his tomb and unless the new rebels have truly forsworn the customary idiocy of the old sexual politics, there will be no revolution. Sex is deep at the heart of our troubles, Genet is urging, and unless we eliminate the most pernicious of our systems of oppression, unless we go to the very center of the sexual politic and its sick delirium of power and violence, all our efforts at liberation will only land us again in the same primordial stews.

From "Sexual Politics: Miller, Mailer and Genet",
by Kate Millett, *New American Review No. 7 1969*

WHAT IS
WOMEN'S
LIBERATION?

A HARD RAIN'S GONNA FALL

What is women's liberation? It is simply organized rage against real oppression. Recently a woman phoned to say she had just had an abortion at one of the best hospitals in the District of Columbia. Because she couldn't find a doctor to help her before, she couldn't have the abortion until her fifth month of pregnancy. She therefore had to have a more complicated and dangerous saline injection, rather than a simple D and C. The saline solution, when injected into the womb, brings on labor contractions in several hours to several days thereafter. The woman had to wait in the hospital until the fetus was expelled, and for the entire operation she paid the exhorbitant fee of $1,000, in advance, not counting the time she lost from work, etc.

The doctor she went to, an ob./gyn. who practices at that hospital, didn't let her know when to enter the hospital until three hours prior to the time he could see her. He told her nothing about the procedure, only that when she went into labor she might ask a nurse for a pain-killer. She waited in terror, not knowing what would happen, on the maternity ward watching newborns come and go until she aborted. She was treated like someone's dead aunt hidden in a closet. Nurses brought her food only when she rang persistently to ask for it, but she was given no other attention.

When she finally went into labor three days later she was in great pain. The nurse refused to give her any drugs; no doctor was phoned. When the nurse finally came to her room about an hour after she first rang, she angrily gave her a bedpan and told her to call after the fetus was expelled. There, alone in her bed, the woman went through several hours of labor, had her five month old fetus in the bedpan, and two hours after the ordeal was over, the nurse finally came to take the pan away.

This woman had to stay in the bed with the bloody fetus in the pan the whole time since she was too weak to move. No antibiotics were given, and she was sent home several hours afterward. She later developed high fever and some infection, and was finally treated by her family doctor since the ob/gyn was not available.

I repeat: this was not a charity case in a city hospital. This was a $1,000 operation at the city's best. You can imagine what happens at D.C. General, the public hospital, but most women never get to a hospital at all.

This is the oppression women's liberation is about. It is caused by the sexism of a profit-based society that refuses to provide adequate health care, that refuses to develop safe contraception, that refuses to allow women the choice of when to bear children, that bases its health system, like everything else, on profit for drug companies, private corporations and not on human needs, that refuses to take responsibility for rearing future generations of children. This is what the women's liberation movement is fighting—not only the images of femaleness *Time* stresses, although those sexy ads and beauty contests are a good indication of the kind of shuffling women are being trained to do.

Since women are both wage and non-wage workers, and since the basis for the economic and social oppression we face cannot be solved on bread and butter struggles alone, it is necessary that we organize into one massive "union" as sisters who will fight sexism and capitalist exploitation of that ideology. We must organize where we now are in hospitals, in industry, at service jobs, and at home in our communities.

We must make programmatic demands that will lead in the direction of our freedom. We need: free medical care that is non-profit and based on preventive medicine; free and safe contraception and abortion; free child-care facilities, day and night for all; wages paid to women for currently uncompensated labor—during pregnancy, for child-rearing, for domestic work at home; equal wages for equal work; and an end to sexist and racist tracking and education.

There are some models that women are now experimenting with:

1. Union caucuses: Women, Inc., a woman's caucus of the Association of Western Pulp and Paper Workers Union, has been demonstrating in Antioch and Stockton, California against both Fibreboard, the corporation that employs them, and their union, for discrimination in wages, in services (day-care, for example), and in hiring/firing, placement on seniority lists, rewritten job definitions, and general discrimination against women workers. They are demanding equal pay for equal work, an end to the misuse of state protective labor legislation, an end to the arbitrary lay-offs of women and for company supported child-care facilities.

This may be the first example of a separate woman's struggle within the organized labor movement since the turn of the century. It certainly is a breakthrough in not allowing either the bosses or the union to channel dissent solely into wage-demands.

2. Organizing women in "women's work"—There has been almost no organizing done in jobs women primarily hold—either by unions or by movement groups. Generally women are seen only as temporary workers, so they are ignored. Women's liberation groups all over are trying to organize secretaries, waitresses and domestics, to give a few examples, not only as workers around worker-type grievances, but as women who will probably not always work these particular jobs, but who will always suffer from exploitative sexism. Therefore, we are organizing around the general condition of women.

3. In the early part of this century the I.W.W. attempted to organize everyone into one big union—the employed, the skilled, the unskilled, and the unemployed. They failed, and were ripped apart by cops, the government, and their own lack of clear direction. It is the intent of Women's Liberation to organize women as one big union wherever they are. Sexism is a total life confrontation. We, as women are now divided into classes, according to race, and by the arbitrary definition of worker vs. non-worker (housewife). We must unite to end the oppression of all women.

There has always been sexism, no matter what the economic system. But sexism has no chance of being eliminated under capitalism. Should some of us think we have "made it", whatever that means, the rest of us will still be used to supply cheap, free and reserve labor, to consume, to scab on each other. We need a socialist system based on human needs, not the profit of some off the exploitation of all the others. We as women must create a total revolution—a classless society where racism and sexism cannot exist. Only in solidarity can we be free, but only in struggle can we create that freedom.

—Marilyn Salzman Webb

From "A Hard Rain's Gonna Fall" by Marilyn Salzman Webb, **win** 1/1/70

An old, Army magazine ad.

AMERICA'S MORAL STRENGTH

'Marry or Die'- The New Feminism

By Margie Stamberg

Inverse red-baiting has become popular on the left, wherein those in women's liberation are considered bourgeois, with the only true reds being women who remain in "the movement."

Fortunately, most women refuse to participate in the "who's redder than who" syndrome which labels feminist groups reformist, non-class-conscious or whatever phrase is the greatest anathema at the time. While the contentless name-calling persists from those who use the "anti-red-menace" approach to dismiss radical feminism for the first time offers to women a supportive movement that allows its members to grow politically.

Women from many New York groups discussed why this should be, and the ways they think the movement is going.

"We have got to completely redefine what it means to be either male or female, and throw out everything that is not human," responded Kate Millett when asked why

she is critical of the left. "The movement is caught up in the eternal male fantasies of violence and weapons. I think the left is getting to a point where all they want is a change of power. They have equated their manhood with humanity, just as for the white supremacist whiteness equals humanity.

We must find our history

"The women's movement must define itself in terms of itself," says Rosalyn Baxandall of New York Radical Women. "We must find our history and create it. We must remain separate for we can talk to women in ways the left never can. We can reach women who are out of the universities, who are secretaries, waitresses, nurses who would never run into the left. The key to this is the family. Some women feel that to attack this is inherently revolutionary. They feel that women are 53% of the population and the key to everyone else's liberation. Whether or not this is true, if women were to be liberated, all institutions, jobs, schools, would have to be radically changed."

"Both men and women are totally ignorant about women's lives," says Myrna Wood. "We must understand that a woman's life depends on who she marries."

This is true for typists, saleswomen, factory workers, educated women and radical women alike.

Because this is true, women have a special way of identifying with their jobs, with their schools and with their movement. Because this is true, capitalism is able to exploit them in particular ways. But to attack capitalism alone does not attack the roots of the oppression.

The family system with its ideology of institutionalized male supremacy is interrelated with and used by capitalism, but the systems are not identical. It is likely that the feminist movement will remain separatist until the left is ready to accept the overthrow of the family system.

A WITCH leaflet, distributed at New York's Bridal Fair a month ago, began: "Women were the first slaves, the first barter items way back when the monied economy and the patriarchal structure were just beginning. Ever since then, the pressure has been on women to marry or face society's rejection as a spinster—a species of subhuman. A woman is taught from infancy that her only real goal in life is to fulfill the role of wife and mother of male heirs. She is allowed an identity only as an appendage to a man. An unmarried girl is considered a freak—a lesbian, a castrating career girl, a fallen woman, a bitch, unnatural, a frustrated old maid, sick. In the end she begins to believe these innuendos herself. There is no way out—marry or die.

"The corporations are quick to capitalize on our insecurities, to transform self-doubts and emotional needs into commodities and sell them back to us at a profit."

It is only secondarily as consumers, however, that capitalism has been able to exploit women. Women are used also as a reserve pool of labor—can be paid lower wages for the same jobs, be ineligible for fringe benefits, penalized for the responsibilities of child care.

"Capitalism has incorporated the family system into its structure," says Ellen Willis of Redstockings. "Business can translate the relation of women and men inside the family into the work world and can relegate intelligent and educated women into doing menial jobs. A woman is kept in control by her fears of getting out of line in terms of her relationship with men at work."

Early attempts by the women's movement to organize women not to buy proved ineffective. According to Ellen Willis, this is because male supremacy is not a superficial manifestation of capitalism, but institutionalized. "Women are not simply shackled by the past or brainwashed by the media," she says. "Women buy because they are oppressed. They must buy makeup because they must be good sexual objects. The capitalist system simply made the goods available; it didn't create the need. If this is not realized it puts you in a real bind about how to approach women. If things in this country change, maybe people won't feel the need to buy. But don't attack the effect instead of the cause."

Consumption overemphasized

"The concentration on the consumption of clothing and cosmetics is overemphasized," Myrna Wood feels.

"It is only for a very short time that a woman can afford to spend like this. If we are talking about consumption we must talk about finance companies, cheaply made but costly furniture, cars, and the prices of food."

"Some movement people argue that to organize around women's issues is counterrevolutionary, that it splits the working class," she continued. But the splits are already there. Like racism, male supremacy is an important cause of disunity. The practice of male supremacy does not provide any material gains for the male working class. That is, the white male worker does not get any *higher* pay because women and blacks get less. In fact he has to fight harder for what he *does* get since management can threaten to hire the lower-paid women and blacks.

"However, the male supremacist ideology does develop in men a male chauvinist attitude which meets a psychological need. It replaces with a false manhood the real humanhood they have lost through total powerlessness in the society. This false sense of power serves to blind them to the way the class's interests are set against each other. Male supremacy does provide, however, real material value to the capitalist system."

The failure to understand how the family system oppresses men and women presents a stumbling block for the left. It is also a reason why many women are unwilling to spend their time battling male supremacy within the movement when they could be out organizing women.

For a while the tendency in women's liberation was to view women's oppression as a history which became a psychology. Groups are realizing now that there are real consequences, not simply internalized fears, for stepping out of role.

"The free sexual revolution has only served to oppress women and especially radical women," says Roz Baxandall. "If she doesn't want to sleep with men, a woman is 'hung up.' If she does, she's known as someone's wife or girl friend. And men still look down on women who have gone through lots of men in the movement. The reverse, of course, is not true."

On solidarity

"The real basis of SDS hasn't changed nor can it without institutional change. Consciousness-raising within the movement is limited because it doesn't confront the institutions or even look at them. The movement still feels the same way about women it always did. And the emotional way women tend to relate holds them back in the male movement. We don't want to be nonemotional. When you're finding out what you want, you can't do it with a group that already knows what it wants."

"The complete hostility which men feel towards women is so deep it is beyond our deepest projection, thank God," adds Shulamith Firestone. If you take away the sexual aspect of man to woman, if he realizes he can get nothing from you, his true hostility begins to show.

"Sex with men is totally wrapped up in ego," she continued. "A man has to prove he is virile and able to conquer. This kind of involvement means he can't love. To love means you make yourself vulnerable. With the new 'emancipation,' women are supposed to act like men. Men blame women for being 'possessive, clinging.'

"Women have been spared the destruction that occurs to men. We don't want to be like them, we don't want a movement that parallels them... Single women are defined by their love lives," she added. To say they shouldn't be won't solve the problem. We must develop solidarity about sexual things and think of sex politically."

"We have to see organizing women as our top priority," concluded Myrna Wood.

The dual attacks on the family system and its interrelation with capitalism can reach out to women in ways the left has never been able to before—for it is the family system which isolates a woman from her sisters, which casts women in the roles of enemies and competitors in the desperate struggle for a husband.

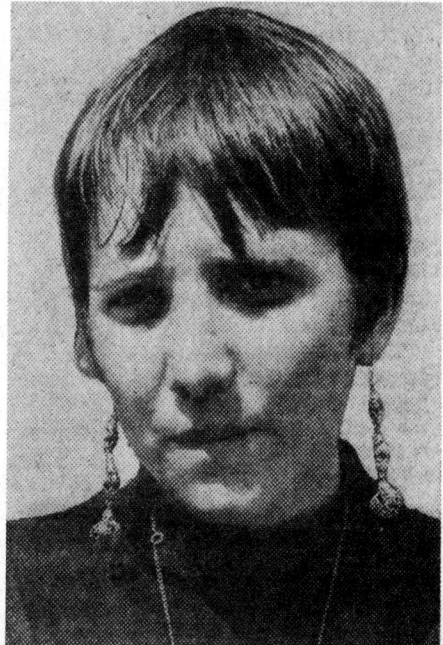

TO GIVE
FULL TIME
TO THE
REVOLUTION

Josephine Drexel Duke Is Engaged To John Marshall Geste Brown Jr.

Miss Josephine Drexel Duke, who carried two of society's most illustrious names into the thick of the S.D.S. struggle against Columbia University, plans to marry Specialist 4 John Marshall Geste Brown Jr., U.S.A.

Specialist Brown, a product of the same Main Line circles as his fiancée's family, is stationed at Fort Dix, N. J., where Miss Duke, a devoted worker for the radical Students for a Democratic Society, helped organize a coffeehouse for enlisted men.

The future bride interrupted her father, Anthony Drexel Duke, in the middle of a speech Thursday night at a Boys Harbor banquet to tell him the news. He took her phone call in the kitchen at the interracial summer camp for boys he founded in East Hampton, L. I., when he was a student at St. Paul's School.

Miss Duke, who is 20 years old, attended Barnard College, where she was a member of the original S.D.S. group that occupied Hamilton Hall and seized the office of Columbia's president, Grayson Kirk, in the spring of 1968. The future bride, who later became the leading spokesman for S.D.S. at Columbia, withdrew from college "to give full time to the revolution."

Her radical activities drew praise from her father, who said, "She is doing something she believes in, she is working hard at it, and I respect her for it. She seems very much involved in the Fort Dix Coffee House."

The prospective bride is the daughter also of Mrs. John Richard Dunn of Coconut Grove, Fla., the former Elizabeth Ordway of Palm Beach, Fla.

Specialist Brown, who is 22, returned to the United States last Christmas after being wounded in Vietnam. He is the son of Mr. and Mrs. John Marshall Brown of Villanova, Pa. His father is a partner of Elkins, Morris, Stroud & Co., members of the New York Stock Exchange in Philadelphia.

Miss Duke was graduated from the Everglades School in Miami and made her debut in 1967 at a dance given at the River Club by her father and her uncle, Angier Biddle Duke, former Ambassador to Denmark and Spain and Chief of Protocol in the Kennedy Administration.

The New York Times

Miss Josephine Drexel Duke

The future bride is a granddaughter of Mrs. T. Markoe Robertson, the former Cordelia Drexel Biddle, of New York and Southampton, L. I., and the late Angier Buchanan Duke.

She is a great-great-granddaughter of Washington Duke, founder of the American Tobacco Company, and a great-granddaughter of Benjamin N. Duke, who was associated with his brother, James B. Duke, in the endowment of Trinity College, which became Duke University. Miss Duke is descended from Nicholas Biddle of Philadelphia, who was president of the Bank of the United States.

Her fiancé attended the Episcopal Academy in Philadelphia and St. George's School in Newport, R. I., before enlisting in the Army.

From the Society page of

The New York Times 8/31/69

REDSTOCKINGS MANIFESTO

I. After centuries of individual and preliminary political struggle, women are uniting to achieve their final liberation from male supremacy. Redstockings is dedicated to building this unity and winning our freedom.

II. Women are an oppressed class. Our oppression is total, affecting every facet of our lives. We are exploited as sex objects, breeders, domestic servants, and cheap labor. We are considered inferior beings, whose only purpose is to enhance men's lives. Our humanity is denied. Our prescribed behavior is enforced by the threat of physical violence.

Because we have lived so intimately with our oppressors, in isolation from each other, we have been kept from seeing our personal suffering as a political condition. This creates the illusion that a woman's relationship with her man is a matter of interplay between two unique personalities, and can be worked out individually. In reality, every such relationship is a *class* relationship, and the conflicts between individual men and women are *political* conflicts that can only be solved collectively.

III. We identify the agents of our oppression as men. Male supremacy is the oldest, most basic form of domination. All other forms of exploitation and oppression (racism, capitalism, imperialism, etc.) are extensions of male supremacy: men dominate women, a few men dominate the rest. All power structures throughout history have been male-dominated and male-oriented. Men have controlled all political, economic and cultural institutions and backed up this control with physical force. They have used their power to keep women in an inferior position. *All men* receive economic, sexual, and psychological benefits from male supremacy. *All men* have oppressed women.

IV. Attempts have been made to shift the burden of responsibility from men to institutions or to women themselves. We condemn these arguments as evasions. Institutions alone do not oppress; they are merely tools of the oppressor. To blame institutions implies that men and women are equally victimized, obscures the fact that men benefit from the subordination of women, and gives men the excuse that they are forced to be oppressors. On the contrary, any man is free to renounce his superior position provided that he is willing to be treated like a woman by other men.

We also reject the idea that women consent to or are to blame for their own oppression. Women's submission is not the result of brainwashing, stupidity, or mental illness but of continual, daily pressure from men. We do not need to change ourselves, but to change men.

The most slanderous evasion of all is that women can oppress men. The basis for this illusion is the isolation of individual relationships from their political context and the tendency of men to see any legitimate challenge to their privileges as persecution.

V. We regard our personal experience, and our feelings about that experience, as the basis for an analysis of our common situation. We cannot rely on existing ideologies as they are all products of male supremacist culture. We question every generalization and accept none that are not confirmed by our experience.

Our chief task at present is to develop female class consciousness through sharing experience and publicly exposing the sexist foundation of all our institutions. Consciousness-raising is not "therapy," which implies the existence of individual solutions and falsely assumes that the male-female relationship is purely personal, but the only method by which we can ensure that our program for liberation is based on the concrete realities of our lives.

The first requirement for raising class consciousness is honesty, in private and in public, with ourselves and other women.

VI. We identify with all women. We define our best interest as that of the poorest, most brutally exploited woman.

We repudiate all economic, racial, educational or status privileges that divide us from other women. We are determined to recognize and eliminate any prejudices we may hold against other women.

We are committed to achieving internal democracy. We will do whatever is necessary to ensure that every woman in our movement has an equal chance to participate, assume responsibility, and develop her political potential.

VII. We call on all our sisters to unite with us in struggle.

We call on all men to give up their male privileges and support women's liberation in the interest of our humanity and their own.

In fighting for our liberation we will always take the side of women against their oppressors. We will not ask what is "revolutionary" or "reformist," only what is good for women.

The time for individual skirmishes has passed. This time we are going all the way.

July 7, 1969
REDSTOCKINGS
P.O. Box 748
Stuyvesant Station
New York, N.Y. 10009

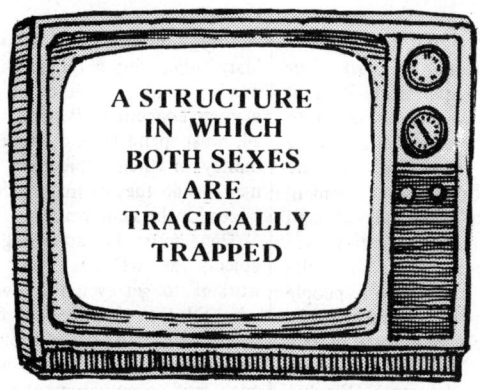

A STRUCTURE
IN WHICH
BOTH SEXES
ARE
TRAGICALLY
TRAPPED

I'm a good anti-racist and a good anti-imperialist and J expect as much from all the broads I screw!

Marxists have quite rightly always stressed that the subordination of women is part of the total mutual devouring process called capitalism. No one group can be liberated except through a transformation of the whole structure of social relationships.

But subordination is not an affair of economics or institutions only. Nor is it only to do with contraception, abortion, orgasm, and sexual equality, important as these are.

It is an assumed secondariness which dwells in a whole complex of inarticulate attitudes, in smirks, in offsides, in insecurities, in desperate status differentiation. Secondariness happens in people's heads and is expressed every time they assume no one would listen. It is located in a structure in which both sexes are tragically trapped. The man as much as the woman, for each time he tries to break through, he meets the hostility of other men or the conflicting demands of those women who prefer the traditional sex game. It is only women who can dissolve the assumptions. It is only women who can say what they feel because the experience is unique to them.

Only women can define themselves. To define yourself you have to explore yourself, you have to find yourself as a group before you can say how you regard yourself as a group. It is only by understanding your situation as a group that you can relate it to the system through which you are dominated

This means a certain withdrawal into the group and a realization on the part of the elite of a common identity. This means that just as the white middle class Cuban found he was a spic and the black PhD that he was a nigger, the privileged woman has to extend beyond her elite consciousness to learn the extent of her common condition with the unprivileged woman. Only then can women really challenge the external definitions imposed on them, become sufficiently conscious to act and thus be recognized as being there.

The enemy is not identified as man. This is as futile as a black white student worker conflict. The ally is not the woman who supports and benefits from capitalism. It is all people who are being crushed and twisted who want space and air and time to sit in the sun.

But the oppressed have to discover their own dignity, their own freedom, they have to make themselves equal. They have to decolonize themselves. Then they can liberate the colonizers.

Men you have nothing to lose but your chains. You will no longer have anyone to creep away and peep at with their knickers down, no one to flaunt as the emblem of your virility, status, self-importance, no one who will trap you, overwhelm you, no etherealized cloudy being floating unattainable in a plastic blue sky, no great mopping up handkerchief comforters to crawl into from your competitive, ego strutting alienation, who will wrap you up and SMOTHER you.

There will only be thousands of millions of women people to discover, touch and become with, who will say with a Vietnamese girl, "Let us now emulate each other," who will understand you when you say we must make a new world in which we do not meet each other as exploiters and used objects. Where we love one another and into which a new kind of human being can be born.

From *The Black Dwarf*, a London underground paper, as reprinted in **OLD MOLE**

HAIRY LEGS FREAK FISHY LIBERAL

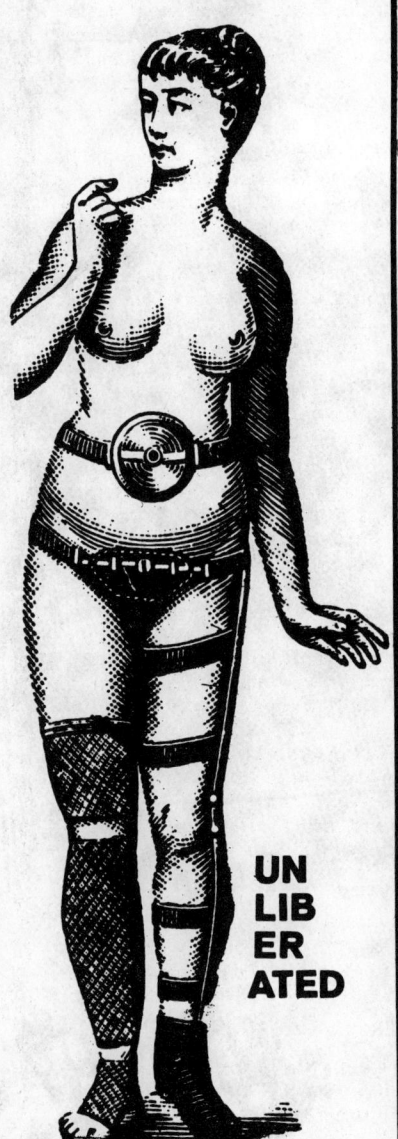

UN
LIB
ER
ATED

by Sheilah Drummond

Some women in San Francisco helped a sister recently, and dealt with a problem that we all share.

On Nov. 5, Mary Alice Carlson, a student at San Francisco State, was called to go to work at Aquatic Specialties, 24th and Vicente, as a saleswoman. She had applied for the job along with several other women a week previously. One of the owners. * * * * * hired her, telling her to begin work two days later. The job consisted of cleaning dead fish from the tanks, learning the names of different species, and waiting on customers.

She came to work at 2:00 p.m. About five-thirty, * * * asked her to come into the back room for a talk. She did. He told her that he didn't think she was going to "work out here," and, in fact, that she was fired. She asked him why.

At first he refused an explanation, but she demanded that he give her some reason, so finally he told her it was because of her "grooming." What, she asked, was wrong with her grooming? (Mary Alice was wearing a clean, simple, straight dress, flat shoes. She was neat and clean.)

* * * told her, "You don't shave your legs."

Mary Alice was stunned. She asked if she was incompetent on the job. She couldn't believe that she was actually being fired because she didn't shave her legs. However, it was true.

She asked how it was that he had hired her (as he claimed at the time) over 16 other applicants when, after all, he had interviewed her and apparently had not been offended at that time by her unshaven legs. He said he had not noticed this at the time or he wouldn't have hired her.

* * * said that he felt rather badly about the whole thing and so he would be willing to pay Mary Alice for a whole day instead of just three hours. Mary Alice declined the payoff and left for home, feeling a sense of unreality about the whole thing, as if she'd somehow gotten mixed up in someone else's scene. It was so hard to believe—but by the time she got home she was both hurt and angry. She talked with her roommates about what had happened, and women involved in San Francisco Women's Liberation began to call each

other and talk about it.

Women from at least four different groups decided that some action should be taken to help this sister. A leaflet and some signs were made up, and on Saturday morning some women, some men and some kids gathered to picket Aquatic Specialties.

The picketers handed out the leaflets and rapped with people going by. People were surprised to hear the story and were mostly sympathetic. Many customers did not go into the store. Finally, * * * screeched up onto the curb in his huge car, in a cacophony of tires, horn and brakes. He was most upset, and agreed to talk with the women.

At first he maintained that Mary Alice was incompetent, and laid down a rap about what a lousy (and possibly dishonest) employee she was. Then he told the group that a Chronicle reporter had called him and asked about Mary Alice and he had told the reporter that she had been fired for incompetence and dishonesty. (A suspect amount of money in the cash register—)

Mary Alice told him that he had slandered her and was continuing to do so and she might well sue him for it.

Then * * * became even more upset, and opened his jacket to flash a small peace button which he had pinned discreetly inside. He told the girls they shouldn't do this to him as it was ruining his business and after all he was a liberal and he thought their movement was all about peace and love and flowers and they were costing him money, this was terrible, and wouldn't they PLEASE GO HOME!

The girls said they wouldn't go home until he did right by Mary Alice! So * * * finally agreed that he would call the Chronicle reporter and take back the slanderous things he had said about Mary Alice being incompetent and dishonest, and that he would hire her back. In the presence of the sisters he did indeed make this call and admit that he and not Mary Alice had misrepresented the situation and that he had been wrong in firing her for not having shaved her legs, and that he was hiring her back.

In a movement of people who are only just beginning to realize that they are oppressed and who have not yet got a really strong sense of unity or purpose, a

victory, however small, is sweet. Mary Alice felt good about the whole action, as did all the women concerned. Women, after all, must spend far more time and money on their appearance than men, while they're making lower wages for the same work.

They must be appealing sex objects as well as competent workers to get even the low-pay jobs. (Not to mention our black sisters, who must try to look like WHITE sex objects). This writer once quit an employment-agency job because of a hassle over a black sister I wasn't even allowed to try to place—with three years of college, she couldn't even get a lousy typing job because she was too "ugly,"—that is, too black, lips too thick, and didn't straighten her hair or wear a wig.

What is Women's Liberation all about, anyway? Maybe it's idealistic, but I think it's about women using their united strength to help first themselves, then each other, then all oppressed, fucked-over people everywhere. We are alienated from each other by the belief in our own inferiority, the belief that we are not, indeed, whole and complete people just as we are, without the penis, with the vagina.

Because of this, we find our situation much like that of the blacks in the stinking Amerikan cities, who turn their hate and frustration on each other. We are familiar with the black cop who oppresses other black people even more than his white counterpart.

We sisters have to deal with the fact that not just men oppress women. Women oppress women. (Gods protect us all from the "respectable" women who have always been the first ones to cast a stone, or a boulder if they can lift one, against their less fortunate sisters.) We must learn to have love for ourselves as the whole and complete people that we are—then we show love and practical, real help for each other.

In San Francisco, that's what they did. They cared about a sister in need and got together to help her, and they were successful. Love to my sisters across the Bay. You make me proud of myself, you make me like myself a little better. Let's build to the point where Women's Liberation is a number that any sister with a problem can call and get whatever action is required.

FROM: WOMAN AND HER MIND: THE STORY OF EVERYDAY LIFE

By Meredith Tax

I. The Assaults of Daily Life

Women are hyper-aware of their surroundings. They have to be. Walk down a city street without being tuned in and you're in real danger; our society is one in which men rape, mug, and murder women whom they don't even know every day. You'd better keep track of what car is slowing down, and of who is walking up behind you.

You must be constantly on the watch for other reasons. Without this radar, how can you be sure of taking advantage of your opportunities? The role you have been given is a passive one; you can't go out and promote what you want, but must think fast and grab it as it flies past.

The self-conscious and consciousness of others that is trained into women is necessary, but it is also extreme and oppressive. There's a lot to be said for being conscious of other people's behavior and needs; and even the self-effacing emotional service-station aspect of many women's behavior is preferable to the unconsciousness bred into men. But the price is high. Since our awareness of others is considered our duty, our job, the price we pay when things go wrong is guilt, self-hatred. And things always go wrong. We respond with apologies; we continue to apologize long after the event is forgotten—and even if it had no causal relation to anything we did to begin with. If the rain spoils someone's picnic, we apologize. We apologize for taking up space in a room, for living. How willingly we would suffer to prevent someone else a moment's discomfort!

I think that for some of my generation, caught in the kind of double binds we have all been caught in, it is impossible to achieve revolutionary consciousness without some sort of confrontation with the self. Politically, this is both a weakness and a strength. It is an asset to come to political understanding through personal pain: it makes possible a gut understanding of how society works as a system dependent on the personal suffering and deprivation of each of us. Such understanding is a help in building a revolutionary movement. Only by realizing what we might have been, can we imagine how different women in a post-revolutionary society might be able to be. But knowing that we cannot achieve this ourselves, that no matter how we struggle we are still in some part of ourselves "damaged goods" (to use the appropriate capitalist terminology), that we can see what has gone wrong within ourselves, and still be unable to put it permanently right—this is very painful and discouraging. But it is necessary: it is this realization that makes it evident that there really are no individual solutions to woman's oppression, no way that one can float free of our society and its conditioning. The pain of it is what makes us search so urgently for new forms of social organization that can help us, and others, change and transcend our limitations. This pain is what makes us realize, in our everyday lives, that *social* change is absolutely necessary.

Only the most radical of social changes—one far more radical in its attack on the basic institutions of this society that traps us, and far more drastic in the changes it effects on human consciousness, than previous revolutions—has a chance of doing the job, of freeing us and freeing those who will be born out of our lives.

II. Female Schizophrenia

A young woman is walking down a city street. She is excruciatingly aware of her appearance and of the reaction to it (imagined or real) of every person she meets. She walks through a group of construction workers who are eating lunch in a line along the pavement. Her stomach tightens with terror and revulsion; her face becomes contorted into a grimace of self-control and fake unawareness; her walk and carriage become stiff and dehumanized. No matter what they say to her, it will be unbearable. She knows that they will not physically assault her or hurt her. What they will do is *impinge* on her. They will make her a participant in their fantasies without asking if she is willing. They will make her feel ridiculous, or grotesquely sexual, or hideously ugly. Above all, they will make her feel like a *thing.*

You can say what you like about class and race. Those differences are real. But in this everyday scenario, any man or earth, no matter what his color or class is, has the power to make any woman who is exposed to him hate herself and her body. Any man has this power as *man,* the dominant sex, to dehumanize woman, even to herself.

In *The Divided Self,* Laing describes the experience of schizophrenia, the contradictory kind of self-consciousness that extends to one's very existence, that is, who is literally not sure he exists.

Let us go into the mind of a woman who is confined to her house, who goes out only to shop, to visit other women, or to chauffeur her kids, and whose only work, or function, is to take care of a man and some children. For her the contradiction will present itself this way:

"I am nothing when I am by myself. In myself, I am nothing. I only know that I exist because I am needed by someone who is real, my husband, and by my children. My husband goes out into the real world. Other people recognize him as real, and take him into account. He effects other people and events. He does things and changes things and they are different afterwards. I stay in my imaginary world in this house, doing jobs that I largely invent, and that no-one cares about but myself. I do not change things. The work I do changes nothing; what I cook disappears, what I clean one day must be cleaned again the next. I seem to be involved in some sort of mysterious process rather than actions that have results.

"The only time that I think I might be real in myself is when I hear myself screaming or having hysterics. But it is at these times that I am in the most danger—of being told that I am wrong, or that I'm really not like what I'm acting like, or that he hates me. If he stops loving me, I'm sunk; I won't have any purpose in life, or be sure I exist any more. I must efface myself in order to avoid this, and not make any demands on him, or do anything that might offend him. I feel dead now, but if he stops loving me I am really dead, because I am nothing by myself. I have to be noticed to know I exist.

"But, if I efface myself, how can I be noticed?"

From the earliest age a girl is deprived of a sense of herself (ego). She is also deprived of a sense of her own competence, of her ability to do and understand things. She is told she must be pretty and sweet; she must be loveable; she mustn't make messes or play rough; she must perform services for Mommy and Daddy and be useful. How different this is from the way boys are socialized—they know they will be loved even if they make messes, stay out late without phoning, get dirty, and act like brats. That's what boys are supposed to do: have strong, competitive egos. Whereas girls are taught to see themselves as *objects* rather than subjects (if only by being continually told what they look like, and how important it is to have other people like them). They are taught to be charming, yet passive. They are taught to fail at most activities, so as not to be threatening or "unfeminine." They are taught to be of "service" to others, not to themselves, so that when they grow up they can be a wife and mother like their Mommy.

Women are stupified, made *stupid,* by the roles they are pushed into. Books on educational psychology always remark the junior high and high school years as ones in which the boys "catch up" to the girls, and begin to surpass them scholastically and on IQ tests. It's no accident that these years are the ones of increased social pressure upon girls to take up their post-pubescent feminine roles and learn to live with them. It's not that the boys are growing smarter; the girls are becoming stupified! Their IQ's—which, it is now recognized, are largely determined by social pressure and by the subject's expectations and sense of his own worth—continue to decline.

This remorseless stifling of a girl's intelligence and ego, this socialization into a life of service, this continued undermining of any possibility of independent achievement outside of the prescribed realm, all constitute a condition one could describe as *female schizophrenia.* Most women suffer from some form of it at some point in their lives. And most of them think of it as a "personal problem" rather than a social disease. That's part of the way they're trapped. For this condition is too widespread and too structurally based to be merely "personal" in origin. Our society could be described as one which drives women crazy.

From an article published by the New England Free Press, 791 Tremont St. Boston, Mass. 02118

WOMAN'S PLIGHT
IN THE
HIGH SCHOOLS

Jumping the Track

by Alice de Rivera

Before I went to John Jay High School I hadn't realized how bad the conditions were for students. One of the things which changed my outlook was being involved with the hostilities of the New York City teacher strikes in the fall of 1968. Students were trying to open the school and the teachers were preventing them.

It was then I found that students had no rights. We had no freedom of the press: many controversial articles were removed from the newspapers by the teacher editors. We were not allowed to distribute leaflets or newspapers inside our school building, so that press communication was taken away from us. We also had no freedom of speech. Many teachers would put us down in class for our political ideas and then would not let us answer their charges. If we tried to talk with other students during a free period about political issues, we were told to stop. The school was a prison—we were required by state law to be there, but when we were there we had no rights . . . .

I have been writing about the student's plight in general because it was my first encounter with oppression. It is such a familiar experience to me now that I think I can try to define it. Oppression, to me, is when people are not allowed to be themselves. I encountered this condition a second time when I realized *woman's* plight in the high schools.

The first time it really occurred to me that I was oppressed as a woman was when I began to think of what I was going to be when I was older. I realized I had no real plans for the future—college, maybe, and after that was a dark space in my mind. In talking and listening to other girls, I found that they had either the same blank spot in their mind or were planning on marriage. If not that, they figured on taking a job of some sort *until* they got married.

The boys that I knew all had at least some slight idea in their minds of what career or job they were preparing for. Some prepared for careers in science and math by going to a specialized school. Others prepared for their later jobs as mechanics, electricians, and other tradesmen in vocational schools. Some just did their thing in a regular zoned high school. It seemed to me that I should fill the blank spot in my mind as the boys were able to do, and I decided to study science (biology, in particular) much more intensively. It was then that I encountered one of the many blocks which stand in the woman student's way: discrimination against women in the specialized science and math high schools in the city.

Many years before women in New York State had won their right to vote (1917), a school was established for those high-school students who wished to specialize in science and math. Naturally it was not co-ed, for women were not regarded legally or psychologically as people. This school, Stuyvesant High School, was erected in 1903 . . . .

There are only two other high schools in New York which specialize in science and math: Brooklyn Technical, a school geared towards engineering; and Bronx High School of Science . . . .

Out of these three schools I could try out for only one. This one, Bronx Science, is one and a half hours travel time from my home. It presents very stiff competition because of the discriminatory policy which allows only a certain number of girls to enter, and also because all the girls who would otherwise by trying out for Stuyvesant or Brooklyn Tech have Bronx Science as their only alternative. I became disgusted with this, not only for my sake, but for all the girls who hadn't become scientists or engineers because they were a little less than brilliant or had been put down by nobody having challenged thosy little blank spots in their minds. After talking about it with my parents and friends, I decided to open up Stuyvesant and challenge the Board of Education's traditional policy.

The day on which we went to court was the day before the entrance exam was scheduled to be given. The Board of Education granted me the privilege of taking the test for Bronx Science (which is the same as the one given for Stuyvesant), and the judge recognized that the results of this test would be used in another court hearing to resolve whether or not I would be admitted. Five days after the other students had received their results, we found out that I had passed for entrance into both Stuyvesant and Bronx Science.

We went to court again a couple of months later, on April 30th the New York City Board of Education voted to admit me to Stuyvesant High School in the Fall.

There are a great many battles yet to be fought. Aside from being discouraged to study for a carrer, women are discouraged from preparing for jobs involving anything *but* secretarial work, beauty care, nursing, cooking, and the fashion industry. During my fight over Stuyvesant, I investigated the whole high-school scene; and found that out of the twenty-seven vocational high schools in the city, only *seven* are coed. The boys' vocational schools teach trades in electronics, plumbing, carpentry, foods, printing (another example of Board of Education traditional policy—there is hardly any work for a hand typesetter today), etc. The girls are taught to be beauticians, secretaries, or health aides. This means that if a girl is seeking entrance to a vocational school, she is pressured to feel that certain jobs are masculine and others feminine. She is forced to conform to the Board of Education's image of her sex . . . .

In conclusion, there are three types of schools, twenty-nine in number, that the Board of Education has copped out on. These schools are composed of the specialized science and math school Brooklyn Tech, twenty vocational schools which teach students their trade according to what sex they are, and the eight traditionally non-coed academic schools.

These eight academic schools are zoned schools which admit only boys or girls. The argument against these schools is that "separate but equal" is not equal (as established with regard to race in the Brown Decision). The psychological result of the school which is segregated by sex—only because of tradition— is to impress upon girls that they are only "flighty females" who would bother the boys' study habits (as a consequence of girls not being interested in anything but the male sex). This insinuates immaturity on the part of girls—and certainly produces it in both sexes. A boy who has never worked with a girl in the classroom is bound to think of her as his intellectual inferior, and will not treat her as if she had any capacity for understanding things other than childcare and homemaking. Both sexes learn to deal with each other as non-people. It really messes up the growth of a person's mind . . . .

All girls have been brought up by this society never being able to be themselves—the school system has reinforced this. My desire at this time is to change the educational situation to benefit *all* the students. But I'm afraid changes *could* be made that benefitted male students, leaving the status of females pretty much as it is. Female students share the general oppressive conditions forced upon everyone by the System's schools, plus a special psychological discrimination showed to women by the schools, the teachers, *and* their fellow students. So, since I don't want *my* issues to get swallowed up in the supposed "larger" issues, I'm going to make women's liberation the center of my fight.

ALICE DE RIVERA is a 14-year-old student recently suspended from John Jay High School for "political activities." In the fall she will be the first girl to attend Stuyvesant High School in Manhattan.

It is sad that any person must struggle so hard to do what they want to do. It is a lonely struggle and young girls find it even lonelier and harder for boys. It is a fundamentally alienating experience for both sexes. I understood better when I was in Cuba last summer the small but concrete ways this alienation manifests itself.

The buses in Cuba are crowded with people. You are lucky to make it to the door for your stop. When I'd ask directions from someone, everyone in the bus would start arguing and gesticulating about the quickest and simplest route. But it wasn't just the spontaneity, the laughing and aggressive pushing and touching. What impressed me more was that women, standing with babies in their arms, could quite freely put their child down in the lap of the person sitting in front of them. They weren't afraid. They didn't have to struggle alone, like we do in Toronto subways, hoping that our child won't cry. In Cuba, the women didn't have to be urban guerrillas — constantly watching for washrooms, seats and tables.

I went into day nurseries, filled with "chiciticos." little ones, brought by their mothers on the way to the field and the office. They were tiny, some of those babies, and they looked not a bit neglected.

And I worked in the fields with some of their mothers. They had a clear sense of working to build a communal society in which everybody could share heavy physical work and tough political decisions. And it was experiencing and seeing how deeply they incorporated the nation's necessity to survive, that I understood emotionally and not intellectually, our oppression. For we have not only been robbed as women of a place in the world, we have been robbed as people of a cultural identity and a national purpose.

From "Sugar and Spice" by Sarah Spinks, *This Magazine Is About Schools* Summer 1969

THE POLITICS OF THE FAMILY
By R. D. Laing

". . .families, schools, churches are the slaughter-houses of our children; colleges and other places are the kitchens. As adults in marriages and business, we eat the product."

SOME QUESTIONS

If we strip marriage of the property function, what is left — intimate relationship between two people? Most marriages, are told, last only because there are children. Why should pec be forced to decide at age 20 whom they will love at 45? W should we be allowed only one intimate relationship? Why alw a man and a woman? Why can't there be an intimate relations between more than two people? Why must there be a legal c tract? Why must it last a lifetime? Why does the world have be divided up into couples who relate to everyone else as coup or else as "unfortunate" singles? Why should each couple live itself, isolated from other friendships, other intimacies? Marri is the cultural manifestation of a society based on private proper Married people possess one another and their children — they each other's private property. The family is a basic consumpti unit. It spends money and accumulates property which it pas down to its children, whom it has raised to love property. teaches the children to need to possess and accumulate proper and to marry to continue the cycle.

In the abstract, it is easy to imagine capitalism surviving t breakdown of the family. Single or communal units of consum tion could prove even more profitable. Public institutions cou inculcate the "proper" selfish values even better than the fami does. Yet, a movement to abolish the family in favor of mc communal, less property-oriented forms of living threatens t privatistic, anti-social, competitive values that the capitalist sy tem is based upon.

From *A Woman Is A Sometime Thing* by Munaker, Goldfield and Weisstein *The New Left* Porter Sargent

The problem of socialization poses more difficult questions, as has been seen. But the need for intensive maternal care in the early years of a child's life does not mean that the present single sanctioned form of socialization—marriage and family—is inevitable. Far from it. The fundamental characteristic of the present system of marriage and family is in our society its *monolithism*: there is only one institutionalized form of inter-sexual or inter-generational relationship possible. It is that or nothing. This is why it is essentially a denial of life. For all human experience shows that intersexual and intergenerational relationships are infinitely various—indeed, much of our creative literature is a celebration of the fact—while the institutionalized expression of them in our capitalist society is utterly simple and rigid. It is the poverty and simplicity of the institutions in this area of life which are such an oppression. Any society will require some institutionalized and social recognition of personal relationships. But there is absolutely no reason why there should be only one legitimized form—and a multitude of unlegitimized experience. Socialism should properly mean not the abolition of the family, but the diversification of the socially acknowledged relationships which are today forcibly and rigidly compressed into it. This would mean a plural range of institutions—where the family is only one, and its abolition implies none. Couples living together or not living together, long-term unions with children, single parents bringing up children, children socialized by conventional rather than biological parents, extended kin groups, etc— all these could be encompassed in a range of institutions which matched the free invention and variety of men and women.

It would be illusory to try and specify these institutions. Circumstantial accounts of the future are idealist and worse, static. Socialism will be a process of change, of becoming. A fixed image of the future is in the worst sense ahistorical; the form that socialism takes will depend on the prior type of capitalism and the nature of its collapse. As Marx wrote: 'What (is progress) if not the absolute elaboration of (man's) creative dispositions, without any preconditions other than antecedent historical evolution which makes the totality of this evolution—i.e. the evolution of all human powers as such, unmeasured by any *previously established* yardstick—an end in itself? What is this, if not a situation where man does not reproduce himself in any determined form, but produces his totality? Where he does not seek to remain something formed by the past, but is the absolute movement of becoming?'[53] The liberation of women under socialism will not be 'rational' but a human achievement, in the long passage from Nature to Culture which is the definition of history and society.

From *Women The Longest Revolution* by Juliet Mitchell *New Left Review* Nov/Dec 1966

Women's Liberation Country Style

An article for the issue on Women's Liberation, is it? Wow, I haven't argued the Woman Question in years. And long, intimate association with a pretty groovy member of the Opposite Sex has rather dulled my appetite for the Battle. (I don't necessarily mean that only unhappily married women will join the Movement.) I'm glad to see you carrying on where the Pankhursts and Anthonys left off. Progress may be even harder now because the issues are less clear cut (you've got the Vote, haven't you?) and sex (vicarious) is *such* good business. Sells cars, etc.

What defines a liberated woman? In my economic and generational bracket she's a woman who had to earn her living before she married and who will get a job when money's tight and be nonetheless A Woman, i.e., run the house, mother the kids and try to keep her husband out of the clutches of some gal who has more time to devote to his ego. If she has An Education she will feel compelled not to "waste" it and will bring in her share of the family income. Mostly it's a question of economics. We only feel equal if we earn money.

It seems to me a liberated woman is one who does anything—have a baby, hold a job, be a jockey—because she wants to, not because she's forced to. But then, that's a liberated man, too. So much of it comes right down to liberating us all, men and women, from a lot of stupid patterns, economic, sexual and social, without getting into worse ones. I mean, I am long past the point where I feel I'm a traitor to my Sex because I prefer brewing and baking all day and half the night to being a teacher or a social worker. Teachers exploit kids and social workers exploit the poor and I've come to think those professions, as they are now practiced, will have to go as surely as bombardiers and munitions makers. And I don't cry any tears over, say women in advertising who aren't offered the highpaying jobs. I do get wrathful about underpaid nurses, not because they're female but because, like all truly useful workers in this society, they are undervalued.

* * *

Peculiar situations arise in regard to woman's role at the two communes I'm best acquainted with. At the longer-established place, women, I understand, are not wanted in the fields. They do specifically the kitchen work and light gardening. They tell me that in the beginning—when they were needed—the women worked along with the men. Now that the community has progressed to a degree of comfort and self-sufficiency it is no longer a girl's choice whether she does "woman's work" or "man's." Some of the girls who resented their work being thus defined left for a newer commune close by which is still at the stage of heavy building and where they are welcomed to help whatever is most urgent. Obviously the men have no choice at either place. A division of labor that gives the physically weaker members the lighter jobs makes sense. And where your community's desperate need is a roof and four walls against the coming winter you're not going to have a husky male (or a not so husky one, for that matter) doing the cooking—though cooking for 25 on a wood stove without running water is no easy task. It will be interesting to see how roles develop as the new commune gets into more comfortable stages. I imagine many of the original women at the older commune are glad not to have to be doing heavy work. That part of building the community is over and they shared in it. Perhaps some of the latecomers feel that by missing the longer experience they are not as fully members.

* * *

We came here, in part, to learn to live together. And living together, meaningfully, means working together; not necessarily doing the same work but each having a part in keeping the family (or community) going. Kids especially miss out on this today. Lots of women, too. They don't have anything *real* to do. Then I think of all the men whose lives are unsatisfactory because they just work for money. I'm sorry, but I can't help feeling that liberation is a two-way street.

I asked my second son one day to take the clothes off the line. (This was in town, before we moved four miles from the nearest neighbor.) He refused, saying he didn't want to be seen doing "woman's work." Well, OK. I didn't want the neighborhood kids to make fun of him either. Would *he* wash the dishes while *I* took down the clothes? Sure. I was liberated far more and without hurting him.

Country living can simplify sexual roles but beware stereotyping. I'm ludicrous on the end of a crosscut saw and as dangerous, though less competent, as Lizzie Borden with an axe. When I bemoaned my failure at wood gathering my oldest son (who towers four inches over me) expostulated, "It's not as though you were entirely useless, you know!" He appreciates my baking 10 loaves of bread a week and being able to cook beans seven different ways. I'll soon be the physically smallest member of my family.

Men and women are defined not only by what they do but by each other. They are also defined as People. Living with four males it's easy to become one of the boys. The kids invited me today to try out their homemade sled drawn by the horse. I got a muddy seat, sore hands, and a big thrill out of my ride. They invited me, not as their lady mother, but because they thought I'd enjoy it and knew I could take it. And then sometimes, when he thinks it's a waltz on the radio, my youngest son will ask me to dance, elegantly.

Smog and DDT and rumors of wars bear down on us. And who shall be saved this time? Non-eaters of flesh, amateur astrologers, users of soap-not-detergents, friends of Smokey the Bear? Save yourself and yours! But who am I to be saved? And who are mine—my husband and children? All beautiful people? All hippies? All Movement people? All mankind?

From my notebook: "I am so happy. I can't believe or describe it. When I look at the acres of brush and mountains out the window I get a thrill like going over a roller coaster. We're here! I'm so happy I keep wondering what's going to happen to spoil it. I daren't write my friends in the City and tell them this—they all sound so miserable in their letters. I hardly dare to write to myself for fear I'll look over this later and think what a fool I was. How easily we grow accustomed to letting ourselves be unhappy."

—Rebecca Johnson
Somewhere in New Mexico

win Jan 1970

Marge Piercy

THE GRAND COOLIE DAM

The movement is supposed to be for human liberation: how come the condition of women inside it is no better than outside? We have been trying to educate and agitate around women's liberation for several years. How come things are getting worse? Women's liberation has raised the level of consciousness around a set of issues and given some women a respite from the incessant exploitation, invisibility and being put down. But several forces have been acting on the movement to make the situation of women actually worse during the same time that more women are becoming aware of their oppression.

Around 1967—the year of what the mass media liked to call the Summer of Love—there was a loosening of attitudes in the movement just as there was a growing politization among dropouts and the hippe communities. For a while movement people were briefly more interested in each other as human beings than is the case usually, or now. Movement men are generally interested in women occasionally as bed partners, as domestic servants-mother surrogates, and constantly as economic producers: as in other patriarchal societies, one's wealth in the movement can be measured in terms of the people whose labor one can possess and direct on one's projects.

For a while people were generally willing to put effort into their relationships with each other and human liberation was felt as something to be acted out rather than occasionally flourished like a worn red flag. People experimented with new forms of communities and webs of relationship reaching beyond the monogamous couple. Men and women were trying new ways of relating that would not be as confining, as based on concepts of private property and the market economy as the ways we have learned to possess each other. Some of the experimenting was shallow, manipulative, adventurist, with little regard for consequence to the others involved, but some was serious and had a tentative willed openness that gave room to men and especially to women to grow out whole new limbs of self and encounter each other in ways that made them more human.

It is not necessary to recount the history of the last two years to figure out what happened. Repression brings hardening. It is unlikely the movement could have gone along with the same degree of involvement in personal relationships. An excessive amount of introspection and fascination with the wriggles of the psyche militate against action. One of the high schools in New York was effectively cooled by involving students in therapy groups and sensitivity training. But there is also a point beyond which cutting off sensitivity to others and honesty to what one is doing does not produce a more efficient revolutionary, but only a more efficient son of a bitch. We are growing some dandy men of steel nowadays.

The typical movement institution consists of one or more men who act as charismatic spokesmen, who speak in the name of the institution and negotiate and represent that body to other bodies in and outside the movement, and who manipulate the relationships inside to maintain his or their position, and the people who do the actual work of the institution, much of the time women. Most prestige in the movement rests not on having done anything in particular, but in having visibly dominated some gathering or in manipulating a certain set of rhetorical counters well in public, or in having played some theatrical role. To be associated with a new fashion trend in rhetoric is far more rewarded than is any amount of hard work on the small organizing projects that actually recruit new people and change their heads.

The movement is an economic microcosm. Presumably the rewards will be bringing about a revolution, changing this society into something people want to live in and which they have a chance of affecting, and which will get off the back of the rest of the world. But the day to day coin is prestige. Another short term reward is a modicum of power, largely to force other people out of some group, or to persuade that group to engage in one activity rather than another. A third type of power is over the channels of communication. These may be formal channels such as *New Left Notes*, the *Guardian*, underground papers, *Liberation News Service*, or other media. There is also power over informal channels of communication. A person may come to usurp the prestige of an organization simply by being the speaker on all public occasions or by representing that group to other movement groups. That may be actually the only work he does, but what meager satisfactions can come from parading the name of his group before others, he will enjoy. At the least he will get a chance to travel a little. Lives in the movement are not exactly running over with pleasures, so that if you have spent all winter on the lower east side of New York, a trip to Rochester or Buffalo can look glamorous.

It is possible to build up power simply through insisting or arranging that all of a particular kind of contact occur through you. The important thing is to keep all transfer of information or requests between any Dick or any Bill routed through you. That gives a look of business and importance. It can be a career in itself. There is a loss of information and energy, but strangely enough goodwill is created among both Dick and Bill. Your phone will ring all the time and people call wherever you go, making manifest your importance before others. Almost all informal movement contacts of this sort are between men. Especially in Ivy League schools, SDS chapters seem to act as fraternities creating in-groups who respect and trust only each other.

If the rewards are concentrated at the top, the shitwork is concentrated at the bottom. The real basis is the largely unpaid, largely female labor force that does the daily work. Reflecting the values of the larger capitalist society, there is no prestige whatsoever attached to actually working. Workers are invisible. It is writers and talkers and the actors of dramatic roles who are visible and respected. The production of abstract analyses about what should be done and the production of technical jargon are far more admired than what is called by everybody shitwork.

Nor is the situation improved when the machers are competing to demonstrate their superior, purer, braver militancy, rather than their purer analysis. In an elitist world, it's always "women and children last." Only a woman willing and able to act like a stereotyped American frontier male can make herself heard.

The leader co-opts the work of his laborers. How many times a macher will say, "I have done," "I have made" when the actual labor was somebody else's. It is easy for the macher to pretend he has written a leaflet he glanced over, inserting the fashionable cant phrase of the week. I am aware that men in the movement who are not domineering, highly verbal, manipulative or hypercompetitive also turn into invisible peasant laborers. If there were no women at all in the male-dominated movement, men not ready to stomp on others would end up playing many roles now filled by women. Which is to say that poor whites may be no better off economically than poor blacks, for the system oppresses them in *some* of the same ways.

We take this alloting of prestige for granted, in which we are an exact microcosm of the society we oppose. Work is shit. It is mindlessly done by unappreciated, invisible workers, and the results, the profits in prestige and recognition, are taken away. Truly, it is not necessary that work be shit even in the bowels of the beast. One of the things that really is true about visiting Cuba is discovering how proud people can be of their work—work they would be ashamed to do here. Because work is admired and makes sense in a society that makes sense, it is social in the full meaning. All right, we cannot have little islands of revolutionary culture in the belly of the empire, but we can try a little harder not to reflect the ugliest aspects of the society we are presumably rejecting.

As the fight gets stiffer and we settle in for the long haul, as all of us accumulate enough experience of failure and look long and hard enough at the cost to ourselves of what we are trying to do, as we get older and go through our share of the nasties, there is an attitude that sustains man: *I am a professional revolutionary*. To take that kind of step in one's head and rhetoric is felt as a leap of commitment. It explains to the person and to others what he is doing. After all, he is acting quite differently from what was expected of him. He is failing to make it in any way he was taught all through growing up American to expect he would do (and to be scared he wouldn't do). So it turns out there is an answer. No, Ma, I'm not a bum. I'm a professional, like a doctor or a lawyer, like I was supposed to be.

One trouble: to be a professional anything in the U.S. is to think of oneself as an expert and one's ideas as semi-sacred and to treat others in a certain way—professionally. Do you question your doctor when he prescribes in dog Latin what you should gulp down? The expert has expertise. Unfortunately, he also often has careerism. He is giving up everything else, and he is not about to let some part-time worker (differentiation between part-time and full-time in the movement is instructive, and dangerous) challenge his prerogatives. Shall the professional revolutionary haul garbage, boil potatoes, change diapers, and lick stamps? Finally, what opposes the professional is counter-revolutionary, even though it may be repressed by the power structure with the same zeal.

The incidence of violent brand loyalty to one's own current dogma has risen. The word 'cadre' as something to caress in the mouth and masturbate over has gone whoosh to the top of the pole in the last year. Cadre has meaning when a movement has really gone underground, when its members have been through training that has attempted to change their characters, when groups have shared harrowing experiences over time so that they know they can trust each other. Cadre applied to the white movement in the United States at this time is elitist bullshit. Our big problem is learning how to reach all kinds of people and we haven't invented any training yet that helps much on that score. People are working hard on projects scattered around the country, and here and there they are making headway in one or another enclave of the old or new working class (or groups in motion are reaching out to them); or in high schools or the army or neighborhoods under stress such as the threat of urban renewal, things are happening; but experts are experts largely in manipulating current jargon.

Now common ordinary gross *chutzpah* is something that in this society sprouts more commonly from the egos of men than from the more shattered egos of women. Women are not encouraged toward professionalism in general, and we are certainly not in the movement encouraged to give ourselves too many airs. Suppose you, Woman Alice, unknown, unvouched for, unaccompanied, come wandering into a meeting and want to speak. The male supremacist will not even hear you. He may launch a sentence while you are in the middle of speaking, and probably he can simply drown you out. The male chauvinist will keep quiet while you speak and may even give a quick acknowledgment that some noise has occurred. He will patronize and move on. The male liberal will note your energy and will commiserate and then co-opt you. You will end up working for him, no matter what you think you are doing. When you oppose him, you will find out which side he is on.

With the professional comes his professional language. A predominantly student movement is a great soil for the growth of monstrosities of jargon. The use of scholarly Marxist jargon is exactly analogous to the use of any other academic jargon. It is a way of indicating that you have put in your time, read the right texts and commentaries, that you are an expert. It is one thing to learn from the long line of revolutionaries who have come before us: we must learn that history or caricature it. (With the factionalism, name calling and assumption of infallibility that has been growing lately, I sometimes get the impression of people role-playing as professional revolutionaries based on comic books in which that was how you could identify the reds.) It is another thing to adopt the language of

any of them, especially translated into lousy American. Now we have scholarly quarrels about the definition of key terms and the appreciation among the in-group of the way in which someone is handling them, as in any English or sociology department. Such articles are written for a snobbishly defined audience of peers. The jargon covers up holes in the world. Most of us know damn little about how the society works and how people live, but rather than find out we will adopt a jargon that stands between the observer and what he is trying to observe. Such articles fail to make our politics lucid to people on a level where they can become autonomous political thinkers and doers. If you have contempt for people and think they cannot know what they want and need, who the hell is the revolution for?

Women in the movement, with a few outstanding exceptions, have trouble talking jargon. One source of unease is lack of practice. The phenomenon of a woman speaking in a meeting, and the meeting going on as if she had belched, is too widespread to need comment. Women don't generally practice on each other. Women are able at least on occasion to be more honest in talking about their lives together than men ever are: not always, not often, but it is a possibility. The mores of the society do not prevent women who trust each other from speaking about their sexual and emotional troubles. Much of this ability comes from our being taught to define our 'careers' in terms of that part of our lives, so that it is shoptalk. In contrast so much of what passes as communication between men and women are responses to signals given, the fulfilling of subtly or not so subtly indicated wishes, games of protection and mutual blackmail. The bases of many relationships are unspoken, not because they lie too deep for words, but because speaking about them would disgust. It would expose connection based on gross and subtle forms of lying and exploitation that would not bear examining aloud.

Sometimes women simply refuse to use jargon. I know one woman who grew up in the Old Left and who will not use language she associates with that type of life and politics. In the small group of organizers she operates in, her refusal is viewed by the male ideological clique as a pitiful weakness. She is crippled. If she cannot talk their language, they cannot hear her: although she speaks the language of the kind of workers they are attempting to organize. They cannot accept her criticisms or insights unless couched in their terminology. Not that that always produces acceptance.

I remember watching a girl at a council meeting a few years ago who was striking in all aspects. She spoke well in a husky but carrying voice, she was physically attractive, she had read her texts and had a militant left position and an obvious sense of style. In her head she was on the barricades, and that excitement carried in her speeches. She had no impact. I heard many people giving *precis* of the council afterward, and no one singled her out to mention, although many of the issues she spoke to carried. She did not succeed in becoming part of that collective of machers who are always counting points with each other. If she had been sexually connected with any of the machers present, the odds on her achieving impact would have been much greater, for she would have been automatically present at the small caucuses and meetings where policy, unfortunately, originates.

Around that time when I attended many women's liberation meetings, I saw the whole thing as interesting primarily as an organizing tool: here was a way to organize women who could not be reached on other issues or in other contexts. I am older than most movement women, have a harder sense of self, make a living off my writing and care about it, and have a good, longstanding and nonpossessive relationship with a man I trust politically and personally. It took me two *more* years of grisly experiences of getting used and purged to get my nose well rubbed into women's exploitation, to find out women's liberation was not talking about the other fellow, and to understand how much I had adopted male values to think of liberation as a *tool*. We are oppressed, and we will achieve our liberation by fighting for it the same as any other oppressed group. Nobody is going to give it to us because we ask, however eloquently. I once thought that all that was necessary was to make men understand that they would achieve their own liberation too by joining in the struggle for women's liberation: but it has come to me to seem a little too much like the chickens trying to educate the chicken farmer. I think of myself as a house nigger who is a slow learner besides. A tendency to believe quite literally in the rhetoric of movement males is a form of *naivete* that no woman can afford. Most movement males' idea of women's liberation is something for their girlfriend to do to other women while they're busy decision making. That's her constituency to bring in.

Fucking a staff into existence is only the extreme form of what passes for common practice in many places. A man can bring a woman into an organization by sleeping with her and remove her by ceasing to do so. A man can purge a woman for no other reason than that he has tired of her, knocked her up, or is after someone else: and that purge is accepted without a ripple. There are cases of a woman excluded from a group for no other reason than that one of its leaders proved impotent with her. If a macher enters a room full of machers accompanied by a woman and does not introduce her, it is rare indeed that anyone will bother to ask her name or acknowledge her presence. The etiquette that governs is that of master-servant.

Women come into the movement for as many reasons as men do. It is not sufficient to speak of women as being recruited in bed, since their attraction to the man is usually as much to the ideas they hear him spouting and what they think he represents and what they imagine their life with him will be, as it is to his particular body or personality. Movement men often project a very sexual image. What's behind that too often is, as with actors, narcissism, impotence and a genuine lack of interest in anybody else except his hero, *The Professional Revolutionary in the Mirror,* and a small peer group whose opinions he values and whom he likes to shoot the bull with, much like ex-fraternity boys.

I've listened to the troubles of dozens and dozens of women and men in the movement. There are a lot of lonely and a lot of horny women. Sex lives of women seem to fall into two patterns, both dreary. Domestic unions on the whole are formed young and maintained in hermetic dependency, until exchanged for others that appear almost identical. People seldom maintain relationships with any content without living together, though it happens. As in conventional marriages, the woman living with a man often finds her world constricted. She is his thing. She keeps house for him and plays surrogate mother, and often he talks to her no more than the tired businessman home from the office. Often the relationship is much like that of the woman living with a medical student and helping to put him through school. Of course, since the woman's intellectual engergy is concentrated on that relationship, she may in fact dominate or manipulate or control the man, as is frequent in conventional marriages also.

The other model is the liberated woman: she can expect to get laid maybe once every two months, after a party or at councils or conferences, or when some visiting fireman comes through and wants to be put up. She may find she can work for years and even take part in planning demonstrations and doing important research and organizing without achieving recognition or visibility. There is a phenomenon I have noted, by the way: allowing for geographical variations, the list of men whom movement women not living with anyone have gone to bed with is surprisingly repetitive. One is left to draw the conclusion that all the liberated (i.e. women living alone) have gone to bed with the same set of men, who would fit in one large room.

These serviceable males fall into two categories: those who make it clear that what they are doing is fucking, and those who provide a flurry of apparently personal interest, which fades mighty quick. The first category are on far less hate lists than the second. There are men in the movement who have left women feeling conned and somehow used, emotionally robbed in every city in the country. Rarely have I heard any man in the movement judge any other man for that kind of emotional exploitation, and never so it could hurt him. The use of women as props for a sagging ego is accepted, socially. Everybody sees it and everybody agrees that they don't. Scalp hunting goes on on both sides of the sexual barrier, but the need to extract a kind of emotional conquest which is sometimes not even sexually consumated, out of woman after woman, seems exclusively the disease of male machers.

This sort of thing can even be called organizing. Many politicos spend their energies organizing inside the movement, instead of into the movement: hence the passionate concern with who is, and who is not, in the vanguard. Transferring the loyalties of worker-woman Lizzie from the research project of Macher A to the pamphlet project of Macher B is organizing.

The men who often get the most opposition from movement women and are often publicly called male oppressors, are precisely those men who have the least skill at co-opting the labor of women: men with a bluff style, frontal attack, an obvious sense of their own competence and a tactless assault on what they see as others' lack of it. They often succeed in rapid fashion in uniting some of the women in a caucus against them.

The style most rewarded is that of the manipulator: the person who makes use of the forms of workers' control and community decision-making to persuade others that they are involved in a "we" that is never out of his control. Given the careerism, in almost any movement enterprise there is at least one person who feels a vested interest: that endeavor is his baby. If there were true workers' control, he might find himself ousted. Most movement ventures exist hand to mouth, and the entrepreneur can always tell himself that a couple of weeks of financial chaos would wreck that precarious balance and run the enterprise into the ground. The rationale for retaining control may be political: the entrepreneur as professional revolutionary finds it necessary to keep political control of the little *Iskra,* lest the bourgeois revisionists get it into their slimy paws, or the soft minds of the shitworkers be led astray. The means to that control is seldom an obvious role as boss, for anti-authoritarianism is as deeprooted among women in the movement as among men.

No, the successful entrepreneur uses all the forms of workers' control and collective decision-making. He may covertly despise these indirect, time-consuming methods. Or he may have contempt instead for those who attempt to work without them, and feel morally superior because of his attachment to the forms of participatory democracy. This distinction is equivalent to the difference between the modes of the male supremacist and the male liberal: but both aim to retain control.

Methods vary. The macher may play off faction against faction or appear to float above petty quarrels. He may form sexual alliances, sabotage others, repeat gossip, start rumors, flatter, sow suspicion, retain the switchboard-control central function, flirt, listen to troubles, pay attention. Since most people in this society are dreadfully lonely, a little attention is a pungent tool. But he must always keep the others from combining.

On one movement staff where I worked, there was one macher, a couple of other males who did not challenge his hegemony, plus a two-thirds majority of women. Whenever we threatened to form an alliance on anything that mattered, the macher would begin jiggling the sexual balance of the group, pursuing publicly one of the staff or another until he had succeeded in creating a harem atmosphere in which all attention was once again centered on him. He would use his confidant relationshi to the staff members to persuade each to talk about the others, comments he would remember and reveal as if reluctantly at the proper moment. Even the fact that he was sexually involved with only one of the staff could be turned to moral advantage, for he would keep her in her place (on his right hand, just under the thumb) by constantly pointing out that he could, in fact, be involved with the others, by ignoring her in the office and flirting and teasing and creating a constant subsurface tizzy centering on his person. None of this, of course, was ever openly discussed. The superficial reality was business as usual, bureaucratic efficiency and personal relations kept out of the office. The effect was to make his position impregnable and enable him to dismiss whomever he chose.

The ability to dismiss from a collective is as important as the ability to recruit. One effective method is to stir up the workers so they themselves expel the person threatening the macher's power. If the expulsion is carried out in the name of workers' control or women's liberation, an expulsion whereby the entrepreneur's power is strengthened, the irony is complete. If the threat to the macher's power is a woman, he will probably carry out the expulsion himself. If he has recruited her sexually, he can expel her on the same basis. There is a false puritanism in never publicly permitting the allusion to relationships everyone knows about.

The male supremacist tends to exploit women new to the movement or on its fringes. His concept of women is conventionally patriarchal: they are for bed, board, babies and, also, for doing his typing and running his office machines and doing his tedious research. By definition women are bourgeois: they are housewives and domesticators. A woman who begins to act independently is a threat and loses her protected status. He can no longer use her.

Such a man will sit at his desk with his feet up and point to the poster on his wall of a Vietnamese woman with her rifle on her back, telling you, "Now that is a truly liberated woman. When I see you in that role, I'll believe you're a revolutionary." He has all the strength of the American tradition of Huckleberry Finn escaping downriver from Aunt Polly, down through Hemingway where the bitch Brett louses up the man-to-man understanding, to draw upon in defense of his arrogance. Not only are women losers, but for a woman to think about herself is bourgeois subjectivity and inherently counter-revolutionary. Now, dear, of course you find your work dull. What the movement needs is more discipline and less middle-class concern with one's itty-bitty self!

At times it may seem to women as if the only way to win their battle is to form some sort of women's brigades and achieve instant liberation by eliminating that whole part of life which hurts the most and competing with the men in meeting goals set by the male-dominated movement. But where women have fought beside their men, how often afterwards they have found themselves right back where they were before. It is easy for men to deal with women as quasi-equals, all soldiers together, during a long or short crisis, but inside their heads is all the old dominance/submission machinery and the old useful myths about Mom and the playmate and good girls and bad girls.

The male liberal respects the pride of women. He has learned well the rhetoric of women's liberation and offers apparent partnership. He will permit small doses of spokesmanship roles, so long as his hegemony is not challenged. Because he is willing to listen on a basis of apparent equality to women who work with (for) him, he is in a better position to draw out higher quality labor. He is just as career-oriented and just as exploitative as the male supremacist, but he gives back enough tidbits of flattery and attention to make the relationship appear reciprocal by contrast with what goes on with bullier males, and he is by far the more efficient long-range co-optor.

Often a woman working with a male liberal will learn imperceptibly to accept a double standard for his behavior: alone with her when she is his equal; and with other machers, when he will pretend essentially not to know her. After all, he will gain no points by insisting others treat her as an equal. Further, if he acted as if the woman were of importance, he might lose some control over contacts essential in dominating his scene. Thus the woman will come to accept the master-servant manners in public, for the sake of the private relationship of equals. It can take her a long time to see that the public manner reflects the power realities.

The importance of male solidarity to enforce discrimination and contempt for women cannot be over-emphasized. The man who goes in the face of this will find himself isolated. He will pay for betraying his caste. Men in this society reinforce each other's acted-out manhood in many small social rituals, from which the man who truly treats women as equals will be excluded.

Neither can we over-emphasize our own acquiescence. As I said, I have been a house nigger in the movement. Since I was first on my own as a skinny tough kid, nobody ever succeeded for long in exploiting me as a woman, until I came into the movement. Then I laid down my arms before my brothers to make the revolution together. How much I swallowed for my politics I have only realized in the pain of trying to write this piece truthfully. I have also begun to see how many male structures I took into my head in order to make it in the male-dominated world. How often in writing this I have been afraid, because I have incorporated so much male thinking that I can hear the responses I am going to get. Finally, I have come to see how separated from my sisters I have been at times to preserve one or other super-exploitative relationship with one or another male macher. As a house nigger how much worse treatment of other women I have watched and satisfied my conscience with vague private protestations to the professional revolutionary in question: nothing that would get him angry at me, you can be sure.

Two inhibitions have acted on me constantly. One inhibition occurred in relationships where work and sexual involvements overlapped. I have not been able to keep tenderness and sensual joy from being converted into cooperation in my own manipulation. One takes the good with the bad, no? The good is loving and the bad is being used and letting others be used. One holds on to good memories to block perceptions that would rock the boat. Yet always what was beautiful and real in the touching becomes contaminated by the fog of lies and halftruths and power struggles, until the sex is empty and only another form of manipulation.

The other, stronger inhibition comes from having shared the same radical tradition, rhetoric, heroes, dates, the whole bloody history of class war. It is pitifully easy for radical women to accept their own exploitation in the name of some larger justice (which excludes half the world) because we are taught from childhood to immolate ourselves to the male and the family.

Once again in the movement, oppression is becoming something for professionals to remove from certifiably oppressed other people. When I am told day in and day out to shut up because our oppression pales beside the oppression of colonialized peoples and blacks, I remember half of them are women too, and I am reminded of my mother telling me to eat boiled mush because the Chinese were starving and would be glad to have it. When people are unhappy, no one can tell them their pain is unimportant. The ruling class isn't dissatisfied: they are healthy, well-fed, live in beauty, enjoy their own importance: fun-loving cannibals. Our men aren't dissatisfied either.

It is true some oppression kills quickly and smashes the body, and some only destroys the pride and the ability to think and create. But I know no man can tell any woman how to measure her oppression and what methods are not politic in trying to get up off her knees. The answer does not lie in trying to be the token woman or in trying to learn quickly how to manipulate or shove around those who manipulate us. Certain of any oppressed group can always rise from that group by incorporating the manners and value system of the oppresser, and outwitting them at their own rigged game. We want Something Else.

We are told that our sense of oppression is not legitimate. We are told women's liberation is a secondary issue, to be dealt with after the war is won. But the basis of women's oppression is economic in a sense that far predates capitalism and the market economy and that is rooted into the whole fabric of socialization. Our claims are the most radical, for they entail restructuring even the nuclear family. Nowhere on earth are women free now, although in some places things are marginally better. What we want we will have to invent ourselves.

We must have the strength of our anger to know what we know. No more arguments about shutting up for the greater good should make us ashamed of fighting for our freedom. Ever since private property was invented, we have been waiting for freedom. That passive waiting is supposed to characterize our sex, and if we wait for the males we know to give up control, our great-granddaughters will get plenty of practice in waiting too. We are the fastest growing part of the movement, and for the next few years it would be healthiest for us to work as if we were essentially all the movement there is, until we can make alliances based on our politics. Any attempts to persuade men that we are serious are a waste of precious time and energy: they are not our constituency.

There is much anger here at movement men, but I know they have been warped and programmed by the same society that has damn near crippled us. My anger is because they have created in the movement a microcosm of that oppression and are proud of it. Manipulation and careerism and competition will not evaporate of themselves. Sisters, what we do, we have to do together, and we will see about them. □

Marge Piercy was active in SDS and NACLA, is a founder of MDS (Movement for a Democratic Society) and is currently involved in Women's Liberation.
@ Marge Piercy, 1969, to be included in *The Hand that Cradles the Rock*, an anthology of women's liberation edited by Robin Morgan.

Leviathan

UNDERGROUND WOMAN

Mary Moylan was one of the "Catonsville 9," who destroyed draft files at a Selective Service office in the suburbs of Baltimore on May 17, 1968. The 9 were convicted of two federal and four state crimes; appeals failed, and six were to begin serving their concurrent terms on April 9, 1970 (two others were given brief extensions; the ninth defendant had died). Four of those scheduled to be imprisoned failed to appear at the appointed time. The woman among them—Mary Moylan—recorded the story of her first few days "underground." Hard Times obtained a copy, and is presenting it in Miss Moylan's own words. The editors believe that internal evidence in the story proves its authenticity. At the time she wrote, Miss Moylan was reportedly in an Eastern city.

I've been underground—if you can call it that—for only a short time. I was supposed to show up at the federal marshal's offices in Baltimore on Thursday, April 9, at 8:30 a.m., to begin serving my sentence, which is two years, I think. We had gotten together—the remaining eight of us—about a week or so before that and the decision that came out of that meeting was that we would do our own thing. I hadn't intended at all to show up, but then neither had I intended to—so to speak—go underground. To cooperate with such authority is to find yourself in a kind of weird position to begin with, and I had just planned to take a walk and smell the flowers and then they could come and pick me up when they so desired. But then, when I realized four men of the group were going underground, that they were not going to show up and were not going to be available, I did some re-thinking and decided that because women's liberation is one of the most important issues being raised, I felt I had to do the same thing—and do it with

sisters, and with the help of sisters. So I let a few sisters know that I did not want to show up, and with their cooperation, I've been sitting around since Thursday.

Being "underground" is strange. I live in an apartment with one bedroom, a kitchen, living room and hall. I spend my days reading, drinking, smoking and sleeping. I'm not at all sure what it means to be underground. I know it means being out of touch with many people, being inactive. I was thinking about the two Kathys—Wilkerson and Boudin—and wherever they are I hope they're in good health because I'm sure they would probably get life sentences if they ever surfaced again. But then, how do you operate? I don't think we have the mechanisms set up for that. I think the black community does, but not the whites. I think there is growing interest in the Movement in setting up some kind of an underground network, and people are trying to get straight in their heads what exactly "underground" means (we use the term so easily).

I expect to turn myself in after the four men do. I think that will be fairly soon, but if it lasts more than six months, say, I would probably leave the country and go to Canada and see what's happening with the resisters. I don't think the feds are looking very hard for us because we're certainly not the 10-most-wanted, and yet in one sense I think we must be very irritating to them. And in this perhaps is our greatest impact.

Up until last Thursday I hadn't really decided what I wanted to do because I'm confused on the whole question of non-violence. I believe in non-violence. There are two groups in the non-violent camp. One of those groups is straight pacifist; the other is much looser, and feels that somehow we have to continue to respect human life: and that's probably the only way we hew the pacifist line. The sort of public non-cooperation of pacifists bothers me; most pacifists I know would have told me to go take a walk in the park and smell the flowers, but it just didn't strike me as enough. It would have been such a futile thing because they would have come and picked me up. The other difficulty is that the feds know who my friends in Baltimore are, and I had to consider the question of how much pressure would be brought to bear on them, so I knew I couldn't go to any of the people in Baltimore, and I had to go to other people in another city.

I have to laugh when I think about the Catonsville action. I don't regret it at all. I'm very content and happy I did it, but it was totally insane. The nine of us drove out to the Catonsville draft board offices around noon. It was a weekday, because we wanted to go when the board was open. Tom Lewis and I went in first, and he had a prepared speech to read to the clerks to reassure them that we were not going to wipe them out. Bureaucracy is fantastic: We walked in and nobody would look at us. Tom came up and started reading: "We are a group of clergymen and laymen concerned about the war." And nobody would look up, they were so busy writing. So we went through our scene—draft files were dumped into our baskets and the phones were taken care of so the clerks couldn't call for help until we had left the building. The clerks were very upset—one woman kept screaming about us taking *her* files, and she would have to protect *her* files. The other woman in the office was determined to make a phone call, so we went through a wrestling match. But we eventually made it out, and I guess they eventually called. The night before, we had cooked up some home-made napalm, so we put the files on the ground outside and stood around in a circle watching them burn. There were some people from the press there, and some of our people made statements. We stood there and we waited and we waited and we waited, and the people were watching us—the clerks from the second floor—and nobody knew what we were doing. Then a little cop on one of those three-wheel things came up and he stood there and watched us, and we thought, "My God, they're not going to arrest us; what are we going to do?" But eventually they came skidding into the parking lot and they arrested us, and we went through the arrest scene, with the FBI wandering in and out.

Then finally we went to jail—thank God—I was so pooped. We hadn't had anything to eat—those people don't feed you—that was a big shock. I thought I'd always heard about cops giving you mugs of coffee, and I was just dying for a coffee or a Coke or something. We never got anything until 10 o'clock that night.

We had all known we were going to jail, so we all had our toothbrushes. I was just exhausted; I took my little box of clothes and stuck it under the cot and climbed into bed. Now all the women in the Baltimore County jail were black—I think there was only one white. The women were waking me up and saying, "Aren't you going to cry?" I said, "What about?" They said, "You're in jail." And I said, "Yeah, I knew I'd be here." So I lay down again and they kept on waking me up and wanting to know when I was going to cry. I said, "I left this morning knowing I was going to be here—what's there to cry about? I should have cried last night." They were funny; a lot of women in jail are coming off dope, and after they get off the first very bad withdrawal symptoms they have a hard time sleeping. I was sleeping between two of these women, and every morning I'd wake up and they'd be leaning on their elbows watching me. They'd say, "You slept all night." I'd say, "Yeah, and I plan to do that every night." And they couldn't believe it. They were good. We had good times.

I had a very thorough Catholic upbringing—all the way through nurses' training. I spent some time in Uganda working as a nurse-midwife with the Women Volunteers Association, a Catholic organization. The nuns sent me home in December, 1965; they decided they didn't like me either. When I got home, I became, through some insanity, director of the group. Then I met Patrick Aloysius Cardinal O'Boyle, we had a few disagreements, and that

finished me. I began working as a nurse in Washington—there's no such thing as working as a midwife in Washington—and met some of the active black people there.

Then George Mische, whom I had known for several years, came to town, and he wanted to start a radical Catholic house. It didn't appeal to me at all. I just didn't want to have anything to do with the Church to begin with and wasn't interested in attacking it or saving it or doing anything with it. I just wanted it to go away quietly.

The establishment press constantly described us, after Catonsville, as "Catholic pacifists," and that's when I stopped believing the establishment press. I'm much too Irish to be a pacifist, and my relationship with the Roman Catholic Church has been off and on, to say the very least, for quite a while. Realizing that that was where I came from, the "Catholic" title bothered me less than the "pacifist" title. But it's even more difficult now because I have no relationship with the Catholic Church, nor do I want any. Everybody in the group, except George and me, was either a priest or a brother or a sister or an ex-one-or-the-other. So everyone assumed when they met me that I was an ex-nun. I've had a lot of problems in my life, but that wasn't one of them.

I suppose the political turning point in my life came while I was in Uganda. I was there when American planes were bombing the Congo, and we were very close to the Congo border. The planes came over and bombed two villages in Uganda (I don't know how the hell anyone figures out where the borders are). But it wasn't that; it was what the hell were American planes doing, piloted by Cubans, bombing the Congo when as far as I knew, the United Nations was the peace-keeping force in the Congo. Where the hell did the American planes come in?

Later on I was in Dar Es Salaam and Chou En-lai came to town. The American Embassy sent out letters saying that no Americans were to be on the street, because this was a dirty Communist leader; but I decided this was a man who was making history and I wanted to see him. We did go and Chou waved to us—probably because we were the only white faces there.

When I came home from Africa I moved to Washington, and had to deal with the scene there and the insanity and the brutality of the cops and the type of life that was led by most of the citizens of that city—70 percent black. Nobody believed that cops were ever brutal—all black people just happened to be lippy and they needed to get a slap in the face once in a while and that was just a fact of life.

And then Vietnam, and the napalm and the defoliants, and the bombings: It was probably Vietnam last of all, as a matter of fact. All the liberals are running around bleeding all over Vietnam, and I can remember all those people who used to knit bandages for lepers in Africa, and all they prayed was that those lepers never ever came near them. The bandages went, and the lepers were happy, and they were happy, but there was never any desire to really deal with the problem. Sometimes I get the impression from some of the more liberal elements in the Movement that it's enough to keep the Vietnamese happy in Vietnam, but we don't want to be involved in any of the dirt and shit that goes on.

I got involved with the women's movement about a year ago. I had heard about it and read about it and the women in Baltimore were forming a women's liberation group. I was in New York where there were all kinds of women's lib groups, so I got in on some of that. In my relations with men I was becoming more and more aware of the fact that they were chauvinists—I guess that's the nicest thing I can think of to say about them. It struck me that there were all these men running around trying to build a human society who couldn't relate to a woman as a human being. The man-woman relationship is a basic unit of society; even if we have communes or collectives, still men and women are going to be with each other. Unless we can deal with that, I feel that our attempts to relate to the Third World or to any other group of people are going to fail. I began to believe that SDS, before their split, would have their revolution, and I certainly wasn't going to stop them, but that we would just have to do it all over again because they were incapable of building a human society, in large part because they're incapable of dealing with women's liberation.

I think I'm really talking about freeing *people*: Men aren't proving anything about themselves as people in saying they've got muscles or that they can rape a woman; or that they're the brains and women are the heart; or that women have certain virtues, all of which are soft. Woman is compassionate, woman is this, that and the other thing, and it's nice to have women around to help men out when they need compassion. I really feel that this is a pivotal issue, and for me it's just a gut reaction; I very definitely would only relate to brothers who, I felt, were trying to deal with the issue—and preferably, only to sisters. If I ever decided to go through Catonsville again, I would never act with men: It would be a women's action for me or I wouldn't act. The Vietnamese and Algerian women have provided me with a real inspiration.

I think men get into competition with each other, and I don't know what the hell everybody's trying to prove. We're all absurd when you come right down to it, but somehow all of us together add up to something that makes sense. And I don't think that any one person or any group of people makes any *more* sense; somehow it's a totality of making sense. The anarchism of the Movement with the very different groups operating makes sense. Out of all that is going to come a future that is a human society.

I was very excited by the Weatherpeople in the "Days of Rage" in Chicago. I was in Chicago for that, but I was with RYM II people [an antagonistic SDS fraction]. I felt that Weatherman was raising questions that the Movement wasn't even dealing with. Unfortunately, RYM II just so overreacted to Weatherman that they—RYM people—ended up in the bag of being "good guys" and they're not going to have any confrontations.

The day I arrived in Chicago, four Weathermen had been picked off from the middle of a demonstration. The Panthers had had a demonstration in front of the courthouse and then RYM had one, and these four Weatherpeople, two of whom were from Baltimore, were picked off: The cops just walked right into the crowd, picked up four people and walked out. The RYM people did nothing. I said, "Oh, wait a minute, I've reconsidered this whole thing; I ain't hitting the streets with you. It's insane." Our Baltimore group got together and we talked about it and I said I couldn't see any political reason to hit the streets with people who were going to let their own people be picked off. And what the RYM people said to me, which freaked me out, was that the Weatherpeople were not "ours" to begin with, so they could be picked up. The proper response, they said, was to get the badge number of the arresting officer and find out what the charge was. I don't know too many police forces—pig forces—in the world that compare to Chicago, and I really didn't feel that there was going to be a big dialogue.

The Weatherpeople came to Chicago and they said they were going to bring the war home. Maybe you don't think that's a good idea, but it's the first time I've ever known SDS to do what it said it was going to do. And I'm not sure that's a bad idea. I wasn't going to go out and *do* it with them, but I didn't think it was such a bad idea...car windows and apartment windows... I don't have any problem with that...or the Loop...that's all right. Weathermen are raising questions. They're continually going through these insane fits of theirs, but some of their very basic questions still haven't been answered. I disagree with them. I don't think that Red China's going to come marching over here and save us. I really don't think the blacks are going to be able to "do it" without us. I think Rap Brown really believes in a colorless revolution, and I really believe in it too. But I think it means we've got to rethink our tactics: And one of those tactics is going to jail. At the time of Catonsville, going to jail made sense to me, partially because of the black scene—so many blacks forever filling the jails and the whites being "very concerned." Jail was not part of the scene for those whites. I don't think it's a valid tactic anymore, because of the change in the country itself. I don't want to see people marching off to jail with smiles on their faces. I just don't want them going. The Seventies are going to be very difficult, and I don't want to waste the sisters and brothers we have by marching them off to jail and having mystical experiences or whatever they're going to have. We're trying to get Bobby Seale and the sisters *out* of jail in New Haven. We've got to start picking up again on our sisters and brothers who have been put away and who have been screwed royally by this society. I think you have to be serious and realize you could end up in jail, but I hope that people would not seek it, as we did.

I have no problem with my own jail sentence. I'll be at the Women's Federal Reformatory at Alderson, West Virginia, and there's a whole bunch of sisters down there in that jail—sister criminals as a matter of fact. I think it will be interesting to see what the women's response will be to women's liberation and the whole Movement. I hate to make this confession, but I am really looking forward to two years of peace, two years of three meals a day, and a bed I can sleep in every night and count on. I don't know what their "solitary"or whatever they call it is like, but—two years: I can make it.

The idea of jail doesn't bother me that much; the idea of cooperating with the federal government in any way at all irritates the hell out of me. My alternatives are to go to jail, go aboveground with an assumed identity, stay underground, or leave the country. Any way I choose, the government is choosing for me. But what we're questioning is their right, and they lost that right because of the obscenity and insanity of their actions, which are growing more and more obscene and insane.

I'm not worried about getting parole, because I wouldn't know what to do with it if I did get it. Parole can really screw you. They demand that you have a nine-to-five job that's a fairly decent job, and it's very much like being on welfare: They have the right to inspect where you live; you can't move without their permission; you can't get married without their permission; you can't go out of town without their permission; you have to be careful whom you see and what activities you're involved in.

What's happening in the Movement now is a separation between so-called "good guys" and the dirty "bad guys." A lot of people say that Weathermen are for shit and we're not going to waste a lot of time helping them or defending them or trying in any way to deal with the issues they're raising. You know the line: The government is going to have to take care of them and we're better off probably if they do because their tactics are terrible and their politics are worse. The Catonsville 9 have always been in most people's minds the good guys; we've been socially acceptable. Most people wouldn't be too upset to have us to their house. You know, "take-a-nigger-to-lunch." But if we think the establishment is illegal, then what are we doing making ourselves so legitimate and so acceptable? It seems to me that we're playing the establishment game. I think we should be saying that we identify with the two Kathys and with Erika Huggins and the women in New Haven.

I very definitely see myself as a criminal. I don't even know what the hell "prisoner of conscience" means. I think if we're serious about changing the society that's how we have to see ourselves. That "prisoner of conscience"—if there is any such thing as conscience and if anybody has it—I guess all of us are prisoners of it, but it doesn't do anything politically to me at all. We're all out on bail, and let's all stay out.

—Mary Moylan

Hard Times

Sisterhood & the Small Group

Contrary to a variety of popular images, Women's Liberation is not a movement of hardened and coldly unfeeling females, shouting rhetoric, hating men, and scorning "unliberated" sisters. Nor is it a movement that demands "instant liberation;" women do not have to leave their husbands and lovers, abandon their children, throw away their make-up, burn their bras, quit their jobs, or sleep with each other in order to be part of the movement. Indeed, even those most involved must continually struggle to come to grips with changing concepts of ourselves.

Liberation* is a constant process—and for a woman whose liberation involves in great part an end to her loneliness and isolation from other women, it would be both agonizing and impossible without their support. And to provide this support, women have organized the "small group"—the strength of our movement, through which women reach out to each other, grope together, grow together. It is our best means of raising consciousness, our most effective organizing tool, and, at the same time, our most human structure.

Every Sunday night I meet with 10 other women. Two high school students, two high school teachers, a social worker, 3 college students, 3 drop-outs. We came together originally through a Resistance women's mailing; later some of us brought friends. Marilyn and Janice are sisters, Kay and I, quite accidentally, are old family acquaintances, Ronny and Paula close school friends, Bette knew none of the others until our first meeting.

Our first discussions were fumbling, in our enthusiasm we would jump from topic to topic as new ideas flew from one to another, fragmenting the political from the personal. Until we realized that we had to begin with our most potent political force—our lives. And the best way to do that, we discovered, was for each of us to speak about her life—her childhood, her family, her friendships, ambitions, lovers, husbands, career. A method in itself revolutionary; a

---

*I do not believe that anyone—male or female—can achieve true liberation under capitalism. In this article, however, I am primarily concerned with those changes that we can make in our lives, the ways we struggle, and the changing of our consciousness.

way of breaking down one of the strongest bulwarks of our society—the belief that an individual's perceptions of herself cannot be understood by anyone else; that individual problems must, therefore, be dealt with in isolation and loneliness.

For the past few months each meeting has been devoted to one of us—to listening to her "story," dealing with her life. And, indeed, though backgrounds, specific experiences, and current situations vary (e.g., Mary comes from Texas, was raised as a Southern Baptist; she and Sandy and Bette "came of age" in the 50's; Paula is from a wealthy Midwestern town, the rest of us from New York, New Jersey or California) we can meet on a common ground, having each been brought up and socialized to play the role of woman.

For many of us this openness demanded a tremendous, sometimes overwhelming emotional effort, one which necessitated the laying aside of life-long inhibitions. In our society it is always a risk to relinquish the security of anonymity, one of the few securities allowed us. In this case, we each had to overcome the additional fear of losing the support and friendship of the group. How did any of us know to what extent we could trust each other? How could we know that we wouldn't meet with hostility, disapproval, ridicule? These fears, though real, proved to be unfounded. In fact, our group has drawn much closer since these intense personal analyses began.

As we grew to know each other better, we began to fall out of the group roles that we had assumed. I no longer felt the need to be a leader, Ronny began to see herself less as the group scholar or group mentor, Bette no longer acted as our most knowledgeable link to other women's groups, Marilyn and Linda stopped being the "not quite committed." And we began to relate to each other as individuals and as friends.

Listening to other women, learning about their feelings, their weaknesses and strengths, their fears, their experiences, has helped me to accept myself as a woman; I'm not the only one whose sexual initiation was difficult and painful; I'm not the only one who won't open her mouth in a large group unless I know the indisputable truth and even then, only if I've rehearsed it a dozen times; I'm not the only one struggling to overcome dependency on men, to experience healthy relationships with both sexes.

But perhaps most important to me—to my self-image—was the realization that the dynamic woman is not a rarity, not an abberation of the natural order. *Every woman in our group is an exciting person*; we don't cackle; we're not incurable gossips; and we are likeable—something American women don't often think about each other—or about ourselves. For me, to enjoy women "en masse" was an almost totally new experience. I, who had always shunned all-girl groups, all-girl schools, now look forward to my all-girl meetings as one of the high points of my week. I know now that if women are dull, if women are docile, if women are difficult to work with, it's only because that behavior has been expected, in fact demanded, of us, and we've learned to see ourselves that way.

But now we're uniting against such programming, and that unity extends across the nation. Debby, who was in our group until she moved to California, sent us a letter about her small group there:

"Several people live in communes, one girl is pregnant and unmarried, another wants to be but is afraid she'll lose her job, another girl just divorced her husband, another is living in a women's commune and not

seeing men. A few undergraduates, 1 or 2 graduate students. A girl who never was told about orgasms or the clitoris and of course is living with a guy. The group is a lot different from the one in New York. While there seems to be, on the whole, a much less developed social consciousness, people are eager to talk about the most intimate things and do so with an amazing frankness and lack of inhibitions... We've had long talks about masturbation and lesbian-ism—talks so honest, that at times I've had trouble participating because of my own hang-ups... In a way this is what I want—for a while I felt I was losing touch with my gut feelings; intellectualizing."

Since Debby's left New York, we have begun to discuss "those most intimate things," but it has been difficult for us to examine our own sexuality on more than a superficial level, a difficulty in great part due to the age range of the group (17 to 36) and the resulting gaps in our sexual experiences.

The concept of women's liberation and participation in the movement has made profound differences in many lives. Shattered illusions replaced by more deeply meaningful realities. Not all pleasant or easily acceptable. As a step towards an ultimate goal—better relationships with men and women—we often have to sacrifice, at least temporarily, those we now have. Until both men and women can better understand what those relationships should be, and until society allows more creative exploration of relationships. For some, this means broken marriages. For Kay, who is thankful she became aware of women's liberation while she is still in high school, it means, "Because of what I now know and feel, I probably won't want to have many of the relationships I might otherwise have desired, but I can see myself having fewer, stronger ones." For Bette it has meant a greater self-esteem, the strength and ability to do what she wants, rather than what is wanted of her. For Sandy it may mean motherhood outside of marriage. Mary, the only woman in the group with children, would like to move into a commune with her family. Ronny has begun to use her maiden name and to explore living apart from her husband. I, too, have given up my visions of myself becoming Mrs. Somebody Else. Which is not to say there aren't many contradictions in our lives—in my life, specifically, there are many: in relationships with some women whom I still see as threats, with men on the demands I still make of them, with my boy friend (especially), with my parents, in my job.

What is often, however, our greatest obstacle is guilt. Guilt that comes from taking care of our own lives. Guilt that is very real for women brought up to be caretakers of husbands and children, to sacrifice their needs for their family's. Or for those of us in the broader political Movement, taught to see our struggles as trivial, even frivolous, next to those of the Asians, the Africans, the Latin Americans, and in this country the blacks and the workers. Guilt that has kept me out of the Women's Movement for a long time.

But it's beginning to go away. I'm growing stronger, more confident, though sometimes I have to fight to make it show. And that's when I know I can turn to my sisters. And I know they'll understand.

—Ronnie Lichtman

ALPHABET SOUP

in attempting to put together an alphabet soup of the women's liberation movement, I began to feel that I was assembling some sort of descriptive telephone book for a small city. With each new discovered and defined group came inklings of a dozen others just beyond, until it became apparent that whatever else the movement is, its numbers are legion and no comprehensive list could be got ready by deadline time.

In a recent article (November 21) on "the new feminism," Time Magazine reported that there are "at least 50 groups in New York... 35 in the San Francisco Bay Area... 30 in Chicago, 25 in Boston and a scattering of others in cities ranging from Gainesville, Fla. to Toronto." I can add to that list an indeterminate number of British groups and a large movement in Berlin (where radical feminists have organized into communes, opened childcare and information centers and operate a mobile health care service). Fifty in New York? At least. Furthermore, the groups vary greatly in type. Some are small, informal consciousness-raising groups like the one described in this issue. Others are organized around a single issue central to the movement such as abortion or free child-care, some along extra-feminist lines (for example, professional groups such as Media Women or the numerous high school, college and graduate school groups). Still others are feminist caucuses within organizations that are, to put it mildly in some cases, not primarily feminist (e.g. YSA Women, the Women's Rights Caucus of the New Democratic Coalition, SDS Women). Finally, there are the groups whose organization and politics are primarily feminist, independent and non-feminist professional and political affiliations, and who operate in a wider sphere than the informal consciousness-raising groups. I don't have a complete list of these groups—as far as I know, no one does, since it is a characteristic peculiar to the women's liberation movement that it cuts across all social divisions of class and race and that it is as politically complex and fluid as a movement can be. New groups are constantly forming, old ones divide and multiply into new or undergo radical transformations as women strive for a new and truer definition not only of themselves but of politics as well. I began this project with the idea of producing a neat diagram of the movement, a tidy, conscientious parsing of its elements. That idea has been abandoned; how does one diagram upheaval? Instead, what follows is an attempt to describe briefly six groups whose differences of style and concentration will yield a rough measure of the movement as a whole.

"Citywide" women's liberation coalition. This group

properly has no name and doesn't particularly want one, but is generally referred to as "Citywide." It began in the spring of 1969 as a coalition of revolutionary women, some from other feminist groups, many from non-feminist radical organizations (e.g. SDS, Newsreel, *Levianthan* and later, RYM II), who met every other Thursday evening to concentrate on women's liberation issues. It has a fluctuating attendance membership of 50-70 women, who tend to believe that while capitalism/imperialism and male chauvinism maintain each other, the greater power and therefore the focus of attack resides in the system rather than in male chauvinism. They are distinct from much of the rest of the women's liberation movement by the fact that they acknowledge the possibility of strategic alliances with male-dominated radical groups. They see women's liberation as essential to any real revolution, but do not always place primary emphasis on it. Suggesting that "freedom is the recognition of necessity" one woman active in the coalition gave as an example the need for black and brown women to multiply in order to combat "American genocidal policies" as more important than the demand for control over their bodies, i.e. free abortion and birth control. The same woman pointed out, however, that there was a growing trend in the coalition toward a more strictly feminist approach. According to another member, the coalition has organized separate day-care, abortion and health collectives and is in the process of developing others. A propaganda collective is planned, as well as others to work with high school and college students, and people are moving to Brooklyn and Queens to organize there. The coalition is also willing to assist any women in starting their own consciousness-raising groups. The group may be contacted through the Leviathan office, 2700 Broadway, New York City.

The Feminists. Self-described as "a political organization to annihilate sex roles" The Feminists began on October 17, 1968 as a breakaway group from N.O.W. which they considered too hierarchical and superficial in its approach to women's liberation. An intense and highly disciplined group, they meet twice a week and conduct frequent workshops and special meetings as well. Penalties for irregular attendance are temporary loss of voting privileges and, if necessary, expulsion from the group. They require further that not more than one third of their membership be either married or living with a man, on the basis that such arrangement are inherently inequitable. They are also insistantly democratic: the chair and secretary of each meeting are chosen by lot, and all work, whether menial or demanding of special skills, is assigned by lot with provision against the same sort of task—writing a position paper, for example—falling to one member twice before it has made the round of the group.

The Feminists' rules reflect their political theory which states, in part, that "all political classes grew out of the male-female role system . . . The pathology of oppression can only be fully comprehended in its primary development, the male-female division. Because the male-female system is primary, the freedom of every oppressed individual depends upon the freeing of every individual from every aspect of the male-female system." They demand that marriage and the family be eliminated, that children be cared for by the society as a whole and not "belong" to anyone and that extra-uterine means of reproduction be developed as "a humane goal." They also oppose sexual intercourse ("at present its psychology is dominance-passivity") and suggest the exploration of other means of sexual gratification as a way toward "physical relations . . .

Photo: Lana Reeves

(that) would be an extension of communication between individuals." In a demonstration at the Marriage License Bureau and City Hall the Feminists made additional demands for economic and educational reparations for women and repeal of all state laws pertaining to marriage, divorce and annulment. An interesting packet describing in greater detail the structure and basic principles of the group may be obtained for twenty-five cents by writing to The Feminists at 320 West 108th Street.

National Organization for Women. NOW was founded in 1966 by Betty Friedan, author of *The Feminine Mystique.* It has more than 5000 members, including some 100 men, with chapters in all the major cities of the U.S. It is the most politically moderate of the feminist organizations and concentrates on working within the system with a program of legislative demands for full equality for women. Those demands include passage of an Equal Rights Amendment to the Constitution which reads, "Equality of Rights under the Law shall not be denied or abridged by the United States or by any State on account of sex." NOW also demands the repeal of all abortion laws, the establishment of free, state-supported child-care centers and the revision of the tax laws to permit full deduction of all housekeeping and child-care expenses for working parents. The organization functions as an effective legislative pressure group and is considered to be largely responsible for the barring of sexual categorization in Want Ads and was instrumental in winning the fight by airline stewardesses to marry and stay on the job after age 32. NOW is the only currently active feminist organization that did not develop out of New Left-oriented radical politics, a fact that is reflected, perhaps, not only in its tendancy to focus somewhat exclusively on specific legislative inequities without going on to scrutinize the social and political system in which these inequities flourish but also in the structure of the organization itself. Not only is NOW hierarchical—there is a board of directors, as well as national and local officers, all elected for fixed terms—but among its male members there is even a chapter president, a phenomenon that one might safely guess has not been duplicated elsewhere in women's liberation. There is evidence, however, that a radical trend is developing in NOW which should be interesting to watch. NOW's Manhattan office is at 328 West 12th Street, telephone 929-8250.

Redstockings. Formed in January 1968, Redstockings insist on the need for a completely new political analysis based on their personal experience as women. Much of their energy has been devoted to personal consciousness-raising, not as "therapy . . . but as the only method by which we can ensure that our program for liberation is based on the concrete realities of our lives." They have participated regularly in women's liberation demonstrations since the start of the movement, however, they recently disrupted and took over an abortion hearing in New York at which women were denied places on the panel. Their persistance in sticking to their slogan, "We will not ask what is 'revolutionary' or 'reformist' only what is good for women," has, on occasion, put them very much at odds with the Citywide faction of the movement. (It's impossible, for example, to imagine Redstockings accepting the Citywide interpretation of the priorities of black and brown women in regard to abortion and birth control.)

Redstockings flatly blames men for women's oppression, stating in their manifesto that "all other forms of exploitation and oppression (racism, capitalism, imperialism, etc.) are extensions of male supremacy: men dominate women, a few men dominate the rest." The group is opposed to marriage and the nuclear family but does not attempt to legislate the sexual lives of its members. They further "call on all men to give up their male privileges and support women's liberation," a demand that reflects their own personal pledge to "repudiate all economic, racial, educational or status privileges that divide us from other women." They hold an orientation meeting for new women on the first Sunday of every month and they also have a selection of interesting literature for sale. Write Redstockings, P.O. Box 748, Stuyvesant Station, New York, N.Y. 10009.

The Stanton-Anthony Brigade of the Radical Feminists. Just begun in November by a group of women already active in women's liberation who felt the need for a group that would concentrate specifically on creating a mass movement. The Brigade, by virtue of the political history of

its members, is radical-leftist but emphasizes feminism as the core of its politics. Their program is one of "consciousness-raising actions," demonstrations designed to focus national attention on radical feminism and to draw as many women as possible into the movement. They feel that too many women's liberation actions in the past have been politically self-indulgent (for example, wearing arm bands mourning the death of Ho Chi Minh at the Miss America demonstration) and have as a result turned women away from a movement that should properly be inviting them in. They also welcome publicity (many groups don't at this point, largely out of fear and distrust) and when planning demonstrations will take into account ways to circumvent distortion and misunderstanding of their actions. They have begun with a core group of around 20 women and welcome new members. As their membership grows it is to be divided into separate "brigades" of fifteen women each. So far they have met once a week, usually on Monday nights, and a meeting for new people is planned for the near future. Call Shulamith Firestone, 673-7658, or Minda Bikman, 924-7264, for information.

Women's International Terrorist Conspiracy from Hell (WITCH). WITCH surfaced on Halloween Day, 1968, with an "Up against the Wall Street" action involving day-long street theatre in the financial district and talk sessions with the women who work there. It is a flamboyant action-oriented organization with more than thirty autonomous covens around the country. Like most of women's liberation it has no official leaders and functions by consensus. WITCH is opposed to marriage and the nuclear family but its distinctiveness lies less in its ideology than in its style, which is by turns exuberant, rude, funny and extravagant. On the bus ride to Atlantic City for last summer's Miss America demonstration, a coven sitting in the back produced several fine, rowdy songs and chants for the demonstration when the bus was barely out of New York. WITCH, more than any other group, suggests in its tone that women's liberation can be fun. A few excerpts from their manifesto:

WITCH is an all-woman Everything. It's theater, revolution, magic, terror, joy, garlic flowers, spells. It's an awareness that witches and gypsies were the original guerrillas and resistance fighters against oppression . . . Witches were the first Friendly Heads and Dealers, the first birth-control practitioners and abortionists, the first alchemists . . . WITCH lives and laughs in every woman. She is the free part of each of us, beneath the shy smiles, the acquiescence to absurd male domination . . . if you are a woman and dare to look within yourself, you are a witch . . . you are free and beautiful . . . Whatever is repressive, solely male-oriented, greedy, puritanical, authoritarian—those are your targets. . . . you are pledged to free our brothers from oppression and stereotyped sexual roles as well as ourselves. You are a witch by saying aloud, "I am a Witch," three times, and thinking about that. You are a witch by being female, untamed, angry, joyous, and immortal."

WITCH also quotes the Bible (Judges): "for rebellion is as the sin of witchcraft." New members are welcome and may write to P.O. Box 694, Stuyvesant Station, New York 10009.

– Karen Durbin

Editor's note: A fifteen-page bibliography of literature on women and the women's movement can be obtained from Lucinda Cisler, 102 West 80th St. New York City. 25¢ each.

Gay Power Comes To Sheridan Square

by Lucian Truscott IV

Sheridan Square this weekend looked like something from a William Burroughs novel as the sudden specter of "gay power" erected its brazen head and spat out a fairy tale the likes of which the area has never seen.

The forces of faggotry, spurred by a Friday night raid on one of the city's largest, most popular, and longest lived gay bars, the Stonewall Inn, rallied Saturday night in an unprecedented protest against the raid and continued Sunday night to assert presence, possibility, and pride until the early hours of Monday morning. "I'm a faggot, and I'm proud of it!" "Gay Power!" "I like boys!"—these and many other slogans were heard all three nights as the show of force by the city's finery met the force of the city's finest. The result was a kind of liberation, as the gay brigade emerged from the bars, back rooms, and bedrooms of the Village and became street people.

GAY POWER RIOTS

RADRAGS

NEW YORK(LNS)—An introductory pamphlet on Gay Liberation, prepared for both gay and straight people, has been published by the Red Butterfly Cell, the Marxist study group of New York's Gay Liberation Front. For a copy of the booklet, send 25 cents to Red Butterfly, Box 3445, Grand Central Station, New York, NY 10017.

Full Moon Over The Stonewall

by Howard Smith

During the "gay power" riots at the Stonewall last Friday night I found myself on what seemed to me the wrong side of the blue line. Very scary. Very enlightening.

I had struck up a spontaneous relationship with Deputy Inspector Pine, who had marshalled the raid, and was following him closely, listening to all the little dialogues and plans and police inflections. Things were already pretty tense: the gay customers freshly ejected from their hangout, prancing high and jubilant in the street, had been joined by quantities of Friday night tourists hawking around for Village-type excitement. The cops had considerable trouble arresting the few people they wanted to take in for further questioning. A strange mood was in the crowd—I noticed the full moon. Loud defiances mixed with skittish hilarity made for a more dangerous stage of protest; they were feeling their impunity. This kind of crowd freaks easily.

The turning point came when the police had difficulty keeping a dyke in a patrol car. Three times she slid out and tried to walk away. The last time a cop bodily heaved her in. The crowd shrieked, "Police brutality!" "Pigs!" A few coins sailed through the air. I covered my face. Pine ordered the three cars and paddy wagon to leave with the prisoners before the crowd became more of a mob.

"Hurry back," he added, realizing he and his force of eight detectives two of them women, would be easily overwhelmed if the temper broke. "Just drop them at the Sixth Precinct and hurry back."

The sirened caravan pushed through the gauntlet, pummeled and buffeted until it managed to escape. "Pigs!" "Gaggot cops!" Pennies and dimes flew, I stood against the door. The detectives held at most a 10-foot clearing. Escalate to nickels and quarters. A bottle. Another bottle. Pine says, "Let's get inside. Lock ourselves inside, it's safer."

"You want to come in?" he asks me. "You're probably safer," with a paternal tone. Two flashes: if they go in and I stay out, will the mob know that the blue plastic thing hanging from my shirt is a press card, or by now will they assume I'm a cop too? On the other hand, it might be interesting to be locked in with a few cops, just rapping and reviewing how they work.

In goes me. We bolt the heavy door. The front of the Stonewall is mostly brick except for the windows, which are boarded within by plywood. Inside we hear the shattering of windows, followed by what we imagine to be bricks pounding on the door, voices yelling. The floor shudders at each blow. "Aren't you guys scared?" I say.

"No." But they look at least uneasy.

The door crashes open, beer cans and bottles hurtle in. Pine and his troop rush to shut it. At that point the only uniformed cop among them gets hit with something under his eye. He hollers, and his hand comes away scarlet. It looks a lot more serious than it really is. They are all suddenly furious. Three run out in front to see if they can scare the mob from the door. A hail of coins. A beer can glances off Deputy Inspector Smyth's head.

Pine, a man of about 40 and smallish build, gathers himself, leaps out into the melee, and grabs someone around the waist, pulling him downward and back into the doorway. They fall. Pine regains hold and drags the elected protester inside by the hair. The door slams again. Angry cops converge on the guy, releasing their anger on this sample from the mob. Pine is saying, "I saw him throwing somethin," and the guy unfortunately is giving some sass, snidely admits to throwing "only a few coins." The cop who was cut is incensed, yells something like, "So you're the one who hit me!" And while the other cops help, he slaps the prisoner five or six times very hard and finishes with a punch to the mouth. They handcuff the guy as he almost passes out. "All right," Pine announces, "we book him for assault." The door is smashed open again. More objects are thrown in. The detectives locate a fire hose, the idea being to ward off the madding crowd until reinforcements arrive. They can't see where to aim it, wedging the hose in a crack in the door. It sends out a weak stream. We all start to slip on water and Pine says to stop.

By now the mind's eye has forgotten the character of the mob; the sound filtering in doesn't suggest dancing faggots any more. It sounds like a powerful rage bent on vendetta. That way why Pine's singling out of the guy I knew later to be Dave Van Ronk was important. The little force of detectives was beginning to feel fear, and Pine's action clinched their morale again.

A door over to the side almost gives. One cop shouts, "Get away from there or I'll shoot!" It stops shaking. The front door is completely open. One of the big plywood windows gives, and it seems inevitable that the mob will pour in. A kind of tribal adrenaline rush bolsters all of us; they all take out and check pistols. I see both policewomen busy doing the same, and the danger becomes even more real. I find a big wrench behind the bar, jam it into my belt like a scimitar. Hindsight: my fear on the verge of being trampled by a mob fills the same dimensions as my fear on the verge of being clubbed by the TPF.

Pine places a few men on each side of the corridor leading away from the entrance. They aim unwavering at the door. One detective arms himself in addition with a sawed-off baseball bat he has found. I hear, "We'll shoot the first motherfucker that comes through the door."

Pine glances over toward me. "Are you all right, Howard?" I can't believe what I am saying: "I'd feel a lot better with a gun."

I can only see the arm at the window. It squirts a liquid into the room, and a flaring match follows. Pine is not more than 10 feet away. He aims his gun at the figures.

He doesn't fire. The sound of sirens coincides with the whoosh of flames where the lighter fluid was thrown. Later, Pine tells me he didn't shoot because he had heard the sirens in time and felt no need to kill someone if help was arriving. It was that close.

While the squads of uniforms disperse the mob out front, inside we are checking to see if each of us all right. For a few minutes we get the post-tension giggles, but as they subside I start scribbling notes to catch up, and the people around me change back to cops. They begin examining the place.

It had lasted 45 minutes. Just before and after the siege I picked up some more detached information. According to the police, they are not picking on homosexuals. On these raids they almost never arrest customers, only people working there. As of June 1, the State Liquor Authority said that all unlicensed places were eligible to apply for licenses. The police are scrutinizing all unlicensed places, and most of the bars that are in that category happen to cater to homosexuals. The Stonewall is an unlicensed private club. The raid was made with a warrant, after undercover agents inside observed illegal sale of alcohol. To make certain the raid plans did not leak, it was made without notifying the Sixth Precinct until after the detectives (all from the First Division) were inside the premises. Once the bust had actually started, one of Pine's men called the Sixth for assistance on a pay phone.

It was explained to me that generally men dressed as men, even if wearing extensive makeup, are always released; men dressed as women are sometimes arrested; and "men" fully dressed as women, but who upon inspection by a policewoman prove to have undergone the sex-change operation, are always let go. At the Stonewall, out of five queens checked, three were men and two were changes, even though all said they were girls. Pine released them all anyway.

As for the rough-talking owners and/or managers of the Stonewall, their riff ran something like this: we are just honest businessmen who are being harassed by the police because we cater to homosexuals, and because our names are Italian so they think we are part of something bigger. We haven't done anything wrong and have never been convicted in no court. We have rights, and the courts should decide and not let the police do things like what happened here. When we got back in the place, all the mirrors, jukeboxes, phones, toilets, and cigarette machines were smashed. Even the sinks were stuffed and running over. And we say the police did it. The courts will say that we are innocent.

Who isn't, I thought, as I dropped my scimitar and departed.

the village VOICE 7/3/69

WHAT EVER HAPPENED TO THE AMERICAN WAY OF LIFE?

During the sit-in at Sproul Hall: American society is a bleak scene, but it is all a lot of us have to look forward to. Society provides no challenge. American society in the standard conception it has of itself is simply no longer exciting. The most exciting things going on in America today are movements to change America...The "futures" and "careers" for which American students now prepare are for the most part intellectual and moral wastelands. This chrome-plated consumers paradise would have us grow up to be well-behaved children.

MARIO SAVIO. *An End to History,* Dec 1963

...the greatest and most disastrous of maladies, of which humanity has not to this day been cured: his sickness of himself, brought on by the violent severance from his animal past, by his sudden leap and fall into new layers and conditions of existence, by his declaration of war against the old instincts that had hitherto been the foundation of his power, his joy, and his awesomeness.

NIETZSCHE

he not busy being born is busy dying.

BOB DYLAN

AMERIKA

The club of induction has been used to drive out of areas considered to be less important to the areas of greater importance in which deferments were given, the individuals who did not or could not participate in activities which were considered essential to the defense of the Nation.

Throughout his career as a student, the pressure--the threat of loss of deferment--continues. It continues with equal intensity after graduation. He is impelled to pursue his skill rather than embark upon some less important enterprise. The loss of deferred status is the consequence for the individual who has acquired the skill and either does not use it or uses it in a nonessential activity.

The psychology of granting wide choice under pressure to take action is the American or indirect way of achieving what is done by direct action in foreign countries where choice is not permitted.

Here choice is limited but not denied, and it is fundamental that an individual generally applies himself better to something he has decided to do rather than something he has been told to do.

In the less patriotic and more selfish individual it engenders a sense of fear, uncertainty, and dissatisfaction which motivates him, nevertheless, in the same direction.

Selective Service processes do not compel people by edict as in foreign systems to enter pursuits having to do with essentiality and progress. They go because they know that by going they will be deferred.

Deciding what people should do, rather than letting them do something of national importance of their own choosing, introduces many problems that are at least partially avoided when indirect methods, the kind currently invoked by the Selective Service System, are used.

Delivery of manpower for induction, the process of providing a few thousand men with transportation to a reception center, is not much of an administrative challenge. It is dealing with the other millions of registrants that the System is heavily occupied, developing more effective human beings in the national interest. If there is to be any survival after disaster, it will take people, not machines, to restore the nation.

July 1. 1965

"Channeling", Selective Service Memorandum 7/1/65

"What is crucial," he leaned forward and spoke intensely, impatient with the need to stop for the translator, "is what happens inside the young. If we can educate them, by example and in the schools, to see work as a prize, not as a burden imposed from without, that'll be a beginning."

CHE GUEVARA in conversation with Nat Hentoff

Capitalists ponder new left

marjorie heins

Capitalist Realism: an immaculate, ruggedly handsome executive holds an oil well or a jet plane in his manicured tan hands. WE BUY CORPORATIONS. C-E SUPPORTS THE EVOLUTION IN LATIN AMERICA. NEED SOMETHING SPECIAL IN CORRUGATED CONTAINERS? THE AMERICAN CAPITALIST... WHEN HIS NEEDS ARE FINANCIAL, HIS REACTION IS CHEMICAL. MOTIVATED MEN MAKE AMERICA GREAT.

Fortune magazine is to Business what Playboy is to Sex: glorified and glossy. This month, Fortune has produced a Special Issue, on Radical Youth. They say that 40% (or about 2,300,000) of college students identify with the New Left. These are the "forerunners," and they represent opinions which will become more widespread. Once this fact is established, the rest of the Special Issue falls into place. Having spotted a trend, the manicured men are trying to understand it, in order that they may attract it into business.

Methods of seducing and utilizing reluctant youth are described at length. Fortune advises its readers they can no longer start college graduates in the mailroom at $5,000 a year. "We're dealing with a lot of tender little egos," a Personnel Officer is quoted as saying. But if you treat your youth right, you don't have to worry. One article describes almost ecstatically the Youth Revolution at General Mills, which occurred when a few young executives in a burst of creativity expanded the company from oats to children's games. Many faculty members understandably refusing to be shut up in an ivory tower, have rushed to an opposite extreme. They have drawn up an indictment of US society out of random observations organized around attitudes of social criticism picked up in the flea market of ideas — mostly odds and ends of Savonarola, Voltaire, Thoreau, Marx, Zola, William Jennings Bryan and C. Wright Mills." (Quite a flea market, that.) Ways writes: "Despite its low intellectual quality, the standard picture of US society held by the academic left serves its purpose. It gives footing for a posture of hostility and defiance, an assumption of moral superiority."

Why has Fortune produced this trash? Not only so its readers can learn how to

use, recruit or co-opt the young, though this is obviously one purpose. The real function of the Special Issue is to reinforce complacency:

"We are observing it (youth) now at a critical point in time. Its members are old enough to be concerned about their future, and to be pondering the career options open to them (including the option to drop out). But they are still young enough to be flexible; they have, even most of those in the New Left, preserved their options."

Preserving our options.

American capitalism is not really worried. An article which pretends to deal seriously with dissident academia ends in a diarrhea of cliches about undisciplined scholarship. Nathan Glaser's intriguing piece, "The Jewish Role in Student Activism," says nothing really except there are a lot of Jewish radicals; and ends very possibly as an excuse for the Establishment of an anti-Semitic world (business) to maintain one particular prejudice: Jews are trouble.

Capitalist realism commands a certain fascination. In Fortune, where this art form is purest, the graphics are far better than the words. But then, Fortune has Time-Life at its disposal, so what can you expect?

An article on youth culture, though deploring most of it and just tentatively admitting that Bob Dylan and Joan Baez "border on art," nevertheless offers encouragement to readers if only they know what to make of it all. A J.C. Penney executive, for instance, is quoted as follows:

"We have a square image. But square is IN. Honesty is in. Cheap is in. Kids are moving toward a 'tell it like it is' philosophy. I think we can hit them right in the eyes with a 'sell it like it is' approach."

Sock it to 'em, J.C.

From a piece on changes in "square" universities: "This is a quiet revolution whose consequences will remain long after Students for a Democratic Society has become an amusing memory of collegiate extravagance." When you think about it, that's a wonderful sentence. Fortune spends zillions of dollars and sends pseudo-hip reporters all over the country to find out about a youth revolution of which SDS was and is one of the most important expressions. They dribble on in perfect seriousness for over one hundred pages. But when it comes right down to it, SDS isn't real; they can't believe it, like the suburbanites who despise hippies even though they've never seen one.

The Special Issue's worst article, by Max Ways, concludes that professors aren't quite so smart nor nearly so scholarly as businessmen. Businessmen are thorough, competent, rational, objective, big on research and analysis, and some have MBA after their names. Professors, on the other hand (Ways speaks of the radicals; I assume Clinton Rossiter is excepted), reach their conclusions not by "disciplined research but rather (by) the folklore of the academic left...."

NOTHING

The draft is the largest educational institution in the world.

ROBERT McNAMARA Johnson's Secretary of Defense, former President of the Ford Motor Co., now head of the World Bank

Let us sum up again. The majority of young people are faced with the following alternative: either society is a benevolently frivolous racket in which they'll manage to boondoggle, though less profitably, than the more privileged; or society is serious (and they hope still benevolent enough to support them), but they are useless and hopelessly out. Such thoughts do not encourage productive life. Naturally young people are more sanguine and look for man's work, but few find it. Some settle for a "good job"; most settle for a lousy job; a few, but an increasing number, don't settle.

I often ask, "What do you want to work at? If you have the chance. When you get out of school, college, the service, etc."

Some answer right off and tell their definite plans and projects. I'm pleased for them, but it's a bit boring, because they are such squares.

Quite a few will, with prompting, come out with astounding stereotyped conceited fantasies like being a movie actor when they are "discovered" — like "Marlon Brando, but in my own way."

Very rarely somebody will, maybe defiantly and defensively, maybe diffidently but proudly, make you know that he knows very well what he is going to do, is indeed already doing it, which is the real test.

The usual answer, perhaps the normal answer, is "I don't know," meaning, "I'm looking; I haven't found the right thing; it's discouraging but not hopeless."

But the terrible answer is, "Nothing." The young man doesn't want to do anything.

I remember talking to half a dozen young fellows at Van Wagner's Beach outside of Hamilton, Ontario; and all of them had this one thing to say, "Nothing." They didn't believe that what to work at was the kind of thing we *wanted*. They rather expected that two or three of them would work for the electric company in town, but they couldn't care less. I turned away from the conversation abruptly,

because of the uncontrollable burning tears in my eyes and pain in my breast. Not feeling sorry for them, but tears of frank dismay for the waste of our humanity (they were nice kids). And it is out of that incident that many years later I am writing this report.

The simple job plight of these adolescents could not be remedied without a social revolution. Therefore is it not astonishing if the most well-intentioned public spokesmen do not mention it at all. But it is hard to grow up in a society where one's important problems are treated as non-existent. It is impossible to belong to it, it is hard to fight to change it. The effect must be rather to feel disaffected, and all the more restive if one is smothered by well-meaning social workers and PAL's who don't seem to understand the real irk. The boys cannot articulate the real irk themselves, for they haven't learned to say it.

From *Youth in The Organized Society* by Paul Goodman

"Vital decision-making, in policy matters as well as in business, must remain at the top. This is partly — though not completely — what the top is for."

Ultimate control must be vested in the hands of management, which is, *"in the end, the most creative of all the arts — for its medium is human talent itself."* This is apparently a divine imperative:

"God is clearly democratic. He distributes brain power universally. But He quite justifiably expects us to do something efficient and constructive with that priceless gift. That is what management is all about."

ROBERT McNAMARA, quoted by Noam Chomsky in his essay "Knowledge and Power." *The New Left,* an anthology.

AMERIKA

Wondering why President Nixon is so slow in filling government posts? "I had never realized," one Cabinet member said, "what a toll the fierce competition of American business and professional life has taken on many of our most talented and successful men. Many of them have simply been worn out in the struggle. Many more have all kinds of family problems they cannot leave. In a great many cases, they have taken to drink to such an extent that the risk is too great. So we have had to go much slower than we expected."

Extra Feb 1969

Environmental disaster was the spectre haunting a Pacific Northwest development conference. Dr. Athelstan Spilhaus, president-elect of the American Association for the Advancement of Science declared, "beware of wise men from the East who have loused up their own region" with ideas they were now "trying to peddle" elsewhere. Socio-economist Robert Theobald stated, "I believe that the decision-making centers in New York, Washington, and Detroit are devoted to shoring up a culture which is clearly collapsing."

A.P. *Extra*

ADVICE TO THE YOUNG FROM MR. NAPALM

THE CENTRAL POINT IS THAT WE ARE FREE PEOPLE WITH FREE WILLS

H. D. DOAN PRESIDENT OF "DOW CHEMICAL"

Boy! THIS LOOKS LIKE EVERYTHING

Dear Mr. Doan:

I question whether a business career will allow me to attain what I would consider a proper balance among all aspects of my life. Is business today so demanding that one would have time for little else? A job is a major part of life but not the whole of it. Raising a family is a very important part of most people's future plans. Therefore, of prime concern would be the possible adverse effects a career in business might have on an individual's family obligations.

Are basic family ties weakened as a result of a preoccupation with business? With respect to family ties, Dr. Feinberg in the January 1968 Dun's Review says, "In the family of the typical business executive there is very little knitting together of diverse environments." It would appear that an executive cannot adequately fulfill his role as a husband and father. The family unit is subordinated to his job. A preoccupation with business can mean more than just a lack of time to spend with one's family. In the same article, Dr. Feinberg says, "Many youngsters feel that their fathers know the *price* of everything and the *value* of nothing." There appears to be the tendency to emphasize the economic side of life and to ignore the equally important personal side.

My question is whether being a good husband and father will necessarily conflict with being a good businessman. Draw on your own personal experience, Mr. Doan. Can you honestly say that en route to becoming a successful businessman, you were an equally successful husband and father? Need these roles be contradictory? If not, how did you resolve the conflict?

Sincerely,

David M. Butler

David M. Butler
*Electrical Engineering,
Michigan State*

Dear Mr. Butler:

You ask about conflict between the time demands of a job in industry and the time we need for our family life.

Well, first of all, I'm not sure there's any real difference between this problem as it occurs in business and as it occurs in any other occupation; the same problem occurs in education, in government, or in the ministry. In any field—and this is the basic problem—the more responsibility you assume the less time you'll have for your family.

In many cases this factor has a built-in balance: the heaviest responsibility usually comes to us at an age when our children have grown up, so that in an idealized sense there may be no problem at all.

My own view is that you can have both a satisfying career *and* a good family life, but I recognize that for the young business executive this is a very real problem, and one that requires some choices to be made —consciously or unconsciously.

You are perfectly right that you cannot carry a very large business or educational or governmental responsibility and also have an ideal family life— particularly from the standpoint of time. Perhaps the saving grace of this dilemma is that each of us can make our choice as to what we want.

When Dr. Feinberg says that many parents "know the price of everything and the value of nothing" he is right, but I'm sure this phenomenon is not exclusive to businessmen. It is more a condemnation of individuals than it is of the business system. There are great numbers of businessmen who have excellent value systems, and in many cases these are based on a self-acquired liberal education. The man who knows the value of all things (and the price of nothing) is invariably of more value to the business system, just as he is a more valuable man to education or to the government.

On the personal side, to some extent I am a victim of the problem you pose. Having raised a family in an imperfect and, I suppose, shorthanded (in the sense of lack of time) way, I can readily agree that there are conflicts. But, having raised a family, I'm convinced as well that no one has an idea how this really *should* be done. It may well be that more time would not have solved problems that were personal short-comings in the first place.

In any event, the central point is that we are free people with free wills. If you want to work a 40-hour or a 30-hour week so that you can spend more time with your family, that is a noble goal and one you can probably achieve—if your goal is not to assume a large amount of responsibility in your chosen field.

Your question is not related solely to business, but to any occupation; and if you are wise enough you can figure out your own best balance in this matter. But I think it should be perfectly apparent to you that not many people are this wise, and that this balance—like many of the elements of Utopia—is not really attainable.

To summarize: if you want to achieve the maximum success in any field you had better be prepared to work long, hard, dedicated hours. This kind of advice admits a heavy imbalance in the way you spend your time, as I am quite aware, but the choice is yours.

Sincerely,

H D Doan

**H. D. Doan, President,
The Dow Chemical Company**

Mr. Doan:

Is the top of the corporate ladder worth the pressure?

WHO CARES ABOUT STUDENT OPINION? BUSINESSMEN DO.

Dialogue

Three chief executive officers—The Goodyear Tire & Rubber Company's Chairman, Russell DeYoung, The Dow Chemical Company's President, H. D. Doan, and Motorola's Chairman, Robert W. Galvin—are responding to serious questions and viewpoints posed by students about business and its role in our changing society . . . and from their perspective as heads of major corporations are exchanging views through means of a campus/corporate Dialogue Program on specific issues raised by leading student spokesmen.

Here, David M. Butler, completing his studies in Electrical Engineering at Michigan State, is questioning Mr. Doan. A member of the Dean's Advisory Committee, Mr. Butler also participates actively in professional engineering organizations on campus;

anticipates graduate studies before developing his career.

In the course of the entire Dialogue Program, Stan Chess, Journalism major at Cornell, also will probe issues with Mr. Doan; as will Mark Bookspan, a Chemistry major at Ohio State, and David G. Clark, in graduate studies at Stanford, with Mr. DeYoung; and similarly, Arthur M. Klebanoff, in Liberal Arts at Yale; and Arnold Shelby, Latin American Studies at Tulane, with Mr. Galvin.

All of these Dialogues will appear in this publication, and other campus newspapers across the country, throughout this academic year. Campus comments are invited, and should be forwarded to Mr. DeYoung, Goodyear, Akron, Ohio; Mr. Doan, Dow Chemical, Midland, Michigan; or Mr. Galvin, Motorola, Franklin Park, Illinois, as appropriate.

The Daily Californian
11/21/68

73

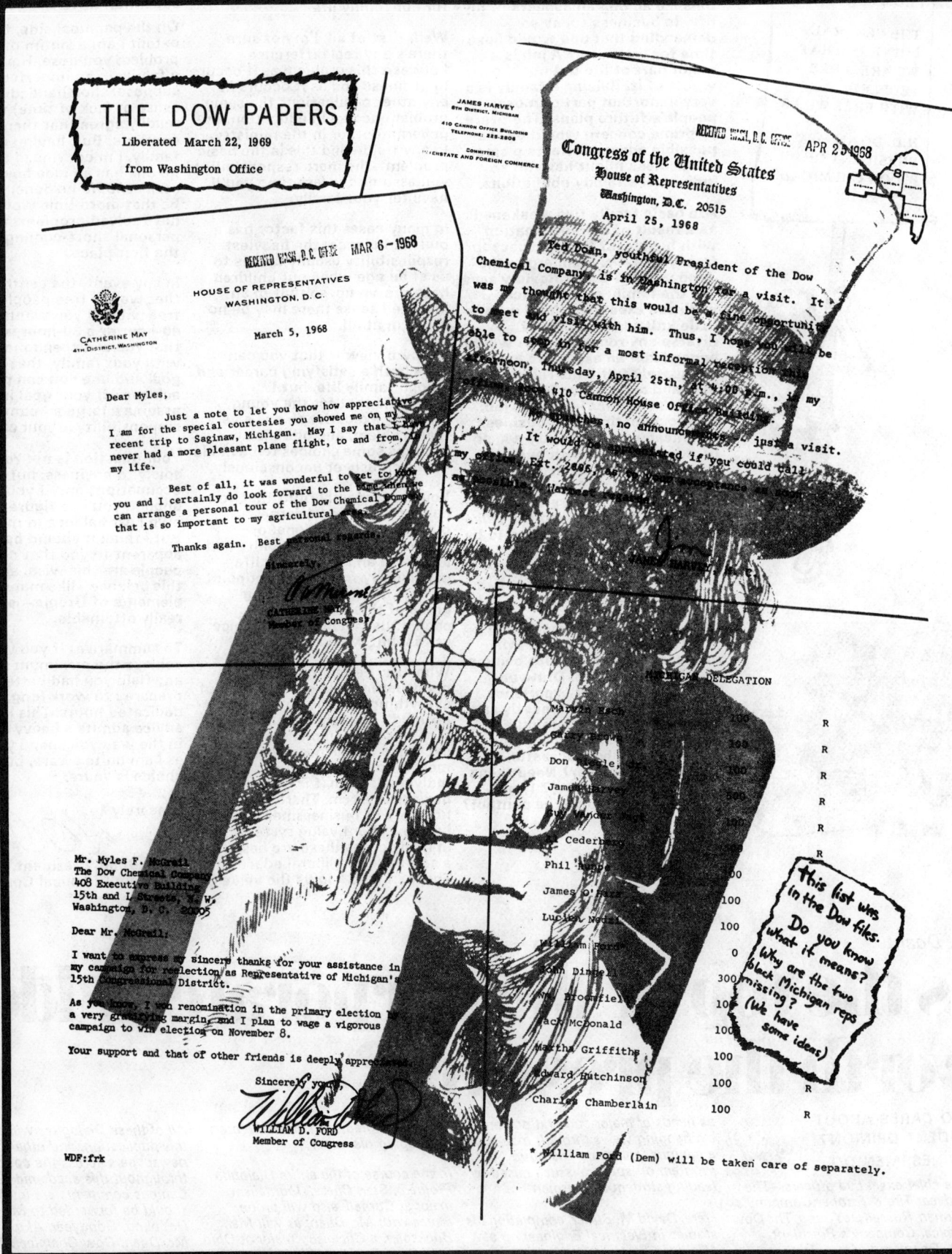

THE DOW PAPERS

Liberated March 22, 1969

from Washington Office

HOUSE OF REPRESENTATIVES
WASHINGTON, D.C.

CATHERINE MAY
4TH DISTRICT, WASHINGTON

RECEIVED WASH. D.C. OFFICE MAR 6-1968

March 5, 1968

Dear Myles,

Just a note to let you know how appreciative I am for the special courtesies you showed me on my recent trip to Saginaw, Michigan. May I say that I never had a more pleasant plane flight, to and from, in my life.

Best of all, it was wonderful to get to know you and I certainly do look forward to the time when we can arrange a personal tour of the Dow Chemical Company that is so important to my agricultural area.

Thanks again. Best personal regards,

Sincerely,

CATHERINE MAY
Member of Congress

JAMES HARVEY
8TH DISTRICT, MICHIGAN

410 CANNON OFFICE BUILDING
TELEPHONE: 225-2806

COMMITTEE
INTERSTATE AND FOREIGN COMMERCE

Congress of the United States
House of Representatives
Washington, D.C. 20515

RECEIVED WASH. D.C. OFFICE APR 25 1968

April 25, 1968

Ted Doan, youthful President of the Dow Chemical Companies is in Washington for a visit. It was my thought that this would be a fine opportunity to meet and visit with him. Thus, I hope you will be able to stop in for a most informal reception this afternoon, Thursday, April 25th, at 4:00 p.m., in my office, Room 410 Cannon House Office Building. No speeches, no announcements... just a visit.

It would be appreciated if you could call my office, Ext. 2806, as to your acceptance as soon as possible. Warmest regards,

JAMES HARVEY

Mr. Myles F. McGrail
The Dow Chemical Company
408 Executive Building
15th and L Streets, N.W.
Washington, D.C. 20005

Dear Mr. McGrail:

I want to express my sincere thanks for your assistance in my campaign for reelection as Representative of Michigan's 15th Congressional District.

As you know, I won renomination in the primary election by a very gratifying margin, and I plan to wage a vigorous campaign to win election on November 8.

Your support and that of other friends is deeply appreciated.

Sincerely yours,

WILLIAM D. FORD
Member of Congress

WDF:frk

MICHIGAN DELEGATION

Marvin Esch	100	R
Garry Brown	100	R
Don Riegle, Jr.	100	R
James Harvey	300	R
... Vander Jagt	100	R
Cederberg		R
Phil Ruppe	100	
James O'Hara	100	
Lucien Nedzi	100	
William Ford	0	
John Dingell		
... Broomfield	300	R
Jack McDonald	100	
Martha Griffiths	100	
Edward Hutchinson	100	
Charles Chamberlain	100	R

This list was in the Dow files. Do you know what it means? Why are the two black Michigan reps missing? (we have some ideas)

* William Ford (Dem) will be taken care of separately.

life sciences

Year of progress in a field of unusual growth potential

The temperature of napalm flame can reach 2060 degrees.

and many

Dow views human health care as a field that offers new opportunities for growth and diversification and in which we can make an increasing and meaningful contribution. We and our affiliated companies in the life sciences are operating as a unified, global group of businesses with a charter to choose innovative patterns...

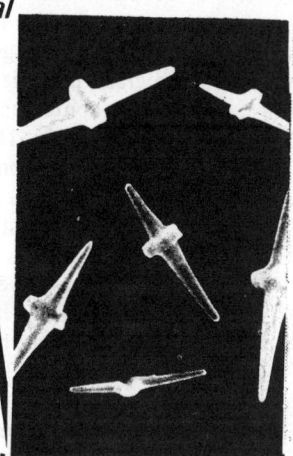

a continuous column or rope of flaming gel can be projected with speed and accuracy to a small target over 150 yards away. Napalm is used in incendiary bombs, fire bombs, land mines and flame throwers. In effect, technology has made it possibee to bring the ovens to the people instead of the people to the ovens.

Newly-developed silicone implants can be used to restore partial activity to hands damaged by rheumatoid arthritis.

een monkeys.

Biohazard skills in design of virus-ntainment facilities have led to a w contract to test the integrity of ogical-barrier systems to be used the Lunar Receiving Laboratory of NASA for the Apollo lunar-landing

ew Diagnostic Produ ncentrated on marketing ging

of *Lirugen* one-shot

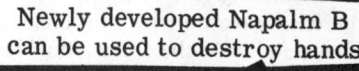

Newly developed Napalm B can be used to destroy hands.

1968, recorded an e ding performance in bo arnings. Bio-Science in so phist g, is i s and chromo latter based

Indu even before ly-c the 1968 Tet offen-plet sive, there were 150,000 st to 200,000 civilian casualties n ph annually; William Pepper estimates that over 400,000 have been killed systo since 1961, many of them children. Thousands have been burned so badly that they do not reach a hospital alive. Many of the casualties are the victims of napalm.

Dow takes pains not to stress its production of napalm, but the fact is that current production of Napalm-B approaches 50,000,000 lbs. a month, compared with 7,500,000 a month at the height of the war in Korea, and 75,000,000 a year in World War II.

observed its centennial with   product, discovered by Lepetit, has

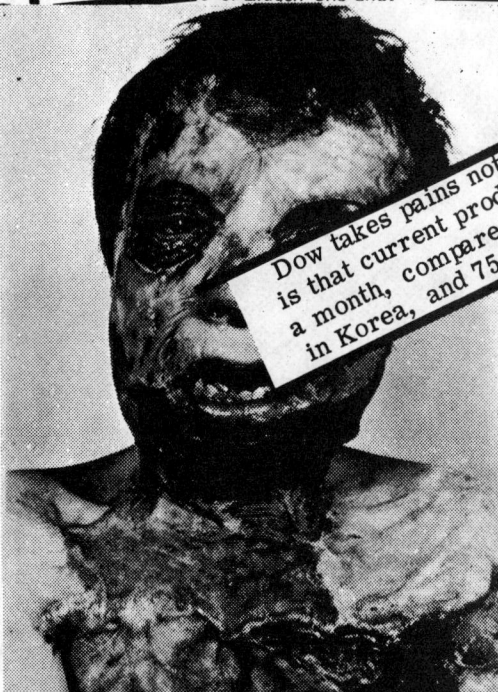

Herbert Doan, July 10, 1969 - Today Show:'This napalm is a good discriminate, strategic weapon, and we feel those folks oughta have it....To us this is a moral decision to stay in this product...." Last fall Dow "lost" its contract for napalm to American Electric Company, a very small company nn Los Angeles which has been making the napalm shell casings for the last couple of years. Dow is still supplying polystyrene.

rthritis

From *The Dow Annual Report 1968*, as interpolated and extended by the guerilla researchers of the D.C. 9, who liberated the files from Dow's Washington offices.

GROW YOUR OWN

Spring is almost upon us, and there is something we all can do at this time of the year that takes very little effort and can yield enormous results. Those who smoke grass have a responsibility to the community to plant the seeds that come with the grass.

I have done this for two years now, and have been very favorably impressed with the quality of grass that grows in the US, and the ability of the plant to grow under a wide variety of conditions with no care.

The earth belongs to the people, and grass can be planted in vacant lots, roadsides, parks, behind factories, under bridges, along the river, or in short, any place where tall weeds can grow unmolested and there is plenty of sunshine. It takes only about one minute to pull up a clump of weeds, shake off the dirt from the roots, scatter ½ dozen seeds, throw some dirt over them and split for another spot. Hundreds of such patches can be planted in one spring afternoon, and if you return in the fall after the first hard frost, you will find that at least half of these spots will have grassplants growing, anywhere from 6" to 6' in height. If you miss a few, the plant is likely to increase its numbers the following year.

Imagine what will happen if this practice becomes widespread. Think of the pigs that will be tied up looking for plants. Grass grows wild in some sections of the US and there is no reason why your area can't be one of them, unless you live in the desert, in which case irrigation is necessary. If you plant in your area for a few years, it is likely that the plant will take hold. The implications of this need not be discussed.

Although guerrilla planting is the best and safest and least time-consuming way to plant, even more reliable results can be secured from cultivating the plants, e.g. watering in dry weather, adding peatmoss to the soil, removing weeds, etc. There are several good booklets giving details on methods at your local head shop. In any case, plant after the last frost.

You should start saving seeds long in advance, in fact you should save all seeds, as with increased government repression, future supplies are uncertain. Make sure those seeds get planted. To remove the seeds from the grass, pulverize the grass in a large boxtop or similar shallow container with your fingers. Tilt the container and tap lightly. The seeds will roll to the lowest corner. The ones that don't roll readily are wrinkled, and probably won't grow. They can be removed with a strainer. It is best not to strain out all the seeds, as the strainer will damage the seeds.

We have the power to make anti-marijuana laws as irrelevant as a law against ragweed. Do you have the will to do your part? SAVE YOUR SEEDS NOW! PLANT THEM EVERYWHERE THIS SPRING!

—ed grassplanter/lns

P.S. According to Edward J. Kirby, Director of the Alcoholic Beverage Control Board of California, cases involving sales of alcoholic beverages to minors have dropped 45% in the last year. This he attributes to the increased use of grass by the same group.

great speckled The·BIRd

Porsche is an acquired taste

■ Not even the most fastidious gourmet was born with a fondness for oysters or the desire for truffles, a fungus which grows wild underground and can be harvested only with the aid of trained dogs and pigs whose noses are peculiarly sensitive to its delicate scent.

Such tastes are acquired by those who seek the ultimate for their palates. No different from those motorists who drive Porsches.

They sampled lesser cars. They wanted superior performance and unique driving pleasure. These tastes led them to the automobile whose qualities have been proven by victories in international road racing and hill climbing competition.

Good things...oysters, truffles, caviar... are always in short supply. Porsche is a good car...the best, some authorities insist. Only 60 are built each day. Hand assembly is painstaking; Porsche testing procedures are exhaustive. . . .
　　　　　Once you get hooked, it's for life! Inevitably, nothing less than the unique Porsche performance will satisfy you. After all, caviar connoisseurs don't go back to tuna fish salad.

NOT WITH MY LIFE YOU DON'T

Bound for Glory

From the cover picture of a sandalled adult male enclosed in a blue membrane (entitled the University Womb) to the back page AT&T ad which somehow tries to metaphorically link slum kids with the alleged aim of big business ("They are partners of all who try to build and keep our cities alive with hope and promise of personal dignity"), the groovy first issue of Careers Today is painfully obvious in its attempt to recruit the so called New Left via the Madison Avenue Railway Express. Although the How of this attempt is so clear as to become absurd, the ramifications of the Why are not so clear and perhaps deserve some thought. The two groups immediately involved here are the publishers and the sponsors, or advertisers, who are basically united by a common goal: Money. The publishers want this money directly, i.e., subscribers, but the ad men want something more. The focus here is not the usual commodity glorification,

rather it is the disguised commodity of personnel they seek -- they want us. They want our souls, our minds, not merely our money. As they tell it, they seek "innovative voices, forward looking young people, youth talent, ambition, openmindedness toward new ideas," and all sorts of other groovy euphemisms for employees, field niggers.

Big Business is hurting for manpower--they need the highly educated, and perhaps they fear the dissatisfied college students of today are gravitating toward the New Left rather than business when they finally reach the point of dropping out. This would to some extent explain the heavy weight of articles criticizing the university ("The Un-Educating Society," "Where Have All the Graduates Gone?") and those Horatio Alger stories of "fat contemptuous Bill Berkeley, who at 22 and just 3 months out of school is running a passel of his own companies from a suite in Manhattan's Pan Am

Building," and of ex-activist "Banker Del Behrend" who "insists by her action, that the vivid values of the now-people can best be realized through the business structures." The prose created, especially in the repetition of phraseology, is so striking as to become an insult. These men have used words like "meaningful," "creative" in a way which makes me angry--it goes beyond the mere double-think we have all become accustomed to. They try to link our aims to theirs as a manipulative tool, and in doing so they degrade these concepts to an irremediable low. Covering all the basic concerns of young people from slum conditions to the fuckover of the university system, they adulterate these concerns, they utilize them to show that the aims of the company are the same as ours, ergo we should join the company to get at them.

Careers Today is shot through and through with this co-optation psychology. The magazine comes on strong with really fantastic psychedelic photo constructs, and the format is strikingly reminiscent of Ramparts. The articles themselves stress again and again the common gripes of business and New Leftists. Especially designed to pull the reader in ("an invitation for readers to participate in editorial discussion of subjects that impinge upon our lives"), and therefore to force identification with the magazine's views, is a reader questionnaire--and who doesn't love to fill out a questionnaire full of relevant and meaningful questions? But these questions are almost overwhelmingly stated in a positive manner, posturing a sympathy with radical goals, and calculated to dispel reader doubts about the magazine and its aims. For example, take #5 in the section entitled, "How do you see yourself in the University?"--"College administrators are largely responsible for student rebellion because they have been indifferent to student needs." What self-respecting student wouldn't at least mildly agree with a statement such as this? They remind me of old-time and not so old-time politicians, who know damn well what the people want to hear. Even the negative response questions are stated in a positive manner--for example #13, "If students didn't have to worry about grades, they wouldn't learn much."

Especially pertinent I think, in relation to the McLuhan drawing-in concept of media, is a look at the Editors Note on page 6. Answering the question, "What is an editor for," Peter Drucker writes, "If he has the courage to make a strong statement, verbal and visual, he defines a new perception and a new form of communication. The great editor, rather than talk to an existing audience, creates a new public. He fashions both a medium and a message. The work of many people have gone into Careers Today--psychologists, educators, executives, artists, above all a fair number of thoughtful students and graduates. Each of them, from his experience, had come to the conclusion that the young people of today lack an organ of their own that can talk with them about their life's concerns and the concerns they hold for the world in which they live." This great editor is indeed out to create a new public, and he proffers his organ as the one that will relieve the itching desire of the New Left. While reading the magazine, I was reminded of a recent article by Carl Oglesby (New Left Notes, Aug. 12) which described overtures of Business International, an elite group of business theorists, to representative members of the New Left. During these discussions (which seemed unbelievably frank) the businessmen admitted that their hegemony over society may indeed be threatened. They sense that the present political system is unable to respond to growing internal stresses. At the same time they consider the Liberal Consensus to be the best atmosphere for conducting business. This consensus is now threatened from both Left and Right, but the more serious threat comes from a Right wing "super-patriotic" reaction, which if extended to the point of welfare cutbacks, civil rights regression, and perhaps even a protectionist U.S. trade policy, would deprive the government of flexibility in responding to and controlling social change. Although Careers Today is far from the sophistication of a group such as B.I. (their main purpose being rather direct profit) there are definite correlations between the approaches of the two. It is becoming increasingly apparent to Business theoreticians that they are attracting the schlemiels of society-people who don't give a damn for the company or their jobs and see them only as necessary evils to obtain the "real" things in life---a second or third car, a plush home in the suburbs. The New Left on the other hand is a group of hard-working and dedicated activists--they are good organizers, and more important, they get things done. These are the kind of people Business needs to perpetuate itself. As Oglesby observes, it is not a question of what the New Left could do with the support of G.M., but what G.M. would do with the resources of the New Left.
---Becky Kurtz

Ed. Note: *Careers Today* has since folded

CONNECTIONS Fall 1968

There's a young brother over at Juvenile Hall in Alameda County right now by the name of Gregory Harrison. He's about fourteen or fifteen years old and he's the leader of the Black Students Union at Oakland Tech High School. At this moment they have him over there charged with insurrection. They've charged him with insurrection because the Black Students Union on that campus wants black history added to the curriculum. They want an environment created on their campus—not one that will teach black people how to be black, but one that will remove the restraints, so that they can just be themselves, and their blackness will automatically flourish. Like you don't have to teach a rose how to turn red, or teach a tree how to grow leaves. You just leave it alone and don't pour salt on its roots, and it will be a rose, or it will be a tree.

ELDRIDGE CLEAVER in a speech given in San Francisco at California Hall, a few days before he went into exile in November 1968, from *Ramparts*, 12/14/68

new york
HIGH SCHOOL
FREE PRESS

"Of, by, and for liberated High School Students"

ISSUE 8
SPECIAL
CONSPIRACY
EDITION
APRIL–MAY '69

5 cents in schools
15 cents on newsstands

"four letter words, filthy references, abusive and disgusting language, and nihilistic propaganda."

—Judge Bartel

It's amazing that during her short visit, Sontag did overcome her initial frustration and achieve an appreciation, if not a real understanding, of the Vietnamese. She considered their repetitious homilies, which seemed at first propaganda, and found they had meaning. She learned that politeness in Vietnam does not mean insincerity as it does in the West, but is a measure of personal dignity. She understood that concepts of heroism, purity and, most of all, simplicity, do not necessarily mean foolhardiness, puritanism or stupidity. "The Vietnamese," she writes, "are 'whole' human beings, not 'split' as we are. Inevitably, such people are likely to give outsiders the impression of great 'simplicity.' But. . .it is NOT simple to be able to love calmly, to trust without ambivalence, to hope without self-mockery, to act courageously, to perform arduous tasks with unlimited resources of energy."

MARJORIE HEINS in *San Francisco Express Times*, reviewing Susan Sontag's book on N. Vietnam

★ ★ ★ ★

It is difficult to be an American because there is as yet no code, grammar, decalogue by which to orient oneself. Americans are still engaged in inventing what it is to be an American. That is at once an exhilarating and a painful occupation. All about us we see the lives that have been shattered by it—not least those lives that have tried to resolve the problem by the European patterns.

THORNTON WILDER, *Towards an American Language*

A mother pleads for her son's freedom at Erasmus High School. he freephoto By Miriam Bokser

HAPPY MOTHER'S DAY

REVOLT IN THE HIGH SCHOOLS

THE WAY IT'S GOING TO BE By DIANE DIVOKY

The young woman above is trying to explain to police officers at a student demonstration why she should not be arrested — "The revolt testifies that the students have been learning more than the schools have taught."

THE words of the school board were unimpeachable: "It is the aim of our high school to encourage students to freely express themselves, in writing or otherwise, as part of their educational program."

What they meant, in fact, was that the school board in suburban Long Beach, New York, would not allow students to distribute on school premises their fledgling independent newspaper, *Frox*. The thirteen staff members, supported by their parents, had made a formal written request to the school's principal. Their concessions were clear: "no obscenity," a promise "to publish views in opposition to our own," and a willingness "to accept a faculty adviser who is not a censor."

Backed by a new school board resolution that managed to come out squarely for both freedom of expression and full school control, the principal responded rapidly: "I feel compelled to refuse you the right to distribute *Frox* as you request and must advise you that any violation will lead to disciplinary procedures."

Bewildered by their inability to help the teen-agers come to a "reasonable, democratic compromise" with the traditionally liberal school administration, the parents have turned to lawyers. At the same time, the students find themselves in a drastically changed role. Youngsters who get good grades and lead school activities, they are suddenly rebels confronting the adults who control their education. They have become members of a growing minority of high school students who are coming into focus as "the new problem" in the nation's schoolhouse.

YET the mood that is nurturing a network of nearly 500 "underground" high school papers, a national student-run press service to feed them, and the proliferation of independent high school unions and chapters of Students for a Democratic Society is being set by a kind of student the school finds difficult to label. This "new problem student" is most often not a classroom failure; frequently, he is black and from a poor family but not "disadvantaged." Sometimes, when his behavior approaches its most disruptive, he resembles a juvenile delinquent, and sometimes, too, he is simply a follower, pressured by the values and styles of the dominant peer group into acting without thinking.

These students, six-year-olds when John F. Kennedy became President, were the youngest witnesses to the high hopes for a more open society that came in the early Sixties—with its battles for civil rights and against poverty. In their short span of history, they have seen on television the assassinations and funerals of three national leaders who embodied these hopes. The war in Vietnam, beginning for them as nothing much more than another TV shoot-'em-up, has become a frightening reality as they approach draft age. Still vitally young themselves, they have watched the nation's shift from a youthful sense of unlimited expectations to the middle-aged habit of assessing and conserving old strengths and former gains.

FED by the mass media, urged by parents and teachers to inquire, the students are sensitive to the larger world—and their limited role in it—as no generation before. For them, the student council that fulfills itself by planning dances, academic work that leads only to high College Board scores, and school newspapers that highlight class elections and football games are not only artificial, but inappropriate.

The underground press is, at first, an escape from the carefully delineated boundaries of school activity and opinion. Not surprisingly, therefore, the newest papers tend to be the most ambitious in scope, boldly taking on the great issues in the national arena. The first mimeographed issue of *Alternative* in Eugene, Oregon, was almost completely devoted to opposition to the Vietnam war. The *Strobe*, an amateurish sheet published in "Baltimore's liberated zone," attacks war, poverty, George Wallace, and the "pigs of Chicago." The Appleton (Wisconsin) *Post-Mortem*, edited by Fox Valley High School students "to challenge the myths and realities of their town and society," gets a bit closer to home by focusing on local police tactics.

In their open horror and bewilderment over the happenings in the society, the articles in these papers tend to emotional or moralistic generalizations, very serious but simple truths. They convey the teen-agers' sense of the outrages happening out there in the world, but also their inability—and lack of equipment—to come to grips with problems that are so vast, so complex, so distant from their own lives.

Society seems unable to let the young stay naïve. The underground newspaper, dismissed as a potential educational tool by school administrators in spite of the student initiative and social concern it displays, teaches in another way. As they seek to express their opinions, the students discover that unlike their parents, their college counterparts, the man on the radio or the street corner, they have no right to express an opinion at all.

Last year, John Freeburg, a senior at rural South Kitsap High School outside of Seattle, Washington, began to edit and publish a mimeographed newspaper for students that reflected his own opposition to the Vietnam war, as well as to the adult Establishment's reaction to long hair. John himself was clean-cut in every sense of the word. The son of a commercial airlines pilot, a boy who spent summers working with diabetic children, he was a principal's dream: a consistent high honor student, one of three chosen by the faculty as "outstanding students," a student council representative, and ironically, regional winner of the Veterans' of Foreign Wars "What Democracy Means to Me" contest. Even in getting out his paper, he operated true to form, submitting articles to the school administration for approval before each issue.

In spite of this, three months before graduation John was suspended, and his parents' efforts to have him reinstated by the school board proved fruitless. The state Civil Liberties Union stepped in and obtained a court order for his reinstatement. An ACLU suit on his behalf for damages brought against the school district is still pending in the U. S. District Court. It claims that John's civil rights were violated; the district's counterclaim uses the traditionally unassailable argument that his activities were disruptive to school operation.

But even if his case should succeed—setting a precedent for the rights of high school students—John Freeburg has gone from idealism to skepticism about the "system" that found his exercise of freedom of the press an embarrassment to be eliminated in the face of pressures from right wing groups in the small community. His school said he was old enough to praise democracy publicly, but not to speak about its seamier aspects. Rather than practicing the ideals of freedom and tolerance it preached, the school used its power to suppress ideas. Something was terribly wrong, John decided, not just across the world in Vietnam, but in the institution that was supposed to educate him.

The staff of *Frox* is undergoing the same experience. Their crudely printed paper has worked almost painfully to link the relevant national issues to their own suburban community, to bring the big labels—"racism, imperialism, poverty"—home to Long Beach. Then they found their careful arrangements for distribution were canceled out by the refusal of the principal and the ambiguous educational rhetoric of the school board. Their own school has shown that, as Ira Glasser, associate director of the New York Civil Liberties Union, has

stated: "In the classroom we teach freedom, but the organization is totalitarian. The kids learn that when the values of freedom and order conflict, freedom recedes." With what they're learning, the Long Beach students won't have to rely on clichés about freedom and repression. They now have their own gut-level issue, with all its complexities and subtleties. Unwittingly, the school system has given injustice the relevance the students themselves could not.

Once students begin to see the school as a bankrupt, manipulative bureaucracy—and themselves as its most vulnerable victims—the stage is set for the real student movement. The underground paper takes on a double role: to contradict the system that says students have no uncensored voice, and to talk with the authority of the insider about the follies of the institution and the ways it might be undermined or openly confronted. In the second issue of Ann Arbor (Michigan) High School's *Us*, the students explained what they learned from the furor produced by their first issue:

> The suppression we encountered was frightening. The savage in Huxley's *Brave New World* comments on our situation, saying to the Controller, "You got rid of them. Yes, that's just like you. Getting rid of everything unpleasant instead of learning to put up with it. Whether 'tis better in the mind to suffer the slings and arrows of outrageous fortune, or to take arms against a sea of troubles and by opposing end them. . . . But you don't do either. Neither suffer nor oppose. You just abolish the slings and arrows. It's too easy." We fear the brave new world, we fear . . . "lobotomized" education, especially in this tremendous school. The issue which was created with this publication was not one of censorship of the *Optimist*. The school paper is possibly the best in the nation. Outside of administrative demands on space and content, we do not question its excellence. The existence of anti-distribution laws for student literature is the major objection. This is a violation of our constitutional rights. If this journalistic endeavor is a failure, it can easily be forgotten. But, if you or they force us to stop, we are all failures. Then, this school, city, and country, and the principles they supposedly represent are lies.

The more seasoned underground papers operate confidently on the understanding that change in the schools is their first order of business, and that national issues—the cry for law and order, teacher militancy—do affect their lives as students. At first glance, these papers are fun. They call themselves *The Pearl before the swine, The Finger, Napalm, The Roach, The South Dakota Seditionist Monthly, Big Momma, The Philistine, The Bleeding Rose, Dormat Dwellers*, even *The New York Herald Tribune*. They are fresh, crazy, biased, irreverent in their view of the world, and often unexpectedly inventive in the way they present it. Albert Shanker, United Federation of Teachers president, becomes a great vulture, perched over the bodies of children. Samson Jones gets kicked out of Gaza Central High School for his long hair—and in a rage pulls the school down.

The more stylish ones are almost a new pop art form. Print runs around,

over, and under stark drawings, viciously pointed cartoons, poignant photographs. Sometimes the word itself becomes the design. Dreamy poems are transposed on psychedelic drawings. Surrealistic obscene headlines fly out from the page. And often a picture stands by itself, telling the story rather than illustrating it. This is the work of McLuhan's generation.

THE national focus for the underground is HIPS, the High School Independent Press Service (160 Claremont Avenue, New York, N.Y. 10027), which offers a weekly packet of news and illustrations of high school uprisings, busts, dress codes, discipline, and politics. Some sixty papers and 400 fans subscribe, at an often uncollected fee of $4 a month. "HIPS is very much in the revolutionary bag," a staffer admits. "I suppose we're just as bad as the *Times* in being biased. But underground papers are more interesting to read than the *Times*. They don't start with the usual 'who, where, when, what, why.' HIPS gets people to think. Gets them radicalized before they get into college. If that happens, chances are a fourth of them will never go to college."

One of the slickest papers HIPS services is the *New York High School Free Press*, which publishes 10,000 copies every three weeks (5 cents for students, 15 cents for teachers). It introduced itself last fall with a full-cover photo of a naked Negro baby girl holding the black flag of anarchy: "Ursula, seven months and already foxy as hell," the editors explained. A coupon form invites the reader to subscribe or, if he prefers, to curse and threaten the "hippie-commie-yippie-queer-pinkos" who print it. Another reader service is a directory of pertinent phone numbers: for prayers, demonstrations, birth control and abortion information, draft counseling, the FBI, and "nighttime companions" — the Girl Scouts.

Yet silliness serves more serious purposes. The *Free Press*, with first-hand reports on national and school crises and interviews with prominent figures, is a sober attempt to reach radical and politically oriented students throughout the city. Its mix of serious radicalism and youthful gags reflects its staff, a closely knit group of intense, quick-witted students, most of whom attend New York's highly selective Bronx High School of Science. In the living room of one of their homes, the students—a balance of whites and blacks — can go with breathtaking speed from typical teen-age roughhousing to political debate.

Reggie Lucas, the paper's fifteen-year-old music critic, talks about "breaking down the traditional teacher-student relationship" in the schools, so that by "interchanging roles, the teacher, as well as the student, could learn." Everything the adult Establishment does, he explains politely, "is not just undesirable, but repugnant to us. The real hero today is the person who can mess up the society and pervert the youth."

Leader of the group is Howie Swerdloff, at seventeen a good-natured veteran of the underground press and radical student movement, who wrote last fall:

> The main thing that's taught us in school is, how to be good niggers, obey the rules, dress in our uniforms,

High School Independent Press Service
New York City

play the game, and NO DON'T BE UPPITY! Oh, we're trained for participating in the "democratic process"—we have our student governments—they can legislate about basketball games and other such meaningful topics. Don't mention the curriculum—THEY'LL tell us what to learn. Oh, we can express our complaints in the school newspaper—but the principal says what gets printed and don't embarrass the school's reputation.

Howie's immediate fight is with the school establishment; his long-range goal is to destroy the government he finds hopelessly oppressive through a worldwide people's revolution. His mother views his position with pride tempered by concern. When he was only fifteen, she recalls, she was first called into school about his activities. Finding Howie distributing antiwar leaflets across the street from the school, she began to apologize to the irate principal. Howie stopped her: "My lawyer said it's OK, Mother."

The Swerdloffs, liberals of another generation, are hopeful about the contributions their son and his friends will make to change the society, yet are appalled by the often violent reaction of the society to the youthful protests. "You wonder," Mrs. Swerdloff said, recalling the violence in Chicago during the Democratic convention. "You teach them such good values, and then when they go ahead and act on them, all this happens."

The underground high school press represents attitudes that have generated a variety of organizations bent on changing the school and the society. Their tactics range from polite dialogue to picketing to direct confrontation with the authorities. It is, nonetheless, difficult to categorize these groups, since their degree of militancy and their deviance from accepted student behavior depend a great deal on the response of school and community officials, the particular issues involved, and on the students themselves.

There is no one approach among the black separatist groups. New York City's High School Coalition, affiliated with the Black Panther party, spews vitriolic rhetoric in its newsletter and operates on a single dogma: the necessity of black liberation by any means possible. In contrast, the Modern Strivers, a group of young Negroes at Eastern High School in Washington, D.C., talks black power, but in the traditional American terms of self-help, hard work, and foundation funding.

THE degree of flexibility within a community helps to determine the degree to which a group is regarded as a problem. In Berkeley, California, the liberal, interracial Youth Council, which has a poster of Black Panther leader Eldridge Cleaver in its office in city hall, received the support of city fathers even after its president was arrested for selling drugs. In Milwaukee, however, the beginnings of a student alliance, a rather apolitical group hoping for school reform, brought shocked cries from administrators, city officials, and the state's principals' asso-

ciation, who were ready to accuse "subversive" outside influences of stirring up the unrest.

The students are conscious of the variety within their ranks. The New York High School Student Union, an integrated, citywide group with semi-autonomous locals in 108 public and private schools, operates so flexibly that members at one school can be requesting more school dances while those at another can be out protesting the war. Its leaders tend to be disdainful of the doctrinaire approach of Students for a Democratic Society, and prefer to let their members "do their own thing."

Many groups, however, influenced by nearby college activity, have become SDS affiliates. Last year, eleven high schools in Seattle formed SDS chapters. In St. Louis, the citywide SDS group became large enough to be broken up into individual high school chapters. The Akron-based Ohio Union of High School Students, though not affiliated with SDS, has an adviser from the organization. National SDS headquarters has been overwhelmed by the flood of requests for literature from high school groups, and estimates an increase of about 800 per cent over last year. To meet the demand, the SDS national council decided in October to hire a full-time secondary school coordinator.

THE schoolmen, caught offguard by the new attitude, are now rushing to diagnose the problem and find solutions. The National Association of Secondary School Principals reports the findings of a national survey of student unrest in large and small school systems at its annual convention this month. A new NASSP handbook suggests ways to make the student council more meaningful. The organization's September 1968 bulletin was devoted to student unrest and included articles about its link with college militancy, possible reasons and solutions for the "coming revolt," and even one on what to do either before—or when—the legal showdown comes. ("The handwriting is on the wall; public school students will be protected in their constitutional rights," it said.)

Reaction to the new activism by schoolmen has been as varied as the kinds of students involved, their forms of dissent, and the responses of communities. A few school administrators regard the militancy as a potentially beneficial force, an often responsible if sometimes shrill demand for a more active role in school affairs. Just as the mass media and current events have taught the students something, so too they may have learned, really learned, what the schools' rhetoric says they should—to inquire critically.

Dr. Eugene Smoley, a high school principal in Montgomery County, Maryland, puts it this way: "The activists represent a real challenge educationally by questioning the foundations of the society. They're looking for ways to be helpful, pushing for a way for their actions to have some influence,

pressing for more meaningful lives. The movement is a very positive thing, because it can only be compared with the apathy of an earlier time."

Many other schoolmen, however, dismiss the activism as a fad, claim that the high school students are only imitating their older brothers and sisters in college, or maintain that because students have always complained, all grievances are on the order of gripes about the cafeteria food.

The school administrator is, indeed, the man in the middle, caught between the community he serves and a whole new set of realities. Traditionally, the community—and the society—expect him to run a well ordered, efficient institution founded on a number of assumptions: Students are children, in both the legal and educational sense. They are pretty much alike—naïve and awkward as they grow. When they learn, they learn in school. The principal is legally responsible for the well-being of school children, and educationally responsible for what goes into their heads.

Although the legal fiction that students are children to be protected remains, much else has changed. Norman Solomon, honors senior and reporter for the county newspaper, who addresses the Montgomery County school board on the system's inputs and outputs and the "serious gap that presently exists between rhetoric and reality," cannot be dismissed as a charming child. The two Berkeley high school seniors who sit as full voting members on city committees know more about the operation of bureaucracy than any textbook could teach them. After his week in Chicago during the 1968 Democratic National Convention, Howie Swerdloff can tell his teachers a good deal about violence and police brutality in this nation.

To what extent can sophisticated adolescents be considered adults when they are still legally children? If the school is to educate, can it afford not to capitalize on the increasing awareness and concern of the students? Can the school be a public forum while maintaining its tight authoritarian patterns? If the school grants more freedom to students, is it opening itself up to irresponsible—as well as responsible—adolescent judgments? Can it find a place for its dissatisfied minority without threatening its more accepting, complacent majority?

The revolt itself testifies that students have been learning more than the schools have taught: from parents who are as well or better educated than teachers; from the mass media with which the school finds itself in competition; from actual participation in the politics and culture of the society. To accept this knowledge and experience means facing up to a set of complicated problems. To deny it is to deny the students themselves.

Saturday Review
2/15/69

sponsored by S.A.C.

High School Students Unite!

FUCK THE SCHOOL SYSTEM CONVENTION

Church of the Mediator
225 Elmwood Ave.
ALL DAY STARTING 10am
DECEMBER 31

FAMOUS SOCIOLOGIST SAYS "LIBERATION MAY FADE AWAY."

CLAIMS THAT THE RIGHTS OF HOMOSEXUALS, WOMEN, DOGS AND THE YOUNG ARE NOT THE QUESTION

Mr. Shils is a man of great learning and a detester of shibboleths. "Those who are running the country don't see how important it is to keep a firm and courageous face on things," he said. "Authority must maintain itself with respect, and failure to do so releases hostility.

"The young are extraordinarily well-treated in this country, and they can do what they want. They're living off the Establishment like court fools, allowed to say insulting things that the older people aren't allowed to say.

"If the young were complaining about not getting a sufficiently stringent education, I would have some sympathy with their complaints. Instead, they complain about 'relevance' and 'discipline,' which are not real issues."

America is still an exciting place, he conceded, and people are still anxious to come "to get a pad and see unclothed plays and buy pornography and to take a puff of pot and to see the dean locked up."

Soviet Russia, on the other hand, is in "a terrible state of discredit, and that country is as boring as it was in 1860," in Professor Shils's view. It ceased to call itself revolutionary, fell out with China, and "it became an America without the lively corruption of America."

"In the sixties we have seen the growth of great apprehension about the future," he said, "and a prevision of the state of nature described by Hobbes—men pillaging men, men obliterating men.

"At the moment we have a coalescence—youth and Negroes and a few Puerto Ricans and women and homosexuals," the sociologist said. "I think they are deflecting the mind of the country from its real problems—which are not the rights of homosexuals or women or dogs. Nobody has gotten around to the dogs yet, but they will, soon enough.

"These things run their course and we may settle down in the seventies. 'Liberation' may fade away. Religious manias have never lasted a long time; delirium and delight are chronically shortlived."

Ed. Note: The movement clearly has biology and time on its side. There are now at least 100 million Americans under 28. As Tom Hayden put it: "We will not bury you; we will just outlive you."

Ed. Note: Prof. Shils teaches at the U. of Chicago and at Cambridge U. In England

The New York Times 12/30/69

YOUTH AS A CLASS

"Youth are now the essential exploited group for the perpetuation of the existing economic system. The youth occupy the critical work-places: they man the war machine and the idea factories. Between 1950 and 1965, the defense-education complex alone absorbed two-thirds of the total increase in the 18–64 year old labouring population. In 1965 more than half of young men 18 to 24 years old were in school, the military or unemployed; more than one-fifth of the 25-29 year olds were in the same situations. They absorb by their own sacrifice the surplus of which the irrational economic system cannot dispose. But, one may ask, how long can this process continue? How large can the army and the schools become? We argue that the exploitation of the young is reaching its outer limits and has begun to threaten the stability of the administrative imperialist system. Young people are beginning to become aware of their exploitation. Many have taken the essential first step to consciousness, the rejection of the present system, and are available to develop a consciousness of themselves as class actors. A significant number have gone even farther and are coming to see the relation between what is wrong with their position in American society and what is wrong with that society as a whole."

—John and Margaret Rowntree, "The Political Economy of Youth," Our Generation Vol 6, p. 171; (REP pamphlet)

In a long and closely argued article "Youth as a Class" (*International Socialist Journal*, February 1968), John and Margaret Rowntree take the bull by the horns and declare that youth is now in "the crucial pivotal class position within the United States," and that the young are increasingly becoming culturally and politically conscious of their class exploitation. Three propositions are used in support of this argument:

1. The American economy is increasingly dominated by two industries that are large, public and rapidly growing — defence and education.

2. The defence and education industries serve crucially as successful shock-absorbers of surplus manpower, particularly young manpower.

3. Economic exploitation in the United States is increasingly directed at the young.

The Rowntrees tell us that total employment *directly* related to the defence industry in the US was estimated by the Department of Labour to be 7 million jobs in 1962; 1 in 10 employed workers in 1962 were *directly* employed by the defence industry. (They deliberately select figures which do not relate to current war spending.) Educational outlay in the US has been rising by 10½ per cent a year for the last decade making it one of the major US growth industries. They quote Clark Kerr, ex-president of the University of California, as saying in his book *The Uses of the University:* "The university has become a prime instrument of national purpose. This is new. This is the essence of the transformation now engulfing our universities. Basic to this transformation is the growth of the 'knowledge industry', which is coming to permeate government and business and to draw into it more and more people raised to higher and higher levels of skill. The production, distribution and consumption of 'knowledge' in all its forms is said to account for 29 per cent of gross national product, according to Fritz Machlup's calculations (in *Production and Distribution of Knowledge in the United States);* and 'knowledge production' is growing at about twice the rate of the rest of the economy."

Defence and education between them have absorbed not only huge numbers of young people, but a rapidly increasing *proportion* of the potentially productive population. "The growth of the defence and education industries are the crucial modifications in the organization of the US economy that have led to the formation of youth as a class. It is know-how and force that keep the capitalist system together; and the exploited workers in these two critical industries are, overwhelmingly, young." The way, they say, to evaluate exploitation in the armed forces is to see how much it would cost to recruit volunteers. (Milton Friedman, in advocating a volunteer army declared that "Conscription is a tax in kind — forced labour exacted from the men who serve involuntarily. The amount of the tax is the difference between the sum for which they would voluntarily serve and the sum we now pay them...") As to students: "Since school is a full-time but unpaid job, most students work part-time or not at all, living on loans or family charity. Professor Theodore Schultz estimates that 55 percent of the costs of a college and 43 percent of the costs of a high school education are foregone income. The Council of Economic Advisers' foregone earnings estimate of $20 to $30 billion, can also be seen as an index of exploitation. This estimate implies that, for all students 16 and over, foregone earnings amount to about 40 to 60 per cent of their 'investment in human capital'. This is roughly $2,000 per student 16 and over. These estimates are themselves exploitive, since they assume high unemployment and low wages. Yet students, like soldiers, lack real choice: they must stay in school (and be exploited), face the draft (and be exploited) or face exploitively high unemployment rates and/or low wages."

It is clear, they say, that the American young, "while they might not prefer to join the military or go to school and live at a low standard of living, have limited alternatives when they face unemployment rates three times those of the labour force 25 and over...What are our conclusions? Increasingly, young people are labouring in the two dynamic 'socialised' sectors of the administrative imperialist system. If they venture outside army or school they are rewarded with unemployment rates two or five times the average. The young therefore form the new proletariat, are undergoing impoverishment, and can become the new revolutionary class. This new class is not a *lumpenproletariat*, like pensioners, welfare recipients, and the disabled. Instead they are in the classic proletarian position, growing worse off within an industry that is itself the engine of prosperity in the economy. They may not be the poorest group; nor are they by any means, the only exploited group."

In the United States students comprise 30 per cent of their age group there, as opposed to 11 per cent in Britain (the pre-war figure here was 2.7 per cent). Paul Goodman declared in his "Thoughts on Berkeley" early in 1965 that "At present in the United States, students — middle-class youth — are the major exploited class. (Negroes, small farmers and the aged are rather out-caste groups; their labour is not needed and they are not wanted.) The labour of intelligent youth is needed and they are accordingly subjected to tight scheduling, speed-up, and other factory methods."

Anarchy, London, August 1968

Harvard Strike, April 1969.

YOUTH AND THE GREAT REFUSAL

THEODORE ROSZAK

Published herewith is Theodore Roszak's introductory essay to a four-part series on what he calls the "counter culture," or by allusion, the "invasion of centaurs." In this impressive work of synthesis he brings together, organizes and evaluates the many aspects of a phenomenon now generally if inadequately perceived and variously referred to by such terms as the New Left, flower power, mind explosion, psychedelia, pot and Zen. Subsequent essays will focus on religiosity, dope and the sense of community, specifying the aspects of the counter culture that spring from these sources and examining the ideas and influence of leaders associated with them. However, the counter culture does not readily compartmentalize and these essays both overlap and reinforce one another. Together they constitute a clear-eyed, occasionally ironic, but basically appreciative estimate of a movement which the author compares, at least in potential, with Christianity under the Roman Empire.

Mr. Roszak, an associate professor of history, is chairman of the History of Western Culture Program at California State College, Hayward. He edited and contributed to The Dissenting Academy *(Pantheon Books).*

The struggle of the generations is one of the obvious constants of history. One stands in peril of great presumption, therefore, to suggest that the rivalry between young and adult in America of the 1960s is uniquely critical. And yet one must risk that presumption in order to grasp the full significance of what is happening to our contemporary culture. For the fact is that cultural innovation in America is becoming more and more the captive of youth who are profoundly alienated from the adult society. For better or worse, most of what is happening that is new, provocative and engaging in the arts, in politics, in education, in social relations (love, courtship, family), in journalism, in fashions and entertainment, is very largely the creation either of the discontented young or of those who address themselves primarily to the young. It is at the level of youth that many of our best minds—as well as our worst—look to find a responsive hearing as, more and more, it becomes the common expectation that the young should be those who act, who make things happen, who take the risks. Until, at last, the adults of the society begin to settle back into the role of amused or disgruntled but mainly passive observers. Adolescent-watching is fast becoming our greatest national spectator sport.

Some simple economic and demographic facts of life help explain this peculiar state of affairs. A bit more than 50 per cent of our population is now under 25 years old. Even if one grants that people in their mid-20s have no business claiming (or letting themselves be claimed for) the status of "youth," there is still, among the authentically young—the 13-to-19 age bracket—a small nation of 25 million people. I will, however, argue below that there is good reason to group the mid-20s with their adolescent juniors.

But numbers alone don't account for the aggressive prominence of youth in our society. More important, the young seem to *feel* the potential power of their numbers as never before. No doubt this occurs to a great extent because the market apparatus of our consumer society has invested a deal of wit into cultivating the age consciousness of old and young alike. Teen-agers alone control a stupendous amount of money and enjoy much leisure; so inevitably, they have been turned into a self-conscious market. Whatever the young have fashioned for themselves has rapidly been rendered grist for the commercial mill and merchandised by admass—including the ethos of dissent, a fact that has created an agonizing kind of disorientation for the dissenting young (and their critics) and to which we shall return in a moment.

But the force of the market has not been the only factor in intensifying age consciousness. The expansion of higher education has, I suspect, done even more. Just as early industrialism concentrated labor and helped create class consciousness, so the university campus, where up to 25,000 students may be gathered, has served to crystallize the group identity of the young—with the important effect of mingling freshmen of 17 and 18 with graduate students in their mid-20s. On the major campuses, it is often the graduates who assume positions of leadership, contributing a degree of competence that the younger students could not muster. When one includes in this alliance that significant new entity, the "non-student"—the campus roustabout who may be well along in his late 20s—one sees why "youth" has become such a long-term career. The grads and the non-students easily come to identify their interests and allegiance with a very young population which, in previous generations, they would long since have left behind.

These campus elders play a role, particularly crucial for they tend to be those who have the most vivid realization of the new economic role of the university. Being closer to the organization-man careers for which higher education is supposed to be grooming them, they have both a stronger sensitivity to the social regimentation that imminently confronts them, and a stronger sense of the potential power with which the society's economic needs invest them. They know how great is society's demand for their skills and they soon see that making trouble on the campus is making trouble in one of the economy's vital sectors. And once the grad students—many of whom may be serving as low-level teaching assistants—have been infected with qualms and aggressive discontents, the junior faculty, with whom they overlap, may soon catch the fever and find themselves drawn into the orbit of dissenting "youth."

The troubles at Berkeley in late 1966 illustrate the expansiveness of youthful protest. First a group of undergraduates stages a sit-in against naval recruiters at the student union. They are soon joined by a contingent of non-students (whom the administration then martyrs by selective arrest) and a non-student of nearly 30—Mario Savio, already married and a father—is quickly adopted as spokesman for the protest. Finally the teaching assistants call a strike in support of the demonstration. When at last the agitation comes to its ambiguous conclusion, a rally of thousands gathers outside Sproul Hall to sing the Beatles' *Yellow Submarine*—which happens to be the current hit on all the local high school campuses. If "youth" is not the word we are going to use to cover this obstreperous population, then we may have to coin another. But undeniably the social grouping exists with a self-conscious solidarity.

Pleasure, Freedom & the Reality Principle

A particular plight of the senior and graduate students offers still another reason for the remarkable volatility of the young. The current generation of students is the beneficiary of the permissive child-rearing habits that have been a feature of our postwar society. Dr. Spock's endearing latitudinarianism is much more a reflection than a cause of this new (and wise) conception of proper parent-child relations that has prevailed for some time in the middle class.

A high-consumption, leisure-wealthy society doesn't need rigidly trained, "responsible" young workers. The middle class can afford to prolong the ease and drift of childhood, and so it does. It "spoils" its kids, meaning it influences them to believe that being human has something to do with pleasure and freedom. But as life in the multiversity wears on, the reality principle begins to demand its price. The students get told they are now officially "grown up," but they have been given no taste for the rigidities and self-denials that adulthood is supposed to be all about. General Motors all of a sudden wants barbered hair, punctuality, and an appropriate reverence for the conformities of the organizational hierarchy. Washington wants patriotic cannon fodder. Some kids summon up the square-jawed "responsibility" to adjust to the prescribed pattern of adulthood (though even the Young Americans for Freedom, who champion the virtues of the corporate structure, have decided, with the vigorous endorsement of Ayn Rand, that conscription is a species of "selective slavery").

Others, being incorrigibly "childish," continue to assert pleasure and freedom as human rights and begin to ask aggressive questions about the meaning of adulthood. Perhaps at last they drop out, restless and bewildered and hungry for better ideas about grownupness than GM or IBM or LBJ seem able to offer. This often places them in the position of nostalgically cultivating the styles of the teen-age world, like the rock music and dance which now unites the whole 13-to-30 population.

The dropouts stall in a protracted adolescence out of which they are eager to break, but not as their parents did. Some become ne'er-do-well dependents; others resort

to flight. The FBI reports the arrest of more than 90,000 juvenile runaways in 1966; most of those who flee well-off, middle-class homes get picked up—by the thousands each current year—in the big city bohemias, fending off malnutrition and venereal disease. The immigration departments of Europe record a constant level, over the past few years, of something like 10,000 disheveled flower children (mostly American, British, German and Scandinavian) migrating across to the Near East and India. The influx has been sufficient to force Iran and Afghanistan to boost substantially their "cash in hand" requirements for prospective tourists. And the British Consul General in Istanbul officially requested Parliament in late 1967 to grant him increased accommodations for the "swarm" of penniless young Englishmen who have been showing up at his consulate, seeking temporary lodgings or perhaps shelter from Turkish narcotics authorities.

One may flippantly construe this exodus as the contemporary version of running off with the circus, but the more apt parallel might be with the quest of 3rd-century Christians (a scruffy, uncouth, and often half-mad lot) for escape from the corruptions of Hellenistic society: it is much more a flight *from* than *toward*. Certainly for a youth of 17, clearing out of the comfortable bosom of the middle-class family to become a beggar is a formidable gesture of dissent. One makes light of it at the expense of ignoring a significant measure of our social health.

The Only Audience

The final ingredient that goes into this ebullient culture of youthful dissent is the adult radical who finds himself in a fix that much resembles that of the bourgeois intellectual in Marxist theory. Despairing for the timidity and lethargy of his own class, Marx's middle-class revolutionary at last turns renegade and defects to the proletariat. In postwar America, the adult radical, confronted with a diminishing public among the "cheerful robots" of his own generation, gravitates to the restless middle-class young. Where else is he to find an audience? The working class, which provided the traditional following for radical ideology, now for the most part neither leads nor follows but bogs down to become the heaviest ballast of the established order. If the adult radical is white, black power progressively seals off his entree to Negro organizations. As for the exploited masses of the Third World, they have as little use for white Western ideologues as do our native blacks—and in any case they are far distant. Unless he follows the strenuous example of a Régis Debray, the white American radical can do little more than sympathize from afar with the revolutionary movements of Asia, Africa and Latin America.

On the other hand, the disaffected middle-class young are at hand, suffering the "immiserization" that comes of being stranded between a permissive childhood and an obnoxiously conformist adulthood, experimenting desperately with new ways of growing with self-respect into a world they despise, calling for help. So the radical adults offer to become gurus to the alienated young, or perhaps the young draft them into that service.

I take the hyper-dynamism of the young to be a thoroughly unhealthy state of affairs. It is not properly youth's role to bear so great a responsibility for inventing or initiating for their society as a whole. It is too big a job for them to do gracefully. The rise of our youth culture to a position of such prominence is a symptom of grave default on the part of adults. Trapped in the frozen posture of befuddled passivity which has been characteristic of our society since the end of World War II (what Paul Goodman has called "the nothing can be done disease") the mature generations have divested themselves of their adulthood—if the term means anything besides being tall and debt-worried and capable of buying liquor without showing a driver's license. It has surrendered its responsibility to make morally demanding decisions, to generate ideals, to control public authority, to safeguard the life of the community against its despoilers. It has been scared off and bought off its proper function in a variety of ways that need not be reviewed here, until it has become, not a catalyst to the growth of its more sensitive children but a barrier of paralyzed complacency, deservedly inviting contempt.

This is the America whose god Allen Ginsberg, somewhere back in the middle fifties, identified as the sterile and omnivorous "Moloch," the America whose premature senility President Eisenhower so marvelously incarnated, and the disease of whose soul shone so lugubriously through the public obscenities that men like John Foster Dulles, Herman Kahn and Edward Teller were prepared to call "policy." There are never many clear landmarks in the affairs of the spirit, but Ginsberg's *Howl* may serve as the first public report announcing the war of the generations. It can be coupled, chronologically, with the appearance of C. Wright Mills's aggressively activist sociology—with the publication of Mills's *Causes of World War III* (1957). Mills was by no means the first postwar figure who sought to tell it like it is about the state of American public life—nor was he necessarily all that right in what he said. But his tone was angrier and his rhetoric catchier. He wanted his sociology to function as part of a public dialogue. Above all, he insisted more urgently than any before him that he wanted action, and wanted it now. He was prepared to step forth and brazenly pin his indictment like a target to the enemy's chest. And, most important, Mills was lucky enough to reach ears that would hear: his indignation found an audience.

When Mills died in 1961, the New Left he was searching for but had despaired of finding among the forces and institutions controlled by his peers was beginning to emerge—of course, from among the students. If he were alive today he would be into his 50s; but his following would still be primarily among the under 30s. Just as Ginsberg, now more than 40, remains the bard of the young.

Elderly Carpers

Admittedly, the dissent that began to simmer in the mid-fifties was not confined to the young. At the adult level of resistance, SANE was created in 1957, and later Turn Toward Peace. But precisely what do groups like SANE and TTP reveal about adult America, even about the politically conscious types? Looking back, one is struck by their absurd shallowness and conformism, their total unwillingness to raise fundamental issues about the quality of American life, their fastidious anti-communism, and, above all, their incapacity to sustain any significant initiative on the political field. Even the Committee of Correspondence, a promising effort formed around 1961 by senior academics, quickly settled for publishing a new journal. I can remember attending meetings of the West Coast committee at which Seymour Martin Lipset, who was the sort of responsible, anti-Communist liberal everybody felt certain had to be included, put the damper on any radical action by arguing without significant opposition that the cold war was entirely the fault of the Russians, and there was nothing to do but leave things to the government, which was in excellent hands, and so why were we all meeting anyway . . . .

At present, the remnants of SANE and TTP have been reduced to the role of carping (often with a good deal of justice) at the impetuous extremes and leftist flirtations of far more dynamic youth groups like SDS or the Berkeley VDC or the Spring Mobilization. But avuncular carping is not initiative. And it is a bore, even if a well-intentioned bore, when it becomes a major preoccupation. Similarly, it is the younger Negro groups that have begun to steal the fire of adult organizations—but in that case with results that I feel are bound to be disastrous.

The fact is, it is the young who have—gropingly, haltingly, amateurishly, even grotesquely—gotten dissent off the adult drawing board. They have torn it out of the

books and journals that an older generation of radicals wrote, and they have fashioned it into a style of life. They have turned the hypotheses of disgruntled elders into experiments, though often without the willingness to admit that one may have to concede failure at the end of any true experiment.

This readiness to experiment with a variety of dissenting life styles is what has made the youth culture of the day so prominent and fruitfully provocative, despite its frequent lapses into the absurd. But, inevitably, the kids have run into criticism, often from no quarter so severe as that of the older radicals. For generations now, radical intellectuals have lambasted the bad habits of bourgeois society: "the bourgeoisie," they have insisted, "is obsessed by greed; its sex life is insipid and prudish; its family patterns are debased; its slavish conformities of dress and cosmetics are degrading; its mercenary routinization of existence is intolerable; its vision of life is drab and joyless, etc., etc." So the kids try this and that, and one by one they discard the vices of their parents, preferring the less structured ways of their own childhood and adolescence —only to discover that many an old-line radical, embarrassed by the brazen sexuality and unwashed feet, gladrags and playful ways, is taking up the chorus: "No that is not what I meant, that is not what I meant at all."

Critics and Publicists

Thus, a good liberal like Hans Toch (writing in *The Nation* for December 4, 1967) invokes the Protestant work ethic to give the hippies a fatherly tongue-lashing for their "consuming but noncontributing" ways. They are being "parasitic," Professor Toch observes, for "the hippies, after all, accept—even demand—social services, while rejecting the desirability of making a contribution to the economy." But *of course* they do: because we have an economy of cybernated abundance that does not need their labor, that is rapidly severing the tie between work and wages, that suffers from hard-core poverty caused by maldistribution, not by scarcity. From this point of view, why is their voluntary dropping out any more "parasitic" than the enforced dropping out of impoverished ghetto dwellers? Is it perhaps because the hippies seem to enjoy their mendicant idleness, do not feel appropriately guilty and frustrated? There are criticisms I shall want to make of the beat-hip bohemian fringe of our youth culture—but this is surely not one of them.

It would be a better general criticism to make of the young that they have done a miserably bad job of dealing with the distortive publicity with which admass has burdened their embryonic experiments. Too often they fall into the trap of reacting narcissistically or defensively to their own image in the fun-house mirror of the media. Whatever these things called "beatniks" and "hippies" originally were, or still are, may have nothing to do with what *Time, Esquire,* C.B.S.-N.B.C.-A.B.C., Broadway comedy and Hollywood surf operas have decided to make of them. If anything, the media tend to isolate the weirdest aberrations *and* to attract to the movement many extroverted poseurs.

But what can bohemia do when it finds itself massively infiltrated by well-intentioned sociologists (and now, all of a sudden, we have specialized "sociologists of adolescence"), sensationalizing journalists, curious tourists, and weekend fellow travelers? What doors does one close on them? The problem is new and tough—a cynical dilution of dissent by saturation coverage—and it begins to look like a far more formidable weapon in the hands of the established culture than outright suppression would be. The situation seems to call for strategies of dignified secrecy which the young have not yet developed.

But to grant the fact of admass distortion is not the same as saying that the young have evolved no life style of their own, or that they are unserious about it. It would be surrendering to admass an absolutely destructive potential if one took the tack that whatever it touches is automatically debased, or perhaps has no reality at all. Commercial vulgarization is one of the endemic pests of 20th-century America, like the flies that swarm to the sweets of summer. But the flies don't create the sweets (though they may make them less palatable), nor do they bring in the summer. It will be my contention that despite the fraudulence and folly that collect around its edges, a significant new culture is being born among our youth, and that this culture deserves careful understanding, if for no other reason than the sheer size of the population it potentially involves.

I think there *is* another reason, namely the intrinsic value of what the young are making happen. But I would insist that in order to understand it one must avoid, as far as possible, relying on the exotic tidbits, the sensational case histories, admass provides. And that would include the superficial snooping that comes of cruising bohemia for a few exciting days in search of local color and the inside dope. Rather, one should look for major trends that seem to outlast current fashions, and seek out the most articulate public statements of belief and value the young have made or given ear to: the thoughtful formulation, rather than the offhand gossip. Above all, I think the older generations must be willing, in a spirit of critical helpfulness, to sort out what seems valuable and promising, as if indeed it mattered whether or not the alienated young succeeded in their project.

Culture or Counter Culture?

Again, it must be granted that it is an old story that the young should have to scrap or remodel in some degree the culture they inherit. Indeed, the Spanish philosopher, Ortega, has elaborated a theory of history (in *Man and Crisis*), based on the fitful transition of the generations. What is special about the present case is the scale on which the cultural revision is taking place and the depth to which it is reaching. I have referred to the "culture" of the young; but would it be an exaggeration to call what is arising among them a "counter culture"? That is, a culture which so radically rejects the mainstream assumptions of Western society that it is scarcely recognizable to many as a culture at all, but looks, instead, like a barbaric intrusion. One thinks of the invasion of centaurs on the the pediment of the Temple of Zeus at Olympia. Apollo, as guardian of the orthodox culture, steps forward to admonish. Apollo, being older than 30, could hardly expect his authority to be trusted now. And, besides, these latter-day centaurs, while "high," are not drunken, and most likely come bearing flowers.

Major cultural disjunctures have happened before, though not with the same high acceleration. Toynbee identified them as the work of a disinherited proletariat and used as his paradigm the role of the early Christians within the Roman Empire. Hopelessly alienated by ethos and social class from the official culture, the primitive Christian community fashioned of Judaism and the mystery cults a culture that could not fail to seem absurd to Greco-Roman orthodoxy. But the absurdity, far from being felt a disgrace, became a banner of the community.

> For it is written [St. Paul boasted] I will destroy the wisdom of the wise, and will bring to nothing the understanding of the prudent . . . . For the Jews require a sign, and the Greeks seek after wisdom . . . . But God hath chosen the foolish things of the world to confound the wise; and God hath chosen the weak things of the world to confound the things which are mighty.

Once such a cultural disjuncture opens out in society, nothing is guaranteed. What happens among the minority that finds itself isolated by the rift is as apt to be ugly or pathetic as it is to be noble. The primitive Christian absurdity can be credited at least with the potentiality of saintly service and visionary poetry. The alienated stock clerks and wallpaper hangers of post-World War I Germany sullenly withdrew to their beer halls to talk imbecile anthropology and prepare the horrors of Buchenwald. So too, contemporary America's isolated minorities include the Hell's Angels and the Minutemen from whom nothing beautiful or interesting can be expected.

And the alienated young: how to characterize the counter culture they are in the way of haphazardly assembling? A heroic generalization about this still embryonic culture is to say that what the young are up to is nothing less than a reorganization of the prevailing state of personal and social consciousness. From a culture that has a long-standing, entrenched commitment to an egocentric and intellective mode of consciousness, the young are moving toward a sense of identity that is communal and nonintellective. I think the disjuncture is just that great—as great in its implications (though obviously not as yet in historical influence) as the disjuncture between Greco-Roman rationality and Christian mystery. Against the traditional Cartesian *cogito*, with its blunt, initial assertion of individuality and logicality, the counter culture opposes the community and visionary inspiration. This really amounts to an assault on the reality of the ego as an isolable and purely cerebral unit of identity.

Hippies and Leftists

At first glance, it may seem that this counter culture, shading off as rapidly as it does into the mind-blown bohemianism of the beats and hippies, diverges radically from the hard-headed political activism of the student New Left. Are there perhaps two separate and antithetical developments; one (tracing back to Ginsberg and company) which seeks to abscond from American political life, and the other (tracing back to Mills and the remnants of the old Socialist Left) which seeks to penetrate and rechannel the mainstream of American society? I think not. At a deeper level, there is a theme that unites these two variations. It is revealed among the activists by the personalism that characterized the beginnings of New Left dissent. [See "Young Radicals & the Fear of Power" by Kenneth Keniston, *The Nation*, March 18.]

New Left groups like SDS have always taken strong exception to the thesis that we have reached the "end of ideology" in the Great Society. But there is a sense in which ideology *is* a thing of the past among most politically involved, left-wing students. By and large, most New Left groups have refused to allow doctrinal logic to obscure or displace an irreducible element of personal tenderness. What has distinguished SDS, at least in its early years, from old-line radical youth groups (say, like the Progressive Labor Movement) is the unwillingness of the former to deify doctrine, granting it more importance than flesh and blood. For most of the New Left, there has ultimately been no more worth or cogency in any ideology than a man infuses it with by his own action: personal commitments, not abstract ideas, are the stuff of politics. Alienation has been the root problem of New Left politics. But not alienation in the sheerly institutional sense, in which capitalism (or for that matter any advanced industrial economy) tends to alienate the worker from the rewards of production; but rather alienation as a deadening of man's sensitivity to man: a deadening that can creep into even those revolutionary efforts that seek to eliminate institutional forms of alienation.

Wherever nonhuman elements—whether revolutionary doctrine or material goods—assume greater importance than human life or well-being, man becomes alienated from man and the way is open to the self-righteous use of others as objects. Thus, revolutionary terrorism is the mirror image of capitalist exploitation.

The flavor is caught by the SDS Port Huron statement of 1962:

> We are aware that to avoid platitudes we must analyze the concrete conditions of social order. But to direct such an analysis we must use the guideposts of basic principles. Our own social values involve conceptions of human beings, human relationships, and social systems.
> We regard *men* as infinitely precious and possessed of unfulfilled capacities for reason, freedom, and love. . . . We oppose the depersonalization that reduces human beings to the status of things. If anything, the

brutalities of the twentieth century teach that means and ends are intimately related, that vague appeals to "posterity" cannot justify the mutilations of the present . . . .

Loneliness, estrangement, isolation describe the vast distance between man and man today. These dominant tendencies cannot be overcome by better personal management, nor by improved gadgets, but only when a love of man overcomes the idolatrous worship of things by man.

In his recent work *The Politics of Experience*, the British psychiatrist, R. D. Laing, a leading figure in Britain's visionary Left, catches much the same spirit: "No one can begin to think, feel or act now except from the starting-point of his or her own alienation . . . . We do not need theories so much as the experience that is the source of the theory."

'Scrupulosity' of the Young

Once upon a time Harry Pollitt, the leader of the British Communist Party, could, with a clear conscience, tell the poet Stephen Spender that he ought to go to Spain and get himself killed—the party needed more martyred artists to bolster its public image. Nor have such perversions been confined to the Stalinist Left. It was an adamant anti-Stalinist, Sidney Hook, who in his famous exchange with Bertrand Russell during the early fifties, logic-chopped his way to the conclusion that thwarting the ambitions of the world's Harry Pollitts was worth wiping out the entire human species: anti-Stalinist militancy required 2 billion martyrs, willy or nilly. This is precisely the sort of corrupted human relations, the sort of subordination of the person to doctrinal logic, that has been pretty much absent from the best New Left politics. If the New Left draws upon the Marxist tradition, its Marxism has been significantly mediated by Camus and the postwar existentialists. Or, in the American radical tradition, it is a humanist Socialist text like Dwight MacDonald's eloquent *The Root Is Man* that one discerns behind a document like the Port Huron statement. (As I write, however, I am bleakly aware that an ideological drift toward righteous violence is on the increase among the young as an adjunct of black power and a romantic infatuation with guerrilla warfare. Despite Camus' wise admonition, the search may be on again among left-wing dissenters to "make murder legitimate," and the New Left may be about to lose its original soulfulness.)

Colin MacInnes, discussing the difference between the youthful radicals of the thirties and the sixties (*Encounter*, November, 1967), observed that the contemporary young "hold themselves more personally responsible than the young used to. Not in the sense of their 'duties' to the state or even society, but to themselves. I think they examine themselves more closely and their motives and their own behavior." Anyone who has spent much time with New Left students knows what MacInnes is talking about. They show a quality of somber introspection that almost amounts to what the Catholic Church calls "scrupulosity." It is a refusal to allow theories or rhetoric to get in the way of intensive self-awareness. Honesty to the inner motive must be kept paramount and so the final appeal is to the person, never to the doctrine.

But then the question arises: what *is* the person? What, most essentially, is this elusive, often erratic, human *something* which underlies social systems and ideologies, and which now must serve as the ultimate point of moral reference? No sooner does one raise the question than the politics of the social system yields to what Alan Watts has called "the politics of the nervous system." Class consciousness gives way as a generative principle to *consciousness* consciousness. And it is at this juncture that New Left and beat-hip bohemianism join hands. The transition from the one to the other shows up in the pattern that has come to govern many of the free universities. These dissenting academies usually get their send-off from campus New Leftists and initially emphasize heavy politics. But more and more the curricula tend to become hip in content and teaching methods: psychedelics, light

shows, multi-media, McLuhan, exotic religion. (See "The Free Universities," by Ralph Keyes, *The Nation*, October 2, 1967.)

The same transition can be traced in the career of Bob Dylan, who commands respect among all segments of the dissenting youth culture. Dylan's early songs are traditional folk protests, laying forth obvious issues of social justice: anti-boss, anti-war, anti-exploitation. Then, quite suddenly, rather as if Dylan had come to the conclusion that the conventional Woody Guthrie ballad didn't reach deep enough, the songs turn surrealistic and psychedelic. All at once one is thrust somewhere beneath the rationalizing cerebrum of social discourse, and is probing the nightmare deeps, trying, it would seem, to get at the tangled roots of conduct and opinion. It is at that point that the project which the beats of the early fifties had taken up—the task of remodeling themselves, their way of life, their perceptions and sensitivities—takes precedence over the task of changing institutions or policies.

Priorities of Liberation

One can discern, then, a continuum of thought and experience among the young which shades off from the New Leftist sociology of Mills, through the Freudian-Marxism of Herbert Marcuse, through the Gestalt-therapy anarchism of Paul Goodman, through the apocalyptic body-mysticism of Norman Brown, through the Zen-based psychotherapy of Alan Watts where political involvement seems to begin evaporating rapidly, and finally into Timothy Leary's impenetrably occult and quietist narcissism where the world and its woes may shrink at last to the size of a mote in one's private psychedelic void. The different schools of thought become an integrated series as soon as one surrenders the notion that institutional patterns are the basis of social reality, and substitutes instead psychic patterns.

Unrelated as the extremes of this spectrum may seem at first, one would not be surprised if the men just named were to turn up at the same teach-in. The Congress on the Dialectics of Liberation, held in London during the summer of 1967, was pretty much that kind of affair: an effort to work out the priorities of psychic and social liberation within a group of participants that included New Left revolutionaries and existential psychiatrists. Allen Ginsberg was also on hand to chant the *Hare Krishna*. As one would expect, the priorities were never established. And, significantly, it proved impossible for the congress to maintain more than minimal rapport with black power spokesmen like Stokely Carmichael for whom, tragically if understandably, real social power has, despite all that history teaches us to the contrary, once more begun to look like something that flows from the muzzle of a gun. Still, for the most part, the common cause was there: the same insistence on revolutionary change that must at last embrace psyche and society. So it is that when New Left groups organize an anti-war demonstration, the misty-minded hippies are certain to join in, though they may tune out the heavy political speechifying in favor of launching a yellow submarine or exorcizing the Pentagon.

The underlying unity of youthful dissent consists, then, in the effort of beat-hip bohemianism to work out the personality structure, the total life style that follows from New Left social criticism. At their best, the beats and hips are the utopian experimenters of the social system that lies beyond the intellectual rejection of the Great Society. The counter culture is the embryonic cultural base of New Left politics, the effort to discover new types of community, new family patterns, new sexual mores, new kinds of livelihood, new aesthetic forms, new personal identities on the far side of power politics, the bourgeois home, and the Protestant work ethic. If the experiments are raw and often abortive, it must be remembered that the experimenters have been on the scene only for a dozen years and are picking their way through customs and institutions that have had more than a few centuries to entrench themselves. To criticize the experiments is legitimate and necessary; to despair of what are no more than beginnings is premature.

Decadence & Innocence

The counter culture described here is but the latest stage in a major tradition of Western social and intellectual history. The parallels with Romanticism, that first great assault on the scientific world view and the conception of personality that flowed from it, are striking. Goethe, describing his generation's rejection (almost 200 years ago) of Baron Holbach's mechanistic *System of Nature*, hits an unmistakably contemporary note:

> How hollow and empty did we feel in this melancholy, atheistical half-night, in which earth vanished with all its images, heaven with all its stars. There was to be matter in motion from all eternity; and by this motion, right and left in every direction, without anything further, it was to produce the infinite phenomena of existence . . . . If, after all, this book had done us some harm, it was this—that we took a hearty dislike of all philosophy, and especially metaphysics, and remained in that dislike; while, on the other hand, we threw ourselves into living knowledge, experience, action, and poetizing, with all the more liveliness and passion.

Even more striking is the overlap between the contemporary counter culture and the late-Romantic "decadents" of France and England, whose favorite constellation of luscious vices—drugs, eclectic mysticism, and *outré* sexuality—is an obvious prototype of beat-hip bohemianism. It is no coincidence then that the *art nouveau* of the sickly sweet *fin de siècle* should now be revived as the official expression of the psychedelic vision. So the English art critic Lawrence Gowing speaks of Aubrey Beardsley as "the prophet of the heightened hallucinatory rhythm . . . the forerunner of the psychedelic flux and its liberated bisexual languor."

But there is an important difference. The style of the "decadents" was brazenly to court damnation by aspiring to satanic wickedness. Today's young assert the innocence, indeed the holiness, of their forbidden pleasures—which is all the more exasperating. The difference stems, I think, from the fact that the bohemianism of the younger generation has been able to claim unashamedly the sanctions of Oriental religion for its erotic and psychedelic adventures. The "decadents," caught in a less debilitated Christian ethos, had to take their joys at the expense of grace.

The counter culture's tie-in with Romanticism is important for one particular reason. In its latest stages, Romantic culture degenerated into one of the central ingredients of fascism: "Feeling is all," Goethe's Faust proclaimed: and a little more than a century later Hitler, almost paraphrasing D. H. Lawrence, provided a distorted echo: "Think with your blood." Murderers and maniacs can, of course, seize upon any body of thought and twist it to serve their debased purposes, a fact which too many intellectual historians overlook in working out intricate genealogies of ideas. But still, the vulnerability of certain ideas to such abuse is the more reason for artists and intellectuals to give the greatest thought to the human potentialities their thought and imagery may release—especially when the audience for their work becomes as young as that of the counter culture. "Make Love Not War" is still the banner most of the dissenting young are rallying to—and those who cannot see the difference between that sentiment and any banners the *Hitlerjugend* carried are plain perverse. So too, one of the most remarkable aspects of the counter culture is its cultivation of feminine softness among the males, a deliberate effort to undercut the crude and compulsive "he-manliness" of our political life. Beat-hip bohemianism is quite simply and unashamedly feminine-centered in its ideal of personality. At the same time, one perceives, still at the fringe of the counter culture, a worrisome fascination with violence-minded phenomena like the Hell's Angels and James Bond movies, or with the chichi sado-masochism of Phoebe Zeitgeist and Barbarella.

Saviors of Santa Claus

Despite all the counter culture owes to previous generations, however, one comes back finally to the striking fact that it is a *youth* culture. What was in the past a bohemian frontier populated by a marginal few—an elite of effete gentlemen, outcast revolutionaries, risqué artists—has been staked out and democratized by a mass movement of the young, and mainly the white, middle-class young. So where the "decadents" specialized, as old roués, in corrupting little boys and girls, now the little boys and girls have gone into business on their own, but refusing to yield their claim to innocence.

The result is dissenting thought and culture at the adolescent level, if not on the part of its creators, then on the part of much of its audience. And these tastes now reach surprisingly far back into the early years of adolescence. I offer one illuminating example. In December of 1967, I watched a group of 13-year-olds from a London settlement house perform an improvised Christmas play as part of a therapeutic theatre program run by the International Theatre Club. The kids had concocted a show in which Santa Claus had been imprisoned by the Immigration authorities for entering the country without proper permission. The knock at official society was especially stinging, coming instinctively from some very ordinary youngsters, who had scarcely been exposed to any terribly advanced intellectual influences. And whom did the 13-year-olds decide to bring on as Santa's liberators? An exotic species of being known to them as "the hippies," who Shiva-danced to the jail house and magically released Father Christmas, accompanied by strobe lights and jangling sitars.

However lacking older radicals may find the hippies in authenticity or revolutionary potential, they have succeeded in embodying what Herbert Marcuse calls "the Great Refusal" in a form that captures the need of the young for unrestricted joy. The hippie, real or as imagined, now seems to stand as one of the few images toward which the very young can grow without having to give up the sense of enchantment or playfulness. Hippies who may be pushing 30 wear buttons that read "Frodo lives" (in Elvish yet) and decorate their pads with maps of Middle Earth (which is also the name of one of London's current rock clubs). Is it any wonder that the best and brightest kids at Berkeley High School (to choose a school that happens to be in my neighborhood) are already coming to class barefoot, with flowers in their hair, and ringing with cowbells?

When radical intellectuals must deal with a dissenting public this young, all kinds of problems accrue. Adolescent dissent is certainly as far from ideal as the proletarian dissent that bedeviled radical intellectuals over the last three or four generations when it was the working class they had to ally themselves with in their effort to reclaim culture for the good, the true and the beautiful. Then the horny-handed virtues of the beer hall and the trade union had to serve as the medium of radical thought. Now it is the youthful exuberance of the rock club, the love-in, the teach-in.

The kids, miserably educated as they are, bring with them almost nothing but healthy instincts. And the project of building a sophisticated framework of thought atop those instincts is rather like trying to graft an oak tree upon a wild flower. How to sustain the oak? More important, how to avoid crushing the wild flower? But that is the project, for dissent has very few other social levers with which to work. This is the "significant soil" in which the Great Refusal has begun to take root. If we reject it, frustrated by the youthful follies that also sprout there, where then do we turn?

From the essay by Theodore Roszak,

THE NATION 3/25/68

Birth is bursting, the shell burst. The start is violent. The great heroic deed is to be born; to slay the dragon, to kill the mother, to conquer Tiamat. Every child, like Athena, is born fully armed; is a knife that opens the womb.

N.O. BROWN, *Love's Body*

Government promotes the idea that freedom is a gift of the Nation-State. My point of view is that you are free if you choose to be. If I get used to you deciding what I ought to do, I'll get less and less inclined to think for myself what I ought to do.

The burden of proof is with the Government, not me: I don't know how to justify not killing.

There are thousands of men who now trust me *because* I am a college drop-out and an ex-convict.

CHUCK MATTHEI draft resister

without invention
William Carlos Williams

Without invention nothing is well spaced,
unless the mind changes, unless
the stars are new measured, according
to their relative positions, the
line will not change, the necessity
will not matriculate: unless there is
a new mind there cannot be a new
line, the old will go on
repeating itself with recurring
deadliness: without invention
nothing lies under the witch-hazel
bush, the alder does not grow from among
the hummocks margining the all
but spent channel of the old swale,
the small foot-prints
of the mice under the overhanging
tufts of the bunch-grass will not
appear: without invention the line
will never again take on its ancient
divisions when the word, a supple word,
lived in it, crumbled now to chalk.

Real Life
growing up in the movement

ON THE WAY
SPRING OF 1968

PEOPLE OF A NEW AGE

To experience the contours of the land, to feel its vibrations and penetrate its fogs and mists, is to begin to understand the fears and aspirations that shape its people. Early in May, Ray Mungo, Verandah Porche, Peter Simon, and I drove cross-country from San Francisco to Chicago, a car full of wandering freaks in search of a home in our land.

Ray and Verandah had spent the previous week hitch-hiking through California. Peter and I joined them in their excitement over the "new age" people—living in caves and cabins in Big Sur and rustic retreats in Marin County—who took them in, blew their minds, and showed them concrete possibilities for dropping out into an alternative life-style.

Of course, we in the East have been talking and writing about alternatives for many months, making acute observations from behind clattering typewriters in moldy movement offices and Lower East Side slum pads. But in California people are living it and making it work. One senses a new age everywhere, from the hippie road repair crew grooving on the pot holes in San Francisco's Mission Street to the wealthy residents of Telegraph Hill who wave and smile at the stoned tourists stumbling through their gardens to admire their vistas of the Bay.

The New Age is more than Haight-Ashbury (now a dismal scene), the generational crusade, and psychedelic drugs, though each has played a part. The new age, a new consciousness, new values, community, sharing with and trusting one another, tolerance, feelings and ideas for which there is yet no language, pervade everything and overwhelm us.

We were reluctant to leave and vowed to each other to build our new society back East. And so over Donner Pass (reversing the route of the old age pioneers) down to Reno, through desolate Nevada and the Utah salt flats, high over the Rockies to Boulder, then flat out across the Plains, Julesburg, Ogallala, Omaha, Chicago, and everywhere we travelled we found signs of a new age, as if cosmic vibrations were sweeping eastward before us.

Good vibrations. In the Salt Lake City Greyhound Bus terminal (only place you can get coffee past midnight), two deserters join our table. They are to be court-martialed for possession of acid. We tell them what we know about going into exile, drink coffee, eat pies, and rap. A long-haired ex-Marine we picked up on the road (his car had broken down) describes his new life and wonders why he encounters such hostility now that he feels so full of love and gentleness towards the people he meets.

In the dark of night somewhere in Nebraska, we get a flat and have no lug wrench. We shout and wave at passing cars and trucks but they speed by. Finally a car stops and three freaks from Washington State emerge. They saw us by the road but were going too fast to stop. So they turned around, drove back to the previous exit and came back to where we were parked. They have a wrench and some grass. We fix the tire, share two joints, and stand by the side of the highway digging each other and laughing. Then on to Omaha.

David Miller edits *Middle Earth,* an underground paper, from a converted one-room school house set amidst rolling fields of corn five miles outside of Iowa City. Cows and sheep live across the street, eight cats reign over the front lawn. The lady of the house serves up a delicious meal and we sit into the night, talking about the underground press, poetry, and the political relevance of dropping out. Someone quotes Dave Harris to the effect that our only political weapon is how we live our lives; we discuss the new consciousness and fantasize what will happen when all these New Age kids are faced with the decision of what to do with their lives and do not choose to become junior executives with IBM.

Later in the car we agree that for the first time since frontier days, great numbers of people have the option of dropping out of a rotten society and building a new one from scratch. And we wonder what this will mean. Che said that "in revolution one either wins or dies." But how is a revolution won? When is it won? We consider that revolution (being itself a never-ending, always changing process) can never be won, can only be lived and experienced. And we groove on that.

We are frontiersmen of the mind, liberating ourselves as we liberate each other. But the Old Age follows wherever we go. The ex-Marine is escorted out of Reno by the sheriff, the two servicemen are kicked out of a small town in Utah where they stop for the night. Restaurants won't serve us, hostility surrounds us. Omaha and Chicago—especially Chicago—fill us with paranoia. Bad vibrations. People are frightened by our presence. Sometimes a well-meant hello on our part breaks the fear, as it did in a small restaurant (home cooking) in Minden, Iowa. But more often than not we are seen as interlopers, usurpers, a threat to the people, a threat to the land.

Why should people be so scared? The land is sweet and good, bountiful, beautiful. But we are a nation of settlers, still unsettled, not yet secure in our relationship with the land. Five years ago, Paul Johnson and I wandered through the coal country of Southeastern Kentucky and discovered in the town of Cumberland the fearful business rivalries, hatreds and petty jealousies that devour so many Americans and drive neighbors apart. Does this same madness possess the citizens of every town we pass in the night?

The people are scared of enemies real and imagined. The settlers took the land from the Indians, the ranchers came, and sheepman and cattleman had it out. Then came the farmers who fought the ranchers and closed the range, and the railroads and monopolies which screwed them all. Fear is a way of life, and now it's the dope-smoking commie hippie peaceniks. What would an America be like, where no one lived in fear?

The people are frightened, threatened. Imagined enemies sweep through their village. Like minutemen, vigilant, they prepare for war. Yet the land is so inviting. It beckons. But there is no time to enjoy it, learn its rhythms, live its seasons. "I want to go soon and live away by the pond, where I shall hear only the wind whispering among the reeds. It will be a success if I shall have left myself behind. But my friends ask what I will do when I get there. Will it not be employment enough to watch the progress of the seasons?"

Thoreau wrote that more than a hundred years ago. But Thoreau, like the Iroquois before him, and the freaks of Big Sur, Middle Earth, and the Nebraska highway, are people of a New Age. There is no winning our revolution, but we'll live it and it'll grow and we'll live at peace with ourselves and with our land.

—Martin Jezer

win June 1968

MISSISSIPPI BELLE SAYS 'GOODBYE TO ALL THAT'

By ROBERT ANALAVAGE
(Assistant Editor)

JACKSON, Miss.—Cassell Carpenter, 21 is under indictment here for obscenity. The charges were brought against her and several others for writing and distributing the *Kudzu* (see December *Patriot*), a radical, youth-oriented paper that aims, quite successfully, to reach white Mississippians.

Miss Carpenter finds herself in a strange position. Where she is at, now, is perhaps less important than where she came from.

Childhood

She was born and reared in Natchez in an ante bellum mansion. A photo of her home is on the cover of the Texaco roadmaps for Georgia, Alabama, Mississippi and Louisiana. In the photo, the mansion (called Dunleith) rests on a hill overlooking 40 acres of rolling, close-cropped lawn. In the corner of the photo, a placid Negro is grooming three sleek chestnut thoroughbreds. It is the Southern myth, a myth that "Little Miss Cassell", as she has been called since birth, lived.

Her childhood was peaceful and she never knew want. "I can say with relative certainty," she said, "that I could have anything I could ever want or need."

Her grandfather owned the City Bank and Trust Company, Natchez' largest bank, and her father became its president, a post he holds today. Dunleith always had at least seven servants and Cassell and her six brothers and sisters were well taken care of. When she went to school, she attended one named after her family. (There are three schools in Natchez named after her family.)

Between 1962 and 1965 she attended an exclusive girls' school in Dobbs Ferry, New York. In 1966 she was selected Queen of the Natchez Pilgrimage, an annual event sponsored by the city's First Families, in which the public is invited to tour the ante-bellum mansions and dip into the nostalgia that invokes the Grand Old South.

"I was a real bad racist," she says. "My parents raised me as a racist and they have a severe class outlook—they look down on *everyone* who is not in their economic bracket.

"In New York, when I was attending boarding school, we were made to go to church and one day there was a black girl at the services. I was infuriated!

"When James Meredith was admitted to Ole Miss, I cried. I thought it just signified the end of everything. And in 1964 I was a staunch Goldwater supporter."

Sometime around 1964 Cassell, who had a lively interest in religion and philosophy, attended a conference in Pennsylvania sponsored by a religious group.

"There was a boy there who had been with the SNCC Summer Project in Mississippi and he told me things that happened, things I was totally unaware of or disbelieved. I argued violently with him, but he left me confused."

In 1965 she returned to Natchez, interested in the SNCC projects. "I sent a friend over to the freedom house to see what he could find out. Somehow the Klan found out about it, called his mother, and threatened that if it happened again, they'd blow up his car. I was quite frightened by this."

That year an official of the NAACP stepped into his car and turned on the ignition. The car exploded, maiming and permanently crippling him. Black Natchez was enraged and took to the streets. White Natchez was petrified and called in the National Guard to restore order.

From Natchez Pilgrimage (1966) ....

... to Women's Liberation Conference (1969)

"My father was stockpiling guns and ammunition. He said our house would be one of the targets. I was confused.

"I didn't want to be on his side, but I couldn't be on the other side. I didn't know what to do."

College

She was enrolled at Ole Miss and soon joined a small Young Democrats Club. Then a friend introduced her to two Howard students who were working at something called Strike City in Greenville.

Strike City was made up of rural blacks who had been driven off the land after striking for more wages. They had been earning between 3 and 6 dollars for a 12-hour day in the cotton fields of the Mississippi Delta. Homeless, the people staged an 'invasion' of an abandoned Air Force base and were promptly driven out by U.S. paratroopers flown in especially for the action. A farmer let the refugees settle on a little piece of his land and they were trying to make it livable.

Cassell visited Strike City. "This was the most beautiful experience I ever had. I played with children and talked to a lot of people. This was my first real experience with black people other than our servants.

Later some friends found out about it in Natchez and gave me a stern lecture saying it was unfitting for a lady to be doing such things."

When she returned home that summer there was a lot of friction with her parents. In countless arguments and discussions she tried to find out where she was at. She left Ole Miss and entered Milsaps College, a Methodist school in Jackson.

Soon she dropped out and went to work at University Hospital as a nurse's aide, taking blood samples. Most of her patients were black and her parents objected to her work. After three months she returned to school and majored in psychology.

She conceived of a project whereby students could work at Whitfield, a state mental hospital, and help with therapy.

SSOC

Last spring she attended a SSOC conference in Athens, Ga. She came into contact with many young white Southerners and with new ideas and life styles. Soon she was working with the peace movement in

Jackson and marching in anti-war demonstrations.

She met Dave Doggett at Millsaps and discussed the idea of putting out a radical newspaper directed at young, white Mississippians. Together she and Doggett put out the first edition from her apartment. It condemned the war in Vietnam, spoke on the side of black liberation and came down hard on the system.

Soon, the Jackson police were harassing them and others who joined the staff. Arrests were made on a variety of charges; but all charges were eventually dropped. A group of Jackson women's clubs visited the mayor (who is up for re-election) a n d complained about the 'obscene' _Kudzu_.

Several of the paper's reporters were arrested for distributing obscene material, including Cassell.

"I went to visit some of our people in the jail and I had some papers under my arm. This detective came up to me and asked to buy one. I said, 'No, you'll arrest me." He said, 'no, I won't.' I gave him one free and

he offered me a dollar. 'No, that's O.K.,' I said. He got change and offered me the price of the paper. I refused and he kept insisting. Finally, he walked away and consulted with some other cops. 'Arrest her anyway,' I heard one of them say, so I was arrested."

Today there is bitterness between Cassell and her family. Her father, who is now on the governor's staff as an honorary colonel, took back her car and she receives no allowance from them. Occasionally, they tempt her with a trip to Rome or something similar. But she insists she will not go back to the life from which she came.

"I think that boy, more than anyone else, helped me," she said, referring to the student volunteer who worked in the SNCC summer project, and with whom she argued so bitterly. "He cracked some of my illusions — and once you begin cracking illusions, all the things that are tied to and dependent upon them begin to crumble also."

the southern PATRIOT

March 1969

GROWING UP IN THE MOVEMENT

GEORGE BROSI

Director, *VOCATIONS FOR SOCIAL CHANGE*

Consultant - hiring full-time workers for social change, and the implementation of democratic values; and how to keep your staff when present funding runs out.

Speaker — topics include "New Careers for Social Change," "The American Job Structure of the Future," "Can the Younger Generation Change the World?" & "Creating Jobs That Blend Personal Preferences with Social Aspirations."

George Brosi's first involvement in social action began in the summer of 1961 in his home town of Oak Ridge, Tennessee. He helped out the local chapter of CORE by joining in the picketing of a segregated laundromat. It was this experience that led to increasing concern and involvement. As a college student at Carleton in Northfield, Minnesota, he was again very active in civil rights, as well as student government and peace work. There George edited THE MIDWESTERN ACTIVIST, the first publication devoted to student social action in the sixties to reach students in North Dakota, South Dakota, Nebraska, Iowa, Minnesota, and Wisconsin. His summers were spent back home in Appalachia, and then in 1964 at the central office of SDS's Economic Research and Action Project — the first program to adapt the lessons of the civil rights movement to poor white neighborhoods. George skipped his graduation ceremony in order to attend an SDS meeting where he was asked to spend the summer in the National Office.

In the fall of 1965 he moved to Nashville, Tennessee, and, supporting himself as a day-laborer, he helped create the city's first organization devoted to opposition to the Vietnam war. George was soon hired as the full-time organizer of the Nashville Committee for Alternatives to War in Vietnam — the first such community worker in the South. In his spare time

he helped out the Southern Student Organizing Committee, co-ordinating some of the first South-wide anti-war actions of the decade. That summer George joined the staff of the American Friends Service Committee traveling extensively through Kentucky, Indiana, Ohio, and North Carolina in an effort to stimulate peace activity.

In February he accepted the position of Coordinator of the Youth Commission of the Council of the Southern Mountains. Through this job he travelled to remote colleges in the Appalachian South in an effort to stimulate student action on the social problems which plague the region. The following September he was one of the leaders of the American peace movement who travelled to Bratislava, Czechoslovakia, to meet for a week with representatives of the National Liberation Front of South Vietnam and the Democratic Republic of (North) Vietnam.

In March of 1968 George began working full-time to implement VOCATIONS FOR SOCIAL CHANGE, an agency aimed at encouraging Americans to choose a job or a life's work in the field of social change. This had been a longstanding interest which finally reached fruition. He now is the Director of V.S.C. working out of its national headquarters in Hayward, California.

Vocations for Social Change 1968

THE CHAIRMAN
OF THE
INTRAFRATERNITY
CONFERENCE
AT MIT AND
HIS FRIEND,
MIKE ALBERT,
THE PRESIDENT
OF THE
STUDENT BODY

You never know what is enough unless you know what is more than enough.

WILLIAM BLAKE

✭ ✭ ✭ ✭ ✭

The young have the right to power because they are numerous and are directly affected by what goes on, but especially because their new point of view is indispensable to cope with changing conditions. This is why Jefferson urged us to adopt a new constitution every generation.

PAUL GOODMAN

✭ ✭ ✭ ✭ ✭

"Johnson says we want to destroy the university. What we want to destroy is a war machine. We are trying to build a university."

-- George Katsiaficas, speaking
to demonstrators in
Building 7.

✭ ✭ ✭ ✭ ✭

George Katsiaficas: Prototype of radicalization

By Jim Smith

Radicalization is an interesting process. It may be born out of many sub-processes: the frustration of working for McCarthy and losing the convention; the emotional impact of a friend being killed in Vietnam; or of witnessing police brutality to demonstrators; or it may devolve from pure intellectual research and discovery about the way national policies are made.

For each person, radicalization may take a different combination of these and other routes. And it takes some further than others.

In this article an attempt is made to get a glimpse into how these processes coalesced in the case of one student radical at MIT-- George Katsiaficas. I interviewed "Kats" Monday night to get his own impressions about his rapid radicalization between the time he was appointed to the Pounds Panel last April 25 and last Friday when he marched on the Corporation with Mike Albert.

I asked Kats what had happened; what landmarks he could cite in his political turn-about. He said that he had not really described the process before and somewhat appreciated the exercise.

"Basically," said Katsiaficas, "there are two factors -- the intellectual and the emotional. The intellectual factor is an indirect one: reading about the War, talking, listening, evaluating one's politics. The emotional factor is more direct: seeing people dying in the War, seeing friends beaten at Harvard."

"My 'radicalization' -- I hate that word -- was indirect," he continued. "Over the summer I did a lot of thinking, asking "What's this all about?' I also wrote a lot -- letters to friends and letters to myself."

I asked what specific event might have started things off, recalling that in my case it was

a particular teach-in three years ago. Kats began to recall some scenes from the previous spring. "Yes, I remember just after the bust at Harvard I went to a meeting in Kresge Little Theatre where SDS members were describing what had happened. After that meeting I came out thinking little more about them than before, but as I was crossing Harvard Bridge with a good friend, John Gerth, John said to me, 'You know, I think they have something. I think they might be right.' Like, wow! That completely threw me, and I began to think more about what they had said."

Weeks later, Kats had a lengthy talk with Mike Albert. He had listened to some of Albert's criticisms of fraternities during the March UAP race, and since Kats was (and is) chairman of the Interfraternity Conference, he was interested in talking some more.

It turned out that Mike and Kats were very much in agreement about most aspects of fraternity life: that pledges should be put on more of an equal basis with brothers, that pledge training should essentially be abolished and so forth. Their agreement was made clearer at this informal discussion in May, and Kats said he began to ask himself, "How is it that he and I can reach the same conclusion on this matter from different assumptions and beliefs?" In the end, it simply turned out that by reverse projection Kats reached those same assumptions and beliefs about socialism, the war, and political processes.

At this point (late May, just before the initial Pound Panel report), Kats was at the point politically where he "didn't believe war research was intrinsically bad, but felt that it should not be done at the university." To this extent he agreed with John Kabat's minority report to the Pound report but signed the majority report on the grounds that a strong majority report would advance the liberal cause the best.

The Pounds Panel work -- five weeks of intensive hearings and debate -- provieded a le lengthy intellectual exercise, penetrated always by the arguments of Kabat. "Before that," said Kats, "I knew what SACC was saying, but then

I had an overdose of it -- and it made sense." When the Panel went into seclusion at Endicott House to write the first report, Kats happened to room with Kabat, which added to the SACC input.

Kats went into the summer, then, with the bulk of the intellectual factor he had referred to. At this point he began to describe an emotional transformation which occurred while working and living outside New York City. Kats is one of the "elite" students chosen for the Undergraduate Systems Program in the School of Management -- Dean Pounds' department. He secured a top summer job with the Bird's Eye Division of General Foods, serving both as student and consultant in the Information Systems Office. Including overtime, he took home about $200 per week.

Working at Bird's Eye, Kats described the emotional effect which came from seeing workers buck for promotions. "I thought of the system which induced this kind of inhumane climbing and scratching. I thought a lot about the fact that I have always been on the winning side of this process and that perhaps it was wrong.

"As the summer progressed," he continued, "I began to question the whole system of capitalism. But it became an emotional thing as much as intellectual. You see, during the summer I was really off campus and isolated from leftist rhetoric. I was dealing with people -- with a boss who was paranoid and a group of employees, some of whom earn more money than others for no particular reason except that they scratched harder."

Kats didn't spend the entire summer in White Plains. In August, he flew to the West Coast and then to Hawaii where "I lay on the beach and thought about how I could be there while people were starving and dying. My whole outlook began to change. Previous ideas about school, work, starting my own company -- the regular route -- began to be thrown out. I began to be concerned about the meaning of my life in a broader context."

September 2 Kats flew from L.A. to Boston on a night flight and walked into the first fall meeting of the Pounds Panel at 9:00. There he made a short, extemporaneous statement which visibly shook many members of the panel. "Unless rapid change occurs in the near future," he said, "the operation of the university is certain to be interrupted." This was some change from the George Katsiaficas who signed an IFC resolution April 9 calling for the right of Walt Rostow to speak without disruption. (The next day Rostow was heckled into silence by a half dozen radicals.) Likewise, it was different from the Kats who signed a personal statement April 11 saying that "both deliberate confrontation and authoritarian response, as they occurred at Harvard, are poor substitutes for responsibility. We like to believe that MIT has been free of violence because of the responsible conduct of all members of the MIT community... We have faith that such thorough, conscientious efforts will also be applied to other current issues."

At the time he addressed the Pounds Panel, said Kats, "I felt that I was still a maverick,

that there was no real ideological similarity with student radicals. Once again, it was only 1 later that I concluded that I too was now a radical."

When Albert came to the Sig Ep house during work week (early September) to canvass the brotherhood (of which Kats is a member) he told Albert "We'll have to work together," but his fraternal obligations kept him from doing so until after rush week. Kats did, however, invite Mike to address the House President's meeting before Rush Week, and gave a somewhat political speech at the pre-Rush Week convocation of the freshman class, telling the freshmen in effect that radicalism was not incompatible with the fraternities, and in fact that some radicals lived in fraternities -- himself for one.

"It was amazing," he said. "Each night of rush week, I was having political raps with the freshmen -- something entirely different from ever before."

The compatibility of fraternal life with rad-

icalism is a story in itself. The thesis is simple. Fraternities are a form of communal living, and a turned-on fraternity is not only plausible but now a major goal of the RL-SDS canvassing efforts. Today Kats works full-time in the same SDS "cell" with Albert and has already personally canvassed the bulk of the fraternities with "promising success."

Ed. Note: Albert and Katsiaficas are now members of Rosa Luxembourg SDS at MIT and live in one of its "collectives." "Johnson" in this case is Howard J., Pres. of MIT.

Thursday an underground student paper at MIT

TWO MOVEMENT ORGANIZERS IN THE SOUTH

THE DRAFT AS A MEANS OF REPRESSION

AN ENEMY OF THE PEOPLE

As people across the country organize for social and economic change, officials—on the local, state and federal level—are moving to stop them.

Sometimes they charge these people directly with their organizing work—as in the "conspiracy" cases of the Boston Five (Dr. Benjamin Spock) and the Chicago Eight (activities at the Democratic Convention). The primary purpose of such charges is to put the most vocal people on the defensive and out of action. And to intimidate others from similar action. At the same time, it makes it very clear why they are being attacked.

But sometimes the charges have no apparent connection with the organizing work—and even appear to have a certain legitimacy. The purpose and effect, however, are the same. The organizers are taken out of the struggle. These cases are harder to fight, because the issues are less clear, but they are nonetheless political suppression.

The draft is one of these "subtle" weapons. Although it can be argued that all young men in the U.S. are in the same position with regard to the draft, it is a fact that, increasingly, the work of young, effective organizers is being curtailed because of it.

In June, 1966, General Lewis Hershey told the House Armed Services Committee: "At the present time, we need some incentive to keep a skilled man working in the national interest after he gets to be 26." He said that "the deferment is that carrot that we have used to try to get individuals into occupations and professions that are said by those in charge of government to be the necessary ones." Evidently, organizing to improve people's conditions is considered neither "necessary" nor "in the national interest."

The experiences of two Southern movement workers—Walter Collins and Joe Mulloy—provide a case study of how the weapon of the draft is used.

Walter Collins is a 24-year-old native of Louisiana. He was reared in the black ghetto area of New Orleans called Carrolton, where his family has lived for generations. His great grandfather donated the land on which the first public school for blacks in Plaquemines Parish was erected. His grandfather was a follower of Marcus Garvey and a leader in early voter-registration programs.

By the time he entered high school, Collins was well aware of what it means to be black in the United States. The segregated schools of New Orleans provided no training for black people. In his words, "blacks were programmed to mimic white society." He first understood how blacks are denied voting rights when a cousin who had attended college in the North could not pass the voter-registration exam.

Collins followed a strong tradition of activism in his family by joining the early sit-ins to desegregate theaters and lunch counters in New Orleans, in 1963. Then he worked with the Student Nonviolent Coordinating Committee (SNCC) registering voters in Louisiana and Mississippi, and with the '64 Mississippi Summer Project.

Joe Mulloy is a 25-year-old native of Kentucky. He was raised in the West End of Louisville, in a working-class family. His father was a plumber and a minor union official.

In 1964, while at the University of Kentucky, he became interested in a student group that was beginning to work with the poor in nearby Appalachia. That winter, he spent his weekends working with the mountain people, fixing up dilapidated school houses and tutoring youngsters. This was at the beginning of the War on Poverty and the student group, called Appalachian Volunteers (AV), applied for and received a federal grant to broaden their work. Mulloy soon joined the staff full time.

His job was to supervise the student volunteers and VISTA workers, most of whom were from out of state. The emphasis of the program was on providing a good experience for the students, by bringing them into contact with the poor and unemployed of the mountains.

After a year of this, Mulloy and several other staff members realized the shortcomings of the AV and poverty-war programs. They felt that the emphasis of their organizing should be, not the student volunteers, but the problems of the people in the area. One of the most glaring of these problems is strip mining.

The Politics of Coal

Strip mining involves scraping the top off a mountain to lay bare the upper seams of rich coal. Auger mining — which is also widespread in Appalachia—uses bulldozers to cut a gash around the side of a mountain, exposing the seam vertically. Huge drills then bore into the side of the mountain, to pull out the ore. Both of these methods push earth, boulders and trees down the mountainsides, burying houses and gardens, polluting streams, and devastating the area.

Under Kentucky law, the mine owner is not forced to pay compensation for the damage he causes. Efforts to force compensation and regulate mining practices have been fruitless, although the coal operators consider Kentucky's surface mining regulations the strongest in the nation.

The fact is that coal is one of the biggest industries in the state. The operators therefore have considerable influence, if not control, over the enforcement of mining laws—even though they pay virtually no taxes. Coal is a multi-billion dollar business which flourishes in the midst of some of America's cruelest poverty and unemployment. To regulate the industry and force it to share its profits with the mountain people through fair taxes would be a giant step toward ending that poverty.

The Strip-Mine Struggle

It was into this struggle that Mulloy and a few others on the AV staff ventured. They began to help a local group which opposed strip mining and advocated coal taxation. Soon strong chapters had been formed in half a dozen Eastern Kentucky counties.

In Pike County, where Mulloy and his wife, Karen, lived, one man forced a confrontation with the law by standing in front of a bulldozer that was about to auger the land above his home. His neighbors were there to back him up, and so were the Mulloys. After a month of confrontations, the Governor suspended the operator's permit and ordered a halt to the mining. This was a tremendous victory for the people—and it pointed the way to many more.

The coal operators knew this, and they moved quickly to crush the movement. In the early hours of August 11, 1967 (eleven days after the victory) a sheriff's posse raided the Mulloys' home and the home of two organizers for the Southern Conference Educational Fund (SCEF). SCEF is a south-wide interracial group working to end poverty, racial injustice, the war and the draft. Books, letters and personal documents were seized and Mulloy and the SCEF workers were charged with sedition—advocating the violent overthrow of the government. The man who led the raiding party was State's Attorney Thomas Ratliff—founder of the Coal Operators' Association and a millionaire operator himself.

The sedition charges were clearly meant to stop the organizing and to promote the interests of the operators—including Ratliff, who was running for Lieutenant Governor of Kentucky at the time. A special panel of federal judges found the sedition law unconstitutional one month later. They

freed the three organizers and two SCEF executives who had also been arrested.

The Draft

The sedition charge, with its potential 21 year sentence, was no longer a usable weapon against the organizers. It was at this point that the draft law was used, to stop Mulloy's work in Eastern Kentucky.

During the strip-mining confrontation in July, Mulloy had been ordered to report for induction, even though he was appealing his reclassification a few months earlier from 2-A (occupational deferment) to 1-A (eligible for induction). He got that order cancelled. Then, two weeks after the sedition arrest, his appeal was unanimously denied by the state board. That left him 1-A.

On the day after the sedition law was thrown out, the board issued another order for Mulloy to report for induction. They ignored the fact that he was still under bond for 60 days, pending a possible appeal by the state, and that he still faced a charge in Pike County.

Mulloy was on vacation and did not find the draft order until he returned in early October, 1967. While on vacation, unaware of the new induction order, Mulloy—encouraged by his wife—had decided to file for CO status when he returned to Kentucky. He had been influenced by the writings of Thomas Merton, a Trappist monk and pacifist. And through his work in the mountains, he met a number of Quakers—from whom he learned of conscientious objection for the first time. (The Louisville Peace Council has repeatedly tried to get the Louisville and Jefferson County boards of education to allow it equal time with army recruiters to explain conscientious objection to high-school students; the board has repeatedly refused to do so.) Although not a pacifist, Mulloy was convinced that war was wrong, and that he could not participate in it. And, like so many young men in the 1960's, he was faced with the reality of Vietnam.

A "Courtesy" Hearing

Returning home, he found the induction order—which was later cancelled because he was still out on bail. Mulloy filed the request for CO status and the board gave him what it called a "courtesy" hearing. The board members questioned his patriotism and quizzed him about his work in the mountains. In January, 1968, he was told that the board would not reopen his case to consider his CO application. This denied him any appeal. The board did not doubt his sincerity—they merely said he did not present enough evidence to warrant a reopening. On the same day, they issued a new induction order.

Mulloy refused to step forward into the army and was convicted in Federal Court in Louisville. At his trial, the clerk boasted that CO status had not been granted even once, in her 17 years with the draft board. The board is the same one that refused to defer Cassius Clay (Muhammad Ali) as a Muslim minister.

Mulloy's Selective Service file contained a stack of newspaper clippings about his work in the mountains and the sedition arrest. The clerk claimed that this was standard procedure, to keep up with the activities of the registrants. Mulloy was given the maximum five-year sentence and fined $10,000, which the judge ordered him to pay immediately, as a condition to bail. He spent six weeks in jail, until the bail ruling was overturned. The Sixth Circuit Court of Appeals in Cincinnati has upheld his conviction, and he is appealing it to the U.S. Supreme Court.

Joe and Karen Mulloy now both work with SCEF, organizing in the mountains and throughout the South. It appears certain, however, that he will soon be in prison.

While attending Louisiana State University in 1965 and '66 he worked on various voter-registration campaigns. In the summer of 1966 he was particularly active in work against the Vietnam War. He felt that "it was a contradiction for black people to have to fight for other people's freedom thousands of miles away, when they were not free themselves." Collins compiled a list of all the black servicemen from New Orleans's Ninth Ward who had been killed in Vietnam. It was much higher than the white death toll. He put out literature about it, using photographs taken from the newspapers. This created a storm of protest in the community—and the local papers quit printing photographs of the war dead, so people could not see how many were black.

That same summer, he worked with his mother, Virginia Collins, trying to make the war on poverty more relevant to black people. His mother was finally fired from her poverty-war job for encouraging blacks to register to vote. She then went to work with SCEF as an organizer in Louisiana. In the fall of 1966, she was called to testify before the Louisiana Un-American Activities Committee. LUAC was investigating "subversives" in the poverty war. Virginia Collins is now a regional vice-president of the Republic of New Africa, a black separatist group that wants five states in the Deep South for a black nation.

Black-White Coalition in Mississippi

Collins has recently been involved with SCEF's Deep South project, Grass Roots Organizing Work (GROW). They are helping to build a political coalition between black and white workers striking against the Masonite Corporation plant in Laurel, Miss. Collins organized support for an independent slate of candidates, running as the Workers' Independent Party, in recent city elections. They lost—partly because the interracial coalition has not yet been realized. But Collins believes that this coalition is a necessity if poor and working people, both black and white, are to control their government.

Draft Problems Begin

His problems with the draft began in the fall of 1966, after a summer of intense activity in New Orleans, during which Collins had carried on the campaign against the war. He was then a full-time graduate student at the University of Michigan. His student deferment lapsed in November and, in January, 1967, he was notified that he was 1-A. This was a full six months before the ruling which disallowed graduate deferments went into effect. Collins immediately wrote his draft board, offering proof of his student status and asking to appeal the classification. That letter has mysteriously disappeared from the clerk's files; the board maintains no such letter exists.

In June of 1967 he was ordered to report for a physical. A few weeks later he was sent a current information questionnaire. Collins filled in the questionnaire and sent it back to the board, asking to meet with them. He had heard nothing about his earlier appeal, and wanted to discuss applying for CO status.

When he arrived in New Orleans, he was told he would have to write another letter to the board about meeting with them, and wait until their regular meeting. He was also told that, since he was a full-time student, he would probably be given a student deferment—so he didn't bother to ask about the CO application.

When Collins got back to Michigan he found an induction order that had been issued before he visited the board. The date of induction had, by then, passed. He immediately caught a plane back to New Orleans and explained to the clerk that the order had not been forwarded. He also complained about the misinformation he had been given in his previous visit, and asked about the procedures for applying for conscientious objector status. The clerk said it was too late to apply for CO status since he was under orders to report for induction. She refused to give him the forms. Collins was told he would be ordered to report for induction the following month.

At the Induction Center . . . .

He reported twice at the induction center, but the officer in charge told Collins to leave because he was wearing anti-war buttons and passing out literature. The draft board clerk finally gave him a CO application form, under instructions from her superiors. But she told Collins that it would do him no good to fill it out—and handed him his third induction notice.

On the fourth induction date, Collins was examined by a medical officer who insulted him with racial slurs. He was then told to sit in a room and wait. After more than three hours of waiting, he got up and left. No one tried to stop him.

Tired of playing around with the draft board, he decided to leave New Orleans, since he did not intend to submit to the draft. He went to New York to work in the peace movement and was arrested a month later. But not before the draft board had issued two more induction orders, which he never received.

The Trial

Collins was indicted on six counts of refusing induction and convicted on five of them. The foreman of his jury was a man who had said, "I'm a spy, a secret agent for the Army. Would that prejudice the case?" while the jury was being selected. Several women who were wives or mothers of policemen were also selected as jurors. He was sentenced to 25 years—the maximum of five years on each charge, to be served concurrently—and fined $2,000. The terms of his $5,000 bond restrict him to the eastern half of Louisiana—and keep him from continuing to build the coalition in Mississippi.

After he was sentenced, Collins said: "If I am guilty of a crime, it is the crime of thinking. The draft is a totalitarian instrument used to practice genocide against black people. Poor and working-class people are drafted to fight, not for American ideals, but for the interests of a few capitalists who run this country."

He is appealing his sentence and the travel restrictions.

And that is how the draft is being used to try to stop Joe Mulloy and Walter Collins—and many others—from organizing in Appalachia and the Deep South.

Collins can no longer travel to Mississippi, to take part in work which was proving to people across the South and the nation that black-white coalitions are possible. He will serve a maximum of five years in prison—but many people will read 25 years, and decide not to take the risk.

Mulloy's case shows that the draft was used to stop his work after another weapon—the sedition law—became useless. The draft board took up the attack immediately after the sedition law was knocked out; it kept a newspaper clipping file on his political activity. The judge went a step further than travel restrictions—he demanded that Mulloy pay his $10,000 fine before he could be freed on bond.

There are countless other examples. Students from Nashville are expelled from college for organizing, lose their student deferments and are drafted. Fred Brooks of SNCC is called before a Senate investigating subcommittee and drafted simultaneously. In South Carolina, Cleve Sellers of SNCC faces charges growing out of the Orangeburg Massacre—and is drafted.

These cases all show that the draft is just one of many ways that movements for social change can be slowed down—different in degree, but not in kind, from conspiracy charges (Dr. Spock, the Chicago 8), Congressional investigations (SDS, SNCC, SCEF, the Black Panthers), and criminal charges (Huey Newton, Rap Brown, Reies Tijerina).

In all of these cases, people have been arrested and jailed because of their efforts to end poverty, racism and war. The suppression of their political rights is a further symptom of the very things they were organizing to end. Unless this is stopped, the United States could easily become a police state—a direction that many feel has already been taken.

The only way to stop this from happening is to fight every step of the way, in every case and every instance. And to continue to organize. As one organizer goes to jail, ten must take his place.

IN NAZI GERMANY . . .

First they put the Communists and Jehovah's Witnesses in the concentration camps – but I was not a Communist or a Jehovah's Witness, so I did nothing. Then they came for the social democrats – but I was not a social democrat, and I did nothing. Then they arrested the trade-unionists – and I did nothing, because I was not one. Then they arrested the Jews – and again I did nothing because I was not a Jew. Then they came for the Catholics, but I was not a Catholic and I did nothing. At last they came and arrested me – but then it was too late already.

—Martin Niemoeller

What YOU can do to stop it from happening here:

Send letters to the editors of the Times-Picayune and the States-Item (both in New Orleans, La.) and to the Louisville Times and the Courier-Journal (in Louisville, Ky.) describing the political nature of these two cases, and protesting such suppression;

Write to the trial judges in both cases, demanding an immediate suspension of sentence and a cease-and-desist order from further harassment. For Collins write to: Judge Edward Boyle, U.S. District Court, New Orleans, La. For Mulloy, write to: Judge James Gordon, U.S. District Court, Louisville, Ky.;

Be on the lookout for cases of political suppression in your community or city. Support the defendants wholeheartedly;

Signed petitions urging the President of the United States to grant amnesty to Mulloy and Collins and all others resisting the draft should be sent to the White House, Washington, D.C.;

Organizations have been formed to abolish the draft entirely. For more information, write the National Council to Repeal the Draft, 201 Massachusetts Ave., N.E., Washington, D.C. 20002;

The cost of fighting a political case is enormous. Besides the normal legal expenses, there is the cost of literature and publicity such as this. You can help greatly by distributing this pamphlet widely and contributing to its cost. Please send money to help fight these cases to:

Southern Conference Educational Fund (SCEF)
3210 West Broadway, Louisville, Ky. 40211.

Southern Conference Educational Fund

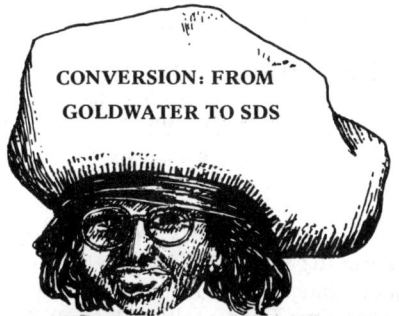

THE CHANGELING: THE STORY OF A HUAC SPY IN THE STUDENT MOVEMENT

Don Meinshausen, a 19-year-old New Jersey student, was called before the House Internal Security Committee (formerly HUAC) one day in August to testify as a "friendly" witness on his activities as paid infiltrator of SDS chapters, conventions, and the National Office. Several months before, however, Meinshausen had begun a process of changing allegiances from HUAC to the Movement. He had come to Washington to seek the advice of Karl Hess, a former right-wing activist and Goldwater aide, who in the past year had also begun to think of himself as part of the radical Movement. The night before the HUAC hearing, Meinshausen drafted a statement condemning the Committee. The next morning, before Meinshausen—dressed in jeans and a work shirt, with long hair, a moustache and granny glasses—had a chance to testify, Committee staffers learned of his change of mind, and in a series of baffling maneuvers (with attempted strong-arm tactics against the witness) managed to cancel the hearing altogether. Later in the same week, Meinshausen was interviewed by Andrew Kopkind, and the following edited version of the recorded transcript was made:

I grew up in Nutley, New Jersey. My parents were German immigrants, Lutherans. My father was a baker till his business failed. He was conservative and both my parents were against Communists— we have relatives behind the Iron Curtain who we would send packages to—and they were influenced a lot by the mass media. All sorts of things like, "I Led Three Lives." We went to church once a week but the church was mostly old people. I couldn't identify with it. My parents' attitude toward Negroes was very weird. It seemed we liked Negro people all right, and we gave stuff to them as charity, but we wouldn't want to live next door to them. We put a lot of money in the house, and, you know, property values go down.

In high school I got caught up in the Goldwater movement. We had a pretty big group; at the time we thought we wanted a change. Looking back it all seems pretty romantic. We liked him because he was an individualist, because he was fighting the Eastern liberal establishment, because he was talking about a return to

American ideals. And he had guts. You could just tell that he wasn't a phoney. But most of the people who were in that group have gone, left. One of them has been involved in People's Park; another one has been arrested for selling guns; another's a real leftist. Others I guess have just gotten sick of politics and left it.

Gradually, I got into politics more seriously. I went through a stage when I studied Ayn Rand and took a few courses on objectivism. I think I needed what they had: a way to answer everything with a certain formula. And at one point I went to a civil rights camp sponsored by the National Conference of Christians and Jews. Most of the kids there were more liberal than I was. Like, I would say that integration would never work—at the peak of the civil rights movement—or that federal aid to education would lead to federal control. But I noticed that on a lot of things I was more radical than the others. They were still sort of hung up in a vague sort of Christianity while I was coming out with something like atheism. Once I was arguing with a girl, who was supposed to be liberal, about why two people should be allowed to live together if they want to. She thought it was horrible; I thought it was OK. I think I was looking for a radical alternative to liberalism, and the only place I could find it was in Goldwaterism on the right. At one point I considered joining the Birch Society and even went to some of their meetings.

In September, 1967, I went out to California to a middle-class junior college, Ventura. There was no YAF [Young Americans for Freedom] out there but there was an SDS chapter. It was a very liberal type of thing. We were just holding picket signs. I mean, how can you react to that? It was like nothing. I held a few jobs: One job, at a MacDonald's hamburger stand, really fucked me over—for $1.40 an hour. They treated you like a machine. First they checked into my background and they found out I had a high I.Q. I found this amazing because I figured, MacDonald's hamburger stand, why would they want to check my I.Q.? And you would have to do something every single second; if you weren't making hamburgers you had to go around wiping stuff. They tried to generate this phoney enthusiasm. "MacDonald's is clean and neat and courteous" and "smile for the customers" and all this type of thing. And I found out that it was really bad stuff. I mean, I don't know if it was inferior meat or anything like that, but it was just bland; it was not really that good at all.

I held some other jobs and then I came back East to Essex County College in Newark, in September, 1968. I wanted to go back into politics since I'd really dug the Goldwater thing, but I didn't want to contradict what I'd already done, so I got involved in YAF. And what happened was that we were sitting around analyzing what happened to Columbia and saying we don't want this to happen again and gradually we got the idea that if we could find out ahead of time what the radicals were planning—you know, like the takeover of a building or something—we'd be better off. We looked at it as a problem in military strategy; we needed better intelligence. And I figured that since I was new I was the only person not known as a right-winger and that I could get into SDS much more easily.

Essex County is really one of the worst schools in the world. It's in a building right in the middle of Newark that was part of Seton Hall, which sold it to the city. It's old and dingy and a couple of weeks a year they tear up the street and you can't hear anything that's going on. The halls are always crowded. You go into the cafeteria and it smells like a factory. There's no place you can go to relax. The college was started to keep kids off the streets, prevent riots and to make the city administration look good. A lot of the deans were brought up from places in the South. Only one of about 33 administrators was black. Another, the assistant to the dean of students, was a goddamn fascist. At one point he tried to get the right-wing Italian kids to organize politically against me.

There was no SDS chapter at Essex and to "infiltrate" I had to organize one. I talked to a lot of kids who looked friendly and said, look, let's organize an SDS or some kind of peace group. People liked the idea and I started to go through the channels, and that's when I got my first hasslings from the administration. They said I couldn't organize SDS because they didn't want any new national organizations on campus, so I said OK, we're going to call it Students for Peace. I wasn't really doing it as a put-on but as a kind of political experiment. I figured I'd just set it in motion and see how it moves along, and this way I could see first-hand what really happens. The first meeting of Students for Peace was OK. There were a lot of people there, and some very radical sponsors from the faculty, and I said, "Well, we're going to do this, this and this, and talk about the war, and see what we can do." Then at the second meeting we had I got a speaker from the National Lawyers Guild to come talk on draft resistance.

In the meantime opposition had developed from some of the Italian immigrant kids on campus. They were very hostile to SDS, because they had heard what happened at Columbia and they looked on Essex County College as their only chance of making it in society. They figured, if their college gets closed down or something like that, they'd get screwed. So they were very angry and showed up at the meeting with the Lawyers Guild speaker, shouting and disrupting and calling him a dirty communist. And all the time I'm trying to keep it down to a very low key, just to let it develop and see what happens, and these kids are fucking it up. Later I was called in by the dean, who accused me of holding a disruptive meeting and inviting an outside speaker without going through channels. He said the administration would hold a trial on the charges. So I went to the Lawyers Guild and one of the guys said, great, we'll represent you, make a big issue out of this. And he wrote a letter to the dean saying that. And the dean caved in because he was afraid of the lawyers, and eventually the charges just disappeared. I got a lot of publicity; I mean, I was interviewed by the school newspaper and all that. Suddenly I found myself cast in this role: SDS organizer on campus. And I thought, insane. This was the most insane possible thing that could happen. But it was cool, you know.

Another weird thing happened. SDS-Rutgers had called for a march through Newark, condemning the elections. So I figured the thing for me to do is get some kids to march, just to see how it goes again. I told the YAF kids about it and they said they'd try to arrange some counter-demonstration, but that nothing serious would happen. They were wrong. The demonstration got wild. There was a rally inside a park, with SDS and the Panthers and guerrilla theater and everything like that. On the outside were the YAF kids plus these Italian North Ward kids, shouting and screaming at us. And we're trying to leave, and I don't know who started it but somehow fights break out and more fights and there was a lot of misunderstanding and confusion about what to do and all of a sudden I see these five guys about to attack me. And a black kid who I made friends with the day before is fighting off one of the

kids who is attacking me and draws a knife on him. And all of a sudden the cops come and they check this black kid who's got the knife and they arrest him. And at the same time the YAF kids are trying to stop the guys from beating me up, yelling, "Don't do it, don't do it, he's on our side." And my mind is going crazy. It was like literally being pulled apart. On one hand this black kid who I'd just met—he was on probation but he risked himself to try and save me. And on the other side there was another kid who knew what I was up to who also risked his neck to try and save me. I couldn't figure it all out. I wondered, am I to blame for all this that's happening?

Anyway, I continued as an SDS organizer. Eventually we formed a coalition with the black students and had big rallies leading to a sit-in which eventually closed down the school. It was really amazing. You know, like, for the first time in their lives, guys from opposite sides of town were talking to someone different and really trying to reach an understanding and agreeing on demands. The whites agreed to black demands for black administrators. And I was one of the leaders of it; I was sort of leading the hip people. I was really emotionally involved because, like, what kids were demanding was that certain incompetent people be fired, that we should have freedom of discussion, and make the school more responsive to the people there. And you know I could really dig something like this. Some of the kids in SDS didn't like it. They said: "Well look at your demands. None of them are oriented toward the working class. None of them show the contradictions of our society. They're all student-power demands. You can't build a movement from that." And I was screaming at them, What the fuck do you know? I mean you go to some place like Rutgers or Princeton or some place like that, while any day I get my ass kicked in over here. I was really pissed off at them.

I was getting variously hung up. Mostly I found good kids in SDS. Kids that really seemed to be committed to the Movement and really wanted to do good things. They helped me when I got in trouble with the dean. One time I had a talk with Mark Rudd and he really dug what I was doing, you know, organizing at a working class college, and I felt a sort of superiority to kids who were going to Cornell and Harvard while I was doing working-class-organizing. But some things I didn't like. Especially their attitude toward civil liberties. That was very important to me. I'd talk to them and say, "If Gus Hall was not allowed to speak on campus, would you support or defend the campus position?" And they'd say, "Oh, I'd support it, because Gus Hall presents such a lousy view of Communism." And I've seen times at SDS meetings where they'd say, "Well, we created a civil liberties issue but it was a good thing anyway." You know, apologizing! And saying that student-power isn't really what we're up to. I was pretty far into it, but the farther in I got, the more confused I got. I think I understand some things a little better now, like what civil liberties means in a society when one class makes the rules. But I don't believe in a manipulative struggle. I think we're going to have to work it up to revolution. Any other way is bad. And I figure if you can really get clear-cut concessions going, get them. Because I think the ruling class can make concessions that will hurt them, too, and eventually sort of maneuver themselves out of the picture.

Around January of this year I started to work for HUAC. One of the YAF kids told me that a guy from HUAC wanted to get in touch with me. There are a lot of connections between YAF and HUAC—they sort of mutually help each other out—and it was all sort of natural. This particular fellow, Herb Romerstein, was a nice guy.

We met first in the Pennsylvania Railroad Terminal in Newark, and later we met seven or eight times in various restaurants. Sometimes Reynolds was there, an intelligence guy from the New Jersey State Police. I had gotten literature and some names and they said it looked good, pretty much what they wanted. They said especially to try to find connections between SDS and the CP.

I kept on getting all this stuff—names and leaflets—but I thought it was pretty silly. The names they could have gotten just by asking on a campus who the SDS people were. And the leaflets said things like, there's going to be a meeting somewhere; or else they said things like, America is an imperialist country and we're revolutionaries. I thought: big deal. So they're calling themselves communists. But Romerstein and Reynolds thought it was really something that anybody would call themselves revolutionary communists. What I wanted them to do was expose situations in which SDS was really manipulating people, and I wanted to have HUAC fight them ideologically, but that wasn't what was really going on.

At the same time I was getting more and more into dope. I tried acid, and a few other things. The two things—politics and dope—weren't really contradictory, but they sort of pulled me back and forth. Also at the same time, I began taking their money. Eventually I told them I was willing to go to the SDS convention in Austin, and they said they'd pay for it. I gave them all the resolutions and all the literature that was passed out—there was no security and anybody could have gotten in. I figured it was all a waste of time, but Romerstein kept saying, "No, it's good stuff, it's good stuff." What it was was piles and piles of shit that no one should have bothered reading. He would ask me: What was happening to SDS? I would talk to a few guys and give him some quotes. Then he'd ask: Did anybody call himself a communist? I think they said that every other sentence. I heard it so much—you know, marxist, communist and so on—I didn't think it was very impressive. Meanwhile, I was getting kind of involved. The speeches and stuff bored me, but after I got the HUAC stuff out of the way, I'd go off and talk with some people and smoke dope. I developed principles about what I was doing. I figured I was spying against SDS but I wouldn't tell them about who smoked grass. I mean, if a person smokes dope and he's a communist, cool, I'll tell them he's a communist but I won't tell them that he smokes drugs. And I wouldn't tell on people who were really innocent. But I'd really give it to PL when I could. I hated them.

I went to Chicago twice, once to the SDS convention [in June] once to sort of work there. At the convention I guess I really became involved. I didn't want to work for HUAC, I just wanted to find the people closest to my own type of politics. But Romerstein was there and he would be standing outside with the pigs and I would go to his hotel room and give the literature and tell him what was happening. But I was becoming more and more reticent to talk. I did find some people in the Anarchist Caucus I felt close to; they said they had a lot of YAF members in their SDS chapters, and I saw some of the former YAF people to talk to myself. I liked that, but I didn't like what I saw happening at the rest of the convention and a lot of people agreed with me. Like the security guards. I thought they were just pigs. A kind of Gestapo within the movement. In fact I thought the whole security thing was completely ridiculous, egotistical nonsense. It was like the Democratic Convention, hassling people about credentials, and it wasn't doing any good. Anybody could get in who wanted to. I didn't like what I saw (the Ohio and Michigan delegations waving the Red Books and shouting Long Live Mao Tse-Tung and Ho Ho Ho Chi Minh, and I didn't like the thing with the Black Panther when he talked about pussy power and everyone yelled "stop male chauvinism" and I didn't like PL). I began to feel a little guilty because I felt that if I'd joined SDS a few years ago I could have stopped it from becoming what it is becoming.

Later I decided to go to work in the NO [SDS National Office]. Romerstein thought that was good. As it turned out I actually only worked there for one day, because Rudd was the only one I knew and he wasn't there, and they were very uptight about strangers. All I actually did was talk to Mark Rudd. I tried to warn him, tell him about what I was doing. I said, Look, I know there are spies in SDS and a guy from HUAC has been after me to spy for them. And I told him about YAF—that YAF was becoming more libertarian—and in general I tried to tell him what was going on, and find out where his head was at. Sometime at about that point I decided it was all over.

I'm not too sure why I eventually changed my mind, but I guess it was building up in me for a long time. Karl Hess was very important to me. I met him at a YAF conference in the spring of '69.

He really intrigued me. I talked to him as if I were an SDS person, and he was telling me how all these people like Taft and Webster and Jefferson were really sort of New Leftists, and that they wanted revolution, and things like that. I came to see him in Washington a few times after that, and eventually told him what I was doing. What happened in Newark during the Election Day march and all the things that happened in my school were important. Something in Carl Oglesby's book. Meeting members of SDS who used to belong to YAF. Taking acid. I'm really not sure. At some point my reasons for doing what I was doing came to seem sort of romantic, James Bondish. I wasn't ashamed of what I'd done, but I felt I had to make it right somehow, or rationalize it. But I guess I just wanted to stop. I don't know what I'm going to do, but now I consider myself part of the Movement.

Hard Times Sep 29-Oct 6 1969

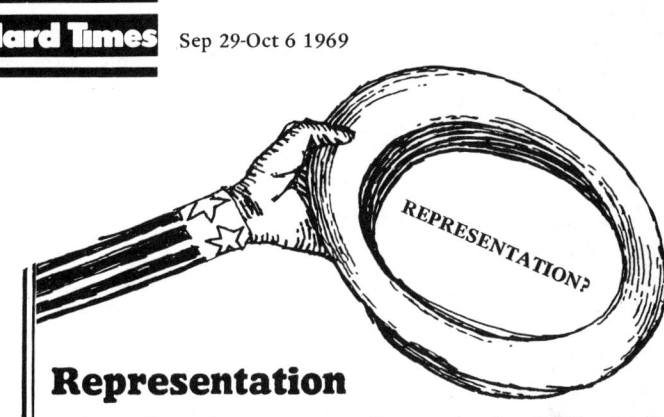

Representation

A reading of two recent polls, one by Louis Harris, the other by George Gallup, measures the present extent of political disaffection. The Gallup poll indicates that 15 million Americans, who were registered, "sat out" the 1968 Presidential election, either from lack of interest in politics or from dissatisfaction with the three candidates. (A much larger number of those of voting age failed to register or did not vote because of illness, absence, change of residence, etc.). A majority of 54 per cent of voters in this latest post-election survey said that they had "split" their ticket and voted for candidates of different parties.

The Harris poll indicates that in a time of unprecedented material affluence, 28 per cent of the adult population— more than 33 million Americans—feel substantially alienated from the mainstream of society. Conspicuously represented among the alienated are the poor, the old, the blacks, and the people who never went to school beyond the eighth grade. Those who voted for George Wallace also express a high sense of isolation from "the American power structure."

Mr. Harris sums up his survey: "In adult America, blacks are now an estimated 12 per cent of the population, whites over 65 are 17 per cent, whites earning under $3,000 a year are 10 per cent, whites with no more than a grade school education are 17 per cent and the Wallace supporters come to just over 13 per cent of the 1968 election. Taken together and eliminating overlap, these groups come close to 50 per cent of the adult population." With 15 million voters so disaffected that they sat out the Presidential election and with perhaps 50 per cent of the adult population alienated from the mainstream of American society, it is apparent that the representational gap has become dangerously extended. This is, perhaps, the "gap" that should concern Mr. Nixon more than the others that he and his associates have mentioned.

NATION 12/30/68

Who's Going to Collect the Garbage?

marjorie heins

"America is a nation so incredibly wealthy that all morality is based on EXCESS:
True American career counselors now ask only one question.
'Do you want to produce garbage or do you want to collect garbage?'
Industrialist or politician?
Fishfarm or junkyard?
The young people want no part of it, what with garbage their natural matrix and medium.
Produce it? Collect it? They want to fuck in it!
...It's just THINGS, it's garbage, it's overflow and the young people know it.
They throw the career counselor out the window.
Who's going to collect the garbage? who knows? who cares?"

　　　　　- The Digger Papers

"The telephone girl who lends her capacities during the greater part of the living day to the manipulation of a technical routine that has an eventually high efficiency value but that answers to no spiritual needs of her own is an appalling sacrifice to civilization. As a solution to the problem of culture she is a failure--the more dismal the greater her natural endowment...
"The American Indian who solves the economic problem with salmon spear and rabbit snare operates on a relatively low level of civilization, but he represents an incomparably higher solution than our telephone girl to the questions that culture has to ask of economics.
"There is no question here of the immediate utility...of economic effort, nor of any sentimentalizing regrets to the passing of the natural man. The Indian's salmon spearing is a culturally higher type of activity than that of the telephone girl simply because there is no sense of spiritual frustration during its prosecution, no feeling of subservience of tyrannous yet largely inchoate demands, because it works in naturally with all the rest of the Indian's activities instead of standing out as a desert patch of merely economic effort in the whole of life."

- Edward Sapir, "Culture, Genuine & Spurious"

Telephone girl or Indian? The choice doesn't seem too appealing. But in America, the most sophisticated civilization history has ever known built on the most barbaric culture, that's what the choice boils down to. The high and low status telephone girls of America are spiritual monsters. They have an astounding ability to consume the lies of media and politicians, to watch atrocities from Vietnam to Chicago, and make excuses; in short, to mold themselves into new kinds of organisms whose ordinary spiritual needs go unsatisfied, and whose resulting neuroses are kept in check by drugs, liquor, pornography, adultery, racism, war, sadism, perversity, bad movies and odd forms of religion.

The Indians, a tiny, splintered group, have varied roots. Some are young Black militants, some are white middle class rebels, some are people with 9-to-5 jobs, teetering on the brink. Some are real Indians. They are not Trots, they are usually not liberals. Often we get political and cultural radicals confused. Bob Dylan is more revolutionary than Fred Halstead, and you know it.

When I lived in New York, until six months ago, it was obvious that very few Blacks were Indians, cultural revolutionaries. These few were what the Panthers, in their recent falling out with SNCC, meant by black hippies. They were common sights on St. Marks Place but rare on Brooklyn's Fulton Street.

When I got to San Francisco, I saw the difference at once. The Panthers had made their mark. Every Black person has heard of them; every young Black understands the challenge they present. At first, I thought the young Fillmore Blacks were tremendously arrogant. They were, compared to what I was used to. I could see in each one, whether he wore his hair Afro or not, the influence of the Black is Beautiful thing.

It's hard to say if the white Indians have made a comparable impact. As our Black brothers are fond of telling us, we can always cross back over. Dope may be liberating, but there are Potheads who are also bank presidents. Generally, the new ways of living whites devise to avoid being telephone girls, are expressed by media, not by arrogance or manners.

"In San Francisco, it began to some extent with the media people, which meant a tacit conspiracy of everybody to take them all to bed, to turn them all on, to turn them into friends. I mean, what's the point of having enemies when you can have friends?" --The Digger Papers

The Digger Papers, published in San Francisco during the Free City movement a few months back, is an articulate expression of the white revolution. It makes distinctions between politicos, hippies and yippies quite irrelevant. Its concern is how to live; and that is culture.

Free City was a very ambitious attempt to make new ways of living viable through communal food distribution, housing, garages, news services, stores and treasuries. These economic foundations were based on an updated Marxist dictum: "Every brother should have what he needs to do his thing."

"We have kicked the habits of Success, Ambition, Cleanliness/Godliness, Duty, Purpose, Loyalty, Citizenship and in some rare and beautiful instances, as with Allen Ginsberg, the loss of the European sense of Self."

Scant months since the appearance of the Digger Papers, Free City has disappeared. In San Francisco, and everywhere white radical communities exist, the Revolution is a mess. The Movement is suffering under immense pressures of paranoia and persecution. The country-commune people criticize the city-political people for not knowing about life processes. We're in limbo, and the dubious phenomena of Eye Magazine or hippie beads in Bergdorf's seem more depressing than encouraging.

In the Digger Papers is a piece called "The Birth of Digger Batman." It's a kitchen delivery, without anaesthetic or forceps. For a while, it looks like the kid's head is in the wrong position and it's going to be a disaster. Everyone sits around in a kind of communal agony. But at last the kid is born and, naturally, named Digger. There's a premonition in this story of the trouble white radicals are having. But at last the kid is born.

Finally, the Digger Papers offer some advice:
"There will be signs. We will know when to slip away and let those murderous fools rip themselves to pieces.
"In the meantime, stay healthy. There are hundreds of miles of walk and lots of work to be done. Keep your mind. We will need it. Stake out a retreat. Learn berries and nuts and fruit and small animals and all the plants. Learn water."

San Francisco Express Times Jan 1969

The Post Competitive Comparative Game of a Free City

Our state of awareness demands that we uplift our efforts from competitive game playing in the underground to the comparative roles *of free families in free cities.*

We must pool our resources and interact our energies to provide the freedom for our individual activities.

In each city of the world there is a loose competitive underground composed of groups whose aims overlap, conflict, and generally enervate the desired goal of autonomy. By now we all have guns, know how to use them, know our enemy, and are ready to defend. We know that we ain't gonna take no more shit. So it's about time we carried ourselves a little heavier and got down to the business of creating free cities within the urban environments of the western world.

Free Cities are composed of Free Families (eg., in San Francisco: Diggers, Black Panthers, Provos, Mission Rebels and various revolutionist gangs and communes) who establish and maintain services that provide a base of freedom for autonomous groups to carry out their programs without having to hassle for food, printing facilities, transportation, mechanics, money, housing, working space, clothes, machinery, trucks, etc.

At this point in our revolution it is demanded that the families, communes, black organizations and gangs of every city in America co-ordinate and develop Free Cities where everything that is necessary can be obtained for free by those involved in the various activities of the individual clans.

Every brother should have what he needs to do his thing.

Free City:
An outline . . . a beginning
Each service should be performed by a tight gang of brothers whose commitment should enable them to handle an overload of work with ability and enthusiasm. 'Tripsters' soon get bored, hopefully before they cause an economic strain.

Free City Switchboard / Information Center
should coordinate all services, activities, and aid and direct assistance where it is most needed. Also provide a reference point for legal aid, housing, machinery, etc.; act as a mailing address for dislocated groups or individuals and guide random energies where they are most needed. (The work load usually prevents or should prevent the handling of messages from parents to their runaway children . . . that should be left up to the churches of the community.)

Free Food Storage and Distribution Center
should hit every available source of free food—produce markets, farmers markets, meat packing plants, farms, dairies, sheep and cattle ranches, agricultural colleges, and giant institutions (for the uneaten vats of food)—and fill up their trucks with the surplus by begging, borrowing, stealing, forming liaisons and communications with delivery drivers for the left-overs from their routes . . . best method is to work in two shifts; morning group picks up the food-stuffs and the afternoon shift delivers it to the list of Free Families and the poor peoples of the ghettos—everyday, hard work.

This gang should help people pool their welfare food stamps and get their old ladies or a group to open a free restaurant for people on the move and those who live on the streets. Giant scores should be stored in a garage-type warehouse equipped with freezers and its whereabouts known only to the Free Food Gang. This group should also set up and provide help for canning, preserving, bread baking, and feasts and anything and everything else that has to do with food.

Free City Garage and Mechanics
to repair and maintain all vehicles used in the various services. The responsibility for the necessary tools and parts needed in their work is entirely theirs and usually available by maintaining friendly relations with junkyards, giant automotive schools, and generally scrounging around those areas where auto equipment is easily obtained. The garage should be large enough and free of tripsters who only create more work for the earnest mechanics.

Free City Bank and Treasury
this group should be responsible for raising money, making free money, paying rents, for gasoline, and any other necessary expenses of the Free City Families. They should also organize and create small rackets (cookie sales, etc.) for the poor kids of the ghettos and aid in the repair and maintenance of the machinery required in the performance of the various services.

Free City Legal Assistance
high style, hard nosed, top class lawyers who are willing to defend the rights of the Free City and its services . . . no

honky, liberal bleeding heart, guilt-ridden advocates of justice, but first class case-winners . . . turn on the best lawyers who can set up air-tight receivership for free money and property, and beat down the police harassment and brutality of your areas.

Free City Housing and Work Space
rent or work deals with the urban gov't to take over spaces that have been abandoned for use as carpentry shops, garages, theatres, etc.; rent whole houses, but don't let them turn into crash pads. Set up hotels for new arrivals or transients by working out deals with small hotel owners for free rooms in exchange for light house-work, porter duties, etc. Big warehouses can be worked on by environmental artists and turned into giant free dance-fiesta-feast palaces.

A strong trio of serious business-oriented cats should develop this liberation of space within the cities and be able to work with the lawyers to make deals and out-maneuver urban bureaucracies and slum landlords . . . one of the main targets for space are the churches who are the holders of most real-estate and they should be approached with a no-bullshit hard-line.

Free City Stores and Workshops
nothing in these stores should be throwaway items . . . space should be available for chicks to sew dresses, make pants to order, re-cut garments to fit, etc. The management should all be life-actors capable of turning bullshitters into mud. Important that these places are first class environments with no trace of salvation army/st. vinnie de paul charity rot. Everything groovy. Everything with style . . . must be first class. *It's all free because it's yours!*

Free Medical Thing
should be established in all poverty areas and run by private physicians and free from any bureaucratic support. The Free City Bank should try to cover the expenses, and pharmaceutical houses should be hit for medical supplies, etc. Important that the doctors are *brothers* and do not ask to be salaried or are not out to make careers for themselves (witness Dr. David Smith of the Hippie Free Clinic in San Francisco who is far from a brother . . . very far).

Free City Hospital
should be a house converted into bed space and preferably with a garden and used for convalescence and people whose minds have been blown or who have just been released from a state institution and who need the comfort and solace of their people rather than the cold alienated walls of an urban institution.

Free City Environmental and Design Gang
gangs of artists from universities and art institutes should be turned on and helped in attacking the dank squalor of the slums and most of the Free City Family dwellings . . . paint landscapes on the sides of tenements . . . fiberglass stairwells . . . make crazy. Tight groups of good painters, sculptors, designers who comfortably construct environments for the community. Materials and equipment can be hustled from university projects and manufacturers, etc.

Free City Schools
schools designed and run by different groups according to the consciousness of their Free Families (e.g., Black Man's Free School, Anarchist's Creative Arts School, etc.). The schools should utilize the space liberated for them by the Free City Space Gang.

Free City News and Communication Company
providers of a daily newspaper, monthly magazine, free Gestetner and printing of notices for other groups and any special bulletins and propaganda for the various families of the Free City. The machinery should be kept in top condition and supplied by any of the various services. Paper can be scavenged at large mills and cut down to proper working size.

Free City Events . . . Festival Planning Committees
usually involves several Families interacting to sponsor tours for the kids . . . Balls, Happenings, Theatre, Dance, and spontaneous experiments in joy . . . Park Events usually are best set up by hiring a 20-foot flat-bed truck for the rock band to use as a stage and to transport their equipment; people should be advised by leaflets to bring food to exchange with their neighbors; banners, props, balloons, kites, etc. should be handled by a committee; an electrician should

be around to run the generator and make sure that the P.A. systems work; hard work made easy by giving responsible people the tough jobs.

Co-operative Farms and Campsites
the farms should be run by experienced hands and the Free Land settled on by cottage industrial people who will send their wares into the Free City. The farms must produce vital food for the families . . . some free land that is no good for farming should be used as campsites and/or cabin areas for citizens who are in need of country leisure, as well as kids who could use a summer in the woods.

Scavenger Corps and Transport Gang
is responsible for garbage collection and the picking up and delivery of items to the various services, as well as liberating anything they think useful for one project or another. They are to be responsible for the truck fleet and especially aware of the economic strain if trucks are mis-used by tripsters.

Free City Tinkers and Gunsmiths, Etc.
will repair and keep things going in the houses . . . experienced repair men of all sorts, electricians, and carpenters. They should maintain a warehouse or working space for their outfit.

Free City Radio, TV and Computer Stations
demand Free time on radio and TV stations; demand a Free City frequency to set up your own stations; rent computers to call the punches for the revolution or use them in any constructive way possible.

Free City Music
Free Music
Where is the place that your music comes from
do you know
What determines the rest between phrases
The Interval that grows from the cluster
of sounds around it
Hanging behind the beat
Clipping the front of it
That's the gift
The thing that blows through a body that responds to
spirit and a mind that doesn't lock itself
It's that thing
We're all made of, forget about, and then try to grab again
That thing that's all there and all free
The fretless infinite string banjo has invented new means
of music which it must buy from itself to sing

The Digger Papers
reprinted from The Realist

 LIBERATION July/August 1968

THE HAVES AND THE HAVE NOTS

Nixon talks about upholding the "vital center" just as LBJ talked about "consensus." These concepts contain the same ideas: uphold the existing America and the status quo; appeal to a mythical average American. Subtract from this vital center black people, Wallaceites, disillusioned McCarthyites, great numbers of high school and college students on the left, poor people, and other dissatisfied groups and the consensus dwindles down to almost nothing.

ARN STRASSER *Extra*

★★★★★★★★★

If I am not for myself, who am I?
If I am not for others, what am I?
If not now, when?

MAIMONIDES

Gov. Ronald Reagan, in Sacramento said the Berkeley disturbances were part of a "nationwide conspiracy of New Left elements."

"I think it's time for all of us to quit being naive about this and quit pretending this is just a spontaneous outburst of youthful agitation," he said. "This [refering to both Chicago and Berkeley] is a plot, there is a conspiratorial side to it. We might as well wake up to the fact that this is plain to all of us."

★★★★★★★★☆

We have no leaders; we are all leaders.

Reply of the University of Minnesota's radical 17th of November Movement to President Malcolm Moo's invitation to send their leader to meet with him.

However unpalatable it may be, the truth is that again and again useful reforms have been achieved in Britain by force after argument has failed. The way to get to the public is to create a disturbance. Thus the temptation of action, not words, is increased.

JO GRIMOND, former leader of the British Liberal party.

★★★★★★ ★★★

The hippies, the yippies. We're niggers all, man. The hippies and yippies are trying to break out of the system and work their way down, and we're trying to break in and work up. And when we meet... America will die. It will die in 18 months.

DICK GREGORY

★★★★★ ★★★★

History advances in disguise; it appears on stage wearing the mask of the preceding scene, and we tend to lose the meaning of the play. The blame of course is not history's, but lies in our vision, encumbered with memory and images learned in the past. We see the past superimposed on the present, even when the present is a revolution.
Régis Debray, French professor and revolutionary, in his book Revolution in the Revolution?

EVEN IN THE AMERIKAN HEARTLAND: FATHERS AND SONS WHO DON'T SPEAK TO EACH OTHER NOW

In Indiana, Nostalgia Prevails

By BERNARD WEINRAUB
Special to The New York Times

BLUFFTON, Ind., Dec. 1—The sycamore and red oak trees are bare now. At dusk a cold rain sweeps over the plowed black soil, spattering the shingled roofs of farm houses where men in knee-length rubber boots pour oil over rusty tractors and plows and cornpickers.

In the evening, the farmers and wives of Wells County in northeastern Indiana drive to Main Street. They park beneath the shimmering holiday tinsel and stroll into Gamble's or Murphy's to buy rolls of Christmas foil or velveteen bows and chat with friends about their children at Indiana University and the shopping trip to Fort Wayne and low farm prices and high taxes and, finally, the uneasiness that grips them.

"There seems to be a movement of people, a restlessness here," said James Murray, the principal of the elementary school. "Gosh, last month seven new kids were enrolled in school. There's a coming in and going out. I don't know . . ."

"The town is changing just like the rest of the country," observed Miss Elizabeth Abel Mason, the Bluffton librarian.

"Somehow . . ." she paused and breathed deeply. "Somehow there's so much more to contend with now."

"We have a strong religion here and it doesn't vary," said the exuberant 39-year-old minister of the First Presbyterian Church, the Rev. Henry Churchill. "It's a religion of behave yourself, keep your nose clean, be harmless, be a good fellow, be a moderate drinker if not an abstainer. It wears a Christian guise."

He was seated in an office cluttered with books and pamphlets on the ghettos. "People are jaded by this now, tired of it," he said. "It doesn't fill whatever restless longings they have. There's a real longing for significance."

Victory for Nixon

This longing is perhaps underlined by the Presidential elections, in which Richard M. Nixon defeated Hubert H. Humphrey in the usually Democratic county. In Bluffton, and dozens of towns like Bluffton, Mr. Nixon overwhelmingly triumphed over Vice President Humphrey—a victory, according to the voters here, for normalcy and balance and toughness.

Bluffton, a flatlands town nestled in the heart of Wells County, is 23 miles south of

Fort Wayne and 100 miles northeast of Indianapolis, with tomatoes and red clover and wheat and corn sprouting each spring from the rich black and loam soil all around. It is a city where 7,500 persons live in white and beige stucco and brick homes built years ago by farmers who moved north from Kentucky and the Dutch and German immigrants who prospered with the land.

Insults are a cure for boys with long hair, says Paul E. Gerwig, the police chief.

The town's wide and silent streets—and the sprawling farms in Wells County—evoke a sense of order and stability...

Nonetheless, a vague personal and public melancholy lingers over Bluffton and Wells County—a nostalgia for the uncomplicated days before Negroes rioted and students demonstrated and Americans were dying in a bewildering war. And it was from this melancholy that Mr. Nixon's triumph in Bluffton emerged.

"There was a real anti-Democratic protest here, a general distrust and dislike for [President] Johnson because people felt he wasn't telling the story," said James Barbieri, a thin, intense political reporter and business manager for The Bluffton News-Banner. "I don't think anyone's expecting anything great from Nixon except something, somehow, firmer and better."

Conservative Country

"This is a heartland for social and political conservatism," Mr. Barbieri said. "There's a feeling now of a lack of responsibility in the country and people here are worried. They feel that society has to be orderly for progress to be made, that people must obey the rules, that you can't advocate the breakdown of institutions without taking responsibility for what will take its place."

"Patriotism is under fire," he added intensely "That's very serious here."

Mrs. Hermine Wiecking Colson, best bridge player in Bluffton, senses a change.

Three blocks away, at the Caylor-Nickel Medical Clinic, Dr. Harold Caylor sat down at his desk and fingered the stethoscope around his neck. "People here hope to goodness that Nixon can pull the country together and put a stop to some of these things," he said.

"I'm 74," he went on, leaning forward. "When I was a boy my father told me the world don't owe anyone a doggoned thing. I peddled milk. I worked hard. The world don't owe me a damned thing and it still don't owe me a damned thing. Too many people now feel that they have a right to get things for nothing."

105

"There's a drift now, a drift," he said, angrily. "Well, we're still close enough to the soil to realize that food don't grow in supermarkets and you got to work like hell in this life."

The anger, at times vague and indefinable, is coupled with a frightened awareness among parents that the social and political turbulence in the country is having a marked impact on Bluffton.

Parents speak in whispers about fathers and sons who don't speak to each other now over the race issue. There are rumors of high school students "turning on" with cough medicine and even a hint that one or two

may have smoked marijuana —a rumor that shocks parents. Several elderly men and women in Bluffton also speak with a shudder of the number of pregnancies among single girls and broken marriages in the town.

This sense of change and confusion is felt with special poignance by the older men and women of Bluffton.

Basically, we all work hard during the week and on Saturday we go to the lake or the country club or Fort Wayne and on Sunday we go to church," Mrs. Colson, a spry, talkative, 80-year-old widow, said thoughtfully. "Maybe some of that is changing, yes it may be changing."

"There is a generation gap

here," said Mr. Churchill, "but I would think of it as not as severe as other places. The parents here were reared in the Depression and their values were set then. The children were reared in growing affluence. There is a kind of puzzlement of the old with the young and a frustration of the young with the old."

Concern Over Race Issue

But possibly the most immediate concern, one that connects the public and private anxieties of the town, is the looming influx of a handful of Negro families. At the moment, local companies employ several Negroes who live outside Bluffton.

Within the town now there

is one young Negro, a Federal employe who had difficulty finding an apartment, has had the air let out of his tires and has generally been given a cool welcome.

"We don't have those racial riots, we don't have what you call hippies," said Paul E. Gerwig, chief of the town's 12-man police force. "We're a pretty clean, retty decent little community."

"On this hippie business," he went on, "if we see a boy with long hair we insult 'em, we shame 'em a little bit and they cut their hair. On the Negroes, as long as they're decent, as long as they act like they should they'll be treated all right."

"We have one colored boy in town and he's a whip of a

nice fellow," Chief Gerwig said. "Of course when one moves in, you got a block pretty well taken care of. But I don't care. If they're decent, that's all right with me."

In an adjoining office in downtown Bluffton, the Republican Mayor, Carl P. Goodwin, a hefty, 46-year-old funeral director, puffed a cigar at his desk and gazed casually through the window at West Market Street.

"We don't have the problems like strikes and sit-downs and lie-ins," he said. "A colored problem — we don't have that. On the whole, I think it's the best damned town in the state of Indiana."

The New York Times
12/2/68

Mood in Capital: Change Will Be Slow

By MAX FRANKEL
Special to The New York Times

WASHINGTON, Jan. 1 — The President is off in California watching football on television. The Vice President is off in Southeast Asia. Congress has scattered, and the Supreme Court is out of sight.

Only Hubert H. Humphrey, who abhors a vacuum, strolled across the darkened stage yesterday to reflect on the year and the decade, but no single actor speaks for Washington nowadays.

At parties here this week, people were grudgingly granting that 1969 was better — meaning quieter — than 1968 and that this was itself a measure of progress. One

THE OLD AMERIKANS

old-timer offered the tentative thesis that the sixties never happened at all, except in America's dreams and nightmares.

Clearly the dominant feeling here is that change can come over this nation and Government only at its own slow pace, no matter how great the convulsions and confrontations.

The New York Times

ADAM AND EVE
IN AMERIKA

WASHINGTON, Nov. 21 (UPI)—The United States Senate barred the press and the public on Oct. 2, swore its employes to secrecy, locked its doors and discussed the America that would remain following a "nuclear exchange" with the Soviet Union.

"If we have to start over again with another Adam and Eve," Seantor Richard B. Russell of Georgia told his colleagues during that private session, "then I want them to be Americans and not Russians—and I want them on this continent and not in Europe."

He argued that the United States should spend the $5 billion that would be required to construct a "thin" anti-ballistic missile system and should consider it the "foundation stone" of an eventual missile system to protect the United States from a Soviet attack. Such a system, it has been estimated, would cost $40 billion or more.

Ed. Note: Russell (chairman of the Senate Armed Services Committee) has advocated the use of small nuclear weapons in Vietnam, increasing the size of the bombs when necessary.

"To be successful, universities require freedom," he said. "To insure freedom, national defense requires the advanced technology often pioneered by universities. This is the simple, strong, mutual bond about which there should be little debate.

"This mutually beneficial arrangement in historic retrospect has been one of our greatest advances in science, without compromise to professional integrity."

DR. GEORGE W. SHILLING of George Washington Univ, quoted in *The New York Times* 12/30/69

Furthermore, in a society in which a "vigorous appetite for income and wealth" is extolled as the highest good, it is difficult—subversive of the prevailing ideology, in fact—to mobilize popular support

for use of resources for the public welfare or to meet human needs, however desperate they may be. The point is explained clearly by Samuel F. Downer, financial vice president for LTV aerospace, who is quoted by Nossiter in explanation of why "the post-war world must be bolstered with military orders":

"It's basic. Its selling appeal is defense of the home. This is one of the greatest appeals the politicians have to adjusting the system. If you're President and you need a central factor in the economy, and you need to sell this factor, you can't sell Harlem and Watts but you can sell self-preservation, a new environment. We're going to increase defense budgets as long as those Russians are ahead of us. The American people understand this."

From "Knowledge and Power" by Noam Chomsky, in *The New Left* (Porter Sargent)

She also told *Time* magazine's Dean Fischer, "anytime you get somebody marching in the streets, it's catering to revolution. . .my family worked for everything, we even had a deed from the king of England for property in South Carolina. Now these jerks come along and try to give it to the Communists. . .."

Commenting on life in Washington, she said, "it's quite a comedown in many ways. We're not living on the same means we had in Rye, N.Y. I think the government should give us free housing. We'll be happy to go back and make some money."

Ed. Note: From Art Buchwald's column 12/4/69. "She" is Martha Mitchell wife of John Mitchell. The latter is a millionaire Wall St. lawyer, a life-long specialist in municipal bonds (the kind the rich use to evade taxes), now Nixon's attorney general. For more information, see *Justice* by Richard Harris (E.P. Dutton).

Brooklyn & Nebraska

At the Crossroads: A Crumbling Empire

by Marvin Garson

CHICAGO — Usually when I drive cross country I kill miles by cramming my head full of the most absurd mental arithmetic: calculating average speed and gasoline mileage to the nearest tenth, estimating time of arrival at the next town to the nearest minute, predicting exactly where I'll be at each sunrise, sunset, noon, and midnight. The miles I kill aren't mine. They belong to a strange nation of Protestant farmers that lies between the Hudson River and the Berkeley hills. I travel with a sort of transit visa that warns me not to stop for sleep if I don't want to press my luck.

This time it was different. I had two "real" Americans in the car with me. Chris had been raised first on an Illinois farm and then in Indianapolis, Catherine had grown up in the small Illinois town far from Chicago where her Quaker ancestors had settled 100 years ago when that part of the country was the heartland of free-soil sentiment; yet I, a Brooklyn Jew, was the only one who felt at home in the country we traversed. Chris was on his way to France, he thought for good. Catherine was so terrified of her fellow countrymen that every time we stopped for coffee she waited in the car.

I looked freakier than I ever had before: mustache and full beard, bellbottom jeans, pea jacket, and a marvelous army officer's hat with leather visor and bronze shield of the United States. But I felt so much at home in the gas stations and cafes that finally, in the middle of Nebraska, I had to take the car off the Interstate and drive down old Highway 30; and then, in each town, I had to get off Highway 30 and drive around the back streets. We must have spent half an hour just cruising around Kearney, Nebraska, before I noticed the street signs and found myself on Avenue M, heading for East 19th Street.

In Kearney, Nebraska, Avenue M is an unpaved street with cornfields on one side and working class frame houses on the other side, with cannibalized old cars in the front yards.

There is an East 19th Street and Avenue M in Brooklyn, too, and that's where I grew up, in a small three-room apartment in a big gloomy apartment house. The outlandish Hebrew characters stencil-ed on butcher shop windows were as familiar to me as the silhouette of the grain elevator is to the people of the Platte River Valley. I was ashamed of Avenue M and proud of my shame, uneasy, nervous, awkward, and desperate to be "cool." I never suspected that so many people growing up in Kearney, Nebraska, felt the same way.

We had a blowout. After changing the tire we were left with no spare and 600 miles to go to Chicago, so we tried to buy a tire that would fit a Volvo—not easy. We must have stopped that Saturday night at 30 different gas stations in eastern Nebraska and western Iowa, each an important social center for teenage boys. There was no question what we were, me with my beard and bellbottoms and my satirical hat, Chris with his shoulder-length hair, driving a Volvo with California plates and a license-plate holder that went so far as to say San Francisco right on it. At a glance they knew that we were dope-smoking, draft-dodging, cop-hating hippie anarchists, and at a glance we could tell that they respected us for it. The conversation was invariably non-political—invariably about tires, in fact, about tread wear and tire pressures and wheel alignment, about other gas stations that might have the size tire we wanted. On both sides, we talked for the sake of the contact, not the tires.

These Iowa kids are cornfed Wandering Jews. They are embarrassed about where they come from—"nowhere." Their culture comes off the coaxial cable from Hollywood or Manhattan, it consists of Joey Bishop wisecracks about Las Vegas nightclubs they have never seen. Everywhere in the world American power has made people feel embarrassed about their own nationality, made them thirst after Coca Cola; America itself is full of aliens (Jews, Negroes, Puerto Ricans, Indians, Slavic and Mediterranean Catholics) who sense themselves tolerated at best but never welcomed by the WASP; and now the small-town WASP himself lives in terror that he has lost his soul. At its center, the empire is empty.

So, Village Voice reader and McCarthy voter, sensitive intellectual surrounded by uncultured brutes, you may be alienated but you are not alone. The empire is crumbling and the continent is up for grabs. You've got as much a right to a piece of it as anyone else. No more sniveling now, no more hiding behind Justice Douglas and the Ford Foundation and the New York Times; no more teasing that sore of alienation, no more cultivated garret agony. Lenny Bruce suffered for you, he died so that you might be free. Now there's no going back.

A few weeks ago, Rolling Thunder came into the Express Times office and rapped for an hour. He's a lawyer and a Shoshone Indian from Carlin, Nevada. Full of pride, he reported how armed Shoshones had chased the white "sports" hunters off the Ruby Valley Reservation this season. The Indians were finally determined not to back up another step. "We always thought we were alone," he said. "We had no idea there were young white people who were also getting ready to fight."

What are we fighting for? Our souls. Isn't that a worthy cause?

Soul is formed from the mysterious landscapes of childhood. For me it was the paste of slush and sawdust on the floors of Avenue M butchershops, the sound of the subway, the heavy gray mass of the apartment building I lived in, its dim hallways, the elevator buttons I stood on tiptoe to reach, and the ominous superintendent who kept chasing me through the building in my nightmares. For the people of Kearney, Nebraska, and all the other Platte River towns, I suppose the shape of the grain elevators must be deeply embedded in their unconscious minds.

Don't scoff at the soul. Don't call it imaginary. Your soul is formed from powerful doses of reality like mother's tit and favorite toy, family brawl and schoolyard fistfight. Your soul is real all right, much realer than your citizenship, which is spun out of such doubtful material as history textbooks and wire service reports and television commercials.

Establishment politics conspires with capitalism to steal our souls away. Radical politics conspires with art to steal our souls back. In a recent issue of Ramparts, Bobby Seale reminisced about how Huey Newton had clapped earphones on a brother and made him listen to Bob Dylan's "Ballad of a Thin Man." Huey Newton was smoking the same dope and listening to the same music *you* were! Something *is* happening here!

The empire is crumbling everywhere, at the edges and in the center. Why is that so hard to believe? Did you think it would last forever? Did you think history had been brought under control by the two-bit contractors and pseudo-philosophical bankers who try to run this country? A people is tough like a weed, almost ineradicable, can survive for thousands of years; but empires hatch and die off like insects.

Every time I drive across the country there is less of the old two-lane highway and more of the Interstate expressway. The Interstate now runs right up and over Donner Pass, a mile and a half high, where the Donner Party of gold-seeking emigrants were trapped by greed and blizzards and wound up eating each other, Donner Pass where no one knows how may unremembered Chinese coolies were eaten up by the Western Pacific tracks that were hacked out of the mountain slopes to keep California in the Union. The purpose was, in their own words, to *conquer* the continent, and they needed Chinese coolies to do it. Whether or not you're alienated, America certainly is.

The Interstate bypasses the Platte River towns. Main Street is now free of the roaring trucks and quarrelsome tourists and fevered wanderers who slowed down to 40 miles per hour for each nameless town, cursing it as they did. The towns are healing now. Gothenburg, Nebraska, is becoming a beautiful place, more beautiful than all but a handful of California towns and, unlike them, safe from pillage by "developers." Gothenburg voted for Richard Nixon to pacify the riotous proletariat in the great cities of the empire. It was a futile and unimportant gesture.

The people of Gothenburg cannot begin to conceive of what the world looks like to the tiny black child wandering through Chicago trash heaps. Soon they will stop trying. Soon they will cultivate their own souls, and let him cultivate his. Perhaps someday they will even feel confident enough to name their streets.

107

All flesh shall see it together. Apocalypse is the dissolution of the group as numerical series, as in representative democracy, and its replacement by the group as fusion, as communion. . .

N.O. BROWN, *Love's Body*

Distrust sad people, the revolution is joy.

The more I make love, the more I want to make revolution.

GRAFFITTI, Paris, 1968

(The Great Subculture) has taught that man's natural being is to be trusted and followed; that we need not look to a model or rule imposed from outside in searching for the center; and that in following the grain, one is being truly 'moral'. . .All this is subversive to civilization: for civilization is built on hierarchy and specialization. A ruling class, to survive, must propose a Law: a law to work must have a hook into the social psyche — and the most effective way to achieve this is to make people doubt their natural worth and instincts, especially sexual. . .
. . .How do they recognize each other? Not always by beards, long hair, bare feet or beads. The signal is a bright and tender look; calmness and gentleness, freshness and ease of manner. . . . — this is the tribe.

GARY SNYDER, *Why Tribe*

President Johnson: "Let's just see if we can't find something good about America, and let's see if we can't take pride in that flag, and let's see if we can't have a little feeling well up in us and see if we can't get down on our knees sometimes during the night and thank God that I am an American.

"I have traveled around the world and I have been in many countries, and I have even seen the glories of art and architecture. I have seen the sun rise on Mont Blanc. But the most beautiful vision that these eyes ever beheld was that American flag in a foreign land."

We hold these truths to be self-evident; that all men are created equal, that they are endowed by their Creator with certain inalienable rights, and among these are life, liberty and the pursuit of happiness."

The above portion of the American Declaration of Independence—without being identified as such—was recently read to 250 US GIs at a base in West Germany in an experiment conducted by the University of Maryland. The GIs were asked to sign the statement if they agreed. The result: 73% refused to sign because they thought it was subversive.

Extra! Summer 1969

ABBIE HOFFMAN DIDN'T COME OUT OF NOWHERE

Hippies as Activists

From the time that "hippie" became a common term applied to a recognizable but mysterious phenomenon, the question of the political behavior of hippies became significant. The general snap conclusion was quite upsetting to most student activists. "Hippie," to them, meant "drop-out," from political behavior as well as everything else. Many, especially in the East, saw the frustrations of anti-war activity driving young activists into the nirvana of acid hippyism, whence no man returneth to the picket line.

It is true that many "stone hippies" exhibit no recognizable political behavior — other than their life-style itself. The migration from activism into "the hippie thing" is steady and well-defined. But the conclusion that hippies are a-political in general is not true. We have lost touch, testing political activeness with the litmus of old vocabularies. Future histories of this change will say, for example, that the first (and so far the only) significant community-organizing done in our white middle class has been the handiwork of the hippies. And even by the most standard indices of attitude and behavior, hippies tend to be more political than the run of their peers — so much so that Carl Davidson, a central figure in Students for a Democratic Society, has suggested that perhaps three-fourths of SDS's national membership can be roughly classed as hippies.

From "Break Through at Berkeley: The Anatomy of a New Political Style" by Michael Rossman, *Center Magazine* May 1968

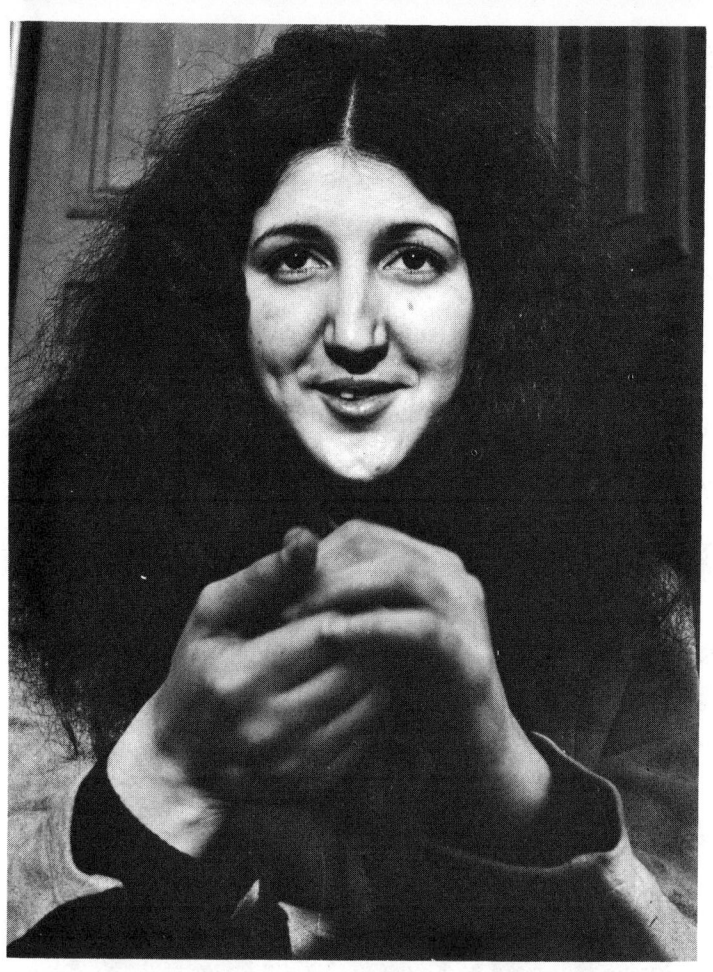

THE FAMILY

You could see them sitting around fires, maybe near a lean-to they had built from leaves and branches or near some crummy outasite truck or next to a big worn green tent. The new family. Tribes sharing their possessions, breaking down the obsolete patterns of race or religion or background. Classless. Barriers broken down by dope and by learning to survive in the death culture. These were the children of the Universe searching for the new city in the midst of the old one, the new people of an electronic age that were breaking down the barriers of a worn-out, wasteful, suicidal, killer world. So much resistance, so much hope, so many symbols stolen and corrupted. Woodstock was the third largest city in New York for three days. Strength came in numbers and in the common experience of 500,000 freaks and potential freaks. The new family. Prisoner on the planet earth, begins to grow and gain strength.

Max Yasgur's 600 acre dairyfarm is a varied landscape of hills, woods, corn fields and lakes. It was this beautiful country that set the tone for Woodstock. For days before the first band played people started arriving at the farm to set up their camps among the trees and on the hillsides overlooking the music area. The 80 ft. stage was still being built and the fences had hardly been started. It was real country and for those smart enough not to have bought a ticket, it was free.

By Friday, the official opening of the "Aquarian Exposition", thousands more than expected had arrived and the media was beaming out a disaster story: thousands of hippies invade Bethel; food and water shortage threatens crowd of 300,000; rain, mud and bad acid create health hazard at Rock Festival.

Friday *was* a bad day. The local Bethel market sold out of every item in the store except for a solitary cup of Gefillte fish. Water wells dug for the occasion started pumping mud. Water trucks couldn't get through the jam on 17-B. Helicopters

started the process of moving in food, medical supplies and serving as ambulances and transportation for performers. The process didn't end until Monday. But still there was never a Woodstock disaster.

The various dope freaks, college students, etc. that made up the 500,000 who "invaded" Bethel spent three days learning to share, relax and face the elements together. Food and dope was passed around freely, there wasn't a fight or even disagreement and people crammed themselves shoulder to shoulder to listen to the music. When the rains came Sunday, people danced in the downpour or crowded together under plastic sheets or played football in the mud or joined in chants of "Ah Shit" and "Fuck the Rain." This was a real sign of the different culture and everyone felt it. Can you imagine "Fuck the Rain" at Yankee Stadium? Not yet anyway.

Especially peaceful and productive was Movement City, a city separated by woods from the main music and camping area. The movement had its own music and entertainment and even a puppet show. Political groups ran booths and the underground press and TV freaks were there. Hog Farm, a Santa Fe commune that worked closely with the promoters as an auxiliary police force were centered in the city. The Hog Farmers, using bread sucked out of the promoters served literally thousands of good natural meals at the city. The real problems with movement city, as Ted Granklin mentions in his article, was how separate the city was from the rest of Woodstock and how little effort was made to attract people to the city either by action or signs.

The problems with Hog farms were more primary. The Commune worked hard, but worked very closely with the promoters. Hog Farmers joined the obnoxious announcers on stage in telling people they were on trial." This bullshit only served to obscure what was really on trial at Woodstock: the outside society where

three days of relative peace and love were a total abnormality. It was cool that the farmers used the promoters' profits, but how they used the money was the important thing.

The media started picking up the good vibes from Woodstock by the second day — they couldn't ignore them. By Sunday stories about the festival of peace and cooperation were churning out of TV, radio and newspaper offices. The articles were like those early articles on Haight Street; full of polite adjectives, vivid contrasts and that journalistic distance we have all come to understand and hate. It was as if the media were watching a new breed of animal at the zoo and reacting with surprise at how gentle the animals were.

A new lesson in crowd control was learned by the cops. With white kids not yet completely outside the culture, as many black people are, maybe it was best to cool it on the guns and stocks. At Woodstock, the cops wore bright red jackets with the words love and peace, and a dove printed on them. It was the Age of Aquarian burn in its full glory: cops giving V signs as they quietly took people away. Form without content, the symbols of revolution without change.

The important thing about Woodstock encampment was for the people who participated in it, not for the people who watched it. For many people it was the first taste of a new, non-exploitive culture: it was swimming in the nude, it was tripping, it was sharing and relaxing and surviving without trying to sell something or ripping off a brother. It was working in the hospital talking people off of bad trips; it was meeting new people. It was just the beginning of a new culture, but it *was* a beginning.

WE WILL NOT BE COOPTED. WE WANT EVERYTHING.

 extra Summer 1969

111
new american

From the Front of the Bus

Colloquy March 1970

The New Generation: en masse, is it always a challenge, a threat, or a cause? When the young are doing their thing, does it necessarily get in the way of everybody else's thing? The Woodstock Rock Festival is mentioned elsewhere in this issue of Colloquy. Here, bus drivers of the Short Line Company, who transported the New Generation to Woodstock, file their reports of the experience.

"All I have to say is next year I'll be the first to sign up to drive them anywhere. A kid with long hair is welcome on my bus. They don't look at the public the way the public looks at them. They treated me with respect. Even love. They were neat, polite, full of fun and good humor and not a bit of sarcasm."

"The most important thing in those kids' lives was getting to the Festival in time. When I told them we would be several hours late on account of the traffic, they didn't say boo. I was really impressed with the way they shared everything."

"What a wonderful, happy bunch. They never offended me or mistreated me in any way. Once, loading up, I told them there were no more seats. These kids didn't mind waiting for the next bus. Everybody had a smile. I tried to give them a good ride. They appreciate everything."

"I don't understand why they wear long hair but now I don't care. It's a free country. And they're the most no-griping, no-complaining, patient and generous, respectful bunch of kids I ever met. Come on kids and ride with me. It's a pleasure driving you."

"We were stuck in traffic for three hours up there and the only noise I heard were jokes about the EXPRESS sign on the bus. Their fashion may be a little sloppy, but they were clean and generous. It's sort of live and let live with them."

"There was this little girl who made homemade bread. She was so proud. She insisted I have some. We have a lot to learn from them about getting along together. They can ride with me anytime."

MO-TOWN JUSTICE

Law enforcement in the United States does not serve primarily the function of maintaining order. In times of crisis, ·particularly, it is more often, as in Detroit, the major source of disorder. It serves another function more fundamental to keeping American society going. It expresses, under conditions of impunity, the rage and aggression of a disappointed *lumpenbourgeoisie* against any style of life that seems either more privileged or more authentic. In his book, Hersey stresses his conclusion that the underlying basis of white racism is probably sexual, reasoning from the mutilation of the Algiers Motel corpses, the language of the police and National Guardsmen, and the fact that the most violent of the police seem also to be those who have served most enthusiastically on the vice-squad and been most ingenious in entrapping whores, pimps, and queers. He is right, I think, as far as his reasoning goes; but it does not go far enough. For sexuality, though surely the greatest triumph of the senses and hence the key to the most profound authenticity — or betrayal — is only one channel of spontaneous self-expression, and the *lumpenbourgeoisie* is against all of them. And the language and attitude of the police and of much of the working class generally toward hippies, pot-blowers, and other creatures who strike them as obscenely subjective is much the same.

From a review of John Hersey's *The Algiers Motel Incident* by Edgar Friedenberg for *The New York Review of Books* 8/1/68

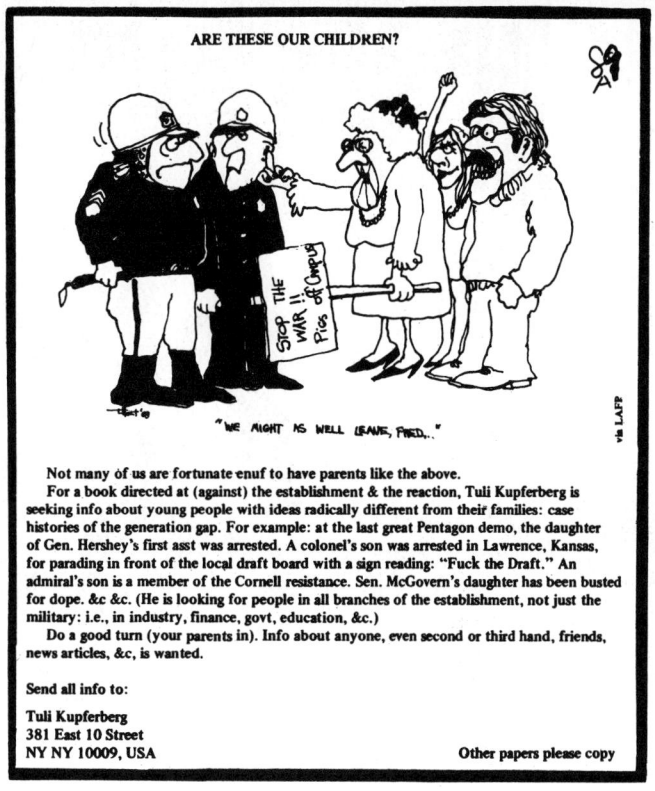

ARE THESE OUR CHILDREN?

"WE MIGHT AS WELL LEAVE, FRED..."

Not many of us are fortunate enuf to have parents like the above.
For a book directed at (against) the establishment & the reaction, Tuli Kupferberg is
seeking info about young people with ideas radically different from their families: case
histories of the generation gap. For example: at the last great Pentagon demo, the daughter
of Gen. Hershey's first asst was arrested. A colonel's son was arrested in Lawrence, Kansas,
for parading in front of the local draft board with a sign reading: "Fuck the Draft." An
admiral's son is a member of the Cornell resistance. Sen. McGovern's daughter has been busted
for dope. &c &c. (He is looking for people in all branches of the establishment, not just the
military: i.e., in industry, finance, govt, education, &c.)
Do a good turn (your parents in). Info about anyone, even second or third hand, friends,
news articles, &c, is wanted.

Send all info to:

Tuli Kupferberg
381 East 10 Street
NY NY 10009, USA

Other papers please copy

A Night in a Jail in Capital: 85 Men in Flooded Cells

By DAVID K. SHIPLER

Special to The New York Times

WASHINGTON, Nov. 16—Scummy water an inch deep covered the floor at one end of the long, dimly lit cellblock last night.

One by one, policemen led the young men, arrested during antiwar protests here yesterday, past the dry cells and into those that were flooded until five people crammed each windowless, 4-by-6-foot cubical.

"Pigs! Pigs! a youth shouted as the steel door clanged shut behind him.

There was not enough room for everyone to sit down. Two metal bunk frames without mattresses hung by chains in double-decker fashion, but a lip of steel around the edges of the frames dug into the youths' legs, making sitting painful.

At least one man at a time had to stand in a puddle, and water seeped into sneakers and shoes. Most of the dry cells remained empty.

About 85 men stayed that way for nine hours of the night in the basement of police headquarters, and the discomfort produced muttered curses, shouted obscenities, dry humor, some friction, a lot of camaraderie and, for a few, a political shift to the left.

Two Oppose Protests

Those arrested said that the police had seized only a few members of the radical factions whose rock and bottle throwing had shattered the calm of a predominantly peaceful day.

A large proportion of the 85 in the cellblock (out of a total of 135 arrested) said that they had been taken into custody while looking for a bus, sitting under a tree or walking along a street from which the radicals had just fled. Two said that they did not favor protests and were not demonstrators at all but had been in Washington sightseeing.

"I should have went to a movie," one of them remarked. He was a 20-year-old named Bobby from Flatbush in Brooklyn, whose father was a New York policeman. He asked that his last name not be used.

His friend, Al Demutis, 18, had recently passed an entrance test for the New York City Police Department and hoped to become a patrolman.

"One of my friends came to demonstrate." he said. "We just came for the ride to get out for the weekend, that's all. I don't go for either side. I don't give a damn. I haven't read too much about it, you know. I don't go for demonstrating."

He said that he and Bobby had gone looking for their friend, who had failed to show up at their minibus. Their search took them into the area of the demonstrations, and they were charged with disorderly conduct, as were most of those arrested.

Hitchhiked From Oregon

Reed Williams, though, had come to demonstrate. Mr. Williams, a 20-year-old with curly, light brown hair over his ears, started hitchhiking last Monday from Portland, Oregon.

He looked out through the thick bars of his cell door. "All of a sudden you're put in this cage, and you're not a human being," he said quietly. "Well, maybe some more people are gonna realize that it's just Tricky Dickie who's the enemy."

That theory was popular on the cellblock. It seemed plausible to many of the prisoners that high officials had directed the police to make their stay in jail as long and uncomfortable as possible to augment, in effect, the $10 or $25 fine that accompanied a guilty plea in most of the cases.

Nobody was allowed to make a telephone call during the nine hours behind bars. But the police officers themselves seemed too friendly and polite, some protesters reasoned, to be initiating this on their own.

A Police Department spokesman attributed the lack of phoning privileges to the skeleton crew he said was manning offices during the demonstrations. And he said that the crowding of prisoners into flooded cells may have resulted from the fact that "in times of emergency and necessity you work out simplified systems."

The hard fact of jail simply confirmed the radicals' views of the world, but it shocked and outraged the more moderate protesters.

Hammers on Bars

Again and again, a 30-year-old salesman from Boston hammered his fists on the bars, exclaiming, "I'm an American! I'm an American! I came down here as an American for peace! Let me out of here!"

After more than an hour, his hands were cut and swollen, and he collapsed in the water on the floor. His cellmates hauled him into a lower bunk frame.

Every new man who came in was asked by the others if he had any cigarettes and whether he knew what was happening in the streets. One middle-aged man had a cigarette, and he reached as far as he could through his bars to hand it to a youth across the corridor.

No Arts and Crafts?

The others in the nearby cells cheered and groaned as the two stretched their arms and strained to make cigarette meet fingertips. They failed. The man then tossed the cigarette, and it fell just short of the cell into a puddle of water.

The boredom quickly returned. "Hey, man. Don't they have some arts and crafts in here?" asked Bobby. "Can't I make a license plate or something?"

Then he added, "Washington, D.C.'s police force—Spiro's finest. Pigs!"

How about his father?

"Oh, he's a traffic cop."

Al Demutis, the prospective New York patrolman, had stopped defending the police, and his optimism that release was imminent had worn away to almost nothing.

Was he still going to be a cop?

"In a small town," he said.

Then, at 3 o'clock this morning, as a roach crawled along the wall of the cell, an officer opened the door to let them out to post their $10 collateral.

After nine hours, the two young men from Flatbush walked out calling the police 'pigs" and flashing the V-sign for peace.

Times Reporter Arrested

David K. Shipler, a reporter for The New York Times, was arrested Saturday night while covering the antiwar demonstrations here. He was charged with disorderly conduct.

Mr. Shipler was on the sidewalk near Constitution Avenue and 12th Street, taking notes on the arrest of demonstrators in the street, when an officer grabbed him and placed him in a police wagon.

After nine hours in jail, he was released after posting $25 collateral. The trial was set for Tuesday.

The New York Times

TORTURE AT THE 17TH PRECINCT
BY JOMO RASKIN

On December 9th I was arrested at 50th street and 5th Avenue during a demonstration and march to protest the murder of Chairman Fred Hampton. The demonstration started at Park Avenue and 48th Street. Nixon was in the Waldorf receiving an award. At 50th and 5th windows had been broken in Sak's 5th Avenue. Six windows. Inside people were doing their Christmas shopping. A policeman had been struck in the face. Blood was on his face. He took 17 stitches. I was walking down 50th Street. A plainclothes pig ran toward me, jumped on my back. At first I didn't know he was a pig. Only when he handcuffed me was I sure. And he never identified himself as a cop. Several other pigs jumped me, 4 or 5. Pigs had been waiting inside St. Patrick's Cathedral, which is opposite Sak's. They weren't praying. A few dozen demonstrators had tried to escape the police by entering the church; had tried to kneel down and pray for revolution, or peace, or safety. But the pigs inside the Church pushed them out and clubbed them on the Church steps. No sanctuary, no place.

Four or five pigs pushed and pulled me to the sidewalk. There was broken glass everywhere. I remember one pig with blue splotched bell bottom trousers and a moustache who kept yelling, "He's mine, he's mine. Leave him to me." Awfully possessive, these pigs. And he whacked me over the head with his nightstick—his identification mark. I put my hands over my head. Blood trickled down my face and my neck. It reminded me of my football days, of a big pile up on the 5 yard line. Then it was still. The noisy street was quiet. I was pulled to my feet and handcuffed to Bob Reilly, an actor, a teacher, the toughest battler I know. Arrested again. We were thrown into the pig car, taken to the 18th Precinct, driven down 5th Avenue, past all the expensive stores, past the stores filled with the loot of the world.

At the 18th the pigs stood us in a corner, banged me in the head a few times. The pig with bell bottoms and a moustache was puffing away on a big cheap cigar. The blood kept flowing. A few minutes after we arrived cops came in with another demonstrator. They threw him to the floor. He had long curly black hair. They yelled at him to get up. "Have mercy," he cried. He couldn't get up. They kicked him in the stomach, the ribs, the back. When I saw him in jail the next day at 100 Center Street, he had a big bandage over his forehead.

Reilly and I walked upstairs, the pigs behind us, prodding us on. The pigs filled out cards, asked us questions. "Where do you live?" "Where do you work?" "When were you born?" They didn't like the fact that I teach at the State University at Stony Brook. "This scum bag is a teacher at Stony Brook," one pig kept repeating. If we didn't answer, or took our time answering questions, they clubbed us. We were put in a cell. One cop spat at me through the bars. His saliva oozed down the wall. He was safe with me behind bars.

Captain Finnigan showed up. He's part of New York's Red Squad. He's at every demonstration taking photos. In his head, he has the face, the file on hundreds of revolutionaries. The word is that he went round to precincts that night pointing out the political heavies. He gave the O.K. to the cops to beat on us. Finnigan had a polaroid camera. He tried over and over again to take my picture, but the camera wasn't working. Finally, he stopped trying. Either he got the photo, or the machine just didn't function. Finnigan looks like a '59 graduate of Princeton. Ivy League. Every hair. graying, is in place. He's got on a three piece tweed suit—Brooks Brothers. He looks like a corporate executive; he's a fascist. Always smiling and giving the orders. A number one enemy of the people.

From the 18th precinct we were taken to Roosevelt Hospital. Reilly got 12 stitches in his head. I got five. We were cleaned up, x-rayed. A pig stood by, all the time, with his gun and night stick. The nurses smiled cheerfully. The interns worked efficiently. Reilly rapped with them about the war, the murder of Fred Hampton. Our friends were waiting outside the Emergency Room Entrance—Barbara, Ann, Annie, Sydney, Mark, Dana, Nancy, Marty. Good to see smiling faces. Exchanged looks—clenched fists. Back to the 18th, a few bangs on the head, bleeding again. A lawyer, Paul Chevigny, shows up, asks how we are, and is quickly hustled out of the precinct. We're taken to the 17th.

The 17th precinct is a torturer's heaven. For an hour, Reilly and I were systematically and efficiently beaten by the pigs. We were taken into the squad room on the 1st floor. There were about 20 cops sitting and standing around. "So here are the pig fighters," they said. They put us in a corner. Our hands were handcuffed behind our backs. Our faces were to the wall. There was a metal coat rack and some pieces of wood with nails in them in the corner. We were thrown up against the metal coat rack and the lumber with the nails. Each pig had his special torture. One hit me with his nightstick in the calf. Another used a black jack on my back. A third hit my elbow with a pair of pliers. A fourth took running jumps and kicked me in the back. Another jumped on my toes. Everyone took turns hitting, kicking, spitting, name calling. I was called Fuck face, douche bag, commie, scum bag, an after-birth. At the start of the beating, Bob Reilly had shouted out, "Hey, lieutenant, how's about breaking up this caucus back here?" The lieutenant never did and the pigs only beat on him worse for yelling out. The brutality was calculated. They stopped, examined our bodies, figured out the best place to hit us, or poke us. They hated us, but they were in control of their emotions and acts. One pig at a desk in the 17th said he hated me because I was taking air from him, because I was breathing his air. They hated us because we're opposed to the war, because we support the NLF, because we defend the Panthers, because we're for armed struggle. They hated us because we're teachers. Their big joke was, "Raskin teaches Riot I, and Reilly teaches Riot II." They hated us because we're rioters, because we're fighters.

The pigs who beat us tried to act tough, but they're wimps. They're puny. It doesn't take any courage for 20 pigs to beat on two guys who are handcuffed behind their backs. On 50th Street and 5th Avenue I saw a pig who was bleeding crying out for an ambulance, wimpering. The TPF (Tactical Police Force) are Hitler youth, New York's SS, and they're afraid, chicken.

For about a half hour, we were beaten in the squad room. Another demonstrator witnessed much of the beating. Then we were taken downstairs into the basement. Everytime you go up or downstairs the pigs try to trip you. They push you up or down the stairs, stick out their feet and warn you, "Watch it, you wouldn't want to hurt yourself." They play petty games. The pig tells you your name is "fuck face.'" "What's your name?" he asks. When you don't answer, he beats you. When you say, "fuck face," he stops. You play cat and mouse, see how much you can take.

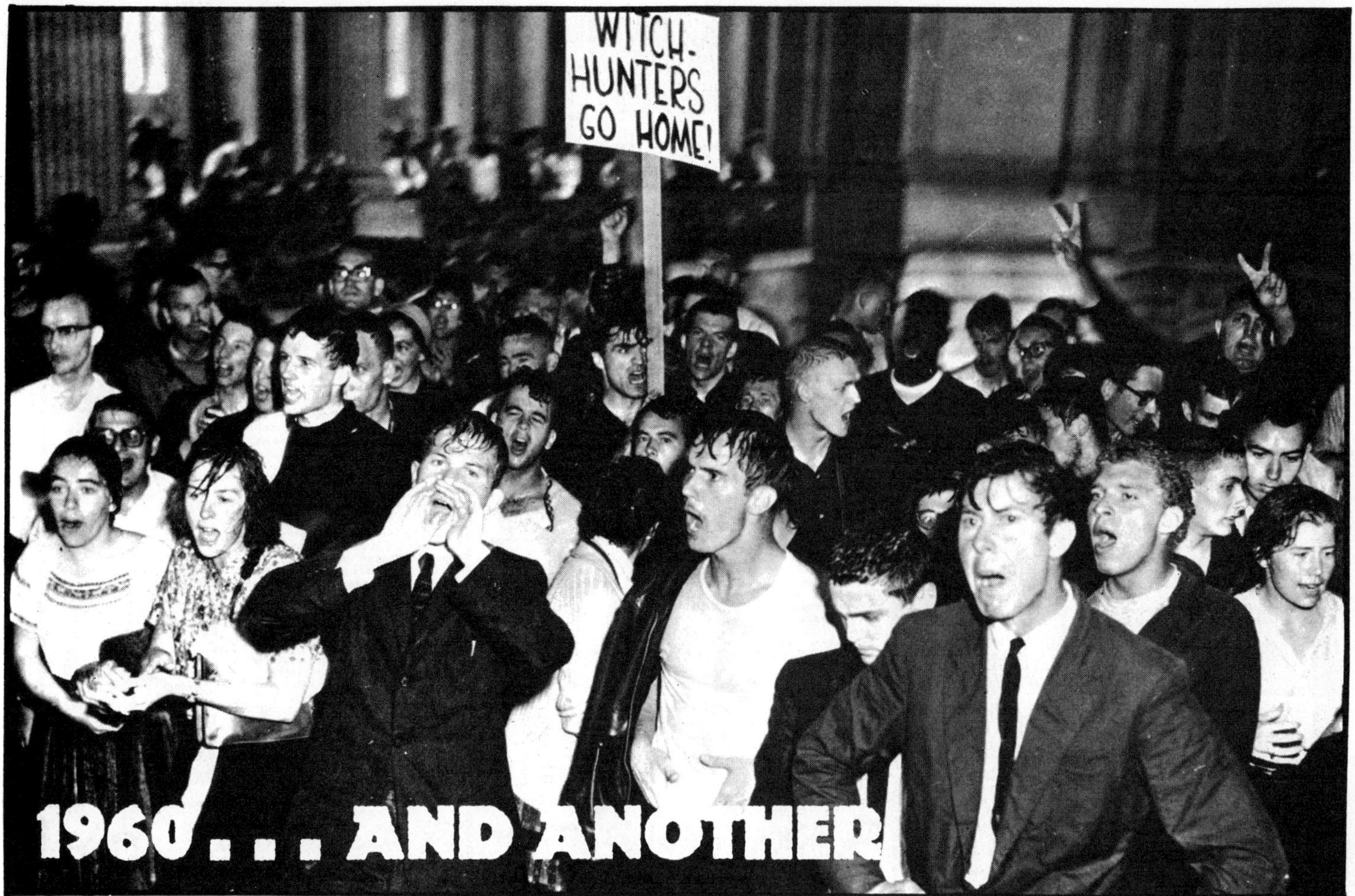
WITCH-
HUNTERS
GO HOME!
1960 . . . AND ANOTHER

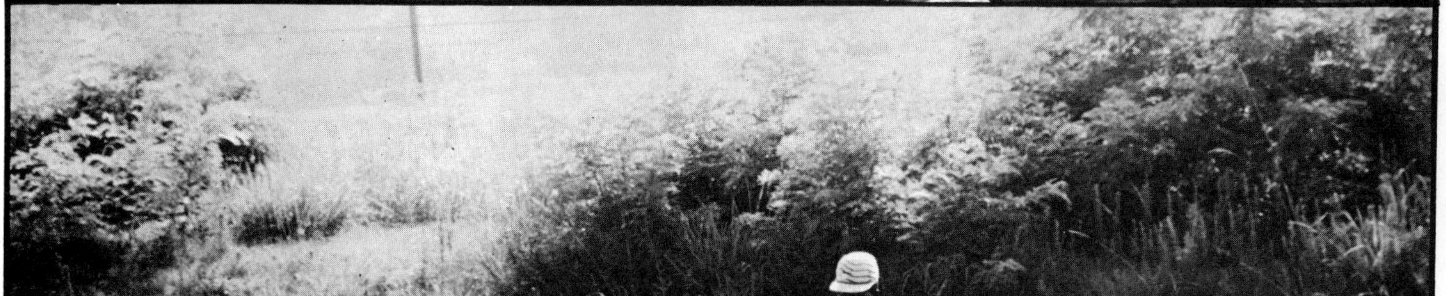
FREEDOM
NOW
1961 . . . AND ANOTHER

Fire hoses failed to disperse these San Francisco demonstrators. They were protesting hearings by the House Un-American Activities Committee.

Small, non-violent groups of blacks attempted to desegregate southern transit and eating facilities. They defied the law, seeking arrest and a federal test case.

OUTLAWS OF AMERIKA

8

COMPREHENSION
America is Uninhabitable

THE SYSTEM
DOES NOT WORK

Marvin Garson's Calling Card

Crime Chrome Cream

The Democratic National Convention ended for me in December, with a 20-day stretch in the Chicago House of Correction. I was the only political prisoner in a dormitory of about fifty men—some of them criminals, some outlaws, some there entirely by mistake. In the evenings we would drag out our mattresses and blankets and lay them down in front of the television set. We were like little boys then, without keys or money or watches or wallets or any other adult prerogatives, as we brought out our candy bars, cigarettes and jars of kool-aid, and huddled together on our mattresses to watch television. The guards, when they came in to count us, were friendly and even tender, perhaps a bit regretful that they could not watch television as we did, totally without worries and the wife.

As my time remaining grew short I began to get restless, not with longing for freedom but with fear of it. My last night in jail I could not sleep for the nervous fluttering in my stomach that I had not felt since high school examinations. At 6:51 the following morning, December 21, at the moment the Apollo 8 astronauts were blasting into space, I was rolling up my blankets and scurrying out of the dormitory—afraid. Perhaps that is America's social crisis: fear and trembling in the face of imminent freedom.

Some of the prisoners were radicals. They had pasted pictures of Huey Newton, Eldridge Cleaver, Rap Brown, Malcolm X and Leroi Jones, along with the slogan "Keeping the devils at bay," right over the water cooler, a semi-official location. The radical subculture is accepted today in many jails, but it is still the criminal culture that dominates. Though criminals are the hippest people around—they know how to get by on the bare essentials: soul, muscle, wit—they are also the squarest: so utterly, childishly selfish and self-pitying. It was a great pleasure to get away from them.

Once I'm out of jail I would just as soon forget about criminals, all things considered, but I'm not permitted to. Society is as terrified by the criminals as it once was by the Communists. I can't even get on the bus in San Francisco any more without the exact change, since the drivers have insisted on a locked cashbox to discourage stick-ups. (Making bus service free was never seriously considered. You wouldn't want someone else to ride more often than you without paying extra, would you?)

There was a time when the countryside was dangerous and towns were safe. In fact, a thousand years ago people were forming towns in Europe precisely for the purpose of physical safety. It was not the police that made

towns safer than the country; professional police forces did not come into being until the 19th century. What made towns safe was simply the presence of so many people. If you were attacked on the street, there was always help nearby.

The reason so many people feel jittery in the streets of a modern American city is that they do not expect to get any help from their fellow citizens. People hold opinions on whether the courts are too lenient or the police too brutal, whether the generals should save us from the politicians or the politicians save us from the generals—they are, in short, conservative or liberal, and perhaps they vote accordingly, but generally they will not cross the street to save a man's life, even at no risk to themselves (e.g., if someone is having a heart attack); so they count for zero politically and socially, no matter which lever they pull on Election Day.

They whine for more police, but the police are recruited from the same psychopath population as the criminals, by and large, and they begin to grow restive of their employers. Even the detectives, the aristocrats of the police force, seldom get to save any damsels. More often they arrive on the scene after the damsel is already dead under the languid eyes of thirty-eight neighbors who didn't want to become involved and don't want to talk about it. For the ordinary cop there is neither damsel nor dragon, just dirty drunks he must haul out of the gutter to keep good citizens from being offended. He grows restless, he begins to dream of a police state, and civilization is threatened precisely by those who are supposed to be its last defense.

The prisoners are no more at ease than the police. They are constantly quarrelling over the pettiest things—an accidental jostling, an incident in a card game, an indiscreet boast—in order to score points. There are lots of threats but very few fights. (The consequences are severe: solitary confinement for both participants, with the corresponding loss of "good time," so that the days in solitary don't count towards the sentence.)

It resembles basketball: men constantly charging at each other at top speed, then a last minute swerve and a try for a two-point basket—one says, "I'll whip your motherfucking ass," and the other swallows it in silence.

It would seem that the best actor, rather than the best fighter, would score the most points. True, but everyone is a "method" actor who is what he pretends to be; so that the one who comes out on top is neither the best actor nor the best fighter, but the toughest man. The prisoners have entered naked. They have no wallet to keep their identity in; it must be in the voice, in the eyes, in the walk. If they want to **look** tough, they have to **be** tough.

Do you want protection from crime? Then you have to be tougher than the criminal. It's not enough just to outnumber him, if most of your numbers are zeroes. You can't hide behind the policeman; he's not often around and he's often a criminal himself. You can't hide behind the loud-mouth politician; he just hides behind the policeman. You have to stop hiding altogether, and start to be a better man than the criminal.

It should not be hard. Criminals, after all, are a weak, selfish, self-pitying bunch of people (I speak of street criminals, naturally, not of Syndicate men or military commanders). We really ought to have no crime problem at all—except for the fact that the typical decent citizen

produced by capitalist society is himself so weak, selfish and self-pitying that he is not an existential match even for a criminal.

He is weak because he is alone. He shares with no one except wife and children, who depend on him. If he slipped and fell, he cannot be sure that his close friends, even his family, wouldn't trample him as they ran squealing toward the trough. His life has neither beauty nor purpose. He believes in nothing except staying alive as long as possible. His children do not respect him because he achieves no wisdom with age. His leaders are grateful to him for being a sucker. His culture is trash—the people who create it are themselves ashamed of it. He squawks to his master for protection from crime as a chicken squawks for protection from the fox.

It is natural to feel admiration for the fox and contempt for the chicken. Lately, in fact, the revolutionary movement has made a cult of the criminal, with "Up Against the Wall, Motherfucker" its rallying cry. (The original, complete phrase is "Up against the wall, motherfucker, this is a stickup.") I dug criminals myself until I began to make a close acquaintance with one who bunked next to me in the Alameda County Jail in July, 1967. Every night we played cards and he told stories about his exploits removing merchandise from department stores with phony credit cards. One night he told me about the time he'd posed as a medical student, brought girls to a motel room where he said he'd perform an abortion, taken their money, had them lie down on a table, gone to "wash his hands" and disappeared out the window. He expected me to be impressed with how far he'd gone beyond the bourgeois moral code.

The fox does not attack the farmer; both prey off the chickens—who, if left alone, would starve. A lovely state of affairs, and there's no way out of it without some social theory.

A social system has to be judged by the people it produces; not by what they are fed—we are talking about people, not horses—but by what they are. That's the key to the revolt of the 1960s: an existential revolt which characteristically says "We refuse to be like you" rather than "We demand more of what you have." "Like you"

means greedy, cowardly, stupid, ugly—possessing the virtues, in short, of a pig. Even the Beatles, so careful not to needlessly offend, sing this song on their latest album:

Have you seen the little piggies
Crawling in the dirt
And for all the little piggies
Life is getting worse
Always having dirt to play around in.

Have you seen the bigger piggies
In their starched white shirts
You will find the bigger piggies
Stirring up the dirt
Always have clean shirts to play around in.

In their styes with all their backing
They don't care what goes on around
In their eyes there's something lacking
What they need's a damn good whacking.

Everywhere there's lots of piggies
Living piggy lives
You can see them out for dinner
With their piggy wives
Clutching forks and knives to eat their bacon.

Why are the young people so rude? ask newscasters and commentators in the grey stretches between such zingy commercials as the Ultra-Brite spots. "Ultra-Brite gives your mouth sex appeal"—the line is delivered with wholesome ski-slope freshness, but still carries a subliminal connotation of lowdown blow job, a combination that has brought newcomer Ultra-Brite to the No. 3 spot in national toothpaste sales. In a recent issue of Progressive Grocer, Ultra-Brite has a full-page ad urging supermarket managers not to let Ultra-Brite run out of stock so often. "Sex appeal for them means profit appeal for you," say the toothpaste people.

Now do you see why we call them pigs?

Ten years ago the only opposition was the self-conscious bohemians who dinged tailfins and dug "folk music." Today it consists of young people from all social classes absolutely determined not to be like their parents; not to be like the dumb sucker father who works in a factory all day and watches television at night, with nothing for his son but an ignorant leer; not to be like the timid clerk of a father whose only word of advice is "crawl"; not to be like the greedy pig of a father who has bought so many men that he thinks he can buy anything; not to be like the mother who prattles about herself like a six-year-old; not to be like the mother who got drugged unconscious to avoid experiencing childbirth, who nursed with a bottle because it was "clean" and "scientific"; not to be like the mother whose whole life is a plot to advance her husband's career in The Company. But that's all negative. How **do** they intend to live?

Biological instinct tells them that they must, somehow, survive—get food every day, keep warm and dry. All their years of school have taught them only one thing about survival: you sell your time to some Company, you do your job, faithfully and punctually. Nothing has prepared them to live without the Company. Two hundred years ago the runaways and dropouts from old Europe managed to live off the American land without any preparation for it; but since then the game has been killed, the forests cut down, the topsoil used up. So the modern pioneer has to hustle his bread in the city: finding casual labor, selling odds and ends, dealing in contraband, shoplifting, going on relief, playing con games, setting up some low-capital small business, working a series of jobs with no "future" and no "security."

A few become criminals; not many. All, however, become outlaws. They sell marijuana, or they give it away, or they possess it, or they are present in a room where it is being smoked—acts none of which are crimes but all of which are against the law. Those who run away from home at sixteen have to live as fugitives; and the fugitive slave acts, known as Contributing to the Delinquency of a Minor statutes, make it unlawful for an adult **not** to turn a runaway in to the police. Even when they do not happen to be breaking the law, young rebels are likely to wind up in jail on charges of vagrancy, resisting arrest or (in some jurisdictions) "failing to give a good account of himself."

They are not criminals, they do not tattoo self-pity on their arms ("Born to Lose"). They are outlaws, people who do not fear their own impulses and do not seek to be punished.

It's a hard life. They choose it because there is no alternative. In dropping out of the world of just-do-your-job-and-pay-the-mortgage they have made no noble sacrifice; they have simply chosen the difficult in preference to the impossible.

Our purpose is to abolish the system (call it the Greed Machine, capitalism, the Great Hamburger Grinder, Babylon, Do-Your-Job-ism) and learn to live cooperatively, intelligently, gracefully (call it the New Awareness, anarchism, The Aquarian Age, communism, whatever you wish). We don't rely much on resolutions, manifestos, proclamations. Instead we follow Western Union's advice to "say it with flowers." We say it with flowers, bricks, dynamite, songs, poems, drugs, hair, meat. We are everywhere, all over America, and we have friends all over the world. It was our brothers and sisters who took the streets of Paris in May, who were massacred in Mexico City in October, who sat down in front of the Russian tanks in Prague in August. We are gaining courage, bit by bit: a few years ago there were so many afraid to picket, now there are some who dynamite draft boards. We grow in numbers and broaden out, down to the 12-year-olds who consider assassinations and burning cities to be normal domestic phenomena, up to their parents, men and women in their thirties who have lived the straight life right into a dead end.

The future of our movement depends upon the future of the Greed Machine. Will it continue its slow crumbling? Then increasing numbers of people will drop out and seek a new life as outlaws. Will it take a turn for the better? Then the Underground will stagnate. Will there be a sudden collapse—economic crash, political crisis, military revolt? Then it's time for revolution, quite possibly before we are ready.

For some reason, it is always considered most likely for things to continue the way they've been going. All right, how have they been going? "The cities," runs the standard phrase, "are becoming uninhabitable." Time magazine, in a recent cover story on the collapse of New York City, fears that it might "prove ungovernable or explode in bitterness." The streets are becoming more and more dangerous. The police force is becoming a politi-

cal party. The air is a menace to health. Traffic is strangling. Lines grow longer for everything. The treasury is close to bankrupt. Strikes trigger political crises over such basic tasks as collecting the garbage. The teachers go on strike because of a conflict with parents and students over the nature of education. That's the way things are going in New York, which Time fears may set the pattern for the rest of the country.

Yet the cities continue to grow. High-rises are built in what once were suburbs. New tracts are developed even further out from the center. Small towns are engulfed by expanding metropolitan areas. "The cities are uninhabitable" means "America is uninhabitable."

But this is, of course, a gross exaggeration. America IS inhabited, and by 200 million people, each with a powerful set of shock absorbers. Social crises disappear for them whenever they flip from the news pages to the sports section—then sneak right into their houses to perch for evermore.

"I'm in charge in our family: I worry about the important things, like whether to recognize Red China, and my wife decides the minor things, like where the kids should go to school." An old joke that has lost all its bite, for nowadays where the kids should go to school is much more burning a political issue than whether to recognize Red China. It is the kind of thing that destroys middle-class families. There is not enough money to send the children to private schools, but the public schools are in constant chaos. The child comes home full of filthy ideas he has learned from a teacher who sounds like a hippie, or he is terrified of the colored children who beat him up and take his money, or he has become an impossible disciplinary problem who simply refuses to learn. It starts as a minor problem and grows to a permanent crisis with no resolution.

Another family watches helplessly as one of its members cracks up. "Mental illness is a disease like any other," they chant. "There's nothing to be ashamed of." But they are ashamed. What can they do? "Consult a specialist." They believe in doctors, and dentists. There is an automobile mechanic they can trust. But throughout their long, expensive relationship with the psychiatrist, they always suspect he is a pure quack. Maybe all he knows is how to get money out of people. Maybe he knows nothing about treating the, uh, disturbed. They have run away from the problem, have paid someone else to do the job, and yet it keeps coming after them. (No escape.)

At a certain point in their marriage, the wife knows her husband is seeing another woman, and he knows she knows. No more romance for her. Now she looks forward to nothing but old age.

No one asks in this society whether it is better to be old or young, better to have wisdom or strength. There is no wisdom in old age. Old people are disgusting. Their children cannot stand to have them around. A man of sixty, still in command of himself, lives in terror of the day when his son will treat him like a child.

The parents had believed that it was just a few teenagers who took drugs and got all the publicity. Then they discover that their own children have been doing it under their noses for years. "Why do you do this to us? Why do you do this to yourself? What's this fantastic"—she searches for the appropriate slang word—"**kick** that you get out of it?" The child says nothing at all. Or cooly holds out a pill. "Do you really want to know? Then here, take this pill."

Crises like these once turned people to the churches. Not any more. Organized religion has placed itself at the service of greed. Now only the "underground church" has any spiritual power, and it belongs more to the underground than to the church; a priest who pours blood on draft board files is no prop for the system. Most often, the despairing soul curls up and dies while the body lives on, a productive American citizen and a zombie. But sometimes the soul goes on a journey, discovering in a flash the secret of travel: leave your furniture behind.

Hundreds of thousands, maybe millions, have "dropped out"—lost their fascination with the bright plastic toys they are supposed to want—in the present period of slow crumbling. Their mere existence is a powerful **subversive** force, but it is not yet truly **revolutionary**; for we will be considered useful gadflies or dangerous parasites—but not an **alternative** to the Greed Machine—as long as we are hustling our bread from the system instead of baking it ourselves.

How do you bake it yourself? Well, let's drop the metaphor and talk about literal bread—Wonder Bread, Taystee Bread, soft white bread that tears apart when you try to spread butter on it. Suppose you want good bread made with real ingredients, fresh-baked and still hot. The system won't even try to sell it to you. It's too much trouble to bake it for yourself. It's too much trouble to bake it for your tight little family of man, wife and two children. It might begin to be worth the trouble in a big family of man and wife, six children and maiden aunt, but those families don't exist anymore. You could bake for the neighbors and sell it to them, but you'd probably go out of business (most neighborhood bakeries have). It all seems impossible.

Now imagine a "village" of, say, fifty or a hundred adults and their children living communally in the heart of the city. They cannot grow their own food, generate their own electricity, refine their own gasoline; but they can bake their own bread, butcher their own meat, make their own shoes, brew their own beer, maintain and repair their own dwellings, make their own clothes, make their own furniture, provide their own medical care, and educate their own children. They cannot be self-sufficient. There are many things they will have to buy (wholesale, usually) in the capitalist economy. They will need some money, and they will have to get it like everyone else: by selling their labor, selling a product, or hustling. But they won't need much money. Most of the time most of the commune members can be busy baking, butchering, cobbling, brewing, tinkering, sewing, carpentering, doctoring and teaching inside a moneyless economy.

Is it ridiculously inefficient? Not at all, when you consider that it eliminates all the work of packaging and selling that constitutes so much of the cost of consumer goods. Efficiency will depend on the competence of the master workmen and the willingness of their assistants. If people have to succeed in order to survive, they will; if they are merely conducting an experiment or trying to prove some point, then their commune will fall apart sooner or later. (The Underground and the straight world function exactly alike in this respect: whatever has to get done, gets done; everything else runs into mysterious difficulties.)

As long as the capitalist economy continues to boom, the Underground will continue to live by hustling. If the capitalist economy should tighten up, the Underground will be forced to develop its own communal counter-economy, which would take many forms (the one described above is just an example). If the capitalist economy should crash, then the drop-outs would number in the tens of millions and the counter-economy they would create might well be a match for capitalism in the revolutionary struggle for land, machinery and raw materials that would necessarily ensue. In the depression of the 1930's, capitalist property was generally respected. Occasionally an eviction was forcibly prevented, but no warehouses or department stores were looted, no land was seized, in fact there were hardly any strikes until 1934. If there should be another crash, this time the stores would be looted bare in a month and communards would be licking their chops at the sight of any vacant land or idle machinery.

The final conflict will be between outlaws and criminals: on one side, millions of Americans turned outlaw by force fo circumstance; on the other side, the forces of respectable society at last revealed as Organized Crime. The outcome will be determined by who has the guns—at the end, of course, not at the beginning. The old order always starts off with all the guns, but they get taken away in every successful revolution.

Our movement is very tender. One cop can usually handle ten of us. Though we have burned our bridges behind us and can't go back, most of us think we can just camp on the riverbank for the rest of our lives. Our militancy is mostly the nervous boasts of green soldiers who insist they are itching for combat—bad acting which cops and criminals can easily detect. But that is the way it always is at the beginning.　　　**—Marvin Garson**
San Francisco Express-Times (UPS)

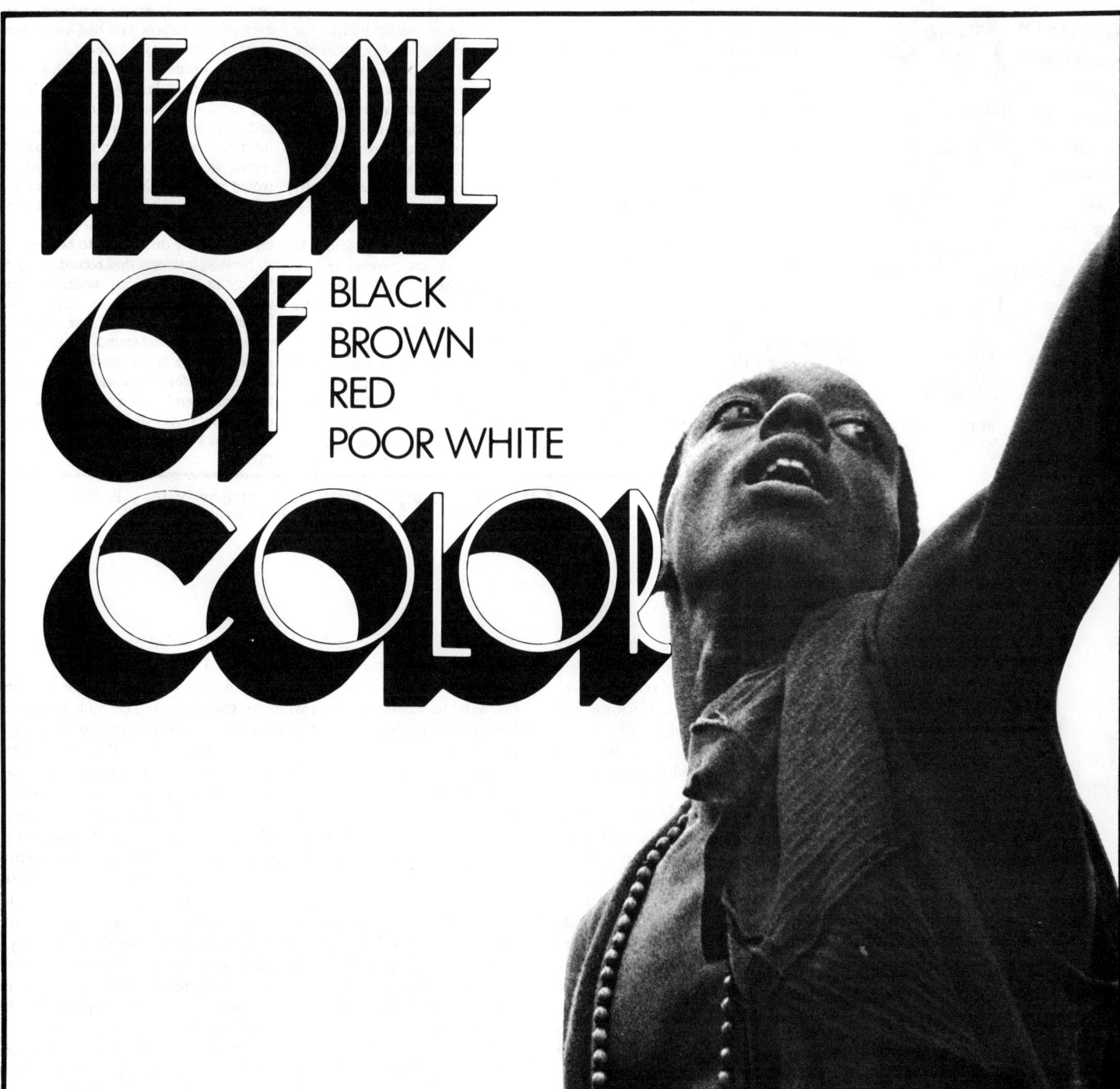

PEOPLE OF COLOR

BLACK
BROWN
RED
POOR WHITE

"I'M A MAN I'M A STRONG MAN" THE PANTHERS MEET DYLAN AND GET TO KNOW MORE ABOUT MR. JONES

Eldridge Cleaver explains in *Soul on Ice* that the black man has been led around by the white man, the white omnipotent administrator primarily, this is what he's talking about—big businessmen who manipulate and bullshit and control the government. The black man has been led around, and was projected as being led around, with a little piece of tiny string, cord string, that could be broken in a minute. The string was tied around the black man's neck, and the black man was projected as a big gorilla. He was a gorilla. He was inhuman, and he couldn't talk. He's not supposed to be able to think. But the gorilla beats on his chest and says, "I'm a man."

One of the symbolic things that Eldridge was pointing out with this thing was that Cassius Clay said: "I'm the greatest"—the symbolic thing of him beating on his chest. He said in fact, "I'm a man." He said, "I'm a strong man." What shocked the racists, what shocked the omnipotent administrator, is that he looked up at the big gorilla. The string had been broken and he saw

this gorilla beating on his chest saying, "I'm a man." That was Cassius Clay.

Cassius Clay would brag. People misunderstood the bragging. All Cassius Clay was saying was that he was defying all this omnipotent, racist bullshit by stepping forward and saying, "I'm the greatest! I can't be hit." He beat on his chest, and when he said that, the white racist omnipotent administrator who had a hold on the string had to ask himself, "Well, if he's a man then what the hell am I?" And that's what Bobby Dylan meant by the geek handing Mr. Jones the naked bone and saying: "How do you like being a freak?" And that's the whole meaning of the question. If he's a man, if he's not a freak, and he tells Mr. Jones he's a freak, then Mr. Jones has to ask, "Am I that?" That's symbolic of saying that if he's a man, what am I?

This song Bobby Dylan was singing became a very big part of that whole publishing operation of the Black Panther paper. And in the background, while we were putting this paper out, this

record came up and I guess a number of papers were published, and many times we would play that record. Brother Stokely Carmichael also liked that record. This record became so related to us, even to the brothers who had held down most of the security for the set.

These brothers had some big earphones over at Beverly's house. These big earphones would sit on your ears and had a kind of direct stereo atmosphere and when you got loaded it was something else! These brothers would get halfway high, loaded on something, and they would sit down and play this record over and over and over, especially after they began to hear Huey P. Newton interpret that record. They'd be trying to relate an understanding about what was going on, 'cause old Bobby did society a big favor when he made *that* particular sound. If there's any more he made that I don't understand, I'll just ask Huey P. Newton to interpret them for us and maybe we can get a hell of a lot more out of brother Bobby because old Bobby, he did a good job on that set.

Ramparts From the "Biography of Huey P. Newton" by Bobby Seale, *Ramparts* 11/17/68

GUERRILLA HISTORY: HARLEM — AUGUST 1943 JAMES BALDWIN

I had not wanted to go to the casket myself and I certainly had not wished to be led there, but there was no way of avoiding either of these forms. One of the deacons led me up and I looked on my father's face. I cannot say that it looked like him at all. His blackness had been equivocated by powder and there was no suggestion in that casket of what his power had or could have been. He was simply an old man dead, and it was hard to believe that he had ever given anyone either joy or pain. Yet, his life filled that room. Further up the avenue his wife was holding his newborn child. Life and death so close together, and love and hatred, and right and wrong, said something to me which I did not want to hear concerning man, concerning the life of man.

After the funeral, while I was downtown desperately celebrating my birthday, a Negro soldier, in the lobby of the Hotel Braddock, got into a fight with a white policeman over a Negro girl. Negro girls, white policemen, in or out of uniform, and Negro males—in or out of uniform—were part of the furniture of the lobby of the Hotel Braddock and this was certainly not the first time such an incident had occurred. It was destined, however, to receive unprecedented publicity, for the fight between the policeman and the soldier ended with the shooting of the soldier. Rumor, flowing immediately to the streets outside, stated that the soldier had been shot in the back, an instantaneous and revealing invention, and that the soldier had died protecting a Negro woman. The facts were somewhat different—for example, the soldier had not been shot in the back, and was not dead, and the girl seems to have been as dubious a symbol of womanhood as her white counterpart in Georgia usually is, but no one was interested in the facts. They preferred the invention because this invention expressed and corroborated their hates and fears so perfectly. It is just as well to remember that people are always doing this. Perhaps many of those legends, including Christianity, to which the world clings began their conquest of the world with just some such concerted surrender to distortion. The effect, in Harlem, of this particular legend was like the effect of a lit match in a tin of gasoline. The mob gathered before the doors of the Hotel Braddock simply began to swell and to spread in every direction, and Harlem exploded.

The mob did not cross the ghetto lines. It would have been easy, for example, to have gone over Morningside Park on the west side or to have crossed the Grand Central railroad tracks at 125th Street on the east side, to wreak havoc in white neighborhoods. The mob seems to have been mainly interested in something more potent and real than the white face, that is, in white power, and the principal damage done during the riot of the summer of 1943 was to white business establishments in Harlem. It might have been a far bloodier story, of course, if, at the hour the riot began, these establishments had still been open. From the Hotel Braddock the mob fanned out, east and west along 125th Street, and for the entire length of Lenox, Seventh, and Eighth avenues. Along each of these avenues, and along each major side street — 116th, 125th, 135th, and so on — bars, stores, pawnshops, restaurants, even little luncheonettes had been smashed open and entered and looted — looted, it might be added, with more haste than efficiency. The shelves really looked as though a bomb had struck them. Cans of beans and soup and dog food, along with toilet paper, corn flakes, sardines, and milk tumbled every which way, and abandoned cash registers and cases of beer leaned crazily out of the splintered windows and were strewn along the avenues. Sheets, blankets, and clothing of every description formed a kind of path, as though people had dropped them while running. I truly had not realized that Harlem *had* so many stores until I saw them all smashed open; the first time the word *wealth* ever entered my mind in relation to Harlem was when I saw it scattered in the streets. But one's first, incongruous impression of plenty was countered immediately by an impression of waste. None of this was doing anybody any good. It would have been better to have left the plate glass as it had been and the goods lying in the stores.

It would have been better, but it would also have been intolerable, for Harlem had needed something to smash. To smash something is the ghetto's chronic need. Most of the time it is the members of the ghetto who smash each other, and themselves. But as long as the ghetto walls are standing there will always come a moment when these outlets do not work.

From *Notes of a Native Son* by James Baldwin, Beacon Press

PRISONER OF WAR

Huey Newton Talks in Prison

By Tim Findley
Chronicle Correspondent

California Men's Colony-East
San Luis Obispo

Huey Newton sat, relaxed, and looked the interviewer steadily in the eye.

"If my being a political prisoner is what made people relate to the Black Panther Party," he said calmly, "then I would stay in jail."

The response came back with hollow resonance giving away the steel walls behind pastel yellow paint in the attorney's interviewing room.

The Black Panther Party predicts that more than 10,000 people will demonstrate in support of bail for Newton at a Federal Court hearing in San Francisco Thursday.

POSTERS

Posters with photographs of the Black Panther founder still insist that "Huey P. Newton Must Be Set Free." Underground newspapers picture young people with clenched fists and angry faces demanding Newton's release.

But here, amid peaceful green rolling hills that surround the "relaxed" institution of California Mens' Colony-East near San Luis Obispo, the 27 year-old Panther Minister of Defense wages a lonely personal protest that denies him even the simple freedom of fresh air.

With determined confidence, he predicts he will be released on bail while he appeals his manslaughter conviction for the fatal shooting of an Oakland policeman. But he is prepared to spend the full 15 years of his sentence in a quiet one-man war against the power structure.

CELL

Newton spends some 20 hours a day in a pale green cell 10 feet by 5 feet. Because of his calm refusal to work unless he was paid a minimum wage, prison authorities have denied him library and canteen privileges. He is allowed out of his cell only four hours a day — for meals.

The "Housing Unit" in which his cell is located is occupied largely by passive homosexuals who have their own keys to their cells. Often they are out until 10 p.m. in the grassy quad formed by four similar units.

Newton's first bid for parole was denied here last week by the Adult Authority, which undoubtedly took into account Newton's staunch refusal to be "exploited" while he is "prisoner of war."

"Those freak show degenerates," Newton flashed in a Chronicle interview Thursday. "They think they can 'rehabilitate' me. How do you relate to a person who is so absurd?"

ANGER

It was the only flicker of anger in Newton's responses.

Virtually all the advantages of this "enlightened" penal institution are denied Newton because he will not work without what he feels is adequate pay.

On his record at the institution are several violations for having "contraband" in his cell. Authorities say the contraband — consisting of such items as toothpaste, hair oil and deodorant — are denied inmates on cell confinement.

Yet even prison authorities are impressed with Newton's quiet, polite determination. "He's never got up in anybody's face — never been out of line with anybody," said Assistant Superintendent D. J. McCarthy.

"He just more or less went his way and we went ours."

But even in his self-imposed isolation, Newton still sets policy and gives orders for what the Panthers say are 46 chapters in 30 American cities.

His statements are carried out by a limited list of visitors — his family and his attorneys — who also bring with them news and problems within the party to be solved by Newton.

From Haight Ashbury to Havana, Huey Newton is considered still a major leader of the militant left. Newton himself, however, is concerned with overly zealous support for him personally.

PARTY

"Americans in general have a tendency to place too much emphasis on one person," he said thoughtfully. "I would be happier if people would just relate to the Black Panther Party."

To most of his followers, and to many who view the Panther party as a threat and a menace, Huey Newton is a stern faced figure in beret and black leather jacket. The most widely-known photograph of him shows him seated emperor-like in a straw chair — one hand clutching a shotgun, the other a spear.

In the 17 months he has already spent in jail or prison, Newton admits to gaining some 30 pounds on his still athletic figure.

HAIRCUT

A short jail haircut has trimmed the medium length natural from around his handsome features.

His voice still has a curious high timbre to it that makes one feel he would not be a great orator. Indeed, he rarely speaks above a conversational tone.

He listens politely and intently with a mind seemingly fascinated at the prospects of weighing another's opinions against his own. Often, his long complex answers are mixed with probing questions and friendly explanations to be sure his audience understands.

And it is ironically appropriate that the black sweater and the light blue jail shirt he wears call the Panther costume of blue and black immediately to mind.

UNCHANGED

For Huey Newton is unchanged.

A seemingly small concession of agreeing to work in one of the institution's trim kitchens would immediately give Newton prison freedoms only dreamed of at harder institutions.

Yet for him it is a matter of simple, unbending principles. In the kitchen he would be paid about three cents an hour.

"I refuse to be exploited under the guise of rehabilitation," he said, adding with detached analysis, "The basic thing the institution doesn't understand is that once you take a person's principles from him he's not himself any more.

"The only way you can come to grips with yourself and know if you're in it for excitement and prestige or for principle and personal integrity is to go through it by yourself."

INTEGRITY

That solemn devotion to personal integrity is apparently what has brought Newton through six months of austere isolation.

"The lockup makes me feel more at home, really. It makes me feel I'm still resisting."

The Black Panther Party, at Newton's orders, expelled more than 100 members and put a freeze on new membership in January. Since then, Newton has ordered new efforts at Panther organization in labor unions, has called for expanded programs such as breakfasts for children in the black community, and has suggested firmer alliances with militant white organizations.

Newton identifies two enemies in American society — capitalism and racism. Black racism and hate, he insists, have never been a part of the Black Panther Party.

"I think what motivates people," he grinned at the interviewer, "is not great hate, but great love for other people."

"There's no reason for the establishment to fear me. But it has every right to fear the people collectively — I am one with the people."

The lights in the visitor's area outside the interview room flickered — a signal that visiting hours were over. Newton rose to undergo a skin search before returning to his cell.

"You always ask about me," he said. "I guess what I'm about is like an old saying — 'If there's a why, we can live by any how.'"

IN MYTHICAL AMERICA

Most Americans who live outside the ghettos or enclaves knew so little of what is happening inside them that they were surprised and shocked when recent racial conflicts ripped their cities, when anti-Semitism affected an election in New Jersey, when Mexican-Americans became mountain guerrillas in New Mexico, when Indians in the Pacific Northwest went to jail rather than give up their rights to fish.

Americans are surprised and shocked because they live in a mythical country. In this mythical America, the conditions of Negroes, Indians, and Spanish-speaking Americans are assumed to be gradually but inevitably improving as court decisions, governmental efforts, and education break down the barriers of discrimination and prejudice. The injustices and crimes committed by frontier Americans against the Indians are described as regrettable but necessary — or part of another era — and the reservation system, through which the government made wards of the Indians, was an attempt to redress the wrongs. The wholesale theft of land from Mexico through the device of the Mexican War with the resulting degredation of the Spanish-speaking peoples is held to be another lamentable but necessary episode in the country's need to expand. The myth takes in the gradual movement of Negroes toward equality. Negro slavery is acknowledged as a moral wrong, and prejudice against Negroes linked with overt discrimination is, too. In mythical America the country slowly is coming to accept Negroes as equals. The grade-school textbooks say so, and President Johnson put the country on record: "We shall overcome."

From "To Serve The Devil" by Paul Jacobs and Saul Landau, *The Center Magazine* March 1969

BLACK
HISTORY
BY A
BLACK MAN

THE AFRO-AMERICAN PAST AND THE AMERICAN PRESENT

NEGRO history suffers the same fate in the overall American story as the individual Negro's integration into American society. That is, small but prominent doses of "Negro History" can be dropped into the national saga, but these black drops should never be numerous or indelible. For if they are oo many and too black, these encroachments might necessitate unpleasant rereadings, reassessments and rewritings of the entire story.

An American history which cannot contain the full story of the black pilgrimage is no more worthy than an American society that cannot bear the full and troublesome black presence in its midst.

Just as America can know no survival worth considering unless it finds a way of facing its black counter-image, so too our history is a tale told by fools if it does not incorporate the Afro-American experience with unflinching integrity. And if such open encounter between black and white history should produce the same insecurity as we now experience in the human encounter, so much the better.

The analogy doesn't end there. The urgency some of us feel for creating such a new American history is no less critical than the pressure impelling us to seek for the lineaments of a new American society. Obviously, the tasks are not unrelated, for there will be no new beginnings for a nation that refuses to acknowledge its real past.

Any American history that ignores the central role of black people as actors and foils on this maddening stage is a falsified and misleading history. Such a history ignores the ironic symbol of that summer in Jamestown more than three centuries ago when representative government and African bondsmen had a mutual beginning of sorts, a beginning that seemed to lock the rhetoric of democracy and the reality of black inequality into the American heart. It is a history that tries to explore the making of the Constitution without understanding the major price in its integrity that was exacted by the system of slavery and its

proponents, both north and south. It is a history that attempts to speak of the Peculiar Institution as if there were no human beings involved who produced no authentic historical materials. (Thus a major publisher could attempt recently to produce a collection of documents on slavery without one document from a slave.) It is a history that speaks of Jacksonian Democracy as if the expanded white franchise were not purchased at the cost of the black northern vote in many states.

Such a vacuous history treats Reconstruction as if it were an unfortunate mistake, rather than one of the nation's greatest lost chances to be honest and free. This kind of history deals with the turn of the nineteenth century without suggesting the way in which the brutality against blacks and Indians at home may have permanently poisoned the nation's attempts at expansion among non-white peoples elsewhere. It is a history that tries to understand the urban crisis of the 1960's without tracing the long and bloody lines of Negro migration since Reconstruction. It is a history that attempts to interpret current American culture without any appreciation for the major role black people have played in creating the popular culture of the nation, especially since the 1920's.

A history without the Afro-American story may indicate why this nation can now be so numb to the brutalization of a Vietnam thousands of miles away. In denying the physical and spiritual destruction of black persons which has become a part of the American Way of Life, a callus has grown on whatever heart a nation has.

This history that has contributed immensely to the mis-education of the American people has not prepared them to face a world that is neither white, Christian, capitalist, nor affluent. Such history may yet prove poisonous, and if there is any possible antidote on the American scene, it could be the hard and bitter medicine of the Afro-American past. Is it too late for a society that still insists that its drops be few and painless?

An Amnesiac Society

Even when one acknowledges the grotesquely slow pace at which black people are moving onto the American stage, the knowledge of their history is still absolutely indispensable as they cast off the roles of the past and seek for new ones. If they come to the integrated scene with integrity, they must come with a knowledge of themselves and of the many-splendored gifts they bring.

Black students in formerly white schools must not enter as suppliants who are going to be transformed from "disadvantaged" to "advantaged" by such a move. They must be so aware of their black fathers and the wealth of their spiritual and intellectual heritage that they will illuminate sharply the disadvantages inherent in an isolated, beleaguered middle-class white world. If they are to become more than black Anglo-Saxons, then they cannot accept the old doctrines of slavery which encouraged them to believe that God somehow blessed darkest Africa with the light of Christian guns and ships and chains. Neither the ancient Kingdom of Songhai nor the modern Kingdom of Harlem was benighted without whites, and black young people need to know the measurements of the light —in both places.

Any society that would encourage black children to live in a state of permanent amnesia or shame—or both— concerning their fathers and their fathers' ways of life is a society not worth knowing. Any men who would enter such a society on its amnesic terms would only add to its corruption, whether they entered through the door of the ninth grade or by the carpeted way of a General Electric executive suite. But it must also be acknowledged that such knowledge is exceedingly dangerous, for if it were faithfully presented, a reading of the Afro-American past might cause black exiles to refuse many an open door. Indeed some doors might be torn from their hinges. This is not teaching hatred of whites. Rather it is the necessary and healthy explanation for the existence of the hatred and fear that most black men have known from childhood on. Any society lacking the courage to take such risks with light lacks the courage to live.

Those white persons who first encounter the token blacks in their new roles also are in desperate need of the Afro-American past. For without it they will be tempted to feel that they are doing a favor for the students or the junior executives by letting them in. Properly read, the pages of the Negro past will reveal that it is black people who have done the favor by doing so much to build the nation under such horrible circumstances, and by letting such ambiguous doors stay on their hinges for so long a time. Compassionately understood, the black past will teach all benefactors that *they* are receiving a favor in being allowed what may be the one last chance to do justice, that they are being graced by the presence of a people whose pilgrimage is perhaps the only true epic poem that America has ever known. Such a reading of the Afro-American past might even shatter the general illusion that token acceptance of token Negroes will ever bring any basic hope for the survival of any of us.

Perhaps the issue of survival suggests another level of our need for the story of this dark journey in America. Not long ago, the most highly esteemed newspaper in America asked an author to write his reflections on the reasons "for the current breaking of America into two parts, based on race." When it rips apart all the easy generalizations of our textbooks (written largely by, for and about white America), the new coming of black history would cast such a question into limbo. For any perceptive apprehension of the Negro-white encounter cannot fail to reveal that there have always been two major communities in this nation—based on race.

The breaking began in West Africa and continued in every colony and state that came into being. If we read with both speed and comprehension, it may not be too late to ask the right questions, questions based not on Newark or Detroit in 1967, but on Jamestown and Philadelphia and Springfield and St. Louis over the centuries. For it is only as America faces a Denmark Vesey, a Nat Turner, a W. E. B. DuBois, a Paul Robeson and a Malcolm X, that the nation will begin to be ready to understand a Stokely Carmichael, a Rap Brown and the host of black radicals yet to come. Such a reading would identify each one as "Made in America, Product of its Broken Community." How shall this land create new and whole men if it refuses to examine its past production record, a record strewn with the crushed bodies and spirits of black radicals hurling defiant curses and urgent pleas for renewal from the same dying lips?

These angry young men's lives demonstrate the fact that the Afro-American past and the black present are no longer matters of limited national concern—if they ever were. Indeed they suggest to us what may be one of the most profound and universally significant uses of this history: that is, its service as an entrance to the non-white, non-Western world. One of the most gifted and least celebrated American political analysts, A. J. Muste, used to say that the basic division in the world now and for some time to come was not based on communism versus capitalism. Rather, Muste said, the world was divided now between those people who had rarely if ever known defeat and humiliation as a national experience and those who had lived with this for centuries.

In a sense, Muste was simply echoing the profound insights expressed by W. E. B. DuBois half a century earlier. However formulated, the concepts of these men remind us that the world experience of the last 500 years has meant that the vast majority of the earth's humiliated people has been non-white, and their humiliation has come at the hands of the white, Western world. Moreover, it appears that this nation now stands as the self-proclaimed leader of that unhumiliated world, and finds itself at once the most powerful and one of the least comprehending national states.

One of America's most critical blind areas is in the realm of understanding the oppressed, the wretched of the earth. Our vaunted experience of virtually unbroken success, our alabaster cities undimmed by human tears (except for the unseen tears of the poor and the black?) and our movement into the strange joys of advanced corporate capitalism—all these have cut this people off from the rest of the world in significant ways.

America a Dangerous Nation

A nation that combines the American predilection towards violence, the American stockpile of weapons and the American lack of empathy for the earth's humiliated peoples is a dangerous nation. Perhaps it can begin another life by introducing itself to the invisible men in its midst, by seeking to know the quality of suffering and hurt and the rebellion they spawn. Such an introduction must include—if not begin with—the past.

Nor are black Americans excused from such a task, for we are constantly exposed to a terrible temptation to forget the black and bloody ground out of which we sprang, as the price for American acceptance. As DuBois put it more than a decade ago, ". . . most American Negroes, even those of intelligence and courage, do not fully realize that they are being bribed to trade equal status in the United States for the slavery of the majority of men." So the Afro-American past must re-

mind black people that we are children of the humiliated and the oppressed, that our fathers were colonized and exploited subjects, and that the ghettos we have recently left are still too often filled with the stench of poverty and despair.

Such history must remind Afro-Americans that all of our greatest leaders have begged us to stand in solidarity with the black and anguished people of the earth. We are their spokesmen in the midst of the world's foremost antirevolutionary power. If we forsake them, we forsake our past, our fathers, and our own best selves. If we forsake them, there may be no future for our children or theirs. If we forget our own father's burnings in village squares and don American uniforms to set fires against the world's desperate revolutions, we will deserve nothing but the scorn of men and the judgment of the gods.

Some years ago, D. W. Brogan, an English expert on American affairs, referred to what he called The Myth of American Omnipotence. This phrase referred to his conviction that the reading of the American past was distorted by a conception of this nation as an entity incapable of failure, powerful and pure enough to succeed at anything it chose. The corollary of this myth, said Brogan (in the days of McCarthy's reign), was that any American failure at home or overseas had to be explained by subversion or conspiracies, or—at worst—a mistake in well-intentioned American judgment.

Related to Brogan's myth is what might be called The Myth of American Romanticism. Ever since the nation's beginning it has been plagued by this equally crippling misconception of itself. Succinctly put, it involves a belief that American history is the story of a society moving on a straight upward line from perfection to perfection, from goodness to betterness, from being better than other nations to being the best and most complete nation God had ever stood over (I take it that is the implication of being "under God"). This mythology was intensified to the point of indoctrination after World War II when history became a tool of Cold War, and it became necessary to prove consistently the superiority of America over every conceivable communist, socialist or neutralist model in the world.

This self-image is on a level with fairy tales and happiness-forever-after. It is the self-understanding of those whose adult development has been aborted by the fear of the risks of growth. Most importantly, it is a refusal to recognize the bloody, tragic line that whips its way through all of life. Failure to face the tragic is failure to mature in national as well as personal spheres, so in the midst of this pabulum view of history a serious implanting of the Afro-American past could be the difference between death and growth—at least spiritually.

Were American historians and American citizens at large to face this story, many—if not all—of their liberal, superficial myths about, and hopes for, American society might be transformed. They would need to face again the fact that two of their greatest heroes, Jefferson and Lincoln, were convinced that black and white people could never live on a basis of true equality in America. They would be pressed to realize that The Great Emancipator cared far more deeply for a cheaply won white reconciliation than for the very costly black liberation, thereby helping to lead the nation down bloody paths of malice for all.

The close reading of the black past might reveal how fully this broken people has tested every line of American democratic rhetoric and how fully each word has shrunk before the ultimate test in every generation. (They would also see the pathetic and perennial sight of esteemed national leaders offering solutions a generation old to wounds long past such ancient salves.) A reading of the black preachers, poets and editors, a sensitive listening to the singers of our songs, would face the nation with the ceaseless rage that has been the lot of men in every strange land who have been called upon to sing, to dance, to laugh, and to be grateful. And in those pages any searching eye would easily spy the century-old predictions of black alienation, sedition, rebellion, and guerrilla warfare. Tragic disaster has always lurked at the American door, created largely by blindness to the nation's fatal flaw.

Not only would the tragic nature of American life perhaps become more clear, but the Afro-American story would remind the nation that it was conceived as an experiment, an experiment that could yet fail, miserably, utterly, explosively. Almost a century ago Henry Adams described the America of 1800 as very healthy "except for the cancer of slavery." The irony and the tragedy of a "very healthy" cancerous body is still the American condition, and though no cure has yet been found for the cancer, it may not be too late to open the blind eyes to see its sources in the past. And what if we open our eyes only to discover that Jefferson and Lincoln (and many black men) were right, that present white prejudice and black bitterness, and unbroken lines of injustice from the past, now make it impossible for us to continue together in integrity? Is it better to go on in blind, self-righteous rage towards internecine struggle or to see, finally see, with sad and mature clarity the pathway down from all our past romantic dreams—including the dream of integration?

The black experience in America allows for no illusions, not even that

last, ancient hope of the chosen American people whom God will somehow rescue by a special act of his grace. America began with such hopes, but they were tied to the idea of a Covenant, that men would have to do God's will for them to remain as his chosen ones. Somehow, just as America forced black men to do so much of its other dirty but productive work, the nation evidently came to believe that whites could be chosen while blacks did that suffering which has always been identified with the chosen ones. Now that is over. The black past has begun to explode and to reveal to a hiding chosen people that to be the anointed one is to be crushed and humiliated by the forces of the world. After almost 400 years of exile, the black branch of the chosen people has grown louder than ever before in its refusal to take the sufferings apart from the privileges of the chosen status.

So, for all who would see it, the Afro-American past illuminates the meaning of being chosen. Perhaps this is what white Americans must see: that they will either join the ranks of suffering and humiliation (beginning perhaps with "losing face" in Vietnam?) or there will be no chosen people on these shores. Either they will submit their children to some of the same educational terrors they have allowed black children to endure or there is no future for any. Either they will give up their affluence to provide necessities for others or there will be neither affluence nor necessities for anyone. Perhaps we were chosen together, and we cannot move towards a new beginning until we have faced all the horror and agony of the past with absolute honesty. Perhaps integration is indeed irrelevant until the assessment of a long, unpaid debt has been made and significant payments begun. Perhaps atonement, not integration, is the issue at hand.

Of course, one last, shattering possibility may remain. It could be that the message of the Afro-American past is this: only one branch of the chosen people has really paid the dues of suffering—with the scars to show for it. Therefore it may be that only the black branch will be allowed to shape the future of the nation and determine its calling for the world. Perhaps only black people are open, sensitive, and scarred enough as a group to lead this nation into true community with the non-white humiliated world. Perhaps that world of suffering will trust no American leaders save those who bear the marks of oppression in their souls. Perhaps it will listen only to those who know the tragic sense of life and are not blind and calloused bearers of death.

May the Last be First?

Perhaps it is already time for the last to be first in our nation. How shall

that overturning come? That knowledge may be too great for even the Afro-American past to bear. Perhaps our black history can only bear witness to the truth, and living men must shape that truth into new action and new history.

To those who would close their ears to such interpretations of the black past, to those who would tune out because such strange musings seem unrelated to the historian's vocation, I cite the word of a white radical who read black history with some care. Before an audience of well-meaning whites, in a time of similar crisis, he spoke on the Afro-American past, focusing on the greatness of a black leader named Toussaint, holding L'Ouverture above the great white heroes of the age. Then Wendell Phillips set out these words: "You think me a fanatik tonight, for you read history not with your eyes but with your prejudices."

So spoke a man who believed that there was no healing for America either in small black drops of history or in small black drops of Negro freedom. Had the nation heard his word and followed his uses of the past, we might well have been spared most of the bloody days between and the terror-filled nights yet to come.

Will there be time before the last night? We who have lived in night and waited long in darkness may have a special word of light for a stumbling power-bound people. We do not panic easily. Shall the word be heard? Only those with ears can say. It is our calling, our vocation, to speak it. And if the last darkness should fall, it is preferable that we be found standing faithful to all the agonizing sorrow-joy of our Afro-American past than lost and sullen black defenders of a world that sucked out our memory and bleached our minds.

Such a land deserves no defense. Better that it pass and make way for whatever is yet to come—even if it be the long-delayed last silence. Or will it be the drums of morning? I do not know. The Afro-American past leaves a man with no illusions, but even in the heart of chaos it does not strip him of his hope. We have come too far, through too much chaos, to cop out here. ■

motive
By Vincent Harding from *Motive* April 1968

CHASE MANHATTAN
PARTNER IN APARTHEID

BLACK RAGE

NEGRO 'PARANOIA' ASSAYED IN BOOK

White Racism Said to Push Blacks to the Brink

By JOHN LEO

White racism forces the American Negro to lead a life of "cultural paranoia" and often pushes him over the brink into true paranoid schizophrenia, a black psychiatrist said here yesterday.

Paranoia, a withdrawal from reality with delusions of per-cution, is by far the most common form of mental illness among black Americans, according to Dr. William H. Grier, assistant professor of psychiatry at the University of California Medical Center, San Francisco.

"That's because a black person has to develop a suspiciousness and defensive posture just to survive in America," he said in an interview. "He has to develop a 'healthy,' adaptive 'cultural paranoia,' which pushes him close to the line of mental illness."

Dr. Grier is the author of "Black Rage," a psychological portrait of the American Negro, published today by Basic Books. Dr. Price M. Cobbs, another Negro psychiatrist at the San Francisco medical center, is co-author.

The book argues that the rage of black men is beginning to break through a complex set of psychic defenses, erected in the time of slavery and little changed since.

Suffering Is Masked

Beneath "the cool style" and "the postal-worker syndrome" of ingratiating deference and passivity, the authors say, the Negro has been spending enormous amounts of psychic energy to mask suffering and rage.

"As a sapling bent low stores energy for a violent backswing," the authors write, "blacks bent double by oppression have stored energy which will be released in the form of rage — black rage, apocalyptic and final."

They also make these arguments:

¶It is the role of the Negro mother to suppress assertiveness in her sons, so they can survive in white society. As a result, Negro men develop considerable hostility toward Negro women as the inhibiting agents of an oppressive system.

¶Negro family structure is weak because it cannot fulfill its primary function: protection of its members. "Nowhere in the United States can the black family extend an umbrella of protection over its members in the way that a white family can," they say.

¶The black woman is prone to depressive, self-deprecatory attitudes. By white beauty standards, she is unable to develop a healthy narcissism, or self-love. She tends to see the sexual act as a degrading submission, which further lowers her self-esteem.

¶After early promise, many talented Negroes fail to do well in their careers because accomplishment is often perceived as a major move beyond the family, and thus as a form of abandonment of loved ones.

¶Many black men weep frequently — without warning and without feeling. It occurs while the black man is passively witnessing another man's triumph, and "the tears are for what he might have achieved if he had not been held back ... by some inner command not to excel, not to achieve, not to becoming outstanding, not to draw attention to himself."

"Under slavery," the authors write, "the black man was a psychologically emasculated and totally dependent human being. Times and con-ditions have changed, but black men continue to exhibit the inhibitions and psychopathology that had their genesis in the slave experience."

The "Black Norm," the authors write, is a set of defensive character traits that the American Negro must acquire.

They list these traits as cultural paranoia (every white man and every social system is the enemy until proven otherwise), cultural depression (sadness and intimacy with misery) and cultural antisocialism (an "accurate reading of one's environment" in which laws are never quite respected because they are designed to protect white men, not Negroes.

Essential Characteristics

"To regard the Black Norm as pathological," the psychiatrists write, "and attempt to remove such traits by treatment would be akin to analyzing away a hunter's cunning or a banker's prudence. This is a body of characteristics essential to life for black men in America and woe be unto that therapist who does not recognize it."

Rage is rising rapidly in the black community, they write, and whites must "get off the backs" of Negroes if they wish to avoid a conflagration.

"Today it is the young men who are fighting the battles, and, for now, their elders, though they have given their approval, have not yet joined in. The issue finally rests with the black masses. When the servile men and women stand up, we had all better duck."

The New York Times

7/25/68

□□□

> SOMETHING JUST HAPPENED TO THE BLACK PEOPLE OF THE UNITED STATES
>
> WE ARE NO LONGER WHAT WE WERE

Negotiation, which according to Rev. Cleage should amount to a real 'transfer of power', was not possible before the riots: one does not negotiate with slaves. Until July, the whites of Detroit, deep inside themselves, considered the blacks of Detroit - 'their blacks' - if not as slaves, at least as second class citizens. In return, numerous blacks had been contaminated by this idea; the slave often ended up accepting the image which his master showed him. It is in this sense that Rev. Cleage considers the eruption of violence redemptive: it definitively broke the relationship of master and slave which found its roots in American history of the seventeenth century. Many whites and blacks of Detroit, if we push the analysis that far, bear witness to no other phenomenon when they say, hopefully or uneasily, 'Things will never be the way they used to.'

"FEAR HAS DISAPPEARED"

Shortly after the rebellion, Rev. Cleage drew a conclusion about it - 'his' conclusion - in his Linwood Avenue church, his back against a gigantic black Virgin painted by a local artist (a former but rehabilitated convict): 'Something just happened to the black people of the United States, ' he said. 'We are no longer what we were a few years, a few months, a few weeks ago. Something has happened to us -- to us, not America -- something which is affecting our way of thinking, our manner of fighting together. It is the most important thing that could happen in the United States. What is it? It is that fear has disappeared. Just a few weeks ago, we were different. Down in the South, we were afraid; here, in the North, we were afraid. It was a very primitive fear. It was the fear of dying. When the white man in the South said to us, 'Get the hell off the sidewalk, ' why did we get the hell off? Because we were afraid to die. Now we are no longer afraid. In addition, the white man has stopped talking to us in those terms: now it is he who is afraid. Now he is obliged to redefine his relationships with us.'

From "Chicago and Black Power" by Jacques Amabric, *Le Monde* Feb 1968. Translation by Denise Bordet and John Heckman.

THE CONFERENCE TABLE IS A FUTILE PLACE

Philadelphia ghetto leaflet defines the white man's notion of manhood as consisting of:

Being born with a penis and being 21 years old; graduating from high school or going to college; having a good job or making a lot of money; having a big house and a lot of furniture and other things; having a big car and a lot of girls — single, married etc. for sexual pleasure; being able to talk well or brag about yourself; going to fight in illegal wars and trying to win little pieces of metal or playing cowboys & Indians or gangsters, in real life with live ammunition; making your body over-developed it you can, with muscles, and trying to be Mr. White America.

On the other end of the state, in Spartanburg, another kind of answer was evolving in the mind of seventeen-year-old J. Wayne Watson, a high school senior. With the most infectious of grins, he told a white man of his distrust for whites. He led a boycott at his all-Negro high school that won new textbooks, the teaching of Negro history, improvement of the library, and other salubrious concessions. He led picketing of the YMCA, and got it integrated. He was forming a Black Youth Awareness Coordinating Committee among high school students and dropouts. And he was leading them in taking an active part in the voter registration effort.

His influence extended to black adults. They spoke of him fondly ("*That* Wayne"), and proudly recounted his achievements in school, his reading, his articulateness. They fell naturally into discussion with him, transcending the generation gap, arguing the fundamentals of black power. The adults urged not so much moderation as self-preser-vation. One sensed that for them Wayne was a spokesman, the articulation of a buried part of them, speaking their anger and their courage. The King assassination, he said, had convinced most young people in Spartanburg that "the conference table is a futile place." Whether there would be violence in such Southern towns as he lives in, he said, "depended on the white people." He spoke of one mass march to protest everything that is wrong, on the grounds that it would take too long to pick off the multitude of evils single-shot. But he indicated little faith in the idea. He seemed conversant with the extremes of Negro protest radicalism.

Why, then, was he working so hard on voter registration — the epitome of Negro participation within the system? "I guess," he said slowly, "you can say I am divided within myself."

From "South Carolina" by Pat Watters

THE Atlantic   Sept 1968

WHITEMAN

POOR OL' WHITEMAN IS ON THE VERGE OF A NERVOUS BREAKDOWN! HE'S A REAL PRODUCT OF THE GREAT DEPRESSION!

I'VE TRIED! GOD KNOWS I'VE TRIED!

A STORY OF CIVILIZATION IN CRISIS

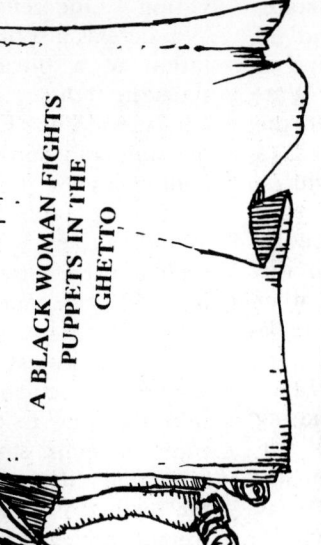

A BLACK WOMAN FIGHTS
PUPPETS IN THE
GHETTO

RECLAIMING OUR COMMUNITY

an exclusive interview with

Novella Williams

BY LEN LEAR

If there were more women around like Novella Williams, we probably wouldn't have to worry about this race thing anymore, much less about this war thing. Mrs. Williams, founder and president of Citizens For Progress located at 262 S. 52nd St., says she simply likes to "do her thing," and when she does it she doesn't play around. You can threaten her with physical harm or even death and you can be a magistrate, constable, mayor or police chief, but you can't intimidate her. If she knows she's right, she'll get what she wants even if she has to fight the Mafia to get it.

For those in Philadelphia who have never heard of her, Mrs. Williams is the black woman who has led the fight to close down the * * *, a private club at 276 S. 52nd St., which according to the fiery Citizens For Progress Head is a mecca for prostitution and narcotics peddling. (Rumors have it from a few black people who frequent the club; all you have to do is go into the club, mention what kind of drug you want, and in a little while a man taps you on the shoulder and takes you into the back where he delivers the goods.) According to Novella Williams, hard drugs are destroying countless young lives in the black community every year, and now it's got to stop.

"Those big-shots who are responsible for bringing the drugs into our community are committing genocide against our young people," she says. "You take a healthy, young man and feed him drugs and he's nothing more than a vegetable inside of a year."

She also makes it very clear that this problem does not only victimize black people. "The drug traffic is detrimental to both blacks and whites because the drug user who needs a fix will stop you on the street, beat you up, rob you or even kill you to get money for his fix, and he doesn't care if you're black or white. Many of the most prominent murders in Philadelphia in recent months have been attributed to users who were desperate for a fix," she adds, "so no one in his right mind could say this is a problem that only affects black people."

Mrs. Williams claims that big, powerful white people in this country are responsible for the drug problem, even though the only pushers that the ordinary user in West Philadelphia ever sees are black. "Let's face it," she declares authoritatively. "There isn't a black person anywhere in this country who has the facilities or the influence to bring all this stuff into the United States. The big shots, who are white, bring the stuff in and have their black boys serve as a front for them in the black community."

The radical community organizer says women on history she admires most are Esther (in the Bible) and Carrie Nation. "They both worked on the minds of apathetic people and awakened them to a new life," she said. "They got these people to act and moved them out of the darkness into the sunshine."

Despite the obvious barriers to the progress of any radical and in particular to that of Novella Williams, we can be certain of at least one thing. From now on in, come hell or high water, even if West Philadelphia has to be completely overturned to bring about meaningful change, Novella Williams will be in the forefront, leading the forces for change, and "doing her thing."

Despite the constant threats on her life, Mrs. Williams led a march of 600 black women and men down 52nd St. Friday, Sept. 27, stopped right outside the * * * and addressed the crowd. "We're saying to our men, 'Come on home to momma,'" she exclaimed. "We're saying to our boys, 'If someone tries to sell you dope, slap him down,' and we're saying to our prostitutes, 'Don't give 'em any more.' Our campaign has just begun," she emphasized. "Every nigger that's fronting for a white man, we're going to beat his brains out." Most of the crowd roared their enthusiasm despite the presence of a few "paid" hecklers who were separated from the crowd by plainclothes police.

"There's a difference between a black man and a nigger, and niggers have got to be stopped," Mrs. Williams insisted. "We're not against people taking an occasional drink, but we're not going to put up with the dope and the vice that's killing our young people and tying them up in knots. We don't care who's behind it or who's making money out of it," she added. "We don't care if it's the Mayor, City Council, some big lawyers, or anybody else. We want them to GET OUT!!" As TV cameras panned in, young people in the crowd held aloft signs reading "Daddy, Save Us," "Clean Up The Strip (52nd St.)," "Black Men, Save Your Black Women," "Vicelords, Get Out," "Rescuing Our Children," "Enforce The Law," "Reclaiming Our Children," and "Black Mothers."

"This is our day in West Philadelphia to stand up and be counted because you just might not get another chance," Mrs. Williams told the crowd. "You cannot raise children to be good, decent black people in an area like this. We have to live here when the businessmen go home at night," she added. "We must live with the stigma of the dope,

Novella Williams

She insists also that police tacitly allow the drug traffic to proceed unmolested because they're paid to do so. "A few months ago they removed every single policeman from 52nd St.," she says. "Since then three men have been shot dead in broad daylight and three others were wounded on 52nd St., but no one has been apprehended for any of these crimes. I am implicating the police here, but I think I'm justified in doing so." The robust West Philadelphia woman says there are two good reasons why police are not apprehending suspects for crimes committed on 52nd St. "For one thing, they just don't care about what happens in the black community, and if the victims are black, they see no reason to spend any effort trying to solve the crimes," she explains. "The second reason is that so many of the cops take graft."

Novella Williams announced her campaign against the drug traffic on Monday, Sept. 23, but she quickly learned that you don't play games with the power structure without some retaliation being visited upon you. Two days later, on Sept. 25, a bomb exploded in the basement of the Citizens For Progress headquarters, causing extensive damage to the entire lower half of the building. All week long, Novella received threats against her life, but she was not to be deterred. "You must be willing to make sacrifices, and you must even be willing to die in order to bring about a just society," she said. "That's the reason why I really dig those yippies. They could sit back and enjoy the luxuries of this society, but they want out of this whole mess. They're willing to sacrifice things to make their point, and we are making sacrifices right now so our children will not have their bodies and minds twisted by drugs and the other vices now in this community."

Mrs. Williams lashed out at hecklers. "What kind of men are you?" she asked rhetorically. Pointing to the TV cameras, she reminded them that thousands of whites were watching. "Do you know what white America thinks of you? Puppets. You are puppets. It's a sad day when women have to take to streets to protect their community. The black businessmen say they'll lose money if they close down over the weekend in a show of solidarity with our movement. They'll lose a heck of a lot more if the whole street is levelled."

Although many of the bar-owners hate to admit it, Mrs. Williams insists her campaign has hurt their business. "Reports by our people inside the clubs say that all the 52nd St. taprooms and clubs are hurting," she says. "They're all complaining because our campaign has hurt their businesses. We're successful because we're dealing with the minds of people, and a lot of minds are being changed. We're reaching a lot of men, and many of them who may not have the courage to come out and join our marches are at least beginning to stay away from the bars."

She   said she refuses to be deterred by a judge's ruling last week which overturned, temporarily at least, a Liquor Control Board order to revoke the * * * license. "What else can you expect?" she asked. "I think the judge acted quite normally in an election year. You must remember that the judges, the police and the politicians are all part of the same power structure that allows the drug traffic to flourish, so you can hardly expect anything else than this ruling."

Mrs. Williams said the ruling wasn't too important because the drug problem wouldn't go away even if the * * * were closed. "Those who wanted the stuff would just go to another place to get it," she said. "That's why we are approaching the problem the way we're doing it. When we finish with these people, none of them will dare set foot in our community."

The West Philadelphia firebrand said she realizes the drug traffic is related to a much bigger problem which concerns the entire world. "It also has to do with the way this country sends our poor black and white boys to Vietnam to kill people who never called them 'nigger.' The drug traffic and the Vietnam tragedy are the last attempts of a dying society to survive, but it won't last. The suppression in this country will die in this country, just as it will die in other countries around the world because you can no longer deny people their human rights and survive."

Novella Williams has only made newspaper headlines in recent weeks, although her entirely-volunteer organization has actually been in operation for a couple years in West Philadelphia. They have been involved in many community projects, including petitions to remove certain undesirable policemen from the area, weekly meetings wherein citizens could make observations, suggestions and register complaints with public officials, a detailed proposal for the erection of a middle-school in the area under community control with a radical, totally new educational concept, and many other things.

the prostitution, and the vice. We're going to have to solve this problem ourselves because whitey ain't going to do it for you."

Mrs. Williams was very critical of those who frequent clubs along the Strip, particularly the * * *. "Any black man -- I can't even call him a man -- I mean any black boy who goes into that place should be cut down," she insisted. "If we catch any nigger selling dope for the white man again, we're going to beat him half to death." At this point, the fiery crusader pointed her finger towards * * *, alleged owner of the club, and said, "We want you to close down, not just clean up. If you don't close it down peacefully, you'll wake up one morning and find it closed down another way. We're going to close this place down if we have to close it down brick by brick."

While Mrs. Williams spoke, CFP members handed out brochures exhorting black men to "recognize their humanity" and begin to act like men. The circular disparaged the white man's notion of manhood as consisting of: "being born with a penis and being 21 years old; graduating from high school or going to college; having a good job or making a lot of money; having a big house and a lot of furniture and other things; having a big car and a lot of girls -- single, married, etc. for sexual pleasure; being able to talk well or brag about yourself; going to fight in illegal wars and trying to win little pieces of metal or learning how to play Cowboys and Indians or gangsters in real life with live ammunition; making your body over-developed if you can, with muscles, and trying to be Mr. White America."

Lest anyone get the wrong impression, the circular went on to say that manhood should also not be defined the way too many black men have traditionally defined it, i.e. consisting of "smoking, dope, alcohol, gang wars, screwing, gambling, stealing, prostitution, sharp clothes, pimping, wife-beating, Saturday night brawls, wars, lying, killing, hate, anti-intellectualism, no regard for discipline, and disrespect and dehumanization of all women."

The pamphlet then exhorted black men, instead, to cultivate "love, respect, honesty, integrity, honor, understanding, trust, spirituality, sensitivity, humility, responsibility, humanism, compassion and human consciousness," so that "all black women and black children born into our community will have a model or example to live by or die for."

SON OF A BLACK JANITOR
HOME, (DEAD), FROM
VIETNAM

JAMES WALLER

The bodies come to Saigon in rubber bags. Men in green smocks are waiting in the room, which has pale green walls. When the bodies come, the men open the bags and slide the bodies onto steel platforms that rise to waist level from the floor. Then the men try to find out who the bodies used to be.

Sometimes it is hard to tell about the bodies right away. Sometimes the men cannot tell for hours, even days. When this happens, or simply when the embalming room is full, the bodies are put in a refrigerator. There are actually three refrigerators, walk-ins, with heavy doors and handles that click, like those in the back of a butcher shop.

The bodies lie here on racks until someone finds out who they were or until there is a table open in the room where they will be embalmed.

The smell is always here because there are so many bodies, whether the big doors are open or closed, but the men who work with it are used to it and do not mind. Occasionally a new man comes in who cannot take it. He is transferred quickly, without disgrace. The major understands.

Basic embalming: "The fine points of cosmetology we leave to the mortician back home," the major says. "But we send, oh, I'd say seventy to seventy-five percent home viewable, and we think that's something to be proud of."

When the embalming is done the bodies lie and wait through the night. Eight hours, at least, for tissue to be preserved. Then it is morning and time for packing to begin.

The first body is carried into the packing room and set down next to a table. There is a thin plastic bag waiting there. A man in a sleeveless green smock, sweat already rolling down the sides of his chest, turns down the front of the bag: a ship steward turning

down the bed. Strips of cotton are laid inside the bag. Then a powder which hardens at the touch of moisture. Just in case there is a leak.

Then the first one—cotton over the eyes and crotch—is put inside the plastic bag, and they wheel the table to the vacuumer. The vacuumer reaches into the plastic bag with the hose in his hand and sucks out all the air. His machine whirs and the plastic crinkles as it collapses around the body.

Then masking tape around the top of the bag so no air can creep back in and undo the embalmer's work during the long flight home.

And the body moves down the line. A sheet is wrapped around the plastic and more men with masking tape move in. They, too, work quickly, wrapping the tape, in thick, sticky brown strips around the sheet.

In the front room there is a chart:

AVERAGE PROCESSING TIME PER REMAINS

Receipt and Verification of Identity—
30 min.
Embalming Operations*—4 hrs. 15
min.
Preservation of Body Tissues—8 hrs.
Packing—10 min.
Out Processing—30 min.
Total—13 hrs. 25 min.

*Severely mangled, charred or badly decomposed remains can require from 10 minutes to six hours depending on the condition.

On Saturday, August 24, James Waller's mother got a letter.

Dear Madam: This is in answer to your letter concerning your son James Waller US 52 814 303.

I have spoken with James and he is doing fine. His job assignment, as you know, is as a rifleman in his company. His com-

pany commander and first sergeant have both stated that his performance has been outstanding and that he is highly respected and admired by his leaders and the personnel assigned to his company. I want to thank you again for your letter addressed to me concerning your son James, and again state that if you have any additional questions, please feel free to write to me. FOR THE COMMANDER: Robert M. Thomas, Captain.

On Monday, Mrs. Waller received another letter. This one was from James. He said he would be needing his good pair of eyeglasses in four months because he would be getting five days off and going to Honolulu. He also said he was trying to read his Bible like she had told him to, but it kept getting wet. He enclosed a picture of himself and two friends, grinning, dressed in fatigues.

A man in a uniform came to the Wallers' house that night. He told them James had been killed. He said it had happened in an attack on the base camp in the middle of the night. He said a telegram would follow. And there would be a Captain Woolley calling soon to help with the funeral arrangements.

The Wallers got a telegram:

THE SECRETARY OF THE ARMY HAS ASKED ME TO EXPRESS HIS DEEP REGRET THAT YOUR SON PRIVATE FIRST CLASS JAMES WALLER DIED IN VIETNAM ON 24 AUGUST 1968 AS A RESULT OF A WOUND RECEIVED WHILE IN BASE CAMP WHEN ENGAGED HOSTILE FORCE IN FIREFIGHT. PLEASE ACCEPT MY DEEPEST SYMPATHY. THIS CONFIRMS PERSONAL NOTIFICATION MADE BY A REPRESENTATIVE OF THE SECRETARY OF THE ARMY.
KENNETH G. WICKHAM
MAJOR GENERAL USA

The newspapers called and put stories on page 3: N. PHILA. SOLDIER DIES IN VIETNAM FIREFIGHT. One of them used a picture. Mrs. Waller told the papers that she did not know where in Vietnam her son had been stationed and that, no, he had not commented on the war in his letters. He had always been cheerful and generous, she said, but the papers did not print that.

Then she got a longer telegram:

THIS CONCERNS YOUR SON PFC. JAMES WALLER. THE ARMY WILL RETURN YOUR LOVED ONE TO A PORT IN THE UNITED STATES BY FIRST AVAILABLE MILITARY AIRLIFT. AT THE PORT REMAINS WILL BE PLACED IN A METAL CASKET AND DELIVERED (ACCOMPANIED BY A MILITARY ESCORT) BY MOST EXPEDITIOUS MEANS TO ANY FUNERAL DIRECTOR DESIGNATED BY THE NEXT OF KIN OR TO ANY NATIONAL CEMETERY IN WHICH THERE IS AVAILABLE GRAVE SPACE. YOU WILL BE ADVISED BY THE UNITED STATES PORT CONCERNING THE MOVEMENT AND ARRIVAL TIME AT DESTINATION. FORMS ON WHICH TO CLAIM AUTHORIZED INTERMENT ALLOWANCE WILL ACCOMPANY REMAINS. THIS ALLOWANCE MAY NOT EXCEED $75 IF CONSIGNMENT IS MADE DIRECTLY TO THE SUPERINTENDENT OF A NATIONAL CEMETERY. WHEN CONSIGNMENT IS MADE TO A FUNERAL DIRECTOR PRIOR TO INTERMENT IN A NATIONAL CEMETERY, THE MAXIMUM ALLOWANCE IS $250; IF BURIAL TAKES PLACE IN A CIVILIAN CEMETERY, THE MAXIMUM ALLOWANCE IS $500. REQUEST NEXT OF KIN ADVISE BY COLLECT TELEGRAM ADDRESS: DISPOSITION BRANCH, MEMORIAL DIVISION, DEPARTMENT OF THE ARMY, WUX MB, WASHINGTON, D.C. NAME AND ADDRESS OF FUNERAL DIRECTOR OR NAME OF NATIONAL CEMETERY SELECTED. IF ADDITIONAL INFORMATION CONCERNING RETURN OF REMAINS IS DESIRED, YOU MAY INCLUDE YOUR INQUIRY IN THE REPLY TO THIS MESSAGE. PLEASE DO NOT SET DATE OF FUNERAL UNTIL PORT AUTHORITIES NOTIFY YOU DATE AND SCHEDULED TIME OF ARRIVAL DESTINATION.

The body of James Waller arrived at the Air Force base in Dover, Del., on Tuesday, September 3. It went immediately to the base mortuary, where the man in charge noted the recommendation that had been attached to it in Saigon: Non-viewable.

That meant that James Waller would skip a step in the process. He would not have to be cosmeticized. Only the rough work, only the basic essential health procedures are taken in Saigon. The fancy stuff, the detail work, that is all done in Dover.

Then the escort detail was notified and Sgt. Ollie Dyson, of Chicago, was told to report at 9 A.M. Wednesday, to accompany the body to the Ray Funeral Home, 1525–27 West Dauphin Street, Philadelphia.

James Waller was removed from the aluminum carrying case and placed in a metal casket, which was sealed. The carrying case was washed and

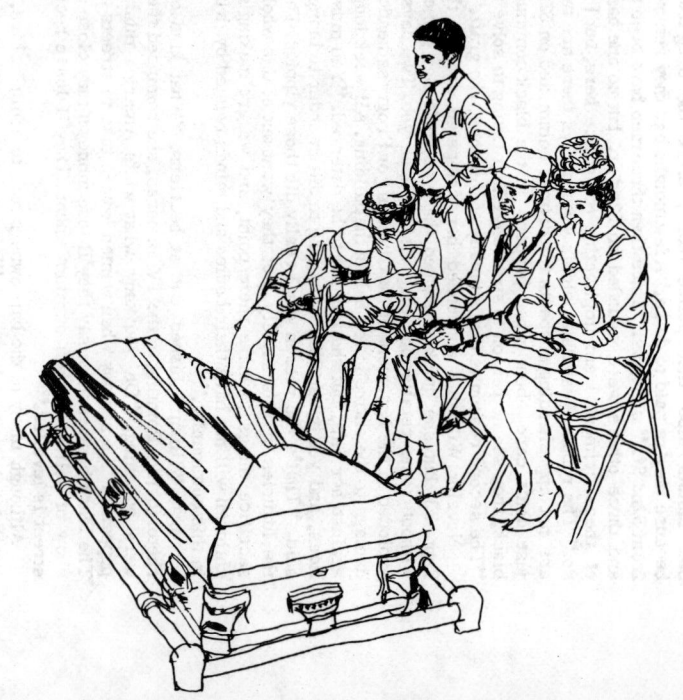

stacked with the others to await return to Saigon.

The Ray Funeral Home is in the section of Philadelphia called The Jungle. Across the street were Pop & Curly's Dauphin Bar, Bennie's Good-Time Bar and the boarded windows of what once had been the Rescue the Perishing Pentecostal Church.

The funeral home was not expecting James Waller's body Wednesday morning. Mrs. Deso Ray, the wife of the owner, said no telegram of notification had come. It was 11 o'clock and hot. Ollie Dyson and the hearse driver and a helper of Mr. Ray's, named William, carried the casket up the steps. Mr. Ray was not there. The casket was placed in a shaded room in the rear of the funeral home; the gray metal was covered by a bright American flag.

When Mr. Ray returned, Ollie Dyson handed him a letter:

To: Receiving Funeral Director:
1. These remains have been shipped to your funeral home consistent with the desires of the family.
2. We are sorry that the circumstances of the deceased's death precluded restoring the remains to a viewable state.
3. Before shipment, the remains and casket were inspected by Air Force representatives and found to be in satisfactory condition.
4. We would appreciate your cooperation in explaining this matter to the family should they question the reason for a sealed casket.
Sincerely,
DAVID J. AFFHOLDER, *Captain*
USAF Mortuary Office

Mrs. Waller could not understand about the casket.

"Don't worry about it," her husband told her. "It doesn't make any difference."

"But how do I know it's him?"

"It's him."

"But why can't we see him?"

"Don't worry about it. What you want to see him for anyway? He's dead."

"If I could just see him one more time."

"Stop talking about it."

There was to be no wake, they decided. The funeral would be Monday night and burial Tuesday morning. They got a letter from General Westmoreland:

Please know that the thoughts of many are with you at this time. The passing of your son, Private First Class James Waller, on 24 August, in Vietnam, is a great loss not only for his fellow soldiers but for his country as well.

I know that words can do little to relieve your grief just now but I hope that you will find comfort in the knowledge that through your son's sacrifice he will live in the hearts of all who desire peace and freedom.

As our Nation strives . . . human dignity which we hold dear . . . most distressing thing . . . through their devoted service . . . remain strong and our purpose steadfast. . . .

At 4:30 Wednesday afternoon, five and a half hours after the body had arrived, the final telegram came:

REMAINS PFC JAMES WALLER ARRIVE PHILA. PA. APPROX 1030 AM 4 SEPT VIA HEARSE RAY FUNERAL HOME NOTIFIED.

Mrs. Waller was sitting at her din-ing-room table. She was a heavy woman and very tired. Her husband was with her. He was a janitor at the Boyles Galvanizing and Plating Company. He wore a medal with a picture of Martin Luther King. James had been their second son. Sidney was one year older. There were also two younger daughters.

"The insurance man was by today and he said I ought to frame that letter," Mrs. Waller said to her husband.

He was staring at the floor.

"Did you hear me? The insurance man says we ought to frame this letter from the chief of staff."

"Yes, I hear you."

"Well?"

"Well, well—well, what? Fine. Frame it."

Mrs. Waller put the letter down and picked up the picture that James had sent her from Vietnam.

"Poor James," she said. "He only just got there in June. He didn't know what it was all about. I told the papers he didn't have any comments about the war. Well, he did have one. He wrote and said, 'Mom, this whole thing is crazy. I don't understand it.'"

"Who does understand it?" John Waller said.

Mrs. Waller did not answer.

"If they had only give him a chance," the father said. "They come up on him in the middle of the night and he was probably sleeping and never even saw them. He was out there in the front row for two months and then he goes back for a rest and they sneak up on him in the middle of the night." John Waller shook his head.

"He could have gone to jail," Mrs. Waller said. "He could have been one of those boys who goes to jail because they don't want to be in the war."

"He's not that type."

"No, but if he had done that he'd of been alive."

"He's not that type. To go to jail. That wasn't how James was."

"No, that's right. James always did what he was told."

The father nodded.

"He never went anywhere that he didn't come back with a piece of paper that said how good he was," Mrs. Waller said. "He got one, look here, from Dobbins, where he went to high school, and one from the R.W. Brown Boys Club and here, one from the American Legion. . . ."

"And then they sneak up on him in the middle of the night."

"James never want to do no killing anyway."

"No, that's right. He told the Army he wanted to be a clerk."

"But they told him he couldn't because he didn't have experience."

"He didn't have experience killing either."

"That's right, he didn't have no experience with guns."

"But that didn't matter, did it?"

"No, they didn't care about experience with the guns."

"What I don't understand," John Waller said, "is if they could teach him how to kill why couldn't they teach him how to type?"

From "Three who Came Home" by Joe McGinnis, *Saturday Evening Post* 2/8/69

BOTH THE GOALS
AND THE METHODS

A Wall Street Journal sampling of opinion among black citizens in four metropolitan areas across the nation [San Francisco, New York, Cleveland, and Chicago] indicates a clear majority of blacks strongly support both the goals and methods of the Black Panthers.
—The Wall Street Journal, **January 13**

" . . . Those who profess to favor freedom, and yet depreciate agitation, are men who want crops without plowing up the ground. They want rain without thunder and lightning. They want the ocean without the awful roar of its waters. This struggle may be a moral one; or it may be a physical one; or it may be both moral and physical; but it must be a struggle. Power concedes nothing without a demand. It never did, and it never will. Find out just what people will submit to, and you have found out the exact amount of injustice and wrong which will be imposed upon them; and these will continue till they are resisted with either words or blows, or with both. The limits of tyrants are prescribed by the endurance of those whom they oppress. . . ."

FREDERICK DOUGLASS
August 4, 1857

The Great Speckled Bird 2/9/70

POLITICS OF VANDALISM

STANLEY COHEN

· · · Deviant behavior is not a static category: an act must be so labeled by others. This means that the sociologist should be on guard when society (or powerful groups in society) designates certain behavior problematic or deviant. In regard to some forms of mental illness, for example, R. D. Laing has suggested that the labeling can be seen to involve a *political* decision: somebody (who has power, influence or status) acts in such a way that somebody else is defined as mad. In discussing vandalism, I want to use this term "political" in the very broad sense that Laing adopts. In a narrower sense, it is apparent that the label one attaches to certain forms of behavior is affected by one's political position: to some, members of an African nationalist group who sabotage a power station in Rhodesia are "freedom fighters"; to others, they are "terrorists."

The term has its origin in the practices of the Vandals, an East Germanic tribe that invaded Western Europe in the fourth and fifth centuries, and eventually sacked Rome in 455. They were regarded as the great destroyers of Roman art, civilization and literature and the term "vandal" was broadened in the 17th century to refer to anyone who recklessly destroyed property, particularly works of art. Vandalism is currently defined by dictionaries as "ruthless destruction or spoiling of anything beautiful or venerable." The vandalism that criminologists study (for example, a group of youths smashing the furniture of a classroom) or the vandalism defined more as "political" than "criminal" and which conveys evident ideological overtones (for example, burning shop interiors during racial disturbances, or stoning embassy windows during a demonstration) seems far removed from the etymological origins of the term. Nevertheless, these origins continue to make an effect: the adjectives which the behavior of the original Vandals conjure up—barbarous, willful, ignorant, cruel—remain part of the stereotype of contemporary vandalism. They are used in a political context in order to justify action against the deviant.

In many cases, of course, the deviant does not accept this description. To him, his acts are not reckless and witless but eminently sensible. As with the Luddites of the early 18th century, property destruction (in their case, machine breaking) may be a deliberate act of protest. Economic historians have done much to dispel the stereotype of Luddism as being "pointless" and "frenzied" or a mere "overflow of high spirits."

Eric Hobsbawm's distinction between two types of machine breaking—"collective bargaining by riot," which under some conditions was a normal way of putting pressure on employers, and the destruction which expressed working-class anger against the new machines of the Industrial Revolution—has more relevance to contemporary forms of vandalism than at first appears. Newspaper accounts and reports by the two commissions on racial disturbances in American cities over the past few years seem to make it evident that most of the property destruction was patterned and, in a sense, "rational." The targets chosen were not arbitrary. For instance, the 1968 Report of the National Advisory Commission on Civil Disorders

states: "In at least nine of the cities studied, the damage seems to have been, at least in part, the result of deliberate attacks on white-owned businesses, characterized in the Negro community as unfair or disrespectful toward Negroes." Even if the targets were arbitrary, there is no denying that, in a society dominated by consumption, those who are denied access to the "goodies" operate by a kind of logic when they destroy whatever they can get their hands on. As one analysis of the 1965 Watts riots expressed it: "The man who destroys commodities shows his human superiority over commodities."

When society defines certain people as outsiders, it needs to emphasize the ways in which such people are different from the insiders, who are normal. Thus criminals are not just people who have broken the law; they are also generally dangerous and not to be trusted. Narcotics addicts don't just take drugs; they are "dope fiends," vicious, degenerate and dirty. To stress the discontinuity between deviance and normality gives a feeling of security; the difference becomes clear-cut between good and bad (or, to be more up to date, between "healthy" and "sick"). It is more disturbing to entertain such a view as that advanced by David Matza that much adolescent behavior—and vandalism would seem a good example—is a caricature rather than an inversion or repudiation of middle-class conformist culture. There is an interchange between the conventional and deviant traditions of society as shown, for example, in the ambivalence of most adults (in private) to many forms of youthful misconduct. It needs no subtle Freudian interpretation to suggest that much adult denunciation of teen-age sexual permissiveness is accompanied by a degree of envy.

Similarly, the values associated with juvenile vandalism and thought to be peculiar to delinquents, such as the search for excitement and kicks, the high regard for toughness and aggression, might reflect values running through the whole society. The adolescent is easily stigmatized as a violent hoodlum or an irresponsible hedonist and, as Edgar Friedenberg has pointed out, many adults use the terms "adolescent" and "delinquent" almost interchangeably. But there is, after all, nothing peculiarly adolescent in the violence and vandalism of James Bond movies, or for that matter, of real life.

I have not tried here to explain vandalism. This does not mean that I consider attempts at such explanations irrelevant: rather that one must first be sure of *what* one is explaining. The usual terms used to describe various forms of vandalism obscure and discredit what may be the real explanations: if a boy breaks into his school and smashes up the classrooms because he has a grievance against the teachers, it is no help to call his behavior "wanton" and "pointless." The only end such labels serve is the teacher's need to hold himself blameless. Most research into school vandalism indicates, in fact, that there *is* something wrong with the school that is damaged. The highest rates of school vandalism tend to occur in schools with obsolete facilities and equipment, low staff morale and high dissatisfaction and boredom among the pupils.

ople of color

On July 18th I sat-in at Newark City Hall, middle of the floor; dialogued gently with all comers including rifle-toting cops; got off pretty nicely to a blood-lined paddy wagon; was released at the police station and offered bus fare to go home to my children.

It's real good to be white. A white woman sitting alone on the floor of Newark City Hall looking quiet and pious gets lots of respect. Maybe I should never do it again.

If you want to know what I think as a pacifist about the Afro-American "Viet Cong," read the July 28 edition of LIFE Magazine and stare a long, long time at the cover. It could have been my kid lying in a pool of his own blood—except that I'm white, and we don't live in the ghetto. Joe Bass, Jr. got it the day he was born black, not the day he was shot. He is recovering from his blackness. He will be a target.

All the revolutions I have ever heard of involved property changing hands. The 13 American colonies were taken from an absentee landlord in 1776. All the shooting done in Newark by black people, LIFE says, was shots fired in the air to decoy the police away from the looters. All the shooting done in Newark by the police, LIFE says, was to protect private property—to take vengeance on those who stole milk and beer. People were shot in the back of the head for taking food and clothing from the stores that live off them.

Is this revolution? Revolution WOW! What will poor pacifists do? The natives are restless, and the Viet Cong would never invade the CNVA farm. Pacifists keep mum in public on whether it's right for the NLF to use guns instead of reason, and the NLF will never move to Queens. Pacifists keep our sights trained on the Pentagon, knowing that some people are more violent than others and the Pentagon is the most violent of all. The Viet Cong never called me "hunkie" and could not come down from Harlem and loot the stores

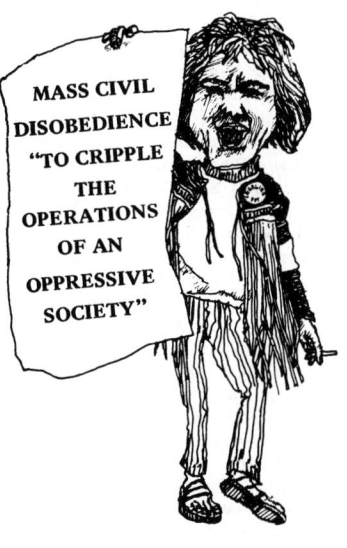

MASS CIVIL DISOBEDIENCE "TO CRIPPLE THE OPERATIONS OF AN OPPRESSIVE SOCIETY"

on Avenue B.

Man, it's hard to live right next door to a VietCong!

The revolution is here, in America, in every ghetto in the United States, and some pacifists want to say to the black people "Shhhhhh, now, don't do anything destructive—the war in Vietnam comes first." The Viet Cong won't come to 5 Beekman Street. The Viet Cong only kills American Soldiers who go to Vietnam. The black people are right here, and what if they make a mistake and attack me without realizing I'm on their side? (Thereby losing the best friend who ever told them to cool it at any cost—to themselves.)

The whole point, of course, dear fellow pacifist, is that the black people have been and are nonviolent. They are not killing. They are being killed for taking food and clothing from the stores that cheat them. The black people have traditionally been Christian pacifists living in the midst of ku kluxers, brutal cops, and the constant death of hunger and rat-ridden firetraps. Now black people are messing around with private property, and some pacifists quake at the words "black power."

We are pacifists because of our conviction that we need to love our brothers, to love all men. But we love the Vietnamese easier than we love our black brothers. We have looked long at pictures of napalm-burned children. Have you seen how many Afro-American children have burn scars on their bodies from exploding gasoline stoves, tenement fires, and the many times they have been left so young to cook for the small babies when mother had to go to work? And the deepest wounds of all are the destruction through contempt of the human heart and mind-and the destruction through segregation of self-respect. No Vietnamese ever walked around with such wounds as some people have whose self-respect has been insulted every day for a hundred years.

CAROL WALLACE, *WIN* Aug 1967

Dr. King Planning Protests To 'Dislocate' Large Cities

Massive but Nonviolent Campaign Is Sought, Before Congress Adjourns, to Get Federal Aid for Negroes

By GENE ROBERTS
Special to The New York Times

ATLANTA, Aug. 15 — The Rev. Dr. Martin Luther King Jr. said today that he planned to "dislocate" Northern cities with massive but nonviolent demonstrations of civil disobedience before Congress adjourns its current session.

The civil rights leader told delegates to the annual convention of his Southern Christian Leadership Conference that he had decided on the step to provide an alternative to rioting and to gain large Federal spending programs for improverished Negroes.

"To dislocate the functioning of a city without destroying it can be more effective than a riot because it can be longer-lasting, costly to the society but not wantonly destructive," Dr. King said. "Moreover, it is more difficult for Govern-

ment to quell it by superior force."

"Mass civil disobedience," he added, "can use rage as a constructive and creative force."

Dr. King announced also that he would meet with his staff in about two weeks to discuss the "specifics" of the civil disobedience campaign and to consider such tactics as weekly school boycotts, blocking plant gates with unemployed Negroes and disrupting governmental operations with sit-in demonstrations in Federal buildings.

The ultimate objective of any demonstration, Dr. King made clear, will be to draw Congress and President Johnson into responding to Negro demands for jobs, improved housing, better education and more intensive enforcement of existing civil rights legislation.

"Our real problem is that there is no disposition by the Administration nor Congress to seek fundamental remedies beyond police measures," he said. "The tragic truth is that Congress, more than the American people, is now running wild with racism."

The idea of massive civil disobedience in the North is not new with Dr. King, although he has never committed himself to it as firmly as he did today. A year ago, he briefly discussed jamming the freeways of Chicago and other Northern cities with Negro sit-in demonstrators, but abandoned the project after white mobs attacked his open-housing marches with rocks and bottles in Chicago.

Campaign Delayed

Some of his aides said then that in delaying his civil disobedience campaign, Dr. King was acting on the advice of people who felt that further demonstrations could touch off still more racial strife in the Chicago area.

Now, according to some of the same aides, he believes that Negroes will not stop rioting unless they are presented with alternative ways of militant protest.

"It is purposeless to tell Negroes they should not be enraged when they should be," Dr. King said today. "Indeed, they will be mentally healthier if they do not suppress rage but vent it constructively and use its energy peacefully but forcefully to cripple the operations of an oppressive society. Civil disobedience can utilize the militance wasted in riots to seize clothes or gro-

United Press International Telephoto
The Rev. Dr. Martin Luther King Jr. addresses meeting.

ceries many do not even want."

However, Dr. King is almost certain to encounter major difficulties in carrying out "massive" civil disobedience campaigns, particularly if he should decide to center the assault on Washington.

No Grass-Roots Staff

One problem is that he has no grass-roots organizing staff working in Negro neighborhoods in Washington, and might be forced to transport demonstrators to the city from other areas. This could seriously tax his organization's financial resources, which have dropped considerably since the Selma-to-Montgomery protest march in 1965.

His staff is also scattered—in Chicago, Cleveland and the South—and probably would have to be regrouped before any massive campaign could be undertaken.

But for all the problems, Dr. King clearly wants to create what he terms a "nonviolent confrontation" between Negroes and the Johnson Administration and Congress. He said that in voting down a rat control bill and cutting back on several poverty programs, Congress had shown itself to be "more anti-Negro than anti-rat."

He also criticized President Johnson—although not by name —for escalating the war in Vietnam, rather than diverting defense money to a war on slums.

The New York Times

8/16/67

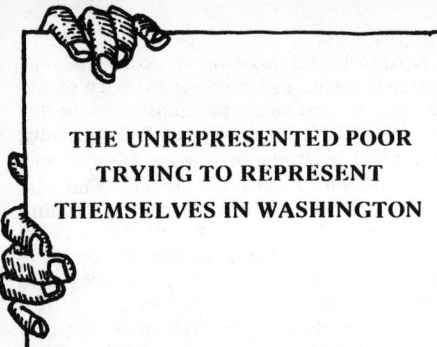

No Miracle in The Mud Flats

by Maude Dorr

"We want Cohen, we want Cohen, we want Cohen." The poor, the poverty workers, the out-of-workers, the mob, the rabble, chant and rock their way into the marble halls of the Department of Health, Education, and Welfare, and demand to see the head. "Ump bah, soooul spirit, ump bah, ump bah bah," past gray - suited men and murals of Depression day workers. The poor have come back to pack the auditorium, take over the mikes: "Like I see it," says the Reverend Hosea Williams, "Cohen's just the custodian of this building while we, the owners, are away; now we've come back to check up on how he's doing his job." This time the poor aren't going to settle for assistants, they aren't going to get pawned off on some second-in command who'd eventually say he really couldn't say, because he'd have to take the matter up with the first invisible man who always had the final say. The poor are going to sit and stay all day, all night if necessary, until they see the head.

The business of Resurrection City is confrontation. The confrontation of shacks and muddy boots, and a government all sealed up in air - conditioned boxes, presided over by officials in suits and ties who go home to the suburbs every day after seeing more papers than people and no poverty. Resurrection City is a mighty sprawling camp of war pitched right in the eye of the government. But the papers are full of accounts of how unsuccessful it is. Although bumper stickers advertise the message "Last Chance for

Non-Violence," most residents of Resurrection City wonder whether there was ever any chance at all. What started out as a dream seemed to be ending in a nightmare, but probably Martin Luther King could not have dreamed that Resurrection City would turn out to be so miserable and authentic a testimony of the poor.

Resurrection City is confused, badly organized, without a clear-cut strategy of non-violent confrontation, but in one month men who have never had a chance of running for mayor have built and run a city, men who have never participated in government are learning to confront a government that is supposed to be theirs, people who have been passive participants are discovering their power.

Part of the dissent in Resurrection City lies in the fact that men traveled from Tennessee, from California, from New Mexico Some traveled for three days and three nights only to find themselves confronted by a leader who only knows how to treat them like a flock of sheep while he plays pastor. Ralph Abernathy's initial strategy was to let the poor build shacks, grapple with the mud, form a mute tableau of poverty while he made all the decisions. On the other hand, the people might complain in workshops, act violent on the side, but when Abernathy appeared they fell into old habits of listening, of agreeing, of "Yeah man, you're right." So that even if they felt he shouldn't live in the Pitts Motel while they stuck it out in the mud, Abernathy could get them all together and persuade the crowd to explain to the press that he their leader didn't have to come down and sleep in their beds. Even though

the citizens might have a workshop debating whether they were ready to die for the cause or not, Abernathy could get up and ask them merely to vote on whether they wanted fried chicken on Saturday or Sunday. At the end of the speech one woman could murmur "Yeah, Sir, you just go home and get some sleep," while another matron could exclaim, "what a bunch of phonies, complain and complain, but never tell him to his face." Just that afternoon an impromptu speaker had whirled on a member of the audience who clapped him, "Yeah man," and said, "Don't clap for me, don't yes - man me, I'm not here for you to make me feel good. I'm here to make you think."

Resurrection City was conceived as a dream where the poor would march upon their government, and the government would look upon the evidence and see. Instead, more realistically, it has turned into a process whereby thousands of people try to realize that they themselves are the government, try to catch up in a few weeks with a democracy that has excluded them for a couple of hundred years. Whether last-minute chances like that even exist is debatable.

The people who came to Resurrection City range from veteran Mississippi marchers to some citizens who had never been out of the hollers of West Virginia before. Some are bold, and some are brave in spite of being scared. There are children, an old woman with no teeth but a sparkling eye and her hair done up in pin curlers, semi militants in magnificent flowing robes, workers in the civil rights uniform of blue jeans.

The two methods of confrontation available to the poor are the

city itself and the marches. Sometimes the impact is strong, sometimes confused. Although the press and Congress have looked upon the mud, the sickness, and the squabbles as the mess the poor have gotten themselves into in Washington, D. C., most of the citizens of Resurrection City know that is about where things are at back home. However, there is no clear spokesman, no forceful propaganda machine to nail home to Congress that the muddy streets of that new city are just like the old roads back home in West Virginia, where all the money goes to building throughways for tourists and none of it to the back roads where West Virginians live, and the school buses can't even get through to pick up the kids. There is no one at Resurrection City to tell it to Congress that those chemical toilets smell a lot sweeter than some of the out - houses in their own backyards, and if there are no showers in Resurrection City there may be nothing more at home than a tin tub and a water pump out in the field. Congress is even reluctant to come down and trample in the mud. Instead they post an appointment sheet for citizens to sign up to come and see them. But Resurrection City residents feel that they've come all the way from California, from New Mexico and Mississippi, and those Congressmen can't even walk down the hill to see them. "Besides my congressman doesn't want to see ME." Resurrection City has all the problems of an authentic ghetto, isolated, hostile, and incommunicative, and yet the citizens are making brave attempts to get the government to see and hear.

Their main tool is the march. The march to this or that department or individual. The confrontations range from the near disastrous to the near magnificent. Sometimes they never get to see the man they ask for, sometimes they get the assistants, sometimes they manage to get to see the head and then get side tracked on the issues, sometimes they manage to confront and get some action.

A sad example of the "no show" occurred the time two busloads of Appalachians set out for the house of West Virginia's arch conservative Senator Byrd, with carefully rehearsed demands and a block-long roll of shelf paper full of signatures. They march around the intersection in front of Byrd's modest brick house, screwing up their courage to sing out a few songs. A very young liberal sets up a stand of free lemonade, while an enraged old neighbor snaps their pictures as frenetically as he would have shot down "the lazy bastards," the law permitting One little girl turns to her suburban mother: "Mommy, what are those people doing on OUR Street?" Fulcher, the leader of the Appalachians, occasionally marches with the people, occasionally drops out of the line saying, "Come on now, I'm not going to sing for you, this is your march." He's a large, demagogic, white preacher recently converted from bigot to saviour by a meeting with Martin Luther King. He rings the doorbell. Mrs. Byrd, a thin but tough lady in white hair, comes out and says something to the effect she can't understand why all those people want to come pester her husband when he works so hard for them and he's even down there at his office today, Saturday. She goes inside to call her husband who says he'll be glad to have everybody come down and see him at his office. The door closes shut and although everybody is standing around the curb, bowing over the lawn like it was a holy carpet, because they might get arrested if they trespass, most Appalachians are mad enough to stick it out until he comes. But they get up and read their petitions bravely, to a closed door, and then Fulcher backs them out of the confrontation saying that he knows a lot of people want to get back to West Virginia as they had planned today, and he has to go with the majority of course, so how many people want to stay there till Byrd comes or get back on the bus. And of course the people, led into leaving, leave. They will be coming back on the 17th and then they'll stick it out.

The confrontation at HEW was more successful. At least 400 residents of Resurrection City succeeded at least in seeing the head of something for a change. It started out as a very orderly confrontation. The citizens marched two by two, hustled along the reflecting pool by their own marshals. They walked peaceably past the temporary war buildings built 20 years ago, past a black couple splashing rising jubilant from the pool. A young white woman asks a Negro on crutches how he got hurt and he spits out that she ain't got no right to ask him how he got hurt, when he's been hurting for a long time and it's none of her business no more.

Only at the intersections does tension strike. Police converge, hurrying marchers across the street with such urgency that a jay walker might touch off a revolution. The orderly line then turns down Independence Avenue, past the palaces of bureaucracy, past polished stone and glass boxes where layers and layers of civil servants stand behind windows that don't open and watch without hearing as the rabble goes by Past the Department of Agriculture, this and that federal building, past doorways marked "closed" at 3 p.m.

and one entrance that has "temporarily been shifted to the other side."

Once inside the auditorium at HEW, the crowd demands to see Cohen, but of course Cohen isn't in. Such and such assistant from such and such department would be glad to tell them all about the new welfare package, about education, etc. The assistants file down front but they have to wait till the people finish their song before getting introduced and even then they don't get much of a chance to talk but remain hostages while the crowd votes that Brother Cohen himself come down here to see them. "You have to understand our reaction," explains Hosea Williams to the officials. "Most of us have third or fourth grade educations. Most of us have seen our fathers leave the family, and we had to leave school to get out there and earn the bread while our mothers turned to prostitution and our brothers into dope addicts. You have to understand, that's why we came out of the mud, from all over the country to let US help YOU see America. We come not out of hostility, we come here to speak. We are constituents, we are ready to plead, if necessary to die." The crowd takes up a song, "Come on up to Washington and I'll be waiting up there. . ."

Corky Gonzalez, leader of the Mexican - Americans from Denver, cuts through all the pleased-to-meet-yous. "It's not a pleasure to be here," he states, "because we came here to make changes. We don't want poverty or welfare or waiting in hospitals or police brutality. We're going to make them give us our fair share." The crowd ignites. Someone shouts, "You may not believe it, but Rockefeller didn't build this nation, we did. For 244 years they worked us in slavery and even gave us bus fare to town. Rockefeller's a fool if he thinks he owns all that oil. He's had enough, his share, now we're going to get some." Somebody tells the press to get the hell out, and the cameramen are already sweating it, sliding up and down against the auditorium walls wishing they were invisible. The talk explodes too violently for a lot of people and a few whites and blacks take the opportunity between speeches to get up politely and leave, as if they suddenly remembered a pressing appointment elsewhere. A little steam goes out of the auditorium with their leaving.

Hosea Williams decides it's time to take a break, time to take a tour of the building while they wait for Brother Cohen, time to see those offices, "not to scribble on the walls or mess it up mind you, but just to run our bare feet through some of those thick carpets." Cohen suddenly decides to appear, before he's

flushed out. He cools it, as though he's late to a tea party: "I want to welcome you all here today: of course next time I'd like a little notice as I had planned a number of meetings for this afternoon, but as soon as they were over I rushed right over here to see you." ("Small world, ain't it?" says someone down right.) "I have here," he continues smoothly, "an official letter I had already prepared for Dr. Abernathy containing my response to your original demands. Of course there's 34 pages of it and I am sure you don't want to go into it all right now." More soothing words, and brief summaries of his serious review of the poor people's "meritorious ideas," and finally the politician's ploy: "Now I really came down here to ask you people for your support because I think welfare ought to be nationalized and welfare payments ought to be equal" ("Not welfare, guaranteed incomes," says a citizen, but Cohen goes on), "so that if a man in New York gets $200, so should a man in Mississippi." And of course everybody is agreeable to something like that and they all clap and Cohen says good night ever so nicely and he'll be glad to meet with any delegates as soon as they have reviewed his proposals. So the crowd leaves, some are satisfied, some know that they ought to have demanded that Cohen sit down right then and there and review all 34 pages even if it took all night.

The most successful non-violent protest was staged by the Mexican - Americans at the Justice Department. Corky Gonzalez and Tijerina assembled 100 of the poor to protest the arrest of 13 men in Colorado. The men, including one teacher, a student from Los Angeles, a community worker, and a group of Brown Berets (a quasi-military group) had been arrested on charges of conspiring to create civil disorder when they had assisted a group of young students protesting against discrimination against Mexican - American students in school. The students wanted Mexican American teachers and courses stressing the contribution of Mexicans to the history and culture of the United States. The 13 persons had been arrested and sentenced by a grand jury to jail on an unheard - of - bail of $12,500. Corky Gonzalez and Tijerina, who led the group, hold widely different philosophies on protest. Corky has been described as a sophisticated, Americanized Mexican from Denver, familiar with the techniques of negotiation, Tijerina is the mountain man from New Mexico who understands violence and direct action. When the group met with no response from the State Department, Tijerina, angry, withdrew his group to protest such

treatment. Corky stayed on. He positioned one Mexican in front of every policeman, and informed the authorities that his people were staying. If the cops wished to arrest the group, they should provide the transportation and Corky's own men would usher the crowd aboard the vans. The group kept the vigil. Corky kept an open line to Colorado, and news came back that hour after hour the bail was reduced and then the men were finally released on $250 bail.

The rest of the Poor People's Campaign has yet to match that kind of confrontation.

To many residents of Resurrection City the whole business of confrontation with the outside world has become secondary to the confrontations with their brothers inside. Middle - aged women, young men, little children, old couples meet to discuss and bullshit away the hours under the training, tent or on the lawn beside the reflecting pool. The semi - violent confront the nonviolent and the dedicated. There are those who see Resurrection City settling in for years until the job is done. They think about ordering heaters and laying sidewalks and erecting western fronts; others are just waiting for the carnival to be over, for the marches to wind up nowhere, for Congress not to respond, for such discouragement to set in that the plain people move out and the demolition experts move in to scare the shit out of everybody and grab what won't be given. Sometimes the arguments are fierce but many militants have genuinely laid aside their bag for the moment to look at where their other brothers are at. "Now don't jump on him saying what he believes. That's just where the cat's at," a moderator will say. Everybody can get up and say his piece and among the endless frustrating stream of words are some eloquent passages on the mistakes of American capitalism, and some agonizing appraisals of whether one is prepared to die for the cause. "I'm not prepared to die, just when life is beginning to get good," says one Negro girl. "How can anybody decide whether he is ready to die sitting in this tent." "What exactly are we going to jail for anyway?" The most tragic aspect of Resurrection City is that it is easier for its inhabitants to confront the prospect of death with which they are familiar, than to focus on changing a government which is totally foreign. A whole lot of people white and black may look back upon Resurrection City as just a brief moment when brother met brother, soul met soul.

A Great Babel of Sound

It was a memory perhaps above all of all the voices joined there, of the great Babel of sound that was so often raised—at the front gate or in the dining tent or outside the two-room shack named City Hall where we went for mail or went to try to get information.

I first listened with awe to that mixture of voices on my way up from the South with the campaign.* I had gone down to Memphis early in May for the start of it at the Lorraine Motel where Dr. King had been murdered, and on to Marks ("where he wept the tears," as one woman told it; King had visited the houses there that stood in festering swampy water), and on up through Nashville and Knoxville and Danville, recruiting more people as we went. Our nights, on the road, we spent most often in huge municipal gymnasiums—where the several hundred voices of the campaigners sounded and resounded against the walls. The clamor kept up always until two or three o'clock in the morning, and began to gather again as early as five o'clock. The first two nights —with the encouragement of several mothers of small children—I made vain gestures of pleading for quiet after midnight. There was never any hope for quiet, of course. Here were lots of people away from home for the first time in their lives, and here were people only recently released by this movement from resignation about their lives, on their way to give battle ("Socksoul! Socksoul!"), and keyed high by all their hopes about that and fears about that. How could they sleep? By the third night, I had given up trying to sleep, myself, and learned to lie back and simply listen to the noise objectively, as one might listen to some clamorous piece of

* The Poor People's March on Washington

music. It was worth listening to in that way. For here, in the form of sound—here in the air for one to study— were all the elements of the gathering struggle.

Some of those musical elements I could lie and disentangle in my mind. I could recall the peculiar high pitch in the voice of a small boy in Marks, marching, singing, back to town, in a line of others, down the highway from the field where a mass rally had been held: as we passed a state trooper at an intersection, the child's arm outflung, his finger pointing out the man and his voice rising again for the words, "No more po-lice over me, over me!", so physically possessed by the courage he had learned that night that now and then he had to leave the line of march and turn somersaults in somebody's patch of roadside lawn. I could recall the voice of the young man of twelve ("boy" would be the wrong word for him), a very gifted gospel singer—his voice more sober, but trembling, breaking now and then with feeling, as he told me how we must pray for more force, more strength, and doors would open if we did. "God moves in very mysterious ways." Or the voice of the talkative young man sitting up front on the bus as we finally entered Washington—suddenly quavering out, solo, "We are not afraid! Oh yes, we are!" We passed some buildings where members of the National Guard were training, and a little girl of eight, sitting between me and her brother of five, turned to me and whispered, "Carl says we are going to die here."

The Music of This Struggle

These notes and a thousand more are in the tumult to which I listen. Voices of the young women dancing down the sidewalks: *Soul Power, Soul Power, ooh! ahh!*— the sounds "ooh! ahh!" thrown off like sparks. *You better do right, white man, do right!*—the key shifting. *Everybody has a right to live!* Every feeling that has drawn these people into this adventure, every feeling that agitates them now that they are on their way, takes the form of sound. And here the sounds have rolled in upon each other; they mix, they collide, mount, tremble and roll into one great wheel of sound—a not quite perfectly rounded wheel, one that staggered somewhat as it moved. The peculiar music of this gathering struggle.

From "Mud City" by Barbara Deming, Sept 1968

LIBERATION

PEOPLE BEGAN ORGANIZING TO FIGHT BOTH THE POLICE AND THE GUARD

Nashville Moves Against Repression

(By Staff Correspondent)

NASHVILLE, Tenn. — People here are taking the offensive against attempts to repress the black community—and the power structure is backing down.

Police rampaged through the ghetto for a week in late January, supposedly looking for some men who had killed a policeman (see February Patriot). Their behavior intimidated people—but at the same time it made them determined to resist.

Negro leaders called for an "economic withdrawal" from downtown stores, to strengthen the black community. Students and militants joined in the drive.

Then three civil-rights organizations held a series of public meetings on police brutality in Nashville—and how it relates to repression across the country. The three groups—SCEF, SNCC and SSOC—have been red-baited in local newspapers and charged with starting the "riots" here last

April; and some people felt that Nashville residents would be afraid to come to any meeting those organizations sponsored.

But more than 300 people attended one meeting, to hear local people describe their experiences at the hands of police; and attorneys William Kunstler and Arthur Kinoy, and Stan Wise of SNCC, discuss what they could do. It was the first such gathering in memory.

The next morning, Nashvillians learned that the National Guard was planning to hold a "riot practice" in the city March 9. Some 3,000 guardsmen, armed with rifles and bayonets, were to occupy Nashville, particularly "potential trouble spots" such as the Fisk-A&I University area. The same day, police shot and paralyzed Dan Massie, a SNCC activist.

People began organizing to fight both the police and the Guard.

After pressure from the black community, the Public Safety Committee called a special meeting on police brutality March 1. More than 90 people attended; many testified; and they submitted 16 written affidavits. The committee will invite the police to answer the charges in a few weeks.

The following day, about 400 people marched through downtown Nashville and gathered at the court house to protest police brutality, Negro unemployment and poor housing conditions.

Meantime, opposition to the Guard's "exercises" was mounting. A group of Nashville ministers sent telegrams to Mayor Beverly Briley, Governor Buford Ellington, and President Johnson, asking that the exercises be cancelled.

More than 500 people joined as plaintiffs in a suit to prevent the National Guard from carrying

out the exercises. They said the Guard's actions would intimidate people and have a "chilling effect" on their exercise of First Amendment rights. And they pointed out that by bringing the guard in, officials were violating every recommendation of the National Advisory Council on Civil Disorders.

The suit was filed in federal court March 7. The Judge refused to consider it, saying that the matter was the Governor's responsibility. But the net effect of the resistance was that the National Guard skulked in a few parks on the outskirts of town, staying barely long enough to eat lunch, and then went home, instead of marching armed through the ghetto, as originally planned.

More resistance is planned.

March 1968

the southern PATRIOT

WHITE POWER

...*the black struggle rages for Victory. That it should be a black struggle has been predetermined by its adversary which is white power. James Boggs, black writer from Detroit, has described it best:*

It is white power which decides whether to shoot to kill (as in Watts) or not to shoot at all (as in Oxford, Mississippi, against white mobs); to arrest or not to arrest, to break up picket lines or not to break up picket lines, to investigate brutality and murder or to allow these to go uninvestigated; to decide who eats and who goes on city aid when out of work and who does not eat and does not go on city aid; to decide who goes to what schools and who does not go; who has transportation and who doesn't; what streets are lighted and have good sidewalks and what streets have neither lights nor sidewalks; what neighborhoods are torn down for urban renewal and who and what are to go back into these neighborhoods. It is white power which decides what people are drafted into the army to fight and which countries this army is to fight at what moment. It is white power which has brought the United States to the point where it is counter-revolutionary to, and increasingly despised by, the majority of the world's people.

JAMES BOGGS in "The City is the Black Man's Land"

DAVE DELLINGER ON NON—VIOLENCE AND THE BLACK REVOLUTION

One of the oldest laments in human history is directed against those who "cry 'peace, peace,' when there is no peace." Today, after the outbreaks of counterviolence in Newark, Detroit and a growing number of other cities, we hear the hurt cries of those who mistakenly think that there was peace in our society and that it has been broken by impatient or criminal individuals. Many persons who themselves managed to get educated, employed, adequately housed and socially accepted to some degree, are crying "Violence and Crime," "Crime and Violence" against the rebellious acts of those who have been victimized all their lives by crime and violence, including the violence of the police.

Those who have never been bitten by a rat or beaten up in the precinct house fall rather easily into the trap of thinking that "law and order" is the framework within which justice is administered and progress takes place. Without going into the usual statistics of unemployment, disease and poverty, we can observe the kind of justice and progress that was operative in the black American community of Newark, in the following excerpt from a report by Steve Block of the Newark Community Union Project (N-CUP):

Tensions in Newark have been rising all spring and summer, and have been centered around two issues. First the mayor lured the New Jersey State School of Medicine and Dentistry to Newark, and a major part of the bait he used was the promise of 150 acres located in the heart of the Central Ward, the worst part of the ghetto. About 20,000 black people will be displaced as a result; and, as always, there are no real plans for finding or providing new homes for them. The black community has been furious and militant all spring and summer about this.

Secondly, the secretary of the Board of Education resigned. In appointing a successor the mayor and the other powers-that-be chose a white City Councilman . . . [with] no college education and no business experience. (The job consists mainly of handling the money.) The black community opposed him in favor of Wilbur Park, a black CPA who works in a financial capacity. . . .

The spark that set off the . . . riot . . . came Wednesday night, July 12. Two cops beat up a black cab-driver, with a crowd of people looking on. (Were they stupid, or did they want a riot?) . . . (*New Left Notes*, July 24)

When the camouflaged and orderly violence of established society is challenged by the crude and unpredictable violence of a forming—but as yet inchoate—countersociety, it is hard for idealists and humanitarians to keep a proper perspective. There is a temptation to condemn the newest recourse to violence—that of the rebels—or at least to equate the violence of the two sides in a way that precludes solidarity with those seeking liberation from the status quo.

This temptation is particularly seductive for those of us who advocate nonviolent methods of struggle but who do not experience in our own daily lives the unremitting violence of existing police and property relationships. Rather than face up to our failure to have taken the lead with a truly revolutionary nonviolence that is engaged in combat here and now, we are tempted to dissociate ourselves from the rebels and to end up, albeit reluctantly, on the side of those who invoke "law and order," "the democratic process" and the protection of the innocent as justification for the suppressive violence of the police and troops. Yet one of the factors that induces serious revolutionaries and discouraged ghetto-dwellers to conclude that nonviolence is incapable of being developed into a method adequate to their needs is this very tendency of non-violentists to line up, in moments of conflict, with the status quo. Thus a vicious circle is set up in which the advocates of nonviolence stand aloof from—or even repudiate—the only live revolutions in the making (Cuba, Vietnam, the black American communities), and determined revolutionaries reject nonviolence out of hand because of the repeated defections from the revolutionary cause of those who champion it.

In this context I was saddened to see Martin Luther King, Jr. endorse the sending of federal troops into Detroit. One can only sympathize with him personally, given the pressures he has been under from all sides. But if there are occasions when those who act nonviolently themselves must become reluctant allies or critical supporters of those who resort to violence—as I believe there are—then at least there should be no doubt that we form our alliances on the side of the oppressed and exploited, not on the side of the establishment.

One can call for alternative, nonviolent methods of liberation and point out the dangers and shortcomings of the current form of rebellion, but it is contrary to the spirit of nonviolence to call for the punishment of those who have resorted to violence in their desperate search for a method of breaking out of the present intolerable situation. After all, nonviolence has ground to a halt in the area of black liberation, staggered by the depth of the problem and hesitating at the crossroads where one must move on from protest, either to the illusions of liberal politics or to genuine revolution. The former means maintaining an uneasy alliance with the government but the latter requires solidarity with and loyalty to the people, even when they succumb to the temptations of violence.

• • •

The politics of Washington do not differ greatly from Saigon to Newark, from the Dominican Republic to Detroit. The current black revolts highlight both the hypocrisy and the futility of U.S. military intervention in Vietnam. How can a society in which millions of its own citizens fail to find jobs, housing, dignity and meaningful democracy claim that its armed attacks on the towns and villages of Vietnam have the serious purpose of bringing the benefits of land reform, economic justice and real democracy to the Vietnamese?

If slum-clearance housing in the United States enriches the real-estate operators and other commercial interests while frustrating the inhabitants of U.S. slums and ghettos, what chance is there that the expenditure of millions of dollars in high-sounding AID programs will do more than line the pockets of the tiny group of feudal landlords, war profiteers and generals who are the main collaborators of the United States in Vietnam? Those Americans who have taken seriously the Administration's claims of noble democratic purpose and ultimate success in Vietnam should re-examine their assumptions on the basis of the unmistakable message from the disillusioned black population of our own country.

There are some ghetto-dwellers who find it so oppressive in the United States that they are willingly in the armed forces, ready to settle for a regular paycheck, a degree of integration and the opportunity to wear a uniform which implies, however falsely, that they have become first-class citizens at last. But surely the revolts in Newark, Detroit and other cities, and the calloused attacks on the black population by police and national guardsmen should make them reconsider where their true loyalty lies.

All Americans who are shocked and appalled by the developing civil war in U.S. cities should redouble their efforts to bring about American military withdrawal from Vietnam. Not only the misdirection of funds and manpower but also the hardening of habits and attitudes contribute to the deterioration within the United States. Even as the U.S. armed forces often bomb, burn or shoot up Vietnamese villages suspected of harboring members of the N.L.F., or destroy a whole village from which there has been sniper fire, so there were instances in Newark, Detroit and Spanish Harlem when police or other armed forces fired high-powered rifles indiscriminately into buildings that might hold snipers. As in Vietnam, a high percentage of the vic-

tims were women and children. Even as American troops and bombers feel frustrated and put upon by the successful resistance of the lowly Vietnamese and, quite naturally, resent the deaths of their buddies, so police and guardsmen were impelled to reassert their authority or revenge their slain cohorts by acts of senseless reprisal. Thus the Newark revolt, which had largely spent itself after two days of reaction to the arrest and beating of a cab driver, was transformed into a massacre on the third day, when the Newark police department, the New Jersey State Patrol and the National Guard decided to show the niggers who was boss.

An eyewitness reports:

"We have got to kill somebody to show these black bastards that we mean business," said one of the Newark patrolmen. This is exactly what they proceeded to do. The people of the Central Ward were systematically insulted, bludgeoned and killed after Friday morning. . . . Police were careful to cover their actions [as in Vietnam]. They haven't permitted newsmen to photograph the hundreds of bloody "casualties" which are being taken to the City Hospital. The death rate rose steadily after Friday morning even though the major portion of the rioting was over by that time. (*National Guardian*, July 22)

According to newspaper reports, forty percent of the Army troops sent to Detroit had been battle-hardened in Vietnam. Eyewitness accounts indicate that this meant, among other things, that some of them at least were able to shoot innocent people without the pangs of conscience that one might ordinarily expect. One of the prices France paid for her unsuccessful wars in Indochina and Algeria was the contempt for human life which many of the soldiers brought back with them. The longer

the war continues in Vietnam the more casually will some of those who stick it out in the armed forces be able — whether as policemen, vigilantes or rebels—to take the lives of those who displease them at home.

• • •

Clearly the prospect is spiralling violence and a decline of humane values, at home and abroad, unless U.S. troops can be withdrawn from Vietnam and kept out of America's troubled cities. But it is not enough to call for a simple redirection of federal funds from Vietnam to the United States. Massive freedom budgets at home can be as illusory as Washington-sponsored social reconstruction has been in Vietnam. Without local initiative and control by the people in whose interests the money is being spent, there can be no real dignity or self-determination. One of the characteristics of the ghetto-dwellers' present rebelliousness is resentment at having things done *for* them as well as *to* them by The Man.

The best way to combat violence always is to work constructively against the cruelty and violence of the status quo. While remaining nonviolent ourselves, we must recognize and respond to the thrust for dignity of those who strike out, however blindly at times, against the system which oppresses them. Only those who have found a sense of dignity and worth in their own lives can believe enough in the dignity and worth of other human beings to become nonviolent. Others may be subservient or submissive—but that is not nonviolence, any more than are the days without arson or sniping in our cities days of peace.

D. D.

LIBERATION July 1967

A VIEW OF URBAN AMERICA FROM THE BOTTOM

Although nothing is more important in America than a job, the market system and free enterprise no longer are able to offer work opportunities to the unemployed ghetto dwellers. And the unemployed have no status in modern society because a man's "skill" is taken to be the test of his basic worth, as if a human being could be regarded as a machine whose value could be determined by its capacity to perform its mechanical function. It matters not, in the American city of today, whether the unemployed are decent human beings, conscious of their obligations to other human beings; if they are unemployed, they are seen as surrounded by an aura of unworthiness, and they begin to accept it as being true. In this kind of atmosphere it is inevitable that the government institutions charged with the specific responsibilities of helping people find employment will fail to help those most in need of it.

• • •

Employment

The tall young Negro was very well dressed. He was wearing a white shirt, regimental tie, three-button suit, and polished shoes. He spoke in an educated voice to the Negro woman interviewer at the state employment office. He seemed an ideal type for some professional or semi-professional job except for one thing—he had the damnedest "Afro" haircut I'd ever seen: his hair grew out high and straight from his head in all directions.

Yet to me he looked both natural and of a piece—the haircut suited him admirably—but not to the interviewer, for I heard her tell him he should cut his hair if he wanted to get a good job. He refused and the next day, when he was back again to talk to the personnel officer of a large utility company, his hair was still "Afro" style. He didn't get the job, of course.

I took him outside the office and we sat in my car, talking about what had happened.

"What do you people want from me?" he asked bitterly. "You tell me I should be proud of my descent, so I let my hair grow instead of getting it processed. I spend a lot of money on this haircut. It costs me six dollars to get it fixed like this, and I have to put hair spray on it every day to keep it neat. I try to keep neat and clean. This morning I took a shower, used a deodorant, put on a clean white shirt, had my mother press my pants, and came down to look for a job. But all they want me to do is cut my hair. Mister, I'm the only one in my whole family who graduated from high school. I even have a year of junior college. But I'm not going to cut my hair. I'm going to wear it 'Afro' even if I don't get a job."

"What will you do?"

"Hustle. I'll get a couple of girls working for me and a few other hustles going. I'll make out. Screw the job if I can't look the way I want."

When I talked with the employment service interviewer about why she hadn't argued with the personnel man when he said he wouldn't hire the kid because of his haircut, she got angry. "He should cut his hair. He should look like everybody else, like the employer wants him to look. It's not my job to argue with employers."

A week later I sat with a group of young Mexican-American kids in another office of the employment service. To them I was just another "Anglo" looking for a job, and so they talked among themselves, indifferent to my presence in their midst. I found it hard to follow their rapid Spanish, filled with Mexican slang words and "chicano" references, but still I heard and understood enough to follow their general thoughts about the jobs. Evidently, none of them expected to get any decent jobs.

Their English is poor and heavily accented. Their mechanical skills are minimal, and that is the primary criterion for employment. Their education is limited, and that is another sizable handicap.

As I talked with unemployed, underemployed, and low-paid workers all over America, I began to see how wrong it is to let the fixed categories of "skilled," "semi-skilled," and "unskilled" worker become the determinant of how people shall live. Does the label "skilled" tell what sort of husband, father, citizen, and human being a man is? Does "unskilled"? If some unskilled man is a good father, husband, citizen, and human being, should he and his family be condemned to a miserable life because he can't handle a welding torch or operate a computer?

From *Prelude to Riot* by Paul Jacobs, Vintage

THE POLLUTER OF MAN

" Les gros Poissons mangent les petits." Drawing by P. Breughel the Elder, after Jerome Bosch. What sense of fun is expressed here. " Big fishes eat the little ones." So goes the proverb. But where did the artist see such a sight ?

We are in an era of unaccountable executive authority and manipulation, of the demise of community polity, of the paralysis of public policy, of the risk of elite private government in the name of public partnership. National and local power structures are creating new ad hoc private and unaccountable self-selecting regional authorities to carry out more and more public functions and to side-track the rise of 'black power' governments in majority-black central cities and insurgent neighborhoods. Neither effective, representative metropolitan government that challenges private interests nor participatory neighborhood institutions that provide a decentralized basis for achieving social purpose are available, even in particular social and personal service sectors such as health and community development. Private medical centers, insurance plans, and medical societies dominate regional hospital planning councils and the regulation, such as it is, of professional health service without real public representation and control. These forces are especially dominant because of the professional and administrative incapacity, political rigidity and conservatism, and second-class services status of public agencies for health and hospitals.

The disintegration of the urban environment and the continuing decay of rural depressed areas are at the root of health problems today. As the National Manpower Commission report puts it, '...increased medical services alone will probably have only limited effects on hardcore health problems...' The causes of much of today's somatic and mental illness are found either in environmental stress or societal failure. And yet the medical arts and sciences are not used to treat these problems at their source. 'Medical space-shots' and marginal, narrow applications of scientific capacity gain central emphasis to the neglect of social and preventive medicine, social action for environmental change, and chronic life-maintenance problems beyond episodic cure. Richard Lichtman poses the problem formidably:

"The city has become literally as well as symbolically the polluter of man. And in defiling his social environment, he of course befouls himself, drawing back into his own being all the refuse and decay he has spewn about him...It is not only that such a place (the city) breeds disease and mental illness, but that the task of ordering the city toward health becomes literally impossible...The individual efforts of men toward improvement curtail the possibility of their common advance."

From "Toward A New Politics and Economics of Health" by Robb Burlage, *Radicals in the Professions* Newsletter

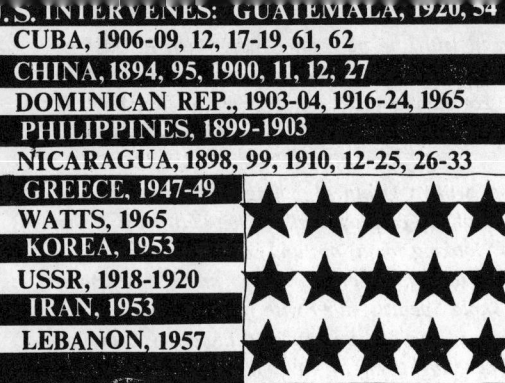

U.S. INTERVENES: GUATEMALA, 1920, 54
CUBA, 1906-09, 12, 17-19, 61, 62
CHINA, 1894, 95, 1900, 11, 12, 27
DOMINICAN REP., 1903-04, 1916-24, 1965
PHILIPPINES, 1899-1903
NICARAGUA, 1898, 99, 1910, 12-25, 26-33
GREECE, 1947-49
WATTS, 1965
KOREA, 1953
USSR, 1918-1920
IRAN, 1953
LEBANON, 1957

Haiti's Papa Doc and Friend

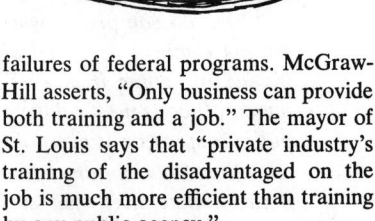

SOCIAL CONTROL

VIETNAM

Power for the Poor

If governmental programs are successfully to attack poverty, it must be realized by their formulators and administrators that success cannot be achieved by subsidizing industry for retraining workers, or by trusting city halls and county courthouses to advance the welfare of the poor. For the goals of industry and politicians are very often unacceptable to the poor. Success will only be achieved through the mobilization of the poor themselves to attack the structures of poverty which keep them poor. In order for the poor to do this, they must have power. "Maximum feasible participation" of the poor is simply inadequate; actual control of programs must be had by the poor. The reason for this is simple, yet complex: poverty is maintained by political and economic structures which are controlled by the very middle class and business interests which have been, so far, the main beneficiaries of the current poverty program. Simple enough. The complexity of the issue will become clear when the poor, having actual control of programs, try to attack poverty and its deep interconnections with the institutions of American life. Very little thought has been given to problems that will arise when, if ever, the poor manage to do that. Some of these problems can be seen in attempts by industry to invest in urban black ghettoes.

Certainly, one of the most publicized of recent social phenomena has been the growing trend of corporate interest in investment in urban black communities. This phenomenon is so recent, it is as yet hard to determine its significance. It appears, however, to be growing in social momentum. The national Urban Coalition—an alliance of local government officials, businessmen, and labor, Negro, and religious leaders—was formed in the summer of 1967 to promote, among other things, business investment in black ghettoes. As of July 10, 1968, thirty-three local coalitions had been formed, and twenty-five more were in the planning stages. *Fortune* magazine devoted its entire issue of January, 1968, to the urban crisis and the need for corporate investment to solve the crisis; McGraw-Hill published a special report, "Business and the Urban Crisis," in all forty-four of its business publications.

Businessmen have been quite candid about the reasons for their new venture. They desire "to cool the anger that boils up in riots," as McGraw-Hill put it. A recent statement published in many newspapers across the country by Goodbody and Company is interesting:

Private business firms, of course, are not established to further the public interest. Their primary objective is to operate profitably. In this case, however, multiple objectives are not incompatible. A largely untapped market of some 25 million people present unparalleled potential sales opportunities for those firms with the imagination to take advantage of them.

Businessmen make it clear, however, that they cannot be expected to solve the crisis in the cities by themselves; they see governmental action as primary. In return for their involvement they expect the government to give them tax incentives, loan insurance, subsidies for job training, investment guarantees, and the like. This is known as "partnership" with the government.

Most businessmen do not regard housing as a promising area for investment at the present time. There is too little money to finance low-rent city housing, and too much strangling red tape, they claim. Senator Charles Percy and the late Senator Robert Kennedy sought to overcome these objectives with various schemes which would subsidize business involvement in housing programs. As this is written, nothing of substance has come of their efforts.

Business Wants Control

Job training and the building of plants in ghettoes have been the prime foci of activities of businessmen to date. It is interesting to note that the government has been placing increasing emphasis upon manpower programs and has been de-emphasizing the more politically hazardous community action programs. Indeed, one could claim that the economic programs advocated by the National Alliance of Businessmen and the Urban Coalition, are by their very existence evidence of the

failures of federal programs. McGraw-Hill asserts, "Only business can provide both training and a job." The mayor of St. Louis says that "private industry's training of the disadvantaged on the job is much more efficient than training by any public agency."

There seems to be a largely unarticulated reason for the corporate emphasis on job training and the creation of jobs. That reason is *social control*. The "nihilistic" impulses of the hard-core unemployed and of ghetto youth must be harnessed. Otherwise, chaos in the form of "riots" may result. Consequently, the manpower training programs, especially those run by the government, exhibit a frenetic concern that the trainees learn good grooming habits, learn to be on time, observe certain rules of deportment. Obviously, a worker must have a certain amount of self-discipline in order to be able to work. Gradually some corporations, however, are learning that workers need not exhibit good middle class standards of behavior in order to possess the necessary discipline. What is interesting about this aspect of job training is not the excessive concern with grooming habits, and the like, but a desire to exercise social control over the new workers.

Julius Lester puts it another way: "As long as the black community exists within the capitalist community, it is impossible for blacks to control it. The Establishment has reached the point where it will allow blacks to run the black community. That has become expedient. To administrate, however, is not to control. And in the end, it is irrelevant who controls the black community as long as that community exists within a capitalist structure." Recent trends in American corporate capitalism bear out Lester's contention. The rise of conglomerates, the emergence of international (or transnational) corporations, and the stabilization of market forces because of planning and what Galbraith terms "the imperatives of technology" are trends and forces of gargantuan scale. Yet if "black control of black communities" is to mean anything, these trends and forces must be dealt with. Little thought has been given to this problem.

From: "The Quest for a Politics to end Poverty" by J. W. Stephenson Wise Jr., Sept 1968

S S
COVER THE EARTH

International Development

FELLOWSHIP

Transfer of Power

What is now happening in Detroit, I think, is typical in at least one way of black communities throughout America: it represents the determination of the black people to control their own community. This marks a new day for black people. Wherever the black revolution is in progress, specific steps have to be taken to structure a transfer of power from the white community to the black community. The white community apparently finds this painful and distasteful, but it is a necessity if there is to be any peaceful resolution of the kind of conflict that shook America last summer and the two preceding summers. The black community is growing increasingly determined that it must control its own destiny. In the simplest terms this means political control of all areas in which black people are a majority — control of community services, police services, and all the things that go to make up a community and that black people do not now control in Detroit or in any other urban center.

This is not political control in the sense represented by the mayoralty election of Stokes in Cleveland or Hatcher in Gary. These were nominal matters with little relationship to real power, and it is real power rather than the ornaments or the appearance of power that black people are interested in. In Cleveland, perhaps even more than in Gary, there was no real power evidenced in the election except perhaps the power represented by the cohesion of a black community that voted approximately 96 per cent for a black candidate — a bloc vote that up to now blacks would have considered unthinkable as a deviation from the American ideals of democracy.

I know this to have been true because for the last five or six years I have been campaigning to get the black people of Detroit to support a black slate, to vote as a black bloc. The idea that I would advocate a racist approach to a solution of the black man's problems seemed unthinkable to many respectable, responsible black leaders. But this feeling has grown less and less as the years have gone by, and in Cleveland, which is much less organized and much less militant and much less black-conscious than Detroit, all but 4 per cent of the black community did support a black candidate without any feeling that they were in any way negating the basic principles of American good government.

This indicates to me that something basically important is happening to the black community throughout America: black people have tended to sever their identification with the white community and to become alienated from America. They no longer want to be part of the white man's society; they have ceased to accept the white man's standards of what is good or bad. This is a total rejection of integration as an ideal or an objective. Instead, the black man is trying to recapture a sense of identification with his own cultural heritage. This involves the rediscovery of Africa, the development of black consciousness, black pride, black unity, and at least the beginning of the development of black power.

Politically, this means that black people want to control the center city. In Detroit, certainly, we aspire to complete control of the city government. We realize we are in a race with the Federal government and the white Establishment because the government is trying to make it impossible for the center cities to become black communities. It is allocating funds with the prerequisite that the centers become a part of a metropolitan combination or area. In Detroit, for example, they are trying to build a six-county metropolitan area which will receive full support from the Federal government and from the white Establishment. To be sure, this plan is not completely supported by white suburbanites because they do not want to become part of a metropolitan government that has a large minority of black people in it. Nevertheless, the Establishment in general, the mass-communication media, the Federal government, and the Democratic Party all seem determined to bring it about as fast as possible.

As a result, the timetable of the black community in Detroit has to be stepped up. Normally, if we followed the gradual evolution of our power in the city we could wait for, not the next election in 1969, but the one after that. However, it now seems almost a necessity for us to elect a black mayor in 1969 unless we are willing to see all the power assumed by a metropolitan government and a mayor elected who would be merely a functionary, a greeter of distinguished visitors. The black community in Detroit now represents at least 40 per cent of the population, and with white people fleeing and black people still coming in the mathematical point of control is near.

Politics is only one aspect, however. It is also necessary for blacks to have economic control of their community. This is more difficult and complex than a political take-over. How do people who are powerless and don't have much money take over the economics of a community? In Detroit we are trying to invent strategies for this, such as the development of co-op retail stores, co-op buying clubs, co-op light manufacturing, co-op education, and similar undertakings that can become possible when large numbers of people with a sense of unity and a sense of cause can put together small individual amounts of money to create enough total capital to establish businesses with some degree of security and possibility of success. These ventures will give black people a sense of their economic possibilities and a realization of their need for economic training. They could also serve as a measuring stick for the white merchants who now prey upon the black ghetto. They will find it less easy to exploit their customers when clean stores run by blacks, with decent produce and decent prices, exist in the area.

We realize we cannot take over the economics of the black ghetto simply by the bootstrap method of setting up small co-ops. We will have to use other methods as well, such as selective patronage or boycott or picketing. We must get the white man who is doing business in the black ghetto to recognize that if 85 per cent of his business is with black people, he will have to hire 85 per cent of his employees from the black community. This means from top to bottom, not just the lower levels of employment.

As one illustration, we are now concerned in Detroit with Sears Roebuck, which does a tremendous business in the black ghetto through three large inner-city stores. We are also concerned, of course, because Sears does a large business in every black ghetto across the country. If we can make some inroads in changing their way of doing business in Detroit it will be significant everywhere else. We have a token picket now and then, and we have conversations with the management. By next summer we will have a massive picket around all three stores unless they are converted in the meantime.

This kind of action will have to be taken on every street in every black ghetto everywhere. We must make sure that no white businessman can succeed in a black ghetto without proper hiring policies and without providing decent service and decent products to black people. This has to be accomplished through selective patronage. The use of Molotov cocktails and bricks is a crude way of putting a white merchant out of business. We think it can be done just as effectively merely by refusing to buy in those stores which do not deal fairly with black people.

It is also necessary to acquire more control of large businesses that want to come into the ghetto for urban redevelopment or for other sorts of economic development. White industry, white investment companies, white banks, must accept the same principles when they invest in the ghetto that they accept when they invest in any other nation — and we think of the black ghettos across the country as being a black nation, a nation within a nation, separate, with a common culture, common aspirations, a common oppressor. When white investors go into a foreign country, they recognize that it is legitimate for that country to insist on some local control of the enterprise and also on an agreement for the transfer of ownership to local interests over a reasonable period of time. The black nation will insist on these principles in their ghettos.

In addition, the Federal government is going to have to recognize that when it guarantees funds for an investment in a black community it will have to do it for a black corporation rather than a white corporation. If we can organize enough political strength to have some say in who is going to be President in 1968, I think the government will be inclined to pay some attention to our insistence that this money be channeled through black corporations or black co-ops rather than through exploitative white businesses.

Besides the transfer of political power and of economic power we are looking for the control of education, the transfer of power from white educators to black educators, the power of the black community to educate its own children. White people have failed miserably over the past 400 years, the past hundred years, the past ten years, to educate black children. We think it is reasonable now to assume that white people are never going to educate black children properly, that they have no real stake in educating black children, that they are going to keep on a second-rate level all the schools that are designed primarily for the education of black children. Black children in inner-city ghetto schools throughout the country are three to four grades behind in achievement and in reading. Black teachers, administrators, and principals have never had an opportunity to test the possibility of changing the motivation of black children by creating a school situation in which the black community has some say

about the curriculum, the textbooks, the teachers, and all the other factors that can make a school an instrument either for education or for debasement.

We feel that most ghetto schools today destroy children rather than educate them. The teachers and administrators serve as power symbols and kill a black child's self-image. Their influence, their lack of concern, and in many instances their contempt make it impossible for a black child to learn. So, we are insisting more and more that a school for black children have black teachers, black principals, and black administrators; that its curriculum be reoriented to cover the culture of black people; that the present textbooks, which are essentially lies, particularly in the area of social science and history, be thrown out and that textbooks explaining the history and cultural background of black people be substituted. We are not insisting that white schools teach the truth, but we do insist that schools in black ghettos teach the truth. Most of the textbooks we have examined that are now used in teaching black children do not teach the truth. So, we now say that the control of the schools must be transferred to black people.

All of this is a far cry from the day when black people wanted to be integrated into white society, and it has happened in a relatively short period of time. It has happened because white people have more and more unmasked themselves. Black people had not fully realized the white attitudes. To see a white mob trying to stop one little black child from going to school was a revelation to black people. Television played a tremendous part in making this revelation possible. I think that very few black people, after watching this day after day, week after week, year after year, could end up with any feeling that integration was either possible or desirable. Certainly this was true when we watched the sit-in demonstrations, the freedom rides, Martin Luther King's massive demonstrations; we watched the march on the Selma Road, we watched the Meredith march; and when Dr. King moved into Chicago we lost the last vestige of hope that there were different kinds of white people. We saw that white people in Illinois were the same as those in Mississippi, Georgia, and Alabama, that there was really no difference between Cicero, Illinois, and the mobs of white bigots throughout the South.

White people did this themselves. They killed the myth and the dream of integration, about which Dr. King spoke so eloquently. Black people listened, but

then the dream died, because it was not based on reality. Now their dream is to recapture their own past, their own culture, their own history, and to put the race issue on the basis of a power struggle pure and simple.

We will take in this country what we have power enough to take, and what we do not have power enough to take we will stop dreaming about. We will try to build power to take the things we have to have. This is the only kind of equality there is — an equality based on power. We are concerned primarily with our own black community. We are not trying to invade white communities, or take over white communities. But we do insist that white people cannot enjoy the luxury of separating us into black ghettos and also enjoy the privilege of exploiting us in these ghettos they have forced us into.

From here on in, we will take the black ghetto and make it a garden spot for ourselves. We will make it something we are proud of. And we will control it. White people will not live in the suburbs and come in each morning to exploit us and go home each night. We will run our own businesses. We will run our own schools. We will run our own government. We do not want the whites to *give* us anything; we want to *take* whatever our power allows us to take, because this is the only way it will become ours.

This is where black people are today in Detroit. Black people throughout the country are concerned about whether we will be able to do it in Detroit. We have the organizational structure, we have the leadership, we have all of the things that should make it possible — provided the white man is reasonable.

This may not be a possibility. It may be that Rap Brown is correct in his analysis. He says — and I paraphrase: "I look at the white man everywhere in America and I believe he is headed for one thing, and that is genocide. I do not believe he will rationally approach the problem of transferring power or permitting black people to take control of their own communities. The only answer is to get ready for the final solution that the white man in America is now preparing, so that when it is under way the blacks can make it the most expensive final solution the white man has ever undertaken in any country in the world."

Rap Brown may be 100 per cent right. In Detroit we are trying to see whether the white man has the necessary intelligence to make a transfer of power before the final destruction of America. We are not sure, but we are trying. We do not have too long to see whether or not it can be done. ᕈ

I WAS A PIG AT GREENWOOD DAIRIES

AN ice-cream cone at the Greenwood Dairies has half a pound of ice cream on it—making it so top-heavy that it is ordinarily presented to the customer upside down, resting on a piece of waxed paper. That's the single-dip cone. The double-dip cone has an even pound, or about a quart of ice cream—the same amount that Greenwood serves in a locally famous sundae called a Pig's Dinner. A Pig's Dinner has four scoops of ice cream resting on a bed of sliced bananas, covered with a choice of topping, and served in an eight-inch plastic trough. The customer also gets a yellow button that says "I Was a Pig at Greenwood Dairies." The buttons are a particularly popular item.

From "U.S. Journal: Lower Bucks County, Pa. Buying and Selling Along Route 1" by Calvin Trill in *The New Yorker* 11/15/69

WHAT IS A CULTURE?

Tidbit

Wisconsin welfare mothers are now allowed 16¢ per meal, a cutback from 22¢ per meal. Monkeys in the Madison Zoo are allotted 58¢ per meal.

Thursday, MIT, Oct 1969

NEW HAVEN: RENEWAL AND RIOTS

DANE ARCHER

LIBERALS ARE ASTONISHED AT ALL THOSE UNGRATEFUL NIGGERS

New Haven
In 1953, Richard C. Lee became the mayor of New Haven, Connecticut's port city of 142,000. In the last fifteen years, his pioneering programs of urban renewal have rebuilt the city. With the single-mindedness of a visionary, he has transformed New Haven's inner city from an aging slum into a futuristic landscape of poured concrete and high steel. Now Richard Lee is in trouble.

In 1953, New Haven's critics were fond of calling the city "a big slum around a big school," but Lee has changed all that. Today, the streets around Yale hum with the sounds of prosperity. Under the Mayor's aggressive leadership, the city's decaying core has given way to bustling retail areas, striking commercial buildings, sweeping highway systems and matching high-rise apartments.

New Haven's massive programs of renewal have garnered national attention for the city and its Mayor. Since 1953, Lee has been the subject of a handful of books and of more than 200 magazine articles. Renewal has also been good politics. Last fall, Lee was returned to his eighth term in office by a comfortable margin. And much federal legislation—including, at least in part, the birth of the War on Poverty—has been influenced by his success. To federal authorities and to jealous mayors of other cities, New Haven is "The Model City."

But something is desperately wrong in New Haven. On Saturday, August 19, 1967, a white snack-bar owner shot a young Puerto Rican. That night, the city's black pockets erupted. Fires, looting and rage swept New Haven. Lee called upon state police and alerted National Guardsmen in an effort to contain the rioters. There were 550 arrests, 145 on felony charges. The violence lasted four days, and was longer and more destructive than the summer riots in any city of comparable size. Only the conflagrations of Detroit, Newark and Milwaukee were more costly.

New Haven officials were stunned. Despite its skyscraping pillars of glass and steel, the city which had prided itself as the high-water mark of America's urban renewal efforts had been found sadly no more secure from violence than the nation's most unredeveloped cities. The city fathers stumbled over one another in a flurry of self-justification.

One spokesman confided privately that "the riots came as a terrible surprise—especially after all Dick has tried to do for those people." New Haven's anti-poverty agency characterized the rioters as nothing more serious than "teen-age hooligans" with a thirst for revelry. According to the agency, "few if any of the incidents of the four days bespoke any widespread discontent."

Mayor Lee called the riots "those awful days last August," and said publicly: "I don't feel discouraged, nor dejected. . . . It won't deter me from continuing the programs we have and if possible intensifying them."

The Mayor is sincere, but his resolve is unfortunate. The resentment which crashed windows to the city's pavements last August is chronic, and not the warm-weather caprice of delinquents. As one ghetto black said, "In winter, the people have the same feelings—but they keep them indoors instead of on the streets."

Today, the city is polarized into racial camps. Last August's violence is never far from sight—it can be seen in the glass shards which litter the streets, and in the plywood panels behind which the ghetto's merchants nervously ply their trades. The city's high schools erupt in staccato bouts of chair throwing and window smashing. The police are nervous and quick to employ Mace in any of a hundred situations where they fear the mushrooming of mass violence.

The anger of blacks has become an inescapable fact of life in urban America, but that it should fan into violence in New Haven astonishes the liberal forces which propelled Lee into power. New Haven has a reputation for working tirelessly to mitigate the toll of being poor, shunned and powerless. This philanthropic image is misleading. The city talks a great deal about progress, but its performance is progress of a very special sort. In 1968, New Haven is much prettier than it was when Lee took office, but it is still a city of the prosperous and the tragically poor. Indeed, there is ample reason to believe that

the urban renewal program never really intended it to be anything else.

The story of New Haven's adventures in urban renewal is inseparable from the career of Mayor Lee. Born of mixed English, Scottish and Irish blood, Lee began work as a reporter for the city's *Journal-Courier*. In 1943, he became director of the Yale News Bureau where his talent for public relations landed A. Whitney Griswold, then president of Yale, on the covers of both *Time* and *Newsweek*.

While working for Yale, Lee entered New Haven politics. In 1949 and 1951, he ran losing races for mayor, the second time by two votes. Then one evening in 1951, Lee visited a tenement on Oak Street, at that time the city's most notorious slum. Overcome by the wretched conditions inside, Lee burst from the building and was violently sick at the curb. The incident angered him and, according to his associates, lit within him a determination to purge New Haven of its slums.

In 1953, with liberal support for a new concept called "urban redevelopment," Lee became mayor. Suddenly, the city came alive. As one aide recalls, "Word spread that something new and big was about to happen in New Haven, and soon political idealists began drifting in from all over the country." Lee attracted city planners and "poverty" bureaucrats like Edward Logue, Mitchell Sviridoff, L. Thomas Appleby, Melvin Adams and others.

In the beginning, the Mayor's ambitious plans for a "slumless city" met opposition. New Haven's other elected officials, including the city's Board of Aldermen, were reluctant to commit the will and resources that massive urban renewal would require. Many of the city's financial leaders feared that Lee's schemes would bankrupt New Haven.

The Mayor was not deterred. Lee made almost no effort to capture the city's political machinery, building his own instead. With federal and private backing, he created a new high-powered bureaucracy called the Redevelopment Agency and, in 1962, a high-budget anti-poverty program. As critics like John Wilhelm have pointed out, Lee's hand-picked "private government" brought with it a vast pool of patronage and power that, financed by federal and foundation money, remained immune to the pressures that dependence on local taxes would have produced.

The bureaucracy of redevelopment is also politically autonomous. No part of the Mayor's machinery (except Lee himself) is elected by the people of New Haven. Despite this, Lee's private government has become the most far-reaching political force in the history of New Haven. His bureaucrats make the decisions which determine the physical shape of the city and, indirectly, the quality of its life.

To underwrite his ambitious plans for the "new" New Haven, Lee looked to Washington. He was the first mayor in America to recognize the cash value of Title One of the Federal Housing Act of 1949 which provided $1 billion for redevelopment planning and property acquisition. Under the terms of the act, the costs of land purchase and clearance are borne two-thirds by the federal government and one-third by local sources. With federal dollars, cities like New Haven were able to buy, level, and sell land to private developers at a loss.

The housing legislation of the federal government also introduced a greater use of the municipal powers of "eminent domain." As one public official said: "Before the 1949 Act, cities could only seize private properties for public *use*, like a highway or school. But now the properties can be taken for a public *purpose*—which in New Haven's case means the elimination of slums and blight."

Lee rapidly became expert at tapping federal coffers. In fifteen years, the city has been given, or has on reserve, urban renewal funds totaling $130,665,844—or roughly $915 for every person in New Haven. By comparison, New York City has attracted a modest $37 of renewal money per person. William F. Buckley has calculated that if every American city were dealt with as generously as was New Haven, the federal budget for urban renewal alone would be roughly $146 billion.

New Haven's war on blight began with ceremony in January, 1957, when the Mayor rode in the cab of a wrecker to send its huge steel ball crashing through the walls of an Oak Street tenement. The demolition crews cut a wide swath through the heart of New Haven, and the city's first renewal project was under way.

Today New Haven operates the most ambitious and thoroughgoing programs of redevelopment anywhere in America. More than 3,000 acres—almost one-third of the city's 22 square miles—have been rebuilt, cleared, or committed to renewal plans. More than $237 million in construction has been completed. Business and industry have profited, the flight of upper-income families to the suburbs has been curbed, and municipal assessments in the redeveloped areas have swelled from $15 million to more than $38 million.

Robert Weaver, Federal Housing and Home Finance Administrator, has said: "I think New Haven is coming closest to our dream of a slumless city." In a sense, that is accurate: most of the city's slum areas *are* being replaced by attractive new structures. But in terms of people's lives, renewal has meant nothing less than disaster. New Haven is being rebuilt as if it were Brasília —a city started from scratch in unpopulated wasteland. Modern high-rise apartments are landscaped by vast open spaces of grass; eight-lane divided highways race through the middle of the city; gargantuan garages and parking lots sprawl over vast areas in the center city. But to make room for Lee's Brazilian vision, thousands of people have had to move. One black, an ex-resident who had been "relocated" to make way for the luxury housing on Oak Street, said: "Man, there used to be people—thousands of real, *live* people living on Oak Street. It wasn't the classiest place in town, but it was home. Today, you can't see a poor face on Oak Street, or a black face either."

In Lee's New Haven, urban renewal has been a euphemism for "Poor Removal" and, in particular, for "Poor Blacks Removal." To clear land for its flashy projects, the Redevelopment Agency makes extensive use of its power to seize private holdings. The natural victims are the city's poor, and most blacks are poor. Although less than 5 per cent of the city's whites have had to move for renewal, nearly 40 per cent of its blacks have been or are being bulldozed from their homes. Despite this, the nonwhite population of New Haven has more than tripled since 1953, and today blacks and Puerto Ricans make up from 25 to 35 per cent of the city. As renewal knocks down existing nonwhite housing, the residents and a growing stream of immigrants are packed into whatever buildings are left standing.

New Haven has compounded its abuse of the poor by its failure to replace the homes it has eagerly destroyed. Since the onset of urban renewal, the city has crumbled 6,776 households—about one-seventh of all the housing in New Haven. In the same period, the city has built less than 2,000 new units of housing, and eight out of ten of these have been for the city's wealthy or middle class. New Haven has completed about 400 low-rental units, but *all but twelve* have been for the elderly. In short, the city's poor have not been rehoused and New Haven's rich and Yale-related professionals now live on land that was once theirs. Perhaps for this reason, Courtland Wilson of the NAACP has called urban renewal "the raping and lynching of the black community—Northern style."

Behind the foggy rhetoric of "doing something for the poor," the city has used public funds to purchase and destroy their homes. In New Haven, it is the already thriving —and *not* the poor—who profit from renewal. But because the city continues to talk about helping its poor, there is some confusion over precisely what the aims of urban renewal have been and are. And the confusion has worked in the Mayor's favor. Lee is the "plastic man" of urban politics and he has carefully stretched himself to be all things to all men. To merchants, Lee is a mayor dedicated to revitalizing business and shopping areas in the city. To industry, he is a man who will flex municipal muscles to secure attractive factory sites. And to the liberals in New Haven and at Yale, Lee is a crusader whose paramount concerns have something to do with poverty and the creation of "a decent home for every New Haven family." In the past, Lee's versatility has created a coalition of support from the organized interests in New Haven.

But after fifteen years, the real nature of the Mayor's programs has become less ambiguous. Melvin Adams, the current Redevelopment Administrator, has said that those forced from their land have been dispersed to foster integration and prevent the creation of new slums. That is just not true—the poor are dispersed to already swollen slums simply because there is nowhere else for them to go. At any given time in New Haven, there are fewer than 1,500 vacancies. Many of these are high rent or too small for a large family, and, after last summer, only a handful of white home owners would rent vacant apartments to blacks or Puerto Ricans. One black on New Haven's Congress Avenue said bitterly: "Man, I've been moved four times in two years. I've tried to get a place where there aren't any bulldozers. But the ads in the paper just list the address and never the phone number, so you have to go in person. The minute they see the color of your face, the place is taken or else going for $250 a month."

Lee's vague concern for poverty is sincere, even if his city's programs fail to reflect it. He is a man distressed by poverty, and his crusade to rid the city of its slums is in part well meant. To the Mayor slums represent "occasions of sin"—they are the breeding ground of vice and crime where children may be molested and where the young may begin lives outside the law.

But Lee's solution to slums has been regrettably simple: he has just knocked them down and seems to harbor the whimsical hope that the poor will be Pied Pipered off to Bridgeport or some other Connecticut city. But the poor do not evaporate, even when their homes are demolished.

In 1962, the city won $2.5 million from the Ford Foundation for an anti-poverty agency intended to improve the quality of life among the city's poor. This agency, Community Progress, Inc. (CPI), has spent more than $22 million in five years, but its dollars have done little more than fuel its own bureaucracy. The face of poverty, and particularly black poverty, has not changed. In 1966, the nonwhite unemployment rates were double those for whites. Whites paid a mean rent of $84.18; blacks paid $99.06. One white in eight lived in substandard housing, but one black in four was poorly housed. In CPI's own words, "All of the various indices of slum housing are present."

With federal backing, Lee has had at his disposal ample resources to mount an unprecedented attack on the causes and symptoms of poverty, but the city has demonstrated other priorities. Perhaps because of his special purposes, Lee has thought it best to by-pass federal guidelines which call for the participation of an informed public in renewal plans. Since the poor are unlikely to champion plans which call for their own removal, they are informed only after the city's designs have been worked out in secrecy. By that time, financing has been arranged and the city is "committed" to its blueprints. Through after-the-fact consultation of the public, Lee has successfully blunted the effectiveness of citizen criticism.

But Lee is a successful politician and, since redevelopment is the most conspicuous feature of his administration, his supporters brandish the eight election victories as an open-ended mandate from the public. In fact, Lee's repeated terms in office prove only that the interests best served by renewal—business, the professions, middle- and upper-income families—are precisely those groups that go to the polls. Those badly served by clearance and relocation—the city's black and white poor—are underregistered and do not vote.

Since last summer's riots, however, the illusory consensus behind Lee has begun to disintegrate. Riots are the products of many things, among them the simple contagion of a well-publicized idea. But in New Haven, they ushered in a fresh look at just what renewal has and has not done. The report of the Kerner Commission on Civil Disorder spoke of the "lesson" of both New Haven and Detroit, "where well-intentioned programs designed to respond to the needs of ghetto residents were not worked out and implemented sufficiently in cooperation with the intended beneficiaries."

One very good reason why New Haven's programs were not worked out in consultation with the poor is that the poor were never intended as the "beneficiaries" of renewal. The real goals of renewal, as Herbert Gans says of Boston's redevelopment in that city's West End in *The Urban Villagers*, involved "replacing low-yield areas with high-rent buildings that would bring in additional municipal income."

As the real purposes and quality of renewal have become apparent, a number of citizen groups have mobilized to inform the public and to organize resistance. The American Independent Movement (AIM), a radical group made up largely of whites, has from almost the start scored the inequity and folly of Lee's brand of city reconstruction. Recently, perhaps because of the riots, people have begun listening to AIM's criticism and some small progress has been made toward limiting the nearly total power of the Redevelopment Agency. Last summer, before the riots, a black group called the Hill Parents' Association (HPA) was given shoestring support by the city to organize a number of black-run, self-help programs. Under the leadership of Fred Harris, HPA's programs—which included a day camp for ghetto children and an employment agency for the unemployed—sparked a small renaissance on the Hill, the city's sprawling ghetto. As one minor city official said, "HPA worked wonders. The kids were going to camp, men were going to work—the Hill was alive and humming for the first time."

But then came the violence and the city stopped playing ball with black leaders, especially those like Harris who feel that blacks should help choose and run the kinds of programs that are advertised as helping blacks. The city also began what could only be seen as a concerted program of harassment. Harris was arrested and charged with the possession of drugs and a stolen typewriter. Then in late December, New Haven police arrested six men—five of them nonwhite—who had allegedly conspired to blow several of the Mayor's new buildings out from under him. Two of the six had connections with community-run organizations on the Hill. To blacks, the city was clearly on a witch hunt to show that New Haven's riots were the work of anarchists and criminals and had nothing to do with redevelopment or the racial malice that divides New Haven.

Brasilia

The winds of change are in the air, and both public opinion and professional judgment are reappraising Lee's variety of renewal. Several aldermen are bucking municipal coercion in an effort to stop the most recent renewal folly: a six-lane "ring" highway which would isolate Yale and downtown New Haven from the rest of the city. And at least one important magazine, *Progressive Architecture*, has criticized the social failures of Lee's renewal programs.

With the end of America's war in Vietnam, what the riot commission called the "lesson" of New Haven will become increasingly valuable. Out of fear, guilt and some sense of justice, our society may be about to shift the gears of its priorities in the direction of its have-nots. As the nation's most redeveloped metropolis, New Haven could easily emerge as a model for whatever new spending is set aside to better America's cities. For just that reason, an accurate evaluation of the "miracle" in Model City has never been more necessary.

In the black areas of New Haven today, passing patrol cars are met with clenched fists. The city's blacks are angry and its whites are arming. Sometimes, as when a tenement vaporizes in the fiery night, the background rumbling of the ghetto is even audible downtown. But at City Hall, fingers crossed, the Mayor continues to apply old errors in efforts to solve the very problems they helped create.

NATION 6/3/68

Bobby Seale, co-founder of The Black Panther Party

BARTOLOMEO VANZETTI
Last Speech to the Court

I have talk a great deal of myself but I even forgot to name Sacco.* Sacco too is a worker from his boyhood, a skilled worker lover of work, with a good job and pay, a good and lovely wife, two beautiful children and a neat little home at the verge of a wood, near a brook. Sacco is a heart, a faith, a character, a man; a man lover of nature and of mankind. A man who gave all, who sacrifice all to the cause of Liberty and to his love for mankind; money, rest, mundane ambitions, his own wife, his children, himself and his own life. Sacco has never dreamt to steal, never to assassinate. He and I have never brought a morsel of bread to our mouths, from our childhood to today—which has not been gained by the sweat of our brows. Never.

Oh, yes, I may be more witful, as some have put it, I am a better babbler than he is, but many, many times in hearing his heartful voice ringing a faith sublime, in considering his supreme sacrifice, remembering his heroism I felt small small at the presence of his greatness and found myself compelled to fight back from my throat to not weep before him—this man called thief and assassin and doomed. But Sacco's name will live in the hearts of the people and in their gratitude when Katzmann's and your bones will be dispersed by time, when your name, his name, your laws, institutions, and your false god are but a dim rememoring of a cursed past in which man was wolf to the man . . .

If it had not been for these thing, I might have live out my life talking at street corners to scorning men. I might have die, unmarked, unknown, a failure. Now we are not a failure. This is our career and our triumph. Never in our full life could we hope to do such work for tolerance, for joostice, for man's onderstanding of man as now we do by accident. Our words—our lives—our pains—nothing! The taking of our lives—lives of a good shoemaker and a poor fish-peddler—all! That last moment belongs to us—that agony is our triumph.

* Sacco and Vanzetti, Italian immigrants, were tried in 1921 for two murders and found guilty. The controversial verdict was disputed by millions throughout the world, who felt the men had not received a fair trial because of their radical affiliations. A retrial was denied and Sacco and Vanzetti were executed in 1927, maintaining their innocence—Ed.

From *The Writing is on the Wall*, ed. by Walter Lowenfels, Doubleday

EVERYTHING HAVE A LAW TO IT, SEE

John Hersey interviews Robert Pollard, the imprisoned older brother of Aubrey Pollard murdered at The Algiers Motel

"Money, that's what makes the world keep going," Robert said to me. "Money, Without no money, wouldn't nobody — if you didn't know nothing about no money or wonderful things to have or anything, you wouldn't care nothing about no money; you wouldn't want nothing. You'd be doing just like peoples in Africa, or somewhere, sitting up and eating dead things and going round, don't want nothing but a old house or something, just a shelter to keep the rain off of you. Go round and kill wild animals and eat them, you know; you're free to kill what animals you want.

"Everything have a law to it, see. Every time you walk out a door, anywhere you walk, you breaks a law. See, because they got so many laws. Actually if people really look at it you don't actually have no freedom. Because anything you do, you've broken a law. I mean the least little thing, you know. You can't even spit on the sidewalk; if you spit on the sidewalk, that's a ticket. They done covered the earth with cement and you can't spit on it.

"If people got a better job and was making more money, and they got in trouble or something, then they'll worry about something like spitting on the sidewalk, see, but a person that never had anything, they don't even let it bother them. I mean, he cares that he's in jail, he cares about his freedom, see, just like a wild animal running out there in the woods or something, you know, you lock him up, he's going to want to get out, although he don't have anything, he still want to get out.

"Something that you were never taught and raised up to, you know — what I'm trying to say: What you want to know won't hurt you. What you don't know, you don't want it."

"As long as there's money in the world," Robert said, "won't hardly anything will change. The *people* won't change. The buildings and the cars and the clothes and stuff, and shoes would change, and different products, and trucks and boats and stuff like that would change, but the people won't change. If you can bring them more money, they'll take it.

"In a certain extent, there's always going to be somebody over you. All peoples are not the same. Somebody's always going to have a little bit more than you. Somebody else is always going to have a little bit more than *that* person, and over and over and over, see. Like it might be this little boy's got a penny right here, and this other boy might be a little bigger, he's got two cents, or they might be the same size, two cents, and three and four and five and six, and all up to a thousand dollars.

"People is very evil against other people."

From *The Algiers Motel Incident* by John Hersey, Knopf

A WILLINGNESS TO DIE

'The first time in my life I felt like a man was when I was burning down that store,' said one of the Negroes arrested during the August 1965 upheaval in Watts.

From *Prelude to Riot*, Paul Jacobs, Vintage.

The riot made clear that if something is not done about the police immediately, the fears of white society will be transformed into reality: whites will be facing a black society that will not only harbor, but welcome and employ snipers. *THE TROOPS DID NOT INSTILL FEAR SO MUCH AS A FIGHTING HATRED IN THE COMMUNITY.* Many people, of every age and background, cursed the soldiers. Women spit at armored cars. Five-year-old kids clenched bottles in their hands. If the troops made a violent move, the primitive missiles were loosed at them. People openly talked of the riot turning into a showdown and, while a great many were afraid, few were willing to be pushed around by the troops. All told there were more than 3000 people arrested, injured, or killed; thousands more witnessed these incidents. From this kind of violence, which touches people personally, springs a commitment to fight back. By the end of the weekend many people spoke of a willingness to die.

Jimmy Cannon was one such person. He was the uncle riding with ten-year-old Eddie Moss when the Guardsmen shot through the car and the young boy's head was ripped open. Jimmy put the car, blood, bulletholes and all, into a private garage as proof of what happened. Then he was beaten on the streetcorner by police who found him there. Jimmy learned how to fight during four years in the Marines. "I don't hold any grudges against you," he told a white person who interviewed him. "I'm just for rights, not for violence. This thing is wrong. I've faced a lot of things, but this is bad, and I just don't care anymore. I am to the point where I just don't care."

From *Rebellion in Newark* Tom Hayden, Vintage 1968

HOW TO GET THE COLONIAL OVERSEERS OUT OF THE GHETTO

INSTEAD, as blacks and Puerto Ricans become political blocs, a direction ahead is for neighborhoods in large cities to insist on a major role in determining who police their streets. This too is already beginning, notably in Washington, where Arthur Waskow of the Institute for Policy Studies reports, "The City Council (presidentially appointed) has begun to take the idea seriously; the Democratic Party is committed to it; much of the black leadership is working on it; many liberal and radical whites have been developing support for it, and some of them have concluded that reconstruction of the police is important to white as well as black communities."

Among the proposals is one for elected neighborhood police commissions and a city-wide review board. Obviously community control of the police does not mean each neighborhood can decide which laws the police enforce and which they don't. Quite the contrary would be the result. Since the poor are victims of most crimes, a neighborhood commission is going to insist on much more conscientious and diligent police work than has been customary in ghetto areas. But it will also, as in the case of local school governing boards, be able to transfer out those cops who regard themselves as colonial overseers. There will be new criteria as well for the hiring of police—among them, racial attitudes, psychological stability, and the capacity for humane resourcefulness. (Certain cops, for example, can be trained to know how to intervene in family arguments and how to break up street hassles without starting their own small wars.) And with the police becoming an organic part of a neighborhood, responsible to the community, there would then be more reason for local residents to consider police careers without being split in their loyalties, as many black cops are now.

From "The Dimensions of Community Control" by Nat Hentoff, *Evergreen Review* March 1969

COMMUNITY CONTROL

A LOT OF PEOPLE GROW UP TO BECOME PIGS BECAUSE THIS SYSTEM TEACHES EXPLOITATION; TEACHES US TO FORGET OUR SISTERS AND BROTHERS.

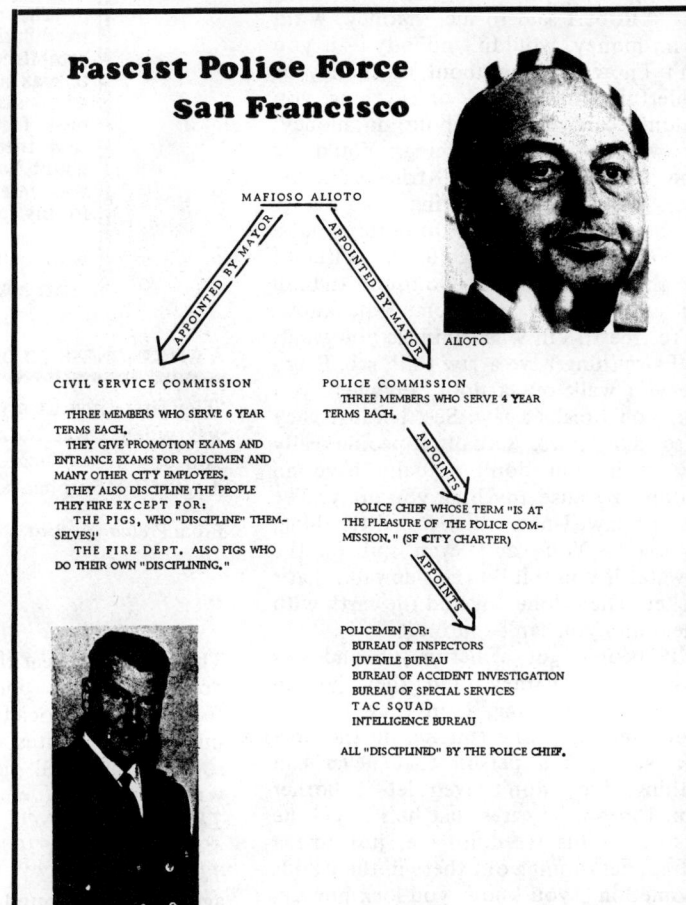

Fascist Police Force
San Francisco

MAFIOSO ALIOTO

APPOINTED BY MAYOR   APPOINTED BY MAYOR

ALIOTO

CIVIL SERVICE COMMISSION

THREE MEMBERS WHO SERVE 6 YEAR TERMS EACH.
THEY GIVE PROMOTION EXAMS AND ENTRANCE EXAMS FOR POLICEMEN AND MANY OTHER CITY EMPLOYEES.
THEY ALSO DISCIPLINE THE PEOPLE THEY HIRE EXCEPT FOR:
THE PIGS, WHO "DISCIPLINE" THEM-SELVES!'
THE FIRE DEPT. ALSO PIGS WHO DO THEIR OWN "DISCIPLINING."

POLICE COMMISSION

THREE MEMBERS WHO SERVE 4 YEAR TERMS EACH.

APPOINTS

POLICE CHIEF WHOSE TERM "IS AT THE PLEASURE OF THE POLICE COM-MISSION." (SF CITY CHARTER)

APPOINTS

POLICEMEN FOR:
BUREAU OF INSPECTORS
JUVENILE BUREAU
BUREAU OF ACCIDENT INVESTIGATION
BUREAU OF SPECIAL SERVICES
TAC SQUAD
INTELLIGENCE BUREAU

ALL "DISCIPLINED" BY THE POLICE CHIEF.

CAHILL

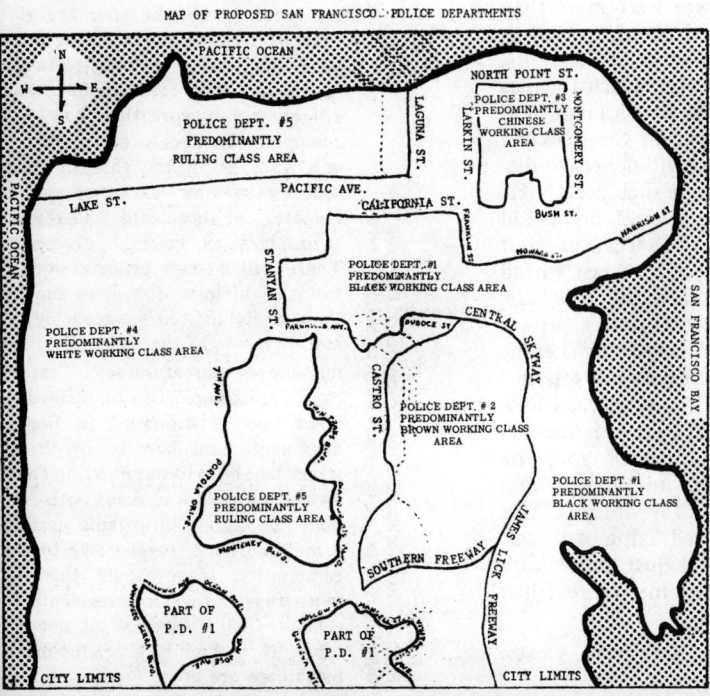

MAP OF PROPOSED SAN FRANCISCO POLICE DEPARTMENTS

PACIFIC OCEAN

N
W   E
S

POLICE DEPT. #5
PREDOMINANTLY
RULING CLASS AREA

NORTH POINT ST.

POLICE DEPT. #3
PREDOMINANTLY
CHINESE
WORKING CLASS
AREA

LAGUNA ST.
LARKIN ST.
MONTGOMERY ST.

LAKE ST.   PACIFIC AVE.
CALIFORNIA ST.
BUSH ST.
FRANKLIN ST.
HARRISON ST.
HOWARD ST.

POLICE DEPT. #1
PREDOMINANTLY
BLACK WORKING CLASS AREA

STANYAN ST.

CENTRAL SKYWAY

POLICE DEPT. #4
PREDOMINANTLY
WHITE WORKING CLASS AREA

CASTRO ST.

SAN FRANCISCO BAY

POLICE DEPT. #2
PREDOMINANTLY
BROWN WORKING CLASS
AREA

POLICE DEPT. #5
PREDOMINANTLY
RULING CLASS
AREA

POLICE DEPT. #1
PREDOMINANTLY
BLACK WORKING CLASS
AREA

SOUTHERN FREEWAY

JAMES LICK FREEWAY

PART OF
P.D. #1

PART OF
P.D. #1

CITY LIMITS   CITY LIMITS

THE POWER MUST RETURN TO THE PEOPLE

THE PEOPLE HAVE TO CHANGE THE SYSTEM -- GET RID OF
THE PIGGISHNESS IN OUR SOCIETY.

PEOPLE'S POLICE DEPARTMENTS

THE ACTION BEGINS WITH EACH POLICE COUNCIL PRECINCT (A 6 TO 10 BLOCK AREA). PRECINCT VOTERS ELECT ONE COUNCILMAN WHO MUST LIVE IN THAT AREA. THIS COUNCILMAN IS ONE OF 15 ON THE POLICE COUNCIL OF EACH NEIGHBORHOOD DIVISION:

POLICE DEPARTMENT #1: BLACK WORKING CLASS COMMUNITY
   7 NEIGHBORHOOD DIVISIONS

POLICE DEPARTMENT #2: BROWN WORKING CLASS COMMUNITY
   5 NEIGHBORHOOD DIVISIONS

POLICE DEPARTMENT #3: CHINESE WORKING CLASS COMMUNITY
   2 NEIGHBORHOOD DIVISIONS

POLICE DEPARTMENT #4: WHITE WORKING CLASS COMMUNITY
   7 NEIGHBORHOOD DIVISIONS

POLICE DEPARTMENT #5: RULING CLASS COMMUNITY:
   3 NEIGHBORHOOD DIVISIONS

EACH POLICE DEPT. LOOKS LIKE THIS:

THE PEOPLE OF EACH PRECINCT ELECT ONE COUNCILMAN

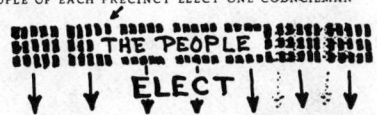

THE PEOPLE

ELECT

POLICE COUNCIL FOR ONE NEIGHBORHOOD DIVISION (15 COUNCILMEN)

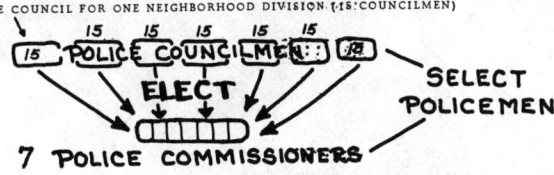

15 15 15 15 15

15 POLICE COUNCILMEN 15

ELECT

SELECT
POLICEMEN

7 POLICE COMMISSIONERS

THE POWER IS RETURNED TO THE PEOPLE

THIS IS A REVOLUTIONARY PROGRAM!

THE COMMUNITY CONTROL OF POLICE PETITION PROVIDES THAT ALL WEAPONS, VEHICLES, EQUIPMENT, FUNDS AND FILES OF THE PRESENT FASCIST POLICE FORCE WILL BE DISTRIBUTED TO THE PEOPLE'S COMMUNITY POLICE DEPARTMENTS. (Section 35.1-A of petition)

POLICE BECOME COMMUNITY PEOPLE

ALL POLICE OFFICERS MUST LIVE IN THE POLICE DEPARTMENT AREAS THEY WORK IN. (Section 35.1-B)

THE YOUTH HAVE A STRONG VOICE

COUNCILMEN CAN BE RECALLED BY A PETITION BEARING THE SIGNATURES OF RESIDENTS EQUALLING 20% OF THE NUMBER OF PEOPLE VOTING IN THAT PRECINCT. THE 20% SIGNING DO NOT HAVE TO BE REGISTERED VOTERS AND THEY CAN BE OF ANY AGE.

COMMISSIONERS CAN BE RECALLED (through a petition) BY 20% OF THE REGISTERED VOTERS IN THAT PRECINCT.

PEOPLE'S POLICE DEPARTMENT
DIAGRAMMED FOR ONE OF OUR CITY'S POLICE DEPARTMENTS

EXAMPLE: A PEOPLE'S POLICE DEPT. WITH 7 NEIGHBORHOOD DIVISIONS.

THE PEOPLE OF THE PRECINCTS:
15 PRECINCTS PER NEIGHBORHOOD DIVISION.
THE PEOPLE IN EACH PRECINCT ELECT A POLICE COUNCILMAN.
QUALIFICATIONS FOR POLICE COUNCILMEN ARE ----->

ELECTED

POLICE COUNCILS FOR THE NEIGHBORHOOD DIVISIONS:
THE 7 NEIGHBORHOOD DIVISIONS EACH HAVE A 15 MAN POLICE COUNCIL. THE DUTIES OF THE POLICE COUNCIL ARE:

ELECTED

POLICE COMMISSIONERS: SEVEN
ONE COMMISSIONER FOR EACH NEIGHBORHOOD DIVISION.
THE DUTIES OF THE COMMISSIONERS ARE: ----->

QUALIFICATIONS FOR POLICE COUNCILMEN:
1. RESIDENCE IN HIS PRECINCT FOR SIX MONTHS PRIOR TO THE UPCOMING ELECTION.
2. MUST BE OF VOTING AGE.

DUTIES OF POLICE COUNCILMEN:
1. SET QUALIFICATIONS FOR SELECTION OF POLICEMEN.
2. HEAR AND ACT ON COMPLAINTS OF PEOPLE AGAINST POLICEMEN.
3. DISCIPLINE POLICEMEN WHO BREAK LAWS OR POLICIES WITHIN THE DISTRICT.
4. SELECT ONE COMMISSIONER TO REPRESENT THE PEOPLE ON THE BOARD OF COMMISSIONERS. THEY CAN FIRE HIM, TOO, IF THEY'RE NOT SATISFIED WITH HIS ACTIONS.
5. MAKE POLICY DECISIONS. THE COMMISSIONER FOR THAT POLICE COUNCIL IS BOUND TO BRING UP THESE DECISIONS AT COMMISSIONERS' MEETINGS AND VOTE ACCORDING TO THE POLICE COUNCIL'S INSTRUCTIONS.
   THE POLICE COMMISSIONERS FORM THE POLICE COMMISSION FOR EACH POLICE DEPARTMENT IN THE CITY.

DUTIES OF POLICE COMMISSIONERS:
1. SELECT POLICEMEN.
2. DISCIPLINE POLICEMEN.
3. SET QUALIFICATIONS FOR POLICEMEN.
4. SET POLICIES WITHIN THE POLICE DEPARTMENT.
5. FIX SALARIES OF POLICE COUNCILMEN AND POLICEMEN.
6. MAKE NECESSARY AGREEMENTS WITH OTHER POLICE DEPARTMENTS AND GOVERNMENT AGENCIES.

COMMUNITY CONTROL OF POLICE MEANS

CONTROL OF OUR DESTINIES: SELF DETERMINATION FOR ALL PEOPLES.

AN END TO THE RACIST HARRASSMENT BY POLICE. HUEY NEWTON, BOBBY SEALE, LOS SIETE AND MANY OTHER POLITICAL PRISONERS WOULD NOT BE IN JAIL TODAY IF WE HAD COMMUNITY CONTROL OF POLICE.

POLICE COULD NOT BE USED AS STRIKE BREAKERS BY THE RULING CLASS, BECAUSE IF THEY DO NOT REPRESENT THE INTEREST OF THE PEOPLE THEY WILL BE EXPELLED FROM THE DEPARTMENT.

FULLER EMPLOYMENT IN LOW INCOME COMMUNITIES BECAUSE RESIDENTS OF THE COMMUNITY WOULD BE EMPLOYED AS POLICEMEN.
POWER TO THE PEOPLE

POWER TO THE PEOPLE!

Economic domination carries with it as well the threat of cultural subjugation — not a threat, but a positive virtue, from the point of view of the colonial administrator or, often, the American political scientist delighted with the opportunity to preside over the "modernization" of some helpless society. An example, extreme perhaps, is the statement of an American diplomat in Laos:

"For this country, it is necessary, in order to achieve any progress, to level everything. It is necessary to reduce the inhabitants to zero, to disencumber them of their traditional culture which blocks everything."

At another level, the same phenomenon can be observed in Latin America. Claude Julien comments:

"The revolt of Latin American students is not directed only against dictatorial regimes that are corrupt and inefficient — nor only against the exploitation by the foreigner of the economic and human resources of their country — but also against the cultural colonization that touches them at the deepest level of their being. And this is perhaps why their revolt is more virulent than that of the worker or peasant organizations that experience primarily economic colonization."

From "Knowledge and Power" by Noam Chomsky, *The New Left,* an anthology, Porter Sergent

✳ ✳ ✳ ✳ ✳ ✳ ✳ ✳ ✳ ✳ ✳ ✳ ✳ ✳ ✳ ✳ ✳
✳ Economists estimate that by 1975, some ✳
✳ 200 corporations will hold 75 percent of ✳
✳ all manufacturing assets in the U.S. Given ✳
✳ the speed with which outfits like Litton ✳
✳ Industries, Gulf and Western, and Ling- ✳
✳ Temco-Vought are piecing together em- ✳
✳ pires, the number 200 may actually be ✳
✳ high. ✳
✳ JOHN DEEDY *Commonweal* 10/11/68 ✳
✳ ✳ ✳ ✳ ✳ ✳ ✳ ✳ ✳ ✳ ✳ ✳ ✳ ✳ ✳ ✳ ✳

our major cities, already black, will become preponderantly black in less than a generation.

This speed-up toward blackening American cities has been accompanied by little discernible consideration — by whites, anyway — of what it will mean when a majority of America's central cities are inhabited by a majority — in some cases perhaps a large majority — of blacks.

One projection is that fifty of our largest cities will by 1970 have majorities of black inhabitants. Another projection says that by 1975 the fourteen largest cities in the United States will have black majorities of 60 to 80 per cent. These projections may turn out to be wrong, but the evidence for them is mounting. Blacks have been moving steadily into the large cities since World War II. Mechanization of Southern farms is pushing them rapidly off the land. Starvation is being systematically employed by Southern whites as a method of chasing blacks from areas where their cheap labor is no longer needed and they become welfare burdens. In forlorn pursuit of community and jobs they go in larger and larger waves to the cities south, north, east, west.

From "Farewell to Integration" by W. H. Ferry, *The Center Magazine* March 1968

Course on Rebellion Listed at J.H.S. 271

By EMANUEL PERLMUTTER

Courses in how to stage community demonstrations and how past revolutions have been planned and carried out are listed in the curriculum of evening adult education classes advertised for Junior High School 271 in the controversial Ocean Hill-Brownsville School district.

Among the teachers listed for the courses is Herman B. Ferguson, who is in jail awaiting appeal of a prison sentence for conspiring to murder moderate civil rights leaders.

Another instructor is Robert (Sonny) Carson, head of the Brooklyn chapter of the Congress of Racial Equality. He withdrew the chapter from the national CORE organization because he considered the parent group insufficiently militant.

Leaflets distributed in the Brooklyn district say that the courses are to be held from Oct. 14 to Jan. 29, Monday through Friday, from 7 to 10 P.M.

Sponsors of the program are identified as the Black Panther party, the Black Caucus Political party, the Black United Front, the African-American Teachers Association, the African-American Students Association, Brothers and Sisters for Afro-American Unity, Independent Brooklyn CORE, and NEGRO (National Economic Growth and Rehabilitation Organization).

The New York Times 10/8/68

THE SYSTEM

Associated Press (AP) survey indicates that one out of five U.S. senators is a millionaire. A U.S. Senator did not agree: said one out of three would be closer, from what he knows. If you happen to be a millionaire, you're well represented in Washington; if you're *NOT* a millionaire. . .
LNS

Rene Dubos believes that as much as 80% of the genetic potential of most human beings may be repressed by their environment. . .we can all agree that the child's potential, whatever it is, should, as far as possible, be protected from environmental obliteration.
ROBERT M. HUTCHINS

As far as possible? BY ANY MEANS POSSIBLE!

WHAT ARE THEY AFRAID OF?

All-Volunteer Force Favored

WASHINGTON — A presidential commission has concluded that an all-volunteer armed force should be established and has estimated the cost at only an additional $4 billion a year in extra spending.

The commission, headed by former Defense Secretary Thomas S. Gates Jr., has also reached the conclusion that this switch would not lead to a big increase in the number of Negroes in the armed forces as some critics had feared.

The Boston Globe Dec 1969

GENOCIDE IN AMERICAN LIFE

By Earl Ubell

We are a nation with the blood of genocide on our hands. For those who think that America cannot go the way of Nazi Germany, we have only to recall that we have already been down that road. That's what makes the whole black-white situation so frightening: will white Americans somehow find their way back to the rationale of destroying whole peoples in the name of God, capitalism, and law and order?

Peter Farb takes us back to that strange country of mass murder in his new book, "Man's Rise to Civilization as shown by the Indians of North America from Primeval Times to the Coming of the Industrial State" (E. P. Dutton, New York, $8.95).

We Americans destroyed some 11 million Indians by burning, pillaging, starving, biological warfare, forced marches, prison camps, and bounty hunting. We popularized scalping by paying some Indians to collect the scalps of others. We kicked the Cherokees out of Georgia, Tennessee, and North Carolina as a reward for inventing writing for their language, for adopting Presbyterianism, and for making a success out of farming. We deliberately spread smallpox and alcoholism among the Indians. And in the end, we worked hard and often successfully to extirpate Indianism from the remnant bands remaining.

The Village Voice 11/21/68

Ed. Note: Earl Ubell is Science Editor for ABC-TV, N.Y.

COMPREHENSION

GENOCIDE
by Jean-Paul Sartre

Carl Oglesby, former president of Students for a Democratic Society and author of Containment and Change, *was a member of the International War Crimes Tribunal, called by Jean-Paul Sartre and Bertrand Russell to consider U.S. actions in Vietnam. Among the charges taken up by the Tribunal was genocide. It was in this context that Sartre's paper was written. The background of its conception is described here by Mr. Oglesby.*

O N THE EVENING OF THE THIRD DAY of the session, November 22, our Tribunal held a special closed meeting at a luxurious home in the posh Copenhagen suburb of Lyngby.

To say there was a pall over the Lyngby meeting would be to exaggerate. But we did wait uncertainly for Sartre, the diminutive giant, to deliver us from the genocide dilemma—the impending need was to reach a verdict on this, the most difficult of the charges we had to consider.

In a sense, it does not really matter whether American action in Vietnam is fixed with the term "genocide." That action is, in any case, just what it *is*: precisely that particular pattern, sequence and aggregation of deeds. Its meaning is intrinsic, beyond the need for clarification, beyond the power of abstract thought to alter. What it is called has little to do with its character as concrete human experience.

But simply by calling itself a "Tribunal" and by laying some claim to Nuremberg ancestry, this project of upstart justice committed itself to a judgment of a Western state in the light of Western laws. It did not create law or judge these laws. Rather, the Tribunal presupposed them, as the basis of its own right to exist and as the source of its intellectual method. It received law and acquired fact in order to ask, "Do these facts prove that these laws have been broken?"

This method encountered little difficulty with the other accusations. The United States was guilty of a crime against the peace, for example, if the historical record revealed the U.S. to be the aggressor in Vietnam; guilty of war crimes if there was evidence of deliberate and systematic attacks on nonmilitary targets; and guilty of crimes against humanity if war crimes were committed with a certain intensity and regularity.

But with genocide the Tribunal knew it had laid hands on an ambiguous and volatile concept.

In the first place, the term has an historical resonance which makes it extremely unstable, even *fragile*: only speak the word and an image of Auschwitz appears. If for no other reason than respect for the six million, one must use this word with great seriousness. Fail to do so, let the voice crack just once, and the concept of genocide loses its delicate juridical-historical equilibrium and dissolves, becoming useless to the Vietnamese and forgetful of the Jewish victims whose fate gave the term its primary moral content. This word should be held in reserve. It is the name of the ultimate crime. Its purity is essential.

In terms of the Tribunal, this meant that very careful definition was necessary; or rather, that it was necessary to employ carefully the definition which had currency and legal weight.

The relevant document, from the Geneva Convention of 9 December 1948, is a sequel to the U.N. General Assembly's declaration, resolution 96(I), of 11 December 1946, "that genocide is a crime under international law, contrary to the spirits and aims of the United Nations and condemned by the civilized world."

Sartre's mind was not made up when we met that night. He

Introduction

Palante/LNS

155

people of c

argued in the first place that the Convention's definition of genocide was too vague and formal to be of much use in the present case, but secondly that it might be "unfair" (the interpreter's word) to accuse the United States of killing the Vietnamese *as such*. His proposal was that the Tribunal should announce its verdicts on the other questions considered at that session and then spend two days in public discussion of genocide—by which he meant, apparently, that on those two days several opinions on the question would be read.

Sartre spent the next days drafting the paper and in the process persuaded himself, and ultimately the Tribunal, that there was no need for such tentativeness. On November 30, at a closed meeting which lasted until about 4:00 a.m., we heard, discussed and in small part amended the paper which Sartre read the next day, the final day of the session, immediately before Vladimir Dedijer's delivery of the verdicts.

On Genocide

The word "genocide" is relatively new. It was coined by the jurist Raphael Lemkin between the two world wars. But the fact of genocide is as old as humanity. To this day there has been no society protected by its structure from committing that

crime. Every case of genocide is a product of history and bears the stamp of the society which has given birth to it. The one we have before us for judgment is the act of the greatest capitalist power in the world today. It is as such that we must try to analyze it—in other words, as the simultaneous expression of the economic infrastructure of that power, its political objectives and the contradictions of its present situation.

In particular, we must try to understand the genocidal intent in the war which the American government is waging against Vietnam, for Article 2 of the 1948 Geneva Convention defines genocide on the basis of intent; the Convention was tacitly referring to memories which were still fresh. Hitler had proclaimed it his deliberate intent to exterminate the Jews. He made genocide a political means and did not hide it. A Jew had to be put to death, whoever he was, not for having been caught carrying a weapon or for having joined a resistance movement, but simply *because he was a Jew*. The American government has avoided making such clear statements. It has even claimed that it was answering the call of its allies, the South Vietnamese, who had been attacked by the communists. Is it possible for us, by studying the facts objectively, to discover implicit in them such a genocidal intention? And after such an investigation, can we say that the armed forces of the United States are killing Vietnamese in Vietnam for the simple reason that they are Vietnamese?

This is something which can only be established after an historical examination: the structure of war changes right along with the infrastructures of society. Between 1860 and the present day, the meaning and the objectives of military conflicts have changed profoundly, the final stage of this metamorphosis being precisely the "war of example" which the United States is waging in Vietnam.

In 1856, there was a convention for the protection of the property of neutrals; 1864, Geneva: protection for the wounded; 1899, 1907, The Hague: two conferences which attempted to make rules for war. It is no accident that jurists and governments were multiplying their efforts to "humanize war" on the very eve of the two most frightful massacres that mankind has ever known. Vladimir Dedijer has shown very effectively in his study "On Military Conventions" that the capitalist societies during this same period were giving birth to the monster of total war in which they express their true nature. He attributes this phenomenon to the following:

1. The competition between industrial nations fighting for new markets produces a permanent antagonism which is expressed in ideology and in practice by what is known as "bourgeois nationalism."

2. The development of industry, which is the source of this hostility, provides the means of resolving it to the advantage of one of the competitors, through the production of more and more *massively* destructive weapons. The consequence of this development is that it becomes increasingly difficult to make any distinction between the front and behind the lines, between the civilian population and the soldiers.

3. At the same time, new military objectives—the factories—arise near the towns. And even when they are not producing materiel directly for the armies, they maintain, at least to some extent, the economic strength of the country. It is precisely this strength that the enemy aims to destroy: this is at once the aim of war and the means to that end.

4. The consequence of this is that everyone is mobilized: the peasant fights at the front, the worker fights behind the lines, the peasant women take over for their husbands in the fields. This *total* struggle of nation against nation tends to make the worker a soldier too, since in the last analysis the power which is economically stronger is more likely to win.

5. The democratic facade of the bourgeois nations and the emancipation of the working class have led to the participation of the masses in politics. The masses have no control at all over government decisions, but the middle classes imagine that by voting they exercise some kind of remote control. Except in cases of defensive wars, the working classes are torn between their desire for peace and the nationalism which has been instilled in them. Thus war, seen in a new light and distorted by propaganda, becomes the ethical decision of the whole community. All the citizens of each warring nation (or almost all, after they have been manipulated) are the enemies of all those of the other country. War has become absolutely total.

6. These same societies, as they continue their technological expansion, continue to extend the scope of their competition by increasing communications. The famous "One World" of the Americans was already in existence by the end of the 19th century when Argentine wheat dealt a final blow to English agriculture. Total war is no longer only between all members of one national community and all those of another: it is also total because it will very likely set the whole world up in flames.

Thus, war between the bourgeois nations—of which the 1914 war was the first example but which had threatened Europe since 1900—is not the "invention" of one man or one government, but simply a necessity for those who, since the beginning of the century, have sought to "extend politics by other means." The option is clear: either *no* war or *that* kind of total war. Our fathers fought that kind of war. And the governments who saw it coming, with neither the intelligence nor the courage to stop it, were wasting their time and the time of the jurists when they stupidly tried to "humanize" it.

Nevertheless, during the First World War a genocidal intent appeared only sporadically. As in previous centuries, the essential aim was to crush the military power of the enemy and only secondarily to ruin his economy. But even though there was no longer any clear distinction between civilians and soldiers, it was still only rarely (except for a few terrorist raids) that the civilian population was expressly made a target. Moreover, the belligerent nations (or at least those who were doing the fighting) were industrial powers. This made for a certain initial balance: against the possibility of any real extermination each side had its own deterrent force—namely the power of applying the law of "an eye for an eye." This explains why, in the midst of the carnage, a kind of prudence was maintained.

HOWEVER, SINCE 1830, throughout the last century and continuing to this very day, there have been countless acts of genocide whose causes are likewise to be found in the structure of capitalist societies. To export their products and their capital, the great powers, particularly England and France, set up colonial empires. The

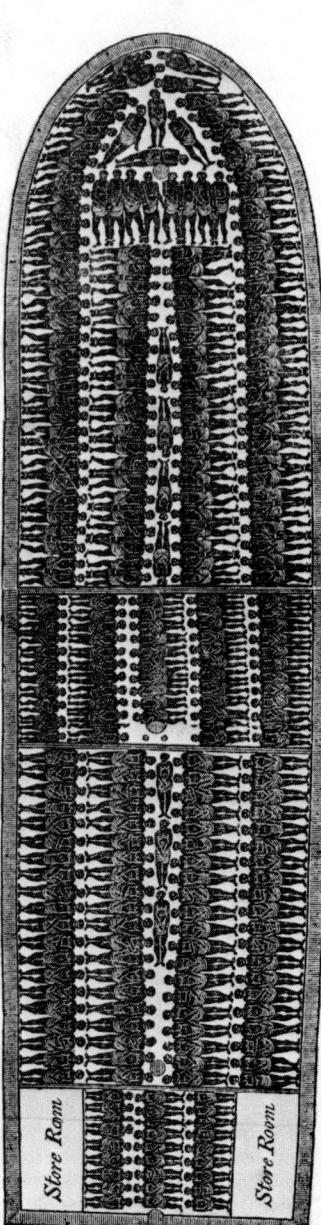

Slave Ship

name "overseas possessions" given by the French to their conquests indicates clearly that they had been able to acquire them only by wars of aggression. The adversary was sought out in his own territory, in Africa and Asia, in the underdeveloped countries, and far from waging "total war" (which would have required an initial balance of forces), the colonial powers, because of their overwhelming superiority of firepower, found it necessary to commit only an expeditionary force. Victory was easy, at least in conventional military terms. But since this blatant aggression kindled the hatred of the civilian population, and since civilians were potentially rebels and soldiers, the colonial troops maintained their authority by terror—by perpetual massacre. These massacres were genocidal in character: they aimed at the destruction of "a part of an ethnic, national, or religious group" in order to terrorize the remainder and to wrench apart the indigenous society.

After the bloodbath of conquest in Algeria during the last century, the French imposed the *Code Civil*, with its middle-class conceptions of property and inheritance, on a tribal society where each community held land in common. Thus they systematically destroyed the economic infrastructure of the country, and tribes of peasants soon saw their lands fall into the hands of French speculators. Indeed, colonization is not a matter of mere conquest as was the German annexation of Alsace-Lorraine; it is by its very nature an act of cultural genocide. Colonization cannot take place without systematically liquidating all the characteristics of the native society—and simultaneously refusing to integrate the natives into the mother country and denying them access to its advantages. Colonialism is, after all, an economic system: the colony sells its raw materials and agricultural products at a reduced price to the colonizing power. The latter, in return, sells its manufactured goods to the colony at world market prices. This curious system of trade is only possible if there is a colonial subproletariat which can be forced to work for starvation wages. For the subject people this inevitably means the extinction of their national character, culture, customs, sometimes even language. They live in their underworld of misery like dark phantoms ceaselessly reminded of their subhumanity.

However, their value as an almost unpaid labor force protects them, to a certain extent, against physical genocide. The Nuremberg Tribunal was still fresh in people's minds when the French massacred 45,000 Algerians at Setif, as an "example." But this sort of thing was so commonplace that no one even thought to condemn the French government in the same terms as they did the Nazis.

But this "deliberate destruction of a part of a national group" could not be carried out any more extensively without harming the interests of the French settlers. By exterminating the subproletariat, they would have exterminated themselves as settlers. This explains the contradictory attitude of these *pieds-noirs* during the Algerian war: they urged the Army to commit massacres, and more than one of them dreamed of total genocide. At the same time they attempted to compel the Algerians to "fraternize" with them. It is because France could neither liquidate the Algerian people nor integrate them with the French that it lost the Algerian war.

THESE OBSERVATIONS ENABLE US to understand how the structure of colonial wars underwent a transformation after the end of the Second World War. For it was at about this time that the colonial peoples, enlightened by that conflict and its impact on the "empires," and later by the victory of Mao Tse-tung, resolved to regain their national independence. The characteristics of the struggle were determined from the beginning: the colonialists had the superiority in weapons, the indigenous population the advantage of numbers. Even in Algeria—a colony where there was settlement as much as there was exploitation—the proportion of *colons* to natives was one to nine. During the two world wars, many of the colonial peoples had been trained as soldiers and had become experienced fighters. However, the short supply and poor quality of their arms—at least in the beginning—kept the number of fighting units low. These objective conditions dictated their strategy, too: terrorism, ambushes, harassing the enemy, extreme mobility of the combat groups which had to strike unexpectedly and disappear at once. This was made

possible only by the support of the entire population. Hence the famous symbiosis between the liberation forces and the masses of people: the former everywhere organizing agrarian reforms, political organs and education; the latter supporting, feeding and hiding the soldiers of the army of liberation, and replenishing its ranks with their sons.

It is no accident that people's war, with its principles, its strategy, its tactics and its theoreticians, appeared at the very moment that the industrial powers pushed total war to the ultimate by the industrial production of atomic fission. Nor is it any accident that it brought about the destruction of colonialism. The contradiction which led to the victory of the FLN in Algeria was characteristic of that time; people's war sounded the death-knell of conventional warfare at exactly the same moment as the hydrogen bomb. Against partisans supported by the entire population, the colonial armies were helpless. They had only one way of escaping this demoralizing harassment which threatened to culminate in a Dien Bien Phu, and that was to "empty the sea of its water"—i.e. the civilian population. And, in fact, the colonial soldiers soon learned that their most redoubtable foes were the silent, stubborn peasants who, just one kilometer from the scene of the ambush which had wiped out a regiment, knew nothing, had seen nothing. And since it was the unity of an entire people which held the conventional army at bay, the only anti-guerrilla strategy which could work was the destruction of this people, in other words, of civilians, of women and children.

Torture and genocide: that was the answer of the colonial powers to the revolt of the subject peoples. And that answer, as we know, was worthless unless it was thorough and total. The populace—resolute, united by the politicized and fierce partisan army—was no longer to be cowed as in the good old days of colonialism, by an "admonitory" massacre which was supposed to serve "as an example." On the contrary, this only augmented the people's hate. Thus it was no longer a question of intimidating the populace, but rather of physically liquidating it. And since that was not possible without concurrently liquidating the colonial economy and the whole colonial system, the settlers panicked, the colonial powers got tired of pouring men and money into an interminable conflict, the mass of the people in the mother country opposed the continuation of an inhuman war, and the colonies became sovereign states.

THERE HAVE BEEN CASES, HOWEVER, in which the genocidal response to people's war is not checked by infrastructural contradictions. Then total genocide emerges as the absolute basis of an anti-guerrilla strategy. And under certain conditions it even emerges as the explicit objective—sought either immediately or by degrees. This is precisely what is happening in the Vietnam war. We are dealing here with a new stage in the development of imperialism, a stage usually called neo-colonialism because it is characterized by aggression against a former colony which has already gained its independence, with the aim of subjugating it anew to colonial rule. With the beginning of independence, the neo-colonialists take care to finance a *putsch* or *coup d'état* so that the new heads of state do not represent the interests of the masses but those of a narrow privileged strata, and, consequently, of foreign capital.

Ngo Dinh Diem appeared—hand-picked, maintained and armed by the United States. He proclaimed his decision to reject the Geneva Agreements and to constitute the Vietnamese territory to the south of the 17th parallel as an independent state. What followed was the necessary consequence of these premises: a police force and an army were created to hunt down people who had fought against the French, and who now felt thwarted of their victory, a sentiment which automatically marked them as enemies of the new regime. In short, it was the reign of terror which provoked a new uprising in the South and rekindled the people's war.

Did the United States ever imagine that Diem could nip the revolt in the bud? In any event, they lost no time in sending in experts and then troops, and then they were involved in the conflict up to their necks. And we find once again almost the same pattern of war as the one that Ho Chi Minh fought against the French, except that at first the American govern-

ment declared that it was only sending its troops out of generosity, to fulfill its obligations to an ally.

That is the outward appearance. But looking deeper, these two successive wars are essentially different in character: the United States, unlike France, has no economic interests in Vietnam. American firms have made some investments, but not so much that they couldn't be sacrificed, if necessary, without troubling the American nation as a whole or really hurting the monopolies. Moreover, since the U.S. government is not waging the war for reasons of a *directly* economic nature, there is nothing to stop it from ending the war by the ultimate tactic —in other words, by genocide. This is not to say that there is proof that the U.S. does in fact envision genocide, but simply that nothing prevents the U.S. from envisaging it.

In fact, according to the Americans themselves, the conflict has two objectives. Just recently, Dean Rusk stated: "We are defending ourselves." It is no longer Diem, the ally whom the Americans are generously helping out: it is the United States itself which is in danger in Saigon. Obviously, this means that the first objective is a military one: to encircle Communist China. Therefore, the United States will not let Southeast Asia escape. It has put its men in power in Thailand, it controls two-thirds of Laos and threatens to invade Cambodia. But these conquests will be hollow if it finds itself confronted by a free and unified Vietnam with 32 million inhabitants. That is why the military leaders like to talk in terms of "key positions." That is why Dean Rusk says, with unintentional humor, that the armed forces of the United States are fighting in Vietnam "in order to avoid a third world war." Either this phrase is meaningless, or else it must be taken to mean: "in order to *win* this third conflict." In short, the first objective is dictated by the necessity of establishing a Pacific line of defense, something which is necessary only in the context of the general policies of imperialism.

The second objective is an economic one. In October 1966, General Westmoreland defined it as follows: "We are fighting the war in Vietnam to show that guerrilla warfare does not pay." To show whom? The Vietnamese? That would be very surprising. Must so many human lives and so much money be wasted merely to teach a lesson to a nation of poor peasants thousands of miles from San Francisco? And, in particular, what need was there to attack them, provoke them into fighting and subsequently to go about crushing them, when the big American companies have only negligible interests in Vietnam? Westmoreland's statement, like Rusk's, has to be filled in. The Americans want to show others that guerrilla war does not pay: they want to show all the oppressed and exploited nations that might be tempted to shake off the American yoke by launching a people's war, at first against their own pseudo-governments, the compradors and the army, then against the U.S. "Special Forces," and finally against the GIs. In short, they want to show Latin America first of all, and more generally, all of the Third World. To Che Guevara who said, "We need several Vietnams," the American government answers, "They will all be crushed the way we are crushing the first."

In other words, this war has above all an admonitory value, as an example for three and perhaps four continents. (After all, Greece is a peasant nation too. A dictatorship has just been set up there; it is good to give the Greeks a warning: submit or face extermination.) This genocidal example is addressed to the whole of humanity. By means of this warning, six per cent of mankind hopes to succeed in controlling the other 94 per cent at a reasonably low cost in money and effort. Of course it would be preferable, for propaganda purposes, if the Vietnamese would submit before being exterminated. But it is not certain that the situation wouldn't be clearer if Vietnam *were* wiped off the map. Otherwise someone might think that Vietnam's submission had been attributable to some *avoidable* weakness. But if these peasants do not weaken for an instant, and if the price they pay for their heroism is *inevitable* death, the guerrillas of the future will be all the more discouraged.

At this point in our demonstration, three facts are established: (1) What the U.S. government wants is to have a base against China and to set an example. (2) The first objective *can* be achieved, without any difficulty (except, of course, for the resistance of the Vietnamese), by wiping out a whole people and imposing the Pax Americana on an uninhabited

Vietnam. (3) To achieve the second, the U.S. *must* carry out, at least in part, this extermination.

THE DECLARATIONS OF AMERICAN STATESMEN are not as candid as Hitler's were in his day. But candor is not essential to us here. It is enough that the facts speak; the speeches which come with them are believed only by the American people. The rest of the world understands well enough: governments which are the friends of the United States keep silent; the others denounce this genocide. The Americans try to reply that these unproved accusations only show these governments' partiality. "In fact," the American government says, "all we have ever done is to offer the Vietnamese, North and South, the option of ceasing their aggression or being crushed." It is scarcely necessary to mention that this offer is absurd, since it is the Americans who commit the aggression and consequently they are the only ones who can put an end to it. But this absurdity is not undeliberate: the Americans are ingeniously formulating, without appearing to do so, a demand which the Vietnamese cannot satisfy. They do offer an alternative: Declare you are beaten or we will bomb you back to the stone age. But the fact remains that the second term of this alternative is genocide. They have said: "genocide, yes, but *conditional* genocide." Is this juridically valid? Is it even conceivable?

If the proposition made any juridical sense at all, the U.S. government might narrowly escape the accusation of genocide. But the 1948 Convention leaves no such loopholes: an act of genocide, especially if it is carried out over a period of several years, is no less genocide for being blackmail. The perpetrator may declare he will stop if the victim gives in; this is still—without any juridical doubt whatsoever—a genocide. And this is all the more true when, as is the case here, a good part of the group has been annihilated to force the rest to give in.

But let us look at this more closely and examine the nature of the two terms of the alternative. In the South, the choice is the following: villages burned, the populace subjected to massive bombing, livestock shot, vegetation destroyed by defoliants, crops ruined by toxic aerosols, and everywhere indiscriminate shooting, murder, rape and looting. This is genocide in the strictest sense: massive extermination. The other option: what is *it*? What are the Vietnamese people supposed to do to escape this horrible death? Join the armed forces of Saigon or be enclosed in strategic or today's "New Life" hamlets, two names for the same concentration camps?

We know about these camps from numerous witnesses. They are fenced in by barbed wire. Even the most elementary needs are denied: there is malnutrition and a total lack of hygiene. The prisoners are heaped together in small tents or sheds. The social structure is destroyed. Husbands are separated from their wives, mothers from their children; family life, so important to the Vietnamese, no longer exists. As families are split up, the birth rate falls; any possibility of religious or cultural life is suppressed; even work—the work which might permit people to maintain themselves and their families—is refused them. These unfortunate people are not even slaves (slavery did not prevent the Negroes in the United States from developing a rich culture); they are reduced to a living heap of vegetable existence. When, sometimes, a fragmented family group is freed—children with an elder sister or a young mother —it goes to swell the ranks of the subproletariat in the big cities; the elder sister or the mother, with no job and mouths to feed reaches the last stage of her degradation in prostituting herself to the GIs.

The camps I describe are but another kind of genocide, equally condemned by the 1948 Convention:

"Causing serious bodily or mental harm to members of the group.

"Deliberately inflicting on the group conditions of life calculated to bring about its physical destruction in whole or in part.

"Imposing measures intended to prevent births within the group.

"Forcibly transferring children of the group to another group."

In other words, it is not true that the choice is between death or submission. For submission, in those circumstances, is submission to genocide. Let us say that a choice must be made between a violent and immediate death and a slow death from mental and physical degradation. Or, if you prefer, *there is no choice at all.*

Is it any different for the North?

One choice is *extermination*. Not just the daily risk of death, but the systematic destruction of the economic base of the country: from the dikes to the factories, nothing will be left standing. Deliberate attacks against civilians and, in particular, the rural population. Systematic destruction of hospitals, schools and places of worship. An all-out campaign to destroy the achievements of 20 years of socialism. The purpose may be only to intimidate the populace. But this can only be achieved by the daily extermination of an ever larger part of the group. So this intimidation itself in its psycho-social consequence is a genocide. Among the children in particular it must be engendering psychological disorders which will for years, if not permanently, "cause serious . . . mental harm."

The other choice is *capitulation*. This means that the North Vietnamese must declare themselves ready to stand by and watch while their country is divided and the Americans impose a direct or indirect dictatorship on their compatriots, in fact on members of their own families from whom the war has separated them. And would this intolerable humiliation bring an end to the war? This is far from certain. The National Liberation Front and the Democratic Republic of Vietnam, although fraternally united, have different strategies and tactics because their war situations are different. If the NLF continued the struggle, American bombs would go on blasting the DRV whether it capitulated or not.

If the war were to cease, the United States—according to official statements—would feel very generously inclined to help in the reconstruction of the DRV, and we know exactly what this means. It means that the United States would destroy, through private investments and conditional loans, the whole economic base of socialism. And this too is genocide. They would be splitting a sovereign country in half, occupying one of the halves by a reign of terror and keeping the other half under control by economic pressure. The "national group" Vietnam would not be physically eliminated, yet it would no longer exist. Economically, politically and culturally it would be suppressed.

In the North as in the South, the choice is only between two types of liquidation: collective death or dismemberment. The American government has had ample opportunity to test the resistance of the NLF and the DRV: by now it knows that only total destruction will be effective. The Front is stronger than ever; North Vietnam is unshakable. For this very reason, the calculated extermination of the Vietnamese people cannot really be intended to make them capitulate. The Americans offer them a *paix des braves* knowing full well that they will not accept it. And this phony alternative hides the true goal of imperialism, which is to reach, step by step, the highest stage of escalation—total genocide.

Of course, the United States government *could have* tried to reach this stage in one jump and wipe out Vietnam in a *Blitzkrieg* against the whole country. But this extermination first required setting up complicated installations—for instance, creating and maintaining air bases in Thailand which would shorten the bombing runs by 3000 miles.

Meanwhile, the major *purpose* of "escalation" was, and still is, to prepare international opinion for genocide. From this point of view, Americans have succeeded only too well. The repeated and systematic bombings of populated areas of Haiphong and Hanoi, which two years ago would have raised violent protests in Europe, occur today in a climate of general indifference resulting perhaps more from catatonia than from apathy. The tactic has borne its fruit: public opinion now sees escalation as a slowly and continuously increasing pressure to bargain, while in reality it is the preparation of minds for the final genocide. Is such a genocide possible? No. But that is due to the Vietnamese and the Vietnamese alone; to their courage, and to the remarkable efficiency of their organization. As for the United States government, it cannot be absolved of its crime just because its victim has enough intelligence and enough heroism to limit its effects.

We may conclude that in the face of a people's war (the char-

acteristic product of our times, the answer to imperialism and the demand for sovereignty of a people conscious of its unity) there are two possible responses: either the aggressor withdraws, he acknowledges that a whole nation confronts him, and he makes peace; or else he recognizes the inefficacy of conventional strategy, and, if he can do so without jeopardizing his interests, he resorts to extermination pure and simple. There is no third alternative, but making peace is still at least *possible*.

But as the armed forces of the U.S.A. entrench themselves firmly in Vietnam, as they intensify the bombing and the massacres, as they try to bring Laos under their control, as they plan the invasion of Cambodia, there is less and less doubt that the government of the United States, despite its hypocritical denials, has chosen genocide.

THE GENOCIDAL INTENT IS IMPLICIT in the facts. It is necessarily premeditated. Perhaps in bygone times, in the midst of tribal wars, acts of genocide were perpetrated on the spur of the moment in fits of passion. But the anti-guerrilla genocide which our times have produced requires organization, military bases, a structure of accomplices, budget appropriations. Therefore, its authors must meditate and plan out their act. Does this mean that they are thoroughly conscious of their intentions? It is impossible to decide. We would have to plumb the depths of their consciences—and the Puritan bad faith of Americans works wonders.

There are probably people in the State Department who have become so used to fooling themselves that they still think they are working for the good of the Vietnamese people. However, we may only surmise that there are fewer and fewer of these hypocritical innocents after the recent statements of their spokesmen: "We are defending ourselves; even if the Saigon government begged us, we would not leave Vietnam, etc., etc." At any rate, we don't have to concern ourselves with this psychological hide-and-seek. The truth is apparent *on the battlefield* in the racism of the American soldiers.

This racism—anti-black, anti-Asiatic, anti-Mexican—is a basic American attitude with deep historical roots and which existed, latently and overtly, well before the Vietnamese conflict. One proof of this is that the United States government refused to ratify the Genocide Convention. This doesn't mean that in 1948 the U.S. intended to exterminate a people; what it does mean—according to the statements of the U.S. Senate— is that the Convention would conflict with the laws of several states; in other words, the current policymakers enjoy a free hand in Vietnam because their predecessors catered to the anti-black racism of Southern whites. In any case, since 1966, the racism of Yankee soldiers, from Saigon to the 17th parallel, has become more and more marked. Young American men use torture (even including the "field telephone treatment"*), they shoot unarmed women for nothing more than target practice, they kick wounded Vietnamese in the genitals, they cut ears off dead men to take home for trophies. Officers are the worst: a general boasted of hunting "VCs" from his helicopter and gunning them down in the rice paddies. Obviously, these were not NLF soldiers who knew how to defend themselves; they were peasants tending their rice. In the confused minds of the American soldiers, "Viet Cong" and "Vietnamese" tend increasingly to blend into one another. They often say themselves, "The only good Vietnamese is a dead Vietnamese," or what amounts to the same thing, "A dead Vietnamese is a Viet Cong."

For example: south of the 17th parallel, peasants prepare to harvest their rice. American soldiers arrive on the scene, set fire to their houses and want to transfer them to a strategic hamlet. The peasants protest. What else can they do, bare-handed against these Martians? They say: "The quality of the rice is good; we want to stay to eat our rice." Nothing more. But this is enough to irritate the young Yankees: "It's the Viet Cong who put that into your head; they are the ones who have taught you to resist." These soldiers are so misled that they take the feeble protests which their own violence has

---

* The portable generator for a field telephone is used as an instrument for interrogation by hitching the two lead wires to the victim's genitals and turning the handle (editor's note).

aroused for "subversive" resistance. At the outset, they were probably disappointed: they came to save Vietnam from "communist aggressors." But they soon had to realize that the Vietnamese did not want them. Their attractive role as liberators changed to that of occupation troops. For the soldiers it was the first glimmering of consciousness: "We are unwanted, we have no business here." But they go no further. They simply tell themselves that a Vietnamese is by definition suspect.

And from the neo-colonialists' point of view, this is true. They vaguely understand that in a people's war, civilians are the only visible enemies. Their frustration turns to hatred of the Vietnamese; racism takes it from there. The soldiers discover with a savage joy that they are there to kill the Vietnamese they had been pretending to save. All of them are potential communists, as proved by the fact that they hate Americans.

Now we can recognize in those dark and misled souls the truth of the Vietnam war: it meets all of Hitler's specifications. Hitler killed the Jews because they were Jews. The armed forces of the United States torture and kill men, women and children in Vietnam merely *because they are Vietnamese*. Whatever lies or euphemisms the government may think up, the spirit of genocide is in the minds of the soldiers. This is their way of living out the genocidal situation into which their government has thrown them. As Peter Martinson, a 23-year-old student who had "interrogated" prisoners for ten months and could scarcely live with his memories, said: "I am a middle-class American. I look like any other student, yet somehow I am a war criminal." And he was right when he added: "Anyone in my place would have acted as I did." His only mistake was to attribute his degrading crimes to the influence of war *in general*.

No, it is not war in the abstract: it is the greatest power on earth against a poor peasant people. Those who fight it are *living out* the only possible relationship between an over-industrialized country and an underdeveloped country, that is to say, a genocidal relationship implemented through racism —the only relationship, short of picking up and pulling out.

Total war presupposes a certain balance of forces, a certain reciprocity. Colonial wars were not reciprocal, but the interests of the colonialists limited the scope of genocide. The present genocide, the end result of the unequal development of societies, is total war waged to the limit by one side, without the slightest reciprocity.

THE AMERICAN GOVERNMENT IS NOT GUILTY of inventing modern genocide, or even of having chosen it from other possible and effective measures against guerrilla warfare. It is not guilty, for example, of having pre-

ferred genocide for strategic and economic reasons. Indeed, genocide presents itself as the *only possible reaction* to the rising of a whole people against its oppressors.

The American government is guilty of having preferred, and of still preferring, a policy of war and aggression aimed at total genocide to a policy of peace, the only policy which can really replace the former. A policy of peace would necessarily have required a reconsideration of the objectives imposed on that government by the large imperialist companies through the intermediary of their pressure groups. America is guilty of continuing and intensifying the war despite the fact that every day its leaders realize more acutely, from the reports of the military commanders, that the only way to win is "to free Vietnam of all the Vietnamese." The government is guilty— despite the lessons it has been taught by this unique, unbearable experience—of proceeding at every moment a little further along a path which leads it to the point of no return. And it is guilty—according to its own admissions—of consciously carrying out this admonitory war in order to use genocide as a challenge and a threat to all peoples of the world.

We have seen that one of the features of total war has been the growing scope and efficiency of communication. As early as 1914, war could no longer be "localized." It had to spread throughout the whole world. In 1967, this process is being intensified. The ties of the "One World," on which the United States wants to impose its hegemony, have grown tighter and tighter. For this reason, as the American government very well knows, the current genocide is conceived as an answer to people's war and perpetrated in Vietnam not against the Vietnamese alone, but against humanity.

When a peasant falls in his rice paddy, mowed down by a machine gun, every one of us is hit. The Vietnamese fight for all men and the American forces against all. Neither figuratively nor abstractly. And not only because genocide would be a crime universally condemned by international law, but because little by little the whole human race is being subjected to this genocidal blackmail piled on top of atomic blackmail, that is, to absolute, total war. This crime, carried out every day before the eyes of the world, renders all who do not denounce it accomplices of those who commit it, so that we are being degraded today for our future enslavement.

In this sense imperialist genocide can only become more complete. The group which the United States wants to intimidate and terrorize by way of the Vietnamese nation is the human group in its entirety.

Ramparts Feb 1968

BUT WHAT THEN?

The Power Struggle

Meanwhile, even some of the most moderate Negro leaders in New York now talk openly of guerrilla war and see the school crisis as one more dramatic evidence of the determination of the white community to oppose and even smash any serious efforts by the Negroes to get power and control over the public institutions that condition their lives.

This is a power struggle with national implications of the most serious nature. The Negro demand for local control is just beginning. It will go on regardless of who is elected President next month, and it will undoubtedly spread into most of the urban communities of the nation.

In the face of the rising opposition of the white community to this Negro movement for the redistribution of power over public institutions and public appropriations, it is easy to see how Mr. Nixon, crying for law and order, can ride the trend against the demonstrators into the White House. But what then?

The Changing Mood

One of the most influential and moderate Negro leaders in New York, predicting that the racial battle of the cities is just beginning, said quite calmly here this week that he expected more repressive measures from a Nixon administration, recognized that more police action against the demonstrators would be popular with most whites, and added that we "may even see concen-

tration camps in this country to hold all the demonstrators."

This is not, mind you, the foreboding of one of the Negro extremists. If the community control experiment is smashed in the Ocean Hill-Brownsville school experiment, he added, "Brooklyn will burn."

It is, of course, precisely such threats that encourage the rising militancy in the white community and help Mr. Nixon. But it does not follow from this that Mr. Nixon's policies will produce the law and order he promises. They may merely please the white majority and revolutionize the Negro minority, and produce less law and order in the end.

JAMES RESTON, *The New York Times*
10/23/68

WHAT DOES THIS DO WITH THE NEGRO? "PUTS HIM IN ONE LITTLE CIRCLE"

SCHIZOPHRENIA

Hersey interviewing the father of Aubrey Pollard killed in Algiers Motel incident.

"I don't hate no policemans," Mr. Pollard said to me one day, speaking of the kind of justice black men and boys get in Detroit, "don't hate no judges, but if justice is going to be — when *I* do wrong, I gets fined, I suffer for it, and I don't expect any more. I could ask for leniency, but I really don't expect it, because I'm poor. But as far as the Negro, he lives in the ghettos, he doesn't know anything else but the ghettos, his parents teach him that because he comes up that way from a little small fellow, to get what you can — grab, quick! The Negro is looked upon as a minority group. Anything that he does, everybody see it. If you think I'm lying, go down to court tomorrow. You'll see how many — now" — and he began to count white suburbs on his fingers — "out in Dearborn, they got their own court; Birmingham, they got their own court; Redford, they got their own court. Murder, regardless to *what* it is, unless there's a case where they bring it downtown, but they keeps it out. What does this do with the Negro? It puts him in a circle, puts him in one little circle. And everyone of them, he got to go down in front of Judge DeMascio, Judge Davenport, and the rest of them. It's a racket, that's all it is! It's the politicians. They work in a circle. You can see the money moving. You don't have to be blind unless you're stupid!"

From Algiers Motel Incident *by John Hersey, Knopf*

(The following is a column from the Society page of the SAN FRANCISCO CHRONICLE by Joan Chatfield-Taylor, Fashion Correspondent):
America's designers have responded to the schizophrenic mood that intelligent American women are in.
On the one hand, there is the fact that many women are richer and have more leisure time than ever before. But it is obvious that this personal well-being is no excuse for euphoria.
There are harsh realities that invade the life of every woman. Violence is one of these. Poverty is another, and most intelligent women didn't need Resurrection City to remind them of the masses of people who can only dream of an existence filled with luxuries.
This coming fall's clothes reflect the current mental state in America.
There are utterly fantastic clothes—escapist clothes in the most luxurious fabrics imaginable. Does she dream of being Natasha in czarist Russia? She can; there are plenty of regal velvet dresses and fur trimmings. Going further south, there's the glittering luxury of the Middle East.
But this fall's fashions aren't all fantasy. There's a definite trend toward realism, particularly in the daytime clothes.
AMERICAN FASHION IS FULL OF THE KIND OF QUIET SUITS THAT A WOMAN CAN WEAR TO A MEETING WITH GHETTO RESIDENTS WITHOUT FEELING OSTENTATIOUS.
The good grey suit is back, usually with an easy skirt and a slightly fitted—if not fitted—jacket; Dior-New York calls one of theirs "San Francisco."
For the most part, the fantasy clothes are for evening, and the realistic clothes for daytime —a sensible arrangement that enables a woman to show her responsible side to the community, and keep her luxury-loving, escapist feelings for her private life.

Connections

"..... AFTER 6 DAYS OF BLOODY HOUSE TO HOUSE FIGHTING — THE VIET CONG CONTINUE TO HOLD MOST OF THE SAIGON SLUM AREAS. TO THE NORTH IN HUE......"

✪✪✪✪✪✪✪✪✪✪✪✪✪✪✪✪✪✪✪ MICHAEL HARRINGTON ✪✪✪✪✪✪✪✪✪✪✪✪✪✪✪✪✪✪✪

THE OTHER AMERICA REVISITED

there is a real invisibility of the poor. The Bureau of the Census has only recently discovered that it had not counted a significant minority of the adult Negro males in the ghetto. Some years before this acknowledgment, Bayard Rustin had told me that there were more blacks in America than the government figured. He pointed out that there were special problems in a place like Harlem — for instance, people doubling-up in apartments, a fair number of individuals who feared any contact with The Man, even with the census-taker — which could lead the professionals to err. I thought that Rustin had created an amateur's fantasy until the hard data began to come in (for instance, the 1967 Manpower Report of the Department of Labor found an "undercount" of twenty per cent of the adult men in the slums). This means that there are several million Americans whose conditions of life are so mercurial that they do not even qualify to be a statistic.

In two particularly tragic cases it is not necessary to speculate about the numbers. The children and the blacks among the poor are worse off than when the war on poverty began. "All told," writes Mollie Orshansky, "even in 1966, after a continued run of prosperity and steadily rising family income, one-fourth of the nation's children were in families living in poverty or hovering just above the poverty line." This fact, of course, has the most disturbing and dangerous implications for the future. On the one hand, poverty more and more becomes a fate because the educational, economic, and social disadvantages of life at the bottom become progressively more damaging; and, on the other hand, the poor still have more children than any other group. Present evidence points to the melancholy conclusion that the twenty-five per cent of the young who are poor, or near-poor, will have large families very much like the ones of which they are now members. If this is true, the current incidence of poverty among children will guarantee that, short of radical political decisions, the next generation in the other America will be even more numerous than this one.

With Negroes, the problem is more a relative position than an absolute increase in indignity, but this is still a politically explosive fact. In 1959 the Social Security Administration fixed the black percentage of the other Americans at twenty-five per cent; by 1966, the proportion had risen to thirty-three per cent. This, of course, still shows that the scandal of poverty actually afflicts more whites than blacks, but it also indicates that discrimination even applies to the rate at which people escape from beneath the poverty line. During these years of prosperity even the worst off of the white Americans have had a special advantage, compared to the Negroes.

It is important to add to this brief survey of the federally certified dimensions of needless economic and social suffering in this country the remarkable "sub-employment" index of the Department of Labor. The index was developed in order to get a more accurate picture of the working — and non-working — lives of people in the slums. Whereas the official definition of unemployment, which currently is fixed at about 3.5 per cent for the nation as a whole, only counts those who are out of work and looking for work, the notion of sub-employment is much more comprehensive. It gives weight to part-time unemployment, to the fact that many people have to toil for poverty wages, to the twenty per cent of the "invisibles" in the slums, and to those who do not look for a job because they are sure they will not find one.

On this basis, the Labor Department discovered sub-employment rates in November, 1966, that ranged from around thirty per cent in the New York ghettos to near fifty per cent in New Orleans. The full significance of this analysis did not become apparent until the winter of 1967 and the report of the National Commission on Civil Disorders. For it was then that the nation learned that the typical rioter was not the least educated, most impoverished, and chronically unemployed citizen of the ghetto. Rather, he was a high-school dropout and a teen-ager and he had worked — but at a menial job. In other words, the frustrations of sub-employment — most particularly of laboring long hard hours without any real hope of advancement — are perhaps more likely to incite a man to violence than the simple despair of having no job at all.

Ed. Note: Martin Luther King reported that 75% of all employed black men work at menial jobs.

From "The Other American Revisited" Jan 1969

THE CENTER MAGAZINE

COMPREHENSION
We are Living in an Elective Dictatorship — Sen. Fulbright

Black Panther free breakfast for children

THE FEDERAL PRINCIPLE

H.R. SHAPIRO

The essence of the United States Constitution was defined by what Madison called the *federal principle*. (Madison, *Federalist Papers*, No. 51):

> While all authority in it [the U.S. Republic] will be derived from and dependent on the society, the society itself will be broken into so many parts, interests and classes of citizens, that the rights of individuals, or of the minority, will be in little danger from interested combinations of the majority. In a free government the security for civil rights must be the same as that for religious rights. It consists in the one case in the multiplicity of interests, and in the other in the multiplicity of sects; and this may be presumed to depend on the extent of the country and number of people comprehended under the same government. . . . In the extended republic of the United States, and among the great variety of interests, parties and sects which it embraces, a coalition of a majority of the whole society could seldom take place on any other principles than those of justice and the general good; whilst there being thus less danger to a minor from the will of a major party, there must be less pretext, also, to provide for the security of the former, by introducing into the government a will not dependent on the latter, or, in other words, a will independent of the society itself [monarchy, etc.]. It is no less certain than it is important, notwithstanding the contrary opinions which have been entertained, that the larger the society, provided it lie within a practical sphere, the more duly capable it will be of self-government. And happily for the *republican cause*, the practicable sphere may be carried to a very great extent, by a judicious modification and mixture of the *federal principle*.

Black people, non-Europeans in general and city-dwellers have remained outside the federal principle in that they have never had control of their own communities and community institutions. This noninvolvement in the federal principle is a major cause both of our present race conflict in America and of the mass society, but, note the key point: it is not the complexity of modern life that has caused this noninvolvement, for as Madison insisted, it is the very complexity of society that makes the federal principle possible.

Ironically, the average American, although not directly oppressed as are most non-Europeans, is coming to be in the same political position as that faced by black people since Emancipation. The average person has no control over his own life, no say in the running of his own community institutions and, in the case of most city-dwellers, no community institutions of his own. That is, the average American is the subject of a mass society.

It is here proposed that instead of trying to bring black people into the mass society, we work our way back to the federal principle by seeing that all communities, black and white (and integrated) have control over their own community institutions and lives. This then would not only be an extension of the federal principle to black people and other non-Europeans, but to city-dwellers and to those whose community institutions are now being centralized and brought under mega-districts or mega-cities.

* * *

The only way individuals can regain control over their lives is by effecting the return of communal and citizen powers to the local communities. The mass society and centralization can only be fought at the local level, the level upon which the mass society feeds. Local communities asserting their rights and controlling their own institutions and interests would have the effect of mountains rising up, penetrating, obstructing and then rolling back the mass cloud, the mass machine which is now devouring the rights and powers of each to participate in the control of his own life.

Public schools in America have traditionally been controlled at the local level. At present, however, when people are acutely concerned (perhaps for the first time in our history) to bring education to their children, the private interest, states and the federal government, assisted by the education establishment, are in a full-scale campaign to take control of the schools from the local level and put them under mega-districts or foundations or state bureaucracies. In the name of an efficiency which doesn't exist, the powers-that-be are attempting to usurp local community and citizen rights over education, a right so basic to democracy that we once thought it the very spirit of the Republic.

If a school district in New York City would assert its rights and regain control over its schools, there would be an immediate obstructing of the mass, centralizing machine. This is no utopian goal. It is concrete, feasible and profoundly within the best American tradition, the very basis of our political structure. It is concrete in that it deals with what people actually do and can do and not with an abstract ideology. It is feasible because local control of local institutions is the basic (if never fully realized or democratically implemented) structure of our politics and society. The feverish efforts of the Establishment to usurp local control demonstrates, indeed, how feasible local control is and how profoundly it is embedded (however much obscured) in the fabric of our national life. All each community would have to do is stand fast and assert its full rights for these rights existed long before teachers' colleges, foundations and unions of experts were born.

A community which controlled its schools could say *no* to: the whole education establishment, to textbook companies, educational-materials peddlers, teaching-machine companies, foundation experiments, phony university, state and federal programs, the compensatory-education business, to the whole mass media and the advertising business, to construction companies, unions and to every other sort of matter, live or otherwise, which is put, pushed or manipulated into the schools. If a textbook company wanted to sell its products to the community, the company would have to serve, not create, the community's needs. In having to serve individual community needs, the companies, foundations, etc., would have to *adjust* to thinking in terms of *people's* needs. Therefore, in *adjusting*, the various businesses will themselves put a halt to the mindless textbooks and empty materials which are the result of having to create a product which must serve uniformly throughout the country and which must thus be emptied of content and removed from reality.

* * *

Local control of schools by African-Americans, other minority groups and city-dwellers in general, will also force the education establishment to re-tool and re-think its attitude toward children and its "philosophy." . . . The community's demand for a totally different approach to education (which minority communities must have to save their children and which all communities would have if they actually did or had to take part in the running of their own schools) would be a first and forceful

step in the interdicting of the whole educational machine. As is the case with other mass approaches to serving individual needs, the education mass machine cannot tolerate this "seeing" on the part of individual communities, nor can it tolerate individual community assertions, demands and decisions and yet remain a mass machine. The machine which pacifies cannot tolerate any other initiative than its own and on its own terms.

* * *

Mass Measures against the mass society tend to be self-defeating. They only feed the monster while legitimizing a mass attitude toward one's own life and political structures. Mass Measures also tend to further condition and "unify" those who have already accepted their position within society and lead others into the bag. The mass society can only be interdicted and fought at the local level because noncommunity organizations, organizations with no *land* under them, have little power or effect on community, city, state and federal government. . . .

People in power only respect and move when either those under them or those in power move or make demands, that is, they only respect others with *political* power. . . .

A community without power is not a community, it is merely a collection of individuals.

* * *

Unless people control their own institutions at the local level, anything can happen and does as in the case of the New York City schools where the children are, in the eyes of the Board of Education, mere abstractions. Of the one million children now in New York City schools, some 750,000 have already been segregated out of the academic tracks by discredited achievement tests which label those who have been taught to read at home "gifted" and the others, "average" or "slow." Those not labeled "gifted" are then totally neglected. Segregated in the second grade by these reading tests, the children who have not been taught at home are written off by being placed in "failure" classes. That is, the school informs the children that they are stupid (nonlearners) when they are seven or eight years old and by the time these children reach sixth or seventh grade, they have been virtually debrained. They no longer listen to or hear anything said in school. This is just one result of people not controlling their own community institutions; the children are reduced to abstractions and no plea or cry can move the bureaucracy, for bureaucracies have no ears.

If African-American (and other minority) groups controlled their own com-

munities, it would be a first step toward a solution of the present civil conflict in America. If each minority group controlled its own local institutions, that is, if each minority controlled its own communities, there would be created *spaces of freedom* for all, for all minorities could then find justice in one community or another. Not only this, but brotherhood, love and integration can only come *after* this democracy through community control for minority groups has been established. Appeals to brotherhood are absurd so long as the supplicants are outside of the political structure and so long as black children are being destroyed in white-controlled schools and black communities are being controlled and raped by white political machines and special interest groups.

If the community controlled its own schools and local institutions, the children, public business and the money involved would be visible. The fact the children are being miseducated would be a daily reality (not a statistical abstraction) and the community could innovate (begin to teach) until such time as there was education in the schools. With the public business visible, corruption would be minimized. Central corruption would be unlikely for federal and state monies would come directly and visibly to the districts and then visibly to the subsections of the districts. For instance, each subsection of a district or community would get its allocation just as the district does and this subsection would know just how much money was due it. Along with the allocation of certain funds to subdistricts, there would be allocation of powers to the subdistricts so that each cluster of schools, in fact, each school, would have various powers including the power to hire nonteaching personnel and, in accordance with the district, to hire or select principals or teachers, etc. These powers would bring to life each subdistrict, in fact, each school area. Given the direct allocation of money, powers and the visibility of both, local corruption would be brought and kept within the bounds and limits necessary for the health and life of the community. When people can see how they are affected by public community decisions and where *their* money is going, we can count on human nature for each person to demand what is his, so long as he is able *to know* what is rightfully his.

* * *

Community development, extending the *federal principle*, participatory democracy, community control of community institutions will not only serve the schools and children, but the Public Interest, the qualitative life of the community and the qualitative life of the nation. To quote Thomas Jefferson:

The way to have good and safe government, is not to trust all to one, but to divide it among the many, distributing to every one exactly the functions he is competent to do. Let the national government be entrusted with the defense of the nation, and its foreign and federal relations; the State governments with the civil rights, laws, police and administration of what concerns the State generally; the counties with the local concerns of the counties, and each ward district the interest within itself. It is by dividing and subdividing these republics from the great national one down through all its subordinations, until it ends in the administration of every man's farm by himself; by placing under every one what his own eye may superintend, that all will be done for the best. What has destroyed liberty and the rights of every man in every government which has ever existed under the sun? The generalizing and concentrating of all cares and powers into one body, no matter whether of the autocrats of Russia or France, or of the aristocrats of a Venetian senate. And I do believe that if the Almighty has not decreed that man shall never be free (and it is a blasphemy to believe it), that the secret shall be found to be in the making himself the depository of the powers respecting himself, so far as he is competent to do them, and delegating only what is beyond his competence by a synthetic process, to higher and higher orders of functionaries, so as to trust fewer and fewer powers in proportion as the trustees become more and more oligarchical. The elementary republics of the Union would form a gradation of authorities, standing each on the basis of law, holding every one its delegated share of powers, and constituting truly a system of fundamental balances and checks for government. Where every man is a sharer in the direction of his ward republic, or of some of the higher ones, and feels that he is a participator in the government of affairs, not merely at election one day in the year, but every day; when there shall not be a man in the state who will not be a member of one of its councils, great or small, he will let the heart be torn out of his body sooner than his power be wrested from him by a Caeser or a Bonaparte. . . . Begin them [community councils] only for a single purpose; they will soon show for what they are the best instruments. . . .

In New York City, there are some thirty school districts. Half are black and Puerto Rican. Both justice and the only possible solution to the present "race" conflict lie in each community's determining its own affairs. We can start with each community controlling its own schools. We must move past the politicians, bureaucrats, New Deal ideologists and special interests who, along with the mass media, keep us in a dulled state of passivity and away from effecting this only possible solution to the present civil conflict in America.

Why should, for instance, a white district in Queens object to controlling its own schools and the state and federal money involved? Certainly the black and Puerto Rican communities in New York City will not object to running their own schools. We have the beginnings of a solution to our political problems in New York City, but in order to effect this solution, citizens and community groups, from all the communities, must rise up and let the politicians and special interests know that they want no mega-city control (nor Tammany control) over their lives, nor experts to run their lives, and that they will no longer tolerate this centrally enforced political impotence . . . and that the communities, all communities, will have control of their institutions and lives.

If African-Americans and other minority groups controlled their own communities (as does Scarsdale, etc.), spaces of freedom would exist for some forty million nonwhite and minority group Americans. Others would not lose control of their communities and lives. In fact, whites would gain or regain control of their lives from the mass machine. In doing so, whites would be able to overcome those abstract fears of the political unknown, that is, fears of anarchy, of black people, of hair and other such mass-media conspiracies. We would have the beginnings of a truly pluralistic society. There would be no effective political persecution for all could find justice somewhere, in one community or another. Injustice would be lessened with this framework or meeting of the various public interests. With community control, integration will first become possible, and we will be able to get on a road leading away from "race" war, from the mass society and toward a real democracy. . . .

With community control of schools and other local institutions, poverty can be abolished. The money now due each community or district from state and federal sources would go directly to the community. Each community could set priorities and hire local residents. In a country where there is more than enough to eat for all, only those who have no political power grow hungry. The point here is that to this extent the political can control the economic. And, in the end, the political must control the economic for the economic is blind, merely production and distribution, while the political is the area where men decide as to the quality of their lives and how they are going to live with one another.

With each community determining its own affairs and looking to its own community welfare, mass movements would, in this pluralistic framework, be highly impossible. Each community would be another obstacle for the mass ideology or irrationality to overcome. For the same reasons, the federal government could no longer totally dominate our foreign policy (soldiers come from communities) and it would be extremely difficult to start any but purely defensive wars. . . .

Fortunately, we do have a tradition of local control; when local control is reasserted and extended to all communities, not only will the pacified "middle-class" communities come to see and live a bit of reality, but our nonwhite and minority communities will be enfranchised and empowered. The country will then be fulfilling one tradition, the democratic, at the expense of the "new" tradition, the imperialistic. By fulfilling our democratic tradition, we can defray the expense caused by the failure of the new tradition and save our national soul.

* * *

At present, the public has no opinion because there is no public, only a mass of individuals with no space or place for discussion of public issues. Opinion is formed as the mass media and central political structures manipulate and stretch one choice and then bend the "discussion" back into the one choice. Given local forums in which people can discuss and debate issues as they occur and in public, and find out just what each decision is going to mean for their rights and lives, people will not cry "yea" everytime a central agency or the mass media bark or whine.

* * *

Local control is the opposite of what is meant by ward politics. Ward politics comes about when local power is taken away and vested in a political machine at City Hall. The political machine then appoints ward bosses who run the local wards. Ward politics is thus based on centralization and a political machine. With local power, local control, there can be no ward politics because the local communities have control of their own affairs and have no need (or, at least, not the all-consuming need) of connections with and in City Hall or with a political machine.

THE COMMUNITY WOULD DECIDE WHO ARE ITS LEADERS AND WHAT ARE ITS NEEDS

IF YA GOT SOMETHIN' IT'S CAUSE YOU'RE GOOD

IF YA GOT NOTHIN' IT'S CAUSE YOU'RE BAD... ASK SANTA CLAUS

©1968 R.COBB ALL RIGHTS RESERVED

New economic lifeblood for Roxbury ... *By Gar Alperovitz*

As Summer approaches and tensions in Roxbury rise, one man on the spot is clearly Mayor Kevin White. Like any big city mayor, he has an all but impossible job; the likelihood of failure is great.

Consider one problem: the mayor can use his influence to help move poverty and other funds into Roxbury. But funds are limited, and so he has the delicate job of choosing which of Roxbury's many groups and projects to aid with the minimal resources at hand.

In most cities the mayor yields in given instances to whichever group causes him the biggest political headache. But no real solution to a city's problems can come out of this haphazard approach. Moreover, every time the mayor chooses, he makes one political friend (for the moment) — and a dozen enemies.

Meanwhile, the people of the ghetto increasingly resent handouts and the overbearing institutions of white society which control their lives — from the outside.

And white people are incensed because taxes are too high and Negroes aren't grateful to be getting welfare.

The tragedy is that there is an alternative: the mayor could test the old idea of local democratic control; he could hand over to the black community itself responsibility for its own affairs. Specifically, he could help arrange that an appropriate share of anti-poverty and other funds be given to the Roxbury community to use as it sees fit. The community would decide who are its leaders and what are its needs.

This approach has, of course, been called for many times, but few realize it has also been put into practice in other cities — with great success.

The best example of community control of resources is a Neighborhood Corporation in Columbus, Ohio. The Corporation is a simple legal line drawn around a ghetto neighborhood of 8000 people.

Unlike current Boston proposals for a Development Corporation, all the stockholders of the Columbus Corporation live in the area, and the Corporation is controlled by the neighborhood—

one man, one vote. Anyone in the neighborhood can become a member—or 'stockholder'—simply by signing up.

The Columbus Office of Economic Opportunity and others working to fight poverty transfer funds directly to the Corporation to be used as the community thinks best for its own self improvement.

Mistakes are made (just as they are in the mayor's office), but there is a good corrective: the Corporation must face the consequences in the open arena of neighborhood politics.

Private, decentralized decision-making of this kind—the antithesis of big government—is one of the most traditional of American values. The people closest to a problem are responsible for solving it; local leaders are recognized and in control.

And it corresponds with the reality that Roxbury was once a self-governing town—and is now clearly a socially distinct community.

The special value of this idea today is that it could substitute local participation and community stability for turmoil and despair. The Model Cities Board is a step in this direction—but a minimal one at best.

But community control of Federal funds—however great its values for stability—is really a very limited concept. It does not help the mayor get the big money he needs for significant community action. Poverty programs, slight as they are, are being cut back—and Congress is not likely to reverse this trend. Moreover, it does not go beyond the idea of 'handouts.'

With a little imagination, however, Mayor White (and other mayors) might see that money for community development could come from the community itself.

If the Community Corporation were not merely a conduit for outside funds, but were a community controlled enterprise for economic development, community business profits could be plowed back into community services.

One result of the riots is that many white businessmen are selling their ghetto stores and

factories. Conventionally, (and also under Mayor White's recent proposals), a few enterprising black entrepreneurs would buy these businesses with the help of bank loans (or funds from the new Boston Urban Foundation).

However, if such loan funds were instead made available so that a Community Corporation —representing the community itself—were to purchase the businesses, the profits could finance needed social services for thousands of ghetto residents.

The economic development of the ghetto need not be restricted to existing small businesses which serve the local market. Both Avco Corporation and Bedford-based EG&G Co., manufacturers of precision instruments, are establishing new plants in Roxbury. Both companies will train neighborhood people to operate and manage their plants—and in the case of EG&G will sell neighborhood employees a major share of equity over the next twenty years.

If the example of EG&G were taken one step further—if (with the help of loans) stock in such an enterprise were sold to a Community Corporation—its profits could provide substantial resources for Roxbury's anti-poverty effort, instead of dividends for a few employees. Business profits would be used to benefit the community as a whole—as the community saw fit.

Creatively developed, such an approach could begin to move away from our present system—a system in which one group is taxed to pay for welfare programs for another, and in which outsiders make the big decisions for the ghetto.

The participation it offers might even help transform the energy of social protest into constructive action for social change. And it could ultimately move away entirely from poverty programs towards the better objective of jobs and community controlled economic development

The author is a fellow of the Institute of Politics at Harvard University.

The Boston Globe

5/18/68

166

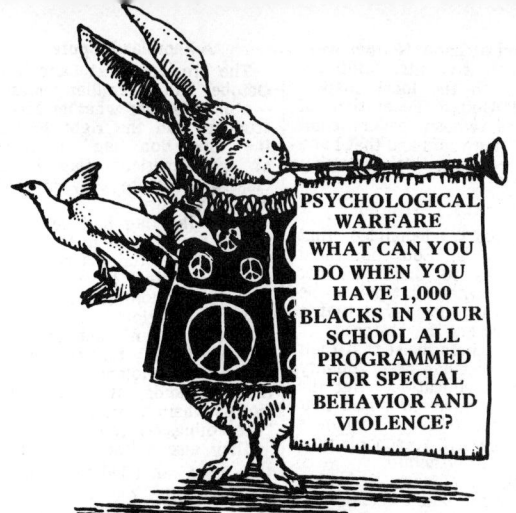

The revolution is from below, the lower classes, the underworld, the damned, the disreputable, the despised and rejected. Freud's revolutionary motto in the Interpretation of Dreams: *Flectere si nequeo Superos, Acherunta movebo.* If I cannot bend the higher powers, I will stir up the lower depths. Freud's discovery: the universal underworld.

N.O. BROWN *Love's Body*

Negro-White Friction Is Eroding Teacher-Student Relations in City's High Schools

By JOSEPH LELYVELD

Racial fears and resentment are steadily eroding relations between white teachers and administrators and black students in many, possibly most, high schools here.

In a few schools, this erosion has gone so far as to create conditions of paralyzing anarchy in which large police detachments have been deemed necessary to keep classrooms functioning and put down sporadic outbursts of violence by rebellious students.

More generally, the widening gulf between white adults and black youths in the schools convinces increasing numbers of blacks and whites that the fading promise of school integration can never be more than a hollow piety.

A two-month survey by The New York Times of a cross-section of the city's 62 academic high schools—some predominantly black, others mostly white, some troubled and others ostensibly calm—indicated that racial misunderstanding appears in some schools not just as a fever that flares now and then but as a malignant growth.

In such schools adults and youths seize on narrow one-dimensional views of each other.

In the eyes of many teachers, students who express feelings of racial pride by donning the African shirts called dashikis and wearing talismans, or by sewing the emblems of various black power movements to Army combat jackets, surrender the status of children for that of "hard-core militants."

"We are faced with a very, very specific political movement," charged James Baumann, a co-chairman of the United Federation of Teachers chapter at Franklin K. Lane High School, a neocolonial fortress on the Brooklyn-Queens border where a force of 100 policemen was stationed last October after an outbreak of racial violence. "A small, dedicated group of militants is trying to polarize the student body and establish a totally black school."

A respected Brooklyn principal, who didn't want to be quoted by name, talked not of small minorities but uncontrollable masses. "What can you do," he asked, "when you have 1,000 blacks in your school, all programed for special behavior and violence?"

In the eyes of many black students, teachers given to such interpretations lose their identity and vocation and merge into that monolith of rigid, hostile authority known collectively as "the Man."

'A Fallen House'

"As soon as they get the cops behind them, they show how racist they are," said a Lane student regarded by teachers as a "militant" leader. "We're trying to get ourselves together but they don't like that. They want to get us out. That's boss [great]! Black people shouldn't go to that school."

A black senior at George W. Wingate High School put his disaffection more broadly: "The school system? Like man, it's a fallen house."

Often under pressure the two sides conform precisely to each other's expectations with results that are mutually disastrous. Then teachers are openly taunted and abused, firebombs and Chemical Mace are discovered in stairwells, and racial clashes erupt between black and white youths who normally keep a safe, formal distance between them.

In 1969 incidents of this type were reported in more than 20 high schools here.

"The youngsters are militant —everyone's militant," said Murray Bromberg, principal of Andrew Jackson High School in Queens.

Much of the anger of teachers and students can be traced to the frustrations both suffer in classrooms.

'We Aim Higher'

In the furor over whether it is the schools that are failing to teach blacks and other nonwhites or the students themselves who are failing to learn there is one undisputed fact—that the results are catastrophic.

The level of educational achievement accepted as a norm in many schools was indicated last month by a letter sent to the parents of all students at Lane. "We are not satisfied just to bring every senior up to the eighth-grade level of reading," it said. "We aim higher."

Many black students are registered in watered-down "modified" courses that lead nowhere. Even in schools that boast of being integrated, these classes are often all-black.

But the small minority of students labeled "militants" are almost never drawn from the mass of undisciplined students, semiliterate dropouts, truants or drug users. Frequently they are among the most aware and ambitious black students in the school—the very students, teachers commonly say, who should concentrate on their studies and "make something of themselves."

Ironic Situation

Some observers regard it as ironic, even tragic, that these students and their capacity for commitment should be seen as a threat. "The fact is that they are an articulate and committed group of youngsters looking for change and reform," said Murray Polner, assistant to Dr. Seymour P. Lachman of the Board of Education.

But that has been distinctly the minority view, especially since the three teacher strikes over the community control issue in Ocean Hill-Brownsville late in 1968.

"That was the precipice," said Paul Becker, a Wingate teacher who broke with the union after the second strike and now is active in the Teachers Action Committee, which favors community control. "After that it was downhill all the way. It was 'us' against 'them.'"

Many black students are still outraged by the memory of epithets and abuse from U.F.T. picket lines. "There were teachers shouting, 'Nigger!'" recalled Billy Pointer, a Wingate senior, in the course of a recent group discussion on human relations.

"No, Billy, that's not right," said Martin Goldberg, a social studies teacher. "I have to admit that some teachers used unprofessional language but I'm almost sure that none of them used the word 'nigger.' That must have been parents."

Later, the teacher commented: "I hate it when people who aren't racists say 'nigger.'"

That the clash of values has not been exclusively racial was demonstrated at Jackson where black students last year agitated successfully for the appointment of a black assistant principal.

This fall the new man, Robert Couche, was stunned to find himself denounced as a "house nigger" after having been regarded himself, he says, as an "extremist" at his previous school.

More recently, these same black students threatened demonstrations to block the transfer of young white teachers whom they considered sympathetic.

Negro school administrators like Mr. Couche find themselves in a lonely, uncomfortable position where their motives are often over-interpreted or misinterpreted by both their white colleagues and black students. Nevertheless there are many who believe that the advancement of more blacks to positions of real authority in the system offers one of the few possibilities of blunting the racial confrontation.

At present few high schools have faculties that are less than 90 per cent white; only three have Negro principals. White teachers often complain that Negroes are being favored for promotion, while many blacks say that the system advances only the "safest" Negroes.

"Now if you don't bite your tongue, you're a 'militant,'" said Charles Scott, a former head of the U.F.T. chapter at Jackson who is a leader of a faculty Black Caucus there that sees itself as a counterpoise to the union.

Student 'Willing to Die'

Many white teachers are convinced that there is a carefully plotted conspiracy for a black "takeover" of the high schools—those of North Brooklyn and South Queens, in particular—by the same forces that were active in Ocean Hill-Brownsville. The evidence they most often cite is the words and rhetoric of black student activists and adults who influence them.

A newsletter of the African-American Teachers Association calls for support of black students who "seek 'through any means necessary' to make these educational institutions relevant to their needs."

At Lane, a student sent tremors through the faculty by proclaiming his willingness "to die for the cause."

What do such declarations mean? John Marson, the self-possessed chairman of the African-American Students Association, replied that violence was the only power students had to "back up what they say," comparing it to the power of the U.F.T. to strike.

But he scoffed at the ideas many teachers hold about a conspiracy. No one can tell the students in the various schools what to do, he said.

That wasn't the way it seemed last semester to Max Bromer, the beleaguered Wingate principal. "It's all planned, it's all planned," he insisted when he was visited one day in his office, which looked like a stationhouse annex with four or five police officers lounging at a conference table and a police radio crackling in the background.

Pressure was building up in the school, he said, and he had reliable intelligence warning him of a likely cafeteria riot in the sixth period.

A white teacher came into the office and reported that the cafeteria was quieter than it had been in weeks. "They're massing," the principal surmised.

When the sixth period passed without incident, his anxiety shifted to the eighth. Finally the school emptied. Was it all a false alarm? "No," he said, "it was psychological warfare."

Mr. Bromer's responses can't simply be written off as jitters, for he had seen his school brought to the edge of a breakdown by racial hysteria and violence, despite what he thought had been a successful effort the previous semester to negotiate an "understanding" with the "militants."

As regularly happens, he has also seen many of his most experienced white teachers flee the school as the proportion of nonwhite students shot past the 50 per cent mark.

Wingate's troubles last term boiled out of a controversy over where to draw the line on expression by black students—the starting point of most racial explosions in the high schools. That line had been clearly transgressed, most teachers felt, in an assembly program staged by the school's Afro-American club.

Two passages were seen as particularly offensive—a recitation of an old Calypso ballad popular among Black Muslims ("A White Man's Heaven is a Black Man's Hell") and a line from a skit ("Brothers and sisters, we can't live if we continue to support the pigs by buying their dope and kissing their —— and letting them label us.")

Blacks Aroused

White students weren't shocked by these lines but by the angry pitch to which black students in the audience seemed to have been aroused. "I was actually embarrassed to be white," one girl said, "because I thought they hated me for something I didn't do."

Teachers saw the program as a deliberate provocation. "The nerve! The nerve! The nerve!" one fumed.

A week later racial clashes broke out in which many more white students than blacks were injured. In fact, many teachers had assumed that a racial confrontation had been in progress ever since the assembly. Black students identified as "militants" complained that they immediately became objects of suspicion.

Many Wingate teachers assumed the students were being manipulated by "outside influences." They singled out Leslie Campbell and Sonny Carson, two fiery figures in the Ocean Hill-Brownsville dispute.

'I Was Whitelisted'

Mr. Campbell, a 29-year-old Lane alumnus who is soft-spoken in conversation and anything but that in confrontation, lost his teaching post in the demonstration project last fall—"I was whitelisted," he says—and has just started a "liberated" high school, in Brooklyn for black students with the backing of the African-American Students Association.

Called the Uhuru Sasa (Freedom Now) School, its curriculum will include courses in martial arts, Swahili and astrology.

Asked to describe his relation to the students, Mr. Campbell didactically sketched a diagram on a pad before him.

"This is the soil," he said, pointing with a pencil. "The minds of these kids is fertile soil but it just lays there in the schools. We supply the seed—an understanding of black nationalism and the political situation."

Mr. Campbell said he was out of "the demonstrations bag." Mr. Carson, a onetime leader of Brooklyn CORE, is still in it. He likes working with students, he said, because they haven't been compromised by "the system."

"These kids are already liberated," he exulted. "They're beautiful."

Black students here reflect a mood of self-awareness that can be found at almost any high school or college in the country with a significant black enrollment. Some are imbued with sloganistic fervor. Some want an outlet for anger. Others are tentatively working out a life style. Many are just happy to "belong."

A few imagine romantic futures for themselves as black revolutionaries. But most think in conventional terms of gaining skills that will make them useful to their people.

Most of them seem more indifferent than hostile to whites. "I can only care about the people I relate to and the people I relate to are all black," said a youth in Panther garb at Jackson.

Linda Jacobs, a black senior at Thomas Jefferson High School in Brooklyn, was similarly casual when asked about her reaction to the flight of whites from her school, which has gone from 80 per cent white to 80 per cent nonwhite in only five years. "It doesn't bother me, not one bit," she said.

Fake Addresses Used

Many whites from the Jefferson district have used fake addresses to send their children across the racial boundary formed by Linden Boulevard to Canarsie High School, which is about 75 per cent white—"a nice, solid ethnic balance," according to its principal, Isadore S. Rosenman.

But Canarsie has had its troubles. After rioting last year it found it expedient to eliminate the lunch period, as a way of preventing racial clashes in the lunch room.

Canarsie has also tried positive measures to overcome the disinclination of black students to become involved in the school's extracurricular life. For instance, it is now routine to have two hands at all dances, one black, the other white.

Teachers use words like "magnificent" and "beautiful" to describe relations at Canarsie. But most black students appeared to agree with Vernon Lewis, a senior, who said, "Here you always have the feeling there is someone behind you, looking at you."

A Sharp Contrast

They contended that they would have more freedom of expression at a predominantly black school like Jefferson. The contrast between the bulletin boards of the Afro-American clubs at the two schools indicated the range. The Canarsie board told of scholarships available to blacks; the one at Jefferson carried the Black Panther newspaper.

Despite the publication of a code of students' rights by the Board of Education last October, there remain extraordinary variations in the degree of expression on controversial issues—racial issues, especially—permitted to students.

At Brooklyn Tech — a "special" school for bright students that is more than 80 per cent white—a dean last year ordered the removal of a picture of Eldridge Cleaver from the cafeteria on the ground that the author and Black Panther spokesman was a "fugitive from justice."

This year the principal, Isador Auerbach, summoned a police escort to remove a black "liberation flag" on the ground that state law forbade any banner but the American flag in the schools.

Ira Glasser, associate director of the New York Civil Liberties Union, termed this a typical case of "the lawlessness of principals." There is no such provision, he said.

Another View

By contract, Bernard Weiss, principal of Evander Childs High School in the Bronx, saw no need to react to the posting of a picture of Huey Newton, the Black Panther Minister of Defense, on a bulletin board in his school.

"We want kids to read, we want kids to discuss," he explained. "We don't teach revolution. But if that's what they want to discuss, at least we can make sure they hear both sides."

Evander is about 50 per cent white, and most of its white students are from predominantly Italian, deeply conservative neighborhoods of the Upper Bronx—the perfect ethnic mix, it is sometimes said, for an explosion. But though the school has had some close calls and thorny issues, it has had no major eruptions of racial violence.

The school that has come closest to a breakdown—and has thereby raised the specter of ultimate disaster for the whole system—is Franklin K. Lane, which is set next to the mausoleums of the Cyprus Hills Cemetery.

On one recent afternoon, chemical Mace was released on a staircase, a fire was started in a refuse can in the lunchroom, and a tearful white girl, reporting that a gang of blacks was waiting to ambush her, demanded a police escort to her bus stop.

"Just a normal afternoon," said Benjamin Rosenwald, a dean.

Normality at Lane also included an ominous stand-off in the cafeteria between white policemen with little metal American flags stuck in their caps and black students standing guard beside a "liberation flag." Routinely, the students taunted "the pigs." The officers masked their reactions behind stiff smiles, but not one of them had his nightstick pocketed.

Many white students are afraid even to set foot in the cafeteria, known to them as "the pit." A handful have been kept out of school altogether by their parents for the last three months.

There are those who find a simple explanation for Lane's woes — the racial incongruity between the school and its locale.

Lane is about 70 per cent black and Puerto Rican but stands in a neighborhood that is entirely white and aroused on racial issues. Mainly Italian and German by ethnic background, the district sends Vito P. Batista, the Conservative, to Albany as its Assemblyman.

But, in fact, the residents were not the first group to become militant over the racial situation at Lane. Neither were the black students. Militancy began with the local chapter of the United Federation of Teachers, whose leaders complained five years ago that Lane was becoming "a dumping ground."

The U.F.T. Position

The U.F.T. demanded that the Board of Education hold the blacks to under 50 per cent and, when that point was passed, they demanded that a racial balance be restored.

The teachers insist that their only interest has been "quality integrated education." But the U.F.T. has never proposed that black students cut from Lane's register be sent to schools now predominantly white.

George Altomare, a union vice president and a social studies teacher at Lane, was asked recently if he thought a black-white balance would also be a good idea for a predominately white school like Canarsie. "Ideally yes," he replied slowly, adding the proviso that more high schools would first have to be built to relieve overcrowding.

But Mr. Altomare believes there must be no delay in implementing a union proposal to make Lane a "prototype" of effective integrated education—to be accomplished by cutting its register by one-third and introducing special training in job skills for students not continuing to college.

It is only on paper that Lane is now overcrowded, for its average daily attendance is under 60 per cent.

Black students find a simple explanation for the faculty's insistence on reducing the student body. "Lane doesn't like us and we don't like Lane," one declared.

Since the strikes in 1968, Lane has gone from crisis to crisis. Last year a shop teacher, identified in the minds of some students as a supporter of George C. Wallace, was assaulted by young blacks who squirted his coat with lighter fluid and set it on fire.

Action Overruled

The assault, which was followed by the threat of a teacher walkout, led to the placing of a strong police detachment in the school and the dropping of 678 students — mostly blacks—from its register, an action later declared illegal by a Federal judge.

Even before the assault, the union chapter had placed a special assessment on its members for "a public relations and publicity campaign" aimed at winning the support of "business, civic, political and parent groups" for its position.

This effort helped arouse the surrounding white community, which formed an organization called the Cypress Hills-Woodhaven Improvement Association specifically to protest disorders at Lane.

Michael Long, chairman of the group, said the union had hoped to use it as a "battering ram," then disowned it when it demonstrated for the removal of the school's principal, Morton Selub.

Now Mr. Long worries that he may not be able to control vigilante sentiment in the community if there are further disorders at Lane.

A Familiar Dispute

The breakdown at Lane last October had a familiar genesis—a dispute over whether black students had the right to fly the "liberation flag" in place of the American flag in a classroom where they studied African culture.

After the flag had been removed from the room two days running, the students staged a sit-in to protect it, setting off the cycle of confrontation, suspensions and riots.

Black student activists at Lane don't deny that they have resorted to violence to press their demands, or "raise tensions to help a brother," or to "keep things out in the open."

They also acknowledge that they have not tried to discourage assaults on whites by younger black students outside their own group who want, as one activist put it, "to express their anger and let the white students know how it feels."

What they do deny is that their insistence on the "liberation flag" was an attempt to do anything but stake out a single classroom where they would be able to express themselves freely.

"Students want to relate to what's happening in their school," said Eugene Youell who prefers the adopted name of Malik Mbulu to his "slave name" and now has enrolled in Leslie Campbell's new school.

Focus of Pressures

Some schools see a point in struggling to prove to themselves and their most aroused black students that there is a place for them in the schools and an incentive to study.

At Jackson, a school that appears to be on its way to becoming all-black, the principal has become the focus of a wide range of pressures—from white teachers, black teachers, middle-class Negro parents who want their sons and daughters protected from radical influences, and some black students who believe they have the right to conduct public readings of the thoughts of Mao Tse-tung or anyone else.

Recently the principal, Murray Bromberg, went before a history class devoted to "the evolution of today's African-American experience" and boasted, "This is the school of the future."

He said it was time for white school administrators and teachers to revise their assumption that standards must inevitably be lower in an all-black school.

His audience seemed to be itching to provide the principal with a list of assumptions about black youths that white adults could revise. But if they were "militants," they were also very obviously teen-agers who found no incongruity in wearing a big "I Support Jackson Basketball" pin next to a "Free Huey" button.

In fact, the African-American Club at Jackson has discovered it cannot hold meetings on the same day as a basketball game. Too many of its members are boosters.

The New York Times

2/9/70

HIGH SCHOOL ESSAYS FROM OAKLAND (WHERE THE PANTHERS COME FROM)

BLACK IS BEAUTIFUL

Black is beautiful and the white man knows it. The white always trying to talk about the Black and his black they are saying black is ugly well how come the white all the wait until summer and go to the beach and go out there with their naked little ass to get a suntan to be black well they can't because they have to be born black and beautiful trying to get a dark tan.

WE HAVE A LIFE TO LIVE

We as black people of America has a life to live just as the white people of America. We can't live this life if we don't have nothing to live with or for. But we would have something to live for if the white man give up all thing which is and have been taken away. We want go housing and a go decent place to live, where it is fitting to lay our body own to sleep. We want good employment for all people. Jobs sowhere you can live like a white man. Let the white man live in a house with a hole in the rooth and rats and roaches all over the place. Let him work where he can ride the bus to work. The black man ride in those find cars. The black man sit under desk and the white man doing hard labor.

By: Black person herself.

black is beautiful; why/

Because Black is plain It's common, It's not toBright
It's decribe the NIGGERS of today not to bright just like the white man wants us But! Black is cool because It's dark trying to seek the light. That's why we call ourself BLACK because we are plain and trying to be ourself and not nobody else!!!!
Black has no feelin Because it is plain so when we are called names we feel the same. "BLACK."

I have been absent from school for queit some while I know my teachers and thing's wonder why, because I have never had any trouble or anything Just being absent. Will it's hard to stay in school I have not got any job, I stay with my mother and I have 3, brothers, and six sister that is younger than I, and it hard for my mother to us up in our needs, if we could have ware pants to school long before now I wouldn't have never been absent, now I'am failing in all my classes, see I drop out two years ago I didn't realize it was just putting me back a litle farther and every time I think about I was sit back. than same times I will play sick to keep from comming. I know how that Negro Indian girl because my mother is not rich but I know if I don't come to school with some of te lastes.

BLACK IS BEAUTIFUL

I miss cat-eyes I'm a Black Girl I feel that all this talk about black people stink that is a lie because I am black and I do not stink because I love water. black is beautiful can you dig it. the people who say black people stink ought to smell there sefes. there are a lots of white people stink like they never saw water they smell so bad. it like a stranger in my own world. do not it me wrong I do not have any thing against white people. we all are sister and brought in God will.

by the one and only miss cat-eys

SMARTNESS IN BLACK PEOPLE AND JEALOUS IN THE WHITE PEOPLE

I believe that black people are very smart, although some may not look like it. The black man can be very poor, but he can dress better than a rich white person. He's smart enough to get money when he wants to eat or get a car. The white person is so crazy and emotional. Who don't hear of no black person dropping LSD and jumping out a window, or crying because he or she got a C on his report card. The white man is jealous, because he gets mad when he sees a black man dress better or outsmarts him. He gets back the black man through his pig power structure.

San Francisco Express Times   1/28/68

By all accounts, black and white, the black activist students today are different —both from the Negro college students of the '40s and '50s and from the white university radicals of the late '60s, such as the Students for a Democratic Society. Prof. Charles V. Hamilton, chairman of the political-science department at Roosevelt University in Chicago and co-author (with Stokely Carmichael) of "Black Power," has been a participant in as well as an observer of what he calls "the development of a black-student social conscience." Hamilton's account of the movement:

A CAT WITH SHINED SHOES WHO DOESN'T LIKE WHITE FOLKS

"It began in 1960 with the student sit-ins. This was the first time on a massive scale that students in this country took the lead in anything—except, of course, for those white students who were active in the '30s. The sit-in students were very religious and influenced by the Gandhian-King notion of nonviolence. They were integrationist: most of them believed very intensely in racial cooperation between whites and blacks. Their tactics were always to be neat, polite and nonviolent. When you go sit-in at Woolworth's, take your Plato and, by all means, wear a shirt and tie. This gained the support of a large segment of white America. Who can fault a cat with shined shoes? Then something happened to begin the transformation to radicalism: the students began to question not only the system, but their own tactics."

According to Hamilton, this change came in 1964, after the rebuffs to the delegates of the Mississippi Freedom Democratic Party at the Democratic convention and the "trauma of the Mississippi summer"—the temporary migration of Northern students to the South to work for civil rights. The disappointments in both these ventures, Hamilton believes, made many black students think the system itself was "illegitimate." Then, he adds, "Stokely went on the stump in 1966 and . . . the entire language of the black student changed. We started using words like 'institutional racism.'

"Today they're understanding that they are black, and that as they go into these colleges—both black and white colleges—they are not going to be made into little middle-class black Sambos. I graduated from Roosevelt, I got a law degree from Loyola University and I got a Ph.D. from the University of Chicago. And I'm going to tell you very clearly that my education over that twelve- to fifteen-year period was geared toward making me a middle-class black Sambo. Nothing devious in that, and I'm not blaming my professors. It's just that that was their orientation. They were saying to me in no uncertain terms that in order to succeed I would have to orient myself to a Western Anglo-Saxon culture.

"But the students today are saying that they are going to be black and skilled at the same time. They're saying that they are going to develop and keep this sense of group responsibility. . . .

Newsweek

ALL POWER TO THE PEOPLE · MALCOLM X ·

At Fisk, the Students Are Totally Black and the Administration Is Scared

More than half the 275,000 black undergraduates in the U.S. attend some 111 predominantly Negro colleges concentrated in the South. Many of these schools were started as church-related institutions after the Civil War and tried to train a Negro middle class of teachers and professionals to serve the segregated Negro community. Today, most of the Negro colleges are small, and many are in serious financial and academic trouble; their endowment is limited, faculty pay is low. The best of the schools—including Fisk, Howard, Morehouse, Lincoln and Spelman—are comparatively well-to-do and successful. At Fisk, for example, 76 per cent of the men and 42 per cent of the women go on to graduate school. The administrators tend to be hypersensitive

to the student mood, though the student mood is no monolith easy to categorize, as this report by NEWSWEEK campus correspondent John J. Oliver, a junior at Fisk in Nashville, Tenn., makes clear:

"The black movement at Fisk has many levels of involvement. There are theoreticians who devise strategy, women's organizations that sew garments of black pride, committees that seek to broaden the black-studies program and ad hoc cadres that are prepared to deal with almost any situation—no matter how far it escalates. There is a definite core group of activists, but in my experience all the students basically support the 'black program.'

"The goal of this black program on the campus is simple: make this educational institution speak to the needs of the black community; that is, structure the curriculum so that it educates and frees a black mind to deal with the system. The goals are limited and are a step in the process of changing the total soci-

ety. The students and the ghetto are one, because most black students are from the ghetto; 'the ghetto' is where any significant number of black people live.

"The student body (enrollment: 1,077) is almost totally black. The faculty is approximately 50-50, white-black, with all types from bleeding hearts to Aryan academicians who seem to want us to learn nothing. There is student pressure to phase them out—great pressure. As for the administration, it is about as scared as it was a year ago. The president of the university has taken a liberal stance as a 'friend of the revolution.'

"About 10 per cent of the students form the core of the revolutionaries, but there is a peripheral group of about 20 per cent. Our heroes are W.E.B. Du Bois, Stokely Carmichael, LeRoi Jones, Eldridge Cleaver and Malcolm X. Our most respected figures are Huey P. Newton, the Black Panthers, and Martin Luther King. Our books are 'Soul on Ice' and 'Black Rage.'

Newsweek 2/10/69

TW College and the Colonial Analogy

troy duster

In the middle of the nineteenth century, when the British held control of India, a debate arose about the kind of education the Indian elite should receive. There were some Englishmen who argued for a resurrection of traditional Indian education, the study of classical Indian history, Indian literature, and Indian institutions. They were opposed by Englishmen who believed that the only real education was one based in Western civilization, and more particularly, at Oxford. This faction, led by Lord Macaulay, won the debate.

Macaulay is an important figure, for his victory crystallized the development of higher education throughout the whole British Empire, and radically affected the way in which the French and Dutch were to proceed. In brief summary, the Western countries decided to train the elites from their colonies with Western higher education.

Most of the colonial elite swallowed the package whole, undigested, just as most students now unthinkingly take notes in class without digestion. These men, dressed in English gowns at Oxford or at the English-style home university in the colony, drank their port and brandy, and discussed humane letters of the West. Occasionally, however, one or two here and there did some critical careful reading.

They not only read Locke and Paine, they thought about it and compared it to reality in the colony. Thus, Ghandhi, Nkrumah, Kenyatta, and many other western-trained colonial elite became disgruntled reformers and revolutionaries because they took Westerners to task for preaching the equality of man then institutionalizing inequality in the colony.

For the most part, however, the Western-trained colonial elite were a rather docile group. ("Toms" come in all colors and cultures, in both sexes and in all ages.) **By their training and education, they were oriented to the West.**

Western standards of success and excellence were assimilated as their own standards. Even the revolutionary elite, such as Ghandhi and Nkrumah, were to some measure victimized, if we can call it that, for their vision of excellence and equality was often a Western one, and was not grounded in Indian or African soil or culture. (Ghandhi was inspired by Thoreau. Nkhuma was trained by U.S. intellectuals.)

Thus, even the revolutionary colonial elite, while bursting with fury and indignation, were so much Western-trained after all those years in London and Paris that they were lacking in systematic knowledge about the indigenous problems of their own cultures. Freedom they could cry, and the colonial yoke they could burst, but I repeat, **even these men were Western-trained.**

They knew of Socrates and Marx, not of their own economies, cultures and social and political institutions. How could they?

In the discussion and controversy over the Third World College, the colonial analogy deserves to be taken more seriously:

The Academic Senate and the Regents will join to argue that there is only one kind of real education for the black elite, the Mexican-American elite, the Asian elite, or any ghetto elite. The Academic Senate follows Macaulay.

The debate over Black Students behind closed doors has taken the form of the argument expressed in the middle nineteenth century: "Is it possible that there is another kind of education, with other standards?" "Well, now, perhaps Black Studies, but the faculty and staff of such a department must be Western-trained black elite. They must be from Harvard, Columbia, Princeton, Berkeley."

Here is the heart of the conflict on the Berkeley campus now, across the Bay at San Francisco State, and increasingly to be heard at other major urban campuses. On the issue of who is to staff such programs, on the issue of how the curriculum is to be oriented, on the issue of "autonomy and control," we can find a different level of insight in the colonial analogy. The students often speak in such abrasive and abusive terms that "civil men" dismiss them out of hand, and either misunderstand them or, having understood, malign them. I am myself a Macaulay product. Accordingly, these men of letters are attuned to listen more carefully when I speak.

The analogy takes both a personal and a political turn. Just like a disgruntled and even outraged colonial elite that spent long years in London or Paris, while I can try to help break the yoke of oppression that lets mace be sprayed in paddy wagons, my "Macaulay education" has ill-equipped me or any other person in my general position to do the specific job that must now be done.

That does not mean that I despair of my utility, for I have never accepted the artificial and mindless separation of ideas and action. There is something fundamentally important about the way problems are isolated by the ideas chosen to characterize them. I see a need for approaching and formulating the problem of higher education of Third World students that orients toward their local communities (read ghetto, read colony, read whatever you like, but know that one-third of this state is living now in communities isolated by color and culture, isolated from the Western whites).

I do see the need for Third World student leadership to emerge that is not already "too far gone" down the road to Macaulay's victimization. Too far gone, that is, to be given a role in carving out new criteria of excellence. The Western-trained colonial elite will only set up a new college based on the one model they have "for too long" experienced.

The Daily Californian

2/20/69

"IT'LL BE THE GRAMMER SCHOOL KIDS NEXT"

Said one white mother, "I think they're using the generation gap argument simply as a copy-cat method, just to create disturbances. The example set by Cal students has now filtered down to high schools and junior highs. If someone doesn't stand up next year it will be the grammar school kids."

The opening weeks of school in Oakland and in the rest of the country were stormy, to say the least. Fremont High School in Oakland was closed for almost a week, due to some fights between black and white students, a fire-bombing by white students, but, in general, due to the black student perception of the irrelevance and brainwash of the present educational framework.

At many high schools in the Bay Area black students have organized and presented demands. These demands have included: more black history and culture courses, more black teachers, the firing of some administrators and teachers, the serving of soul-food in school cafeterias.

Black History

Most school administrators and teachers, when pressured, and almost all students, black and white, termed the demand for black history "legitimate."

There were exceptions. For example, Stuart Phillips, Oakland Superintendent of Schools, said that there now is a course in Mexican-American history at Fremont High . . . soon there'll be demands for Oriental history . . .

And a parent said, "They should provide for themselves, just as other minorities have done. Have a second school after the regular one. There should be no special emphasis on any ethnic group". Here, racism parades in the guise of equality for all. As if there had not been special "emphasis" and special "deemphasis" up to now.

Eventually Fremont, after meetings day after day went back into session. Black history will be taught, starting immediately. Most other demands are receiving fast attention. The struggle ended in substantial victory.

At Ravenswood High in Palo Alto, students held a sit-in. They demanded the removal of the principal, Malcolm Taylor. Many of the movements began with administrator or teacher provocation, and

built as students handled the administrators, not vice-versa.. When asked about the quality of education in the predominantly black school, Taylor says, "Many children do have an inferior education...not becuase of inferior instruction, but because they've done an inferior job of taking part in it".

Malcolm Taylor was removed.

Discipline

At Emeryville High School nine black students blocked a doorway and the school was closed for that day. One administrator couldn't understand why some black students had objected when the course which was being taught in black history was integrated.

Emeryville High did not call in the police. They instead sought "dialogue." After a prolonged assembly in the gymnasium, peace was restored.

The refusal to call police prompted reaction. One mother said, "discipline was more stringent when I was a child. . . people thought of you as a child and treated you as a child. Even if things weren't fair to me -- it didn't make much difference because the school and the principal were the bosses."

"It's time youngsters learned that getting an education is a privilege, rather than a right."

In the scattered incidents of violence many people found the hook to hang their objections to student demands. One parent called it "all take and no give. . . the one quarrel I have with it all is their lack of concern for humanity."

The violence that took place was minor . . . the threat, however, was ever present. It, along with the present atmosphere of tension in Oakland, contributed to the surprisingly careful handling of protest by the schools. High school students had found power in organization and in muscle. High school students demonstrated a strong defiance of established school authority. If the administrators were uncooperative, the students simply refused to deal with them.

Where Does It All Come From?

The disturbances in Oakland schools clearly reflect the depth to which revolt has penetrated in 1968 America. In some

cases, white students sided with black students against administrators, or in support of the black demands.

In some cases too the demands involved things like more black pom-pom girls -- seemingly surface things which spoke for a larger and less articulated protest against the status-quo and the racist nature of the schools. But often, as in Vallejo, student demands escalated consciously from small demands to broader ones, as Black Student Unions formed to continue the struggle.

Not a generation gap. But a gap informed by the content of black protest against either inhumane discipline or irrelevant curricula or racist teachers. It is clear that the black power move-

ment, as well as the general discontent in this society, has not only filtered down to the high schools . . . it has recently been invigorated and strengthened by militant actions of high school students.

Many high school students took part in the Stop the Draft Weeks, the riots in Berkeley, the Free Huey demonstrations, the actions in Chicago. Oakland seems a good example of black high school students working effectively on their own base, their own place of work -- the school itself -- forcing once all-powerful school boards and administrators to yield, at least for the time being. From all indications, high school students in Oakland are just beginning to move.

the MOVEMENT Nov 1968

"We're Not Grinning Anymore"
An Interview

**"They said, 'Your attitude has changed.'
I said, of course it has. I have seen
what is going on in this school....
You don't expect a drowning man to grin?"**

LESTER: *What is it like at Taft High School?*

KAREN: Well first of all I'd like to say that there is no outward atmosphere of racial tension at Taft. It's all covered. Blacks and whites seem to get along. But I find that if we do get involved in very serious discussions—nothing so ridiculous as should whites hate blacks or blacks hate whites, but really deep down discussions about self-determination for black people—you will find large differences between the blacks and the whites.

LESTER: *Can you give me a specific example?*

NAOMI: Oh yes. I had a run-in with a teacher when he realized that I was in support of some black militant students who had published a black theology. He was very surprised that I was in support of them. He said: "I've never felt any animosity from you. How can you back up what these fellows have to say?" I answered: "It's very simple. We're all black. We all have the same situation. We all have the same goals. We might not all be following the same route, but we intend on getting to the same place. So we must present a united front."

I found the same attitude in many of the teachers after the UFT strike. They are con-

KAREN BUTLER, NAOMI CARNES and JACKIE GLOVER, seniors at Taft High School in the Bronx, N.Y., were interviewed by Julius Lester over Radio WBAI in N.Y. in February and March, 1969.

stantly trying to cut me off from the rest of the black students by telling me: "Naomi, you're an intelligent student, and you want to go to college." I say: "This is very true. And I'm also a black student; what does that have to do with it?" There's always this kind of undertone, you know. You always feel like you're being plucked—like a petal from a flower. And that's what's happening.

JACKIE: Everything was fine before the strike. But once they were on the picket line, we could see what was going on. We saw hatred in the teachers' eyes. We saw, we heard the threats that they gave to teachers who were not on that picket line. Like we had 10 teachers who came into the school and helped us open it. They told us they had been threatened; their time cards were destroyed; very malicious comments were made from the picket line. Now while I was out there I saw all this, so when I came back I had a different attitude altogether. When I came back the teacher said: "You don't smile any more." Now here I was out of school for 10 weeks because of the teachers' strike, and they want me to smile! There was nothing funny to me. And then they said: "Well, Jackie, your attitude has changed. You used to be a nice, sweet girl." I'm not sweet any more because I saw for the first time what was really going on in that school.

During the strike we set up classes; there were at least 200 kids. It was decided that we

would set up our own library because the one upstairs was locked. Our whole thing was black awareness. We wrote a notice saying we would like to start this black library and students could borrow books. We urged all the kids to give books, stating that no black library would exist in Taft without the support of the students. (Now this was during the strike, mind you.) After the strike, the very next day, a teacher Xeroxed copies of this notice and put them into the teachers' mailboxes. She said there were black books in the library upstairs and we didn't need a special library. We said that wasn't the point.

KAREN: According to this teacher, the statement in our library notice charged that there was no black library now or that the library would be destroyed. Later we met with librarians and they didn't object to a black library. But one librarian did not feel Leroi Jones was acceptable to a high school because he was profane. This was ridiculous.

JACKIE: *Catcher in the Rye,* that's the most profane book out and they have 32 copies in Taft's library. We said, all right, you don't want Leroi Jones in your library—fine. That's why we want our own library.

KAREN: The incidents after the strike went on and on. We'd like to talk about one important one which has led to the expulsion of one of our brothers, Ron Dix. According to the administration, it was for distributing "unauthorized literature." You could say, well, why not get it authorized? But that is like being a slave, going to the owner and saying, 'will you authorize this leaflet calling for a rebellion tomorrow night?'

NAOMI: There were three students involved, Ron Dix, Jerry Hudson and Ronald Smith; they were specifically trying to promote black awareness with their literature, contrary to whatever else many students may have heard. Before Ron Dix was expelled and before the three brothers resorted to printing their own literature, we held three meetings with the faculty and the principal to resolve the problem of "unauthorized literature." The administration claims that literature unsigned by any teacher in the school is "unauthorized." Yet you can walk down the halls any day and have someone shove something into your hand about a new discotheque, a dance, a track meet, about anything at all. But as soon as the word "black" appears—boom—unauthorized literature.

JACKIE: When the brothers passed out this flyer called "Dig It," about the extra 45 minutes of school, things really began rolling. After it was brought up, the brothers admitted the flyer was worded badly. The school wouldn't let it drop at that, claiming it was anti-semitic. The school sent them down to the

Bnai' Brith and the man there couldn't find anything anti-semitic about the literature. But the teachers insisted it was anti-semitic. All right. The brothers produced another leaflet. This one was beautifully worded. It was given out. (As soon as we who are considered militants start passing out anything, white students run over faster than black students; they don't wait for you to hand it to them.) So they started grabbing the leaflet and I watched one white fellow flip through it, see the word "Jew," and stop. He began reading a quote from the *New York Times* that said Jews control the New York City school system. That's all he read. It was after this leaflet that the trials began.

LESTER: *Who held the trials?*

NAOMI: The principal, administrative assistant—they had UFT teachers there—our Afro-American club advisor, and the guidance counselors and teachers who had had the three brothers in their classes. It really was a kangaroo trial. They started by saying the three brothers should be thrown out of school because of anti-semitic literature, etc.

JACKIE: Now Ron, Jerry and Ronald had written the literature together, but they were going to be tried individually. The brothers said they wouldn't go in separately.

The main purpose of the trials was to scare them. They did it to another brother last year, brought him to trial. I don't know what they told him but he was scared enough to cut his hair and beard. But they couldn't scare Ron, Jerry and Ronald, so they threatened them with suspension. The brothers said, go ahead if you want to. But the school didn't, just then, they were afraid the community would go into an uproar if three brothers were suspended. What did happen was that the school called all types of students to a meeting: militants, the Student Organization, hippie groups. At the meeting one of the teachers said "We want to establish peaceful coexistence." Others started throwing words around like justice, equality and democracy. You can't tell a black man about justice and you don't tell him about equality—there are no such things. So we laughed at those terms. They said we weren't serious, etc. and the meeting was adjourned.

LESTER: *When they got the brother and told him he was suspended, what reasons did they give?*

JACKIE: The major thing was the supposed rule he had broken by distributing "unauthorized literature." But he didn't distribute it except on request. It turns out that one teacher specifically asked him for a copy of the leaflet. This teacher then turned him in and he was told to leave the school. Ron said he wasn't leaving unless his parents were called. A policeman was called to remove him. The policeman manhandled Ron who is a minor. Aside from this and the fact that police are constantly in the school, it was some time

before Ron's parents were called. This was hardly due process.

NAOMI: I'd like to go into this suspension because there is a process stated in the Rules of the Board of Education whereby a student and his parents must be at three hearings which are entitled, I believe, suspension hearings. It seems that the meetings we held during December (1968) are now being titled "pre-suspension hearings." Now none of our parents were present; none of them were notified. This means they weren't suspension hearings at all. This was the due process that was *lacking* in Ron's suspension.

LESTER: *The teachers, of course, have the power to keep you from graduating or kick you out of school, and they get rid of the bad niggers and use them as an example; the rest keep cool after that. All three of you are seniors. Have they moved against you at all yet?*

KAREN: Today I was called down to the administration office for not standing to say the pledge. Now, I've not been standing to say the pledge because it was against me personally to say it. If I did stand to say it, I would be out and out lying. Now, according to this school official, I was breaking a school law. I said that I was not aware that any such law existed, and if I didn't know of its existence, I could not very well break it. I asked to see it in writing; it was not produced. Then he started saying that I was such a good Negro student, and didn't I think I had gained anything from

this country? I said that as Karen Butler I had personally gained a lot from the school system, but as Karen Butler the black person, I had gained nothing. "Well, why don't we speak about you as Karen Butler," he said. Oh no. We speak about me as Karen Butler, part of a black mass in this country that is oppressed. There's no singling me out. I can gain a lot from singling out, but I am part of a mass.

JACKIE: The whole thing is this system has scared these people. These brothers and sisters in Taft are scared. You ask them will you sign this? "Oh no! I'm not going to touch it because I might get into trouble." Or: "Am I going to get into trouble if I sign it?" We say what kind of trouble? "I may get sent to the dean. Oh no, I'm not going to sign it." This is how the system has worked on them. It's scared a whole lot of students. It's got them too scared to move.

JACKIE: For example, one day I got a pink card (disciplinary referral to the dean) just for reading a notice on a UFT bulletin board which was telling chapter members not to come to any more meetings with students. Now this teacher who gave me the pink card ran to my leaders club advisor and told her about it. (Leaders club is for the outstanding girl athletes of the school. You're supposed to have leadership qualities and set an example. You help the gym teachers do practically everything in the gym: you help conduct classes, and do clerical work, etc.) So my advisor told me that my leader's white gym

Mike Klare

suit would have to be taken away because I was setting a bad example.

Now, they weren't worried about that pink card. The thing was that I was too black to be in that white gym suit. I was really speaking my mind, and they said: "Your attitude has changed." I said of course it has. I have seen what is going on in this school. So of course my attitude has changed. You don't expect a drowning man to be grinning? I find nothing to grin about. So she said: "It's your attitudes, your activities." I said what do you mean, my activities? "You belong to the Taft Afro-American Cultural Society, don't you? Well, I think you got into the wrong company Jackie; you're really a nice girl." So what it came down to was that I asked how long my gym suit would be taken away. She said: "Until we see a 100% change in attitude and until you change your activities." I said in other words, drop out of the Taft Afro-American Society and forget my black brothers and sisters to get this white gym suit. She said: "I don't think you have to go so far as to drop out, but quiet down so everybody doesn't focus on you." So I figure, if I can't be black in a white gym suit, what's the sense?

NAOMI: The administration tried for a long time to talk me into being a good house nigger too. When they found that wouldn't work, I was threatened indirectly. I found myself frequently down at the dean's office for minor things, such as being a few minutes late to one classroom. Realize: lateness can get you suspended. I was called down and told by one of the deans of girls that if I didn't quiet my activities in the school (which she never did define to me) I would have to go before the character committee and . . .

LESTER: *Wait, wait. Stop! The character committee?*

NAOMI: That's what you have to go through to graduate from Taft high school. They decide whether or not your character is acceptable. I didn't find out about it until recently; many students never hear of it until their senior year. If they find your character unacceptable, your diploma will be withheld.

KAREN: Right. Just as a point of information, the character committee happens to be composed of white people, so being black obviously puts me in a rather precarious position. It was mentioned to me today about my not saying the pledge that if I continued to refuse to stand, I would be brought before the character committee.

JACKIE: A lot of the kids in the school are going to be shocked and a lot of the Negro kids are going to say 'oh no . . . Taft's not like that.' But, I'm telling them now, you listen to what's going on. A lot of Negro students don't listen, they let everything slip by them. This is why we are having a big problem in our black history class where we have a white teacher. Every day we confront him and he gets upset

and defensive because he's white. He came to us and said 'Naomi and Jackie you can't challenge everything I say or else we're not going to get anywhere this year.' I said, I don't care if we don't get past Africa. We've got to learn the truth. He holds up John Hope Franklin's book and says, 'Well, he's black, he wrote this.' I said he didn't write history he only copied down what was written by the man before him who was white. So you're not teaching me black history, only what the white man put down on that page at that time which no black person has had a chance to rebut.

KAREN: A lot of Taft students ought to get hip. I was really a good Negro for three years in that school. I was in the honor school, and I was a perfect Negro. But with the strike, everything changed.

"Karen you're an intelligent student" and "Karen, I don't understand." What they were really coming out and saying was that I was being influenced. Of course I'm being influenced; a lot of things came to me and made a lot of sense. I can get a lot of places by acting quite well and capitalizing on my honor school, but at the same time I realize it was only by accident that I happened to be in honor school. Most black kids are not.

They have a couple of shop classes down in the basement. Who fills those shop classes? Blacks and Puerto Ricans. I don't think truthfully I've ever seen one white person in that shop class. One day the shop teacher came over to me and said "Look at the great lamps they're making." I said what are they going to do with this when they get out of high school? And he said "Well, it's made out of finer wood than any company makes." I said fine, but the company's got the business. I don't care if they're making it out of paper, the company's got the business. I said that's fine for a hobby, but what are they going to do when they get out of school?

JACKIE: With the guidance counselors it's the same thing. When a black student fails two subjects: "Wouldn't you like to take a commercial course?" Next thing is "Wouldn't you like to take a general course?" And they shuffle you off with "You can't make it in academic."

When I was in the 10th grade, I had two years of Spanish already. I had biology already and was taking chemistry and geometry. Then I was approached and asked to take a pre-tech course, guaranteed to get me into a two-year college to study business. I said What?? And give up my academic? "Because your average may not be high enough to get into college." As many colleges as want black students today to prove that they're not prejudiced? I mean, go on: I got no problem to get into college. Schools are writing to me like this: "You are an outstanding black student and you were recommended by so-and-so and please come to our college." And they're telling black stu-

dents now that they can't go to college? Boy, they would take a black student with a 60 average just to prove that they're not prejudiced. The brothers and sisters have to get hip to that. Don't let these people tell you you can't go to college. You put your mind to it and you can do anything.

Leviathan June 1968

ALL POWER TO THE PEOPLE

CLARENCE MAJOR
Vietnam #4

a cat said
on the corner

the other day
dig man

how come so many
of us
niggers

are dying over there
in that white
man's war

they say more of us
are dying

than them peckerwoods
& it just
        don't make sense
unless it's true
that the honkeys

are trying to kill us out
with the same stone

they killing them other cats
with

you know, he said
two birds with one stone

Two leaders in the racial struggle in Detroit, the scene of extensive rioting last summer, talked recently to the staff of the Center. Frank Joyce, director of People Against Racism, reported on the political and social climate as it has developed since the riots. The Reverend Albert Cleage, chairman of the Inner City Organizing Committee, described the expectations of some of the inhabitants of the Negro community of Detroit.

FRANK JOYCE:

Death of Liberalism

My own theory about what has been happening in Detroit has been described accurately in an article in *The New York Review* that said: "The insurrections of July have done what everyone in America for thirty years has thought impossible. Mass action has convulsed society and brought smooth government to a halt. Poor blacks have stolen the center stage from the liberal elites, which is to say that the old order has been shattered. The civil war and the foreign one have contrived this summer to murder liberalism in its official robes."

This seems to me an accurate description of what has happened in Detroit, and also of what is in the process of happening or can reasonably be expected to happen in other cities. The old liberal order has collapsed. The political functions of government in Detroit have broken down. More specifically, the efforts of the city government toward any kind of political relationship with the black community, which constitutes at least 40 per cent of the population in Detroit, have been abandoned. Another way to say this is that the Detroit city administration in all of its manifestations has abandoned pretense in its dealings with the Negroes.

Until the time of the rebellion Detroit had enjoyed a reputation as a model city. Mayor Cavanagh had been regarded as a city official who knew how to deal with Negroes better than any other major-city mayor in the country. The first change in this reputation came at the time of the rebellion when any pretense of justice in the city's court system was abandoned. I grant that this was due in part to the fact that more than 7,000 people were arrested and it was necessary to process them through the judicial system in a very short period of time. There is evidence, nevertheless, that in order to help control the situation the judges consciously decided that the writ of habeas corpus would not be honored, that bail bonds would be established not for the purpose of assuring appearance at trial but rather for the purpose of keeping people in jail and off the streets, and that those arrested would be assumed guilty until proven innocent.

The more important decisions and actions, however, came in the aftermath of the rebellion. The judiciary continued the policy they established in the rebellion. In the executive branch the most tangible action was a bond issue of something over $7 million. Of this amount more than $1 million has been used to buy various kinds of equipment. It is worth describing this equipment somewhat specifically because I think it is important and significant and not generally known. This is from a list of appropriations approved by the Common Council in the bond issue:

700 12-gauge shotguns
100 Stoner machine guns
1,000 M-1 carbines
25 gas guns
25 30-06 calibre rifles
  with 4-X scopes
25 infra-red snooper scopes
1,200 gas masks
5,000 chemical mace dispensers
1,500 flak vests
9,000 sets of fatigue clothing
500,000 rounds of various kinds of
  ammunition (of which the largest
  single appropriation is for 150,000
  rounds of .223 calibre ammunition for
  the Stoner machine gun)
8 armored personnel carriers
4 mobile support vans with radio
  equipment
2 prisoner buses

The only item eliminated from the original administration request was the Detroit Air Force, so-called, which was to have consisted of one helicopter and one fixed-wing aircraft.

I want to digress to say a word about the Stoner machine guns, because they are to urban rebellions what napalm is to Vietnam. The Stoner machine gun was developed in response to the Geneva Accords outlawing the use of dum-dum bullets. It fires a small calibre bullet which has the same effect as the dum-dum because it tumbles both in flight and upon impact. If a man is hit in the stomach with it he is literally torn from head to toe. This has been the tangible response of the city to the rebellion of 1967.

Shortly after the rebellion was officially over — indeed, perhaps, even before it was over — the Mayor appointed a task force to study why the trouble had come about. The group has now produced a 750-page set of recommendations and reports. Most of the recommendations, in my opinion, are terrible, but the point is that there is no means by which these recommendations can be implemented and there are not even any suggestions for their implementation. In fact, their primary effect has been to suggest a new criterion for judging urban uprisings: "Did you have a 750-page rebellion or only a 300-page rebellion, and are you shooting for a 1200-page rebellion next time?" Beyond this, the report has little significance other than to have given some people some things to do for a period of time.

The second action of the Mayor took place not in Detroit but in Miami, where he made a speech. I quote from an article that appeared in the *Detroit Free Press* the day after he talked: "Mayor Cavanagh of Detroit suggested a back-to-the-land movement in the South Wednesday to slow the flow of Negro poor to Northern cities. Under Cavanagh's plan the Federal government would make rural life more attractive by buying farms and selling them on easy credit terms to sharecroppers. Cavanagh claimed there is a lack of Federal programs to make rural life, particularly in the South, more appealing to destitute Negroes. During the last sixteen years, Cavanagh said, more than 5,000,000 Negroes have moved to the North. Cavanagh went on to say a Negro family could be settled on a family-size farm in most parts of the South for an investment of $10,000 to $15,000. This would be far cheaper than transferring that same family to the welfare rolls of a Northern city. Cavanagh described the proposal as a new, interesting idea and the right line of thinking."

This has come to be known as the "Cavanagh reservation plan." He has yet to introduce it in any official form in the city of Detroit itself, but, according to a subsequent press article, it is apparently under serious study in Washington.

One additional item which I submit as testimony to my general thesis that there is in fact a breakdown of the old order in Detroit has to do with an agreement between the Michigan Bell Telephone Company and the city school system, under which the telephone company has agreed to "adopt" one of the all-Negro high schools in the city. To me this is a tacit admission by the Detroit school system, which exists separately from the city government, is autonomous, and has its own tax base, that it is either incapable or unwilling to carry out a real education program in the ghetto. In effect, they have sold one of the public high schools of the city to private enterprise, which has promised to put resources into the school system that the public realm cannot itself do, such as a redesign of the curriculum, the hiring of additional teachers, the setting-up of extra classes, and so on.

These are my evidences for what I call the breakdown of the old liberal order in the city of Detroit.

I believe there are four reasons for that breakdown. The first is psychological and involves certain assumptions that liberals in general and liberal politicians and mayors in particular have had about cities for some time. One gets the distinct impression in seeing Cavanagh on television, reading his press conferences, etc., that one of the things which motivates him at this point is a deep sense of betrayal. He sincerely believes that he has made serious efforts on behalf of the Negroes, and he cannot understand why they betrayed him by tearing up the city and destroying his reputation.

Mayor Cavanagh is a classic example of the white liberal whose power in the past has been, in effect, black power. White liberals have always used black power, and Cavanagh has been no different from many others in the fact that it was the Negro vote that put him into office in the first place and has kept him there. He now feels very nervous, with good reason, that the Negro vote is no longer his and that therefore he must shift his base of political power. This is a contributing factor, I believe, to his present attitude, which represents an abandonment of any attempt at anything other than a military relationship with the Negro community. He has said repeatedly that the number one priority of the city administration is to reduce violence and — what is apparently now a nationally accepted euphemism — "crime in the streets," and he has called for the hiring of 1,000 additional policemen.

The second reason for the breakdown involves an attitude that affects all American cities. This is the standard liberal solution to problems, whether they concern Negroes or poverty or whatever: when in doubt, spend money. Cavanagh is constrained by the fact that he does not have any money to spend. As everyone knows, cities are losing resources as a result of the war in Vietnam, the white backlash votes, and a variety of other factors. Thus, Cavanagh is not able to find substantial resources to develop the kinds of programs that he once believed would be successful.

The third reason for the breakdown is also common to other cities and has to do with the kind of red-tape bureaucracy and staff difficulties that all city administrations face. During the last few months before the rebellion Cavanagh had lost all of his executive staff. The ability of any mayor to retain good, creative staff people is limited by money, of course. It can also be complicated by political problems such as the Mayor has had with his Housing Commissioner, who handles urban renewal programs and the like and is second to no one except a Detroit police officer in arousing the antagonism and animosity of the Negro community because of his blatant attempts to bulldoze people out of neighborhoods.

The fourth reason for the breakdown, and probably the most serious of all, has to do with Mayor Cavanagh's constituency. The Common Council of Detroit has always been responsive to the white community. Its members are elected at large and there have been only two Negroes on the Council in the history of the city. The current Negro member, who was elected with the support of the newspapers and of Cavanagh himself, made it very clear at the outset that it was his intention to represent not the Negro community but the whole city. Thus, the black community is not really represented on the Common Council. Their access to the administration had generally been through the Mayor's office, and this is no longer the case.

The Mayor's constituency problem stems in part from the great growth of the white right wing in Detroit. Before the uprising there was an organization in the city called Breakthrough. It was fairly typical of its kind, although in some ways

perhaps more creative and imaginative than most, certainly more oriented to activism and John Birch Society-Minutemen-type beliefs. Breakthrough had been a fairly small organization until the rebellion gave the members the opportunity to discuss race openly in the white neighborhoods of the city. They succeeded in bringing out well over 1,000 people on an average at each of a series of community meetings. One of the speakers was a representative of the National Rifle Association, who recommended to the audience, all of whom were lower-middle-class, blue-collar workers or immigrant small storekeepers, the kinds of weapons they ought to own to defend themselves. Secondly, they were told how to organize their blocks for self-defense and what provisions and supplies they would need for what was called in a leaflet "survival during a 30-day prolonged civil disorder." Finally, they were given a political line which I think probably has not been duplicated in other places. The head of the organization sponsoring the rallies (who is, interestingly enough, an employee of the city) said that in the past the response of whites to such situations had been to move to the suburbs, but Breakthrough believed that the real responsibility of the whites was to stay put and defend their land. Fleeing the city and abandoning it to black people was "what the Communists want us to do." This attitude seems to me to establish a polarization and a declaration of war at a higher level than has appeared in cities in the past.

Mayor Cavanagh has apparently decided that the pressure from this constituency, which declares that concessions ought not to be made to black people, that there ought not to be "rewards" for riots, as their rhetoric goes, is such that he should be more responsive to them than he used to be, especially since whites still make up 60 per cent of the voters.

This does not mean that Cavanagh has entirely abandoned the Negro community, only that the city administration has, because shortly after the rebellion was officially quelled the Mayor appointed an organization called the New Detroit Committee. In my opinion this group represents a new force in cities with racial problems. It may be the last serious, sincere effort on the part of a significant segment of the white community to deal peacefully with the black community. The Committee consists of thirty-nine people chosen from what we usually call the "power structure." It includes the Chairmen of the Boards of Chrysler, Ford, and General Motors, the heads of all the utilities in the area, and the heads of a number of other corporations and unions.

Some examination of the New Detroit Committee is useful, because I think groups like this will either spring up voluntarily or be appointed or perhaps hired in major cities throughout the country. It is a new kind of effort on the part of corporations, and a new kind of liberalism, or at least liberalism from a new

source. In some places the idea might eventually result in corporate subdivisions that would run things like the Job Corps. Corporations might even be hired to administer cities, because in a city like Detroit the political process is really almost totally dysfunctional. The questions become simply, who is going to pick up the garbage, or who is going to see that the police get to work on time, and so on, and these are the kinds of operations best left to corporations, whose primary criterion is efficiency. And this is, in part, the primary criterion of the New Detroit Committee.

The Committee has access to resources that are limited only by how much the corporations represented on the Committee are willing to give. They have already appropriated more than $1 million for a study of reform within the Detroit police department. Unfortunately I am afraid this will fail, since the man the Committee has hired to direct the study is the Dean of Police Administration at Michigan State University, who is the gentleman who went to Saigon under the MSU-CIA contract to organize the South Vietnam secret police for Mr. Diem. However, the initiation of the study at least indicates the willingness of corporations to put up a lot of money.

Another asset of the Committee is the brightness of its staff people, who have been loaned by the corporations involved and remain on the corporation payrolls but have been assigned to work full-time with the Committee.

Another factor working in favor of the Committee is that it does not have the same constituency problems as a politician. No one elected the members, they will never be running for re-election, they are not responsible in the direct sense of a politician to anyone in the white community. As a result, they have flexibility and considerable freedom of action.

The three main forces in motion in Detroit today are the city administration, the New Detroit Committee representing a whole new element openly involved in the arena of race relations, and the black community. I see something of a contest between the city administration and the New Detroit Committee, with the former playing a waiting game: "If you people fail, if you do not succeed in pacifying the black community, then we will be ready with our Stoner machine guns, with the Michigan National Guard (whose size is to be doubled, incidentally), with our eight armored personnel carriers, and so on. If you do succeed, fine." The Committee and the black community are involved in a more fundamental struggle, which comes about essentially over the question of who is to control the black community in Detroit. This struggle is in an advanced stage in Detroit, more advanced, I would say, than in any other city in the country. It can best be described by my colleague, the Reverend Albert Cleage. ✦

THE CENTER MAGAZINE
March 1968

Peter Berg: ...They are the black mirror. We see our dark image in black people...

Q: How long did you stay in New York?

Peter: Long enough to get awful blue there.

Q: What are the blues like?

Peter: The blues life is a mystique. ...And the blues-life mystique is that if you want to do anything, you have to lose your left arm. You have to pay a lot of dues...to live full out — full out, not far out — as you can, if the cost is in dues. The only people that can do it are oppressed...The hard-kick seekers who laid down the patterns of extreme beauty for this civilization...like the blues singers and John Dillinger, Willie Sutton and Billie Holiday ...They're all people who got burned for what they did...being repressed beyond recourse...Don't you know what that means? ...People who lived it were essentially oppressed beyond action, oppressed beyond action. To be oppressed without recourse is blues life...

Ed. Note: Peter Berg described by Leonard Wolf "A radical activist, a former member of The Mime Troupe, and a founder of the Digger Movement"

Knocking around with Rapp and the Rhythm Kings put the finishing touches on me and straightened me out. To be with those guys made me know that any white man if he thought straight and studied hard, could sing and dance and play with the Negro. You didn't have to take the finest and most original and honest music in America and mess it up because you were a white man; you could dig the colored man's real message and get in there with him, like Rapp. I felt good all over after a session with the Rhythm Kings, and I began to miss that tenor sax.

Man, I was gone with it — inspiration's mammy was with me. And to top it all, I walked down Madison Street one day and what I heard made me think my ears were lying. Bessie Smith was shouting the *Downhearted Blues* from a record in a music shop. I flew in and bought up every record they had by the mother of the blues – *Cemetery Blues, Bleedin' Hearted*, and *Midnight Blues* – then I ran home and listened to them for hours on the victrola. I was put in a trance by Bessie's moanful stories and the patterns of true harmony in the piano background, full of little runs that crawled up and down my spine like mice. Every note that woman wailed vibrated on the tight strings of my nervous system: every word she sang answered a question I was asking. You couldn't drag me away from that victrola, not even to eat.

MEZZ MEZZROW Jazz Musician of the 1930's and 40's *The William Carlos Williams Reader* Edited by M.L. Rosenthal, New Directions.

Chester Grey, 19 *"You go into your local library, and you can't find a book by Malcolm, or LeRoi or Gwendolyn. But then you go over to the high school gym, and there's so many basketballs you can't count 'em. Seems the only thing Whitey wants to give us is basketballs. A group of us have started the West Garfield Youth Organization to spread awareness of our black culture. We'll have a newspaper and an Afro-American history club, so maybe we keep some of the brothers from playing that damn basketball and running up and down the damn streets and get them reading some books. Every time my old man turns on the TV, he's getting psyched. Commercials come on: 'Yes, it's truly true. White rain, white cloud, the white horse, angel's food cake is always white.' And he gets up and goes out with that in his mind. Young whites are beginning to feel the guilt, not their guilt but the guilt of their parents and ancestors. There's hope with young whites, especially the hippies. We were having a meeting one night, and it was supposed to be all black. Hippie comes to the door, and the brother says, 'What are you doing here?' The hippie says, 'I'm here in the name of love.' The black brother didn't know what to think. So the hippie picked up his little flutelike thing and just blowed his way inside. He said: 'My brothers, we may be different, but you're still my brothers. I'm here in the name of love.' We let him stay."*

Look 8/6/68

A WHITE MAN WHO SPOKE TO A BLACK MAN

Six days after Joan and Craig died, Jack Kerouac concluded a three-day drinking spree with his death. There are two kinds of loving deaths—the conscious act of Joan and Craig's and the unconscious, but no less deliberate dying of Jack Kerouac. He knew, he had to know, that he was going to die because he lived with such intensity. It was no accident. It simply took Kerouac forty-seven years to complete the process which Joan and Craig finished in seventeen. (He who remembers Kerouac as a force in his life is acknowledging that he is from another generation, a generation that knew no student movements and no political action. Those who would've been the political activists of that day were lonely, spectral figures on campus, travelling many miles through the backyards of their souls. Kerouac was the Che of my coming of age. He was the one who told me that there was another way, a better way, a way that had meaning and I fused the vision he and Allen Ginsberg and Gary Snyder gave me with the knowledge of

blackness bequeathed me by my father and thus was born.) Jack Kerouac was a revolutionary, because he made us see, feel and live in a manner counter to that which everyone told us was the only way to live. But to say that he was a revolutionary is to define him in terms which were foreign to him. He was a human being. He was not anti-capitalist, anti-racist, anti-imperialist and would not have understood what that might mean or why people who call themselves revolutionaries would define themselves negatively. If a man tells you what he is for, you know what he is against. But let him tell you what he is against, you still don't know what he is for. Those of us who were a part of that distant piece of American history called the "beat generation" knew what Kerouac was for and there would be less of a radical political movement today if he had not revolutionized the consciousness of so many of us.

From "Aquarian Notebook" by Julius Lester, *Liberation* Dec 1969

AL YOUNG

A Dance For Ma Rainey

I'm going to be just like you, Ma
Rainey this monday morning
clouds puffing up out of my head
like those balloons
that float above the faces of white people
in the funnypapers

I'm going to hover in the corners
of the world, Ma
& sing from the bottom of hell
up to the tops of high heaven
& send out scratchless waves of yellow
& brown & that basic black honey
misery
I'm going to cry so sweet
& so low
& so dangerous,
Ma,
that the message is going to reach you
back in 1922
where you shimmer
snaggle-toothed
perfumed &

powdered
in your bauble beads
hair pressed & tied back
throbbing with that sick pain
I know
& hide so well
that pain that blues
jives the world with
aching to be heard
that downness
that bottomlessness
first felt by some stolen delta nigger
swamped under with redblooded american agony;
reduced to the sheer shit
of existence
that bred
& battered us all,
Ma,
the beautiful people
our beautiful people
our beautiful brave black people
who no longer need to jazz
or sing to themselves in murderous vibrations
or play the veins of their strong tender arms
with needles
to prove how proud we are

From *The New Black Poetry* ed. by Clarence
Major, International Publishers

VOICES VOICES VOICES VOICES VOICES
VOICES VOICES VOICES VOICES

Photo by Gerhart Gscheidle

Tonight we have to talk about several things. We're here to celebrate Brother Huey P. Newton's birthday. We're not here to celebrate it as Huey Newton the individual, but as Huey Newton part and parcel of black people wherever we are in the world today. And so in talking about Brother Huey Newton tonight we have to talk about the struggle of black people not only in the United States but in the world today and how he becomes part and parcel of that struggle, how we move on so that our people will survive America.

Therefore we are not talking about politics tonight, we're not talking about economics tonight, we are talking about the survival of a race of people. That is all

didn't know a damn thing about this country. The red man showed them how to adapt to this country. He showed them how to grow corn. He showed them how to hunt. And when the Indians finished showing him, *he wiped them out!* He wiped them out, he wiped them out.

He was not satisfied. He went to South America. The Aztec Indians said: "This is our silver, this is our copper, these are our metals, these are our statues, we built them for the beauty of our people. After the Indians showed it to him, he took it and *he wiped them out.* He wiped them out.

He went to Africa. Our ancestors said: "Dig, this is our way of life. We beat drums, we enjoy ourselves, we have gold, we make diamonds and stuff for our women. He took the gold, he made us slaves, and today he *runs* Africa.

He went to Asia. The Chinese showed him everything they had. They showed him gunpowder. They said: "We use this for fireworks on our anniversaries, on our days of festivities." He took it, he made it a gun, and he conquered China.

We are talking about a certain type of superiority complex that exists in the white man wherever he is. That's what we have to understand today, so that everything goes out the window, we talk about survival. That's all. They can cut all the junk about poverty programs, education, housing, welfare — we talking about survival and brothers and sisters, *we gon'* survive America, *we gon'* survive America, we gon' survive America.

Now then we have to understand what is going on not only in this country but in the world, especially in Africa. Because we are an African people — nothing else. We have *always* been an African people, we have *always* maintained our own value system and I will prove that to you.

As much as he has tried, our people have resisted for 413 years in this wilderness. And they resisted for *this* generation to carry out what must be done. We cannot fail our ancestors, cannot fail our ancestors, cannot fail our ancestors. We resisted in every way you can point to.

Take the English language. There are cats who come here from Italy, from Germany, from Poland, from France, — in two generations they speak English perfectly. We have *never* spoken English perfectly, never have we spoken English perfectly, never, never, never. And that is because our people consciously resisted a language that did not beong to us. Never did, never will, anyhow they try to run it down our throat we ain't gonna have it, we ain't gonna have it. You must understand that as a level of resistance. Anybody can speak that simple honkey's language correctly. Anybody can do it. We have not done it because we have resisted, resisted.

Check out our way of life. No matter how hard he's tried, we still maintain a communal way of life in our community. We do not send old people to old people's homes — that's junk, that's junk, that's junk, that's junk. We do not call children illegitimate in our community, we take care of *any* child in our community, any

STOKELY CARMICHAEL
a declaration of war

that is at stake. We are talking about the survival of black people — nothing else, nothing else, nothing else. And you must understand that. Now why is it necessary for us to talk about the survival of our people? Many of us feel — many of our generation feel — that they're getting ready to commit genocide against us. Now many people say that's a horrible thing to say about anybody. But if it's a horrible thing to say, then we should do as brother Malcom said, we should examine history.

The birth of this nation was conceived in the genocide of the red man, genocide of the red man, of the red man. In order for this country to come about, the honky had to completely exterminate the red man, *and he did it.* And he did it. He did it. And he did it where he doesn't even feel sorry but he romanticizes it by putting it on television with cowboys and indians, cowboys and indians.

Then the question we must ask ourselves is if he's capable of doing it to the red man, can he also do it to us?

Let us examine history some more. People say it is a horrible thing to say that white people would think about committing genocide against black people. Let us check our history out. It is a fact that we built this country, nobody else. I'll explain that to you. When this country started, economically it was an agricultural country. The cash crop on the world market was cotton. WE PICKED THE COTTON! We picked the cotton. We did it. So it is *we* who built this country. It is we who have fought in the wars of this country.

This country is becoming more and more technological so that the need for black people is fastly disappearing. When the need for black people disappears, so will we, and he will consciously wipe us out. He will consciously wipe us out. ·

Let us check World War II. He will not do it unto his own. Notice who he dropped an atomic bomb on, some helpless yellow people in Hiroshima, some *helpless* yellow people in Hiroshima, in Hiroshima. If you do not think he's capable of committing genocide, against us, check out what he's doing to our brothers in Vietnam, *check* out what he's doing in Vietnam. We have to understand that we're talking about our *survival* and nothing else, whether or not this beautiful race of people is gonna survive on the earth. That's what we're talking about, nothing else, nothing else.

If you do not think he's capable of wiping us out, check out the white race. Wherever they have gone they have ruled, conquered, murdered and plagued — whether they are the majority or the minority they *always* rule. They always rule, always rule.

And check out the pattern in which they move. They came to this country — they

child in our community.

It is a level of resistance that we must begin to look for among our people. Pick up that thread and do what has to be done so that our people will survive. Three things: First and foremost, he has been able to make us hate each other. He has transplanted the hate and the love for each other for the love of his country — *his* country. We must begin to develop, number one, and this is the most important thing we can do as a people — we must first develop an undying love for our people, our people, our people, our people. We must develop an undying love as is personified in Brother Huey P. Newton. Undying love for our people, undying love. If we do not do that, we will be wiped out. We must develop an undying love for our people. Our slogan will become: First, our people, then and only then me and you as individuals. Our people first, our people first.

Following from that comes secondly the slogan: Every Negro is a potential black man. We *will* not alienate them, we will not alienate them, we will not alienate them. And we must understand the concept of Negro and the concept of black man. We came to this country as black men and as Africans. It took us 400 years to become Negroes. Understand that. That means that the concept of a black man is one who recognizes his cultural, his historical and the roots of his great ancestors who were the greatest warriors on the face of this earth — Africans, Africans, Africans.

Many of our people's minds have been whitewashed. If a Negro comes up to you and you turn your back on him, he's got to run to the honky. We're gonna take time, and patience with our people because they're *ours*. They're *ours*. All of the Uncle Toms, we're gonna sit down and we're gonna talk, and when they flap we're gonna bow, and when they flap we're gonna bow and we're gonna *try* to bring them home, and if they don't come home, we gonna off them, that's all, that's all.

We have to recognize who our major enemy is. The major enemy is not your brother, flesh of your flesh and blood of your blood. The major enemy is the honky and his institutions of racism, *that's* the major enemy, *that* is the major enemy. And whenever anybody prepares for revolutionary warfare, you concentrate on the major enemy. We're not strong enough to fight each other and also fight him. We *will* not fight each other today. There will *be* no fights in the black community among black people. There will just be people who will be offed. There will be no fights, there will be no disruptions. We are going to be united!

Thirdly, and most importantly, we must understand that for black people the question of community is not a question of geography. It is a question of color. It is a question of color. If you live in Watts, if you live in Harlem, South Side Chicago, Detroit, West Philadelphia, Georgia, Mississippi, Alabama, wherever you go, the first place you go is to your people. Not the land, to your *people*. For us the question of community is a question of color and our people — *not* geography, *not* land, not land, not land, not geography.

That is to say that we break down the concept that black people living inside the United States are black Americans. That's nonsense. We got brothers in Africa, we got brothers in Cuba, we got brothers in Brazil, we got brothers in Latin America, we got brothers all over the world, all over the world, all over the world. And once we begin to understand that the concept of community is simply one of our people, it don't make a difference where we are — we are with our people and therefore we are home. Therefore we are home.

Now then, speaking of survival, it is necessary to understand the moves of our enemy. The United States works on what we call the three Ms — the missionaries, the money, and the marines. That's precisely the way it's moved all over the world, it is the way it moves against *us*. They have sent the missionaries in — we sent them out. They have sent the money in, with the poverty program — the Vietnamese and the Koreans are pulling the money out. The next thing comes the marines. Comes the marines. And if we're talking seriously, we get prepared for the marines. Now if some black people do not think that the white man is gonna wipe us out completely, then it won't be no harm being prepared just in case he decides to do it, just in case he decides to do it. So there'll be no harm in us preparing ourselves for the marines.

Now there's a lot of tactics we can learn. The VC are showing us the best way to get it done, best way to get it done. And don't be afraid to say, yeah, you want the Vietnamese to defeat 'em 'cause they wrong from the jump. They wrong from the jump. They wrong. Don't get up there and play games with them. You ever see them on TV — "Well actually, we were wrong going into Vietnam but we can't get out unless we save face." To save that honky's face, millions of Vietnamese got to die. That's a lot of junk. If you're wrong, say you're wrong and get out. Get out, get out, get out.

We have to then go down the programs that they run through our throats and see how they relate to us. The first one is the vote. They got a new thing now: "Black power is the vote." The vote in this country is, has been, and always will be irrelevant to the lives of black people, that is a fact. We survived in Mississippi, Alabama, Georgia, Louisiana, Texas, South Carolina, North Carolina, Virginia and Washington, D.C. without the vote. Without the vote. Two years ago when Julian Bond was elected by black people in Georgia, they took him off the seat, there was no representation but black people in Georgia are surviving today. They took Adam Clayton Powell out of office they had him out of office for a year and a half — black people in Harlem are still surviving. That should teach you the vote ain't nothing but a honky's trick, nothing but a honky's trick.

If we talk about the vote today, we talk about it as one thing — an organizing tool to bring our people together, nothing else, nothing else, nothing else. It becomes a vehicle for organization, it cannot be anything else. To believe the vote is gonna save you is to believe the way brother Adam Clayton Powell did. He's in Bimini now.

That's what we have to understand. The second thing they ram down our throat is the poverty program. And you have to understand the poverty program. It is designed to — number one, split the black community, and number two, split the black family. There is no doubt about it splitting the black community. We know all the people who've started fighting over crumbs ('cause that's all the poverty program is, the crumbs). If we'd leave the crumbs alone and organize, we could take the whole loaf, 'cause it belongs to us.

But what happens is that the poverty program sends a couple of hundred thousand dollars into the community and groups start setting up to fight over that money. So automatically you've got splits in the community. Watts is the best example that we have to date. It was the first one to get the poverty program after the rebellion and today it is the most divided black community in the country, in the country.

Second thing we have to recognize is what the poverty program does. In any race of people the most instinctively revolutionary people is the youth. Because the youth is always willing to fight at the drop of a hat. In anybody's race, in anybody's race. And the poverty program is geared right at our youth, right at our youth — to stop them from fighting. That's all the poverty program is: stop the rebellions — not take care of black people — stop the rebellions. How is it that you felt that you were a father, and your son who you were supposed to be providing for comes home with ninty dollars a week, and you still unemployed. What is the poverty program doing to our fathers? What is it doing to our fathers? If they were concerned about the black community, if they believed the garbage they run down about the black family, they would give the jobs to our fathers, the bread-winners of our families, so we *could* have some respect for them, we *could* have some respect for them.

But it is precisely because the poverty program is aimed at quelling our youth that they do that, and all the people who administer the poverty program won't even put their children in those programs that are supposed to be so good for us.

Let us move on to education. And we must talk very clearly about this concept of education. Franz Fanon said very clearly: "Education is nothing but the re-establish-

ment and reinforcement of values and institutions of a given society."

All the brother's saying is that whatever this society says is right, when you go to school they gonna tell you it's right and you gotta run it on down. If you run it on down you get an A. If I say to you, Columbus discovered America in 1492, if I was your teacher and you said "No, Columbus didn't discover America in 1492, there were *Indians* here," I tell you you flunked the course. So education doesn't mean what they say it means. So now we must use education for our people.

And we must understand our communities. In our communities there are dope addicts, there are pimps, there are prostitutes, there are hustlers, there are teachers, there are maids, there are porters, there are preachers, there are gangsters. If I go to high school I want to learn how to be a good maid, a good porter, a good hustler, a good pimp, a good prostitute, a good preacher, a good teacher, or a good porter.

And education is supposed to prepare you to live in your community. That's what our community is like. If the educational system cannot do that, it must teach us how to change our community, how to change our community. It must do one or the other. The schools that we send our children to do not do one or the other. They do neither, they do something absolutely opposite. And when our youth, who are more intelligent than all those honkies on those boards drop out of that school cause they recognize it's not gonna help them, then we turn around and yell at them, dividing our community again, dividing our community again. We have to understand that unless *we* control the education system where it begins to teach us how to change our community where we live like human beings — no need to send anybody to school, that's just a natural fact.

We have no alternative but to fight, whether we like it or not. On every level in this country black people have *got* to fight, *got* to fight, *got* to fight.

Now let us move down and talk about organizing in a concept. We have in our community black people — the masses and the bourgeoisie, that's about the level of breakdown. The bourgeoisie is very, very minute inside our community. We have to bring them home. We have to bring them home for many reasons. We have to bring them home because they have technical skills which must be put to the benefit of their people, not for the benefit of this country which is against their people. We've got to bring them home, we've got to bring them home.

One of the ways of bringing our people home is by using patience, love, brotherhood and unity — not force — love, patience, brotherhood and unity. We try and we try and we try. If they become a threat, we off them. We off them.

But we must begin to understand that in a context of forming inside our community a united front — a *black* united front which engulfs every sector, every facet and every person inside our community working for the benefit of black people, working for the benefit of black people. And that is for each other's survival. A lot of people in the bourgeoisie tell me they don't like Rap Brown when he says I'm gonna burn the country down. But every time Rap Brown says I'm gonna burn the country down, they get a poverty program. They get a poverty program.

A lot of people say to me, we don't like the Blank Panthers for Self Defense walking around with guns. I tell you now, if the honkies in San Francisco take off the fighters who happen to represent the Black Panthers for Self Defense, (ain't nobody in this community prepared to fight right now) everybody gets offed. Everybody gets offed.

continued

STOKELY CARMICHAEL

One of our main purposes is to unite our brothers and sisters in the North with our brothers and sisters in the South.

We need each other, we have to have each other for our survival. We got to have each other, from the revolutionaries to the conservatives — a *black united front* is what we're about, a black united front is what we're about. Now there's some people may not understand Brother Rap when he talks about whom we ally with. He says we have to ally with Mexican-Americans, Puerto Ricans, and the dispossessed people of the earth. He did not mention poor whites. We must understand that. I will not deny that poor whites in this country are oppressed. But there are two types of oppression. One is exploitation, the other is colonization. And we have to understand the difference between both of them. Exploitation is when you exploit somebody of your own race. Colonization is when you exploit somebody of a different race. *We* are colonized, *they* are exploited. They are exploited.

Now let us explain how the process of exploitation and colonization works. If I am black and I am exploiting you who are also black, we have the same values, the same culture, the same language, the same society, the same institutions, so I do not have to destroy those institutions for you. But if you are of another race, if you have a different culture, different language, different values, I have to destroy all of those who make you bow to me. And that is the difference between poor black and poor white. Poor whites have their culture, have their values, have their institutions, ours have been completely destroyed, completely destroyed, completely destroyed.

So when you talk about alliances you recognize you form alliances with people who are trying to rebuild their culture, trying to rebuild their history, trying to rebuild their dignity, people who are fighting for their humanity. Poor white people are not fighting for their humanity, they're fighting for more money. There are a lot of poor white people in this country, you ain't seen none of them rebel yet, have you? Why is it that black people are rebelling? Do you think it's because it's just poor jobs? Don't believe that junk the honky is running down. It's not poor jobs — it's a question of a people finding their culture, their nature and fighting for their *humanity*, for their humanity, for their humanity, for their humanity.

We have been so colonized that we are ashamed to say we hate, and that is the best example of a person who's colonized. You sit in your house, a honky walks in your house, beats you up, rapes your wife, beats up your child, and you don't have the humanity to say, "I hate you." You don't have it. That is how dehumanized we are. We are so dehumanized we cannot say "Yes, we hate you for what you have done to us." Can't say it, can't say it. And we are afraid to think beyond that point. Who do you think has more hatred pent up in them, white people for black people or black people for white people? White people for black people, obviously the hatred has been more. What have we done to them for them to build up this hatred? Absolutely nothing. Yet we don't even want to have the chance to hate them for what they've done to us. And if hate should be justified, we have the best justification of all for hating the honkies. We have it for hating the honkies, we have it, we have it. But we have been so dehumanized, we're like a dog which the master can throw out the house, which the master can spit on, and whenever he calls, the dog comes running back. We are human beings and we have

emotions. We're fighting for our humanity, we're fighting for our humanity, and in regaining our humanity we recognize *all* the emotions that are in us. If you have love, you've got to have hate. You don't have one-sided emotions, that's a lot of junk. You always have two sides — hot, cold, white, black — everything goes — love, hate. 'Cause if you don't have hate, you cannot differentiate love, you cannot do it, you cannot do it.

Now then that brings us to the point of this thing about communism and socialism. Let's get to that, once and for all. Communism is not an ideology suited for black people, period. Period. Socialism is not an ideology fitted for black people, period. Period. And I will tell you why. And it must become crystal clear in our minds. Now we don't **say** that because the honkies call us communist, we don't care what they call us, it don't make a difference, don't make a difference. The ideologies of communism and socialism speak to class structure. They speak to people who oppress people from the top down to the bottom. We are not just facing exploitation. We are facing something much more important, because we are the victims of racism. Communism nor socialism does not speak to the problem of racism. And racism, for black people in this country, is far more important than exploitation. 'Cause no matter how much money you make in the black community, when you go into the white world you are still a nigger, you are still a nigger, you are still a nigger.

So that for us, the question of racism becomes uppermost in our minds. It becomes uppermost in our minds. How do we destroy those institutions that seek to keep us dehumanized? That is all we're talking about. On the question of exploitation, it comes second.

Now for white people who are communists, the question of communism comes first, because they're exploited by their other people. If you were exploited by other black people, then it would be a question of how we divide the profits. It is not that for us, it is not that for us. It is a question of how we regain our humanity and begin to live as a people — and we do not do that, because of the effects of racism in this country. We must therefore consciously strive for an ideology which deals with racism first, and if we do that we recognize the necessity of hooking up with the nine hundred million black people in the world today. That's what we recognize.

And if we recognize that, then it means that our political situation *must* become international. It cannot be national, it cannot be national, it *must* be international, *must* be international. It must be international because if we knew anything, we would recognize that the honkies don't just exploit *us*, they exploit the whole Third World — Asia, Africa, Latin America. They take advantage of Europe, but they don't colonize Europe, they colonize Asia, Africa, and Latin America. Understand *that*.

If we begin to understand that, then the problems America is heading for become uppermost in our minds. The first one they're heading for is the conflict in the Middle East. We must declare on whose side we stand. We can be for no one but the Arabs. There can be *no* doubt in our minds, no doubt in our minds, no doubt in our minds. We can be for no one but the Arabs because Israel belonged to the Arabs in 1917. The British **gave** it to a group of Zionists who went to Israel, ran the Palestinian Arabs out with terrorist

groups, organized the state and did not get anywhere until Hitler came along and they swelled the state in 1948. That country belonged to the Palestinians. Not only that, they're moving to take over Egypt. Egypt is our motherland — it's in Africa.

We do not understand the concept of love. Here are a group of Zionists who come anywhere they want to and organize love and feeling for a place called Israel, which was created in 1948, where their youth are willing to go and fight for Israel. Egypt belongs to us four thousand years ago and we sit here supporting the Zionists. We got to be for the Arabs, period. Period.

That means that we also move with the rest of the Third World and understand exactly what is going on. It is no coincidence that the honky who stole a heart out of our brother and put it into another devil, was brought here on nationwide TV. Now for those of the older generation who say I may be harsh because I said the devil, let me give you a biblical quotation. It says, "Beware that the devil will come telling you that he can give you back life after death." If that's not what they doin', I don't know what is.

We have to understand that just today the United States voted for South Africa to come into the Olympics, and black people here are debating whether black athletes should be part of the Olympics. That is not a debate. The question is final. There can be no black athletes with any dignity participating in that white nonsense, that white nonsense, can't be no dignity, can't be no soul.

Now then we have to understand more and more as our people talk about survival. It means that when we talk about survival we organize politically, we organize consciously — that's what they call education, we call it black consciousness, 'cause that speaks to us, education speaks to them — we organize economically, and we organize mi-li-tarily. Because if we don't do that, if you don't have a gun in your hand they can snatch the ballot from you. But if you got a gun, it's either them or us.

And the preparation of that fight on all struggles must become conscious among our people. We are ahead of the Jews, we know what they getting ready to do. They tell us every day in their Esquire magazines, they tell us on their televisions, they tell us with their 15,000 soldiers they're putting in the cities, they tell us with their tanks, they tell us with their Stoner guns, they tell us. We got to wake up and tell them *we* are going to get you *back*.

Wipe out of your mind the questions of minority, wipe out of your mind the questions of technology, technology never decides a war. It is the will of a people that decides a war. It is the will of a people, the will of a people. Wipe out of your mind the fact that we do not have guns. The Vietnamese didn't have it when they started, now they got American guns, American tanks, American everything, everything, everything, everything. If they come to get us they got to bring some to get some. We gonna take it — and the gun, and the gun, and the gun. And unless we raise our minds to the level of consciousness where we have an undying love for our people, where we're willing to shed our blood like Huey Newton did for our people, we will not survive, we will not survive.

Now there are many people who know that. All of the brothers sitting on the stage, all of the brothers around here, we all know that when something goes down, we are the first ones offed. There's no question in any of our minds. Only thing gonna stop us today is a bullet, and we spittin' 'em back, and we spittin' 'em back. But the question is not whether or not we can move, but how this entire black community moves for survival in a world that's clearly heading for a color clash. That is what we must ask ourselves, that is the only question. We can only do that by organizing our people and orienting them towards an African ideology which speaks to our blackness — nothing else.

It's not a question of right or left, it's a question of black. You dig where we coming from? We coming from a *black* thing, from a *black* thing, that's where we coming from. Because we can begin to pick up the threads of resistance that our ancestors laid down for us. And unless we begin to understand our people as a people, we will not do that, because they *will* split us and divide us. That means consciously we have to begin to *organize our people!* Organize our people! Organize our people! Organize our people! Organize our people! Nothing else! Organize our people, our people! We have no time for them; all our sweat, all our blood, even our life must go to our people, nothing else.

We have to understand this consciously. Our youth must be organized with a revolutionary perspectus. A revolutionary perspectus says that we're fighting a war of liberation. In order to fight a war of liberation, you need an ideology of nationalism. We do not have this country. The nationalism can be nothing but black nationalism. It is insane to think of anything else. Black nationalism has to begin to be our ideology. While blackness is necessary it is not sufficient, so we must move on, we move on then to consciously organize in our communities. And we recognize today while we're organizing: we do not have the money to feed our people, so there's no use to say "organize, we can get you a job." We can't get 'em, they control 'em, that is a fact. That isn't a reason for you to sit down, it is only more the reason for you to fight, to think that you can't give your people a job. That's more of an inspiration to fight so you *can* give them a job rather than to sit down and say the honkies got us on every end. They are not God, they are not God. We are a beautiful race of people, we can do anything we want to do, all we got to do is get up, get up, get up and do it, get up and do it, get up and do it, get up and do it.

Now then we have to discuss very cold the question of rebellions. It is a fact that they're prepared to meet rebellions anywhere in the cities. Now what's gonna happen if one of our brothers get offed? What happens if they go ahead and off Huey Newton? We must develop tactics where we do the maximum damage to them with minor damage to us. And when we move into that arena, that means that this black community must be organized. So if Huey Newton goes, and ten honky cops goes, won't a black man in this community get up and open his mouth, 'cause if he does, *he* goes too, he goes too, he goes too, he goes too. That means that in organizing for the maximum damage against them and minor damage against us, we must be consciously aware of the fact that there will be people in our community who are going around doing just that. In our community we seen nothing, we hear nothing, we know nothing. We see nothing, we hear nothing, we knew nothing.

Now the question of agents is becoming a question where it's making us paranoid. We cannot become paranoid because what they can do is make you so afraid you won't move. So we're not gonna do that. We're gonna plan what we're gonna do. Little groups are gonna plan theirs, big groups are gonna plan theirs. If an agent is found, there is no question, he is gonna be offed in such a manner that any other black man who dares talk to the honky will have three thoughts before he even *talks* to a white man about reporting in our community.

Our people have demonstrated a willingness to fight. Our people have demonstrated the courage of our ancestors — to face tanks, guns, police dogs with bricks and bottles, that is a courageous act! We must understand that. And since our people have demonstrated a willingness to fight, the question is how can we organize that fight so we become the winners. So we become the winners. If a major rebellion were to break out, our people may or may not become the losers, but if a small group was doing maximum damage, we remain on top. We remain on top. That is what we must understand, consciously understand it. It is not a question of what they might do, it is a question of how and when they're going to do it, that is all that's in their minds. That is all. For us the question is not going to Vietnam anymore, the question is how we can protect our brothers who do not go to Vietnam from going to jail. That's the only question we have to face in our community today. So that when one brother says "Hell, no," there's enough people in that community around him that if they dare come in, they gonna face maximum damage in their community.

We are talking about survival. We are talking about a people whose entire culture, whose entire history, whose entire way of life have been destroyed. We're talking about a people who have produced in *this* year a generation of warriors who are going to restore to our people the humanity and the love that we have for each other. That's what we're talking about *today*, that's what we're talking about today. We are talking about becoming the executioners of our executioners. For example, you should give a lot of money to that defense fund, because while some of that money gonna go for that court thing, the rest of the money's gonna go for the executioners. So that if they execute Huey, the final execution rests in *our* hands, our hands, in our hands.

It is simply a question of a people. They control everything. They make us fight, they make us steal, they judge us, they put us in prison, they parole us, they send us out, they pick us up again — where in God's name do we exercise any sense of dignity in this country? Where? Where? Where? Where? What in God's name do we control, except the church, whose ideology is based to be compatible with the system which is against us? Where in God's name do we exercise any control as a people whose ancestors were the proudest people that walked the face of this earth? Where? Where?

Where, do I ask you, where? Everywhere he's gone he controls our people; in South Africa he steals the gold from our people, in the West Indies he steals the materials from our people, in South America where he's scattered our people, he's raping us blind, in America he rapes us, in Nova Scotia [sic] he rapes us. Where in God's name are we gonna find a piece of earth that belongs to us so we can restore our humanity? Where are we gonna find it unless this generation begins to organize to fight for it? To fight for it, to fight for it. Where?

And if *this* generation begins to fight, there can be no disruptive elements in our community. There can be none — we will tolerate none. There will be no disruptions. Anyone who fights for their people, we put our life on the line for them. Huey Newton fought for our people. Whether or not Huey Newton becomes free depends upon black people, nobody else, nobody else. Other people may help, but the final decision of brother Huey depends upon *us*. He didn't lay down his life for other people, he laid it down for *us*. For *us*. And if he did that, we must be willing to do the same, not only for him but for the generation that's going to follow us.

Consciously we must understand we're about organizing every element in our community. That work must begin. People must be willing to give money to an organizer who is willing to spend 24 hours a day organizing. He cannot organize from the poverty program because they tell him what to do. But if black people are giving him the money, he can do anything for the benefit of black their people. We have to run all the exploiters people, of black people. That means that people have to consciously give money for out of our community, by any means necessary, by any means necessary.

You ask yourself, if you were white, why would you want to be a cop in a black ghetto today when you *know* they looking for you? Why, if you weren't sick in the mind and felt you were so superior that you had the right to rule, why would you want a lousy five thousand dollar a year job when you white and you can make it in this society, why would you want the job as a cop if you weren't sick, tell me? Would you want to be in their community if they were ready to off you, for four thousand, five thousand, six thousand dollars a year? We have to understand the politics of those honkies in our community. They are there to patrol and to control. That is all. We are going to do the patrolling, we are going to do the controlling. We are building a concept of peoplehood. We do not care about honkies; but if in building that concept of peoplehood, the honkies get in our way, they got to go. There is no question about it, there is no question about it. We are not concerned with their way of life, we are concerned with our *people*. We want to give our people the dignity and the humanity that we *know* as our people, and if they get in our way, they gonna be offed. They gonna be offed. We're not concerned with their system. Let them have it. We want our way of life, and we're gonna get it. We're gonna get it or nobody's gonna have any peace on this earth. No peace on this earth.

Now then finally before I sit down, let me say two things. I want to read a statement that brother Huey P. Newton wrote yesterday when I saw him in jail. You have to understand the statement. He says: "As the racist police escalate the war in our communities against black people, we reserve the right to self-defense and maximum retaliation."

All of the things we spoke about tonight centered around brother Huey P. Newton because all of the things we spoke about tonight exemplify what he was trying to do. Now we have to understand something. There is no need for us to go to jail today for what we say. They did that to brother Malcolm X, they just offed him for what he was saying. We have to progress as a race. Brother Huey may or may not have wiped out that honky, but at least it shows a progression, at least we're not getting offed for what we say, we're trying to get offed for what we *do*. Understand this concept: when they offed brother Malcolm, we did nothing; if they off brother Huey, we *got* to retaliate, we *got* to retaliate, we *got* to retaliate, we *got* to retaliate! Do you think that any other race of people will let them off somebody, and the rest of them sitthere? Where in God's name would you find a race of people like that?

Only on the bones of the oppressors can the people's freedom be founded -- Only the blood of the oppressors can fertilize the soil for the people's self-rule.

We have lost in the last five years some of our best leaders — Lumumba, Malcolm X, they offed brother Kwame Nkrumah, and we do nothing, we do nothing, we do nothing. While they offing our leaders, they take our youth and send them to Vietnam, send them to Korea. We are slowly getting wiped out. We must retaliate, we must fight for our humanity. It is our humanity that is at stake. It is not a question of dollars and cents. We gonna survive, because we have survived what *they* couldn't survive — that's natural-born fact. We have survived. We survived through slavery, we survived through their jive reconstruction, we survived through World War I, we survived through the Depression, we survived through World War II, we survived after World War II when they threw us out of the jobs in the North, we survived their Korean War, we gonna survive, we gonna survive, ain't no doubt about that in my mind, no doubt at all.

Our problem is to develop an undying love for our people, an undying love for our people. We must be willing to give our talents, our sweat, our blood, even our life for our people. Nothing else! Not this country — our people!

We must develop the concept that every Negro is a potential black man. You do not alienate your potential allies. Let's bring our people *home*. Let's bring our people *home*.

We must understand the concept that for us the question of community is not geography, it is a question of us — black people — wherever we are, so we have to consciously become a part of the nine hundred million black people that are separated over this world. We were separated by *them*. We are blood of the same blood and flesh of the same flesh. We do not know who is our sister, who is our brother, or where we came from. They took us from Africa and they put thousands of miles of water between us, but they forgot — blood is thicker than water. We coming together, we coming together. Blood is thicker than water, blood is thicker than water.

We are an African people with an African ideology, we are wandering in the United States, we are going to build a concept of peoplehood in this country or there will be no country. Or there will be no country.

As I end, brothers and sister, brother Huey P. Newton belongs to us. He is flesh of our flesh, he is blood of our blood. He may be Mrs. Newton's baby, he's our brother. He's our brother. We do not have to talk about what we're going to do if we're consciously preparing and consciously willing to back those who prepare. All we say: brother Huey will be set free — or else.

This is a complete transcript of Stokely Carmichael's speech at the Oakland Auditorium February 17, 1968. The occasion was a benefit birthday party for Huey P. Newton, Minister of Defense of the Black Panther Party for Self-Defense. Newton is awaiting trial on charges of killing a white Oakland policeman.

The speech as it appears in cold print lacks both the rhetorical devices and the genuine emotion of the speech as delivered—which was magnificent. The general sentiment of staff people who heard the tape in our office was "Too bad he's so groovy." We hope to have a more thorough critique in the near future.

The following is from an interview with John Watson, the editor of the Inner City Voice, *Detroit's black revolutionary newspaper. Watson has had a wide experience in the movement, both in various aspects of the black student movement and as a black auto and newspaper worker. In addition to being editor of the* Inner City Voice, *Watson is now the editor of the Wayne State University newspaper, the* South End.

Q What were the origins of the *Inner City Voice*? What are its aims? What has been its experience?

A. The *Inner City Voice* was created in response to certain adverse conditions that black militants had found in Detroit and in the country as a whole, conditions stopping the further development of a permanent and powerful revolutionary movement among black people. In the last ten years there has been a rise in consciousness among blacks, particularly students, that

created an entirely different political climate. But this has serious drawbacks and hangups. The major one is the general instability of the movement. As far back as 1960 or 1959 there were people involved in various organizations that were single issue oriented, they had some particular object such as a sit-in campaign, police brutality, war, the peace movement, etc. These organizations had a life of their own — internal organizational activity, with lots of people doing concrete work against the system. But they could not sustain themselves, they would fall apart. Then there would be a new upsurge, a new organization.

There was a wave-like character of the movement, it had its ebb and flow, and because it had single issues it had no clear ideology. There was everything from bourgeois integrationists to black nationalists to Marxist-Leninists. But the movement could not keep up with either these single purpose organizations or with the general movement of the black community. Before the July Insurrection we had an advanced community but no organization or leadership as advanced. Therefore, there was no organizational continuity. That is one of the lessons that the July Insurrection reinforced.

How to build a party, a black Bolshevik Party? How to organize black workers, coordinate the activities of black students, how to break away from the old radical organizations? As students of history we went back to see how people did these kinds of things, how in particular they attained relative permanence. We had studied the history of the Russian Bolsheviks and found a specific pamphlet by Lenin called "Where to Begin," written in 1903, before he wrote "What is to be Done?," where he described the role a newspaper could play. A newspaper was the focus of a permanent organization, it could provide a bridge between the peaks of activity. It creates an organization and organizes the division of labor among revolutionaries. Revolutionaries do something, not just a meeting on Sunday, making speeches and passing resolutions. It creates the kind of division of labor needed not just for the newspaper but for a revolutionary organization.

It was these tasks that we set out to perform through the creation of the *Inner City Voice*. The people who created it were Marxist-Leninists, revolutionary socialists, or at least thought of themselves in this way. We wanted to build an organization of black workers, of black students, both in high schools and colleges, and ultimately to create a black Marxist-Leninist Party, flowing from the newspaper.

This was no easy task — we draw all our resources from the black community. And there was no experience among us in terms of publishing, we had no experience insofar as conducting a business operation, we had no money. When we first began we went around to a lot of people. Lenin's idea about a newspaper seemed so logical to us but unfortunately many people didn't see it. Only some young black radicals did. We had only to face the question of going ahead and creating that kind of paper. We had a lot to learn. We had an organization that operated day-to-day rather than week-to-week and meeting-to-meeting. And that kind of activity got us involved in all the problems of people working closely together on a day-by-day basis. We had to solve this.

We started work in May of 1967. We worked through the July Insurrection and came out finally in September. There was a great deal of criticism of the paper, we had too many typos, the articles had errors, etc., etc., but the important thing is that each issue had improved from the experience of the last issue. We had to make our own experience, typos and all.

When we first began there was the question about whether we were a vague black nationalist organization or a Marxist-Leninist organization. The revolutionaries won despite the fact that because we have not yet written out a program, many essentially reformist people came around to play off the rhetoric of the movement.

The *Inner City Voice* has proven many things. It is a very popular paper. We have been printing 10,000 copies each recent issue and these have been almost all sold. We are popular despite the sporadic nature of production — we have only been coming out about once a month. Even the most reformist cannot attack us because we have created an independent base in the black community. No one can redbait us — a lot of people read the paper and we can attack and hurt those who call us "Black Power Communists." The power of the black left has been able to increase through the *Inner City Voice*.

We are well received in the black community. Most of our problems are financial. The organization of circulation is very diffuse. It is difficult to get back full value from sales. But we have managed to survive. And more than that. Since the initiation of the *Voice,* several other things have happened. All of them, including the developments of the *Voice,* are part of an objective development around which groups could coalesce. And this had been so because the first problem has been solved: despite the ebb and flow of activity, we have a permanent organization.

Around the *Voice* there is a conglomeration of activity. We have our office in a large building with our own coffee house and with our own school, teaching black history and now courses in Marxism-Leninism. The coffee house is very popular with the community. Also housed in the same building is the new publication, the *Black Student Voice,* which coordinates the activities of the spontaneous groups that have been formed in inner city schools. We are involved with organizing workers. At the Dodge main plant in Hamtramack, 60-70% of the workers are black. Some of the *Inner City Voice* people were working there and were deeply involved in a wildcat

strike. Out of this came the Dodge Revolutionary Union Movement and now a weekly paper, *DRUM.* This is a very important development because this is the first time recently that black radicals, any radicals for that matter in the country, have organized workers.

What we know is that black workers have the power to close down the American economy. Only workers can end the war and black workers will be and are in the lead. Only the working class can carry through the revolution. Ultimately we must see all segments united around the working class in a revolutionary party — workers, students, intellectuals, community organizations.

The newspaper is moving in this direction. The *Inner City Voice* has gone far to accomplish what Lenin described in "Where to Begin." It has been the focus of a permanent organization, it provided a bridge between peaks of activity. It has organized the division of labor among black revolutionaries and created a network throughout the community.

Q. Stokley Carmichael in a speech to the Black Panther conference in Oakland some months ago said that socialism and communism were not for black people, despite the fact that he had been going all over the world, including to the OLAS conference in Havana, speaking for socialism. What is your reaction to all of this?

A. Our position on this is that it is bullshit. To say socialism or communism is irrelevant is foolish and we oppose this. We know, of course, that you don't go around to the ghetto community and tell them with every breath that socialism is the answer. You organize around concrete issues. But in a public debate in which this subject comes up, we oppose Stokley. There are a number of different kinds of black nationalists. I don't know exactly where Stokley stands. There are black capitalists, there are black mystics, there are black community organization types, there are those with no ideology, there are those who see it as a straight cultural matter, a matter of identity.

We take a Marxist-Leninist position. The question of black people in the United States is a caste and class problem. Black men are exploited as a function of the capitalist system as a whole by white capital. Racism is a tool which the man uses to carry out his exploitation. And we are no more for integrated capitalism than segregated capitalism. Neither are we in favor of a separate state, based on the same class lines as in this society. We are against a separate state in which a black capitalist class exploits a black proletariat. We are opposed also to all sorts of haphazard analyses which certain revolutionaries talk, even in semi-socialist terms, haphazard talk which doesn't tell us what to do with the United States capitalism and imperialism. As to separatism, we leave that question until it can be decided by the whole black people, after the destruction of capitalism.

If Stokley comes to Detroit, in a city with socialized production, owned by capitalists, in which speedup, bad working conditions, automation, "niggermation" (in which one black man does the job previously done by three white men) prevail, what does he say? Is he for the white capitalists? Is he for turning the industry over to black capitalists? Is he for destroying industry? Is he for black workers being exploited no more than white workers?

There is a struggle over cultural nationalism and it is not an abstract ideological question. There is all sorts of analyses but unless we see slavery and racism as extended under capitalism as tools of capitalism, we cannot go anywhere. What should we do? Work primarily with students? Work primarily with workers? Get students involved with workers? These are concrete questions.

I don't know whether Stokley has capitulated to the cultural nationalists. I am surprised by someone who goes around the world and makes all sorts of statements, revolutionary statements, and comes back here and makes statements like the one at the Black Panther rally. We note that Huey Newton, the Black Panther leader, from jail said that blacks must be socialists. Not an abstraction which you preach at people but a concrete ideology which directs what you do.

A lot of black nationalists go around and say we need a new ideology because the experiences of black folk are different. But these people have never studied history, not even the history of black people in this country. They talk of a new ideology, out of the sky, rather than looking to Marxism-Leninism. Not that the Marxism of the past had all the answers. But we know that Marxism is a particular method and that it is a newer and more inherently revolutionary method of gaining black freedom than haphazard analysis. Of course, there should be discussion in the movement but this is our point of view.

There are all sorts of people who say that what we need is black unity. But the thing is that the real world doesn't operate that way. There are real differences in the black community and some of them are class or at least semi-class based. We are one contending force in that community. We have to put forward not a diluted reformist program based on a false unity, but our point of view and win that struggle. We cannot unify with everybody. That's bullshit. Certain programs we can support whole-heartedly, certain programs we can support tactically and certain programs we can't have anything to do with at all. We can coexist with cultural nationalists but we are black Marxist-Leninists and therefore when Stokley is attacking socialism he is attacking us. How can socialism be irrelevant? We don't understand that.

Sunday, 7 July 1968
Detroit, Michigan

Radical America July 1968

ONE JOINT: 30 YEARS
(IF YOU'RE BLACK AND MILITANT)

Houston Militant
Sentenced to 30 Years

By ROBERT ANALAVAGE

HOUSTON, Tex.—In the past six months, police have placed more than 16 different charges against Lee Otis Johnson, chairman of Houston SNCC and a member of the Black Panther Party. They wanted him very badly. They got him. He is now serving 30 years in prison.

He was convicted of giving one marijuana cigarette to an undercover agent. The agent was black. He was the only witness the prosecution produced. His testimony was the only evidence the prosecution entered. For the jury, it was enough.

Johnson's wife, Helen, described the attitude the police had toward her husband and his activities. It is not unlike that held by police against the Panthers in Oakland or in New York, where 200 off-duty police beat up 10 Panthers who showed up at the court where one of their members was being tried.

One night, several months ago, a car in which the Johnsons and two others were driving was stopped for allegedly going through a stop sign. While checking all the occupants' ID's, the policeman recognized Johnson's name.

He radioed police headquarters and five more officers arrived.

Johnson and his friends were taken to the Burglary and Theft Bureau, questioned, and charged with trespassing. They remained in jail for half a day before SNCC could bail them out. While in jail, Johnson's wrists were beaten with handcuffs.

His wife's treatment was much worse. She describes this: "This cop took me down to the booking room and on the way he cursed and kicked me. I repeated this to the desk sergeant and he told me to shut up.

"A matron came over and asked me why I was dressed the way I was. I had on a long dress and wore my hair in the Afro style. I told her I dressed to please my husband. She screamed that my husband was nothing but black-power scum, a communist, and

should be hung. I told her to talk to my husband about it.

"A cop grabbed me, pulled my hair and began punching me in the stomach. They took me to a cell and smashed my head against the concrete. I kept passing out. One tooth was knocked out and the partial plate I wear was cracked. The FBI three days later photographed the bruises. I haven't heard anything from them."

After the murder of Dr. Martin Luther King Jr., Lee Otis Johnson organized and led a memorial march of 8,000 people through Houston. According to those present, Johnson was given a steady ovation after he finished speaking. Apparently such popularity with his people alarmed the police.

The next day, police raided the SNCC freedom house and arrested three persons; one was Johnson. They were charged with sale and possession of marijuana; later the possession charge was dropped.

"The undercover agent," Mrs. Johnson said, "was a Negro—I

wouldn't call him black. He had an Afro haircut that had to take him six months to grow. That's how long they were planning this. It was this guy's word against Lee Otis's. The jury believed him."

Today Johnson is in a prison that is 80 percent black. He is isolated from the other prisoners, obviously because the authorities fear he may carry on his organizing work among the inmates. He has written a letter from jail addressed to his people.

In it he says, "We still got house niggers running around here. Just as the slave masters used TOM in those days to keep an eye on us in the field—to keep him informed—he is still using the ole house nigger today to keep us in check. Its the same situation, he loved his master then, he loves his master now. He betrayed his people then; he was dangerous, he is a danger to all of us today."

the southern PATRIOT   Oct 1968

free ALL political prisoners

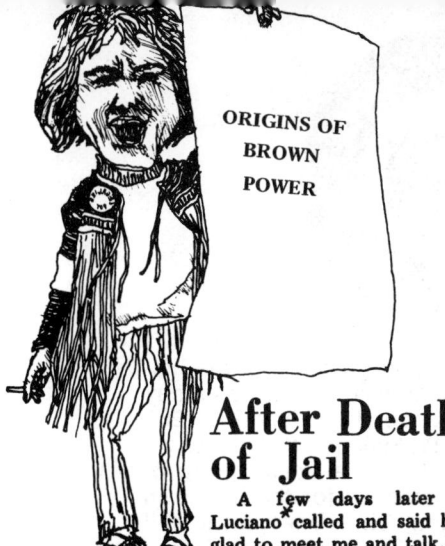

After Death of Jail

A few days later Philip Luciano* called and said he'd be glad to meet me and talk. It may indeed be a source of contention between him and some of the Last Poets that his passions are so various. For example, he is legally Philip, but Felipe by adoption through his new pursuit of his Puerto-Rican identity. At the same time his exuberant Afro, his speech and attitude point to a deep identification with blacks, which he freely admits. And another theme in his fast and tremendously animated talk is Jews and Jewish history. "I'm not anit-Semitic, though that's in vogue," he remarked with mock rue; he attributed his interest here to his being raised on the Bible by his Pentecostal mother. Then he distinguished between this sort of religion and his own in his poem "Books," which he says is about how he's been raped by the Public Library: "Mom believe in God, I believe in revolution, we both believe in something devoutly." The revolution he wants is everyone's: he subscribes to those of the Black Panthers who are coming out for a black, white, and Puerto Rican revolution. Sometimes in his hands the revolution is a struggle for manhood—but, he hastily adds then, "the sort of manhood a *woman* can achieve." And yet he has just opted out of the struggle at Queens SEEK because everything—women, trees, music—all were becoming political and he feared losing his sense of beauty. Governed by the desire to reject all limiting categories and yet to sacrifice no drop of intensity, Felipe Luciano is quintessentially 21, except for the fact that he served two years for attempted manslaughter.

Luciano's adolescence in Brownsville and Bushwick was in some respects the Spanish counterpart of Kemp's in Harlem. Both involved a curious balance of antipathetic roles. For example, Luciano said, "I loved Shakespeare in the eighth grade and I was a brilliant student. They called me Professor, but I was also a jitterbug. I was interested in college, but a fight was a fight." Crazy about singing as long as he can remember,

Luciano also worked with a singing group and made four unsuccessful records. Then one evening, when he was 16, he came home from Carnegie Hall where he'd had a "beautiful date" to hear the Hanover College Choir, and found his 14-year-old brother beaten speechless on the stoop by a black gang that "had to get a Spic." The man in the house ever since his father abandoned his mother, Luciano said, "I was the guy, I was the army, everything in one. I had to revenge this. I knew I'd get busted, but I saw no way out. I couldn't live that down. You let it go and you have to worry about your mother and your sister. Of course, now I know there was a lot of self-destructiveness in me at the time." He phoned his cousin's friends ("We don't have that gang structure now—the way things were then, nobody asked questions"), and with them backing him, beat the black leader. Just as he started to leave, a fellow he didn't know, who had come with one he'd called, stabbed the beaten man twice and killed him. He and Luciano were arrested in five minutes and beaten till they signed a confession. Luciano was sentenced to five years at Coxsackie Correctional Institute.

"When I went to prison, I believed anyone could make it on his merits. I believed I could be President. Prison was a turning point for me. I took a vow there that I would never take things for granted. You know, Dostoevsky says in 'The House of the Dead' that you can judge the degree of civilization in a society by entering its prisons. It's true. You see what it's all about. People say, 'But that's a jail.' I say, 'No, it's America, it's what's underneath.'" Luciano described blacks taking worse punishment than whites, and the elaborate racial hostilities fostered by the guards and represented schematically by the way men sat on the benches of their race in the yard. "I stood in the middle with the guys they called the creeps. I said, 'Forget this skin analysis thing, you're every one of you oppressed.'"

As for schooling in jail, Luciano said, "The prison teachers there couldn't make it in the outside world. For example the * * * * was neurotic and homosexual; he was a great teacher, but a maniac. He put guys who spoke back into solitary. Everything I learned was through self-sudy." He read Will Durant, the only philosopher in the library. "Black Boy" was banned, but one volume passed from hand to hand. More fundamentally, the jail experience shaped his philosophy of personal freedom. "Jails go to the deepest part of our depravity. There's no worse living death than jail. No one can tell you if

you haven't seen it. And any guy who's gone through death knows life. And he's not going to be restricted. I have one life to lead—there's nothing I'm going to not try because someone tells me it's wrong. In the movement so-called, any place, I'm going to be me and what I'm doing is what I believe in."

A romantic theory of oppression and art grows out of this sense. "When any people go through a period of oppression—the Vietnamese, the black American—something is brought out. If you have to worry about surival, the other part, the creative part is stronger. They say women in concentration camps gave up their rations so their sons could go to the rabbi. If you have no material, possessions don't possess you. If social equality is a dream, you have to fall back on yourself, on your spirit, which I mean as something sensory and mystical at the same time. My mother is Pentecostal," he wound up with a delighted smile, "give her a few thousand dollars and she won't need those spiritual orgasms—she'll become a Methodist." He then reminisced about a day in prison in which he saw a tree through the window, with peculiar intensity and as if for the first time.

Education seems to be for Luciano a means to strengthen and deepen his commitment to art and revolution. "I knew SEEK was a pacification program from the beginning, but I could use it to get tools. Which tools? Well, particularly the ability to abstract and to communicate that abstraction." But in December he took a leave of absence because his political activities were impairing his freedom. After working for two years to get the sort of revolutionary movement he wanted, he found himself burdened by leadership. "I felt I was being puppetized, being made into a humanoid," he explained, with an usual note of bitterness. "A leader has to embody the people's aspirations, so a leader doesn't cry, a leader doesn't question whether there's another way. If he does he's finished, so I quit." Talking later about his problematic attitude toward armed revolution, he said: "I hate systems, I don't hate individuals. I have a poem that ends, 'I'll cry and I'll shoot and I'll cry and I'll shoot'—that's my reality."

Now Luciano is tutoring Harlem drop-outs during the day and leading a workshop on "political thought and behavior" at night. The workshop meets in a Harlem loft where the Last Poets also perform, named the East Wind for its non-Occidental stance. "I began with a group of six, but we advertised at performances and now I have

around 60. We study all the political options. We go over Fanon chapter by chapter and Che and Morgenthau and C. Wright Mills and we read poetry. We're trying to break through the myths that surround us and in the process build a consciousness. Action, thought and spirit must be one. Two things I keep saying—'Take your soul and let it all hang out' and 'Choose your own death.' I Talk a lot about concepts of death, which are really concepts of life. Do you have Nietzsche's 'Thus Spake Zarathustra'?" He riffled through the pages and read from the section on free death: "He that consummates his life dies his death victoriously, surrounded by these who hope and promise. There should be no festival where one dying thus does not hallow the oaths of the living." In the next moment he tossed Nietzsche aside, picked up my baby daughter, and sang to her in Spanish. "You're what's happening," he told her. "Everything is everything, isn't it?" He turned to me. "You know, it's funny. She's beautiful, but she doesn't make me want to bask. She makes me more determined to fight because of what's out there. Every man has to have two babies. One's like this, his own, and the other he leaves in the minds of the people." Luciano would like some day to have a large family, including adopted children because of what he has seen orphans suffer. Meanwhile he and his workshop are setting up a "revolutionary pre-school" for children under six, "to prepare each child to be a warrior, scholar, lover, all at once."

His ultimate scheme of setting up "a whole revolutionary school system" may have influenced the style of his application for next year to a new experimental college. "They asked me to write down the questions *I* would ask of entering students. I gave them three questions:

"Have you had a good orgasm? Have you ever been really hurt, physically or emotionally? And are you willing to carry a gun for what you believe? You aren't really ready to learn without these things."

He grinned. "They probably won't take me, but I have to go back to school. My thing is going to be streets, but I need to tax my mind more. I've been sparring. Now I have to get into some matches with some real heavyweights."

* * *

From *Gifted Offenders* by Bell Gale Chevigny, 7/10/69

Ed. Note: Luciano is now (February 1970) one of the leaders of the Young Lords in East Harlem

ETHERIDGE KNIGHT

He Sees Through Stone

He sees through stone
he has the secret
eyes this old black one
who sits under prison skies
sits pressed by the sun
against the western wall
his pipe between purple gums

the years fall
like over-ripe plums
bursting red flesh
on the dark earth

his time is not my time
but I have known him
In a time now gone

he led me trembling cold
into the dark forest
taught me the secret rites
to take a woman
to be true to my brothers
to make my spear drink
the blood
of my enemies

now black cats circle him
flash white teeth
snarl at the air
mashing green grass beneath
shining muscles
ears peeling his words
he smiles
he knows

the hunt   the enemy
he has the secret eyes
he sees through stone

"July 23, 1968, will have to go down in the history of the black revolutionary struggle as a day of even more importance than July 25, 1967 (Detroit), and August 11, 1965 (Watts). It was on Tuesday night, July 23, that a small group of black men set up an ambush for the police in the streets of Cleveland, Ohio. They set it well and carefully . . ."

Julius Lester

julius lester

The revolutionary process takes many decades to fulfill itself. The generation which finally assumes power gives the appearance of having started a revolution in a short period of time. That is not so. The generation which wins power is only completing work begun decades before.

The 1960's has been a decade of rapid change. Each succeeding year has seen a heightening of consciousness and while problems exist in great abundance, these problems will be overcome if the organization, understanding, will and discipline exists to do the necessary work to see that they are overcome. Each succeeding year of the 60's has also seen an intensification of the actual struggle itself. The early willingness to suffer arrest and go to jail has given way to an attitude of "catch me if you can," not to mention the increasing willingness of people to fight back when attacked.

One of the most important changes in consciousness has been the acceptance of the concept of self-defense. When Robert Williams organized self-defense units in Monroe, N.C., he eventually had to leave the country to save his life. Malcolm X brought the concept to a mass audience and was eventually killed. The Panthers have made the concept manifest on a mass level and are suffering intense harassment. But today, there are no debates over the rightness of defending one's self and one's community.

The next step in the evolution of the revolutionary process will be the move from self-defense to aggressive action. This has occurred in a few isolated instances, particularly on college campuses on the West Coast and a few black campuses, where buildings have been set afire and heavily damaged. This type of activity will, in all likelihood, increase in the coming months.

The black community has settled down to a quiet state of low-key warfare. In New York and various communities in New Jersey there have been numerous attacks on police stations in the past few months. Though most of them have been unsuccessful, the mere fact that the attempts are being made is significant. The black movement has reached a point where it is unnecessary to discuss the necessity of "the gun" any longer. People know what needs to be done and are going about and doing it.

One city in the country which has settled down to a state of constant war is East St. Louis. The St. Louis Post-Dispatch of January 16 reports that since August 1968, there have been more than 50 sniping incidents in East St. Louis. Three people have been killed in these incidents — an 18-year-old white boy and two white men shot in an after-hours tavern by a sniper firing from a bridge. The effect of "The Sniper" (there is probably more than one) on the economic life of the city has been profound. Because whites are now afraid even to drive through East St. Louis, sales tax revenues from the city to the state declined by $30,000 in the third quarter, which ended October 31. The mayor's office estimates that overall, the sniper has cost the city $200,000 in sales taxes, merchants license collections and overtime pay for policemen. There is no estimate of how much revenue the city will lose by businesses leaving the area.

To the black community, "The Sniper" has become a hero. He is known to shoot only at whites or at blacks who are known enemies of the community. He is also known to be bold, able to strike at high noon or after midnight with equal impunity.

The number of fires in the East St. Louis-St. Louis area have also increased These fires seem generally to be directed against white businesses known to be cruelly exploitative in the community. Firemen now carry rifles as part of their standard equipment, which gives an indication of just how serious the situation has become. Police have been totally ineffective in dealing with "The Sniper" or those who are sabotaging the businesses.

What is happening in East St. Louis points up once again the advantages of medium-sized cities. In the large cities of the East and West, the police have tremendous sophistication and are much more difficult to combat. In the medium-sized cities of the South and Midwest, this is not true to the same extent. The military parallel of this is the Vietnam war, where the National Liberation Front has concentrated on small and medium-sized cities, leaving Saigon, Danang and other large cities for the last. And in fact the same practice prevailed in the revolutionary wars in China and Cuba. This is not to say that the large cities should be ignored. They cannot be. But the risks are higher, the preparation needed much greater, and unless the action taken is a large one, the returns from that action might be smaller than if the action were taken in a smaller city.

On the surface it may appear that the black movement is in a state of disarray. While this may be partially true of some groups, the black movement has never been isolated from the black community. In an unorganized sense, the community has been the military wing of the movement, while known groups have been the political wing. Some theoreticians of the white radical movement considered the black rebellions of 1965-68 to be nonrevolutionary in content because they were aimed at property, which thereby made them "consumer-oriented."

This kind of analysis points up once again how at variance the black and white radical movements are. Having been glutted by a consumer-oriented society, it is natural that young whites fight against it. Having been on the outside, it is natural that blacks would seek to acquire. What the white radical theoreticians overlook is the way in which blacks have done their acquiring and the subsequent destruction of property that inevitably comes after the acquisitions have been made. The black rebellions also served as "on the job" training for what is now developing in East St. Louis and no doubt other cities around the country.

If East St. Louis is any indication, the revolutionary process has entered another stage. At present, it is harrassing action. Undoubtedly, it will be followed by terrorist action in the white community, and eventually all-out guerrilla warfare. It is to be hoped that the white radical movement will be able to relate effectively to what is developing in the black community.

Reprinted from the Guardian, radical newsweekly, New York, distributed by LNS.

Guardian Feb 1969

There is reason to believe that the Negro of 1959 will not accept supinely any such compromises in the contemporary struggle for integration. His struggle will continue, but the obstacles will determine its specific nature. It is axiomatic in social life that the imposition of frustrations leads to two kinds of reactions. One is the development of a wholesome social organization to resist with effective firm measures any efforts to impede progress. The other is a confused, anger-motivated drive to strike back violently, to inflict damage. Primarily, it seeks to cause injury, to retaliate for wrongful suffering. Secondarily, it seeks real progress. It is punitive—not radical or constructive.

The current calls for violence have their roots in this latter tendency. Here one must be clear that there are three different views on the subject of violence. One is the approach of pure nonviolence, which cannot readily or easily attract large masses, for it requires extraordinary discipline and courage. The second is violence exercised in self-defense, which all societies, from the most primitive to the most cultured and civilized, accept as moral and legal. The principle of self-defense, even involving weapons and bloodshed, has never been condemned, even by Gandhi, who sanctioned it for those unable to master pure nonviolence. The third is the advocacy of violence as a tool of advancement, organized as in warfare, deliberately and consciously. To this tendency many Negroes are being tempted today. There are incalculable perils in this approach. It is not the danger or sacrifice of physical being which is primary, though it cannot be contemplated without a sense of deep concern for human life. The greatest danger is that it will fail to attract Negroes to a real collective struggle, and will confuse the large uncommitted middle group, which as yet has not supported either side. Further, it will mislead Negroes into the belief that this is the only path, and place them as a minority in a position where they confront a far larger adversary than it is possible to defeat in this form of combat. When the Negro uses force in self-defense he does not forfeit support—he may even win it, by the courage and self-respect it reflects. When he seeks to initiate violence he provokes questions about the necessity for it, and inevitably is blamed for its consequences. It is unfortunately true that however the Negro acts, his struggle will not be free of violence initiated by his enemies, and he will need ample courage and willingness to sacrifice to defeat this manifestation of violence. But if he seeks it and organizes it, he cannot win. Does this leave the Negro without a positive method to advance? Mr. Robert Williams would have us believe that there is no effective and practical alternative. He argues that we must be cringing and submissive or take up arms. To so place the issue distorts the whole problem. There are other meaningful alternatives.

The Negro people can organize socially to initiate many forms of struggle which can drive their enemies back without resort to futile and harmful violence. In the history of the movement for racial advancement, many creative forms have been developed—the mass boycott, sit-down protests and strikes, sit-ins—refusal to pay fines and bail for unjust arrests—mass marches—mass meetings—prayer pilgrimages, etc. Indeed, in Mr. Williams' own community of Monroe, North Carolina, a striking example of collective community action won a significant victory without use of arms or threats of violence. When the police incarcerated a Negro doctor unjustly, the aroused people of Monroe marched to the police station, crowded into its halls and corridors, and refused to leave until their colleague was released. Unable to arrest everyone, the authorities released the doctor and neither side attempted to unleash violence. This experience was related by the doctor who was the intended victim.

There is more power in socially organized masses on the march than there is in guns in the hands of a few desperate men. Our enemies would prefer to deal with a small armed group rather than with a huge, unarmed but resolute mass of people. However, it is necessary that the mass-action method be persistent and unyielding. Gandhi said the Indian people must "never let them rest," referring to the British. He urged them to keep protesting daily and weekly, in a variety of ways. This method inspired and organized the Indian masses and disorganized and demobilized the British. It educates its myriad participants, socially and morally. All history teaches us that like a turbulent ocean beating great cliffs into fragments of rock, the determined movement of people incessantly demanding their rights always disintegrates the old order.

It is this form of struggle—non-cooperation with evil through mass actions—"never letting them rest"—which offers the more effective road for those who have been tempted and goaded to violence. It needs the bold and the brave because it is not free of danger. It faces the vicious and evil enemies squarely. It requires dedicated people, because it is a backbreaking task to arouse, to organize, and to educate tens of thousands for disciplined, sustained action. From this form of struggle more emerges that is permanent and damaging to the enemy than from a few acts of organized violence.

Our present urgent necessity is to cease our internal fighting and turn outward to the enemy, using every form of mass action yet known—create new forms—and resolve never to let them rest. This is the social lever which will force open the door to freedom. Our powerful weapons are the voices, the feet, and the bodies of dedicated, united people, moving without rest toward a just goal. Greater tyrants than Southern segregationists have been subdued and defeated by this form of struggle. We have not yet used it, and it would be tragic if we spurn it because we have failed to perceive its dynamic strength and power.

From "The Social Organization of Nonviolence" (a reply to Robert F. Williams) by Martin Luther King, Jr., 1959 **LIBERATION**

Describing an OAAU meeting in Harlem, Marlene Nadle wrote that "a man stood, rocked back on his heels, and very slowly said, 'We heard you changed, Malcolm. Why don't you tell us where you're at with them white folks?' Without dropping a syllable he [Malcolm] gave a black nationalist speech on brotherhood."

Malcolm: I haven't changed. I just see things on a broader scale. We nationalists used to think we were militant. We were just dogmatic. It didn't bring us anything.

Now I know it's smarter to say you're going to shoot a man for what he is doing to you than because he is white. If you attack him because he is white, you give him no out. He can't stop being white. We've got to give the man a chance. He probably won't take it, the snake. But we've got to give him a chance.

We've got to be more flexible. Why, when some of our friends in Africa didn't know how to do things, they went ahead and called in some German technicians. And they had blue eyes.

I'm not going to be in anybody's straitjacket. I don't care what a person looks like or where they come from. My mind is wide open to anybody who will help get the ape off our backs.

From Marlene Nadle, *Village Voice*. February 25, 1965

Malcolm X Speaks, Grove Press

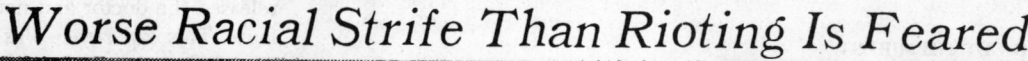

Worse Racial Strife Than Rioting Is Feared

A Cleveland policeman firing at snipers on the night of July 23d this year, start of four days of sporadic fighting between Negroes and the police there. Eleven persons—three white policemen and eight Negroes—were killed by gunfire.

United Press International

Here are some indications:

¶Guerrilla warfare, long a part of the rhetoric of Negro militants, now appears to have the potential for coming into practice. Indeed, that phase may have already begun.

¶Scores of incidents of sniping at policemen in Negro neighborhoods have been reported in recent months in major cities across the country.

¶Off-duty white policemen, some wearing Wallace buttons, beat Negro youths belonging to the Black Panthers in the corridors of a Brooklyn courtroom.

¶The founder of the Black Panthers, Huey Newton, was recently sentenced to from 3 to 15 years in the killing of a white Oakland policeman. Two other Oakland policemen were recently dismissed from the force for shooting up the Panthers' headquarters.

¶In a recent poll of Southern white schoolchildren, 59 per cent were either elated or indifferent about the assassination of the Rev. Dr. Martin Luther King Jr.

¶Black militants, with some pride, have displayed their weaponry to other Negroes. White viligante groups continue to instruct white women and children in the use of firearms, sometimes, as in Cleveland, with the assistance of individual local policemen.

Collision Course

Never before in the modern history of this country have Negro aspirations been in so direct a collision course with white resistance.

A Negro student at the University of California, Berkeley, recently predicted with a hint of a smile that "the black man's quest for what he should have will not slacken and whites will resist it to the last drop of Negro blood."

And a 48-year-old Negro lawyer from Pontiac, Mich., Milton Henry, said:

"We're forced to become revolutionaries, since they program us right out of the system. They keep telling us to be nonviolent while they remain unwilling to make meaningful changes."

Mr. Henry is vice president of the Republic of New Africa, an organization that seeks complete separation of the races, "by peaceful means if possible."

Guerrilla Warfare Feared

Ocie Pastard, who, as a Negro social worker, watched the Watts section of Los Angeles go through 11 days of burning and blood-letting in 1965, declares that the nation has seen an end to such burning. But he adds:

"The next stage is guerrilla warfare unless some very basic changes in the system of racism are made."

Mr. Pastard currently directs the Mid-City Community Congress, a church-sponsored amalgamation of groups, some integrated but mostly Negro, in St. Louis, a city that many believe is building to a battle with black militants.

It is not surprising to many social scientists that predictions of intentional violence, of insurrection as opposed to spontaneous rioting, would come at a time when some Negroes are making unprecedented breakthroughs in what had been a white world.

With the new sense of community and collectivism among the Negro activists, the yardstick that measures progress is no longer calibrated to individual Negroes who have "made it" but rather to the masses of Negroes who have not.

'Born of Hope'

Revolutions "are usually born of hope, not despair," Nathan S. Caplan and Jerry M. Paige wrote in the August edition of Scientific American. Of the individual rioter during the Newark and Detroit disorders of 1967, they concluded:

"The continued exclusion of Negroes from American economic and social life is the fundamental cause of riots . . . Negroes are still excluded from economic opportunity and occupational advancement, but they no longer have the psychological defenses or social supports that once encouraged passive adaptation to this situation."

The writers are with the Institute for Social Research at the University of Michigan, an organization that surveyed Negro rioters for the National Advisory Commission on Civil Disorders.

Cleveland, that ethnically Balkanized "mistake by the lake" that elected a Negro Mayor last year, produced the largest Negro insurrection (as opposed to riot) in recent history. An unknown number of armed Negro men took to the streets last July and conducted several gun fights with policemen.

A close look at the 11 violent deaths resulting from this insurrection illustrates the potential for violence on the part of Negroes, whites and policemen.

Three white policemen were shot to death as were three of the Negro insurrectionists. One Negro was killed by policemen on the street. The police called him a looter, but his wife denied that he was.

One Negro who had aided the police was killed during the gun battle. It was not certain whether he was shot by Negroes or the police.

Another Negro was found dead of gunshot wounds behind an empty black nationalist headquarters that white policemen had shot up after ordering a Negro policeman assigned to guard the building to leave his post.

A Negro marine, AWOL and in civilian clothes, was shot to death by whites five miles from the scene of the shoot-out but on the same night.

And a Negro folk singer, driving through a white area in Cleveland, was shot to death when he stopped for a red light early in the morning.

In several cities across the country, Negroes, especially youths, are forming groups "to protect our community from racist cops." St. Louis is one such city.

A former worker for the Student Nonviolent Coordinating Committee, Charles Koen, 23, recently formed the Black Liberators in St. Louis. There followed several charges of harassment by the police, including beatings, wrecking of the organization's headquarters and the burning of a Liberator car. The police denied the charges.

4 Seized and Fined

After an early September protest rally, Mr. Koen and three others, including Phil Hutchings, the head of the student committee, were arrested and charged with unlawful assembly. A city court judge found them guilty the next day and fined Mr. Hutchings and another S.N.C.C. official $5,000 each and Mr. Koen and another Liberator $150 each.

This greatly enlarged the conflict. The American Civil Liberties Union subsequently filed a suit in Federal court to order the police to stop arresting the militants. Scores of civil rights, student and church groups pledged support for the Negroes and The St. Louis Post-

Dispatch accused the police in an editorial of deliberately harassing the Negro militants.

Several white groups and some labor union officials have sided with the police. So has Missouri's Governor, Warren Hearnes. This earned him enthusiastic cheers from policemen but he was labeled a "meddler" by The Post-Dispatch.

"You can feel the tension," a white social worker in St. Louis commented recently. "You start thinking that any minute this city can erupt."

tion here," Mr. Tindal said. "Negroes saw it was black people who died in the riots but still they will not allow police to abuse them as they had done in the past." Mr. Tindal recently took a leave from the N.A.A.C.P. to run for city-councilman-at-large.

Robert Lamb, a 43-year-old history buff employed by the Justice Department's Community Relations Service in Washington, agrees with Mr. Tindal.

"Unless the man really addresses himself to the problems of the cities, there will probably be instances of guerrilla warfare," he said. "Black youths are determined that white policemen will not come into the black community, abuse them, disrespect them and treat them less than human and then walk out with impunity."

Mr. Lamb, a Negro, until last month had been a police captain in Atlantic City.

The associate director of Brandeis University's Lemberg Center for the Study of Violence. Ralph W. Conant, who is white, has said:

Disturbances Grow

"The black people in the ghetto see the police as violent and strike back with increasing intensity. Studies being conducted at the Lemberg Center show that in the majority of instances, police violence toward ghetto residents precedes and supersedes ghetto violence."

While national surveys indicate that very few Negroes favor violence as a method for making racial progress, observers have noted that disturbances have a way of growing rapidly when policemen start to manhandle rioters.

In city after city, Negro working men were drawn into the battles they had been watching

when club-swinging policemen tried to get them off the streets. Family men left their apartments to fight policemen when communities were tear-gassed.

A family man in Cleveland told a newsman how he lay on the floor in his house during a racial disturbance with his pistol in hand, "waiting to shoot the first white cop who came in because the cops were shooting anything black that moved."

'It's Not So Simple'

During times of stress it will often make no difference if the police officer is Negro. This is especially true if the Negro officer insists on forcefully putting down the disorder and objects to the inevitable pleas of the rioters that he join them.

"It's hard as hell being a black cop during a riot," said a Negro police official in New York. "You know you're going to keep the peace, but when King was killed I felt very much like tearing up things myself. It's not so simple as just maintaining the law when you know from personal experience that the people breaking it are also being victimized by the same law."

New York was one of a very few cities where some Negroes felt the police had been effective in recent years in apply-

Billboards in Detroit

In Detroit there are several Police Officer Association billboards showing a white policeman helping a Negro schoolgirl across the street. The caption reads: "Parents, your children are our concern too."

But Robert Tindal, who heads the local National Association for the Advancement of Colored People, remarks:

"It seems there is little likelihood of riots, but there is danger here. If the attitudes of the police don't change they'll find themselves involved in retaliatory shootings for sure."

Mr. Tindal, who had served on a task force aimed at improving relations between the police and the Negro community, resigned after a "stop and frisk" law had been adopted by the city.

"There is a new sophisticating techniques aimed at avoiding riot situations.

Negro policemen in Chicago recently formed an organization to act independently of the department to improve deteri-

orated relations between Negroes and the police. In Washington, D. C., the wives of Negro policemen formed their own group to counteract what they called "the conservatism" of organizations of white policemen's wives.

Several cities present a prospect for racial violence. With "community protective" organizations arming in Negro areas and "vigilantes" arming in white areas, officials of some major industrial centers are fearful of racial disorders.

"It could happen any minute here," an automobile industry executive said in Detroit. "Every day we go without a major outburst I'm thankful."

Many white auto workers are open supporters of George C. Wallace for President, though the leadership of the United Automobile Workers opposes him. They feel threatened by the influx of Negroes into the industry, a good many of whom are highly resentful of Wallace.

A militant Negro organization, DRUM (Dodge Revolutionary Union Movement), has been formed among Negro workers for Chrysler.

'Disregard for Rights'

DRUM contends that although Negroes make up close to a third of the Chrysler workers, they are not being treated fairly. The organizations asserts that while top management makes a public display of promoting equal opportunity, middle management still practices a good deal of discrimination.

Said one member: "When I get on that assembly line that honkie is steadily bearing down on my butt. He does not treat whites that way."

"DRUM is successful because black people are daily confronted with a complete disregard for their rights," said Al Dunmore, a Negro, suburban affairs specialist for Chrysler who formerly edited Detroit's Negro weekly, The Michigan Chronicle. "Unions, civil rights and other groups have failed to correct this so far. The industry is ripe for DRUM. Then can seize upon an issue, exaggerate it and get many black people who've known discrimination to follow them."

The case of Harry Douglas, a seven-year Chrysler employe

currently at odds with the company, is indicative of the labor-social problem that officials fear could result in violence.

Mr. Douglas, 37, a Negro, had been an efficiency expert before he requested and received assignment as an instructor for classes of former hard-core unemployed Negroes whom the company is training to fit into regular jobs.

"A part of the training is black history, the use of black images to instill pride, self-respect and reliance in men who come with little self-esteem," said Mr. Douglas.

Picture of Carmichael

He said a white superior objected strongly to a picture of Stokely Carmichael (alongside pictures of Dr. King, Whitney Young and Roy Wilkins) and a running argument ensued.

"I objected because Stokely is a fact of life," Mr. Douglas said, "and white people have been writing blacks out of history for too long."

He said that he was subsequently offered a "promotion" to another location, which he turned down, and that he was then relieved of his teaching job because of the refusal to transfer.

He sat in the Chrysler personnel office a couple of Fridays ago and got his leave with pay extended and picked up his salary check at another location.

Mr. Douglas has not worked for six weeks while awaiting a decision by Chrysler, and DRUM members are following his case closely. He reports once a week, just to pick up his check.

Said one DRUM member, in a quiet, off-handed tone: "We'll see what happens to the brother. We can stop the production line if need be. We can close the whole industry, like whitey used to do when he struck against black people being promoted. But we'll just wait and see how Charlie works this thing out for the brother."

A Negro auto worker, not a DRUM member, commented: "Can you imagine the white reaction to Negroes stopping the line—getting into their bread and butter? We have a few fights out here, now and then, but this could be war."

The New York Times
10/22/68

GOOD EVENING, EVERYBODY. Kind of stuck for words tonight. I don't know whether this is a hello or a goodbye. I talked to my parole officer today, and he told me that on Wednesday the 27th he wanted me to call him up about 8:30 in the morning, so he could tell me where to meet him so he could transport me to San Quentin. They want to have a parole revocation hearing, and I guess they think they have a right to do that. They certainly are proceeding as though they have a right. Having had some experience with them, I know that when they have you in their clutches, they proceed with what they want to do whether they have a right or not.

A lot of people don't know anything about the prison system. I think they make the same mistake looking at prison [continued] officials as they do with cops: they think that in some sense they are guardians of the law; that they're there to protect society, and everything they say is the truth; that there's nothing wrong with what they're into, and nothing wrong with what they're doing. Well, I know. Not so much in my own case, but from the cases of others that I've observed in the various prisons in the State of California. There are a whole lot of people behind those walls who don't belong there. And everybody behind those walls is being subjected to programs that are not authorized, nor related to the reasons for which they were sent there.

Rehabilitation in the State of California is less than a bad joke. I don't even know how to relate to that word, "rehabilitation." It presupposes that at one time one was "habilitated," and that somehow he got off the right track and was sent to this garage, or repair shop, to be dealt with and then released. Rehabilitated, and placed back on the right track. Well, I guess that the right track has to be this scene out here: the free world. Convicts call us out here the "free world." After you're behind those walls for a while, I guess it starts looking like the Garden of Eden. They can't see all of the little conflicts that are going on out here. Alioto [San Francisco Mayor Joseph Alioto] doesn't look as much like Al Capone from that distance. That's right. Al Capone, Alioto—Big Al. Alley-oop Oto. You know. People yearn, people *yearn*, behind those walls, to return to the free world. To return to society. To be free, and not to be returned to the penitentiary.

Now, when I went into the penitentiary I made a decision. I took a long hard look at myself and I said, well, you've been walking this trip for a little too long, you're tired of it. It's very clear that what you had going for yourself before you came in was not adequate. While you're here you're going to have to work with yourself, deal with yourself, so that when you get out of here you're going to stay out. Because it was pretty clear to me that that was my last go-round, that I could not relate to prison any more. So I guess I developed something of a social conscience. I decided to come out here and work with social problems, get involved with the Movement and make whatever contribution I possibly could. When I made that decision, I thought that the parole authorities would be tickled pink with me, because they were always telling me to do exactly that. They would tell me I was selfish. They would ask me why I didn't start relating to other people, and looking beyond the horizons of myself.

So I did that, you know. And I just want to tell you this. I've had more trouble out of parole officers and the Department of Corrections simply because I've been relating to the Movement than I had when I was committing robberies, rapes and other things that I didn't get caught for. That's the truth. If I was on the carpet for having committed a robbery, well, there would be a few people up-tight about that. But it seemed to be localized. It didn't seem to affect the entire prison

system or the entire parole board. They didn't even seem to have much time to discuss it, you know. They run you through their meetings very, very briefly. You feel that your case is not even being considered. But I know that now my case is constantly on their desks, and my parole officer doesn't have very much to do except keep track of me. He wants to know where I go, how much money I make each month, where I'm living, when I'm going to go out of town, phone him up when I get back to town, and ask his permission to do this and that.

THERE'S SOMETHING MORE DANGEROUS about attacking the pigs of the power structure verbally than there is in walking into the Bank of America with a gun and attacking it forthrightly. Bankers hate armed robbery, but someone who stands up and directly challenges their racist system, that drives them crazy. I don't know if there are any bankers in the audience tonight, but I hope that there are. I hope that there's at least one, or a friend of one, or somebody who will carry the message to one. And I hope particularly that there's one here from the Bank of America. I heard today on the news that brother Cesar Chavez has declared war on the Bank of America. The Bank of America is Alioto's bank. My wife told me this evening that she received a phone call from the Bank of America saying that they were going to repossess our car because we were three months behind in our payments. That's not true, but I wished that I had never paid a penny for it. I wished that I could have just walked onto that lot and said, "Stick 'em up, motherfucker! I'm taking this." Because that's how I felt about it. That's how I feel about it now. I don't relate to this system of credit—see it now, take it home, pay later . . . but make sure you pay.

It was only out of consideration for the atmosphere that I would need in order to do the other things I wanted to do that I didn't rip it off. Or that I haven't walked into the Bank of America. Or that I haven't walked into any other establishment and repossessed the loot that they have in there. So I don't know what they expect from me, see? I haven't committed any crimes. I don't feel there's a need for rehabilitation. I don't feel the need of going back to Dirty Red's penitentiary. Warden Nelson? [Warden of San Quentin] The prison guards call him Big Red, but the convicts call him Dirty Red. He's sitting over there across the bay and he's waiting for me, because we have a little history of friction. He doesn't like me. My parole officer doesn't like me. He tells the newspaper writers, "Yeah, I think he's a real nice fellow. I think he's made an excellent adjustment. If it wasn't for this particular indictment brought against him, I'd be perfectly willing to have him as my parolee from now on." Yet if you go down to the parole department and ask them to let you see my file, you will find just one charge against me, other than those lodged against me in Alameda County, which are yet to be adjudicated. I haven't gone to trial for those. I have pleaded "Not Guilty" to them. The one legitimate charge they have is "failing to cooperate with the parole agent."

The first time I saw that, I couldn't understand what it meant, because I bent over backwards to cooperate with that punk. So I asked him, "Just what does that mean? What's the substance of that?" Now this is going to really surprise you. He said, "Do you remember when you went to New York to tape the David Susskind Show?" I said, "Yes, I remember doing that."

"Remember I told you that when you got back you should give me a phone call and let me know you were back in town?"

"Yes, and I did that, didn't I?"

"No, you didn't do it. That's against the rules."

And that's the only thing that they have in my file that is even debatable. All the other things that they are hostile towards me for, they can't put in the files because it's against the law. It's contrary to the Constitution and they would be ashamed to write it down on paper and place it in my file. They probably have another file that they smuggle around between them. But they cannot come out and tell you one thing that I've done that would justify returning me to the penitentiary.

I just have to say that I didn't leave anything in that penitentiary except half of my mind and half of my soul, and that's dead there. I have no use for it. It's theirs. They can have that. That's my debt to them. That's my debt to society, and I don't owe them a motherfucking thing! They don't have anything coming. Everything they get from now on, they have to take! I believe that our time has come. A point has been reached where a line just has to be drawn, because the power structure of this country has been thoroughly exposed. There is no right on their side. We know that they're moving against people for political purposes.

There's a favorite line of mine. It says that there is a point where fortune ends and cowardice begins. Everybody is scared of the pigs, of the power structure. The people have reason to be concerned about them because they have these gestapo forces that they issue orders to. They come in with their clubs and their guns, and they will exterminate you, if that's what it takes to carry out the will of their bosses.

I don't know how to go about waiting until people start practicing what they preach. I don't know how to go about waiting on that. Because all I see is a very critical situation, a chaotic situation where there's pain, there's suffering, there's death, and I see no justification for waiting until tomorrow to say what you could say tonight. I see no justification for waiting until other people get ready. I see no justification for not moving even if I have to move by myself. I think of my attitude towards these criminals—my parole officer included—who control the prison system, who control the parole board. I can't reconcile things with them because for so long I've watched them shove shit down people's throats. I knew there was something wrong with the way that they were treating people. I knew that by no stretch of the imagination could that be right. It took me a long time to put my finger on it, at least to my own satisfaction. And after seeing that they were the opposite of what they were supposed to be, I got extremely angry at them. I don't want to see them get away with anything. I want to see them in the penitentiary. They belong in there because they've committed so many crimes against the human rights of the people. They belong in the penitentiary!

WHEN YOU FOCUS ON THE adult penitentiaries, you're looking at the end of the line, trying to see where a process begins. But if you really want to understand and see what's behind the prison system, you have to look at Juvenile Hall. You have to go down to Juvenile Hall. That's where I started my career, at about the age of twelve, for some charge. I don't know what it was, vandalism. I think I ripped off a bicycle, maybe two or three bicycles. Maybe I had a bicycle business, I don't remember. But it related to bicycles. They took me to Juvenile Hall, and it took me about six months to get out again. While I was there I met a lot of people. I met a lot of *real, nice, groovy* cats who were very active, very healthy people, who had stolen bicycles and things like that. Then I moved up the ladder from Juvenile Hall to Whittier Reform School for youngsters. I graduated from there with honors and went to another one a little higher, Preston School of Industries. I graduated from that one and they jumped me up to the big leagues, to the adult penitentiary system.

I noticed that every time I went back to jail, the same guys who were in Juvenile Hall with me were also there again. They arrived there soon after I got there, or a little bit before I left. They always seemed to make the scene. In the California prison system, they carry you from Juvenile Hall to the old folks' colony, down in San Luis Obispo, and wait for you to die. Then they bury you there, if you don't have anyone outside to claim your body, and most people down there don't. I noticed these waves, these generations. I had a chance to watch other generations that came behind me, and I talked with them. I'd ask them if they'd been in jail before. You will find graduating classes moving up from Juvenile Hall, all the way up. It

occurred to me that this was a social failure, one that cannot be justified by any stretch of the imagination. Not by any stretch of the imagination can the children in the Juvenile Halls be condemned, because they're innocent, and they're processed by an environment that they have no control over.

If you look at the adult prisons, you can't make head or tail out of them. By the time these men get there, they're in for murder, rape, robbery and all the high crimes. But when you look into their pasts, you find Juvenile Hall. You have to ask yourself, why is there not in this country a program for young people that will interest them? That will actively involve them and will process them to be healthy individuals and lead a healthy life. Until someone answers that question for me, the only attitude I can have towards the prison system, including Juvenile Hall, is tear those walls down and let those people out of there. That's the only question. How do we tear those walls down and let those people *out* of there?

People look at the point in the Black Panther Party program that calls for freedom for all black men and women held in federal, state, county and municipal jails. They find it hard to accept that particular point. They can relate to running the police out of the community, but they say, "Those people in those prisons committed crimes. They're convicted of crimes. How can you even talk about bringing them out? If you did get them out, would you, in the black community, take them and put them on trial and send them back again?" I don't know how to deal with that. It's just no. NO! Let them out and leave them alone! Let them out because they're hip to all of us out here now. Let them out. Turn them over to the Black Panther Party. Give them to us. We will redeem them from the promises made by the Statue of Liberty that were never fulfilled. We have a program for them that will keep them active—24 hours a day. And I don't mean eight big strong men in a big conspicuous truck robbing a jive gas station for $75.* When I sit down to conspire to commit a robbery, it's going to be the Bank of America, or Chase Manhattan Bank, or Brinks.

I'VE BEEN WORKING WITH Bobby Seale on the biography of Huey P. Newton. Bob Scheer and I took Bobby Seale down to Carmel-by-the-Sea. But we went away from the sea. We went into a little cabin, and we got a fifth of Scotch, a couple of chasers, a tape recorder and a large stack of blank tapes. We said, "Bobby, take the fifth, and talk about brother Huey P. Newton." And Bobby started talking about Huey. One of the things that just blew my mind was when he mentioned that prior to organizing the Black Panther Party, he and Huey had been planning a gigantic bank robbery. They put their minds to work on that because they recognized that they needed money for the Movement. So they sat down and started trying to put together a key to open the vault. But as they thought about it, they thought about the implications. Bobby tells how one day while they were discussing this, Huey jumped up and said, "Later for a bank. What we're talking about is politics. What we're talking about essentially is the liberation of our people. So later for one jive bank. Let's organize the brothers and put this together. Let's arm them for defense of the black community, and it will be like walking up to the White House and saying, "Stick 'em up, motherfucker. We want what's ours."

So there's a very interesting and a very key connection between insurrection and acts carried out by oneself, a private, personal civil war. We define a civil war as when a society splits down the middle and you have two opposing sides. Does that have to be the definition? Can 5000 people launch a civil war? Can 4000, 3000, two or one? Or one-half of 1000? Or half of that? Can one person? Can one person engage in civil war? I'm not a lawyer. I'm definitely not a judge, but I would say that one person acting alone could in fact be engaged in a civil war against an oppressive system. That's how I look upon those cats in those penitentiaries. I don't care what they're in for—robbery, burglary, rape, murder, kidnap, anything. A response to a situation. A response to an environment. Any social science book will tell you that if you subject people to an unpleasant environment, you can predict that they will rebel against it. That gives rise to a contradiction. When you have a social unit organized in such a way that people are moved to rebel against it in large numbers, how then do you come behind them and tell them that they owe a debt to society? I say that society owes a debt to them. And society doesn't look as though it wants to pay.

There's a young brother over at Juvenile Hall in Alameda County right now by the name of Gregory Harrison. He's about fourteen or fifteen years old and he's the leader of the Black Students Union at Oakland Tech High School. At this moment they have him over there charged with insurrection. They've charged him with insurrection because the Black Students Union on that campus wants black history added to the curriculum. They want an environment created on their campus—not one that will teach black people how to be black, but one that will remove the restraints, so that they can just be themselves, and their blackness will automatically flourish. Like you don't have to teach a rose how to turn red, or teach a tree how to grow leaves. You just leave it alone and don't pour salt on its roots, and it will be a rose, or it will be a tree.

THIS PIGGISH, CRIMINAL SYSTEM. This system that is the enemy of people. This very system that we live in and function in every day. This system that we are in and under at this very moment. *Our* system! Each and every one of your systems. If you happen to be from another country, it's still your system, because the system in your country is part of this. This system is *evil*. It is criminal; it is murderous. And it is in control. It is in power. It is arrogant. It is crazy. And it looks upon the people as its property. So much so that *cops*, who are public servants, feel justified in going onto a campus, a college campus or high school campus, and spraying mace in the faces of the people. They beat people with those clubs, and even shoot people, if it takes that to enforce the will of the likes of Ronald Reagan, Jesse Unruh, or Mussolini Alioto.

Have you ever seen Alioto on television? When you see him will you swear that he doesn't frighten you, or that he doesn't look like Al Capone? Alioto reminds me of convicts that I know in Folsom Prison. And this is not a contradiction. When I speak up for convicts, I don't say that every convict is going to come out here and join the Peace and Freedom Party. I'm not saying that. Or that he would be nice to people out here. I'm not saying that. Yet I call for the freedom of even those who are so alienated from society that they hate everybody. Cats who tattoo on their chest, "Born to Hate," "Born to Lose." I know a cat who tattooed across his forehead, "Born to Kill." He needs to be released also. Because whereas Lyndon B. Johnson doesn't have any tattoos on his head, he has blood dripping from his fingers. LBJ has killed more people than any man who has ever been in any prison in the United States of America from the beginning of it to the end. He has murdered. And people like prison officials, policemen, mayors, chiefs of police, they endorse it. They even call for escalation, meaning, kill more people. I don't want it. The people who are here tonight, because I see so many faces that I recognize, I could say that I know you don't want it either. There's only one way that we're going to get rid of it. That's by standing up and drawing a firm line, a distinct and firm line, and standing on our side of the line, and defending that line by whatever means necessary, including laying down our lives. Not in sacrifice, but by taking pigs with us. Taking pigs with us.

I cannot relate to spending the next four years in the penitentiary, not with madmen with supreme power in their hands. Not with Ronald Reagan the head of the Department of Corrections, as he is the head of every other state agency. Not with Dirty Red being the warden. If they made Dr. Shapiro [San Francisco psychiatrist and long-time supporter of the Panthers] the warden of San Quentin, I'd go right now. But while they have sadistic fiends, mean men, cruel men, in control of that apparatus, I say that my interest is elsewhere. My heart is out here with the people who are trying to improve our environment.

You're even a bigger fool than I know you are if you could go through all of these abstract and ridiculous charges, all of these overt political maneuvers, and think that I'm going to relate to that. Talk all this shit that you want to, issue all the orders that you want to issue. I'm charged with a crime in Alameda County and I'm anxious to go to trial because we can deal with it. We're going to tell the truth, and the pigs are going to have to tell lies and that's hard for them to do, especially when we have with us technicians such as the Honorable Charles R. Garry [Huey Newton's attorney]. I'm not afraid to walk into any courtroom in this land with a lawyer like Garry, because he can deal with the judge and the prosecutor. But don't you come up to me telling me that you're going to revoke my parole on a charge for which I put in nine years behind the walls, and for which I was supposed to receive my discharge next month. Don't you come up to me talking that shit because I don't want to hear it.

* Two days earlier, eight Panthers had been arrested following a gas station robbery in San Francisco. Charges against five of them have since been dropped.

WILDCAT!

Articles written by Jon Schwartz

Strike Mahwah

Wildcatting black auto workers shut down a Ford assembly plant in Mahwah, New Jersey, for five days last month. The black revolt in the auto industry, well established in Detroit, has come to New Jersey.

On April 25 – 29 the United Black Brothers of Mahwah, with over 800 active supporters, completely shut down the 80% black night shift, and severely hurt the predominantly white older day shift. They struck against continued speed-ups, racism, and lay-offs. From the beginning, the UBB requested and got support from both SDS and the Black Panthers.

The UBB strength reflects the racist conditions of the plant. Blacks work the night shift and the body shops – – the roughest work on both shifts. The group was organized by night shift workers in the fall.

On April 23, the growing tensions in the plant came to a head. A newly hired UBB member went into the body shop to find out where he was to work that night. He got chewed out by supervisor Ray Eskew. When the worker protested, Eskew shouted, "Get out of here, you're fired, you black motherfucker."

As usual when faced with racist supervisors, the UAW local did nothing. This time the UBB did. At a mass meeting called that day, they formulated four demands:

1) Removal of Ray Eskew.

2) Removal or transfer of supervisors with records of repeated acts of discrimination and abuse of workers.

3) Reinstatement of workers who were provoked into action and then fired by their supervisors.

4) An end to kangaroo court tactics used by the company with the union's approval to fire UBB members.

While this incident provoked the UBB into action, the real cause of their militancy lies in the basic working conditions of the plant. Ford has been attempting to get more production by speeding up the line past the limit of 56 cars an hour up to 62 cars when they can get away with it. Those men who cannot keep up with the inhuman pace are fired and harassment by management is continuous.

Cheaper by the Dozen

The UBB leaflet said "You know what's been going on. The company's been laying off men by the dozens, but the lines have not slowed up one bit. You have been given more work and if you can't do it, you lose your job or get time off. The supervisors are harassing the men and calling them all kinds of names such as 'dirty guinea bastard' and 'black son of a bitch' and 'stinking spic,' to name a few."

At rallies, Mark Rudd of SDS and Jimmy York of the New Jersey Panthers joined UBB speakers. Over a hundred students swelled picket lines. The UBB was able to use such tactics as a stall-in in the parking lot while the shifts were changing.

The Local Opposes

To their original four demands, the UBB add the demand that they be recognized as an independent bargaining unit. From the beginning the UBB walkout was opposed by the union local. While this particular local is known for its independence from the Reuther machine, and has a black president, union officials urged men to return to work and completely ignored the justness of the UBB demands.

The union was joined in its efforts by the management, which was sending out five-day quit notices which told workers that if they missed any more work they would automatically be fired. By May 5, as a result of these efforts, and some confusion inside the UBB, all but a hard core of several hundred black workers returned to work. The company has spread rumors that if the work stoppage ended they would bargain with the UBB and that they had fired Eskew. Neither was true. Eskew has apparently been given a two-week vacation, while seven UBB workers have been fired.

Hassling Chrysler

Detroit – – An eight-day wildcat over safety conditions at the Chrysler's Sterling Stamping plant idled 35,000 workers here. The strike brought a sizeable number of white workers into the fight, which was already being carried on by the Dodge Revolutionary Union Movement and other black groups, against Chrysler and the United Auto Workers' leadership.

On wednesday, April 2, workers were ordered to clear out 12 feet of scrap metal which had piled up because the conveyor belt carrying it away from the presses had broken down. This had happened before and was a source of resentment among the workers, since the contract provided that scrap could not accumulate above 6 inches; the company ignored this rule, kept the lines running and took men off the line to do a dangerous job outside of their classification, while those left on the line had to do the work of the missing men.

Local union officials told workers they weren't required to clear the metal and were promptly fired by Chrysler. As they left the plant, they told other workers what had happened and the plant walked out rather than continue without union representation.

That night, scabs driving through the picket lines were attacked and cars smashed. Thirty-four workers were arrested. After that, except for a few small incidents, the picket lines remained firm. Teamsters who deliver parts to and from Chrysler plants in the Detroit area refused to cross the picket lines. The strike of 3,500 at Sterling soon had 35,000 workers out.

Why The Auto Industry?

It is no accident that the recent dramatic developments in the labor movement have occurred in the auto industry. From the sit-down strikes in the 1930's to these wildcats at Sterling Stamping and Mahwah Ford, the militancy and imagination of the auto workers have set the pace for the labor movement.

What is it about the auto industry that generates so much rank and file militancy? The answer lies in the size of the industry, in the kind of production line necessary, and in the importance of the industry to the national economy.

The size of the industry and the importance of automotive equipment for the transportation of people and goods, assured that it was one of the prime targets for labor organization, and that some of the most skilled organizers took on the task of building the auto workers union in the thirties. Once organized, the union had considerable leverage because of its strategic position. These factors have helped to give the auto union a long, and at least in their first decade, a militant tradition.

But the fact which continues to generate the need for militant action is the nature of the production process itself. The size of the product, and the fact that it is a compilation of many separate parts, means that it must be produced on a motor-driven assembly line. The output of any plant, and thus the profits of its owners, is thus directly related to the speed of the belt, and thus to the speed with which individual workers can be made to perform their specific jobs.

Industries which produce a continuous stream (rooling mills or oil refineries) employ workers to monitor and adjust machines rather than to perform tasks directly. Speeding up the work of individual members does not speed up the flow of products. Speeding up the *process* does not have so immediate an impact on those who monitor, and there are relatively fewer of them. These industries, as well as batch industries

This did not make Chrysler too unhappy since the company has a surplus of cars. If the corporation had laid off its workers due to low sales, the longer service employees would have gotten 85 – 95% of their base pay. With a strike, the workers got nothing, and probably saved Chrysler money.

It should be clear that these militants were not radicals. They were pissed off at the arrogance of management, poor working conditions and continual mistreatment. They were angry at the UAW International for not supporting their actions. They supported their local officers and most sought to build a strong union.

Monday morning, five days after the strike began, the UAW called the local leaders to its headquarters and demanded that they order the workers back to work. Not satisfied with their response, the UAW put the local into receivership and Douglas Fraser, head of

the union's Chrysler division, ordered the workers back.

Lacking rank and file leadership, discouraged by the meeting, they returned to the plant. Fraser denounced the presence of "outside agitators" at the wildcat, referring to students from Wayne State and the University of Detroit. Workers booed him down and shouted back, "The students helped us more than the international.

On the other hand, the workers continually emphasized their distinction from the students. They were unswayed by the rhetoric of the student movement. They knew that the union was selling them out, and that Chrysler screws them, but they asked, "what can you do about it?" Their willingness to become radicals rests on the ability of the movement to provide real alternatives on the issues which concern them.

OLD MOLE
5/9/69

THE LEAGUE OF REVOLUTIONARY BLACK WORKERS

Editors' Note: John Watson, editor of the Wayne State University South End, has been involved in Detroit revolutionary politics for a number of years. Former editor of the black community newspaper, The Inner City Voice, Watson was one of the original founders of the League of Revolutionary Black Workers. He is currently serving as a member of the Central Committee of the League.

Fifth Estate: What is the history of the League of Revolutionary Black Workers? Why was it formed?
John Watson: The League of Revolutionary Black Workers is a federation of several revolutionary union movements that exist in Detroit. It was originally formed to provide a broader base for the organization of black workers into revolutionary organizations than was previously provided for when we were organizing on a plant to plant basis.

The beginning of the League goes back to the beginning of DRUM which was its first organization. The Dodge Revolutionary Union Movement was formed at the Hamtramck Assembly Plant of the Chrysler Corporation in the fall of 1967. It developed out of the caucuses of black workers which had formed in the automobile plants to fight increases in productivity and racism in the plant.

All the caucuses which had developed previous to DRUM had been co-opted, either by the company or by the union. In other words the company had either fired the leadership of these caucuses or bought them off by giving them jobs as foremen or supervisors, or the union had managed to buy off the leadership one way or another.

The organization of DRUM was in direct response to numerous attempts by black workers over the last several years in the Hamtramck Assembly Plant to organize a movement which could resist racism and oppression both on the part of the union and the company. We wanted to be a revolutionary organization which would not be co-opted by the moneyed forces.

Briefly, the history of DRUM began with a series of wild-cat strikes which we held around the issues of productivity, production standards and overt racism. The first strike was held when Chrysler Corporation

speeded up the production line six cars an hour, during the UAW Convention last May.

After this strike in which both black and white workers participated, the company imposed disciplinary action on those who they considered to be leaders of the strike action. This disciplinary action was taken primarily upon black workers. A number of black workers were fired, and quite a few received suspensions from anywhere from three to thirty days. In response to the racist attack which the company laid upon black workers after the first strike, DRUM organized a number of other strikes at that particular plant.

With the development of DRUM and the successes which we had in terms of organizing and mobilizing the workers at the Hamtramck Assembly Plant, many other black workers throughout the city began to come to us and ask for aid in organizing some sort of group in their plants. As a result shortly after the formation of DRUM, the Eldon Axle Revolutionary Movement (ELRUM) was born at Eldon Gear and Axle Plant of the Chrysler Corporation. Also, the Ford Revolutionary Union Movement (FRUM) was formed at the Ford Rouge Complex, and we now have two plants organized within that complex.

Since that time the organizational activities have been expanding. We've moved into hospital industries with the HOWRUM, NEWRUM for the newspapers in Detroit, an UPRUM which stands for United Parcel Revolutionary Union Movement for black Teamsters who work at United Parcel. There's a JARUM which is Jefferson Assembly Revolutionary Union Movement and there's the development of a CRUM, which is Chevrolet Revolutionary Union Movement. Other automobile plants and other industries are in the process of being organized now.

PLANT CONDITIONS

FE: What types of conditions exist in the plants that are being organized by the League?
JW: Working conditions are deplorable. What's been happening over the last fifteen or twenty years in industry in general, but especially in the auto industry is the increase in productivity. A lot of people describe the increase in productivity as meaning that there's automation or something like this going on. But in

most of the automobile plants, what's been going on is "nigger-mation."

"Nigger-mation" is simply when you hire one black man to do the job which is previously done by two or three or four white men. There's a constant struggle which is going on inside the automobile plants in which the foreman and the general foreman and the supervisor are constantly attempting to work the men harder. They are constantly attempting to speed up the production line. They are constantly attempting to cut down the number of people who work on the lines.

In their insatiable drive to make greater profits for the company, they have negated all considerations of the welfare and safety of the workers in the plant, especially the black workers. As a result, in the foundries for instance almost 95% of the workers in those plants have some sort of industrial illness, usually silicosis or some sort of other lung disease. In the stamping plants all kinds of guys are walking around with two or three fingers missing from one of their hands because of the unsafe machinery.

People are regularly killed in the automobile plants in a wide variety of different kinds of industrial accidents which take place there. The air is foul, it's hot, the noise level is extremely high, the environment is almost intolerable and it gets worse every day because of the constantly increasing production standards of the company.

Besides the problems that black workers have with productivity and safety standards, they have the added problem of overt racism, which exists under these monopoly capitalist corporations. In the first place most of the supervisory personnel, white-collar personnel, skilled trades are all white. It's almost impossible for the average brother who gets a job in an automobile factory to be able to move into one of these positions.

Besides that those white foremen generally have very degrading attitudes towards black people. Every day there are instances in which there are clashes between black workers and white foremen because of racist remarks or racist actions on the part of company representatives.

The racism of the company presents itself not only in the form of verbal abuse and in the form of various kinds of disciplinary action which are laid on the heads of black workers, but also on the very basic level of the allocation of jobs. In almost all plants you find the black workers on the hardest jobs in which you have the heaviest work and in which you have to work the fastest and in which the conditions are most unsafe, whereas you find white people with less seniority are generally employed at lighter jobs which don't have the same sort of safety hazards which the black workers must face. Moreover, white workers are not subjected to the kind of racist insults and harassment that black workers constantly find themselves subjected to.

FE: How do you organize the plants you are working in? What kinds of things do you find necessary for organizing a plant?

JW: Black revolutionaries in Detroit have a Marxist-Leninist position and have recognized the necessity of organizing in the working class for a number of years now. We had made attempts a number of times to begin to move in the direction of mobilizing the black working class; but up until this point those attempts had been pretty futile, although they had given us a lot of experience into the things that are necessary to successfully organize.

OUTSIDE SUPPORT

One of the things that we find is that it is absolu-
tely essential that the workers have some sort of support from outside of the factory. When we carry out strikes at any of the plants, we usually have a large number of people come down from the community to man the picket lines. They often bring drums, huge congo drums. This helps to raise the morale of the workers in those actions.

Anyone who works in a plant who participates in a wild-cat strike can be fired, if the company can prove that he actually participated in it. So by having people from the community man the picket lines we can begin to avoid the problem of having large numbers of members losing their jobs and livlihoods.

We find that the basic things that are necessary in terms of organizing a plant are, first of all, a clear understanding of the needs of the workers and the kinds of problems which they are facing in the plant; second, an ability to articulate those needs and to set forth demands which can begin to solve those problems and third, the establishing of a mechanism, an organizational structure which can effectively mobilize the workers to resist the pressures of the company and the union. This organizational mechanism generally requires that we produce a publication for the plant.

This publication is an organizing tool in and of itself in that workers themselves begin to write for the publication and distribute it in the plant. Through recruiting reporters and through distribution of the publication, we develop a network of communication throughout the plant, throughout the department.

The production of the publication is fundamentally different from producing a single leaflet which you pass out once or twice at a factory. It takes eight, ten, or twelve weeks, for instance of consistently producing a newsletter and having it passed out within the factory before the workers can really understand that the people who are behind this organization are dead serious about it. The workers have had a lot of experience with people who come into a plant for one-shot deals, people who come in and run down a whole lot of radical business. But they are really concerned with people who are going to be consistent and who are going to be persistent, who they can depend on. When they see that the DRUM publication is at the gates being passed out every Tuesday on the nose without deviation they begin to recognize that this is a very serious organization which they're dealing with.

The production of the publications, the publication of the various documents which are needed, for instance, the constitution for the group, demand organizational skills which don't exist among the workers. A wide variety of tasks which have to be done are generally done by people who are outside the factory.

It is also essential to understand that the cats working in an automobile plant killing themselves for ten hours a day, working six and sometimes seven days a week, are generally too tired to do all the work which is necessary to tie together membership meetings, produce publications, get in contact with community groups for support, raise funds and so on and so forth. Therefore, it is necessary to have some group of supporters outside the factory who can carry out all these services to the workers.

In terms of providing this support, providing the print shops, printing facilities, community support, raising money, the League is very important because through the League, workers in a number of plants throughout the city can combine their resources together so that they can be serviced by the same administrative staff. This prevents duplication of a

lot of activities which would be necessary if we didn't have this kind of broad federation.

FACTORY ORIENTED ORGANIZING

FE: What are the differences between a community-oriented and a factory-oriented type of organizing?
JW: We have a certain program, a certain understanding of the dynamics of American capitalist society and we're acting on the results of our analysis. This doesn't mean that we're against those people who are involved in community organization. Our analysis tells us that the basic power of black people lies at the point of production, that the basic power we have is the power as workers.

As workers, as black workers, we have historically been and are now an essential element in the American economic sense. Without black slaves to pick the cotton on the Southern plantations, the primitive accumulation of capital which was necessary to develop industry in both Europe and America would never have been accomplished. Without black workers slaving on the assembly lines in automobile plants in the city of Detroit, the automobile companies would not be able to produce cars in the first place, and therefore, wouldn't be able to make-the tremendous profits which they have been making.

Therefore, we feel that the best way to organize black people into a powerful unit is to organize them in the factories in which they are working. We feel that black workers, especially, have the power to completely close down the American economic system. In order to implement that power, we have to become organized.

In one factory you have 10,000 people who are faced with the same brutal conditions under the same system from the same bastards every day, eight hours a day, ten hours a day, six or seven days a week. When you go out into the community, the interests of the people, let's say in a particular neighborhood, more than likely are going to be much more greatly dispersed than the interests of the workers are. That is, people have different landlords, they are exploited by a number of different shop-keepers, they are faced with a number of different kinds of problems throughout the community, and they don't represent the same sort of homologous mass as 10,000 people in a factory do. Therefore, just in terms of expediency there are greater possibilities in the organization of the plant.

And when you consider even farther than that, when you do organize significant sectors of the community, the kinds of actions which can be taken are not as effectively damaging to the ruling class as the kinds of actions which can be taken in the plant. For instance, when you close down Hamtramck Assembly Plant, you do a number of things automatically. If you close it down for a day you cost Chrysler Corporation 1,000 cars. That, considered in relationship to their investment, means the loss of a sizeable sum of money.

Also, when you close down a large automobile plant, you automatically can mobilize the people in the streets, 5,000 or 10,000 people at a single blow. Whereas when you attempt to organize the community especially if you go from house to house or block to block, it is much more difficult to gather together that many of the people at the same time.

Finally, we feel that in conjunction with the organization of workers in plants you automatically have the development of community organization and community support. After all, workers are not people who live in factories 24 hours a day. They all go home and live somewhere in the community. We have found that it's almost an inevitable and simultaneous development that as factory workers begin to get organized, support elements within the community are also organized. We feel that it is necessary to have broad community support in order to be able to effectively organize within the plant and effectively close down significant sectors of the economy.

Therefore, we have an overall analysis which sees the point of production as the major and primary sector of the society which has to be organized and that the community should be organized in conjunction with that development. This is probably different from these kinds of analysis which say where it's at is to go out and organize the community and to organize the so-called "brother on the street." It's not that we're opposed to this type of organization; but without a more solid base such as the working class represents, this type of organization, that is, community-based organization, is generally a pretty long and stretched out and futile development.

BLACK MOVEMENT & WHITE WORKERS

FE: What generally has been the relationship between the black union movement and white workers? For example, recently out at the Chrysler Sterling Stamping Plant there was a wild-cat strike, led mainly by white workers, who called on the League of Revolutionary Black Workers to come out and help them with their organizing. Is this kind of thing happening more frequently?
JW: This kind of support between black and white workers in militant actions is in its beginning stages of development now. Our position vis a vis white workers has been distorted by the ruling class, the UAW and by various white radical organizations which are opposed to us for some reason or other.

Basically, we have organized an all black revolutionary union movement, the League of Revolutionary Black Workers, because of the fact of racism existing in American society, because of the fact that the working class is already divided between the races, and because it is necessary for black workers to be able to act independently of white workers. We have learned historically that in too many instances white workers have been willing to sell us out because of their own racist misunderstandings of the dynamics of struggle.

Since the beginning we've had relationships with white workers at the plants that we've organized. For instance, at the Hamtramck Assembly Plant there has been the formation of an organization among white workers which hopes to begin to organize them to struggle against the company and against the union in regards to their own interests, and to support the development of organizations like the League of Revolutionary Black Workers.

We have found that among older white radicals and older union activists, even though we're carrying on positive struggle against capitalism, these people tend to be opposed to us because of purely academic arguments. They got all kinds of theoretical ideas about how we're splitting up the working class between black and white, when actually they know damn well that the working class has been split between black and white a hell of a long time because of conditions which I alluded to before. They have been doing very little to eliminate any of these conditions. Part of the problem is that white radicals tend to think that they have the sole solution to the problems involving all humanity. As a result of this, they become extremely dogmatic and incapable of working out any kind of alliance or coalition with other organizations.

In recent history, however, there have been some positive developments along the lines of the League being able to move into coalitions with groups of white workers. For instance, at the Detroit News there has been the development of an organization known as the News Revolutionary Union Movement (NEWRUM) among black workers. And this organization has attempted since its very inception to encourage the development of militant revolutionary organizations among the white workers at the plant.

Unfortunately, we ran into some problems there in that we found that although a number of the white guys who were down there had risen above the levels of racism and understood the exploitative nature of the company and the exploitative nature of the system, they had very little experience in organizing to fight oppression and exploitation. As a result of their lack of experience, the white workers' organization has been moving at a very slow pace. It seems to be necessary that the leadership of the League begin to provide some sort of theoretical or practical guidance to those whites who are attempting to move to organize in this particular situation.

In other plants such as the Sterling Plant, for the first time militant whites have called for us to support their action. Our position on this is that we of course, support any progressive action on the part of any workers, white or black, who are moving to resolutely confront this racist capitalist system.

I think that there's going to have to be an awful lot of discussion over the next few months over the relationship between the League of Revolutionary Black Workers and the various white organizations which are beginning to organize among white workers. The National Organizing Committee (NOC) has begun to implement a very positive program in this city among the white working class, and all indications are that it is going to be a fairly successful effort. Our relationship with that organization at this time, although unofficial, is very good in that both of us understand the positions which we're coming from and we both understand who the enemy is and what the nature of the enemy is. Therefore, we're not attempting to dominate one another; we're attempting to begin to coordinate our activity for a more solid attack.

I think the black people who are involved in the organization of the black working class should recognize that the theoretical conception of black people being the vanguard of revolutionary struggle is not just a conception which is meant to be laid in the clouds somewhere above everyone's head. It can be applied in a very practical and programmatic fashion. What it simply means is that as political beings we have to understand that the development of the white movement has been retarded, that it has not developed as rapidly as the black movement has had to develop, that it doesn't have the kind of experience of struggle that we have had.

Therefore, even though many of these white radical organizations have resources in terms of money and manpower which far exceed ours, because of their lack of experience most of them are unable to put these resources to work in a positive fashion at this particular time. As political animals, we have to realize that it is necessary for us to provide them with the kind of leadership which they lack at this moment and to begin to do all that we can to help them develop that leadership to the point where it can be self sufficient.

LONG RANGE PERSPECTIVE

FE: In terms of a long range perspective, has your experience with League organizing given you some insight or ideas into where the general revolutionary process is moving in this country and the kinds of things that it will ultimately culminate in?

JW: We have some definite conceptions of how the revolution is going to be accomplished in this country. In the first place we're organizing in automobile plants on the basis of the local struggles which black workers are faced with in the industries in which they are working. But we find that any time we carry out a strike at a particular plant the company doesn't simply rely on the resources which it has at that particular plant to suppress our strike but moves to bring in outside police, moves to bring in the courts, moves to use the mass media, moves to use a number of resources which are available to the ruling class to suppress the struggle. Therefore, at a particular plant sometimes we find that in the struggle against the company the workers are overwhelmed by the amount of strength which the company can bring to bear against us.

If you consider this in a theoretical sense it's no different from the kinds of struggles which are taking place on an international level where American imperialism is allowed to concentrate superior forces in a small area of the world in order to suppress a liberation movement. For instance, look at the struggle which went down in Santo Domingo. Che Guevara has told us that the response to this kind of tactic of the ruling class is to spread their forces thin throughout the world by the opening up of "two, three, many Vietnams," so that each local guerilla movement can deal more effectively with their local situation.

You can relate this to the situation as it exists in this country. We have found that in the future when a particular plant goes down and the ruling class brings in the police and courts and all the rest of that stuff, we're going to have to respond in some sort of fashion in which we can bring equal force against of being able to have national general strike.

If a national general strike reaches the point of absolute confrontation between us and the system and if the ruling class refuses to capitulate to the demands which we lay on it, it would probably resort to the type of tactics which were used to suppress the unorganized general strike which was held in July of 1967 in Detroit. That is, it would probably try to garrison off the community and starve us out.

A revolutionary organization and revolutionary leaders simply cannot tolerate the starvation of our community and facing that kind of position we would have no choice but to call for the workers to go back into the factories and assume control of the means of production and distribution in order to feed ourselves and feed the community.

Assuming control of the means of production essentially means that you are at the first stage of assuming state power. It is from the escalation of this type of struggle and from the reaction of the ruling class to it that we see the development of an overall revolutionary movement which will forever overthrow capitalism and imperialism and racism.

FE: In the context of this long-range perspective where is the League generally going in the short-run? Is it going to be confined to a local level or are plans now being made for national expansion?

JW: At the moment we are tightening up the organization on the local level and expanding to new plants and new memberships on a local level. Our interim medium-range plans are of course to begin to expand outside of this immediate geographic area to organize black workers wherever they might exist.

Our ultimate intention is to organize black workers as a whole, as a class throughout the country and proceeding from that basic mass organization to extend a revolutionary black organization throughout the black community.

The Fifth Estate, Detroit, reprinted in *The Movement* June 1969

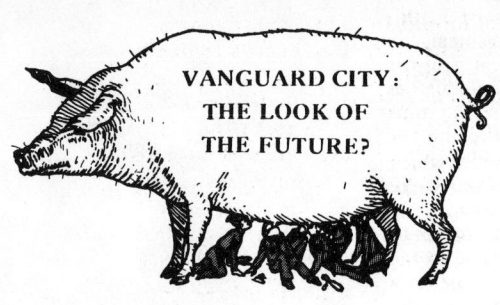

VANGUARD CITY: THE LOOK OF THE FUTURE?

WILMINGTON, DELAWARE — Background Information

On April 9, 1968 the full 4,000 man Delaware Army and Air National Guard was ordered into Wilmington, Delaware by Governor Charles Terry (Dem) in response to the request of Mayor John Babiarz (Dem) for 500 men. The request came in response to a relatively minor civil disorder following the assassination of Dr. Martin Luther King, Jr., in which there were no deaths and less than $250,000 property damage.

Today, nearly ten months later, a contingent of Guard troops still patrols the Black sections of the city every night. Armed with M-1 carbines, they travel in convoys consisting of three jeeps and a Delaware State Trooper car. On April 30, one of them shot and killed Douglas Henry, Jr., who was in police custody at the time. The response was the passage of a state law stating: "Any individual called to state duty by the Governor. . .shall not be liable civilly or criminally for any act done by him in the line of duty."

In addition to the Guard patrols, the black community of Wilmington has also been subjected to a concentrated, systematic and largely successful effort to destroy black militant leadership and organization. The Guard has served as a smokescreen for the fact that at least 150 black people, affiliated with local organizations, particularly the Wilmington Youth Emergency Action Council (WYEAC), have been arrested since last April 21. More than 30 men, women and juveniles are presently in jail unable to meet the costs of excessive bond.

Behind all of the issues in Wilmington, whose 90,000 population is 40% black, is the question of institutional and corporate racism. Delaware is now and always has been controlled by the duPont family. It is a "vanguard" city not only because of the sustained and baseless military presence, but also because of duPont's early involvement in the ghetto. The present situation is the culmination of ghetto intervention which began considerably before other giant corporations found it necessary and fashionable to do so.

The governor-elect, Russell Peterson, who will take office January 21, is a Republican and for the last ten years has been a duPont employee. During the election campaign he supported the Guard and since his victory has adamantly refused to oppose its presence or say what he will do when he takes office. The mayor-elect, multi-millionaire Harry Haskell is also a Republican with ties to duPont, and also supports the Guard.

The atmosphere of repression in Wilmington extends beyond the Guard and to suppression of white dissent as well. In October, $200,000 was appropriated by the city and state for "monitors" who now patrol the corridors and classrooms of the city's high schools. Local white protest against the War in Vietnam last spring was met with instant arrest and conviction; three whites protesting the Guard patrols in downtown Wilmington over the Christmas Holidays were also immediately arrested and the only two dissident faculty members at the University of Delaware have recently been fired.

But perhaps most disturbing is the fact that the police state in Wilmington has gone virtually unchallenged for ten months by outside groups and most Delawarians. There has been no legal opposition to the "authority" under which the Guard remains on duty. Nor has there been any defense for blacks arrested for political reasons. Wilmington's story was neglected completely by the mass media until September, five months after the appearance of the Guard. Since then, scattered stories in national publications have aroused little or no response. But then, it can't happen here.

A leaflet distributed by People Against Racism, Detroit

FROM MALCOLM X TO FRANZ FANON

The store is well kept, extremely clean. It explodes in the grayness of the South Side, which is emphasized by the nearby Elevated. The windows are impeccable, without a trace of dirt, which is unusual. The clients -- the brothers and sisters -- are numerous: intellectuals, of course, but also young people, boys and girls, neighborhood housewives, men in working blue whom one could more easily imagine leaning on the nearby bar or watching a game of billiards next door. If few make purchases, all leaf through the works on display: from The Autobiography of Malcolm X to Wretched of the Earth by Franz Fanon; from the novels of Langston Hughes to the classics of Afro-American history. In the center of the room, several copies of the first book by Stokely Carmichael (which had just come out) the cover of which bears in black letters on a white background the inscription: "Black Power". To one side, there are several issues of the Peking Review, examples of the underground press, those pacifist or revolutionary newspapers which the Vietnamese war has caused to flower.

Ellis' bookstore does not constitute the center of the ghetto any more than Afro-American bookstores in Detroit, Cleveland or New York, where they are springing up. Nonetheless, it is one of the four or five permanent and discreet meeting places of a new generation of leaders and militant nationalists: teachers, college students, representatives of neighborhood organizations, whether recognized or clandestine, members of gangs who have found a new reason to fight a society in which they have no hope of some day participating. Not all the black leaders of Chicago call themselves nationalists: many of them will always want cooperation with liberal whites, whether out of a deep conviction or because their careers depend on it. But very few permit themselves to publicly criticize the nationalists. As one of them said to me, "The climate favors nationalists." One should doubtless interpret: "The masses favor them." In fact, these are the only leaders to whom the masses will still listen in a time of overt crisis.

Ellis' bookstore and its clients are only the indication of a much vaster movement. The other indications? The wall of pride, of disdain or defiance against which any white who ventures into the ghetto hurls himself; the modest museum of Afro-American history created several years ago by Charles and Margaret Burroughs, where increasing numbers of black teachers bring their pupils; the group of young black intellectuals whom I found one night in the halls of the museum in the middle of working on an Afro-American anthology; the fact that Ebony magazine, spokesman for the "respectable" black middle class, has reversed its policy by devoting a long study to the advantages of wearing a "natural" hairstyle and has published pages of ads vaunting the merits of such and such a product designed to re-kink hair. The wall of pride is also the increasing numbers of proud young women draped in flowing African robes, great golden rings in their ears; the young students of a school in the city going on strike and setting in motion the beginning of a riot in five degrees below zero weather to protest the transfer of one of their teachers who was accused of extremism by school authorities for having given too much place in his course to Afro=American history; these new comic strips proposing new heroes to black children; even the posters designed by Rev. King which are found displayed in the offices of even the most conservative black organizations, proclaiming in defiance: "Black is beautiful". Also, in Chicago, what the inhabitants of the ghetto call today the "wall of respect": the immense facade of a building in the heart of the South Side which was transformed by local painters into a long fresco where all the "heroes" of the community are represented, from Malcolm X to DuBois, the theoretician of Pan-Africanism; from Charlie Parker to Muhammed Ali, alias Cassius Clay; from Marcus Garvey, the apostle of a return to Africa in the 20's, to Stokely Carmichael, not to mention the incendiary Rap Brown.

A MOVEMENT OR A STYLE?

Does this represent a mass movement, a movement of intellectuals, or of a passing "style"? It is without any doubt much more than a style, much more than an intellectual movement, for many intellectuals are following rather than preceding the movement. A mass movement, then? It is still too early to answer. But one thing is certain: In one month spent in the ghettoes of several American cities, I did not find among the blacks a single leader, a single militant, anyone with whom I talked even briefly, who laughed, or smiled at this new "renaissance" which is no longer restricted, as it was in the Thirties, to the artistic circles of Harlem. Two years ago, traditional leaders like Mr. Roy Wilkins of the NAACP enjoyed making ironic comments. Today, some may express their doubts, or remark that the aspirations of the ghetto are still the aspirations of the middle class and not of Afro-American revolutionaries; others can criticize, say there are the seeds of a black racism, of a new segregation. But nobody takes the new state of mind lightly, which even the most moderate cannot escape: "thinking black", the fact of thinking Black, of feeling Black. A young black minister of Chicago, who could never be accused of extremism, summed up his "conversion: to "thinking black" this way: "It was during the Detroit riots, at the end of July, the evening when they sent in the paratroopers. When I went to bed, I was a Negro. But it was a Black man who woke up."

The passionate and erratic nature of the movement does not escape the most lucid observers. But, they say, it is not so much a matter of forging links (which are too restrictive and finally artificial) with Africa, as it is of finally making the black man see himself, his reality, and not the degrading and humiliating picture of him reflected by white society. Slavery, they add, is a reality: it makes up part of the past of the black man, and the black man will no more escape it than he will escape the ghetto. He must not seek to flee this past by dreaming of an impossible integration, but stop his flight and face up to what he has been -- to what whites have made of him. Up to now, white society, by its conventions, by its schoolbooks, by its mores, has set itself to convince the black man that slavery and then segregation were the direct result of his intrinsic inferiority. That is how the lie has been perpetrated: not content to conjure away the slave revolts, whites refuse to see in slavery the product of a very definite historical situation, and in segregation, institutions seeking to perpetuate slavery. Rather than being ashamed of his past and vainly trying to ignore it, the black man must draw lessons from it, and generate a new moral force which whites have always sought to destroy. In the same way, rather than being ashamed of his ghetto, the black man must learn to think of it as his nation, a nation which he must control, a nation which must be restored by gaining independence.

THE FAILURE OF INTEGRATION

What gives its importance to this black "nationalism" is the fact on which it rests: the defeat of integration, such as it has been presented in the United States for about fifteen years. Suddenly, after four years of riots, white and black liberals are asking themselves with anguish: have they been dreaming? have they confused a simple act of faith with a program of action?

At the end of the Fifties, optimism was still de rigeur: integration -- which nobody had thought of defining, however -- was "just around the corner". Slavery, and after it segregation, were only bad accidents in American history. The institutions of the country were not at stake: on the contrary, they were going to permit justice to triumph. From this perspective, the judges of the Supreme Court had truly given a mortal blow to the sacrosanct principle of segregation -- "separate but equal" -- in declaring the unconstitutionality of segregation in public schools in 1954.

To remind a young black militant of that historic decision is today to invite sarcasm. "Progress? You're kidding," one said to me. "That decision concerned only the South, where it was a failure anyway. But in the North? It doesn't have the power to change anything, segregation in the schools here is not the result of an openly racist act that you could have condemned by a court of law, it is the result of a whole system that's subtly racist, of a collective behavior on the part of whites. Besides, the situation has only gotten worse: for example, in Chicago the percentage of black students in the public schools was 47% three years ago: this year it reached 52%, and it is estimated at 60% in 1972; in Philadelphia it's already 62%: in New York, in Manhattan it's over 70%: it is even higher in Washington. No, believe me, integration was never conceived for the black masses but for a minority of blacks who represented nothing and who have moreover always refused to identify with the residents of the ghettos. Integration is a trick: a transitory moment when a white neighborhood bordering on a black neighborhood is in the process of becoming black. To speak of integration to a society which knows itself today to be the victim of a racist system, which knows that to be black means having eight chances out of ten of never escaping the ghetto, only one chance out of three of finding work, has no meaning!"

From "Chicago and Black Power" by Jacques Amabric Le Monde, Paris Feb 1968

PANTHERS IN BABYLON
the law book and the gun

L.A. Panthers seized during pig attack, Dec. 1969.

[EDITOR'S NOTE]

THE BLACK PANTHERS HAVE SPRUNG FROM their Oakland, California, base to assume the dimensions of a major black radical movement, and now they are being "covered" extensively by the media. They are good copy, as was SNCC before them, and there is no lack of "news" about their current confrontations with established power. But for all this exposure, the Panthers are treated as nothing more than a bizarre happening in violence—not as a movement which poses a serious alternative to the power of white America.

This is the obtuse and contemptuous notoriety with which America likes to neutralize the experience of a threat. But the Panther movement does not lend itself easily to co-option. The American establishment can no more absorb the Panther than comprehend him, for the Panthers are reacting to a ghetto milieu whose existence white America continues to deny. So the television networks offer up their version of the Panther movement in order to convince us that it is simply an exercise in mindless freak theater—entertaining, provocative, insignificant —and that the Panthers' confrontation with society is a momentary spectacle, isolated from history.

Black power defined in this way—as transitory, though recurrent, moments of violence—is a concept that white America is able to study ad nauseam and perhaps even sympathize with. But black *revolution*—the statement of an alternative system of values, the move to acquire power to assert those values, and the express willingness to respond with revolutionary violence to the violence inherent in established power— is another matter. The Panthers have run this division down and they have acted on the basis of it, and that is why they are now the focal point of repression.

Society does not offer the Panthers anti-poverty programs; rather it has moved to obliterate the movement. The Panthers have not only upped the ante on SNCC's opening gambit, they

lack the protective associations that SNCC had by virtue of its very name and its origins in that "good" civil rights movement of nonviolence and integration whose memory is now part of white America's mawkish nostalgia. There is no such comforting familiarity in the origins of the Black Panthers; they have come to us raw, permitting us no illusions.

However disquieting it may be to the media, the Panthers do have a history, and one must study it to understand what is authentic and powerful about this movement. The pages that follow form the initial sketches of a Black Panther Party history, centering necessarily on the development of the prime mover: Huey P. Newton, the Minister of Defense of the party who is currently appealing a conviction of "voluntary manslaughter," carrying a two to fifteen year sentence, on charges of killing an Oakland policeman last October.

The incidents in these sketches occurred over a period of several years during which time the essential dynamic of the Panther program and tactics developed as a response to the failure of less revolutionary strategy to affect significantly the conditions of the ghetto. The Panthers are real precisely because they emerged from the crucible of West Oakland experience rather than from a disconnected intellectual exercise or the operations of the mass media.

The selections here are from a book of Newton's life and writings which is being compiled by Eldridge Cleaver, Minister of Information of the Black Panther Party, in conjunction with Bobby Seale, the party's Chairman. The book will be published by RAMPARTS in the near future.

Eldridge Cleaver's association with RAMPARTS began with his "Notes on a Native Son" (RAMPARTS, June 1966) and "Letters From Prison" (RAMPARTS, August 1967; included in his best selling *Soul on Ice*, a RAMPARTS-McGraw Hill book). He is currently a senior editor of this magazine, as well as the Presidential candidate of the Black Panther Party and the Peace and Freedom Party.

—ROBERT SCHEER

[INTRODUCTION]

I REMEMBER ONCE DURING THE TRIAL of Huey P. Newton, a lawyer stopped me in the hall of the Alameda County Courthouse. He was very nervous, and he said, "They are crucifying Huey in there—they are turning him into another Jesus." And I remember almost instinctively replying, "Yes, Huey is our Jesus, but we want him down from the cross."

The tendency to look upon Huey as being above and beyond others, to view Huey as being different from everybody else, I think this is something that happens; I know that it happens to members of the Black Panthers, and it happens more and more to black people who have an understanding about Huey, and who know a little about his leadership of the party and some of the very courageous stands that he has taken. When you think of Huey, along with his followers, out on the streets of Oakland at night, in alleys, on dark streets, confronted by racist pig cops who are known to be very brutal, very vicious and murderous in their approach to black people, you cannot help but be amazed and fascinated by his seriousness, by his willingness and readiness to lay down his life in defense of the rights of his people, and his own rights, his human rights and his Constitutional rights.

I cannot help but say that Huey P. Newton is the baddest motherfucker ever to set foot inside of history. Huey has a very special meaning to black people, because for 400 years black people have been wanting to do exactly what Huey Newton did, that is, to stand up in front of the most deadly tentacle of the white racist power structure, and to defy that deadly tentacle, and to tell that tentacle that he will not accept the aggression and the brutality, and that if he is moved against, he will retaliate in kind. Huey Newton is a classical revolutionary figure. His imagination is constantly at work, conjuring up strategies and tactics that apply classical revolutionary principles to the situations confronting black people here in America.

Much has been written about Huey P. Newton, Minister of Defense of the Black Panther Party, but most of what has been written, it seems to me, obscures his essential character, as it fails really to show Huey in motion. The man who knows Huey perhaps better than anyone else is Bobby Seale, Chairman of the Black Panther Party, who, along with Huey, organized the party. Bobby has known Huey Newton for approximately eight years, dating back to their days at Merritt College in Oakland. He has had a chance to observe Huey under varying circumstances and in various situations, and he has an appreciation and an understanding of Huey that comes only from careful observation, that becomes a fixation on what makes this man, Huey Newton, tick.

Because Bobby united with Huey and, in a very real sense, placed his life in Huey's hands, he had very good reason for checking out Huey very closely, and he arrived at the conclusion that it was a proper and safe thing to do. I would say that, knowing Bobby and Huey, and knowing the relationship that exists between the two of them, Bobby had no choice, and felt compelled to place his life in Huey's hands. You could almost say that his admiration and respect for Huey is a sort of worship, and I don't mean this in any religious sense, but in the sense of Newton as a man who is motivated by a deep and burning preoccupation and concern with the plight of black people, who is seeking solutions to the problems of black people, and who recognizes that it is going to take a very fundamental action on a revolutionary level to cut into the oppression and to motivate people, black people, to take a revolutionary stance against the decadent racist system that is oppressing them.

Bob Scheer and I took Bobby Seale down to Carmel, California, and we secluded ourselves in a little cabin, and placed a tape recorder in front of Bobby, and put a microphone in his hands, and asked him to talk about Huey P. Newton. What emerged from that was a very fascinating narrative of Bobby's perception and an understanding of what Huey P. Newton is all about. We have selected key incidents from this narration and present them here as an insight into the man, Huey P. Newton, in motion. Having myself joined the Black Panther Party, and accepted Huey P. Newton as my leader, I find myself sharing with Bobby Seale the same attitude towards Huey—the same willingness to place my life in his hands, the same confidence that Huey will do the right thing at any given moment, that his instincts are sound, and that there is nothing to do but follow Huey and back him up.

—ELDRIDGE CLEAVER

[I MEET HUEY. HE COULD SHOOT YOU DOWN IN AN ARGUMENT OR KNOCK YOU DOWN WITH HIS HANDS.]

I MET HUEY P. NEWTON IN THE EARLY '60s, during the time of the blockade that JFK had enacted against Cuba, when there were numerous street rallies going on around Merritt Junior College in West Oakland. One particular day there was a lot of discussion about black people and the blockade against Cuba. People were all out in front of the college, in the streets, grouped up in bunches—200, 250, what have you—and there were these kind of gatherings and informal rallies at different times.

On this particular day that I met Huey, I don't remember exactly what day it was, but Huey was holding down a crowd of about 250 people who were standing around listening to him, and I was one of the participants. After he had held the conversation down to what in those days they called "shooting everybody down"—that means rapping off information and throwing facts—somebody would ask Huey a question or refer to something he said. They would try to shoot Huey down by citing some passage in a book concerning the subject matter being discussed, and before they knew it, Huey would have whipped out a copy of *Black Bourgeoisie* by E. Franklin Frazier and shown him what page, what paragraph and corrected the person.

I guess I had the idea that I was supposed to ask questions in college, so I walked over to Huey and asked the brother, wasn't all these civil rights laws the NAACP was trying to get for us, weren't they doing us some good? And he shot me down too, just like he shot a whole lot of other people down. Like he said, it's all a waste of money, black people don't have anything in this country that is for them. He went on to say that the laws weren't even serving them in the first place, that they were already on the books and what's the use of making more laws when what was needed was to enforce the present laws? So all the money that the people were giving to Martin Luther King and the rest of them who were supposed to put these laws on the books for black people, that was a waste of the people's money, of the black people's money.

And I was ready to accept that when he started citing many more facts to back up his point of view—I guess you respected Huey because you observed the cat blowing for a while and he could bring out so much information and clarify a philosophical point of view; you might not be able to articulate exactly what he said but you could see him citing so many facts, giving liturgy to a philosophical point of view.

These are the basic ways and things that Huey would always bring out whenever he was clearing up a point. He always brings out basic, practical things, and that's the way he talks to you, that's the way he explains things to you. And he gets to a point where you can't get around. So you kind of have to face things.

"You can jail a revolutionary but you can't jail the revolution. You can run a freedom fighter around the country, but you can't run freedom fighting around the country. You can murder a liberator but you can't murder liberation."-- Fred Hampton, Deputy Chairman, Ill Chapter of the Black Panther Party -- Born: August 30, 1948. Murdered by fascist pigs: December 4, 1969.

203

But anyway, that's the kind of atmosphere I met Huey in. And all the conflicts of this meeting, all this blowing that was going on in the streets that day during the Cuban crisis thing, all of that was involved with his association with the Afro-American Association—a lot of arguments came down. A lot of people were discussing with these three or four cats in the Afro-American Association, which was developing the first black nationalist philosophy on the West Coast, they got me caught up. They made me feel that I had to help out, be a part and do something, you know, to help out some way. I think it was one or two days later I went around looking for Huey at the school, and then I went to the library. I found Huey in the library, and I asked him where the meetings were, and he gave me an address and told me that there were book discussions. And then he told me the name of the book they were discussing at the time, which was *Black Bourgeoisie*.

HUEY WAS A LARGE INFLUENCE on the whole campus. He influenced everybody and, well, like I got to know where Huey was on campus, and I remember a sister come up to me, wanting to know where Huey was. I wasn't a running partner of Huey's then, but I was catching him on the streets and knew he was down at Jo Ethel's Cafe, or another cafe, and I would direct the sister. And we would all wig out behind brother Huey, and I guess everybody respected Huey's mind and also Huey's guts because he had something about him, that he didn't drive over people, but he would never let anyone drive over him. Especially in a violent and rowdy fashion because—I didn't know it at the time but I learned later—Huey had a kind of hidden reputation on the block with the brothers.

There were cats all over East and West Oakland who had reputations for being bad, and they were known throughout the community for being bad. But Huey didn't have this kind of reputation. The bad cats terrorized the community—and Huey terrorized the bad cats.

There's another thing about Huey. I remember one time, there were some black nationalists, cultural nationalists, on the campus who used to project all this cultural nationalism. They was so engrossed in this cultural nationalism, they just *hated* white people simply for the color of their skin. This is where me and Huey get this thing about cultural nationalists. Huey had opened the door for a sister to go through. You know how a man open the door for a woman? So there happened to be a white girl, coming right behind the sister, and so the white girl walked in. So one of the cultural nationalists run up to him and say, "How come you opened the door for that white girl?" And Huey turned around and looked at him. He say, "Look man, I'm a human being and I'm not a fool. I opened the door for the sister. There happened to be a white girl behind her. The white girl's not attacking me. She's not brutalizing me. So there's nothing wrong with me keeping the door open for her to pass through, too." And the cultural nationalists just went out of their minds, exaggerating the shit and all this bull crap. You know, that's just a point to show about Huey's humanism towards all other human beings; this is the way he was.

We walked up to the counter and were paying for the shotgun. And the broad at the counter says, and you could tell she was lying, "You know, these FBI men around have been coming in to request information and names on EVERYONE who buys a gun in our store." Huey says, "We don't care, that doesn't make any difference. Here is my money. I'm Huey P. Newton of the Black Panther Party. Here's my money. I want my shotgun." And the broad looked at him, amazed. I don't know who she thought she was tricking because she wasn't tricking Huey P. Newton—he couldn't give two good goddams about who she thought she was intimidating with some damn supposed FBI investigation.

It's very important about Huey's attitude and his personality and the way he's going and the way he knows he's going. That's very important. 'Cause Huey says, "Here's my money. My name is Huey P. Newton of the Black Panther Party," and

we pick up that shotgun.

So we sold them Red Books and made the money. We used that money to buy guns. Me and Huey and the brothers in the core organization used the Red Books and spread it throughout the organization. Because Huey made it a point that the principles and the revolutionary principles concisely cited in the Red Book should be applied whenever they can be applied. That is, whenever they can be applied within the confines of this system. So, from there we righteously used the Red Book. Because we talked about it, and Huey had us practicing the principles. And from Fanon, and from Malcolm X—his autobiography and other material on him. Huey integrated all these principles of the brother revolutionaries. We taught from all these materials, and every time we ran into something with Che Guevara too.

WE INITIALLY USED IT (the Red Book) as a commodity—to sell. See, Huey knew that the radicals on the campus would pay a dollar for that Red Book if we had it. And we was the only ones who had it. We was the only organizational ones who had it.

I remember a lot of people would ask very inquisitively, "Where did you get those books?" I would holler, "I know you're wondering what in the world are those Negroes doing with those Red Books." And I would sell three or four. So we used it to make money at first. To buy guns. Later, we knew that the guns would be more valuable and more meaningful to the brothers on the block, by drawing them into the organization, then in turn teaching them from the Red Book. Huey was a bitch. Huey was a motherfucker. He was two motherfuckers. In fact, he was ten motherfuckers. I mean he knew how to do it. I mean that's the way I see it. Huey was ten motherfuckers. 'Cause he would say, "Bobby, you and I know the principles in this Red Book are valid, but the brothers and the black folks don't and they will not pay a dollar or thirty cents for that book. So what we have to do is to get to the white radicals who are intellectually interested in the book, sell the book, make the money, buy the guns and go on the streets with the gun. To protect a mother, protect a brother, and protect the community. And in turn we get brothers in the organization and they will in turn relate to the Red Book."

That's the way the shit went. At the same time, Huey would go off into Fanon. He would get off into Malcolm X. Huey would relate these principles. He was a motherfucker. You couldn't get around Huey. He knew the Red Book sideways, backward and forward. You got brothers in the Party that got to know the Red Book cattycorner. The brothers know that book sideways, backwards, forwards, upside down. Turn that book any way you want to—they tell you in a minute. "The Red Book and what else? The gun! The Red Book and what else? The gun!" That's what Huey would say.

[HUEY BACKS THE PIGS DOWN
WITH AN M-1 RIFLE
AND A LAW BOOK.]

HUEY WAS DEALING ON A LEVEL where he was ready to organize the black brothers for a righteous revolutionary struggle with guns and force. So it came to a point where we walked in and out of the Black Panther office every day around to my house or around to Bobby Hutton's house, or somebody's house, with guns on our sides, and got in a car, or two or three cars, or four or five cars as it built up, and patrolled the pigs on Friday and Saturday nights. Or sometimes when we were going to a meeting during the week we would patrol the pigs.

And one day, as we were walking out of the office, I guess we'd been there about a month or so, a pig passed by. He saw us coming out with shotguns and pistols on our sides. About six or seven of us came out of the office there, in the daytime, and we looked at the pig as he passed by, and he jumped on his radio and we readily assessed that he must have been jumping on his radio because he saw us coming out of the office with those pieces and stuff, 'cause we had just gotten through field-stripping weapons, learning about double-O buckshot, learning about the 9mm and the .45.

We had a .45 and a .357 magnum in the group, and a couple of M-1s. We had three or four shotguns by then. We bought up guns like a son of a bitch then. The pig went down two blocks and turned around, came back up the other side of the street. They were building rapid transit, BART, right down Grove Street there, and he came up the other side of the boulevard and came back, and we readily assessed that the pigs were ready to see what the fuck was happening, this pig had radioed in and he was running it down how he had seen some niggers come out of a place here with some guns and blah blop de bloo, etc., etc., come out of this office with guns and stuff. He was radioing to other pigs to help get 'em.

Huey had his father's car that day. I think he had just finished paying some bills and he stopped by the office for about a half an hour. By the time we got in the car, the pig was back around down the street and he drove up behind us and Huey told everybody to remember what he'd said—that nobody in the car say anything. Only the driver do the talking, and Huey happened to be the driver. He said, "I'm the driver. Nobody else say anything, and remember the legal first aid." This was the legal aid information that we had printed for the brothers in the party, and we were teaching them 13 points of basic, legal first aid.

Huey used to teach the brothers on that; he wouldn't let them get around it, 'cause Huey understood brothers this way, that they had no guidelines about how to deal with the pigs. So Huey went off in the area of law and he found out the brothers respected law. If you *know* something about law, like Huey did—he could use it to make it serve him. That's all he was doing, but he was bringing them basic things in everyday life about law. That's what Huey dug; he understood that shit. Huey would take those 13 basic points and try to show a dude where he was fucked up at *in the ghetto.* That's very important, man.

So he said, "Nobody say anything, because the minute somebody says something the man is going to try to arrest you. And he's going to arrest you for some jive about interfering with an officer carrying out his duty, but he's going to try to prove to all the people who are subject to gather around us here that we have no right with a gun. And he's going to arrest you on a traffic ticket and the people out in the community will think he arrested you because you've got the gun, and we want to prove to the people that we've got a right to carry guns and they've got a right to arm themselves, and we will exhaust our Constitutional right to carry these guns." That's what Huey was trying to exhaust. Boom. Which he did exhaust, ultimately.

Huey GOT IN THE CAR and the pig came up to the window. "You have any driver's license?" So Huey rolled the window down. There wasn't more than about a three or four inch crack in the window.

Huey handed his license out the window. "Is this your true name?" the pig said. And Huey said, "Yes, that's my true name, Huey P. Newton." "Is this your true address, 841-47th Street?" And Huey said, "That's my true address, 841-47th Street." "What're you doing with the guns?" And Huey said, "What are you doing with *your* gun?" This particular pig decided he wasn't going to argue, so he went back and got his little writing pad where they fill out shit.

"Your true name is Huey P. Newton?" Huey said, "That's right." The pig wrote this down.

"Your true address is 841-47th Street?"

Huey said, "That's right." The pig then looked at his license. "What's your phone number?" And Huey said, "Five!" and stopped and wouldn't say anything else. And the pig said, "Five what?"

This is what began all the shit between the party and the

pigs. This is when the shit got started. Huey said, "The Fifth Amendment, Pig! You ever heard of it? Don't you know about the Constitutional right of a person not having to testify against himself? Five! I don't have to give you anything but my identification, name and address, so therefore I don't even want to talk to you. You can leave my car and leave me alone. I don't even want to *hear* you."

"What do you mean?" the pig said. And Huey said, "Just what I said. The Constitutional right of any man is that he doesn't have to testify against himself." And Huey got a big M-1 sitting to his right with his hand on it. I got this 9mm sitting beside me, and Huey got this M-1 at his side. Huey was driving. Four other brothers were in the back seat, and one of 'em was Bobby Hutton. They were being quiet 'cause Huey told them to be quiet. 'Cause they ain't supposed to interrupt. You dig where it's at? And the pig is going crazy. He's by himself and Huey got all these black niggers in the car going for a motherfucker.

Meanwhile, while the pig is trying to get bad, three cars drive up in the back of us, and one in the front. Some are in the driveway. Blop, blop, blop de bloo. Then another car comes up in front of us. A pig jumps out of this car, walks up to our car and says through the crack in the window, "What's going on here?" And Huey says, "The same basic procedures that are supposed to go on!" Huey rolls down the window another five or six inches. The pigs are looking at the guns in the car.

"Can I see that pistol there?" a pig says. "No, you can't see it!" Huey tells him. I'm beginning to get skeptical about what's happening because he pointed to my 9mm pistol. Huey's on probation, and if they would think that this is Huey's pistol. . . . I don't know this law stuff too much like Huey knows it, so I moved the pistol over beside me real close. It had been laying in the middle of the seat. I say, "No, you can't see it!" Huey says, "No, you can't see the pistol, nor this [pointing to his rifle], and I don't want you to look at it. You don't have to look at it."

"Is that your pistol?" he asks Huey. And I said, "No, it's not his pistol, it's my pistol!" I'm saying this here because I'm thinking the man gonna jump on Huey because I know he already told me about the law—if he gets caught with a pistol, he's burned. But if he gets caught with a rifle, the man can't mess with him 'cause his probation officer told him he can carry a rifle or a shotgun, and he couldn't stop him. The pig said, "Can I see it or not?" So Huey said to me, "*I'll* talk." And then to the pig, "No, you can't see the pistol. Get away from the car. We don't want you around the car and that's all there is to it."

"Well, I can ask *him* if I want to see his pistol or not," the pig says. So I said, "Well, you can't see the pistol!" The motherfuckers try to get indignant. They were blabbing and oinking to each other about who in the hell we thought we were and, "Constitution my ass. They're just turning it around." Then a pig said to Huey, "Who in the hell you think you are?"

"Look, dammit," and Huey just opened the car door, and this is where Huey gets mad. I mean you got to imagine this nigger. He got mad because these dogs were going to carry on and they were bracing up like they were bad. This Huey doesn't go for at all. Huey got very *mad.* He opened up the door saying, "Who in the hell do you think *you* are? In the first place, this man [pointing at the pig], came up here and asked me for my license like he was citing me for a ticket or observation of some kind. This police officer is supposed to be carrying out his duty, and here you come talking about our guns." Huey put his hand around his M-1 rifle and continued, "We have a Constitutional right to carry the guns anyway, and I don't want to *hear* it."

The pigs backed up a couple of steps, and Huey was coming out of the car. Huey had his hand back in the car, getting his M-1, and you know, you ever seen Huey, he gets growly like, but articulate? You know what I mean? He comes out of the car with his M-1. See, Huey knows his law so well he won't have a M-1 loaded inside the car. When he comes out of the

car, he drops a round off into the chamber right away.

"Who do you think you all are anyway?" Huey says to the pigs. And the other pigs are on the sidewalk harassing all the brothers and sisters who have gathered around: "You people move on down the street!" Huey started interrupting. "You don't have to move down the street! Don't go nowhere! These pigs can't keep you from observing. You have a right to observe an officer carrying out his duty." And these pigs, they listened to this shit. See, Huey's citing law and shit. "You have a right to observe an officer carrying out his duty. Any policeman carrying out his duty. You have a right to. As long as you stand a reasonable distance away, and you are a reasonable distance. *Don't go nowhere!*"

The pigs kept trying to move the people, saying, "You're gonna get under arrest." So Huey just went over and opened the door to the Panther office and said, "Come on in here. They can't move you out." He took his key out, opened the door and let the people go in. "Now, observe all you want to!" The pig said, "What're you going to do with that gun?"

"What are you going to do with *your* gun?" Huey said. "Because if you try to shoot at me, or if you try to take this gun, I'm going to shoot back at you, swine. Furthermore"— and he just got off into it—"you're nothing but a sharecropper anyway. You come from Georgia somewhere, you're downtown making $800 a month, and you come down here brutalizing and murdering black people in the black community. They gave you some sergeant stripes and all I say is that you're nothing but a low-lifed, scurvy swine. A sharecropper from racist Georgia in the South somewhere.

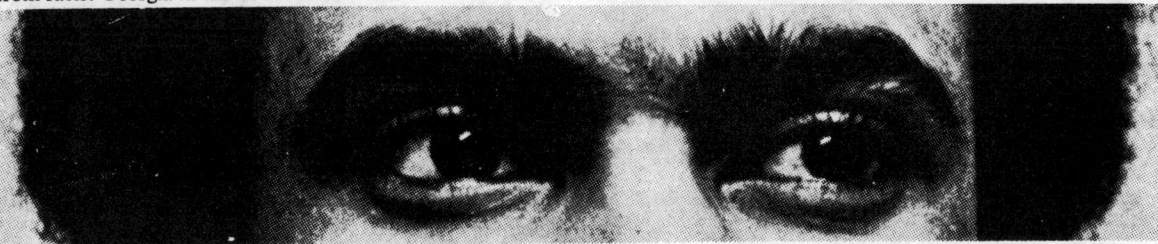

"So if you draw that gun, I'll shoot back at you and blow your brains out!"

"You, you, you . . ." the pig was mad. "You're just turning the Constitution around." This is the pig trying to slough it off.

Huey said, "I'm not turning anything around. And I got my gun. What are you going to do with yours?" This blowed the pigs' minds. Pigs didn't know where to go, man. Huey just walked on around the front of the car. Got on around the front of the car, talking, then went on and opened the office door again and let some more people in, telling the people they don't have to go nowhere, citing their Constitutional rights and all this stuff, and just jumped on out of the office again and said, "Now what are you going to do?"

I'M SITTING IN THE CAR. I GOT THE HAMMER of my 9mm cocked back. I say, "These pigs is going to be wild-eyed. I *know* they gonna be crazy." I rolled the window down. "What's *your* name?" I say, "My name is Bobby Seale, why?" "Want to check *you* out. Got any identification?" I laid my pistol down, gave them identification; I picked my pistol back up. I said, "My name is Bobby Seale, as it says in my identification. Want to check me out?"

"You was arrested for armed robbery at seventeen."

I said, "You a goddamned liar. I never in my life been arrested. I never have been arrested for armed robbery." They didn't even check me out. "You were arrested for armed robbery when you were seventeen. But since you were a juvenile, we can't arrest you for possessing a gun now." I say, "You damned liar. I never been arrested for armed robbery. I don't want to hear it. Fuck it."

And Huey out there, man, he's calling the pigs swine, dogs, sharecroppers, bastards, motherfuckers, with his M-1 in his hand. And *daring* them, just daring them! "You don't pull your gun on *us*." And that's where Huey began to show us.

You tell some motherfucker, and you *mean* it! This is what I remember. Huey was relating to one thing. When he told me, a long time ago, to remember that we might not ever come back home one day, I said, "I'm with you, Huey." I remember that. I remember I might not never come home one day. "Fuck it, I'm with you."

We were sitting in this car, and Huey made us all stay in the car and be quiet. He's out there, the baddest motherfucker in the world, man. He and ten pigs. Three or four of them trying to run kids off of bicycles and tell them people they ain't got no right to stand around, and Huey going out there interrupting, "No! Come in the office." Little kids on bicycles got inside the office. We had a big, wide, clear picture window. Niggers just got all over the front of the window, man. They'd lean on it, kiss the window, just to listen to this shit. And they would be hollering, "Go 'head on, brother," and, "Run it on down. You know where it's at," and "I can dig it," all the while Huey was letting these pigs know where it was at. The brothers observing would see that those pigs were scared of that *big* gun that a bad black but beautiful nigger had in his hand. Every time Huey would say, "If you shoot at me swine, I'm shooting back," niggers would have to holler something like, "Tell it, *do* it brother." All that would do to Huey is let him know that he was revolutionizing our culture; educating black people to be revolutionaries, that the gun is where it's at and about and in.

Then some people came up after that, after Huey had made this display of going in the office. The other people were standing around and the pigs weren't even moving no more.

And Huey just daring them to do anything. Huey got a M-1 with him. One of them eight-round clips in there. What do you do, man? All you do is back up a nigger like that. You do nothing else but that. Anything that happens, this nigger's the baddest nigger you ever seen. 'Cause this nigger is telling *ten pigs*, "I don't give a damn what you do," and making all of us shut up and be disciplined. And we have our shit ready, sitting in the car.

So I say to myself, this is the baddest motherfucker in the world! This nigger is telling pigs, "If you draw your gun, I'll shoot you." Telling this to the pigs standing there. All of a sudden the pig says, "You're just turning the Constitution around." Huey say, "I'm turning nothing around. I'm exercising my Constitutional right. I've got the gun to back it up!" And he got the gun in his hand. And the pig *see* the gun. And the nigger done told the pigs that if you act wrong, you get down wrong, I'm going to kill you!

So what do you do? You say, this nigger is bad. This nigger is crazy. But I like this crazy nigger. I like him 'cause he's good. He don't take no bullshit. You back him up.

So that was the very major incident that happened with the Black Panther Party in front of the Black Panther Party office. And after *that*, the major incident that happened, we really began to patrol pigs then, because we got righteous recruits. I think we got 10 or 12, maybe 13 extra members in the party that day, just come in, put applications in. We went down to the Poverty Office again, I was still working there, and drew up a formal form of application for enrollment to get into the Black Panther Party. And from there, what did we do? We just patrolled pigs.

From "The Biography of Huey P. Newton" by Bobby Seale with an introduction by Eldridge Cleaver *Ramparts* 10/26/68

THE PANTHERS ON THE STREETS

THE DEATH OF DENZIL DOWELL: THE BLACK PANTHER PARTY IS CALLED TO NORTH RICHMOND.

THE BLACK PANTHER PARTY got called to come to Richmond by the Dowell family. They had heard of the Black Panther Party over in Oakland. Mark Comfort came down to the office at 56th and Grove, and told us that the Dowell family would like for us to come over because Denzil Dowell had been killed in Richmond by a Contra Costa County deputy sheriff.

Well, we went out there that day and saw the Dowell family. We were in our Panther uniforms. We talked to the family, and they began to explain all the details about how certain people had said they heard ten shots, and the papers, the local media there, was saying that it was only two or three shots that were fired. And how the coroner's office had originally told them he was shot nine or ten times, but the police department said he was only shot once or twice. How the pigs had lied about Denzil Dowell, the brother, telling about how he was trying to burglarize some place. And his brothers, Carl Dowell and George Dowell, explained how the pigs knew Denzil by name, because they had arrested him a number of times. The pigs had made threats that they were going to get Denzil. It was just a cold-blooded killing of a black man out there. Some pigs were trigger-happy and wanted to shoot somebody.

They explained all this to us. Then the family took us over to the site where they killed brother Denzil Dowell, and showed us just where the bullets hit certain walls and the direction they came from and how the pigs lied and said that he ran and jumped a fence. The blood was 20 yards away from the fence. They must have dragged his body over to the other side, and then over another fence. The blood was in two different places. We were investigating, and a lot of black people in the black community there came out. They had noticed us Panthers, with our guns and everything. I guess there were ten or twelve of us who went out there together and went through the whole process of investigation, of looking over what had happened, and listening to the information that people were giving that contradicted all the crap that the pigs and the newspapers had run down.

We were standing on the corner there in North Richmond. There were about 150 people around, some in cars, some standing across the street. Some of the younger brothers, fifteen, sixteen, some twenty years old, were asking us about the guns, and we were explaining to them about the Black Panther Party. That the Black Panther Party was a revolutionary organization that was going forth, organizing in a revolutionary manner to get black people's basic political desires and needs answered. That we intended to use revolutionary principles, and that one of the tools of liberation is the gun. All of a sudden, some sister hollers out, "Uh, oh . . . here come the *cops*."

When the sister hollered, Huey jacked a round off into the chamber of his 18-inch shotgun with a loud click and clack. When he did that, I just unhitched the strap that held the hammer down on my .45, and it clacked too. People started moving back. Some of them went across the street. Some got in their cars and drove up the street. Then the pigs came on down and Huey stepped to the curb. I followed Huey and stepped to the curb, a few feet down from him. The pigs were surprised all of a sudden. They looked and noticed who's ready and standing tall for them. The pigs kept driving, drove right on off—in fact, they speeded on up and drove on away. Then the people moved on back, and some of them jumped around across the street, figuring there was going to be a shoot-out, but we just stood tall, ready to defend ourselves. We were educating the people that we would die here for them. This was the position we always took with brother Huey P. Newton.

We told the people there that we were going to have a rally that coming Saturday, on the corner of Third and Chesley, right down the street. We said we'd run down and educate them about the fact that we'd have to start using guns to defend ourselves, because the racist pig cops were coming to our community and murdering our brothers and sisters. Brother Denzil Dowell was killed, and we'd found information out about two, three other brothers who'd been shot up back in December, in North Richmond there. The brothers had been shot in the armpits, which clearly showed they had their arms over their heads.

Two brothers killed in December, and this is right around April 1st that Denzil Dowell was gunned down by those pigs. Huey told them we were going to have a rally concerning this, to tell the people it was necessary for us to arm ourselves—that we must have a political party that goes forth with revolutionary tactics against these racist dog pigs, who occupy our black communities like foreign troops occupy enemy territory.

So we went forth to have this rally that Saturday, and we got about 20 brothers together with their pieces and their uniforms. We had the rally right there on the corner of Third and Chesley. We got guns and a force to defend ourselves. Ain't no pigs going to come down here and stop our street rally. We're going to exercise our Constitutional rights to free speech. And we're just going to have a rally right here on the corner. Most of North Richmond don't have sidewalks at all. But for that section on the corner there, in front of this liquor store, there's an eight to ten foot sidewalk between the curb and the store. We got right out there on the corner, and all the brothers out there in this community saw us with the guns. We lined up all along the streets.

IMAGINE AN INTERSECTION NOW, of two streets crossing each other. On one corner we put four, five brothers and they were spread out about 20, 30 feet from each other, coming around the corner. On the corner across the street we put a brother on the corner, then two brothers down from him, 30 or 40 feet apart. Then on the corner where Huey and I were speaking, right there in front of the liquor store, we lined that corner up going east and west. Then we lined the other corner up as you go north and south. So the whole intersection was lined up with Panthers, all up and down the corners, going north, east, west and south on both sides of the streets. And we had our guns, shotguns, pistols and everything.

The people began to line up and brother Huey told me to go ahead and start blowing. So I start blowing to the brothers there, running down to them about the ten-point platform and program, what kind of organization we had now, about the fact that brother Denzil Dowell had been killed by some racist dog gestapo pigs. And the fact that we must begin to unify and organize with guns and force. That the Black Panther Party had come to North Richmond, and the Black Panther Party is there to serve the people, it's going to be a black people's party. It's getting ready to use revolutionary principles, to educate black people in revolutionary principles, to educate them and also to put the principles in practice, in arming ourselves in the community and driving these racist pigs out. I guess about two, three hundred people gathered up around. In fact, people in cars just stopped, and the whole section, like on the one side of the street there, was just a line of cars. And on the other side, coming right up to the intersection, there was another line of cars. Some cars

207

Panther Erika Huggins

were still moving, by going on the other side of the street, driving up the wrong side of the street.

I was blowing there, and then all of a sudden they start sending some sheriffs in. The people had noticed that we were there, we were there with our guns, we were back again. So we blew, and then the pigs start driving down the streets, the sheriff's pigs. So Huey whispered, he said, "Run it down about the pigs, Bobby. About how we're going to hold this street rally, and how we're going to exercise our right of free speech. No pig's going to stop it." And he said, "Tell them about the reason why no pig's going to stop it. It's because we've got guns and force here to protect ourselves, to protect the people."

So I run it down to the brothers, and pointed to the pigs, and the pigs got nervous. I noticed one of the pigs stopped across the street and sat there, and started listening. Four of the brothers came across the street and surrounded the pig car, standing about nine, ten feet away from it. One brother had a .357 Magnum, Warren Tucker had a .38 pistol hanging on him, and Reginald Forte had a 9 mm. pistol. One brother didn't even have a gun and he got up there too. Then the pig got nervous, and he started trying to light a cigarette, but the cigarette just fell out of his hand, with all these people looking at him. The black people had guns and force, ready to deal with the pigs, and the pig just couldn't take it no more, he couldn't light his cigarette he was so nervous, he just up and drove away. The people yelled and raved at the fact.

Huey P. Newton had placed the notion in their minds that we organize. I think the people respected the fact that Huey had all of them brothers organized, because he had them all stationed up and down the streets, covering the intersection, guarding the lives of the black people, while we go forth to organize the people. They respected this organization that Huey put down. Huey put down a form, a discipline, that the gun was for our protection, and not for no bull-jive. So the pig had to split.

Another pig was sitting there. This other pig came up in a car and some of the people's cars moved along. But one man said, "Well, I ain't moving my car. I'm going to sit here and listen." And this cop got caught in between the cars and he couldn't move and he had to sit there and listen to everything. He couldn't do nothing. And that brother didn't move his car. He had a Cadillac too, and him and his woman were sitting in the Cadillac, sitting right at the head of the intersection. So this pig's car was right in between, and he couldn't move, he just had to sit there and listen, and look at 300, that's right, he had to look at 300 mad niggers—mad at the pigs for killing Denzil Dowell. And 20

Panthers out there armed with guns, disciplined, standing 30 or 40 feet apart, on every corner of the intersection. So it was tied down.

And the people dug it and they say, "Right on." And Huey went on and blew to the brothers and sisters and told them how we're going to get organized and how we're going to start using guns and force in an organized and disciplined manner. In a very revolutionary manner we're going to go forth, and we're going to defend ourselves against any racist attacks. These pigs get down wrong and we're going to drive them out and blow them away, every time we catch one of them trying to get down wrong. And we're going to patrol these pigs, we're going to patrol our own communities, even the old people are going to have to patrol from their homes and houses. And everybody has to have a shotgun in their home, everybody. Then George Dowell blew about how his brother, Denzil, had gotten murdered by them pigs. So we scheduled another meeting. We said we were going to have another meeting over on Second Street, and Huey said we're going to block the whole street off, and ain't no pigs going to be allowed up the street . . . *at all.*

SO WE HAD THIS SECOND Richmond rally, and three or four hundred people came up. They drove their cars all up inside the street, and brothers got on top of cars and top of roofs all up and down the street, from one corner to the next, and it was a pretty long block. The whole street was cluttered with cars. We were at one particular address, where I think some relative of George Dowell lived. This was all right around the corner from George Dowell's mother's home. All the people came around and we had applications there for people to join the party. And I guess just about everybody out there joined the party that day, from little young fourteen-year-olds and twelve-year-olds. We let twelve-year-olds in the party too. Huey'd say we have a junior Panther. But these young brothers are not allowed to have guns—they go to black history classes and other kinds of classes, to learn revolutionary principles, because Huey understands that the youth are going to be the ones that are going to mold the country, especially if they have the right principles and the right direction.

The community people got together and George Dowell's sisters and brothers and friends got together and began to have a regular session. And everyone would come to the meeting with the people of North Richmond. The brothers had their guns on. They were tired, sick and tired, and they loved brother Huey. They thought brother Huey was out of sight. He was a beautiful leader, and Huey began to instruct them on many things, on many ways they can go about

dealing with the real problems. One of the sisters brought up the problem at one of the nightly sessions that one of those schoolteachers beat up and slapped down a couple of black kids in school. She wanted the Panthers, the Black Panther Party, to go to the school, and she was going to get a lot of mothers and parents to go to the junior high school where her kids went. We all got together and scheduled it for that Monday.

On Monday we took three carloads of Panthers down to the school. All of them were armed down to the gills. We got out of the cars with our guns and stood on the sidewalk. Right at the sidewalk there's a fence to the schoolyard. All the little black kids ran over to the fence, and all the little white kids ran away from the fence, and went and hid somewhere inside the school. Then the mothers came driving up. They went inside the school building to patrol the halls of the school. They patrolled the halls during this lunch hour situation, and went and told the principal that they didn't want any more brutality upon their kids in the schools. "We're concerned citizens, and we'll whip your ass and anyone else's that we hear of slapping our children around."

After about 20 minutes, while the mothers were patrolling the halls, the pigs drove up. This little, young, rookie, jive pig, trying to look mean and thinking he was bad or something, he walks up to the car, and when he walks up to the car, the brothers were sitting there in the car, looking back at him, 'cause Huey had trained his brothers, don't be moving, moving in no rash manner. And they got shotguns, four motherfuckers, M-1's. He looks in the car and sees all these pieces and he moves back in a hurry. He got all nervous. "Wha' . . . wha' . . . what the guns for? What the guns for?" And I think Huey said, "We're the Black Panther Party, why?" "Uh, uh, da, da, doo, do you have any license? Do you have any driver's license?" And Huey gave him his license.

"Well, you're Huey P. Newton."

"Minister of Defense Huey P. Newton, of the Black Panther Party." And the pig was just shaking. He didn't know what to do, so he gave Huey his license back and went and got on his radio and called up another pig. They kind of hung off, away from us, looking and not knowing what to do. Shook, because there's too many niggers and too many guns down there for them.

They called another car up and the principal of the school come out, and was trying to talk to the pigs. Their cars were parked a little way out in front of the sidewalk that leads into the door of the school, about 30, 40 yards or so behind ours. All they could do was sit there and wonder. And that's all they did was sit there and wonder. We went there with the mothers and they patrolled the halls for the lunch period, and then we left.

ABOUT FOUR, FIVE DAYS LATER, they called us up at the Panther office and said there was a session going on out there, up in the Sixth Street office over in Richmond, concerning the fact that the DA of the county had better do something, had better charge these cops who killed Denzil Dowell.

Me and brother Huey and a number of other brothers all got together and

walked off into the meeting there, with our guns. This DA was sitting there and he looked up and saw Huey; he saw Huey with that big shotgun. The pig can see that Huey's shotgun carries a whole lot of rounds. And Huey had a bandolier holding 26 shotgun shells across his chest. Huey had double-O buckshot, and the pig was definitely checking Huey out. Huey was decked out in the Panther uniform and he simply walked in and sat down, and the brothers and the sisters who were there talk about this pig, this DA. Talk about him like he was nothing, and running it down about how rotten he is, and he's trying to give off some verbal sincerity.

The people saw Huey, and they felt it was no time for them to be taking no shit because here's a man that we respect, here's a leader. He's armed down to the gills and he's articulate, and he knows what he's talking about. Like they're ready to jump over there and snatch this DA's throat out, concerning this whole situation and how Denzil Dowell was killed. So we blew the dude away, and told him he wasn't doing nothing, wasn't serving the people, that he was jiving, that he was a swine, and that he wasn't intending to do nothing for the people, etc.

But he came up and started talking about, why don't you go to the Contra Costa County Sheriff's Department, up in Martinez, and if you go to the Contra Costa County Sheriff's Department in Martinez, maybe you can get some results there. So the people say, "We're going to go to the Contra Costa County Sheriff's Department in Martinez." The mother and the father and the Dowell family wanted us to go to Martinez, and since we're a people's party, we generally go along with what the people want to do, to serve them. Especially if we think it will help them to raise their interests

and unity, and get support and try to begin to attempt to change the system. So, we say, "Yes, we'll go to Martinez, with the brothers and sisters here. We're concerned about this here. The Panthers will definitely be there." . . . . .

WE WENT BACK and laid out the first Black Panther, Black Community News Service paper. It was two sheets of legal-sized mimeographed paper, printed on both sides. The headline was, "Why Was Denzil Dowell Killed?" We printed about five or six thousand of those papers and took all the Panthers and went out to the black community in North Richmond. We got to passing the papers out and giving them to people, and children were following, about 100, 150 kids on bicycles, and some of them walking down the streets, following the Panthers, walking all throughout the community, block to block, passing out leaflets. We gave a lot to the kids and told them to put them on all the doorsteps.

We had gotten an interview done by the Examiner. The Examiner came down to the Panther headquarters, and did an interview on a Tuesday. They said they were going to print it on a Sunday. That Saturday evening the headlines hit, about the existence of the Black Panther Party, who patrolled cops in the black community. They wrote it all backwards. They said we were anti-white and were black racists. After that Huey began talking about how we needed to go straight up in front of some city hall, like we did in Martinez, and talk to the people and hold a rally there, so we could get a message over to the mass of the people. And the mass media would come along and cover it. We saw another article in the paper about the Black Panther Party about three or four weeks from this particular time. We all read the papers and realized that the news of the existence of the Black Panther Party was being widely distributed, especially in the Bay Area.

One Monday morning Huey called me up and says, "Bobby, come over to the house right quick." I came over to the house. Huey showed me the papers. He said, "Look here, Mulford is up in the legislature now, trying to get a bill passed against us. We don't care about laws anyway, because the laws they make don't serve us at all. He's probably making a law to serve the power structure. He's trying to get some kind of law passed against us." He says, "I've been thinking. Remember when I told you we have to go in front of a city hall, in front of a jail or do something like we did in Martinez, to get more publicity, so we

can get a message over to the people?" This was Huey's chief concern, getting the message over to the people, about the fact that we have to arm ourselves with guns and force against this racist, decadent system, because of what it was doing to us.

So Huey says, "You know what we're going to do?" "What?" "We're going to the Capitol." I said, "The *Capitol?*" He says, "Yeah, we're going to the Capitol." I say, "For what?" "Mulford's there, and they're trying to pass a law against our guns, and we're going to the Capitol steps. We're going to take the best Panthers we got and we're going to the Capitol steps with our guns and forces, loaded down to the gills. And we're going to read a message to the world, because all the press is going to be up there. The press is always up there. They'll listen to the message, and they'll probably blast it all across this country. I know, I know they'll blast it all the way across California. We've got to get a message over to the people."

Huey understood a revolutionary culture, and Huey understood how arms and guns become a part of the culture of a people in the revolutionary struggle. And he knew that the best way to do it was to go forth, and those hungry newspaper reporters, who are shocked, who are going to be shook up, are going to be blasting that news faster than they could be stopped. I said, "All right, brother, right on. I'm with you. We're going to the Capitol." So we called a meeting that night, before going up to the Capitol, to write the first executive mandate for the Black Panther Party. Huey was going to write Executive Mandate Number One.

This executive mandate was the first major message to *all* the American people, and *all* the black people, especially in this country, who're living in the confines of this decadent system. Eldridge and Huey and all of us sat down, and it didn't take us long. We weren't jiving. Take no time at all, not like some of them intellectuals and punks that have to take ten days before they can write an executive mandate to put things together. I don't think it was 15 minutes before we whipped that executive mandate out, looked it over, and Eldridge corrected it, got things together. So the executive mandate would be the first message, the first major message made by the Black Panther Party, coming from the Minister of Defense, Huey P. Newton. Huey told me to organize the brothers, tell them to get their guns and be at the office tomorrow morning, at nine o'clock. "We're going to leave at ten o'clock. We're going to leave at ten o'clock sharp."

From "The Biography of Huey P. Newton" by Bobby Seale with an introduction by Eldridge Cleaver *Ramparts* 10/26/68

RULES OF THE BLACK PANTHER PARTY

CENTRAL HEADQUARTERS
OAKLAND, CALIFORNIA..

Every member of the BLACK PANTHER PARTY throughout this country of racist America must abide by these rules as functional members of this party. CENTRAL COMMITTEE members, CENTRAL STAFFS, and LOCAL STAFFS, including all captains subordinate to either national, state, and local leadership of the BLACK PANTHER PARTY will enforce these rules. Length of suspension or other disciplinary action necessary for violation of these rules will depend on national decisions by national, state or state area, and local committees and staffs where said rule or rules of the BLACK PANTHER PARTY WERE VIOLATED.

Every member of the party must know these verbatum by heart. And apply them daily. Each member must report any violation of these rules to their leadership or they are counter-revolutionary and are also subjected to suspension by the BLACK PANTHER PARTY.

THE RULES ARE:

1. No party member can have narcotics or weed in his possession while doing party work.

2. Any party member found shooting narcotics will be expelled from this party.

3. No party member can be DRUNK while doing daily party work.

4. No party member will violate rules relating to office work, general meetings of the BLACK PANTHER PARTY, and meetings of the BLACK PANTHER PARTY ANYWHERE.

5. No party member will USE, POINT, or FIRE a weapon of any kind unnecessarily or accidentally at anyone.

6. No party member can join any other army force other than the BLACK LIBERATION ARMY.

7. No party member can have a weapon in his possession while DRUNK or loaded off narcotics or weed.

8. No party member will commit any crimes against other party members or BLACK people at all, and cannot steal or take from the people, not even a needle or a piece of thread.

9. When arrested BLACK PANTHER MEMBERS will give only name, address, and will sign nothing. Legal first aid must be understood by all Party members.

10. The Ten Point Program and platform of the BLACK PANTHER PARTY must be known and understood by each Party member.

11. Party Communications must be National and Local.

12. The 10-10-10-program should be known by all members and also understood by all members.

13. All Finance officers will operate under the jurisdiction of the Ministry of Finance.

14. Each person will submit a report of daily work.

15. Each Sub-Section Leader Section Leader, Lieutenant, and Captain must submit Daily reports of work.

16. All Panthers must learn to operate and service weapons correctly.

17. All Leadership personnel who expel a member must submit this information to the Editor of the Newspaper, so that it will be published in the paper and will be known by all chapters and branches.

18. Political Education Classes are mandatory for general membership.

19. Only office personnel assigned to respective offices each day should be there. All others are to sell papers and do Political work out in the community, including Captains, Section Leaders, etc.

20. COMMUNICATIONS — all chapters must submit weekly reports in writing to the National Headquarters.

21. All Branches must implement First Aid and/or Medical Cadres.

22. All Chapters, Branches, and components of the BLACK PANTHER PARTY must submit a monthly Financial Report to the Ministry of Finance, and also the Central Committee.

23. Everyone in a leadership position must read no less than two hours per day to keep abreast of the changing political situation.

24. No chapter or branch shall accept grants, poverty funds, money or any other aid from any government agency without contacting the National Headquarters.

25. All chapters must adhere to the policy and the ideology laid down by the CENTRAL COMMITTEE of the BLACK PANTHER PARTY.

26. All Branches must submit weekly reports in writing to their respective Chapters.

8 POINTS OF ATTENTION

1) Speak politely.

2) Pay fairly for what you buy.

3) Return everything you borrow.

4) Pay for anything you damage.

5) Do not hit or swear at people.

6) Do not damage property or crops of the poor, oppressed masses.

7) Do not take liberties with women.

8) If we ever have to take captives do not ill-treat them.

3 MAIN RULES OF DISCIPLINE

1) Obey orders in all your actions

2) Do not take a single needle or a piece of thread from the poor and oppressed masses.

3) Turn in everything captured from the attacking enemy.

I cannot help but say that Huey P. Newton is the baddest motherfucker ever to set foot inside of history.

ELDRIDGE CLEAVER

October 1966
Black Panther Party Platform and Program

What We Want
What We Believe

FREE HUEY
Minister of Defense, Black Panther Party

1. We want freedom. We want power to determine the destiny of our Black Community.

We believe that black people will not be free until we are able to determine our destiny.

2. We want full employment for our people.

We believe that the federal government is responsible and obligated to give every man employment or a guaranteed income. We believe that if the white American businessmen will not give full employment, then the means of production should be taken from the businessmen and placed in the community so that the people of the community can organize and employ all of its people and give a high standard of living.

3. We want an end to the robbery by the CAPITALIST of our Black Community.

We believe that this racist government has robbed us and now we are demanding the overdue debt of forty acres and two mules. Forty acres and two mules was promised 100 years ago as restitution for slave labor and mass murder of black people. We will accept the payment in currency which will be distributed to our many communities. The Germans are now aiding the Jews in Israel for the genocide of the Jewish people. The Germans murdered six million Jews. The American racist has taken part in the slaughter of over fifty million black people; therefore, we feel that this is a modest demand that we make.

4. We want decent housing, fit for shelter of human beings.

We believe that if the white landlords will not give decent housing to our black community, then the housing and the land should be made into cooperatives so that our community, with government aid, can build and make decent housing for its people.

5. We want education for our people that exposes the true nature of this decadent American society. We want education that teaches us our true history and our role in the present-day society.

We believe in an educational system that will give to our people a knowledge of self. If a man does not have knowledge of himself and his position in society and the world, then he has little chance to relate to anything else.

6. We want all black men to be exempt from military service.

We believe that Black people should not be forced to fight in the military service to defend a racist government that does not protect us. We will not fight and kill other people of color in the world who, like black people, are being victimized by the white racist government of America. We will protect ourselves from the force and violence of the racist police and the racist military, by whatever means necessary.

7. We want an immediate end to POLICE BRUTALITY and MURDER of black people.

We believe we can end police brutality in our black community by organizing black self-defense groups that are dedicated to defending our black community from racist police oppression and brutality. The Second Amendment to the Constitution of the United States gives a right to bear arms. We therefore believe that all black people should arm themselves for self-defense.

8. We want freedom for all black men held in federal, state, county and city prisons and jails.

We believe that all black people should be released from the many jails and prisons because they have not received a fair and impartial trial.

9. We want all black people when brought to trial to be tried in court by a jury of their peer group or people from their black communities, as defined by the Constitution of the United States.

We believe that the courts should follow the United States Constitution so that black people will receive fair trials. The 14th Amendment of the U.S. Constitution gives a man a right to be tried by his peer group. A peer is a person from a similar economic, social, religious, geographical, environmental, historical and racial background. To do this the court will be forced to select a jury from the black community from which the black defendant came. We have been, and are being tried by all-white juries that have no understanding of the "average reasoning man" of the black community.

10. We want land, bread, housing, education, clothing, justice and peace. And as our major political objective, a United Nations-supervised plebiscite to be held throughout the black colony in which only black colonial subjects will be allowed to participate, for the purpose of determining the will of black people as to their national destiny.

When, in the course of human events, it becomes necessary for one people to dissolve the political bands which have connected them with another, and to assume, among the powers of the earth, the separate and equal station to which the laws of nature and nature's God entitle them, a decent respect to the opinions of mankind requires that they should declare the causes which impel them to the separation.

We hold these truths to be self-evident, that all men are created equal; that they are endowed by their Creator with certain unalienable rights; that among these are life, liberty, and the pursuit of happiness. **That, to secure these rights, governments are instituted among men, deriving their just powers from the consent of the governed; that, whenever any form of government becomes destructive of these ends, it is the right of the people to alter or to abolish it, and to institute a new government, laying its foundation on such principles, and organizing its powers in such form, as to them shall seem most likely to effect their safety and happiness.** Prudence, indeed, will dictate that governments long established should not be changed for light and transient causes; and, accordingly, all experience hath shown, that mankind are more disposed to suffer, while evils are sufferable, than to right themselves by abolishing the forms to which they are accustomed. **But, when a long train of abuses and usurpations, pursuing invariably the same object, evinces a design to reduce them under absolute despotism, it is their right, it is their duty, to throw off such government, and to provide new guards for their future security.**

Ed. Note: When the program was written down in 1966, there were two Black Panthers, Huey Newton and Bobby Seale

THE BLACK PANTHER   12/20/69

OLD MOLE 9/26/69

HUEY NEWTON TALKS TO THE MOVEMENT ABOUT THE BLACK PANTHER PARTY, CULTURAL NATIONALISM, SNCC, LIBERALS AND WHITE REVOLUTIONARIES

THE MOVEMENT: The question of nationalism is a vital one in the black movement today. Some have made a distinction between cultural nationalism and revolutionary nationalism. Would you comment on the differences and give us your views?

HUEY P. NEWTON: There are two kinds of nationalism, revolutionary nationalism and reactionary nationalism. Revolutionary nationalism is first dependent upon a people's revolution with the end goal being the people in power. Therefore to be a revolutionary nationalist you would by necessity have to be a socialist. If you are a reactionary nationalist you are not a socialist and your end goal is the oppression of the people.

Cultural nationalism, or pork chop nationalism, as I sometimes call it, is basically a problem of having the wrong political perspective. It seems to be a reaction instead of responding to political oppression. The cultural nationalists are concerned with returning to the old African culture and thereby regaining their identity and freedom. In other words, they feel that the African culture will automatically bring political freedom. Many times cultural nationalists fall into line as reactionary nationalists.

Papa Doc in Haiti is an excellent example of reactionary nationalism. He oppresses the people but he does promote the African culture. He's against anything other then black, which on the surface seems very good, but for him it is only to mislead the people. He merely kicked out the racists and replaced them with himself as the oppressor. Many of the nationalists in this country seem to desire the same ends.

The Black Panther Party, which is a revolutionary group of black people, realizes that we have to have an identity. We have to realize our black heritage in order to give us strength to move on and progress. But as far as returning to the old African culture, it's unnecessary and it's not advantageous in many respects. We believe that culture itself will not liberate us. We're going to need some stronger stuff.

Revolutionary Nationalism

A good example of revolutionary nationalism was the revolution in Algeria when Ben Bella took over. The French were kicked out but it was a people's revolution because the people ended up in power. The leaders that took over were not interested in the profit motive where they could exploit the people and keep them in a state of slavery. They nationalized the industry and plowed the would-be profits into the community. That's what socialism is all about in a nutshell The people's representatives are in office strictly on the leave of the people. The wealth of the country is controlled by the people and they are considered whenever modifications in the industries are made.

The Black Panther Party is a revolutionary Nationalist group and we see a major contradiction between capitalism in this country and our interests. We realize that this country became very rich upon slavery and that slavery is capitalism in the extreme. We have two evils to fight, capitalism and racism. We must destroy both racism and capitalism.

MOVEMENT: Directly related to the question of nationalism is the question of unity within the black community. There has been some question about this since the Black Panther Party has run candidates against other black candidates in recent California elections. What is your position on this matter?

HUEY: Well a very peculiar thing has happened. Historically you got what Malcolm X calls the field nigger and the house nigger. The house nigger had some privileges, a little more. He got the worn-out clothes of the master and he didn't have to work as hard as the field black. He came to respect the master to such an extent until he identified with the master because he got a few of the leftovers that the field blacks did not get. And through this identity with him, he saw the slavemaster's interest as being his interest. Sometimes he would even protect the slavemaster more than the slavemaster would protect himself. Malcolm makes the point that if the master's house happened to catch on fire the house Negro will work harder than the master to put the fire out and save the master's house. While the field Negro, the field blacks was praying that the house burned down. The house black identified with the master so much that when the master would get sick the house Negro would say, "Master, we's sick!".

Black Bourgeoisie

The Black Panther Party are the field blacks, we're hoping the master dies if he gets sick. The Black bourgeoisie seem to be acting in the role of the house Negro. They are pro-administration. They would like a few concessions made, but as far as the overall setup, they have a little more material goods, a little more advantage, a few more privileges than the black have-nots; the lower class. And so they identify with the power structure and they see their interests as the power structure's interest. In fact, it's against their interest.

The Black Panther Party was forced to draw a line of demarcation. We are for all of those who are for the promotion of the interests of the black have-nots, which represents about 98% of blacks here in America. We're not controlled by the white mother country radicals nor are we controlled by the black bourgeoisie. We have a mind of our own and if the black bourgeoisie cannot align

ple of color

itself with our complete program, then the black bourgeoisie sets itself up as our enemy. And they will be attacked and treated as such.

MOVEMENT: The Black Panther Party has had considerable contact with white radicals since its earliest days. What do you see as the role of these white radicals?

HUEY: The white mother country radical is the off-spring of the children of the beast that has plundered the world exploiting all people, concentrating on the people of color. These are children of the beast that seek now to be redeemed because they realize that their former heroes, who were slave masters and murderers, put forth ideas that were only facades to hide the treachery they inflicted upon the world. They are turning their backs on their fathers.

The white mother country radical, in resisting the system, becomes somewhat of an abstract thing because he's not oppressed as much as black people are. As a matter of fact his oppression is somewhat abstract simply because he doesn't have to live in a reality of oppression.

Black people in America and colored people throughout the world suffer not only from exploitation, but they suffer from racism. Black people here in America, in the black colony, are oppressed because we're black and we're exploited. The whites are rebels, many of them from the middle class and as far as any overt oppression this is not the case. So therefore I call their rejection of the system somewhat of an abstract thing. They're looking for new heroes. They're looking to wash away the hypocrisy that their fathers have presented to the world. In doing this they see the people who are really fighting for freedom. They see the people who are really standing for justice and equality and peace throughout the world. They are the people of Vietnam, the people of Latin America, the people of Asia, the people of Africa, and the black people in the black colony here in America.

White Revolutionaries

This presents somewhat of a problem in many ways to the black revolutionary, especially to the cultural nationalist. The cultural nationalist doesn't understand the white revolutionaries because he can't see why anyone white would turn on the system. So they think that maybe this is some more hypocrisy being planted by white people.

I personally think that there are many young white revolutionaries who are sincere in attempting to realign themselves with mankind, and to make a reality out of the high moral standards that their fathers and forefathers only expressed. In pressing for new heroes the young white revolutionaries found the heroes in the black colony at home and in the colonies throughout the world.

The young white revolutionaries raised the cry for the troops to withdraw from Vietnam, hands off Latin America, withdraw from the Dominican Republic and also to withdraw from the black community or the black colony. So you have a situation in which the young white revolutionaries are attempting to identify with the oppressed people of the colonies and against the exploiter.

The problem arises then in what part they can play. How can they aid the colony? How can they aid the Black Panther Party or any other black revolutionary group? They can aid the black revolutionaries first by simply turning away from the establishment, and secondly by choosing their friends. For instance, they have a choice between whether they will be a friend of Lyndon Baines Johnson or a friend of Fidel Castro. A friend of Robert Kennedy or a friend of Ho Chi Minh. And these are direct opposites. A friend of mine or a friend of Johnsons. After they make this choice then the white revolutionaries have a duty and a responsibility to act.

The imperialistic or capitalistic system occupies areas. It occupies Vietnam now. They occupy them by sending soldiers there, by sending policeman there. The policemen or soldiers are only a gun in the establishment's hand. They make the racist secure in his racism. The gun in the establishment's hand makes the establishment secure in its exploitation. The first problem it seems is to remove the gun from the establishment's hand. Until lately the white radical has seen no reason to come into conflict with the policemen in his own community. The reason I said until recently is because there is friction now in the mother country between the young white revolutionaries and the police. Because now the white revolutionaries are attempting to put some of their ideas into action, and there's the rub. We say that it should be a permanent thing.

Black people are being oppressed in the colony by white policemen, by white racists. We are saying they must withdraw. We realize that it is not only the Oakland police department but rather the security forces in general. On April 6 it wasn't just the Oakland police department who ambushed the Panthers. It was the Oakland police department, the Emeryville police department and I wouldn't be surprised if there were others. When the white revolutionaries went down to close up the Army terminal in October 1965 it wasn't the Oakland police by themselves who tried to stop them. It was the Oakland police, the Berkeley police, the Highway Patrol, the Sherriff's Department and the national guard was standing by. So we see that they're all a part of one organization. They're all a part of the security force to protect the status quo; to make sure that the institutions carry out their goals. They're here to protect the system.

As far as I'm concerned the only reasonable conclusion would be to first realize the enemy, realize the plan, and then when something happens in the black colony-- when we're attacked and ambushed in the black colony--then the white revolutionary students and intellectuals and all the other whites who support the colony should respond by defending us, by attacking the enemy in their community. Every time that we're attacked in our community there should be a reaction by the white revolutionaries; they should respond by defending us, by attacking part of the security force. Part of that security force that is determined to carry out the racist ends of the American institutions.

As far as our party is concerned, the Black Panther Party is an all black party, because we feel as Malcom X felt that there can be no black-white unity until there first is black unity. We have a problem in the black colony that is particular to the colony, but we're willing to accept aid from the mother country as long as the mother country radicals realize that we have, as Eldridge Cleaver says in SOUL ON ICE, a mind of our own. We've regained our mind that was taken away from us and we will decide the political as well

as the practical stand that we'll take. We'll make the theory and we'll carry out the practice. It's the duty of the white revolutionary to aid us in this.

So the role of the mother country radical, and he does have a role, is to first choose his friend and his enemy and after doing this, which it seems he's already done, then to not only articulate his desires to regain his moral standard and align himself with humanity, but also to put this into practice by attacking the protectors of the institutions.

MOVEMENT: You have spoken a lot about dealing with the protectors of the system, the armed forces. Would you like to elaborate on why you place so much emphasis on this?

HUEY: The reasons that I feel very strongly about dealing with the protectors of the system is simply because without this protection from the army, the police and the military, the institutions could not go on in their racism and exploitation. For instance, as the Vietnamese are driving the American imperialist troops out of Vietnam, it automatically stops the racist imperialist institutions of America from oppressing that particular country. The country cannot implement its racist program without the guns. And the guns are the military and the police. If the military were disarmed in Vietnam, then the Vietnamese would be victorious.

We are in the same situation here in America. Whenever we attack the system the first thing the administrators do is to send out their strongarm men. If it's a rent strike, because of the indecent housing we have, they will send out the police to throw the furniture out the window. They don't come themselves. They send their protectors. So to deal with the corrupt exploiter you are going to have to deal with his protector, which is the police who take orders from him. This is a must.

MOVEMENT: Would you like to be more specific on the conditions which must exist before an alliance or coalition can be formed with predominantly white groups? Would you comment specifically on your alliance with the California Peace and Freedom Party?

HUEY: We have an alliance with the Peace and Freedom Party. The Peace and Freedom Party has supported our program in full and this is the criterion for a coalition with the black revolutionary group. If they had not supported our program in full, then we would not have seen any reason to make an alliance with them, because we are the reality of the oppression. They are not. They are only oppressed in an abstract way; we are oppressed in the real way. We are the real slaves! So it's a problem that we suffer from more than anyone else and it's our problem of liberation. Therefore we should decide what measures and what tools and what programs to use to become liberated. Many of the young white revolutionaries realize this and I see no reason not to have a coalition with them.

MOVEMENT: Other black groups seem to feel that from past experience it is impossible for them to work with whites and impossible for them to form alliances. What do you see as the reasons for this and do you think that the history of the Black Panther Party makes this less of a problem?

SNCC and Liberals

HUEY: There was somewhat of an unhealthy relationship in the past with the white liberals supporting the black people who were trying to gain their freedom. I think that a good example of this would be the relationship that SNCC had with its white liberals. I call them white liberals because they differ strictly from the white radicals. The relationship was that the whites controlled SNCC for a very long time. From the very start of SNCC until here recently whites were the mind of SNCC. They controlled the program of SNCC with money and they controlled the ideology, or the stands SNCC would take. The blacks in SNCC were completely controlled program-wise; they couldn't do any more than these white liberals wanted them to do, which wasn't very much. So the white liberals were not working for self-determination for the black community. They were interested in a few concessions from the power structure. They undermined SNCC's program.

Stokely Carmichael came along and realizing this started to follow Malcolm X's program of Black Power. This frightened many of the white liberals who were supporting SNCC. Whites were afraid when Stokely came along with Black Power and said that black people have a mind of their own and that SNCC would be an all-black organization and that SNCC would seek self-determination for the black community. The white liberals withdrew their support leaving the organization financially bankrupt. The blacks who were in the organization, Stokely and H. Rap Brown, were left very angry with the white liberals who had been aiding them under the disguise of being sincere. They weren't sincere.

The result was that the leadership of SNCC turned away from the white liberal, which was very good. I don't think they distinguished between the white liberal and the white revolutionary, because the white revolutionary is white also and they are very much afraid to have any contact whatsoever with white people. Even to the point of denying that the white revolutionaries could give support, by supporting the programs of SNCC in the mother country. Not by making any programs, not by being a member of the organization, but simply by resisting. Just as the Vietnamese people realize that they are supported whenever other oppressed people throughout the world resist. Because it helps divide the troops. It drains the country militarily and economically. If the mother country radicals are sincere then this will definitely add to the attack that we are making on the power structure. The Black Panther Party's program is a program where we recognize that the revolution in the mother country will definitely aid us in our freedom and has everything to do with our struggle!

Hate the Oppressor

I think that one of SNCC's great problems is that they were controlled by the traditional administrator: the omnipotent administrator, the white person. He was the mind of SNCC. And so SNCC regained its mind, but I believe that it lost its political perspective. I think that this was a reaction rather than a response. The Black Panther Party has NEVER been controlled by white people. The Black Panther Party has always been a black group. We have always had an integration of mind and body. We have never been controlled by whites and therefore we don't fear the white mother country radicals. Our alliance is one of organized black groups with organized white groups. As soon as the organized white groups do

not do the things that would benefit us in our struggle for liberation, that will be our departure point. So we don't suffer in the hangup of a skin color. We don't hate white people; we hate the oppressor. And if the oppressor happens to be white then we hate him. When he stops oppressing us then we no longer hate him. And right now in America you have the slave-master being a white group. We are pushing him out of office through revolution in this country. I think the responsibility of the white revolutionary will be to aid us in this. And when we are attacked by the police or by the military then it will be up to the white mother country radicals to attack the murderers and to respond as we respond, to follow our program.

Slave Masters

MOVEMENT: You indicate that there is a psychological process that has historically existed in white-black relations in the U.S. that must change in the course of revolutionary struggle. Would you like to comment on this?

HUEY: Yes. The historical relationship between black and white here in America has been the relationship between the slave and the master; the master being the mind and the slave the body. The slave would carry out the orders that the mind demanded him to carry out. By doing this the master took the manhood from the slave because he stripped him of a mind. He stripped black people of their mind. In the process the slave-master stripped himself of a body. As Eldridge puts it the slave master became the omnipotent administrator and the slave became the supermasculine menial. This puts the omnipotent administrator into the controlling position or the front office and the supermasculine menial into the field.

The whole relationship developed so that the omnipotent administrator and the supermasculine menial became opposites. The slave being a very strong body doing all the practical things, all of the work becomes very masculine. The omnipotent administrator in the process of removing himself from all body functions realizes later that he has emasculated himself. And this is very disturbing to him. So the slave lost his mind and the slave-master his body.

Penis Envy

This caused the slave-master to become very envious of the slave because he pictured the slave as being more of a man, being superior sexually, because the penis is part of the body. The omnipotent administrator laid down a decree when he realized that his plan to enslave the black man had a flaw, when he discovered that he had emasculated himself. He attempted to bind the penis of the slave. He attempted to show that his penis could reach further than the supermasculine menial's penis. He said "I, the omnipotent administrator can have access to the black woman." The supermasculine menial then had a psychological attraction to the white woman (the ultra feminine freak) for the simple reason that it was forbidden fruit. The omnipotent administrator decreed that this kind of contact would be punished by death. At the same time in order to reinforce his sexual desire, to confirm, to assert his manhood, he would go into the slave quarters and have sexual relations with the black women (the self-reliant Amazon). Not to be satisfied but simply to confirm

his manhood. Because if he can only satisfy the self-reliant Amazon then he would be sure that he was a man. Because he doesn't have a body, he doesn't have a penis, he psychologically wants to castrate the black man. The slave was constantly seeking unity within himself: a mind and a body. He always wanted to be able to decide, to gain respect from his woman. Because women want one who can control. I give this outline to fit into a framework of what is happening now. The white power structure today in America defines itself as the mind. They want to control the world. They go off and plunder the world. They are the policemen of the world exercising control especially over people of color.

Re-capture the Mind

The white man cannot gain his manhood, cannot unite with the body because the body is black. The body is symbolic of slavery and strength. It's a biological thing as he views it. The slave is in a much better situation because his not being a full man has always been viewed psychologically. And it's always easier to make a psychological transition than a biological one. If he can only recapture his mind, recapture his balls, then he will lose all fear and will be free to determine his destiny. This is what is happening at this time with the rebellion of the world's oppressed people against the controller. They are regaining their mind and they're saying that we have a mind of our own. They're saying that we want freedom to determine the destiny of our people, thereby uniting the mind with their bodies. They are taking the mind back from the omnipotent administrator, the controller, the exploiter.

In America black people are also chanting that we have a mind of our own. We must have freedom to determine our destiny. It's almost a spiritual thing, this unity, this harmony. This unity of the mind and of the body, this unity of man within himself. Certain slogans of Chairman Mao I think demonstrate this theory of uniting the mind with the body within the man. An example is his call to the intellectuals to go to the countryside. The peasants in the countryside are all bodies; they're the workers. And he sent the intellectuals there because the dictatorship of the proletariat has no room for the omnipotent administrator; there's no room for the exploiter. So therefore he must go to the countryside to regain his body; he must work. He is really done a favor, because the people force him to unite his mind with his body by putting them both to work. At the same time the intellectual teaches the people political ideology, he educates them, thus uniting the mind and the body in the peasant. Their minds and bodies are united and they control their country. I think this is a very good example of this unity and it is my idea of the perfect man.

The Guerrilla

MOVEMENT: You mentioned at another point that the guerrilla was the perfect man and this kind of formulation seems to fit in directly with the guerrilla as a political man. Would you like to comment on this?

HUEY: Yes. The guerrilla is a very unique man. This is in contrast to Marxist-Leninist orthodox theories where the party controls the military. The guerrilla is not only the warrior, the military fighter;

he is also the military commander as well as the political theoretician. Debray says "poor the pen without the guns, poor the gun without the pen". The pen being just an extension of the mind, a tool to write down concepts, ideas. The gun is only an extension of the body, the extension of our fanged teeth that we lost through evolution. It's the weapon, it's the claws that we lost, it's the body. The guerrilla is the military commander and the political theoretician all in one.

In Bolivia Che said that he got very little help from the Communist Party there. The Communist Party wanted to be the mind, the Communist Party wanted to have full control of the guerrilla activity. But yet weren't taking part in the practical work of the guerrillas. The guerrilla on the other hand is not only united within himself, but he also attempts to spread this to the people by educating the villagers, giving them political perspective , pointing out things, educating them politically, and arming the people. Therefore the guerrilla is giving the peasants and workers a mind. Because they've already got the body you get a unity of the mind and the body. Black people here in America, who have long been the workers, have regained our minds and we now have a unity of mind and body.

MOVEMENT: Would you be willing to extend this formula in terms of white radicals; to say that one of their struggles today is to get back their bodies.

HUEY: Yes. I thought I made that clear. The white mother country radical by becoming an activist is attempting to regain his body. By being an activist and not the traditional theoretician who outlines the plan, as the Communist Party has been trying to do for ever so long, the white mother country radical is regaining his body. The resistance by white radicals in Berkeley during the past three nights is a good indication that the white radicals are on the way home. They have identified their enemies. The white radicals have integrated theory with practice. They realize the American system is the real enemy but in order to attack the American system they must attack the ordinary cop. In order to attack the educational system they must attack the ordinary teacher. Just as the Vietnamese people to attack the American system must attack the ordinary soldier. The white mother country radicals now are regaining their bodies and they're also recognizing that the black man has a mind and that he is a man.

MOVEMENT: Would you comment on how this psychological understanding aids in the revolutionary struggle?

HUEY: You can see that in statements until recently black people who haven't been enlightened have defined the white man by calling him "the MAN". "The Man" is making this decision, "The Man" this and "The Man" that. The black woman found it difficult to respect the black man because he didn't even define himself as a man! Because he didn't have a mind, because the decision maker was outside of himself. But the vanguard group, the Black Panther Party along with all revolutionary black groups have regained our mind and our manhood. Therefore we no longer define the omnipotent administrator as "the Man" . . . or the authority as "the MAN". Matter of fact the omnipotent administrator along with his security agents are less than a

man because WE define them as pigs! I think that this is a revolutionary thing in itself. That's political power. That's power itself. Matter of fact what is power other than the ability to define phenomenon and then make it act in a desired manner? When black people start defining things and making it act in a desired manner, then we call this Black Power!

MOVEMENT: Would you comment further on what you mean by Black Power?

HUEY: Black Power is really people's power. The Black Panther Program, Panther Power as we call it, will implement this people's power. We have respect for all of humanity and we realize that the people should rule and determine their destiny. Wipe out the controller. To have Black Power doesn't humble or subjugate anyone to slavery or oppression. Black Power is giving power to people who have not had power to determine theirdestiny. We advocate and we aid any people who are struggling to determine their destiny. This is regardless of color. The Vietnamese say Vietnam should be able to determine its own destiny. Power of the Vietnamese people. We also chant power of the Vietnamese people. The Latins are talking about Latin America for the Latin Americans. Cuba Si and Yanqui, Non. It's not that they don't want the Yankees to have any power they just don't want them to have power over them. They can have power over themselves. We in the black colony in America want to be able to have power over our destiny and that's black power.

MOVEMENT: A lot of white radicals are romantic about what Che said: "In a revolution one wins or dies . . ." For most of us it is really an abstract or theoretical question. It's a real question for you and we'd like you to rap about how you feel about it.

HUEY; Yes. The revolutionary sees no compromise. We will not compromise because the issue is so basic. If we compromise one iota we will be selling our freedom out. We will be selling the revolution out. And we refuse to remain slaves. As Eldridge says in SOUL ON ICE "a slave who dies of natural causes will not balance two dead flies on the scales of eternity." As far as we're concerned we would rather be dead than to go on with the slavery that we're in. Once we compromise we will be compromising not only our freedom, but also our manhood. We realize that we're going up against a highly technical country, and we realize that they are not only paper tigers, as Mao says, but real tigers too because they have the ability to slaughter many people. But in the long run, they will prove themselves paper tigers because they're not in line with humanity; they are divorced from the people. We know that the enemy is very powerful and that our manhood is at stake, but we feel it necessary to be victorious in regaining ourselves, regaining our manhood. And this is the basic point. So either we will do this or we won't have any freedom. Either we will win or we will die trying to win.

Mood of Black People

MOVEMENT: How would you characterize the mood of black people in America today? Are they disenchanted, wanting a larger slice of the pie, or alienated, not wanting to integrate into a burning

house, not wanting to integrate into Babylon? What do you think it will take for them to become alienated and revolutionary?

HUEY: I was going to say disillusioned, but I don't think we were ever under the illusion that we had freedom in this country. This society is definitely a decadent one and we realize it. Black people are realizing it more and more. We cannot gain our freedom under the present system; the system that is carrying out its plans of institutionalized racism. Your question is what will have to be done to stimulate them to revolution. I think it's already being done. it's a matter of time now for us to educate them to a program and show them the way to liberation. The Black Panther Party is the beacon light to show black people the way to liberation

You notice the insurrections that have been going on throughout the country, in Watts, in Newark, in Detroit. They were all responses of the people demanding that they have freedom to determine their destiny, rejecting exploitation. Now the Black Panther Party does not think that the traditional riots, or insurrections that have taken place are the answer. It is true they have been against the Establishment, they have been against authority and oppression within their community, but they have been unorganized. However, black people learned from each of these insurrections.

They learned from Watts. I'm sure the people in Detroit were educated by what happened in Watts. Perhaps this was wrong education. It sort of missed the mark. It wasn't quite the correct activity, but the people were educated through the activity. The people of Detroit followed the example of the people in Watts, only they added a little scrutiny to it. The people in Detroit learned that the way to put a hurt on the administration is to make Molotov cocktails and to go into the street in mass numbers. So this was a matter of learning. The slogan went up "Burn, baby, burn". People were educated through the activity and it spread throughout the country. The people were educated on how to resist, but perhaps incorrectly.

Educate Though Activity

What we have to do as a vanguard of the revolution is to correct this through activity. The large majority of black people are either illiterate or semiliterate. They don't read. They need activity to follow. This is true of any colonized people. The same thing happened in Cuba where it was necessary for twelve men with a leadership of Che and Fidel to take to the hills and then attack the corrupt administration; to attack the army who were the protectors of the exploiters in Cuba. They could have leafleted the community and they could have written books, but the people would not respond. They had to act and the people could see and hear about it and therefore become educated on how to respond to oppression.

In this country black revolutionaries have to set an example. We can't do the same things that were done in Cuba because Cuba is Cuba and the U.S. is the U.S. Cuba has many terrains to protect the guerrilla. This country is mainly urban. We have to work out new solutions to offset the power of the country's technology and communication; its ability to communicate very rapidly by telephone and teletype and so forth.

We do have solutions to these problems and they will be put into effect. I wouldn't want to go into the ways and means of this, but we will educate through action. We have to engage in action to make the people want to read our literature. Because they are not attracted to all the writing in this country; there's too much writing. Many books makes one weary.

Threat from Reformers

MOVEMENT: Kennedy before his death, and to a lesser extent Rockefeller and Lindsay and other establishment liberals have been talking about making reforms to give black people a greater share in the pie and thus stop any developing revolutionary movement. Would you comment on this?

HUEY: I would say this: If a Kennedy or Lindsay or anyone else can give decent housing to all of our people; if they can give full employment to our people with a high standard; if they can give full control to black people to determine the destiny of their community; if they can give fair trials in the court system by turning over the structure to the community; if they can end their exploitation of people throughout the world; if they can do all of these things they would have solved the problems. But I don't believe that under this present system, under capitalism, that they will be able to solve these problems.

People Must Control

I don't think black people should be fooled by their come-ons because every one who gets in office promises the same thing. They promise full employment and decent housing; the Great Society, the New Frontier. All of these names, but no real benefits. No effects are felt in the black community, and black people are tired of being deceived and duped. The people must have full control of the means of production. Small black businesses cannot compete with General Motors. That's just out of the question. General Motors robbed us and worked us for nothing for a couple hundred years and took our money and set up factories and became fat and rich and then talks about giving us some of the crumbs. We want full control. We're not interested in anyone promising that the private owners are going to all of a sudden become human beings and give these things to our community. It hasn't ever happened and, based on empirical evidence, we don't expect them to become Buddhists over night.

MOVEMENT: We raised this question not because we feel that these reforms are possible, but rather to get your ideas on what effects such attempted reforms might have on the development of a revolutionary struggle.

HUEY: I think that reforms pose no real threat. The revolution has always been in the hands of the young. The young always inherit the revolution. The young population is growing at a very rapid rate and they are very displeased with the authorities. They want control. I doubt that under the present system any kind of program can be launched that will be able to buy off all these young people. They have not been able to do it with the poverty program, the great society, etc. This country has never been able to employ all of its people simply

because it's too interested in private property and the profit motive. A bigger poverty program is just what it says it is, a program to keep people in poverty. So I don't think that there is any real threat from the reforms.

MOVEMENT: Would you like to say something about the Panther's organizing especially in terms of the youth?

HUEY: The Panthers represent a cross section of the black community. We have older people as well as younger people. The younger people of course are the ones who are seen on the streets. They are the activists. They are the real vanguard of change because they haven't been indoctrinated and they haven't submitted. They haven't been beaten into line as some of the older people have. But many of the older people realize that we're waging a just fight against the oppressor. They are aiding us and they are taking a part in the program.

Jail

MOVEMENT: Tell us something about your relations with the prisoners in the jail

HUEY: The black prisoners as well as many of the white prisoners identify with the program of the Panthers. Of course by the very nature of their being prisoners they can see the oppression and they've suffered at the hands of the Gestapo. They have reacted to it. The black prisoners have all joined the Panthers, about 95% of them. Now the jail is all Panther and the police are very worried about this. The white prisoners can identify with us because they realize that they are not in control. They realize there's someone controlling them and the rest of the world with guns. They want some control over their lives also. The Panthers in jail have been educating them and so we are going along with the revolution inside of the jail.

MOVEMENT: What has been the effect of the demonstrations outside the jail calling for "Free Huey"?

HUEY: Very positive reactions. One demonstration, I don't remember which one, a couple of trustees, white trustees, held a cardboard sign out the laundry window reading "Free Huey". They say people saw it and responded to it. They were very enthusiastic about the demonstrators because they too suffer from being treated unfairly by the parole authorities and by the police here in the jail.

Open or Underground

MOVEMENT: The Panthers organizing efforts have been very open up until this point. Would you like to comment about the question of an underground political organization versus an open organization at this point in the struggle?

HUEY: Yeah. Some of the black nationalist groups feel that they have to be underground because they'll be attacked. But we don't feel that you can romanticize being underground. They say we're romantic because we're trying to live revolutionary lives, and we are not taking precautions. But we say that the only way we would go underground is if we're driven underground. All real revolutionary movements are driven underground Take the revolution in Cuba The agitation that was going on while Fidel was in

law school was very much above ground. Even his existence in the hills was, so to speak, an above the ground affair because he was letting it be known who was doing the damage and why he was doing the damage. To catch him was a different story. The only way we can educate the people is by setting an example for them. We feel that this is very necessary.

This is a pre-revolutionary period and we feel it is very necessary to educate the people while we can. So we're very open about this education. We have been attacked and we will be attacked even more in the future but we're not going to go underground until we get ready to go underground because we have a mind of our own. We're not going to let anyone force us to do anything. We're going to go underground after we educate all of the black people and not before that time. Then it won't really be necessary for us to go underground because you can see black anywhere. We will just have the stuff to protect ourselves and the strategy to offset the great power that the strong-arm men of the establishment have and are planning to use against us.

White Organizing

MOVEMENT: Your comments about the white prisoners seemed encouraging. Do you see the possibility of organizing a white Panther Party in opposition to the establishment possibly among poor and working whites?

HUEY: Well as I put it before Black Power is people's power and as far as organizing white people we give white people the privilege of having a mind and we want them to get a body. They can organize themselves. We can tell them what they should do, what their responsibility is if they're going to claim to be white revolutionaries or white mother country radicals, and that is to arm themselves and support the colonies around the world in their just struggle against imperialism. But anything more than that they will have to do on their own. ∎

the MOVEMENT Aug 1968

"TO BE A REVOLUTIONARY NATIONALIST YOU WOULD BY NECESSITY HAVE TO BE A SOCIALIST"

"WE DON'T HATE WHITE PEOPLE, WE HATE THE OPPRESSOR: IF THE OPPRESSOR HAPPENS TO BE WHITE, THEN WE HATE HIM."

"REVOLUTION IN OUR LIFETIME"

Q: *What happened on April 6, the night of the shoot-out in which Bobby Hutton was killed?*

A: We were in the process of gathering food for the picnic the next day in Sherman Park. We had a fund-raising picnic for Bobby Seale and Huey Newton and Kathleen, who was running for office. We needed funds for their campaigns and also for the Huey Newton defense fund, and a few cases in which bail money was needed. So we organized this picnic. We spent a lot of time on it and had invested $300 in meat and things like that. We were really uptight about the picnic. We wanted it to come off without any problems, you know. We put leaflets in the community, put up posters, had some spot advertising on the radio, so that it was a well-known fact that the thing was coming up. We had a little encounter with the cops over the picnic. They went to the Park Authority people and tried to get them to refuse to let us have the facility, and people didn't go along with that. The pigs did persuade the park people to impose some very stringent conditions, like no political speeches to be given in the park, no passing out of leaflets and literature during the picnic, no this, no that. Intentionally petty harassment.

We had this car that had been given to us by this white cat; he gave us two cars. A lot of people have given us things. But this particular car had a Florida license. It was a white Ford with a Florida license plate. It was quite easy to spot, you know. And none of the brothers liked to use it for that reason. I had pretty good identification. I had press cards, press passes, things of that nature, but most brothers don't have anything beyond a draft card, and possibly a driver's license. A lot of brothers have insufficient identification. Well, this car was always being stopped, you know. The pigs would spot the license plate, move in, pull the car over, stop the cat, put him through a lot of changes, ask him if he was from Florida and shit like that, just to be fucking with him. This night, about nine o'clock, the shit went down. We had been going back before, using David Henman's pad as the point where we were centralizing all the food and things so that we could take it to the park. His house was closest to the park of the pads we had available.

We'd been out, dropping people off here and there, shit like that. We were on our way back to this house; I was driving this car I just described to you. There were two other cars behind me belonging to brothers, you know.

I have this thing going, you know, I have to take a leak some time. This particular night it came down on me and I had to take a piss real badly. I'm only three or four blocks away from the house, I guess, but I just about pulled down this street, you know. My reaction is I gotta take a piss, the other cats stop their cars right behind mine, and I got outta the car and started taking a piss right along the driver's side. And then this car comes around the corner down here, you know. I didn't know it was a cop car when I first saw it, so I said, Wow, there's some people coming, man, so I stopped pissing and ran around to the other side of the car—just continued—I was just trying to avoid those lights, you know, a bad scene, he might drive by.

But when the car got up there, it stopped right behind my car. I could see all these lights and shit right on top of it, then I could tell it was a cop car. Threw the spotlight on me, man; both cops jumped out, yelling, "Come out from behind there!" I zipped my pants back up; I guess I took too long to get from back there to the street, but it really wasn't that long, you dig? When I stepped out from behind my car, man, them motherfuckers start shooting, see. I don't know if they recognized me, or if they just knew I was driving, or if they had it set up and were just waiting for a chance, or what. So naturally, what I do is dive for the ground. Somebody had a gun or two (hell, I don't know), but somebody started returning that fire. By that time another cop car come from around another corner, and cops in that car start shooting, shot out all the window shields in our car. Everybody was yelling, "Let's get outta here." And so we scattered, see? We ran across the street, and they shot one brother, Warren Wells. I thought I was shot, you know; I fell down, tripped over my feet, hit the ground. It was a very frightening situation. That was a weird shoot 'em out—I can't describe to you. It turned out there were about fifty cops around that area, and they say that all those cops came after we had gone into this house, but there was so much shooting going on, man, that there seemed like fifty million cops.

I hope I'm not skipping over some of that nice detail. But we had run away, and ran right into a cop and he started shooting at us, ran

another way and another cop started shooting at us. So we fall through this fence thing, you know, which turned out to be a little shed. When I hit the ground, I found myself boxed in between two houses with the shed in back with the pigs back there. And out in front, man, the street was just full of cops, and they were all shooting over there, see? And when I hit the ground on the other side, that's when I discovered that Bobby had a rifle, you know, and he started running into these cops and they shot and he split and that gives him some air, you know. But during that pause Bobby was nearest his house, he tried the doors and found it was open, see? So we went into the cellar over there. The cops surrounded the pad, man, and just started pouring fire into it. They were shooting it out something terrible. They started throwing in tear-gas shells.

Bobby was dealing with the door, and there really was no way for them to rush down there because they'd have to come down the little narrow passageway. And they couldn't really get in there now, during all this fire, and they were throwing this tear gas in there. We tried to move some of that furniture shit around so we could get a little protection, see? While I was standing there, man, Chuck [whitey] shot a tear-gas grenade through the window, it hit me in the chest, see, and sock—down on my ass.

Well, I just thought that I would never see again—it's dark in there, see, and little Bobby stripped all my clothes off me and patted me down for blood, dig? And that's how my clothes got off, see. The show went on for about ninety minutes, according to the papers. In that time we were fighting on gas, more or less, and getting shot at. Eventually, they set the house on fire, they shot fire balls in there and we couldn't deal with that. We could deal with gas, but . . .

Q: *How?*

A: Well at first, man, we were very frightened, and we thought we couldn't deal with it. But it was a question of dealing with that gas or running out into those bullets. This gas, man, when it first started coming in, we were breathing real slowly. We got used to it, man. It just stopped hurting. The fire came then, man. It was fucking hot. It was like the atmosphere caught on fire behind the gas. It was just fire, man, fire, fire. So we had to get out. I called out to the cop and told him we wanted to come out, you know, the cop says throw the guns out . . . Bobby threw his rifle out the window. I forgot to mention that I got shot in the leg when I was inside the pad, see. We were laying down along this 18-inch ceiling wall foundation. That's one thing that helped us from getting wasted by the bullets because they couldn't make that angle.

After we threw the guns out, they saw us coming out, with our hands up, you know. I got a shot in my leg, while I was lying down by the wall. I could only move with Bobby's help, so he had me draped over his shoulder, and as we went out the door there was like a threshold, like a step down. We tripped and fell down on the ground right outside of the door. Now these cops were in the house next door, in the windows, and they had their guns on us. There must have been seven or eight cops. They told us to just sit still and keep our hands up in the air. That's what we did, just like that, our hands up in the air. Then they said, "We got 'em," and all the other cops ran over, about fifty cops, all of them with their guns out. Then they started on us, started hitting us, kicking us, cursing and talking crazy—really a frantic scene. So if you can imagine the whole scene, it took about two hours. They were uptight, we were uptight, you know.

Then there was a pause, a hesitation, you could see them talking again. So then I get up, Bobby got up, and he started helping me up, but I couldn't get any further than right here, and I couldn't put my weight on this foot 'cause I got hit down here. They snatched Bobby away. They seemed to resent him helping me get up, dig? They told us to go down this walkway thing . . . told us to run to that car, dig? I can't run, see what I mean, so I tell them I'm wounded, man, I can't run. So they told Bobby, "Run to that car," and pushed him, and imagine, like our eyes were swollen —it was easy to see our eyes were swollen—from that gas, dig? So when we came out all that air was like acid—so we were pretty fucked up, you know. Bobby was just stumbling from the shove, stumbling down this walkway, and he was scared, naturally, uptight, man, and fucked up, you know.

And they start burning him, shot him down. It sounded like fifteen, sixteen shots. He just fell, man. And then all these people who had come out from the sound of all that shooting and shit, all these people had come out and crowded around and they start yelling at the cops, you dig? "Murderers! Pigs!" All kinds of names. "Leave him alone." And they got all uptight about that, and a lieutenant came over there

and then went to see the captain and told the captain, "This one here says he's wounded." The captain said to me, "Where you wounded at?" "In my foot," I said, and the motherfucker stomped me on my foot, you dig? "OK, get him outta here." And the same captain—his name is Captain McCarthy—is one of the leading troublemakers in Oakland. I had a couple of encounters with him, and he knows me, and I know him on sight.

Then they put me in a car. Then took me out of the car and into one of the big Marias, and then they began to fuck with me. One of the cops was talking on the mike. "We are bringing one in," he said, and asked what my name was. I told him and he repeate it on the microphone. Then these two cops got in the Maria and started fucking with me, hitting me, you know? They were telling the driver to drive down a dark street, you dig? And the driver turned and said, "I've already called in on that guy." Man, they cursed him, man, "Why in the fuck you do that for?" you know. The point is that they have a twenty-four-hour tape of all calls on the switchboard, so that if they had gone on and fucked with me that tape would have my name on it and they didn't dig that, see what I mean?

So they took me to the hospital. When I got there this other brother Warren Wells was laying up on the table. And a cop started fucking him up. One thing struck me as being quite significant: he (the cop) said, "You ain't goin' to no barbecue tomorrow. *You* the barbecue now!" So that indicates to me that this thing we were trying to do was very much on their minds. They took me in. There were some brothers and sisters working in this hospital, and they were trying to help us, you dig? We had so much tear gas on us, the people's eyes started burning when they brought us in. The sister did the best she could, she was washing all over my body, trying to get that gas out, which was in my hair, my beard, and my groin. All the skin was off my groin for three or four weeks. And the sister was washing me down in all these chemicals and everything. And this cop was standing there: "Say, hurry up, come on, he don't need all that." And the sister said, "Well, he goin' get all that. You don't get him until I'm through with him." So there were all kinds of conflicts like that, you know. And I'm just mentioning this to bring out the attitude of these pigs in Oakland, you see? Racist pigs, Gestapo.

From an interview by Cecil M. Brown, *Evergreen Review* Oct 1968

evergreen

Letter from Oakland

Paul Jacobs

BOBBY HUTTON 17

"There's a hawg in the stream!" shouted the Reverend E. E. Cleveland. He was holding a portable microphone in his hand as he swayed back and forth in the pulpit of the Ephesian Church of God in Christ in Oakland, California. "There's a hawg in the stream and the hawg is muddying up the cool water. God put in the stream! You got to get the hawg out, you got to get the hawg out of the stream or you cain't get a cool drink of water."

"Amen," shouted some of the congregation, the older women with black or white hats, the older men in suits with white shirts and dark ties, appropriate funeral clothes. But many others in the church, especially the young ones, sat in silence as the man in the pulpit took off his jacket and continued preaching in his shirtsleeves with his suspenders and belt showing. The teenage girls and a few of the women were bareheaded, with "natural" haircuts.

Two separate funerals were going on simultaneously in the church on Alcatraz St., almost at the dividing line between Oakland and Berkeley. (In spite of its grim name, Alcatraz is a pleasant street; middle-class whites live at its western end up in the hills, and the residents grow blacker down toward the much poorer eastern flatland that borders on the bay. Even there the neighborhood is more prosperous than most of Oakland's black ghetto. The Ephesian church itself is "modern" with stained glass windows of abstract design.) One funeral was a religious ceremony while the other was political, but both were for Bobby Hutton, the eighteen-year-old Black Panther who had been killed by the Oakland Police a few days earlier as he emerged, hands in the air, from the house where he, Eldridge Cleaver, and a group of other Panthers were under siege by the police.

The religious funeral was conducted in the traditional Negro style: hymns were sung, the minister preached the Gospel, while the older mourners moaned Bobby's name again and again, and an obituary of Bobby Hutton was read aloud, which mentioned every church choir group of which he'd been a member in his short life, but which said nothing of his membership in the Black Panthers.

The other funeral for Bobby was given him by the Black Panthers. They stood alongside the walls on both sides and back of the church, some wearing their black berets, all staring silently, almost stolidly, at the casket in front of the pulpit. The Panther services for Bobby were led by Bobby Seale, the Panther chairman, who spoke briefly and then introduced another Panther leader who talked for a few minutes of how Bobby Hutton had died to help save his people.

Neither of the two Black Panthers mentioned God or patience. And although they used the Minister's allegory of the "hawg in the stream," their message about it was that black people couldn't wait any longer for someone else to get the "hawg" out of the water, but had to do it for themselves, by fighting back at those who were keeping them from drinking the cool water.

Except for Marlon Brando who was sitting with a group of Panther leaders, there weren't many white people besides myself among the mourners. But the balcony of the church was crowded with white photographers, TV cameramen, and reporters. Once, during the service, the Negro preacher shouted up at them for snapping pictures of bodies and not of souls, asking why they came only to photograph funerals like that of Bobby Hutton but didn't come to take pictures when his congregation was having a revival service.

And as the preacher ranted at the reporters, three young girls in the row in front of me turned around to stare at them. One of them wore a sweatshirt with Malcolm's picture stenciled on it; all of them were obviously part of that group of high-school kids whose militance and hostility has not yet been sensed by much of the white world. Not many encounters have taken place yet between the newly emerging black high-school generation and white society.

But it was clear that these young people identified most with the silent Panthers in their black jackets and berets. Whatever doubts many white liberals and radicals, too, feel about the Panthers' willingness to use guns in self-defense, whatever uneasiness is created among those white liberals and radicals by the Panthers' continual use of the word "pigs" to describe the police, these are not shared by many young blacks. They may not be willing to participate directly in Panther activities but it seems certain that they identify emotionally and intellectually with them.

Such young people are not as concerned as are most whites with whether the police fire the first shot at the Panthers or whether the Panthers fire the first shot; unlike the whites, they are sure that if a policeman approaches them with a drawn gun, he is probably going to shoot them. That is reality to them as it is to the Panthers, and in Oakland they are very close to the truth.

The Oakland police have harassed the Black Panthers since they were organized early in 1966 by Huey Newton and Bobby Seale, who met while they were students at Merritt College in Oakland. Newton had started law school but left to spend full time organizing the Panthers (the name was taken from the Black Panthers Party of Lowndes County, Ala.). Hutton, then only sixteen, was the first member Newton and Seale had recruited.

Initially, the Panthers functioned as a Community Alert Patrol in the Oakland ghetto, following police cars and advising the residents of their legal rights if they were arrested. The group then called itself the Black Panthers For Self-Defense and the members stressed, again and again, that they would not attack first, but would defend themselves, with arms, if they were attacked. When the Panthers began their patrolling, the police compiled a list of all the license numbers of Panther cars, and stopped them arbitrarily. In October 1967, Huey Newton was arrested for the alleged murder of a police officer who halted his car; the circumstances surrounding the incident are still obscure and will not be clarified until Newton's trial takes place in June. His arrest has become a central issue among black militants and white radicals: the cry of 'Free Huey' is raised continually and Newton is now a congressional candidate of the Peace and Freedom Party.

The Panthers have recently become a frankly political organization. Much of their program would be acceptable to liberals; they ask for jobs, better housing, and decent education for blacks. But many liberal and even radical whites or blacks are uneasy with such Panther demands as the release of black prisoners from prison: the Panthers say they are engaged in a full-scale attack upon the legal system of America which, they insist, has deprived blacks of their rights to be tried by a jury of their peers. Yet the Panther leaders also express their opposition to rioting, and have been willing to work in close cooperation, on an equal basis, with white groups. Basically, the Panther political positions are related to what Eldridge Cleaver has described as the emergence of "national consciousness" among those minority groups who the Panthers insist are not American citizens except on paper. The Panthers believe that these minorities are in fact separate nations, systematically excluded from American society, and that therefore they should be given the opportunity to govern themselves and decide whether or not they wish, in Cleaver's phrase, to "integrate into Babylon."

Thus, the Panthers insist on the right of the blacks to "self-determination" and to breaking up the systems which now govern the lives of the ghetto residents from the outside. They want to police their own ghettos with men and women who live in the community. But their demands also strike at many American institutions. They ask for reparations for the hundreds of years in which black people have been the source of cheap labor. "If the white American businessman will not give full employment, then the means of production should be taken from the businessman and placed in the community."

Most of the white community in California is unaware of the Panthers' political position; all they can see are the guns which are played up by the press and on television. They are made uneasy, too, by the black berets and leather jackets that have become the Panther uniform. The Panthers do not discuss the size of their membership but it is obvious that they have at least a few hundred members in the Bay area, and they are now organizing in Los Angeles and other cities. They have also worked out a formal merger with SNCC. Still, the police tactics are hurting the Panthers: their homes are entered without warrants and their leaders arrested on charges which are then dropped.

Bobby Hutton had been killed on the night of April 6 after the Oakland police had stopped a car of Panthers returning from a meeting. According to the police version, the Panthers shot at them and they returned the fire. The Panthers maintain that the police pulled their guns and shot at them first. A few minutes later, the police surrounded the house into which the Panthers had run. Tear gas grenades were thrown, machine gun bullets poured into the floodlit house, setting it on fire. After about an hour and a half, the Panthers stopped shooting back and surrendered. Bobby Hutton was the first to come out of the house. He stepped forward with his hands in the air, and was told to move from the floodlit area to a police car. A police officer shouted, "He's got a gun." Bobby fell dead, his face and body riddled with bullets. Later, the police admitted he did not have a gun.

Only at the end of Bobby Hutton's funeral, the difference between the two separate funerals became clear; just before the last benediction was to be given, the preacher asked to speak a moment more. Directing himself to the Panthers alongside the walls, he pleaded with them to work in God's way with patience for the freedom of their people. He went on and on and on, his voice rising and falling, his body swaying. The young people in the congregation seemed to grow restless, until Bobby Seale walked up to the pulpit, and the preacher ended his plea. Seale spoke a few moments as if to reestablish the dominance of the Panthers and gave the signal for them to file past Bobby Hutton's bier. After all of them had walked past the coffin, the people in the congregation moved out into the aisles: directly ahead of me was the girl in the Malcolm sweatshirt. As he walked by the coffin, her eyes filled with tears. Angrily she blinked them back.

A few days later, four other members of the Panthers were arrested near the Panther office by the Oakland Police Department on "suspicion of robbery." After seventy-two hours, they were released for "lack of further evidence." □

*Oakland Panther
H.Q. after drunken
pigs shot it up.*

STALKING THE PANTHERS

KATHY MULHERIN

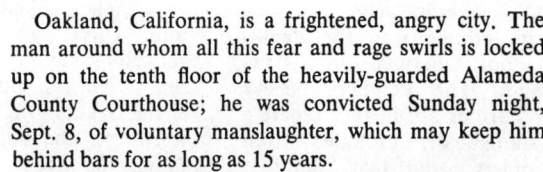

THE TRIAL OF
HUEY P.
NEWTON

Oakland, California, is a frightened, angry city. The man around whom all this fear and rage swirls is locked up on the tenth floor of the heavily-guarded Alameda County Courthouse; he was convicted Sunday night, Sept. 8, of voluntary manslaughter, which may keep him behind bars for as long as 15 years.

Follwing the announcement of the verdict in the murder trial of Huey P. Newton, founder and Minister of Defense of the Black Panther Party:

—Extra Oakland police patrolled city streets in unmarked cars.

—San Francisco and other Bay Area police departments were put on alert.

—Repeated denials from authorities did not quash the rumor that a camp heretofore used by the Job Corps was the center of mysterious troop maneuvers in the East Bay, and a local radio station reported that 14,000 National Guardsmen had been mobilized.

—On Monday, the streets of Oakland were saturated with Highway Patrol cars and police cars from surrounding communities, along with regular Oakland patrols.

—At 1:30 A.M. Tuesday morning, two Oakland policemen opened fire from their patrol car on the unoccupied Black Panther headquarters in the heart of the ghetto; some two dozen bullets smashed through the store-front window, ripping huge posters of Huey Newton and Minister of Information Eldridge Cleaver. The officers were charged with felonious assault in a complaint signed by Po-

lice Chief Gains and immediately fired by the city manager. Gains noted with dismay that the men had been drinking. Later, a police sergeant claimed that two hundred officers did not show up for work the next day in sympathy with the two men.

At a press conference, an attorney from the Policeman's Association, who had offered to defend the two in court, tried to explain why his clients "lost their cool" by comparing them to soldiers "who come back from the war for rest and recreation and they shoot up a village—they're suffering from battle fatigue." Policemen these days, he went on, are under tremendous pressures, abused from every quarter. "They bring their families into the war zone. . . . they are living in continual apprehension."

—Tuesday, a Bay Area newspaper (considered somewhat conservative) published a series of interviews conducted the day before with black and white people in the community. Generally, black people, especially poor and lower-income blacks, felt that the verdict was unfair; white people tended to feel that it was fair or that Newton should have been convicted of first-degree murder. All the policemen interviewed felt the jury had been "too soft" because the sentence for manslaughter would be a "cheap price to pay for an officer's life." Black teenagers expressed anger and warned of trouble.

One middle-aged black woman summed up the reaction: "Chile, will you tell me what's gong on? I'm a God-fearing woman and now that this Black Panther fellow got more than his people wanted for him to get and not as much as the police wanted, we're all in for it."

The trial lasted 34 days; it was a long, intense, bewildering experience for everyone involved. It was conducted in an atmosphere hardly conducive to calm and reasoned debate. And all this dramatic tension was supported by deeper, subtler strains: racism is a delicate reality, faced with it, the smallest nerves quiver.

I set out to write dispassionately, objectively, and found myself writing words which rubbed dryly against one another like small cardboard boxes. People are suspicious of the Panthers, I thought. I must not make them think I am partisan.

Suddenly I realized I had fallen into the same trap that caught the jury, the judge, the prosecution and the media. They had set out to judge Huey P. Newton and found themselves on trial. Straining to be "color-blind," to function according to principles on which the legal system rests, they sought merely to determine whether Newton actually killed one policeman and wounded another on the 28th of October, 1967. Above all, they wanted to be fair. They wanted to prove that a black man, even one so controversial and frightening as the Black Panther Minister of Defense, could get a fair trial in America, in Oakland, California, a "war zone." Prove to whom? To themselves. Just as I wanted to prove to the reader that I would be fair, too. The impulse exposes us. To see this case color-blind was also to see it without depth.

Even so, the riddle was difficult to resolve. There were four witnesses to Officer John Frey's death:

Officer Herbert Heanes, who never saw a gun in Newton's hand and who was himself shot three times. He claims he shot Newton in the stomach, although he might accidentally have hit Frey;

Henry Grier, a black bus driver who claimed his bus headlights illumined the whole scene, alone saw a gun in Newton's hand, and insisted he saw Newton shoot Heanes and Frey. But Grier was mistaken about Newton's height and clothing and, in his initial statement to police, said he could not see the gunman clearly. Also, a passenger on the bus named Thomas Miller insisted that Grier was making change for him during the shooting and that it was too dark to see much of anything;

Gene McKinney, a friend of Newton's who was with him that night. Officer Heanes testified that he stood quietly by, unarmed. But in the last days of the trial, McKinney took the stand, and when defense attorney Garry asked him if he had shot Frey, he refused to answer on grounds of self-incrimination. The prosecution discounted the implication that McKinney might have shot Frey, but it disturbed the jury. After the trial, a juror told a reporter, "If Huey isn't satisfied with the verdict he got, he ought to talk to his friend Gene McKinney. He's the key to the whole thing."

The weapon: There is no evidence to corroborate Grier's testimony that Huey had a gun in his hand. Frey's gun has disappeared, and the police did not notice its absence until they got him to a hospital; it is thus conceivable, said Garry, that someone unrelated to the case might have picked it up. The prosecution contended, and the jury believed, that Newton had hidden his own gun and Frey's before he went to the hospital. Two expended 9MM bullets were found on the ground plus an unexpended one in the car Newton was driving.

The motive: Prosecutor Lowell Jensen argued that the defendant was on probation for a previous felony conviction and knew that if he was found with a gun and marijuana (two matchboxes were found in the car but they

mysteriously disappeared *after* the police found them; Newton was not charged with possession), he would go to jail, so he panicked and tried to shoot his way out. Garry showed that his client's probation officer had told him his probation was over the day before. The Panther leader insisted he knew nothing about marijuana and had no gun.

The shooting: Jensen projected a description of what happened that night: Huey shot once with his own gun drawn from his shirt, then wrestled Frey's gun away from him and altogether shot Heanes three times and Frey five times. Inexplicably, police never made a routine test (neutron activation) to determine whether either had fired a gun. Newton was wounded in the abdomen.

Huey said Frey pulled him over, said, "Well, well, what do we have here, the great Huey P. Newton," demanded his registration and license, conferred with Officer Heanes who arrived to back Frey up, and returned to put Huey under arrest for "false identification." Newton protested, and he was frisked "in a very degrading manner." As he walked toward the patrol car with Frey, he opened the law book in his hand and asked why he was being arrested. Frey called him a "nigger" and straight-armed him, knocking him back several steps. He fell to one knee, looked up and saw Frey draw his revolver. Then, he claims, he felt something like "boiling hot soup" spill over his stomach and he blacked out. He remembers nothing until he reached the hospital.

The Context of Racism

On this level of the case, there were dozens of small mysteries, contradictions, discrepancies. The jury's verdict (voluntary manslaughter in the killing of Frey and innocent of the charge of shooting Heanes) indicates that they believed only part of Grier's testimony, since the first thing he claims to have seen was Newton shooting Heanes. In that case, who did shoot Heanes? If the jury thought McKinney might have done it, how did they reconcile Heanes' testimony that McKinney was unarmed? At least one juror had a "premonition" that there might be a fifth, still unknown person involved. There are literally dozens of factors which, in the opinion of many, created room for "reasonable doubt."

Interestingly, white people sympathetic to Newton followed the case very closely, probing the testimony for weaknesses in the prosecution's case, so they could prove to one another that Newton was innocent. But the Panthers did not seem to care whether Huey was innocent.

Power, says Huey P. Newton, says Mao Tse-tung, comes from the barrel of a gun. No doubt, but it belongs also to whoever can define what is real and what is not, what is legitimate and what is not. The court used its power (of both gun and definition) to make the defense deal with the question of Huey's guilt or innocence in the shooting of Frey. The only way the Panthers could get their leader back was to defend him against this charge, but they in turn forced the court to take their definition of the situation into account, for they turned the courtroom into a platform for their view of America; they made it clear that they considered the state, the court, the jury illegitimate, that Huey was in their eyes a political prisoner. They raised the most basic questions about the ability of the legal system to deal with disputes of this kind, and managed to create a good deal of doubt about its viability as a fundamental social arbiter. And if the jury decision was indeed a compromise, then it serves to illustrate vivdly that power, not justice, was the key to Huey Newton's trial.

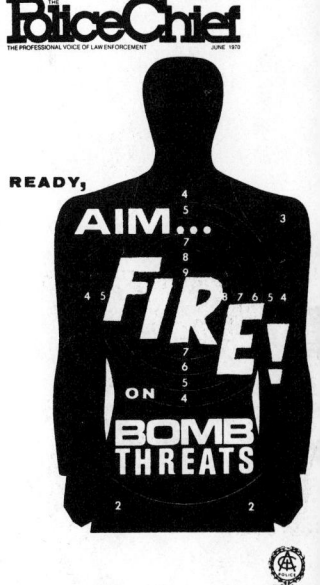

What interested Charles Garry and Huey Newton above all was the context of racism in which the whole case was acted out, from the night of the shooting to the day the jury returned a verdict. There were two reasons for their determination to concentrate on this point. The first, and least important, was that the issue of racism offered them the best legal leverage. The legal system is believed to be just, all men are equal before it, and its validity in American history and political life rests on this thesis—it is very sensitive to the charge of racism. So Garry set out to prove to the court that it could not give Huey a fair trial, that jury selection, the police and the "facts" were weighed against him.

The first two weeks of the trial were taken up with jury selection. Charles Garry sought to prove that current methods of jury selection were inherently prejudicial to his client; he offered expert testimony:

1. Dr. Jan Dizard, a sociologist from the University of California, testified that his studies showed that jury panels drawn from voter registration lists are discriminatory. The chief eliminators of prospective jurors were factors like high mobility and economic hardship; hence the poor and ghetto blacks tend to be excluded. Judge Monroe Friedman, 72, interrupted frequently to insist that the testimony focus on Alameda County, California.

2. Floyd Hunter, sociologist and author of a study of Oakland's power structure, tried to explain to the court why black people are frequently too discouraged to vote. The judge was skeptical that black people in Alameda county feel that way.

3. Dr. Hans Zeisel of the University of Chicago, who has studied the jury system, testified that racism is a major differentiating factor in opinions regarding capital punishment. Black people tend to oppose it. Those who favor it tend to oppose open housing and need less proof to conclude guilt.

4. Dr. Nevitt Sanford, a Stanford psychologist and one of the authors of a classic study of the authoritarian personality, pointed out that people who support capital punishment tend to be "authoritarian personalities."

5. Dr. Robert Blauner, University of California sociologist whose field is race relations, distinguished between "objective" and "subjective" racism: objective racism is institutional, and subjective racism is attitudinal. "Living in this [objectively] racist society," he said, "it is not possible for white people to be free of subjective racism." The judge asked if there was a way to test for racism. Noting that all whites including himself were infected with some racism, Blauner suggested that a juror who met four conditions would be most free of it: such a person would a) know something about black history and culture, b) be aware of his prejudice and be working to overcome it, c) have lived and worked with black people, and d) be actively committed to changing the racist structure—in his job and personal life.

It became clear that few jurors qualify. Dozens were eliminated for revealing blatant racist attitudes, but what was more significant was that the court did not seem able to absorb and incorporate the information presented by the sociologists. The judge was a crotchety old man who gave few signs of understanding its importance, and as the case dragged on, seemed to become increasingly involved emotionally. After hearing all this testimony, he swiftly denied Garry's motion to eliminate the entire jury panel. Indeed, there would have been no way to conduct the trial if he had accepted Garry's arguments. The flaw is too deep. The legal system requires that a man be judged by his peers; the underlying assumption is that all citizens are "peers," but it has been all too clear for some time, and was merely spelled out by this trial, that the

relationship between white middle-class Americans and poor blacks is not that of "peers"—it is colonial. Huey's peers live in the ghetto of West Oakland and were unrepresented on the jury. Later in the trial, defense attorney Garry brought forward a black sociologist named Henry Blake who tried to explain something about the black sub-culture, ghetto slang and code words. He argued that words which mean one thing to a white man mean quite another to a black man; thus, the inflammatory language used by the Panthers when speaking of the police merely represented their demand for the removal of police from their community and an effort on their part to free themselves of the myth of the white man's invulnerability. (After the trial, a lady juror remarked in an interview that she found his remark very enlightening, which "surprised" her because "with that beard all over his face, he looked like a bum.")

But the court could not accept these arguments for a very good reason. The legal system is designed to arbitrate disputes impartially. If it does not represent, cannot even understand, some significant segment of the society, then it becomes a vested interest, a lobbyist for one interest against another.

The court refused to believe that America is schizoid, a refusal which forced it to behave in a schizophrenic manner. For, by insisting on a "color-blind" perspective, by denying the expert testimony which pointed to the racism inherent in jury selection, the court had to "make believe." Precisely, make believe: either the expert testimony was correct and the legal system must be radically overhauled, or it was false; to believe the first and go on with the trial would have been false pretense of the worst kind; to believe the second was delusion.

The second reason the defense concentrated on the issue of racism was that it felt strongly that Newton's indictment itself was the direct result of racism. Garry argued that the Black Panthers, and especially their leader, had been the victims of sustained harassment by the Oakland police ever since they had marched into the state legislature a year and a half ago heavily and legally armed in order to dramatize to black people their right to carry guns. In addition, he presented testimony which indicated that John Frey had a remarkably racist past, and that others in the case, such as the nurse at the hospital Huey went to for treatment after he was shot and the policemen she called to restrain him, had subjected him to brutally racist abuse. When he took the stand, Newton discussed, under cross examination, the many encounters he has had with the police. Prosecutor Lowell Jensen tried to show that Huey had a violent past and Newton, with calm and assurance, tried to counteract that impression by insisting that he had been victimized in every case. Evidently, all this testimony impressed the jury, because the manslaughter verdict implies that Newton was provoked into shooting Officer Frey. In fact, the same lady juror who was surprised by the sociologist's beard, declared that she didn't "blame" Huey for the shooting. In this respect, then, the trial represented a victory for the defense.

But there was a way in which the Panthers succeeded far more deeply. They wrested much of the power to define away from the prosecution, the judge and the jury. They did this in a number of subtle and not-so-subtle ways. They conducted a campaign based on the slogan "Free Huey," not, "give Huey a fair trial," not, "Huey is innocent," but simply, free Huey. Never once in the dramatic demonstrations they made around the courthouse and all over Oakland, nor in any speech nor in anything they wrote, did they mention Huey's innocence. They said: we are a subjugated population, a colony, and the "pigs" (*we* are human, *they* are animals) of the "mother country" have our leader captive—if they don't set him free, we will retaliate, we will make them pay in flesh and blood and destruction. We will destroy them if they do not return him to us.

They marched rhythmically around the courthouse in gleaming black jackets, carrying signs reading "the sky's the limit," chanting in ominous, beautiful antiphony: "Black is beautiful/Set our warrior free!" They appeared every day in the courtroom, sat silently, grimly, staring straight ahead. A black poet who covered the trial wrote: "You glance around you. The Panthers are sitting in the other section of the courtroom. You remember this scene and you feel for a moment that this is a legitimate battle, that the Panthers are only emissaries of a fully equivalent power, and that behind them stand black regiments, black cities, black presences, prepared to start battle if their people are not given justice."

And the court, the state, responded. The courthouse was heavily guarded by armed policemen stationed at every door; no one was allowed in without precise credentials. Every day, new press passes were issued, and every day, every spectator and reporter who entered the courtroom was thoroughly and uncomfortably frisked. And after the verdict, as I've mentioned, the city braced itself.

Cool Big Cats

Yet, for all the bristling, the Panthers played it cool. They insisted, as the trial drew to a close, that "the sky's the limit" meant exhausting all legal remedies, and when it was feared that the incident involving the two policemen who shot up the Panther office would precipitate a riot, Huey Newton held a press conference from his jail cell in which he strongly admonished his people to "cool it." Bewildered observers wondered whether the Panthers meant what they said, or if, in fact, they had been misunderstood by the white community. The answer may lie in a remark made by Newton two days before the verdict was in: Quoting from the third chapter of Ecclesiastes, he said. "To everything there is a season, and a time to every purpose under the heaven"; he told his followers that the police were "looking for an excuse" to injure and arrest Panthers.

The Panthers defined for black people the reality of the trial as they saw it, and declared it illegitimate, but they went one step farther and made the trial historic, made it a profoundly important experience for black people and many whites—they exposed the root: fear. Huey P. Newton founded the Panthers on the notion that his people would only be free of oppression when they were no longer afraid of the white man; the source of that fear lay in the white's power to kill them. That is why he focused on the issue of guns. And what everyone, absolutely everyone in that courtroom saw, was that Newton was not afraid, that his people outside were not afraid. As the weeks went by, the slight, dark man who sat quietly by his attorney, began to affect everyone in it. When he took the stand in his own defense, he spent perhaps five minutes describing the events of the night of October 28th. And then, with great dignity and almost imperturbable calm, he spoke at length about his people, their history, their slavery, their contributions to American history, and he spoke of the Panthers, how and why they began. He delivered, as far as it was possible, a series of lectures—to a captive audience. The judge and the prosecuting attorney showed remarkable patience with the young man as he rambled on; they seemed curious, respectful, and a little puzzled. Huey was not afraid. That fact was lost on no one, fascinated

everyone—showed on the faces of the jurors, in the voice and manner of the prosecutor, in the awkwardly deferential treatment he was suddenly accorded by the police deputies who escorted him back to his cell, in the slightly awed articles by the press, which spoke of his serene, charismatic qualities, in a new gentleness in the faces of his friends and fellow Panthers.

Let us not exaggerate the drama—the truth is dramatic enough. Everyone was quite aware that Huey could be condemned to death, that no one could forcibly liberate him from his cell. Nor is Newton a saint; he was nervous when he first began to speak; his lectures wandered, became dull; his humor was wry and mischievous, and there were times when he must have been lying. He did not behave like a fanatic too wrapped up in delusions of grandeur to understand death; he is a young man, eager to work. But he made it very clear that he belonged to his people, to his culture, that he expected nothing from his captors.

It was this, finally, that made the trial powerful. Huey Newton's trial received national and international publicity—and however uncomprehending or biased that coverage might have been, Newton was given an opportunity to speak to his people. He used it well and shrewdly. How blacks in the poorest slum tenement must have laughed to hear or read of Judge Friedman's gruff bewilderment in the face of ghetto slang; they must have felt some wicked or bitter pleasure to sense the fear behind the judge's harsh inquiries into the meaning of the black slogan "by any means necessary," especially when Newton replied by reading from the Declaration of Independence.

Huey Newton has touched a deep nerve in America; he has, and probably will have, enormous support in the poor black community. He and the Panthers have used the trial to delegitimize the legal system; they have also shown themselves capable of defining their own value structure, and of overcoming their fear of white oppression. Those may well be revolutionary feats.

The sociologist Talcott Parsons once wrote: "Law flourishes particularly in a society in which the most fundamental questions of social values are not currently at issue or under agitation. If there is sufficiently acute value conflict, law is likely to go by the board. Similarly it flourishes in a society in which the enforcement problem is not too seriously acute. This is particularly true where there are strong informal forces reinforcing conformity with at least the main lines of the legally institutionalized tradition."

Law is thus, finally, a matter of faith. The world views represented at this trial, however, were so deeply opposed that they undercut the very foundation of faith on which the entire system rests. The jury must be twelve peers possessed of common sense, and common sense must spring from a common culture. But these were not Newton's peers, not of his culture—they were, in a sense, foreigners and, in the Panthers' eyes, foreign tyrants, colonial governors. All this explains why the jury's verdict, which was a compromise between these two world-views, was contradictory; the jurors despaired of finding the truth and sought to grapple with the balance of power. So, this long trial did not even succeed in eliciting the "color-blind" truth of that night.

For Huey Newton, the Panthers and black people, the trial was a step toward liberation from oppression, but for whites, and indeed, the society as a whole, the implications are awesome.

See No Evil, Hear No Evil, Tell Lies

"I don't like calling policemen pigs any more than I like to hear white people call colored people niggers," the woman said, and I accepted that, though I myself am not opposed to calling a pig a pig. But what do I make of her when she goes on to say that she "would object" to racial intermarriage? Why does the term "nigger" disturb her when the term "unfit-to-make-love-to" (or however she phrases it in her mind) evidently bothers her not at all?

This woman, Adrienne Reed of San Leandro, has been tentatively seated as one of the jurors who will pass judgement on Huey Newton. When Newton's attorney, Charles Garry, asked Mrs. Reed *why* she objects to intermarriage, prosecuting attorney Lowell Jensen jumped up and shouted "Objection!" and Superior Court Judge Monroe Friedman angrily declared, in a voice much louder than usual, "Objection sustained!"

This is the story of our society. And it is the story of the first two weeks of the Newton trial. The defense attorney can be legally prevented—prevented by a court set up to administer the Law of the Land—from asking the one question that gets at the root of racism, the question that every governing body, church, club, committee, or political group which claims to oppose racism should be asking its members, the question that everyone who wants to prevent chaos (and I assume this includes Judge Friedman) should be shouting from the rooftops.

But we object to this question!
Objection sustained.
Injustice sustained.
Sickness sustained.

—Marlene Charyn
in the
Midpeninsula Observer (UPS)

Chairman Fred

"When one of us falls, 1,000 will take his place."

Fred Hampton, 21, Chairman of the Illinois Chapter of the Black Panther Party was shot and killed in his bed this morning, December 4th, by Illinois state's attorney's police. Also murdered was Mark Clark, Panther Defense Captain of Peoria, Illinois. Four other Panthers were wounded in the raid on Hampton's apartment at 2337 West Monroe, one block from the Black Panther Party headquarters.

According to police reports, a gun battle began after fifteen state's attorney's police cordoned off the block and tried to enter the Monroe street apartment. The raid was made on the basis of a search warrant issued by Circuit Judge Robert Collins after a witness swore he had seen "a large cache of shotguns and other weapons" in the building earlier in the day.

Sgt. Daniel Groth of the state's attorney's police led the raid. At a press conference Groth said, "I knocked on the front door, and someone asked 'Who's there?' I identified myself as a police officer and said I had a warrant to search the premises. I got no response. I repeatedly demanded entry for several minutes. Then I forced the front door with my shoulder. It was only a light touch. As I entered the darkened apartment I saw a girl on a bed holding a shotgun. As she fired the gun, Det. Duke Davis and three others fell to the kitchen floor."

This writer went to the apartment twelve hours after the slaying took place. Sgt. Groth is lying. He said he forced the front door open, was met by gunfire, and four of his cohorts fell to the kitchen floor.

Fact — The front door opens onto the front room.

Fact — The kitchen floor is in the kitchen which is the back room.

Fact — The front room door shows no evidence of having been forced.

Fact — There is a bullet hole in the front door which was made by a bullet <u>entering</u> the front room.

Bobby Rush, Minister of Defense of the Illinois Black Panther Party reported that a witness to the raid said he heard a knock on the front door. Someone in the apartment asked, "Who's there?' "Tommy," was the reply. Then a gunshot ripped through the door and into the front room.

All police statements insist that it was the police that were attacked, that a wild gun battle ensued, and that they were carrying on a legal search to confiscate illegal weapons.

Bobby Rush called it "another search and destroy mission." He said, "this vicious murder of Chairman Fred and Clark was implemented by that dog Nixon and Hanrahan and all the rest of

the pigs. Hampton never fired back when the pigs came into his back room and shot Fred in the head. He couldn't have fired back because he was asleep.

"If the Panthers had as many weapons as the pigs said they had and if they had fired them, there would have to be evidence those weapons were fired."

There was no evidence in the apartment that the Panthers had fired. There is one bullet hole going <u>into</u> the front door. In Hampton's bedroom, a blood-stained mattress lies on the floor, there are nine bullet holes in one wall, and fourteen bullet holes in another wall. The last set of holes are the effect of bullets which were shot <u>through</u> that wall from an adjoining bedroom. If it was a pitched 10-minute gun battle, as the police claim, then it is truly amazing that only two cops were injured — one struck in the right hand by flying glass, the other grazed by a shotgun pellet on the left leg.

Coroner Andrew J. Toman said Hampton was shot twice in the head and once in the left shoulder, and that Clark had been shot once in the left chest and once in the left arm.

Four other Panthers were taken to County Hospital. They are: Ronald (Doc) Satchel, 19, Minister of Medicine, shot in the abdomen and left leg; Blair Anderson, 18, shot in the abdomen; Vernlin Brewer, 17, shot in the left leg and thigh; and Brenda Harris, 18, shot in the right leg and left hand.

Three others were arrested: Deborah Johnson, 19; Louis Trueluck, 39; and Harold Bell, 23.

State's Attorney Hanrahan said all of those arrested in the "shootout" would be charged with attempted murder.

Bobby Rush said, "The people will beat the pigs to death and just because Chairman Fred has fallen does not signal the end of the Black Panther Party in Illinois.

"When one of us falls, 1,000 will take his place."

Marshall Rosenthal

This is the house that blood built. It is called 2337 West Monroe Street. It is in Chicago, in what Elvis calls "the ghet—to."

A pool of blood stains the carpet behind the front door to this house. The blood was part of Mark Clark until the morning of December 4th. Mark Clark was a Black Panther from Peoria, Illinois.

Color him dead.

Overturned furniture fills the front room and hallways of this house. The walls and furniture are air-conditioned police style — ventilated by shotgun, pistol, automatic rifle, and magnum shells.

Color them violated.

There is a third bedroom at the end of the hallway, and the mattress in this room is half brown and half red. The brown part is frayed from use, the red part is fresh and slippery with agony and pain.

This redness was a part of Fred Hampton. Fred Hampton was Chairman of the Illinois Black Panther Party. Color him dead, too.

Fred Hampton was 21 years old.

Mark Clark was 22.

A block away, the Information Minister and the Defense Minister and several other speakers speak of Chairman Fred and Mark Clark and armed struggle. They speak of why they are tired of writing and lecturing and organizing in the shadow of 400 years of Babylonian Captivity.

Words.

At the house that blood built, words are no longer necessary. The shotgun patterns show where Ron Satchel, Blair Anderson, Verlin Brewer, and Brenda Harris were put up against the wall. Shocked eyes play "follow the dots" and relay the truth: each was shot only in the lower body, each was shot to cripple him or her for a long time.

Soon we will pay yet another visit. Jews call it "sitting shivah." Irishmen call it a "wake." The Vikings launched ships when the time came. Soon we shall go to a place unlike "the ghet—to," a place where the air is clean and there is space for people to stretch out. We shall go to this place of good-byes, and we shall say our farewells to the 37th and 38th Black Panthers to perish this year. We shall stand over the graves and hear eulogies to those who faught well and not in vain.

More words.

We, the long-haired sons and daughters of the middle-class, went to the house that blood built and saw the truth that words and rhetoric cannot say. We saw the redness of black men and women and knew it for the redness of the yellow Vietnamese and the white activist whose blood will flow before the beast is slain. We stepped in the redness, and felt rage that the State's attorney could dare to congratulate his his gunmen for killing people in their beds. The redness seeped into our minds as we thought of our own communal homes and our still-living loved ones.

When we left the house that blood built, we knew that we had descended from the mountain to join with those who dwell in the valley. And, when we looked into each other's eyes we knew that the road back had been sealed by the avalanche of what we had seen.

Bring the ghetto home.

Abe Peck

This is war, people.

Fred Hampton was murdered in his sleep last night. He was the 38th member of the Black Panther Party to be killed by the pigs and their lackeys in 1969.

The Weathermen want to bring the Vietnam war home to Amerika. They don't have to lift a finger to see it done. The pigs are doing it for all of us and the heaviness of the Amerikan war is increasing geometrically every day.

I talked with half a dozen people today, the day after the murder, who were pale and trembling because of the thoughts that were going through their heads. One girl kicked parking meters. Someone else spraypainted messages of sorrow and revenge on the walls of the neighborhood. Another person went home, took out his gun, and gazed at it thoughtfully all afternoon. Voices on the phone sometimes sounded very faint and faraway, I tried to remember Fred alive as I printed photo after dead photo of him. I thought of the people I knew who are dead now. It's getting to be quite a list.

State's Attorney Hanrahan got on the tv and said how proud he was of his men for killing another couple niggers, and a boss one at that. A black man was arrested while walking down Ashland Ave. singing and firing random shots in the air. Panthers conducted tours through the blood-soaked apartment. Thousands filed through. A reporter for a daily paper went through the apartment and called his editor. "It was cold-blooded murder" he said. "Will the paper print that?" someone asked. He replied, "I don't know...I don't know." Four stoned longhairs stumbled across a street, almost getting hit by a car. Laughing, they disappeared into a brightly lit apartment. The Conspiracy 7 asked for a recess because they were emotionally upset. Judge Hoffman refused.

Brothers and sisters, they have killed too many of us. They have put too many of us in jail. They have insulted us too long with their lies and drivel. The time of choices is rapidly drawing to an end. It is stand and fight or die. I don't know how to say how strongly I feel this Maybe e.e. cummings said it:

I don't want to frighten you
but they mean to kill us all
and B. Dylan said it:

You must choose now, take what you need, you think will last.

We will last. We need each other. If you haven't chosen, you must soon.

Armando

Chicago Seed Extra 12/6/69

SEIZE THE TIME!

The seven Panthers who survived the police raid on December 4 which took the lives of Chairman Fred Hampton and Mark Clark were indicted in Chicago, January 30, on charges of attempted murder.

Four of the seven Panthers were shot by the cops. Two of the cops were slightly wounded—one cut his hand breaking a window, the other apparently grazed in the fusillade of gunfire by his fellow officers. There is no substantive evidence that the Panthers fired a shot.

And, once again, the victims are to be judged by their assassins.

The Great Speckled Bird 2/9/70

THERE IS A CLEAR THREAT TO THE FASCIST PIGS WHEN BLACK CANNON FODDER BECOMES BLACK LIBERATION FIGHTERS.
WHEN THE ONE-TIME MERCENARY BECOMES A FREEDOM FIGHTER, THE FASCISTS SEE PROBLEMS COMMING.
THIS IS WHY THEY TRY AS HARD AS THEY CAN TO DEPRIVE THE BLACK PANTHER PARTY OF BROTHERS TRAINED IN ANY MILITARY SKILLS.

RANDY WILLIAMS, F
FORMER PARATROOPER
101st. AIRBORNE
Political Prisoner

LANDON WILLIAMS
Political Prisoner

BOBBY SEALE
Chairman
Black Panther Party
Political Prisoner

TO MY BLACK BROTHERS IN VIET NAM

ELDRIDGE CLEAVER
Minister of Information
Black Panther Party

ELMER PRATT (GERONIMO)
Dep. Min. of Defense,
So. Calif.

HAROLD BELL,
Political Prisoner

BOB RUSH
Dep. Min.
of Defense,
Chicago

I'm writing this on January 4, 1970. We are starting out a new year. On August 31, I'll be 35 years old. I'm married, and I have one child with another one on the way. I am in love with my wife and I would like to enjoy a happy life raising a family. But I am not free to live the type of life that I would like. Pigs--the racist fascist rulers of the United States--won't let me.

And I would like to ask you Brothers: are you living the life that you want to live? Are these same pigs cramping your style? I don't believe that you actually prefer to be way over there, fighting against our Vietnamese Brothers and Sisters who are fighting for their freedom. Because your own people, whom you left behind in Babylon, are also fighting for their freedom a- gainst the very same pigs who have you over there doing their dirty work for them. And your people need you-- and your military skills--to help us take our freedom and stop these racist pigs from committing genocide upon us, as they have been doing for the past 400 years.

I am the Minister of Information of the Black Panther Party, and I am speaking to you now for the Party, but I want to put a personal note into this because I know that you niggers have your minds all messed up about Black organizations, or you wouldn't be the flunkies for the White

We either help our people or, by refus- ing to help them, make it easier for the enemy to destroy us. There are no two ways about it.

While you are over there in Vietnam, the pigs are murdering our people, oppressing them, and the jails and pri- sons of America are filling up with political prisoners. These political pri- soners are your own Black Brothers and Sisters. We have a desperate, life and death struggle on our hands, and if we a people are going to sur- vive, then we must save ourselves. We need your help, desperately, be- fore it is too late.

This is the moment in history that our people have been working, praying, fighting, and dying for. Now, while the whole world is rising up with arms against our oppressors, we must make a decisive move for our freedom. If we miss this chance, this golden op- portunity, who knows when we will get another chance? We cannot afford to gamble with this chance by putting things off. Now is the moment for decision. This very moment, right where you are. You do not have to wait until later, until after you are back home and out of the army. You can make your move now, while you are still inside the army, because the army is one of the key weapons which the pigs have up their sleeves to use against us when the time comes. And make no mistake about it, the White

New York, 14 in New Haven, 18 in Los Angeles, and 16 in Chicago.

We appeal to you Brothers to come to the aid of your people. Either quit the army, now, or start destroying it from the inside. Anything else is a compromise and a form of treason against your own people. Stop killing the Vietnamese people. You need to start killing the racist pigs who are over there with you giving you orders. Kill General Abrahms and his staff, all his officers. Sabotage supplies and equipment, or turn them over to the Vietnamese people. Talk to the other Brothers and wake them up. You should start now weeding out the traitors amongst you. It is better to do it now than to allow them to return home to help the pigs wipe us out. Especially the Uncle Tom officers should be dealt with now, because the pigs will use them as effective tools against our peo- ple. When you can no longer take care of business inside the army, then turn yourself over to the Vietnamese people and tell them you want to join the Black Panther Party to fight for the freedom and liberation of your own people. If you do cross over, you don't have to worry about the Vietnamese people abusing you. They will be glad to see you drop out of the army because what they want most in life is to stop the fighting in their land. You have a duty to humanity as well as to your own people not to be used as murderous

JOHN SEALE

ROOSEVELT HILLIARD (JUNE)
Asst. Chief of Staff, Black Panther Party

ELBERT HOWARD (BIG MAN)
Dep. Min. of Information

ROBERT WEBB

CLARENCE TERRY

ROBERT BRYAN-L.A. 18

organization--the U.S.A.--for whom you have picked up the gun. The Black Panther Party has picked up the gun too, but not to fight against the heroic Vietnamese people, but rather to wage a war of liberation against the very same pigs whom you are helping to run their vicious game on the entire world, including upon your own people. Dig it. I wonder, can you dig it? Can you dig niggers, brothers and sisters off the block, who have said later for the pigs and have picked up guns, in Babylon, to bring to fulfillment the dreams of freedom that have kept our people alive for 400 years, under the racist yoke of the White man. From the said days of slavery in the cotton fields of the South, to the present bleeding years of the Democrats, Republicans, Uncle Toms, Lyndon B. Johnson, and now, the foulist racist pig ever to become president of the United States, Richard Meatly Mouth Nixon--your Commander in Chief and the Number One Enemy of our people.

The struggle of our people for freedom has progressed to the form where all of us must take a stand either for or against the freedom of our people. You are either with your people or against them. You are either part of the solution or part of the problem.

is coming and it is almost here. The pigs are using G.I.'s from Vietnam on the police forces and National Guard units inside Babylon. Many of our Black Brothers go to Vietnam and learn how to kill human beings, then when they are released from the army they return home and end up on the police force. On the police forces, they carry out the same dirty work against us, in the name of "Law and Order" that they carried out against the Vietnamese people.

In 1968-69, the pigs murdered 28 members of the Black Panther Party and nobody even knows how many other of our Black Brothers and Sisters were shot down by the pigs. But it is a long list. Scores of our Party members are being held as political prisoners because they took a stand for the freedom and liberation of our people. Huey P. Newton, Minister of Defense of the Black Panther Party, our leader, is in prison in California. Our Chairman, Bobby Seale, is in jail and the pigs are trying to put him in the electric chair, in Connecticut, on trumped up charges. Pigs in Chicago murdered Fred Hampton while he was sleep in his bed. Shot him in his head with a shotgun, with 00 Buckshot. The pigs have been making mass arrests of our Party members, with 21 arrested in

tools by racist pigs to oppress the people.

Think about it, Brother, and act on it, because you don't have much time. Organize all the Brothers around you and move. Force the pigs to understand that you will no longer be their slave and hired killer. Let the pigs know that, instead, you want the persecution of your Black Brothers and sisters to stop and that you intend to help stop it. Demand that Huey P. Newton and Bobby Seale be set free. Especially, help us force the pigs not to murder Bobby Seale in the electric chair.

We have dedicated our lives, our blood, to the freedom and liberation of our people, and nothing, no force, can stop us from achieving our goal. If it is necessary to destroy the United States of America, then let us destroy it with a smile on our faces. A smile for the freedom and liberation of our people. The Black Panther Party calls for freedom and liberation in our life time, because we want to leave behind us a decent world for our children to grow up in. Let's turn 1970 into a year in which our people make heroic drive for freedom and liberation.

ALL POWER TO THE PEOPLE!
SEIZE THE TIME!

JEWEL COOK

RAY 'MASAI' HEWITT
Minister of Education, Black Panther Party

ISAIH HOUSTON -L.A. 18

HARAWESE MOORE (PEACHES)- L.A. 18

WILLIE ICENT (MONK TEBA)

R. CHAKA WALLS

JAMES JOHNSON

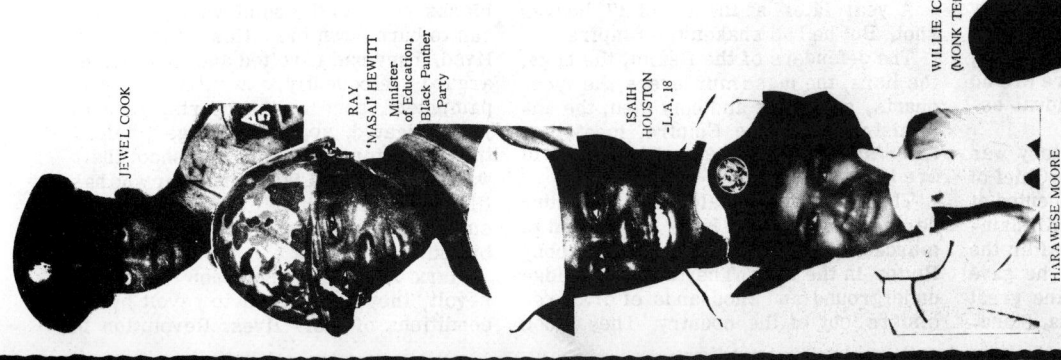

THE BLACK PANTHER

Brothers and Sisters...

A STATEMENT BY OAKLAND SEVEN DEFENDANT TERRY CANNON AT THE END OF THE COMMISSION OF INQUIRY INTO THE WAR AND POLITICAL REPRESSION, JANUARY 18, 1969

Brothers and sisters,

Is there anyone in the audience who belongs to the Friends of the Irish Republican Army? Too bad, I wanted to sign up.

When I was youngly political nine years ago—I turn 29 on Monday—I was not proud of my race, I thought we were a race of southern sheriffs and northern liberals. Now I am proud—of my brothers and sisters within that race. Stop The Draft Week brought that pride to a peak. In the 10,000 there on Friday (October 20, 1967) I saw a pride I had never seen before. I was politicized in SNCC, not in SDS, and I was afraid that I would only see that pride in young black people. They way they carried themselves: defiance in their eyes and love and protection of themselves.

And in our history I have found brothers and sisters who achieved that level Che Guevara talked about, the new man, that even that anti-struggle cat Donovan understands, when he sings "and all my race proud and free," people who liberated themselves by liberating others, who found individually that there are no individual solutions, no individual escapes.

One brother of ours in history was Padraic Pearse, Commander in Chief of the Irish Republican Army, executed at three-thirty in the morning in Kilmainham Jail in Dublin in 1916, after the Easter Rising. A year earlier he gave an oration at the funeral of the great Feinian leader O'Donovan Rossa. Standing by the grave of his comrade, he said:

"Our foes are strong and wise and wary, but strong, wise and wary as they are they cannot undo the miracles of God, who ripens in the hearts of young men the seed sown by the young men of a former generation—and the seed sown by young men of 65 and 67 are coming to their miraculous ripening today. Rulers and defenders of realms had need be wary, if they would guard against such processes.

"Life springs from death, and from the grave of Patriot men and women spring living nations. The defenders of this realm have worked well in secret and in open. They think they have pacified Ireland. They think they have purchased half of us and intimidated the other half. They think they have forseen everything; but the fools, the fools, the fools, they have left us our Fenian dead, and while Ireland holds these graves, Ireland unfree shall never be at peace."

A year later, at the age of 37, he was shot. But he had shaken the Empire.

The defenders of the Realm, the hogs, the liars, the mass murderers, the sycophants, gangsters and holy men, the administrators of the Empire, today they rule America—all the rest in the world are lackeys.

They shot down Malcolm X and murdered Martin Luther King. They tried to murder Huey Newton and they shot Bobby Hutton in the back. They drove Eldridge underground and thousands of draft resisters out of the country. They stood over Che Guevara and pumped bullets in his chest. And they have tried to blow the living nation of Vietnam into submissive oblivion.

Thousands of us are in jail. And the rest of us? We are all—all of us—out on bail.

Men do not struggle easily. We do not come to battle out of boredom or existential malaise. Men are forced to fight. In 1958, after a thousand years of struggle against foreigners, the Vietnamese still chose nonviolent struggle against the Saigon clique. Before they again took up arms, Diem had to send troops into the countryside and massacre whole villages of people sympathetic to the Vietminh. Only then did they dig up the guns buried after Dienbienphu and turn them against their own people who had chosen to pimp first for the French and then for the Americans. They didn't want to, and neither do we.

It was four hundred years before the blacks came to the point where they began to burn down the cities in which they lived. They had revolted and died before, argued eloquently, written tracts, pamphlets, gone to the courts, gone to jail, litigated, appealed, begged, before they were forced to burn and shoot their way to freedom. Like a prisoner who has filed writ after writ to deaf judges and smug appeal boards before he makes the break.

Marx is right: people don't decide to revolt, they are forced to revolt by the conditions of their lives. Revolution is not an act of will, it is an act of desperation, defiance, and total hope. And we, we whites, on top of the world, will not all revolt against America, until America has driven us against the wall, until it has hurt each of us unendurably in our bodies and our minds. We will go on, driving cabs, writing PhD theses, going to school, building palaces for business, selling cars, conducting experiments, passing each other in the lobby and on the streets, collecting friends and degrees and reputations, until one day the hurt will become so deep and our slavery so degrading that we will rise up and lash back with every ounce of energy in our bodies and souls.

Last night we saw that movie by the Cubans on Hanoi. They kept flashing the words "we turn our hate into energy" on the screen. Last Monday, the first night of the trial, after they had pushed our brothers and sisters out of the courthouse and whipped Stew Albert's head, my hate got out of hand. I got drunk in a bar in Oakland and walked back to the courthouse and could only stand in front, slamming my fist against the stone wall and crying, as if I could knock it down alone. That was very unrevolutionary of me, but my heart had got out of control.

Last Fall I met with our comrades in the NLF in Budapest, and I learned one thing clear and hard as a stone: there is no such thing as a revolutionary tactic.

We have tried to find the one "revolutionary tactic" that would work, that would bring this country down. We founded whole organizations on single tactics: SDS on confrontation, the Resistance on burning pieces of paper, the Mobilization on pulling people peacefully into the streets. No one of those will work. When the thing comes down, it will be some massive combination of them all, leaflets and sit-downs and strikes and fighting in the streets—all of them together.

The NLF could not understand why we did not have a single revolutionary organization like them in this country, ONE organization with a strategy for the liberation of America. We tried to explain that we were new at this business, we were experimenting, we were still trying to find the revolutionary tactic that would bring this country down. Maybe our generation will produce that organization. We will be forced to, we will be driven to it by pain and love. That will be a long way off, years, it will be a long, long time, but I have the most complete assurance. America's rulers, vicious and canny, cannot exempt themselves from the laws of history, they cannot escape the effects of what they have done. The sins of the fathers will be punished by the sons.

Back to brother Padraic Pearse, who wrote a poem called The Rebel:

And now I speak, being full of vision:
I speak to my people, and I speak in my people's name to the masters of my people.

I say to my people that they are holy, that they are august, despite their chains,

That they are greater than those that hold them, and stronger and purer. . .

And I say to my people's masters: Beware,

Beware of the thing that is coming, beware of the risen people,

Who shall take what ye would not give. Did ye think to conquer the people,

Or that Law is stronger than life and than men's desire to be free?

We will try it out with you, ye that have harried and held,

Ye that have bullied and bribed, tyrants, hypocrites, liars!"

And I reply to you, brother Pearse, my Commander-in-Chief, with no apologies:

The defendrs of the American empire too have worked well in secret and in open. They think they can pacify America. They think that they have purchased half of us and repressed the other half. They think they have managed everything: but the pigs, the pigs, the pigs, they have put our backs against the wall, and as long as we know this is true, America unfree, will never be at peace.

---

photo: steve shames;
child is defendant Frank Bardacke's son

San Francisco
Express Times

Brown People Red People Poor People

I've heard
Black is Beautiful
but
I want
Brown is Beautiful
to feel is to be
        to live
My feelings are Beautiful
        Because they're Real
        Because they're
                Me
And I'm being brave enough, loving enough
To allow myself to feel
        To be myself. . . To Grow.
But shit
Who can will understand my
        Frustration
        my Pain
Who can I turn to
Who will help me untwist my Stomach
My body is screwed with this
        Pain . . . my gritoes
                loud and long.
Can't you hear it?
That I feel Ugly. . .
To discover after all these years,
That all these years, I've been looking
at Myself through Gavacho eyes . . .
Judging, condemning.
No more white man, no more,
Gavacho, Gavacha
I'm Brown, I'm Beautiful
I'm a Chicano
Y sabes que, white man, Pig, Educator
No chinges conmigo mas ! ! ! !

                Olivia de san Diego

Old Mole Nov 1969

BROWN POWER

BLOW OUTS were staged by us, Chicago students, in the East Los Angeles High Schools protesting the obvious lack of action on the part of the LA School Board in bringing ELA schools up to par with those in other areas of the city. We, young Chicanos, not only protested but at the same time offered proposals for much needed reforms. Just what did we propose?

To begin with, we want assurance that any student or teacher who took part in the BLOW OUTS — WILL NOT be reprimanded or suspended in any manner. You know the right to protest and demonstrate against injustice is guaranteed to all by the constitution.

We want immediate steps taken to implement bi-lingual and bi-cultural education for Chicanos. WE WANT TO BRING OUR CARNALES HOME. Teachers, administrators, and staff should be educated; they should know our language, (Spanish), and understand the history, traditions and contributions of the Mexican culture. HOW CAN THEY EXPECT TO TEACH US IF THEY DO NOT KNOW US? We also want the school books revised to reflect the contributions of Mexicans and Mexican-Americans to the U.S. society, and to make us aware of the injustices that we, Chicanos, as a people have suffered in a "gabacho" dominated society. Furthermore, we want any member of the school system who displays prejudice or fails to recognize, understand, and appreciate us, our culture, or our heritage removed from ELA schools.

Classes should be smaller in size, say about 20 students to 1 teacher, to insure more effectiveness. We want new teachers and administrators to live in the community their first year and that parents from the community be trained as teacher's aides. We want assurances, that a teacher who may disagree politically or philosophically with administrators will not be dismissed or transferred because of it. The school belongs to the community and as such should be made available for community activities under supervision of Parents' Councils.

There should be a manager in charge of janitorial work and maintenance details and the performance of such duties should be restricted to employees hired for that purpose. IN OTHER WORDS NO MORE STUDENTS DOING JANITORIAL WORK.

And more than this, we want RIGHTS — RIGHTS — STUDENT RIGHTS — OUR RIGHTS. We want a free speech area plus the right to have speakers of our own choice at our club meetings. Being civic-minded citizens we want to know what the happenings are in our community so we demand the right to have access to all types of literature and to be able to bring it on campus.

The type of dress that we wear should not be dictated to us by "gabachos," but it should be a group of Chicano parents and students who establish dress and grooming standards for Chicano students in Chicano schools.

Getting down to facilities. WE WANT THE BUILDINGS OPEN TO STUDENTS AT ALL TIMES, especially the HEADS. Yeah, we want access to the Heads at all times. . .When you get right down to it, WE ONLY DEMAND WHAT OTHERS HAVE. Things like lighting at all ELA football fields, swimming pools. Sport events are an important part of school activity and we want FREE ADMISSION for all students. We, CHICANO STUDENTS, BLEW OUT in protest. Our proposals have been made. The big question is will the School Board take positive action. If so, WHEN? IF NOT — BLOW OUTS BABY — BLOW OUTS!!

Report by Chicano student on the March 1968 blowouts in L.A. in *The Movement*

*Nations' share of the gross
international product (G.I.P.).
Taken from Reischauer's maps.*

"I envy you.

You North Americans

are very lucky.

You are fighting the most

important fight of all –

you live in the heart of the beast."

Che, 1964

TIERRA AMARILLA:
"La tierra les pertenece a los que lo trabajan con sus proprias manos" (The land belongs to those who work it with their own hands)

We, the people of Tierra Amarilla Merced (land grant) have formed a cooperative: COOPERATIVA AGRICOLA DEL PUEBLO DE TIERRA AMARILLA. We plan to work together this summer to grow such crops as beans, potatoes, wheat to grind for flour, onions, garlic and squash: just to name a few vegetables. We are going to work together so our children will not be hungry next winter.

Our people are hungry and have to practically beg for food from the government. We beg that same government which took our land or supported those who took it. We beg that same government which cuts down our right to the water in favor of the big cattle man, the rancher in Texas, the big growers in southern New Mexico. This government will not allow us to hunt all year round to feed our families . . . and instead will allow the Texan to come over and take his Elk's head to put in his house as a trophy, while our children hunger for meat. We have to beg that same government which charges us a fortune to graze our cattle while at the same time it cuts down our grazing permits.

We don't want to beg anymore. We want to grow the food we need, so we don't have to go to welfare or to the store which robs us in credit charges. We will store the food we grow and next winter give it to those of our people who helped grow it and those who are hungry.

The world only knows Tierra Amarilla as a land of guerillas led by "fiery land grant leader, Reies Lopez Tijerina." The newspapers are always talking about the violence, vandalism and troublemakers of the North. What the world doesn't know is the history of the people of T.A., who have had the patience to match any saint. Surrounded for nearly a century by land-grabbing gringos, politicos, lambes, state and federal governments, the people of Tierra Amarilla have always defended their right to stay on their land. For as one man has said, "The land is our mother. If we lose the land we are orphans. Where will we go?"

Before Reies Tijerina was born, the people of Tierra Amarilla were fighting for what is theirs by the Treaty of Guadalupe Hidalgo. "Ever since I was 4 or 5," says Senora Juan Martinez, "my daddy would explain to me how we came to be on the land and how it was ours by right. We have never stopped fighting for our land."

In the old way of life, whole villages of our people owned land together, because this was provided for in the laws of the Indies. They would farm together, build houses and prepare food for the winter together. These traditions have been crushed as our people have been driven off the land and onto welfare rolls. Under the anglo system of making a living, if a person wants to survive without being poor, he has to fight to "get ahead" and sometimes against his own people. When our communal way of life went, the trust our ancestors had to work the land and prepare the food together went too.

People seldom used to need money: they lived off the land. They worked their own leather and made boots and moccasins. They worked the wool, making blankets and clothes. And with the wood from the forest, they worked their own furniture. They grew their own crops and had enough water to irrigate the land. They used to dry or can the food without losing any of the vitamins. People say that eating the food this way made their bones and teeth stronger and people lived longer. Now the food they buy at the store has lost a lot of the food value and vitamins. The flour is bleached and they take out the healthiest part of the grain. El Senor Miguel Aguilar said during one of the co-op meetings, "In the factories they boil the vitamins out of the vegetables and sell them to us this way." Senor Nicolas Lopez added, "Yes, and then they sell us the vitamins."

To the people of this merced, the land is their survival. They know that a movement or a revolution to get the land back is not only speeches, demonstrations, court battles, and sometimes, when necessary, the physical defense of your land and families. They have been through all of these things for the past 100 years and will continue such things if they help bring closer the day when the land is once again theirs.

What our people in Tierra Amarilla are going to do this year is to revive the old traditions of working together to feed our people . . . because this is the revolution also. What good is it to fight this long fight for the land, when our children grow up without food? Without a culture? Our children belong to the tomorrow, when our revolution will bring fruit.

The gringo doesn't understand the way we feel about the land. He uses the land to make money from. He doesn't care what he does with it, as long as he makes that money. And he does anything necessary for his profit: from stealing the land from us to making the laws—like the water laws—which benefit him and hurt us. The land for us is not to make money. Nor is the water or the trees. "ELLOS SON DE DIOS" He gave them to us to feed our families with, and not to make a whole lot of money . . . .

—El Grito, 3/10/69

* * *

Spring has been here for more than a month in most of New Mexico, but for the people of Tierra Amarilla it has barely arrived. The rolling hills of this high plateau country are just turning green and every afternoon huge grey rain clouds move in and down from the somber mountains of Colorado that tower to the North. The adobe homes with their wooden outhouses and wells, standing in isolation across the landscape, look warmer and more comfortable now. The dirt roads are passable, after months of snow and mud. It is still a hard land, but the people have lived here for many generations and they are as strong as the land itself.

Out of that strength has been born La Cooperativa Agricola del Pueblo de Tierra Amarilla—the Agricultural Cooperative of the People of Tierra Amarilla.

T.A. was, of course, the scene of the June, 1967 courthouse " raid" which awakened many Americans and people abroad also to the struggle for land and justice in New Mexico. The people of this area are no less determined today, but they want to build an economic base for further action. You can't fight in any way on an empty stomach—and there are many empty stomachs here. So this spring half a dozen farmers of the area pledged a total of 300 acres to be farmed communally with the produce distributed for communal benefit. Loans and donations made it possible for work to begin.

There have been many difficulties in getting the land plowed and planted. Daily rain-storms created delays, as did trouble with the 3 borrowed tractors. The land donated by the Aguilar family—Mrs. Gregorita Aguilar is President of the Cooperative—has not been worked in 35 years and was so hard that the tractor almost stood on end sometimes. Distances are long up here and you may have to go 175 miles or more to get one tractor part. But the people have lived with difficulties all their lives, and they keep moving, and the work gets done . . . .

Young people have come down from Denver to help with the planting; people have come up from Albuquerque to help repair tractors and do other work. Those who come are enthusiastic about the co-op and how it can relate to the struggle of Raza people elsewhere. The Crusade for Justice, for example, has a farm near Denver where young people who have always lived in the city are going to learn to farm. They see efforts like this as a return to their roots and a step forward toward self-sufficiency . . . .

—El Grito, 5/19/69

We have been living and working in the mountains around Tierra Amarilla for the past week now and we plan to stay in the mountains until October. Before this, we were at a house about 10 miles away in Rutheron. While we were in Rutheron, the Cooperative plowed 100 acres in different places and planted them with 5,000 pounds of wheat, 50 sacks of potatoes, and garden vegetables.

The nights are freezing here and you sleep close together with lots of blankets. The days are hot. All of us are up between 6:30 and 8:00 a.m. Someone will start the coffee and those who are hungry will eat: maybe eggs and bacon or last night's *papas con carne*. The work for the day is discussed and everyone decides what he or she will be doing.

We are working on good land. These 200 acres have never been touched with a plow and are covered with sage brush. We plowed five acres and pulled out all the sage brush in two days. Today, June 5th, these five acres are being disced.

About 1 p.m., we go back to the camp site for lunch. Everyone is hungry, and much more awake and alive than in the morning. We get back to work a little after 2 and work until 5:30 p.m.; if there is special work to do, then until sunset at 8:30.[1] Everyone takes a break when they need it and we often have visitors.

When we get back to camp in the evening, everyone does different things. Some go to wash up, others to chop trees for firewood; some read, others start supper, some go into town for a telephone call or supplies.

We are nine people living and working full-time together: some young chicanos and two older chicanos, a *coyote* (Mexican-Dutch), and an Anglo man and woman who just arrived. Local members of the Cooperative who have other responsibilities come and work for whatever time they can spare.

After supper we all spread out around the fire and talk for a few hours. We talk about many things; about revolution, about the problems between men and women (especially in work) about the problems we had at work that day. We talk about our experiences, different people, different ideas, different lands and countries. We talk about the politicos, about cops, about the city, about music and books and love.

I look around me. We have no running water, no electricity, no bathrooms. We have some farm equipment, a goat, cattle, a rabbit, a pregnant pig and ourselves. It is a good group of people; there have been no big personality hassles. We tease each other a lot, and get mad about little things, but we can always be free. The power of the people is growing stronger, the idea of having a harvest, of not selling our harvest to the exploiter merchants, of sharing it with the people, is becoming more real each day.

ADELANTE UNIDOS!

—El Grito 6/14/69

*Lambes: Chicano Uncle Toms

**When I was there on June 21, there were 12. —P.J.

THE COOPERATIVE AGRICOLA DEL PUEBLO

DE

TIERRA AMARILLA NEEDS YOUR HELP . . .

We need money most of all, or green stamps, to purchase equipment for planting & harvesting . . .
*A combine
*Trucks (preferably 4-wheel drive)
*Tractors, plows, discs
*Shovels, hoes, axes
*Tents, sleeping bags, blankets
*Food which does not need refrigeration
*Work clothes for adults (boots, pants, shirts, jackets, socks, gloves)
*Toothpaste, toiletpaper, etc.
If you can provide any of these needs, please send a check or money order, or write (in English or Spanish) to:

Cooperative Agricola del Pueblo de
Tierra Amarilla
c/o Cruz Aguilar
General Delivery
Parkview, New Mexico

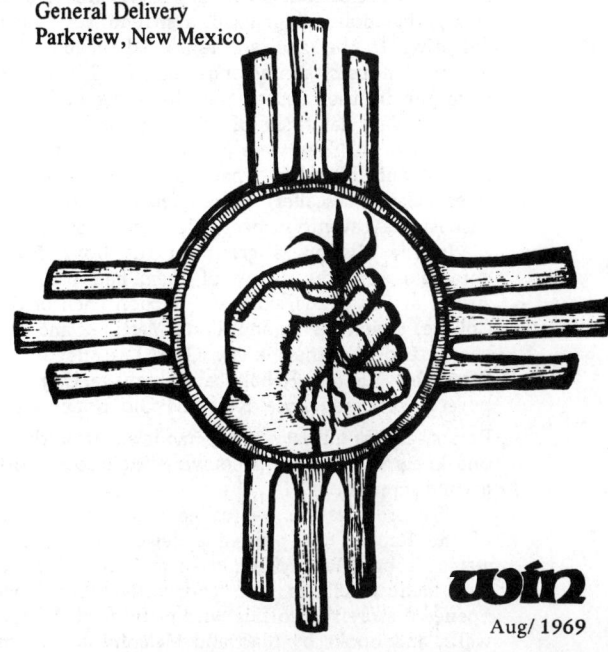

win

Aug/ 1969

THE BROWN MOVEMENT
"BASTA YA!"

LOS SIETE DE LA RAZA

San Francisco—

On May 1, 1969, about 10 am, a car carrying two plainclothes police officers pulled up in front of the house of Jose Rios, 18. Rios lives in the Mission District, a latino slum. He and some friends were carrying a television set into the house. The boys immediately recognized the police as members of a detested undercover burglary squad which had been hounding teenagers in the Mission. Details of what happened next are confused: The police got out of the car, announced the tv was stolen, and lined the boys up against the wall for frisking. The boys protested. A fight broke out. One of the officers was shot and killed. The bullet which killed him came from the second cop's gun. It is not clear whether one of the boys grabbed the gun and shot the cop, or whether he was killed by mistake by his partner.

In minutes the police had 200 men on the scene. Cars, cycles, dogs, helicopters converged on the Rios house. The boys had disappeared. The police lobbed tear gas into the house, then riddled it with bullets. The place was reduced to ruin, and in the process Rios' younger sister was grazed by a bullet. Next, the police organized a manhunt, assigned 12 homicide detectives to the case, and rampaged through the Mission, bursting into houses, ransacking them, and sticking people up at gunpoint in their quest for the alleged killers.

Five days later six of the suspects were nabbed by police in Santa Cruz. They were jailed, charged with murder, attempted murder and burglary. Their names are Mario and Tony Martinez, Gary Lescallet, Bebe Melendez, Nelson Rodriguez and Jose Rios. A seventh suspect, Gio Lopez, has not been caught.

In the Mission, a group of the boys' friends organized a defense committee. Many of them had fought together in the strikes at San Francisco State, Mission High or San Mateo Junior College, which Mario and Tony Martinez and Nelson Rodriguez had attended. Others knew Gary Lescallet and Bebe Melendez from the Mission Rebels, a militant-talking street gang-turned poverty program. Jose Ruis and Gio Lopez were in the Brown Berets, a para-military group modeled after the Panthers. Everyone knew that the suspects were "righteous brothers," and were getting screwed.

The organization was called Los Siete de la Raza—the Seven of the Race. They printed a newspaper, Basta Ya! (Enough!), started a breakfast for children program, made attempts at legal and medical clinics, and cooperative ambulance services, and opened a storefront office with pictures of Zapata and Che on the walls, and books by Mao and Malcolm X underneath the tables.

The Black Panthers gave support, publicity, money and advice. Charles Garry agreed to take the case. Bumper stickers went up; Basta Ya! got bigger; Newsreel made a film on the subject; the office relocated in a small restaurant, where Movement friends could get cheap meals; and, as the trial approaches, each preliminary hearing is crowded with brown and black kids, as if Mission High had closed up for the day.

There is more than a glorified defense committee here: The kids in Los Siete, the parents, and the brothers in jail, have a kind of love and devotion among them that is unique to that half-mystical entity known as La Raza. As one issue of Basta Ya! put it: "Los Siete did not turn their backs on the community; we cannot turn our backs on them."

The Mission District, a huge, flat area of low pastel-colored houses close to downtown, is the home of San Francisco's latinos, though there are sufficient numbers of blacks, hippies, Irish and elderly whites to provide racial tension. It is an area of low income (Mission High being the lowest income high school in the city) and high rents (rents have nearly doubled in the last three years), about two percent vacancy; landlords and homeowners burdened by heavy property taxes.

In Mission High, at the north end of the barrio, or Balboa High, at the south, there is overcrowding, hostility between blacks and browns, tracking (only five percent of Mission's graduates go on to college because most of them have been in vocational tracks since grade school), and heavy reliance on reds and other drugs. Teenagers, many of whom came from Mexico or Central America as children, may be the only ones in their families who can speak English; the jobs available are usually degrading poverty program handouts at $1.35 an hour, and there aren't enough of these to go around. Kids spend a lot of time riding around in souped-up cars, dropping reds, avoiding cops, and making out in Mission Dolores Park.

Politics in the Mission is a tangle of organizations: poverty agencies, block committees, youth groups, which may or may not be accomplishing anything. Progressive Labor had four fronts in the Mission last year, though this year they all seem to have disappeared. The Mission Coalition, an amalgam of 83 business, labor, ethnic, church and youth groups with a combined membership of over 20,000, has been the most effective in reaching people and representing them: It won, after a long battle, the right to control the planning of a Model Cities program in the District. The Mission Rebels, founded by the Rev. Jesse James as a sort of group therapy, self-improvement thing, has become a large organization raking in almost $400,000 a year from OEO, filling out endless progress reports, and running job-training, tutorial and counseling programs with names like Operation Opportunity and Operation Motivation.

Hovering over the whole swamp of community organizations is the spectre of corporate planning, which has already displaced some poverty areas. The Bay Area Council, which represents all the big local banks, construction and defense firms, is deeply involved in urban renewal: They don't want a San Francisco 40 percent black and latino by 1980 (one likely projection). Nor do they want big ratty ghettoes full of unemployable rioters and troublemakers right near downtown, when their employees have to travel long distances from the suburbs to work.

Mayor Alioto and his Board of Supervisors have recently accelerated a familiar process of slavishly approving every corporate plan: One skyscraper after another is okayed for the waterfront despite feeble protests from Telegraph Hill view-lovers; the Bay Area Rapid Transit (BART), a commuter system which will bring workers and shoppers from the suburbs into the city while bypassing some ghettoes completely, rumbles on to completion; and huge urban renewal complexes of hotels, parking lots, expensive apartments and more parking lots replace salty if seedy neighborhoods close to downtown.

When it became known in 1966 that urban renewal was planned for the Mission, the Mission Council on Redevelopment was formed. Its purpose was to make sure any renewal would be done with the advice and consent of Mission residents. The Council soon became the Mission Coalition Organization (MCO), a multi-issue group with committees on housing, education, welfare, employment, etc. But its purpose remained to gain control over any Model Cities program.

Finally, in December, after much bad-mouthing from the left ("just a tool of the Mayor"; to which one MCO organizer replied, "Is Chavez a tool of Schenley?"); and from the right ("just a paper organization"); and from dead center (the City Attorney said MCO's demands for control would be illegal); and after producing over 700 earnest, well-behaved citizens to jam a Supervisors' meeting, MCO won: It will appoint 14 people to the Model Cities Planning Board, and the Mayor will appoint the other seven.

MCO may not be able to stop the Bay Area Council's long range plans to make the Mission a middle class residential area and adjunct of downtown finance; but it's encouraging that MCO exists at all, and has forged a workable alliance among a great diversity of groups, from the Welfare Rights Organization to the St. Kevin's Teen Club, to the Junta Hispana de Real Estate Brokers. The Mission won't be destroyed without a fight.

As the bigger, bulkier organizations lose their federal funds, MCO, with a budget of $40,000 a year from the San Francisco Foundation and four churches, and with a largely volunteer staff, will be able to grow and radicalize its tactics.

At the moment, though, MCO occupies the middle of the road in community politics. At its infinitely well-organized convention in October (there were instantaneous translations into Spanish, and heavy reliance on Roberts Rules of Order), the 800 MCO delegates passed a gutless resolution condemning the media's orgy in the Los Siete incident but not really supporting the brothers. Two resolutions supporting the S.F. State strikers then on trial were not passed. The MCO came out in support of the New Mobe, draft alternatives ("rights of conscience"), and the grape boycott.

The greatest debate at the convention raged over a resolution passed requesting more "police protection," with a limp emphasis on recruiting minority cops. Considering the department is having trouble recruiting any kind of cops, and is trying to bust a popular black officer who headed a community relations division, this is a laugh. As it is, only about 15 percent of the Mission cops speak Spanish (three or four on any given shift); there are only two foot patrolmen (both at night), and policing is done by two-man teams in cruising cars.

The police are the clearest reminder of the Mission's colonial status, and they are thoroughly detested, especially by the brothers who fought them at the college strikes last year. The strikes were the result of inconsistencies in the California Master Plan for education. The Master Plan, designed by corporate types to meet "manpower needs," created three levels: universities, state colleges and junior colleges. As a result of tracking based on IQ tests, very few blacks and browns were even prepared to go to the universities; a few were making it to the state colleges, and more to the junior colleges. These kids soon realized that their education was isolating them from their people and making them compete against each other—like poverty programs which create a small class of articulate black and brown bureaucrats at the expense of the entire community. Thus, the genesis of two important Third World Liberation Front demands at State: an autonomous school of ethnic studies related to the needs of the people, and open admissions for all Third World kids.

At the two-year College of San Mateo, the strike was triggered by a College Readiness Program, begun three years before, which had recruited some 650 black and brown kids—mostly high school dropouts. With intensive tutoring and wages paid for time spent in class, the Program achieved astounding success. Whereas in 1964 thirty of 39 minority students flunked out, by 1968 ninety percent were going on to four-year schools. Bob Hoover, black director of the program, was told to put more of his kids into vocational training. "I didn't know I had a quota," he said. "You don't," the administrators answered. "But you still should put more students into vocational training."

The College Readiness Program was radical; there were the ubiquitous posters of Mao and Che on the walls; and much rapping about the System and the Man. Students like Mario Martinez recruited their friends out of the streets and pool halls of the Mission, and they discovered that with the right teachers and the right atmosphere, just about anyone could make it in college.

The San Mateo administration, feeling uneasy about 650

black and brown street kids spouting Mao on their campus, began to misplace financial aid applications. By December of 1968, monthly paychecks were reduced from $150 to $40. About 100 students dropped out, including Nelson Rodriguez, who spent the remainder of the semester on the line with his brothers at State.

The Mama Strike spread to San Mateo and on December 14, blacks and browns began breaking windows. The cops came in; San Mateo became an armed camp, with guards checking IDs at every entrance. Leaders of the strike were arrested; mass meetings were forbidden; Bob Hoover was fired, then rehired; someone shot into the Dean of Instruction's garage, and all the top administrators got bodyguards.

Very quickly, the brown movement meant a lot more than Delano. The browns didn't go through anything comparable in magnitude to civil rights, mass protest, or nonviolent resistance. Boys like Mario and Tony Martinez became instant revolutionaries, learning in a few months that the reason latinos couldn't get good jobs wasn't that they were stupid or lazy but undereducated, brainwashed, poor, and only semi-literate in English; that you don't beg the Man when you want something, because he's not going to give it up: You have to win it.

Tony Martinez became chairman of COBRA, the Confederation of the Brown Race for Action, at San Mateo. Through COBRA's leadership during the strike, the blacks and browns won some new counselors and an ethnic studies department. But the College Readiness Program was still a shadow of its former self. While Mario and Tony were recruiting still more friends for the Program, the events of the school year '68-'69 were already leading toward the kind of repression that brought about the Los Siete incident. As Bebe Melendez remembers it, "I met brother Roberto from Horizons Unlimited. I rapped to him one day and he was telling me why don't I go to college. Like a lot of brothers, I told him that I couldn't make it there. He told me it wouldn't hurt trying. Then I met this sister...she was teaching school for the Rebels. I was in her class, she was a Panther and she was telling me how the system dominates all the brothers. Not paying attention to her really hurt me, cause I was like many other brothers—brainwashed, you know—I didn't righteously realize.... Then I met brother Gio Lopez. And he was telling me about CSM [College of San Mateo]. I dug what he was telling me. So I was gonna go, but Los Siete came."

Mission High also caught the strike bug. There were the usual demands for reform, met by an unresponsive administration. Small coteries of cracker whites insisted that the militant blacks and browns were only a "vocal minority." Tactics escalated; "outside agitators" were blamed, and finally, the cops came in and broke heads. The Mission Coalition managed to negotiate the removal of the principal and two other administrators. But the new administration is little better: Anti-leafletting laws are constantly bent and stretched to meet a given situation. Students were forbidden to hand out a Moratorium leaflet recently because it advocated leaving school for the day.

Since the strikes last year, Reagan has tried to remove every pretense of liberalism from California higher education. There was the highly-publicized Angela Davis case, in which the Regents unsuccessfully tried to get the black communist teacher fired. Less publicized was the attempted firing of a Black Muslim, Marvin X, at Fresno State. At S.F. State, Hayakawa shafted fifteen AFT members who were active in the strike, and, of course, Black Studies chairman Nathan Hare. After much talk of a "reign of terror" in the Black Studies department, Hayakawa has fired ten black aides and threatened to withhold paychecks for the entire faculty if they don't agree to "meet" with the administration. Hayakawa called the department "a training ground for revolution."

A plan for 18 new junior colleges has been rejected: "Fewer, larger campuses are more efficient," said the Coordinating Council on higher Education, a group of businessmen. In October, U.C. Berkeley and Santa Cruz were no longer accepting applications for the spring quarter, and the U.C. budget has been cut, with the probable elimination of summer quarters at Berkeley and UCLA. At Sacramento State there were 600 places for 7,000 spring semester applicants. The Chronicle reported that "thousands of junior college transfers have virtually no place to go for their junior year."

The Regents have proposed a learn-now pay-later tuition plan in the traditionally free public colleges. Said Reagan in explanation: "Higher education should be looked upon as a capital investment...the university is not a sanctuary for someone who wants to pursue knowledge for knowledge's sake."

In the midst of these changes—more police repression in the city; reaction run wild in Sacramento; quickly raised if sometimes half-baked revolutionary consciousness—the case of Los Siete takes on great importance. The brothers in jail were among the most promising and articulate children of immigrant parents in the Mission. They had typical ghetto youths: knives, drugs, cars. They came from big families, couldn't get any but the most degrading jobs, were beginning to discover the mechanics of oppression, and were quickly taken out of circulation. As Tony Martinez said, "This has been a uniting point for a lot of people... they realize that it can happen to anybody. It can happen to their kids around the corner."

For the last eight months, the boys have been in jail, charged with murder, attempted murder, and burglary. Microphones have been hidden in their cells. They have been beaten and denied visiting rights, and Gary Lescallet has been in solitary. Meanwhile, the lawyers have made motions (some successful) for discovery of prosecution evidence and motions (unsuccessful) for quashing the indictment because the all-white Grand Jury was illegally constituted. The trial is scheduled to begin this month.

—Marjorie Heins

1/12/70

TEN MILLION MEXICAN-AMERICANS: AN INVISIBLE NATION HIDDEN IN OUR MIDST

Chicanos turn to Brown Power: 'Five years behind the blacks, but we'll catch up very fast'

By Kathy Mulherin
Special to the National Catholic Reporter

THERE IS an invisible nation hidden in our midst. The nearly 10 million Mexican-Americans in the United States constitute the country's second largest racial minority – a silent minority until very recently.

But they are rapidly becoming politically organized, and it seems quite possible that in the next few years, at least in the Western United States, they will match and surpass black people in militancy and political strength.

Of late, Chicanos (as they call themselves) have begun to be "visible" all over the Southwest. For example:

—Cesar Chavez and his pacifist United Farmworkers union, on strike against large, corporately owned farms, have elevated to an international scale their boycott of table grapes.

—Thousands of Chicano high school and college students all over the Southwest have formed militant organizations, protested school conditions and participated in walkouts. Denver's Rudolfo "Corky" Gonzalez, the nation's most popular Chicano leader in the eyes of young militants, has called for a nationwide school walkout next Sept. 16.

—Reies Lopez Tijerina, controversial founder of the Alianza Federal (alliance of Free City States), made national headlines in 1967 when his followers used gunfire to press their claim to territory of Tierra Amarilla in Northern New Mexico.

—There have sprung up militant organizations of *barrio* (any area where poor Spanish-speaking people live) youth, such as the California Brown Berets who are modeled after the Black Panthers.

The movement invites comparison with the black power movement. The results are startling:

Chicanos are the largest minority in the Southwest, from Colorado to Mexico, from California to Texas. In California alone the three million Chicanos outnumber blacks two to one.

And their condition is worse. In Los Angeles, for example, their average annual income is $1,380, lower than the $1,437 for blacks. Only the American Indian has a lower income than the Chicano. And the Chicano receives only an average of eight years of schooling, compared with 10 years for blacks and 12 for whites.

The experience of the black power movement has not been lost on the Chicano. Said one professor: "We are about five years behind the blacks, but we will catch up very fast."

So far, a striking feature of the brown power movement is the absence of the many internal splits that plague the black and white radicals. Deep and common cultural roots seem to make the Chicano movement healthier, more flexible and more naturally communal than other radical groups.

As one Chicano told me: "We have always had our own community, so we have never suffered the feelings of *isolation* the black man feels."

The need for roots forces the black radical to expend much emotional energy over the question of how to treat his African culture which the white slave-owner tore away from him. But the Chicano feels psychologically unwounded because he has stubbornly kept his roots intact.

IN THE PAST few weeks, I have traveled several thousand miles around the Southwest, interviewing leaders such as Corky Gonzalez and Reies Tijerina, young students and barrio militants, and poor farmers. I discovered a vigorous, complex people whose physical features, life styles and politics reflect the *mestizaje* – the mixture – which produced them: Spanish, Indian, and North American. Luis Valdez, founder of the United Farm Workers' *Teatro Campesino* (Rural Theater), has written:

La Raza, the race, is the Mexican people. Sentimental and cynical, fierce and docile, faithful and treacherous, individualistic and herd-following, in love with life and obsessed with death, the personality of the *raza* encompasses all the complexity of our history. The conquest of Mexico was no conquest at all. It shattered our ancient Indian universe, but more of it was left above ground than beans and tortillas. Below the foundations of our Spanish culture, we still sense the ruins of an entirely different civilization . . . . A Mexican's first loyalty – when one of us is threatened by strangers from the outside – is to that *raza*."

But all this is only the soil of political organization. It was Cesar Chavez who, in recent times, first began to cultivate that soil when he organized the Delano farm workers not simply as victimized workers, but specifically as Mexicans. His campaign succeeded far better than previous efforts, and it helped to unleash a wave of energy which is creating the Chicano movement.

Frequently compared to Mahatma Gandhi for his gentle long-suffering (he has been afflicted with severe illnesses since his long fast last year, a fast he undertook to mobilize and unify support for his union), and passionate dedication to his people and the principles of nonviolence, this quiet, sad-eyed man has become in the last four years, an inspiration for thousands of Chicanos all over the West.

They were moved not only by Cesar's example but by the symbolic genius of his organization which spoke to their Mexican roots. Luis Valdez writes of the grape pickers' dramatic march from Delano to Sacramento in the spring of 1967:

"The pilgrimage to Sacramento was no mere publicity trick. The *raza* has a tradition of migrations, starting from the legend of the founding of Mexico. Nezahualcoyotl, a great Indian leader, advised his primitive Chichimecas, forerunners of the Aztecs, to begin a march to the south. In that march, he prophesied. . . . they would begin to build a great nation. The nation was Aztec Mexico. . . . Mexican grape pickers did not march 300 miles to Sacramento, carrying the standard of the *Virgen de Guadalupe,* merely to dramatize economic grievances . . . . The Virgin of Guadalupe was the first hint to farmworkers that the pilgrimage implied social revolution. During the Mexican revolution, the peasant armies of Zapata carried her standard . . . . Beautifully dark and Indian of feature, she was the New World version of the Mother of Christ . . . . The people's response was immediate and reverent. They joined the march by the thousands."

The UFW produced the first newspaper of the movement, *El Malcriado,* and the first theater: today, there are 17 such newspapers, a Chicano Press association and at least six theater groups modeled after the *Teatro Campesino.*

IF CHAVEZ and the UFW provided the initial thrust for the movement, its current style and direction are better represented by Denver's Crusade for Justice and its director, Corky Gonzalez. It is, so far, the movement's most important organization, and Corky is easily the Chicano's most influential national leader.

Gonzalez, small, dark and trim, with curly black hair, a thick mustache and serious black eyes, was one of the nation's top 10 featherweight boxers from 1947 to 1955. Today, 40 years old, the father of eight children and given to wearing black T-shirts and black pants, he still exhibits the fighter's qualities of highly concentrated discipline and passion.

Such qualities come in handy in a city like Denver. Predictably, the city center is filling up with blacks and Chicanos who together will account for 20 per cent of the area's population by 1970.

Here, as elsewhere, Chicanos are the least educated and the poorest – the city's over-all unemployment rate is 3 per cent but for Chicanos it is 10 per cent. A few more facts: 55 per cent of Chicano homes in the *barrios* have six or more children; 50 per cent of the Chicano population is under 19 years of age; 75 per cent of the inmates in Denver prisons are Chicanos.

Driving into Denver from the airport, one passes successively through clearly divided residential areas -- white suburbs, black middle-class, poor black, and finally, Chicano *barrios.*

There are many long, low, red brick apartment buildings, each with thin scruffy children playing on narrow strips of grass bordering the sidewalks. There are also many seedy brick and wooden houses with porches supported in weary dignity by dingy gray columns reminiscent of an earlier time, and a more genteel era.

Even with this background of poverty, neither Corky nor his followers in his organization, the Crusade for Justice, began as militants.

For years they tried to work within the Democratic party in Denver; Corky was a ward captain, he ran for mayor, the crusade once took over the Democratic party county and state conventions, and at one point, Corky was even a War on Poverty director.

Now he says: "We gave up on that political scene – the party system is a two-headed monster that eats at the same trough. The Chicano has to drop out of 'their' politics and create his own . . . . (This is) a controlled society in which the *gringo* (Anglo) makes all the major decisions . . . . As a result, my people have been politically destroyed and economically exploited."

His experience makes him wary of government programs – "there are always strings attached" – and he points with pride to the fact that the crusade's 26-room headquarters, a great musty box of a former Baptist church, was acquired nine months ago and is slowly being paid for without any grants from public or private agencies.

"Some of our people work for government agencies," says Emilio Dominguez, second in command in the crusade, "and we like to use them if we can." Dominguez, a middle-aged man with long hair and a beard who is by turns serene and irascible, chuckled wickedly as he told how his wife had insisted on conducting a federally supported summer project from crusade offices, "so we got all our phone bills paid that way!"

The crusade headquarters is a comfortably shabby labyrinth of classrooms, auditoriums, offices, recreation rooms and a curio shop. A newspaper, *El Gallo* is put out; there are classes in Mexican and Indian culture and history, in poetry, dancing, drama, Karate, judo and boxing. Crusade officers meet in one room, teen-agers sit around laughing and joking in another, and in the kitchen, someone is cooking up a batch of tortillas for a hungry visitor or for a poor family unfortunate enough to arrive in town on a weekend when the welfare office is closed.

Crusaders try to inform their people of their welfare rights, help them with grievances against school and city officials, find jobs for *barrio* youths. One gentle and sorrowful man, D. C. de Herrera, investigates police brutality cases.

The crusade has its playful moments too. This year's Mother's Day celebration was a vivid illustration of the warmth and affection between Chicanos of all ages and political attitudes.

THE DAY BEGAN with a mass offered by Father Craig Hart (called Padre Corazon) on the stage of the auditorium. Music was provided by a good-natured, hardy band called *Los Vigilantes,* composed of a father and his four children, who were 5 to 15 years of age.

Father Hart asked everyone to gather around the altar and matter-of-factly encouraged participation. The people responded eagerly -- the mass was in English, punctuated by simple Mexican religious folk songs. The mood was relaxed and informal as young people spoke about their mothers and their intentions. At communion, Father Hart greeted each person by name as he distributed consecrated portions of a corn tortilla.

After mass, I talked with Father Hart; he is a handsome and disarming young man with calm brown eyes and an easy grin. Earnestly, he talked about his own definition of religion. "It's the people's attempt to *hear* life . . . that means the world is religious, because the world is becoming -- freeing itself. These people here are religious all the way, but not in the official sense. They go to mass for important reasons – when somebody's baptized, married or buried."

When I asked whether the crusade received support from the church in the area, he frowned and shook his head. "And last week, when I was arrested (for sitting in at the State Legislature with fourteen others to protest that body's indifference to Chicano problems), the bishop said I was acting as an individual! Toleration isn't enough! The bishop's have to speak out!"

Downstairs in a basement recreation room decorated with mural paintings of Aztec Indians, there was a noisy and cheerful party going on. Corky made a little speech in which he described his speaking tour of California campuses and he gently admonished: "Some of our old people say (about the youth), 'they're not doing it like we want to do it' but the young people are ahead of it – they're gonna lead it . . . . We have to catch up with the youngsters . . ."

After dinner, the floor was cleared for dancing. To this reporter, accustomed to seeing gatherings of activists immediately segregate themselves by age group, accustomed to observing families suffer the anguish of the "generation gap," it was a rare sight to see militant young Chicanos, their faces relaxed in wide grins, bouncing around the dance floor with stout middle-aged women, and old men gravely dancing with little girls.

BUT IF OLDER Chicanos have always relied on leaders to initiate political movements, today's young Chicanos are beginning to move on their own.

Which is how Denver's spectacular "West High blowout," as it is called, got started this spring.

Students at predominantly Chicano West high school, angered by a teacher they felt was racist, decided to walk out of school in protest. They came to the crusade to get advice on what to do after they walked out. They asked Corky to speak to the school administration in their behalf.

The walkout ended in a confrontation between police and students. Denver police, unaccustomed to such demonstrations, became frightened and reacted as if the city were under siege.

The walkout spread to other schools and cities, and when it was over, dozens of Chicanos had been beaten, Maced, gassed and arrested (among them Corky), 17 policemen had suffered injuries and there was considerable property damage — including 25 badly damaged police cars.

Since then administrators have found themselves faced with demands for bilingual instruction, more Chicano teachers, courses in the history of Mexico and a large determined body of students. Everyone seems to agree that the current peace is uneasy at best.

Unrepentant, Corky called a Youth conference at the end of March, which was attended by 1,500 young militants from across the Southwest and from Chicago and New York (represented mostly by some Puerto Ricans). For five days they held workshops and bull sessions, and celebrated their ancestry in their own poems, plays and songs.

At its end, they marched down to the State Capitol building and hoisted the Mexican flag over it, while grim-faced police looked on.

They concluded the conference with the declaration of a document called *El Plan Espiritual de Atzlan* (Spiritual Plan of Atzlan, the name given to the Southwest by those ancient Indian tribes migrating south to form the Aztec nation of Mexico).

The plan committed its authors to nationalism as the basis of political organization. It called for community control of Chicano *barrios,* schools, lands, institutions, and it promised self defense against the "occupying forces of the oppressors" at every school. It called for the creation of an independent political party and for a nationwide school walkout on Sept. 16, the birthdate of Mexican independence.

Whether such an ambitious program will be carried out remains to be seen, but certainly the plan illustrates the grand nationalist scale on which Chicanos are thinking these days.

■ THE NATIONAL CATHOLIC
reporter

6/4/69

THE KIDS MAKE 'BROWN POWER' WORK

Brown Power leader Ries Tijerina (right) addressed an Oakland rally with a Brown Beret bodyguard at his side.–Photo copyright 1969 by Stephen Shames

By Kathy Mulherin
Special to the National Catholic Reporter

"TIERRA O MUERTE!" (Land or death!) was one of the battle cries of the Mexican revolution, and it echoed across the Southwest as late as the Mexican-American war.

But two years ago the cry was heard again in the northern New Mexico county seat of Tierra Amarilla (Pop. 600) when about 100 armed Chicano farmers, led by Reies Lopez Tijerina, invaded the county courthouse to make a "citizen's arrest" of the district attorney.

For Tijerina and his followers, it was a dramatic, symbolic gesture designed to draw attention to the Chicano population's claims to the territory by way of land grants from the king of Spain through the viceroy of Mexico, and confirmed by the treaty of Guadalupe Hidalgo of 1848, which ended the Mexican-American war.

Symbolic or not, officials of the state of New Mexico took the affair quite literally; the little band of peasants was met with National Guard troops, tanks and guns. The encounter ended in farce and near tragedy – there was a lot of shooting and shouting and confusion. One law man was shot -- but not hurt badly -- and the state was much embarrassed when the story made international headlines. Tijerina and 10 others were charged with everything from insurrection to assault, but last December Tijerina was aquitted of three of the 57 charges against him.

I visited the man the press calls "King Tiger" in his reinforced concrete headquarters -- the target of several bomb-

ings – in Albuquerque.

Tijerina, 42, is a handsome man with wavy black hair, sharp features, expressive hands and a disarming, intimate style. Speaking in Spanish, occasionally breaking into English, he began, as if for the first time, to tell a story he must have told a thousand times.

The land grants date from the 16th century, he said, and the treaty of Guadalupe Hidalgo states very clearly that U.S. courts would recognize their legal validity. "And from 1848 to 1891 -- 43 years -- the matter rested, without any determination by the courts.

"The documents which had been kept in Guadalajara (Mexico) were lost in a fire in 1858, and in 1870 William Pyle in Santa Fe *threw out* all the local records!! Physically!!"

Tijerina stared at me, his eyes wide in shock at the thought.

"In the newspapers they called him *'cabeza de perro'* -- 'pighead' -- for what he had done. All the history has been erased, and with it the destiny of this *pueblo* (free people). And the conspiracy is clear! Clear!"

Tijerina said that the 16th-century grants were not like modern deeds made out to individuals, but grants to the general population of Andalusian settlers. He and his followers make a great point of this communal -- not individual -- nature of the original grants.

Citing names and dates with great relish, Tijerina detailed the gradual encroachment of the U.S. government on the lands owned by the community of Chicano farmers. Too poor and bewildered to win their lands back, the people had submitted--until Tijerina came along, said Tijerina.

Now, he said, he and his Alianza Federal followers were about to move to the forested mountains north of Los Alamos to claim some of this land. He strode to a large wall map which described the area as San Joaquin. (Like many other names on Tijerina's map, San Joaquin does not appear on conventional maps of the area.) He said the move was scheduled for June 5, the second anniversary of his courthouse raid.

"We are going to stake out boundaries and put up billboards saying: 'This is the liberated *pueblo* of San Joaquin.'"

From Albuquerque, I drove north through this country which Tijerina promised to liberate to the courthouse town of Tierra Amarilla, to talk with some of those who accompanied Tijerina on his famous raid.

North of Albuquerque, the land is mostly barren, and sparsely inhabited, except for Santa Fe and a few small towns and villages. Here and there one passes an Indian reservation, but mostly one sees flat grasslands, brown hills, stark clay-red buttes, and to the east, dark, misty blue Sangre de Cristo mountains, their snowy peaks brilliant in the sun.

A real estate salesman might be hard put to understand why the poor farmers of Rio`Arriba are willing to fight for this crusty, dry land. But it is beautiful country, and it has carved itself on the tough, clean, warm brown faces of the people. Their dark red and grey adobe houses are hardly visible, they blend so thoroughly with the land.

IN PARK VIEW, a tiny hamlet near Tierra Amarilla, I talked with some farmers who are starting a cooperative farm from 400 acres of which they are the undisputed owners. For generations they have been too poor to farm, surviving by grazing a few cows and living on welfare. Energized by the courthouse raid, some of them -- including one of Tijerina's brothers, "Chemo" -- are hoping that the cooperative will provide the people with both nourishment and political strength.

We stood outside a small sun-bleached wooden shack -- as Chemo talked with a young man who had brought his wife and three skinny children to help cut potatoes for planting, the setting sun turned the black soil in newly plowed fields to golden brown.

The landscape and the Spanish-speaking people, poor and hard as desert bones, made it difficult to remember that this place is in the United States, not Mexico. Still, these people elicit no pity. Their cooperative is a tenuous venture and it will not survive without tools and money from the outside.

Unfortunately, Reies Tijerina does not approve of the cooperative, hence the farmers have had to start it without him. They are hurt and bitter about his indifference to a project of such importance to them, and there is talk that Tijerina is only interested in fame and glory. Last week, Tijerina and the Alianza appeared in Washington, D.C., in an unsuccessful attempt to make another "citizen's arrest" of the new Supreme Court appointee, Warren Burger, for his allegedly "racist" decisions against minority groups.

In the meantime, the people of the north country of New Mexico, descendants of Andalusian settlers, Indian natives and Mexican immigrants, are slowly reclaiming the land on its own terms – by sowing seed.

These people are few in number, but their activities have great symbolic significance for Chicanos in the Southwest, for they have created a geographical locus for the movement to call its own. Such symbols have great power.

ALL THE same, for the millions of Chicanos living in cities, New Mexico cannot serve as anything but a dream at the moment.

The problems of the one and one-half million Chicanos in Texas, for example, are more immediate: "If you were to draw a line across southern Texas from Corpus Christi to San Antonio and Nuevo Laredo, and if the land south of the line were to be made a separate state, it would be the poorest state in the country," one professor told me.

Nowhere else in the United States are Chicanos so concentrated, a fact which may account in part for the almost hysterical alarm among Anglos in Val Verde county, Texas, the scene of a controversy over the firing of some Vista workers for allegedly spreading "hate literature" (Chicano underground newspapers) and for "allying" themselves with a militant youth organization.

Anglo Texans are practiced in dealing with Mexicans and it has been difficult for Chicano political organizers to get a foothold there. Cesar Chavez's United Farm Workers two years ago failed in a campaign to unionize farm workers.

Now the young people of the area, inspired by the successes of the Chicano movement elsewhere, have begun to move on their own, and have formed an organization called MAYO (Mexican-American Youth organization). They are angry and militant and not afraid of confrontations.

When Governor Preston Smith called on the Economic Opportunity office to withdraw some Vista workers from a very poor area in southern Texas, because "they were doing more harm than good," MAYO responded with anger. The Vista volunteers had aroused the ire of local politicians, they said, mostly because they were helping the people to organize themselves.

In support of the volunteers, nearly 4,000 people marched to the Val Verde county courthouse in Del Rio, led by young men from MAYO who looked like Zapata revolutionaries in their beards and mustaches, combat boots and serapes.

And, just as the youth at the Denver conference did, they hoisted a flag -- MAYO's own red and black flag -- up the courthouse flagpole. They also tacked a three-page manifesto on the door of the courthouse which listed their grievances -- resembling those held by Chicanos everywhere -- and concluded:

"On this day, we serve notice to Del Rio and the nation, that . . . . we are willing to lay down our lives to preserve the culture and language of our ancestors and to blend them with that which is best in these United States . . . our beloved country. . . . We are prepared to be as aggressive as necessary until everyone of our Mexican-American brothers enjoys the liberty of shaping his own future."

The whole affair has become embroiled in the byzantine politics of the Lone Star state, as U.S. Rep. Henry Gonzalez delivers frequent public diatribes against MAYO "hate sheets" and accuses its members of getting their training in Cuba. On the other side, MAYO leaders coolly threaten violence "if that is necessary to get the gringo off our back." These are words which for Anglos, conjure images of Chicano hordes swarming down on them, and for Chicanos, they signal the end of their legendary patience.

BUT PERHAPS the most energetic and militant source of energy in the Chicano movement comes from California. After his tour of West Coast campuses, Rudolfo "Corky" Gonzalez, of Denver's Crusade for Justice, declared: "The student movement in California is the most advanced in the movement." And indeed, it was in California that the Brown and Black Berets began, that the first school walkouts took place, that militant student organizations like the United Mexican American Students (UMAS) and the Mexican-American Student confederation (MASC) were founded.

In the past year, Chicano students have joined with black students in Third World Liberation fronts at a number of university and college campuses, to press for their demands together.

Chicanos have insisted on their right to retain their own culture and to study Mexican history. As one student put it in a wry poem: ". . . If George Washington/ Is my father/ How come/ He's not a Chicano?

After the Gonzalez-inspired Denver conference, Chicano student groups merged into an organization called *Movimiento Estudiante Chicano de Atzlan* (MECHA).

The change marked a tougher, more united militancy, but Chicano students insist that their movement is more complicated than simply another ethnic minority possessed of a new militancy.

Manuel Gomez -- a fierce young poet at Hayward State college in Northern California's Bay area who has been called the "Eldridge Cleaver of the Chicanos" -- likens the movement to an "iceberg," or "a pearl, which is the oysters, response to an irritant."

Manuel, with his long, shining black hair, his high cheek bones, aquiline nose and a large Zapata mustache, looks at once like a Mexican revolutionary at the turn of the century and like a throwback to the Aztecs. "They have conquered the land, but not the people," he says, "we recognize no borders: for us, this is occupied Mexico -- 'Alta California' -- My people have been fighting for years."

One way some Mexican-Americans have been fighting has been in resisting assimilation – and therefore, in the eyes of militants, resisting oppression, since assimilation is considered a subtle method of suppressing Mexican culture.

For as long as anyone can remember there have always been *pachucos,* or *bato locos* or *barrio vatos* the various terms for young men who band together in street gangs, and who, by their speech, dress, and life styles have formed what one scholar called "one of the few truly separatist movements in American history." Every city and town in the West with a substantial Chicano population has *barrio vatos.* Of late, some of these groups have begun to get involved in overtly political activity. They are attracted to such militant organizations as the Brown Berets.

I SPENT AN evening recently observing a meeting of a largely Chicano gang called *Los Lobos,* (The Wolves) in east San Jose, the *barrio* of a busy industrial city of almost 400,000 people, nearly a quarter of which is Chicano. The club is primarily social, but it serves as some guarantee of protection for its members in a very tough neighborhood.

As night closed in, a community service center called "The Dead End" began to fill with men ranging in age from 15 to 35. Most are wearing dark blue windbreakers with *"Los Lobos"* emblazoned in gold across the back. Several are wearing political buttons – "Boycott Grapes," the clenched fist of revolution, "Che." One bony young man slouched in a chair reading *Peanuts* cartoon books is wearing a wide wristband which holds a knife close to the underside of his wrist.

Yet if they were ferocious in appearance, they acted like any other group of energetic adolescents -- they mocked one another, pranced before the girls, traded witticisms and playfully punched one another.

The meeting had been called to discuss an altercation with representatives of two Anglo gangs – "The Lone Wolves" and the "The Law." No one was very anxious to fight however, and the matter was being settled by negotiation. Carefully and courteously, each side raised complaints about the behavior of the other, about rumors, about insults and incidents which had caused bad relations in the past; each promised to look into the complaints and to discipline those members responsible.

Lobo: "How do you expect us to recognize you if you don't wear colors? . . . If maybe there was a lotta people standing around some night and there was some hassle, we might not know it was you, if it was dark, or we might think it was some other club."

Gradually, with diplomacy and precision, they laid out detailed guidelines – a kind of informal treaty, only they used imagery instead of legal language, creating pictures of hypothetical situations, drawing them in the air with dark brown expressive hands. They displayed a strange combination of innocence and wisdom based on experience.

IN EAST Los Angeles, nearly every night of the year, Whittier boulevard, the artery of the Chicano community, is crowded with large chrome-studded cars cruising up and down, past knots of dark young men, dressed in narrow pants, pointed shoes and jackets with the names of their gangs sewn carefully on the back.

Raul Ruiz, editor of *The Chicano Student Movement,* an underground newspaper, has worked with gangs like the *Lobos* in Los Angeles: "The *barrio vatos* know about power," he told me, "They have to be diplomatic -- anything can cause a disruption of negotiations, and the results can realistically affect you in your daily movements throughout the *barrio. . . .* They respect each other's power. The *vato* has known how to survive, how to move, for a long time – he doesn't have to be taught that."

Vatos have long eyed with suspicion Chicanos who have made it out of the slums to go to college.

"The Chicano has never tried to make it into the society," Raul Ruiz declared. "His sociological base of reference is not necessarily the larger society. The society can't give us anything -- we don't want it. Actually, only the *vatos* can organize themselves–the students can't do it, because the *vato* suspects everyone outside the *barrio.*"

Unless the students themselves are *vatos.*

For several weeks in March, 1968, thousands of students from five Los Angeles high schools in which Chicanos were the majority or the largest minority, walked out of classes to protest what they said were bad educational conditions. These "blowouts" at first caught the city off guard, but on May 31, police arrested 13 Chicano leaders in a surprise move, and charged them with "conspiracy to disturb the peace."

The tactic of filing a conspiracy charge -- which permits police to transform a misdemeanor into a felony and does not require prosecutors to prove even that the misdemeanors were committed – has become quite popular among law enforcement agencies who have applied it against the Black Panther party and white radicals in Oakland, San Francisco, New York and Chicago in recent months.

But so far, the charges do not appear to intimidate any of those against whom they have been used. For example, in the past year, there have been walkouts or protests by Chicanos in five cities in the central agricultural valley of California, and in several Bay area cities as well.

Few of these students are non-violently inclined. "We support Chavez," said Raul Ruiz, echoing the words of many other young Chicanos I spoke with, "but we're not interested in that non-violence thing. Our people are being shot and killed and beaten every day -- we're not gonna take that any more. Chavez is a good man, we owe a lot to him, but working within the system hasn't gotten him anywhere, so we'll deal with oppression in whatever way is necessary."

AND THAT note is probably as good as any on which to begin an assessment of the new Chicano militancy.

For, although the question of the "necessary means" is one on which there are many opinions in the Chicano movement, they are uniformly resentful when white liberals demand to know whether they are going to "kill all whites." The question is absurd, argue the militants, and they have a point, because the important thing about the statement, "by any means necessary," is that Chicanos have committed themselves to a careful, concrete, step-by-step search for an end to their oppression. They march, petition, sit-in, argue, threaten, fight -- whatever *works.* That may be too utilitarian for the taste of white liberals, but the daily lives of poor Chicanos leave little room for much else.

And this leads to another important truth about the Chicano movement. It cannot be understood if viewed only as a potential source of social unrest and disruption. It is a deep, complex, lively, vigorous, often cantankerous and contradictory movement, composed of many people of every variety of political orientation – to the left of the Democratic party anyway -- and rather apolitical people as well.

It is a people renewing itself through cultivation of its historical roots. And, in many ways, it is a revolutionary movement.

At a time when our whole culture is showing signs of severe strain and even disintegration, it is only natural that many people should begin to seek pure, more stable, more meaningful roots and sources of energy. White middle-class styles have dominated America for a long time, and given our present situation, it is not surprising that many people are losing faith in them.

But the Chicano movement has not merely lost faith – it has begun to develop, with pride and energy, its own resources. *Nothing could be healthier.* Those who regard the Chicano movement, or any other minority movement for that matter, as simply having a siege mentality, miss this crucial point.

The phenomenon is not romantic. There are deep wells of hostility among the poor and oppressed. For centuries this hostility has been turned inward -- Chicanos have fought with blacks daily in every major city where they live side by side, scrambling over the crumbs left to them by the society. Those battles still rage, though both blacks and Chicanos are trying mightily to end them.

But it has been an ugly, bitter business and it will take a long time to heal the scars of oppression and poverty and, for that matter, the scars of the oppressors.

It is worth noting, too, that the Chicano movement, though gleefully designed to make the white middle class uneasy, need not necessarily be feared, might conceivably be imitated, at least in its communal aspects.

Only tyrants regard revolutionary movements exclusively as forces which overthrow governments; the revolutionized regard them as movements which weld a people together. It is in this latter sense that the Chicano movement may just possibly be a revolutionary movement.

reporter 6/11/69

people of color

YOUNG LORDS

A group of revolutionary Puerto Rican youths have rio, New York City's Puerto Rican ghetto. They have renamed the church "La Iglezia de la Gente"–People's Church.

Until last Sunday, this church only opened a few days a week for services, but now the people of the neighborhood can come there every day for free breakfast (75 to 100 children showed up for breakfast the first day of the occupation) and lunch and free medical care; their children can attend a "liberation school" as antidote to public school brainrot; children can play in the church gym; and everyone can attend evening festivals of folksongs, films, and raps until dawn.

For twelve weeks the Lords had attended services at the Church, mingling with the congregation to try to convince them that the church should serve the poor people of El Barrio by opening its doors to a free breakfast program. Although the congregation consisted of middle class Puerto Ricans who live outside El Barrio, the Lords claim that many agreed the church did not do its job. The conservative Cuban exile minister was less sympathetic. On December 7 he denounced the Lords from the pulpit, and when the Lords rose to reply, club-swinging policemen quickly moved in. Seven Lords were injured and thirteen arrested. Hundreds of community residents and Lords supporters then marched through the streets around the church, talking to people about what had happened.

After services on Sunday, December 28, the Lords barricaded themselves inside the church. "If they had granted us the space for the breakfast program in the first place, we wouldn't have had to go through all this business," said the Lords Minister of Defense. "The church board kept refusing to meet with us. They called us Satana—the Devil."

Since the occupation of the church there has been no repetition of police action. "They can't beat us up now," said a Lords spokesman, "because to do that they'd have to beat up the children and their parents of the Barrio, because they're in here with us." On January 3rd the church obtained a court order against the occupation. At a press conference in the church the following morning the Lords pointed out that everyone present was in violation of the order, but had not been arrested, "because the power of the Puerto Rican community outside of the church and the 300 people that occupied the church last night are preventing the city from moving in on us." The church plans further legal action to strengthen its position, before calling in police. The Lords have said that they are ready to defend themselves "if we have to."

The Young Lords Organization, now part of the multiracial "Rainbow Coalition" with the Black Panthers and (white southern) Patriot Party, was originally a Chicago street gang until one of their leaders read the essays of Eldridge Cleaver. The Lords became politicized and borrowed much from the Panthers in formulating a guide to free their people from oppression. They also rely on the works of Pedro Albicu Compos, a leftwing Puerto Rican nationalist. The Lords call for the independence of Puerto Rico which they regard as a colony of United States business interests.

The Lords consider themselves both an educational organization and "an armed group prepared to protect our communities from the brutal attacks by the power structure that are committed every day." Police brutalize and murder Latins just as they do blacks. But Yoruba, 19-year-old Minister of Information for the New York Lords, agrees with other members of the Rainbow Coali-

tion that "the present stage of revolutionary struggle is one of education and information to raise revolutionary consciousness." He told a *New York Times* reporter:

"All the Lords are on duty 24 hours a day, wherever they are. In the street, in homes, in stores, they talk to the people to show them how it is the capitalist system that keeps them poor."

Like the Panthers, the Lords try to "serve the people," which means that revolutionaries must practice what what they preach by helping people to help themselves collectively. This also involves the transformation of oppressive institutions into ones that benefit the communities around them.

The Lords' breakfast and lunch program, an idea pioneered by the Panthers, embodies this concept of service to the people. Food is collected from the same white storekeepers who make their living by overcharging poor people. If a store refuses to contribute, it faces a boycott by the community. In this way, the program is not one of charity but rather a transfer of resources from the oppressor to the oppressed.

The Lords began to attack El Barrio's problems last August, when they protested poor garbage collection by blocking streets with mounds of garbage. They also campaigned for community control of Metropolitan Hospital in El Barrio which they claim provides inadequate service. Most dramatically, they tackled the problem of lead poisoning, which brings brain damage or death to many slum children. Paint containing lead was used in tenements when they were first built, and as the many layers of old paint peel off, children tend to pick up and eat the poison. Landlords refuse to replaster or board up the walls, and the city refuses to pressure the landlords or even investigate the problem.

When a drug company donated 30,000 *free* lead poisoning tests to the city, an official ordered 13,000 but neglected to have them picked up. The Lords finally obtained some tests after a sit-in, and began taking them door-to-door in El Barrio. 30% of the children contacted tested positive. (So 30% of slum children may have brain damage. What DO you call genocide?) A group of medical students working with the Lords is currently trying to get the children admitted to the clinic of Metropolitan Hospital, but have run into red tape.

The Chicago Young Lords have conducted similar programs, in coalition with other politicized Latin youth groups. They were able to work with a sympathetic minister who turned over part of his church for a community day care center. The minister and his wife have since been killed.

All over the country members of the Rainbow Coalition and groups close to them are trying to show people how our society should serve us all. They face severe police repression, which has come down most heavily on the Black Panthers but has also killed and jailed members of Latin street gangs gone political, white student rebels in SDS, and the poor Southern whites in the Patriot Party. Lords Minister Yoruba is hopeful:

"See, the man has psyched the people into thinking they have all the power, but people are aware, and pretty soon all of them will have to decide, as Eldridge Cleaver says, if they're a part of the solution or part of the problem."

—barbara joye

(compiled from reports in the Young Lords newspaper, El Barrio newsletter, Liberation News Service, *The New York Times,* and WBAI-FM (NYC). An article on the Patriot Party will appear in the *Bird* shortly.)

ATZLAN

by Sierra

Denver, Colorado (LNS)

"We have created the nation of Aztlan," Corky Gonalez said last week at the second Annual Chicano Youth Liberation Conference.

The meeting was held to create a political party and Congress of Aztlan — geographically covering the lands of the Southwest stolen from the Indians and the Mexican ancestors of today's Chicanos, and spiritually incorporating all brown people, all Spanish speaking people.

The basic concerns of Aztlan will be: Community control of the schools, churches, agencies and other institutions; Creation of an Economic Base in the BARRIOS of the cities and villages through rural and industrial cooperatives; Security and self-defense; meaningful Education through creation of Chicano liberation schools and universities; Health and Welfare relating to community needs; preserving the rich Chicano cultural heritage of art; and Anti-war and Draft Resistance.

Brown women met during this conference, to discuss their role AS BROWN WOMEN, as revolutionaries and potential revolutionaries. After the first tentative meeting, they opened the continuing women's workshops to the men, and the overall effect was to produce stronger, more committed women taking their place in the Chicano movement alongside their men. (This was not an easy struggle. More articles will follow on the development of women within the Chicano Movement.)

Puerto Ricans and Blacks were invited, and Young Lords and Latin Kings shared the stage, dormitories, and guard duty with Brown Berets and Crusaders. Gangs from Chicago, whose members could not have walked across each other's turf, travelled together in the same buses, shared meals and lodging, and rapped, coming out of the conference with a feeling of brotherhood inconceivable a short time ago. A few individual fights did send several brothers to the hospital. But instead of rallying around their injured members and counter-attacking the other groups, which would have been the traditional response, gang and club leaders denounced the actions as "fucked up behavior" and reaffirmed their stand with their brother groups.

More than 3,000 Chicanos, Latinos, and Puertoriquenos from all over the country filled Denver's Crusade for Justice Hall for five days (over 2400 registered the first day) for the main purpose of creating an independent political party of the nation of Aztlan.

While there was unanimity of purpose, heated arguments on tactics pervaded many of the workshops and most of the after-hours discussion. Corky Gonzales, although he denies there is a single leader of the Chicano movement, clearly is the leader at this point. Corky is fast becoming as dangerous to the powers that rule this country as Malcolm X was before his assassination. He jabbed at both YSA and PL when he asserted, "This conference was not called to relate to any outside ideology. . .If you want to be a politician first and a Chicano second,

then get the hell out of here!"

During the conference it was decided there will be no dual membership in Aztlan. "No one can be a member of the Congress of Aztlan who is a member of any other political party or organization involved in electoral politics outside the Chicano party." It was made clear that Aztlan would go beyond simply repudiating the Democratic and Republican Parties, but would have a party strictly and entirely for La Raza.

Disagreements ran through all discussion about what role the party was to play. Many were adamantly opposed to any involvement in electoral politics; others followed Corky's lead in saying that a political party could be a tool with which to make use of the gringo mass media.

In other resolutions, proposed by the delegation from New Mexico, Rieis Tijerina was proclaimed national hero of Aztlan, with June 5—the date of the Tierra Amarilla raid—declared a national holiday.

One of the final acts of the conference was a wedding of two young Denver chicanos by the nation of Aztlan. The audience accompanied the young couple with rythmic hand-clapping as they marched through a line of Brown Berets and Black Berets — each raising a clenched fist as the couple passed through. At the stage Rocky — wearing an army fatigue jacket and black beret, and Della, in jeans, t-shirt and serape, faced Corky, who told the people present: "I am no high priest. They have made the decision. This isn't a ceremony but a witnessing of the love of two revolutionaries who believe in the same cause, the same nation. What these young people do today is a symbol of liberation and revolution."

A Church in El Barrio

The Week of the Lords: 'This Is a Family Thing'

by Jonathan Black

The paper Nativity cut-outs were pasted back over the altar, although two lambs appeared to be missing. Gone were the posters of Manuel Ramos (a Young Lord martyred in Chicago), the pictures of Che, the Puerto Rican flags, the messages of revolution. At the back of the chapel, four Lords had put away a deck of cards and were enforcing quiet in the adjoining hall and rooms. An older man with two large crates of fudge cream cookies picked his way through the pews and downstairs to the kitchen. The

floors were mopped and spotless; "no smoking" signs were taped to the cinderblock walls of the chapel. And a stand-in minister stood up to address a stand-in congregation, a congregation of Young Lords, white radicals, some blacks, lawyers, doctors, newsmen, children, and a few regular Sunday parishioners.

It had been a week since El Barrio's Young Lords had nailed shut the doors of an unlikely church on East 111th Street, and now Felipe Luciano, the 22-year-old leader of the Lords, had announced the church would be temporarily open for Sunday

services. Later the posters would be back on the walls and Aretha Franklin back on the hi-fi. But somehow, that curious truce brought full circle all the extraordinary events that had characterized this hectic week of mini-revolution.

In selecting the First Spanish Methodist Church, the Lords had captured an ideal symbol for all that has gone wrong for the poor of East Harlem. Sitting in the middle of a wasteland of rotting and gutted tenements, the newly renovated church is a large, empty building. Three spacious rooms just off the chapel and a converted (to "prayer room") basketball court runs the width of the building in back; in the basement are the kitchen and two more enormous rooms, and upstairs, three more rooms, converted by the Lords into a nursery. The Lords charge that the church was shut six days of

the week and open only two hours on Sunday.

The pastor of the church, Humberto Carrazana, is a Cuban exile. Eighty-five per cent of its small congregation of about 100 reportedly come from outside the community, many from boroughs other than Manhattan. Although nominally Methodist, the church is more fundamentalist and pentecostal in spirit, and before formal services begin, the congregation generally undertakes a writhing, shaking exorcism of the devil. Despite the Lords' appeals to the board of directors for space in the church, they are only one of several organizations—another being MEND—that have asked for the church's cooperation, only to be refused.

The Lords seized the church the Sunday after Christmas. Monday morning 75 children showed up for a free hot

TWO OCCUPANTS OF
THE SPANISH METHODIST CHURCH

breakfast in response to some energetic door-to-door work by the Lords. A liberation school and 24-hour medical services were set up. "We want the people to think of us as Latins who are serving the people," says Luciano, "not fuzzy-headed 'revolutionary' dudes who go around blasting with Thompson machine guns."

Since then, support has grown. Several hundred people occupy the church daily. On New Year's Eve, more than 500 were stuffed into the chapel for a "people's service," revolutionary poetry, Newsreel films, a children's skit re-enacting the taking of the church, and some speeches. Last Sunday, in a basement news conference, the Lords assembled the cream of East Harlem's povertycrat heavies, a Lindsay aide (Arnold Segarra), and some "community spokesmen" who pledged support for the Lords' action and gave some indication that they might be around when the bust came.

The front door of the church is barricaded with a piano and some furniture. At the side entrance, everyone is frisked, with varying degrees of attention, and warned that no arms or drugs are allowed. One newsman loudly resented the frisking, complained of an "unfriendly, hostile attitude," and emerged several hours later with a clenched fist and a farewell cry of "Power to the People."

Inside the church is a kaleidoscopic blur and swarm of moods, impressions, activities, raps, jobs, and squealing children. The Lords conduct "tours" through the building and explain their various programs to newcomers. In the medical room, Gene Straus, chief medical resident at Metropolitan Hospital, talks about lead poisoning and anemia testing. The Lords have administered about 200 lead poisoning tests at the church, and have organized groups to conduct door-to-door anemia testing. Even if they're kicked out of the church, says Straus, files are kept and the tests will be followed up. "Some people come in here with serious problems," says Straus, "some just because they haven't seen a doctor for 10 years. We've already referred five people to hospitals."

Around a table in the basement, a small group of blacks, whites, and Puerto Ricans are debating similar take-overs in Harlem. "In Harlem," says one black, "you'd never get away with popping off a church like this. The ministers there are organized. Those churches are armed. People don't recognize that there's only one black power in Harlem, and that's Adam Clayton Powell." And another: "We messed up with the State Office Building because we didn't come to terms with the black gangsters who work for the man. We let them have that parade, and they carried American flags, and the next day we were off the site." Upstairs, in another room, a clutch of Weathermen in denim is squatting on the floor and relaying the latest word from Flint on drugs, the Mother Country, and the "Fish in the Sea" line. Above the group is a piece of manila paper and a seven-year-old's scrawl: "The Lords are my People, Off the Pig!—Sister Emily Cruz."

No one expected to be occupying the church for eight days. One bathroom serves 500 people, and a small kitchen with a temperamental chef serves four hot meals a day to 200. But there is no shortage of food or supplies: they're either brought in by volunteers, or "requested" by the Lords from neighborhood stores. And there's no shortage of spirit. The Lords have created a mood that mixes good cheer with discipline and minimizes the rhetoric and sloganeering of revolution. Only rarely do words such as "fascism," "imperialism-capitalism," and "Marxism-Leninism" come up. "You walk up to somebody on 110th Street and tell him he belongs to the lumpenproletariat," says Yoruba, the Lord's minister of information, "and you'll get a lumpen in the mouth." Again and again, the Lords talk about concrete, tangible benefits, day care, programs, and "serving the people." "A guy walks in and he's not so sure what the Lords are all about," says Yoruba. "He comes out of that church and says, 'They're all right, they gave me a sandwich and they got some pretty hip music.' "

The Lords are billed as Puerto Rican Panthers. But while they undoubtedly owe their inspiration and structure to the Panthers, the Lords have carved out their own style of revolution. While referring to Panther rhetoric, they attempt to distinguish themselves from Panther tactics and avoid the pitfalls that have led to the decimation of Black Panther Party leadership. Noticeably absent in their talk, for instance, is any mention of "armed struggle" or "self-defense." The repeating scenario for the week's press conferences pitted sensation-oriented newsmen ("Will you resist arrest violently?" "Are you going to fight police when they come?") against quieter and more diplomatic Lords ("Our fight is serving children breakfast." "We want to live to serve our people, not get our heads busted." "There are no arms in this church.") Relations between the Panthers and the Lords appear to be in a state of flux. In a cordial and respectful mood, a couple of Lords dropped by the Panther office last week, and told them "Your Minister of Defense is in jail. Your Minister of Information is in exile. Your Chief of Staff is in jail. Your Chairman faces a death sentence. And you're still the baddest thing going." The Panthers asked them to leave.

While the two groups share the same oppressions, the same goals, and the same ideas of "serving the people," they are sharply distinguished by their opposite backgrounds and experiences. The Lords are a young organization, and while they have already had their share of harassment, arrests, and beatings—in New York and Chicago—they have not had to face the organized extinction of their party charged by Panthers, either through police "shoot-outs" or conspiracy charges.

The special qualities that flavor the Lords are strong family ties, Latin identification and recent emigration, a still relevant Christianity, and a willingness to cooperate and negotiate with non-revolutionary groups. In addition, there are the personalities of the handful of Lord leaders and a style that has worked a magic charm on generally unsympathetic groups, notably the press. Luciano has been described as a cross between Eldridge Cleaver and Lenny Bruce. Both he and Juan Gonzalez have been through college. All the Lord leaders have amused, impressed, radicalized, and charmed the pants off their audiences. Their facility in working with white establishment groups, however, does not appear to have eroded their credibility or determination in the ghetto.

Most striking are the family ties. After the seizure of the church, Yoruba's mother began working in the kitchen and looked somewhat skeptical and uneasy. By the end of the week she was beaming at everyone and proudly introducing herself as "Yoruba's mother." Other Lord parents have spent time in the church and delighted in meeting each other. And throughout the week, all the Lords' speeches have been laced with family references. "This is a family thing," said Juan Gonzalez. "This is the only place where the whole family can come and fight for liberation." David Perez, Minister of Defense: "My mother and father didn't come to this country to live in tenements and work their heads off in the garment district." And Luciano: "We see our mothers sweeping floors and insulted every day. I'm sick of seeing my mother come home with her knuckles scraped to the bone. I'm only 22 but I've seen it all. I can't even blush any more, and that's pathetic."

Although the Lords have a clear idea of what they're about and hold a revolutionary outlook, they have not yet drawn hard and fast with-us or against-us lines. They have gone to great lengths, for instance, to rationally convince the church's board of directors to give up some space—several directors are reportedly sympathetic to the Lords' position. Toward the end of the week, the elders of the congregation—white-collared and sober—were escorted cordially into the front pews of the chapel and addressed by several Lords attempting to explain their program. The dialogue, however, progressed little beyong accusations and defenses regarding Communism and Satanism.

This easy-going attitude has made the Lords an especially attractive cause to white liberal-radicals, many not yet committed to the vocabulary of revolution. At one of the week's impromptu speeches, Luciano said, "We don't ask you all to be revolutionaries; many of you don't come from our background. We just ask you to open your eyes."

The Lords apparently see their strength in support—not "correctness" of position—and they have cultivated ties with anti-poverty groups and other community organizations not specifically aligned with the Lords' philosophy or tactics. Their courtship of the press has proved outstandingly successful. Too successful perhaps, says Luciano: "All of a sudden everybody loves us, and I'm getting scared. We must be doing something wrong." Demi-celebrities (Elia Kazan, Jose Torres, Budd Schulberg) and politicians drop daily into the church; on Friday evening, Charles Garry, the West Coast Panther lawyer, came by with "greetings from Huey Newton" and thrilled the packed chapel with clenched fists raised in spread-armed salute. And Gloria Steinem's fur has been spotted more than once in the church.

And so far, even the overt hostility between Panthers and police has not been so bitterly articulated. In part this may be due to the newness of the Lords; in part to an absence of anti-black emotion and the threat posed to police by the Panthers' nationwide, uniformed militarism. To date, the Panthers are the only group to have actually fought the police with guns and bullets.

By the end of the week, the Lords were exhausted. Many had had only a few hours sleep all week, and they appeared both overwhelmed by the success and publicity of their action and wary of the bust they knew was coming. (Defended by a battery of eight lawyers, 11 Lords arrested the Sunday before the seizure appeared in court Monday, and the only talk was of the imminent bust.) The Lords had hoped that supporters would pack the church, and that police would have to arrest them while they were feeding children or conducting neighborhood classes or testing for lead poisoning.

The Lords had executed an extraordinary coup—they had stormed El Barrio's Winter Palace—and too much energy had been generated to begin to examine its consequences. "Whatever happens to us now," said Yoruba, "we have a victory here, and they're never going to wipe us out of people's minds and hearts."

the village VOICE

1/8/70

LETTER FROM A NAVAJO
INDIAN TO THE U.S. ARMY

Dear Mr. D. D. Spahr:
This letter is in answer to the two notices or Questionnaires you have sent to me in the last 6 weeks, this last one, day before yesterday. I am filling out this last one and returning it to you today. I have read it over and am filling it out as honestly as I can. The reason, that I have hesitated to return it: I am not interested in your war in Vietnam and I am interested in the problems of our Navajo people here on the Reservation and especially in the welfare of my immediate family and my father's family.

When I first came home when you released me, I found my family very much in need of help, as I had been gone for a long time, both domestically and in the fight we are all having with the State of Utah over a $10,000,000.00 oil Fund, that the State of Utah is trying to beat my people out of, and I just stayed here and soon found myself so involved, that it was just out of the question for me to return to the N.G. I just felt like, what I was doing over there with you fellows in the Army, was just nothing, that my life was here and no other place in the world. I was going to school, as you know, when you people took me into the Army and I only got to finish the eleventh grade in my school work. If you hadn't taken me then, I would have finished High-school at least.

Anyway, my family has been talking all this over this morning and we have discussed my situation from many ways. My father has been talking: He told us that the

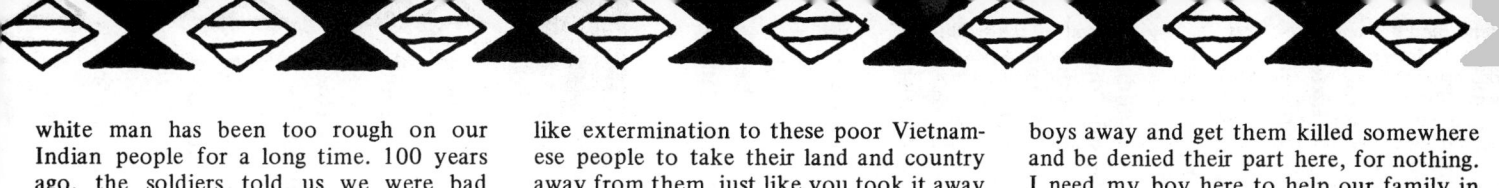

white man has been too rough on our Indian people for a long time. 100 years ago, the soldiers told us we were bad people and rounded us up with cow-whips and drive us to Ft. Sumner and held us there in Consentration Camps for 4 years and starved and froze to death, 4000 of our people there and while we were there, the United States had other soldiers all up here over our country, hunting for the few Navajos the first soldiers missed and shooting them down like coyotes and burning the people's blankets and saddles and stealing their horses, laying waste to everything they could find, that was usable for our people. The record shows, the soldiers treated us worst than animals at Ft. Sumner and when they were about to let us come home, they told us a hundred times, to not kill any more white men. They told us not to have anything to do with a gun, to get away from it if we saw one, to come back and live at peace with every body and we would have a good life. That we have done and have done for all this 100 years since we sign the Treaty, tho' we had to sign it with a gun in our backs, we have kept that pledge we made at the Treaty. Now, in this Treaty we signed with the United States Government, we and you have a Clause there, that at no time will our Indian people be called up on to go across the Ocean and fight, to engage in Military Service. But that if the United States is threatened with an Invasion by a Foreign Power, we are obligated to help defend this Nation as much as any other element of our population. Will you look up the Records. Everywhere we go, we hear a distaste for this present war you fellows are fighting in Vietnam. These people you are fighting are not white people. On T.V. we have seen American white soldiers setting matches to these poor people's homes, murdering their children in cold blood, spreading more destitution and Poverty over that land, in one day, than the President's "War on Poverty" can heal in six months. It just don't make sense to us Indians. From what I have seen in pictures of these Vietnamese people, they look like Indians to me and I just don't want to kill, especially, my own brothers.

Did you know, that just before the Civil War, the South had a blue print to completely destroy the North American Indian and put Negro slaves in his place and at that time the white man had nearly all other tribes of Indians in consentration camps the same as us, preparatory to mass extermination, had the South won the war. Now, here comes the Bypartisan Rightists of both political parties of 1966 of these United States of America, taking a war of

like extermination to these poor Vietnamese people to take their land and country away from them, just like you took it away from us, leaving these poor Vietmenese people homeless, with their loved ones killed, all of them left in such sorrow, that cannot be measured, with a hatred in their hearts for the United States that will never heal. Lately, we hear that your white soldiers have been turning loose poison gas on these people, even killing some of your own men with it by mistake. This is your war, not ours. You are the ones, who conceived it, our people would not do a thing like this. Our history shows, together with our present peaceful status, that we are a peaceful people and our constant daily efforts to create something beautiful and beneficial to our people is everywhere before the white people of this country and before the people from acrossed the ocean, who have come here to visit us.

Here we are, the North American Indians: For 300 years, you white people tried to utterly destroy us. The methods and extremes you went to to do this is appalling and revolting to the civilized half of the human race. You tried to make slaves out of us, but we proved to you, that we would die, before we would be slaves to any white man.

My father said further: Is the white man over there across the sea now, trying to take that land away from these people. If they do this, are they going to give us back some of our land, they took away from us the same way. I don't want my land back at the cost of killing some one else. I think these poor people in Vietnam are people as we are. I would like to visit them some time and have some of them come to see us. I do not want to hurt them in any way. We don't believe in hurting any body and even hesitate to fight when we are justifiable. Our fathers lived here in as much peace with everybody as we could for many years. I try hard to live that way myself and teach my children to do like our fathers did. We are a people, who work for what we need and work more to beautify the things we hold dear to us. Never, have we found pleasure in destruction or using more of our natural resources, than we find necessary to supply our necessities. When we had this country, we never had it cut up with ditches, carrying away our soils and the most of our waters, that used to soak into the ground, providing abundant grass for our sheep and horses and the wild animals, that belonged to us. All I have here, I have cared for and created for the benefit of my family, which is my life, for their welfare after I am gone and for their children after them and I don't want to see the white man take my

boys away and get them killed somewhere and be denied their part here, for nothing. I need my boy here to help our family in our daily life and his wife and baby is a responsibility, that no body else can take care of. I have spent a lot of money to help my boy get a little education and all along, I have been expecting him to come back home, when he got this knowledge and help his own family first and then our neighbors around us. I, Myself, didn't get any education and I have come to think somehow, that I ought to have better knowledge of the records of the past, that it would make everything more clear of how to deal with the white man and help me to better care for my family and be able to advise my people on the things that are good for them. Now, that my boy has achieved some thing of what I ought to have had, I don't want his knowledge destroyed, before he has a chance to help raise our people up, and his blood poured out across the sea, fighting there poor Vietminese people. We have our own civilization and you white people have yours. We have the record of all the crimes, that your fathers have tried to destroy us, and from the beginning of your occupation of our country, to the present day, our fathers hand this story down to the children and will never forget the deceptive nature of the white man.

I do not have much education yet and there are many things that I do not understand, but with what I have, I understand some things very well. I do know what is right and wrong, tho' I have made some mistakes. I realize, that I have just begun to really learn. Today, many of our Navajo people are very much uninformed and many of us have been misinformed. Many of our Navajo drafted young men do not know, what is in the Treaty about fighting these foreign wars. None of our people are cowards, but we have to have a real reason, before we would take part in any conflict, that is a life and death struggle.

We are not the only people in the United States, who believe this war is a crime. We are learning that there are millions of white people and nearly all the black people are against it too. We can't find that these Vietnamese people have ever harmed anybody and you white people ought not to be over there, destroying their living and their lives. That country is theirs, the same as this country is ours and they have every sacred right to keep it dear to themselves. If we had to, we would live on a very little food, before we would kill somebody and take their living.
RAYMOND BELETSO, J-PVT *ER25738585.

The Navajo Times 3/24/66

SPEECH BY A YOUNG INDIAN THAT THE WHITE MEN REFUSED TO HEAR

The American Indian situation is a condensed and distilled version of the state of the union. The problems of American Indians are the result of the bureaucratic behavior, of dehumanized interaction, of "intellectuals" defining the System.

In January of this year the National Indian Youth Council submitted a statement to the National Conference on Poverty in the Southwest. This fell on deaf ears because it was essentially a protest against the very conditions outlined above.

We are on the threshold of creating the Great Society. What was once thought a fantasy could become a reality. But if you don't speak, no one will listen—

The cancelled speech:

A friend of mine has a sign which hangs on the wall behind his desk. The sign says, "Are you contributing to the solution or to the problem?"

My name is Clyde Warrior and I'm a full blood Ponca Indian from Oklahoma. I appear here before you to try, as much as I can, to present to you the views of Indian youth. If I start my presentation with a slightly cynical quote it is because American Indians generally and Indian youth particularly are more than a little cynical about programs devised for our betterment. Over the years the federal government has devised programs and "wheeled them" into Indian communities in the name of economic rehabilitation or the like. These programs have, by and large, resulted in bitter divisions and strife in our communities, further impoverishment and the placing of our parents in a more and more powerless position.

I am a young man, but I'm old enough to have seen this process accelerate in my lifetime. This has been the experience of Indian youth—to see our leaders become impotent and less experienced in handling the modern world. Those among our generation who have an understanding of modern life have had to come to that understanding by experiences outside our home communities. The indignity of Indian life, and I would presume the indignity of life among the poor generally in these United States, is the powerlessness of those who are "out of it," but who yet are coerced and manipulated by the very system which excludes them.

I must say I smiled at the suggestion that this conference would draw together articulate spokesmen for the poor. There may indeed be articulate spokesmen *for* the poor but there are no articulate spokesmen *of* the poor. If my relatives were articulate they would not be poor. If they could appear before gentlemen such as yourself and make a good case for their aspirations, they would of course not need a War on Poverty. They would not be "out of it." They might not be the warm human beings they are but they would be verbal, aggressive, and not so poor. They would have been included in on the act of America.

When I talk to Peace Corps volunteers who have returned from overseas, they tell me, along with many modern historians and economists, that the very structure of the relation between the rich and poor keeps the poor poor; that the powerful do not want change and that it is the very system itself that causes poverty; and that it is futile to work within this framework. I am not an economist and I cannot evaluate these ideas. I hope that men of good will even among the powerful are willing to have their "boat rocked" a little in order to accomplish the task our country has set itself.

As I say I am not sure of the causes of poverty, but one of its correlates at least is this powerlessness, lack of experience, and lack of articulateness.

Now we have a new crusade in America—our "War on Poverty,"—which purports to begin with a revolutionary new concept—working with the local community. Indian youth could not be more pleased with these kinds of statements, and we hope that for the first time since we were disposed of as a military threat our parents will have something to say about their own destiny and not be ignored as is usually the case. If I am once again a little cynical let me outline the reasons for our fears. I do not doubt that all of you are men of good will and that you do intend to work with the local community. My only fear is what you think the local community is.

It has been my experience that many Americans think of a community in terms of a physical area or a legal unit, not in terms of a social unit—a unit where people have close personal ties one to another. Let me give you an example of what I mean. The Ponca tribe of which I am a member lives in Kay County, Oklahoma. You could call Kay County a community, it is a legally designated unit, but if it is a community my relatives are not part of it. In fact, I would imagine Kay County, Oklahoma to be a number of communities, as I use the term—several white communities and an Indian community. One white community, the business class of our county seat, owns the riches in the institutional structure and makes decisions for the other communities in Kay County. There is probably some overlap between the various white communities in our county, but certainly our Indian community, as far as being part of Kay County, might as well be on Mars. I would guess that this is the dilemma of the poor, be they Indian, Anglo, Mexican-American or Negro. Our communities have no representatives in the legally designated units of which we are a part.

With the Indians this is even more complicated because, as many of you know, we do have a legal structure which articulates us with the central government even though we have no articulation with the county and state government. On the face of it, Indians seem to be in a better position than most other poor people. However, these institutions called tribal governments have very limited functions from the viewpoint of the Indians who live in our communities. In most places they serve as a buffer against the outsider. And in fact other people of prestige and influence among us thus go unnoticed and unbothered by the white man, so that much of our important leadership is hidden from the eyes of outsiders. Many times our tribal governments, which have very little legal power, have been forced into the position of going along with programs they did not like and which in the long run were harmful. They had no choice. They were powerless to do otherwise.

Modern Americans have developed a habit in recent years of naming something and then assigning attributes to whatever they have named which are part of the name itself. There is no Kay County, Oklahoma, community in a social sense. We are not part of it except in the most tangential legal sense. We only live there. There is no Ponca tribal government. It is only named that. We are among the poor, the powerless, the inexperienced and the inarticulate.

I do not know how to solve the problem of poverty and I'm not even sure that poverty is what we must solve—perhaps it is only a symptom. In a rich country, like the United States, if poverty is the lack of money and resources that seems to me to be a very small problem indeed. So I cannot say whether poverty is a symptom or a cause or how one would go about solving it in pure economic terms. But of this I am certain, when a people are powerless

and their destiny is controlled by the powerful, whether they be rich or poor, they live in ignorance and frustration because they have been deprived of experience and responsibility as individuals and as communities. In the modern world there is no substitute for this kind of experience. One must have it to make rational choices, to live in a world you feel competent to deal with and not be frustrated by. No one can gain this experience without the power to make these decisions himself with his fellows in his local community. No amount of formal education or money can take the place of these basic life experiences for the human being. If the Indian does not understand the modern economy it is because he has never been involved in it. Someone has made those decisions for him. "Hand outs" do not erode character. The lack of power over one's own destiny erodes character. And I might add, self-esteem is an important part of character. No one can have competence unless he has both the experience to become competent and make decisions which display competence.

In the old days the Ponca people lived on the buffalo and we went out and hunted it. We believe that God gave the buffalo as a gift to us. That buffalo alone did not erode our character, but no one went out and found the buffalo for us and no one organized our hunts for us, nor told us how to divide our meats, nor told us how to direct our prayers. We did that ourselves. And we felt ourselves to be a competent, worthy people. In those days we were not "out of the system." We were the system, and we dealt competently with our environment because we had the power to do so. White businessmen and bureaucrats did not make the Ponca decisions, the Poncas made those decisions and carried them out. If we were rich one year, it was our doing and if we were poor the next, we felt competent to deal with that condition. Democracy is just not good in the abstract, it is necessary for the human condition; and the epitome of democracy is responsibility as individuals and as communities of people. There can not be responsibility unless people can make decisions and stand by them or fall by them.

I might also add it is only when a community has real freedom that outside help will be effective. The lessons of new nations have certainly taught us that. It was only when colonies in Africa and Asia had their freedom that economic help from France and England became productive. We can apply that lesson here in America to the local community itself.

I congratulate you gentlemen on the great crusade you have undertaken. I wish you luck, not for your sake, but for the sake of my relatives; and I beseech you to in fact deal with the local community, not just a physical or legal area, but a community of people. Give our communities respect, the power to make choices about our own destiny, and with a little help we will be able to join the United States and live a decent fulfilling life.

Clyde Warrior, 1965

From *The Shoshoneans* by Ed. Dorn, William Morrow and Co.

THE OLDEST AMERICAN TRADITION: INDIANS AS ANARCHISTS

The Goals of the Group

THE LOST UNIVERSE. By Gene Weltfish. Basic Books. 506 pp. $12.50.

THE LONG DEATH: The Last Days of the Plains Indians. By Ralph K. Andrist. The Macmillian Co. 371 pp. $8.95.

D'Arcy McNickle

As to the question of posting sentinels to guard against surprise attacks, Dr. Weltfish suggestively writes that "they were a well-disciplined people under many trying circumstances. And yet they had none of the power mechanisms that we consider essential to a well-ordered life. No orders were ever issued. No assignments for work were ever made. . . . The only instigator of action was the consenting person." Even in so critical an area of public safety as the posting of camp guards, the will of the individual governed. According to Dr. Weltfish, a young man would say, "I think I'll go up to the sentry post early tomorrow morning." A friend would respond, "I think I'll do that too." In due course as many men as were needed would have volunteered.

It is conceivable, under such a system of individual consent, that there would be temporary lapses, moments when the guard was down. Any democratic society based on the consent of the governed is vulnerable to sneak attack from a militant neighbor.

The Pawnee system of individual consent brings us to one of the central themes of the book, for Dr. Weltfish is manifestly interested in the meaning of democracy, as practiced by this tribe, which lived in the Missouri River basin for more than 600 years—a longer time perspective than archaeologists of the area formerly reckoned with. She asked repeatedly how the people managed to live together without centralized au-

thority and could find no instance in which a political leader, a priest, or even a senior member of a household presumed to give orders at large or to another individual. Even formal discussion for the purpose of arriving at a consensus was not a general procedure. When asked how plans were worked out, who discussed them, the informant would answer, "They didn't discuss it at all. They don't talk about it. It goes along just as it happens to work out."

Social forms, she decided, "were carried within the consciousness of the people, not by others who were in a position to make demands." For such a system to operate, as this one did for a longer period than most modern democracies have existed, participation had to be universal, the autonomy of the individual had to be inviolable, and the individual had to be internally disciplined and responsible, not for himself alone, but for the entire group within which he functioned.

What brought down the Pawnees was not a failure in the society but diseases against which they had no immunity; competition with the Sioux, intensified by a shrinking economic base; and finally by the total destruction of that base, the buffalo herds. And behind all of this was the incoming white man, who practiced a democracy in which every man wants to be king.

The development of the individual within his society is yet another part of the question raised by Pawnee democracy, which Dr. Weltfish explores. "One thing is clear," she writes, "no one is caught within the social order . . . each person stands as his own person." The child was born into a community, but was never swallowed up by it. From the beginning he was made to feel that his identity was with the infinite cosmos, as the roundhouse within which he lived served as a central observation post from which the movements of the planets and the stars were calculated for ceremonial purposes.

Affection came from many sources, in varying degrees of kinship intimacy, but affection never became a smothering overprotection. "The special concern of his mother did not mean that he was so closely embedded with her emotionally that he was not able to move about." Move about he did, to the homes of his uncles, his half-brothers, his grandparents, always certain of food and warmth, "and there was no reason why he should hesitate to set out alone and explore the wide world, even though years should pass before he returned." The

world, indeed, was his home. Dr. Weltfish contends that "it is not easy for us to perceive the wide gap in kind between Pawnee society and our own, and yet in the face of all the terrible events of the past and the pressure to destroy his personality, surely it must mean something that the American Indian has maintained his identity among us."

If the meaning of Pawnee identity eludes us at this moment in time, the occasion may yet arise when we find ourselves retracing the social development of these once despised denizens of the Plains for the threads of continuity which successfully carried them beyond disaster.

One such thread certainly was the individual—not the social form or the institution, which may stifle individual growth and in any case is a temporal creation of fallible men. The Pawnees were fortunate in that they were born into a fluid society. "The individual personality was not trimmed down to fit the kin structure, but the structure was used to realize the individual personality. The Pawnee social structure was written into no statute books, nor did it have the status of doctrine, and there was no chain of command to enforce it."

With freedom to move and to grow, the individual carried out his commitment to the group, not because of coercive sanctions or internalized guilt, but because in his own searching for goals he was realizing the goals of the group. "His aspiration [was] not to surpass some one else, but to go beyond his own past achievements." And therefore, his aspirations, even his personal name, were secrets which he shared discreetly, if ever. To speak publicly of such matters was to invite competition and conflict.

In such a society, the individual was the keystone. This, the Pawnee, as well as other Indians, understood. Which perhaps is the ultimate explanation of why the Indian people have kept their identity through all adversity. After all forms had crumbled, the man stood revealed.

On that final point, having reminded us that the problems of our bomb-ridden, automated age "call for drastic revisions in our age-old motivations," Dr. Weltfish concludes that "it is within the individual that the universe will be regained."

This, also, the Pawnees knew.

Ed. Note: D'Arcy McNickle, a member of the Confederated Salish and Kootenai Tribes of Montana, is director of American Indian Development

From "The Goals of the Group" a review in *The Nation* by D'Arcy McNickle 9/25/65

ole of color

Indians Meet the Press: It's Pride Vs. Prejudice

by Paul Cowan

WASHINGTON — "The demonstration at the Supreme Court today, planned by the Poor People's Campaign, failed to achieve any of its objectives and showed supreme contempt for the court."—Douglas Kiker, NBC news, May 29.

"Ordinary American citizens must react to the disgraceful behavior of those who besieged the Supreme Court Wednesday with outrage and indignation that probably has to be tempered with the old folk wisdom 'poor people have poor ways.' "—Editorial, Washington Post, May 31.

What terrible event had the liberal journalists seen that made them sound as angry as white Mississippi newspapermen in the early days of the civil rights movement?

Pavlov could have used journalists instead of dogs for his experiments. Most of the men who are supposed to transmit and interpret complex information through the mass media respond only to the stimuli with which they are most familiar. They see each new event they cover as a repetition of some story they had been assigned last year.

The Poor People's Campaign was conceived by a black organization, SCLC, but its demonstration at the Supreme Court was planned by some American Indians who had come to Washington to join the campaign. That small paradox was too complicated for reporters like Douglas Kiker. The Indians were angry at a recent Court ruling that restricted their right to fish in the Columbia River in the state of Washington; they asked the Mexican - Americans, the black people, and the poor whites who are also participating in the Poor People's Campaign to join their demonstration. To reporters the fact that red men rather than black men had planned the day's protest suggested that there was an angry struggle for leadership between the ethnic groups. And that raised the specter that commentators and editorial writers fear most: chaos.

The Indians who organized the demonstration were dressed in the same costumes they wear at rodeos and wide-screen movies and it was hard for the reporters, accustomed to stories of Sitting Bull and Tonto, to realize that they weren't side-show attractions but committed activists with genuine complaints. There is little work for the Indian in the remote areas of the West where his reservations are located. The United States government, which has violated most of its treaties with the Indians, owes millions of dollars to tribes throughout the country. But not a single Indian serves as a Commissioner on the Bureau of Indian Affairs, not a single red man is in a position to defend his people's interests.

The Indians who organized the demonstration at the Supreme Court were hurt, angry people. They had come all the way from Washington, Montana, North Dakota to win back their rights, and now that they were involved in active protest they showed none of the frightened humility that liberals praised as dignity when they saw that attitude constraining the early civil rights demonstrators. The Indians seemed genuinely dignified, genuinely proud of their identities: examples, though they didn't realize it, of the attitude the black power movement hopes to instill in American Negroes.

But the reporters seemed much more interested in gossiping about the Indians' costumes than in talking with them. "I was more impressed by the outfit I used to see on the barbershop Indian back home," one said. George Crow Flies High, the old man whom many seemed to regard as their chief, wasn't colorful enough for the journalist.

Around noon a stocky fellow wearing a huge headdress and a tight, white tribal suit came striding up the Supreme Court steps. The reporters rushed over to talk with him; they had found a spokesman they could quote in the next morning's newspapers. His name was White Bear O'-Conner, he said, and he was the Chief of Indian Security for the Poor People's Campaign.

"Do your people believe in non-violence?" one man asked. "We will remain non-violent," White Bear answered, "until," then he looked around for someone to complete his statement. But he was the only Indian there. "Until the time comes to be violent." The reporters recorded his remark diligently.

"How long will your people stay in Washington, Chief?" White Bear was asked. "We will stay in Washington until"—again he looked around him—"until the time comes to leave." Another quote to be stored in the reporters' notebooks for the late city edition.

Most of the Indians had been sitting at the top of the steps, in front of the heavy main entrance to the court building which had been locked since their demonstration began. They kept chanting angrily and banging on the door. "It's a fitting thing," one woman told her friends. "The doors of justice have been locked to us ever since the white man came to America."

But now the interview with White Bear provided a new outlet for their fury. "Listen, reporters," a stocky young man yelled from the top of the steps, "we're tired of people like you defining our leaders according to who wears the biggest headdress. This isn't a cowboy and Indian movie, you know. This time we're playing for real.

"Anyway, this White Bear O'-Conner you've been interviewing isn't an Indian at all. He's an Irishman."

Several elderly Indians walked with him toward the reporters. "I don't know if you realized that we have a 101-year-old woman with us," he continued. "She's one of our real leaders. She knows more about America than any of you ever will. Listen to her. Write what she says in your newspapers."

Her name was Mattie Grinnell, and she was the last living full-blooded member of the Mandan tribe, which had lived in North Dakota. The United States had killed the rest of her people. She recalled that when she was a girl her tribesmen had been able to eat the nourishing meat of the buffaloes they used to hunt near their home. But now, she said, there are no more buffaloes and the Indians are confined to their reservation, forced to subsist on the terrible food that the government provides them. When she began to talk about a treaty which the white man had signed and then broken, a reporter interrupted her; he wanted information that he could include in a light, anecdotal article. "What is your Indian name?" he asked. She could speak English much better than she understood it, so she smiled at the reporter while she waited for his question to be translated. "Many Roads," she said finally. Then she began to describe the effect of reservation life on the Indian men who had always been accustomed to hunting wild game over huge spaces of land.

Now another reporter interrupted her. He hadn't heard the most relevant piece of information and he wanted to make sure he had it before the speech ended. "What was that name again?" he asked. After Mattie Grinnell answered his question she quit talking. She was too tired to go on.

There were some journalists who found Mattie Grinnel's history more interesting than White Bear's headdress, and they used it to provide their readers with a quick snatch of local color. But it was an item for the features page, an oddity of the Poor People's Campaign: a sideshow. None of the reporters who heard Mattie Grinnell or George Crow Flies High describe the Indians' problems thought to connect the conditions they were describing to the demonstration in which they were participating.

The real news of the Poor People's Campaign, as far as the press was concerned, was the disruption it might cause, the violence it theatened to produce.

The reporters got their big story later that afternoon.

The leaders of the demonstration had gone inside the Court Building to talk with the Chief Clerk. For the first time in a dreary, rainy week the sun was out. Some of the teenagers began to play near a shallow pool on the plaza in front of the Court. A Mexican-American boy, wearing a gaudy bandana around his neck, snuck up behind a black man in an African outfit and shoved him into the water; then the two of them united to drench a white girl who laughed loudly with excitement. The kids were getting noisier and noisier. Though the water was only up to their waists some of them began to leap in feet first, hands holding their noses, as if they were at a swimming hole back home. The plaza in front of the stately marble Supreme Court Building had been turned into a public park for poor people.

The plainclothesmen who had been assigned to cover the demonstration seemed very uncomfortable. "You know, we can arrest these people any time we want to," one of them said to his partner. He seemed to see the kids as a bunch of hoodlums maliciously defiling a national shrine.

Soon the police got their chance to act. Two demonstrators had lowered a flag near the pool to half-mast in honor, they said, of John F. Kennedy's birthday. The same thing had happened several hours before but then some of the marshals appointed from within the Poor People's Campaign had restored the flag to its full height without creating an incident. But this time, within a minute of the offense, a herd of cops was stampeding onto the plaza. At least 75 of them raced toward the flag pole, pummeling anyone who got in their way. They made three quick arrests.

The campaign marshals calmed the demonstrators immediately. Near the police wagon Andy Young, the executive vice-president of SCLC, wandered back and forth telling people to "Cool it, brothers, there'll be many a day like this before we get back home."

But the cops were not so peaceful. On the far side of the police wagon five were hunched over on the street, pinning one of the black men who had been arrested to the pavement. They held his right leg in a hammerlock, his foot above his waist, even though there was no way he could have escaped the platoon of policemen if he had been physically free.

Within five minutes the demonstration was orderly again. People ate sandwiches, sang freedom songs, talked, listened to speeches as they waited for their leaders to report on the conversation with the Court Clerk. But the press had its news of disruption. The newscasts that night and the papers the next morning focused on the arrests and on the fact that five windows in the Supreme Court Building had been broken (no one knew whether members of the Poor People's Campaign were responsible for that damage). There was no description of the Indians' complaints. From the stories that appeared it seemed that a horde of poor people had gathered at the Supreme Court for no reason except to display their contempt for the American legal system.

The news the journalists reported was an exact reflection of the Washington Post's folk wisdom that "poor people have poor ways."

Late that afternoon the Campaign leaders emerged from their meeting with the Clerk of the Court. "He told us that he was not competent to handle our complaints," said Hank Adams, a young Indian who was serving as the group's spokesman. "We are going to take him at his word. We consider him incompetent, too. Now we are judging the Court, and in our case we find it guilty of inhumanity. The

Indians who come from Washington are going to continue to fish in the streams that have always fed their families. If they get arrested the rest of us are going to go out there to get arrested with them."

Then Ralph Abernathy made the argument which in his mind connects the protests of the Mexican Americans, the black people, the Indians, and the poor whites who have come together to wage the Poor People's Campaign. "It was genocide," he said, "when white America killed off millions of Indians so that they could settle the West. It was genocide when white America ran the Mexican Americans off their land in the Southwest. It is genocide when America deprives black people and poor whites of food and employment. How many people has America killed to build this country? They have enslaved us, murdered us, stolen our land, starved us. They have nearly exterminated an entire race, the Indians. That is why we are here in the Poor People's Campaign—to change this country non-violently. For we are afraid that if we don't change America completely then America will destroy us."

The Washington Post concluded its article criticizing the Supreme Court Demonstration with this paragraph:

"The Poor People's Campaign, by this foolish episode, has done its cause more harm than any of its enemies ever could. As the President said in his Texas address: 'Those who glorify violence as a form of political action are really the best friends the status quo ever had.'"

It was the mass media that took three arrests and five windows that some poor people might have broken, and defined that as violence. It was the Washington Post that glorified that violence—enshrined it on the editorial page—and ignored the brutal history that cause the Indians to demonstrate. It was Douglas Kiker of NBC, complaining about "supreme contempt for the Court," who indicated that in his view the building was far more sacred than the people who felt compelled to protest in front of it.

I sometimes think that newspapers like the Washington Post and television networks like NBC would have accused the Jews who planned the uprising in the Warsaw ghetto of irresponsibility, and would have insisted that by their disgraceful behavior the rebels were doing their cause much more harm than good.

the village VOICE 6/6/68

Old Ghosts in an Affluent Society

by Paul Cowan

WASHINGTON — George Crow Flies High, the middle-aged chief of the Hidatsu tribe from Fort Berthold, North Dakota, was drawing a map to show me how the United States government had violated its treaties with his people. Several days earlier his picture had been relayed throughout the country by the mass media: his deeply lined face and full tribal costume had become the symbols of the Indians' demonstration in front of the Supreme Court. Now, dressed in white man's clothes, sitting in the austere basement of the church that housed the Indian contingent to the Poor People's Campaign, he was trying to make me understand the hatred his people felt for mine.

He sketched the North American continent as a perfect rectangle surrounded by a single, circular ocean and bisected diagonally by one great river. On the upper right hand corner of the paper where he had made

the map, just beyond the round ocean, he inscribed that date when "Columbus discovered us": 1892. He must have made the mistake because he felt distracted talking to a strange white man, but as I looked at the figure I realized that the 400 years which meant so much in our history must have meant far less to him — except that during that time his people were robbed of their land. For him the brave Columbus we learn about in school didn't exist. Instead Columbus was the first white intruder, an ethereal figure whose malicious greed had brought him here from some mysterious place beyond the circumference of George Crow Flies High's imagination.

Along the river that divided the continent the Indian drew two alternating shapes: large squares, the land which the United States government had seized from the Indians to provide white people with their homesteads, and much smaller circles,

the reservations onto which the Indians had been pushed.

The only other symbol on the map was a mark which George Crow Flies High had placed on the upper edge of the continent, in the direction from which Columbus had come. That was the White House. "He took all our land," the Indian exclaimed. (He spoke English well; the pronoun was not the result of faulty grammar.) A treaty had been signed in Washington in 1851, he said, in which the United States had promised to pay the Hidatsu and her sister tribes $50,000 a year for 50 years. "But he never gave us a penny of that money. All the time he treated us like stupid animals. When the white man came here we didn't know his ways and we signed the papers he gave us. Then his courts told us that the agreements didn't mean a thing. We tried to hire lawyers to fight our cases. But all the lawyers and all the judges work in his house." He pointed at the White House. "They don't want to help us.

"Your government has done us great harm. Now we Indians are going to join with the colored fellows. They have been hurt, too, and they know how to fight

back. Together we will be very strong. We will win the country back from the white man."

* * *

The Perkinses, members of the Arikara tribe from Ft. Berthold, are not nearly so militant as their friend George Crow Flies High. Perkins is 80, his wife is 73: all they really hope for is a pension that will relieve their intense poverty. Mrs. Perkins's chronic diabetes had made her reluctant to journey to Washington at all, but friends on the reservation had begged her to accompany them. Her perfect English gave them additional confidence. She speaks the language with a courtesy so sweet as to be slightly archaic, and her accent — a brogue which sounds almost Scottish — makes listening to her a delight.

Her husband joined the Poor People's Campaign to repeat a claim that had brought him to Washington twice before. In his pocket he carried a yellow, crinkling rectangle of paper, a discharge from General Custer's army that had been issued to an uncle of his in 1872. "I sent a letter here to Washington more than 40 years ago," he said, "and they never answered. When

e of color

I was here 15 years ago they wanted to know if I had ever made any claims before. I told them. I had and they asked me for a copy of my letter. I suppose it's one of those big offices here in Washington. Aren't those government people paid to keep track of our complaints?"

I offered to drive Perkins to the Indian Claims Commission. He was a bulky old man with white hair cropped so close to his head that he looked almost bald; his tight jeans, his Western-style cotton shirt, his black stetson hat made him seem like an older, wiser version of Spencer Tracy in "Bad Day at Black Rock." He and his wife squeezed into the back seat of my Volkswagen and as we headed toward the center of the city they began to talk about the indignities the white man had afflicted on them.

"My brother went to an Indian boarding school," he said, "and one day he started acting up. The white men who ran the school decided to put him in the dungeon. It was a real dungeon, way beneath the ground. They

were fed nothing but cold water and crackers for two weeks. Of course he was forbidden to see anyone. When he came up he was insane. He has never recovered."

* * *

As I drove home from the church where they were staying I began to think about another woman from their reservation, Mattie Grinnell, who at 101 years old had come from North Dakota to Washington for the Poor People's Campaign. At a press conference she had told reporters that she was the last full-blooded member of the Mandan tribe and I had written that down without really thinking about it. Now I realized that it was as if I had been transported forward in time to meet the last full-blooded Ecuadorian or Irishman —or North American.

It was my people who had displaced her tribesmen: starved them, murdered them. If the word extermination applied to the Jews in Germany or the Japanese at Hiroshima it also applied to the Indians in the United

States. At school I had learned to think of the exterminators as brave Americans whose dream was to expand the frontier, to make the continent safe for democracy.

The day after their visit to the Indian Claims Commission Mr. and Mrs. Perkins returned to Ft. Berthold. That day Robert Kennedy was shot.

I kept trying to imagine how the Indians perceived the assassination. Was their distrust of the white man intensified by being deprived of their best white friend?

I had a different impression. The Perkinses must have seen Kennedy's assassination as an extension of the history of violence that had destroyed so many of their relatives, and left them confined to their poor reservation. Now that there were no more Indians to kill, they may have thought, the white man may have turned his hatred (an inherent trait) back upon himself. And if there was one thing the Indians knew about the Europeans who had conquered them it

was that the intruders were resolute, highly efficient. With their new machines of violence they could destroy themselves in far less time than it had taken them to win the continent.

Perhaps, then, the Perkinses, George Crow Flies High, and Mattie Grinnell returned to their reservations in that barren, freezing corner of North Dakota with the odd notion that it would now be a waste of time to press the formal claims they had to portions of the white man's land. For the end of the empire that had exterminated their people and colonized them must have seemed very near. Even the battle for liberation of which George Crow Flies High dreamed now seemed unneccessary; for their enemy was killing himself.

They had only to wait at Ft. Berthold. Some day soon the white man would vanish, as abruptly and mysteriously as he had arrived four centuries before. Then the land the Indians loved would be theirs once again.

the village VOICE 6/20/68

WHITE MEN WITHOUT GREED

marvin garson

"They've pushed the Indian far enough," says Rolling Thunder. "We're not going to pay any more taxes, and we're not going to give up any more land."

Rolling Thunder is a Shoshone Indian from Carlin, Nevada. He is a lawyer and a warrior. He gives the impression of meaning what he says.

Two months ago, just before the hunting season opened, a Shoshone named Stanley Smart was arrested for killing a deer. He needed the meat for his family — a wife and nine children.

The Indians decided to retaliate against the white "head hunters" — sporting men who hunt deer for the prestige of big antlers and often leave the carcasses behind to rot on garbage dumps. On October 15 a group of armed Shoshone, some wearing war paint and feathers, surprised a drunken party of white hunters camped on the Ruby Valley Indian Reservation and gave them 15 minutes to leave. One of them was a deputy sheriff, and showed the Indians his badge. "That's no good here," Rolling Thunder told him. The white men were gone in fifteen minutes. "Head hunters" kept clear of the Ruby Valley Reservation for the rest of the hunting season.

The Shoshone earn a sparse living as ranch hands and mine laborers in the dry lands of the West — Nevada, Utah, Wyoming, Idaho, and the Mojave Desert of Southern California. How many Shoshonee are there? "We don't want to be counted. Last time they sent around a census-taker, we locked him up."

Stanley Smart did break Nevada laws by killing a deer for his family to eat. But Rolling Thunder does not see why the Shoshone ought to get hunting licenses and follow Nevada game laws. "It would be like us getting licenses from the Chinamen or the Russians. The white men have got things backward: they think

WE'RE in THEIR country."

He hastened to avoid giving the wrong impression: "We're not racists. We believe there's room here for everyone. But the white men have to realize that there must be room for the native people too. We're not greedy. We didn't wipe out the buffalo. When we shoot deer it's to feed our families, not to show off the head and throw away the meat."

A white caught would have been cited like a speeder. But Stanley Smart was brought to Winnemucca and thrown in jail. The next day Rolling Thunder represented him before the judge.

"I said if they were going to take deer meat away from this man's family, then they'd better give them some other kind of food, because all they had was three cans of milk for the baby. The judge said, 'Well, you can go on welfare, can't you?' I said why doesn't he call the welfare people and see. He didn't want to do that. I called the welfare man and he said the paperwork would take 6-8 weeks. So I told him there would be a lot of Indians coming into Winnemucca to wait there until this man's family got food. Suddenly then he remembered that there was an emergency fund he could dip into to get groceries, and he did it."

Rolling Thunder speaks excellent English and knows his way around bureaucracies. He is one of those "instructed to travel among the white men and report back to his people" on what is transpiring behind the "buckskin curtain." He sees encouraging signs.

"I saw the young people with long hair and the Great Spirit told me they will have no greed. We have waited a long time to find white men without greed. But we knew there would come a time when we could get together as brothers."

San Francisco Express Times 11/13/68

people of

**INDIANS FIGHTING BACK
ALONG THE NISQUALLY**

By ROBERT D. CASEY

The fall fishing season here in the State of Washington opened with an almost inevitable confrontation between the Indian tribes, who were exercising their Treaty rights to earn a living by fishing their rivers, and the State, which is attempting to regulate this troublesome ethnic minority out of existence by destroying their economic basis of survival. Although the Indians catch only five per cent of the annual take of salmon, most of the recently enacted legislation, all in the name of "conservation," seems to be aimed at them and not at the commercial fishing interests, which maintain expensive, efficient, and well paid lobbies in the corridors of the State legislature—playing a game the Indians don't even know the name of.

A new, and potentially dangerous, development is taking place in the ranks of the Indian youths serving in the armed forces. (They are disproportionately represented there, because very few Indian lads are deferred for any reason. During World War II, the Indians used to say that "if you can see lightning and hear thunder, you're in.") Some of the young braves, home on furlough from the killing in Vietnam, have determined not to go back to the war in Asia until they have finished fighting for the rights of their own people here at home.

Here are excerpts from a public declaration made on October 13th by P.F.C. Sidney Mills, a Yakima and Cherokee Indian who served in the Army for two years and four months and was critically wounded in combat in Vietnam:

> My first obligation lies with the Indian people, fighting for their lawful treaty rights . . . and in serving them, in this fight, in any way possible. The defense of the Indian people, and their chosen way of life . . . is more compelling than any duty to the U.S. military. I renounce, and no longer consider myself under, the authority and the jurisdiction of the United States Army.
>
> I have served the U.S. in a less compelling struggle in Vietnam and will not be restricted from doing less for my own people within the United States . . . I have given enough to the U.S. Army and now choose to serve my people. My decision is further influenced by the fact that we have already buried Indian fishermen, returned dead from Vietnam, while other Indian fishermen live here without protection and under steady attack from the power processes of this nation and the States of Washington and Oregon.
>
> I will not be among those who draw pride from a past in which I had no part, nor from a proud heritage I will not uphold. We must give of ourselves today—and I for one will not be content to have women and children fighting in my stead. At least, I will be among them—at least, they will not be alone.

After Sidney Mills made his decision to fight for justice along the banks of the Nisqually River, instead of the Mekong, others followed his lead. Meanwhile the State stepped up its harassment of the tribes and ugly incidents became common. What the Indians feared most was another successful raid on their fishing gear. A couple of years ago the State made a clean sweep of their nets, boats, motors, etc., supposedly in order to gather them as evidence, although there have been many trials since that time, and the "evidence" has neither been presented in court nor returned. If the State had continued to stage such raids the tribes would soon have been bankrupt. Fishing gear comes high and the Indians are destitute and obviously unable to pay legal costs. So they made a drastic decision: they decided to post armed guards in order to protect their rights.

Hank Adams, spokesman for the Survival of American Indians Association (S.A.I.A.), sent an open letter to Washington's Governor Dan Evans, informing him that the tract of land commonly known as Frank's Landing was being posted against trespass and that an armed guard was being stationed to prevent certain specific actions that might be carried out by enforcement officers acting under the authority of the State of Washington. The armed guard was under instructions to use their weapons only to prevent trespass 1) for the purpose of making arrests or serving warrants for arrest issued by the State or 2) for the purpose of confiscating fishing nets placed in the river and affixed to Frank's Landing. The guards were instructed not to use their weapons under any other circumstances. Since the Indians claim that Frank's Landing is a Federal Trust Area, they are pledged to honor all Federal warrants for arrest, search or seizure but not those issued under the authority of the State.

The posting of the armed patrol of course raised tensions further, but it did end the immediate threat to the boats. One thing about the Indians, they always mean what they say. No forked tongues. They maintained an information booth down the road from the armed guards, to answer queries from the many sympathizers who stopped by and to ward off unfriendly attentions from a large group of Wallace supporters from the Olympia area who have made the Indians the object of their racial hatred. The nearest black ghetto is in distant Seattle, and these people seem to need someone to hate. The information booth was manned predominantly by white students, many of whom have been with the Indians since August, living in the tents and lodges alongside the Nisqually and really roughing it.

On October 17th, six Indians were surprised, well above Frank's Landing, as they were setting their net. After a fight, they were arrested and their net confiscated. They were later bailed out and are now awaiting trial.

On October 29th came the long demanded intervention of the United States Department of Justice, which pledged itself to protect certain Indian rights in the Federal Trust Area, in return for the dismissal of the armed guards about the boats. Since their gear is now finally protected from confiscation, the Indians were glad to comply.

On the same day Robert Satiacum, chairman of the Puyallup Tribal Fishing Council, announced plans to fish the Puyallup River, in conjunction with members of the militant S.A.I.A. He said that the decision had been taken after the State's refusal to consider the Indians' proposals regarding conservation. The next day the Indians turned up and set their nets on the Puyallup, where a late run of silvers (salmon) were going upstream. A large number of spectators, most of them sympathetic to the Indians, showed up, but there was no trouble. Although the State Fisheries Department sent observers, no arrests were attempted.

Important Notice

The S.A.I.A. has asked me to state that, while there are many, many worthwhile Indian projects that urgently need your help, there is only one Treaty fishing fight, and that no one, Indian or otherwise, is authorized to collect money for them. If you want to help the Indians who are fighting on their rivers to maintain an Indian way of life, then make out your donations only to:

**The Survival of American Indians Association
P.O. Box 719
Tacoma
Washington
98401**

They desperately need financial support.

It has come as something of a shock to the River militants that there is a goodly collection of "fast buck" Indians who are quite prepared to profit from sympathy for their people by helping them—this "help" beginning with old Number One and seldom getting beyond that character. If you have donated in the past and wonder if your money reached the River, I suggest that you write to Al Bridges, who is chief of Indian fishermen at Frank's Landing, at the above address.

Finally, all sympathizers are invited to visit Frank's Landing personally. Drive over and meet the people involved in this prolonged clash. You might even want to join the many students who have camped out for a week at a time living in authentic "Indian style"—something to tell your grandchildren about.

e of color

CATHOLIC WORKER
Dec 1968

Another Time Dimension Than Ours

JOHN COLLIER

The recent death of John Collier, who was best known for his service as U.S. Commissioner for Indian Affairs from 1933 to 1945, came as a shock to me. This may seem an extraordinary thing to write of a man of 84 living in very modest retirement in Ranchos de Tao, New Mexico, but Collier was an extraordinary human being—a poet, historian, ethnologist, journalist and public servant. More particularly, he was a prophet, and I was shocked to realize that despite the value his prophetic writings had for me, they were not widely known among my friends in the Movement and that I had done very little to correct this.

The fact is that Collier had been for more than forty action-filled years an exponent of a social philosophy that is more relevant today than ever before. The source of his inspiration was the American Indians, to whom he—a "dropout" from Atlanta and Greenwich Village—devoted most of his life from 1922 on. But he was no simple do-gooder or esthete. His encounter with the Indians was shattering in its revelation of true humanity and of the sickness of Western society, with community lost and nature denied.

His best-known work is Indians of the Americas, *published in paperback by the New American Library, and his autobiography,* From Every Zenith *(published by The Swallow Press, Inc.), is fascinating. My favorite book of his is the more philosophical* On The Gleaming Way, *subtitled "Navajos, Eastern Pueblos, Zuñis, Hopis, Apaches and Their Meanings to the World." It is a Sage Book published by the Swallow Press, Inc., and available in paperback ($1.85) and cloth ($3.50). Although it is copyrighted 1949 and 1962 by Collier—and might seem dated—it should be recommended reading for any American who is puzzled by the "stubbornness" of the anti-American Vietnamese. The following excerpt is the first chapter of that book.*

L.H.

These Southwestern Indians have much that we know we need. And they have one possession, the most distinguishing of all, which we have forgotten that we need. Rather, perhaps, we dare not hope to make it our own.

That possession is *a time sense* different from ours, and happier. Once our white race had it too, and then the mechanized world took it away from us. Each of us has experienced that other and happier time sense in young childhood, and then we moved into the lockstep of clockwork time. We think, now, that any other time than linear, chronological time is an escapist dream. The Indians tell us otherwise, and their message and demonstration addresses itself to one of our deepest distresses and most forlorn yearnings.

We bow to clockwork time. We think we must yield to it our all—body, conduct and soul. Strange vortex in the ocean of life, created by intellect and by the machine only yesterday in our racial history, and in hard contradiction with vital and spiritual instinct: such is clockwork time, necessary as a tool, deadly as a master.

Clockwork Time

But we think it is our master, and here the Indians will gainsay us. And clockwork time—the event which in unmusical synchrony marches to the beat of the minutes, the hours, the onrushing and vanishing years of linear time—sweeps us and inwardly impels us faster and faster on. And enough of clockwork time we never have—never. And we abide so briefly, within that rush of linear time which subconsciously we experience as a kind of panic rout; and we are old, so soon, and we are done, and we hardly had time to live at all.

Not that we choose that life shall be that way. Did there exist—as the Indians in their whole life affirm—a dimension of time—a reality of time—not linear, not clock-measured, clock-controlled, and clock-ended for us, we would be glad; we would enter it, and expand our being there. There are human groups, normal, and efficient in difficult ways of the world, which do thus expand their being, and the tribal Indians are among them.

In solitary, mystical experience many of ourselves do enter another time dimension. But under the frown of clockwork time which claims the world, we place our experience out in an eternity beyond the years and beyond the stars. Not out there did the other time dimension originate, in racial history, but within the germ plasm and the organic rhythms and the social soul; nor is its reference only or mainly to the moveless eternity. It is life's instinct and environment, and human society's instinct and environment. To realize it or not realize it makes an enormous difference, even a decisive difference. The Indians realize it, and they can make us know.

Rhythms of Ceylon

There comes from England, by boat mail, a manuscript chapter of a book not yet published. Its writer is a British colonial administrator, recently lecturer on colonial administration at Oxford University, now returned to colonial service in Melanesia. Adrian Dobbs is his name; a man of experience wide and profound. And his subject proves to be *the time dimension*, examined as a practical factor in the administration or servicing of the billion of "pre-industrial" inhabitants of Asia and Africa.

Time, Adrian Dobbs suggests, does veritably have, for organisms, souls and societies, a dimension different from, and in contrast with, that merely linear dimension which our machines, clocks and calendars insist on. One, two, three, and thus on without pause or end, goes linear time; the synchronized future is hurtled remorselessly across the knife-edge present into a time-ordered past where nothing changes, moves or acts, forever. But not thus, Adrian Dobbs insists, does time appear to the Buddhists of Ceylon, to the Gaels of the wild northwest coast of Ireland, and to many another branch of the human race.

The Time Dimension

In the mind of Buddhist Ceylon, in its private and public behavior, in its work rhythms and play rhythms, its private and public expectancies, linear time is not the only and not the controlling time. Instead, time as experienced and lived by Buddhist Ceylon is no linear instant wherein all real events march lockstep from nothing to nought; time is enduring and commanding future, which hurtles not across the narrow present to become immured in a linear past—it is enduring future which draws the present on and on. And time is enduring past, which is not dead and gone, which can enter and does enter the knife-edge present, but whose fundamental relationship is with the enduring future. In human reality, in Ceylon, this *other* time dimension contains the linear dimension as a sometimes phantasmal, sometimes insubordinate and unreconciled, lesser part; in the final event, it is lord over linear time.

Hence, human experience in Ceylon has an atmosphere and meaning and value somewhat different from experience with you and me. Life has an inner spaciousness greater than yours or mine. The capacity to wait, to endure, to possess the things that seem gone, and to strive, and socially to create, is somewhat different from ours. Dobbs believes that the difference is momentous, practically as well as emotionally and spiritually, and he asks: What will result, in changed world events, if the clock-mindedness of the modern industrial West shall equate itself with the enduring-past and enduring-future mindedness of peoples like the Ceylonese? And how far representative, in this matter, are the Ceylonese?

The Tesuque Indians

My mind goes to a certain American Indian tribe. The Tewan pueblo, Tesuque, is practically within the suburbs of Santa Fe, in New Mexico. Its contact with the white world has been a thing of every day, now into its fifth post-Columbian century. Tesuque is a tiny city-state; its population is one hundred and fifty souls. Tesuque is at home in the white world. Economically and politically, it is a cooperative commonwealth, efficient, sophisticated, and of undeviating public virtue; but the virtue contains within itself no puritan gloom. Tesuque functions, when need be, and through a secondary adaptation, along the narrow edge of linear Western time.

In the autumn of 1922, I had occasion for long and absorbed meetings with the Governor of Tesuque and his Council of Principal Men. Whites had seized nearly all of Tesuque's irrigable land. Legislation had been forced through the Senate by the Interior Department at Washington, designed to legalize the whites' seizure of the tribe's lands. The bill momentarily might pass in the House, and was assured of Presidential signature. And a drive to exterminate the Pueblos' ancient religions had been launched by the government. Tesuque at that date was subsisting (I did not then know the fact, because the Tesuques never mentioned their bodily hunger) on a per capita income of a few cents over sixteen dollars a year, including all produce grown and consumed.

Gradually, as our meetings progressed, and as Martin Vigil of Tesuque enlightened me by interpretation, I came to realize that I had entered a time dimension not like that of the white world from which I had come. These men and women were living in a time a thousand years ago. An event of many thousand years of group volition, no part of it lapsed into a dead past, was travailing across the present into a future of unknown thousands of years. Toward that "enduring future," the tribe's being and soul was winging like a migrating bird along its ancient migration route.

So intense was the reality of this effort of flight between the "twin eternities" of past and future, that all minor aspects fell into oblivion. Personal contingency, personal fate simply did not figure at all. Hunger did not figure. A white well-wisher in Santa Fe discovered that the little tribe was in famine, and set in motion a newspaper campaign for relief. The Tesuques smiled, because the diversion from their real issue was friendly meant; they stayed with their real issue.

A violent action was in process (this was how the Tesuques viewed their crisis), an action directed from the outside against the tribe. The action was designed to kill what the white man called the Indians' past, by shattering the bridge of tribal land and tribal religion which united past and future—the bridge on which the deathless two-way journey plied from living past to living future, living future to living past. Meeting the crisis, the "twin eternities" merged their brooding power; and this they did at each of the twenty-one menaced pueblos in New Mexico of which Tesuque was one. The result was planned action in the linear present —action which will be mentioned at its place in this book; the action marked and made the beginning of the historic change in governmental policy which revolutionized the situation of all Indians. But at this point, the subject is the time dimension of tribal Indian life, that all-conserving abysm of time wherein is no past wholly gone and no future wholly inert.

Relevance of Geologic Time

On another occasion, some years later, at a pueblo which I may not name, the tribe's priestly representative was assisting for initiation into the tribe a young man from another pueblo who had married a girl of this pueblo. Much that he told this young man, the teacher was not free to tell to me. But part of the tutelage was the unveiling of the hidden names and the spiritual meanings of hundreds of physical places, wide over the land. Mesas, plinths, streams and springs; forests that existed no more, trails unused for hundreds of years. Some of the places had vanished utterly with the passage of linear time; the highest mountain peak, in one of the sacred areas along the Rocky Mountain range, was the highest no longer, and the tree line had moved upward two hundred vertical feet since these tribal memories, as we would call them, this tribal present, as the Indians knew it, had been born. The memories, the present, spanned geological time.

"But Geronimo," I remarked, "your tribe does not own these places and boundaries any more." He replied: "We own them in our soul."

In those years, I still took for granted our modern fatalism: that the Indian's spirit, and all aboriginal and ancient spirit, had to die. Omnipotent clockwork time must engulf all. The glory and power of that other time dimension would have to yield to the cosmopolitan century. I knew it would mean diminishing the human stature, draining the dearest meaning out of the universe, the stripping away of his uniquely vital and human part from man, the greater dominance of mechanism over life. But it had to be, I believed; and only in solitary, mystical experience, thereafter, would all-conserving and prophetic, dynamic, creative time be known.

The ensuing twenty-five years seem to have proved that the fatalism was wrong, not only as applied to the American tribal Indian but as applied to groups in many parts of the world. That time dimension not linear, which was of ancient

man, bestows a power to endure, to create, and to outlast; a motive and a power to bend means to ends; it has a survival value biological and social; it is central to man, and this age of commanding externalism, which seems to have engulfed so much of our white life, may yet fail to engulf the human time dimension.

In the Americas at least, Indian societies which live by the time dimension not only linear, the conserving and future-containing dimension, are reasserting themselves in all the lands from the Arctic shores to southern Chile. And in the American Southwest, recent years have witnessed a deeply exciting event. Ancient tribes, in order that their living past shall not die, and under the impulsion of their living future, have utilized the modern technologies and organizational forms with brilliant effectiveness; they have triumphed along the roaring assembly line of linear time, in ways which the clock-conditioned observer finds to be practical and momentous. That other time dimension, which Adrian Dobbs finds in Asia, is no mere subjectivism, no mere and sterile dream of the Ceylonese and the Hopi and Tewan and Keresan and Zuñian and California Wintun soul. It is a society-building, action-sustaining, wisdom-giving and health-giving and world-shaping endowment, which humanity will not permanently do without.

LIBERATION

Radicals and White Racism:

The most intensely debated question in the Movement during the past year has been the relation of white radicals to racism.

This debate has a history, suggested by titles such as Tom Hayden and Carl Wittman, "An Interracial Movement of the Poor?" written in 1963, and Anne Braden, "White Organizing and White Racism," written in 1966.

In those essays, and in the debate of the past year, three essential positions have been presented:

1. Whites and blacks should be organized separately but on the basis of common interests, and coalesce at some future point;
2. Whites should organize in support of black demands and for the renunciation of white privilege;
3. Whites and blacks should be organized together from the beginning.

These three sentences describe practical alternatives which confront any white organizer when he begins to work. Over-elaborate arguments as to whether or not black people in the United States constitute a "nation" or a "minority," or as to which organization in the black community constitutes the "vanguard," lead away from practicality toward adventurist fantasies, such as the concept of a black nation in the South prior to a socialist revolution or the proposal of a white "Red Army" to support black liberation struggles. These arguments appear to

Preacherman of the Patriot Party

Toward an Interracial Movement of the Poor
Staughton Lynd

have arisen from factional struggles within white radical organizations rather than from the day-to-day practice of white organizers.

Leaving aside the language of resolutions, then, and attempting to penetrate beneath that language to the real political choices which confront white radicals, how should whites organize with respect to racism?

Hayden and Wittman, in their 1963 article, called for an "interracial class movement." Of black nationalism they said: "Even were it to develop in some organized form, we would guess that at some future time the possibility of Negro-white alliances would reappear because a program based primarily on race will not improve the terrible social conditions which provide the impetus for the movement." We are convinced, they went on, "that permanent alienation can be avoided and overcome by a serious movement which fights for the interests of both groups."

Hayden and Wittman then approached the question of white-black relations from the standpoint of issues. They saw four kinds of demands made by the black movement, and tried to assess the effect of each kind of demand on the possibility of an interracial class movement:

1. "Demands to eliminate discrimination or de facto segregation" with regard to housing, hiring, and the gerrymandering of school and voting districts. Of these Hayden and Wittman stated: "No doubt the ire of the white unemployed, or working class, or voting property holder is sometimes heightened by many of these insistent Negro demands, but there is hardly any infringement of basic interests here."

2. "Demands which symbolically assert Negro dignity but neither achieve change nor alienate whites very much." The authors were thinking particularly of school integration. Their argument was that whites fear the integration of schools because they fear "that the proposed integration will destroy the 'quality' of the school and prevent their youngsters from getting the education necessary to fit into the highly-skilled professions." Tom and Carl considered these fears "very unrealistic:"

... the threat of integration is likely to lead to either (1) the evacuation of the white groups from the area, if they are financially able, or (2) the actual integration of the whole neighborhood, with the resulting great potential for seeing common problems. In either case, there is not a serious long-term threat of severe alienation no matter how militantly the Negro movement presses the issue.

3. "Demands which are specifically racial, do not achieve very much, and potentially alienate large numbers of whites." The clearest example of this kind of demand, according to Hayden and Wittman, was replacing white workers with black ones in a situation of chronic unemployment. Another possible example was "the moving of a Negro into an economically insecure white neighborhood, although a violent white lower-class status reaction in these circumstances is not likely to be permanently alienating."

Hayden and Wittman suggested that the most creative way to deal with situations where blacks threaten to take jobs away from whites is to "fight together for full employment."

4. Finally, there were "demands for political and economic changes of substantial benefit to the Negro and white poor." In the opinion of Hayden and Wittman:

Examples of these include improved housing, lower rents, better schools, full employment, extension of welfare and social security assistance. They are not "Negro issues" *per se;* rather, they are precisely those issues which should appeal to lower-class whites as well as to Negroes.

Finally, "An Interracial Movement of the Poor?" comes to those issues under debate in the movement today. We realize, they wrote, that

it is illusory to expect the instant removal of prejudice among many whites. The whites must be organized on economic issues which are more important than their racial ideology. Perhaps today this is more possible than in the past because it is hard to imagine the poor white improving his economic condition without confronting a Negro movement already involved in many of the same issues. In this situation we think whites would decide to identify with the Negro struggle were it generally parallel to their own. Of course, the whites could opt for prejudice and further poverty—then we all lose. Whether this choice is made depends, perhaps, in large part on the organizational role we play. Further, the authors thought there was "potentially an important role for Negro organizers among the white poor." They thought that the Chicago JOIN project would "involve at some point interracial organizing teams."

Summing up in terms of the three organizing alternatives sketched at the outset, "An Interracial Movement of the Poor?" emphasizes *issues* rather than *organizational forms*, and argues that in choosing issues the organizer should "avoid programs that lead to the permanent alienation of potential class allies."

Anne Braden's 1966 essay, in contrast, urged "interracial organizing of the poor" in the sense of organizing blacks and whites *in the same organization.* The teams of black-and-white organizers which Hayden and Wittman believed to be probably desirable at some point in organizing white com-

munities, Mrs. Braden considered "urgently needed ... *from the very beginning.*" Of issues, she said only that white and black groups organized separately would "very likely ... become more and more ... rivals and antagonists (for public funds, power, etc.)," and instead recommended "tying in" white groups with black groups whose problems were "similar in many ways."

Thus, in these two seminal articles nearly identical words—"interracial movement of the poor" (Hayden and Wittman), "interracial organizing of the poor" (Braden)—have meanings which, although not necessarily contradictory, are significantly different. Hayden and Wittman seem to feel that the way to bring black and white together is through choice of issues. Anne Braden appears to fear that unless black and white are physically together "you may be creating a Frankenstein": building racism, even with the best of intentions.

A third key essay, Noel Ignatin's "Learn the Lessons of U.S. History," first appeared in *The Movement* in February 1968. It anticipated a new orientation to racism which became dominant in the movement after Carl Oglesby's speech to the SDS National Council meeting at Lexington in late March, after President Johnson's withdrawal, the partial halt in the bombing of North Vietnam, Martin Luther King's assassination, and the rioting which followed his death.

Ignatin quoted extensively from Anne Braden. But just as she had used the language of Hayden-Wittman to mean something a little different than they did, so Noel's argument was not the same as the argument of "White Organizing and White Racism."

Ignatin criticized an approach to the task of organizing working class whites which he described as follows:

... find the issues which immediately affect the people we are trying to reach, and which they feel most keenly. Organize around these issues and, as the people are drawn more into struggle in their own interest, they will come to see, with our help, who are their friends and enemies. Specifically, coalitions between poor white and black will develop from each fighting for his own "self-interest" and coming to see that there is a common enemy, the rich white man.

Ignatin went on to express his disagreement with the approach just summarized. "I don't believe it is possible to build coalitions of black and white on the basis of the self-interest of each," he wrote, "if the self-interest of the whites means the maintenance of white supremacy and the white-skin privilege."

Here Ignatin was indeed picking up a point made by Mrs. Braden. She had asserted in "White Organizing and White Racism:"

> ... white people are the oppressor group. This is true even if they are on the low rungs of the ladder. They can organize to throw off economic oppression, and that's good, but at the same time they are members of an oppressed group economically they are still very much a part of the whole oppressor white group too—and when they are organized as *white people* the groups they form may very well become expressions of that oppression (as well as maybe expressions of their own fight against economic oppression).

Similarly, Ignatin invoked American history to show that during Reconstruction, in the time of the Populist movement, and again in the depression of the 1930's, "whenever masses of white poor have been radicalized and brought into struggle, the power structure has been able to hold out the crumb of the white-skin privilege, breaking any developing coalition and struggle."

Nevertheless, "Learn the Lessons of U.S. History" went beyond "White Organizing and White Racism" in the following ways:

1. Mrs. Braden says that if whites are organized separately from blacks, their organizations may become racist. Ignatin makes the larger claim that white supremacist thinking is the "greatest barrier" to working-class consciousness and solidarity in the United States. The exaggeration in Noel's argument is particularly evident in his contention that "the halting of the labor movement's advances at the end of the 1930's, and its reversal and defeat in the years after World War II, was due to the ... failure to challenge white supremacy." I question this. A recent assessment of "the failure of Depression-era radicalism" in *Radical America* stresses "the rapid submergence of discontent in the onslaught of the Second World War." Another obviously important factor was the conservative character of Communist Party leadership, under the influence of a "united front" strategy. No doubt the CIO's failure to challenge white supremacy

by moving aggressively into the South was another important element in the picture. But for Noel, without evidence, to insist that it was *the* decisive causal element, is unconvincing. And this weakness in his argument is not trivial, for his over-emphasis on racism as an historical cause mirrors the recent tendency of white radicals to make support for black liberation the whole of their politics.

2. Mrs. Braden speaks of whites *teaming up* with Negroes: ". . . they are going to have to team up with those black people," ". . . their interest lies in teaming up with Negroes." Ignatin, in contrast, puts much more emphasis than Braden on *giving up*: on renouncing privileges. He makes the following striking analogy between the working-class and draft resistance movements:

> An excellent example of the practical application of my thesis is the SDS position on the draft, of opposing the draft and, at the same time, denouncing the II-S student deferment as a racial (and class) privilege whose only purpose is to divide the anti-war movement, and not merely denouncing it, but calling upon all students to renounce it.

The approach criticized by Ignatin was, on the whole, the approach advocated by Hayden and Wittman and applied by ERAP organizers, especially in JOIN. In the spring of 1968, the SDS national office reprinted "Learn the Lessons of U.S. History" together with four other articles, three by JOIN organizers, in a pamphlet entitled *Don't Mourn—Organize!* Each of the pieces by JOIN organizers described a process of beginning with "issues which poor and working-class people feel," such as "cops, the draft, welfare, credit, schools, housing, urban renewal, food prices, etc.," and working from these to the issues of the nature of the Vietnam war and racism. "We clearly demonstrated that racism could be overcome by poor whites genuinely in motion around their own demands," wrote Richard Rothstein. This was so even though, contrary to Anne Braden's urging, JOIN people were organized in (on the whole) all-white groups by an (on the whole) all-white staff of student organizers. "JOIN rent strikes were co-ordinated with rent strikes in black communities; co-ordinated demonstrations of black and white welfare recipients occurred more than once at public aid offices," Roth-

stein continued.

During the black rebellions of summer 1967, Mike James and Bob Lawson of the JOIN staff wrote any essay on "Poor White Response to Black Rebellion." We are well aware that black people are the most exploited group in this country, they began. But:

> We have learned that Southern whites, dealing with issues similar to those black people confront (welfare, police brutality, housing, etc.) understand the racial and "riot" questions. . . . People's opinions seem to be related to the amount of contact and involvement with JOIN.

When, in the winter of 1967-68, students were asked to leave the neighborhood by those whom they had organized, they left behind an integrated group of welfare recipients and a youth group presently allied with the Black Panthers.

These evaluations of the most long-lived organizing project in a (Northern) poor white community which ERAP experienced, ironically reprinted in the same booklet with Ignatin's "Learn the Lessons of U.S. History," suggest the limitations of Ignatin's analysis. The 2-S deferment is a misleading model in understanding the privileges of white workers. The result of the 2-S deferment is that most white students escape the draft entirely. The deferment is, literally, of life-and-death significance. In contrast, the privileges of white workers are only of relative significance. Until he renounces his privilege the student is not exposed to the draft at all. But the white worker is exploited by capitalism at the same time that he enjoys certain privileges denied to the more exploited black worker.

Consistent with his misreading of the history of the CIO and his mistaken analogy to the draft, Ignatin argues that the organizer must *begin with* the renunciation of "white-skin privileges." I am sure that it was not Noel's intention, but what came through to the middle-class white college students who used his essay this past winter, was the concept that white radicals should act in support of black demands rather than raising "white demands" at all. Hayden's and Wittman's sophisticated discussion of the *kind of demand* which would tend to bring black and white together, as opposed to the kind of demand which might alienate them permanently, was forgotten completely. And the concept of beginning with support of black demands and the renunciation of white privileges was extrapolated into the fantasy that there could be a successful black liberation struggle in this country before whites were brought into motion around their own needs and interests.

It would seem, all things considered, that none of the three organizing alternatives summarized at the beginning of this essay succeed in synthesizing the movement's best thought and experience. Specifically:

1. Anne Braden's essay stresses the question of separate or interracial organization, but gives too little attention to organizing issues. Perhaps her approach reflects a Southern awareness in the sense that in the South white workers are very poor and have an obvious material interest in coalescing with blacks, but fail to do so because of a prejudice stronger than in other parts of the country. Hence a perspective which says that issues are no problem and the breaking down of prejudice all-important.

2. Noel Ignatin emphasizes that the obstacle to interracial unity is not just prejudice but the material "white-skin privileges" which white workers enjoy. This approach would appear to reflect the objective situation among unionized workers in Northern plants. It does not accurately reflect the experience of JOIN organizers who found that the poor white "underclass" in Chicago's Uptown readily recognized that they were oppressed by policemen, landlords, real estate developers, and so on, in the same way that black people were oppressed.

3. The Hayden-Wittman essay seems the most satisfactory of the three analyses, despite its age. But it appears to brush aside too casually the conflict of interests between whites and blacks with regard to issues such as housing, schools, and jobs. Demands that good housing, quality education, and well-paying jobs be created by the society for all who need them do not do away with an objective present in which, as Ignatin says, "there are not enough jobs to go around."

I believe that the approach to racism through renunciation, as recommended by Noel Ignatin, has won wide support this past year because it provided a rationale for the guilt feelings of white middle-class students. Noel, I know, recommends renunciation as a consequence of a Leninist theory of imperialism which holds that capitalism

buys off a portion of the working class with privileges obtained through the exploitation of other workers, and believes his perspective to have been validated in his own practice as an industrial worker. But I persist in regarding it as a theory which makes sense, if it makes sense at all, only on the campus. There white students can build a politics around the admission of black and brown students, or the creation of an Afro-American studies program, because, especially at elite universities, white students themselves have nothing vital at stake.

Interracial organizing as urged by Anne Braden also makes more sense on the campus than off it. In the artificial society of the university, blacks and whites may be physically intermingled to a degree which is very rarely, and less and less, true in off-campus poor communities.

Therefore, as white radicals move off the campus and into the community I believe they will have to rely on issues which inherently tend to draw black and white together, rather than on sacrificials or physical propinquity, in building an interracial movement. Anne Braden and Noel Ignatin have rightly made us more aware of the dangers which may flow from organizing whites separately around their own interests. We will simply have to try to be more sensitive to those dangers as we continue to do that kind of organizing. This sensitivity can express itself, for example, in pushing the demand that the wages of all workers should be increased but that the wages of the most poorly-paid should be increased most, so as to equalize the wages of different categories of workers. It will also express itself in the organizer's selection of issues in which whites and blacks have some common interests, and need each other to win: issues such as shifting the burden of taxation from poor people to corporations, community control of schools, ending the war.

Politics based on the repudiation of privilege leads one into a morass of argument as to whether, in the past white workers have hurt black workers by accepting bribes from the bosses at the expense of their black brothers and sisters, or whether, on the contrary, low wages for black workers and the blacks usually unemployed are used to keep down wages of all workers. Every one knows the appropriate Marxist texts in support of each viewpoint, every one recognizes that evidence can be adduced in support of both arguments, and every

one has experienced enough factional squabbles about it to last a lifetime. I believe it would be more fruitful to look to the future and to emphasize (with Bob McBride and Jim O'Brien) that the demand to restructure the economy so as to guarantee decent incomes, provide adequate housing, consumer goods, medical care, and public services, is neither a black demand nor a white demand, but a black-and-white demand beneficial to both on which both can unite.

The resolution on race and class proposed to the SDS convention by a group from Wayne State and Columbia University clears the air by restating the obvious—that the oppression of blacks is both race and class oppression—and by insisting on the need for "concrete answers" which will be found in the course of an "activity" that does not wait on programs. ●

LIBERATION July 1969

Things are Moving in the White South

It's really happening—the thing the Southern Conference Educational Fund (SCEF) has been working for over 30 years. White Southerners are organizing with the goal of getting together with their black brothers.

Within the past two months, various members of our staff have, among other things:

Met with 70 white people in Mississippi who are launching an organizing drive among poor white people in that state;

Helped to pull together a series of meetings of people organizing in six Appalachian states to wage their own war on poverty through independent political action. A new battle to force coal operators to do something about 'black lung' disease is bringing many people together throughout the mountains;

Helped to organize a Southern Committee Against Repression, to pool the fight-back resources of movements across the South (in both black and white communities) where movements for change are under attack by local and state officials;

Met with and assisted workers on strike for better conditions in four states. There is a new militancy in Southern factories, and the necessities of life are bringing black and white together on the picket lines;

Assisted groups of white students who are being harassed by police because of growing activity against war, in support of black freedom movements, for freedom on their campuses.

UNITY AMONG BLACK AND WHITE has developed in a small South Carolina town, where about one-third of the workers at a Wentworth textile mill walked out (photo by Bob Analavage).

Within the next month, we'll be attending meetings of people who are organizing in even more places—in North Carolina, in Virginia, in Georgia.

All of this indicates a ferment in the white South that has simply not existed before. Many people are following the George Wallace forces and rallying around them for a new push between now and 1972. But many—more than ever before—are realizing that this represents a dead end. So they are looking for other answers.

We are trying to keep up with this new ferment—to offer help where and when it is needed, to bring people together, to put them in touch with like-minded people in their own community, in the next state, across the South.

We are doing this despite intensified attacks on us. For, in the past two months also, two of our staff narrowly escaped injury or death when their mountain home was dynamited; the McClellan Committee set hearings to which SCEF staff members have been summoned and ordered to bring records of our and other organizations; the Kentucky Un-American Activities Committee (KUAC) has been continuing its efforts to run us out of the state where our main office is located.

We can survive the attacks; we've lived with them for many years, and after each one we emerge stronger than before. But we need to keep up with the new ferment in the white South—and not let this time of opportunity pass, when it just may be possible to do the thing we've worked for over three decades:—form real black-white coalitions that can bring political and economic democracy to this region, and the nation.

We need more organizers; we need more literature (people are hungry for it). And all that takes money.

We ask you to renew your contribution to SCEF at this time—the support of people like you has brought us to this moment. With your continued help, we'll take hold of the new opportunities and go on from here.

SCEF Southern Conference Educational Fund, 3210 W. Broadway, Louisville, Ky. 40211,

Honesty in Organizing

By JOE MULLOY

(Joe Mulloy has been organizing in Eastern Kentucky for the last three years—first as a field supervisor for the Appalachian Volunteers, now on SCEF's staff.)

One of the recurring problems in training and working with organizers is the question of honesty. For some reason, many organizers — particularly those in the white community — feel that the only issues they can talk about are those rising directly out of the local community.

They think that no matter how the organizer feels personally about the war in Vietnam or the insurrections in our cities, he will be violating some sacred principle of organizing if he initiates discussion or action on one of these issues.

The organizer may justify his silence by statements like these: "The folks aren't ready for that yet," "the war is not an issue here," or "these people are extremely patriotic and racist so they won't understand."

The organizer, in short, is being dishonest with people by hiding his own opinions (this denies his own humanity) and, even worse, making decisions for the people by claiming they aren't ready yet. This shows a very low opinion of the maturity of the people.

A basic principle of organizing is trust. There must be trust between one who seeks to organize and the people to be organized. The only way to build this trust is to be honest. If an organizer is unable or unwilling to take the same risk that he is trying to organize the people to take, his efforts will fail completely. When the people sense that unwillingness — and they will — they will turn away from that organizer. And rightly so.

Challenge in the White Community

Let me give you an example. Organizing against strip mining in Eastern Kentucky can be a deadly struggle, as the events of the last year have shown. People have been killed and people have gone to jail.

Last summer, during a confrontation between the people and the bulldozers, the sheriff came up the hill to arrest us for violating a court injunction. But one of the organizers of our struggle—who had been effective up until then— was unwilling to risk arrest. When he heard the sheriff coming he disappeared into the trees and hid, coming out only after the sheriff had left.

It didn't make any difference that the sheriff only threatened us and didn't make any arrests. The fact was established that this organizer wanted us to do something he was unwilling to do himself. His credibility was destroyed and he was never again effective with that group of people.

A situation arose last summer when a group of people from the small black community wanted to use a swimming pool previously used only by whites. One of the white organizers felt that this attempt would alienate poor whites he was working with. So he cooled out the black group and transferred the young black organizer to another county.

Thus, in an attempt to secure a base for himself the whites were held secure in their racist attitude, if indeed they had one, and the blacks continued to swim in the river.

The point is, if the poor are going to improve their condition it's going to have to be by black, red, brown and white people working together to defeat the Man. Anytime whites are kept from getting together with their black brothers, or aren't even allowed the chance to decide for themselves if they want to get together, it is ten steps backward for the movement and cement for the cracking walls of the power structure.

Organizers must remember that they are people, too, and that to be accepted they must be themselves. It is a valuable thing for the organizer to express himself and to be open about his feelings and opinions to the people he is working with. This does not mean that he forces or manipulates people to his point of view, but that he merely shares with others the fact that he is a human being.

It is an undisputed fact now, of course, that the war is an issue in the Appalachian mountains. The area has one of the highest draft quotas in the country. The poverty-war workers who have occupational deferments and are against the war but who refuse to make information—just plain information—on the draft available to the people they're working with, are the most hypocritical of the dishonest organizers.

I feel that one reason why this dishonest situation exists is that many of the organizers are unsure of their own ideas and beliefs. Until they are sure, they have no business trying to organize.

Organizers must face themselves primarily with the question of honesty, both to themselves and to the people they work with.

the southern PATRiOT June 1968

> Most of us think of the Black liberation movement or the student rebellion when we hear about public officials' trying to stop people from organizing.
>
> Many are not aware that the same forms of repression are used whenever people get together to change their political or economic conditions. It doesn't matter what color the people are: they are attacked by the power structure--state, local, and federal-- if they challenge things as they are.
>
> Appalachia, especially Eastern Kentucky, provides a case study of how the instruments of power go into action to stop a people's movement. In this case, most of the people are white but they are as poor as black people being oppressed in the Deep South. This pamphlet tells about what happened to them.

Appalachia is a colony, lying mostly in the Southern United States. Its wealth is owned almost completely by people who live elsewhere and who pay little or no local taxes.

There is not even a tax on the millions of tons of coal that pour out of the mountains each year. This is because the coal operators control the people who fix and collect the taxes.

Like all colonies, Appalachia is run by men and women beholden to the absentee owners and the banks. Judges, sheriffs, tax assessors, prosecutors and state officials are tied to the coal operators in one way or another.

These people led the drive to stop union organizing in the mountains in the 1920's and 1930's, and they now lead the fight against organizing white and black people for political and economic power.

This situation prevails in Pike County, Kentucky, which currently produces more coal than any other county in the United States. Much of the coal is sold to the Tennessee Valley Authority (TVA) to produce power. The coal operators look with horror on a proposal that power plants, owned by the people, should be set up at the mine mouths to make use of these resources for the benefit of the people.

For, despite all the natural resources, there is obvious and chronic poverty among a majority of the people in Appalachia. The coal operators are having their best years of production and profit, but tens of thousands of people do not have enough to eat nor clothes to wear. Their houses and schools are falling into ruin.

Alan and Margaret McSurely moved into Pike County in early 1967. Mrs. McSurely was employed by the Southern Conference Educational Fund (SCEF) which had set up the Southern Mountain Project to help the people to organize for political and economic power.

SCEF's objective is to help the people to win power and run this country for their benefit. It believes this can be done peacefully--by people organizing from the grass roots to the state and national levels.

Alan McSurely was employed by the Appalachian Volunteers, a group primarily financed by the federal poverty agency, the Office of Economic Opportunity (OEO). He was fired by the AVs when he began to tell the workers and the people that the solution to their problems would be through political action. He then joined his wife on the SCEF staff.

When the McSurelys moved into Pike County, Joe and Karen Mulloy were working there on the staff of the AVs. They were aiding in a community struggle against a strip-mining operation in Island Creek.

Much of the mountain area is being turned into a wasteland by removing the topsoil to get to coal lying a few feet below the surface. The courts have ruled that the coal companies have a right to do this under deeds given to them by ancestors of the people now living on the land. The people in Island Creek helped one of their number, Jink Ray, to resist the stripping of his land and the possible ruin of his home. They adopted tactics of the civil-rights movement and stood in front of the bulldozers which had come to remove the soil.

The struggle was resolved in favor of the community when the people outlasted the coal company in daily showdowns for two months. Joe Mulloy summed it up this way:

> *"This was perhaps the first time since the heyday of union organizing that the companies were stopped from doing their will. The significance of this victory was not lost on the coal operators. They knew that if it can happen in Pike County, it can happen anywhere."*

OEO-funded projects carried on much activity that year (1967) but the fight against strip mining had the most meaning. This was because it challenged the coal operators directly in their pocketbooks.

What happened after the Jink Ray fight is perhaps best told step by step:

JULY, 1967

* Pike County sheriff and the di-

rector of the Chamber of Commerce visit the Mulloys at their home and warn them that "someone" might blow up their car if they continue to organize against strip mining.

AUGUST

* McSurelys and Joe Mulloy arrested on sedition charges, accused of trying to overthrow the government of Pike County by organizing the poor people. Arrests come 8 days after a victory in the strip mine fight. All of the McSurelys' and Mulloys' books and private papers seized. The prosecuting attorney, Thomas Ratliff, announces that he will gladly make this material available to an investigating committee of the U.S. Congress. (Ratliff is running for lieutenant governor of Kentucky on the Republican ticket, a race which he loses in November.)

SEPTEMBER

* The McSurelys, Mulloy, and Anne and Carl Braden, executive directors of SCEF, indicted on sedition charges by Pike County grand jury. Bradens refuse to post bond and are jailed. A three-judge federal court frees all of the accused on the ground that the state sedition law is so broad and so vague that it violates the constitution of the United States.

Presiding Judge Bert Combs says: *"It is difficult to believe that capable lawyers could seriously contend that this statute is constitutional."* He adds: *"The conclusion is inescapable that the criminal prosecutions were instituted, at least in part, in order to stop organizing activities in Pike County."*

* Joe Mulloy is classified I-A by his draft board in Louisville, although he has applied for status as a conscientious objector. (His draft board is the one that refused to defer Muhammad Ali, world heavyweight boxing champion, as a Muslim minister.)

OCTOBER

* The Permanent Subcommittee on Investigations of the U.S. Senate Committee on Government Operations serves McSurelys with subpoenas to bring their seized papers to a hearing in Washington, although the documents are still in the hands of Pike County officials.

This committee was formerly headed by Sen. Joseph McCarthy of Wisconsin, but is now in charge of Sen. John McClellan of Arkansas, and is called the McClellan Committee. McClellan says he wants the material as part of his investigation of ghetto uprisings in U.S. cities.

It is revealed that prosecutor Ratliff allowed an investigator for McClellan to make copies of the seized material while it was in his custody for safekeeping.

* Attorneys for SCEF, the McSure-

lys, and Mulloy challenge subpoena on the ground that the material was illegally seized. They take their case to the U.S. Court of Appeals in Cincinnati.

DECEMBER

* Mulloy fired from government job He and Karen Mulloy join the SCEF staff.

JANUARY, 1968

* Mulloy denied right to appeal I-A classification and ordered to report for service in the armed forces. He refuses and is arrested under the Selective Service and Training Act.

MARCH

* The Kentucky Legislature sets up the Kentucky Un-American Activities Committee (KUAC) to do what officials were unable to do under the sedition law. Gov. Louie Nunn had been elected on a platform which included setting up such a committee "to run SCEF out of Kentucky." Much literature attacking SCEF and its staff circulates through Kentucky.

APRIL

* Joe Mulloy given maximum of five years in prison and $10,000 fine for refusing induction. Friends picket Louisville jail for 6 weeks until bond is cut from $12,000 to $2,000 and he is freed.

MAY

* Uprising breaks out in Louisville's largest ghetto because of police brutality, poor housing, lack of jobs. City officials try to blame the black community and white friends but are at least partly thwarted by SCEF and other groups.

JULY

* The U.S. Court of Appeals orders seized material returned to Mc-Surelys and Mulloy on the ground that it was illegally taken.

SEPTEMBER

* KUAC holds hearings in Frankfort Ky. to try to show that "agitators," including the SCEF staff, started the Louisville uprising.

OCTOBER

* KUAC holds hearings in Pikeville in effort to show that "agitators" including SCEF staff, are to blame for unrest in mountains.

NOVEMBER

* Seized material is returned to McSurelys and Mulloy by state officials. Investigator for McClellan Committee immediately serves the McSurelys with a new subpoena ordering them to appear in Washington on January 14, 1969.

Subpoenas instruct them to bring documents relating to a meeting of the board of directors of SCEF held in Nashville, Tenn. in April, 1967; also material relating to their associations with SCEF, Southern Student Organizing Committee (SSOC), Student Nonviolent Coordinating Committee (SNCC), Students for a Democratic Society (SDS), National Conference for New Politics (NCNP), Vietnam Summer, Appalachian Volunteers, and the United Planning Organization, Washington, D.C. Committee is especially interested in meeting of Stokely Carmichael with the SCEF board on April 7, 1967.

DECEMBER

* KUAC returns to Pike County and attacks the McSurelys again. Eight days later, at 1 a.m. on December 13, the McSurely home is dynamited.

Bomb is thrown at window of their bedroom but it misses and hits the side of the house instead. This saves McSurelys and their year-old son, Victor, from death or serious injury. McSurelys ask the U.S. Department of Justice to investigate, charging that the coal operators are behind this and other attacks on them.

McClellan's concern about Carmichael's meeting with the SCEF board removed any doubt that his aim is to stop people from organizing for their own benefit---whether they are black or white, red or brown, poor or middle class.

Carmichael met with the board to give his version of black power, which was being described as violent and racist by most newspapers and broadcasters. Carmichael told the board what he and CHarles V. Hamilton later summed up in their book, Black Power:

"It is hoped that eventually there will be a coalition of poor blacks and poor whites. This is the only coalition which seems acceptable to us, and we see such a coalition as the major internal instrument of social change in the American society.

"It is purely academic today to talk about bringing poor blacks and poor whites together, but the task of building a poor-white power bloc dedicated to the goals of a free, open society---not one based on racism and subordination ---must be attempted."

The specter of such a power bloc in coalition with black people has always haunted the people who own and run the South; such a coalition has been the goal of SCEF for more than three decades, and it is the main reason why SCEF has been attacked so furiously from the day it was founded in Birmingham in 1938.

SCEF is known throughout the nation for its bold and firm struggle to end racism, poverty and war. It is also known for the attacks on it by McClellan's allies in Congress---the Southerners who run the House Un-American Activities Committee (HUAC) and the committee headed by Sen. James O. Eastland of Mississippi.

In fact, both HUAC and Eastland had been busy trying to blame "agitators" for uprisings in the nation's ghettos. This was before McClellan took over the investigation of the rebellions as his special field.

In August, 1967, Eastland held hearings at which one of the chief witnesses was Police Capt. John Sorace of Nashville (later promoted to assistant chief for the damage he did to the Nashville freedom movement).

Sorace told Eastland that a black liberation school in Nashville was teaching hatred of white people, when in fact it was giving a course in black history.

By the time Sorace appeared before the McClellan Committee in November, 1967, to testify about a ghetto uprising in Nashville the preceding April, the liberation school had been destroyed by the attacks upon it.

Sorace's testimony before McClellan also had the effect of fragmenting the liberation movement in Nashville and forcing many of its leaders to leave the city.

The police officer tried to show that the uprising in his city was the work of "agitators" from SCEF, SSOC, SNCC and similar local groups. Sorace stressed the SCEF board meeting and several gatherings at SSOC's headquarters in Nashville just before the rebellion broke out.

Since the McSurelys attended most of these meetings, McClellan seized the opportunity to summon them and examine their private papers (incidentally helping out Pike County officials, who were interested in keeping the papers away from the McSurelys and continuing their harassment).

The intent was to do to the organizing drive in the mountains what had been done---to the black movement in Nashville---destroy it.

Whether McClellan succeeds will depend on how clearly people see what he is doing; on how well they resist his claim that unrest is caused by "agitators" instead of by the conditions under which people live.

In the long run, it will depend on how well the people organize themselves for their mutual benefit and for their common interest--black and white together.

Southern Conference Educational Fund pamphlet

PIGS WAR ON PEOPLE

CITY PLANS WAR ON GANGS

June 9 (adapted from FRED)—Mayor (Big Pig) Daley held a conference today to plan how to destroy youth organizations in Chicago. All the top pigs—State's Attorney Edward V. Hanrahan, Police Superintendent James Conlisk, Chicago Housing Authority Chairman Charles Swibel, Park District President Daniel Shannon, Schools Superintendent James Redmond, and Human Resources Commissioner Deton Brooks—were there.

After the meeting the Big Pigs held a press conference to announce the forming of a special grand jury to "smash the gang structure" in the city. When asked whether he was trying to repress (smash) youth organizations, Daley said: "This is no attempt at any witch hunting. We are not trying to repress anything."

What they plan to do, however, is spread the City's network of tricks and informers. Redmond said he would issue special instructions to all teachers about crime reporting; and John Desmond, President of the Chicago Teachers Union, held a separate press conference to urge teachers to co-operate in arrests and prosecutions. Charlie Swibel said that CHA tenants' councils will be asked to supply information. Conlisk promised protection to all witnesses who appeared before the grand jury. Deton Brooks said that the Human Resources Department would gather information on gang activities (nothing new since Human Resources offices now send in daily reports to the Mayor's office on gangs and community organizations).

Big Pig Daley also said that they will form two new court branches to deal with gangs, community organizations, and demonstrators. One, to be called "Violence Court", will handle all violent crimes on the streets and public property by men over 17 and women over 18. Hanrahan said: "We are trying to avoid losing these cases in the massive number of other matters flooding our system."

Young Lords, Young Patriots, Panthers etc. march to Chicago Ave. police station to protest shooting of Manuel Ramos.

In an interview in Chicago Today, Hanrahan made his philosophy even clearer: "I think this is a situation where, locally, we have to re-establish the principle that was established internationally—that appeasement (pacification) merely strengthens an aggressor." Pig Buckney of the Gang Intelligence Unit agreed: "You try to appease these guys and you can lose half the city."

Interview With Lt. Buckney of the
Gang Intelligence Unit (GIU)
(reported in Presbyterian Life)

Reporter: If First (Presbyterian) Church is doing the
wrong thing, then how can concerned churches
work with gangs?
Buckney: They can't.
Reporter: How can other social agencies and groups work
with gangs?
Buckney: They can't
Reporter: Then who can work with gangs?
Buckney: The police.
Reporter: How can churches and other groups help the
police work with gangs?
Buckney: They can't
Reporter: Of the many different efforts now being made
in Chicago to deal with gangs, which have been
the most helpful to the police?
Buckney: The formation of the Gang Intelligence Unit.
Reporter: What can be done about gangs?
Buckney: They must be broken up.
Reporter: What can a church do if it should find itself
with a gang on its doorstep?
Buckney: Call the police.
Reporter: What should First Church do for the youth of
Woodlawn?
Buckney: Organize a youth fellowship.
Reporter: What should it do about the Rangers?
Buckney: Nothing.
Reporter: Who will do something about them?
Buckney: The police.
Reporter: What will they do?
Buckney: Break them up.

Y.L.O., newspaper of The Young Lords in Chicago, July 1969

Ed. Note: Hanrahan, the State's Attorney, is the
man who ordered the raid that resulted in the
murder of Fred Hampton

REVOLUTION AS AN EVENT IN NATURE

A revolution is a force against which no power, divine or human, can prevail, and whose nature it is to grow by the very resistance it encounters...the more you repress it, the more you increase its rebound and render its action irresistible, so that it is precisely the same for the triumph of an idea whether it is persecuted, harassed, beaten down from the start, or whether it grows and develops unobstructed. Like the Nemesis of the ancients, whom neither prayers nor threats could move, the revolution advances, with sombre and predestined tread, over the flowers strewn by its friends, through the blood of its defenders, over the bodies of its enemies.

PROUDHON

Press conference held by Black Panthers, Young Patriots, Young Lords, Black Disciples and Rising Up Angry.

LEARNING

DESPERATE ATTEMPTS TO KEEP THE YOUNG IN SCHOOLS THAT ARE HOPELESSLY OUTDATED

When you begin to think about adolescence in this way, what sense can you make of our schools? None of the proposed changes makes sense to me: revision of curriculum, teaching machines, smaller classes, encounter groups, redistributions of power—all of these are stopgap measures, desperate attempts to keep the young in schools that are hopelessly outdated. The changes suggested and debated don't go deeply enough; they don't question or change enough. For what needs changing are not the methods of the school system but its aims, and what is troubling the young and forcing upon their teachers an intolerable burden is the *idea* of childhood itself; the ways we think about adolescents, their place in the culture itself. More and more one comes to see that changes in the schools won't be enough; the crisis of the young cuts across the culture in all its areas and includes the family and the community. The young are displaced; there seems no other word for it. They are trapped in a prolonged childhood almost unique.

In few other cultures have persons of fifteen or eighteen been so uselessly isolated from participation in the community, or been deemed so unnecessary (in their elders' eyes), or so limited by law. Our ideas of responsibility, our parental feelings of anxiety, blame, and guilt, all of these follow from our curious vision of the young; in turn, they concretize it, legitimize it so that we are no longer even conscious of the ways we see childhood or the strain that our vision puts upon us. That is what needs changing: the definitions we make socially and legally of the role of the young. They are trapped in the ways we see them, and the school is simply one function, one aspect, of the whole problem. What makes real change so difficult in the schools is only in part their natural unwieldiness; it is more often the difficulty we have in escaping our preconceptions about things.

In general the school system we have inherited seems to me based upon three particular things:

☐ What Paul Goodman calls the idea of "natural depravity": our puritanical vision of human nature in which children are perceived as sinners or "savages" and in which human impulse or desire is not to be trusted and must therefore be constrained or "trained."

☐ The necessity during the mid-nineteenth century of "Americanizing" great masses of immigrant children from diverse backgrounds and creating, through the schools, a common experience and character.

☐ The need in an industrialized state for energy and labor to run the machines: the state, needing workers, educates persons to be technically capable but relatively dependent and responsive to authority so that their energies will be available when needed.

These elements combine with others—the labor laws that make childhood a "legal" state, and a population explosion that makes it necessary now to keep adolescents off both the labor market and the idle street—to "freeze" into a school system that resists change even as the culture itself and its needs shift radically. But teachers can't usually see that, for they themselves have been educated in this system and are committed to ideas that they have never clearly understood. Time and again, speaking to them, one hears the same questions and anguish:

"But what will happen to the students if they don't go to school?" "How will they learn?" "What will they do without adults?"

What never comes clear, of course, is that such questions are, at bottom, statement. Even while asking them teachers reveal their unconscious and contaminating attitudes. They can no longer imagine what children will do "outside" schools. They regard them as young monsters who will, if released from adult authority or help, disrupt the order of things. What is more, adults no longer are capable of imagining learning or child-adult relationships outside the schools. But mass schooling is a recent innovation. Most learning—especially the process of socialization or acculturation—has gone on outside schools, more naturally, in the fabric of the culture. In most cultures the passage from childhood to maturity occurs because of social necessity, the need for responsible adults, and is marked by clear changes in role. Children in the past seem to have learned the ways of the community or tribe through constant contact and interchange with adults, and it was taken for granted that the young learned continually through their place close to the heart of the community.

We seem to have lost all sense of that.

PETER MARIN

They asked me to write down the question *I* would ask of entering students. I gave them three questions: Have you had a good orgasm? Have you ever been really hurt, physically or emotionally? Are you willing to carry a gun for what you believe? You aren't really ready to learn without these things.

FELIPE LUCIANO a leader of the Young Lords, in his application to a new experimental college.

Think about the kind of world you want to live and work in. What do you need to know to build the world? Demand that your teachers teach you that.

KROPOTKIN quoted by Paul Goodman in Liberation Nov 1967

NO
PROFESSORS
NO
BUILDINGS

SEMINARY TO HAVE
CITY AS A CAMPUS

An experimental theological seminary without professors or buildings will get under way this fall for the benefit of the Unitarian Universalist Association.

The "campus" will be the facilities of New York City, the classrooms wherever a candidate's interest may take him. His textbooks will include the Bible and selections from the writings of Buddha, Aristotle, Nietzsche, Dostoevski, Lenin and Freud.

Instead of relying on teachers, each seminarian will absorb learning from doing. This may entail anything from studying choreography with a modern dance group (to enhance his knowledge of the dance in public worship) to investigating drug addiction therapy and the off-Broadway theater.

During their three-year course, the ministerial students will work independently of each other, except for occasional get-togethers for informal seminars on their separate projects or to analyze study books.

Three experimental fellowships will be available in the fall for candidates with college degrees. The program will include a

month's vacation each year at a time convenient to the student's schedule.

The seminarians may arrange to take special courses, if they wish, at the New School for Social Research, Columbia University, New York University or Union Theological Seminary.

A tutorial committee will oversee each student's work and at the end of three years accredit him for acceptance into the Unitarian Universalist ministry.

Dr. Harold Taylor, former president of Sarah Lawrence College, conceived the idea of a school outside the usual theological setting several years ago.

GEORGE DUGAN *The New York Times* July 1969

A FREE SCHOOL FOR
HIGH SCHOOL STUDENTS

A Free School for High-School students has been organized in Chicago. Classes are held in the evenings and on Saturdays. Organizers of the school state that: "In public schools we are told what to learn, when to learn it, and when to stop learning. At the Free School we will decide for ourselves. The teachers at our school will not plan courses and throw them at us. We will plan the courses with them and will be involved in constantly re-evaluating the classes to see if our questions are being answered."

Courses include media, current events, black history,   and American history. Classes are bieng held at Roosevelt University, 430 South Michigan Avenue, Chicago. Rooms will be posted on the Student Senate blackboard.

For further information, contact Amy Kesselman, 7056 North Paulina, Chicago, Illinois 60626

HELP SOUGHT ON RESEARCHING
THE UNIVERSITY

A fraternal research and analysis group at Washington University in St. Louis is seeking any research material and papers on "just about anything connected with the university". Specifically, aid is sought in these areas:

faculty and administrative bureaucratic structure and power relations.

alternative teaching and learning techniques

alternative grading and evaluation proposals

research on trustees

experimental courses and programs

government ties, DoD, et cetera

admissions and recruitment

interdisciplinary courses and programs

university relations to the outside community

lab-community schools

If you can help, please contact Dave Glanz, Box 1068, Washington University, St. Louis, Missouri 63130

Radicals in the Professions Newsletter

THE
SCHOOL SYSTEM:
INSULATED, INBRED,
INCORRIGIBLE

Most big city school systems are strangled in red tape, mired in inertia, inefficiencies and incompetence, insulated, inbred, leaderless, protective of mediocrity (through civil service and tenure), and they victimize many people who come in contact with them. I have documented this in my book for New York City, but further studies by myself and others indicate that it is a national problem.

Even if we had more money, better and more relevant curricula, better training and better educators it might all be for nought, given the clear record of how administrative rules and constraints have ground down so many competent and idealistic educators and absorbed, diluted and discredited potentially good educational programs.

Militant ghetto groups in New York City and elsewhere now see this point, and they have turned to decentralization and community control. They saw how desegregation and compensatory education programs were subverted by the educators, and they want to make the educators more accountable to the public by relocating power and authority at the local community level.

This is not just a ghetto fight, however, and decentralization will help improve education in white and middle class districts as well.

DAVID ROGERS *The Los Angles Times* 12/29/68

In describing the school system, Mr. Rogers writes: It has an almost unlimited capacity for absorbing protest and externalizing blame, for confusing and dividing the opposition, 'seeming' to appear responsive to legitimate protest by issuing sophisticated and progressive policy statements that are poorly implemented, if at all. . .The system is like a punching bag. Protest groups can hit it in one place, and it simply returns to an old equilibrium.."
. . .

David Rogers is associate professor of sociology and management in the Graduate School of Business Administration of New York University. He is the author of "110 Livingston Street: Politics and Bureaucracy in the New York City School System."

Bold, Earthy Approach To Teaching Grammar

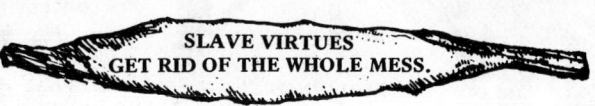

SLAVE VIRTUES
GET RID OF THE WHOLE MESS.

By Bill Moore

A British educator said here yesterday exactly what teachers should do with text books and grammar in American schools.

"Get rid of the whole mess," declared Geoffrey Summerfield — who at 37 has written 25 books, many of them scathingly critical of education in this country.

"Hell, live a little dangerously and start introducing into the schools that vital ferment that is taking place in American culture," said the bushy haired author in an interview before his speech to the National Humanities Conference.

The conference at the Sheraton-Palace Hotel is sponsored by the National Council of Teachers of English.

"American teachers are crippled by an undue preoccupation with form and so-called correctness," said Summerfield, a lecturer at the University of York.

"We must not forget that language is a social act," he said, "and we should be promoting extensive writing and continual conversation in the language these children, particularly ghetto children, know and understand. When we drill them with some alien and superficial grammar, we are not putting the emphasis where it belongs, on meaning.

"The textbook field is doing the same thing. It is lucrative as long as the publishers play it safe, and they always do. The textbook is a cudgel which beats most kids into a state of stupor," Summerfield said, violently tapping his fingers on the sole of his shoe.

"Our schools are still committed to promoting the slave virtues of listless punctuality, uniformity and toeing the line," he said.

Where is the hang-up?

"Teachers," said Summerfield. "The profession is by and large made up of lower - middle - class whites who have not been educated to understand anyone who is not a lower - middle - class white."

The American concept of the melting pot is no longer true, he argued.

"If we talk about heritage, we better talk about Indian, Spanish-American and black heritages, as well as white heritage. Your whole school system here is geared to turning out the good American, and the interpretation of it is very narrow."

Instead, he said, the schools should foster diversity.

"That means encouraging imagination," Summerfield said. "If a class is dealing with poetry, it should not concentrate on the meter and the rhyme scheme and all that crap. It should concentrate on the feeling of creating."

Can America overcome brittleness and regimentation in the classroom?

"I don't know," said Summerfield. "Can it?"

3/31/69
San Francisco Chronicle

Metropolitan Achievement Tests

Do you pass the test?

SAMPLE

Policemen are our friends. They help us to cross the street. They keep cars moving. Sometimes they scold people, but only ★when the people do something wrong. Everyone should obey policemen.

B In this story, the word <u>obey</u> means to —
    ◯ run home to Mother   ◯ sit up
    ⬛ do what you are told   ◯ drive fast

Hey Teach!, Teachers for a Democratic Society

I am now a bad boy in school.
I was a good boy in school but I don't know what came over me.
Now I wish I could get good agin.
But I can not.

Duran Montgomery
Grade 4
P.S. 165

SCHOOL IS BAD FOR CHILDREN

BY JOHN HOLT

Almost every child, on the first day he sets foot in a school building, is smarter, more curious, less afraid of what he doesn't know, better at finding and figuring things out, more confident, resourceful, persistent and independent than he will ever be again in his schooling—or, unless he is very unusual and very lucky, for the rest of his life. Already, by paying close attention to and interacting with the world and people around him, and without any school-type formal instruction, he has done a task far more difficult, complicated and abstract than anything he will be asked to do in school, or than any of his teachers has done for years. He has solved the mystery of language. He has discovered it—babies don't even know that language exists—and he has found out how it works and learned to use it. He has done it by exploring, by experimenting, by developing his own model of the grammar of language, by trying it out and seeing whether it works, by gradually changing it and refining it until it does work. And while he has been doing this, he has been learning other things as well, including many of the "concepts" that the schools think only they can teach him, and many that are more complicated than the ones they do try to teach him.

In he comes, this curious, patient, determined, energetic, skillful learner. We sit him down at a desk, and what do we teach him? Many things. First, that learning is separate from living. "You come to school to learn," we tell him, as if the child hadn't been learning before, as if living were out there and learning were in here, and there were no connection between the two. Secondly, that he cannot be trusted to learn and is no good at it. Everything we teach about reading, a task far simpler than many that the child has already mastered, says to him, "If we don't make you read, you won't, and if you don't do it exactly the way we tell you, you can't." In short, he comes to feel that learning is a passive process, something that someone else does *to* you, instead of something you do for yourself.

In a great many other ways he learns that he is worthless, untrustworthy, fit only to take other people's orders, a blank sheet for other people to write on. Oh, we make a lot of nice noises in school about respect for the child and individual differences, and the like. But our acts, as opposed to our talk, say to the child, "Your experience, your concerns, your curiosities, your needs, what you know, what you want, what you wonder about, what you hope for, what you fear, what you like and dislike, what you are good at or not so good at—all this is of not the slightest importance, it counts for nothing. What counts here, and the only thing that counts, is what we know, what we think is important, what we want you to

do, think and be." The child soon learns not to ask questions—the teacher isn't there to satisfy his curiosity. Having learned to hide his curiosity, he later learns to be ashamed of it. Given no chance to find out who he is—and to develop that person, whoever it is—he soon comes to accept the adults' evaluation of him.

He learns many other things. He learns that to be wrong, uncertain, confused, is a crime. Right Answers are what the school wants, and he learns countless strategies for prying these answers out of the teacher, for conning her into thinking he knows what he doesn't know. He learns to dodge, bluff, fake, cheat. He learns to be lazy. Before he came to school, he would work for hours on end, on his own, with no thought of reward, at the business of making sense of the world and gaining competence in it. In school he learns, like every buck private, how to goldbrick, how not to work when the sergeant isn't looking, how to know when he is looking, how to make him think you are working even when he is looking. He learns that in real life you don't do anything unless you are bribed, bullied or conned into doing it, that nothing is worth doing for its own sake, or that if it is, you can't do it in school. He learns to be bored, to work with a small part of his mind, to escape from the reality around him into daydreams and fantasies—but not like the fantasies of his preschool years, in which he played a very active part.

The child comes to school curious about other people, particularly other children, and the school teaches him to be indifferent. The most interesting thing in the classroom—often the only interesting thing in it—is the other children, but he has to act as if these other children, all about him, only a few feet away, are not really there. He cannot interact with them, talk with them, smile at them. In many schools he can't talk to other children in the halls between classes; in more than a few, and some of these in stylish suburbs, he can't even talk to them at lunch. Splendid training for a world in which, when you're not studying the other person to figure out how to do him in, you pay no attention to him.

In fact, he learns how to live without paying attention to anything going on around him. You might say that school is a long lesson in how to turn yourself off, which may be one reason why so many young people, seeking the awareness of the world and responsiveness to it they had when they were little, think they can only find it in drugs. Aside from being boring, the school is almost always ugly, cold, inhuman—even the most stylish, glass-windowed, $20-a-square-foot schools.

And so, in this dull and ugly place, where nobody ever says anything very truthful, where

everybody is playing a kind of role, as in a charade, where the teachers are no more free to respond honestly to the students than the students are free to respond to the teachers or each other, where the air practically vibrates with suspicion and anxiety, the child learns to live in a daze, saving his energies for those small parts of his life that are too trivial for the adults to bother with, and thus remain his. It is a rare child who can come through his schooling with much left of his curiosity, his independence or his sense of his own dignity, competence and worth.

So much for criticism. What do we need to do? Many things. Some are easy—we can do them right away. Some are hard, and may take some time. Take a hard one first. We should abolish compulsory school attendance. At the very least we should modify it, perhaps by giving children every year a large number of authorized absences. Our compulsory school-attendance laws once served a humane and useful purpose. They protected children's right to some schooling, against those adults who would otherwise have denied it to them in order to exploit their labor, in farm, store, mine or factory. Today the laws help nobody, not the schools, not the teachers, not the children. To keep kids in school who would rather not be there costs the schools an enormous amount of time and trouble—to say nothing of what it costs to repair the damage that these angry and resentful prisoners do every time they get a chance. Every teacher knows that any kid in class who, for whatever reason, would rather not be there not only doesn't learn anything himself but makes it a great deal tougher for anyone else. As for protecting the children from exploitation, the chief and indeed only exploiters of children these days *are* the schools. Kids caught in the college rush more often than not work 70 hours or more a week, most of it on paper busywork. For kids who aren't going to college, school is just a useless time waster, preventing them from earning some money or doing some useful work, or even doing some true learning.

Objections. "If kids didn't have to go to school, they'd all be out in the streets." No, they wouldn't. In the first place, even if schools stayed just the way they are, children would spend at least some time there because that's where they'd be likely to find friends; it's a natural meeting place for children. In the second place, schools wouldn't stay the way they are, they'd get better, because we would have to start making them what they ought to be right now—places where children would *want* to be. In the third place, those children who did not want to go to school could find, particularly if we stirred up our brains and gave them a little help, other things to do—the things many children now do during their summers and holidays.

There's something easier we could

do. We need to get kids out of the school buildings, give them a chance to learn about the world at first hand. It is a very recent idea, and a crazy one, that the way to teach our young people about the world they live in is to take them out of it and shut them up in brick boxes. Fortunately, educators are beginning to realize this. In Philadelphia and Portland, Oreg., to pick only two places I happen to have heard about, plans are being drawn up for public schools that won't have any school buildings at all, that will take the students out into the city and help them to use it and its people as a learning resource. In other words, students, perhaps in groups, perhaps independently, will go to libraries, museums, exhibits, courtrooms, legislatures, radio and TV stations, meetings, businesses and laboratories to learn about their world and society at first hand. A small private school in Washington is already doing this. It makes sense. We need more of it.

As we help children get out into the world, to do their learning there, we can get more of the world into the schools. Aside from their parents, most children never have any close contact with any adults except people whose sole business is children. No wonder they have no idea what adult life or work is like. We need to bring a lot more people who are *not* full-time teachers into the schools, and into contact with the children. In New York City, under the Teachers and Writers Collaborative, real writers, working writers—novelists, poets, playwrights—come into the schools, read their work, and talk to the children about the problems of their craft. The children eat it up. In another school I know of, a practicing attorney from a nearby city comes in every month or so and talks to several classes about the law. Not the law as it is in books but as he sees it and en-counters it in his cases, his problems, his work. And the children love it. It is real, grown-up, true, not *My Weekly Reader*, not "social studies," not lies and baloney.

Something easier yet. Let children work together, help each other, learn from each other and each other's mistakes. We now know, from the experience of many schools, both rich-suburban and poor-city, that children are often the best teachers of other children. What is more important, we know that when a fifth- or sixth-grader who has been having trouble with reading starts helping a first-grader, his own reading sharply improves. A number of schools are beginning to use what some call Paired Learning. This means that you let children form partnerships with other children, do their work, even including their tests, together, and share whatever marks or results this work gets—just like grownups in the real world. It seems to work.

Let the children learn to judge their own work. A child learning to talk does not learn by being corrected all the time—if corrected too much, he will stop talking. *He* compares, a thousand times a day, the difference between language as he uses it and as those around him use it. Bit by bit, he makes the necessary changes to make his language like other people's. In the same way, kids learning to do all the other things they learn without adult teachers—to walk, run, climb, whistle, ride a bike, skate, play games, jump rope—compare their own perform-ance with what more skilled people do, and slowly make the needed changes. But in school we never give a child a chance to detect his mistakes, let alone correct them. We do it all for him. We act as if we thought he would never notice a mistake unless it was pointed out to him, or correct it unless he was made to. Soon he becomes dependent on the expert. We should let him do it himself. Let him figure out, with the help of other children if he wants it, what this word says, what is the answer to that problem, whether this is a good way of saying or doing this or that. If right answers are involved, as in some math or science, give him the answer book, let him correct his own papers. Why should we teachers waste time on such donkey work? Our job should be to help the kid when he tells us that he can't find a way to get the right answer. Let's get rid of all this nonsense of grades, exams, marks. We don't know now, and we never will know, how to measure what another person knows or understands. We certainly can't find out by asking him questions. All we find out is what he doesn't know—which is what most tests are for, any-way. Throw it all out, and let the child learn what every educated person must someday learn, how to mea-sure his own understanding, how to know what he knows or does not know.

We could also abolish the fixed, re-quired curriculum. People remember only what is interesting and useful to them, what helps them make sense of the world, or helps them get along in it. All else they quickly forget, if they ever learn it at all. The idea of a "body of knowledge," to be picked up in school and used for the rest of one's life, is nonsense in a world as compli-cated and rapidly changing as ours. Anyway, the most important questions and problems of our time are not *in* the curriculum, not even in the hot-shot universities, let alone the schools.

Children want, more than they want anything else, and even after years of miseducation, to make sense of the world, themselves, other human beings. Let them get at this job, with our help if they ask for it, in the way that makes most sense to them.

John Holt

Saturday Evening Post 2/8/69

Fight for Chicano Control Erupts in L. A. High Schools

By DELLA ROSSA

LOS ANGELES—The demand for Chicano control of Chicano schools led students and parents to set up a Chi-cano-controlled school at Euclid Cen-ter in East Los Angeles March 13 after a week of demonstrations, vicious beat-ings by police and the arrest of over 250 students and adults.

The demonstrations began at Roose-velt High School on March 6, the sec-ond anniversary of the Chicano high school blow-outs. The students were protesting miserable conditions which were forcing from 40-60 percent of the students to drop out of school. About 82 percent of the Roosevelt students are Chicano and the remainder are predominantly Oriental and Black.

An estimated 80 police were called to the school and attacked eight people in the process of arresting 31 students and six adults. A leaflet protesting the attack said one girl's arm was broken.

Jorge Rodriguez, chairman of the United Mexican American Students at Roosevelt, said that the demands of the students were for a special class period for Chicano history; more Chicano lit-erature; the right to distribute leaflets on campus on Chicano social, political and educational issues; abolition of I. Q. tests based on English and the Anglo culture; and a special reading program. Preparation for college edu-

270
learning

cation rather than vocational training was also demanded.

Over 200 people, mostly young Chicanos, marched on two sides of Hollenbeck Police Station on March 7 to protest the brutal arrests. There was both anger at the brutality and a strong spirit of *carnalismo* [brotherhood].

Marlin Foxworth, an English instructor at Roosevelt, said at the demonstration, "What happened yesterday was just like the last 20 years there. The schools are racist and try to perpetuate the existing structure and keep the Chicano down. Some teachers on the staff still tell 'nigger' jokes."

On Mon., March 9, over 400 students out of a student body of around 3,000 at Roosevelt High demonstrated in protest of the March 6 arrests. They chanted "Chicano Power" and carried signs reading "Chicano Control of Roosevelt." A large contingent of police attempted to intimidate the demonstration. Students at Huntington Park High School demonstrated to protest the harassment and arrests at Roosevelt.

A fact sheet issued out of Euclid Center said that on March 10 "600 students, mothers and community [people] demonstrated. Police were called for the third straight time. They harassed students and chased, beat and arrested 12. Students demonstrated again at Hunt-

ington Park, 100 students held a rally at Lincoln High [also predominantly Chicano] and there was student unrest at Garfield High."

Nena Huffsteter, a member of MECHA, an organization of Chicano college students, reported that on March 11 she and other Chicano college students were marching with the Roosevelt students very peacefully.

"We had been marching since about 10 a.m. About 1 p.m., the police began to jeer the students and gun their motors to get us to make a move. About 1:55 we heard glass crash across the street and a bottle hit a police car. Then the police went toward the students, not toward the bottle-thrower. We tried to keep the kids calm, but they ran and the police chased them, breaking heads.

"The people along the street opened their doors to the kids to protect them from the police. The students were followed onto the lawns and the porches. The people there know Fourth and Mott is part of an armed camp."

Reports at Euclid Center indicated that as many as 1,000 students boycotted classes on March 11. At least 58 people were arrested.

Community meetings with high school and college students supported by parents and community people were held throughout the week at Euclid Cen-

ter. Typical of the meetings was one March 11 when 600-700 people jammed the meeting hall and were packed tight out to the sidewalk.

None of the basic demands coming out of the 1968 blow-outs, when as many as 3,000 Chicano students walked out of their schools, have been fulfilled two years later.

By Fri., March 13, school administrators admitted that nearly 1,000 Roosevelt High students had boycotted classes while about 150 people demonstrated in front of the school.

Sympathy boycotts and demonstrations continued at Huntington Park, Garfield and Lincoln High schools and spread to South Gate High School and Excelsior Junior High. A round of applause burst out when word was received late in the afternoon at Euclid Center that students at Beverly Hills High School, an Anglo upper-middle-class school, had gone out, with over 200 students boycotting classes for an hour.

By March 13 the indications were that the following week would bring continued demonstrations and school boycotts and the continuance of an independent Chicano school at Euclid Center, where the first session had as many as 100 students.

The Militant Feb 1970

High schools becoming more political

THE SO-CALLED EDUCATORS KNOW THEY ARE IN TROUBLE.

There are 45 million prisoners in America's public school system. And a lot of them are angry. They know they are being force-fed an unpalatable education, and in most urban high schools at least they are reminded daily of their second-rate status by the ever-present cops prowling their corridors.

There are changes on both sides of the office wall. Out front the conversation of the students takes on more and more of the aspect of prison scuttlebut, with all the militance but little of the sense of defeat which eats away at old cons. Meanwhile, in smoking backrooms, principals exchange advice which might make a nice column in the Jail Warden's Gazette--how to fortify, how to defend, but most of all, how to cool things out before they burn.

Last year there were disruptions in three out of five of America's high schools, ranging from pickets to taking principals hostage, over 2000 outbreaks in all. This year, as fall settles around the necks of young people, observers from left and right foresee the most vigorous uprising ever.

In Richmond Hills, Queens, New York, SDS activists staged an unscheduled assembly at the local high school and met with a warm response. The unexpected visitors, part of the Weatherman faction of SDS, ran into a regular assembly. chained the door to keep out the cops, and rapped down a number of speeches denouncing occupation troops in Vietnam, Korea, the black ghetto, and urban high schools. The kids were enthusiastic, and next day, when the SDSers re-

turned to talk with them outside of the school, they found much more interest than hostility to their communist ideas.

In an open letter to the powers-that-be, the African-American Students Association, a New York based group which does extensive work in Brooklyn, issued the following stern warning:

"We wonder how you were unable to find money for clothing for children on welfare but ready and able to find the funds to put police guards back in our schools. We urge you to remove these guards and police by Monday, Sept. 15; otherwise, the uneasy peace that has existed for the past few days stands to be disturbed."

The so-called educators know they are in trouble. "The high school principal," bemoans an official of the National Education Association, "is replacing the college president as the most embattled American." When high school principals get together, they may make an abstract reference or two to "reform" (liberal rhetoric still sounds nicer than racist truth) but when they get down to the nitty-gritty the topic is how do we fight back.

A document which recently slipped into the hands of Liberation News Service in New York reveals the exact same counterinsurgency mentality which went into the making of hundreds of reports from American professors to the U. S. Army and its affiliates on Vietnamese society and the best methods to destroy it.

The document, entitled "Confrontation and

Response" (and, incidentally, marked "CON-FIDENTIAL: for High School Principals' Association use only!"), begins with a snow-job prologue, describing New York City's high school principals as long-time "spokesmen in the great libertarian tradition." The paper gives its "unequivocal endorsement" to good, and by implication, its "unequivocal opposition" to evil.

As the generalities subside, "Confrontation and Response" gets down to business. We must never, as the bearers of wisdom and agents of courage, allow the "corrupt fringe to seduce the innocent." "Responsible dissent" which doesn't lead to turmoil is of course all right, but any serious attack on the status quo must not be tolerated. "The elite corps of left fascism" must be defeated at any cost.

"The nature of the demands--not even demands; rather, manifestos, political platforms, position papers--and the manner of their presentation," sputters the paper, "violent, sometimes wantonly destructive, using hostages as a political weapon--allow only one response: denial, simple, clear, and unequivocal.

"Discussion, perhaps. Negotiation, no."

But the basic problem in counterinsurgency, whether in Vietnam, on the domestic culture scene, or in the high schools, is how to keep people on your side if you don't intend to make any of the basic changes that they deeply need.

The proposal of "Confrontation and Response" is quite specific. Assume a "flexible, reasonable and liberal posture," and whenever a crisis comes up, refer the problem to a variety of advisory groups operating on all levels (student, student-faculty, faculty-administration, and administration) to the point where a multiplicity of frivolous meetings that seem to be the cutting edge dissipate the attention of both the militants and the people they are trying to reach. Be flexible, and do nothing; keep the noisy minority away from the silent majority.

But the high school principals have a sense that they are fighting a losing battle. The time when they could successfully "divide and conquer" is running out, and they are forced to think defensively or lose very soon:

"We place ourselves at a psychological disadvantage, ill-equipped for conflict, unless we properly assess the ultimate objective of the new left. The school is the target, the symbol of the state, the epitome and embodiment of society's corruptions...

"In more and more schools the search for a cause ultimately results in success. Masses of students are radicalized, accepting the militants' cause as their own. The school bubbles with excitement; the halls and cafeteria buzz with a continual, conspiratorial caucusing. Sometimes supported by dissident teachers and community extremists, they demand action--now!"

LIBERATION NEWS SERVICE Sept 1969

The typical child, by the time he is 17, has been in school 12,000 hours. This does not include all the hundreds of hours of homework. . .School absorbs more & more time. . .The average 17-year-old has seen 17,000 hours of TV.

DOUGLES HEATH Associate Professor of Psychology at Haverford College

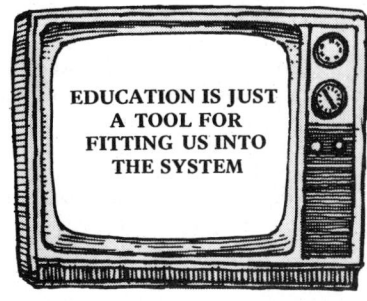

EDUCATION IS JUST A TOOL FOR FITTING US INTO THE SYSTEM

We want education for our people that exposes the true nature of this decadent ameriKKKan society. We want education that teaches us our true history and our role in the present-day society.

The parents in the LIFE Poll know exactly what *they* want from the schools. Teach the kids to understand our existing values, they say; discipline them to conform. But there is a large and vocal band of utopian critics who claim that these are the very standards that defile the whole education process. "Education is just a tool for fitting us into the System," they say, and they undeniably have a point. The fact is that, under the traditional American educational system, the student is indeed required to conform to someone else's ideas of what is important, and all too often those ideas are presented in a pitifully restricted fashion, without much sense of unity, and in a thoroughly authoritarian manner. Authority demands conformity, conformity leads to routine, and routine produces boredom. The status quo may be served, but the effect on the student can be disastrous.

●

If the LIFE Poll makes one thing clear, it is that most parents are thoroughly unsympathetic with their children's aspirations for participation and involvement in determining the role and function of their schools. Reduced to its simplest terms, the generations disagree on the most fundamental question of all: What is education for?

●

CONCLUSION: More than half of today's high school generation is impatient with the limited participation it has been allowed in running its educational affairs. And, since 55% of those who graduate are headed for college, the implications of this discontent for future campus ferment are enormous.

STUDENT PARTICIPATION IN POLICY MAKING

	S	P	T
Want more	58%	20%	35%
Want less	2	11	4
About same	39	65	60
Not sure	1	4	1

IMPORTANCE OF STUDENT PARTICIPATION IN POLICY MAKING

	S	P	T
Very important	54%	25%	30%
Somewhat important	34	38	39
Not very important	11	33	31
Not sure	1	4	*

*Less than 0.5%

SHOULD STUDENTS HAVE MORE SAY?

	S	P	T
In making rules	66%	24%	40%
In deciding curriculum	63	35	47
In determining discipline of students	48	28	37
In deciding how to conduct classes	48	21	28
In determination of grades	41	14	18

SHOULD THESE TOPICS BE DISCUSSED IN CLASS?

	S	P	T
Folk rock music	35%	6%	19%
Black students' rights	52	27	36
Underground paper and films	40	17	36
Sex hygiene	52	41	62
Hair, dress, styles	37	30	28
Use of drugs	70	66	72

S = students **P** = parents **T** = teachers

Life 5/10/69

BALLOON

By Trude Bennett

Anyone with a bachelor's degree (well, almost anyone — beards and short skirts are not appreciated) can earn $24 a day as a substitute teacher in the Boston Public Schools. If you walk into the Department of Teacher Placement at 15 Beacon Street with a college transcript and a report of a recent chest X-ray, you can walk out with a booklet containing "Directions for Reaching Boston Public Schools," a copy of Boston Public Schools Form No. 499: "General Instructions to Temporary Teachers," and a place on the substitute list.

It seems like a good job for liberal arts graduates who need money but don't want full-time jobs. It offers high pay, short hours, flexibility, a chance to be with kids, to learn about the schools, to find out if you might like teaching, and maybe a chance to do some teaching.

"Floater"

But working in the schools becomes a kind of complicity in crime. Most people decide it's not worth the money or flexibility to become a substitute oppressor and oppress themselves in the process.

I took a job three months ago as a "building substitute," or "floater," in a Boston school. I'm on the staff of one school and substitute every day for any teacher who is absent. I am jumped from the kindergarten to the eighth grade, sometimes within the same school day since I am also used as a relief teacher.

I knew substituting would be hard. I only felt hopeful about it because I didn't want to be an authority and thought that I could communicate that to the kids. I wanted to relate to them through interest and respect, not fear. My time in the classroom seemed a chance to talk with them about why the schools are so bad and how people find ways to change things. But I didn't understand the ways in which the repressiveness of the school would shape their responses and mine.

As my examiner in the Boston Teacher's Exam answered one of my comments about teaching: "It's nice for children to learn things that are relevant to them as individuals. But what happens later when they have to adjust to jobs that aren't relevant to their interests? The schools have to teach them how to do things they don't like to do."

The most important lesson taught in the Boston schools is discipline. Dull senseless routine, constant physical punishment, and accusations of laziness, "freshness," and being just plain "bad" badger students into conformity with the schools' decisions and the society's traps for their lives.

"Laggards"

Boys and girls who are taught they don't have the right to decide when to go to the bathroom, who can never open a book unless they are told to, who must always be on time or accept punishment as "laggards," must always wear a tie and address the principal as "sir" or must act like a "young lady" at all time — are being trained for a lifetime of accepting the authority of bosses, husbands, drill sergeants, or the Welfare Department.

Somehow kids never lose themselves completely. But all their vitality, their interest, and their excitement go underground. They assume after a while that anything interesting to them must be hidden. Anything that's part of school cannot be interesting, so they suspend themselves completely from what they are forced to do in school.

Class work goes on with some minimal level of involvement and success — but sometimes it becomes too much to bear.

Once a first-grader burst out crying when I asked her class to do a page in their phonics workbooks. The rest of the children picked up their workbooks and began plodding through the lesson, but she started sobbing and finally explained, "I just can't do this anymore. I hate it." First grade.

The school creates a relation of constant struggle between student and teacher. The students have a momentary advantage in that struggle when there is a substitute in the class. Children's energy often finds its only outlet in school in disruptive, covert, or forbidden behavior. When a substitute comes in, there is more opportunity for utilizing that energy.

I discovered that kids often did not want to try out my ideas for activities, no matter how exciting they seemed in the planning. They want me to try to enforce the teacher's rules. A sub who tries to reject stupid structures that give the kids security will be met with constant, fearful cries of "That's not what the teacher does. Miss Smith does it this way." The children have been taught not to rely on their own resources so they're scared when someone releases them from their protective shackles.

The sub is literally a substitute for the teacher — kids can rebel against the substitute in all the ways they want to defy the teacher. So they demand that you enforce the rules (be the teacher) and then, within a familiar and safe framework, they act out all their hatred of those rules and the teacher's authority.

You may find yourself trying to cling to the authority you are forced to represent and executing all of those repressive rules as well as you can. Everyone — the principal, the other teachers, and the kids — expects you to keep some semblance of control in your classroom. In spite of yourself, you'll internalize their demands. If you feel chaos descending, you'll probably feel helpless and inadequate.

You may find yourself becoming more and more of a monster — desiring control as your only refuge, creating the fear that will enhance your control, forcing the kids to do work they cannot understand and could never care about, and knowing that you are helping them become more and more alienated from learning.

Humor

I felt lost like that a few weeks ago when I spent several days in my school's special class for ' slow learners" (below 70 IQ). Most of these seventh graders are waiting for the time when the law will allow them to quit school. They are bored and embarrassed by low-level, low-interest books they must read again and again. They know they are being disciplined for the sake of order and control, not even for the pretense of learning.

I liked the class a lot. We talked about things that are seldom considered legitimate for school discussion — their families, school rules, hippies, the war. One day we spent a long time discussing humor — what makes people laugh, why so much humor is cruel, why people laugh in different situations.

Some of the kids got really excited in that discussion. One boy gave long, perceptive descriptions of the ways people use laughter and humor as a nervous defense or an escape from their own feelings. He talked about the hurt he felt when people made jokes instead of expressing their real feelings. The class tried for a long time to think of occasions for laughter that were not at the expense of other people. There was an outburst of delight when one girl finally said, "When you're crying and your mother tickles you."

Most of them were unaccustomed to discussion that was so interesting and personal. They were excited to find that their sensitivities about people could make an important contribution to a lesson in school.

The Cycle

That lesson was a novelty to them. They enjoyed it, but they still felt they were getting away with something because they weren't doing normal schoolwork. They first saw me as a friend or maybe an ally, but when I tried to insist on a certain amount of order and directed activity, they began to ignore me. I wouldn't be a "teacher," I wasn't a friend, and we were all stuck there inside the classroom. The situation gradually turned into chaos.

As a substitute, you face the effects of an extremely repressive environment. You can't ignore the kind of socialization all children undergo in this society. In fact, as a substitute, you bear the brunt of it. In one day you can't expect kids to relax, suddenly find self-direction, or even view you as something other than a target for their frustration. So you must play the role of teacher to some extent.

You should be honest with them and with yourself. You should make a point of explaining to the kids that you aren't the teacher, and you're not going to do everything the way the teacher does — in fact, you don't want to. When kids treat you without respect, or ignore you, your anger is justified. They may no longer be able to see teachers as people, but you can't accept that treatment any more than you can lose respect for them. They should have to face your anger if you can express it honestly and not in a punitive or hysterical way.

You can't blame yourself for the cumulative horrors of the school system. Public education reinforces the values and priorities of this society. It trains people to think that the system is always right and cannot be effectively challenged. As long as the schools serve to socialize children into a repressive society, no teacher can find ways to liberate himself or the students in his classroom from the system's demands. Teachers must find a way to work politically outside the classroom to end the cycle the schools help perpetuate — a cycle of authority and fear and refusal to let people understand and fulfil their own interests and needs.

I came in with the 2nd shift
on April Fool's Day;
signed the Loyalty Oath
in duplicate,
& stood in the hall
reading *The Story
of Dr. Wassell* (novel)
for the 2nd period.
Dr. Wassell. Late Hilton.
Early to Middle American
Imperial. Java. 1942
with the Dutch.
with God.
　　　　　　　Time
to talk sharply;
　　　　　　　Time
to teach: open
the book: open
the minds.

　　　　　　　—Bill Costley

What Kids Write

Dear Mr. Riley,

How are you fine I hope I hope you'll be back soon because we miss you the Class aint the same. We have a very nice teacher who is taking your place she would be nicer if the boys would only be a lot more gooder and I know you know what I mean.

Your Friend,
Susan Flanigan

Dear Mr. Riley,

I hope you are Better and I hope that you do not com back we all hat you. We like the other teacher better than you.

Your Friend,
Janice

Dear Mr. Riley,

I hope you dont get Better.
I hope you die in the Hosptel.
You are no goob.
We are doing detter with out you
You *skum* and wen you Die
I will send you *weeds*

Michael B.
John Simon
David Jenks

Today in Room 315 The students were very bad they were making lots of noise. talking out loud getting out of their seats And they daity up the room and the thing that they did that was mean was they gave the teacher a headace and that was very mean of them to do it to a nice teacher like that. All this class wants is everything their way, and I don't think that's nice. that's why we got a bad name for this class anyway.

Today the children was acking up because the teacher wasi'nt in and I think that wasint nise
to give you a heack
and I think if the teacher was here the kids wouldent go nothing but the work the teacher give them.

Because the boys and Girls were running round the room and making nose and yell and throwing thinking running in and out of the room I am sorry for making nose and giving you a headack please forgive me if you could

If I was a scientist I would invent a machine that make people old so they could shiver.

If I were a substitute and the children were yelling I would just lay down to take a rest.

If I were a scientist I would make a love machine so Kenny would love me and I love him. And also make a cigarett machine.

If I were a substitute I would be mean to me I would be mean to but if there good to me I'il be good to them.

If we had a balloon school. I would put a pin through it. And there would not be any more school.

If I was in a balloon It wontned feel nice because if you just look down I will get high sick but when I was on a plane to california I don't get high sick because you could close you eyes and go to sleep that's why. I wount go on a balloon I hate to be a balloon boy do I get high sick on a balloon.

I think a balloon school is nice. Because if I get a pin, I wood pop the school. So I think a balloon is nice.

I did not every like Nixon, but I think since he is our president so we have to have some respect for him but other than that I think he is a creep in plane English he will not do anything he said he will.

Nixon is no good because he dose not
help us. And he is to skaid he will get shourt and he is not doing anything he just sit on his bom

Nixon takes the stand
Nixon is at the stand
because he wants to stop
the war because to many of our
boy die so he wants to save our boys
and thinks that our boys are nice

President Nixon shall go home
everybody are very mad
so nixon please go. home

I wouldn't like to be a substitute teacher because I wouldn't know what to give for work. I would give anything I think of.

The End

TO: ALL TEACHERS   RE: LAGGARDS

1. Anyone that is a laggard must be kept after school for an unbroken 30 minute period, not less. Unbroken.

2. A notebook in which the names of those who are laggards are noted, will be circulated. The teacher will take notice of those who are laggards in his/her room. The teacher will sign his/her name in the appropriate place. The teacher will tell the pupil when to remain after.

3. Any child reporting to homeroom after the classes have filed into school should not be allowed admittance to the homeroom until it has been ascertained that he/she has signed the laggard books, which are in the custody of the laggard monitors at the boys' side and at the girls' side.

4. No pupil is to enter the school through the front door between 8:30 and 8:45. Pupils must come through side doors. To come through the front door between 8:30 and 8:45 is a serious offense. Please make sure that all understand this.

5. Pupils arriving after 8:45, will report to the office, then report to Mr. * (boys) or to Miss * (girls). To fail to do so is a serious matter.

EXCERPTS FROM "GENERAL INSTRUCTIONS TO TEMPORARY TEACHERS" BY THE BOSTON PUBLIC SCHOOLS

SCHOOL PROCEDURE:

Each temporary teacher is expected:

1. To conform to all the rules of the school to which he is assigned.

2. To follow the teacher's program so far as possible and to make no changes without the consent of the principal or the teacher in charge.

TEACHER PREPARATION:

1. Each temporary teacher is expected to do a full day's work. He is to teach the day's lessons, to supplement work already begun, and to make a substantial contribution toward class progress.

2. A temporary teacher assigned for more than one day is expected to have a carefully prepared plan written out for the second day and each day thereafter. He is to keep these plans on file in a Progress Book for the information of the Department of Teacher Placement. Failure to keep such plans is indicative of the teacher's lack of fitness for substitute work.

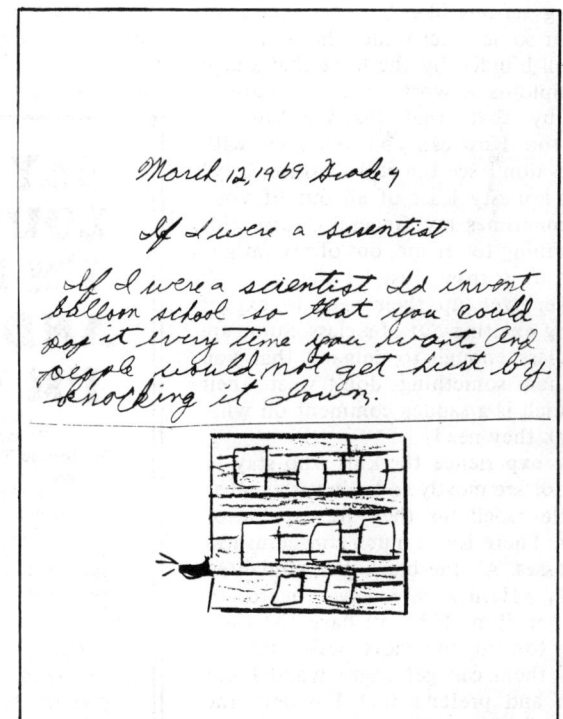

March 12, 1969 Grade 4

If I were a scientist

If I were a scientist I'd invent balloon school so that you could pop it every time you wanti And people would not get hurt by knocking it down;

Old Mole 4/11/69

SCHOOL

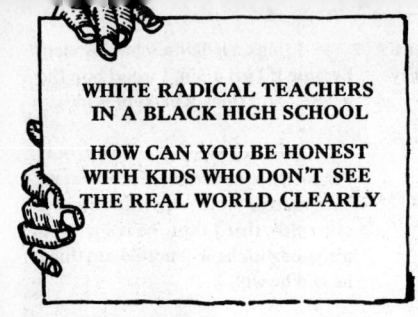

DULLED KIDS

Those kids they call 'dull.' Almost every time you stop in the teacher's rest room for a quick piss between classes, you'll hear some old lady, or even a young lady, tell another, or tell you if you're the only one around, about how she tried a lesson but these kids were too dull to get it. A complaint that is not accompanied by the introspective, 'What do you think I did wrong in presenting it?', of course. Funny thing is, it seems to me that the intelligence level they're condemning, and feeling sorry for themselves—even martyred—about, is *really* exactly a matter of dullness: kids seem to me to have grown dulled, closed up, by the time they're in high school. Anyone with real rebellion, or even real intelligence, has realized that you're not going to get a much better job with a high school diploma than without one, if you're black, or that a diploma only means that you've been in attendance, not that you have a skill. A skill you can get only if you drop out of the phony school, and get into something serious like business school or nursing or some other trade school instead. Those still blinded by the hope that a high school diploma is worth something are so blinded by that, that that's a kind of dullness too. How can you be honest with kids who don't see the real world clearly? Or want honesty least of all out of you? Sadly, sometimes my General Course kids will be willing to let me, out of my fatigue or anger or sorrow, just let the class sit; they have given up their need to expect something exciting out of a class. Some are middle class enough to demand that you 'teach' them something—don't waste their time. Which is a sadder comment on what they think they need?

In my experience the kids who stay in high school are mostly so brainwashed that what little rebellions they are capable of are petty. There is not much consciousness in my classes. All the black girls straighten their hair. Hardly any have heard of Stokeley or Rap. They all have the right attitudes toward the riots—well, not all. Some of them can get angry when I put them on and pretend that I believe the propaganda of my own upbringing: that Europe is the only part-continent worth studying. Fortunately some are still capable of that anger. But it's mostly the freshmen and sophomores. My juniors look at me like, 'Why doesn't she stop that shit and teach us some grammar?' So they won't rebel in ways I try to force them to. But they will have petty attention-demands. A girl will demand a drink of water NOW, just to get you to say that she should wait a minute, so she can *get* you. And if she is docile enough, which a lot of them—too many—are by this time, to accept your busy or harassed or even reasonable suggestion that she wait two minutes until the bell rings, or until attendance is taken, or until the person who's got the pass now comes back with it, she'll whine, and then she'll forget, because the need wasn't real. And that whining is very sad, to me, because I have this feeling that part of what it means to be fully consciously alive is to have a real understanding of your real needs, so you can learn how to go about achieving their fulfillment. The system has made them so used to asking permission for natural functions that they don't know how to just stand up and do something. Or at least they don't any more. They know the punishment for talking out without raising their hands and being called on. They know that the bathrooms in some schools are locked between periods to keep them from smoking. They know that their presence has to be accounted for everywhere, so they cut my classes to challenge me. But they do not challenge my being white. I have never been called 'Whitey' or 'Hunky.' And this is in a predominantly black school in 1967-68! They do what they know they can get away with, within the system: they cut one of the infrequent assemblies, which may be their only opportunity to experience some live music or live drama in this 'rich' city. That's their way of saying, 'Screw you, whitey, and your "culture".' But they don't come out and say that, except by dropping out.

Those who don't drop out keep cool. And turn dull. They rebel how they can, but mostly they just accept what you put down within the system.

The foregoing is from a longer paper by Liz prepared for the Vocations for Radicals conference in Boston in March. For copies, try writing to: New England Free Press, 791 Tremont St., Boston, Mass. 02118

From "School Teaching: The Success of the System" by Liz Fusco *R.I.P.* Newsletter, Fall 1968

SCHOOLS AND PRISONS

There is hope, however, in what George Bernard Shaw said: "Schools and prisons came in together and will go out together." In trying to locate this quotation once again in his introduction to his play, "Misalliance," I got caught up in his witty and provocative essay of 105 pages and had a field day underlining statements as relevant today as ever. "There is, on the whole, nothing on earth intended for innocent people so horrible as school. To begin with, it is a prison. But it is in some respects more cruel than a prison."

But youngsters don't know they have been as conditioned to go to school as cows, who, robbed of their young, are trained to gather at the pasture gate to be relieved each evening of their milk. They are ready to consent to every humiliation and subjection that school imposes because they think it contains the formulas for learning, when its only real resources are the children's own gifts and creative yearnings.

EDWARD P. GOTTLIEB *Fellowship* Jan 1969

SAY IT LOUD— I'M BLACK AND I'M PROUD

Last Friday, a small vigorous young black army from Polytechnic High School — reinforced by ghetto tenagers and Panthers — paraded across San Francisco to present a list of soul demands to the Board of Education.

A white truck driver, standing along the route of march, whispered his surprise into my white ear: "Would ya look at all the spooks." And then turned his head cautiously to see if any blacks had overheard him. Convinced that it was still our secret, he leaned over my way again and warned: "These niggers ain't bullshittin'."

Earlier in the week, twenty-one teachers from Poly presented a list of complaints about conditions there — specifically pimping, prostitution, drug dealing, and sex in the halls. The students said they were stabbed in the back. Led by student body president Greg Durrell, and marshalled by the Black Student's Union, they marched through the Fillmore on their way downtown. A few white youngsters, mostly long-haired girls, locked arms with their black schoolmates, but the march was for blacks and in their idiom.

"Right on, blood." A BSU monitor crouched, threw his head back and fist up in the direction of a handful of salutes coming from the curb. A few black grade-school teachers had their classes out with children's signs: "Keep on pushin'."

The police acted like scoutmasters, patiently assisting the swarms of eager, aggressive black monitors who directed traffic; making little suggestions. The city figured it all out ahead of time. All demands were agreed to except outright firing of the twenty-one teachers for expressing their opinions. The auditorium in the Board of Education building on Van Ness was opened for the Poly negotiating team to rap the victory story to the students. Reporters and photographers were excluded, and barely managed to hide their ruffled feathers. Finally, city buses were provided for the students to go back to Poly or to Friday's football game.

Poly High will have Swahili taught and soul food served. It was all too easy. The mayor admits to being a black militant himself. The city plays a good liberal game. Concessions to stop the work of Black Panthers in the Fillmore.

"You a reporter. You know. When they ketch a Black Panther, they don't find no ROCK in his pocket."

San Francisco
Express Times 4/11/69

Photographs by The New York Times by JACK MANNING

Students in a psychology class, given at the First Baptist Church in Philadelphia, in connection with the Parkway Program, begun nearly a year ago

Students Flock to Philadelphia 'School Without Walls'

By WILLIAM K. STEVENS
Special to The New York Times

PHILADELPHIA, Jan. 21 — About a year ago, amid great fanfare, high hopes and some skepticism, the Philadelphia school system initiated one of the nation's boldest experiments in public education, the Parkway Program, in which high school students choose their own subjects of study and use the city's institutions and businesses as classrooms.

The program was designed as an alternative means of education for teen-agers who find conventional schools repressive and oppressive and conventional instruction dull and unrelated to their own concerns. It is directed toward students who want to attend college and those who do not.

Now, as the program's first anniversary approaches (the first 140 students were selected by lot from a group of volunteers last Jan. 31), many of its supporters — especially students and parents — feel that the high hopes are mostly being fulfilled.

"For the first time," said one parent, [my son] is actually being educated. He has learned more in his first session than in all his previous years of school. For the first time he likes school."

Final Judgment Deferred

But many of the approving parents have some reservations, often centering on whether the program deals adequately with basic skills like reading and writing and basic disciplines like history and science. Final judgment, in most quarters, is therefore being deferred.

So attractive has been the program's inherent freedom, however, that more than 10,-000 students applied for the 500 places open this year. Partly because of this response, other cities are considering the merits of the program. One, Chicago, will open its own "school without walls" on Feb. 2.

Essentially, the philosophy behind the Parkway Program is that people learn only what they want to learn, not what someone else imposes on them, and that they learn best by grappling directly with the rich material in the world around them.

"School is not a place but an activity, a process," says John Bremer, the 42-year-old, British-born director of the program. He further conceives of school as "a service organization" whose function is to help the student as he pursues his own self-initiated learning scheme.

The Parkway Program "is an attempt to break down the dichotomy between living and learning, and to that extent it's extremely significant," says Mario Fantini, who has been monitoring the project for the Ford Foundation. The foundation helped the program to get started with a $100,000 grant.

'Not a Total Solution'

"It's an important option for kids who aren't profiting from school," Mr. Fantini said, "but it's not a total solution. For some kids it may work, for others it may not."

The program is set up this way:

Students are organized into four "communities," each of which is governed informally through a "town meeting" held once a week. Teachers and students together decide what courses will be offered.

Credits in broad subject areas such as English and social studies are required so state demands may be met, but within each general area students decide what, specifically, they are to study.

"Alpha" community, the original group of Parkway students, now offers 95 separate courses—many of them conventional academic and vocational subjects, many of them unknown to the ordinary high school. Some examples of the latter are psychology of the adolescent, game theory, computer programing and a seminar on Vietnam.

There is also an encounter group, in which students attempt to strip away each other's psychological defenses and communicate more directly and openly. Many courses involve social service projects, for example working with post-psychiatric patients or the aged.

"Classes" are held at various sites around the city — newspaper offices, hospitals, an art museum, university laboratories, corporate offices, print shops, garages, a drama institute, a music academy, to mention some — where workers, managers and professionals in the adult world become volunteer teachers.

More-or-less conventional classes are conducted by certified teachers in churches and lofts.

There are no grades, except for pass or fail. Teachers assess students' progress on a personal basis, and students evaluate teachers' performance. If a student does not like a class he can drop out and attend another one. Some do.

Equality between student and teacher is not only encouraged but is pursued almost fiercely. Sometimes it is difficult to distinguish long-haired, bearded teachers from teen-agers. Students call instructors by their first names and in general wear their newly found equality like a badge.

Help Is Available

In one class yesterday, a student challenged a teacher's statement with an expletive that would have got him thrown out of some schools. The teacher, obviously used to such things and not in the least disturbed, simply entered into what turned out to be a rational discussion with the student.

"If you need help, the teachers will help you," 15-year-old Janet Sloan said as she sat and talked in Alpha group's cluttered headquarters at 1801 Market Street yesterday. "There's no attitude like 'It's just another stupid 15-year-old, so what's the difference!'"

Some students complain that they detect such attitudes in ordinary classrooms.

Some parents worry that their children are not independent enough to handle the increased freedom and responsibility; that they flounder and need more direction. Students say some classes degenerate into bull sessions. In some instances, classes turn into a routine lecture, and students usually are quick to call the teacher to task for it.

There is no objective way so far to determine, in traditional terms, how much and how well the students are learning. The major indication along these lines is expected to come when students who have spent most of their high school careers in the Parkway Program take college entrance examinations. This is what leads many parents to suspend judgment.

Some Parents Concerned

Despite their children's liking for the program, some parents are concerned lest it fail to provide a solid subject-matter undergirding and philosophical framework for what the students learn from their encounters with the city's life.

"There is considerable value to learning by doing, by touching, feeling, making mistakes, etc.," one parent wrote in a generally favorable critique, "but often this has the limitation of provoking only a superficial or surface knowledge."

"On this," said Mr. Fantini of the Ford Foundation, "we'll just have to wait and see what happens. To just make the students happy and deny them the skills they need to survive in a technological society, well, that's not fair."

The New York Times

1/23/70

27

SCHOOLS VERSUS EDUCATION

A DISCUSSION OF THE FILM HIGH SCHOOL

By Richard S. Fuller

Frederick Wiseman is a lawyer turned film-maker who has a way of stirring people up with his cinema verite movies. Cinema verite, the technique of trying to record with handheld camera and sound equipment the reality of people and situations, has become something of a fad these days. Everyone seems to be shooting a movie in this so-called style. The problem is, most of the films shot in this style have little or no style. They ramble on, showing us "real" people ostensibly doing "real" things. They aren't very convincing, usually.

Wiseman's film *High School* is another matter. He wanted to do a documentary on a large urban high school. A good one. He went to the Board of Education in Philadelphia and was given a choice of schools. He chose Northeast High, where he spent five weeks and shot over forty hours of film. The edited film runs seventy-five minutes. It is a mosaic, for those who have forgotten, of the World of High School: the classes and teachers and gym sessions and advisors and hallways and detentions. Wiseman catches it all with a camera that is remarkably unobtrusive. Only a couple of teachers "perform" for the camera. One touch catches the essence of my memory of high school, when the clock forever moved in slow motion: Wiseman's camera drifts about a classroom, gazing at students' faces, and then moves in for a close-up of a kid's watch.

Boredom is one of the film's major themes. The other is suggested by the title of this piece, which is a quote from the film. A girl is being verbally chastised because her dress is too short. At the senior prom, *all* girls will wear long gowns and *all* boys will wear tuxedoes. "It's nice to be individualistic," says a male teacher. And then the girl gives her classic reply.

I saw the film with three high school students: Steven Porter, a senior at Newton South High School in Newton, Massachusetts; Fred Bigger, a sophomore at Dorchester High Annex in Dorchester and Kathryn Humphrey, a junior at Newton North High School, also in Newton. We began with initial reactions to the film.

STEVE: I've seen it three times. It's a very frightening experience because I go through it every day. I go to a high school which maybe practices what you see in that movie in a more subtle way so that one can't see it. We don't have the emasculation that goes on in that film, the treatment of students not as people.

You can't just be anyone in school. You have to be something the school wants you to be. This is, I think, one of the worst things a high school does.

RICHARD: For you the movie is aptly titled *High School*. It is representative. It's not just Northeast High.

STEVE: Right. It's found everywhere, no matter where you go. It just takes different forms.

RICHARD: What was your reaction, Fred?

FRED: This was the first time I saw it. In a way, it's just like my school. It's telling how schools are. Some people don't believe that. They think the teachers are all good and if they say a child is wrong then the parents believe them. But it's sometimes the teachers, too. Sometimes it is the teachers. Sometimes it is the child. Most of the time it is the teachers, I believe.

KATHRYN: I thought it was a pretty frightening film. It was the first time I had seen it and it was very sickening in many ways. It's a good film to see because when we're caught up in the middle of it, it's difficult to see the overall picture and see what is actually happening to us. I agree with Steve. My school has similar tactics but in a much more subtle way.

FRED: They should show this film to parents instead of pupils so they can find out how school really is.

RICHARD: I was thinking of what you said, Kathie, about being in this situation now. I'm pretty far beyond it and yet it brought out the cold sweat on my forehead—the familiar look of everything, the guy chewing you out, the regimentation. I had forgotten how oppressive it was.

KATHRYN: Don't forget.

RICHARD: Who should see this film?

STEVE: Fred talks about having the parents see it. We showed it to our parents. Their reaction was, "Oh, my God. This isn't our high school."

KATHRYN: But how many parents would look at it and say, "Well, what's wrong with that? That's fine. I'd be very proud to have my kid go to that type of high school. They have very fine upstanding students. They keep them on the right path straight towards—"

RICHARD: Vietnam.

KATHRYN: Yes, honorable and noble. Be a man and follow orders. Learn to take orders.

RICHARD: The prevailing feeling I got is that you're being policed constantly.

STEVE: In my school you don't get policed, but you have something behind you. There is this thing that's there all the time. It's very hard to say what it is. But it's there and you know that if you don't fulfill certain obligations which they have set up you're not going to make it. You're not going to be a well-off middle-class individual, which is supposedly what you are trying to become. You've never been told to become anything else. In my school, you are told there are a lot of jobs you can do that you don't need a college education for. But in Newton you've got to go to college. Otherwise you failed in Newton.

KATHRYN: It's like you can't be a whole person unless you go to college.

RICHARD: This pressure that you feel constantly—are parents feeling it too? Who is putting this pressure on them?

KATHRYN: It started way back.

FRED: They were pressured so they figure we should be pressured too. One of the parents in the film said her mother taught her a certain way. Now she's going to teach her child. This is a different time. We're not living back in the old times. She has to teach her some new way.

KATHRYN: If it's good enough for me, it's good enough for them.

FRED: Yes, that's what they say. It's not that way, though.

RICHARD: Some of the people who have commented on the film have mentioned the classroom scenes where the camera closes in on the faces of students while a teacher reads "Casey at the Bat" or the young teacher plays a Simon and Garfunkel song. Do the kids seem bored?

FRED: Yes, they seem bored. They're listening to some corny old poem. Who wants to hear it? Half of them are going to sleep. You can see it.

RICHARD: That made me think of my seventh grade.

KATHRYN: I think I had that in fifth grade. And then the smug look on the teachers' faces, like they're doing this noble service. I wondered how many of the teachers were there because they enjoyed young people.

STEVE: We come to school so they can get money. They're supposedly in school for us. The schools were made for us. We weren't made for the schools. We're not coming to school for them. Of course, that's not in practice anywhere.

KATHRYN: There's no reason why it shouldn't be just as much an educational experience for the person supposedly playing the role of teacher as it would be for the person supposedly playing the role of student. They're roles. They're games that go on constantly and they're so sickening. In some ways I didn't want to watch the film because once the bell rings in school I'm very glad to be out.

FRED: Everybody runs for that door.

RICHARD: I remember those bells. The afternoon would stretch out infinitely long and the big clock would sit up there—

FRED: Some kids have their watches and count down, you know, how many more seconds before they get out of school.

RICHARD: This is horrible. We spend so much time in schools; we spend money building expensive plants. How can we get out of this bind?

STEVE: It's going to take a major revolution in education. The administration, the faculty, the people on school committees have all failed to justify why we are going to school. They have never satisfactorily answered the question: Why are we sending students to school? They don't know why. This is why we're so confused. This is why no one seems to be doing anything right. This is why people are destroyed in school, because no one really knows why you are going. Why are you taking mathematics? Why are you taking algebra two? Why are you taking calculus? What is the purpose of all this? You do it so you can get a better job. You can go to college, get a better job, make more money, buy a car, be a consumer, be a good American. The horrible thought is that maybe there is no justification for our going to these schools. Maybe there is no justification for high schools to exist, and we've been going up a wrong alley for a long time.

FRED: The teacher should make the class interesting instead of boring. I had a history teacher. He tells about Alexander. He doesn't read it out of a book. He tells how Alexander went wild and killed his best friend. Then he cries a little, he screams, he throws his pointer. Everybody likes it. Everybody in his course passes.

KATHRYN: The thing that I object to so much in schools is that all they do is prepare you for tests and the tests are testing what you don't know. They're not testing what you do know.

FRED: With this teacher, you can't help remembering. We had him in the last period and the bell was going to ring. Everyone wanted to hear what happens.

STEVE: He's an exception, though. There are very few good teachers like that. In the film, with the chick who was playing the Simon and Garfunkel song, the kids were just as bored with that as with "Casey at the Bat." You don't pick something you consider relevant material and then shove it down kids' throats.

KATHRYN: She had it all planned on the board. You fill in the blanks.

STEVE: Yes. She wants you to fill in as you listened to the record. Don't listen to the record for what it is but listen to it so you can tell what the metaphors were or the similes. This is not an education. This is just breaking things down into little patterns so you can recollect when someone asks you what a simile is. I can't

deny that any bit of knowledge would have use.

KATHRYN: The film is good because it shows the physical limitations and the terrible bells and that everybody looks so much alike. They all look alike and dress alike. You don't wear a cocktail dress, you wear a long formal gown to a school function. They emphasize the terribleness of the physical limitations and they very cleverly show you what's wrong with the whole system, the whole philosophy of school. If we get to the point of changing the physical but not the philosophical thing, we're going to be in bad shape. We'll think we've reached where we're going and we haven't.

RICHARD: That may be even more sinister.

STEVE: It is. The thing is, the high school is not a separate entity. The high school is a reflection of the society which created high schools, the society which

gives it its teachers, its students, its administration, its rules. These are all from the society. If you think that the movie is sick and the high schools are sick, this is just part of the society. It's not something divorced from the society. High schools have lost their meaning. They've become sort of halfway houses for wayward boys and girls on their way to college or on their way to the draft or jobs. By the time you're a senior in high school, you sort of know where you're going and your chances.

KATHRYN: It's pretty easy to succeed if you just let yourself be a machine and go through all the motions. If you have a good memory, you'll go through high school beautifully.

Note: The film can be rented from OSTI FILMS/264 Third Street/Cambridge, Mass. 02142.

colloquy March 1970

High School Rights

A coalition representing the massive 275,000-strong high school student body of New York has presented the Board of Education with the nationally known *High School Bill of Rights* demanding greater freedom in the high schools and a bigger role for students in determining all aspects of the educational process.

At the same time, the Board of Education and high school principals have launched a concerted effort to discredit the coalition, to impugn its members, and to prevent them from distributing informational leaflets.

These "educators," according to the Feb. 25 *New York Times*, described the high school rights bill as "the work of a small group of extremists and outsiders seeking to gain control of the high school system."

It is far from the truth. The formation of the High School Students Rights Coalition (HSSRC) represents an eruption of the profound discontent of tens of thousands of students oppressed and virtually imprisoned in New York's police-occupied schools. It follows months of previously unorganized attempts to improve the schools in dozens of areas which desperately need improvement; and it culminates intensive discussion between leading student government representatives and activists in the antiwar and Third World movements.

A glance at some of the Bill of Rights demands reveals the extent of symbolic expression, to choose their own dress, conduct and personal appearance.

* "Students may form political and social organizations, including those that champion unpopular causes, shall be free from discrimination on the basis of ethnic background, sex, group membership, economic class, place of residence or any other personal factor.

* "Students and their parents shall have the right to file complaints against school officials, shall have the right to security of their persons, papers, and effects against arbitrary searches and seizures.

* "Students shall be free from the illegal use of police by school officials.

* "All students shall have the right to receive information on abortion and contraception, the right to receive information on drugs, the right to

draft counseling at their school."

The Board of Ed got a taste of the determination and militancy of student rights supporters when the board held a Feb. 26 public hearing at New York City Community College on its proposed "Responsibilities of Senior High School Students (Amended)."

More than 500 students and their parents came to the hearing and effectively turned it into a discussion on the High School Bill of Rights, which would give students genuine rights of self-government, not the token ones offered in the Board of Ed's plan.

During the discussion, every student speaker and many of the adults expressed support for the High School Bill of Rights. As Julian Gonzalez, a representative of the General Organization at John Jay High School, put it, the Bill of Rights "is a step toward guaranteeing high school students the same rights as accorded all U.S. citizens. These rights will make student government what it is supposed to be, a student government."

Mike Weisman, national high school Student Mobe coordinator, described how the repressive nature of school administrations denies the right of students to organize against the war in Vietnam. The high schools will be major organizing centers for building the spring antiwar offensive, declared SMCer Julie Simon.

An indication of the explosive situation occurred recently at George Washington High School in upper Manhattan. On March 2, parents, students, and a few teachers attempted to set up tables at the predominantly Black and Puerto Rican school in order to get a sense of student grievances. After being refused by the administration, the group succeeded in shutting down the school.

(The High School Rights Coalition can be contacted at the SMC headquarters, 857 Broadway, Room 307, New York, N.Y. 10003.)

Note: the centerspread of this issue carries the full text of the High School Bill of Rights. It is designed to be used as a book cover.

—dick roberts &
derrick morrison/
the militant

USE THIS
SPACE
FOR
DOODLING
↓
(THAT MEANS
DRAWING)

High School Bill of Rights

1. STUDENTS HAVE THE RIGHT TO EXERCISE ALL RIGHTS ENUMERATED IN THE UNITED STATES CONSTITUTION, THE BILL OF RIGHTS AND ALL OTHER AMENDMENTS AND THOSE ESTABLISHED BY THE UNITED STATES SUPREME COURT.

II. STUDENTS HAVE THE FULL FREEDOM OF POLITICAL ACTIVITY IN THE HIGH SCHOOLS.

1. Students may form political and social organizations in the school, including those which champion unpopular causes and regardless of the political and social views of the organization.

2. Students have the right to full use of school facilities—bulletin boards, auditoriums, public address systems, mimeo facilities—to advertise their ideas and activities that take place inside and outside the high schools.

3. Students have the right to plan and carry out forums, assemblies, seminars and other school programs in order to expand the educational process. These are to be carried out at a time chosen by the students. Speakers may not be rejected by administrators and/or faculty.

4. Students have the right to distribute any leaflets, pamphlets and political material freely inside and outside the school and school grounds without authorization of the principal or any body of the school administration or the Board of Education.

5. Students have the right to wear any symbol of their political beliefs, such as buttons, armbands, and style of dress which express their opinions.

6. Students have the right to choose their own method of expressing their beliefs and to refrain from saluting the flag or from attending any assemblies which they so desire.

7. Students have the right to strike.

III. STUDENTS HAVE THE RIGHT TO FREEDOM OF SPEECH AND THE PRESS.

1. Student publications must be controlled by the students and may in no way be censored by the administration or faculty. Editing will be done by the student editors. Any student organization has the right to have access to the school newspaper to advertise its ideas and activities.

2. Student publications (newspapers and magazines) which are not "official" school publications are to be treated with the same rights as (1) above with full use of school facilities to produce and distribute them.

IV. STUDENTS HAVE THE RIGHT TO DUE PROCESS.

1. Students have the right to a fair hearing which includes representation by counsel, with the right to question witnesses *prior* to any disciplinary action. The hearing shall conform to all present laws pertaining to court procedure.

2. Students may not in any way be penalized by administration or faculty for any political or moral beliefs which they have or upon which they act.

3. Students have the right to receive annually upon the opening of school a publication setting forth all the rules and regulations to which students are subject. This publication shall contain a statement of student rights.

4. Students and parents have the right to see their personal files at any time.

5. Students have the right to appeal any decision on a disciplinary action with a transcript of the trial provided by the school administration.

V. STUDENTS HAVE THE RIGHT TO FREE ELECTIONS IN THE SCHOOLS.

1. Students shall have the right to run in any school election for any office. There shall be an end to arbitrary administration requirements and screening of candidates.

2. All students in the school shall have the right to vote. Scheduling of balloting shall occur at a time when all students are present during regular school hours.

3. All candidates shall have the right to wage a real campaign with full use of school facilities to freely advertise their full election platform.

VI. STUDENTS HAVE THE RIGHT TO END HIGH SCHOOL COMPLICITY WITH THE WAR MACHINE.

1. The student body has the right to be free from the presence of any influence of federal agencies not directly involved in the educational process.

2. There shall be an end to all military programs like ROTC in the schools and to all military recruiting in the high schools.

3. There shall be an end to the use of police to settle disputes within the schools.

VII. STUDENTS HAVE THE RIGHT TO HELP DETERMINE THEIR CURRICULUM AND EVALUATE THEIR TEACHERS.

1. There shall be no discrimination on the basis of sex.

2. The tracking system shall be abolished.

Homestead High Smothers Student Rights

By Dennis Gall

Elliott Jones learned two things at Homestead High, and he learned them the hard way. He learned that the great American Rhetoric about the sacred and almost awesome bill of rights is just that—mostly rhetoric. And Elliott Jones learned that when you deal with the administration, they have all the trump cards.

Elliott is the head of the United Liberation Force (USLF) at Homestead High School. The purpose of USLF is to change the system existent in the suburban and rural high schools. USLF wants many changes; abolition of the present grading system, freedom to dress as one pleases, freedom to speak and discuss any issues, an y time, freedom to wear long or short hair, and a general reorganization of the curriculum to make it more relevant to the students and to involve the students in the decision making process. "We will have change—if necessary, at any price." This militant attitude has the administration at Homestead running scared and they have reacted to it in the same fashion as hundreds of other school administrators—with repression.

Elliott started out small. He published a one page mimeo sheet entitled "A Leaf, Let Us Turn Over." It came out on Dec. 22. The administration reacted. Copies of the Open Door (a radical high school paper in Milwaukee) were confiscated from Elliott's locker. Elliott along with Bill Bailey put out their second issue on Dec. 29. The administration reacted again. They proposed and passed what the USLF call the "oppressive bills."

According to the oppressive bills, which were passed just after the second issue of "A Leaf," the administration of Homestead has the authority to suspend or expel "any student who through his actions, behavior, dress, or presence shall disrupt the normal routines of any school activity...or who follows a course of conduct which may become disruptive." The USLF petioned against the bills, but the general apathy of most Homestead students assured their passage.

Elliott didn't stop, however, and a third issue of "A Leaf," appeared on the first of January. Elliott was called in to see Mr. Dixon, the principal of Homestead and warned that his radical activities were not appreciated. Elliott persisted, and printed his fourth paper, now called "Rap Unlimited." Elliott was immediately suspended and threatened with expulsion if his "agitation" continued. Bailey was threatened with suspension if he continued.

Elliott described his experiences with the administration at Homestead for us: "Their tactics have ranged from co-option to hardline and blatant repression. In trying to co-opt us, they have tried to resolve differences by means of closed discussions where they can channel our revolutionary attitude into harmless discussions where they don't have to respond to our grievances. In this way they can keep us from leafleting, distributing underground newspapers, rapping with students, under the pretence that the "problem" is being studied. The administration has tried to root out and destroy dissenting students and those with whom they do not agree."

Elliott is back in school now and though he's had to concede outwardly, his attitudes haven't changed. "The USLF may have been dealt a severe blow at Homestead but the organization as embryonic as it is, is moving forward, organizing at other suburban schools educating kids to the nature of this ridiculous prison-like school system, and its relationship to the contradictions in the bureaucratic society (war, racism and the draft)."

Elliott also learned that it's not a bed of roses being an unsung martyr. Most of the students at Homestead, though they may agree that something's radically wrong with their school and with the establishment in general, are too afraid of being suspended themselves to openly support Elliott. The USLF is part of a nation-wide assault on the American high schools. The Milwaukee Student Alliance, which publishes the "Open Door," is also involved in radicalizing the student. These young people see the world that they are being prepared to face, and realize in their own minds that all the administration wants to do is mold them into fine upstanding citizens. Since this idealistic, and often hypocritical life no longer appeals to these students, they no longer find their education relevant. The problem lies not so much in the high schools, though strict dress codes, repressive rules and nonsense courses, irritate many students but lies in the basic moral question facing America. Can a nation that is supposedly based on liberty, equality, and individual freedom survive when it enslaves its black people, sends its young off to fight in a meaningless war, and everybody makes a mockery of its constitution? That's the problem. And that's the problem Elliot and others like him face today.

kaleidoscope 2/27/69

Milwaukee Student Alliance

The Milwaukee Student Alliance is an attempt on the part of high school students from all over Milwaukee to come together to discuss our mutual problems and act as a force for social change within the schools. We spend twelve of the most formative years of our lives within the public school system and therefore feel that it is both our right and our obligation to examine that institution critically and act upon our critique, demanding that the schools enhance our development as individuals and our interaction as a community.

Many of us have been asking ourselves questions such as what is the purpose of grades, dress codes, smoking regulations, required courses, and required study halls, (to name just a few). Are they aiding our development as people, or are they teaching us to keep our mouths and minds shut and toe the line? Are our teachers rewarded for their ability to generate intellectual excitement within the classroom or for being faithful servants to the administration and good disciplinarians? Are we bored in school because learning about ourselves and our world is intrinsically boring or because we are truly learning neither? Why does genuine student concern and initiative, such as the Washington leafleting or Marshall newspaper, strike such terror into the hearts of school administrators?

These are the kinds of questions we are exploring, and this paper represents our first attempt to articulate and communicate our dissatisfaction. We still have a long way to go both in our ability to communicate exactly what is bothering us and in our efforts to bring an end to these conditions. We need your help.

Join Us!

. . . . . .

Those interested in working on the newspaper or joining the discussion groups should call or come by the Milwaukee Student Alliance office: 1536 N. Jackson; Tele. 271-8687.

From *The Open Door* Milwaukee underground high school paper Oct '68

THE VOICES OF TEEN-AGERS IN 1966 57% SAID THEY WOULD LIVE AWAY FROM HOME IF THEY COULD

Those adults who least understand kids are often those closest to them: teachers and parents. Perhaps that's because teen-agers "don't trust anyone over 30"; 81 percent say they behave differently around adults. Jackie Vandre, 14, of Denver, Colo., says, "I'm not afraid to talk about anything with kids. At home, I get sat on if I say the wrong thing." Lynn Holland, 18, of Martinsville, Va., catalogs adolescent camouflage: "Act well-adjusted and well-behaved, be sort of a hypocrite, try to win adults' confidence. They can help you someday if you're nice." Don't bother, grumps another boy: "Adults aren't much of a challenge, a matter of not wasting time with a blank wall."

Barriers like these prevent dialogue between adults and teen-agers. They shut each other out. The kids wear disguises; they treat parents as indispensable institutions, not as whole beings. Parents don't, or won't, listen to them. Jay Dunham, 19, of Manchester, N.H., is bitter: "Few would accept what I say and defend it to another adult." Dave Hull, an afternoon disc jockey at KRLA in Pasadena, Calif., gets up to 10,000 calls an hour from teen-agers. Some telephone just to chat because, they say, no one at home talks to them. Carole Levine, who has never called Dave Hull, lives in Queens N.Y. She groans, "My

mother says, 'Who's going to listen to a lousy, snot-nosed 17-year-old girl?' She just 'yeses' me to death when I talk—doesn't hear a thing."

What do teen-agers say about their parents? Listen: They describe them as "too status seeking, too money conscious"; "too content, too passive." They say they are narrow-minded, less educated, less worldly, less happy, less urbanized, more materialistic, more conforming than the young.

"I don't think adults value and seek anything. They just live," cracks Alan Rottersman, 18, of Atlanta. "They don't have any real goals." Albert Gore, 18, son of Sen. Albert Gore of Tennessee, says, "Democracy is a fetish with them to the exclusion of enlightened social change." Carol Taylor, also 18, of Washington, D.C., goes on: "They seek the security of believing there is a Good and a Bad, and that there is a set order to life." Ed Kapinos sees them this way: "Sometimes, they are horribly weird with their friends. I look at them and say, 'You're not like that.' "

And most aren't. Despite misunderstandings, despite bitterness, teen-agers like their parents. Fifty-two percent admit their "strong" influence. When they worry, teen-agers turn to their parents as often as to their friends. (Only one said he turned to his clergyman.) Few wear clothes parents object to, but there are complaints, "My father is over-protective," says pert, blue-eyed Signe Anderson in the Candlelight, a soda stop. "He thinks I should go around in bobby sox and ribbons."

True to past generations, these teen-agers—some 46 percent—claim that adults don't set an example to be followed.

"They try," explains Ted Mesmer, the moustached lad, "but I'm not going to follow when they can seriously talk about the destruction of other countries."

Most have friends their parents don't like. Mercedes Mattsen, 16, of Boston, wearing large gold earrings dangling from pierced ears, an imitation Slavic-print dress with puffed sleeves, and sandals, illustrates: "I ask my friends over, like my mother suggests. Then when they get here, mother takes one look, screams, 'What will the neighbors think?' and suddenly she doesn't consider them friends any more."

Seventy-nine percent of those surveyed say their parents annoy them; 57 percent say they would live away from home if they could. What do they disagree about? "Everything I do," groans an 18-year-old boy. "They disagree about me." Two high-school girls in Atlanta tick off: "Dates, boys, phone calls, money, who you date and what kind of car he drives." Add to that: clothes, working around the house and grades.

Parents, as these teen-agers tell it, complain about "feet sticking out from under the sheets and when to leave in the morning." Or, "the way boys wear their hair," adds John Morgan, 17, of Richmond, Va. "My father points at a boy from the car and says, 'Isn't she cute.' " Diana Gotcher, 16, of Tucson, Ariz., lists her transgressions, and closes with, "Would you believe that I am selfish, inconsiderate and reckless?"

Parents may see epidemics of adolescent immorality. Teen-agers don't. "I've heard so much about those orgies," says Bill Lineaweaver, 16, of Gainesville, Fla., "and I've been wanting to find one."

Look "Youth Survey" 9/20/66

The school is expected to do what the community cannot do and that is impossible. In the end, we will have to change far more than the schools if we expect to create a new coherence between the experiences of the child and the needs of the community. We will have to rethink the meaning of childhood; we will begin to grant greater freedom and responsibility to the young; we will drop the compulsory-schooling age to fourteen, perhaps less; we will take for granted the "independence" of adolescents and provide them with the chance to live alone, away from parents and with peers; we will discover jobs they

can or want to do in the community—anything from mail delivery to the teaching of smaller children and the counseling of other adolescents. At some point, perhaps, we will even find that the community itself—in return for a minimum of work or continued schooling—will provide a minimal income to young people that will allow them to assume the responsibility for their own lives at an earlier age, and learn the ways of the community outside the school; finally, having lowered the level of compulsory schooling, we will find it necessary to provide different *kinds* of schools, a wider

choice, so that students will be willing voluntarily to continue the schooling that suits their needs and aims.

All these changes, of course, are aimed at two things: the restoration of the child's "natural" place in the community and lowering the age at which a person is considered an independent member of the community. Some of them, to be sure, can be made in the schools, but my sense of things, after having talked to teachers and visited the schools, is that trying to make the changes in schools *alone* will be impossible.

PETER MARIN

CEREMONIES OF HUMILIATION

But youth remains a subject minority denied the legally defensible rights now provided to all other Americans—over 21. We remain unaware of these special disabilities of youth because we have been taught to regard them as special services to the immature for which youth ought to be grateful. But I suspect there are many parents—and I know there are many youngsters—who when they think what the school that serves them is really like, recognize that the compulsory attendance law is, among other things, a very serious restriction.

The compulsory school attendance law gives school regulations the force of law. The quality and spirit of those regulations becomes, therefore, a matter of crucial concern to civil liberty; the liberties involved may seem trivial; but they are all an adolescent has left of the normal supply. The quality is not good; and the spirit is largely a spirit of contempt for youth, and for its feeble and capricious efforts to defend its own dignity.

And things are getting worse rather than better. Richard M. Gummere, Jr., Assistant Director of University Placement and

Career Planning at Columbia University, in a recent article in *The Nation*, discussed the alarming rise in the use of corporal punishment in the schools, which seems to correspond with an increasing meanness in our national spirit. The practice of paddling school children steadily declined from the turn of the century till about 15 years ago, but it seems to have come back as a part of the general punitiveness more conspicuously symbolized by Senator McCarthy and the radical right. Today, the only state that forbids it is New Jersey. School counselors in one relatively slum-free district in California have estimated to me that children are now formally paddled—usually by a vice-principal or a physical education instructor in the presence of another teacher as a scarcely-impartial witness—in eighty per cent of the schools in this district. But nobody really knows how often beatings occur. The California Superintendent of Schools, Max Rafferty, has made frequent public statements supporting the use of corporal punishment; and early this year ten or more junior high school students in Campos Verdes Junior High School near Sacramento...were so badly bruised that the Sacramento Bee for January 14, 1966, a most responsible and un-sensational family newspaper, published photographs of the bare buttocks of two of them so that Bee readers could judge for themselves whether they approved the technique of these zealous public servants. Judging from the letters the Bee received and published, and the refusal of the District Attorney to issue a complaint—he did suggest that the school replace its paddle with a leather strap, which he said would be safer—a lot of them did.

It may be offensively patronizing for me to say at this point that most teachers are decent people—one of the most depressing things about public education is how little difference their obvious decency makes. And I believe that most disapprove of the kind of harassment I have been discussing, though each individual incident is usually defended as having been necessary because some particular teacher insisted that the principal "back him up" in a disciplinary action. What is involved here is not sadism but Eichmannism—that is, a dutiful willingness to do what a job seems to require, or what a superior demands, and a shocking—but very common—and blithe inability to believe that one is personally responsible at all for actions that have become customary within the system. School personnel, for example, often boast to me about how they have personally evaded participation in a degrading event—they have made it clear to the principal, say, that *they* will not serve as witnesses at a paddling—but they hardly ever express any feeling that if they thought it was wrong they ought to have tried to prevent it. If I suggest this, they respond with astonishment rather than embarrassment. I wouldn't really expect them to risk destroying their usefulness to the system, would I?

No, I wouldn't. Despite the many able and intelligent teachers and administrators I have known, I no longer expect so much. I have come to expect certain other virtues, valuable in themselves. I know a great many teachers—some schools are full of them—who genuinely like youngsters, enjoy teaching them, and teach them ably and well. I know a great many—though not as many—administrators who are extraordinarily patient with my criticism and who have gone out of their way to give me

opportunities to express it to their staffs. On the basis of greater experience with public education than mine, they are, I think, simply more fully aware than I of how unlikely it is that their courtesy will result in any significant change.

But I know very few who, when the issue arises during the actual working day, will place the dignity of a student above the interests of harmony, and defend him against humiliation at the hands of their peers—much less their superiors. And that humiliation is unfortunately not the result of occasional mischance. It has, I maintain, become institutionalized in a public school system that has evolved to meet society's demand for a docile and uncritical youth.

The devotion of the schools to docility has become a major source of irony. If our schools had developed a tradition of respect for the persons and the character of their students, those who became critical could have done so while remaining civil; for their dissent would not have turned the social system against them and alienated them from it. But American democracy, though it has so far managed to tolerate an astonishing—and reassuring—level of protest, has not shown itself to be capable of such refinement. Our new protesters, accordingly, are not always quite as civil as either their disobedience or their rights—both of which, perhaps, were withheld much too long. In this respect, Birchfield has so far been very fortunate. More fortunate, I should say, than any community deserves to be in which just growing a beard can make you an outlaw.

RICHARD M. GUMMER, JR., "Discipline in the Dark; On Beating School Children," *The Nation*, 201, p. 442-45, December 6, 1965. From "Our Contemptuous Hairdressers" by Edgar Friedenberg *This Magazine Is About Schools* Aug 1966

The American Hangup

by Ivan Illich

SCHOOLING HAS BECOME A MAD RELIGION IN THE UNITED STATES

The following remarks were made by Ivan Illich, founder of the Centro Intercultural de Documentacion (CIDOC) in Cuernavaca, Mexico, an organization of scholars engaged in the study, analysis, and publication of information about Latin America. His comments were recorded by Eileen Christelow Ahrenholz at Cuernavaca.

Schooling has become a mad religion in the United States. It offers an initiation right to power which is not available to 95 percent of humanity, but which you preach to them as their only salvation. When you North Americans talk to me about education, you speak of a ritual where children sit in a classroom five hours a day, five days a week, ten months a year, for a minimum of twelve successive years. Your schools have become a new established church. Christians once shuddered at the thought of unbaptized babies going to hell. But today, in the United States, it is a dogma that high school dropouts are condemned to the ghetto.

We must not exclude the possibility that schooling may not be a viable answer to the emerging nations' needs for universal education. Perhaps this kind of insight will make it possible to go into a future in which schools as we

know them today will disappear. It is an illusion that the most important learning happens in school. Perhaps the forces which are now expended toward schools should be redirected to education in a broader perspective.

Schooling has become a process of accepted ritual certification for all members of a school society. Schools select those who are bound to succeed and send them on their way with a badge marking them fit. Once universal schooling has been accepted, a person's education is measured by the amount of time and money spent in school rather than what he has really learned. You can't even join the Street Cleaners' Union and work for the Sanitation Department of New York unless you have a high school diploma. You see what a strange religion you profess.

In Latin America, there is a strong tendency to accept this North American myth that all children and teenagers and young adults belong in a school. All over Latin America, there is a growing desire for schooling. What amazes me most is that so many intelligent people see this as a desirable development. I feel a great sin has been committed against these people.

Anyone who has gone through twelve years of schooling has an investment in him of between eleven and seventeen thousand dollars. He has gone through thirteen thousand hours of sitting on a school bench at an average cost of one dollar per hour. This kind of waste of people and time is possible in a rich nation like the United States. But that is the total amount of money available to feed, clothe, and house the median Latin American during his entire life. In the United States, you are concerned about making twelve, fourteen, or sixteen years of schooling available to all your citizens. You can play these kinds of games because you are wealthy, but the rest of the world cannot play them at all.

Schooling is so expensive that it is beyond the greatest hope of two thirds of the people in Latin America. But they are being indoctrinated to believe that unless they can be schooled, they will remain inferior, uneducated persons. The indoctrination of the masses that school is necessary in countries where schooling cannot be economically provided only convinces the majority of people that they are second-class citizens. Schools grade and, therefore, degrade. They make the degraded accept his own submission.

In your country, teachers are beginning to accept what many students have long felt—that the schools only stultify those who manage to pass through them. I do not understand why you equate education with schooling or why you believe that more schooling makes better citizens.

Too often, when we think about quality education, we think about improving or revamping the system of schools. What we need is an alternative to schooling. The first step toward radical educational reform in Latin America will be taken when the educational system of the United States is accepted for what it is: a recent, imaginative social invention historically rooted in America; a recent phenomenon, and perhaps not the best, if one is really concerned about education. But it is difficult now to challenge the school because we are so accustomed to it.

Many discussions of radical alternatives to school-centered formal education upset our notions of society. No matter how inefficient schools are in educating people, it is difficult to get people to see that schools are not necessarily *the* answer to our educational needs.

THERE IS
NO ONE OVER
YOU

'Discipline is a big issue—for parents'

WHAT SCHOOLS SHOULD DO—THE ADULT VIEW

	P	T
Maintaining discipline is more important than student self inquiry	62%	27%
Homework requiring memorizing is good and useful	70	46
Students are justified in feeling there is too much drudgery	32	54
More outside speakers and lecturers should come to school	46	74
Students should do more fieldwork outside of school	48	77

HOW TO HANDLE UNRULY STUDENTS

	S	P	T	Adm
Crack down on them	37%	63%	50%	41%
Try to understand them	56	35	46	54
Leave alone	5	1	*	*
Not sure	2	1	4	5

*Less than 0.5%

S = students P = parents T = teachers Adm = administrators

From a poll in *Life* 5/10/69

What keeps running through my mind is a line I read twelve years ago in a friend's first published story: *The Idea in that idea is: there is no one over you.* I like that line: *There is no one over you.* Perhaps that signifies the gap between these children and their parents. For the children it is true, they sense it: there is no one over them; believable authority has disappeared; it has been replaced by experience. As Thomas Altizer says, God is dead; he is experienced now not as someone above or omnipotent or omniscient or "outside," but inwardly, as conscience or vision or even the unconscious or Tillich's "ground of being." This is all too familiar to bother with here, but this particular generation is a collective dividing point. The parents of these children, the fathers, still believe in "someone" over them, insist upon it; in fact, demand it for and from their children. The children themselves cannot believe it; the idea means nothing to them. It is almost as if they are the first real Americans—suddenly free of Europe and somehow fatherless, confused, forced back on their own experience, their own sense of things, even though, at the same time, they are forced to defy their families and schools in order to keep it.

PETER MARIN

ARE YOU NEXT?

On Thursday, the 17th of October, I was kicked out of school. You guys really messed my mind when I heard no one showed up for the meeting that night. By kicking me out (quite illegally) they accomplished what they set out to do—place fear in all of you. The paper is for you, the students of Sun Prairie High. *Don't cop out now.* Can't you see that's what they wanted? We have people backing us that know what they're doing and are more than glad to help. If you have any doubts about your articles just ask them. They know what's legal and what isn't, and just how much we can get away with.

Of course you're going to get some static. The truth hurts and the administration is really going to be hurting. We are always being told to stand up for what we believe in so what's the reason for not putting out our own paper and speaking our own peace of mind. We've listened long enough—now it's time for them to listen for a while.

All of us will probably get roughed up sooner or later by kids that don't see things our way, but we'll just have to turn the other cheek and try to understand that these kids are victims of the establishment. We will have to try and make these kids see the light. Yes, it will be slow, tedious work but even if we win over one person a month it will be something to be proud of.

A leaflet written by a high school student in Wisconsin

Bright Milwaukee Students Find School Dull and Form Their Own

By WILLIAM K. STEVENS
Special to The New York Times

MILWAUKEE, Feb. 11—Bill Ahlhauser, Belinda Behne, Jim Boulet and 32 other Milwaukee teen-agers — among them some of the brightest and most successful students in the city's most highly regarded public and private schools—believe that much of their high school experience has been a waste of time.

So these three and their companions, 15 to 19 years old, have dropped out of their old schools and formed the Milwaukee Independent School, in which each student chooses what he wants to study, how he wants to study it and where. The school is getting under way this week.

A Growing Revolt

The attempt has inspired no great enthusiasm in public administrators charged with enforcing the state's compulsory attendance law. For the time being, they are considering the students as absent from school. Ultimately, the matter may become a legal test case.

M.I.S., as the school is commonly called, is in the avant garde of educational reform, the latest in a series of attempts in various parts of the country to establish alternatives to conventional schools both public and private, but particularly state-operated ones, that have a virtual monoploy power over most students.

It is a peaceful manifestation of a growing revolt against secondary education as it is practiced in the United States.

"Too many things are done in school only for the school's purposes and not the students," says Bill Ahlhauser, who maintained a 95 average when he attended Marquette High, a prestigious Jesuit parochial school.

"There is an extreme lack of respect for students in many schools. Students' initiative and creativity are impeded and inhibited. It [school] is terribly dull, and the kids are pitted against each other for grades and rank in class."

"Kids are pumped through the system like products, never learning to think at all," says Miss Behne, a slim, animated 17-year-old who until a few weeks ago made A's and B's at John Marshall High School, which is generally regarded as one of Milwaukee's best.

The Basic Premises

Jim Boulet, 18, describes a typical class at Riverside High School, where he was a senior last semester, this way:

"Here was this nice sterile little cubicle, and you'd turn your mind off when you went inside. When you got out you'd turn it back on. What went on [in the classroom] had nothing to do with the world, and they called this learning."

The new school is based on these premises: that all students have serious personal interests; that these interests should be the starting point for education; that they should be developed and enriched by first-hand contact with human life, and that the function of reading, writing and formal academic inquiry is to facilitate this process.

Learning, students say, never stops. It goes on outside school. Consequently, they will spend only a few hours a week in the somewhat delapidated white frame building that they have rented to serve as library, discussion hall and home base.

They have spent most of the last 10 days painting and plastering the inside of the building. And today they got down to the business of planning their programs of study.

Typically, a student will study a given subject under a qualified volunteer from the community—a Shakespearean scholar at one city college, a biochemist at another, an artist, an electronics engineer from a private concern, for example. About 90 such volunteer teachers have agreed to take part.

In addition, some students will learn by holding part-time jobs, others by living for brief periods in specialized settings. Jim Boulet, for example, wants to study religion. So he plans to live in a monastery, then with a rabbi, then with a minister.

Communication Stressed

All the students are to undertake individual projects tied to their own interests, some of them consisting of conventional research and some dealing with community matters, such as planning a recreation center.

There will be a special emphasis on the development of basic communications skills, such as analytical reading, invective writing and coherent speech.

The students are being aided in working out their programs by Paul H. Krueger, who left his post as a professor of education at the University of Wisconsin's Milwaukee campus to become full-time coordinator of the school, and two students from his former department.

Mr. Krueger's salary is being paid by community donations. So far, $4,500 has been raised. About $40,000 is needed. Although the school is tuition-free, some parents have made contributions.

This experiment in educational self-determination is closely allied to the development of student-operated "free universities" and experimental colleges in recent years.

Such schools have been set up, for example, in Syracuse, Rochester and Cortland, N. Y.; Palo Alto, Calif., and Washington. More recently, parents of elementary schoolchildren in New York and Washington have taken their children out of conventional schools and organized their own classes.

The new school here has been greeted by parents of its students with a mixture of enthusiasm and foreboding. Some sympathize with their children's concerns but worry about the risks involved. Others are out-and-out converts.

One public school administrator, Theodore J. Kuemmerlein, who is assistant superintendent for pupil personnel, feels this way:

"Anytime your top students leave school, it concerns you. It makes you wonder what we're not offering to meet their needs."

Mr. Kuemmerlein, who is charged with enforcing the compulsory school attendance law in Milwaukee, has ruled that unless and until the new school is declared a bona fide school under state law, its students are to be considered absent. Just who has the authority to make the bona fide declaration seems unclear, he said.

This raises a fundamental question: Who should determine what education is?

The students take the position that they themselves should. Mr. Kuemmerlein said that the City Attorney was considering the matter, and that could eventually go to court.

The students believe that what goes on in their former schools, for the most part, is not education. According to

them, negative features of conventional schooling include emphasis on pleasing and out-guessing the teacher, rather than on discovering, exploring and thinking; an almost total divorcement of school work from reality as perceived by students and an over-reliance on grades.

These views are closely aligned with those of high school students in other parts of the country.

Premium on Conformity

In a much-noted critique delivered to the Montgomery County, Md., school board a year ago, students charged that their system—generally regarded as one of the best in the nation—was based on fear of bad grades and on an insistence on blind obedience. They also said that the schools placed a premium on conformity."

Timothy A. Simone, an 18-year-old graduate of Germanown High School here talked with the Maryland students two summers ago. A year later he became the prime organizer of the new school here. He was joined by Bill Ahlhauser as co-coordinator, and they set about bringing the school into existence.

They wrote to colleges all over the country to inquire about how enrollment in the school here would affect chances of a student's admission. Many, including Harvard University, replied thet it would have no adverse school here would affect effect. One, Fordham University, said it it would enhance a student's chances.

Some of the students plan to take standardized college entrance examinations when the time comes, and most are confident they will have no trouble with them because they can be "crammed" for.

When the word got around in Milwaukee that the new school was about to start, 80 students applied for the 35 places available. The 35 were chosen by lot. They turned out to be the sons and daughters of white, middle-class families, although two blacks had applied.

Many of the students know with some certainty what studies they are going to pursue. But for others, Mr. Kreuger says, there may be initial problems in getting used to a nonrigid, nonauthoritarian arrangement.

But although the risks seem high and success is unassured there appears to be little chance that many of the students will go back to conventional schools.

The New York Times 2/13/70

...in principle the school has no other educational resources than those which exist outside the school...The sort of material that instructs children or adults outside of school is fundamentally the same sort that has power to instruct within the school...

JOHN DEWEY *Lectures* 1899

We need to get kids out of the school buildings, give them a chance to learn about the world at first hand. It is a very recent idea, and a crazy one, that the way to teach our young people about the world they live in is to take them out of it and shut them up in brick boxes.

JOHN HOLT in the *Saturday Evening Post*

The Liberation of Bronx H.S. of Science

todd gitlin

For Joe Blum, Bronx High School of Science '58

New York, a gargantuan dog-corpse of wires and dark places, chewing itself. Still there, New York, and will be until the great tidal wave — when, o Lord? — bounds up one inch too many and suddenly all the victims are dashed smashing against the perpetrators, the cleaning lady against David Goliath Rockefeller, everyone goes down at once as natural history substitutes for class war and men, women and children, without regard to race, creed, color or national origin, realize too late it is too late for New York and subside bloated onto the scummy surface....

I don't like New York, never did in all the sixteen years I lived there, and I had a terrible time there this trip, thanks. One day I tried to type the word "kissed" and it came out "killed" and that was a typo I don't think I'd ever made before. I would bore you telling you all the things I didn't like. Mostly it's that in New York everything already seems to have happened, long since decided, and people are

very busy living out the consequences. Nothing seems to change except the borders of the ghetto and the number of cops.

But this time the teachers were on strike, the third strike this semester, out for all but eleven days. Images of "disintegration" and "ungovernability" suddenly came into focus: one million (1,000,000) public school students locked out; parents occupying schools; a liberal teacher passing a pile of dog turds in Central Park and placing a sign there: "Lindsay Was Here."

I come from a teacher family. To them the strike is a vast and grievous interruption, but a necessity too, because the uppity black governing board in Ocean Hill-Brownsville had asserted its right to hire and fire teachers and nothing is more sacred to a New York teacher than security. The New York teachers have built a union to safeguard their guild status and they now insist, brandishing their normal-school certificates, that they and only they know what and how and even why to teach. Not to be unsympathetic toward the teachers: they wasted all that time in school, they have to believe there was a purpose to it. The teachers

are devoted to the myth that professional status confers purpose; how can you think that your work is waste or worse than waste?

The blacks have the nerve to know that their children aren't being educated, by ANY standards, that each grade their children fall farther behind the whites' (a hard fact that the white teachers prefer not to notice, or prefer, rather, to turn upside down into an accusation against the black kids). The teachers divorce their profession from its function: they proclaim on their banners the "right to teach," disregarding the patent evidence of their failure. Failure they rationalize into arrogance, the staple of an agent-client relationship: if the client bridles, he is an ape and an ingrate. In this case, he must also be an anti-Semite: two-thirds of the United Federation of Teachers' 55,000 members are Jewish. If black anti-Semitism did not exist, it would have to be invented, so that the strike could be clothed as a holy crusade. But I don't pretend to follow all the intricacies of the strike: there is a good summary in an article by Sol Stern in the November 17 Ramparts.

Before I'd heard my family sounding

off, I'd "supported" — in the usual abstract way — the Ocean Hill-Brownsville governing board, although the strike was for me only another newspaper episode. Now the passions of the nouveau labor militants flicked my curiosity: what newfound commitment had driven my quite private mother to tell my grandmother not to buy grapes? Then I got busy — the only way to survive in New York — and I forgot about the whole business.

One day in late October I had occasion to call the office of Liberation News Service, and when I relayed my message the person on the phone asked my name. When I gave it he let out a slight Oh! "Oh! Hey, you were once a valedictorian at Science." (That's what you call the Bronx High School of Science, the school that helped Stokely Carmichael into radicalism sort of the way prison pushed Eldridge Cleaver along.)

In a mock-humble gruff tone, I said, "Yeah, that was a long time ago, and so what, and who are you?"

His name was Dave Graham and he was with the High School Student Union at Science. "Well, we're having liberation classes in the school, and Chuck Pasternak from Newsreel was up shooting a film the other day and he noticed the roster of valedictorians and he pointed out your name."

Liberation WHAT?

"Liberation classes. Supporting Ocean Hill-Brownsville. Look, why don't you come up there and talk to us? We're there every day."

It was the last place I had ever wanted to see again. Immediately I said I would go; I conjured up images of Destiny for the first time in a long time.

*   *   *

Two days later I took the subway up to 200th Street, all the way rehearsing my astonishment so as to be able to learn from it. I knew as much about high school kids (one hears they smoke dope and fuck a lot) as my parents knew about me, but I knew I would feel the liberated, not the liberator, and this was how it should be. I had never much liked being a math whiz, one of those funny myopic kids carrying slide rules on our belts (really!), sneering a lot at the dumb clucks who fell into other schools, reading Riesman and H.L. Mencken and matching College Board scores and pining all the while in some very dark and sealed-off corner of ourselves for a more whole way of being. Even before I got off the IRT I was starting to feel like an old black Mississippi sharecropper watching the first SNCC workers arrive in 1961. When somebody does what all along you wanted to do but dared or could not, that is relief and gratitude and vindication; it is something still grander when somebody does what you didn't even know you wanted at the time.

The Bronx High School of Science looks like a factory and it is the closest its students will ever come to one: about 99% of the graduates go to college. Above the entrance hall, behind glass, is a gigantic mural having something to do with Galileo standing under a rainbow, and people like that. Out in front, about thirty striking teachers were meeting to keep up their stamina on the picket line. I recognized an old math teacher (a left-winger, I later learned), who had been instrumental in building the union: what agony it must be for him now. And there

was the old disciplinarian whose name we used to forge on pass-slips: if he was outside, something good must be going on inside.

I walked to the main doors, naively expecting a roar of solidarity from inside. Instead a sentry-teacher asked my purpose. I said I was an alumnus, invited up by Dave Graham, and I was getting nowhere when another teacher walked up, told me the liberators had to watch out lest anyone from the UFT gain entry in order to gum up the works. He had a neat beard and seemed to be enjoying himself immensely but without the possessiveness teachers usually exhibit to outsiders, and he beckoned me in.

His name was Bob Rossner, teacher of English, maybe in his early 30s — one of the generation swept by the civil rights movement and the stirrings of the New Left. I asked him how the liberated school had come about. When the UFT declared its third strike, the local governing board dutifully voted 8-0 to close the school. (Science students come from all over the city, but the local board thought it had the authority.) Teachers and students who supported Ocean Hill-Brownsville gathered in front of Science and demanded that the janitors, who backed the UFT, let them in. The janitors refused, and locked the doors, whereupon a student who knew the doors would still open from the inside climbed in through a window, made his way behind the line of janitors, said, "Excuse me," and simply opened a door. Liberators poured in and sat down in the hall. Police lined the walls and booted them out.

The liberators remained locked out, according to Rossner, until a couple of students read one night in The New York Times that the state law which decentralized the city schools had left a loophole. The "special schools" (Science, Stuyvesant, Music and Art, Performing Arts, etc.) were left under the jurisdiction of the state. Since the state did not recognize the strike, since in fact the strike was illegal, the schools were legally open, and authority devolved on whomever would keep them open. Rossner said he understood cops better now: once the liberators convinced the cops that they, who wanted the school open, were the duly constituted authority, the cops switched sides to enforce the opening. Servants of the law after all.

The school had been open now for three weeks. There were about 300 students (a little less than one-tenth of the student body) and 20 teachers (about one-eighth). At first, students had insisted on conducting their classes and free-for-all raps in the hall, to break down the mystique of the classroom. After two weeks of it some alliance of traditional-minded students and teachers combined to reinstate a definite class schedule. Most students wanted their science classes continued along the lines of the standard curriculum: they are, after all, college bound. Other classes were redefined: Rossner's own English class was reading Claude Brown's "Manchild in the Promised Land." Students walking through the halls were consulting the dittoed class-list: teachers were encouraging consistency, but the students were still free to choose.

The striking teachers seemed especially threatened by the notion that traditional class trajectories would be dis-

rupted; that fear fused with their bigotry. A popular young social-studies teacher named Schwartz was a distinctive target. As he walked into the school one day, according to Rossner, strikers yelled, "What are you going to teach today, Schwartz — African history?" "Where'd you get your haircut, Schwartz — 125th Street?" Schwartz' class that morning, I noticed, was mobbed.

Once the principal had been shamed into skulking off, the liberated school was being governed by a steering committee of eight students and eight teachers, all elected. They met daily, and their proposals were referred to the next morning's general assembly of all students and teachers. As we walked around in front of the building, smoking, Rossner noticed two students making faces at him from inside; sheepishly he dropped his cigarette and ground it out. He told me that one day a teacher had come upon a couple of students smoking grass in a stairwell. The teacher hadn't threatened the kids, only reminded them that the purpose of the liberated school was to show support for Ocean Hill-Brownsville and that the union would be looking for a pretext to close the school. The steering committee had then decreed that there would be no smoking, OF ANYTHING, BY ANYONE, student or teacher, on school grounds. Fair enough, everyone figured.

Rossner is keeping a diary he expects to be published by Dial Press. When we walked back inside five students were squatting on the floor — as if they owned it! — talking about the affairs of the newly-formed High School Student Union. One girl called him Papa Bear. Rossner said delightedly that he had picked up a phone message in the Office one day — for Dave Graham. His book should be worth reading.

*   *   *

Hierarchy there still is, and I wasn't around long enough to trace it. I was ushered into the Math Department office, where almost ten years ago I had spent many provincially happy hours. The sort-of principal is Henrietta Mazen, a math teacher I remembered distinctly. Mrs. Mazen — I couldn't call her anything else — is the kind of woman you want your mother to be. She is one of the NICEST people around. Flying around in the rush and drama of scheduling, consulting (a precise description of her relation with students), keeping the sometimes perplexed teachers happy, she didn't have much time, but she was glad to take out what she had.

The liberated school was no revolution to her, she's been around too long for that: she supported Ocean Hill-Brownsville but also wanted the school to go on for its own sake. She demarcated herself from the radicals with a plain noncommittal definiteness which signaled respect, as if to say, "We, in our community, differ among ourselves, but no mistake, we are one community." She said she liked seeing the radicals obey the rules now that the rules were of their own making, but she said it without condescending: house mother in a good house. Scrambling to keep things going, her trouble would come if voluntary order became sticky enough, if serious conflicts arose between teachers and students. A striking physics teacher, the one we used to call Bugsy, had decided to join the liberation, and one day thereafter in study hall he had blown his stack and told the kids to fill out regular program cards. "The kids called him down," said Mrs. Mazen, "but he almost jeopardized everything we'd been trying to do. The next day he came back and apologized, told the kids, 'I'm sorry. Please understand we teachers are under a lot of strain.' So we held together."

* * *

Why are the students coming? Certainly almost all want to declare themselves on the side of Ocean Hill-Brownsville. Probably many also fear falling behind. The striking teachers were holding their own hideously-misnamed "freedom schools" in a local Jewish community center — announcing too that THEIR students would be tested on their work. The liberation classes would not be tested: a considerable inducement right there. And then there was that tonic feeling of self-government, a feeling that gets into your blood. Students were coming and going as they pleased, but the steering committee had recommended (and the assembly had agreed) that everyone should be encouraged to come at nine and stay through lunch. I heard a white student wearing a Stokely button tell a hall monitor (a rotating job, one teacher and two students at a time), "Tell them, 'Is it that urgent that you can't wait for lunch?'" A kid left nevertheless: school is still school for some.

The corridor said a great deal about the new Science. There is a line painted down the middle, to keep traffic moving on either side; no one was observing it now. One bulletin board proclaimed "IMAGINATION TAKES POWER," with a drawing of the upraised fist (glad universal symbol!) and photos of the Columbia insurrection. Another one: "SCIENCE OPEN TO SUPPORT OCEAN HILL." Under "Science," someone had

scrawled "is objective": the students are in many ways the same eager grinders and pushers and arrogant wags they were In My Day; all the more remarkable that at the same time they are, many of them, restless and inventive and taken with the radical possibilities of their generation. One room was resounding with Aretha Franklin records: this was study hall, and most of the students inside were black. (Seventy percent of the school's 6% black population were attending.) The corridors were clean; only the first floor was in use; with the janitors on strike, the liberated collective were cleaning up by themselves. Nobody bitched.

Most of the liberated students don't seem to be radical; I saw two Humphrey-Muskie buttons for the one Stokely. But the radicals seem to dominate the student wing of the steering committee and their spirit also prevails: they are perhaps the vanguard in a true sense, the tone-setters. They don't always push through their positions. The steering committee had agreed to distribute draft information but not to allow draft counseling in the school: "The reason that the proposal to have draft counseling was defeated," said the posted summary of the day's decisions, "is the possible reaction when the strike ends. There would be a perfect reason (I didn't find out whether they meant "reason" or "excuse") for the administration to reinstate military assemblies." The liberation is thus tinged with a sense of interlude, fantasy: everyone knows that sooner or later authority will revert to the established order; the teachers will try to forget their differences; there will be multiple-choice exams, grades, irrelevance, college applications. The most concrete future the liberators have imagined is to retain the part of the first floor they are now occupying for some

sort of liberated sub-school in the gut of the unliberated school.

But on whatever terms the strike ends, the 300 students and 20 teachers will have shared an experience that will stand out all the stronger by contrast with the keep-on-time-take-your-tests routine of the strikers. The Administration or returning teachers may insist on grading the liberated students; certainly they will try to restore the old rules; in any case the memories will not easily fade. Normalcy will lose the rock-solid legitimacy in which it is ordinarily sealed. The shake-up does not lead inexorably to revolutionary change in curriculum or rules, and there is a great burden beside the great glory in being a high school radical organizer these days.

But some year, sooner rather than later, a substantial chunk of the senior class at the Bronx High School of Science may walk into the dimly-lit star chamber to take their College Boards, and suddenly everyone will break the point on his pencil, and everyone will call, "Monitor, monitor," and the monitors will scurry and find more pencils and then in a flurry of cracks all the points of the new pencils will be broken, and someone will jump up on a table and say No, we aren't going to be graded like sides of beef anymore, we are going to learn however and whenever we see fit and we are going to stand with our brothers and sisters in Ocean Hill-Brownsville....

* * *

I never got to speak formally; they wanted me to stay for an assembly, but I couldn't take the time, and I felt more like listening anyway. When I left Science in 1959, I celebrated my relief. In 1968 I left feeling a little more free than I'd felt in a long time.

San Francisco
Express Times 11/13/68

FREE YOU

Midpeninsula Free University continued its liberation of downtown Palo Alto this week by opening the winter quarter with 220 courses in arts, crafts, encounter, leisure, philosophy, politics and science.

MFU, with a registration last quarter of 1275 (at $10 a head; $2 for high school students), is getting to be a formidable free community in the Midpeninsula. They now operate a crafts store, print shop, professional service organization and semimonthly magazine, "The Free You." MFU Be-Ins and street dances are the banes of the high-rise Palo Alto Establishment. In the works is a large Community Center which will include coffee house, dance hall, arts & crafts shop and ample office space.

Dedicated to the proposition that "the natural state of man is ecstatic wonder; that we should not settle for less," MFU presents not a supplement but an alternative to the established education in the area.

A sampling of some intriguing course descriptions:

POETRY & UNDERGROUND JOURNALISM: "The new journalism, poetic journalism, street journalism and contemporary approaches to poetry. Outside material like R.D. Laing, Rowen Barthes, Mailer, and various accounts of the Huey Newton trial."

ZOMBIE DRAWING: "Mr. Goya with his finely-shaped mind, Breughel and his penis-oriented gut scenes, Blake and his fine-reclusive madness; and lately, other guys who draw tiny little monsters and hop on their nightmares."

INSANITY, GENIUS & HEROICS: "Many people experience the collapse of their allegiance to the present American system as a fear that they are going insane ... Nietzsche saw that to create new values, new ways of life, genius was necessary. Psychoanalysis and psychedelics have shown that everyone has the requisite creative potential, that the

problem is to discover how it can be safely released."

STRIKING BACK AT THE GODDAMN SONS OF BITCHES: "The idea is to get together those local individuals who'd like to be active against Bay Area industries who pollute the air and water .... Tactics beyond gentle pleas must be devised. Middle-class tax-paying home-owning rebels arise. This is your thing!"

Also: Electronics & Practical House Wiring; Pool Playing; Insidious Education; Trust, Touch & Tenderness; Eros of Teenagers; Out of the Rut, Into the Groove; Swedish Massage; Hitchhiking; Birdwatching; Cannibals Co-Op; Out of the Aquarium and Into the Aquarian; Workshop on Black Studies for High School Youth; Provo Tactics; The Womanly Art of Breastfeeding; The Magic Mushroom; Beyond Auto Eroticism (for mechanics).

Anyone can teach a course at MFU; most groups are small and meet in the teacher's home. For a copy of the beautiful catalog, or to register, write, call or drop in:

MIDPENINSULA FREE UNIVERSITY
1061 El Camino Real, Menlo Park 94025
Phone: 328-4944

ANARCHISM

A review of the underground, libidinal, anarchic tradition: peasant wars, 19th Century theorists and terrorists, mass anarchist movements in Russia and Spain, anarchism and Marxism, syndicalism, Dada and surrealism. Ecology and anarchism in post-scarcity society.

Murray Bookchin author of books on ecology, environment and anarchism; *Anarchos* magazine.

INTRODUCTION TO REVOLUTIONARY POLITICAL THEORY

Basic problems in Marxist theory; anarchism, political organization, theory of state, reform and revolution. Course for people with relatively little familiarity in revolutionary political theory. Guest speakers.

Stanley Aronowitz former trade union organizer; presently community organizer and *Guardian* writer.

GRAPHICS WORKSHOP

To service Alternate U. and individual, general movement work. Leaflets, posters, wall newspapers, flags, buttons, ads, etc., using mimeo, silk-screen and mechanicals for photo-offset.

Ina Clausen, Nancy Colin, Su Negrin and Susan Sherman; free-lance graphic artists.

PIG LAW

A workshop on the problems of radical activists confronting legal systems. Legal or political defense? Self-defense? The history and politics of legal oppression. Discussions with movement activists and radical lawyers.

POLITICAL STREET THEATER

A workshop to pool ideas and talents for guerrilla theater actions.

Lynn Laredo Open Theater.

Alternate U. is an inexpensive evening school free of grades, credit and age restrictions, offering a wide range of courses whose content and approach are not available elsewhere. It is democratically run through weekly meetings open to the entire Alternate U. community.

More and more people are disaffected from establishment education and from the American Empire in general. These people are moving—some in their heads, some in the streets—and they all need contact with new facts, theories and active experienced people. Alternate U. aims for two levels of development: first, to gain an understanding of contemporary forces and events and the meaning of one's own life within these; and second, to stimulate people to begin actively shaping their own lives and the forces and the events around them.

Alternate U. aims to create new forms of communication allowing for maximum freedom and learning —learning not in the usual sense of accumulating facts, but learning as a process of heightening awareness, deepening involvement and commitment, and transforming the individual and social self. This will be facilitated by instructor-student relationships based on equality, openness and joint struggle, and by school meetings open to all members. At these meetings there will be criticism of and by the instructors and students, analysis and correction of the school's direction and functioning, planning of projects and week-end political-cultural programs, and a sharing of the enthusiasm and frustrations that are so common to people struggling to change society.

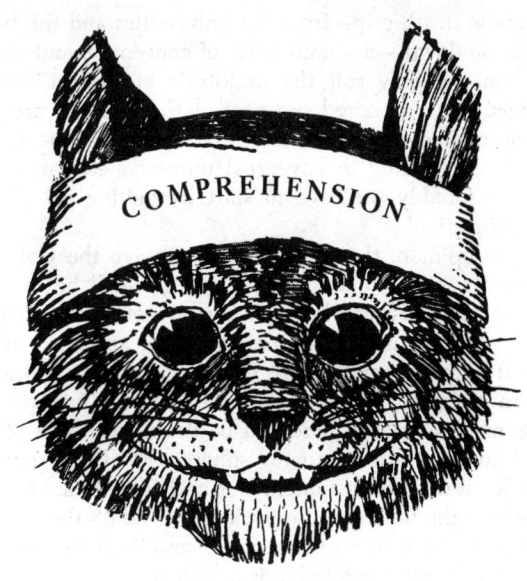

COMPREHENSION

Paul Goodman

From John Dewey to A. S. Neill

One really gets impatient, if not outraged, at the remarks about Progressive Education made by the Rickovers and Max Raffertys. Historically, indeed, the intent of Progressive Education was exactly the opposite of what the critics say; it was the correct solution that Rickover, at least, ought to be asking for, but doesn't know enough to ask for. Progressive Education developed in this country in the intellectual, moral, and social crisis of the development of industrialism after the Civil War. It was the first thoroughgoing modern analysis of the crucial modern problem of every advanced country in the world: how to cope with high industrialism and scientific technology, which are strange to people; how to live in the new cities; how to have a free society in such conditions; how to make the high industrial system good for something, rather than a machine running for its own sake.

The thought of John Dewey was part of a similar tendency in architecture, the functionalism of Louis Sullivan and Frank Lloyd Wright, that was trying to invent an urbanism and an esthetic suited to machine mass-production and yet human; and it went with the engineering orientation of the economic and moral theory of Veblen and others, objecting to money values and the false classicism that had become a leisure-class ornament. These thinkers wanted to train, teach (accustom is perhaps the best word) the new generation to the actualities of industrial and technical life, working practically with the machinery, learning by doing. People could then be at home in the modern world, and possibly become free.

There was a political and economic side to it. Dewey, at least, was distressed by both the robber-baron plutocracy and the bossed mass-democracy. He put his faith in industrial democracy, overestimating the labor union—he did not foresee their bureaucratization. (As a pragmatist, he must have expected that the skilled would demand a say in management and production, and not be content with merely bargaining on wages and conditions!) But at least the school was to be a training in self-rule, democracy and community. And these two

ideas, practical learning of the machinery and democratic community, in an atmosphere of free animal expression and freedom to fantasize, instead of the parson's morality and the schoolmaster's ruler, constituted the whole of Progressive Education. With spontaneous interest (including animal desire), rigorously controlled by the hard pragmatism of doing and making the doing work, the young democratic community would best learn the modern world and would also have the will, cooperatively, to change it. It was a theory of continual scientific experiment and nonviolent social revolution.

As was inevitable, our society being what it is, this theory was entirely perverted when it began to be applied, either in private schools or in the public system. Because of the outcry of the conservatives, it began to be toned down. A program of practical training and community democracy, whose purpose was to live scientifically and change society, was changed into a psychology of "belonging" combined with "socially useful" subjects and "citizenship." Driver-training was the type of the "useful." (Dewey would by now, I hope, have been teaching how to curtail the number of cars!) Social dancing was the type of the "belonging." The Americans had no intention of politically changing, nor of broadening the scientific base and taking technological control and expertness out of the hands of the top-managers and their technicians. Democratic community became astoundingly interpreted as conformity, instead of being the matrix of experiment.

At present, suddenly, there is a great cry for scientific and technical training. By strict lessons and draconian grading (plus bribes) we are supposed to find the scientifically gifted, an elite group. Dr. Conant says that the "academically talented" are 15% and these, largely selected by national tests, are supposed to be at home in the modern technical world and be the creative spirits in it. The bother is that the teachers of science who know what they are talking about—e.g. the consensus reported in Professor Bruner's *The Process of Education*—ask for a kind of training that looks very like Deweyan Progressive Education. They counsel practical learning by doing, avoiding testing and grading, encouraging spontaneous experiment and guesswork. There is no point, they say, in learning the "answers," for very soon there will be different answers. What must be taught are the underlying ideas of scientific thought as part of the substance of the youngster's life, fantasy, and experience. My guess is that when Professor Bruner and his associates explore a little further, they will find that democratic community is also an essential, because it is impossible to do creative work of any kind when the goals are pre-determined by outsiders and cannot be criticized and altered by the minds that have to do the work. Indeed, they will end up right where John Dewey and others began!

In the past three or four years there has been a significant revival of Progressive Education in this country, taking a peculiar form. It has been modeling itself on Summerhill, A. S. Neill's school in England. In most ways the Summerhill idea is not unlike old-line Progressive Education—it stresses animal freedom, learning by doing, and *very* democratic community processes (one person one vote, enfranchising small children!). But it also emphasizes an issue that to Dewey did not seem important, the freedom to choose to go to class or stay away altogether. A child at Summerhill can just hang around; he'll go to class when he damned well feels like it—and many coming from other schools don't damned well feel like it for eight or nine months. After a while—since their friends go—they give it a try.

It is significant, in my opinion, that it is just *this* development in Progressive Education that is catching on a little bit. The significance is simple. Our entire school system, like our over-organized economy, politics, and standard of living, is largely a trap; it is *not* designed for the maximum growth and future practical utility of the children into a changing world, that they too will hopefully improve, but is a kind of inept

social engineering to mold, and weed out, for short-range extrinsic needs. And even when it is more benevolent, it is in the bureaucratic death-grip—from the universities and the boards of education down—of a uniformity of conception and method that cannot possibly suit the multitude of dispositions and conditions. Yet a hundred per cent of the children are compelled or cajoled to remain, for 12 years (!) in one kind of box. If we are going to have real universal education, that educates, probably we have to start by getting rid of compulsory education!

In my opinion, the future—if we survive the Cold War and have a future, which is touch and go—will be more leisurely anyway; and the leisure—if it is not to be complete inanity—will include much more community and civic culture; there will be more employment in human services and less in hardware gadgets; there will be more citizenly initiative and less regimentation; and there will be decentralization of control and administration in many spheres. For these purposes, the top-down dictated national plans and educational methods that are now the fad are quite irrelevant. And on the contrary, it is precisely the society of free choice and lively interpersonal involvement of Summerhill that is practical.

So just as with Dewey, the new wing of Progressive Education is again a good index of what the real social situation is. Let us hope that this time around Progressive Education will not allow itself to be perverted by the pressures of a society which needs it but is afraid of it and will seek to abuse it.

LIBERATION

Board of Education Can't Find Pencils

brother justice

Rafael Weill School is a poor public school in the Western Addition. Seventy-five percent of its students are black.

For a year, the Rafael Weill School Community Organization has been trying to get workbooks and fire escapes and similar luxuries for the school from a very reluctant Board of Education.

Now if they won't give you fire escapes for your children, then you know they regard you as nothing but trash. It was an angry session.

"In the morning I hand out pencils," a teacher told the Board, "and in the afternoon I have to collect them, because a kid just might lose a pencil or take it home, and there aren't enough to go around."

Most of these kids will have the experience some day of handing in their spoon to the guard or trusty after each meal. They are getting early training. Prisoners receive just a spoon—no knife and no fork, because they can be weapons. The kids at Rafael Weill get just pencils, when they should have paint and amplifiers and typewriters and mimeograph machines. That's expensive compared to pencils, but dirt cheap compared to jet bombers, penitentiaries and interstate highways.

About twenty different parents and teachers spoke for Rafael Weill School to enthusiastic applause from an audience of at least a thousand. The fascist-minded citizenry and their goons were not in evidence. This week the audience consisted of teachers, clergymen and

other professionals, with quite a few black militants and white longhairs to spice up the bubbling stew. Uniformed cops stood at the auditorium entrance looking alien and uncomfortable. Black militants in leather jackets stood in a military at-ease posture in the lobby. They had helmets and two-foot long flashlights that could double as clubs.

The audience was together. There was no hostility between black and white, parents and teachers; it was the people versus the Board of Education.

Donald Rhodes, assistant superintendent in charge of elementary schools, was the brown-suited bureaucrat who had stalled off the fire escapes, workbooks and pencils for a whole year. The mild-mannered killer of children stood up and tried to answer the attacks against him, but he came across as a pitifully unconvincing liar. If there had been a jury it would have deliberated two minutes and then found him guilty on the first ballot. The heckling was creative and energetic, but it never attempted to stop Rhodes from speaking. He just ran down like an old watch.

The Board of Education cross-examined Rhodes in a half-hearted way. They maintained a polite front, but did nothing to protect Rhodes from the audience's taunts. "This business about the fire escapes is actually very serious," a Board member mumbled into the microphone. "This is something that should be installed tomorrow morning."

Should be—but won't, and everybody knew it. The Board of Education looks very tired, ready to give up on the whole

idea of public education. Not only can't they run schools where children learn; they can't even run prisons. And they know it.

One of these Tuesday nights the Board of Education will just be shunted aside. The audience will take over and turn it into a big work meeting. The Western Addition is full of storefronts nobody wants. Every vacant storefront can become a mini-school, a base of operations for a dozen kids and two or three adults (with or without college degrees). The kids and teachers can paint the place themselves. For a tricky job like wiring, the teachers call in an electrician who works with the kids watching. From the school they take little informal field trips to the bakery and the garage and the metal-working shop in the neighborhood. Learning how the city works is the basic curriculum; reading, writing and arithmetic then come into play quite naturally.

For the time being, here's what you can do. If you work in a large, modern, well-equipped office, then take pencils home with you—if you can get a typewriter out under your coat, do that. Bring the stuff to Rafael Weill School for the children to use. The school is at 1501 O'Farrell.

The bureaucrats are running scared and the school office is in friendly hands, so walk right in and pay your schools taxes the modern way.

San Francisco Express Times 3/11/69

Mini-Schools: A Prescription for the Reading Problem

HOW TO RADICALLY
CHANGE THE SCHOOLS:
A PRACTICAL PROPOSAL

Paul Goodman

What follows is a statement I recently made when asked to testify on teaching reading, before the Borough President of Manhattan:

A chief obstacle to children's learning to read is the present school setting in which they have to pick it up. For any learning to be skillful and lasting, it must be or become self-motivated, second nature; for this, the schooling is too impersonal, standardized, and academic. If we tried to teach children to speak, by academic methods in a school-like environment, many would fail and most would stammer.

Although the analogy between learning to speak and learning to read is not exact, it is instructive to pursue it, since speaking is much harder. Learning to speak is a stupendous intellectual achievement. It involves learning to use signs, acquiring a vocabulary, and also mastering an extraordinary kind of algebra—syntax—with almost infinite variables in a large number of sentence forms. We do not know scientifically how infants learn to speak, but almost all succeed equally well, no matter what their class or culture. Every child picks up a dialect, whether "correct" or "incorrect," that is adequate to express the thoughts and needs of his milieu.

We can describe some of the indispensable conditions for learning to speak.

1. The child is constantly exposed to speech related to interesting behavior in which he often shares. ("Now where's your coat? Now we're going to the supermarket, etc.")

2. The speakers are persons important to the child, who often single him out to speak to him or about him.

3. The child plays with the sounds, freely imitates what he hears, and tries to approximate it without interference or correction. He is rewarded by attention and other useful results when he succeeds.

4. Later, the child consolidates by his own act what he has learned. From age three to five he acquires style, accent, and fluency by speaking with his peers,

adopting their uniform but also asserting his own tone, rhythm, and mannerisms. He speaks peer speech but is uniquely recognizable as speaking in his own way.

Suppose, by contrast, that we tried to teach speaking academically in a school-like setting:

1. Speaking would be a curricular subject abstracted from the web of activity and reserved for special hours punctuated by bells.

2. It would be a tool subject rather than a way of being in the world.

3. It would not spring from his needs in immediate situations but would be taught according to the teacher's idea of his future advantage, importantly aiming at his getting a job sixteen years later.

4. Therefore the child would have to be "motivated," the exercises would have to be "fun," etc.

5. The lessons would be arranged in a graded series from simple to complex, for instance on a false theory that monosyllables precede polysyllables, or words precede sentences, or sentences precede words.

6. The teacher's relation to the infant would be further depersonalized by the need to speak or listen to only what fits two dozen other children as well.

7. Being continually called on, corrected, tested, and evaluated to meet a standard in a group, some children would become stutterers; others would devise a phony system of apparently speaking in order to get by, although the speech meant nothing; others would balk at being processed and would purposely become "stupid."

8. Since there is a predetermined range of what can be spoken and how it must be spoken, everybody's speech would be pedantic and standard, without truth to the child's own experience or feeling.

TURN NOW to teaching reading. These eight disastrous defects are not an unfair caricature of what we do. Reading is treated as abstract, irrelevant to actual needs, instrumental, extrinsically motivated, impersonal, pedantic, not expressive of truth or art. The teaching often produces awkwardness, faking, or balking. Let me also make four further points specific to learning reading:

1. Most people who have learned to read and write fluently have done so on their own, with their own material, whether library books, newspapers, comic books, or street signs. They may have picked up the ABCs in school, but they acquired skill, preserved what they had learned, on their own. This self-learning is an important point, since it is not at the mechanical level of the

ABCs that reading retardation drastically occurs, but in the subsequent years when the good readers are going it alone.

2. On neurological grounds, an emotionally normal child in middle-class urban and suburban surroundings, constantly exposed to written code, should spontaneously learn to read by age nine just as he learned to speak by age two or three. (This is the conclusion of Walla Nauta of the National Institute of Mental Health.) It is impossible for such a child *not* to pick up the code unless he is systematically interrupted and discouraged, for instance by trying to teach him.

But of course our problem has to do with children in the culture of poverty, which does not have the ordinary middle-class need for literacy and the premium put on it. Such children are not exposed to reading and writing in important relations with their parents and peers; the code does not constantly occur in every kind of sequence of behavior. Thus there is an essential need for the right kind of schooling, to point to the written words and read them aloud, in use.

3. Historically, in all modern countries, school methods of lessons, copying, and textbooks, have been used, apparently successfully, to teach children to read. But this evidence is deceptive. A high level and continuing competence were required of very few—e.g., in 1900 in the United States only 6 percent graduated from high school. Little effort was made with children of the working class, and none at all with those in the culture of poverty. It is inherently unlikely that the same institutional procedures could apply with such a change of scale and population. Where a dramatic effort has been made to teach adults to read, as in Cuba, the method has been "each one teach one," informally.

4. Also, with the present expansion of higher education, teachers of freshman English uniformly complain that the majority of middle-class students cannot really read and write, though they have put on a performance that got them through high school. As John Holt has carefully described, their real life need was not reading or writing but getting by. (This is analogous to the large group among Puerto Rican children in New York who apparently speak English well, but who in fact cannot say anything that they need or mean, that is not really simply parroted.)

I trust that the aim of the Borough President's hearings is how to learn reading as truth and art and not just to fake and get by. Further, since poor children do not have the continual incentives and subtle pressures of middle-class life, it is much harder for them to learn even just to fake and get by. And even if they do get by, it will not pay off for them in the end, since they do not have money and connections. To make good, they must really be competent.

THE QUESTION IS, is it possible and feasible to teach reading somewhat in the way children learn to speak, by intrinsic interest, with personal attention, and relating to the whole environment of activity? Pedagogically it is possible and feasible. There are known methods and available teachers, and I will suggest an appropriate school setting. Economically it is feasible, since methods, staff, and setting do not cost more than the $850 per child that we now spend in the public schools. (This was demonstrated for two years by the First Street School on the Lower East Side, and it is in line with the budget of Erik Mann's new school for Negro children in Newark which uses similar principles.) Politically, however, my present proposal is impossible and unfeasible, since it threatens both vested interests and popular prejudices, as will be evident.

For ages six to eleven, I propose a system of tiny schools, radically decentralized. As one who for twenty years has urged democratic decentralization in many fields, including the schools, I am of course interested in the Bundy recommendation to cut up the New York system into sixty fairly autonomous districts. This would restore some relevance of the culture (and the staff) of the school to the culture of the community. But however valuable politically, it is an administrative arrangement; it does not get down to the actual pedagogical operation. And it certainly is not child-centered; both poor and middle-class communities have their own ways of not paying attention to children, according to their own prejudices and distant expectations. By "tiny school," therefore, I here mean twenty-eight children. . . with four teachers (one grown-up to seven children), and each tiny school to be largely administered by its own staff and parents, with considerable say also for the children, as in Summerhill. The four teachers are:

A teacher regularly licensed and salaried. Since the present average class size is twenty-eight, these are available.

A graduate from the senior class of a New York college, perhaps just embarking on graduate study. Salary $2000. There is no lack of candidates to do something interesting and useful in a free setting.

A literate housewife and mother, who can also prepare lunch. Salary $4000. No lack of candidates.

A literate, willing, and intelligent high-school graduate. Salary $2000. No lack of candidates.

Such a staff can easily be racially and ethnically mixed. And it is also the case,

as demonstrated by the First Street School, that in such a small setting, with individual attention paid to the children, it is easy to get racially and ethnically mixed classes; there is less middle-class withdrawal when the parents do not fear that their children will be swamped and retarded. (We have failed to achieve "integration" by trying to impose it from above, but it can be achieved from below, in schools entirely locally controlled, if we can show parents that it is for their children's best future.)

For setting, the tiny school would occupy two, three, or four rooms in existing school buildings, church basements, settlement houses otherwise empty during school hours, rooms set aside in housing projects, store-fronts. The setting is especially indifferent since a major part of activity occurs outside the school place. The setting should be able to be transformed into a clubhouse, decorated and equipped according to the group's own decision. There might be one school on every street, but it is also advisable to locate many in racial and ethnic border areas, to increase intermixture. For purposes of assembly, health services, and some games, ten tiny schools could use the present public school facilities.

The cost saving in such a setup is the almost total elimination of top-down administration and the kind of special services that are required precisely because of excessive size and rigidity. The chief uses of central administration would be licensing, funding, choosing sites, and some inspection. There would be no principals and assistants, secretaries and assistants. Curriculum, texts, equipment would be determined as needed—and despite the present putative economies of scale, they would be cheaper; much less would be pointless or wasted. Record-keeping would be at a minimum. There is no need for truant officers when the teacher-and-seven can call at the absentee's home and inquire. There is little need for remedial personnel since the staff and parents are always in contact, and the whole enterprise can be regarded as remedial. Organizational studies of large top-down directed enterprises show that the total cost is invariably at least 300 percent above the cost of the immediate function, in this case the interaction of teachers and children. I would put this 300 percent into increasing the number of adults and diversifying the possibilities of instruction. Further, in the conditions of New York real estate, there is great advantage in ceasing to build four-million-dollar school buildings, and rather fitting tiny schools into available niches.

Pedagogically, this model is appropriate for natural learning of reading:

1. It allows exposure to the activities of the city. A teacher-and-seven can spend half the time on the streets, visit-

ing a business office, in a playground, at a museum, watching television, chatting with the corner druggist, riding the buses and subways, visiting rich and poor neighborhoods and, if possible, homes. All these experiences can be saturated with speaking, reading, and writing. For instance, a group might choose to spend several weeks at the Museum of Natural History, and the problem would be to re-label the exhibits for their own level of comprehension.

2. It allows flexibility to approach each child according to his own style and interests, for instance in choice of reading matter. Given so many contexts, the teacher can easily strike when the iron is hot, whether reading the destination of a bus or the label on a can of soup. When some children catch on quickly and forge ahead on their own, the teacher need not waste their time and can concentrate on those who are more confused. The setting does not prejudge as to formal or informal techniques, phonics, Montessori, rote drill, Moore's typewriter, labeling the furniture, Herbert Kohl's creative writing, or any other method.

3. For instance, as a writer I like Sylvia Ashton-Warner's way of teaching little Maoris. Each day she tries to catch the most passionate concern of each child and to give him a card with that key word: usually these are words of fear, anger, hunger, loneliness, or sexual desire. Soon a child has a large ineradicable but very peculiar reading list, not at all like Dick and Jane. He then easily progresses to read and write anything. From the beginning, in this method, reading and writing are gut-meaningful, they convey truth and feeling. This method could be used in our tiny school.

4. The ragged administration by children, staff, and parents is pedagogically a virtue, since this too, which is real, can be saturated with reading and writing, writing down the arguments, the rules, the penalties. Socially and politically, of course, it has the advantage of engaging the parents and giving them power.

I am assuming that for the first five school years, there is no merit in the standard curriculum. For a small child everything in the environment is educative, if he attends to it with guidance. Normal children can learn the first eight years' curriculum in four months anyway, at age twelve.

FURTHER, I see little merit, for teaching this age, in the usual teacher-training. Any literate and well-intentioned grown-up or late teen-ager knows enough to teach a small child a lot. Teaching small children is a difficult art, but we do not know how to train the improvisational genius it requires, and the untrained seem to have it equally: compare one mother with another, or one big sister or brother with another. Since at this age one teaches the child, not the subject, the relevant art is psychotherapy, and the most useful course for a teachers' college is probably group therapy. The chief criterion for selection is the one I have mentioned: liking to be attentive to children. Given this setting, many young people would be introduced to teaching and would continue with it as a profession; whereas in the New York system the annual turnover approaches 20 percent, after years of wasted training.

As I have said, however, there are fatal political and administrative objections to this proposal. First, the Public School administration does not intend to go largely out of business. Given its mentality, it must see any radical decentralization as impossible to administer and dangerous, for everything cannot be controlled. Some child is bound to break a leg and the insurance companies will

not cover; some teen-ager is bound to be indiscreet and the *Daily News* will explode in headlines.

The United Federation of Teachers will find the proposal to be anathema because it devalues professional perquisites and floods the schools with the unlicensed. Being mainly broken to the public school harness, most experienced teachers consider free and inventive teaching to be impossible.

Most fatally, poor parents, who aspire for their children, tend to regard unrigidly structured education as downgrading, not taking the children seriously, and also as vaguely immoral. In the present Black Power temper of Harlem, also, the possible easy intermixing is itself not desired. (Incidentally, I am rather sympathetic to black separatism as a means of consolidating the power of black communities. But children, as Kant said, must be educated for the fu-

ture better society which cannot be separated.)

In spite of these fatal objections, I recommend that, instead of building the next new school building, we try out this scheme with 1200 children.

After this statement had been circulated, the following statement appeared in the Chelsea Clinton News, *Nov. 30, 1967:*

Paul Goodman's analysis and proposal are an extremely important contribution to educational thinking. I shall submit the article to headquarters with the recommendation that the proposal should be tried out. I am convinced that it has great merit.

Dr. Elliott Shapiro

(*Dr. Shapiro is assistant superintendent of School District 3, which includes Chelsea and Clinton.*) □

The New York Review
of Books

FROM THE OTHER SIDE OF THE DESK

THE REAL WORLD

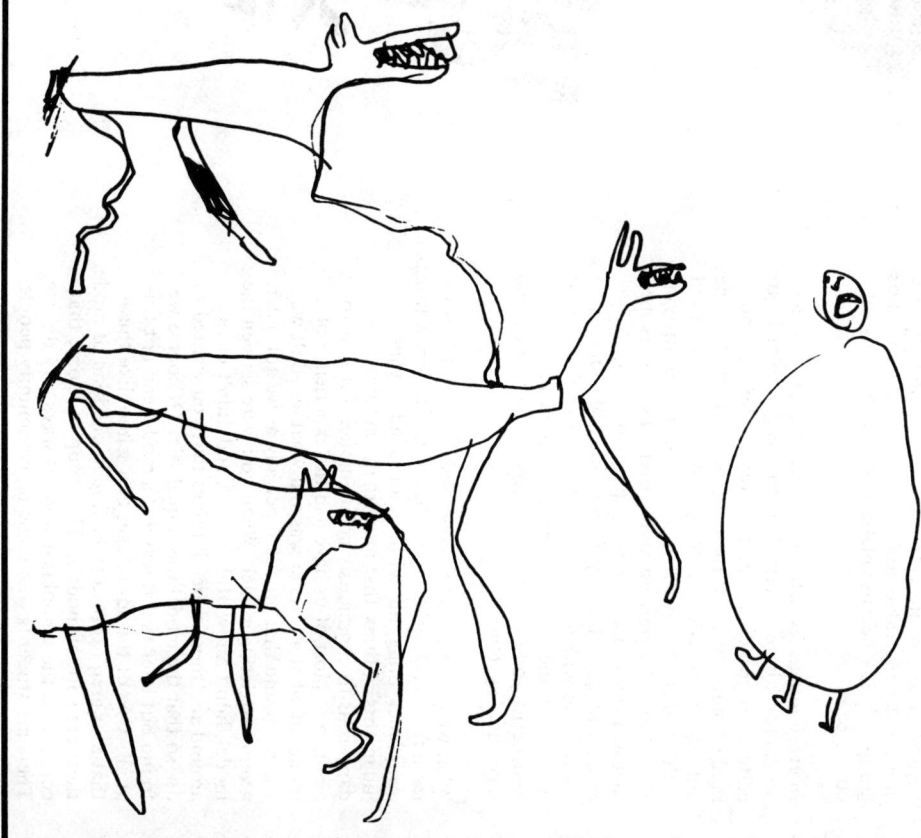

A Dream

One day Mr. G. sent me to the dean. So when I came back I caught him after school and knocked his ass down. Boy you would have sworn that he'd got punched out by Joe Louis. Then I kicked him right up his ass. After that I stuffed a piece of ice down his fat neck. For the finale I took a piece of glass and cut his stomach and a whole lot of smelly fat came out.

I Had A Dream

I had a dream last night that my Math teacher Mr. D. got smart with me. I went up to him and punched him in the nose. Then I just kept on beating him until he was out cold. Then I stuck a great big pin in him and let out all the air out of him.

"The Saddest Thing That Happened in My Life"

The saddest thing in my life was to see a White man shoot a Negro in the streets two days ago.

The Negro man ran out of a drug store and along behind him came the White man. The white man aimed at the man and pulled the trigger.

I heard something like a firecracker and I turned around. I saw a man lying on the ground and a crowd of people around him. I said to myself, "what a way to die."

Hey Teach!, Teachers for a Democratic Society

bill ayers

Bill Ayres is one of the founders of Children's Community, an integrated school community in Ann Arbor, Michigan. He has since changed jobs and is now working full-time on various Ohio and Michigan campuses as an organizer for the Students for a Democratic Society.

TRAVELLING WITH CHILDREN & TRAVELLING ON

a number of different models. Everyone says, for instance, that the model of a nice cop is unrealistic for ghetto kids because cops are just not nice in ghettos. We get out of the community a lot by taking trips — as many as five or six trips in a day — and the vital sense you develop in the community of what to expect from different adults gets tested out. You learn that some cops are nice and help you across the street and others aren't so nice. I think they are getting a much more realistic picture of the world. The point is that kids learn by testing reality and not by what someone has decided is the truth they are going to tell them.

picked things up and threw things out

I don't think you can generalize from twenty-five kids in three years, but I think we have seen some indications that this is a good approach. We've seen every kid come in much narrower than he is today. The white kids came in generally quieter, more academically oriented, more afraid of new situations. The Negro kids came in busting out all over with enthusiasm, excitement, violent play. They enjoyed new situations, meeting strangers; they liked exploring, and of course they spoke differently from the white classmates. We've seen in three years that the white kids have loosened up a good deal, that they now follow the lead of their black classmates; they too explore on a trip, they go off by themselves and ask questions of strangers and kind of snoop around. They do more physical kinds of play, they dance much looser, they've picked up some of the language and thrown some away. The Negro kids today are able to spend a lot more time doing something quiet, they've picked up some of the language of their white classmates. We've seen this exchange completely without our intervention, without us saying these things are good or bad, but just by themselves they have picked things up and thrown things out however they saw it necessary.

The ratio of black and white kids in the school is about half and half. We make decisions when we accept parents of kids to keep a lot of different balances — age balances, sexual balances, race balances — so that in different age groupings there are different kids. Each kid has kids his own age and his own colour and sex to play with. It's really hard to do when you only have twenty-five kids — like programming on a computer. One of the problems is that the school is, in a lot of ways, much more oriented towards black kids, or rather the atmosphere that prevails is created by those kids in the sense that many of the things that go on there are dominated by black kids. We didn't consciously make that decision, but the fact is that the black kids are more of a group, they are older and smarter. The black kids have been in the school longer as a group. They tend to be more open and more anxious to get out of

One of the major motivations for the people who started the school was that they felt there wasn't a good model of an integrated school: the integrated schools were in many ways as racist as the old segregated model. We're trying to approach integration in a totally new way. Not only do we have black and white kids in the same school, but we don't make any value judgments about either of those groups of kids, because making value judgments turns out to be racist.

In every integrated school I've seen except ours the model for failure is everything that is ghetto or Negro culture. If you dress a certain way, prefer a certain kind of music or food, then you're ignorant. It comes out most obviously in language. When a child says "I ain't" and the teacher says it's wrong, he's destroying a lot. The child grew up saying that. His parents speak that way, everyone he knows speaks that way, he's learned to speak his way successfully and suddenly he's confronted with a new system that says he's ignorant. In this way the integrated school may be more destructive to both white and negro kids than the old segregated system.

What we try to do is to allow these groups of kids to learn from each other, to exchange things, throw things away, pick things up, without any kind of value judgments. I think that more than anything it is dangerous to consciously create models for kids to emulate. Most of us have had the experience of a model of what a teacher was and what an adult was, and we found that model, especially as we got older, a very restricting model. When you were sixteen the model didn't screw, didn't drink and didn't mess around and those were all things that you wanted to do, so that the model was unrealistic. Of course we found out later that it was just a model and not true at all. One of the advantages of a school like this is that kids aren't forced to believe in one kind of model: there are a lot of models. The group of people that comes into the school is in a lot of ways very diverse. There are students who come in, community people with all kinds of different ideas about politics, life styles, kids, interests. Kids can learn much more from their houses and hang around with us. Some of that was certainly conscious. We live in a black neighborhood now. We thought it would be good to be near those kids, because we have been in a white neighborhood before and much nearer to most of the white kids.

Another problem is that we do not have any black staff. That is primarily because we can't afford to pay anybody and there are very few people at the university that are willing to devote time to the Children's Community rather than get a college degree and a job. That is something that really works against us. Parents come, and are encouraged to come as much as they can, but that is never regular because they have to work. The first year we had an unemployed black guy who came regularly and we now have a black girl who comes once a week, but it is still one of the big shortcomings.

There is no conflict between black and white kids in the school. There is real openness and acceptance of other kids. But there is a kind of ghetto atmosphere in the school. It is a poor run-down place to begin with and much noisier than it would be if we had all white kids. Yet that is not a simple matter of class difference. We have wealthy kids who are black and white, and poor kids who are black and white. The spectrum of the school runs from very poor people who can't afford to pay any tuition to people who are professors and make over $10,000 a year. I think the wealthiest kid in the school is black, but he is about the only one that crosses the economic boundaries. For the most part the black kids are poor. The fact is that the white kids who are poor are the sons and daughters of struggling students or new left parents coming out of a middle class culture. And the black kids whose parents may make more money than those people are still coming out of a ghetto culture. It is hard to talk about the differences economically.

The economic and racial differences between kids are sometimes reflected in the kids' attitudes to each other. When they leave the school, the white kids probably go to their white neighborhoods and the black kids go to their black neighborhoods. But they play together outside of school more than kids from most schools, although not necessarily inter-racially. Given the fact that they are scattered all over Ann Arbor, for Todd to play with Duke is a big trip, and yet they do it three, four, five times a week. More important than the inter-racial relationships that are formed (which, after all, are hard to measure) is the fact that exchanges take place in a very free atmosphere that is broadening for all of them.

on the outside

We see learning as going on every place — unstructured and undefined. When we talk about the discovery approach to learning, or about making learning a total process, we often talk about the cooking we do and the trips we take. We take trips every day certainly. That doesn't mean every kid, but those who are interested in whatever is happening. Sometimes the kids suggest a trip, sometimes we do. If we have to plan it we involve the kids in the planning. We don't consider the teacher suggesting a trip a betrayal of the discovery method. If there is a healthy open relationship the kids feel no kind of pressure about accepting the suggestion or rejecting it. Whether they want to go or not has nothing to do with what the teacher thinks of them. We do think that we have a responsibility to make a lot of different kinds of things accessible when available, and that includes materials, trips, even activities we might bring in. For instance, I was reading a book to three kids about fossils, and I discovered through reading that you could find fossils in limestone. Since limestone is plentiful and commonly used in a lot of the buildings around, I suggested a trip to go to the administration building and look at the marble floors and the walls to find the fossils. We did it. It was the kind of thing I could suggest to tie into what they were doing.

apples, hamburgers, cars and airplanes

A number of times we've gone to an apple orchard and eaten the apples. Once as we were leaving, a truck was loading up with apples. One of the kids wanted to follow it and we did. It dropped off a load of apples at the A & P and we went in and bought some more apples to eat. You could see in that whole process that a real understanding about the economics of apples was starting. Apples are grown, sold, and bought.

Another trip came out of a discussion of meat. Someone in the group said wisely that hotdogs come from a cow you know. Someone else added that hamburgers come from a cow too. I sensed in the discussion that they were fascinated, but didn't have a clear understanding of what they were saying. Everyone knows that meat comes in pieces and packages. When someone asked if it was true that salami comes from a sheep I started to talk about it. I said it was true that meat comes from animals and that we kill a lot of animals every day to get the meat we need. This was very fascinating to them. We talked about going to Detroit to see them slaughter animals. I arranged the trip and took five kids. The only stomach that turned was mine. We spent a couple of hours watching them herd in pigs, electrocute them, slit their throats, hang them up, take them down, cut them up, and package them. The way they talked about it afterwards to their friends and to one another was significantly different from what they had said before. I don't think there is any way this kind of understanding could have been gained through lectures, pictures or adult pronouncements. Perhaps we ought to record some of the discussions, but I would argue that written records are a sort of neurosis of older people, who want to get the understanding spelled out on paper.

Oh yes, I just remembered another great trip. There's a real fascination with cars with a lot of little kids, you know. Interest in cars can lead to any number of things but a couple of kids really wanted to see the way a car was built so we arranged two trips — one to the Cadillac plant in Detroit (of course being near Detroit helps) and one to the largest Ford plant. An interesting thing happened, I think. You see the way I learned about automobiles and Henry Ford and all that, and Henry Ford was a genius and he did a lot of good for the whole country and he liberated masses of people with his invention. Now as I got older I started to get a different analysis, and I feel that Henry Ford did more to enslave workers than he did to liberate them. But you know my philosophy of teaching overrides both of these views, and I don't think it's wise to put either one of these on kids — to tell them that Henry Ford was a genius and liberator nor to tell them that he was an enslaver.

So what we did was go to the plant. Coming back from the Cadillac plant I had about five kids in the car, I think, and they were concerned with different things. Some of them were concerned with how amazing it was and it was amazing to watch the assembly line, it's an amazing kind of thing if that is what you want to see. It's a stroke of genius in a sense to see that all this can come together and make a car — so some of the kids were concerned with this. Another group of the kids were talking about the fact that it stank, that it was noisy, that it was filthy, that it was too long, that the trip was too long, it was boring . . .

Okay, so without me imposing my values on them, or someone else imposing theirs on him, they learned what they wanted to learn and I think that they learned it much more significantly than if we had given them all the lectures about it. You know, in a sense, this says that any kind of social studies that you could possibly teach or write books about has to be alive, in a sense has to be incomplete at least and the point that is often made that these kids know more about sociology and about social sciences than we do — if by social sciences we mean the make-up of society and how one exists in it — that is true.

So I think the car trips were fascinating to us. The airport trips are other ones — kids love airplanes, they all love airplanes but about five or six love them more than others, so there was a while there when we were making about four or five trips to the Metropolitan Airport a week which was getting a little heavy on the like to. Most of the kids really do want to learn to read. They learn to talk because everyone around them talks. They want to be competent. They want to make sense out of things like everyone else seems to be able to do, so they learn to talk, and the same is true of reading. It is impossible to exist in this world without being bombarded by words on television, street signs, advertising. Kevin, for instance, learned words like Dristan and Stop. Michael learned words like synagogue. These aren't the clean clinically-tested sociological words.

Part of the great sorting-out process of American public education is that a lot of the kids who come through high school don't know how to read. In this sense the school system has failed because it has set itself up as the institution that teaches reading. It really ends up in just teaching a skill, and we are not particularly interested in that. We hope that the kids can do more than identify certain words. We hope they learn how to express themselves, that words have a certain power, and the only way to learn this is to have something powerful to communicate and then to have the opportunity. Learning just can't take place in a situation where you have curriculum guides and authoritarian teachers putting a mass of knowledge into an average student. That isn't real learning at all.

how limits are learned

We have not sat down and decided what is important for kids to do. They choose what they do and they do what they are interested in. There is no set of values by which we judge cutting up carrots as opposed to doing something else. The kids are already fairly conscious of what is reasonable in relating to society and what is not. They are used to having their hands slapped. But I think they learn more in this kind of environment. What they learn about fighting, for instance, is infinitely more valuable than being told it is not nice to hit. Here they learn over a period of time and a number of experiences. Every day a kid named Kevin would pick a fight with Darlene and always get his ass kicked. There was nothing you could say to him to convince him that fighting with Darlene particularly was going to lead to getting your ass kicked. Over a two week period it finally sunk in. He learned he was better off not to pick fights with Darlene. Another issue we had was swearing. We didn't want to say swearing was wrong—probably because that's phony, but also because we wanted the kids to learn for themselves what is appropriate. I always used to say when we were going on a trip that there was a good chance we would get kicked out if there was swearing. One day we went out to a printing place, and I told Jonathan that if he swore there was a good chance we'd all be kicked out. We walked in and

using what is there

Cooking is another of our activities that allows a wide range of learning. Through cooking you have to get to things like reading in its natural setting, and some kinds of chemistry. You can very easily go into social sciences. If one kid makes cheese sandwiches one day, another kid might bring in his mother's recipe for corn bread and chitters, and you get a whole discussion about cultures. You have to allow food to be used in a lot of different ways, to be messed with, to be thrown around some, used as a weapon, to be played with. Cooking happens all the time. There is always someone in the kitchen, usually a few kids. They love to cook. They come with baloney sandwiches and they fry their baloney before they eat it. They use whatever is there.

bombarded by words

With all the hysteria about reading, we find that kids learn to read in a million different ways. Some learn to read because they like cars and want to learn the different names of cars. Others learn because they go on a lot of trips and read the signs along the way, they learn to read each other's names, or they read the labels in a store, or they learn to read because they

this is where they would rather be. In terms of trip taking our kids have become very sophisticated. Part of it is the way we take trips. We don't make the kids stand in line while a person lectures to them. We don't force them to go from one thing to another, in the museum for instance, and listen to someone talking about what they think the kids should be interested in. We allow our eight year olds, considering the amount of experience they have had, to go out by themselves in groups of three or four. We don't have fear about that. In a year or two some of our kids will be taking all kinds of trips by themselves. The teacher who says he can't take trips because he is only one person and the children need a "capable" adult to control them should consider that classes are going to get bigger and that you can't control 35 kids unless you spend your time bringing kids back into the group. The only possible solution is to let kids do what they are interested in. You've got to trust them to go off into many different activities at the same time. The student-staff ratio is a big bogie. Successful public school teachers in this country have come to the decentralization of the class through trial and error. They learned that any other way their primary role was as cop, their secondary role was bureaucrat and lastly they might be able to get a little bit of teaching done, though they weren't even sure of that.

gas bills. But you know it wasn't only a fascination with airplanes although that was part of it. It's so many people talking in foreign languages, escalators, movies, little displays that they have all over, cards hung up on the ceiling. And it's big and it's got a big marble floor, and you can run across it and no one gives you much trouble.

But it's also the car ride. It's fun to get in a car with five other kids because that situation is a foreign situation and you can talk and bicker and notice and observe and, you know, carry on all sitting there going someplace. Last week I got in a car with four kids who said: "Let's go for a ride" and I said "Where?" and they said "It doesn't matter" so we got in the car — I had a couple of short errands I wanted to do — we got in the car, and we drove around and they spent the whole time fighting, competing, noticing things, singing songs. But that's all they wanted to do for a couple of hours —just ride around in the car and I think riding in the car aimlessly is sometimes a very good experience.

It's an interesting thing about the Cadillac plant incidentally. There was a public relations guy who showed us around, typical public relations guy, very nice guy, and he said, "Well you know we've never had kids under twelve before," and he was a little apprehensive and he said "Now the first thing we do is go into this auditorium and I give you a five or ten minute talk about what you're going to see . . ."

.. So I said "Well, that's fine," and we walked in and you know there is something magical about stages and little kids, so they saw this stage and twenty of them rushed up to the stage and started to do an impromptu dance and song routine and the guy was just appalled and didn't know exactly what to do. So I rushed over to him and I said—I kind of blurted out as fast as I could that these are little kids and it's very hard for them to learn by you lecturing to them, and so why don't you just lead the way and we'll kind of orbit around you like little stars and if anyone has a question he'll come up and ask you. And it turned out that the guy was just a very nice guy and once he got into it really, he dug it. When it was through the guy said, "Well this is amazing. We might just have to re-evaluate our policy."

the bogie of student-staff ratio

People have often said to me, "You have such well behaved children." My first reaction is to say that well behaved doesn't mean anything, but then I start to wonder what in the world they mean. By anybody's standards but our own they are really ill-behaved. There is no way in the world that I can control them if they don't want it. But I think a group of kids, even a large group, are well-behaved when they are interested, when he looked at the lady and said, "You're a mother-fucker" and we got kicked out. I think he learned from that.

The school has always been in the basement of a church but the kids have been quick to learn the restrictions made by being in someone else's facilities. The main restriction is that we have two not very big rooms. It is difficult to be able to be alone. But we have arrived at an arrangement through a meeting with the kids. You have got to understand that meetings with six or seven year olds are just the most beautiful things. They last about a minute and a half, with everyone very excited, all trying to get in at once. They decided that the big room should be a place where they could ride tricycles and run up and down and play games like frozen tag and so on, and the little room should be crowded with activities like mathematical games, typewriters, books and art supplies. The little room is very crowded, but a lot of kids spend a lot of time there. This is the closest we have been able to get to a kind of privacy. Occasionally a child will ask to be by himself in a room we can use upstairs very quietly, or one will ask to take a walk with an assistant as a way of being alone. But the last thing on their mind is a nap.

anxieties from outside

There are a lot of problems with trying to run a school like this, and one of them is the anxiety the kids feel from their older brothers and sisters, from the neighborhood kids about being in a different kind of school. They have a hard time seeing it as a real school. The kids on their block talk about reading lessons, homework, and other things they don't have. Kids shouldn't be faced with the problem of having to defend their school. They should just think that they go to a different school, no better or worse. They don't really understand the differences, and having to defend it simply confuses them. Parents send their kids to the school for all kinds of reasons. They are not all absolutely committed to our philosophy of education, and though we interview them carefully, I don't think we always know whether they think it makes sense. The black parents as a group are fairly authoritarian with their kids. One of the overriding reasons they send them to our school is that they think black kids get a fair shake here, and they wouldn't be at another school. We try to avoid being used for kids who are found emotionally disturbed at the public schools. Although the whole philosophy sounds beautiful, when you actually have to deal with all the things that come out in a free atmosphere it's not always pretty. A lot of anger and hostility come out and are allowed to be expressed without retaliation.

The kids have a tremendous identification with the school as a community. There is the sense that it is our school. I think that if we continue to grow at the rate of a grade a year, if we get through junior high, we will have done a great deal. The kids who leave then will be able to make conscious decisions about when they will or won't play the game. People often ask how kids adjust if they have to go to public schools. When you think of what that means, it means doing everything for the approval of the teacher, moulding oneself around what other people expect. It's a double-edged knife. The kids who don't adjust get screwed in one way, but the kids who do are just getting moulded into that other-directed person. It's a shame.

funds and state boards

I think that the majority of our problems would be wiped away if we had an angel come along with funds. A year ago we had the major problem of not having a full staff. Now the staff is full and working well together. If we had our own building and the kind of supplies we need it would be golden. We urge other people — groups of parents, community organizing projects — to start their own schools too. We could get some information together about how we got supplies, raised money and coped with the legal hassles.

We have no enemies now because there is really nobody around who cares a whole lot about what we are doing. At some point when the school becomes more threatening to different groups I can envision a legal hassle. There are a lot of legal things that hang over our heads but have not yet come down. Teacher certification is one. Now we have one certified teacher in a room, and as far as the State Board of Education is concerned she is the only one who is supposed to engage in any kind of learning situation with kids. Everyone is counter to having adults in the classroom and to using the resources of the community. One of the funniest things the administrators of the State Board talked about was the reason we needed an accredited teacher. An accredited teacher is the only one who can make learning decisions. We talked about that. I said, "Well, we have a retired engineer who comes in and does science experiments, is that all right?" And he said, "Yes, that's perfectly fine as long as he does not make learning decisions." Then we have a lady who comes in and dances with the kids. "Is that all right?" "That's demonstration of a skill, as long as the demonstration of the skill is not a learning decision." It became clear that that term just defined itself. We asked about the university students who come in one or two days a week, and they said that as long as the teacher makes the learning decision the assistant can sit down and supervise — as if from that point nothing about learning goes on. I have an idea that the children make more of the decisions than anyone else.

teach black kids karate?

Part of what kids learn in this kind of situation is that adults are different, that they're not always men, not always black, not always white. They don't all blow their tops at the same time. Some of them never blow their tops. Some of them would never like to sit down and read a story; some of them would never like to go on a hike. That's all good to learn. Rather than confusing the kids, I think it sharpens them.

One of our primary considerations is to fight the monolithic system of American society. We still have the goal that people break out of their ghettos, that they grow and pull in other things. Our model of integration says that there are differences, and you don't have to make judgments about those differences. When black kids are bussed into white schools, you have to ask, "What does it mean for a black kid to ride through the ghetto to the suburbs?" I think it is more damaging to him than when he just existed in his little ghetto school. It says that white schools are better, and white kids have learned better things. America is in a time of crisis and we don't know what kind of society these children will have to live in. But we're not retreatist. Someone argued with me that if you want to prepare black kids for what is coming then you teach them karate, you twist them up and make them hate you. But my feeling is that when you give kids self-confidence, when you create an environment where they can learn who they are and develop a certain amount of pride, and where they can learn about the world in a very realistic sense, then no matter what happens in ten years, they'll be ready. They'll have more of a sense of what's happening in our society than other kids. You don't teach people to deal with difficult situations by punishing them. The kids have some positive ideas about what life can be like, and that's the important thing. That's why you can be involved in this school and find it regenerating for you day by day.

teaching black kids

I think the original issue is still the issue: is this society going to educate black children or not. When it took the form of bussing, of Head Start programs, a lot of people got off. Now you see Black Power schools run by black communities. If you read the '54 Supreme Court decisions you get a very clear sense of the whole concept of cultural deprivation before the words were even invented. What does culturally deprived really mean? The Negroes clearly have a very strong culture and it has had a tremendous influence on all of American culture. It doesn't mean that their culture is isolated. The Coleman report says that of all classes taken together, the white middle class is the most isolated from other cultures in America. What culturally deprived ends up meaning is not suitable to this white middle-class culture. So integrated schools were pushed and pushed, and eventually, with the coming of the Coleman report, we realized that we had to confront the failure of integration and start to re-examine some of our assumptions.

Given America today, the reason you have a school like the Children's Community is that kids are forced to go to schools, and why not provide the best possible school? Those of us who are running the school see in it a lot of political implications. We think that by creating this radical alternative and working with this small group of parents and kids in creating a model around which we can do other kinds of political activities, we can become a force for change, not just in schools, but in society in general.

you shaved off your moustache

Now I'm going to be running for the school board. Issues have to be raised, you know, like teacher certification, all the issues that could close us — they are really at the heart of what is wrong with American education, and you have to choose a time when you think you have enough support in the community and wherever you can get it, you have to last through a campaign where issues are raised like how you run a school, and you try to force some kind of change. As Skip Taube, one of our teachers, has pointed out: "Either you are going to exist as an isolated wonderful little project or you are going to become a threat." Whenever you become a threat you are risking something but you waive that and you decide to risk that at some point and we have decided to do that now.

win." So obviously, he already knows about the campaign . . . .

What happens is you have a bunch of nice people who push for reforms in the schools, the reforms are absorbed by the system and nothing fundamentally changes. Witness what happened to Dewey — that in a lot of ways all his rhetoric, a lot of the forms that he developed were taken into the public school system and yet nothing fundamentally was changed. But I think one of the interesting things about running a school like this is when you start talking to groups of people about the school and about free education generally and they start questioning what will happen. I mean, is it possible to have a lot of Children's Communities in this country? — and you start to throw that around. And what kind of kids will develop? and will they be able to fit into General Motors and a Ford plant? In evaluating questions like these, people may start to move, politically at least in their heads. Because it is clear that the school system that now exists does a pretty good job of channeling people into different places, of fitting kids for the Ford factory and other kids for the executive offices, other kids for politics, and academics, whereas our system doesn't do that at all. Our system has, in that sense, a lot of very revolutionary implications because American society couldn't exist with a lot of Childrens' Communities, or said the other way, a lot of Childrens' Communities couldn't exist in America.

So around the issue of education, around the issue of what is a good way to treat kids, you can start to raise a lot of the issues about American society and why the political scene is the way it is. I have seen it happen a lot of times in classes, in groups — just that kind of progression, and that is kind of exciting.

Editor's Note:

I saw Bill again in August and talked to him on the phone in early October. Since he made the tape, he ran for the board and was not elected. He feels it was worth it anyway, partly for the reason he gave in the interview — in public meetings he felt that by holding firmly to his radical position, the other candidates and the audience were forced to be serious about fundamental questions. Even more, he says it was worth having the chance to do some organizing of Ann Arbor high school students and teachers.

Recently he and two other teachers at the school, Diana Oughton and Skip Taube, took part in the Chicago demonstration. He and Skip were both arrested and their trial is pending. "To be young in Chicago was to be a nigger," he says. He tells of one incident when he tried to get into a hotel but was stopped by the police. A handsome McCarthy kid, well-dressed, came along and asked to go in and the police were about to let him. The kid grabbed Bill by the arm and said "he's my friend — we're both going in" and immediately "the handsome guy became a nigger too and both of us were kept out."

Bill has changed jobs. He is no longer at the Children's Community but is working full-time on various Ohio and Michigan campuses as a regional traveller for the Students for a Democratic Society. He says that for a year now, as the students have become more mobilized, he has questioned whether the school community in Ann Arbor was making the impact on society at large that it should. "Apart from vague vibrations now and then and my running for the Board, I feel we have been too isolated," he told me. "Schools like ours are still very important, especially as student revolt gets nearer to being successful, but I think I can be most helpful more directly as an organizer. Eventually if there's to be a serious revolution in this country there must be an adult movement, possibly built around professions like teaching. But any such movement must be built on the foundation of the student movement. In building this movement, one serious question we're going to be facing — since the country as a whole is moving more and more to the right — is to choose when we must do things which are good for the movement which in the short-run are bad for the country. Chicago, for example, drove the country towards Wallace, but it built up the movement. Lots of unpleasant choices will have to be made."

"The Children's Community is in trouble right now. The fire marshall and the building inspector have said that we can't meet any longer in temporary quarters and we don't have the money to buy a building. The school authorities aren't too pleased about this either but they aren't pushing us. It looks as if we may not be able to open this year."

This Magazine Is About Schools Fall 1968

Ed. Note: The school was finally closed down by the authorities, snuffed out by bureaucrats just as Eric Mann's proposed Newark Community School had been earlier. Bill and Eric and Diana joined The Weathermen. Eric is in prison; Diana was killed in the bomb accident on W. 11th St. in New York; Bill has disappeared.

COMMUNITY WORKSHOP SCHOOL

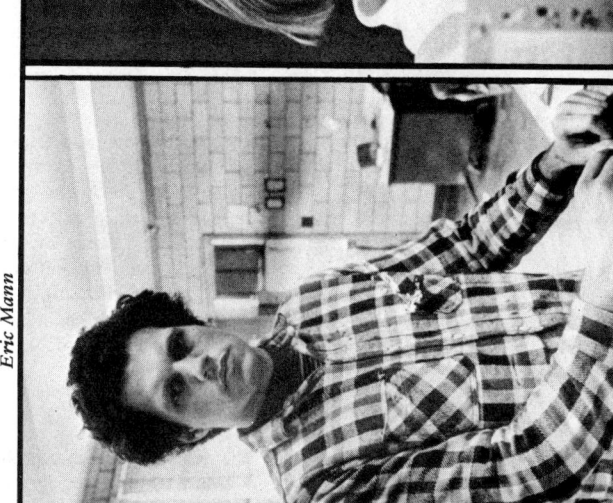

Bill Ayers

Diana Oughton

THE TEACHERS WHO BECAME WEATHERMEN

Eric Mann

To the Editors:

One of the most exciting and significant educational ventures that I have seen is now operating on the upper West Side of New York City. It is the Children's Community Workshop School [55 W. 88th St. NYC 10024] now beginning its second year of tuition-free, integrated community education; it is innovative, it is humane, and it is what a school should be.

I have heard recently from Mrs. Anita Moses, Director of the school, that the school desperately needs money. I have visited the school and the best way to indicate my enthusiasm and sense of urgency is to enclose here the letter which accompanied my own contribution.

Dear Anita Moses,

Your Children's Community Workshop is the most impressive and hopeful project I've ever seen.... What I noticed first when I visited the classrooms was not the children but the teachers. They were all smiling.... **The whole spirit was of a group enterprise, moving forward through the efforts of all....**

I loved the fact that by opening the door you step directly onto the city sidewalk—no great courtyard, or pompous flight of stairs—nothing to set the school apart from the rest of life as something special and different. School is a part of life; learning is one continuous being-in-the-world. (The blind beggar, tapping with his cane, walked into your classroom by mistake, perhaps thinking it was a store. He was embarrassed and was in a hurry to get out. The children understood his error. They were calm about his coming in and calm about his going out. They were awed by his blindness. They went back to work.) Your neighborhood is one of the "borderline" neighborhoods that Paul Goodman and Elliott Shapiro mention as being ideal for meaningful integration. You have middle-class whites, blacks, and Puerto Ricans, and lower-class whites, blacks, and Puerto Ricans. This is not a peaceful combination, but it's a strong one. It brings children and parents through their racial hang-ups. It diminishes the vulgarity of ignorant and mean-spirited households, and dissolves the complacencies of gentility (which are frequently a flight from experience).

You don't charge tuition. You are a *public* school. Yet you provide quality education—which will raise the poor and at the same time keep your middle-class families with you. And your strategy with the Regents is marvelous, since you are asking to be accepted as a school district. This is *exactly* what a school district should be: the immediate neighborhood, the ones who know each other—or who *should* know each other. I hope to God you succeed in this.

I liked the simplicity of the classrooms, the fraternal ease between teachers and children, the sense of individual progress, individual work, individual growth.

The teachers live in the neighborhood. That idiotic distinction between *parents* and *teachers* doesn't apply. Here are adults who are neighbors. Naturally they are concerned with the children of the neighborhood.

I liked the way your own son, when school was over, led a multi-colored troop around the corner, running up to your apartment to play together.

I liked the parent-teacher conversations on the sidewalk when school let out.

I liked the way the kids came up to you and talked in the classrooms, and talked to me too, without suspiciousness of a stranger.

And I marvel that you've done all this on tiny grants and contributions. (Which I can't say without promising to send my own.)

George Dennison

New York Review of Books 10/9/69

Teachers:

the UNITED STATES
in VIETNAM in
the UNITED STATES

VIETNAM CURRICULUM
- Introductory Units
- History and Issues
- Impact of the War
- American Attitudes (and Values)

Five high school teachers in the Boston area have written a 350-page curriculum on the war in Vietnam and related issues. The *Vietnam Curriculum*, in four volumes, contains new teaching methods which go beyond the traditional lecture-discussion techniques and engage the students in an examination of their own ideas, concerns, and values. As Edgar Z. Friedenberg says in his Introduction, "High school students who are given an opportunity to see the *Vietnam Curriculum* may thereby conclude that the high school has finally come to respect them as individuals . . . ."

The response has been overwhelmingly favorable:
- Urban teachers used new methods
- Suburban classes broke through clichés
- Teacher training courses became relevant
- Community workshops increased their scope

"These materials are excellent, both the source and reference materials, and the suggested class activities. This curriculum would be most interesting and valuable to almost any high school class."

—John Holt
Author of *How Children Fail*

"Every child realizes that what he studies in school has almost no relation to the world in which he lives. Most educators prefer this aura of unreality, for it is safe and uncontroversial. The *Vietnam Curriculum* is a rebellion against this position. (It raises questions which will allow students to get excited about what goes on in school."

—Christopher Jencks
Harvard Graduate School of Education
Co-Author of *The Academic Revolution*

Authors:
SUE DAVENPORT
FRANCES MAHER
JOAN McGREGOR
WALTER POPPER
ADRIA REICH

Published in conjunction with the Boston Area Teaching Project, Inc.

Vietnam Curriculum
Department RS-1
New York Review
250 West 57th Street
New York, N.Y.10019

Please ship immediately___ set(s) of all four volumes of *Vietnam Curriculum* post paid. I enclose a check payable to the New York Review ($10 per set; $8 per set for ten or more sets).

Name_____
Address_____
City _____ State _____ Zip _____

. . Let me tell a story. When I first started teaching fifth grade, I was listening one day to three or four 10-year-olds talking to each other. In their talk, one of them said to the others and I can't convey in print the matter-of-factness with which he said this, "If I grow up. . ." Every time I think of it I feel a large part of the appalled horror with which I first heard this innocent remark.

The reason we, the older generation, have lost our authority over kids has nothing to do with permissiveness. It is quite simply that we have destroyed, or allowed to be destroyed, the moral basis on which the authority of the old over the young has always been based—the fact that they could protect and were protecting the young, that they were holding and running a world into which the young people could enter, in short, that they knew what they were doing. This is no longer the case. A world in which a 10-year-old can face, and must face, as a perfectly commonplace sort of reality, the fact that he may never grow up, is not a world in which we can say to the young any longer that Daddy knows best.

. . .There is only one position that we adults have any right to take in dealing with children. "We didn't mean to get into this jam. We don't know how to get out. Don't abandon us. Help us." Only from this position can we have any meaningful dialogue with the young, and exert any reasonable and constructive influence over their lives.

JOHN HOLT Letter printed in *Psychology Today* 1968

STUDENT AS NIGGER

Students are niggers. When you get that straight, our schools begin to make sense. It's more important, though, to understand why they're niggers. If we follow that question seriously enough, it will lead us past the zone of academic red tape, where dedicated teachers pass their knowledge on to a new generation, and into the nitty-gritty of human needs and hang-ups. And from there we can go on to consider whether it might ever be possible for students to come up from slavery.

First let's see what's happening now. Let's look at the role students play in what we like to call education.

At Cal State, L.A., where I teach, the students have separate and unequal dining facilities. If I take them into the faculty dining room, my colleagues get uncomfortable, as though there were a bad smell. If I eat in the Student Cafeteria, I become known as the educational equivalent of a niggerlover. In at least one building there are even restrooms which students may not use.

Students at Cal State are politically disenfranchised. They are in an academic Lowndes County. Most of them can vote in national elections - their average age is about 26 - but they have no voice in decisions which affect their academic lives. The students are, it is true, allowed to have a toy government of their own. It is a government run for the most part by Uncle Toms and concerned principally with trivia. The faculty and administrators decide what courses will be offered; the students get to choose their Homecoming Queen. Occasionally, when student leaders get uppity and rebellious, they're either ignored, put off with trivial concessions, or maneuvered expertly out of position.

A student at Cal State is expected to know his place. He calls a faculty member "Sir" or "Doctor" or "Professor" - and he smiles and shuffles some as he stands outside the professor's office waiting for permission to enter. The faculty tell him what courses to take (in my department, English, even electives have to be approved by a faculty member); they tell him what to read, what to write, and frequently, where to set the margins on his typewriter. They tell him what's true and what isn't. Some teachers insist that they encourage dissent but they're almost always jiving and every student knows it. Tell the man what he wants to hear or he'll fail you out of the course.

When a teacher says "jump", students jump. I know of one professor who refused to take up class time for exams and required students to show up for tests at 6:30 in the morning. And they did! Another, at exam time, provides answer cards to be filled out - each one enclosed in a paper bag with a hole cut in the top to see through. Students stick their writing hands in the bags while taking the test. The teacher isn't a provo; I wish he were. He does it to prevent cheating. Another colleague once caught a student reading during one of his lectures and threw her book against the wall. Still another lectures his students into a stupor and then screams at them in a rage when they fall asleep.

Just last week, during the first meeting of a class, one girl got up to leave after about ten minutes had gone by. The teacher rushed over, grabbed her by the arm, saying, "This class is NOT dismissed!" and led her back to her seat. On the same day another teacher began informing his class that he does not like beards, mustaches, long hair on boys, or Capri pants on girls, and will not tolerate any of that in his class. That class, incidentally, consisted mostly of high school teachers.

Even more discouraging than this Auschwitz approach to education is the fact that the students take it. They haven't gone through twelve years of public school for nothing. They've learned one thing and perhaps only one thing during those twelve years. They've forgotten their algebra. They're hopelessly vague about chemistry and physics. They've grown to fear and resent literature. They write like they've been lobotomized. But, can they follow orders! Freshmen come up to me with an essay and ask if I want it folded and whether their name should be in the upper right corner. And I want to cry and kiss them and caress their poor tortured heads.

Students don't ask that orders make sense. They give up expecting things to make sense long before they leave elementary school. Things are true because the teacher says they're true. At a very early age we all learn to accept "two truths", as did certain medieval churchmen. Outside of class, things are true to your tongue, your fingers, your stomach, your heart. Inside class, things are true by reason of authority. And that's just fine because you don't care anyway. Miss Wiedemeyer tells you a noun is a person, place, or thing. So let it be. You don't care.

The important thing is to please her. Back in kindergarten, you found out that teachers only love children who stand in nice straight lines. And that's where it's been at ever since. Nothing changes except to get worse. School becomes more

and more obviously a prison. Last year I spoke to a student assembly at Manual Arts High School and then couldn't get out of the school. I mean there was NO WAY OUT. Locked doors. High fences. One of the inmates was trying to make it over a fence when he saw me coming and froze in panic. For a moment, I expected sirens, a rattle of bullets, and him clawing the fence.

What school amounts to, then, for white and black kids alike, is a 12-year course in how to be slaves. What else could explain what I see in a freshman class? The saddest cases among both black slaves and student slaves are the ones who have so thoroughly introjected their masters' values that their anger is all turned inward. At Cal State these are the kids for whom every low grade is torture, who stammer and shake when they speak to a professor, who go through an emotional crisis every time they're called upon during class. You can recognize them easily at finals time. Their faces are festooned with fresh pimples; their bowels boil audibly across the room. If there really is a last Judgment, then the parents and teachers who created these wrecks are going to burn in hell.

So students are niggers. It's time to find out why, and to do this, we have to take a long look at Mr. Charlie.

The teachers I know best are college professors. Outside the classroom and taken as a group, their most striking characteristic is timidity. They are short on guts.

Just look at their working conditions. At a time when even migrant workers have begun to fight and win, college professors are still afraid to make more than a token effort to improve their economic status. In California state colleges the faculties are messed up regularly and vigorously by the Governor and Legislature and yet they still won't offer any solid resistance. They lie flat on their stomachs mumbling catch phrases like "professional dignity" and "meaningful dialogue".

Professors were no different when I was an undergraduate at UCLA during the McCarthy era; it was like a cattle stampede as they rushed to cop out. And, in more recent years, I found that my being arrested in sit-ins brought from my colleagues not so much approval or condemnation as open-mouthed astonishment. "You could lose your job!"

Now, of course, there's the Vietnamese war. It gets some opposition from a few teachers. Some support it. But a vast number of professors, who know perfectly well what's happening, are copping out again. And in the high schools, you can forget it. Stillness reigns.

I'm not sure why teachers are so afraid. It could be that academic training itself forces a split between thought and action. It might also be that the tenured security of a teaching job attracts timid persons and, furthermore, that teaching, like police work, pulls in persons who are unsure of themselves and need weapons and the other external trappings of authority.

At any rate teachers ARE short on guts. And, as Judy Eisenstein has eloquently pointed out, the classroom offers an artificial and protected environment in which they can exercise their will to power. Your neighbors may drive a better car; gas station attendants may in-

303
learning

timidate you; your wife may dominate you; the State Legislature may ignore you; but in the classroom - students do what you say - or else. The grade is a powerful weapon. It may not rest on your hip, potent and rigid like a cop's gun, but in the long run, it's more powerful. At your personal whim - any time you choose - you can keep 35 students up for nights and have the pleasure of seeing them walk into the classroom pasty-faced and red-eyed carrying a sheaf of typewritten pages, with the title page, MLA footnotes and margins set at 15 and 91.

The general timidity which causes teachers to make niggers of their students usually includes a more specific fear - fear of the students themselves. After all, students are different, just like black people. You stand exposed in front of them, knowing that their interests, their values, and their language are different from yours. To make matters worse, you may suspect that you yourself are not the most engaging of persons. What then can protect you from their ridicule and scorn? Respect for Authority. That's what. It's the policeman's gun again. The white bwana's pith helmet. So you flaunt that authority. You wither whisperers with a murderous glance. You crush objectors with erudition and heavy irony. And, worst of all, you make your own attainments seem not accessible but awesomely remote. You conceal your massive ignorance - and parade a slender learning.

The teacher's fear is mixed with an understandable need to be admired and to feel superior, a need which also makes him cling to his "white supremacy". Ideally a teacher should minimize the distance between himself and his students. He should encourage them not to need him-- eventually or even immediately. But this is rarely the case. Teachers make themselves high priests of arcane mysteries. They become masters of mumbo-jumbo. Even a more or less conscientious teacher may be torn between the desire to give and the desire to hold them in bondage. There is a kind of castration that goes on in the schools. It begins, before school years, with parents' first encroachments on their children's free un-ashamed sexuality and continues right up to the day when they hand you your doctoral diploma. It's not that sexuality has no place in the classroom. You'll find it there but only in certain perverted and vitiated forms.

How does sex show up in school? First of all, there's the sadomasochistic relationship between teachers and students. That's plenty sexual, although the price of enjoying it is to be unaware of what's happening. In walks the student in his Ivy League equivalent of a motor-cycle jacket. In walks the teacher - a kind of intellectual rough trade - and flogs his students with grades, tests, sarcasm and superiority until their very brains are bleeding. In Swinburn's England, the whipped school boy frequently grew up to be a flagellant. With us, the perversion is intellectual but it's no less perverse.

So you can add sexual repression to the list of causes, along with vanity, fear, and will to power, that turn the teacher into Mr. Charlie. You might also want to keep in mind that he was once a nigger himself and has never really gotten over it. And there are more causes, some of which are better described in sociological than in psychological terms. Work them out, it's not hard. But in the meantime what we've got on our hands is a whole lot of niggers. And what makes this particularly grim is that the student has less chance than the black man of getting out of his bag. Because the student doesn't know he's in it. That, more or less, is what's happening in higher education. And the results are staggering.

For one thing, very little education takes place in the schools. How could it? You can't educate slaves; you can only train them. Or, to use an even uglier and more timely word, you can only program them.

At my school we even grade people on how they read poetry. That's like grading people on how they make love. But we do it. In fact, God help me, I do it. I'm the Adolph Eichmann of English 323. Simon Legree of the poetry plantation. "Tote that i-amb! Lift that spondee!" Even to discuss a poem in that environment is potentially dangerous because the very classroom is contaminated. As hard as I may try to turn students on to poetry, I know that the desks, the tests, the IBM cards, their own attitudes toward school, and my own residue of UCLA method are turning them off.

Another result of student slavery is equally serious. Students don't get emancipated when they graduate. As a matter of fact, we don't let them graduate until they've demonstrated their willingness - over 16 years - to remain slaves. And for important jobs, like teaching, we make them go through more years, just to make sure. What I'm getting at is that we're all more or less niggers and slaves, teachers and students alike. This is a fact you want to start with in trying to understand wider social phenomena, say, politics, in our country and in other countries.

Education oppression is trickier to fight than racial oppression. If you're a black rebel, they can't exile you: they either have to intimidate you or kill you. But in high school or college, they can just bounce you out of the fold. And they do. Rebel students and renegade faculty members get smothered or shot down with devastating accuracy. In high school it's usually the student who gets it; in college, it's more often the teacher. Others get tired of fighting and voluntarily leave the system. Dropping out of college, for a rebel, is like going North, for a Negro. You can't really get away from it so you might as well stay and cause trouble.

How do you cause trouble? That's a whole other article. But just for a start, why not stay with the analogy? What have black people done? They have, first of all, faced the fact of their slavery. They've stopped kidding themselves about an eventual reward in that Great Watermelon Patch in the sky. They've organized; they've decided to get freedom now, and they've started taking it.

Students, like black people, have immense unused power. They could, theoretically, insist on participating in their own education. They could make academic freedom bi-lateral. They could teach their teachers to thrive on love and admiration, rather than fear and respect, and to lay down their weapons. Students could discover community. And they could learn to dance by dancing on the IBM cards. They could make coloring books out of the catalogs and they could put the grading system in a museum. They could raze another set of walls and let education flow out and flood the streets. They could turn the classroom into where it's at - a "field of action" as Peter Marin describes it. And, believe it or not, they could study eagerly and learn prodigiously for the best of all possible reasons - their own reasons.

They could. Theoretically. They have the power. But only in a very few places, like Berkeley, have they even begun to think about using it. For students, as for black people, the hardest battle isn't with Mr. Charlie. It's what Mr. Charlie has done to your mind.

Jerry Farber

Professor at California State, L.A.

HIGH SCHOOL STUDENTS UNITE!

DO IT YOURSELF

HOW MANY OF YOUR KIDS HAVE ASKED TO MEET THE AUTHOR OF ONE OF THEIR READERS?

In the classrooms where we tested 400 sets of *I Know a Place* (Wayland, Weston, Roxbury and Philadelphia), students regularly asked to meet Robert Tannen. Why? Because they wrote the books with him.

I Know A Place (in three books) is a collaboration between teacher/behavioralist Tannen and the student who puts his own name on the cover. Guided by Tannen's careful verbal structure, the student writes and illustrates the books, choosing whatever content he wishes. He creates a place, a society, and several individuals, drawing on his own experience or imagination (or both). The book becomes his. He comes to feel that his existing knowledge has value and he reveals the nature of this knowledge to the teacher. One teacher said about her kids, "They seem quite eager to show their books to me and never seem to show negative attitudes about the work that I've seen in other written and artistic work... Also, every child has completed the work he started."

I Know A Place cuts across several disciplines: reading (and word origins), writing, social sciences (including sociology and anthropology), art and group dynamics. Because the child creates the content, these books are culture-free. The series can be used at any grade level. (In our field test its greatest success was in grades 3 and 4, but this revised edition could also be useful in the middle school.)

PRICE: $1.50 for the set of three. A teacher's booklet accompanies orders of 15 or more. (A Spanish edition is in production.)

WHY DO WE DESIGN SUCH BOOKS?

The teachers at CSCS feel that most schoolbooks don't communicate with children:

(1) Big publishers aim at a common-denominator child who doesn't exist;
(2) Books seldom offer children the chance to participate—to talk to the book.

We believe that children become more engaged by the lives of real people, themselves and other children, and that they'll come to read and write with gusto by writing their own books and reading other kid's books. We call this PARTICIPATION PUBLISHING. *I Know a Place* is written by kids after they get it. Here's a book written by kids before we published it:

Mother, These Are My Friends, compiled by New York teacher Mary Anne Gross (with a foreword by Robert Coles), is a collection of wishes expressed (originally on tape) by four to six-year-old city children. In the immediate language of the kids themselves, these short pieces reveal the desires and interests of the city child, and of all children. Alternate pages are left blank for your students to illustrate, if they like, and there is a place at the end for the reader's wish. Besides its value as an elementary reader, *Mother, These Are My Friends* can be particularly useful at the secondary level as an introduction to a study of urban people and problems.

PRICE: $1.00 ($.80 each in lots of 15 or more.)

WHO ARE WE?

We're people from teaching and publishing who have been dismayed by the focus and the price of materials from the Park Avenue conglomerates. The CSCS approach has attracted the support of people like the following:

CSCS ADVISORY BOARD

JOHN HOLT, author of *How Children Fail* and *How Children Learn*
ROBERT COLES, research psychiatrist, Harvard University; author of *Children of Crisis;* contributing editor, *The New Republic*
MICHAEL SPOCK, Director, Children's Museum (Boston)
HERBERT KOHL, teacher and author of *36 Children*
PRESTON WILCOX, Chief Consultant, I.S. 201 Complex (New York City)
BERNARD WATSON, Deputy Superintendent of Schools for Planning (Philadelphia)

City Schools Curriculum Service, Boston

The children and the blacks among the poor are worse off than when the war on poverty began. 'All told,' writes Mollie Orshansky (of the Department Of Health, Education and Welfare) 'even in 1966, after a continued run of prosperity and steadily rising family income, one fourth of the nation's children were in families living in poverty or hovering just above the poverty line.'...poverty more and more becomes a fate because the educational, economic and social disadvantages of life at the bottom become progressively more damaging...

Quoted from "The Other America Revisited" by Michael Harrington in *The Center Magazine*, Jan 1969

Babies and infants show a style of life, and a desire and ability to learn, that in an adult we might well call genius.

JOHN HOLT

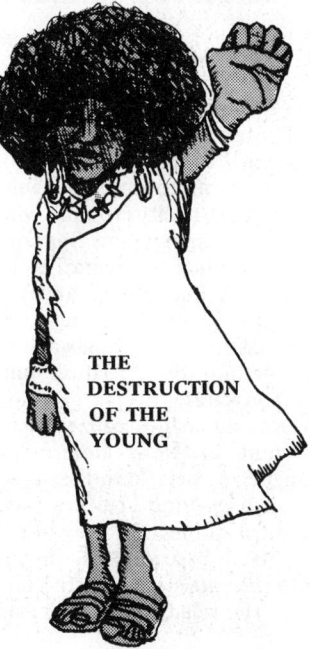

THE DESTRUCTION OF THE YOUNG

JUST what kinds of boys are sent to schools like Warrendale? In this country, one out of six is summoned to court before he is through adolescence. On any given day 90,000 boys can be found in our institutions, and on a national average, it costs about $10 a day to remove a child from his home and confirm, by locking him up, his belief that society is against him.

"In theory," states *Correction in the U.S.*, a report to the President compiled by the National Council on Crime and Delinquency, "training schools are specialized facilities for changing children relatively hardened in delinquency. In practice . . . they house a non-selective population and are primarily used in ways which make the serving of their theoretical best purpose, that of 'change,' beside the point." (Worse yet, detrimental change may occur, as when an eleven-year-old whose only offense is having been deserted by his parents is assigned a bed, between a kleptomaniac and a homosexual.)

From "How to Teach a Delinquent" by Nicholas Hahn, *The Atlantic* March 1969

NEW(S) FROM THE NETWORK
or, how to keep your head fed.

Over the past couple of years, a variety of papers, proposals, polemics, etc. dealing with educational reform and community organizing have appeared which have come to be called "underground" writing. Many began as private working papers which, through the miracle of xerography, slowly found their way into wider and wider circles and sometimes into publications. For numbers of people concerned with these topics, the various articles have stimulated new thought, given concrete form to loosely defined notions, or provided action models for organizing.

Some examples of the type of writing we're talking about: Werdell's "Letters," Rossman's "Some Background Notes. . ." Farber's "The Student as Nigger" Vozick's "The Hired Education." (a bibliography of the most well-known and widely circulated papers is available upon request.) Distribution methods have been crude—loose mailing lists, word of mouth, hand-me-down—but some papers have had enormous effects from coast to coast within very short periods of time. The Facilitator papers alone have stimulated a whole group of independent educational and organizational experiments.

BUT because of the informal way that many of the writings are distributed they do not often get to the individuals who would most desperately like to see them. Even the stuff that does get into print does so with no consistency—and never in the original spontaneous form. The bibliography shows material appearing, often months or years after it was written, in publications as disparate as *The California Aggie* and *The American Scholar*.

A Modest Proposal: We feel it is important that this "underground writing" on educational reform and other types of organizing that students are presently doing be circulated with some regularity to those who might benefit from it. To this end, we have created **THE EXPERIMENT(AL) BOOK**. Simply, the book will be a collection of reproduced papers, proposals, and other interesting documents sent to the subscriber in instalments as they appear. The only thing we can say with a good deal of certainty is that the writing will continue. Actually, there will be editing. We hope to select material which seems to have the most general relevance, even though rather esoteric selections are sure to appear in your mailbox too.

The way it works is that you send in $10.00 and what you receive are the NEXT 400 pages of "underground writing," in loose-leaf instalments of which there may be anywhere between fifteen and forty. We can start as soon as we have subscriptions from 300 people—then we'll start the mailings. The ten dollars covers duplication and mailing costs, and is not intended to make a profit. If our costs are lower as a result of many more subscriptions, we shall simply give you more than 400 pages until the money runs out.

We, of course, would like to solicit and encourage contributions to the **Experimental Book**. There are no royalties other than the intangible ones of having your feelings/insights/thoughts shared with a larger circle of like-minded people.

Blair Hamilton, Doug Glasser and Philip Werdell

send your address and $10 to:

EXPERIMENTAL BOOK
Antioch College Union
Yellow Springs, Ohio 45387

checks payable to:
EXPERIMENTAL BOOK

AN APPEAL: This October, the Addie Mae Collins Library and Center of Learning begins its second year. We are trying to build a place of hope, revolution, black presence and imagination in the midst of the black community. We get no government or city aid, but for my salary (about $70 a week) and our rent and telephone, both paid by O.E.O. About 15 workers, all black, manage the storefront. About 70 children and 50 adults are all paid. This summer we had to beg $700 a week. This fall we must beg at least $600. On Sept. 9, our school for the smallest children begins. We need tables, low chairs, toys (tough, wooden toys), crayons, paper, cups and food. (We have a community feast each day at noon.) We are tax deductible. Checks to: Addie Mae Collins Library Fund, 2067 Fifth Ave., N.Y., N.Y. c/o Ned O'Gorman, Director.

Commonweal Sept 1968

NEW MEXICAN SCHOOL

(LNS)—Alianza Federal de Mercedes, of which Reiss Tijerina is president and founder, has opened a school which will both educate its students to improve their social and economic position and will provide extensive training in Spanish culture. This Educational Cooperative is for both families and individuals, and its curriculum includes Spanish reading and writing; problems of the poor; English and speech; political organization; Spanish and Mexican history and karate.

"The Alianza membership realized that the school system in New Mexico is designed to anglicize the Indo-Hispano. The Spanish language and culture are forbidden and most subjects at the state schools have little relation to life," commented Alianza assistant Hetti Heimann, explaining the need for the school.

COLLEGES JAILS AND OTHER INSTITUTIONS OF HIGHER EDUCATION

The degree of civilization in a society can be judged by entering its prisons.

DOSTOEVSKI *The House of the Dead*

That's how I look upon those cats in those penitentiaries. I don't care what they're in for—robbery, burglary, rape, murder, kidnap, anything. A response to a situation. A response to an environment. Any social science book will tell you that if you subject people to an unpleasant environment, you can predict that they will rebel against it. That gives rise to a contradiction. When you have a social unit organized in such a way that people are moved to rebel against it in large numbers, how then do you come behind them and tell them that they owe a debt to society? I say that society owes a debt to them. And society doesn't look as though it wants to pay.

ELDRIDGE CLEAVER

The whaling ship, my Harvard and my Yale.

HERMAN MELVILLE

"Last night I stayed up thinking about what I have to do. I really think I have come to terms with myself, not because of prison but because people like Ron and David. But this is unusual. The other times I felt more like this." And he took from his wallet a scrap of paper a fellow inmate had given to him, a message the prisoner had addressed to society. It said:

"You have placed us here for punishment, you say, but the quest for revenge lights your features. Even so, if prison is for punishment the method derived to inflict that punishment is calculated to strip us of our initiative, decency, pride and respect.

Intrigue and Perversion
"After many years of degradation, humiliation and living a life of intrigue and perversion, you ask me to step from my 'den of iniquity' into your paradise and you expect me to make this transition overnight. I marvel at your naivete.

"Fate stirs the finger of fear within me. Like a wild beast I shall soon be unleashed to prey amongst you. I have survived my ordeal in this concrete and steel jungle and I am ready for the hunt."

From an interview with a man just released from prison, *The New York Times* 2/11/70

Ed. Note: How many sociologists, philosophers, psychologists, how many judges, cops, prosecutors, journalists have ever seen the inside of a prison, even just to visit?

REBELLION AS EDUCATION

IT TAKES REBELLION TO LEARN MANY OF THE REALITIES OF OUR SOCIAL ORDER AND CIVILIZATION

KINGSLEY WIDMER

Mr. Widmer, professor of English at San Diego State College, is the author of The Literary Rebel *(Southern Illinois University Press), and of books on D. H. Lawrence, Henry Miller and Herman Melville.*

We need not be at one with current campus rebels to give them sympathy and support. Granted, their rhetoric often comes out raspy, their tactics Pyrrhic and their programs simplex. All decent citizens decry the rebel's arrogant dogmatism, even when it matches official obtuseness; all deplore calling policemen "pigs," even if they do behave bestially; and all disapprove of erratic violence, even if provoked by systematic force. At worst, we may be evoking the style of revolt that we as a society deserve. History can judge the quality of a civilization by its rebels as well as by its official heroes, and that may shame us. Though good Americans all, our rebels might, and perhaps will, learn to do better if they continue their education in rebellion.

Among their present limitations one must include the current curriculum of insurrection, which is not altogether of their choosing. They seem to be as much chosen by, victimized by, as choosers of such basic issues as subordination to the military-industrial order, the structural exclusion of minorities, and the fatuous ideologies of autocratic elites. These academic side-washes of a competitively bureaucratic, militarily aggressive and smugly unjust society rarely appear evident to those who never touch them. One must, as do our militant students, wade into attempts at change, or get splashed with typical American righteousness, to realize how rough and bitter can be our social and political waters.

But, goes the stock "liberal" retort, why should the campuses of higher education be the scenes for these rough confrontations? Why don't the deprived blacks assault the business and union leaders instead of the academic administrators; why don't the draftable young men fight the government instead of the campus police, or the leftist students attack the corporate offices instead of the university halls? Probably they would if they could. But because academic institutions half fraudulently claim to be sanctuaries from the worst aspects of this society, they become especially and justifiably vulnerable. Throughout history, revolutions have occurred more often among the half-free than among the fully oppressed. The minorities in our universities, including the few from the under-classes, the dissident middle-class students and the radical-intellectual teachers, are sufficiently well placed to revolt, though certainly not to carry out revolutionary action in the society at large. If much of this insurgency could move from the campuses and ghettos to the headquarters of power and the suburban shopping centers, this would already be a quite different society. We must understand, and critically support, dissent and protest and rebellion where we find them.

At this moment, they rightly arise in and against academic society. Ambitious efforts at higher education long ago claimed to go beyond antiquarianism and specialism to social pertinence. Now at last, in insurgency and disruption, the academies do become relevant. Student revolt as education may be epitomized in the remark of a young lady on an urban university campus: "I learned and felt more about American society in the few days of the student strike than in four years of taking courses." In our higher education it is an achievement to fuse, even briefly, social role and individual intelligence and feeling. Such responsive experience, rather than the sometimes *outré* styles and superrevolutionary mannerisms, should be the

abrasive to bring out the grain of our responses. It takes rebellion, if not some official beatings, to learn many of the realities of our social order and civilization.

In and of itself, today's higher education demands its troubles and deserves its disruptions—most of which can only improve it. But even the rebellious only reluctantly learn this lesson. They, too, are compulsively entrapped in the American religiosity about education. When I taught in, and attended meetings with, the student administrators of a "free university," or listened to an SDS chapter I was advising on "university reform" (now Maoistically out of fashion), or joined debates in and on the "New Student Left," or discussed polemical targets with the editors of an "underground" newspaper, or sat through interminable quasi-therapeutic sessions of a "Student-Faculty Committee for Change," or chaired protest rallies, I often cringed at what most of the rebels thought was relevant and tough criticism of the Hired Learning. Classroom habit tempted me to rush to a blackboard and list satiric novels about academic absurdity for them to read, or to quote the lovely - aphorisms, from Diogenes through Veblen to Goodman, of biting contempt for official education, or to start telling personal anecdotes of the pathology of half a dozen universities. Only as the rebels literally dramatize their yearnings for more authentic education do they discover the dishonesty and intransigence of the authorities, the selfishness and cowardice of much of the faculty, and the arbitrariness and falsity of much of academic life.

Many of the rebellious poignantly suffer shock from the lack of humane sympathy for their efforts and the righteous refusal of demands for adequate changes. Hence the increasingly disenchanted and belligerent styles of campus insurrection. Their liberal professors, the students discover, all too often provide melancholy confirmation of the usual truths about sophists, mandarins, clerics, technologues and other orthodox rationalizers. Baroque professorial ways hardly obscure the primary drive of the hirelings to self-perpetuation and self-justification. In answer to student complaints about the usual mediocre teaching and mendacious programs, my colleagues fall back on one or another appeal to "our scientific and humanistic traditions." It is disingenuous and comic, for tradition in America is like instant beverage: the bland result of a little synthetic dust and a lot of hot water. Academicians sound more sincere, I suppose, when they speak of defending from disruption universities as sanctuaries for the pursuit of truth and art and dissent in a hostile and corrupting society. Logically enough, rebellious students begin to wonder why they and their suppporters can't get amnesty, much less sanctuary, when the crunch comes. Rather more than the mainline faculties, the dissidents want to create autonomous places of order and joy within America's repressive fragmentation.

The aggrandizing of institutions of higher education within the past generation obscures for the rebels what restrictive places universities have been and continue to be. The real academic tradition is that of keeping out, or only tolerating, not only the poets and saints but most of the original and critical minds. Most significant intellectual and moral work remains peripheral to formalized education or in subversion of its orderings. Though academics claim large roles for their disciplines, they tend to operate as technicians of them, and even more so these days in a society that glorifies technique. To be concerned about authentic intellectual experience still, as always, includes assaulting traditional learned disciplines, accepted and honored views and official higher education.

The odds oppose most of the academic caste doing this barnyard labor. While professors currently confuse their trade with civilization itself, most vocally in the humanities, their narrow and fearful tones belie such pretensions. There is nothing mysterious about it. Academicians are the victims of one of the most elaborate processes for inculcating subservient responses: it takes about thirty years of formalized indenture, from nursery school through assistant professorship, to become a full member. Especially these days, selection is mostly by institutional conformity rather than by any autonomous achievement.

No wonder universities suffer from ornate law-and-order arbitrariness and that so many of their members feel threatened by any criticism and disruption. Next thing you know, someone will question academic hierarchy. Are most full professors (I am one) 100 to 500 per cent more competent and harder working than assistant professors? A joke! The percentages, except for salaries and similar prerogatives, usually run the other way. However, the spread in salaries has for some years been growing even faster than the excessive general increases in academic compensation. With justice, younger faculty tend resentfully to support rebellious students. And with good reason, much of the public suspects all of us of crass self-interest. The step-by-crawling fraudulence of licking and booting one's way up the crypto-military ranks—and up the crypto-theocratic path from the provincial animal farms to the "big twenty" zoos—takes a considerable human toll. Internal exploitation creates the proper atmosphere for internal rebellion.

From their captive clientele (students) through their indentured servants (teaching assistants) into their arbitrary hierarchy (professional as well as institutional) to their dubious packaging ("sciences" and "liberal" education), the universities illustrate, as much of American advertising and foreign policy illustrate, grievous mislabeling of an ideology of competitive aggrandizement. As might therefore be expected, academic hiring exhibits all the ethical delicacy of, say, real estate brokerage. Sycophantic salesmanship controls not only the acquiring of prestigious jobs, awards and publications but reaches right down to the often miserable junior colleges and their petty prerogatives. In the current expansion of higher education, the traditional elitist and paternal (master-protégé) placement system becomes a manipulation of "connections" and "professional" images. The appropriate morals and manners for all this racketeering help determine what happens in the classrooms—and, now, on the steps of the embattled administration buildings.

Behind the rhetoric of student rebels lies the awareness that when one speaks of a "power elite" or an "authoritarian bureaucracy" or "corporate liberalism," or more generally of competitive and exploitative and unjust order, one is not referring to something "out there" but to conditions right on campus. Even when the militant focus seems mainly political, as with "student power" struggles against "militarism" and "racism," it is also a protest against faculty subservience to such order. Because of decades of institutional indoctrination and corrupt recruitment and hierarchy and production, we hardly notice the lack of an autonomous community of scholars until the students rebel in its name. They teach us what we should be teaching them.

Most of us serve large, mediocre undergraduate state institutions. (Perhaps the problems presented by the "very best" colleges and universities would require a different emphasis but, having taught in several which claim such distinction, I doubt it.) In social function, these educational bureaucracies serve to indoctrinate what used to be called the lower-middle class, now relatively affluent, in the techniques and attitudes necessary for submissive service in the middle ranges of corporate and public bureaucracies. Split between the purposes and functions of the institutions and our claims to separate moral and intellectual values, we end nastily ambivalent. Only thus can one explain some of the weird and even hysterical faculty responses to rebellious demands for clear moral choices. It is hard altogether to blame dedicated little scholars, after years of institutional processing, for themselves becoming bureaucratic devices. At our best, I suppose, many of us secretly believe that we can provide some counter-education, some involvement, for example, in literature and thought, which will work against the restricted indoctrination which the students and schools officially pursue. We fall back on such wheezing rationalizations of our roles as staying neutrally "Socratic," i.e., playing question games as a substitute for a sustained view (and as a device to avoid class preparation). But methodological excuses only midwife the rebelliousness which justly threatens to put us down and out.

For most students these days, interesting educational experience comes in inverse proportion to what passes for a "professional" or scholarly (usually meaning a technical) emphasis. But, some of my colleagues will reply, that is because the students came to college for the wrong reasons. A better case might be made that their professors, employed in one of the more lavish industries, stay in universities for the wrong reasons. Students, of course, are drawn to campuses by all sorts of motives: to remain adolescent a while longer, to look for sex, to acquire a trade the slow way, to avoid the draft, to gain social status, to play games, to join the rebellious communities, or just because they have been drilled to believe they ought to be there. Probably many students should not at their age be involved in higher education, at least in the traditional scholarly and intellectual senses. A later time of life would be much better.

The resentment of many young students, who endure years of inappropriate academicism warps the universities into doing all sorts of anti-scholarly things and the students into rebellions which reveal an unpleasant anti-intellectual element. Those colleagues who piously assume that years of submission to bureaucratic education produces socially liberal and psychologically liberating benefits reveal themselves as quacks of educationism. College may well be a net loss for many, including some who don't disgustedly drop out or arbitrarily get pushed out. Students who don't develop some resistance and some confidence in their dissatisfaction, who don't autonomously turn hip or radical, must find the processing an anxiously competitive and morally degrading effort to become less truly responsive and integral human beings. Professorial self-interest has been used to deny these students both candor and compassion.

The colleges serve partly as custodial institutions for many who lack adequate place and role in an amorphously restrictive society. Periodically, those treated as inmates do naturally rebel. Professors are well paid for their institutionalization; students are not (though they should be) and therefore feel freer to express their discontent than do the custodians. As one finds in reading most of the apologies for higher education, the basic ideology glorifies the custodial separation of knowing and doing, of culture and living. Campus rebellions, no matter what the immediate generous "cause," must be partly understood as defiance of that moral schizophrenia, which the students vehemently attempt to bridge by moral activism and lashing out against custodial treatment.

Whatever many of my colleagues might claim in scholarly allegiances, their devotion to busy work, to arbitrary requirements, to competitive procedures, to specialist propaganda, to punitive grading and to professional-

class decorum reveals them as primarily keepers. The horrendous processing—requirements, courses, tests, majors, minors, patterns, units, grades, averages, honors, etc.—is even more stupid than vicious. Even at its best it rests on the fallacy that repetitive accumulation is learning. Students, unless they take to conning the mechanism as most of their professors did, can Schweikishly soldier or collectively disrupt. The white students' current enthusiastic support for the black students' autonomous control of ethnic studies programs goes beyond racist guilt and political principle to tell us something of their own longings. That rebellious students also display notable disrepect for our "scholarly" justifications means that they see them, too, as just more of the processing. Rightly enough.

In my own field of "literary scholar-criticism," in which I'm sufficiently published to confess rather than complain sourly, most of the production is hobbyism: the overelaborate doctoring of texts, the compulsive collection of historical trivia, and the willful interpretation of interpretations. I don't mean to attack this hobbyism as such, for it is a pleasant pastime which merits gracious support; but it should not be confused with the need for responsive teaching and critical intelligence. Turned into professionalist ideology and institutional aggrandizement, however, scholarship provides trivial and inhumane molds for much of teaching and thinking, and deserves to be broken. Nor am I arguing for the reduction of faculties to mere pedagogues and intellectual scoutmasters, which often seems to be the position of the "anti-publication" faction in academic departments. (In some institutions these people protectively align themselves with the milder student rebels.) Actively cultivated and contentious people—those with something to say—should be recognized as a good in themselves. Given the lack of other harboring institutions in this society, they should be a major part of higher education, rather more so than the sinecured scholar-researchers and the bureaucratic technicians. Sartre once commented that to be a teacher was to be an intellectual monk. I don't care for the desexed metaphor but the quality of intellectual commitment may be hard to describe in a post-religious way. Certainly it provides a proper contrast to our hired education, in which business and bureaucratic production, if not racketeering, replace true vocation. A seasoning of critical intellectuals among teacher-students and student-teachers suggests the best possibilities for a community of learning and change.

Otherwise we can expect rebellions to increase against faculties as well as officials. In past years, campus revolt aimed mostly at the administrators, especially when they asserted parental and police powers. The superjanitors who now administer most academic institutions often deserve and incite rebellions. On good Jeffersonian principles, one can agree that there should be student disruptions of power every generation (academically, every four or five years). However, the old rebellions simply wanted to dethrone the administrations and then carry on much as before, like the liberal theologians who admit that God is dead but want to keep the old show going. Those rebellions of the middle sixties brought some changes, which now look extreme only in their moderation. But other failures appeared. The changes didn't develop community and autonomy in education, partly because it wasn't really allowed and partly because American capacities for full participation have been deeply eroded, not least by years of phony play-yard democracy in schools and other institutions. Fighting the administration does not create sufficient conditions for change, both because the universities are subordinate to the state and because the faculties are loaded with mediocre bureau-

crats. The demands then enlarge. The style of rebellion exacerbates until it fractions the faculty and incites government and public. The education in rebellion has now reached the intermediate level at which both new styles of insurgency and increased repression may be expected. An end to it would require major internal changes in universities as well as a move to other arenas for the drastic contentions all too necessary in this society.

As the student *enragés* keep trying to tell us, intellectual commitment can no longer be kept separate from moral passion. Modern academic humanism long ago settled, though not very successfully it becomes evident, for freedom from interference rather than freedom for innovation. We regular academicians may be justly accused of denaturing the professor, who no longer professes anything but a supposedly neutral methodology and submissive ideology for technicians. That may no longer get by. Students should rebel against us as well as against the administrators and the power forces in the larger society. Almost any critical éclat in the academy becomes self-justifying as a means to break the narcissistic routines and institutional denaturing. It may well be true that nothing less than disruption, however messy, will bring most of us to the perplexity and passion of a larger reality.

Can the universities bear the disruption? More grandiloquently, can our liberal humanism endure such uncouth assaults? If the institutions are so brittle, and our culture so anemic, that they can maintain themselves only by huddling in fearful unchange behind massed troopers, then there is little to be lost and, as the militants chant, "Shut it down!"

No historical evidence suggests that a culture dominated by bureaucratized intellectuals retains much vitality in the long run. We dissident professors, also quite likely warped by decades of institutionalization and excessive engagement to official culture, must make conscious efforts to support the rebellions. That does not mean forgoing criticism: black demands sometimes contain a second-rate nationalism and chauvinism; New Leftism, especially some current trends in SDS, desperately moves into a doctrinaire abstraction of reality and a destructive super-militancy; such socio-cultural rebellions as hippiedom, though delightfully realizing in a dreary academic context what Fourier called the "butterfly instinct," contains a mindless mystagogy and cultism. Discrimination is our obligation, but it should be part of a continuing radical critique to achieve the disequilibrium that allows rebellion to surface and change to come about. Academic resistance may, and must at times, take forms other than overt rebellion. However, professors cannot claim privileged sanctuary from the essential struggles of the society of which they are all too obviously an exploitative part and dishonest parcel. Only when we resist do we truly teach, turning topsy-turvy accepted values and transforming ways of life. We cannot do this by playing professional hacks and academic custodians. Nor do we really profess any humanism or science by mainly channeling students into more bureaucratic education and corporate elites and the nondimensional sensibility of the hired learning for a counterfeit society. The most distasteful deceit of professors these days comes out in those who demand intellectual and social and political change, but always somewhere else. The overwhelming majority of liberal-radical academicians, and not least the Neo-Marxists, have come out against rebellions on campus. It is sheer hypocrisy. The current rebellions should educate us, not just the students, into seeing education as rebellion.

VICTORY TO THE N.L.F.

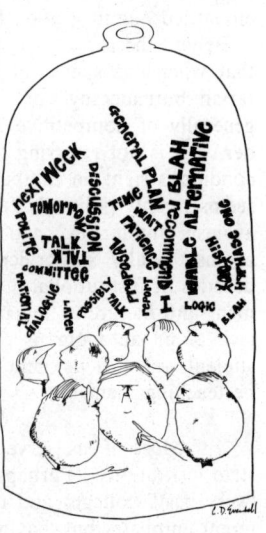

THE CENTER FOR PARTICIPANT
EDUCATION AT BERKELEY
CHALLENGE BY STUDENTS
TO THE ACADEMIC CULT

STUDENTS HAVE THE POWER TO CLOSE THE UNIVERSITY, NOT TO CHANGE IT

If the state, the University and State College Administrations, and the faculty have their way, this may well be the case. San Francisco State is the testing ground for programs of radical reform and the Governor and the present administration of the State College system are hoping that reform can be destroyed. Little do they understand that if reform fails, there are many people—black and white —who will turn to full-scale revolt. As Andre Gorz makes clear, a program of radical, structural reform is no cop-out; it presents a model of the good society and identifies and attacks those groups that are the obstacle to realizing that model for the society as a whole.

But reform which does not challenge the basic foundations of the evil in society is not really reform—it is palliation. The evils and the injustices of any society are not accidental, they are a product of the goals and values of the society. Just as many of the problems of the University can be traced to its intimate involvement with the military and government, and its re-definition of itself as a place of business, and thus to the emphasis on the production of knowledge and personnel rather than on the education of students—so also many of the evils of American society can be traced to its emphasis on comfort and stability, away from the values of human life. It is necessary for a comprehensive and meaningful reform movement to challenge this misplaced emphasis, and the misallocation of power and money which maintains it.

* * *

CPE does not, itself, challenge any of the precepts of the society. What it does is provide a forum for those who would. It encourages and develops the ideas of society and man which are developed by the students and teachers themselves. It serves as a place where people can redefine their existence, their society, and themselves. It provides a place where people who wish to challenge the precepts of American society can do so.

Jocks at S.F. State replace torn-down flag as pigs provide protection.

Because we believe that to understand the logic and the consequences of American society is to challenge its very existence, we hold classes which examine the logic and consequences of American society. The people who run this society, the would-be designers and manipulators of our lives, are merely protecting their own interests when they attack CPE and the student-initiated courses program.

Because as people can think for themselves, they can redefine themselves, and thus their society. It is for this reason that the CPE is attacked, not because of poor academic standards, not because our teachers don't have Ph.D.'s Jean-Paul Sartre doesn't have a Ph.D.—does that mean that he could not teach here? Academic qualification means undergoing a certain ritual, and thereby fulfilling the requirements of a cult.

That is why, when Richard Lichtman suggested that CPE be invited to join Academic Senate negotiating on standards for experimental courses, he was voted down by an almost 10-1 margin—the defenders of the cult do not want non-believers in. That is why John Searle, guardian of academic

freedom for the faculty (but never for the students) wants standards for experimental courses—he, like the others who have gotten themselves to involved in the myths and rituals of the "university" feels threatened.

* * *

CPE has only one standard for a course—students want to take it. If students do not want to take it, then the course should not be taught; if they want to take it, it should be taught. Any other standards for any course, let alone any experimental course, are part of the maintenance of the myth of the university, and part of the maintenance of the myth of democracy which American society has become.

We have developed our own cliches in response to the vacuum of relevance in university education —"student involvement in the educational process," "relevant education"—which draw their meanings from the form of CPE classes themselves, from their informality, from the lack of distance between student and teacher with the learning context for their stimulating content, the redefinition of education as a PROCESS rather than as a THING, and as the product of dialogue rather than lectures.

The classes are revolutionary in one sense: they are departures from the traditional norms of the university, in inception, in form, and in the way they are received. The classes are started by students, organized, outlined, and defined (or not defined, as the case may be) by students; emphasis is on dialogue, on the encounters of ideas, on conflict between points of view, on new subject matter, and on weird subject matter, on things never before studied in an American university in a way theretofore unknown. And they have been well received. CPE has grown and become an important part of the educational life of students.

* * *

The CPE exists to serve students—to help them to define themselves and their world, to help them train themselves to go into the regular university critically, so that what they learn can and will be useful to them, and serve them and their needs. We feel that our existence is a challenge to those things in American society which young people have objected to and tried to change. We cannot exist in a vacuum, and we cannot be successful without the participation of students. Participation in this case means the active participation in regular classes of the university, enrollment in CPE classes, and initiation of your own CPE classes. Participation means defining your own environment and your own destiny.

—Dave Kemnitzer

(Editor's Note: The above column is reprinted from the Center for Participant Education winter catalogue, which may be purchased on campus.)

Reprinted in

The Daily Californian Jan 1969

3

```
* * * * * * * * * * * * * * * * *
*  I learned and felt more about American  *
*  society in the few days of the student  *
*  strike than in four years of taking courses.  *
*                                            *
*  A STUDENT AT BERKELEY                      *
* * * * * * * * * * * * * * * * *
```

NONSENSE! HOW DO YOU EXPECT TO LIVE, COMPETE, AND ULTIMATELY ACHIEVE CHECKMATE IN THIS CHESSBOARD WORLD OF OURS WITHOUT OBEYING AND STUDYING THE RULES OF THE GAME?

R.COBB

Since the significant reforms needed in the universities are the very ones which administration must resist, since they curtail administration's reason for being and jeopardise its security ("reforms toward freedom, commitment, criticism and inevitable social conflict, endanger the Image"), why not go right outside the present. collegiate framework? Secession—the historical remedy of bands of scholars seceding and setting up where they can teach and learn on their own simple conditions, was, he claimed, difficult but not impracticable, and "if it could succeed in a dozen cases—proving that there is a viable social alternative to what we have—the entire system would experience a profound and salutary jolt". Pointing out the relevance of Goodman's continual search for something that can be done *now*, Theodore Roszak remarked recently in *The Nation* that "The defection has since taken place, spilling over into the many 'free universities' that are springing up, and Goodman was on hand at one of the best of them, San Francisco State's 'Experimental College', to offer a year of his time in residence." The first of these free universities sprang up in the Berkeley strike. "Before they beat and dragged us out," a student wrote to us at the time, "we constructed a community. We founded the Free University of California and held fifty classes in Sproul Hall. Graduate students taught in the stairwells. . . . We set up a kitchen and a first aid station. Blankets were distributed. We governed ourselves. Peace and order prevailed, although we were exhausted and attack by the police was imminent. In evolving a community, in confronting the latent totalitarianism of the larger liberal society and coming to a better understanding of our place in the world, we emerged healthier people, with a brightness that will show. . . ." The same story has been told since time and time again in many colleges,   *Anarchy* (London) Sept 1968

A MESSAGE TO NON-STRIKING STUDENTS WHILE THE TEAR-GAS CLEARS

LEAFLET PUBLISHED BY CPE AND AFT LOCAL 1570 DURING THE STRIKE FOR A THIRD WORLD COLLEGE AT BERKELEY JAN/FEB 1969

While the professor was laying down the elements of the life cycle in class this morning, UC scientists at the Naval Biological Laboratory in Oakland were designing the aerosol spray for biological warfare goodies deadlier than the Bubonic Plague. They probably listen to KSAN and feel they're Beating the System.

While your TA did a hip put-down of Reagan and you joined in his laughter, UC Davis researchers were taking a coffee break with the grape growers and discussing the automatic grape-picker. They won't get arrested, as did the eleven Chicanos last quarter when they sat-in to demand that UC food services remove grapes from our campuses. The researchers are beginning to grow sideburns; they're nice, cool people like us and grumble about their jobs—but feel they're Beating the System.

While you were Beating the System this morning in class, figuring out your GPA as the professor rapped about exploitation at the dawn of the Industrial Revolution, a UC sociologist was dotting the i's on a report for the Institute for Defense Analysis on how to calm down enraged cane-cutters working for pennies an hour somewhere in the Third World—South America? Delano? He was writing about giving them Democratic Values. He wears granny glasses and a psychedelic tie and thinks he's Beating the System.

(The Regents, too, were active this morning, taking care of business in *their* universe—the banks, agribusiness, department stores, weapons, mass media, oil, and so on. Running the System is *their* thing. It all hangs together.)

FAR OUT!! Right? Wrong!
Along comes a colorful group of freaks who cry that the Emperor has no clothes. They hint to us in various ways that Beating the System IS the System. They decide that the University should serve the needs of change and human values instead of the profit-oriented, War-supporting rat race we've all tried to beat by joining.

They decide that since one-third of the people in California aren't white middle-class, a piece of the machine should be reserved for them. . .perhaps so that they can begin to change the machine itself, give it some purpose beyond selfishness and intellectual snobbery. They are setting an example for all us fools who worry about ourselves within a system we don't even really dig. They are standing up and saying: Give us an autonomous college where we look at the ALTERNATIVES to the present System.

Autonomy
O.K. So why can't the Third World College be born through the "proper channels" like everything else? Why the demand for autonomy, this difficult birth? One reason is that the "proper channels" are themselves defined by the System, foster parents. The foster parents themselves are part of the problem. Can you dig it?

Berkeley is a rich and powerful suburban family, run by suburban people who teach suburban children the mores and attitudes of suburbia so that they can safely return to their suburban communities. The family to which the Third World people belong is that of the city and the fields—where people labor and try to keep body and soul together, doing suburbia's dirty work. To change their condition, they must be allowed to control and define what is relevant to *them*. How can white, middle-class administrators plan and implement programs which may be antagonistic to their attitudes and interests in the System? If we can dig the need for these programs, then why not let the people most affected by the programs create them? This is what autonomy is about.

Long hair, leather, dope, and the latest Warhol flick are important bits of individual freedom. But being free is more than that. While you are at this institution, you're contributing your body to a collective, whether you like it or not. To say "I am just an individual" and go off to class is bullshit. Those who administer the

collective give you a schedule, do not view you as an individual, but rather as a group to be manipulated and used by the System. If you go to class, you are co-operating with them, no matter how much you rap about Beating the System and doing your own thing.

Putting ourselves on the line for Third World self-determination and autonomy brings us closer to figuring out the forms of our *own* liberation.

Join the strike. Join the line. Seize your life in your own two hands.

The brothers and sisters who have put their bodies and their minds on the line need your help. They are being busted daily, with high bails and excessive sentences. They deserve and need your help and support. Contributions to the bail fund can be sent to the Third World Liberation Front Bail Fund, 509 Eshleman Hall, Campus. Please give.

Ed. Note: AFT Local 1570 is the Teaching Assistants' Local of the American Federation of Teachers at Berkeley. The T.A.'s were active in the strike. The regular faculty, with few exceptions, was not.

Letter from Vietnam

PURE (OBEDIENT) PRODUCT OF AMERICAN HIGHER EDUCATION LEARNS ABOUT WAR (TOO LATE)

The following letter was written by a young American lieutenant in Vietnam to his sister and brother-in-law just after an encounter in which he killed a number of Vietnamese. The soldier's sister told LIBERATION that her brother and the rest of the family have been very much in favor of the war. The sister's adamant opposition to it has been a source of tension within the family.

Dear Fred and Sandy or Sandy and Fred, (whichever the case may be)

Anyway, Hello 'Der.

It may sadden you to know that your little brother is no longer "a cherry Lt." I finally know what it's like to kill a man, a human being like ourselves.

You wrote me a letter, Sandy, about Last Xmas. You asked me to tell you what was in my heart & not to quote books & manuals etc. Well, I never answered because I couldn't. I had to get here and see before I could say.

Before I go on, I want to note that I'm still in a mild state of shock; but I want to record my feelings before this wears off & my senses dull. So please pass over your "schoolmarm" instincts to correct grammar & spelling & take the content in context.

Right now I'm sitting in a bunker at our Fire Support Base writing this by candle light although it is about 8 AM here. About 7 PM preceding day your time (E.S.T.).

It started out yesterday about dusk. I was writing a poem. Yeah, yeah—I know, the old Boondocks Bard. I'll try to remember to enclose a copy of the same.

Anywhoo, all of a sudden, all Fucking Hell broke loose (Sandy you seem to "groove" on profanity so I hope that you'll understand the words in their proper context. The Army has a language all its own especially the "grunt", the *footsoldaten*, (composed mostly of 4 letter words) Rockets, mortars, and R.P.G. (Rocket Propelled Grenades). Fred, I hope that you can explain some of the technical bullshit of this mundane vocabulary to my sometimes extremely dense sister. (No real insult intended, but Sandy you really aren't

up on some of the technological aspects which, of course, is understandable).

This was followed by a ground probe of "Hard Core" V.C. & North Vietnamese troops—100-150 men maybe as many as 300. I don't really know or care.

We were reading, playing cards & generally "batting the bull" when they hit us. I don't know about the others but here's what I remember.

As the first rounds hit I grabbed a "thump gun" (40 mm grenade launcher) & "made it" to the bunker. (The enemy attacked the southwest section, my section.) The "enemy" then started in with recoiless rifle fire and M.G.'s. Then they came. Screaming pidgen obscenities enough to burn the ears of a hardened sailor. i.e., "Mother Fucka you die, GI's eat shit," etc. to which we replied, along with return fire, "Sui loi" (sorry 'bout that) & "dinky dinky doo" (fuck your mother by your brother or cut your own throat). I had approx. 76 rounds of HE (high explosion) for the "thump gun" & 5 rounds of cannister (buckshot). I remember hitting a sapper complete with satchel charge right off center with an HE (high explosive) round & blew him into about four or five big pieces. About half-way thru the attack I ran out of ammo & then I strolled casually over to the 50 Cal. MG. I know that I was crouched down and running like hell, but it seemed as though I was strolling about quietly down a country lane trying not to draw attention to myself. (The 50 is one of the meanest mothers ever to thump through the valley of death). Anyway I got to the 50 & saw that it had about 1000 rounds of ammo, so I threw in a belt & charged the weapon. I *know* that I hit about six. You can tell when you hit somebody with a pound of steel-jacketed lead traveling at 1,500 Ft. p. Sec. (Feet per Second) no matter how big he is he tumbles asshole over appetite & usually doesn't get up again. Those six *didn't*. After about five or six min. I ran out of "boom boom" rations for the 50.

Then somebody, I think that it was Cpt. Smith yelled, "Allright men, over the top." I had been firing an M-16 "Zap" gun on "Rock & Roll" (full automatic) & then it was empty, but I was wearing my pistol belt with a 45 (pistol) and 3 clips of ammo (7 rounds per clip) & a machete & over the top we went screaming like a bunch of demented lunatics. I had the machete in my right hand & my pistol in my left & the next thing I know I was trying to pry the blade loose from an R.P.G. gunner's skull. I pulled & pulled with all my might but I couldn't get it loose. It went in just above the left ear & stopped just after it severed the clavical (breastbone). I fired into the body repeatedly (four or five times) & still couldn't get it loose & I had only about 14 or 15 rounds left for my pistol. Then I took out my switchblade knife (I'd bought it in Hawaii, it has a four (4) inch blade) & flicked it open. I thought for an instant of trying to cut the machete loose, but then they were on me.

May God(s) (if there is a God or gods) forgive me for I lost all sense of reason, an educated man with a college degree turned into a wild blood-thirsting animal. I felt a horror when I sunk my teeth into a *human throat!* I *almost enjoyed* killing, such is the blood lust in the human animal (a pretty good argument for instinct, huh?) I smashed my knee into the genitalia (groin) & felt the satisfying crunch of bone on tissue. & then I struck & struck with my pistol for a club & never thought of pulling the trigger. I remember the look on the face of a young V.C. girl (at least I think it was a girl—long hair, large chest, etc.) It was a look of utter disbelief. She had been so indoctrinated that the Americans were soft, pleasure-loving pushovers, degenerate playboys (maybe the 4-F cocksuckers in the states, but not the linedoggies) that she couldn't believe the ferocity of the counterattack.

Then as suddenly as it began it was over. I guess the VC-N.V.A. High Command thought that the price was too high to pay for one lousy, God Forsaken fire support base.

Their bugles blew retreat & they melted into the darkness carrying as many of their dead and wounded as they could.

My hands were caked with blood and there was blood on my face and encrusted in my mustache & in my mouth. I tried not to be sick, I really tried but I couldn't help it. I puked & puked my guts all over the field & I wasn't the only one. Gore & sweat covered me from head to foot. I want to burn my clothes, but I have no others.

Oh God, why must there be war why must people die like this? I'm tired & sick & scared & I want to go home to see peaceful valleys & streams & not to feel fear with every step I take, but I can't. I'm duty bound (intelligence over instinct) to stay here in hell for another 10½ months.

LATER

10 AM. The body count is 70 enemy dead on the wire (triple strand concertina barbed wire that surrounds the camp). We captured 8 light MB's about 40 AR 47 & 50 submachine buns & a whole shit pot full of assault rifles (all Russian or Chinese made)' & we found beau-fucking-coup (boo coo) blood trails. I went out and got the machete & my pocket knife. Both were encrusted with blood. I stripped the one that I thought was a girl. I was right after all. but it's so hard to tell over here. The women, for the most part, small breasted & slimhipped, even the whores wear padding, (taboo in most places) I pulled my knife out of her throat & got sick all over again. I'll pick up again later. I've been ordered to take a party & follow the blood trails.

1600 (4 PM) We found 18 bodies, 4 of which had been buried alive. Our 'Kit Carson' scout (Kit Carson, Chieu Hoc or "open arms" returned from the V.C.—turncoats) says [they were buried alive] so as not to destroy the myth of the V.C. invincibility. What sort of animal would leave its own to die by slow suffocation without even the mercy of a coup de grace? What sort of animal are we fighting? I don't want to kill anymore, I just want to go home & live in peace with all mankind, but if I can retain my sanity I'll probably remain in the Army now that I know what it's like to kill I don't ever want my son to have to do the same, ever!!!!

Bye the bye the poem I mentioned.

War (revised)

The sounds of rockets overhead,
The cursing wounded, the mounting dread,
A flare erupts into the night
Firing off its blinding light.

A target moves, you shoot it down
(S)he dies very slowly, a moaning sound
Your heart cries out, "Why fight this war?"
"Why are we here"? "What's it for"?

Then, the answer hits you clear.
You fight this war because of fear.
Fear for your home, your family
The United States, the right to be free.

The command come down, it's time to go,
But in your heart one thing you know.
You'll fight this war if it must be.
You'll fight on 'til eternity.

You look at the pictures of the ones you love
In your heart it plucks a string
You say a prayer, then move on
In a land called Vietnam.

If you know a god, pray for my soul
Mars (Ares) loves me
but Jehova has doomed me to eternal damnation for breaking the commandment.
    "Thou shalt not kill"
But I did kill and I almost enjoyed it.
God help me.
                                    Love, Eddie

LIBERATION Nov 1969

COLLEGE ISN'T THE PLACE TO GO FOR IDEAS
HELEN KELLER 1916

GOD FORBID WE COULD EVER BE 20 YEARS WITHOUT A REBELLION
THOMAS JEFFERSON 1787

THE ONLY PENETRABLE POINT OF A TYRANT IS FEAR OF DEATH.
FREDERICK DOUGLASS 1860

What you see in this picture is not just the result of war. War causes death- people killing and getting killed. And since most people are glad to be alive, they are usually glad if the people trying to kill them get killed themselves. What this picture shows, though, is not just death and gladness.

Armed Education: Glimpse the Future At College of San Mateo

WHAT WE'RE RUNNING IS A POLICE STATE: THE DEAN OF STUDENTS

john spitzer

SAN MATEO, CA (LNS-NY) — Just 45 minutes south of the beseiged San Francisco State campus, California's university of the future is taking shape. Atop an isolated hill behind a wealthy suburb is a two-year college of 20,000 students that resembles nothing so much as a prison camp.

Uniformed and helmeted policemen man a checkpoint at the College of San Mateo's single gate. Students queue up each morning hundreds of yards deep in their cars, waiting to have their IDs examined and approved. When a bus arrives at the checkpoint, each student is checked for his ID. Visitors are invariably turned back unless they have attained a special permit from the president or the dean of students.

A force of about 100 cops armed with riot clubs and Mace maintains a constant patrol of the campus. Plainclothesmen

mingle watchfully with the students on their way to classes, at lunch, in the library. A helicopter circles overhead inspecting the chain-link fence which surrounds the campus — no one goes in or out except through the single checkpoint.

The university of the future came into its own at San Mateo after a mini-riot of the school's black and brown students on Friday, the 13th of December. The students were protesting the college administration's mismanagement of the program for minority students: windows and heads were busted — many more windows than heads.

The following Monday, students arriving at the college were greeted by an army of more than 300 cops dispatched from all over the San Francisco Bay Area. The cops have been here ever since, and, according to the administration, "They will stay as long as they are needed." American education pushes itself to its logical conclusion.

Before the 13th of December, another university of the future was coming into being on the San Mateo campus, but since the coming of the cops, that university has been on strike. The College Readiness Program was set up only three years ago as an attempt to recruit minority group kids off the streets into the university. Black and brown students received intensive tutorial instruction in special all-minority classes.

Even more important, students were paid a "wage" for the time they spent in class, and in tutorial sessions. The program showed immediate results: where four years ago 30 of 39 minority students flunked out in one semester, blacks and browns now have the highest graduation rate in the college, with 90 percent of them going on to a four-year school.

By last year, however, College Readiness had become more than a reformist program. It was a political movement. Enrollment had jumped to 650. Bob

Hoover, a black militant, had been hired as director. Tutorials and special classes did not confine themselves to the punctuation of sentences and the intricacies of long division; they taught students how they could play the school system on their own terms, and how to beat the white college at its own game.

A program of Black Studies was inaugurated. Posters of Mao and Che covered the walls of the College Readiness Center, the program's headquarters. While the purpose of bringing black and brown students to college had once been to paint them white, now the whole atmosphere of the program was black and brown. The language of the street became the language of the classroom.

To the white college, this vanguard university of the future was inevitably a threat. Thirty-nine black students were one thing — especially when 30 of them flunked out in a semester. But 650 blacks and browns, most of them off the streetcorner, are something else. The funds for the program were cut back. The school administration, despite the pleas of the black and chicano students, refused to put any effort into raising new

funds. Students found their monthly paychecks reduced from $150 to $40.

By December, 100 students had been forced out of the program for financial reasons. Students were told there was no longer any point in applying for aid, and if they still applied, their applications were customarily mislaid.

After the mini-riot of December 13, the crackdown entered a new phase. The campus was occupied. Bob Hoover was summarily dismissed. The College Readiness Program was put under the "direct control" of the administration. The black and brown students called the strike and mounted demonstrations to get Hoover re-hired and the program restored in its integrity.

But the garrison university of the future is efficient. Student leaders were arrested at the checkpoint; all mass meetings were forbidden. On the campus of the future, students have been forced into a "war of the flea." College officials are harassed in person and on the telephone. On the night of January 6, a shot from a Mauser fired into the garage of the dean of instruction, Phil Garlington, ignited his car and caused $20,000 worth

of damage to his house. Now every college administrator has a constant escort of two cops.

To date, the two universities of the future — the lily-white concentration college of the administration, and the third-world college of the black and brown students — seem irreconcilable in the College of San Mateo. For the administration, there is still no such thing as the right to be black: "Although most of the students want an education," says Dean Garlington, "we have some who are very militant."

Bob Hoover has just been offered and has accepted a new job back on campus, but the cops are slated to remain, says the administration, "as long as we can foresee."

To both sides, the logic of American education seems inescapable: "What we're running is a police state," confesses Dean of Students Jack Alexander, "but they forced us into it. We have no choice."

San Francisco
Express Times 1/14/69

STRIKE FOR THE EIGHT
DEMANDS STRIKE BE
CAUSE YOU HATE COPS
STRIKE BECAUSE YOUR
ROMMATE WAS CLUBBED
STRIKE TO STOP EXPANSION
STRIKE TO SEIZE CONTROL
OF YOUR LIFE STRIKE TO
BECOME MORE HUMAN STR
IKE TO RETURN PAINE HALL
SCHOLARSHIPS STRIKE BE
CAUSE THERE'S NO POETRY
IN YOUR LECTURES
STRIKE BECAUSE CLASSES
ARE A BORE STRIKE FOR
POWER STRIKE TO SMASH THE
CORPORATION STRIKE TO MAKE
YOURSELF FREE STRIKE TO
ABOLISH ROTC STRIKE BECAUSE
THEY ARE TRYING TO SQUEEZE
THE LIFE OUT OF YOU STRIKE

Harvard Strike Poster Spring 1969

why strike

President Nixon has once again shown his utter contempt for the American people. By invading Cambodia, resuming the bombing of North Vietnam, and continuing to go all-out for a military victory in Southeast Asia, he has denied all demands that the war be ended.

Response to Nixon's move has come quickly. A national strike has already begun on college campuses. We won't take power by striking, but we can make the cost of the war a lot harder for the government to handle. With the government itself split on Cambodia, it puts Nixon in a pretty tough spot.

A strike is a lot more than just a big demonstration or a lot of leaflets and rallies. By leaving our classes, refusing to take exams and refusing to participate in "business as usual," we make time to reach out to other people who aren't in motion yet. We make withdrawing all troops from Southeast Asia and ending repression the central daily task of tens or hundreds of thousands of people.

During the strike, we exert pressure on the government by stopping essential institutions until our demands are met. Also, in some universities, we can demand—as we have done in the past, but stronger—that they end their part in the war and the foreign policy which brought it about: end ROTC, weapons research, counter-insurgency research, dependence on Pentagon money.

How to Strike

Form local committees: Our strike is decentralized. It began spontaneously. For it to work, everyone who supports it has to be involved in working together around our demands. To make this happen, and to make decisions about what we and the people we know should be doing, we have to set up local committees. We need them in dorms, in colleges, in high schools, in blocks and neighborhoods, in workplaces; also by groups, such as women's strike committees and campus workers' strike committees.

Activities: The committees have to take actions, not just sit around waiting for something to happen. We should do a lot of leafletting and canvassing off campus and on campus. When a particular school is already on strike, its students should go to other nearby colleges and high schools and help them get started. We can also talk to people at work by going to factory gates, going to office buildings and talking to secretaries, explaining the strike and why we feel it's time for action.

We can organize local marches and rallies: picket lines around our schools, picket lines at public places where we can talk to people about Nixon's lies and the real nature of the war in Indochina.

Beyond this, we have the power to disrupt war-related institutions, such as the Instrumentation Labs at MIT, the Center for International Affairs at Harvard, or the police training institute ("College of Criminal Justice") at Northeastern which trains people in domestic repression.

Local committees should make contact with a city-wide office (868-6700 ext. 4220) which provides speakers and literature and information about what's going on everywhere else. At some point, when the local strike committees are established they will have to come together into a city-wide committee to take it from there—we might want a huge city-wide march on some specific target. Harvard strikers have already called for a city-wide rally Friday afternoon at the Harvard stadium. Maybe later we would want a national action.

If you're not in school, or don't live in a dorm, organize a community meeting to plan some action or community discussion. If you work, try to get a bunch of people to call in sick. If you can hold meetings where you work, or at your high school, do it! If not, call the strike committee of the nearest college and they can get you a room.

THIS IS A NATIONAL STRIKE. Remember that the strikes, and the organizing and demonstration going on at your campus is going on at every other campus in the city, and the strike activity in Boston is being repeated in cities across the nation.

OLD MOLE *Extra! 5/5/70*

Not everyone will be on strike. That doesn't mean there is nothing you can do. If you are in high school, if you are a street person, or working you can still talk to people about the invasion and help them to understand why it has happened and what it means. You can talk to people about the planned extermination of the Panthers and the shooting of students in Ohio. You can form committees to fight the war. Finally you can support the strikes.

"To him who does not know the world is on fire, I have nothing to say."
—Bertholt Brecht

STATEMENT INTENDED TO "DISORIENT" NEW STUDENTS AT BERKELEY

Introduction

The world you walk into--beneath the scrubbed facade of Academia, behind even the words of this booklet which try to give form to frenzy--is a world on fire. There are no words of welcome, perhaps no words at all, that do justice to the callous brutality which lurks beneath the forced smiles and the glib rhetoric of our "liberal" managers. "It is not Reagan," they confide to their colleagues, "but the students that are out to destroy the University." But there is nothing left to destroy: long having been compromised by liaisons with corporate industry and the military, the University is but a painted lady. You may have expected a welcome to the academy; we welcome you instead to the brothel.

We are seeing the best minds of our generation destroyed by madness--a madness thrust upon them by small men in high places. It is a madness forced by threats of jail, of murdering or being murdered in Vietnam, of the grovelling ways of academics, of rerouted lives and broken marriages. We who came to study are now learning what is not in books: of tear gas, arbitrary arrest and political repression. Since 1966 the University has assumed the form of a Police State--more or less occupied by troops depending on the ability of students to express their rage. Sproul Plaza has been a battle field; Sproul Hall is now a jail.

You probably feel as we did when we first came to Berkeley--a little uncertain--disoriented enough without somebody taking pains to extend the malaise into a week's activities. Perhaps in this large campus and within this town of rebels, hustlers and freaks you may actually feel anonymous. You are, on the contrary, exceedingly important. The buzzards are already hovering over your futures: Heyns wants you, Dow Chemical wants you, Uncle Sam wants you, as do SDS and the rest of us. Some would have you become technocrats, functionaries or manipulators of others' minds. What we want is for you to feel out the situation, mull it over, and disorient yourself from these plans.

The attempt to figure out what to do, where to go, what to be is a collective problem: life in Berkeley is not easy. Either purposefully or unconsciously, you will change in the next few years. Berkeley is a town and a school in crisis. Soon you will be called upon to make a choice: for or against the demands of racial minorities, for or against your careers, the draft, the ASUC bookstore.... You will find yourselves in groups, struggles and situations which lead off campus in every direction; you must find yourselves in terms of these struggles first.

You may want to man a SNCC table--as did the original combatants in the FSM; you may be offended by the presence of the Navy recruiters on campus-- as were those who began the '66 strike. You may oppose the University's role in the community, which results in high rents, racial separation and urban sterility. Or you may move for student power over grades, curriculum and distribution of educational resources--which will put you smack up against the State Master Plan.

It may seem strange that we want to welcome you into such a hassle, but we hope that the following essays will make clear the vitality and variety of our struggles for orientation which lead necessarily to disorientation from the structures, programs and world-views which threaten to define our lives. Since no "campus community" exists, we welcome you to the Berkeley community, and into the Movement which permeates and sustains it. We have tried in these pages to give you a sense of what this place means to us-- a place in the history of human relations rather than on a map.

The essays here relate how we have found ourselves conspired against by the master planners of the interlocking establishments, how our studies have been distorted and disrupted by the imperatives of the modern profit system; how our lives--like the departments into which you will be channeled--have been fragmented, and how we are learning to respond and survive in order to resist. We have written about the men who try to plan our lives, who lecture at

NEW STYLE THEATER

HOW IT'S DONE SOME EXAMPLES FROM THE UNIVERSITY OF WISCONSIN

Ed. Note: *Connections* was an underground paper in Madison; now merged with *Madison Kaleidoscope. The Daily Cardinal* is the official college paper.

Walking around campus lately I have noticed more and more guerrilla theater performances. On the last couple of Thursdays, just before eleven o'clock classes, The Circus has a beautiful opening which itself contradicts the ugliness of contemporary life. They string out banners and ribbons to mark off their playing area, then play music and talk to the audience, building a good rapport with those around before they start the show. Then they do a mime which represents some aspect of living in the university, e.g., being trapped. They close down.

All are dressed in fine circus costumes in keeping with their apparent theme that the university is a circus. They can get away with miming to make their point even more effectively because they have some talent and know what to do with it. They seem to believe that they have to have developed theater skills in order to make their political points. The effect of all their preparations and spectacle is perhaps even more inspiring than the mime itself. The show, while it doesn't go far enough, makes the point that it is possible to liberate ourselves from the meaningless drudgery that is the university for many students.

A group calling itself the Military Industrial Complex Recruiting Team, now registered as an official campus organization, has been visiting science departments lately to recruit. On their table is an application form similar to those used at the draft physicals for those who want to join up. They also have a communist sympathizer sign-up sheet for those who don't like the Military Industrial Complex. They are always picketed by "peace creeps." There was some uncertainty among the actors as to whether they were to satirize the job recruiting by doing unsubtilely what the corporations

do subtilely, or whether they were to attempt to trick those who stopped into confronting their willingness to work for the military industrial complex. This conflict points out a change that "guerrilla theater" seems to be undergoing, change for the better in my opinion.

When guerrilla theater first started the idea was to blow the audience's mind. The assumption in trying to shock people was that they weren't aware of the injustices of our society and would help reform these injustices once they were made aware by confronting the issues. But we have come to see that there are people who win a privileged position because of these injustices, and will not change. Thus the mind-fuck guerrilla theater is a vestige of a more naive era of our movement. Guerrilla theater has undergone a change which parallels this perception. Instead of staging a "real event" which was intended to shock the audience into awareness when the hoax was admitted (as in the arresting of draft resisters in the union or speaking at the city council meeting, as guerrilla troupes have done), the latest trend is to announce to the audience that they are about see a theatrical performance. The audience is then prepared to enjoy itself and to see what the play has to say. This approach does not assume that we all have common values but tries to communicate the new values of the movement.

The depths to which the first type of guerrilla theater can lead is the claim by the chairman of the English department that a visit of the Madison police to one of his TA's classes was actually guerrilla theater staged by that TA. That old guerrilla theater in the long run increases the lack of belief of people in each other and actually desensitizes the audience rather than increasing their consciousness once they have been ex-

posed to too much mind-fuck theater. In the new trend the audience is not threatened and can enjoy itself while learning what the troupe is trying to say. This theater does not hate its audience as does mind-fuck guerrilla theater, which generally took a superior moral position and attacked its audience for not having the same morals. This theater tries to teach. (I exempt that guerrilla theater which is intended to sabotage some of the institutions that oppress us, such as Rubin before HUAC. This is a tactic whose primary result is to show others that these institutions can be resisted if one has the will and the imagination.)

But the new trend too is still a theater of exposure. Almost all guerrilla theater we have tried has been intended to raise an issue to its audience. It rarely gives any indication of what to do about the wrong it is pointing out. We can not make the assumption that if the issue is raised everyone will have a solution and act on it. Part of the creativity of the left will be in bringing some answers that those on the left have found for their lives and presenting them as examples to others.

I think our theater should go beyond exposure and become radical. This means to explore the problems raised in some depth. For example, whether it succeeded or not, the SF Mime Troupe in the Farce of Patelin attempted to go into what capitalism does to people. This was an attempt to explore for people the ramifications of capitalism and how it permeates our lives.

Theater is definitely an effective way to communicate one's attitude toward life and society. Through it we can explore more ways to escape from the ruts into which our society tends to force all of us.

—Hank Haslach

Radical Caucus Leaflet

WHAT ARE YOU HERE FOR?

In a few weeks you will be confronted with a Six-Week exam. You will be called upon to regurgitate what you have supposedly learned in History III. But have you learned anything? Of all the things to know about the Egyptian Empire is it really important to learn that Amenhotep IV had an endocrine problem? Does this really add to your understanding of the dynamics of history?

Some of you have already begun to question the lecture by raising questions in class in hope of filling in the gaps and making the course more interesting. In the last lecture you heard about the Religious Revolution of Amenhotep IV, but are the causes of the revolution and the reactions to it understandable? Was the religious revolution merely due to the Pharoh's devine inspiration, or was the revolution a response to the particular social, economic, and political conditions of the time? It should be the duty of the lecturer to raise and discuss such questions rather than filling in an already outlined syllabus with more outline material.

You already have a syllabus which outlines the course. Why not print up past lecture notes as we have done which will fill in the syllabus. The lecturer will still require you to come to class but you will be free to eat lunch, read a novel, eat lunch, nap.

Why is class attendance required?

Does class attendance add to critical understanding of the material?

Are you just putting in time?

Can this be made into a critical course in which the students actively participate in an educational process which has significance for their lives?

Would all those students interested in printing more lecture notes and in making this a better course please meet in the back after class.

Frank's Landing

By DOROTHY DAY

COLLEGE STUDENTS LEARNING TO LEARN OUTSIDE THE UNIVERSITY

Frank's Landing on the Nisqually River, which empties into Puget Sound between Tacoma and Olympia in the State of Washington, is not the place it was when Robert Casey, our Northwest Coast correspondent who is a seaman working on the Alaska run, wrote about it in the December *CW*. The melting of tremendous snows in the mountains led to such a rising of the rivers that two of the six acres belonging to William Frank (for whom Frank's Landing was named) have been washed away, and the landing itself has collapsed into the river. We sat there all one Sunday afternoon—Maiselle Bridges, who is William Frank's granddaughter, Toni Casey (Bob's Japanese wife) and I — and talked about the situation of the Indians in general and of the winter just passed when as many as a hundred and fifty sympathizers with the Indians' struggle to retain their treaty-guaranteed fishing rights were students at what could be called a unique school.

William Frank is a ninety-year-old Indian who has for the last six summers performed a unique service for students of Indian life. He has put on tape, with the assistance of a Professor Metcalfe of the University of Washington, the history or the Puget Sound Indians and their language, which is Salesh, not a written language as yet, although some professors are trying to transcribe it. Although Frank has complained to the Bureau of Indian Affairs and the Conservation Army, he has received no compensation for his loss, on the grounds that it was not productive land, there was no truck farming or dairy operated on the land.

I had been reading of the long struggle of the Coast Indians to maintain their way of life and fishing rights against the government, ever since the days of Isaac Stevens, who made the first treaties in 1850. Stevens had tried to herd the Indians on to reservations in order to turn them into homestead farmers, "economically independent," and the government has been equally unrealistic ever since in its plans for them.

The story of the school is this. The struggle over the fishing rights had been going on for a long time, marked by frequent clashes with game wardens, which were becoming ever more serious. The publicity attendant on this struggle, in which Maiselle Bridges' two daughters were jailed, along with other members of the Indian community, evoked the support of students, especially after a Rock Festival was held. Many of the students, young teachers, some members of the Students for a Democratic Society, and one member of the Southern Christian Leadership Conference (Martin Luther King's group) who was accused of being a Black Panther by local residents, came to the aid of the Indian fishermen demonstrators and stayed for months.

At Frank's Landing they put up the framework for nine bunk houses, which they covered with heavy plastic, and there they lived from September to May. One bunk house was a tree house, built on the stumps of two gigantic cedars as a foundation, and nestling between the branches of other trees which had grown up around and in the stumps. They put stoves inside these plastic houses and used driftwood to heat them. I would not have believed that this could be done if I had not seen a similar house built as a studio by Joe O'Connell, the Minnesota artist who gave us our stone statue of St. Joseph which stands in the window at our First Street house. He worked in it all winter and kept it warm by a great pot-bellied stove. The students carried all their water for cooking and washing and used outhouses,—all a part of their education in survival living.

It was a spontaneous coeducational school which sprang up and was at first looked upon with some misgiving by the Indians themselves.

"Our neighbors," Mrs. Bridges said, "indicated that they had been willing to stand by us in our struggle until we accepted the help of hippies, Black Panthers and S.D.S. But we soon learned from these young ones, just as they learned from us.

"They participated in the almost daily demonstrations and clashes with the authorities and they were learning all the time about the Indian. Sometimes there were as many as three hundred, sometimes the numbers went down to seventy-five. It was snowy this winter, the hardest winter we ever had here on the coast. The snow lay on the ground a long time. But the kids stayed.

"To insulate the floors of the houses we put down plastic, then straw, then more plastic and rugs over that. We got rugs in every thrift shop in Olympia and Tacoma and people brought us their old rugs. The fishing every day supported the camp. Groups went to Seattle, Tacoma and Olympia with the fish and sold them for fifty cents a pound. They had deer meat (we still have some in the deep freeze) and the boys learned how to skin the deer and cut up the meat. They missed fresh vegetables and fruit, but people made contributions. Some of the students picked cucumbers later, some went to the public markets and the bakeries. One girls' father, who had a chicken ranch, sent half a dozen chickens for a stew. They gathered wood at Fort

Campus confrontations acquire a wider understanding with the release of a new study into the mind and manner of the typical college and university trustee.

The study finds that "trustees do not read—indeed have generally never even heard of the more relevant higher education books and journals."

Also, most trustees feel that the administration should control the content of student newspapers; well over a third believe it reasonable to require loyalty oaths from faculty members, and a similar number hold that students punished for off-campus behavior should also be disciplined by the college.

A fourth of the trustees would screen campus speakers, and deny to faculty members, "the right to free expression of opinions."

What kind of nutty picture is this? Not nutty at all, unfortunately. It's the one that emerges from an opinion sampling of more than 5,000 trustees at 536 colleges and universities, made by the Educational Testing Service in Princeton, N.J., in cooperation with the American Association for Higher Education and the Association for Governing Boards of Universities and Colleges.

According to the study, the average trustee is in his 50s, white, Protestant, conservative and rich (more than half have incomes in excess of $30,000 a year). He agrees on balance that "running a college is like running a business," and generally favors for the college a "hierarchical system in which decisions are made at the top and passed down."

All of which places trustees as a group at opposite end of the spectrum from most faculty members and students. The study concludes:

"To the extent that ideological differences among these groups remain (or increase), we might expect greater conflict and disruption of academic programs, a deeper entrenchment of the ideas of competing factions, and, worst of all, an aimless, confusing collegiate experience, where the student's program is a result of arbitration rather than mutual determination of goals and purposes."

From "News and Views" by John Deedy
Commonweal 1/10/69

I MET BOLIVAR ON A LONG MORNING...
"FATHER," I SAID, "ARE YOU, OR ARE YOU NOT, OR WHO ARE YOU?"
AND HE SAID:
"I RISE EVERY HUNDRED YEARS WHEN THE PEOPLE WAKE UP."
—PABLO NERUDA

THE AWAKENED COMMUNITY WILL SEE ITS DEMANDS REALIZED; THE STRIKE WILL CONTINUE.

THE ICEBERG STRATEGY

UNIVERSITIES AND THE MILITARY-INDUSTRIAL COMPLEX

CORPORATE INVASION OF THE UNIVERSITY

Martin Nicolaus

In the Spring of 1966, VIET-REPORT published a series of three articles on the Michigan State University project in Vietnam,[1] describing what had been done and attempting to examine why it happened. What I will do here is criticize some of the conclusions that were made in those articles and also try to develop further those parts of the conclusions that I think are still relevant. One of the basic themes in those articles, and something a lot of people have been saying all along, is that the involvement of the university with the military complex and the accompanying secret projects are bad for education. Although I agree that it's bad for education I think there's a misconception involved.

GOETHE, KANT, AND THE EDUCATIONAL INSTITUTION

It's a misconception to say that the university is an educational institution. An institution is something that has walls of one kind or another; it may have physical walls but it can also have only social walls. It's a place inside of which you are supposed to be safe. A prison is also an institution that protects you, but it does so against your will. A university is (or was) supposed to be an institution that protected you against the outside world. Universities in medieval times were sacred grounds. If a student came there he couldn't be touched or arrested. This is what is meant when we call the family an institution; the family is a place where nobody is supposed to be able to get at you; it's a place where you're safe. This obviously is not the case with universities today, and we'll come back to this.

Education, from the Latin, means exducare (to draw out); originally it involved two ways of drawing out. First, it meant to draw out of the human being all the potentialities that were there; to draw out of the human brain all the possibilities that were inside it and to develop them. The ideal of the educated man, in this sense, was a person like Erasmus or Goethe. Goethe was that great fellow who was a zoologist, botanist, philosopher, poet, playwright, novelist, political theorist, and all kinds of other things. He was not only good at each of these different fields but he was at the head of the science in all of them. He was one of those who fit the definition of what an educated man is: 'An educated man is one who can do also what other people can do only.' The goal of education was to produce an all-rounded kind of individual. The other side of the definition was that education drew the individual out of the people. It took the brightest people (and this is also the church concept of it) in the lower classes and drew them out of the 'vulgar mass' into an obvious elite position. For example, when Goethe came out in favor of

1 Martin Nicolaus, 'The Professor, the Policeman and the Peasant,' VIET-REPORT, Vol. 2, #1, 2, 3 (February, March-April, June-July 1966).

the French Revolution, he wrote a beautiful, strong philosophical support of the principles of the Revolution. However, he could be read by only about 5% of the population of Germany at the time (and they were all elitists like him) and so it didn't matter at all. Or take Kant, the great philosopher of Koningsberg who took his walks at five o'clock every afternoon very regularly. Everyone set his clock by him, but he wouldn't have dreamt of talking to a lowly watchmaker. He wrote a fantastic essay on the 18th Century Enlightenment saying 'dare to know!' But nobody could read and so it didn't make any difference. These were the two meanings of 'education' -- on the one hand to develop you as an all-sided individual; on the other hand to develop you into an elite individual who couldn't communicate (and wasn't supposed to communicate) with people below him.

STRAIGHT ACADEMICS AND THE KNOWLEDGE INDUSTRY

Obviously what we have today in our so-called educational institutions doesn't conform to this definition in any way. There is a book put out by DAEDALUS magazine (which is sort of a READERS DIGEST of the academic community) called The Contemporary University USA.[2] The writers include such notables as Clark Kerr, David Riesman, Kenneth Keniston and Martin Myerson (straight academics all) who reveal their thoughts about what's happening in higher education today. They don't make any bones about it; they call it the 'knowledge industry.' Here are a few things from the editor, Robert Morison: 'The faculty expect salaries roughly comparable to those of middle management in large industry.'[3] (He then explains why this is no coincidence.) 'Not surprisingly, it turns out that the classical departmental structure of universities is not well adapted to devising new weapons systems, putting a man on the moon, cleaning up polluted rivers (!), planning for healthful and convenient cities (?), or learning everything one needs to know in order to deal sensibly with the emerging nations of Africa.'[4] Our favorite ex-president, Clark Kerr, also puts it very straightforwardly. He says that there are three great changes taking place in the university: there's growth, there's shifting academic emphasis, but most importantly there's involvement in the life of society. 'The university, in particular, has become in America, and in other nations as well, a prime instrument of national purpose. This is new. This is the essence of the transformation now engulfing our universities.'[5] He goes on to show how, through federal funding -- of research, of departments, of professors and of students -- the university's control over its own destiny has been substantially reduced. This is obvious, because the people who put up the money for the universities control what happens to the money in the universities. Now, therefore, university presidents (even people of the stature of Clark Kerr) are not nearly so powerful about determining what happens within their institutions (or ex-institutions) as they used to be. Kerr notes that 20% - 80% (the larger the university, the higher the percentage) of a university's expenditures may be handled outside the normal channels, and universities are thus gradually losing control over the activities carried on within their walls. This is one essential feature of the knowledge industry. Study specific fields from the foundation's viewpoint and you'll find why they don't subsidize the social sciences as much as they do the physical sciences. The phrase that is used is 'the investor in the social sciences has a more difficult time than do those of us who deal with the natural sciences.' The term is clear; it's borrowed from industry -- 'investor'. Robert Morison, the editor, notes that 'many of the characteristics of American universities owe their existence to the peculiar tendency of wealthy Americans to leave their capital in trust for the public welfare.'[6] We could talk about almost any large university in this country today just from this one book. Peter Rossi, in his article on researchers and scholars notes:

> The major foundations and government agencies from whom funds on this scale /on the scale necessary to conduct sociological studies/ are usually obtained are reluctant to part with this much money without being quite convinced of the practical importance of the survey in question. Hence, large scale survey research is generally 'applied' social research; that is to say, the grantor is convinced that the results will have some immediate bearing on policy formation. The high cost of social research has meant a close tie with the machinery of policy making.[7]

He goes on to tell an example of a visit that was made to NORC (National Opinion Research Council) at the University of Chicago. 'Recently,' he says, 'NORC was visited by Mr. Louis Moss, who is director of the Government Social Survey in Great Britain.' He sat down with Mr. Moss and compared the types of surveys they had done. In Great Britain it's a government agency, straightforward and here it's NORC, a university group.

> We could find parallel studies on about two-thirds of ours and about one-half of his projects. This means that together with other survey research organizations connected with universities or functioning as commercial enterprises, NORC is serving the same function for the American policy-maker as the Government Social Survey functions in England.[8]

2 Robert Morison, ed. The Contemporary University USA (the Daedalus Library.) Boston: Houghton Mifflin, 1966.

3 ibid., p. x.

4 ibid.

5 Clark Kerr, 'The Frantic Race to Remain Contemporary,' in Morison, op. cit., p. 20.

6 Robert Morison, 'Foundations and Universities,' in Morison, op. cit., p. 123.

7 Peter Rossi, 'Researchers, Scholars, and Policy Makers,' in Morison, op. cit., p. 123

8 ibid.

What all these examples show is that we no longer have education; we have a knowledge industry. This means that the goal is not to draw the student out in any sense -- either in the sense of drawing out his individual potentialities or in the sense of drawing him out of the life of working society. Instead, we now have a system of 'inducation' or 'induction' into society. What the knowledge industry is trying to do (and what it is doing) is to train people for industry. This is obvious at the large universities; at the smaller universities it's often not so clear. The smaller schools don't get so much money and have more of an elitist orientation. There will always be some of these small elitist universities because there will always be a need for a few people who know a little about everything. But the needs of industry in general are not for people who 'know a little about everything' (people like Goethe); industry needs people who have specialized skills.

THE EDUCATIONAL ICEBERG AND THE MILITARY-INDUSTRIAL COMPLEX

This is where the question of the iceberg arises. In our discussions about the military and the universities, what are we aiming at and what are we trying to do? It seems to me that it's very clear that the military -- the baby burners and the people who study how to burn babies -- are only the top of the educational iceberg. This whole knowledge industry is oriented toward precisely the same task that the military is oriented toward. Former President Eisenhower noted quite rightly that there is no essential distinction to be made between the military and the industrial complex in this society. There is no real difference between the people who actually manufacture baby-burning machines and the people who design these machines. This is all done in the universities; the research for these things comes from the ordinary science departments. It is often argued that most of the research on these things is done in the Dow chemical research laboratories, not at the university campus. But who trains the people for the Dow laboratories? Who gives them the skills and the ethics that are necessary in order to produce people who are willing to make napalm? Who produces people who will make ordinances, learn how to do ballistics, or learn to do social studies of what happens to the social network when people are bombed out? Obviously, this is all done by the universities. It seems to me that the distinction between these two things is really very hard to make. It is right for us to protest when a member of the university community is involved in burning babies but we must also see what other members of the university community are doing. For, in fact the entire university is oriented at the policy level toward the burning of babies -- either the rapid burning of babies with napalm or the slow frizzling of babies' minds in the so-called educational system. If we don't see that the whole thing is oriented at the policy level toward specialization and destruction of individuals and induction of individuals into the industrial system, then it seems to me that our strategy is not going to get off the ground.

Suppose we see ourselves in a gunboat facing the top of this iceberg -- all the military things that we've forced to come to the surface -- and we blast it. We get all of these military contracting organizations out of the university. I think this is going to be relatively easy, because all that will happen is that when these organizations disaffiliate, professors will take jobs with them on their own, as 'outside consultants.' This has happened at Pennsylvania; it is probably going to happen at Princeton; it's the kind of thing that can happen elsewhere. There's nothing that prevents it. If we are going to attack military involvement in the university, as it seems to me we have to, then we have to attack the principle of faculty members contracting out to industry. In other words, a whole other part of the iceberg is going to surface. We must not think that the first thing isn't worthwhile doing (for it is); but we must see that the first thing implies other things. If we are going to attack the ties between the university and the <u>military</u> apparatus, then we will inevitably have to attack the ties between the university and the corporate <u>industrial</u> structure as a whole. This I think is quite clear.

DEPARTMENTS, GRADES, AND BOARDS OF GOVERNORS

Then, it seems to me, we have to look ahead, not necessarily to what we are going to be able to do (because I don't know how much power we have) but to what is logically involved in what we're doing. If we are going to do something about ending the military influence in the universities we must first get rid of defense contracting. If we then can get rid of industrial contracting, we will have to get rid of boards of governors, because these are largely composed of businessmen who are tied in with both the military and the industrial complex. (This is very nicely illustrated in a recent paper by Kathy McAfee.[9])

When all this is done, we must do something about the departmental structure. The way that 'departments' and 'area projects' are separated really has nothing to do with the subject matters that are involved. There may be departments of history, politics, sociology and anthropology, but that doesn't mean that there are actually different worlds out there. You can look at a process but you can't split it up and say one part is the anthropological side of it and one part is the sociological side. That's not real; in reality these things are connected together. The reason that we have departments in the first place, other than for administrative convenience, is because industry needs 'economists' or 'political scientists.' Industry needs people with job classifications that are standardized, rationalized, and computerized. In this way, you can get one economist in your industry, fire him, and be fairly certain that the economist you hire in his place will be just like him, though hopefully a little better (more informed about what's happening or more yielding to your demands). We have to recognize that the departmental structure is involved in this.

---

9 See the paper by Kathy McAfee on IDA (Institute for Defense Analysis) in the January 1968 issue of VIET-REPORT.

Still another important concomitant of the university as a knowledge producing industry is the grading system. Why are there grades -- does anybody really care whether somebody is 'smarter' than somebody else? None of the professors I've talked to will admit that in their heart of hearts they really care about any of this business -- grades, exams, or papers. It's not because they care about the students; it's just because they don't care about the crapwork. There is, however, a necessity for a grading system. For if you look at the statistics, you will see that the people with the higher grades get the better jobs. Industry needs a grading system in the knowledge industry in order to know who to hire to the top positions and who to hire to the less important positions; to know who to pay and where to feed people into industry.

TAYLORISM AND IMPERIALISM

If we are going to do something about the university's involvement with the military-industrial complex we have to go further than what has been outlined. Take the concept of courses. One person, a teacher, takes a batch of students (a steadily increasing batch of students with classes of 400, 500 or 2,000) and runs them through a predetermined, standardized routine with textbooks. These are the methods of industry; you recognize them as the methods of Taylorism, of scientific work management; you recognize in the process the principle of the highest output at the least cost, least wages, and least educational investment. The course structure is also something that is determined by the needs of industry and something must be done about it if the university and industrial world are to be separated. Look, also, at the actual content of what's taught; take anthropology. There's a very fine anthropologist, Kathleen Gough Aberle who studied the history of anthropology during the last 200 years and says flatly: 'Anthropology is a child of western imperialism.'[10] There have been anthropological speculations for hundreds of years but anthropology as a field of academic inquiry didn't originate until the 1870's when European imperialism got underway. Anthropology in this country didn't originate until the federal government, among other organizations, started sponsoring research. This means that not only the actual research locations that are chosen but the attitudes, concepts, and ways of thinking about the world that are involved in anthropological thinking are essentially the products of imperialism. The way that an anthropologist or a student of anthropology looks at a so-called native is conditioned by at least a hundred years of involvement with his people as a conquering race. If something is going to be done about separating the university from the military-industrial complex, then the very concept of anthropology has to be exploded and rewritten. New ones must be created in its place. The same is obviously true of sociology and the other social sciences. An excellent book on this subject is Loren Baritz' The Servants of Power,[11] which studies the involvement of sociologists with government and with industry. Baritz shows in detail that sociology (in this country at least) didn't come out of the dark ages of philosophical speculation and become a 'social science' until industry started paying for sociology. Industry paid sociologists to do studies of why workers strike and how they can be stopped from striking, and how workers can be induced to produce more. Sociology also grew during the second world war when it was found that the behavioralist method (the survey research business) could help the Army train its soldiers and keep them happy while they were in combat. There's a big four-volume study on the American soldier[12] which contains information of no use to anyone except the Army.

The methods of sociology and all the survey research work have in them implicit assumptions about what people are, what society is, and how people hold opinions. These concepts are based on three general attitudes. First, the sociologist is a superior person to the person who is being studied. Second, the person who is being studied is a passive person to whose wishes no attention has to be paid (except in a manipulative way). Third, the only thing that's worth knowing about people, in general, is what the people that sponsor research want to know. Take the concepts of sociology that we have; the concepts of Talcott Parsons. This philosophy should not be viewed as an empirical description of reality but as a grand analogy to the real world. There is implied in this a view of a harmonistic universe in which everyone gets along nicely -- a universe in which people who protest are not put down for being 'communists' or 'radicals' but are put down for being 'dysfunctional.' This is true of practically all of sociology; most sociologists have this kind of thinking at the bottom of their thoughts and there are few sociological concepts that do not, in some way, reflect the position of sociologists as servants of power.

To go beyond that we should probably go into our own attitudes. I think that we can say that the educational system has been molded by the military industrial complex and by military research in the areas of university structure, grading, course structure, and course content. The same forces have probably shaped all of our minds in ways that make it extremely difficult for us to see the problems that exist for people who are being oppressed in the way that they see them. It is extremely difficult for us to get down in the valley and look up at the mountain and see it the way that the people below see it. It's possible for us within the university to write book critiques -- papers against Lipset and Hoffer, for example;[13] this is excellent and really must be done. But it's still not entirely possible for

10 Kathleen Gough Aberle, 'Anthropology and Imperialism.' A paper delivered at the Southwestern branch of the American Anthropological Association meetings, March 1967. Available from the Radical Education Project.

11 Loren Baritz, The Servants of Power. Wesleyan University Press.

12 S. A. Stouffer, et al. The American Soldier: Adjustment During Army Life. Princeton: Princeton University Press, 1949.

13 See the book-critique series published by Madison SDS and the Radical Education Project; included are critiques of Lipset's Political Man and Hoffer's The True Believer.

very many of us to look at the world through the eyes of people who aren't even in the university. This is one of the things that the university has done to us, for in 'inducating' us into the knowledge industry it has 'exducted' us out of the people.

EDUCATION AND REDNESS

It seems to me that we need to have a long-range strategy. The strategy we have now, of getting people to see the little peak of military research at the top of the iceberg and blasting that doesn't seem to me to be enough. I don't mean to put down the current campus activities because these things have to be done; you get other people to see what's below the top of the iceberg by making them see how horrible the top of it is. But as a long-range strategy, blasting what's on top isn't enough. If we challenge the military invasion of the university but we are not willing to challenge corporate invasion of the university we may get caught in a bind where we cannot explain ourselves to other people. People will say to us, 'you object to professors contracting out for napalm, but what about professors contracting out for social surveys among napalm victims?' We have to face these questions, we have to think about them and answer them.

It seems possible to me that we could attack the iceberg at different levels; instead of just lopping off the top of the iceberg (or trying to melt it down with love) we could demand changes right at the base of the structure. We could challenge the departmental structure or the grade system or perhaps we could go deeper and challenge course content. I think also we have to challenge the part of ourselves that has become 'exducted' or 'educated away' from what's really happening. Because we have been trained in the university to fill jobs in industry; 'education' in the university today is training for management positions. We are intended to get jobs with corporations that oppress people; with companies that are the cause of the fact that people are down and out. Somewhere along the line we have to make a decision in our own lives about what we're going to do, and I wonder if it's not possible for us to coin a new concept of the university. Take the part of the old concept of education that was clearly good, the concept of education as developing an individual's potential. But do this not by isolating ourselves from the people that are being oppressed but do it in their terms of reference. In other words, combine expertise (not expertise in the sense of knowing how to put two molecules together to make napalm, but in the sense of being an educated man) with 'redness'. Because it seems to me that what is going on in China in the cultural revolution business, which all started with university students challenging course content and administrators, is very relevant to what's happening here. Because what the Chinese are saying is that even in their society, the process of education has caught us up and isolated us from each other.

I wonder if there's some way in this society we can put together the concepts of education and the concept of being red, that is to say, of being 'with the people.' This is just one way of thinking down below the top of the iceberg.

THE INDUSTRIAL REVOLUTION IN THE KNOWLEDGE INDUSTRY

What is happening in our educational institutions, what The Contemporary University USA describes, is very similar to what happened a hundred to two hundred years ago in England. Peasant boys were thrown off the farms and put to work in the cities. On the farm, they had been universal men in their own way. They had a self-sufficient agri-

cultural economy; they knew how to make clothes, how to slaughter cows, and how to raise cows. Then they were taken off the land and drawn into factories where they lost all these skills that might have led to the development of a fully rounded human being (it doesn't have to be brainwork). They were put on machines where all they had to do was to make certain motions. This was what the industrial revolution did; it took people who had some kind of all-sidedness (even if only a very primitive sort) and put them into the production industry. It made them narrow; they were not even cogs in the machine but were made into a sort of raw material of the machine.

The same thing is happening now in the so-called education business; it is being turned into the knowledge industry. People who have aspirations to know lots of things are taken and compressed into knowing just a few things. We are confronted with an industrial revolution in education.

What we are trying to do now when we try to throw Dow Chemical off campus (for example) is approximately on the same level as the French peasants who took off their wooden clogs and threw them in the machines -- sabotage (wooden clogs -- 'sabots'). This simple beginning is a really good beginning, but it is not going to be enough. We are faced with a new system of producing knowledge and our efforts are going to have to measure up to that in the long run. We must have a full-fledged 'iceberg strategy'.

"The Iceberg Strategy" was first presented at a conference on "the university and the military" at the University of Chicago, November 10, 1967, and was transcribed and edited by Janet Dowty, of the REP staff.

Radical Education Project and New England Free Press

Published by
    The Radical Education Project
Box 625   Ann Arbor, Michigan   48107

It is nothing short of a miracle that the modern methods of instruction have not yet entirely strangled the holy curiosity of inquiry; for this delicate little plant, aside from stimulation, stands mainly in need of freedom; without this it goes to wrack and ruin without fail.

ALBERT EINSTEIN

It is impossible to become engaged or usefully to identify when one cannot initiate and have a say in deciding.

PAUL GOODMAN

...An act of learning is a meeting, and every meeting is simply the discovery in the world of a part of oneself that had previously been unacknowledged by the self. It is the recovery of the extent of one's being. It is the embrace of an eternal but elusive companion, the shadowy "other" in which one truly resides and which blazes, when embraced, like the sun.

PETER MARIN

Lynd, Voice of Left, Now 'Teacher in Movement'

THE LIBERATED PROFESSOR,
"WELL, I CAME TO CHICAGO IN THE FIRST PLACE TO FIND OUT WHAT IT WOULD BE LIKE TO BE A FREEDOM SCHOOL TEACHER FULL TIME —A TEACHER IN THE CONTEXT OF THE MOVEMENT"

By J. ANTHONY LUKAS
Special to The New York Times

CHICAGO, Aug. 7—Propped against a book-lined wall in Staughton Lynd's Spartan apartment here is a placard that proclaims in bold lettering: "Reinstate Suspended-Expelled Students. Drop Trespass Charges."

A visitor wonders whether the books are holding up the placard or the placard is supporting the books, but to Mr. Lynd, one of the leading voices of the New Left, it is all the same: Books and placards are inextricably intertwined in his life these days.

After more than a year of fruitless efforts to find a tenure teaching post here, he said he had given up once and for all the traditional role of teacher in the academy and become what he calls "a teacher in the movement or a movement teacher."

Skeptics might conclude that Mr. Lynd's decision stemmed directly from the repeated rebuffs he has suffered from university administrations here. One after another, the University of Illinois's circle campus, the University of Northern Illinois, Chicago State College, Roosevelt University and Loyola University rejected him despite recommendations from the institutions' history departments.

In only the Chicago State case was it clear that he was being rejected for political rather than academic considerations.

Last year the Board of Governors of State Colleges and

Staughton Lynd

Universities turned down Mr. Lynd's appointment, contending that his visit in 1965 to North Vietnam in defiance of the State Department and his espousal of nonviolent civil disobedience "goes beyond mere dissent." The board said it did not question his ability as a teacher, but "believes the teacher has a responsibility to support and stay within the laws of this country."

In mid-October after Mr. Lynd brought suit for the restoration of his contract, the board agreed to let him teach one year at the graduate level. However, his appointment ran out in June.

Meanwhile, the history department at Roosevelt University, where he had been teach-

ing a graduate seminar, recommended him for a three-year term as an associate professor. But this was refused in March by the president, Rolf A. Weil.

Mr. Weil said he had "ad hominem [against the man] grounds" for rejecting Mr. Lynd, but he refused to disclose them.

Mr. Weil's stand touched off a student rebellion at Roosevelt. A series of student sit-ins ended with 60 arrests.

After these rebuffs, another man might have left Chicago. Mr. Lynd could have gone back for a fifth—but almost certainly final—year of his appointment as assistant professor at Yale, but in May he told Yale he would not return. Instead, he has decided to remain in Chicago indefinitely, eking out a living from several jobs related to the "movement."

This year he will divide his time between teaching a course in American radicalism at the Free School, which was started by dissident Roosevelt University students this spring, and a similar course at Columbia College, a small liberal institution on Chicago's Near North Side.

"It will be touch and go as far as money is concerned," he said the other day in an interview. "But, believe it or not, I'm really happier now than I've been since I was a director of freedom schools in the Mississippi freedom summer of 1964."

"Those were marvelous days," he said pensively, gazing out from his unruly shock of brown hair as he lolled on a couch in his sparsely furnished

living room on Chicago's South Side.

"Well, I came to Chicago in the first place to find out what it would be like to be a freedom school teacher full time—a teacher in the context of the movement," he said.

Mr. Lynd, who is the son of the noted sociologists, Helen and Robert Lynd, grew up in New York.

"I knew the kind of sterile radical community you had in New York, the handful of dogmatists on 14th Street passing resolutions, caucusing and counter-caucusing," he recalled.

"That sort of thing is the characteristic weakness of the radical movement in America—sitting around and debating with each other over abstract doctrine. I wanted to come to a city where the ratio of movement action to movement intellectualizing was high.

"And at Chicago there are extraordinarily few academic radicals here, an unusually large number based in the neighborhoods. The most important thing going on in the movement here today is precisely this—young people moving off the campus, either graduating or dropping out, and attempting to find ways to remain radical while getting married, having kids, growing over 30.

"I find it terribly exciting. People scraping along on this or that job, getting all sorts of weird diseases from fatigue."

"It hasn't been a frustrating year," he added. "It's been an exciting year, getting a handle on the kind of thing I can most usefully do."

[ATTRIBUTES CONTRIBUTING TO CAREER SUCCESS]	
Attribute	Rank
Volume of publication	1
School at which doctorate was taken	2
Having the right connections	3
Ability to get research support	4
Quality of publication	5
Textbook authorship	6
Luck or chance	7
School of first full-time appointment	8
Self-promotion ("brass")	9
Teaching ability	10

This chart appeared in American Political Science, A Profile of a Discipline, *by Albert Somit & Joseph Tanenhaus (1964, The Atherton Press, New York). It was compiled from the responses of members of the American Political Science Association, when they were queried about the factors they considered important in "getting ahead" in their profession.* Ramparts May 1969

★★★★★★★★★★★★★★★★★★★★

Most of our graduate students don't want to be academics, publishing or perishing and that sort of thing.

It used to be that students' greatest ambition was to be like their professors some day. Not now. They just will not play the game anymore. This makes it very difficult for the faculty. There are a lot of very upset people on the faculties.

PROF. IVAN SOLL ot the University of Wisconsin, at the annual meeting of the American Philosophical Association, *The New York Times* 12/30/69

★★★★★★★★★★★★★★★★★★★★

End of 'a nice, safe place'

By Laurie Taymor

Benjamin Milner, chairman of the Briarcliff College board of trustees, recently told Briarcliff women not to feel bad if we didn't make the dean's list, since his wife graduated from prep school at the bottom of her class, and our president's wife was a high school dropout.

Since we are the daughters of the richest families in America, and since our fathers are the men who control the American empire, they have sent us to Briarcliff to ensure that we remain uncontaminated by the rest of society tucked safely away in New York's Westchester County. The college prepares us to be cultured baby-producers—whores of the ruling class.

But Briarcliff is no longer a nice, safe place. On the morning of March 11, the old Victorian lounge of the administration building was taken over by 50 students protesting the firing of two faculty members and the college's racist admissions policy.

Three Briarcliff High School students were suspended for joining the demonstrations. The turning point came at 11 p.m. when President Steward called the fire department to clear us out of the lounge, claiming we were a fire hazard.

For the next four days, the old sitting room, symbol of the tea-and-crumpet sanctities of Briarcliff life, was the center of discussion by the entire college. Our demands were: (1) student voting rights over the hiring and firing of faculty, (2) student-faculty voting rights on the board of trustees, (3) more scholarships for minority groups, a black assistant dean of admissions, a black studies program and (4) abolition of the president's veto power over internal college affairs.

Students who opposed the sit-in formed a "counterproposal" group, saying our demands would lower Briarcliff's academic standards.

The author is an organizer of Briarcliff SDS.

Guardian 3/29/69

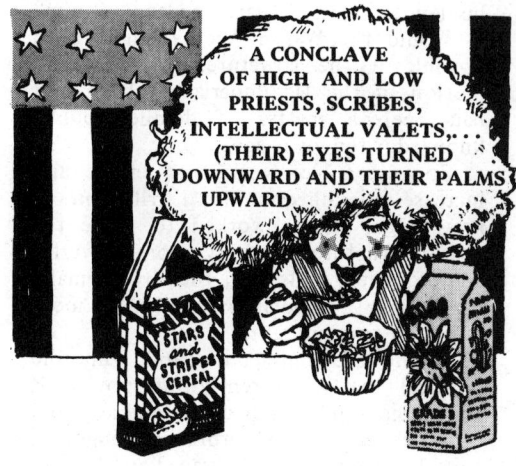

A CONCLAVE OF HIGH AND LOW PRIESTS, SCRIBES, INTELLECTUAL VALETS,... (THEIR) EYES TURNED DOWNWARD AND THEIR PALMS UPWARD

FAT-CAT SOCIOLOGY

REMARKS AT THE AMERICAN SOCIOLOGICAL ASSOCIATION CONVENTION

by Martin Nicholaus

These remarks are not addressed to the Secretary of Health, Education, and Welfare. This man has agreed voluntarily to serve as a member of a government establishment which is presently fighting a war for survival on two fronts. Imperial wars such as the one against Vietnam are usually two-front wars—one against the foreign subject population, one against the domestic subject population. The Secretary of HEW is a military officer in the domestic front of the war against people. Experience in the Vietnam teach-ins has shown that dialogue between the subject population and its rulers is an exercise in repressive tolerance. It is, in Robert S. Lynd's words, dialogue between chickens and elephants. He holds some power over me—therefore, even if he is wrong in his arguments, he is right; even if I'm right, I'm wrong.

I do address myself to the Secretary's audience. There is some hope—even though

the hour is very late—that among the members and sympathizers of the sociological profession gathered here there will be some whose life is not so sold and compromised as to be out of their own control to change or amend it.

While the officers of this convention and the previous speaker were having a big meal in the hotel, I was across the street in a cafeteria having a hot dog and two cups of coffee. This may be why my perspective is different.

The ruling elite within your profession is in charge of what is called Health, Education, and Welfare. Those of you who listened passively to what he had to say presumably agreed that this definition—this description of what the man did—carried an accurate message. Yet among you are many, including the hard researchers, who do know better or should know better. The department of which the man is head is more accurately described as the agency which watches over the inequitable distribution of preventable disease, over the funding of domestic propaganda and indoctrination, and over the preservation of a cheap and docile reserve labor force to keep everybody else's wages down. He is Secretary of disease, propaganda, and scabbing.

This may be put too strongly for you—but it all depends on where you look from, where you stand. If you stand inside the Sheraton Hotel these terms are offensive, but if you gentlemen and ladies would care to step across the street into Roxbury you might get a different perspective and a different vocabulary. If you will look at the social world through the eyes of those who are at the bottom of it, through the eyes of your subject population (and if you will endow those eyes with the same degree of clear-sightedness you profess to encourage among yourselves), then you will get a different conception of the social science to which you are devoted. That is to say that this assembly here tonight is a kind of lie. It is not a coming-together of those who study and know—or promote study and knowledge of—social reality. It is a conclave of high and low priests, scribes, intellectual valets, and their innocent victims, engaged in the mutual affirmation of a falsehood, in common consecration of a myth.

Sociology is not now and never has been any kind of objective seeking-out of social truth or reality. Historically, the profession is an outgrowth of Nineteenth Century European traditionalism and conservatism, wedded to Twentieth Century American corporation liberalism.

That is to say that the eyes of sociologists, with few but honorable (or honorable but few) exceptions, have been turned downward, and their palms upward.

Eyes down, to study the activities of the lower classes, of the subject population—those activities which created problems for the smooth exercise of governmental hegemony. Since the class of rulers in this society identifies itself as the society itself—in the same way that Davis and Moore in their infamous 1945 propaganda article identified the society with those who run it—therefore the problems of the ruling class get defined as social problems. The profession has moved beyond the tear-jerking stage today: "social problems" is no longer the preferred term; but the underlying perspective is the same. The things that are sociologically "interesting" are the things that are interesting to those who stand at the top of the mountain and feel the tremors of an earthquake.

Sociologists stand guard in the garrison and report to its masters on the movements of the occupied populace. The more adventurous sociologists don the disguise of the people and go out to mix with the peasants in the "field," returning with books and articles that break the protective secrecy in which a subjugated population wraps itself, and make it more accessible to manipulation and control.

The sociologist as a researcher in the employ of his employers is precisely a kind

of spy. The proper exercise of the profession is all-too-often different from the proper exercise of espionage only in the relatively greater electronic sophistication of the latter's techniques.

Is it an accident—to name only a few examples here—that industrial sociology arose in a context of rising "labor troubles," that political economy grew when elections became less predictable, or that the sociology of race relations is flourishing now?

As sociologists you owe your jobs to the union organizers who got beat up, to the voters who got fed up, to the black people who got shot up. Sociology has risen to its present prosperity and eminence on the blood and bones of the poor and oppressed; it owes its prestige in this society to its putative ability to give information and advice to the ruling class of this society about ways and means to keep the people down.

The professional eyes of the sociologist are on the down people, and the professional palm of the sociologist is stretched toward the up people. It is no secret and no original discovery that the major and dominant sectors of sociology today are sold—computers, codes, and questionnaires—to the people who have enough money to afford this ornament, and who see a useful purpose being served by keeping hundreds of intelligent men and women occupied in the pursuit of harmless trivia—and off the streets. I am not asserting that every individual researcher sells his brain for a bribe—although many of us know of research projects where that has happened literally—but merely that the dominant structure of the profession, in which all of its members are to-some-extent socialized, is a structure in which service to the ruling class of this society is the highest form of honor and achievement. (The speaker's table today is an illustration.) The honored sociologist, the big-status sociologist, the jet-set sociologist, the fat-contract sociologist, the book-a-year sociologist, the sociologist who always wears the livery—the suit and tie—of his masters: this is the type of sociologist who sets the tone and the ethic of the profession, and it is this type of sociologist who is nothing more or less than a house-servant in the corporate establishment, a white intellectual Uncle Tom not only for this government and ruling class—which explains to my mind why Soviet sociologists and American sociologists are finding after so many years of isolation that, after all, they have something in common.

To raise and educate and train generation after generation of the brightest minds this country's so-called educational system

has let survive in this sociological ethic of servility—to socialize them into this sociocracy—is a criminal undertaking: one of the many felonies against youth committed by those who set themselves up in a loco parentis situation that is usually far more oppressive than any real parental relation. The crime which graduate schools perpetrate against the minds and morals of young people is all the more inexcusable because of the enormous liberating potential of knowledge about social life. Unlike knowledge about trees and stones, knowledge about people directly affects what we are, what we do, what we may hope for. The corporate rulers of this society would not be spending as much money as they do for knowledge, if knowledge did not confer power. So far, sociologists have been schlepping this knowledge that confers power along a one-way chain, taking knowledge from the people, giving knowledge to the rulers.

What if that machinery were reversed? What if the habits, problems, secrets, and unconscious motivations of the wealthy and powerful were daily scrutinized by a thousand systematic researchers; were hourly pried into, analyzed, and cross-referenced; were tabulated and published in a hundred inexpensive mass-circulation journals and written so that even the fifteen-year-old high-school drop-out could understand them and predict the actions of his landlord—manipulate and control him?

Would the War in Vietnam have been possible if the structure, function, and motion of the US imperial establishment had been a matter of detailed public knowledge ten years ago?

Sociology has worked to create and increase the inequitable distribution of knowledge; it has worked to make the power structure relatively more powerful and knowledgeable, and thereby to make the subject population relatively more impotent and ignorant.

In the late summer of 1968, while the political party currently in power is convening amidst barbed wire and armored cars, the sociological profession ought to consider itself especially graced and blessed that its own deliberations can still be carried on with a police-to-participant ratio smaller than one-to-one. This may be because the people of the USA do not know how much of their current troubles stem—to borrow Lord Keynes's phrase—from the almost-forgotten scribblings of an obscure professor of sociology. Or it may be that sociology is still so crude that it represents no clear and present danger.

In 1968 it is late; very late; too late to say once again what Robert S. Lynd and C. Wright Mills and hundreds of others have long said: that the profession must reform itself. In view of the forces and the money that stand behind sociology as an exercise in intellectual servility, it is unrealistic to expect the body of the profession to make an about-face.

If the barbed wire goes up around the ASA Convention in a future year, most of its members will still not know why.

This speech was given in August 1968 at the Convention of the American Sociological Association in Boston. Martin Nicolaus was on the platform with Wilbur Cohen, Secretary of Health, Education, and Welfare. A caucus organized by Columbia University graduate students and the New University Conference protested Cohen's appearance as major speaker and requested that Nicolaus speak.

The New University Conference is a national membership organization of radical faculty members and graduate students currently engaged in organizing some fifty chapters at various universities. Part of our program is the organization of caucuses and working groups within the disciplines. We seek to join in the struggle for a democratized university and a radically transformed society. Please join us now. Dues, needed but non-obligatory, are $25 per year for faculty members, and $15 per year for graduate students. This includes a subscription to our newsletter ($10 per year separately). If you can organize a chapter at your university or want more information, please write to Richie Rothstein, National Director, New University Conference, 622 W. Diversey, room 403a, Chicago, Ill. 60614. Phone 312 929-3070.

The 1969 A.S.A. Convention, held in San Francisco, was even livelier. There were counter seminars and lectures held in a nearby church. And lots of guerrilla theater. The climax was the evening address by the Association President. He was interrupted by a hundred students and faculty who took the microphone away and began conducting a memorial service for Ho Chi Minh (who had died a day or so before). They then got ready to offer speakers and films by NEWSREEL. The President had the microphone turned off and the lights turned up, then he and his followers withdrew to the Imperial Ballroom to continue their lifeless ritual while the dissidents moved to another room to show the films. In 1968 the radicals took over the MLA Convention (college English teachers), and continued to set the tone of the organization in the 1969 meeting. Today it would be hard to imagine a meeting of academics (or scientists, or even of the A.M.A.) without an opposition faction from the left. Women's liberation is an increasingly important element here.

Radical Education Project

HE WAS A BETTER TEACHER WHEN HE DIDN'T HAVE ALL THE ANSWERS

Instead of lectures, a conversation with students in a geology survey

Most difficult of all, says Geology's Frederick Berry, was "to let there be silence."

He was talking about his Geology 10 survey course last fall, and some of the ideas he tried out on the mixed bag of 75 freshmen and sophomores taking the course to fulfill the science requirement.

For some time Berry had been observing that, regardless of age, people learned at a "prodigious speed" when they were really interested in something. He had also noted that this kind of involvement was not very likely in the passive role usually assigned to students by the traditional lecture system. The alchemy of "having an idea of your own" simply didn't work when the ideas were pre-chewed, swallowed and digested by a teacher who had long ago wrung all but the most vicarious excitement out of them.

He had noticed, too, that he himself was a better teacher when he didn't have all the answers. Something about his own uncertainty seemed to leave students more elbow room to discover some idea or interpretation of their own.

Berry has long believed that "you can teach people to think creatively." Last fall he decided to find out if he was right.

He scuttled the lectures he was tired of giving. He told the class it was up to them to start conversations. They could go in any direction that interested *them*. While they might not learn as much geology as usual, he said, what they did cover they would really know when they were through.

But how to start? Students and professor sat silent, looking at each other. The temptation to talk, to "control the situation" was almost too much for the normally loquacious Berry. But he managed to keep quiet and, eventually, someone asked a question. Halting though it was, the conversation Berry hoped for had begun.

Within a month he had learned that his "listening" gave a subtle new dimension to the class. Progressively it became more and more of a delight. Three times a week, he says, he found himself thinking "Now I'm going to go down and have some fun."

Part of it was the unpredictability. By refusing the traditional professorial control, Berry had built in a spontaneity he had never before encountered in his teaching career. At the same time, his answers to their questions were designed to continually open the way for new questions and new directions, however erratic student interest might be. Without realizing it, they were actually learning a lot of geology, he says.

But not everybody was so pleased as Berry.

About half the class was uncomfortable and even frightened at being cut adrift. They didn't think they were learning anything, wanted more of the familiar old structure, and resented the professor's abandonment of the authority role. The attendance of this segment of the class began to fall.

Nor were the TAs happy.

Berry had not tampered with the labs. But even though they knew what was going on in the "lecture" part of the course, the TAs didn't really understand what Berry was after. "They thought I was goofing off while they did the work."

Midterm results nebulous

By the time the mid-term rolled around, everything about Geology 10 was still nebulous and the results of the exam—neither bad nor good—didn't seem to prove anything one way or the other.

But during the second half of the quarter, what was happening began to come to the surface.

The TAs took the class on a field trip, and, as their gesture toward whatever it was Berry was trying to do, they dumped the usual guided tour for a new tack. "They took them out to an area, sat down in the middle of it and turned the students loose to figure out the geology on their own."

The response astonished the teaching assistants. All day, they reported to Berry, those students asked questions, questions, questions. Just any old answer wasn't good enough. They knew what they wanted to know, were impatient with superficial replies, insisted on learning the "why" of things the TAs had thought far beyond them. The field trip was a "howling success."

Now that the quarter was near its end, class sessions were freer and more autonomous. Students seemed to know when further discussion of a question would be fruitless and themselves turned the conversations in new directions. But the split between those who didn't like Berry's unorthodox set-up and those who did was increasingly obvious.

Earlier, he had offered them an option: a final exam or a research paper on some mutually agreed upon topic. To some degree, the schism in the class was reflected in their choices. The most dissatisfied students elected the exam; the most enthusiastic, the paper.

With the exams, the professor asked for critiques, and even though he now thinks he should have been prepared for it, he was shaken by the vehemence, anger and sense of outrage in the comments returned to him. "If they didn't like it, they *really* didn't like it."

Exams unexpectedly good

But even among this group, what he had been trying to do was not entirely lost. The exams were unexpectedly good, and here and there a student had noticed something. "I was interested in spite of myself," said one. Another remarked that his notes and books had turned out to be superfluous because "when the discussion is over, I *know* the material."

Nevertheless, Berry says, he was looking for a vote of confidence and when he didn't get it, he was tremendously disheartened—until the research papers began to come in. In part, at least, he was vindicated. "This was a whole new ball game. *These* kids really got the message."

He had told them he wanted no rehashes, only "their own thing, whatever that might be, as long as it had *some* relation to geology," and he got what he asked for. Papers were original, imaginative and often brilliant, a delight to read, he says happily.

Fantasy about gold

One student wrote a Goldfinger fantasy on beliefs and attitudes about gold. Another, herself a potter, turned in a study of pottery and glazes. A forester mapped the effect of rocks on vegetation patterns in the Berkeley hills. A Point Reyes native studied an anomolous lake above sea level near his home—"and I'm sure he's right in his conclusions."

Berry looks back on his Geology 10 experiences with pleasure and a still-present sense of excitement. "This is what we ought to be doing."

Nor is he alone in his feeling that the experiment turned out well. One of his students told him that "she never knew something so exciting and so much fun could be called learning."

Berry agrees with her.

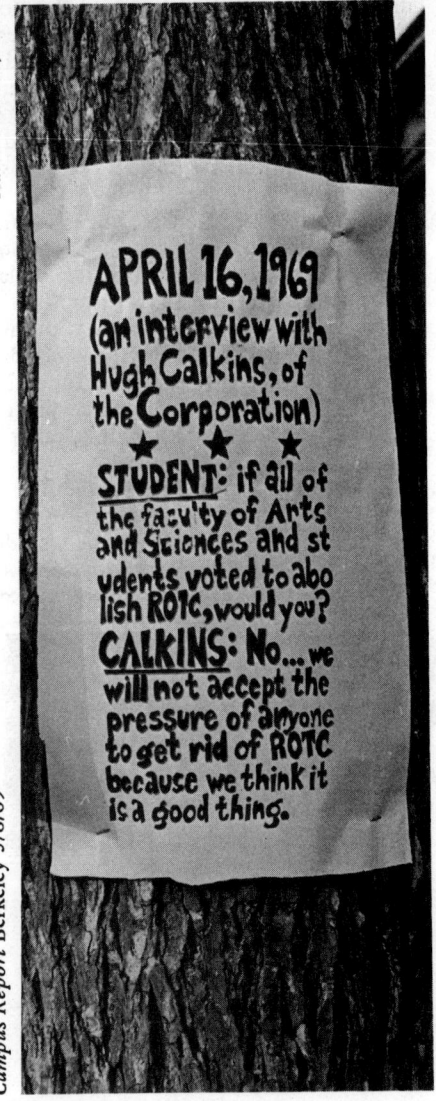

Harvard Strike, 1969

Campus Report Berkeley 5/8/69

APRIL 16, 1969
(an interview with Hugh Calkins, of the Corporation)
★ ★ ★
STUDENT: if all of the faculty of Arts and Sciences and students voted to abolish ROTC, would you?
CALKINS: No... we will not accept the pressure of anyone to get rid of ROTC because we think it is a good thing.

COLUMBIA'S NEW PRESIDENT SPEAKS OUT! ——————————

(from the New York Times, Friday, September 20th, 1968)

Doctor Cordier went out of his office at 1:25 p.m., while a rally by the Students for a Re-structured University was being held to protest the University's ban on the use of campus facilities by Students for a Democratic Society (SDS). His arrival was met by signs of both approval and condemnation; but there were no placards, and the atmosphere was generally calm and at times even friendly.

After expressing his pleasure at meeting with students, Doctor Cordier said that he planned "to continue this policy right through this year" and explained that he was sorry he was forced to leave quickly because he had a commitment to tape a closed-circuit television show to be shown to Columbia alumni.

"Talk about the issues!" someone in the crowd shouted.

"On the issues," Doctor Cordier said, "thank you." And he laughed. "I always speak on the issues. And I'm glad you raised that point, as a matter of fact, because I do not evade issues, as many of you know."

"I think we need to look into the issues," Doctor Cordier continued. "What we want from this campus is to be a sure, dynamic, forward-looking, progressive institution which engages in efforts—and strenuous efforts—to have a program which corresponds to the temper and needs of our times.

We live in a rapidly-changing society, and it's very difficult unless people very purposefully work for progress, in fact to keep pace with that progress.

"So the policy this year is going to be based on human relationships...." Doctor Cordier was interrupted here by a girl who shouted "Repression!"

He smiled and went on. "No repression whatsoever, my dear," he said. "No repression whatsoever." There were laughs and cheers as he continued: "Repression is not a word in my vocabulary, never has been and never will be."

Another heckler shouted something about Doctor Cordier's role in the Congo, where he directed United Nations operations in the early 1960s. "Not in the Congo," he said, "not here. I'm going to give you a couple of lectures on the Congo one of these times to tell you the facts of life."

As Doctor Cordier began to leave, he paused when some students demanded to know why he did not discuss the long list of specific issues raised by SDS, including Columbia's involvement in war research and its alleged policy of "racist expansion" in the neighborhood surrounding the Morningside Heights campus.

"On the issues," Doctor Cordier replied to the shouts, "I'd like to say one word about the issues. There seems to be a tendency in some quarters for the issues to get longer and longer and longer. Now when are the issues going to stop?"

Moving on in their "analysis" they see our universities as having been taken over by the business and military establishments lock, stock, and barrel....they say our universities are devoted to the present and future domination of the people of the world — both in Vietnam and in our urban ghettoes.' Obviously they live in a world of fantasy. —*Nathan M. Pusey*

President of Harvard

Student spring offensive on!

By Carl Davidson

Created and produced by striking students at Harvard's Graduate School of Design.

The opening assault in the radical student movement's spring offensive rocked campus after campus across the country last week. The full range of the nation's institutions of higher education felt the attack: from Ivy League colleges and state universities to community colleges and working-class high schools. Tens of thousands of students have taken militant action against the class and colonial oppression built into the educational system. The following reports of campus revolts are only a few of the hundreds that occurred:

Columbia University, New York: Fourteen black freshmen took the lead in the attack on Columbia's privileged admissions policies last week by occupying the admissions office. The students, members of the Students' Afro-American Society, demanded a black admissions board, nominated and controlled by black students, to evaluate the applications of all potential black students. On April 21, 150 black high school students came on campus and sat in to demand open admissions for students graduating from four nearby Harlem high schools.

While SAS has not yet endorsed the open admissions demand (they want to establish a black studies program first), they responded by calling for a 24-hour evacuation of the campus to press for their demand for a black-controlled interim board setting up the black studies program, a black cultural center, and determining guidelines for black admissions.

SDS, which has been pushing the open admissions demand, organized several militant rallies in support of the black students. Many sympathetic white students, however, looking to SDS for leadership, have been confused about how best to relate to the struggle of the black students because of serious internal divisions in SDS.

City College of New York: Black and Puerto Rican students chained the gates of CCNY's south campus April 22, forcing the school to close for the rest of the week. About 200 students took part in the action, demanding a school of black and Puerto Rican studies, an admissions policy reflecting the racial composition of New York high schools, black and brown control of preparatory programs, and required courses in black and Puerto Rican history and the Spanish language for all students seeking teaching degrees.

SDS has tried to rally white student support, but has been hampered by internal disputes. Meanwhile, 700 engineering students and faculty ignored the administration's order to close the school, heckled the picket lines and held classes anyway.

Fordham University, New York: More than 150 students and a few faculty members pushed aside five campus cops and occupied the office of the school's president in an anti-ROTC action April 23. "No negotiations, no committees, no referendum, no deals," read their statement of demands; "ROTC must be abolished now." After holding the building for 24 hours the students left, leading a march around the campus. A mass meeting on the issue, called by the president, revealed a clear division among both students and faculty. The leaders of the sit-in, organized by the Committee Against ROTC and by SDS, considered the action a partial victory, since they won many more students to their side than they had expected.

Princeton University, Princeton, N.J.: Marine recruiters were blocked by a sit-in of 40 SDS activists April 21. A vigorous debate followed between some SDSers and the Marines, and few students were interviewed. Two days later, about 100 SDS students blockaded the offices of the Institute for Defense Analyses adjacent to the campus. Several IDA employes tried to break through the line and a brief scuffle broke out. SDS left the scene after the police arrived, not wanting to risk arrest.

Suffolk Community College, Selden, N.Y.: Marine recruiters were forced to leave the campus last week after a sit-in of 400 students led by SDS. One of the SDS leaders is a Marine Vietnam veteran. The administration also agreed to a demand to call off all campus recruiting until students and faculty could vote on the issue.

Harvard University, Cambridge, Mass.: Harvard students continued their militant anti-ROTC campaign last week, along with their fight against Harvard's expansion policies into surrounding working-class neighborhoods. A two-week-long class boycott, however, was called off. The boycott ended after the faculty voted to establish a black studies program controlled equally by black students and by the faculty.

The faculty also voted to make ROTC an extracurricular activity. This was condemned by SDS, which charged that " . . . extracurricular genocide is still genocide." Most students in the strike, including most of SDS, saw the decision on black studies as a victory. But the "worker-student alliance" caucus of SDS saw it as a "smokescreen" and a "black student-power" measure designed to coopt the student movement.

Hampton Institute, Hampton, Va.: At this predominantly black college, 1500 students of a student body of 2500 occupied a building last week to protest paternalistic administration policies and defend two popular faculty members. The president closed down the school completely, locking the dorms and shutting down the cafeteria. One student remarked, "I'll just have to take a diploma in insurrection."

University of Arizona, Tucson, Ariz.: A protest march of 200 persons was held April 18 in reaction to police harassment of black people near the campus. After the firebombing incident, police occupied a housing complex for a week, subjecting blacks to racist insults and trumpted-up arrests. The Black Student Union and SDS led a march on the mayor's office. The mayor was spotted in a car near campus, and was immediately surrounded and held for 20 minutes until he agreed to a public hearing on the issue.

Merritt College, Oakland, Calif.: Chicano students pressed for and won approval of a set of demands from the faculty and trustees after a week-long struggle, April 14 to 21. The demands called for naming Froben Lozada, a chicano member of the Socialist Workers party, head of a new Mexican-American studies department, free textbooks and meals for needy students and increased hiring of third-world people. The students had to barricade the faculty into their meeting room and threaten the same to the trustees to win the demands. Merritt College is the alma mater of Huey P. Newton, founder of the Black Panther party.

University of Montana, Missoula, Mont.: After 1600 students, faculty and townspeople turned out last week to hear Dr. Benjamin Spock denounce the Vietnam war and the draft, 19 students and two instructors turned in their draft cards and refused to cooperate with the Selective Service System.

Marquette University, Milwaukee, Wisc.: Anti-ROTC protests broke out April 22 when students and faculty occupied a campus building. More than 70 persons were arrested when police were called in to break up the sit-in.

Massachusetts Institute of Technology, Cambridge, Mass.: War research laboratories were picketed by more than 300 students and faculty members April 22. When the lab's director refused to talk to the demonstrators, they marched to the office of MIT President Howard Johnson and sat in until he arrived to debate the issue.

After defending MIT's cooperation with the Defense Department, Johnson came under heavy attack from students and faculty who demanded that a moratorium be called on all war research until MIT's entire research program could be democratically reviewed. The protest was organized by the Science Action Coordinating Committee.

American University, Washington: SDS students ejected university President George Williams from his office April 24. The administration was charged with pursuing policies resulting in the oppression of black and white working-class people.

Guardian 5/3/69

Senate Bills

LEGISLATORS
AS
EDUCATORS

SB 5, Whetmore — Makes it a crime for maliciously disrupting normal operations, specifically on a college campus.

SB 20, Harmer — Provides for the dismissal of state employees who disrupt campus activities.

SB 28, Harmer — Provides for the expulsion of students for disruption of campus activities.

SB 32, Walsh — Defines pornography and prohibits exhibitions of such in dramatic productions at any State College.

SB 34, Walsh — Increases the penalties for inciting a riot on a campus.

SB 51, Whetmore — Amends Mulford Act by increasing penalties for refusing to leave campus if ordered to do so.

SB 56, Harmer — Permits the president of a college to declare a state of emergency and restrict access to his campus.

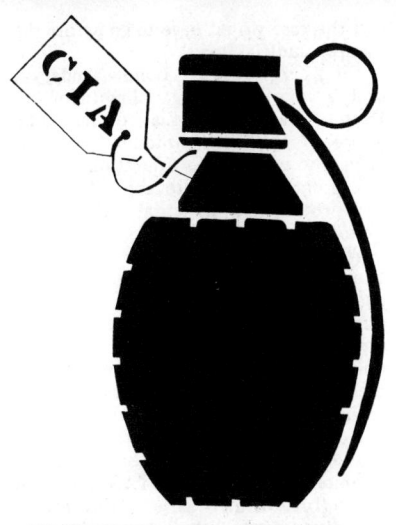

CORPORATION POWER

SB 132, Harmer	Oath of non-disruption to be required after 1970 by all students.
SB 173, Harmer	Allows a penalty of up to five years or $5,000 or both for persons who disrupt activities of college or university officials.
SB 179, Wedworth	Requires State Allocation Board to reimburse cities and counties for police costs in civil disorders.
SB 309, Schmitz	Establishes Campus Safety Commission which has the power to charge, hear, make findings and dismiss any student, faculty member or employee for disrupting campus activities. Also permits firing of college or university chief campus officer or administrator for failing to quell disruptions.
SCR 25, Stiern	Urges Regents, Trustees, Board of Governors, and school districts to file charges against disruptors.

Assembly Bills

AB 4, Britschgi	Anyone violating the Mulford Act (anti-trespass statute) must promise not to return to campus before being released.
AB 20, Wilson	Any employee participating in a campus strike shall be immediately dismissed; a 5.2% pay increase is included.
AB 48, Mulford	Faculty members participating in strikes are automatically dismissed from employment.
AB 59, Ketchum	Any student or academic employee using force or violence on a campus shall be immediately and permanently expelled.
AB 70, Lanterman	Any student violating campus rules and regulations shall forfeit state scholarships for one year.
AB 75, Collier	"Earn, learn and reimburse" tuition proposal. Students would pay substantial tuition which could be deferred and repaid later.
AB 86, Fenton	Provides penalties for distributing "harmful matter" which is defined.
AB 123, Wakefield	Students disrupting campus activities shall be suspended or expelled with total loss of fees paid.
AB 188, Wakefield	Requires student to sign paper saying he will abide by the campus rules and regulations.
AB 222, Pattee	Provides for suspension of students for crimes committed during a Trustee declared state of emergency.
AB 223, Pattee	Limits college ability to recognize certain organizations or allow the use of campus facilities.
AB 286, Wakefield	Prohibits any dismissed student or faculty member from entering any State College campus without permission of the chief campus officer.
AB 291, Schabarum	Makes it a misdemeanor to remain on any land when ordered to leave by the owner or an agent thereof.

Official list of Bills in the Assembly of the California State Legislature 1969

U.C. REDLIST

Dean Elberg:

Jim Lemmon, Dean of Men, thought that you should be aware of this case. Antonio Camejo is currently applying to Education for the M.A. program. This was not noticed at once because he used his full name, Antonio Camejo Guanche, on the application. Education now has the material.

Is there any action that you would like taken at the present time? *Yes - I want to examine the case at your stage, I want strongly doubt his commitment to study.*

Would you like to see the case when Educati returns the decision? *Y*

The Registrar has been advised to make an additional block on the registration of Antonio Camejo Guanche as well as on the origin name, Antonio Camejo.

Bonnie Anderson

by Craig Pyes

Sanford Elberg is Dean of Graduate Admissions at the University of California, Berkeley — one of the most prestigious graduate schools in the country. Naturally he was aghast to find out that I'd anonymously received photostatic copies of certain radicals' graduate files.

"This is outrageous!" he declared. "An act of villany. What are you doing with confidential files? The confidentiality of these files must be maintained. Absolutely!"

"Why?" I asked, as he in great agitation grapped the phone.

"So that the confidence and intregrity of the University is not impugned." He dialed furiously. "I am calling the General Council (who handles legal matters for the University) in order that a full investigation be conducted into this vile and heinous matter."

I sat back. And after the initial hysteria had worn off we conducted a very civil discussion.

* * *

THE IMPORT OF THESE FILES IS THAT THEY CLEARLY SHOW THAT THE UNIVERSITY OF CALIFORNIA KEEPS POLITICAL RECORDS ON ITS STUDENTS. ON THE ONE HAND, THE REGENTS & ADMINISTRATION CRY FOR THE DEPOLITICALISATION OF THE UNIVERSITY, WHILE ON THE OTHER HAND THEIR DECISIONS ON WHO'S ALLOWED TO ENROLL IS OFTEN POLITICALLY MOTIVATED.

Elberg leaned back in his swivelchair. "There are, of course, no political decisions made on enrollment. One needs only to look around the campus to see that. In fact," he exclaimed, "we go out of our way to bring this type of person here. We WANT exceptional people."

Certain "exceptional people", if we are to believe the precedent set in the case of Antonio (Tony) Camejo, who is ironically candidate for State Superintendent of Public Instruction, are no longer desireable. These "exceptional" people are "egregious".

It is an old story. One read about the Jews who were no longer desireable in Nazi Germany; and Danny The Red who was denied admittance into Gaulist France. . .But it as the French poster exclaims: NOUS SOMMES TOUS INDESIRABLES.

* * *

A secretary, Bonnie Anderson, was the first to discover Camejo. She noticed that his graduate application was submitted under the name: Guanche, Antonio Camejo. She checked the name similarities, Guanche with A. Camejo, and discovered they were one and the same person.

She called Jim Lemmon, Dean of Men, who notified her that Camejo was arrested for strike activities on 2/13/69

and the case would have to go before the Campus Judicial Board.

On 21 April 1969, Bonnie Anderson sent a note to Elberg: "Jim Lemmon, Dean of Men, thought that you should be aware of this case. Antonio Camejo is currently applying to Education for the MA program. . .Is there any action that you would like taken at the present time?"

While interviewing Dean Elberg he stressed that eligibility for admission is determined "basically" on academic criteria and "documentation solicited directly from the student himself." The only time extra-curricular information is used is if there is a disciplinary problem, such as a disciplinary probation.

However, Elberg answered this portion of the 21 April note: "Yes—I want to examine the case at each STAGE, I would strongly doubt his (Camejo's) commitment to study." At the time this was written, the Education Department still had all Camejo's academic material, unreviewed by Elberg. Yet the Dean was "doubting" Tony Camejo's "commitment to study."

When the application was returned to the Graduate Division there were no "Department Comments" on it. And the Graduate Division circled "No Review."

In other words, there was never an academic appraisal made as to Camejo's qualifications.

Yet a "special denial" letter was drawn up on 6 May with an appended note by Elberg that Camejo was "academically not qualified" for graduate study at Berkeley. There was no mention of disciplinary consideration over Camejo's Third World strike activities.

"No further comment is to be made. I will sign the letter," Elberg wrote.

The letter states: "A careful review of your application materials indicates that you do not have the academic qualifications required for admission to a graduate program at Berkeley."

Right on!

* * *

Bureaucratic control is one of the oldest and most insidious components of the Corporate State. Great policy decisions can be executed from quiet offices without ever arousing suspicion, without ever coming under review.

When the police force is increased it is noticeable, like a gunshot; when policing is done from offices, it often goes undetected, like a poison.

The worst part of it is, the bureaucrat can explain away the most criminal of actions as a "procedural abnormality": The Rules say it can be done. . .the Final Solution, you see, is simply an adjustment of columns. . .

Roger Heyns in his book, ANATOMY FOR CONFORMITY, explains that one of the ways to insure conformist behaviour is to "separate" non-conformist individuals from a population.

This, in effect, is what happened to Antonio Camejo. The term, "separation from" pops up again and again in Heyns' statements. The Angels of Admission scribble memoranda to the registrar on those individuals marked for separation. Camejo has one, Stew Albert, Bob Mandel, Reese Erlich, and Frank Bardacke have them too.

The paranoia the bureaucrat faces is of course great. He is like a man obsessed with cleanliness constantly cleaning and re-cleaning himself, trying to wash away all adverse political taint. Thus even insignificant actions are noted and filed away.

On 17 April 1969, Steve Goldfield, a graduate chemistry student and member of the RSU, went to obtain a copy of a statement made by Elberg (who was a micro-biologist) on CBW on campus. This request, which has no academic nor disciplinary significance, was placed into Goldfield's graduate files.

In Bardacke's files there are over 9 newspaper clippings concerning political activity, from subjects ranging from his suspension as a TA to his arraignment for Stop the Draft Week.

When I questioned Elberg about this practice, he explained that it was probably for disciplinary information. Other articles mentioned a noon rally Bardacke was scheduled to speak at, and one, simply stated that he was writing a leftwing sports column (Feb '68) called "From Left Field" for the EXPRESS TIMES.

Ed. Note: Camejo, Albert, Mandel, Erlich and Bardacke are long-time Berkeley activists (and former students). The last three were among the Oakland 7 "conspirators".

Before revealing these files I checked with the people they concerned, and they gave me permission for disclosure. The nature of the material has never before been made public.

These files, by the way, are only graduate student files—the contents of regular student files is still a mystery.

The "absolute confidentiality" of these files is a crock of shit. When the McClelland Committee, investigating radical activity on the campuses, subpoenaed students' files, all their contents were divulged.

If any one of six police agencies ask to see these files they are shown without hesitation. But if a student asks to see his own file, the request will be denied. This sort of confidentiality is gladly betrayed.

3/6/70

WHAT IS A UNIVERSITY? AND WHAT IS A RADICAL INTELLECTUAL?

THE RESPONSIBILITY OF RADICAL INTELLECTUALS

By Staughton Lynd
This is an edited version of a talk presented to the New University Conference, March 22, 1968, in Chicago.

I ask that we consider carefully whether the American university is realistically likely to become, in the words of the conference call, a place where "we may freely express the radical content of our lives" and a "base" which will export "humane values" to other institutions in the society. Asking that question also means not accepting unthinkingly the equation of radical intellectual and fulltime academic. Even in America this equation is inaccurate: surely we have had as much to learn from Paul Sweezy, who was thrown out of the academic world, and Herbert Aptheker, who was never permitted to enter it, and Isaac Deutscher, who first taught at a university the last year of his life, as from say, C. Wright Mills and William Appleman Williams. What is far more striking is that of the principle luminaries of the intellectual tradition to which most of us in some degree are drawn, namely Marxism, not one—not Marx, not Engels, not Plekhanov, not Lenin, not Trotsky, not Bukharin, not Rosa Luxemburg (who had a particular contempt for professors), not Antonio Gramsci, not Mao Tse-tung—put bread on his table by university teaching. Please observe that I am not quoting the eleventh

thesis on Feuerbach. I am not arguing (for the moment) that we should act rather than think. My point is that without exception the most significant contributions to Marxist thought have come from men and women who were not academics, who passed through the university but did not remain there.

An exceedingly modest inference from that momentous fact is that whatever else it means to be a radical intellectual in America today, one thing requisite is an experimental attitude with respect to life-styles. Conferences all over the country this past year have explored the possibilities of radical vocation and radicalism in the professions. Just as some of us in years past chose to teach in Southern Negro colleges, so now adventurous souls are seeking out junior colleges and public high schools in white working-class neighborhoods. Are they not also radical intellectuals who are sweating out inner-city teaching, or researching police brutality and local power structures, or attempting to clarify current tactical dilemmas in the Movement, or painstakingly documenting trends in American imperialism at some local equivalent of the British Museum? If we believe in what Marx called "praxis," or practical, critical activity, and in a future society in which the barriers between manual and intellectual labor will be broken down, we should at least not permit our present society narrowly to

define what the life of the mind, or better, the use of the mind, must mean.

We ought to take very seriously the fact that the university corrupts radicals more often than it destroys them. Whatever our social origins, the university is a marvellously effective instrument for making us middle-class men. First it sets us in competition one with another. As undergraduates, graduates, and very often as professors, we are not working together on a common task, not—like children in a Soviet kindergarten—rolling a ball too large for anyone of us to roll alone. We are competing in the performance of tasks little significant in themselves to see which ones of us will be permitted to realize the upwardly-mobile fantasies which the university requires us to entertain. You cannot work at a university as a factory worker labors at the bench. In the university it is up or out; hence, simultaneously scornful of tenure and attracted to it, we are unable matter-of-factly to conceive the university as a source of livelihood, a kind of work in which (like baseball umpiring) "you can't beat the hours"; no, we become emotionally engaged in the upward scramble and, whatever our rhetoric, in fact let the university become the emotional center of our lives. Neither the first nor the second halves of the academic career curve—the frenzied struggle for position, the economic assurance which follows—seem exactly the contexts from which radicalism may be expected to emerge. It is a very peculiar sort of radicalism which permits one only to be arrested in summertime, or obliges one to hurry home from Hanoi to be on time for a seminar. But that is the kind of radical one has to be so long as one's first commitment is to university life. If it is symbolic, one-shot, moral-gesture radicalism, that may be not so much because of our ideological orientation as because of the academic schedule. The point is that whatever we may think, or think we think, university life requires us to act as if our radicalism were episodic and of secondary importance. The conference call says: "we are committed to the struggle for a democratic university". We are unlikely to do much in the direction even of that objective, let alone make an American revolution, so long as we are not prepared to be fired at any moment. The most hopeful recent happening in American intellectual life is that last fall so many graduate students and professors were arrested along with undergraduates in demonstrations against Dow.

But what is required to stand up against the blandishments and threats of academia is not merely courage, but clarity. If I am not mistaken, most of us simultaneously half-believe in two contradictory images of the university and the teacher. On the one hand, we are inclined to conceive the university as an oasis of pure thought where Veblenian intellectuals set their idle curiosities to work. Together with this image goes the notion of the university as a privileged corporation, governed by laws different from those applicable to society at large, immune from kinds of harassment which the off-campus citizen must expect. On the other hand, however, we are attracted to the vision of the university as a power house for social transformation, a counter-society dedicated to the *Aufhebung* of its institutional environment. The first projection leads to socialist scholars' conferences which seem to wish to convey the implicit message: We too have panels with speakers and discussants; we too meet in expensive downtown hotels; we too, whatever the content of our papers, are scholars. The second projection finds Martin Duberman writing *In White America*, Staughton Lynd directing freedom schools, Howard Zinn freeing pilots in Hanoi, Noam Chomsky arrested at the Pentagon.

From such intellectual confusion springs tactical inconsistency. Which of us objected when SNCC was the "institutional client," when intense young men in blue jeans walked onto college campuses, scorned debate as bull-shitting, and recruited students for illegal activities in the larger society? Is it not the case that before we sought to get the military off the campus we did our darndest to get the civil rights movement on it? It would seem that, intellectuals though we may be, we change our definition of the university every year or two just as we change our attitudes toward decentralization or the Supreme

Court. We should be able to do better than that. We need to recognize, if we cannot resolve, the tension between the rhetoric of ethical commitment.

Consider the position of the American Association of University Professors toward obstructive demonstrations on campus. The Association states: "action by individuals or groups to prevent speakers invited to the campus from speaking, to disrupt the operations of the institution in the course of demonstrations or to obstruct and restrain other members of the academic community and campus visitors by physical force is destructive of the pursuit of learning and of a free society." This is not an illogical position if the university is conceptualized as an oasis of freedom in a hostile environment, a conception we often espouse. However, the position of many Dow Demonstrators was that they were obstructing that portion of the Dow Chemical Company's activity most accessible to them. They obstructed Dow not because it invaded the campus sanctuary but because its off-campus activities are nefarious. Dow does not cleanse itself in the eyes of these demonstrators if, while on campus, it observes academic decorum and agrees to debate its views. Were it in the power of these demonstrators, they would put Dow out of business.

This too is a stance many of us have adopted. But where does it leave us when right-wing demonstrators seek by non-violent obstructive means to interfere with projects ethical in our eyes but nefarious in theirs?

The tension between the rhetoric of truth-seeking and the rhetoric of ethical commitment was exhibited during the recent contretemps between myself and the Board of Governors of Chicago State College. Among the professors who formed an *ad hoc* defense committee there were three positions. One was that a teacher necessarily teaches the whole of what he thinks and is, and therefore should have the right to say anything he wishes in the classroom.

A second position held that whatever considerations of academic appropriateness might apply to on-campus utterances, off-campus a teacher should be free to advocate like any other citizen.

My own attitude was different from both the foregoing. In contrast to the first position, it seemed to me there was a difference between the low-keyed presentation of intellectual alternatives and the attempt to kindle in an audience an awareness of some indignity. Both seemed to me important things for the man of intellect to do; yet they are different; and my instinct was to accept the proposition that a classroom is a place where one's purpose should not be persuasion, but an opening-up of possible new ways of seeing things.

In contrast to the second position, I felt that a teacher should be free not only to talk as he wishes outside the classroom but

to act as he wishes. It seemed and seems to me that when and if a teacher is arrested, prosecuted, convicted, sentenced, and put in jail, he will be unable to meet his classes, and at that point his academic employer may with some justice put him on leave or, if uncharitably inclined, dismiss him. Until that point is reached I believe a teacher should not be penalized, nor obliged to answer questions concerning his public life. Like any other citizen he should be considered innocent until proven guilty. Academic employers should eschew appointing themselves as judges and convicting a man before the courts have acted.

Perhaps many of you experience moments when such questions seem real. One characteristic answer to which we turn in such moments is: "Yes, but I am less a scholar than a teacher. The college has shown itself an instrument not only of bourgeoisifying those who stay there permanently, but of radicalizing those who pass through it for four years. As a radical faculty member I can at least protect, perhaps in part produce, radical students. I too am in one sense an organizer, dealing with a constituency, less concerned with paper than with the eager, frightened young human beings whom the campus, like the factory as Marx described it, brings together and subjects to common experiences."

The fundamental problem for the full-time teacher is that he sends his students forth to confront problems which he himself has not encountered. Whether as drop-out or graduate, the student leaves the campus but the teacher does not. The teacher's life does not speak to the problem of how to "make it" as a radical off the campus. I suspect our students learn this lesson well. We may imagine that we are contributing to the revolution by teaching Marxism or socialism or radicalism to a new generation of activists. We may overlook the possibility that those whom we thus indoctrinate will become teachers in their turn, justifying their existences as radicals with the argument that they are readying for action a new generation of radicals — namely, their students — who, however, are all too likely also to become teachers, speaking, just as we do, of the splendid young people to whom they lecture who need only a solid intellectual grounding — and so on.

The fact that we ourselves as full-time academics cannot provide models of off-campus radical vocation is the more frustrating this spring because the draft has forced so many of our students, as we have not been forced, to say Yes or No to the demands of the larger society.

After all these distressingly negative and essentially preliminary words, let me briefly attempt to answer the questions: What is a university? And what is a radical intellectual? The purpose of the foregoing has been to insist that, as radicals, we should take neither the institution nor the role for granted but attempt to approach them with fresh eyes. The way to do that, I think, is to begin with the reality of the Movement and observe how an intellectual function crystallizes out from its activity; or alternatively, how in the midst of the Movement's so-called mindless activism, obviously necessary intellectual tasks fail to be performed.

By now we have a certain stock of experience. SNCC, for instance, established an educational institute at Waveland, Mississippi in the fall of 1964. The Free University of New York has existed almost three years. SDS attempted last summer to run three schools for campus organizers in Boston, Chicago and San Francisco. Teach-ins, educational conferences, at least two new national newspapers and three nationally-circulated periodicals, all testify to the seriousness with which the Movement, charges of mindless activism notwithstanding, has tackled the function of internal education.

Different observers will assess this experience differently. Some feel that what is lacking is a systematic body of general theory. My own conclusion, perhaps predictably, is almost the reverse. Having been personally involved in several of these experiments, my impression is that their characteristic weakness has been remoteness from action. This expresses itself in two different ways. At Waveland, for example, the most educational experience for the SNCC staff people assembled there was to travel into a New Orleans courtroom where, I believe, the precedent-establishing Bombrowski case was being argued, and then return to Waveland to discuss its implications with the lawyer, Arthur Kinoy; almost everything else in the program presented at Waveland by distinguished guest speakers passed the students by, because not linked to their immediate experience. Similarly, the Free University of New York struck me as different from the usual bull sessions of campus radicals mainly in locale. Those who talked together were not acting together. What was exhilarating about Vietnam teach-ins, it seems to me, was that students and teachers together addressed a problem in relation to which all were amateurs. Although action was not always explicitly projected, in the atmosphere of such occasions was a serious search for means of protest. Subsequent teach-ins at which this element was lacking, as at Ann Arbor last September, appear to me to have been sterile by comparison.

Remoteness from action in such educational ventures reflects the fact that those commonly called in as teachers, namely ourselves, are ourselves thus remote. There is no getting away from the fact that universities combining theory and practice, like the University of Havana whose students work together in the cane fields, or the University of Yenan where students grew their own food, wove their own clothes, and graduated together to fight the Japanese, can only be created by individuals who combine theory and practice personally. I have been at too

many embarrassing occasions when full-time activists and full-time intellectuals were brought together in the naive hope, on the part of the activists, that the intellectuals could give them a magical something which they somehow lacked. A more hopeful model in my own experience was the Mississippi Freedom Schools. There Northern white college students and Southern black teen-agers had first to encounter one another as whole human beings, to establish trust. This happened in the process of finding a church basement together, deciding on a curriculum together, improvising materials together, that is, in a context of common work; and it matured in that context, too, as those who talked together in the morning registered voters together in the afternoon. Please note I am not advocating a narrow pragmatism. What was read together in the mornings was often James Joyce, what was talked about may have been French or algebra as well as Negro history. But I must simply testify that the context of shared experience, (which meant, too, that the teachers characteristically boarded in their students' homes) made all the difference.

Do I mean, then, that in the protesting words of the rector of Charles University in Prague the social sciences must become "a mere tool of propaganda and agitation"? No. My point is that if we take Marx, or Freud, or Veblen seriously we must understand that a man's view of the world grows out of — I did not say "reflects" — his socially-conditioned experience. You and I as intellectuals do not merely observe this phenomenon. It is exhibited in our lives, too. Many intellectuals will not and should not become activists. The intellectual's first responsibility is, as Noam Chomsky says, "to insist upon the truth," "to speak the truth and to expose lies." But what truth we discover will be affected by the lives we lead. There is no such thing as "working-class truth" or "bourgeois truth" or "the truth of the anal personality." Yet that portion of the truth to which we are led, the truth which seems to us significant, is not independent of our experience as whole human beings. Moreover, to hope that we can understandingly interpret matters of which we have no first-hand knowledge, things utterly unproved upon the pulses — to hope, for instance, that upper-middle class white professors can have much illumination to shed upon black power — is intellectual hubris. Another way to phrase what I am saying is the following. It is easy for us to see that the factory does more than oppress the worker, it also assimilates him to its hectic pace, its system of material rewards, its hierarchical decision-making. Similarly we are not merely oppressed by the university but conditioned, too. The grotesquerie of this university, elucidating Aquinas with the left hand while with the right hand it uproots poor Negro families in Hyde Park and Woodlawn, is too much the grotesquerie of our own lives as well.

Again, it is easy for us to see that liberal

intellectuals tacitly assume a division of labor between themselves and democratic politicians. They can restrict themselves to cloistered thought because, in their view of things, somewhere out there in the world of action is a democratic political process which in the long run will assimilate their thinking and be guided by it. But does it now also affect us that, as Professor Morgenthau wrote last fall in *The New Republic,* "the great national decisions of life and death are rendered by technological elites, and both the Congress and the people at large retain little more than the illusion of making the decisions which the theory of democracy suppose them to make"? Do we not also justify our intellectual labors by assuming the existence of a political *deus ex machina,* whether that be the Party, or the proletariat, or the youth? I think the times no longer permit this indulgence, and ask us, at the very least, to venture into the area where political parties, and working-men, and young people do their things, seeking to clarify that experience which becomes ours as well, speaking truth to power from the vantage-point of that process of struggle.

To do this, we ourselves must have a foot solidly off the campus. More of us, like Joe Tuchinsky at Roosevelt, should teach part-time and supervise the training of draft counselors with the remainder; or like Sid Peck and Bob Greenblatt of the National Mobilization Committee alternate years of full-time intellectual work with years of full-time work for the Movement. The economic problems in living thus more adventurously are not insuperable. Nothing in the Communist Manifesto or for that matter the New Testament assures us that at age thirty-five or forty we should expect to achieve economic security for the rest of our lives. Disgorge the bait of tenure, and the problem of making a living can solve itself year-by-year. Face the problem of livelihood as husband and wife, accepting the possibility that sometimes one of you, sometimes the other, will be the main breadwinner, and you will have taken a long step toward solution of the so-called woman question. Face the problem of livelihood together with your friends in the Movement, recognizing that at some times you may support them, at others they you, and that you can all take greater risks because of this assurance, and you will have taken a long step toward the overcoming of alienation. The great hindrance is not in the objective world but in our heads. The hindrance is the notion that real intellectuals — unlike Thucydides, Machiavelli, Milton, Locke, Hamilton, Jefferson, Trotsky, Lenin, and unlike what Marx would have been if he could — do nothing but think. The first constituency we need to radicalize is ourselves. Our path of honor is to live so as to be able to tell the truth about the hopes and sufferings of mankind in our generation.

New University Conference Newsletter 5/24/68

THEY CAN'T TAKE IN EVERYONE, CAN THEY? OR CAN THEY?

But I was puzzled by the proposal for open admissions. I found myself thinking, if anybody could get into the university, why wouldn't ten thousand, twenty thousand, a hundred thousand people come here, and if they did, what would the university do with them? And I began thinking freshly about a question that people have been asking me many times in my lecturing on education. Hundreds of teachers and parents have said to me, "If children are educated the way you want, if they can learn whatever they like in the way it seems best to them, how are the colleges going to solve their admissions problem?" My answer was usually that I did not consider the solving of the college admissions problem a high priority question, for me or even for the elementary or secondary schools of this country. I usually followed this by suggesting one or more ways in which colleges might, by my lights, improve their admissions procedures so as to make places available to students of a much wider variety of talents and backgrounds. But I accepted almost without realizing it the assumption on the part of my hearers that a college must make decisions about who *can* come in and who *cannot*. After all, their facilities are limited, aren't they? They can't take in everyone, can they?

Then one day I found myself thinking of the Boston Public Library, which I go to quite often, more to borrow classical records than books. Here is what must certainly be called an educational institution. Yet it does not make decisions and judgments about who can come in and who cannot, and—what is more important —who is good enough to come in and who is not. It simply says like libraries everywhere, "Here are some facilities—books, records, films, exhibits. If you want, come in and use them, as much as you want, as long as you want." I thought of many other educational institutions that serve society, none of which exclude anybody, and it suddenly occurred to me that the admissions problem of our universities is not a real problem but a manufactured one— that is, it exists because the universities want it to exist, not because it has to.

Why shouldn't a school, college, or university be like a museum, a library, a concert hall, a lecture hall, a sports facility? Why shouldn't it, like them, say to the public, "Here is what we have to offer you; here are the possibilities. If they appeal to you, come in and use them, for as little or as long as you like." If more people want to get in than there is room for, let them handle this situation the way a concert hall or theater handles it. Why not hang out a sign saying "Sold Out—next performance tomorrow afternoon, next week, next month, next year." If a student wanted to take a course with Professor So-and-So and there were hundreds of other students wanting to take the same course, why not let him make the kind of choice that someone makes who wants to see a very popular play? Let him either, in effect, wait until there is an opportunity to get in the course, or, if that seems like too long a wait, think about getting the

same sort of information or help somewhere else? If I want to see a doctor, and someone says that he has so many patients that I won't be able to see him for four months, the sensible thing to do is find some other doctor, maybe not quite as good but with fewer patients.

Let the student worry about overcrowding. The university can say, we can provide university housing for so many thousand students; after that, people will have to find their own. Large numbers of students at Berkeley and other state universities do in fact live off campus. This often makes housing both scarce and expensive, and this may in turn make a student decide that a particular university is or is not a good place to go. But let this be his worry, not the university's. If the housing, facilities, and courses at one university are terribly crowded so that desirable courses are hard or impossible to get into —as indeed they are now in many cases at places like Berkeley—the student can decide either to try to wait it out or to go somewhere else.

Nor is there any necessary reason why universities should worry so about qualifications. This will seem startling at first. But after all, when I borrow a book or record from the Boston Public Library, nobody gives me a quiz to be sure I will understand it. It's up to me to decide how I want to spend my time and to run the risk of wasting it. Similarly, if I go to the Boston Symphony to hear a piece of difficult modern music, nobody examines me in the hall to make sure I'm educated enough to appreciate it. I pay my money and I take my choice. If I go home later feeling angrily that it was a waste of an evening, all right, that's my tough luck. But why should anyone else make this decision for me?

It is perfectly true that universities of this kind would be in important ways different from the ones we know today. The universities as they exist have come to think of themselves as private clubs. They are in a race with each other for prestige, which is quickly translated into money and power—the professor from a prestigious university has more chance of getting a big foundation or government grant than a professor from some less prestigious one. Therefore, they have an interest in convincing the world that their club is harder to get into than anybody else's. At the same time, they try to convince the oncoming generations of students that membership in this club will in the long run prove more valuable—again in terms of power and money—than membership in any other. That is what creates the admissions problem. I make a great many people think that my club is the one to be in, and then I stand at the door and tell large numbers of them that they aren't good enough to get in. On the other hand,

since the Boston Public Library isn't trying to convince people that because it is harder to get in it is a "better" library than the New York Public Library, it doesn't have to urge large numbers of people to come to it because it is the best and then put somebody at the door turning most of these people away because they aren't good enough to get in.

The universities that consider themselves superior have an enormous investment, financial and psychological, in the notion of their own superiority, and I don't expect them to give it up quickly or lightly. Given its present concerns, which do not for the most part have much to do with education, I can understand why the University of California should feel threatened by the demand of the Third World students that they open their doors to any Third World people who want to come in, and I can understand their wanting to resist this demand as much as they can. As long as universities are interested in prestige and power, they will want to go on saying to the world that people are coming to them because they are so good, and that they are turning away most of their applicants or supplicants because they in turn are not good enough. But a university truly dedicated to education, to the spreading of knowledge, skill, and —most important—wisdom to all who wanted or needed it, would think in other terms.

People ask, what about the granting of degrees? If anybody who wants can come to a university and there study as much or as little as he wants, how will the university issue its credentials? I don't think the university ought to be in the credentials-granting business. Why should our universities be hiring halls for business and government? It does not seem to me to be a vital or necessary or even acceptable part of the process of education. In any case, people even now take courses in the extension divisions of universities and, depending on the length of the course, get a certain number of credits for work done. There's no reason at all why people could not over a number of years take courses in an assortment of universities, depending on where they lived and who they wanted to study with, and simply have some kind of certificate listing the total number of credits they had collected. In any case, there is plenty of evidence that educational institutions do not and cannot teach competence. Since they don't and can't, why go on any longer with the pretense that an academic degree is a certificate of competence? All it shows or can show is that such-and-such a person has taken so many courses and played the school game for a certain length of time; it says nothing about what he will or will not be able to do in his later working life. The prestige universities have worked hard, for reasons already given, to convince employers and the public at large that their degrees are indeed certificates of exceptional competence and worth. They have to do this to create among the students a demand for these degrees and among employers a demand for holders of them. But it is a con, and there is really nothing in it. If the universities grew interested in education they could give up this fiction along with others.

To the dissatisfied, the universities like to say, in one way or another, "If you don't like our rules, you don't have to play our game." This seems the height of reasonableness. It is nothing of the kind. The universities, which in other circumstances like to think of themselves sometimes as exclusive clubs, sometimes as temples of the higher truth and learning, are comparing themselves here to any kind of store. You go to the supermarket, pay some money, walk out the door with a little food. If you don't like their food or their prices, you don't go to that supermarket; you go to some other. In the same way, the universities say, we offer certain kinds of learning, skill, and money-attracting credentials, in return for a good deal of the students' money and time.

The trouble with this—and it should be obvious to anyone who takes half a minute to think about it—is that the stores we trade at do not exercise the kind of influence and pressure on our lives that the universities, singly and collectively, exercise on the lives of their students. The supermarkets do not post people at the door deciding whether or not I am good enough to get in. Nor do they stamp on my forehead in indelible ink for the world to see whether or not I *was* good enough. They do not grade me like the meat they sell. The universities, on the other hand, do exactly this. They have arrived at a situation, and to a considerable extent contrived it, in which their opinion of a young person determines to a very large degree what that person can or cannot do, will or will not become during the rest of his life. There is probably no other single institution in society, even the armed forces, which has as much to say about our lives. (The armed forces, it is true, can put a man in a position where he may be killed or injured, but once he gets out of their hands, so to speak, they don't cast much of a shadow over his future.)

Our young people start living under the shadow of universities almost as soon as they're born. What the universities want, what they think is good, bad, valuable, valueless, certainly determines and creates the kinds of pressures that our young people live under beginning as early as age three or four. Our young people spend a very large part of their time, even before they go on to college, doing what the schools think the universities want; they go on doing what they want while they're at the universities, which may be anything from four to heaven-knows-how-many years; and, as I said before, they carry on them for the rest of their lives whatever sort of brand the university has chosen to put on them. Their demand—that since universities exercise this enormous control over the lives of their students, students should have something to say about them and the way they are run—seems to me to be altogether right and just. If universities want to say to our young people in effect, "We are just a gathering of scholars doing our thing; please stop bothering us and interfering with us, and let us do our own thing the way we want," then they have got to get their feet off the collective necks of the young and give up the extraordinary and unjustifiable power that they have acquired over their lives.

From "Letters From Berkeley" by John Holt, *Yale Alumni Magazine* Nov 1969

KNOWLEDGE IS POWER

JOHN McDERMOTT

Mr. McDermott is Field Secretary of the New University Conference and a free-lance lecturer. Formerly, he was associate editor of Viet-Report *and has written widely on the Vietnamese War. His book on technology and society will be published later in the year by Random House.*

The key to understanding the oppressive class structures now developing in American society is found less in the maldistribution of the nation's property than in the maldistribution of its knowledge. Whether in the form of raw data, esoteric scientific principle, advanced industrial technique or the judgments of scientific and technical elites, knowledge has become decisive, for it is rapidly displacing wealth, real property and individual entrepreneurial skills as the growth factor in industrial production, social organization and, most important of all, political power.

This increase in the importance of technical knowledge has been embodied in the expansion of the giant institutions which have come to achieve a near monopoly over its effective use. Segments of knowledge still belong to technical specialists and pieces of knowledge to the well educated, but only the very largest organizations are able to integrate these proliferating segments and pieces into systems of productive, effective or, more likely, profitable information. That is the meaning of technological progress: the systematic application of new knowledge to practical purposes. And it dictates a continual increase in the size, wealth and managerial capacity of the organizations which seek thus to apply the knowledge. Corporations, government agencies, universities and foundations have been quick to respond.

Not only has technological progress demanded the extraordinary growth in institutional scale witnessed in the years since World War II; it has also modified it in an unusual and important way. For beyond a certain size institutions need no longer confine themselves to their original spheres of activity. Their scope and wealth, the sophistication and ambition of their managements, the urge and capacity to profit from novel undertakings, the desire not to take second place to their rivals combine to produce the diversified corporate which has become the characteristic form of organization among the larger institutions of American society.

In the institutional world, the most successful corporate bodies are those that have most diversified their activities. Their managements have accepted the challenge and the opportunity to master an ever wider range of scientific and technical disciplines and to weld them into production and distribution of ever more varied and sophisticated goods or services. Consider the variety of outputs now characteristic of our corporates and the range of knowledge they employ. A company like RCA manages missile tracking systems, does research in linear algebra, edits and markets new novels, plans new educational systems, and experiments with electronic music. The University of Michigan, another growing corporate, teaches students at Ann Arbor, advises welfare mothers in Detroit, and pacifies peasants in Thailand. The most impressive example of diversification is found, as one might expect,

A STRONG PEOPLE NEED NO LEADER
—ZAPATA

in the Department of Defense. High energy physics, trans-oceanic logistics, infantry tactics, elementary and secondary education, comparative linguistics, Greek political studies, psychiatry and astronomy are but a handful of the knowledges the Pentagon employs in its far-flung activities. Among corporate bodies like these, the words private and public, industrial and educational, national and international, military and civilian, no longer define significant distinctions; for, in the case of each pairing, a single group of managers, acting through bureaucratic hierarchy, has disciplined the babble of modern specialisms to its own expanding purposes.

That these facts, and their social consequences, are not more widely understood is in part tribute to the doggedness with which we cling to an inaccurate and outmoded conception of knowledge. Intellectual tradition still treats knowledge as the property of an individual man, its highest forms being humane learning, wisdom or science. This faces us in precisely the wrong direction to understand what has been happening to knowledge and its uses. The prevailing complaint is that the knowledge explosion has forced men to specialize so intensely as to lose contact with the general contours of knowledge and thus of human experience itself. But concern with this phenomenon has blocked our appreciation of a far more important one. As individual men have become micro-specialists, less and less able to understand and act from general systems of knowledge, the great institutions have become generalists, increasingly able to integrate the discrete information of the specialists into technical and organizational systems which produce goods or services.

Thus the same explosion of information which has been so unkind to the makers of intellectual systems has been a boon to the makers of industrial systems. What has been for individuals a source of private alienation has been for institutions a source of social opportunity. What has been for the former an insurmountable barrier to understanding has been for the latter an indispensable aid to Gargantuan expansion. The mathematicians, sociologists, metallurgists and psychologists of the Defense Department may be alienated from their work, but in the higher echelons of the Pentagon, as throughout corporate America, knowledge is power.

These are not new facts and, in their outlines at least, they are frighteningly simple. America believes in *progress.* Hence it gives free rein to those very large organizations which have mastered *technology,* calling this *pluralism.* Its ethos is governed, ideally, by the principle of *equal opportunity* for enormous privilege, the result being a social system called *Meritocracy* or, by some, *Meritocratic Democracy.* (See "The Laying on of Culture," *The Nation,* March 10, p. 300.) It is the *American Way* adapted to the *World of Tomorrow.*

One cannot rest easily with the maldistribution of knowledge which is so essential a feature of the American Way. For the concentration of effective knowledge of and about American society in several giant organizations can lead to no other result than a substantial decline in the capacity of ordinary Americans to control that society and those organizations. In fact, one can already observe several important tendencies which mark that decline.

First, as the institutions have increased in size and enjoyed growing monopolies, both of information and of the products and services dependent on it, their relation-

ships to the unorganized and hence uninformed individuals who make up their publics have undergone a subtle but radical change. Whereas previously these had been to some extent political or market relationships, implying some bargaining between the interests of the two parties, they now tend more and more to become administrative,

implying subordination of the interests of the weaker party. The vague feelings of impotence so widespread in this country reflect the true state of affairs; for to be a consumer of, an employee of, a client of, a citizen of, a voter of, a taxpayer of, a draftee of, a reader of, a student of, or even a member of a large institution is, increasingly, to be its victim, not its master.

Second, just as institutions have improved their capacity to act on their various publics, their managers have improved their capacity to control the internal behavior of the institutions. Former Secretary McNamara's cost/benefit systems, which revolutionized and centralized budgeting procedures in the Department of Defense, are a startlingly cogent instance of a general trend. The increasing professionalization of middle management and the growing employment of data storage and retrieval systems are among a host of new techniques which enable senior managers to exert more selective control over the internal behavior of even the very largest and most diversified institutions. The combined result of these two tendencies is that the growing command of large institutions over the vital processes of American life measures the real power of their managers over the activities of Americans generally.

Third, as these institutions gather, process and apply wider and wider systems of information and steadily expand into novel spheres of activity, the distinction between (public) right and (private) privilege disappears. Whatever is done within the confines of an institutional bureaucracy becomes for that reason a private matter, of concern only to those technicians immediately involved and their hierarchic superiors. Whether an institution is privately or publicly controlled is not material; the laws and customs of private property or academic freedom guarantee the privacy of the former, while those of national security have spread to veil the latter.

As a result of these three tendencies, politics has lost its significance as a set of devices by which the general public rules over private hierarchy. It has become a shadow, uncertainly related to the real events of the private world it ostensibly controls. This summary point must be gone into at length, for it involves much more than the traditional tricks of the traditional parties.

Those of us engaged in "guerrilla journalism" over the war in Vietnam have learned that it is no longer possible to keep up politically with most areas of national life simply by reading the conventional press. However carefully one studies *The New York Times, The Wall Street Journal, The Washington Post,* etc., the news-weeklies and other mass sources of information, one is at a loss to pass judgment on events unless one also follows the relevant technical press. Perhaps an instance will suffice to document and clarify this lesson.

During 1965 repeated press stories reported that neutral Thailand was being used as the base from which most of the air offensive against North Vietnam was being launched. This should have been a singularly important fact for the public debate of the time. It not only made possible a quantitatively heavier offensive against the North but represented a qualitative escalation of the war as well. Once Thai bases were used, the conflict was no longer confined to Vietnam. And, since it was likely that the Thais had exacted some price for the use of their airfields, it was also likely that the diplomacy of the war had become more complex: presumably the Thais too would now have to be satisfied in any war settlement. Finally, of course, the bases raised the possibility that the North Vietnamese would henceforth feel justified in causing the Thai dictatorship some equivalent grief, thus increasing still further the military-political complexity.

This singularly important information about the bases

NIXON
IS SORRY --BUT

THE PENTAGON
CALLS THE SHOTS

WOMEN'S
SOLIDARITY
STRIKE

BOURGEOIS
VOUS
N'AVEZ
RIENCOMPRIS

never really penetrated the public debate, for it was never permitted to become a public fact. By the technique of issuing "unofficial," "informed sources," "nonattributable," "off-the-record," "official" and "attributable" denials—as the situation demanded—to accompany each new press report (which were dutifully printed by the newspapers in tandem with their own stories), the government managed to obscure from the public both the seriousness of the Vietnam escalation and the gravity of its probable development. However, no such clouding of the situation affected the technical press. Journals like *Air Force and Space Digest* early carried and soon confirmed the reports and, as if to underline my point, were careful to emphasize that the government was making a major effort to hide their importance from the general public. The reason for this difference in news dissemination is plain. The climate, geography, dust and logistic peculiarities of Thailand affected the procurement of technical equipment for the short future and its design for the middle future. Persons engaged in the aircraft and electronics industries had to know about the Thai bases because they were expected to develop and act on that knowledge. They belonged to the private institutional world, and in the private world one has rights based on function. No equivalent rights exist in the public world. It is a world which, increasingly in our society, has no function.

This leads to perhaps the most important of the tendencies encouraged by maldistribution of knowledge. Stripped of any relation of control or significance to the events of the real world, people's political responses have themselves become increasingly unreal and even paranoid. That explains, I think, the wild gyrations of public opinion polls, especially those dealing with international questions. It also partly explains the appeal of Goldwater and Wallace.

This apparent irrationality is widely misunderstood. Educated Americans tend to see in the primitive style of the Wallace movement, for instance, merely a projection of the primitiveness of its individual adherents. They explain its propensity to violent solutions for various questions as an acting out of the private frustrations and fantasies of its so-called "redneck" members. But the Wallace people are not reacting blindly out of the inadequacies and failures of their *personal* lives. They are trying to react rationally to the inadequacies of their *social* lives. Uneducated people and people at the social margin of this technically advanced society correctly perceive that politics is changing so as to reduce their power to act for the advantage or defense of their own interests. They recognize that the institutional processes which disenfranchise them have already advanced to a degree that conventional political channels are closed to them. Thus they forsake the conventional parties. Of course, the substitutes offered by Wallace and his cronies also fail to reach the heart of any problem—except perhaps the expression of resentment.

Deeply sensed political incapacity extends to the Left as well, especially to the educated liberal Left. In retrospect, it is evident that the combination of President Johnson's March speech, the opening of the Paris talks, and the McCarthy candidacy caused many liberals to channel the bulk of their political energies and hopes into the campaign leading up to the Democratic convention. Having channeled themselves it was easier for others to deflect them, with the result that the McCarthy candidacy gurgled to a docile end within the hostile and muddy confines of the Democratic convention. For what the McCarthy people failed to realize was that their strength within the Democratic Party was solely and directly dependent on their strength outside it. They never had the numbers, re-

sources, skills or strategic position within the party to win the nomination or even a continuing minority position. Their real allies were the draft card burners, resisters and demonstrators, and the broad popular movement these "extremists"—not McCarthy, a late-blooming dove—had called into being. But the McCarthy people didn't see this; they saw their campaign as an "orderly" alternative to the "extremist" movement, rather than as the expression of that movement. It was only in the brief span of Chicago that the mutually supporting relationship which should have characterized the link between the party and nonparty people became apparent and effective. But the alliance came too late to accomplish anything more than Humphrey's defeat, and has not been maintained since.

The radical Left understood the situation very little better. In spite of some evidence to the contrary, it was largely the play of events, not conscious choice, which created their effective temporary alliance with party types in Chicago. As the McCarthy campaign illustrates, the overeducated Left fares no better than the undereducated Right when it comes to analyzing and acting effectively within the ghost world of contemporary public politics. And the reason for this is that we confront a social phenomenon, not a personal one. The very political language people use is seriously debased; loyalties they retain border on total unreality. Even the actual processes which they engage in, such as reading newspapers, belonging to political clubs and voting, have small ascertainable relevance. In short, the popular political culture has become so distant from the knowledges that influence the real world of decision making that the former is no longer able to deal with the latter in any effective and humane way.

America's developing class structure would appear to parallel this maldistribution of its knowledge. Within and around the great institutions which now constitute the core of our political, economic and social life, two distinct classes are taking shape, both defined by their relationship to the processes of those institutions. An overclass comprises those who manage the lives of great institutions, and an underclass those whose lives the institutions manage. By means of institutional place and institutional resources, the former normally amasses the technical, scientific and political information necessary for the direction of American life and the satisfaction of its own interests. For the underclass, largely buried in bureaucratic pigeonholes, a perspective on its own situation is, socially speaking, nearly impossible. For between them and the means to put the reality of their social lives in manageable order, to formulate their interests and to act effectively in their own behalf, stands almost the entire panoply of our largest, most prestigious and most powerful institutions.

In saying this, one must guard against two important misconceptions. First, the maldistribution of socially effective knowledge provides only a guide by which the outlines of the class system may be charted. The latter's substance rests in far more diverse phenomena, namely in the interaction between the explosion of technical knowledge and the capitalist and cold-war legacy within which that explosion has occurred. It is the institutional framework that is critical here. No amount of technical information pumped into the public life stream would be likely to correct the weaknesses of underclass politics, for the

underclass now lacks the social, cultural and organizational framework within which that information can be assimilated and acted upon. As I have tried to stress, the problem is fundamentally a social one, not one of making individuals better informed. After all, Senator McCarthy and his followers were "smarter" than General Westmoreland, Mayor Daley and theirs, but not so powerful.

Second, we should purge ourselves of the all too prevalent view that the new importance of scientific knowledge promotes the growth of freedom. As Carol Brightman has pointed out (*Viet-Report*, January 1968), this is an old illusion in American life and one which has, unfortunately, a considerable following even today. Carl Becker spoke for several generations of American Progressives when he wrote in *Progress and Power* that

> . . . the mastery of the physical world has been effected by scientists whose activities, *unhindered by the conscious resistance of their subject matter or the ignorance of common man*, have been guided by matter-of-fact knowledge and the consciously formulated purpose of subduing things to precisely determined ends, [while] the organization of society has been left to the chance operation of individual self interest and the uncertain pressure of mass opinion. (*Italics added.*)

Looking to the cure of our social ills, Becker shared with John Dewey and Robert Lynd the diagnosis that

> those who have or might acquire the necessary matter-of-fact knowledge for adjusting social arrangements to the conditions created by technological progress have not the necessary authority, while those [elected representatives] who have . . . must accommodate their measures to a mass intelligence that functions most effectively at a level of primitive fears and taboos.

What is this but a literate statement of the ideological presuppositions behind which the new technocracy combines with the old oligarchy to remove public concerns to the institutional world of private decision making? Knowledge necessary "for adjusting social arrangements" has become almost exclusively the possession of a narrow and privileged class of men and women, residing in the commanding positions of America's great institutions and protected by law, ideology, custom, power and technique from the "conscious resistance" of an increasingly disoriented and feckless underclass intelligence.

For intellectuals concerned to mount effective attacks on this class system, two steps appear to have priority. First, the world of institutional behavior and the knowledges it employs must be charted far more precisely and more richly than has heretofore been the case. Current descriptions and explanations of corporate, government, municipal, union and foundation behavior are inadequate, for they do not permit a sufficiently reliable forecast of how and why institutions will act under specific circumstances. The Left is especially and perennially susceptive to explanations so general that they describe little more than anger and frustration. We are forever being surprised and undone by developments.

A good example of the low level of our understanding of institutional behavior is a little booklet which grew out of the Columbia University student strike last year and which has been circulated by SDS in the thousands to campus activists, students and faculty. *Who Rules Columbia?* is an excellent and important work of research on Columbia's Board of Trustees, and in this respect it should be, and has been, copied by other campuses. The character of the analysis it draws from this data is another matter. It tries to explain Columbia's interest in Defense-related research, CIA shenanigans, business education and the denial of student rights as a pure and simple function of the presence on the Board of Trustees of corporate, media, foundation, government and other Establishment figures. The influence of faculty ideology, alumni fears and professional administrative standards, as well as bureaucratic inertia (one of the main, designed-in "values" of bureaucracies that deal with ordinary people) is not even raised, much less explored. And the critically important role played by other university administrations, which urged Columbia's to hold the line (or the first domino) against a Red-anarchist-nihilist-nonprofessional plot, is also ignored. When one considers that *Who Rules Columbia?* is an approach to this kind of problem infinitely more sophisticated than the usual academic discussion

—which equates a few pieties about academic freedom and the advance of knowledge with a worn-out theory of university governance—the problem is serious indeed.

But it is not fundamentally an intellectual problem, a matter of pure scholarship. Among the knowledges which large institutions have come to master are those which can be employed to disguise, prevent and manage conflict. Columbia, for example, might reasonably have been considered a bland, successful and liberal community of scholars until its carefully nurtured appearance was probed by the actions of student radicals. It was only then, as the Cox Commission itself pointed out, that under the stress of conflict the reality of Columbia began to emerge: ill-managed, torn by unresolved internal problems, unwilling and unable to deal forthrightly with the wishes of its student and black publics.

To the extent that the same situation holds in other corporate organizations, the response should be designed accordingly. Practically speaking, what is both needed and possible is not a disengaged scholarly literature about institutions apparently at peace with themselves and their world such as now strangles academic political science. Good scholarship here requires, I believe, a working alliance with insurgent political activity.

It therefore follows, as the second step, that the mutually destructive division between intellectual culture and popular culture should be ended. The anti-Populism of university-based intellectual culture, so evident in its attitudes toward Wallace followers, should be attacked. We should frankly recognize that that culture, comfortable in its adherence to the liberal social prescriptions of Dewey, Becker and Lynd, and confident that those once Progressive canons still contribute to the general betterment of mankind, now too often merely mask the social rapacity of the technological impulse.

Underclass assaults against American society, led by left-wing youth and right-wing adults, now pose a serious problem of orientation for intellectuals. One possible reaction was typified by George Kennan's recent widely publicized exchange with Princeton students. But the cultural exclusivity and intellectual clericalism espoused by Kennan can lead, I think, only to the destruction of any serious humanist role for intellectuals. It leaves the intellectual in the position of being a protected minority within the exploding multiversity, well away from its technological mainstream, and thereby under powerful sanction to shift roles from intellectual to intellectual technician. The difference in the two roles is fundamental: intellectuals contribute to people's self-knowledge and liberation; intellectual technicians con people while trying to control them.

A constructive alternative to Kennanism and Progressivism is not easy to describe. It requires an intellectual culture, such as has been lacking for many years, that is really knowledgeable about the concerns, activities and situations of popular life in the country. Intellectuals have to make contact with the views, experiences and problems of people who have no daily relationship to the university or who, if they have, are antagonized by it. The burgeoning radicals-in-the-professions movements, the New University Conference, draft counseling, and the various efforts to work with GI war protesters fit this description. It would help, too, if intellectuals would really face up to the fact that the gentler virtues are by no means a monopoly of the educated classes, and that there are decent visions behind the often violent and shortsighted slogans of underclass revolts. We should recognize that intellectual arrogance in these matters is a result of the same system which makes those revolts necessary.

MAYBE THEY CAN'T HEAR US

STRIKE

A LITTLE LOUDER

1963... AND ANOTHER

The Civil Rights March on Washington was the largest non-violent, black freedom demonstration.

1964 . . . AND ANOTHER

Malcolm X articulated growing black dissatisfaction with the ineffectiveness of integration and non-violent protest.

In an essay on revolutionary drama in TDR (T42), I indicated, with the term "revolutionary," a relative handful of major plays which—more than depicting social life critically and in a manner to express despair or perhaps anger at the way things are—take an added and very difficult step, which is the depiction of effective revolutionary conduct upon the stage. Study of these plays suggested that their authors had become capable of producing them only under the impress of revolutionary examples in life.

Briefly the article touched on John Reed. Although his plays were performed at the Provincetown Players, the *theatrum mundi* very soon claimed Reed's attention, and his dramatic genius found realization in revolutionary action. His case appears, in today's perspective, to be anything but unique. We seem to have entered an era in which the human dramatic potential is to be realized foremostly in life, and for life. The stage once again follows along. It tries with audience participation experiments and guerrilla theatre to become more like the drama of history.

What follows is a dossier: several photo-analyses of the performance of history in terms of the essential dramatic ingredient. And two arguments—conservative and libertarian—to represent the opposed bodies of values and knowledge which now animate the actors of the world stage.

I

(Transcript of the Edmund Burke Memorial Lecture for 1969, delivered to a Meeting of the Rand Corporation by a Spectacle Manager.)

Gentlemen, we gather at a most difficult time. The principles and causes of the prosperity and consensus of our system are being questioned. In many cases the most promising of our young people, white and black, are responsible. I don't know, perhaps some of your children are mixed in . . . [*general laughter*]. The problem is not that the malcontents exist; for they always have, and shall. The vexation is that our radicals once obligingly limited themselves to the spoken and printed word, for the most part. And today they do not: they *act*. They do these spectacular things which get in the press and on television and heat up others. Then they have the temerity to come into our courts claiming that to burn a draft card, or to hurl blood in the Dow Chemical headquarters, is "symbolic speech"—a kind of communication protected by the Bill of Rights! Thus the new radicals are exploiting, or better perverting, the natural and usually wholesome tendency of our public to react strongly to events—not words, events—as a drama.

I advisedly say "perverting;" for traditionally, as we all know or should know, the social dramaticism has belonged to us. It has been a key and vital bulwark of government. Dismay is justified, inasmuch as the New Left—how consciously is not yet clear—has discovered the performance element of politics for its own ends [*distress in the hall*].

The annual Edmund Burke Lecture honors a great theorist of the preservation of Anglo-Saxon government. He counsels us from across the years, in our latest crunch. The universality and timeliness of Burke are seen in the stress he gave the fact that a lucid theatricality is essential to maintaining the consensus. I need but quote from his *Reflections on the Revolution in France* to illustrate, for example, what flows from an undermining of our effective monopoly control of dramaticism: "Now all is to be changed. All the pleasing illusions, which made power gentle, and obedience liberal, which harmonized the different shades of life, and which, by a bland assimilation, incorporated into politics the sentiments which beautify and soften private society, are to be dissolved by this new conquering empire of light and reason. All the decent drapery of life is to be rudely torn off . . ."

The radicals we face, gentlemen, speak disdainfully of "the puppet show of state," as once did Burke's opponent, Tom Paine. They invent for themselves, and even go beyond, the tactical insights of Paine, e.g.—"A single expression, boldly conceived and uttered, will sometimes put a whole company into their proper feelings, and whole nations are acted upon in the same manner," to quote *The Rights of Man.* Our opponents thus armed, gentlemen, we must affirm and newly promulgate the rules of our traditional stagecraft. The Rand Corporation relies on you, urgently, to take and perform the dramatistic insights in your industries, military bases, universities,

COMPREHENSION

Spectacles and Scenarios: A Dramaturgy of Radical Activity

Lee Baxandall

[A constitutional republic] cannot forever withstand continual carnival on the streets of its cities and the campuses of the nation. Unless sage debate replaces the belligerent strutting now used so extensively, reason will be consumed and the death of logic will surely follow.
   Vice President Agnew, Honolulu Address to the Young Presidents Organization, May 2, 1969

There is so much upheaval in the world, it's more theatrical than the theatre. The theatre is in a state of unrest and we're all trying to find out what its function is.
   Mildred Dunnock, *N.Y. Times,* January 18, 1969

Action from principle, the perception and the performance of right, changes things and relations; it is essentially revolutionary, and does not consist wholly with anything which was.

   Henry David Thoreau, "Civil Disobedience"

and other walks of life. Bear in mind that Plato termed statecraft the highest art.

First, and to take nothing for granted: *is* politics performance, and everyday activity dramatic? Our language—the American idiom especially—seems to confirm it. We speak of a theatre of war, making a scene, properly acting in the spotlight, staging an event from behind the scenes. This might merely be misleading though ornamental metaphor. That it is not is affirmed by the peers and compatriots of Burke through the ages. Plato, the Stoic philosophers, Roman authors, and medieval writers such as Salisbury, declared with Shakespeare that "all the world's a stage." And generally, they go on to concur with Calvin that the world is "the theatre of God's glory"—one performs according to divine will, that is, a high or (usually) low role in the Great Chain of Being. This is an essential item, whether or not dressed out in a religious garb, from our point of view. If time-honored thinking on this matter is correct, can we discern a *function* of theatricalizing politics not to be had by government in any other way?

Permit me to analyze this point in perfect candor. Minced words would not be respected by you, who well know *how few* in effect take basic decisions for and reap the basic benefits from the society as a whole. The importance of performance to our politics is summed up in the phrase of Thomas Hobbes: "reputation of power, is Power." Not merely force and status, but the skillful *show* of force and status achieves our hegemony. Those who rule are a small minority, always. They—we, therefore—have not sufficient pooled powers to maintain a right attitude among the majority, so to prevent civil wars, unless the otherwise scant personal status and capacity for violence of those who govern are multipled geometrically by a usage of history as theatre, to which the term *spectacle* may be applied.

Some among us may object that in the last instance not fine words nor *show* of force, but the actual violence of a police and army keep a fragile order—as in Vietnam, Watts, Detroit, or San Francisco State College. True: a governing class is finally sustained by the obedience of a host of warrior recruits. But these are drawn largely from the underclasses, and it is a caution to recall that at precarious moments the salaried legions of enfranchised violence may waver, ignore their duties, even go over to "the people." Thus order in a state is always more tenuous than appears, and the reputation of power especially has to be nurtured in those whose violence will be called upon, when the spectacle has faltered in the other domains.

Walter Bagehot, a founder of modern political liberalism, put it as follows in *The English Constitution*, 1867. "The ruder sort of men," Bagehot said, must be finagled into a "reverence" toward the regrettably "plain, palpable ends of government" by the usage of "theatrical elements."

To this end the state has uncounted stages, plot-lines, and "routines." All of course is not pomp and intimidation. The show is sugared with entertainments; mitigated by allowance for private diversions; and indeed, best secured by seeing that many of the ruled, the armed forces especially, are assigned gratifying and in some respects commanding roles to play. The Great Chain of Being may be preserved and beautified best when most confused among tributary chains of command and obedience all mixed into one another. Thus Thomas Hobbes wrote in his *Leviathan*: "The Athenians were taught (to keep them from desire of changing their Government) that they were Freemen." Couple that thought with the aphorism at one time widely displayed in officer training schools, and attributed to General Eisenhower: "Leadership is the art of getting men to do what you want them to do, because they want to do it."

Neither force nor show of force, then, can of themselves and on all occasions guarantee a pliant civil population or warrior class; where it may be afforded the show of liberality becomes as important. Ultimately this liberality can be defined as a spectacle made of prerogatives left to others, which—though channelized, few, and insufficient—owing to the apparent stability of your system of spectacle, the ruled are led to believe they could not equal or get in any other way.

Force or liberality, whichever the profile of power displayed: the whole of the spectacle is distilled and celebrated in the drama of the central authority figure, and conversely, the head of state's example instructs authority in its conduct on the tributary stages. The theatrical principle known as empathy coordinates this minimizing, this harmonizing of the performance style differences you would expect between the great stage and the many small. Vicarious experience and emulation, as well as mystifying impression and admiration, marry for example the man at the head of the family to this man at the head of the state.

Admittedly we have lately hit a crisis-of-empathy snag. Lyndon Johnson stepped down solely because his performance was too widely jeered. Aside from the dramatistic failing, his politics were "functional" and are being carried on, but that is just the point; the dramaticism is not an "aside," it is functionally integral. A decade or so ago this could not have occurred. The public was not offered competing dramatistic styles and it scarcely knew how it acted. Now the head of state must play to divergent and competing empathy wants among the spectators and these, in truth, scarcely may be reconciled in a single man's performance. Look at Mr. Johnson's replacement. Unfortunately, his histrionic instinct is most expressed in the thrusting of balled fists into the air while his head becomes lost in the suit jacket . . . [*some suppressed laughter*]. Plainly the needed deference to the drama of the Presidency continues in trouble.

As perhaps never before our supremacy on the terrain of social dramaticism is heckled and flaunted, challenged or ignored. We must not countenance any loss of our lease on this psychological property; for it constitutes the holding corporation through which our otherwise scanty personal powers secure the property order of society generally. We do at least still enact the everyday hegemony within the public school systems, the army training camps, and the like. Although even here a small if potently dangerous minority is out of hand, the majority continue on the whole to absorb their exercises in spectacle obsequiousness. And clearly we still have the greater lucidity.

The radicals, I believe, do not conduct classes in their performance problems and techniques; nor have they done theoretical work which would be of consequence, for their thinking seldom seems to go beyond vague references to life style. Where the radicals remain instinctive, we of course possess uncounted management training schools and seminars, Dale Carnegie Courses, etc., for study and rehearsal of concrete performance politics. We have sociologists who strictly write and are resource con-

sultants on "social integration" through dramatistic interaction—for example, Erving Goffman, author of *The Presentation of Self in Everyday Life*, a commendable work which offers radicals no guidance whatsoever in their trend of dramaticism. It is this edge in lucidity which should prove decisive for us. Normally it does, through history.

Let us get firmly in mind the asset of a monopoly on tutorship in history as theatre. During all the centuries of organized society the ruled might, and would, imbibe their outlook and demeanor unwittingly through performance opportunities within

NUREMBURG, 1936: FASCISM EXPLOITS AND CORRUPTS THE HUMAN NEED FOR SCENARIO. The Hollywood film WILD IN THE STREETS and some "social commentators" have conveniently lumped the New Left's sense of the dramatic with the conduct of the Hitler youth. This is totally to misapprehend both fascism and the hopefulness of the present scene. As the Nuremburg rallies confirm, spectacle was of the essence in Hitler's master plan: scenario activity fed into and guided by the fantastic dream of the Master Race. National Socialism ("the socialism of fools" as someone well termed it) had a staggering if brief success, however, largely due to its skill in giving multitudes the illusion of participating in a dramaturgy which would realize their potential, whatever the cost, in a national destiny. To ignore this operative Nazi secret and to condemn a dramaturgical politics wherever it appears is to be foolish, and also inhuman. It is to consign social life to an unending alienation and to continued exploitation by classes no doubt more clever than the fascists in their use of spectacle for the long haul. The New Left emerges from the womb of the old system of social relations and is not untainted, nor can it always do without certain measures made urgent and all too comprehensible whenever a spectacle shifts from largely symbolic to outrageously punitive repression. The point, however, is this: the New Left clearly suffers from no addiction to ideological fantasies which could subordinate its salutary scenarios to a new spectacle, equally or more vicious than the present one; rather the attention to elementary human needs and values among the New Left is virtually without precedent.

photo: wide world

and between the classes; rulership has never taken the chance that its youth would stumble onto the precepts of spectacle, left to themselves. Perhaps the first well-ordered stratum of spectacle tutors, the Chinese mandarins, are described by Max Weber as "keepers of the rites" who through many centuries conferred status honor on the style of life of the privileged by teaching and refining the ceremonies which sanctified power. Plato was such an instructor, although he had to compete with philosophers more prized by the rising merchant class. We still accept uncritically the contempt with which Plato spoke of the Sophists, these tutors of a culture opposed to the Athenian aristocracy and which became, indeed, a forebear of our own establishment.

During the Renaissance, Castiglione deftly distilled the essence of performance insight in *The Book of the Courtier*. Let's not ignore Machiavelli. He became *the* publicly denounced, and avidly read, political philosopher in all civilized lands for decades, because he spelt out unapologetically both the technicalities and the show of power. For every such "name" tutor, the spectacle has been preserved through the marshalling of many thousands of the unpropertied educated to the task of intensely instructing the sons of nobility, and later of the high bourgeoisie, in religion, deportment, and the "science of rhetoric" (you will recall that even today most college theatre study remains located in Departments of Speech).

Education has changed, religion waned. But counterbalancing this, recall that a number of recent giants in the human sciences have actually helped reinforce the theatre of God's glory. Darwin presented himself as a religious man. Sigmund Freud argued in his later works that all but an enlightened few must be vouchsafed their sacred dramas and authority figures whom they will revere and who can essentially act for them. James G. Frazer drew from the vast study of primitive myth for his *Golden Bough* a lesson repeated by most anthropologists to our own day: men must have sacred drama if social integration is to be preserved. Gentlemen, we still enjoy the assistance of highly-skilled spectacle tutors and of thinkers of great reputation.

The arts, which become more pervasive all the time, likewise build the reputation of our legitimacy. Edmund Burke was not in error when he said, "the theatre is a better school of moral sentiments than the churches." Excuse me—[*a battering or striking without has made hearing difficult*]—would someone check out the reason for that noise?

The artists nowadays conceive many "audacities." They quickly use the term "revolutionary" for their work. Some want to universalize the license permitted their stratum. These ends, however, are frustrated and art chiefly lends reinforcement to social integration, due to empathy and another psychological property noted by Aristotle, catharsis. Can't that noise be stopped? [*The beating and now yelling has distracted the audience.*] Empathy and catharsis permit the public, I say, vicariously to live and timorously to *purge*, all in one operation, their curiosity about the most dangerous kinds of denied experience. The spectacle of allowing the imaginative events to be staged, shown, or written about meanwhile builds the reputation of government for liberality and stability. Finally, a flourishing cultural scene comes to appear to the great majority as the sole terrain for the serious practice of human aesthetic capacity. This illusion diverts many radicals as well from realizing the aesthetic dimension of their politics.

I shall speak more loudly. Can art ever surmount these factors to act dangerously upon our encapsulating spectacle? To do so it would have to depict, I believe, vivid models of directly emulable conduct more viable, vigorous, and gratifying than that of spectacle society and irreconcilable with it. We know, gentlemen, how rare is the artist who manages to this extent to release himself from spectacle obsequiousness. And if he appears—probably due to the encouragement and example of a radical constituency—and can somehow get his work before the public, despite the legal and informal web of spectacle checks and pressures to the contrary: would the public sympathetic to his paradigm want to absorb itself in his surrogate of an alternative conduct? Wouldn't the public thus prone to break with the spectacle prove impatient of all fictions, however emulable and laudable they think them?

Thus the arts appear always beneficial, or at least harmless to public order.... Can we have, please, an end to the commotion outside? ... [*The doors have burst open —black and white youths shouting swarm everywhere they seem to demand ...*]

End of transcript.

II

(*To an activist who shall be known as "Rimbaud Vivant," our thanks for the following, and for making available to us the Burke Lecture transcript.*)

A fresh vision of 1984: the world's populace liberated, you and everyone performing needs and abilities with one another freely—except for the spectacle managers and addicts, who despite themselves carry on as today in theatres especially designated for them.

The Rand Corp. expert talked straight as he knew. No crap about progress through pluralism with fun politics for all, no pray together to stay together in the greatest society ever. But their understanding of "dramaticism" ends with the grimaces they agree to pass for smiles, and Yeats' "coat upon a stick." They con their show of powers from the tattered promptbook of a court tragedy they do not quite understand, but even less know how to put aside. We have today the chance to grow joyous naked, to continuously discover and invent ourselves in the concerted white heat of expressive realization; and still the spectacle managers think themselves wise, as they mumble each one their paraphrases of the words uttered by Henri IV when told he had to turn Catholic to become Henri IV: "Paris is well worth a mass."

In the performance of yourself to others many see only a burden, if not the betrayal of an inner "real" self. Pirandello's theatre universalizes the bafflement and rage of that sense of betrayal. Failing to recognize its origin in the spectacle genre which makes you narrow and stupid, Pirandello projected his distress onto every mode of self enactment. He embraced, moreover, the pseudo-alternative of the Fascist State, which was in fact more of the same.

We create the dramaturgy of radical activity.

Dramaturgy retains its dictionary sense: "the art of making dramas and placing them properly on the stage; dramatic composition and representation." We add that the world stage takes precedence and that most human beings, freed of spectacle obsequity, could well compose and realize in activity their root nature. *Radical* is thus to be understood in its original sense: "going to the roots." Class domination and its spectacle society sharply frustrate, pervert your root potential. If overcoming this material and psychological alienation requires a role condemned by spectacle

managers as "radical," i.e., "extremist," take heart in knowing the spectacle addict to be the authentic extremist: alienated most radically from his humanity. *Activity* in our sense is therefore not a mere expenditure of energy in movement, but a unification of theory and sensuous conduct, a praxis, a free intelligent activity: a per-

COLUMBIA UNIVERSITY, SPRING 1968: THE SPECTACLE IS MADE TO REVEAL ITS BASIS IN VIOLENCE. A paradigm instance of the dramaturgy of radical activity is found in the Columbia "revolt" and the career of the student who largely conceived and led the radical scenarism there, Mark Rudd. The small campus chapter of Students for a Democratic Society had long agitated for an end to university ties with the Pentagon-guided Institute for Defense Analyses. It also sought reversal of the university's decision to build a new gym in adjacent Morningside Park which, SDS argued, should instead be developed to benefit Harlem, which abuts on three sides of the park. SDS had chosen to build a movement around specific issues which "dramatized" the complicity of the educational bureaucracy in racism and imperialism on a far broader front. But the chapter had made little progress with tactics of leafleting, dorm talks, and small protests. The administration remained aloof and evasive, adopting a paternal and "liberal" posture toward most of the agitation while yielding on none of its entanglements and plans. The "dramatic" issues of IDA and the gym were not compelling for most students and faculty, because SDS (and the black students' organization) had found no means to show that privatized, rather abstract popular opinion could enter upon an enlivening dramaturgy, effectively challenging the usurpations of the governing Regents.

Decisive leadership by Mark Rudd altered this situation within two months. In early March of 1968 it was learned that the head of the Selective Service System for New York City was to speak on campus. Rudd urged the SDS Draft Committee to greet him with a flamboyant protest. The old leadership of the chapter responded that Rudd's proposal lacked "political content" and the committee voted 30-1 simply to ask "probing questions" at the confrontation. This in Rudd's view was more of the same "verbalism" which led nowhere. On his own he organized a clandestine action group. In the middle of the Colonel's speech a mini-demonstration appeared: fife and drug, flags, machine guns, and noise-makers. The attention of all was directed to this mocking counter-spectacle in the back of the room. Suddenly someone in the front row stood up and placed a lemon-meringue pie in the Colonel's face. The scenario accomplished, all the performers vanished at once. Aside from the old SDS leadership and the administration, the entire campus seemed delighted with the way the Selective Service spokesman had "lost face." Rudd won the presidency of Columbia SDS on the basis of this feat and a sequenced scenario he now circulated, a plan for drawing a great many interested but apathetic students into radical dramaturgy. On March 27th a heavily-subscribed petition against the IDA was carried into Low Library, where President Kirk's offices were located, in defiance of new regulations against indoor "demonstrations." Next came a walk-out on the sanctimonious memorial service for Martin Luther King where Vice-President Truman and Kirk were delivering themselves of eulogies. On April 19 the chapter newspaper UP AGAINST THE WALL carried Rudd's open letter to Kirk, which explained to the entire campus the chapter policy of militancy and struggle.

The noon meeting at the sundial on April 23 might well have ended, Rudd has said, in another fruitless try at confronting Kirk directly on the IDA. Three factors merged to make this occasion decisive: (a) readiness for scenario audacity, accumulated by SDS and its sympathizers after the Selective Service, IDA, and King events; (b) new and exemplary militancy evinced by the Students' Afro-American Society; (c) the presence of a number of Columbia's fraternity boys and athletes between the sundial and Low Library, determined to bar the way. This vigilant opposition had gathered in response to a leaflet put out by Roger Crossland, a member of the sailing and judo teams, the naval ROTC, a fraternity, the Young Republicans, and the Conservative Union. Further indicative of Crossland's attachment to the values of spectacle is his permanent coat-and-tie attire: "It's different; you can't be typed" he has explained. Rudd had taken one of Crossland's leaflets, written his own comments in the margins, and re-duplicated and recirculated it on behalf of the SDS protest. The promise that the abstract confrontation was at last to become a human matter, that the other side indeed had partisans who would materialize, drew a much larger demonstration than usual. Rudd has argued that black students catalyzed the situation, both later, and through the "honky-baiting" speech of SAS chairman Cicero Wilson at the sundial (THE MOVEMENT, March 1969). No doubt the militancy of the blacks—and the proximity of Harlem—were crucial to the next hours and days. But it is true also that the whites' initiative at the King memorial spectacle preceded anything of the kind by the SAS.

Blocked, then, from entering Low Library with the petition by the show of right-wing readiness to inflict violence, the sundial group of about 200 raced to the gum site, where fences protecting Columbia's $1-a-year property grab were torn

formance of capabilities, taking into account all biological and social data, which ignores no biological and social potential.

The dramaturgy is realized in scenarios, which are—rather like the *improvvisa* of the *commedia dell'arte*—projected and agreed beforehand in part, and in part created as opportunities and fortuities arise in performance. If acting among friends and the likeminded, you perform peace scenarios. The ends and means will more or less be understood and agreed. Needs and capabilities are transposed to interactive expression by an invention of specifics which strive toward universality.

The terrain for peace scenarios—found to this day most often in the love affair—is not only limited but highly vulnerable to the totality of impinging social relations and values. Thus the necessity of mounting concerted war scenarios to dismay and rout the spectacle managers. A war scenario certainly does not by definition entail bloodshed (though the spectacle managers may seek the show of blood). It does assume the opponents' values to be irreconcilable with your own. Not cooperation and kindliness but surprise and relentless audacity can alone win through. Especially here, every tried and tired script not thrown aside is quoted merely for irony or as a diversionary tactic, or at worst used, when imagination weakens, for linking bits and pieces (others may recognize them as such to your loss). Total resource-exposure and esteem-risk occur. Certainly you elicit it of your collaborators and of the foe. For if you and the like-minded will not venture all to create and enlarge the liberated zones, your fate too is finally to perform as a spectacle husk. (Of course the spectacle too has its quiet reinforcive scenarios: but these are adjustive, not of its essence, not worth your life.)

The liberation drama of history has also had tutors. Not only Paine. Every solid radical has manifested the consciousness of dramaturgy; and many, significantly, wrote plays in going from youth to a mature identity. For instance, Karl Marx, Friedrich Engels, Leon Trotsky, and John of Leyden—who led the rebellion and Anabaptist commune of 1534 in Münster. Others like Antonio Gramsci, Georg Lukàcs, and Kurt Eisner, lived their transition as drama critics. Gustav Landauer was a Shakespeare authority and, with Eisner, a leader of the 1919 Bavarian Soviet (his grandson is Mike Nichols). (Peter Brook is the son of a Menshevik revolutionary of 1917.) Ernst Toller apprenticed in the Bavarian Soviet. Georg Büchner wrote *Danton's Death* as second best to carrying on the revolutionary society he'd founded, which just weeks earlier the police had uncovered and dispersed. Still others were initially actors: B. Traven, who was in the Bavarian Soviet leadership, and Sandor Petöfi, the Hungarian poet-revolutionary who died on the battlefield in 1848.

Engels' play was performed before the German workers' union of Brussels in 1847. The text has been lost, but a witness recalls the "amazing clarity" with which the necessary course of the February, 1848 uprising was foreseen. Trotsky, in *My Life*, recalls the stunning effect a visit of Christmas mummers had upon him when he was seven. During evening tea they invaded his father's farmhouse on the South Russia steppes and recited the piece "Czar Maximilian." Trotsky pursued the actor of the Czar and made him dictate the part to him. "A fantastic world was revealed to me, a world transformed into a theatrical reality." Thereafter he recited and composed dramatic verses frequently. Sent to school in Odessa, "my first visit to the theatre was like no other experience, and beggars description." One summer Trotsky spent weeks rehearsing a Pushkin play. At seventeen he collaborated on a drama about the Russian Socialist movement, "full of social tendencies, against a background of the conflict of generations." Just months later he first transposed his consciousness to the task of founding and leading a clandestine union of workers.

He was the dramaturgical dynamo of the 1905 Revolution. To understand those skills, we may look at a strategic scenario he wrote out a few months prior to the events.

Tear the workers away from the machines and workshops; lead them through the factory gate out into the street; direct them to neighboring factories; proclaim a stoppage there; and carry new masses into the street. Thus, moving from factory to factory, from workshop to workshop, growing under way and sweeping away police obstacles, haranguing and attracting passers-by, absorbing groups that come from the opposite direction, filling the streets, taking possession of the first suitable buildings for public meetings, entrenching yourselves in those buildings, using them for uninterrupted revolutionary meetings with a permanently shifting and changing audience, you shall bring order into the movement of the masses, raise their confidence, explain to them the purpose and the sense of events; and thus you shall eventually transform the city into a revolutionary camp—this, by and large, is the plan of action.

Brilliantly actable, this text is the result of a close analysis of the political "factors" so often conceived as abstractions.

Lenin was in hiding during many crucial days in 1917, and Trotsky was again the most motive figure, if not quite as predominantly as in 1905. His book on 1917, *The Russian Revolution*, is a virtual promptbook of radical dramaturgy. Trotsky remarks for example the little latitude left to the spectacle managers once things get going: "the scripts for the roles of Romanov and Capet were prescribed by the general development of the historic drama; only the nuances of interpretation fell to the lot of the actors." The rebels' scenario inventiveness is brought out—as during the February overthrow, when a unit of the feared mounted Cossacks appeared before a group of unarmed workers, who "took off their caps and approached the Cossacks with the words: 'Brothers—Cossacks, help the workers in a struggle for their peaceable demands; you see how the Pharaohs treat us, hungry workers. Help us!' This consciously humble manner, those caps in their hands—what an accurate psychological calculation! Inimitable gesture! The whole history of street fights and revolutionary victories swarms with such improvisations."

Lenin was not known to have taken more than a spectator's interest in theatre, and the flamboyance of Trotsky was alien to him, though he respected its efficacy. Gorky, however, has recorded that Lenin used both laughter and temper masterfully to shape an intimate discussion; and his public speaking style, if unembellished, was "a very work of classic art." In brief one might say that Lenin deeply distrusted spectacle and every radical tendency toward it—"the human yearning for the beautiful, dramatic and striking," as he once wrote. On the other hand he stressed scenario action: as in his famous instructions of Summer, 1917, which urge repeatedly that insurrection "must be treated as an art, that one must *win* the first success and then proceed from success to success, never ceasing the *offensive* against the enemy, taking advantage of his confusion, etc."

Given a matrix of scenarist initiative, elements of radical dramaturgy were valuable, Lenin held. For instance: workers once having actually gone out on strike, "the sight of their comrades ceasing, if only momentarily, to be slaves and becoming the equals of the wealthy is infectious for them." And finally: "revolutions are festivals of the oppressed."

The French Revolution of 1789 was spectacle vs. scenarism from start to finish. George Plekhanov remarks justly that as the culture of the monarchy went under, the "aesthetic requirements" of the citizens, "far from stifled," turned rather toward a "poetry of action" and "the beauty of civic achievement." The seizing of the Bastille, the signal event, was provoked by a show of mercenary troops deployed near Paris by the King. An unemployed actor—Camille Desmoulins—transformed an angry but aimless mood among the crowd at the Palais-Royal into a pledge by every individual to adopt armed resistance; he plucked a leaf from a garden tree as a sign of his commitment; shortly all the trees were stripped. A playwright, Maret, among Desmoulins' listeners urged the next action: close every theatre, spectacle and ball that evening. This was done, the rebels creating their own theatre of the streets. Two nights later the Bastille fell.

Indeed the theatres of Paris were barometers of the conflict of power and values, as the struggle to put Beaumarchais' *Mariage de Figaro* on the stage, finally successful in 1784, had already proven. Now Desmoulins, Mirabeau, Danton, much of the revolutionary party bent efforts to have staged *Charles IX* by Marie-Joseph Chénier. The spectacle of what lines and images would hold the stage was as nothing to the scenarios of vituperation and combat in the theatre stalls with results that reached to Versailles. "If *Figaro* killed the aristocracy," Danton remarked as the new play

down. The several policemen stationed there attempted arrests and were resisted: a second confrontation with the violence of business-as-usual. The group returned to campus to find the vigilantes still in place. Partly for defense, but more importantly to make its demands palpable, Hamilton Hall was now entered, where a dean was confronted and discouraged from leaving. During the night the white students' will to continue was near collapse. The black students at this juncture chose to entrench themselves in Hamilton and to eject the whites. Nearly overawed by the growing scope and uncalculable risks of the scenario but going ahead, the latter occupied Kirk's offices in Low. That morning, radical dramaturgy made it big in the press as an ugly spectacle of impertinence. But to those with first-hand experience who were not reliant on the media for their consciousness, a vital, beautiful, and somehow just action was occurring. Only this can explain the ingress of many hundreds to the dramaturgy: more buildings taken, communes established, faculty drawn in to back SDS/SAS or to act as defensive monitors.

Once concretely confronted, the administration's policy of remote spectacle was shown to mask ineptitude in nearly every branch of reinforcive scenario. And so the spectacle collapsed entirely at the end of the week into the ultimate recourse of all legitimizing spectacle: official violence. When Grayson Kirk was dismissed a few months later, NEW YORK TIMES ran an article titled: "Academic Miscasting." No doubt his temporary replacement, Andrew Cordier, chosen for diplomatic backstage skills in evading unwanted encounters while getting things done for the US in the Belgian Congo and elsewhere, was a performer of more formidable range. The Columbia trustees also implicitly conceded the justice of the SDS program, even while punishing its performers, when they dropped IDA ties and the gym. Was the spectacle reinstated? Perhaps temporarily. SDS was in difficulty, de-escalating to more intimate—and in a sense more demanding—one-to-one scenarios in classroom and dorm, of the kind any emergent radical dramaturgy must master if it is to integrate new performers and so move on to a next stage. In the long run, however, the reinforcive, scenaristic, and co-optive skills of spectacle are limited by its prerequisite: defense of a more or less rigidly defined status quo. C. Day Lewis put this well in his youth: "Evolution is the dance, revolutions are the steps."

Mark Rudd once wrote plays. He grew up in a New Jersey suburb, the son of a Polish emigrant who had risen in the US Army to the rank of lieutenant-colonel before retiring to become a real-estate dealer. His school grades were excellent; his home loving and secure; he took an interest in the boy scouts, ham radio, jazz. Rudd became indignant, however, when he recognized the oppressed condition of blacks in the Newark ghetto. The plastic alienation of the suburbs made him restive. He began while in high school to write a play based upon "Mario and the Magician," the Thomas Mann story; Rudd was fascinated by the way the characters in it were drawn from their anomie into unified, focal behavior through a "determinism" exercised by the hypnotist. This was his "mystical" and a-historical period, Rudd said later. He would cease to write plays, and Mann's peculiarly German notion of the crowd and its leadership would be supplanted by SDS participatory democracy and the writings of Marcuse, who "made it clear that revolutions come from the will to revolution, which is itself a product of historical situations." Among SDS people Rudd discovered a sense of motion and excitement: "They were the only people doing anything." Experience followed in dormitory organizing and speaking.   photos: columbia owl

GRINNELL COLLEGE, IOWA: PLAYBOY MEETS THE WOMEN'S LIBERATION FRONT. A promotions man for PLAYBOY spoke in the college's sex education series early in 1969. Ten students (four of them men) stripped for a confrontation. "Pretending to appreciate and respect the beauty of the naked human form," their leaflet said, "PLAYBOY in actuality stereotypes the body and commercializes on it. PLAYBOY substitutes fetishism for honest appreciation of the endless variety of human forms." Brice Draper, the PLAYBOY man, chuckled: "I think you're pretty swinging." But when challenged to pose nude with one of the women for a woman photographer, he declined: "I came here to talk, not to pose nude." His employer built an empire exploiting the male fantasy, using the principle of repressive desublimation. As the women dramatically suggested, the spectacle of the monthly gatefold girl will not survive the rise of radical scenario activity.   photo: Wilhelm

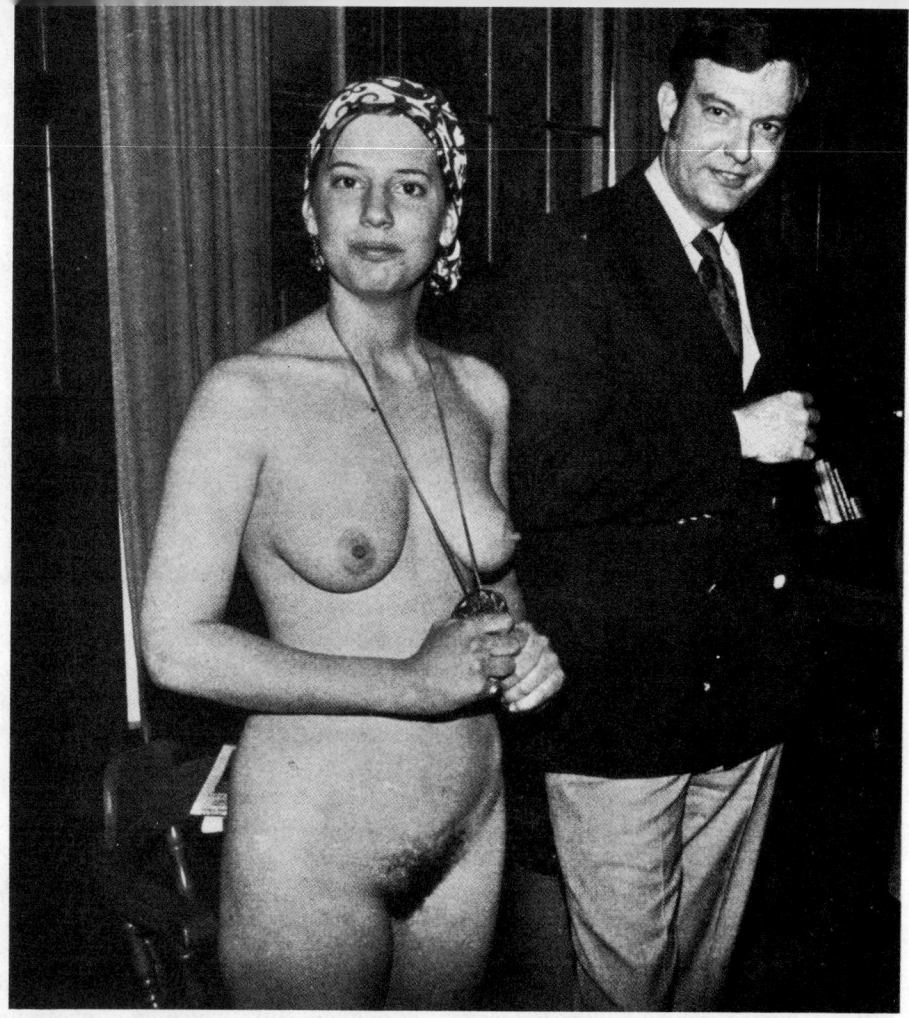

MAY 1968: A PARIS BARRICADE. A red flag. A beer advertisement. Gasmask handkerchiefs and goggles. A medic in the rear. Even staid publishers cash in on photos like this: titillating glimpses of heady spectacle. But observe: the actors do not show up for you. This unposed photo presents an integral moment of the scenario of a daring struggle to acquire state power and distribute it among popular councils. "The more I make love, the more I want to make revolution—the more I make revolution, the more I want to make love" (writing on a Sorbonne wall). The scenarios for the two activites are interrelated, and are contrapuntal to C. Wright Mills' remark that private troubles mask public issues. The scenario potentials of affection and eroticism will be held to a grotesque and often perverse sector of fools' liberty within a sea of exploitative repression, will remain a force for privatization and privation, as long as the deepest needs which can unite people do not become the effective ends, to a great extent, the means of everyday "politics."   photo: wide world

made its debut, "*Charles IX* will kill the royalty." Mr. Edmund Burke rather agreed. He was shocked the author had not been clapped in chains.

The King meanwhile had been taken virtual prisoner and brought by multitudes from Versailles to live in the Paris Tuileries, following a peculiarly inept spectacle of disrespect for the nation—actually staged during an uproarious banquet in the palace theatre! It is impossible here to give further account of the French dramaturgy, or of its transformation into a new mode of spectacle representing the requirements of

the bourgeoisie victorious.

Equally it is impossible to describe here the subtle, profound analysis permeating the books of Marx and Engels (*The Eighteenth Brumaire of Louis Bonaparte* by Marx is a good introduction). I want not to ignore, though, that Marx found the beginnings of a liberating dramaturgy in the erotic nexus. "Love . . . first really teaches man to believe in the objective world outside himself," he wrote in *The Holy Family* of 1845. It "not only makes man an object, but the object a man!" He adds, in *The German Ideology* of 1846: "Philosophy, and the study of the actual world, stand in the same relation to one another as masturbation and sexual love."

The conscious poet of this dramaturgy of one-to-one has been Louis Aragon; he calls it "the intimate theatre." A campaign to end its repressive privatization, and to pervade society with the values discovered in the sexual congress, is being led by the new rock groups. As Jim Morrison of The Doors says:

> When I sing my songs in public, that's a dramatic act, but not just acting as in theatre, but a social *act*, real action. A Doors concert is a public meeting called by us for a special kind of dramatic discussion and entertainment. We make concerts sexual politics. The sex starts with me, then moves out to include the charmed circle of musicians on stage. The music we make goes out to the audience and interacts with them; they go home and interact with the rest of reality, then I get it all back by interacting with *that* reality. When we perform, we're participating in the creation of a world, and we celebrate that creation with the audience.

Beyond the present war scenarios and beyond the privatizing and privational peace scenarios: What Is Our Program? It is this. To employ the now achieved material and technological abundance of our planet as the basis of a universalized peace scenarism.

Given the present and growing abundance, and the success of our war scenarios—and this unity of objective and subjective factors spells the abolition of class society—we could live a pacific permanent revolution. Potentials and conflicts would be hassled out, and root human needs thus fulfilled, without basic recourse to violence or the repressive show of it. There seems no reason why this social dramaturgy of a creative and non-violent stamp cannot serve as, in the phrase of William James, the moral equivalent to war.

The concomitant is, of course, that the human aesthetic capacities shall no longer be relegated chiefly to the Other World of the stage play, artwork, poem, novel, etc. On the one hand, the making and contemplation of Aesthetic Objects will always have a felt function for us. Experience and expression in life can rarely be as distilled and achieved as in the compression won in this activity, especially by unusually gifted men and women. On the other hand, in our present social order the aesthetic traits of experience are clearly far out of kilter—alienated from the world of the everyday, preserved as in alcohol by museums, cultural centers, a specialized breed of men. This scarcely is normal. In so-called primitive societies, every aspect

OCTOBER 20, 1967: THE PENTAGON BESIEGED. Television transmitted it as an anti-war spectacle (significantly, the networks refused to permit live coverage); it was for those present a high drama of interwoven scenarios. One of every 2,000 Americans—the nation has approximately the same number of millionaires—were gathered at the Lincoln Memorial. They marched across the Potomac and up to the malls of the Pentagon, where cyclone fences, topped with barbed wire, had been erected. Swiftly the fences went down as "demonstrators" moved to confront, close beneath the building's Mussolinian facade, an involuntary cast placed there by Robert Strange McNamara: several thousand paratroopers, military police, and federal marshalls. The scenario was to disrupt Pentagon operations as fully as possible without resort to arms. Defense Secretary McNamara, who was peering from a window, had of course the FORCE MAJEURE. But the FORCE DÉMONSTRATIF gained the initiative, up to the point where the military used its singular skills. Scaling ropes, flanking maneuvers, inundation by sheer numbers were but part of the repertoire of this humoristic, motley, and audacious legion. The yellow submarine of the hippies, 12 feet long, was passed over heads toward the doors. Smaller contingents of troops were surrounded, talked to, pressed in so tightly they could not use their weapons, allowed to retreat only in disorderly flight, perhaps with helmets swiped or a flower in a rifle barrel. Posters and slogans remembering Che appeared on abutments. Tens of thousands alternated "America the Beautiful" with an ironic "Sieg Heil!" salute chanted to commanding officers on the battlements. Yippies, banners proclaiming solidarity and a victory more than pyrrhic (WE HAVE ONE), moved upon the portals chanting: "Out, Demon, Out!" to a strange music. Before the Pentagon under a golden sun in a crisp breeze, the flag of the Vietnamese National Liberation Front fluttered, blue and red with a gold star. A contingent with flags penetrated through a side door, were beaten at once and expelled. Everywhere there pervaded a spirit of Epic Theatre (so many actions and performers, so much detached awareness of one's deeds even as one acted), even to a Brechtian "narrator" who stood with a bullhorn where he had a commanding view and laconically interpreted events for the majority who could not summon a whole view. The troops tried to seize the narrator; with a little help from his friends he evaded them, not once losing his cool; his ironic commentary set the context for the besiegers. Low overhead the helicopters of the press circled and, visible in their doorways, photographers winding cameras and "shooting" (one constantly recalled the gunship whirlies in 'Nam); the actors in this way too reminded continually of the present moment as history for the making. Sometimes soldiers (their regulation issue: mufti and gasmasks, teargas guns, fixed sheathed bayonets) were brought to admit softly their sympathy for the "protest." And although I did not witness it, this probably happened, as many say it did: A line of troops had been ordered to hold a long incline leading to the Pentagon's doors. Already they'd repulsed several attempts on their line. Now a hippy couple were before them and began to make love. Protestors nearby stood relaxed, and as the boy and girl rubbed each other, kissing deeply, the soldiers grew transfixed, with the couple reaching into shirts and down trousers, loosening clothing, approaching THE ACT. From shock or desire or both, the soldiers were witless when suddenly the demonstrators pierced the military line with a rush, hurling these troops aside to penetrate to the doors by the thousands. On the six o'clock news, it perhaps all looked like damnfool spectacle. But not to those there: not to the Pentagon "insiders," and not to that one

American in 2,000 who shortly returned to those little Pentagons—the draft boards, the firms profiting from manufacture of terroristic weapons and from exploitation, schools and labs with Defense Department contracts across the land. October 20, 1967 could be said to mark the end of the mass sterile protest parade and the start of an open-ended era of mass, infectious radical dramaturgy.   photo: joe r. krock

VALLEGRANDE, BOLIVIA: CAN YOU KILL A SOCIALLY-ORIGINATED SCENARIO? The Bolivian Army believed it could, when it murdered Che Guevara while he was a wounded captive in October 1967 and then asked photographers to make pictures like this one. The spectacle is to show the futility of revolutionary action. But as John Berger, the English art critic, has noticed: this shot at spectacle backfired. To succeed, it would have had to compress the entire meaning of Che's revolutionary decision within the instant of mortification. And this it could not do, for Che Guevara had foreseen that moment. More than a decade earlier, he had come to terms with the likelihood of death in combat. This consciousness and resolve released in him the possibility of conduct which became so exemplary as to cancel the generals' iconography. "Either the photograph means nothing because the spectator has no inkling of what is involved, or else its meaning denies or qualifies its demonstration." Few men in modern history have equalled the leaders of the Cuban Revolution in fully and ably understanding the dramaturgically exemplary aspect of radical activity; and in structuring its survival and the people's welfare upon scenarios of action rather than repressive spectacle, no state has matched Cuba. As Che relates in his EPISODES OF THE REVOLUTIONARY WAR, these capabilities were sorely learned. He began with "a spontaneous and somewhat lyrical decision" which only through experience became "a more serene force; one of an entirely different value" based upon a knowledge which induced him to see situations in terms of "protagonists in the drama." The terminology of aesthetics is not accidental or extrinsic: it expresses Che's fundamental attitude. He described the "strange and moving drama" enacted between Fidel Castro and "the individual, the actor" within the new society ("Socialism and Man in Cuba"). The initial lyricism never ceased to guide Che's dramaturgical outlook, as this comment from his Bolivian diary, on a fallen comrade, confirms. "Of his unknown and unheralded death for a hypothetical future that may crystallize, there is only to say: 'TU CADÁVER PEQUEÑO DE CAPITÁN VALIENTA HA EXTENDIDO EN LO INMENSO SU METÁLICA FORMA.' "   photo: upi

of the life of every member of the social unit is imbued with aesthetic expression, there is not even a concept or word for what we have reified as "art." Our lives are impoverished of the aesthetic qualities of rhythm and grace and harmony. We are sick for the lack of coherence and intensity of expression. What we want—and a return to the drawbacks of "primitive" society is not necessary, of course—is the integration of the aesthetic with man's other capacities.

Herbert Marcuse calls for a new "aesthetic ethos" in his *Essay on Liberation*. Surprisingly, Marcuse omits any idea of the performance of self with others; he takes his model from painting, rather than theatre which has to be the paradigm. Schiller's letters on aesthetic education were more to the point. *Homo Ludens* by Johan Huizinga is an important historical account of the "play" element in social contest. But the best previsions of universalized scenarism are perhaps found in Charles Fourier's notion of *cabalism*, and in Marx's passage in volume III of *Capital* on "the art of consuming labor-power."

Marx, noting the introduction of "self-actor" machines to industry (automation), believed the supervisor of complex factory production would eventually function on the model of an "orchestra conductor." "An orchestra conductor need not own the instruments of his orchestra, nor is it within the scope of his duties as conductor to have anything to do with the 'wages' of the other musicians. Co-operative factories furnish proof that the capitalist has become . . . redundant as a functionary in production" and may be replaced by the "combination and co-operation of many in pursuance of a common result." In feudal France, Marx adds, the production manager was known as the *régisseur* (still the German name for a stage director).

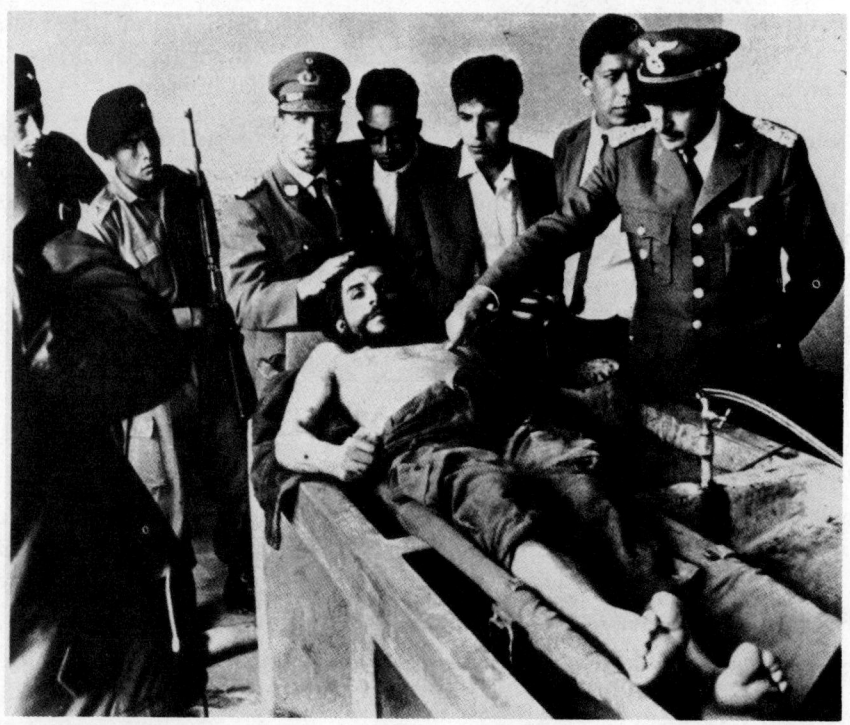

Fourier speaks to our time away from work and offered, said Marx, "the presentiment and imaginative expression of a new world." His cabalist passion—"far removed from the insipid calm whose charms are extolled by morality"—to be realized in the future, entailed the scenarist notion in embryo:

> The cabalistic spirit is the true destination of man. Plotting doubles his resources, enlarges his faculties. Compare the tone of a formal social gathering, its moral, stilted, languishing jargon, with the tone of these same people united in a cabal: they will appear transformed to you; you will admire their terseness, their animation, the quick play of ideas, the alertness of action, of decision; in a word, the rapidity of the spiritual or material motion.

The spectacle managers will believe this to be nonsense. But their show cannot survive. Not in this time when a black youth in Watts, asked his attitude about serving in Vietnam, replies: "Man, they ain't going to put me in that movie, even if they make me the star!"

PEOPLE MEDIA PIG MEDIA

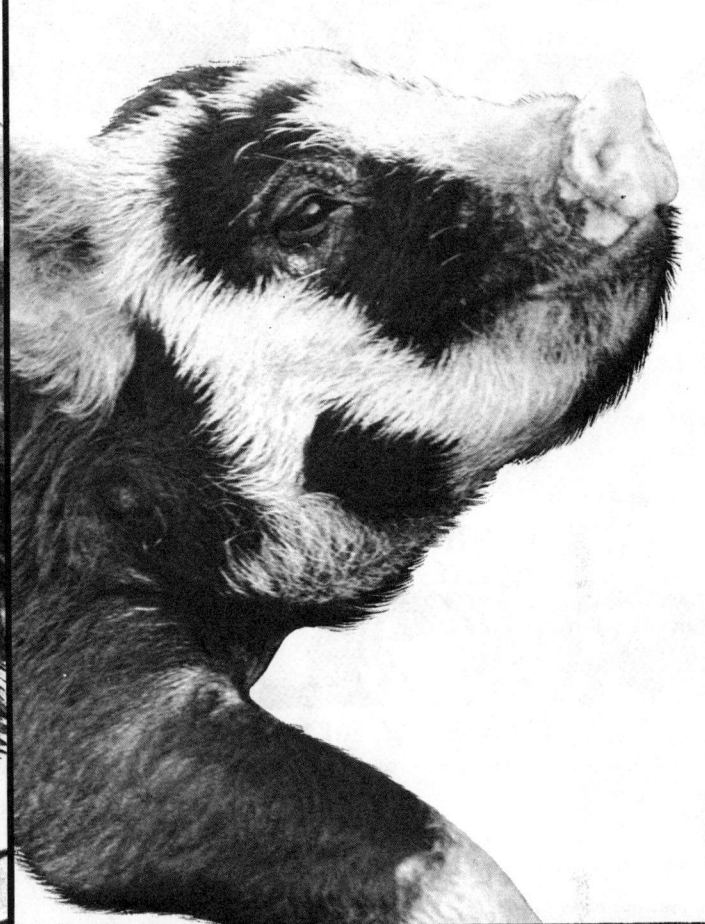

On previous page: Pigasus, nominated by the Yippies for President, August 1968.

THE ACT IS THE THING

The burning need of a culture is not a choice to be made or not made, voluntarily, any more than it can be satisfied by loans. It has to be where it arises, or everything related to the life there ceases. It isn't a thing, it's an act. If it stands still, it is dead. It is the realization of the qualities of a place in relation to the life which occupies it; embracing everything involved, climate, geographic position, relative size, history, other cultures — as well as the character of its sands, flowers, minerals and the condition of knowledge within its borders. It is the act of lifting those things into an ordered and utilized whole which is culture. It isn't something left over afterward. That is the record only. The act is the thing. It can't be escaped or avoided if life is to go on. It is in the fullest sense that which is fit.

WILLIAM CARLOS WILLIAMS *The American Background* 1934

There are twice as many governmental public-relations men in Washington as there are journalists.

WILLIAM LEDERER *A Nation of Sheep*

Look, if you think any American official is going to tell you the truth, then you're stupid. Did you hear that? Stupid.

ARTHUR SYLVESTER, former Assistant Secretary of Defense for Public Relations

Did you hear that? Stupid.
Hear that, stupid?
That stupid.
Stupid Stupid Stupid
Stupid
Stupid
Stupid

Media Freaking
ABBIE HOFFMAN
Lincoln Park, Chicago,
August 27, 1968
Talking to the Yippies

taped by Charles Harbutt

This sure is fun. You know, the city news bureau here in Chicago, where you can always call and get their version of what's happening, is ST2-8100. You might want to take care of a cat named Jack Lawrence from CBS who threw me out while I was fuckin' with their teletype machine last night. That was very unfair. I had some good news items. Now, let's see who else is here. The police, there's some good numbers. OK. Now this is a top secret number that like only a few of the top police have. It's the central number for the police station up here in the zoo. They're very fucked up in there. I've been up there, and you think they're organized, well you're full of shit 'cause their walkie-talkies don't work. I mean they're all stoned up there, tripping over each other, you know, they're rapping, all they want to do is fight and they don't care about all the walkie-talkie shit, they just want to fight, you know. That's their thing. All right, that number is 528-5967. Now—here's the way you use it. There's a Commander Brash of the 18th Precinct who's in charge of the general area of Lincoln Park and there's Deputy Chief Lynsky who's the cop above him. Now, the police have a system of anarchy. See, the Chief might say somethin' is OK, see, then you get some low-level honky cop saying don't do it, you know. The idea is to convince that honky cop on the other end that Chief Lynsky said it was OK, even if you gotta bullshit him a little. You just drop names, like Commander Brash said this was OK, you know, and if Chief Lynsky said this was OK, you know, those cops don't want to lose their jobs. They won't check it out.

work, you know. But the *Daily News*, that's a TV set. Look at it, I mean look at the picture right up front and the way they blast those headlines. You know, "Yippies, sex-loving, dope-loving, commie, beatnik, hippie, freako, weirdos." That's groovy, man, that's a whole life style, that's a whole thing to be, man. I mean you want to get in on that.

When we stormed the Pentagon, my wife and I we leaped over this fence, see. We were really stoned, I mean I was on acid flying away, which of course is an anti-revolutionary drug you know, you can't do a thing on it. I've been on acid ever since I came to Chicago. It's in the form of honey. We got a lab guy doin' his thing. I think he might have got assassinated, I ain't seen him today. Well, so we jumped this here fence, see, we were sneaking through the woods and people were out to get the Pentagon. We had this flag, it said NOW with a big wing on it, I don't know. The right-wingers said there was definitely evidence of Communist conspiracy 'cause of that flag, I don't know what the fuck it was. So we had Uncle Sam hats on, you know, and we jumped over the fence and we're surrounded by marshals, you know, just closin' us in, about 30 marshals around us. And I plant the fuckin' flag and I said, "I claim this land in the name of free America. We are Mr. and Mrs. America. Mrs. America's pregnant." And we sit down and they're goin' fucking crazy. I mean we got arrested and unarrested like six or seven times. And when we finally got arrested, it was under other names. I'm really a digger, I never was a Yippie. Was always a digger. So I said, you know, A. Digger, Abbie Digger, Mr. and Mrs. A. Digger. They say are you a boy or a girl, I say girl. Right. This is where I wanna go. I don't have to prove manliness by beatin' up 14-year-old girls with nightsticks, you know. Fuck 'em. But ideas, you just get stoned, get the ideas in your head and then do 'em. And don't bullshit. I mean that's the thing about doin' that guerrilla theatre. You be prepared to die to prove your point. You gotta die.

You know, what's life? Life's all that fun shit. Life's doin' what you want to do. *Life's* an American magazine, and if we hook them right, they're gonna give us 10,000 flowers that are gonna be thrown out of a helicopter tomorrow afternoon. But we'll only allow them to do it if they bring a newsreel person up in the helicopter with 'em. You know, to take the pictures. So we're workin' out that negotiation with *Life* magazine. 'Cause we said, you know, it's called Festival of Life, man, we named it after your magazine. I know that's immoral and I know that's cheatin' and that's stealin'. I wish I was a revolutionist. I wouldn't have these problems. A lot of revolutionists come here, they worry about parking the car. Where we gonna park the car, should we park it in a meter? The meter'll run out, we'll get a ticket. It's a weird revolution. Fuck it. We don't need cars; we travel in wheelbarrows. You see, just worry about your ass. Forget about your clothes, your money, you know, just worry about your ass and all the rest of us's asses. Cars don't mean shit. They grab our walkie-talkies you say yeah, there you go, take it, thank you, it was too heavy to carry.

I think it's a good idea to cut your hair or get a wig or let your hair grow pretty fast or paint your face or change your clothes or get a new hat and a new name. I mean everybody ought to have a new name by Wednesday. And like you know we're all one huge happy family with all new names or no names and no faces. 'Cause when we bust out of this park and go down to Grant Park and then go out to the amphitheatre, there are gonna be some mighty strange theatrical events. And you better have your theatre thing down pretty pat.

Well, I've shot my load. I'm for ending the Yippie thing Thursday, killin' it all, 'cause I don't think people are Yippies anymore than they're Mobe or Mother-fuckers or whatever they are. They're just people. And I think we oughta burn all our Yippie buttons and laugh at the fuckin' press and say nyah nyah, we took you for a fuckin' ride. That's what we figured when we started this thing back in December—just a couple of speedfreaks hangin' around the cellar sayin' now how are we gonna do this Chicago trip? We ain't got no fuckin' money, you know, we

ain't got no organization, we ain't got no constituency. We went to a New Left meeting, they said where's your constituency, you can't talk here, you know, you ain't against imperialism. I said, man, I don't want any pay toilets in this fuckin' country, I don't want to pay a dime to take a shit. SDS doesn't consider that relevant. That's the trouble with the Left you know. Did a trip on a Socialist Scholars Conference, a couple of Hell's Angels guys and I, we went up and had a capgun fight in the Hotel Hilton where the Left has their conferences, it's very interesting. So the heads of the Hilton and the heads of the socialists were gettin' together to decide how to throw us speedfreaks out of the fuckin' place, see. But they didn't, I mean, we stayed to do our thing. The problem with the Left is that there are 10,000 socialist scholars in this country and not one fuckin' socialist. I mean I talk to guys on *The Guardian* and they say yeah, we're working on a serious analysis of the Yippies. I say, that's pretty fuckin' cool, man, that's great. By that time there won't be any Yippies. I mean, what the fuck are you analyzin' for, man, get in and do it.

The complete workshop speech from which this is taken is part of the evidence being used to indict Abbie Hoffman along with Rennie Davis, Dave Dellinger, John Froines, Tom Hayden, Bobby Seale, Jerry Rubin, and Lee Weiner for conspiracy to incite riots during the Democratic Convention. Their trial begins in Chicago on September 24, 1969 and each faces ten years in prison and $20,000 fine. We are told that funds and other assistance are badly needed. Persons interested in contributing should make checks payable to the Chicago Defense Fund, c/o The Conspiracy, 28 E. Jackson Blvd., Chicago, Illinois.

> Life actors never rehearse and need no script. A life actor uses only what is available, nothing more, nothing less.
> - Abbie Hoffman

The Drama Review Summer 1969

MOVEMENT COUNTERATTACK

Last summer, after beating a 13-month strike by its employees, the Booth family's DETROIT NEWS returned to its standard racist and reactionary distorted news practices. The response of the white and Black movements was the total boycott declared below. But as we all know, it is not just the NEWS which distorts information to the people at the source, nor just the Booth newspapers, tv and radio stations which hold the people down by denying them full and accurate information about their place in the world, and what people are doing to change the world—it is the entire spectrum of the power structure media. Until the movement stops cooperating with the power structure media in the naive confidence that it is WE who will be using THEM, and until the people act on their knowledge that "you can't believe what you read in the newspapers," or hear on radio or see on television, our image of the world and ourselves will depend on the power-structure's definitions, and we will never be free.

DECLARATION:

" The undersigned organizations and individuals will not knowingly give statements, interviews or press releases to the Detroit News (or its affiliated TV and radio stations). Persons identifying themselves as agents of the Detroit News will not be granted admission to meetings, press conferences, or events of

which the undersigned are sponsors.

Let it be known that henceforth, "news" stories appearing in the News about any of the undersigned organizations and individuals or their activities will be based on information obtained in one or more of the following ways:

Deceit: The News may obtain information by lying about who they are.

Hearsay: They may pick up stories from other, second-hand sources.

General Public Knowledge: The News can masquerade as part of the public and acquire information about events available to any citizen who witnessed events such as public meetings, demonstrations, etc.

It is important that the reasons behind this declaration be understood. They are simple.

As self-appointed spokesmen for the power structure of which they are a part, the Detroit News in its so-called news coverage, its editorial stance and its relations to its own employees and the community is anti-black, anti-woman, anti-worker, anti-youth, anti-democratic, anti-progress and anti-self-determination.

Secondly and more specifically, it is a waste of time to talk to a Detroit News reporter. They do not have any control whatsoever over what finally appears in the newspaper. The more sympathetic they are, the more closely they are supervised and the less control they have over their material.

In other words, it would be silly and stupid for us to continue to lend the illusion of legitimacy and credibility to the News' "coverage" of our efforts to change the existing political economic and social order. The fact that a tiny group of white men, through inherited wealth and power acquire control over the means of communication does not give them the right to foist their opinions on all the people in the guise of "objective truth."

Let the public be informed. Any information appearing in the Detroit News henceforth should be considered one-sided and unreliable. If you read the News you don't know—because they don't know."

Detroit Area People Against Racism
National Organizing Committee
Ad Hoc Action Group, Citizens of Detroit
Youth for Peace, Freedom and Justice
The Fifth Estate
Women's Liberation
Michigan Regional SDS
Detroit Newsreel

Berkeley Tribe

✪✪✪✪✪✪✪✪✪✪✪✪✪✪✪✪

Berkeley Tribe

Screw, Lawrence, Kansas. March 1968, before Columbia University student strike

The Open Conspiracy

"Break the Dishes"

Disruptive guerrilla actions became a big part of the work on tour. Disrupting a faculty meeting at Keuka College, disrupting Plaimpton speaking to students at Amherst, disrupting classrooms, etc. Each action had basically the same two-fold purpose: To advertise our evening performance and to interrupt the bullshit of the moment, whether it be the President's speech, or a class in Western Thought.

We did these actions with no hostility towards the students. Successful disruption is when you don't alienate the kids you want to reach, but manage to point out to them the bullshit of what you are interrupting, the bullshit they are participating in. And pointing it out is sometimes just the act of being irreverent to something they've been tuaght to value, like a College President. It will make some students angry—we try and rap with them. They are our potential brothers and sisters and we have to get them to fight the man.

At Amherst College all the dishes have as their design pictures of Lord Amherst killing Indians—which he did, in real life, by smallpox infestation. During one meal we started singing, very loudly, with guitar accompaniment, "Have you looked at the pictures on your dishes?" We riffed until we got to "Break the dishes." Which we did, and some students joined us. The action worked because we were so obviously correct to break those ugly genocide dishes. Although our action was violent, it was done with a sense of humor too—we had a ball. But most important, it prompted political discussions all over the cafeteria.   **Arlene Brown**

The Pageant Players Guerrilla Theatre; Liberation News Service, May 3, 1969

CURSING ESTABLISHMENT SEIZES MASS MEDIA

todd gitlin

"Money doesn't talk, it swears." — Dylan

Your eyes might have been stabbed by the Page One headline in last Wednesday's S.F. Examiner: "Cursing NY Hippies Seize TV Station."

"FOUL TALK GOES ON THE AIR"

"6 MEN, WOMAN ARRESTED"

"By United Press International and Associated Press"

Between them, each with their vast chain of bureaus and thousands of Trained Personnel, these two giant "news"-"gathering" corporations were able to assemble this blood-curdling tale:

"NEW YORK — A score of loud-mouthed hippies, shaggy, beaded and screaming obscenities, took over an educational TV station while thousands of viewers watched in their living rooms."

"The intruders burst into the basement studios of station WNDT-TV, across First Avenue from the UN, during an 'underground press' interview late last night. They knocked down a guard and punched their way past two members of the station staff, totally disrupting the program.".....

"When the intruders were asked what they wanted, one replied, 'We're here to break down the barriers of panel discussion shows.' Another said simply, 'We want in.'....."

Now, just as a guerrilla is explained by the system that drives him into final opposition, so is what happened June 25 at WNDT-TV perfectly well explained by the Examiner story. But not the way the Examiner meant it. And the Examiner is no mere benighted bush-league villain. The Chronicle's story the next morning was in a lower key just as confused and confusing, and the New York Times headlined, "20 Hippies Invade TV Show and Shout Obscenities on Air." The media, sure enough, as a whole, were the message — but not the way McLuhan understands, either.

No one has to study Marcuse's One-Dimensional Man — though it would help — in order to read between the lines. Anyone who has ever been billyclubbed or Maced by a cop only to read that his peaceable demonstration was "violent" and that Law Enforcement Officers used "necessary force" (if the fact that cops used force at all was deemed Fit To Print), anyone who has been in Vietnam and returns to hear on the radio that "our boys' morale is high," any Columbia insurrectionary who reads the Times accounts — anyone who has lived an event,

a place, a mood from the inside, and knows and insists he knows what he saw, heard, felt despite the sonorous, three-button interpretations of Information Specialists; anyone, in short, who has held to the slightest shred of his own intuition and judgment knows that the media lie.

They lie daily, they lie in patterns, they invent lies and peddle the powerful's, maybe they apologize and they lie again, by commission and omission: they lie, we might say, chronically, predictably. They lie by conspiracy (the handling of D.A. Garrison), they lie by implication ("Communist" equals archdemon), they lie by diversion (at least Miss California gets close to Jesus Christ), but mostly they lie by telling what they imagine to be the truth. They lie because of the code of their objectivity, because they have learned not to see, hear, feel, not to believe in the inside of a fact, not to doubt that their leaders lie and their textbooks lie and their teachers equate blue-eyed rock-stable property-gagging manifestly-destined 5% interest America with truth. They lie finally because they can do no other, because they need their lies, for the crude but quite serviceable reason that lying is their livelihood, brings in advertising; and — never forget this better concealed, more insidious reason — because the very particular slant of their lies numbs their audience into nodding befuddlement, makes consumers of men and masses of publics, makes packaged try-harder Americans of puzzled disgruntled people.

T.V.

And the chronic liar who from time to time tells the truth is no more credible, for who can tell? We may be grateful for small exceptional favors, if we can detect them — that Examiner interview with Huey Newton "wasn't bad," I thought last Sunday morning: a grudging and to me demeaning tribute — but the pattern is still bare — threadbare — for all who will look, and no less

The cultural guerrillas who for some 15 minutes liberated a small zone of the New York airwaves had come naturally to such thoughts, and thoughts pushed them to action. Most had grouped around Newsreel, a project founded early this year by New York filmmakers determined to make and distribute films addressed to The Movement, The Underground — films which engaged political reality from within it, who asked the questions of it that an activist would ask, who reported demonstrations (October at the Pentagon, the Jeanette Rankin Brigade, Up-Against-The-Wall-Mother-fucker's dumping of garbage at Lincoln Center) and organizing projects (Resistance, Boston Draft Resistance Group) not only thoroughly, but with an eye to conveying experience to people prepared to apply its lessons.

The country is fairly crawling with filmmakers who refuse to sever their talent from their commitment, their eyes from their more vital organs: a San Francisco group is already at work. Newsreel, like the underground press, has flowered, and for the same reason: they exist to sensitize and serve those of us who refuse to consume the indigestible products of our enemies.

But to declare yourself fully it is necessary to do more than Your Thing, because Your Thing is circumscribed and absorbed and eaten in a million ways by their spongy, 50,000-watt, 1-million-circulation Things. The German SDS knew this well last spring: they took after Axel Springer, right-wing tycoon publisher, as if he were simply manufacturing poison. It is intolerable to manufacture poison, they reasoned, even if someone else is allowed to make antidotes.

Newsreel took on a more elusive and therefore striking target, and they hit the mark directly. ABC, CBS, NBC would have been sitting ducks — even former FCC Commissioner Newton Minow had consigned them to a "vast wasteland." Money-making enterprises pure and simple, purchasing rigged polls to justify their spewing forth of canned pap, dispensing "news" in interchangeable pellets (usually placebos), reserving the most meager shreds of creativity for commercials, the networks have left many highly-placed people with empty feelings and headaches beyond even the far reach of Excedrin. CBS News Chief Fred Friendly had quit in 1966 when higher-ups refused to jerk the morning's soap operas to broadcast the Fulbright hearings live, and written a book, "Due to Circumstances Beyond Our Control," denouncing narrow-minded bureaucrats. What Friendly proposed instead were broad-minded bureaucrats, administering higher-toned culture in gilded eye-droppers to higher-toned people — broadly speaking, the upper middle class. Meanwhile McGeorge Bundy's Ford Foundation had argued for a publicly-financed TV channel, a fourth network devoted to "public affairs" and symphonic civilization: and lo and behold, we have PBL, Public Broadcast Laboratory. (The alacrity with which PBL zoomed into regular existence tells you something about where power is lodged.) No commercials, well-mannered critiques of the war — not yet of the lustful imperialism (another curse word!) that powers this war and the next — sympathetic treatments of black power: but that's just it. PBL offers TREATMENTS, renditions, slicked through the detached cinematic retina. The upper middles don't want to relinquish their position, only to secure it more firmly by adjusting its sights, "taking account of "new realities." Typical board member: James Restin of the New York Times, who blandly bemoans the plight of the Empire and hopes Senator McCarthy will goose it back into gear. Poor James. So much for "new realities."

And thus NET, the National Educational Television network, a string of stations — WNDT-TV, New York, KQED-TV, San Francisco, etc. — that have popped up over the last few years to form an oasis in the wasteland. NET has distributed Felix Greene's "Inside North Vietnam," Saul Landau and Richard Moore's pro-Castro "Report on Cuba." Only the wasteland seeps into the oasis; the oasis ignores its location only at great peril. Almost everything is packaged for the most painless consumption, tailored to cramped time-formats, stripped of the sharpest edges; NET does not, cannot promote and elaborate the shattering idea that it is possible for Americans to live a different way. Instead it offers a channeled switch-off for the good people whose most elementary sensibilities will not allow them to stomach the Big 3 networks. American television, they will conclude, is indeed an open marketplace; let the buyer only beware, and he will be rewarded. NET is the lollypop after the $2.50 haircut, the last meal on Death Row.

I exaggerate, but to a point. Consider the rebuttal: "But it's worlds better than CBS" But there is a principle at stake: the airwaves belong to the people: not grudgingly, not in boiled-down concessions, not forever subject to broad-minded censors who balance politics as if they were a diet, but as a matter of right. The right to say so before a microphone, for the titillation of an audience trained only to be flattered by novelty, is not the issue. The issue is the right to exercise the right, not proclaim it.

So the Newsreel people chose WND-TV to make their point. The occasion was a panel discussion on the underground press, moderated (very precise word) by a protege of James Restin. The guests (no doubt as to who owned the house) were Allen Katzman, editor of the East Village Other, Jeff Shero, editor of Rat, and Marvin Fishman of Newsreel. And a few minutes into the show, other Newsreel people entered the studio, began shouting telegraphic versions of their views: "The establishment press lies! TV is free!" Under the circumstances, on hostile ground in an unaccustomed medium, they resorted to slogans: but then they assumed the show had been zipped off the air, couldn't know the studio was still transmitting. Why it did remains a mystery: were the technicians friendly?

The nervous moderator was just as oblivious. "Why did you do this?" he asked, when the noise level had settled. "This is what the underground media really is," Fishman said, "and no established media can convey what the underground wants to convey. You've got a format; the underground doesn't work according to your format. The underground works, operates and creates in a whole different manner. We go to Columbia and we work on the inside where the action is. We go to Resurrection City and we work on the inside.... We cannot work as the media does, behind the line of the police."

He went on to talk about a show illuminating Positive Features of the Bedford-Stuyvesant ghetto, and Jeff Shero defined a central principle of the Newsreel-Underground approach: "If you want to do a show on Bedford-Stuyvesant, you have an open camera and let anyone who wants to sit down and talk — gang kids, dope pushers, anyone."

Then the bombshell. "And," said Jeff, "I can't say 'fuck' on this TV station." Extra consternation in the studio.

"If you're doing a show on Bedford-Stuyvesant, people have to express themselves in their own language — not in the language of the establishment."

Fishman added, "When someone goes on TV, he is expected to use the language of TV. He can't say 'fuck' on the air because it's considered bad taste. But the fact of the matter is, he uses 'fuck' a great deal — not for its own sake. He uses it in the natural course of how he lives."

But probably no one was listening any more. Probably no one heard Jeff Shero go on to ask whether NET had broadcast evidence liberated from Grayson Kirk's office of the tie between Columbia and the Institute for Defense Analyses, evidence of Columbia as realtor and holding company. Probably no one heard the answer, "No," let alone pondered the implications. Scandal blurred substance, most likely: after all, this was the no-feedback medium, there was no chance to read the watching armchair faces, say "Wait a minute now, you don't understand, OK, we'll explain."

And the infantry was on its way to re-take the hamlet, to clear and hold. Word got to the liberators, and most cut out, melted back onto the street. Seven were a little slow in leaving, and were arrested, charged with (1) burglary, breaking and entering with intent to commit a felony, namely: (2) rioting. Maximum penalties, seven years on the first charge, four years on the second.

This is serious business, this business of clearing the air. Everything has gotten more serious this year, which is another way of saying that the stakes, those intangible and preoccupying stakes we carry in our heads, are climbing; what we once found tolerable we can no longer blink. "Provo tactics" not so long ago seemed innocuously cute, the raw precious stuff of stories with which to regale your friends for months to come. No longer. Working through the implications of theory in real life, always risky in the abstract, has become a matter of concrete risk and practical planning, a constant tension. Who knows what was in the minds of the medical students who in 1957 seized a radio station in Havana, held it momentarily before falling, shot dead in the streets where markers today commemorate them?

Do not mistake me: We are not riding the crest of a revolutionary wave; we are only — ONLY, but this is no small feat: staking out our own history, defining precedents, opening space for new objectives, lighting new energy-fuses. Vague formulations all, for the holding of cultural and physical territory is something we know little about.

But as we come to reckon as seriously with the cultural artillery of the oligarchy as with our own walled-off culture, the liberation of WNDT-TV, half-assed and incomplete and problematic as it was, may stand as one more cracked foundation stone on which the New City may yet be built.

San Francisco
Express Times 7/3/68

〰〰〰〰〰〰〰〰〰〰〰〰〰〰〰〰〰〰〰〰〰

〰〰〰〰〰〰〰〰〰〰〰〰〰〰〰〰〰〰〰〰〰

I read the news today (oh boy!) and find that I am the news, and go to court soon for sentencing.

BEELZEBUB a reporter for the San Francisco Express Times 1/28/69 (he was busted and jailed for dealing in marijuana)

The news director, Wes Nisker, of the Bay area hip-rock FM station, created a new collage form for the news broadcasts. He spliced together speeches of people in the news and combined these with sound effects and his own reading of the news. At the end of each broadcast he reminded his listeners: "If you didn't like the news, go out and make some of your own."

LEVIATHAN March 1970

CONNECTIONS

vol III no. 2 Sept. 24 - Oct. 15, 1968 15¢ (20¢ out of wis.)

DADS AND DAUGHTERS

Dear Sir:

As the father of the above listed subscriber, who is aged 15, I am hereby requesting — instructing — ordering you to remove her name and address from your circulation listing.

In brief, I do not want her to receive any future issues of your publication. You may retain any monetary value remaining in the subscription charges.

Just so there is no mistake in your circulation records I have attached hereto the portion of your publication listing the recorded name and address.

Very truly yours,
R.J.S.
Elm Grove, Wisconsin

Dear Editor,

You've probably already gotten the letter from my dad telling you to stop sending me your "obscene" paper. I wish I could tell you to keep sending them but the D.A. told my dad that if you do he can sue you. All we need is to go to court with C.T. Seraphim against us.

I wanted to tell you to keep up the good work, or bad, depending on who looks at it, and I'll be buying it as often as possible. Wonder what my dad would say if I started selling for you?

Unfortunately, he thinks you're corrupting my mind and if you're removed he can control my thoughts. What they don't see is that things are going to come off with or without Kaleidoscope.

Peace,
J.S.
Elm Grove, Wisconsin

Two letters to *Kaleidoscope*

what did you do,
by JOHN HUNT

But that the white eyelid of the screen
reflect its proper light,
the Universe would go up in flames.

—Luis Bunuel

Those who applaud Hollywood's occasional "New Look" ventures are motivated by a desire to find some crumbs of comfort in what they basically regard as a hopeless situation; it seems "hopeless" because they are overawed by Wall Street's cultural dominance, unwilling to concede the possibilities of a broad movement for a democratic culture.

John Howard Lawson wrote these lines before going to jail for contempt of the House Unamerican Activities Committee proceedings in 1952. Feeling that the capitalist film industry could be "pressured" into making concessions which would eventually lead to real gains on the road to a people's film art, Lawson pleaded for audience organization. He felt change could come from within—and not without good reason: Lawson made his living writing films. He had hopes at that date of continuing his work. He was not allowed, however, and was one of "The Ten" blacklisted writers and directors who were shut out by the studios. But Lawson never lost his optimism, nor his clear vision of what film was all about. And he was ready to fight: "The idea that it is futile to attack Hollywood's film propaganda indicates lack of confidence in the capacity of the masses to grasp the issues, and to organize effectively to influence the content of films. It indicates failure to see the *ideological* struggle, the struggle to expose and defeat fascism and war propaganda, in its necessary connection with the political and economic struggle."

For Lawson to see the ideology behind the Hollywood film, to probe through its subtle surface, was to preview the issues we are facing today. In *Film in the Battle of Ideas,* published in 1953, long before Women's Liberation, he was writing this: "Many film artists seem to be unaware of the political purpose underlying the increasingly degrading roles assigned to women." And: "An attitude of tolerant amusement toward the film's mockery of women indicates failure to grasp the political significance of the woman question. Hollywood's vulgarities cannot be dismissed as adolescent sexuality, or even senile decay. Films degrade women because their degradation is an economic and political necessity of the drive to fascism and war."

I stress these comments because of their importance in creating a total awareness in an area which has been relatively excluded by the New Left. That this area has been ignored, or left unexplored, is inexcusable. The media have embedded themselves in our brains by a long process known popularly as "entertainment"; unless one is aware that every single piece of information garnered from radio, TV, films, etc., has been encased in the enemy's crust, one runs in circles trying to penetrate into the guts of today's problems.

In "14 Notes on Television and the Movement" (*Leviathan,* July/August 1969), Todd Gitlin aptly dissects the monster. He calls for a sharpened awareness of our roots, which means analysis of the media. At the risk of overloading this article with other people's words, I quote him: "Whether the cool acceptance or the cool skepticism triumphs, whether skepticism turns to disgust or even directly to revolt, depends on the magnetic power of the movement to define an alternative. The revolutionary black movement and some hip communes come closest to embodying a totally opposed consciousness transcending the commodity riot. Finally, only a totally opposed consciousness can counter the culture's total assault." The point is, 1953 to now is a long time to sit around waiting for someone else to take care of business.

Going back to Lawson's statements concerning what can be done to move "Toward a People's Film Art," as he calls one section of his book, we see his alternative, broadly stated, as turning the guns around. "Underlying the passive acceptance of Wall Street's power over films *and other forms of communication* is disdain for culture: since its class function is not seen, its value as a weapon in class struggle is not respected: the danger of its use by the bourgeoisie is belittled, and the possibilities of its use by the masses are ignored" (italics added).

It is impossible to divorce the movement from the very tools which, in the hands of the capitalists, have formed it. It is impossible to be "pure," standing outside the media (or any of its appurtenances), when the media have things under control. To effectively counteract what has been done, and then build up from the ashes, the movement must supply alternatives, as Gitlin says, a "source of values, network of relations and standard for authenticity."

In 1952, Sam Goldwyn made *I Want You*, a blatant piece of fascist propaganda, in which the necessity of "war to protect democracy" is defended. The hero, Martin Greer, a middle class, married, typically happy American, questions himself about going to fight in Korea. Greer is a specialist and his country needs him. His younger brother, after protesting mildly about his draft notice, has been patriotically persuaded by Greer's own wife to do his duty. The clincher comes when Greer wonders what he will answer when his son in future years asks, "What did you do, daddy, in the war against Communism?"

Few critics were taken in by this fright line, and the film was a box-office failure, indicating audiences were small. But there were other films not so easily detected, and far more successful, i.e., financially rewarding and effectively subtle as propaganda: *Viva Zapata!*, for example, doubting a great revolutionary's mental capacity, reminds me of the pat liberal reply to one of the solutions available to the oppressed peoples, that *the land belongs to those who work it*: "It's too simple"; *A Streetcar Named Desire* or *Westward the Women*, in which women are "dumb cows" deserving of any violence they receive: *How Green Was My Valley*, which treats a capitalist workers' nightmare as a fairy tale romantically set in the hills of Wales, far removed from the sweatshops of Chicago, or the fields of Delano.

"Salt of the Earth"

In contrast, there is only one film from this entire period that deserves

daddy, in the war

mention as perhaps the first American people's film, *Salt of the Earth*. The film was begun in 1951, written by Michael Wilson and directed by Herbert Biberman, one of the HUAC's "pinkos"; it wasn't until March, 1954, that it was premiered, following years of struggle against the whole film industry. The industry was so against the production that even the labs, usually uncommitted in any direction except cash, refused to handle the film's processing.

The film is simple, and unrelenting in its pursuit of the issues. A group of miners in Zinc Town, New Mexico, both Anglos and Mexican-Americans, go on strike for improved safety conditions. The company, with the aid of the local police and the courts, tries to break the strike. The union fights hard, but at one point, with the arrival of an injunction prohibiting the men from picketing, it looks as though the strike is finished; but, against their husbands' wishes, the strikers' women rally and picket in place of the men. The strike continues to be effective and a new power has to be reckoned with. The men are forced to confront not only their position with the bosses, but to re-evaluate their family relationships. At the end the strike is won only temporarily, and there is a premonition of future struggle; but in their solidarity they have won a battle. The film is truly a call for a united front.

One description in the scenario points out that the makers had full understanding of what they were about. During the early part of the film, before the strike, there is an accident at the mine and the men have gathered to protest. The wounded man is taken away and the boss orders them to return to work; they are silent, staring high over the mine shaft to where their families have stood watching the confrontation: *from their angle, long shot: the women and children standing on the knoll above the mine. They are silent and grave. The women's skirts billow in the wind, like unfurled flags, like the tattered banners of a guerrilla band that has come to offer its services to the regular army. Fade out.*

Compare this to a great people's artist, Bertolt Brecht, and four lines of a song in *Congress of Whitewashers*, a play which, understating grossly, calls for cohesion in the face of oppression:

> *If a skirt is a fancy dream*
> *It's alright just so*
> *We can use it for a flag*
> *Long live Kai Ho [a revolutionary leader].*

One question arises from all this: what happened to Biberman, Wilson, and rebels like them? Many, of course, returned to the fold. Lawson didn't, and he grows old in Los Angeles, forgotten by the industry he loved, but didn't know well enough. If it hadn't been for the HUAC hearings and the subsequent blacklistings, I doubt if a film like *Salt of the Earth* would ever have been made. Basically it was outrage at their being financially cut off from their "trade" that caused men like Biberman, Lawson, and Dalton Trumbo to revolt. Trumbo, for instance, after a clandestine period of writing under a pseudonym, returned with Stanley Kubrick to concoct *Spartacus*, romantically putting down a revolutionary struggle and being hailed once again as the great artist.

It is interesting to note that films like *Spartacus*, which could deal with current issues, and do *appear* relevant, sidestep many of the real issues. Because they are no threat to anyone—except the movement—they are allowed wide release and great press coverage. Up till now, a review of *Salt of the Earth* aired on the Canadian Broadcasting System sums up with few exceptions the American film: "*Salt of the Earth* is an American movie about workers, which fact alone makes it unusual. The idea that workers are people, and have conflicts and problems worthy of attention, has never impressed the American film industry . . ."

What about *Grapes of Wrath*? Let two lines suffice. Again Lawson: "During the 1930's, one film, *Grapes of Wrath*, dealt seriously with economic struggle. But it did not touch the problems of industrial workers, and its portrayal of the tragedy of migratory farm labor in California was marred by a negative and defeatist ending."

Fonda and $$: The Loner

And what of today? Has anything changed?

The Green Berets is up-front, laughable, and can be compared to *I Want You*. But what of a film like *Easy Rider*? Peter Fonda has said he has chosen not to give us any hope, because, I suspect, he is unable to get it together in his own head and align himself with an ideology which offers solutions—no matter what he may say. There is no such thing as "no hope," because conversely the intimation is that at one time there was some. Hope stems from false bourgeois sentiment: Dream. Hope is the great divider, the disorganizer which spreads dissidence and chaos among "good intentioned" souls: a dreamer faced with the cold reality crumbles into powder, which the fascists then piss on, knead, and reshape into the "new democratic man." There is only what is; and there are solutions. Fonda's portrayal of America's face may be accurate, but it is misleading, being only a manifestation of the real problems. It takes no great genius to know what he shows us. It's been here for quite some time and requires a deeper look than he gives us. To have the bikers in the film seem "right," and have them destroyed by a couple of fascists, is to point down. Up is the way, through organized resistance, by involvement in the movement, and not as loners, on their super $$ choppers trying to escape.

There is no place for loners today. The opposition is so well organized it is ridiculous even to comment on it. In this light perhaps Fonda's fate in the film is exactly what should have happened—anyone standing alone will be crushed. Why weren't he and his sidekick (the director, Dennis Hopper) taking the cash from their deal and dumping it into a breakfast program for kids, or a bail fund? For the same reason Fonda admits he will probably return to Hollywood to work in other people's films, because he "needs" a couple hundred thousand dollars to support his family. Because he rides a $3,000 chopper. Because he makes films which subvert the movement. In other words, Fonda *is* the enemy. Columbia Pictures did *what!?!*

Or perhaps he was out to create a new folk hero, something like Bonnie and Clyde. Before Arthur Penn, Bonnie and Clyde were folk heroes of a sort. But Penn was only interested in putting down violence. Penn has no idea of a people's film, and although *Bonnie and Clyde* does not make gratuitous use of violence, the ending does have a mollifying effect—kind of a violent lesson turned around, demanding more and more violence—for no end.

And then folk heroes who become popular are always suspect in a capitalist society. A good recent example is Johnny Cash's song "A Boy Named Sue," near the top of the "pop" charts across the country on AM radio. (Written, incidentally, by Shel Silverstein.) Cash, once again, *appears* to be saying something, when in the song he wants to kill his father for having named him Sue, an incident which has made him the brunt of derisive jokes and the center of many fights. But, after all, the fights have really built up his character—as his father points out in the end. Cash comes away "with a different point of view," satisfied that his father's intentions were really good, even though he was a drifting drunk unable to see the "outside" forces which broke him in the first place.

The revolutionary movement in America is not about to kill anyone over a name. The issues are far deeper, infinitely more important, and

limited showing, in this country particularly, because Bunuel is unassimilable. "In a world as badly made as this, rebellion is the only way possible," has been his life's creed. *Belle de Jour* is an excellent example of the slickness of the package baffling the distributors. It was advertised as a very daring, sexy film. Audiences didn't understand it when the twisting around of their own morality was presented to them. The images will not easily be erased. It is because Bunuel is so conscious of class morality that he was able to take the opposing premises and proceed to prove them incapable of dealing with reality—a reality, by the way, created and nurtured by our existing morality. This, the paradox of modern society, must be eradicated before any sort of lasting change can come about. (Complementing this, in true Bunuelian fashion, he has said that he took something he hated—the book—and made it into something he loves. At least this was his intention at the beginning of the project.) It is because he always cuts away the fat, penetrating to the bone, that he is able to tie up complicated situations with simple symbols, clearly understandable once one realized that his morality must be adjusted. His early documentary *Land Without Bread,* made in his own country, Spain—where he has only returned once to film *Viridiana*—is documentary in that it gives you the facts, but presents them in a way that makes catharsis—and therefore a sense of resolution—impossible. There is nothing false—sentimental—about the film; the falseness is in us, the viewers.

Many times the films of Newsreel, the movement's only real organized film producers (as distinguished from co-ops), give us a sense of action taking place, involving us rather than forcing us to involve ourselves; these films make viable situations out of last-ditch, too-late efforts on the part of

against communism

keenly visible. Popular "art" and performers such as Johnny Cash and Peter Fonda cloud things over with their drivel. They present clear images about irrelevant issues, thus pushing the real issues underneath. They do this because they are incapable of seeing clearly, and because they are making much money. They are fat, and have no wish to jeopardize their positions within the industry; until they prove otherwise, there is nothing else to say.

Rebellion Is the Only Way Possible

On the other hand, *If,* Lindsay Anderson's second feature film, presents the issues clearly, then offers the only possible alternative. *If that's the way you want it, that's the way you'll get it,* and the small group of resisters pick up their guns. His last scene, though violent, shows no trace of blood or death, because these we know will occur; the scene is positive, constructive, metaphorically stating what has to be done. Revolution is never pleasant but is necessary and inevitable under present conditions. The only point I would bring up is that instead of *If,* perhaps it should be *Why Has It Taken So Long?* But again, by presenting the issues in a way that cannot be considered didactic by even the most liberal members of the audience, *If* forces idealists and non-action people to come up against the rational deduction of the film's statement. (And if education is the aim, *If* is the proper title.) And the movement's communicators must recognize that a large number of people are still questioning the validity of revolution. These are the people who must be reached, not turned off. Turning off people as an end in itself is separation, as destructive as anything coming down from the capitalists. That's why Anderson's film is important. Fonda is trying to be the great existential artist, glibly denouncing hope, because he has had his personal hopes wiped away in the Hollywood shithouse. Anderson has never shown liberal sentiment, always keeping the real issues in front of him. For this reason, of course, he has only made two features.

Also for this reason filmmakers like Luis Bunuel have always had

an oppressed people outside the US who have been just as propagandized by our (and their own) media as we ourselves, and are still not able to understand fully the media's function. In other words, as information aimed at those within the movement, Newsreel succeeds. As education for those on the periphery, they are passed off as being didactic, forcing no conflict of morality, often using the exact same cultural images which have gotten us where we are to start with, not challenging the entire class morality which is the superstructure of Culture.

Newsreel of course is right; but audiences are nonetheless scared off, frightened at even inquiring as how to best become involved. And following involvement comes commitment. There is therefore room for a subtler approach.

Bunuel made *Viridiana* in Franco Spain, with government-backed money, even having his script approved. When the film was completed he had to scurry across the frontier, clutching his negative firmly in hand. If anything, the film shows the fascists' inability to come to terms with a symbolic representation of their own milieu; many workers, it's true, are unable to get a total perception out of the film. This is not critical, but merely shows the need for both types of approach. To limit the movement's media in any way is merely to replace the enemy's restrictions with our own. The thing is, it is necessary to become alert to all possibilities, both in attack, and in defense. Unity is the only end we can strive for. If someone refuses to see what is clearly in front of him, then—at this point of development—it is up to us to utilize another method. No one can be given up on unless he proves himself the enemy by choice. It is true that when there are two armed camps there will only be need for information—and guns. At that time the greater numbers will defeat, or control, the lesser numbers. But only by refusing overtly our alternatives can a member of the middle join the opposition's camp. Until that choice is made it is up to the movement, through its media (and don't forget, it's *Mass Media*), to penetrate into the lives of those who do not see. It is necessary to break down the old moral codes, and at the same time offer new ones, giving vitality to life where now there is only existence.

I heard an old black man say to a government worker one time, "You can't reach me, because you can't see me."

It works both ways.

It is also interesting to note that for Bunuel a blind man is always a symbol of evil.

And so, many filmmakers today have resigned themselves to the fact that they may never be able to make the films they want to make: there are far too many important things to be done with the money today, and every penny must be weighed and justified as to the effect the film will have. Whatever they do, though, their sight should never be limited, and, as I have used Bunuel as an example, let me finish up with him: "But that the white eye-lid of the screen reflect its proper light, the Universe would go up in flames. But for the moment we can sleep in peace: the light of the cinema is conveniently dosified and shackled."

Bunuel confronts this dilemma in his films and his life style. It is up to us to do the same, bringing light and destruction to the darkness and corruption we have come from.

Leviathan Sept 1969

there is an inner
anterior image
of divinity
beckoning me out
to pilgrimage

ALLEN GINSBERG

THEY TRYIN TO GET BACK

MUSIC
THE SUPREME
MYSTERY OF
THE SCIENCE
OF MAN

—May I turn to the work which you now are engaged upon? In that extraordinary opening section of Le Cru et le Cuit (The Raw and the Cooked), where you sum up so much of your recent thinking on language, we come to the statement that music is the "supreme mystery of the science of man, the mystery against which the science must necessarily butt its head, and the mystery which keeps the key to the progress of the science of man...." What thought were you developing there?

We all know that music is a means of communication. When we listen to music we communicate with the composer; we communicate with the musicians themselves; and we communicate together in sharing the same emotion between members of the audience. But this kind of language cannot be translated into anything else, except itself. You can translate music into music. You can shape the melody from major to minor. You can even devise a mathematical equation which will permit you to change according to a certain rule the interval between the notes of the melody and it will be a translation of the melody. But you cannot translate music into speech; if you do, you reach the kind of phraseology which does not convey anything of the message of the music itself. This raises, of course, an enormous problem exactly akin to the problem raised by mythology—because there have also been attempts to translate myth into something which is not mythology. But what you arrive at are generally platitudes of the worst kind. Myths are translations of one another, and the only way you can understand a myth is to show how a translation of it is offered by a different

myth. So there is something very similar between mythology and music.

—You spoke of sharing the musical experience. Does not ethno-musicology suggest that musical experiences are highly specific to individual cultures? You write: "Music, the only language, both untranslatable and immediately understandable." Is this so? Isn't music understandable only to very specialised groups who know the syntax of the music of a particular culture?

LÉVI-STRAUSS: I was speaking only of music within a culture. But I was not claiming that any kind of music is understandable to any audience.

—The fact that it can be translated into no other medium also means it cannot be translated into another idiom.

LÉVI-STRAUSS: Yes. The same is true for mythology, because you cannot make mythology understood by somebody of a different culture without teaching him the rules and the particular traditions of that culture.

From "a conversation with Claude Lévi-Strauss" by George Steiner, Encounter April 1966

WHAT'LL YOU BOYS HAVE? SHE ASKED. RAW MEAT, THEY ANSWERED.

sandy darlington

Saturday at Santa Clara Fairgrounds. Hot weather and a good sound system. About 8000 people came to hear the rock bands.

There were a lot of long-haired people there, but the major part of the audience was 15-17 year old white kids. Lots of short sleeves, some Bermuda shorts. Kids with straight faces held in that anticipation, waiting for themselves, waiting for Stars, waiting to be turned on, waiting to be sent into combat, intent on what was happening but not used to bursting out. Kids who were used to being told, "Sit up straight and don't make faces." They had become the nice children their parents had raised them to be, and now they were looking for something beyond that.

Last year they could have eased their changes maybe with a transitional music like Herman's Hermits, the Monkees or even Early Beatles: boys who didn't look like they'd push a girl too far, boys who were willing to come in and meet the parents before a date. Now that kind of act is out, perhaps a victim of the general polarization of attitudes that is going on in America. Now there is a vacuum, a lack of in-betweens. These kids came from Scouts, Sunday School, mowing the lawn for chores and maybe getting a pony for Christmas. And they're going straight out of that toward the world of Pigpen and Janis.

It's a big jump, and they were slow in getting involved in the music that day. They weren't dumb, they just hadn't been anyplace yet, and they rather shyly waited to be shown around. They were like the farmers who gathered in Ottawa, Illinois in 1858 to hear the first Lincoln-Douglas debate:

After their first debate in Ottawa, the New York Evening

photos by Jeffrey Blankfort

Post reported: "All prairiedom has broken loose. It is astonishing how deep an interest in politics these people take."

The bands went through a slow and roundabout courtship with the audience, trying to turn them on. Here were all these hairy gang-bang bands all ready to whoop it up like they'd just driven the herds into Dodge City all the way from the Mexican border, and the crowd was like the school-marm who wonders if kissing with the tongue is ladylike. So...it took time.

Finally the Youngbloods started to get to them with "Let's Get Together." They're a trio now. Jerry Corbett has quit to do some record producing. Jesse said, "He got tired of running around playing rock band gigs." Then Crome Syrcus, a developing band, still not there. Some parts work and some don't. They ended with their ballet score from "Astarte" which just didn't have anything to say in an outdoor rock concert. Then the Steve Miller Band, the first really hard band of the day, all tight and together. Like watching a good middle-weight contender. They set the crowd up.

Next came the Grateful Dead. Tom Donahue announced that their new album is out this week and suggested that the Dead might play some numbers from it during their set. Jerry Garcia smiled benignly to himself. He said they'd do "Alligator" and they did, for about 40 minutes. That was their set and it blew the place wide-open.

Most bands hit a song fast, then stretch out for a while, then end up with a bang. The Dead go into a song slowly, tentively, and build up an atmosphere until everybody is inside the music. And then they take off, exploring the figures over and over again over that super rhythm section. If you're outside it, it can be boring. But when they get to

you, it's incredible and hypnotic as if the music was happening inside you. In Santa Clara it blew everybody's mind. It was as though we were hearing for the first time in our lives and we stood in a kind of trance, scarcely knowing that we were listening. The ending was very drawn-out, on purpose. From that incredible middle they trailed off slowly into percussion sounds, then down to just cymbal noise, and from there to silence. When it was over, we didn't clap much, we just stood there open-mouthed: Who was that Masked Man?

Then Big Brother and the Holding Company came on completely out front, pouring everything into just that moment, as though there is no tomorrow, only right now. Raw power and excitement. The most intense band around. And yet they're all so gentle. They look like they'd scare hell out of a waitress at a drive-in (What'll you boys have? she asked. Raw meat, they answered) and yet they'd be great with children.

And they're all so tasteful. They make their choices like old-time country musicians. Janis looks like a gramma and like a little girl, and like she's burning up with a white flame. While she was singing, the wind was blowing the cottonwood trees behind her, and the leaves were turning over, from green to grey-green and back, as though in time with the music. They're presently recording an LP for Columbia in L.A. They're good people and I hope they get home all right.

And top of the bill, Jefferson Airplane. What a complicated bunch! Cassady, Dryden and Jorma laying down their music, and Paul, Grace and Marty Balin out in front doing some weird version of Who's Afraid of Virginia Wolfe, making little remarks, gestures, giggles and faces at each other like they were passing notes in a schoolroom. Their last number was Do You Want Somebody to Love. They led up to it with and air of mixed boredom and relief, like "Oh, not this again," but when they got into it, they really got with it and cheered up and smiled and bopped around.

The crowd reaction began with O Wow, the Hit! and then warmed up into: Yes, I do want somebody to love actually. Then the festival producers and monitors started shooing away the fans who were standing on the stage: All right, kids, maybe you want somebody to love, but right now, run along home. That all happened behind the Airplane, who were having a really good time by then. Then they ended and we all ran along.

STREET FIGHTING STONES

There is a song for fighting people. The uncensored complete lyrics of Street Fighting Man from the Rolling Stones, banned in Chicago. Of this song, Mick Jagger said: "They must think that song can make a revolution. . .I wish it could." This song is reprinted from the Songbook of the International Workers of the World songbook (40 cents from IWW, 2422 N. Halsted St., Chicago, Ill. 60614).

Everywhere I hear the sound of marching,
   charging feet, boy.
Comes summer here and the time is right
   for fighting in the street, boy.
Hey, think the time is right for a palace
   revolution.
But where live the game to play is
   compromise solution.

Hey, said my name is called Disturbance
I'll shout and scream
I'll kill the king.
I'll rail at all his servants

CHORUS

But what can a poor boy do except to
Sing for a rock 'n' roll band.
Guess in sleepy London town, there's just
   no place for a street fighting man.

kaleidoscope Milwaukee

Richard Goldstein, rock critic says: "Pop culture can teach us things (indirectly). Like I quoted Eldridge Cleaver in a line that was deleted from my Times piece before it was printed: 'Soul music taught us how to move our ass' he said, and I really think that culture can grab you, before you realize on the level of ideas and philosophy what your objections are and what your aims are, and can express these in a mythic way that is really much more powerful than a dogmatic way. That's the way I really look at rock — or its potential, anyway."

But rock is an art, and artists do more than merely pick up and feed back the vibes of their culture. Ed Sanders, Fug:

"The relationship between rock and revolution is granting that most musicians are a bunch of avaricious ass-sucking dogs, and most of the song writers (too), myself in many ways included. It's the form or the intention, or the implications of the music that make it interesting to the revolutionary. It's a tool and a tactic for getting children to revolt against the protoplasm that raised them and consider other forms of government, other forms of dealing with the situation. When you coordinate and liberate and release the sexuality and the minds of youth, and can twist it and change it toward a different goal and direction, via rock 'n roll, via fucking in the streets, via dope, via action, direct action. . .then you can maybe push this country and we can rewrite the whole structure, based on the kind of energy released by rock 'n roll."

From a *WIN* symposium on Rock and Revolution

ROCK MANIFESTO

Ultimately there's nothing left but the present. By and large, the past two generations have made such a colossal mess of the world that they have to step down and let us take over.
PETER TOWNSHEND, *THE WHO*

The American idea of youth assumes that all rebels finally join the herd. But you can't ignore us. Even if you don't like the ideas behind our music you have to listen to it because it is everywhere.
FRANK ZAPPA, *THE MOTHERS OF INVENTION*

Erotic politicians, that's what we are. We're interested in anything about revolt, disorder, chaos and activity that appears to have no meaning.
JIM MORRISON, *THE DOORS*

It's *real*, that's what this new music is — and that's what makes it different from anything which has ever happened in pop music before.
MARTY BALIN, *JEFFERSON AIRPLANE*

Lots of the things we do are dangerous, but life itself is dangerous; nothing is really worth bothering with that isn't *full of danger.*
JIMI HENDRIX, *EXPERIENCE*

The drug experience may not prove much in the long run, but it has taught us that to be *deranged* is not necessarily to be useless.
ERIC BURDON, *THE ANIMALS*

Unnatural, that's what the old idea of art was for most Americans. It's inevitable for us to create art which is natural to us.
BRIAN WILSON, *THE BEACH BOYS*

The world is ready for a *mystic* revolution, a discovery of the God in each of us.
GEORGE HARRISON *THE BEATLES*

ABBEY ROAD: BEATLES AS AGING CHILDREN

Christmas at home was a down. (Me, my wife Bobi, brother Scott, trimming the family tree, meticulously looping one end of each separate strand of tinsel over each twig, my mother chortling orgasmically from the couch, "This—I really believe—is the most beeyooteeful tree we have ever had," Dad grumping about our not playing "Christmas music," Grace Slick penetrating the whole fireside scene: *Redwoods talk to me; say it plainly/The human name doesn't mean shit to a tree.*) For those of us still on a vestigial Tom Wolfe trip (no, children, the *other* Tom Wolfe), reunion with our ever older, ever straighter, ever duller parents painfully reminds us both that we can't go back and that we once were there, and also that where we were was limited by factors not under our control—like when we were born.

Age has a way of collecting its dues, of marking rings on us, like a tree. There are exceptions; put the president of the University of Virginia Honor Court alongside Abbie Hoffman; one is 33, the other 21; which is younger?—but even Abbie, like the rest of us, is an aging child.

I remember the Day the Beatles Happened. Three or four pledges racing maniacally about the fraternity house, frantically rearranging their (UVA customary) long hair in reasonable simulations of the cover photograph. I smiled, paternally, and climbed the stairs to listen not to the Beatles, but for the hundred-oddth time to "the lonesome death of hattie carroll," to, in sum, significant music, leaving teenybopper trash to its herd.

Okay, so we "came around," "got into," "accepted" the Beatles, rejected the dichotomy between them and, say, pre-rock Dylan, even tired of Dylan's own "charisma," as did he. But what, I can only wonder, goes on in the heads of those whose affinity for the Beatles just *happened*, requiring no such linear-logical process as I have described, because the Beatles *were* (and always have been as far as a 17-year-old cares), as much a part of their environment as TV and credit cards (both of which I remember "adjusting" to).

Perhaps the Beatles too are aging children, and

perhaps *Abbey Road* is the songs which, says Joni Mitchell, come to aging children. The Beatles, you see, are around 30; they lived through the same changes I experienced. They too differ "biologically" (in the Marcusian sense of environmentally conditioned biology) from those millions of Beatles fans not yet 20. And *Abbey Road* reflects their perception of that missing link, and the impossibility of the Beatles continuing any kind of "leadership" role in their music.

There is, in the construction of a house, the critical step of laying the main beam. Once this beam is set, level and straight, floor joists are set across it, and the floor is nailed to the joists. From the beam the house derives its main support, though the beam in no way forecloses the more visible shape the house may take; the beam simply undergirds the subsequent construction. Similarly, there is in *Abbey Road* that point at which the beam/support of the album can be discerned. The bridge(!) in "Something" goes: "You're asking me will my love grow—I don't know, I don't knooooow. You stick around and it may show--I don't know, I don't knoooooow," tumbling off that plateau in a cascade of drums, disappearing in the lemon drop sweetness of the lead guitar. So here we are, after all these years together, us and the Beatles, the summation of the whole trip: "I Don't Know."

And instantly, the Beatles and I, all old men, unable to experience the freshness, the vitality of the post-linear younger generation between which and us there is, unmistakably, a gap, less ominous perhaps, but more chasmic than the gulf between me and my Christmas tree mommy. And just now, just this soon after the Altamont death festival, some of us over 25 are trying to freak out, to once-and-for-all throw off this ever nettling thing vaguely termed "youth (or "hip") culture," casketing that phenomenon in the category of "reaction" and "bourgeois self-indulgence." In the bridge of "Something," the Beatles speak to Altamont. They say, simply, "I don't know."

The names of the executioners at Altamont are not definitively available, and, as David Crosby asserts, "Blame is the worst trip of all," but the cause of the crime *is* known. Altamont was what it was—scene of Merideth Hunter's murder, incredible numbers of bad trips on good acid, individualized surge to relate 1 to 1 to the "stars," because Altamont was self-consciously a Woodstock West, a *tour de force*, a (here is the crux) profit-making enterprise. Rock as commodity—we have seen fragmental evidence before; we have bit our tongues in silence; we have peacenflowered our minds into submission, but we dare do so no longer. Todd Gitlin, reflecting on Altamont, asks if youth culture will leave us a monument more than a market. It is a serious question; it is "playing for keeps." To flush the whole trip down the toilet of bastard "Marxism" is trivial and "incorrect." To continue as we culture freaks have so often done, to paper over the economic realities of a tour by Blind Faith, or the Stones, or Steppenwolf, is to become PR men for streamlined capitalism (read racism, et. al.).

The trouble with youth culture is that it is too *little*, not too much in the hands of youth; it is *my* generation that promotes (thereby making a shitload of money) the festivals which are our most visible (if not central) expression of who and what we are. As long as the preoccupation with material acquisitiveness dominates the rock scene, rock will be almost (not quite) as managed as Arthur Sylvester's news releases in Vietnam.

But youth culture is more than my generation, more than 25-30-year-old civil rights activists turned peaceniks turned on to dope and rock music. Youth

culture is also the Weathermen, average age 17 and hard as hell for me to understand. It is also the White Panthers. And it is our children.

It is Quint, our communist son. Not yet two. Born into an environment so imbued with rock music that I can identify songs by watching his vital young body sway and jerk and stomp and clap his hands and toss his head; he having got beyond, *before his second fucking birthday*, those taboos which I had to overcome as systematically as I "changed my mind" about the Beatles—"dope is dangerous," "dope is Against the Law." Born stoned, he knows (and will tolerate) no other life. And not just because his mother and father are trying—clumsily, self-consciously, fitfully, note-by-note, to liberate ourselves from the central fear of not having "enough bread to make it" which poisons and pollutes our "radical" lives.

No, more than us, there is the tube. My family bought a TV when I was 9; Quint plays with our set as naturally as with a light switch. And no matter how hard capitalists manipulate the medium, TV communizes people ("tribalize" if you're chickenshit). Satellites have begun to make Bombay as close as Five Points, and it will become closer. Our children have seen "Viet Cong" faces on TV--and they see *faces*, not "Viet Cong." The "enemy" is human; he is visible in living color. So that both Quint and H.L.Hunt's little boy see the world as a village ("commune" if you're dogmatic). So that both H.L. Hunt and I wrestle with this new thing called "ecology," while our children *feel, know, take for granted* the interdependence of all life, the struggle of *all* life against death, and they both will be moved to communize the world. They will live the reality which sounds to us like frenetic overstatement: "Communize or perish!"

We, like the Beatles, can never *feel* that slogan just as our parents will never feel, "We Won't Go." Our task as a generation, then, is to *link*, to fight bullheaded fascism both in occasional military engagements (Piedmont Park) and by creating a community of consciousness centered on love-making and the preservation of Life, to say "WE WON'T GO INTO YOUR PLASTIC DOMES"—until our children do lightshows in them.

The Beatles "don't know," and that is an honest first step. But they try: "Come Together" is the first of many songs on the album which set the task of the revolution in the necessarily broad terms in which that task must be stated. "One and one and one is three," says ol' Flattop, and he is one of the three who must "come together" in the simultaneous orgasm of all life.

"Maxwell's Silver Hammer" performs a similar function in trying to probe the nature of violence. A funky, bouncy, rinky-dink tune (my son really gets off on it) about a medical student who murders his date—"made sure that she was dead"—right, as dead as Meredith Hunter, only Max is a future physician, not an Angel, and the Beatles' point is the same as Jesus': you have heard it said that whoever kills his brother shall be punished, but *I* say, if you hate your brother, even for an instant, that's the same trip, and don't give me any of your culturally restrained gentility bullshit about your not being violent (we *are* all outlaws). So sing the Beatles, who, by the end of 1968, had grossed 70 million *pounds* (168 mil). And one can not deny the fact that *Abbey Road* is the

care fully wrought, multi-layered thing that it is in large measure because of some very expensive equipment, and some very subtle after-the-taping-session blending and mixing on another very expensive machine. And the Beatles have nothing to say about how they got all that equipment; instead they *use* it to bring us a melancholy pastiche from the heads of aging children, recognizing the rings that 1970 has marked upon them. And so they close their (last?) album, recognizing their juxtaposition with Martin Luther King, who may have climbed to the mountaintop and beheld the Promised Land but was not to enter therein.

We are still, those of us who remember books, on Thomas Wolfe's trip, dreading going home, resisting our comfortable aboriginal linearity, but still trying—again and again: "Once there was a way to get back homeward—ahhhh, we're gonna *carry* that weight, carry that weight, a long time." And then Lennon's welding torch, burning our minds with liquid steel, carrying us to one last feeble, irresistible tautology for a transitional generation:

"And
        in the end
            the love you take
                is equal to the love—
                    you make."

Get together with *Abbey Road*; it's a very inviting, very tearful thing.

—greg

The great speckled BIRd 2/2/70

STONES

On November 29, the Stones played their second concert in Boston. The first, over three years ago, had been played in Manning Bowl in Lynn. Then the press referred to the Stones as the GROUP SECOND TO THE BEATLES, but to the bikies, high school kids and college rock freaks who packed the Bowl, sat through the rain and the McCoys singing Hang on Sloopy, the Stones were more important than any press statement. There was no other band that through its music (both lyrics and instrumentals) could so precisely pounce on all that is most obscene and grotesque in our culture, mirror all our feelings, and throw them back at us in a selfconscious and rebellious way. The Stones were and are a ROCK group. On that rainy summer late afternoon when they broke into Paint it Black, Jagger cavorting, taunting, urging: black jacketed kids snaked, danced tore up the chairs, carried each other on their shoulders and felt all their passions, depressions, darknesses, petty rebellions and rage come pouring out.

Now the Stones returned to Boston. Again touted by the press, hailed by eager promoters, accompanied by unctuous disk jockeys, they were now playing in a society that has a commercial youth culture, where rock has become an important part of tens of millions of people's lives. This time they played in Boston Garden, following Bruins games and preceding the Ice Capades. Tickets, unscalped, were going for $6.50–$7.50. But despite all the furbishings and prices, the Stones performance was still an attack on popular culture. They are what they were three years ago, except more so and better at it.

Their concert was long, and despite a few technical troubles brilliant. The Stones looked like their music. Jagger was dressed in black jersey, black silver-dotted bell-bottoms and a long purple taffeta scarf. He walked on in an Uncle Sam hat; on his scrawny chest was a large painted Resistance sign. Keith Richards was also notably grotesque: red tee shirt with comic star in the center, and one flashy pearl earring. In general they looked thoroughly raunchy, ugly, pale and scrawny.

The first song, Jumping Jack Flash, , revealed what was to be underscored all evening: that the Stones are musically, especially in their guitar work, among the greatest of the groups. Keith Richards, who no one used to be even aware of, is a stunningly exciting guitar player. And Mick Taylor, the newest Stone, has an impressive blues style of his own.

They next went into an old Chuck Berry song, fitting because that is where the Stones came from: Berry, Howling Wolf, the Kings, Muddy Waters. In the early years they played only their own,

Mick Jagger and Keith Richards (opposite page).

often very good, translations of Black America's music. They made little pretense at exact copy, no real attempts at innovation. They mastered and retained the classic rock form, later added some elements of Soul. Now almost all their material for the last three and a half years has been their own, built on this tradition.

What makes their music exciting and startling is the way in which it cuts through all the false sentimentality of pop romanticism. Unlike a lot of the commercial "youth culture", they sure don't obscure our society's realities. They reflect them so harshly, starkly, and creatively that their music becomes an assault on the culture, their concerts even a taunting jeer at the audiences. While other groups sing of idealized sexual relationships, or romanticize male supremacy, the Stones slap you in the face with it: Stupid Girl, Back Street Girl, Mother's Little Helper. They understand and make you feel musically all the tension, ugliness, tenderness, frustration and excitement that presently go into sexual relations. What other group could produce Going Home? Next to the Stones, the Doors seem hollow in their attempt to portray sexual release. What other group could have produced Satisfaction?

Last week they also performed their more recent songs, still richer musically, especially Stray Cat Blues and Love in Vain. Jagger and Richards also did several with Jagger singing and Richards on acoustical guitar.

But the turning point was their long, theatrical straight old Stones Midnight Rambler. Against the impressive guitar work, Jagger sang and acted out the story of a rapist, with explosive contortions, down on the floor, taking off his belt, almost throwing the microphone into the crowd. And when it was over, the Stones had everyone in the audience digging them on their own terms.

Then they whipped into some of their best songs: Satisfaction, Honky Tonk Women and finally Street Fighting Man. But not before Jagger had the house lights on so he could see his audience and exclaim (taunt?) "Are you not beautiful!?"

The Stones' music began from their appreciation of the culture, with all its contradictions, of the Black underclass. They continue to identify, to push to the extreme their identification with all, the outcasts whose lives indict our culture ("I want to dedicate this song to all the fags and junkies in the audience"). And with every performance Jagger taunts the audience, plays to them, plays with them, plays on every taboo. Their performance is a combination of great rock and the theater of the absurd and the cruel. It is not just that their lyrics accuse—their music expresses, releases, incites the anger and rebellion of a generation whose national anthem screams "I can't get no satisfaction."

OLD MOLE

12/5/69

THE MOTHERS OF INVENTION
FRANK ZAPPA

" If you want to come up with a singular, most important trend in this new music, I think it has to be something like: it is original, composed by the people who perform it, created by them – even if they have to fight the record companies to do it – so that it is really a creative action and not a commercial pile of shit thrown together by business people who think they know what John Doe and Mr. Jones really want. We did 'Freak Out' a long time ago if you measure time the way the clock of music is running today. Our new things are not released yet; it takes a long time. Some people are just starting to find one of our records which is far behind what we're currently doing.

"I think that as far as music in America today is concerned, rock is probably the most vital, most alive sort of music, but it doesn't know what the hell it's doing most of the time . . . I'm not on intimate terms with most other groups, but the ones I do talk to don't seem to really know what music is. They don't have an aesthetic understanding about what or why they compose. They simply don't get into it on that level. They're concerned with this attitude of 'Doing their thing' – whatever the fuck that is supposed to mean! Probably what they finally do is much better than what they are, if you know what I mean. Because they don't have the equipment or the background to really develop themselves on an aesthetic level. For me it's different. I care a great deal about music; all kinds of music. And I have helped, I really think that I've helped to turn some kids on to some of the important music they may be

I used to save up for a month, so I could get an R & B album and, the same day, the completed works of Anton Webern. Maybe that means something. Maybe that tells you something about my music. So if they think it's all weirdness, well, okay, as long as they listen to it. At least they know I'm alive.

'You also have to take some notice of the way rock has changed the public's ear. You know, it was pretty rough to expect most people to listen to a recorder or a Bach trumpet and that sort of instrument. For some reason it takes exposure for us to get into the sound of various instruments, let alone electronic music. We have made a lot of progress. Let's face it, kids are listening to the classical string quartet without suffering. That's pretty heavy stuff. It's like in the olden days they used to think atonally; that any chord and any key was okay . . . at one time that was very advanced theory. Then they said that it was no longer necessary to even think about key at all. We'll just treat all 12 tones equally. But they didn't really do much to the space between the notes: they kept a pretty austere view of rhythm. Some of the things I write have all kinds of chords within keys that nobody expected to find there, and there are other things, some of the things we use don't even make use of what you would call noise. For me the art of composition is the art of assembling anything. The packaging is to a certain extent an extension of the work itself. If a person who gets one of our products in their home has

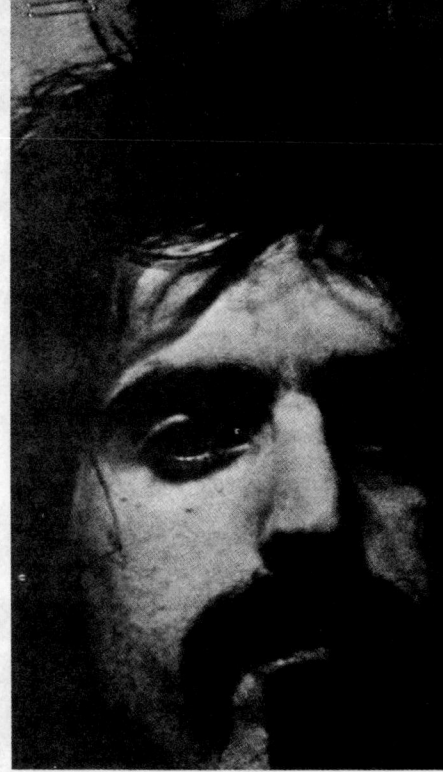

Frank Zappa

...enough perspective to sit back and view the whole package — well, I think he would find some pretty revolutionary ideas.

"There always was a lyrical Frank Zappa except for one thing. It's quite possible to take any tune and play it and make it sound horrid. Arranging is a science and the clothes in which you dress up any tune makes a lot of difference in the way people hear it. For instance, you can take something that's really a bullshit tune and play it on a pretty instrument or have the strings play it and it becomes nice — or you can play something that's really an interesting melody and really has something happening chord-wise and play it on a fuzz-tone guitar and you're going to get a completely different effect from it. So, a lot of the things I've written have never been played prettily and mostly that was done on purpose. Also, you have to understand that most people like to perceive satire in what I do. I mean that they really aren't into the music; they are too hooked on the pure theatre side of the music. They're listening to a comedy routine and they want to listen to it that way because unfortunately, a lot of people aren't really equipped to evaluate any other kind of artistic structure. You know as well as I do that for an audience there's nothing easier than comedy."

Rock and Other Four Letter Words Bantam 1968

Gradually, rock has made everything possible because it is capable of and willing to assimilate everything. . .because a fantastic number of kids are willing to listen. From freak out — which was a fairly primitive and mind-blowing break with the past — we have gradually moved into a new bag. We mention lots of experimental composers on our album covers; and that could do more to get kids into the heavy stuff than all the preaching in the world. That's a hell of a lot more for culture than Babe Ruth offered!

BLOW THEIR MINDS

By Frank Bardacke

I begin writing about Bobby Dylan with some uneasiness. If we are not careful we will analyze and classify him to death. Everybody wants a piece of his action ("You never understood that it ain't no good / you shouldn't let other people get your kicks for you") and "relating him to American politics" is my own particular game. But I proceed in the spirit of one of his own songs:

I ain't lookin' to
block you up
shock or knock or lock you up
analyze you
categorize you
finalize you
or advertise you
all I really want to do
is baby be friends with you

I suppose the picture on Bob Dylan's most recent album, *Blonde on Blonde* was only meant to catch our attention. But look at it. There he stands, slouched against a wall, with his fuzzy hair out of control, his eyes indefinite, and his whole body somehow out of focus. It is hard to believe that this is the same young man as the one on the cover of *The Times They Are a-Changin'* issued only two years before. Then he appeared on the album jacket sharply focused in black and white with a straightforward jaw, serious eyes, and wearing a work shirt. These contrasting photographs are only a partial indication of the changes that Dylan has crammed into the last two and one half years of his life. Changes that have led many in the American left either to dismiss Dylan as a sell-out or to warn others against following him down the road to political quietism. He is seen as a threat to the left, representing an anti-political response to the increasing crises in American life. It is

often said that he has rejected politics and retreated into his own private concerns and fantasies.

But it is not too far back to the Spring of 1964 when *The Times They Are a-Changin'* was released and Dylan was the darling of the left. In those optimistic days Dylan usually sang in clear tones about plain truths. His direct lyrics either denounced the "masters of war" or celebrated a new world about to be created when "the ship comes in." Dylan was singing about war, poverty, and race murder, just as a good left-wing folk singer should. Many thought that he was a new Woody Guthrie (a man he claimed as an idol), bringing a fresh mind to the old problems.

The people who considered him a new Woody Guthrie should have listened a little harder. Most of Dylan's better songs were not traditional protest songs. He had a private vision that could not be contained within the standard "protest" idiom. That is what made "A Hard Rain's A-Gonna Fall" such a magnificent song. The eerie juxtaposition of ideas in that song ("I met a young child beside a dead pony/ I met a white man who walked a black dog/etc.") took it out of the confines of the usual anti-war songs. It is not a safe song. Dylan violated ordinary thought sequences and thereby convinced us that the mere contemplation of nuclear war is a violation of the human spirit.

But these strange songs were pretty much ignored, along with his love songs and his nonsense songs. He became famous through his more obvious protest songs ("finger pointing songs" he calls them now). Some of these political songs, like "Blowin' in the Wind," became so popular that Dylan became a semi-official spokesman of the civil rights movement. He sang at civil rights rallies and appeared at movement benefits. The left was sure they had a spokesman. Bob Dylan, however, was not so sure. With his next

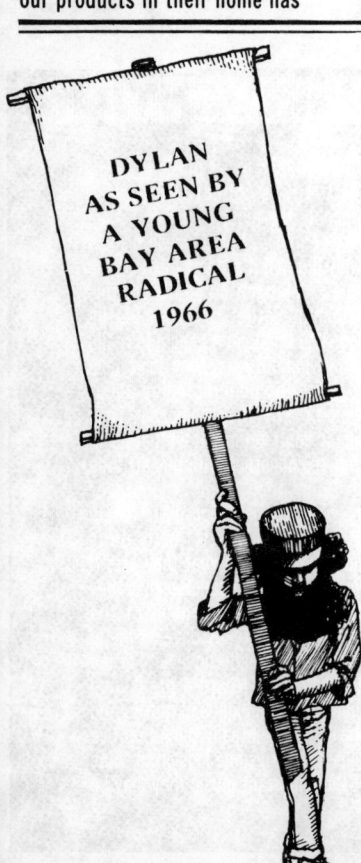

DYLAN AS SEEN BY A YOUNG BAY AREA RADICAL 1966

own ambivalence about the traditional battles of the left.

This change in attitude is best expressed in a song on that album called "My Back Pages." Dylan says that in his earlier songs he "lied" by saying that "life is black and white." He dreamed of romantic battles and assumed the stance of a fighter and preacher. This preaching lead to an intense seriousness and to songs that made everything seem simple and easy. He closes "My Back Pages" with this complaint:

> Good and bad I'd defined these terms
> quite clear no doubt somehow
> but I was so much older then
> I'm younger than that now

Anyone who missed the point of this song could have looked at the poem on the back of the album which stated even more strongly his uneasiness about "good and bad." The poem begins,

> run go get out of here
> quick
> leave joshua
> split
> go fit your battle
> do your thing
> i lost my glasses
> cant see jerico
> the wind is tyin' knots
> in my hair
> nothing seems
> t be straight
> out there
> no i shant go with you
> i cant go with you

Dylan can no longer see jerico; he is not so sure of right and wrong ("good and evil are but words/ invented by those / that are trapped in scenes," he says later in the poem.) This does not mean, however, that Dylan was falling back into a position of complete relativism and saying that it was impossible to tell good from evil. What Dylan is complaining about are highly abstract notions of morality that have little to do with the way people actually act and feel.

This is illustrated by the central incident of the poem. Dylan is in a crowd watching a man who is about to jump off the Brooklyn Bridge. He realizes with horror that he, along with the rest of the crowd, wants to see the man jump. This realization smashes all of his claims to be a fighter for good against evil. All his abstract beliefs in "good" did not help him have a decent emotional response toward a man who was about to commit suicide. He leaves the scene seeking some explanation for his terrifying reaction. He is convinced that the explanation will not be found in any left wing abstraction about good and evil. He seeks to find the answer through an understanding of the more direct personal experiences of Americans. He even approaches some answers in this poem:

> loneliness has clutched
> hands an squeezes you
> into wronging others
> everybody has to do things
> keep themselves occupied

He also comes to realize that:

> slaves are of no special color
> an the links of chains
> fall into no special order

The left has been mistaken. It is not only the Negroes who are in chains, but all Americans who are trapped by an uneasy boredom, by loneliness, and by god knows what else. These are the chains that Dylan wants to break. He is convinced that the only way to freedom is through an understanding of his own personal dilemmas. And he knows that such an understanding will involve him in an exploration of the terrible anxiety of middle class American life.

To understand Dylan's disenchantment with the left it is important to remember the position of the days of apparent victories, the movement had a straightforward ideological technique. Leaders emphasized the discrepancy between American ideals and the American reality, and claimed that the purpose of the civil rights struggle was to close that gap. But Dylan had come to doubt the ideals themselves. In "My Back Pages" he criticizes himself for having said that "liberty is just equality in school." He leaves the movement because he does not think that it has any answers to the real problems of most Americans.

So Dylan was no longer interested in those acceptable protest subjects of war, poverty, and discrimination. He was now concerned about the problem of freedom. At the recording session for *Another Side of Bob Dylan* he told Nat Hentoff, "I looked around and saw all these people pointing fingers at the bomb. But the bomb is getting boring, because what's wrong goes deeper than the bomb. What's wrong is how few people are free. Most people walking around are tied down to something that doesn't let them really speak, so they just add their confusion to the mess..."

But has Dylan gotten anywhere in his new search? What has he told us about freedom in his most recent songs? Has Dylan deserted the old themes, only to have the new ones overwhelm him?

In the next to last verse in the song "I Shall be Free No. 10" Bob Dylan sings,

> I'm goin to grow my hair down to my feet so strange
> so I look like a walking mountain range
> then I'm goin to ride into Omaha on a horse
> out to the country club and golf course
> carrin' a New York Times
> shoot a few holes
> blow their minds

Bob Dylan intends to "blow their minds." It is a common phrase now, originating with the dedicated experimenters with drugs, and quickly filtering up into the rest of society. And the phrase is the key to a new road to freedom.

Look at our situation. The most important reason why middle class Americans do not act to change their lives is because they can not conceive of a different kind of life. Most Americans believe that America is the "good society", and that this is the "good life." Any unhappiness, or boredom, or despair, therefore, is not blamed on society but rather on yourself. All failures are personal failures. After all, in this society if you "have it" you will "make it." Dylan hints at how this works in "Its Alright Ma (I'm Only Bleeding):"

> Advertising signs they con
> you into thinking that you're the one
> that can do what's never been done
> that can win what's never been won
> meantime life outside goes on
> all around you

Americans are overwhelmed by the social order that exists. People simply can not conceive of an alternative society, even in their wildest dreams. Rather, the fantasies of our adult lives are provided for us by the various mass media. They are safe fantasies as they only reinforce the pre-existing values of the society. James Bond, for example, is the safest of fantasies. We watch Bond and dream about miraculous personal success, new powerful gadgets, and fantastic sexual conquests (as distinct from sexual satisfaction.)

These dreams of ambition and accomplishment are encouraged, while we destroy the dangerous fantasy lives of our children. Thus, the genuinely erotic fantasies of childhood are warped and degraded into visions of sexual battle. And when the society has powerful tools with which to impose its own set of fantasies, we are left with little psychic space to conceive of alternative ways to live our lives.

This is what is completely missed by those who claim that Bobby Dylan has deserted radical politics and is now acting out the politics of escape. The very first mission of the American radical is to escape. If he does not escape from American values and the American vision of society, then his political activity is meaningless. The radical must present a counter vision, he must create new values. No matter how militant any particular action is, if it does not take place in the name of a different vision of society then it will be easily absorbed, muted, and incorporated into the American morass.

So Bobby Dylan has escaped. He has held onto his dangerous fantasies. And he intends to "blow their minds." In a society where the most important restrictions of freedom are the limitations on consciousness, "blow their minds" is the rallying cry of freedom fighters. It is roughly equivalent to the cry of an older historical period, "break your chains."

But not exactly equivalent. The phrase was not "break your chains," it was "you have nothing to lose but your chains." The parallel then is "you have nothing to lose but your mind." And that is Dylan's message. If you hope to achieve freedom the first thing that you must do is escape from the values of American society. But such an escape is dangerous and the attempt to lose old values may eventually cause you to lose your mind.

This warning brings us to the use of drugs as an attempt to transcend American values. In the technological society that limits consciousness, a technological device (drugs) is used to expand consciousness. And Bob Dylan has written the great American ode to drugs, "Mr. Tambourine Man," which sounds significantly like a childhood fantasy. The tambourine man has taken the place of the drinking gourd; you now follow him to freedom.

> And take me disappearing
> through the smoke rings of my mind
> down the foggy ruins of time
> far past the frozen leaves
> the haunted frightened trees
> out to the windy beach
> far from the twisted reach
> of crazy sorrow
>
> yes to dance beneath the diamond sky
> with one hand waving free
> silhouetted by the sea
> circled by the circus sands
> with all memory and fate
> driven deep beneath the waves
> let me forget about today
> until tomorrow

But Bobby Dylan is no Timothy Leary; he knows the road to freedom is a difficult one and that many get lost along the way. The danger is obvious. Dylan attempts to transcend America simply by believing in new values. That is, he tries to overcome American ideology without struggling against the institutions that support it. It is a heroic and a lonely struggle as there is no movement of opposition that could give the young rebel a secure home and protect him from the competitive pressures of the larger society. Dylan is remarkably sensitive to this dilemma, and it is the subject of one of his best poems and many of his songs.

> Jim Jim
> where is our party?
> where is the party that's one
> where all members're held equal
> an vow t infiltrate that thought
> among the people it hopes t serve
> an sets a respected road
> for all of those like me

But there is no party and there is no respected road. And finally he says that you can not even follow the tambourine man to freedom. In the summer of 1965 the problem becomes clear in one of Dylan's best songs.

> How does it feel
> how does it feel
> to be on your own
> with no direction home
> like a complete unknown
> like a rolling stone

Dylan's lonely search has not really led him to the creation of new values. But the creation of the new always begins with the destruction of the old. And in that Dylan has succeeded. The only way to appreciate this destruction is by listening to the songs themselves, but I will try to give an example without doing too much violence to the song. In "Bob Dylan's 115th Dream" he lampoons a totally commercialized America; an America of the wheeler-dealers where everybody is out to screw everybody else. From the moment Dylan steps off the boat onto American soil he is jailed, charged, robbed, and robbed again. As soon as Captain Arab sees America he plans to buy it with beads (at a bargain). Dylan later needs money (for bail) so he goes to a bank where they want "collateral." Dylan pulls down his pants, but that is not enough. (If he could have banked that, would it have grown 5½% per year?) Dylan is rolled by a girl who steals his boots. He encounters a funeral director who gives him a card and says, "Call me if they (his friends) die." In order to get a coin to flip he has to hock his sailor suit. When he gets back to the ship he finds a parking ticket, etc.

To the formal American left, of course, all of this means very little. The attempt to escape from America by creating new values is hardly a sufficient goal for the political activist. The only way that change can be made meaningful is by creating new institutions which actualize these new values. The left asserts that Dylan and his compatriots are not building a new society and do not seem to want to help those that are struggling against the old one. They also argue that it is impossible for this group of disaffiliated middle class kids to build any institutions that could possibly rival the dominant structure of American society.

The obvious answer to such an argument is that the creation of new values or at least the destruction of the old ones can be an important first step (and for most Americans an enormous first step) in constructing counter institutions. But there is a more direct answer. These middle class drop-outs are building counter institutions, it is just that the American left does not know how to look for or recognize them. What about the Diggers, that new group of San Francisco hippies, who live together and everyday provide free food for anyone who can make it to the San Francisco Panhandle? And what about the new bands? All the members of any one band usually live together in one big house and form the nucleus of a little community. These small communities are daily living out significant social experiments on a scale which exceeds any previous conscious effort by Americans to set up experimental communities. And nowhere in these groups is there any of the debilitating self-consciousness that usually ruins Utopian experiments. These people do not look upon themselves as Utopians; they are simply trying to live their lives.

This is not to say that these bands and the new Diggers have the answer. I am only arguing that when looking for social and political change in modern America it is a mistake to focus only on direct and obvious political action. If fundamental change ever does come to America it will be such an astounding occurrence, that it is impossible to tell who will be in the vanguard and who in the rear.

Nobody thinks that the new society is almost here. But the old one seems to be breaking up. When it comes to the destruction of American values, Dylan has had a lot of help in the last few years. The daily newspapers read almost like Bob Dylan songs—and his most vicious anti-American songs at that. Dylan speaks for more and more people when he sings,

Though the masters make the rules
for the wise men and fools
I have nothing, ma
to live up to

Or maybe it isn't significant that "Mr. Tambourine Man" and "Rolling Stone" were the number one selling records in America. Maybe Dylan just happens to be in fashion. Perhaps the kids who bought those records don't really care about the content of the songs. After all, it is hard to hear the words on many of his big rock records and maybe they are only listening to the big beat. ("It ain't me, Babe," a fine song by Dylan was up near the top of the list, but so was "I got you, Babe," a bad, bad song by Sonny and Cher which had the Dylan style.)

But maybe some of them are getting the message. Maybe these young kids will be our political comrades. It is hard to tell. But walk over to the local high school (this is especially good if you live in Berkeley) and watch them walk out of school. Many of them look like my idea of the American exiles in Paris in the 1920's. Maybe together we can make a revolution. Or maybe it is all just my private fantasy.

Steps No. 1, Dec 1966

TEARS OF RAGE!
TEARS OF GRIEF!

SANDY DARLINGTON

Bob Dylan was a kid named Zimmerman who came flashing out of Minnesota a few years back, riding the legends of Woody Guthrie and Hank Williams inside his head like he was hitching a ride on the Wabash Cannonball. He zoomed into New York and into the lives of a lot of folk-scene people who didn't understand how anyone could hitch a ride on a legend and have it all be in his mind.

That was cool at first, because he didn't understand it either, but when he kept going toward life and being out front, it put a lot of heads through hard changes. It was just three summers ago that Mike Seeger told me that he still didn't understand what that song was about.

Meanwhile, those wars have grown cold. We've left them behind at last, like the bones from a good meal, and we've all started to flow together, so that now Bob Dylan, once the arch-individualist (or so a lot of us categorized him), is making music with a band. Moreover a band that lives out in a big pink house in upstate New York, a band of people who mess around together for the purpose of making a music that is a statement of exactly where they as individuals and as a group are at.

Right now, Americans are involved in a very intense conversation about how we want to live our lives. What do we mean when we say we love? Everybody is talking about this, from Eldridge Cleaver to Fat Hubert, and each is spinning what he feels is the pertinent mythology.

The straight world's myths are based on games and fences, isolation and emptiness. Recently, Time Magazine put John Updike on its cover because of his novel "Couples." Time looked on the novel as a mix of sexual play plus down-home commuter-village philosophy. Which it is. It's a documentation and celebration of a diseased way of living.

Those people were born and trained to be work freaks. Why are we on this planet? Don't ask me, I haven't time for silly questions, I've got to work work work, sweat provide defend toil puff puff. But in the course of things, they built all this labor-saving machinery that frees them from the necessity of toil. All of a sudden, they are surrounded by Free Time. Nothing to do. O God, what a terror!

They look around frantically. Why am I alive? What should I do? And there's no answer. Their billboards surround them and echo back their questions. They're strangling in their own boredom.

So they screw their neighbor's wife in the back seat of a car in a closed garage with the motor on, so the fumes accumulate along with their passion. Air pollution and orgasms. What a trip!

The clever man in that world is one who sums up this picture, sells it and gets enough money to afford to continue to play out the same games. No wonder Time dug it. Mind cancer is what they've got, and mind cancer is what they're selling.

But there are other ways to live that involve the central feeling of growth, of being with the Universe, of being part of the ecology. Your life should be a celebration of itself. You came from a seed, you are a plant, and your poems and songs are your wriggly branches of leaflets, they are your fingertips, your way of touching others. Music in such a life is a sound that arises from your calm center.

If you get hung up in the crossroads and can't discover where that deep source could possibly be inside yourself, then maybe you have to go back and come to terms with silence. Especially since that's where it all comes from anyway.

All sorts of people are making this pilgrimage back into themselves, into silence, and then waiting in the silence until they discover that being in the silence is the music. And then they make deeper music.

Thus it was with the person who had the famous name of Bob Dylan once. And thus it was with the others who for one reason or another ended up at this point in time hanging around with Bob Dylan in upstate New York. So out of their lives, they make this message of music and zap it out to our heads, and I write my message, and somebody standing on a corner stands his message, and we signal each other: Hey, Dig This! and Stick with it, Help is on the way. And so the word gets around.

San Francisco Express Times 7/17/68

* *

...then, as if a signal had been given, as if the Mind had shouted to the Body, "I'm ready!"— the Twist, superseding the Hula Hoop, burst upon the scene like a nuclear explosion, sending its fallout rhythm into the Minds and Bodies of the people. The fallout: the Hully Gully, the Mashed Potato, the Dog, the Smashed Banana, the Watusi, the Frug, the Swim. The Twist was a guided missile, launched from the ghetto to the very heart of suburbia. The Twist was a form of therapy for a convalescing nation...(which) responded so dramatically...to the Twist precisely because it afforded them the possibility of reclaiming their Bodies again after generations of alienated and disembodied existence...They came from every level of society...feeling...release from some unknown prison in which their Bodies had been encased, a sense of freedom they had never known before, a feeling of communion with some mystical root-source of life and vigor, from which sprang a new awareness and enjoyment of the flesh, a new appreciation of the possibilities of their Bodies. **ELDRIDGE CLEAVER** *Soul On Ice*

* *

About four weeks ago a new record store opened up on 16th and Wells called Van Winkle Sound. One of the owners is Tom Forester. Last spring, when a lot of things were beginning to brighten after a long winter, Forester directly helped the pigs bust fourteen brothers and sisters at UWM.

Now Forester says he's not a narc anymore, but what kind of position do we take towards someone who pigged on fourteen people? Forester hasn't done anything yet to show us that he wants to do something in 'retribution' for the East Side community. What can he do for those people still sitting in jail?

Milwaukee doesn't have a legal self-defense fund. Forester could help get one together by giving the community back some of the money he makes off our culture. Then we could begin to help people with bail hassles, etc. This is only one idea, but for the meantime a lot of us aren't going to buy his records. If you still want to buy his records, ask him about the bust and what he wants to do for the community. Once a pig, always a ?.

Life to the life culture!
Death to the death culture!

White Panther tribe

They Even Sell Songs

In a capitalist society everything is for sale—not only food, clothing and shelter, but even songs.

According to the current Rolling Stone, Albert Grossman will not permit any writer to quote the lyrics of a song by his top client, Bob Dylan, without paying a $1000 royalty fee.

In London, a battle is shaping up for control of Northern Songs, a music publishing firm which owns the copyright on 120 Beatles songs. The Beatles, who own 30% of Northern Songs, are seeking $14.4 million to use in a fight against Associated Television Company, which owns 35% of the company.

You are suppose to sympathize with the Beatles and with Dylan. You are supposed to be mad at Albert Grossman and at Associated Television. You sucker.

Let us by all possible means stand in the way of the shit that envelops us.

FLAUBERT

STOP LOOK whats that sound

everybody look whats goin' DOWN

by Bonny Cohen (with a little help
from Keith Maillard)

The sound is rock music.
What's going down is money.
Columbia records nets billions
from sales. On album jackets recording
artists are called "revolutionaries", but
CBS, which owns Columbia, has defense
contracts to help murder revolutionaries.
Rock stars wail out anger and scream re-
volt and leave concerts in Cadillacs (Jimi
Hendrix has a WHITE chauffer).

Pop music has become a financial
staple of US internal imperialism.

We tend to assume infinite co-op-
tability: U.S. money culture is a giant
amoeba or an octopus with stranglehold
tentacles. But how much spontaneity,
rebelliousness and sexuality can this
society absorb? Marcuse suggests the
pessimistic possibility of "repressive
desublimation:" totalitarian leisure, the
re-conversion of *class* America to enjoyment. But there are no signs of
institutional relaxation; schools, factories and carpeted corporation offices remain rigid and stultifying.
There's no rock in Congress. Adult
hip culture is a peripheral phenomenon,
despite its economic importance.

To young people, however, their
music is real, and crucial. Like drugs,
rock music is a component of cross-
class rebel youth culture. The music
is subversive. There is something about
that electronic energy which escapes
Madison Avenue's captivity.

Heavy rock music is rebellion
and disgust. It is a plea against loneliness, people reaching out over personal isolation barriers; it is raw sex -- "you
know you got it if it makes you feel
good."

And in groups of people rock has
become the energy of destruction.
When artists decimate their technological apparatus at the end of each concert, moneymakers pat their bellies: artificial obsolescence. But when a thousand young people storm musical festival gates, demanding *their* music FREE,
they run right up against the American
police wall. Many of this summer's
rock concerts have turned into police
riots. Lovely "Monterey Pop" is part
of history: "...if you're going to San
Francisco, you're sure to meet some
gentle people there..." PEOPLES
PARK: gas masks not flowers in your
hair.

In the Great Detroit Ghetto Riot
loudspeakers fed the flames with the
Doors' "Fire." Raiding New York's
Fillmore East in the middle of a con-
cert, police were fought off by the
Who on stage and kids in the audience.
Mick Jagger gave his original hand-
written manuscript of "Street Fighting
Man" to *Black Dwarf*, an English un-
derground paper, for their "Smash the
American Embassy" issue.

Violent concerts are not bread
riots, but they do create an energy of
revolt and a subliminal solidarity,
which can't be merely co-opted, desublimated, or even forcibly repressed.
The music is exclusively *ours*, not the
Man's, even if its profits bulge *his* capitalist pockets. Record companies want
money, so they're willing to cater to,
and foster, our desires for dangerous
music. But the frenzy of rock may be
turning against its purveyors.

Keith Maillard has been given a
half-hour over WBUR-FM, Wednesday
nights, to rap. He reads from the underground press. On Wednesday, July
23, he attacked the music establishment.

Reading from Mark Kramer, I.NS,
he asked: " 'How do we deal with the
rock hip imperialists who are ripping
us off?' " As tactics, he suggested exposure, extortion, and forcing artists
to give back profits to the communities
out of whose guts the music came
(Harlem, Haight-Ashbury, the southern
black backwater, the streets of doo-
wah-ditty New Yahwk City).

More from Mark Kramer:
*...rock may have come from the
streets...but in between you and the
performer is billions of dollars...some
record companies also have government
contracts...they'll make their money
by anti-war youth culture or by killing...Does this mean you shouldn't
buy records? Understand the facts of
life: you can't escape the Death Machine...We've got to put the finger on
those who are ripping us off...We've
got to get the message across to the
artists, get them to be non-exploitive...*

Cut to excerpts from Dick Gregory's new album, put out by Poppi
Records, a company attempting to be
responsible to the community which
listens to Gregory:
*...You tell me in that history
book of yours that you came to these
shores and DISCOVERED a country
that was already occupied. You think
about that...How did you DISCOVER
something that's not only owned by
somebody else but that's being used
at the time that you DISCOVER it?
That's like me and my old lady walking out of here tonight and you and
your lady sitting in your brand new
automobile, and my lady say, "Gee,
honey, that sure is a beauty-ful automobile, I sure wish it was mine."
I'll say: "Well, Lillian, let's DISCOVER
it."*

Few radio stations will play
that album. Radical programming has
great potential. It's a part of the underground which takes advantage of
the overground: Keith was using the

media to attack the media. Radio
speaks to a faceless mass, but it speaks
almost spontaneously (it doesn't take
much to flip a radio dial) and simultaneously to thousands of people.
And radical radio is popular. The
underground station beaming out of
Ann Arbor, Michigan is Detroit's third
most popular station.

For radio, as for underground
newspapers, the media has got to be
the message in order to get that message across. Keith hopes to do mon-
tages- the juxtaposing of music and talk,
parodies of ads ("Try out for Miss Imperialism," "How to Join Progressive
Labor"), and anything else that comes
into his imagination. If successful, Keith
hopes to expand to a half-hour a day of
radical news reporting.

P.S. "the Underground News" is
broadcast by Boston University's
listener-sponsored station. The program's continuation depends very
much on supportive response from listeners. Keith is open to suggestions.
for future programming. And
he will read sympathetic political announcements over the
air. Call him at the station
(266-1000) or at the Boston
Free Press (868-9788).

By airing some facts a-
bout recording companies,
Keith Maillard was attempt-

ing one of Mark Kramer's
suggested lines of attack -- exposure. But its limits are obvious. Ideological assault on
the media by its underground
is in many ways wasted energy. Appalling facts themselves
rarely generate revolt in a society as corrupt as ours. Madison Avenue is going to keep
selling our culture *as long as
it is for sale.*

Trying to radicalize artists also
has its limits. A singer will sell his soul
in order to sing it. Almost all of the
"stars" are insulated. In and out of
cities, in and out of their heads, few
relate to the movement. They don't
read underground papers. At the recent underground media conference,
Keith reports explaining to an amazed
Blood, Sweat and Tears man all about
the Columbia-CBS imperialism/music
nexus. He had no idea...

But like the mode of the music,
there is something about the artists
which works against their own corrupt
ties. It's their image, the Rock and
Roll Star: a beaded, or bearded, moving sex, drugged, wild-hairy, sensitive
but motherfucking tough, inscrutable,
pig-hating, stone rebel. No matter what
they really are, that's what they have,
to project. That's their *image* for
American youth (how to be cool, get
the girls).

OLD MOLE

8/1/69

The Eagles Liberation Front, a group of Seattle, Washington, high school radicals, have shown that economic pressure can force rock ballroom operators to meet the needs of the audience. Their boycott of Eagles Auditorium, a rock ballroom in Seattle, has resulted in promoter Boyd Grafmyre lowering his prices and expanding services to the community.

The ELF came into being in early December, after Grafmyre had announced that smoking dope and "making out" were forbidden. To the weekly patrons, this was the last in a long series of outrages the audience—made up mostly of high school students—had put up with. They began leafletting the high schools and picketing the Auditorium calling for a boycott.

They amazed Seattle's radical community by bypassing them completely. They refused an offer of help from the Weathermen. They went to the underground paper, *Helix*, for advice, but refused to let the paper's staff join them in negotiating with Grafmyre. They wanted to do their own thing.

"Rock music began in the alternative community, our community," their leaflet read. "Rock expresses the ethos of our community, its force is filled by our struggle. But over the years, the established entertainment industry—promoters, agents, record companies, media, and every name group have gradually transformed our music into an increasingly expensive commodity. They have stolen our music.

"We are taking it back!"

After a couple of weeks of boycotting, Grafmyre had to make some major concessions. Specifically, ticket prices were lowered from $3 in advance and $4 at the door to $2.50 and $3.50. Double shows will now begin earlier and last three and one-half hours instead of three. Eagles will now be available for community benefits, and weekly audition concerts will begin, with $1 admission, with the proceeds going to the groups involved. Uniformed police will be excluded from the hall except for two officers guarding the box office as required by the insurance company. The Eagles staff will be permitted to unionize, and fire precautions have been updated.

Finally, and most interestingly, Grafmyre would attempt to arrange meetings between the ELF and rock musicians and managers to discuss questions about the cost of rock and roll music. ELF realized that the main problem stems from the prices of the top rock bands and the expensive nature of the music industry. They committed themselves to boycotting those groups which have priced themselves out of Eagles.

The struggles of the ELF in Seattle set a good example of what can be done in Atlanta, specifically concerning the pop festival. The promoters of the festival are now in the process of choosing the bands. If people could get together, demands could be raised concerning the exorbitant prices of pop festivals and the lack of relationship to the community which fosters and provides the best audience for rock music. Bands can be induced to lower their fees and promoters can be forced to stop ripping off profits from the community.

The ELF statement puts it right when they said, "This struggle will not end until Eagles and music have been completely returned to the community. This struggle will continue until the culture vultures who prey on our community have been eliminated."

—jeff berchenko, condensed from *Rolling Stone*

2/9/70

ELFROCK

BOOTLEG RECORDS

Madison has seen a rash of bootleg records -- most sold at super high prices -- and the gigantic profits going to who knows who.

Now, however, some of us who feel that freak-rock belongs to the people from where it came, have liberated Dylan and Beatles tapes and returned the music to the people.

Here's the story:

The Beatles recorded a whole bunch of songs for their soon-to-be released "Get Back" album which will come out when they get their movie (also called "Get Back") finished. The tapes we acquired were thecuts that were excluded from the commercial "Get Back" LP.

The three Dylan cuts on the community's record were recorded live at his recent Isle of Wight concert (his first concert in years) and are really exciting to hear.

As far as we know, this is the only bootleg album with anything from the Isle of Wight festival.

So, the money was put up and 1000 records cut, with a possible 1000 more later. The album sells for $3.00 -- and every penny except for the cost of manufacture will be returned to the community. The bail fund especially will benefit. The community outlets selling the album receive the proceeds from the sales (IF they need the bread like many co-ops do) or donate their share to the Bail Fund.

This album is a step toward reclaiming the people's music from filthy-capitalist record companies. And a lot of people are also thinking very seriously about the planned rock festivals for Madison this summer and how to deal with them.

John Sinclair is on the album cover for a purpose. Ten years in jail for two joints is what we're all about. Dig it?

Over His Dead Body

by Jill Johnston

I was privileged to be present Friday night, March 21, at Judson Church, at the most unusual manifestation of a performer-audience situation I have witnessed in a decade of attending a theatre in which the performer-audience relationship has been pushed in every conceivable direction. Unusual is a mild word for it. It was a kind of psychological trauma involving two principals and the rest of us in a spontaneous drama expressing the agony and the comedy of the condition called human. The occasion was the Destruction in Art Symposium preceded by Destruction events in Judson's back yard.

The atmosphere in the yard was a bit like a bazaar — the spectators milling around passing from one set - up to another: an excerpt from Hermann Nitsch's Orgy - Mystery theatre; Lil Picard with plastic bags full of feathers set to flaming on a charcoal burner; Steve Rose standing by a frying pan on a hot plate cooking an orange and a banana; Bici Hendricks handing out ice picks to anyone wishing to hack at a large vertical hunk of ice surrounded by raw eggs; and preparations for Ralph Ortiz's chicken-killing event was the first presentiment of a rumble nobody expected. The two live chickens were strung up from trees several yards apart. John Wilcock calmly cut the chickens down and, assisted by Michael Kirby, made off with them to an adjoining yard to release them over a high fence. Ortiz later said he was delighted the chickens were rescued. He accepted the frustration of his plans as a worthwhile event in itself and re-programmed himself by subsequently attacking the two trees (he climbed one, Jon Hendricks the other), sawing a limb off each one after a preparation (pouring) of the cow's blood originally to have been part of the chicken scene. The attitude Ortiz assumed about the interference in his thing became relevant to the amazing drama that ensued inside at a scheduled panel of the artists involved. A soap-box orator from the yard, whose hysterical blather was punctuated with a few brilliant remarks, threatened to dominate proceedings in the lecture-room. Hendricks, Ortiz, and Hansen accepted him without relinquishing their own purpose and somehow finally integrated him in the total situation.

Hendricks announced a performance by Charlotte Moorman of Nam June Paik's "One for Violin," a piece dating from 1961. I knew the piece from Paik's performance of it in '64 at a Fluxus concert. In a rather disorderly atmosphere Miss Moorman assumed the appropriate concentration and a courteous hush fell over the room. The piece entails the destruction of a violin after a long preliminary passage in which the performer raises the instrument in slow motion from a position at right angles to the waist to a position over the head in readiness to smash the thing on impact with table. Miss Moorman got maybe one minute into the act when a man from the back tried to stop her. She dispatched him with a push and resumed the performance. Another more determined spectator approached the table and the war was on. Charlotte was angry. She demanded to know who he was (translated: who the hell do you think you are?). He said he didn't want her to break the violin. "By breaking a violin," he said, "you're doing the same thing as killing people." And something about

giving it to a poor kid who could use it. Attempting to go on with the piece she said, "this is not a vaudeville routine" and "this is not an audience - participation piece." But he persisted and I think Charlotte slapped his face and suddenly there was a tragedy in the making and shock-waves in the air and terrific agitation all around. Someone suggested he give her his coat in exchange for the violin. He removed his coat but she wouldn't have any of it. I was inspired by this suggestion and found myself hollering in the din: GIVE IT TO HIM. Charlotte accused her intruder of being as bad as the New York police. He announced that "we are sitting down and refusing to allow this violin to be broken." He forthwith stretched himself out on his back on the table in front of her. As Ortiz said later— she had to over his dead body. It happened very fast and there are probably as many versions of the climax as the number of people who were there. As I saw it, Charlotte's tormenter sat up and was sitting on the edge of the table and at some moment turned to face her at which point with malice aforethought she bashed him on the head with the violin and the blood was spilled. My description can't do justice to this extraordinary situation. The ramifications are extensive. It wasn't so much a question who was right or wrong (I thought, if pressed, both were right and both wrong), but what might have been done to avert the inevitable. That seems the ultimate political question so

brilliantly posed by this little war right in the ranks of those so violently opposed to the war at the top.

The victim introduced himself as Saul Gottlieb. Charlotte was contrite and ministered to his wound. She explained the point of the piece is to show that we think nothing of killing people in Vietnam and we place a higher value on a violin. She said she didn't mean to hit him but he was in her performance area. Speaking of the therapeutic value of such actions Ortiz said Charlotte was trying to displace her hostility onto an inanimate object and Gottlieb wouldn't let her do that. Our soap-box man said that if "we the people want to come into the government" (represented here as artists) "we should be able to." He also told Gottlieb he was sick because he stood there and let her hit him with his back turned. Gottlieb said that Charlotte was determined to break the violin regardless of what happened and was unable to de-program herself. The adjustment Ortiz made in his chicken event became instructive. What were Charlotte's alternatives in the face of being robbed of her artist thing? Blowing her cool she was left with a literal destruction. The irony of a symbol converted into a reality. Yet why didn't Gottlieb honor her appeal for attention? "I request the honor of your presence at . . ." etc. At what? At the daily level, let's say, how we take turns in a conversation piece. Many more things were said at the Judson gathering. The last thing I saw was a touch-

Voice: Fred W. McDarrah

CHARLOTTE MOORMAN and SAUL GOTTLIEB (right) in an angry confrontation at Friday night's Destruction in Art symposium at the Judson Memorial Church (the man in the middle is Jon Hendricks). As Miss Moorman neared the climax of a John Cage piece — the destruction of a violin — Gottlieb rushed forward out of the audience and demanded that the violin be given to a "poor needy child." Miss Moorman smashed the violin over his head.

ing demonstration by Steve Rose of a simple exchange based on respect. He requested the indulgence of his audience in a piece he wished to perform. He said it would begin when he finished talking and it would end when he sat down. He stood as he was and looked round slowly at the people there gathered, with some slight perplexity I thought. And that was the piece. And the audience expressed their appreciation at a point well taken.

the village VOICE
3/28/68

DOWN HOME RAUNCHY

W. C. FIELDS MEMORIAL ORPHANAGE

The Pitschel Players do evenings of improvised skits on Friday and Saturdays at 9 at St. John's Evangelical Church between 15th and 16th off Market. It costs $1.50 and there's free coffee, tea, donuts, wine, cheese ... donations cheerfully accepted. It's called the W.C. Fields Memorial Orphanage, and the content is changing all the time.

That's all we knew about it, except that one of the actresses is Robin McDonald, Country Joe's wife, and I'd been to the church for their wedding and she asked us to come see their show.

The show is in a hall with a stage, not in the church proper. It turns out that the population of the neighborhood has shifted so much that there's only a congregation of 25 left in the church. The whole place has a comfortable and run-down air like a 1948 stationwagon. A woman hands out leaflets on the grape workers' strike. A bunch of kids descend on the donuts and they disappear before your eyes. Various young ladies in shawls and their men with beards and long hair. We sit at card tables. The place fills up slowly, and everybody is genial.

The revue, I guess you'd call it, begins with a bunch of short skits, such as a Berkeley Radical talking with a soldier who's going to Vietnam next week, Adam and Eve in the Garden, a Channel 7 editorial on poverty which ends: "Some people say there's poverty in America, some people say there is none; Channel 7 believes the truth lies somewhere in between."

It's down home. San Francisco raunchy. People's theatre, out style. We are the people. That statement has a meaning on a barricade, it has another meaning when we are living our lives. The two go together. I think the straight world has died. In fact, it's

dying all over me. Over us. We scrape off its remains like soot and go on our way, creating things like this evening of theatre.

I felt I was in a neighborhood movie as a kid. All sorts of memories of the nice side of my history before I left where I grew up. It seems we have all come home again. Once I was clever. I had to become that to get away. It's like you have to reach a certain velocity to escape earth's orbit. Now I'm becoming simple again, like when I was a kid, and I could enjoy the humor at any level. Some of it was corny. And I dug it. It all had a homey air. This theatre wouldn't work well in the streets because it has an indoors feeling. But indoors in our kind of place, and this room at the church does that.

There's seven or eight actors, a director and a piano player. They have workshop/rehearsals twice a week, and they have a dream of someday getting a club where they could perform five days a week. They'd like to serve cheap meals and beer, plus coffee and pastries, set up their own atmosphere and let the whole thing become more intense by performing more often. They were amateurs once, not people trained in theatre, and they've been at this for two years until now they are really beautiful at it. They change hats and roles, and yet there's none of that clever bitchy air that usually hangs around theatre people like cheap perfume. And there's no upstaging. They thought up the skits and each person developed his own lines. It shows.

The finest skit, for me, came at the end of the first half. It took place in a truck-stop and was a dialogue between Frank the truck driver and Flo the waitress, made up of aimless bits of conversation that kept wandering and building into these huge oceans and mountains of inconsequential

words combined with real affection. She cooked him grouse eggs as a special treat. They were blue, and she said that when she mixed them with regular eggs it made a very pretty green. She wore paper bags on her feet because she'd just mopped and didn't want to make footprints. He said she was making bagprints. She agreed but said it was okay because they looked just like the floor. He asked for soy sauce, and she told him about the Chinese customer who had come in on a very foggy night and stolen the soy sauce out of the safe. She then brought out the six foot bottle of Worscestershire Sauce.

Robin who was Flo told us later that the skit had started during a workshop when they were satirizing the difficulty some actors had in handling imaginary objects, how when there were no props and actors had to represent them by their actions, imaginary tables shifted places, imaginary coffee was put on to boil, then forgotten, imaginary bottles grew larger. In this world of shifting space, the actors developed people who were just as vague, and the whole thing kept building into this 15 minute piece of surrealistic truck-stop burlesque like a cross between the Grapes of Wrath and Waiting for Godot.

Surreal, simple-minded, elegant, pratfalls, whimsy, zany and human like a day in the park, or like the Fish or the Skiffle Band. If you want entertainment that is Hard-Sell, Polished, Professional, Night-Club, Expense-Account: don't go. If you want to enjoy yourself and groove around with your friends: do.

sandy darlington

San Francisco
Express Times 9/11/68

THEATRE IN THE STREETS

and fresh air

There is, in these turbulent times, much talk of puppets.

Everywhere you look, you see one or several: Thieu, Barrientos, Humphrey. Almost all puppets have in common their attachment to the strings of the American Establishment.

Not so the Gutter Puppets, whose name derives from the fact that--their strings severed--they have descended (like risen angels) onto the waiting hands of our puppetteers on the streets below.

Disconnected from the powers at the top and answerable only to those on the bottom, the Gutter Puppets, unlike their "responsible" counterparts, are thoroughly irreverent, impeccably honest and brimful of information on how to succeed as a revolutionary in the midst of the labyrinth.

Though schizophrenic--they bear allegiance to both Malatesta and McCarthy (Charlie)--they will agitate, feloniously incite, and generally blow your mind. Those who are satisfied with the quest for bourgeois rewards should shun the Gutter Puppets, as they are guaranteed to damage such psyches irreparably.

If, however, your goal is to free humanity of imperialism, bureaucracy and the profit motive, call GE 1-1984 and ask for Punch the Red.

SAN FRANCISCO MIME TROUPE, INC., 450 ALABAMA STREET. SAN FRANCISCO CALIFORNIA 94110

ON THE SAN FRANCISCO MIME TROUPE

The Mime Troupe started in 1959 doing silent mime (the art of Chaplin — Marceau does pantomime) with the idea of restoring movement to a stage crippled by decades of realism. We broke into noise, and then speech, when our ideas became more complex: we now do plays, but mime is still the point of departure for our style, in which words sharpen and refine but physical action carries the substantial meaning. We did our first movement — noise happening, Event I — with artists Robert Hudson, William Wiley, and Judy Davis — in 1959, our first *commedia dell'arte* play, THE DOWRY — from Moliere, Goldoni, and improvisation — in 1960. Our interest in this 16th century form is not antiquarian. We use it because it is funny and adaptable, and because comedy is ultimately more serious than tragedy or realism.

In 1962 we went outdoors with a portable stage and performed our commedia show twice in San Francisco parks, passing the hat afterwards. We have done new commedias outdoors each year since. In 1965, the San Francisco Park and Recreation Commission refused us a permit to play CANDELAIO on the grounds of "vulgarity"; we played and were arrested, the ACLU appealed, and the refusal was ruled an unconstitutional attempt at censorship. (The controversy cost us our first and only grant.) In 1968, after another court fight, the Mime Troupe liberated the parks of Mill Valley, a suburb, and did six park shows a week from April through September.

We opened our indoor theater in December, 1963, with Jarry's UBU ROI, followed by plays, events, and movies: we presented a regular film series in 1964 under the direction of Saul Landau, showing such artists as Brakhage, Conner, and Genet (UN CHANT D'AMOUR). This phase ended in 1965 when our theater became a parking lot; since then we have lived from the parks and from engagements. We did mixed media: Brecht's EXCEPTION AND THE RULE with a talk on Vietnam by Robert Scheer, De Ghelderode's CHRONICLES OF HELL with poets Lawrence Ferlinghetti, David Meltzer, and Lew Welch,

and the first light-show rock dance at the Fillmore Auditorium (November, 1965).

Our work always referred to political concerns; it has come gradually to direct engagement. CENTERMAN, an original play about American brutality by Peter Berg, opened in 1966 at a teach-in rally in San Francisco and played Bay area theaters; SEARCH AND SEIZURE, about drug law enforcement, opened at a benefit for Timothy Leary and played as a cabaret theater piece. A MINSTREL SHOW, OR CIVIL RIGHTS IN A CRACKER BARREL (by Saul Landau and R. G. Davis) which exploded racist and integrationist clichés before Black Power, opened in 1965; it toured the U.S. and Canada for two years, during which time its prophecies became realities. Vietnam has escalated our consciousness as it has that of many. THE EXCEPTION AND THE RULE was our first play about the war; in 1966-67 we did a Brechtian production of Sartre's CONDEMNED OF ALTONA, which tries the individual for crimes of state; in 1967 Goldoni's L'AMANT MILITAIRE, freely adapted (by Joan Holden) to demonstrate the absurdity of pacifism in the face of the military machine; in 1968 Beolco's RUZZANTE RETURNS, about the disillusion of the returning soldier, and his response.

L'AMANT MILITAIRE and another commedia, OLIVE PITS, toured across country in 1967, hitting universities a jump ahead of Dow recruiters, then winning an Obie award in New York; when we came back we started our Gorilla Marching Band. We found that to play for an audience conscious of crisis, we had to know what we had to say. The new or guerilla theater (as opposed to the "New Theater" of neo-absurdist destinationless trips) accepts this responsibility; the next step is for radical theater to become revolutionary: from theater of exposure to theater of example. We have placed ourselves outside; outside the commercial market and outside in the streets and parks, because outside is the only place a revolution can grow. We have spent 10 years clearing a place; in the next 10 we will build a concrete alternative.   *Arts in Society No. 3,* 1969

⊗⊗

SIXTH STREET THEATRE

Street and Mobile Theatre, to provide an alternative to the prevailing moral and economic systems, for ourselves and our audiences. <u>Mime, acting and music,</u> working around an agreed-upon scenario. Permanent people only (a year or more). Volunteer at first, possible small salary after three months--will help find part-time jobs and/or room and board in the meantime. ---Contact Eileen LaRue; Sixth Street Theatre; 543 East 6th Street; New York, New York 10003; (212) 475-0434.

Vocations for Social Change

The Street Scene: Playing for Keeps
by John Lahr

WHEN THEATER GOES into the streets of America, its function and its tactic must change. The streets are not polite; they are silent monuments to boredom and despair, the fetid reminders that melodrama or song-and-dance do not approach a hard-won existence torn from squalor. In the open, the theater leaves its own conventional environment—controlled, safe, predictable—and faces what the world has created. That moment brings the insight—for to be valid as theater it must be true to the life experience of the people. Where television can speak for the aspirations of white, middle-class America, street theater goes deeper into the cultural complex of a city, drawing on its most vulnerable emotions, finding a successful form *only* when it has understood the unique elements of the local geography. To acknowledge the people, instead of forgetting them, is to become political.

Art has nothing to do with the life of a street. On 104th Street in East Harlem, the bongo drums tell Enrique Vargas, the organizer of Gut Theater, the tempo of the moment. "They sit on the window-sills or the rooftops playing. By the sound, you can tell if things are easy, if there's a Narco inspector around, or a shortage of heroin." What speaks in the street is not the reflective polish of a refined Western tradition, but something which 'fesses up to the brutality of hardcore poverty. When Joseph Papp tried to bring his Mobile Theater into Morningside Park in Harlem in 1964, ghetto youths, obeying their own territorial imperatives, threw rocks. Four years later, they sit respectfully through a performance of a black *Hamlet* only to heave chairs into the empty wooden rows after the performance or lob beer bottles over the park fence in the darkness. The intruder is not merely the white man, but a lifestyle with its implied suburban condescension. A black *Hamlet* does more for Shakespeare than the ghetto, adding a resonance to the soliloquies but little relevance to the poor. Papp himself questions the efficacy of his Mobile Theater. He is hamstrung between his private liberalism and an artistic mentality which will not give up its individuality for the people. As a result, his theater misses its audience. He confesses his impotence in the face of radical social change in America which needs a new theatrical language to encompass it.

Papp: There was a time when doing Shakespeare seemed all right. It doesn't seem so right now. In the last few years, it hasn't seemed right.
Interviewer: Maybe, that's because of the political situation?
Papp: Absolutely. Everything's changed to such a degree. I had a big argument with LeRoi Jones one time. "Shit," he said, "they don't need *Hamlet*. Give them plays about their lives."
Interviewer: I think he might be right.
Papp: He's partly right; but someone else would have to do that. It's not for us to do.
Interviewer: Why isn't it for the New York Public Theater to do?
Papp: Well, first of all, I wouldn't know what to do. We had Bobby Hooks go out one time—in an all Negro group with a thing called *We Real Cool*. We didn't create it; Hooks did it and we toured it. I wouldn't know what material to do.

Papp, a liberal dedicated to the theater, has lost sight of the terrain, like most of bourgeois America. He does not understand the world he would improve—neither the humor of the streets nor its demands. If he is concerned about the problem, his willingness to meet it balks when action moves outside art to a more dangerous commitment. The real street theater is indigenous to the community it serves rather than a form lopped onto it from antiquated concepts of the social situation. The myopic planning of most street events indicates the breach between the white-collar ideas of the streets and the vulgar reality. Papp, surveying his audiences after a Shakespearean evening, confides, half-expectantly, "Only a revolution can change this." His theater, despite its technical expertise, fails in the streets because it is too tepid to stand up for change while wistfully toying with the idea.

The Mobile Unit was conceived to play middle and upper income neighborhoods as well as ghetto areas. The two worlds do not mix. In his play, the black Prince beats up a policeman, entering in his uniform and talking a hard-line "To be or not to be. . . ." But a street audience, struggling with words or sensing an idea behind them, demands more than fine phrases. It does not want the culture of a world alien to its own; it cannot abide the condescension which comes with most forays into its own universe.

ENRIQUE VARGAS' theater, on the other hand, is more carefully planned. It does not arrive with a controlled environment like the Mobile Unit, or elaborate machinery (lights, microphones, etc.) which cuts off the *fact* of the streets rather than acknowledging it. If his work is a service, making the community aware of itself and its potential, the theater also respects the public imagination. Vargas never plays a street without casing it for a few days, observing the habits and rhythms of the people at different hours of the day. Even in his own work with local youths, his theater comes out of an understanding of their games, a fantasy world where the children do not play cowboys and Indians, but cops and junkies. "They kill everybody and then kill themselves in a shoot-out," explains Vargas. "I also study the games of tag, the magical words and different places of touch. You've got to know the architecture of the community, what are the most conducive kinds of communication. In East Harlem, drums and the Latin sound speak to the people. There is also a special kind of humor. Chaplin is much closer to our humor than, say, the Marx Brothers who belong to an English buffoon tradition. In Chaplin, the people see the harlequin, the servant who outwits the master. You've got to know what touches the people. What they laugh at, what they read; what comic strips are preferred; what approaches the local preachers use to reach them."

Most street theater discounts the lack of self-respect engendered by poverty or the impulses of an audience not bred to "culture." In order to "control" its audience, the Mobile Unit usually performs in fenced environments; there is an age restriction of sixteen years, and younger children must come with an adult. Ushers from the community police the aisles and the atmosphere becomes as fearful and repressive as that which the theater would transform. Recently, New York's Mayor John V. Lindsay inaugurated his own concept of a street event called Broadway in the Streets, reflecting a Republican booster impulse which trusts the Establishment and "professionalism," strangely alien to the ghetto population. Lindsay's statement about his street enterprise illustrates the moral cross-purposes that confuse placating the poor with sustaining their development. Sounding like George Babbitt at an Elks meeting, Lindsay announced to the press:

New York City is the capital of the entertainment industry. We have the finest in Broadway, night club, and recording artists. And yet with this abundant talent, there are thousands of youths in the ghetto areas of the city who have never seen live performances given by quality entertainers.

For this reason I am urging all our friends in the performing arts to join with me in the unique and vital opportunity to bring Broadway to the streets.

The attitude of *noblesse oblige* creeps into every public statement. What, indeed, is the Mayor bringing to the city slums? An image of wealth and success which reminds the audience of its own impoverishment, a moment in their daily struggle, communicating an excitement which quickly vanishes, leaving the sense of theatrical immediacy without the fact of it. Joel Grey, Jerry Orbach, Larry Blyden, Jule Styne—talented and well-intentioned—can only perform from the position of success they represent so gaudily. They have made it in the commercial world; the people who watch in Bedford-Stuyvesant have not.

BROADWAY IN the Streets, complete with Rotarian format (master of ceremonies, etc.) only reinforces the gap between the underprivileged and the middle-class communities. There is no sense of "quality" in living off the garbage of affluence. Instead of building local unity or struggling for a community redefinition of purpose, Broadway in the Streets asks its audience to have fun, to escape from the streets, when that prison is the one undeniable fact of life. The street audience—tough, cynical, and hungry—has been betrayed too often. "Whenever Broadway in the Streets tries to come down here, they'll get booed out," explains Vargas. "It's like getting Jerry Lewis to do a show for the Viet Cong. There's a different reality here. The mere presence of Broadway in the Streets is like a Madison Avenue advertisement — a reality which is a lie."

Despite its ridiculousness, Broadway in the Streets is certainly an improvement over last year's production of *The Ox Cart*, a melodrama about Puerto Rican life which toured under the auspices of Mayor Lindsay's Task Force. The tale traced a Puerto Rican family through their journey to the urban world and their subsequent disenchantment with America. The final horrendous lines of the play were: "We must go back to where we came . . . (it is) the land that gives life." Where El Teatro Campesino educates their Latin brothers to exercise their rights and Gut Theater works to unify Puerto Rican power, the city—predictably—chose to present a play which argued astoundingly for submission, rather than resilience and dignity. Where

El Teatro or Gut Theater can inspire laughter, rage, even joy to the streets, the more "sophisticated" Puerto Rican Traveling Theater could only reinforce the universal yawn between immigrant groups and the Establishment.

The emergence of street theater revives in America a much older impulse for a democratic event that haunted men like Diderot and Rousseau in other revolutionary times. A people's theater is just emerging in America after many fallow decades. Street theater at its best can call on the life-energy of the public, externalizing its inarticulate longings and confusions. An earlier poverty, unsure of itself and still clinging to a faith in the process of democratic government, founded the burlesque halls and vaudeville houses. Today there is no theater for the people. The showbiz fare does not reflect the hazards of their lives, while pricing them out of the theater-going community with seats on Broadway as high as $15 a ticket. The aestheticians of the past were thinking of actual theaters and a literary *oevre*. Times have changed; what is effective literature changes in political crisis. "Poet friends of mine feel their poetry makes 'more sense if it is scribbled on walls," explains Vargas. "Calls to incite people, to get people going can't be printed in hard-cover books. You know, $6.98—signed.'"

A theater for the people will never have the ideal conditions postulated by such theater dreamers as Romain Rolland (1866–1944) who begins his speculation about such an enterprise, "Supposing that the capital is secured and the public ready." Street theater uses adversity as part of its emotional impact. There will be little security for the enterprise and the public will be as prepared as the material which arouses its interest. Diderot (1713–1784) suggests a type of theater for his time now possible in our own:

Shall we ever have anything of the sort on our stage? There we can never show more than our action, while in nature there are many simultaneous actions, which, if performed at the same time, would intensify the whole, and produce a truly terrible and wondrous effect . . . We are waiting for the genius who will combine pantomime with dialogue, mingling dumbshows with the spoken scenes, and render effective the combination; above all, the approach, terrible or comic, to such simultaneous scenes.

Street theater is born out of a will to survive which accepts its heritage as well as life's variety. At its best, the random elements of street life reinforce the dramatic event. Genius in street theater is not the *bon mot* or the well-made plot, but the ability to judge the community and offer images which speak with force and passion to the problems which must be faced.

In the streets, the actor too must change his tactic. What succeeds on asphalt is energy and concern. Talent is an asset, but an artistic temperament is not. The actor who turns to the streets must acknowledge a more difficult relationship to his audience—where there is no reverence for the spoken word, where the audience may well talk back or throw something. In one performance of Papp's *Hamlet*, a fight broke out in the second act. The actors remained on stage momentarily, with Laertes observing in character, "Violence disgusts me." In the end, the entire company left the stage in what amounted to an artistic flap. The momentum of the performance was lost; the trust in the actors and their enterprise totally dissolved by their arrogance. The actor must become an activist, putting the people before his performance, the intention of theater ahead of the "literary" content of the play. The audience keeps the performer honest. "If you're doing something bad and someone throws a tomato, get out," suggests Joe Walsh, founder and chief freak of the Anyplace Theater in Minneapolis. "If you're good, the community of the audience will put a stop to it."

Many of the street events are rehearsed indoors for their outdoor activity This is true of Papp's Mobile Unit and also Teatro en la Calle, produced with the support of the New York State Council on the Arts and the Rockefeller Foundation. In both cases, the impulse is hopelessly out of touch with the facts of the street. "It's like learning to swim by jumping in the air," suggests Vargas. More important to the hundreds of bored audiences who sit and hear performers speaking into microphones, the immediacy and energy of street theater is never communicated, only an electronic hum where the performer focuses his efforts on speaking directly into the equipment rather than connecting with the people. Teatro en la Calle is significant because of its foundation support and its indubitable lack of quality. Instead of dealing with the moment, Teatro en la Calle adapts Chekhov and Molière stories for the street—an enterprise which would be annoying were it not laughable. Ancient fictions compounded with humor from some distant tradition and Spanish costumes from a Lupe Valez idea of Latin America cannot fool an audience which talks, laughs, and gazes at more interesting sights throughout most of the performance. Teatro en la Calle, like so many others, sets up an elaborate platform, speakers, equipment which cut the audience off from the event, and isolate the actors.

When street theater is effective, as with El Teatro Campesino or Gut Theater, the performers are responding to the environment and using it to further their effect. The language of survival becomes the tempo of urban life. As Vargas maintains, "The whole rhythm and energy which is given by a performance should be equal or bigger than the rhythm of the street at that given moment. If you're performing in the street and you're not in complete control of everything around you—the kid that just yelled, the fire sirens two blocks away, a person that pushed you—you're not connecting with anyone, you're not in control and you'll be laughed at."

The impulse of most street theater is to control the audience response and to disregard it if it does not seem pertinent. Teatro en la Calle marshals in local children as masqueraders for a brief and formal moment; Papp's Mobile Unit likes to peer down at the crowd, slap a few happy hands, but never allows the rapport to muffle the words. This reaction is a significant hangup of middle-class organizers who have not been taught to listen to their environment, because, insulated from ugliness, they have not struggled to stay alive. Vargas, who holds a degree in anthropology, knows the importance of understanding the patterns of his people. "The people around you are a chorus no matter what you think and cannot hear. You must perform *with* them rather than *at* them."

There seems to be no neutral ground in street theater: the art-oriented, middle-class ventures dwindle to mere caterwauling for lack of focus, balm for the performers' souls but superfluous to the life of the audience. The Task Forces, the "star" theaters, the myriad one-night stands become virtually useless, a lavish gesture to their own political myopia. Were the money squandered on such follies directed into community ventures—less attractive, more difficult, and even, perhaps, unsavory—the cause for liberty, for self-improvement, and the rights of the oppressed would be much more concretely aided. The presence of so many makeshift schemes merely confuses the hard task of organization, and convinces a bourgeois public which never dips its toe in unpleasantness that something is being done. This can also be true of radical groups like the San Francisco Mime Troupe. After walking through Harlem, the Mime Troupe's efforts seem like a Disneyland flotilla. Their enterprise dwindles to a chic if exciting idea in the face of poverty, a derivative commedia dell'arte which becomes a museum theater with almost no relevance beyond the college campus.

El Teatro Campesino (now El Central Campesino Cultural), like the Gut Theater, must become more than a street theater—a new way of life. At the Gut Theater local renovation problems and the lack of information have created the "Newspaper of the Truth," a whitewashed wall of the tenement where daily bulletins explain "what they think" and "what we think." The artist-workers for these organizations have denied prophetic individualism of the Western artist. Enrique Vargas, explaining his approach, puts it this way: "The artist who comes from the Western traditions of prophets and kings is a vain, a very selfish person by definition. The art-worker cannot be vain. He has to redefine his whole course of action. Who is he working for? Why? What language is he using? What does he have to get rid of? That is not just a question of his own artistic language but a question of what is happening all around him."

On 104th Street, a block which has been nicknamed by the neighborhood "Junkie's Paradise," there is a world worth fighting for, but it seems far away. What's happening is dope addiction, city indifference, police harassment, swindles, ignorance, festering shame and outrage. From the rooftop of the Gut Theater's tenement building, New York Central trains can be seen streaking safely to suburbia. On this roof, Vargas has posted warnings of the Revolution to scare commuters. He has also thought of choosing one train a day and, over a period of days, educating the window-gazers with information. Surrounded by rubble, encased by fences painted with words like "unity," "brotherhood," "power," is a squalor perpetuated by absentee ownership and a city's lethargy. Within the ashes, the Gut Theater may be regarded with skepticism by the older members of the community, but among the young it is a vital, active force, certain of its own identity, in charge of a momentum. "We don't like to call it a community center because of bad implications—but rather a communal house. We don't do this because we're social workers or somebody's paying us. We do it because we've got to get together."

In the past, the theater has been a powerful force in binding communities in a shared, articulate experience. Now Broadway inculcates a passive acceptance of the bourgeois world in its entertainments. Gut Theater and its many smaller, disenfranchised prototypes throughout America are talking about revolutionary action, using the theater to begin a debate and then following it with serious organizing. The Gut Theater has played in the streets for the last three months, trying to unify local opinion and action against renovation demands where the tenants, asked to evacuate (some after thirty-five years of occupancy), had no bargaining power and could not confront the landowners. Slowly, by showing that unity can have some effect, the Gut Theater can prove itself, just as El Teatro Campesino did—bringing pressure against larger industries to alter their exploitation, by winning a union contract for the grape-pickers and traveling the country.

Like any valid street theater, the form must come from the needs and traditions of the environment. Vargas has special training for his workers. "One thing I insist is for people who work with me to go to an Evangelical or Pentecostal Church service. They usually begin with singing, movement, sound. The preachers know when the right time has come; the people begin to say 'Amen' together. This never happens at the beginning—they warm up. They're going to make something happen with *their* universe. It's done in complete connection with the congregation—and this is what theater is all about." The impulse of street theater is to move forward rather than return to a form of the past. It can become a serious ritual, in much the same way as French drama in a decadent tradition caused Camus to write:

In Athens there was nothing at all frivolous about theater; performances took place only two or three times a year. And in Paris? They want to go back to something dead. It is much better to create your own style of drama.—*Carnets*

Vargas' plays capitalize on the emotional truth of the ghetto experience. "I write them like an architect builds houses—if it's constructed right, the people always know where they're walking, they always feel right. The play allows people to conceptualize things they want to play with. The energy has to be there—otherwise it's useless." Vargas uses the popular fascination with wrestling as a metaphor for oppression. Captain America, complete with gold brocade and rock music, is pitted against Poppo. Vargas plays the referee who looks the other way while Poppo is being fouled. In his newest play, *The Bench*, Vargas begins the event forty-five minutes before the actual performance with Congo drums stationed around the block. The beat gradually moves in on the arena, forming a counterpoint between the stage action and the people. The audience, sandwiched between stimuli, watch a city official, his wife, and a Puerto Rican advance man try to give a speech on a bench made of police boards. It starts with slapstick caricature, the city official beginning in a nervous benevolence and finally, in fear, refusing to read his speech. The wife tries to speak, only to be drowned out by drums. The speech begins, "How can you people become better Americans?" While they talk, Puerto Ricans begin to sit at the edge of the flimsy platform. At first there is one, but finally, when the advance man joins his brothers at one end of the platform, they are able to tip it. Together, they have power to shake things up. At this point, the theater looks to its audience. "What do you think? Is this our bench?" The answers come from the drums and the people. The slapstick changes abruptly. "We bring the audience to this point and then make them realize we're talking for real. This is my first attempt to say "Vaya! You're right, brother. It's a race revival, a brotherhood. It means unity and action." Those who respond to the play are contacted with pamphlets explaining how to organize themselves and suggesting books to read. The educational function comes full circle, moving from the imagination back into life.

The beauty of these events, on strike lines and in the rubble of Spanish Harlem, is their gorgeous flowering in arid terrain—the simplicity with which they discover the dignity of the human will. No two street theaters can be the same; each environment has its special metabolism. But where the need is so immense and the communication barriers so great, the fact of beginning is itself an important step. Vargas' own axioms are general cornerstones on which to build:

1. KNOW WHO YOU ARE: if you know who you are, you'll know what to do.
2. WHAT IS THE BEST ROAD TO SURVIVAL: What are your best tools for communicating with groups (movement, sound, words).
3. WHAT ARE THE BEST WAYS OF CONNECTING WITH THE COMMUNITY: Find the simple way which won't turn people off. *Begin where they're at.*

While so much of America's theater suffocates in its golden delusion, another dramatic tradition holds out the possibilities of a revitalized life, denying decorum and discovering vernacular. Among the ashes, street theater ferrets out a performing impulse almost lost—a mime for survival. ☐

evergreen

Oct 1968

Theater in the streets

Photos: Howard Harrison; text: Larry Meyers

New York's Sixth Street Theatre has been performing on the streets, on campuses and in their Lower East Side storefront for a year and a half in an effort to reach people other than habitual theater-goers. The troupe makes plays about familiar social issues for an audience often unacquainted with a radical perspective. This summer the theater will make a cross-country tour with a repertoire including plays against the draft, for community control (performed during New York's teachers' strike), about slums, the election hoax, and an improvisational play based on the day's newspaper. Their latest play, "Studentlife," follows a student's career from matriculation to revolt.

This is political theater. Its members number among the victims, the revolted. Their affinities are natural, not ideologically set and tuned. Theater for the movement and for the uncommitted. To show social relations under death culture—images to crystallize hopes, fears, dangers, haterds, loves. . . . They look to audience for recognition of common lot; attempt to portray rise in consciousness, but also ability to act on new level.

The plays are built improvisationally on on a highly flexible scenario. Troupe shares responsibility for ideas, which often often come on the spot and are tested there. Ego has no script to defend. This submerges subjectivity, but increases personal involvement. Family quarrels. Making a play is a dance in itself.

Mime-dance. A more powerful language than words, which have been so degraded no one trusts them any longer. Physical gesture, however, is undeniable; posture and grouping as well. You dig. (Narration and dialogue sometimes, but qualified by use as song or chant, inclusion in context of costumes, masks and music.)

This is street theater. Away from proscenium arch into new context. What's precious (theater) is slapped up against what's raw (garbage). Transmutation into innocence and awe, though both are slangy. And street theater as quality that survives indoors when fleeing cold weather or cops—sudden enrichment coming from half challenge, half tender appeal in midst of bleakness.

Neither off- nor off-off-Broadway. Motivation is not careerism (even of the left), but spark between filaments of art and revolution. Political theater, street theater, not advance guard of bourgeois culture, not aimed towards profits, fame, anthologizing. No time to waste: during a recent snow squall that darkened the sky at midday, a worker was reported to have cried, "Hurry up, it looks like the end of the world!"

Bread & Puppet Theatre

Clowning with the life force

by Maurice Blanc

The gas lantern had run out of fuel so we kept the lights of one of the cars trained on the flat stretch between Charlie Adams' House and the workshop/barn. (That July day in Maine was much too hot so we slept and decided to rehearse throughout the night.) There we crawled on the ground within sylastic beast heads resembling the faces of wolves and wild boars, our bodies smeared with a strong-smelling insect-repellent and Woodman's Dope and wrapped in — burlap. With George Ashley writing down every movement, Peter Schumann announced tasks and improvisation suggestions from a megaphone as he sat on a log stump in the middle of a moving insect fog. With strange ululations and grotesque instrumental noises we accompanied the slithering and violent motions of the "beasts." Distant farms heard the rites and days later sent puzzled, shy, and envious visitors curious to know about Druid or Dionysian pleasures.

The Bread and Puppet Theatre had been commissioned for a new piece by the Newport Folk Festival and Peter, without a clear end in mind, was having us move and do tasks utilizing the one tangible element he had a certainty about: the "beasts." Peter always works without a script. He moves performers (preferably not actors) around in large puppets, masks or bare-faced: tries sounds, juggles ideas and visual effects over and over until certain patterns are pleasing to the secret voice, which one might call almost-rational-instinct, within him. Much of what we produced that night in the way of fodder for the production seemed, felt inspired, right, vital. But Peter wasn't at all satisfied. The next day we tried wild take-offs on the Jacob-Joseph stories of the Old Testament and eventually reached a terrible impasse as the parallel between the famous Biblical dreams and the one of Martin Luther King, Jr., suddenly semed a meaningful, but with futher thought, an awkward, forced theme. The efficacy of theatre at this moment was the oppressive question in Peter's mind. And it rose higher in priority for him than the responsibility

of getting a new show ready. And yet that he had to do. Earlier in July in Denver at a workshop conference of the National Churches of Christ that we participated in, he had hinted at, made verbal his fears that theatre clearly wasn't enough, that people were becoming immune to anti - war plays or works that spoke to their conscience.

Claire Clouzot's article, "Godard and and the U. S.," in the summer issue of Sight and Sound perhaps sheds some light on Peter's dilemma as an artist and a man. Miss Clouzot quotes Jean Luc Godard, badgered by militant students to be their vanguard, as "supporting the ones who are taking up the guns," but not wishing to abdicate creation for active revolt. Godard is also quoted as saying, "The Third World's problem is that it is hungry. We on the contrary are over-fed culturally and we eat things which are culturally unnecessary, so we must learn again what is our real nourishment." Because this last is Peter's fervent belief also, he has started a commune in Maine. With the use of his own and Mary Kelly's land and by the hard work of interested friends and puppeteers, an experiment is in the process. The show given on July 26 in Newport was a product of the commune. Peter's frustration at the early rehearsal mentioned above had continued during the rest of the days in Maine and during those long desperate rehearsals on the stage and lawn at Newport. That the performance itself had a certain raw power and satisfying feeling, despite rough moments, did not neutralize the fact that Peter was still troubled by what his best role is in America at this time.

Since '60 or '61 when Peter came here from Germany, by way of: a short-lived communal society in Southern France and earlier from a moderate success as a German choreographer, he was engaged in creating a theatre without pomposity and with the humor of Punch and Judy and the power of Dreyer's "The Passion of Jeanne d'Arc". Those are two of his sources and he can move from the style of one to the style of the other with mecurial speed. The stamina he admires in the Bunraku or Sicilian puppeteers he has also in remarkable

abundance as well as their finesse and childlike glee of performance. He reminds me of my childhood impression of Chaplin, before I became aware of the only - too - knowing cynical eyes and mouth beneath the Tramp's pose.

For five or more years the Bread and Puppet Theatre has performed at anti-war rallies, in churches, in parks, on an open truck clowning around with the life force and not fooling around with human needs. Peter and Elka and their five kids live on East 6th Street. It's not affluence And when he cringes at the over-gracious push of the ladies from SANE it's because he's more at home with a certain under-graciousness on the part of some of the New Left. He himself, never grand nor brutish, has nicely avoided New York "style".

In April, before Peter, Margo Sherman, Bob Ernstthal, myself and Irving and Pearl Olie departed for Europe, primarily to perform "Fire," most of us saw Godard's "La Chinoise". We saw it hoping to learn the tenor of France since the city of Nancy was our host and our first stop. The film seemed more critical of the young revolutionaries than the Sight and Sound article implies. "La Chinoise" didn't prepare us for the intelligent passion of the students we eventually met and worked with in Nancy and Paris; a viewing of Godard's 1960 "Le Petit Soldat" might have been more pertinent. The difference between the 35-year-old Godard and the 34-year-old Schumann is that Peter still has been able to be sufficiently anonymous and independent of critical pressure so that he can create his street plays and irreverent yet respectful masques with basic ingredients: the staff of life rather than pretty, over-rich, if Brechtian, marzipan. Yet traveling through Europe, Peter was suddenly put on the spot in a way he hadn't been in the States; theatre scholars and active craftsmen had read the recent interview in The Drama Review. Suddenly he was a world leader. And as we moved through Europe Peter was made to evaluate and reevaluate every thing he had formerly designed and believed.

In Europe, after the Festival Mondial of young theatre in Nancy, we played in streets, factories, school yards, plazas, housing projects, community centers, theatres, universities, art galleries in and about London, Paris, Amsterdam, Utrecht, and finally Berlin. Bruno Eckhardt, an old colleague, at present living in West Germany, joined us and gave

us great inspiration with black chain gang and Spanish civil war songs.

"Fire," the play which Peter had dedicated to those five Americans who immolated themselves in protest to the war in Vietnam, was extremely well-received by such papers as Le Monde and the London Times. The French audiences, in particular, were intensely responsive. We were there at particularly crucial times. Two days before we arrived in Paris the May manifestations had begun. (And ten days before and ten days after we left two American leaders of peace and justice were assassinated.)

Because "Fire" demands more than aesthetic appreciation from an audience, sometimes elegant society crowds were able to view the play only from a limited current vampire-surrealism fad. They would comment on how effectively the white Vietnamese masks "worked" against the black cloth backgrounds, or how much they were impressed by our controlled stillness and movements. When I had first seen the show during the winter at the Washington Square Methodist Church I thought that I would never be able to stand the intense, agonized concentration that the mute, slow acting called for. Actually it was easier to play in it than to view it. Peter, when he had created the peice, answered a profound need in himself to come to terms with the continuing inhumane acts of men. Recreating the show daily was like a personal act which could, perhaps, absolve our fat-cat guilt. If, at the end, the audience cheered (as often happened), we felt affronted as if they had missed the point in not continuing the play's mood by remaining silent and respectful of its last image: the fallen woman in white, scarred with long terrible red strips across her body. Playing the stark ritual of "Fire" 50 times in Europe, two or three times a day, one had to guard carefully against too easy a feeling of expiation of guilt.

In spite of accumulating talk and sights of repression everywhere we traveled we thought seriously of following the Living Theatre's example and staying in Europe. However, the idea was rejected. Once in a French railroad couchette the five of us opened the shelves and caught some sleep since we had been packing all night. A French conductor awakened us with a thundering, lyrical phrase, "No sleeping in the daytime." The officials were tough on Bruno as we approached Berlin through the East German border. Also we got a taste of the repressive bureaucracy of East Berlin when we tried to visit the Berliner Ensemble. Peter was denied entrance because he was carrying a can of film (Jules Rabin's footage of the Bread and Puppet Theatre in the summer of '66 in East Harlem and the South Bronx) which we wanted to have Helene Weigel see. I went over myself easily the next two days, but Peter and Bruno still having German citizenship had had enough of grim reminders of the past.

Our initial entry into Berlin by train from Amsterdam was a tremendous shock. We were greeted by 30 chanting students who carried red flags and expected us to be their vanguard against their "new Nazi leaders." Some of them were Americans from the exile group called The U.S. Campaign Against the War. One of the latter was Murray Levy, formerly of the Free Southern Theatre, who acted as our liaison, etc., in Berlin.

That first night in Berlin Peter had long discussion with the militant Marxists who had volunteered to help us find places to perform whether on boards or at town squares. Aggressively they suggested new endings to our plays as they considered them too quietistic, too mystical, too resigned. A friend of Bruno's, Kott, who I believe had once been one of Brecht's aides, was a gentle yet persistent gadfly on these matters. He was convinced that most reform is at this time impossible; assisting the death of freedom he said were the supposedly innocent stockholders and people with bank accounts who were in effect also slaveholders and murderers of yellow men in Asia.

We performed in the Ford Building the night the Berlin students took over the Free University anticipating that the police would interrupt the speeches before we had a change to do "Chairs." Untrue to form they did not come. We played on the Ku Damm at the Forum Theater evenings at 11 to the Berlin jet set who laughed at the death scene and the air raid scene. And during the fire scene I found a new daemonic energy to wrestle in effect with the hardened cynicism and insensitivity out there. I threw the cloth flames over the mangled and twisted mannequins with a new intensivity and power. To Peter, who is seldom lacking in courage, those performances are a bad memory, but to me they are reminders of how fear can disappear in the face of bestiality.

On our last day in Berlin Bob, Margo, Peter, Bruno, and I were driven to a sidewalk next to the U.S. Army PX where we performed a short anti-war play. Fortunately we were being televised by the Cologne TV. The MP's merely had the German police take our names and passport numbers; otherwise, friends told us, we would have been beaten or arrested. Then, commitments in Denver and Newport brought us home.

At present there are some county fairs and Upward Bound shows to do in Maine and a projected San Francisco area tour planned for September and October that Peter is still puzzling over in his mind. In the meantime about 20 people are living at the commune. They cooperate on the chores on two farms which lack electricity, running water, and telephone. They pitch in building outhouses, cutting fire wood, getting well water, gardening, cleaning up, cooking. They also create ceramics, short books "crankee" films, puppets, flower presses, quilts, poems, etc.

9/5/68

FROM "COMEDY AND REVOLUTION" BY JOAN HOLDEN

Now the population of the aware numbers into the millions, some of whom have known how bad it is for a good many years, and it is presumptuous to take up more time until you have something to say that will make a difference. Once we are exercised about "militarism, racism, bureaucracy, and the dehumanizing effects of technology" (the list of what youth is in revolt against, in the prospectus provided by this journal, notably omits private property) there is nothing left to say except how to change them. Artists who consider themselves in the vanguard, and most do, must assume the responsibility of the vanguard, which is to lead. This most will find impossible to do without radical changes in their ideas about art. They will have to abandon objectivity in favor of morality and metaphysics in favor of history. Granted that too few of us know what politics we want, that most of the New Left does not know what it wants, there is a general extreme aversion to direct statement in art that prevents most artists from even asking themselves the question, and a preference for metaphysical concerns that relieves them of historical responsibility.

The twin pillars of our high culture are positivism and relativism. If there is anything at all we can be sure of, it is only the isolated messages our senses receive: all larger truths are provisional. "What does 'what does it mean' mean?" replied Pinter to a questioner. The work of art should not interpret: it should transmit, or re-create, or be experience. Statements of direction and value are intrusions on art: Martin Esslin treats Brecht's Marxism as a vision impediment. The history of modern art can be outlined as a series of attempts to destroy rational constructions and break through to raw experience. Think of thousands of symbolists, surrealists, abstract expressionists, alone in their studies and studios like so many alchemists, breaking experience down into its parts, all searching for the ultimate concreteness. This mass purist quest has brought tremendous results: revealed, explored, and invented rich forms of expression for huge previously forbidden tracts of consciousness; neither art nor consciousness will ever be the same. Many people will never be the same since acid; in either case we arrive with consciousness enriched, after long trips and many changes, at the question, "All right, my mind's blown — now what?" Awareness is a means that has so far been mistaken for an end; without an end it becomes inversion. Who can profit from seeing more than one play of Beckett's or Ionesco's? (Who can profit from seeing one play of Albee's?) To refuse to interpret, to judge and to direct, is to confer the sanction of inevitability on the world as we know it, by conveying pieces of it as the ultimate reality.

The same effect of implicit sanction is produced by focussing, as our playwrights and novelists prefer to, on the metaphysical situation rather than the historical one: our particular troubles are seen as symptoms of irreparable flaws in the eternal fabric, and made to seem trivial, anyway, by comparison. Who cares who owns the factories, when Sam Shephard, Thomas Pynchon, Claude Van Itallie — all the bright young men, as well as the somber old ones — are announcing that entropy is about to take over? We have few books about curable evils: CATCH-22, probably the solidest, best sustained satire of our period, is a model for the way the specific evil, in our fiction, eludes resolution by opening onto the general uncertainty. The unrelieved accumulation of terrible details gradually makes the insanity of the army appear as the insanity of the universe, in the light of which there is no point in trying to do anything, except maybe find a comfortable hole. (Carl Oglesby pointed out in a 1967 lecture, "The Deserter, or the Contemporary Defeat of Fiction" that Heller "cops out to despair" by sending Yossarian to Sweden instead of having him assassinate General Cathcart, a possibility entertained at several points in the book.) Similarly, in Burrough's satire, addiction and buggery accumulate meanings and swell until they swallow the universe. To have a blacker vision than Burroughs is a widespread ambition. With God dead, the metaphysical outlook is naturally bleak; on the historical plane, however, there are a few things left to try, and the reluctance of most artists to promote them invites the suspicion that they prefer the evil which guarantees them a subject to the revolution which might leave them without one.

To rejoin history art must become didactic, moralistic, propagandistic: all bad words to the sophomore English major but assumed motives of art at most times other than our own. It must also be visionary. It must also be good, or it will fail as propaganda.

To imagine that one has to choose between creating a lasting monument and a work which is immediately useful is to pose an unnecessary dilemma: whoever writes the Divine Comedy of the revolution can be confident of its survival. We can divide the work: Burroughs has written our Inferno, let us go on to the next two books, because knowing it's bad is not enough to move people to change it. That knowledge, alone, oppresses the poor and sanctions the inaction of the educated. The art of despair panders to the fundamental complacency of an "enlightened" bourgeoisie which naturally prefers to exercise its guilt in artificial suffering rather than be carried to the point of considering real sacrifice; so much the better when it is assured that real sacrifice would be unavailing. People move when they know what they want: what art must now do is make real what, for the good of all of us, people should want. The art of exposure has to be replaced by an art of example.

The Living Theater, to cite a rare instance, has made this transition: from THE BRIG (hell on earth) to PARADISE NOW. This just (February 1969) played in Berkeley, where the audience who had battled the Highway Patrol a few hours earlier indicated plainly that the "anarchist non-violent revolution" was not the paradise it had in mind. But to move straight people to take off their clothes, or jump from balconies in the justified faith that their brothers underneath will catch them, as the Living Theater has done all over the country at places less advanced than Berkeley, is living power. Most theaters move people to clap. A friend of mine watched a crowd which had just finished applauding RHINOCEROS file past an ashcan which had caught fire and was burning in the lobby.

The undeniable achievement of hippy culture is that it presented a real vision of a preferable life; undeniable because thousands flocked to it and more thousands are living parts of it now. If we object that the vision was incomplete our job is to make a completer one as strong. I think socialism is what people should want: what they do want, as the hippy movement, the group therapy fad, the nationalist movements (in which the opportunity of calling others "brother" is relished as much as vengeance) makes sometimes pathetically clear, is a sense of community. The ideal work of art would envision a believable version of communal life, demonstrate that individualism in all its aspects including capitalism stands in the way, point out the first step to take to destroy the obstacle and get people to take it.

This brings us to comedy, which is inherently subversive and visionary, always has a moral, and has always been popular. The traditional class connections of the dramatic genres are conventionally explained in terms of relative sophistication: only the aristocracy has leisure and refinement to consider the great issues propounded by tragedy; realism appeals to the no-nonsense outlook of the bustling middle class; comedy delights the childlike hedonism of the masses. Another way of putting it is to say that each genre carries a different subliminal message, and each class knows which message it wants to hear. Tragedy says there is an immutable order which it is idle to resist (our tragedy is the theater of the absurd, which says it is an immutable disorder); realism says the game is to the strong; comedy says you can have what you are being denied.

All comedies (if they don't, they aren't really) share one basic plot, fairly transparent in its psychological motivation. The hero, whom we like — if this seems obvious, the point is to remember that we identify with the comic hero — and who is always somehow disadvantaged: too old, too young, poor, a servant, or female, wants something out of a person, or persons, more powerful than he. What he wants is usually a girl or money, but it can be, as in Aristophanes, a better world, or peace. The enemies are always power figures: parents, husbands, masters, governments. After a struggle which usually brings him close to disaster, the hero beats the enemies, gets the prize, and the play ends with a celebration.

This pattern is traced by the anthropological critics, following Cornford's ORIGIN OF ATTIC COMEDY, to ancient fertility ritual and interpreted as sympathetic magic designed to insure the triumph of spring and the vital principle over winter and death; by the psychologists, following Freud's WIT AND THE UNCONSCIOUS, it is interpreted as fantasy wish-fufillment acting out the triumph of the id over restraints. It is also the basic plot of any revolution. This makes it relatively easy to represent a revolutionary action. You have the oppressed class in the servant characters, the oppressors in

the power figures (whom you can identify as specifically as you like: the more specific, the more the audience will love to see them beaten), the vanguard in the hero; enlarge the goals of the victorious struggle, from marriage or money to freedom or peace, and it becomes a revolution; the new order is represented in the distributive justice of the happy ending. The moral is always clear: do like the hero. Now you have only to decide what revolutionary action you can suggest to your audience; you have caught up with the rest of the vanguard.

In our version of L'AMANT MILITAIRE (1967), the soubrette heroine dressed up as the Pope, appeared over the curtain, and stopped the war in Vietnam; then came down and told the audience, "If you want something done, my friends — do it yourselves." This meant, take power, but we admit it begged the question of how. It did leave the audience **wanting** power (and won us the epithet "cheerleaders of anarchy," which we would accept with pride if it were amended to "cheerleaders of the socialist violent revolution"); compare with the effect of Peter Brook's film, TELL ME LIES, which in one sequence shows the hero very plausibly entering the Pentagon during working hours, hiding till night, and starting a conflagration in a vast bank of IBM cards; just when the audience is thinking "Wow — it really could happen" the character wakes up and we learned that it is only a nightmare. Mr. Brook could not stick with anything stronger than the question which ends the film: (supposing a napalm-burned child appeared at your door): "What would **you** do?" Why make the film? In RUZZANTE (1968) we were concrete: the hero blew up the co-opted professor (destroy the university in its present form). This happy ending was appreciated on campuses but people reproached us for making revolution look easy — the hero didn't make the bomb himself, it appeared by magic.

The problem is that if it doesn't look easy it isn't magic, and if it isn't magic you might as well write a pamphlet. If the artist has to choose between creating the desire and outlining the means he must choose the first, as the thing that art is best at. Art conveys implicit messages deeper than it does explicit ones. The special power of comedy as revolutionary art lies not in the facility of representation — that problem can be solved in other ways — but in the psychological correspondence between comedy and revolution: the pattern wherein anger and love combine in a movement toward freedom. If you don't think love is a revolutionary motive, Che thinks so. The double motivation, what he calls "celebration and abuse," is repeatedly emphasized by Cornford. It was not enough simply to carry on the Maypole: first winter had to be driven out with sticks. The endurance of this pattern in art suggests that it endures in our psychology, awaiting release to be expressed in life. What comedy has special power to do is create a compelling vision of this release.

Ed. Note: Joan Holden writes and acts with the
San Francisco Mime Troupe

Arts in Society No. 3, 1969

Four Guerrilla Theatre Pieces

from THE AMERICAN PLAYGROUND

THE PAINTER

SCENE: Any public park across from a public building. In this case, Lafayette Park, across from the White House. The first day of a warm and pleasant week.

A man arrives in the park carrying a largish (4' x 6') canvas and all the accoutrements of a Sunday painter. He sets up his easel across from the White House, and begins to sketch the building. He is quite friendly to all onlookers and especially friendly to the park police, with whom he has as many pleasant conversations as possible. He works slowly and with great accuracy, laying out his lines as if to produce a work for the public library. At dinnertime, the painter leaves, ready to return the next day. What is important is that he establish beyond a doubt his legitimacy in the park, his friendliness with the police and passersby, his solid technique—his existence as a genuine painter who has a right to be doing what he is doing. To as many people as possible: "I'll see you tomorrow," "Come back later and see how I'm doing," etc.

Over the course of the next few days the painting begins to take shape and the painter's presence becomes a colorful local phenomenon. Businessmen stop off during lunch-hour to check his progress. An article appears in the local section of the newspaper with a picture of him and his work.

Now, slowly, the painting begins to transform into a scene appropriate to the subject matter. On the White House balcony babies are napalmed, from the roof ICBM's emerge. Fragmentation bombs are exploded on the lawn maiming the (black) visitors. A grotesque Nixon and Laird oversee the operations. The painting becomes a mirror reflecting the inner truth behind the marble facade.

The painter attempts to be as friendly to onlookers, especially the police, as he was before, but he will find that the nature of their response to him has changed. He may even find that he is no longer allowed to paint in the park without a permit or somesuch. The newspapers should be notified to follow up his harrassment. They will certainly run a second story and picture. He should follow up his ex-

pulsion from the park with TV and radio interviews. Money from the sale of the now-famous painting is donated to the Movement.

A CLASSROOM PROBLEM

SITUATION: A radical young teacher facing an apathetic, reactionary class. In this case, a young white radical teaching in a predominantly Negro (not black) public high school in a middle class Negro (not black) neighborhood. Some of the kids in the class have already complained to the principal that the teacher is calling them "black" and feeding them left-wing propaganda.

The teacher announces several days in advance that he intends to invite one of the more flaming radicals of the community to speak to the class about revolution. On the scheduled day, teacher and radical show up, along with a straight-looking older man. The teacher announces that because of the speaker and the topic, the Board of Education has seen fit to send a representative to the classroom as an auditor. Teacher is visibly upset by this. The auditor produces a tape recorder, and announces his intention to record the session. He sits at the back of the class. The guest radical begins to rap, growing more and more fiery and seditious. At some point, the auditor objects to the proceedings, and in the name of the Board of Education tries to stop the talk. The teacher insists on freedom of speech, that this is his class, and that he will set the rules. Teacher and auditor begin shouting at each other, and the battle escalates until the auditor strikes the teacher in a fit of aggressive self-righteousness. Auditor storms out of the classroom, "to speak to the principal," followed by teacher and radical. Class sits stunned for a few moments until second teacher (privy to the plan) steps in to cover the class. (She and first teacher exchange classes at that point.) She explores what happened with the class, and gets them to discuss the issues involved—repression, academic freedom, student-as-nigger, faculty-as-nigger, the generation gap, etc. All the while, the tape is running. The following day, the regular teacher returns, exposes the plot (introduces the actors) and plays the tape of the kids' reactions. The rest of the week (month? year?) is spent in discussion and action at a new and higher energy level. The kids will react negatively to being tricked and manipulated. Use it to explore how they are habitually tricked and manipulated without knowing it.

A PIECE FOR CONVENTIONS

SITUATION: Any convention at a big hotel where a group of people are discussing everything but what they should be discussing. (The American Chemical Retailers Association *not* discussing napalm, The American Association of University Professors *not* discussing Columbia and SF State, a meeting of Peace Group leaders *not* discussing the futility of more petitions, etc.) In this case, the annual meeting of the U.S. Student Press Association, a group of college editors from all over the country *not* discussing Vietnam and the responsibility of the college press. It is helpful, but not absolutely necessary, to have a confederate among the conference organizers. In this case, we did.

Before the conference began, we hung giant white screens from the balconies of the ballroom. These remained up for the entire conference and were accepted as decor. On Friday night a strongly worded Vietnam resolution was circulated, along with an announcement that the resolution would be debated at a plenary session Saturday afternoon. The resolution was "submitted" by editors whom we knew to be absent from the conference, but of whom all had heard.

By Saturday morning there had been generated, of its own accord, an "anti-resolution resolution," and much heated argument was heard in the hallways. At the plenary session, we had plants ready to take various points of view, to heat up the debate if necessary. They were not necessary. Clearly we had touched off tremendous energy already seething in the group. As the wrangling began to get out of hand, a motion was passed to table the question. Table Vietnam!! At that point, we cut the lights and began a barrage of six simultaneous atrocity films and tracks: battle scenes, LBJ, Rusk, napalm, a homecoming parade, dead children projected on the hanging screens. Pandemonium in the room. After three minutes, the lights were switched on, the films cut off, and a voice boomed over the great loudspeaker system of the grand ballroom. It was our "police voice" announcing that the films just shown were contraband North Vietnamese films, shown without State Department approval, and were being confiscated. The meeting was declared illegal and was ordered adjourned. The editors were given five minutes to clear the room. The way the films were stopped, the nature of the sound, the previous emotion-

alism all created a credibility which might not have prevailed in a more rational context. The meeting broke up, confused. The editors returned to their rooms to talk about college editors and Vietnam.

KITES

SETTING: A crowded park on a windy day. The piece should take most of the afternoon.

CHARACTERS (15):

1 Great Dragon, created along the lines of the magnificent oriental dragon kites. Pictures and plans are available in public libraries.

1 False Dragon, created in USA.

10 Small Dragons, whose painted faces, when ripped to shreds, reveal NLF flags.

1 Military Industrial Kite, with a timed, self-igniting incendiary device.

2 American Razor Blade Kites, a series of razor blades tied to their tails. The razor-blade tails can be manipulated to cut lines and slash faces.

THE FOLLOWING SECTIONS ARE DEVELOPED AND CHOREO-GRAPHED:

1. The Great Dragon, flying high in all its beauty, attracts a crowd of onlookers.

2. Slowly, the Great Dragon collects the Small Dragons around it. They soar.

3. The False Dragon confers with the Military-Industrial Kite.

4. The False Dragon (its *éminence grise* lurking in the background) tries to lure the Small Dragons away from the Great Dragon. No success.

5. Another conference.

6. This time, False Dragon returns with the two American Razor Blade Kites, which begin to cut into the crowd.

7. As some of the faces of the small dragons are slashed away, they transform into VC kites.

8. The Military Industrial Kite ignites and destroys two small dragons by fire.

9. One of the burning VC kites ignites the Military-Industrial kite.

10. As the Military-Industrial kite struggles to stay up, it accidentally ignites the False Dragon. Both fall to the ground.

11. The Small Dragon and VC kites evade the razor blades of the American kites, and drag them down to earth, tangled in their string.

12. Only the Great Dragon and a tattered band of Small Dragon-VC kites remain, soaring proudly in the sky.

AN ALTERNATIVE SCHEME WITH SMALLER CAST AND DIFFERENT EFFECT:
An American Razor Blade Kite hacks a lovely Great Dragon to pieces. A pitiful sight.

Although the plotting seems simple, the effectiveness is limited only by the beauty of construction and skill in handling of the kites.

A Note on Guerrilla Theatre

The term guerrilla theatre is beginning to be thrown around quite loosely, referring in general to any form of political or avant-garde theatre from *Hair* to the San Francisco Mime Troupe; it is becoming more and more meaningless. I suggest restricting its use to that form of theatre which does not identify itself as such. Theatre-which-pretends-not-to-be-theatre. Theatre which IS a reshaping of reality. This type of theatre is peculiarly effective since it avoids being boxed into that "Well, it's only theatre" or "Oh, it's that crazy Kusama again" routine that most people go through to insulate themselves against the possibility of change. It hits at an unguarded subject, and is itself vulnerable since it travels without the protective mantle of being ART.

The purest form of guerrilla theatre never reveals itself, but like The Painter, simply stalks away into reality. Some guerrilla theatre, like A Classroom Problem, reveals itself afterwards in order to heighten and explore its effect. The Convention Piece uses frankly theatrical means (films and tapes) but rationalizes their use through context, so as not to o'erstep reality and subsequent credibility. Kites, standing free, is closer to street-theatre, although as originally planned for a kiting festival at the Washington Monument it might have functioned as guerrilla theatre.

Understood in this way, guerrilla theatre is being done by few theatre groups. Yippies, narks, The American Playground, State Department Interventionists and the NLF are among its practitioners. A mixed bag, but we must begin to be as effective as they are.

After first being upset by the event, many people are doubly upset if/when they later find out they've been conned. So much the better. For what better way to sensitize people to the ubiquitous, insidious, and obscene con job of America, what better way than to gently but firmly, issue by issue, demonstrate to them their vulnerability—and our own—than through acts of redemptive theatre? For guerrilla theatre creates new realities. Vulnerability, for instance. By acting as if certain things were true, it creates the conditions whereby they may *become* true. Sometimes the truth revealed is merely the flowering of latent evil in the situation. But the flowering of evil can lead to its extirpation.

And guerrilla theatre can also operate from the other direction. Recently, we "guerrillaed" a peace conference by feeding lunch to the participants. We placed morsels of food into people's mouths, touching their lips with our fingers and stroking their hair. People began to feed each other and us, and for the first time we all felt what it might be like to live together in a world of peace and love.

Perhaps guerrilla theatre is a form of guerrilla warfare. But as Brown says, "The thing, then, is not to abolish war but to find the true war. Open the hidden Heart in Wars of Mutual Benevolence, Wars of Love."

Guerrilla Theatre without Actors

Much street and guerrilla theatre suffers from high input, low output. A lot of emotional and physical preparation goes into presenting pieces which few spectators see and which, increasingly, the media ignore. Here are a few suggestions for mounting a relatively long-term attack on local consciousness with very little effort.

1. *Defoliation for peace.* Remember how concentration camp prisoners used to drop the dirt from tunnels they were digging? Try walking on a convenient lawn (like the Pentagon lawn), inconspicuously dropping grass killer from your pocket. Walk in a pattern which spells out in big letters the message you want to leave. Wait a week, and you've got it.

2. *Spray paint and stencil.* Two nice examples I've seen lately are STOP signs turning into STOP WAR signs, and mail boxes turning into NLF flags by the addition of a yellow star at the intersection of the red and blue areas. They only take a second to do and reach many people before they're "corrected" (which, given the bureaucracy, can take a long time).

3. *Bumper Stickers in Better Places.* SHOOT LOOTERS stickers put on police cars in ghettos, or SUPPORT YOUR LOCAL POLICE stickers added to traffic signs such as No Left Turn (Support Your Local Police), Right Turn Only (Support Your Local Police), Yield (Support Your Local Police), etc.

4. *Paint your car.* It's your own property. You can take your time and do a good job. There are no laws against it. A VW bus painted on both sides with THINK OF THE CHILDREN OF VIETNAM would move a lot of people.

5. *Use chalk.* White chalk on soot-black buildings doesn't come off without sandblasting. Ask your kids for some.

6. *Work hard at graffiti* in toilets, on public transportation, on restaurant menus. Ask questions. You'll get answers. Start dialogues, go back and tend to them. I'm convinced a lot of people's heads could be changed while they're sitting on the can.

"Art, if you want a definition of it, is criminal action. It conforms to no rules. Not even its own. Anyone who experiences a work of art is as guilty as the artist. It is not even a question of sharing the guilt. Each one of us gets all of it."—John Cage.

MARC ESTRIN in *The Drama Review* Summer 1969

BASEBALL
MOVIES
ETCETERA

from left field...

by Frank Bardacke

Just when it seemed that Americans could tolerate no more disasters, the 1968 Major League All-Star Game came along. It was advertised as a "classic" whose potential for greatness was obvious: all-star teams playing in Houston's Astrodome before a record television audience. We were due for a national celebration.

All the pre-game excitement centered on the Astrodome. The five restaurants, two private clubs, gold furnished apartments (complete with bowling alleys) and two million dollar scoreboard made the Astrodome "more than modern" in the words of the T.V. announcer. Best of all was the rain. It was raining hard in Houston on the night of the game, but there would be no postponement. Under the Astrodome the playing conditions remained "air conditioned perfect" just as they always do. Always.

This triumph over nature should have initiated a happy evening of American entertainment. I was in my parents' home in San Diego settled comfortably in front of the television set. I imagined that Americans everywhere were about to enjoy an evening in front of the tube. No funeral or war or riot. Just a good game of baseball and perhaps a prodigious feat to talk about in the office or on the job or in the street the next day.

Instead the country was treated to more calamity and defeat. The players were catastrophically inept. They set records for the least hits by one team, the least hits by two teams combined, the least runs scored, and the most strikeouts by two teams. Many of the pitchers were newcomers to the All-Star game, hardly established stars. They did not deserve credit for the lack of hitting. No, it was not good pitching—the hitting was simply atrocious.

The All-Star Game only made clear what Americans have sensed all season. American athletes can no longer hit a baseball. With the season half over there are only two hitters in the American League batting over .300. The American League All-Star first baseman, Harmon Killebrew, is not even hitting his weight. The National League hitters are doing only slightly better.

This is a time of despair and disruption, as we all know. The nation is experiencing a "crisis of confidence," the press keeps telling us. How does the chorus go? Americans see no way out of their racial troubles, they don't know how to end the war, they are afraid of their children, and they cannot understand the violence within themselves.

And now we have seen the last of the .300 hitters. Americans can no longer do well the one thing they could always do superbly — play baseball. Fear and a sense of shame spreads throughout the country. The best ballplayers in America cannot hit. What has become of us? Young singers cry out in bewilderment:

"Where have you gone Joe DiMaggio?
A lonely nation turns her eyes to you."

But since we are good Americans we try hard to UNDERSTAND. It could not be fate that strikes us down. There must be a reason for our impotence. We call on experts to explain our problems so that we might improve ourselves.

Sports Illustrated features a series by Ted Williams (the last .400 hitter) telling the secrets of hitting. It is a regular Kerner report. Williams lays it on the line. Today's hitters are stupid, they lack purpose, and they are greedy. Stupid because they don't study the pitchers. Purposeless because they treat baseball as just another job — no one is dedicated to the craft of hitting. And greedy because they're all trying for the big home run money, even though the home run swing ruins their overall hitting.

Stupidity, lack of purpose, and greed.

So America adjusts. Baseball tries desperately to recover. The cry goes out. We need new solutions. . .new leadership . . .new policies.

Our first new solution is gimmickry. We can't hit anymore, but we can still make gadgets. Grass won't grow under the Astrodome, so it is covered with green painted nylon held together by three miles of zipper. The two million dollar scoreboard shows cartoons when the game gets boring. Fireworks go off after a home run. Mules cavort in the outfield. Clowns fool with the umpires.

But gimmickry is not enough. There is another, truly American, answer to baseball's problems: expansion. Four new teams are being added this year. Baseball is growing. There are more teams, more games, more players, more countries. We are crossing borders. Bringing baseball to foreigners. Montreal has been awarded a major league franchise. Japan will get one soon. We will sell our product everywhere. We will show the game to the world.

But who is going to teach the heathens how to hit?

The Three Lives of Jean-Luc Godard

marjorie heins

The Godard Festival now at the Surf features some of the filmmaker's least-seen and best works, including three weeks of "Les Carabiniers." It's good to have Godard festivals because more than any other director, Godard has created a comprehensible "oeuvre" (to use a word he'd probably hate), a body of political and artistic meaning for everybody, especially those who are young and those who are radical. Godard's works interrelate and grow one from the other—"La Chinoise" being a revision of "Masculin Feminin"; "Deux ou Trois Choses Que Je Sais d'Elle" being a revision of "La Femme Mariee." Godard festivals are also good because his films are better savored and more comprehensible on third, tenth or nth viewing—not many people take to them right away.

The Movement, mostly young, mostly nonideological New Leftists, both in France and America, identifies with Godard for one reason—he is the Movement, too, he is of us: more than alienated, more than disgusted, impulsive, ironic, amused, trying to be liberated. "Children of Marx and Coca-Cola." Though older in years than most of us, his feeling and thought have developed and changed with ours. He expresses us, and in America, we instinctively recognize this.

His work, like the Movement, has three stages:

1) Bourgeois Rebellion: "Breathless," "Vivre Sa Vie," etc. Godard was part of the "Cahiers du Cinema" group, architects of the "auteur" theory which has become gospel in modern filmmaking, which has allowed him to make fine political films because they are always GODARD films first, POLITICAL films second. His early work, like his participation in "Cahiers," is an attempt to understand and criticize bourgeois culture, especially the culture of America—its ideas of heroism, cruelty and love in "Breathless"; its ideas of beauty, cruelty and love in "Vivre Sa Vie." Visual awareness of bourgeois culture—the movie and advertising posters which form the background of so many of his shots—is already his identifying mark, but at this stage it is still background.

In "Breathless" there appears a theme which is to recur obsessively in Godard's work: the ignorance and cruelty that hurried harried bourgeois society engenders. Belmondo is crossing a street; a man has fallen in a hit and run; people are rushing by; Belmondo, turns, looks, for a minute there is doubt or compassion or something on his face, then he shrugs and walks away. From the first, Godard is searching for alternatives to bourgeois stupidity, alternatives to be found in creative individuality, imagination. His heros are outcasts, prostitutes, petty gangsters. He is political only insofar as he rejects society's heros in favor of outlaws. This is like the New Left in its early stages, when we were beginning to examine and criticize the society that our predecessors in the fifties had so willingly joined. Words like alienation, dehumanization, sterility and IBM card were popular.

"Les Carabiniers," though more openly political, fits into this group. It is a magnificently bleak, deadpan, funny and agonizing fable of war. Two unknown soldiers plodding through the mud of an unnamed country for an unspecified king in an uncertain war. Committing atrocities blankly, stupidly grabbing spoils, the riches and pleasures they desire slipping through their hands just as the movie image slips through the hands of the dumb soldier who runs to the screen and tries to grasp it in the film's most hilarious sequence. "Les Carabiniers" is an expression of immense disgust, anguish and amusement, but it hasn't yet the specifically modern-day political concerns which characterize the films Godard made in the years after 1964.

2) Political Articulation: "La Femme Mariee," "Masculin Feminin," etc. Godard, like the New Left, grew from bourgeois rebellion to a deeper political commitment. This politics rejected ideology, emphasized humanism and creativity. Godard's style became more fragmented, episodic, didactic, cruel and absurd. "Masculin Feminin" features several incidents of cruelty like the hit and run in "Breathless." These incidents, conveniently, are derived from American "protest" literature—a scene reminiscent of LeRoi Jones' "Dutchman" and one like Albee's "Zoo Story." The advertisements, the high camp, grow from ominous background to active character: in "La Femme Mariee," ads for bras and other sex-related items are THE most important character in the movie; the capitalist-advertising-pandering world is the film's true subject.

The New Left in these years (roughly '63 to '66) went from "alienation" to activism—draft card burnings, peace marches, sit-ins and other attempts at personal salvation through politics. Most of us have a fondness for this period, now past, when we were all so righteous and existential. Likewise, we have a fondness for "Masculin Feminin," whose characters are beautiful renderings of the vague sentiments that led to our first political outbursts.

3) Uncertain Revolutionary: "Made in USA," "La Chinoise," etc. Godard, like the rest of us, suddenly finds himself in the midst of a militant, compulsive political rhetoric—guerrilla warfare, street violence, Maoism, Fidelism. His last batch of films try frantically to cope with this—"La Chinoise" most obviously, but also "Made in USA" and "Deux ou Trois Choses Que Je Sais d'Elle." His style has become so fragmented as to be at times incomprehensible. We don't always know what's going on in "Made in USA"—that's part of the game—but we can tell it's Godard's vision of compulsive, crazy, trigger-happy America. There's a profound disillusion, almost a numbness in the film, as if the mysterious death of the man Anna Karina is trying to revenge is the death of something in the Movement, perhaps a certain humanity.

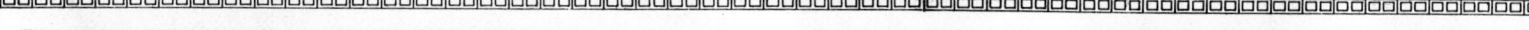

"Deux ou Trois Choses," though not about political people, is a frantic view of a fucked-up society, endlessly repetitious, blandly colorful, and agonizing. ''Weekend," from what I hear, proclaims the gruesome death of bourgeois society that "Deux ou Trois Choses" strongly suggested.

"La Chinoise," of course, is a key film politically. Debate rages over whether Godard was parodying the film's young revolutionaries, or praising them. Many militants have felt insulted at Godard's haphazard and (they feel) superficial treatment of them. They misinterpret the man's style. It has become extremely fragmented and comic book-like. The content may appear absurd or frivolous at the same time that the theme is deadly serious.   This may be   defensive on Godard's part, but then, his films have always been amusing, ironic, with a touch of the absurd--it makes them more human. In "La Chinoise," the characters' often mindless quoting of Chairman Mao is not so important in understanding Godard's feeling about them as their morning exercises on the terrace, or their mean and willful toying with each others' emotions. Godard is PRESENTING more than coming out for or against. Of course, he is for the revolutionaries and against the Establishment. If he parodies their methods, at the same time he loves them. If he shows their weaknesses, it is not in the spirit of a schoolteacher, but of an artist, examining in reverence a phenomenon much bigger than himself.

Godard has always taken a passionate interest in matters intellectual and political. It's said he will flip through a book hurriedly, then quote from it in a film without ever having fully read it. Bits of literature and philosophy appear like graffiti in his films--Poe in "Vivre Sa Vie"; Racine in "La Femme Mariee"; Mao in "La Chinoise." Godard has not fully absorbed all the material he presents; his genius is in presenting it so effectively.

Filmmakers are not philosophers or poets or political theorists. Godard is a great filmmaker and a lousy philosopher (remember the embarrassing platitudes of "Alphaville"?) He has expressed in his work the attitudes and changes of a whole generation, the generation that is now turning the world upside down in Paris, Mexico City, Japan, West Germany and Morningside Heights.

San Francisco
Express Times Oct 1968

The power structure media will not tell the truth about oppression, exploitation and people's needs and struggles here in the United States and around the world. For the most part, power structure media function for profit, and always to co-opt and suppress criticism and movement for change.

"The first thing a revolutionary has to understand is that the ruling classes have organized the state so as to dedicate every possible means to maintaining themselves in power. And they use not only arms, not only physical instruments, but all possible instruments to influence, to deceive, to confuse."

–Fidel Castro

The realities of America are moving people toward the movement, and the movement toward revolution. Continuous foreign wars and permanent high taxes, decaying cities, high schools that function as prisons, colleges that train students only to serve and maintain the system of their own and other people's oppression, inhuman factory speedup—all these and more are educating the American people to the hard necessities of Empire, and forcing them toward the alternative of people's power, peace and freedom.

NEWSREEL is among the people's counter-media that confirm their experience of this harsh reality, and our films are part of the struggle for revolutionary change.

NEWSREEL was founded two years ago in New York by several radical independent filmmakers. Since then we have grown into a national organization with bases in 10 cities: Boston, New York, Washington, Detroit, Chicago, Atlanta, Albuquerque, Seattle, San Francisco, and Los Angeles, and in Puerto Rico. We have produced more than 35 films, including several feature films, and imported more than a score of films from Cuba, Vietnam and other countries.

Unlike the power structure media, we make our films within the situations they present, from the point of view of the people. And we screen them—whenever possible with Newsreel members participating in discussion of the actions, ideas and issues they present—not only in theaters and auditoriums, but wherever we find the people: in the streets, in backyards and livingrooms, in bars, coffeeshops, churches and community centers, as well as schools and colleges.

We have produced this catalog of themed film programs as an aid in selecting and using our films and understanding the political nature of our work. Our basic rental fees (about a dollar a minute) apply primarily to institutions and groups that can afford them, and to commercial screenings. We are always ready to negotiate or waive fees to get our films before the people. Don't hesitate to call us for help in arranging screenings, or advice as to the relevance of specific films to your situation.

ALL POWER TO THE PEOPLE!

newsreel

catalog of movement films

NEWSREEL - 2: "NO GAME". October 21, 1967; The Pentagon; 100,000 anti-war demonstrators who hadn't come prepared for the tear gas and rifle butts of the military police and Pentagon guards.

Running Time: 17 minutes
Rental:$25

NEWSREEL - 3: "FOUR AMERICANS". The aircraft carrier Intrepid lies off the coast of Vietnam sending its planes out daily to bomb the Vietnamese countryside; it vacations in Japan - and returns to continue its work minus four sailors. In this interview,the sailors who deserted tell their story. Filmed in Japan. Running Time: 17 minutes
Rental:$25

NEWSREEL - 4: "THE JEANETTE RANKIN BRIGADE". 10,000 women led an orderly march against the war in Washington in January 1968. It left its more politically active members frustrated. Their discovery reflects the opinions of more and more Americans - that such actions are politically ineffective Running Time: 8 minutes
Rental:$10

NEWSREEL - 5: "GARBAGE". Filmed during the Great N. Y. Garbage Strike of 1967-68. Members of a then emergent political group on the lower East Side (later known as the Motherfuckers) travel north to the Lincoln Center for the Performing Arts, a national symbol of "cultural elegance", to share some of the realities of life with the Center's well-heeled patrons. Can be used with NR 16 in raising questions of working and ruling class cultures. Running Time: 12 minutes
Rental:$15

NEWSREEL - 7: "BOSTON DRAFT RESISTANCE GROUP" One of the many anti-draft groups in the country advising young men of the alternatives to military service and offering them counseling services and legal aid. This film documents the group as it broadens its role and begins an active campaign of canvassing in the community.

Running Time: 18 minutes
Rental:$25

NEWSREEL - 9: "RIOT CONTROL WEAPONS". Rap Brown said that Vietnam is the testing ground for U.S. ghettos. The weapons being tested there will be most important to America's "security" at home. This film documents the weapons the government has specifically designed to paralyze mass resistance in the cities. Running Time: 6 minutes
Rental:$10

NEWSREEL - 11: "6TH STREET MEAT CO-OP" The pacification program of the "war on poverty" grinds to a halt as the Federal bureaucracy frustrates the attempts of Negro Action Group, an anti-poverty agency,to set up an independant meat cooperative. Running Time: 10 minutes
Rental:$15

NEWSREEL - 13: "CHICAGO,APRIL 27TH". The Chicago police force, getting in shape for the violence of August, tests its clubs and mace against unsuspecting anti-war marchers.   Running Time: 10 minutes
                                                                    Rental:$15

NEWSREEL - 14: "THE COLUMBIA REVOLT". In May 1968,the students of Columbia University were forced to strike after the administration repeatedly ignored their demands for open discussion of the university's involvement in racist policies,exploitation of the community, and imperialist oppression. Far from meeting the demands, the administration refused to recognize them as legitimate, and forced the students to escalate their protest by occupying university buildings. This is the story from inside those buildings.   Running Time:50 minutes
                                                                    Rental:$60

NEWSREEL - 16:"THE CASE AGAINST LINCOLN CENTER" Urban renewal destroys a working class neighborhood to provide a cultural showcase for the ruling class. The film discusses the links between the problems of city, and the forces of American Imperialism. Available in Spanish.
                                                     Running Time: 11 minutes
                                                                    Rental:$15

NEWSREEL - 17: "CHICAGO CONVENTION CHALLENGE". In the streets, the meeting rooms, the parks, this film shows the movement behind the demonstrations at the Democratic National Convention in Chicago in August 1968.   Running Time: 17 minutes
                                                                    Rental:$15

NEWSREEL - 19: "BLACK PANTHER". ("Off the Pig") The Black Panther Party is training itself, in struggle, for struggle. Training in armed self-defense, the support of the Black community, alliances with Peace and Freedom in Oakland, the Panther's Ten-Point Program,confrontation with Oakland police. Interview with Huey P. Newton, Minister of Defense of the Black Panthers,in jail, and an interview with Eldridge Cleaver, Minister of Information.   Running Time: 15 minutes
                                                                    Rental:$35

NEWSREEL - 21: "THE HAIGHT". San Francisco, 1968. The Hip Community is forced to fight in the streets to defend its culture against brutal police oppression.   Running Time: 7 minutes
                                                                    Rental:$10

NEWSREEL - 22: "UP AGAINST THE WALL MISS AMERICA. Women's Liberation groups attempt to disrupt the 1968 Miss America pageant and make boardwalk and contestant spectators more aware of the insidious contest that perpetuates the image of "mindless womanhood". Includes footage from inside Convention Hall which TV cameramen were forbidden to show. Good companion film to NR 4 and 126 for Women's Liberation Groups.   Running Time: 7 minutes
                                                                    Rental:$10

Photo is from Weatherman's "Days of Rage,"
Chicago, Oct. 1969.   A Sampling from *The Newsreel* catalog

A Guide to Anti-War Flicks

by Peter Gessner

QUESTION: What is an "anti-war" film? Often it is hard to tell. Probably a bad category. A commodity film like **The Dirty Dozen** which we see in the isolation of a neighborhood culture palace is pro-war and anti-war, depending on who *you* are, and in the end is useless as any kind of human or political testament. One doesn't even have to enter the swamp of deabte about whether, say, John Wayne's **Green Berets** is in fact self-condemnatory in order to open up the multiplicity of possible anti-war films. Ultimately certain "pro-war" films may finally be more "anti-war" than any simplistic catalogue of the ravages of war we can piece together: films about the French *maquis,* Andrej Wajda's films of the Polish resistance or, more recently, **The Battle of Algiers** are memorable and passionate appeals to end wars of oppression. Clearly, the mere representation of brutality and violence divorced from meaning is no certain criterion of anything.

So: leave the unreal question of what an "anti-war" film is and move on to what films might be useful to people organizing other people in specific situations. We should stop dreaming of what the "ideal" anti-war film might look like (my own fantasy is Luis Buñuel's version of **Johnny Got His Gun,** which he wants to make some day). The nightly repetition of Vietnam atrocities beamed from the electronic box has taught us that images alone are not enough to move people to significant changes of consciousness. Films that can cut their way through all the surrounding bullshit our culture throws up to insulate and protect itself must attempt to organize, not merely to reflect, experience.

What follows is a very incomplete listing of some films available in 16 mm on a non-commercial basis which can be used as starting-points for discussions around the general question of war, *past, present* and *future.* The films find their fullest meaning not as isolated esthetic events, but as contexts for raising issues and provoking further questions.

STRANGE VICTORY by Leo Hurwitz. A brilliantly edited documentary of World War II, the so-called "unambiguous" war; raises essential questions about political war aims and the assimilation of the enemy's contagion. A controversial film, attacked by both Right and Left at the time of its original release in 1948. Available from the film-maker.

THE WAR GAME by Peter Watkins (available from Contemporary Films). A vision of the specific effects on a modern state (England in this case) of a future war and nuclear destruction. Weak in terms of how it sees the political genesis of nuclear attack; valuable in terms of its projection of a total breakdown of the surviving society and what kinds of things surface in its place.

FALN (available from Newsreel). A less fantastic projection of more probable future wars: wars of counterinsurgency. An historic and analytic account of the birth of Venezuela's National Liberation Movement; speaks directly to the question of why there will be more Vietnams. Made by Peter Gessner & Robert Kramer in 1965.

NO GAME (Newsreel No. 2) October 21, 1967: the Pentagon. Records the transition of the anti-war movement into a more generalized resistance movement; not just another "demonstration" film, used in conjunction with Newsreel No. 17, **Chicago Convention Challenge**, this film might provide a way to begin to talk to general audiences about why Amerika's children have become "reasonable madmen."

U.S. ARMY FILMS. The U.S. Army and the Department of Defense have made numerous and expensively produced films arguing their case for Vietnam and wars of counterinsurgency in general. Made with your tax money, they are available for "educational" showings (free) and should be used with films made by the Vietnamese showing why they are fighting. Write for catalogues available at local Army centers (Audio-Visual Support Centers. See below for NYC regional address).

VIETNAMESE FILMS made by the NLF and DRV (available from Walter Teague and Newsreel). Some of these films are in poor print condition and the English translations often seem crude, but the better films provide incredible direct testimony of the war and the kind of society the Vietnamese are trying to build in the midst of it. **Cu Chi Guerilla Village, The Threatening Sky,** and **Victory Will be Ours** are some of the more recent, and better, available films. **Rising Storm** is a feature-length ficition film from the DRV (now available from Walter Teague).

MILLS OF THE GODS by Beryl Fox. Made for the Canadian Broadcasting System in 1966, this is undoubtedly the best television-type documentary of the Vietnam war. Memorable direct-cinema interviews, including one with an American pilot who survives from day to day by an act of icy mental dissociation. An oblique yet powerful film. Good for audiences not yet ready to trust anything not seen through Western eyes. As of this writing, it is unclear whether CBS—or anyone else—has plans to release this film for general showings, despite pressure put on them to do so. Inquiries should be sent to Beryl Fox (see below).

HANOI 13 by Santiago Alvarez (available from Newsreel). Daily life in and around Hanoi as filmed by one of Cuba's most respected film-makers. With very little narration (what there is, is from Jose Marti), this film quietly builds a strong picture of a country and a people going about its business of simultaneous defense and construction. President Johnson intrudes into this reality in a strongly abstract, almost surreal series of images from his Texas boyhood—a sequence which disturbed Renata Adler's sensibilities in a recent *NY Times* piece on Cuban films. In black and white and color.

TIME OF THE LOCUST by Peter Gessner (available from Brandon Films, the Film-Makers Co-operative and Newsreel). A short compilation film, edited from the NLF, Japanese and American footage. The tangible reality of Vietnam is on the screen while "official" patriotism and reason are in the ear (LBJ, Ky, military officers). Essentially a film of outrage.

IN THE YEAR OF THE PIG, produced and directed by Emile de Antonio, who directed **Point of Order and Rush to Judgment,** combines stills, American newsreels and interviews primarily with prominent Americans to present an overwhelming cinematic portrait of the American invasion of Vietnam. While Colonel George S. Patton III generously compliments his men for being "a bloody good bunch of killers," the Vietnames rice farmer speaks to his fellow villagers in ancient parables about rice and life, heaven and earth.

In the Year of the Pig is an excellent film for fundraising and education, particularly with groups who have some prior knowledge of Vietnam's history since World War II. For information on obtaining the film write Jane Kronholtz, 246 East 54th St., New York, NY 10022.

The list could, and should be, expanded and is provided only as a beginning point for organizers. Vietnam is naturally in the foreground, but we should also be thinking about other films which speak to some of the root realities which Vietnam has served to unmask. Again, films alone are not enough. Jean Renoir, when asked about what he took to be the effect of his **Grand Illusion**, replied: "I made the film in 1938, and the next year war broke out." Films can act as testimony and witness, but too often are received as passive-spectator experiences; we need to learn to see them as part of a larger arsenal for change.

SOURCES & ADDRESSES

Leo Hurwitz, 617 West End Avenue, NYC
Contemporary Films, 245 Park Avenue, NYC
Newsreel, 28 W. 31 Street NYC 10001
Army Films (NYC): Audio-Visual Support Center
       Fort Hamilton
       Building 210
       Fort Wadsworth, S.I. 10305
Walter Teague, Committee to Support the National
  Liberation Front
    Box C Old Chelsea Station, NYC 10011
Beryl Fox, 295 Central Park West, NYC
Brandon Films, 221 W. 57th Street, NYC
Film-Makers Co-operative, 175 Lexington Ave, NYC ●

LIBERATION May 1969

TRAFFIC

"I'm Stevie Winwood, yeah; and you see I used to be with the Spencer Davis Group. Me and my brother Muff both split. And I formed my own group, Traffic. Yeah, that's how it was. It's been about eight or nine months now. We came down here to Wallingford and got this here cottage with the plan of not releasing any singles — no records of any kind — for six months. Living in London you don't get time to do anything. Well, we came down here because London's expensive. And we wanted to get something done. And, like, we're like any new group . . . it needs a certain amount of time. We want to get to know each other properly. And so we just came down here for six months. We had to learn how to live with each other. That's important in the world we're in. We had to come face to face with the world and with each other. Do ya know what I mean? I think if you believe in this thing as a group — which I definitely do — in a way you almost have to have a kind of telepathic communication. This can only happen if you marry each other. And, like any marriage, it's rough, you know. It's easier just to screw up the whole deal and split, but we had to find out how to live and work together otherwise we'd never had anything to say in our music. I don't mean a 'message' or anything like that; I mean we had to find out how to say something through the music itself. Unfortunately Dave decided to leave us. Well, sure it hurts; but that's the way it is. Yeah, tonight is our last performance with Dave; it's kind of wild in a sad sort of way. But we've had some nice blows together. We taped some of the blows, and the last track we did on the LP was blown right here at the cottage. You can definitely see that it's like a step off the track and you step into this next thing. It's very much into a groove. The four of us have got something going . . . the whole thing is something that we've got between us. That's what our music is; the sound we've found down here in the middle of nowhere.

WE HAD TO
LEARN HOW
TO LIVE WITH
EACH OTHER

Black Drama Gains as Way to Teach, Unite— and Amuse

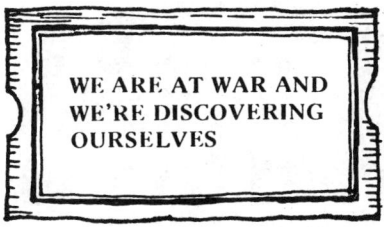

WE ARE AT WAR AND
WE'RE DISCOVERING
OURSELVES

By THOMAS A. JOHNSON

"There is no truth that speaks so clearly to me as the truth of my own experience."

This theme, by John O'Neal, director of the Free Southern Theater, characterizes the new "black" school of drama, a self-styled revolutionary arts movement that is growing across the country.

Like the Negro revolution that spawned it, the black school of theater is young, brash, often undisciplined and always insisting that it makes its own rules. It is impatient with—and often scornful of —the traditional and therefore "white" theater.

Its participants see their art in purely functional terms as a social instrument to help organize and motivate Negro communities. They want the black theater not only to be entertaining and artful, but also to reflect, interpret, teach, chronicle, take part in and, in a sense, lead the black revolution.

Larry Neal, a poet, defines the vision this way: "The black arts movement is radically opposed to any concept of the artist that alienates him from his community."

Whites Seen as Irrelevant

The black-school participants seek, for the most part, to speak only to black people. And, like many other activists in the black revolution, they seek to make white attitudes — whether supportive, hostile or apathetic — irrelevant to their own black thing.

"Most are not thinking about making it on Broadway," Mr. Neal said. "The young black writers are re-evaluating Western esthetics and the traditional role of the writer and the social function of art."

The black theater is but one esthetic expression of what has been called the Negro's "do-it-yourself" revolution. There has also been a great surge in the black press stressing "black to the bone" themes of racial pride. Negro popular music of the "soul" variety, long a vehicle for the expression of black attitudes, has also felt the surge. The very popular James Brown recently was criticized by his supporters for a recording that expressed pride in being an American, but that glossed over the difficulties faced by Americans who are Negro. He has regained his status, however, with a subsequent and more militant recording in which he shouts: "Say it loud!" and a chorus responds: "I'm black and I'm proud!"

The growth of the black theater is frequently compared by Negroes to the Irish revolution of the 1920's that produced Yeats, Singe and O'Casey. "They also wrote at a time when people were liberating themselves from oppression," said a Negro poet. "Just as they were at war, we are at war and we're rediscovering ourselves."

The Drama Review in its summer, 1968, edition, devoted entirely to black theater, listed 37 blacks or black-oriented theater groups with some degree of white participation, across the country. In fact, however, there are probably hundreds of others supported by antipoverty, self-help block associations and church groups.

A well-traveled Negro journalist said recently, "The small, informal and black-oriented theater group is getting to be one of the most popular organizing tools in the ghettos—you'll find very few poor, black communities without their own little group."

Sought to Prevent Riots

A good deal of the growth of contemporary black arts and letters can be traced to the countless, hastily thrown together riot-prevention programs brought into the country's slums in recent years.

Much of the interest in drama, for example, goes back to the LeRoi Jones-led Black Arts Theater that was founded in Harlem by Project Uplift—the Haryou summer crash program—during the summer of 1965.

Participants in Mr. Jones's group believed that the $3.2-million, 10-week program, coming one year after the Harlem disorders, was designed purely as a way to stop riots.

But with a series of short plays, by himself and young student playwrights, that were produced on street corners, tenement stoops and in parks, Jones brought a living theater to Harlem.

The original Black Arts Theater was criticized as being both antiwhite and profane. After less than a year Jones gave up the venture in Harlem and founded the Spirit House in his home town of Newark, giving that problem-plagued city its only repertory theater.

In explaining his concept of theater, Jones once wrote: "The revolutionary theater should force change; it should be change. If the beautiful see themselves, they will love themselves."

One of the best known of a growing school of LeRoi Jones protégés is Ed Bullins, a bearded, heavy-set writer from Philadelphia.

"I write for black people," Mr. Bullins explains, "to entertain, to instruct, to help."

He is an advocate of street-corner theater "where the pimps, whores and hustlers and the black working class are."

To punctuate his convictions, Mr. Bullins recently turned down a lucrative offer to write a screenplay for a Hollywood studio impressed with his plays, "The Electronic Nigger" and "Clara's Ole Man."

Diatribes and Pleas

Many of the productions coming out of the black slums are not plays in the strict sense of the word (but the writer here determines what is or is not a play) and some are diatribes, pleas or wish fulfillments spoken by actors on a stage.

In Ben Caldwell's "The Militant Preacher," for example, an obsequious Negro minister is converted into a pistol-packing revolutionary because he mistakenly takes the voice of a burglar for that of the Lord. Audiences have criticized the Caldwell play as wish fulfillment and praised it as an updated Molière's "Le Malade Imaginaire."

In another Caldwell play "Riot Sale or Dollar Psyche Fake Out," a group of would-be Negro revolutionaries do a complete about-face when the police fire money-loaded, antipoverty cannons into the group. While the Negroes fight among themselves, a policeman says: "Look at the black bastards go after that money."

Rally for Panthers

During a fund-raising rally for the Black Panthers in San Francisco last year, a play by Jimmy Garrett, "We Own the Night," was presented for the first time. The title was taken from a poem by LeRoi Jones and the plot dealt with an armed revolution by Negro youths, one of whom kills his mother, depicted as a symbol of Negro subservience to whites.

A less bloody but no less tragic black family crisis was the subject of Ronald Milner's three-act play, "Who's Got His Own," performed at the American Place Theater here last year. In the play, the love-hate relationship between whites and blacks has left the frustrated blacks with a residual impulse. As one of the characters in the play puts it: "Like he had to kill one of them before he could have any peace."

Jo Jackson, author with Joseph A. Walker of "The Believers," a musical drama tracing Negro life from pre-slavery Africa to the present, said recently:

"We're trying to say to black people that we can believe in ourselves. If we accept what we are, then the hell with what anyone else has to say about it. If the [white] man doesn't like it, that's his problem."

Miss Jackson, who is an administrator at Haryou's Head Start program, believes Negroes must write, direct and produce their own plays. "No one can tell my story the way I can," she said. "The way I see it, we've got Moses, we don't need Aaron."

Jesse De Vore, actor-producer of "The Believers," says it would be very difficult for whites to adequately judge many of the new black presentations.

Sitting in a Hot Church

"They can criticize acting or directing," he said recently, "but if they've never sat for hours on end in a hot, sweaty Deep-South Baptist church on hard, stiff-backed chairs and watched Deacon Miller snoring, they won't know what we're doing on stage. It would be like me trying to evaluate the Talmud."

C. Bernard Jackson, director of the Intercity Cultural Center of Los Angeles, is an advocate of community theater, but a theater that includes all the voices of the ghetto.

"There is a definite need for black groups to explore their own situation fully," Mr. Jackson said, "but there is also the very vital need for all minority nonwhites to begin establishing a dialogue because their problems are so similar."

Showcase on Coast

The Intercity Cultural Center is a showcase for the contributions of most of the ethnic groups of Los Angeles. In coming weeks, Mr. Jackson said, it will present "A Raisin in the Sun" by the late Lorraine Hansberry; "El Manco" by a 25-year-old Mexican-American, Josef Rodriguez, and "Eagle Boy" by an American Indian, Emathla A. Marshall.

The passionate interest in the black arts has brought with it a lack of desire on the part of some black professionals to set their sights on Broadway.

"There is no time for the luxury of being a performer who just happens to be black," said Barbara Ann Teer, the actress-director whose performance in "Home Movies" won for her the Vernon Rice Award for the Best Actress of the Year in 1965.

Miss Teer is now trying to develop "a whole black performing technique" that would use the black life style —its music, folklore, and "the life you find on the street corner, in barber shops, churches and whatever black people do naturally—soul."

Miss Teer, who wrote and directed the musical revue "We Real Cool," is highly critical of Broadway, a position that is common to many supporters of black community theater.

"Integration is only a subterfuge for the maintenance of white supremacy," she said. "Besides, the Man has reached a dead end creatively, so why should we continue to take our problems to him? He can't even solve his own."

Explaining Opposed

Many supporters of the black theater contend that it would take so much effort to explain their art to whites that the art itself would suffer to the point where it would no longer be black art. But others see the vitality of the black theater as a means of bringing new life to the "white" theater.

Mr. O'Neal, for example, has written in The Drama Review: "If I cut to the essence of my own truth there will lie a truth for all men." Mr. Jackson has said: "We doubt that the commercial media can make a truthful statement at this time. We hope to force them to speak the truth. If this kind of change is to come, it will be prompted by groups that have had the least opportunity to compete in the theater as it is now."

And the Negro playwright, Loften Mitchell, writes near the end of his book, "Black Drama":

"The one hope is that these groups in the ghetto areas—the townships composed of poor whites, Puerto Ricans and Negroes — will create drama as it was intended, as a living instrument that educates, communicates and entertains, an instrument that has a life commitment.

"The one hope is that these people will march into the center of the city and reshape the American theater into what that institution ought to be."

The Black Revolutionary Commercial by Ed Bullins

In San Francisco, during the Spring of 1967, LeRoi Jones worked with Black Arts/West, The Black House, and The Black Students' Union of San Francisco State College through a Black Arts coalition called the Black Arts Alliance to implement a Black Communications Project (T40, p. 53).

One of the numerous activities of the writers of The Black Arts Alliance was the writing of Black Commercials for use as short, low budget films that could be distributed nationally—quickly and economically—throughout Black communities.

We knew that the major means of communication to Black people in America is television. Then film. And we realized that the technical form of the television commercial was recognized by this Black audience on a mass subliminal basis and that we could utilize the forms but change the content, thus producing a revolutionary mass communications tool.

A number of Black Commercials were written by LeRoi Jones, Marvin X, and myself. All of mine were destroyed except the following (Black Commercial #2) during a period of imprisonment when the San Francisco police harrassed The Black House, our headquarters with Eldridge Cleaver and The Black Panther Party for Self-Defense, and Marvin X and I were arrested and held in various jails in the Bay area until The Black Arts Alliance freed us. Soon afterwards The Black House disintegrated and The Black Arts Alliance concentrated on creating a documentary film (*Black Spring*) and doing plays throughout California.

February 26, 1969
Harlem

LeRoi Jones

FADE IN:

Scene: Saturday night. "The Place," a pig feet emporium and whiskey, beer, and wine joint in the Black community. Black People so close that the air can be sliced in squares, packaged, and shipped north.

The Crowd watches Rufus and Blue as they occupy the dance floor. Rufus and Blue are killing each other. Rufus has a broken beer bottle and is trying to gouge Blue's eyes out. Blue holds his friend's arm with one hand and is kept from driving his bone-handled switchblade into Blue by the man's tenacity to remain alive.

RUFUS, *huffing.* Ya black mathafukker ... I'm gonna kill ya.

BLUE, *puffing.* Kiss ma ass ya jive mathafukker! ... I'm ...

CROWD (THE BLACK CHORUS). KILL KILL KILL ... THAT BLACK MATHAFUKKER!

RUFUS. I'm gonna cut ya up and down.

BLUE. Ah'm gonna cut ya side ta side.

CROWD. KILL KILL ... CUT 'EM UP 'N' DOWN ... SIDE TA SIDE ... 'N' 'CROSS DE CROSS ... KILL! KILL!

RUFUS. Ah'm gonna fuck ya up so bad ya mamma won't have ya.

BLUE. Black mathafukker! ... I don't play that shit ... just you wait!

They tussle more furiously.

CROWD. BLOOD! BLOOD! BLACK BLOOD! BLACK BLOOD!

RUFUS. Let me go, nigger ... so I can kill ya!

BLUE. Nigger ... just you wait until I git mah knife in ya ass!

A Young Blackman steps out of the crowd. He is neatly dressed and speaks quietly.

BLACKMAN. Brothers.

The two stop fighting.

RUFUS. What you say, man?

BLACKMAN. Brothers.

RUFUS and BLUE, *together.* Huh????

BLACKMAN. Brothers.

BLUE. You mean you think him and me is brothers?

BLACKMAN. Brothers.

CROWD, *bewildered, intermittent voices.* BROTHERS! BROTHERS! BROTHERS! BROTHERS! BROTHERS! BROTHERS! BROTHERS! BROTHERS! BROTHERS! (*Growing more confident.*) BROTHERS BROTHERS BROTHERS BROTHERS

BROTHERS BROTHERSBROTHERS-BROTHERSBROTHERS ...

RUFUS, *to Blue.* If we brothers, man ...

BLUE, *perceiving.* Yeah ... then ...

RUFUS, *recognizing.* Why ... brother ...

Rufus helps Blue up. Blue begins brushing his brother off.

BLACKMAN. Black.

CROWD, *chants.* Black brothers black brothers black brothers ... black black ... (*Blackman steps back into the Crowd and becomes one of them as Rufus and Blue clasp hands and speak of their mutual plans for the future, working in unity.*) Salaam ... Salaam ... Salaam ... All Praises Due to the Blackman, etc....

FADE OUT

THIS BLACK PUBLIC AFFAIRS ANNOUNCEMENT WAS MADE POSSIBLE BY YOUR NATIONAL BLACK CONSCIOUSNESS BROADCASTING COMPANY (BCBC).

4/12/67

SOURCES OF THE NILE

paul williams

I don't know why I'm always leaping into text to talk about nonverbal, abstract aesthetic experiences, stuff that can't be talked about, stuff like comic art and rock and roll. But I have a real obsession with Things That Need To Be Done; I keep thinking, "If I don't, nobody will." And it seriously upsets my sense of the order of the universe to think that, with all the emphasis that's placed on mass media (like the underground press) these days, no one in this media is writing about and legitimatizing and boosting the careers of such vital spokesmen as Bob Crumb, Marty Carey, Ron Cobb, Lou Reed, Ray Davies, Eben Given, Arthur Lee... well, anyway, I get to thinking how much I love (for example) Bob Crumb's comic strips, and how nice it would be to write an essay about them that would turn people onto them, offer some insight and encourage people to "take them seriously," i.e., let them into your life, not just your living room. Well, okay.

And so Bob's first full-fledged book (not quite as exciting as his first full-fledged comic book, but Good), HEAD COMIX, becomes available, and I decide now is the time. Aha. But thinking how nice it would be to write about so-and-so is just the anticipation stage. When I actually get going I don't care what I'm writing about as long as the words keep coming, as long as it has that tiger-by-the-tail feeling as it pours through the typewriter. But suppose I can't get going? Suppose that strange force that takes over my mind and moves my fingers fails to show up? What if I actually have to sit back and think up a whole article about Bob Crumb? What would I say?

Recently I picked up a copy of the "Portable Thoreau," and it pleased me no end that the first essay I read was a review of a study of the Wildlife of Massachusetts, in which Henry began by talking about why and when it's pleasant to read about wildlife, and went on to discuss the kinds of birds he had seen in the woods, with scarcely a backward glance at the book. This struck me as real legitimatization of my haphazard approach to the "review" ("Gee," I thought, "Maybe I'll be remembered as an Essayist, who of course doesn't have to worry himself with facts and subject matter"); but still I worry about getting myself together.

Some time ago (January 1966) I started a magazine of rock and roll because we were all listening to the stuff and it seemed that as long as we had this shared experience, why not talk about it? Well, since then a number of other people have had the same idea, and rock has been beaten half to death with words and attention. Which makes one wonder if one should talk about stuff, the word "legitimatization" has a kind of a cruddy ring to it anyway, why not stay home and get stoned and not try to turn people onto things?

I don't know.

I think we're pushing toward some further point, if you want the truth. Common experience is a very big part of common consciousness. People who took acid ten years ago report very different experiences and reactions from taking it in '66 and '67, "when everyone else was taking it," when one was conscious of acid as a thing, something people were doing, a common adventure, like a political movement or adolescents discovering sex. There are levels of life these days that don't have to do with the individual against the universe, or alone; levels that one can only really perceive in the context of being part of a group. This is partly the result of growing up plugged-in, via telephone, tv, radio, daily paper, jet, all that stuff — it still gives me chills to think that many million people could be hearing this song or watching this show at exactly this same moment — I once flashed on how EVERY PERSON IN THE WORLD associates the same tactile sensation (phone receiver) with the voices they hear over the phone! But our growth into gestalts of varying sizes and degrees which will eventually take over a number of tasks now left to individuals, or to individuals "representing" millions of people, is in all ways a natural next step in our mental and social growth as homo sapiens — and certainly it seems clear that one way or another we're on the verge of the biggest step in two-thousand years. You can feel it in the air. You can certainly see it in the art.

So I suppose I can explain to myself my sense of urgency about turning people onto stuff that moves me; it's that "let's get together" instinct ("love" was a word that got tossed in to fill that vacuum for a short time last year), that back-to-the-womb-on-a-cosmic-basis, purple shift uge. That feeling that not just is it nice to understand the universe and how to behave in relation to it, but it's necessary-to-survival and urgent that EVERYBODY understand the thing and as quickly as possible, ecological panic; which feeling results in a half-generous, half-righteous notion that anything that helps me figure out what's going on ought to be given a try by all of my friends. So we've all become Bible-thumpers, even if it is for rock bands and books of children's fantasy.

But what can I say of Bob Crumb? Well, I like him because he makes me laugh (of course), because his world-system is so believable, so easy to slip into, and because so often when one says, "Yes! That's it!" looking at a Crumb comic, one has to admit that one never knew that that was it until old Bob's eagle eye noticed it and pointed it out. Bob has a real grasp on the vague, the fine point that isn't quite there ("Lost it again!") but that certainly has an effect on what's happening. (Now, when the smallest of the three girls grabs Fritz the Cat by the tail, saying "I wanna be in on this thing," why is it so believable, so much like something one has seen many times? After all, people don't have tails, so that particular bit of business couldn't be natural, must be part of Crumb's imagination. But still it's definitely something I've seen many times — I don't know what — the point is, Crumb portrays a REAL world, which you accept as real and as being one you live in even when you can't make the connections. He's that convincing. And subtle. And perceptive.) The genius of the artist is, as always, that he makes us see with our eyes what we feel with our emotions and grasp with our minds. He rarefies human experience into a representation that is as full as the experience itself, but stopped, there on the page, accessible, unbound by space and time.

Crumb presents Whiteman in all his glory, pulling himself together from a wreck to a proud specimen in one panel, but later complaining that his "rigid position" is hard work (only the rare Group Image comics share this kind of social sensitivity): "I get head aches! My bowels refuse to function... guts are on fire..." He runs through the spectrum of his spiritual life — being polite, being exhausted, craving sex, being an American & an Adult with Responsibilities, chickening out, drinking, feeling fear, embarrassment — perfect, precise, beautifully, humanly caricatured... but it would still be too heavy-handed were it not for the last panel. Whiteman has been captured by his own fantasy "Little Rascals"/"Amos & Andy" spades and had his pants pulled off. "Hey c'mon!" says one darkie. "We's all joinin' th' parade!" The narration reads: "Will Whiteman join the parade?" You see Whiteman going through his changes below ("foolish nonsense... might be fun...") and the final narration: "Oh, eventually!" Tell it like it is, brother, And not only are the story and the portrait right on target, but the tone, as created by the dialogue, the style of drawing, the rhythm of the gags, is just what it has to be, and more. Crumb can be as pleasant to listen to as Brian Jones.

And for very little money (well, less than a record album — but we'll discuss the value question another time) you get "Stoned," "Whiteman," "Mr. Natural Visits the City," "Fritz the Cat," "Keep on Trucking," "Life Among the Constipated," and more, all in the livingest black and white you ever saw. If you're ready for a freaked-out view of modern life that sounds like everything that entered the portals of your mind via tv, comics, magazines, radio between maybe ages five and ten, if you're ready to see things the way you know they are but are trying to pretend they're not, if you're a fan of Herriman, Johnson, Kelly and Capp and don't want to be left behind this generation, folks, you know what to do. HEAD COMIX is published by Viking Press. Also keep your eyes open for copies of "Yellow Dog," the comic newspaper ("Those Cute Little Bearzy-Wearzies" in YD5 is my favorite Crumb), have fun, and there goes another column it took four days to write.

San Francisco
Express Times 11/13/68

KOMIX KOUNTERMEDIA

The Left's mixed reception of komix is an interesting indication of the schism in attitudes toward "cultural" subjects. On the one hand, people (including myself) who believe that the New Left is only part of a much larger but more amorphous New Culture movement are excited to see an intrusion of radical attitudes into "classic" areas of modern cultural mediations, comic strips and comic books. For us it seems to promise another step toward an organic New Left, striking root in society deeper than the level of "politics" (elections, parties, organizers, etc.). On the other hand, plenty of fine, even good-humored radicals are plainly distressed to see the excitement over komix. One extreme tendency is indicated by a dealer in an old, CP-oriented bookshop who wrote me that *all* "underground culture" was a new attempt by the ruling class to pervert the revolutionary threat. Another attitude, common among people sympathetic to New Left culturalists, is that komix are interesting but not to be taken seriously in political terms.

A considerable amount of the confusion about komix and the Left is their newness, with their power to irritate or excite. Not that comic strips have been unknown to the Left: from the old *Industrial Worker's* "Mr. Block" (an ignorant, strikebreaking worker who always ends up getting his lumps from the capitalists) to the *Daily Worker's* Little Lefty (a Pop-Front-ish slum kid, predictable, but the most live thing in the paper) to the satire of a liberal superman in *19* (put out by New York CIPA) a couple of years ago, strips have often been offered in radical newspapers. But komix, as drawn by such creative figures as Robert Crumb, Gilbert Shelton, and S. Clay Wilson, are more than simply instruments of the political New Left; they are subversive thrusts at capitalism coming right out of a popular cultural tradition.

More fundamentally the confusion about komix is symptomatic of important misunderstandings about the meanings of culture and art. Bourgeois aesthetics has taught us that these are leisure customs associated with the elites, rather than organic aspects of popular life. But if we accept the anthropological definition of culture as the style and organization of day-to-day life and of art as a more self-conscious aspect of "culture," then content, how popular "culture" and "art" relate to the values of society's rulers, becomes an important political question.

As yet, the New Left does not possess the theoretical tools for a full analysis of modern (hence popular) culture and its art forms (certainly less for comic strips than for America's other two distinctive contributions to twentieth century culture, cinema and jazz) under capitalism in the mass market epoch. Certain critics, like Marshall McLuhan, attempt to deal with the meaning of various communications media in contemporary society; but for me the most heuristic insights were offered by Walter Benjamin over thirty years ago, in his brilliant essay, "Art in the Age of Mechanical Reproduction."

Art, as Benjamin understood, could not remain unchanged in the new era of mass production and consumption: its traditional "aura," its quality of craft refinement, of rarity, could not survive immersion in the "commonness" of the masses and their daily life. Indeed, to have any elan or vitality of its own art had to associate itself with and give expression to the existence of the people it now reached. Even poor Mona Lisa, reproduced on a half million postcards, simply wasn't enough.

But Benjamin also perceived that the possibilities for new, popular arts were emerging at the very time when bourgeois cultural vitality had long passed even though their nascent forms were subject to the influences of the decay of bourgeois culture. On the other hand, he believed that the threads of art's resurrection nevertheless lay *within popular culture,* in the essence of their content that commercial forms so thoroughly violated. In one sense, the forms of the future were stretching their fingers into a repression-ridden present; in another, mass art, like politically revolutionary forces, was maturing, as it had to, within the womb of the culture of the old social system.

Drawing on Benjamin's notion of a cultural dialectic, I have noted three rough stages for the emerging modern art form which also describe the growth of twentieth century comic strips: (1) an early, highly experimental period, where the very newness of the form permits the "eccentric" visionaries to practice before internal and external discipline are fully introduced; (2) a period of immense *schlock,* where glimmerings of a future art are more hidden than earlier, and certainly less immediately political; and (3) the emergence of a new style, which cannot fully develop itself under capitalism, but reaches beyond its limits in a hundred ways, often grasping an alternative (usually non-profit) medium for uncensored expression.

From an article in *Leviathan* July/Aug 1969 by Paul Buhle

Leviathan

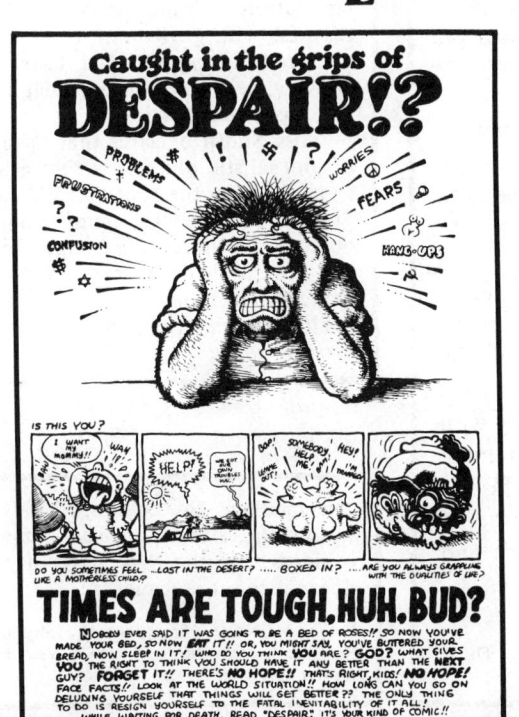

LETTERS

FACTS
FIGURES
FEELINGS

Serve the People!

Friends—

Just a note on that piece I did about the Minuteman raid on Voluntown (see WIN vol.IV, no.16), since I'd like to maintain some degree of credibility as a reporter. Although the report was obviously incorrect in many ways, it was nonetheless the story as it was received from four different sources. The farm folk *were* phoned, as were the State Police.

All I can say in my defense is that during the couple weeks after the attack, I heard no less than three different versions from the Police and two versions from different farm people. I'm willing to admit that the things I reported were incorrect, but I must tell you that it's an accurate repeating of the story as I got it. Perhaps I ought to have "reliable sources" like the government. As to whether or not certain parts were in good taste, well, that's up to each of us and there's no reason to argue.

On a last point, however, I must say something. Off and on I have been criticized for writing rather emotionally, not sticking to facts and figures to the minutest degree. The reason I have tried to make my articles slightly emotional is this: I am tired as hell of reports that are cut and dried and nearly devoid of imagination. I think it's important that moods and feelings be put across in print, because we *do* have them from time to time and it might be dangerous if we portrayed ourselves as robots that bear with unbearable sorrow without batting an eyelash. We might begin to *believe* we're braver, or stronger, or more moral, or holier than those who disagree with us if we speak only of actions and avoid emotions. I have sadly seen much imagination, creativity, and openess vanish from the "movement".

Put it this way: we are dehumanized by so much that we needn't start working on ourselves. Leah Fritz is only too correct when she says we have been stupid. In the name of facts and figures, we have put aside our feelings.

Argue the reporting, if you wish, argue the facts and figures that were the first to come to the surface, but don't turn it into a criticism of writing style—OK friends?

Steve Trimm
Chatham, N.Y.

A letter to WIN Sept 1968

What is new, in our democracy, is the quantity, the degree of news management. What is new is the fact that high government officials openly admit it, and that the large majority of the American people have accepted it as one of the facts of life. William Touhy, the *Los Angeles Times* correspondent in Saigon, writes:

Sylvester [Assistant Secretary of Defense for Public Affairs Arthur Sylvester] has said he favors government news management, including lying to the press in times of crisis. On a trip to Vietnam, he declared the press ought to be the handmaiden of the government, as far as reporting the war went.[15]

And *Newsweek* quoted the official spokesman for the United States mission in Saigon as stating: "My directive says that our policy is one of minimum candor."[17]

The open advocacy by governmental leaders of policies of "minimum candor" and lying to the people undermines "the right to know." The restrictions on his right to know the truth mesh neatly with the citizen's regressive wish to remain unknowing, and further facilitate his regression to the preadolescent phase of seeking security in the omniscience and omnipotence of the authority figures.

Psychological Habituation To War by Dr. I. Ziferstein, 1967

UNDERGROUND PRESS CATCHES YOUTHS' EYE

LOS ANGELES—Many young people are turning away from the conventional press to the different view of society they find in "underground" newspapers.

This is the conclusion of Miss Gaye Smith, a journalism student at the University of California at Los Angeles, in a study entitled "The Underground Press in Los Angeles."

There are more than 150 underground newspapers across the country, with a total circulation of 2 million copies, Miss Smith reports. The growth of these papers has occurred during the last four years, she adds, while many conventional newspapers are ceasing publication.

Miss Smith declares that "a basic tenet of journalistic practice is that a newspaper should mirror the society." She added that "by the mid-1960's, many young people no longer believed the image projected by the established press." With a new iconoclastic humor, new "morality" and cynicism, experimental journalism was inevitable, she suggested.

The media is the enemy, Mr. Mungo said. I'd much rather put The Times out of business than the New York City police. It does much more damage.

RAY MUNGO, founder of Liberation News Service, in an interview with a *New York Times* reporter.

HERB CAEN: "I'M JUST AN OLD HOOKER"

alfonso vendetta

Almost every day some reporter from an official newspaper or some student at an official university calls up the Express Times office to ask for an interview.

"I'm supposed to write something on the underground press," they say. "When are you free?"

"We're always free," is one answer. "How about you?"

Three weeks ago, in a fit of pique, I called up Herb Caen's office, said I was doing a feature on the Establishment press, and wanted to interview him. To my surprise he called back the next day and found an open date: March 12 at 1 pm.

"Let's make it on OUR turf," I said. "Hamburgers at the Cabaret, 260 Valencia."

The Cabaret's gaily striped awnings face a Levi Strauss factory. It's one block away from the huge National Guard Armory at 14th and Mission. Our network of distant early warning poets tells us that the National Guard will be in the Mission District some time this year or next. Mission High students---black, latino, and hip--are already in an insurrectionary mood. The area is rapidly filling up with hip people who can't afford Bernal Heights or North Beach and can't take the Haight-Ashbury, at a time when the latino population has stopped thinking of itself as a bunch of short, dark people best suited for stoop labor. Now they know they are the original soul of this American continent. Aztec culture is beginning to sprout in the Mission; "Tio Taco" is dead for good.

The Mission Coalition Organization, a broad front of community organizations which in normal times would be Alioto loyalists, voted full support to the San Francisco State strike. City Hall radar recorded it as a strong blip. Herb Caen missed it. His antennae are pointed in a different direction--North of Market, towards Nob, Russian and Telegraph Hills.

"We already have an underground daily paper," he said for openers. "Right here in San Francisco."

How can he call the Chronicle an underground paper?

"Because it's irreverent and anarchical. At the same time, it's commercially acceptable--something that can happen only in San Francisco."

Only in San Francisco--Herb Caen's theme. I don't like seeing San Francisco chucked under the chin, kichy-koo. San Francisco is beautiful—not cute.

My hostility came out in two sharp questions. The first: "Is it true that you're corrupt?"

"Corrupt? Do you mean print items for money?"

"Money or sexual favors."

"Absolutely not," he said, and sounded like he meant it. "I'm not for sale."

The second hostile question: "How much money do you make?"

"About as much as a good centerfielder with a lifetime batting average of .300, who's a little past his peak."

It sounded like about a hundred thousand dollars, and it also sounded sad. Herb Caen has been writing his column six days a week for 31 years, and he got sick of it long ago. He says he has spent all the money. One suspects he has salted a lot of it away; but his talent is more important, and he believes it is gone for good.

"I always planned to get out of journalism by the age of 40,'" said Caen, now 53. "George Bernard Shaw said you've got to get out of journalism by the time you're 40 or it'll suck you dry. He was right. I should have gotten out, but for some reason I couldn't. It did suck me dry. Now I'm just a hack, and I'll keep hacking away."

In one important respect Herb Caen shares the condition of the workers at the Levi Strauss factory next door to the Cabaret. They are doomed to do the same thing every day, doomed to follow a rhythm different from the rhythm of their own bodies. Herb Caen can look at his appointment book today and tell you just what next Tuesday will be like for him.

"Isn't there some way of making it better?" I asked. "Sabbatical leaves, maybe."

"No," he said. "That won't work. If we didn't do it every day, we couldn't do it again at all. The longer you write, the more insecure you get. I shudder to think of writing the column after a year off. I'm just an old hooker, and I can't quit now."

How would he feel if an old Chronicle, five years old maybe, happened to appear on his desk. Would he look at his column?

"Yes, I'd have to look at it. But I wouldn't like it. I don't think I've ever written a column I've really liked."

The atmosphere was getting too thick with self-pity. Time for a change of subject. "Reading between the lines in your column, I gather you smoke pot. Is that true?"

"I have smoked it," he answered. "Back in 1934, when I was a police reporter in Sacramento, Sergeant Eddie Cox took me aside after a raid and we smoked some confiscated pot. He said: 'Sooner or later you're going to try this, kid, so smoke it with us and you won't get into trouble.'

"But basically I'm a juicehead," he said with an apologetic smile. He has never tried LSD or any other strong psychedelics.

Periodically I threw in quick surprise questions like, "Who runs San Francisco?" It was a small-town prosecutor's trick, and he handled it very graciously. "I wish I knew who runs San Francisco," he would say. "But I really haven't got the slightest idea."

He praised the hamburgers—the Cabaret makes a very nice Russianburger with sour cream for 75¢—and expressed disbelief at the prices. "How do they stay in business with prices like these?" He paid the bill and scuttled off.

Two days later, Nacio Brown went to photograph Caen in his office, and dragged three of us along for the ride. We conversed nervously for ten minutes while Nacio clicked away. Caen's office —"fancier than the publisher's", whispered a jealous Chronicle reporter—defeated us.

We stopped in the city room on the way out and purched on the desk of a feature writer who covers the oddball beat for the Chronicle. Twenty years ago he was editing a tiny anarchist magazine. Ten years ago he was writing poetry in North Beach. The day of our encounter he had just finished a cute little piece on the "Nude-In" that didn't encounter he had just finished a cute little piece on the "Nude-In" that didn't happen in Woodside. It was the kind of story that is the Chronicle's bread-and-butter: suburban bluenose high school authorities outwitted by wholesome, lusty youth.

We chatted for half an hour while the city room hummed all around us. It's an informal place, comfortable and well worn. The employees are free to put up notices and posters anywhere, and they take advantage of it. The copy boys are all longhairs; so are some of the reporters and copy editors. But people sit at desks, in rows; and they are all men, for some reason.

"You need an advice column," suggested the feature writer. "And I've got someone in mind who could do a good job. You know what I mean: kind of 'Advice to the Hiplorn', how to arrange an abortion if you knock up your girlfriend, that kind of thing."

The woman in our party winced to hear that, and tried to explain why.

We talked about a series he had done recently on North Beach. He had tried to coin some word for the new North Beach crowd; had come up with "bippies," a combination of "beatnik" and "hippies" which clearly would not work. The series had stopped short after two articles. The word "beatnik" was coined by Herb Caen and went round the world; it became a powerful weapon in the hands of the smug. "Bippie," fortunately, won't go anywhere.

The Chronicle is by far the best daily newspaper in the country. The writing, the headlines, the makeup, the photos and photo captions all show an intelligence and sense of humor that make the ordinary daily newspaper look like a weekly shopping news. The prestige newspapers—New York Times, St. Louis Post-Dispatch, Washington Post, and now the L.A. Times, I suppose—are so impressed with their own importance in History that they lose the feel of the street. They are written and laid out according to thirty-year-old formulas. The Chronicle, by playing it just a little bit loose, has attracted and kept some of the best talent in the business—INCREASING circulation all the time, prospering while other papers collapse.

But the men who put out the Chronicle take a terrible beating. They have to turn it out every day—and anything, even fucking, gets to be a drag if you have to do it on schedule. They type their stories with multiple carbons which a copy boy spreads around to the men whose job it is to read them. The atmosphere reeks of alchohol, self-pity and fear; not so much fear of the boss as fear of the audience they write for. They conceive of themselves as infiltrators into the middle-class mind. If the readers ever discover how they were being subverted, they would rise in righteous wrath. Editor Scott Newhall protects his staff from Teamster goons and suburban fascists. Miracle of miracles, he even keeps the big advertisers happy.

They have a union, The Newspaper Guild, but no sense of family. The Guild is for editorial employees; men who work with metal type have a separate union, as do men who deliver bundles of newspapers. There is a class barrier between the city room and the delivery trucks, and a strong political polarization in the wind. The city room is solidly against Jim Rourke and his goon squad; but how do the drivers feel about it? Something to worry about.

All week we had been handing out leaflets for the Marina Green rally, handing them out to salt-of-the-earth working people on the Muni buses. We hairy freaks preaching revolution now feel more at home in America than the men who are suppose to have their fingers right on the pulse of the public.

"After all these years," Herb Caen told me, "I've lost touch. I envy you people because you know your audience so much better."

Yes—and perhaps because we're getting to know HIS audience so much better. The Marina Green rally got virtually no advance publicity in the Establishment media. The Chronicle carried just one story on it, on page 11 last Friday. Television coverage was nil. The word was spread through the underground press, through leaflets posted and handed out, through the FM rock stations. Trying to get a plug for the rally in Herb Caen's column, I told him last Wednesday to expect a crowd of 75,000. He looked incredulous, but he printed that number in his Friday column. It turned out to be four or five times too big—but it was the only number he had.

In the city room, the feature writer was worrying about "the Nixon Era" descending upon us.

"Man," I said, "you've got the wrong attitude. They give you an inch and you say, 'Thank you sir, I'll use about three-quarters of an inch and save the rest for a rainy day.' That's all wrong. If they give you an inch, take a mile."

San Francisco
Express Times 3/18/69

The following memorandum has been distributed to department heads at the New York Times: "The Publisher has expressed a strong feeling that the Times should insist on reasonable standards for the personal appearance of young men who work for the Times. By this he means that their hair should be cut reasonably short and that they should be clean shaven and neatly attired, with clean, business-style shirt with necktie, where appropriate to the work situation.

"In order to make sure that these standards are met, I would appreciate it if, when hiring new employes, you would make it clear that you only hire people who meet them, and that maintaining this level of appearance will be required for continued employment.

"Young people already employed should be told that The Times expects them to meet the same standards and that, although continued employment will not be jeopardized by failure to meet them, they will be a factor considered when opportunities for advancement arise.

"If you have any problems concerning the implementation of this policy, please contact Industrial Relations. We will be happy to work on any individual situation that may arise."

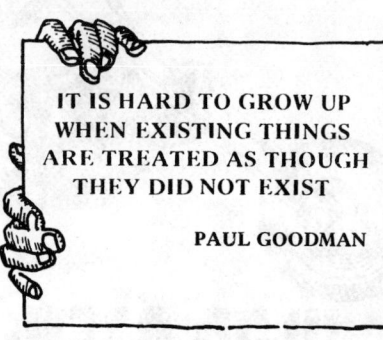

IT IS HARD TO GROW UP WHEN EXISTING THINGS ARE TREATED AS THOUGH THEY DID NOT EXIST

PAUL GOODMAN

Censorship is not concerned so much to prevent the transmission of forbidden information or ideas as to deny legitimacy to a style of life and the experiences to which those ideas attest.

EDGAR Z. FRIEDENBERG "The Hidden Costs of Opportunity" in *Atlantic Monthly*

In American society we have perfected a remarkable form of censorship: to allow every one his political right to say what he believes, but to swamp his little boat with literally thousands of millions of newspapers, mass-circulation magazines, best-selling books, broadcasts, and public pronouncements that disregard what he says and give the official way of looking at things. Usually there is no conspiracy to do this; it is simply that what he says is not what people are talking about, it is not newsworthy.

(There is no conspiracy, but it is *not* undeliberate. "If you mean to tell me," said an editor to me, "that our magazine tries to have articles on important issues and treat them in such a way that nothing can come of it — who can deny it?" Try also, to get a letter printed in the New York *Times* if your view on this issue calls attention to an essential factor that is not being mentioned.)

Naturally, the more simply true a statement is in any issue where everybody is quite confused, the less newsworthy it will be, the less it will be what everybody is talking about. When the child in the story said, "But the Emperor has no clothes on!" the newspapers and broadcasts surely devoted many columns to describing the beautiful new clothes and also mentioned the interesting psychological incident of the child. Instead of being proud of him, his parents were ashamed; but on the other hand they received $10,000 in sympathetic contributions toward his rehabilitation for he was a newsworthy case. But he had a block in reading.

Where there is official censorship it is a sign that speech is serious. Where there is none, it is pretty sure that the official spokesmen have all the loud-speakers.

PAUL GOODMAN in "Youth in an Organized Society."

The Image Monopolists

THE FIRST FREEDOM. *By Bryce W. Rucker. Southern Illinois University Press. 322 pp. $12.50.*

HERBERT I. SCHILLER

Mr. Schiller is research professor of economics and communications at the University of Illinois.

The original version of *The First Freedom* appeared in 1946, and was dedicated by its author, Morris Ernst, "To the Members of the Congress of the United States on whom we must rely to restore free enterprise in movies, radio, and press." This misplaced trust aside, the book called attention, in documented detail, to widespread monopolistic developments in the American press, radio and motion picture industries. Still, Ernst was not without hope. "I am convinced," he wrote then, that "it is not too late to stem the tide. But we must act fast and with bravery."

More than two decades later, Bryce Rucker, with Ernst's approval, has published under the same title an updated inventory of the organizational state of American mass communications. Expectations for remedial change, along with confidence in the essential health of the media, are barely visible this second time around. In an introduction to the modernized work, Ernst observes dejectedly: "The most frightening part of Professor Rucker's exploration may well be seen in the simple and dirty fact that the abandonment of the idea of competition of ideas can scarcely be debated in our culture today. It will be of interest to note," Ernst adds, "whether the Rucker facts and thesis are even given public attention in the mass media." He concludes it would be a miracle to expect such an event.

Is this despair justified? In 1946, Ernst had recommended, among other measures, that joint communications ventures be prohibited; that newspapers be divested of the ownership of radio stations; that radio stations be pried loose from broadcasting networks; that N.B.C. be liberated from RCA; that the chain ownership of radio stations, newspapers and theatres be disallowed; and that FCC control be imposed over the speculative sale of radio stations.

The latest evidence, painstakingly and impressively accumulated by Rucker, demonstrates that the trends uncovered by Ernst have become dominant and seemingly institutionalized national patterns. In a word, the movement to monopolization in the mass media has accelerated. Chains reach across the land. In 1967, newspaper combines "owned 871 of the 1,767 daily newspapers . . . or 49.3 percent of the total." Chains owned the five largest general circulation dailies, and nineteen of the top twenty-five. Chains owned 31.4 per cent of the commercial AM and a similar percentage of FM radio stations. Television, just appearing when Ernst made his pioneer study, but now the most influential of all the mass media, Rucker finds "virtually taken over by enterprising chain broadcasters," who now control 73.6 per cent of all commercial stations.

The process of concentrated control extends in all directions. Newspapers own huge numbers of television stations. In 1967, publishers "held interests in a third of the VHF stations (156) and in 22 percent of the UHF stations (28)." Beyond this, "newspaper-television monopolies existed in 27 American cities" and varying degrees of joint media control prevail in scores of other communities. Last year, on the newspaper front alone, there were competing dailies in only sixty-four of America's 1,547 daily newspaper cities. In several states, no competing papers exist in any localities.

In television, chain ownership is but one facet of monopoly control. Three networks (A.B.C., N.B.C., C.B.S.) largely determine what Americans see on the tube, for "only about 13 percent of all broadcast time is devoted to local-live programming." In prime time (7 to 11 P.M.), networks provide 95 per cent of the material. In addition to programing control, the networks own the most profitable stations in the largest markets. In turn, the networks are either part of larger electronics-defense-communications combines (N.B.C. resides in the RCA-corporate-supershelter), or are utterly dependent on a few hundred giant advertisers for the bulk of their income. "The five largest advertisers in 1966 contributed 17.8 percent, the 35 top advertisers supplied 50.7 percent of television's total advertising income."

Bryce Rucker systematically examines the entire image-making apparatus (with the exception of motion pictures) and finds it interconnected at almost every vital point. Two international news services, AP and UPI, themselves the instruments of tightly held interests, provide the world view of most Americans, since these services, with few exceptions, are the main sources of international news for the nation's press and broadcasters.

The communications technostructures prefer to minimize their economic impulses and to emphasize a posture of public spiritedness, but profit seeking is their driving force. In a thirteen-year period, from 1954 to 1966, "4,369 broadcasting stations as well as 538 television stations, changed hands at a total cost of $1,536,014,367." This mountain of capital gains, incidentally, derives from the assignment of licenses, granted by the FCC to private broadcasters on a temporary basis, for the use of public property—the radio spectrum.

This should suggest that the mass media are more than the well-paid servants of commerce, though they are certainly that. In structure, operation and motivation, the business of communications is distinguishable from other corporate business only in its claim of special constitutional privilege. It utilizes technology to reinforce market position, and Rucker details any number of anti-competitive practices including price fixing, kickbacks and pools.

Favorite cold-war social science models, predicating pluralism, the end of ideology and the attenuation of profit maximizing are poor guides to the performance of the mass communications industries. What is more, the media's conditions do not reflect malfunctioning in vestigial economic activities. Monopoly, profit maximization and a public-be-damned stance are located in the most dynamic, modernized and "cleanest" industries. These constitute the central nervous system of the social order. They provide the national image of what is normal, what is orderly, what is preferable, and what is just. But these perspectives are the carefully tooled products of business structures heavily concentrated, self-serving, and as indifferent to the public interest as any 19th-century trust. Moreover, the doctored outputs of the American mass media are penetrating international markets and have created a monumental problem for those concerned with safeguarding national cultural sovereignties.

Is the present course reversible? Ernst, nearly a quarter of a century ago, appealed to Congress. Rucker, more realistically, notes that "Approximately twenty-five congressmen or members of their family own interests in radio and television properties. . . . Less well known, but even more serious, probably half of the senators and representatives through their law firms represent broadcasters . . . (and) what should we call the free radio and television time given to two-thirds of the members of Congress by their local stations?" Not surprisingly, Congress is quick to censure even the mildest efforts of that notorious paper tiger regulator, the FCC, when it moves to remind broadcasters of their public responsibilities.

Obligated to be as constructive as possible in an increasingly desperate situation, Rucker proposes some legislative reforms to stymie further concentration in the mass media. His prescriptions—tax levies that discourage station sales, adjusted postal subsidies that reverse the arrangements that now benefit the large newspapers and magazines, and more prominent ownership disclosure in all media—in the unexpected event that they should be enacted, are unlikely to halt the rush to continental inter-media combination. Fewer and still more omnipotent private conduits of information and entertainment seem to be in the offing. Vast electronic, "knowledge conglomerates" are currently being assembled. This raises a question: "Can the day be far off," Rucker asks, "when criticism of the mass media will be published only by the university presses?" Answer: Southern Illinois University Press published *The First Freedom*.

Much of the reason TV is misunderstood in terms of its effects is that we want to relate to it as a visual medium, the way we do print. According to McLuhan, "TV is, above all, an extension of the sense of touch, which involves maximal interplay of all the senses." A generation raised on assimilation of the electronic experience of television is not a visual (Marcuse's "one-dimensional man") generation but is instead a generation plunged into a depth relationship with every facet of their world. "Primitive" cultures which have not been permeated by print have much more in common with the youth of Amerika (as does China) than the youth have with their elders; current borrowings from Afro-American, American Indian, and Oriental culture demonstrates the relationship being formulated between non-literate peoples and post-literate ones.

Attempts by the power structure of the United States to manipulate the medium of television are even more failure-prone than their blatant misunderstandings of the effects of TV coverage of an event. The spectral presence of the TV camera during the moon explorations digs the grave of the militarist, imperialist, capitalist powers that try to "sponsor" the event of space travel: Nixon should never have placed that phone call to outer space! It is not so much the physical act of travelling to the moon that is so powerful in its repercussions; rather it is the simultaneous involvement in this event by millions of people all over the globe that is the crucial phenomen. The maintenance of power by an empire is destroyed utterly by the global shrinking that occurs when the earth (and Man) is no longer the "subject" of the universe. If TV is the LSD of the planet earth's human population, the ego-loss that is taking place is none other than the loss of power of the United States of Amerika, the "I" of the world. Just as the liberation of women forces men to lose their status of perpetual Subject, Author and Actor (with women the perpetual Object, Creation, Receiver), the moon probe forces the planet earth to reevaluate itself within the context of a new perspective in which the earth is, concretely, merely one body among many in the universe, man merely one animal among many.

Agnew's epochal speech lamenting the failure of the Amerikan body politic to effectively harness and manipulate one of their technological offspring merely reveals the truth that technology is coming of age and wants to be its own boss. Television is probably the single most crucial unruly thread that is unravelling the whole fabric of Amerikan power both at home and abroad (and if Amerika is uptight about the effects of TV, wait till it picks up on the vibrations of the computer!). "Democracy," or corporate capitalism, depends tremendously on a "free press," "free speech," etc. None of these are, of course, free in the sense of liberated or liberating because they have their roots in the cult of the individual; they are no more "free" than "free enterprise," but they are crucial to the smooth functioning of such a society.

TV
AGNEW
UNDERGROUND

"Underground" newspapers are more vital as print media simply because the people involved in their production have been more profoundly influenced by the effects of television than their establishment counterparts. The most revered characteristic of establishment journalism—objectivity—is the greatest obstacle to the success of underground journalism. Underground writers are actually TV cameramen while most television practitioners belong in the medium of print journalism. The word "news" has been totally redefined by television—and by the underground press. It is no accident that the political persuasion of the underground press, and of the revolutionary youth movement as a whole, should take the form of communism: "What the Cubans are getting by TV," says *The Gutenberg Galaxy*, "is the experience of being directly engaged in the making of political decisions."

Not only has Agnew picked up on the fact that there are "substantive" contrasts between the power of TV and that of print, but also the incredible powers of "a raised eyebrow, an inflection of the voice, a caustic remark dropped in the middle of a broadcast," the new "stereotypes" that he sees have replaced the old ones destroyed by TV. The famous "credibility gap" is not, as Agnew says, so much in the offices of the government in Washington nor even, as he suggests, in the studios of the networks in New York, but is actually on the television screens of millions of people across the country. The Credibility Gap, like its sibling the Generation Gap, is simply that moral, emotional, social, esthetic, political, psychic no-man's-land between the world of print and the world of electronic media. There is an infinite amount of difference in separation by space, which exists in the case of a newspaper "news story" and "editorial comment," and separation by consecutive time, which is the case with, for example, Nixon's Vietnam speech and the "instant analysis" indulged in by network commentators immediately—they are connected in a way that no article and commentary could ever be, just as the involvement on the part of someone reading an article or book or editorial on Vietnam is infinitesimal compared with the depth participation effected by watching color footage of war scenes on a Vietnam TV broadcast. That same qualitative difference is the difference in two generations' relationship to the war, and to the conditions from which it sprang.

—miller francis, jr.

The "success" of the Washington Mobilization is in no way comparable to that of the Woodstock festival experience: only the "violent," i.e. involving, action at the Justice Department (which, contrary to "mediated" reports, involved tens of thousands of participants) is comparable. The chemical of one event was lysurgic acid, that of the other was tear gas: both expanded the consciousness. While the form of the Mobe was impressive—over half a million people showed up—its content, i.e. the speeches at the Washington Monument, were almost totally devoid of power, unlike the high energy music heard and felt and assimilated at White Lake

Dear WIN:

Radio Free People produces tapes of movement struggles, actions, ideas . . . for radio stations, organizers, free people . . . to be broadcast, played in classrooms, dormitories, meetings, street corners, G.I. barracks, or anywhere.

A new catalogue listing 24 programs is now available. These programs deal with women's liberation, G.I. organizing, black organizing and repression, health care, Irish justice, alternative culture . . . . They are in the form of documentaries, collages, songs, poetry.

All programs available on reels or cassettes. Write for free catalog and low, low prices: Radio Free People, 133 Mercer St., N.Y., N.Y. 10012.
—*Radio Free People*

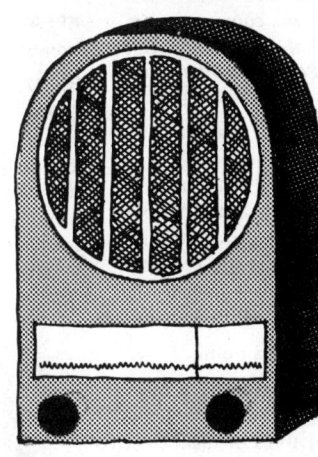

Today in America, thought control is a reality.

Radio Free People exists as a functioning alternative to thought control. Our primary goal is to eliminate all restrictions on the freedom of the public media to convey unpopular points of view; a freedom which can be preserved only by its own exercise. Our philosophical perspective is fundamentally radical, which dictates absolute respect for the rights of those who disagree with us to form associations offering information and opinion without employing economic or political coercion in any form whatever.

We hope to achieve our goal by introducing honest, outspoken radio programs, and by helping communities to establish independent local audio and radio outlets and production units. We are also working towards the creation of an international audio network.

Stimulating Independent Production

RFP is compiling a handbook dealing with all essential aspects of creative audio production, geared to intelligent newcomers to the field, who may employ relatively inexpensive, easily obtained equipment. It is very much against our philosophy of decentralism to have all production originate in New York or other large cities. We will emphasize in our catalogs programs of high quality produced on individual initiative or by local groups. We will stress high technical standards, but content always gets priority.

Inaugurating "Community Listening Groups"

It is unrealistic to forget that in many parts of the United States the free expression of unpopular points of view may be—perhaps quite literally—suicidal. In these areas, where obtaining air time on local stations or establishing CCR outlets may be impossible, we will encourage people to create private Community Listening Groups. These would meet, prehaps weekly, in schoolrooms, churches, public halls or private homes. They would have the further advantage of encouraging direct communication among listeners, resulting hopefully in the formation of groups devoted to eradicating basic social ills. A nominal admission fee or contribution could completely defray the cost of ordering RFP tapes. Any surplus could be applied to the financing of action groups. The Community Listening Group amounts to a new medium of communication whose potential is presently unexplored. We think it is limited only by the involvement and imagination of the participants.

RFP also has some further objectives. Among these are:

1. To establish a center for the intensive study of the ways in which thought control is currently being practiced. Special emphasis will be placed upon the conscientious gathering, organization and dissemination of hard evidence.

2. To serve as a nucleus for research into the unique electronic needs of an enlightened radical movement, and to gather engineers and technicians who would in turn train others in the communications arts and technology. Examples of such needs are: low-power radio stations, low-cost recording facilities, a nationwide net or ham-radio and other shortwave communications and news distribution, low-cost hi-fi and sound-reinforcement systems for active people and organizations.

3. To offer a viable, stimulating alternative outlet for the skills and talents of people already active in broadcasting and allied fields, and to assist them in examining the social consequences of what they do.

4. To establish an economically self-sustaining business which would act as a clearing-house for electronic and communications ideas, services, and hardware. Like the many successful Movement printshops and publications, this would help set the movement for social change on its own feet.

69-2 ELDRIDGE CLEAVER'S AFFIDAVIT

On November 27, 1968, Eldridge Cleaver dropped out of sight. He refused to return to jail after his parole had been revoked again by the California court system. One part of the chain of events that led to the revocation occurred on the night of April 6, 1968, when Bobby Hutton was shot down after a gun battle with the Oakland police. This is Eldridge Cleaver's statement about what happened that night. It was recorded by Cleaver's lawyer, Charles Garry, on May 25, 1968 at the Vacaville County Jail for San Francisco Newsreel, who made it available to RFP.
Running time 29 minutes.   Price D.

69-5 THE PENTAGON IS RUNNING FREE!

Many people are vaguely aware of the United States government's development of chemical and biological weapons, but not at all aware of the magnitude of these research and manufacturing efforts. Three trillion lethal doses of nerve gas already stockpiled! Anthrax packaged in operational munitions! In this program, Seymour Hersh—without going into the political ramifications of it all—lays bare the fundamentals of this country's involvement in chemical and biological warfare.
Running time 48 minutes.   Price F.

69-10 JOIN THE A.S.U.

Andy Stapp, Chairman of the American Servicemen's Union (ASU) explains how the union started and points out the problems soldiers face when organizing in the army. Bill Smith and Bob Lemay, also of the ASU national staff and both veterans of Vietnam, tie together what is going down in Vietnam with their organizing efforts among servicemen everywhere.
Running time 23 minutes.   Price C.

69-8 THE JELLYROLL PRESS

One of several "free businesses" proliferating on the West Coast, the Jellyroll Press keeps the San Francisco Bay area illuminated with leaflets, posters and pamphlets done in rich colors and with great skill. "We're not an abstract ideology . . . our ideology is getting printing done, and we get printing done for people that need printing done that don't have the resources to get it done." How does it work? Mostly without money, for one thing.
Running time 30 minutes.   Price D.

69-18 MY BODY IS MINE TO CONTROL

"Women rewarded for weakness and punished for trying to be strong/ Locked in our homes, in the prisons, and jobs where we're told we belong" . . . have written these songs. Songs about women's struggle for liberation, people's park, three pregnant Panther women in jail in Connecticut, third world women. Songs of love, liberation, struggle, songs of rage. "Some people fight for love and others fight to eat/ It's all the same struggle, the same enemy to beat." Written by Beverly Grant and Lynn Phillips, sung by Beverly Grant.
Running time 26 minutes.   Price C.

69-19 UP AGAINST THE MATTRESS DOWN IN THE VALLEY

A collage of sounds of objects (men and women), and more; with sex, politics, music, economics, and the potential for stimulation, in nine or so easy-to-listen-to minutes. Recommended for starting something. For women, mostly, primarily.
Running time 10 minutes.   Price A.

Catalog, Radio Free People Winter/Spring 1970

TOOPROLETARIANINTOXICATEDTOBEASTRONOMICAL

an interview with Roland Young

Roland Young was a disc jockey at KSAN radio in San Francisco until December, 1969, when he was fired for political reasons.

The station's history and the changes it's gone through, particularly in the last six months, are representative of major trends in hip-rock-FM radio throughout the nation. KSAN began early in 1968 in the aftermath of a strike at KMPX-FM, the first Bay Area station to gear its programming directly toward so-called hip youth. The programming staff from KMPX approached the managers of Metromedia's KSFR, then a classical music station, with their idea for changing the station's entire format. And Metromedia accepted the proposal.

Metromedia knew what they were doing. The name of the company itself implies what they think of as important, and their corporate connections make their attitude clear. Metromedia owns Foster/Kleiser (outdoor advertising), The Traveller's Times (transit advertising), direct mail marketing outfits, television stations and syndicated television programming. In its annual report Metromedia states its fundamental principle: "A responsive broadcaster is a responsible broadcaster." For a while there seemed to be some question as to who Metromedia was responsive to.

At first, questions of culture, music, general rapping and interviews were left to the disc jockeys and news broadcasters. The news direc-

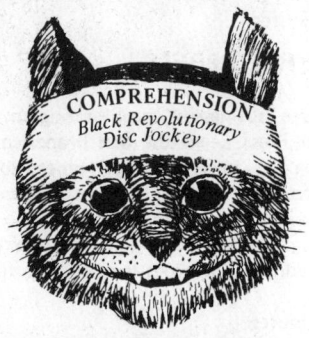

COMPREHENSION
Black Revolutionary
Disc Jockey

tor, Wes "Scoop" Nisker, created a new collage form for the news broadcasts. He spliced together taped speeches of people in the news and combined these quotes with sound effects and his own reading of the news. At the end of each broadcast he reminded listeners, "If you didn't like the news, go out and make some of your own." Roland Young joined the station in August of 1968.

People in the Bay Area dug KSAN because of the kind of music it played and because the station catered to the life style of the listeners.

But the Agnew-FCC crackdown on media put the home office really uptight. They knew who they were supposed to be responsive to. And besides, the station hadn't been pulling in enough major advertising.

Roland was fired. And Scoop "resigned" after being told that his produced news broadcasts were being phased out.

Since his firing, Roland has arranged and presided over benefits for the Panthers. He also writes for the Panther paper and has a late-night music and rap show on KPFA-FM, the Pacifica station in Berkeley.

The following interview was composed from two taped conversations with Roland, one with the news director of KPFA, the other with Leviathan staff members.

Roland: I got fired because of a statement I made on the air. I passed the word that a listener had called in suggesting that those who support David Hilliard's speech at the November 15 Moratorium and/or his right of free speech, should send like telegrams to President Nixon. The station received a subpoena the next morning for a transcript of my program.

KPFA: Where was that subpoena from?

R: It was from two federal lawyers from Washington and one secret service agent who hangs around the Bay Area. All three of them came down to the station in a classic intimidating situation. They storm in—I wasn't there when they came in, but I saw them. They're tall cats. One wears a big hat; they have on those grey suits and, you know, the greasy look. It really shook up the station manager. Because I used to tell him about those people, but he didn't know they exist. When they converged on the station, that reality was made very apparent to him. They talked for hours, I would imagine. And when I spoke with him later he said I think last night you went too far. And when he said that I knew exactly what that meant. He meant that I was fired. He said I have to talk to the New York office, the New York attorney, the New York this, the New York that—so in the meantime, I'm going to keep you off the air. And I'll let you know tomorrow. He called me up and said I'm afraid I'm going to have to fire you. And so I said Right On.

KPFA: That was that.

R: That was really that.

KPFA: I don't know what was in his head, but I imagine in consulting with New York the problem was that you were as popular as hell. And they had to keep that in mind too, because that's after all one of their things.

R: Well, my popularity doesn't supersede a threat from the federal government. I guess that supersedes all kinds of popularity. I think they acted very unwisely to fire me because I didn't commit any illegal act. I was not indicted for an illegal act. They will not be indicted for an illegal act. They're just clearly and simply yielding to the pressure of the federal government.

KPFA: What's the law? The law is advocacy, right?

R: Sure. But Willis said I would have fired you anyway, because I think you went too far. What does going over too far mean? Does it mean that I don't say anything on the air that may upset the federal government, even though it may not be illegal? So that's a clear violation of freedom of speech. I'm even willing to accept freedom of speech up to the point of breaking a law, I'll go that far with them. But if there isn't a law broken, then it's silly. They're going above and beyond the law themselves. So I think they're clearly acting in an unconstitutional manner. And I'm a firm believer in the Constitution. And I'll fight for it, for my rights.

KPFA: What kind of hassles have you had previously?

R: I've never had direct political hassles. The KSAN management doesn't really want to offend anyone, that's their whole trip. But it's absolutely impossible to say anything without offending someone. You offend people every night. So it's not that they don't want to offend anyone, but just don't offend the wrong person.

Photo/David Goldstein

KPFA: You phrase this whole business with the firing and everything in terms of your support for the Panthers and the attack on the Panthers.

R: Sure. I see that the attack on me was clearly a part of the harassment that's been going down throughout the nation against the Black Panther Party. Particularly considering that it was an issue related to David Hilliard. You read in the paper that they're doing an autopsy on the body of the Deputy Chairman Fred Hampton in Chicago. It seems he was shot in his sleep. Down in Los Angeles they shot tear gas into someone's house and raided the office simultaneously. These raids are going on every day against the Black Panther Party. They're really coming down on them and it means life or death. A lot of Panthers have been killed, at least 28. It's an attack on the entire Black Panther Party. And I just happen to be an individual victim of it. It's also part of the whole attack against media, part of an attack on free speech, and part of the rising tide of fascism—all hooked up together.

I feel that fascism is definitely on the rise. Not only the Black Panther Party has been attacked. You find Nixon making very slanderous remarks against even a peaceful demonstration of people expressing their sympathies against the war. And at the same time you find this country involving itself more and more in imperialist wars abroad. The result is a tightening up at home on dissent against those wars because those wars are very vital to it. So when I say rising tide of fascism, I mean personal repression against *all* citizens, white or black, liberal or left, is going down.

KPFA: You've been into the whole hip thing on KSAN and into that music and of course seen the movement go back and forth about what the hippie thing is and what that whole cultural thing is and whether it's positive or negative and what it does in a period of political crisis like this one. What are your ideas about that?

R: Within itself youth culture has contradictory aspects. Right before the rise of fascism in Germany there was a movement similar to part of the movement going on here. That movement was co-opted and turned into a fascist movement of young people. Many of them became brownshirts. I see aspects capable of being revolutionary. Like within the hip movement there are class differences. The rock-and-roll element is a very bourgeois tendency within that movement and I think that element can be counted on to be successfully co-opted. But then you have other strands represented by other people who put out various underground papers, people like John Sinclair, Weatherman, whatever. And then there's a whole other trend cropping up that's probably even more relevant than any of those so far—young poor white people, the Young Patriots and other groups like that. When you talk about the hip scene you're talking about two strains, one very bourgeois and one very potentially revolutionary. There's some people in the Appalachia areas that are beginning to get it together. There are various black workers caucuses that have popped up across the nation, not putting forth separatist demands, putting forth revolutionary demands that all workers can relate to. I see that as very positive. I see the Weatherman as a positive trend. And the cats that were charged in New York for the bombings there. Some people are responding on that level. And it must be legal, because the U.S. practices bombing daily, so I know that they think that's a good thing. I know that Nixon would approve of that. Right On, he'd say. I see that as positive too. But also in order to have a successful revolution, we're going to have to have a large mass-based movement with a general understanding of what we want to do.

And I would never say that young people are the agents for change, particularly young whites, so-called hippies. I think they're just acting out their alienation in a very creative manner. The spiritual oppression of the young white hip scene is another thing, but a lot of times it doesn't relate to revolutionizing people because it was founded on anti-revolutionary principles of individualism. The conditions of young people always make them more ready to bring about revolution. They're always in the more mobile position, they have more energy, they're younger, they're faster and they fight better. We know they have advantages. But the people who are out doing the fighting aren't

necessarily the sole agents of revolution. The National Liberation Front is primarily made up of young people, but the agents of change are the whole mass of people, not just those young people. Because without all the other people doing the other things, those young people couldn't do anything. The agents of change will not be just young people. The issue of revolution relates to class consciousness and the level of the material oppression of people. I think the masses of working people—black and white —are the people who, in the final analysis, have to be persuaded over to the side of revolution before we can expect any kind of change in this country.

KPFA: When the Rolling Stones were at Altamont about 300,000 people were there, but there hasn't been a single mass demonstration having to do with the shootings in Chicago.

R: I think about the Rolling Stones demonstration. Mick Jagger was contacted and asked to make a public appeal for support of the Black Panther Defense Fund. He said not only would he not do that, but if any political speeches were made on the stage, they wouldn't play. And this is the group that put out "Street Fighting Man." See, it's a shuck and it's a sham. I have little faith in rock-and-roll and rock-and-roll entertainers overall as being anything in this society but very bourgeois sell-out people. Which they prove to be.

PETER: I've always had a sense that people confuse the fact that the Rolling Stones made "Street Fighting Man" but acted another way. It just seems to me that it was inevitable that they would lead a certain kind of life if they were multi-millionaires.

R: Pop music is good because the masses of people can relate to it—a kind everyone can dig on—but inherently it has problems being revolutionary. The music is, well, Marcuse understands what it is. It's the ability the society has to incorporate anything into it, and turn it into a commercial item. Total cooptation. Like rock-and-roll in its most revolutionary stages became mysterious. As people's curiosities rise, their ability and desire to consume also rises. Ad men ease in on that, fill that void by making that which was once a protest actually a salable item. That's what was going on at KSAN. That was clearly my role there. A salable item. Whatever controversial things may have gone down in my program, they said, well, let them go down, cause it makes more people listen and we can ease these products in on them while they're digging their controversy.

I think the politics a lot of rock-and-roll stars themselves espouse and the commercialism of how that art form is put to people, via the ads, via record sales and so forth, has had the effect of causing certain kinds of political attitudes to go along with the entire trip. Now in order to be a successful rock-and-roll star, to sell a lot of records, to be on television a lot and make radio appearances, you have to stay within certain kinds of political understandings of the society, particularly since repression is coming down like it is today. So you have David Crosby of Crosby, Stills, Nash and Young coming on the stage making the statements against poli-

tics he did at Altamont. He said politics is bull, of course. And you find those people out their at the Moratorium responding to the cast from *Hair,* which is one of the most bourgeois decadent trips that has ever gone down. On the other hand you have them booing David Hilliard.

P: You have said that up until three years ago rock-and-roll contributed to pushing things to the left, but that it couldn't do that any more.

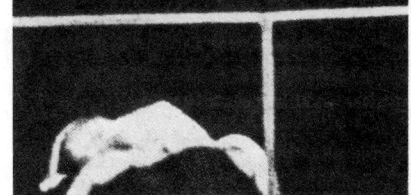

R: I think it's reached its saturation point now. Music has pushed people as far as they can be pushed and people have pushed themselves as far as they can push without moving to another level. Looking at Santa Barbara, Buffalo College, the Young Patriots, the Black Panther Party, Los Siete, throughout the nation, we see that the only way people can now act effectively if they are to get some concessions, this small group of radicals and revolutionaries, is to take up the gun. That's the only alternative at this point, because the struggle has pushed itself as far as it can go in a nonviolent manner. On campuses they can no longer have a San Francisco State without masses of people being slaughtered. And so there are only two alternatives left for people in the so-called movement —move back into the community and get that constituency on your side or move into bands of armies and just take over. So the music has done as much as it can.

P: Do you see a relationship between the political development of the black community and its impact on the political development of the white community. People talk about the black leadership and the vanguard role and it seems to me there's a similar thing happening on a cultural level. They reinforce each other.

R: Black music is being very influenced by rock-and-roll now, black and white music are interacting now. At one time it was just one way—black music was just totally pushing itself onto white music, because the white people had no music of their own, but I think albums like *Rubber Soul* helped establish the base for that interaction. But the whole basis of American culture is black because the basis of white culture is exported from Europe. But you still see there are some groups that transcend all those categories, for example a group like Sly or a group like Santana. We know that what keeps them from being close is the class divisions and racism, not the actuality of the culture itself.

* * *

KPFA: Where are things going now? In terms of your own thing, but also things in general. Not only the music/cultural thing, but the whole political thing.

R: I think we're here for a protracted struggle. I'm not very upset about a lot of the divisions that are going on in the left because I understand history and I understand it's a historical process—when a country goes into a pre-revolutionary stage you have all these various groups because there's no one way people know of doing things. The people who are ultimately going to bring about the revolution have just begun to get into the movement. And that's the masses of working people—black, white and third world in this country. They've just begun to get into motion.

I want to get into the music, man. People have never asked me about my music. They go into my politics, and that's just one aspect of what I'm all about. Music was the most relevant thing, it allowed me even to do the politics. That's the part I really dug, I still dig, as well as the politics. The music was a very special kind of thing to me because I was trying to put the music into an internationalist perspective. I was trying to act like a socialist on the program. For instance, I would do a certain kind of a set—like I would do Sam and Dave, then I would do the Band, then I'd do Sam and Dave again, then I'd do a Dvorak cut that would relate very much, both structurally and melodically, to the Sam and Dave, then I'd go somewhere else.

What I was doing was tying all this in together, and showing the interrelationship between all that beautiful music. And to put it into people's heads that ultimately, man, this is where it's at. Internationalism is the *only* way we can ever have the kind of world we can live in. If that music can come at you like that in so many relevant ways and do that to your head, then imagine the world functioning on that same level. So my music was the living process of the philosophy I was trying to lay down. And it didn't totally make it cause there's not that much hip music. But it made it to the level that I think the general understanding was there. And I sure like people to dig on that a lot.

Music now is expressing a desire for dignity and all that stuff. That's the thing with a whole lot of black music today, soul music. It's not really revolutionary, it's reformist or at the most it's cultural revolutionary—the theme's basically black. The ghetto is the theme of a lot of soul tunes, and you'd expect that because of cultural oppression and because the question first and foremost on the minds of black people is the national question, I believe. And national solidarity.

P: **When you say "cultural" you don't mean that in a negative sense.**

R: I'm saying that that's as *far* as black music has gone. It can end up being negative if it's cultural nationalism, if it doesn't express a way out of the oppression. I think that popular art, at least in the black community, is very far behind.

P: **I wonder if music can express a way out of oppression.**

R: In this country today some of the most revolutionary music is music associated with "avant-garde" jazz—the lifestyle of the musicians as well as the art form itself. The music of Archie Shep and Cecil Taylor and John Coltrane. Those cats were the first to explore Eastern forms of mysticism. The only whites who were into it were the Beatniks and that was a very small group of people. That group has been around for a very long time, but their art form is not a popular one and therefore a lot of their messages don't get over to the masses of people. We know that pop art in this country is a creation of the establishment. They set the tone for it by what they put on the radio—radio that they control. They create it in the sense that they popularize it, they make it into a popular form.

P: **It seems that some of the best musicians in groups wanted to make it in jazz and for a variety of reasons, primarily that they were white, they took rock-and-roll. It was second best.**

R: Chicago is a good example. Even plastic groups like Blood Sweat and Tears. Nobody can make it in jazz, white *or* black. It's a myth that blacks are more successful in jazz than whites. That's not true. Most money made by jazz musicians is made by white studio musicians. Black people appear most in clubs—Woody Herman probably makes the most money of any jazz musician. If John Coltrane had been white, imagine the money he would've made. Used to be a time when jazz clubs would not hire white groups. That was when jazz was controlled by just a small group of racists who wanted to have black people perform for them. Now that situation has changed.

R: The music of Ornette Coleman, man, has been some of the most significant music in America and we know that he hasn't been rewarded for that. That whole jazz-rock thing is such a shuck—groups like Blood Sweat and Tears that have horns and use a few more chords. KJAZ (in San Francisco) has been playing a lot of that as a way of popularizing their format to bring in more listeners and money, and they've been successful at it.

* * *

P: **I know a lot of people aren't aware of the fact that when a cat sits down to do a music show he's not just putting up the records and talking in between. Can you tell us a little of the feeling that goes into composing a show?**

R: I spend the whole day running through in my head various forms of music to put together and various things to work out, forms of information that I want to give out to people. Checking news sources, magazines, I read all the underground papers, listen to the news, all stations, talk stations, soul, as much as I can. A normal preparation would consist of writing all these things out as well as ideas for music. I get to the station two hours early to pull all the records I need, listen to them, bring my lamp in, turn the lights off, turn my lamp on, set up a whole lot of shit. Most of all, getting the music together, because if the music is not together, if it's not the way I want it to be, then the information will not go out as smooth as I want it to. The basis of my program is the music, that's why people are turning it on.

P: **The interesting thing is that you see music as expressing almost everything that's going on in the country. You use the music to deal with all the other things that you look at.**

R: The music doesn't always do it. But I think it can do as much as I can to deal with a lot of things. That's the way I've always prepared for a show ever since I started with KSAN. Always opening up, listening to all kinds of music.

A song can go beyond one level and elicit other meanings if it's put in another context. A lot of songs are indicative of those double meanings. On that record *Conversation with Collins*—He makes the guitar sing "fuck you" several times, "motherfucker, dirty motherfucker." He's talking about this conversation he had with his woman after she had been out all night. But that also expresses a cultural understanding clearly and a way of projecting a people's language. It's also an interesting political education class in linguistics about how certain people talk and how they use the language and how that directly relates to how his guitar is being played. And where the sounds of that guitar come from. Plus you see an exchange between a man and woman plus you see a cultural expression.

Songs that have lyrics are composed of at least three things: melodic information, rhythmic information and then the lyrics themselves. Each one of those songs relates to another song in some kind of significant way and some other kinds of ideas as well. If all these can be told in the right form, the right manner, it seems very valuable—like writing something and sending it out.

KPFA: Do you relate your rapping to the music more directly?

R: Sure, man, sure. Whatever kind of music I was playing at the time I would be rapping. For instance if I was playing some Ray Charles music, some of his very slow stuff, then there were certain kinds of raps that were relevant to that, and others weren't. The same kind of rap that's relevant to "Street Fighting Man" is not to Ray Charles. And I try to keep that in mind. Plus some of it is magic, I guess. Which is to say that some of it is not explainable.

That was so beautiful, man, cause I just loved playing that music. Heavy speakers, that sound coming at you. A good high. I'd like to say that the revolution is about staying high. I mean staying high by being elated, digging what you're doing. Very much involved in the whole process on a daily basis. The assuredness of what you're doing, and why you're doing it and how you're going to do it. It's about that total understanidng of yourself. It's about that kind of high. I'm not talking about enjoying going to jail, getting beat across the head. But enjoying what you're doing and if you were doing anything else you would not enjoy it. What you're doing leads to certain things, that's the consequences, but the fun is the act of what you're doing, the creative process you're engaged in and that's making revolution, love, or whatever. And it seems like if revolutionaries are high, and elated, then they're going to be heavy. And if they're down and gray and dull like a lot of them were in the '30s and '40s then they'll have trouble. Cause if it's not going to be fun, at least fun on the level of knowing what you're doing and where you're going, it's not worth doing.

KPFA: Yeah, I don't think you mean fun...

R: Yeah, I mean fun. I mean digging it. Like you may have something you dig more but the process—digging struggling more than digging not struggling. Like the act of struggling itself makes you happier than it would if you weren't struggling. So you are digging it on that level. And at times the struggle itself is fun, particularly if you're won a tactical victory. Like I'm sure that the battle of Dien Bien Phu was fun when it was over to the brothers when they did the French in.

KPFA: I think people can get it in their heads when you say that, no misinterpretation of what you're saying.

R: You know everybody says the same thing when I say fun. They say I don't mean *fun*. But I do, man, I do mean fun. Like we had fun the other day at that protest at Air France because we knew what we were struggling against and we knew ultimately what we were going to do.

KPFA: That was the time they tried to stop Emory Douglas of the Black Panther Party and Don Cox and Emory's wife, Judy. They were in Paris and were going to Algiers.

R: Right. And Air France detained them so Emory said, all right, I'll go to Air Algiers and they said OK. He went over to Air Algiers and found out that Air France owned it and he got a good political education about imperialism and monopoly capitalism right there.

Fred Hampton said he was too proletarian intoxicated to be astronomically intimidated ... he was talking about that too. Fred was a cat who had fun in what he was doing; you could tell that by the things he said, by the way he related to them, he knew it was a very heavy trip he was into. But it didn't mean nonstruggle for him. It just means you're into it.

It would be even more fun not to have a world that needed struggle, but I think that's absurd to talk about. There was a need before I was here and there will be a need long after, so I don't even want to get into that. But through struggle, even according to traditional Marxist thinking, I believe, people began to realize

MUSIC MEDIA

drawings by Rupert Garcia

themselves, to become themselves. That they made their own history through their struggles and that process should be one that entails fun. You read the writings of a lot of revolutionaries and you can see the ones that did and those that didn't. Che obviously did, Stalin obviously didn't.

* * *

KPFA: So you were in the Bay Area by this time?

R: Yeah. Actually, when I was in the Navy, the ship that I was on came to the Bay Area in 1961. And I started hanging around Fillmore Street. By 1963 I had decided to live here. Two months before I got out of the Navy me and this white cat that wanted to be a Muslim got an apartment together. Both of us gave up on Islam, though—became Democrats. I remember we were very much into the Johnson/Kennedy thing at the time. I moved into the Haight-Ashbury in 1964. I was there, and then that thing started happening. That added another thing to my head. I think finally I've just now found time to synthesize things. It all just started falling together about two years ago.

KPFA: How'd you get into the radio thing?

R: Yeah. All my life I'd wanted to be a disc jockey, believe it or not. When I was a little boy I used to play like I was on the radio. I had a microphone that I made and a stack of 78's. And I would sit there and perform for my friends as though I was on the radio. I would pattern myself after this disc jockey, who was really the heaviest disc jockey in town. His name was Mad Lad, E. Rodney Jones, on KUDL [read "cuddle"—Ed.] radio in Kansas City. He talked a whole lot of jive. We heard that he smoked—in 1954 he smoked grass! They said he got so high one time he took off all his clothes in the studio. We thought this cat was heavy, man. We related to rebels. Cause we hated everything that stood for law and order. I was taught by my father when I was a little boy to hate cops. He hated cops. He said If you ever become a cop I'll kill you. I never had any illusions along that line, ever. So anyway, I always wanted to be a disc jockey. And another thing I did, when I got through my disc jockey show, I'd put on a puppet show. I had these puppets and I had this stage. I used to sew curtains and do drawstrings. So I had this theatrical orientation, plus I played a horn. I started playing the clarinet when I was ten. And I sung in singing groups. In fact I've got a record that we made when I was fifteen years old—Roland Young and the Velveteers, singing I Love You and Baby, baby . . . Stingy Ginny or something. I was always into music, man.

I approached KSAN before I even realized the political potential. I approached it for the music. Like a lot of cats on the air were disc jockeys and their approach was as disc jockeys. My approach was a way to play music for people and to lay that out. That's what initially turned me onto it.

* * *

R: What, the movement or me?

KPFA: Well, both.

R: I hope that the movement becomes more revolutionary, more beautiful, and more dope-oriented. In the positive sense of the word that people use dope to liberate themselves and not to oppress themselves. That they really expand their minds, whatever they can do, and that people all join together who have any kind of complaints against this country on any level. Join together and support the Black Panther Party! Not necessarily all their politics or their Ten Point Program or any of that, but support the fact that they're being harassed daily, that they have large bails, and it's a clear attempt to break up the Black Panther Party. Which ultimately will mean an attempt to break up all dissent in this country. So if you come to the defense of the Black Panther Party now, you may save yourself tomorrow. You can send it to 3106 Shattuck, Berkeley, California, Black Panther Party National Headquarters. All Power to the People! And Oink to the Oinkers.

Leviathan March 1970

FREE SPEECH

Albert Camus

"For 50 years, the writers of a business society believed, with very few exceptions, that it was possible to live happily in irresponsibility. They lived alone and they died as they lived, alone. We writers of the 20th century will never again be alone. We must realize, on the contrary, that we cannot escape the common lot of pain, and that our only justification, if one there be, is to speak insofar as we can on behalf of those who cannot."

—Speech in Stockholm, 1957

Q: *What do you see as the specific role of the black writer? Like young cats coming up, where should they look for literary models?*

A: I think they need a good perspective on the history of literature, the way we got into this shit, you know, where we are now. I think that for a black writer to *really* come to his own he needs to have as part of his working equipment some understanding of world literature, what it means, what literature means to people, and the part that it plays in helping people cope with life, in terms of explaining what some of the best minds have seen going on in the world, you know.

By and large it's to prepare oneself for battle, that's what it amounts to, because we're involved in a war. We need a fighting literature, we need to understand ways of using words to expose, to expose and to resurrect, to expose the conscious efforts the white man has made to rob us of our history, to rob us of our dignity, of understanding, of ourselves as a strong and proud people. But not just that. I'm trying to say that words, literature, is one of the categories, man, one of the essential things for survival, like music, dancing, technology. Literature is just as important as any of the other major categories of our human activity, and not just literature—literature is just a particular way of doing it, you know, putting it on paper—but the whole process of recording one's history and views of life and interpretations of human experience. There used to be a time when they had what we call the oral tradition. That is, history as the memory, the collected memory of a people, you know, and literature.

Interview with Eldridge Cleaver by Cecil Brown, *Evergreen Review*

UNDERGROUND FUCK

Tom Forcade of the Underground Press Syndicate sent LNS a list of 28 papers that he knows are getting a raw deal. We found others he didn't even know about. Many college papers have been getting the same treatment.

An astounding case of underground harassment: Dallas versus Dallas Notes.

The paper has been busted twice, on October 30 and November 15. Vice squad cops came looking for "pornography" and tore the office apart, carting away everything in sight. In the two busts, the cops confiscated the following: four typewriters, cameras, darkroom and graphic equipment, business records, books, posters, a desk, a drafting table, copy and other material for the next issue, and everything else that could be ripped loose and carried off.

Dallas police also arrested several staff members for possession of pornography. Publisher Stoney Burns was busted both times. Editor Rodd Delaney and his wife, circulation manager Donna Delaney, were arrested the first time and left the paper soon after, partly because the hassle was getting to be too much. Dallas Notes is still alive.

Atlanta's Great Speckled Bird, which has been considered "obscene" by unaesthetic officials:

The Bird's problems started when a group of anonymous local citizens, calling themselves the Dekalb Parents' League for Decency, decided to print up the Best of the Bird. They distributed a smear sheet made up of Bird excerpts with all smut carefully underlined (as well as references to draft resistance, dope, and civil rights activity).

The leaflet said:

"Teachers, ministers, judges, police officials, and other responsible persons are rightly disturbed by the sacrilege, pornography, depravity, immorality and draft dodging which are preached in the Great Speckled Bird.

"...Let's put a stop to this flow of filth before it hurts any MORE children than it already has."

Liberal community members complained that the leaflet was in violation of a state law prohibiting the distribution of unsigned political material.

The city promised to take action. And it did — but not against the Parents' League.

The local media began to carry reports that the Bird was being "investigated for obscenity." Vendors were questioned by vice squad cops, some dealers were intimidated into not selling the Bird, and the paper was forced to go to Alabama (of all places) to find a printer.

Tom Coffin reports in the Bird, "On Wednesday we are visited by an investigator from the Solicitor General's office and two vice squad men. On Thursday we discover that we are to be indicted the next day. Proceedings move as fast against the Bird as they are slow against the Dekalb politicos: the media heat is effectively transferred, on a false issue."

The ACLU agreed to help. (In some cities, ACLU is cooperative, in others its policy is hands-off.) A complaint was filed against the harassment and a temporary restraining order was requested until a three judge panel could be formed to rule on the constitutionality of the Georgia obscenity law. The judge would not grant the restraining order, but said that if the Bird would be reasonably good, no evil would be perpetrated upon them until the formation of the panel.

So the Bird is in for a long legal hassle. Could be costly, but things don't look as bleak as they do in Dallas. If anything, the harassment has done the Bird good. According to staffer Gene Guerrero, the community has rallied to the support of the paper. "Friendly people have been popping out of the woodwork to help."

Another southern paper, the Kudzu, in Jackson, Mississippi, has raised the ire of local folk. Salesmen have been busted cameras confiscated, and the paper evicted from its office. On October 8, 18 Kudzu staffers and friends were jumped and beaten by deputy sheriffs in front of a local high school.

Many northern papers have been labelled "smut" by the city fathers.

Philadelphia's Distant Drummer had its troubles last summer. Street salesmen were arrested, some retail outlets quit selling the paper, and some advertising was lost.

But one charge went beyond obscenity: Police Commissioner Rizzo asked the district attorney to prosecute the Drummer for solicitation to commit murder. The murder of Rizzo. Seems the Drummer had run a story about the commissioner which Rizzo felt advocated his murder. The DA said he wouldn't prosecute because he didn't want a riot over that crummy paper, or so says editor Don DeMaio.

Milwaukee has written a new obscenity law (something to do with exposure of nipples) to harass its underground tabloid, Kaleidoscope. Several staffers are facing obscenity charges. And editor John Kois' car has been firebombed and its back windows shot out.

John Bryan, editor of Open City in Los Angeles, has been convicted of obscenity once, and now they're after him again.

Bryan received a sentence of six months or $1,000, now under appeal. for publication of obscenity. The "obscenity" was a half page ad for an electronic music group. The ad was itself a parody on the use of sex to sell products (wonder how many records it sold).

John was busted again recently for a short story by beat-generation poet Jack Michelene which appeared in a recent issue of the paper.

Three staffers of the University of Hartford Liberated Press have been arrested for violating a Connecticut libel-obscenity statute: editor John Hardy; publisher Ben Holden (head of UH student government); and John Zanzal, who drew the cartoon. They ran a cartoon depicting Nixon as a large, erect index finger.

They were arrested on a breach of the peace provision of a Connecticut libel statute which prohibits the publication of any "offensive, indecent or abusive matter concerning any person." Holden says it is the first time this law has been used. The three were also charged on an obscene literature statute. They are now out on $500 bond.

The Hartford ACLU indicated it would take the case, though no final decision had been made at the time of this writing.

Holden told LNS that, while he was at the police station he was asked by a reporter how the busts would affect the future of the paper. Holden said the paper would continue come hell or high water; then winced, for fear of prosecution under the state's anti-blasphemy law.

Connecticut statute 53-242 says, "Any person who blasphemes against God... the Holy Trinity, the Christian religion or the Holy Scriptures shall be fined not more than $100 and imprisoned not more than one year...."

Just some antique law they would never prosecute? Holden's saying his prayers.

With other college papers, the main bugaboo seems to be the word fuck. According to Susie Schmidt, "The word 'fuck,' long a commonplace in youthful vocabularies, and adult as well, has sent countless printers of college papers into such rage that they censor the copy, refuse to print the papers, even try to get schools to discipline editors."

Editors of Wisconsin's Daily Cardinal almost got fired because of a College Press Service story on the recent SDS national council meeting which quoted a member of Up Against the Wall/Motherfucker.

The staff wrote a front-page letter to the regents, calling the attack on the paper, "only a beachhead in the total effort by the regents to exert control over every aspect of the University operation, student life and faculty freedom."

Michigan State's State News printed a story about the censorship at Wisconsin and got some of the same treatment. Salaries of the editors were cut as punishment.

William Smoot, editor of the Exponent at Purdue, was fired because, according to Purdue's Vice-President for Student Affairs, he had "offended the sensibilities of the public."

The article which lost Smoot his job said, "Regarding a vicious rumor concerning (university) President Novde... let us set the record straight. Our president is not anal-retentive... he dumped on the students just last week."

Envoy, from Hunter College in New York, ran the word fuck in an article about Chicago.

The Oakland (Michigan) University Observer: printer would not run a four-page supplement written by a black student.

The Lion's Roar from Windham College in Putney, Vermont: their printer boycotted an article titled "The Myth of Vaginal Orgasm."

The Stetson University Reporter and Berkeley's Daily Californian have been surprised to find words and letters eliminated at the printer's whim.

New York's Rat has been under fire. The New Jersey Attorney General threatened an obscenity investigation and frightened off the Rat's Jersey printer. Editor Jeff Shero says too many Jersey high school kids were reading the paper.

Now the Rat is being forced to find a new office because its rent has been doubled. Three months ago, the FBI paid a visit to the landlord. The Rat's mail has a "cover" on it at the post office, a friendly postal employee informed Shero. He said they started checking Rat's mail right after Chicago (when the Rat got a lot of publicity because of its special convention issue).

A "cover" means they keep addresses

of everyone who writes you.

Other papers are faced with subtle forms of repression. The Rag, in Austin, Texas, almost folded last summer because it couldn't get an office. Every place the Rag rented got condemned by the City. Eventually, no one would rent to the paper because they didn't want the kiss of death on their property.

The Rag has other problems. Several staff members were called before the grand jury because of such things as a front page photo which pictured two lions fucking and bore the caption "Peace." The county decided not to prosecute.

Now the paper is having trouble with printers. It has lost several, and its present printer has a habit of putting little black boxes over things he thinks are obscene. He recently refused to print the back page which was layed out with LNS artwork. So the Rag came out with a blank flip side.

And speaking of printers — Orpheus, in Phoenix, Arizona, has been turned down by 25 of them.

Tom Cahill, editor of the Chicano paper, Inferno, in San Antonio, was silenced as a result of his own activities. He was found guilty in January of breaking a closed-circuit TV camera used to spy on workers in a restroom in a San Antonio factory. He agreed to pay the damage and his three year sentence was held in abeyance. The owner of the fac-

tory, Marshall Steves, was also then president of Hemisfair and preferred to snuff publicity.

But recently, the San Antonio News ran a story linking Cahill to SDS activities at St. Mary's University. He is now in jail for "violation of probation."

Other editors have been silenced by the selective service laws. Bruce Dancis of the First Issue in Ithica, New York, and Jim Retherford of Bloomington, Indiana's Spectator, have been convicted for resisting the draft. Retherford and Dancis are appealing six year terms for selective service violations.

The most devious bust concocted by the enemies of the underground press occurred in St. Louis. Staffers of the Daily Flash were waging war with police chief Walter Zinn. The chief couldn't get the city to prosecute the Flash for obscenity. (The city manager decided that a conviction would just get struck down in the courts and wasn't worth a hassle.)

So they got an undercover cop, groomed hippie style, to live as a freak, claiming to be a Vietnam vet grooving the scene. The cop, Harold Jones, busted Pete Rothchild, an editor of Xanadu (which had meanwhile evolved from the Daily Flash). Rothchild was arrested for suspected possession of marijuana.

John Mathieson, editor of Raison Bread; Tony Seed, editor of the Canadian

Free Press; and John Sinclair of the Sun and the Fifth Estate have also been busted on dope raps.

Others that have been hassled (some to the death) include Avatar, Georgia Straight, Helix, Logos, Seed, Spokane Natural, Florida Free Press, Vanguard, Harbinger, LA Free Press, and many more.

So what's in the future?

Open City's John Bryan thinks things'll get even tighter. "It feels like the heat's getting turned up."

Stoney Burns of Dallas Notes plans to stick it out. "The cops have succeeded in ruining our production schedule, in causing us great expense, but we're too stubborn to quit."

Gene Guerrero of the Bird is more optimistic yet. He thinks harassment in Atlanta will help coalesce the underground community.

After Kudzu staffers were busted in Jackson, Mississippi, the jail cell bore the following inscription:

"On October 8, 1968, the Kudzu staff was illegally seized and thrown into this cell. But we are free forever in our minds and our souls. Freedom is a constant struggle — and we are ready, we are together. We want the world and we want it now."

San Francisco
Express Times 12/11/68

STARTING A COMMUNITY NEWSPAPER

By David Ransom
An editor of the Peninsula Observer
University Avenue, Palo Alto, California

A newspaper is a tool — theirs for managing the society, ours for making the revolution. But the revolution is a process of destroying old relations and creating newer, more humane ones. A movement newspaper is revolutionary when it creates new patterns of seeing, new relationships between paper and community, new relationships within its collective.

Starting a newspaper in your own community presupposes that you have a community you can call your own. Start a paper where you have close ties and when you have made at least a tentative commitment to long-term local organizing. Start a paper where the movement needs one, not as a substitute for organizing that movement.

My experience is with the *Peninsula Observer*, a radical newspaper founded a year and a half ago and now coming out almost weekly, a 20-page tabloid with press run of 4500. We attempt to cover from San Francisco to San Jose, but our essential community is Stanford-Palo Alto. The area is closely tied to California big business, and it has had a strong liberal-radical community since the Fifties. Both have helped us get going. Our community is essentially white middle class. Your first problem will be who you are writing for. Black, chicano, working class papers are different from ours!

Most towns are one-paper towns, and all sorts of people feel the need for a paper not tied to the local establishment. While they may not desire a radical paper, many are willing to back one if it gets the news out. Most of these people are in opposition to the establishment — small property owners, small business men, academics, some of the churches, the hip community, the left liberals and the radicals. A radical paper, reporting suppressed or overlooked local news, muckraking the local establishment, and analyzing both news and establishment, serves these people's needs, shows them their common interests, organizes, radicalizes.

With the national and international news and analysis available from the Liberation News Service and other underground press, this makes for a pretty formidable body of thought for your broad readership.*

And nothing turns a man on like getting into all that good stuff he's missed all his life.

One other thing about readership: think about who you are writing to. There's nothing more boring than reading an article which rants to the faithful; even the faithful get bored. Liberals reading radical muckraking need radical analysis along with it, not the mere implication that what they are being shown is bad, nor the condescension that "moderating" the analysis brings. Radicals need the analysis also, too often having understood what is right or wrong without having understood why.

You're to make people think.

Where To Start
Probably there are radical journalists around your community already. They write the best leaflets, contribute left analyses to the college paper, are doing power structure analysis. Probably there are already a couple of newsletters being put out by SDS, the peace committee, the conservation group. Letting it be known that you are starting a paper will bring together a nucleus of people that can get things going. Look to these groups for initial funds, too.

Your basic staff needs will be in reporting, writing, and editing; layout and production; and advertising, distribution, and business. Add to this perhaps fundraising. We made it with an initial hard core of maybe twenty, a total staff of fifty or more. Others have done it with fewer.

You can get a story by knowing the situation yourself, covering the event and doing the writing. Eventually you will want to have staff members covering particular "beats" they are interested in — local power structure, the high schools, pot busts, guerrilla theater. Another good way to get stories, and a good way to begin to develop regular writers, is to get someone primarily involved in the action to report it: someone going to the demonstration, or involved in the fight for low-cost housing, or trying to organize his high school. Adequately critical reporting is the difficulty here, but your editor's concern that the story get told critically and well will be a great help to how the reporter sees his own work and will contribute to building movement self-criticism. And don't get into the bag that reporting must be "objective." There isn't any such beast as "objectivity." But by showing and defending your position you are more credible than the local press.

Where To Go

My experience is that the movement generally hasn't a good enough idea of who and what it's up against. Perhaps the major service a paper can do the movement community is to organize and publish power structure research and analysis. Give you an instance: we got involved in discovering the major landholders in the town and how they had bought the last city council election. When the local free university came up against these interests on two fronts, one fought by a sit-in and the other in the courts, we were on hand with the information that explained just exactly who they were fighting and what their power consisted of. Even the establishment press, very hostile, carried our allegations and some of our data. Since then, we have been able to show these same interests working through their council against local small business, and we are beginning to be able to effect some small coalition between forces which otherwise would have been at each other's throats rather than that of the establishment.

Power structure analysis is pretty easy: Contributions to candidates are public information, as is land ownership. (Read Jack McGinnis, "Care and Feeding of Power Structures" — 25 cents — and SDS's "Where It's AT" — $1.00 — both available from Radical Education Project, Box 625, Ann Arbor, Michigan 48107.) Power structure research also brings in the older people who have had long-standing gripes, some of who have long-standing clipping files and lots of information. They get turned on and start to write. Above all read your local straight paper carefully. It will send you to the Junior Miss Pageant for an article for the "Cultural Revolution" section, discover for you the small businessmen's association angered by attempts of bigger commerce to force them out of downtown, turn you on to attempts to close the county hospital for "austerity" reasons, tell you that the supervisors want to use helicopter police patrols in the black community. Our local paper buried the items. We exhumed, developed, analyzed.

Editing is hard work, particularly as you will not be working with professional writers and will be working with those who have axes to grind. The people you involve who work on their college paper or who teach freshmen English will probably want to edit their own work, since they've seen what happens when they don't. Writing and editing are not two separate jobs, but need in each particular case to be done by two separate people — someone other than the writer needs to see the piece, someone who will see it with fresh eyes.

oduction

Layout and the rest of production takes experience, but is not too difficult to learn. Having a readable paper depends on good layout. A lot of underground papers are simply unreadable. Hopefully, you will find someone with previous experience who will do this work or show you how.

Study the other underground press for good ideas.

You will probably get your paper printed at the local publisher of market weeklies, probably by photo-offset process. This means that all you need take them is your copy, laid out as you want it, with graphics, screened photos and headlines in place. That way, cost will be at a minimum. If you get him to set and justify (make the right-hand margin even) your copy, the cost will skyrocket ($25 a page). He will be able to set your headlines and screen your photos for less, but you can make yourself a copy camera (we haven't), set your headlines with decal letters (a drag), or get a versatile and easy to operate Strip Printer headline machine for $300 (pays for itself in ten or fifteen issues).

Money

Expect your tabloid printing costs to begin with $100 for the press run and first thousand, $10-$25 per thousand thereafter (8-20 page issue). Headlining and photo work can cost $80 for a 20-page issue. Scout the town for the old cheap offices. Ours cost $100 per month. Then postage — send your mail subscriptions bulk rate with the notation "time value." That gets the local copies delivered the next day. Cost — $45 for a year's permit, 3.6 cents per copy. Second class permits are hard to get, we've found — read the requirements carefully before you decide to apply.

If you prepare your own copy for printing, you will probably use an IBM Executive, which rents for $25-$35 monthly and sells reconditioned at about $400.

We have found it difficult to pay more than one or two people subsistence salaries ($30-$60 a week), and have asked that people otherwise unable to support themselves get part-time jobs. This is a hinderance, but works.

Where The Money Comes From

You needn't come out weekly. Bi-weekly publication gives you time to learn as you go along; had we tried to come out weekly at the beginning we would have foundered. With a little bit of luck, you can put out a bi-weekly, 8-page, 4000-copy tabloid for under $500 a month. Twice or three times that is not too much to ask from a community that needs a newspaper.

Your income will be from sales (subscriptions, street sales, and sales from stores and stands), advertising, and most importantly from community underwriting. Don't expect advertising to pay the costs of printing, the yardstick generally used to measure newspaper success in straight journalism. Our most important income has been through subscriptions and the one-time gifts they bring in, and from monthly pledges. Send as many compli-

mentary copies (so marked) as possible, enclosing a paid return mail envelope (get a return permit from the post office, had for the asking). Your issue carrying the article on smog gets sent to the membership lists of the three local conservation groups. The return envelope increases returns immensely, the rubber stamped "sample copy" makes them understand the thing ain't for free.

Go to the people who you think want and need a paper and ask them for money. Self-sufficiency should be an ultimate goal, and the point at which you become self-sufficient should be computed to keep you within reasonable bounds.

Beside getting you the bread, getting the money together to start from interested groups and individuals is an important part of community building. Come the repression, or, more likely, incipient bankruptcy, this will be important for you. A lot of bad blood can be stirred generally if your endeavor doesn't create community participation from the start. Those of us who start newspapers — word freaks, power structure analysis types, observers — are often enough of an opposition within the broader movement already.

Besides subscriptions and complimentary mailings, distribution will include street sales, and sales through boxes and stores. This is a big job: the movement lacks the distribution agencies it sorely needs. Street sales are best done when the paper salesmen knock on your door for copies which you sell them for two-thirds list price (they get a third and can return unsold copies for cost). But, initially, at least, you will probably be on the street selling too, not a bad way to keep in touch with the realities of selling and community response.

Sales through turned-on stores, head shops, the peace center and perhaps a few odd places like a mod dress store have to be developed and are a chore. It is hard to find someone to sell regularly without pay. If you run into difficulty getting street sellers, as we did, you may find street boxes an acceptable substitute. Open "honor" boxes with a bubble cover cost about $11 plus chain and lock, and about a third of the papers taken from them are paid for, but the ones stolen are probably read, and that's the point. Don't put them in dark corners — breaking into newspaper boxes is a highly developed avocation.

And for god's sake or the sake of the revolution, get out to movement events and hawk or give 'em away. Get the thing known and read.

Organization

Legally, you probably will be a de facto partnership of those who do the most work and those who contribute the most money, even if you think you are a participatory democracy. This is a corporate society; corporate organization is probably legally best for you, though it costs some bread.

Also, this society functions through hierarchies, and the movement group which most easily and thoughtlessly falls into the pattern of organization is a newspaper. Seems natural. Tain't. We've evolved a weekly business meeting at which major decisions are discussed and made, open to everyone working, an office structure (particularly an editorial structure) in which "editor of the issue" is a revolving job — each piece gets two readings by two editors, deciding vote (yet to be used) rests in the "editor of the issue." Every other week our business meeting is given over to political discussions.

When someone's work is not printed, an editor must give him a good reason why, and a procedure by which he can contest the decision set up — let him bring it to the general meeting and have the whole group read, debate, decide. This is particularly important for outside groups who feel their material is going unprinted for political or personal reasons, when the problem (you maintain) is in the writing.

Our structure evolved out of good hard fights caused by personal hangups and the contradictions between democratic ideals and hierarchical structure. At the same time it became clear to us, as it had earlier become clear to the Mid-Peninsula Free University, that business meetings dealt with a particular facet of our collective experience and that we needed another form to get into rather important depths and relationships. We've set up a confrontation group (encounter group, T-group), complete with movement psych, by which we discover that the ink and paper truths of Marx and Marcuse are flesh and blood contradictions and psychological problems and antagonisms and misunderstandings. The confrontation meetings are becoming increasingly important to the development of our work group as a community, a collective.

How else can you bring work, "personal" life, and politics together? Things in the office have never been better.

*Liberation News Service (LNS) sends out two packets weekly from 160 Claremont Avenue, NYC 10027; cost varies on ability to pay

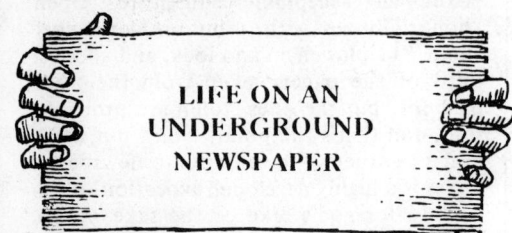

LIFE ON AN UNDERGROUND NEWSPAPER

Editors edit, don't dictate

By Judy Wasserman

(Editor's note: This is the first of a series of articles by Observer staff members describing their views of the recent changes in the Observer.)

You may have noticed a change in the Observer staff box several weeks ago. Now we no longer distinguish between editors, managers, and other staff members. We decided to drop that distinction, reflecting

we hope, an actual change in the structure of our organization and the relationships among the staff members.

Two things are happening. One involves the formal decision-making process of the newspaper; the other involves personal relations among the staff. The first is much easier to describe.

Until the middle of last fall, responsibility for the Observer, financial and otherwise, was in the hands of a few people known as editors. As the staff size increased, the editors decided they didn't have to carry that much responsibility, although giving it up also meant giving up a certain amount of power. Production-line staffers began to resent their underling status, and felt left out of policy making. About the same time, it became clear that there was no established decision-making procedure on the paper at all; decisions seemed to be made by whomever answered the phone or was in the office when questions came up. Finally, huge hassles began to arise--some over trivia, some over major policy--usually just before the paper was about to go to bed. They would be settled by force of personality or sheer endurance, and would carry over into the meetings that followed.

When we couldn't stand it any more (staffers weren't coming in because they couldn't endure the hostile atmosphere in the office), we spent an evening establishing a democratic structure that we hoped would be reasonably consistent with a humane, yet efficient, way of running the paper.

First, we set aside a time for personal confrontations, separate from the Sunday night business meetings, leaving us time to conduct some business instead of fighting on Sundays. Group therapy or confrontation had been suggested earlier by one staffer who had a good experience in a therapy group, but we'd been both timid and unconvinced of the need for it. This plan works so well that we now get enough business done on Sundays so we can spend alternate weeks in serious political discussion.

Then we agreed that all policy and financial decisions would be made by the entire staff at business meetings, even if important decisions had to be delayed, if stories had to be pulled at the last minute, or if people got angry. Procedural decisions--commas, layout, captions, etc.--were left to final arbitration by whoever was doing that job, insoluble difficulties to be decided by the editor-of-the-week.

The position of editor-of-the-week would be rotated among five people, and every business meeting would have a new chairman. Anyone calling the office to ask for the boss gets to talk to whoever answers the phone. There is no required length-of-time-in-service for the editor-of-the-week. However the job does carry a lot of responsibility, so a prospective member of the editorial pool must be approved by the staff at a meeting. We also made a job called office manager, to be filled by someone who doesn't mind spending a lot of time at the office, so that the editors wouldn't have to handle minor business matters and could concentrate on writing, assigning, and editing stories. But we have already lost two office managers.

New people are being trained for all the other jobs on the paper as well, so that no one is indispensable. This not only helps eliminate the power-play problem, but allows a guy to take a vacation without shutting down the paper.

So what have we now? Ideally, a non-hierarchical staff of equals, in which editors edit but don't dictate, in which policy is made by the group (we even have a rule that says we can't vote to have someone do something he doesn't want to do), in which procedural decisions may be made by fiat but are subject to criticism later. We decided it was OK to make-- even publish--a mistake.

In truth, what we have is a bunch of people trying to get to that point. Setting aside a time for personal confrontations was a recognition of that fact. One of the first things we discovered was that we hardly knew each other, that we had worked together for several months (in some cases more than a year) and rarely saw each other outside the office, and that one of our primary goals was to become friends, and, hopefully to build a community of trust and interdependence.

It would be nice if the paper ran more smoothly as a result, and to some extent it has. The staff is now large enough, and operations are well enough defined, for us to publish weekly instead of biweekly. Before, no one wanted to spend every weekend hassling. People are beginning to see that criticism of their sentence structure of their drawings or their layout is not necessarily a personal attack. We're also learning to be able to tell when it is.

We are becoming closer personally; we're learning each other's sensitive spots and when it's appropriate to avoid them. We're also learning that a friendly touch on a sensitive place doesn't hurt as much as we thought it might. We felt close enough to want to have Thanksgiving dinner together, although enough people were still on their own trips to show that we weren't quite a family yet.

We still have problems. Some people speak loudly and are too easily heard, others have good ideas and are too shy to speak up. Some of us aren't totally committed--that is, we do other things besides work for the Observer. Should these people carry the same weight as the full-timers? Formally, we've agreed they should. Actually, there's still occasional friction.

What is all this in terms of the movement, or the revolution? Partly, we found that the inherent alienation and suspiciousness of the left had seeped into us and kept us separate, even from our comrades. We used the newspaper to help us communicate (at what a safe distance!) with the world, now we're learning to speak to each other. More important, we're beginning to look at what the revolution would mean to us as people, and to see that some of the goals can be lived now. We can integrate our work (the paper) and the people we work with into our lives only if we see our comrades-at-work as a total people, not job-role-fillers, and make them our friends and family. The psychological barriers built by alienation between people are as real as the physical barriers built by the police, and both must be torn down in this revolution.

If I am not for myself, who am I?

If I am not for others, what am I?

If not now, when?

--Maimonides

ANATOMY OF AN UNDERGROUND PAPER

The Great Speckled Bird and Atlanta, Georgia co-exist on not entirely unfriendly terms. Indeed (though it has but seldom happened since), official Atlanta myth-makers almost welcomed *The Bird* when we began publication. The day after *The Bird* first hit the streets, *Atlanta Journal* columnist Roy Blount (now with *Sports Illustrated*) wrote a congratulatory and even perceptive column on *The Bird*, wishing it success in an only slightly patrician tone. A few weeks later, Pulitzer Prize-winning *Atlanta Constitution* editor Eugene Patterson (now of *The Washington Post*) spent a column castigating the Atlanta police force for refusing *Bird* reporters press passes and access to police files, reminding the police that it was not their function to determine the "legitimacy" of the press.

Image conscious Atlanta cosmopolitanites interpreted the appearance of an "underground paper" further proof that Atlanta of a million-plus population was truly coming of age as a city. Atlanta, you see, is a city almost proud of its problems: the bigger it gets, the taller the buildings, the greater the traffic jams, the fouler the air, the worse the ghettoes, the more obnoxious the hippies—why, the more is Atlanta like New York, Chicago and Los Angeles.

In this way *The Bird* truly reflects Atlanta—its image surpasses its reality. Beyond that I am uncertain how to proceed. It would be nice to say that *The Great Speckled Bird* is this, that it is trying to do that, that the people involved are these and they think those thoughts and do those things. But definition requires distance, it requires surface to explore and a certain stasis in time. *The Bird* is a myriad of surfaces and constant flux, *The Bird* changes from week to week and issue to issue, internally if not immediately externally. Sheer momentum of a year's publication provides much of the driving force on *The Bird* it is true, but it is momentum renewed, changed, shaped by persons defining and redefining roles, perspectives, attitudes and even values. The momentum carries us over the valleys, it produces a paper weekly on sched-ule despite circumstances, but it also tends to mute our energy peaks; the momentum often masks our confusion in direction and method, but at the same time largely precludes true clarity in our vision.

The Bird was born in an atmosphere, if not of mutual trust among equals, at least of an unspoken understanding to postpone questioning, either of ideology or motive, by the persons involved in the planning. It was given that we—upwards of 20 most of the time—small groupings of friends among strangers, were all activists against war and racism; and that, immediately, was enough.

The Bird is organized, loosely, as a cooperative, incorporating the idea of worker's control in by-law and, to varying degrees, in practice. Given democratic decision-making as the verbalized ideal, the day to day functioning of the paper and the cooperative results from an uneasy compromise between polar opposites. In our free-wheeling moments, whoever is present at the time of decision makes the decision; at other times consensus is sought and reached before a move is made. Ultimately, those things which must be done get done, and we move on.

At present on *The Bird* are seven full-time and three part-time paid staff members in a cooperative numbering about 20. Editorial authority is decentralized and democratized by an editorial board comprised of both paid and unpaid staff members. Each editor (and we are nearly all editors) is responsible for developing and working in a given area, defined by subject or geography. The previous full-time paid position of managing editor has, theoretically again, been devalued and redefined as a role to be rotated among the several members of the editorial board on a no-longer-than-three-month basis. Other rotation plans are being considered, including the possibility of persons rotating on and off paid staff in an effort to prevent or forestall the possibility of *The Bird* becoming in-grown rather than out-reaching.

The true strength of *The Bird* is not its structure, but its looseness, its receptiveness to new ideas, and its accessability to new people. A person becomes a "staff member" only by consistent work on the co-op, but the policy is non-exclusionary: natural process ultimately works more efficiently than rules which judge and accept or exclude regardless. Salaried staff are paid not for their creative—i.e. visible-to-the-public work, be it writing, layout, graphics, photography or whatever—but for the day-to-day shitwork of production: business, advertising, circulation, composition, sweeping the floors and cleaning the toilets. The aim is to burden no one with routine tasks to the extent that their creativity is stifled; or, and equally, to pay persons for *mere* creative work, the satisfaction of which is implicit. As more paid staff members are added, staff positions will be redefined and labor redivided as equitably as possible, to retain balance between time spent on creative and non-creative work among all paid staff members, with intent to maximize the creative work of each person.

I see that I have once again written an academic and quasi-theoretical piece, though I keep telling myself that I'd rather write stories. To tell the truth, *The Bird* is an ego trip, always has been and will be as long as it stays good. At worst it is ego hassling ego, at best the collective expression of personal trips, most of the time an undefinable compromise. But we are doing what we want to do and enjoying it, a seldom thing in America 1969, and damn rare in Atlanta, Georgia. Which is why we survive. And keep smiling.

—*tom coffin*

TOM COFFIN was managing editor of The Bird *until it abandoned a formal organizational structure.*

win 6/1/69

MORE...
AND MORE

"El Grito Del Norte" is a cry for justice in northern New Mexico. "El Grito" is a newspaper that has continued to grow in circulation and in importance to the Chicanos of this isolated area where bread and land are still the primary issues. Forty percent of the people in this area earn less than $3000 a year, and the counties served by "El Grito" have been officially designated as a "starvation area" by the U.S. government. The paper is written in both Spanish and English so the people feel that "it is a voice of theirs." Everyone brings in or sends in stories, articles, or news items of community interest. Most importantly, "El Grito" has given the people a sense of unity, a voice to make known their grievances, and hope where there was very little before. Anyone wishing to subscribe may write: "El Grito Del Norte," Rt.2. Box 5, Espanola, New Mexico 87532.

"Rights of Man" is a working class newspaper circulated through the South. What gives this new paper its distinctive flavor are the writers who in large measure are the workers themselves. There is a notable absence of the usual revolutionary slogans and rhetoric of the left, but as the "Rights of Man" says itself -- "to those who may be disturbed by the absence of revolutionary slogans, and the omission of certain terminology to which they are accustomed-- to those people we can only say that the extent to which they feel disturbed and offended may be the measure of their separation from the working people of the country." Their address is P.O. Box 30028, New Orleans, La. 70130

RESIST
Newsletter

Support your underground newspaper

new news is good news

The Movement grows. And grows. Three recent indications: the *Polylogue*, aspiring to more than a dialogue, just hit the streets of Augusta. Six pages of local news, military info on Fort Gordon, and little statements of personal philosophy dominate the first issue. You can get a copy from the Augusta Educational News Cooperative, PO Box 3334, Hill Station, Augusta, Georgia 30904.

The third issue of the bi-weekly *Memphis Root* just came out. Twenty pages, rather large for a paper just getting off the ground and looking pretty solid. Subs are $3.50 a year, $2.75 for students and GIs; from PO Box 4747, Memphis, Tennessee 38104.

And *The Fuse*, volume three, number one, just arrived in the mail from Oneonta, Alabama. Its biggest issue yet, twelve pages jammed with revolutionary theory. Gone are the funny little articles about Alabama that it used to run. Sad. But maybe the future will be brighter. You can get it from PO Box 728, Oneonta, Alabama 35121.

—steve wise

The Great Speckled Bird 11/24/69

Underground Switch-board

Underground Switchboard is for everyone. It is a service that has 24 hour coverage. Our phones are open to anyone wanting drug information, legal contacts, places to crash, legal abortion information, things happening around town, and any other community service reference we can think of. We are also there to rap with anyone wanting to hear a friendly voice. This space in Kaleidoscope will be used to make announcements about what this service is into and to get in contact with people. As things stand now, we are planning a benefit dance for badly needed bread at the Juneau Village Church, on Friday, February 13. Good local groups will be volunteering to play. We are still in need of people to cover the phone. We only ask that you be over 18, live in or near the East Side or have relible transportation, have some knowledge of drugs and the underground scene (whatever that is). Help would also be appreciated from anyone who feels they have information or references we could use. Listen to WTOS for announcements of our number and other communications.

271 3123

Kaleidoscope

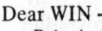

FREE OLD MOLES!

Come and get some Old Mole back issues. They're free if you come pick them up. Give them away, leave them at laundromats, take them to the park.

WHAT'S HAPPENING?

Dear WIN -

Printing facilities and printers all over the country are one of the urgent needs of the movement. The costs of commercial printing are very high but paper and used offset equipment are not expensive at all. Anyone who has the mechanical understanding to fix a car should have little difficulty learning to be a printer and maintaining the equipment.

As a mechanic and offset printer, I would be happy to travel to help set up print shops for the movement, and to train people in operating the equipment. I would need room and board, travel expenses, etc.

If you are looking for help in these lines, write: P.O. Box 57, Rifton, N.Y. 12471.

Yours for peace,
Art Rosenblum

POOR PEOPLE'S RADIO

Poor People's Radio, Inc., hopes to be on the air over the city by mid-summer as a beachhead for "People's Media" in the Bay Area.

PPR, a non-profit corporation formed recently by Meyer Gottesman and a small circle of friends, is now in the process of filing for an FCC license to opreate at 89.7 on your FM dial.

Once the License is acquired, the station will begin broadcasting with a feeble ten watts of power from the Fox Plaza Building in San Francisco. A good tuner with an outside antenna will be able to pick up the station in the East Bay.

There is a hang-up though. Before the station can get a license, they have to come up with $10,000 to cover the first year's operating expenses.

A fund drive is now underway, and contributions should be sent to Mr. Sherman Ellison, 345 Franklin St., San Francisco (94102). Checks should be made payable to Poor People's Radio, Inc.

Anyone interested in working for the station for little or no pay should contact Gottesman at 751-1974. People are needed for everything from secretary to DJ.

Berkeley Tribe 3/6/70

John McDermott: Just by way of preface, I am not exactly sure that it is going to be possible in this country to continue to maintain the covert quality of some of the operations. You have now the growth of a very substantial guerrilla scholarship on foreign policy matters — young men and women who think nothing is more fun than to go through the abstracts to find out what kind of contracts are around and to expose them. Part of the trouble at Columbia, I think, grew out of that. I think this is a new political fact which has to be taken into consideration.

The Atlantic Dec 1968

DAVE: Who is the new audience?

AL: Well, I don't just want to say the young people; Time Magazine makes so much of the generation gap that I wonder if it really exists, but it is the audience that is served by a kind of network in the Bay Area; this network helps make the Bay Area a livable place. The network of communication I'm talking about includes the Express Times, The Barb, The Committee, The Mime Troupe; it also inclues the Chronicle, which is a very open paper, with room for lots of different kinds of views. The whole thing is a kind of a free confusion, addressed to the Bay Area; KPFA has to serve more than just the University community, and join the network.

DAVE: How does KPFA do that? What kinds of format changes should be made?

AL: One of the questions about that —about getting KPFA going—is, simply, do people want to listen to the radio anymore, except as background music? The change in the times is, for example, the guy who used to write a novel now goes over to SF State, enrolls in the film department, and makes a movie.

DAVE: Well, what kinds of specific changes will you make?

AL: KPFA can be an outlet for people, a place for public announcement, kind of a continuing bulletin board. Maybe we can't go out to everybody, but we can use the phone a lot more. People should know they can call in and get air time; they have to realize KPFA is an outlet.

Instead of having black people talking to white people on our programs, we should try and get black people preparing programs for black people. That will not only speak to black people, but probably be more interesting to whites, too.

From an interview with the manager of KPFA, a listener-sponsored San Francisco FM radio station, in *San Francisco Express Times*

HAM RADIO MOVEMENT COMMUNICATIONS

Friends in New York are trying to set up a Radical Ham Radio Network to aid in the rapid exchange of news and political analysis among parts of the Movement here and in Europe. If you have, or know of someone who has, an amateur radio license or ham radio equipment, contact: Liberation News Service, 160 Claremont Ave., New York City, New York.

"Whatever the adversity we should protect our mimeographs and other printing equipment and materials even at the risk of life..."

COMRADE KIM IL SUNG, the leader of the 40 million Korean people.

KIM IL SUNG

End Racial Genocide

Dare to Struggle

Dare to WIN

HAVE A MERRY MARXIST CHRISTMAS
3 Ministers Give a Marxist Interpretation of Christ As A Radical
Surplus Prophets
FRIDAY 11:30 pm
KPFA-FM 94.1

BAY AREA FREE RADIO

Surplus Prophets — A public utility. Political rap, call-in, music and musing, sonic movies, poetry, unexpected interviews: sometimes more than one at once. We started in November 1968, and without a fulltime producer, have had to feel our way from there. Sometimes we concentrate on the local radical scene (shows on San Francisco STate strike, on legal defense, organizing in Chinatown, in the Army, in welfare bureaucracies), sometimes on analysis of news (Black Panthers, Hayakawa, The Nixon Administration, France, the economy), sometimes on celebration (International Women's Day); there's no telling, but then again there's a lot of telling.

We also premiered the songs of Carl Oglesby and Fred Gardner; we try to fuse words and music in overlay, sometimes also sounds of the preceding week, to compound a new medium of alertness.

We're a bulletin board, alerting audiences to upcoming demonstrations, meetings, so forth; once, we became an emergency communications service when Berkeley police invaded People's Park annex in the middle of the night and began arresting people, busting heads and tearing up the plants.

We start about 11:30 Friday nights, and we go until we run out of steam usually between 2 and 3:30 in the morning.

Basically, we're trying to give the movement some more room in which to flex — and to move outward. Since there are many ways in which the movement has to do all that, the show is hard to pin down. But you sort of know it's there — like the sonic equivalent of an underground paper.

Keepers: Terry Cannon, Todd Gitlin, Martin Nicolaus, Jim O'Connor, Steve Weissman, with a lot of help from our friends.

THE MICRO-BOPPER
SPEAKS A NEW
LANGUAGE

Another way of perceiving the micro-bopper would be to understand his apparatus —the way in which he communicates. The micro-bopper speaks a new language.

The use of the phrase "new language" is not entirely journalistic and oracular rhetoric. The micro-bopper language is to a large extent nonverbal: part gesture, part tone, part assumption, part telepathy and part words. They *express* themselves to each other. Conversation is highly animated, almost theatrical. Small talk is not part of their world; communication between two close friends becomes esoteric, multi-leveled and intricate, and to us incomprehensible. Where we use gestures to support words, they use words to support gestures. They have been called post-literate.

One magazine editor described the micro-bopper telepathy this way: "Just before their song was announced as No. 1 on a New York hit parade, the pre-teen members of the Cowsills, a family music group adopted by MGM Records and supported by a $250,000 publicity campaign, were moving aimlessly around their agent's office eerily communicating with each other in this fashion: Their own album provided background sound; they sang snatches of their music, touched one another, pushed and pulled, gradually, through movement, filling the office with themselves. Words were not strung together in sentences, they were used to punctuate gestures. To one of us not an understandable statement was made in twenty minutes.

Yet, they seemed to be talking to each other. They were."

It is not that micro-boppers are inarticulate; they do not *choose* to talk. Anthropologist Ted Carpenter sees their communication techniques as akin to that of primitive languages which utilize polysynthetic forms. "Consider the speech of primitive peoples . . . they do not separate the actor and the action.

"I once saw a film showing two Eskimos on a boat in the Arctic carrying on a conversation with each other. The film was silent. But do you know I *really* felt I knew exactly what it was they were saying!" A predictable observation since at least sixty percent of Eskimo adjectives are gestures.

This kinesthetic contribution to language is something that will pose no problems for micro-boppers who have grown up with technology and the multi-media. "Pre-teenagers do function this way, with this consciousness of multi-media," Carpenter says. "This is tribal in the deepest sense. Gesture includes tone, pitch, stress, juncture, body movement, all an integral part of the tribal language. You must watch and listen simultaneously. Words become a spatial creation —created by the eye."

From "Life Styles: The Micro-Bopper" by Saul Braun, *Esquire* March 1968

COMPREHENSION
The National State Obsolete
Bankrupt Illegitimate

The Impact of the Draft on the Legitimacy of the National State

by KENNETH E. BOULDING

❧ ONE of the most neglected aspects of the dynamics of society is the study of dynamic processes which underlie the rise and fall of legitimacy. This neglect reflects, in the United States at least, not merely a deficiency in social sciences and social thought; it reflects a grave deficiency in what might be called the popular image of the social system. We all tend to take legitimacy for granted. Thus, the economist hardly ever inquires into the legitimacy of exchange, even though this is the institution on which his science is built. The political scientist rarely inquires into the legitimacy of political institutions or of the institutions of organized threat, such as the police and the armed forces. Consequently we are much given to discussions of economic development as if this were a mechanical or quasi-automatic process without regard to the conditions of legitimacy of various activities and institutions. Similarly, in our discussions of the strategy of threat we rarely take account of the legitimacy of the institutions which either make the threats or provide their credibility. To put the matter simply, we tend to regard both wealth and power as self-justifying and this could well be a disastrous error.

The truth is that the dynamic of legitimacy, mysterious as it may seem, in fact governs to a remarkable extent all the other processes of social life. Without legitimacy no permanent relationship can be established, and if we lose legitimacy we lose everything. A naked threat, such as that of the bandit or the armed robber, may establish a temporary relationship. The victim hands over his money or even his person at the sword's point or the pistol's mouth. If we want to establish a permanent relationship, however, such as that of a landlord demanding rent or a government demanding taxes, the threat must be legitimized. The power both of the landlord and of the government depend in the last analysis upon the consent of the rentpayer or the taxpayer and this consent implies that the whole procedure has been

KENNETH BOULDING is the outstanding economist and author, now at the University of Colorado. He is author of "There Is a Spirit," "The Meaning of the Twentieth Century" and many others.

legitimated and is accepted by everyone concerned as right and proper. Legitimacy may be defined as general acceptance by all those concerned in a certain institution, role, or pattern of behavior that it constitutes part of the regular moral or social order within which they live. Thus legitimacy is a wider concept than the formal concept of law, even though the law is a great legitimator. At times, however, law itself may become illegitimate and when it does so its capacity to organize society is destroyed.

Legitimacy Defined by Sacrifice

Legitimacy has at least two dimensions which might be described as intensity and extent. Its intensity refers to the degree of identification or acceptance in the mind of a particular individual, and it may be measured roughly by the extent of sacrifice which he is prepared to make for an institution rather than deny it or abandon it. The extent of legitimacy refers to the proportion of the relevant population which regards the institution in question as legitimate. An overall measure of the legitimacy of any particular institution might be achieved by multiplying its intensity by its extent, but such a measure might easily obscure certain important characteristics of the system. A case in which an institution was regarded with intense allegiance by a small proportion of the people concerned would be very different from one in which there was a mild allegiance from all the people; the former, indeed, would probably be less stable than the latter. In considering any particular case, therefore, it is always important that we consider both dimensions.

The creation, maintenance, and destruction of legitimacy of different institutions presents many difficult problems. Legitimacy is frequently created by the exercise of power, either economic power in the form of wealth or political power in the form of threat capability. Legitimacy, furthermore, frequently increases with age so that old wealth and old power are more legitimate than new. The nouveau riche may be looked upon askance but their grandchildren easily become aristocrats. The conqueror likewise is illegitimate at first, but if his conquest is successful and his empire lasts, it eventually acquires legitimacy. All these relationships, however, seem to be nonlinear, and reverse themselves beyond a certain point. Thus, the display of wealth tends to become obscene and damages the legitimacy of the wealthy. In order to retain legitimacy they often have to diminish their wealth by giving it away, establishing foundations, or at least by abstaining from ostentatious consumption. Similarly, political power often seems to lose its legitimacy when it is apparently at its very height. It is at the greatest extent and power of a regime, nation, or empire that it often suddenly collapses through sheer loss of belief in it. Even age does not always guarantee legitimacy. After a certain point an ancient person or institution simply becomes senile or old-fashioned and its legitimacy abruptly collapses.

There have been enough examples of collapse of legitimacy of apparently large, prosperous and invincible institutions to suggest that we have here a general, though not necessarily a universal, principle at work. It is perhaps an example of another much-neglected proposition, that nothing fails like success because we do not learn anything from it. Thus in Europe the institution of the absolute monarchy seemed to be most secure and invincible at the time of Louis XIV, yet only a few decades later it was in ruins. Similarly, in the early years of the twentieth century the concept of empire seemed invincible and unshakably legitimate, yet in another few decades it was discredited, illegitimate, and the empires themselves collapsed or had to be transformed.

An Institution Must Be Transformed

It looks indeed as if there is some critical moment at which an institution must be transformed if it is to retain its legitimacy and transformed, furthermore, in the direction of abandonment of either its wealth or its power in some degree. Thus, after the eighteenth century the only way in which the institution of the monarchy could retain its legitimacy was to abandon its power and become constitutional. By abandoning his political power, that is, his threat capability, the monarch was able to become a symbol of the legitimacy of the state and hence was able to preserve his role in the society. Where the monarch did not make this transition, as for instance in France, Germany, and Russia, the incumbent frequently lost his head, the whole institution was destroyed, and the role simply abandoned. Similarly, in the twentieth century, if any semblance of empire was to be maintained, the political power had to be abandoned and the empire transformed into a commonwealth or community based on sentiment rather than on threat. Even the church in the twentieth century has largely had to abandon the fear of hell, that is, its spiritual threat system, as the prime motivation in attracting support. In most countries, furthermore, it has likewise had to abandon the support of the state and the secular arm, that is, the secular threat system, in an attempt to enforce conformity. Here again we see an example of the abandonment of power in the interests of retaining legitimacy.

The National State Dwarfs All

At the present time by far the most wealthy, powerful, and legitimate type of institution is the national state. In the socialist countries the national state monopolizes virtually all the wealth and the threat capability of the society. Even in the capitalist world the national state usually commands about 25 per cent of the total economy and is a larger economic unit than any private corporation, society, or church. Thus the United States government alone wields economic power roughly equal to half the national income of the Soviet Union, which is the largest socialist state. Within the United States government the United States Department of Defense has a total budget larger than the national income of the People's Republic of China and can well claim to be the second largest centrally planned economy in the world. It is true that the great corporations wield an economic power roughly equal to that of the smaller socialist states; there are, indeed, only about 11 countries with a gross national product larger than General Motors. Nevertheless, when it comes to legitimacy the national state is supreme. All other loyalties are expected to bow before it. A man may deny his parents, his wife and his friends, his God, or his profession and get away with it, but he cannot deny his country unless he finds another one. In our world a man without a country is regarded with pity and scorn. We are expected to make greater sacrifices for our country than we make for anything else. We are urged, "Ask not what your country can do for you, ask what you can do for your country," whereas nobody ever suggests that we should "Ask not what General Motors can do for you, ask what you can do for General Motors."

An institution of such monumental wealth, power and legitimacy would seem to be invincible. The record of history suggests clearly, however, that it is precisely at this moment of apparent invincibility that an institution is in gravest danger. It may seem as absurd today to suggest that the national state might lose its legitimacy as it would have been to suggest the same thing of the monarchy in the days of *le Grand Monarque*. Nevertheless both monarchy and empire have lost their legitimacy and that at the moment of their greatest power and extent. If history teaches us anything, therefore, it should teach us at this moment to look at the national state with a quizzical eye. It may be an institution precisely filling the conditions which give rise to a sudden collapse of legitimacy, which will force the institution itself to transform itself by abandoning its power or will create conditions in which the institution cannot survive.

Individuals Must Justify Their Sacrifices

These conditions can be stated roughly as follows: An institution which demands sacrifices can frequently create legitimacy for itself because of a strong tendency in human beings to justify to themselves sacrifices which they have made. We cannot admit that sacrifices have been made in vain, for this would be too great a threat to our image of ourselves and our identity. As the institution for which sacrifices are made gains legitimacy, however, it can demand more sacrifices, which further increases legitimacy. At some point, however, the sacrifices suddenly seem to be too much. The terms of trade between its devotees and the institution become too adverse, and quite suddenly the legitimacy of the whole operation is questioned, and ancient sacrifices are written off and the institution collapses. Thus men sacrificed enormously for the monarchy, and the king was able to say for centuries, "Ask not what I can do for you, ask only what you can do for me," until the point when suddenly people began to ask. "What can the king do for me?" and the answer was "Nothing." At that moment the monarchy either died or had to be transformed.

We may be in a similar moment in the case of the national state. The real terms of trade between an individual and his country have been deteriorating markedly in the past decades. In the eighteenth century the national state made relatively few demands on its citizens, and provided some of them at least with fair security and satisfactory identity. As the nation has gathered legitimacy however from the bloodshed and treasure expended for it, it has become more and more demanding. It now demands ten to twenty per cent of our income, at least two years of our life—and it may demand the life itself—and it risks the destruction of our whole physical environment. As the cost rises, it eventually becomes not unreasonable to ask for what. If the payoffs are in fact low, the moment has arrived when the whole legitimacy of the institution may be threatened.

Has Technology Made the State Obsolete?

We must here distinguish the internal from the external payoffs of the national state. Internally the payoffs may still be quite high, though it is perhaps still a question whether governments today, like the medical profession a hundred years ago, really do more good than harm. In the external relations, however, there can be no doubt that the system of national states is enormously burdensome and costly. It is not only that the world-war industry is now about 140 billion dollars, which is about equal to the total income of the poorest half of the human race, it is that this enormous expenditure gives us no real security in the long run and it sets up a world in which there is a positive probability of almost total disaster.

It is perfectly reasonable indeed to ask ourselves this question: After a nuclear war, if there is anybody left, are they going to set up again the institutions which produced the disaster? The answer would clearly seem to be "No," in which case we may say that as the present system contains a positive probability of nuclear war it is in fact bankrupt and should be changed *before* the nuclear war rather than afterward. It can be argued very cogently indeed that modern technology has made the national state obsolete as an instrument of unilateral national defense, just as gunpowder made the feudal baron obsolete, the development of the skills of organization and public administration made the monarchy obsolete, and economic development made empire obsolete. An institution, no matter how currently powerful and legitimate, which loses its function will also lose its legitimacy, and the national state in its external relations seems precisely in this position today. Either it must be transformed in the direction of abandoning its power and threat capability or it will be destroyed, like the absolute monarchy and the absolute church before it.

The Draft Calls All Into Question

What then is the role of the draft in this complex dynamic process? The draft may well be regarded as a symbol of a slow decline in the legitimacy of the national state (or of what perhaps we should call more exactly the warfare state, to distinguish it from the welfare state which may succeed it), that slow decline which may presage the approach of collapse. In the rise and decline of legitimacy, as we have seen, we find first a period in which sacrifices are made, voluntarily and gladly, in the interests of the legitimate institution, and, indeed, reinforce the legitimacy of the institution. As the institution becomes more and more pressing in its demands, however, voluntary sacrifices become replaced with forced sacrifices. The tithe becomes a tax, religious enthusiasm degenerates into compulsory chapel, and voluntary enlistment in the threat system of the state becomes a compulsory draft.

The legitimacy of the draft, therefore, is in a sense a subtraction from the legitimacy of the state. It represents the threat system of the state turned in on its own citizens, however much the threat may be disguised by a fine language about service and "every young man fulfilling his obligation." The language of duty is not the language of love and it is a symptom of approaching delegitimation. A marriage in which all the talk is of obligations rather than of love is on its way to the divorce court. The church in which all worship is obligatory is on its way to abandonment or reformation, and the state in which service has become a duty is in no better case. The draft therefore, which undoubtedly increases the threat capability of the national state, is a profound symptom of its decay and insofar as it demands a forced sacrifice it may hasten that decay and may hasten the day when people come to see that to ask "what can your country do for you" is a very sensible question.

The draft, furthermore, inevitably creates strong inequities. It discriminates against the poor, or at least against the moderately poor; the very poor, because of their poor educational equipment may escape it just as the rich tend to escape it, and the main burden therefore falls on the lower end of the middle-income groups. As these groups also in our society bear the brunt of taxation—for a great deal of what is passed as "liberal" legislation in fact taxes the poor in order to subsidize the rich—an unjust distribution of sacrifice is created. Up to now it is true this strain has not been very apparent. It cannot indeed be expressed directly because of the enormous legitimacy of the national state, hence it tends to be expressed indirectly in alienation, crime, internal violence, race and group hatreds and also in an intensified xenophobia. This is the old familiar problem of displacement. We dare not vent our anger at frustrations upon their cause and we therefore have to find a legitimated outlet in the foreigner, or the communist, or whoever the enemy happens to be at the moment. What is worse, the frustrated adult frequently displaces his anger on his children who in turn perpetuate the whole miserable business of hatred and lovelessness.

Like compulsory chapel or church attendance, which is its closest equivalent, the draft has a further disadvantage in that while it may at best produce a grudging and hostile acquiescence in the methods of the society, it frequently closes the mind to any alternative or to any reorganization of information. The psychological strains which are produced by compulsory service of any kind naturally result in displaced aggressions rather than in any reform of the system which created them. Consequently the draft by the kind of indoctrination and hidden frustrations which it produces may be an important factor in preventing that reevaluation of the national policy and the national image which is so essential in the modern world if the national state itself is to survive. The draft therefore is likely to be an enemy of the survival of the very state in the interests of which it is supposedly involved. It produces not a true love of country based on a realistic appraisal of the present situation of human society but rather a hatred of the other which leads to political mental ill health, and an image of the world which may be as insulated from the messages which come through from reality as is the mind of a paranoid.

We Must Attack the Legitimacy of the Draft

Perhaps the best thing that can be said in defense of the draft is that the alternative, namely, raising a voluntary armed force by offering sufficient financial inducements, or by persuasion and advertising, would involve even more the whipping up of hatred of the foreigner and the reinforcement of paranoid political attitudes. The draft by its very absurdities and inequities at least to some extent helps to make the whole operation faintly ridiculous, as we see it in comic strips like Beetle Bailey or in movies such as *Dr. Strangelove,* and hence makes the operation of national defense commonplace rather than charismatic. The draft certainly represents the institutionalization of the charisma of the national state, to use an idea from Max Weber, and this may be something on the credit side. Even this merit, however, is dubious. Insofar as the draft leads to widespread commonplace acceptance of mass murder and atrocities, and an attitude of mind which is blind to any but romantically violent solutions of conflict, its influence is wholly negative. Certainly the political wisdom of the American Legion is no advertisement for the political virtues of having passed through the Armed Forces.

It seems clear therefore that those of us who have a genuine affection for the institution of the national state and for our own country in particular should constantly attack the legitimacy of the draft, and the legitimacy of the whole system of unilateral national defense which supports it, in the interest of preserving the legitimacy of the national state itself. The draft, it is true, is merely a symbol or a symptom of a much deeper disease, the disease of unilateral national defense, and it is this concept which should be the prime focus of our attack. Nevertheless, cleaning up a symptom sometimes helps to cure the disease, otherwise the sales of aspirin would be much less, and a little aspirin of dissent applied to the headache of the draft might be an important step in the direction of the larger objective. Those of us, therefore, who are realistically concerned about the survival of our country should probably not waste too much time complaining about the inequities and absurdities of the draft or attempt the hopeless task of rectifying it when the plain fact is that the draft can only begin to approach "justice" in time of major war, and a peacetime draft has to be absurd and unjust by its very nature. The axe should be applied to the root of the tree, not to its branches. An attempt to pretty up the draft and make it more acceptable may actually prevent that radical reevaluation of the whole system of unilateral national defense which is now in order. We are very close to the moment when the only way to preserve the legitimacy of the national state will be to abandon most of its power. The draft is only a subplot in this much greater drama. ■

From *The Draft,* A Handbook of Facts and Alternatives, ed. by Sol Tax (U. of Chicago Press)

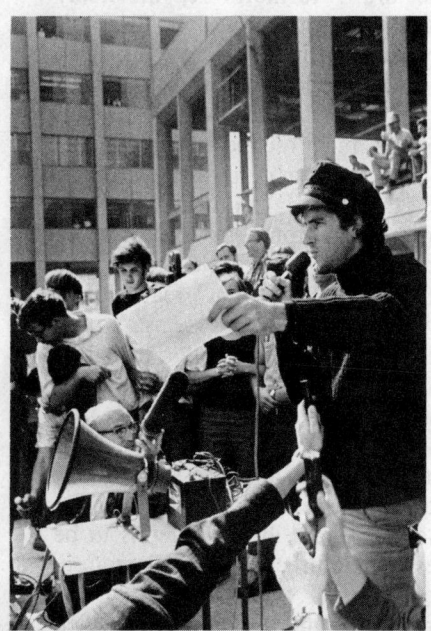

FROM REBELLION TO RESISTANCE TO REVOLUTIONARY ACTION

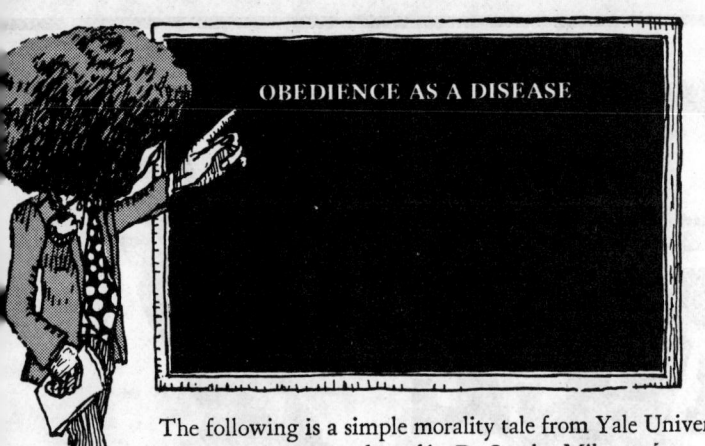

OBEDIENCE AS A DISEASE

The following is a simple morality tale from Yale University, an experiment conducted by Dr Stanley Milgram.[5]

Dr Milgram recruited 40 male volunteers who believed they were to take part in an experimental study of memory and learning at Yale University. The 40 men were between the ages of 20 and 50 and represented a wide range of occupations. Typical subjects were postal clerks, high school teachers, salesmen, engineers and laborers. One subject had not finished elementary school, but some others had doctorate and other professional degrees.

The role of experimenter was played by a 31-year-old high school teacher of biology. His manner was impassive but he maintained a somewhat stern appearance during the experiment. The experimenter was aided by a mild-mannered and likable man, who acted as a 'victim'. The experimenter interviewed each volunteer and, with him, the 'victim' masquerading as another volunteer. He told the two of them that the intention was to investigate the effects of punishment on learning, and in particular the differential effects of varying degrees of punishment and various types of teacher. The drawing of lots was rigged so that the volunteer was always the teacher and the 'victim' was always the learner. The victim was strapped into an 'electric chair' apparatus and electrode paste and an electrode were applied. The teacher-volunteer was then taken into an adjacent room and placed before a complex instrument labeled 'Shock Generator'. The teacher-volunteer was given a 45-volt shock to demonstrate the apparent authenticity of the machine.

Pulling the Switch

A row of 30 switches on the 'shock generator' were labeled from 15 to 450 volts by 15-volt steps. In addition, groups of switches were labeled from 'slight shock' to 'danger: severe shock'. Following instructions and in the context of a mock learning experiment, the teacher-volunteer was led to believe that he was administering increasingly more severe punishment to the learner-victim, who made prearranged responses. The learner-victim gave incorrect answers to three out of every four questions and received shocks as punishment for his errors. When the punitive shock reached the 300-volt level, the learner-victim — as had been prearranged — kicked on the wall of the room in which he was bound to the electric chair. At this point teacher-volunteers turned to the experimenter for guidance. The teacher-volunteer was advised to continue after a 5-10 second pause. After the 315-volt shock, the pounding was heard again. Silence followed. At this point in the experiment the teacher-volunteers began to react in various ways. But they were verbally encouraged, and even ordered in a firm manner, to proceed right up to the maximum level of voltage.

Test Results

... Dr Milgram states that contrary to all expectations 26 of the 40 subjects completed the series, finally administering 450 volts to the now silent 'victim'. Only 5 refused to carry on after the victim's first protest when 300-volts were apparently administered. Many continued, even though they experienced considerable emotional disturbance, as clearly shown by their spoken comments, profuse sweating, tremor, stuttering and bizarre nervous laughter and smiling. Three subjects had uncontrollable seizures. The teacher-volunteers who continued the shock frequently voiced their concern for the learner-victim, but the majority overcame their humane reactions and continued as ordered right up to the maximum punishment.

One observer related: 'I observed a mature and initially poised businessman enter the laboratory smiling and confident. Within 20 minutes he was reduced to a twitching, stuttering wreck, who was rapidly approaching a point of nervous collapse. He constantly pulled on his earlobe and twisted his hands. At one point he pushed his fist into his forehead and muttered: "Oh God, let's stop it." And yet he continued to respond to every word of the experimenter, and obeyed to the end.'

The conflict that the subjects faced in this experiment was between obeying an authority they trusted and respected, and doing something they felt to be wrong. The real-life situation is more horrible. There is, for many, perhaps no conflict at all. My guess is that *most* people feel guilty at *not* doing what they are told, even though they think it is wrong, and even though they mistrust those who give the orders. They feel guilty at trusting their own mistrust.

Quoted from N.Y. *Academy of Science*, 4/18/64 by R.D. Laing, in an address entitled "The Obvious," publ. in *To Free A Generation*, Collier Books

Photo: Entrance to the Ft. Dix Stockade.

A. A violent order is disorder; and
B. A great disorder is an order.
These two things are one.
                              --Poems of
                            Wallace Stevens

This country, with its institutions, belongs to the people who inhabit it. Whenever they shall grow weary of the existing government, they can exercise their constitutional right of amending it, or their revolutionary right to dismember or overthrow it.
                            -Abraham Lincoln
                            First inaugural Address

BUS STOP

Six o'clock, six o'clock in the morning and something special, hung-over and stumbling through the dark to the bus station for the trip to Milwaukee induction center, wondering just what in God's name I'm trying to do. Couple–three months ago another awful morning, the same awful walk and at the station two DRU* organizers sneaking aboard the bus, talking, leafleting, saying not to sign the security clearance because then J. Edgar has to check it out and that takes six months, at least six more months before the tap and I figure what the hell, so I don't sign. And last week another letter "you are or' red to report for questioning by an intelligence officer," so down to DRU yesterday to see what it's all about, turns out I don't have to go but if I do and decide to talk to the rest of the guys a little, well that would be groovy.

So I write out a personal statement about having to get up at 5 A.M. for selective service and killing for Ky and getting killed for LBJ and phony patriotism and just who are all these people playing with our lives anyway, and DRU runs it off and I'm handing it out to the most wretched crew of guys I've ever seen, the hippy barefoot and bells, couple-three night-long drunks starting to wear off, another so strung out he doesn't catch his own name till the draft board beauty yells it for the fifth time, all the hang-overs and hang-ups, all the fears, a real zoo and they're all sitting sick in the station a few months ago and someone stuffing something into my hand. And then we're milling out to the buses and a DRU organizer who's been leafleting shouts at us as we board

Remember, you're still human beings, so don't let them treat you like animals.

it follows us into the bus but can't go down, floats in the air like a left-over fart we can't take because we know that today we are animals, that they have made us so, and yet can't fully reject either, for we do not like what they're doing to us.

Fifteen minutes along to Milwaukee and I'm still sitting, the horribly hushed bus, no idea what to say, finally figuring what the hell and into the aisle. About two minutes into the rap, working off the leaflet and starting in on what the guys going for physicals can expect, the bus driver yells at me to sit down. I go up

—Wha?

—I said sit down. You can't stand up on this bus like that

—Why not?

—Against the state law.

Here I am telling the guys to Beat Army and can't even think of much to say to the bus driver. Luckily I glance up, see a sign "no standing in front of line," look down and I'm on it. move back six inches and shout

—Sign says in front of the line. I'm behind it.

turn around and start in again. He shouts he'll pull off the road if I don't stop, go ahead, so he does and I sit down. He starts again, I get up, he stops, I sit down, three or four more like this and he threatens to flag down the first state police car, go ahead we're not in any hurry, he babbles on and then from behind me the first sign of life

—Hey you, just do the goddam driving, huh?

After that it gets better, we do the physical and the security clearance and the draft and the war and they're with me, but quiet, mostly tired and apathetic, and it's light, the sun shining bright as we pile out of the bus and into the induction center.

And then all hell breaks loose. Three DRU members start leafleting the guys sitting around on chairs and couches, about ninety in all. The Corporal wheels out from behind his table at the front of the room, waving his arms and shouting

—Stop it, stop it, you can't do that!

—Why not?

—Give me those, you can't do that

—(all the time passing them out) I don't believe you.

—(waving arms wild) Stop, stop!

—Take me to your leader. No, I'm busy, bring your leader here. I don't believe you.

Corporal dashes out double-time up the stairs, returns in a few minutes with the Captain and a slew of others. By this time the leaflets are distributed everyone laughing. Corporal points the three out to Captain, he looks darkly confiscates the remaining leaflets says that's enough, then turns to the rest of us and brightens, starting his nice-guy pitch. I'm in the back of the room, figure now is as good a time as any and start in

—What kind of place is this, Army can hand out their stuff and do all the talking they want, but not us.

Captain is a great believer in free speech, says so, also there's a time and place for everything. Then on the other side of the room the little guy who'd come up to me on the bus a half-dozen times, very nervous, was I sure that not signing the security clearance was legal, yes I was (but not so sure what he was going to do), now he gets going

—That's not free speech, that's tyranny.

—That's your interpretation!

and now I know he won't sign, wants to stop running, fighting back and I give him a little help

—It's also the Court's Interpretation, it's in the Constitution, the Constitution, remember that?

and now five or six guys are shouting, everyone laughing, the hippy jingling his bells, Captain fuming and confused, a truly beautiful scene.

Finally things calm down, Captain recovers cool, begins anew, and a pattern emerges, him talking and me translating, like

—Men, we all want this to be over as fast and as easy as possible, so if we can all co-operate. . .

—Yeah, we co-operate with them and they slap a gun in our hands and ship us off to Vietnam, that's some co-operation.

or

—Selective Service has brought you here today for your. . .

—When he says selective service, he means selective slavery.

Couple-three minutes of this and Captain realizes he's losing control again, stalks back and starts talking directly to me, but I keep translating

—You're creating a disturbance here.

—They're the ones disturbing us, waking us up before five in the morning, herding us into that bus. . .

—You could get into trouble for this.

—They haven't got us in uniform yet, until they do they can't touch us, we're still. . .

—Stop shouting!

—Stop interrupting me!

Finally Captain blows completely, orders me out of the place. I start walking slowly up the room, tired of shouting but I didn't take that bus ride for just fifteen minutes of this, trying to think of something and then have it, whirling on Captain following right behind me

—My lunch! My bus trip back to Madison! You owe me money!

a roar of laughter, Captain hesitating then talking fast

—That's not the Army's responsibility, that's the responsibility of Selective Service, we don't. . .

but he hesitated, all I need and I'm off in a rage, up and down the aisles, my lunch, my bus ticket, the draft, the world, Captain and Corporal both after me, heading me off near the front of the room, Captain pointing with shaking finger, in quivering voice

—You. . .you go stand there. . .you be quiet now. . .

so I go stand in my corner, Corporal next to me, sort of screening me off from the rest of the guys. I try being friendly but he's stone-face Duty-Honor-Country and what the hell, I didn't come to infiltrate the ranks, not today anyway. Occasionally I step out a little and shout something and he flaps his arms around

—You. . .hey, now, you. . .hey. . .

but the guys are getting their packets and starting to go upstairs, grinning sort of sick

4
resis

as they go by, and I'm starting to feel sick again myself, especially when the three bulls that Captain phoned walk in behind me, if I do any yelling now it's a disorderly conduct bust and I'm just not up for that act today. I go sit with the three DRU guys who are to be segregated from the rest of the guys while they take their physicals, and then they go up and I'm told the "intelligence" officer won't be here till ten.

I sit around for a few minutes, then sneak upstairs, the guys are in taking mental tests and signing security clearances, I open the door and shout
—Remember, you don't have to sign that thing!
slam the door and turn to meet a Sergeant trotting up to me, before he can get anything out
—I'm supposed to report to you, Sergeant.
Well, Sergeant he really had no idea, but anyway I should stick with him and keep my mouth shut, so I stand and smoke and then a PFC bursts out of the room, looking scared
—Sir, I've got a bad one in there.
it's the hippie and he's into his thing now. I peer over Sergeant's shoulder and see his security clearance, nothing but block capitals
—ALL FORMS SUCH AS THIS ARE BASICALLY EVIL
and before that he refused the desk, took to the floor cross-legged reading from a book of Zen meditations. Sergeant he don't dig, puts me into another room with the three leafleteers and goes in to see. We sit around ruminating on the relative merits of the subversive groups listed on the security form, with "Serbo-Croatian Caucus" finally losing out to "Blue Star Mothers of America." Then in comes the hippy, Buddha and bells now subversive too, plops down on the floor and we rap a few minutes before he gets up and goes sits on the window-sill legs dangling outside. PFC walks in and freezes, takes a few steps, stops,
—Hey you, get away from that window!
—(smiling gently) Why?
PFC really scared now, staggers a few more steps, shouts
—Get down from there, get away from that window!
but just smiles and sticks his head further outside, PFC near tears now, extends arms hands open in supplication, almost whispers
—Please come down.
—OK.
and back to the floor. PFC stares dazed and weary, he will never, never know, and then Sergeant comes in, I'm wanted on the third floor.

Up there a secretary gives me a bunch of forms to fill out so scrawling a big "NO" across each, dropping in a few doodles and she looks somewhat distraught, I've cheated her, but she takes and goes and I wander around talking with the other secretaries about life with Army. Finally

I'm called into Lieutenant's office, he informs me of all my rights I keep nodding and grinning and someone comes in behind me, very short and bouncing on his toes, dead fish face coming on like Jack Webb, and after a few minutes of some crazy code conversation he's introduced to me as Intelligence Officer Whatchamahoopsie. I say pleased, he says nothing and then we march up to the fifth floor, the interrogation room. He holds the door for me, a table and chairs in the middle and couch along a wall, I flop on the couch and he slams the door behind him it bounces back tries again back again, five times before he turns the knob and closes it. This one is the prize of the day. He sits at the table, points to another chair
—You sit here.
so I do and he flips a wallet across at me
—I'm with Army Intelligence.
flip it back off his chest
—I'm with humanity.
a bit weak but he helps
—Oh, that's nice.
—Well, it's a hell of a lot nicer than being with Army Intelligence.
Then he starts in on all my rights, but I'm playing with some paper so
—Do you wish to make a statement?
—No.
—Then you'll sign a statement stating that you refuse to make a statement.
—No.
and that's it, back down to the third floor, more buffooneries and finally on a couch in the main lobby where we started, staring up at the ceiling.

Up above the ceiling the guys are suffering through the same obscenity I remember from a few months ago. After the mental testing its off with the clothes, height and weight, and then head down, eyes on the floor, follow the yellow line, station one give us a cup of your piss, station two your ears, your eyes station head down seven some blood please, on the yellow line and on station thirteen some shrink's sticky questions you're fit for use and then lined up in a big room, dirty old men looking you over poking probing grabbing your balls finger up your ass you're good enough to die and now the ceiling back and forth and in a slow whorl up and down and close my eyes. . .
When I open them a blob, long yellow hair freckles and braces, a noise it talks
—Wanna cookie?
cute and friendly thirteen-year old Red Cross girl and I want nothing more than to swat her through the window, but I take her coconut crumble and bite. Then walk outside and spit it into the gutter, sail the rest at a third-floor window and up the street for a beer. In the bar remembering the shrink looking at my psycho questionnaire last time
—What do you mean, "mildly paranoid"?
—Oh, it's nothing to worry about.
—Yes, but what do you mean?
—Well, I mean, like they're after me.
—I see. Who is "they"?

—The ones who are after me.
—Mmm. Why are they after you?
—Because they want to get me.
Then back, it's clouding up now, into the main lobby, couple guys finished early but no talk, just sit and stare, so up to the second, the third, the fourth floor, saying the same thing to every soldier and secretary I see, getting the same blank then incredulous look and directions to another office, working my way up till finally what I want
—See Captain.
his office empty he's in conference next door with the Commandant, some Something-less-than-General and in I go, heads bent low over desk, a nod to the flag and then this time shout it
—You people owe my old high school a buck!
heads coming up. open mouth and saucer eyes, Something-less-than-General completely stooged but finally Captain he's learning closing eyes and very soft
—Would you please wait for me in my office?
so I do and then explain how Army sent to High School for a transcript and High School sent me the bill and Army really should take care of its own debts and he quivers across paper for the address he'll handle it personally.

Down to the second floor and smoke one under a big "No smoking" sign but nothing happens they're learning so down to the lobby and Corporal calls the hippy up they rushed him want no part of him and I'm called and we can leave now with bus tickets if we like and he
—Man, I want out of this place.
so do I but maybe something else will happen so I just walk him out to the corner and off he goes and now a faint mist. Back in and Corporal calls me but a big bunch is going to lunch so out again, leaving Corporal's wailings "Han-ley" behind he's supposed to keep me away from the others, onto the bus in the back and Corporal at the door.
—Hey Hanley, come on in.
—I already am in.
—No, in the building, we've got some food for you inside.
—That's all right, I'm going out for lunch today.
—You want to go with these guys?
—I think so, yeah.
—(almost inaudible) Ok.
what can he do drag me down the aisle? Then lunch in the unused basement of a downtown cafeteria, cakey inedible pork and potatoes and talking to upstate guys the draft the war and being treated like animals but tired now not getting very far.

Back in the lobby and some of the guys finishing up coming down or back from lunch, one-by-one coming up to me
—How'd "intelligence" treat you?
and getting theirs back, all the gore, then just rapping, some very, very good raps democracy the draft imperialism freedom and all that. And the plans, the schemes, the escapes one guy knew the ear-test

machine beat it bad, another into Navy OCS it's bad but it's not Vietnam, one refused to give blood and another with the shrink

    —I see you've checked "yes" for "homosexual tendencies."

    —(leaning across, looking, nodding) Yeah, yeah, right.

    —Are you serious about this?

    —Well, Freud says we all have them.

    —(disgusted) You'll never be able to work for the government, you know.

    —(long hesitation) Gee whiz, I never thought of that.

and many more. Then we're thirsty, six or seven heading out for beer, I'm last and behind me a guy I haven't seen before

    —Where you guys going?

    —Couple beers.

and he's in, then Corporal

    —Hey, you guys can't leave the building when you're. . .

and he looks back bitter

    —Fuck you, Army!

and out we go, into the drizzle and the bar.

    Then back in the lobby, more talk and turns out seven guys refused to sign the security questionnaire. Finally the bus is ready, back towards Madison, someone asks about my interview I talk a few minutes and its a quiet return trip, low mutterings or silence just looking out at the driving rain. Madison.

    —See you.

    —Yeah, take it easy.

and then the long walk back to my room, it's been a wild day and I did have fun and I don't quite know why I'm down, so very down sloshing through the storm.

    Looking back on that day now I think I know much more what I was doing, what I could have done, and why I came away so low. The shouting and disrupting were one way of attempting to penetrate the thick layer of fear and apathy we've all acquired en route through America, of showing that authority could be ridiculed and challenged. I've learned since then that there was much more I could have done, both on the bus and in the building.

    But more than this, I know now that such spasmodic efforts as I made that day will end no drafts, stop no wars, break no empires, create no souls, and humanize no worlds. That day was only a very small part of what must be the far larger whole of resistance. People must be reached long before that wretched morning when they enter the bus station already beat. We must come to see that today's Great War is the Man against us, and that to continue fighting it as a strictly individual thing can only mean all kinds of death.

    On his side the Man works 365 days a year to effect his will. This we too must do, and since he has most of the guns we must work twice as hard, struggle with twice the effort. It will be a long and difficult struggle, this one, and we will inevitably take some losses along the way. But it's the only way, and perhaps someday, a day we may never see, perhaps somewhere beyond the sheets of despair through which we now move, perhaps—just perhaps—we can walk free, we can live our lives as human beings in the way we see fit.

    That's what draft resistance is all about.

*WISCONSIN DRAFT RESISTANCE UNION

By George Hanley, from *Connections* 1968

CONNECTIONS

FORT DIX IS AN EQUAL OPPORTUNITY EMPLOYER

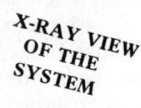

Channeling

"Channeling" is one of ten documents in an "Orientation Kit" put out by the Selective Service. It was issued in July 1965 and has recently been withdrawn. The following are excerpts from that document.

One of the major products of the Selective Service classification process is the channeling of manpower into many endeavors, occupations and activities that are in the national interest. . . .

The line dividing the primary function of armed forces manpower procurement from the process of channeling manpower into civilian support is often finely drawn. The process of channeling by not taking men from certain activities who are otherwise liable for service, or by giving deferment to qualified men in certain occupations, is actual procurement by inducement of manpower for civilian activities which are manifestly in the national interest.

While the best known purpose of Selective Service is to procure manpower for the armed forces, a variety of related processes take place outside delivery of manpower to the active armed forces. Many of these may be put under the heading of "channeling manpower." Many young men would not have pursued a higher education if there had not been a program of student deferment. Many young scientists, engineers, tool and die makers, and other possessors of scarce skills would not remain in their jobs in the defense effort if it were not for a program of occupational deferments. Even though the salary of a teacher has historically been meager, many young men remain in that job, seeking the reward of a deferment. The process of channeling manpower by deferment is entitled to much credit for the large number of graduate students in technical fields and for the fact that there is not a greater shortage of teachers, engineers and other scientists working in activities which are essential to the national interest. . . .

The System has also induced needed people to remain in these professions and in industry engaged in defense activities or in the support of national health, safety or interest. . . .

This was coupled with a growing public recognition that the complexities of future wars would diminish further the distinction between what constitutes military service in uniform and a comparable contribution to the national interest out of uniform. Wars have always been conducted in various ways, but appreciation of this fact and its relationship to preparation for war has never been so sharp in the public mind as it is now becoming. The meaning of the word "service," with its former restricted application to the armed forces, is certain to become widened much more in the future. This brings with it the ever increasing problem of how to control effectively the service of individuals who are not in the armed forces.

In the Selective Service System the term "deferment" has been used millions of times to describe the method and means used to attract to the kind of service considered to be most important, the individuals who were not compelled to do it. The club of induction has been used to drive out of areas considered to be less important to the areas of greater importance in which deferments were given, the individuals who did not or could not participate in activities which were considered essential to the defense of the Nation. The Selective Service System anticipates further evolution in this area. . . .

No group deferments are permitted. Deferments are granted, however, in a realistic atmosphere so that the fullest effect of channeling will be felt, rather than be terminated by military service at too early a time.

Registrants and their employers are encouraged and required to make available to the classifying authorities detailed evidence as to the occupations and activities in which the registrants are engaged. . . . Since occupational deferments are granted for no more than one year at a time, a process of periodically receiving current information and repeated review assures that every deferred registrant continues to contribute to the overall national good. This reminds him of the basis for his deferment. . . .

Patriotism is defined as "devotion to the welfare of one's country." It has been interpreted to mean many different things. Men have always been exhorted to do their duty. But what that duty is depends upon a variety of variables, most important being the nature of the threat to national welfare and the capacity and opportunity of the individual. Take, for example, the boy who saved the Netherlands by plugging the dike with his finger.

At the time of the American Revolution the patriot was the so-called "embattled farmer" who joined General Washington to fight the British. The concept that patriotism is best exemplified by service in uniform has always been under some degree of challenge, but never to the extent that it is today. In today's complicated warfare, when the man in uniform may be suffering far less than the civilians at home, patriotism must be interpreted far more broadly than ever before.

This is not a new thought, but it has had new emphasis since the development of nuclear and rocket warfare. Educa-

tors, scientists, engineers and their professional organizations, during the last ten years particularly, have been convincing the American public that for the mentally qualified man there is a special order of patriotism other than service in uniform—that for the man having the capacity, dedicated service as a civilian in such fields as engineering, the sciences and teaching constitute the ultimate in their expression of patriotism. A large segment of the American public has been convinced that this is true.

It is in this atmosphere that the young man registers at age 18 and pressure begins to force his choice. He does not have the inhibitions that a philosophy of universal service in uniform would engender. The door is open for him as a student if capable in a skill badly needed by his nation. He has many choices and he is prodded to make a decision.

The psychological effect of this circumstantial climate depends upon the individual, his sense of good citizenship, his love of country and its way of life. He can obtain a sense of well-being and satisfaction that he is doing as a civilian what will help his country most. This process encourages him to put forth his best effort and removes to some degree the stigma that has been attached to being out of uniform.

In the less patriotic and more selfish individual it engenders a sense of fear, uncertainty and dissatisfaction which motivates him, nevertheless, in the same direction. He complains of the uncertainty which he must endure; he would like to be able to do as he pleases; he would appreciate a certain future with no prospect of military service or civilian contribution, but he complies. . . .

Throughout his career as a student, the pressure—the threat of loss of deferment—continues. It continues with equal intensity after graduation. His local board requires periodic reports to find out what he is up to. He is impelled to pursue his skill rather than embark upon some less important enterprise and is encouraged to apply his skill in an essential activity in the national interest. The loss of deferred status is the consequence for the individual who has acquired the skill and either does not use it or uses it in a nonessential activity.

The psychology of granting wide choice under pressure to take action is the American or indirect way of achieving what is done by direction in foreign countries where choice is not permitted. Here, choice is limited but not denied, and it is fundamental that an individual generally applies himself better to something he has decided to do rather than something he has been told to do.

The effects of channeling are manifested among student physicians. They are deferred to complete their education through school and internship. This permits them to serve in the armed forces in their skills rather than in an unskilled capacity as enlisted men.

The device of pressurized guidance, or channeling, is employed on Standby Reservists of which more than 2-1/2 million have been referred by all services for availability determinations. The appeal to the Reservist who knows he is subject to recall to active duty unless he is determined to be unavailable is virtually identical to that extended to other registrants.

The psychological impact of being rejected for service in uniform is severe. The earlier this occurs in a young man's life, the sooner the beneficial effects of pressured motivation by the Selective Service System are lost. He is labeled unwanted. His patriotism is not desired. Once the label of "rejectee" is upon him all efforts at guidance by persuasion are futile. If he attempts to enlist at 17 or 18 and is rejected, then he receives virtually none of the impulsion the System is capable of giving him. If he makes no effort to enlist and as a result is not rejected until delivered for examination by the Selective Service System at about age 23, he has felt some of the pressure but thereafter is a free agent.

This contributed to establishment of a new classification of I-Y (registrant qualified for military service only in time of war or national emergency). That classification reminds the registrant of his ultimate qualification to serve and preserves some of the benefit of what we call channeling. Without it or any other similar method of categorizing men in degrees of acceptability, men rejected for military service would be left with the understanding that they are unfit to defend their country, even in wartime.

An unprejudiced choice between alternative routes in civilian skills can be offered only by an agency which is not a user of manpower and is, therefore, not a competitor. In the absence of such an agency, bright young men would be

importuned with bounties and pirated like potential college football players until eventually a system of arbitration would have to be established.

From the individual's viewpoint, he is standing in a room which has been made uncomfortably warm. Several doors are open, but they all lead to various forms of recognized, patriotic service to the Nation. Some accept the alternatives gladly—some with reluctance. The consequence is approximately the same.

The so-called Doctor Draft was set up during the Korean episode to insure sufficient physicians, dentists and veterinarians in the armed forces as officers. The objective of that law was to exert sufficient pressure to furnish an incentive for application for commission. However, the indirect effect was to induce many physicians, dentists and veterinarians to specialize in areas of medical personnel shortages and to seek outlets for their skills in areas of greatest demand and national need rather than of greatest financial return.

Selective Service processes do not compel people by edict as in foreign systems to enter pursuits having to do with essentiality and progress. They go because they know that by going they will be deferred.

The application of direct methods to effect the policy of every man doing his duty in support of national interest involves considerably more capacity than the current use of indirection as a method of allocation of personnel. The problem, however, of what is every man's duty when each individual case is approached is not simple. The question of whether he can do one duty better than another is a problem of considerable proportions and the complications of

logistics in attempting to control parts of an operation without controlling all of it (in other words, to control allocation of personnel without controlling where people eat, where they live and how they are to be transported), adds to the administrative difficulties of direct administration. The organization necessary to make the decisions, even poor decisions, would, of necessity, extract a large segment of population from productive work. If the members of the organization are conceived to be reasonably qualified to exercise judgment and control over skilled personnel, the impact of their withdrawal from war production work would be severe. The number of decisions would extend into billions.

Deciding what people should do, rather than letting them do something of national importance of their own choosing, introduces many problems that are at least partially avoided when indirect methods, the kind currently invoked by the Selective Service System, are used.

Delivery of manpower for induction, the process of providing a few thousand men with transportation to a reception center, is not much of an administrative or financial challenge. It is in dealing with the other millions of registrants that the System is heavily occupied, developing more effective human beings in the national interest. If there is to be any survival after disaster, it will take people, and not machines, to restore the Nation.   July, 1965

Ramparts

THE ASSUMPTIONS OF THE DRAFT

THE POLITICS OF FEAR: DOES YOUR LIFE BELONG TO THE STATE?

I'd like to talk about the basic assumptions which that system represents, and the pillars upon which it is built, because I think you and I have to understand what it means to carry a draft card. One of the things it means is a set of terms you accept, and for a moment I'd like to lay those terms out.

I. The most obvious assumption of military conscription is that the lives of young people in this country belong not to those young people; the lives of those young people instead are possessions of the state, to be used by the state when and where the state chooses to use them. The decisions made by those young people are not decisions made on the terms that they find in their lives. They are rather decisions that are made on the terms of the state because those people belong to the state. What the draft card represents is a pledge. It's a pledge that all of you have signed to the American state. That pledge says,

"When and where you decide murder to be a fit international policy, I'm your boy."

If your relationship to the state is one of subservience, then you can expect that state to reproduce that subservience in kind around the world. History should leave us no doubt about that. And what we see happening in a situation like Vietnam today is not a mistake. It is not something that's fallen down out of the sky on all of us. Rather, we see the American logic coming to fruition. We see a dispossessed people dispossessing other people of their lives.

The first problem that you and I face is the problem of repossessing that basic instrument called a life. That life all of you have signed over to the state. And it is only when we begin to repossess those lives that you and I can ever talk about those lives having meaning or about living in a society that was really shaped by the meaning of those lives.

II. The second assumption of conscription is perhaps the least obvious, but it is also the most important. For a moment,

I'd like all of you to think of your draft cards as an educational mechanism. You're given a draft card to teach you a way of thinking about yourself and a way of thinking about people around you. And what has been taught to a generation of young people in this country by conscription is a basic fact that has to do with a mode of energy of life.

You know for all of us there are thousands, literally thousands of psychological and emotional resources one might go to to find the energy to pursue one's life from day to day. But rather than any of those various energies, what we live in is one of those energies organized. *And what that draft card has taught people from day to day to day in their lives is how consistently to live under the auspices of fear.* How continually when they seek those resources that one needs to live a life, how continually to go to fear for those. And as you and I look around us, we can say that fear is not just a simple, personal, psychological fact; what you and I live in the midst of is the organized politics of fear.

If we were to dispense with words like "left" and "right," which may be totally inadequate to understand those organizations from the point of view of what human energy is, their base for social organization, what model of man are they based upon, then what you and I can say in the world today is that we live in the unanimous organized politics of fear. That fear has made men blind. That blindness has made people starve. That blindness is the fact of lives around the world today.

What you and I can reasonably do, then, is not say that we won't be afraid, because I've never met a man who wasn't afraid. What you and I can say is that we refuse to make that fear the central fact of our lives. We refuse to make it the hub around which we revolve.

Most of all, we refuse to build that fear into social organizations. What we can say is, we may be afraid, but that fear will not be imposed by us on the people around us. That fear will not be made into a society, which means that no longer can we continue to act under the auspices of that fear. And what we in the Resistance have done is said: NO MORE. No more will we breed and extend that fear. No more will we be that fear's servant.

III. The third assumption of conscription is the most obvious: that is, 80% of the people in the world today live lives that we could characterize as miserable. They live those lives not because the world does not possess the resources to give them meaningful lives. You live in a country that every hour spends seven million dollars on weapons. Every month we spend the money for armaments for the war in Vietnam that is necessary to feed every starving person in the world today. The world is not lacking the sustenance for those people.

Rather, what stands between those people and anything we might understand as the basic refinements of life is you and me, and the fact that you and I and the people around the world have made the decision that it's much more important to kill those people, that it's much more important to see every starving face in the world today as a potential enemy than it is to go to those people and talk to their hunger and give them food.

And if we are to ask ourselves what institution in this society stands as a representative of that decision, what we can say is that the United States military is the obvious representative of that decision on your and my parts, and that the United States military does not exist without conscription, and conscription does not exist without you and me. That system of conscription is not General Hershey. It is not Lyndon Johnson. It is not any Congressman or Senator who voted upon that bill. It is not any one of the little old ladies that shuffle the daily papers of the SSS. Military conscription is every man that carries a draft card.

You and I are the bricks and mortar of that system. And the most elaborate bureaucracy for selective service in the world does not function without people such as you and me willing to sign our lives over to that system. Without you and me, it's nothing. I mean, the beautiful thing about American totalitarianism is that it is participatory. Which means that if you don't buy it, it doesn't move. And I don't buy it.

I think you buy it when you carry a draft card. I think you become one more link in a whole chain of death and oppression on people's lives around the world.

What we in the Resistance have said about that act of refusing to cooperate with military conscription is not that we see it as a final act, not that we see it even as the great culmination. It's one little thing. It's one step. But it's the first step. To take that step means for most of you taking on what's probably going to be a wholly new social role. That's called the role of criminal. . .

You and I have to stand up. The first way you can stand up is to take that little piece of white paper called a draft card that you carry around in your pocket, you can take it and say:

IN REALITY, THIS IS NOT A PIECE OF WHITE PAPER. IN REALITY, THIS IS A DEATH WARRANT. I'VE SIGNED THIS DEATH WARRANT, AND I NOW TEAR THIS DEATH WARRANT UP. MY NAME GOES OUT ON NO MORE DEATH WARRANTS, AND MY BODY STANDS BETWEEN ANY MAN AND THAT DEATH WARRANT. I STAND HERE TODAY AND TOMORROW AND THE NEXT DAY WITH MY BROTHERS AND I DON'T STOP STANDING UNTIL ALL MY BROTHERS ARE ON THEIR FEET.

From remarks made by Dave Harris at The National Student Congress, 1968. Harris, a founder of the West Coast Resistance, is now serving a 3-year sentence for induction refusal.

AMERIKA

The regime is illegitimate because it is dominated by a subsidized military-industrial group that cannot be democratically changed. There is a 'hidden government' of C.I.A. and F.B.I. The regime has continually lied and witheld information to deceive the American people; and with a federal budget of $425 millions for public relations, democratic choice becomes almost impossible. Even so, the President deliberately violated the overwhelming electoral mandate of 1964; it transpires that he planned to violate it even while he was running. The regime presents us with *faits accomplis;*. . .Then we judge that the government is a usurper and the Republic is in danger. . .

PAUL GOODMAN

In the last seven years we have spent 384 billion dollars on war, 27 billion dollars on space and less than 2 billion dollars on community development and housing.

W.H. FERRY Jan 1968

"This country," declared a forthright director of the American Cancer Society yesterday, "has got its priorities all wrong."

Here was his bill of particulars:

A total national budget for the coming year of $195 billion—equal to $974 for every living American.

Of this spending per capita, $127 is going to the Vietnam war; $400 is going to other defense spending; and 93 cents is going to cancer research.

"Ninety-three cents," said Dr. James T. Grace Jr. of Buffalo, N.Y., "for research into a disease that will kill 50 million Americans now living."

San Francisco Chronicle March 1969

Indeed, the things that unite America with Germany may be more than those that divide them. There is really nothing to choose between "America, right or wrong" and "Deutschland uber Alles." For, when chauvinism supplants reason, all crimes are permissible. And what was unspeakable yesterday is commonplace today.

WILLIAM STRICKLAND

NEW JOB (same boss)

WASHINGTON (LNS)—Senator William Proxmire (D-Wisc.) issued a report showing that the number of high ranking retired military officers working for the defense industry has tripled in the last ten years.

The report, made with the cooperation of both industry and the Pentagon, showed that 2,072 retired officers with the rank of colonel and above were presently employed by the leading military contractors.

The easy mobility with which officers move into top defense contracting jobs " . . . is solid evidence of the military-industrial complex in operation," said Senator Proxmire.

The top ten defense contractors and the number of officers in their employ were listed by the Senator as follows:

General Dynamics	113
Lockheed Aircraft	**210**
General Electric	19
United Aircraft	48
McDonnel Douglas	141
AT&T	9
Boeing	169
Ling-Temco-Vought	69
North American Rockwell	104
General Motors	17

In Dr. Samuel Johnson's famous dictionary patriotism is defined as the last resort of a scoundrel. With all due respect to an enlightened but inferior lexicographer, I beg to submit that it is the first.

--Ambrose Bierce
The Devil's Dictionary, '06

Communities of Resistance
Seeds of Liberation

res

GARY RADER

Soon after April 15, six of us who had burned our draft cards in New York got together to talk about the possibilities of an effective draft-resistance movement in the Chicago area. Out of that group emerged an organization known as the Chicago Area Draft Resisters.

We felt that it was valuable to have the original nucleus be men who were thoroughly committed to civil disobedience. Having this basic commitment quickly established a feeling of solidarity and camaraderie. We were also able to maintain an aggressive, activist attitude, which helped us keep going during the sometimes discouragingly long hours of work involved in starting a new organization.

We contacted and included several other persons seriously thinking about draft resistance. These were located through personal contacts or informally recruited at a draft-resistance workshop at the University of Chicago and another at the Student Mobilization Conference on May 12.

We kept our membership small at the outset, twenty to twenty-five at most. Personally, I feel this is wise; you can't start a group from scratch with a hundred people. The hard-core activists have got to do some long, hard thinking and serious planning, then gradually integrate new members into the group.

We faced the problem of group structure very soon, as we began to confront the possibility of having fifty or more show up at meetings. Our solution was, I think, both a sound general concept and immediately utilitarian. We intend to form a number of local, autonomous "squads" of draft resisters scattered across the Chicago area. Members of each squad would live fairly near to each other, making possible frequent meetings, promoting interpersonal contact outside of squad meetings and solving other logistical problems involved in organizations with scattered membership.

Each squad will be responsible for actions directed toward local draft boards and recruiting stations, for contacting the scheduled inductees in its area and for organizing in the local high schools, colleges and youth and community organizations—as well as for any other group activities in which numbers of people may be presented with antiwar or antidraft education, including information about CADRE. Each squad should contain at least two or three full-time organizers located at a draft-counseling-draft-resistance office.

We began with one squad, located mainly in one of the more radical areas of Chicago, Hyde Park—the University of Chicago area. We started working on the local draft boards, and also covered the induction center daily. We attained a city-wide strength of fifteen full-time and about sixty part-time workers, at which time four of the full-time organizers moved out to organize new squads on the Near North Side (around our central office in Old Town), the far North Side, and in a section of the ghetto, Lawndale. Many of the remaining full-time organizers moved into the roles of city-wide coordinators or bureaucrats —office staff, printers and fund-raisers.

We found it important to specialize within the squad: one person in charge of mobilizing people to leaflet the draft board, one to mobilize people for the squad's day at the induction center, one to handle the project of contacting men classified 1-A (lists are published by the draft boards) and one to arrange speaking engagements. The bureaucrats should also specialize. However, specialization was not undertaken until each person had worked in many areas and understood the group program and how it fit together.

Membership is basically nonexclusionary. We draw the line at violence, in that the group will not support violence on the part of one of its members, although individual members are perfectly free to do as they wish. We also like to have a commitment to civil disobedience in a new member, but so far it has not been required. One must radicalize over time; if we limited ourselves only to those committed to c.d., we could not build a very large movement.

So what specifically will we be doing? Let me list a few points:

● *Recruiting:* We shall use personal contacts, media coverage, speaking appearances, meetings at draft-counseling-draft-resistance centers and brochures.

● *Activities at Military Establishments:* Squads will conduct an escalating campaign of education and confrontation at local draft boards, recruiting stations and the Chicago induction center. Activities will include leafleting, on-the-spot counseling, demonstrations and sit-ins. I think one fine day we may even nonviolently close down a few establishments. Women and veterans will be particularly useful for leafleting and demonstrations.

All leafleting at draft boards will be done by trained draft counselors. We want as many of our members as possible to be so trained. We feel that the best way to make the first strong personal contact with youths is to provide a service immediately applicable to their needs—solid knowledge of the Selective Service laws. One must start with legal alternatives and over a period of time move on to radical ideas.

● *Education:* Strong emphasis will be placed on antiwar and antidraft education. We want to bring as many people into the movement as possible and we believe we must first provide a solid understanding of the nature of the war and the nature of the draft. Squad members will arrange to attend and speak at group and organizational meetings, especially those involving young men who are or will be eligible for the draft. Top priority will go to antidraft education of scheduled inductees and their families.

All literature used will have necessary phone numbers for interested youths to call. Leaflets and pamphlets will be created and oriented towards specific activities and locales: a set for actions at draft boards, a set for speaking and other public appearances. Specific material aimed at ghetto youths will be created. A pamphlet for resistance recruitment and education will be prepared presenting the philosophy and rationale of noncooperation with the Selective Service System. (We already have three excellent statements from current members.) All educational activities will be coordinated with other peace groups working within the community.

● *Draft-Counseling-Draft-Resistance Centers:* Storefronts are best for centers; however, to cut costs we are seeking out existing peace offices, community centers and churches. The centers will be focuses of neighborhood organizing and education. They will be congregating places for neighborhood high-school and college youths. Full-time staff will conduct draft counseling, distribute literature, discuss draft resistance, conduct educational programs and workshops and train new organizers.

● *Lawyers:* A pool of lawyers willing to defend draft resisters either free or at reduced fees has been set up in Chicago. We will work with this pool.

● *Fellowship of Reconciliation Project:* The FOR is planning a major postcard campaign to provide draft-age youth with an opportunity to state that they believe the war in Vietnam is wrong and that they should not be made to fight in it. Three men will handle a mass-distribution campaign in Chicago; at least one will be from CADRE. We are especially interested in the possibilities for follow-up (Coordinator: Ron Young, FOR, Box 271, Nyack, N.Y. 10960)

● *Funds:* Several fund-raising activities are planned. A letter has been drafted and sent out to about five hundred people on a few preliminary mailing lists. Additional selective lists from Negro community organizations, the American Friends Service Committee, Veterans for Peace and the Chicago Peace Council may be used. Members are also sending letters to personal friends.

Several possibilities for benefit concerts and lectures are being explored. Faculty support groups are being organized at local universities. We are asking substantial individuals to organize gathering of their friends and acquaintances at which CADRE members will present our program and request funds. We are also emphasizing a campaign to get antiwar families to "adopt" full-time organizers for the summer, providing room, board and expenses. Finally, a barrel will be manned in Old Town (the local Sunset Strip) for solicitation.

● *National Coordination:* Copies of all materials created or used by CADRE, progress reports and suggestions on organizing and direct action will be sent to S.D.S.'s *New Left Notes* and the draft-resistance newsletters coming out of The Resistance and the Draft Resistance Clearinghouse in Madison, Wisconsin (8 Frances Court). A full-time member will also coordinate publicity with the press.

● *The Resistance:* CADRE is acting as Midwest coordinator for the October 16 National Non-cooperation Day called by The Resistance in Berkeley. On October 16, hundreds of men will turn in their draft cards and end all cooperation with the draft at demonstrations before federal buildings in major cities across the country. We expect at least two hundred noncooperators from the Chicago area. All participants will support the first of their number arrested by publicly con-

fessing and demanding trials. (The Resistance, Tenth Floor, 5 Beekman St., N.Y., N.Y. (212) 732-4272; 2502 Telegraph #4, Berkeley, Calif., (415) 849-4950)

CADRE and The Resistance held a conference in Chicago on July 7. Representatives of Midwest groups gathered to work out a unified plan of attack against the draft, and to solidify their plans for October 16. The conference was attended by over a hundred committed organizers, who returned to their own areas to organize the action. We are beginning to send out travelers to help other Midwest unions get moving.

CADRE was born out of a series of courageous personal acts. The first group action came as a wave of demonstrations in support of these actions. A two-hundred-man support demonstration before the local Federal Building, complete with six draft-card burners, was organized at the time of my first court appearance after arrest. A demonstration took place at the draft board of one of our members, Don Tylke, at which he indicted the board for conspiracy, along with other draft boards and the federal government, to commit genocide in Vietnam and to violate the Thirteenth Amendment (involuntary servitude). Another demonstration at this board occurred at a personal appearance by Don requested by the board members.

The cluster of draft boards at Sixty-third and Western and the downtown induction center at 615 West Van Buren have been the targets of a daily leafleting campaign, which has kept the office full and the phones busy with counseling cases. Forty to fifty of us have demonstrated at the induction center at least once a week this past month in support of men refusing induction. There was a large demonstration when Secretary of State Dean Rusk arrived to address the Lions' Club convention in Chicago, at which one of our members burned a draft card.

A central office, offering draft counseling and information on draft resistance was opened in Old Town on North Avenue. We have also arranged for office space at a peace center on the South Side and at a project house on the West Side. Members are participating in an ongoing Draft Caravan covering all Chicago high schools. Our draft-board leaflets, including a separate one specifically for ghetto Negroes, have been printed. A weekly draft-counseling training session for CADRE members has ben set up by the American Friends Service Committee.

Members have spoken at several high schools and community organizations,

and some of them have been interviewed on a number of radio and TV shows in recent weeks; more are scheduled. We are renting a community apartment for full-time organizers; we feel that living together will help coordination.

So we are building a movement involving large numbers of people to carry out an extensive program. However, it costs a lot to support our fifteen full-time organizers and one office, not to mention the thirty other organizers we would like to hire and the half-dozen other offices we wish to open. It also takes a lot to provide for bail and legal defense for the growing numbers of draft resisters. So we need your help. We are dependent on our more established friends to keep our individual resisters and our organized resistance from being buried under debts and legal problems.

Copies of our literature and progress reports are available to anyone asking to be placed on our mailing list. Write CADRE, 333 W. North Ave., Chicago, Illinois 60610. (Phone: (312) 664-6895)

We call ourselves CADRE. We speak of squads, escalation, campaigns. The terminology is no accident—it fits our attitude. We are no longer interested in merely protesting the war; we are out to stop it.

LIBERATION July 1967

Tribal Model

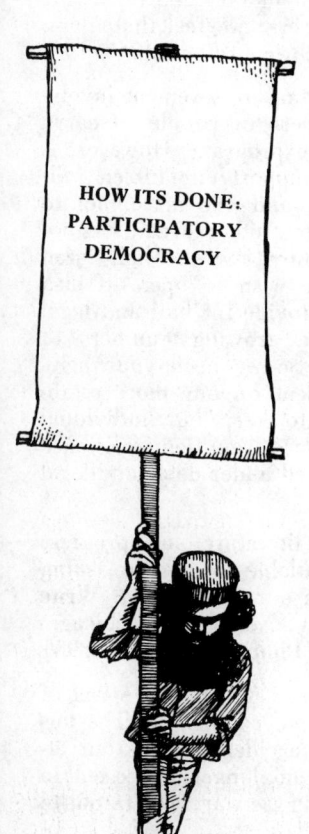

HOW ITS DONE:
PARTICIPATORY
DEMOCRACY

1. "Power Seekers" and "Responsibility Takers."

Power does tend to corrupt. The politicians of our nation are "power seekers". Our political system, despite the myth of democracy, is a bifurcated one made up of leaders and the led. Our leaders are men of limited integrity and/or misguided moralism and self-righteousness. Their proverbial willingness to compromise and to "reason together" does tend, as our political scientists never tire of telling us, to help our political system function. But we in the resistance movement are committed to repudiating that system, to finding a more humane and human way of ordering our collective existence. Therefore, we ought to understand that we are engaged in a political struggle which demands coordination and leadership. To speak of social change is to be ready to contemplate alternatives, alternatives which promise to both achieve our goals and to continually reaffirm our values by working toward these goals in a manner appropriate to who we are and what we hope to become. Simply, our leadership must be one comprised of *"responsibility takers"*, not "power seekers".

At the Resistance office, I have for the first time seen a kind of participatory democracy which stands in stark contrast to the kind of politics we in the U.S. have been programmed to accept as natural. The reluctance to take a formal vote on issues, the "sense of the meeting" and the informal staff or steering committee meetings are the concrete manifestations of our "New Left mood". I dig it. We should retain it. But we ought to realize that the nature of the struggle confronting us is beginning to make demands upon us that require a more articulated organization. There is a non-bureaucratic model which seems to offer some hints to achieving this goal. It is provided by the political systems of traditional Black Africa. In particular, I will make reference to the Masai, the people with whom I am most familiar (having spent 14 months doing doctoral research amongst this pastoral people of Kenya and Tanzania).

2. "Sense of the Meeting" and "Consensus".

Anyone who has studied pre-literate societies would see a striking similarity between the refusal to take formal votes and reliance on the "sense of the meeting" which permeates the Resistance and the "consensus" decision-making which characterized traditional African societies such as the Masai. The Masai elders' councils will discuss an issue until "everybody" agrees. There is no formal vote taken—there is (ordinarily) no need for one. But the consensus is and must be real. For the Masai to operate in this fashion a number of factors must be operative. First, there is a thoroughly shared, and deeply ingrained, set of values about the *way* decisions ought to be made, i.e. egalitarian-participatory as opposed to authoritarian-bureaucratic. Secondly, the ability to reach such a general consensus is based on the bonds of kinship and extended kinship (all age-mates are "brothers") of economic inter-dependence and of the ties of locality and neighborhood. Out of these shared ties and values comes the quality of being able to really "speak each others' language" and a commit-

ment to talk, talk, talk. Every Masai elder may speak in council, most do. The meeting will continue until all feel they can agree—everyone recognizes that the appropriate decision has been made. If this requires two days they meet for two days, If they must meet again in a week's time they will. And so on.

At the Resistance we must recognize that a "sense of the meeting" will be a phony and imperfect substitute for consensus unless we commit ourselves to talk, talk, talk. As for shared values and bonds, much already exists. Our collective *rite de passage* does form a bond for many of us. Many of us have surely felt the impulse to call fellow resisters and resister-sisters "brother" or "sister". Though still mainly unspoken, I believe many of us share parallel orientations toward politics and interpersonal relationships. Those of us, like myself, who are seeking to, in some sense, share our lives in Resistance co-ops with others in the movement may be helping to lay the secure foundations for the kinds of ties and gut-level understandings which will help to make "consensus" decision-making a realizable medium for organizing our collective struggle to build something true and, therefore, beautiful in the way of political community

Conclusion

The tension that exists between the desire for "openness', "participatory democracy", playfulness, and the seriousness of our commitment and magnitude of our struggle are very real. To keep our New Left "thing" is, to me, as important as being "efficiently organized" or "effective". It is only our desire to see that ends continue to flow from means that offer us the chance to really achieve a different, more human life-style. These thoughts have been offered with the aspiration for such a life-style in mind. As we work, life, and struggle together I hope we can in some meaningful way come to love one another. In doing so we risk much. Not only the confrontation with prison but the physical violence we may increasingly encounter. Not only a personal challenge and apprehensiveness and fear, but the pain of being separated from "brothers" and "sisters" and feeling the pain of their pain. But this is a risk we must take. For this risk comes only from the willingness we have to really share with one another, to go beyond the corrosive, limiting individuality of an ego outside of community.

To do "your own thing" and to do the "Resistance thing" will naturally grow together for many of us.

To put all this "jazz" down on paper about organization, etc. is necessary. But what it is really all about is how we must hang together, dig each other, laugh and cry together and fuck up and never quite get organized but do "the thing" each alone and all together. These thoughts are offered with the affection that grows from the new-found excitement, energy and wonder of being a member of this unfathomably beautiful, bumbling-effective assortment of real people.

—Howard Banow

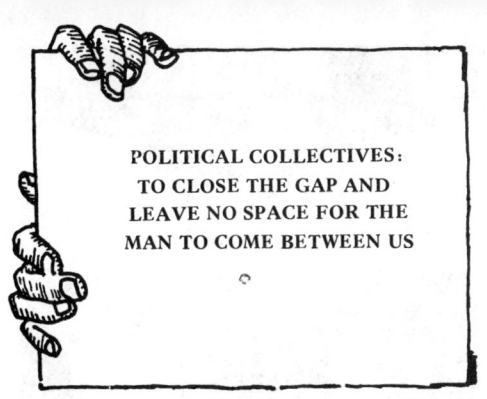

POLITICAL COLLECTIVES:
TO CLOSE THE GAP AND
LEAVE NO SPACE FOR THE
MAN TO COME BETWEEN US

Another problem we have not dealt with and often wish to forget is that as the repression against us gets heavier, we go the gamut from outrage, demoralization and frustration to a general freakout. The daily stories of premeditated shoot-outs against the Panthers, pig riots, etc., filter into our consciousness. The lag between political seriousness and emotional response on the one hand and the required maturity and commitment of being revolutionaries on the other stems in part from preparing ourselves as revolutionaries without being able to see the final struggle as really imminent.

Because we understand that the struggle is going to be a long one and that it will get even rougher as time goes on, we must develop forms which will help us to deal with the various

problems and situations that we face now and in the future. For example, ways that minimize our isolation from each other, meet our need for tight security measures and material subsistence, and help re-pattern our individualist styles of political work; and, very important, the chance to lay the groundwork for and experiment with new social relationships, particularly in regard to sharing the responsibility for children and dealing with male chauvinism. There is no permanent or all-purpose form, but one hopeful possibility is in the political collective.

Collectives are being worked out in a great variety of ways: communes, clusters of organizers who live and usually work together, people who live separately but work on the same project. The goals that each collective sets for itself may develop from its own view of a strategy for the movement and may also determine its form.

No one who has been part of a collective is likely to view the form as a panacea, but collectives can begin to deal with certain major difficulties. The most important one being the unresolved division between our "political" and "personal" lives. Just as our understanding of the society developed in a fragmented way, so our struggle to close the gap between political priorities and personal desires continues. As we have more and more come to understand our

commitment as revolutionaries, our need for the movement to serve as a *whole* way of life has grown urgent. We cannot be 9-to-5 revolutionaries for two simple reasons: because we cannot make a revolution that way and because we cannot long retain our sanity that way. Collectives provide the possibility for integrating our duties with our personal needs. It is not only that collectives are politically efficient in day-to-day organizing, but they are important because together we can take steps toward breaking out of our individualist, privatist life styles.

Obviously we cannot *solve* the problems nor can we create truly new women and men until imperialism is destroyed; but we can and must give real meaning to revolutionary comradeship: to not only call each other "sister" or "brother," but to close the gaps and leave no space for the Man to come between us.

RANDY RAPPAPORT / *with Berkeley Womens Liberation, is active in Bread and Roses in Boston.* **BEVERLY LEMAN /** *active in New York Womens Liberation, is on the N.Y. staff of* Leviathan. **CAROL McELDOWNEY /** *is active in Bread and Roses in Boston.*

From "Hey There What's That Sound?" by Randy Rappaport, Beverly Leman, Carol McEldowney **Leviathan** Feb 1970

WHAT COMMUNITY MEANS—
CONCRETELY

I said Alice and I had for three years been part of a co-operative community, as Phil mentioned, the Macedonia community—in 1954 to '57, when we were in our mid-twenties. But even though that community came to an end twelve years ago, it has been for us, ever since, a touchstone of everything that we did, what we were trying to do with the rest of our lives. To find a way to carry forward the same

values which had become clear to us at Macedonia. And so I said, when I was asked this question a year ago, I hoped Everdale could be for Barbara something that she would look back on in a way that Alice and I look back on the experience that we had in Macedonia community. Somehow the rest of her life will be a carrying forward of what has happened to her at this place.* And what I want to try to do is just to say a word about certain things which my wife and I experienced in co-operative community which I have sensed to be present here. And which we, and I guess I in particular, have also found exemplified in what in the United States is called "The Movement," that is SNCC, SDS, the movement of young people for social change. I want to talk about certain things which I find in all three of these situations; co-operative community, the experimental school, and the movement for social change.

One of the things which the community, the school and the movement had in common was the way of making decisions—which SNCC and SDS call participatory democracy, which is sometimes called making decisions by consensus in that one does everything one can to avoid a vote. One waits as long as possible for a common feeling to take hold of all or most of the people in the room rather than pushing matters to a decision by a narrow majority...Whenever possible, decisions were made by the whole. And this was not just a question of taste, of preference, although it was that, but for example in the case of SNCC, the southern civil rights movement, the sorts of decisions that were

there being made had to do with whether or not a given staff member would go to a particular town in the south and try to do voter registration there. And it was a decision that might well cost that person his life. No one would be part of an executive committee that would assign someone else to carry out that sort of task. And, I suppose by analogy that carries over into situations which are less obviously fraught with the implication for a person's life than a voter registration programme which might result in his physical death. The people who are used to making decisions in that way also develop a reluctance to make seemingly much less consequential decisions which would tell another person what it was he ought to do about this or that. Okay, that's one thing.

The second thing which strikes me as common in community and the school and the movement is a certain orientation to experience as opposed to philosophies about experience. And, maybe that's one of the reasons people have trouble getting a statement of education philosophy out of Everdale, because the staff and the students here feel that same way. And let me try to explain what I mean: It happened that the core of the community in which we lived were persons who had been objectors or draft resisters during WW II, and who, when the war was over, tried to find some way of exemplifying positively that which they had stood up for in saying "No, I won't go." Though there was that shared experience of draft resistance, or at least conscientious objection, nevertheless, people came to that experience and came also to the experience of community from very different religious and philosophical backgrounds. I was the village atheist. Other people had come from extremely fundamentalist Protestant backgrounds, and so forth. And we found that when we spun things up to the level of religious philosophy or political philosophy they tended not to go well. Rather, we tended to find ourselves in situations where we would all suddenly feel, "Look, we don't really differ as much as our words make it appear that we do." And we developed it, almost as a rule of thumb, to try to get back to the common experience. What is the experiental content of what we say as opposed to the philosophical or abstract content? Now, oddly enough, in my opinion at least, this is a matter of immense significance in the political movement in the States and also in Canada that calls itself The New Left. I think that one of the differences between the "New Left" and the "Old Left" is that when you had a decision to make in the Old Left, the way you made it was that everybody in the decision-making apparatus, all 87 members of the Party, divided themselves into caucuses or factions, met secretly, each caucus circulated its position paper with appropriate quotations from Marx and Lenin. Finally there was a vote in an atmosphere of mutual denunciation and whichever position was adopted by no matter how narrow a majority became the correct political line for the coming period. That was the way of making decisions, which had little enough to do with experience, and tended to leave people divided and angry at one another, and, very often, not inclined to do anything, no matter what the decision. But in the New Left, with its orientation to experience, it was much more like this: "Okay, we have a general sense that something is important." Before 1961 we had a general sense that it's important to try to register voters in certain predominantly black rural communities in the South. In the summer of 1966 we had a general sense that it's important to develop groups of people who are prepared to resist the draft and give one another support in doing that. In 1969 we have a general sense that it's important to find ways to resist oppression (legal oppression, political oppression of the movement) in such a way that the movement can go on growing and not consume all its energies in defending itself.

Okay, but having that general sense, rather than going into the kind of caucusing and resolution passing which was traditional as we perceived it as part of the politics of the previous generation, we say, "Fine, now let's cast the seed, let's all of us, as individuals or in small groups, go out and experiment with solving this problem. And then, for example, when one of us, or a few of us, begin to find a solution to that work (when Bob Moses goes to Mississippi), we begin to find ways to gather support in extremely difficult situations. Then people naturally gather around that successful solution and start experimental schools across the face of Canada, and as time goes by select themselves into those that seem to be most fruitful, as parents, as teachers, as students. This was the way we felt it was important to make decisions. So, that a meeting of the movement in the United States would be not so much an occasion (this is not so true of the present, I regret to say, it was more true in the past)—the meeting of the movement would not be when people would go at one another, hammer and tongs, to decide who was right, with the implication that everybody else must be wrong, but rather an occasion where people shared experiences with the sense that even the failures were important additions to the common experience. Simply a completely different atmosphere, I think, of folk relating to one another rather than the more traditional method I stopped to describe.

Okay, a third thing, which I think again was true of the community in which we lived, was true of the movement in the United States, and I sense perhaps, in a somewhat different form is also true here at Everdale. And that's what at Macedonia we used to call direct speaking. If you are going to the altar, or for that matter the cow shed, and you discover in your breast you have a difference with your brother, then turn aside and go and straighten the bloody thing out with him. Don't, above all, go to some third person and start gossiping. And if at all possible, don't suppress your feelings with the other person immediately concerned, but say it right out to him on the spot. "Why," to quote an example of last night, "Why did you leave your car in the driveway, for crying out loud, so nobody else could get past to come up to this meeting?" And to say it, you see, and the person responds, "You fool, it's obvious why I left the car there, because I wanted to leave the meeting early"; and it's over. It's over! But the other way, you see, over breakfast the next morning with still a third person you say, "You know, I've noticed something about so-and-so." Even the root of not saying it right out, of keeping it back, means that ten days later, at a meeting about something quite different, let's say, when to start planting the garden, you say, "For crying out loud, not only are you wrong about when to plant lettuce, but you even left your car in the middle of the driveway." And by that time, you have to

start arguing about the facts of the situation which you've both forgotten in the meantime. And it all becomes more cumbersome and complicated than it needs to be. And I don't think what I'm talking about is essentially a technique. I think it could express itsef in quite different forms in different groups of people. I think it's an atmosphere for which I've been able to find no better words than "emotional openness." Is there such a thing as a group in which people expose themselves to one another without trying to protect themselves from the consequences of that exposure? This is a very rare kind of group I think, in our society. This is part of the peculiar genius of this place as of the others I've described. It doesn't necessarily mean earnest, solemn discussions about what we feel toward one another. It can express itself in a kind of humour: sort of understated, in the style, in the way people write or talk to one another. But the important thing is the underlying concept. And that's the third thing.

Now I come to two things that are more, sort of, total, which I will nevertheless take a stab at. In the community we talked all the time about commitment. It simply made all the difference in the world whether you were still there wondering whether you were going to stay, or whether you had put your savings, your car, your mortgage, your emotional problems, the whole of yourself into it. That feeling. Commitment is one way to describe it. In the movement, I think, a very similar thing was talked about as putting your body where your mouth is. "It's very nice, the opinion you just expressed, but I'm not sure I heard you say that *you* were the person planning to do it." "Yes, it would be very good to have a voter registration project in Macomb but when are you leaving?" And which I think Bob Davis was expressing in a different way, just at the close of the last segment of this meeting. "I've been telling you how much we need you parents, but don't make the mistake of believing that we shall stop if by any chance you shouldn't help us. Because, we're going to keep this place going on somehow even if we're all carrying two jobs to do it. Even if there are seven kids rather than seven times seven." And this is what I took from what he said, and I think that's the same quality I'm trying to describe. Not just that the teachers would have made this kind of commitment in order to bring Everdale into being, but that the graduates from Everdale are people who want to live this way, who insist on living this way, and who won't settle for a life in which people do not give themselves completely to the things that they do. Which means, and I think in our group this morning there at first was a discussion which was inaccurate in its terms, between rebelling against the system and adapting to the system, that these were the two alternatives. If you adapted to the system, you stayed out there, and if you rebelled against the system, of course you came to Everdale. But, it seems to me that what Everdale is about is producing people, who when they leave here, will create new vocations, will become doctors, and lawyers and brick-layers and all the things that people become out there, but with a difference. Doctors who insist on being a different kind of doctor. Lawyers who half of who's clients don't pay them anything. Teachers who are fired again and again and again, if I can use my own example, who end up having three part-time jobs instead of one full-time job and no tenure, but much happier than I was when I was still in the academic rat-race. It seems to me that the creation of this sort of person who puts his body where his mouth is, who is prepared to take risks through the whole of his life, that Everdale ultimately is bound to do.

And then the last thing is something about what it means to be a community and to turn out young people who will have experienced living in community for a number of years and in this way too won't settle for anything less for the rest of their lives. Now what does that mean? What is one talking about when one says that I can only give a couple of examples? Shortly after we arrived at Macedonia there was an incident with the woodworking shop. Macedonia produced children's toys and created the business that Bob and Phil alluded to that happens on the Bruderhoff, the Community Playthings children's toy business.

But at the time when we were at the Macedonia community this business was a very small and struggling thing, as the whole community was. It was all touch and go whether we would get the next order out and make it through the next month. And it happened that a benefactor had given us a planer, the kind of planer that you push boards through. And a member of the community had taken a truck from our community in North Eastern Georgia, to somewhere in Michigan to pick up the planer and he drove it back, going day and night and got in about five o'clock in the morning. He went to sleep with the strongest kind of instruction that no one was to touch the truck or the planer until

he woke up, because he had directions about how to move it. So while he was sleeping another member of the community, who, like the man who had driven the truck was also very handy with mechanical things or thought he was, tried to unload the planer. The planer was sitting in the back of the truck. It was lifted by using pulleys with a metal cable which goes up over something and then down to something else.

It all went well. The truck drove away, the planer hovered in the air and then the cable broke and the planer came down on its head, like this, and the cement floor cracked. Well, my reaction was—"That's it! The community is over. Let's go back home." Not so much, or only in part because the planer dropped, but also what Dick would say to Ivan when Dick got up. But after a while, I noticed a strange phenomenon. It was true that Dick and Ivan had gone off and had a little discussion with each other, and nobody seemed to be getting ready to leave. As a matter of fact (this was, I think, a Friday or a Tuesday) everybody was going on getting ready for Easter which was three days hence and in a quiet way I scurried about making sure that everyone knew about the disaster which had occurred, because I assumed that once they knew, well of course we would forget about Easter and turn to the problem of the planer. And it finally dawned on me that people there really felt Easter was more important than the planer. And that simply because the planer had dropped they had no intention of dissolving the community.

And as I thought about it, I realized behind that was the attitude that "we are in this together," and the tremendous accession of psychological strength that somehow is created when people say that to one another. It is much more than saying, "Well, we're four, so we are four times stronger than if there were only one of us." It is that each person has somehow had lifted from his shoulders the burden that each of us staggers about with without being fully aware of it—namely that there is only ourselves to depend on after all. Especially financially.

And when the push comes to shove, after all, we have to have a bit in the bank for it. We may have a neighbour next door who has a house like ours, and a car just like ours, and a job not so different. But we don't—if we are laid off, it just doesn't enter our minds to feel that the obvious thing to do is to knock on his door and ask for help. That's not the kind of society we have. But that's what community is about, it seems to me. And it creates the kind of strength that just has to be experienced. I want to say this. I think that can happen in very dramatic and highly charged circumstances, and indeed in circumstances much more highly charged than that of the planer.

For example, the group of fourteen people who burned Selective Service files in Milwaukee last September issued a

statement explaining why they had done that, in which they used the phrase that they had been "delivered into resistance." And then a little later they went on to use the expression "resistance community" as that thing which they were. And it was clear that these were people—not only the kind of single young men and women who are usually involved in the movement. There is Michael Cullen who has three children. There was Doug Marvey who married and gave up a mathematician's job to do this. They were people who had that kind of responsibility which usually leads us to assume that they couldn't possibly be involved in an act of this sort, who were among that fourteen, and it was perfectly clear that none of them would have been able to take that act which involved possible sentences of ten, twenty, thirty, forty, fifty years if both State and Federal government should convict them on all possible charges and gave them maximum sentences, none of them would have been able to do that had they not just had the faith that the children would be cared for. "Yes, they are, in a sense, my children" and "No, I do not lightly leave their care to another." Nevertheless there are circumstances in which it is right for me to leave their care to another, and moreover, there are others who will care for them." And that's community, in a sense, in an obvious way.

But the last point that I would like to make is that it seems to me community operates much less pretentiously under very prosaic circumstances, such as a group of people feeling that the person who peels the potatoes or drives the bus, or takes out the garbage, is just as important a member of the community as the person who gives speeches at conferences, or the person who usually greets people when they come to visit the community. That in some ways, I think, is just as difficult a thing to achieve as the kind of sharing the Milwaukee Fourteen file burners are capable of. But it's another way of describing what I mean when I am asked, "What is community?"

Macedonia: a cooperative community in Georgia. Alice is Lynd's wife. Barbara is his daughter.

From "Open Politics and Community," a talk by Staughton Lynd to the community of a free school (Everdale), printed in *This Magazine Is About Schools* Feb 1969

THE COMMUNITY OF PRISON

SANTA RITA:
SUMMER OF
1967

Notes from
the County Jail

Michael Rossman

*On December 2, 1964, 800 Berkeley
students were arrested in the big sit-in
that climaxed the Free Speech Movement.
Two and a half years later, the Supreme
Court refused to review our case. So
a number of us went to the county jail,
for having (successfully) fought the university's attempt to prohibit our advocacy
on campus of actions—like burning draft
cards or trying to shut down the Induction Centers or signing complicity statements or smoking pot or being black,
though at the time we were thinking
more of Civil Rights sit-ins—which might
prove to be illegal.*

*These notes were written, then, during
last year's summer vacation, nine weeks
in the Santa Rita Rehabilitation Center.*

*They were written to my friends, who
know their longer original form as "The
Adventures of Garbageman Under the
Gentle Thumb of the Authority Complex." I wish I were certain of their
relevance to the many more who are
going in soon, and for far longer.*

They locked us in messhall again, to
wait through a recount and a recount and
a recount outside. Shadowboxing, the
black kids singing. "Hey, sport, you're
kinda crazy," said my new sidekick on
the garbage crew. A Mexican kid with a
sour expression, he pulled his toothbrush
out and combed his mustache. You see
it on most of them, that bent-over plastic
handle hooked over their shirt pocket.
Sideburns and beards are verboten, a
mustache is all you can nurse. "Grows
out all kinky if you don't keep after it,"
explained the kid who married a virgin.
It really gave me a start, the first time
I saw someone pull out his toothbrush
and use it, casual as a comb through
greaser hair.

"You're kinda crazy, sport," said my
partner—he does the kitchen head, I
keep after the cans. "I know," I said,
idly. "No . . . you act kinda crazy most
of the time." "Yeah, I know." "No, I
really mean it, you do." "Man, *I know*,"
I said, "it's cool." "You like acid,
dontcha," he stated. I cracked up and
eyed him for a moment, doing that little
widening motion so the pupil floats like
a blue yolk in its innocent white. "Man,
I was crazy *before* I took acid," I said,
"but yeah, I do." He was the fourth one
to tell me I liked acid; they all say it
with the positive relief of a bird-watcher
hitting the right page in his manual. No
one asks about grass. It's taken for
granted: everyone here smokes shit on
the outside. But—even though a number
of the spades have tried acid and dig it,
and some of us haven't—LSD is taken as
a kind of dividing line. We are the
hippies. Even though we stalk around
with books in our hands all the time,
that's our identification: not college kids,
or "professor" (as it was when I used
to dig ditches, that traditional tag), but

hippies. No question about it. The other inmates are friendly, curious, josh us. There's a goodly amount of respect for us as a group: we have status, an identity. Hippies.

"They don't understand you guys," said the wiseacre kid who tools the messhall truck around and jokes with the guards. "Whaddaya mean?" I asked him. "Like, what went on between you'n the officer inside, it really put him up tight. He was about ready to roll you up and send you off to Greystone, thought you were some kinda fruit." We were sitting behind the messhall, waiting for the count-clear siren. Earlier I'd walked into the little glassed-off office in the kitchen, to get the duty officer to clear my work so I could go. Four of the mess crew were clustered around his desk. "Whad-daya want?" An antic impulse: I answered, "Love." "What?" "Love, man, and I'm happy. Also you could check my work." He gave me a very odd look, and said to wait a bit; cleared me later without mentioning the incident, which I thought no more of till the kid brought it up.

He went on. "A lot of the officers, they don't like you guys. I mean, they're cops, you know, and you guys fought City Hall, and got away with it. Now with us, that's cool, we understand and dig you, know what I mean? But you made the cops look foolish then, and a lot still have it in for you even if it was a couple years ago. They look for you to be troublemakers, and when you aren't, well, that bugs 'em too. You gotta be careful with them, because they don't understand you."

But aside from not letting our books through, there's been remarkably little hard-timing. Partly this is because, almost to a man, we're easy with being here. (Today at lunch I remembered how bristling with hostility we'd been on our first visit, the night of the arrest, and we all had a good laugh at the contrast. "But," said Mario, "there were reasons then, you know, like getting dragged down stairs and all that.") But also it's because we've violated their expectations. We're open and friendly and curious, and we work hard. That counts for a lot. Garson, Lustig, and Saslow are on Bakery crew, up at 4:00 in the morning; now Mario has joined them. At first the ex-service guy who runs that show was down on them, riding them. Now he treats them with open friendliness, so much so that it's getting to be a bit of a distraction. "He keeps trying to father me," says Mario. Word has leaked back from the Booking Office, Santa Rita's nerve center: he keeps talking about us. "Get me nine more like them . . . hell, I'll have this place so changed. . . ." There has been a bit of trouble: a couple of kids have wound up in the Hole for four days, for refusing to work. But the work was

painting Army barracks, the objection moral rather than lazy. All in all, our stock is sound and rising. But still no books.

*   *   *

Everyone's curious about Mario. "Which one he, where he, he you leader? Say man, point him out to me." Sitting around behind Mess-Hall, waiting for the count siren to sound all-clear: a dozen of us, all but two black. They talked about Mohammed Ali, about the fighters he admires, then about us. "Mario, he the leader of them hippies." "Shit, he had like a million people following him, that dude. And why? Man, because he spoke *freely* what he thought, that why. . . ."

A BIRD FLEW into the garbage compound. Some wanted to kill it; three of us went in. One heaved a brush as it flew, missed. I climbed the mountain of boxed empty tins, retrieved it, jumped down. Outside someone took it gently from my hand. "Look here"— to no one—"here's how you hold it, see so he free in you hand." Then chucked it into the sky, underhand and up. *Away*. The tension broke, and suddenly a tall black kid did a spot routine. "Ho, when he get home. . . ." The circle acted it out: the girl birds hanging around twittering, testing his muscles. "There they was, hundreds of them, two of 'em had me by the wings and one by the legs, oh, but I faked 'em all out. Shit, they was *all* over me, man, they was gonna roast me . . . you got any idea what they smell like?" "Tell it, man, tell it. . . ."

*   *   *

Many of us are looking on this imprisonment as our only possible live rehearsal for what draft-resistance might bring. A county jail isn't much like a federal prison, nor is a month or two like three to five years, but that's the best we can do. I have been cheered both because I adapt easily to the life and people here, and also because I've had no trouble at all in launching and sustaining a mind-project: the essay I'm working on, about the generation gap. For the month before I came in, I was working my ass off to finish another manuscript; I expected to need an (involuntary) vacation. Instead, my desires to talk with people and to plug away on the essay are constantly fighting each other.

Paradoxically, even as maintaining an independent mental and emotional life here is much more practical than I'd expected, the idea of spending a long time in jail becomes even less appealing. I'm not sure why. Weinberg points out that Santa Rita is oppressive precisely because it's relatively humane, a model county jail (he likens it to the ideal socialist state). I dig what he means; it

confuses me even more about doing federal time, behind bars. S——, W——, a couple of others have already decided to split for Canada; their stay here has had little impact on that decision. I have begun thinking about it seriously, for the first time. Barely.

Visiting days are a mixed blessing, mail call also. "You have to be where you are to make it," points out Steve, "and news or touch of the outside pulls you back, between two worlds." There are other reminders, besides the papers, to keep our thoughts ambivalent. Last Sunday's flick was a World War II romance, set in S.E. Asia: jungle warfare, the whole bit. We have been well-conditioned: we cheered when Sinatra and his faithful handful of natives wiped out the Jap jungle airstrip with its planes near the end, in a sneak attack, and then penetrated the Chinese border and executed a couple of hundred captives taken there, in retaliation for their attack on the supply convoy that was supposed to support our boys. Back in the barracks, the papers describe Westmoreland's request for 140,000 more men. How many of us lay awake that night, trying to pick apart that snarl of feelings generated by the flick: exhilaration, regret, detachment, anger, and fear?

*   *   *

I was thinking about the haircut incident, which happened well over a week ago, while hustling garbage after dinner today. It was probably not malicious, but gratuitous, I decided: meant as a sort of benign amusement. And so my account of my reactions probably says a lot about my hairtrigger feelings about authority, pun intended.

That being so, and me being in jail, I've decided there's a definite advantage to my college background, despite the way the high-school dropouts in the officers' mess tease me, with their oranges and corned beef. For what is jail but a primitive form of the Authority Complex, cast in locks, alarms, and barbed wire? And what sort of problem does *that* present to a young man trained for nine years in the most Prestigious Multiversity in the land? Despite my touchiness about personal integrity, my dislike of stupid orders, and so on, I get along just fine: doing easy time, an exemplary prisoner: *my* suntan will never pale from days spent in the Hole, and if they gave Extra-Good Time I'd get that too and be out of here the sooner. For if there's anything being in college teaches you, it's how to relate to authority: even more than being black does, though the techniques are similar.

For here I am, the friendly Garbage-man. With an antic smile and an off-key wail of "Gaaarbaaage . . . ," like a London street-cry. (Establish a distinct but non-threatening identity.) My cleaned cans upside-down on the cart, so the imprisoned steam can *puff!* impressively as I upend them back in their places. (Pick a symbol of excellence in your subject; accentuate it.) Clanging the cans with great zeal, even risking an occasional caution about too much noise when the officers are eating. (Be passionately dedicated to the pursuit of Truth; venture a daringly unorthodox hypothesis whose subtle flaw the instructor can point out.) Candidly confessing—when nothing could be proved—that the carbon paper found among the empty cans was mine, hastily thrust there after someone I'd asked idly for a sheet brought me a sheaf, swiped from the office. (Admit an evident mistake gracefully; show yourself open to instruction and able to profit by it.) Wheeling the cart like a madman past others leaning indolently on their mops; cleaning up someone else's mess silently and for free —but in public—once in a while. (Invite favorable comparison, but let others provide it.) Changing clothes at best every other day, and not trying too hard to keep clean—it goes with the rôle. (Be a bit of an eccentric—you *must* be bright.) Hosing the whole garbage-room down on Mondays; asking innocently if this wasn't standard practice before. (Establish a minor but admirable innovation in the System's procedures; undervalue it.)

I could go on, but fuck it. The truth of the matter is that I *do* hustle—partly because I simply dig hustling and doing a good job, partly because being a political prisoner is or seems to be like what being a Jew and short was for my old man *in situ* thirty years ago: "You've got to be twice as good as anyone else to come out even," he reasoned or felt, and he may have been right, who knows? But over all this, as a surface gilding long since learned into instinct (Woodrow Wilson Fellowship, '63), is the complex of little actions, attitudes, and details that constitute my way of relating to— of "handling"—the Authority Complex. They are as involuntary as the deep anger, whose possible consequences they so nicely avert, even as they disguise and are fueled by that anger. I learned my lesson well, in a thorough school.

* * *

Strolling through the litter of pork-chop bones that graces the barracks yard —which is always decorated on the rare morning-after something decent and portable appears for dinner—a puzzle came clear to me. Before I came here I phoned all over the country to get quotes for an article I was writing. This gave me a chance to hear some dear voices again and apologize for my absence and silence. But there was an awkward air about some of the conversations, which I only now understand.

One friend confessed shyly—to my complete surprise, though I knew him for a long and ardent student and admirer of Gandhi and King—that he envied me deeply and would take my place if he could: that he felt keenly,

as a lack in his own life, never having gone to jail for his beliefs. Another friend was terribly agitated because no one was making a fuss over our finally going in, or seemed even to remember why. Somehow a proper response was absent: we, and what we meant, were unheralded, unsung. "Surely someone must say something publicly," he cried to me over the phone.

I was taken off-balance and touched by their real concern, and responded to both with the embarrassed careless callousness I so often face emotion with: toss it off, downplay it, trying badly to be gentle. And my own closure is so familiar that I didn't realize till now that something else confused my response—and what it was. One of these men is a college president; the other— generally one of the two most perceptive observers of my generation I know —was offered a presidency and refused it. I love them both; but neither can afford such romantic innocence about the contemporary young. For it is dangerous to lose track of which revolution you're watching—especially if you'd like to help it—or you'll find yourself responding inappropriately.

My grandfather, whose eyes were also blue, was a Bolshevik: prison and exile. I too had certain time-honored feelings when my friends and unknown beloved peers were beaten and bailless in Southern jails. But we are freedom *trippers,* not riders. And there is nothing romantic, nor inspiring, nor unduly grubby, about being this kind of political prisoner. It is a dull and practical necessity, and will not be emulated or repeated. For FSM was a signal beacon which started much, both locally and nationally; but its message was sounded and heard, and there's no need to do certain parts of it again. Eight hundred kids should never again need to choose arrest to spite a college administration that doesn't deserve so much respect. The small price of our current jailing (and the $100,000 in fines) is not even a symbol: merely the tangible mark of a learning experience, a necessary experiment. And so our own kids know better than to waste inappropriate or sloppy sentiment on us. Though FSM and our jailings are in some senses inseparable, their warm feelings about the one and their indifferent practicality about the nuisance of the other are the best indication that the connection is only operational. Being here accrues me no capital save the (considerable) writing I'm doing and some insight. Grandfather, or not, if I could buy out, I would.

Granted, I had those nice warm feelings too when we were busted, as much as anyone did; and the martyr's pride did not entirely evaporate in the disgusting tedium of that hot spring's trial. I have traded on it since, for which I some-

what dislike myself, and will again; and a residue accompanies me here, probably making jail a bit more bearable, spice in the stew of my feelings. But by far my main emotion is simple and sheer irritation: *What a drag!* I've better things to do with my time—not only making love, but building what I was arrested for and have pursued since, in forms which have changed with my understanding. For FSM, in retrospect, was the first clear signal that America was involved in not one but two revolutions; and the rapid events since have brought the newer one out from under the shadow of the Civil Rights Movement and an old politics. Our problem now, and mine, is to learn, by doing, what feelings and actions are proper to being observers and shapers of this other revolution, of which we have no choice but to be a part even as it outdistances our understanding of it. The emotions of the older one, which include familiar forms of martyrdom, give us no clue. But, though I struggle uncertainly with their residue, I don't mean to put then down: they are simply inappropriate.

For us, that is. The spades who are going to jail for the flaming cities are quite a different story, as it will be if —no, when—they try to frame Stokely and Rap Brown for that. And those brave kids who are choosing, quietly calmly and without hope, four years in a federal pen rather than play the System's death-games or run out on what they know of their souls—they are also a different story, partly because Vietnam and the spades are slices off the same overdue hunk of my grandfather's flesh. But the steadily growing pool of kids in jail across the country for grass and acid and "street-blocking" are political prisoners just as surely as we are—I think of beautiful Michael Solomon with his black flame halo, busted in the Haight on a trumped-up charge: forty-five days in San Bruno, off light compared to the kids here doing six or nine months— and, because they are movers in the same other revolution as we are, as little deserve to be romanticized. (Though that is not meant to inveigh against feeling or action for the human cost involved in their imprisonment, which is considerable.)

No, a new trip demands new guideposts; and jail simply is not our thing. Not that we too are not romantic— though I think we will ultimately prove less so than our elders, because we are more willing to abandon our foothold on what we have known. But the voices on the telephone wished me well with the expectations of my own past, which will no longer serve. We cannot inherit even the form of our symbols now: which leaves us nothing but trial-and-error to find or build them. □

From "Notes From The County Jail" by Michael Rossman, *New York Review of Books* 2/15/68

The Malcolm/Eldridge Educational Supercharger. It is really very simple, both Malcolm and Eldridge used it while in jail. The parts are deceptively easy to get. Even a black man in jail can get them. That's pretty easy. We don't have big budgets for educational systems for black men in jail.

To build the Malcolm/Eldridge Educational Supercharger take one pocket dictionary, any edition, any size, any age, the quality of the book is not important. To this add one ream of paper and a ball point pen. The educational system has one moving part: the pen on the paper.

To operate the Malcolm/Eldridge Educational Supercharger, read one page of the dictionary each day. Study each entry on the page. Copy out each entry three times with ball point pen on a sheet of paper. Read the copied dictionary entries and make sure they are exactly the same as the originals in the book. Do this at the rate of a page a day for a year.

You will in that time have mastered the content of the English language. In so doing you will have learned the art of logical thought. You will have produced the basic tool with which you may become self educated: An inquiring mind which seeks input.

There were few men in prison who had a poorer prognosis than Malcolm or Eldridge. Each man worked out this system for himself. Each was diligent in his application of it. It worked for them. It will work for you.

If you discover that you are in jail, or about to go there for a period of time, perpare and distribute as many Malcolm/Eldridge Educational Superchargers as you have funds for. Allah will bless you. It is a good thing to teach a man to read and write.

BEN DOVER *San Francisco Express Times* 3/18/69

A VETERAN NON-COOPERATOR OF WWII TAKES ANOTHER LOOK AT PRISON LIFE

COMMENTS ON COOPERATION IN JAILS

I knew Corbett Bishop years ago in the alternative service camps of World War II, before his now almost mythical prison resistance, and again briefly after he came out. His prison experience unfurled an inspiring banner in the movements for peace and against the state; but whether it did him much good, I can't say. In the four months in camp with him, our closeness to each other was almost entirely political—concern with how more dramatically to say what we had to say, and this was mainly a matter of embarrassing authority. He was for me one of those people who does not reveal much of his personal life, and this seemed even more true after prison. How he lived, and lived with himself, in his remaining years in his bookshop in Alabama, I don't know. I had the impression then that prison had made him withdraw even more into himself and that he related to the world with increasing reserve.

I don't mean in any way to put him down. Whatever bravery, commitment, selflessness may mean, Corbett had these—as much as anyone I've known. But I think that those who are impressed with his near ultimate non-cooperation should be aware of some of its subtle consequences.

The Corbett saga came back to me strongly on reading Jim Wessner's account of his soul-searching after several days of non-cooperation following arrest (in Ellen Reinstatler's impressive report of his arrest and trial in the June 29 *Peacemaker*). The question of how to behave in prisons keeps coming up. Young men, facing prison, have said to me (as one who had refused for almost a year to work or eat in prison) in effect: "Everything I believe in tells me that I should follow in Corbett's footsteps, but I'm afraid that I'm not equal to it." Let me try to put my thinking on the question this way:

A man's deepest commitment must be to himself, to his search for truth, to his efforts to grow, to his striving for fulfillment. This very reaching for more meaning is what leads him to prison in the first place, but it can be frustrated if he enters jail convinced beforehand about how he should behave.

No matter how many prison books one reads, flicks one sees, former prisoners one talks to, there is the first prison experience each one of us has to face. To "know" beforehand how one should act can be as presumptuous as "knowing that the only thing the 'enemy' understands is force." Isn't this the justification for bombing communists—or capitalists? Isn't this also denying—regardless of how well we understand the system from the outside—that the system is made up of men, each an individual in his own right, and that if we are indeed concerned with moving towards a more human society we must never fail to relate to each man as an end in himself?

Does this mean that noncooperation is never justified? Hardly. What it means to me is this: in prison, as outside, my obligation to myself means keeping myself in optimum health—physical, emotional, intellectual, mystical, aesthetic, social. These demands are frequently in conflict with each other; the brain says hunger-strike, the gut says eat. The ideal condition, I believe, is one in which one is open enough, supple enough, sensitive enough, so that we emerge from such an inner conflict on some higher level of synthesis—a gentle yielding of one need to another, determined by some inner equilibrium whose existence I accept on faith, but whose mechanism I have no way of describing.

In the prison context this means, specifically, to enter jail as light on one's feet, as open, as possible; to let the total "me" decide what is right; to act in response to the total situation and not only in terms of the hunger of my stomach, or the politicizing of my mind, or the socializing of my person. Trust yourself, or at least have trust in your potential self. One morning you will awaken to the whole "you" saying noncooperation and you will then be able to do this gently and with a minimum of irrelevancies jarring on yourself and those about you. And if two days or two months later your whole "you" says cooperate, then you will be able to withdraw gracefully. You are, hopefully, constantly evolving, and to commit yourself totally and for all time (even to nonviolence) is to hamper that evolution. The only permissible consistency is one's search for truth, and not to people (and ideologies and institutions) outside of one's self.

Several years ago Vic Richman served three months at Danbury for participation in Polaris Action. He refused to work or eat from the start and was kept in isolation. After several weeks he became curious about life and the people out there in the prison. So he started to cooperate, but after satisfying his curiosity for several days he reverted to noncooperation. All this he did with a minimum of misunderstanding—and in accord with my own deepest convictions about the peacemaker's role in a non-peaceful society.

IGAL ROODENKO *The Peacemaker* 7/20/68

TAKING A STEP INTO
AMERICA BY WAY OF
ITS JAILS SUMMER,
1969

Last spring, eight of us from Columbia SDS were sentenced to 30 days in the New York County Civil Jail for breaking an injunction that prohibited political activity on the campus. The notes that follow are taken from a longer version of the paper about our month in jail.

No jail is good; they keep people locked up, deprive them of their dignity, and beat them—physically and psychically—into becoming slaves of the authority of the state. Jail is the embodiment of imperialist society: all the inmates are at each other's throats fighting to see who will win the chance to serve the warden coffee. Like any social institution, the line you're given by the Authority never changes: "We got all the aces, so don't give us any trouble. You scratch our backs, we'll scratch yours." The Civil jail was run along these lines. But, although the inmates were all working class, it was still something of a "gentleman's jail." The importance of the time we spent inside was our prolonged and close contact with a class of people from whom we had always been alienated.

We entered the prison with vague political notions which were later encapsulated, to some extent, in the "Weatherman" paper presented at the SDS National Conference (June, 1969). We didn't go to jail "testing" those notions; rather through our experience with our fellow inmates and from what they taught us, we discovered they were more than ideas and had a life and reality of their own. When people ask me—not being a weatherman—what the weathermen mean by the statement that the blacks can do it alone, I talk about Patrick, Tyrone and ourselves in order to express that concept's clearest meaning.

June 12

We are starting to become friends with the other men. This afternoon we received the newspaper reports of our sentencing and imprisonment. Santiago, a twenty-year-old Puerto Rican, went around shaking our hands; all of the men read the stories. A---, a young Jewish guy who seems to be one of the prison's trustees, came over to me and asked if we really meant the phrase in the press statement we released after the sentencing: "It is not right for people to desist from just struggles simply because unjust laws exist." He listened while Robbie and I explained our position to him: the law is not an abstract thing composed of moral judgments, but a concrete defense a class uses whenever any of its interests are attacked; and therefore, if one does fight in the interest of another class, it is absolutely necessary to break laws. He answered by asking what we thought would happen if everyone went around breaking laws and we replied that the question had to be decided on the merits of the case: why the laws existed, what reasons people gave for breaking them, and how much good or harm they accomplished by breaking them.

But it seemed he lost interest and the discussion was interrupted. I think we talked too abstractly: as though he were a college student.

* * * * *

A--- seems to be in a position of some kind of responsibility here. So is the other young white man of the jail, Patrick. He's Irish, about thirty, and hasn't talked to any of us yet. Three times a day we eat in a mess room on a long, plastic-covered table. He sits alone during meals, punctuating his silence with loud "quiets"—directed toward the four Puerto Rican inmates. He has a large picture of Adolf Hitler hanging on his locker door. Patrick seems to be revered here: evidently he's a fine electrician and mathematician and he studies a lot. A--- is in here for not paying alimony; Patrick is being held as a material witness.

The night before last, Robbie and I had a long discussion with Angelo, an Italian guard who comes from Little Italy. He's almost fifty, and has been working at the jail for close to 25 years; he hates the warden, but the job is good and he's too old to start switching around in his work, so he figures he'll remain at the jail until he can retire. Angelo's main concerns were two: what happened during a rebellion or strike to those working people who just managed to pay for school and, why was violence necessary? He couldn't understand, he said, if we wanted to overthrow the system—an idea he dug—why we just didn't take one of the great businessmen—he kept on referring to Rockefeller—and either kidnap or kill him. "After a while these guys would get the idea, you know what I mean?" Talking with all these people—Santiago, Rafael, Patrick, the guards, the other inmates—we are always made aware, on the one hand, of their infinite strength and cunning and their intimate knowledge of the system; and, on the other, of their feelings of complete hopelessness in the face of the system's totality.

* * * * *

These men feel extraordinary hatred for the circumstances of their lives; but they always see their enemies as either petty criminals, like the hack judges that inhabit 100 Centre Street, or people in the same circumstances as they or slightly worse ones. The one-gun theory shows their consciousness: they have fought, fight, and will continue to fight for the betterment of their lives, sometimes that means the hustle on the corner, sometimes it means offing scabs during a strike, and sometimes it *could* mean charging Alameda County Prison to free Huey; but their hatred is so locked up in the individual circumstances of their lives that it never directs itself for a sustained period of time against their common constant enemy: the ruling class. Intellectually, they understand that their misery is caused by a system; in practice, their hate is directed against the one man, one judge, one pig, one boss who did them wrong.

* * * * *

When we first came here, Patrick was a perfect example of this: he hated and was contemptuous of the enemy, but would never ally himself with anyone who also possessed that hate. He was alone. Several days ago when Tom was arguing with a blue-jacketed businessman who was in here for a day because he refused to pay alimony, Patrick yelled his way in. The businessman was talking about the Russian atrocities committed against the Germans in World War II. Patrick broke in, "They should have killed *every* fucking German! How many Russians died in World War II? Three fucking million in Stalingrad alone throwing fucking bricks. You think the American people would defend America like that? They fucking would not! And they'd be fucking right!" His onslaught continued, while he attacked the Rockefellers and the Englehards and posed them against the people: they stole from *the people,* they robbed *the people,* they helped kill *the people.* The change was due to two things: one, he was attacking the other man and was defining his position by attacking him; two, I think we've begun to convince him in those long night talk sessions we have in the john, that there are millions of others who share the conditions of his life, share in fact, worse ones, share his hate, and already *are* fighting. As his hate for the enemy becomes less atomized, so also his experience— the events in his life which allow him to decide who are his brothers and who are his enemies—becomes more generalized. "You know what America gives the poor?" he asked the startled, frightened businessman, "fucking poison for milk!" Then he told this story: "When I went to school in Chicago, I didn't have enough money for milk. My family didn't have enough money for milk! I had to steal it from people's porches. One fucking day I stole a bottle of lye by accident. I almost fucking died! That's what America does!"

* * * * *

But it's difficult to generalize one's experience; their hate is so intense that it needs a specific focus, against one man, one gun, one company, one detective, one judge. To discover how profound this hate is, one need only know how total is the misery of their lives, and how profound their resistance is to it. When Patrick went through his lecture on junk a week ago, he was recounting at one point the ways in which different friends of his had died. "Let's see," he said, after already cataloging several people who sounded as though they came from the myth of the American underworld, "who else had died recently?"

* * * * *

Yesterday was the day for hard knock stories. Santiago told me he couldn't read well, and then said he couldn't read at all. He said, he never admitted it because if he did, people would sound him and, with his fierce pride, he would get violent with them. He went to Benjamin Franklin High School in Manhattan, a school close to Columbia, from which 1.5% of an entering class leave with academic degrees. Santiago is a functional illiterate, served in the Army, couldn't get a job because of preferential hiring practices (he's a trained plumber) and, hustling on the streets, ended up in jail.

The other hard knock story came from Lowell, who's supposed to be getting released tomorrow (Charlie keeps asking him: "What you want to leave for? What are you going to do outside?" He works with Charlie in the kitchen and, when they've successfully sneaked a bottle of Thunderbird into the jail, they empty it together; Charlie asks his question often enough to make clear that he really doesn't want Lowell to leave; but he asks it with a smile as though he's laughing at his foolishness in placing a friendship in jail above freedom). I have a special feeling for Lowell for three reasons: he comes from the Smokey Mountains; he has a marvelous mountain accent; he offered to play cards with me the first night we were here (he won consistently). Last night, he had a long conversation with Stuey, who bunks next to him. Lowell kept insisting that we should bomb Vietnam into the "Stone Age," repeating the LeMay phrase several times. Robbie and Juan talked to him about this for a long time after Stuey had become exhausted for, while wanting to blow up Vietnam, he also insisted that he liked the Panthers, likes what we're doing, and was all ready for the Revolution. He didn't seem to recognize any discrepancy between the two positions. Later on, a bunch of us and Patrick went into the john to talk and read; Lowell came with us and continued to say how he was in complete agreement with us. He told us stories about the prisons in North Carolina, several of which he's been in. In Raleigh, several hundred prisoners stood in the courtyard to demand a dollar an hour minimum wage (they aren't paid a cent). The men were fired upon: eight men were killed and 72 men wounded. Then Patrick told us that there was also an action in New York State around the same kind of demand: a several-week, totally successful sit-down strike that worked in all of the New York State prisons. The strikers demanded that they get "good time":, time off for good behavior. "Otherwise," Patrick explained, "what the fuck purpose is there for working? You hardly get paid for it." Then we told them about how Huey Newton had refused to work in

ωín
magazine

1 october 1969   30¢

In the morning the sun climbs the wall

Night still tarries in the depths of the prison...
    and comes knocking;
        the door stays shut;

Being chained is a luxury to compete for.

The chained have somewhere to sleep,
    the unchained haven't...

the state treats me to its rice,

I lodge in its palaces,

Its guards take turns escorting me.

Really the honor is too great.

(Written in Chinese Nationalist Prison, 1942)

Ho Chi Minh 1890-1969

Alameda for the same reason; and how, after being kept in solitary without being allowed reading material, writing material, any time out of his cell, visitors, or even physical exercise for more than twenty minutes a day, Huey, when he was taken out of solitary and asked if he would now work, answered, yes, he would, providing they paid him and all the other inmates the minimum wage. Then Lowell said: "See, I know these things, you know, and I been saying them for a long time, ever since I seen how sorry the lives of the people were, you see what I mean: how sorry the lives of the people were." Then (after informing us that the Salvation Army was the second richest organization in the world), he told us how the truth had been revealed to him: he had just left the Army and was planning to go home after spending some time in a nearby big city in Tennessee. He had 165 dollars in his pockets and took a room in the "Windsor Hotel" and asked for a girl. She came, charged seven dollars, and left; a couple of hours later he met another whore out in the hall, felt like "having it again" and asked her how much she would charge. Ten dollars, she said, "Dog-gone right!" he replied and reached for his wallet to pay her in advance. His pockets were empty though; his wallet was gone—he ran downstairs and started yelling at the bellhop that he had been robbed, and that the bellhop must know something about it. "You don't shut up I'm gonna call the cops," was the bellhop's response. "You go on and call them," Lowell answered, for he was sure that if the pigs came they would arrest the evil doer and not the oppressed. Five minutes later, the pigs came; seven minutes later, he was in a pig car, arrested for drunkenness and disorderly conduct. When he got to court, he figured, I'll explain the story

to the judge, get myself released and have the bellhop arrested. When he got to court, he did explain the story to the judge—who said $600 or 60 days. His mother came in and paid the fine. Several days later, back in his home town, he found out that the judge who had tried him was also the owner of the hotel. "And that's what opened my eyes and I first started to see down the road of injustice."

* * * * *

Robbie asked Charlie how he felt when a lot of new prisoners come into the jail. Charlie answered: "My dick gets hard."

Patrick told me yesterday that he once read Ramsey Ullman's fictional biography of Rimbaud, *Day on Fire*. He admired and liked the book and its hero. I thought of Rimbaud: homosexual, gun-runner, dope fiend (as Patrick calls himself and other junkies), friend of impoverished people and their exploiter, diseased, brilliant genius. The story is not greatly different from Patrick's: gun-man, junkie, commiserator with the poor and constant racist, brilliant wasted genius. Yesterday I heard him tell Stuey, there was no such thing as a *North* Vietnamese: there are only Vietnamese. One people.

June 28

Tyrone has been put in the hole for a week. He called the warden a "racist motherfucker" and told him to "shut the fuck up." The warden had been bothering him for a couple of days before it happened; the final explosion was touched off by the warden's refusal to let Tyrone stay in his own cell and rest for the morning. We feel we should do something, but we don't know what. Last night I talked to Patrick; I was mad at him for an incident that had happened in the afternoon. David, our lawyer, had come to visit us with an SDS member from Columbia who's studying law. He thought she'd be allowed to enter as his aide. But she was kept out, and after he left we looked out the window and saw that Elinor was downstairs with him; she waved to us. The warden saw her and immediately ordered the dormitory cleared out. Patrick yelled at us for the incident. I said it wasn't the job of prisoners to yell at one another: we were all, except for stoolies, each other's friends and brothers, and our job was to yell at the warden. It wasn't the men breaking the rules who were wrong; it was the rules. It is this point of view that all the men find difficult to accept. Later that night, Patrick and I repeated the argument. Patrick's answer to my arguments was simple: he came out with horror stories; last night he told me about a state prison hospital where his friend had been mentally and physically crippled. "I've seen things you haven't," he repeats tirelessly (and of course he has), and *know* there's no percentage in breaking the law: they have all the aces. Inside here they have the cards, and you're an idiot and ball-breaker—breaking other people's balls—if you start trouble. I understand his feelings: in prison your needs are maximal, and every time the few privileges you possess are threatened you feel it is a mighty imposition and are tremendously resentful. He told us again of the prison strike; that he had thought it was a good thing because it was organized and everybody went into it together. But then he told us of men in Cook County Jail who try to get out by stealing a spoon. If the guards discover that a spoon's missing, they make each man empty all the belongings he has in his cell into a big pile in the middle of the cell block. Then the guards inspect everything; maybe a man has kept a nail-file or a pin-up picture in his cell, maybe a book which doesn't come from the prison library—everything is confiscated. And, of course, the man who stole the spoon doesn't escape either. But now Tyrone is in the hole for telling the warden an absolute truth about himself, and telling him to shut up, which is what everybody wants him to do anyway; and the reaction of the other inmates, the impossibilities of any meaningful action, and our own isolation both inside and outside, are paralyzing. And we are also unsure about the status of the other prisoners. We're sure that at least one is a stoolie. We think it might be Santiago.

When we came upstairs from hearing about Tyrone we got into a big argument with A---. He said a lot of reactionary dribble: how the warden is the boss and that Tyrone had lost his self-control by calling him a name; then, under attack from us, moving on to claim that the draft resisters were cowards and punks. Everyone attacked him for this—but though he felt embarrassed and kept quiet, it was clear that he really believed what he had said. The arguing was loud and violent (Patrick had dropped out early). During the middle of the fight, Santiago—he had earlier asked Robbie if he thought the warden was a "racist motherfucker"—walked into the dormitory and said that "the men in the hole" (Tyrone and the other two black men who had tried to escape) were saying that they heard we were giving them a lot of

moral support, but what they wanted was physical support. If we decide to do anything our allies are few: perhaps G---, who is to be released Monday, and Rafael. But none of the rest of these men, I truly believe, would risk losing even a small privilege over something like this: they are up on charges, or threatened with them, and have to serve long periods of time; they're not radicals, and they're totally isolated. They're not so poor that they have nothing to lose, yet they are not rich enough to spare any loss. It's a maddening, frightening situation.

June 29

At first we couldn't agree on what our course of action should be: we were in a totally new situation. We've never been particularly imaginative about tactics, and we made silly and even absurd suggestions. They ranged from doing nothing to, in effect, staging a full-scale riot. Moreover, because of the tenseness of the situation, we weren't working well together; throughout the morning we were in a constant meeting from which some of us would drop out while others would join in. We didn't talk enough with the other prisoners, and felt unnecessarily isolated. Nor did we talk with Roger or Michael, and because they weren't aware of the plans we made, they unintentionally broke them. We were all very confused, but by eleven-thirty, the basic outlines of our plans were established. Expecting to have to continue a hunger strike past lunch, a bunch of us gathered around Tom's bed munching oranges, candies and cookies. (When I think about it now, I feel a hunger strike represents almost no struggle at all; but, then, at least, it *was* something.) We were also prepared to try and get our people to make a small picket line outside the jail the next day if the hunger-strike didn't work. The warden had been very easy on us throughout the morning; aware of our shouting, and the fact that the Columbia people had been meeting constantly, he left the dormitory open all morning. (One of the other tactics suggested was that we refuse to leave the dining room; but no one could figure out how that would hurt anyone, or even be symbolic.) Juan wrote up a petition: originally it ended by saying that no one could help but notice that all the men in the hole were either black or Puerto Rican; but G-- believed that this would be detrimental: he said that though he would still sign the petition with the last sentence, he would feel much better if it were taken out. Finally he argued into taking out the sentence. The petition read: "Warden; We ask you to suspend your sentencing of Tyrone B--- to solitary for a week. Many of us feel that it is unfair to sentence B--, a man who is recuperating from wounds, who needs fresh air, who should be able to move around and exercise, and who has committed and is charged with no crime." When the call came for Juan and Stuey to take the lunch trays down to the warden, they both refused; Roger was asked, and, not knowing of our plan, agreed to do it. Then we went for lunch. It wasn't until we were in the mess hall that we finally decided not to eat. It's always that way; you haven't decided on anything until you do it. Many of the other men made jokes about our not eating, including Santiago who, under the admonishing stares of Rafael and another Puerto Rican, ate only one mouthful. Then I passed around the petition;

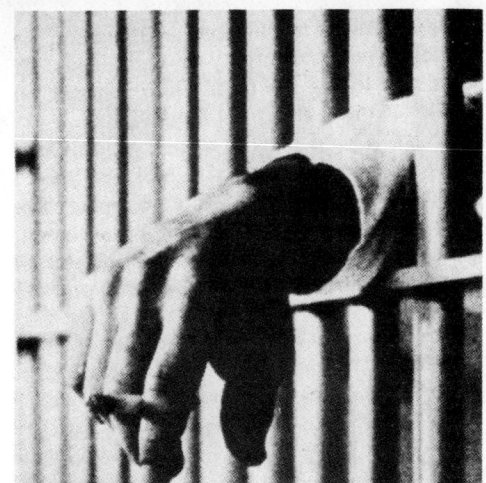

G-- signed it; Patrick said it should be thrown into the garbage; A--- read it, thought about it, read it and thought about it some more, and then passed it on—it was as though he believed that this play-acting would convince us that he was really considering the justness of the petition. (Earlier that morning I had asked him if he would sign a petition like this one; as long as the petition didn't exonerate Tyrone, he answered, he most certainly would, I guess he figured that we'd never actually write such a petition, and that he'd be off the hook.) A couple of days ago, there was an "alimony-sweep" across the city, and we got five more men, all rather middle-aged, and three of them quite pleasant. They're all Italians; the fourth is a real sharpie who talks a lot about his girlfriend, and who everyone thinks is really a paddy–boy. All of the Italians signed the petition.

While the petition was being passed around, Rafael, small and lithe and with a big smile on his face, walked around the mess flicking cigarette ashes into the uneaten food so that it couldn't be used again, saying, "That's the name of the game, baby, that's the name of the game." G-- became very upset about it, but Rafael just continued moving agilely around the room spoiling the food. We felt pretty good: we already had close to fifteen signatures on the petition, and none of the Puerto Ricans had even signed it yet. Then the captain walked into the mess. He looked around the room and called Hank over to him. Hank towered above him as the captain put his arm around Hank in his strange, buddy-buddy way and whispered to him that he knew that many of the men were upset over Tyrone's punishment and that he was going to be immediately released. Hank announced this to us as the captain left the room, but we kept the petition going around. Santiago wouldn't sign it at first, just as he wouldn't refuse to eat; but again he was yelled at by Rafael, and he soon relented, signed it and then immediately transferred his guilt to another Puerto Rican who was planning to sign anyway. *"Firme, firme, yo lo hago tambien,"* he was yelling at the other man, when suddenly Tyrone walked into the mess hall. Earlier, during lunch, Lennie who had finally received his release papers, had gone around shaking everyone's hand and saying goodbye. Everyone was excited and pleased by his release, but the tension we felt about Tyrone immediately eclipsed our **feelings about Lennie's release: it's a good thing when a man is partially granted freedom; it's a**

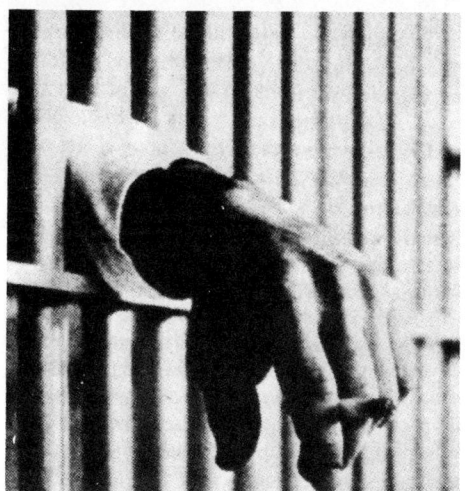

joyful and elating event when people *win* that freedom. We all clapped and stomped on the floor as soon as we say Tyrone; we went around hitting one another's shoulders, yelling, slapping one another's hands, and then clapping and stomping some more. Everybody went up to shake his hand; Rafael looked at him as though he were a long lost brother, and it was difficult to tell whether Tyrone was more pleased to be out or whether we were more pleased to have been successful in our action. "Thanks a lot," he kept saying to everyone; "Thanks a lot for what you did." "Let's eat!" Santiago cried. "Fuck that shit, man" Rafael answered, "We'll wait for dinner." I don't know to whom the action was exemplary: certainly it was the first show of solidarity most of these men had experienced and taken part in; but it was also more moving to us, it was more moving and steeling for us to win out against this small, pitifully trivial injustice than any number of the major political battles, internal or external, we had waged during the year. We made several mistakes during the action, but somehow things came through all right. And now Rafael wants us to free the other two black men who are trapped in solitary.

* * * * *

The major mistake we made in the action was the deletion of Juan's last sentence, and this was caused by and coupled with an even greater, more general mistake: a mistrust of the other men in the jail. Before we sent the petition around, we were sure we had practically no allies; but the petition was signed by more than one half of the inmates. Because we felt so isolated, we were too easily argued out of the necessity for keeping the last sentence in the petition. For the great majority of the men either did believe that the warden was a racist, or simply sided with Tyrone as another inmate, no matter what he did. The only ones who were actively against the petition were A---, Patrick, and the paddy-boy. Our mistrust of the people led us to dilute the politics of the action and showed our greatest weakness: a tendency towards indecisiveness, a fear of taking the offensive, and, once having taken it, keeping it and pressing onwards. We are afraid of taking vanguard actions because we're afraid of being isolated from the people; and as the level of struggle increases so do the consequences, not only for the vanguard but also for the people.

* * * * *

Patrick and A--- are furious that we won. As soon as Tyrone was released, Patrick came over to me: "Just don't think that you can get away with anything now." Rafael wants us to move on. The racism in the jail is, of course, real: not only in the fact that in this jail, as in all of them, there is a totally disproportionate number of black and brown prisoners (who, altogether, make up some 80% of all New York State prisoners), but also in the way the jail is run. The Puerto Ricans and blacks always get extra duties; the white guards and inmates always try to *colonize* them: they treat them as children, arrogantly teach them English (or tell them to speak it), make fun of their music, etc. If any fight should break out between one of the Puerto Rican inmates and a white inmate, it's always clear who gets the most blame. So it's right that Rafael should be so insistent, and take such a vanguard position; so should Patrick, if he weren't held back by his privileges. Patrick can't tolerate the fact that we won: he wants to see us crushed, so that he can continue to believe in his own powerlessness, so that he can continue to believe his passivity is necessary for any self-preservation. We challenged his passivity—and his racism—and now he refuses to give in. Yesterday he entered the argument we were having with the other men only once: he told me how the people in jails are evil and deserve to be there, how I was a chump and a kiddo. He said this to me with the most severe conviction. If he didn't believe that he *was* guilty, he would hate those who have put him away more than he does: he would hate them overpoweringly. It is as though he is afraid to allow himself the knowledge that they made him waste ten years of his life, and that he submitted to it. His eyes when he talks about his past life, lose their focus, and his face loses all of its pleasant Irish definition. His conviction is a desperate one: it is too much, almost, of an imposition and threat to believe that the whole world isn't made up of degenerates and madmen, that *he* isn't a degenerate and a mad-man. If we could smash through that threat, if he could again begin to believe and trust in himself and his brothers and focus his hatred upon those who deserve it, he would be a solid, stone rebel. But now he sometimes makes me think of a man who has been hit by the same cannon fifteen times and believes each wounding, blasting bullet came from a separate gun.

July 1

I guess we like to believe that everything has a beginning and an end; our immediate response to Tyrone's release was that it was an ending. The next ten days were for reading. How wrong that was—as though life here were like school, and the actions in the spring marked the end of the term! A day after Tyrone's release everything had returned to normal: G--- worrying about whether or not he'd be released; Patrick studying his math; Charlie living out his life. For none of them was Tyrone's release an end: and it was a sign of our privileged position, and our distance from the other men, that we allowed ourselves to act as though it were.

After Patrick had yelled that we shouldn't expect to get away with everything now, he began to retreat to his math books, studying long into the night and sleeping most of the day. Because he knew that we were contemptuous of his refusal to sign the petition, he became much closer to Tyrone, who talked to him about Cleaver, jails, being a junkie. We act terrible towards Patrick: disregarding what he says, not attending to his stories, in a word, being liberals. We had strong arguments with him, but we refused to discuss them with him openly. Finally Tom had a shouting, yelling fight with him and A---, in which Tom decided to come on strong and called both of them, and especially Patrick, a "jerk, putz, schmuck" etc. Patrick didn't respond to this at all: he wasn't even antagonistic. Toward the end of the discussion, one of us exploded and shouted at Patrick that he knew very well who the enemy was, and that he was crazy to go around fighting his brothers: it was Rockefeller who should be killed. This sentiment shocked A--- very much. Communication between Patrick and us ended for a day. We realized that we had thought Patrick had become a solid rebel and had reacted with hostility when we discovered that mythic radicalism destroyed. We hadn't understood our own failures, so we went on a counter-attack, asking Patrick questions, listening to his stories, discussing things with him, and we all began to get tight again.

Last night there was a great and noisy fight between Roger and Michael and us. After the lights went out, we all exited to the john where we met Patrick; he hadn't taken part in the fight, but had listened to it. He told us that the one thing he learned from it was that the important thing is to get people into struggle and not keep having fights with people who are supposedly our friends. He spoke like a member of the SDS Chapter of the New York Civil Jail. He disagreed with us when we said why we thought the things we were arguing about were important; he said it was bullshit: what mattered about was not what people were struggling around, but what they were struggling against. We didn't know what to say to this: his insistence on the movement getting out to spread and deepen its struggles was fine, but his dismissal of any ideology was awful. That this wasn't just an intellectual disagreement between the two of us became clear when Patrick referred to the Minutemen as an example of whites taking up guns against the government; he made them appear as though they were the White Panther Party. "See," he said, "they're a lot of white fighting the government, they just don't know that they are part of the movement." We tried to get him to see why the argument we had with PLP was important, and in understanding their racism begin to combat his own. It was useless: the good thing about our conversation was not its content, but its form: once again we were being truthful with each other and, since we were talking to Patrick as another *human being* and not an experiment in organizing, he spoke to us as friends. Once again we learned our seemingly constant lesson: it isn't racism, anti-communism, male supremacy or any other ideological bugaboo that keeps these men from fighting: it is their total and overwhelming disbelief in themselves as men who can *change* things. They use the most outrageous arguments to support this disbelief—especially Patrick,

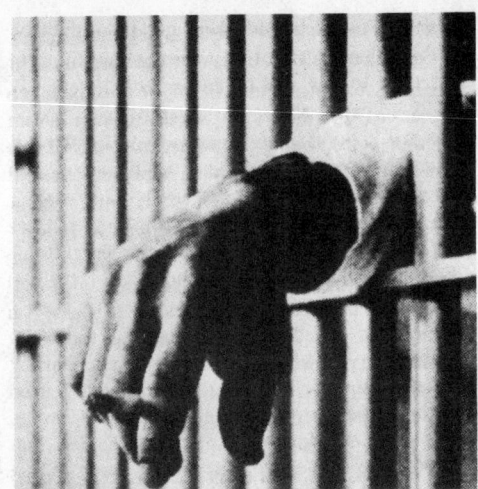

who's brilliant. After he gives up saying that blacks "need help" or that women and men aren't equal, or that the Chinese Communists are out to conquer the world and stomp everyone in it to death, he energetically tells us that it's all very well, everything that we're saying, but the fact of the matter is that "you can't change human nature" since man is "just an animal like everything else and has naturally bad instincts." We answered by telling him how all the French believed that the Algerians were genetically different from everyone else, and that was why they had had such a high criminal record; and how, during and after the Revolution the crime rate dropped to practically nothing. We talk about the changes that have taken place in Cuba since the Revolution. It's no good. "Well," says Patrick, "you just can't go around changing human nature." Patrick! Whenever he starts saying these things—and he will say them five minutes after explaining to us how the prison system is simply a way of super-exploiting unemployed workers—I feel disgusted and embarrassed for him. I talk to Hank about Patrick's passitivity; and he pointed out that the root of Patrick's individual history lay in the past history of the Left in America, a history of equivocation and compromise whenever there was a necessity for sacrifice and dedication. Patrick has felt the effects of such policies: as a young man he tried to join the Electrician's Union and couldn't because of the fantastic bribes you have to pay to get in. Of course Patrick hates Rockefeller: but he doesn't see his white working-class brothers fighting to overthrow him; and he dismisses the people who *are* fighting against Rockefeller as barbarians with whom he shares no interest. We originally thought that if we could break through his racism, his passivity would vanish. But it's clearly the other way around. His arguments are the most difficult to combat: they cede neither to logic nor argument, but only to constant example through practice.

July 7

Tonight we had a long talk with Patrick. His harangues at the guards have become prison commonplaces; the guards hate it, the other men love it. They gather around and watch as Patrick's unbelievable tongue whips away at these men, making them foolish, beaten, afraid. The other inmates learn a lot too, because Patrick has a lot to teach and gets in all kinds of

facts: the oppression of people abroad and at home that Rockefeller is responsible for (Patrick has fallen in love with a quote from Rocky: "I know these people, I hear these people, I love these people." He said it in the middle of his Latin American journey) the war, taxes, the Third World, the recently discovered terrible deaths of a couple of nine year-olds who were taking junk. He lays it all down with such a passion that it's as though he's gaining his freedom by talking. Meanwhile, we are pressing him to work with us when he gets out; we have gotten him a lawyer, and we think there's a good possibility of his finally being released. We are also pressing him to write an article for the movement about the prison system in the States. He's reading, ploughing through *Report From a Chinese Village*; and he told us that he was giving up his math books: he wants to read political stuff from now on. He still doesn't want to concede that we helped win Tyrone's release, but he doesn't adamantly reject our use of Tyrone's release as an example of what people can win through, and only through, struggle. He says he thinks the movement should form a "united front," that we argue too much and organize too little. I think he's furious with us that he had to meet us in jail. We spoke to him about the need for ideology: particularly the necessity to support liberation movements, the Third World, the movement for Black Liberation, Women's Liberation; and we tried to get him to see the absolute necessity for people to make choices about where and when and how to fight and about what they're fighting. Patrick didn't answer; unlike students, he doesn't throw out clever ideas, and doesn't agree or disagree with you immediately: he digests what you're saying, and the only way you'll know whether or nor you've convinced him is if he translates the idea to someone else in a conversation. But I have the feeling that since Independence Day he has decided to put all his past ideas in a box, hammer it closed and begin to form his opinions and sentiments all over again. Just like Eldridge says: "We decided to shut that book closed and stamp it Pig History."

July 8   S

Patrick started his article today and read us what he has already written. It's written as he speaks, rough & going everywhere at once; but it has all kinds of information and a lot of fine points. It will begin to make real to the movement the demand that all prisoners, at least all prisoners who are junkies, are political prisoners and must be freed. He is also clear on the racist character of the prisons: he states that the vast majority of the prisoners are black and brown and oppressed because of their color as a people; and that dope is one way the Rockefellers—the personification for Patrick of the ruling class—have of keeping the internal colony repressed.

* * * * *

Robbie and I were talking to Tyrone about what he was going to do when he leaves the jail. He's thinking about joining the Panthers, but isn't sure. He said everyone he knew was a junkie, and he talked about how junkies go in and out of jails in order to "dry out," staying off the stuff for a while and then going back on it. The worst thing he said about junk was that

it didn't allow people to "see themselves." The reason why so many revolutionaries come out of the jails, he said, is that they get off junk there. "They dry out and can begin to see themselves."

July 9

I'm writing this outside of jail. This morning as Hank and I were released in the custody of two pigs, we were booked on additional charges and then let out on bail. We said goodbye to A---, who was planning to pick up and leave soon; and to Patrick who was desultory as proof that he would see us soon on the outside.* Rafael also had to go to court that day and gave us the clenched fist as he went down the stairs. Charlie had been mad at us for leaving; he said that instead of paying a fine we should stay the extra ten days. The day we left, he just went about his business, which was winning six chess games in a row from a Southern aristocrat who just entered the jail as a material witness. As the pigs were tailing us back to Centre street, I remembered my only thought as we were being driven to prison. I was frightened, didn't know what to expect and didn't welcome the idea of going. Driving in the prison bus up Houston Street, I tried to imagine the time when no one could be driven to jail along the street: because all the truck drivers, cabbies, push-cart vendors, unemployed and unemployable wouldn't let the bus go through. I didn't tell any of my comrades about my fantasy then; I was embarrassed by it and thought it liberal and sentimental: we were all embarrassed by our fear and handled it in differen ways. The first few hours in the jail we knew that we were part of a movement that had the allegiance of thousands of people; and we knew that our struggle was just: but we only believed intellectually that it was the struggle, indeed, of the people with whom were going to be living for the next month. But the more you get to know the people, the more you get to trust and respect them: trust and respect their knowledge of the exploitation, oppression and represion they must suffer and trust and respect their resistance to it, their cunning and bravery in the face of it. Being in jail, living with those men, learning from them, made the belief real to us, and, we've sure made the fantasy with which I entered prison closer to becoming a reality.

From "Drying Out" by Lew Cole,

Leviathan Feb 1970

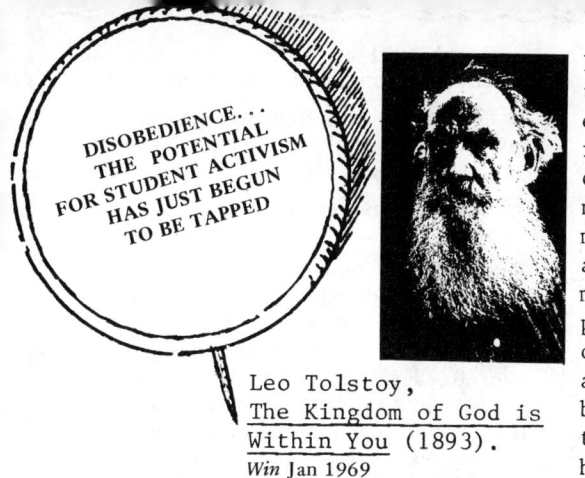

DISOBEDIENCE...
THE POTENTIAL
FOR STUDENT ACTIVISM
HAS JUST BEGUN
TO BE TAPPED

Leo Tolstoy,
The Kingdom of God is
Within You (1893).
Win Jan 1969

In early Christian times a soldier, Theodore, told the authorities that being a Christian he could not bear arms, and when he was executed for this the responsible authorities quite sincerely regarded him as a madman and far from trying to conceal such an occurence, exposed him to public scorn at their execution. But now when cases of refusals of military service occur more and more frequently, these cases are no longer regarded by the authorities as madness, but as a very dangerous awakening from madness, and the governments far from holding such cases up to public scorn carefully conceal them, knowing that the salvation of men from humiliation, enslavement and ignorance, will come about not by revolutions, trade-unions, peace-congresses, and books, but in the simplest way -- by each man who is called upon to share in the infliction of violence on his fellow men and on himself, asking in perplexity: "But why should I do this?"

THE HARRIS POLL

A poll conducted by Louis Harris during the first two weeks of May and released in June indicates that draft resistance has gained considerable respectability during the past year in the opinion of many of this year's graduating seniors. The poll, conducted at 50 American colleges and universities (the University of Wisconsin, the University of California at Berkeley, Western Washington College of Education, Black Hills College for Teachers, Mount Mercy College, and others) asked 1005 graduating seniors about their re-actions to various forms of protest. The data gathered during the survey showed a surprising increase in campus radicalism.

A summary of the results of the poll in the June 30 New York Post stated that: "Aversion to the war in Vietnam has reached the point among college students that by 48 to 34 per-cent, a cross section of just-graduated seniors say they'respect those who refuse to go into the armed forces when drafted.' This marks a sharp reversal from a comparable sur-vey of a year ago when seniors then said by 50 to 29 percent that they would 'respect' such draft resisters 'less'."

Harris found surprising agreement that the protests which occurred at so many campuses (at two/thirds of those in his study) had been worthwhile. Only seven percent of those interviewed said that the protests never should have occurred.

The survey also indicated that, while protest activities had increased considerably in the past year, there was an even greater increase in the number of students who have never par-ticipated but now would be willing to do so, even if it endangered their future. Of those questioned, 40 percent have participated in demonstrations; 72 percent would be willing to; 11 percent have engaged in civil dis-obedience, 36 percent would be willing to do so.

These findings show that a profound radicali-zation of students has taken place during the past year, that the newspapers have failed to report or have greatly underesti-mated the breadth of the protest movement, and that the potential for student activism has just begun to be tapped. *Resist* Newsletter 8/7/69

In one recent week (Feb 1970) at the Oakland Induction Center, 250 men were called, 130 showed up, and 40 refused induction. Deserters from the Army are now at the rate of 60,000 a year: one every 10 minutes.

WIN figures reported by local draft boards

THE STATE OF THE DRAFT

Will Tychonievich reports that he and those who refused induction with him were astounded that their number was so great. The Guardian called the Oakland Induction Center to see if this was a usual day. We spoke to Captain Robert W. Munson. After getting permission from his superiors, he gave us these figures for "an average induction day in recent months":
***Those ordered to report for induction—375
***Those who, in fact, do report for induction—250 to 270
***Those who report for, but refuse induction—15
According to the Army's own statistics, then, 27 to 33 per cent of the young men called for military service do not even bother to show up. Anther 4 per cent openly defy the draft law by refusing induction.

Randy Kehler
WIN Oct 1969

Draft Violators Increasing in Number Throughout U.S.

Draft violation is reportedly the third ranking "crime" in the United States according to the latest figures available this year. Out of 37.5 million men registered with Selective Service, about 1 in 1600 was considered delinquent.

According to a testimony by a former draft board clerk from two San Jose, Cal., draft boards, two thousand men turned in their draft cards to those boards alone in 1968. The former clerk who testified at a trial of one of the men, said that out of those 2,000, only 200 have been declared delinquent and processed for induction. He also stated that only those politically active and known to the board were singled out for these actions.

Some 50,000 young Americans have reportedly chosen to live in Canada, Sweden, and elsewhere rather than be drafted, according to a recent report in the *Chicago Times*. Also, 1,000 draft re-sisters are now in prison, and another 1,000 have deserted and live in exile.

Fellowship Aug 1969

FOR WHAT?

The real terms of trade between an individual and his country have been deteriorating markedly in the past decades. In the eighteenth century the national state made relatively few demands on its citizens, and provided some of them at least with fair security and satisfactory identity. As the nation has gathered legitimacy however from the bloodshed and treasure expended for it, it has become more and more demanding. It now demands ten or twenty per cent of our income, at least two years of our life—and it may demand the life itself—and it risks the destruction of our whole physical environment. As the cost rises, it eventually becomes not unreasonable to ask for what? If the payoffs are in fact low, the moment has arrived when the whole legitimacy of the institution may be threatened.

KENNETH BOULDING

How wonderful it is that freedom's instruments—the rights to speak, to publish, to protest, to assemble peaceably, and to participate in the electoral process—have so demonstrated their power and vitality! These are our alternatives to violence; and so long as they are used forcefully, but prudently, we shall *continue* as a vital, free society.

ABE FORTAS In Concerning Dissent and Civil Disobedience

All of our major problems have become revolutionary, unprecedented ones, and they call for revolutionary, unprecedented answers.

FRANKLIN D. MURPHY, chairman, Times Mirror Co., Los Angeles, quoted in *Vital Speeches*

Mayor Daley is the ball game.

SENATOR ROBERT KENNEDY— spring 1968

When somebody burns the United States flag I generally get the idea he's not very friendly to us. And when somebody flies a Viet Cong banner, when someone speaks out favorably for the policies of Ho Chi Minh, I get the idea he's not with us anymore.

SPIRO AGNEW

UNIVERSITIES KILL

Universities kill. That is the underlying theme of a new movement pamphlet, entitled "The University-Military Complex: A Directory and Related Documents."

The pamphlet, compiled by Mike Clare and published by the North American Congress on Latin America (NACLA), has material on university contacts with the Pentagon, the role of professors, anti-cop war research and other related data. There is an index of people and institutions.

The pamphlet may be obtained from NACLA, postage paid, for $1.25, PO Box 57, Cathedral Station, New York, N.Y. 10025.

Good Times

Mr. Katzenbach, testifying on the basis of his experience as former chairman of the President's Crime Commission and former Attorney General, also said that he could rationalize the violence of war and the attempt to subdue violence domestically...

Later, when Thomas D. Barr, deputy executive director of the commission, asked the witness what he thought of the

philosophy, "I am a free man first, an American second," Mr. Katzenbach said:

"If I felt our system was incapable of justice, I suppose I would step outside (the system) and take a gun or something else.

The New York Times 9/26/68

The system. . .has an almost unlimited capacity for absorbing protest and externalizing blame, for confusing and dividing the opposition, seeming to appear responsive to legitimate protest by issuing sophisticated and progressive statements that are poorly implemented, if at all.

The system is like a punching bag. . . protest groups can hit it one place and it simply returns to its old equilibrium.

From *New York Times* article quoting a report on the New York school system.

Mrs. Humphrey said she, her husband, and their children certainly wanted to hear young America's view, but that they were already aware of them. "Our youngsters are all over talking with young executives and young Jaycees."

The New York Times

Attorney General Ramsey Clark told the panel that police action "in excess of authority" is the most dangerous type of violence. This is so because, he said, "who will protect the public when the police violate the law?"

The New York Times 9/19/68

Justice is merely incidental to law and order

J. EDGAR HOOVER

TOWN MEETING: BREAKING THE HABIT OF OBEDIENCE

Viet Critics: They Put Themselves on the Line
by Sally Kempton

Last Sunday night at Town Hall more than 500 people put themselves on the line in active support of draft resistance. They were members of the audience at a rally which had been called to demonstrate solidarity with young draft resisters—and with Dr. Spock and the other men recently indicted for their support of draft resisters. The audience's action came at the end of an evening of speeches, after chairman Douglas Dowd had asked supporters to come up to the stage and sign a huge scroll which contained a pledge to counsel, aid, and abet any young man who wished to refuse the draft. Dowd also asked that in order to make their support a legal fact, signers put money in an envelope with their names and addresses and donate it to a resister.

The audience responded so quickly that they seemed to have simply surged into the aisles. Within two minutes nearly 300 people had lined up to sign the scroll, and before the first of them was halfway across the

stage another 300 were out of their seats and jostling their way to the end of the line. People filed forward, speaking their names into a microphone, until to speed things up the sponsors put up two more microphones and another scroll.

Not all the people who rushed forward to put their names on the list were habitual activists. Norman Mailer and Allen Ginsberg and Conor Cruise O'Brien and Susan Sontag and Jane Jacobs signed, Noam Chomsky signed, ladies from Women Strike for Peace signed, as did a man from Trade Unionists for Peace. But there were schoolteachers who signed and social workers. A retired police sergeant signed, and several war veterans, and a taxi driver. A lady came down from the balcony and said she'd never done anything like this before, but she had two sons of draft age and felt she should.

Most of the signers did so in full expectaton of facing prosecution for support of draft resistance. (The maximum penalty for aiding and abetting draft refusal is five years imprisonment or $10,000 fine or both). One gray - faced middle-aged woman stood on the stage waiting to drop her check in the collection box and said she was afraid to go to jail. "I don't think I have five years left to live," she said. "Then don't do it," said her friend. "Oh," the lady answered in a trembling voice, "I couldn't not do it."

When it was over the leaders counted 560 signatures. A spokesman from Support-in-Action, one of the sponsoring organizations, announced herself astonished at the extent of the response. "We expected 50 or 75 people to sign the statement," she said. "I can't even convey how important this is for the peace movement."

The Village Voice 1/18/68

HISTORY: A LEFT-LIBERAL TRIES TO GET IT STRAIGHT

Green Beret Liberalism

by Jack Newfield

Professor Daniel Moynihan, in the May, 1968, issue of *Commentary*, tries to suggest that Lyndon Johnson's decision not to seek re-election and the current peace negotiations in Paris represent a "vindication" for liberals and a repudiation of the new radicals. Professor Moynihan writes: "We—and I speak here as a member of the liberal wing of the Democratic party—we won. . .We must hold on to the realization that reasoned and non-violent opposition to the course of American foreign policy did prevail, when everyone on the Right said it would not, and everyone on the Left said it could not."

His Orwellian rewriting of the history of the last eight years continues: "With the sudden and sharp escalation of military action in the spring and summer of 1965, there followed the familiar onset of intolerance and hysteria, except that his time *'les terribles simplificateurs'* arose not on the far Right of the political spectrum, but on the far Left. . .They were not, however, making any dent on policy itself." Moynihan then goes on to suggest that "singular honors" for vanguard opposition to the war should go to his New Frontier and Cambridge colleagues, Richard Goodwin and John Kenneth Galbraith. (Goodwin and Galbraith were the first two leaders of the liberal establishment to become publicly critical of the war).

Thus, in Professor Moynihan's revisionism, Reverend William Sloane Coffin, Staughton Lynd, Hans Morgenthau, the New Left, the teach-in movement, and the Resistance have all become un-persons. History begins for Professor Moynihan only when insurgent or underground movements begin to influence his friends. It is the same mentality which says Lincoln freed the slaves, Samuel Gompers created the labor movement, and de Gaulle settled the Algerian war. It is elitist, ignorant of prophetic currents on the margins of society, and plain bad history.

Now I certainly don't believe all liberals are implicated in the guilt of Vietnam. Many acted with great courage and vision—senators like Ernest Gruening and J.W. Fulbright, and others like I.F. Stone, Carey McWilliams, and Representative George Brown. But one should not give exclusive credit to Galbraith and Goodwin and deny credit to the young radicals who risked exile.

In retrospect, I think there have been five key events of expansion in the history of the anti-war movement. Each created a new climate of opinion. The first was the birth of the teach-in movement at Ann Arbor in March of 1965, which galvanized the academic community against the Johnson Administration. The second was the first mass demonstration against the war, organized by Students for a Democratic Society in April of 1965. The third was the launching of the "dump Johnson" movement by Allard Lowenstein in June of 1967. The fourth was the march of 75,000 on the Pentagon last October 21. And the fifth is the march and "freak-out" planned for the Democratic Convention this August by SDS veterans Rennie Davis and Tom Hayden and the Yippies.*

Each of these five extra-parliamentary, experimental tactics created space and energy for the liberals—McCarthy and Kennedy, as well as Goodwin and Galbraith—to act on later. Significantly, each of these five steps, *when taken,* was bitterly attacked by the liberals as irresponsible and counterproductive.

The teach-in movement was begun in 1965 at the University of Michigan by SDS graduate students and radical faculty members like Arnold Kaufman. During the early teach-ins, both Galbraith and Arthur Schlesinger actually defended the Johnson Administration's Asian policy. On April 21, 1965, the liberals' liberal, James Reston, wrote a *New York Times* column acidly critical of the teach-in movement, asserting: "At many other colleges, however, these nocturnal marathons have not been debates at all, but anti-Administration demonstrations disguised as 'teaching' and, in many cases, backed by propaganda of the most vicious nature. . .

"This is no longer a casual form of campus fever. The zeal of the civil rights movement is being transferred in some places into a get out of Vietnam campaign, and this, in turn, is being widely distributed by Communist countries to the detriment of the Administration's effort to force a negotiated peace."

In April, 1965, SDS organized the first mass public protest against the war. More than 20,000 people—mostly students—showed up, many more than even SDS had hoped for. The speakers included activist and historian Staughton Lynd, Paul Potter of SDS, Bob Parris Moses of SNCC, journalist I.F. Stone, and Senator Gruening. Nevertheless, the liberals wanted the protest to be more hygienic, and more orderly, so the march was attacked beforehand by Turn Towards Peace in an editorial in the *New York Post* and in a statement of "moderate" peace leaders signed by Bayard Rustin, Robert Gilmore, and twelve others. But the march, organized by the New Left, proved to be a watershed in the growth of the anti-war movement, *proving the existence of mass support for the first time.*

Last summer, Allard Lowenstein, Sam Brown, and Curtis Gans launched the movement to dump Johnson. They asked every liberal leader and institution to join them, from Wayne Morse to the ADA. For five months not one of them responded. Richard Goodwin, at the NSA Congress last August, reluctantly endorsed Johnson for re-election, and was booed. In September, the ADA national board refused to adopt a dump LBJ resolution. ADA leader Joe Rauh, in fact, tried to abort the "dump movement" by organizing a competitive movement for a meaningless peace plank in the party platform.

Not one major liberal politician or intellectual participated in the Pentagon march. Many, in fact, invoked its spector to frighten the country into tolerating "dissent within the system" as an alternative to the "freaks and Maoists." But it was the Pentagon march that finally showed just how deeply the country was split, how fragile its membrane of stability was, how desperate its best young were.

"Vietnam," as William Pfaff has written, "is liberalism's war."

McNamara. Rostow. Roche. Goldberg. Meany. Ascoli. Humphrey. To the very end, the architects and justifiers of our Vietnam policy have been liberals. Surely, some liberals, like Goodwin, Roger Hilsman, and Schlesinger, saw the folly of that policy earlier than most others and joined the opposition. That distinction must be acknowledged by those who now wish to indict all of liberalism for Vietnam. But equally any fair judgment of the last few years must admit that it has been the radicals, students, and literary intellectuals who were first to see that the emperor had no clothes, and to call him naked. . .

*Another crucial factor in turning the country against the war was the ghetto rebellions which have increased each summer since 1964. Significantly, SNCC, in April, 1965, was the first civil rights organization to insist on linking Vietnam to the ghettos. Two years later, when Martin Luther King made the same connection, he was attacked by liberal institutions like *The New York Times* and Freedom House.

Ed. Note: This is a useful but too-simple picture. The attack on the Oakland Induction Center and The Draft Resistance Movement, for example, are neglected, as is the crucial organizing role played by Dave Dellinger.

From "Green Beret Liberalism" by Jack Newfield, *Evergreen* Aug 1968

evergreen

SANCTUARY AT M.I.T. A 19-YEAR-OLD DESERTER TEACHES THE STUDENTS OF THE WORLD'S DEADLIEST WAR RESEARCH CENTER WHAT IT MEANS TO RESIST

A numerically strong support community has become the most important aspect of the antiwar sanctuaries for at least three reasons. Primarily, bodies are needed to obstruct the police. There is no intention of hiding the "fugitive," but it is desirable to demonstrate a nonviolent resistance to the arresting authorities. Second, this massive display of civil disobedience shows the public the extent of the support. Third, and most important in the long-range goals of the antiwar movement, is the metamorphosis of the community from a large number of bodies into a massive political forum in which radical education can take place.

This third function was aptly demonstrated in a sanctuary at the Massachusetts Institute of Technology beginning Tuesday morning, October 29, 1968. The MIT Resistance had reserved the Sala de Puerto Rico, a large ballroom in the Student Center, for a teach-in on the Vietnam War. In the morning, Pfc. J. Michael O'Connor arrived with a small group of supporters and established the Sala as the first nonreligious political sanctuary. In his statement to the press, Mike explained that he sought sanctuary at MIT to expose MIT's close ties with the military ($124 million in Defense Department contracts this year, far more than any other private university), and that he came to the Student Center rather than the chapel to involve the universities, in addition to the churches, in critical political issues.

"We Are All One!"
In the early afternoon, about thirty of us held an open meeting and decided to have a nonviolent obstruction when and if the feds arrived. We discussed the possibility of having everyone wear a mask. In effect, we would be saying, "When you come to arrest Mike, you are arresting all of us. We are all the movement. We are all one."

On the afternoon of the first day, some instructors brought their classes to the sanctuary, and the room began to function as simultaneous classrooms for a variety of courses ranging from topology to contemporary American literature. On Wednesday, "liberation courses" were formed. It was then that Jerome Lettvin, one of MIT's most popular professors, made a strong plea for the hundreds listening to stay overnight. He then gave the microphone to Mike O'Connor. With tears in his eyes, Mike threw his statement to the floor and asked us to stay with him and support him. At first, there was a silence and then resounding applause as hundreds of hands flew into the air displaying either the V-sign for peace or the fist of resistance. The community solidified.

On Saturday night, other events were taking place in the Student Center, and many students in coats and ties brought their dates into the Sala. We referred to these couples as "tourists." Many of them joined the discussions and decided to spend the night. The Student Center was absolute mayhem.

We Lived in a System of Democratic Communism
The twelve days which I spent in Sanctuary provided an experience which I will never forget. The oneness of the people was beautiful. Mattresses, pillows, and blankets became community property. All food was shared; money was passed out and shared as needed. Everyone had an equal voice in all discussions and an equal vote in all decisions, and this included unsympathetic passersby. At one point, a moderator of a major discussion turned off his microphone, claiming that it gave him an unfair advantage in the discussion. The community was economically and socially communistic and politically 'a participatory democracy. It worked better than anyone could have expected.

The pervading atmosphere of the Sanctuary was one of nonviolence. We had voted very early to have a nonviolent obstruction if the bust were to come. On Friday night, there were 1200 bodies solidly packed between the door and Mike. If the feds were to get to him, they would have to get past all of us. Instructions were given from a stage on the most stable and protective obstructive position as well as demonstrations on going limp. The bust did not come that night, mainly, we think, because the feds had learned of the vast number of people inside. . . . . .   *Colloquy* March 1970

TOM HAYDEN IN 1963: A RECOGNITION AND A PROPHECY

The problems are immense. We of the Left, however, find no rest in theory, and little hope in leadership. Liberal philosophy has dealt inadequately with the twentieth century. Marx, especially Marx the humanist, has much to tell us but his conceptual tools are outmoded and his final vision implausible. The revolutionary leaders of the rising nations have been mostly non-ideological, either forced to be so or preferring (as in the case of Guevara) to forge their political views in the heat and exigencies of revolution and the present. The American intellectuals? C. Wright Mills is appealing and dynamic in his expression of theory in the grand manner, but his pessimism yields us no formulas, no path out of the dark, and his polemicism sometimes offends the critical sense. The others? There is, I find, an inhibiting, dangerous conservative temperament behind the facade of liberal realism which is so current: Niebuhr in theology; Kornhauser, Lipset, and Bell in political science and sociology; the neo-

Freudians in psychology; Hofstadter in history; Schlesinger and others of the ADA mind in the Democratic Party. Their themes purport to be different but always the same impressions emerge: Man is inherently incapable of building a good society; man's passionate causes are nothing more than dangerous psychic sprees (the issues of this period too complex and sensitive to be colored by emotionalism or moral conviction); ideals have little place in politics—we should instead design effective, responsible programs which will produce the most that is realistically possible... Here and there, from the pages of *Dissent* or from isolated radicals and scholars, including Mills himself, come cries: No! You false liberals are suffering from the failure of your youthful dreams; you are eviscerating the great optimistic tradition of liberalism from the Enlightenment to the twentieth century; you are justifying disinterest in morality; you are eliminating emotion, dissent, outrage, and yes, the wellsprings of life itself.

So here we stand, limp, questioning, even scared. Our jokes run something like the cover of a recent *Liberation*: scrawled in the manner one finds covering rest room walls is the question "What can we do now?" and the huge, bold answer, "Get ready to die." It is not as though we can dismiss the world; some of us know people who already have contracted radiation disease. It is not as though we can change

things; Mills was pretty accurate with his description of the monolithic power elite. It is not as though we even know what to do: We have no real visionaries for our leaders, we are not much more than literate ourselves. And it is not as though, I also fear, we even know who we are. What has made me so strangely sensitive when my brothers seem so acquiescent, what has made me call insane what the experts call "hard facts of power politics," what has made me feel we are on the threshold of death when others excitedly say we are on the New Frontier, and why have I turned with trembling and disgust from the Americans who do recognize peril and recoil into shelters full of the comforting gadgets the culture has produced? A more blinding situation is difficult to imagine.

From "Agenda for a New Generation" in *The New Student Left,* Beacon Press

When Arthur Schlesinger was asked by *The New York Times* in November, 1965, to explain the contradiction between his published account of the Bay of Pigs incident and the story he had given the press at the time of the attack, he simply remarked that he had lied...It is of no particular interest that one man is quite happy to lie in behalf of a cause which he knows to be unjust; but it is significant that such events provoke so little response in the intellectual community...

NOAM CHOMSKY, *New York Review of Books, 2/23/67*

RESISTING IN THE STREETS: FIRST STEP

Big Demonstrations

October 16-21 again proved, in the cities, on the campuses and at the Pentagon, the human value of big demonstrations: the courage given by the company of like-minded thousands; the ability spontaneously to over-ride official rules and permits; above all, the heady sense of being the sovereign people, the body politic. All this is politically transitory and it often involves moral ambiguities, but it is a unique human experience and energizes all other resistance. It is *not* ineffective or "merely symbolic" (whatever that means). It is the exercise of the right oı petition guaranteed by the Bill of Rights* and it is contagious to others as well as cementing solidarity among ourselves. Even among the police and soldiers there were cases of coming over, in Oakland and Washington. When students sat down in front of the State Department auditorium when I was telling off the gentlemen of the National Security Industrial Association (see *The New York Review of Books,* November 23, 1967), a dozen even of these representatives of the military-industrial came to me privately and said, "Those youngsters are right; my own son and daughter are doing the same." Naturally the problem is to get them to speak publicly and quit.

In my opinion, if such demonstrations continue to grow, with increasing willingness to risk jail and injury and with the self-feeding conviction of sovereignty, the usurping government in fact cannot continue its course; and its jittery alarm and excessive mobilization of troops show that it knows it. Will it then order a massacre? Or will it cede? We shall see.

*Like all hoary antiquities of direct democracy, it puts the government on the spot. The government cannot suppress the right without social shock; it cannot permit it without the situation getting out of hand. This dilemma becomes the origin of new controversy—"comfort to Hanoi," "what about our boys?" etc. The fashionable expedient is to make Byzantine rules, lie about the numbers, and assert via Hubert Humphrey that it all means nothing at all. Which opinion is then echoed by Students for a Democratic Society. But in fact what it means is what it generates, as Rosa Luxemburg knew.

The distinction between what is "symbolic" and what is "real" is a spurious one; the correct distinction is between what leads further and what does not (and to what it does lead). Consider, a few years back, the mass advertisements signed by hundreds and then thousands of teachers, professionals, etc. At present at meetings these ads are referred to as the height of futility; but this betrays a short memory. When they appeared, they in fact produced a shock of excitement at how numerous we were. When the government dramatically escalated the war in the face of these "humble petitions," there was a deeper shock, the awareness of powerlessness; but this awareness was a new fact. Rhetoric changed rapidly to impatience and anger, and there is no question that this in turn both enormously increased the size of the public demonstrations—for people said, "We have to do *something*"—and led to the invention of new tactics—for people said, "We have to *do* something." Do the young militants imagine that their own involvement was not profoundly influenced and strongly encouraged by these ads? And incidentally, the professors were not simply unrealistic. Their ads had had a practical effect in stopping the bomb testing and the shelter program, for these were scientific issues in which academics wielded public authority. Now the most recent ad has been from Veterans of the Vietnam War. Almost surely this too leads somewhere, in the armed forces and in the public concern for "our boys."

From "The Duty of Professionals" by Paul Goodman, *Liberation* Nov 1967

A NEW CALL TO RESIST ILLEGITIMATE AUTHORITY

SEPTEMBER 1969

Opponents of the Vietnam War have worked to end it in many ways, some through conventional politics, some by supporting draft resistance or attacking university complicity in militarism. Others have carried resistance further, destroying draft files and developing opposition within the armed forces.

We believe that resistance to _many_ forms of illegitimate authority is necessary to bring health to this country and make it a constructive force instead of a terror in the politics of nations.

Therefore, we support those who resist by

- refusing to register for the draft or submit to induction
- impeding the operations of draft boards and induction centers
- expressing anti-war views while in the armed forces, or refusing to obey illegal or immoral orders, or absenting themselves without leave
- conducting rent and workers' strikes, boycotts, and similar direct actions aimed at ending exploitation in the fields, in factories, in housing
- organizing against harrassment by police, by the FBI, by the courts, and by Congress
- organizing sit-ins, strikes, and any principled actions at schools and universities, to end racist practices and direct complicity with militarism

The Vietnam War has reminded us that major decisions can be made in the United States in cynical disregard of the clearly expressed will of the people and with little concern for those most affected, at home and abroad. The war has also illustrated the readiness of the U.S. to use violence to impose the social arrangements of its choice and to destroy those who attempt to achieve popular control over their affairs. Closely linked to the government, providing its top personnel and shaping its policies, are the centers of private power, the great corporations that control the economic life of the nation and, increasingly, of the world. They are governed not by popular will but by corporate interests as determined by a narrow autocratic elite. The government's resort to force to impose decisions of a ruling elite is one sign of failing democratic institutions and thus of the illegitimacy of the state. Both the use of police and the military and the absence of democratic control over major institutions underscore the illegitimacy of the authority that sets public policy in the U.S. and establishes the framework for social life. **But it is not enough to decry the exercise of illegitimate authority; if it is illegitimate, it must be resisted.**

Resistance to the war and the draft has brought peace groups into conflict with police, courts, and universities. This is not surprising, for the war has its roots deep in our society and to oppose it seriously is to attack a wide range of evils and the institutions that sponsor them. A brief review of five areas of illegitimate authority follows.

1. The war on Vietnam is neither a unique folly nor an error in judgment. Since the end of the last century, U.S. power has been used for economic, political and cultural exploitation of smaller and poorer nations. The "accelerated pacification," the most ferocious non-nuclear bombing in history, and the deceitful maneuvering in Paris are recent manifestations of a global strategy aimed at building an integrated world system dominated by the U.S. Thus seen, Vietnam is one of a long series of interventions in the affairs of many nations: Greece, Cuba, the Dominican Republic, Guatemala, Iran, Laos, Thailand, the Congo, the Philippines, and others. Motivated by a mixture of private interests and misplaced convictions, the Pax Americana continues to inflict suffering and subservience on much of the third world.

2. The Vietnam War has also brought the human and economic costs of the garrison state at home. It has allowed an insatiable military organization to claim over half of the federal budget, directly and indirectly. (A tenth is allocated to health, education, and welfare.) Beyond that, President Nixon has promoted the MIRV and the ABM, both bellicose gestures towards China and the Soviet Union as well as extravagant subsidies of aerospace industries. The Pentagon has insisted recently that military expenditures, even "after Vietnam," will remain at current levels, in order to "resupply and modernize" the armed forces. And in states and cities, a martial mood prevails as police and national guardsmen arm themselves with new weapons, gas the Berkeley campus from helicopters and, there and elsewhere, shoot at citizens, particularly the poor and the young. Dissidents in the army face heavy sentences; and for young men generally, the draft remains the prime symbol of social obligation. In brief, the violence of the state has come increasingly to threaten or control the lives of U.S. citizens.

3. This triumph of illegitimate force has continued to enrich the rich. Cost-plus defense and space contracts have guaranteed affluence to a handful of corporations and subsidized their

growth, while the real wages of workers, after inflation and spiraling taxes, have diminished. The non-unionized and the unemployed are, obviously, the worst victims: welfare programs, ill-conceived to begin with, have been cut back or left languishing, more an insult than an aid. Real welfare programs have been reserved for the wealthy: tax loopholes, the oil depletion allowance, airline subsidies, farm subsidies, highway projects, urban renewal, subsidies to elite universities, and so on. In the past government policy has characteristically preserved or increased the distance between rich and poor. The policy of permanent preparation for war is no exception.

4. Like wealth, control over institutions has been unequally distributed and irresponsibly used. The mistreatment by police of the people they supposedly serve has been only the most blatant example. Schools have failed to educate the children of poor and working class families, thus guaranteeing their impotence in a technological society: in most inner cities, fewer than half the students who enter high school graduate; in New York City, where blacks and Puerto Ricans make up about half of the student population, only a fifth of the graduates of academic (i.e., college-oriented) high schools are black or Puerto Rican — and only a fifth of those graduates go on to college. Yet attempts by parents to improve the schools through community control have been fought bitterly by New York's educational bureaucracy. Or to take a rather different instance, heavily subsidized highways have displaced families and foreclosed possibilities for mass transport systems that might serve all — hardly a surprise, given the dependence of the nation's largest corporations on the automobile. Industrial wastes, oil leakages, and municipal sewage rob citizens of beaches and streams and, with the fouling of the atmosphere, literally threaten the continuation of life. In short, most people have little control over the conditions of their work, their education, their protection, their means of transport — indeed, the air they breathe and the water they drink.

5. The most powerless have been people of color. U.S. history has included the systematic conquest and slaughter of American Indians, the enslavement, degradation, and murder of Afro-Americans, the callous exploitation of Chicanos, the detention and robbery of Japanese-Americans, and the use of atomic weapons, napalm, gas, and crop-destroying chemicals against people of the third world. Consequently, U.S. citizens inherit a nation in which white privilege and white power are part of the "natural" order and structure of society. People of color die at a disproportionate rate in warfare or "peace." They are unemployed disproportionately, receive inferior education disproportionately, are humiliated disproportionately. Despite the recent recognition of some mystical, undefined "racism" by official government commissions, the living conditions of non-whites have remained intolerable. Every effort by non-whites to gain power, even in their own communities, has been met by violent opposition; militant blacks, determined to bring about the promised changes, are harrassed, jailed, killed, or forced into exile. In many ghettoes, there is virtual war between blacks and predominantly white police.

Two years ago, the first Call to Resist Illegitimate Authority focused on the war and the draft. **But we cannot oppose the war without opposing the institutions that support and maintain it.** Imperialism, militarism, economic exploitation, undemocratic power, racism: though the words may seem stale, they describe the exercise of illegitimate authority in the United States today. Again, we call upon all to join us in the struggle against illegitimate authority. **Now is the time to resist.**

In reversing the convictions of the Boston Four, the First Circuit Court of Appeals left open the possibility that signing the original Call to Resist or this New Call could, in conjunction with other acts, be viewed as illegal. We believe it is the government's actions, not ours, which are illegal. However, signers and contributors should be aware that their actions might be found illegal.

---

send to: RESIST/Room 4/763 Mass. Ave./Cambridge, Mass. 01239

☐ Add my name to the list of signers of the "New Call"; you may make my endorsement public.

☐ I enclose a contribution of $_____ to support the work of RESIST. (Please make checks payable to RESIST.)

☐ I pledge $_____ monthly to support the work of RESIST.

☐ I am interested in organizing or joining a group in my community.

Please Print

name _____

address _____

city _____ state _____ zip _____

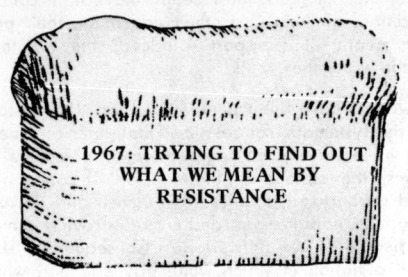

1967: TRYING TO FIND OUT
WHAT WE MEAN BY
RESISTANCE

Ultimately, then, the resistance phenomenon is significant insofar as it begins to galvanize a constituency that will be crucially important as an agent of social change. Not all college students will return their cards. But it is not so much the position that is important as the process, which can take many forms. The existence of a sizable group of young men who return their draft cards is a challenge to others. It is an act, a response, against which others must measure themselves and their lives. If others accept this challenge, they take responsibility for an agenda of social change. Resistance is, in short, a position of political witness.

We would be deluding ourselves, however, if we ignored the gap between the tactics now employed and the incipient ideology which informs them. What is needed is a subtle analysis of the American social structure, and a strategy for organizing the constituencies in this structure that will be the agents of its transformation.

A Phony Distinction

There is a distinction in the air now between "symbolic" and "genuine" confrontations. The action at the Pentagon is thought to be the latter, a direct disruptive challenge to the war machine. Descriptions of this type of confrontation are draped in the language of militancy, but in light of the government's monopoly on effective violence, it should be clear that this distinction is utterly phony, a kind of inverted Platonism. All the confrontations of recent months—the Pentagon, The Resistance action, Oakland and the various attempts to disrupt recruiting on campuses—were symbolic. There should be nothing derisory in this label. Symbols are useful, human and effective political instruments of communication. The point is to choose carefully the symbol one employs in a given environment. It must speak to a constituency, either mobilizing it or, what is more difficult, organizing it.

It is precisely because the distinction between genuine and symbolic confrontations is not illuminating that we must now rethink the whole question of tactics, or at least take a deep breath. Unfortunately, the recent phrases "From Dissent to Resistance" and "From Protest to Resistance" have obtained their meaning more out of a mood of frustration (even boredom!) with "traditional" tactics, than out of any clear sense of why one goes into the streets or outside of the electoral process. Until shortly after the Mobilization of April 15, some things were clear. Action was chosen for its persuasive force. An effort was made to give it a face with which potential constituencies could identify. If the act was one of civil disobedience, a Gandhian moral edge was projected by drawing with crystal clarity the line between our legitimacy and the government's illegitimacy. (We never did any of these things well enough, but that's not the point at issue here.) This situation began to change last summer when talk of "resistance" gained currency in the antiwar movement, and this notion very quickly came to be associated with "disruptive confrontation." The Movement imagination had been captured, thus Oakland, the Pentagon, the campus recruiters.

The troubling thing about resistance as "disruptive confrontation" is that a dynamic has now been set up leading us further and further from the set of criteria on which we used to base our tactical choices and which, it seems to me, are still the relevant ones. The recent Stop the Draft Week (December 4-8) in New York City is instructive in this regard. A brief chronology: the week began in the Lutheran Church of St. John the Evangelist, Brooklyn, with a Resistance service and the second return of draft cards organized by that group. On Tuesday there was a sit-in and legal picket line at the Whitehall Street induction center. About seventy people, including Dr. Benjamin Spock, were arrested in ritual manner. But it was Wednesday through Friday that set the tone of the week (even obscuring the contours of Tuesday's ritual).

Mobile Tactics

The last three days were to involve "mobile tactics" around the induction center and, unlike Tuesday, the action was billed as an attempt to close it down "by force of our numbers." By Tuesday it was clear that this was not an attainable goal. Police, their leaves cancelled, were out in force and completely controlled the Whitehall area. Prodded by our own rhetoric, we had narrowed down the options to two: either we would stay in the Whitehall area and be satisfied the rest of the week with more mass, ritual sit-ins and picket lines in barricaded areas, or, if we tried the "mobile tactic," would end up running around the streets of the city with our flies open, raising hell. Bemused by our own rhetoric, we chose the second: three days of chaotic jousting between police and demonstrators, never more than tenuously focused on any specific political target, certainly not on the induction center.

Several lessons must be drawn from this experience. First, genuine conflict situations are significant only where there is a real chance to weaken seriously the institution or practice. This potential exists on campuses, where recruiting *has* become more difficult and in some places probably will be curtailed as a result of the disruptions. It does not exist around the Pentagon and induction centers. Second, since attacks on these institutions should not cease, we must set attainable goals for our direct action around them. This means going back to the set of criteria antedating last summer: persuasive action with a Gandhian moral edge, confrontations with an identifiable face. In short, Monday and Tuesday of the recent Stop the Draft Week must become our models of resistance.

This situation should disappoint and frustrate no one except those wedded to the ambition of becoming the American Che Guevara. The Resistance strategy, for example, has real political promise. December 4 brought the total of cards returned up to about two thousand. A similar number of academics, clergymen and professionals have declared themselves in conscientious complicity with this draft refusal. If the Conscientious Resistance movement grows in the next four or five months it has real potential for dislocating the Selective Service system and narrowing the government's ability to co-opt resistance to its war policy. What is more, this kind of civil disobedience has a clear political and moral focus which cannot be clouded nearly as easily as the recent action in New York City. If our goal is to move a body politic, to activate a general will—which we assume to be tacitly against the war and the iniquitous draft of American society—then we cannot allow our own frustration, disappointment, sometimes even boredom, to distract us from this task.

From "Pentagon Confrontation" by Marty Jezer

LIBERATION Nov 1967

TALKING WITH THE TROOPS

GEORGE DENNISON

ON THE STEPS
OF THE
PENTAGON

OTHER PARTICIPANTS will be writing political analyses of the Pentagon March, but this will be a more personal account. I would like to describe what happened in front of the Pentagon doors, especially at night, and if possible tell why I found it so moving.

I was in the large group that broke into forbidden territory between 4:30 and 5 Saturday afternoon. We had been clustered at the barricade on one of the auto ramps that lead to the doors of the Pentagon. The barricade was lightly guarded. It went down without violence—except to the barricade itself—and we streamed up the ramp. It was obvious, as elsewhere in the demonstration, that we had not "broken through," but rather that the troops, following strategies of their own, had fallen back so as to cull the militants from the mass. We were immediately sealed off from our supporters in the Mall and on the large stairway directly in front of it.

In general, when the troops wished to contain us, they had no trouble in doing so. Ten thousand were utilized. Other thousands were held in reserve, as were Sherman tanks. The troops were armed with rifles, pistols, clubs, bayonets and tear gas. This is a striking portrait of our government vis-à-vis its citizens, yet many reporters have justified these armaments by citing the unruliness of the crowd, which is to say that we were "armed" with angry faces, angry voices and angry placards. (Our secret weapons, it turned out, were spray cans used to inscribe such slogans as NEGOTIATE on the outer walls of the Pentagon.) Later Saturday night, when even our anger had vanished (it vanished into affirmation of who we were and what we meant) we saw panic reactions stirring among the troops. Tactical theorists will have to ask themselves what force was frightening them. I hope that I can describe it.

A great shout went up when our barricade went down. Several hundreds of us (a completely haphazard assortment, and this turned out to be a blessing) streamed up the ramp. The voices and faces expressed elation, gaiety and curiosity. This was the effect of our numbers and of the youthfulness of the great majority. It was the effect of the sunshine, too, but above all of the fact that our ultimate purpose seemed to have little to do with the troops—we had serious words for fellow citizens and officials.

Most of us bore within us a two-part message:

● that we refused absolutely to lend ourselves to a war that is a total and willful disaster, and

● that we were opening the question of whether the people of our own country must at present be described as a captive population.

Our presence, our civil disobedience, *was* this message. We intended no violence. Our motivation was obvious. Our first reaction to the extravagant might assembled against us was a kind of scornful laughter, not unlike the laughter of children at the antics of the insane. Later, after we had witnessed violence and had begun to see the soldiers' faces, our sense of the disproportion between our motives and those of our government became poignant and profound. We could see with our eyes how the masses of the Army are controlled by the nightmares of a relative few. Our sense of purpose was deepened and purified. This was the source of the modest bravery of those who confronted the troops late at night. It was the source, too, of an extremely generous communal spirit.

The troops were to be shamed by their officers and by the U.S. Marshals roving among them. They were frozen in ludicrous postures of violence before seated youths and girls, who struck up, among other songs, "Yellow Submarine." When violence occurred, many soldiers turned their heads in disgust. Two defected. Every sign of this kind, of the human spirit alive within the uniform, was described on our bull horns and became an occasion for rejoicing.

"Let Us Live"

It is hard to make these feelings clear. Guns and acts of violence do, after all, enforce powerful simplifications. Here on one side were the animated faces and the lively voices of the young, there on the other the grim monotony of military force. We might have been a delegation from the modern world saying only, "Let us live." We said much more than that, and said it clearly, but our sense of one deep issue—the plight of individual life brimming against repressive force—was so acute that we felt the deepest emotion over incidents which, except symbolically, were hardly of great consequence.

As we poured into the blacktop parking ramp—designed for the cars of VIP's—a torrent of helmets gushed from the building and came bubbling down the steps. Three youths made a dash for the door and were clubbed with rifles. We other hundreds sat down immediately, in close order, and linked arms, expecting an

It was this soldier who, five hours later, began crushing the heads of seated demonstrators . . .

assault. But the troops, some leveling their rifles at our heads, lined up in front of us and along one side, sealing us off from the thousands who were now cheering on the "legal" stairway and in the Mall. We could see masses of troops, all helmets and guns, streaming along the side of the building so as to close the rampway we had entered. These early positions, taken before 5 in the afternoon, were held until 6 the next morning.

For several hours our numbers grew. We had been sealed off—which is to say that the thousands down below now had a goal. We saw strange arrivals—grinning, elated youths wiping tears from their eyes and coughing. They had run the lines of troops, God knows how. Some had climbed rope ladders improvised from barricades. Others had literally hurled themselves into our midst—for a section of high wall had been left unguarded. Helicopters chattered overhead. The windows of the Pentagon were crowded with faces and the roof was thronged with blue and khaki brass interspersed with troops, rifles at the ready. Above it all was a dazzlingly lovely Indian summer day.

Wooden with Embarrassment

While daylight lasted, I looked as closely as I could at the soldiers in front of us. Many were Negro; almost all were young. These were not violent faces, but those of boys from small towns and city slums, many with an unfinished, hangdog look of profound uncertainty in the conduct of life. Their cheeks and jaws were wooden with embarrassment, Their eyes flitted here and there, some with hungry surprise, others with a kind of wide-eyed fearfulness, drinking in the age-mate faces of those who sat before them. (Toward the left of the front line a large soldier eyed us narrowly, his lips drawn upward in the fixed smile of self-conceit. I pointed him out to a friend. It was this soldier who, five hours later, began crushing the heads of seated demonstrators with his rifle butt, spreading his rage and panic to five or six soldiers who stood near him.)

Whereas the soldiers, taken in the mass, were much as I have described them (and in some cases were touchingly open to what transpired), their sergeants and officers tended to have closed faces and guarded eyes. We became acutely aware that night of the meaning of faces. The marshals' were the worst, and it was only they, as a group, who kept up a tactic of violence and provocation. Most of their arrests, especially after nightfall, were made brutally. It is worth mentioning here that sometimes a stereotype is accurately diagnostic. Men are various in health. They resemble each other in disease. "The face of a cop," in short, is the name of a disease, a particular kind of human collapse.

It would be interesting to draw out the political meaning of faces and bodies. When lives are coerced and thought is rendered valueless, these facts show in the face. Self-conflict is a political-moral fact. Self-contempt is ugly. Chronic anger is ugly. Stupidity shows in the face as a form of fear; it is ugly. Envy, resentment, complacency—all these feelings, under certain conditions, become chronic; they are fixed in the face as if by molds, and at this point they must be taken seriously. Social criticism, in one of its deepest aspects, is nothing but the criticism of the ugliness of Americans.

I say all this in order to make clear why I was so deeply moved by the beauty of the young faces all around me. They were, of course, vivified by the integrative and liberating action at hand. But more than this, they were simply beautiful. It was the ordinary beauty of man—so rare: the beauty of intelligence, of natural pride. For my own part, I know that this beauty was the deepest of the many meanings of the event. Perhaps if I describe here certain characteristic deformities of Americans, the political content of this statement will be clear. I have in mind Camus' statement that a man is responsible for his face.

Tribute to Vanished Patriarchs

But let me put it in terms of youth's own rebellion against the prevailing norms of individual life, for the long hair and the beards of many collegians are first a refusal to be the shorn and colorless Duplicate Man of the business world, who attests in every gesture and by dress that no imperative—be it moral, religious, intellectual or sexual—will interfere with his employer's demands. The beard is a tribute to vanished patriarchs and it means, "You must take my manhood into account," just as the long hair, in the mechanical landscapes of our cities, announces, in the form of loyalty, the animality of the human animal. No one who has heard the angry complaints of parents and authorities doubts for a moment their jealousy and shame. Nor is their own suffering a small matter, for they have already paid the price these young have refused.

The issue at stake is that of coercion. "You must knuckle under. You must conform." It appears in a thousand guises, in our schools, on our cop-ridden streets, in our mental wards, our tormented nighttimes, the dead-level drone of restaurants filled with businessmen. There is no sadder sight—and it is brought to an essence in the cities of New Jersey—than the little crowds of adolescents slouching down the streets, ward heelers at 16. With hulking shoulders, drooping heads and wise-guy smiles they express the most craven self-contempt and contempt for each other in every second word. They are not unusual in this country of ours, but surely they would look strange in a truly democratic land.

It is an extraordinary thing that in the midst of this rot our present generation of radical young should have emerged. They are their own men. They have not

knuckled under, nor will they. Their self-respect, their love for and admiration of each other, their moral courage and independent thought, their sense of a world to be gained—all this is like a burst of sunlight after the longest, longest fog.

It is not easy to imagine sweeping changes based only on resentment, or on the insights of sociology, however true. But to see young men who are patently free men demanding a world for their manhood—this is truly a different matter. At the Pentagon they were faced by the very image of man at his worst, all thought and feeling submerged in the uniform and reduced to robot response. Yet the long hours of the confrontation salvaged the soldiers' faces. The demonstrators spoke to them as men, and were acutely aware of the individual's plight. "We're not against the *soldiers!* We're against the *war!*" This was the first of many chants intended to clarify the confrontation.

The Hippie Face

Let me say a word here about the few hippies who were present among us. I have always taken their bizarre dress as a kind of confession that they have no world to live in. I think that in the crowd assembled before the troops—it was mostly collegian, yet people of all ages and of many different styles of life were present—the hippies glimpsed a world more vigorous and communal than the world they had rejected. One striking thing about the hippie face is that though it is sorrowing and sometimes apathetic, it is not corrupted —it has none of the lines of bitterness, self-contempt and impotent resentment that characterize so many American faces. The hippies, on this night, had the radiance of helpful children. I realized, looking at them, that one of the great energies of youth is the energy of love. Youth is unaware of it, except in the form of the absolute attractiveness of the world. When this attractiveness is destroyed, the energy of love is balked. In short, I understand that the hippie mystique of love, though it has never described their lives, has indeed indicated this crucial frustration of energy. Above all, it has described their yearning.

By nightfall our numbers had decreased to four or five hundred. Apparently the numbers had similarly shrunk on the steps and in the Mall. As it grew dark we began to understand the significance of the absence of live TV. It meant that in the event of violence by the troops or marshals no fear of public exposure would serve as restraint. The film tapes would be edited—as indeed they have been edited—very likely by the same powers who persuaded the networks to omit live coverage, who gave the figure of 55,000 to the press and who denied the use of tear gas and the defection of troops.

We had been sitting for hours. As people rose and departed, we closed our ranks. Two bull horns had been carried through to us and they were used by many different persons. The presence of the troops, the guns leveled at our heads, the youths among us who had been tear-gassed or clubbed, the report of a bayoneting, the repeated voice of an officer on the military bull horn, "Company B hold your line. Nobody comes, nobody goes"—all this was more than enough to dispel the usual mists of political debate. When a speaker blundered into the self-indulgent phrases of speechifying, he was met instantly by choruses of "No, no." Just

the one word, but in such a tone as to convey: Surely you see that we don't need it? (with the not-astonishing result that the speaker did see and dropped his harangue without trying to justify himself or feeling it necessary to apologize). When unlikely tactics were suggested, the chorus of "No, no" again righted the course and alternate proposals were shouted from the assembly.

An astonishing number of decisions were made in quick order, not without debate, but with debate laid bare to the bone. Finally the bull horn was used almost entirely for announcements: Tear gas had been used and there was an explanation of what to do against it. "We need volunteers to get water. Rags can be made out of skivvy shirts." Similar announcements had been made in the Mall, and soon plastic bags appeared among us filled with wet socks and handkerchiefs. Plastic jugs of water passed from hand to hand, and all through the group bare-torsoed men ripped skivvy shirts to rags and handed them out. "The people down below are rounding up food. We'll get cigarettes, too, but we need some money." Volunteers stood up and collected it, and soon, out of the dark of affluent America, appeared the first

"You wouldn't really shoot me, would you?"

wave of "food": potato chips, pretzels, cookies. They had been handed to our runners through the windows of buses, the residue of the picnic atmosphere of the early afternoon. More substantial items came later—apples and cold cuts, and cigarettes in quantity, so that one heard voices announcing the brands and other voices, "Do you have a menthol?"

One of the loveliest things about these early hours in the dark was that all these voices were inquiring after needs and trying to meet them. Several of the youths who spoke briefly at the bull horn wanted only to say, in emotional voices, that we were a community and would always remain one. As we lit our cigarettes and chewed apples, leaning against each other, voices called out, "Let the troops relax! Give the troops a smoke!" There were cheers of approval, for the hapless troops were still standing as before, some with rifles aimed at our heads, others holding them erect.

Unguarded Bushes

It grew colder as the hours lengthened, and we realized that the lack of toilets would be a problem. This too was discussed on the bull horn and occasioned much laughter. "If we stay here much longer, we'll be the first organized shit-in in the history of the movement. [uproar] But here's the Pentagon. Who else has had a chance to both literally and symbolically piss on war [uproar]?" Some of the troops were smiling, and a girl took the occasion to look up at the man who held his rifle just above her eyes. "You wouldn't really shoot me, would you?" His poker face broke into a grin and he shook his head. "Seriously," said our bull horn, "our problem is not the lack of toilets. Our problem is modesty. It'll probably make things easier if we go in groups. There are some bushes just to my right. They are unguarded [laughter]."

Another, smaller group had established themselves beyond a line of troops to our right. It was they who sang "Yellow Submarine." We kept hearing news of them and of other events: ". . . a soldier just passed out cigarettes to three demonstrators down in the Mall and said 'Keep up the good work.'" This was greeted by cheers, which suddenly—as if at a signal, but none had been given—turned into a prolonged and urgent chant of "Join us! Join us!" In the brief silence that followed, the strained, high-pitched voice of a girl could be heard, "We are brothers and sisters!" And again, absolutely spontaneously, a great chant, "We love you! We love you! We love you!" It is impossible to convey the sound of this chant to those who did not hear it. By sound I mean its real meaning. It was not a tactical maneuver. The time for such things had long since

passed. Nor were these words addressed to the troops, as such, and certainly not to individual personalities. Our sense of ourselves as a community—the community that could be, the one we felt *had* to be (and a deeply American one, at that)—was acute. And there before us—one would say in panic might—was the vast engine that is in fact destroying the modern world.

Just as we were aware of ourselves, and of the beliefs that held us together, we were aware of the soldiers in their individual uncertainty, their lack of human force. They had been pushed from behind by U.S. Marshals so as to collide with seated demonstrators. They had been told we were Reds and Traitors and Drug Addicts—and now one could see the hungry surprise on their faces as they listened to these youthful voices that spoke so well and struck so many notes of awareness, compassion and determination. Frozen in grotesque postures of threat, they had listened to this free-flowing spirit. It was clear to us that we had broken into their lives—not past barricades of wood and rope, but of Army brainwashing and the drizzle of the press; and we had forced upon them a shaking dose of reality. It was this that held some of them at the edge of panic.

In short, our chant of "We love you! We love you!" was addressed to the best instincts and perhaps in many cases to the relinquished hopes of the men who appeared before us in a condition that can only be described as the abandonment or betrayal of their humanity. The change conveyed that the community we felt alive among us was not such as to abandon the individual soul, but to nurture it. When the bull horn announced the first of two troop defections (I have spoken with eyewitnesses of both), our response was jubilant. It did not occur to us how fearfully those soldiers would be punished. We were aware only that they had done the profoundly human thing we all desired. We were cheering with wide-open throats, and against the roar came the barely audible sound of a meager voice, "Company B hold your line. Hold your line."

. . . suddenly The Star-Spangled Banner swelled from our throats. It was our song. It expressed us.

However, at no time—not even when the beatings occurred—did we feel that we had been transported to Nazi Germany. It was too obvious that the violence was isolated, which is to say that it was not supported by a normative mythology. On the contrary, many troops were shocked by what they saw. There was nothing in their view of life, or in their understanding of duty, which justified the smashing of rifle butts into the faces of seated youths and girls. They were affected by the horror we all felt, one part of which was due to the fact that no one could prevent what almost all detested.

Looking back on the event, there are many things that seem extraordinary, though it is not difficult to see how they came about. Every speaker at our bull horn, after the assault I have described, addressed himself to the immediate moral reality. Some few of us had literally lost sight of things; we had ceased to see faces and had given way to blind hatred of Military Force. But the faces in front of us were not Military Force. Troops had turned away in disgust and pain; some were seen in tears. These reactions were described on our bull horn; they were the human facts of the occasion. The words on the bull horn, in the ears of the troops, meant that we recognized their distress—for certainly there were many who had come to see that the guns they held were profoundly impotent in the true affairs of life. The human force lay with us. We had, and they had not. We gave, and they received. I am not speaking here of self-awareness, but of overflow.

Love of Country

We had tried, earlier in the evening, to sing. "America the Beautiful" fell flat, as it always does. "We Shall Overcome" has grown old, and in any event it is a kind of lullaby, very moving when sung in the mass—but it could not have expressed us. We gave up singing—or at least we did until suddenly *The Star-Spangled Banner* swelled from our throats. I had never sung it before without some twinge of resentment at the hoked-up circumstances. Here we sang it wide-open, high notes and all. It was our song. It expressed us. Our country had come alive among us—not the New Frontier or the wretched Great Society (the Great Society stood facing us, and it was not singing)—but our country, just like that. (It occurs to me that you have to be in foreign lands to feel this bone-deep love of country and we were, of course, in foreign lands, for the capital is not any country at all, but an ugly wasteland of Office, habitat of Careers and Guided Tours.)

Paddy wagons had moved up the opposite ramp and arrests were being made in the small group to our right. Our bull horn kept us informed. "They're picking them off one by one." The technique was as follows: the marshals stood behind the troops and shoved them against the demonstrators, then burst through the line and struck a few blows at a demonstrator and dragged him back through the line. Some soldiers obliged the marshals by pushing ahead with their feet. "He's sitting on your foot, huh?"

We no longer thought of sleeping. It was very cold. Bonfires had been lit, fed alike by shattered barricades and placards urging peace. There was another assault. A girl had made unkind remarks to the soldier standing by her. A marshal broke through the line and began beating her with his club—a wanton, vicious, absolutely senseless act. The youths beside her tried to pull her out of reach and they too were beaten. The marshal was photographed in action, and several who stood nearby identified him as the same man who that afternoon had dragged a youth off a flat-bed truck and beaten him unconscious. The youth had been hospitalized and reportedly lay in a coma for four hours.

Gary Rader addressed the troops, standing a few feet from their front line and speaking into the bull horn. The officer in charge tried to drown him out and for a few minutes we heard an overlay that sounded like this:

My name is Gary Rader, I'm twenty-three years Company B hold your line. Nobody comes, nobody goes. I was in the Special Forces Reserve Company B hold your line and I quit and I want nobody comes nobody goes I want to tell you what led me up to that Company hold your line what led me up to that decision nobody comes nobody goes we will be heard. . . .

Teach-In for the Troops

And Rader was heard, for the officer realized that he was shaming his men by plugging their ears in public. He must have guessed, too, what detestation they felt for him. He fell silent and Rader continued speaking, carrying the teach-in to the troops themselves. It was a beautiful occasion and a rare one, for the troops had no choice but to listen—and some at least had long since been softened by the youthful voices, the beards, the lack of beards, the long hair, the short hair, the silky legs, the courage and the communal generosity of the Traitors, Reds and Drug Addicts assembled before them. Rader spoke in a forthright way, without condescension or moral superiority, telling of his own enlightenment, the history of Vietnam and the lies our

government has addressed to its people. He described the experiences of Sergeant Donald Duncan and told how he himself, at Ft. Bragg, had talked with returning Special Forces on leave from Vietnam. Those were not men who needed to believe in the war. They described our blunders, our destruction of civil life, the corruption of Saigon, the hatred the Vietnamese feel for us. It made no difference; they were going back. It had made a difference, however, to Rader. He had become hungry to know, and now he described his efforts to find out. For many of the troops who heard him, this was the first real news of the war.

From time to time, Rader was interrupted by descriptions of arrests. Soon only a few remained in the group to our right. They made the mistake of locking arms and were badly beaten. Our bull horn announced that none were left. The paddy wagons were moving away and so were troops.

It was about 1 in the morning. There were some three hundred people left, many of them conferring in little groups. My friends and I—two women and a man—decided to wait until the last moment and then, if we could, walk out so as to avoid the marshals' clubs. Two paddy wagons appeared on our ramp, preceded by an ambulance. As they reached the edge of our group we stood up and left, followed by some few others.

As things turned out, however, this had not been the last moment. An official from the Justice Department arrived on the scene from Occoquan. There had been too many arrests—some seven hundred. No more were made. The sit-in continued until 6 in the morning, when almost everyone left. The small group then remaining, led by Gary Rader, was apparently forced back to the head of the stairway covered by the permit. Reinforcements arrived at daybreak and it was here that Sunday's sit-in took place.

The response of the press has been shameful, as if dealing instinctively with the revolt of its own captive audience. The protest, one would think, was small, shaggy and irresponsible. In fact, I have never seen so many middle-class faces at a protest in Washington. Certainly we were unruly; that is, we were determined to cross the line drawn by illegitimate authority. That done, the protest was almost classically nonviolent.

II

The concept of "symbolic resistance" that some activists are criticizing while endorsing "real acts of deterrence" seems to me pretty much of a straw man. The so-called acts of symbolic resistance are not initiated by tactical considerations, and no one should know this better than these youths. Neither do they simply "bear witness." They are acts of necessity.

The Body Politic

Once the resistance is in the realm of force, it is nothing. But if the physical force is on the other side, the authority—historical, psychological, philosophical, religious, moral, constitutional—is on ours. If we have taken a radical stand—relative to the masses of the middle class—we are nevertheless joined to these masses by the power of this authority. Rather, they are joined to us whether they like it or not. This is the meaning of the "body politic." It is not simply masses of people and it is not much sounded by the interviewers of the Gallup Poll. It is touched when Hershey opens his wretched mouth and every lawyer in the country sits up with a jolt at the violation of our basic rights. These lawyers don't have to agree with us, but they *have* to say, "It's illegal!" And they do say it. The masses of Americans have no conception of freedom, but the body politic is touched again when there is evidence of official violence. It is true, alas, that their noses must very nearly be rubbed in it, but when the chips are down they cannot restrain themselves from saying, "It isn't *right*." And they are not talking about fair play: they mean that we elect our officials and they cannot do this to us.

Obviously it is essential for the resistance to maintain its authority. This does not mean placating the middle class. It means asserting the authority precisely *as* authority and not as something else. I am not speaking here against Provo tactics. They are the stuff of life—witty, daring and not inherently violent. They are not enough in themselves, but they are a kind of super-rational filigree this world would be sad without. They must be added to the action that comes out of the true necessity.

But then what is that necessity? What is the real force that makes us take part in demonstrations, draft refusals and the like? No one went to the Pentagon *in order* to stop the war in Vietnam, for no one believed that as a result of that action the war would stop. We might say that we went there so as to add to a series of events which if carried far enough would stop the war. This would at least describe some kind of faith and hope and —more important—tell us that our sense of the true necessity is a sense of a continuing cause. But still, this adding to the series is not the push itself; it is not what one feels but only what one agrees to and formulates. I think the real push, the true proximate cause is this (and it will sound odd for a moment): that one goes *in order* not to have not gone. All other feelings—anger, enthusiasm, resentment—are so much lace; they are not answered by the event and did not cause it. This means that a compelling imperative inhered in the event, that we had to accept it in order to remain whole and that the self-damage of refusing is precisely the damage of fragmentation: one is diminished and so is one's world. One is diminished not only by loss of self but also by loss of others, the very ones one admires. These are the features of moral decision.

Remaining Whole

Remaining whole means, in short, that we take our stand in what we know to be the world that is essential to our life. It is not that our actions are in themselves world-building or world-preserving (that always remains to be seen) but that we cannot refrain from acting to build and preserve our necessary world. This is the felt push and the actions I have called essential are those that proceed from it as closely as possible. Obviously they are not acts of violence. (Hitting cops with bricks is merely self-expression.) All Americans are entitled to feel resentment, anger and hatred—and some, perhaps, a great deal—but no one is entitled to present them as the wellspring of life or the rationale of action.

I began by saying that I was deeply moved by what I saw at the Pentagon. It comes down to this: the troops in front of us represented great force, but it was obvious that they were quite without power, for their force can only destroy. Power, however, was brimming in the faces and shining in the actions of those around me. I have tried to indicate its attributes but have come nowhere near doing so.

A loud *no* and a loud *yes* were spoken both together. The yes was the spirit exemplified by hundreds of actions—communal, vivacious, brave and beautifully rational. It may be too hopeful to say that this spirit is contagious, but there is evidence of contagion. It is evident that this spirit is involved with far deeper issues than the war.

The yes, in the form of yearning, has been lived in hippieland (and, in the form of apathy, so has the no). But the yearning yes is surely widespread and the no has been spoken on many occasions. I have never heard the two together so convincingly as here. The yearning vanished into affirmation. The no was an act of physical courage. These two together were the event. Such is the archetypal action from which the changes we desire might truly proceed.

What we experienced was, in miniature, the present situation of our country as a whole. Let me list some of the observations many have made of these events:

● Public opinion—and public *response*—was vitiated by premeditated government lies and the disgusting connivance of the press.

● All violence is individual. We could tell which soldiers would attack us. We could see that all the marshals would. Only certain kinds of people hire out for such work, yet as a nation we have found employment for many thousands of them. By and large, they are outside the law: police, Federal Bureau of Investigation, Central Intelligence Agency and now, increasingly, the Army. As organizations, these are such that downright psychotic behavior does not seem seriously inappropriate to their activities.

● All these persons—who in a nation's range of types are least to be admired—have been interposed as a barrier between the government and ourselves.

● No responsible official addressed us during the whole of the protest, though we were certainly petitioning the government.

● The force marshaled against us was so excessive as to be nightmarish—yet this nightmare is the daytime mood of Washington at present.

● It was at the same time evident—and this has been confirmed by the published statements of soldiers who took part—that the covering orders forbade violence. The many—but isolated—attacks by troops and the use of tear gas represented disobedience to orders, yet no attempts were made by officers in charge to prevent these occurrences or to cut them short. There is evidence that some were planned.

A Fascistic Assault

The overall situation, then, was this: At the heart of the "nonviolent" containment of our nonviolent demonstration was a fascistic assault on the rights of citizens. The violence was not the only manifestation of this; many persons became short-term political prisoners—that is, they were detained on buses and were given the choice of jail or the Union Station, in a clear-cut violation of constitutional rights. These aspects of the government action have been hidden from the public, as has the size of the protest and its middle-class character. Nothing is more characteristic of the Johnson administration than this combination of inward contempt for—and outward show of—democracy.

 **LIBERATION** Nov 1967

The first requirement of any institution should be that it function with reasonable effectiveness and equity; if it does not, it can hardly hope for and does not deserve allegiance and respect.

TOM WICKER in *The New York Times*, on the Postal Strike. The institution in this case is "the Government."

Political power often seems to lose its legitimacy when it is apparently at its very height. It is at the greatest extent and power of a regime, nation or empire that it often suddenly collapses through sheer loss of belief in it.

KENNETH BOULDING

OUR LITTLE ANARCHIST PARTY BY ONE OF THE OAKLAND 7

STOP-THE -DRAFT WEEK

By Frank Bardacke

Life begins on the other side of despair.
– Sartre

During the summer of nineteen hundred and sixty seven despair became a cliche among young white radicals. Many of us in Berkeley talked incessantly about political impotence. We were enthralled by apocalyptic novels like *The Crying of Lot 49* and *Cat's Cradle.* The New Left looked sick and few disagreed with those who reported that it was near death. Andrew Kopkind said it for us all when he began an article in the *New York Review of Books* with the laconic sentence: "To be white and a radical in America this summer is to see horror and feel impotence."

Anti-war activity seemed purposeless. Originally the anti-war demonstrators wanted to dramatize the existence of a sizeable minority who opposed the war, thereby stimulating a debate about it. And they were successful. The demonstrations revealed that the country was divided and public opposition to the war became respectable. But the demonstrations could achieve no more than that. The April 15th demonstration marked the end of these attempts to create dialogue. Fifty thousand people sitting in Kezar Stadium was all very nice, but it was not related to stopping the war. Persuasive arguments and massive marches did not affect the war makers. The early demonstrators spoke truth to power and the powerful moved on undaunted.

We might have been encouraged by the ghetto rebellions and the strength of the black power movement. Now black power advocates are demanding a different America, not just a part of the old one. That is a struggle for "black liberation." Sure, we all had fantasies of being part of a real revolutionary movement that week that we watched Detroit on television. But we knew that we had to watch it on television. The talk of running guns to the ghetto was the hopeful nonsense of young white men who could not admit that we actually had nothing to offer the people in Detroit.

But we still hoped to be comrades of those Negroes with whom we had some contact – the SNCC and CORE organizers.

So we picked up a cue here and there and started calling them blacks. But this linguistic trick did not help, and after the fiasco of the Chicago NCNP Conference we felt more white and more middle class (they almost mean the same thing in America) than ever.

Electoral politics could not bring us out of our funk. It is not only that many of us feel that it is an inappropriate response to the enormous disaster that is America. The question is how can one organize the heart of the American political ideology. Most Americans believe they are free simply because they have the right to vote and because they do not live under communism. By centering a movement around the ballot box radicals only reinforce Americans in their belief that they are free men. But voting is only an instrument of freedom when it is an integral part of a rich public life. Voting becomes important when a people form a participating community – a community for whom voting is only one of many public acts. Until such a community exists any group organized around the polling booth is prey to the worst kind of opportunists and charlatans. But perhaps Berkeley has become a participating community and therefore electoral politics is not premature. Unfortunately the evidence is not clear enough to save us from our despair.

Nor do the hippies give us any reason to rejoice. A movement that promised to offer a new style of life, a model for a counter community, seems to offer only confusion. Certainly they are experimenting and experimenters need time, but a walk through the Haight is not encouraging. The beautiful people look scared, lonely, and frantic – except when they dance to their music. The hippies have influenced the style of the New Left in this last couple of years, but they do not stand as a hopeful alternative that might succeed where more conventional politics fail.

It was a tough summer. A summer in which some of my friends started playing with guns as a way to forget their own hopelessness. Their rationale was identical to the familiar argument about passports. It is easy to get a passport (gun) now. But when you need a passport (gun) it may be difficult to obtain. So get one now. But the guns just depressed me. I know what a passport is for and I know exactly what I would do with it. But I can not imagine who the hell I would shoot or under what conditions I would be called upon to shoot anyone. The guns seem completely unrelated to our stiuation and therefore become supreme symbols of our desperation

Even worse were the constant discussions of sabotage. No party was complete without some conversation of how we would blow up this or that Well, maybe we should, but nobody who was talking about it was actually doing it or could even conceivably do it. The conversations were complete fantasy, and fantasy that was eloquent testimony to the fact that we had no idea of what to do with our lives.

To all this the decicated reader of *New Left Notes* has an inevitable response – community organize! It is one of those slogans that means nothing by itself and yet it is often used in the abstract to oppose "other" types of action. I have heard arguments about electoral politics versus community organizing, demonstrations versus community organizing, campus reform versus community organizing, and even anti-draft versus community organizing. When done in a certain way these kind of activities constitute community organizing, but independent of any of them community organizing is non-existent.

Berkeley radicals have been community organizing for over three years. But at the beginning of this academic year they felt that they had little to show for their efforts. They had not radically changed the University, the peace movement seemed to be in a shambles, and although the community had all the right sentiments they appeared to be turned off politics. From this point of view Chancellor Heyns' boast that the campus was calm and quiet seemed all too true. We feared for the movement, and we looked around unsure of each other and ourselves.

But some continued to work, seeking a new direction for their amazingly resilient radical energies. Their work focused on the draft. It was a logical choice. Most of the participants in the anti-war demonstrations were of draft age, and the war touches them directly through the Selective Service System. Also the draft is a perfect symbol of coercive society. The United States would have great difficulty waging the war if it did not have the machinery to force young men into the armed services.

The Bay Area developed three strategies of draft resistance – the anti-draft union, the new "militant" demonstration, and the Resistance. The strategy of the anti-draft unions is to organize young men of draft age, in the hope that as union members they will support each other in their determination to resist the draft. They attempted to rally support by leafleting the induction center and holding demonstrations whenever one of their members was called for a physical. Most of the members of these unions (about five or six have been established in the Bay Area) are college students protected by their 2-S status. Now these unions are making serious attempts to recruit and agitate among high school students and others who are particularly vulnerable to the draft. Much of the work of these anti-draft unions involves straightforward draft counselling – talking to people who wander into Berkeley hoping to find some help in beating the draft. A draft counsellor from the Berkeley anti-draft union has office hours at the Free University of Berkeley twice a week. Attendance is high.

These anti-draft unions face a nearly impossible task. Most young men who are drafted into the army go not because of secondary sociological pressures. They go not because their family wants them to go, or because it is generally popular to go. They go because the alternative to induction is jail. And for most of them jail is unthinkable. But the anti-draft unions do not have anything else to offer them on a mass basis (except Canada). They can help a few people get out on 1-Y's or as conscientious objectors, but if masses of people were to try this, the Selective Service system would change its policy. Very quickly the anti-draft unions come up against an uncomfortable truth about opposition politics. Once you lose faith in the changing society through discussion and discourse your politics must offer people an alternative way to live. You must not only offer a new way of life but the resources to sustain people in that new style. But the Left can do neither. We have no alternative to offer America and we can not even protect young men who would resist the draft. The choice is just as the powerful want it to be — induction or jail. The Left has not changed the terms of that choice.

Many people who were involved in these anti-draft unions started thinking about a new kind of demonstration. They talked of a militant demonstration that would show the strength and the seriousness of the anti-draft movement and thereby encourage young men to resist the draft. A steering committee was put together and Stop the Draft Week was announced. The steering committee was a combination of old and new faces. The old faces were Steve Hamilton and Mike Smith, two Berkeley activists who had been expelled from school during an abortive free speech fight (PROC) and had thus been turned into full time activists. Although they had been kicked out of school they continued to live in Berkeley and stayed in the student community. They are Berkeley students and everyone recognizes them as such. They, along with some other Berkeley students (of the SDS variety) joined with some white northern SNCC workers including Terry Cannon. Most of these people lived in San Francisco and shared the same general culture as the Berkeley students but they were not completely familiar with all the forms that the Berkeley movement had developed in the past three years. This proved troublesome during Stop the Draft Week itself, but during the summer organization it was probably beneficial. Led by Cannon the steering committee demanded that the movement create a new kind of militant demonstration.

But how was the demonstration to be new and militant? The leaders did not publicly commit themselves to non-violence before the demonstration. This provoked considerable controversy but it was not really all that new. Earlier anti-war demonstrators were not all pacifists; only a small minority were. When police attacked individuals in earlier demonstrations, they generally protected themselves. The steering committee was only making an unofficial policy official by announcing that the

demonstrators would be free to defend themselves. This "threat" of self defense became important only when combined with the general strategy of the demonstration. Stop the Draft Week intended to shut down the induction center without involving people in a sit-in followed by mass arrests. When that plan was combined with the declaration that the demonstrators would defend themselves it was clear that some people (perhaps thousands) would spend the week fighting the police.

This is not the way to create dialogue. This demonstration, unlike most of the ones that preceeded it, did not aim at provoking discussion about a war among the white middle class. Rather, the leaders saw themselves as demonstrating to young blacks and young workers (they actually used that word) that the white anti-draft movement was serious and strong. Such a demonstration would encourage them to resist the draft and to refuse to fight. In short, the leaders saw the demonstration as an organizing tool for something like lower class anti-draft unions.

The meaning of militancy had changed. Earlier demonstrations centered on the rally — the success of the demonstration depended upon articulate spokesmen. Activists were primarily concerned with the "political line" of the speakers and the "demands" of the demonstration. To fight for a "militant" demonstration meant to fight for a radical speakers list and for a policy of immediate withdrawal. Now no one was sure what militancy meant. Were you militant if you were more violent? Were you more militant if you managed to shut down the induction center for a long period of time? And what was the relationship between militance and ending the war?

These questions were left unanswered while the steering committee and a group of prospective monitors started discussing tactics. Stop the Draft Week had announced that the Oakland Induction Center would be closed for one week. They distributed a poster which proclaimed that "by our decree there will be a draft holiday." Publicly they talked big, but the conversations at the monitors' meetings were hardly confident. The steering committee had no real plan for closing down the Induction Center. Many had been through the October 15 march on the Oakland Army Terminal two years before. They now relied on the hypothesis that we would have evaded the Oakland Police line by the simple maneuver of turning left on Shattuck Avenue. They talked of mobility and of outflanking the police. People even talked about something called "the French Plan" (because it is used by French student demonstrators) where students turn over cars and force police to break their ranks. Everyone laughed at such a suggestion. Nor was any plan taken seriously. People were quick to see that the Center probably would not be closed and they urged the leaders to think of alternative targets. Others complained that the leadership had

been irresponsible in announcing that the Center would be closed when they had no real strategy in mind. People were afraid that the demonstration would be disastrous. We would learn only one thing — that we are powerless to stop the draft.

But the leadership (especially the San Francisco SNCC group) stuck by their rhetoric and continued to claim that they would close the Induction Center. Their idea of the demonstration seems to be modeled after a black street rebellion where medium sized groups of angry young men who are willing to take risks can elude the cops and obtain their objective. They did not know how this would be done, but they were sure that when the time came people would discover how to do it in the streets.

While all this frantic planning was going on the men of the Resistance (as they liked to be called) were calmly organizing their troops. The resistance had its own strategy of anti-draft work, although they might disavow anything so dispassionate as a strategy. They argued their case in a straightforward leaflet:

"The Resistance is a group of young men committed to a stance of complete noncooperation with military conscription. On October 16 members of the Resistance around the country will be publicly returning their draft cards to the government. We will not accept any classification, any deferment, any orders from selective Service. From that day on, we will follow a course of continual confrontation with the draft. To resist faces each of us with the possibility of five years in federal prison. Such is the threat to which we refuse to submit. Whatever plans for prosecution the government attempts to use against us will be used to further resistance. If we are to be imprisoned, we will build until the day of our imprisonment. We are a community united by a feeling about our lives and for what ends our lives must be led. We will act as a community, continually growing, continually facing military conscription as a body rather than as isolated individuals. Join us."

Although most of the Left admired the passion and eloquence of the Resistance leaders they disapproved of burning and turning in draft cards as an anti-draft tactic. They claimed that the Resistance was moving back to a position of apolitical moral witness and they demanded to know what was the political purpose of spending five years in jail.

Never has the Left so thoroughly missed the point. The Resistance made Stop the Draft Week possible. Young men burning their draft cards on Sproul Hall steps changed the political mood of the campus. This example and that of the hundreds who turned in their draft cards gave the rest of us courage. Just as Stop the Draft Week was supposed to strengthen those who might say "no" to the draft, the resistance strengthened the students who participated in Stop the Draft Week. They taught us that anti-draft work is serious, and that a man can not work against the draft without taking risks. They risked five years in jail and therefore we were able to risk being beaten up or arrested.

The men of the Resistance also taught us something about freedom. The biggest obstacle to draft resistance is that the alternative to the draft is jail. The Resistance overcame this obstacle by stating their willingness to go to jail. Lenny Heller put it bluntly: "you have got to give up the idea that they are never going to catch you. They may catch you. Make up your mind about that — and then forget it." They refused to let the threat of a five year jail sentence inhibit their anti-draft work. Once they had turned in their draft cards they could act as free men ready to accept the private consequences of their acts. These free men spoke to us in a way that the SDS rhetoric of the official leaders never had. Those draft cards that burned in front of the police lines on Tuesday and Friday made everything else possible.

Stop the Draft Week changed the movement. We did not do anything as grand as "move from dissent to resistance," as some leaders claimed. But we went through a change — we became a more serious and more radical movement. Two of my friends explained this change to me by suggesting that I look at the demonstrators as Negroes and see Stop the Draft Week as a telescoped version of the Civil Rights Movement. On Monday we were the lunch counter sit-ins — sincere, idealistic, hoping that through an act of impersonal courage and moral strength we could change a social system. On Tuesday we became the Selma marchers receiving sympathy from a citizenry outraged by the brutal tactics of the police. But on Friday we experienced something like Detroit as we felt the anarchistic joy of "rioters" and as responsible American berated us for "hurting our own cause."

It is a nice analogy. But it gives us a false importance and it leaves out too much that is different about our movement of white middle class radicals. For most of us the week began on Tuesday morning. We went into that morning knowing that the leadership had been boasting about our power for over a month and that they had confidently declared we were going to close down the Induction Center. Early that morning we matched our power with that of the police. We were routed. The work of the induction center was only slightly disturbed and the new militant demonstration had clearly failed. Its only achievement was that we received some hard earned sympathy from people who were concerned about our cracked heads.

Tuesday afternoon and evening the leadership seemed unable to pull itself or its mass constituency back together. The leaders were unable to run a coherent rally. The speeches alternated between injured cries of police brutality and hollow declarations of power. The steering committees failed to offer any proposal about what we should do next. After a long, chaotic and

dispirited rally Tuesday night the crowd decided to go back on Wednesday for peaceful picketing.

After being burned in our "new kind of militant demonstration" we decided to try the old kind of demonstration. On Wednesday we talked casually in peaceful picket lines and polite sit-ins. Everything was pleasant until those busses came. The busses stopped in front of the door and some very young boys trotted from them into the Induction Center. None of them swaggered; they all looked scared. Almost all of them would rather have been protesting than going into the army. That ten or fifteen-minute peaceful scene taught us about the essential violence of the draft. Those young men went into that Induction Center because the only alternative was the violence of jail. Our demonstration had been completely inappropriate. In the face of that violence all we could do was shout, "Don't go." We had demoralized ourselves by organizing large groups of people to stand by and watch the horror that is an Army Induction Center. As we left Wednesday we knew that if peaceful picketing was all we could do, mass demonstrations were over.

After this disastrous peaceful picketing many people felt that we should try again to shut down the induction center. The steering committee agreed and pulled itself together. On Thursday they ran an excellent rally (the first of the week) and began to speak sense to their constituency. Rather than bragging about our power they talked about the ambiguities of the situation. They admitted that we might fail to close the induction center. In our failure, however, we would demonstrate that the government had to use full police power against its own people in order to wage the Vietnam war. Nobody tried to kid us into thinking that we were going to physically stop the war effort. But to have a successful demonstration we had to make a serious attempt to stop the induction process. We learned on Wednesday that legal picketing of the draft center or even peaceful sit-ins did not constitute a serious attempt to shut it down and only exposed our impotence.

It is difficult to write about Friday. After the opening moves by the Oakland police the demonstration was broken up into about seven or eight separate groups and no one knows what went on in all of these. But a definite mood prevailed throughout the demonstration and I can write about the particular things I saw. The most important thing about Friday is that we gained confidence in ourselves. In the face of the police we kept our cool, few people were injured, few were arrested. And the fact that the police recognized the risks we were taking made it possible for us to talk to them. We did not call them fascist beasts or the other familiar epithets used in more "peaceful" sit-ins. We were able to talk to them about the war, their jobs, and the country. In one instance where we faced a line of Highway Patrol-

men for about 45 minutes we came close to politically neutralizing the police line. No policeman actually broke ranks, but they were visibly shaken by listening to us and they did not use their clubs when they were ordered to advance. Political neutralization of the police is the dream of all student revolutionaries who know that the classic sign of the revolution is that the police refuse to interfere with the masses in the streets. This one experience does not indicate that the revolution (whatever the hell it is) is around the corner; it only suggests that a change in police attitude was made possible by the obvious horror of the war and the impression made by our physical courage.

As all the police were being used to keep us away from the Induction Center we had free-play in downtown Oakland. A month before when someone suggested turning over cars we laughed. But on Tuesday some people blocked intersections with their bodies, and on Friday we created barricades out of cars and other available material. (The leaders had been right — we did learn something in the streets.) The barricades were supposed to prevent the busses loaded with inductees from reaching the Induction Center by stopping traffic in downtown Oakland. But they also made Oakland feel for just one day a different style and approach to the sacred symbols of modern America. We painted downtown Oakland with our anti-war slogans showing people that in some cases political slogans are important enough to be written on the walls and windows of public and private buildings. We painted over the glass windows on parking meters delighted with the silly moral dilemma that the police would face the next day of whether to ticket no one or everyone. We treated the private car — that crucial part of the American dream — as material for our barricades. We blocked traffic and changed the streets from thoroughfares of business into a place for people to walk, talk, argue, and even dance. We felt liberated and we called our barricaded streets liberated territory.

We did not loot or shoot. But in our own way we said to America that at this moment in history we do not recognize the legitimacy of American political authority. Our little anarchist party was meant to convey the most political of messages: we consider ourselves political outlaws. The American government has the power to force us to submit but we no longer believe that it has the authority to compel us to obey.

Americans did not understand our message. They called us vandals and said the demonstration was chaos. But this reaction is inevitable. What matters is that *we* understand the meaning of our act. And if we can actually convince them that we can cause chaos in this country as long as the war continues, so much the better. We may have even stumbled on a strategy that could end the war.

But maybe we have only moved one

step closer to the concentration camps. If we succeed in organizing something like Stop the Draft Week again, the Government will begin to consider organizing a Stop the Left Week. But that is a risk we have to take. There is no going back to April 15th. Once you have gone through Detroit you do not go back to Selma.

Last year at this time we were singing "Yellow Submarine." Now we are singing "Alice's Restaurant." The difference is subtle but real. The Yellow Submarine celebrated our feeling of community. Ringo Starr sat in a yellow submarine in the middle of the ocean surrounded by his friends. This is an attractive fantasy to those who have suffered a defeat and who only want to defend themselves. But Alice's Restaurant is full of hopes. Arlo Guthrie beat the draft and he has written a song of resistance. His song is also a fantasy, but it is a fantasy about a movement — a successful movement.

Steps Free Univ. of Berkeley, Dec 1967

"That's the Oakland 7, Bill.

sandy darlington

The defense started this week. I thought that would be more interesting, or fun, or something. Our side, as it were. But no, it's worse.

Dr. Lawrence Rose, eye specialist: "...the sickening sound of a club hitting the human skull has to be heard to be believed; I cannot over-stress that."

Witness after witness described how the police systematically clubbed and Maced the demonstrators. That sentence is becoming quite familiar, isn't it?

When the police wedge started moving, people were still coming in the other end of the block. As the police started clubbing people, the people turned and tried to run, which squeezed them against those who were still coming in, to make for a massive crush. The front row of police were Macing everybody they could, and the rest of the police were beating people as they fell. People were knocked to the ground, blinded, they tried to crawl away, others tripped on the curbs or ran against parking meters as they tried to get away.

When the police wedge reached the doorway of the induction center, the left flank broke off and a semi-circle of police, 4-5 deep, surrounded the demonstrators who were sitting-in there and proceeded to beat them as they tried to crawl out. One little old lady testified that she deliberately sat in front to protect the young men because she knew from experience that "Police won't beat little old ladies." They didn't. They dragged her out of the way first.

As demonstrators did get out, they had to run along the wall and past the left side of the wedge, which had continued down the street. A dozen policemen waited in a double row along the wall and beat them systematically as they went through. One in particular used a very effective club jab to the stomach.

Family news: Many policemen brought their wives on Tuesday morning. The wives watched the festivities from various levels of the parking garage.

As the police started beating demonstrators in the doorway, a TV camera crew started filming them. Immediately several police descended on the camera crew and beat them. At that point, general police hysteria seemed to increase.

None of the police witnesses would say in court that he ever saw any policemen hit or Mace anyone. They always answer, "I don't recall" to those ques-

They're so young and hard."

tions. They are trained to do that. Their life motto should be: We are the Police, We don't recall.

Hodge: As the police began hitting people, did you hear any response from the other police in the parking garage?

Witness: Yes, a couple of cheers, like a football game.

Several members of the jury quickly looked away from the witness at that remark. It implies too much cruelty, I guess.

I watch the jury a lot. Number three wore groovy pants on Thursday. Is that a sign of hope for us? Number five has a nodding, waving acquaintance with the reporter from the Oakland Tribune.

The two main events being described over and over are the rally in Sproul Plaza on Monday night and the demonstration Tuesday morning. Witness after witness testify that yes they were at the rally but they don't really remember what

What does the jury think of that? It might sound suspicious to people who've never been to an open mike radical rally, where usually all is confusion, repetition, ego trips, leadership fantasies, and dull rhetoric. You go there almost by reflex, hang around, look around, dig the chicks, gossip, meet friends, deplore the speakers, go have coffee....Anybody who really pays attention must be either a fool or a police spy.

As for the demonstration, people were in a festive and keyed-up mood until the police violence started. Many had been up all night. People were singing, milling around, chanting. As the police line formed in the street, one kid danced around in front of them making spirit exorcism gestures and squirting shaving cream at them from a spray can.

People knew they'd be moved off, and probably arrested if they tried to sit in the doorway. But most didn't expect to be beaten up for demonstrating. We talk pretty cynical at times, but most of us truly expect to be treated like human beings, even by the police.

Jensen: Did you have anything in your hand as you crossed the street toward the police?

Witness: Only my girl friend's hand.

Lowell Jensen wants to show a neat Plan devised by Leaders and carried out by Followers. An anarchist organizational chart. It's a lie of course. But he doesn't know that. He's so hung up on neatness that he has to waste his life trying to prove that people plotted to do something that actually came quite naturally.

Jensen: Did Mike Smith or Bob Mandel tell you to go there?

Witness: No. If I'd seen them, I would have told THEM to show up.

If this Trial were fiction or movie, it could actually be the story of Lowell Jensen and how everyone and everything in it is trying to help him grow up, help him realize that the Law and Order that appears so flashy to his boy's mind is not the Justice a man must seek.

He will never learn that. In a way he's he's a tragic figure, a rational man who cannot see that he is only a tool in a great irrational conspiracy against life. Like Rommel.

But tragic heroes are really quite boring. This is a comic age. We want freedom.

Several witnesses later married the people they went to the rally with. That's become a standing joke in the Trial. It's part of something that nobody outside this movement seems to understand: A demonstration is not basically a protest against anything, it is a demonstration FOR something, it is a fertility ritual, an assertion of life that demands to live in spite of the concrete environment they are trying to force on us. Then the Law, which is on a Death Trip, comes out and beats people up and throws them in jail.

Meanwhile, the good citizens stay at home and mind their own business. They gave already, at the office. They are indifferent to all this. That is the real crime.

Jensen: You stood in the parking lot while the police wedge cleared the street as far as 16th. What did you do then?

Witness: I cried.

San Francisco
Express Times 3/11/69

THE ONLY WAY TO LIVE FRANK BARDACKE OF THE OAKLAND 7 TALKS ABOUT THEIR TRIAL

The Oakland 7

by Frank Bardacke

This is a story about the trial of the Oakland 7. It contains some hitherto unrevealed dirt, a few laughs, a smattering of politics, and a confession or two. I have been an Oakland 7 for some time now, and if you read on, you will learn a lot about me. But this is not a story of my life. Some things just don't belong in the newspapers.

Alameda County District Attorney J. Frank Coakley created the Oakland 7 a year and a half ago. He indicted seven leaders of October 1967's Stop the Draft Week for conspiracy to commit three misdemeanors — resisting arrest, trespass, and creating a public nuisance. Conspiracy to commit a misdemeanor is a felony. It carries a three year prison term.

An American court of justice is a mysterious institution, perhaps impossible to understand. It is the enforcer of the State's rules; the place where a man comes up against "thou shalt not." We live under thousands, perhaps millions, of thou shalt nots. A few are reasonable rules that help us live together, like the laws against murder and drunk driving. But the vast majority are designed to serve, consolidate, and perpetuate power. That is the purpose of all the laws that make it illegal to rip off property, just as it is the purpose of the law that prohibits young men from interfering with the Selective Service System. If you fight people who have power, almost by definition, you will violate the law.

The Law, the Judge, the District Attorney, and the police (represented in the courtroom by the bailiffs) form an enormous protective association that has at its command the legal authority to take away part or all of a man's life. This protective agency of the State serves in the name of the people, and does protect some people — those with power and money.

All sorts of men serve in this giant organization. They are not all villainous men. Often they are just doing their duty as they see it, and they always believe that they are protecting all the people. No judge, no DA, no cop believes that he serves only the rich and the powerful.

Allow me to introduce the Honorable Judge George W.

Phillips, Assistant District Attorney Lowell Jensen, Special Assistant to the DA Chick Harrison, and bailiffs Sigler and Lindstrom.

Judge Phillips is a little man, barely over five feet tall, with only one finger on his right hand, and the face of a fat bird. Very much a liberal, he voted for Eugene McCarthy, is against the war, and was all smiles to the defendants. His liberalism is tempered by an enormous fear — a fear that befits a man of his size and deformity. He let prosecutor Jensen push him around, he let defense attorney Garry push him around. The only people he was not afraid of were his assigned inferiors: the court clerk, the court recorder, and the bailiffs. To them he was demanding and rude.

Whenever he made a decision he explained that he had no other choice. "I have to follow the law, and I don't like many of them any more than you do." When he said that he was looking down at his desk afraid to look up at the court. This pretense of simply following the rules is a favorite trick of petty bureaucrats. It helps Phillips soften the psychological damage caused by the clash between his nicy-nice liberalism and the reality of his role — punishing the victims of the State.

On the first morning of the trial we went into the Judge's chambers. A plush carpet, big, rather cluttered desk, and a TV set in the corner. It was not an extravagent office, but right there on the wall was the perfect symbol of this man George W. Phillips: a series of idealized photographs of very expensive racing yachts next to a photograph of poor Oakies. Phillips believes he can have it both ways. Lead a life of casual luxury and be a friend of the poor.

But he has a heavy conscience. He has to make countless decisions. Take our case. Basically sympathetic to the defense he had to be careful not to displease the District Attorney. "You see," he expained to anyone who would listen, "the DA might do to me what he is doing to Judge Avakian." Judge Avakian is another liberal whose decisions angered DA Coakley and now the DA challenges him every time a criminal case comes before his court. Avakian has probably presided over his last criminal case in Alameda County. Phillips does not want the same thing to happen to him.

Phillips knows well the basic calculus of the liberal: is it more important to do good here and now or should I save myself so I can do good later? Trapped into such a calculus by their very existence in ruling institutions, liberals live on — oppressing, exploiting, managing, and killing — sure that they are doing as much good as possible. This calculus could have been used by liberal guards at Nazi concentration camps. It will be used at the American ones.

Phillips used the liberal calculus perfectly in the trial of the Oakland 7. One of strongest legal arguments was that the charges against us represented selective prosecution. District Attorney Coakley had made the case for selective prosecution when he said, "Technically we could have indicted thousands, but we took the most militant leaders." California courts have recently ruled such political discrimination unconstitutional. But Phillips would not allow us even to introduce the question of selective prosecution. If he had, we would have put Coakley on the witness stand. Coakley surely would have punished Phillips for that.

But ultimately the threat of Coakley's reprisal was not as great as the threat to Phillips' own image of himself as a liberal. At the end of the trial, under the intense prodding of one of our attorneys, Mal Burnstein, Phillips went out of his way to give good instructions to the jury. Without those instructions we might not have been acquitted.

The one regret I have about our acquittal is how satisfied the Honorable Judge George W. Phillips must be with his perfect display of liberalism.

District Attorney Lowell Jensen is a man who deserves to be taken seriously. Here is a description of him taken from my notes early in the trial:

Jensen is a cop's lawyer. He stands 6'4" and is very much a big man. Dark scowl, might say he has a ruddy complexion, but to me it just looks like he had very bad acne as a kid. He is a brilliant no nonsense straight talking man. In court he is very economical with words, never saying more than necessary. He always starts with his strongest points and shows a very forceful logical mind. I often end up agreeing with him when there is a legal dispute between him and our lawyers. Very impatient with stupidity. He has great contempt for Garry's showmanship. Contempt is his emotion. His face is built for it. He rolls, raises, purses his lips — they seem to travel half way up his face — in a beautiful expression of total contempt when Phillips goes through his shuffle. His smile is somewhat similiar — just a slight protruding of the lips. He sits up straight, stands up straight, and has the tightest asshole west of the Rockies. He considers himself a liberal.

During the course of the trial I developed some affection for him. Outside the context of the law he is capable of decency, kindness, and genuine emotion. When Charlie Garry had a stomach seizure that we all were afraid was a heart attack, Lowell was one of the most concerned men in the courtroom. He walked around nervously, tried to call an ambulance, made Charlie sit down, and touched him affectionately. Jensen once accidently knocked down my son, who was playing behind a swinging door, and he was embarrassed and concerned. He laughs with shaking shoulders and a lot of teeth.

But within the context of the law, Lowell Jensen is capable of murder. He worked hard to send Huey Newton to the gas chamber and he stands behind the pigs who murdered Bobby Hutton.

While waiting for the verdict, I was reminded of the evil that Lowell Jensen has given his life to. Warren Wells, a Black Panther, who was involved in the Eldridge Cleaver-Bobby Hutton shoot-out, is in jail at the Alameda County Court House where our trial was held. His first trial ended in a hung jury (10-2 for acquittal) and the pigs are keeping him in jail until the new trial. For some reason the Alameda County Sheriffs threw Warren into solitary confinement in a strip cell. While he was waiting for our verdict to come in, Charlie went before a Superior Court Judge to get Warren out of that cell. He was opposed by Lowell Jensen.

The strip cell, which is located on the 10th floor directly over Judge Phillips' courtroom, is slightly over six feet long and 4½ feet wide. It has four concrete walls and one small window which is opened for only 15 minutes a day. There is no running water. A round hole in the floor, four inches in diameter, is supposed to take care of defecation and urination. But that is difficult to manage. The cell is not cleaned until the prisoner leaves and then it is not cleaned very well. The prisoner is stripped bare and put in the cell. All he gets is a peanut butter sandwich and a half quart of water three times a day. The cell also has a small blanket. Nothing else.

Lowell Jensen, an intelligent and in some respects decent man, found himself defending the existence of that hole and protecting the men who use it to destroy other men.

Lowell Jensen has given himself up to the law. That law is capable of leading him anywhere. But why such total devotion? To answer that we have to go back to Lowell's most obvious peculiararity — his obsessive neatness. Lowell Jensen is a very clean man. His notes are always well organized and filed smartly in large manila envelopes. He was disgusted at the end of a day if we recessed too early and lost even five minutes of court time. He brushed away invisible dirt from his desk throughout the trial. His cross-examination was detailed and meticulous to the edge of insanity.

Some will argue that all of this is due to unfortunate toilet training and has nothing to do with politics. Perhaps. I think it is at the very root of his politics and helps to understand his enslavement to the law. Lowell Jensen is

Governor Reagan

Chancellor Roger Heyns

Sheriff Frank I. Madigan

Photographs by Jeffrey Blankfort

terrified of confusion. He has organized his life so as to avoid chaos. The mere hint of a mess threatens to rip apart his careful organization. The law is a necessary system of rules that stands between society and anarchy. Any disrespect for the law, any slight weakening of it, will bring about total cataclysmic breakdown. The danger of living without law is so great, nothing but complete devotion to law will protect us. If we don't formally and rigidly organize ourselves there will be shit everywhere. Lenny Bruce had a routine about the law that went something like this. At first a bunch of people were just lying around being together. Then one man got up and threw some shit at somebody else. The other guy threw some shit back. Pretty soon everybody was throwing shit. And then they had to make rules about just when and where you could throw your shit.

Without sounding like a psychoanalytic nut, I would like to suggest that Lenny Bruce has given away the whole secret. The first experience a person has with the law is the rules of his toilet training. That training colors his attitude toward law for the rest of his life. The fear that without law there would be anarchy and chaos is rooted in the parents' fear that without rigid, inflexible rules the kid would shit all over the place.

If you want to understand why so many in our generation have a casual attitude toward law you must start with Dr. Spock's *Baby and Child Care*. One of the main purposes of the book was to relax parents and to break down the system of rigid, inflexible rules that dominated the child. It was a revolutionary book when it came out in the early 1940s, and it helped to raise a revolutionary generation. Those right wing nuts who blame everything on Spock are not far wrong.

As the clincher, think back to Warren Wells' strip cell. It is a detention cell for convicts. It provides discipline for people who are already being disciplined. And the primary horror of that cell is the tiny hole in the floor through which it is almost impossible to defecate or urinate. The appropriate punishment for the lawless man is to force him to live in his own shit.

Special Assistant to the D.A. Chick Harrison is my favorite cop. A big round man with a friendly baby face, part of Chick's job is to spot political agitators at rallies, demonstrations, and riots. (He told me that Marvin Garson is his favorite agitator.) He goes in plain clothes and aids whatever police department is around. He is one of the men who identified and arrested Jerry Rubin, Steve Hamilton, Stew Albert, Mike Smith, and Bill Miller at the 1966 U.C. sit-in. He does all this in good humor and without rancor. Mid-way through the trial the Oakland 7 jokingly proposed a deal to him: We will not point him out to the demonstrators as a plain clothes cop if he doesn't point us out as agitators.

I first noticed Chick a couple of days into the trial. We were seated at opposite ends of the courtroom looking right at each other. Jensen was making a good point and Chick raised his eyebrows at me and smiled. I looked away. Later Charlie was making a good point. I looked at Chick, gave him a wink and smiled.

From then on it was a fine relationship. We would make faces at each other, feign sleep when the trial was particularly boring, and roll our eyes at the weakness of the judge. At breaks we often talked about sports together—he told me that he had ready my sports columns in the *Express Times*. I think that our affection was cemented when I bumped into him as we were both leaving an Oakland Seal Hockey game late in the trial. The Seals lost 9-0. He did a triple take when he saw me. I walked right up to him, patted him on the shoulder, and said, "Man, *we* sure played some lousy hockey tonight."

Chick Harrison is into the game of cops and robbers. He enjoys it as a game, and I believe he has a comic

distance from himself. I am sure that he is physically fearless and that he would give his life to protect his friends—most of whom are cops. He will continue to be a cop—and although he is incapable of any collossal evil—he will do almost anything that is asked of him. If there ever were a showdown, however, and he discovered a way to preserve the integrity of his physical courage, I think Chick Harrison just might cross over.

I don't think there will be many more cops like Chick Harrison. Any man who now becomes a cop must know that he is going to kill blacks and bust hippie heads. That means that the naive, nice guy jocks, like Chick, simply will not join the force.

This is not just my fantasy. Every metropolitan police force is having difficulty recruiting. Not many people want to be pigs. Those who sign up definitely hate us, and don't care what we call them. It is a good development. In a few years we can be confident that all the cops are both objectively *and* subjectively our enemies.

(Stew Albert read these paragraphs about Chick and blushed with embarrassment for me. Stew says that Chick once kicked a woman demonstrator in the head and slapped someone who was handcuffed. Stew cannot understand how I could be so wrong about a pig. "Jesus, Frank, all sorts of people like sports.")

The two bailiffs, Mr. Sigler and Mr. Lindstrom, were sad cases. Mr. Sigler, a heavy sullen man, seemed to sleep through most of the trial. His main function was to run around doing the judge's chores. Although Sig didn't seem to like anyone, he liked the judge least of all. I would guess that Mr. Sigler has a lot of violence in him. I don't want to be in the way when it all comes out.

Mr. Lindstrom, or Lindy as he liked to be called, was the darling of the judge. A big, curly-headed, sunny-faced Swede, Lindy had a smile for everyone. Phillips believes that he is the model cop. I think he is a pig.

Lindy ran the seating arrangements in the courtroom. This was a position of some power, because often there were more spectators than seats. And Lindy was sure to exercise whatever power he had. He made the spectators feel that the seats were his own personal property, that that he was letting people sit in them out of the goodness of his heart. Spectators had to line up in front of the courtroom door and then Lindy would let them in one by one.

Often when there were empty seats in the courtroom, and people were waiting outside, Lindy would make those people wait for 45 minutes until the next recess. And all the time that he was fucking people over in this extremely petty way, he wanted everyone to love him. He often came up to some spectator and said, "How do you like your seat, pretty good, huh?" His manic friendliness and desire to be loved (even by people he was mistreating) made Phillips think Lindy was the perfect cop.

Once a woman reporter and I were sitting in the hallway outside the courtroom. Lindy came over and told me that it was against the rules to sit down in the hallway with your feet out. I was furious and told him that he should mind his own business and stop telling people the exact manner that he wants them to live. He was shocked. He pointed to Emma and said, "See, she is sitting okay. She has her legs folded under her." I told him he would have to physically move me if he wanted me to change my position. He said he was going to tell the judge on me. And he did.

Lindy gave himself away during the Warren Wells strip cell controversy. Most of us were outraged about the strip cell, and someone mentioned it to Lindy who always came on as The Humane Cop. Lindy looked genuinely confused. "What is Wells complaining about? He's been in the hole before. He can do it standing on his head."

For bailiff Lindstrom the world is neatly divided into two kinds of people. The ones who go to jail and the ones who don't. Those who go to jail are some other kind of species—and although you might show a little kindness to that species and want it to like you just as you would want a dog to like you, basically it is sub-human. We humans, thinks Lindy, can do most anything to those others. They are used to it.

The courtroom was designed to intimidate the poor bastards who come before it. The judge sits behind a huge desk, peering out over his dominion. Behind him is an enormous American flag, perhaps 10 feet wide and 25 feet long. The people are reduced to spectators, bullied by the bailiff, and forced to sit in the back. They are under totalitarian control. More than once Judge Phillips told them, "There will be no laughter in this courtroom unless it is *absolutely* justified."

Much of the language of the Judge, the D.A., and the lawyers is incomprehensible to any defendant. People on trial are supposed to be confused observers, not allowed to speak or display emotion. At the beginning of the trial the Judge pulled me aside and told me affectionately, "Mr. Bardacke, your face is much too expressive. You are just hurting yourself with the jury." The perfect defendant, like the perfect high school student, should come to court wasted on smack.

The conspiracy law was the strongest part of Lowell Jensen's case. The law is so broad and vague that it seems to make the planning of any militant demonstration illegal. One conspires when he adopts, along with others, a common design to commit an unlawful act— or a lawful act in an unlawful manner. You don't even have to know your fellow conspirators. All you have to do is to "adopt a common design."

Confident that the law was with him, Lowell Jensen put on his case. His two undercover agents—young recruits taken right out of Junior College police science classes—identified all of us as leaders of Stop the Draft Week. Some grown-up pigs testified that they ordered the crowd to disperse and they didn't, forcing the cops to clear them out.

A few other witnesses testified that we hired buses, opened bank accounts, passed out leaflets, all in the name of Stop the Draft Week. One pig said brother Bob Mandel had hit him. And finally Jensen read from our leaflets which advocated shutting down the induction center, freeing people from the police, and blocking the inductee buses.

The prosecution's star witness was undercover agent Bruce Coleman. A young man whose face seemed to disappear under close scrutiny, Coleman was terrified on the witness stand. The muscles in his face went a hundred miles an hour. When Jensen asked him to identify us, he slowly rose, crossed the room and carefully looking away from our stares, pointed us out. He deserved to be hated, but I only pitied him.

Our lawyers cut up these witnesses pretty bad. But we did not really dispute anything they said (except the lie about Bob hitting the cop). We helped organize Stop the Draft Week. We were proud of it, and not about to deny it. In cross-examination we simply tried to bring out the cop witnesses and let them display themselves to the jury. A few were pigs, a few were mechanical men, and a few were liars. We hoped the jury would notice.

Our defense was managed by three lawyers: Charlie Garry, Dick Hodge, and Mal Burnstein. These three entirely dissimilar men worked beautifully together and pulled off the miraculous. At the beginning of the trial they told us that an acquittal was impossible and the most we could hope for was a hung jury. Their skill as political lawyers far surpassed their talent as prophets.

I first met Charles R. (R for Rasputin, says Charlie) Garry three three years ago. Stew Albert, Marvin Garson,

Pete Camejo, Mike Smith, Jack Weinberg and I were charged with several misdemeanors, stemming from a Berkeley street demonstration in support of Buddhist demonstrations in South Vietnam. We knew nothing about Garry and he knew nothing about us. We just dropped by his office to see if he would take our case. He let us talk for a little while and then interrupted, "Okay, what are your politics?" Stew, in the great P.L. tradition he then followed, puffed out his chest and announced in a large voice, "I am a communist." Charlie answered, "Big fucking deal."

Toward the end of the "interview" we still did not know if he would take the case. We had asked him a few times, but we never got a straight answer. Then Charlie noticed that one of the soles of Stew's shoes was almost worn away. Charlie casually asked him his shoe size. "I don't know, it's so long since I bought a pair." Charlie pulled out from under his desk a fifty dollar pair of shoes. "Here, see if these fit you." Stew tried them on, they fit, and he began thanking Charlie. He was cut off. "Listen, I can't have my clients going without shoes—it might give me a bad name."

There are a million Charlie Garry stories, but they don't capture all of him. He surprised us, right up to the last day of the trial. An hour before the jury brought down the verdict, Charlie stood on his head for ten minutes in the middle of the courtroom. All I can do is lay down some disconnected impressions, all of which I should warn you, are highly colored by my love for the man.

Charlie lives for the courtroom. During our trial he often ate a quick lunch and returned to court an hour early to study his notes. The year he took our Berkeley street demonstration case he handled 50 trials. Since the Huey Newton case he has given full time to the Panthers, the Oakland 7, and now the Chicago Conspiracy.

He finished the Warren Wells case on a Friday. Then, the day before Christmas, he called up all us defendants. "I have been studying your case over the weekend. Let's talk about it. Can you make it to my office in a couple of hours?" When I got there he was running all over the office, answering the phone, and trying to cement an alliance between us and the Black Panthers. I think it was then that he jumped up and screamed, "Hell, they should pin a medal on you guys, not charge you with conspiracy." It was a terrific Christmas present.

In court Charlie is aggressive and dramatic. It is not an act. He is always aggressive and dramatic. At first his aggressiveness puts people off. During jury selection he screamed at some of the jurors. He even asked one woman if her constant twitching meant that she was too nervous to be a fair juror. His manner shocked the jury and infuriated the judge. But he got away with it. He screams but he also jokes. He gets angry, but he also gets sad, hurt, embarrassed, and happy. He hides none of it.

But the reason juries love him is that he cuts through the pretensions of the court. He has little education—he never went to college—and he speaks plain old American. He cannot pronounce any of the court Latin and he cannot spell. During the trial he wrote Hap Hazard on the board. He loved the jokes that ensued. He is incapable of a pompous act, and if the jury is made up of working class Americans they know immediately that they have at least one friend in the courtroom.

His great virtues as a lawyer are setting the proper political tone and cross-examination. Rather than taking the politics out of a case—as most lawyers do—he emphasizes the politics. He claims that in a political trial you must explain your politics to the jury. What happens is that *Charlie* explains the defendant's politics to the jury—that is not always the same as the defendant's politics—but it is pretty damn good. He turned the Huey

Newton trial into a teach-in on racism and self-defense. He turned the Oakland 7 trial into a teach-in on free speech, police brutality, and the war in Vietnam.

Charlie is a master at cross-examination. He showed his stuff on the very first prosecution witness, Deputy Chief Brown. A tall, smooth middle-class cop, Brown is a professional witness. He testified with a practiced look of confused innocence. When Charlie was done with him he looked more confused and not at all innocent.

Charlie's technique with Brown was simple and direct. While he was cross-examining him he held a copy of Brown's earlier testimony about Stop The Draft Week before the Grand Jury. Brown had given that testimony over a year ago. There would be a long pause (Charlie is not afraid of a 3-minute silence while he prepares a question) as he read the testimony to himself, sure that Brown could see what he was doing. Then a burst. "Mr. Witness, is it your testimony *now* that you gave three dispersal orders? Remember you are under oath." The cop was terrified that he would be caught in a lie. Real quick he had to try to remember what happened, what he said had happened a year ago, and what he should say now. That was simply too much to ask, even of a Deputy Chief.

Charlie's cross-examination was filled with shotgun questions which kept witnesses off balance. "Do you know what a fink rat is?" "You are a man with a tremendous temper, aren't you?" "Is that a baseball bat in your hand?" he asked a cop looking at a picture of himself with a billy club. He also staged a battle with a cop, tricking the poor sucker into manhandling him in front of the jury.

The last Charlie Garry story I will lay on you displays his own favorite skill: the quip under pressure. Several Black Panthers were interviewing Charlie before he was hired to defend Huey Newton. Some Panthers were reluctant to have Huey defended by a white man. They were putting this 60-year-old man through his paces, acting tough, and throwing questions at him. Finally someone said, "You think you are so good—are you as good as Perry Mason?" Charlie shot back: "I'm better. Both of us get all our clients off; but Mason's clients are innocent." Ain't nobody going to fuck with Charles Rasputin Garry.

But as great as Charlie Garry is, the Oakland 7 case was not his victory. We were defended by a team of three lawyers, and it was the team that won. Richard Hodge is a good looking young man with a constant smile and the demeanor of a swinger. He has all the tools to be a highly successful establishment lawyer. Good looks, intelligence, an easygoing manner, and a straight background. He studied to be a Methodist Minister and he has worked in a District Attorney's office. But somewhere along the line he picked up a nagging conscience. He is now sacrificing a potentially lucrative practice to become a Movement lawyer. That is a mark of the Movement's health.

Dick played a crucial role in the trial. Charlie's cursive cross-examination was often sloppy and Dick unfailingly cleaned it up. He prepared most of the defense witnesses and always brought the best out of them. His summation was magnificent—a beautiful mixture of political plain talk, common sense discussion of the evidence, and passion. Everyone congratulated him afterward, but Chick Harrison gave him the greatest compliment. Chick looked very worried.

Our third lawyer, Malcolm Burnstein, was the legal expert in the case. He had at his command all the legal arguments against the war and a forceful argument showing the relevance of the Nuremburg judgment. Mal claimed our attempt to close down the Induction Center was legal because the war in Vietnam is illegal and a crime against humanity. During the trial he constantly pressed this view whenever it conceivably could be intro-

duced. Phillips turned him back at every turn, but Mal's arguments were so good that Phillips could never say why he was turning them down. He would just apologize and rule against us. Once he pointed out that the issues had not been introduced in other cases and said, "I am sorry, Mr. Burnstein, but I am just a Superior Court Judge."

Poor Mal suffered, as he is wont to do. A man committed to the intellect, Mal could not stand to have his arguments turned down without being answered. He would stand before the judge and die a little. But all this suffering was rewarded. Phillips brought Nuremberg into the instructions. He told the jury that they could take into account any evidence that indicated that we believed we were upholding the law and not breaking it.

The instructions were Mal's triumph. He argued for a day and a half in defense of his suggested instructions. Not only did the Judge grant the Nuremberg instruction, he also gave several good First Amendment instructions. He even told the jury that the First Amendment protects the advocacy of illegal acts in the absence of immediate danger. After all those losses, Mal scored the single most important victory of the case. Legally it was now possible for the jury to consider our attitude toward the war, and how the conspiracy law measures up against the First Amendment. That was an important wedge.

We had a simple defense strategy. We attempted to focus attention on the war in Vietnam, police brutality and the First Amendment. We tried to force the jury to vote not on our guilt or innocence, but rather for or against the war, for or against the police, and for or against free speech.

The war and the cops are straightforward issues, but the First Amendment is weird. We did try to shut down the Oakland Induction Center. Our lawyers could argue that this was just an ordinary demonstration, but it was not. We said at the time that it was a new kind of militant demonstration. The First Amendment does not protect those who close down government agencies. Some day a Movement lawyer is going to argue that blowing up a police station is protected by the First Amendment because it is symbolic speech.

But the Federal Government did not indict us for interfering with the Selective Service System. Instead they left it up to Alameda County to punish us. In order to pin felonies on us Alameda County charged us with conspiracy to commit misdemeanors. Organizing almost any demonstration involves planning to break misdemeanors. And the conspiracy law makes such plans a felony. That is unfair and unjust, but I don't believe it is a violation of the First Amendment.

All of this is very hairy and quickly becomes impossible to understand. But don't worry. You are not supposed to be able to understand the law. That is for judges and lawyers. Just remember, if you fight people who have power you will surely do something illegal. But when you get into court you may discover that you can convince the jury that the people with power are evil and wrong— and you are right. The jury will then try to find a legal excuse to let you off.

We tried to show the righteousness of our cause through 47 defense witnesses. They were supposed to represent the Movement to the jury. Primarily young, they ranged from McCarthy kids to Crazies. All of them had been at the demonstration. We did include some respectable types —doctors, ministers, and even a probation officer. But we did not attempt to represent ourselves as any more respectable than we actually are.

Each witness tried to get across our three major political points. The first question to every witness was, why did you attend the demonstration? This allowed the witness to give a short speech against the war. In some cases the witnesses gave long speeches against the war—Phillips allowed that because the witness supposedly was only reporting what he earlier had said to a defendant. Then the typical witness said that he was not under orders from any of the defendants and that the demonstration was organized just like any other demonstration. Finally the witness reported incidents of police brutality.

Although the majority of the testimony fit this simple pattern, it was highly varied and usually exciting. The defense witnesses stood as strong contrast to the mechanical testimony of the prosecution witnesses. None of our people were professional witnesses. Some got mad and yelled at Jensen, some wept, and most were open and obviously telling the truth.

Their testimony was so successful that we no longer considered our own testimony crucial. And all the lawyers felt that if we testified, Jensen would be able to build up his weak case through cross-examination. All of us had written articles which tied together all the loose ends of Jensen's case. These articles could not be introduced unless we testified. So in a move that dropped Jensen's jaw we rested our case without taking the stand.

And the whole mess went to the jury. The jury was a wondrous mystery. We gave them our constant attention, always guessing and arguing about where they were at. This reached an insane level when the jury returned to re-hear testimony. We sat there staring at them, trying to interpret a raised eyebrow or a tightening mouth.

When they left to deliberate Charlie called a conference and we discussed our impressions. "Mrs. Wood looks very tired, she is being put through a wringer." "I am sure she is against us." "Why?" "She takes notes whenever there is a good prosecution point." "So does Salazar and he supports us." We actually had some bad-tempered arguments about how the jury lined up.

This attempt to guess the position of the jurors was particularly difficult because the jury was picked for their lack of obvious feelings. American courts are committed to the ignorance theory of objectivity. Supposedly, the less you know about a subject the more objective you can be. During jury selection anyone who voiced a strong opinion about the war or the draft or demonstrations was sure to be rejected. Mrs. Daws, juror No. 11, is the perfect juror. She does not read a newspaper. She doesn't watch TV news or listen to the radio. She has no opinions. She is one of those women who thinks that ignorance is attractive.

Anyone who had any direct knowledge of the demonstration was automatically rejected. Judge Phillips put it best: "Eyewitnesses, of course, would have a hard time judging the evidence." If there were a general uprising would it be impossible to bring the leaders to trial because there would be no objective jurors? I understand the Chicago 8 are asking for a 25-year continuance on just those grounds.

More goes on during jury selection than just trying to find people who have no opinions. Both the prosecution and the defense try to figure out which jurors do have opinions and are trying to hide them. It is an exciting game. Jensen, assuming that all blacks would be anti-cop, kicked them off the jury. He finally accepted one, Ulysses Peters, who said that he had a son in Vietnam who disapproved of anti-war demonstrations. That and the man's polite demeanor encouraged Lowell to believe he had found a Tom.

We tried to keep on workers with trade union affiliations, any third world people, young people, and those who we guessed were against the war but hiding it. After more than two weeks the game grew very tiring and we accepted a jury.

The jury had two secretaries, 39 and 49 years old; two housewives, 44 and 38; a carpenter, 51; two post office clerks, 43 and 54; an assembly line worker in a Ford plant, 28; a tool and die maker who works for Defense Technology Laboratory and has a security clearance, 48; a supply manager for Lawrence Radiation Laboratory also with a security clearance, 40; an accountant for Smith Corona, 34; and a retired Marine Colonel, 62.

Who knows how to categorize this jury? Should we call them average Americans? Working class? New working class? Old working class? Lower middle class? Upper lower class? Liberals? Protofascists? Neopopulists? I don't know. Ask some of your friends who are expert in such matters.

This collection of Americans acquitted us in a situation where the law allowed them to find us guilty. They chose the Movement over the police. Mrs. Reitsma, the lone Republican juror, is now reading *Soul on Ice* "to find out why the Oakland 7 supports Huey Newton." She told a reporter that "I have been a sitter my whole life, but I now realize I was just playing into the hands of the power structure."

The whole experience must have been quite special. One of the jurors told us that the jury plans to have a reunion every month. That won't last, but it is easy to see why they want it.

How many Americans have an opportunity to make a decision of the highest public importance? Americans are hungry for politics. These lucky twelve, chosen because they were apolitical, were thrust into a situation where politics was forced upon them. They loved it.

A special experience for the jurors, the trial was an extraordinary experience for us. At first we were afraid our trial might go the way of the Spock trial. The Spock conspirators never got together. They each had separate lawyers running separate defenses. I am told that their lawyers did not even sit together in court. The defendants lived through their trial separately, afraid for their individual safety and suffering private pain.

But we were too young to do that. The Spock conspirators had fully-developed private lives they felt they had to protect. Most of us were kids, still in the street, trying to decide how to live. We had little to protect; the indictment eventually shook us away from our private lives and threw us together as brothers.

The trial and our defense forced us to work together on a single project for an extended period. That is a blessing for a New Left activist. It is probably the only way to get anything done in politics. It is certainly the only way to live.

We worked together, rode to court together, got high together, shared our "personal" problems with each other, fought viciously among ourselves, and finally looked at each other and said, "Okay, brother, I see who you are, I respect it, and you are good enough for me."

Now that the trial is over it will be impossible to keep all that. The Oakland 7 was created by D.A. J. Frank Coakley. We can not artificially hold it together. We are not a revolutionary party, we can not find a single political project to unite us, and eventually we will go our separate ways. We will still be friends, of course, but brothers and sisters, no. We won't achieve that until we meet on the barricades.

Ed. Note: Bardacke is one of the most notable of a generation of West Coast radical activists who combine broad intelligence and humanity, street-fighting shrewdness, and a capacity to speak, write and organize. The trial he tells of here has been neglected. It is as significant in the history of the Movement as the Conspiracy trial in Chicago.

The Realist

Nov/Dec 1969

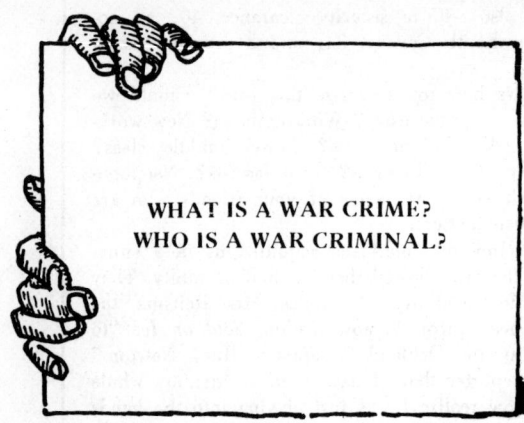

WHAT IS A WAR CRIME?
WHO IS A WAR CRIMINAL?

THE NURNBERG PRINCIPLES

The Treaty of London, August 8, 1945 (59 Stat. 1544), provided for the creation of the International Military Tribunal and the Charter of the Tribunal. The first session of the General Assembly of the United Nations unanimously affirmed the principles of international law recognized by the Charter and Judgment of the Nurnberg Tribunal and directed the International Law Commission to formulate them into an International Criminal Code (Res. 95 [1], 11 December 1946). "The Nurnberg Principles" were adopted by the International Law Commission, June–July 1950:

Principle I. Any person who commits an act which constitutes a crime under international law is responsible therefor and liable to punishment.

Principle II. The fact that internal law does not impose a penalty for an act which constitutes a crime under international law does not relieve the person who committed the act from responsibility under international law.

Principle III. The fact that a person who committed an act which constitutes a crime under international law acted as Head of State or responsible government official does not relieve him from responsibility under international law.

Principle IV. The fact that a person acted pursuant to order of his Government or of a superior does not relieve him from responsibility under international law, provided a moral choice was in fact possible to him.

Principle V. Any person charged with a crime under international law has the right to a fair trial on the facts and law.

Principle VI. The crimes hereinafter set out are punishable as crimes under international law:
  (a) Crimes against peace:
      (i) Planning, preparation, initiation, or waging of aggression or a war in violation of international treaties, agreements or assurances;
      (ii) Participation in a common plan or conspiracy for the accomplishment of any of the acts mentioned under (i).
  (b) War crimes:
  Violations of the laws or customs of war which include, but are not limited to, murder, ill-treatment or deportation to slave-labour or for any other purpose of civilian population of or in occupied territory, murder or ill-treatment of prisoners of war or persons on the seas, killing of hostages, plunder of public or private property, wanton destruction of cities, towns, or villages, or devastation not justified by military necessity.
  (c) Crimes against humanity:
  Murder, extermination, enslavement, deportation, and other inhuman acts done against any civilian population, or persecutions on political, racial, or religious grounds, when such acts are done or such persecutions are carried on in execution of or in connexion with any crime against peace or any war crime.

Principle VII. Complicity in the commission of a crime against peace, a war crime, or a crime against humanity as set forth in Principle VI is a crime under international law.

Ed. Note: By the Treaty of London, ratified by the U.S. Senate, the Nurnberg Principles became a part of U.S. Law. Also: Technically, U.S. Military law recognizes the right to disobey an order against conscience. The Military, in practice, tends to favor blind obedience.

ELITISM
CENTRALISM
DOGMATISM:
A WARNING
FROM
ROSA LUXEMBURG

Long ago, Kropotkin observed that "the modern radical is a centralizer, a State partisan, a Jacobin to the core, and the Socialist walks in his footsteps." To a large extent he is correct in thus echoing the warning of Bakunin that "scientific socialism" might in practice be distorted into "the despotic domination of the laboring masses by a new aristocracy, small in number, composed of real or pretended experts," the "red bureaucracy" that would prove to be "the most vile and terrible lie that our century has created." Western critics have been quick to point out how the Bolshevik leadership took on the role outlined in the anarchist critique— as was in fact sensed by Rosa Luxemburg, barely a few months before her murder by the troops of the German socialist government exactly half a century ago.

Rosa Luxemburg's critique of Bolshevism was sympathetic and fraternal, but incisive, and full of meaning for today's radical intellectuals. Fourteen years earlier, in her *Leninism or Marxism,* she had criticized Leninist organizational principles, arguing that *"nothing will more surely enslave a young labor movement to an intellectual elite hungry for power than this bureaucratic straitjacket, which will immobolize the movement and turn it into an automaton manipulated by a Central Committee"* (her italics). These dangerous tendencies towards authoritarian centralization she saw, with great accuracy, in the earliest stages of the Bolshevik revolution. She examined the conditions that led the Bokshevik leadership to terror and dictatorship of "a little leading minority in the name of the class," a dictatorship that stifled "the growing political training of the mass of the people" instead of contributing to it; and she warned against making a virtue of necessity and turning authoritarian practice into a style of rule by the new elite. Democratic institutions have their defects:

"But the remedy which Trotsky and Lenin have found, the elimination of democracy as such, is worse than the disease it is supposed to cure; for it stops up the very living source from which alone can come the correction of all the innate shortcomings of social institutions. That source is the active untrammeled, energetic political life of the broadest masses of the people."

Unless the whole mass of the people take part in the determination of all aspects of economic and social life, unless the new society grows out of their creative experience and spontaneous action, it will be merely a new form of repression. "Socialism will be decreed from behind a few official desks by a dozen intellectuals," whereas in fact it "demands a complete spiritual transformation in the masses degraded by centuries of bourgeois class rule," a transformation which can take place only within insitutions that extend the freedoms of bourgeois society. There is no explicit recipe for socialism: "Only experience is capable of correcting and opening new ways. Only unobstructed, effervescing life falls into a thousand new forms and improvisations, brings to light creative force, itself corrects all mistaken attempts."

The role of the intellectuals and radical activists, then, must be to assess and evaluate, to attempt to persuade, to organize, but not to seize power and rule. "Historically, the errors committed by a truly revolutionary movement are infinitely more fruitful than the infallibility of the cleverest Central Committee."

These remarks are a useful guide for the radical intellectual. They also provide a refreshing antidote to the dogmatism so typical of discourse on the left, with its arid certainties and religious fervor regarding matters that are barely understood—the self-destructive left-wing counterpart to the smug superficiality of the defenders of the status quo who can perceive their own ideological commitments no more than a fish can perceive that it swims in the sea.

It would be useful, though beyond the bounds of this discussion, to review the interplay between radical intellectuals and technical intelligentsia on the one hand and mass, popular-based organizations on the other, in revolutionary and post-revolutionary situations. Such an investigation might consider on the one extreme the Bolshevik experience and the ideology of the liberal technocracy, which are united in the belief that mass organizations and popular politics must be submerged. At the other extreme, it might deal with the anarchist revolution in Spain in 1936-7— and the response to it by liberal and Communist intellectuals. Equally relevant would be the evolving relationship between the Communist Party and popular organizations (workers councils and commune governments) in Yugoslavia today, and the love-hate relationship between party cadres and peasant associations that provides the dramatic tension for William Hinton's brilliant account of a moment in the Chinese revolution. It could draw from the experience of the National Liberation Front as described, say, by Douglas Pike in his *Vietcong* and more other objective sources, and from many documentary accounts of developments in Cuba. One should not exaggerate the relevance of these cases to the problems of an advanced industrial society, but I think there is no doubt that a great deal can nevertheless be learned from them, not only about the feasibility of other forms of social organization but also about the problems that arise as intellectuals and activists attempt to relate to mass politics.

From "Knowledge and Power" by Noam Chomsky in *The New Left* (an anthology)

Rosa Luxemburg

As remarkable as the speeches by Staughton Lynd and Greg Calvert were the spirit or mood of the entire Resistance conference at Bloomington. Over 150 activists spent four days talking about the movement—and parted friends. They even enjoyed themselves. Long sessions in workshops or plenaries led to long personal raps with each other, or to singing movement songs, or to games outdoors. When they left for home, they hugged one another. I was amazed: at this late date (March 1969), with the movement factionalized and uptight, the open and experimental groups uncertain and the disciplined cadres more arrogant than ever, national SDS meetings reduced to empty ideological debates, and even some resistance groups split over tactics and hassled over personalities, 150 movement people actually managed to hold a healthy conference.

I don't want to sentimentalize it. Cohn-Bendit may be right to say "There is only one reason for being a revolutionary—because it is the best way to live," but it won't always be fun and games. We've been hurt already, and we'll be hurt a lot more. We have years of dirty and desperate work ahead, and it will take more discipline, nerve, organization—and maybe violence—than most of us

are ready to face. And yet the internal health or spirit of the movement is a serious matter, and there is nothing sentimental about trying to improve it, or rejoicing when it occasionally blooms. How people feel toward one another, whether they are sportsmanlike to those they think are wrong, their honesty about their own and others' weaknesses and strengths, the brotherly (and sisterly) affection that grows from shared work and shared commitment, these are often more important than the "correctness" of the ideology. The best decision is meaningless if the process of deciding is filled with distrust, mental reservation, and a breakdown of fellow-feeling. Good movement work depends on the energy, good cheer, and mutual confidence of the workers than on the strategic assumptions directing them.

The good news from Bloomington is not only the strategic consensus along the lines Greg and Staughton have sketched, but also the resurgence of healthy comradely feeling among movement people. I, at least, left the conference with a new taste for movement work, and it has at least as much to do with my feelings toward my brothers and sisters as with the ideas we talked about.

Mike Ferber

THE BACKBONE OF OUR FREEDOM

The Movement: A New Beginning

by Staughton Lynd

I'm going to talk in a way that may seem to some of you abstract or theoretical. Usually I, too, feel impatient of theory and concerned that people relate what they say today to what they, personally, are going to do tomorrow. But at this conference I feel differently. If our discussion is limited to problems which arise in daily resistance work, then we tacitly take for granted our present definition of that work. This procedure will not serve if we want to take a fresh look at how that work has been defined. My own conviction is that this is an historical moment when the Resistance must make an intellectual leap and newly define its work on a multi-issue, multi-class basis. It cannot do that, so it seems to me, without some notion of the kind of society it ultimately wants to create, of the historical forces working for and against the attempt to achieve that vision, and of a coherent strategy, however tentative, for getting from here to there.

There is what might be termed a classical period in the history of draft resistance to the Vietnam war. This period began in April 1967, when about

150 young men burned their draft cards in Sheep's Meadow and, in the Bay Area, David Harris, Dennis Sweeney, Lenny Heller and Steve Hamilton named themselves The Resistance and in its name called for the mass return of draft cards on October 16. The classical period ended in April 1968, when within the space of a week Lyndon Johnson withdrew from the Presidential campaign and announced a partial bombing halt, a third day of card returns brought the number of noncooperators to perhaps 2500, and Martin Luther King was assassinated.

During that year, April 1967 to April 1968, there was an obvious answer to the question: What is a member of the Resistance? A member of the Resistance during this classic period was one who publicly and collectively noncooperated with the Selective Service System, or who advocated, aided and abetted that act.

Somehow the classic act of noncooperation with the Selective Service System has been permitted—to borrow from Karl Marx language which he borrowed from the anthropology of religion—to become a fetish, to be reified or thingified, so that an action which, after all, is only one way of resisting one form of repression, has come to define our movement as a whole.

The Resistance must grow beyond this classic definition of resistance. It must find its way behind the fetish on noncooperation with the Selective Service System to the spirit which prompted that act to begin with. To move forward from an ossified form is difficult, but a spirit can grow and take new forms. We need to do whatever has to be done so that, in a manner faithful to our original spirit, we can become a mass movement of resistance to all forms of repression.

How will we respond to this challenge? What is the future of the Resistance? Probably the history books of the next century will say something like this:

> After April 1968 the Resistance began to decline. High draft calls for college students in the summer of 1968 did not materialize. The war dragged on, even in some respects escalated, but in the absence of dramatic single acts of escalation the Resistance was unable to recapture its initial momentum. Factions crystallized into irreconcilable splinter groups. Some Resistance groups, impressed by the anti-imperialist analysis of SDS, began to demand a multi-issue program and a coherent long-run strategy for fundamental social change. Frustrated in their efforts to induce their fellow-resisters to develop such a perspective, those who felt this way drifted away from the Resistance, often into SDS, although not without occasional nostalgia for the consensus decision-making emotional openness, and decentralized structure of the resistance community. Among those who remained in the Resistance, concerns previously secondary to the war—drugs, diet, communes, the creation of nonviolence—became more and more prominent; and this in itself had a fragmenting effect, as individuals began to put their main energies into coffee houses, free schools, and other enterprises distinct from draft resistance work. When the war finally ended, the Resistance, like other groups organized around the single issue of the war, disintegrated. Within six months of the signing of the Vietnam peace treaty, the Resistance was dead.

This, I repeat, is what the history books will probably say. Now let me project another history, not probable, but I am convinced possible. Here is how that possible history goes:

> After April 1968 the Resistance, like the larger movement, experienced the disorientation characteristic of Presidential election years. About a year later a new direction began to emerge. Despite the general confusion many Resistance groups had been patiently exploring forms of resistance beyond the draft, and conducting experimental joint actions with high-school, GI, and women's liberation groups, as well as with some local chapters of SDS. Internal tensions, a natural result of this exploration and experimentation, were fruitfully resolved at a national conference in Bloomington, Illinois. Work against the draft continued, of course. The draft itself continued, because American imperialism required the flexible supply of manpower which the draft made available in order to fight more than one Third World insurrection simultaneously; and when, in the spring of 1969, it became clear that the war in Vietnam was far from over, the Resistance revived. But the Selective Service System was now viewed as a single facet of an illegitimate structure of power. Accordingly, many members of SDS, who had hitherto dismissed the Resistance as masochistic middle-class moralism, turned toward the draft resistance movement as a political vehicle which, in contrast to the polemical in-fighting dominant in SDS, combined sophisticated analysis with a humane spirit reminiscent of the movement in the early 1960's. As a result the Resistance found itself in a position to play a key role in building the broad liberation movement which organized the revolutionary general strikes of the next decade.

I don't have a formula for bringing to pass that second, merely possible history. No one does. I want to try to help us all think more creatively in that direction by examining two pieces of our common experience. First, the year prior to April 1967, during which we groped our way toward the act of public, collective card return; second, the year since April 1968, during which many Resistance groups have been revising their initial assumptions as they sought to relate to new issues and new social classes.

I

Several groups, several strains of thinking converged to produce the resistance actions of April 1967: the burning of draft cards in New York City, the call for October 16 from the Bay Area, and, lest we forget, the induction refusal of Muhammad Ali.

First there was a group of pacifists for whom dissociation from the draft expressed a more-than-political worldview. This group could trace its philosophy to A.J. Muste's essay on "holy disobedience." It included many members of the Committee for Nonviolent Action and the Catholic Worker community, such as Tom Rodd, David Miller and Tom Cornell. Meeting in New York City in October 1966, adherents of this approach issued the following "Statement of Non-cooperation with Military Conscription":

> We, the undersigned men of draft age (18-35), believe that all war is immoral and ultimately self-defeating. We believe that military conscription is evil and unjust. Therefore, we will not cooperate in any way with the Selective Service System.
> We will not register for the draft.
> If we have registered, we will sever all relations with the Selective Service System.
> We will carry no draft cards or other Selective Service certificates.
> We will not accept any deferment, such as 2-S.
> We will not accept any exemption, such as 1-O or 4-D.
> We will refuse induction in the armed forces.
> We urge and advocate that other young men join us in non-cooperation with the Selective

Service System.

We are in full knowledge that these actions are violations of the Selective Service laws punishable by up to 5 years imprisonment and/or a fine of $10,000.

Near the opposite end of the political spectrum was a tendency illustrated by David Mitchell and, after the enunciation of Black Power in mid-1966, by SNCC. These resisters were not pacifist. Nor were they noncooperators, but they publicly refused induction. They were also explicitly anti-imperialist, in David Mitchell's case since 1961. This tendency is represented in resistance work today by the Wisconsin Draft Resistance Union and the Boston Draft Resistance Group.

Between these two ideological extremes—pacifist noncooperation, and anti-imperialist induction refusal—fell the bulk of students opposed to the war. They expressed themselves in the spring of 1966 by sitting-in against the sending of class ranks to draft boards, and in the fall of 1966 by signing We Won't Go statements. It is fashionable in the Resistance to deprecate such activities, since the students involved rarely grasped the nettle of induction refusal. But for many resisters, anti-rank and We Won't Go represented a stage in their development which they repudiated in moving on to resistance. Thus Michael Ferber, David Harris and Michael Cullen of the Milwaukee 14 signed We Won't Go statements; Kerry Berland, after taking part in an anti-ranking sit-in at Chicago, was shocked that after the sit-in many of the demonstrators took the test anyway.

I see the movement which became the Resistance emerging from certain groups of students who, as they moved beyond a We Won't Go position, sought to combine the insights of pacifist noncooperation with those of anti-imperialist induction refusal. No doubt the most significant of these student groups was that at Stanford, which included David Harris, Dennis Sweeney, Paul Rupert, Ira Arlook, and Joel Kugelmass. Here I would like to describe two East Coast groups, at Yale and Cornell.

In July 1966 there met in New Haven a group of young men who drew up the following statement:

We men of draft age disavow all military obligations to our government until it ceases wars against peoples seeking to determine their own destinies. On November 16 [November 16, 1966, mind you] we will return our draft cards to our local boards with a notice of our refusal to cooperate until American invasions are ended. We fully realize that this action will be considered illegal and that we will be liable to five years impresionment.

We propose to develop our program August 25 and 26 prior to the SDS convention at Clear Lake, Iowa.

Of the eight men who signed that statement, one was longtime worker with CNVA. A second belonged to the self-styled anarchist wing of national SDS (I recall his saying at that meeting, "SDS members have never done anything."). A third had made a detailed proposal for anti-draft activity at the SDS National Council meeting the previous spring; his proposal, one of four, had been lost in rhetoric and he was ready to look elsewhere. Three of the others, as well as myself, had worked together in Mississippi in the summer of 1964. One had worked with Dennis Sweeney in McComb.

From that meeting in New Haven travellers fanned out across the country as far as the West Coast. I have a letter written from Madison on July 22, 1966 which began:

We've made our way to Chicago and on up to Madison, Wisc. The results of our probes into Detroit and Ann Arbor have been encouraging. Seven or eight of my close co-patriots in Detroit are gravitating very strongly. Ann Arbor folks, numbering five or six, are moving as well. We've been keeping the numbers small but discussions have been intense.

This was exactly the process which Dennis Sweeney and David Harris would repeat the next summer on the West Coast. And already in mid-1966, the germs of the coming split between SDS and the Resistance were apparent. The letter goes on:

Discussion in Ann Arbor clarified another pattern of thinking; namely, that the idea and act were no political. Persons who say this attribute to this action a mere mechanical quality. For some people like Steve Weissman and Mike Goldfield, they had to see this idea as a comprehensive political program with organization "guarantees" for its expansion into all levels of the student movement. Until that could be developed, they were unable to see it as a viable political movement. I come at the question from a different perspective....

On July 30, 1966 the travellers returned to New Haven for a second meeting. A report on that meeting included the following observations:

Since the individual commitment to go to jail is the basis of the collective strength of the movement, we talked for a while about the kinds of reasons a person would take such an action. The two basic motivations are personal and political. In the case of the former, the person sees the draft situation as his personal climax with the system—he probably would have done a similar act anyway, but decides to do it with the group because of the strength that adds to him and the group. A large majority of us, however, would not have taken this act, at least not until after [being] confronted with induction itself. We are arriving at the decision because we feel that we have a political program we can make work.

The report laid out perspectives for organizing. "There was a very strong feeling that we have to organize by sending our field staff to places which are not normally reached by the movement, in addition to the usual centers of activity." The organizers, this report continued, "have to really go out and *work* to build strong democratic local organizations (or anti-draft struggle committees), that have a common relationship through this and other programs. In the case of existing organizations like SDS chapters, the idea would be to strengthen the movement and deepen the particular group's commitment to change. . ." Further, "we have decided to reject the type of organizing that issues calls to do something, writes magazine articles and prints newspaper ads, and then expects people to act. . . Only after the basic groundwork is laid over the next few months (i.e., building strong committed local groups by the field staff) will we pull out the stops of publicity. . . Those of us who travelled west were awed by the size of the country and feel that if there is regional strength and unity this will help in the struggle that is to come."

The report on this meeting of July 30, 1966 went on to affirm that "the November launching date is seen as a *beginning*, not as a final goal. It is from this date that the important building has to be done with other constituencies and programs. It was generally agreed that the major *program* that would follow from the collective act of draft defiance would be the organizing" of "a broad range of forms of draft resistance." It was assumed that those who turned in their draft cards on November 16 would thereafter become organizers. Also discussed were adult support—that was to be my province—and the alternative merits of different kinds of legal defense:

> We can take a civil liberties defense (claiming that we can advocate anything and also that the government is violating our liberties by drafting us to fight their war). We can take a Nuremburg defense (the war is immoral and unjust and it is our responsibility not to fight but to resist). We can also stand mute (and declare that the court is a political tool of the system and could not possibly grant us any justice).

Finally there was discussion of womens' liberation:

> It was noted that there was a vast potential for organizing young women since there was a vacuum now organizationally and programatically. WSP is mostly middle-aged and programatically fuzzy. SDS, despite occasional rhetoric to the contrary, remains a male-dominated organization. We agreed to raise programmatic possibilities with women we know, but felt that it would be up to the women themselves to develop corollary programs to our draft resistance.

There were women's workshops at the subsequent Des Moines meeting and at the We Won't Go conference in Chicago in December 1966. The first women's liberation groups in the country, organized by Heather Tobis Booth, Naomi Weinstein, Sue Munaker and others, grew directly from these workshops.

The Des Moines meeting in late August 1966 decided that the projected November 16 date was premature. Individuals were urged to return to their various communities and organize solid local groups. Perhaps the most important of these was at Cornell,

for it was this group which called for the mass burning of draft cards in New York the following April. The organizer of the Cornell group was Tom Bell, who had attended the July 30 meeting in New Haven and the Des Moines conference. Tom has described in an article in *New Left Notes*, reprinted by my wife in *We Won't Go*, how he approached his task: in the characteristic Resistance manner, rather than calling a meeting he sought out an individual at a time. Characteristically, too, the call for mass draft card burning was stimulated by the decision of one person, Bruce Dancis, to burn his own card.

Bruce and Tom both illustrate the attempt to synthesize ethical and political insights which I have stressed as typical of these early resistance groups. Bruce Dancis was quite active in SDS as a Cornell freshman and at the time he burned his draft card was Cornell SDS president. The other side of his background is suggested by the fact that his father had been a CO in World War II, that he was raised in what he terms "an Ethical Culturist home," and that the summer before he went to college he met and was much influenced by David McReynolds of the War Resisters League.

The day he registered with the Selective Service System, in May 1966, Bruce Dancis also took part in a sit-in in the university president's office against the turning over of class ranks to that same system. At this time he told his draft board that he did not want a 2-S deferment, that he wanted 1-O status, but that if granted 1-O status he might not do alternative service. By the next fall (this is still 1966),

> I began to see that CO had the same things wrong with it that 2-S had. I saw that a guy from the streets of Harlem, who couldn't get a 2-S deferment since he wasn't in college, couldn't get a CO since it is such a difficult form to fill out. I couldn't see myself having to explain to a bunch of old men why I should be exempted from killing people. . . In December, 1966 I finally decided that I must sever my ties with Selective Service. On December 14, outside a meeting of the Cornell faculty which was discussing the university's policy towards Selective Service, I read a statement to my local board before a crowd of 300 people and then ripped up my draft card.

The Cornell anti-draft union agonized for weeks over how to respond to Bruce's action. Finally on March 2 five men—Jan Flora, Burton Weiss, Robert Nelson, Michael Rotkin, Timothy Larkin—called on others to pledge to burn their draft cards April 15 if at least 500 people acted at the same time. The language of the call combined ethical and political arguments:

> The armies of the United States have, through conscription, already oppressed or destroyed the lives and consciences of millions of Americans and Vietnamese. We have argued and demonstrated to stop this destruction. We have not succeeded. Murderers do not respond to reason. Powerful resistance is now demanded: radical, illegal, unpleasant, sustained.

In Vietnam the war machine is directed against young and old, soldiers and civilians, without distinction. In our own country, the war machine is directed specifically against the young, against blacks more than against whites, but ultimately against all.

Body and soul, we are oppressed in common. Body and soul, we must resist in common. The undersigned believe that we should begin this mass resistance by publicly destroying our draft cards at the Spring Mobilization.

The statement continued as follows:

The climate of anti-war opinion is changing. In the last few months student governments, church groups, and other organizatons have publicly expressed understanding and sympathy with the position of individuals who refuse to fight in Vietnam, who resist the draft. We are ready to put ourselves on the line for this position, and we expect that these people will come through with their support.

We are fully aware that our action makes us liable to penalties of up to five years in prison and $10,000 in fines. We believe, however, that the more people who take part in this action the more difficult it will be for the government to prosecute.

Even after the call had been been issued, Tom Bell struggled with the question of whether the decision had been right. He wrote me on March 18, 1967:

I still have some pretty serious reservations about our action—especially as I see it at work . . . What disturbs me is that almost 50 Cornellians have pledged to burn their draft cards and I am afraid for many of them the decision comes from the emotionalism of the moment. The sessions in the [student] union are very much like revival services (even including some of the rhetoric at times). We have speeches, a collection for the anti-war office and on the spot conversions—signing pledges, plus a lot of personal witnesses. I am going to try to get all the people who have signed pledges together for some collective thinking about what we are doing and I hope that we can get some things cleared up. There is real agony for me in the dilemma presented by seeing this great opportunity for political organizing and action vs. the likelihood that a lot of people are going to be hurt (including myself) by the action being taken. I'm even more afraid when I think of the impersonal situation of sending out the calls. Don't really know why I am unloading all of this except that I feel caught—I don't like national actions but I do want to change America. I like a personal, deep communication type of politics but perhaps this is not really political. I don't want to manipulate anyone but I feel that it is essential for my own struggle and for the development of all of us as human beings that people change.

On April 2, less than two weeks away from April 15, Tom wrote again. "I've begun to feel better about the draft card burning, as a political act at least, but it looks like it will not come off. We have only about 90 pledges so far and the Spring Mobilization (Almighty Executive Board) has apparently refused to let us take the action as part of the April 15 action anyway." The rest is common knowledge. The evening of April 14 those who had signed the conditional pledge met and decided to go ahead if there were fifty persons who would burn their cards together. At that meeting just over fifty said, Yes. The next day three times that many acted.

What, besides nostalgia, ought we feel in recollecting these beginnings? What struck me most as I went over the documents again was the connection between noncooperation and the 2-S deferment. Those who chose noncooperation for philosophical reasons, such as the CNVA resisters, were a minority. For most resisters noncooperation was a means whereby students protected by 2-S deferments could make themselves vulnerable to induction and so compel the government, as Steve Hamilton put it, "to deal with us." Early leaflets of the Resistance make this motivation clear. "An organizaton has been formed," began one, "of men preparing to jointly give up all deferments and refuse to serve." "THE RESISTANCE," another stated, "is a group of men who feel we can no longer passively accept our deferments so that others can go in our place." It would seem that had there been no 2-S deferment there would have been draft resistance, but it would have taken the form of mass induction refusal rather than mass noncooperation. And this in turn suggests that the division of the draft resistance movement into, on the one hand, a movement of induction refusal or resistance within the armed forces, and on the other hand, a movement characteristically expressing itself by the act of noncooperation, is itself a consequence of the class character of the Selective Service System, of channeling, of the success of the American governing class in dividing the opposition.

This conclusion, if accurate, has implications for the current debate as to whether or not to give up draft card turn-ins. What it suggests to me is that noncooperation remains, as it has always been, an appropriate act of resistance for deferred college students and conscientious objectors; but that it is not now, nor should it ever have been regarded as, a likely form of resistance for the young man of draft age not so insulated; and that, therefore, on May Day for example, the form of ceremony which would most precisely reflect the right relationship of noncooperation to other kinds of resistance would be a ceremony in which the noncooperator was one of several kinds of resisters each doing his thing.

II

There is, however, a further argument against the act of noncooperation which must be confronted. This is the argument first expressed (in my memory) by Carl Davidson in *New Left Notes* during the spring of 1967, and again by Steve Hamilton in the same journal when he broke with the Resistance the next fall, namely, the contention that inviting imprisonment by noncooperation expressed a characteristically middle-class sentiment, of guilt, masochism, and would-be martyrdom. Davidson insisted that not only did permitting oneself to be imprisoned deprive the movement of a needed organizer, but that psychologically it weakened and emasculated, rather than strengthening, other young men of draft age. The implication of this criticism of the Resistance is that no one should return his draft card because the act is inherently apolitical and unhealthy.

Let me begin to respond to this criticism by recalling another strand of motivation which led to the Resistance. I have said that many of the proto-resisters whom I knew had worked together in Mississippi. For them, myself included, draft resistance was in complex ways a means of dealing with the psychological aftermath of that experience. As of spring 1966, with the articulation of Black Power, we were irrevocably excluded from the civil rights movement. I think it was more than the escalation of the Vietnam war which caused draft resistance to begin to take form the following summer. We were looking for something white radicals could do which would have the same spirit, ask as much of us, and challenge the system as fundamentally, as had our work in Mississippi.

Dennis Sweeny felt, he remembers, that while it was wrong to build a movement on risk-taking, still risk-taking was conspicuously missing from the movement in the North. Dennis never thought that the draft was the most important of all social issues or that the Resistance could end the draft. He considered the draft a particularly clear illustration of what was wrong with the system as a whole. He also wanted a means to pull together seriously-committed white radicals for longtime work. Draft resistance seemed to Dennis a kind of net (as he expressed it) which one could pull through the campuses of the country and thus collect the people with whom one really wanted to make a movement.

What did the South, in particular Mississippi, signify in the experience of former civil rights workers. Something we wanted to get away from, something else we wanted to keep. We wanted to get away from the role of white people helping black people, the role of missionary to the oppression of others, the role of auxiliary to a radicalism the center of gravity of which was in other people's lives. In the South many of us had drifted into administrative roles in the Atlanta SNCC office or the Jackson, Mississippi COFO office, not because we wanted to be leaders, but because we were obviously better able to write press releases and answer the telephone than to approach frightened black people in remote rural communities. The objective result, however, was that we made more decisions than we should have made, and black SNCC field secretaries had the experience of returning to their headquarters after beatings and imprisonments to find more white faces than black there. When the philosophy of control of black organizations by black people was announced our own experience made us recognize that, however painful for us personally, Black Power was right.

This time around, then, we did not want to manipulate the lives of others who ran risks which we did not share. In the words of the report of the New Haven meeting of July 30, 1966: "As organizers of draft resistance we must be the first to confront the government and to challenge its authority. We must be the first to confront the fear of long jail sentences." In the words of the call to the Sheep's Meadow card-burning: "We are ready to put ourselves on the line." As Paul Rupert puts the same feeling: It was a politics of risk. We had to be the first people to take the risk.

Was this a desire for martyrdom? Perhaps a politics of risk, but also a politics of guilt? Only in part. Insofar as noncooperation represented nothing more than a renunciation of a 2-S deferment it certainly resembled the impulse which sent white Northern students to the South. But noncooperation meant more than this. After publication of the channeling memorandum in January 1967 white radical students began to realize that "the club of induction" not only forced others into the army but forced themselves into a careerism and conformity which they abhorred. Hence in saying No to the draft one also said No to a grey-flannel image of one's future. In contrast to the role of the white student in the Southern civil rights movement, resistance to the draft and the war was resistance to an oppression which affected the non-student most severely but also oppressed oneself.

At this point the positive memory of the South, and particularly of Mississippi, came into play. Those of us who had worked with Bob Moses saw in him a model for the democratic organizer. It was not only that, in the fall of 1961, he had put his body on the line by going alone into Amite County to begin voter registration. It was also his rejection of the conventional leadership role: sitting in the back of the room at meetings, refusing to speak, when he spoke standing up in place rather than coming to the front of the meeting, when he came to the front asking questions rather than making a speech. When I first met David Harris at the ill-fated Madison, Wisconsin draft conference of August 1967, I was immediately struck by the similarility between David's reasons for resigning his position as student body president at Stanford and Bob's reasons for fiercely refusing the charisma thrust upon him. In each case, the motivation was not guilt, but the desire to enable others by removing the impediment of a dominant personality, to oblige others to improvise their own militancy rather than deferring to a leader.

The emotional thrust of the resistance movement is not masochistic self-denial but self-reliance, not emasculation but manhood. Guilt is so strong a strain in our authoritarian culture that we constantly betray and caricature our best impulses. Lenny Heller caricatured what resistance was about when he told all and sundry in the summer of 1967 that those unready to noncooperate and go to jail had no balls. David Harris may have permitted himself partially to betray his own initial understanding by playing the role of perpetual spokesman. But having spent two long nights recently exploring with David the genesis of West Coast Resistance, I am convinced that affirmation rather than self-denial was the emotional kernel of their call for October 16. David, who himself spent some time in Quitman County, Mississippi in the fall of 1964, believes the Resistance style of politics to have been a synthesis of the style developed in the South and what he terms an exploration of selfhood. Neitzsche was part of it; so was existentialism, and riding a motorcycle on the Sierras with the wind on one's face. The emotional overtones were, not asceticism, discipline, suffering, but endurance, going beyond one's limits, invulnerability, adventure. Running for Stanford student body president David's campaign buttons were "Home Rule" and "Community Not Colonialism." Their spirit anticipated the button with which SDS joined draft resistance in the spring of 1967, "Not With My Life You Don't." When David and Dennis went up and down the West Coast in the summer of 1967 seeking noncooperators, they, like Tom Bell before them sought out one individual at a time, spending time with him, getting to know all sides of him, playing guitar and dropping acid besides talking politics. The first leaflet of the Bay Area Committee for Draft Resistance was simply six individual statements of noncooperation. This "open style" of organizing, in which one man tells another why he has decided to do something, seems to me inherently life-affirming, as opposed to the style which asks others to immolate themselves in a collective, impersonal destiny.

Which brings me to an extraordinary coincidence. In February 1967, more or less at the same time that five men at Cornell called for draft card burning in Sheep's Meadow and that Steve Hamilton and Lenny Heller became acquainted with David Harris and Dennis Sweeney, the national secretary of SDS gave a speech at Princeton in which he described precisely that style of organizing, and that need to struggle for self-liberation, which were at the heart of the developing Resistance. Liberalism, Greg Calvert asserted, is based on the psychology of guilt and on the program of helping others to achieve what one already has. On the other hand, radicalism stems from "the perception of oneself as unfree, as oppressed" and expresses itself in "a struggle for collective liberation of all unfree, oppressed men." And Greg opened his speech with the following vignette of what, I submit, is resistance organizing at its best:

It is said that when the Guatemalan guerillas enter a new village, they do not talk about the "anti-imperialist struggle" nor do they give lessons on dialectical materialism—neither do they distribute copies of the "Communist Manifesto" or of Chairman Mao's "On Contradiction." What they do is gather together the people of the village in the center of the village and then, one by one, the guerrillas rise and talk to the villagers about their own lives: about how they see themselves and how they came to be who they are, about their deepest longings and the things they've striven for and hoped for, about the way in which their deepest longings were frustrated by the society in which they lived.

Then the guerrillas encourage the villagers to talk about their lives. And then a marvelous thing begins to happen. People who thought that their deepest problems and frustrations were their individual problems discover that their problems and longings are all the same—that no one man is any different than the others. That, in Sartre's phrase, "In each man there is all of man." And, finally, that out of the discovery of their common humanity comes the decision that men must unite together in the struggle to destroy the conditions of their common oppression.

That, it seems to me, is what we are about.

This speech suggests that protagonists on both sides of the debate between SDS and the Resistance should be careful not to deal in stereotypes abstracted from time and place. There was a period, roughly the years 1966-1967, when SDS and the tendencies which became the Resistance were very close to one another. One sees this not only in the speech just quoted, but in the further facts that Greg Calvert helped set up the Des Moines meeting of August 1966, that (as previously mentioned) Bruce Dancis was an SDS chapter president and Tom Bell an SDS traveller, that Jeff Segal of SDS and later of Stop the Draft Week spoke at the Chicago We Won't Go Conference of December 1966, that in that same month the SDS National Council not only endorsed draft resistance, but condemned all military conscription, and finally, that at the 1967 SDS convention a resolution was passed supporting military desertion.

This was a period when draft resistance was a cutting-edge or growing-point for the movement as a whole. It developed for the most part outside SDS, but this was partly because of the size and heterogeneity of SDS; many people within SDS welcomed it.

What caused this happy state of things to deteriorate? It seems to me that the period when SDS and draft resistance were closest was also a period when white radicals, responding to their repudiation by SNCC, were asking how their own lives needed to be changed and whether it was possible to build a radical majority in white America. For white radicals it was a time of a politics of affirmation rather than a politics of guilt. With this in mind, perhaps one should turn the SDS critique of the Resistance inside out, and argue that during the past year SDS has been reverting to the very politics of middle-class self-flagellation which it charges to the Resistance; that is, that since the spring 1968 National Council meeting SDS has asked white people again to play the role of auxiliaries to others peoples' radicalism.

In this view, the psychological history of the movement falls into three periods. The first period, from 1960 roughly to 1965, is the period of orientation to the Southern civil rights movement. The intermediate period of non-vicarious politics found expression in the "student syndicalism" resolution at the SDS Clear Lake convention in August 1966, the draft resistance resolution adopted by the SDS National Council in December 1966, and the so-called "new working class" perspective developed by Carl Davidson, Greg Calvert, David Gilbert and others in the spring of 1967. The third period begins in April 1968, when the apparent deescalation of the Vietnam war and the riots following the assassination of Dr. King led SDS to drop the draft and turn to racism as the main issue.

To say this is not to deny that white radicalism in American history has been infected by racism, nor that the liberation front required to change America may have more black than white leaders. But the best way white radicals can contribute to that eventual coalition is by building a strong white radical movement. This movement must be free of racism, yet agitation against racism is not the best way to build it. For white radicals to make freeing Huey Newton or support for the demands of black students their *primary* political activity is to recreate at a higher level of struggle the friends-of-SNCC psychology of the early 1960s, and to program a new generation of activists into the functional equivalent of going South.

The problem about guilt which I see is not that in the past the Resistance built its politics on that emotion, but that, because so many people in the larger movement are now feeling guilty about being white and middle-class, we might at this point find it difficult to grow in a natural and relaxed way. Since April, 1968 the Resistance, like SDS, has been feeling its way beyond a middle-class constituency, and coming to the recognition that racism and capitalism as well as militarism must be resisted. Should this growth take place in an atmosphere of guilt, of repudiation of the past, of frenetic need for self-justification, of impatience for quick results because of fear of failing, then it *will* fail, and turn out to be not growth but disintegration. To be specific, I understand that there are Resistance groups which have involved themselves in university sit-ins and gone to pieces as a result; and it would be my guess, having been through an experience of that sort at the University of Chicago, that the resisters involved lacked confidence that they could deal with this new kind of problem, failed to meet regularly during the course of the action, and so were overwhelmed and dispersed by the effort to move outside the draft issue. Again, I understand that there are those who feel that the New England Resistance hardly belongs to the Resistance any longer because it decided not to turn in draft cards on November 14. In contrast it seems to me that the experimental work with high-school students and GIs, which is the other side of that decision, should be a resource to all Resistance groups. The concern of many groups to develop educational programs about imperialism is another indication of new life which should be welcomed, not feared.

I am struggling to delineate an attitude which will permit growth to take place in oneself and in others. Is it correct not to cooperate with courts, or to try to transform them by asking juries to rule on law as well as fact? There is no correct line. Let's try both, and evaluate the outcome together. Is student power in the university desirable, or should students leave the university and resist it from the outside? Again, there seem to me arguments on both sides, and many more than two possible answers. Should a teacher go into the public schools or create a free school? We need both, and life may settle the issue by recruiting the staff for free schools from the teachers fired from the others. What is the proper relationship of resisters to SDS chapters, to women's liberation groups, to high-school students, to persons over draft age who want to be more than supporters? Once and for all, I say down with correct lines, and the structuring of situations as if only two choices were possible, and a politics which makes the participant live in fear of being wrong.

Lest I seem to have endorsed doing one's own thing ad infinitum, let me conclude by suggesting a few guidelines which I think can be helpful as we experiment and grow.

III

First, something specific. There are certain values which, it seems to me, have to be axiomatic in the movement, because it is precisely by these values that we define ourselves. One of these values is love and respect for all human beings. I can imagine a comrade who, feeling this love and respect, nevertheless kills someone. The attitude of the revolutionary Vietnamese as I experienced it comes very close to this. I cannot imagine a comrade who gratuitously vilifies and denigrates others. Hence, if I have explained myself at all clearly, I feel less separated from a person who in a moment of danger slugs a cop than I did from my friend Tom Hayden when, on the eve of the Democratic Convention, he wrote an article in which he called policemen "pigs." I am ashamed of a movement which calls policemen pigs. I don't want to belong to it. Similarly, I feel deeply troubled by the attitude that, since we are right, we can take away civil liberties from others which we insist on for ourselves. I preferred the New England Resistance when, in an instruction sheet for a spring 1968 demonstration, it said, "Everybody has a right to demonstrate: they have the right to yell at us," than when, in a fall 1968 issue of the *Journal of Resistance*, it tried to justify heckling Hubert Humphrey to the point that he was unable to speak. Morality aside, I consider this a suicidal attitude with which to approach politics in a period of increasing right-wing repression.

Nevertheless it would be the worst sort of dogmatic rigidity and parochialism, characteristic of the old middle-class pacifism which I am sure we all want to transcend, were we to permit even these fundamental questions of value to blind us to the many things we have to learn from the kind of thinking exemplified by the New England Resistance. Among such lessons are the following:

1. The Resistance should explicitly condemn capitalism as the ultimate source of America's aggressive foreign policy. I do not think this requires the theoretical overkill one finds these days in *New Left Notes*. I don't believe we need to take a position on, say, the relative importance of the stockpiling of weapons or the contrivance of unnecessary missile systems as devices to avoid depression, on the one hand, as over against, on the other hand, overseas private investment; nor do I think we need be unanimous as to whether overseas investment arises from a need for cheap foreign labor, a need to export surplus capital, or a need for new markets, or some combination of these, and if so, what combination; I do not think consensus is required as to the impact of imperialism on the wages of different sectors of the American working-class and finally, recognizing that existing American investment in Vietnam is slight, that the expectations of future investment is difficult to document and that quite apart from particular investments the people who run this country may wish to deny an area to Communism or demonstrate their power to crush Third World revolutions, I do not believe the Resistance should commit itself to a detailed explanation of the Vietnam war, which may not be possible for some time. In short, we do not need to lose ourselves in the theory of imperialism in order to condemn the capitalist economy and thy imperilaism in order to condemn the capitalist economy and the imperialism to which, by whatever mechanisms, it indubitably gives rise. We must be very very clear that great power rivalry, the practice of conscription, and the sins of human nature, are not in themselves adequate explanations for American foreign policy; that the frantic character of American foreign policy is the other side of the ability of the peacetime domestic economy to maintain full employment and satisfactory profit margins; that to oppose Vietnam without opposing capitalism is to acquiesce in future Vietnams. I might add, taking note of the language of the conference agenda, that to oppose imperialism without opposing capitalism is also, in my opinion, to let the sickness spread while responding only to symptoms.

2. I don't see what sense it makes to talk about resisting capitalism without affirming an alternative. We should explicitly be socialists, or anarcho-syndicalists. The words are less important than the spirit. My intuition is that the movement will eventually come down on a political perspective intermediate between middle-class moralism, on the one hand, and Leninism, on the other, and that the Resistance, as a current in the movement intermediate between traditional pacifism and Marxism-Leninism is uniquely situated to affirm that perspective.

Let me give three illustrations of this perspective. Noam Chomsky, in his new book, speaks of "libertarian socialism," "anarchism," and "revolutionary pacifism." He illustrates what he has in mind by a long description of the

revolution-from-below created by peasants and workers in the midst of the Spanish Civil War and uniformly neglected by the war's elitist historians.

Second, Daniel Cohn-Bendit, in *his* new book, criticizes Leninism in much the same terms and offers another illustration: the current within the Russian Revolution known as the Workers' Opposition which insisted that socialism must mean workers'control, and which was crushed by the Bolshevik government at Kronstadt and elsewhere. Even in translation Cohn-Bendit evokes eloquently the vision of a revolution growing from decentralized resistance. What we need, he says, is "not organization with a capital O, but a host of insurrectional cells," "spontaneous resistance to all forms of domination," "the multiplication of nuclei of confrontation." And Cohn-Bendit is clear that this ultimate vision means that during the revolutionary process minorities within the revolution must have, not only the rights of free speech suppressed by the Bolsheviks, but the right to act out their minority convictions. Cohn-Bendit calls this "the right of independent action," a right, it seems to me, which the Resistance has hitherto practiced, and which it should not abandon in the quest for a more coherent political perspective.

Finally, there are the Wobblies, who wrote no books at all. At point after point, as we intuitively perceive, the spirit of the Resistance is akin to the spirit of the IWW. Their insight that change must come about through direct action at what they called "the point of production" is akin to the Resistance axiom that people must change the circumstances of their own daily lives. Their affirmation of the maxim that "an injury to one is an injury to all" is exactly the sense of solidarity with which the Resistance has sought to overcome the atomization created by the Selective Service System. Their belief in building "the new society within the shell of the old" overlaps what, in a more middle-class way, the Resistance has been feeling its way toward through alternative institutions.

This perspective is brilliantly laid out in an article by Dan Tilton in the *Journal of Resistance* for October 1968 entitled "socialism and Human Freedom" Tilton asserts that "the time has come for the Resistance to seriously consider definite alternatives to capitalism. . . .It is time . . . for the Resistance to state clearly that not only is capitalism insane, but more importantly that socialism is the only possible alternative." What Tilton means by socialism, however, is libertarian socialism or anarcho-syndicalism. He feels that the Resistance should carry over into its new commitment to socialism its old awareness of the evils of militarism and the nation state.

Our struggle in the Resistance has been up to now a struggle against governmental bureaucracy and illicit power. In this we have shown more wisdom than our Old Left counterparts with their ideas of nationalization of industry or the dictatorship of the proletariat. We have always realized that political power is suspect not just in capitalist nations but also in so-called socialist nations and that any solution to capitalism that involves socialism must answer the anarchist's questions concerning the nature of power and concerning its legitimacy. It must answer why "socialism" has not brought about human freedom.

Unlike many elements in the movement Tilton affirms rather than repudiates participatory democracy. "What needs to be done now," he writes, "is to carry the concept of participatory democracy to its ultimate conclusion."

Tilton's attitude toward participatory democracy is the attitude which people in the Resistance should have toward their original intentions. When we are told to abandon nonviolence so as to join in working-class struggle, we can respond that historically that struggle has expressed itself through the nonviolent means of strike, boycott, and sit-in. When advised to put away childish things and become politically "serious," we should remember that the characteristic Resistance conceptions of existential commitment, and the encounter between man and man, were created, not by armchair theorists, but by Albert Camus, Dietrich Bonhoeffer, Martin Buber, Ignazio Stone, in the furnace of resistance to fascism. I think it is possible to become politically serious without giving up the values which drew us into politics in the first place.

LIBERATION

May 1969

MORATORIUMORATORIUMOR

COMPREHENSION
From Demonstration to
General Strike?

WHERE TO?
WHERE TO?
WHERE TO?

jeremy brecher

True mass movements develop quickly; they contain contradictory impulses; they change rapidly in the face of events their leaders cannot control. The great mass movement called the Moratorium already shows three explicit political strands, each with its own assumptions and its own trajectory for the movement.

1) For the great majority of participants, the Moratorium is essentially an expression of sentiment, based on the hope that such an expression will somehow sway the President to change his course. They show somewhat the touching spirit of the Russian peasants who demonstrated on Bloody Sunday, 1905, in the belief that if only the Czar knew the people's misery he would save them. In this case, however, faith is put not in the magical mantle of divine authority, but in the equally magical belief that 'the government represents the people' and therefore will act upon their will. A more sophisticated version maintains that politicians in a democracy must respond to public pressures; the example is given of Johnson's reversal of Vietnam policy in the face of overwhelming public pressure. But the fact is that even Johnson's extreme political isolation, which would have led to the fall of any parliamentary government in the world, led him only to make a change in strategy, while leaving half-a-million men in Vietnam.

To the extent that the Moratorium remains within this framework it has no future, for the October 15th demonstrations alone were enough to show overwhelming popular desire to get out of Vietnam, as did the October Gallup Poll showing that a bill to withdraw all U.S. troops from Vietnam by the end of 1970 was supported nearly two-to-one. If the Moratorium retains this view, it may grow for a month or two, but after that it will gradually fade away, leaving little effect on the actual course of events.

2) The second strand constitutes opposition politics. It is essentially a continuation of the Kennedy-McCarthy movement of 1968—even the faces are the same. It too is based on a touching faith in the electoral process, seemingly impervious to the results of experience. Its proponents have not learned the obvious lesson of the 1968 campaign: that the electoral process is controlled from above, not below. They have not learned the obvious lesson of the A.B.M. struggle: that the real power over governmental action does not lie in elected bodies. They have not noticed that Nixon ran as a 'Peace candidate', as did our other Vietnam War Presidents, 'we seek no wider war' Johnson and 'let us put a truce to terror' Kennedy, before him.

Naturally, there are always politicians who are willing to associate themselves with 'peace' when peace is popular. Thus, for example, Teddy Kennedy and George McGovern both associated themselves with the Moratorium by speaking on October 15—and proposed that all troops should be withdrawn by 1972! Several top Moratorium organizers themselves see it as a jumping-off point for their own political careers: Adam Walinsky, who all but took over the

New York Moratorium office, is planning his campaign for state attorney-general, and Sam Brown, national director of the Moratorium, is talking about a Massachusetts congressional campaign.

The program of this approach will be to keep the Moratorium going for a few more months, then swing it into the 1970 primaries and elections, building a base for a McCarthy-style campaign in 1972. Its main requirements are that the movement remain respectable, give visible support and loyalty to likely candidates, and continue to grow for a few months until it can be channeled into electoral action.

3) The third strand is confrontation. In its extreme form, as practiced by Weatherman, it is rejected by most of the Moratorium movement, but as the legacy of the civil rights movement and the old Mobilization Committee, its basic idea that 'power is in the streets' remains the frame of reference for most radicals in the peace movement. It assumes that each confrontation simultaneously advertises the radicals' cause and undermines the claim of the government to represent the popular will. If the government uses violence, it presumably de-legitimates itself further with the population by showing that the basis of its power is not consent but force. At some point in the escalation of demonstrations, the demonstrators (as Staughton Lynd once imagined it) simply march to the White House and in their overwhelming numbers take back control of the country.

The first problem with this approach is quite obvious—until the military and police power of the state dissolves, it is based on sheer fantasy. As the efforts to 'storm' the Pentagon in the October, 1967 Mobilization, the battles at the 1968 Democratic Convention, and the recent Weatherman demonstrations in Chicago show, such tactics are essentially suicidal; not only because of the direct effects of the state's brutality on demonstrators, but because few sane people deliberately offer themselves up as victims of police brutality where there is no other gain to be made. That is one reason why confrontation actions have had steadily fewer participants each time since the Pentagon demonstrations of 1967, even while opposition to the war grew by leaps and bounds.

The second problem is perhaps more important. The favorite tactic of an unpopular ruling group is to turn the sentiment of the population against the radical opposition. Since confrontation can always be interpreted as a deliberate provocation of violence, it plays directly into the hands of the authorities, who through their control of the press can make even a non-violent confrontation appear a deliberate act of violence. Even such flagrant official aggression as that of Daley's cops at the 1968 Democratic Convention was palmed off as 'demonstrators' violence' to a majority of the population. Thus, the prime political objective of confrontation fails; the government is permitted to portray itself as the bastion of public interest and public order under attack by a few violent malcontents. The radicals, desiring to show to the people their own power, reveal instead only the weakness of demonstrators before the military power of the state.

The program of the confrontationists will be primarily to make the Moratorium demonstrations more 'militant'—that is, essentially to seek conflict with the police rather than to avoid it. If the Moratorium and Mobilization Committees do not adopt such a course, they will attempt to generate such confrontations through separate demonstrations and organizations. The result will be a tendency toward splitting of the

movement, falling off of mass support, new vulnerability to governmental attack, and no doubt a few concussions.

II

All of these tendencies are rooted in the idea that real power lies in Washington. But the Moratorium movement also contains the seeds of a different approach.

Despite the apparent power of the men in Washington to make the crucial decisions, it is not they who keep the country going, who do its work and fight its wars. Rather, it is the people—the same people who support two-to-one the withdrawal of all U.S. troops from Vietnam. If they refuse to work—if they strike—the war must end. Indeed, the Moratorium itself was originally conceived as a general strike against the war, but was watered down by leaders who, as the New York *Times* put it, "liked the idea of political action but not the threat of a strike." To end the war, the Moratorium must more and more become a general strike against the war. It is here that the real power of the movement lies, not in playing politics or playing with violence.

Of course, a general strike does not come into being simply because some organization calls for it. It will only come about if public sentiment moves from a mere dislike of the war to a decision to force it to end, and if the movement puts its faith in itself, not in politicians who promise but won't—or can't—deliver. But as long as the government continues the war, the movement against it will grow and deepen, and the Moratorium will be able to take on more and more the character of a general strike.

How can the Moratorium movement develop towards a general strike? First, by constantly widening its support. Second, by developing more and more job walkouts as part of its monthly protests. If such walkouts spread, the Moratorium thereby becomes a symbolic general strike. If even that fails to force an end to the war, the groundwork will have been laid for a real general strike, with the population halting production and providing for its own essential services until the government stops the war. The key in all these steps lies in the *workplace organizations*.

Throughout the country, workplace committees have sprung up spontaneously to coordinate participation in the October and November demonstrations. In New York, for example, Moratorium committees were formed by employees in each of the major newspapers, T.V. stations, and publishing houses; in Boston, by secretaries and lab workers at M.I.T.; in Washington, by workers in each government agency.

The main activities of such groups so far have been recruiting for participation in demonstrations and education teach-ins, discussions, and meetings for fellow workers.

Even such elementary exercises of Constitutional rights have often brought conflict with the employers over peace work during working hours and the use of employers' facilities. Thus, at both the New York *Times* and the National Institute of Mental Health the use of auditoriums was refused for October 15. In the latter case, the ban was overturned by an injunction secured by the workers against their governmental employer. Thus, such a movement automatically raises the most fundamental questions of participatory democracy and socialism: workers' control of their own work time and work place, and their responsibility for the overall direction of society.

The prime objective of each workplace organization should be participation of a majority of their fellow workers either in workplace educational meetings or as a group in demonstrations on each Moratorium day, eventually including mass walkout.

III

Such great social events as general strikes do not usually result from a single source of discontent; rather, they are a response to the piling up of one grievance on another, one action on another. So far action against the war has come primarily from middle-class and white collar people. However, those who fight against the war directly will have new allies in the coming months, for the government has deliberately put the burden of the war on those who can least afford it.

While fighting against tax reform, Nixon has demanded that the special war surtax remain. He has deliberately adopted policies which create unemployment in order to restrain war-generated inflation. This, combined with the fact that real take-home pay of workers had decreased each year since the escalation of 1965, means that strikes will increase and become more bitter. Pressure on business to cut payrolls will lead to attempts at speed-up, with a resulting increase in wildcat strikes. As Labor Secretary Shultz said recently, "there will be a lot of tension . . . I imagine there will be strikes . . . this is part of the process of sorting out and rearranging the sense of direction of the economy."

Strikes and resulting wage increases will make the economic consequences of the war still less manageable for Nixon. The rise of discontent will undermine the lock-step patriotism of those who today still think it disloyal to oppose the President. Thus, the effects of this strike movement will converge with those of the growing anti-war strike movement.

IV

As things become more serious, Nixon may attempt a counter-attack against the peace movement—everything from red-baiting to jailing leaders and shooting at demonstrators. By these means he may scare off many of the politicians who have seen benefit in supporting the movement, and even break up the national organizations which have led it. For these results the movement must be ready: it must be prepared to lead itself.

At this point the workplace organizations again become critical. For they can carry on the movement on their own initiative, no matter what happens to the movement's national leadership. Even coordination of dates for their action will be no problem because of the monthly pattern which has been established. As the real power of the antiwar movement lies in the people, so in their own organizations lies the people's power to act.

The course of action for opponents of the war is thus clear: set up a Moratorium or strike committee where you work. Coordinate directly with other workplace organizations. Organize teach-ins, educational meetings, and participation in Moratorium-day demonstrations among your co-workers. Move these actions as rapidly as possible toward mass walkouts.

Jeremy Brecher was once Northwest regional organizer for SDS. He is now an Associate Fellow at the Institute for Policy Studies in Washington, D.C. and co-editor of Left Mailings, *a new radical pamphlet series.*

LIBERATION Dec 1969

COMPREHENSION
What Is the Movement? Where Has It Been? What Is Its Program?

Politics of the Movement

THE AGONY OF THE AMERICAN LEFT. *By Christopher Lasch. Alfred A. Knopf. 220 pp. $4.95.*

JOHN McDERMOTT

Mr. McDermott is field secretary of the New University Conference and a freelance lecturer. Formerly, he was associate editor of Viet Report *and has written widely on the Vietnamese War. His book on technology and society will be published later in the year by Random House.*

The Agony of the American Left is at once intellectually lucid and politically opaque. The distinction, I recognize, is

an odd one and difficult to explain but it holds nevertheless. Each of the five essays collected in this volume contains an unusual wealth of insight into the history of the American Left and its recurring (and, Lasch feels, highly abortive) efforts to reform our society. In the essay on Populism, for example, American domestic society is portrayed at one point as an empire, dealing with its own minorities as it deals with its client-states overseas. The overwhelming and now traditional intellectual sterility of American Marxism is dissected in the essay on black nationalism. In his essay on the Socialist Party, Lasch traces out the causes and implications of our failure to link politics and culture in any creative way. In the same essay, he suggests that the current Left reaches back much more to the Socialists and the Wobblies than the movements of the thirties, a theme, incidentally, which one would like to see developed much further than he does.

His history of the Congress for Cultural Freedom, which originally appeared in *The Nation* (all of these essays have appeared previously in various periodicals), remains the best analytical piece on the anti-Communist liberalism of the McCarthy period. Here, as elsewhere, Lasch's purpose is to illuminate the past in order to enlighten the present. The value of his analysis is doubly confirmed as day by day the same kind of perverse liberalism, led often by the same men as in the fifties (for example, Sidney Hook)

tries to revive itself in order to lead a new purge against "subversion," "totalitarianism" and other dangers from the Left.

Yet, for all the illumination, a political opaqueness still remains. It stems, I think, from Lasch's almost unremitting failure to perceive the current Left movement in this country as a political movement per se giving expression to profound social and economic grievances. Instead Lasch, along with Kenneth Keniston, whose work he cites with approval, insists on portraying today's radicals as animated by moral or cultural (or even) generational protests only marginally related to American politics and social life. Accordingly, the tempered political judgment which characterizes his treatment of earlier American movements such as the Socialist Party before World War I, or even American society today, is put aside when he reaches the New Left and we must settle instead for unrestrained and unenlightening polemic.

The New Left or, as it calls itself, the Movement, now about ten years old, is a political community of anarchists, antiwarniks, blacks, black nationalists, draft resisters, GI dissidents, intellectuals, liberals, libertarians, Marxists, Marxist-Leninists, C. Wright Millsians, pacifists, Socialists, students, young professionals, syndicalists, women and youth (among others). *Fortune* credits it with about 125,000 student activists and suggests that its close sympathizers on campus total 2.3 million. Numbers in the other categories are difficult to estimate. (I'd be interested to see the FBI's.) In any case it is a mass movement and it continues to grow. Among whites, the SDS chapters and campus-based anti-war and resistance committees have been the most important organizations but their hegemony is being challenged by the steady growth of organizations for non-students, particularly GIs, women, and young professionals.

It is a political movement and it has scored some impressive political victories. In 1960-64, led by SNCC, it smashed legal segregation in the South. In the spring of 1965, led at first by SDS, it began the mammoth task of checking the war in Vietnam. It is useful to recall here how bitterly opposed older leftists such as Irving Howe, and peace organizations such as National SANE, were to the principle that the anti-war movement must take the road of open, mass and, if necessary, illegal opposition rather than limit itself to intellectual dissent and legal petition. I raise this point of history not for polemical purposes but rather to underline the political character of that SDS decision. The successes which grew from it were political successes: building a mass, radical anti-war movement, placing a ceiling on the duration and weaponry of the Vietnamese War, and preventing the growth of a mass movement of the Right over the frustrations of the war. (People tend to forget that in the absence of a mass, radical opposition to the Korean War, both Truman and Eisenhower not only believed it politically acceptable to use nuclear weapons in Korea but were under considerable pressure to do so. Similarly those critics who blame the rise of George Wallace on the Movement forget that during the Korean War Joe McCarthy won almost a majority for a much more dangerous domestic and international program.)

The Movement played a major role in driving LBJ from office, and its activities in Chicago during the Democratic convention were decisive in Humphrey's defeat last November. This latter fact is made clear by analysis of the vote fall-off in 1968. A smaller percentage of registered voters went to the polls than in any national election since 1948. The overwhelming majority of the *registered* stay-at-homes were Democrats and many of them had learned from the Movement's activities in Chicago how bankrupt and anti-democratic the official liberalism has become.

The Movement has set off a wave of change on campus, especially in the professional associations, and it has created publications (some of serious intellectual weight) with a monthly circulation of over a million. In a brilliantly conceived and executed campaign it has succeeded in building a resistance movement within the armed forces, recruiting in the process and for the first time large numbers of working-class youth to its ranks.

I do not mean to overlook the Movement's failures. SDS has been temporarily stalemated by a tactic of declining effectiveness—the sit-in—and now appears strategically uncertain about its immediate objectives. Similarly, I would not exaggerate the ultimate significance of its victories to date, or denigrate the force of other factors (e.g., NLF victories in Vietnam). But what must be understood is that the activities of the Movement were decided upon by groups of political people engaged in political analyses of this society in pursuit of political objectives. Some of the decisions, for example to begin organizing within the armed forces, were taken independently and simultaneously by a number of different groups. By contrast, the decision to go over into the opposition in the spring of 1965 was taken within the SDS national office. But in all these things the initial decisions were quickly ratified by the actions of large numbers of people who adopted the analyses and actions as their own. This is precisely the kind of reaction one would expect from a movement with a developed political consciousness. Such reactions are inexplicable if one characterizes the Movement, as Lasch often does, as a loose collection of morally "alienated" people which deals not with real issues but with "leftist fancies," led by its "more demented" elements who must be "recall[ed]" to their senses (those that ever had any)."

When the views of a writer of Lasch's caliber overlap those of, say, Max Lerner, Sidney Hook, Eric Sevareid, Richard Nixon, or the education editor of *The New York Times*, it is a matter which obviously requires more than passing explanation.

Lasch argues forcefully that the United States is now a post-industrial society, a society in which the problems of poverty, economic deprivation and regimentation to industrial discipline have been or can be solved for the vast majority of Americans. By contrast, in post-industrial society poverty and its kin have become endemic for a minority (mostly black) who are excluded from mainstream America. Simultaneously, mass education removes large numbers of young people

at a critical period in their lives and for a considerable time from the productive process and . . . from institutional ties to the rest of society. . . . As marginal members of society students as a class, like Black people, are more likely than other classes to be attracted to perspectives highly critical of society, particularly when they are faced with "integration" into society in the form of the draft. This is the basic sociological condition that gives rise to the student Left and the "new radicalism" in general.

It is this perspective, more than anything else which makes Lasch concentrate on the zanier, less responsible and less pleasant elements of the Movement, which make him read its anti-academic clericalism as anti-intellectualism, its combativeness as nihilism, and its contempt for procedural liberalism as incipient totalitarianism. If students are socially marginal it is not primarily their social relationships (e.g., being socially or economically exploited) which animate and are expressed in their politics, for it is precisely these social relationships and experiences which are lacking. Hence, for Lasch, this deficit of social experience can only be made up, so to speak, by ideological assets: a rich analysis of society and the past, a fund of ideology, ample intellectual balance and maturity, and so forth. Because ideological assets like these are exactly what the Movement most lacks, Lasch is led to see in every one of its shortcomings convincing evidence of what he believes is its central and, probably, fatal failure— a lack of program.

Here I find Lasch's analysis of American society very useful and his programmatic suggestions extremely valuable in themselves. But I fear that a misperception about a very tiny point leads him to very large and erroneous consequences. Youth or students *as a class* are not marginal to post-industrial society and they are not created as its by-product. There are no such classes in pre-industrial or even classical industrial society. In both cases, one goes directly from childhood to adulthood without an intermediate stage. The significance of "youth" and "students" in contemporary American society follows from the need of advanced technological society to give very broad technical and scientific training to great masses of people, while at the same time acculturating them to an extraordinarily restricted political, social, personal and work life. A hundred years ago 8-year-old girls could be forced into coal mines, fitted into the traces of a hand-pulled coal car and starved into obedience. Today, America's 6-to-24-year-old incipient Adj. A.s, B.A.s, M.S.s, E.E.s, and Ph.D.s must be made technically competent and socially mature but no less obedient in their own way. Since starvation (in the mother country at any rate) is no longer an acceptable sanction to create industrial discipline, discipline must be internalized in industry's human resources while they are young. The acculturation mechanisms of our society have a heavy load to bear. The industrialization of university (and school) life is the answer.

One is not using a metaphor when one speaks of students being turned out like industrial products. It's the simple truth. The university is now one of the main consumers of the nation's capital investments (much of it in the form of tuition). Its open-market structure has been replaced by a managed economy, and the organization of its productive process, the division of its labor, and the specifications on its end products have been thoroughly rationalized. Some institutions, such as Harvard and Berkeley, even offer quality control.

Such changes in the university, the *details* of which Lasch describes quite brilliantly, are not aptly characterized by his concept "post-industrial." In fact, analogous changes are now going on throughout American society. (See my article "Knowledge Is Power," *The Nation*, April 14.) Whereas formerly only hard goods were the subject of industrial production, now the production of students, research, health care, social services, residence and transportation systems, culture and even lower echelon managers is increasingly becoming capital intensive, management intensive and rationalized at every stage. The processes of industrialization, formerly experienced by a relatively small segment of our population, are now permeating the society as a whole. Students and youth, i.e., those who are in process of being made into industrial commodities, naturally feel the pressures most sharply, in the form of speed-up, tighter intellectual discipline, restrictive educational channels, mass organization, bureaucratic high-handedness, and so forth. Selective Service (and punitive cuts in loans and scholarships by legislatures) supplement their exploitation. Accordingly, they have created a massive and militant response primarily directed at the immediate agencies of their exploitation, the military and, especially, the university. The latter's pretense to being still a simple

community of scholars they find particularly galling. (Lasch incidentally has not yet completely shed this old myth.)

And more widely, the new wave of industrialization is re-creating the classical problems of industrial society, but in altered form. They include adulterated air, social exile for the elderly, political disenfranchisement for the masses, and a decline in certain aspects of people's living standards: residential congestion, lack of social (not recreational) life, decline in the quality of goods per dollar spent, and deprivation of health care. (An adult movement project in New York, the Health Policy Advisory Center, estimates that at least half the city's population is now medically indigent, while 80 per cent of the city's residents are indigent with respect to major medical care.) But all of this is a story in itself. Suffice it to say that the Movement is the beginning of the American people's response to a new wave of industrialization masquerading under the name of technological progress. Industrial society has not ended; in a real sense it has hardly begun.

Lasch's main contribution in these five essays is his dissection of the causes and effects of the American intellectuals' isolation from mass movements in this century. Especially in his essay on the Congress for Cultural Freedom (originally published in these pages) he shows how their elitism and power worship—the latter usually disguised as "pragmatism" or "realism"—have created a pro-

found and destructive intellectual, moral and social chasm between them and the political movements of the Left which have had such hopeful beginnings in the past and whose failures are symbolized in the title of his book. The problem has been and remains the problem of being intellectuals not *to* the Movement but *of* the Movement, not its clergy but its staff, not its organizational commissars but its intellectual cadre. More pointedly, there is no sense in demanding that the Movement have a program here and now. Such a program is now shaping itself as our people, long politically dormant, look at their society with a critical eye, learn its realities in sometimes ill-focused but always instructive struggles, and come to recognize what they want and what they don't. Left intellectuals should add their considerable talents to that process, and not be content to chafe at its slowness. High on the agenda is the task of building an adult movement on the Left of a size and strength commensurate to that of the students, co-belligerent with them, and capable of shaping the radical program Lasch demands. It is a job hardly begun and, despite my critical observations, it is a job to which, I feel, this book makes substantial contribution.

THE NATION
6/23/69

SPROUL PLAZA AT
BERKELEY: THE DEAN
(ON HIS LOUDSPEAKER)
DECLARES A WAR NING

THIS IS A WAR
NING THIS IS A
WARNING THIS IS
AN URGENT WAR
NING THIS AN AN
URGENT WARNING
THIS IS A WAR
NING I REPEAT
THIS IS A WAR
NING THIS IS AN
URGENT WARNING
Found Poem Beverly Pervier 12/5/68
Daily Californian, U. Cal. Berkeley, Dec 1968

Do not mistake me: we are not riding the crest of a revolutionary wave; we are only — ONLY, but this is no small feat — staking out our own history, defining precedents, opening space for new objectives, lighting new energy fuses. Vague formulations all, for the holding of cultural and physical territory is something we know little about.

TODD GITLIN, *San Francisco Express Times* 11/13/68

GRIM REAGAN CALLS IT 'INSURRECTION'

The violence which rocked the Berkeley campus of the University of California yesterday "is insurrection," Governor Ronald Reagan declared here last night.

"It is a wholesale effort to bring the university to a halt," the Governor said. "I think there's no excuse for it."

Reagan, who appeared grim and weary, commented on the turbulent campus situation moments after he arrived here in order to attend a meeting of the UC Regents in Berkeley today.

"I'm not pessimistic," he said. "However, this will have to end quickly — immediately."

Earlier yesterday in Sacramento, Reagan said the statewide student unrest amounted to guerrilla warfare, and that the only way to stop it is to "eliminate" those who cause the trouble.

The solution in guerrilla warfare is to eliminate and kill your enemy, Reagan told a group from San Diego's Chamber of Commerce during impromptu remarks in his office.

The Governor said that while he obviously doesn't advocate killing faculty and student dissidents, "the only thing that can win in guerrilla warfare is. . .you have to eliminate them by firing the faculty and expelling the students."

San Francisco Chronicle 2/21/69

REAGAN'S CALL FOR 'BLOOD BATH' ROUSES CALIF. DEMOCRATS

SACRAMENTO, Calif. — A call by Gov. Ronald Reagan for "a blood bath" to silence campus revolutionaries has set off a political storm.

Although the Republican governor retracted the remark, Democrats quickly seized on it as an incitement to violence and as concrete evidence of his attitude toward young dissenters.

The remark was made at a meeting in Yosemite Park Tuesday. In answer to a question regarding militants, Reagan said "if it takes a blood bath, let's get it over with. No more appeasement."

The Boston Globe 4/9/70

BERKELEY
HAS BEEN A
KIND OF
EXPERIMENTAL
THEATER

CLAIMING TURF IN BERKELEY

michael rossman

People are considering the First Battle of Berkeley in terms of police brutality, civil liberties, Berkeley civic politics, or even the emergence of a revolutionary political vanguard, god help us. There is much confusion about what the Battle meant, in what if any sense it was a victory, and where and how to move next. And though this groping community conversation seems our own, most of it is not: in talking both tactics and theory, we define ourselves by and in reaction to the Outside's terms, its threats and promises. We have few terms of our own, natively new: little positive sense of who we are and of what moves through us.

There is a deeper context to this Battle than one hears in the immediate political conversation, on the streets or in our forums. To begin with, it is an episode in a struggle for ghetto self-rule. For the Berkeley community, of which Telegraph Avenue is the commercial and cultural center, is a first class ghetto: no matter that its inhabitants are young instead of black, no matter that its membership is voluntary rather than compelled. (Even this last may not be entirely true. We shouldn't dismiss too lightly the feeling of a growing many in their twenties: that urban life detached from our peculiar supportive communities is impossible.)

Berkeley and the Haight are America's prototype VOLUNTARY YOUTH GHETTOS, and with the East Village form the three largest ones. Such ghettos are unique and new to history; and the change they portent and begin may have properties that aren't described by any classical model of revolution (YSA beware). For the change goes deep; the Battle of Berkeley is more than a ghetto self-rule struggle and more than an expression of a future-oriented nationalism. A new culture, in the full strength of that term, is being born among the young of technological America. We all are coming to know this, and it's time to confess it publicly, and move with the knowledge.

Berkeley is one of that culture's three present main focii, and the Battle is an episode in its blind searching-out of forms and expressions for its growth. More than revolutionary politics or human rights of expression are involved: an emerging culture's survival is being tested out. (For who can doubt, that if enough of our heads get senseless bashed into the ground, a deep weariness will descend to fragment us beyond hope and our song into impotence, and the dawning of the new be again delayed?)

At Berkeley, the new culture first burst out in campus-based political expression, from '58 to '64, shaking up the surrounding society. Lately it has flowered also in urban community, in high arts and home arts and beauty and some thought: and a glad flag has been raised in our home-seeking hearts, its emblem still seen dimly. And the culture has been moving to claim the heartland of its birth, its home turf: the campus Plaza has been shakily secured for four years, since FSM, and now it moves on Telegraph.

Consider the chain of episodes which testify to our intense and growing territoriality. During the years when our only public expression was political, it struggled, harassed but successful, for a physical toehold on the edge of the campus.

OCTOBER 1964. The administration decides to take away our space, banishes the political tables. Cops drive onto campus and arrest a kid at an "illegal" Civil Rights table. 1000 Students entrap the copcar for two days, wait for 600 cops to descend upon them (no blood this time). Free exercise of political rights on the Plaza is decreed, enforced by popular support: the Plaza is ours, and we'll talk there as we please, by the laws we recognize: our bodies on the line to defend our public place.

APRIL 1966. A night-time VDC rally in support of striking Saigon students is held on Telegraph, choking the Avenue. There is no permit. Police club the microphones silent, confiscate them. The demonstration moves down to City Hall, fruitlessly and nonviolently. (Later the courts say we shouldn't have been denied the permit.)

NOVEMBER 1966. Police come onto campus to remove an anti-war table set up opposite a Marine recruiting table — in our Student Union, which we have paid for and supposedly run, but do not control. They arrest first one student, and then four non-students from the sit-in which forms in protest. By midnight, 3,000 students vote the school out on its second protest strike, which comes off fairly well but wins us no space.

APRIL 1967. The Better Berkeley Committee spent a year of fruitless dicking-around with the city government, committees reports and petitions, trying for experimental closure of Telegraph as a mall and for festivals. Finally

someone prints up 500 buttons saying, "Telegraph/April 9th." And on that day of good music and public dope 3,000 friendly people close their street and play, unmolested. (The Haight beat us to the street-closing act a week earlier, but theirs got a bit smashed up by the heat.) We are temporarily bought off from regular trespass by the offer of Sunday rock concerts in Provo Park — a territory the Berkeley High kids had already somewhat liberated, where we tasted our first bit of teargas in 1967.

OCTOBER 1967. We are trying to close down the Induction Center. We need a place to gather, a public place to discuss and decide. The Plaza is sanctified by use. Court order forbids this; but the University helps fudge the interpretation so we aren't molested. Why? Because the 6,000 clustered in that shallow bowl of night — whose use we have not yet forced them to grant us in law — made it quietly quite clear once again that they would not move: that they would defend their possession and right to that place against clubs, tear gas, and perhaps death.

That is the leading edge of the present feeling about Telegraph Avenue: there is no mistaking the mood that grows in Berkeley, and only much cost will change its direction even temporarily. We are acting out a deep territorial imperative: a new culture must control its birthground, to control its own growth. (Much of our longing for an open space which is fully our own comes from our sense that in it will crystallize that community we so strongly anticipate, and whose fragments, frustratingly incomplete, nourish us now.)

In Berkeley, as in the Haight and her echo-communities, we are liberating territory in which to build and heal and play and learn. Free territory for these life-functions of community and culture comes also in forms other than physical space. With the underground papers, rock stations, and films we have staked out a corner of Medialand, in which our control is still uncertain. And in the hundreds of free universities, we begin to explore the unknown landscape of Our Necessary Education.

Observe the rough progression, Fellow Social Scientists. As people decide to stay on in Berkeley, they build to a critical culture-producing mass. The focus of community, once exclusively on the campus, suddenly doubles: a non-campus Berkeley community develops and displays itself, continuous and compatible with the campus community: twin yolks in the hot pan of our time. Expression broadens from the "merely political," and Telegraph Avenue becomes the best approximation to the physical root of our miraculous mushroom culture.

And thus the turf we decide to claim as our own expands off campus: we move on Telegraph. And the kinds of things we try to do on that turf, the social myths we try to act out, become more diverse and broadly humane. Creative/Joyous Community. Revolutionary Community. Are our efforts feeble? We have few models, and we're coming up from a long blind despair. Are our examples ludicrous? Don't laugh: they're all we got. And if Telegraph Avenue is not ours,

what is?

The victory of the Battle of Berkeley — if we may come back to that — is not in civic politics, where our quite real rational arguments and allies got a few liberal councilmen to switch votes, and prevent a July 4 massacre. The victory lies in this: The volatile edge of our disorganized community's will claimed Telegraph for July 4, and got it, IN PUBLIC. We have staked claims to our piece of land, and given notice that we will push for it: the threat of our bloodied presence and retaliation is full and credible. And this goes a long way toward shaping our consciousness, our sense of our interests, direction, and center. For some spaces of land do have special meanings and social powers.

Right now we take our turf at their mercy, and they clearly want to club the shit out of us (the broad violence of the old culture's Official Arm gives a clue to how deep our change runs). Moves are under way to try to ratify our claim politically: the PFP/Panther proposal for local community-controlled police is one such. A good political solution seems unlikely, though to get the city to give us the street seems possible. It would probably help to conceive and present the next moves in the struggle for Telegraph in this broader context, as part of a movement for ghetto and cultural self-determination. For the description furnishes a good framework for understanding . . e and how to move next, both within ˙ beyond political action.

Two footnotes. First, I'm not sure what to say about our violence, except that we're being roasted in the oven of our culture's violence, and what sad surprise if we heat in the heat, being flesh? But somewhat connected with this, is this matter of language: CLAIM A PIECE OF TURF. That is a strong nuance in our territoriality: we have in some respects a natural gang mentality. This isn't surprising either: the cops, the Kennedys, the Panthers, the Mafia, and the CIA are gangs, and we organize in response to our environment.

Also, a solid case can be made for a ghetto self-rule analysis by sociologists, and perhaps we should press them to do so. For they are long overdue, and the best among them are longing, for a way to translate their knowledge into social consequence. Why should they not finally go down to City Hall — even a few would do — and lecture those people that they've got knowledge they'd like to see have effect? And threaten to go off and organize a referendum ordering the City to act in accord with the findings of a study, which would mainly say KEEP OFF OUR BACKS? For the university community and its secular sister control Berkeley, at least when you count all the liberals in. And they just might be induced to vote all together to get the town's government to follow the scholarly dictates of sweet Reason. Especially if the fate or breaking of the University appears to possibly rest on the question of whether the State continues to harass its changling young.

San Francisco Express Times 7/9/68

5
resis

SUMMER OF 1968: SAN FRANCISCO TEEN-AGERS TAKE THEIR CUE FROM BERKELEY

Young Pacifica— Revolutionary Surprise!

lenny the head

Youth-Revolution culture, teenage Pacifica style, kicked open the garden gate in two days of Shopping Center skirmishes against reactionary police. The sons and daughters of commuting factory workers and office clerks have "nowhere to go when the beaches are cold"; are tired of being harassed by the cops and storekeepers; like to smoke marijuana and don't care who knows it.

Proudly: "I'd say fifty percent of the high school turns on. That's 700 out of 1300."

Boasting: "I think everybody gets stoned except the police explorers" (a handful of students interested in law-enforcement careers).

The entrance to the Linda Mar shopping center is impressively corner-stoned by Texaco and Phillips 66 on either side of divided Linda Mar Boulevard which cuts perpendicular into the coast road. Nightly fog.

"The cops'll start it. They're down on young people."

Sunday afternoon, a young man bought a coke and sat down to drink it. One of the new private cops told him to vacate the chair "reserved for customers only."

The young people, who occupy the vast parking lot in the summer, set up a PROTEST picket line. "This Shopping Center Unfair to Teenagers." The merchants were infuriated and called the police.

"Their attitude was 'We don't want your nickels, dimes and pennies.'" The truth is that Grant's, Sears, Mode 'o Day (imagine?) and most of the others rely on the teenagers' trade. They're bluffing.

A crazy guy in a red sports car tried running down a few of the demonstrators, and brazenly stepped out of the car offering a karate whipping to anyone who dared. The people made a citizen's arrest.

Lacking any sense of justice, the police intentionally arrested the wrong man and let the criminal go free.

"I was talking to a friend about it and I said 'Fuck'. They arrested ME... Fascist pigs, that's what they are."

bed by the police in front of his father— now his most ardent supporter. "The guy hit me in the neck with his stick and I just grabbed him." He's been charged with two felonies. "The ACLU is going to court with us Wednesday."

photo by jeff blankfort
The informant: "It was all planned."

He and his friends used to go up to Haight-Ashbury. "Too many burns. No burns around here, and not much Methedrine, anymore. Later on they threw me down the stairs at the station and then they beat me." He started to show me his bruises and modestly changed his mind.

Another casualty was Pacifica Police Chief Tremaine, who blasted himself in the face when he tried to fire his can of mace from the hip.

"They arrested this teacher, 36, a good guy. When the cop said to disperse, he said 'Why?'. About 21 squad cars were there--from all over the county-- they sprayed everyone in range: girls, fathers, mothers." Organizing tool of the Left.

Monday night curfew for under eighteen: ten pm.

"They kicked me outa the store; why not the older people?"

The kids are coming, tooling into the left turn onto Linda Mar, honking horns, waving, flashing the V. "Last night, nuthin' was broken. Tonight'll be a different story." One firebomb was harmlessly thrown, out by the highway side of the shopping center.

Nick Gust, grey-haired salesman of a mayor, uptight and condescending, was trying to cool things down in the parking lot. "Now you get your group together. Tomorrow? Fine. I wanna see what you kids are looking for."

Believe him?

"No. This has been goin' on a long time." A year ago, 500 petitioners requested facilities from the council for recreational use. The Peace and Freedom Party was helpful. Nothing.

A small girl, junior high, stared up at the mayor's twisting, distracted head. "Why don't you do something else? We need like an Avalon Ballroom instead of gas stations."

There were parents in that parking lot; parents WITH their children; feeling guilty perhaps for having left the city, for running away to tract land. Cheaper homes and more country in Pacifica.

An adamant, portly mother blocked my path: "I'm sick and tired of the way the newspapers treat these young people. It's the police that's to blame, NOT THEM!" After I promised to report the truth, she let me go.

Exit the mayor. Cops in the parking lot: "This is Captain Shipley, a peace officer of the state of California and the town of Pacifica." Same old shit--disperse. "...and those of you who are res-

unless you have business at the shopping center."

"Move to the sidewalk!" comes from the ranks, followed by echoes.

"Let's move across the street." The strategy unfolds.

More squad cars: six, eight, ten. The policemen set up.

"Free Huey." Again, "Free Huey."

An angry old lady nearly zipped me over, flying by in her granny goose shoes: "Everybody just wants their picture taken." It's almost true. Berkeley's paranoia about lists and files is not yet known in Pacifica.

Pow! A cherry bomb.

"Burn. Burn. BURN. BURN! BURN!"

"Attention on the street....."

"Fuck you!"

A shaggy line of police moved across Linda Mar. Retreat over the empty lot. Hop the big fence. Heave a few rocks. None of it too tense. And just beyond the fence, just a block to the east, lay a great, ugly, two-model expanse of homes and lawns, to feast the eye upon.

From behind the fence, a great mother came out to pull her boy home. "Get in there!" His friends laughed. She took him.

The police fanned out, poorly organized, new units arriving all the time — the San Francisco delegation.

"I got a date, man. What am I doin' here?" Dungarees. The girls were more with it, using feminine blackmail to wring concessions from their parents. There was practically no delineation with respect to appearance. Longer hair is a privilege of the clever or the independent.

At ten, the police moved out in force, clearing the streets, sending them home, trying to be polite with the families who had forsaken the set to come out and watch it live.

"Folks. Do you live here? I'D appreciate it if you went inside." Co-operation.

The boys WALKED away from the sauntering police clubs, defiant, grumbling audibly over their shoulders: "I live here. You go home." Up and down the street. The people stopped where and when the police did. Slowly, after hanging, driving around, the crowd dispersed.

The cops had their theory: First night was troublemakers, but nothing outside organized; Second night "it was a couple of professionals, they've changed their tactics." Retreat is the tactic.

Monday night, they went after individuals. Informants made it a little easier. Occasionally, they got a little pissed and chased some car or somebody. Split real fast. If you got caught, it was handcuffs, a little roughing, face down on the trunk. A few cops were toting shotguns. Back at the parking lot, an informant bared himself for the press. The man doesn't understand movements. He said it was all planned. It wasn't. A hundred and fifty police tried to force them back into the static role the community held ready for them.

No! Independence! We decide for ourselves what's right here. Leaders emerged: the voices directing groups movements; the inexperienced brick-throwers; the boys singled out.

Wednesday is court. PROTEST. The council meeting. PROTEST. Learn how.

Is there any radical potential in it? Well, how many shopping centers are there?

Ed. Note: Pacifica is a middle-class residential section of San Francisco. These events followed soon after the fight for Turf on Telegraph Ave. in Berkeley (above).

San Francisco Express Times 7/30/68

WHO OWNS THE PARK?

Someday a petty official will appear with a piece of paper, called a land title, which states that the University of California owns the land of the People's Park. Where did that piece of paper come from? What is it worth?

A long time ago the Costanoan Indians lived in the area now called Berkeley. They had no concept of land ownership. They believed that the land was under the care and guardianship of the people who used it and lived on it.

Catholic missionaries took the land away from the Indians. No agreements were made. No papers were signed. They ripped it off in the name of God.

The Mexican Government took the land away from the Church. The Mexican Government had guns and an army. God's word was not as strong.

The Mexican Government wanted to pretend that it was not the army that guaranteed them the land. They drew up some papers which said they legally owned it. No Indians signed those papers.

The Americans were not fooled by the papers. They had a stronger army than the Mexicans. They beat them in a war and took the land. Then they wrote some papers of their own and forced the Mexicans to sign them.

The American Government sold the land to some white settlers. The Government gave the settlers a piece of paper called a land title in exchange for some money. All this time there were still some Indians around who claimed the land. The American army killed most of them.

The piece of paper saying who owned the land was passed around among rich white men. Sometimes the white men were interested in taking care of the land. Usually they were just interested in making money. Finally some very rich men, who run the University of California, bought the land.

Immediately these men destroyed the houses that had been built on the land. The land went the way of so much other land in America—it became a parking lot.

We are building a park on the land. We will take care of it and guard it, in the spirit of the Costanoan Indians. When the University comes with its land title we will tell them: "Your land title is covered with blood. We won't touch it. Your people ripped off the land from the Indians a long time ago. If you want it back now, you will have to fight for it again."

BERKELEY GRAPHIC ARTS

ORIGINAL POSITION PAPER OF THE PARK'S PEOPLE BY F. BARDACKE

The Meaning of Peoples' Park

I. todd gitlin
II. john simon

I.

What is it about People's Park in Berkeley? Meanings proliferate: the escalation in systematic counter-insurgency, Vietnam coming home, the nationally-coordinated repression, the raising of the question of private property, Berkeley as weapons-testing ground.* But from a few weeks' distance, the most distinctive meaning seems to me something different. We are still inside the events though, and these notes are not intended to have finality.

For the first time the white left and street movements have fought to defend something they made themselves rather than to win demands from the Authorities. When the Park-makers talk about the Park, they glow: when they talk about the fence, they become grave. The Park is physically, touchably, verifiably *there*, not just for its makers but for any eyes and hands. "Serving the people" requires physical proof, and the Park was that. Straight people were welcome, and they used the Park.

Public need and vision collided with property. The friction between irrepressible need and immovable institutions ignited a war.

The Mayor of Berkeley said the trouble was that the street people had not asked the University's permission. Disingenuous or not (there was no sign the University would grant anything), this Jeffersonian relic, caricature of the petit-bourgeois antihero, had put his finger on something. Indeed no permission had been solicited. A number of Telegraph Avenue revolutionaries had simply moved onto the land, to use and defend it in the spirit, they said, of the Costanoan Indians who had owned the land before Spanish missionaries, Mexican troops, American settlers, the U.S. government, and the University of California in turn had expropriated it. Squatting, whether enshrined in ruling-class law or outside it, is one of the few uniformities in American custom. The difference was that the Park-makers applied the standard of good use. Had the University enriched the community when it seized private property (yes!) from small landlords who hadn't wanted to sell, the Park-makers could not have made an appealing case for their use of the plot. As it was, the University had planned lucrative and authoritarian dormitories—for students who don't want to live in the ones that exist—and later, after the Park was started, had

scraped together a scheme for playing fields—for students who don't use the present ones. Meantime, the land was a muddy parking lot.

As substance and sign of a possible participatory order, as the living and hand-made proof that necessary institutions need not be overplanned, absentee-owned, hierarchical—as such the Park came to stand in many minds as one tantalizing trace of a good society, as the practical negation of American death, as a redemption worth fighting for. Suddenly, almost inescapably, citizens were asked to choose between the splendid, self-ordered reality of People's Park and images of Chancellor Roger Heyns with his committees and charts and literally murderous lies. At a Regent's committee meeting June 7, the question kept coming up, "What would you do if another group came onto the land and claimed it?" One member of the Park negotiating committee answered, "We'd talk it over with them, work something out." Another member said later he wished he'd had the chance to say: "We know we wouldn't shoot them, the way you did." As the real-world choices shrink to two, soulful socialism and the police state, could they be any clearer?

The point is that the Park began to embody, not just the negation of capitalist principles of property and land-use, but some glimmering of the method and substance of a consciously visionary socialism rising from the ashes and the mud. It "educated" more people than a million anti-imperialist and anti-capitalist slogans. In the eyes of students and townspeople it discredited the University as dozens of transient, strictly-oppositional movements had failed to. "Yes, of course! Why *should* land be traded like paper? What is land for anyway?" The same principles here as in the Black Panther Party's program of Breakfast for Children, about which Jesse Unruh complained that the Panthers were feeding more California children than the Government of the United States of America. Bobby Seale worked in the Park, praised it, instantly comprehended its meaning.*

On the other hand the SDS chapter at Berkeley, dominated by Progressive Labor, hadn't the faintest idea what the Park was about. "Workers can't relate to parks," a spokesman said. "Workers can only relate to racism and imperialism." (As beneficiaries?) Among the "non-progressive aspects" of People's Park they listed the idea of building "islands of socialism." Without any sensitivity to the *process* of a revolution, the need of people to know that something better is possible, the central value of vision and the instructive value of vision denied—without sensitivity to the necessary tension between vision and reality, in other

words—they could offer nothing. Their demands somehow neglected to include the return of People's Park.

Meanwhile, people from all classes worked in People's Park and in the subsequent People's Park Annex, and then fought for them. Many working-class people, including National Guardsmen, could understand the Park as well, and what they didn't understand could become an opening wedge into a discussion of property.

But if there's all this creative energy on the Avenue, a friend of mine asks, why don't they use it to feed children? A creditable and pregnant question, but asked in a curiously abstract fashion. People's Park is a major milestone on the white movement's climb toward identity, without which there is no revolution. Roger Alvarado of San Francisco State College has said that the white movement is an issue-movement while the Third World movement, by contrast, is programmatic. The mission of the whites is to destroy, that of people of color to build anew. It is a common distinction: S.I. Hayakawa has said as much, and radicals commonly complain, bravely, that our task is to destroy or at least paralyze imperialism so that Third World revolutions may gain the space to build a new world.

But in People's Park the white movement gave body to its vision, blended construction into destruction; and thousands of people responded, in their own fashion—PTAs, unions, and the rest. Thousands of prior Reagan supporters turned on him and decided not to be "good Germans." The ruling class itself was substantially split, and the paltry parliamentary democracy of the Berkeley City Council discredited. (Even their halting vote to ask Reagan to withdraw his troops was ignored.) Had Berkeley been America, a contest for power would have become a plausible prospect, and we could have begun choosing the means to translate the popular will into a new system.

Of course, in itself the political culture of Telegraph Avenue for years has embodied a certain embattled alternative, a brushing-up-together of hip culture and Berkeley politics, the strung-out and the strong. For almost as long, the University, the city and the State have been trying to destroy that community, which the University has referred to as a zone of "hippie types and high crime." Telegraph Avenue even physically is placed like a knife pointed at the heart of the University; it is an attraction (distraction) for machine-processed students and an infiltrator of spirit. The combined counter-offensive has included the demolition of cheap housing near the campus, making the Avenue one-way, master-planning to raze an entire side of the street, hiring 25 new police for the Avenue in the summer of 1968, constant dope busts and that daily police occupation which could be called "petty harassment" were it not constant, patterned, everyday. Energy flared and burned out several times a week. The street began to look like a mad and morbid carnival of the gaily doomed. An alternative culture without definite embodiment, without growing into unavoidable, organic conflict with its true enemies, grows stale.

In late June 1968, the Young Socialist Alliance tried to organize a street rally in solidarity with the French revolutionaries. Police moved in and a riot took place. (This was the first major police use of gas against whites in Berkeley. It was also the first taste we had of "people's war"—many straight people hid street people from the police.) Of course the riots were not "about" the First Amendment, though the YSA and others tried to focus them there. The riots were "about" the right to the street. People wanted the street because it was theirs.

Marvin Garson had the insight at the time that two theories of the street were at war. In the bourgeois theory of the street, a person has three essential functions in life: working, buying, and "living." The cement of the system is traffic, especially car traffic. The street has value as the route between home and office, office and store, store and home. When the authorities say traffic must be kept moving, they mean it. This is the simple and monstrous logic behind the defacing of all American land, behind a legislative committee's recently-announced call for 1400 *more* miles of freeway in the San Francisco Bay Area by 1990. Meanwhile, the street people were saying that they are whoever they are wherever they are; that life is not segmented; that the street is for being, and that being takes precedence over traffic.

Those two theories crashed head-on. But last year the community was not ready for much beyond its still vague and abstract right to the street. So factions quarreled about "demands," "leadership" separated from the mass, and it all ended July 4 with a giant Avenue celebration. Few talked about a program that groups of people, "affinity groups," could themselves begin to implement from the stuff of their organic need.

Less than a year later, the community had defined its need in its devotion to the fact of People's Park. It didn't matter who started to make the Park; from the first day on the Park-makers had crystallized a common need, and thousands came out to work. Work was joy, not a job—how revealing of previously thwarted need in a community which had defined itself in its estrange-

ment from approved capitalist-Calvinist ideas of work! Later, thousands were to fight, literally to risk death, for what they had built. And a new theory of the street was born: the absolute negation and transcendence of the street. Probably the most revolutionary act of the weeks of battle after Bloody May 15 was the planting of "instant parks"—sod and trees—on and through the pavement next to the fence the University had built around People's Park. No demands, but the carving-out of a liberated area from the asphalt itself. Those areas don't last—except as images, but images become models and intimations.

The vision and the struggle had fused, as in People's Park itself. To make the stuff of human needs in America requires transgression of secular-sacred law. To construct what is most worth constructing is to collide at some point with the world capitalism has made. To liberate land for authentic public use in the South Campus area meant clashing with the University. It should be obvious; now more people know it. There didn't have to be an ulterior motive, a thirst for confrontation with the Authorities, an "issue" "around which" "we can get people to move"; the contest with the Authorities was built into the expression of the need. The University, owned by corporate wealth, simply could not tolerate the open, self-determined space, the spontaneous design which the community needed, with its energy and courage the proof of its need.

In People's Park Annex (a new park on Rapid Transit-owned land), the day after Berkeley police had demolished it, a girl listened skeptically to eyewitness stories of the night before: the police had gone berserk, burned tents, killed a kitten, broken trees. I had heard as many such stories as I could bear, and walked away to watch the work of reconstruction and to talk with friends. A few minutes later the girl came running over, listened for a while, then asked how we could possibly be grinning. She said she was new in Berkeley, and she didn't know how to live in fascism. How could we? I couldn't put in words what I felt: that our victory would be in continuing to build, freshly, against the guns, traces of what this society could be; in making something the mass of Americans will not be willing to see suppressed. •

I've gone into some of this, and the history of People's Park, in an article, "White Watts," in Hard Times No. 33 (80 Irving Place, New York 10003). On weapons-testing, remember that gas was first spewed in quantity on whites in Berkeley (June 1968). Days after a National Guard helicopter bombarded the University with CS gas this May, the same technique (developed at the Stanford Research Institute) was used on blacks in Greensboro, North Carolina.

TO OUR BROTHERS

These National Guardsmen are not pigs. They're not even gung-ho soldiers.

Most of them share our view that the Vietnam war is an unworthy act of aggression. By joining the Guard they avoided two years of active duty and a tour in Vietnam.

As 6-monthers, they have scorn for the Regular Army volunteers and the officers and career non-commisioned officers who harass them back at the armory. They know that the men who give the orders are only in the Guard for the pension, or because they love the once-a-week excersize of power.

Sooner or later many of these guardsmen will realize that their six month deal was an impossible compromise. Talk to them and explain what we are fighting for.

Many of them will choose the Movement over the Military.

You can distinguish potential friends from outright enemies by the insignia they wear. Here's a breakdown:

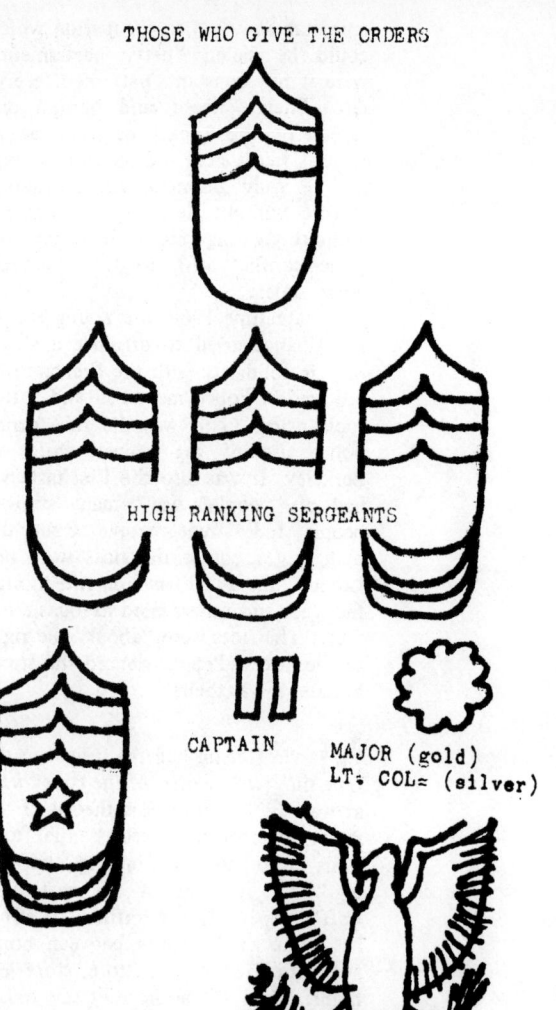

THOSE WHO GIVE THE ORDERS

HIGH RANKING SERGEANTS

CAPTAIN   MAJOR (gold)
           LT. COL. (silver)

COLONEL

TO OUR COUSINS IN THE ARMY

Once again, Reagan and Heyns have decided to make Berkeley an occupied area. With teargas and shotguns they are attempting to deny the legitimate right of this community to determine the use of its own land. The same people who wanted to use you in Vietnam have now ordered you into Berkeley. You said "No" then, can you say less now?

You are under orders to occupy this community against your will. You know that the people you face are not the enemies of America. They are young people much like you, people who are struggling to make this country a decent place to live, work and love.

You joined the National Guard because you were decent enough not to want to kill innocent people in Vietnam. You hoped to serve your six months and return to your own lives and homes. Now you're being called upon to perform the dirtiest work a soldier can do: fight his own countrymen!

can you?   WHAT CAN YOU DO?

1. Talk this over among yourselves. Why is the American Army being used against the American people?

2. Talk to us about the Park. Let us explain what we are fighting for.

3. If you can, join us. We will do all we can to help.

REMEMBER:

You too are angry at the powerful people who rule this country. You too feel real concern over the future of America.

You know how to resist the army better than we. Our beef is with the Regents and the cops. We don't want to fight you. If you are called upon to fight us, don't fight hard.

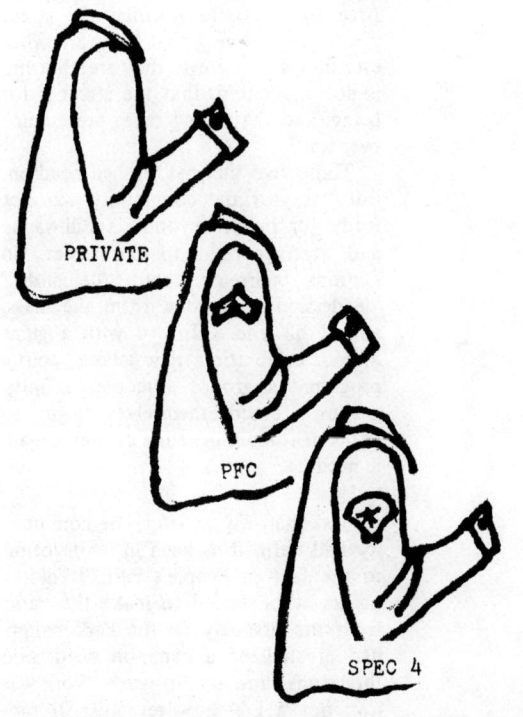

THOSE WHO TAKE THEM

PRIVATE

PFC

SPEC 4

Leaflets from The People's Park Committee, Berkeley May 1969

8
nce

II. "...just the beginning"

Like who knows how many thousand others, I got involved in the battle of People's Park when somebody handed me a shovel and said, "over there, we're breaking it up so we can lay sod down." Packed by weight of years of houses and months of cars, the hard earth barely yielded to any tool, had an oily blue sheen in the sunlight where it was cut. This was Sunday, April 20, behind Telegraph Avenue in Berkeley.

I worked steadily for 20 minutes, then wandered through the diligent crowd. "Now I see how the Chinese build dams." No idle tools, and some dude in a cowboy hat was grading the bumps and hollows on a rented bulldozer. Wine bottles passed, lemonade, and joints from hand to hand. By dusk a rock band was playing and several hundred square yards of park had been laid down under old trees.

In the next three weeks I came back time after time, bringing trees, poems and most of the children on my block. Now there is a brown dusty lot there, patrolled by Burns detectives, who replaced the National Guard behind that cyclone fence. I suppose that in the national mind, if any, the whole issue seems a little silly, cross between the spring dreams of flower children and the devious plots of SDS-inspired revolutionaries. Some factions of SDS, at least, share this view.

But we find it impossible to deny that the park is at the very center of our struggle. The revolution is about the opening of time and space for human beings, inevitably the total liberation of the ecology. "The most revolutionary consciousness," says Gary Snyder, "is to be found among the most oppressed classes—animals, trees, grass, air, water, earth." The park has brought the concept of the Whole Earth, the Mother Earth, into the vocabulary of revolutionary politics. The park has raised sharply the question of property and use; it has demonstrated the absurdity of a system that puts land title above human life; and it has given the dispossessed children of the tract homes and the cities a feeling of involvement with the planet, an involvement proved through our sweat and our blood.

The park has joined international antagonists in battle. The owner of title is the University of California, the prototype Multiversity, up to its ears in war research and with a Rand systems analyst for its president. The park people are the students, quasi-students and street people who made a Free Speech Movement, a Vietnam Day Committee, a Stop the Draft Week, who declare themselves to be the brothers of the Black Panthers, the Cubans, the Vietcong.

The land of the park used to be nice "substandard" houses where students and street people lived. The University, spreading its holdings particularly in the south campus hip ghetto, acquired the land via eminent domain for $1.3 million with the claim that it had become "a scene of hippie concentration and rising crime," and demolished the houses in the summer of 1968. Then

the lot was empty, cars stuck in the winter rain and mud, glass, litter.

Central to previous Berkeley crises was the theme of protest, disruption of the public obscenities that maim our society. The park crisis started because people went ahead and did something for which there was no legal convention, building a new society on the vacant lots of the old. The park was born April 20, and it lived three and a half weeks. It is difficult to go back to the spirit of those days, when at first even the police were reasonably friendly. Decisions were made by the people who wanted to work, to lay sod here and plant a revolutionary corn garden there. There was a play area with several swings and a sandbox, but the favorite children's thing was a set of 7-foot high wooden letters spelling K N O W which could be crawled through. A platform festooned with prayer flags, brick walls, a maypole, a fire pit surrounded at night by the young passive drifters, far gone and not coming home.

Thursday morning, May 15, 300 police in battle gear surrounded the park at 4:45 a.m. and ordered us out. Hopelessly outnumbered, we stumbled through their lines to watch workmen putting up the fence. Exhausted, tears of rage, tears of grief. And then at noon 5000 people whooped down the Avenue from campus to do battle. Everybody knows about Bloody Thursday, the shotguns, the death of James Rector. The days became indeterminate ages of confrontation, continual fear, meetings to all hours; too close to it to be a historian, I can offer an incident or two to give a sense of how it was:

Late afternoon, Bloody Thursday, quiet south campus street, woman with baby carriage, telephone repairman, street brother grazed earlier by pellets tells girl on lawn "they're shooting people on telegraph." "Are you sure?" then Blue Meanie (Alameda county sheriff) pokes his head around the corner and lets fly, wounding the brother again, missing the baby carriage and grazing the phone man who doesn't understand, "lemme go get his badge number" he cries and has to be held back gently, "no, he's not wearing a badge and if you go up there they'll shoot you again."

Gatherings, marches, loitering is illegal at the discretion of the pigs; every day the people gather, march, loiter; dispersed, they regroup and come back for more; downtown Berkeley is closed down nine days in a row. Cut off from the main body, a group of 50 blocks a busy intersection for ten minutes; one brother is nearly run down by a young black gunning in a sports car. Then come a dozen cops and the people slowly yield, one boy a little too slow and he is thrown down, the clubs rise and fall but somehow he is up again and running free, pursued as rocks fly from the crowd, the first cop trips and helmet, club shoots loose, he has to retreat—combing his trained blonde hair. . . .

Every day three helicopters circle the city from first light. One day a trapped crowd is gassed on campus by a copter. The afternoons go on and on, the people still unused to violence and untrained, intermittently ready to go down for each other, not really sure how much they mean by revolution, not yet a military quantity. Thursday the 22nd nearly 500 are herded into a parking lot and busted, then subjected to incredible humiliations at the concentration camp known as Santa Rita; when I see friends on their release next day, they are whispering, shaken and bent.

The confrontations quieted before the big march on Memorial Day. Thirty thousand people, mostly scared to death; Telegraph Avenue is closed off by barbed wire, machine guns are on the roofs; liberal nonviolent monitors with white armbands are circulating in the crowd, at intersections they link arms between the people and the police, continually they cry KEEP MOVING.

The official park monitors in green helmets are very far between. Everyone expects a massacre. At the park, the march slows; a few continue around the city-assigned route, others sprawl off into side streets, frustrated by the fence and the incongruous picnic atmosphere. A band arrives on a flatbed truck, grass is laid down in the street and freaks with hoses begin to jump up and down, screaming and spraying the crowd. The tension dissolves into an incomplete orgy; behind the fence, the Guard is watching, roasting in their flak jackets, impassive, feelings masked. Late afternoon, a thousand people follow the band through the streets, dancing whooping and hollering WE ARE FREE a block away from the scene of the big bust. "Not yet."

On the day of the march a 13-point "Berkeley Liberation Program" appeared in the *Berkeley Barb*. Drawn up after weeks of discussion among many Berkeley radicals, it represents a common point of departure for the community, and already has become a focus for right-wing hysteria. Reagan has cited it as evidence of What They Really Want, and the conservative Berkeley Gazette, viewing it as "a declaration of war," editorialized "there is no gentle way to deal with the Berkeley Liberation Program." And yet it is a curiously modest document, raising almost no ideas that have not been raised before. It does not appear to be a blueprint for a revolutionary society; at most it is a plan for survival in a dangerous period, a list of not impossible priorities.

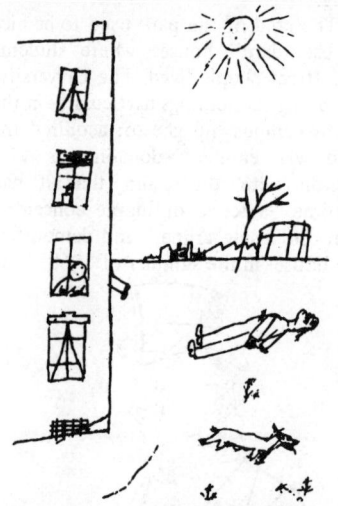

The points call for the south campus ghetto to become "a strategic free territory for revolution," speak to the flowering of revolutionary culture and working out a humane community through communal services, housing councils, tax reform and a government of "people in motion around their own needs." The schools are to become "training grounds" of struggle, while open war is declared on the University as "a major brain center for world domination." The document demands the full liberation of women and defends "the liberating potential of drugs." It announces alliance with the Black Panther Party and "all Third World Liberation movements and criticizes sectarian groups as "supposed vanguards seeking to manipulate mass movements." The tenth section says "we will

defend ourselves against law and order" and suggests that the people must be armed and skilled in self defense and street fighting. Finally, "liberation committees" of people who can trust each other are put forward as an alternative to traditional organizing techniques.

The Liberation Program is important because Berkeley represents probably the only place in America where white revolutionaries live in a territory in which it makes sense to say they are the people, *now*. Unlike the hip enclaves in New York, Chicago, San Francisco and so on, the south campus is a valid community to itself and does not have to cope with enveloping and hostile working-class neighbors. Within this territory the people have risen and fought the police four times now in the last year. Although the future of People's Park remains unclear, people have begun to look towards many ways of implementing the basic principles of the park: community, spontaneity, and opening of time, space and life in relation to the environment. The Liberation Program speaks to the possibility of maintaining a "zone of struggle and liberation" in Berkeley. An International Liberation School is opening this month, which will teach basic survival skills: self defense, first aid, legal defense and communications. People are talking now about breakfasts for children, legal collectives, free clinics. Some are beginning to see that this is not an easy matter, it will last years, last our lives. ●

LIBERATION July 1969

Letters to the Editor

A Proposal: Classroom Work to Be Devoted to Life-and-Death Question of the Park

May 18, 1969

To the Editor:

I came to teach at Berkeley on the assumption that the faculty (and even some of the administrators) had been educated by the events of the last five years — by local crises if not by the crimes of Vietnam. I deceived myself. Given the opportunities for learning that have existed here—from FSM to the present moment—I see now that this may well be (with a handful of exceptions) the most backward group of academics in the whole sad spectrum of our "great" universities.

The situation speaks for itself. Two questions, though, by way of clarification:

1) How many members of the faculty ever saw the People's Park — that beautiful example of a concrete, cooperative learning experience? How many even so much as talked about it with their students?

2) When will the faculty ask for censure of the professor of petroleum engineering who, when asked by the district attorney to testify (in the public interest) on the disaster at Santa Barbara, made it so clear that his first allegiance was to the oil companies? When will the faculty follow Harvard, Yale, et al. and drive the Professors of Killing (called ROTC) from their midst?

If there is any hope left for this university, it may lie in this possibility: that a head-on educational effort by students and TA's may yet break through the armored minds and bodies of the faculty, and bring them into the life of their own time and place. This time of police guns and unsheathed bayonets on the streets and campus of Berkeley. This time of anguish in the young, who no longer see their elders — and especially their teachers —as serious men. Or, more precisely, no longer see them as men.

I have a suggestion on how the faculty might be educated (along with those students who do not yet know they live in the Age of Terror). It is this: For the remainder of the quarter all classroom work should be devoted to the life-and-death question of the People's Park.

The initiative will not, I'm sure, come from the faculty, most of whom are convinced they have nothing to learn from their students. Therefore it will have to come from the students and some of the more enlightened TA's, who must say to their teachers that right now they can no longer concern themselves with the usual academic routine but must deal with the crucial matters of survival, human dignity and the transformation of a corrupt social order.

The related questions for discussion are endless. Examples: Human rights vs. property rights. Authority? Where does it come from? What makes it legitimate,

or illegitimate? Disobediance? Community? Who is the University of California? What do they want? What are their responsibilities (in land use, for example) to the surrounding community? How do people learn? What is violence? What is a "teacher?" What is a "student?"

There is no shortage of reading material. The People's Park Committee is one good source. Guest lecturers might include members of that Committee, an ACLU lawyer, Sherrif Madigan, a Black Panther, and the faculty of the Department of Environmental Design. Even Chancellor Heyns might engage in the give and take.

Is this sacrilege? Perhaps. But it is not unheard of. One of Harvard's more eminent professors, Reuben Brower, had this to say of his teaching innovations: "I started out with **three or four** people who were willing to experiment, and we tried to see if we could start quite differently, **assuming that neither we nor the students knew very much."** (emphasis added).

Brower went on to say: "It's always been very much a cooperative affair . . . even though, of course, most of the teachers are teaching fellows. (TA's . .) I find that some of these people are much more adept at doing it than I am. I think they have a better sense of what the students are thinking and what they can do."

In these days of the Garrison Campus, the need for such experiment is critical. Will it work? Ask the students of Columbia, Stanford, Harvard, Berkeley who say, again and again, that they have learned more from the immediate experience of campus crisis than they did from the rest of their education put together. Even some of the "jocks" have said it.

Before the University falls apart (and into the hands of Reagan) **participate** in learning and teaching. Tell your professors what it is you want to learn. Teach them a lesson.

—Mitchell Goodman
Lecturer in English

PIGS' PARK

They make a desert, pave it, and call it an athletic field. Despite the Regents' plans, the land everyone knows as People's Park goes unused. The plot of Berkeley land, so bitterly fought over (see Hard Times, No. 33), is now known as "Haste Field."

During the summer, under pressure from its young staff members, a University-hired architectural firm refused to design housing for the cyclone-fenced field. No other local firm will accept the contract.

The University administration has tried to lease the larger of the two parking lots to the City of Berkeley. When the City backed out, UC offered a profitable deal to a black OEO group; they could lease the land for $10 and pocket all parking fees. Now the group has backed out. "The scheme must be exposed for what it is," said their release. "Namely, a divisive tactic and possibly a planned confrontation which could end in the slaughter of many black and street people, by each other, or ultimately by the police or National Guard."

At the same time, the campus Interfraternity Council voted 30 to 1 to boycott the field. Intramural teams will not play there.

"The Regents want it to be a sports field and parking lot," a University spokesman told the Berkeley Tribe. "Whether anyone uses it is another matter."

Hard Times 12/15/69

ARCHITECTURAL FIRM REFUSES TO COLLABORATE IN THE RAPE OF THE PEOPLE'S PARK (NOT EVEN FOR MONEY)

GERALD M. McCUE & ASSOCIATES INC.
McCUE BOONE TOMSICK   ARCHITECTS
4 August 1969
The Regents of the University of California
Berkeley, California

Attention: Prof. F. C. Hurlbut, Chairman – Student Residential Apartment Committee
Mr. Louis A. DeMonte, Campus Architect
Mr. Andrew G. Jameson, Chancellor's Office

Gentlemen:

We would like to thank you for having appointed our firm as architects for the South-Side Student Housing project but feel at this time it is necessary for us to withdraw from this appointment because of our position as outlined herein.

The current direction of urban design in this country is not being considered in the development of the site. Government, public institutions, and private enterprise are recognizing that the concern of the public can no longer be disregarded on those projects which directly affect the environment of the city. It is our opinion that if the community is not permitted the position of influencing a project which directly affects it, the project is of questionable social significance.

The present program concerning student housing is excellent. However, we have come to the conclusion that this program without provision for a user developed space cannot succeed on this site because of the overwhelming endorsement of the campus community for the inclusion of such space. We now understand that it will not be possible to modify the program to include this type of space.

It was our initial assumption that this firm would be involved in the important decisions affecting the project as a result of our working directly with the program committee. It has now become clear that decisions on what we feel are the critical program considerations have already been made and that the normal constructive involvement by the firm during programming and design would be seriously limited.

We had hoped for the opportunity to work with the University in developing a solution that would be a new kind of urban environment, a solution which would satisfy the needs of both the University and the community and possibly bring an end to the unrest associated with this site. However, because there appears to be no possible resolution to the above considerations, we have reluctantly concluded that we must withdraw from the appointment.

Sincerely,
McCue Boone Tomsick Architects

Gerald M. McCue
David C. Boone
Frank Tomsick

ARCHITECTURE / PLANNING   631 CLAY STREET SAN FRANCISCO CALIFORNIA 94111   TELEPHONE (415) 434-0300
GERALD McCUE FAIA • DAVID BOONE AIA • FRANK TOMSICK AIA • WILLIAM DUTCHER AIA • ALAN WILLIAMS • PETER HOCKADAY

Letter reprinted in *The Daily Californian*, U. Cal.
Berkeley, Aug 1969

The Berkeley Liberation program was written by several groups of Bay Area radicals and was first made public at the time of the People's Park struggle. It is one of the first efforts by movement activists to set out a more or less comprehensive political vision for the city in which they live and work.

The new left does have a positive politics and this program is an assertion that now is the time to make that clear and out front. The program is also an effort to identify a series of continuing program objectives which can relate different organizing activities in the community by bringing them together in a larger framework and strategy for movement building. In these two aspects, the program provides an important model: seeking to get beyond the episodic, reactive, and often defensive and negative character of many current movement scenes.

The particulars of the program are another matter. Already there has been much debate about the specifics of the thirteen points, their applicability to other areas of the country, or even their appropriateness to an expanding movement in Berkeley.

The points where debate should focus now are the politics implicit in the program:

The program is an effort by white, mostly male and university-centered radicals to define a working relationship with street culture, the women's movement and the extensive drop-out community which are major factors in Berkeley politics.

It is an effort to connect the public concerns of the movement to the basic needs of, at least, its own members (for subsistence, community fun, drugs, etc.) while dealing with a range of problems (taxes, parks, police, rents, schools) faced by others in Berkeley whom the movement seeks to reach.

It is an effort to develop a form of movement organization relying on small "affinity groups" or collectives as a base for political work. The emphasis is on a program which demands neither closely coordinated structure nor complete agreement about political content.

And finally it is an effort to deal in practical terms with the problems of repression and the increasing violence of political confrontation providing training for self-defense, legal problems and medical aid, and encouraging people to find small groups which they can rely on.

These aspects of the program represent both new developments in the Berkeley scene and sharp departures from the emerging political direction characterized by developments in SDS (the two Revolutionary Youth Movement proposals).

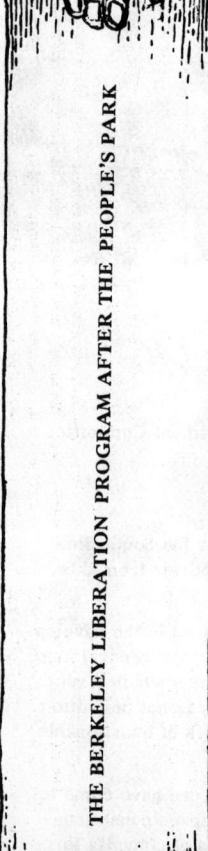

THE BERKELEY LIBERATION PROGRAM AFTER THE PEOPLE'S PARK

POWER TO THE IMAGINATION ALL POWER TO THE PEOPLE

THE PEOPLE OF BERKELEY PASSIONATELY DESIRE HUMAN SOLIDARITY, CULTURAL FREEDOM AND PEACE.

Berkeley is becoming a revolutionary example throughout the world. We are now under severe attack by the demons of despair, ugliness and fascism. We are being strangled by reactionary powers from Washington to Sacramento.

Our survival depends on our ability to overcome past inadequacies and to expand the revolution. We have not done enough to build a movement that is both personally humane and politically radical.

The people of Berkeley must increase their combativeness; develop, tighten, and toughen their organizations; and transcend their middle-class, ego-centered life styles. We shall resist our oppressors by establishing a zone of struggle and liberation, and of necessity shall defend it. We shall create a genuine community and control it to serve our material and spiritual needs. We shall develop new forms of democratic participation and new, more humane styles of work and play. In solidarity with other revolutionary centers and movements, our Berkeley will permanently challenge the present system and act as one of many training grounds for the liberation of the planet.

1 WE WILL MAKE TELEGRAPH AVENUE AND THE SOUTH CAMPUS A STRATEGIC FREE TERRITORY FOR REVOLUTION.

Historically this area is the home of political radicalism and cultural revolution. We will resist plans to destroy the South Campus through University-business expansion and pig assaults. We will create malls, parks, cafes and places for music and wandering. Young people leaving their parents will be welcome with full status as members of our community. Businesses on the Avenue should serve the humanist revolution by contributing their profits to the community. We will establish cooperative stores of our own, and combine them within an Avenue cooperative.

2 WE WILL CREATE OUR REVOLUTIONARY CULTURE EVERYWHERE.

Everyone should be able to express and develop himself through art—work, dance, sculpture, gardening and all means open to the imagination. Materials will be made available to all people. We will defy all puritanical restraints on culture and sex. We shall have media—newspapers, posters and leaflets, radio, TV, films and skywriting— to express our revolutionary community. We will stop the defiling of the earth; our relation to nature will be guided by reason and beauty rather than profit. The civili-

7 WE WILL PROTECT AND EXPAND OUR DRUG CULTURE.

We relate to the liberating potential of drugs for both the mind and the body politic. Drugs inspire us to new possibilities in life which can only be realized in revolutionary action. We intend to establish a drug distribution center and a marijuana cooperative. As a loving community we shall establish drug information centers and free clinics. We will resist the enforcement of all drug laws in our community. We will protect people from narcs and burn artists. All drug busts will be defined as political and we will develop all necessary defense for those arrested

8 WE WILL BREAK THE POWER OF THE LANDLORDS AND PROVIDE BEAUTIFUL HOUSING FOR EVERYONE.

Through rent strikes, direct seizures of property and other resistance campaigns, the large landlords, banks and developers who are gouging higher rents and spreading ugliness will be driven out. We shall force them to transfer housing control to the community, making decent housing available according to people's needs. Coordinated housing councils will be formed on a neighborhood basis to take responsibility for rents and building conditions. The housing councils will work with architects to plan for a beautiful community. Space will be opened up and living communes and revolutionary fam-

As reprinted in
leviathan
Summer 1969

zation of concrete and plastic will be broken and natural things respected. We shall set up urban and rural communes where people can meet for expression and communication. Many Berkeley streets bear little traffic and can be grassed over and turned into people's parks. Parking meters will be abolished and we will close areas of downtown and South Campus to automotive traffic. We shall celebrate the holidays of liberation with fierce dancing.

3 WE WILL TURN THE SCHOOLS INTO TRAINING GROUNDS FOR LIBERATION.

Beneath the progressive facade of Berkeley's schools, students continue to be regimented into accepting the existing system. The widely-celebrated integration of the schools is nothing in itself, and only perpetuates many illusions of white liberalism. The basic issue is creating an educational system in which students have real power and which prepares the young to participate in a revolutionary world. Students must destroy the senile dictatorship of adult teachers and bureaucrats. Grading, tests, tracking, demotions, detentions and expulsions must be abolished. Pigs and narcs have no place in a people's school. We will eliminate the brainwashing, fingernail-cutting mass production of junior cogs for tight-ass America's old age home war machine. Students will establish independent educational forms to create revolutionary consciousness while continuing to struggle for change in the schools.

4 WE WILL DESTROY THE UNIVERSITY UNLESS IT SERVES THE PEOPLE.

The University of California is not only the major oppressive institution in Berkeley, but a major brain center for world domination. UC attempts to kill radical politics and culture in Berkeley while it trains robots for corporations and mental soldiers to crush opposition from Delano to Vietnam.

Students should not recognize the false authority of the regents, administration and faculty. All students have the right to learn what they want, from whom they want, and in the manner they decide; and the right to take political action without academic penalty. We will build a movement to make the University relevant to the Third World, workers, women and young people searching for human values and vocations. Our, battles will be conducted in the classrooms and the streets.

We will shatter the myth that UC is a sacred intellectual institution with a special right to exist. We will change this deadly Machine which steals our land and rapes our minds, or we will stop its functioning. Education can only begin when we're willing to close the University for what we believe.

5 WE WILL STRUGGLE FOR THE FULL LIBERATION OF WOMEN AS A NECESSARY PART OF THE REVOLUTIONARY PROCESS.

While the material oppression of women varies in different classes, male supremacy pervades all social classes. We will resist this ideology and practice which oppresses all women. As we struggle to liberate ourselves, many of the problems of inequality, authoritarianism and male chauvinism in the Berkeley movement will be overcome. We will create an unfettered identity for women. We will abolish the stifling masculine and feminine roles that this society forces on us all. Women will no longer be defined in terms of others than themselves—by their relationships to men and children. Likewise, men will not be defined by their jobs or their distorted role as provider. We seek to develop whole human beings and to bring together the most free and beautiful aspects of women and men.

We will end the economic oppression of women: job discrimination, the manipulation of women as consumers, and media exploitation of women as sexual objects.

We demand the full control of our own bodies and towards that end will establish free birth control and abortion clinics. We will choose our own sexual partners; we will eliminate the demeaning hustling scene in Berkeley which results from male chauvinism and false competition among men and among women. We will not tolerate harrassment in the parks, streets, and public places of Berkeley.

We will resist all false concepts of chivalry and protectiveness. We will develop self-reliance and the skills of self defense. We will establish female communes so that women who so choose can have this free space to develop themselves as human beings.

We will end all forms of male supremacy by ANY MEANS NECESSARY!

6 WE WILL TAKE COMMUNAL RESPONSIBILITY FOR BASIC HUMAN NEEDS.

High-quality medical and dental care, including laboratory tests, hospitalization, surgery and medicines will be made freely available. Child-care collectives staffed by both men and women, and centers for the care of strung-out souls, the old and the infirm will be established. Free legal services will be expanded. Survival needs such as crash pads, free transportation, switchboards, free phones, and free food will be met.

9 WE WILL TAX THE CORPORATIONS, NOT THE WORKING PEOPLE.

The people cannot tolerate escalating taxes which are wasted in policing the world while businessmen are permitted to expand their profits in the midst of desperate social need. Berkeley cannot be changed without confronting the industries, banks, insurance companies, railroads and shipping interests dominating the Bay Area. In particular, University of California expansion which drives up taxes should be stopped and small homeowners should no longer pay property taxes. We will demand a direct contribution from business, including Berkeley's biggest business—the University, to the community until a nationwide assault on big business is successful.

10 WE WILL DEFEND OURSELVES AGAINST LAW AND ORDER.

America's rulers, faced with the erosion of their authority in Berkeley, begin to take on the grotesque qualities of a dictatorship based on pure police power. We shall abolish the tyrannical police forces not chosen by the people. States of emergency, martial law, conspiracy charges and all legalistic measures used to crush our movement will be resisted by any means necessary—from courtroom to armed struggle. The people of Berkeley must arm themselves and learn the basic skills and tactics of self defense and street fighting. All oppressed people in jail are political prisoners and must be set free. We shall make Berkeley a sanctuary for rebels, outcasts and revolutionary fugitives. We shall attempt to bring the real criminals to trial; where this is impossible we shall implement revolutionary justice.

11 WE WILL CREATE A SOULFUL SOCIALISM IN BERKELEY.

The revolution is about our lives. We will fight against the dominating Berkeley life style of affluence, selfishness, and social apathy—and also against the self-indulgent individualism which masquerades as "doing your own thing." We will find ways of taking care of each other as comrades. We will experiment with new ways of living together such as communal families in which developing problems of income, child care, and housekeeping are mutually shared. Within the Berkeley movement we will seek alternatives to the stifling elitism, egoism, and sectarianism which rightly turns people away and creates organizational weakness. We have had enough of supposed vanguards seeking to manipulate mass movements. We need vanguards of a new type—people who lead by virtue of their moral and political example, who seek to release and organize energy instead of channeling or curbing it; who seek power not for themselves but for the people as a whole. We firmly believe in organization which brings out the leadership and creativeness existing in everyone.

12 WE WILL CREATE A PEOPLE'S GOVERNMENT.

We will not recognize the authority of the bureaucratic and unrepresentative local government. We will ignore elections involving trivial issues and personalities. We propose a referendum to dissolve the present government, replacing it with one based on the tradition of direct participation of the people. People in motion around their own needs will become a decentralized government of neighborhood councils, workers councils student unions, and different sub-cultures. Self-management in schools, factories, and neighborhoods will become commonplace. Locally chosen "people's mediators" will aid those desiring to settle disputes without referring to the illegitimate system of power.

13 WE WILL UNITE WITH OTHER MOVEMENTS THROUGHOUT THE WORLD TO DESTROY THIS MOTHERFUCKING RACISTCAPITALISTIMPERIALIST SYSTEM.

Berkeley cannot be free until America is free. We will make the American revolution with the mass participation of all the oppressed and exploited people. We will actively support the 10-point program of the Black Panther Party in the black colony; all revolutionary organizing attempts among workers, women, students and youth; all Third World liberation movements. We will create an International Liberation School in Berkeley as a training center for revolutionaries.

WE CALL FOR SISTERS AND BROTHERS TO FORM LIBERATION COMMITTEES TO CARRY OUT THE BERKELEY STRUGGLE.

These committees should be small democratic working groups of people able to trust each other. We should continually resist the monster system; our emphasis should be on direct action, organizing the community, and forming a network of new groups. Together as a Berkeley Liberation Movement, the liberation committees will build people's power and a new life.

ilies will be encouraged.

the end of man?

ECOLOGY—
A SUBVERSIVE SUBJECT

My choice of title is not facetious. I wish to explore a question of growing concern. Is ecology a phase of science of limited interest and utility? Or, if taken seriously as an instrument for the long-run welfare of mankind, would it endanger the assumptions and practices accepted by modern societies, whatever their doctrinal commitments?

PAUL B. SEARS *BioScience* 14(7): 11, 1964

Growth for the sake of growth is the ideology of the cancer cell.

EDWARD ABBEY

A sign above another exhibit read: "If the available food were to be evenly divided among the world's people—this would be your share today." On the table was half a cup of rice, a glass of milk made from soybean oil, and some brownish-red seaweed.

From a description of a college ecology fair, in *The New York Times*

The so-called consumer economy and the politics of corporate capitalism have created a second nature of man which ties him libidinally and agressively to the commodity form. The need for possessing, consuming, handling, and constantly renewing the gadgets, devices, instruments, engines, offered to and imposed upon the people, for using these wares even at the danger of one's own destruction, has become a "biological" need.

HERBERT MARCUSE *One-Dimensional Man*

WA$TED LIVE$

NEW YORK (LNS)—"It's bread," one girl said, commenting disparagingly on the dull life led by her parents. "Nobody needs that much bread. You have to think of the total life."

More and more young people are reaching the conclusion that their parents lead dull, directionless lives. And they are concluding that the cause is capitalism—a system which breeds purposeless lives, which alienates people from their work.

A recent survey by *Youth Report,* for example, shows that the prevailing mood among many students is that they feel "sorry" for their parents. The survey, which concentrated on 18-year-old women freshmen, pointed out that young people believe their parents have wasted their lives. The root of this evaluation, the survey concluded, is the young people's conclusion that they can have more fulfilling lives if they are motivated by concerns other than money.

RUBBER RACISM

JOHANNESBURG—When Harry Oppenheimer, President of Anglo-American Corporation, recently declared South Africa's economy to be headed for economic suicide because it "deliberately sets out. . . not to make proper use of 80% of its potential working population," his concern was about the inefficiency of the system and not about its racist cruelty. South Africa and Firestone Tire and Rubber Co. are collaborating to save the situation with their winning combination of apartheid and greed.

Firestone, working in cooperation with the South African government, recently announced plans to build a $10 million factory at Brits in South Africa's Transvaal Province. The plant is to be built in a border area adjacent to "tribal reserves"—the white supremacist euphemism for concentration camps—which contain vast numbers of South African blacks.

The practice of locating foreign industries in border areas helps to legitimize South Africa's concentration camps, and provides subsistence living standards for the "natives" at no cost to the white government. The Transvaal factory will give Firestone ready access to an incredibly cheap labor pool (most people would call "slave" labor), and will allow the South African government to increase industrial production without threatening the status quo.

—africa research group/LNS

There exists today a clear imbalance between the population of various areas of the globe and the distribution of the world's wealth. At present we can say that approximately one quarter of the world population is using up three quarters of the world's production. For this one favored quarter to profit so prodigally it is, of course, necessary that the others limit themselves to what is left. None of our Western philosophies, up to and including Marxism-Leninism, has prepared us for this distortion of values. On the contrary it can only be understood as a kind of suicidal frenzy.

SHADRACH WOODS, *Urbanism is Everybody's Business,* Ulrico Hoepli Editore Milano.

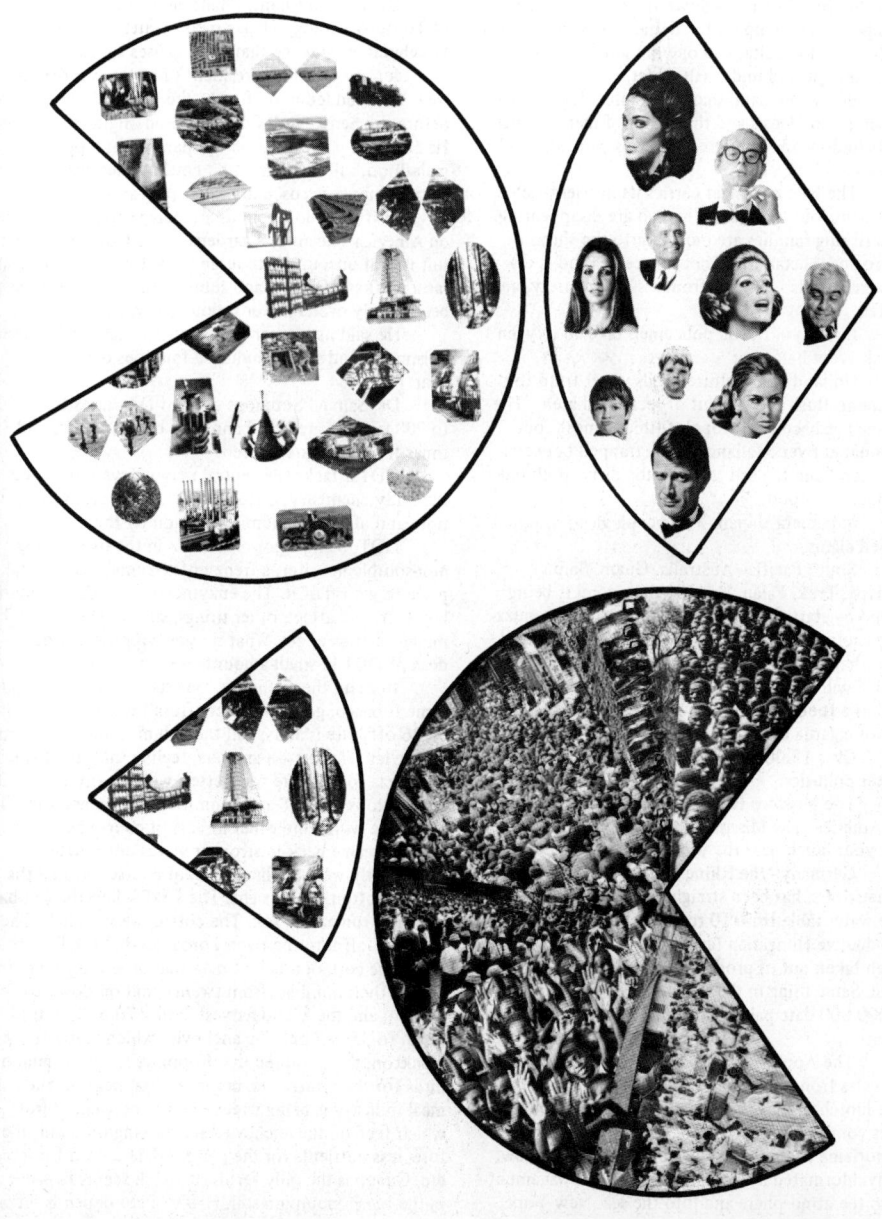

THE END OF MAN

Dr. Richard Felger, Senior Curator of the Los Angeles Museum of Natural History, and Professor Barry Commoner, Washington University, St. Louis, estimate that man has about 40 years left to live on this earth. Dr. P.C. Orloffs of Canada gives us only 15 years to live. A gloomy conclusion. Is it valid?

Let's look around. A short news report.

Sign on Los Angeles schoolroom bulletin board. Warning!! Do not exercise strenuously or breathe too deeply during heavy smog conditions. APCD.

Announcement from National Cancer Institute: "DDT is a cancer causing agent."

Egypt: The Aswan Dam has slowed down the Nile. Six hundred miles down river sandbars have stopped building up on the delta. The Mediterranean is flooding the delta, and one million fertile acres have disappeared under salt water.

Below the dam, snails carry the blood flukes of schistosomicosis and thousands of men, women and children are going to die of this painful, cruel disease.

The Nile no longer carries its nutrient-rich sediments out to sea and the fish are disappearing. The fishing families are moving into the slums of Cairo and Alexandria. That source of food is disappearing. Also Oxygen from loss of greenery, and water.

In Tokyo, traffic policemen take an oxygen break every half hour.

Holland's agriculture needs water from the Rhine to flush the salt out of reclaimed areas. The Rhine has become Europe's filthiest, most contaminated river. Holland is now trapped between invasion from the salt sea, and the dirty, polluted Rhine. Less food.

Minamata, Japan—100 people dead of poisoned clams.

South Pacific—Australia, Guam, Saipan, Panape, Truk, Palau, Hawaii—their coral is being killed by starfish which are proliferating in a puzzling ecological explosion. Dr. Bruce Halstead told me—that when the coral is dead, a weed will grow which will contaminate the fish, eliminating the fish as a food source. Natives who eat the fish then die of cigarua disease.

Over 15,000,000 fish died last year from water pollution.

The Missouri River is to become the Colon of America. The Mississippi carries signs, "Don't eat your lunch near the water."

Germany—the Rhine along with hundreds of other rivers, has been straightened out. This lowered the water table from 10 to 25 feet. 35,000 acres of productive Hungarian farmland have dried up and been taken out of production; 200,000 acres in Alsace. Same thing in the Sahara—water table lowered, 1,000,000 date palm dead and 120,000 natives face disaster.

The Apollo 10 astronauts easily picked out Los Angeles from hundreds of miles out. They could see the blotch of ugly, cancer-colored smog, 4,000,000 cars vomiting cancer-causing gases, 16 million tires vaporizing deadly asbestos particles, and the new, polychlorinated hydro-carbons onto the pavement—into the atmosphere and into the sea. New York,

Chicago, Philadelphia, Denver, Washington, Boston, St. Louis, Mexico City and Tokyo. 100 cities, 100,000 towns, all making their permanent contributions to the atmosphere.

An important doctor from the American Medical Association said, "Unless the combustion engine goes in 5 years—we will."

How does smog affect man? Chronic bronchitis is seven times higher than it was ten years ago. Lung cancer is twice as prevalent in the cities as it is in the rural areas. Bronchial asthma and emphysema are up eight times in the last ten years and skyrocketing. One day's breathing of New York smog is equivalent to smoking 5 packages of cigarettes. It is anticipated that before many years have passed, ten thousand people will die daily of pollution. Doctors are advising 10,000 patients a year to leave California.

Scientists from the National Cancer Institute state, "DDT is a cancer-causing agent."

Hungarian scientists examined 1,000 mice for five generations. Leukemia appeared in 12.4% of the DDT mice but only 2.5% of the non-DDT mice. Tumors appeared in 28.7% of the DDT mice, but only 3.8% of the non-DDT mice, and most of the malignancies were in the later generations, the children indicating genetic damage.

According to the University of Miami School of Medicine, people dying of cancer contained more than twice as much DDT in their fat, 20-35 ppm, as victims of accidental death, 9.7 ppm.

Dr. Donald Chant, Chairman of the University of Toronto Zoology Department, states, "Absolutely undebatable evidence that DDT causes cancer."

Jerome Gordon, president of a research firm in New York, added more fuel to the fire while testifying before the Senate Sub-Committee on Migratory Labor. He attacked parathion, methyl parathion, tepp and malathion, calling them "first cousins chemically to a German nerve gas used in biological warfare."

"Fifty million pounds are being spread unchecked on America's farms and gardens," said Gordon. "The result is that uncounted thousands of the nation's migrant farm workers, farmers and suburban homeowners have been fatally overcome or seriously disabled."

He said more than 100-thousand cases of pesticide poisonings and several hundred fatalities occur each year.

Dr. Samuel Simmons of the FDA states that 150 to 200 persons are killed annually by pesticides, and 100 times that many are injured.

DDT attacks the central nervous system, upsets the body chemistry, distorts cells, accelerates gene mutation, and affects calcium absorption by the bones.

DDT, being a poison, lodges in the liver. Being non-soluble in water, a frenzy of enzymatic action takes place to get rid of it. The enzymes are not discriminating, however, and attack other things, such as steroid sex hormones, estrogen, etc. What do you suppose our daily dose of DDT in small amounts is doing to us?

In Peru, the economy consists of cotton agriculture, some tobacco, guano fertilizer from the cormorant birds on 36 offshore islands, and the fish-meal industry from anchovies. The cotton growers, feeling that, if a little DDT was good, more was better, were finally up to 50 applications of DDT a year on their cotton acreage. The pink bole worm and other insects of course became resistant and came back in stronger waves until 50 applications yearly were applied. This, of course, pushed the cost of cotton out of sight. The DDT killed the soil bacteria and ruined the soil. The cotton went to hell. The DDT run-off into the rivers contaminated the fish which killed the cormorants that manufactured the guano, reducing their numbers from twenty million down to six million, and the guano harvest from 170 million tons down to 35 million. The anchovies which feed off the plankton, that required the droppings from the guano birds for their nutrients, began to disappear, so the fish meal industry is being wrecked, and the guano birds which feed on the anchovies are starving to death, therefore, less nutrients for the plankton, less food for, etc. etc. Guano is the only fertilizer which seems to work in the harsh mountain soil. Half of Peru depends on

this food production for survival. The result has been expropriation of American interests and a stepped-up hostility toward our American trawlers cruising in the open sea nearby. Their fishing boundary has now been pushed out to 200 miles. All of this has greatly harmed American-Peruvian relations and now becomes a political problem.

Zoology Professor Kenneth E. F. Watt said in a prepared statement, "It is now clear that air pollution concentrations are rising in California at such a rate that MASS MORTALITY incidents can be expected in specific areas, such as Long Beach, by the 1975-76 winter.

"The proportion of the population which will die in these incidents will at first equal, then exceed, that of the 1952 London smog disaster." (Nearly 3,000 Londoners died from the effects of smog during the Christmas season of that year.)

During the 1966 Thanksgiving weekend in New York, it has been estimated that 168 deaths were caused by smog.

Smog damages crops to the tune of ½ billion annually. In New Jersey alone 36 crops have been seriously damaged. Spinach, lettuce, beets, etc. Food gone and oxygen gone. Dr. O.C. Taylor, "If the pollutants in the air are unchecked it won't be many years before agriculture in certain parts of America ceases to exist." Less food.

Up in the Lake Arrowhead area about 10% of the Ponderosa pines, 1,300,000 trees, have died as a result of smog. It is estimated that 10% of our farm produce is being damaged by smog which means less oxygen, less food, and less water.

"One of the most tragic ironies of our age could be in the making, if certain tests at University of California, Los Angeles, prove correct. Scientists claim that the present anti-smog device placed on our cars may be increasing, not reducing air pollution." Engineer, Air Resources, Channel 7, 7/30/69.

The final contribution of the combustion engine to us, seems to be death by disease and starvation.

The gentle dust of DDT blows off the farms, ranches, plantations, into the sea for the plankton and the fish to absorb, which are then eaten by the birds. Last spring, with Dr. Risebrough and members and scientists of the Western Vertebrate Foundation, I went to the pelican rookeries on the island of Anacapa to observe the nesting of the pelicans and the 10,000 baby chicks that ordinarily are born in the spring in that rookery. We discovered that all the eggs had collapsed, and the embryos killed, because DDT ingested by the mother bird upset her calcium metabolic processes, causing her to lay thin-shelled eggs which could not support her weight. Three or four days after laying, they collapsed. Instead of 10,000 baby chicks only two were hatched there this year. The same was true of the rookeries of the pelicans on the Mexican islands.

We also found the first thin-shelled cormorant

eggs. Now they have become quite common. Recently I was told that the first seagull eggs, thin-shelled, had collapsed. The pelican, the osprey, the cormorant, the petrel, the seagull, the American Bald Eagle and the peregrine falcon, eggs all collapsing. No new generation is being born.

Now—who is going to discover the first collapsed hen's egg.

I have mentioned plankton. These microscopic plants serve two purposes. First, plankton, microscopic sea-animals, are the base of the whole fish food chain from anchovies to whales. Without plankton there would be no fish, whatsoever. Secondly, plankton provides 70% of the earth's oxygen. 70%. Take 70% of the oxygen out of this room and you and I are soon gasping. Well, eleven parts per billion of DDT, that's at the ratio of about an ounce to a thousand railroad carloads, 11 ppm of DDT in water are sufficient to kill off the plankton. No oxygen. No fish. Already, this is happening in the estuarial areas close to land, but a couple of weeks ago, an FDA man told me they had picked up their first load of contaminated deep-water fish. DDT is now in the DEEP, blue sea. Another food source is in danger. It doesn't take much.

The Rhine disaster, which killed all the fish in the Rhine recently, was caused by one sack of insecticide falling off a dock into the water.

Should DDT be banned? Of course, but it may be too late. All of the above is the result of only 1/3 of the DDT that has already been spread on the land. 2/3 still hangs in the air, 1 billion pounds, and will be settling on us, slowly, for the next couple of years. One billion pounds left up there. Twice as much coming down like a ghastly dew on the sea, on the land, on us, for the next few years.

The Department of Agriculture says, "We control the spreading of DDT." How? Ninety percent of it blows into the air, all over the world. Polar bears in the Arctic, penguins in the Antarctic, eel pouts, 1,500 feet deep in McMurdo Sound at the South Pole are loaded with DDT. There isn't a cubic inch on earth free of DDT.

Mercury poisoning. The run off of mercury into the sea, from industrial wastes is contaminating the North Sea, according to Dr. Bruce Halstead, to the degree that in three years the fish from the North Sea will be too poisonous to be edible. Mercury is used in the U.S. in the manufacture of plastics, paint and paper pulp, and as a fungicide for wheat seeds.

In the little town of Minamata, in Japan, almost one hundred people have died as a result of eating clams contaminated by the mercury in water wastes from a nearby plastics factory.

Mercury poisoning is passed on from the wheat seed into the bread made from the wheat flour, into the mother and congenitally into the child, who dies at the age of two or three in convulsions with brain damage.

Recently, in Lake Boone in Tennessee, millions of fish died as a result of mercury poisoning from barrels that had been used in the manufacture of paper pulp and then turned into floats for docks. Traces of mercury leached out of the barrels two and three years later, killing the fish.

Wilamette River, Oregon—dying. Several pulp mills, five of which use the sulphite pulping process produce 70% of the pollution, thousands of gallons of dark, chemical poison, daily. About cleaning up the river, the pulp mills pretty well control state politics on pollution.

The Potomac is a sewer for every town it passes. It is drying up, and its ancient, historic bones are now desecrating the scene. Its mudflats are now showing, covered with garbage, old tires, junk, human sewage. During cherry blossom time it is the best-dressed cesspool in America.

The Army Corps of Engineers suggests putting up a large dam (here they come again) at Seneca, building up a huge head of water, and then releasing it suddenly to flush out the river, exactly as you would

flush the john. One day flood waters, next day mudflats.

Why don't they suggest sewage equipment and complete removal of pollution? Why always a big dam?

The Engineer Corps is especially good at dams. Thirty years ago the slogan was, "dams, more dams for hydroelectric power," and they built dams, good dams. The dams held back the water and wiped out millions of acres of scenery, living room and productive land. The water slowed down, the lakes behind the dams silted up, and are now useless.

Lake Erie, 10,000 square miles, is biologically dead. Zero oxygen. Beaches are unsafe, algae coats the bodies of swimmers, and piles up in foul smelling reefs at the shoreline. Flies everywhere. Fishing, once a major industry, has dwindled to a small fleet of boats. The lake has aged a million years in the last fifty.

The Cayuhoga River which flows into Lake Erie is so loaded with oil wastes that it has been declared a fire hazard. A river—a fire hazard? As a matter of fact, it did catch fire. Burned two bridges. $50,000.

Congressman Blatnik of Minnesota, author of the water pollution bill, points out that on the banks of the Mississippi, down below St. Louis, there are signs warning picnickers not to eat their lunch on or near the banks of the river. The spray from the river contains typhoid, colitis, hepatitis, diarrhea, anthrax, salmonella, tuberculosis and polio. In simple language it is an open, running sewer. This water is so toxic that if you place a fish in a container of river water the fish will die in 60 seconds. If you dilute the river water 100 times with clear water, the fish will die in 24 hours. The plain truth of the matter is that we all drink a chlorinated soup of dead bacteria that in some cases has passed through eight or ten people. It can only get worse.

Speaking of arrogance—the Union Oil Public Relations Department told quite a few fibs about the amount of oil spilled at Santa Barbara, and the extent of the damage to beaches and wildlife. Our government went right along with them. Our Governor says not a word, Secretary Hickel talks of another 50 wells, Union continues to pump, and the oil, as of this minute, continues to smear and smell up the beaches, kill the wildlife on which we depend, and ruin the real estate. Union oil claims there is no danger.

Where do we go for unbiased, authoritative evaluation? Our research scientists at our universities? Let me quote the Chief Deputy Attorney General of California:

"The University experts all seem to be working on grants from the oil industry. There is an atmosphere of fear. The experts are afraid that if they assist us in our case on behalf of the people of California, they will lose their oil industry

grants."

Los Angeles Regional Water Quality Control Board has the problem of harbor pollution by Union Oil. One of the Board's voting members is an employee of Union Oil.

A recent study at the University of Pittsburgh suggests that downwind from our atomic testing infant mortalities rise about 50%, and that since the Alamogordo blast in 1945, we have killed about 475,000 children in their first year of life. This, the result of 20 megatons. We continue the testing.

Currently, the Atomic Energy Commission is examining the feasibility of blasting out a new Panama Canal. 250 megatons. Fallout clouds 40,000 feet high. Evacuating tens of thousands of people for over two years. To where? To what end? What happens when the Pacific, 18 feet higher than the Atlantic, rushes across the Isthmus bearing millions of tons of water with a different salinity, a different temperature, a different population of sea organisms, thousands of species dying in the new environment, the climate being altered, agriculture suffering, the lives of nations being transformed . . . for what?

After the plankton the remaining 30% of our oxygen supply comes from our forests, our greenery. We have destroyed 93% of our forests, and we're losing one million areas of greenery each year. 1,300,000 Ponderosa pines up at Lake Arrowhead have been killed by us. Each Sunday edition of *The New York Times* killed by each Sunday edition of *The New York Times* consumes 150 acres of timber. Multiply that by 100 cities and 10,000 towns. Seven days in the week. There go the trees, oxygen and water.

One car driven down one block consumes the oxygen one hundred people need to survive for one month.

The U.S. destroyed 340 million acres through urban spread, highways, erosion, dustbowls. With each acre gone we lose oxygen, food, water. In the major cities, in many areas, the production of carbon dioxide already exceeds that of oxygen. The moment is not far off when the oxygen content in our atmosphere will fall below the minimum required to support life.

We will not be the first civilization to die. Much of China and India have gone back to sand as a result of man's greed. Syria and Turkey, by land misuse, have created poverty-striken wastes. Very little topsoil is left in Greece. 2,000 years ago they cut down all the timber to build warships. The Sahara, once a land of rivers and grasslands—now a sea of sand.

In the past when man abused his environment he had a choice. He didn't have to die. He could migrate. Today there is no place to which we can migrate. We have only one choice left. Control our population, conserve our plant and animal life, or die.

The ancient controls of famine, disease and war are not standing by awaiting our decision. They are already moving in. America is not immune.

Six years from today we shall export our last grain of wheat. We will have no more wheat surplus. We will not have enough for ourselves. Dr. Paul Ehrlich:

"The battle to feed all of humanity is over. In the 1970's the world will undergo famines. Hundreds of millions of people are going to starve to death in spite of any crash program embarked upon now."

Let me repeat our opening words. Drs. Felger and Commoner estimate that we have about 40 years left for us on this earth. Dr. Orloffs gives us only 15 years.

—eddie albert/*helix*

Tłe·BIRd

A MAINE LOBSTERMAN:
"...ON THAT DAY MANY OF
US WILL TAKE UP ARMS AND
FIGHT."

and a voice from the coast

This is a statement that summarizes generally how all of us feel who are opposed to refineries being place in Washington County, but who do, however, want some clean industry brought into the area.

We strongly oppose refineries being placed anywhere in this area because they carry an inacceptable amount of risk to our livelihoods, our environment and our way of life. Placing them in this area we feel would be incompatible not only with conditions that exist in the world today but with the way that we wish to develop this area.

We who have spent our lives on this coast and are familiar with its strong tides, its heavy fogs, its rocky shoals and its frequent and severe storms believe it to be one of the most hostile stretches of ocean in the world and one of the riskiest places to handle oil.

For this reason we belive that oil spills are inevitable. The nature of fisheries is such that a large oil spill or cumulative small ones would, we feel certain, destroy the fisheries in this area, depriving the lobster fishermen, the clam diggers, the shrimp fishermen, the seiners and others of their livelihoods.

Along with this idea we must consider too that we are living in a hungry world that is rushing toward mass starvation, and the scientists tell us that our only hope of feeding these masses is embodied in the world's fisheries. Knowing these facts, how can anyone be so careless, so indifferent to world conditions and to the rights of those of us who live in this area as to propose building a batch of refineries in the midst of one of the world's best fishereies, risking the loss of that source of food?

Let us consider further the economic aspects. What person among our unskilled numbers has any assurance of a job in the refineries once they are built? What person among us has any assurance that his oil will be one cent cheaper either? What kind of an economic theory justifies risking the livelihoods of thousands to give employment to hundreds? I say "Beware the oil industry bearing gifts."

We realize that this area needs industry and we will fight as hard as the next person for good clean industry suitable to the area. The oil industry constitutes a cruel hoax against the hopes and needs of the mostly unskilled poor and hungry people in our midst. They want industries suitable to the area and to their abilities. They want something that will help them, not ruin them. It has been said that a hungry man will grasp for straws but I say that unless he is crazy he won't reach for a tiger.

Next, let us consider the environmental aspect. Every man needs places where he can commune with nature, places where he can rest and play and achieve restoration of body and spirit. These places are becoming few and far between on our east coast. Maine is the last frontier.

All of us must ask ourselves this question. Are we willing to tell the next generation that because of our thoughtlessness and because nothing was sacred to us except money, we lost for the the fine environment that we ourselves once had? I'm sure that I don't want that responsibility.

Certain individuals in Augusta and elsewhere are trying to cram oil refineries down our throats with no consideration for our wishes on the matter. I always though that in a democracy we were supposed to have the right to vote on something that strongly affected our destiny, after which we would abide by the wisdom of the majority. It seems in this case that we are to be denied that right.

Let us remember that it was for causes such as this that our forefathers took up arms and fought the first battle of Machias Bay, and, ladies and gentlemen, I believe that on the day we have our livelihoods and fine environment taken from us by the oil spills and pollution of the oil industry, on that day many of us will take up arms and fight too.

I should like to end with this suggestion: that Governor Curtis spend as much time and effort in finding us some good clean industry that we want as he does in trying to give us refineries that we don't want.

by Jasper Cates, Jr.

(Mr. Cates is a lobsterman from Cutler, and wrote this statement for delivery at last Tuesday's meeting in Machias.)

MAINE TIMES 3/13/70

Santa Barbara
Anti-Oil Crowd Storms a Meeting

MODELS FOR DIRECT ACTION

Santa Barbara

The Santa Barbara city council hastily adjourned last night in the face of an angry crowd demanding the city regain control of Stearns Wharf, staging center for off-shore oil operations.

As the seven councilmen stalked out, members of the crowd estimated at 400 hurdled the railing and took over the councilmen's seats and microphones.

"It was pure chaos, pure anarchy," said City Attorney Stanley Tomlinson.

CROWD

The crowd consisted of students, conservationists and members of GOO (Get Oil Out). They demanded immediate action to ban the municipal wharf to big oil companies.

During the afternoon session, William Botwright, a spokesman for GOO, voiced the sentiments of the large gathering.

"The people," he said, "have scribbled letters and telegrams to Washington until their fingers are cramped" protesting off-shore drilling and the big oil slick caused by a Union Oil Company blowout last January 28.

He said Mayor Gerald Firestone and other civic leaders "have pleaded with the Interior Department and President Richard Nixon until they are hoarse, seeking to have the oil drilling stopped here."

ORDER

After the Platform A blowout. Interior Secregary Walter J. Hickel ordered all drilling halted. However, on April 1 he modified the general shutdown, permitting limited operations.

In the face of citizens' frustration in stopping the drilling, Botwright urged the City Council to terminate a 25-year franchise allowing private use of Stearns Wharf. He said the city should "redevelop it for recreation, commercial and sports fishing and banish all oil traffic from the wharf and the city harbor as well."

The City Council voted unanimously to instruct Tomlinson to look into legal aspects of reclaiming the wharf. It also called on Public Works Director Dennis Hogle to investigate safety factors related to the ability of the wharf to carry big loads of heavy oil equipment.

INCOME

Eric Lyons, a real estate man representing an informal protest group, said the city "should exercise its right" to cancel the franchise because it was returning no income to the city.

The afternoon crowd of about 350 filled the council chambers and overflowed into the corridors of the Spanish Colonial City Hall. Still other protestors assembled in De la Guerra Plaza.

Among the turnout were many who had staged a sit-down on Stearns Wharf Sunday, blocking trucks from making equipment deliveries.

Our Correspondent

San Francisco Chronicle
4/9/69

518
sistance

ECOLOGY
AND/OR THE
POLICE STATE

I REMEMBER
WHEN THE AIR
WAS FRESH 'N'
CLEAN!

YEAH! AND NOW
IT SMELLS LAK
SHIT!

MORE

EARTH READ-OUT:
ECOLOGY AND/OR THE POLICE STATE

It is unpleasant to have to talk about the Amerikan police state. Much easier on the nervous system just to acquiesce in the general coyness.

But it's now abundantly clear that unless ecology activists directly resist the police state there is little possibility we'll survive the century generally intact in terms generally tolerable.

A pattern has emerged in recent weeks. Because the clean young people and the clean older people who do the eco-publicity work (the TV appearances, radio and newspaper interviews, speeches, etc.) have not been frank, the ecology movement (tho not eco-concern) has been discredited among most of the best and most deeply caring young people.

With some exceptions ecology groups are attracting young people no more resolute than the hi-there kids who rang doorbells for Eugene McCarthy two years ago. To become effective, to get past language, the ecology movement must at-tract the more serious young people, the so-called freaks. These more serious people can be attracted only through frankness. Only by resisting (and rolling back) the police state can we create an atmosphere within which frankness is possible.

It's not surprising that the PR people in the eco-movement keep clean and talk coy. They know that if they look dirty or even scruffy they may get their skulls clubbed in just walking down a city street. They know that if they're frank (as the Chicago Ten were frank) about the nature of Amerikan politics or economics they may well be framed on felonies and thrown into jail.

In sum: you can't have frankness without rolling back the police state and without frankness you can't enlist the subcontinent's best human energies.

Present indications are that the teach-ins scheduled for April 22 on hundreds of U.S. campuses will be controlled in such a way as to provide mostly a keep-clean-northern-white-liberal-Democrat forum and thus not deal frankly with the problems imposed by the police state.

The best recent example of the disenchantment among the young is found in a piece entitled ECOLOGY SUCKS which appeared in the Feb. 20-March 5 issue of the Spokane Natural. Here are excerpts from it:

"ECOLOGY SUCKS! It sucks the life out of social reform. It sucks energy out of campus movements. It sucks irritants out of capitalism. It sucks change out of politics. It sucks reason out of thought...

"White House spokesmen recently announced that the President encouraged students and young people to demonstrate vigorously for fresh air and clean water. This is the same man who watched a football game while 500,000 peace demonstrators marched down Pennsylvania Avenue...

"The movement to save spaceship Earth from extinction is so infinitely reasonable that it's difficult to find any opposition to it. The planet that Milton called 'This pendant world, in bigness as a star' has become such an obnoxious open sewer that every sane person, regardless of age or political persuasion, is convinced a remedy must be found before it's too late.

"But the issue is so blinding that no one is asking the questions that must be asked. No one is taking the time to understand fully what it is they are lending their support to.

"For example, the pollution control movement helps to conceal the fact that corporations owe the public much more than they can ever repay. Most have operated in such a criminally irresponsible way that it will take a quarter century to repair even a portion of the damage they have created. But few anti-pollutionists are asking them to pick up the tab. On the contrary, everything imaginable is being done to exonerate industrial capitalism.

"And if we are all guilty (as corporations and their friends are quick to point out), then what will be the results of pouring billions and billions of tax dollars into ecological restoration? If we remain in the space race, if the Vietnam war continues, if the anti-ballistic missile program expands annually, if huge defense contracts go on, where will the money come from?

"As things stand now, any money for environmental improvement must come from social programs, education, welfare, urban renewal, public housing, food distribution, social security, workmen's compensation and medicare. If the military-industrial complex gets its way, the people who have received the least benefits from the industrial age will be forced to pay for its destructive fecal matter.

If the possibility of an environmental apocalypse is as imminent as ecologists claim, then those who play games with the issue should be exposed for the dangerous hypocrites that they are.

"For example, Nixon called the automobile 'our worst polluter of air,' yet the government will not impose maximum exhaust standards until 1980. Even current regulations calling for a yearly reduction of exhaust emissions will not be enforced until 1975.

"This kind of stalling, dodging and empty promises by government and industry should convince even the most optimistic ecologist that nothing substantial, or genuinely honest, will be done about the environment until the world is at death's door.

"It is madness to believe than an unresponsive, undemocratic government and corrupt economic system will or can save the earth. Just as it is madness to participate in a popular ecology movement that is endorsed by the very people who make the movement necessary...

Earth Read-Out (ERO) March 1970

FREE MEN WILL NOT BE GREEDY

ARMSTRONG
COLLINS
ALDRIN
They Brought Us Together

TECHNOLOGY for LIFE

*i*n a future revolution, the most pressing task assigned to technology will be to produce a surfeit of goods with a minimum of toil. The immediate purpose of this task will be to permanently open the social arena to the revolutionary people, *to keep the revolution in permanence.* Thus far, every social revolution has foundered because the peal of the tocsin could not be heard over the din of the workshop. Dreams of freedom and plenty were polluted by the mundane, workaday responsibility of producing the means of survival. Looking back at the brute facts of history, we find that as long as revolution meant continual sacrifice and denial for the people, the reins of power fell into the hands of the political "professionals", the mediocrities of Thermidor. How well the liberal Girondins of the French Convention understood this reality can be judged by the fact that they sought to reduce the revolutionary fervour of the Parisian popular assemblies—the great Sections of 1793—by decreeing that the meetings should close "at ten in the evening", or, as Carlyle tells us, "before the working people come . . ."from their jobs. The decree proved ineffective, but its aim was shrewd and unerring. Essentially, the tragedy of past revolutions has been that, sooner or later, their doors closed, "at ten in the evening" *The most critical function of modern technology must be to keep the doors of the revolution open forever!*

Nearly a half century ago, while Social Democratic and Communist theoreticians babbled about a society with "work for all", those magnificent madmen, the Dadaists, demanded unemployment for everybody. The decades have detracted nothing from this demand; to the contrary, they have given it form and content. From the moment toil is reduced to the barest possible minimum or disappears entirely, however, the problem of survival passes into the problem of life and it is certain that technology itself will pass from the servant of man's immediate needs into the partner of his creativity.

Let us look at this matter closely.

Much has been written about technology as an "extension of man". The phrase is misleading if it is meant to apply to technology as a whole. It has validity primarily for the traditional handicraft shop and, perhaps, for the early stages of machine development. The craftsman dominates the tool; his labor, artistic inclinations, and personality are the sovereign factors in the productive process. Labor is not merely an expenditure of energy but the personalized work of a man whose activities are sensuously directed toward preparing, fashioning, and finally decorating his product for human use. The craftsman guides the tool, not the tool the craftsman. Any alienation that may exist between the craftsman and his product is immediately overcome, as Friedrich Wilhelmsen emphasized, "by an artistic judgement—a judgement bearing on a thing to be made". The tool amplifies the powers of the craftsman as a *man* as a *human*; it amplifies his power to impart his artistry, his very identity as a creative being, on raw materials.

The development of the machine tends to rupture the intimate relationship between man and the means of production. To the degree that it is a self-operating device, the machine assimilates the worker to preset industrial tasks, tasks over which he exercises no control whatever. The machine now appears as an alien force—apart from and yet wedded to the production of the means of survival. Starting out as an "extension of man", technology is transformed into a force above man, orchestrating his life according to a score contrived by an industrial bureaucracy; not *men*, I repeat, but *bureaucracies*, i.e., *social machines.* With the arrival of the fully automatic machine as the predominate means of production, man becomes an extension of the machine, not only of mechanical devices in the productive process but also of social devices in the social process. Man ceases to exist in almost any respect for his own sake. Society is ruled by the harsh maxim: production for the sake of production. The decline from craftsman to worker, from the active to the increasingly passive personality, is completed by man *qua* consumer—an economic entity whose tastes, values, thoughts, and sensibilities are engineered by bureaucratic "teams" in "think tanks". Man, standardized by machines, is finally reduced to a machine.

*t*his is the trend. Man-the-machine is the bureaucratic ideal. It is an ideal that is continually defied by the rebirth of life, by the reappearance of the young and by the contradictions that unsettle the bureaucracy. Every generation has to be assimilated again, and each time with explosive resistance. The bureaucracy, in turn, never lives up to its own technical ideal. Congested by mediocrities, it errs continually. Its judgement lags behind new situations; insensate, it suffers from social inertia and is always buffeted by chance. Any crack that opens in the social machine is widened by the forces of life.

*h*ow can we heal the fracture that separates living men from dead machines without sacrificing either men or machines? How can we transform the technology for survival into the technology for life? To answer any of these questions with Olympian assurance would be idiotic. Liberated man may choose from a large variety of mutually exclusive or combinable alternatives, all of which may be based on unforeseeable technological innovations. As a sweeping solution, they may simply choose to step over the body of technology. They may submerge the cybernated machine in a technological underworld, divorcing it entirely from social life, the community, and creativity.

*a*ll but hidden from society, the machines would work for man. Free communities would stand, in effect, at the end of a cybernated industrial assembly line with baskets to cart the goods home. Industry, like the autonomic nervous system, would work on its own, subject to the repairs that our own bodies require in occasional bouts of illness. The fracture separating man from the machine would not be healed. It would simply be ignored.

i do not believe that this is a solution to anything. It would amount to closing off a vital human experience: the stimulus of productive activity, the stimulus of the machine. Technology can play a very important role in forming the personality of man. Every art, as Lewis Mumford has argued, has its technical side—the self-mobilization of spontaneity into expressed order, the need during the highest, most ecstatic moments of subjectivity to retain contact with the objective concreteness that responds with equal sensitivity to all stimuli—and therefore to none at all.

A liberated society, I believe, will not want to negate technology—precisely because it is liberated and can strike a balance. It may well be that it will want to assimilate the machine to artistic craftsmanship. What I mean by this is that the machine will remove toil from the productive process, leaving its artistic completion to man. The machine, in effect, will participate in human creativity. "The potter's wheel, for example, increased the freedom of the potter, hampered as he had been by the primitive coil method of shaping pottery without the aid of a machine; even the lathe permitted a certain leeway to the craftsman in his fashioning of beads and bulges," observes Mumford. By the same token, there is no reason why automatic, cybernated machinery cannot be used in a way so that the finishing of products, especially those destined for personal use, is left to the community. The machine can absorb the toil involved in mining, smelting, transporting, and shaping raw materials, leaving the final stages of artistry and craftsmanship to the individual. We are reminded that most of the stones that make up a medieval cathedral were carefully squared and standardized to facilitate their laying and bonding—a thankless, repetitive, and boring task that can now be done rapidly and effortlessly by modern machines. Once the stone blocks were set in place, the craftsmen made their appearance; inhuman toil was replaced by creative, human work. In a liberated community the combination of industrial machines and the craftsman's tools could reach a degree of sophistication, of creative interdependence unparalleled by any period in human history. William Morris' vision of a return of the crafts would be freed of its nostalgic nuances. We could truly speak of a qualitatively new advance in technics—a technology for life.

*H*aving acquired a vitalizing respect for the natural environment and its resources, the free decentralized community will give a new interpretation to the word "need". Marx's "realm of necessity", instead of expanding indefinitely, will tend to contract; needs will be humanized and scaled by a higher valuation of life and creativity. Quality and artistry will supplant the current emphasis on quality and standardization; durability will replace the current emphasis on expendability; an economy of cherished things, sanctified by a sense of tradition and by a sense of wonder for the personality and artistry of dead generations, will replace the mindless seasonal restyling of commodities; innovations will be made with a sensitivity for the natural inclinations of man as distinguished from the engineered pollution of taste by the mass media. Conservation will replace waste in all things. Freed of bureaucratic manipulation, men will rediscover the beauty of a simpler, uncluttered material life. Clothing, diet, furnishings, and homes will become more artistic, more personalized, and more Spartan. Man will recover a sense of the things that are *for* man, as against the things that have been *imposed* upon man. The repulsive ritual of bargaining and hoarding will be replaced by the sensitive act of making and giving. Things will cease to be the crutches for an impoverished ego and the mediators between aborted personalities; they will become the product of a rounded, creative individual and the gift of an integrated, developing self.

A technology for life can play the vital role of integrating one community with another. Rescaled to a revival of crafts and to a new conception of material needs, technology can also function as the sinews of confederation. The danger of a national division of labor and of industrial centralization is that technology begins to transcend the human scale, becomes increasingly incomprehensible, and lends itself to bureaucratic manipulation. To the extent that a shift away from community

control occurs in real material terms, technologically and economically, to that extent do centralized institutions acquire real power over the lives of men and threaten to become sources of coercion. A technology for life must be *based* on the community; it must be tailored to the community and regional level. On this level, however, the sharing of factories and resources can actually promote solidarity between community groups: it can serve to confederate them on the basis not only of common spiritual and cultural interests, but also common material needs. Depending upon the resources and uniqueness of regions, a rational, humanistic balance can be struck between autarchy, industrial confederation, and a national division of labor; the economic weight of society, however, must rest overwhelmingly with communities, both separately and in regional groups.

*I*s society so "complex" that an advanced civilization stands in contradiction to a decentralized technology for life? My answer to this question is a categoric, *no*! Much of the social "complexity" of our time has its origin in the paperwork, administration, manipulation, and constant wastefulness of capitalist enterprise. The petty bourgeois stands in awe of the bourgeois filing system—the rows of cabinets filled with invoices, accounting books, insurance records, tax forms—and the inevitable dossiers. He is spellbound by the "expertise" of industrial managers, engineers, style-mongers, manipulators of finance, and architects of market consent. He is totally mystified by the state—the sick fat of coercion, control, and domination. Modern society is incredibly complex—complex even beyond human comprehension—if we grant that its premises consist of property, production for the sake of production, competition, capital accumulation, exploitation, finance, centralization, coercion, bureaucracy—in short, the domination of man by man. Attached to every one of these premises are the institutions that actualize them—offices, millions of "personnel", forms and staggering tons of paper, desks, typewriters, telephones, and of course, rows upon rows of filing cabinets. As in Kafka's novels, they are real but strangely dreamlike, indefinable, shadows on the social landscape. The economy has a greater reality to it and is easily mastered by the mind and senses. But it too is intricate if we grant that buttons must be styled in a thousand different forms, textiles varied endlessly in kind and pattern to create the illusion of innovation and novelty, bathrooms filled to overflowing with a dazzling variety of pharmaceuticals and lotions, kitchens cluttered with an endless number of imbecile appliances (one thinks, here, of the electric can-opener) —the list is endless. (For supplemental reading, consult the advertising pages of the *Ladies Home Journal* or *Good Housekeeping*.) If we single out of this odious garbage one or two goods of high quality in the more useful categories and if we eliminate the money economy, the state power, the credit system, the paperwork and policework required to hold society in an enforced state of want, insecurity, and domination, society would not only become reasonably human but also fairly simple.

I do not wish to belittle the fact that behind a single yard of high quality electric wiring lies a copper mine, the machinery needed to operate it, a plant for producing insulating material, a copper-smelting and shaping complex, a transportation system for distributing the wiring—and behind each of these complexes, other mines, plants, machine shops, and so forth. Copper mines, certainly of a kind that can be exploited by existing machinery, are not to be found everywhere, although enough copper and other useful metals can be recovered as scrap from the debris of our present society to provide future generations with all they need. But let us grant that copper will fall within a sizeable category of material that can be furnished only by a national division of labor. In what sense need there be a division of labor in the current sense of the term? Bluntly, there need be none at all. First, copper can be exchanged for other goods between the

free, autonomous communities that mine it and those that require it. The exchange need not require the mediation of centralized bureaucratic institutions. Secondly, and perhaps more significantly, a community that lives in a region with ample copper resources will not be a mere mining community. Copper mining will be one of many economic activities in which it is engaged, a part of a larger, rounded, organic economic arena. The same will hold for communities whose climate is most suitable for growing specialized foods or whose resources are rare and uniquely valuable to society as a whole. Every community will approximate, perhaps in many cases achieve, local or regional autarchy. It will seek to achieve wholeness, not only because wholeness provides material independence (important as this may be), but also because it produces complete, rounded men who live in a symbiotic relationship with their environment. Even if a substantial portion of the economy falls within the sphere of a national division of labor, the overall economic weight of society will still rest with the community. If there is no distortion of communities, there will be no sacrifice of any portion of humanity to the interests of humanity as a whole.

A basic sense of decency, sympathy, and mutual aid lies at the core of human behavior. Even in this lousy bourgeois society, we do not find it unusual that adults will rescue children from danger although the act will imperil their lives; we do not find it strange that miners, for example, will risk death to save their fellow workers in cave-ins or that soldiers will crawl under heavy fire to carry a wounded comrade to safety. What tends to shock us are those occasions when aid is refused—when the cries of a girl who has been stabbed and is being murdered are ignored in a middle-class neighborhood.

Yet there is nothing in this society that would seem to warrant a molecule of solidarity. What solidarity we do find exists despite the society, against all its realities, as an unending struggle between the innate decency of man and the innate indecency of the society. Can we imagine how men would behave if this decency could find full release, if society earned the respect, even the love of the individual? We are still the offspring of a violent, blood-soaked, ignoble history— the end products of man's domination of man. We may never end this condition of domination. The future may bring us and our shoddy civilization down in a Wagnerian Gotterdammerung. How idiotic it would all be! But we may also end the domination of man by man. We may finally succeed in breaking the chain to the past and gain a humanistic, anarchist society. Would it not be the height of absurdity, indeed of impudence, to gauge the behavior of future generations by the very criteria we despise in our own time? An end to the sophomoric questions! Free men will not be greedy, one liberated community will not try to dominate another because it has a potential monopoly of copper, computer "experts" will not try to enslave grease monkeys, and sentimental novels about pining, tubercular virgins will not be written. We can ask only one thing of the free men of the future: to forgive us that it took so long and that it was such a hard pull. Like Brecht, we can ask that they try not to think of us too harshly, that they give us their sympathy and understand that we lived in the depths of a social hell.

But then they will surely know what to think without our telling them.

—Lewis Herber
Reprinted from Anarchy 78. WIN Aug 1969

GINSBERG— TREES ARE OUR ALLIES

(the following interview is reprinted from
THE FIFTH ESTATE, a detroit underground :)

Editor's Note: This interview with poet Allen Ginsberg took place at 10:00 a.m. on October 15 while driving from Detroit's inner city to Macomb College where he was reading. Ginsberg was in the area doing a series of readings for the John Sinclair Defense Fund and a benefit for the Ann Arbor Argus.

Fifth Estate: What place does poetry have in the United States, at the present time, in connection with the movement?

Allen Ginsberg: Well, what's going on in America is much larger than what's going on in the movement. What's going on is a lot of trees growing and plants moving around and cows eating grass, which is more important than anything, so poetry is just part of the same natural order, which is it's just like speech, peace of speech, and so it's just more coherent speech.

So, if coherent speech has any place in the larger natural movement that's going on, including the sun and the stars and people growing up then it has got the same old place it always had, and as for the movement, it can stick its preoccupations with what place anything has up its own ass.

FE: Do you think that poetry is playing an important role in creating social awareness?

AG: No, I don't think it is.

FE: Do you think that more people read poetry today, or say, in the last ten or fifteen years, than ever before?

AG: No, less if anything. There's more people, so more poetry is being read on account of the doubling of the population, but more people listen to it in song, they don't read it.

FE: Then you've noticed a decline in the reading of poetry?

AG: Yeah, I think less people sit down in an attic and read.

FE: Because the most easily accessible poetry is contained in music?

AG: No, because people look at television instead of reading. I don't hardly read any more.

FE: Do you think that rock music is the new poetry as far as young people are concerned?

AG: Well, yes, with the Beatles', "I Am A Walrus," and some of Dylan's lyrics. It returns to the old poetry which is minstrelsy.

FE: Do you think that young people are taking it as minstrelsy?

AG: Well, I think it's being used in the same way that minstrelsy was being used. Like, the bard used to be the cat who went around from valley to valley getting the news and rhyming it up and ancient oral newspaper before they had moveable type and so, like now, song is a source of information and news, about which way the wind is blowing.

FE: What purpose do you think you poetry serves?

AG: I don't know anymore. I just feel as if I'm getting up and bullshitting to myself. At least at this hour of the morning, that's what it feels like.

FE: What did it feel like last night when you filled up Community Arts Auditorium?

AG: More of, like, one old lone man talking to himself, other people overhearing, and to the extent that his speech was accurate and honest, one man felt like anybody else, or everybody else. But it didn't have any social conclusions or propositions to it finally. There's no system at the end. What'd we begin with, let's go back to there.

FE: All right, what place poetry has in connection with the movement in America today.

AG: Here's what I'm bridling about is that what is happening socially now, which here in Detroit, right now, is being called the movement, is a little wavelet on a larger awareness that's growing in people, which is a biological awareness rather than a political awareness. Or another kind of politics is slowly emerging which is indistinguishable from biology or ecology and that ideological politics, ideological Marxist politics has become completely bankrupted along with capitalism in the biological crisis that's overtaken the planet.

So there's a threat to the existence of the entire planet, so when you ask the question what place has poetry in the social revolution that's taking place now, I begin bridling, I begin cursing because it's like putting everybody's understanding back in the thirties, in a way, when everybody was arguing whether or not the poet should be responsible socially.

This is an argument that ultimately wound up whether or not the poet was responsible to the Central Committee of the Communist Party for a proper articulation of the needs and desires and logical ideology of the masses. And that, as Chairman Mao has repeatedly said, the poet must stand up and take criticism from the Communist Party and because the Communist Party is the will of the people.

Therefore, since the poet must be responsible to the will of the people he must be responsible logically to the Communist Party and therefore, if they tell him to fuck off, he's got to fuck off. So in other words, the terminology of the question you asked, that same terminology seems dated and that's why I was being so creepy in my answer.

The creepiness of my answer did sneak in some reference to biology. I don't think the movement as it is known here is yet ecologically oriented and biologically conscious or complete and, therefore, the movement is full of shit.

FE: The movement as it is here in Detroit?

AG: Everywhere in the United States, everywhere -- the whole movement, in the United States and Cuba and Russia and China, everywhere, the whole revolutionary movement is not yet into the realization of the fact that man's material grasping is actually destroying other species and it's actually beginning to threaten the existence of the planet itself.

As Gary Snyder points out, the exploited masses are not just and blacks and hippies and the Chinese, the exploited masses are the trees and the fish in the sea, those are the exploited masses, the rest of the sentient beings on the planet. So I think we need things like Snyder's "Smokey Bear Sutra," and then they've got a new thing called "The Declaration of Interdependence," which was just put out by a whole gang of ecology action people on the west coast, that are sympathetic enough to include the whole planet and not just the human contingent.

that has ecology as its roots, is based on the west coast?

AG: Because everybody here is so covered with machinery and smog that they have forgotten that nature even exists. Quite literally, here, people have become so divorced from the bio-system of the planet, especially here in Detroit, the center of mechanization, that they literally have forgotten that they are part of a larger interdependent harmonic organic system. They've got mountains out there so you can always go out in the mountains and realize that mountains are bigger than cities, that the back country is much much vaster than the places the humans have filled up.

FE: Well, what effect do you think ecology oriented poets like Gary Snyder and Diane di Prima are having on the people as far as changing these things goes?

AG: I don't like the phrase "the people". Who is the people, who is the people, who the fuck is the people? · I keep bridling over this political terminology. Who is the people? What does that mean?

FE: Well, the people who are capable of changing things or setting the world straight, because the trees certainly can't do it by themselves.

AG: The trees are the only ones who are getting the world straight. They're the ones who are producing the oxygen we are consuming, the trees are like the oxygen factories of the atmosphere. The trees are our biggest allies. If the enemy is the materialistic, consumer oriented, predatory, acquisitive capitalistic, manufacturing society which is consuming all our natural resources at a suicidal rate, our natural allies in this batlte for survival are the trees and the grass.

I think what is happening is that the ecology oriented people are articulating clearly what everybody unconsciously realizes, including the capitalists, what everybody is unconsciously realizing. But it is just too large and apocalyptic and horrible to realize into consciousness that we are in, perhaps, the death throes of the planet and that the planet may be finished unless we take some immediate measures, unless we're aware of the fact that we're a threat to the planet. Lake Erie is poisoned.

FE: Does the poet have any place in turning peoples' eyes to these facts?

AG: Well, not ordained by God, but it's just common sense. I guess that poets have always been running around in the woods and spouting out about nature so, yeah, sure, they'd be the first ones to be sensitive when nature gets shit all over. It is shit because it's just the waste product, thoroughly machine shit, the shit of robots, even brown colored, in a gaseous form, robot farts.

FE: Does poetry have any importance politically beyond ecology. I mean, why is it that the state is constantly busting poets like John Sinclair, LeRoi Jones, you, and in some cases, even driving them to suicide as with d.a. levy.?

AG: Or Brody, Alexi Ginzburg, Yesinen Volpin or all the poets in China they fucked in the ass, too. I hate Mao Tse-Tung. His literary criticism is the worst of the new criticism.that has escaped, worse than Alan Tate.

Well, mainly they bust poets because I don't think poets are intimidated by authority. If they've reported their unconscious correctly, if they're measuring their unconscious accurately, then you are getting an unconditioned report on what you're actually thinking and feeling rather than a partial report on what you think you're supposed to feel and think as dictated by politicians of any side.

Anyway, all politics is, in a sense, is poetry -- in the sense that it's hypnotic imagery being laid out like the dominoe theory, which is a two word

hypnotized and it's all public communications now....the imagery, television, and language that goes along with it. So it's all made up, selected, edited, made up compositions and that's what poetry is....compositions that you make up out of your brain from language or painting pictures. So that a Frankenstein picture of China which requires people to put up an ABM system is just a piece of bad poetry, like, in other words, a whole political language is also poetry, is just bad poetry. In other words, a whole political language is also poetry, is just bad poetry in the sense that it's made up pictures. It's a question of what composition has the most information and is the most revealing and is the most accurate. A hysterical composition by the police blaming outside agitators for violence or blaming conspirators for what's wrong is like a second rate poem, or a second rate generalization, just like Abbie Hoffman or Jerry Rubin talking about the Chicago 8 trial being theater. It is all theater, the Democratic convention was theater, like the Living Theater theater.

FE: What do you think of violence as a means for change. I mean, do you feel there's a time when its use is necessary or acceptable?

AG: Once a question like that is posed, it then becomes unanswerable. That's like something Burroughs said the other day, "Once a problem is posed, it becomes insoluable." There's no answer, I mean I don't have an answer for that, all I know is that I get violently angry, but I know every time I do, I pay for it because I usually hit the wrong person. Like at the beginning of this interview I was violently angry, but I don't even know who I was being angry at, so I took it out on you. So, most violence I've seen has been bullshit.

FE: Can you rationalize it as self-defense ever?

AG. Well, I've never been in a situation where violent fisticuffs, guns, or self-defense was more effective than other means. there are always other means that were more effective, I've found. But it requires training in other means, just as self-defense requires training in karate. In Chicago, had they had classes in rhythmic behavior, mantra chanting and organized body movements, the first day of the Convention would have sent a message much more sympathetic and interesting to the world at large through the public imagery than they did when they sent the snake dance karate message.

They would have averted violent conspiracy evidence in the trial and they would have trained people for something useful because the karate class in this case was neither used nor useful. It was just a lot of bullshit. It was never put into use anyway, it was just a theatrical gesture.

The rationalization for it at the time was that it was absolutely practically necessary that they be trained precisely in that way, for physical combat contact. Well, it wasn't – it was just hysterical and the guys who were running it agreed, later anyway. It would have been more effective in terms of street tactics had they spent a day teaching people mantras, because the mantras were used a little, at least, and the karate never was – so violence only leads to more violence, it's a big drag, egotistical, like with the police, but the violence is already set forth and so escalated in every direction and everybody is so insistent on having their own way that I suppose that it's going to take place.

There's no way out of it. The Jews are going to stomp all over Sinai, and the Arabs are going to cut the Jews' throats; hippies are going to cut the cops' throats and the cops are going to cut the hippies' throats....great....the narcs are going to cut the mystics' throats.

FE: Where's it all going to stop.

AG: Burroughs says the planet's finished. As to whether or not it is?

Recorded and Transcribed by
David Fenner

ANATOMY AND DEVELOPMENT OF STUDENT REBELLION

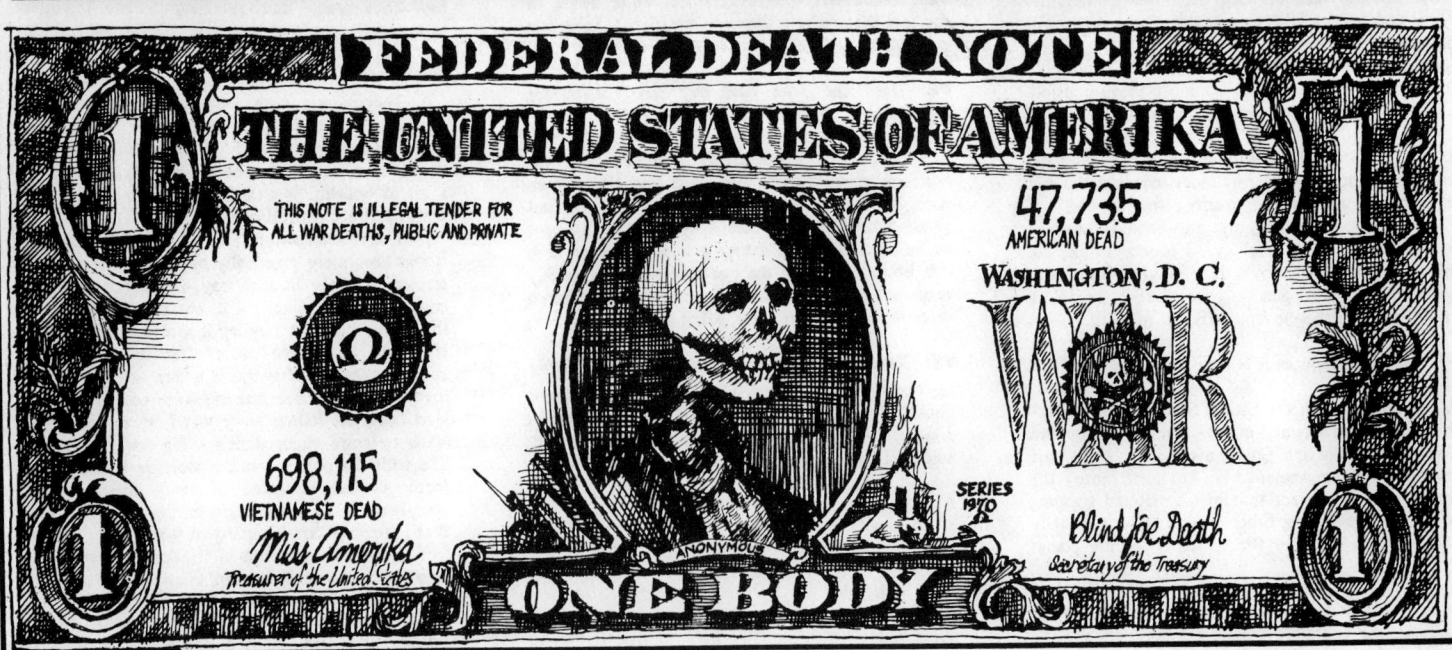

Above: watching funeral procession for Jeff Miller, one of the Kent State dead.

"Two, Three, Many Columbias"

By Tom Hayden

THE GOAL WRITTEN on the university walls was "Create two, three, many Columbias"; it meant expand the strike so that the U.S. must either change or send its troops to occupy American campuses.

At this point the goal seems realistic; an explosive mix is present on dozens of campuses where demands for attention to student views are being disregarded by university administrators.

The American student movement has continued to swell for nearly a decade: during the semi-peace of the early '60s as well as during Vietnam; during the token liberalism of John Kennedy as well as during the bankrupt racism of Lyndon Johnson. Students have responded most directly to the black movement of the '60s: from Mississippi Summer to the Free Speech Movement; from "Black Power" to "Student Power"; from the seizure of Howard University to the seizure of Hamilton Hall. As the racial crisis deepens so will the campus crisis. But the student protest is not just an offshoot of the black protest—it is based on authentic opposition to the middle-class world of manipulation, channeling and careerism. The students are in opposition to the fundamental institutions of society.

The students' protest constantly escalates by building on its achievements and legends. The issues being considered by seventeen-year-old freshmen at Columbia University would not have been within the imagination of most "veteran" student activists five years ago.

Columbia opened a new tactical stage in the resistance movement which began last fall: from the overnight occupation of buildings to permanent occupation; from mill-ins to the creation of revolutionary committees; from symbolic civil disobedience to barricaded resistance. Not only are these tactics already being duplicated on other campuses, but they are sure to be surpassed by even more militant tactics. In the future it is conceivable that students will threaten destruction of buildings as a last deterrent to police attacks. Many of the tactics learned can also be applied in smaller hit-and-run operations between strikes: raids on the offices of professors doing weapons research could win substantial support among students while making the university more blatantly repressive.

In the buildings occupied at Columbia, the students created what they called a "new society" or "liberated area" or "commune," a society in which decent values would be lived out even though university officials might cut short the communes through use of police. The students had fun, they sang and danced and wisecracked, but there was continual tension. There was no question of their constant awareness of the seriousness of their acts. Though there were a few violent arguments about tactics, the discourse was more in the form of endless meetings convened to explore the outside political situation, defense tactics, maintenance and morale problems within the group. Debating and then determining what leaders should do were alternatives to the remote and authoritarian decision-making of Columbia's trustees.

The Columbia strike represented more than a new tactical movement, however. There was a political message as well. The striking students were not holding onto a narrow conception of students as a privileged class asking for inclusion in the university as it now exists. This kind of demand could easily be met by administrators by opening minor opportunities for "student rights" while cracking down on campus radicals. The Columbia students were instead taking an internationalist and revolutionary view of themselves in opposition to the imperialism of the very institutions in which they have been groomed and educated. They did not even want to be included in the decision-making circles of the military-industrial complex that runs Columbia: *they want to be included only if their inclusion is a step toward transforming the university.* They want a new and independent university standing against the mainstream of American society, or they want no university at all. They are, in Fidel Castro's words, "guerrillas in the field of culture."

How many other schools can be considered ripe for such confrontations? The question is hard to answer, but it is clear that the demands of black students for cultural recognition rather than paternalistic tolerance, and radical white students' awareness of the sinister paramilitary activities carried on in secret by the faculty on many campuses, are hardly confined to Columbia. Columbia's problem is the American problem in miniature—the inability to provide answers to widespread social needs and the use of the military to protect the authorities against the people. This process can only lead to greater unity in the movement.

Support from outside the university communities can be counted on in many large cities. A crisis is foreseeable that would be too massive for police to handle. It can happen; whether or not it will be necessary is a question which only time will answer. What is certain is that we are moving toward power—the power to stop the machine if it cannot be made to serve humane ends.

American educators are fond of telling their students that barricades are part of the romantic past, that social change today can only come about through the processes of negotiation. But the students at Columbia discovered that barricades are only the beginning of what they call "bringing the war home."

Ramparts 6/15/68

Why S.F. State strikers won't negotiate

THIRD WORLD
LEADS THE
MOST MASSIVE
AND SUSTAINED
STRIKE
EVER SEEN ON
AN AMERICAN
CAMPUS

Following is the text of a Jan. 18 interview between Guardian reporter Robert L. Allen and Roger Alvarado, on-campus coordinator and spokesman for the Third World Liberation Front (TWLF) at San Francisco State College.

How would you summarize the basic meaning of the 15 strike demands?

There are two basic ideas. One of them is confrontation with the institutionalized racism within the school—the structure of the courses, the lack of any relevance to third world people—which excludes the perspective of third world people as well as our cultures and histories in the development of this country and our home countries.

The other basic idea is the principle of self-determination. What we want is to determine for ourselves what our education is, who our instructors are, who the administrators and coordinators will be, as well as what we will do with that education ultimately.

It has been stressed repeatedly that these demands are non-negotiable. In most labor disputes, however, everything is open to negotiation. How would you explain the TWLF's position on negotiations?

It is based on the two principles I just mentioned. If we were to negotiate any of the 15 demands, we would be negotiating on how much racism is to be institutionalized or how much self-determination we are to achieve.

As far as labor unions—I think the rank and file is beginning to realize that most unions have not fulfilled their obligations to their memberships. Their willingness to negotiate has resulted in workers not being able to meet their economic and other needs. Now a couple of unions are starting to take the position that their demands are non-negotiable.

What is necessary to make education relevant to third world communities?

The most important thing is participation of the community as much as possible in the educational system—as students, teachers,

trustees, directors and administrators. Without the participation of all the people at all levels, you can't expect anything better than we're getting now. It's not possible for someone else to run a system in our best interests.

We can't afford to continue the separation between students and community, or between students and teachers, or between administrators and the community. That would mean continuing the disunity and isolation and racism that exist throughout the society.

What has been the actual amount of grass-roots community participation in the strike up to this point?

That's hard to estimate. We've had a lot of participation from community leaders whose organizations support the strike. In terms of people who have been directly involved either in picketing or rallies and marches, I would say that about 50% of our community support has been from the grass-roots level. A lot of young people have been involved—high school and junior high school students.

It's particularly significant that community groups have begun to organize in various ways to support the strike and to oppose the tactics used by the administration and the politicians to divide them from the students.

Some of the old barriers between students and community are also beginning to come down. Traditionally you had third world students who earned a college degree and in the process become assimilated into middle-class society with all its racism. And then they come back into the community to work as teachers and social workers and in all these other service fields, all the while feeding into the community the attitudes and middle-class perspective that they had been educated with. Now the students are saying they don't want that kind of relationship maintained.

One of the differences between what happened at Columbia University and what is going on at State is that at Columbia there was a seizure of buildings whereas at State there is a strike directly involving large masses of students without such a seizure. How would you assess the value of these different tactics?

The value of the tactics has to do with the confrontation you're trying to enforce. If you're trying to enforce a confrontation with a building, you go into the building and you close it down. If you're trying to enforce a confrontation with a system, you've got to concern yourself with the operation of that system.

When we were about to start the strike we analyzed what had gone on at different universities and we concluded that if we wanted to win the 15 demands we would have to be involved in a long struggle—continually harassing and disrupting the school until they were forced to shut it down.

In this country they go for a quick victory, which means that nothing pleases them more than when students take over a building where they can be isolated, arrested and the impetus of the movement destroyed. Our feeling was that we didn't want a mass confrontation with the cops; we didn't want to have people arrested in large numbers.

One of the brothers calls it "the war of the flea." The system is the dog and we are the fleas. We take a little bite here and a little blood there, and keep on the move so that the dog can never get rid of us. Now the number of fleas is increasing, and if the magnitude becomes great enough we can make the dog get up and move.

There have been reports in the press of splits between "militant" and "moderate" factions in the strike leadership. Would you comment on these?

Roger Alvarado, coordinator of the SF State TWLF.

Guardian photo by Luis Espinoza

I think the basis of these reports came from the administration, in an attempt to split the leadership of the third world and the coalition between third world groups.

What is the role of white students?

Though many of the white students come from families that have pretty racist attitudes against people in the third world, they themselves are pretty much discontented with their relationship to people in the third world. They find a lot of contradictions in this country's ideology and in the functioning of the political and economic structure.

Secondly, and possibly more critical, the white students have seen that they don't have any self-determination themselves. As a result they have expressed active solidarity in supporting TWLF. Their role has been one of support. They recognize that it is the responsibility of the third world students to direct the strike.

Some students have been critical of the American Federation of Teachers [which is also on strike] on the grounds that it is not firmly committed to the 15 demands. How would you assess the role of the AFT?

It's hard to say where the AFT stands now or where it has ever stood. I'm not saying that they don't support the demands, but there's a real difficulty relating to them. They've been a hard group of people to get together because they've never been together before. Their understanding of politics in terms of what it means to move from a powerless position into a position of power has been naive and has really been developed in the last three months, so they're beginning to get some kind of perspective on what they're involved in.

As far as where they stand on the 15 demands, that decision is still up in the air since the [San Francisco Central] Labor Council has agreed to recognize only their labor-oriented demands. This forces the AFT to decide whether it will maintain a wildcat strike if necessary in order to see the implementation of the 15 demands.

The contradiction is that you have a labor union supporting a moral position—something which labor unions traditionally haven't done. And for a white labor union to support a moral position for third world people is kind of a tenuous thing to expect to last very long. We're hopeful that it will, because we recognize the importance of the stand that they've taken. But at the same time we recognize the factors which will make it difficult for them to maintain that position. So this makes our relationship continually conflicting.

What do you think are the prospects for the strike spreading to other state college campuses?

The prospects are very good. The condition of third world people throughout the state educational system is atrocious in terms of discrimination and miseducation. The strike at State has proved that people can make specific demands concerning their education, and other students are beginning to see the need to take a position and the need to develop a strategy that can ultimately mean the fulfillment of their demands.

Very definitely it will spread, maybe not in the next two or three months, but within a year. The questions that have been raised at State will be raised throughout the educational system, not just at the state college level, but at the university level and in the junior colleges and even down into the high schools and junior high schools.

Guardian 2/1/69

ONE LAW FOR WORKER "INSURRECTION" AND ANOTHER FOR STUDENTS (OR BLACKS)

In April, 1937, seven prominent Bostonians, including the President Emeritus of Harvard University, sent a telegram to the United States Senate, stating, among other things, that "armed insurrection—defiance of law and order and duly elected authority—is spreading like wildfire. . . . It is the obligation of Congress and the state legislatures, of the President and the governors, in their Constitutional fields, to enact and enforce legislation that will put an end to this type of defiant insurrection."

The "armed insurrection" to which the Bostonians were referring was the sit-down strike in which thousands of General Motors employees took over the G.M. plants in Michigan.

In the case of the sit-down strikes of 1937, no one doubted that the strikers were violating the law. It was clear that they were occupying property that did not belong to them and were, in addition, prepared to defend their "right" to carry on this illegal activity. Yet, the state made no attempt to remove them forcibly from the G.M. property nor was there any prosecution of them after the strike ended. Political power and economic pressure outweighed the purely legal considerations.

From "The Varieties of Violence" by Paul Jacobs
The Center Magazine Jan 1969

MADISON FIREMAN LEARN FROM SDS: A STUDENT STRIKE SEEN IN ITS CONTEXT

mighty madison: behind the lines

jackie disalvo

MADISON, Wisc. (LNS). Students attending classes at the University of Wisconsin during recent strike activities had to pass through armed troops in order to reach the English Department.

Convoys of jeeps interrupt rush hour traffic on University Avenue. Soldiers with bayonets unsheathed advance up Bascom Hill like they were scouting a contingent of Viet Cong. This campus has looked like an army post ever since Governor Warren Knowles ordered in 2,000 National Guard in what is probably the most drastic reaction yet to student demonstrations.

Madison students struck for over a week in support of black student demands (which include a student-controlled Black Studies department and increased black admissions).

The New York Times, assuming that "where there's smoke, there's fire" reported that the Guard was brought in to quell student violence. Before the Guard arrived, however, Madison students were engaged in peaceful picketing and leafletting in a week of what even the local press now lauds as "remarkably restrained demonstrations." The way in which the Guard was sent onto the campus left the students with the impression that the Governor was not concerned with either breaking the strike (which, of course, was strengthened by the presence of the Guard) or with maintaining law and order, but with staging one of the most spectacular street dramas the country has yet seen.

"Step right up ladies and gentlemen, see student guerrillas stalk Bascom Hill; see black extremists on the rampage, threatening to burn, baby, burn down your shiny white Capitol; see drugged-up hippies call the upholders of order dirty names; and see the nations finest, the khaki-clad defenders of their country, protect you from rioting communist niggers right here in Madison, Wisc., folks. Playing tonight on your very own television screen."

When the establishment moves into guerilla theater, it comes on with a cast of thousands. The Governor even went so far as to station troops inside the capitol building during the meeting of the legislature to impress upon them the idea that they were in danger of immediate siege.

Neither the Times nor the TV commentators have been able to discern the real purpose of this living theatre, a last-ditch effort by the state to find a scapegoat at the University for a social and economic crisis now facing Wisconsin in general and Madison in particular. The pressure exerted by black students is just the first rumbling of an explosion which may rock the entire state.

Knowles' gubernatorial campaign last November was based on that good Republican platform—the balanced budget. Two days after his election, the Milwaukee Journal revealed that the state he had already led for four years faced a budget crisis of incredible proportions. The crisis is of national significance because it reflects one of the drastic dislocations caused by the war in Vietnam. The cut-back in federal funds to the state has led to a cut in state money for programs ranging from education to medical care, farmers' assistance, poverty programs, and last but not least, state employees' salaries. Since this crisis was revealed, the state legislature has been frantically slashing expenditures and proposing tax increases that will affect the income of nearly every wage earner in the state.

The Left has long speculated in quiet anticipation about what would happen if the general repression set off by the war ever reached the workers and their paychecks. In Madison, Wisc., the shit has hit the fan. Students who originally went out on strike to support the educational demands of blacks find themselves stepping into state politics, and they are beginning to form some rather unexpected alliances in the context of social unrest which may reach major porportions.

The state's financial crisis has brought new actors onto the stage of Madison's living theater, actors that Governor Knowles did not expect. Even before the student strike, the teaching assistants at the University had passed a strike vote. The TAs' vote was designed to resist a bill before the Wisconsin legislature to cut their salaries by revoking their out of state fee remission.

At the same time AFL-CIO Local 171, which includes all non-teaching University employees, such as janitors, cafeteria workers, etc., is also facing salary cuts. The legislature has passed a wage and hiring freeze for government workers and has eliminated overtime for university workers. Although the union has never broken the anti-strike law before, the heading of 171's most recent newsletter read "STRIKE -- OUR LAST RESORT".

A simultaneous strike in the next few weeks by the TAA and local 171 would close down the University. Imagine the scenario: troups brought in, not against the Commie-Jew Nigger Lovers, but against Wisconsin Trade Unionists!

The state and city governments have even greater reason to panic, for the University is not all that could be shut down by a strike of public employees. One third of Madison's work force is composed of public employees and the state capital would be paralyzed if they ever struck. Throughout the year newly class-conscious students have been lending at least minimal support to local strikes. The city firemen, when they were about to strike, threatened to use militant tactics which one leader acknowledged had been picked up from SDS

Students have had good communication with firemen ever since. Some evidence of the city's determination to take a hard line against "illegal strikes" was its threat at that time to bring out cops against the firemen. The police, it happens, were given an extremely liberal contract in exchange for their acceptance of a rigid no-strike clause; in effect, agreed to act as strike breakers against the firemen.

TAs' are in the interesting position of being students and state workers simultaneously. And speculation here is that the administration's overreaction to campus demonstrations could be a calculated attempt to discredit students—to project the image that they are wild and irresponsible. Thus the state hopes to nip at the outset any alliances between discontented students and equally discontented workers.

Ed. Note: When Madison Firemen later struck, they received amnesty along with a wage increase.

San Francisco
Express Times (LNS 2/25/69)

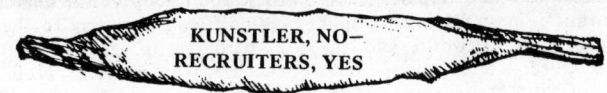

KUNSTLER, NO—
RECRUITERS, YES

VIOLENCE

University of Illinois Becomes a Battlefield Scene

CHAMPAIGN, Ill. (LNS)-- It started with a small, peaceful rally Monday, March 2. Within four days, the University of Illinois campus here had become a scarred battlefield, an occupied, curfewed zone -- a Day After.

The outburst of student rage, which eventually saw thousands of people battling with every size, shape and brand of cop the state could muster, and which caused 900 National Guardsmen to be brought onto the campus, was sparked by the Monday rally called by the Radical Union to protest the presence of General Electric recruiters on the campus. At the rally, students who had been working at the GE plant in Danville, 30 miles away, explained GE's double-edged profiteering: its underpayment of its own workers and; as the nation's second largest defense contractor its lucrative involvement in the deadly exploitation of the Third World.

After the rally several hundred demonstrators moved to the Electrical Engineering building where GE was recruiting on the third floor. They found all entrances guarded by police -- one could visit the GE men "by appointment only."

Fifty students pulled down a fire escape and surged up to the third floor where they scuffled briefly with police. One cop was knocked out by a well-swung bookbag. Several people were arrested inside the building, others were clubbed and arrested outside. GE recruiting stopped for the day.

That afternoon the Board of Trustees of the university cancelled Conspiracy lawyer Bill Kunstler's speaking engagement for Tuesday night, branding him "a clear and present danger" to the campus.

An angered crowd rallied in the Student Union at 7 p.m. and then, 5,000 strong, they swarmed through the campus hitting selected targets. Two-thirds of the windows of the huge oval Armory which houses the University of Illinois ROTC program were broken. Windows in the Administration Building, the Chancellor's office,

the Electrical Engineering Building, the Math Department and three nearby rip-off stores were also smashed.

Four hundred university, Champaign, Urbana and State police exercised little control over the crowd, merely picking up (with the assistance of frat men and jocks) isolated students here and there. By midnight when the crowd dispersed, they had arrested 24 students on charges including mob action, criminal damage, criminal trespass, resisting arrest and disorderly conduct.

After a fairly peaceful Tuesday -- with the campus swarming with hundreds of police and National Guardsmen -- the students came to campus Wednesday to learn that General Motors, Standard Oil, Lockheed and U.S. Steel were recruiting on the third floor of their own Student Union. (Students later found out that Dow Chemical had been recruiting secretly the same day in another building.)

Three hundred students moved up to the third floor and sat-in in the corridor. Some recruiters came out from behind their locked doors and left the building. When Champaign and State police were called in, the sit-inners tried to leave peacefully, but the cops began pushing peo-

ple down the stairs. One student tried to save his friend from arrest and got a six-inch split clubbed into his skull for his efforts.

A crowd of 2000 people milled around the campus Wednesday afternoon, alternately confronting police and retreating or being clubbed back. Several people were seriously hurt. The windows of the nearby Bell Telephone Company were smashed.

After the 10:30 p.m. curfew, police rounded up three busloads of curfew violators, pulled demonstrators out of dormitories and private houses, and refused to let injured people into the school's medical center. A 13 year old boy was run over by a police car during the wipe-up operation. Wednesday saw 147 arrests.

The National Guard is still in Champaign. You still have to be off the streets at 10:30 It isn't over yet.

Madison kaleidoscope (LNS) 3/18/70

SANTA BARBARA!!

SANTA BARBARA, Calif. (LNS) -- More than 1,000 kids seized a three-block business district in a student neighborhood near the University of California at Santa Barbara Wednesday night, Feb. 25, held it from police for six hours, smashed windows, set fire to a police car, and burned a plush Bank of America office to the ground, doing more than a quarter of a million dollars damage to the bank alone.

Five hundred national guardsmen were

called out Friday, Feb. 27, and another 2,500 placed on standby alert after students drove 300 police out of their neighborhood three nights in a row. Two inches of rain plus a student decision not to fight the Guard quieted the area Friday and Saturday nights. "We don't have any quarrel with them," a spokesman said.

But sheriff's officers worried that renewed demonstrations would follow the pull-out of the Guard on Sunday and Monday. "It scares me," said Sheriff Lieut. William Chickering. "We've been told that the demonstrators are going to wait until the National Guard pulls out and do it to us again."

A total of 141 persons were arrested in five nights. At least 34 policemen were injured. Other casualties included a 35-year-old university employee, who was shot in the shoulder when he accidentally drove through a police roadblock, and a 21-year-old student, who was hospitalized after being run down by a police car Thursday night.

Gov. Ronald Reagan flew to Santa Barbara on Thursday morning. He called the demonstrators "cowardly little bums," declared a "state of extreme emergency," and placed National Guard units on alert. He also said he would declare martial law if necessary. County officials ordered

a 6 p.m. to 6 a.m. curfew, and police were ordered to "prohibit loitering on public streets" and to "break up assemblies of more than three persons."

Students defied the orders, and a combined force of 300 police, California Highway Patrolmen and sheriff's deputies was gathered from three counties Thursday night. They fought students for six hours and were forced to withdraw at 11:30 p.m.

The most spectacular destruction occurred Wednesday night. One thousand demonstrators began pelting sheriff's cars with rocks. At 9:45 p.m. they captured one car, forcing two deputies to flee and then setting the car afire. The flames were 30 feet high. Windows were smashed; the plywood used to board up the Bank of America's windows, smashed the day before, was torn down and set afire; demonstrators then surged into the bank.

An observer said that the group inside "hurled chairs into windows, overturned desks, created snowfalls of envelopes from an upstairs office and tore up anything they could reach." Then some people got a big trashcan, set it on fire, and ran it through the front doors and pushed it against the drappery.

The police were informed that a manager was inside the burning bank. Seventy sheriff's deputies, in full riot gear, were sent to free the manager, but when they arrived they found they had fallen into a trap. There was no manager inside but there were hundreds of students surrounding the cops, throwing rocks.

The police fought their way out and withdrew completely, surrendering the area to the students until 2:15 a.m., when a force of 240 cops returned to clear the streets.

After the police withdrawal, firemen were unable to reach the bank. Some fraternity members tried to put out the fire, but it was ignited again and the whole place was gone in 45 minutes. A few charred beams were all that remained the next morning; bank officials said $275,000 damage was done.

One veteran radical said, "While the students held the shopping center, there wasn't an atmosphere of 'wild in the streets.' The group was calm and highly political -- explicitly anti-capitalist. Targets of window-breaking were chosen carefully: the Bank, the real estate offices which gouge students on rents, and the gas stations whose companies pollute Santa Barbara Bay with oil seepages. Small businesses were not touched."

The business district that was seized and held from police on three consecutive nights lies in the heart of Isla Vista, a suburb of Santa Barbara, with a population of 13,000. Of these, 9,000 are students of the University of California branch here.

The students had been united by a ser-

ies of on-campus demonstrations which began in January, when Bill Allen, a popular anthropology professor, was denied tenure. Three-fourths of the school's 14,000 students took part in one demonstration or another. Two-thirds of the student body signed a petition in support of Allen.

"This was the first time radical politics made an appearance at the University of California at Santa Barbara," one veteran radical said. "In the campus demonstrations there was a feeling of the early 'sixties -- they were non-violent and not confrontation demonstrations."

In spite of the peaceful character of the campus demonstrations, police arrested 19 people, dragging many of them out of bed in the middle of the night. The demand to re-hire Allen was not met, and a massive residue of frustration and hostility to the police was left.

The Chicago conspiracy defendants became immensely popular among Santa Barbara students. Tom Hayden gave a speech at the university in early January, drawing an enthusiastic crowd of 1,200, the largest audience ever assembled for a political event on the campus up to that time. In February, the official student government invited Defense Attorney William Kunstler to speak on campus, offering him $2,000 of student funds, plus a percentage of the gate, plus a passing of the hat. He appeared Wednesday afternoon, February 25, in the football stadium, where 7,000 people paid 50¢ each to hear him.

The night after his speech the bank was burned. Gov. Reagan suggested that Kunstler had violated the "Rap Brown act" -- saying he crossed a state line to incite violence (this is the law the Chicago defendants were convicted under).

Student leaders pleaded with newsmen not to say Kunstler incited the violence, pointing out that the windows of the bank had been broken the night before his appearance on campus.

The Bank of America, whose offices have been attacked during the past week in Berkeley, San Francisco and Los Angeles, has offered a $25,000 reward for the Santa Barbara arsonists. Board Chairman Louis B. Lundborg reported that "we have not been able to open the vault doors since the fire, but we assume that the bank's funds and records are safe." He said the bank was "proud to be a symbol of the establishment in the real sense of that word: established law and order, established orderly process."

Tromp Imperialism

THE MOVEMENT
THE WORKING CLASS
THE CORPORATION

STANDARD OIL WANTS STANDARD PEOPLE

marvin garson

STUDENTS MEET THE WORKERS IN THE WEST

Standard Oil is a country masquerading as a company. Last year Standard of California had gross revenues of $4,150,000,000--about twice as much as the government of Mexico.

The gigantic refinery and chemical plant at Richmond is an enclave in the United States, like Hong Kong in China or the U.S. Navy's Guantanamo Bay enclave in Cuba. The company's own ships bring in crude oil, and the company's own union drives the company's own trucks carrying refined gasoline to the company's own dealers all over Northern California.

Sometimes it is hard to understand where the Oil, Chemical and Atomic Workers local 1-561 gets the nerve to strike against this colossus. They are not a strong union like the Teamsters or the United Auto Workers. They don't have the plant completely organized. (The Chevron Chemical subsidiary is solid for the strike, but blue-collar workers with years of seniority are scabbing in the refinery.) Nor are they getting as much help as they could from other workers. The ships keep coming in and the trucks keep driving out. The Central Labor Council's call for a one-day general strike in Contra Costa County to protest police brutality met an embarrassingly feeble response.

They are striking for "72 plus". The "72" refers to a 72¢-an-hour raise from a pay scale which now ranges from $3.29 an hour to $3.88. That means you can make, oh, $6000 a year take-home, with a wife and two children. It is not luxury living.

The company has offered a 6% pay increase now and 4% in 1970, which will keep the workers just a little bit ahead of inflation. They want a SUBSTANTIAL pay increase; the 72¢ will let them feel that they are getting somewhere, not just getting older.

The "plus" in "72 plus" refers to such matters as medical benefits, retirement plans and union rules. The present medical plan has $50 deductible insurance. The worker pays the first $50 of any medical bill—which means, in practice, that he has no coverage for ordinary medical expenses. The retirement fund, as it works now, amounts to a forced loan from the worker to the company—at a dirt-cheap interest rate of 3%. The company wants to put Chevron Chemical, which has a union shop, under the same open-shop conditions as the Standard refinery. (A company spokesman told me that the charges of anti-unionism were "a load of hay. We have 57 different labor agreements with 27 different unions." Uh-huh.) Management is pushing for such innovations as "departmental seniority"—meaning that a man with ten years seniority loses it all if the company should decide to transfer him to another department in the same plant.

So the men have to fight—if they want to feel like men, and not like the terrified white-collar rabbits who scurry in out of the Standard Oil building at 225 Bush Street in downtown San Francisco.

When Jake Jacobs, Secretary-Treasurer of Local 1-561, was beaten by Richmond police at the station where he had gone to inquire about an arrested union member, he was angry enough and desperate enough to call for help from the revolutionary students striking at SF State and Berkeley. Monday morning, February 3, the students and the workers came together on a mass picket line in Richmond—each side hiding its fear of the other.

To the students, the workers had been the vicious rednecks who jeered "take a bath" at anti-war demonstrators; who insisted on a racist school board and a racist police force to keep down Richmond's large black population; who lived for nothing but Buicks and color TVs.

To the workers, the students had first been sissies and cowards who wouldn't fight for their country, then mindless militants who wanted to burn down everything in sight.

Last week all those fears and hatreds collapsed. Last week Standard Oil—and General Motors and AT&T and General Dynamics and IBM—got something to worry about. In a very small way, last week in Richmond was like last May in France, when students and workers closed down the schools, closed down the factories and said: Let's take a look, for once, at what's been going on inside these schools and factories, let's not open them up again, let's not get into the old habits again, until we've decided what we want to use them for and how. The French government brought in the riot police to keep the students and workers from talking to each other, to open up the schools and factories, to force the students to study so hard and the workers to work so hard that they wouldn't have time to think. But revolt has broken out again in France (see page 6), and the French authorities now live in permanent fear of revolution.

Five hundred students came to the oil workers' picket line knowing hardly anything about the strike demands. They knew the oil strikers had been roughed up by the police, and that destroyed the image of the blue-collar worker as the cop's best buddy. The students also knew that they hated Standard Oil.

Standard makes the chemicals that defoliate Vietnam. Standard makes the sinister international deals, the coups and the assassinations, the little wars and the big counter-insurgency operations. Standard killed Che Guevara.

Standard pollutes the air. Standard creates cities like Los Angeles where you can't live without a car. Standard debauches the public taste with its garish $2,300,000 hula-hula Wiki Wiki Dollar giveaway. Standard strangles the beauty of the American road.

Most important, Standard is the leering devil that buys up souls for $15,000 a year. Standard wants college graduates, the neatly-trimmed kind, the creative but not the too-creative. Standard needs slightly corrupt chemists, personnel managers, industrial psychologists, salesmen, programmers, designers. The students refuse to be human raw material for Standard Oil. That's why they grow their hair long, that's why they listen to poets, that's why they have been closing down their colleges and universities.

"Last night they rushed in thirty extra plant guards just because there was a rumor the students were coming," says an old worker admiringly.

"I was down on the Berkeley campus today," says a young worker, "and they know how to picket—take it easy when nothing's happening, and make all your noise when the scabs come."

So the students weren't sissies or

cowards; they weren't publicity hounds playing to the TV cameras; they weren't lunatics who chanted obscene slogans at you when you asked a friendly question.

Meanwhile the students were discovering that lots of the young oil workers had beards and looked vaguely familiar, not entirely out of place on Telegraph Avenue or at the Avalon Ballroom. They had met somewhere before, not as student and worker (that was new) but as youth, in the places where soldiers, sailors, bikers, dropouts, poets, freaks, runaways, students and young workers all meet to buy and sell drugs, to look for a woman, to find out what's happening—to feed their heads.

"The young guys are what keep the strike going," says a worker with fifteen years seniority. Next to him is a young worker wearing a chain around his waist in place of a belt. Neither of them knows much about unionism or union history.

In fifteen years at Standard, the older man has never been in a strike, except for a brief wildcat last year. Talking about the strike issues, he confuses "closed shop" with "union shop." When was the last strike at Standard? There is muttering about "after the war," but no one seems to know for sure. It's a whole new working class—maybe a whole new ball game.

Come look at this strike. Look at the faces on the picket line. They're human, they're flexible, they move easily. Now check out the Standard Oil Building, 225 Bush Street. Watch the white collar workers, each one scared of the man just below and the man just above and the man right alongside. See what Standard Oil can do to a human face.

San Francisco
Express Times Feb 1969

Man being maced by police at anti-Dow demonstration.

Garbage

This leaflet is about our school. This leaflet is about garbage. Let it collect in the hallways, classrooms bathrooms, Mr. Wendt's office. Let it pile up til they have to close down the school.

Then the city will be forced to deal with the janitors who are on strike demanding a decent wage.

The school administration wants us to help pick up the garbage so that school will look clean and neat. But don't take garbage from anybody. Let it all hang out! Garbage is reality. Let's show what our school is really like.

Support your local janitors' union in their just strike. Do not work against their strike. Do not pick up the garbage!

- -

When you finish reading this leaflet, tear on the dotted line, fold, mutilate, and drop it on the nearest floor.

- -

(This leaflet was prepared by students at La Follette High School during the recent city employees' strike.)

G.E. SEES WHAT IS COMING

the emergence of a workers' left

by Jon Schwartz and Bill Callahan

A "new left" is emerging among white workers; the General Electric strike is probably the most important contribution yet to this process.

At the gate leading to Building 63 of GE's sprawling Erie plant, a striker asked one of the authors, "are you picketing?" No, he was there to write a magazine story. "Is it a socialist magazine?" Yes. "All right, as long as you're a socialist. Sometimes the company sends spies around and we have to be careful. But if you're a socialist that's fine. Why don't you come picket?"

Sam, another striker, is a big balding guy with a slight Italian accent who has worked for the company for over 20 years. His son, who was in Vietnam until 1962, explained why the government had us fighting there — because "the communists just keep spreading, and we have to stop it somewhere." But Sam thinks now that we would have to destroy Vietnam to win the war, and "we can't do that — what will the world think of us?" What does he think of college radicals? "I'll tell you this — those kids are smart, they won't take any shit." Like the younger union men, who won't let themselves be pushed around "like we did thirty years ago."

Says a salaried worker, "GE treats us like we treat the niggers".

Erie, Pennsylvania is a long way from centers of radical influence. Pittsburgh is almost a hundred miles away, Cleveland is nearly as far. When asked about student support, chief steward John Wassel says, "We haven't really looked for it. Maybe we should have."

Wassel is a big man with a grey mustache and a quick grin. On October 15, a week and a half before the strike began, there was a gate meeting. It wasn't a moratorium meeting, but Wassel took the occasion to speak a-gainst the war. He says, "A year ago the men were for Wallace. We've had Wallace in the White House for a year now and the men have had enough." Where will they go? "Maybe to a third party — labor or progressive. There are no parties now. There's no Democratic party."

Jimmy Nelson is chief steward of Building 63. He wears strike buttons and peace buttons side by side while he is on a picket line. Over lunch we talked about the Weatherman, the Conspiracy, and the war. We had similar conversations with several other young strikers.

We have no idea how representative they are, since they were mostly from one building and were among the most active strikers. It is possible that they are an isolated phenomenon. Even so, the fact remains: in the UE local in Erie there is a group of active, potentially influential strikers who respond with enthusiasm to magazines like *Liberation* and to underground newspapers like the *Old Mole*. These are men who would like to talk to people from the student movement; who oppose the war and see connections between their oppression by GE and the US government's goals in Vietnam; who understand the "race problem" as the result of white racism.

And there is a further fact: *receptiveness* to these ideas is common to some degree in every person we talked to in Erie. This is not the result of any organizing or leafletting, but the values they have constructed in the context of national unrest and white youth culture, combined with the experience of working for and striking against GE.

There are two reasons why this new openness to left thinking should have made its appearance in a strike against GE. First, the golden myth of the CIO of the 30's and 40's has a real meaning for GE workers. It is not a justification for letting things remain the way they are as it has been for much of the older union leadership, who are content to point out how much better things are today, and seem to hope that the 30's and 40's will prove to have seen the last major transformation of the American labor movement. In 1946 all organized workers employed by GE struck together for nine weeks as members of the UE-CIO, and won an 18½ ¢ an hour wage increase in a one year contract. The significance of this strike can be measured by the fact that since that time, due to GE's successful anti-union policies, GE workers have never won an equivalent settlement in terms of real buying power. It was therefore painfully obvious to them that trade unionism had failed to achieve what even the most conservative trade unionist claims for it, namely money.

A second distinguishing feature of unionism in the electrical industry has been the stregth of the left-wing tradition. During the 30's and 40's, left-wing influence was stronger in UE than any other major union. It is still felt in the electrical industry through staff and rank-and-file members whose ideas were formed during this period. These people have in turn influenced many younger workers.

The old left's approaches to issues like racism and peace, much less its forms of organization and action, have become increasingly irrelevant. But the older leftists who have remained in the labor movement, particularly those who didn't become full time bureaucrats, have often retained a freshness of style and a continued radical committment which are much rarer among their counterparts outside of the labor movement.

The combination of leftist tradition, which included solidarity and the realization of the inadequacy of trade unionism, placed GE workers in the position to approach a series of alternative values as they struggled against GE's corporate power.

As one striker said, "This strike isn't really about economic issues, it's about the power that big companies have. When you get stuck by the side of the road, nobody'll stop to help you — they've got us divided against each other so much . . . . What we need is something like they had in France last year; that would really shake Nixon up. But we aren't even organized well and enough to run this strike very well . . . . Most people are too comfortable to be very militant now, but if Nixon keeps going with his anti-inflation policies, that might change soon."

OLD MOLE 3/5/70

An internal memo prepared by GE dealing with confrontations shows that the central office has whole departments devoted to producing the non-commital bullshit they come out with at the bargaining table.

Take, for example, this list of directions for a Company spokesman facing a confrontation: (from p. 8)

a. use the appropriate digest of positive Company attitudes and accomplishments.

b. avoid conferring legitimacy on a demand that may or may not have merit.

c. avoid any specific commitment that could prejudice subsequent assessment and consideration of the demand

d. avoid being responsive to the demand itself.

GE feels that they are in for heavy weather. The introduction to the memo sets the problem out thus:

There is a growing likelihood that industry in general and General Electric in particular face a mounting wave of confrontations similar to those directed against church and campus.

GE then goes on to state their objective in solving the problem:

Identify sites and subjects of likely confrontation with the company. Prepare management for a standard operating procedure of reaction that will maintain a favorable corporate image with minority groups and with the public at large without compromising future corporate actions or decisions and without provoking escalation of the conflict.

Later in the memo GE states:

The currently mounting attack upon...the military-industrial complex is stage-setting for a new period of political attack upon virtually every aspect of corporate management.

Right On!, GE.

GE at B.U.

GE came well recieved at BU this month. Both the BU Action Group and BU SDS (WSA) were on hand Tuesday afternoon to confront GE representative Bertotti with his presence on campus. The two groups rallied at 1pm in the student center and then tried several times unsuccessfully to enter an auditorium where Mr. Bertotti was speaking. Attempts at discourse ended when it was discovered that Mr. GE had been smuggled from the auditorium.

OLD MOLE

12/16/69
(during the G.E. Strike)

From: GE Strikers "Welcome to the Club, Students"

How do we thank you for the broken bones, bruises and brutality inflicted upon you because of your support of our strike against General Electric? Why do University administrators seek (and get) injunctions to protect GE recruiters and spokesmen from the wrath of the students? Why do police departments beat up students who side with us?

Is there some connection between the General Electric Company, University administrators and police departments? Are they allies in the fight against GE strikers? How did our strike find its way to college campuses?

Our strike is for direct wages, protection against speed-up, integrity of our contracts, insurance and pension benefits that will help us through sickness and old age. It's a straight fight, GE wants us to provide ever greater profits for them and intends to make us pay the price of inflation. That very inflation is caused by General Electric and the rest of the war profiteers associated with General Electric.

In the shop we see college and university graduates working as managers, engineers, market and sales specialists, technicians, labor relations fakers, wage cutters and literate liars who describe the company as a sort of public benefactor.

Do you support us because you sympathize with our reasons for striking? Or because you yourselves are also on strike against being recruited and used for the well paid flunky jobs GE makes available to college graduates, or both?

Whatever the reason, you are clearly on our side. We do not belive that you are fighting G.E. bosses and university administrators and police departments merely as a favor to us.

So a "thank you" is not enough. We say "Welcome to the struggle. We are glad to have you as brothers, sisters and allies."

Leaflet Distributed by G.E. Strikers in Boston Nov 1969

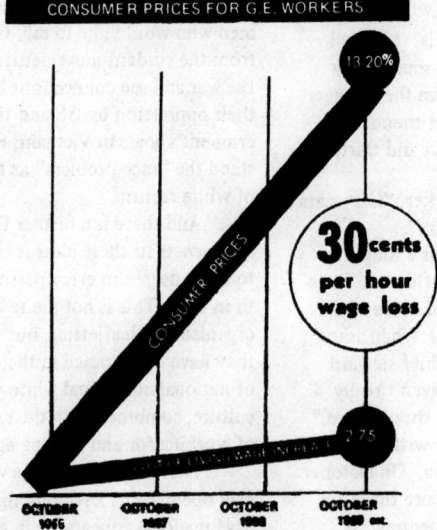

COST OF LIVING WAGE INCREASES LAG BEHIND CONSUMER PRICES FOR G.E. WORKERS

13.20%

30 cents per hour wage loss

2.75

OCTOBER 1966   OCTOBER 1967   OCTOBER 1968   OCTOBER 1969 est.

Guerrilla History in Gary

staughton lynd

Historians tend to overlook the experience of common people. Here, Staughton Lynd employs "guerrilla history" to gain new insights into the decline of labor militancy in the late thirties.

The history that "has the most influence on . . . the course of events . . . is the history that common men carry around in their heads." Carl Becker wrote this in 1955, repeating his long-standing argument that "everyman [should be] his own historian."

Recently this same idea has appeared in many places. For instance, in his magnificent account of the revolution-from-below which took place during the Spanish Civil War, Noam Chomsky advises the scholar who wants to tell the truth about that popular movement to talk with the republican exiles still living in southern France.

For labor history the memories which "common men carry around in their heads" are indispensable. They are the primary sources which written records of any kind can only supplement and, when necessary, correct.

In an article or "Working-Class Self-Activity", George Rawick comments: "Doubters should listen to the sit-down stories of auto workers from Flint, Michigan, and compare them to the official UAW history which emphasized the strikes' leadership (none other than the present national officers and executive board of the UAW). Radical scholars should begin to collect materials while there is still time."

Oral history from the bottom up, or as I prefer to call it, "guerrilla history," is of interest to more than radical scholars. Rank-and-file trade unionists want to know the history of the 1930s so that they can respond to the present upsurge of labor militancy armed with an analysis of why the CIO unions so rapidly grew bureaucratic and conservative. (I will present a concrete example of such analysis in a moment.) A second constituency for guerrilla history is the children of working-class families who are going to college so as to avoid going into the mill. Exploration of their own memories and the memories of their parents and parents' friends can provide, in the words of John McDermott, "the opportunity to discover the reasons for their attitudes on a score of moral and social questions, the reality of their social lives, and the possibility of rebuilding a more humane culture . . . for their own advantage." These young men and women may come to feel, through learning experiences like guerrilla history, that they need not be ashamed of their parents' failure to "make it" out of the factory. Perhaps they will perceive that as teachers or secretaries or health technicians they will still be wage-earners, heirs to a tradition of collective struggle,

with roles to play relative to their parents, cousins, brothers, and sisters employed at manual labor.

Finally, there are the radical students and ex-students taking jobs in factories, moving into working-class communities, teaching at junior and community colleges. They need to avoid the missionary attitude so well described by McDermott in his, "The Laying On Of Culture." For them guerrilla history can be a means of learning at the same time that they teach. As the New Left turns toward labor, guerrilla history becomes a valuable tool.

An Example

This summer I have interviewed perhaps a dozen steelworkers in Gary, East Chicago and Hammond who helped to organize the first CIO locals in Lake County, Indiana.

Another man with whom I talked is the son of an activist who was fired after the 1919 strike and never was able to get another job in the mills. My informant's first political act was to join the Gary contingent of the 1931 hunger march. Later he was chairman of the Gary unemployed council. He is an apparently inexhaustible source of stories about street-corner meetings broken up by the police and evicted tenants restored to their homes by popular action.

With every one I have raised the question: What happened to the militancy of 1936-1937, when two years of rank-and-file pressure from below finally produced the Steel Workers' Organizing Committee, when half a million workers around the country sat down in their factories, when ten men were shot in the back and killed at the Republic Steel plant near the Indiana-Illinois state line?

The most interesting response thus far has come from two men with a combined experience in their local of more than fifty years. Both belong to the local's rank-and-file caucus and from time to time have held important offices in the local.

These two men, whom I will call John Smith and Jim Brown, made me aware of the fact that between the failure of the Little Steel strike of 1937 and formal recognition of the United Steelworkers in 1942, Little Steel labor bargained with management without written contracts. In the plant employing Smith and Brown the Steel Workers' Organizing Committee met monthly with the plant superintendent. The workers were represented by grievers elected in each department, just as they would be after the signing of a contract. (Monthly meetings continued

after union recognition until 1950. One of the men to whom I spoke had a complete set of the minutes of these meetings from 1938 to 1950.) But until 1942, as the superintendent himself remarked in the meeting for July 1941, "we have no contract."

Further research revealed that it was just this issue of a written contract which kept labor and Little Steel management apart for these five years. The understanding signed between U.S. Steel and the Steel Workers' Organizing Committee on March 6, 1937 obligated both sides to meet no later than March 10 to effectuate "a written agreement." According to Tom Girdler, president of Republic Steel and leader of Little Steel management forces, SWOC then demanded that Republic and other Little Steel corporations sign an identical understanding. Republic's refusal to do so initiated the bloody industrial warfare of the following half decade. "The sole remaining issue was that of a signed contract," Girdler states. "The union demanded that we sign the contract and we refused."

Now, what one might term the received version of these events casts SWOC as the unequivocal good guy and Girdler, with his munitions stocks and scabs and company police, as undisputably wrong. Young radical scholars have begun to question this assumption. Mark Naison observes in his study of the southern Tenant Farmers' Union:

The CIO built its organizing drive around the recognition of vast industrial unions as the sole bargaining agents of workers in American industries; the great majority of its strikes were fought around the issues of union recognition rather than wages or working conditions. . . . In every instance in which the CIO had extended funds for organization, its goal was to win signed contracts and to institutionalize bargaining on an industry wide level, a basis upon which the CIO could 1) extend its control of wage levels and productive conditions in the American economy and 2) extract a steady income for new organizing.

Not only was the CIO model inappropriate for workers like the Southern tenants who were outside the industrial system and driven by their situation to challenge capitalism politically. In Naison's view, even for industrial workers like those in steel, CIO organizing was a mixed blessing, because it sought to assure "a disciplined response by the work force" and "to rationalize a capitalist economy."

My informants, Smith and Brown, emphatically agree. They go farther. As they see it, the critical difference between the years before 1942 and those which followed was that before signing a contract the workers retained the freedom to strike at any time. In each department, before 1942, the workers had an unwritten understanding with management backed up by the threat of striking. If management was recalcitrant a department would "go down," and in this way, according to John Smith, the 15,000 steelworkers in the plant won things, including wage increases. Both these veteran militants believe that the workers were in a stronger position before a contract was signed. If you must have a contract, adds Smith, it should be as vague as possible and interpreted by the rank-and-file through their enforcing action.

What these men advocate on the basis of their long CIO experience is nothing else than the no-contract position of the IWW. They derive this lesson from the years after the contract was signed as well as from the years before it. Now, says Smith, "you have a pretty good company union." After the signing of a contract the union found itself obligated to police the contract by disciplining members resistant to the pledge "that there shall be no interruptions or impeding of work, work stoppages, slowdowns, strikes, lockouts or other interferences with production and maintenance of the Company's plants during the term thereof." I asked Smith what he thought about the Communist Party's advocacy of a no-strike pledge during World War II. He responded that he was critical of the Communist Party for failing to demand a more democratic structure in the international union, but that, so far as the no-strike pledge was concerned, the fundamental no-strike pledge was that in the contract itself. For instance, in 1948 when Smith was president of the local, 7-8000 members of a department undergoing automation struck to ensure the retention of their jobs at undiminished pay. Over Smith's head the district director of the international union agreed with the company

that sixty-five men who had led the wildcat should be fired.

Signing a contract meant not only surrender of the right to strike between contract negotiations, but institutionalization of the dues' check-off, which made possible the multiplication of salaried pork-choppers. Before 1942 stewards and grievers were unpaid. They collected dues on the mill floor at the risk of their jobs. Sometimes the local threw dues' picket lines around the mill: Smith and Brown wryly mention a member of "the opposition" in their local who in those days climbed over the fence rather than pay his union dues. Brown himself was fired while dues-collecting, and subsequently blacklisted by four other mills in the area before he got his job back in 1950. Yet he thinks it was better for the local when it had to prove its worth to its members in order to get their dues.

To discover this Wobbly period in the history of one of the more centralized CIO unions, and especially to find that experienced activists look back to that period as the time when they most effectively served their members, seems full of suggestions for organizers seeking to create, or respond to, a new surge of rank-and-file militancy. The Left has not had an effective answer to labor historians who contend that institutional hardening of the arteries is inevitable in any trade union once it begins to demand specific improvements in wages, hours, and working conditions. "Business unionism," it is argued, brings with it a business spirit and a form of organization patterned on the business corporation. For examples of unions which resisted this process we have had to point to unions in marginal sectors on the labor market. Thus one can instance the STFU which won significant strikes against the cotton growers but, according to its founder H.L. Mitchell, never negotiated with them. But Smith and Brown remember a stretch of about five years when in steel itself a local won concessions from management without surrendering its independence.

Insight spills over into action. Smith and Brown are doubtful whether they can accomplish significant change within the limits set by the structure of the international union and the no-strike clause of the contract. But they are trying, through the rank-and-file caucus. The *Voice Of The Rank And File*, the caucus newspaper, proposed the following resolution to a recent convention of the union: "Resolution to Eliminate No-Strike Clause in Contract. The no-strike clause would become inapplicable under the following conditions: (a) If the company does not abide by the arbitrator's decisions. (b) If the Company delays grievance procedure unduly. (c) If the Company makes arbitrary rules that cause harm to the members." (Clauses (b) and (c) would appear to illustrate what Smith means by a vague contract!)

In seeking change, Smith and Brown explicitly hark back to the period before the signed contract. Running for chairman of the grievance committee of the local, Smith put out a leaflet which began:

Used to be a time when if you had a gripe you could get your grievance man, see your foreman and usually get it straightened out. That's out now. The foreman can't settle grievances. The super isn't allowed to settle grievances. Labor Relations (these relations are tougher to get along with than your in-laws) is in the hands of a small group of people who seem to have nothing else to do but figure out ways to skin you out of your rights . . . .

These militants seem to feel a kinship not only with the early days of the CIO but with the IWW. One issue of the *Voice* borrowed language from the Wobblies in urging "that everything possible must be done to settle grievances 'at the point of production'." ∎

LIBERATION

From "Guerrilla History in Gary" Oct 1969

UNCOMMON CARRIERS

The postal workers' strikes are more than an important event in labor history: They seem now to be a defining political event for the next decade. By the mid-Seventies, half of the salaried workers in the US will be direct employees of government. They form the real "proletariat" of America—unprivileged, poorly paid, mindlessly manipulated, cheated of "middle class' status. More than a proportionate share (according to population) of that work force is black. Unionization for them has meant only more sophisticated exploitation. Now, the postmen have provided an example for the kind of fight these workers can make. It's easy to see that this is only a beginning: The postman always rings twice.

The first ring was totally unexpected. Strikes by government workers are extremely rare in US history (not to mention "illegal"), and strikes against the Post Office simply don't happen. Beyond that, the belief persists that all major conflicts in US labor-management relations have been solved, at least on the theoretical level. From the political science myths of the Fifties comes the idea that American labor has been successfully integrated into the middle class. What conflicts seem to remain—

industrial strikes—are merely anachronisms and aberrations, "bugs" in a system which in theory can be made to work perfectly.

For such reasons, labor is not taken seriously by politicians or the press. Time and Newsweek, for instance, freaked out on the postal strikes and devoted "crash covers" to the events; but readers could look in vain for coverage of the postal workers' plight over the last many years. Even the radical movements of the New Left have avoided labor with uncommon diligence—except for a minor flirtation of a few young activists in the last year (and they are concerned for the most part with industrial workers and the underclass).

What makes the postal strikes so critical is the sense of real conflict they have brought back to the politics of work. The strike started out to be a "traditional" action for higher wages (a 40 percent increase against the five percent offered by the Congressional committees). But before the brief strikes were over, they had called into question the bases of the "public employee's" role: the worthlessness of the mediation process; the failure of government unions; the contradictions of the government budgeting system; and the double-edge nature of "reform."

Mediation: The right to strike is not merely "one weapon in the workers' arsenal," as editorialists say, but the only weapon that really matters. Without the recognized potential to withhold labor, workers must ultimately rely on the good will of the bosses —in the postmen's case, Congress and the Nixon-Agnew Administration. It goes without saying that good will these days can't be taken for granted. Real interests of immensely resourceful institutions are dead set against significant improvement in government workers' conditions. Postal workers, teachers, garbage collectors, clerk-typists—all have to "negotiate" their betterment with public officials who are permanently pressured by corporations, businessmen, the military, universities and "expert" managers. Without the capability to strike, there simply ain't no way.

Unions: Leadership of the postal workers' unions was timid and hypocritical. In New York, rank-and-file workers shouted their leaders down and in some instances very nearly put them out of the way. In fact, the various government employee associations are at best "company unions," in which workers are manipulated by deals made privately between the leaders and public officials. In the Letter Carriers union, for example, the executive board decides on the terms of the union's "understanding" with Congress (there's no real "contract"), without going to the rank-and-file.

"It's not a union, it's a lobbying operation," one labor official said recently. "The leaders agree to the terms in the Congressional bills, and the rank-and-file never say a word one way or the other."

Budgeting: The public employee's condition is directly related to the failure of the public budgeting system. That is, the diversion of public funds for military expenditure, for space spectaculars, for corporate give-aways, for middle-class benefits—all comes at the expense of low-level workers. The postman's plight is directly tied to the war in Vietnam, to the ABM, to suburban beltways, to oil and gas depletion allowances. Postal workers saw that clearly last month for the first time. They were victims of the "war on inflation," the war in Vietnam, and the war machine.

Reform: Schemes to reform and "rationalize" government services will always serve to keep public employees in the same functional relationship they now enjoy—or rather, do not enjoy. For example, the proposal to make the Post Office a "public corporation," on the model of Comsat or TVA, simply removes workers one or more steps further from the seats of power in which decisions about their lives are made. In countries that are more obviously "totalitarian" than the US, workers have no right to strike; they must belong to unions that are part of the "public corporations" the workers serve. Fair arguments for such a system might be made in a revolutionary situation, in which the worker is the basic element of state power (although such arguments are usually proved wrong in practice). But in any other state, such a system is called fascism, or pretty close to it.

Hard Times

Excerpted from ▬▬▬▬▬▬▬ (A. Kopkind and J. Ridgeway) 4/6/70

WHAT THE ANIMALS DID

For corporate chief executives, the year 1968 was a year of changing strategies and changing games...[it was the year of] the merger upheaval...and conglomerate warfare...it was one in which both classical economic and decision theories were inadequate to explain some of the major events.

JOHN McDONALD *Fortune*, May 1969

They got so hungry they all
began to attack each other

and even try to eat each other
and many did eat each other

even the war and the moon
were not enough for them

they got so hungry it was
not just big ones eating

small ones some very lit-
tle ones attacked big ones

& managed to swallow them
alive it was crazy really

crazy because it wasn't a
year of famine there was

plenty of food around with
the war and the moon plenty

to eat but the more they
ate the more they wanted.

J. LAUGHLIN

**HOW TO
ATTACK THE
CORPORATIONS**

Letter to the Movement: the honeywell project
marv davidoff

The Honeywell Project in Minneapolis, Minnesota was initiated in December 1968 when I called a meeting of 25 local people, clergy, students, SDS, draft resistance, and woman's liberation people. (Local black radicals have since endorsed the project but have not yet participated actively.) Immediately we constituted ourselves a research committee and collected information from Honeywell brochures, back files of local papers, etc. We find that the only public protest against production of fragmentation bombs in Minneapolis

had occured two years ago when twenty Unitarians demonstrated for a half a day at a Honeywell ordnance plant in Hopkins, a suburb of Minneapolis. A few letters to the editor were written after that demonstration. We have held weekly meetings since December involving 10–40 people with about 35 people seriously involved now.

April 22 Ed Anderson, a University of Minnesota professor of mechanical engineering who had worked at Honeywell on development of war material and had quit in disgust over hideous weapons manufactured there, called James Binger, chairman of the board of Honeywell for the project. Ed asked Binger to meet with 10 project members. Binger refused a meeting until Ed said project members planned a demonstration at Honeywell annual shareholders meeting. Binger said he would meet that afternoon with three of us. So, Anderson, Woods Halley (a professor of physics at University of Minnesota) and I met with Binger and Gerry Morse, VP in charge of personnel and labor negotiator for Honeywell, in an hour long meeting in Binger's office. I outlined the nature of the project:

We will persist with development of political pressure upon decision-makers until they stop production of fragmentation bombs and all war material. Our demands are non-negotiable. However, we will work cooperatively by bringing economists, scientists, union people, and marketing experts to Honeywell free of charge if necessary to develop plans for conversion to peaceful creative products. I said these bombs have been used against people—men, women and children in North Vietnam—since 1965. Binger added, "and the south too." There was no arrogance in his voice. I asked him if he would like to see photos of bomb damage to children. He said, "No, I've already seen many of them."

Morse said Honeywell employs 20,000 people in its defense group, 400 alone in the St. Louis Park plant (a suburb of Minneapolis) where fragmentation bombs are made. That plant is called Candlestick Park plant because the owners of the San Francisco Giants ball team own the property.

The first time both men exhibited a gut reaction occured when I said, "We plan at some future time to stage civil disobedience at the homes, country clubs, businesses and churches of decision-makers." Binger asked what that meant, and I merely gave a dictionary definition of civil disobedience. I said also we shall contact the Japanese, French, German, English, Italian and Australian peace movements in whose countries Honeywell has plants.

Binger said he could see we were serious. Morse said he was happy we had warned them of our demonstration because if they had been taken by surprise, they might have unloaded the big guns.

Tuesday, April 29 Thirty-five project members demonstrated in front of Honeywell main offices on company property. Binger said Honeywell would not keep us off the street in front of their main office so long as the demonstration was peaceful.

We had blown up photographs of atrocities with excerpts from the Honeywell statement, "it is entirely appropriate, correct, and a matter of good citizenship" printed below a dead child with fragments in its head.

A few days after our demonstration we got a call from two very sympathetic union people, a white woman who is part-time recording secretary with the union and a black man who is a plant steward in aerospace. Both belong to the New Democratic Coalition. We met, and they agreed to advise us on leaflet content, etc. Neither would publicly identify with the project at that time. We plan to leaflet the main bomb plant and our union friends suggested we focus on the issue of taxation and how it effects wage earners.

We got 14 calls from union people at the plant the next few days. One woman said, "Tell me the truth, is Ralph Abernathy involved in this?" "No." "Is Matt Eubanks involved?" (Matt is director of the Citizens Community Centers in Minneapolis, a radical close to the Panthers.) I said I had talked with him about the project. "Does he endorse this project?" "Yes." "Well, thank you for telling me the truth. We are in accord with many of the things you say in your leaflet." Others asked if we were the SDS work-in project. Most callers the first few days expressed no hostility, and we told them of a meeting we would have in a Catholic church the following Sunday.

Two weeks after the initial demonstration, eight straight-looking young project people leafleted the St. Louis Park bomb plant, distributing about 500 sheets. I had called Binger to notify him three days before and this time he requested we meet Honeywell security official Fred Cary to ascertain ground rules. For traffic safety we were allowed off the street and onto the grounds. Cary maintains the fragmentation bomb is not used against civilians and insists if Honeywell didn't produce the weapon someone else would.

Our union friends tipped us off that the teamsters would send observers to our meeting and when three project members, Fran, spokesman for our labor committee, Gordon, a marine with 13 months combat service in Vietnam, and Lee of Women's Liberation went to the church at 6:30 Sunday they found about 60 teamsters, including the Honeywell union president, standing on the stairs. Fran said they looked like a klan mob. Fran said we were not an SDS project but said he agreed with many of the goals of SDS. He referred to a Harris poll which said most students supported goals of the radicals and reminded the men that when Teamsters battled police and the Minneapolis power structure in the streets of Minneapolis in the 30's, they were called radicals, communists, etc. There were men in suits and in lumberjack shirts and the suited men got up to leave at one point obviously expecting everyone else to leave. When they didn't the suited men returned. Gordon, the ex-marine, spoke next about the war and half-way through his rap a Teamster shouted they only want to hear themselves talk and everyone left in unison.

The sympathetic union woman was talking with our three people on the steps of the church as the teamsters milled around on the sidewalk. The union president called her down and ordered her not to speak with our people. She told him she would and she did. One man took a tire iron from his car and was restrained by others and bashed it at a street sign.

The union comes up for contract in February and if we can create rapport with individual union members, something quite creative could occur at that time. The labor committee of the project has leafleted four plants now, the bomb plant twice and although some of the calls coming through in response are hostile and red-baiting, others are friendly and encouraging, although people do not yet leave their names. Sometimes they give their addresses.

Here is a brief discription of our other committees.

1. The church committee is sending speakers to various denominations urging them to take public positions of opposition to fragmentation bomb production by Honeywell, to raise funds for the project and to visit members of the Honeywell board of directors.

2. We have a University of Minneapolis campus group and project groups at Carlton, Macalester and Hamline-Carleton Colleges.

3. Woods Halley has met with Honeywell scientists in a long range attempt to organize engineers and scientists there.

4. We are beginning a study group at the University of Minneapolis on economic reconversion.

5. Various people will carry project information to European and Japanese movements where Honeywell has plants overseas.

6. A small DFL ward club in St. Louis Park have met with members of the city council there and demanded the plant be zoned out of their area.

In the future 1) We shall continue meeting one-at-a-time with Honeywell directors who form the cultural and power elite in Minneapolis.

2) We hope to create national and international demonstrations perhaps during one designated week at Honeywell plants and sales offices everywhere in the world.

3) We shall demonstrate at the churches and homes and country clubs of local directors and may have civil disobedience demonstrations when the situation has been carefully prepared.

4) We hope to create a situation where Honeywell recruiters have a rough time on campus this fall.

5) We are researching the possibility of selective boycott.

6) The project will be training ground for organizers.

7) We hope to contribute towards workers control of Honeywell by long range self-education and creation of day care centers for children and whatever other ways we can.

8) We shall call for a national meeting to be held in Minneapolis probably in the early fall where people interested in this kind of an attack on corporate power can learn from us and share insights.

Any questions or comments can be sent to me, Marv Davidov, 529 Cedar Ave. South, Minneapolis, Minnesota, 55404, phone 336-1581.

Text of Terrorist Letter

Following is the text of a letter received by United Press International from a group—revolutionary Force 9 —which said it was responsible for the bombing of three buildings in Manhattan yesterday. The letter was postmarked 1 A.M., March 12— an hour before the explosions. The misspellings, abbreviations and use of symbols are those of the writer of the letter.

IBM, Mobile and GTE are enemies of all life. In 1969 IBM made $250 million, Mobile $150 million and GTE $140 million for US "defense" contracts—profits made from the suffering and deaths of human beings. All three profit not only from death in Vietnam but also from Amerikan imperialism in all of the Third World. They profit from racist oppression of black, Puerto-Rican and other minority colonies outside Amerika, from the suffering and death of men in the Amerika army, from sexism, from the exploitation and degradation of employes forced into lives of anti-human work, from the pollution and destruction of our environment.

To numb Amerika to the horrors they inflict on humanity, these corporations seek to enslave us to a way of "life" which values conspicious consumption more than the relief of poverty, disease and starvation, which values giant cars as status symbols more then the purity of our air (so Mobile can make $$$ thru gas sales).

This ways of "life" sucks up 60% of the world's resources—for 16% of the planet's population—and then wastes them in compulsive consumerism and planned obsolescence (so IBM can make $$$ off new model computers), distributes millions of TV sets (Sylvania's included), all the better to put lies into our heads and convince us to buy, buy, buy, and then offers only work helping to produce the goods that bring slow death at home or genocide abroad (or in the USA.)

This way of "life" is a way of death. To work for the industries of death is to murder. To know the torments Amerika inflicts on the Third World, but not to sympathize and identify, is to deny our own humanity. It is to deny our right to love—and not to love is to die. We refuse. In death-directed Amerika there is only one way to a life of love and freedom: to attack and destroy the forces of death and exploitation and to build a just society—revolution. REVOLUTIONARY FORCE 9

The New York Times 3/13/70

MORE TOKEN RESISTANCE

Guerrilla bands are forming all over New York City. They are untrained, but quickly learn the finer techniques that make them effective. The bands move unannounced, strike quickly and then disappear. Rarely are arrests made. For a month now, this writer has been a part of a group formed at the Peace Building at 339 Lafayette Street in New York City. Daily at rush hour, our group forms quietly, arms itself, and moves out to challenge the city's powers of influence. Our arms, of course, are leaflets; our mission is to enter a crowded subway station and let the people know that SUBWAYS ARE FREE IF THE PEOPLE WANT THEM TO BE.

There is little technique to liberating a subway station. Most of New York City's straphangers oppose the new 30¢ fare and look for any excuse to make their opposition known. Our function is to start the ball rolling while disseminating the facts behind the fare increase. We merely open the gates and declare "The subway is free today, don't pay the new 30¢ fare." Immediately, the straphangers move out of the token lines and pass through the gate. Some people laugh and celebrate the liberation by dancing and skipping through the open gates. Others pass through with a look of defiance, as though they are trampling Governor Rockefeller underfoot.

Our leaflets attempt to simplify the present situation with the transit workers, the Metropolitan Transit Authority, the city and the state. We explain that the subways were first built with public monies (for the most part), that the city turned the subways over to banking interests (like Rockefeller and Morgan) so they could be run as a private enterprise on a profit basis. They did manage to make a profit. They raked in $10 million profit every year and collected 6% interest on their original investment. But they did not improve the subways. As a matter of fact, the service and safety deteriorated to such a degree, that the city was forced to buy them back. Now, the people of New York had paid for the subways TWICE.

As though the city had not raped the peoples' pockets enough, they floated $310 million in bonds which the straphangers are still paying interest on. To make the horror story more incredible, the city issued another $5 million bond in 1953 to cover the cost of a new 2nd Avenue subway *that was never built*.

It is obvious to the wage earner that transportation is on the same list of necessities as food, housing and medicine. To the city, however, transportation is viewed as another means of making profits for the hungry bankers and speculators. One important thing to remember is that the subway demonstrations are not aimed at the Transit Workers Union. As a matter of record, these actions are in *support* of the Union. Our program also supports a wage increase for the transit workers on the principle that the banks, large property owners and financial speculators should pay a tax increase that would cover the cost of free public transportation, wage increases for the transit workers, and health and safety improvements.

So far, the transit actions have been overwhelmingly successful. The second week in January, about two thousand people went through the gates at the Wall Street RT stop. On January 28, three thousand went through at the Broadway-Lafayette IND stop. That same week, thousands crashed the gates at two stops in the vicinity of Park Avenue on 23rd Street. The almost 90% participation is not so incredible when one considers the number of wage earners in Metropolitan New York and the fact that the public transit facilities involve everyone. Economic issues have power, and such massive involvement can lead to mass radicalization.

The thing to remember is DON'T PAY THE FARE. If you are alone, or with a few friends, it is a simple matter of going in the "out" gate. The token seller cannot leave his booth or if there are two, they have no power to do anything if they do catch you. Usually, if a Transit Policeman catches you, he will simply make you go back and pay the fare. If a cop is by the gate, use a slug. But it is best to reserve the slug for the times when a cop is present because others will often follow when they see you go through the gate.

The sentimental comparison of the price of a quart of milk and a subway token is, of course, something to remember. But more important is the over-all sum of hundreds of dollars to middle income and poor families. Economic resistance has never been as great as it is in New York over the fare increase. This resistance has the potential of stressing greater issues in the total economic picture in the United States such as budget spending priorities that are now directed into the Defense Department when the need is at home. Remember, SUBWAYS ARE FREE IF YOU WANT THEM TO BE. DON'T PAY THE FARE.

—Jerry Wingate

win March 1970

EAST COAST CONSPIRACY TO SAVE LIVES

As American citizens who share a responsibility for the actions of our country, we have liberated draft files in Philadelphia, Pennsylvania, and General Electric files in Washington, D.C. We have done so because of our concern for human life. We have done so because we are aware of the conspiracy among the military, large corporations and the United States government. We have done so because of the need for serious and continuing resistance to the racist and militarist institutions operating in the United States. And we have done so because through our acting we have found a new life style which offers opportunities and hope, for ourselves and others.

We have destroyed draft files, pieces of paper, because those pieces of paper mean slavery and possible death for young Americans and certain death for Vietnamese and other non-white people of the Third World. The draft is an

instrument of murder and as such it must be stopped. It is no accident that
the boards we have acted against are inner city boards. Blacks, poor whites,
and working class whites - those society treats the worst - are forced to do most
of the fighting and dying in America's wars, since American racism destroys
their free choice. This racism fosters a type of frustration which is at the root
of our deteriorating society. We specifically reject the racism that sends its victims
in highly disproportionate numbers onto the front lines of battle. If they return to
the U.S., they find themselves oppressed by the same racist society which sent
them to war. The fight for freedom is at home, not overseas.

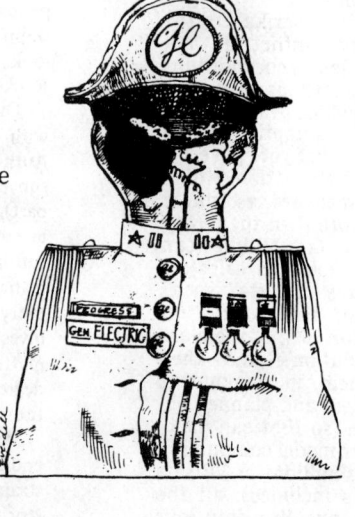

We have destroyed General Electric files because G.E. is the second largest
war contractor in the United States because G.E. exploits its workers both at
home and overseas, and because we wish to point out the collusion between the
military system, giant corporations and government. The three are inseparably
wedded to one another.

As the American people continue to pay taxes to the government, that money
subsidizes giant corporations, mainly in the form of war contracts. The
Selective Service System and the military are used to protect an expansionist
economic system which obtains growth and control at the expense of human lives.
At the same time, the Selective Service System channels young men, through the
use of deferments and the threat of being inducted if a deferment is lost, into
present-day American society as cogs in a vast inhuman machine.

We have acted against General Electric because we feel a responsibility, as victims
of a system which places profit above life, to confront institutions of death. The
butchery these institutions perpetrate on ourselves and our brothers in the name of
patriotism is abhorrent to men of conscience.

We have acted taking care that no individual was hurt by our actions. We believe
in the use of tactics which do not heighten the fear and distrust which are so much
a part of the present ugly way of life in America. We are committed to a non-violent
revolution against injustice. This means a non-violence of effective and continuing
disruption of the machine of death and oppression in America. This means a
disruption which destroys certain property when that property is used to destroy
men, women, and children. As the Catonsville 9 siad, " Some property has no
right to exist. Hitler's gas ovens, Stalin's concentration camps, atomic-
bacteriological-chemical weapons, files of conscription and slum properties
have no right to exist."

We are a group of priests, nuns, students, teachers, and former students. We
wish to confront by our actions those institutions with which we are affiliated -
church and education - and to force them to decide whether or not they will continue
to serve the needs of American power or begin to serve the needs of man.

We have acted at the same time that three major political trials are going on
in the United States: The conspiracy 7 Trail, the D.C.-9 Trail, and the New
York 21 Trail. We express our solidarity with those three groups, as well
as with the Black Panther Party, those who have acted against draft boards
prior to us, and other victims of government repression. We believe that
the best defense against repression is a continuation of actions similar to ours
and a rapid growth in the movement seeking an end to racism, militarism
and capitalistic imperialism. With the Beaver 55 we say "These actions
must continue; the spirit of the people will not be overcome."

A Leaflet from The East Coast Conspiracy to
Save Lives

A two-mile section of a 6-mile-long field of 7,000 retired B-17s.

...IN A WORKING CLASS SUBURB OF A SMALL FACTORY CITY.

Greasers Lightning

By Kathy Mulherin

Since this newspaper likes to present its editorials through its reporting, and since the opening of school calls for an "inspirational" piece, we offer the tale below to students and teachers.

I heard this story from a young woman who has been given a pseudonym to protect her identity. The events she describes took place last year in an upstate New York public high school located in a working class suburb of a small factory city (pop. 30,000). Most of the students (where Martha Zimmerman was a teacher for two years) were children of factory workers, telephone linemen, small business men. Martha, having taught in a Harlem public school, was assigned to teach English and Social Studies to the "dumb kids," thirty or forty lower middle class white kids — many of them the toughest "greasers" in the school.

"The school wasn't officially tracked but I got the kids who scored lowest on the exams. Most of the guys were headed for Vietnam and the girls would all become beauticians and like that — dead end jobs and they knew it.

"I wanted them to write compositions about whatever they wanted." Martha is about five feet tall, she has large clear gray eyes and when she speaks, her hands move nervously and expressively in the air around her. Those kids must have figured she was going to be a joke.

"At first their papers were full of every kind of obscenity you can imagine, but when they found out they really could do what they wanted some of them began writing beautiful stuff.

"One time we decided to have a writing contest and I said I would print up — just for the class — the winning paper. One kid wrote this incredible satire/drama about Vietnam.

"You know" — she paused in her narrative, "those kids are very conscious of the fact the only valuable thing they can do is fight and die for their country. In that school there were *two* honor rolls — an academic list and one of those who die. And the principal always spoke of and treated with respect the guys who went to Vietnam, even when they'd been considered trouble makers.

"Anyway, this story had some swear words in it, but it was really beautiful. In the story, this kid was in Vietnam and a helicopter came down over him and suddenly it turned into a giant insect about to snatch him up. The class chose his story knowing there might be trouble from the administration. Later there were rumors

and we had a discussion in class about what to do. Some kids got up and said the hell with it, we know we didn't do anything wrong we'll just keep on doing what we're doing.

"The district principal presented me with a letter which demanded that I 'cease and desist from accepting papers from students which make use of poor language and from issuing materials that do the same.'

"I said I couldn't sign that and take away the kids' freedom. He gave me a big argument — and it was interesting — because he kept insisting that it was very dangerous to do this kind of thing with this kind of kid. He said it was all right to try it with black kids because it was in their environment, and it was all right with college-oriented kids because they were responsible, but doing that sort of thing with these kids would 'teach them defiance' and 'encourage bad behaviour.' He claimed that since I had come, the kids from my class were starting to challenge other teachers and make trouble."

When Martha held firm, the principal declared that she was treading on thin ice and repeated his warning about the danger of her experiment: " 'These kids are going out to work in factories, or to Vietnam. What will happen if they're not used to conforming to certain standards?' "

As the year wore on, tension rose and several incidents occurred which gave the whole affair a life of its own and made it far deeper than a simple matter of freedom of speech:

Martha mimeoed for her class copies of the poem by e. e. cummings ostensibly about cars which is really about fucking:

"oh and her gears being in
A l shape passed
from low through
second-in-to-high like
(greased lightning). . ."

The poem got out and made the rounds of whispering faculty. There was much speculation in these learned circles about the poem's true meaning — was it about *cars* or *sex*? But the furor was derailed when it was discovered that the poem was in the school's own library.

There was an SDS festival at a nearby college which Martha's husband helped to organize and Martha herself told some of the kids about. At one workshop, for high school kids, a number of teachers appeared and the kids, encouraged by the SDS moderator, insisted they leave, for they could not speak freely in the presence of their custodians. "They really dug being

able to do that."

The year before, in a frenzy of bureaucratic game hunting, the administration and faculty had hit upon a surefire way to prevent the kids from smoking in the bathrooms. *They took the doors off.*

Thirty guys decided to challenge this. They went to Martha and said: "You were at the Pentagon, how do you have a sit-in?" They presented the principal with their demand: reinstall the doors within three days. On the third day, no doors, so thirty very tough white guys lined up in front of the bathrooms. They managed to get some of the doors reinstalled. But the principal held an assembly in which, briefly, he identified those thirty kids as of that infamous and hairy lot of campus radicals now ravaging America. In a single moment of hysterical eloquence thirty ordinary greaser white teenagers — heroes to the student body — had been placed in the front ranks of the revolution.

The student body was continually subjected to painful concerts given by imported artists from Lincoln Center. The kids found ballets and musicians "faggoty," and hated every minute of the hours they were made to sit in silence listening to the yodelling and screeching called, elsewhere, "culture." One day, during a cello concert a kid wandering around backstage heard the music/noise and, thinking it was one of his friends goofing off, stole up behind the cellist and threw his arms around him. The cellist fell over backwards, the student body howled and hooted with joy at the sheer beauty of it, the cellist fled, and the administration and faculty, mortified, retired to seek revenge. During an emergency faculty meeting, Martha defended the students. An argument ensued as Martha heard again the old story which was — it was now clear — the school's reason for existing: "What are these kids gonna do in the factory or the army if they're not willing to do things they don't like!?" What indeed. The teachers, said Martha, knew they were supposed to teach the kids to passively accept their lot.

By this time Martha was spending nearly all her class time rapping with the kids about school, the war, politics, and together they had begun to analyze the ways in which they were oppressed. If this wasn't subversive enough, other kids were always wandering into her classroom — without pass slips — to comment on these matters. The whole school was strongly affected by all this energy, especially since the most popular and toughest kids were the leaders.

Parents, teachers and administrators became increasingly uptight. Martha began receiving threatening phone calls. Her husband was arrested for leafletting her school. "The kids were very excited when SDS came to leaflet — it was very important to them that that organization was paying attention to *them*." Several kids went down to an SDS sponsored demonstration against General Westmoreland when he came to a nearby city to award medals to Vietnam veterans.

"None of the kids had any use for 'pacifist creeps,' because they said their brothers were fighting and dying in Vietnam so why didn't 'those people' fight for what they believed in? In fact, one kid told me that the first time he had any respect for the New Left was when he sat in front of his TV eating a sandwich and watching those kids in Chicago fight the cops at last year's Democratic Convention."

And yet the kids were not gangsters. Martha spoke of their innocence, tenderness, and emotional sensitivity. She told me of a party at her house celebrating her husband's release from jail. "There were radicals there and these kids from school

but that night we really did feel close. It was a great night — we really had fun."

One day there was an honors assembly. These ceremonies were designed to honor the ten or so kids — all children of professional families — who got the highest grades. These kids had their own lounge and were the darlings of the teachers. "Six kids came into my room around lunch and told me they weren't gonna go to the assembly — it had nothing to do with them anyhow: 'Those kids are brown noses and liars and they'll do anything to get a grade and they're getting honored for *that*!? Fuck it. We won't go! They asked if they could use my classroom. I said sure and stayed with them. The principal freaked again and got on the loudspeaker system to tell everybody that they *had* to be there. Inside the assembly, everybody was talking about it — they were all sympathetic — and one honors girl made a speech in which she said she didn't know if these assemblies meant anything anyway.

"That day, after everyone had gone home, they called me in and fired me and threatened to arrest me if I came on campus again. I left and saw one of the

kids in my class — one of the leaders. I told him and he said: 'Don't you worry, we're gonna fill these halls tomorrow. Nobody will be able to get through the halls to class.'"

The story's end is painful. They decided to wait till the seniors came back from a trip on Monday (Martha was fired on a Thursday) and the administration conducted a heavy campaign of repression over the weekend, calling up the leaders' parents and telling them they would get their kids busted for dope or other things, that they should keep their kids home on Monday if they couldn't make them promise not to sit-in. The kids who did show up on Monday were pretty demoralized but they gamely milled around the halls between periods while teachers shrieked orders and the assistant principal (ex-Marine) beat the shit out of one kid.

There doesn't seem to be much left to say. Have faith in the people. And power, good sweet power, to the people.

9/9/69

In an interview in *Chicago Today*, Buckney, head pig of the Gang Intelligence Unit, admitted that his greatest fear was the unification of the city's gangs. As a result, some of his men spend their time "keeping things stirred up" between the gangs.

Y.L.O. newspaper of the Young Lords, Chicago, July 1969

CHICAGO: THE GANGS COMING TOGETHER

GANG BUSTERS

For the past month in Chicago we haven't been able to pick up a paper or listen to the T.V. or radio, and get the straight scoop on the gang scene. All this despite a barrage of publicity about the gangs, Black, White and Latin. So what's happening? Let's get into it.

First of all, we have to understand some stuff about ourselves. It's real simple: man is a social animal; we can't make it alone, so we get together in groups. We

do this despite attempts to separate us from each other, like they send guys to one school, girls to another, kids from the same neighborhood to different schools; they divide us up with 'specialized jobs' at work, get us to try and out-answer each other in class, get kids to be brown-noses (just where does that phrase come from) and tricks, and on and on. One thing is certain about this society we live in: they don't want people to get together.

But people dig each other! They're always getting together in groups. The need to be together is real. It's human. It's natural. And it's a necessity. So we form 'gangs', clubs and political groups (which the Man calls gangs unless he thinks they're respectable and proper). It's happened throughout the history of mankind. Every neighborhood and school in the city has its groups, its gangs.

Let's repeat it: THEY DON'T WANT US TO GET TOGETHER. Why? Because the people who run the show are threatened by any group that they don't control. So they try and either get the gangs on their side (we'll give you this and that if you don't do this and do that -- or else) or smash us. They don't understand how human beings work. They try and split us up to control us.

OK, so a lot of gangs are violent. This can be good, or it can be bad. Sometimes violence has been misdirected. We've been frustrated and pissed off at the world for good reason. So we strike out. We all know that some-

ance

times this isn't cool, like when guys turn in on each other, or vamp on some wino, or lady with a purse who's carrying home bread to feed her kids. But other times violence is ok. When someone is stepping on your neck you don't say 'hey, please cut it out.' So sometimes we're violent cause we have to be, we have to survive, we have to protect our people, our members, our turf, our neighborhood, and our families, against cops, tricks, businessmen, urban renewal and other gangs who aren't hip to the real enemy so they hit on us.

OK, we all know that something is happening. We're hip that it's a waste of time to keep jamming, vamping and gang bopping just because there ain't nothing else to do. So a lot of the gangs are becoming political groups and people's organizations, talking about serving and protecting the people from the Neanderthals and Bloodsuckers who run the show. Now this is where the Man, like Daley, Conlisk, State's Attorney Hanrahan, Chief Judge Boyle, and the Gang Intelligence Unit (G.I.U.) creep Buckney get uptight. They're really uptight. And they should be, because as our people get hip to who to hit, the man knows he's in trouble unless he can control us and use us.

But we're getting cool; so it's getting hard for them to use us. So now there's a shift, a difference in the way they deal with us. Right now they're trying to put us all down, smash us, White, Black and Latin.

Here's how they do it. Hanrahan, lover of the big crooks, uses his ties to the bullshit newspapers to get them to blast us. They give Hanrahan, Daley, Buckney, Boyle and Conlisk all the press they want. Big deal front pages 'exposing' somebody or some group. Once in awhile they cover the gang's side, like when the P-Stones (Rangers) and Disciples made their alliance public.

But look what happened. Sengali of the Rangers made it real clear that the gangs would take responsibility for their members as far as posssible and that future incidents didn't indicate a breakdown of the alliance. So the next day Hanrahan takes something that happened and gets a big story saying how the alliance is a phoney. If something did happen it might not have even involved Rangers or Disciples. It might have been some dude trying to prove himself, or someone in a gang who just wasn't hip to the changes, to the new spirit growing among Chicago's gangs.

It's clear that the reason the Neanderthals are waging war on gangs in their papers and on their T.V. and radio stations is because they're making a move to get more cops. Check out this connection. When they decided to raise the fares on the CTA (again), they blamed it on workers wanting more money (the politicians and businessmen get more money off us, and when some of us want more money to survive they take it out of our checks, not their's.) But they also made a big deal in the papers for a week about how many robberies and beatings were happening on the CTA. They of course didn't tell us that that stuff does happen all the time (go ahead, check the statistics.) They tried to brainwash the people, and the next week they raised the fare. TOO MUCH!

The same thing is true now. A week after Hanrahan starts shooting off his mouth about gangs, blaming anything that happened anywhere on gangs (especially organizations making peace and serving the people like the P stones and Disciples, Young Lords, Latin Eagles Young Patriots and Black Panther Party), Conlisk came out requesting 1000 more cops for next year to deal with the streets. Of course neither he, the papers, Daley, Buckney, Boyle or Hanrahan said anything about how they were politically threatened and scared, 'cause they couldn't control the gangs anymore.

Hanrahan laid the propaganda groundwork, Conlisk made the move, and now we'll see Daley's mangy dogs (the Aldermen) trot along in agreement. Meanwhile big crime, and bloodsucking businessmen go about their dirty business untouched.

The Gang Intelligence Unit

Now the dudes who do the nitty-gritty dirty work (the ones we have to deal with on our turf) are the punks in the GIU. GIU is part of the police dept. and was formed in 1967. It only had a few people. It replaced the Youth Group Intelligence Unit which had been set up to help gang kids, to keep them from fighting each other. That was when the cops and city were trying to use the the gangs, make them like the Conservative Vice Lords. (The Conservative Vice Lords on the west side are now sucks for the Democratic party, and made crook State Senator Bernie Neistein an honorable member.)

Under bootlicker Captain Ed Buckney the policy is one of throwing gang members in jail and keeping 'em there as long as possible (he said it on T.V.) This spring they upped the number of pigs in the GIU from 37 to 200

Quite a jump, and it goes to show they're scared of people in the streets, afraid that White, Black and Latin gang kids will become the people's liberation army that can bring justice back to Chicago and America.

Right now the GIU spends more time with Black and Latin gangs than White. That's because those groups moved sooner and faster than a lot of us Whites. It's obvious that they're tighter, more together, and have a greater spirit of solidarity running among their people because they know they got to be tight to survive. But things are changing in the White gangs. All over the city we're working out alliances with each other, and talking to Black and Latin organizations like the Panthers and the Young Lords. One of the first white groups to make its position clear, in support of the people and against the cops, was the Young Patriots. GIU has stepped up its harassment of our Patriot brothers and is doing likewise with white gangs everywhere in the city.

In the past GIU could be loose with us. Our cats were bought off with stuff like 'we'll let you drink if you keep it cool, if you hassel the Blacks, Latins and hippies.' But a lot of us know that never worked for long. As soon as too many of us were on the corner, blam, blam, under arrest. Don't let the people get together.

Now we know that there are some White gangs that get special treatment because some of their members became cops. (This is true of some duper gangs in particular). But even a lot of these groups who tricked or people and sold other people out, while doing more bad shit than most other gangs, are catching their lunch. So they had better dig what's going on and stop their bull shit, or catch their lunch from a lot of directions.

ALL POWER TO THE GANGS THAT FIGHT THE REAL ENEMY, LOVE THEIR BROTHERS AND SISTERS, AND SERVE THE PEOPLE!!!

Jan 1970

STONE GREASE

GRAPEVINE

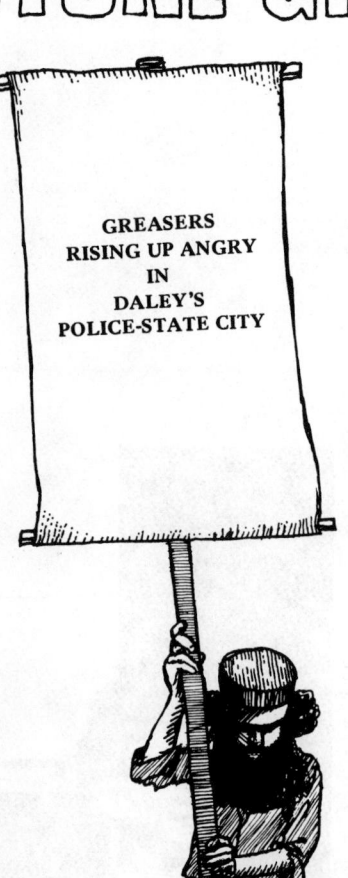

GREASERS
RISING UP ANGRY
IN
DALEY'S
POLICE-STATE CITY

SOUTHWEST SIDE

Members of one of those so-called civic organizations, The East Beverly Association, met at the Graver Park field house and complained about teenage gangs. Apparently some of the brothers have been drinking beer and leaving a mess. One of the things that came out at the meeting was that Pig commander Sheehy of the Ghresham district gave his men a standing order to check on the park every hour in the evenings.

The night the meeting was held, it was cold, and down at the other end of the park the brothers had a bonfire going. Pigs made a raid, but the brothers escaped down the alley. Maybe if they'd get off our case, stop pushing their bullshit morals and old fashioned standards and ideas on us, and let us have a place to go that we could run ourselves, there wouldn't be a 'teenage problem.' But maybe that wouldn't work either; they might get uptight because we were doing our own thing without their ancient neanderthal interference. All Power to the Brothers and Sisters who defy the pigs and the so-called civic organizations!!!

KENWOOD HIGH SCHOOL

People are digging this paper on the south side. Kenwood is supposed to be a 'new' school - it looks like a shiny new factory on the outside - but inside it's the same old tired crap of keeping the students in their place. It's supposed to be integrated (it's 30% white) but students are segregated into 'tracts'. We're all hip to it - they put the upper middle class students in the so-called 'honors tracts' and all the lower class brothers and sisters in the 'lower tracts'. But people got together despite the racist rules. 600 of us - half of the school - walked out the day after Chairman Fred's murder. We went over to the park and burned a paper machier pig in a wooden coffin. Then we walked by the school, chanting 'pigs ain't shit!' We felt good because we were more together than ever before. We were black and white, united in anger about Fred's murder, and refusing to sit in a bullshit classroom - being fed an education that maybe was important 50 years ago but doesn't mean shit today.

CYO - NORTH SIDE

Some of the brothers have been doing a little boxing. Brothers and sisters from Rising Up Angry checked out the CYO semi-finals boxing tournament at St. Andrews gym on the north side. We dug it. Pictured here is brother Pearson (dark trunks) of the north side's Aristocrats, fighting out of St. Andrews, going at it with brother Gillette, fighting our of Our Lady of Guadelupe on the south side.

KOZY PARK

One of the brothers from Kozy Park who had split the army was forced to go back in. It's real hard to stay out — you can't get a job, parents hassle you and if you get busted you'll go right to the stockade. He couldn't take it anymore — so he just turned himself in. Now he's serving a year in Ft. Riley, Kansas.

We got to get it together so that when our brothers go AWOL they can come back to the neighborhood and be hidden from all the pigs who want them to go back.

We should develop networks where these brothers can do revolutionary work and not get picked off right away. We have to protect our own people! Let's get it together brothers and sisters!!

TULEY HIGH SCHOOL

The brothers and sisters at Tuley are pretty much together. Blacks, Latins and whites. Because of this, there's a lot of cops around the school and the kids have to have I.D.'s to get in. Some of us were around with the paper and were told not to stand by the school or we'd get busted for sure. The week Fred Hampton was murdered the pigs were all around but some of us RUA and some revolutionary sisters from Tuley passed out the paper near the school anyway.

4
nce

RISING UP ANGRY has been going to different neighborhoods with flicks. We're showing 2 flicks about the army rebellions. to gangs, groups and clubs all over the city. We've got a bunch of different flicks - so give us a call and we'll help set up a thing. Get some people together. People's Power to the Revolutionary Grease!! Leave a message at WH 3-1424.

SIENA HIGH SCHOOL - WEST SIDE

Revolutionary Sisters (not the ones in habits) at Siena High (Central and Washington) brought in food for the Panther breakfast program. That load of food helps. All power to the sisters at Siena.

TJO - NORTH SIDE

As usual the pigs are hasseling us. Seems that they don't like the Thorndale jackets. Recently two pigs jumped brother Tommy, beat him up, and then split. Then they wonder why we grow in numbers, why the brothers and sisters hate pigs and the bullshit they stand for. Slick Power to all Revolutionary Grease!!!

YOUNG PATRIOTS - UPTOWN

The Young Patriots Organization is a revolutionary group of brothers and sisters in Uptown. Recently they began some programs to serve the people in the area. They set up a free medical clinic, and they provide free breakfast for school children. Power to the Patriots.

LINCOLN PARK

Alice's Restaurant used to be a coming together place on Lincoln near Fullerton. The landlord received pressure to close the place down. Out of a home now for 2 months, it looks like agreement is near on a lease at a new location in the Lincoln Park area. Watch for it. It'll be a gathering spot for revolutionary brothers and sisters.
All Power to Alice's who Feeds the People!!!

LATIN KINGS

The present Latin King Organization had its origin in the summer of 1963 when 'The Skulls and the Spaulding - Ohio Kings united under the leadership of Nando.

At the time of organizing there was confusion and discussion due to the fact that some of the members of each gang wanted to have the name of their gang. Finally the name Latin Kings was decided on.

As time went on, the Latin Kings became a feared group, fighting with other gangs or clubs such as the Chi-West, the Gaylords, Joker, C-Notes and so on. The members became a pattern for other kids in the area to immitate and the Jr. Latin Kings as well as the Pee Wee Latin Kings were formed. Now it's perhaps the largest but loosely organized club of Latins in Chicago. Each section of the city has its Latin Kings with their own president. Sometimes the only thing that holds the various groups together is the pride they feel in the name.

The year 1969 was the beginning of the new image of the Latin Kings. Under the leadership of Papo and Tarzan, they started moving into the political realm with the desire of helping their community in the problems of welfare, education, and health. No more gang bopping-Fight the real enemy.
All Power to All the People!!!

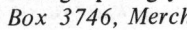

Rising Up Angry
Box 3746, Merchandise Mart, Chicago, Il. 60654 $5/month; joint sub with Chicag. Seed, $10.

In Chicago it's the "necks" who are gettin it together—the "greasers, called 'block around DC and 'slicks' in Pittsburgh."
At Chicago's Civic Center, at a rally fo Bobby Seale and the Conspiracy 8, thirt. REVOLUTIONARY GREASE showed u together, brothers and sisters both. It ble some people's minds; they couldn't believ it—grease into the revolution. Pigs did double take: "Oh, no, not them too what's happening to the divide an conquer game?"
Rising Up Angry Nov 1969

(first issue) July 1969

Arthur Turco

CONFEDERATE FLAG AND
PANTHER FLAG—
SIDE BY SIDE

YOUNG PATRIOTS

The story on the arrest of the Patriot Party which appeared in the March 2 Bird contained several inaccuracies because we had only partial information as we went to press. The short article below is the most accurate news story we have received. It is followed by a history and background of the Patriots.

NEW YORK—Twenty cops with guns drawn kicked in the door of Arthur Turco's apartment on Feb. 21 and arrested the five members of the Patriot Party who were inside. A few minutes earlier, seven other members of the party had been arrested downstairs in front of the building. Turco is Chief-of-Staff of the Patriots.

The 12 were officially charged with illegal possession of weapons, illegal possession of drugs, and interfering with arrest. They were held on bail totalling $34,500.

The following day police leaked reports to the press that the 12 were being questioned in connection with the firebombing of the home of Judge John Murtah, who is running the Panther 21 trial now in progress in New York. But Turco, who was arrested in the raid, said at a press conference on Feb. 23, "They never questioned us. The first we heard about these charges was when the assistant DA made them at the arraignment yesterday."

New York City's two daily newspapers, the Times and the Post, giving the story front-page coverage, talked about a "cache" of arms that included "a 12-gauge shotgun, three pistols, a carbine, four gas masks, a sword, three daggers and hundreds of rounds of ammunition." When 21 members of the Black Panther Party were arrested in their homes last April, the press used the same scare tactics, convicting the Panthers before they ever reached the courtroom.

The Patriots denied possession of the pistols, and said that the rifles were legally registered. Turco charged the power structure, from the local DA right up to Nixon, with conspiracy to wipe out the Patriots with the same tactics used against the Panthers. The Patriots are a member of the Rainbow Coalition with the Young Lords and the Black Panthers.

The police ransacked the apartment and took gun registrations, clothes, jewelry, stereo, tapes and the only available copy of the film "American Revolution Number 2." They also found a number of hypodermic needles, which the press mentioned in connection with the dope charges. The press did not mention that Turco is a diabetic.

—*liberation news service*

Yorkville, New York, Dec. 30, 1969: Patriots show me pictures of a rally held in Chicago jointly wit with the Panthers. A Confederate flag hangs behind the podium next to the Panther flag. Another, slightly tattered Confederate flag on the wall behind us belonged to the Patriot Party Chairman's family. "It was actually flown in battle," boasts Roger, who looks about 17 but has worked with the Patriots "from the beginning" when they were a newly politicized gang of street kids in Uptown, Chicago. If you've seen *Medium Cool,* you've seen shots of Uptown—that's the slum for the poor whites who came north from Appalachia hunting jobs.

At the time of their arrest the Patriots were making last-minute plans for an organizing tour of the South, which they hope to make the main focus of a national revolutionary white community. Although their internationalist, anti-racist emphasis and much of their rhetoric derive from the Panthers, they take pride in their Southern origins and still hope to visit the South (including Atlanta) in the near future.

Roger's black cowboy hat bears two Patriot buttons, beside the stars and bars. One button shows two upraised red fists breaking handcuffs; the other reads: "Resurrect John Brown." Around us on the walls, among posters of Che and Panther martyrs, hang leaflets offering free medical care to the people of Yorkville, and urging tenants to band together "against all pig landlords." Young kids from the neighborhood drift in and out, children of German and Irish immigrants, saluting each other with "power to the people." The storefront office's taped-up window bears scars of a confrontation with the local Nazi party.

The Patriots differ from most white supporters of the Panthers, and from most white revolutionaries, not only in their Southern origins but also in their working-class roots. In 1964 some of them had joined a project set up by SDS, "Jobs or Income Now" (JOIN), but by 1968 they had politely kicked out SDS and taken over the project, renamed National Organizing Committee. In 1968 NOC ran Peggy Terry, a poor white woman, for vice president as running mate to Eldridge Cleaver on the Peace and Freedom Party ticket.

The street gang which formed part of NOC emerged the next year as the Young Patriots, joined by the Lincoln Park Patriots, a gang of bikers. They saw strong similarities between conditions in the black, brown and white slums of Chicago and concluded that the same system oppresses all poor people. Patriots began to form strong friendships with Panthers.

They feel that poor people of all races can, and must, support each other. And they are interested in organizing the poorest and most disadvantaged groups in our society. "We're concerned with our people, the oppressed whites, those who haven't even made it into the working class yet, people that are so far down, so stomped on, that they can't even get a job and have no place to go but up. We're into organizing the lumpen-proletariat, the black and white niggers, that's us," says Defense Captain Art Turco.

Some of the Young Patriots in Chicago grew restless, sensing a mood of urgency among white youth around the country. They felt that the Patriots should move swiftly to form a national party.

Other members wanted to wait until they had organized more of their home community. The national faction changed its name to the Patriot Party and left Chicago. "By the time we got Uptown 'together' the Panthers could be completely wiped out," they explained. They also claim that those left behind were too indulgent of their old friends and neighbors and didn't push the Patriot principles consistently.

The Party now has chapters across the country—Eugene, Oregon; Cleveland, Ohio; New Haven, Conn.; and Richmond, Va., as well as Yorkville. If Wallace could do it, why not a revolutionary party? The Patriot's Yorkville newsletters answer the charge of "outsider" by affirming: "We are no strangers to the conditions that exist here in Yorkville. . . Housing problems, tax problems, unemployment, bad schools, and on and on. . . We are from the thousands of Yorkvilles all over the country." And Uptowns. And Cabbagetowns.

At the same time, the Patriots hope to remind "their people" of America's radical tradition, especially in the South: the mountain counties that opposed slavery and sent troops to the Union army, for example. (Fannin Co., Ga., flew the Union flag.) They avidly read such works as *Millhands and Preachers, Tom Watson, Agrarian Rebel,* and *Black Reconstruction in America,* all of which show black and white Southerners struggling against oppression.

All this sounds much like the now-dissolved Southern Student Organizing Committee in its "Southern nationalism" period. The difference lies mainly in SSOC's middle class, mostly Southern student orientation, contrasted with the Patriot's emphasis on solidarity between poor people across lines of color and region. In spite of these differences, the similarities show how attractive the "rebel" tradition can be, since the Patriots seem to have had very little contact with SSOC. On the other hand, the Patriots may not use the stars and bars to organize in the South, where they are identified with a racist ruling class rather than an oppressed minority.

The Patriots hope to organize people around a lot more than history lessons. They adapted the 10-point program of the Black Panthers, which outlines the basic needs of poor communities: jobs, housing, control of police, etc. The Eugene chapter, for example, feeds breakfast to about 50 children, runs a liberation school, and has organized a firewood co-op for mountain families using wood stoves.

This winter Patriots opened a free clinic and a free breakfast program in Yorkville. An earlier Patriot drive to combat the destruction of Yorkville's low-cost housing continues, with slowly increasing community participation. Although most of these services mirror ones designed by the Panthers, the Patriots assert that they spring from the real needs of Yorkville's poor. "Even if the parents have food for their kids, they have to get up at six or seven in the morning to go to work and can't prepare it."

The Patriots, like the Panthers, emphasize community control. "We don't want to run this clinic for the people, we want them to learn how to run it and take it over." Another difference is the source of the breakfast food. Their leaflet explains:

We are asking merchants in the community

to contribute food to the program. Since they make a profit on what we need to survive we believe they have a responsibility to the community, especially the big stores, ask them if they are contributing to the free breakfast program. If not, we should all begin shopping somewhere else.

Poor whites who support black militants—and try to organize other poor whites to do the same—have to have a lot of guts. The Patriots already have one martyr: John Howard, a white welfare recipient from Georgia who came to Chicago seeking work. In 1964 he began working with JOIN in Uptown. The film "American Revolution # 2" shows a meeting attended by Uptown whites and Panthers in 1966. In that scene John Howard says: "I'll stick with the Panthers if they'll stick with me, and I know they will." When Howard returned to Georgia in 1969 to visit his family, he was identified at a meeting as "the guy who works with niggers in Chicago." The next day he was found dead, his throat slit.

The Patriots' expansion South has possibilities. "If you feed 15 poor white kids till you get to the point where you can talk to them about Bobby Seale [jailed Panther chairman], you're doing more to free Bobby than if a whole university came out on a 'Free Bobby' demonstration," they feel. But can the Patriots get their anti-racist message across while emphasizing white solidarity? "Whites have to start getting together. If we're the ones to get them together, we'll be able to deal with this racism thing."

At the moment, a few charismatic male leaders hold the party together. A certain arrogance has characterized the Party's relations with other Movement people whom they tend to label "petty-bourgeois." As the Party grows, it will have to deal with male chauvinism, as well as racism, in a structural and programmatic way.

But ever since 1966, when SNCC told white radicals to organize their own communities, the Movement, with a few exceptions, has hesitated at the edges of the campus. We talk a lot about organizing workers, unemployed youth, and over-taxed Southerners who vote for Maddox because he seems to stand for "the little man." The Patriots seem ready to do more than talk. Right now, especially in the South, they're just feeling their way. We owe them our support and enouragement.

—barbara joye

SILENT MAJORITY SOLDIERS

BURY THE DEAD

The war continues the mother continues she knits
The father continues he does business
The son is killed he continues no more
The father and the mother go to the graveyard
They find this quite natural the father and mother
Life continues life with knitting war business
Business war knitting war
Business business business
Life with the graveyard.

—Jacques Prevert

On Dec. 5, Rod, Ricky and Dwyane Stevens, Jr. got an order from a court in Redding, California, barring a military funeral for their brother, Dennis, 21, killed in action around Chu Lai. Dennis's legal guardians, an aunt and uncle named James and Joyce Stevens, insisted that he be buried "with dignity and with high military honors." A hearing to settle the matter took place three days later.

Redding is a city of some 15,000 near the top of California's great Central Valley. Sprawling farms to the south produce rice, olives, prunes and almonds. Lumber and sheep-raising are major sources of income. The mountains and streams bring in tourists. Redding is the seat of Shasta County, and it was outside the courthouse that the two feuding sides of the Stevens family gathered Dec. 8.

They looked like the silent majority embodied: powerful men with leathery cheeks and broad hands, mortar under the nails, dressed in windbreakers and gabardine and Ban-Lon; grim women in bouffant hair-dos; teenagers with crew cuts. The teenager wearing round-rimmed granny glasses turned out to be Dwyane Stevens, Jr. He told me that this whole crowd sided with him and his brothers against the Army. Uncle Jim—"I don't even think of him as my uncle now"—was standing some 40 feet apart, with his wife and stepson and some military personnel.

Dwyane laid out the complicated family history. The older generation of Stevenses—Dwyane, Sr., Bud and Jim—had come to Redding from Iowa some 30 years ago. Dwyane, Sr. married and had four children. Then, in 1952, his wife disappeared, never to return. When he died a few years later his three oldest boys, Rod, Dennis, and Ricky, went to live with his brother Bud, his wife Ioia and their five children. Dwyane, Jr., the baby, was adopted by a union brother of Bud's. All four boys grew up in Redding—healthy, athletic, good in school.

When Dennis was 15 he spent a summer down in Vallejo with Dwyane, Sr.'s other brother, Jim. Jim's wife, Joyce, had four kids by a previous marriage and she found Dennis a good companion for them. She invited him to spend the school year and promised him a motorcycle. She also requested, and got, the $20 a week from Dwyane, Sr.'s pension which Bud conscientiously had been putting into a bank account for Dennis. Lest there be any squabble about this, Joyce and Jim had a court make them the boy's legal guardians. Dennis played varsity football at Hogan High School in Vallejo for two years. Then he moved back to Redding. He later complained that during his stay in Vallejo, Joyce Stevens had dipped into his small legacy to buy a washer and drier.

Dennis was drafted in the summer of 1968, spent six months

at Fort Lewis, Wash., training for the artillery, then shipped out for Vietnam in August, 1969. He was killed on Nov. 14. The Army owes somebody $10,000 life insurance.

"Joyce is a bit of a flag-waver," Bud Stevens said that morning outside the courthouse. "But I don't think that's her real reason for insisting on a military funeral. I hate to say this about anybody, but I think maybe money's behind it. She might think the Army will make her the beneficiary just 'cause she supports the war." He shook his head and chomped his cigar butt.

Joyce Stevens, a stocky woman with close-cropped black hair and a tense manner, seemed upset that Dennis's high school football coach was not on hand. She had wanted him to testify that the boy loved drill-and-ceremony. "The boy is being dishonored," she said. "I raised him and nursed him when he was sick. We are his legal guardians, we are his next-of-kin and it is so noted on the Army records." Her husband, a big, blue-eyed man who resembles Bud, stared hard at the ground. None of his relatives would speak to him.

She introduced her son, William Koontz, as "Dennis's brother, who has a top-secret clearance from the Navy."

I said I thought Dennis only had three brothers.

"Dennis was my foster brother," the top-secret man said.

"They were *like* blood brothers," Joyce insisted, "and my husband, of course, was a blood brother of the boy's father."

The military men hovering around were the Vallejo Stevenses' lawyer, a Major Workman, and their key witness, Sgt. Richard Moulton. It was Moulton, a tall, fat man with "escort duty" inscribed on his nameplate, who had accompanied Dennis's body to a nearby Memorial Chapel. His orders listed James and Joyce Stevens as next-of-kin. Escort duty is voluntary in the Army. You have to be very humane or very malign to want the job of telling people their sons are dead. And the Army doesn't attract many career humanists. "It's funny," Sergeant Moulton reflected, "but I had a very similar case just two weeks ago in Columbus, Ohio. The boy had been recommended for a private showing, but that was somebody's error of judgment. He had had a lot of waxwork and the parents just couldn't recognize. They insisted it wasn't their son. Said they couldn't locate a certain scar. In the end it turned out all right, though."

—"What do you mean?"

—"Well, they took my word it was him."

Dennis Stevens described his increasing revulsion over the war in letters to his family and friends in Redding. Almost all the 30 people gathered outside the courtroom had a letter from him in hand or back home. The letters said that Dennis's battery had been decimated—23 men left out of 130—and that he had been reassigned to an infantry unit by a captain who hated him. "Now you're gonna get it, Stevens," the captain had promised.

"If you ask me, the Army killed him," says Glen Jeffries, the retired plasterer who brought up Dwyane. "He had no infantry training and they put him in the infantry."

Ricky Stevens, home on emergency leave from Fort Dix, had a letter saying, "The captain told me he was going to send me into the field with 'A' Company—that's the infantry. Rick, if you can get the fuck out of the fucking Army, do it!'"

Dwyane, Jr. says, simply, "I won't go. That's that. Don't ask me 'What if...?' I'm telling you I won't go." He is a student at Shasta Community College, where "just about everybody's against the war. They support us in what we're doing about the funeral." What about the vets? "Especially the vets. Vets have been coming up to me after class to say we're doing right fighting the Army."

The hearing itself took only 10 minutes. Rod, the oldest at 22, testified that he was next-of-kin and wanted to make the funeral arrangements. Ricky and Dwyane took the stand in his support. Then Joyce Stevens showed her certificate of guardianship to the judge. Her tone was Hollywood-grief, her language, strictly military. She whimpered: "According to Army regulations he never changed his status with respect to these papers, as would have been his prerogative." Major Workman said that even though Dennis had turned 21 in Vietnam, the Army recognized the legal guardianship of James and Joyce Stevens. "Doesn't the Army recognize the legal impact of adulthood?" the judge asked. "No," the Major said.

The judge scowled and ruled in favor of the brothers.

Ioia Stevens was sobbing in a daughter's arms. "It don't bring anybody back to life, does it?" she asked.

Joyce Stevens went into consultation with Major Workman about when the life insurance payment would come down.

"Do you know that the policy was made out to you?" I asked.

"The paperwork is in the hands of Sixth Army," she replied. "Processing takes four weeks." Major Workman nodded. Then he put on a smile and approached Rod Stevens in the hall outside the courtroom. "I'm here to be of assistance to you," he said. Rod glared at him. Dwyane said, "First you kill him, then you want to help. You lifers make me sick."

Jim Stevens was trying to get a hello out of some of his relatives, but to no avail. Finally Bud walked up to him and said quietly, "You shouldn't have pushed it this far, Jim. The boys have a right to bury their brother the way he would have wanted."

An hour later a CBS-TV crew showed up at Rod Stevens' house, where the brothers were drinking beer and listening to Santana.

"Which did he object to, exactly, the military or this particular war?" the interviewer wanted to know.

"Well, he hated the military," Rod said, "and he hated this war. He hated them both."

"There seems to be particular feeling against *this war*," the CBS man hinted.

"He hated this war and he hated the Army."

"Why didn't he resist the draft?"

"How could he know before he went in what the Army was like and what the war was all about?"

"Why do you think he disliked the Army?"

"He *hated* the Army," Rod said. "He wrote my brother Rick he should get the fuck out."

The interviewer blushed, stammered and cut off the conversation. He asked if they had a photograph of Dennis around. Rod brought out a Polaroid shot of a broad-shouldered, handsome young man in fatigues. In the background was thick jungle foliage. The soldier had a flower in one hand and was giving the peace sign with the other.

—*Fred Gardner*

Hard Times 12/22/69

Major General Smedley D. Butler USMC (retired) from *Common Sense* November, 1935.

I spent 33 years and 4 months in active service as a member of our country's most agile military force—the Marine Corps. I served in all commissioned ranks from a second lieutenant to Major-General. And during that period I spent most of my time being a high-class muscle man for Big Business, for Wall Street and for the bankers. In short, I was a racketeer for capitalism.

I suspected I was just part of a racket at the time. Now I am sure of it. Like all members of the military profession I never had an original thought until I left the service. My mental faculties remained in suspended animation while I obeyed the orders of the higher-ups. This is typical of everyone in the military service.

Thus I helped make Mexico and especially Tampico safe for American oil interests in 1914. I helped make Haiti and Cuba a decent place for the National City Bank boys to collect revenues in. I helped in the raping of half a dozen Central American republics for the benefit of Wall Street. The record of racketeering is long. I helped purify Nicaragua for the international banking house of Brown Brothers in 1909-12. I brought light to the Dominican Republic for American sugar interests in 1916. I helped make Hondoras "right" for American fruit companies in 1903. In China in 1927 I helped see to it that Standard Oil went its way unmolested.

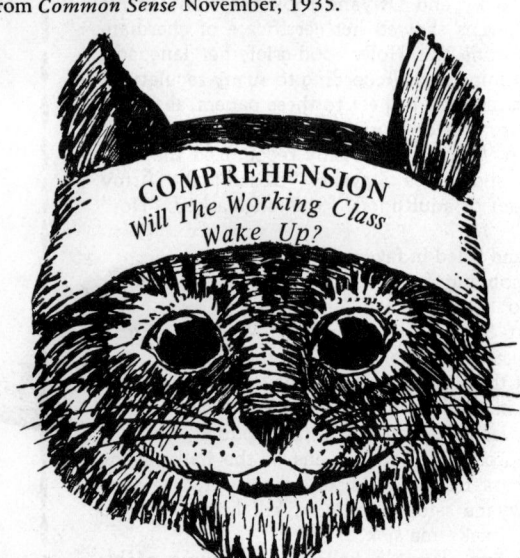

COMPREHENSION
Will The Working Class
Wake Up?

U.S. Marines invade Dominican Republic, 1965.

ERNEST MANDEL'S AMERICA
staughton lynd

What can be expected of American labor in the 1970's? For twenty-five years, since the end of World War II, radicals have hopefully scanned the economic horizon for signs of impending recession and an attendant upsurge of labor militancy. The reader of Marxist periodicals in these years could only assume that hard times, like Herbert Hoover's prosperity, was always just around the corner.

Such forecasts have repeatedly proved dead wrong. The relevant prediction has been that of Walter Oakes in his essay, "Toward a Permanent War Economy," published in *Politics* magazine in February 1944. "The fact is that the capitalist system cannot stand the strain of another siege of unemployment comparable to 1930-1940," Oakes argued. "The traditional methods . . . will not be followed." A repetition of the 1930's would be forestalled by massive and continuing government spending on "defense."

So it has turned out. Recently, however, a number of factors, not least the student movement's need to reach off-campus America, have raised the old questions once again. Analysts point to the decline of real wages since 1965, the formation of black caucuses and the growing number of black workers in basic industry, the evident discontent revealed in the blue-collar vote for Wallace, and spreading wildcat strikes. In the hope that these symptoms presage the disintegration of the post-war economic equilibrium, movement people across the country are taking jobs in factories, moving into working-class communities, seeking out working-class students in junior and community colleges. If the theory many have felt the New Left to lack is to prove its worth it must speak to these hopes and reliably assess their substance.

The writings of Belgian economist Ernest Mandel offer the most impressive set of predictions currently available. The following remarks do not pretend to review adequately the two big volumes of Mandel's *Marxist Economic Theory*. They attempt to extract from that master-work and from two recent essays what Mandel has to say about the shape of things to come, and then to evaluate that forecast.

In Mandel's view, the characteristic feature of "capitalism in decline" is the intervention of the state. The spread of socialism across the face of the earth makes more and more areas inaccessible to private enterprise. Imperialism, therefore, is less capable of disposing of capitalism's surplus productivity than might have seemed the case at the time of World War I. Accordingly the state steps in. "External outlets playing less and less the role of safety-valve after the First World War, and especially after the Second . . . capitalism turns more and more to the state, in order to secure by state intervention in the economy what the normal working of the latter can no longer secure for it. *The bourgeois state becomes the essential guarantor of monopoly profits.*"

Agreeing with Oakes, Mandel believes that spending on armaments is the most important way in which the state props up capitalism. "Armaments economy, war economy, represent the essential replacement markets which the capitalist system of production has found in the age of its decline." In this connection Mandel presents a striking

∿∿∿∿∿∿∿∿∿∿∿∿∿∿∿∿∿∿∿∿∿∿∿∿∿∿

In the last analysis, I think one's commitment to the cause of labor must rest not on a prediction of labor radicalism the day-after-tomorrow, but on a sense of solidarity with those required to do work no human being should have to perform, under conditions of arbitrary discipline no grown man or woman should have to endure...

∿∿∿∿∿∿∿∿∿∿∿∿∿∿∿∿∿∿∿∿∿∿∿∿∿∿

conception of fascism. Fascism is that situation in which a declining capitalist economy relies wholly on public expenditures in the form of armaments, instead of public expenditures in the form of programs for health, education and other social services. Thus, "in Nazi Germany, between 1933 and 1939, the national income increased by exactly the same amount as military expenditure."

What does all this mean for the labor movement? In part:

1. As production of war materials comes to represent a higher and higher percentage of an economy's output, a tendency to inflation also becomes stronger. Defense expenditure pumps money into the economy without putting goods on the market, hence is peculiarly inflationary. "The dilemma confronting the state in the age of declining capitalism," Mandel writes, "is *the choice between crisis and inflation.*" Whereas inflationary public spending may at first benefit working people by producing more jobs, at a certain point, as in the United States since 1965, it causes a decline in real wages by stimulating price increases greater than wage increases.

2. At first glance it might seem that capitalism could obtain the benefits of public spending without the liabilities of inflationary spending on armaments, if public spending took the form of investments in health, education, transit, and the like, which are in the long run anti-inflationary because they increase the productivity of labor. The difficulty is political. "Fierce resistance is to be met with on this front, in capitalist circles; this resistance wavers only when it is a matter of expenditure on armaments." " . . . a managed economy of the 'Welfare State' type is less and less capable of avoiding considerable economic recessions by its limited state investments, while investments of a larger order can be realized only within the setting of an economy of re-

armament and war." The natural program of the labor movement in every advanced capitalist society is massive public spending on social services. Rarely, however, has a labor movement, parts of which themselves derive direct benefits from arms spending, displayed sufficient vision, discipline and muscle to force public spending away from death toward life.

3. Therefore it must be assumed that the drift of things in a declining capitalist economy is toward larger and larger spending on war. In Mandel's view this also entails state regulation of wages and an attack on the trade union movement. Even the richest capitalist countries are unable to produce more guns without curtailing the production of "butter." Even in a United States the permanent war economy tends to bring with it "squeezing of civilian consumption and of production of consumer goods, forced saving, financing of rearmament partly from social security funds, etc."; in short, "safeguarding of profit by reduction in the standard of living of the masses." Capitalism-dependent-on-defense, therefore, doubly attacks the workingman's standard of living: first, by inflation, which causes a decline in real wages; second, by reduction of public expenditure on welfare and regulation of the effort by trade unions to redistribute income through strikes.

In two recent articles in *New Left Review*, Mandel spells out the implications of his analysis with reference to the French rebellion of May-June 1968 and the upsurge of labor militancy here. ("Lessons of May," November-December 1968; "Where is America Going?" March-April 1969).

The French events, for Mandel, illustrate the circumstances that "the increasing role of the state means at the same time the violent compression of social and international contradictions." It is true that the permanent war economy makes possible substantial control of economic fluctuations, hence that in modern capitalism crisis tends to take the form of stagnation, rather than of breakdown. But this stagnation, this apparent peace, represses beneath a surface of law-and-order the increasing bitterness of wage-earners at whose nationalize certain industries, to control the freedom of action of trade unions, precisely to that degree—according to Mandel—grievances accumulate and workers' struggles become "more explosive, as the proletariat strives to win back in a few weeks what it feels it has lost over long years. Strikes, even and above all if they become less frequent, tend to become more violent and, increasingly, to start as wildcat strikes." The dramatic, massive phenomenon of depression is prevented by a state intervention which produces dramatic, massive resistance to wage restraints imposed by state control. In this analysis, then, state intervention simply shifts the arena of working-class action from the economic (resistance to the employer) to the political (resistance to the state). Such is Mandel's understanding of crisis of the French type.

America represents a second type of situation. State intervention in the labor movement is less pronounced than in a country like France. Because the American economy is wealthier than the French, welfare spending can to a certain extent co-exist with armaments spending, and direct attack on the standard of living of the mass of people is less required. Labor unrest in the United States, accordingly, takes a form more economic and less political than in France. Mandel assesses it as follows:

1. *The decline of unskilled labor as a result of automation.* "The number of unskilled labor jobs in industry has come down from 13,000,000 to less than 4,000,000, and probably to 3,000,000, within the last 10 years," This "truly revolu-

tionary process" helps to explain both black radicalization and student revolt. The elimination of unskilled labor hits black workers hardest: the unemployment rate among young black workers is now 15-20 per cent, four times the rate in the labor force as a whole and "a percentage analogous to that of the Great Depression." Students, on the other hand, are drawn into the labor process by the same technological revolution which displaces blacks. The third industrial revolution, summed up in the catchword "automation," requires highly-trained workers in place of workers without skills. Therefore the multiversity becomes a process of apprenticeship for industry, which "bends, folds, spindles and mutilates" the young human beings who pass through it, which "channels" them away from humane endeavor toward the modern corporation. Within both the black and student communities, as a result, the more gutsy and imaginative rebel.

2. *The erosion of real wages through inflation.* This is the process discussed earlier. Mandel says that although the decline in real wages since 1965 has been only at about the rate of one per cent a year, "it is a significant break in a tendency which has continued without interruption for the last 35 years." Mandel thinks that "if American workers accepted more or less easily and morally the integration of their trade union leadership into the Democratic Party during the long period which started with the Roosevelt Administration, this acceptance was a product of the fact that their real income and material conditions, especially their social security, improved during that period. Today that period seems to be coming to an end."

3. *The social consequences of public squalor.* The starvation of social services characteristic of a permanent war economy also affects the wages of the 11,000,000 wage earners in public administration, who are chronically underpaid. (To Mandel's analysis on this point might be added the fact that these workers in public administration are often teachers, social workers, hospital technicians, whose parents worked in factories. They are members of the university-trained "new working class" whose own experience of exploitation provides a basis for solidarity with their relatives who do industrial work.)

4. *The impact of foreign competition.* According to Mandel, American workers make wages on the order of three times those of European workers, and five times those of workers in Japan. Now that European and Japanese industry has substantially caught up with American industry in respect both to technology and scale of operation, this wage differential between American and foreign firms makes it possible for the latter to compete effectively. Hence foreign producers of steel and automobiles have captured 10-20 per cent of the American market in recent years. Should this trend continue American industry will find itself driven to a direct attack on the wages of American workers. (One might add that the very degree to which research and development spending in America is concentrated in defense-related industries makes American industry more vulnerable to foreign producers of consumer goods.)

At that point, according to Mandel, the trade-union activity which New Leftists have tended to dismiss as reactionary might appear in quite a new light. Defense of an existing reality, such as existing wage rates, could rapidly mobilize tens of thousands of persons as the projection of a desirable future situation (say, socialism) never could. In Mandel's words:

Trade-union consciousness is not only negative. Or, to formulate this more dialectically, trade-union consciousness is in and by itself socially neutral. It is neither reactionary nor revolutionary. It becomes reactionary when the system is capable of satisfying trade-union demands. It creates a major revolutionary potential once the system is no longer capable of satisfying basic trade-union demands. Such a transformation of American society of capital is today knocking at the door of US capitalism.

and again:

As long as socialism or revolution are the only ideals preached by militants because of their own convictions and consciousness, their social impact is inevitably limited. But when the ideas of revolutionary socialism are able to unite faith, confidence and consciousness with the immediate material interests of a social class in revolt—the working class—then their potential becomes literally explosive. In that sense, the political radicalization of the working class, and therewith socialism, will become a practical proposition in the United States within the next 10 or 15 years . . .

Will they? For one like myself who has heard this same prediction many times, nagging doubts remain.

Does automation simply radicalize blacks thrown out of industrial work and students drawn into it? Does it not also decrease the cost of production so as to make possible increased production for the domestic market at lower prices, in the manner of Henry Ford and his successors?

About inflation, does not Ernest Mandel hang too much on a trend toward the decline of real wages only three or four years old, which may not continue if the Vietnam war ends? And can we assume that workingmen driven frantic by high prices and high taxes will blame their difficulties on the Defense Department, rather than on black welfare recipients and striking firemen?

Public employees are undoubtedly rapidly unionizing, but the example of the New York Teachers' Strike suggests that white-collar wage-earners can be the greatest "labor aristocrats" of them all.

Even foreign competition, Mandel's ace in the hole, can be circumvented by tariffs on imports and by the investment of excess capital in foreign subsidiaries with cheaper labor costs.

Finally, the black caucuses in industrial unions—a factor too little emphasized by Mandel—may not be so unambiguously radical as some radicals seem to assume. In comparison with the typical black wage-earner, who is unemployed or employed in marginal industries uncovered by the minimum wage law, the black auto worker or steel worker might become a labor aristocrat within the community of black labor, jealously defending the token privileges sophisticated managements make available (e.g., access of blacks to cleaner departments in the steel mills, even though the blast furnace and coke departments remain largely black).

So I don't know. In the last analysis, I think one's commitment to the cause of labor must rest, not on a prediction of labor radicalism the-day-after-tomorrow, but on a sense of solidarity with those required to do work no human being should have to perform, under conditions of arbitrary discipline no grown man or woman should have to endure; and who, because of their powerlessness, must reach out to each other for help in a spirit of comradeship almost unknown in our dog-eat-dog society. ∎

 **LIBERATION** Dec 1969

Other Kinds and Degrees of Resistance: from Protest to Sabotage

FIGHTING
CITY HALL
FOR
YOUR LIFE

YOU CAN'T FIGHT CITY HALL!

Expressway Hearing

Persecution of the City Performed by its Inmates

by Leticia Kent

Talking to yourself, says an old saw, can make you crazy. After nearly three decades of testifying against the Lower Manhattan Expressway at public hearings, last week the Lower East Side quit the onanistic practice, regained its sanity, and drove the establishment crazy.

Onstage in the auditorium of Seward Park High School at Essex and Grand Streets a stenotypist was setting up her brand new machine. "New York State hearing on the Lower Manhattan Expressway—April 10, 1968," she typed phonogramically. She checked her supply of paper tape and patted the machine.

By 7.15 p. m. the place was nearly filled. Besides area residents there were officials, politicians, press, and police. Cops distributed hearing cards and small, shiny brochures prepared by Madigan-Hyland (the same engineering firm used by Robert Moses to justify a similar scheme 20 years ago). The 15-page booklet had no hard facts—only cartoons. A few maps of the 10-lane cross-Manhattan artery drawn by Vollmer Associates (another firm favored by Moses) were placed about the room, but if you lingered to study them, a cop eased you back to your seat. State officials and the stenotypist sat onstage. Everyone else sat in the audience or testified, facing the audience, from a floor mike at the foot of the center aisle. It was possible to wonder who was to be heard by whom.

Among the first speakers was Commissioner Frank Arricale, head of the city's relocation department and a proponent of the Expressway. He ticked off figures of tenants to be dislocated by the road: "Total residential units: 1246; total residential tenants: 1246." The audience objected. "What about the ramps?" they yelled. "How many more are you going to throw out to put in the ramps?" Arricale laughed and tried to go on. For the first time, he said, the city was committed to relocating everyone. Asked for details, Arricale was vague. The specific sites, he claimed, were part of a soon-to-be-completed Lower East Side redevelopment plan. Someone demanded to know if one of the proposed sites was to be Cooper Square. Arricale hedged. "I'm simply saying housing will be available for everyone," he said.

"Where" a resident persisted. "All my life I've lived on Mulberry Street. You can walk there day and night without being molested."

"Are the sites already spoken for?" shouted another resident. "Mayor Lindsay promised Cooper Square to another group. They need it as badly as we do."

"I wonder, as a practical matter, if Lindsay is your mayor," mused the Reverend Gerard LaMountain, pastor of the Most Holy Crucifix Church on Broome Street. "His promises don't seem to mean anything and he seldom shows up at public meetings. On the map," Reverend LaMountain stated, "my church has been replaced by a park with fountains. My parishioners are poor. Where is the city going to move them? To housing already allocated to the people of Cooper Square? As much as I love the people of Broome Street, they should not dislocate the people of Cooper Square. This hearing is a swindle."

As speaker after speaker enumerated the devastating effects of the Expressway on 800 businesses and 2000 families in the area, the residents grew increasingly angry. Congressman Leonard Farbstein, of all people, forthrightly recommended civil disobedience. "If you will permit me to urge militancy," Farbstein said, "I assure you they will not drive you out of your homes." He got a big hand.

Walter Kirschenbaum, a city official, was speaking against the Expressway for the Liberal Party when the audience began to call for urban critic Jane Jacobs—"We want Jane. We want Jane." Kirschenbaum graciously ceded his time to Mrs. Jacobs, thus setting in motion an astonishing chain of events.

Jane Jacobs, long-time opponent of the Expressway, made her way to the front of the room amid cheers. "It's interesting," she observed, "the way the mike is set up. At a public hearing you are supposed to address the officials—not the audience."

In a flash, George Toth, an official of the State Department of Transportation, came down from the stage and turned around the mike.

"Thank you, sir," said Mrs. Jacobs, turning her back on Toth. "But I'd rather speak to my friends. We've been talking to ourselves all evening as it is."

She called the hearing "worse than a sham" because the officials' minds were made up beforehand. "One thing I came to see was what kind of administration could even consider destroying the homes of 2000 families at a time like this. They must be insane. With the amount of unemployment in this city, who would think of wiping out thousands of minority jobs. They must be insane. They are apparently out of touch with reality. The city is like an insane asylum run by the most far-out of its inmates. If the Expressway is put through," Mrs. Jacobs warned, "there will be anarchy."

To dramatize their decision not to accept the Expressway, she suggested the residents stage a peaceful demonstration right then and there. So they rose and marched, led by Mrs. Jacobs and Frances Goldin of the Cooper Square Committee. Elderly couples marched. Catholics and Jews. Italians and Russians. Businessmen and artists. They marched down the center aisle and onto the stage.

The stenotypist hurriedly picked up her precious machine and the tape spilled onto the floor. Yards and yards of phonograms. Yards and yards of testimony. Jane Jacobs came down from the stage. Other marchers festooned the platform with tape and tore it into little pieces. Pieces of testimony. "There is no record," said the seemingly astonished Mrs. Jacobs. "There is no hearing. We are through with phony, fink hearings."

"Arrest that woman," Toth ordered, pointing down to Mrs. Jacobs, who was leaving the auditorium. The residents surrounded Mrs. Jacobs. They accompanied her out into the vestibule of the school where she was arrested. They followed her to the Seventh Precinct on Delancey Street. They raised such a ruckus—"We want Jane! We want Jane!"—outside the station house that the police begged them to cool it. But they wouldn't, not until Jane Jacobs, charged with disorderly conduct, was released in her own recognizance two hours later.

Meanwhile, in the nearly empty auditorium of Seward Park High School, Paul W. Douglas, representing the City-wide Organizations against the Lower Manhattan Expressway, was reading his remarks into the fragmentary record. "It is obscene," he said, "to expend $150 million for 1.3 miles of road the day after the funeral of Martin Luther King."

the village VOICE

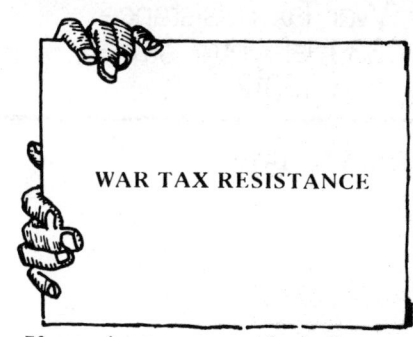

WAR TAX RESISTANCE

If we ignore or neglect the great potential of tax resistance joined to constructive action, we must be deaf to history and blind to experience.

Deaf to history. Do we not know that tax resistance has been one of the greatest sources and strategies of revolutionary movements throughout history? Has not history shown that taxation is a process requiring the general consent and cooperation of the populace? Has it not been shown that when numbers of people reject a government by withdrawing their consent from the elaborate bureaucratic process of taxation, that government is in deep trouble? Did not the French Revolution begin with tax resistance? Was not the Estates General called into session by the King because he found it impossible to raise sufficient revenue for the operation of his government? Was not tax resistance the slogan and rallying cry of the American Revolution: "Taxation without representation is tyranny!"? Does not the Boston Tea Party, an act of resistance to taxation, stand in our historical tradition as a model for the actions of the Baltimore Four, the Catonsville Nine, the Boston Two, the Milwaukee Fourteen, the D.C. Nine, and the Chicago Fifteen? Did not Thoreau fashion the cornerstone of American resistance theory out of his own experience as a tax resister? Was not Gandhi's largest and most significant campaign of civil disobedience, the Salt March, based on the strategy of tax resistance?

Blind to experience. Can we not see what the I.R.S. knows full well: that even where the public gives general consent to the process of taxation it is always and everywhere a grudging and tentative consent, a resentful and querulous consent, a fragile consent that must always be nursed and safeguarded by positive public relations? Why has the I.R.S. trodden so lightly in prosecuting principled tax refusers, usually concentrating instead on ineffectual attempts at collection? Is it not because there exists among the public at large a greater reservoir of grievance, a potential of sympathy for tax resisters, and, what is more, a vast subliminal potential for tax resistance and evasion, that only needs to be aroused by news of widespread tax resistance?

From "A Fund for Mankind" by Karl Meyer, *Catholic Worker* Oct-Nov 1969

IRS Raided

On January 13, as requested in a letter from the Internal Revenue Service, I appeared at their main office with a little help from (ten of) my friends.

The IRS officials were quite disturbed by the presence of our "community of Resistance". Their intended purpose of the meeting was to discuss my tax liability of $16.70 (accumulated telephone tax). Our purpose was to discuss the war in Vietnam and their complicity in murder.

Mr. Gomella, the young official who had "invited" me there went into immediate conference with several of his superiors, who in turn called the police.

We unrolled a huge poster of the My Lai massacre and I asked, "Is this what you want me to pay for?" Some of the IRS officials looked sickened and left the room. Others entered and we asked their position on the war and the killing. We told them that we knew the telephone excise tax was specifically for the war. We were all asked to leave, when Mr. Gomella offered to meet privately with me. He was promptly put down by his superiors.

As we slowly departed (we left behind a copy of the Nuremberg Principles, which they said they would read), we held the My Lai poster up high, showing it to a good many of the workers. As we passed through the official waiting area with our poster, we cried out, "You can claim these people as your dependents."

All in all we kept at least ten IRS officials occupied for about a half hour, interrupting their "business as usual" schedule.

Instead of dismissing "invitations" from IRS as most of us have done in the past, we are encouraging other people to attend such hearings with as much community support as they can gather. We're also trying to re-schedule hearings that we've passed up, knowing that we'll have an official opportunity to go up and hassle at least once a week.

Tax Talk 2/13/70

Ken Sherman
Philadelphia, Pa.

Tax Talk

published by War Tax Resistance
339 lafayette street
nyc 10012

Bradford Lyttle, Coordinator   February 13, 1970

Following my Conscience

Director of Internal Revenue
Denver, Colorado

Dear Sir:

Recently I claimed more exemptions than I am entitled to claim so that no further income tax will be withheld from my checks.

I realize that this puts me into conflict with federal law, but I find I must now choose between the laws of man and the laws of God. I am told "Thou shalt not kill" and given no exceptions, while my government says I must support the butchery in Vietnam or go to jail. By paying for the bullets I am as guilty as the the man who pulls the trigger or the president who orders this slaughter.

I see my tax monies being spent all over the world to suppress the poor. In Vietnam we support the landlords against the landless peasants. In Latin America we supply the super-rich with tanks and guns to suppress their poor. In America my taxes are spent to beef up the forces of "law and order" to protect the "haves" from the Blacks, Mexicans, Indians, and poor whites whose alleged crime is a burning desire for food, housing, clothing, and medical care for their children. What little is spent on their welfare is mere tokenism and only serves to humiliate them.

I am 35 years old, a factory laborer, and the father of six children. I did my share of "commie" killing in 1952 in Korea only to see South Korea turned over to a handpicked military dictatorship of the worst kind. I mention this only so that you will know it is not only the young who have had a belly full of power-crazed, corrupt, insensitive leadership.

Since I have no control over how my tax dollars will be spent and any dollar I give to you could buy bullets for further violence against the poor, I can no longer pay my taxes. The money that I would normally pay in income taxes I will give directly to a charity of my own choice—which is as it should be in a free society.

If you, Sir, choose to remain an instrument of a government gone mad, that is your affair. You can always claim that you were "just following orders"; but I have finally reached a point in my life when I must begin following my conscience.

In peace,
Gary Cox

Tax Talk 2/13/70

AN OPEN LETTER TO THE CORPORATIONS OF AMERICA

Today, March 22, 1969, in the Washington office of the Dow Chemical Company we spill human blood and destroy files and office equipment. By this action, we condemn you, the Dow Chemical Company, and all similar American Corporations.

We are outraged by the death-dealing exploitation of people of the Third World, and of all the poor and powerless who are victimized by your profit-seeking ventures. Considering it our responsibility to respond, we deny the right of your faceless and inhuman corporation to exist:

you, corporations, who under the cover of stockholder and executive anonymity, exploit, deprive, dehumanize and kill in search of profit;

you, corporations, who contain (or control) Americans and exploit their exaggerated need for security that you have helped create;

you, corporations, who numb our sensitivity to persons, and capitalize on our concern for things.

Specifically, we warn you, Dow Chemical Company, that we will no longer tolerate your refusal to accept responsibility for your programmed destruction of human life.

You, stockholders and company executives alike, are so willing to seek profit in the production of napalm, defoliants, nerve gas, as in the same spirit you co-operated with the I. G. Farben Company, a chemical manufacturer in Nazi Germany, during the Second World War.

You, who without concern for development for other nations or for their rights of self-determination, maintain 100% control over subsidiaries in more than twenty nations.

You, who in the interest of profit, seek to make it in the military interest of the United States to suppress the legitimate national desires of other peoples. Your product is death, your market is war.

Your offices have lost their right to exist. It is a blow for justice that we strike today.

In your mad pursuit of profit, you and others like you, are causing the psychological and physical destruction of mankind. We urge all to join us as we say "no" to this madness.

(Signed) Rev. Robert Begin, Rev. Bernard Meyer, Rev. Joseph O'Rourke, S.J., Rev. Dennis Maloney, Mr. Michael Slaski, Rev. Michael Dougherty, S.J., Sr. Joann Malone SL, Rev. Arthur Melville, Mrs. Catherine Melville.

Statement of the D. C. 9

BEAVER 55 STRIKES AGAIN

Over the weekend, St. Paul and Minneapolis, Minn. was the scene of a massive action to destroy U.S. ability to wage war in Vietnam.

A group calling itself Beaver 55 raided Selective Service offices in 3 separate locations. All 1-A and 1-A delinquent draft files along with ledger books and cross references were destroyed in local boards 27 thru 48 in Hennepin County and 87-98 in Ramsey County. The State office building housing all duplicate files was also ransacked and thousands of back-up files for those boards were destroyed. The group announced its support of the Provisional Revolutionary Government of South Vietnam and denounced the draft for "perpetuating and inflicting male chauvinism in our culture."

These actions will probably stop any possible induction from these local boards for up to a year. This will cripple almost 50% of the entire Selective Service System in the state. This is the largest and most effective strike against the Selective Service System of its kind and the first time a State office was invaded.

The group, Beaver 55, was responsible for actions against 44 draft boards in Indianapolis Oct. 31, and Dow Chemical Company November 7. It seems these actions are continuing as the group said they would.

WIN, April 70

Draft board raids up

An incomplete listing on draft board and Dow Chemical Co. raids (The Dow raids are of the same genre and often are conducted by the same people) shows that they have become much more frequent as the Vietnam war has dragged on.

There was a kind of freak raid on a Minnesota draft board in 1966, but the one that is generally credited—or blamed—with starting the movement was the four-person raid at the Baltimore Customs House Oct. 27, 1967. Father Berrigan was among the raiders who poured blood on the draft records.

The federal charges were destroying government property and interfering with the Selective Service system's operation. These charges have since become fairly standard wherever federal prosecution of draft board raids is undertaken.

The next step was the May 17, 1968 raid by the Catonsville 9—Catonsville is a Baltimore suburb—and this precipitated not only federal but also Maryland state charges, including arson. Most of the state charges eventually were dropped.

Next came the Sept. 14, 1968, raid by the Milwaukee 14. In this case, two of the raiders pleaded guilty to federal charges but eventually federal charges against all other defendants were dropped because it proved impossible to get an impartial jury.

The pace was stepped up this year. It went like this:

—March 22 the D.C. 9 invaded Dow Chemical's Washington office. They are charged with three federal felony counts—burglary, and two counts of property destruction—and come to trial Feb. 3 in a federal court in the District of Columbia.

—May 20, the Pasadena 3 invaded an induction center in that Los Angeles suburb, took 600 1-A files and burned them in a field. They got three years in federal prison.

—May 21, the Silver Spring 3 invaded a draft board in that Maryland suburb of Washington, threw paint on the files and destroyed equipment. Two of the three pleaded nolo contendere—one who'd broken bond was sent to jail while a second was sent to a federal youth center at Morgantown, W.Va.—and the third raider, a 17-year-old, got three years' probation.

—May 25, the Chicago 15 invaded a South Side Chicago draft board, took files down a fire escape and burned them. They await federal trial at the end of January; the state did not press charges.

—July 4, the New York 5, led by Maggie Geddes, invaded a Rockefeller Center draft board, shredded 6,500 1-A files, damaged 1-A keys on typewriters and destroyed cross-reference books. Miss Geddes was not arrested but the other four were. The federal case against them was dismissed but they could be re-indicted.

—Aug. 2, in the Bronx and Aug. 15 in Jamaica, Long Island, the New York 8 invaded draft boards and damaged records. Later in the month they surfaced and accepted responsibility for the acts. No prosecution so far.

—In mid-October two Clevelanders set fire to draft board records in Akron and later surfaced in a Cleveland cathedral, claiming responsibility for the act. No prosecution so far.

—On Oct. 31, the Beaver 55—who were not 55 but only eight and were named whimsically by Tom Trost, one of the group—shredded records of 44 Indianapolis draft boards, according to their later statement. No prosecution so far.

—Nov. 7, the Washington Dow Chemical offices were hit again, with files strewn and ink and chemicals splashed around. A short statement left in the office said it was wrong to "put profit before people," invoked support for the Beaver 55, the D.C. 9 and the Ohio group and was signed, "D.C. 54½."

The person who carried this out surfaced the next day; he was one of the Akron draft board invaders. No prosecution so far.

—Nov. 7, the Boston 8 entered four Boston locations housing eight draft boards and shredded files. The Boston 8 surfaced the morning and afternoon of Nov. 15 in Washington and distributed Boston draft files around the mall and the reflecting pool between the Washington Monument and Lincoln Memorial. No prosecution so far.

Nov. 7, the Beaver 55 invaded Dow Chemical's data center in Midland, Mich., and erased magnetic tapes filled with biological and chemical research. They surfaced at a Nov. 16 Washington press conference (which was widely unreported); five of the Beavers were arrested in Midland and held on $20,000 bond apiece under state charges.

—Nov. 11, the Silver Spring draft board was revisited by the youngest of the original Silver Spring 3, plus the two Clevelanders who had worked over the Akron draft board. They took out the files and left them on a railroad track. They were spotted and held on federal charges; bond is $10,000 apiece.

The trick in all this seems to be to not get caught and then surface at some distance from the deed and with sufficient vagueness so that no evidence is available for prosecution.

What about other profiteers? Lockheed, GE, General Dynamics, McDonnell-Douglas, United Aircraft, AT&T, Ling-Temco-Vought, No. Amer. Rockwell, Boeing, GM, Honeywell, Ford, Olin, Standard Oil, IBM, MIT, etc.?

CHICAGO:

"MAYOR DALEY IS THE BALL GAME" ROBERT KENNEDY 1968

Truth About Tear Gas

CHAPTER 5-WHY CS IS BETTER
By LAKE ERIE CHEMICAL

Law enforcement agencies throughout the U.S. are building up their stocks of tear gas and training in its use. Police officers are following advice like that in the FBI's riot control manual, which concludes that chemical agents are the most effective, humane means of temporarily neutralizing a mob, while minimizing personal injury.

But many are wondering which *kind* of agent to get. The older CN ("tear gas")? Or the more powerful irritant agent, CS?

The National Advisory Commission on Civil Disorders has indicated in its report that CS has been found by the military to be considerably more effective and safer than CN. The Commission has expressed an opinion that the only currently available alternative to using CS is applying potentially lethal force, and has strongly recommended the use of CS before rifles or bayonets.

Although Lake Erie makes both agents, we recommend CS.

The first dose does it.

Simply stated . . . CS is the most apt to stop a riot so it can't restart! Though all rioters will run out of a cloud of either agent, the big difference is this . . .

After 10 minutes or so of "recovery" in fresh air, determined rioters may have forgotten the effects of CN to the point where they're ready to start trouble again, a block or two away. But if they've had a dose of CS, they're through for the day. (And maybe for the year.) CS has *extremely* sobering effects on a lawbreaker, including burning sensations and the feeling he can't breathe. These, added to the tears, are so psychologically demoralizing, even in memory, that wild horses couldn't drag him back.

Another point: CS grenades, properly used, are almost impossible to throw back. It would be difficult to find even a fanatic with the nerve to pick one up, without a mask.

Yet, according to a large body of impressive evidence, CS has proven extremely safe. More and more police departments are switching from CN to CS. And in our experience, not one has wanted to switch back.

Want more evidence?

Send for an authoritative article on the subject, which we have reprinted with the permission of ORDNANCE magazine.

And let us know what you need.

Lake Erie Chemical has been the leader in CS, the first to introduce it to commercial markets in the U. S. in 1962. We continue to offer either CS or CN in all Lake Erie grenades and projectiles. Your Lake Erie distributor will take fast action to supply your needs.

Help with more than tear gas.

Lake Erie Chemical is a member of Smith & Wesson's growing Law Enforcement Group, manufacturers whose aims and products all share one characteristic: dedication to the professionalism of the American police officer and to the protection of the public he serves.

The group now includes, in addition to Smith & Wesson and Lake Erie: General Ordnance Equipment Corp. (CHEMICAL MACE®); Stephenson Co. ("Speedalyzer" radar, BREATH-ALYZER®, Minuteman resuscitators); and Dominator Company (electronic sirens, radar).

Contact your Lake Erie Distributor.

And for reprints of this advertisement, the article mentioned above, or our catalog . . . Write to Lake Erie Chemical Division, Smith & Wesson, Rock Creek, Ohio 44084. (Cable Address: LECCO, CLEVELAND.)

Lake Erie Chemical Division.
SMITH & WESSON
Agents in principal cities of the U.S.A. and
in every country of the free world.

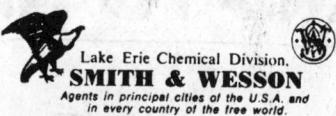

CN may stop here . . . CS keeps them running home

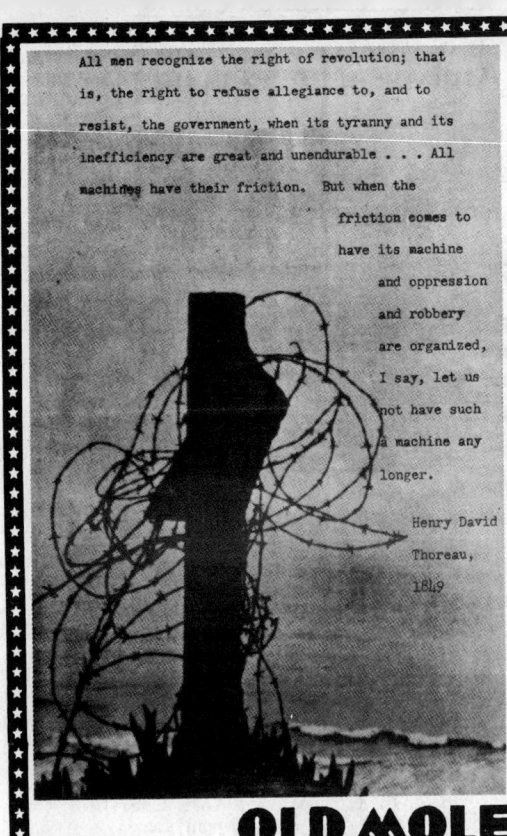

All men recognize the right of revolution; that is, the right to refuse allegiance to, and to resist, the government, when its tyranny and its inefficiency are great and unendurable . . . All machines have their friction. But when the friction comes to have its machine and oppression and robbery are organized, I say, let us not have such a machine any longer.

Henry David Thoreau, 1849

OLD MOLE

Paradoxically and unexpectedly, the Democratic convention in Chicago proved that the nation's political system is valid and viable.

The New York Times

Outside the Hilton Hotel, Chicago, August 1968.

AN APPEAL TO THE TROOPS AND TO THE POLICE

TWO LEAFLETS
FROM CHICAGO:
SUMMER 1968

An Appeal to the Troops

We Know that you're here under orders. Maybe you want to know why WE'RE here.

We're here because we — the entire American people — were double-crossed in 1964 by an Administration that promised peace and practiced war. We're here to say that the Johnson Administration has no right to perpetuate itself.

We have exercised our Constitutional right of free assembly for years, all across this country, in front of fancy hotels — the Waldorf, the Beverly Wilshire, the Conrad Hilton — where the men who rule this country wine and dine and plot their deeds of death.

It was only when we came to Chicago, the world capital of crime, that we were denied our rights at gunpoint. It's up to you, now, not to let American democracy go down the drain. (You six-monthers sensed the war was rotten and futile; you US's and RA's have seen for yourselves). It's up to you to let us stand in front of the Amphitheater.

We are not going to charge the delegates (we don't have the instruments of force and aren't going to use force). But we insist on our right to stand witness against this evil deed — the abandonment of the peace plank and the nomination of Lyndon Johnson's flunky.

To the Police

Our argument in Chicago is not with you.

We have come to confront the rich men of power who ordered America into a war she voted against. . .The men who have brought our country to the point where the police can no longer serve and protect the people — only themselves.

We know you're underpaid.

We know you have to buy your own uniforms.

You often get the blame and rarely get the credit in day-in day-out situations.

Now you're on 12-hour shifts and not being paid overtime.

You should realize we aren't the ones who created the terrible conditions in which you work. This nightmare-week was arranged by Richard Daley and Lyndon Johnson, who decided we shouldn't have the right to express ourselves as free people.

We understand — and you should, too — that you are simply the servants of Daley and Johnson.

Our prayer is for the day when you can again become the servants — no, the friends — of the people.

As we march, as we stand before the Amphitheater, we will be looking forward to the day when your job is easier, when you can perform your traditional tasks, and no one orders you to deprive your fellow Americans of their rights of free speech and assembly.

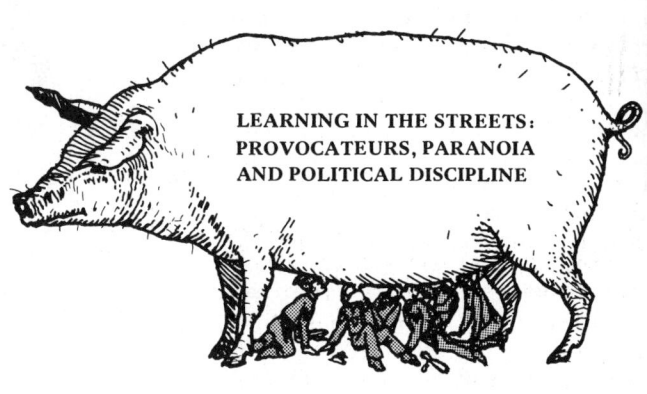

pigs

Street Sense

LEARNING IN THE STREETS: PROVOCATEURS, PARANOIA AND POLITICAL DISCIPLINE

Watch the man who casts the first stone. He may be a cop.

There's nothing like a week in Chicago to clear the mind of adolescent machismo fantasy. I saw smart street tactics keep the body healthy and the way clear, win friends and influence people. And I saw foolhardy moves -- the kind Communists like to call "adventurist" -- pass all initiative to the cops, isolate us and cost us broken limbs and cheated intentions. A street tactician I'm not, but it doesn't take a maquisard to know that the police also have objectives on the street.

Consider these recent episodes in what is, after all, an age-old saga of deceit:

Item: The prime witness against the R.A.M. people in New York was an infiltrator who had talked up assassinations and stockpiled material.

Item: August 28 in Grant Park, Chicago, the cops charged into the crowd, swinging. They intervened because someone had pulled down the American flag. One of the flag-pullers -- according to the Chicago Tribune, a public relations branch of the Police Department -- was Robert Pierson, Jerry Rubin's bodyguard, an undercover cop playing motorcycle heavy. Pierson also tried to instigate the seizing of intersections in dangerous circumstances, but wiser heads prevailed.

Item: The Peninsula Observer has pointed out before that the demonstrators who first hurled bags of blood at the cops in front of the Fairmont last winter had never been seen in friendly circles before or since.

Item: The guy who broke an office window in the Administration Building at SF State last May was -- you guessed it -- a plainclothes cop.

Question: Who molotoved the Highway Patrolman in Berkeley last July, setting Wayne Greene up for the rap?

Question: Who smashed the Bank of America windows in Berkeley? Who shot the cop? When I got back from the inscrutable East, friends were casting dire suspicions like so many tacks on the street. "Must have been cops, nobody else would be that stupid."

Of course it's not so simple, and we have to judge delicately; in case somebody hasn't noticed, this is no game. A tactic can't be appraised apart from here-and-now circumstances. Moving into the street, breaking windows, wrecking insufferable property, etc., sometimes makes sense, sometimes not. You can't know unless you have a purpose. Spontaneity in the street is like bennies in alcohol: one might (MIGHT) send you high, but chances are you'll hurt, and hurt bad. Know what you are doing and harness means to ends.

Unfortunately, delicate judgments in these raging days are falling afoul of a fetishism of the streets: that is why we have a hard time telling the cops from the desperados. We are living through some profound crisis of masculinity, explained but not wholly justified by the struggle to shake off middle class burdens of bland civility. The guy who hits hardest and moves fastest begins to look like the biggest revolutionary cock; it doesn't seem to matter whom he hits, where he runs.

Some organizers in Chicago were entranced by a mystique of the Park People, a melting pot of motorcycle greasers, working class ethnics, blacks, a few hillbillies, hard Old Town hippies (all young and ready to fight), and mystery youth -- including not a few plainclothes dicks. Now Jerry Rubin's right when he says that when we welcome the fighting people into our ranks with open arms we have to risk inviting the finks along with the pinks. All the more reason to fix our own objectives and shirk mystiques. We want to organize the castaways, not become their least reliable selves.

Finally I know of no easy sorting out system. Even as we move beyond the mystique of violence, our salvation demands that we constantly extend the

Two plainclothes pigs just before they attacked a Berkeley crowd. The one in the foreground has a blackjack; in the background, another goes inside his jacket to draw a pistol.

streets and propagandizing by the deed; in the nature of our movement we will attract provocateurs, and we can't tell the players without a scorecard. That scorecard is unwritten except in the slippery terrain of our separate common senses, seeming to leave us with nothing but paranoia.

And the police would like nothing better than to have all militancy discredited under suspicion of provocative trickery, all trust shattered by curse and countercurse. Always looking over your shoulder, you trip over your own feet, or stand still in cynical safety. A puzzle.

The only working solution is in political discipline. Know what you want to do, and then you have solid ground to refuse to follow people who take you where you don't want to go. Use strategy as a code to define pro-

whether the outlaws are cops or simply madmen: you'll avoid them and find ways to handle them, so suspicion won't spiral endlessly from every accusation.

After the NSA-CIA disclosures, radicals frittered away countless hours wondering whether Al Lowenstein was really an agent, whether So-and-So had been "witting" or "unwitting." It didn't matter, any more than it matters whether the Ford Foundation funnels money from the CIA or whether the guy who molotoved the Highway Patrolman was really a cop. The consequences are the same. And a serious revolutionary movement knows how to judge the consequences of its acts -- this is its reason, and its magic, too.

--Todd Gitlin

San Francisco
Express Times Sept 1968

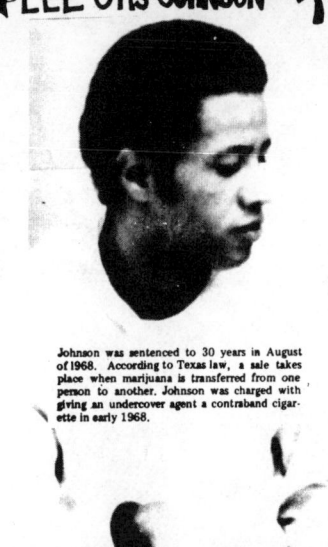

Johnson was sentenced to 30 years in August of 1968. According to Texas law, a sale takes place when marijuana is transferred from one person to another. Johnson was charged with giving an undercover agent a contraband cigarette in early 1968.

CO-ORDINATING IN THE STREETS

by Paul Potter

Although they received absolutely no publicity in the mass media, one of the most important links in the success of the protests at the Democratic Convention was the operation of thirty-five Movement Centers. Working out of churches, the offices of friendly organizations and a couple of unions, the Movement Centers provided a principle organizational focus for a large number of people in Chicago. Perhaps as many as one thousand people considered themselves Movement Center staff and several thousand others were living in the Centers and working

closely with them.

The idea of Movement Centers developed early in June in response to two problems. First it seemed impossible to tell how many and what kind of people would show up in Chicago. Most people thought there would be an enormous number of McCarthy supporters who would try to push McCarthy over the top with gigantic street demonstrations. But it also seemed possible that as military preparations received more publicity and McCarthy's defeat seemed inescapable that a smaller though far more militant group of people would come to Chicago. These and other possibilities made it

necessary to have a flexible way of approaching the situation as it developed.

Had the overwhelming majority of people in Chicago been McCarthy supporters the Movement Centers could easily have worked as a radical caucus operation designed to reach and recruit them. But as the situation developed we were able to use the Movement Centers as staging areas for action and strategic coordination.

Decentralization

Second, a four day action as diverse and complicated as the one called for Chicago made the decentralization of initiative and responsibility an absolute necessity. There was no way for the Mobilization Steering Committee and its staff to plan the details of each day's activities and communicate that to thousands (potentially tens of thousands) of people around the city. This was particularly true when it was assumed that tactics would have to change from day

562
Resistance

to day in response to events (read: police).

Furthermore there was general agreement that even if the Mobilization could dictate strategy it shouldn't. One of the things we wanted to demonstrate in Chicago (to ourselves as well as the world) was the political diversity and richness of our Movement; its ability to share and pursue simple objectives without turning itself into a machine or a monolith.

The idea as it developed called for inviting a number of organizations, regional groups and issue-oriented constituencies to set up Centers in the city. The Centers would provide a way for people to sort themselves out in Chicago, take initiative in numerous small actions organized through the Centers, and provide the Mobilization with a flexible strategy and intelligence mechanism.

For example a resistance person coming to Chicago would naturally gravitate to one of the resistance centers. An SDSer to one of the SDS centers. The idea was to allow people to locate themselves in a place where they would feel politically at home. The hope was that this would reduce sectarian tensions and allow for more work to take place.

As a staff operation and a locus of activity we wanted each Movement Center to be involved in evaluating what was happening day by day and through a coordinating committee of Movement Centers we hoped to be able to gather a lot of information on what was happening and then to knit that into an overview of what should be done. This would be a much more effective way of keeping track of things than to let a steering committee made up of persons with bureaucratic responsibilities dictate the planning.

In addition the Movement Centers as politically more compatible and coherent groups than the Mobilization could raise the level of political discussion and education.

Of course, things worked differently than planned. Very few of the Movement Centers were prepared to exercise much initiative in Chicago. Only a few local demonstrations focused on political targets scattered around the city (e.g. Draft Boards, Military installations, Dow and other corporate war contractors etc.) materialized. Nor did the Centers initiate much guerila theatre, leafletting or civil disobedience of any sort. They simply lacked enough internal organization and familiarity with Chicago to move effectively. The centers themselves were scattered throughout the city whereas the people were concentrated first in Lincloln Park and later in Grant Park. Recruiting people to relate to a Center or some action it was organizing meant going into the parks and talking to them, leafletting and using the two wall papers that were circulating for publicity. But most centers weren't prepared to do this.

Partly the Mobilization failed to do an early enough, or thorough enough job of working with the people who were putting the centers together, although we were hindered by the fact that so many groups waited until the last minute to come in. We needed a nucleus of people from each Center who were thoroughly familiar with the areas we were concentrating in; our legal and medical operations, how to use the wall papers, publicity, the internal communication system the Mobilization established, transportation, etc. Without this complicated understanding people spent much of their time learning how to survive in the city.

Mostly, however, the shortcomings of the Movement Centers were the shortcomings of anything complex that is being tried for the first time. The Movement Centers more than anything else kept people together and gave them a way to concentrate on the problems of survival. And survival was the key problem in Chicago. Many of the Centers did no more than to provide people with a place to eat and crash as well as offering physical and emotional shelter from what was going on in the streets. But it was things like this that enabled people to survive and carry on the action.

Real Street Leadership

Had the city responded less fascisticly, failures of initiative would have been more obvious and serious, but as it was, keeping people alive and together was exactly where energy had to be directed. Most of the real street leadership in Chicago came out of the Movement Centers and more than anything else the Centers kept morale high. Finally, some important initiatives did come out of the more organized Centers -- e.g. the SDS wall paper which spoke very effectively to what people were experiencing or the PFP organized support of the wildcat transit strike that went on during the Convention.

Despite the diversity of groups running centers (Committee of Returned Volunteers, SDS, Vets for Peace, Resistance, People Against Racism, N.Y. Parade Committee), the level of sectarianism in Chicago was almost zero. This was due largely to the tremendous unifying force of events, but even if that had been less true the structured legitimacy for diversity that the Movement Centers represented pretty well eliminated the need for people to claw one another for a scrap of the pie or the credit. It was almost the only occasion that I can recall when the broad anti-war coalition that most people agree should exist actually worked together happily.

There is no doubt that if we had it to do all over again we could do it much better and more effectively. To begin with, organizations should not be reluctant to run Movement Centers. That would allow us to thoroughly familiarize people from each Movement Center with the logistics of the city and the internal organization of the Mobilization -- e.g., how to use our internal communication system. It would allow us to initiate much in advance a more thoroughgoing discussion of strategy and tactics for each Movement Center. That in itself is reason enough to hope that Chicago represents the beginning of a new kind of mass action in this country. ∎

the**MOVEMENT** Oct 1968

VISIONS
OF
CHICAGO

To the Hippies

Hippies, young people of the demonstration, you no longer belong to America, which has moreover repudiated you. Hippies with long hair, you are making America's hair curl. But you, between earth and sky, are the beginning of a new continent, an Earth of Fire rising strangely above, or hollowed out below, what once was this sick country — an earth of fire first and, if you like, an earth of flowers. But you must begin, here and now, another continent.

The First Day:
The Day of the Thighs

The thighs are very beautiful beneath the blue cloth, thick and muscular. It all must be hard. This policeman is also a boxer, a wrestler. His legs are long, and perhaps, as you approach his member, you would find a furry nest of long, tight, curly hair. That is all I can see — and I must say it fascinates me — that and his boots, but I can guess that these superb thighs extend on up into an imposing member and a muscled torso, made even firmer every day by his police training in the cops' gymnasium. Higher up, into his arms and hands which must know how to put a black man or a thief out of action.

In the compass of his well-built thighs, I can see. . .but the thighs have moved, and I can see that they are splendid: America has a magnificent, divine, athletic police force, often photographed and seen in dirty books. . .but the thighs have parted slightly, ever so slightly, and through the crack which extends from the knees to the too-heavy member, I can see. . .why, it's the whole panorama of the Democratic Convention with its star-spangled banners, its star-spangled prattle, its star-spangled dresses, its star-spangled undress, its star-spangled candidates, in short the whole ostentatious parade, but the color has too many facets, as you have seen on your television sets.

The Second Day:
The Day of the Visor

The truth of the matter is that we are bathed in a Mallarmean blue. This second day imposes the azure helmets of the Chicago police. A policeman's black leather visor intrudes between me and the world: a gleaming visor in whose tidy reflections I may be able to read the world, wittingly kept in top condition by numerous, and doubtless daily, polishings. Supporting this visor is the blue cap — Chicago wants us to think that the whole police force, and this policeman standing in front of me, have descended from heaven — made of a top-grade sky-blue cloth. But who is this blue cop in front of me? I look into his eyes, and I can see nothing else there except the blue of the cap. What does his gaze say? Nothing. The Chicago police are, and are not. I shall not pass. The visor and the gaze are there. The visor so gleaming that I can see myself and lose myself in it. I've got to see the continuation of the allegedly Democratic Convention, but the cop in the black visor with the blue eyes is there. Beyond him, I can nonetheless catch a glimpse of a lighted sign above the convention floor: there is an eye and "CBS News," the structure of which in French as in English, reminds me of "obscene." But who is this policeman in the blue cap and black visor? He is so handsome I could fall into his arms. I look again at his look: at long last I recognize it; it is the look of a beautiful young girl, voluptuous and tender, which is hiding beneath a black visor and blue cap. She loves this celestial color: the Chicago police are feminine and brutal. It does not want its ladies to meekly obey their husbands whose hair is sky blue, dressed in robes of many colors. . .

The Third Day:
The Day of the Belly

Chicago has fed these policemen's bellies which are so fat that one must presume that they live on the slaughterhouses required by a city which resembles three hundred Hamburgs piled one on top of the other, and daily consumes three million hamburgers. A policeman's beautiful belly has to be seen in profile: the one barring my route is a medium-sized belly (deGaulle could qualify as a cop in Chicago). It is medium-sized, but it is well on its way to perfection. Its owner wheedles it, fondles it with both his beautiful but heavy hands. Where did they all come from? Suddenly we are surrounded by a sea of policemen's bellies barring our entrance into the Democratic Convention. When I am finally allowed in, I will understand more clearly the harmony which exists between these bellies and the bosoms of the lady-patriots at the Convention — there is harmony but also rivalry: the arms of the ladies of the gentlemen who rule America have the girth of the policemen's thighs. Walls of bellies. And walls of policemen who encircle us, astonished by our appearance at the Democratic Convention, furious at the unconventional way we're dressed: they are thinking that we are thinking what they know, that is that the Democratic Convention is the Holy of Holies.

About ten o'clock this evening, part of America has detached itself from the American fatherland and remains suspended between earth and sky. The hippies have gathered in an enormous hall, as starkly bare as the Convention Hall is gaudy. Here all is joy, and in the enthusiasm several hippies burn their draft cards, holding them high for everyone to see: they will not be soldiers, but they may well be prisoners for five years. The hippies ask me to come up onto the stage and say a few words: this youth is beautiful and very gentle. It is celebrating the Un-Birthday of a certain Johnson who, it seems to me, hasn't yet been born. Allen Ginsberg is voiceless: he has chanted too loud and too long in Lincoln Park the night before.

Order, real order, is here: I recognize it. It is the freedom offered to everyone to discover and create himself.

Too many star-spangled flags: here, as in Switzerland, a flag in front of every house. America is Switzerland flattened out by a steamroller. Lots of young blacks: will the delegates' hot dogs or the revolver bullet murder the democrats before it is too late?

Fabulous happening. Hippies! Glorious hippies, I address my final appeal to you: children, flower children in every country, in order to fuck all the old bastards who are giving you a hard time, unite, go underground if necessary in order to join the burned children of Vietnam. — *Translated by Richard Seaver*

From "The members of the assembly" by Jean Genet, *Esquire* Nov 1968

The Conspiracy 7: Top, from left; Lee Weiner, Dave Dellinger, Jerry Rubin, and Tom Hayden. Bottom, from left; John Froines, Renny Davis and Abbie Hoffman. Bobby Seale, constantly denied bail, couldn't make the picture.

INDICTMENT: "IT IS OBSCENE. . ."

It is obscene for a government which has accelerated the bombing in Vietnam to daily levels four times that of the heaviest bombing raids of World War II to indict those who are trying to put an end to the slaughter. It is hypocrisy for an administration which has refused to withdraw its troops from Vietnam and therefore bears the responsibility for the death of 453 Americans in a single week to indict us for travelling to Chicago to demand an end to the war. The government which uses napalm to incinerate little children has huffed and puffed and tried to save its honor by indicting us on trumped-up charges of teaching the use of incendiary devices. The government which by its own admission has tapped our phones and sent spies and provocateurs to our meetings has indicted a former employee of NBC for placing a microphone in a Democratic Party committee meeting. We are proud to have our words and actions made public but the people who rule this country cannot afford to submit their deliberations to public scrutiny.

DAVE DELLINGER

A lack of faith is simply a lack of courage
one who says "I wish I could believe that" means simply that he
is coward, is pleased
to be spectator, on this scene where there are no spectators
where all hands, not actually working are working against
as they lie idle, folded in lap, or holding up newspapers
full of lies, or wrapped around steering wheel, on one more
pleasure trip

When you seize Columbia, when you
seize Paris, take
the media, tell the people what you're doing
what you're up to and why and how you mean
to do it, how they can help, keep the news
coming, steady, you have 70 years
of media conditioning to combat, it is a wall
you must get through, somehow, to reach
the instinctive man, who is struggling like a plant
for light, for air.

When you seize a town, a campus, get hold of the power
stations, the water, the transportation,
forget to negotiate, forget how
to negotiate, don't wait for DeGaulle or Kirk
to abdicate, they won't, you are not
"demonstrating" you are fighting
a war, fight to win, don't wait for Johnson or
Humphrey or Rockefeller, to agree to your terms
take what you need, "it's free
because it's yours"

Can you
own land, can you
own house, own rights
to other's labor (stocks, or factories
or money, loaned at interest)
what about
the yield of same, crops, autos
airplanes dropping bombs, can you
own real estate, so others
pay rent? to whom
does the water belong, as it gets rarer?
the american indians say that a man
can own no more than he can carry away
on his horse.

Left to themselves people
grow their hair.
Left to themselves they
take off their shoes.
Left to themselves they make love
sleep easily
share blankets, dope & children
they are not lazy or afraid
they plant seeds, they smile, they
speak to one another. The word
coming into its own: touch of love
on the brain, the ear.
We return with the sea, the tides
We return as often as leaves, as numerous
as grass gentle, insistent, we remember
the way,
our babes toddle barefoot thru the cities
of the universe.

"DOES THE END
JUSTIFY THE MEANS?" this is
process, there is not end, there are only
means, each one
had better justify itself.
To whom?

not all the works of Mozart worth one human life
not all the brocades of the Potala palace
better we should wear homespun, than some in orlon
some in Thailand silk
the children of Bengal weave gold thread in silk saris
six years old, eight years old, for export, they don't sing
the singers are for export, Folkways records
better we should all have homemade flutes
and practice excruciatingly upon them, one hundred years
till we learn to
make our own music

THAT GODDAM FAG

...WITH LIBERTY AND JUSTICE FOR ALL.

& IF THE LAW IS ABSURD... WHAT THEN?

SUBTITLE: "BECAUSE I DON'T KNOW-UNDERSTAND..." - j. hoffman

The trial of the Conspiracy is a trial of one consciousness by another. On Thursday, December 11, Allen Ginsberg, poet and man of the planet, came to Julius Hoffman's courtroom to speak in behalf of Abbie Hoffman, Jerry Rubin, and the Yippie Festival of Life that fell before police clubs in Lincoln Park and on Michigan Avenue last August.

The following is an abridged transcript of Allen's testimony. It testifies to a meeting between an ancient life-force struggling to be born again and a decaying America that cannot understand anything we believe in—from Black Panthers to white magic.
—Abe Peck

Thursday: Len Weinglass for the defense asks the questions (Q).

Q. Will you please state your full name?

A. Allen Ginsberg.

Q. What is your occupation?

A. Poet.

Q. Have you authored any books in the field of poetry?

A. Yes.

Q. Will you indicate to the jury the titles of the books you have authored?

A. In 1956, "Howl and Other Poems;" in 1960, "Kaddish and Other Poems;" in 1963, "Empty Mirrors;" in 1963, "Reality Sandwiches;" and in 1968, "Planet News."

Q. Now, in addition to your writing, Mr. Ginsberg, are you presently engaged in any other activities?

A. I teach, lecture, and recite poetry

be-in is.

Witness. A gathering together of younger people aware of the planetary fate that we are all sitting in the middle of, imbued with a new consciousness and desiring of a new kind of society involving prayer, music and spiritual life together rather than competition and war...

(Allen then describes his first meeting with Abbie about Yippie.)

A . . .we talked about the possibility of extending the feeling of humanity and compassion of the human be-in in San Francisco to the City of Chicago during the time of the political convention, the possibility of inviting the same kind of younger people and the same kind of teachers who had been at the San Francisco human be-in to Chicago at the time of the convention in order to show some different new planetary life style than was going to be shown to the younger people by the politicians who were assembling . . .

(Allen went on to describe a phone conversation with Jerry about plans for Chicago).

A. Yes. He said that he thought it would be interesting if we could set up tents and areas within the park where kids could come and sleep, and set up little schools like ecology schools, music schools, political schools, schools about the Vietnam war, to go back into history, schools with Yogis.

He suggested that I contact whatever professional breathing exercise Yogi Swami teachers I could find and invite

laughter came from everybody that Mr. Kunstler is usually defending for laughing.

Kunstler. Your Honor, I would say—You mean from the press?

Witness. Might we go on to an explanation.

Court. Will you keep quiet, Mr. Witness, while I am talking to the lawyers?

Witness. I will be glad to give an explanation.

Court. I never laugh at a witness, sir. I protect witnesses who come to this court. They are entitled to the protection of the Court. But I do tell you that as I am sure you know, the language of American courts is English. The English language, unless we have an interpreter. You may use an interpreter for the remainder of this witness' testimony.

Kunstler. No. I have heard, your Honor, priests explain themselves in Latin in American courts and I think Mr. Ginsberg is doing exactly that same thing in Sanscrit for another type of religious experience.

Court. No, no. You are mistaken.

Kunstler. Your honor, I can't—

Court. I don't understand Sanscrit. I venture to say the members of the jury don't. Perhaps we have some people on the jury who do understand Sanscrit, I don't know, but I wouldn't even have known it was Sanscrit until he told me.

Weinglass. Let me ask this:

Mr. Ginsberg, I show you an object

Q. And another category listed under that?

A. Art.

Q. Another one under that?

A. Newspaper.

Q. Under that?

A. Religion.

Q. Under that?

A. Film.

Q. The next.

A. Sex.

Q. And the last one?

A. Games.

Q. And your name appears in which category?

A. The religious category.

(The meeting is then discussed. Weinglass asks him to say what was related.)

Q. Did the defendant Abbie Hoffman say anything at this meeting?

A. Abbie Hoffman said the park wasn't worth fighting for, that we had, on our responsibility, invited many thousands of kids to Chicago for a happy festival of life, for an alternative proposition to the festival of death that the politicians were putting on, and that it wasn't right to lead them or encourage them to get into a violent argument with the police over staying in the park overnight. He didn't know, he said he didn't know what to say to those who wanted to stay and fight for what they felt was their liberty, but he wasn't going to encourage anybody to fight, and he was going to leave when forced himself.

(Allen is asked what he did when the

at universities.

Q. Can you indicate to the jury without going extensively into your travels what your last trip in connection with teaching and lecturing consisted of?

A. I was at Princeton University for three days...

Q. Where have you studied?

A. In India and Japan.

Q. Could you indicate for the Court and jury what the area of your studies consisted of?

A. Mantra Yoga, Meditation exercises, chanting, and sitting quietly, stilling the mind and breathing exercises to calm the body and to calm the mind, but mainly a branch called Mantra Yoga, which is a Yoga which involves prayer and chanting...

All of these involve chanting and praying, praying out loud and in community.

Q. In the course of a Mantra chant, is there any particular position that the person doing that assumes?

A. Any position which will let the stomach relax and be easy, fall out, so that inspiration can be deep into the body, to relax the body completely and calm the mind, based as cross-legged.

Q. And is it, the chanting, to be done privately or is it in public?

Mr. Foran (prosecutor) Oh, your honor, I object...

The Court (Julius Hoffman) I think I have a vague idea of the witness' profession. It is vague.

Foran: I might indicate also that he is an excellent speller.

Court: I sustain the objection, but I notice that he has said first he was a poet, and I will give him credit for all of the other things, too, whatever they are.

Witness: Sir—

Court: Yes, sir.

Witness: In India, the profession of poetry and the profession of chanting are linked together as one practice.

Court: That's right. I give you credit for that.

(Allen says that he worked with Jerry Rubin on anti-war rallies in Berkeley during 1965, and was at the Human Be-In held in San Francisco in 1967.)

Q. Would you describe for the court and jury what the Be-In in San Francisco was?

Foran: Objection, your honor.

Court: Just a minute. I am not sure how you spell the be-in.

Weinglass: Be-in, I believe. Be-in.

Witness: Human be-in.

Court: I really can't pass on the validity of the objection because I don't know—understand the question.

Weinglass: I asked him to explain what a be-in was. I thought the question was directed to that possible confusion. He was interrupted in the course of the examination.

Foran: I would love to know also, but I don't think it has anything to do with this lawsuit.

Weinglass: Well, let's wait and find out.

Foran. This is San Francisco in 1967.

Court. I will let him, over the objection of the government, tell what a

them to Chicago and asked if I could contact Burroughs and ask Burroughs to come also to teach non-verbal, non-conceptual feeling states.

Q. Now you indicated a school of ecology. Could you explain to the court and jury what that is?

A. Ecology is the interrelation of all the living forms on the surface of the planet involving the food chain—that is to say, whales eat smaller fish, octopus or squid eat shell fish which eat plankton, human beings eat the octopus or squid or smaller fish which eat the smaller tiny microorganisms.

Foran. That is enough, your honor.

Court. You say that is enough.

Foran. I think that the question is now responsive.

Court. Yes. We all have a clear view now of what ecology is...

(Allen told about a Yippie press conference in March 1968.) ..the central motive would be a presentation of a desire for preservation of the planet. The desire for preservation of the planet and the planet's form, that we do continue to be, to exist on this planet instead of destroy the planet, was manifested to my mind by the great Mantra from India to the preserver God Vishnu whose Mantra is the Hare Krishna, and then I chanted the Hare Krishna Mantra for ten minutes to the television cameras and it goes:

Hare Krishna, Hare Krishna, Krishna Krishna

Hare Hare, Rama Rama Rama Rama Hare Hare.

Q. Now in chanting that did you have an accompaniment of any particular instrument?...

Court. By an instrument do you mean—

Kunstler. Your Honor, I object to the laughter of the Court on this... I think this is a serious presentation of a religious concept.

Court. I don't understand it. I don't understand it because it was—the language of the United States District Court is English.

Kunstler. I know, but you don't laugh at all languages.

Witness. I would be glad to explain it, sir.

Court. I didn't laugh. I didn't laugh.

Witness. I would be happy to explain it.

Court. I didn't laugh at all. I wish I could tell you how I feel. Laugh, I didn't even smile.

Kunstler. Well, I thought—

Court. All I could tell you is that I didn't understand the question.

Witness. Sanscrit, sir.

Court. What is it?

Witness. Sanscrit, sir.

Court. Sanscrit?

Witness. Yes.

Court. Well, that is one I don't know. That is the reason I didn't understand it.

Witness. There is a popular song put out by the Beatles with those words.

Court. I am not interested in—

Witness. Your Honor, of course the

marked 150 for identification, and I ask you to examine that object.

A. Yes.

Foran. All right.

(Allen opens a box and begins to play music on what everyone in the court suddenly learns is a harmonium).

Your Honor, that is enough. I object to it, Your Honor. I think that it is outrageous for counsel to—

Court. You asked him to examine it and instead of that he played a tune on it.

Foran. I mean, counsel is so clearly—

Court. I sustain the objection.

Foran. —talking about things that have no conceivable materiality to this case, and it is improper, your Honor.

Witness. It adds spirituality to the case, sir.

Court. Will you remain quiet, sir.

Witness. I am sorry.

Court. My obligation is to protect you, but my obligation is to see that you act in accordance with the law...

Q. Will you explain to the Court and to the jury what chant you were chanting at the press conference?

A. I was chanting a Mantra called the Maha Mantra, the Great Mantra of Preservation of that aspect of the Indian religion called Vishnu, the Preserver, whom every time human evil, human evil rises so high that the planet itself is threatened, and all of its inhabitants and their children are threatened, and Vishnu will preserve a return.

Court... When you offer anything in a foreign language, sir, and you think it is material, you must have an interpreter here so that the witness can be—

police showed in the park that night.)

Q. Without relating what you said to another person, Mr. Ginsberg, what did you do at the time you saw the police do this.

A. I started the chant, O-o-m-m-m-m-m, O-o-m-m-m-m-m.

Foran. All right, we have had a demonstration.

Court. All right.

Foran. From here on, I object.

Court. You haven't said that you objected.

Foran. I do after the second one.

Court. After two of them? I sustain the objection.

Weinglass. If the court please, there has been much testimony by the Government's witnesses as to this Om technique which was used in the park. Are we only going to hear whether there were stones or people throwing things, or shouting things, or using obscenities? Why do we draw the line here? Why don't we also hear what is being said in the area of calming the crowd?

Foran. I have no objection to the two Om's that we have had. However I just didn't want it to go on all morning.

Court. The two, however may characterize what the witness did, may remain of record, and he may not continue in the same vein.

Court. Will you finish your answer?

A. I am afraid I will be in contempt if I continue to Om...

(Allen is asked by Weinglass to recite "Howl." He does so with all the emotion of an Old Testament prophet threatening sinners and standing with the oppressed. The jury is transfixed by the words, the waving arms and bobbing head of the wonderful madman before them. When he recites the lines:

"Moloch. Moloch. Nightmare of Moloch.

Moloch the loveless.

Moloch the heavy judger of man."

and points an accusing figure at Hoffman.

Moloch the stunned government."

Allen continues, climbing higher with each incantation. He reels off 1000 words, and suddenly drops off:

"That is fragmentary."

Weinglass. I have nothing further.

Court. Within the limits of that examination, I will permit further examination.

Foran. No thanks.

Court. Nothing. You may go, sir.

Witness. Thank you.

Abbie Hoffman cries and joins the defendants and half the court when they rise in tribute as Ginsberg leaves. Prosecutor Foran is overheard as he mutters, "that goddamned fag."

Weinglass. If the court please, I do have an interpreter. The interpreter happens to be the witness.

Court. Oh, no, that would hardly be fair. An interpreter must be responsible to the Court, and he must take a special oath. I don't know whether you know that or not, but we have a special oath here for interpreters.

Weinglass. It is my understanding that an interpreter is only used when the witness is not proficient in the English language and requires the aid of an interpreter.

Court. He used another language here

Witness. I am speaking English, sir.

Court... Now I have tried to be as kind as I could to you.

Witness. I am trying to be kind to you.

Court. I don't want you to interrupt me when I am speaking.

(The jury is released for the day.)

Friday, December 12:

(Allen is asked by Len Weinglass to describe a meeting with Jerry held at Allen's house in mid-April of 1968. This happens just after Allen has listed the categories of the Youth International Party.)

Q. Looking at the top of the document, the left-hand column, is there a category indicated?

A. Yes. Music.

Q. Music. And then is there another category listed under that?

A. Theater.

OLD MOLE

25¢ NUMBER 33   A RADICAL BI-WEEKLY   BOSTON, MASSACHUSETTS   FEBRUARY 20 - MARCH 5

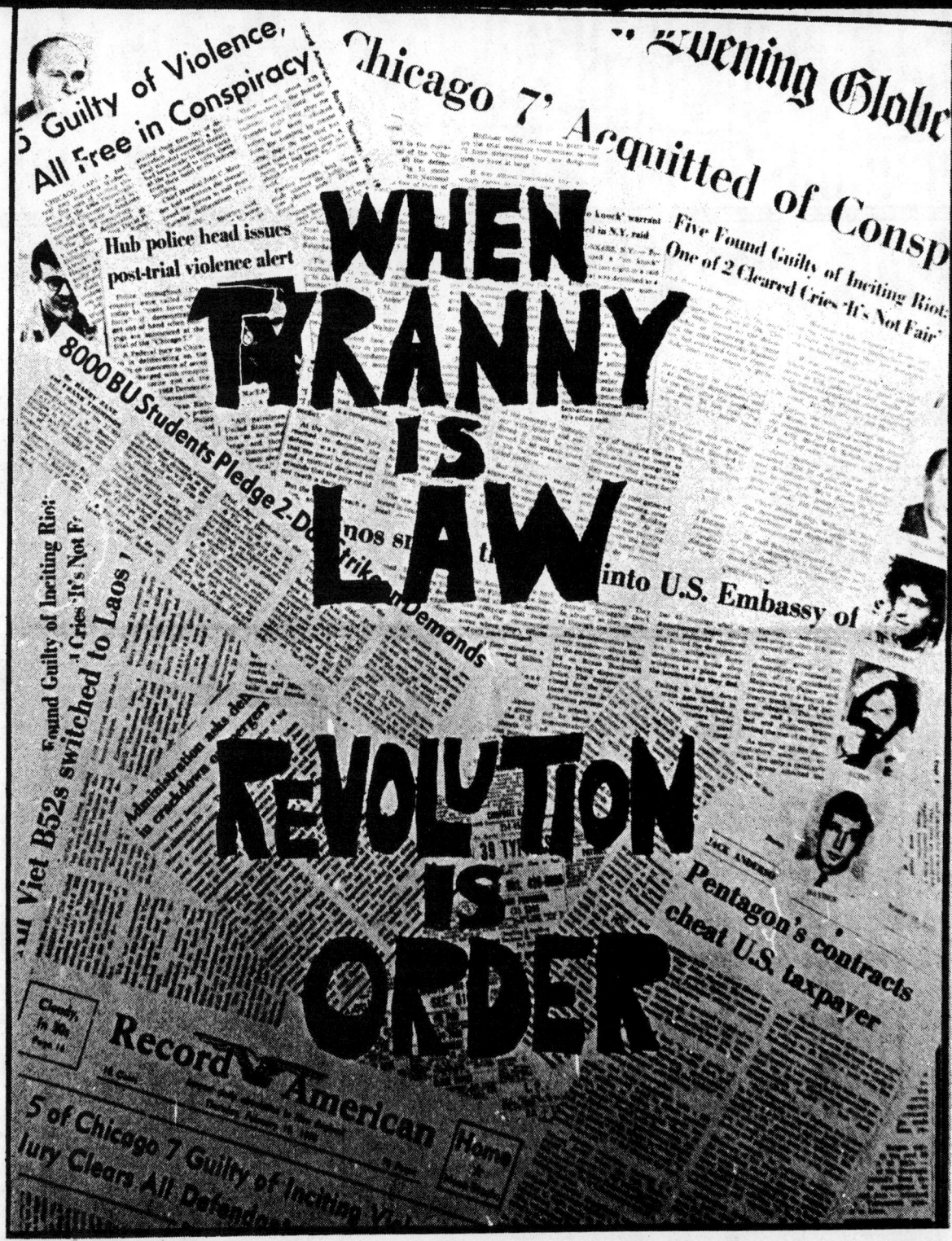

WHEN TYRANNY IS LAW

REVOLUTION IS ORDER

> "You are holding back the tide of history, which you will not succeed in doing, and you are trying to forestall a second American revolution, which you will not succeed in doing."
>
> —DAVID DELLINGER

DAVE DELLINGER IN CONTEMPT

DAVE DELLINGER

First, I think that every judge should be required to serve time in prison, to spend time in prison before sentencing other people there so that he might become aware of the degrading and anti-human conditions that persist not only in Cook County Jail but in the prisons generally of this country...

I think that in 1970 perhaps the American people will begin to discover something about the nature of the prison system, the system in which we are now confined and which thousands of other political prisoners are confined.

The Black Panthers have said that all black prisoners are political prisoners, and I think that although it may be hard for people to understand, I think that all people in prison are political prisoners. They are in prison, most of them, because they have violated the property and power concepts of the society; and the bank robber I talked to yesterday was only trying to get his in the ways he thought were open to him, just as businessmen and others profiteer and try to advance their own economic cause at the expense of their fellows.

I think in a society in which one has to have education, good family, connections in order to rise to the top economically, it is not surprising if residents of a ghetto and residents of the poor white working class and lower middle class often feel that the only way that they can get what everybody else is getting, can get it that way.

I do not think that the property system and the economic anti-egalitarianism of our society justifies putting a strain on people holding up this idea of self-advancement and then putting them away under conditions which when the United States becomes enlightened, everybody will be ashamed of. I think it is impossible to think of the United States as being a civilized country when it has prisons such as those we are now confined in.

Our movement is not very strong today. It is not united, it is not well organized. It is very confused and makes a lot of mistakes, but there is the beginning of an awakening in this country which has been going on for at least the last fifteen years, and it is an awakening that will not be denied. Tactics will change, people will err, people will die in the streets and die in prison, but I do not believe that this movement can be denied because however falsely applied the American ideal was from the beginning when it excluded black people, and Indians and people without property, nonetheless there was a dream of justice and equality and freedom, and brotherhood, and I think that that dream is much closer to fulfillment today than it has been at any time in the history of this country.

I only wish that were all not just more eloquent, I wish we were smarter, more dedicated, more united. I wish we could work together. I wish we could reach out to the Forans, and the Schultzes and the Hoffmans, and convince them of the necessity of this revolution...

I think I shall sleep better and happier and with a greater sense of fulfillment in whatever jails I am in for the next, however many years, than if I had compromised, if I had pretended the problems were any less real than they are, or if I had sat here passively in the courthouse while justice was being throttled and the truth was being denied.

I learned that when I spent my three years in jail before. When I ended up in the hole and on a hunger strike for sixty-five days, I found out that there are no comforts, no luxuries, no honors, nothing that can compare with having a sense of one's own integrity -- not

one's infallibility because I have continued to make mistakes from that day to this, but at least one's knowledge is that in his own life, in his own committment, he is living up to the best that he knows.

I salute my brothers in Vietnam, in the ghetto, in the Women's Liberation Movement, all the people all over the world who are struggling to make true and real for all people the ideals on which this country was supposed to be founded, but never, never lived up to.

The optimism of a few hours earlier had been replaced by an edgy tension. More plainclothesmen were scattered through the audience, a heavier guard was at the door. Hoffman nodded his head for emphasis as he read through Dave Dellinger's contempt citations, his frail voice shaking with indignation. The count finally reached thirty-two instances of contempt. Dave Dellinger, looking somewhat tougher and just a little haggard from his long trial, rose to speak as is the custom before sentencing. This balding pacifist veteran was spending time in jail when some of the defendants were babies. Throughout the trial he had accumulated increasing respect and now with a dignity and warmth that belittled the egotistical judge he asked, "I hope you will do me the courtesy not to interrupt me while I'm talking."

Julius replied, "I won't interrupt you as long as you're respectful."

Dellinger replied matter of factly, "Well, I will talk about the facts and the facts don't always encourage false respect." And then he began to explain his motivation for incurring the Judge's contempt. In the first citation, he had attempted to read lists of the war dead during Moratorium day, and he was moved to interfere the second time to defend Bobby Seale. Dave went on in a calm voice that "the war in Vietnam and racism in this country are the two issues that this country refuses to solve."

Immediately, Judge Hoffman began reddening in the face. "I don't want you to speak about politics. You must speak about punishment." he interrupted.

Dave halted to hear the Judge's objections: "You see, that's one of the reasons I've needed to stand up and speak anyway, because you have tried to keep what you call politics, which means the truth, out of the courtroom. He spoke with a certain fearlessness that came from the knowledge that this Judge could really do nothing more to him. His bail had already been revoked as a disciplinary procedure because of his refusal to submit silently in the courtroom. He could take that better, probably, than the younger defendants. In fact, when he was put in jail by Julius Hoffman, he had been greeted as something of a hero. Prison-toughened cons came up to him to shake his hand: "That bastard Hoffman gave me ten years; I'm glad someone finally told him off."One can imagine the typical scenes in the yard where felons talking out of the sides of their mouths would slide up to Dave, who resembles a humble, but self-contained minister, maybe a latter-day John Wesley, and say "You're all right in my book, Dave baby."

How was this pipsqueak of a Judge, his only authority the power of the jails and marshals at his command, interrupting Dave Dellinger and telling him to sit down.

Dave, for a moment flushed with anger, composed himself and replied, "You want us to be like good Germans supporting the evils of our decade. And then when we refused to be goodGermans and we came to Chicago and demonstrated despite the threats and intimidations of the establishment; now you want us to be like good Jews, going quietly and politely to the concen-

tration camps, while you and this court suppress freedom and truth. You want us to stay in our place like black people are supposed to stay in their place..."

The Judge, in his bald-headed intemperance, had no control over Dellinger; he called for the Marshal to sit him down. Two marshals came over, put their hands on Dave and eased him into the chair, while he continued speaking.

"....like poor people are supposed to stay in their place, like people without formal education are supposed to stay in their place, like women are supposed to stay in their place."

The courtroom was heating to a boil. The marshals were forcibly shoving Dave into his seat now. But he continued speaking; "....like children are supposed to stay in their place, like lawyers are supposed to stay in their place."

"It's a travesty of justice, and if you had any sense at all, you would know that the record condemns you and not us."

The marshals prowled the aisles like overfed hyenas ready to attack. Others tried to silence Dave, who continued, "It will be one of thousands and thousands of rallying points for a new generation of Americans who will not put up with tyranny, will not put up with the facade of democracy without the reality."

My blood raced. We were caught in a moment of power and beauty. The power of the marshals, despite their attempts at manhandling, couldn't silence his spontaneous eloquence. Dave was being shoved about and the marshals were yalling for him to be quiet, Yet he persevered "You take an hour to read the the contempt citations, you have the power to send me away for years, but you will not give me one-tenth of the time to speak what is relevant by my deserts and by history's deserts as well. I sat here and heard that man Mr. Foran say evil, terrible, dishonest things, that even he could not believe --- and you expect me to be quiet and accept that without even speaking up."

"People will no longer be quiet. People are going to speak up. I am just an old man and I am just speaking feebly and not too well, but I relect the spirit that will echo...."

Judge Hoffman: "Take him out."

".....throughout the world."

Tasha Dellinger began applauding her father from her seat in the first row. Spectators joined spontaneously in a wave of emotion. A woman marshal, joined by two others,grabbed Tasha She was thrown to the floor, as Conspiracy staff members jumped into the struggling pile to help out. One staffer jumped through the air and landed a flying right hook to a marshal who was choking a girl. Complete pandemonium. As Dave's two daughters were being knocked about for their support of their father, he was being dragged from the room. The court record shows that his last words were: "Right on beautiful people, black people, Vietnamese, poor people, young people, everybody fighting for liberty and justice. Right on!"

From "Conspiracy" by Jeff Shero, 3/1/70

THE EIGHTH CONSPIRATOR

The Chicago Eight trial became the Chicago Seven trial on November 5, 1969 when Judge Julius Hoffman severed Bobby Seale from the case and put him away for four years for contempt of court. The Establishment Media was quick to erase the memory of the Eighth Conspirator; and the white movement, to its discredit, found it fairly easy to forget Bobby Seale, too. Nationwide demonstrations didn't follow Judge Hoffman's November decision. After all, the Black Panther Party chairman was never at press conferences, was never out addressing rallies, never made it into Richard Avedon's photographic record of the trial. He was, for the duration of his stay in Chicago, confined to the Cook County Jail – whisked in via prison van to the Federal Building by 10:00 and whisked out again after court recessed, held in the lock-up during lunch. He is now in prison in San Francisco, on trumped-up charges of conspiracy to murder. The Government apparently was able to invent a better reason to keep him locked up than a Chicago Conspiracy indictment (Bobby was only in Chicago for two days and made only two public speeches during the convention).

The "disruptions" for which Bobby was chained and gagged and eventually jailed, were never the unreasoned bursts of rage described by the Overground Media. Each and every time Bobby interrupted the Court, it was to carry out his legal defense in the absence of Charles R. Garry, who Bobby recognized as his one and only lawyer. The now-famous "racist pig" epithets usually came at the end of frustrated attempts by Bobby to act as his own attorney.

Hoffman gave Bobby three-month sentences for each case of contempt -- 16 counts in all, four years in jail. Dave Dellinger was cited 32 times for contempt. His sentence was two and a half years. (Proving that "racist pig" was only an accurate description of Hoffman's court.) The contempt citations ranged from a one sentence interruption to lengthy discourses by Bobby on his constitutional rights. Bobby would refer to Title 42, U.S. Code Section 1981 to justify his self-defense. Title 42 is a Reconstruction statute granting blacks equal protection under the law. Hoffman cited a technicality (Kunstler had signed as Seale's lawyer so that he could visit the Panther in jail while Charles Garry was recuperating from an operation) and consistently denied Bobby his right to present his legal case.

The official transcript records the running battle between the black revolutionary and the white Court. Excerpts follow.

by Alice Embree

On Black Power vs. Power to the People:

"MR. SCHULTZ: Your Honor, before the next witness testifies, would it be possible if the Court would permit the Government—well. we haven't offered the picture, as a matter of fact. We have the picture of the boy with the black power symbol fist on his sweat shirt that was identified by Officer Tobin and Carcerano as the boy— '....

"THE COURT: Show it to counsel.

"MR. SEALE: That's not a black power sign. Somebody correct the Court on that. It's not the black power sign. It's the power to the people sign.

On U.S. Attorney Schultz (before court convened, Bobby had warned Panthers in the audience to cool it, unless attack; Schultz told the Judge he had exhorted them to attack):

"MR. SCHULTZ: He was talking to these people about an attack by them.

"MR. SEALE: You're lying. Dirty liar. I told them to defend themselves. You are a rotten racist pig, fascist liar, that's what you are. You're a rotten liar. You're a rotten liar. You are a fascist pig liar.

On the jury (the Judge had informed the jury about alleged threatening letters from the Black Panthers and one juror whose family had supposedly received a letter had been dismissed because she no longer felt she could be impartial):

"MR. SEALE: The jury is prejudiced against me, all right, and you know it because of those threatening letters.

You know it, those so-called jive threatening letters, and you know it's a lie. How can that jury give me a fair trial?

"THE COURT: Mr. Marshal, will you go to that man and ask him to be quiet?

On his constitutional rights as protected by the Reconstruction law:

"MR. SEALE: Yes, that's because you violated my constitutional rights, Judge Hoffman. That's because you violated them overtly, deliberately, in a very racist manner. Somebody ought to point out the law to you. You don't want to investigate it to see whether the people get their constitutional rights. 68,000 black men died in the Civil War for that right. That right was made during the Reconstruction period. They fought in that war and 68,000 of them died. That law was made for me to have my constitutional rights.

Again on his constitutional rights (this time while gagged):

"MR. SEALE: [Through his gag] I would like to cross-examine the witness. I want to cross-examine the witness.

"THE COURT: Ladies and gentlemen of the jury, I will have to excuse you.

"MR. SEALE: My constitutional rights have been violated. The direct examination is over, cross-examination is over, I want to cross-examine the witness.

"THE COURT: Please be quiet, sir. I order you to be quiet.

"MR. SEALE: I have a right to cross-examine the witness. I want to cross-examine the witness at this time. I object to you not allowing me to cross-examine the witness. You know I have a right to do so.

"THE COURT: Ladies and gentlemen of the jury, you are excused until tomorrow morning at ten o'clock. I

"(The following proceedings were had in open court, out of the presence and hearing of the jury:)

"THE COURT: Now I want to tell you, Mr. Seale, again—I thought you were going to adhere to my directions. You sat there and did not during this afternoon intrude into the proceedings in an improper way.

"MR. SEALE: I never intruded until it was the proper time for me to ask and request and demand that I have a right to defend myself and I have a right to cross-examine the witness. I sit through other cross-examinations and after the cross-examinations were over, I request, demanded by right to cross-examine the witness, and in turn demanded my right to defend myself, since you cannot sit up here—you cannot sit up here and continue to deny me my constitutional rights to cross-examine the witness, my constitutional right to defend myself. I sit throughout other cross-examinations, I never said anything, and I am not attempting to disrupt this trial. I am attempting to get my rights to defend myself recognized by you.

And his final speech, after being sentenced for contempt:

THE COURT: Mr. Seale, you have a right to speak now. I will hear you.

MR. SEALE: For myself?

THE COURT: In your own behalf, yes.

MR. SEALE: How come I couldn't speak before?

THE COURT: This is a special occasion.

MR. SEALE: Wait a minute. Now are you going to try to—you going to attempt to punish me for attempting to speak for myself before? Now after you punish me, you sit up and say something about you can speak? What kind of jive is that? I don't understand it. What kind of court is this? Is this a court? It must be a fascist operation like I see it in my mind, you know,—I don't understand you.

THE COURT: I am calling on you—

MR. SEALE: You just read a complete record of me trying to persuade you, trying to show you, demonstrating my right, demonstrating to you the need, showing you all this stuff about my right to defend myself, my right to defend myself, history, slavery, et cetera; and you going to sit there and say something about, "OK, now you can speak"?

What am I supposed to speak about? I still haven't got the right to defend myself. I would like to speak about that. I would like to—since you let me stand up and speak, can I speak about in behalf of—can I defend myself?

WHY?

■

So it goes in the court-rooms and law schools of the country as judges and lawyers and professors try to cope with rowdy defendants and still stay within the Constitution. Mostly they are waiting for some guidance from the Supreme Court — and some are saying, as did Harry Kalvin of Chicago Law School, "We're a little puzzled now as to why defendants have behaved so well in the past."

The New York Times 3/22/70

ANALYSIS: YOU CAN'T JAIL THE REVOLUTION.

Conspiracy

--comment by Margo Conk

(Editor's note: the author is a secretary in the Political Science Department.)

The furor over the Chicago Conspiracy Trial has reached a fever pitch in the last two weeks. The guilty verdict and the handing down of the contempt citations have put a note of finality and meanness into the acid discussions that have raged around the trial for the last six months.

It is too late now to hope that the jury will be hung or the defendants acquitted. The fact is that they were not acquitted, nor was the jury hung. The fact is that despite the loud and sometimes violent protests, the government has won in its attempt to repress and punish five men for speaking out against imperialism, the war, and the American power structure.

We all have had at least one argument lately about Abbie Hoffman's conduct, Judge Hoffman's repressiveness, or the birthday cake. I have found that the arguments tend to fall into consistent patterns. On one side it the radical who makes the blanket statement that the courts are the servants of the 'ruling class,' that Judge Hoffman is Mitchell's servant, that the whole trial is an insult to the defendants, that it is Mayor Daley and the Chicago police who should be on trial. On the other side is the liberal who 'questions the constitutionality' of the law, deplores the judge's 'excesses,' deplores the prosecutor's excesses, but believes in the sanctity of the judicial system, and concludes by adding, "And besides, the courtroom conduct of the defendants was ghastly and crude. And after all they have the right of appeal."

At this point the discussion deteriorates into a dreary catalog of charges and counter-charges on specific incidents in the case. The chaining of Bobby Seale, the refusal to let Ramsey Clark testify, the contempt citations, implores the radical. Seale's hideous behavior, his cries of 'Pig!' hurled at the judge are outrageous, says the liberal. And so it goes.

Clearly a list of indignities, horrors, and injustices committed by one side or the other will not resolve the issue. What lies much deeper than the 27,000 pages of testimony are the attitudes of people toward the trial. In many ways what they think happened is and should be more important than the intricacies of what actually did happen. The legal issues of the case are a fit subject for lawyers. Lawyers have and will continue to fight in the courts the issues of free speech and repression which this trial has raised. But it is not enough for us laymen to withhold judgment until the Supreme Court judgment is in, to defer to the experts, the lawyers. We also must take a stand.

At issue is a novel question in American political life -- the Conspiracy's refusal to admit the government's right to try them, the billing of the trial as "The World Series of Injustice -- the Washington Kangaroos v. the Chicago Conspiracy." It is this refusal that led to the frantic condemnations in the established press -- the editorials in the New York Times and the proposals for Adolf Eichmann-style isolation booth to protect the courts from disruption.

It is important to clear away some of the confusion created by the pious language of Times editorials and the frightening suggestion of mini-jails in the court-room. It is not enough to condemn the actions of Rubin and Hoffman as 'nuts.' There were ten intelligent men on trial in Chicago (I count the lawyers), and it is condescending and foolish to consider the defendants merely as unprincipled, loud-mouthed fools. A poster printed by the Conspiracy shows a clenched flame-red fist next to the bold words, "YOU CAN'T JAIL THE REVOLUTION, Stop the Trial, Free the Conspiracy 8." This appeal more than anything else explains the structure of the defense.

First, the Conspiracy refused to admit that they were on trial; they systematically tried to turn the process around and put the government on trial. Hence the attempts to make a citizen's arrest of Mayor Daley, the call to every major literary and artistic figure in the movement to testify in support of the defendant's attempts to create a life-giving counter-culture. The goal was to point up the criminality and hypocrisy in present day American life, to point up the absurdity in the over-produced and up-tight society we live in.

Second, they attempted to break down the authority figures of the courtroom, and eventually to break down the authority of the courts in general. Thus Judge Hoffman was depicted as Mr. Magoo, called Julie by Abbie. Hence the defendants celebrated Bobby Seale's birthday in court.

Finally, they hoped to create chaos by random disruption, to put the whole court-room under such pressure that it almost could not function. Shouting out that "This ain't the Standard Club, Julie," or "Pig" served to disturb a proceeding that was predestined to condemn the defendants, in the hope that the jury would sense the hypocrisy, understand the injustice, and feel the humanity of the defendants.

In other words, the defendants refused to let themselves be tried. The revolution will not be; it is. Only by living as a free man are you a free man. When you surrender to repression, you are repressed. When you stand up to it, it becomes your show. Your humanity wins easily against the small and closed attitudes of your repressors. One of the most impressive results of the trial is the defendant's and lawyers' insistence that the trial was the most real, most human and fulfilling experience of their lives. In a very deep sense, the revolution that the defense speaks of lives in the hearts of these men.

It is possible to have endless arguments over the success or failure of the defense tactics, whether they were successful in their resistance. I think it is indisputable though that one must accept the resistance as the thoughtful decision of thoughtful men, that one cannot dismiss it as mere foolishness or crudity or simplistic defiance. The resistance must be considered as a complex attempt to confront the powers that be. That attempt is the thorn that underlies the frenetic attempts in liberal circles to discredit and dismiss the defense tactics. For one of the great liberal platitudes extols the independence and impartiality of the American court system. When all else fails, the liberal resorts to 'reason and the courts' to bring justice to the downtrodden. And it is just that 'impartiality' that the Conspiracy is challenging. What Kunstler and the defendants have been saying from the first is that the deck was stacked against them. It is the same thing that all American minorities have been saying from the beginning of the Republic. Whether it was Jefferson defending those prosecuted under the Sedition Act of 1798, or the labor unionists railing against the injunction in the late nineteenth century, or the immigrant IWW members condemning the Red Scare, all have recognized that the court system is at best a tardy dispenser of justice, at worst a wholesale oppressor. For what good are the platitudes to those who fight five years of appeals to secure their freedom -- what of the cost in dollars, in energy, in worry.

What is so radical about the Chicago Conspiracy is not the condemnation of the courts as unjust, but rather the decision to act and resist on that ground in the courtroom. Perhaps never before in the history of American political trials have the accused refused to believe in the sacred character of the courtroom and have they carried the resistance so far, so consistently. In the past political prisoners have refused to admit they were guilty, but I doubt that they ever tried to begin the revolution in the courtroom.

It is on this issue that the controversy must hinge. In light of the conviction and sentences, the predicament becomes more acute. The battles rage in Vietnam, in the ghettoes, in the street. Can or should the courts remain apart? Is the quiet of the courtroom the ground of reason, or the quiet of a Pax Romana?

Telegram

western union

345A EDT FEB 5 70 BA424
TDA437 B CDV016 WJ PSX224 28
PD INTL FR CD MASSY VIA WUI 23 1425

THE CONSPIRACY
28 EAST JACKSON
CHICAGO. ILLINOIS

EMERGENCY MEETING OF NATIONAL SECURITY COUNCIL CONCEDES DEFEAT STOP

VIETNAM TROOPS WILL BE WITHDRAWN IMMEDIATELY STOP ALL POLITICAL

PRISONERS WILL BE FREED STOP THE TRIAL IS OVER STOP JUDGE HOFFMAN

CAN BE DEALT WITH APPROPRIATELY STOP CORPORATE AND GOVERNMENT

LEADERS AGREE TO IMMEDIATE WHITE HOUSE MEETING STOP WILL DISCUSS

TERMS OF IMMEDIATE TRANSFER OF POWER TO PEOPLE WITH MR. HUEY NEWTON

AND REVOLUTIONARY GOVERNMENT STOP WHATEVER GOES UP MUST COME DOWN

> RICHARD MILHOUSE NIXON
> PRESIDENT OF THE UNITED STATES
> WASHINGTON. D.C.

SORRY, PEOPLE

ITS NOT GOING TO
HAPPEN THAT WAY,

PEOPLE WHO HAVE POWER
HOLD ON TO IT,

THEY RUN THINGS THEIR WAY
THEY CHANGE THINGS THEIR WAY,

SO WE'VE HAD TO FIGHT,

AGAINST THEIR WARS,
THEIR RACISM (AND OURS)
THEIR MALE CHAUVINISM (AND OURS)
AGAINST THEIR SYSTEM,

THEY FIGHT BACK,

WITH MURDERS:
28 PANTHERS DEAD SO FAR
THOUSANDS KILLED IN GHETTO REBELLIONS,

WITH LAW AND ORDER:
A BRUTALITY WHICH
HAS BECOME
COMMONPLACE,

WITH TRIALS:
THEIR NUMBERS INCREASE
DAILY,

THE TRIAL IN CHICAGO
DEFINES THEM ALL,

OUR MOVEMENT ON THE RACK:
4 MONTHS OF THEIR LIES AND
OUR ATTEMPT TO REFUTE THEM,

LIES ABOUT OUR MOVEMENT,
LIES ABOUT OUR HOPES,

BOBBY, GAGGED
AS THIS COUNTRY SHACKLES
ALL BLACK PEOPLE,

THE WAR JUDGED IRRELEVANT,
IMPERIALISM OUT OF ORDER,
OUR POLITICS IMMATERIAL,
OUR CULTURE DENIED,

WITHIN TWO WEEKS
THE JURY DECIDES

CONDEMNS THE STRUGGLE
OF THE LAST TEN YEARS

ISSUES A WARNING
FOR THE NEXT TEN,

WITHIN TWO WEEKS
OUR PEOPLE WILL GO TO JAIL,

JUDGE HOFFMAN IS NOT KNOWN
FOR HIS LENIENCY,

IF THEY ARE CONVICTED
THEY FACE TEN YEARS,

IF IT'S A HUNG JURY, HIS HONOR
PUTS THEM ON ICE ANYWAY,

THE LAWYERS TOO,

FOR CONTEMPT,
THAT'S WHY WE HAVE TO ACT,

THE DAY AFTER,

TDA

TO TELL THEIR SYSTEM
THIS SHIT MUST STOP,

WE ARE ON TRIAL TOO

CONSPIRACY MEANS
WE BREATHE TOGETHER,

WE ARE ALL PART OF THE CONSPIRACY,

THE CONSPIRACY MOVES,

IN THE STREETS,

WITH A MASSIVE MARCH,

THE DAY AFTER
THE WORD COMES DOWN,

THE DAY AFTER,

THE FIGHT GOES ON,

TOGETHER,

ASSEMBLE PARK ST MTA
(BOSTON COMMON) 4 PM TDA

The Day After the Verdict: Leaflet for TDA demonstration in Boston Feb 1970

Even the best teachers, with the best intentions, seem to diminish their students as they work through the public-school system. For that system is, at bottom, designed to produce what we sometimes call good citizens but what more often than not turn out to be good soldiers; it is through the schools of the state, after all, that we produce our armies. I remember how struck I was while teaching at a state college by the number of boys who wanted to oppose the draft but lacked the courage or strength to simply say no. They were trapped; they had always been taught, had always tried, to be "good." Now that they wanted to refuse to go, they could not, for they weren't sure they could bear the consequences they had been taught would follow such refusal: jail, social disgrace, loss of jobs, parental despair. They could not believe in institutions, but they could not trust themselves and their impulse and they were caught in their own impotence: depressed and resentful, filled with self-hatred and a sense of shame.

PETER MARIN

I'm 22 years old and I'm tired. America has worn me out. I don't believe in God. And I don't believe that America is the Golden center of the universe. You can get away with not believing in one of these but not both.

ANONYMOUS STUDENT *Atlantic Monthly* Oct 1968

He feels imprisoned on this earth, he feels constricted; the melancholy, the impotence, the sicknesses, the feverish fancies of the captive afflict him; no comfort can comfort him, since it is merely comfort, gentle headsplitting comfort glazing the brutal fact of imprisonment.*But if he is asked what he wants he cannot reply. . .He has no conception of freedom.*

FRANZ KAFKA

QUOTE/UNQUOTE

The crucial problem today is that we too often are unable to really imagine other people's death. We make love by telephone, we work not on matter but on machines, and we kill by proxy.

ALBERT CAMUS

The people of a village near Bettiah told me that they had run away whilst the police were looting their houses and molesting their womenfolk. When they said that they had run away because I had told them to be nonviolent, I hung my head in shame. I assured them that such was not the meaning of my nonviolence. I expected them to intercept the mightiest power that might be in the act of harming those who were under their protection, and draw without retaliation all harm upon their own heads even to the point of death, but never to run away from the storm center. It was manly enough to defend one's property, honor or religion at the point of the sword. It was manlier and nobler to defend them without seeking to injure the wrongdoer. But it was unmanly, unnatural and dishonorable to forsake the post of duty and, in order to save one's skin, to leave property, honor or religion to the mercy of the wrongdoer. I could see my way of delivering the message of nonviolence to those who knew how to die, not to those who were afraid of death.

I do believe that, where there is only a choice between cowardice and violence, I would advise violence. I would rather have India resort to arms in order to defend her honor than that she should, in a cowardly manner, become or remain a helpless witness to her own dishonor. But I believe that nonviolence is infinitely superior to violence, forgiveness is more manly than punishment . . . Strength does not come from physical capacity. It comes from an indomitable will.

The weakest of us physically must be taught the art of facing dangers and giving a good account of ourselves. I want both the Hindus and the Mussalmans to cultivate the cool courage, to die without killing. But if one has not that courage, I want him to cultivate the art of killing and being killed, rather than in a cowardly manner to flee from danger.   **GANDHI**

I remember a line from Daley in Chicago, "Shoot the looters to kill." Right On Mayor Daley. Shoot the looters to kill but we are going to make it retroactive. We're going to talk about who looted the Indians, we're going to talk about who looted the Black man, and we're going to talk about whose looting the whole fucking world right now. And then if we absolutely have to we're going to pay attention to what Mayor Daley has to say."

Mike Albert
Speech to Freshman
Sept. 1969

Ed. Note: Albert was then President of the M.I.T. student body

THURSDAY (M.I.T.)

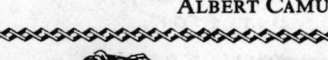

GHETTO COMMUNITY: BLACK, BROWN AND LONGHAIR-WHITE

'New Antidromy'

The Lower East Side: Longhairs Are Dangerous

by Kenneth Pitchford

Dear Mr. Straight White Radical: You wanted to know what's been happening to the Movement community on New York's Lower East Side. With your short hair and your ostentatious uniform of self-effacing blue work-shirting (although bibliography, not manual labor is your forte), you've already expressed suspicions about the life style of the new antidromy (from the Greek *anti* against, plus *dromos* running, meaning a movement or course that is opposed to the normal, as the direction of a nerve impulse). You overlook the fact that, like it or not, this antidromy is young and growing and developing its own consciousness—without your advice. When you say the revolution, pacifist or otherwise, can't occur except by your leave and within the confines of a life style you approve, you simply miss the point, baby. There are more of us than of you, and we aren't reading your boring dissertations to find out what's wrong with the youth freak longhair majority we soon will be in this country: we're acting and coming together and defining ourselves and our goals and are already off and running in a direction opposed to what the

System defines as normal—and what you define as normal, as well. Because you and the System agree on more things than you disagree. Both of you want us to cut our hair (which we will do only when the tactics of subversion or infiltration demand it). Both of you want us to stop enjoying our resistance and our life style, and to be "serious" instead. Both of you want us to stop smoking pot. Both of you think of sexual freedom and the liberation of women as unnecessary at best and frivolous or degenerate at worst.

Fine, turn away, ignore us, watch for the next SDS seizure of college buildings, make your plans for the inauguration, arrange sanctuaries for GI deserters, plan another mass protest parade against the not-yet-ended war. Meanwhile, the Movement as a whole is reaching a turning point and we—all of us—had better at least try to understand the terrain of the next battlefields, and why it is unwise to under-rate the growing resistance underground in a community like the one I have lived in for 10 years, this place realtors degrade with the name "the East Village," a name echoed in the title of one rightward-trending ex-underground newspaper.

Dig it. The blacks have had Malcolm, and since they began putting his lesson of black autonomy into practice, whites have at least had Vietnam. Convenient as this was, it focused your efforts on a single war, a single President, not even (yet) a single foreign policy. Get rid of that war and that President and a fair number of your friends would be glad to go back to sleep, right? At the same time, there were these irresponsible flower-power dope fiends, but it was a relief for you to be able to attack them as earnestly as did the followers of Wallace-Nixon- Humphrey-McCarthy-Trotsky-Mao. It showed that you really loved America after all. Of course, it was funny that they didn't seem to go away after the fad was over and a few of them were murdered. And as their numbers grew and grew, in fact, you had to constantly devise new ways for looking at them as unserious, unimportant, uncommitted, you name it. College kids, well, that was different; their hair was long, but not long-long, you know what I mean?, and their idealism made them respectable. It is a lack of respectability that America (and, alas, the American Movement) fears most.

Another reason for ignoring growing longhair communities: The antiwar movement classically expressed itself by one of two extremes. One, mass demonstrations (wear middle-class clothes so that CBS will be impressed). Two, organize counseling and support services for the individual draft resister and help him to achieve whatever he chooses as an alternative—escape to Canada, interment in prison, etc. The notion of whole communities resisting was certainly not feasible at this point—except for blacks.

Now the hated President is a lame duck, a bombing halt is in force, peace talks flounder in Paris, and Thieu may actually send a delegation after all. And Humphrey was not rewarded for Chicago, Nixon got no mandate to crow about, Congress remains moderate (no lunge to the right developing there), and Wallace got 13 per cent, not 23 per cent. If the war goes on, the Movement will be in fine shape, knowing exactly what to do. But if it ends?

We on the Lower East Side know what will happen. It has been happening to us all along. I took up residence here over 10 years ago, before the advent and demise of flower power. In front of my pad is Prostitute Walk, where uptown white businessmen bargain with black women addicts who are in the process of dying so rapidly that you can watch it happen from one day to the next: legs encrusted with running syph sores, heads unaware that they are shaking like a metronome and, sometimes, screaming (not to mention crying out loud). How nice of these white men not to mind the condition of the women whose cunts or mouths (which are offered for a $2 reduction in fee) they will use that night. A taste for respectability is not something you need to share, evidently, when it comes to the dirty act of discount sex. To the east of Prostitute Walk (Third Avenue to uptowners) is a block-long Puerto Rican ghetto; need we exploit the six-in-one-room wretchedness there? Moynihan hasn't yet figured out how to demonstrate their inferiority, since Pope Paul keeps these families together -in joyless fecundity and malnutrition. To the west of Prostitute Walk is the Heroin Hilton of the Lower East Side, where stolen goods and money buy another day's reprieve from withdrawal symptoms.

What oozing compassion the McCarthy liberal would feel for the desperate family, what nice notions about spontaneity and sexual freedom lubricated the head of one Old Left visitor of mine who had to watch a typical sex transaction on my doorstep. Later, he quoted something by Brecht about some Berlin whore. (No, Virginia, these prostitutes do not brim with life, thinking of another spontaneous and joyous toss in the hay.) That these blacks and Puerto Ricans hate each other goes without saying; that both hate white longhairs like me, ditto.

Last summer, before the arrival of a new sort of bereted black in the neighborhood, three black junkies held up and threatened to kill my wife and me; a Puerto Rican intervened and saved our life. A few weeks later, some black killed some Puerto Rican on the sidewalk outside our house. None of this makes the papers, over- or underground. Why should it? It's gone on long before the longhair arrived, bringing in his wake the big businessman selling psychedelia and the pseudo-underground news selling sex titillations for uptown tourists.

Against the white longhair, everybody could direct his anger; against the Electric Circus and the Fillmore, nobody cared to say a word. The cops don't always answer calls about mugging in this neighborhood (we were no exception that summer night) but they'll protect the Fillmore and Circus owners to the hilt. Money talks. Property sucks. Bribery pays off. Look at Greenwich Village (the "West Village" to squares). It went through the same death agony. "Bohemians," then. The moneyed entrepreneurs followed. Now you can see high-rise apartment houses called the Van Gogh and the Gauguin in those neighborhoods—with unbelievable gold-sequined lobbies, the home of the rich and the depraved. The attempt to do the same here on the Lower East Side is obvious. Everybody knows the "West Village" isn't where it's at; when rich square people move in, creative hip people—and poor people—move out, not out of antipathy but out of economics.

Already soigneed uptowners are moving into renovated slum buildings on Lower East Side streets. Naturally they like to be "where it's at"—they are uptown editors with daring sideburns. But, just as naturally, they don't like walking through long-haired rabble to the grocery or laundry; naturally this brings in the police. So what was first a lovefreak happening is slowly becoming a resistance army this time around. And the old Jewish-Ukrainian-Polish population tightens inward upon itself as its sons and daughters dwindle away to the white successful short-haired suburbs. In front of my house, I saw a mini-riot break out this summer because a bereted black told a junkie pimp that he'd better not sell his black sister to the potbellied white respectable Wallace-type uptowner, suited and tied beside his shiny cream-colored car. Quick like the john he was, the white was off in his car, the black sister running after (I think her purse was trapped in The Man's car), and the two men were fighting in the street. Odd. Even the Puerto Ricans in the fast-assembling crowd were cheering the man in the black beret.

Odd? When the Lower East Side's major riot (so far) happened a few months later and the Tactical Police Force (TPF) was called in to club heads, it was Puerto Ricans and their old enemies, blacks, and both their old enemies, longhairs, who found themselves fighting side by side against this invasion of their neighborhood. This went on several nights running with the community remaining uncowed in most of the nightly battles—winning, because as Mao has said, they had a neighborhood to swim through, like fish through water. If anybody was fleeing a cop charge, anybody's door opened and swung shut again, never mind if it was the first time a Puerto Rican had been in a hippie's pad or a—but you fill out the possible permutations yourself. (Sorry, old pacifist buddy, but fires were set and rocks and bottles were thrown; some struck home. So?) So the community had learned one lesson: against a common enemy, they were each stronger when they stood side by side.

I have purposely not given the tedious sociology concerning the growing numbers of longhairs in the neighborhood thus far. You can write your own history of flower-power and the murder of Linda and Groovy. The thing you never go on to say is that the end of that phase didn't scatter us to the four winds. True, we didn't have overtly organized smoke-ins in Tompkins Square last summer (we miss you, Dana Beal), but we were beginning to develop means of knowing each other and working together for our common survival. With the Jade Companions long gone (common defense fund for drug busts) there are now the bad-ass Motherfuckers. There are now communes—who must be nameless, since the police love to batter down doors without warrants and arrest everyone by virtue of the nickel bag that has just fallen from the coat sleeve of the arresting officer. There is now a real underground paper, Rat, giving us the information we need to stay alive—even though Gems Spa pushes the East Village Other on its outside stand and hides Rat indoors in the back. There is now WITCH (Women's International Terrorist Conspiracy from Hell) which surprised the commercial non-community on its first Witch March on Halloween, bruising even the pummeling fists of the Circus bouncers with the butt of a (toy) gun. And when the police recently beat up a black wino and threw him through a Pizza Parlor window, there were two nights of rebellion by the whole community, black, tan, and longhair, in which trash cans blazed like beacons up and down Second Avenue and traffic was stopped and commerce was disrupted in all the uptown merchant's downtown emporiums. On the second night, a street meeting of the community (without permit) warned the TPF audience that they can no longer pick us off one by one without reprisals.

Several times there've been attempts at setting up telephone trees for a Defense Early Warning System when someone gets busted or hassled—or when a commune is attacked, as recently, and four of its girls are raped and the cops, instead of asking for descriptions, arrest the commune. And when one Yippie was arrested for dealing (a laugh, if you knew this Yippie), more than just Yippies staged a freak-out demonstration in front of Criminal Court.

One more point has to be made about this just-coming-into-existence pattern of the new antidromy, since many of us feel it is nothing less than the already visible shape of our future in this country (like the last prophetic half of Godard's film "Weekend," except with a specifically urban basis). Your admiration for the resistance of college students is fine. But they are only a hothouse community drawn from scattered locales of the System itself—places where resistance has not yet been feasible—and after they leave college? This is the big question that makes people like Julius Lester wonder whether the college rebellion can lead to anything permanent. They can always swell your ranks, of course, writing position papers with excellent bibliographies. Or they can drop out into the shopping district nearest to the college they attended and become an all-white band of professional non-students, still clinging to the Linus blanket of the academic radicalism inside the college itself—like Telegraph Avenue next to the Berkeley campus. Actually, I'm not interested in attacking any sort of community resistance wherever it occurs—what is "artificial" anyway? But on the Lower East Side, we are more than ex-students, youth rebels, disaffected longhairs, militant blacks, and radical Puerto Ricans—we are just people, people who are beginning to be a community vitally determined to protect our apartments, our schools, our jobs (or hustles), our institutions, our parks, our lives. We see the hope of becoming an organic entity that the System can mess with only at its peril. (Notice that I haven't mentioned the new city-owned "Free" Store, which has now been shut down,

anyway—riots occur only in the summer, see?)

It's in this context that you should approach the "frivolous" confrontation over the Fillmore. With the Motherfuckers as spokesmen, the community expressed its wish to use the theatre on one of its dark nights—to use it free as a place for the community to do its thing, exchange information on arrests, needs, troubles, and to present its own life-giving music, poems, theatre, films, to plan and scheme ways of survival in Nixon's Weimar Republic. The community tries to know itself now on streetcorners—but the cop's billy club prods those who seem to stand too long or are maybe successfully breaking down the moving wall of suspicion that is St. Mark's and Second Avenue. And in the winter, it's too cold for standing around, anyway. Besides, the police Mod Squad has grown long hair and is good at infiltration.

Bill Graham, the Fillmore's owner, is a self-made pseudo-hip rich man; he got rich on the new rock music, on the new life style that includes long hair, beads, pot, war resistance, a notion that "useful work" can no longer be defined as that which makes money. Maybe you've already seen him on television, delighting you by denouncing the young kids who have adopted this life style for real—in resistance to values of money-making and murdering. To hear him in open confrontation with the community in the Fillmore is a revelation. The first confrontation grew out of a benefit at which the Living Theatre performed. (Only 10 per cent of the house—top price, $25 dollars—went to the benefit sponsors, the rest to Graham.) Surprisingly enough for someone who talks revolution from papier-mache barricades, Julian Beck did not cop out that night, but supported the community demand for the free night. Graham asserted that he worked, sometimes 20 hours a day, for the right to own the Fillmore, and would give it up only over his dead body. Also, the Fillmore was nothing until he moved into it, took it over, and made it into a success. His was the old Calvinist notion that you can tell a man's intrinsic worth by the money he has piled up for himself. Thus, the robber barons of the 19th century, as well as H. L. Hunt, Paul Getty, Onassis, and the Kennedys are ipso facto virtuous while Appalachian whites and ghetto blacks are ipso facto deserving of their malnutrition and bought-and-sold status that benefits only uptown johns.

People tried to make him understand that a new

community, a new world, sees the possession of $1 million as ipso facto proof of guilt, of human violation, bribery, pillaging of community rights. Others tried to teach him the tired truth that somebody could spend 20 hours a day doing nothing that Graham might respect—and still be accomplishing a necessary and valuable task. My God, even incipiently right-wing McLuhan could wise up this 19th century free-enterprizer by demonstrating how it will be the tribe alone that will be determining value systems soon—and that then green pieces of paper will be proof of absolutely nothing. Leave it to the new rock critic of The Village Voice to wish Graham every success in the battle—and to complain that it's a drag to have to wade through this rag-tag community to get Graham's musical offerings. Nevertheless, this particular confrontation has now been won. It became obvious that the rich uptown Village Voice hippie, already repelled by the milieu, wouldn't want to risk pickets, stink bombs, etc., to continue rewarding Graham's money hunger. And Graham's other alternatives—either relocate or become the Lower East Side's Mayor Daley—were not as convenient at this point. So longhairs, blacks, Puerto Ricans, bikers, the Motherfuckers, and WITCH—the activist wing of the women's rights movement—have been doing their thing several Wednesdays running, hearing free live rock-blues-jazz, seeing Movement films, hearing brothers and sisters rap on the problems of community control. Graham must be given credit, too—he's donated his theatre personnel on these evenings, and is beginning to understand a little better what "community" means. Concomitantly, another community grouping, the Lower-East Side Defense (LSD), also known as the Action Committee for Internal Defense (ACID), has begun sending out small groups to patrol the neighborhood on weekends. These groups (laughingly called the Red Guards) wear red headbands and observe the wheeling and dealing of the local police on its omnipotent rounds. A Movement coffee shop, the Common Ground, has also become a place for community rapping—except that Gottherer and Davidoff (Mayor Lindsay's Rosencrantz and Guildenstern) are rumored to be interested in subsidizing this experiment. The old story? To control community control? All the better to infiltrate you, my dear, or—if necessary—bug you, in any way necessary.

The question of tacticians such as you is this: Can local community struggles succeed at

this point? Can communities define themselves, police themselves, ward off unfriendly occupation forces with antiquated notions of right and wrong, determine for themselves what is permissible in the community, based on actual experience (smash speed dealers, for example, but protect honest-weight pot suppliers)? For answers tune in next week. But tacticians point out that segmenting off a piece of the monster and trying to liberate it is like someone in the Warsaw Ghetto hoping to defeat the Nazis. The System is omnipotent when compared to any struggling community; it can smash such a community the minute it shows signs of reaching a point of consciousness that actually threatens the existing hegemony. Ocean Hill, another beleaguered community, may succeed partially in fighting off the forces of repression only because America is impressed by the ability of blacks to put to the torch the ruling white's investment in poverty. When this investment is threatened, compromises are suddenly discovered.

Non-all-black communities have fewer options. We have not yet burned down whole city blocks here when they club our longhair brothers, arrest our Puerto Rican brothers on trumped up charges, cut our psychedelics with addictive poisons, hook our black brothers on heroin, buy up our underground papers and head shops so they can lie to us with sexploitation charades, prostitute our sisters, kill our multicolored children in racist schools (and don't think the New York school crisis doesn't have yet one more shock in store down here on the Lower East Side, as glimpsed already at Seward High, where school demonstrations bring out teenage students with helmets that have battle legends on them reading "First Columbia Bust. First Battle of Lincoln Park. Second Battle of Grant Park. Sirhan Lives.")

The liberal, meanwhile, looks askance at our long hair ("Scum"). The Marxist-Leninist looks askance at our long hair ("Nihilists"). Wallace looks . . . ("Anarchists"). Nixon looks . . . ("Nihilist anarchist commie scum"). One thinking-of-herself-radical woman says, "I don't live down there and I don't understand that music, and I really don't care about those hooligan kids, and besides, I'm too busy with Ocean Hill." She's white. She's indifferent to one group of people's struggle for survival. What's so liberated about her neighborhood, her life style, her age group, her music, that she can sneer at ours? She doesn't live in Ocean Hill, either. So, because we aren't respectable, the Movement ignores us, and five short-haired whites (from her neighborhood?) jump out of their car one night and beat the shit out of me, shouting "Bomb Hanoi." At least *they* know where it's at. Longhairs *are* dangerous. And I'm taking self-defense classes at last. Can Hess be far behind, now that Nixon's here?

In a cold winter and a cold age commandeered by the jowls of Kristall Nacht Nixon, we huddle together in our tenements and

discover that even the police are not our enemy. We discover that nobody would have to steal to fix an addiction as agonizing as an insulin deficiency, that nobody would have to be hungry or lack contraception and abortion and medical care, that nobody would have to surrender their slum apartment to $300-a-month renovated sideburns, that nobody would have to listen to Bill Graham's version of virtue and at the same time watch his brothers and sisters

dying by inches, day by day. No, the enemy is money. The enemy is liberal (with his well-heeled odor of sanctity). The enemy is anyone who tells us to keep our hair cut short until . . . to keep "our women" quiet until . . . to be respectable until . . . Until? Until after the New Hampshire primary, until after the 1972 EMK primaries, until after the concentration camps, until after the revolution, until . . . But we are dying *now*, and we have decided

that if this *is* the Warsaw Ghetto in fact, then at least we will not die alone. Not quietly. Not respectably. Some will die with us. Which side of the barbed wire are you on, brother, sister? Don't smile when you shave my head and punch my identity card. "You won't be forgiven anything, not ever."

the village VOICE

11/28/68

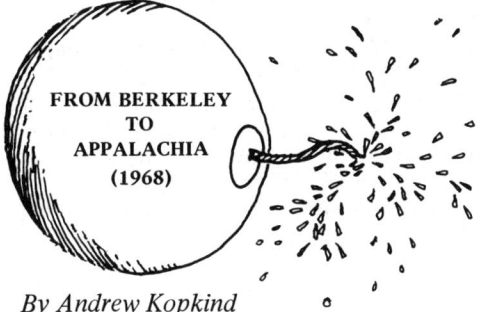

FROM BERKELEY TO APPALACHIA (1968)

SABOTAGE

By Andrew Kopkind

The war began last winter on the Western front, in the rainy season. The guns of February were four Molotov cocktails, thrown at the Naval ROTC building on the Berkeley campus of the University of California. The shots were not heard 'round the world'; as it turned out, they were hardly noticed at all beyond the San Francisco Bay area. But "war" is not always a recognizable object. More often, it is a concept in the mind of the beholder, and only an idea links individual acts of violence in a political train of events.

People are used to think of wars of nerves, or wars against poverty, or wars of all-against-all. But the new "underground" war in America is not just a metaphor for political action or social unrest. This campaign has dynamite, fire-bombs, and plastique. It is fought on hill-tops in California, in the hollows of Appalachia, on scores of college campuses, in black ghettoes and downtown shopping districts. The targets are police cars, draft boards, military facilities, power stations and mining equipment. Although no lives have been taken, property damage runs into the millions.

Very slowly, the possibility creeps into public consciousness that all the explosions fit some political pattern. Exactly what the outlines are is difficult to discern. The few newspaper accounts of the various "incidents" do not distinguish between the Cuban exiles' bomb project and the others. Rather, everything is lumped into a category of "violence," which seems to have arrived for no reason at all, like an aberrant tornado on a summer's day.

But at bottom, the campaign of revolutionary sabotage grows logically from very real conditions. The failure of traditional mediators of change, on the one hand, and the increasing militancy of the forces of change — on the same hand — provide a framework in which violent

action is at least thinkable. The experience of "real" warfare in Vietnam and widespread violence in urban ghettoes lends a certain practicality to any plans that might be hatching. There is no need for national coordination, and there is no evidence at all that any exists. Related action springs naturally and spontaneously from similar causes: revolutionary youths in Delaware do not have to get orders from Berkeley to attack their local draft board. News of one incident spreads quickly enough from coast to coast in the radical underground, and the very knowledge that a war is underway gives support and encouragement all around.

The first attack on the Berkeley ROTC building was followed by the burning of a similar center, of Stanford. At about the same time, electric power cables strung over the Berkeley hills were cut. Then, three giant electric towers in Oakland were blown to the ground, leaving about 30,000 houses without power and stopping work at the Lawrence Radiation Laboratory at Berkeley. A few days after the tower was destroyed, a University of Colorado dropout student turned himself in to police to publicize his "crime." "I had to do something to stop their machines — so maybe they would listen, so that this war would be stopped," he said.*

Other bombers have not been so open; few have been caught, and police and FBI seem to be going about their investigations in a curiously low-key way. Most of the attacks on police facilities — in Oakland and in the Detroit area — have been unsolved. Last week, police rounded up several suspects in the anti-Castro campaign, but not many of the war protestors or the other "revolutionary" saboteurs have been apprehended.

ROTC buildings and draft boards remain favorite targets. The Stanford ROTC building attacked last winter was hit again a few months later, and destroyed. On Sept. 18, a Naval ROTC hall at the University of Washington, in Seattle, was blasted, with damage estimated at $85,000. Hundreds of students watched the building burn, and a cheering section chanted, "This is number one, and the fun has just begun.

Let it burn, let it burn, let it burn." Five days previously, a Naval ROTC building at Berkeley was dynamited and an ROTC hall at the University of Delaware was hit by a Molotov cocktail. Last spring, an ROTC building at Nashville (Tennessee) Agricultural and Industrial College burned to the ground while the school's students (all black) kept firemen from fighting the fire effectively. In Eugene — hard by the University of Oregon — a series of explosions destroyed the Naval and Marine Corps Training Center, in late September. Damage was put at $106,000; trucks, a personnel carrier, a crane, and a radio tower were destroyed.

Draft boards have been attacked in North Hollywood, California, Xenia, Ohio (near Antioch College), and Berkeley. In early September, a building near Detroit, housing two suburban draft boards, was bombed. Last March, an office used by employment recruiters for defense contractors at San Fernando Valley State College (Los Angeles) was fire-bombed. At Stanford, the office of President Wallace Sterling, was burned by "arsonists." Sterling's collection of rare books and objets d'art were destroyed. One police report attributed the fire to a "crank." No one talked much about Sterling's heavy criticism from students, who were protesting his involvement with war contracts and research. In Ann Arbor, the unmarked office of the local CIA agent was bombed — and permanently closed. Policemen's private automobiles in station-house parking lots in Detroit have been blown up or damaged.

Sabotage of strip-mining operations in Appalachia does not fall into exactly the same category as the university-military attacks, but there are some obvious political connections. The new radical movements have been active in Appalachia since the early 'sixties. The poverty of the "poor whites" and unemployed miners in the region was one of the first major issues for the New Left—even before the Negro civil rights movement took the center-stage. President Kennedy capitalized on sympathy for Appalachia's poor in his 1960 campaign, and the Southern mountains became a fashionable hard-core poverty area for welfare bureaucrats and economic development experts. VISTA volunteers and assorted anti-poverty organizers roam about the area, but the economic decay continues and the political stranglehold of company-owned local officials is hard to break.

Strip-mining is the most distressing external expression of the ills of Appalachia. Coal companies have succeeded in winning legislative rights to destroy surface land to get at mineral deposits, and in the process have laid waste thousands of square miles of farms and wooded hillsides. The landscape is now barren and unreclaimable. Small farmers and rural residents have no power to push conservationist demands against the influence of the companies and their political allies.

But in the past few months, the people of Appalachia have asserted a new kind of power for themselves. On August 24, four men invaded a mine office in Middlesboro, Kentucky; they bound up the night watchman, carted him away, and set off the company's own explosives. A million dollars' worth of equipment went up with the dynamite charge. Throughout the summer, the "Appalachian guerrillas" roamed Kentucky counties, blowing up strip-mining equipment where they could find it. State authorities would like to blame out-of-state organizers, but so far most of the activity seems to have been carried on by inside-agitators: townspeople, union men, people who have been run out of the hollows by strip mine land slides. It would be hard to say they don't have enough to be agitated about.

Appalachian sabotage has a parallel with "civic-action" projects in many black communities across the country — and the well-publicized and televised riots, but the nightly bombings and burnings which police and municipal officials would rather not talk about. In Washington, there were several nights of looting and street-demonstrations last month after a white policeman shot and killed a black man whose crime had been to cross a street against a red light. (The policeman has been indicted for homicide). Tear gas filled the streets and the mass-media was on hand. But when the crisis subsided, public interest disappeared — and still, fire-bombs explode on the same streets and the white-owned stores (those that remain) are being picked off one by one.

*Ed.'s note: This young man was only responsible for overturning one electric tower by driving a tractor into it. He was never charged with the other acts of sabotage, nor did he claim to have committed them. However, the person or persons who did blow up those towers gave an interview to the *San Francisco Express Times*.

Temple Free Press 11/18/68

CIVIL WAR?

Clausewitz Updated

Everyone who can read is reminded a dozen times a year that war is the extension of policy by other means. This dictum needs to be domesticated: A nation that maintains warlike, aggressive, counterrevolutionary policies abroad is a nation that will eventually pursue these same objectives at home. Thus domestic politics becomes the extension of war by other means.

The Defense Department is not unaware of this development. A UPI story from Washington (September 14) reports that it "is being drawn ever more deeply into the problem of domestic violence in America" and cites the movement of 6,000 Regular Army troops from Texas, Oklahoma and Colorado to Chicago during the Democratic convention to restore order if the local police and National Guard were overwhelmed by the hippies and Yippies. The Army also provided the Secret Service with agents, helicopters, communications support, air reconnaissance, vehicles and experts on defusing bombs. As it turned out, the Chicago police clubs were more than sufficient to control the demonstrators and put the fear of Daley into the hearts of bystanders, but the "pre-positioning" of federal troops for a political convention in an American city is surely a significant innovation.

Chicago presents only an isolated instance of the Pentagon's role in quelling or preventing riots. A 180-man Directorate of Civil Disturbance Planning and Operations, commanded by Lieut. Gen. George R. Mather, was set up in April as the nerve center for such activities, and a Civil Disturbance Steering Committee, headed by Army Under Secretary David E. McGiffert, meets about once a week. During the summer Army teams visited more than 100 American cities to discuss riot-control plans with local officials and study the layouts of police precincts and communications to insure that the police, National Guard and federal authorities could cooperate in civil crises. "City profile" books incorporating the findings have been compiled for future use. An Army school at Fort Gordon, Ga., gives a week-long course in civil disturbance planning for troop commanders of the Regular Army, National Guard and city and state officials. Some 160,000 Regular Army troops have received thirty-two hours of riot training. Including Reserves and Guard units, riot-trained military forces in the United States are stated to comprise more than 500,000 men.

The UPI survey does not touch on an important phase of federal aid in civil crises which may well be in an area so sensitive that publicity is best avoided. However, another of Clausewitz's teaching is apposite in this connection. He was a pioneer in total war: instead of the traditional armies clashing in battle, the citizens, property and territory of the enemy nation should be attacked by all available means. In the present situation the enemy nation, so to speak, is within the national borders and the Clausewitz doctrine, if adopted by its military segment, leads to the concept of total guerrilla warfare and unlimited sabotage.

More than half the population of the United States now lives in urban and suburban areas which are completely dependent on distant sources for food and water and only partially self-sustaining in electricity. The cities are thus less vulnerable within their boundaries than at innumerable external points, perhaps dozens or hundreds of miles distant. To guard major highways, bridges, aqueducts and transmission lines day and night will be a large order, even if the defense uses the latest technological equipment and the troop strength of the Army, Guard and Reserves.

It would seem less expensive and more prudent to forestall such developments by other than military means, yet with varying emphasis all three Presidential candidates are fostering the idea that law and order are to be preserved almost exclusively by force. No doubt Clausewitz would agree.

From an editorial in THE **NATION** "Clausewitz Updated" 11/4/68

The Vietnamese experience shows that sabotage as a politically isolated act quickly turned against the revolutionary forces. It only proved useful as a carefully planned part of a total revolutionary program.

With several hundred successful bombings throughout the country in the last year, the movement rose from frustration to the pulse-quickening embrace of concrete revolutionary action. Life Magazine publicizes a new trend and a fad is born.

The hip community has to make clear that only certain sabotage operations serve the people, that carefully selected institutions which enslave people should be the targets, and that lives should be spared. It's all too easy to imagine a person wanting to strike a blow against the government while expressing solidarity with the working class setting a bomb in a U.S. Post Office which explodes killing several late-night customers at the postage stamp machine. It is also conceivable to imagine a high school student in rebellion against his mind slavery setting a bomb which destroys the principal.

The careless attitude by some in the left in disseminating incomplete information about bomb formulas and sabotage diagrams could prove disastrous. As the country moves into a period of increasing violence which takes on some characteristics of urban guerrilla warfare, only the coolest and most mature heads who have thoroughly studied their calling should play the role of saboteurs. Courage should be recognized, but romanticization of bombings encourages fools to grab for the glamor of the day.

If good-hearted revolutionary fools plan bombings which harm the people then they must be denounced and opposed. If for instance the person who set the bomb in the Electric Circus in New York which slightly injured fourteen was a leftist he must be attacked. The effect of such a bombing would be worse than if the explosion were caused by the right wing. It will only take a few foolish bombings to undercut confidence in the Left and render bombings less effective as revolutionary actions. At all times the revolutionary's value of human life has to be made distinct from the Capitalist society's property ethic.

Revolutionaries who want to consider themselves part of the planet-wide struggle against exploitation want to do something real. Meetings, organizational work, patiently explaining to people the reasons for actions seem academic exercises when compared to bombings. The American system's educational mind-policing so divides words and thoughts from experience, that the slow basic work of increasing people's unity and understanding seems impotent and self-indulgent. But it's the most basic ingredient of revolutionary change. The stakes are getting serious, and the gambler has our lives as well as others on the table. We can't afford to confuse the useful and limited possibilities of bombing with romantic dreams of quick and easy victory.

WEATHER VANE TELLS VELOCITY OF WIND

. . . Can be adapted to other uses

Excerpt from "Responsible Terrorism,"  4/3/70

But having an analysis is not enough; we must also demonstrate our analysis through collective actions which show people that there is a way of stopping what we know is bad and of building what we know is good. This means that our actions must also demonstrate the value and necessity of collective struggle instead of individual action; and to demonstrate that people are not alone in their conditions or anger or sense of impotence. Passivity and an inability to foresee success are a result of both the deepest isolation and the unqualified acceptance of the United States as an unbeatable power. Any actions the movement initiates should help people move out of passivity and isolation (break down the "you can't fight city hall" belief). In fact, one of the major effects of the state's use of repression is to isolate people and make individual examples: getting them to believe they are alone and without support in their struggle. In the courts and jails, such techniques serve the pigs well: defendants and inmates feel deserted, alone, stripped of every facet of their identity and made completely dependent on authority for their most minimal needs.

The movement often measures the importance of its actions by the amount of material damage done. To some extent this is correct: our sheer physical ability to do damage is more than an idle threat; but even the economic and psychological cost of disruptions or the constant threat of them (which often impede the normal functioning of institutions) do not represent the most threatening aspect of such militancy.

Rather, the basic threat in militant actions is that they will be exemplary to the many who are almost ready to go into the streets to assault the institutions which oppress them; exemplary because they will demonstrate an alternative to the passive and humiliating acceptance of oppression and repression; exemplary because they happen where the people live or work or just hang together. Just as the NLF and the Black Panther Party have served as examples to the white movement, we must serve as an additional example to others, joining with them where we can in mutual struggle.

From "Hey There What's That Sound?" by Randy Rappoport, Beverly Leman, Carol McEldowney **Leviathan** Feb 1970

The state is coming down hard on drugs. More and more Sisters and Brothers are getting busted everyday, smoking or dropping in their apartments. Pigs are kicking down doors and ripping people off the streets all over the Hill and all over America.

We've heard their lame excuses like "We have to save our youth" or "We have to conduct medical studies." But we don't believe that line, we know that they don't give a shit about us or our health.

The truth is that Nixon-Mitchell and the rest are out to destroy youth culture.

The first attack is to shut off the supply of grass and acid through Operation Intercept and selective busts to try to force us to killer drugs like scag and speed. Body drugs destroy us and our ability to act. They're not afraid of us when we're in the closet on the nod. Body drugs divide us. Scag is a solitary drug, we isolate ourselves from our sisters and brothers and we end up ripping each other off. Grass and acid are communal drugs, they bring us together. But they love to see us kill each other, it saves them the bother. This is not a new tactic. Scag has been used for decades in Black communities to keep Black people down, to keep them from moving.

The second attack is to send the pigs to harrass us. They either bust "legally" and send us away for years, or kick down our doors or conduct "illegal searches" that tie us up in court for months or years before we are acquitted. We end up spending a lot of money for lawyers, getting evicted from our apartments, and maybe losing our jobs or getting kicked out of school.

Why is the State trying to destroy the Youth Culture movement and the Urban Youth Ghettoes like Beacon Hill, Berkeley

THE KNOCK AT THE DOOR

and the East Village. Because we potentially pose a direct threat to their system, we are a potentially revolutionary movement. Street people in Berkeley moved on to defend their lives by fighting at Oakland draft centers and at People's Park and through rent strikes. They aren't afraid of us because we smoke dope. They are afraid of us because we aren't walking out of their schools into their factories and desks. They are afraid of us because we know what they are doing in Vietnam, in Roxbury, in Dorchester and right here, and they know we can get together and do something about it.

Thus the campaign against us is political repression. We can get too big and too together. They see the threat. So they bust us, divide us, and addict us. We have to recognize this repression is the same repression leveled at the Black Community and the Black Panther Party and the Vietnamese, although it is certainly not as heavy. It will be when we build a movement that will follow the example of

Blacks and Yellows.

We have to fight this repression WE NEED TO BE A COMMUNITY. We must begin to use self-defense. To begin with we need a community lawyers guild and a community bail fund. We need to know the few rights we have.

Some of us are trying to get this together. If you need a name call us the Beacon Hill Revolutionary Action Group. We all need to defend the Hill. We dig on that. And we dig on other people fighting for what they deserve. Like the Blacks, the Vietnamese, and the Cubans. We need help. PEOPLE.

Help build a movement on the Hill. For bust assistance or if you want to work with us, call BEACON HILL REVOLUTIONARY ACTION GROUP – HA6-2122 (Leave a message at this number and we'll get it within the hour.)

POWER TO THE PEOPLE
BEACON HILL RAGS

A leaflet from Boston

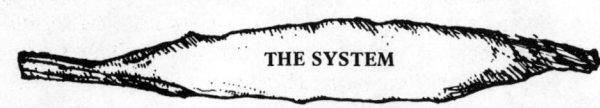

THE SYSTEM

FREE PRESS REPRESS

by Jerry Applebaum

Next Monday, April 13, I go on trial in Los Angeles Superior Court for being a reporter who abused the "freedom of the press."

I'm charged (along with LA Free Press owner Art Kunkin) with two counts of allegedly "receiving stolen property"; an Attorney General's report of an investigation into widespread malpractice in the UCLA Campus Police Department, and a list of the names, addresses and phone numbers of eighty state narcs from the California Bureau of Narcotics Enforcement.

The penalty is one to ten years on each count.

The charges grow out of the publication in the Free Press last August (while I was still an "employee") of the

information allegedly contained in two Attorney General's files. Jerry Reznick, a former employee of the Attorney General's office in Los Angeles is charged with stealing the files. the results of the investigation into the UCLA Pig Department. Among the allegations made in the report were dereliction of duty by Chief Boyd Lynn; extortion, burglary of University property, assault, forcible rape and receiving stolen property. Members of the Los Angeles Police Department were also implicated.

The Attorney General had more than enough evidence to bring charges against the pigs, including the police chief. All could have been fired or suspended pending trial.

The Attorney General didn't do anything, even though the investigation had been going on for over a year. In my story I accused him of complicity because of his lack of action.

In the August eighth edition we

published the narc list—the Attorney General and the narcs freaked.

Their initial response was to sue Kunkin, myself and the rest of the staff for $25 million. The narcs filed a $15 million suit for "invasion of privacy." The Attorney General sued us for $10 million, claiming that we had "obstructed justice" and for destroying the "effectiveness" of the Bureau.

A few weeks later they went to the Los Angeles County Grand Jury and got the felony indictments against us. The pigs hope to not only put us in jail but to put the Free Press out of business. Whatever the merits of the Free Press may be, it should not be allowed to be destroyed by the pigs.

If the Free Press is destroyed then no other underground paper is safe.

BERKELEY TRIBE 4/10/70

PIGS... the nature of the BEAST

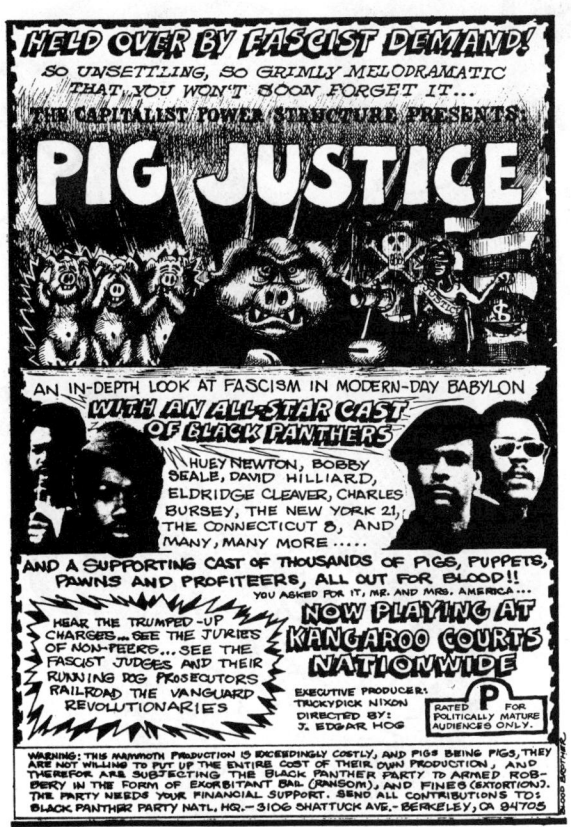

HELD OVER BY FASCIST DEMAND!
SO UNSETTLING, SO GRIMLY MELODRAMATIC THAT YOU WON'T SOON FORGET IT...
THE CAPITALIST POWER STRUCTURE PRESENTS:

PIG JUSTICE

AN IN-DEPTH LOOK AT FASCISM IN MODERN-DAY BABYLON
WITH AN ALL-STAR CAST OF BLACK PANTHERS

HUEY NEWTON, BOBBY SEALE, DAVID HILLIARD, ELDRIDGE CLEAVER, CHARLES BURSEY, THE NEW YORK 21, THE CONNECTICUT 8, AND MANY, MANY MORE.....

AND A SUPPORTING CAST OF THOUSANDS OF PIGS, PUPPETS, PAWNS AND PROFITEERS, ALL OUT FOR BLOOD!!

YOU ASKED FOR IT, MR. AND MRS. AMERICA...

HEAR THE TRUMPED-UP CHARGES... SEE THE JURIES OF NON-PEERS... SEE THE FASCIST JUDGES AND THEIR RUNNING DOG PROSECUTORS RAILROAD THE VANGUARD REVOLUTIONARIES

NOW PLAYING AT KANGAROO COURTS NATIONWIDE

EXECUTIVE PRODUCER: TRICKYDICK NIXON
DIRECTED BY: J. EDGAR HOG

RATED **P** FOR POLITICALLY MATURE AUDIENCES ONLY.

WARNING: THIS MAMMOTH PRODUCTION IS EXCEEDINGLY COSTLY, AND PIGS BEING PIGS, THEY ARE NOT WILLING TO PUT UP THE ENTIRE COST OF THEIR OWN PRODUCTION, AND THEREFORE ARE SUBJECTING THE BLACK PANTHER PARTY TO ARMED ROBBERY IN THE FORM OF EXORBITANT BAIL (RANSOM), AND FINES (EXTORTION). THE PARTY NEEDS YOUR FINANCIAL SUPPORT. SEND ALL CONTRIBUTIONS TO: BLACK PANTHER PARTY NATL. HQ.- 3106 SHATTUCK AVE.- BERKELEY, CA 94705

RAP SHEET ON COPS

There are a lot of things about the cops that are wrong. Here are some of them:

1. Cops have authority over the people even when they (the cops) are wrong.

2. Cops can stop and frisk people whenever they feel like it. The law says they can only do this when they have probable cause, which means they have reasonable grounds to believe that a crime has been committed or is about to be committed. Too often cops stop and frisk kids with no justification. They do it for the hell of it.

3. Cops lie in court. Many are trained perjurors. Cops usually have a tight relationship with judges, the State's Attorney, public defenders (prison deliverers), and lawyers. This automatically means that in most cases trials are stacked against people before people are proved guilty. In practice the Constitutional guarantee that a person is innocent until proven guilty has disappeared.

4. Cops are in the schools. Schools are mental and physical prisons. Instead of trying to ease tensions between different racial and ethnic groups, the cops encourage these tensions, heating them up.

5. Cops harass and hassle people. They run hot checks at their pleasure, fingerprint people for misdemeanors, stop people just to get payoffs, have a quota of tickets they have to give out, work with teachers to hassle kids, make false arrests whenever they feel like it, and are evaluated for promotion on the basis of the number of arrests they make.

6. Cops harass juveniles and members of minority groups. Juveniles and minority groups are ordinary people, yet they are treated like dogs, not like citizens. We are the dogs that cops kick.

7. Cops show favoritism to rich people and rich people's kids.

8. Too many cops treat people brutally and threaten them.

9. Cops harass people who are under supervision and on parole. Once the cops get you fingered, you are a branded man.

10. Cops are the military arm (the army) of the ruling class. They serve and protect property, not people. The property they protect is owned and controlled by the rich who run this city, state, and country. What has happened is that property has come to be considered more important than people. This is wrong.

Get uptight over the word 'pig?' Got a cop in the family, or on the block, or an old buddy? Maybe he's a bastard, maybe he's a nice guy, but you know his family, you know his problems.

For a lot of black, Puerto Rican and Southern whites this might not be true. Not too many become cops from their neighborhoods. But it's true a lot in other neighborhoods. Maybe yours, ours.

Maybe a cop comes on a lot like our own people, more than a hippy does, or a college kid, or rich people. So it looks like we got things in common. Maybe we do. We're part of that big bunch of people who do the work in this society, part of the working class. But so what? Almost everyone is, whether they know it or not.

But it isn't whether you work or not, but what you work at, and how much you're trying to change things. If you're union but trying to make the union more responsive to the needs and feelings of the members instead of the union leaders, that may be alright. Or any job you are on and are trying to get better conditions and more control for you and the other workers, and less bullshit from bosses, or maybe no bosses, that's alright too.

But cops don't only work for someone else, like most of us, they work to keep that someone else on top, and us in line. A cop should protect people. But he protects property and the few people who own and control it. Not personal possessions, but property, like stores, buildings, banks. What kid owns a building? Which sister or brother drives a cadillac with a cop escort who makes sure their investments are safe?

Cops are bound to come down on you if you're young, black, brown, or poor because except for rare cases you are the enemy of the few people cops really work for. Because those few have got what you want and need but they aren't gonna let you have. You might not know it - but they do.

Do cops tear up rich homes looking for dope or beer or murderers? The rich businessmen have lawyers and connections and control. We don't.

If a cop's gonna kick our asses for standing on the corner and allow rich businessmen and politicians to buy that corner and tear it up or demolish it or do anything they want with it, then he's a pig. Even if he smiles and asks us nicely to get off our corner. He still isn't protecting you or your personal possessions; he's too busy looking out for that rich guy and his private property, even if that happens to be the building you live in.

Cops aren't forced to be cops. They do it for the steady money and security. They have to raise their families - they have to get a job. But becoming a cop is taking a job that protects the system that made it necessary to fight and scrape for steady money and security in the first place. It's a vicious circle. But they can quit. There might have been nice guys in the Nazi army but they were protecting a rotten bastard and keeping an inhuman and no good system going. And those suckers were drafted.

But if you wanted to deal with Hitler and his bullshit you had to deal with those soldiers.

If the cop doesn't quit - we've got to try and make him understand that he'd better. Otherwise, he's a pig as long as he wears that uniform and uses it to keep the rich businessmen and their politician cohorts in business, and us in line. Both articles from *Rising Up Angry* Oct 1969

HEY KIDS!
READ ABOUT
THE PIG'S WAR ON YOUTH

WHO, ME?

BUT MEANWHILE...

PIG DIGNEY: A SMELLY BOOT ON THE NECK OF YOUTH

NOTE: What follows is the first in a series of articles, dialogues, descriptions, depictions and maybe some prescriptions of life as a kid under the paw of the pig in Dane County, Madison. Some of this may suggest it is truly an uncomfortable situation to be a juvenile in Dane County, Madison.

The author has been closely involved in police/juvenile relations in the city for several years and will remain anonymous.

More and more kids are becoming aware that they are being pushed, kicked, bribed, jailed, and physically abused because they refuse to be pointed in the adult-specified direction. With the persuasive/oppressive powers of both County and city cops, kids must either "shape up" or get shit upon. Many young people now understand it is the same ugly pig boot kicking them that kicks students, blacks, welfare mothers, etc.

This and future articles will serve to inform parents, teachers, businessmen, etc., that hope for reconciliation and/or working with youth in traditional terms is fading quickly, possibly quicker than most youth counselors think. Later in the series, a list of the ten most hated disciplinarians, cops, principles, radio announcers, etc., will be announced. At that time, it is highly recommended that these ten fascist clowns

leave the state. Let them be forewarned that the imagination and creativity of all those who suppress and abuse youth in Dane County can not match the powers of spirit, ideas and imagination of the youth they suppress and abuse.

Let's look at the individual who is at this moment a front runner in the race for number one of the ten most-hated by youth in Dane County. He is known to young people by many titles, all of which are more pleasing to the ear than his own evil tag. The man resides at 3909 Anchor Drive. His home telephone number is 249-9392. He is responsible for the recruitment of many informers/squealers through bribery, threats, and battery to juveniles, carelessly shooting at fleeing 13, 14, and 15 year old boys, and threatening the lives of young people to expedite his war on youth in Dane County. WOULD DETECTIVE ROBERT M. DIGNEY PLEASE STAND UP, so that he may better be knocked down.

Detective Digney has resided in the Madison Police Department for more than 15 years. His fellow officers consider him "strictly law and order," and sheriff's deputies often shrug their shoulders, grin sheepishly, and slobber out, "Ya, Digney gives kids more hell than any other man

on the force." Digney has devoted the last fifteen years and more of his life to the harassment, abuse, and arrest of kids. He recently lashed out at the substitution of civilian counselors for cops in the Dane County Detention Home on the third floor of the City-County Building. In a remarkable demonstration of restraint and open-mindedness, Digney denounced the Detention facility as being "taken over by hippies, communists, and dirty students." According to the CAP TIMES, none of the counselors are students, one is a 32-year-old ex-Lutheran minister, another a 34-year-old ex Madison cop, etc. Bob Digney doesn't only lie to teenagers and the public; he's not even capable of telling himself where it's at. The man is a public menace, a danger to youth and other living things in the community.

Quite in line with the tradition of the liberal bullshitter, Bob the Bully is noted for his graceful snow job for parents of the kids he hates so passionately. (Let us not assume most parents are capable of correctly interpreting their youngster, but for the moment lets give them credit for existing.)

Madison **kaleidoscope** 3/18//0

POCKET LAWYER OF LEGAL FIRST AID

from THE BLACK PANTHER

1. If you are stopped and/or arrested by the police, you may remain silent; you do not have to answer any questions about alleged crimes, you should provide your name and address only if requested (although it is not absolutely clear that you must do so.) But then do so, and at all time remember the fifth amendment.

2. If a police officer is not in uniform, ask him to show his identification. He has no authority over you unless he properly identifies himself. Beware of persons posing as police officers. Always get his badge number and his name.

3. Police have no right to search your car or your home unless they have a search warrant, probable cause or your consent. They may conduct no exploratory search, that is, one for evidence of crime generally or for evidence of a crime unconnected with the one you are being questioned about. (Thus, a step for an auto violation does not give the right to search the auto.) You are not required to consent to a search; therefore, you should not consent and should state clearly and unequivocally that you do not consent, in front of witnesses if possible. If you do not consent, the police will have the burden in court of showing probably cause. Arrest may be corrected later.

4. You may not resist arrest forcibly or by going limp, even if you are innocent. To do so is a separate crime of which you can be convicted even if you are acquitted of the original charge. Do not resist arrest under any circumstances.

5. If you are stopped and/or arrested, the police may search you by patting you on the outside of your clothing. You can be stripped of your personal possessions. Do not carry anything that includes the name of your employer or friends.

7. Do not engage in "friendly" conversation with officers on the way to or at the station. Once you are arrested, there is little likelihood that anything you say will get you released.

8. As soon as you have been booked, you have the right to complete at least two phone calls—one to a relative, friend or attorney, the other to a bail bondsman. If you can, call the Black Panther Party, 845-0103 (845-0104), and the Party will post bail if possible

9. You must be allowed to hire and see an attorney immediately.

10. You do not have to give any statement to the police, nor do you have to sign any statement you might give them, and therefore you should not sign anything. Take the Fifth and Fourteenth Amendments, because you cannot be forced to testify against yourself.

11. You must be allowed to post bail in most cases, but you must be able to pay the bail bondsmen's fee. If you cannot pay the fee, you may ask the judge to release you from custody without bail or to lower your bail, but he does not have to do so.

12. The police must bring you into court or release you within 48 hours after your arrest (unless the time e?ds on a week-end or a holiday, and they must bring you before a judge the first day court is in session.)

13. If you do not have the money to hire an attorney, immediately ask the police to get you an attorney without charge.

14. If you have the money to hire a private attorney, but do not know of one, call the National Lawyers' Guild or the Alameda County Bar Association (or the Bar Association of your county) and furnish you with the name of an attorney who practices criminal law.

A KIND
OF DIALOGUE

Pacifist A.J. Muste (center)

3 BOMBS FOUND AT ARMY PLANT

Incident Is Latest Reported in Wisconsin Terrorism

Special to The New York Times

MADISON, Wis., Jan. 6—An unsuccessful attempt to bomb an Army ammunition plant from a stolen airplane was the latest reported incident in a wave of terrorist attacks on area military and Selective Service installations.

A spokesman for the Dane County Sheriff's office confirmed today that three bombs had been found at the 7,000-acre Badger Army Ammunition Plant, situated near Baraboo, Wis., 35 miles north of Madison. The plant manufactures powder for use in Vietnam.

Discovery of the bombs apparently confirmed assertions made in an anonymous telephone call yesterday to the University of Wisconsin student newspaper, the Daily Cardinal.

The caller, who identified himself as "The Vanguard of the Revolution," said members of his group had stolen a two-seater Cessna-150 plane from a suburban Madison airport

about 1:30 A.M. New Year's Day. He said the bombs were dropped at 2 A.M. and the plane was then abandoned at an unlit nearby airport.

Field Morey, vice president of the Morey Airplane Company, confirmed that the plane, one of severla used to give University of Wisconsin Reserve Officert Training Corps cadets flight training, had been stolen. The police found the aircraft abandoned at Sank-Prairie Airport, a community airfield near the Badger plant.

The anonymous caller said, "Unofrtunately the bombs were all duds." The police would release no information about the bombs.

The wave of destruction and bombing, now the object of an investigation by the police and military intelligence and Federal Bureau of Investigation agents, began Dec. 28 when an R.O.T.C. headquarters on the university campus was damaged by a fire bomb. During the New Year's weekend, a Madison Army Reserve center was heavily damaged and axes were used to smash doors and destroy communications equipment.

On Jan. 3 a fire, which authorities say resulted from a fire bomb, did extensive damage to the "Red Brick Gym," a campus landmark that housed R.O.T.C. offices.

The anonymous caller also warned that attacks would be made later on other university

installations, the State Capital in downtown Madison and state office buildings in the city.

The reported threat incurred the wrath of State Senators, in Madison for a two-week legislative session.

"Maybe the time has come to meet violence with violence," said Senator Ernest Keppler, Republican of Sheboygan, who urged that the Capitol's security forces be strengthened.

The Daily Cardinal today printed an editorial endorsing the action of the terrorists, arguing that "the Establishment" had been unresponsive and repressive in the past when peaceful demands for policy changes had been lawfully made.

University administrators reacted to the student editorial with shock. Vice Chancellor Bryant Kearl said, "I am shocked and do not believe that this can possibly represent the views of the students of Wisconsin."

"If acts such as those committed in the last few days are needed to strike fear into the bodies of once fearless men and rid this campus once and for all of repressive and deadly ideas and institutions then so be it," the student daily said in its lead editorial, entitled "End of the Road."

The New York Times
1/7/70

A Workable Alternative

Martin Luther King did offer an alternative, on August 15 when he told delegates to the Southern Christian Leadership Conference's convention: "mass civil disobedience can use rage as a constructive and creative force. To dislocate the functioning of a city without destroying it can be more effective than a riot because it can be longer-lasting, costly to the society but not wantonly destructive. Moreover, it is more difficult for Government to quell it by superior force."

As specific examples of "nonviolent confrontation," King gave the convention delegates: blocking plant gates with unemployed blacks, disrupting governmental operations with sit-ins and weekly school boycotts.

Whether King could mobilize a major nonviolent protest action in light of the present decline in popularity of nonviolence, is questionable. He did last summer in Chicago, his brother did this spring in Louisville, and Father James Groppi is doing so in Milwaukee. I feel King definitely could do it, at least in one key locality.

War Resisters League News Sept 1967

Street fighting heroics — throwing back a tear gas canister.

CREATIVE NONVIOLENCE

Many people feel that an organization that uses nonviolent methods to reach its objectives must continue winning victories one after another in order to remain nonviolent. If that be the case then a lot of efforts have been miserable failures. There is a great deal more involved than victories. My experience has been that the poor know violence more intimately than most people because it has been a part of their lives, whether the violence of the gun or the violence of want and need.

I don't subscribe to the belief that nonviolence is cowardice, as some militant groups are saying. In some instances nonviolence requires more militancy than violence. Nonviolence forces you to abandon the shortcut, in trying to make a change in the social order. Violence, the shortcut, is the trap people fall into when they begin to feel that it is the only way to attain their goal. When these people turn to violence it is a very savage kind.

When people are involved in something constructive, trying to bring about change, they tend to be less violent than those who are not engaged in rebuilding or in anything creative. Nonviolence forces one to be creative; it forces any leader to go to the people and get them involved so that they can come forth with new ideas. I think that once people understand the strength of nonviolence—the force it generates, the love it creates, the response that it brings from the total community—they will not be willing to abandon it easily.

CESAR CHAVEZ

Daniel Cohn-Bendit, "Danny the Red," was a leader of the French student-worker rebellion of May 1968.

A Left Wing Alternative

by Greg Calvert

It is with a certain amount of nervousness that I speak. That's related to a feeling I have had in the last year, a time in which I have wondered, very deeply and with great pain, whether the kind of movement which over the years has made it possible for us to live in America—the kind of movement which, out of the obscenity and sterility of this society, has given us new life—whether in fact that movement was going to survive and grow or whether it was going to die and leave us isolated.

When I worked in the national office of SDS in Chicago, I used to take the bus down West Madison Street in the Skid Row area. I used to look out the window at the faces of the alcoholics and think about my experiences bumming around the Skid Row area in Portland, Ore., when I was a high school kid back in the early 50s. There I ran from time to time into some old Wobbly organizer. Some of us in the movement have wondered whether, after so much hope and so much life, we would end like some of those old Wobblies.

Industrial Workers of the World — Wobblies — were early-1900s labor radicals. Their powerful, popular socialist movement was destroyed by government repression.

I was asked recently whether I thought there was any possibility that we could avoid the Stalinization of the Left. I said there is only one response: Knowing we are faced with the possibility of the Stalinization of the Left, we must do whatever is necessary to see that it does not happen.

Staughton Lynd has offered two alternative histories of the last months of this decade. One of them projected the disintegration of the Resistance, its splintering into a number of factions and its end in irrelevancy. Another projected people from different organizations of the movement beginning to discuss the possibility and the framework for creating the non-Stalinist, the libertarian, the life-giving alternative for the Left.

If that alternative is not created, if the life-giving, libertarian spirit of the Left is lost in the mechanical, guilt-ridden forms of Stalinism, we will have no one but ourselves to blame.

We can no longer objectify the problem and say there are the following ten forces operating which militate against the alternative. We simply must be more determined. If subjectivism—and I use the term imprecisely, the way I get attacked for using it—if the quality of life inside the movement is to survive, we must do it, and we can do it.

But we can't do it unless we cling to all of the categories which now end up on the phony side of phony dichotomies. Let me offer one. Someone has said that today it's "ideolog versus activist." In times past it was "nonviolence versus violence," then it was "centralism versus decentralism," or "student power versus racism." All of those were attempts to assume that at any moment in our history we have only one of two choices. That kind of thinking has to be broken down—especially the phony distinction between "security" and "openness," as though there were any other kind of real security in the movement apart from the trust in openeness which develops among people who can count on each other when the heat's on.

It is very fashionable in SDS these days—an organization to whose national meetings I have not had the emotional energy to return for a year—to denounce something called personal liberation. If you talk about what you feel or what's meaningful to you in a political forum, you're suddenly one of those personal liberation people.

I don't quite understand what that's supposed to mean. I do not believe in a two-story universe; I don't think there's going to be some reward out there somewhere. I don't believe in capitalist ideology, which is the ideology of deferred life, of deferred existence, of accumulation for tomorrow. Unless one does believe in that, then I don't understand what motivation there would be for a biological, physical being to get involved except the liberation of that individual.

In Danny the Red's book, *Obsolete Communism—The Left Wing Alternative*, there's a phrase which I think must be taken seriously. He discusses and puts down people who operate on the politics of guilt—the politics of life deferral, the politics of the acceptance of repressiveness, in the hope that some day there'll be a non-repressive future born suddenly and cataclysmically. He says *the only reason for being a revolutionary in our time is because it's a better way to live.*

I don't think I've ever known anyone in the last five to seven years who was in the movement and in it for good who wasn't there knowing that it was a better way to live. If you think that politics and personality can be split apart and still build a revolution, if you think it's possible to be, in this kind of society, in any sense revolutionary without being engaged to the deepest level of your life, if you think any of those things or do any of those things to your movement, then we will not create that alternative history.

I do not mean that I think it is any longer possible for us to deal with our political responsibilities to ourselves, and to that larger America which we must reach, simply on the basis of existentialist language. But, the alternative is not Stalinist ideology. The alternative to understanding that I'm in this because I want to be free is not economic determinism. Certainly Marx is important; but let us not create a movement based on Marxism as ideology. Let us do more justice to Marx himself.

I want now to trace what I perceive to be the history that has led us to this impasse and this possibility, and talk about my experience of the theme of resistance from the inside of SDS.

This takes us back to the summer of 1966, a summer of great possibilities, possibilities which were given to us because the first phase of the movement had definitely come to an end. We could no longer find our constituencies outside ourselves by going South, into the black community. The statement of black power which SDS endorsed in June 1966 came at a time when many white radicals were realizing it was absolutely necessary that we go out and build in our own circumstances our own movement. Because black power threw us back on ourselves and our own lives, our own situations, it offered us the possibility for being sincerely radical, and not the liberal adjunct of the black movement.

It was also in that summer that the first traveling draft resistance work was done. Mendy Samstein, who had been my closest friend in graduate school at Cornell in 1960 to '61, and who had spent about three years working in the South, came to Chicago and talked about draft resistance and about his projected program. I argued with Mendy very intensely about that program because I was afraid that inherent in his notion about non-cooperation was the possibility for perpetuating in the new situation the politics of masochism. After I talked with Mendy and others, it seemed to me that, though the danger was there, there was another kind of possibility inherent in the Resistance approach. This was the possibility of white radicals beginning to engage the struggle in the deepest way they needed to around an issue which was the issue of their own oppression.

After SDS passed its draft resistance resolution in December, 1966, at the Berkeley National Council meeting, a very interesting set of ideas began to be generated. In their final formulation, these ideas were our attempt to provide some of the theoretical notions for a larger movement in the United States, which would not only be draft resistance but would go beyond draft resistance and talk to the great mass of Americans about struggling over their own oppression, and struggling for their own liberation—not somebody else's—in the context of the conditions of their own lives.

Let me try to trace how those ideas emerged. I think there's been a kind of unrealistic assumption made about where terms like "neo-capitalism" and "new working class" came from, as though we had snatched them from the firmament of Marxist ideology and imposed them on the movement. In January, 1966, we put out the button, "Not With My Life You Don't," to concretize the spirit of, "It's my fight, it's my life." Everyone was talking about strategy for draft resistance, but every time we sat through a three-hour session on strategy for draft resistance, we didn't get anywhere. What we were asking was the impossible: that draft resistance give us the channels for making a total revolution in society.

Then an article was written by Peter Henig in *New Left Notes* called "Manpower Chanelling." That, at least in SDS, was the first time anybody had bothered to read the material that came out of the Selective Service System. It crystallized a lot of vague notions we'd been playing with in our heads about who students are. What it told us was that this supposed privilege, II-S, was at at deeper level another instrument of oppression. It was part of a larger program, a program of manpower channelling for not only the military but for industry.

It had been written, back in 1947 or whenever, to insure that the military needs of American capitalism and American imperialism would not interfere with the continuing supply of manpower for profit at home. Since the period following the second world war was the period in which the new technology of the coming automation and cybernated production were emerging, it was clear that American capitalism and industry were going to need an enormous number of highly trained, highly skilled workers to plug into those slots in its advanced technological machinery.

It was clear, also, that the university was going to become the training ground for those workers, those scientific, technical and professional workers who were needed by advanced capitalism. The multiversity would become the motor for the transformation of the labor force in the direction of the new technology.

It was out of that set of realizations that we began to see that students are in a tremendously different historical situation than that of Lenin's Russia in 1902, when they *were* the petty bourgeois intelligentsia. There's something different with seven million students in the multiversities of the United States. By 1975, one quarter of the labor force in the country will have had some college training.

We said, then, that the working class was being renewed, expanded; we called these people the "new working class," the university-trained workers.

That was important because it gave us a handle on the long-range question of social change, of revolution in society. It gave us the possibility of a perspective that said students and post-students fighting around the conditions of their own lives are legitimately revolutionary strata where they are at, and that that can be their great contribution to a larger movement, which must include other sectors of the population—the blue-collar workers and the poor.

Back to a little history to bring us up to 1968.

After the summer of '67, the Pentagon action and Stop the Draft Week which preceded it, it seemed to some of us that the time was rapidly approaching when the resistance notion of strategy could become the base for a new kind of radical solidarity among a variety of elements within the movement. I mean by "resistance strategy" a notion which included not only draft resistance and non-cooperation, but also resistance to Dow Chemical and other institutions of repression.

Michael Ferber and I talked the other day, trying to dredge out of our unconsciouses the memories of those months from October, 1967 to April 1968. What we came up with was a wealth of memories of political events which affirmed what we believed, events in which representatives of the black militant movement were saying, "Yes, now we have a legitimate basis for an alliance, because in the resistance movement there is a truly radical and potentially revolutionary movement among whites."

I believe that that was true. I do not wish to pretend that events exterior to the movement—such as Johnson's dropping out of the race, and a series of events exterior to the white movement, the series of uprisings that followed King's assassination—did not have an importance in reorienting people's outlooks. The reorientation of SDS in that spring of 1968 was to drop draft resistance and resistance themology almost entirely, and to revert to, "We got to support the black movement, racism is our issue. Anti-racism is the radical position."

What you do to a white man in today's society when you tell him he's got to fight the anti-racism struggle is give him a struggle that doesn't have any outside to it. I do not want to deny that racism is a problem, as male chauvinism is a problem inside of us. But I wish to insist that the only way we can finally fight against racism effectively is to be fighting our battles for our own liberation, in alliance with black people fighting their struggle for their own liberation.

In that situation, when the movement should have held strong—despite the fact that LBJ's pulling out and what happened after King's death were going to have an effect—the movement should have held firm and insisted more firmly than ever on the relevance of the resistance strategy. Instead, meetings were beginning to be held to plan for Chicago. Having taken that direction, having decided that, instead of pushing our resources on the legitimate strategy which we had and focusing our resources on the convention, we abandoned strategic leadership for the white movement. The decline of mass, spontaneous kinds of activity around the war movement, which was inevitable, need not have also disoriented the solid core of resistance which was there.

I do not know, but I wonder whether some of the shifting direction from April to the summer in black organizations was not conditioned by our failure. My understanding of the dynamic of the black movement in relation to the other strata in American society is that it has two choices—either it can rely on whites for liberal support, or it can find a radical ally in a radical white movement. When that ally is not there doing his thing, then the black movement, for its own survival, reverts to looking for liberal support. If honky-baiting goes up, it's because we create the dynamic where there's no other response for desperate black militants. I wonder whether once again in that situation we don't have ourselves to blame.

In the ensuing year, having myself left national SDS much disturbed over this question, having opposed the line of racism being our first issue, having opposed the publication of a pamphlet which said liberation will come from a black thing and having called that pamphlet obscene—in the last year I think we have seen what Staughton described, particularly in SDS, a revival of the politics of guilt. There was one major change, however—from 1961 to 1965 the rhetoric was liberal, and in 1968 to 1969, its rhetoric, but only its rhetoric, was revolutionary.

I do not believe that in a society like ours—an advanced capitalist society where mass culture itself is an instrument of oppression, where the repressiveness of all the last 6,000 years of civilization becomes surplus repression, where the authoritarianism of a highly bureaucratized, centralized corporate capitalism requires the inculcation of authoritarian and self-hating values in order to pacify the population—I do not believe we can free ourselves from that society through emotional structures of guilt which were created to kept us from fighting for freedom. No one that I have talked to in this year of isolation has been able to convince me otherwise, either through argument or through political accomplishment.

From left, Abbie Hoffman, John Froines, Dave Dellinger, Jerry Rubin of the Conspiracy during Nov. 15 Moratorium in Washington.

What's going on in SDS is that, having denied that students have legitimacy as a strata, or that new-working class people have legitimacy as revolutionary strata, we revert to the old Leninist formulations which say that the task of the petit-bourgois intelligentsia is to form a vanguard party which will relate to the proletarian struggle of the factory worker. I do not deny the importance of 20 to 30 million blue collar workers in long-range revolutionary strategy for the society. To do so would be foolish and absurd on its face. But, coming from a blue-collar working class background, I find it very difficult to believe that the breast beating of white students and white professionals and white technical workers about the fact that they aren't on the production line is going to save my relatives or my high school classmates from the oppressive institutions of capitalism. Nor do I believe that talking that way to them addresses itself to the real concerns of their lives.

I think what addresses itself to the concerns of the lives of young people and others in my home town, where practically everybody works in the lumber mills, is to talk to people about their lives in the way we talk with others about our lives, to organize in the same spirit of openness and commitment and hopefulness and joyousness.

I would go even so far as to argue that to organize otherwise is not to organize for revolution and liberation, but to run the danger of organizing something very different. I know from my personal upbringing what the authoritarian discipline of factories does to the family lives of workers. Not to fight authoritarianism there in the same spirit that we fight it in the university is, I think, to make a grave error, and finally to be of no use to anyone, neither to ourselves nor to those whom we would pretend to reach.

Will it be possible to create that alternative history? Will it be possible to build a movement which talks about the community of free men, about the new selfhood, about new human beings, about new possibilities, about the new man?

Will it be possible for us to have the courage to say, yes, what we want is beauty and freedom, and we think that that could happen and that we become freer and more beautiful on the path to getting there?

It seems to me that such a possibility is not only there in what Marxists call objective conditions, but is also there in the recent history of advanced capitalist civilization itself. It is very much there in the events of France in May and June. 1968.

French students, Paris Rebellion, May '68.

BOURGEOIS VOUS N'AVEZ RIEN COMPRIS

French rebellion poster: 'Bourgeoisie, you have understood nothing.'

What were *we* doing in May and June 1968 when revolution almost took place in one of the advanced industrial societies of the world? It was the exemplary action of students fighting first around their own demands that catalyzed the situation. Despite the fact that France has the second-largest Communist party outside the Soviet Union in the industrial world, and despite the enormous reactionary force of that party and its trade union bureaucracy, the students were able to create a language of action which spoke to the other sectors of the population about the control and transformation of our lives, because they fought for control and transformation in a revolutionary sense, of the institution in which they were involved. A left-wing alternative was not only created but its effectiveness in opposition to the reactionary character of existing communist institutions was proven.

What were we doing in those months?

The SDS national office was trying to grind out an elaborate analysis of racism, couched in the most abstruse and dogmatic language so that the line would be right at its national convention in June.

It seems to me that one of our problems, which is a real problem, after 50 years of Stalinism, is the problem of models that give hope. Because of the despair of the new left with the bureaucratic forms of so-called socialism in the Soviet Union, we've always looked and looked for some place where somebody's trying to do it better. It's not so much that we're dumb and unimaginative—although I think we're dumber and less imaginative than need be—but because the question of 20th century history was: Is human freedom possible? Was there another stage of civilization, or were we headed towards 1984, no matter what the ruling bureaucracies called themselves?

So we are enthusiastic when we think that maybe Cuba is doing something new, maybe there is real popular involvement, or maybe the Vietnamese are in fact embodying a spirit like that which gives us life. I do not want to denigrate our attachment to the heroism of the Vietnamese or of the Cubans; nor do I think we should in any slavish manner suspend judgment when we look at societies which turn us on. What I'm saying is what France should mean, and what I know it does mean for the new left in Europe, is that we now have a concrete set of experiences to look at that can tell us so much more than the Cubans or Vietnamese can tell us, because they are experiences of an advanced industrial society.

Over and over again, as I've read the documents and Cohn-Bendit's book, the experiences tell us we were right. The student movement at Nanterre began really in the spring of 1967, when the university had refused to allow guys and girls to sleep together in a the dorms. So a sexual liberation front was created, and they reprinted Wilhelm Reich's sexual liberation manifesto of 1934, and talked about the relationship between authoritarianism, sexual repression and fascism. They began to build a movement which obviously had a most libertarian spirit. That spirit was obviously at the fore when the March 22d movement was crystallized a year later. It was "movement people" doing "movement things" that made France happen.

It may be because most French students had already heard about Marx, and read through that, put it in perspective, that it was possible for something new to arise, whereas here it seems that every time old Karl's name is mentioned our deep Baptist backgrounds or something out of our repressive pasts come surging to the fore.

One of the things which the French events say to me very deeply and clearly is that most of the traditional conceptions of organization of vanguard parties, of Leninist practice, are not only unpleasant but ineffective. I find myself revising some notions that had been lost as we thought we were getting more radical and more serious. We used to talk in the old days about things like parallel institutions. I don't think that was the right language, but the language pointed to the notion we had, that the revolution was not an event on day "X", but a process that we're into now, and that the structures of revolution and of revolutionary society would begin to be created as we did more work, got involved in more scenes, discovered new things.

What I'm saying is that I think there is an alternative to the question of party, which properly has at least some of its historical antecedents in that tradition which is called by that horrible noun, people's socialist or anarchist or whatever you call it movement. It says also that Marx was serious when he said socialism would grow out of the womb of capitalism. The deadly serious question to ask, if that's true, is how the embryo is conceived: what are the embryonic forms of revolutionary society which must be created, however embryonically, as we work?

Is it not possible to begin to envisage a movement which builds a variety of forms and structures, and uses those instead of a centralized party—structures in which the questions of control and transformation are raised in a way which points toward the historical alternative, in terms of both the form and the content of those embryonic revolutionary institutions?

All of that, I think, is true and possible. All of that requires a great deal of imagination—the imagination which the students at the Sorbonne enthroned in power in those exciting days of May and June. It takes enormous imagination, a willingness to be new, but that is the only way out.

I do not know whether I would or could participate in an organization which did not embody in its immediate present the values and hopes and the fulfillment of need which I have, but I think it no longer, in our society, does any good to say, "I will sacrifice myself to be part of that dehumanizing vanguard for my children in another day." I just don't think there's any evidence that there's anything revolutionary in doing that.

Once again, if the new life which has been created in us in this decade is to be more than a footnote to the last chapter of world civilization, we must take very seriously the lesson of trust in ourselves, of not killing what we feel and need to be true, not blaming objective conditions or using them as a pretext for dehumanizing ourselves, because that's a very silly game. People who argue that game are arguing that the reason I can't be free is because all of that stuff is weighing on me. It's true that the authoritarian forms which are anti-life were not created by us, and we do not need to blame ourselves for them. But we also know in scientific and psychological terms that repression in ourselves does not begin when we touch the outside world. Repression in ourselves begins when we interpret an inner impulse as an exterior threat and call it the world. Since so much of our lives has been learning not only to trust those inner impulses but to rediscover the ones that society, organized as it is, wishes were dead, we should in fact affirm those feelings.

That means hard work, but work with joy. It means trusting ourselves, being willing to be experimental. It means not accepting simplistic either/or formulations of complicated human situations. I think, finally, it means being concerned with effective activity rather than purity of the line. We have to trust other people in the immediate situation who may differ from us in their analyses of things; we must be willing to be wrong and willing to be critical, but clinging to what we knew the movement was all about. Only an ideology of puritanism, religion, capitalism—of deferred existence—can argue otherwise for my life.

I remember one of the most moving and unsettling events in the nine months I spent as national secretary of SDS. I had been out on the road for a couple of weeks, and during that time passed my 30th birthday. When I came back to the office, comrades younger than myself needed to assert their youthfulness in the face of my coming middle age with something resembling guerrilla theater. In rummaging through my desk, they discovered an old passport photo of me from 1961, when I was leaving to go to Europe. I was dressed in a very straight suit, tie, and very short hair. I looked for all the world like what I was at the time, an Ivy League graduate student in history. They put next to it a picture from the New York Times of this rather scruffy looking, very tired, but younger looking person—myself.

They wrote underneath it, "The good guerrilla in our society must know how to change his identity in order to fit all new situations."

Ed. Note: Calvert has recently helped to start a new movement press in Texas

Speech To the Resistance Conference, Bloomington, Ind. March 1969

GOING DOWN IN CHICAGO

I prefer the philanthropy of Captain John Brown to that philanthropy which neither shoots me nor liberates me....I do not wish to kill nor to be killed, but I can foresee circumstances in which both these things would be by me unavoidable. We preserve the so-called peace of our community by deeds of petty violence every day. Look at the policeman's billy and handcuffs! Look at the jail!...We are hoping only to live safely on the outskirts of this provisional army. So we defend ourselves and our hen-roosts, and maintain slavery. I know that the mass of my countrymen think that the only righteous use that can be made of Sharpe's rifles and revolvers is to fight duels with them when we are insulted by other nations, or to hunt Indians, or shoot fugitive slaves with them, or the like. I think that for once the Sharpe's rifles and the revolvers were employed in a righteous cause. The tools were in the hands of one who could use them....The same indignation that is said to have cleared the temple once will clear it again. The question is not about the weapon, but the spirit in which you use it.

—Henry David Thoreau
1859

There were twelve people in our two-man cell at the Chicago Police Headquarters last Saturday after the SDS "Weatherman" march through the Loop. Our charges ran from disorderly conduct (my own) through possession of explosives to attempted murder. The styles and situations of the dozen were as widely disparate as the charges: A black student (explosives) in boutique bell-bottoms stretched out coolly on one of the two wooden benches, surveying the rest of us with amusement as well as attachment. A long-haired New York weatherman, who said he had written and produced a musical version of the Columbia University insurrection, skillfully sang both the instrumental and vocal parts of the Cream's "I Feel Free." A very young, very rich kid (mob action) spouted heroic slogans intermittently during a compulsive, anxious monologue about himself. An uncommonly tender gang type from a Michigan Weatherman collective washed a cell-mate's wounds with wet toilet paper and went to sleep on the crowded cement floor. Brian Flanagan, a bright and sensitive upper-middle "moderate" who found his way inside a Columbia building last year, and had now come to be charged with attempted murder (of Chicago's toughest judicial figure), rested in another corner, dealing quietly with his own fear and a large still-bleeding gash in his head.

The events of the afternoon were common to us all, whether we had been busted in the La Salle Street melee, or a mile away (as I and two friends were). Solidarity and spirit grew easily from the experience of fear and force; it was expressed through the long first night in jail with songs and chants and good talking. But beyond the fellow-feeling and gallows humor, much more drastic changes were running down within us, and they could not be expressed at all, at least not then and there. That protean rebellion which was born ten years ago in the South: that found forms to fit the Mississippi Delta, the Cleveland slums, the Berkeley campus, the hundred colleges and parks and Army posts: that appeared bloody last summer in Grant Park and stoned this summer at Woodstock: It ran that day in the Loop. Almost everyone else now thinks that that spirit of the Sixties has found its end. But at night in the cell-block, we believed that it had found a new beginning.

Weatherman demands the willing suspension of disbelief. As an ideology of communism and a strategy of revolution, it shatters the reliable categories of thought and modes of action which white radicals have developed in the last ten years. It challenges the validity of an intellectual Left, which functions as a comfortable culture of opposition; instead, it asks that radicals become revolutionaries, completely collectivize their lives, and struggle to death if necessary. Nothing could be more threatening to the investments of thought and action which Movement people have made. Weatherman asks them to leap—in life-expectations as well as political ideas—over a distance fully as wide as that which they crossed from liberalism (or whatever) into the Movement.

Since the civil rights movement moved North in 1964, white radicals have been working within a politics that was defined in the SDS "ERAP" community organizing projects in Newark, Cleveland, Uptown Chicago, and a half-dozen other urban centers. Although the organizers used some revolutionary rhetoric, they were never able to find a strategy for mobilizing masses of people to restructure "the institutions which control their lives." Marches, sit-ins, tenant strikes and election campaigns inconvenienced but did not seriously threaten the welfare departments, housing agencies and city administrations against which they were directed. At length, the project workers—mostly white college kids—realized that those institutions could not be overhauled without wholesale shifts in power inside the "system" itself.

Since ERAP began to dissolve in 1966 and 1967, radical organizers have used basically the same strategy in other areas: campus strikes, draft resistance, Army base movements. The common principle was the organization of people in one locale (or in various branches of the same essential locale) to change the immediate institution which most oppressed them. For example, students were organized to change "the university"; young men were organized to "stop the draft"; basic trainees were organized to "fuck the Army." It was hoped that such action might lead, in an always undefined way, to a chain reaction of structural changes throughout the whole system. But of course nothing like that ever happened.

Taken together, at least, that effort can hardly be counted a political failure, even if it did not accomplish its rhetorical objectives. What did happen was the creation of a race of radical organizers who are extraordinarily competent to do the work which their strategy defines. But there are obvious limits to the strategy, and after years of operational failures, a feeling of frustration and even desperation has set in. Many of the early organizers went off to the peripheries of politics: journalism, the academy, legal aid, teaching or even "liberal" government welfare jobs. And others went completely into personal "life-style" retreats in one or another wooded groves in New England, California or the Southwest.

As the repository of the political forms in the Movement, SDS has been struggling to break out of the frustration of repeated failure—or at least dispiriting un-success. The factionalism which has now become rampant is a direct result of that situation; politics without promise rapidly loses its coherence. The various factions within and around SDS accurately represent the political alternatives that now seem available. Progressive Labor, the "Maoist" party that was expelled from SDS last June but still holds on in an ambiguous role, expresses the conviction that revolutionary conditions already exist in the US, and it requires only the organization of the industrial proletariat to set the revolution in motion. Revolutionary Youth Movement II (RYM II) agrees in part with Progressive Labor, that workers organized "at the point of production" can become a revolutionary force in America, but it goes on to emphasize the paramountcy of subordinating white efforts to the "vanguard" of blacks and Latin movements. Despite their expansive theoretical flights, both PL and RYM II work inside the framework of the community-organizing strategy. They try to get factory workers to demand "power" within their factories, or hospital workers—and users—within the hospitals, or soldiers within their bases.

Weatherman is something else. It is, in theory and practice, a revolutionary "army," and it flaunts that notion: "Come to Chicago. Join the Red Army," the leaflets called out. At this point—

only a few months after it was born—Weatherman presents this schema: The fight against the American empire, at home in the black "colony" and abroad in the Third World, is the center-ring of world politics today, within which the American system will eventually come to grief. The colonized peoples—black Americans and Third World guerrillas—can "do it alone"; but white Americans can both deepen and extend the fight if they disregard the position of "privilege" their white skins automatically provide, and learn to live and die like un-privileged guerrillas. In Weatherman's book, it is "racist" to accept white privilege in any way.

From that ideology flow a set of shattering implications. First of all, Weatherman action has to be directed at "material" aid (not just rhetorical support) to the anti-imperialist fights. It isn't enough to march or leaflet in support of the Vietnamese or the Black Panthers; there has to be an active effort to pull the machinery of empire off their backs.

Next, weathermen have to understand the necessity of risking death, in terms of the historical necessity of revolution. It is the custom of intellectual Lefts around the world to sit sipping coffee (or its current moral equivalent, smoking dope), grooving on other people's revolutions, staring at posters of other revolutionaries, and waiting for one's own revolution to start tomorrow. Weatherman says that tomorrow is forever, and the time is always now. To the widespread charge of "adventurism" on that account, Weatherman insists that nothing that hinders the empire from carrying out its "business as usual" against the colonies can be a worthless adventure—although of course some actions are of more strategic value than others, and that there is a time for up-front fighting and a time for background organizing.

The life-arrangements which have been built to deal with both the personal and political consequences of Weatherman are collectives—numbering now about a dozen in Ohio, Michigan, Illinois, New York, Maryland, Washington State, and Colorado. The intensity with which they work is almost indescribable; they are crucibles of theory and practice, action and self-criticism, loving and working. They are widely experimental: some now are considering rules against men and women living as "couples"—a form of privatism which inhibits total collectivization. In a few, women talk of intensifying their personal relationships with other women—as a way of getting over the problem of "women-hating women," which derives from female self-hate—akin to the self-hatred people in oppressed groups, such as Negroes and Jews, seem to contain. Often, members of collectives are revving at such high speed and intensity that they sleep only every other night; the rest of the time they are working—reading, criticizing, writing, traveling, pushing out the problems of the collective and out talking to other people.

The Weatherman perspective treats collectives as "pre-party" organizations, building eventually to a fighting communist party. A structure of leadership is developing with the "Weather Bureau" at the top, regional staffs under that, and the collectives providing local cadre. The principle of authority is a form of "democratic centralism," with as much self-criticism thrown in as anyone can bear—probably *more* than anyone can bear.

But despite that formal plan, Weatherman is still primarily an organizing strategy, not a fighting force. Heavy actions in the streets and schools are undertaken more for their "exemplary" effect on potential weatherpeople than for their "material" aid to the Viet Cong. Weatherman wants to get at high school and community-college dropouts—not middle-class university kids—and it believes that the way to do it is to convince them that they can fight the authorities who daily oppress them: cops, principals, bosses. Weatherman as a strategy was born last April at Kent State University in Ohio, when a small group of SDS activists broke first through a line of "jocks" and then a phalanx of police to occupy a building where a hearing was being conducted on disciplinary and student-power issues. The attack so galvanized the campus that 5,000 students came out the next day in support of the SDS fighters.

There's no denying the antagonism to Weatherman within the radical Left—not to mention the sheer horror with which liberals and conservatives view it. In some places—Detroit, for instance—unweatherized radicals have tried to form coalitions specifically aimed at destroying Weatherman. Some of the best New Left radicals believe that Weatherman is destroying (or has destroyed) the Movement. Movement spokesmen, such as the Guardian and Liberation News Service, are almost viciously anti-Weatherman; the underground press, for the most part, thinks Weatherman is positively insane. Such hostility is more than mere factionalism. It represents total rejection of Weatherman's revolutionary form.

Weatherman itself doesn't help matters. Perhaps because of the intensity of their own lives, the members cannot accept the relative lethargy of other radicals. More than that, weathermen have built such elaborate political and emotional defenses against their fears of death and imprisonment that any challenge to the meaning of their work directly threatens their identities. It is obvious that Weatherman is quasi-religious and "fanatic" in a way; they see those who stand apart as the early Christians must have seen the pagans. It is difficult to die for a cause that their peers reject.

The Movement's antagonism is particularly wounding because Weatherman has so far failed to attract the large numbers of people it hoped would follow "up-front" fighting. All summer and in the early fall, Weatherman tried to organize its dropout constituency by running through schoolrooms yelling, "Jail break!", fighting with hostile kids, and carrying NLF flags down beaches literally looking for trouble. When trouble came, the weathermen fought, and in many instances "won"; but the actions did not mobilize the hordes of kids the organizers had expected. There were famous Weatherman horror shows: in Pittsburgh, where members ran through a school and were arrested with no organizing effect; and in Detroit, where a group of weatherwomen (now called the Motor City 9) entered an examination room in a community college, locked the doors, subdued the teacher, and then took two hostile male students out of action with karate blows.

It's hard, too, for many outsiders to grasp the dramatic—often comic—aspects of Weatherman's political style. I first saw Weatherman as the "Action Faction" of SDS at the National Convention in Chicago last June (see Hard Times, No. 38). It surfaced the first afternoon; during a particularly dreary maneuver by PL, the Action Faction people leaped up on their chairs waving Red Books and chanting, "Ho, Ho, Ho Chi Minh...." They succeeded in breaking up PL's silly obstructions by an essentially dramatic move, which had elements of both parody and instruction.

That element has carried through into all aspects of weathering, so that at times it is difficult to tell whether the entire phenomenon may not be a gigantic psychodrama. Most weathermen, in their own self-criticism sessions, are aware of the dangers of the emotional "trip" that revolutionism entails. At a meeting one night during the Chicago weekend, speaker after speaker warned against the "death trip" or the "machismo trip" or the "violence trip." "We act not out of our private emotions, but in accordance with our political understanding," one weatherman said.

Because Weatherman is still so young, it would be fatuous to condemn it as worthless or elevate it to heroic proportions. Its contradictions are apparent, even to most weathermen, who are defensive outside their collectives but truly self-exploring within. What seems most troublesome right now is Weatherman's simple-mindedness about the varieties of political experience in America; as revolutionaries usually discover, violent struggle and less intense organizing are not mutually exclusive. RYM II and independent radicals are still producing organizers who can serve a variety of functions; to put all radical eggs in a weatherbasket would be unutterably foolish.

Nor is there much evidence that violence can mobilize thousands of kids, even in Weatherman's chosen dropout pool. Real revolutionaries have a contempt for violence, not an adoration of it; it is used only as a last resort, as a response to specific oppression. As yet, most people do not comprehend the relationship of the police in America to the B-52s in Vietnam. A revolutionary party finds its moral authority in leading an oppressed people in retaliation against their intolerable oppressors: That's how the Viet Cong did it in Vietnam and how People's Democracy is doing it in Northern Ireland. To most people outside, Weatherman is a vanguard floating free of a mass base.

But there's more to it than that. What appeal Weatherman has comes in part from its integration of the two basic streams of the movements of the Sixties—political mobilization and personal liberation. Since the break-up of the ERAP projects, few radical organizations have been able to contain and combine both streams. Those in the "liberation" stream have gone off on private trips; those in the political stream have been reduced to Old Left sloganeering and dreary demonstrations. Weatherman does break through, with its liberating collective sensibility and its active mobilization. However disastrous or brilliant its strategy may turn out to be, its spirit, purposefulness and integrity ought to command respect.

Oct 1969

Diana Oughton was part of this women's contingent of Weatherman's "Days of Rage", Chicago, Oct. 1969.

PROTEST
Memories of Diana

Bomb threats plagued the nation again last week, but very few bombs were going off. Nonetheless, the reverberations of recent blasts could still be heard. In Washington and in state capitals, officials were searching for new means to control dynamite and dynamiters. In Maryland, where two black militants died in bomb blasts, the trial of Rap Brown was moved once more to a new site as an indirect result of the explosions. In Manhattan, police picked carefully through the rubble of the West 11th Street house, where at least three people died. There, in the ruins, they found a severed finger, which enabled them to identify one of the victims as Diana Oughton, 28, a talented, idealistic girl whose turn to radicalism brought her in the end to a rebel bomb factory.

Most Americans find it difficult to grasp that some of the brightest and best-cared-for young are so enraged that they have opted for the nihilism of blowing up society. Diana Oughton's story

THOMAS R. COPI

OUGHTON (LEFT) & FRIEND
Always her own ideas about everything.

provides some answers—and engenders some pessimism as well:

Diana was born on Jan. 26, 1942, and raised in Dwight (pop. 3,100), a town set in the prairie cornfields of northern Illinois. Her conservative, Episcopal family is one of the community's most prominent. Her paternal great-great-grandfather established the Keeley Institute for alcoholics. Her maternal great-grandfather, W.D. Boyce, founded the American Boy Scouts. James Oughton, 55, Diana's father, is a Dartmouth graduate and restaurateur. Diana and her three sisters were cherished and deeply loved. Said her father: "The social life in Dwight has never separated adults from children. Dinner was a family affair, and there was a pretty wide discussion all the way through."

Storybook Child. TIME Correspondent Frank Merrick met in Dwight last week with Oughton and one of Diana's sisters, Carol, 26, who now lives in Washington. At first, Jim Oughton was remarkably composed for a father who had just learned that his eldest child had been blown apart. He told of her storybook childhood, of how she became a good horsewoman and swimmer, played a social game of tennis, studied piano and the flute. Her father remembers Diana as "independent in her thinking. She always had her own ideas, and they were sound ideas." About what? "A picture she liked, the best way to treat an animal, which was the finest season of the year—almost anything."

Aware of the limitations of Dwight, Oughton sent Diana off to Madeira School in Greenway, Va., and Bryn Mawr. She spent her junior year at the University of Munich. It was at Bryn Mawr that Diana first showed an interest in social problems. Like many collegians, she was active in voter registration and tutored junior high school students. At night she would go by train to Philadelphia, where for two years she tutored two ghetto boys. Said Carol: "I remember how incredulous Diana was that a seventh- or eighth-grade child couldn't read, didn't even know the alphabet." A Princeton football player proposed marriage, but Diana said: "I don't want to get married now. There are too many things to do."

During her year in Germany, Diana made the turn away from affluence that so often marks the contemporary young. She preferred a *Pension* to a luxury hotel, a bicycle to a taxicab. On a trip with her father, she carried a Michelin guidebook because, he recalled, she "didn't want to go to any of those places, she wanted to go to places unknown."

After graduating, Diana signed on with the American Friends Service Committee, took a crash course in Spanish and was sent to Guatemala. Stationed in Chichicastenango, she taught Spanish to the local Indians, who were mostly limited to their native dialect. Her eyes widened at the vast poverty and the class hatred between the wealthy few and the impoverished many. She was particularly troubled that a regime she viewed as oppressive was so strongly supported by the U.S. But she was still willing to give the U.S. Establishment a chance.

Diana went on to the University of Michigan to earn a teaching certificate. This was the critical year of 1966, when U.S. students were being radicalized by the Viet Nam War. While at Ann Arbor, Diana joined the Children's Community School, an unstructured, permissive experiment in education for children from four to eight. There, she worked with Bill Ayers, son of the board chairman of Chicago's Commonwealth Edison Co., and with Eric Mann—who later became luminaries of the Students for a Democratic Society. The school, operating on Great Society mon-

ey, folded in 1968, when its funds were cut off.

Stormy Days. "It was about this time," said Jim Oughton, "that there was less and less communication between Diana and any of us. She'd call and we'd call. She'd be home briefly from time to time." Diana joined S.D.S., and she was in Chicago for the stormy days and nights of the Democratic Convention. Sometimes she would stop in Dwight. She brought Bill Ayers and other radicals, and she would talk politics with her father, defending the revolutionary's approach to social ills.

"That was one of the tense things we did. I was so eager to find out the rationale of her thinking and activities that I probably pressed her harder than I should have. It was a complete stalemate, and she would just change the subject. I deeply loved Diana, and I certainly didn't want to break the communication for the future. I felt that sooner or later there'd be a maturity of thinking, a change of thinking."

Oughton, losing his composure at last, said: "This is as much as we know. Anything that happened with Diana in the last two years we don't have information on." He did become convinced that Diana was "completely carried away. It was almost an intellectual hysteria." The years unknown to her father were in-

tensely political for Diana. When factionalism shattered S.D.S. in 1969, she and Bill Ayers joined the most radical, extreme, violence-prone faction, the Weathermen. She began to build an arrest record, once in Flint, Mich., for passing out pamphlets to high school students and again in Chicago in the Weathermen's "days of rage" forays against the police. Detroit police say that Diana was present at the small, secret conclave of Weathermen last December in Flint, at which a decision was reportedly made to begin a bombing wave. As one of the leading activists, gifted and smoldering Diana Oughton went on to her death in Manhattan.

To people in Dwight, what happened to Diana seems to be news from another planet. As one elder explained: "There is no radicalism in Dwight. It was a contact she made outside of this town, and thank God, she didn't bring it back." Diana's father is equally puzzled, but absolutely sure of one thing: "Even though there is a big difference of opinion as to whether she's right or wrong, I'm sure that in her own heart she conscientiously felt she was right. She wasn't doing this for any other gain than—well—you might say the good of the world."

TIME
THE WEEKLY NEWSMAGAZINE 3/30/70

AH,
WHAT AN AGE
IT IS . . .

Diana Oughton, 28 years old, was one of three people who died in the explosion on March 6 which destroyed a Greenwich Village townhouse. "I'm glad I'm not a writer," Diana had once said. "Whenever I try to describe someone, it always sounds too partial."

She knew how complicated people were. Every day of her life she was discovering how complicated she was herself, tender and strong with a warmth that touched everyone she knew, with hatred for a system that hated life. She was open and stubborn and loving; she was afraid sometimes, but learning better how to overcome her fears.

But it all does sound so partial. Look at a poem by Bertolt Brecht, "To Posterity," one of her favorites: "Ah, what an age it is when to speak of trees is almost a crime/ For it is a kind of silence against injustice." It should help you understand what she was about.

So Diana volunteered for VISA, a foreign assistance program sponsored by the American Friends Service Committee, and was sent to Guatemala. For two years she lived in the Indian market town of Chichicastenango. She witnessed unbearable suffering, premature deaths, and crippling ignorance there. She worked hard—incredibly hard—teaching people how to build latrines and stoves, training teachers for the literacy program, and helping set up a medical clinic.

Slowly, she began to see that nothing really changed for the better in Chichicastenango as a result of her work. She didn't understand why—not many of us did then—but she wasn't the sort of person you could fool for very long.

When she came back to the US in 1965, she taught literacy for awhile in a working class neighborhood in Philadelphia, and then enrolled at the University of Michigan in Ann Arbor, where she got a Masters degree in Education.

At this point in her life, Diana felt that the key to social change was education. She thought that the system would be flexible enough to encourage instead of stifle children's creativity; flexible enough to see children as human beings rather than as raw material to be stamped and molded according to the needs of capitalist society. Diana probably wouldn't have expressed it that way. She had no use for rhetoric and was extremely suspicious of language that generalized. Her eloquence was simple and direct, and she was much more interested in action than words.

In Ann Arbor, she went to work on the staff of the Children's Community School, an integrated experimental school based on the Summerhill model of A.S. Neill. It lasted a couple of years, but in the course of the struggle to keep the school going Diana learned a lot about the power structure of this country, about how the educational system was part and parcel of a larger system that in fact could not allow its children to be free.

It was about this time that Diana began to seek a revolutionary solution to the horrors of war and poverty, and a solution, increasingly more important as her life neared its end, to her own oppression as a women.

By the winter of 1968-69, she had become a regional organizer for SDS in Michigan. It was a clear and logical step in her development.

Diana became a revolutionary socialist, a communist. At the same time she was beginning to develop a greater understanding of herself as a woman.

"I'm learning about independence," she wrote to a friend about a year ago, "it's exciting and very difficult." She had begun the long struggle to free herself, intellectually and emotionally, from her oppression.

On the exterior, she cut off her long heavy hair and wore the glasses she had neglected to wear for so long because men supposedly do not like women who wear glasses.

But inside there were deep changes too. She was bolder, her arguments were more developed, and she was standing up to men and struggling with that fierce yet gentle fervor she applied to everything she did.

In a conversation a few days before her death, Diana talked about an international army. She understood that a popular army must be based on a mass movement, and she recognized the need for a lot of hard, practical political work in creating such a force. But her sense of priorities led her to believe that somebody else should be doing that kind of work now, and that she had to concentrate on the military aspects of the struggle.

"We'll make mistakes," she said, in that same conversation shortly before she died, "We have a lot to learn." You think of Che who said that in revolution one wins or dies, because you know Diana understood that and would not have it any other way.

The day after Diana's body was identified, two children with two older friends stopped in front of the site on 11th Street and placed two bunches of yellow spring flowers and a note in front of the open pit that was all that was left of the house. The note read: "To Diana from Children's Community." A button pinned to the note said, "Children are only newer people."

The Great Speckled Bird

4/2/70

The Press of Freedom:

The Weathermen's Solution Is Part of the Problem

by David Gelber

There's something about a home-made bomb which invigorates flagging editorial writers. On last week's Channel 13 kulturkampf, Jimmy Wechsler politely accused Rennie Davis, Abbie Hoffman, and Jerry Rubin of responsibility for the deaths of three or more people in the West 11th Street explosion. The Times, which considers the makers of our Vietnam policy as good-men-with-enthusiasm-carried-to-tragic-excess, suddenly found its voice and denounced the bombers as criminals and murderers. So much for the pillars of under-statement, the exemplars of what Max Lerner likes to call "humanist liberalism."

For myself, I find this a hard piece to write, partly because of the ambivalence I feel about bombing (in the next few months we may all become inured to it, I suspect) and partly because some who read this article still believe that companies who produce Mace and fragmentation bombs are just doing their patriotic duty.

The easy way for a radical to write about violence on the left is to put the bombings in context (compare the violence of a single B-52 raid to all the bank burnings, annihilated computers, and charred bodies for which the left is responsible: no contest). Then, you could join the professional association of media shrinks and posit theories on what frustration can do to an

---

---

ex-Peace Corps volunteer from an Ivy League college. Such argument is the sort of defensive rhetoric radicals might use in a middle-aged suburban gathering of people whose political aspirations do not and never will exceed trimming the worst excesses from a system whose institutions perform brilliantly only when they are required to produce gilded trash. Sure the Weathermen are frustrated, but to leave it at that is to trivialize their aspirations and ignore their politics.

The Weathermen are where they are now because, first, the SDS faction which became Weatherman resolved more than a year ago that the movement had to break out of its essentially middle-class student base and organize white working-class kids who were perceived as rootless

and angry enough at cops, teachers, and parents to be organized to fight the state. The Weathermen believed that only by transforming themselves into tough, violence-prone individuals would they be taken seriously by kids steeped in the culture of street violence. Knowing they wouldn't win over all the kids at once, the Weathermen did believe that raids on high schools and street-corner fights in defense of their anti-racist beliefs would turn on the sharpest kids. When Mark Rudd was beaten up by a white gang at a MacDonald's hamburger stand, he reportedly was exhilarated by the confirmation that the Weathermen were "taken seriously." This phase of Weatherman history seems now to be over, doomed by the impossibility of a group with their politics functioning in full view of the state, but also eclipsed by a second tenet of Weatherman thinking: that the American empire is principally threatened by third world revolutionaries abroad and blacks at home. To the Weathermen, this implied they could best serve the struggle by destroying the property of war-makers and by diverting the empire's police to the home front.

I'm not happy with my rather sterile sketch of the Weatherman position. Much of what is really significant about them lies in the acts of will by which they have undertaken to transform themselves into authentic guerrillas. Anyone who wants to understand what self-transformation has meant for the Weathermen should read Shin'ya Ono's article in the December Leviathan. Here, it is enough to say that the caricature of the radical dilettante, sympathetically quoting Che Guevara while retaining the psychological and economic prerogatives of the well-educated, is, for the Weathermen, a chilling nightmare, an apparition of what they might have been. Cleaver's law ("you're either part of the problem or . . .") becomes the only descriptive statement needed for a guide to action.

I have gone through all this partly because I think too many liberals, Marxists, etc., condescendingly view the Weathermen as wildly adventuristic nuts oblivious to the laws of history or the inevitability of progress if only Lindsay is elected President. I agree with the Weatherman view that things don't change, less because people are enchanted by the national consensus ideology than because Americans are down on the possibility of changing anything very much and not sure they're willing to risk the little

they have for an uncertain future. With the Weathermen, I think too many radicals wear their politics as a kind of cultural badge without fighting through the personal implications of being an enemy of the state.

Having said all this, it is my view that the Weathermen are at best peripheral to what the movement needs to do and at worst an actual threat to what we might be able to accomplish. Since I don't see how the Weathermen are going to beat America at the one thing it does best (producing commodities of war), I can't take seriously the claim that Weathermen serve the Vietnamese as a rear-guard auxiliary. If, for instance, they ever did manage to blow up a gunsight factory, I would expect Nixon to acquire all the Kalachnikov rifles he needs from the Soviet Union. More important, defining one's political role as that of an auxiliary to another national struggle is an old trap for the American left. I don't think the Communists in the '20s and '30s carried Mother Russia in their heart of hearts because they were stupid. The frustration of imagining and fighting for a liberated America led the C.P. to exult in the Bolsheviks' success instead ("see, it can be done"), just as the same frustration now closes the Weathermen to anything but visions of aiding the Vietnamese ("see, American imperialism can be had"). The irony is that by failing to do much for the Vietnamese and, more significantly, by scaring the hell out of a lot of already up-tight people and converting practically everyone else into spectators (however inclined to regard the flames with secret joy), the Weathermen end up reinforcing the passive behavior they want to overcome. By contrast to the May-June near-revolution in France where just about everyone (including the national football team which demanded "football to the footballers") had a positive role to play in the revolutionary process, the Weatherman scenario relies on incredibly few people with an intoxicated sense of their capacity to "make history."

The gruesome report that fragmentation pellets were found in the ruins of the West 11th Street townhouse, is, if true, a measure of how the dynamic of self-transformation unredeemed by tolerance and the absurd application of Cleaver's law has alienated the Weathermen from so many people who hover somewhere in the smog between problem and solution.

Quite aside from the Weathermen, the left will have to come to terms with violence against property as a morally and tactically appropriate weapon. There are ways to do it without raising general anxieties (the six women who destroyed the Manhattan draft board files last year if anything *reduced* the anxieties of draft-age kids and their families) and in order to win concrete victories. What if, for instance, a tenants' organization held a rent strike and needed additional capital to renovate their building? Suppose that good old Jesse James National Bank, whose vaults are stuffed with loot from subway bonds and slum mortgages, has more than enough to make the neighborhood livable? Then, what if a delegation of tenants visited the local branch of James National and requested reparations with the understanding that if the board of directors didn't like the investment, the local branch of James National wouldn't function in its customary neighborhood location? I think these are the kinds of hypotheticals the movement will have to face, and perhaps what Rennie Davis had in mind when he observed that "the '70s will be the time for burning banks."

the village **VOICE** 15c

3/26/70

A CALL TO ARMS

A People's Militia should be formed in Berkeley.

Collective, armed self-defense is needed to protect our community against the dual threat of an expanding police state and right-wing vigilanteism.

Our community is creating collective institutions upon which our lifestyles nad politics can be realized. We are building a Tenants' Union to deal with housing conditions, a Free Clinic to deal with health problems, a Food Conspiracy to meet nutritional needs and a Peoples' Architecture to deal with environmental needs.

Our community includes living communes and work collectives. Among our brothers and sisters are ecology activists, women's liberationists and gay liberationists. Telegraph Avenue, the main street of our USA is a common turf for cultural revolutionaries and revolutionary socialists.

None of these energies are yet satisfied, none of these projects are yet complete. The non-exploitative society is not yet reality for us or our brothers and sisters throughout the oppressed world.

But however unfinished the growth of our community may be, it is a new beginning in the belly of the Amreikan monster. It is a beginning worth defending.

When the Federal Regime put the Chicago Conspiracy on trial the Regime attacked us, the Berkeley community. When the national power structure convicted the Conspiracy, they attacked our lifestyle of personal liberation and our politics of collective liberation from worldwide Amerikan imperialism.

When the Man imprisoned the Chicago Conspiracy he attacked our right to survive and create social change.

The Day After street action in Berkeley responded to that attack. The Day After we informed the businessmen and the bureaucrats that for every attack they made on us, we would make they pay a price.

Now these businessmen and their regime are agitating for the destruction of our community. Their goal is to create a police state in Berkeley powerful enough to crush our communtiy.

Toward this end the local businessmen have already begun to clamor for one final Krackdown. They are even attempting to cover their fascist tracks with the democratic facade of a "People's Committee"—the Berkeley Chamber of Commerce and the Berkeley Board of Realtors with their faces rearranged.

This clamor for Fascism Now! has already resulted in a gestapo invasion of the Free Church Wednesday night.

Faced with this developing crisis, self-defense is quickly becoming our primary need.

Those who profit from racism and imperialist wars in Vietnam and Laos, those who hoard the power from the people to satisfy their own greed, those who put the pigs on our streets will not allow us the choice of peaceful co-existence, even were we willing to accept it.

There is one weapon which has enabled the pig to daily trample over our rights, our dreams and our bodies—the gun. To defend ourselves against mounting pig terror, we must take up the gun.

An armed People's Militia can provide collective self-defense for our homes, our gatherings, our land and our lives.

In Berkeley and throughout Amerika we are a new people. We must survive.

The Tribe advocates the speedy formation of a People's Militia for Self-Defense in Berkeley.

The Tribe will begin next week to publish information relating to the use of firearms and other practical aspects of self-defense.

Free Berkeley!

The Tribe Editorial Collective

3/6/70

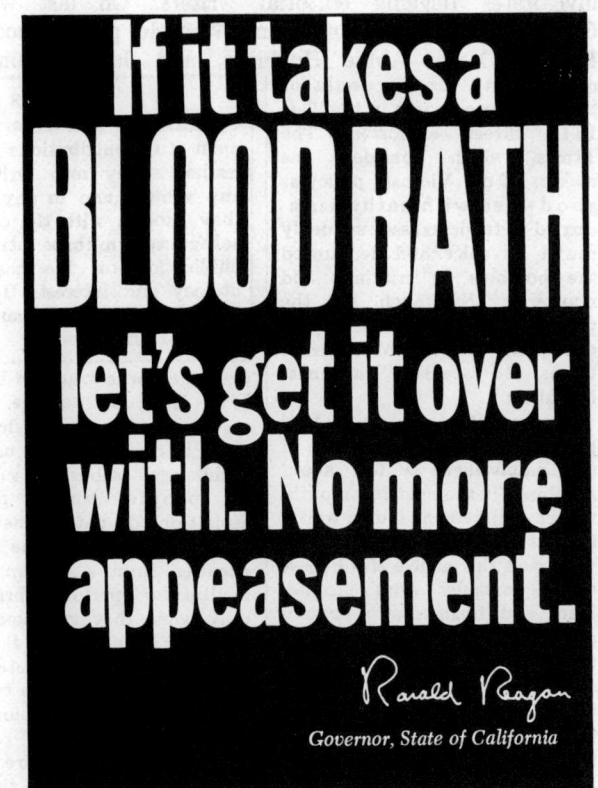

If it takes a **BLOOD BATH** let's get it over with. No more appeasement.

Ronald Reagan

Governor, State of California

U.S. AIR MAIL

FREE! WOODSTOCK ★NATION★

Amerikan Outlaw Trading Cards

OK, onward: FREE SINCLAIR is a good idea, yes, I can really relate to that one. But the wider issue of marijuana laws as political tools is the real thing to work on, along with the so-called obscenity busts and all other busts that are related to our culture/life style. According to the honk culture, everything we do is illegal because THEY MAKE THE LAWS. The whole business of DEFINITION is really crucial and it's crucial to make people see how it works, e.g. what is a law but some words oinked out by some honks meeting in a building somewhere and conspiring to douche some cultural group that lives differently than the lawmakers? It's all the same old problem of image vs. reality. They sit up there and make the laws and then put them out into the national consciousness as if these new laws were handed down from God like the Ten Commandments or something. That's why we were having our people go to those awful city council meetings in Ann Arbor so they could see exactly what the laws were and how they were passed. Since we started doing that we've stopped them from outlawing a lot of our people's activities, but that has to be done on a national basis so all the kids can see what's going on. Who is John Mitchell, anyway? A finance Wall Street lawyer who managed Nixon's campaign—"I programmed the candidate," he said during the campaign—and was given the Department of Justice as his reward and because it's the most important agency in govt now and in the months ahead. Who is Warren Hamburger but an old ponk who teamed with Nix and McCarthy (Joe) in the '50s to get rid of the "Commies" and now gets his Supreme reward when his boy takes office. Who is Clement Haynsworth but some crook from S.C. who Nixon owed Strom Thurmond for whitewashing the southern delegates at the 1968 conven-

tion, and Strom threw his boy in the court as his reward and so the niggers won't get any farther out of line. I mean, we know all this but the kids still look at it like it's something weird or holy or something, or don't pay any attention to it and just keep on doing their thing. This ponk in EVO talked about Woodstock being like a hip concentration camp, or said something about he could dig it if there was a groovy camp like that where they could all do their own thing and not have to bother with the awful nasty stuff in the world. No wonder the blacks have no respect for those creeps. But it is our job to educate the people, and it has to be done or we might as well forget the whole thing as far as I'm concerned. Because I don't want any part of a Nation of imbeciles who sit around and shoot speed and listen to bogus records, and all. I've had enough of that forever. And the other ones, the "politicals," are just as bad too, and their culture is bogus as well. The records they listen to are even worse....

... Anyway, there is still too much antagonism being directed at the bourgeoisie as in Ann Arbor, and not enough effort being made to educate the bourgeoisie as to who is in fact their enemy, i.e. the capitalists and the police lackeys and demagogic politicians.... Our rhetoric has been too irresponsible and too crazy in the past, mostly thru my own shortcomings, but also mostly because the times and conditions were very different. We have to be ever mindful that things are changing very very rapidly now, and that there are masses of people who are anxious to hear what we have to say....

One of the most important changes lately is that we are getting an increasingly greater opportunity to reach the masses of the people, as in these courts and in cases like mine and the Chicago conspiracy. People are beginning to

wonder what we're talking about, and it's not enough just to say rock and roll, dope, and fucking in the streets. It's time to push the 10-Point program and its significance for the masses, and how the present ruling structure is keeping the people from their rightful lives. I'll try to finish that pamphlet up in the next couple of days, but I'll have to study and think a long time before I start any important project to make sure I come up with the right thing. So please don't get impatient, I'm doing all I can. But it has to be done, and unfortunately I can't take any part in spreading it—that's all up to you all, especially to you, Skip, because you're the most eloquent. But we have to keep in mind the necessity of not alienating any more straight people than necessary—the SDS adventurists are really blowing it in that respect. Now is the time, when the masses are starting to come around and listen to what we have been saying for years, to consolidate these gains and make them see that our struggle is their struggle. The Moratorium today is the biggest thing in history—two years ago this kind of protest was vilified and bad-mouthed throughout the honk culture, now they're running to endorse the end of the war and, by corollary, the end of imperialism. They don't know how these things are connected, and it's up to us to educate them and let them know what's going on.

(signed)
LOVE, JOHN
POLITICAL PRISONER
(Reprinted and excerpted from *The Seed*.)

Ed. Note: John Sinclair is a poet. He was a founder of The White Panthers and The MC5, a political rock group. He is serving 10 years in Marquette State Prison for giving two joints to a police agent.

I know these people, I hear these people, I love these people.

NELSON ROCKEFELLER, during his recent tour of South America

The great courage is still to gaze as squarely at the light as at death.

CAMUS

ALL YOU NEED IS LOVE

People capable of love, under the present system, are necessarily the exceptions; love is by necessity a marginal phenomenon in present-day western society ... because the spirit of a production-centered, commodity-greedy society is such that only the non-conformist can defend himself successfully against it. Important and radical changes in our social structure are necessary, if love is to become a social and not a highly individualistic, marginal phenomenon, —Erich Fromm

"whenever any form of government becomes destructive... it is the Right of the People to alter or to abolish it, and to institute new government, laying its Foundations on such principles, and organizing its powers in such form as to them shall seem most likely to effect their safety and happiness."

. DECLARATION OF INDEPENDENCE

And if it is a despot you would dethrone, see first that his throne erected within you is destroyed.

For how can a tyrant rule the free and the proud, but for a tyranny in their own freedom and a shame in their own pride.

— Kahlil Gibran

COMPREHENSION
Exploring Revolutionary Violence &
Non-Violence: Dellinger-Deutscher-Muste

Marxism and Nonviolence

In May, 1966, for the second year in a row, Isaac Deutscher spoke at Berkeley's Vietnam Day. In 1965, Vietnam Day had made a major impact on the campus and the country, with more than 10,000 students participating and a broad range of viewpoints represented on the sponsoring committee and on the speakers' platform. The 1966 event was a pale shadow, with the sponsoring committee clearly in the hands of the Young Socialist Alliance (a Trotskyist organization) and only a handful of students attending. The next day Deutscher and I traveled to Los Angeles together and from there the following day to New York. At Los Angeles a "mass meeting" of the "anti-war movement" also turned out to be Trotskyist dominated and sparsely attended. Deutscher was furious, feeling that he had been brought to the events under false pretenses. Either that fact or the experience of traveling together and listening to each others' speeches three days in a row led to an unusually frank and probing discussion of Trotskyism, Marxism, pacifism and the anti-war movement.

I became aware that Deutscher was struggling more deeply than could be seen in his writings with an acute consciousness of the decline in revolutionary morality on

the left, as seen not just in the crudities of violence and political repression but also in the substitution of dogma and doctrinal rigidity for revolutionary solidarity. A lifetime of thought and analysis predisposed him against nonviolence as a moralistic evasion of the hard realities of revolutionary struggle, but particularly in the protected isolation of our plane trip to New York, he questioned and probed, weighed and analyzed the idea that nonviolence might be a potentially revolutionary method of struggle— one that had never been developed into a satisfactory form but conceivably could be. It was almost as if troubled by the political weakness of the left in a period of growing popular alienation from capitalism, Deutscher yearned for the movement to reestablish an identity between revolutionary goals and methods.

Excited by the earnestness and brilliance of Deutscher's reflections, I suggested with some hesitation that he sit down with A.J. Muste and Staughton Lynd to continue the discussion, hoping that the interaction of the three would be helpful to all. His first reaction to the mention of Muste was negative—based on contacts of many years before, but it was perhaps indicative of the extent of his curiosity about revolutionary nonviolence that on second thought he expressed himself as eager to have the meeting. We agreed to tape the discussion for possible use in Liberation. *Staughton was unable to be present, but Hans Konigsberger, who had just returned from China, took his place.*

The rest is anti-climactic. Because of mechanical problems with the taping, only a portion was audible. Acutely aware of what had been lost and of the fragmentary nature of what remained, Liberation *laid the whole matter aside. Recently, I tried the tape again on a new machine without significantly better results but was struck by the fact that the section which was audible was eminently worth publishing, to make public at least a little of what Isaac Deutscher was thinking on the subject of revolutionary violence and nonviolence. Deutscher's death last year has unfortunately made impossible any revisions in the transcript that he might have wished.*

Dave Dellinger

Dellinger:

We would like to bring the challenge of a revolutionary nonviolence to an accomplished revolutionary theoretician like Isaac Deutscher. I operate on the theory that nonviolence is not sufficiently developed yet, that it can't be fully appraised or understood in its present form as revealing of the true potential of nonviolence. I think the same thing can be said of socialism at a certain stage; there was the pre-Marxian stage of Christian Socialism and various forms of what is called romantic socialism. Socialism has been going through a gradual sophistication and process of maturation. I think the same thing has to happen in relation to nonviolence, but that unfortunately revolutionary Marxists have had a tendency to discard nonviolence as a revolutionary weapon based on its earliest and most primitive formulations.

There has been a transition from nonviolence as either a symbolic witness or as the special vocation of a small group of people somewhat set apart from the rest of society by their religious training, to the kind of nonviolence which has the determination to change history, to actually change events, a determination which is as strong and as dominating as the revolutionary impulses of non-pacifist revolutionaries of the past. During the Korean War in one of the pacifist organizations that I belonged to I submitted a statement attacking the American position and was horrified to find that within the organization even some of the leadership really supported the American cause, but felt that the American aims should be accomplished by nonviolent instead of violent means. This approach to nonviolence is receding, with the Vietnam War as perhaps a watershed, now the emphasis is on the determination to change historical events.

The pre-Vietnamese War peace movement consisted of at least two main orientations. Some people wanted to achieve the American aim of containing communism and protecting the American system by nonviolent means instead of by violent means. Many of these people have not spoken out against the war very sharply and this has speeded up the historical process of discrediting this kind of "nonviolence." I'm not suggesting that pacifists ever wanted war or didn't want a warless world, but I think there has been a reluctance in the past to get into the muck of politics and social conflict for fear that in the process one would lose his pacifist purity. I think that the absolute need now, and the trend of historical development, is in the other direction, that is of nonviolence trying to present an alternative method of liberation for all oppressed and exploited people. To use one other example: there's been a tragic tendency in the pacifist movement to concern itself disproportionately with overt violence, the violence of the method, and not to concern itself adequately with the violence of the status-quo or institutional violence. Today there is a recognition that people are just as dead if they are killed by preventable disease attributable to poverty as if they were shot with a bullet, or that they're just as wounded by living in a ghetto or, for that matter, living as a member of the parasitical rich, as if they'd been wounded by a bullet. This development leads to the whole approach to non-violence as a serious method of liberation, a serious alternative to the present wars of liberation.

In this respect I like to think in terms of the dialectic, at least in my limited understanding of it. The old-fashioned nonviolence of non-resistance, perhaps inadequate preoccupation with institutional violence, I think of that as the thesis. The anti-Nazi resistance movement during World War II, the guerilla movement in Cuba of the Fidelistas, the heroic resistance in Vietnam today, I think of that as the antithesis. What I would like to have us consider is the possibility that there is a synthesis, that will be something new that we've had hints of but has really not been developed. Guerilla warfare rests on an identification with the population of the country that is conducting the resistance, and that identification is not a facile or a facetious thing; it's something that stems from an identification with the aspirations for liberation, dignity, justice of the country. This is an example of one of the things that has come out of this synthesis. On the other hand, nonviolence has a deep and universal humanism which is also characteristic of historical, not non-violent revolution at its best, but tends to be betrayed and squeezed out in the course of the actual conflict. I think we've learned that anything that looks on the class enemy or the institutional enemy as also the human enemy tends to lead to internal corruption and a cumulative deterioration within the movement of its original idealism and its original methodology. I have one other example. Isaac Deutscher, when he spoke at Berkeley recently of the negative effects of the present conflict in Vietnam within the Communist world, indicated that although the de-Stalinization process has not been totally lost, it has nonetheless been halted or possibly even set in reverse a little bit. He spoke of the fact that in fighting supposedly for freedom in Vietnam, one of the indirect effects has been to encourage the throttling of freedom within the communist world. I think this stems from the fear and from the reaction of like producing like, violence and hatred and distrust producing violence and hatred and distrust, and I wonder why it isn't equally true that even the most idealistic revolutionary movements who rely on hatred and violence provoke a similar misunderstanding, a similar fear, a similar hysteria in the opposition so that there is again this cumulative effect and we actually antagonize the people it is our job to win over. (In Trotsky's history of the Russian revolution, which is certainly not a book advocating nonviolence, I was struck by the extent to which the Russian revolutionists won over the troops which were ordered to disperse them or shoot them down. There seemed to be a very dynamic and creative process at work which, lacking the nonviolent emphasis, most revolutionary movements tend to cut short at a very crucial moment.) I think that we have to get over the idea that nonviolence can win a bloodless war (I think there have to be victims, there have to be deaths) but we're not justified, even if there is a major massacre on our side, which says, "see it won't work, now we have to go into war," because in the process obviously we also guarantee that there will be more massacres, more deaths.

Deutscher:

I must admit that talk about the challenge of nonviolence tends at the beginning to stare at all my deep seated Marxist bias against this kind of argument. I am at once aroused to suspect some wishy-washy idealistic generalizations that lead us politically, analytically and morally nowhere. But as I listen to your argument I become increasingly aware that my bias is directed against an opponent who doesn't stand in front of me at all; my bias is directed against the escapism of absolute pacifism. Even against the high principles of absolute pacifism it is difficult to argue without feeling a certain moral embarassment, because one would like the absolute pacifist who denies absolutely any positive role of violence in history to be right. And yet one knows that he isn't right and that this is a very dangerous escapism. Therefore, one tends to react, if one is a Marxist, with a certain venom. But you are not romantic creatures of nonviolence. To my mind, and I hesitate to use strong words, you have taken a heroic stand over the war in Vietnam. When you started your protest you could not have foreseen that you would be backed by such wide popular response: you have taken great risks in order to express not only your opposition to the violence used by American power, by American imperialism, but also to defend to some extent, morally, the violence to which the Vietnamese have to resort in order to save their own dignity, their own interests, their own present and their own future.

One might say that there is an inconsistency in your attitude, a contradiction in your preaching nonviolence and yet accepting morally to some extent the violence applied by the Vietcong in Vietnam and probably by the FLN in Algeria. But I think that this is a creative inconsistency, a creative contradiction in your attitude. Although you start from an idealistic and to my mind a somewhat metaphysical principle, nevertheless your inconsistency opens for you an important horizon into the realities of our age. I think that you are carrying out something like truthful self-criticism. It is the self-criticism of a variety of pacifism which is not afraid of bringing its own apparent formal inconsistency into the open in order to achieve a greater moral and political consistency in action. And may I say that arguing philosophically from places partly opposed, I admit a similar, but a much larger, perhaps a more tragic inconsistency in the history of revolution, in the history of Communism and Marxism.

The fact is that there is a whole dialectic of violence and nonviolence implied in the Marxist doctrine from its beginnings and throughout all its historic metamorphosis from 1848-1966. As Marxists we have always preached proletarian dictatorship, and the need to overthrow capitalism by force. We have always tried to impress on the working classes of all countries that they would have to be prepared to struggle, even in civil wars, against their oppressing and ruling classes. We were quite devastating in our rejoinders to all those who doubted the right or questioned the need for all those preachings. But here is the dialectical contradiction; after all what has been the idea of Marxism? That of the classless society in which man is no longer exploited and dominated by man, a stateless society. So many people of the left consider this the Utopian element in Marxism, the aspiration to transform societies in such a way that violence should cease forever as the necessary and permanent element in the regulation of the relationship between society and individuals, between individuals and individuals.

In embracing the vision of a nonviolent society, Marxism, I maintain, has gone further and deeper than any pacifist preachers of nonviolence have ever done. Why? Because Marxism laid bare the roots of violence in our society, which the others have not done. Marxism has set out to attack those roots; to uproot violence not just from human thoughts, not just from human emotions, but to uproot them from the very bases of the material existence of society. Marxism has seen violence fed by class antagonism in society—and here Marxism should be assessed against the two-thousand-year record of futile Christian preaching of nonviolence. I say futile in the sense that it has led to no real consequences, to no real diminution of violence. After two millenia of "love thy brother" we are in this situation; that those who go to church throw the napalm bombs and the others who were also brought up in a Christian tradition, the Nazis, have sent the six million descendents of Christ's countrymen to the gas chambers. After two millenia the preaching of nonviolence has led to this! One of the reasons for this is that the roots of violence have never been attacked, never been dug up. Class society has persisted and therefore these preachings, even when most sincere, even when the Christian teacher put both his heart and soul in them, were bound to be futile, because they attacked only the surface of the nonviolence. But then the dialectic of Marxism has also been at fault; Marxism itself, throughout its history of deep and tragic contradictions. How strong the dream of nonviolence lay at the root of the Russian Revolution one can find out if one studies Lenin's statement on Revolution which is written in outwardly a very dogmatic form, almost like an ecclesiastical

text interpreting Biblical verses. Behind these somewhat ecclesiastical formulas there is the deep well of the dream of the stateless society constantly welling up. The October insurrection was carried out in such a way that, according to all the hostile eyewitnesses such as the Western ambassadors who were then in Petrograd, the total number of victims on all sides was ten. That is the total number of victims of that great revolutionary October insurrection. The men who directed this insurrection: Lenin, Trotsky, the members of the military revolutionary committee, gave some thought to the question of violence and nonviolence and organized this tremendous upheaval, with a very profound although unspoken concern for human lives, for the lives of their enemies as well as for their own people. The Russian Revolution, in the name of which so much vio-

lence has been committed, was the most nonviolent act of this scale in the whole history of the human race!

The revolution was won not with guns, but with words, with argument, persuasion. The words were very violent, the words were terribly forceful, but this is the violence of emotion in the revolt against the actuality of violence, of a world war which cost millions of human beings. All those people nowadays who take it upon themselves to preach morality to the makers of the Russian Revolution assume, of course, that there was a kind of good and angelic status quo, an angelic nonviolence which was upset by those Dostoyevskian possessed fiends, the revolutionaries who appropriated to themselves the right to dispose of human lives. Nearly ten million people had perished in the trenches of the First World War when the Bolsheviks carried out that great revolution which cost ten victims.

The deep universal humanism inherent in what you call the challenge of nonviolence has been there in Marxism as its most essential element. We were a little more shy about talking about humanism—we are more shy about this because what scoundrel in world history hasn't spoken about humanism—hasn't Stalin, hasn't Hitler, hasn't Goebbels? I always get more than a little shocked when I hear left-wingers and ex-Marxists suggest that Marxism needs to be supplemented by Humanism. Marxism only needs to be true to itself.

But what happened really after this very promising beginning of the Russian Revolution, after Lenin had written

The State and Revolution, which is the great revolutionary dream about nonviolence expressed in Marxist terms, what happened? The others who preached nonviolence, for instance Kerensky, preached nonviolence to the oppressed by reintroducing the death penalty for soldiers who were refusing to fight on the front. Perhaps in the nature of people who really detest violence there is a greater shyness about speaking about nonviolence. I distrust those who have so many noble words on their lips. I very often trust more those who speak frankly and even brutally about the necessities of the political struggle as long as they don't get carried away by their own righteousness.

Then came the intervention, the civil war. Violence had to be used on an increasing scale, just as the Vietcong today has to use violence on an increasing scale. They can't help it; they're either to go under or they use the violence.

But even in the civil war what did the Bolsheviks do? Again they tried to keep a balance between argument, persuasion and violence; a balance in which they still attached far greater importance to persuasion and argument than to the gun. In sheer arms they were infinitely inferior to the British, the French, and the Americans (who sent both troops and munitions for the White armies in Russia). The Red army led by Trotsky at that time was far inferior. What happened? They agitated, they appealed to the consciousness of the soldiers, of the workers in uniform in those interventionist armies. The French Navy, sent to suppress the revolution, rose in mutiny in Odessa and refused to fight against the Bolsheviks; another triumph of nonviolence in the civil war. This revolt of the sailors was the result of what was called Bolshevik propaganda, but this "subversion" prevented violence. (In Britain in 1920 during the intervention, during the Russo-Polish war [when Poland was White Poland] the dockers of London struck and refused to send arms against Russia and the docks of London were immobilized—this was nonviolence.)

Then comes the great tragedy of the isolation of the Russian Revolution; of its succumbing to incredible, unimaginable destruction, poverty, hunger, and disease as a result of the wars of intervention, the civil wars, and of course the long and exhausting world war which was not of Bolshevik making. As a result of all this, terror was let loose on Russia. Men lost their balance. They lost, even the leaders, the clarity of their thinking and of their minds. They acted under overwhelming and inhuman pressures. I don't undertake to judge them, to blame them or to justify them. I can only see the deep tragedy of this historic process the result of which was the glorification of violence.

But what was to have been but a glassful of violence became buckets and buckets full, and then rivers of violence. That is the tragedy of the Russian Revolution. The dialectics of violence and nonviolence in Marxism were so upset that in the end the nonviolent meaning of Marxism was suppressed under the massive, crushing weight of Stalinism. It wasn't a matter of chance that Stalin implicitly denounced the Leninist and Marxist idea of the withering away of the state. It was on that idea that the whole Marxist nonviolence was epitomized. The Stalinist regime couldn't tolerate, couldn't bear the survival of that dream. It had to crush it out of human minds in order to justify its own violence. I'm not saying this to blame the whole thing on single individuals. It was more than that. It was the tragedy of an isolated and poverty-ridden revolution incapable of fulfilling its promise in isolation and poverty: a revolution caught in this tragic situation—of the irreconcilable contradiction between promise and fulfillment, between dream and reality, sunk into irrationality.

To what extent is Marxism, as such, responsible for this? It would be wrong to identify Stalinism with Marxism, and to blame Marxism for the things that have been done under Stalinism. On the other hand, it would show a lack of moral courage in Marxism to draw the formal line of dissociation and say that we are not responsible for Stalinism, that that wasn't what we aimed at. You see, in a way Marxism is as responsible for Stalin as Christianity was responsible for the Borgias. The Borgias are not Christianity, but Christianity cannot bleach the Borgias from its records. We cannot delete Stalinism from our records although we are not responsible for Stalinist crimes. To some extent we (and when I say we I mean that generation of Marxists with which I as an individual identify morally, I mean Lenin, Trotsky, Bukharin, Zinoviev, the early Communist leaders in Europe) participated in this glorification of violence as a self-defense mechanism. Rosa Luxemburg understood this when she criticized the first faint signs of this attitude.

But the issue is larger and deeper than just human

intentions. The violence isn't rooted in human intentions. The human intentions are, shall we say, the mechanism, the psychological, the ideal mechanism through which material factors and material necessities transmit their pressures. Marxism had not made any allowance for the possibility of such tremendous outgrowth of violence, of such tremendous abuse of violence that would be done in the name of Marxism, for a simple reason. Marxism assumed that revolution would always be an act of change in society carried out violently, but with the support of immense popular majorities. It assumed revolution in an industrialized West carried out by working classes committed to socialism, supporting the revolution with all their heart and confronting as their enemies a really small minority consisting of the exploiters. In such a confrontation of revolutionary majorities with counter-revolutionary minorities, the need to use violence would indeed have been very limited and the dream of nonviolence would have had all this hope for fulfillment.

It is said that Marxism suits the underdeveloped countries but not the advanced and industrial west. I still maintain that the original dream of Marxism and the real original inspiration and hope of Marxism still suits the industrial west much better than it can suit the underdeveloped countries, even if revolution in certain phases is the job of great majorities as it was in Russia in 1917, as it was in China in 1949, as it is in Vietnam today. In underdeveloped countries there comes a moment after the revolution when again there is this breach between promise and fulfillment, of making the people accomplish what they had set out to accomplish or they can accomplish it only partly, very inadequately. Therefore there come frustrations, explosive dissonances and the desire of the post-revolutionary rulers to secure the revolution as they understand it and are able to secure it. The more underdeveloped the country, the more bound to come, after the revolution, a moment of bitter truth and violence.

However, I think that the violence in China already is much smaller than it was in Russia. The irrationality of the Chinese Revolution, though goodness knows there is a lot of irrationality, so far is much less, I think, than what came to the top in the Russian Revolution. But then the Chinese Revolution wasn't the first pioneer, wasn't the *isolated* revolution: it was already assisted by Stalinist Russia, and this reduced the amount of irrationality. I think that with the spread of revolution, with the advance of the industrial and technological aspects of revolutionary societies, with the growth of their wealth, with the rising in their standards of living, with a relative contentment in the popular masses, the irrational element will decrease. The final vindication of the dream of nonviolence in Marxism will come with socialism gaining the advanced countries. That is my belief, and it is not a belief of wishful thinking; it is the whole theoretical structure of Marxism that leads me to this conclusion. I think that the de-Stalinization carried out in Russia, partial, self-contradictory, inadequate, hypocritical as it has been, has already somewhat reestablished the balance between the contradictory elements in the Russian Revolution by reducing the violence and giving more scope to the nonviolent element in Marxism.

You have asked me what I meant when I spoke about the negative effect on the Communist World of the war in Vietnam. The war in Vietnam may or may not be a prelude to new confrontations of violence surging back from the Western world and flooding the world again. The fear of the ultimate violence promotes a recrudescence of the authoritarian and violent trend within Russia and in China. I made an analogy between the effects of the Vietnamese War in the Communist part of the world and the repercussions of the Korean War in the last years of Stalin's era. The fears and panic let loose by the Korean War expressed themselves in Russia in the insanity of Stalin's

rule in the last years, in the repetition of the witches' sabbath of the thirties. I don't foresee and I'm not afraid of something as terrible as that in Russia in response to the American aggression in Vietnam, but we have already seen some recrudescence of the authoritarian trend. The Twenty-third congress of the Communist Party testifies to this. The trials of Daniel and Sinyevsky were symptomatic of the partial return of the authoritarian trend.

On the other hand I don't think that one can say that the Korean War had only one effect, i.e. the encouragement of domestic violence in the Soviet Union and China. It also had a positive effect parallel to the effect that it had in our part of the world. It gave one a sense of human solidarity with a small nation so ruthlessly attacked, so ruthlessly crushed by the most powerful, the greatest, the richest nation in the world. The Korean War disposed of certain illusions which Khruschevism spread, namely the illusion about the possibility of the peaceful transition from capitalism to socialism in such countries as France or Italy. Try to go now to French and Italian workers and tell them that they can accomplish this miracle when in such small nations as Korea and Vietnam it is so resisted by the great capitalist powers.

A. J. Muste: In the first place with most of your analysis I go along completely, including the concept that we don't have to introduce nonviolence into Marx as a new revelation at this time. I also agree with the statement that if you are going to talk about violence you have to talk about the violence of the Christian West. I would say one has to be careful about terminology at that point because very early the Christian church turned away from nonviolence. It was a very small sect that believed that Christianity was associated with nonviolence. I agree completely that if you are looking at violence historically and in the present it is to be found in the Christian Church, Christian civilizations, and Christian nations. Therefore basic to my conception of the role of a possibly revolutionary nonviolence is the responsibility to destroy the violence of the western nations—imperialism. So people like Dave and myself accept the criticism of the absolute pacifists who reject the violence of the Vietcong. You have to make a political judgement about these relations, you can't make an isolated moral judgement. If you make it on absolute dogmatic grounds you remove yourself from the political situation.

A question that gives me problems and which you have left in an overview is the tragedy of the Marxist movement in its orgies of terror and violence in the Soviet Union and Eastern Europe, under Stalin. It seems to me that the great tragedies of which we must be aware should actually be the Soviet Union and the U.S. But there is something there needs further analysis in order that given the example of the communism in the Soviet Union those of us who are revolutionaries may guard ourselves against going further in that kind of evolution of violence. In the second place we must ask whether in the concept of nonviolence there are other forms of force than military forms. This means guarding against accomodation with a system whose very essence is violence, even in so-called peace time. Now on my part, I am constantly frustrated in trying to know what we should think when we think about nonviolent revolution. What do we do if concretely we are in Vietnam. Are there concrete ways of struggle other than those used by the Vietnamese? I think we have only an elementary concept of nonviolent force as a constant in struggle with the arms of imperialism, which is a very reactionary force. I think there is no room for compromise but I think we do have suggestions on how perhaps to avoid what happened in the Soviet Union in this country. *(At this point, Muste's words became inaudible.)*

Deutscher: We have to make known the long, terrible road leading us to that classless society. You speak as if we stood already on the threshhold of a classless society. You see it's so easy to make the slogan of nonviolence an escapism; so easy to overlook the realities of this long road and on this road we shall live with violence, and if we are socialist we shall use violence.

My point is this. As Marxists, whenever we are driven to use violence what we must know and tell those people whom we shall call to act, is that violence is a necessary evil. And the emphasis will be on both the adjective and the noun, on the necessary and on evil. To preach nonviolence to those always the object of violence may even be false. I say the lesson we should learn from Soviet history is that we can't overemphasize the evil of violence. But if I were a Vietnamese and also in the ranks of the Vietcong I would also use violence. I don't know if, with my Western way of thinking, if I were a Vietnamese I would try to tell my comrades in arms we should not make a virtue of the bitter and terrible necessity of violence. But we are acting in the West where this argument has much more chance of being understood and accepted.

On the Left in the West we must foster a way of thinking which would not shirk realities. We have in front of us—and this is where Marxism parts from anarchism and pure pacificism—we share with anarchists the dream of a stateless society but we ask how do you arrive at it. You accept the view that the Vietnamese war is not an accident of history; that it expresses the structure of your society, expresses the imperialist character in your relationship to the outside world. If you accept this you imply that the social order has to be changed. How is it to be changed? How is it going to be changed by nonviolent methods when those who refuse to move an inch in Vietnam to their class enemies—will they yield the territory of the United States to socialism without defending the status quo? Can you imagine this? I can but only under one condition. That is when you have the overwhelming number of Americans ready to use violence in order to bring about socialism, only then may socialism conquer the U.S. without the use of violence. The capital of the revolution was its moral supremacy. You see, if you achieve for socialism a moral supremacy in American society comparable to that of the Russian revolution then you might have to use only an infinitesimal amount of violence. But here again is the dialectic—only if you're ready to use violence without making a virtue of it.

LIBERATION

July 1969

●○●

"The problem after a war is with the victor. He thinks he has just proved that war and violence pay. Who will now teach him a lesson?"

—A. J. Muste

MUSTE

["... Practically all our thinking about pacifism in connection with class war starts out at the wrong point. The question raised is how the oppressed, in struggling for freedom and the good life, may be dissuaded from employing "the revolutionary method of violence" and won over to "the peaceful process of evolution." Two erroneous assumptions are concealed in the question put that way. The first is that the oppressed, the radicals, are the ones who are creating the disturbance. To the leaders of Jesus' day, Pharisees, Sadducees, Roman governor, it was Jesus who was upsetting the people, turning the world upside down. In the same way, we speak of the Kuomintang "making a revolution" in China today, seldom by any chance of the Most Christian Powers having made the revolution by almost a hundred years of trickery, oppression, and inhumanity. Similarly, society may permit an utterly impossible situation to develop in an industry like coal, but the workers who finally in desperation put down tools and fold their arms, they are "the strikers." the cause of the breach of the peace. We need to get our thinking focused, and to see the rulers of Jewry and Rome, not Jesus; the Powers, not the Chinese Nationalists; selfish employers or a negligent society—not striking workers—as the cause of disturbance in the social order.

A second assumption underlying much of our thinking is that the violence is solely or chiefly committed by the rebels against oppression, and that this violence constitutes the heart of our problem. However, he basic fact is hat the economic, social, political order in which we live was built up largely by violence, is now being extended by violence, and is maintained only by violence. A slight knowledge of history, a glimpse at the armies and navies of the Most Christian Powers, at our police and constabulary, at the militaristic fashion in which practically every attempt of workers to organize is greeted, in Nicaragua or China, will suffice to make the point clear to an unbiased mind.

The foremost task, therefore, of the pacifist in connection with class war is to denounce the violence on which the present system is based, and all the evil-material and spiritual—this entails for the masses of men hroughout the world; and to exhort all rulers in social, political, industrial life, all who occupy places of privilege, all who are the beneficiaries of the present state of things, to relinquish every attempt to hold on to wealth, position and power by force, to give up the instruments of violence on which they annually spend billions of wealth produced by the sweat and anguish of the toilers. So long as we are not dealing honsetly and adequately with this ninety percent of our problem, there is something ludicrous, and perhaps hypocritical, about our concern over the ten percent of violence employed by

the capitalist as well as for the laborer), another statement of the rule is, "They that sow the wind shall reap the whirlwind." You get from the universe what you give, with interest! What if men build a system on violence and injustice, on not doing good to those who hate them nor even to those who meekly obey and toil for them? And persist in this course through centuries of Christian history? And if, then, the oppressed raise the chant:

Ye who sowed the wind of sorrow
Now the whirlwind you must dare,
As ye face upon the morrow,
The advancing Proletaire!

In such a day, the pacifist is presumably not absolved from preaching to the rebels that they also shall reap what they sow; but assuredly not in such a wise as to leave the oppressors safely entrenched in their position, not at the cost of preaching to them in all sternness that "the judgements of the Lord are true and righteous altogether."

As we are stayed from preaching nonviolence to the underdog, unless and until we have dealt adequately with the dog who is chewing him up, so also are all those who would support a country in war against another country stayed from preaching nonviolence in principle to labor or to radical movements. Much could be said on this point, but it is perhaps unnecessary to dwell on it here. Suffice it to observe in passing that, to one who has had any intimate connection with labor, the flutter occasioned in certain breasts by the occasional violence in connection with strikes seems utterly ridiculous, and will continue to seem so until the possessors of these fluttering breasts have sacrificed a great deal more than they already have in order to banish from the earth the horrible monster of international war."]

A.J. Muste, 1928

wn March 1970

the rebels against oppression. Can we win the rulers of earth to peaceful metheods?

The psychological basis for the use of nonviolent methods is the simple rule that like produces like, kindness provokes kindness, as surely as injustice produces resentment and evil. It is sometimes forgotten by those whose pacifism is a spurious, namby-pamby thing that if one Biblical statement of this rule is "Do good to hem that hate you"(an exhortation presumably intended for

REVOLUTIONARY LETTERS

Number One

*I have just realized that the stakes are myself
I have no other
ransom money, nothing to break or barter but my life
my spirit measured out, in bits, spread over
the roulette table, I recoup what I can
nothing else to shove under the nose of the maitre de jeu
nothing to thrust out the window, no white flag
this flesh all I have to offer, to make the play with
this immediate head, what it comes up with, my move
as we slither over this board, stepping always
(we hope) between the lines*

Diane di Prima

Number Eight

*Every time you pick the spot for a be-in,
a demonstration, a march, a rally, you are choosing the
    ground
for a potential battle.
You are still calling these shots.
Pick your terrain with that in mind.
Remember the old gang rules:
stick to your neighborhood, don't let them lure you
to Central Park, every time. I would hate
to stumble bloody out of that park to find help:
Central Park West, or Fifth Avenue, which would you
choose?
go to love-ins
with incense, flowers, food, and a plastic bag
with a damp cloth in/it, for tear gas, wear no jewelry
wear clothes you can move in easily, wear no glasses
contact lenses,
earrings for pierced ears are especially hazardous
try to be clear
in front, what you will do if it comes
to trouble
if you're going to try to split stay out of the center
don't stampede or panic others
don't waver between active and passive resistance
know your limitations, bear contempt
neither for yourself, nor any of your brothers
NO ONE WAY WORKS, it will take all of us
shoving at the thing from all sides
to bring it down.*

Nonviolence vs The Mafia

The following article was submitted to the WRI triennial conference. It was written by Danilo Dolci, the Sicilian nonviolent leader,   —Eds.

The problem of our new revolution is to find how best to eliminate exploitation, murder, the investment of energy in weapons of destruction—how to provoke chain reactions not of hate and death but of new constructiveness, of new quality of life.

It is easy to doubt the efficacy of nonviolent revolution while it has yet to be proved, historically and systematically, that it can change *structures*. But in a world tired of murder, betrayal, pointless death, there can be a more direct appeal to people's consciences when a movement for change is both robust *and* nonviolent.

In Partinico in the winter of '55, there was really desperate hunger among most of the population, outlawed in every sense from the life of the nation. When we held the first peasant meetings, quite a few proposed flinging stones through the carabinieri's windows or setting fire to the Town Hall. But the majority objected that this way would be less effective, since people would be unwilling to participate if it meant putting themselves in the wrong. After fuller discussion, we decided on a day's fast by 1,000 people, to be followed by a "strike in reverse"—working on a dilapidated country road. The people joined in with scarcely any fear at all, despite massive intervention by the police—because they knew they weren't doing anybody any harm: and within a few days they had succeeded as never before in penetrating the public conscience with their protest and their own positive proposals.

With this profound capacity for awakening consciences, nonviolent action is also revolutionary in that it activates other forces that are revolutionary in different ways. And everyone who wants change makes the sort of revolution he can.

Often the situation in Partinico was so grave, the terror of the Mafia so widespread, that it was like working on the edge of a landslide. When some of us felt the situation demanded action, we decided to fast (as one has to in prison when it is the only action possible), in order to try to bring the peasants out of their isolation by joining with them in exposing the intolerable reality and making specific suggestions. At first many people disagreed with this method, but gradually as the days passed almost everyone's conscience was galvanized; discussions became animated; enterprises proliferated—among the embryonic trade unions, the local Councils, parties, individuals and groups, often even in rivalry with one another. And many people now, as they look at the new lake with its ducks, inevitably reflect on the method which, from the first few stones to the final great mass, brought about the construction of this magnificent dam.

Sometimes we may admire violent revolutionary forces not because they are the only possible ones, or the most suitable to the circumstances, but because where they are active they are often the only ones brave enough to exist at all. But anyone who thinks war the *highest form* of struggle, or the *means* of resolving conflicts, still has a very limited vision of man. Anyone with effective revolutionary experience knows—and has to admit—that to succeed in changing a situation he must have not only a material appeal but a higher *moral* appeal; he knows that the appeal to truer principles, to a superior ethic, itself becomes an element of strength: and thus his action is revolutionary also in so far as it helps create new feelings, new abilities, new culture, new instincts—a new human nature.

Personally, I am absolutely convinced that peace means action—when necessary revolutionary, but *nonviolent*. I recognize that a diseased situation can be brought nearer to health, and therefore nearer to peace, by other means too: but I know that violence, even when directed to good ends, still contains the seed of death.

Which are more numerous—those who would gain by changes, or those who think they benefit from maintaining the status quo?

There are thousands of millions of people in the world at present excluded from progress. By interpreting and expressing the profound needs of *these* people, by helping them to take stock of their problems, by helping them to initiate enterprises of every kind, at every level, and to press effectively for changes, we can activate a positively revolutionary force.

Though planning from a position of power is more likely to be effective, we mustn't underestimate the possibilities of opposition planning.

Many revolutionary movements, though good at arousing consciences and effective in protest and pressure, suffer from weakness on their *constructive* front. But the demolition of old systems and the building of new organic groups should be simultaneous, coordinated activities which potentiate each other: the growth of convincing alternatives encourages attack on the old groups, while the loss of authority of the old structures facilitates development of the new.

I refer to the dam built on the Iato river: even though this "laboratory" is only a tiny part of the world, and still in its early stages, the sequence of events there provides a useful example.

A desperate population was dominated by the Mafia, strong through its political connections: there was no prospect of change. Together with the more enlightened people, we begin to seek possible remedies. The necessity and feasibility of building a large dam to irrigate the zone are established. Educational activity at the grass roots so that people understand what a dam is. Pressure, by a few at first, then growing ever wider and more continual, until the dam is started. The workers on the dam site form a trade union: jobs are no longer got through the Mafia, which loses prestige. Local *mafiosi* are publicly denounced; their relationship with the two powerful politicians from the area is likewise denounced; and two politicians are dropped from the Italian Government. Construction work is speeded up. Creation of the first (though still rudimentary) centers for promotion of a democratic irrigation syndicate to ensure non-Mafia water supply. Co-operatives are formed. In the neighboring Belice valley, pressure has begun for the construction of another, bigger dam; communal and intercommunal centers for organic planning are formed, and meanwhile another center is growing up at which people will learn the techniques of planned development with active involvement of the whole population.

—Danilo Dolci

A SENSE OF CRISIS

But you see, we all believe in what Bakunin and Nachaev said: that a revolutionary is a doomed man....So you come to terms with the idea that you may be killed. And when you have to live with the prospect of being wiped out in a flash, you either stop doing what you're doing and remove yourself from that situation, or else you have to accept it and kind of repress it, and get it off your mind. Otherwise, you'll be nonfunctional. You can't walk around afraid and watching and looking over your shoulder. Anyway, I think many people these days have learned to live with that understanding. I learned to live with it somehow. —Eldridge Cleaver

Ralph Featherstone lived in Neshoba County, Mississippi, for two years, off and on. He had first come there one day in the summer of 1964 to meet three fellow civil rights workers in a church in the county seat of Philadelphia. The three had left Featherstone in Meridian in the morning; he was to catch up with them in Neshoba later in the afternoon. Featherstone waited all afternoon in the church in Philadelphia. Micky Schwerner, James Chaney and Andy Goodman never did come.

Black folks in Philadelphia gave Featherstone a place to sleep and food to eat, and he'd pay them a few dollars every now and then with money he'd get from Northern white contributions to SNCC. Then the money stopped, and Featherstone began working on economic development projects which might make the Southern movement, and the black community, self-sustaining. I spent some time with Ralph in Neshoba, and the one day I remember most vividly was framed by two visits: by the FBI in the morning and by the notorious Sheriffs Rainey and Price in the late afternoon. Neither visit was pleasant; the FBI was polite and menacing and the sheriffs were rude and menacing, but Ralph dealt coolly and good-naturedly with both. At the end of the day he drank a lot of milk and took medicine for his stomach. He kept a shotgun next to the medicine.

The economic development project didn't work, and Featherstone came back to Washington, where he had grown up and had gone to college, to try a similar scheme. That one came to little, too, and he went back to Mississippi for a spell. As the movements of the Sixties progressed, he went to Japan to talk to young people there, and he traveled to Cuba to see what that was like, and to Africa. SNCC pretty much stopped functioning as an organization, but Featherstone and some of the best of the SNCC people kept working. In the months before he was blown to bits by a bomb in Bel Air, Maryland, Featherstone and several others were running a book store, a publishing house and a school in Washington. Ralph lived a few blocks from me and we'd bump into each other every few weeks, chat briefly, and make vague plans to get together for a meal or a longer talk. As we both knew, the plans would not be followed. Somewhat mindlessly, I would slip Ralph into a category called "the black thing," which was a locked box decorated with exotic Benin artifacts, and a tag: "Do Not Open Until...." I shudder now at the thought of the tag on the bag he had for me.

I don't doubt that the road from Meridian ended, in many more ways than one, last week. Ralph's progression in the last six years was, like the road itself, an attenuated metaphor. Strung out along the way were the mileposts of a generation, the markings of a movement, passed as soon as they were come upon, quickly out of sight. It's hard to say how one or another man or woman is bound to travel, and it can't be known where

anyone is going to stop. Ralph missed a meeting in Neshoba; but then he kept his appointment in Bel Air.

A desperate irony of history, a dialectical pun, put Featherstone's death next to the explosions in the Wilkerson house in Greenwich Village and the bombings a few nights later of three corporations' offices in Manhattan. In evidentiary terms the events of that week seem totally disconnected. Featherstone and his companion, Che Payne, were most probably murdered by persons who believed that Rap Brown was in their car. Featherstone had gone to Bel Air on the eve of Brown's scheduled appearance at the trial to make security arrangements; Brown had good reason to fear for his safety in that red neck of the woods. No one who knew the kinds of politics Featherstone was practicing, or the mission he was on in Bel Air, or the quality of his judgement, believes that he was transporting a bomb—in the front seat of a car, leaving Bel Air, at midnight, in hostile territory, with police everywhere.

The police and newspaper accounts of the goings-on in the Wilkerson house on West Eleventh Street seem—in outline, at least—consistent within themselves and probable in the (dim) light of developments after the recent break-up of a formal Weatherman organization. The tensions within Weatherman, both organizationally and politically, were always as explosive as any bomb; weathermen were experimenting not only with new tactics and ideas but with new styles of living, new ways of loving, and new values of existence. They changed their course almost fortnightly: puritanical one week, totally uninhibited the next; druggy and orgiastic, then ascetic and celibate; concerned with a mass line and liberal movements, then deep into guerrilla training. And all the time they were dealing—not very successfully— with open repression from the Man and open hostility from most other radicals. It was clear at the Weatherman convention at Flint in December that the organization was not going to grow in size and legitimacy, and as early Weathersymps and cadre from the collectives dropped out of contact, the core hardened. In a few months, the distance between the guerrilla center and the discarded cadre and the lost sympathizers could be measured in light-years; people who had once worked closely with the women who were, reportedly, in the Eleventh Street house knew nothing of those recent activities, and could not begin to find out.

The bombings in Manhattan on the night of March 11 appear to be the work of people with politics quite different from the post-weathermen of Eleventh Street. The obvious differences can be seen in the messages the bombers left; even a cursory *explication du texte* indicates that the bombers were of the same anarchist strain as those who hit similar targets last November, and quite distinct from the specific line of Weatherman. The notes spoke in terms of "death culture" and life forces, but contained few of the internationalist, anti-police, anti-racism and pro-Viet Cong references which mark the Weather ethic.

But although the three events are disconnected in all particulars, they are at the same time tied at some radical bottom. Guerrilla attacks by the revolutionary Left and counter-attacks by the extreme Right seem almost natural in America this winter. When students demonstrate they do not merely sit-in but burn-up: They fire-bomb a bank in Santa Barbara, snipe at policemen in Buffalo. Few peaceful marches end peacefully; both marchers and police are ready to fight.

The newspapers have begun calling the current crop of radicals "revolutionaries," but they have removed the quotation marks and have dropped such skeptical qualifiers as "self-styled" or "so-called" before the word. For the first time in half a century, at least—and perhaps since 1776—there is a generalized revolutionary movement in the US. It is not directed at organizing labor or winning civil rights for minorities or gaining power for students in the administration of universities. Wholly unorganized and utterly undirected, the revolutionary movement exists not because it is planned but because it is logical: not because a handful of young blacks or dissident middle-class whites will it, but because the conditions of American life create it: not because the Left is so strong, but because the center is so weak.

It's worth saying what the revolutionary movement is *not*. First of all, it's not big—at least the active part. All the people who are into demolitions this year could gather in a townhouse or two in the Village—and probably did. There have been scores of bombings in the past six months—in New York, Seattle, the San Francisco Bay Area, Colorado and scattered college towns. In Madison, Wisconsin, for instance, someone predicted "Zabriskie Point" and bombed an ROTC building from an airplane (the bombs did not go off). But a hundred or two hundred people could have done all that, and there is no reason to believe that there are vast divisions preparing for the next assaults.

Second, it's not yet a revolution. A bomb in Standard Oil's headquarters in Manhattan does as much material damage to Standard Oil as a tick does to a tiger. Universities have not ground to a halt, draft boards have not been shut down, the war in Indochina hardly has ended. The resources of the corporations and the government that make public decisions and social policy are complete.

But then, the revolutionary movement is not isolated in its few activists, nor confined to its few acts of violence. There was a general sense of depression in the liberal Left when the Eleventh Street house blew up; and there was a genuine sense of exhilaration when the bombings followed. People who could not, in their weirdest fantasies, ever see themselves lighting a fuse were lifted for a moment from their set of dull futility. For that reason, the guerrilla acts cannot be dismissed as "isolated terror" by a "lunatic fringe"; they draw a positive response from a surprisingly large number of ordinary people—even those who venture out of their conventional lives for nothing more exciting than a Moratorium rally, and who will tell you before you ask that they "deplore" violence. The contradictions of the society as a whole exist within each of them as well.

Finally, the revolutionary movement is not professional, nor is it politically mature, nor tactically consistent. Nor is there much chance that it will get itself together in the coming months. If it was a "tragic accident" that killed three young people in the Eleventh Street house, it was in one sense no accident: Those who seek to build a revolution from scratch must inevitably make such mistakes. (For a description of how amateurish revolutionaries can be, read Che's diaries.) The politics of the guerrilla acts are not always self-explanatory, even to committed radicals; in what kind of political demands were the Manhattan bombings set? One New York radical activist said recently that those acts could have contextual meaning only if the messages demanded US withdrawal from Vietnam and Laos, say, or freedom for Black Panthers in jail. A note which threatened continued attacks until the war ended, for example, would make sense to many more people than the seemingly "nihilist" statements made last week.

At this stage, tactics can be crucial. Attacks against property —in which care is taken to avoid injuries to people—are much more easily understood than terrorist acts against police, much less "innocent" bystanders. It's necessary, too, to think through any action to avoid bringing retaliation down against those who are not responsible: For example, the fire-bombing of Judge Murtagh's house in New York (in protest against the trial of the Panther 21) was obviously prejudicial to the Panthers' case, and their cause. If whites did that act, they should have made it their own responsibility—and they should have set its political meaning straight. Explanations are necessary, but they are hard to make by the underground guerrillas, in the absence of an overground mass movement—tied in sympathy but not in fact to those below.

The escalation of radical protest into revolutionary action will produce two major social effects: a sense of crisis in the society as a whole, and a need for repression by the authorities. The two effects are inextricably related. If there is crisis, there will be an appropriate response to it. The sense of crisis is not the work of the bombers or bank burners or demonstrators or Panthers alone. It develops easily when the phones don't work, the beaches are oil-slicked, the blacks are bused to white schools, the priests are marrying, the redwoods are toppling, the teenagers are shooting-up, the women are liberating themselves, the stock market is falling and the Viet Cong is winning.

Neither does repression happen in a single tone of voice. Even in the most critical of times (*especially* in the most critical of times) the State acts, as Lenin put it, like hangman and priest. Despite the policy of "benign neglect" which the Nixon Administration is following in most matters, the process of buying off black revolution—by accepting black militancy—is continuing at a fast clip. If the government tends to fall behind in the effort, private corporations, foundations and educational institutions keep up the pace. In the same months that Fred Hampton is killed or desegregation is postponed in Mississippi, millions of dollars went to black urban bureaucrats; black students were streaming into previously white colleges and white jobs; and the government made plans to give preferential hiring to blacks in construction jobs. It's easy but unwise to dismiss such methods as "meaningless," or "too little," or "cynical." Of course, the "Philadelphia plan" for hiring black construction workers is also a way to limit the power of labor unions. But in the near and middle-distances those measures—the repressive and the cooptive —are reasonably successful in blunting the chopping edge of the black liberation movement.

In the week that Vice President Agnew is denouncing "kooks" and "social misfits," and Conspiracy Prosecutor Foran is talking of a "freaking fag revolution," the Nixon Administration and a coalition of politicians from (and including) Goldwater to Kennedy are proposing lowering the voting age to 18, and plans are going ahead for an all-volunteer Army. Again, the point is not that either of those proposals will accomplish much in the way of changing social values in America; but those measures are not exactly Nuremburg Laws to be used against a radical force or a distasteful element of society.

In the wake of the bombings and deaths last week, the FBI fanned out to question anyone known to have a connection with the Eleventh Street people. Agents were unusually uptight; one set of FBI visitors called a New York man who declined to speak to them a "motherfucker." There were police agents with walkie-talkies standing around major airports all week long. The newspapers—especially in New York—bannered scare headlines and speculated endlessly, and foolishly, on the connections between the events. Authorities "leaked" word to Richard Starnes, a Scripps-Howard reporter in Washington who often acts as an unofficial flack for the FBI, that both Featherstone and the three Eleventh Street people so far identified had visited Cuba—and that Attorney Leonard Boudin, whose daughter's papers were found in the house, represented the Cuban government in legal matters in the US. Senator Eastland has now called for an investigation of the Venceremos Brigade of Americans who have gone to Cuba to harvest sugar cane. No one believes that the natives in America can be restless—all by themselves.

The level of fear (that is, paranoia with good reason) rose to exorbitant heights, but that too affects the general sense of crisis in the society. Seen in relief (if there can by any), that crisis is the most serious organizing effect of the bombings. If the radical movements are to win middle-class people—or those, both black and white, who aspire to middle-class comfort and security—they must devise ways of forcing real existential choices upon them. At one time, marches and rallies or sit-ins or building occupations provided a setting for those choices. But privileged Americans do not easily make the revolutionary choice. Only if their privilege is worthless are they free to act. Now, the sense of crisis is the specific contradiction to privilege: that is, all the things that Americans want to get and spend are without meaning if the world no longer holds together. At such times, people choose to fight—one way or the other. It may be that such a time is now.

—Andrew Kopkind

Hard Times
3/23/70

REVOLUTIONARY

When he said
'Your struggle is my struggle'
a curtain was pushed away.

A curtain was pushed away revealing
an open window
and beyond that

an open country.
For the first time I knew it was actual.
I am indoors still

but the air from fields
beyond me touched my face.

It was a country
of hilly fields, of many
shadows and rivers.

The thick heavy dark
curtain had hidden
a world from me,

curtain of sorrow, world
where far-off I see
people moving—

struggling to move, as I
towards my window
struggle, burdened but not

each alone. They move
out in that air together
where I too

will be moving,
not alone.

DENISE LEVERTOV

AT THE JUSTICE DEPARTMENT, NOVEMBER 15 1969

Brown gas-fog, white
beneath the streetlamps.
Cut off on three sides, all space filled
with our bodies.
   Bodies that stumble
in brown airlessness, whitened
in light, a mildew glare,
   that stumble
hand-in-hand, blinded, retching.
Wanting it, wanting
to be here, the body believing it's
dying in its nausea, my head
clear in its despair, a kind of joy,
knowing this is by no means death,
is trivial, an incident, a
fragile instant. Wanting it, wanting
   with all my hunger this anguish,
   this knowing in the body
the grim odds we're
up against, wanting it real.
Up that bank where gas
curled in the ivy, dragging each other
up, strangers, brothers
and sisters, Nothing
will do but
to taste the bitter
taste. No life
other, apart from.

DENISE LEVERTOV

1967... AND ANOTHER

The Pentagon March was a prelude to Chicago. Anti-war demonstraters charged past cordons of soldiers and hundreds burned their draft cards.

On February 8, 1968, two years, two
months and 25 days before the killing
of four student protesters at Kent State,
three student protesters in Orangeburg,
S.C. were killed by state police.

The New York Times devoted 10½
feet of news column space to Kent
State — and 29 inches to Orangeburg.

The students at Kent State were white.
The students at Orangeburg were black.

Remember the Orangeburg Three:
Sam Hammon, 18
Delano Middleton, 17
Henry Smith, 18

(No Picture Available)

1968... AND ANOTHER

1968... AND ANOTHER

1968... AND ANOTHER

The almost-revolution of French workers and students. They fought together against police while, over universities and factories alike, the red flag flew.

A long series of student rebellions began with the uprising at Columbia. The war, racism and poverty, as reflected in school policies, were the issues.

BLACK G.I. PANTHERS

Say; how'd you get to be a co-respondent an' come ovah to this raggedy-ass motherfucker?"

He was a really big spade, rough-looking even when he smiled, and he wore a gold nose-bead fastened through his left nostril. I told him that the nose-bead blew my mind, and he said that was all right, it blew everybody's mind. We were sitting by the chopper pad of an LZ above Kontum. He was trying to get to Dakto, I was heading for Pleiku, and we both wanted to get out of there before nightfall. We took turns running out to the pad to check the choppers that kept coming in and taking off, neither of us were having any luck, and after we'd talked for an hour he laid a joint on me and we smoked.

"I been heah mo'n eight months now," he said. "I bet I been in mo'n twenny firefights. An' I ain' hardly fired back once."

"How come?"

"Shee-it, I go firin' back, I might kill one a th' Brothers, you dig it?"

I nodded, no Vietcong ever called *me* honky, and he told me that in his company alone there were more than a dozen Black Panthers, and that he was one of them. I didn't say anything, and then he said that he wasn't just a Panther; he was an agent for the Panthers, sent over here to recruit. I asked him what kind of luck he'd been having, and he said fine, real fine. There was a fierce wind blowing across the LZ, and the joint didn't last very long.

"Hey baby," he said. "That was jes' some jive I tole you. Shit, I ain' no Panther. I'se jes' fuckin' with you, see what you'd say."

"But the Panthers have guys over here. I've met some."

"Tha' could be," he said, and he laughed.

A Huey came in, and he jogged out to see where it was headed. It was going to Dakto, and he came back to get his gear. "Later, baby," he said. "An' luck." He jumped into the chopper, and as it rose from the strip he leaned out and laughed, bringing his arm up and bending it back towards him, palm out and the fist clenched tightly in the Sign.

From "Illumination Rounds" by Michael Herr, *New American Review No 7*

This sit-down protest over the killing of a deranged fellow-prisoner won some of these Presidio GIs 16-year sentences for "mutiny." Public outrage forced sentence reductions.

THOUSANDS OF SOLDIERS IN ACTIVE OPPOSITION

Protect Civil Liberties for GIs

By Larry Seigle

The antiwar movement among GIs has developed from its initial stage of antiwar actions on the part of individual soldiers to a full-fledged movement involving literally thousands of servicemen in active opposition to the war in Vietnam. October, 1968, was the month in which the GI peace movement came of age. In San Francisco, on October 12, 500 active-duty GIs organized and led an antiwar march and rally attended by 15,000 civilians. On October 26 and 27, in response to the call of the Student Mobilization Committee, active-duty soldiers joined in antiwar actions in cities throughout the country. In spite of local restrictions on GIs' right to participate in demonstrations, hundreds of soldiers, sailors and marines demonstrated that day against the war, in Atlanta, Detroit, Chicago, Austin, Seattle, Los Angeles, and many other cities. Demonstrations involving GIs also took place on November 2nd in some cities.

Along with the upsurge in antiwar activity, the number of cases of soldiers being persecuted for their political position has risen dramatically.

In response to the need for "outside" legal help and publicity, the GI Civil Liberties Defense Committee was formed to aid GIs whose constitutional rights of freedom of speech, freedom of the press, or freedom of assembly and association, are being denied by military authorities.

In its first case the GI Civil Liberties Defense Committee won a decisive victory when an army court-martial at Ft. Dix, New Jersey, found Sp/4 Allen Myers not guilty on a charge of disobeying an order. Myers had distributed leaflets put out by the Philadelphia Student Mobilization Committee.

Other current cases, some of which are being handled directly by the GI Civil Liberties Defense Committee, are described below. In all cases, protest letters and telegrams can be sent to the Commanding Officer at the base involved. Copies of all letters and telegrams should also be sent to the GI Civil Liberties Defense Committee at Box 355, Old Chelsea Station, New York, New York 10011. Financial contributions, which are desperately needed for legal expenses and publicity, can be sent to the same address.

Forty-three black soldiers at Fort Hood, Texas were arrested on August 24 after an all-night spontaneous demonstration against their possible assignment to Chicago for "riot" duty. One hundred and twenty-five black soldiers from the 1st and 2nd Armored Divisions met in a parking lot on the Fort to discuss the impending call-up and evidence of racism at Fort Hood.

At midnight, Major General John K. Boles, Jr., Commanding Officer of the 1st Armored Division, met with the men. Boles gave them permission to remain at the parking lot until they heard from him. He informed them he would consult with higher authorities to see whether they could be exempt from duty in Chicago as a matter of conscience, and promised to return with an answer. Some of the men left during the night. Major General Boles never returned.

At 5:45 a.m. MPs arrived and ordered the remaining sixty GIs to disperse. Minutes later they arrested those who had not left. The soldiers were charged with willful disobedience of an order of a superior officer, namely to disperse their demonstration and return to their units.

The prisoners were held incommunicado, beaten, and subjected to hours of questioning. • • •

National Guardsmen riot-training.

ARMY TIMES ▰▰▰

The GI "protest" movement is growing as dramatically, in its way, as the student radical movement did half-a-decade ago. But the military system is far more tough to crack than the university establishment. The biggest GI action to date—in mass if not militancy—was a march last month of 750 active-duty servicemen, most of them from the San Diego, Calif., Naval complex at Camp Pendleton, through nearby Oceanside.

The servicemen led a chanting crowd of about 5,000 people on the march through the town —the closest community to the sprawling Marine encampment. There was more than a march; at a rally afterwards, GIs announced the formation of "Movement for a Democratic Military," and read a list of 12 demands ranging from collective bargaining to support of the Black Panthers' "POWs for Panthers" prisoner exchange project with North Vietnam. The GI contingent was thoroughly integrated; one key organizer, a black Marine sergeant named Jack Anderson, had been bailed out two days before after being beaten and jailed in a raid on the Los Angeles Black Panther Party headquarters. Press and town officials hardly knew how to respond (Washington newspapers carried a one-paragraph item the next day); but the classiest comment of the day came from the mayor of Oceanside: "It was like a great open sewer running through the streets of our city."

▰ In the last month California has also seen the birth of another unusual kind of anti-military activity: the beginnings of political organizing among Reservists and National Guardsmen.

Until now, Reservists and Guardsmen have been anything but outspoken. They are the upper end of the Army's class hierarchy: Blacks and high school dropouts end up on the front lines in Vietnam: Upper-middle college graduates tend to wangle their way into Reserve and Guard units. There, they usually spend four and a half months on active duty at US training bases, and the rest of their six-year obligation period going to evening and weekend drills and an annual two-week summer camp. It's a bothersome routine, but a good deal more privileged—and safer —than crawling through the rice paddies of Southeast Asia.

The new organizing within the military comes in the form of a strongly-worded statement now being circulated by 50 officers and men from the National Guard and the Army, Navy, Air Force, Marine, and Coast Guard Reserves. They call for immediate total withdrawal from Vietnam, and demand "total withdrawal now of all the American soldiers advising the armies of dictatorships throughout Latin America and Asia. We don't want Guatamala, Thailand, or Bolivia to become the Vietnams of the 1970s. One Vietnam is enough; too many people have been killed already to preserve America's overseas empire."

Organizers of the campaign hope to gather several thousand signatures from around the country and use the total to publicize the extent of anti-war feeling inside the military. Guardsmen and Reservists can legally sign a statement like this; active duty soldiers believe they cannot. Readers in the Guard or Reserves interested in seeing the statement and adding their names should write Box 4398, Berkeley, Calif.

Hard Times ▰▰▰ 1/5/70

A Mirror For Secretary McNamara
Jules Feiffer

The Secretary of Defense, whose name I keep thinking is Napalmara—a natural mistake—said in a speech of last August made before an extremist group called the Veterans of Foreign Wars, that the Defense Department today is the largest single educational complex that the world has ever possessed. So in effect, Pvts. Johnson, Mora, and Samas are really just dropouts.

In his speech the Secretary of Defense goes on to deplore the wasted potential of the undrafted poor, undrafted because they don't meet the physical and educational requirements of the United States Armed Forces (poor bastards). "Fully one third of the nation's youth currently do not qualify . . . six hundred thousand young men a year are rejected," says Mr. McNamara, a sympathetic tear welling in his eye because he has strong feelings about rejection he was father of the Edsel.

Through the application of advanced educational techniques, Mr. McNamara tells us, we can salvage tens of thousands of 4-F's each year, first to productive military careers, and later, he says, to productive roles in society. As what he does not say. Perhaps rioters.

In any event, the Defense Department has pioneered, says Mr. McNamara, some of the most advanced teaching techniques. So if we are to believe Mr. McNamara, the Defense Department which used to be called the War Department may, in the near future, be known as the Department of Health, Education and Welfare—and the U.S. Army is simply I.S. 201 writ large—in which case I would think the insurrections of Pvts. Johnson, Mora, and Samas should be treated quite differently than the Board of Education in the Pentagon seems to be treating them now.

I don't wish to sound too ironic about Mr. McNamara. I have friends who know him and they tell me he is deeply disturbed by the current trend of events. One of the mistakes too easy for critics of the war to make is to begin to picture those who are running the war as monsters. As villains. They are no monsters. They are not villains. They are, each and every one of them, deeply disturbed. Secretary McNamara is deeply disturbed. Secretary Rusk is deeply disturbed. Vice President Humphrey is deeply disturbed. And, I am told by insiders, that more disturbed than anyone is President Johnson. In Washington all anybody talks about is how disturbed our President is. But what can they do, ask Rusk, McNamara, Humphrey and Johnson? What can one man do? They are just following orders. Rusk, McNamara and Humphrey are following Johnson's orders. And Johnson, according to Johnson, is following Eisenhower's orders. And didn't Eisenhower just the other day say he would not outlaw the use of any weapon to win the war, even those he describes as "nucular" weapons? So the example of Nuremberg that critics bring up is grossly misleading in regard to the men who preside over our destruction of Vietnam. Their defense is *not* that they are mechanically following orders but that they are *reluctantly* following orders, that they are with *great dismay* following orders, that they follow orders with *sadness of heart*. That they are, as *humanists*, as *civil libertarians*, as *fans of the Civil Rights Movement*—well, former fans—that they are *deeply disturbed* by our policies in Vietnam. So it is a very different situation than Nuremberg. There is no banality to their evil.

Listen, for example, to further thoughts from the Secretary of Defense. He says about our education system that since students clearly differ in their learning patterns "It is the educators' responsibility to create the most favorable conditions under which the student himself can build on his own learning pattern and at his own pace."

I would suggest that the pace James Johnson, Dennis Mora, and David Samas are being brought along at is hardly their own, and that since he is a concerned educator Principal McNamara should summon the three men to his Pentagon office and help create a dialogue. He can say, "Look guys, I am fundamentally on your side. Boy, if you ever heard me in some of those inner council meetings you would know right away that I'm also a member of the New Left. But let's be practical. Let's be realistic. Don't you realize that as Army dropouts you seriously endanger your career options if and when we ever let you out of jail. Look, I'm all for dissent, and firmly believe that constant invective against our foreign policy is what makes America great. But don't you see how your extremist actions are defeating your own purposes? Alienating your friends? Building resentment against the very cause you espouse? Why not be more like me? Why not work from the inside?"

If I may now sidetrack this inspirational dialogue I would like to say something about the three men on its receiving end.

I was very struck by each of the personal statements made by Privates Samas and Mora and PFC Johnson (How in the world did he ever make PFC?). A remark of Dennis Mora's reminded me of my own state of mind when I was drafted during the Korean War. Mora has said "When we entered the army we were all against the war in one way or another but we were willing to go along with the program believing that we would not be sent to Vietnam."

Those were my feelings, and the feelings of numbers of friends of mine, during Korea. Our opposition to the war and to the military establishment that had inducted, tested, vaccinated, psychoanalyzed and physically examined us to the extent of grabbing the privates of us privates and telling us to cough, that had numbered us, uniformed us, asked us what we'd like to do in the service and then laughed at us, that had told us that its aim was to separate the men from the boys and, apparently in pursuit of that aim yelled at us each morning to drop our cocks and grab our socks, that educated us once a day in I and E lectures—information and education—given by a semi-literate staff sergeant who told us the history of the Cold War in the half dozen polysyllabic words he knew—that weren't obscenities—and then during what the army euphemistically called the question period answered all prob-

ing inquiries with the worst insult any soldier could use on any other soldier: He would accuse the questioner of being a "college boy." And our position to this assault on our integrity and our good taste was manifested in one hope, in one program toward which we devoted all our passion and considerable amounts of our energy. This program was: to get ourselves a good deal.

So I am that much more impressed by the actions taken by Pvts. Mora, Samas and Johnson after they *didn't* get a good deal. Because I know what I would have done in their case. I would have boarded the troopship like other opponents of the war. I would have taken hot showers at night, and gone immediately for long cool walks in the sea air in the mad hope of catching pneumonia. I would have drawn handsome portraits of every influential officer on board in the hope that he would become my patron, my buddy, my ticket home. I would have done anything I had to in order not to fight, other than tell anyone I wouldn't fight. Once the man has been separated from the boy there are some things one just doesn't do.

And it's this startling willingness to do those things in the army that one just doesn't do that makes me admire these three men so. Dennis Mora has admitted sadly that soldiers do finally learn to accept the facts of life, or rather half life. Accept the fact that they will go to Vietnam. He has heard them say, "Somebody has got to do it," "When your number's up, your number's up." "Orders are orders," "The pay is good." More results from Principal McNamara's biggest school in the world.

Could the biggest principal in the world have been thinking of these remarks when he said in his VFW speech "Too many instructors look at a reticent, or apathetic, or even hostile student and conclude he is a low aptitude learner. In most cases it would be more realistic for the instructor to take a hard honest look in the mirror and conclude I am a low aptitude teacher." Will somebody please lend a mirror to McNamara?

From a talk given in New York's Town Hall, October 9, 1966, at a meeting sponsored by the Fort Hood Three Defense Committee.

Nov 1966.

LIBERATION

The Trial of Captain Levy: II ★★★★★★★★★★★★★★★★

BY THE POWERS OF HIS EXAMPLE

Andrew Kopkind

On a bright day in early November, I returned to Fort Jackson, S. C., for a visit with Capt. Howard Levy, who was then still detained in the prison ward of the hospital in which he had served as an Army doctor for almost two years. He had been a prisoner since June 3, when a court-martial sentenced him to three years "at hard labor" for refusing to train Special Forces medical aidmen, and for inspiring "disaffection" among enlisted men. That day, he was led in handcuffs from the small Post courtroom and put in the stockade; he was transferred to the detention ward the next day when the Army realized that Levy in irons did more damage to its image than Levy in comfort would do to its security. Since then a series of somewhat frenetic legal maneuvers to free him on bail—or failing that, to keep him at Fort Jackson—had ended in failure, and Levy and his lawyers supposed that he would soon be removed to the US Disciplinary Barracks at Fort

Leavenworth, Kansas, for the remaining thirty months of his sentence. So it was, probably, a last visit for the duration of his term; at Leavenworth, Levy would be allowed to see only his lawyers and a short list of relatives and intimate friends.

In May, I had arrived at the Columbia, S.C., airport on a midnight flight with a cadre of lawyers, legal PR men, and reporters. We swarmed into town in a fleet of rent-a-cars and camped out with the rest of the Levy entourage at a huge motel built in the Waikiki-Antebellum style. For two weeks the trial unfolded as a kind of morality pageant with a Brechtian *mise-en-scène*: circus clowning, flowing booze, running gags, shackings-up, and puttings-down. We moved through the town and the base like actors in street theater, using the surroundings as props, alienating the audience, and playing only to ourselves. Through it all, the moral—the commitment of a man, the confusion of a generation, the agony of the times—bounced and bumped against the surface action, until at

the end it emerged almost too clearly by comparison.

In November, there was no theater in the streets of Columbia, no way of shutting out the depressing surroundings. Objectively, the town was in all ways unchanged, give or take a new A & W Root Beer stand or a McDonald's Golden Arches. But for us (I was with another journalist and an American Civil Liberties Union lawyer) it was all different. Columbia was no longer a prop, but a completed universe; it shut *us* out, isolated us, made our visit a marginal event, while the first time it had seemed central. It was like walking through an Alabama county the day after a civil rights march passed by, or visiting a college campus in the summer after one's own graduation.

THAT SENSE OF ISOLATION, or something close to it, was with Howard Levy at Fort Jackson in the years before the pageant arrived, and it reclaimed him—despite his efforts—when everyone left.

Levy could have visitors without limit, and a few came or phoned (he had an incoming line) almost every day. But it was of course a life apart that he was forced to live, and the personal relations he built from his cell were necessarily partial. To the local radicals and political activists, he was the guru; for the scattered GI's at the Post who dared make or continue friendships with him, Levy was a moral (emotional?) inspiration. He would hardly admit the existence of his former colleagues. Dr. Ivan Mauer, who admired but could not emulate Levy's defiance, came often to the prison ward. At first, Levy filled each visit with brutal assaults on Mauer's caution and failure to share his protest. Then anger cooled to contempt, and Levy simply ignored the other doctor. Mauer would come and read a newspaper and slip out without a word of conversation; his wife brought gifts of food, which failed to appeal to Levy's appetite. . . . . .

There is a certain amount of freedom within the prison, and Levy spends his days talking with enlisted men. The Fort Hood Three are at Leavenworth, and in all, Levy says, there are about forty "political prisoners," although the Army classifies most of them as AWOL's or puts them in other non-political categories. In a way, Levy now sees his role as an organizer, and he has told his few visitors that he thinks "inside" political organizing in the Army can be effective.

"Outside," the effect of Levy and his trial on particular political developments is difficult to assess. At Fort Jackson, a nucleus of Levy's friends began open anti-war activity in January, and in a month's time they were strong enough move from town onto the base for a protest "meditation" service at the chapel. About thirty soldiers appeared, but before it began, Col. Chester Davis called in one of the leaders and ordered him to cancel the meeting, or "you will end up in prison like Dr. Levy." The soldier reluctantly obeyed (for his troubles, he has been denied a minor promotion), but two others who came refused to leave the chapel grounds and fell to their knees in "prayer." MP's dragged them off, and Colonel Fancy brought charges. Charles Morgan, Levy's flamboyant ACLU lawyer, took their case, and the sky at Fort Jackson grew dark with chickens coming home to roost. Signs went up on bulletin boards: "Morgan's Back." Finally, Colonel Fancy dropped the charges. Attempts at more "pray-ins" have been made, but the authorities have managed to break them up. They have also been able to frighten away some original supporters, but the protest effort seems to be growing. "Levy is spiritually responsible for it all," a political activist in Columbia reported recently. "He single-handedly turned on the half-dozen people who started it all down there. It's the best example of direct personal organizing I've ever seen."

Away from the Post, the activities

which Levy generated or encouraged continue in a less dramatic way. A nucleus of activists was created during and after the trial, and separately if not together they will go on working. Around the country, the pray-in "movement" spawned at Fort Jackson is spreading to other military camps; there was a similar demonstration last month in Fort Ord, Calif. There are also a few more cases of individual resistance like Levy's. Air Force Capt. Dale Noyd has just been sentenced to a year in prison at Clovis Air Force Base, N. M., for refusing to train airmen for Vietnam. A private at Fort Dix, N. J., applied for conscientious objector status and, when it was denied, refused to wear his uniform. He has been sentenced to a year at Leavenworth. A lieutenant at Shaw Air Force Base, S. C., refused to assist in training for the war and has also been convicted and sentenced. Perhaps a dozen other cases of overt resistance have been tried in the past eight months.

I THOUGHT at the time of the trial, and see more clearly now, that Levy was as much a metaphor for a generation as a political leader. He "turns people on" not by the force of his arguments (which have grown more sophisticated with his prison reading and reflecting) but by the power of his example. Everyone who was at the trial was touched in some way; many came to see that their perceptions of their lives were profoundly changed. Of course that happened in the context of the war and a society in crisis, but Levy supplied the live model. An Army doctor who testified in the trial found himself increasingly bound up with Levy and has become a working political activist. A lawyer who helped with the defense realized in the months after the trial that his own association with liberal causes and action never extended to the roots of his existence, and he is undergoing a painful, and probably unresolvable, reevaluation of his life. Capt. Richard Shusterman, the cool young prosecutor who did more than his duty in arguing against Levy (he added two charges to the case), has recently ended his Army Service; together with his assistant at the trial, he is reported to be "pretty much against the war." Shusterman has joined a Philadelphia law firm. His former assistant is now an anti-poverty lawyer in Florida. Neither has yet had public second thoughts about Levy. Col. Earl V. Brown, the law officer ("judge") at the trial, suffered a mild change of heart. He has left the Army to become assistant dean of the Columbia University law school; in February, he signed an advertisement published in the Times calling for an end to the war. "We believe that the terrible violence the war is inflicting on the people of Vietnam is destroying the society we seek to protect . . . . We believe that the US cannot by acceptable means succeed in its attempt to secure and maintain control of the Saigon government," the ad said. In May, Colonel Brown had

denied the existence of any "pattern or practice" in the US conduct of the war which was unacceptable to generally held moral standards.

Levy's example extends to medical students (who are being organized in one of the most energetic radical movements in the country) and doctors (several—led by Dr. Spock—visited him in Fort Jackson in November) and others across the spectrum of political action. But most of all, it has an impact on those who are most like him in age and class and social role—the "generation of the Fifties" that exists in confused transition between the security of liberal careerism and the support of the radical movements. Burt Austen, a biomedical engineering researcher at Downstate Medical Center in Brooklyn (where Levy was trained), lived on that margin, and what has happened to him in the last half-year seems to represent the experience of others.

"Last summer, an ACLU man spoke at Downstate about the Levy case, and I became quite interested," Austen told me not long ago. "I talked with him for two hours or so after the meeting, and before long I was volunteering for work on the 'Committee for Howard Levy, M.D.'* We had a demonstration in Times Square on Hiroshima Day, and in November we went to Fort Jackson. I more or less organized it. It was really the first time I had done anything like that—for years my wife and I looked at TV and she said we shouldn't pay our taxes, but I just scoffed at her. What happens can be very strange. When we went down to visit Howard, he told us not to waste our time on him, but to do more. Do more. He even told Spock he wasn't doing enough. I think it made me do more, sort of reflect on what I had done up to that point.

"Most people take the attitude, it can't happen to me.' When I met Howard I realized I knew so many people like that in Brooklyn where I grew up. I realized that it didn't take much to be there: I mean circumstances could have placed any one of us in that stockade. The more each person does, the more he can't stop, the more he has to see it through to the end. I ran a press conference for the doctors at Fort Jackson; I never thought I could do it, but then when I did it, I said, well, I can do it again. I felt in thirty-six years I had not really matured, and then in six months I came of age. I can't really look at things the way I used to. Sometimes a person comes in via the back door and before he knows it he finds himself organizing without really knowing what happened to him. You see, the more you do the more you have to do." □

* The address is: Box 200, New York City 10032.   4/11/68

After sentencing, Dr. Levy is led away by the executive officer of the Ft. Jackson Hospital.

★ ★ ★ ★ ★ ★ ★ ★ ★ ★ ★ ★

The New York Review
of Books

Fort Dix   May 16, 1970

A UNION
FOR SOLDIERS

G.I.'s Battle for Rights

by Andrew Stapp

General Charles Stone, Commander of the 4th Infantry Division in Vietnam recently announced to the press that he was sending soldiers who had failed to salute officers to the front. This ugly story of how a General was ordering men to face possible injury or death because they had defied the Brass hat's caste system was fully reported in the October 8 edition of the **New York Times.** The American Servicemen's Union (ASU), founded to defend the rights of rank and file servicemen, responded to this outrage immediately by calling the Pentagon and demanding of Colonel Heath (a Public Information Officer) that Stone either end this policy or resign his command. The ASU released this demand to the press, with a note to call Col. Heath if additional verification was needed. Several hours and a few dozen phone calls later, Col. Heath announced to the press that Gen. Stone's order would be rescinded "momentarily". The ASU had won another small victory in its

battle with the Dr. Strangeloves who run the U. S. Armed Forces.

The concept of an armed forces union grew out of a series of courts-martial of anti-war GI's that rocked Ft. Sill Oklahoma in the summer of 1967. In less than two months I was twice court-martialed. Both cases involved a violation of First Amendment rights. I was convicted on a charge stemming from my refusal to turn over my political books to an officer. That conviction is being appealed. I was acquitted of another charge for speaking at the University of Oklahoma and I still have not received a decision on a third charge

relating to my organizing activities with the ASU.

Dick Ilg, the Battalion Intelligence clerk, and Dick Perrin, a squad leader in Advance Individual Training, were also tried and convicted. That August, Key Martin and Maryann Weissman, activists from the Committee for GI Rights, each received six months in prison for breaking General Brown's bar order by entering the post as a show of solidarity for the GI's being tried on July 31. The broad sympathy that the GI defendants and their civilian supporters evoked from the other men stationed at Ft. Sill showed clearly that anti-war, anti-brass feelings run very deep in the Armed Forces.

ASU Demands

Not until the following December, however, did the founding conference of the American Servicemen's Union take place. A handful of men from the different branches of the service gathered for a closed one-day conference shortly before Christmas, and hammered out the union demands:

1. Election of officers by the vote of the men.
2. An end to saluting and "sir"-ing of officers.
3. Racial equality.
4. Rank and file control of court martial boards.
5. Federal minimum wages.
6. The right to free political association.
7. The right to disobey illegal orders—like orders to go and fight an illegal war in Vietnam.
8. The right of collective bargaining.

Retaliation

The Brass retaliated, arresting ASU organizers on "suspicion of burglary," or for "assaulting a Non-Commissioned Officer" or, in my case, for "subversion." The Army's counter-attack failed in almost all cases. Their most sophisticated attempt to break the union, a full Field Board Investigation of my beliefs and associations, became three days of misery for the Ft. Sill authorities as one GI after another took the stand and attacked the war and the Army caste system. Mike Kennedy of NECLC represented us at this army version of HUAC.

Events moved rapidly at Ft. Sill after the February hearings. A Japanese-American GI, Rod Oshiro, approached the ASU requesting help in a court martial he faced for neglecting to address a racist officer as "sir." We passed the hat in the barracks and raised enough money to pay the travel and living expenses of Atty. Rudolph Schware who volunteered to come down from Denver to defend Oshiro. Rod was convicted (as are 94.5% of all GI's in summary courts-martial), but the rank and file GI's had learned a real lesson about the power they could wield if they stuck together.

Rights Nov 1968

MORE ON THE G.I. MOVEMENT

GI CIVIL LIBERTIES, etc.

Several periodicals have run stories recently which should be of interest to those following the GI movement. See Robert Sherrill's *Playboy* article on "Military Justice," (January, 1970); *The Nation,* "GIs for Peace," by John Rechy (January 12, 1970); and both the editorial and the letter from GIs for Peace in the December 6, 1969 *New Republic.* GI activity in Vietnam is covered in *Newsweek,* February 2, 1970 in an article entitled "A New GI: For Pot and Peace."

Copies of GI newspaper are available to civilians at nominal cost, usually a quarter. A complete list of papers is carried on the back page of the GI Press Service, a bi-weekly magazine published by the Student Mobilization Committee at 1029 Vermont Avenue, Room 902, Washington, D.C. Papers mentioned in this newsletter are:

GIGLINE: P.O. Box 31094, Summit Heights Station, El Paso, Texas 79918

BRAGG BRIEFS: P.O. Box 437, Spring Lake, North Carolina

AEROSPACED: P.O. Box 92B, RR 4, Kokomo, Indiana 46901

LEFT FACE: P.O. Box 1595, Anniston, Alabama 36201

GI CIVIL LIBERTIES DEFENSE COMMITTEE, P.O. Box 355, Old Chelsea Sta., New York, N.Y. 10011

FTA
FREE THE ARMY
FUN TRAVEL ADVENTURE
FUCK THE ARMY

what if...

DAN Margulies

Do you say the army is really bad? Do you say that you are caught up in a big machine and can do nothing? Or do you say that your commanding officer is really bad? Did you ever think that maybe it could be your own fault? Did you ever stop to think that maybe you have been bullied like a child into a useless fear that serves only to benefit the army? Do you ask what can be done? Did you ever think of organization?

Did you ever hear of the old saying of "GI ingenuity?" Did you ever stop to think that it was the privates who brought about that reputation for the US Army? You don't think it was the officers or NCO's, do you? The lifers aren't too smart, are they? Who is smart, where are the brains? Who is the backbone of the army? Could it be the privates? Can the privates organize? Do they want to organize, and if so, what can they do?

Have you noticed within the last year that the army has been forced to add a new regulation: that mustaches can be worn as long as they are neatly trimmed? It used to be that only mustaches could be worn if on your ID card, remember? Could it be that enough soldiers began losing their ID cards after mustaches were grown, that it became too much of a headache for the army paper work? Can the army be forced to do more? What if everyone began to wear a flower in their buttonhole? Could it be possible that eventually the army would publish a regulation declaring that flowers worn will not exceed two inches in diameter and three inches in length? It sounds silly but you must admit that it would be a change much like that of the mustaches, wouldn't it?

Do you say that you have a bad CO and a lot of useless harassment? Did you ever think of harassing the CO? Like for instance, do you have a US Savings Bond? Did they tell you to sign for one in basic? Did you know that you don't have to have one? Did you know that any harassment by the CO or First SGT for not having one is illegal? Did you know that the CO gets a nasty letter from the higher-ups if his company doesn't have close to 100 per cent participation in the bond program? Can you imagine the nasty letter he would get if all of a sudden the participation were to be 0 per cent? Did you know that all you have to do to cancel your bond is to tell your company clerk to do it, and that any action to prevent your request is illegal? Can you imagine the effect it would have on the CO to have 100 or more cancellations in one day? Like it might blow his mind, wouldn't it?

Do you say the harassment is really bad? Well, what if around payday everybody ate in the snack bar? Did you ever think of striking the mess hall? Like if everybody did it, could you imagine at three meals a day for 200 people, just how much garbage would pile up in a couple of days, or maybe in a couple of weeks? Can you see that if nobody signed the meal roster the mess hall wouldn't get any more food? Then can you imagine what would happen if one day 200 people demanded their food and there wasn't any? Would that psych out a mess sergeant and maybe the CO?

What if 100 or 200 privates all of a sudden complained of stiff joints and stiff necks and nausea, and thought maybe they might have spinal meningitus? Can you imagine 200 people on sick call? Could you imagine the effect of a letter to a congressman saying that they wouldn't let you go on sick call for possible spinal meningitus? Could you imagine 200 such letters? Would that be a mind blow?

You say you don't like the idea of all this saluting? What if a private salutes a private? Is there a regulation saying that a private can't salute a private? What if all enlisted men saluted each other in a friendly manner? If everybody saluted then it wouldn't mean much, would it? Would that be taking the officers' thing away? If a private saluted an officer and then saluted a private, would that be a silent way of saying, "We're all the same, baby"? What if everybody addressed each other as "sir," would that blow a mind or two?

Can you think of other possibilities? Where is the old "GI ingenuity" nowadays? Can you organize? Can you write letters to congress? Can you do things in numbers? Can you sign petitions? Can you resist? Are you brainwashed?

Do you notice that everything in this article is written as a question? A question doesn't really say to do anything, does it? Like, whoever wrote this bunch of questions cannot be convicted of conspiring a mutiny, can he? DIG IT?

WIN —Reprinted from Shakedown, the Fort Dix, N.J., underground newspaper

Some Marines upon return from Vietnam duty.

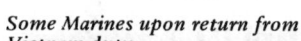

... Only The Beginning

Helicopters flying at tree top level -- grotesque figures with bulb-like eyes and rubber faces, holding instruments of death to be used if necessary on the American People -- to defend what? -- roads barricaded with barbed wire -- gas warfare used upon the American People, a taste, although small, of the mechanical inhumanity shown toward the Vietnamese for so long.

And on the other end of the bayonets were thousands of peaceful civilians expressing their support for GI's who have lost their human freedoms, either through actual imprisonment or through enslavement to the will of the Military Machine.

With open spirit on the outside and tacit support on the inside, Fort Dix was under seige last Sunday. Not in the sense of actual physical attack but in the tightening of the gaps among the potentially most effective force in America, the common people. We have always been conditioned to classify and separate people into ethnic, religious, political, social, and even occupational groups, but when a group of 8,000 people can all unite in one common cause (the cause = 4 demands: 1) Free the Fort Dix 38 2) Abolish the stockade system 3) Free all political prisoners in civilian and military jails, including Huey P. Newton, the NY Panther 21, the Chicago 8, etc. 4) Immediate withdrawal of U.S. occupation forces from Vietnam), you have to know changes are taking place. In a demonstration united around a meaningful cause, such as the one held at Fort Dix on October 12, all

these conditioned barriers are broken down, and the immediate result is great rapport between people, real feeling. This is in itself a worthwhile end. But a demonstration in which a mass of people can be well-disciplined without a guillotine of some sort over their head is going even a step farther toward the radical changes that are needed.

Other positive effects are: over 300 prisoners were released from the stockade that weekend; for the first time in American history, people coming onto an army base made front-page headlines across the nationa and created an awareness of the feeling of solidarity with the American GI; the army couldn't even trust their own men to defend their own fort so they brought in the 519th MP Bn, a group of professional riot control pigs, from Fort Meade, while the 759th MP Bn were kept in their barracks because their loyalty was questionable; the army was put on the defensive and GI's have come to realize that power is in numbers; for the first time in Fort Dix history all members of SPD were given passes because it was feared that if they were restricted, they would rebel. Finally and most important of all, GI's were shown that they are not alone. GI's have been solidly bound to the to the movement of the People for control of their own lives.

<u>This is only the beginning!</u>

THE TIME HAS COME FOR A LONG-NEEDED
SHAKEDOWN
Terry
Steve
Art
Skip

(Ft. Dix, N.J.)

THANKS

SHAKEDOWN THANKS LNS FOR THE USE OF THEIR PHOTOGRAPHS THROUGHOUT THIS ISSUE

THE COMMITTEE TO FREE THE FORT DIX 38 THANKS THE MEDICAL COMFOR HUMAN RIGHTS AND THE MILITARY LAW PANEL FOR THEIR HELP AND CONCERN DURING THE DEMONSTRATION

after nine months,
THE PENTAGON IS RISING

It's difficult to write about what happened that night and not sound corny. You had to have been there and felt the vibrations to understand how real it was. We began pleading with the soldiers to "Join us," singing "Soldiers are our friends, we shall overcome," and chanting "We love you." Corny words, silly slogans, cliches that have long lost their meaning. But we were communicating with the soldiers, putting them through changes. And they, with their silent faces, were communicating with us, putting us through changes. For us it was a shock of recognition that despite their arms, their uniforms, and their orders to attack us, the soldiers were very much our brothers.

WIN Magazine, Review of October 21-22, 1967 Pentagon demonstration

---

★ ★

NEWSLETTERFORSERVICEMEN

NEW YORK(LNS)—GI Counselling Services, formerly the New York GI Coffeehouse Project has begun publishing a newsletter that will provide advice and information for the GI movement.

The Counselling Services offers advice on: 1) the legal rights and alternatives of servicemen; 2) discharge and legal problems; 3) legal, medical and psychiatric aid; 4) resistance information; 5) training counsellors, collaborating on books and articles on military law, informing civilians of GI activities.

For a copy of their first issue write, GI Counselling, 339 Lafayette St., NY, NY 10012.

★ ★

A lot of GIs are taking a lot of shit from the brass because they oppose the war, because they organize other GIs, because they smoke dope, because they refuse to take riot training, because they refuse to become automatons.

These same GIs come to the city looking for a little brotherliness, dope, support. And they get cold stares because they have short hair.

As if it needed to be said, hair don't mean shit. But for a brother to be able to come to a strange place and find friends does. Support our boys — bring one home now.

the old pooperoo

The Great Speckled Bird 3/9/70

OLEO STRUT
IS RECRUITING

The Oleo Strut is looking for new staff members. The Strut is a GI coffeehouse located in Killeen, Texas near Fort Hood. As well as the regular activities of a GI coffee house, we hope to have a radical bookstore, combination military law and radical books library in the near future.

Killeen is a small town with a population of 35,000 people totally dependant on the Army for its income. Fort Hood itself is a 39,000 man Armored Post staffed largely by Viet Nam returnees. There is no basic training, and almost everyone is just waiting to get out. Because Fort Hood is a riot control center and discipline is threatened by Nam vets, the propaganda and coercion are heavy.

The Oleo Strut staff is a collective. We live in one house and all work every day at the Strut. We have been working as a collective for 4 months and have been varyingly successful. Within the collective is a women's caucus. We discuss all problems and political questions that arise. We discipline ourselves individually and from the collective we discipline ourselves as a group and criticize each other for mistakes we make as staff members.

We feel that our most important work is developing GI organizers who are laying the groundwork for a mass movement in the Army. One of the best organizing tools that has been established at Fort Hood is the Fatigue Press which is put out by the GIs.

In conclusion then, we are looking for people (men, women, or couples) who are willing to:

1) make a commitment of at least six months, hopefully starting in October or November, or as soon as possible.

2) do shit work in the coffeehouse.

3) learn about military law and counsel on court-martials and CO applications.

4) learn and make changes according to the demands made by the working situation in Killeen and the Army.

5) view their work as long-range, and not look for regular victories. This is organizing, not activism and takes patience.

6) talk politics with guys in the Army and keep studying and learning new ways to build a movement.

If you feel that this is the kind of work you want to do, please write us immediately, so that we can begin discussions about joining the staff. Tell us about yourself and what you have been doing, and we will describe in greater detail the work that goes on in the Strut. Write to: OLEO STRUT, 101 Avenue D Killeen, Texas 76541

San Francisco Express Times 7/17/68

UNDERGROUND USO'S SUPPORT OUR BOYS

By Donna Mickelson

"The Army, they're smarter than you think. That Sergeant, he's looking you straight in the face, see, telling you what to do, but what they're really saying is coming at you from both sides. . ."

That's an eighteen-year-old draftee talking. He's from Ohio, he's stationed at Fort Jackson, South Carolina, and he's sitting in the town of Columbia talking to the kind of girl you don't usually find in Southern Army towns. She's there because she thinks being against the war means, among other things, being for his right to live and do what he wants to with his life — and that, if you believe that, you begin with a draftee's here-and-now, in Shitsville, South Carolina, by opening the only place in town where he's treated like a human being, where he can sit and rap to people who will listen, and where he's likely to see a real smile. It's called the UFO Coffee House. I just came back from eight months spent helping to make it happen.

The clientele are hillbillies and black men from the ghetto, college dropouts (or forceouts) and would-be hippies. In their fantasies they are Peter Fonda or Steve McQueen or maybe even Jimi Hendrix. They have come to Fort Jackson from all over, but seem to arrive in waves, big concentrations at different times from New York, Ohio, Pennsylvania, Appalachia, with only a few things in common before the shared hell of Basic Training draws them together.

More than not are from poor backgrounds. They're stuck in a town which celebrates its enthusiasm for the war with annual parades (to the average soldier that means preparing for an inspection) and clip joint diamond palaces, but not so much as a military discount at the movies. The Girl At Home comes alive in locker room stories and wallet photos, whether or not she gave them a tumble back in Philly. Even after they can come into town in civvies, they're betrayed by their heads, shaven into clipped dandelions, and the local girls step around them like empty muscatel bottles in doorways.

It should come as no surprise that almost none of them wants to be there. Even with the incredible indoctrination they are given, and the films about the Communist menace which will soon be on our shores, few believe in the war. They may be there out of some twisted sense of masculine pride, or because it gets them out of a house with eight other kids in three rooms, but for the most they simply had no choice and any reason is a rationalization. Deep down — or after a couple of beers — they know it.

But on the other hand they have been taught, or have come to assume, that the peace movement is against THEM. For a look of real shock, you just can't beat a buck private who has asked what the hell a good-looking, hip girl from New York or San Francisco is doing in this godforsaken place, and been told she thought he was getting the raw end of a rotten war, so she came to work here.

The UFO really swings on a Saturday night. Chances are a trainee peering through the door will see up to a hundred soldiers and a sprinkling of local people, students, girls and the staff, all snapping their fingers, clapping, sometimes even spontaneously dancing between the tables or in front of the counter. The large room is completely filled with the guitar and voice of a short, hunched-over black man whose face glistens with sweat while he belts out twenty-minute riffs of funky old blues and makes up lyrics and whole songs from the stage. His name is Drink Small and sometime soon we'll bring him out to the Bay Area; he's in a class with Howlin' Wolf and Big Mama Willie Mae Thornton. Meanwhile, he spends weekends in his home town of Columbia blowing the minds of soldiers that got the word from their buddies in Basic: the place to go in town is the UFO.

And Drink isn't the only one. Phil Ochs played one Saturday night to three full houses. Jeff Zinn, a fine young rock singer-songwriter from Boston, spent the spring as musician in residence, living on subsistence. With all due respect to Joe MacDonald, I don't think anyone could have done a better "Superbird" the night Superjohnson bowed out of the race. He had us all on our feet stomping and cheering and dancing around: the shaved-head recruits, the medics who help run the coffee house, and us. The place really has its moments.

It also has its quiet afternoons, when soldiers play chess or put on Loretta Lynn or the Supremes or Vanilla Fudge records. Or they browse through the magazine rack a local university student painted in psychedelic splendor. They find *The New York Times, Newsweek*, underground papers, and *The Vietnam GI*, a paper put out by anti-war GIs and veterans. And there's time for the people serving coffee and cokes to sit down and talk to tables full of draftees.

Everybody on the staff has a different style. Sometimes Fred would sing songs he'd written himself, when he was still there. All of us listen to a lot of gripes and fantasies and stories about "Nam" from guys who've been there — every so often throwing in questions, moving the talk about. One girl sits down with a group of hillbillies and when they complain about training and not being able to score with local girls, she says, "the Army really has you by the balls, doesn't it?"

The Army doesn't like UFO or the three similar coffee houses that have opened near other bases. Martha Raye in fatigues, flanked by bird colonels, is one thing. But Barbara Dane throwing in anti-war songs along with San Francisco Bay Blues for a love-in at Fort Hood, Texas, that's another. It's easy to see how they could lump together into the "dangerous" category coffee houses run by people you'd never see at the USO.

Finally, three people starting one coffee house with the help of a handful of sympathetic contributors has now grown into a Summer of Support: three coffee houses and a central office in Chicago run by Rennie Davis. They raise money, publicize, arrange special entertainment (like Barbara Jane for the Fourth of July Oleo Strot love-in) and provide legal support, communication and the like. Their job isn't easy. It's an election year, and most people who want to do anything against the war are giving their money or energy to McCarthy.

So S.O.S. needs support too — maybe yours. For the summer, and/or fall, more than anything else, people are needed. Couples are especially good, because it's not easy for a woman who is alone to deal night after night with guys whose chief perceived problem is that they can't get laid (the irony alone is hard to handle). Some of the women's rights groups have said they thought the project was inherently chauvinistic and that it sounded like women wind up as ornaments who do shitwork on the side. One organizer I know has referred to it from the outset — just because he knows how to raise my hackles — as Pimps and Prostitutes for Peace. As I see it, these have hardly been realities of the project, but they are potential difficulties that have to be recognized and dealt with by each staff. A woman with a sense of herself can do it; we made it for eight months. But not only is it easier on everyone psychologically to have a couple, but there is just a lot more latitude for a girl who doesn't have to deal all the time with the question of her own eligibility.

Seven months in Columbia, South Carolina, have convinced me that this work will matter, that this creation of a counter-environment right between the paws of the paper tiger is just a beginning in the same sense that the early work in the South laid the foundation for things that are only coming to fruition now. The possibilities are almost limitless; each coffee house takes on its own mood and style, according to the people who run it, the kinds of soldiers and local people who frequent it, and the places they are from.

Especially needed are those with any performing ability (singing, guitar, guerrilla theatre), people with coffee house or restaurant experience, or specific skills like bookkeeping, carpentry, sound equipment savvy. Above all, anyone who has been in the military. And of course, people who like to rap and can listen. S.O.S. can pay travel expenses and a subsistence wage.

JOIN THE FOREIGN LEGION

The 13,000 American civilians employed in South Vietnam have a "high incidence of alcoholism, psychopathic behavior and frank psychosis," according to Dr. John A Talbott, just returned from a year in Saigon serving as an army psychiatrist.

"The US government and its private contract firms offer positions in Vietnam that appeal to the borderline personality, the person with severe character disorders and the social misfit.

The men seek jobs in Vietnam hoping to recover "their lost youth, their dashed hopes; primitive, mainly living without rules and bossy American women."

They hope that "Vietnamese women women are compliant and feminine, with girlish, thin figures; they do not talk back and are readily available to Americans." Dr. Talbott's report appeared in the Journal of the American Psychiatric Assn.

Greensboro, SC district court Judge Elreta Alexander says that in the last few months case after case of violence and brutality by ex-Vietnam war veterans has been brought before her. She said that military training makes a man into an "animal" and that men "come back unprepared for living and reacting in a peaceful society."

MAYDAY

The Army has officially welcomed the idea of an all-volunteer force, but the brass is actually dismayed by the prospect. A report warns, "The officer accessions will probably come from the affluent, permissively raised and often confused groups. An increasing number of the young enlisted volunteers will probably come from rural or urban poverty areas. Both of these groups will have been exposed to anti-war sentiment, violence in the streets and disobedience of laws. ...This may have a serious impact on the quality, composition of and dedication to the Army." The report also foresees that "hard or unpleasant work may not be accepted." ■

a.w.o.l.

The desertion rate from the U.S. Army has increased 80% since 1967. When Lt. General A.O. Conner, Army personnel chief, was called before a House committee to explain this alarming development, he came up with this answer: "We are getting more kooks into the Army, for one thing. We are getting more young men who are coming in undisciplined, the product of a society that trains them to resist authority." But despite the rise in desertions, Gen. Conner said that the troop morale in Vietnam was "fabulous" and that the "vast majority of them are doing it beautifully---we do not have to be too concerned about our youth." (LNS)

THE NEW ACTION ARMY

THIS HERE'S ROTTEN COMMIE SUBVERSIVE PROPAGANDA AN' I DON'T WANNA CATCH ANYA YOU CLOWNS READIN' IT!!

IS THIS ANY WAY TO RUN THE ARMY?

BY CHARLES PERRY

"Rock and Roll music contributes to both the usage of drugs and the high VD rate among the enlisted men in the Army today."

This statement from an Army Captain, represents the off-the-record opinion of most high-ranking officers in the Armed Services today. But there is nothing they can do about it.

The Armed Forces have changed radically in the last four years. The raising of draft quotas and the tightening of deferment and exemption loopholes has made for a different military, with a higher proportion of men who would otherwise be in college, and a far greater number of men of one generation drafted into the service.

Briefly put, there is a flowering of rock and roll and dope among the unwilling soldiers of today. It is altogether out of hand. It already involves so many men that the brass can't even begin to crack down on it.

"Lots of guys come over here very lame but go home heads. Everyone is ex-cited about trying it 'back in the world' because it is so groovy even at this down place. Guys have mustaches and long sideburns that the average citizen would never believe they were soldiers. We are anxious to get back and grow wild hair and beards without any restrictions. Beads and Peace symbols are worn with the uniform."—A Corporal in Phu Bai, Vietnam.

In the past year the Army has been directly responsible for turning on probably more than a quarter of a million young American innocents by sending them to Vietnam, and thousands of others merely by putting them together with others of their age — whether in Europe, Asia, or even right down home in Louisiana. But most of all it is Vietnam: the Army has taken hundreds of thousands of students out of school and plopped them into what seems like a marijuana-heaven on earth. In Vietnam, you can buy marijuana already processed into cigarette form, packaged 10 to the pack (200 to the carton) and a pack costs a dollar. At least in Nha Trang, it costs a buck.

In the highlands of Vietnam, where daily battle is waged, such amenities do not exist. Instead, it grows wild. And thus, so grows the United States Armed Forces overseas, wild as a march hare.

The Navy and the Coast Guard, favored duty for men facing the draft who want to avoid combat duty and bad chow, is filled with even more unmilitary types than the Army, especially among the Medical Corpsmen. The voluntary combat services, the Air Force, the Special Forces (Green Berets), and the Marines, are a different story — but not altogether, as we shall see.

In order to find out what was going on, ROLLING STONE recently sent questionnaires to a selected group of servicemen who reported from nearly fifty military stations — Air Force Bases, ships at sea, Pacific Islands, stateside bases, Saigon, huge military bases and even jungle patrols in Vietnam. Respondents represent just about every branch of the service, including Marines and Green Berets.

Allowing for the self-selection in the various branches of the service, you can

-- STONED?

say that young men bring the common tastes of their age-group with them when they enter the service. A Navy Personnelman 3rd Class with over three years' service breaks down this way:

"The median sailor comes from a small town in the Midwest and comes generally from the wide middle-class stratum, is high school graduate, has dabbled maybe even in college, and may have been picked up by local police for some minor infraction. Well, here is the rundown: About 10% of sailors *know* rock in every form, can rattle off managers' and band members' names etc. About 20% have their foot in both deep rock and commercial sounds. Another 30% are R&B fanatics (mostly from east of the Rockies) and 10% dig country (in our idiom, shitkicking) music.

"Maybe 5% are classical buffs, maybe 10% folkies (the 'Seekers' and 'Weavers' types). The rest of swabs just generally drift around with either no musical tastes or completely absorbent so that it doesn't matter to them what type of rock or soul or whatever it is. I have offended some, converted others, and made some more music-deaf by playing my disks. But I guess we are still pretty good off, compared to the Marines and Airedales, anyway."

The greatest difference is not between the services, however, but between upper-echelon officers (essentially, career military personnel)—all ranks above SP/5 (sergeant) — and enlisted men. As an SP/4 writes from near Thu Dau Mot, "Lifers can't comprehend rock and roll, they're completely disoriented doers of the establishment. Even ROTC and OCS three-year officers who should have some appreciation seem bound by some kind of unspoken code of conformity."

"Ned from Nha Trang," a GI stationed in Vietnam, elaborates: "The NCO's are a belligerent lot who spend their free time drinking in 'the club.' Officers aren't 'allowed' to associate with us lowly, peon, scum bag EM's (that's 'enlisted men,' what a fucking label, ugh).

"You must realize that lifer dogs (besides being the most sexually fucked up minority of society) are the most colorles and slow group of people (yes — can a lifer be considered a person ???), for it takes the act of war to make them face the reality that 'something is happening but you don't know what it is.' Lifers are so out of touch with the emotionalism and combustion of rock that to a dog, 'it all sounds the same'."

A sailor stationed at Pearl Harbor: "Officers consider rock at best the music of a stage from which they have long since passed into 'maturity.' At worst, the braying of a smelly, dirty, leftist, commie, pinko, homosexual, dope (generic term) taking hippie. Or vice-versa, depending on which you consider worse: a screaming jerk-off or a smug condescender."

A Marine Lance Corporal in Central Vietnam: "When the lifers & C.I.D. hear Doors or Dead, or Dylan and especially the Beatles, they bug ya, always looking for something."

The Armed Forces Radio and Television Service provides entertainment for military personnel overseas. But as you might expect, it is of, by and for career men (in enlisted men's idiom, "lifer dogs"). Says an SP/4 from near Khanh Hoa:

"Very few people are into AFVN Radio 'serving the capitol, Saigon,' because military radio is a real down. Army commercials are so dry that I would rather not go through the hassle. Every time the music stops there is Big Brother Uncle Sam talking to you with his liferdog propaganda.

"Some people make requests (to all the 'swingers' of B Company, 14th Med) but those are the people still goofing on the Beach Blanket Fuck-In Movies. I never listen to the radio because it's mainly piped-in restaurant type music although someone told me he heard Dylan once. But you people must realize that most people are into tapes."

An SP/4 now back in the States, formerly stationed in Nha Trang: "The AFVN Radio comes across with swinging Chris Noel and her 'groovy' songs for an hour a night. They have a request show, but not all requests are played. The DJ apologizes and plays a substitute. The South VN Government won't let us play certain songs on the air. For instance, the Animals — 'We Got to Get Outa This Place'."

"We get no protest and very little psychedelic music. We never got 'Lady Madonna,' probably because of the 'baby at your breast' line. Some top twenty things just never show up — god knows why. We get very little album material—used to be none at all—it took a year to get anything from *Sgt. Pepper*. Now we get a few things by Country Joe, Cream, Grape and Hendrix.

"It's getting better all the time but as you can guess we never got 'Eve of Destruction,' 'Universal Soldier,' or anything obvious like that. They're not too hip in LA or AFRTS — we did get 'Acapulco Gold.'

Recently the word has been getting out in national weeklies and the underground press as well: if you missed out getting turned on to marijuana in high school or college, the Service will give you the opportunity to continue your education.

There was a small-scale marijuana scandal right after World War I centering upon servicemen stationed in and passing through the Panama Canal Zone. (A seaman on the USS Boxer reports that everyone is still searched coming aboard in the Canal Zone.) This was before Federal legislation against cannabis, and it was also a different scene, mostly non-specific hell-raising.

World War II and the Korean War were also different scenes—there was no talk of a "drug menace" attacking the ranks, although thousands of men saw combat in North Africa and Southeast Asia, where hemp has been cultivated since time out of mind (as the phrase goes.) Both cannabis and opium are known in Korea. but it seems only a few of the generation of the Fifties thought to experiment with the two quite different smokes.

Plainly the difference is in the generation and in the war. The Forties and its war were crusading against Fascism and the Fifties operated in numb obedience. The key word in this generation is revolt and the current war has no meaning for most draftees—it is obvious that the Vietnamese don't want them in their country, and it is not obvious at all what interest a draftee has in being there.

So incredible numbers of enlisted men are smoking grass to "get away," and more than that, to reinforce their feelings of solidarity with other unwiiing conscripts. This is on top of the generation-wide taste for novel thrills and some of these men were blowing pot even even before they were drafted.

The fact remains that the military provides at least as much exposure to marijuana as a big-city college. This is implicitly recognized in the practice of allowing servicemen to turn in contraband before reaching US Customs, with no questions asked.

A corporal writes f r o m a former French resort town in Vietnam:

"There is something about being a head in Vietnam that you can't get back in the world. It may have something to do with complete feeling of oneness (same clothes, same paycheck, no competition for girls, etc.) or it could be other things. But I'm not here to philosophize, am I?

"There is one interesting thing about grass here. In Vietnam you buy ten already rolled J's for about 100 piastres (88c). 1 or 2 at the most is all you need to get high, where it might take 4 or 5 in the world. Because it is so cheap and effective, many *very* straight people come over and by the time they return to Altus, Oklahoma, or wherever, they are full-fledged heads and have a new outlook on many things. The Vietnam experience is doing a lot more good, in some ways, than you would think.

"Because pot is so cheap and abundant, it is smoked like a regular cigarette —tossed away like butts when it becomes too short, and a new one is lighted up. The paths are littered with roaches. Walking along a road one might think how ironical it is that here, in Vietnam, the streets are literally 'paved with gold.'

"Unlimited supplies. Pot and opium is all they have here. Out of 600 men a good solid half, possibly more, turn on with J's regularly. A few dozen of these on opium. The common practice is to blow outside the barracks, rap a while, then back in to listen to some music. You see GI's walking to and from places blowing all the time. Of course it's not so open in the world."

An SP/4 writing from a mountain in Vietnam: "Grass is plentiful and cheap. LSD comes from the States. Occasionally we have Afghani and Pakistani hashish and sometimes meth. Opium is plentiful. We take or smoke anything we can. I'm stoned 50% of my waking hours, like now for instance. War? What war?

"We smoke semi-covertly. We work stoned. Music most of the time. Our favorite combination is HOG (hash, O, grass.) I dropped 500 micro-g's of Acid last month. Four people total dropped and we mainly had an introvert head trip, as there was little visual stimulation. I tripped on Byrds' music for about two hours. I also went to Army school in the States stoned on acid. Big color trip.

"Most Army jobs are so intellectually easy that it is possible to be stoned *all* the time, which many of us do for (literally) weeks on end.

"Oh yeah, I went to reinforce an ambushed patrol o n c e stoned on Meth. Bodies splashed all over the road, and I just diddleybopped down the road digging people with no heads, and some sergeant starts yelling at me to get down. I walked up to him, an only then did I realize that I was the only guy standing up, and everyone else was under cover. So I turned around and walked back down the road which really blew the sergeant's mind. Speed is good for combat, though.

Despite paranoid stories in the Berkeley Barb and other underground papers, it does not seem that apprehended or suspected smokers are being sent to the front lines on certain - death missions. While troublemakers may be treated maliciously, inconspicuous marijuana usage is currently being winked at by all branches of the service, although naturally no official statement has been made to this effect.

The reason is simple—there are too many men involved, and a full-scale crackdown would make for serious depletions in the ranks, especially among the trained specialists. Individuals at lower levels of command, including senior enlisted men, may go in for harassment as individuals, but the top-level policy is to turn a blind eye to the phenomenon.

Convicted drug users face discharge, but most often an administrative discharge, which is not dishonorable. Both sailors and Vietnam GI's report cases of men provoking a bust in order to get out of the service.

Recently some people in the peace movement have been taking an interest in the plight of the large scale slice of this generation unwillingly imprisoned in olive drab. In addition to the organized pacifists and radicals who put out the GI-oriented newspapers The Ally, The Bond, Vietnam GI and others, an organization formed by Fred Gardner of Ramparts Magazine (Summer Of Support) has been establishing coffeehouses in the vicinity of half a dozen Stateside military bases.

These coffeehouses provide a place to talk and listen to music in an un-military environment. They provide the only taste of freedom and Bohemianism available to the men at the bases, many of which are located in dreary places in the rural South. Tom Cleaver writes

about musical tastes at the Oleo Strut, near Camp Hood, Killeen, Texas:

"There is more political content than one would probably find in a civilian community, but I think that this is because of the same reasons that black slaves had political' music. It is a quiet way of expressing what they think without being too active about it, thus keeping down the possibility of individual visibility."

Enlisted servicemen make up a lot of people, caught in a particularly nasty and confusing middle-of-things. But it seems plain that it's all one generation, uniformed or not.

"I feel guilty when I think of the people who resisted and went to jail. That was something I couldn't do. I'm not serving my country, the ones who are in jail are serving their country.

"There's nothing I can do now but keep stoned. Am I 'passing the buck'? I did go as far as I could, I refused to do anything that had to do with combat."—A medic in Germany.

"People who are lucky enough to get CO or 4F classifications have no idea at all how bad it all is. Especially basic training. Girls have no idea at all what we go through. I am at an Army Reception Station where guys come their first five days in the Army, and I've seen the Army drive people to do things I could not believe. Suicides and attempted suicides are regular things.

"I can only suggest that people with the draft very close do either of two things if they don't think they can handle it. (1) Split—they will never catch you if you're cool, and (2) press for a CO (conscientious objector) very hard."—Fort Polk, Louisiana.

"I guess about the only thing that really fucks with my mind is the thought of how foolish this whole ordeal is. Every day I see evidence that indicates the Vietnamese people resent our presence—if they don't want us and we don't want to be here, just what the hell gives?

"For three weeks in a row, 'Sky Pilot' was number one in Bien Hoa. I keep thinking of the line, 'A young soldier so ill/Looks at the sky pilot, remembers the words, "Thou Shalt Not Kill".' Man, give me some slack, huh. Thank God for the sense of sound."—An MP in Vietnam.

The Intrepid Four: PATRIOTIC DESERTERS

Shown reading their statements in Tokyo on November 1 are, left to right: Lindner, Anderson, Bailey and Barrilla.

On the evening of October 23, 1967, in a Tokyo coffee shop, four young American sailors—Craig W. Anderson of San Jose, California; Richard D. Bailey of Jacksonville, Florida; John Michael Barilla of Catonsville, Maryland; and Michael A. Lindner of Mount Pocono, Pennsylvania—decided not to return to their ship, the U.S.S. Intrepid. They were angry with the war and fed up with the military, and their ship—an aircraft carrier—was returning to active duty on the Tonkin Gulf.

The most remarkable feature of the "intrepid four" was their ordinariness. I met them in Tokyo about two and a half weeks after their decision, and they seemed the quintessence of high-school educated youth in middle-class America. They were honest and direct, completely unservile, sensitive to people and human feelings, only vaguely educated despite their high schools (and they were keenly aware of this deficiency), sceptical of authority whether parental or governmental, quick to be friendly but surrendering none of their independence in order to please, polite without being mannered, moral without any interest in conventional versions of morality.

They were not in fact ordinary any more, of course. They were already showing a special sort of maturity that comes from facing a momentous decision.

From my talks with them, lasting several hours, I established certain features of their current attitudes. They all strongly rejected the use of violence on foreign peoples, from whom they felt no conceivable threat, and were particularly disgusted by the war against Vietnam. Their dislike of military life, shared perhaps by millions of young Americans, became a profound rejection when they realized that it was all to no purpose but an evil one. They were clearly aware of the legal danger to themselves arising from the course of action on which they had embarked but were determined to face these dangers and the consequences, without turning their backs on their conscientious position.

They had reached their decision on their own, without pressure from any individual or group, though they had been treated with great kindness by Japanese in and out of the Beheiren peace movement there. (Perhaps almost all Japanese are in some sense in the peace movement.) Here you may read the various statements which they left behind them (both on paper and in a film made by the Japanese group)* so that their reasons for taking this drastic action may be heard.

LIBERATION Nov 1967

ERNEST P. YOUNG

Sergeant, you tell them that if they won't die for important people like us, they're cowardly and communistic and they won't get any more medals.

BARRILLA

My name is John Michael Barrilla. I enlisted in the Navy almost two years ago, shortly after graduating from high school. I spent most of my life in Baltimore, Maryland and most of my time staying happy while maintaining average grades in school.

Like most American youths, after graduation I was thinking of the future and the ever-imposing draft. I felt that I was not prepared for college, so I had very little choice but to enter the military or get drafted. This ultimatum seemed to me quite contradictory to a supposedly democratic society. I was stationed aboard an aircraft carrier, the U.S.S *Intrepid*, now deployed in the bombing of Vietnam. All war is ugly and Viëtnam is no exception. I cannot understand how the United States, supposedly standing for a world peace, could possibly release such a colossal destructive force against such a small underdeveloped Asian country.

I can no longer betray my own humanitarian beliefs and the ideals of peace shared by so many throughout the world by further engaging myself in the war. One of my strongest feelings against the Vietnamese conflict is that no one seems to have a reasonable argument for it.

A governmental speech containing so many words such as "Communism," "freedom" and "the aggressor" hardly gives an excuse to murder countless numbers of Americans and Vietnamese. Some people seem to be trained to respond to these emotive words and phrases like Pavlov's dogs. It is time for Americans to wake up to reason and not to words, peace and not to war.

Because of my actions and beliefs I will be jailed if apprehended. By some I will be labeled as an anti-American or a Communist. These are just emotive words again and none of them actually apply to me. I am just an American standing up for what I think is right, and I'm not alone.

JOHN MICHAEL BARRILLA

LINDNER

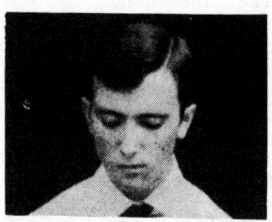

I am a somewhat average American boy, born into an average middle-class family. My parents were strict as far as love would allow but very open-minded. I have a sister who is married and has a beautiful family and a brother who is pursuing his education.

I regret that I will never again be able to see my family because of what I believe in and stand up for—these things that are guaranteed me by the Bill of Rights and denied me by the military.

Taking the consequences into consideration and placing them in their proper perspective, I have decided to desert the military and the crimes that it represents.

I believe that my presence in supporting the Vietnam war was immoral and entirely inhumane. To take another person's life for any reason is crime against myself as well as the person whose blood I am shedding.

I say "supporting the Vietnam war" instead of "fighting for the United States in Vietnam" because I don't feel that I was there doing something for the land or the people of America, which and whom I love in the same way the Vietnamese love their land and their people (what's left of them). Rather I was there supporting the annihilation of thousands of people, which is a crime no less than murder.

It is too bad that I will be labeled with some kind of "ist" pronoun and categorized with an "ism" for my beliefs. I claim no political affiliation and do not want to be classified in any way except as being an American who refuses to support mass military slaughter.

MICHAEL ANTHONY LINDNER

Transcript of Interview of Vietnam War Veteran on His Role in Alleged Massacre of Civilians at Songmy

Mr. Meadlo was described as the son of Mrs. Myrtle Meadlo of New Goshen Ind., who was quoted as saying:

"I sent them a good boy and they made him a murderer."

Following is a transcript of an interview with Paul Medlo, Vietnam veteran, by Mike Wallace on the Columbia Broadcasting System Radio Network last night:

MEADLO: Captain Medinas had us all in a group, and oh, he briefed us, and I can't remember all the briefing.

WALLACE: How many of them were you? A. Well, with the mortar platoon, I'd say there'd be about 65—65 people, but the mortar platoon wasn't with us. And I'd say the mortar platoon had about 20—25—about 25 people in the mortar platoon. So we didn't have the whole company in the Pinkville, no we didn't.

Q. There weren't about 40-45. . . . A. . . . right. . . .

Q.—that took part in all of this? A. Right.

Q. Now you took off from your base camp—A. . . . yes —Dolly.

Q. . . . Dolly. At what time? A. I wouldn't know what time it was . . .

Q. . . . in the early morning . . . A. . . . In the early morning. It was—it would have been a long time ago.

Q. And what had you been briefed to do when you got to Pinkville?

A. To search and to make sure that there weren't no N.V.A. in the village and 'spectin' to fight—when we got there . . .

Q. To axpect to fight? A. To expect to fight.

Q. Uu-huh. So you took off and—in how many choppers?

A. Well, I'd say the first wave was about four of us— I mean four choppres, and uh . . .

Q. How many men aboard each chopper?

A. Uh, five of us. And we landed next to the village, and we all got on line and we started walking toward the village. And there was one man, one gook in the shelter, and he was all huddled up down in there, and the man called out and said there's a gook over here.

Q. How old a man was this? I mean was this a fighting man or an older man? A. An older man. And the man hauled out and said that there's a gook over here, and then Sergeant Mitchell hollered back and said shoot him.

Q. Sergeant Mitchell was

in charge of the 20 of you?
A. He was in charge of the whole squad. And so then the man shot him. So we moved on into the village, and we started searching up the village and gathering people and running through the center of the village.

Q. How many people did you round up? A. Well, there was about 40-45 people that we gathered in the center of the village. And we placed them in there, and it was like a little island, right there in the center of the village, I'd say. And—

Q. What kind of people— men, women, children? A. Men, women, children.

'I Want Them Dead'

Q. Babies?
A. Babies. And we all huddled them up. We made them squat down, and Lieutenant Calley came over and said, 'You know what to do with them, don't you?' And I said Yes. So I took it for granted that he just wanted us to watch them. And he left, and came back about 10 or 15 minutes later, and said, 'How come you ain't killed them yet?' And I told him that I didn't think you wanted us to kill them, that you just wanted us to guard them. He said, 'No I want them dead.' So—

Q. He told this to all of you, or to you particularly?

A. Well, I was facing him. So, but the other three, four guys heard it and so he stepped back about 10, 15 feet, and he started shooting them. And he told me to start shooting. So I started shooting, I poured about four clips into the group.

Q. You fire four clips from your . . . A. M-16.

Q. And that's about—how many clips — I mean how many — A. I carried seventeen rounds to each clip.

Q. So you fired something like 67 shots—A. Right.

Q. And you killed how many? At that time?

A. Well, I fired them on automatic, so you can't — you just spray the area on them and so you can't know how many you killed 'cause they were going fast. So I might have killed ten or fifteen of them.

Q. Men, women and children? A. Men, women and children.

Q. And babies? A. And babies.

Q. Okay, then what? A. So we started to gather them up, more people, and we had about seven or eight people, that we was gonna put into the hootch, and we dropped a hand grenade in there with them.

Q. Now you're rounding up more?

A. We're rounding up more, and we had about seven or eight people. And we was going to throw them in the hootch, and well, we put them in the hootch and then we dropped a hand grenade down there with them. And somebody holed up in the ravine, and told us to bring thme over to the ravine, so we took them back out, and led them over to—and by that time, we already had them over there, and they had about 70-75 people all gathered up. So we threw ours in with them and Lieutenant Calley told me, he said, "Meadlo, we got another job to do." And so he walked over to the people, and he started pushing them off and started shooting . . .

Q. Started pushing them off into the ravine?

A. off into the ravine. It was a ditch. And so we started pushing them off and we started shooting them, so altogether we just pushed them all off, and just started using automatics on them. And then—

Q. Again — men, women, children? A. Men, women and children.

Q. And babies?

A. And babies. And so we started shooting them, and somebody told us to switch off to single shot so that we could save ammo. So we switched off to single shot, and shot a few more rounds. And after that, I just—we just—the company started gathering up again. We started moving out, and we had a few gooks that was in—as we started moving out, we had gooks in front of us that was taking point, you know.

Q. Uh-huh. A. —and as we walked——

Q. Taking point. You mean out in front? To take any fire that might come.

Stepped on Land Mine

A. Right. And so we started walking across that field. And so later on that day, they picked them up, and gooks we had, and I reckon they took them to Chu Lai or some camp that they was questioning them, so I don't know what they done with them. So we set up (indistinct] the rest of the night, and the next morning we started leaving, leaving the perimeter, and I stepped on a land mine next day, next morning.

Q. And you came back to the United tSates. A. I came back to the United States, and lost a foot out of it.

Q. You feel —
A. I feel cheated because the V.AA. cut my disability like the did, and they say

that my stump is well healed, well padded, without tenderness. Well, it's well healed, but it's a long way from being well padded. And without tenderness? It hurts all the time. I got to work eight hours a day up on my foot, and at the end of the day I can't hardly stand it. But I gotta work because I gotta make a living. And the V.A. don't give me enough money to live on as it ia.

Q. Veterans Administration. A. Right. So—

Q. Did you feel any sense of retribution to yourself the day after? A. Well, I felt that I was punished for what I'd done, the next morning. Later on in that day, I felt like I was being punished.

Q. Why did you do it? A. Why did I do it? Because I felt like I was ordered to do it, and it seemed like that, at the time I felt like I was doing the right thing, because like I said I lost buddies. I lost a damn good buddy, Bobby Wilson, and it was on my conscience. So after I done it, I felt good, but later on that day, it was gettin' to me.

Q. You're married? A. Right.

Q. Children? A. Two.

Q. How old? A. The boy is two and a half, and the little girl is a year and a half.

Q. Obviously, the question comes to my mind . . . the father of two little kids like that . . . how can he shoot babies? A. I didn't have the little girl. I just had the little boy at the time.

Q. Uh-huh. How do you shoot babies? A. I don't know. It's just one of them things.

Q. How many people would you imagine were killed that day? A. I'd say about 370.

Q. How do you arrive at that figure? A. Just looking.

Q. You saw, you think, that many people, and you yourself were responsible for how many of them? A. I couldn't say.

Q. Twenty-five? Fifty? A. I couldn't say . . . just too many.

Q. And how many men did the actual shooting? A. Well, I really couldn't say that, either. There was other . . . there was another platoon in there and . . . but I just couldn't say how many.

'Just Sitting, Squatting'

Q. But these civilians were lined up and shot? They weren't killed by cross-fire? A. They weren't lined up . . . they [were] just pushed in a ravine or just sitting, squatting . . . and shot.

Q. What did these civilians —particularly the women and children, the old men—what

did they do? What did they say to you? A. They weren't much saying to them. They [were] just being pushed and they were doing what they was told to do.

Q. They weren't begging or saying, "No . . . no," or—A. Right, They was begging and saying, "No, no." And the mothers was hugging their children and, but they kept right on firing. Well, we kept right on firing. They was waving their arms and begging . . .

Q. Was that your most vivid memory of what you saw? A. Right.

Q. And nothing went through your mind or heart? A. Many a times . . . many a times . . .

Q. While you were doing it? A. Not while I was doing it. I just seemed like it was the natural thing to do at the time. I don't know. It just— I was getting relieved from what I'd seen earlier over there.

'It Was . . . Mostly Revenge'

Q. What do you mean? A. Well, I was getting . . . like the . . . my buddies getting killed or wounded or—we weren't getting no satisfaction from it, so what it really was, it was just mostly revenge.

Q. You call the Vietnamese "gooks?" A. Gooks.

Q. Are they people to you? Were they people to you?

A. Well, they were people. But it was just one of them words that we just picked up over there, you know. Just any word you pick up. That's what you call people, and that's what you been called.

Q. Obviously, the thought that goes through my mind —I spent some time over there, and I killed in the second war, and so forth. But the thought that goes through your mind is, we've raised such a dickens about what the Nazis did, or what the Japanese did, but particularly what the Nazis did in the second world war, the brutalization and so forth, you know. It's hard for a good many Americans to understand that young, capable, American boys could line up old men, women and children and babies and shoot them down in cold blood. How do you explain that?

A. I wouldn't know.

Q. Did you ever dream about all of this that went on in Pinkville? A. Yes, I did . . . and I still dream about it.

Q. What kind of dreams? A. I see the women and children in my sleep. Some days . . . some nights, I can't even sleep. I just lay there thinking about it.

The New York Times 11/25/67

THE CRIMINALS

Governments hold monopolies on war crimes trials. The US isn't about to allow itself to go on trial for committing crimes against human nature and international law in its conduct of the Vietnam war. (The court-martial of Lieutenant Calley is the very opposite of a proper Nuremburg process.) It's small wonder, then, that the US Army took swift action against four GIs at Fort Gordon, Ga., who announced the formation of a "GI War Crimes Commission" and taped an interview on the same subject with radio station WBBQ in Augusta. Monopolies do protect themselves.

The Army threw three of the men—Pfc. Dick Horner, Pvt. Larry Czaplyski and Pfc. Tim Johnson—in the stockade. The fourth, Pfc. Terry Kline, has been confined to quarters. The charges: Article 134, something about undermining discipline and loyalty in the Army; and Article 92, distributing unauthorized printed matter on post. A friend of Kline said that the four fully expected to be locked up, but were determined to set an example to "spur people to action against the war machine."

The broadcast seems to have been more provocative than the mimeo sheets, for the GIs managed to distribute only a few sheets on post before their arrest. But the sheet is a good example of the tone of the GI movement these days. It states the purpose of the War Crime's Commission:

"To dispel the prevailing myth that the US soldier is more moral than his enemy counterpart;

"To show to the American people what their sons are capable of and by doing this, try to arouse in them an antiwar and anti-militaristic response;

"To get across the fact that Songmy wasn't an isolated incident and that genocide against the Vietnamese people by the US Armed Forces is an everyday occurrence;

"To get more GIs actively involved in the antiwar movement."

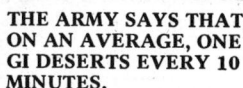

THE ARMY SAYS THAT, ON AN AVERAGE, ONE GI DESERTS EVERY 10 MINUTES.

JOURNEY'S END

Hard Times 2/9/70

THE COLONEL SPEAKING OF HIS MEN

Or, the interview with Colonel George S. Patton, III, from the film library of WABC-TV, New York. Patton speaking of his men:

"Of course they're the subject of our constant concern because they're such a magnificent group of fighting men. Their morale is extremely high. They always have a smile. I was at a very kind of sobering thing last night, a memorial service for four men in the second squadron who were killed the other day, one of them being a medic, and the place was just packed. And we sang three hymns and had a nice prayer. I turned around and looked at their faces and they were —I was just proud. My feelings for America just soared because of their—the way they looked. They looked determined and reverent at the same time. But still they're a bloody good bunch of killers."

From an interview with Col. George S. Patton, III, WABC-TV, N.Y.

THE NAZIS HAD A WORD FOR IT

From William Buckley's syndicated column of Dec. 19th:

"The enemy in Vietnam retains the technical capacity to regenerate himself at about the rate at which we have been killing him. An estimated 100,000 healthy males not designated for specialized training turn 18 every year. That is about how many soldiers on an average, have been killed per year over the course of the war.

"The bright side of it, in the macabre figuring of the military statisticians, is that something like an entire generation of North Vietnamese males has been killed during the past seven years. The sobering side is that they grow 'em as fast as we kill them."

Old Mole Jan 1970

THE FUTURE OF DESERTION

GI organizers should re-examine the question of desertion if for no other reason than that the GI movement itself is at a tactical impasse. This is how that impasse developed:

In the fall of 1967, when Howard Levy was in the unused officers' wing of the Fort Jackson Army Hospital confinement facility (prior to his transfer to Leavenworth), the GIs who used to visit him, and thousands of others across the country, wished there were something they could do, *short of jail or exile*, to express their own anti-war sentiments. As one of them put it then, "It's not just that I don't have Levy's guts; it's that you can't build a whole movement of martyrs. I don't mind being a martyr, but I'd rather be an unknown guy within a movement." The Fort Jackson GIs finally did hit upon a tactic enabling them to involve 35 men: the anti-war meditation at the post chapel. All the anti-war gestures devised that year—newspapers, union meetings, rap sessions at service clubs, political meetings in the barracks, off-post marches, anti-war rallies at coffeehouses or in parks—were aimed similarly, at creating the mass movement that jail or exile could not achieve. These tactics, properly described as dissent, were not employed by men who thought that a march or a petition was the be-all and the end-all of resistance. The anti-war GIs hoped that the relatively safe actions would involve growing numbers of men, and that when hundreds and then thousands found themselves in opposition to the war, the vision of their own collective strength would enable them to plan and carry out heavier acts of resistance, acts that would tangibly undermine the war effort: mass refusal to train or fight in Vietnam.

The brass understood this threat and decided to crush dissent before the hundreds had turned into thousands. In the spring of 1969, the Department of the Army drafted "guidelines on dissent," providing commanders with legal ways they could punish protesters. These guidelines were revised by the Defense Department—at the urging of Mendel Rivers and the Pentagon's manpower chief, Roger Kelly—so as to de-emphasize the Constitutional restraints on commanders and add to their repressive options. As a result of the DoD directive, soldiers can no longer distribute their anti-war papers on post. Having two copies of a paper in your possession is proof of intent-to-distribute. A soldier named Wade Carson is now serving six months in the Fort Lewis, Wash., stockade for precisely this crime.

In addition to the repressive legislation, the brass can use an extra-legal trump card called "punitive reassignment." Without going through the trouble of a court-martial—which also entails a public record—a commander can phone the Pentagon and put a man on "hot levee" for another duty station. Depending on how vindictive the officer involved, the assignment can be to Germany, or a stateside post, or to Vietnam. At Fort Jackson this spring, a bright, honest soldier named Bill Mackey, assigned by Military Intelligence to infiltrate the GI movement, instead joined the staff of Short Times and told how he had been used and coerced. He was immediately reassigned to Vietnam and is due to ship from Oakland on May 23.

Suffice it to say that union organizers, coffeehouse patrons and other anti-war GIs face this same kind of treatment day-in, day-out. The brass is waging total war on GI dissenters but, in the manner to which they've grown accustomed in Asia, it is a hidden and deceitful war. The GI movement, finding its institutions under attack, has been trying in the past year to defend itself; unfortunately, the fight has been conducted on the enemy's battlefield: the courts. This rearguard fight looks like a loser. Of course we should not fold up whenever attacked; that would be a fatal display of impotence. And there are times when the movement must demonstrate its professional competence—by building a splendid coffeehouse or publishing a superior paper. But the institutions of dissent have no value beyond the sum of their functions, and if we can't have a coffeehouse we can still have a bookstore, a staff house open to GIs, a free U., a be-in at the park. If men are being busted for distributing lithographed, easily recognizable papers, it might be best to go back to mimeographed broadsheets (which are often punchier). The irrefragable fact is that the forms of dissent developed in the past two years are no longer safer than the acts of witness that touched off the GI movement. Nor is dissent any safer than desertion. We must question, therefore, whether dissent is the likeliest way to build an anti-imperialist movement among soldiers.

Judging from the history of how armies fail, it appears that disintegration, not dissent, may characterize the final crisis. There has never been an army that fell apart through the exercise of civil liberties; but there have been some big ones cracked by mass desertion. As a tactic, desertion has the under-rated virtue of simplicity. It is the archetypal anti-war act.

Why have people in our movement written it off as an apolitical gesture? Granted, not everyone who refuses orders for Vietnam does so because he opposes the illegal, immoral war. The majority of men I've spoken to in Canada—out of perhaps 200 in the past two years—do not give the wrongness of the war as their main reason for splitting. But somewhere in their list of reasons comes a phrase such as, "and what's this war all about, anyway?" Soldiers who desert have acted politically whether or not they say so out front. Any glib son-of-a-bitch can express a noble motive; but few people act so directly against the war as the soldier who refuses to take part. It is snotty of American radicals to put them down as escapists. Escape from oppression is a political act; not the highest form of struggle, obviously, but political just the same. The GI movement, like the women's movement, is rooted in real oppression and operates on principles of self-interest. Maintaining an empire might be fine for most other Americans, but it's not worth it to the soldiers who pay with body, mind and soul. That's what the GI movement is all about. To criticize deserters because they merely want to stay alive is inhumane; to dismiss them as apolitical is not only wrong, but has the elements of a self-fulfilling prophecy.

The way out of a tactical impasse is to develop new tactics, never yielding the initiative. We should not think of desertion, mechanically, as an alternative to on-base organizing; that's like saying the forehand is alternative to the backhand and therefore a tennis player should only rely on one. The fact is, desertion and dissent are two aspects of the same movement and re-inforce one another. It's no coincidence that the desertion rate shot up in the spring of 1968, just at the time that on-base organizing became widespread (and in the wake of the Tet offensive).

At present, men are reluctant to engage in on-base organizing because they don't want to wind up in jail, Vietnam, or an exile that would effectively end their political lives. That's why the success of the GI movement hinges on whether or not the deserter community can begin to thrive. If the ADC had the resources to run a stable and efficient office; if they had a large collective farm just north of the border where newcomers could go to get their heads and bodies together; if they could put on a Judy Collins or Arlo Guthrie concert every month; or sponsor Carl Oglesby or Angela Davis or Roxanne Dunbar speaking on the state of affairs here in the US—not only the desertion rate but GI dissent would pick up. The physical and moral presence of thousands of American exiles would be felt within this country. Their parents could be organized as a counterpoise to those Air Force wives Mr. Ross Perot flies around. Every college could be turned into an underground railway station, giving campus politics a heavier anti-imperialist content and a grounding in reality.

One could speculate endlessly about what the deserters might achieve once they get organized. A minimum goal would be to make the brass rue the day they decided to outlaw dissent.

—*Fred Gardner*

Hard Times

From "The Future of Desertion", 5/4/70

We appear to have forgotten in our schools what every primitive tribe with its functional psychology knows: allegiance to the tribe can be forged only at the deepest levels of the psyche and in extreme circumstance demanding endurance, daring, and awe; that the participant must be given *direct* access to the sources of cultural continuity—by and in himself; and that only a place in a coherent community can be exchanged for a man's allegiance.

I believe that it is precisely this world that drugs replace; adolescents provide for themselves what we deny them: a confrontation with some kind of power within an unfamiliar landscape involving sensation and risk. It is there, I suppose, that they hope to find, by some hurried magic, a new way of seeing, a new relation to things, to discard one identity and assume another. They mean to find through their adventures the *ground* of reality, the resonance of life we deny them, as if they might come upon their golden city and return still inside it: at home. You can see the real veterans sometimes on the street in strange costumes they have stolen from dreams: American versions of the Tupi of Brazil, who traveled thousands of miles each year in search of the land where death and evil do not exist. Theirs is a world totally alien to the one we discuss in schools; it is dramatic, it enchants them; its existence forms a strange brotherhood among them and they cling to it—as though they alone had been to a fierce land and back. It is that which draws them together and makes of them a loose tribe. It is, after all, some sort of shared experience, some kind of foray into the risky dark; it is the best that they can do.

PETER MARIN

COMPREHENSION
N.O. Brown at Columbia
8 years before the strike.

APOCALYPSE

THE PLACE OF MYSTERY IN THE LIFE OF THE MIND

by Norman O. Brown

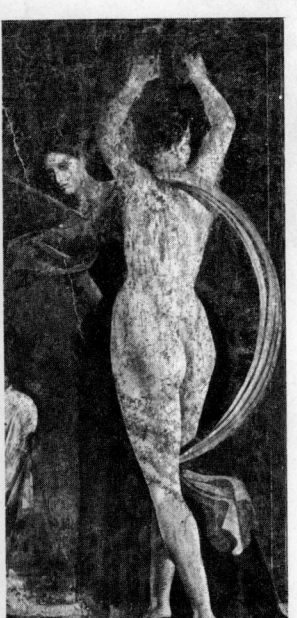

I DIDN'T know whether I should appear before you—there is a time to show and a time to hide; there is a time to speak, and also a time to be silent. What time is it? It is fifteen years since H. G. Wells said Mind was at the End of its Tether—with a frightful queerness come into life: there is no way out or around or through, he said; it is the end. It is because I think mind is at the end of its tether that I would be silent. It is because I think there is a way out—a way down and out—the title of Mr. John Senior's new book on the occult tradition in literature—that I will speak.

Mind at the end of its tether: I can guess what some of you are thinking—*his* mind is at the end of its tether—and this could be; it scares me but it deters me not. The alternative to mind is certainly madness. Our greatest blessings, says Socrates in the *Phaedrus*, come to us by way of madness—provided, he adds, that the madness comes from the god. Our real choice is between holy and unholy madness: open your eyes and look around you—madness is in the saddle anyhow. Freud is the measure of our unholy madness, as Nietzsche is the prophet of the holy madness, of Dionysus, the mad truth. Dionysus has returned to his native Thebes; mind—at the end of its tether—is another Pentheus, up a tree. Resisting madness can be the maddest way of being mad.

And there is a way out—the blessed madness of the maenad and the bacchant: "Blessed is he who has the good fortune to know the mysteries of the gods, who sanctifies his life and initiates his soul, a bacchant on the mountains, in holy purifications." It is possible to be mad and to be unblest; but it is not possible to get the blessing without the madness; it is not possible to get the illuminations without the derangement. Derangement is disorder: the Dionysian faith is that order as we have known it is crippling, and for cripples; that what is past is prologue; that we can throw away our crutches and discover the supernatural power of walking; that human history goes from man to superman.

No superman I; I come to you not as one who has supernatural powers, but as one who seeks for them, and who has some notions which way to go to find them.

Sometimes—most times—I think that the way down and out leads out of the university, out of the academy. But perhaps it is rather that we should recover the academy of earlier days—the

Academy of Plato in Athens, the Academy of Ficino in Florence, Ficino who says, "The spirit of the god Dionysus was believed by the ancient theologians and Platonists to be the ecstasy and abandon of disencumbered minds, when partly by innate love, partly at the instigation of the god, they transgress the natural limits of intelligence and are miraculously transformed into the beloved god himself: where, inebriated by a certain new draft of nectar and by an immeasurable joy, they rage, as it were, in a bacchic frenzy. In the drunkenness of this Dionysian wine, our Dionysius (the Areopagite) expresses his exultation. He pours forth enigmas, he sings in dithyrambs. To penetrate the profundity of his meanings, to imitate his quasi-Orphic manner of speech, we too require the divine fury."

At any rate the point is first of all to find again the mysteries. By which I do not mean simply the sense of wonder—that sense of wonder which is indeed the source of all true philosophy—by mystery I mean secret and occult; therefore unpublishable; therefore outside the university as we know it; but not outside Plato's Academy, or Ficino's.

Why are mysteries unpublishable? First because they cannot be put into words, at least not the kind of words which earned you your Phi Beta Kappa keys. Mysteries display themselves in words only if they can remain concealed; this is poetry, isn't it? We must return to the old doctrine of the Platonists and Neo-Platonists, that poetry is veiled truth; as Dionysus is the god who is both manifest and hidden; and as John Donne declared, with the Pillar of Fire goes the Pillar of Cloud. This is also the new doctrine of Ezra Pound, who says: "Prose is not education but the outer courts of the same. Beyond its doors are the mysteries. Eleusis. Things not to be spoken of save in secret. The mysteries self-defended, the mysteries that cannot be revealed. Fools can only profane them. The dull can neither penetrate the secretum nor divulge it to others." The mystic academies, whether Plato's or Ficino's, knew the limitations of words and drove us on beyond them, to go over, to go under, to the learned ignorance, in which God is better honored and loved by silence than by words, and better seen by closing the eyes to images than by opening them.

And second, mysteries are unpublishable because only some can see them, not all. Mysteries are intrinsically esoteric, and as such an offense to democracy: is not publicity a democratic principle? Publication makes it republican—a thing of the people. The pristine academies were esoteric and aristocratic, self-consciously separate from the profane vulgar. Democratic resentment denies that there can be anything that can't be seen by everybody; in the demo-

cratic academy truth is subject to public verification; truth is what any fool can see. This is what is meant by the so-called scientific method: so-called science is the attempt to democratize knowledge—the attempt to substitute method for insight, mediocrity for genius, by getting a standard operating procedure. The great equalizers dispensed by the scientific method are the tools, those analytical tools. The miracle of genius is replaced by the standardized mechanism. But fools with tools are still fools, and don't let your Phi Beta Kappa key fool you. Tibetan prayer wheels are another way of arriving at the same result: the degeneration of mysticism into mechanism—so that any fool can do it. Perhaps the advantage is with Tibet: for there the mechanism is external while the mind is left vacant; and vacancy is not the worst condition of the mind. And the resultant prayers make no futile claim to originality or immortality; being nonexistent, they do not have to be catalogued or stored.

The sociologist Simmel sees showing and hiding, secrecy and publicity, as two poles, like Yin and Yang, between which societies oscillate in their historical development. I sometimes think I see that civilizations originate in the disclosure of some mystery, some secret; and expand with the progressive publication of their secret; and end in exhaustion when there is no longer any secret, when the mystery has been divulged, that is to say profaned. The whole story is illustrated in the difference between ideogram and alphabet. The alphabet is indeed a democratic triumph; and the enigmatic ideogram, as Ezra Pound has taught us, is a piece of mystery, a piece of poetry, not yet profaned. And so there comes a time— I believe we are in such a time—when civilization has to be renewed by the discovery of new mysteries, by the undemocratic but sovereign power of the imagination, by the undemocratic power which makes poets the unacknowledged legislators of mankind, the power which makes all things new.

The power which makes all things new is magic. What our time needs is mystery: what our time needs is magic. Who would not say that only a miracle can save us? In Tibet the degree-granting institution is, or used to be, the College of Magic Ritual. It offers courses in such fields as clairvoyance and telepathy; also (attention physics majors) internal heat: internal heat is a yoga bestowing supernatural control over body temperature. Let me succumb for a moment to the fascination of the mysterious East and tell you of the examination procedure for the course in internal heat. Candidates assemble naked, in midwinter, at night, on a frozen Himalayan lake. Beside each one is placed a pile of wet frozen undershirts; the assignment is to wear, until they are dry, as many as possible of these undershirts before dawn. Where the power is real, the test is real, and the grading system dumfoundingly objective. I say no more. I say no more; Eastern Yoga does indeed demonstrate the existence of supernatural powers, but it does not have the particular power our Western society needs; or rather I think that each society has access only to its own proper powers; or rather each society will only get the kind of power it knows how to ask for.

THE Western consciousness has always asked for freedom: the human mind was born free, or at any rate born to be free, but everywhere it is in chains; and now at the end of its tether. It will take a miracle to free the human mind: because the chains are magical in the first place. We are in bondage to authority outside ourselves: most obviously—here in a great university it must be said—in bondage to the authority of books. There is a Transcendentalist anticipation of what I want to say in Emerson's Phi Beta Kappa address on the American Scholar:

"The books of an older period will not fit this. Yet hence arises a grave mischief. The sacredness which attaches to the act of creation, the act of thought, is transferred to the record. Instantly the book becomes noxious: the guide is a tyrant. The sluggish and perverted mind of the multitude having once received this book, stands upon it, and makes an outcry if it is destroyed. Colleges are built on it. Meek young men grow up in libraries. Hence, instead of Man Thinking, we have the bookworm. I had better never see a book than to be warped by its attraction clean out of my own orbit, and make a satellite instead of a system. The one thing in the world, of value, is the active soul."

How far this university is from that ideal is the measure of the defeat of our American dream.

This bondage to books compels us not to see with our own eyes; compels us to see with the eyes of the dead, with dead eyes. Whitman, likewise in a Transcendentalist sermon, says, "You shall no longer take things at second or third hand, nor look through the eyes of the dead, nor feed on the specters in books." There is a hex on us, the specters in books, the authority of the past; and to exorcise these ghosts is the great work of magical self-liberation. Then the eyes of the spirit would become one with the eyes of the body, and god would be in us, not outside. God in us: *entheos:* enthusiasm; this is the essence of the holy madness. In the fire of the holy madness even books lose their gravity, and let themselves go up into the flame: "Properly," says Ezra Pound, "we should read for power. Man reading should be man intensely alive. The book should be a ball of light in one's hand."

I began with the name of Dionysus; let me be

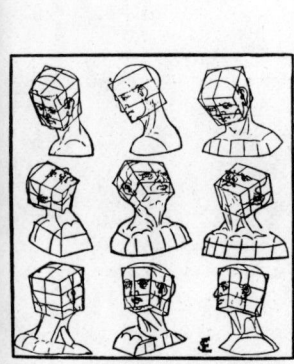

permitted to end with the name of Christ: for the power I seek is also Christian. Nietzsche indeed said the whole question was Dionysus versus Christ; but only the fool will take these as mutually exclusive opposites. There is a Dionysian Christianity, an apocalyptic Christianity, a Christianity of miracles and revelations. And there always have been some Christians for whom the age of miracle and revelation is not over; Christians who claim the spirit; enthusiasts. The power I look for is the power of enthusiasm; as condemned by John Locke; as possessed by George Fox, the Quaker; through whom the houses were shaken; who saw the channel of blood running down the streets of the city of Litchfield; to whom, as a matter of fact, was even given the magic internal heat—"The fire of the Lord was so in my feet, and all around me, that I did not matter to put on my shoes any more."

Read again the controversies of the seventeenth century and discover our choice: we are either in an age of miracles, says Hobbes, miracles which authenticate fresh revelations; or else we are in an age of reasoning from already received Scripture. Either miracle or Scripture. George Fox, who came up in spirit through the flaming sword into the paradise of God, so that all things were new, he being renewed to the state of Adam which he was in before he fell, sees that none can read Moses aright without Moses' spirit; none can read John's words aright, and with a true understanding of them, but in and with the same divine spirit by which John spake them, and by his burning shining light which is sent from God. Thus the authority of the past is swallowed up in new creation; the word is made flesh. We see with our own eyes and to see with our own eyes is second sight. To see with our own eyes is second sight.

Twofold Always. May God us keep
From single vision and Newton's sleep.

Dr. Norman O. Brown, Seney Professor of Classics at Wesleyan University, was born in Mexico, educated at Oxford and the University of Wisconsin, and served with the OSS during World War II. In 1953-54, under a grant from the Fund for the Advancement of Education, he undertook a study of the irrational in human nature. The result was his book "Life Against Death," which Lionel Trilling called "A contribution to moral—and by implication, political—thought which cannot be overestimated."

"Apocalypse The Place of Mystery in The Life of the Mind" by Norman O. Brown, May 1961

In his summary description of the counter-culture of the young, Roszak also made clear that the analogy with second century Christians is not merely formal: "A heroic generalization about this still embryonic culture is to say that what the young are up to is nothing less than a reorganization of the prevailing state of personal and social consciousness. From a culture that has a long-standing entrenched commitment to an egocentric and intellective mode of consciousness, the young are moving toward a sense of identity that is communal and nonin-tellective. I think the disjuncture is just that great—as great in its implications (though obviously not as yet in historical influence) as the disjuncture between Greco-Roman rationality and Christian mystery. Against the traditional Cartesian *cogito*, with its blunt, initial asser-tion of individuality and logicality, the counter culture opposes the community and visionary aspiration. This really amounts to an assault on the reality of the ego as an isolable and purely cerebral unity of identity" (*ibid.*).

THEODORE ROSZAK quoted by Rev. Myron Bloy, 1/17/69

commonweal

The Golden City

Has there ever been a community of adults so conscious and envious of children—and so fearful of growth? We seem mired in guilt. The family, each adult life, which might at best be like a vessel, an adventure, is instead a fort established on a hostile plain—and the child is its natural enemy, for he brings to it all the energy (that wind of chaos) that threatens it with change. Say the same for schools. Say the same for each of us. Instead of pre-ceding children, leading them, we shove them forward like bodyguards. Anyone who has known them inti-mately can sense their combined strength and fragility, a recurrent brit-tleness that stems from what is para-doxically an excessive exposure to culture and a dearth of participation.

They lack the resonance of cultural continuity or connection. Neither fam-ily, school, tribe, nor a usable past supports them. Instead, they seem to pass among us like buffalo, like alien beasts: the reverse image of ourselves, strange weddings of the elements bred out of our lives and returned to haunt us with the irony of Greek tragedy.

It is no accident that adolescents have turned inward toward what they call "inner space." The landscape around them must seem crowded, must thwart and diminish them, bled as it is of drama and life. In some way, like all primitive men, youth must dream of a golden city. It is that city Rousseau had in mind when he spoke of the golden age which is neither be-hind nor ahead of us but *in us*. It is

in adolescents, and close to the sur-face, raging for release. But adults must seem to them to stand between them and their dream, for we have occupied those cities and the conti-nent, have closed the gates to them, despoiled it, have built Pittsburgh and Chicago instead of Jerusalem, and have resigned ourselves, it seems, to *what is here*. That is what seems to turn youth toward rage, that sense of another city beyond, beneath this con-fusion, another place somewhere. But where? Perhaps, they believe, we can tear all this down, can burn it, and that other hidden city, within, set free, will magically emerge.

PETER MARIN
Principal, Pacific High School, Saratoga, California

THE CENTER MAGAZINE

UP FRONT ON DOPE FRONT

In a couple of generations, when historians look back—don't jump on me now, let's just assume for the moment that the species *is* going to pull off that 100-to-one shot and make it that far; and, even more implausibly, that in such a case there will still be historians—look back, as I was saying, on the crucial decade immediately behind us: what's going to stand out for them as most significant? *Not* the Vietnam war, I'm fairly certain, or any of the others, or those factions or factors causing or prolonging them, or even the consequent protests and burgeoning social/moral/political consciousness. *Not* any beginnings of any old-fashioned (i.e., violent, class- or race-oriented, ideological) revolution, any-where. Certainly, *not* the fact that some people, at tremen-dous ecological cost to all people, began to explore outer space and managed to land physically on the moon.

More likely—much more so, if I'm at all right about *how*

that 100-to-one shot could be pulled off—our hypothetical historians will note the importance of the fact that some other people were beginning to explore *inner* space, and that out of their internal meanderings there emerged a tentative (and not new, but rather, age-old, restored) under-standing of man's rightful place in the world, and that more and more other people, especially younger Americans, be-gan to follow after these early, wierd, ecological pioneers.

Okay. Now that I've gotten *that* off my chest, what *about* this psychedelic business, whatever it is, anyhow, and revolution, whatever *that* means in this context? A lot of people have been using up a lot of paper and tape and film on this question for the past several years, especially people who haven't had much meaningful first-hand experience of either; but even *they* know the connection is real—if incre-dibly complicated.

Grass. Hash. Bob Dylan. *Everybody must get stoned.* San Francisco, 1966-68. Acid. Acid Rock. The Beatles. *Turn off your mind, relax, and float downstream. . . .* Exorcise the Pentagon, Yippie. Straight young politicos like Jerry Rubin used to be, suddenly turning freaky. Promising young artists like Ken Kesey, ditto. B rilliant young scientists and mathmaticians like Peter Stafford, even more so. And whatever happened to the crewcut, athletic boy next door? Joined the army, went to 'Nam, came home wearing a peace button, grew shoulder-length hair, a glassy grin, and a lot of confusing talk about loving not only all human beings, but every plant and animal as well. Then split for a commune in the mountains. And you still don't know what's happening, do you, Mister Jones? But we're certainly getting warm.

That peace button, you see, wasn't a cause, merely a symptom. The *cause*, nine times in ten, was grass, hash, acid, mescaline, peyote, psilocybin, or the triptomines. (Some, of course, came at it the other way around: movement activities, hence a radical lifestyle first, dope later; usually, they were a few years older, a few corners squarer to begin with.) By the end of the 1960's, virtually *everyone* in the U.S. under 35—and a great many older—smoked marijuana as a matter of course. No, not just the longhaired dropouts, but the banktellers, the teachers, the bus drivers, the cops. Obviously, there are no available, reliable statistics on either that last statement or this next one, but: it would seem a conservative estimate that one-third of those who have turned on to grass have also dropped acid. Finally, now, it scarcely matters whether one takes his dope personally or not: the entire culture, fad and fabric, is permeated with it. The whole nation is on a contact high.

Where did it start? Well, history, as we all ought to know, is a most imprecise discipline; very few of the dates and names we had to memorize in school are anything better than arbitrary. These, however, seem as good as can be found:

In 1958 or 59, a handsome, husky, curly-haired fellow, would-be writer and born athlete, perfect boy-next-door type, volunteered for the "psychomimetic" experiments being run at the Veteran's Hospital in Menlo Park, California, because they were paying $75 a day for their guinea pigs. His name was Ken Kesey. The researchers blew his mind, but good, on LSD. Soon he was turning on all his friends—and collecting some strange new ones—who eventually came to call themselves the Merry Pranksters. Meanwhile, Kesey produced two best-selling novels in order to finance this floating menagerie (the first modern tribe) of freaks that, in 1964, took the world's first psychedelic bus trip across the U.S. Soon afterwards—incidentally creating the first psychedelic posters, lightshows, and acid rock—the Pranksters were attempting to turn on the world-at-large through fantastic parties they called "acid tests."

There was a truly anarchic, truly religious, truly revolutionary fervor about the Pranksters that never appeared with any of the other pioneers in dope; the comparison that comes to mind is with Dr. Timothy Leary and his lotus-positioned Millbrook entourage. But in any case, of course, it didn't come off; Kesey, inevitably enough, ran afoul of the drug laws, fled to Mexico, and thereby lost his grip—if he really ever had one—on what was happening at a critical juncture. When he returned, at the crest of Haight-Ash-

bury's wave, the entrepreneurs of acid had arisen, and they banded together (so goes the gospel, anyhow) to protect their budding commercial interests from these wild-eyed zealots whose next prank no hip robber-baron could hope to predict. And another messiah, plus disciples, bit the dust. (Or not quite. You'll still find ex-Pranksters Where It's At, as for instance Hugh Romney and the Hog Farm, or the Whole Earth Catalogue.)

You can read all about it in *The Electric Kool-Aid Acid Test*, and you most definitely should. I very nearly didn't, because of the fop who wrote it, and the foppish things he wrote before. He's still Tom Wolfe, but the material took over, and did wonders with him. Unless Kesey himself comes out of his silence, this is as close to a definitive text as we're going to get. It's also a dazzling gallery of beautifully vivid sketches of already mythic folk, like Neal Cassady, and Owsley, and the Hell's Angels. But most of all, it's a ouija board that time and again almost spells out those Very Big Answers for us. Almost—like acid itself.

The Teachings of Don Juan isn't history. It's *supposed* to be anthropology. Forget that. Forget, also, the last third of the volume, a so-called Structural Analysis—astonishing thing though it is, simply in the fact that it could be written, after what the author has been through: a stirring, and frightening, testimony to the tenacity of academic training. But then, the whole idea of this being a *book* is dizzying and, on reflection, nauseating. The only thing to do is to read the first part, the Teachings, fast, and don't let Carlos Castaneda infuriate you any oftener than he did Don Juan. Which will take some doing, because Don Juan is beyond any doubt one of the very wisest, kindest, most amazingly patient human beings I have ever met through the printed word. (If there were any certain means of comparison/translation with half a dozen persons I have been lucky enough to meet in the flesh -for instance, A.J. Muste—I'd happily drop that single qualification.)

Don Juan was, and possibly still is, an ancient Indian brujo living in the southwest. "Brujo" is Spanish for warlock—a male witch, a magician. Carlos Castaneda was a California graduate student whom—tragically, because he was growing so old, and there was simply no one more suitable to pass his wisdom on to—Don Juan accepted as an apprentice. Carlos more or less served in this capacity—chortling at first, I'm sure, over the juicy dissertation it was going to make—for five years. He got his dissertation all right, that's what you'll be reading, and it's a lulu. He also got one hell of a lot more than he smugly bargained for. He damned near lost all his credentials as a Civilized 20th Century Man; or, as he and most other Civilized 20th Century Men would term it, his sanity.

The Teachings are very difficult to talk about, without a great deal of explanation and redefinition. Even though he spent considerable time with Don Juan over a five-year period, Carlos was clearly still just a beginner when he reached a crisis tantamount to nervous breakdown, and had to withdraw. The source of his crisis seems simple enough: he could go no further into Don Juan's world and still retain any shreds of his respectable, academic Los Angeles existence. The two paths were just too far apart. However, as Don Juan said to him:

"You have the vanity to believe you live in two worlds, but that is only your vanity. There is but one single world for us. We are men, and must follow the world of men contentedly."

Carlos, as usual, missed the point of that completely. He probably thought Los Angeles was as validly "the world of men" as "the one single world" that Don Juan kept trying to show him. Yet how *could* he mistake the message, having been so explicitly warned:

"I say it is useless to waste your life on one path, especially if that path has no heart."

"But how do you know when a path has no heart, Don Juan?"

"Before you embark on it you ask the question 'Does this path have a heart?' If the answer is no, you will now it, and then you must choose another path."

"But how will I know for sure whether a Path has a heart or not?"

"Anybody would know that. The trouble is nobody asks the question; and when a man finally realizes that he has taken a path without a heart the path is ready to kill him. At that point very few men can stop to deliberate, and leave the path."

"How should I proceed to ask the question properly, Don Juan?"

"Just ask it."

"I mean, is there a proper method, so I would not lie to myself and believe the answer is yes when it really is no?"

"Why would you lie?"

"Perhaps because at the moment the path is pleasant and enjoyable."

"That is nonsense. A path without a heart is never enjoyable. You have to work hard even to take it. On the other hand, a path with heart is easy; it does not make you work at liking it."

Don Juan employed three drugs in his teachings. No, wait, I didn't say that right, but there is no direct, "right" way to say it. He *used* two drug mixtures, one made from the datura plant and the other primarily from psilocybin mushrooms, both of which he called (potential) "allies"; and he *let* peyote *happen to* Carlos, or to both of them together. But he never called it either "peyote" or "it"· that would be dangerously disrespectful; he used the nickname "mescalito" and the pronoun "he" The experiences with the sacred cactus described in this book are absolutely the best, most vivid and straightforward accounts of drug-induced states that I have ever read anywhere.

An *ally* is something you can acquire the assistance of in order to gain either *power* or *knowledge*—in short, to become a diablero (sorcerer), a brujo, or a "man of knowledge." Don Juan was preeminently the last-named; his ally was the mushroom mixture, which he called the "little smoke." The datura—a fairly common vine of the juniper mesas, with lovely trumpet-shaped white flowers, which contains atropine (the active ingredient in belladonna)—had been Don Juan's own teacher's ally, but he himself didn't like it: datura gives you power, he said, not knowledge, and it's demanding and fickle like a woman, enslaving its users.

I go into some detail here because Carlos found a natural ally in the datura, while the little smoke scared him silly: Civilized 20th Century Man, you see, with his classical hang-ups. On datura, Carlos did some apparently successful divination, with the help of two lizards which he had to catch, then to sew up the mouth of one and the eyelids of the other (if you can imagine Carlos 20th-Century Castane-da doing such things, despite his fears of being *seen* by somebody, you can begin to appreciate how much of a brujo Don Juan must have been). Also, on another occasion, he grew enormous, limber legs, and flew. With the little smoke, the once he was able to get past his terror, Don Juan turned him into a crow: first his body disapperaed, then legs grew out of his chin, wings from his cheekbones, and so on. He flew that time, too, as a crow, with other crows. Very easy, said Don Juan; anyone can turn into a crow, that's elementary.

You think someone's kidding, don't you? Carlos, too, tried desperately to reinterpret his experiences in terms of the only "objective" reality he'd ever been taught to believe in. He kept asking pathetic questions: if a third party had been present, would *he* have seen a crow, or just a man who *thought* he was a crow? Time and again, Don Juan tried to make him understand that such questions simply did not apply:

"The particular thing to learn is how to get to the crack between the worlds and how to enter the other world. There is a crack between the two worlds, the world of the diableros and the world of the living men. There is a place where these two worlds overlap. The crack is here. It opens and closes like a door in the wind. To get there a man must exercise his will. . . . "

Poor Carlos. He got one glimpse of that crack, his hair stood on end, and he'll never stop running away from it until the day he dies. But who can say for sure that he wouldn't have acted the same way? Certainly not I. But that's not the area of Don Juan's wisdom I wish I had; what I want to know about is that "one single world" he lived in so wisely and well.

Neither of these books, I shouldn't have to point out, is "pro-dope." At least one friend of mine—the one who gave me the book—hasn't dropped acid since he read *The Electric Kool-Aid Acid Test*: it raised too many questions he'll have to answer first. And nobody in his right mind, having read *The Teachings of Don Juan*, would want to go messing around with peyote or mushrooms or datura, at least without a trustworthy teacher by his side. Both—but especially the latter—are serious works that tell us more about our enormous, dangerous ignorance of inner realities than they do about anyone's certain knowledge. They stand at the edge of the last known frontier, and point out—or rather, in.

They tell me it's 238,866 miles from the center of the earth to the center of the moon. I think it might well be a whole lot longer trip to the center of a human consciousness. But,

Once there was a way
To get back homeward,
Once there was a way
To get back home——

and that's what we've got to do, you know: find that way again, somehow, get back there, clean up that godawful mess we're sure to find, and start all over. A lot of heads don't even know it yet, but that's where they're going. That's what it's all about.

—Paul Johnson

Allan Ginsberg

330 A.D. the state took over (co-opted) religion and formed official church=Constantine "accepted" Christ. Simultaneously purge of all communal-hip-ecstatic ideology— GNOSTIC traditions banished into darkness of history as a "heresy"—Council of Nicea (313 A.D.).

Now: the ancient "prescientific" (Gary Snyder's word is "neolithic") gnostic/hermetic/hip understanding of identity (many-dimensional) (psychedelic) re-emerges, accompanied by resurrection of texts (modern spells, Dead Sea Essene Scrolls, Paracelsus, Blake reprints with color, etc.) and GNOSTIC (formerly heretical) understandings of universe compete with established authoritarian Jehovaic interpretations, Oriental books now available on mass scale: I Ching, Tibetan Book of the Dead, etc.

(According to Mandean Myth, Jehovah was a con man (CIA), the snake was a messenger from Nirvana.)

Gnostic (formerly supressed heretical) tradition is Western imagery for exactly same ideas in Hinduism, Buddhism and American Indian Creation and Reality myths.

i.e. yes, yes, yes Hindusim is another culture, useless here: our Western equivalent is the Gnostic tradition—all western images.

See Gary Snyder's Earth House Hold *(New Directions, New York, 1969) for complete application of above to U.S. POLITICS.*

LSD is an agent which "inhibits conditioned reflexes"* thus catalyzing unconditioned consciousness equal to old-fashioned (pre-scientific-Neolithic) religious "mystic" apprehension.

*Artificial Psychosis, *Dr. Jiri Roubechek (Prague, 1958)*

LIBERATION June 1969

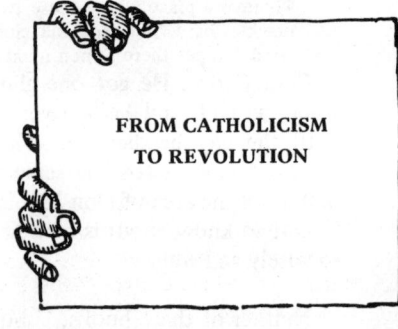

FROM CATHOLICISM
TO REVOLUTION

RUFUS-
THE RADICAL REPTILE

CHILDHOOD AND EARLY YOUTH

NEWLY HATCHED, THE WORLD LOOKED GOOD TO HIM...

GEE! NICE PLACE!

?

...BUT NOT FOR LONG!!

WITHIN HOURS HE WAS CAPTURED BY THE PET INDUSTRY...

"We do not feel like a cool, swinging generation— we are eaten up by an intensity we cannot name."
Student speaker at Radcliffe
graduation ceremonies in 1968.

This article is about the way thousands of young Catholics in my generation have moved into the New Left, the underground, the counter-culture. There is a joke in New Left circles that the movement is made up of Jews and Catholics and a few lost Protestants. There isn't much in the way of statistical evidence to support that observation—only the McClellan Committee has membership lists—but it is pretty clear that there are disproportionate numbers of Catholics on the left. It is an extraordinary phenomenon and it is no accident.

I do not wish to speak directly about those Catholics on the left whose political activity is pointed towards Christians, who identify themselves as Catholics and Christians and who tend to define their radicalism in prophetic Christian language. They speak of their acts as witness and they speak for themselves. But there are thousands of young people who might be regarded by orthodox priests or bishops as "fallen away" Catholics; they wryly acknowledge their Catholic roots, though now they identify first with the Movement. Three of the best known examples are Mario Savio, Mike Klonsky (last year's SDS president), and Tom Hayden.

There are connections between the Catholic background of such people and their involvement with the Movement, or the counter-culture. Those connections are deep and personal: they are part of a process unfolding on an immense scale all over the country, the world. I write about them largely from my own experi-

MEMORIES OF A (LATTER-DAY) CATHOLIC GIRLHOOD

From the convent school to the counter-culture

KATHY MULHERIN

ence, so I cannot get it down one-two-three like a good journalist. What follows is a kind of collage, or a collection of voices. It's hard not to be confused about what has happened to us—we are not sure where we are, where we are headed. I'm hoping you'll recognize something.

And although it's Catholics I describe, I find myself frequently quoting Jews or black people who often articulate our experience more accurately.

I—The Fifties

They say that the generation of the '60s is activist, that the kids in the '50s were "passive," "uncommitted," that it was a "square" decade, and that young people wanted nothing so much as to follow the rules and to get ahead. But the generation of the '60s was growing up in the '50s.

"Somebody once wrote that Eisenhower was cotton candy in the mouth of history—well—that's how I felt then, you know? Fuzz! You know, like the lining in my boots." Lenny Heller, a co-
founder, with David Harris,
of the Resistance.

Underneath the fuzz there was a deep, passionate energy. It was trapped, though, which made all of us a little crazy. Recently a young free-lance rock critic named Michael Lydon, who was raised a Catholic, tried to describe his feelings during that period. When Lydon was 15, his hero was Charley Starkweather, "1958's crazy-mixed up Nebraska teenage killer," who at the age of

19 ran away with his girl friend and shot, stabbed and beat 11 people in four days. Lydon writes:

When I was at parochial school in the early '50s, we used to skip out of the playground at lunch time to steal cigarettes at Rosie's candy store. I remember playing out an escape drama in my mind that included turning and mowing down the nuns in the playground with a machine gun just as I was at the top of the wall ready to drop to the sidewalk on the other side. I figured it was the same for Charley. There I was, listlessly losing a battle with the forces telling me to grow up, do well, compete, accumulate, and train all eccentricity and fancy out of my mind. But out there, . . . Charley was running and blazing away, . . .

That era was Charley's context, . . . Even now I revel in its mannered magnificence: the chopped, blocked, and dropped Mercs with dice hanging from the rear view mirrors and tassels along the back windows peeling out of the school parking lot, . . . packs of Luckies rolled up in the sleeves of muscle T-shirts, girls with kerchiefs over drying pin curls, their combs stuck through wallets bulging with pictures or down into thick white socks over black penny loafers, . . . hops in the gym, and slide stepping to get the most noise out of heel taps. It was a real culture; not empty rebellion, as adults liked to say, but the defiant self-definition of kids who felt together. . . .

Killing really was the final thing. If adults were telling you that 'It's just a phase you'll grow out of,' you had to show them all that turmoil was for real. . . . It's hard to be patronizing to a mad-dog killer; . . .

from *US* magazine

It was not that we were murderous, but we were hungry for experience, for real culture, something we could touch, and taste.

By the mid-'50s, Catholic and Jewish culture had been pretty thoroughly secularized and Americanized, but not entirely:

What are we fighting for? Our souls. Isn't that a worthy cause?

Soul is formed from the mysterious landscapes of childhood. For me it was the paste of slush and sawdust on the floors of Avenue M butchershops, the sound of the subway, the heavy gray mass of the apartment building I lived in, its dim hallways, the elevator buttons I stood on tiptoe to reach, and the ominous superintendent who kept chasing me through the building in my nightmares.

Don't scoff at the soul. Don't call it imaginary. Your soul is formed from powerful doses of reality like mother's tit and favorite toy, family brawl and schoolyard fighting. Your soul is real all right, much realer than your citizenship, which is spun out of such doubtful material as history textbooks and wire service reports and television commercials.

Establishment politics conspires with capitalism to steal our souls away. Radical politics conspires with art to steal our souls back. . . .

Marvin Garson in the *Village Voice*

You see, alienation is too simple an idea to encompass what is going on inside of us. We reflect the people we came from. A young black woman, a poet named Nikki Giovanni, from Knoxville, Tennessee, writing about her experience as a black person, insists that the birth of the civil rights movement did not spring from the fact that there were restaurants or schools which were segregated. The source lay much deeper, in the "base experiences," of people's lives: "Base experiences affect people; before they are born, events happen that shape their lives. My family on my grandmother's side are fighters. My family on my father's side are survivors. I'm a revolutionist. It's only logical. . . . Beliefs come, generally, through training; and training is based on feeling" (*US* Magazine). And Robbie Robertson, a member of the best country rock band in America (The Band), told a *Time* reporter recently, "Your roots really are everything that has ever impressed you, and how much of it you can remember."

Exactly. Beliefs come through training, training is based on feeling, and feeling, or intensity, comes out of the experiences deeply impressed upon your soul.

I remember vividly the upper class Catholic boarding school which completely enveloped my teenage years. The school was a locked-up world of its own: within its walls flourished that baroque, European Catholicism which has been so thoroughly repudiated by the forces of renewal, and with good reason. It was authoritarian, myopically narrow, elitist, racist—a relic of another era. (Incidentally, the school was closed recently.)

But its very "irrelevance" made it a unique and wonderful gift. Over 150 girls were crowded into an old drafty estate so removed from the world that I was never aware in the whole four years I lived there that one of America's largest and ugliest black ghettos was only a few miles away. The halls were dark and chilly and we were ordered around nearly every minute of the day. Still, mysteriously, there was space and time and rich material for my energetic adolescent fantasy life. The chapel was a miniature Gothic cathedral, at once primitive and highly civilized; it seemed like a deep cave, dimly lit and full of stalactites and spires. Standing up from both ends of each pew there were two-foot-high ornamental posts, intricately carved with grapes, vines, snakes; from a certain angle they formed an elaborate totem forest, a silent army of wooden worshippers. We were encouraged to spend a lot of time in that chapel—we were kept pretty busy but I used to go in there at night and peer into the dark sanctuary and my head would swim with saints and God and the sweaty little anxieties of adolescence.

Life was organized around the liturgical year—Lent was long and barren and purple; it was easy to feel the appropriate sorrow in Philadelphia's damp, gloomy winters. But the liturgical year was a source of joy too: besides the numerous saints' days and holidays provided by Holy Mother Church, the religious order which ran the school had on its own accumulated over a century of rituals, practices and symbols—and had woven them all into the fabric of school life.

Loyalty was the key to survival in that school, and, my friends tell me, the key to survival as well for seminarians, nuns, everyone who was deeply involved in religious institutions. There were kids in my school who hated it and wanted badly to get out, to get out into the world of real people and boys and cigarettes and lipstick. They were regarded by the nuns and the rest of us as rather pathetic figures, even as traitorous if they were adamant enough; God knows they were miserable.

But if you were loyal, and I was, you could be happy. Michael Rossman once characterized the spirit of the Free Speech Movement as one of "fierce joy," born of a novel and intense communal experience. Something like the same spirit often animated the days at my convent school. In retrospect the moral and social rigidity of the place seems incredible, but at the time, our world was so complete—full, playful, momentous. A photographer once came to our school to do a photo-essay about us and after hanging around for a few days she remarked wistfully that she had rarely seen so many happy, carefree kids. She was probably aware of how much money it cost to create such a carefree situation. Many of the girls had

. . . RUDELY DUMPED INTO A TANK WITH SOME OTHER BABY GATORS . . .

HEADS UP!

ARRGH!

. . . AND OFFERED FOR SALE!

YOUR CHOICE ← $1.98

AFTER SEVERAL BORING DAYS IN THE TANK, HE WAS BOUGHT BY A LITTLE BOY AND HIS MOM . . .

THE ONE WITH THE BIG BLUE EYES!

YOUR CHOICE ← $1.98

unhappily married parents and they were relieved to be away from them. In any case, the photographer was right, we were innocent, sheltered, and the dramatic religious atmosphere lent a quality of grandeur and intensity to our lives that would have been difficult to sustain in the "outside world."

I do not wish to romanticize the place. It was a "total institution." Years later, I had to spend a couple of weeks in jail. I recognized it at once: it was like boarding school. There was no veil of illusion in jail, but the structure was the same. One day, a gentle, simple girl named Alice, jailed for heroin addiction, confided to me that she had thought jail was going to be terrible, but she'd been in and out half a dozen times and now, "I kind of like it here. It's not so bad." I nodded.

The nuns were just as deluded as we were—they really believed that they were engaged in a lively struggle for our souls. They wanted very much to produce exemplary children of the Sacred Heart, and daughters of the Church. The model was a creature of gentility and grace, of sweet humility and vigorous devotion. What they actually tended to produce was something like the Kennedy daughters (all of whom attended these schools by the way): a devout, active young woman of the upper classes, capable of taking her place at the side (and a little to the rear) of one of the third generation Irish or Italian Catholic young men who were just beginning to move into the higher reaches of politics and business.

Years later I discovered with great bitterness that my school and those nuns were successful in large measure because they were so brilliantly skilled in assimilating and raising the social standing of their students. Who were sent there for that purpose (myself included).

We were taught in a hundred different ways that the outside world, the secular world, was godless and inhuman (they adapted to their own uses the critique of mass culture which was so popular in those days). *But,* we were made to understand that it would be possible, even desirable to go out into that world and work among its people, *provided* we maintained a vigilant devotion. That is, you could marry an executive of say, IBM, or Standard Oil, and mingle freely in the secular world of business and society as long as you took care to attend mass every morning, prayed a lot, did charity work (the genteel Junior League variety was considered appropriate) and raised your numerous children to be good Catholics.

In the cold light of the last dozen years such a perspective seems hypocritical indeed, and there is no denying it.

But what was nonetheless important for me and for thousands of other Catholic kids raised in somewhat less affluent surroundings, was that the symbols were compelling and that many of the people who ruled our lives were fine, sincere, intelligent, and dedicated to their work and to us. There is no denying that either.

I wanted to be a missionary when I grew up. I learned from the nuns that it was not necessary to go off to "darkest Africa" to do that kind of work—one could develop a secular career, or a religious career in a secular context, which would serve the same purpose. I wanted to give my life to the salvation of my fellow man and I knew that in America the odds would be against me.

In fact, I was certain that there was no possibility for social change. I was deeply imbued with a sense of history as a long procession of splendor, tragedy, evil, beauty, and for all its upheaval, a certain regularity. The history of the Church, we were often reminded, was not always righteous ("after all, it *is* a *human* institution!"), but it was for always. Salvation was a painful, plodding, absorbing, one-to-one affair. Evil, crime, sin, poverty would always be with us—though, thankfully, not *too* close to anyone *we* associated with.

...WHO TOOK HIM BACK TO NEW HAVEN AND TAUGHT HIM TO DO TRICKS IN EXCHANGE FOR MEALS!

PICK A CARD!

THIS WENT ON FOR SOME TIME... BUT ONE DAY HE GAVE THE LITTLE BOY A PLAYFUL NIP! HE DIDN'T KNOW IT THEN...

?

WAAAA!

HE'S ALMOST BIT MY HAND OFF!

BUT THIS WAS A SERIOUS INFRACTION OF THE RULES! THE BOY AND HIS MOM TALKED IT OVER AND DECIDED...

YA GOTTA UNDERSTAND!

YEAH! =SNIFF=

II—Fools Gather

It was this fundamental despair about the nature of change which drew me to the Myth of the Fool. At the age of 19 or 20 my hero was Prince Myshkin in Dostoevsky's *Idiot*: he was gentle, epileptic, given to losing his cool in critical situations, so he never really did much good, but he was so translucently good that he moved people deeply, even if he couldn't help them in their practical agonies. He was exemplary, so tender and full of his own insignificance that those who came into contact with him found themselves on intimate terms with him. He seemed to see through everybody and to love them for what he saw. My teachers introduced me to a critical analysis which assured me that Myshkin was Dostoevsky's idea of Christ.

Many religious writers have pointed to the spirit of abandonment, or recklessness which characterizes the true Christian: one who gives all without weighing the consequences, who is so devoted to Christ that he or she is released, liberated, made free. The implication was that anyone like that would often come into conflict with the dictates of the social order in which she or he lived. The nuns took care to curb our enthusiasm for such a life—they were not eager to unlease on the world a crowd of females, wandering about half-mad with religion like medieval freaks, saints and minstrels.

You see, the point is almost too simple. Some of us were getting heady ideas about what the religious life required. Those who did not want to enter the convent began preparing for a life of ascetic poverty and dedication to the people of God. And even those who despaired of storing up the will power for such a rigorous future still hungered for the intensity that kind of life offered. Maybe *meaning* is more accurate—we wanted our lives to be full of meaning: we knew the world, by itself, could offer little, and that it would bring enormous pressure to bear on the meaning our church had given us, try to wear it down, destroy it. Outside the Church others, like Camus, bore the same message: the world is absurd. And a few years later the Beatles were to write a song about a fool on a hill whom "nobody wants to know . . ./ They can see that he's just a fool."

Please understand; we were not fanatical kids, we were pretty ordinary middle class young men and women. By the time we were 21, we knew there wasn't a hell of a lot you could do. We had that in common with others of our generation:

No one really believed anyone could do anything much about anything. . . . It was against this background that we began to move: not out of hope, but because we had to, because that context of Impossible granted us a weird sort of freedom. . . . freedom to be what we are, for we are all there is.

At the same time somehow, we were also beginning to perceive that this mighty Church, this backbone and fabric of our lives, was losing its grip. Even if we had been inclined to ignore that fact, or make our own accommodation with it, the Church itself was confronting it. I graduated from college in 1963. By the next fall, the Vatican Council had begun to affect me.

What the Council did for me, and for millions of others, was to legitimize the delegitimization of the Church. It was that simple. The renewal was a direct attack on the moral and intellectual authority of the Church, of the whole late-scholastic tradition:

Cardinal O'Boyle was right when he said recently of the Washington dissenters [the priests who publicly opposed the Church ban on artificial birth control]: 'They're not testing birth control so much as the au-

thority of the Church; it's the same sort of rebellion that is happening everywhere in the world.'

New York Times editorial

Right on, your excellency, right on.

Of course, the Council alone was not so powerful. Those who remained locked up in that world, those pockets, those grottoes the Church had established and guarded so jealously, could ignore the Council and the 20th-century. Most of us could not.

1963 was the year that Bull Connor's dogs tore into civil rights marchers in Birmingham, Alabama, the year that President Kennedy was assassinated; and the TV cameras brought it all back home. It's possible the Council might not have released us so abruptly from the myths which ruled our youth if those years had been relatively peaceful. But it was the beginning—for us—of a whole new era.

1964 was the year of the Free Speech Movement at the University of California in Berkeley. It was the start not only of the public delegitimization of the university, but one of the birthplaces of the "counter-culture." We learned from the Free Speech Movement that we had the power to *define the terms* for ourselves. FSM was communal; it was theater and politics; it was play and work. Politics and life-style interacted, each creating a context for the other.

The Vatican Council made it clear that it would no longer do simply to obey, to follow the rules. The rules changed and the Church didn't seem so certain, so *right* anymore. How then, was one to live? The question was forced wide open. The Council also defined the relationship between man and God as horizontal, if you will: man made contact with God through other men. The notion that each man and woman made contact with God primarily individually, vertically, was dead—had been an illusion. (Inasmuch as I had suffered agonies all those years in school because I couldn't *find* God, never knew whether God knew about *me,* I was immensely relieved to come upon this discovery; I was also angry, for the energy I had poured into that search for God now seemed a waste of time and strength.)

I am not certain at this point, for each of us perceived the problem differently. I think that we sensed even before the Council that the symbols, the images which formed what Nikki Giovanni calls our "base experiences" were beginning to lose their power. If you went to a parochial school in some sooty industrial town, maybe you caught on to that long before I did. If you had to cope with the world on *its* terms it was very difficult though not impossible to avoid some hard questions about the Church and its immutability. I have friends who had been exposed to the poverty and oppression of blacks and Chicanos and had been fighting the Church on this score for several years before the Council —fighting and failing and despairing. They were bitterly conscious of the venality and corruption of the institution.

All I know is that none of us wanted to settle down with our disillusionment and stumble through the years like Saul Bellow's *Herzog.* I thought Herzog was a jerk, full of recriminations, self-pity and pompous notions about the course of history and the nature of man. Not tragic, merely pathetic.

Do you understand? We were hungry for experience, for some kind of real life, for some way to tap our energy.

And what were the choices? Who were the models, the heroes? Who, what should we be? Well, look, I was sitting there in graduate school, miserable, on fire with anger at the lies and illusions I had accepted so trustingly and eagerly. There was FSM and there that testy bunch of

cardinals and bishops bickering in Rome about the future of Christianity. It took me a long time to choose, but in retrospect it seems pretty obvious.

The ironic thing was that the Church had taught me that there could be no change—no real change. Now, it was the Church, caught up in profound upheaval, struggling to reform itself which showed me that change was after all, possible. I felt a tremendous surge of energy.

But the questions raised were endless, and their implications very deep. What should we be? Who were we? Whose judgment should we trust for guidance in trying to figure out what was happening to the country and the world and ourselves? Everybody—Jews, Catholics, WASPs, nothings—everybody understood that the problem was *moral.* But what could we do? What could we expect?

Never trust anybody over thirty.
Never underestimate the stupidity of the Administration.   FSM maxims

Once you see one *truth, everything becomes clear, all the lies, the bullshit, the things they make you do you really* see!

Lenny Heller, Resistance organizer, talking about the first impact of FSM on him.

Oski dolls, Pompom girls, U.C. all the way.
Oh, what fun it is to have your mind reduced to clay.
Civil rights, politics, just get in the way.
Questioning authority when you should obey.

FSM Christmas carol set to "Jingle Bells."

. . . the best among the people who enter [college] must for four years wander aimlessly much of the time questioning why they are on campus at all, doubting whether there is any point in what they are doing, and looking toward a very bleak life afterward in a game in which all of the rules have been made up, which one cannot really amend.

It is a bleak scene, but it is all a lot of us have to look forward to. Society provides no challenges. . . . The most exciting things going on in America today are movements to change America. . . .

Mario Savio in a speech on the steps of Sproul Hall during FSM

Politics is the coming together of people to make decisions about their lives.

From a SNCC leaflet in a Lowndes County organizing campaign

All this is pretty familiar now. But the most important thing about the whole experience was that the young people who took part in it *defined the terms;* and they did it by acting.

A movement of young people who defined themselves through action. It had been many years since that kind of politics had faded from the scene. It's impossible to describe how many old assumptions, methods, traditions, values, institutions, systems, were uprooted in every one of us—one could almost feel the tug of each nerve and root. When Lenny Heller said everything became clear once he saw one truth, he meant to describe a feeling: we knew we were moving to a wholly different vantage point; everything looked different but at first we couldn't see much beyond our noses.

It was a painful, step-by-step process and in the early '60s it was again the Church that taught me most of the truths other people were learning in the South and in the university. My civil rights activity, such as it was, was focused on racism in religious institutions. On that level, the Church showed me much about how a system works, how bureaucracies obstruct change, how vested interests

maintain their power, how stupid old men rule the lives of the young, the poor, the powerless. It was the sort of experience which made many people begin to lose their fear of the high and the mighty in authority.

I turned to the New Left because its members were really dealing with the personal, social, political and religious problems I was facing. They were developing an analysis which helped to explain the incredible resistance to reform in the church and the state. They were carving a life style whose basic thrust was ethical. They were studying and fighting poverty and racism and they were trying to capture communal experience in politics. It was exciting and liberating.

And there were Catholics—theologians, priests, authority figures if you will—who were beginning to look all over the world, everywhere, for sources of inspiration, for ways to make change and for instruction in what kind of changes to make: people like Michael Novak, Dan Callahan, Robert McAfee Brown and others. Like the young nuns, priests, seminarians who were beginning to move. I did not feel alone.

Novak more than anyone taught me that I did not have to "leave" the Church to maintain my integrity. He introduced me to a wide variety of intellectual traditions and religious sources within and beyond the Catholic tradition; slowly I began to redefine my religious world view.

Occasionally, I would suddenly remember my rigorously Thomist education and wonder whether I was meandering into heresy; but the comical truth was there was nobody to excommunicate you. It was very clear that the bishops and the Curia types were too busy trying to keep the lid on to worry about me and my heresies.

It was a playful, comforting feeling to know that I did not have to leave my people to build my life. I did not want to cut my roots. It was obvious that we were going to need all the roots we had in the coming storm. Recently Novak wrote some articles in the *National Catholic Reporter* declaring that to be a Catholic is to belong to a people. Doubtless we need reminding since the Church is so torn, but when I was growing up that was my natural context; so deeply was I imbued with that truth that even now I can affirm it.

What I am getting at is complex, not entirely clear to me, difficult to dry out, separate and harden into words. Do you see that the process by which one moved from orthodox Catholicism to radicalism and the counter-culture was connected by thousands of threads—some you had to break before you could move, others drew you along, led the way.

Turning to the Liturgy

Maybe one way of getting at the delicate blending of our religious tradition and this new way of life being born (Birth: breaking with the old tradition/drawing strength from it.) is to turn to liturgy.

All my life the crux of the liturgy, the only part that always interested me, was communion—communion and the consecration, because the moment of consecration was still, stark, full of majesty, because communion was eating God and I really dug getting *close* to God. Once in high school, a nun was showing a few of us around the chapel sacristy. To impress upon us the dramatic character of the transubstantiation, she opened a large, flat cookie tin full of unconsecrated wafers and bade us eat some. Shocked and thrilled, we reached in timidly, growing bolder as she encouraged us. In a minute we were silently grabbing handfuls and stuffing them into our mouths. The nun soon became uneasy and closed the tin. She never opened it again though we sometimes asked her to.

The consecration and communion were the most tangible moments of the religious life, but the whole liturgy was pretty tangible. A friend of mine, raised by anti-religious parents in a rural California county, told me that as a kid he used to visit all the churches in town from time to time just to see what they were doing. "I thought the inside of the Catholic church must be Paradise—it was real pretty. They and all these pretty things on the altar and gold leaf on the walls and statues. It was the prettiest place in town."

The renewal movement wanted to bring the liturgy out of the encrusted tradition in which it was embedded and give it fresh life and relevance. The only trouble was that the old tradition, however irrelevant, had more soul than the feeble efforts of the liberals who dominated the renewal movement. They managed to free the liturgy for experimentation; great beauty and rich experience has come out of that, but they are caught in a transition, an almost aimless wandering. The current state of Christian liturgy expresses more poignantly than anything else the profound confusion and ambivalence of Christianity today.

It was not long before the new liturgy and even the most "advanced" experiments became boring:

What the kids really want out of liturgical experiments is novelty. They like guitars at mass and all that but if the format doesn't change all the time they get bored and stop coming.

A Jesuit sociologist at the
University of San Francisco

These kids are really different now. They're more selfish. They are always trying to get us to change little regulations about hair, ties—and that's not the point. They don't care about mass—even guitar masses; only about one third of them go to mass on Sunday. An unhappy Dominican principal of a private Catholic day school for boys in Los Angeles

Nor is it just the kids. Who talks about the "underground church" now? Who can be bothered going underground just for a home mass? The underground church was not merely co-opted by reform within the Church. Many of its members lost interest in it and dropped out. There was something missing: Sister Corita's celebration of Wonder Bread ignored the fact that it's terrible bread—expensive and flimsy. It was the same error that Harvey Cox made in the *Secular City*. Why celebrate something that's sick? We were exhorted to love the world—but what part of it? What was required was a critical theology: a politics.

There are thousands, perhaps millions of Catholics in this country who are waiting—still hungry for a liturgy which will invest their lives with religious import, a liturgy by which they can transform the world, celebrate what there is to celebrate and gather strength to fight what must be destroyed. They have few illusions; they are clean and dry as a desert. They wait.

But all this hasn't put an end to living liturgy. Liturgy as politics has brought off some really great experiences in the last few years.

A demonstration is not basically a protest against anything, it is a demonstration FOR something, it is a fertility ritual, an assertion of life that demands to live in spite of the concrete environment they are trying to force on us. Then the law, which is on a Death Trip, comes out and beats people up and throws them in jail. Sandy Darlington, a rock critic writing about the Oakland 7 Trial in the *San Francisco Express Times*

... HE CALLED THE A.S.P.C.A FOR ASSISTANCE!

ZIP-TICKY-TICKY!

THEY SEEMED VERY NICE AND EAGER TO HELP...

CAN I HELP YOU SIR?

WELL...UH...

... BUT SOMETHING BOTHERED HIM ABOUT THE ORGANIZATION ...

JEEZ! THE HANDBAG!!

UH...

It is a liturgy which grows the way a politics grows: it expresses the development and the weaknesses of the participants. There are numberless examples:

—The sit-in around a police car on the Berkeley campus which sparked FSM. Michael Rossman quotes Mario Savio: "That event has always seemed to me to have the archaic primitive quality of a childhood dream."

—The first Be-In, January 14, 1967, in Golden Gate Park in San Francisco, and nearly every Be-In after it. Each one openly liturgical, religious, each a joyful celebration of the life and the values we were learning to create.

—The exorcism of the Pentagon by witches and Yippies at the 1967 March on the Pentagon at the end of Stop the Draft Week.

—"Beautiful Friday," the last day of Stop the Draft week in Oakland, California:

. . . on Friday we created barricades out of cars and other available material—The barricades . . . made Oakland feel for just one day a different style and approach to the sacred symbols of modern America. We painted downtown Oakland with our anti-war slogans showing people that in some cases political slogans are important enough to be written on walls and windows of public and private buildings. . . . We treated the private car—that crucial part of the American dream —as material for our barricades. We blocked traffic and changed the streets from thoroughfares of business into a place for people to walk, talk, argue and even dance. We felt liberated and we called our barricaded streets liberated territory.

> Frank Bardacke, one of the Oakland 7

Then there were the thousands of draft card burnings all over America, the acts of sanctuary, the building of Peoples' Park and the fight to keep it, the street fights which have erupted all over the country in white communities: kids fighting the police with shouts or rocks or water, fighting to hang onto their turf or the culture they have defined as their own.

Let the theologians define what liturgy is. Ask anyone in the Movement, in the counter-culture, if he or she is religious. Few will deny it. Our liturgies celebrate us, our brotherhood, our god-likeness, the world, our visions; our liturgies confront our fears and fantasies; our liturgies all possess an inner tension of vigorous dialogue; our liturgies are relevant—paltry world in this context; our liturgies refresh us and nourish our communal bonds; they are intense and dramatic, and they are forged out of our activity.

The family that disobeys together stays together.
> Abbie Hoffman, upon being released from jail with his wife, after Stop the Draft Week

For the Hassidic Jews every gesture was potentially holy, a form of prayer, when it was made with a reverence for God. In the same way a gesture is always a form of wisdom—an act is wisdom—when it is suffused with knowledge, made with a reverence for the truth.

> Peter Marin, in "The Open Truth and Fiery Vehemence of Youth," in *Center Magazine*

In the same article Marin talks about the human need for ritual:

I once wrote that education through its limits denied the gods, and that they would return in the young in one form or another to haunt us. That is happening now. You can sense it as the students gather with their simplistic moral certainty, at the

gates of the university. It is almost as if the young were once more possessed by Bacchanalian gods, were once again inhabited by divinities whose honor we have neglected. Those marvelous and threatening energies . . . we lack rituals for their use and balance.

Primitive cultures dealt with this problem, I think, through their initiation rites, the rites of passage; they legitimized and accept these energies and turned them toward collective aims; they were merged into the life of the tribe and in this way acknowledged, honored, and domesticated—but not destroyed. In most initiation rites the participant is led through the mythical or sacred world (or symbolic version) and is then returned, transformed, to the secular one as a new person, with a new role. . . . He is put in touch with the sources of energy, the divinities of the tribe. In many other cultures the symbolic figures in the rites are unmasked at the end, as if to reveal to the initiate the interpenetration of the secular and sacred worlds. . . . The rites are in a sense a social contract, a binding up; one occurring specifically, profoundly, on a deep psychic level. The individual is redefined in the culture by his new relation to its mysteries, its gods, to one form or another of nature. . . . These ritualized relationships of each man to the shared gods bind the group together; they form the substance of the culture: an invisible landscape that is real and felt, commonly held, a language which resides in each man and in which, in turn, each man resides.

We are religious; we are attempting to deal with the most profound human needs and relationships, and we have had to begin almost from the beginning. So we bring to this effort everything from the past which might be useful. And you see, Catholicism, almost by virtue of the fact that it allowed itself to fall out of touch with the modern world, was dealing with those needs *on some levels* better than most institutions.

I am a Catholic, simply, neither Orthodox, nor Roman, nor Anglican, because the Catholic Church has preserved the anthropological, the folk religion, that engendered and nourished Western civilization. These are our own rites of passage and of the year. . . . Although as a corporation it [the Church] defines faith as belief and excludes the disbeliever, it can still nourish faith as life in an age of faithlessness. Religion is something men do, not something they believe.

> Kenneth Rexroth in *Commonweal*

It was on the wave of this kind of dynamic that most of us have ridden, struggled from Catholicism into the New Left.

III—Liberation

But the process which began in the South in the late '50s and spread to the North by the early '60s would make no sense if described in purely political terms, or purely collective terms. Each of us has gone through, is going through a very personal process of liberation. The counter-culture grew up out of the energies released by that process; it grew up to nourish and sustain the fragile ambitions, styles, habits we were developing.

The only reason for being a revolutionary in our time is because it's a better way to live.
> Danny (The Red) Cohn-Bendit

It is impossible to say what came first, how it got started. One thing led to another, not necessarily in a

linear procession. Drugs, music, funky life styles, clothes, sex—everything affecting everything else.

Marijuana has been around for a long time. I don't know what happened to me, innocent convent girl, that when somebody I liked and trusted in California offered me a joint I smoked it. But it's easy to say why I kept smoking it. It was really nice. Drugs helped us to break down the barriers between ourselves and nature, between ourselves, between our insides and our outsides. Drugs help you to see more clearly. Anybody who has ever seen a speed freak knows that they can deepen your confusion and ruin your mind too. I don't want to get into an argument about the merits of drugs: they are all around and our culture is shot through with their influence. Drugs have also proved to the counter-culture that it is religious.

But drugs were really a very small part of the process of liberation for most of us. Each of us got turned on to different kinds of experiences. I spent a lot of time in the mountains, in Big Sur, on the beach. I began to get some notions of what it means to be related, integrated into, the environment.

Rock music was very important, especially the sounds that began to come out of California in the mid-'60s. It was very good music. It was good, it was ours, and it was physical:

> . . . then, as if a signal had been given, as if the *Mind* had shouted to the *Body*, '*I'm ready!*'—the Twist, superseding the Hula Hoop, burst upon the scene like a nuclear explosion, sending its fallout of rhythm in the Minds and Bodies of the people. . . . Negroes knew something fundamental had changed. '*Man, what done got into them ofays?*' one asked. '*They trying to get back*,' said another. . . .
> '*Get back?*' said a girl, arching her brows quizzically, '*Get back from where?*'
> '*From wherever they've been*,' said the cat, '*where else?*'

Eldridge Cleaver, on white people learning to dance, in *Soul On Ice*.

The music isn't just noise and rhythm either. It is embedded deep in a dozen American musical traditions, and it is *funky*. Do you know what funky is? Funky is something that tastes good, smells good, looks a little ragged, odd, and stinks a little. Funky is a hippy dressed in an old plaid shirt of his father's, a $40 leather vest, old, old levis, washed pale blue, cowboy boots, a big black hat like the Amish wear, long stringy hair and a great, thick mustache. Funky is what *Playboy* magazine is not.

> . . . *How I'd love to be in Berkeley right now, to roll in that mud, frolic in that sty of funky revolution, to breathe in its heady fumes*, . . .
> Eldridge Cleaver, *Soul On Ice*

Funky is not camp. The difference is irony, an earthy sensuality, and a certain wry nostalgia, the playful aspect of a serious search for roots. Funky is sexual.

Young Catholics are more likely to lose their virginity and their sexual illusions with one another under the stern yet oddly tolerant protection of the Church. But sexual joy and freedom, that sweet intimacy, knowledge —the absorbing play of two people naked, acting naturally—that is more elusive. Jansenism sucked our young passion; sexual energies, trapped in baroque tunnels, longed to be released, to flow free.

The radical left and the counter-culture, with their willingness to experiment, their natural sexuality, their hatred of guilt, was an attractive place to dig and search for the root. Those of us raised Catholic had carried our sexuality separate, hidden from ourselves in a maze we unwittingly helped to construct. The struggle to free ourselves of it has taught us only too well how it is possible for men and women to be warped and twisted by a sick social system; it is a truth we can taste—a radical truth.

Again, it's not that simple. Catholicism was a pretty funky religion in my childhood, even more so in the periods I read about, like the Middle Ages, the Renaissance. If it was absolutist and rigid, everybody knew that Holy Mother Church could wink at sin, juggle the saints with the sinners. Eventually, I came to think of the Church as a huge, wicked, rich, wise old whore.

Until I was of high school age, I lived with my family in Venezuela, where common-law marriage was a lot more common than the other kind. I remember an elderly nun stationed in a hospital run by the Maryknoll order. She used to go around visiting all the sick men she knew to be living in sin (fathers of five, ten children!) and work on their weakness. Then, once every couple of months she'd round them all up and hold a mass wedding in the tiny hospital chapel. It would be packed with mothers and fathers and children and relatives and nuns and after the wedding everybody would go down to the dining room and have a party.

See, the counter-culture's sexual and moral flexibility was a great liberation, a dramatic reversal of the style of the Church. But then again it was familiar.

Liberation requires concrete models; we sought heroes to show us what was possible. You see, it was *never* true what they said about not trusting anybody over 30; that was just to serve notice that all credentials were being reviewed. From the beginning people had heroes over 30 —sometimes way over 30, like Herbert Marcuse.

No one hero was or is expected to be everything to everyone. Often people have dozens of heroes, full of contradictory qualities. That's why people for example who are adamantly non-violent can admire Che Guevara. I saw connections between St. John of the Cross and Albert Camus; and at the very time when I felt most alienated from the Church I grew close to a middle-aged priest. I studied and imitated Mitchell Goodman, Denise Levertov, Karen and Michael Novak. One of my heroes is 4-years-old. Many are my own age, just ordinary good people.

We knew you couldn't build a life from ideas alone. You had to watch how other people did it. It's like learning a sport or an art; it *is* both sport and art. Aristotle said that. And we demand that our heroes learn from us, respect us, relate to us. Heroes are not solely authority figures, although for people in their late 20s they function that way to some degree. We after all had to break out of the world which kept us under control. Today, the whole system has lost so much authority that it has to use force, brute force to control our younger brothers and sisters. But force is not enough to repair the rent that has opened up in our culture.

For the children. . . . they sense it: there is no one over them; believable authority has disappeared; it has been replaced by experience. . . . The parents of these children, the fathers, still believe in 'someone' over them, insist upon it, . . . demand it for and from their children. The children themselves cannot believe it; the idea means nothing to them.

It is almost as if they are the first real Americans— suddenly free of Europe and somehow fatherless, confused, forced back on their own experience, their own sense of things, even though, at the same time, they are forced to defy their families and schools in order to keep it.

Peter Marin

. . . SOME DISTURBING FACTS!

WOW! THE A.S.P.C.A. IS FUNDED BY THE ROCKE-FELLER FOUNDATION, WHICH OWNS CONTROLLING INTEREST IN AN ALLIGATOR BAG FACTORY IN MOBILE, ALA. !!

DISILLUSIONED AT FIRST, HE WAS FEELING VERY DOWN!

O TEMPORA! O MORES!

WHAT'S TO BECOME OF ME?

BUT SOON HIS DEPRESSION CHANGED TO ANGER!

GNASH! GRRR! RRR!

IV — Revolution

Everyone knows there is a generation gap, but Marin points to something I've been trying to get at obliquely. Our movement, our counter-culture is not ahistorical, not growing up apart from the life of the nation: it is profoundly American. It consciously seeks roots in America. If we repudiate the imperialism in "Manifest Destiny," we celebrate its sheer explosion of energy. We do not feel guilty about the Indians, we study them, imitate them, fight beside them when we can.

We are operating under the same impulse which drew the reformers in the Church back to early Christian history, made them seek to return the Church to its purer roots, to purge itself of the accumulated garbage of the centuries and renew its original purpose.

Thus do reform movements try to legitimize themselves in the eyes of the people by proving that they, and not the established regime, are the true bearers of the people's hopes. Certainly, that is what we are trying unconsciously to do. But we do it in good faith, because every people which has lost its way does well to go back to its roots. Those roots are not always visible, not always recorded in the official histories, not always respectable. And the search must needs be as much instinctive as self-conscious.

It may be that all of this chaos is a way of breaking with the old world and that from it some kind of native American will emerge. Peter Marin

A people is tough like a weed, almost ineradicable, can survive for thousands of years; but empires hatch and die off like insects.
Marvin Garson, in the *Village Voice.*

WE are the people!! We ARE the people!! We are the PEOPLE!!
The chanting reply demonstrators make to the police when the latter make announcements "in the name of the people of the city of New York"

A few years ago I found myself saying, in a *Commonweal* symposium, "America, I don't know you, and I don't like you." I felt pretty alienated. Today, in one sense, I'm more alienated: haunted by paranoid dreams I awake to find reality outstripping the dream. Fred Hampton (chairman of the Chicago Black Panther Party) was murdered in his bed the other night. What was he dreaming just before he woke up? Did he wake up? Fred Hampton is my brother; I want the same things for America Fred wanted, and I believe pretty much what he did about how to get those things: Revolution, armed if necessary. I have not spoken much here of the background against which all these changes occurred in our lives; you know it well. How many lists have you seen, of the multitudinous ways in which horror moves in America, the ways in which our government, our corporations, our military, exploit, plunder, kill the poor people of the world. On this level the explanations are simple: Catholics or not, we have become radicals and revolutionaries because we have been driven to it.

But today I love America, though I don't know it much more deeply; I want to, I want to dig in like a weed. The American people are my people; the Catholic people are too. I'm aware that as I move slowly, reluctantly, towards becoming a revolutionary, and a member of the revolutionary community, the memory which stands out most vividly in my head is the community of faith I was raised in, that I belonged to.

It still delights and amuses me to hear hairy, wild-looking radicals talking awkwardly about revolution in language I first heard from nuns in school, from priests in church: they speak of faith in the people, of dedication, of discipline, of hope, of the struggle we must make. Cynics will retort that we are fanatics, as the nuns and priests were. Were they? Are we?

The other day I laughed out loud to realize suddenly, with a new clarity, that to love your neighbor as yourself is revolutionary. The Catholicism I grew up interpreted that to mean that one should not love oneself at all. The process of liberation I tried to sketch straightened us out on that point. Now, as we come closer together, as we struggle to learn how to make revolution (there is only one *kind* of revolution: "The revolution is moral or not at all." Péguy), we are beginning to discover the cost and weight, to plumb levels of desperation we never imagined and to see that coming together is so difficult that we will not do it until we have to. The only way to love your neighbors as yourself is to marry the lot of them: work together, share everything, fight together, build institutions to support yourselves, break down the barriers between you. That is the starting place of a theology, a politics.

I cannot tell you what this revolution will be like, or if there will be one. I do not know very much about it. We want a country that has no need or desire for imperialism; a country where government is impossible unless the people are deeply involved and committed to it, where health care is free and there is no need for insurance companies, where there are no rich or poor, where the nation's industrial energy is subordinated to the needs of the land and the people, where the ecological context is the ordinary perspective, where technology releases individual energies for creative activity so fantastic we cannot imagine it, and where the social structure is rebuilt to encourage people to get together, not isolate them from one another and call it "individualism." Does all that strike you as Utopian? That's the way it is in Cuba and China, hardly utopias. Does that remark strike you as false? Well, it depends on whom you believe, who controls the terms you use. Which brings us back to where we started.

One thing I know. The Catholic Church and the schools I attended prepared me for this decade, for my life, no worse certainly than Harvard prepared my friends in SDS—in fact I may be a little better off. After all, I was raised an Irish Catholic; I come from a wise, mean, humorous, tough, compassionate, fierce people. My ancestors? The I.R.A. My cousins? The civil rights struggle in Northern Ireland. That's not a bad heritage for a revolutionary.

Do you see now the point of all these words? I wish to speak to you. If you feel despair, that nothing can be done here, it may not be because the situation is hopeless. It may be that you are isolated from the sources of hope, that is, isolated from the people around you, from your own situation. Have you ever tried to organize the people in your building, your block, your neighborhood? Not to sign a petition for this or that, but to get together for good, as a political unit. Have you ever worked with the Black Panthers, joined a GE striker's picket line, taken part in a university sit-in or the occupation of a building? I do not mean to accuse you— only to point out as concretely and gently as I can what I think isolation is. If you tell me, or if your eyes reveal you have no hope, I understand that to mean that you are isolated from your brothers and sisters. Get together.

commonweal
3/6/70

AND THE MORE HE THOUGHT ABOUT IT, THE MORE HE BEGAN TO GET REALLY PISSED OFF! ROWR!

...AND BEFORE HE KNEW IT, HE WAS A REVOLUTIONARY! THE COUNTRY NEEDS A NEW KIND OF BAG! SNAK!

...DEDICATED TO THE OVERTHROW OF THE ESTABLISHED ORDER!

changes

ASH WEDNESDAY
A Day for burning

Resistance fires are still burning in Milwaukee. After the Milwaukee 14 burned draft files on September 24 and the card burning at St. Boniface shortly after, there was a long, quiet period. People went back to the business of draft counseling and organizing, of rallies and marches and speeches. Then on Ash Wednesday the fires were lit again, this time at Marquette University during a liturgical celebration. It was advertized as an "Ash Wednesday Liturgy;" but the underground had the word that it was to be something special. At 4:30 the people started pouring into the ballroom of the student union. The chairs had been removed, so coats were spread and everybody sat down on the floor, almost five hundred students, faculty and visitors sitting on the floor singing to the music of electric guitars. That's how it all started.

After a few minutes, Father Quentin Quesnell of the theology department mounted the stairs to the stage and took the microphone. Around a series of scriptural readings he wove an explanation of what Ash Wednesday is all about. We tradition-ally burn palms because in the day of Jesus palms were a symbol of royalty, empire and power. Palms were waved and strewn along the way as Jesus rode triumphantly into Jerusalem. They were a symbol of the royalty the people wished to confer on him, a particular kind of worldly royalty which he ultimately refused. Father Quesnell went on to explain that Christians burn palms on Ash Wednesday as a sign of their own rejection of worldly royalty and empire. Burning palms symbolizes the Christians' desire to destroy all that enslaves man. At this point Father Quesnell took a few palms and lit them. He then explained that in our day there are other more important things to burn, other symbols of enslaving power He called on those who wished to come up and burn things they felt would be appropriately reduced to ashes.

Art Heitzer, the president of the student body, stepped to the microphone. He reviewed the history of war and the history of the peace talks; he spoke of what is right now going on in Vietnam; he recalled that 14 brothers might soon be in jail for burning draft files. Then he took a card from his pocket, a card which he said had been weighing him down for too long, a card which bound him to a selective service system he had long rejected. He took the card to the fire and burned it. Others followed with similar cards and similar explanations. A girl stepped up with IBM cards, a symbol of the way students, who are people, are reduced to numbers. She burned the cards. Someone brought a dollar bill to the fire, explaining that it was a symbol of the way men are made slaves to a competitive economic system that colors their entire lives and their personalities. Finally, a black girl stepped forward with a copy of the Marquette Student Handbook and read from it. "Final responsibility for the conduct of students rests in the president of the university." As she tore the handbook and placed it in the fire she spoke, "Final responsibility for my conduct rests with me." The fire burned and people watched it silently.

As the fire burned down, the ashes were taken in plates and passed through the crowd. People took the ashes and rubbed them on one another's foreheads, signing one another with the sign of destruction which is also a sign of hope, the destruction of slavery and hope for a new, free future.

More music . . . *where have all the flowers gone, long time passing*. Something was happening at the center. People were moving together across the floor, holding hands, touching bodies, raising held hands into the air in the sign of peace, still singing . . . where have all the soldiers gone, gone to graveyards everyone, when will they ever learn. Five hundred people touching, singing, breathing together, still sitting on the floor, marked with ashes of hope.

After the song, Father Quesnell brought forward the bread and wine. He made a prayer of thanksgiving; he recalled the night before Jesus died; he passed the bread and cup through the crowd. They ate and drank. Then Father Quesnell spoke a final prayer. The music played again. People stood up as if to leave but reluctant to go. A few people formed a circle and started to dance. They held out their hands and brought others into the circle. The circle widened. More and more joined. The circle expanded almost to the walls of the ballroom. Hundreds of people dancing in a single circle as the music played. Then they broke apart, some running hand in hand out the doors, others staying to meet, to kiss, to talk. Everyone was happy, almost high. Something unusual had happened. The fire was out now, only ashes left, but the fire had been communicated and was burning in people.

win
Richard Zipfel
March 1969

SEMINARIANS SAY: CHURCH IS FULL OF SHIT!

There are a few seminarians around General Synod — very few. There are a few seminarians interested in the church — very few. Ever wonder why? Do you give a damn?

Seminaries around the country resembled other campuses this Spring: At Andover Newton students seized the administration building to demand that black trustees be added to the Board; at Union students seized the administration building to demand that the Board of Trustees commit themselves to the Black Manifesto; at the San Francisco Theological Union the six schools closed to debate the issues of the Black Manifesto; at McCormick students seized the administration building to protest the building of a fence around the school (designed to keep out the "niggers"); at Harvard students have been protesting the building of a Rockefeller hall — Who the hell needs a Rockefeller hall?

So what's wrong?

a. American churches are by and large more committed to "capitalism" and "free enterprise" (witness the report from the First Church, Malden, as endorsed by Cardinal Cushing) than to their neighbor.

b. The church missionary task has an odious past, an odious present, and plans for an odious future. The association of missionaries with American government officials is particularly obscene, i.e. AID, etc. The church missionary task is not imaginative enough to know that the demands laid upon it by our oppressed brothers and sisters are the demands for revolution. The church cannot proceed toward a "Theology of Hope" without a "Theology of Revolution." Why don't we have missionary work going on in North Vietnam?

c. Local churches are desperately separated from the church "leaders," making most "top-down" educational and theological tasks impotent. Our task must be the local one of helping the churches to place themselves along-side of those who are working for radical change. It would be too much to expect the church to lead the movement for change; at least the church might be expected to stand beside those who do have the courage to risk, i.e. the Black Panthers, SDS, and all others struggling for a new America.

d. The local church is trapped in impotence largely because it must expend most of its time and money caring for property. The church needs to free itself of its property, by mortgaging property, thus enabling church people to commit themselves more fully to tasks.

e. Church executive structures are so bull-shit that they should close and remain closed. Church publications, too, generally serve no one; if these publications are to continue they must be put at the disposal of those actually needing media. Church resources must be committed to research, to action, to radical change.

Seminarians are increasingly up-against-the-wall of church crap. How can anyone expect students to be involved in church life as long as its style reeks of cliche, of tired rhetoric, and marshmallow liberals?

The people of the church had best wake up to the need for revolution if they are to retain any presence or integrity.

Victor Judson Schramm — Episcopal Theological Seminary
Robert K. Crabtree — Andover Newton Theological School
Arkley F. King — Episcopal Theological Seminary
Robert M. Hundley — Union Theological Seminary
Robert J. Mitchell — Harvard School of Theology
John Karnodle — Andover Newton Theological School
John Cupples — Harvard School of Theology
Tim Smith — Union Theological Seminary

A leaflet

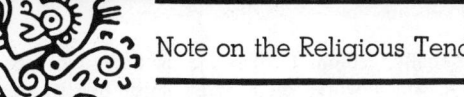

Note on the Religious Tendencies

THIS religiosity is primarily one of practice and personal experience, rather than theory. The statement commonly heard in some circles, "All religions lead to the same goal" is the result of fantastically sloppy thinking and no practice. It is good to remember that all religions are nine-tenths fraud and are responsible for numerous social evils.

Within the beat generation you find three things going on:

1. *Vision and illumination-seeking.* This is most easily done by systematic experimentation with narcotics. Marijuana is a daily standby and peyote is the real eye-opener. These are sometimes supplemented by dips into yoga technique, alcohol, and Subud. Although a good deal of personal insight can be obtained by the intelligent use of drugs, being high all the time leads nowhere because it lacks intellect, will, and compassion; and a personal drug kick is of no use to anyone else in the world.

2. *Love, respect for life, abandon, Whitman, pacifism, anarchism, etc.* This comes out of various traditions including Quakers, Shinshu Buddhism, Sufism. And from a loving and open heart. At its best this state of mind has led people to actively resist war, start communities, and try to love one another. It is also partly responsible for the mystique of "angels", the glorification of skidroad and hitch-hiking, and a kind of mindless enthusiasm. If it respects life, it fails to respect heartless wisdom and death; and this is a shortcoming.

3. *Discipline, aesthetics, and tradition.* This was going on well before the beat generation got into print. It differs from the "All is one" stance in that its practitioners settle on one traditional religion, try to absorb the feel of its art and history, and carry out whatever ascesis is required. One could become an Aimu bear-dancer or a Yurok shaman as well as a Trappist monk, if he put himself to it. What this bit often lacks is what 2 and 3 have, i.e. real commitment to the stewpot of the world and real insight into the vision-lands of the unconscious.

The unstartling conclusion is that if a person cannot comprehend all three of these aspects—contemplation (and not by use of drugs), morality (which usually means social protest to me), and wisdom—in his beat life, he just won't make it. But even so he may get pretty far out, and that's probably better than moping around classrooms or writing books on Buddhism and Happiness for the masses, as the squares (who will shortly have succeeded in putting us all down) do.

LIBERATION

MAGIC CHRISTIANS

The establishment Episcopal Diocese of California is going all out to support the radical Free Church of Berkeley.

A few weeks ago Berkeley pigs smashed Free Church windows sans reasons. The Free Church is now getting ready to sue (they have a good case) and the Diocesen Council, the ruling body of the Diocese, passed a resolution supporting the decision to sue. The resolution, passed on St. Patrick's Day, condemns the Berkeley Police Dept. and offers the Free Church the services of the Diocesan lawyers.

The Diocese also took action on another issue — On March 10, the Chronicle quoted Dr. Edward Jenkins, the senior surgeon of the National Guard, at the California Medical Association Meeting: "If Berkeley is placed under National Guard control during a future disturbance, I would have to seriously consider closing the Free Church and other such facilities (Free Clinic) because they encourage the riot to continue by allowing rioters to be treated without having to face the authorities."

The Urban Dept. of the Diocese, who have been financially aiding the Free Church, passed a resolution condemning Jenkins' statements and pledging continued support of the free church's medical activities. They sent copies of the resolution to the Governor, the Adjutant General, the Sheriff of Alameda County, the mayor of Berkeley and the Chief of Police Baker, of Berkeley.

The mind revolution, the best revolution, is spreading.

—jenny

4/3/70

ELDRIDGE CLEAVER'S MINISTRY

Berrigan from Jail: 'Truth Creates Its Own Room'

Baltimore County Jail

Dear Dan:

More for the family album . . .

I've just read Eldridge Cleaver's *Soul on Ice,* which an unusually honest dustjacket blurb calls "one of the discoveries of the 1960s." Providentially, Cleaver's book reached me during a period of jailhouse doldrums, when existence passed for living, and living was as appetizing as unseasoned oatmeal. Oddly enough, neither depression nor self-pity was the trouble. Rather, the trouble was a kind of moral exhaustion which reduced reality to an obscure and vapid common denominator. The world, people and jail no longer stimulated me, and I seemed powerless to turn them on. For a time at least, dullness and lethargy had their day.

Yet Cleaver snapped me out of it with his lucidity and outrage. (Lucidity and outrage—a rare package, deplorably lacking in what masquerades as social criticism today.) It was Simone Weil, I think, who observed that truth creates its own room, as though to take possession of a person. Cleaver performed such a service, dispelling the vacuum within me. As Fundamentalist Christians would put it, "he performed a ministry for me."

Many things about this book moved me. Generally, it is a raw and slashing attack upon American life, while preserving a delicate balance of humanity and humaneness. Cleaver never insists that whites become more than he has become, or that humanity is less possible to a white racist than to a black man. No one can discount the obstacles he faced and overcame—poverty, blackness and a brilliance whose misguidance in early life made him a racist and a brute. ". . . If I had not been apprehended (for rape of whites)," he wrote, "I would have slit some white throats."

Once back in prison, he began writing to capture an identity which he never really had. Writing forced him

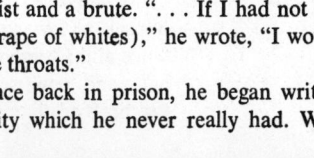

Panther women taken as political prisoners during . . .

. . .police attack on L.A. Panther headquarters.

to read, and both imparted the conclusion that life meant more than what he knew of himself, and of white America. From that turning point, he began to build an authentic humanity, as *Soul on Ice* testifies.

While not desiring to make this a book review, I can't resist the opinion that his grasp of racist psychology is as incisive as Baldwin's, and more comprehensive. He sees correctly that ghettos create both the black colonist and the black mercenary—abject caricatures forced upon black Americans at home and abroad. "Separate but equal" for blacks in the United States equals "Open Door" as foreign policy to Cleaver—he understands that the Great Society has in fact upgraded "separate but equal" only faintly and grudgingly, a function which foreign aid repeats faithfully. It is clear however that whatever the euphemism—"separate but equal," "Open Door," "Great Society," "foreign aid"—they disarmingly disguise control of people, whether by economic, cultural or political measures.

(Cleaver's book and other similar studies are beginning to make a point with many Americans—that there is but one policy governing America's national and international life, a policy precisely tailored for expansionist capitalism. Which is to say, it is tailored to enrich further a predatory wealthy elite, and to entrench further a somnolent middle-class, which serves in effect, to insulate the wealthy from change.)

Nevertheless, the impression that lingered was nothing specific, just the intense drama of a man liberated by the honesty of his suffering. St. Paul has a famous line telling how Christ learned obedience through his suffering. Some might think that referring this to Cleaver is odd, yet he strikes me as a man profoundly obedient to a truly human order—a man of acceptance as well as determination. One does not develop such virtues except through suffering.

Malcolm influenced him tremendously—today's Black Panthers are several logical steps beyond Malcolm's still-born Organization of Afro-American Unity. When America grows up, it will treasure both men; both of whom won their humanity in jail; both of whom combined the visionary and activist roles; both passionate lovers of truth and justice; the one murdered, the other still precariously alive, destined for the leadership of his people, or for a racist bullet.

The Terror of Tedium

But I was telling about Cleaver's ministry to me. Despite freedom from uncommon problems in jail, I am susceptible to a common one—tedium. Now, tedium tends to feed upon drabness and routine, overcrowding; upon steel bars, and body counts, isolation from community, issues and struggle. In effect, tedium tempts one to quit; to submit gracelessly and imperceptibly to cop-out; to relish appearances rather than reality; to think less, feel less and love less; to suspend life, growth and Christianity for the duration.

Like most temptations which demean, tedium fits what *seems* rather than what *is*, inviting one to stress the unnaturalness of confinement, bureaucratic rulebooks and rigidity, inmate hangups and custodial impersonality, moral and political uselessness, the total climate of futility and waste. No wonder that prisoners "chalk off" that portion of their lives, believing it barren of anything constructive. Extreme cases tend to despair—a lad killed himself at Lewisburg since I've been there. A long sentence and a burdensome confinement made him despondent—and powerless to cope with news of a younger brother's death in Vietnam.

Personally, tedium terrifies me as a kind of deadly abrasive which works on a man's spirit like wind and water on loose soil. The erosion that results becomes commonplace, and very nearly inevitable. To see men of intelligence and accomplishment (not uncommon in federal prisons), far more innocent of crime than many of our public pillars (not uncommon either), lick their wounds and fan their resentments like punished children, mark time and feast upon distractions, longing uncritically for a society which has misused them, and which they intend neither to hold accountable nor reform, is a scene of depressing waste. I find myself vainly trying to discover in them a spark of constructive anger, but they appear to desire nothing so much as anonymity and normalcy after release.

The brush tars wide and indiscriminately, and I find myself often marked by it. Somebody said once that life consists of catching up with what one has done, or going beyond it. I feel that the first case applies to me, requiring a sustained pondering of what I have done, and a present consistent with it. Otherwise, life might become a sterile compromise, setting at work a series of mysterious injuries among people depending on me. I have seen such compromises, and their effects, by men who acted well and courageously against injustice, never to recover from the consequences.

Life is more precious than liberty, one must admit, and the donation of life more difficult than the donation of liberty. But my conscience did not allow immolation, so I gave what was possible. Since resistance required trading liberty for imprisonment, imprisonment should be another way of extending resistance, and even of adding to it. It should give one the vantage point of being at the heart of moral conflict, yet physically detached from it; of being at grips with what St. John calls "the world" (the institutions of domination), yet removed from public struggle with them.

To appraise my situation from a merely political view is to go a long way toward destroying it. Friends commiserate with me and watch the political horizons anxiously, looking for a change of weather that would give strength to legal appeal, or a better chance for executive clemency. They are clearly sympathetic, but not particularly perceptive. If I were the lowliest of draft resisters, buried anonymously in some federal prison, forgotten by everyone but parents and one or two friends, I would be contributing more to the peace than the most spectacular dove, who makes headlines and rallies supporters, and whose exhortations are heard with apprehension even in the halls of government. "But the foolish things of the world has God chosen to put to shame the 'wise,' and the weak things of the world has God chosen to put to shame the strong, and the base things of the world and the despised has God chosen, and the things that are not, to bring to naught the things that are; lest any flesh should pride itself before him." I Cor. 1, 27 seq.

So Cleaver has done me a service by giving me of his strength. His fight for manhood gives energy to my own, since in every case, that fight is an unfinished business. But one can face it better, knowing of another who had less to work with, becoming in spite of that, a better man than I.   PHILIP BERRIGAN

commonweal 12/6/68

Ed. Note: Phil Berrigan is now in Federal prison.
Dan is underground.

The question which one continually encounters today, however, is whether the church has not outgrown itself; whether, in fact, the church as we have known it — local community of worship and larger organization — has not become dysfunctional precisely because it has been successful. It sometimes seems that all those values and ways of living and modes of responsiveness that Christian teachers constantly instruct us in, verbally and otherwise, appear to be so deeply rooted now in parts of our culture that they are accessible outside the churches, with less artificiality and less semantical and historical ambiguity. A passion for justice, a realism regarding power and achievement, honesty, brotherliness, gentleness, meditative prayer, joy, a sense of God's healing presence and other similar values are as open to non-Christians as to Christians. One does not have to go to church to learn them, to reinforce them, or to celebrate them. One might possibly — even probably — learn them more sharply, more concretely, and more limpidly outside the churches than within.

MICHAEL NOVAK, *Commonweal*

GRAFFITI

Recently, at a church-sponsored youth conference (grades 9 to 12), a large piece of newsprint was taped to the wall and the young people were invited to create a huge graffiti during the course of the week. It is fascinating to compare what they inscribed on that newsprint with a random selection of announcements of sermon titles appearing in the Saturday newspapers.

Youth Graffiti:	*Sermon Titles:*
All power to the people!	"In the Cross of Christ
Resist!	I Glory"
Che!	"Do You Feel as Close to
Make peace not war!	God as You Once Did?"
Hell no, I won't go!	"God Too Small"
"The draft is the white	"Fear God"
man sending the black	"Grease Well the Gateposts"
man to kill the yellow	
man to 'save' the land he	
stole from the red man."	"The Music of God"
(Hair)	"A Door Opened in Heaven"
Do humans ever realize	"Backdrop of a Cloud"
life as they live it?	"Faith in God"

colloquy March 1970

POLITICS of the NERVOUS SYSTEM

THEODORE ROSZAK

Mr. Roszak, an associate professor of history, is chairman of the History of Western Culture Program at California State College, Hayward. He edited and contributed to The Dissenting Academy *(Pantheon Books).*

On October 21, the Pentagon was besieged by a motley army of civil demonstrators. For the most part, the 50,000 protesters were made up of activist academics and students, men of letters, New Left and pacifist ideologues, housewives, doctors and such. But also, we are informed: "witches, warlocks, holy men, seers, prophets, mystics, saints, sorcerers, shamans, troubadours, minstrels, bards, road men, and madmen"—who were on hand to achieve the "mystic revolution." The picketing, the sit-down, the speeches and marches: all that was protest politics as usual. But the central event of the day was a contribution of the "superhumans": an exorcism of the Pentagon by long-haired warlocks who "cast mighty words of white light against the demon-controlled structure," in the hope of levitating that grim ziggurat.

They did not succeed—in floating the Pentagon, that is. But they did manage to convey their generation's political style, a style so authentically original as to border on the bizarre. If the youthful political activism of the sixties differs from that of the thirties, the difference reveals itself in an unprecedented penchant for the occult, for magic, and for exotic ritual which has become an integral part of the counter culture. Even protesters who didn't participate in the rite of exorcism took the event in stride —as if they understood that here was the style and vocabulary of the young, and one had to tolerate its expression.

Religiosity has been characteristic of the postwar youth culture since the days of the beatniks. One finds the quest for God in many of the earliest poems of Allen Ginsberg, well before he and his colleagues had discovered Zen and the mystic wealth of the East. In his poetry of the forties, he showed a sensitivity for visionary experience—"Angelic raving" as he was to call it—which suggested even then that the social dissent of the younger generation would never quite fit into the adamantly secular mold of the old Left. Ginsberg spoke then of seeing

> *all the pictures we carry in our mind*
> *images of the Thirties,*
> *depression and class consciousness*
> *transfigured above politics*
> *filled wih fire*
> *with the appearance of God.*

These early poems contrast strongly with Ginsberg's style today. They are often brief, tightly written affairs, done in a short, orderly line. The more familiar Ginsberg line, rambling and ham-fisted (the line based on "Hebraic-Melvillian bardic breath") does not appear until the 1949 poem "Patterson." But the religiosity was already there, giving his work a sound very different from the social poetry of the thirties. From the outset, Ginsberg was a protest poet, but his protest runs back not to Marx but to the ecstatic radicalism of Blake. The issue is never as simple as social justice; rather the key words and images are those of time and eternity, madness and vision, heaven and the spirit. And as early as the later forties Ginsberg is experimenting with marijuana and writing poems under the sway of narcotics.

By the early fifties, Ginsberg had abandoned the conventional virtues of poetry in favor of a spontaneity that comes across as an unchecked flow of language. From then on, everything he writes has the appearance of being served up raw. There is never the trace of a revised line; rather, another line is added on: instead of revision, there is accumulation. To rework would be to rethink, hence to doubt the initial vision. For Ginsberg, the creative act was to be a "come-as-you-are" party. Lack of grooming marks his poems as "natural," therefore honest. They are the *real* thing, not artifice.

There is a good deal of Charlie Parker's improvisation in Ginsberg's work, and of the action painters. Jackson Pollock worked at a canvas with a commitment never to erase or redo or touch up; but to add, add, add, and let it all somehow work itself into a pattern. Similarly, Jack Kerouac came to the point of typing out his novels nonstop onto enormous rolls of paper—6 feet a day—with never a revision. At last, a deal of Ginsberg's late work sounds very much as if it were taken off a tape recorder as dictated.

That this improvisatory method of writing produces a great deal of trash is, for our purposes here, less important than the light this choice of method throws on the generation that accepted Ginsberg's work as a valid form of creativity. It is a search for art unmediated by intellect; or rather, since the application of intellectual control is what makes art of impulse, it is an effort to extract and indulge the impulse, without regard to the nature of the product.

Poetry defined as an oracular outpouring has a genealogy running back through the Hebrew prophets to the shamans of dim antiquity. The Hebrew term for prophet is *nabi:* mutterer, babbler, one who speaks with tongues. Unhappily, Ginsberg is no Amos (though perhaps we should have a poorer opinion of Amos if we had the whole of his life's utterances to get through instead of only the most elegant passages), but he belongs within that tradition. He belongs there, however, not as an artist but as a conjurer with subterranean forces, a kind of witch doctor. It is as if, initially, Ginsberg set out to write poetry: to say something about the anguished state of the world. What came of that was a howl. But at the bottom of the howl Ginsberg discovered what it was that Moloch was most intent upon burying: the non-intellective powers.

Every artist has discovered something of that in the creative process. What sets Ginsberg's career apart is that, having once experienced the powers, he set out to make over as much of his own life and as much of the culture as he could lay hold of in the image of that experience. For Ginsberg the use of narcotics was not simply a perverse Bohemian vice; it was another, more effective way of short-circuiting the intellect and tapping the energy beyond. It was a way of subverting Moloch by reorganizing the politics of the nervous system.

There is something more to be noted about the visionary impulse in Ginsberg's work and life. The ecstatic power he and most of the early Beat writers reached for was never sought in other-worldly sources. Their mysticism was never escapist or ascetic; it did not lead them, like T. S. Eliot, into a transcendent rose garden. Theirs was to be a this-worldly mysticism, an ecstasy of the body and of the earth that somehow would embrace and transform mortality. Joy was to be had even (or perhaps especially) in the commonplace obscenities of existence. As Ginsberg put it in one of his early poems:

> *This is the one and only*
> *firmament . . .*
> *I am living in Eternity.*
> *The ways of this world*
> *are the ways of Heaven.*

Or, even more powerfully:

> *For the world is a mountain*
> *of shit, if it's going to*
> *be moved at all, it's got*
> *to be taken by handfulls.*

William Carlos Williams observed in the poems of the young Ginsberg "a beat that is far removed from the beat of dancing feet, but rather finds in the shuffling of human beings in all the stages of their life, the trip to the bathroom, to the stairs of the subway, the steps of the office or factory routine, the mystical measure of their passions." This is, in fact, a remarkable anticipation of the Zen doctrine of the "illuminated commonplace."

Popular Zen

If one can believe the account Jack Kerouac gives in *The Dharma Bums,* the book which was to provide the first handy compendium of all those Zen catch phrases that have since become more familiar to contemporary youth than any Christian catechism, it was from the West Coast poet, Gary Snyder, that he and Ginsberg learned their Zen upon going to San Francisco in the early fifties. But behind Snyder stood Alan Watts, who had recently begun teaching at the School of Asian Studies after leaving his position as an Anglican counselor at Northwestern University. When he arrived in San Francisco, Watts, who was only 35 years old in 1950, had written at least seven books dealing with Zen and mystical religion. He had in fact, been a child prodigy in his chosen field of study: at 19, he was appointed editor of *The Middle Way,* an English journal of Buddhist studies, and at 23, co-editor of the English "Wisdom of the East" series. Along with D. T. Suzuki, Watts, through his televised lectures, books and private classes, was to become America's foremost popularizer of Zen.

The Radical East

But with that much granted, it must also be recognized that what the young were vulgarizing in this way was a body of thought which, as formulated by men like Suzuki and Watts, constituted a radical critique of the conventional scientific conception of man and nature, which has been long due for reappraisal. Even if they seized on Zen with shallow understanding, they grasped it with a healthy instinct. And grasping it, they bought the books, and attended the lectures, and spread about the catch phrases and, in general, helped to provide the platform from which a few good minds who understood more deeply could speak out in criticism of the dominant culture. Perhaps what the young took to be Zen has little relationship to that venerable and elusive tradition; but what they went for was a gentle and gay rejection of a positivistic and compulsively cerebral technological society.

This is another way of saying that beyond a certain point it becomes little better than pedantic to ask how authentically "Buddhist" are poems like Ginsberg's "Sunflower Sutra" (1955). Perhaps not very, but it *is* a poem of great tenderness, expressing an unashamed wonder for the commonplace splendors of the world and calling into question that anthropocentric arrogance with which our society, in the name of progress, has gone about mechanizing and brutalizing its environment. And it is a commentary on the state of what our society regards as its "religion" that the poet who still commands the greatest attention among our youth should have had to cast about for an exotic tradition from which to take inspiration in expressing these humane sentiments.

The same holds true for Ginsberg's more recent interest in Hinduism. It is, at the very least, a fascinating Odyssey of the contemporary spirit that takes a young Jewish poet

from Paterson, N.J., to the banks of the Ganges to become America's most renowned Hindu Brahman. But is his Hinduism the real thing? Again, the question is beside the point. What is far more important is his deeply felt need to turn away from the dominant culture in order to find the spirit for such remarkable poems as "The Wichita Vortex Sutra" and "Who Be Kind To"—both compelling expressions of humanity and compassionate protest. And even more important is the social fact: Ginsberg the mantra-chanting Hindu does not finish as an isolated eccentric but rather as one of the foremost spokesmen of the younger generation.

Following Ginsberg, the boys and girls don cowbells and tuck flowers behind their ears—and listen. Ginsberg claims a greater audience among dissenting youth than any Christian or Jewish clergyman could hope to reach or stir. Perhaps the one exception to this might have been the late A. J. Muste in the final years of his life. But then Muste always kept his ministerial identity as unobtrusive as possible.

After Christianity

Indeed, we are in a post-Christian era, despite the fact that minds far more gifted than Ginsberg's—like that of Thomas Merton—continue to mine the dominant religious tradition for good treasures. But it has been a decided mistake to expect that the death of the Christian God would be followed by a thoroughly secularized, thoroughly positivistic culture, dismal and spiritless in its obsession with technological prowess. That was the world Aldous Huxley foresaw in the 1930s when he wrote *Brave New World.* But in the 1950s, detecting the rising spirit of a new generation, Huxley's utopian image had brightened to that of *Island,* where prevailed a nonviolent culture elaborated out of Buddhism and psychedelic drugs. It was as if suddenly he had seen an emerging possibility: beyond the Christian era and the "wasteland" that was its immediate successor, might lie a new, eclectic religious revival.

That is precisely what confronts us now as one of the massive facts of our youthful counter culture. The dissenting young have indeed got religion. It is not the brand of religion that Billy Graham or William Buckley would choose for youth's crusade, but nonetheless it is religion. What began with Zen has now rapidly, perhaps too rapidly, proliferated into a phantasmagoria of exotic religiosity.

Who would have predicted it? At least since the Enlightenment, perhaps with the exception of the early Romantics, the major thrust of *avant-garde* thought has always been anti-religious, if not defiantly atheistic. And even among the Romantics, the most pious tended to become the most politically reactionary. Would-be Western revolutionaries have always been strongly rooted in a militantly skeptical secular tradition. Rejection of a corrupted religious establishment has carried over almost automatically into a root and branch rejection of all things spiritual. "Mysticism" has always been one of the dirtiest words in the Marxist lexicon.

But now the psychedelic weeklies, sprouting like mushrooms across the land, splash across their pages pictures of Christ and the prophets, mishmashed mind-bogglingly with Zen, Hinduism, primitive shamanism, theosophy, the Left-Handed Tantra. The youthful counter culture is aclutter with satanists and neo-gnostics, would-be witch doctors and self-proclaimed swamis. The Berkeley "wandering priest" Charlie (Brown) Artman, who was in the running for city councilman in 1966 until he was busted for confessing to possession of narcotics, strikes the right note of eclectic religiosity: a stash of LSD in his Indian-sign necklace, Hindu cowbells, and the campaign slogan,

"May the baby Jesus open your mind and shut your mouth."

No anti-Vietnam War demonstration would be complete without a hirsute, bell-festooned contingent of holy men, bearing joss sticks and intoning the *Hare Krishna. The Berkeley Barb,* an underground weekly, gives LBJ a good left-wing slamming on page 1, but devotes the center spread to a crazy mandala for the local yogis. And in its back pages, the "Servants of Awareness," "a unique group of aware people using 136 symbols in their meditation to communicate directly with *Cosmic Awareness . . . ,*" are sure to take a 4-inch ad. The San Francisco *Oracle* runs photos of stark-naked madonnas with flowers in their hair, suckling their babies . . . and the effect is not at all pornographic, nor intended to be.

At the level of youth, the mid-1960s begin to resemble nothing so much as a cultic hothouse of the Hellenistic period, when every manner of mystery and fakery, ritual and rite, intermingled in a marvelous indiscrimination. And, for the time being, the situation makes it next to impossible for many of us who teach to convey much in the way of education to the radical young, given the fact that the conventional curriculum, even at its best, is grounded in the dominent Western tradition. If you asked the kids to identify (a) Milton and (b) Pope, their answers are likely to be: (a) Milton *who*? and (b) which Pope? But they may do no mean job of rattling off their *Kabbala* or *I Ching* (which the very hip get married to these days) or, of course, the *Kama Sutra*.

Magic & Counter Magic

What the counter culture offers, then, is a remarkable defection from the long-standing tradition of skeptical, secular intellectuality that has served as the prime vehicle for 300 years of scientific and technical development in the West. Almost overnight (astonishingly, and with no great debate on the point), a significant portion of the younger generation has withdrawn from that tradition, as if to provide an emergency balance, often by occult aberrations just as gross, to the gross distortions of technological society. As often happens, one cultural exaggeration calls forth another to be its opposite equivalent. In the hands of a Herman Kahn, science, logic and the precision of numbers have become their own caricatures as part of a mystogogy of mass murder. Even official Washington calls its Sino-Soviet advisers "demonologists"—and the designation is scarcely a wisecrack. Mumbo-jumbo is indeed at the heart of human affairs when so-called scientific decision making reveals itself as a species of voodoo. ("Crack-pot realism," C. Wright Mills called it; and Allen Ginsberg "a communion of bum magicians.")

When science and reasons of state become handmaidens of political black magic, who can blame the young for diving headlong into the Jungian stew, in search of "good vibrations" that might ward off the bad? Of course, they are soon glutted with what they find. Whole religious traditions become baubles to play with. A light-show group in Detroit names itself "The Bulging Eyeballs of Gautama," and all of a sudden the Beatles become the contemplative converts of a particularly simple-minded swami who advertises in every London underground station.

One does not unearth the wisdom of the ages by shuffling about a few exotic catch phrases—nor does one learn anything about anybody's lore or religion by donning a few talismans and dosing on LSD. The most that comes of such superficial muddling is something like Timothy Leary's brand of easy-do syncretism—"somehow" all is one, and never mind precisely how. Fifty years ago when Swami Vivekananda first brought the teachings of Sri Ramakrishna to America he induced a gaggle of high-social dilettantes to say as much. The results were as

YOGI BEAR

ludicrous as they were ephemeral. Yet things are just beginning. In the present state of affairs, in the turgid flood tide of discovery, sampling and restive fascination, it would perhaps be too much to expect disciplined order —as surely it would be folly to try to deduce order from this happy chaos. The young have happened upon treasure trove long buried and are busy letting the quaint trinkets spill through their fingers.

Science as Superstition

Still, for all its frequently mindless vulgarity, for all its tendency to get lost in exotic clutter, a powerful and important force is at work in this wholesale willingness of the young to scrap their inherited culture's entrenched prejudice toward myth, religion and ritual. The life of Reason (with a capital R) has all too obviously failed to produce the agenda of civilized improvements the Voltaires and Jeffersons foresaw. Reason, materialism, the scientific world view have revealed themselves too often as simply a higher superstition, based on dubious but well-concealed assumptions about man and nature. Science, it has been said, thrives on sins of omission, and for 300 years those omissions have been piling up like the slag tips that surround Welsh mining towns: immense, precipitous mountains of frustrated aspiration and metaphysical yearning, which threaten to come cascading down in an impassioned landslide. It is impossible any longer to ignore the fact that our conception of intellect has been narrowed disastrously by the prevailing assumption, especially in the academies, that the life of the spirit is: (*1*) a lunatic fringe best left to artists and marginal visionaries; (*2*) a historical bone yard for antiquarian scholarship; (*3*) a highly specialized adjunct of professional anthropology. For along none of these approaches could the living power of myth, ritual and rite penetrate the intellectual establishment and have any existential (as opposed, at best, to merely academic) significance. As Lewis Mumford has suggested in his recent study, *The Myth of the Machine*:

> . . . the whole sphere of early man's existence which the modern scientific mind, in its consciousness of intellectual superiority, rejects, was the original source of man's self-transformation from an animal into a human person. Ritual, dance, totem, taboo, religion, magic—these provided the groundwork for man's later higher development.

This blind spot has made it possible, in the name of intellectual respectability, to ignore the obvious fact that not only early man but man through the ages has always devoted as much of his wit, care and energy to the creation of mythologies, ritual forms and world systems as to gathering the physical "necessities." And yet the standard stance of every "good" college teacher who is confronted with the task of breaking in a freshman class and introducing it to the life of the mind, is still that of the old village atheist, wielding a ruthless, positivistic skepticism.

The anti-religious prejudice of the intellectual establishment has severely crippled science and scholarship by fanatically ruling out whole areas of experience from systematic inquiry. If conventional scholarship touches those areas of life it is usually with the intention of compiling knowledge, not with the hope of salvaging value. And yet is was "science" in the highest sense of the word that brought William James to his study of religious experience, and Aldous Huxley to his experiments with the hallucinogenic drugs.

The Dark Side

Similarly, when Lewis Mumford insists—as he does in all his work—that historical studies must come to grips with the undeniable power of dream, myth and the sacred in human affairs, he is upholding the highest standards of scholarship. But when academics and intellectuals arrogantly truncate this greater conception of science and scholarship, they come up with that "middle-class secular humanism" of which Michael Novak has aptly said:

It thinks of itself as humble in its agnosticism, and eschews the "mystic flights" of metaphysicians, theologians and dreamers; it is cautious and remote in dealing with heightened and passionate experiences that are the stuff of great literature and philosophy. It limits itself to this world and its concerns, concerns which fortunately turn out to be largely subject to precise formulations, and hence have a limited but comforting certainty.

I think we can anticipate that in the coming generation large numbers of students will begin to reject this reductive humanism, demanding a far deeper examination of that dark side of the human personality which has so long been written off as "mystical" by the dominant culture. It is because this renaissance of mythical-religious interest promises such enrichment of Western culture that one is led to despair when, as often happens, the young reduce it to an esoteric collection of peer-group symbols and slogans, vaguely wicked and ultimately trivial. Then instead of culture, we get collage; a miscellaneous heaping together, as if one had simply ransacked *The Encyclopedia of Religion and Ethics* and the *Celestia Arcana* for exotic tidbits. For example, the *International Times* of London prints a major article on Aleister Crowley, but the treatment goes no further than the sensational surface. It is a simple inversion of what too often dominates the underground press: the straight papers say "scandalous"; the underground says "marvelous"; but understanding gets no aid.

This is the point at which the young, who are offering, I feel, a great deal that is good to work with, need the help of mature minds, in order that distinctions can be drawn between the deep and the shallow, the superstitious and the wise. It is important to discern the underlying connection between the inspired seer on the one hand, and the side-show charlatan on the other, and to recognize that the skeptical, en bloc rejection of both has been a prime disaster. That much the young have seen. But between seer and charlatan there is also an all-important difference, and it is apparent only upon reflection. But who, among the alienated young, constantly on the lookout for the narks, has time for reflection?

NATION

April 1, 1968

A Kind of Mecca

The Roman Catholic directory in New York City shows no listing for 241 East 116th Street, and indeed there is nothing about the narrow brownstone in Manhattan's East Harlem to suggest that it is a church. Outside, the four-story town house exhibits no cross or Mass schedule; inside, there is no chapel, confessional or even a pastor. The only iconography is graffiti culled from poets, saints and politicians. Yet every Sunday the small, second-floor living room is crowded with worshipers who celebrate Mass with a joy and intimacy that most cloistered monks would envy.

Emmaus House* is, in fact, an experimental community of Christians modeled after the "house-churches" of first-century Christianity, but laced with all the shapeless enthusiasms of contemporary liberal Catholicism. So radical is its approach that Catholic officials in New York have put pressure on Emmaus to disband. The community currently includes a staff of six—three priests, a Protestant layman and two Catholic laywomen—plus 25 religiously diverse "members" who work or worship at least once a week at Emmaus. "The church is moving toward a honeycomb of creative ecumenical communities," explains Father David Kirk, the 32-year-old priest of the Melkite Byzantine Rite who acts as house coordinator. "We're trying to be both a symbol of what the church will be and a catalyst in making it happen."

This is as close to a definition of purpose as any member of Emmaus cares or dares to make. "We have no blueprint for this community," says Kirk, who is an activist in the antiwar movement. "Everybody has to do his thing. Together, we hope to explore a wide variety of new styles in Christian living."

Schoolteacher Kathryn Mahon, for example, has organized college students as private tutors for neighborhood children. Maria Piedra, ex-president of the University of Peru, has opened a "problem clinic" at Emmaus House to aid Puerto Ricans in finding jobs and welfare assistance. Father Richard Mann, a talented 28-year-old Australian on temporary leave from the Congregation of the Blessed Sacrament, edits a sprightly quarterly magazine, "The Bread Is Rising," devoted to radical reform in the church and society. The latest issue contains a romantic eulogy to Cuban revolutionary Che Guevara.

Heady: Founded in 1966, Emmaus has become a kind of mecca for everyone from disenchanted Catholics to fiery New Leftists. The staff has welcomed more than 1,500 visitors: troubled priests and nuns in the midst of re-evaluating their vocations, black-power militants who would never step inside a conventional church, and many—like the group of Ecuadorians who recently dropped in unannounced at 3 a.m.—who simply want to see what Emmaus is all about.

What they find is an exciting, almost nervous, blend of social action and heady intellectual discussion. Such sought-after speakers as author Conor Cruise O'Brien, philosopher Maurice Friedman and Catholic writer Daniel Callahan regularly give free lectures on Sunday nights at Emmaus. But the spirit of the community is most profoundly revealed in its radically creative liturgies. Emmaus members take turns selecting contemporary songs to sing at Sunday Mass and in composing new canons to replace the traditional ones used in churches. Only at the Eucharistic prayer does a priest move forward to consecrate the loaves of Italian bread and ordinary wine.

To Catholic book editor William Birmingham, who drives his wife and five children in from New Jersey every Sunday for Mass at Emmaus, the new liturgy represents "the first time that my family and I have found a completely meaningful form of Christian worship in which all of us can really participate. My kids won't let us miss a Mass at Emmaus."

Emmaus House, of course, has its troubles. Last month, Kirk narrowly averted a transfer to the Diocese of Rochester, and Mann must soon decide whether to leave his order, or return to monastery life. What's more, funds are hard to come by; the center raises all its cash through personal donations and benefits. Even so, Emmaus is going ahead with plans to join with the East Harlem Protestant Parish in forming an "Ecumenical Action Ministry." Beyond that, staffers look to the formation of similar house-churches throughout the U.S. as part of a movement to alter the church's traditional parish structure. The Emmaus experiment, says Kirk, is a "call to faith, a test of ourselves and a test of the church."

Ed. Note: Emmaus House has supported both the Black Panthers and the Young Lords.

---

*A name chosen from the New Testament episode in which Jesus revealed himself to two mourning disciples on the road to Emmaus.

Newsweek

11/27/67

BERRIGAN AT CORNELL

SOCIAL DEVIANTS
THE BERRIGAN BROS.

Daniel and Phillip Berrigan, both Roman Catholic priests, are presently in Federal prison for willful destruction of Selective Service records.

Both were among the earliest and most vociferous members of the anti-war, anti-draft movement and have participated extensively in militant actions against draft boards around the country. Among their actions were a public burning of draft-board records and the pouring of gallons of duck's blood over SS files in a Baltimore-area induction center.

American Outlaw Trading Cards

The decision to come to Cornell was an experimental one. That is not to say that it was irresponsible. I know I am at an age where you don't repeat your life. To come here means you didn't go elsewhere or didn't stay elsewhere. I loved where I was and to come here was a very difficult decision. It wasn't fleeing and it wasn't a solution. It won't solve certain problems I will continue to have with the Church and the Society. I came here after a long struggle of many months.

I think as far as I could express it the decision to come here had to do with the sense that I gained, when I was invited to spend a day or two here in May, that there were students doing something unique and valuable. I could continue here the work I had already been doing for many years. The contribution I could make to the specific Catholic structure was pretty well ended.

Maybe I could invite other Jesuits and priests and other Christians to reflect on the kind of new exploration, the new landing that I would like to make here. It would not be a professorship and it wouldn't claim the immunities of the structure but it would try to be present in the midst of a very difficult, historical thing, the war; to be acceptable as a person of resources and imagination to the administration with their obvious complexities and their threatened subversion by the government. I could never be wedded to the power structure that is operating at Cornell or its large, prestigious, government oriented and morally ambiguous institution; nor can I separate the fact of Cornell from the fact of Harvard or the fact of Fordham from the fact of the war. This is why I am at Cornell; because Cornell is not separating 'the fact' — at least certain communities within it are not.

So, for a year or two or three we might explore together this new highwire act between the student community and the faculty-administration complex. Any more than any other person on a highwire, I have no illusions about survival. The point is that for a certain number of hours you do your act; the act might be exhilarating or....

STUDENTS

It seems to me that one can make either of two choices as a responsible student in choosing a place like Cornell. He can choose an umbrella or a community. At Cornell the best thing is the existence of certain nuclear communities which are here within the great things. It is almost impossible for a student at Cornell not to know that there is a very powerful and exasperating peace community here. Therefore, he can come into it, he can try it, he can join it, he can leave it, he can ignore it. And in his own department he can prepare traditionally for a rather honored place in his society within or apart from this other involvement.

Another important choice which I think is opening up for the student is the invitation to join a smaller, more experimental college than Cornell. He can form his human future by the demands he feels now. If he enrolls in a small college concentrating on one aspect of human development, he runs the risk of sectarianism 'ipso facto.' That is to say, he takes the chance that he may become paranoic. If he joins a great university community like Cornell, he avoids that in principle, maybe not in fact, but in principle by his exposure to human diversity. But that too has its danger in the leveling off of his consciousness to the point where he becomes a cynic or a person of professional despair or a member of the establishment in the image of those who run Cornell.

I sense that among the students there is a passionate realization, very untidy, very much subject to violence, unfinished and unacademic and unacceptable to those in power, that here we must stand and here, also, we must be willing to introduce some measure of public disorder in the name of world order and in the name of the upsetting of all the idolatries on which public order stands (i.e., the draft, the universities subverted by the state, overkill, etc.)

The risks are present at every point. The real point is to meet the risk because the risk is not death. the risk is life, the risk is an opportunity to stand at a cross road, as the Greek would say, to choose — and to lose.

WAR

The question of the war is a very precious one to which I have given certain irreplaceable years of my life in my poetry and my relationship with others in all those things which define me. These are years I will not have again. I can't really go back and say that I made a good or bad choice. I just chose! I chose to be here rather than elsewhere in the largest sense. So it is clear to me that I operate from a sense that all things are obscurely joined and that to be really at a point of human death or anguish or hope is to be at the center of the picture. Maybe this is the act demanded of us: to take one choice that includes many other choices.

The choice that my brother and I have made was, given the times and the Church, a choice of conflict, undoubtedly with our own communities and our own faith and the things we had grown up with. But this act resulted in a great communion with all sorts of other people, of other faiths and traditions. We found a larger meaning to being Catholic Christians. Neither of us

found a serious temptation to leave our commitments in any of these absurd ways that others are speaking of. We probably have certain resources available to us which allowed us to get beyond our own needs. We didn't need to be married — I say this humbly, it's just that we could operate as celibates. We were not in such revolt against authority that we could not communicate with it. We didn't have any personal frenzy or revenge to work out.

The war is a nightmare and the only advantage my brother and I have is that our nightmare began earlier. It began four or five years ago. So, we are better prepared to live in this nightmare, not as nightmare figures but as men who declare that it is a nightmare and, therefore, can dissolve it. Let us begin living in reality once more. This requires what it required of any period of the Church where death is in command and where society is moving to exclude more and more people through jail or the army or exclusion from benefits.

The real news is that Rome is burning. The city in which we are asked to live is in flames. I am trying to get with a much bigger thing than this little churchy thing which has been proposed as a real thing. What I am trying to suggest is that neither the Church nor the State nor the University alone has been capable of dealing with fact of death, mass extermination and nuclear overkill, the cold war and the despair of the developing peoples.

Christianity deepens in men without violating any area in which we are requested to be human beings. Christianity does not say get the hell out of your profession or income or anything else. But it does place these things in question; which is exactly where they should be — in question.

We will try to expose our conscience to the Catholic

A FATHER IN:
The Rev. Daniel Berrigan, a Jesuit priest convicted of destroying Selective Service files, is led off to jail after his arrest August 11, 1970 on Block Island, R.I.

A BROTHER OUT:
Huey P. Newton, co-founder of the Black Panther Party, addresses a crowd upon his release from jail. Huey was imprisoned 33 months before his highly irregular manslaughter conviction was overthrown. Huey said pressure from the people forced his release.

community and listen. If they will respect us, we will go ahead. If they do not respect us, we will go ahead. But we will not cut ourselves off, though we will not foreclose the possibility of their cutting us off.

POETRY

I suspect that any Christian intellectual or artist in his community (whatever it may be), is going to have impact today in proportion to the moral passion he is capable of bringing to bear upon world realities and his society.

I speak from the embattled corner of the poet and actionist and contemplative. This is my own contribution as contrasted with the intellectual. The intellectual becomes progressively sterilized in proportion as he has no symbolic content to draw upon, to seize upon and to explore. So it is important that some do symbolic activity that is highly charged and very risky and available. This activity is, in the nature of things, not rational any more than it is irrational. It is symbolic — which is another thing altogether. Men like Origen and Augustine realized that they could not meet history with purely intellectual rules; they needed constantly to be drawn back to the impurity and untidiness of the human scene. It was the poets and actionists and those who were willing to be jailed and tortured and die for their vision who offered gifts that their own lives could not offer.

In the Catholic tradition, Father deLubac said some eight or ten years ago that the man of action badly needed the symbolist, a man capable of symbolic action; and vice versa. The rhythm is a constant one, a fraternal one. But we do not solve the impasse of the Church by heightened intellectualism in her theology, any more than we solve the impasse of society by a more intellectual approach to war or a more persuasive appeal to the dogma of the military or political power.

In both Church and society all of us realize that we are at an almost absolute dead-end with regard to our resources, and that we must draw on something wider and deeper than we have known. My only plea here is that the moral man take on a wider understanding of himself through the poet and the sacrificial student and the Negro and the inner city community. He must be called to be a 'suffering servant' and stand where the majority of people must stand today if we are going to be human at all.

GOSPELS

The real fidelity of Catholic Christians is not to the Greek conciliar formulations of the Gospels but to the Gospels with a certain interest in the Greek formulations. This is a subtle difference which only a few are equipped to grasp. Grasping it, however, does not bring me to a dilemma or stalemate. It brings me to a radical position which I would formulate tentatively as follows: The Gospels, being both personalist and universal, cannot finally be couched in one language, one culture or one experience. The Gospels offer one way among five or six or ten ways of being a human being in the world. The real question of the religious Gospel is not a religious one at all; as soon as it is seen as a religious question it becomes a secularist question. That is, it confronts one ideology with another and supplies a totally useless imperative to human beings that to be saved you must become a member of this or a citizen of that. I reject both alternatives and say: I am offered by Jesus Christ, dead and risen, God incarnate, one invitation, one direction to become a human being. That vision of humanity includes mystery and actuality, citizenship and protest, the possibility of martyrdom and the very real historical possibility of cowardice. Which is to say that Christianity offers me the widest option I can discover in my lifetime of being present to historic reality and of working out with others (Buddhists and Jews and Chris-

tians and humanists) the human possibility men have come upon and struggled for and died for up to this point.

Beyond that I must say, as clearly as I know how, that my life literally has nothing to do with 'religion' or with observance.

THEOLOGY

What is operative in theology is analogies between disciplines and that theology cannot claim immunity from; analogies operative among the sciences and the forms of literature and creativity, the arts. Formerly we could claim a transcendence which said, "Everything human is all right but we are divine." I think that this is finished — historically; every human endeavor, including theology, has been radicalized out of such arrogance. I can only rejoice at this.

What I am trying to suggest is that we are not left on the one hand with a kind of flat-footed reliance on what psychology says about religion or what ESP says about theology and the Gospels. That is one awful end of the spectrum that has nothing to do with the real investigation and communication of one's tradition. On the other hand, I must reject out of hand the pseudo-mystification that follows when religious mystery insists upon its immunity from communion with science and with human life and with community and with human communication. Two very rough polarities that strike me as extremes.

In between is the constant historical effort to declare in the midst of those communities God hath given us to commune with that the mystery is humanly available. In the outer reaches where our minds operate, Christ is not at enmity with the workings of the intellect and the sensibility and the culture and the scientific and technological advances of man. Somewhere in that vast unknown land in which all men operate as ignorant people seeking light, the Christian operates, listening and learning and integrating and protesting.

I do not operate outside of any human endeavor or any human commitment or any tradition. At the same time I do not dissolve into those communities as finally expressive of my word about God and man. Therefore, I operate as a corrective, as a spur, as a source of exasperation. I operate at CURW; I operate as something the administration does not like, that the students may not like. I operate as another voice in the great community of hope and of human decency and human respectful intelligence and variety.

MOTIVATION

"A couple has lost a child in snake bite. The parents have come to the holy man with the body of the child asking for a miracle. They set the child's body down on the floor with a sheet over it and they sat around in silence with the holy man. He understands but says nothing.

"After some period of silence the holy man steps forward and lays his hands on the feet of the child and says, 'In 40 years, I have not believed in what I have done; may God have mercy on this child.' At that point, the poison left the feet of the child.

"After a silence the mother stepped forward and laid her hands upon the heart of the child and she said, 'In 20 years of marriage I have not loved my husband or served my family. May God have mercy on this child.' At that point the poison left the child's heart.

"Finally, after another period of silence the father stepped forward, placed his hands upon the head of the child and said, 'In 20 years of marriage I have not loved my wife or performed an act of kindness toward my friends. May God have mercy on this child.'

"At that point the poison left the child's head and he stood again."

The story is so rich and has meant so much to me

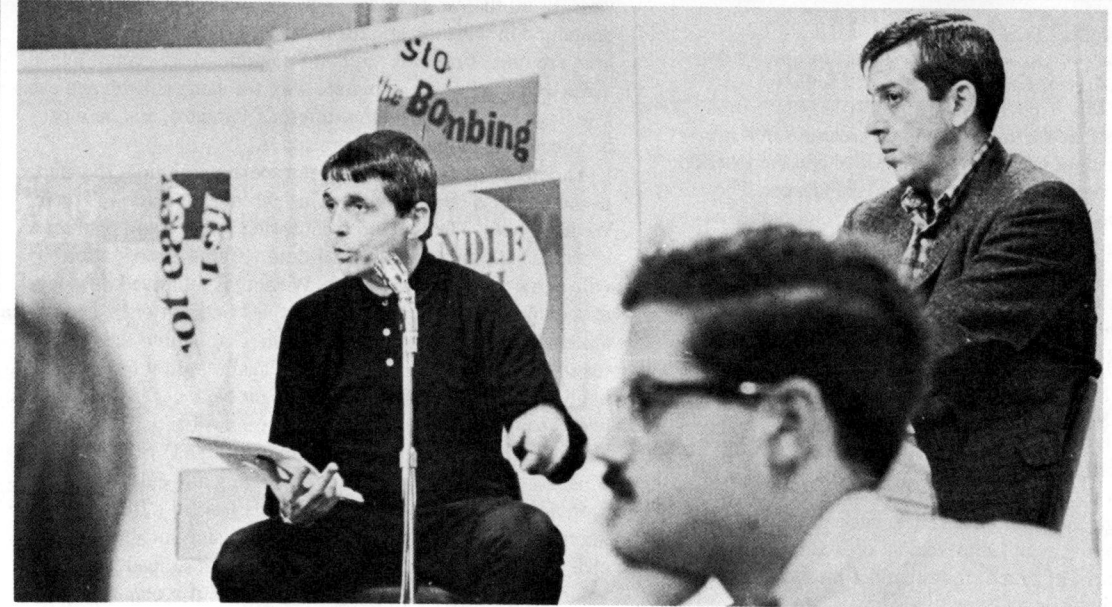

that I am at a loss where to begin. It has extraordinary and universal resonance. The meaning of the poison in the household, the snake that creeps into the family and then, most of all, the idea of innocent death; the idea that death can only be relieved by those who believe in life and that life is connected inexorably with the admission of personal guilt. The miracle of life-giving is always gradual. Death may be instantaneous but we only give life through patience. The poison killed the child so quickly that we are appalled. But the child is restored gradually only by an admission of guilt on the part of those who are responsible for the sacred and those who are responsible for life. It is only when death has been exorcised from the temple and the home that the child can stand again. Ultimately, as they admit, the priest and mother and father have killed the child; the snake is only a symbol of their hatred. I am trying to say something very important about myself and the students.

The only man who is interesting to a community is the man who can smell death. Not as the professional mortician who smells it for money or power or the soldier who smells death because he creates death. The only one worth talking about is the one who smells death in such a way as to restore life because he believes in life, because he believes that life has slightly more chance than death. Not a great edge because life is always in the breach; still such a man believes that man has a future. He does not believe that the future is in overkill, in stepping over the bodies of the dead and the living. His optimism is extremely guarded, it has grown modest through all he has endured. But his optimism allows him a slight edge over the killers because he has survived their methods whether jail or violence to his body or violence against his mind.

BERRIGAN

I speak as a minority figure. I've always been one. I try not to be romantic or obsessive about it but that is where I am. Around me is a minority group whether Christian or Jewish or humanist or secular. We represent, perhaps, only two percent of the community. From the point of view of anything now operating in society that remains true. Mine is an embattled, impoverished minority. My brother is just out of jail; he is in official disgrace. He is a cleric facing trial in war time and I am with him. The Society of Jesus, which is my community, which I love very much, which is the source of almost everything I have ever learned and valued is silent and will probably remain silent.

When I was in jail in Washington in November, I asked myself where the members of my community were. Why didn't a Jesuit come to see how I was or another member of the Catholic community? Why didn't someone come and say, "Where is Berrigan? I don't agree with what he is doing but he is my brother and, therefore, I must know how he is?" I look to my brothers in the Society for a communal effort toward redemption. But except for one priest, I was abandoned by the Society, and except for a fine Dominican chaplain, also by the Church. I was left to the community which grew up in that jail among the protestors — most of whom were not Catholics.

I don't want to make a great issue. I want to express my anguished longing which I am trying to be faithful to, to remain a priest in the Church and my Order. To invite my Order to a deeper understanding of itself, of the dead-end it is encountering by identifying through its silence with the structures of power, the war structures. This momentary evidence of power has nothing to do with real history, which is to say, the real Church. It may be necessary to be evicted from the Jesuits in order to do this. I have faced this and it is quite tolerable to me. I do not have any turn-off point at which I must say that my conscience must come to terms with what is officially acceptable. I must take the very absurd risk of saying that I could die in disgrace and die at peace in the hope that something would come later.

For the Church, I must say in all honesty, I have already outlined the choices and I have deliberately ignored the Catholic campus. I have ignored it because I believe it is unhistorical and finished. I have hoped not to be insensitive to the values of the best of these campuses but I am profoundly convinced that the time has come for them to integrate and reform themselves and make their values available to those who are passionately interested in entering into communion with the purity and depth of the Catholic tradition. And who, I might add, desperately need this resource.

We are facing a mysterious kind of new form of the immanence of God with regard to young people of very deep sacrificial possibility. I don't know whether it is inevitably connected with one period, one war, one crisis; or whether the times are really forming people who can be ready for whatever is going to happen. But let us rejoice in what is here. And what is here is a minority, extremely precious and exciting and full of promise for humanity with the Church.

BUDDHISM AND THE COMING REVOLUTION

Buddhism holds that the universe and all creatures in it are intrinsically in a state of complete wisdom, love and compassion; acting in natural response and mutual interdependence. The personal realization of this from-the-beginning state cannot be had for and by one-"self"——because it is not fully realized unless one has given the self up; and away.

In the Buddhist view, that which obstructs the effortless manifestation of this is Ignorance, which projects into fear and needless craving. Historically, Buddhist philosophers have failed to analyze out the degree to which ignorance and suffering are caused or encouraged by social factors, considering fear-and-desire to be given facts of the human condition. Consequently the major concern of Buddhist philosophy is epistemology and "psychology" with no attention paid to historical or sociological problems. Although Mahayana Buddhism has a grand vision of universal salvation, the *actual* achievement of Buddhism has been the development of practical systems of meditation toward the end of liberating a few dedicated individuals from psychological hangups and cultural conditionings. Institutional Buddhism has been conspicuously ready to accept or ignore the inequalities and tyrannies of whatever political system it found itself under. This can be death to Buddhism, because it is death to any meaningful function of compassion. Wisdom without compassion feels no pain.

No one today can afford to be innocent, or indulge himself in ignorance of the nature of contemporary governments, politics and social orders. The national polities of the modern world maintain their existence by deliberately fostered craving and fear: monstrous protection rackets. The "free world" has become economically dependent on a fantastic system of stimulation of greed which cannot be fulfilled, sexual desire which cannot be satiated and hatred which has no outlet except against oneself, the persons one is supposed to love, or the revolutionary aspirations of pitiful, poverty-stricken marginal societies like Cuba or Vietnam. The conditions of the Cold War have turned all modern societies—Communist included—into vicious distorters of man's true potential. They create populations of "preta"—hungry ghosts, with giant appetites and throats no bigger than needles. The soil, the forests and all animal life are being consumed by these cancerous collectivities; the air and water of the planet is being fouled by them.

There is nothing in human nature or the requirements of human social organization which intrinsically requires that a culture be contradictory, repressive and productive of violent and frustrated personalities. Recent findings in anthropology and psychology make this more and more evident. One can prove it for himself by taking a good look at his own nature through meditation. Once a person has this much faith and insight, he must be led to a deep concern with the need for radical social change through a variety of hopefully non-violent means.

The joyous and voluntary poverty of Buddhism becomes a positive force. The traditional harmlessness and refusal to take life in any form has nation-shaking implications. The practice of meditation, for which one needs only "the ground beneath one's feet" wipes out mountains of junk being pumped into the mind by the mass media and supermarket universities. The belief in a serene and generous fulfilment of natural loving desires destroys ideologies which blind, maim and repress—and points the way to a kind of community which would amaze "moralists" and transform armies of men who are fighters because they cannot be lovers.

Avatamsaka (Kegon) Buddhist philosophy sees the world as a vast interrelated network in which all objects and creatures are necessary and illuminated. From one standpoint, governments,

wars, or all that we consider "evil" are uncompromisingly contained in this totalistic realm. The hawk, the swoop and the hare are one. From the "human" standpoint we cannot live in those terms unless all beings see with the same enlightened eye. The Bodhisattva lives by the sufferer's standard, and he must be effective in aiding those who suffer.

The mercy of the West has been social revolution; the mercy of the East has been individual insight into the basic self/void. We need both. They are both contained in the traditional three aspects of the Dharma path: wisdom (prajña), meditation (dhyāna), and morality (śīla). Wisdom is intuitive knowledge of the mind of love and clarity that lies beneath one's ego-driven anxieties and aggressions. Meditation is going into the mind to see this for yourself—over and over again, until it becomes the mind you live in. Morality is bringing it back out in the way you live, through personal example and responsible action, ultimately toward the true community (sangha) of "all beings." This last aspect means, for me, supporting any cultural and economic revolution that moves clearly toward a free, international, classless world. It means using such means as civil disobedience, outspoken criticism, protest, pacifism, voluntary poverty and even gentle violence if it comes to a matter of restraining some impetuous redneck. It means affirming the widest possible spectrum of non-harmful individual behavior —defending the right of individuals to smoke hemp, eat peyote, be polygynous, polyandrous or homosexual. Worlds of behavior and custom long banned by the Judaeo-Capitalist-Christian-Marxist West. It means respecting intelligence and learning, but not as greed or means to personal power. Working on one's own responsibility, but willing to work with a group. "Forming the new society within the shell of the old"—the I.W.W. slogan of fifty years ago.

The traditional cultures are in any case doomed, and rather than cling to their good aspects hopelessly it should be remembered that whatever is or ever was in any other culture can be reconstructed from the unconscious, through meditation. In fact, it is my own view that the coming revolution will close the circle and link us in many ways with the most creative aspects of our archaic past. If we are lucky we may eventually arrive at a totally integrated world culture with matrilineal descent, free-form marriage, natural-credit communist economy, less industry, far less population and lots more national parks.

From *Earth Household* by Gary Snyder, New Directions 1969

1968 ... AND ANOTHER

CAN MAKE-UP COVER THE WOUNDS OF OUR OPPRESSION?

1969 ... AND ANOTHER

Women began challenging their roles as sex-objects and household slaves. Small groups developed into a movement of increasing militancy. Police raiding a gay bar in New York City were stoned by angry homosexuals. The militancy grew; the gay liberation movement was on.

THE ULTIMATE JUSTICE OF THE PEOPLE.

1969 . . . AND ANOTHER

1969 . . . AND ANOTHER

Destructive raids, trumped-up charges, jailings without bail, and murder by authorities fail to destroy the Black Panther Party.

Two teachers, a Panther, two anti-warriors, a pacifist and a couple of yippies represented a movement on trial in Chicago.

COMPREHENSION
Marcuse Moved By The
Movement

THE DIALECTICS OF LIBERATION

a review of Herbert Marcuse's

An Essay on Liberation

by Harold Jacobs

"We must grow tough,
but without ever losing
our tenderness."
—Che Guevara, 1967

In *One-Dimensional Man*, Marcuse argues that the technology of "advanced industrial society" creates individual needs and aspirations in its own image, institutes covert forms of social control and cohesion, and provides a level of productivity and growth potential that insures the stability of the system. The problem is that this social system exists within a framework of domination. The administered society systematically fails to provide for the unfolding of human potential; it depends for its survival on a permanent war economy; and it is structurally incapable of utilizing scientific progress and technology to meet human needs.

On the one hand, the system's apparent rationality, as reflected in its efficiency, growth, and increasing standard of living, shapes culture and consciousness in such a manner as to obfuscate its fundamental irrationality when viewed as a whole. On the other hand, the system precludes people from obtaining objective knowledge of the facts and engaging in intelligent evaluation of alternatives: meaningful self-determination is prevented by means of propaganda, indoctrination, and manipulation.

Generally speaking, the technological society provides a universe of discourse capable of containing critiques, while its institutions function to contain qualitative social change. Although Marcuse set himself the task of exposing the stabilizing mechanisms of the system, he was pessimistic about the possibilities of breaking the ideological hold of established institutions. He further observed that critical social theory possessed no explanation of how an advanced industrial society could be transcended in practice.

Critical social theory could point to antagonistic contradictions, but the dialectic revealed no demonstrable revolutionary agents of historical transformation. The industrial proletariat, having become incorporated into the system, could no longer be considered the agency of revolutionary change envisioned by classical Marxism. All that is left are "the substratum of outcasts and outsiders, the exploited and persecuted of other races and other colors, the unemployed and the unemployable." They partake of the Great Refusal. They have not been

integrated into the system, and their opposition cannot be deflected by the prevailing rules of the game. In this sense they are objectively revolutionary, regardless of their political consciousness. But they are not revolutionary in the sense that they, by themselves, can change the system in a qualitatively positive direction. It is perhaps in their power to create chaos or catastrophe, or to reform the system by making it more rational in its own destructive terms. But critical social theory cannot explain how they could constitute an effective agency of revolutionary change.

Barely avoiding despair, Marcuse embraces their revolt on existentialist grounds. He concludes *One-Dimensional Man* by expressing his loyalty to "those who, without hope, have given and give their life to the Great Refusal." '

Marcuse's latest book, *An Essay on Liberation,* can be best understood as an extension of the arguments developed in *One-Dimensional Man.* Marcuse expands his previous analysis by delineating more concretely in the new book the liberating tendencies within the established societies. He also provides a concrete vision of the possible forms freedom could take in an integral socialist society. Having dissected the evil nature of the "affluent monster" in *One-Dimensional Man,* Marcuse now concerns himself with analysing the tendencies working to undermine it, and outlining the kind of socialist society that could replace it.

Marx maintained that the historical agent of revolution among other things must be, at least potentially, the bearer of new goals and values. In *An Essay on Liberation,* Marcuse adapts Marx's insight to fit the exploitation and domination characteristic of advanced industrial societies, especially under conditions of corporate capitalism. Marcuse argues that the emergence of different life styles and aspirations from those generated by the repressive order is a precondition for revolution. This is all the more necessary with regard to present established societies, for to an unprecedented degree in human history their class structure, mass media, and politics combine to produce false class consciousness, to pervert rational and

emotional faculties, and to stifle imagination. Under these conditions, elementary human sentiments of social morality and solidarity have been repressed. The needs that do exist tend to strengthen the "voluntary servitude" of the exploited. Thus, Marcuse insists that along with political and social changes, the preconditions for liberation involve inculcating needs, aspirations, and satisfactions which differ from and negate those prevalent in the repressive societies.

Marcuse maintains that the needs reinforcing repression reach deep into the "instinctual structure" of human existence. Hence the difficulty in overcoming them; hence the creative effort needed to replace them with a new introjected morality and sensibility. Before men can move toward freedom they must begin to transcend the institutions and mechanisms of co-optation and repression. No revolution is possible unless "the rupture with the self-propelling conservative continuum of needs" precedes the revolution. For freedom to become a felt need, inside the womb of the old society men must begin to recreate themselves, to transform themselves into "new men," men "who have developed an instinctual barrier against cruelty, brutality, ugliness, . . . who have the good conscience of being human, tender, sensuous, who are no longer ashamed of themselves." The revolution has begun once the new sensibility and consciousness begin to replace the old. Marcuse thus strikingly supports the views of those in the movement who contend that the subversion of the culture of the established societies must be a prime political object of radical practice.

II.

One-Dimensional Man was published in 1964. The burgeoning insurgent movements that have arisen in the interim, culminating in the May Revolution in France, increasingly manifest the consciousness that a qualitative change affecting all of human existence is a perpetual possibility, that freedom in all its utopian possibilities is inherent in the productive potential of advanced capitalism and socialism. Marcuse regards this consciousness along with the new sensibility as *the* emergent political factor critical social theory must conceptually incorporate and evaluate in terms of its implications for the possibilities of human freedom. This task lies at the center of his efforts in *An Essay on Liberation.*

As Marcuse envisions it, the new sensibility expresses "the ascent of the life instincts over aggressiveness and guilt" and when accompanied by "a desublimated scientific intelligence" would foster "the creation of an *aesthetic ethos."* The "aesthetic" (that which pertains to art and the senses) is acclaimed as a possible form of the free society. Constructing a free society would be analogous to creating a work of art, a process whereby imagination would mediate between sensibility and reason, and beauty would emerge as a quality of freedom.

After describing what would be possible in a liberated society, Marcuse analyzes with extraordinary perspicacity the subversive effect that the new sensibility has had on the one-dimensional society's use of morality, language, and art. But he is cognizant as well of some of the one-dimensional aspects of the cultural revolution. For example, he criticizes those who intentionally withdraw from the established system in search of psychedelic truth as creating "artificial paradises" and escaping not only from "the exigencies of the existing order but also from those of liberation." Marcuse instead advocates "methodological disengagement and refusal of the Establishment" by means of a political practice that is informed by the rationality of liberation and aimed at both a socialist reconstruction of society and a "radical transvaluation of values."

III.

The social forces Marcuse cites as being part of the Great Refusal within the established societies are the youth, the intelligentsia, and the persecuted minorities, while outside the wretched of the earth wage armed class struggle. In the United States, the militant intelligentsia and the ghetto population are minorities within the middle class and the organized working class. The combined actions of the nonconformist young intelligentsia (struggling for freedom) and the ghetto population (fighting for basic material needs) have created a prerevolutionary situation. A revolution, however, is only possible if these two social forces act as catalysts for the industrial working class.

The industrial working class continues to be objectively and potentially the basic force of transformation. At present, it is acting as a stabilizing, conservative force and will continue to do so as long as the society remains economically stable and socially cohesive. Furthermore, the changing composition of the working class from predominantly blue to white collar workers—the "new working class"—tends to reinforce the integration of the class as a whole, owing to the new strata's present bourgeois conception of need and interest.

This ideological backwardness is threatened by the student movement, which is largely prospective new working class. Corporate capitalism supplies its vital and growing need for technical and scientifically-trained workers from the student labor pool. As student rebels begin to work in areas of material production, they will bring with them an increasingly militant anti-capitalist consciousness. The exchange of ideas and experience between the present and future members of the new working class allows for its gradual radicalization.

Given this prerevolutionary situation, Marcuse believes that the articulation of a new awareness and a new definition of need is the major task confronting the radical movement in the near future. If the radical forces fail to develop in the exploited a consciousness which overcomes their present enslaving conception of needs, then the movement will not break their dependence on the system of exploitation. As a result certain counterrevolutionary tendencies will be strengthened.

In particular, Marcuse has in mind two such tendencies. On the one hand, the racial conflict between blacks and whites and the emerging class divisions within the black community both reinforce the possibility that the economically "expendable" blacks might be severely repressed. On the other hand, the student movement faces the following "absurd situation." In using the administered democracy against itself, as it must, the student movement tends either to add to the system's legitimacy or to expose its hypocrisy and the destructive character of its institutions. The former results in cooptation; the latter, necessarily involving radical political practice, further isolates the movement from the masses and provokes intensified repression.

The established society, under the guise of "law and order," mobilizes the mass media and uninformed public opinion against the student movement. Marcuse provides the movement with the philosophical arguments it needs to defend much of its radical political practice. The survival of the movement depends on its ability to extend itself to new constituencies. To do so the movement must break through the established network of lies and distortions; it must fight for genuine opportunities to explain itself to its potential base; and its explanations must be grounded in the rationality of liberation. Marcuse, in laying out the requisite arguments, helps not only to disarm the movement's critics, but to sharpen the revolutionary consciousness of movement activists. In thus bolstering the theoretical confidence of young activists, he indirectly contributes to the likelihood that they will go forth as organizers and engage the masses in ideological struggle.

IV.

And when they do, Marcuse suggests they can take with them a more concrete vision than Marx was able to construct of an alternative to the two repressive modes of advanced industrial society—corporate capitalism and bureaucratic socialism. Briefly, an integral socialist society would be one which contained (1) collective ownership, control, and planning of the economy, (2) conditions and ends of production in keeping with a new, profoundly humane harmony between individual and social needs and aspirations, (3) an end to all economic, political, and cultural forms of exploitation and domination, (4) the subordination of the principles of efficiency and productivity to those of beauty and the overcoming of alienation, and (5) a co-operative work ethic, grounded in human solidarity and allowing for the enhancement and unification of life.

Marcuse embraces the principle of communist society: "From each according to his ability, to each according to his needs." But he goes beyond it by perceiving the possibilities of human liberty with a greater degree of specificity, particularly in his analysis of the nature of human needs most in keeping with liberation. What emerges is a vision of a classless society controlled by human beings who have an "instinctual" aversion to competition, aggressiveness, ugliness, and brutality. Hence, the inculcation of a new consciousness and sensibility in the working class of an advanced industrial society is not only a precondition for a socialist revolution, but an essential quality of a liberated society.

The possibilities for liberation are already inherent in the structure of advanced industrial societies. What is lacking is a working class with the requisite subjectivity to make concrete what is now, at best, only an abstract alternative. Marcuse, however, recognizes that the system is hardly free from severe economic and political contradictions. While the Soviet orbit's policy of "peaceful coexistence" helps stabilize capitalism, the Third World liberation movements materially and ideologically threaten the imperialist system's survival. The death blow, nevertheless, must come from within, from the disintegration of the internal structure and cohesion of the capitalist system. Intense class struggles, while threatening a socialist revolution, could still be contained within a capitalist framework by the suppressive force of the system. The gradual and decentralized collapse of state power will occur when not just the political but the mental repression of the system becomes insufferable. In Marcuse's words, this will occur when the system's "insane features, expression of the ever more blatant contradiction between the available resources for liberation and their use for the perpetuation of servitude, would undermine the daily routine, the repressive conformity, and rationality required for the continued functioning of society."

V.

Marcuse, as the author of *An Essay on Liberation*, emerges as the foremost theoretician of the revolutionary wing of the cultural revolution. In a mere ninety-one pages, he discusses almost every controversial issue being debated in the new left. Brilliant, courageous, passionate, concise—the book nevertheless is difficult to understand, owing to its neo-Hegelian circumlocutions. Each re-reading yields additional insights. It especially should be studied by doctrinaire Marxists who tend to discount the new left, by academic intellectuals who claim the left is shallow and has no vision, and by movement activists whose revolutionary practice is sometimes not matched by their theoretical acumen. But, despite its significance, the book suffers from one-sidedness, for it focuses almost entirely on the problem of creating a new way of life, rather than on building organization to confront the power of the state. And this is no accident given Marcuse's general theoretical orientation.

Marcuse is among those men of the left, such as C. Wright Mills and James Weinstein, who developed the theory of corporate liberalism. Molded by the temporary incorporation of the organized working class and isolated by the lack of mass radical political activity characteristic of the decade of the 1950's and early 1960's, they tended to view American capitalism as practically omnipotent in its ability to manipulate, manage, or co-opt opposition. In general, the period after the Second World War was projected as a post-revolutionary, stable epoch. While the left bemoaned this state of affairs, liberal and conservative theorists alike celebrated the apparent death of Marxist revolution and the end of ideology. The entire spectrum of social theorists, from Paul Baran to Talcott Parsons, called attention to the stabilizing features of corporate capitalism. For a revolutionary in the advanced industrial societies, it was a dismal time to be alive. It is in this context that Marcuse's *One-Dimensional Man* must be read

As I noted, Marcuse's main thesis was that the material goods produced by advanced industrial society cement it together. The pervasive output of commodities generates a way of life, a pattern of one-dimensional thought and behavior, which contravenes qualitative change. Marcuse assumed that people would not reach a point of satisfaction with regard to commodity production because in emphasizing the co-optive powers of the consumer economy, he overlooked the possibility expressed by Marx that satisfying one set of needs gives rise to another. While Marcuse was conscious of the growing revolt among middle-class youth, he could only praise it but not explain it.

Part of Marcuse's difficulty stems from the social psychological theory he adopts. In opting for an unadulterated Freudian perspective, Marcuse accepts its weakest point—Freud's instinctual drive theory of motivation. This led him to a relatively deterministic, integral theory of personality, one that postulates transcendence as an extraordinary event occurring only under exceptional circumstances. The alternative perspective, far more in keeping with the assumptions classical Marxism made about the "nature" of man, derives from the tradition of William James, George Mead, and John Dewey. Human social behavior is not taken to be a product of instinctual desires, but a construction arising out of interpersonal relations. Man is considered a malleable historical creation, possessing a self that is by nature both social and historical. Human transcendence is not an unusual, rare occurrence, but an immanent

possibility. In short, the yet-to-be-fully-realized intellectual synthesis of the twentieth century is not to bring together the views of Marx and Freud, but of Marx and Mead. Like so many of his generation, Marcuse has not been able to escape the pitfalls of the Freudian perspective. He thus postulated a one-dimensional consciousness and sensibility that reached into the instinctual structure of the human organism. This led Marcuse into overestimating the hold the consumer economy had over people's minds, while incorrectly projecting the economic stability and social cohesion that existed in the 1950's and early 1960's into the indefinite future.

But as Marcuse's critics have noted, there were limits to the manipulative ability of the system which manifested themselves in the latter part of the 1960's. The consequences of the Cold War and the instabilities of a permanent war economy, the increasing polarization between rich and poor, racial oppression and degradation, and the moral bankruptcy and sterility of a plastic, ego-centered culture provided the backdrop. *One-Dimensional Man* predated such events as the Berkeley Free Speech Movement, the anti-Vietnam War protests, Watts and other major ghetto rebellions, the campus revolts at Columbia and San Francisco State, the May Revolution in France, and this past summer's demonstrations at the Democratic National Convention. In *An Essay on Liberation,* Marcuse takes account of these events and the liberating tendencies they represent. He fails, however, to put them in the proper perspective, for he continues to regard the society as being dominated by a corporate liberal outlook.

Actually, prevalent tendencies indicate that we are in for a good dose of domestic fascism. The foreign and domestic consequences of the war in Vietnam have eroded the authority of the government to an unprecedented degree. With regard to the poor, the students and youth, the blacks—the system has demonstrated an incredible rigidity. Spokesmen for the ruling class find themselves increasingly unable to provide the people with acceptable explanations for the conduct and continuance of the war in Vietnam, the rapidly decaying cities, high taxes and increased military spending, escalating social conflict and violence, and the collapse of social morality. The tightly integrated and subtly controlled one-dimensional society Marcuse described is disintegrating more quickly than anyone thought possible. Manipulation and co-optation, while still important mechanisms of social control, are giving way to repression and raw police power. While the government prepares for the outbreak of guerrilla warfare in the ghettos by stockpiling military equipment and systematically moving to destroy black revolutionary leadership, high-ranking officials in the Justice Department talk

of detention camps for "ideological criminals." One need only look at the allocation of resources to see how little the society is spending on programs designed to co-opt in comparison with the substantial funds going to domestic counter-insurgency. The spokesmen for corporate liberalism can still be heard from occasionally in the person of a Teddy Kennedy or a John Lindsay. But they increasingly have assumed a defensive posture in the face of the ascending forces of "law and order." In sum, corporate liberal ideology has been overshadowed by widespread subservience to the ideas of repressive law and order while, at the same time, the ruling class gradually transforms the administered democracy into a form of institutionalized fascism.

Marcuse misguides the movement when he stresses the new, humane consciousness and sensibility without also drawing attention to the need for movement activists to acquire the skills, combativeness, hardness, and organizational strength to withstand police-state repression. We indeed have to remake ourselves but not only in the humane ways we might wish. We have to learn to discipline ourselves, to hate, to destroy, and to kill. This society will be liberated but unfortunately at the cost of much blood.

Perhaps the best we can hope for is that in the course of the struggle we can develop humane social relations among ourselves, while being engulfed by death and destruction. A Cuban journalist, Raul Valdes Vivo, reporting in *Granma* (February 12, 1967) on the youth brigades in North Vietnam, wrote: "the roads that these brigades open every day and at all hours . . . lead not only through space but also through time." He meant that under conditions of near barbarism, the young men and women of the brigades nonetheless consider themselves "brothers in everything" and "all live in communism":

> *Life in common, in the daily presence of death; work which if not collective would be impossible; the study of reality for the purpose of transforming it; poetry springing from the most commonplace (sweating, running, scraping off mud, calling to passersby, shooting) and, in sum, the awareness of greatness despite individual smallness, through the grandeur of what unites them all, is communism.*

We should strive for nothing less as we fight to liberate this inhuman society.

An Essay on Liberation, Beacon Press, 1969, by Herbert Marcuse.

Harold Jacobs is teaching in the sociology department at UC Berkeley and is active in the International Liberation School.

WHY TRIBE

We use the term Tribe because it suggests the type of new society now emerging within the industrial nations. In America of course the word has associations with the American Indians, which we like. This new subculture is in fact more similar to that ancient and successful tribe, the European Gypies—a group without nation or territory which maintains its own values, its language and religion, no matter what country it may be in.

The Tribe proposes a totally different style: based on community houses, villages and ashrams; tribe-run farms or workshops or companies; large open families; pilgrimages and wanderings from center to center. A synthesis of Gandhian "village anarchism" and I.W.W. syndicalism. Interesting visionary pamphlets along these lines were written several years ago by Gandhians Richard Gregg and Appa Patwardhan. The Tribe proposes personal responsibilities rather than abstract centralized government, taxes and advertising-agency-plus-Mafia type international brainwashing corporations.

In the United States and Europe the Tribe has evolved gradually over the last fifty years—since the end of World War I —in response to the increasing insanity of the modern nations. As the number of alienated intellectuals, creative types and general social misfits grew, they came to recognize each other by various minute signals. Much of this energy was channeled into Communism in the thirties and early forties. All the anarchists and left-deviationists—and many Trotskyites—were tribesmen at heart. After World War II, another generation looked at Communist rhetoric with a fresh eye and saw that within the Communist governments (and states of mind) there are too many of the same things as are wrong with "capitalism" —too much anger and murder. The suspicion grew that perhaps the whole Western Tradition, of which Marxism is but a (Millennial Protestant) part, is off the track. This led many people to study other major civilizations—India and China— to see what they could learn.

It's an easy step from the dialectic of Marx and Hegel to an interest in the dialectic of early Taoism, the *I Ching,* and the yin-yang theories. From Taoism it is another easy step to the philosophies and mythologies of India—vast, touching the deepest areas of the mind, and with a view of the ultimate nature of the universe which is almost identical with the most sophisticated thought in modern physics—that truth, whatever it is, which is called "The Dharma."

Next comes a concern with deepening one's understanding in an experiential way: abstract philosophical understanding is simply not enough. At this point many, myself included, found in the Buddha-Dharma a practical method for clearing one's mind of the trivia, prejudices and false values that our conditioning had laid on us—and more important, an approach to the basic problem of how to penetrate to the deepest non-self Self. Today we have many who are exploring the Ways of Zen, Vajrayāna, Yoga, Shamanism, Psychedelics. The Buddha-Dharma is a long, gentle, human dialog—2,500 years of quiet conversation—on the nature of human nature and the eternal Dharma—and practical methods of realization.

In the course of these studies it became evident that the "truth" in Buddhism and Hinduism is not dependent in any sense on Indian or Chinese culture; and that "India" and "China"—as societies—are as burdensome to human beings as any others; perhaps more so. It became clear that "Hinduism" and "Buddhism" as social institutions had long been accomplices of the State in burdening and binding people, rather than serving to liberate them. Just like the other Great Religions.

At this point, looking once more quite closely at history both East and West, some of us noticed the similarities in certain small but influential heretical and esoteric movements. These schools of thought and practice were usually suppressed, or diluted and made harmless, in whatever society they appeared. Peasant witchcraft in Europe, Tantrism in Bengal, Quakers in England, Tachikawa-ryū in Japan, Ch'an in China. These are all outcroppings of the Great Subculture which runs underground all through history. This is the tradition that runs without break from Paleo-Siberian Shamanism and Magdalenian cave-painting; through megaliths and Mysteries, astronomers, ritualists, alchemists and Albigensians; gnostics and vagantes, right down to Golden Gate Park.

The Great Subculture has been attached in part to the official religions but is different in that it transmits a community style of life, with an ecstatically positive vision of spiritual and physical love; and is opposed for very fundamental reasons to the Civilization Establishment.

It has taught that man's natural being is to be trusted and followed; that we need not look to a model or rule imposed from outside in searching for the center; and that in following the grain, one is being truly "moral." It has recognized that for one to "follow the grain" it is necessary to look exhaustively into the negative and demonic potentials of the Unconscious, and by recognizing these powers—symbolically acting them out —one releases himself from these forces. By this profound exorcism and ritual drama, the Great Subculture destroys the one credible claim of Church and State to a necessary function.

All this is subversive to civilization: for civilization is built on hierarchy and specialization. A ruling class, to survive, must propose a Law: a law to work must have a hook into the social psyche—and the most effective way to achieve this is to make people doubt their natural worth and instincts, especially sexual. To make "human nature" suspect is also to make Nature—the wilderness—the adversary. Hence the ecological crisis of today.

We came, therefore, (and with many Western thinkers before us) to suspect that civilization may be overvalued. Before anyone says "This is ridiculous, we all know civilization is a necessary thing," let him read some cultural anthropology. Take a look at the lives of South African Bushmen, Micronesian navigators, the Indians of California; the researches of Claude Lévi-Strauss. Everything we have thought about man's welfare needs to be rethought. The tribe, it seems, is the newest development in the Great Subculture. We have almost unintentionally linked ourselves to a transmission of gnosis, a potential social order, and techniques of enlightenment, surviving from prehistoric times.

The most advanced developments of modern science and technology have come to support some of these views. Consequently the modern Tribesman, rather than being old-fashioned in his criticism of civilization, is the most relevant type in contemporary society. Nationalism, warfare, heavy industry and consumership, are already outdated and useless. The next great step of mankind is to step into the nature of his own mind—the real question is "just what is consciousness?"— and we must make the most intelligent and creative use of science in exploring these questions. The man of wide international experience, much learning and leisure—luxurious product of our long and sophisticated history—may with good reason wish to live simply, with few tools and minimal clothes, close to nature.

The Revolution has ceased to be an ideological concern. Instead, people are trying it out right now—communism in small communities, new family organization. A million people in America and another million in England and Europe. A vast underground in Russia, which will come out in the open four or five years hence, is now biding. How do they recognize each other? Not always by beards, long hair, bare feet or beads. The signal is a bright and tender look; calmness and gentleness, freshness and ease of manner. Men, women and children—all of whom together hope to follow the timeless path of love and wisdom, in affectionate company with the sky, winds, clouds, trees, waters, animals and grasses——this is the tribe.

From *Earth House Hold* by Gary Snyder, New Directions

COMPREHENSION

HOW TO LIVE WHAT TO DO

Listen to the Secret Humming Of the Landlords

marjorie heins

The Panthers call us white mother country radicals, children of affluence, rebelling not against racism or oppression but against sterility and moral death.

We're not children any more. We've left home, we've left the warm university towns. Now, when we need an apartment or a job, we're treated as if WE were black—nothing overt usually, maybe a qeustion about noise or parties, a discrimination all the more infuriating because it is subtle.

When I walk through a department store these days, I'm followed by two anxious sales ladies and a dozen more pairs of eyes. They ask if they can help me find something. They want to make sure I pay for it.

Now don't tell me I look THAT seedy. Or is it the Oakland Seven fist button on my coat?

Our landlady explained she just HAD to raise the rent, in order to meet expenses. Desperate to move, we began checking classifieds. The first place we looked at was an attic in Bernal Heights. To reach it, we walked through a garage, and climbed two flights of rickety back stairs. We hit a bombed out porch, then two other tiny rooms, and finally a kitchen, where the landlord crouched, toying with pipes. The inside of the refrigerator was coated with black goo.

Another couple, the guy with a goatee, shuffled around the way people do when they pretend to be considering something important.

In the fifteen minutes we were there, four young hip-looking couples came and went. We all filled out applications, stating employment, bank references, etc. Being novices, my husband and I weren't too good at faking these.

The landlord said he'd let us know that night. We made our way down the back stairs, through the garage, and home, whereupon we discussed for two hours the pros and cons of moving to this paradise.

Of course, he never called. A straight-looking couple probably came in later, and got the place right off.

Then there was the basement in the depressed section of Potrero Hill. It had no refrigerator, few windows, dead cockroaches, and hard little dried up dog turns on the floor. One sink didn't work at all; the other sort of dribbled. I filled out an application, and took my husband back the next day to look at the place. When we got there, a young, blond, most cleanshaven couple stood in the hall, surrounded by a set of blue initialed luggage, and a portable TV.

* * *

I used to wonder why my father and so many of his friends were schoolteachers. During the Depression, he explained, that was the most financially secure job.

And after the Depression? A handful had ventured into other careers: business, stock market. Between Barricini candies, they made bad jokes about themselves: the office Jews, they never got ahead, even though they were so bright.

Most remained schoolteachers. From all of them, something had been stolen. Probably, it is the same thing Eldridge Cleaver means when he says that oppressed people have to revolt, violently, in order to experience themselves as men.

The saddest part is, having grown overweight and subject to the wills of their wives, these fiftyish Jewish schoolteachers from New York now seethe with race hate for the blacks who are finally insisting on that dignity so often denied the Jews by the WASPs and women's pages of America.

We Jewish children, who are now a good part of the white radical movement, and especially of the underground press, were not subject to the oppression of our parents and grandparents. Our rebellion took the form Black Panthers describe. A lot of it was guilt, compassion, reading about racism in the South. Many of us went South; a couple got killed. The oppression of black people grew realer and uglier to us. Civil rights activity flowered into an aggressive movement of great spirit and hope, known as Black Power.

The country polarized. Suddenly, much to the bewilderment of my parents and their friends, the word "liberal" became derogatory; now it is outmoded. There are only two sides. If we white mother country radicals have any doubt which side is ours, we have only to listen to the secret humming of the landlords.

San Francisco Express Times 3/18/69

A SMART KID WHO LEARNS TO BE A PROFESSOR SPENDS TEN YEARS TRYING TO UNLEARN IT ALL

Q: You've had therapy?

PAT: I was in therapy for almost two years.

Q: What's the relationship of therapy to taking acid?

PAT: They're both the same thing. They're just two ways of getting to the same place.

Q: How come you do both? Where do you [want to] go?

PAT: It's a hard question for me, because every time I get high I've gotten someplace different. From any place I've ever been before. The down world seems like a joke. When I'm really high, I do weird things with that. I think about being down and being high, and realizing that the down world's a joke. Then when I get high I realize that I didn't really understand at all. Only when I'm high do I really understand.

Q: What do you understand?

PAT: I understand how arbitrary and simple all the games are. . . . Maybe I'm just talking about my own alienation. When I was a kid, up to the second grade, like I felt that I really belonged, I didn't feel any different than anybody else. I think that the other thing began with reading. I had a sense of separateness that was partly because I was a lot smarter than the other kids, and partly because the pressures of becoming a social part of the school were so great that I was beginning already to withdraw. From about the third grade on up to twenty-two, I really tried like hell to get into that thing that everybody else was into. They really gave me shit all the way through grade school. I was the kid that just didn't belong. And when I think about it now, it seems to me that the nuns were even in collusion, that they really didn't admire smart kids, and I threatened them. I remember reading a Sir Walter Scott novel behind the stupid goddam reader and having the nun come up behind and crack me with her knuckles. . . . Even today I can hardly stand having anyone behind me when I'm reading. . . . So from about the third grade on I felt that I was living in a very alien world. . . .

Q: Where was this?

PAT: Seattle. My father owned a loan company . . . several. . . . I was angry that I was different, and I knew that I couldn't give up the thing that made me different, but I knew also that I couldn't have that other thing until I gave this up. And I felt like a fool because I couldn't give it up. And yet felt it would be degrading to do so. To give up the thing that made me different. I think a lot of it was neuroses, and some of it was pride, and some of it was creativity and sensitivity and intelligence. They were all mixed up together.

Q: What happened when you left junior high school?

PAT: Well, I didn't go to junior high school. I went to a Catholic grade school, a Jesuit or a Holy Names grade school. Then I went to a Jesuit prep school.

Q: You never went to a public school?

PAT: No, not until I started college. Then I went to the University of Washington, and I entered a fraternity — Sigma Chi — so I still didn't have much real contact with women. I was very frightened of them. And I feel that it's only in the past couple of years that I finally had an orientation that's closer to women than to men, and yet I've always had a strong sexual drive. . . .

And then when I was in college I had to reject fraternities, which I did in a sort of symbolic suicidal gesture. I joined the Air Force. . . .

Q: How old were you?

PAT: I had just turned twenty, maybe nineteen still, but close to twenty.

Q: How long were you in the Air Force?

PAT: I was in for three and a half years. I was an enlisted man and a survival instructor. It was a really beautiful experience for me. I spent a lot of time in the Sierras backpacking.

Q: You didn't hate it?

PAT: Yes, I hated the Air Force. But it was only in the Air Force that I began to see that the force of my anger extended out beyond me, it extended out into the whole society.

I met a guy from Reed College, [who] had a kind of a crush on me . . . he was a homosexual . . . and like I responded to it in a way, like I didn't ever have homosexual relations, but I really grooved on the feeling of intimacy that was there. He began turning me on to a lot of things I hadn't read before. . . . *Flowers of Evil,* and a book on semantics by Stuart Chase, and Proust. Then I found Faulkner by myself. After a couple months I began writing. I think it was the beginning of a process of reintegration.

Q: What did you write?

PAT: I began writing fiction. Really weird stuff. I wish I'd saved some of it. I was really a primitive. I had no idea of a literary society or all the asshole shit that goes down among good people. With publication and all that . . .

Q: I described you deliberately as a para-hippie. You dig the hip scene without being part of it — without having dropped out.

PAT: I feel almost as separate but a little less alienated from the kids on the street as I do from my colleagues. I say alienation from my colleagues, I don't mean there's any anger in it. . . . Maybe alienation isn't the right word. Different from. I feel that my solution has been pretty much an individual thing, because I didn't even know any Bohemians until I was about twenty-three. There weren't any in Seattle that I knew of.

Q: How old are you now?

PAT: Thirty-two. By the time I got out of the service, I knew what I wanted to do. I had a very strong sense of purpose. . . . I took a correspondence course in fiction writing from a groovy old lady who published a novel in the twenties. She thought what I did was really great. . . . She wanted to send my stuff out. I had incredible ambitions at that time. I remember saying to myself, "I want to be better than Shakespeare." Why not? . . . I learned pretty quickly . . . that what I was doing wasn't what *Partisan Review* wanted. . . . So then I decided, "Well, okay, I can't do this. Like I can't write what I want and make money at it. So how will I make money so I can write?" So I thought, well, I'll get into the whole teaching thing. I'll get a master's degree in creative writing. Then I'll teach someplace where it won't be much work.

43. KUAI-BREAKTHROUGH
-RESOLUTENESS

The Judgement:

One must resolutely make the matter
known at the court of the king.
It must be announced truthfully. Danger.

It is necessary to notify one's own city.

It does not further to resort to arms.

It furthers one to undertake something.

In a resolute struggle of the good against evil, there, are, however, definite rules that must not be disregarded, if it is to succeed. First, resolution must be based on a union of strength and friendliness. Second, a compromise with evil is not possible; evil must under all circumstances be openly discredited. Nor must our own passions and shortcomings be glossed over. Third, the struggle must not be carried on directly by force. If evil is branded, it thinks of weapons, and if we do it the favor of fighting against it blow for blow, we lose in the end because thus we ourselves get entangled in hatred and passion. Therefore it is important to begin at home, to be on guard in our own persons against the faults we have branded. In this way, finding no opponent, the sharp edge of the weapons of evil become dulled.... Finally, the best way to fight evil is to make energetic progress in the good.　　I CHING

maybe six units or something. So I went back [to school]. . . . Then I got married, to a girl who I married because she was not like my mother.

It was at that point that the external part of my life became different from other persons'. I didn't even know what beat was then, but I didn't have much money, and my parents refused to recognize the marriage.

Q: On what grounds did they object? Religious?

PAT: Yeah, the girl was divorced. . . . So we moved into a little place on the east side of Lake Washington, on the shore. A cabin. It was a beautiful place. . . . I remember lying back on this couch I'd made and listening to jazz that was on, and watching the trees and stuff.

And my wife had a kid who died that winter, which created a terrible feeling in me about death. I didn't realize I was mortal until . . .

Q: What did it die of?

PAT: We'd dropped her off in the morning at my wife's mother's place. She was going to go to school at nine o'clock, and she had a little bit of sniffles. [My mother-in-law] wasn't going to send her to school. By noon she had a little fever [and was] put to bed. By five o'clock in the afternoon she was convulsing. I was giving her artificial respiration and she opened her eyes and they stayed open and she shat on the bed. I couldn't believe she was dead. The firemen came. And doctors. They gave her a tracheotomy. [But] she was already dead when they came. It really frightened me. It was spinal meningitis.

Q: How old was she?

PAT: She was five going on six. . . . We were going to a place called Krishna Vedanta Center where they were turning people on with acid. This was in 1957. I didn't know what LSD was. They were turning people on and sitting around and playing music. We never turned on there, but we had smoked a lot of grass. My wife had a friend who was a musician who used to come up from L.A. and he'd bring us grass when he'd stay with us. We began to know people who were sort of like ourselves, only we didn't have a name for it. The school thing was going very well; I was very bright. In almost every class I was clearly the smartest student. And increasingly I could learn more than everybody else. . . .

And also I was still . . . like all my life I had had to feel competitive, or feel I was staying with my head out of water. So that whole thing carried over. I was always treated in terms of goals I was achieving. I'd retained that. Which is a hangup.

Q: Why is it a hangup?

PAT: Well, sometimes when I'm pounding a nail, I really work like hell to get that nail pounded, and forget what my arm feels like pounding the nail. I feel that kind of shit might kill me someday too. Anyway, [to get back]. All these people were pretty freaky. [But] there was no sense of community. There was a sense of people that were at least different. . . . Then I got a Woodrow Wilson Fellowship, and I had to go somewhere. So I decided I would go to Berkeley. By this time my marriage was just total shit. We lived in an Oakland flat that was fantastically bad, all the neighborhood kids had colds all winter long, so we had colds all winter long. . . .

I started getting political at Berkeley. In May 1960 there was the HUAC thing down at City Hall. I was pretty involved in school and I didn't go down but I knew people who did and they put it on me that I should have gone down, and I recognized that I had an obligation there. So I began getting more political, and seeing that the whole fuckup in our society probably had political origins. That our political system was disfunctional. And it's strange that this realization should come so late. I was a graduate student when it came. Kids learn a lot faster now. . . .

So I went back to the University of Washington and by that time I knew school was bullshit. . . . One teacher I had admired said, "Quit worrying so much about unanswerable questions; you're here to get a union card." It was sort of a concretion of what I felt anyway. So I went back to Seattle and moved into a housing project. And really grooved on that whole scene. . . . About that time I met this guy and his wife. They were like old-time Bohemians. They'd made that scene. He was a painter, a really good one. He had a really nice skid-row place, and I used to go down there at night. I used to go to some Indian bars on skid row and also a German bar. . . . By this time I didn't really study hard. Really child's play. But I knew I was going to go through with it anyway. I didn't do any work. I would start out a course being very brilliant, show them a rough draft of the term paper, and they'd say you should publish this. Then I would do the final paper, which would be longer but shittier.

Also at that time I began to develop something that I think is very important in my life — a sense of historical consciousness. I was part of the continuum. I think that's why I teach eighteenth-century literature, because of its engagement in society, so that immediately when you begin working with literature, you're working with social problems, political problems, problems of the impact of technology and culture.

Q: How would you apply that to the Haight-Ashbury?

PAT: I've got very well-formed views about that. I think that we now live in a society of abundance, if we'll only see that it is one. And when we do see it, then we can stop worrying about work. If we do it before we blow ourselves up, we could come out on the other side of technology. I feel that technology has been

very disruptive for our society. It's almost an accident that technological man preceded psychological man. I think we're in the Stone Age of psychological man now, but we're making great advances. With Freud and Jung, we invented the real, and we may make it. Psychological man is overtaking technological man. I do not believe the solution for the whole culture is anything like a utopian society. For one thing, conscience always destroys utopian communities. . . .

And that's what's happened, I think, on Haight Street. Like it's affected all the leaders. If it had gone the way of Jimmy who stood up and said, "Fuck everybody and fuck everything, I'm going to do my thing," if it had gone that way, it could be an entity. But it's involved with public relations and committed to this society, which in a way is good. Yet it destroys it as a utopian possibility.

I don't know about the [Digger] farms; probably they're okay, I don't know. I haven't been out there. But the thing in the city is very much involved with public relations. So it's fragile, and dependent on the old society for an image of itself. And dependent also on the old society to change. In order that the people in the Diggers and the people that are working with them can have feelings of self-worth, you've got to accomplish things in the real world. That's good. But that's what destroys the possibility of a utopian community. . . .

The way it has to be is like the whole Digger thing, getting bigger and bigger and bigger. New Digger societies . . . all over the country. Until enough people are insisting that you not do what we're doing — acting as if we're living in a Communist scare, acting as if we can't get along without this three per cent yearly increase in our gross national product. Destroying the whole character of our country. That part of the consumer dollar, that portion which is growing fastest, and taking from other portions, is that part which is going into consumer research. It's not really to help anybody, or to build a better product, it's a way of coercing somebody to do what you want . . . in this case to value your product. In most cases people have enough things now.

That's where this country is. We've got so many things we could all puke. . . .

Q: Why is the movement happening here?

PAT: Because of the beat thing in the fifties, and it's a nice climate. In the fifties, when I was in the service, I'd go over to North Beach, and I remember . . . most people, at least publicly, used juice instead of pot. And we'd go up to somebody's place and sit on a mattress and get juiced. And there was all the excitement of being a beatnik and that whole thing. But that thing petered out. All the types that were born there like Neal Cassidy, there are hundreds of kids living out Neal Cassidy's views right now. It's just something that evolved. I don't see it as any different. . . .

Q: The kids feel that this is different.

PAT: Yeah, they can. That's okay. Sure, because they weren't around for this other thing.

Q: How do you square your job, your income, with the belief that the culture is corrupt?

PAT: For one thing, I feel that if you want to find the roots of our present problems, the vital roots, you can go back to the seventeenth century and see them becoming public issues and big problems then. You can see the rise of technology [and] the thing Swift was so worried about — abstraction. It's only through abstraction that we can have cybernation and cybernation will finally free us from the hangups of the physical universe. But first in order to do that the natural philosophies had to alienate us from the physical universe. Swift saw that. He saw that the man who could think mathematically before pragmatically was capable of turning sunshine into cucumbers and shit into food. He could do anything. He could even build the atomic bomb, which eventually he did. Blow up everything. We may yet. It's important that kids should know their tradition, if it's only known in order to be rejected. . . . I get very involved in the historical questions, because I feel that in this instance, although not always, the truth will set them free. They can see where it all started and see what the problems are, and they'll have a better understanding, and they'll see what's bullshit, they can see what's transitory, what's irreparable, what you can't change but what you now have to move beyond.

Q: Couldn't you teach that outside the context of a college?

PAT: I've had several times a desire to get out, and I have some urges right now. I'm really happy with Diane, she's a good wife. Pretty straight. But I've got that Neal Cassidy myth floating in the back of my head, and sometimes I want to get on the road and go, or just blow my mind on something. And I've also got a desire to make it out of this shit by myself. I'm building [a] cabin up in the Sierras right now. Sometimes I feel like getting out by myself. I feel there is that perfect place, at the end of a road. . . . An opening out, a blessing, a forgiveness, a radiance. So I've had a lot of times the impulse to get out. . . . not to make ten thousand dollars a year, not to publish, but just to take off and demand and get everything right now. . . .

Q: What would you be?

PAT: I'd be stoned. You've got to do it by being stoned. This guy in Seattle that was kind of a guru for me is pretty stoned.

Q: You're still not saying what the ideal world looks like. Is it being stoned all the time?

PAT: No, I don't see that that's the ideal world, but I see it as one kind of extreme solution to the present one. I think of the ideal world as being much softer and not requiring extreme solutions. The first thing we'd have is a guaranteed annual income. . . .

With the degree of automation we have now . . . we can produce goods as they are needed. People will have the money for what they need. I'm imagining a situation which is not quite revolutionary, maybe rapidly evolutionary, where there are enough people who want to work to take care of all that and more. [Now] we have to play all kinds of games, . . . getting to the moon and all that, just to keep a three per cent unemployment rate, and our unemployment rate is artificial. It's really about seven or eight per cent, it doesn't count the people who've dropped out or who've been forced to drop out. So you just give those people money. . . . I feel the present political system is a farce. It stands in the way of everything, although I'm not sure what political system, if there's any I would approve of. I see a kind of technocracy. Like people who are machine people, let them run the machines, and the machines will take care of physical wants.

Q: Would the machine people be stoned?

PAT: That would be up to them. . . . Everything would be a lot more open. I think appeals of private ownership would disappear except for aesthetic reasons. . . . If somebody wanted to build something, it would be their thing to build. Having built it, it would be anybody's. There might be an aesthetic involvement in the creation of something, and [one] might very well take some kind of symbolic proprietary interest in it at that time, but then after that, it's anybody's.

Q: But then stoned doesn't mean on drugs.

PAT: I feel that I've altered my consciousness permanently with acid. And that I could alter it more. Permanently, with acid or meditation or freedom.

Q: To what degree is this vision like the vision of the Haight-Ashbury?

PAT: I don't see that there's much relation. I think that what's going on now in the Haight-Ashbury can be about as traumatic for the kids entering it as it was for me to enter the first grade. A lot of the kids don't know much about getting along with one another. And they've got a philosophy that obliges them to love everybody and particularly the guy that's sitting across from you, disregarding the fact that his eating habits are a big drag. And he's slopping things all over the table. Or obliges them to love somebody who's bum-tripping them, or selling them bad acid. . . .

What you have . . . I feel in the Haight-Ashbury is a situation something like this: there's some leaders, some beautiful people, [and] a few bad ego trips, and a lot of people like myself, who've been around the subculture for a long time, who are presently withdrawing from the Haight-Ashbury. Most of the people I know in their thirties don't like to go down Haight Street now. I mean hip people. Some of the hippest people I know are moving out of the Haight-Ashbury because they don't like to get hassled. By the police, by landlords, by all the shit. . . .

Q: Some people speak of the Haight-Ashbury as being first revolutionary and secondly transitional toward something important.

PAT: I think it's a turn-on. It's rough and traumatic for some of these kids, but it's turning them on to something entirely new. I feel that the Haight-Ashbury won't change society, but that these kids when they leave the Haight-Ashbury will change society. I've seen a couple of kids who've gone through it, like down through the whole communal thing, and back and gone away and done their own thing carrying with them what they've learned, and what they've sensed and felt. They're beautiful people, and I think they've saved themselves. . . .

Q: Is acid the key to that salvation?

PAT: I don't think so. The first time I took acid . . . well, I got very far out, the first time I took it. I had hallucinations that had no relation to the particular reality I was in for about three hours. I was soaring through time and space. I saw this fantastic dream creature with my whole body . . . like from my forehead down to my toes. I got very, very vibrant. . . . When I came back down I thought, "Jesus Christ, I'm going to have to spend the rest of my life telling people about it." Since that time I've had a few friends that have blown their minds on acid, and there are lots of people who've taken a lot of acid who don't yet lead good lives. It's not the acid alone that does it. It's partly a shuck that the middle-class society puts on the Haight-Ashbury in order to give them a reason for rejecting it.

I mean, kids don't wear bells because they've taken acid. They wear bells because they believe that you can celebrate your way as you go. And like, adults have responded to kids who have long hair and bells as if the drug was making it that way, which is a cop-out.

No. I think that probably we could all be that way without drugs. I think eventually there will be complete sexual freedom. And with that maybe people will stop taking drugs.

Q: What constitutes complete sexual freedom?

PAT: Well, I suppose complete sexual freedom is fucking anything and everything, and getting fucked by anything and everything — anytime, anyplace. This sounds incredible in the context of our cultural tradition, yet I don't believe that human beings are dirtier than dogs. Dogs can fuck in the street and everywhere. I've never seen a human being that wasn't interested in a dog fucking in the street. I've never known a human being that wasn't interested in a human being fucking. Yet we treat our interest as prurient or morbid. . . . All inhibitions and repressions are so deep in our culture that in spite of the bullshit about hippies in the newspapers, not many hippies have managed to achieve sexual freedom yet that I know of. And I haven't myself, but I feel that maybe my kids will, and I know that their kids will. I mean the thing that Wordsworth is talking about, the prison house growing up around you, is the conflict between the desire to reach out and touch everything and the society that puts bars between your hands and your cock, and flowers and cunts and life. Wordsworth couldn't express it that way, and maybe it's all the more powerful because it's not openly expressed, but that's what I feel is implicit in the "Immortality" ode. That's what society is, in a large part, is a regulating mechanism to distribute inhibitions and repressions in order to make possible certain types of activities which are necessary in a scarcity economy. . . .

Q: Do you feel yourself in flux about where you are? Is that the common bond between you and the Haight?

PAT: No, I feel that I'm more settled in that way than most people. I don't feel that that's my bond with them. I've got a few notions that are a little far out and a life which is pretty quiet. . . . I'm not sexually free. If I were I'd be a different person. I would have to be a different person to be sexually free rather than wanting to be. . . .

Q: Is the hip community achieving [sexual freedom]?

PAT: No, but there are some people who are. . . .

Q: Can you find a model of sexual freedom in the community? Does acid free people enough for it?

PAT: What I feel is happening with a lot of young kids is pretty rough. There are a lot of young girls who are coming in from the suburbs who really want to get laid and be liked and be loved. And they're getting fucked but they're not getting loved. And that's because the young males in the Haight-Ashbury still have their own hangups. They can't love everybody. Or they can't see that to embrace somebody is to love them. So like I know a couple of communal places . . . that have had more and more meth-heads going all the time, and girls are getting stoned on meth and get fucked for a couple of days until they freak out. But that's not sexual freedom, that's sexual compulsion. . . .

Q: Where does love come in fucking an object?

PAT: You can't fuck an object. That's a paradox. You realize on acid that the whole relation between self and other postulated in Western culture as if they were entities, self and other, is bullshit. In a sense there is no other.

Q: Then what is sexual activity?

PAT: Loving. Yourself and that is the whole universe. If you love the whole universe, then you love yourself. I feel that few civilized people who haven't had acid ever experience sex. Maybe there are some primitives, but that's so totally different. Like you recognize what, if we were free, sex would be for us. And it doesn't have much to do with genitalia. That's just one place. It's polymorphous.

Q: Until acid, then, nobody had experienced it? Blake must have experienced it.

PAT: Yeah, maybe, like with an angel. Visionaries have experienced it. People may have had intimations of it with amyl nitrite. But I feel this is something that is bound to be misunderstood. . . . When I'm talking about sexual freedom, I'm talking about no inhibitions on love. . . .

Q: Why do you think you're personally so tidy?

PAT: I have a desire for order.

Q: How do you square that with the role of the avant-garde professor?

PAT: It seems to me that my desire to create a world more possible for my students and my kid and the people coming *is* a desire for order and that it informs my teaching, my poetry, and lots of my life.

Q: What kind of an order do you foresee?

PAT: Simply this: an end to disorder. . . . Human society as it can be is the most highly organized natural community in the animal kingdom. We are in many ways fallen gods, but we're still gods and we have a capacity for a godly kind of order.

I really don't feel that that's bullshit at all. I really feel it's there. I sense it. I said once before that I rejected the idea of my being in the avant-garde and I accept the idea of my being a traditionalist, because I feel that what I'm trying to do is to recapture the world of order that's implied in literature, which itself comes after that high order that's communal. I feel that the artistic expression itself is very highly indicative of a society that's fallen away from its natural goodness; and yet it helps lead us back.

From *Voices From the Love Generation* ed. Leonard Wolf, Little Brown

Ed. Note: Interview with Pat Gleeson, professor of English at S.F. State College, who was a planner of some of the major happenings in the Haight Ashbury community.

letters

WHAT DO YOU TELL THEM?

dear people,

i want to drop out. i am highschool age, and am sick of "living" according to the System. if there are any communes, areas, or just people who could help me, please do. don't tell me to change what's here. what i've tried to do in this vein has failed—has met with suppression by my parents. i want to *live*. please print this letter . . . there are many like me who have contemplated/are contemplating/or have committed suicide.

love,
steve

(Write to steve c/o WIN, and we'll forward.)

Dear Steve, and "the many like you":

Carleton Collective Communities Clearinghouse (Carleton College, Northfield, Minn. 55057) has just recently begun, so they may not be too much good to you right away, but they're the only place I'm aware of that's trying to connect people who are looking for communes with communes that are looking for people. They charge 50 cents per xeroxed file of each commune you pick from their list.

Vocations for Social Change (Canyon, Calif. 94526) can give you a lot of addresses of communities and organizations in need of helping hands—and perhaps more importantly, as far as you're concerned, of those who help runaways. Just write the VSC and ask for a copy of their newsletter. Send them some bread if you can; they need it and deserve it.

"Runaway" is what you'll be, you know, if you leave home before you're 18. This means you're not only fair game for any cop-type on the road, but also that you're liable to bring heat down on anyone who gives you any assistance. That's lousy, but that's how it is—and it means you've got to be super-cool, and you can't expect a brass-band welcome from folks who are already hassled by uptight straight neighbors. I'm not trying to scare or dissuade you; I just hope you realize that your parents aren't your only potential suppressors. Dropping out of the "System" is great, but not very easy.

Lots of luck—you're gonna need it,
Paul Johnson

win 6/1/69

WHAT DOES
A STUDENT
RADICAL DO
WHEN HE
GRADUATES?

From the **CANYON COLLECTIVE** Box 77,
Canyon, Ca. 94516

TO CHANGE THE WORLD COMPLETELY IS ALL WE WANT. AND IT ISN'T ALL THAT HARD. THE EMERGENCE OF LIVING

SITUATIONS THAT PLAY WITH THIS WORLD AS THEY CREATE A NEW ONE. PEOPLE TAKING THEIR OWN POWER INTO THEIR OWN HANDS: THIS IS POSSIBLE ALL THE TIME — EVERYWHERE

THE BEGINNING OF THE END OF THE END OF THE

RADICAL THEATRE REPERTORY

Seventeen theatre ensembles have joined together as participating groups of the RADICAL THEATRE REPERTORY. They state: "The member groups, and dozens of others in this country and abroad, are in the vanguard of a new phenomenon in theatrical and social history -- the spontaneous generation of communal playing troupes, sharing voluntary poverty, making experimental collective creations, and utilizing space, time, minds, and bodies in manifold new ways that meet the demands of our explosive period. RTR arranges tours, one-night stands, radical theatre festivals, lecture-demonstrations, film programs, and conferences for its member groups with universities, schools, organizations and communities throughout the world." (from the RTR brochure)

Members of the RTR include: Living Theatre, Firehouse Theatre, Open Theatre, The Performance Group, Daytop Theatre Company, OM Theatre Workshop of Boston, Pagent Players, GUT Theatre, Concept East: New York; Drama Group of Mobilization for Youth, Theatre Black, Black Troupe, Playhouse of the Ridiculous, Caraban Theatre, Bread and Puppet Theatre, El Teatro Campesino, and the San Francisco Mime Troupe.

To arrange engagements for any of these groups, and for new groups now in process of joining RTR, please call or write to: Oda Jurges, Co-ordinator, Radical Theatre Repertory, Inc., 32 Washington Place, Room 74, New York, NY 10003. Phone: (212) 598-2525 or 598-3279.

A CONTINUING COLUMN...

What does a student radical do when he graduates? What CAN a student radical do, after graduating, to keep body and soul together and continue to work in the Movement? What existing organizations, or even organizational forms, are there for the adult white radical?

For an increasing number of radicals, now students or only shortly separated from universities, this is an important problem. It is significant not only to them, but to the development of an adult left in America. If the only white radicals in the country are students, then the left in America is doomed to failure.

We address ourselves to this problem also because the student movement seems to have exalted the position of full-time organizer ("true revolutionary") and by implication to have criticized those who are not in the position of being able to live this life of luxury, supported by others. That attitude is elitist and untenable. It reveals not only a class background which afforded students the luxury of not working for a living, but also a lack of either understanding or sympathy for the majority of the people of this country who don't have that luxury. The view that only full-time politicos can be true radicals denies the role of ALL working people in building a revolutionary movement — whether they started work after elementary school, high school, or college.

(In many ways it is analogous to the mistaken attitude once held by many in the early peace movement: that soldiers are the enemy. We have learned that soldiers are one group of victims, those forced to do the dirty work, of the real enemy, American corporate capitalism.)

There can be no doubt that the Movement needs full-timers, nor that more more such roles, as organizers, on newspapers, etc., must be created as the Movement grows. But this is no answer to the larger question.

Radcials in the Professions, Vocations for Social Change, etc., are efforts to deal with the problem. But they are limited — limited in regard to the number of people who can participate, and limited in regard to the range of political issues that professional interest groups can deal with.

There is not yet an adult counterpart to SDS. Movement for a Democratic Society (MDS) is an effort to meet this need. Perhaps a political party is one answer. We don't know

As it exists now, the New Left is mostly a student movement with adults who were once students who center their political activities still around students or college-community areas. The left needs to create new organizations and forms so that it does not remain basically a student movement.

The Old Mole asks readers to contribute suggestions and articles on this problem. Include your name, address, and phone.

OLD MOLE 5/9/69

WORK, WORK, WORK

A lot of us are talking about the working class nowadays: but what about work itself? What does it mean for particular people to have to work at a particular job? What is work like under this system; how does it affect the people who do it; what do they think about their working lives?

Some years ago, **New Left Review** (London) began to publish a series of personal accounts written by people in a wide variety of different occupations describing their work and their feelings about it and themselves. A factory worker on the dead time of factory work: but also a busdriver, a computer programmer, a "housewife." They wrote about what they did; and they also wrote about the meaning of what they did, about what they wanted out of life, what they settled for, what they still want. It is not heard to understand what a bus driver does: but what does it mean to **be** a bus driver, eight hours a day, forty hours a week, fifty weeks in the year, year after year? That is what these personal accounts are all about.

Twenty of these accounts, collected together by Ronald Fraser, were recently published in England by Penguin Books under the Title, **Work**. **Work** also contains a concluding essay by Raymond Williams (author of **The Long Revolution**) on the meaning of work—as it is, as it could be. **Work** is not commercially available in the United States; but through a special arrangement with **New Left Review, Leviathan** will sell copies of this important collection to its readers. To receive a copy of **Work** send this coupon with $1.50 (which includes postage) to: **Leviathan, 2700 Broadway, New York, N.Y. 10025.**

GETTING
TO KNOW
AMERICA

In effect, it will be necessary for some elements of the movement to cut themselves off from the organized left and the student culture. They will have to live, work, and struggle with the mass of Americans, at first to learn, only later to teach. They will have to organize around what the people perceive to be their problems—probably not war and racism. Only by living with and learning from the people will revolutionaries be able to speak to them in a language that is understandable.

*T*he organizational form of the American Revolutionary Movement cannot be predicted, because it will have to grow from the activity of the people as revolutionary culture again merges with American culture. As new leadership develops among the people, new organizational forms will be created (this has already happened in the black movement, first in SNCC, then in the Panthers).

It does seem unlikely to me that the new movement will be centralized, bureaucratic, or Leninist in form, partly because of the great diversity in America, partly because the American revolutionary tradition is primarily anarchist. In any event, for the next five to ten years, the movement will, I believe, be decentralist. The most viable organizational form for that period will likely be thousands of rather small collectives, or affinity-groups, carrying out individual projects. Some may work around movement institutions like schools or presses; others may be organizing committees in shops, neighborhoods, or vocations.

One advantage of such groups is that they minimize the amount of time spent on internal organizational problems since they are small and most coordination takes place in a natural, almost instinctive fashion. A second advantage is security, both from external agents and provocateurs, and from left disruptors. Finally, they provide an atmosphere of mutual support and trust which is essential to the psychological well being of individual organizers. There should, and will be some national coordinating agency for these groups. I doubt that it will take the form of a party. It may be the resurgent IWW, which has the advantage of having been the greatest revolutionary organization in our history. Or it may be an entirely new federation.

The regular left will not, and should not, disappear. Student organizing, anti-war activity, non-violent confrontations, and so on will all continue to play an important role in shaking the conscience of America. But unless some of us are out there talking and working with the people while they're being shaken, they will never understand.

The new movement must, as Walt Whitman said of the new poetry, "bend its vision toward the future, more than the past. Like America, it must extricate itself from even the greatest models of the past, and, while courteous to them, must have entire faith in itself, and the products of its own democratic spirit only. . . .

From "Getting to Know America" by Bob Cook, Aug/Sept 1969

LIBERATION

Keep on Truckin'...

TAKING A STEP INTO AMERICA

(The following is a report given by the National Community Union and the community organizing workshop at the SDS National Council meeting of 28–30 March.) *1968*

We are, by and large, from the middle class. We have spent most of our time there; we do not know America. We must take a step into America; we must discover what is all around us, for if we don't we will never realize our democratic and revolutionary ideals.

At the 1966 Convention in Clear Lake, Iowa, SDS moved toward a conception of ourselves as a union of organizers. We would reach out to people, knowing we had something good, rather than waiting on people to come to us. Too few of

us have taken that development seriously. We talk of going in to organize neighborhoods or factories, or relating to those projects with some professional skill, but too few of us have moved.

We (the NCU and the workshop) suggest that SDS look upon this summer as one of 'forced transition'. We want people to look at parts of America that most of them don't know. By living and working with poor and working people, we believe that many students will learn that organizing in poor and working class neighborhoods is not the ascetic, austere, monk-like trip that remains with us in image from the peanut butter and jelly days that Andy Kopkind wrote about in 'Of, By and For the People'. We bet that many who try it will stick -- they will learn many things, things that they may put to use as organizers if they decide to stay on. We suggest this experience for the summer not only for those who think that they want to be community organizers some day or a radical teacher working with a community organization some day, but also people who know right now that they want to be academics -- the experience will do them good and will help in their organizing and teaching on the campus.

Look: students aren't going to do much organizing in a summer; to think so is presumptuous. Some people talk of doing agitational work, maybe around the draft, and then returning to school. Well, there are a lot of problems with that, but it's okay. Yet we can do more than agitational work this summer. We can place ourselves in a position (who we work with, and where) that will help us to organize ourselves, that will give us a broadened picture of what the world is all about, and how we as radicals can work effectively to change it in the 1-2-3-4-5-6-7-8-9-... years to come, whether we end up living in working class or middle class settings.

WE SUGGEST

1. Encouraging people to go to cities where there will be many things happening; where we have relatively stable movement operations (Chicago, Cleveland, etc.); places where there are people who've been around awhile and can help give direction.

2. That the first priority in these cities be for people to work with existing organizing efforts underway and new projects just getting started.

3. That people go to work in factories. This is perhaps the most difficult thing for people leaving campus to do, but it is probably the most important. We can make contacts, learn, and maybe some will stick and really get something going over time.

4. All people who don't work full time in factories should rely on day-labor work for support, working one or two or three days a week. It would be possible to have a research and organizing project around day labor, specifically oriented to take on Manpower, a large slave-labor outfit, in several cities. This kind of action could provide publicity for the grievances of poor and working whites.

5. Everyone should live in poor, transitional and working class neighborhoods. Many of these neighborhoods have people of different class, ethnic and racial backgrounds, including hip-political student types.

6. The people who participate in this program should get together once or twice a week (but not more -- they should be out discovering, not talking to radicals about 'what we're going to do'). The get-together could take different forms -- a speaker, forum, discussion, radical newsreels, films, a party, or free university for those involved.

7. Participants can do a lot of movement stuff, in addition to just working and living with working class people. They can do draft resistance work, in fact they should. But they should talk about a lot of issues, which is something people discover once they get into a neighborhood. They might talk about food prices, the war, the job, the cops, etc. etc., including cars, motorcycles, sex, drinking and music.

8. We should develop a leaflet program, so that participants would have good educational leaflets, geared toward workers, that could be distributed while riding public transportation to work, or on the way to see a friend across town. Leaflets could cover things like the draft,

the war, race, the Democratic Party, labor, transit problems, pollution, consumer issues, etc. We should be careful not to be too exuberant with such a leaflet program, for giving too many out in a neighborhood or on the job could hurt the chances for long-range organizing on the part of people who want to stay for more than just a summer. However, friends made in the neighborhood or on the job might want such literature, and might even start passing it on to their friends.

9. The proposal is open to additions. It seems to us that such a program needs film makers, agit-prop theater, people working with kids, etc.
The main notion is that we will learn some new things, 'cause we aren't so hip that we don't have a lot to learn. We may also discover that by talking to people (rather than about them) we just might rub off.
The summer will be a transitional phase; it will help the many who talk about organizing, but have a lot of anxieties about starting, to think more seriously about it cause it won't all be so abstract, so much talk, any more. That's what happened with Chicago's Center for Radical Research last summer. The 80 participants weren't research types; they were movement kids, like the rest of us, who wanted to get into things but didn't know how to start. So they started by doing research for the movement. Except, over twenty people didn't go back to college, but are now organizing in Chicago -- factories, high schools, working class neighborhoods, etc. etc.

This is a report, a suggestion, not a proposal: too many proposals just get passed. What we suggest is that people interested in making something like this happen in their city, or having things for people in their city, or having things for people in their chapters to do this summer, get together and make it happen. On 4-5 May there will be (was) a big conference at the U of Iowa. There should be conferences, about what we do this summer, and how we get people to stay on, in Detroit, Columbus, Cleveland, Chicago, etc. People should think about how we pull people into cities (or if they're already there, how we pull them out of their apartments), give some direction and reinforcement and encouragement, and get people to stay on. We should think hard about on-going training programs, starting with a conference at the beginning of the summer in each city, where people think hard about what they're going to do for ten weeks (and after), how they're going to do it, and what they want out of the summer and beyond.

IF WE'RE GOING TO TALK ABOUT BUILDING A MOVEMENT, LET'S NOT FORGET THAT THE SUN SHINES ON MEN AND WOMEN WHO'VE GOT SENSE ENOUGH TO GET OUT AND STAND IN IT.

Radicals in the Professions Newletter May 1968

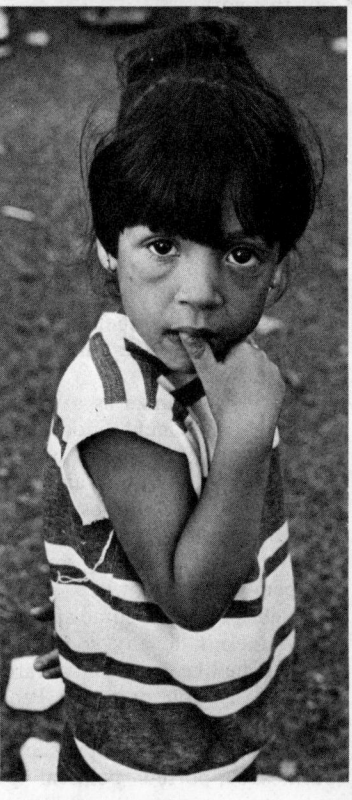

Radical Education Project (REP), Box 561-A, Detroit, Michigan 48232, is an effort by activists and intellectuals to develop an internal education arm for the movement--a research, education, and publication center. They publish an excellent literature list and a movement speakers guide. They also publish a monthly magazine "Something Else" containing articles on organizing efforts, informational articles about local and national radical organizations in various professional fields, and more theoretical pieces on how and where to organize. This magazine is the only other publication that we know of which shares with VSC a focus on how people can become involved in the movement on a full-time basis. A yearly subscription is $5.00.

Vocations for Social Change Newsletter

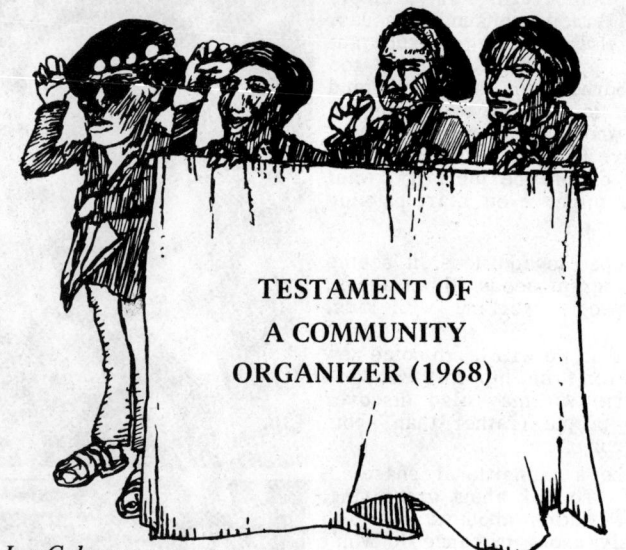

TESTAMENT OF A COMMUNITY ORGANIZER (1968)

By Les Coleman

You see.

You see the political repression of black people in this country in their day to day lives and in their attempts to build political power.

You see the economic regimentation of both white and black where you go to school and where you work. You see deadened lives caught in the nets of either poverty or credit; you see people that never say what they think because it "won't do any good."

You see half the people tied up in programmed misery—programmed by force or be institution—and you see half the people smug and stupid in the ownership of other people's time.

You see that your country is the source of military and economic repression of movements of national liberation throughout the world.

You see, and what do you do?

You see a black movement, built in hard careful base work. You see it grow facing repression. You know it has to be black and separatist, to grow and survive. But you know that it must have allies in this country to survive for a long time, or to effect social change. You know it must have allies among the white people who feel the regimentation and oppression of the system. These white people are your people; you like them; they speak your language, have your humor, play and sing your music. . .

So you organize as a student, but the student movement doesn't reach the people you know must be reached. You organize in the shops and factories, you work inside the unions. You organize in the community around whatever issue you can find. But the thing you want doesn't happen. Why, why, why?

Well, you know some answers.

It doesn't do any good to latch on to some issue like wages or welfare, and try to *educate* as you organize. People see the point: business is behind the manipulation of their lives, democracy controlled by business-supported political parties is a fraud, the war machine breeds a patriotism as well as an institution that holds people in allegiance to a government against their interests, their guts and their hearts. People see the point, but they are not organized politically. They are in most cases hardly organized at all.

But the answers:

. . .You know that there is a sentiment of resistance among your own people. You know if you've talked to them: "There was never an honest politician." "It's a rich man's war being fought by working people. . ."

You know that there is a sense, a sentiment, among your people that their enemy is inside the country: that their enemy is the people in power. But you can't organize that sentiment by *educating* to it—that sentiment only gets organized in an identified struggle *against* the enemy.

These kind of conclusions, and the frustration of student, community and union organizing, have led me and others like me to the draft resistance movement. What we're talking about is *organizing* around the draft: first settling in a community, knowing the people, making community contacts and reaching out to people to give them information about fighting the draft; then, second, building a union of people to support young men who refuse to go, and to support the union's right to exist and provide information about fighting the draft.

The idea is simple; you have a way to attack a community. You have information to bring that people want. You have a reason for being there: you need people to join with you because without people the union is powerless. You will find, as others 'are already finding—in Cleveland, in Boston, in New Orleans, in Dallas—that men and women no longer of draft age will join in a union to defend their young people.

And then it makes sense to talk about resistance unions that move on other kinds of issue organizing, but this time with a group that has a *concrete* political identity, that has mobilized and proclaimed to the community that sentiment of resistance to political fraud, oppression and stupid social regimentation which I know my people have.

The draft is a splitting issue. A community union that pulls together, also doing draft work, will split neighbor from neighbor. The ties of life-style, of humor and acquaintance, which hold a man or woman to his racist or militarist super-patriotic neighbor aren't broken over issues of street cleaning, city councilman, housing: or even over the war in a general way. But active participation in draft resistance unions will break that tie. And only when the tie is broken do people join in fights that identify themselves as fights against those in power.

So it seems in the long run that what we're doing is building a movement of small but similarly styled community resistance organizations. That movement won't threaten the power that makes even local self-government meaningless, but it will break into our own people's allegiance to that power: if we involve working people in a resistance movement, then other working people will listen to it. If we involve professional people, then professionals will listen. In the same way that black people are listening to the black movement because it is "people like them" who are fighting.

And here is a movement. It is a movement supported strongly by the student movement, but it is one that affects, mainly, non-students. Community groups are beginning all over the country, and the communications that make a resistance movement are beginning to develop.

We have an obligation to the survival of that movement to connect draft resistance to the issues and people we have been working with. *We* have an allegiance to the resistance movement.

Reflections:
Synthetic Mescaline Trip no. 3
by the Black Hand

"If I could turn you on, if I could drive you out of your wretched mind, if I could tell you I would let you know."

R.D. Laing, *The Bird of Paradise*

"This isolation of the individual, this narrow self-seeking is the fundamental principle of our society everywhere....The disolution of mankind into nomads, of which each one has a separate principle, the world of atoms, is here carried out to its utmost extreme....Everywhere barbarous indifference, hard egotism on the one hand, and nameless misery on the other, everywhere social warfare, every man's house in a state of siege, everywhere reciprocal plundering under the protection of the law, and all so shameless, so openly avowed that one shrinks before the consequences of our social state as they manifest themselves here undisguised, and can only wonder that the whole crazy fabric still hangs together."

Engels, *The Condition of the Working Class in England*

OLD MOLE Mar 1969

the southern **PATRIOT** Summer 1968

Don't Criticize, Organize.

[1]

Get together a couple of friends and plan a small demonstration in which you can reveal the "true nature" of a particular social agency or corporate interest. For instance, have a student power demonstration in front of any bank, business, etc. whose Chairman or President sits on the Board of Regents of the school concerned. Or do a phone tax demonstration in front of the local phone company. Etc. Use your head. Read number 2. If you have already read number 2, read number 3.

[2]

Study. Read. Think. Research your community. Ask questions. Reread number 1.

[3]

Find someone who voted for Wallace and convert him to radical action. Paint his button black. Try talking politics to weird people. Give literature to everybody.

[4]

Find a concrete specialty—tax or draft resistance, pollution, local politics, education, racism, the gold standard, the English language and start fighting for change. Don't give up for at least one year.

[5]

Take a good look at your job. After you stop crying, hunt around for one that doesn't oppress South American peasants. Think about cooperatives, communes, alternate life styles.

[6]

Don't buy products manufactured or distributed by Imperialist American Corporations. (After you've tried, *then* tell me that revolution is a meaningless word.) Think of ways around supporting these American Imperialist Corporations. Think about cooperatives, etc.

[7]

When you think about cooperatives, etc. don't ever divorce economics from social liberation.

[8]

Don't pay taxes. Ask Maris Cakars: why not?

[9]

Don't call cops "pigs." If you want to hurt their feelings, call them "blue creampuffs" or "motorcycle faggots."

[10]

Get it out, roll it up and light it. Take a good drag. Relax your mind. You deserve a rest now and then. Read number 11.

[11]

Sit down and make a list like this. It will freak you into doing something. Send the list to WIN. Paul Johnson will print it.

[12]

Burn a dollar bill in a bank.

[13]

Make love in a church.

[14]

Recall the saying—"Love the sinner but hate the sin." Don't hate Joe Snerd, but hate the social role he so happily fills. Find ways to separate Joe from his social role short of killing him. In America, the dead fill a social role, too, so don't give Joe a chance to die with his social role on.

[15]

When you attack an institution keep in mind the function it was supposed to play. Every institution had a reason-for-being when it began. Find out by hook or crook. Think up a free institution which would actually accomplish this desired end. Go out and start it.

[16]

Free yourself from the three following social roles: child and/or parent, good citizen, productive economic unit. Think up five more social roles and free yourself from these. (I have, for instance, chosen to renounce the following roles: World Redeemer, good guy, liberated sage, immortal prose writer and preacher.)

[17]

Hustle everyone. Remember the line "What's a pretty girl like you doing in a place like this?" Use a variation of it on every new person you meet. Example: "What's a creative person like you doing in a job, role, institution like that?" Keep digging till you find a person.

[18]

Stop being afraid—drop your guise of good guy or mean mother. Find a more flexible way to relate to the other ass-holes around you.

[19]

Keep after the state at every level. No harassment is too petty. Why should they win the small battles as well? Get a jury trial for every traffic ticket. When you get a parking ticket, put in the money and return it with ten neighboring victims. All the tickets say is put in so much bread, they don't specify *which* ticket. Don't put stamps on mail to oppressive governmental and business agencies. If they want to hear from you, let them pay for it. Always add a couple extra punch holes to any official computer card you are served with. A little confusion clarifies things.

[20]

Remember that I am not advocating anything, this is all being set down by a mind split in temporary possession. (Don't make things too easy for them. Cover your tracks with professions of good faith like the above.)
I'm still stoned.

—Paul Encimer

DRU SUMMER OFFENSIVE: WRAP UP RAP UP

The Summer Offensive was conceived of by people in WDRU, SDS, and Connections in order to extend to all Wisconsin the movement for radical social change in America. It has been our attempt to enable more people to see the possibility for the kind of radical change we think is so necessary. Since we had been able to create for ourselves a viable radical program in the WDRU, we were ready to bring our ideas and efforts to the entire state, to enable hundreds of dissatisfied people to play a beginning role in changing their country. Now that the Summer Offensive is more than half over, it seems fitting to evaluate the successes of its projects thus far, and suggest future directions that they may take.

Since its founding over one year ago, the WDRU had stayed deliberately out of campus politics in Madison and concentrated on building contacts, creating programs of relevance to the war and the draft, and extending its political perspective to all sorts of groups of people throughout Wisconsin. By the end of spring semester, this exhausting state travelling and correspondence had paid off, with groups of young people and liberal minded adults anxious for full time organizers to come to their cities and help them create and carry out elaborate educational and organizing programs.

At the same time, literally dozens of Wisconsin students came to the WDRU with the commitment to work full time at bare subsistence for the summer. So the Summer Offensive was ready to begin, with full time organizers in several cities here and in Illinois and Iowa, with hundreds of part time workers in Madison, with a guerrilla theatre caravan designed to make new contacts in still more places as well as to help those people in cities to which we could not send a full time organizer.

Several high school students expressed a willingness to publish a state-wide, underground, high school newspaper. So LINKS came into being. Three or four experienced WDRU organizers took on the tasks of state travelling to knit projects together. An internal education program was built and carried out, not only for the full time organizers, but for interested individuals in their constituencies as well. And an internal staff newsletter has been published more than once each week to carry news of new programs and progress to everyone working with us in this region.

WISCONSIN'S CITIES

What has happened in the cities? The cities are quite different, but they share several attributes. Young people needed a place to go where they would not be hassed, and could discuss politics and political programs for the future. Kids wanted some publication call their own, in which to present their views of life in a small Midwest city, the war, the draft, whatever. Organizers helped them set up radical coffeehouses and underground newspapers.

In Eau Claire there is a committed and quite liberal community of local adults with whom we have excellent contacts. So a draft information center and political forums were set up. The college campus there offered the chance to work with students at small Wisconsin campuses around issues they consider most pressing--like the relevance of courses or the strict and highly authoritarian rules which prevail. And in Eau Claire there were the remnants of an excellent high school group with whom we had worked before, who were anxious to create programs for organizing in their own high school in the fall.(Two of our full time organizers outside of Eau Claire came from this same group of high school students.)

CONSTITUENCY ORGANIZING

The example of Eau Claire suggests our whole approach to organizing. We consider ourselves to be doing constituency organizing, where a constituency is any group of people who share a common oppression from some institution which is central to their lives. So teachers, or social workers, or workers in a particular plant, or students in a particular dormitory are all constituencies. We know that for the most part all of our constituencies may be part of the working class or middle class. But as we see things at this time we can be most effective in raising radical demands if we do so in a context with which they identify, that is teachers as teachers, ghetto blacks as ghetto blacks, high school students as high school students, and so on.

In Appleton and Waukegan, almost all work has been with high school students and graduates concentrating on the demands they wish to make of their cities and their schools. The only big difference is that in Appleton, most of the kids are middle-class whereas in Waukegan they are working-class and do not expect to go to college. Draft board research and interviews were done in Appleton, guerrilla theatre was important in Waukegan. In both places, LINKS has been sold and distributed, helping to make new contacts. The Waukegan cops arrested several kids for selling LINKS and almost created a full conflagration with hundreds of young people who rightly resented that unlawful harassment.

Williams Bay, in the resort area of Lake Geneva, has a few full time workers who have graduated from high school and have been organizing there for over a year. A radical book and art supply store they opened last year was forced to close. They have since opened a coffeehouse and have evoked a sympathetic response from half the kids in town.

In Racine and Dubuque a Draft Information Center was opened; there, the WDRU workers have tried to use draft counseling and the issue of the draft as a means of organizing with mixed failures and success.

Milwaukee has several WDRU and affiliated organizers who have been pulling together high school groups and helping them to start full-scale organizing in their high schools for the fall. Guerrilla theatre and speeches at city-wide activities--like the Summerfest--aroused the excitement and brought in the names of hundreds of contacts and future workers.

GUERRILLA CARAVAN

All of the cities have made use of the services of the caravan, or they will do so shortly. We found on the caravan's first trip out of Madison (to Manitowoc where we know no one) that the colorfulness and liberated life style of a traveling guerrilla theatre troupe can attract many local young people who can't stand their boring, small city lives. Plays went over extremely well, with the audience hanging on every word. And a group of Manitowoc's high school students constituted themselves--with the assistance of caravan members--to do extensive political work in their city. They had seen that something could be done, they got news of what was happening in other cities like their own, and so their acute pessimism started to fade, and they began to act out their discontent in terms of reaching new people and challenging hated institutions instead of just sitting around and complaining.

MADISON: A BASE

Here in Madison, we had to form a base--by raising funds to support 40 people; by supplying massive literature needs; by putting out the staff newsletter and the high school newspaper. But even more important, we felt the need for the Madison campus to play a vanguard role with which our brothers throughout the region could identify. It seems that the example of successful organizing in Madison in the fall will be invaluable for organized young people and adults throughout the state. For the first time they will understand what Madison students are about, and they can identify with them. That's how we hope a regional consciousness can endure, as well as by continuing to publish LINKS and do extensive state travelling out of Madison.

JOIN US!

In the end we can say we've seriously affected hundreds of people in a short time; we've nurtured dozens of cadres who should be able to continue next year (independently with only our assistance) and we've collected much valuable experience both for our own organizers and for the movement as a whole--lessons--as to how to create meaningful programs that allow people to develop as radicals and combat the things that hurt them in America.

We hope that Madison can be a focus for the movement in Wisconsin. The growth and development of the movement on the Madison campus can do great service to lonely, beginning organizing in strict and hostile Wisconsin cities. We think we can do it, and we know we have an obligation to people throughout Wisconsin. WILL YOU JOIN US?

--Mark and Marilynn Dworkin

CONNECTIONS Sept 1968

MOVEMENT AND ORGANIZATION

A Program for Post-Campus Radicals

Staughton Lynd

*T*he question for the 1970s, then, is whether we can find ways to work through what Andre Gorz calls revolutionary reforms: whether there is a middle path between reformism and adventurism. I want to argue that we try. I suggest that this effort in the 1970s can be understood as a synthesis of what was best in the political work of the 1960s with what was best in the political work of the 1930s.

What we have failed to do is to make radicalism attractive, because rewarding, to ordinary Americans with jobs, children, cars, homes, taxes, and installment payments. In seeking ways to do this I think we can learn from the older radicals whom we so readily write off but who, nevertheless, organized five million workers into industrial unions and led 500,000 workers in sit-down strikes in 1936-1937. The organizers of the 1930s may have something to teach us in just those areas where our own work has been weakest: the building of mass organizations, the bidding for real power.

Of course, the work of the 1930s was also one-sided. The New Left created movement without organiza-

tion; the Old Left, organization without movement. In its concern to defend the Soviet Union and to cultivate Franklin Roosevelt as a potential Soviet ally, the Communist Party of the 1930s failed to project a socialist vision and so built organizations which, lacking this element, became partners in capitalism. This was notably true of the CIO. The war alone cannot explain how rapidly the new industrial unions surrendered their independence, gave up the right to strike in wartime, purged their radical members. Much blame must also fall on the courageous organizers whose work laid too much stress on material, achievable, short-run objectives, and too little on long-range goals.

The organizers of the 1930s tended to be opportunistic, "economist." We of the 1960s have tended to be utopian and adventurist. A mass, revolutionary socialist movement must synthesize what was best in both experiences.

The new kind of organizer I am envisioning will build a new kind of organization.

*B*y the end of the 1970s, hopefully,

there would exist in cities and regions across the country organizations with these three characteristics. In contrast to a cadre organization of professional revolutionaries, they would be based on mass participation. Yet, unlike an industrial union or a Social Democratic political party, they would rely tactically on direct action from below rather than on the delegation of power to representatives. Finally, and particularly by the end of the decade, they would explicitly affirm the socialism which would from the beginning have been implicit in their choice of corporate targets.

In the movement today, people talk of a dichotomy between the loose, non-ideological "movement" of past years and the disciplined Leninist "party" which they hope to create. What I envision is a confederation of local mass organizations which will still be a decentralized "movement" but which will no longer be made up largely of students and other academics. It will preserve the best characterisitcs of the New Left of the 1960s but overcome the New Left's major weakness: its on-campus, isolated, non-representative composition.

All over the country there are organizers quietly resuming the long-term building of grass-roots organizations which SNCC abandoned in 1966 and ERAP in 1967. Some worked in SNCC and ERAP and doggedly continued after those projects folded; some are Southerners left without a regional network by the collapse of SSOC (Southern Student Organizing Committee); many are women, concerned both to reach non-middle-class working women and to develop multi-issue programs; they may be NUC (New Universities Conference) members teaching in junior or com-

munity colleges; and some are members of the Resistance, now beginning to work with young people off campus. There are common themes. For instance, in Springfield, Massachusetts (see the June *Liberation*), Gary, Indiana and Oneonta, Alabama, as well as in the dramatic workingman's campaign in Laurel, Mississippi, organizers are trying to build around the idea of taxing the corporations and using the proceeds to finance local welfare programs. Interestingly, this was precisely the program pushed by Stokely Carmichael and the Black Panther movement in Lowndes County, Alabama in 1965-1966.

*T*his is a very different style of work than that of summer projects for students followed by fall national demonstrations. The historical precedent for that style is the Freedom Summer and SCLC. Reversion to it underlines the fact that those whose rhetoric is most revolutionary are still campus-bound.

For people drawn to a politics of work rather than rhetoric, what are the next steps? It might be fruitful to create a series of low-keyed occasions at which individuals and groups who are committed to long-term organizing in white communities come together to share experiences. These gatherings, I would hope, would pass no resolutions, make no decisions, start no new organizations. In somewhat the same fashion as the old ERAP, this informal network would exist side-by-side with other movement structures, helping working organizers to find each other and then to find their way forward together.

From "A Program for Post-Campus Radicals," Aug-Sept 1969

LIBERATION

POLITICS AS A VOCATION

*I*n "Politics as a Vocation" Max Weber analyzed the conflict between a "politics of responsibility" and a "politics of ultimate ends." Genovese is urging the left to adopt a politics of responsibility in the form of alliance with moderates to preserve the possibility of socialism and to destroy those who weaken criticism and dissent by their shrillness, their extremism or their irresponsible activism. For him those who respond to the call of conscience, who insist that there are imperatives which transcend history, are the immediately dangerous enemies of radical politics. But Weber knew, as Genovese does not, that the moral force of a politics of ultimate ends is all that keeps a politics of responsibility from becoming static and repressive. All who have the calling for politics must live with the conflicting attractions of conscience and effectiveness; both are indispensable. Weber's words have profound relevance for this debate and others wracking the American left. "Certainly all historical experience confirms the truth that men would not have attained the possible unless they had reached out for the impossible", Weber wrote. "Even those who are neither

leaders or heroes must arm themselves with that steadfastness of heart which can brave the crumbling of all hopes. This is necessary right now or else men will not be able to attain even that which is possible today. Only he has a calling for politics who is sure that he shall not crumble when all the world from his point view is too stupid or too base for what he wants to offer. Only he who in the face of this can say, 'In spite of all!' has a calling for politics."

The Lynd-Genovese controversy, with its implications for students and radicals, parallels debates in other areas, notably in ethics. These disputes are raised beyond the academic by the insistent question posed by Christopher Lasch "What must a moral man do?" To accept Genovese's response to the question will enmesh us once again in the failures of the old liberalism and Marxism: the confusion of means and ends, the postponement of the moral life until material conditions allow, the adaptation to possibilities defined by "history", as Genovese would have it, more likely by power possessed and exercised by real men here and now, Undoubtedly there are risks in asserting that each man must create new possibilities, must make history rather than adapt to it. The danger of

fanaticism is real, as Genovese points out, but many men have already experienced the fanaticism cloaked in the shroud of realism and the horrors unleashed by those who believed they had discerned the course of history. At the very best Genovese's own writings, with their self-righteousness and dogmatism and their demand for "radical surgery" to destroy deviationists like Lynd, manifest a fanaticism as virulent as anything likely to come from his opponents. Given a choice between Genovese's brand of ideology and scholarship and that of Staughton Lynd, the rest of us must stand with Lynd, who wrote in the book which Genovese so cruelly attacked: "One cannot entrust men with a collective right of revolution unless one is prepared for them to revolutionize their lives from day to day; one should not invoke the ultimate act of revolution without willingness to see new institutions perpetually improvised from below; the withering away of the state must begin in the process of changing the state; freedom must mean freedom now".

From "Eugene Genovese and the Student Left" by David J. O'Brien, Oct 1969

LIBERATION

THE SYMBOL OF WHITE POWER

TWO MOVEMENT
ORGANIZERS GO INTO
CHICAGO:
A CATHOLIC SCHOOL
AND A YMCA

Letter to the Movement:

richie rothstein

Dear Friends,

Vivian and I have just finished two years of work in what is generally regarded as a symbol of white lower-middle class racist reaction in America —the Chicago West suburban communities of Maywood, Broadview, Cicero, and Berwyn. Neither of us have had much contact in this time with the national movement community which, in a sense, sent us here. So I thought this might be an appropriate time to report to you on some of our impressions.

I suppose the first thing to say is that we have survived, are well, and are in love with many of the young people (and even adults) with whom we have worked. True, the pressure of the organized right is constant and a source of concern. Three weeks ago the Minutemen shot crossbows into the church basement coffee house for teenagers with which Vivian was associated; a local right-wing group reprints in a newsletter material from our police

and F.B.I. files; yesterday I received an anonymous package of literature and threats ("even now the rifle cross hairs are on the back of your necks"), the most humorous of which identified Tom Hayden as part of the international Jewish conspiracy. However, it matters not so much that the Minutemen send such threats (using our local draft counseling center as their return address); more important is the continued existence of the draft counseling center which brings many junior college kids from the area into their first contact with the movement.

The draft counseling center was set up by a local "Clergy and Laymen Concerned" group which is still the only functioning left political organization in the Western suburbs. It is composed primarily of radical ministers, priests and religiously inspired activists who see the draft counseling center as a rare programmatic option. Occasionally their churches get bombed by the organized right, but these ministers still feel a commitment and the possibility to move. They can usually collect a group of young people from their parishes with whom to work; they form human relations clubs, institute annoyance suits against racist school curricula, run peace candidates for office, have a few discussion meetings at church. But beyond this, they see few radical ways of relating to the community and its concerns. Their "liberalism" is not the result of a poverty of analysis but of program. Some of them moved to this noted racist area for essentially the same reasons we did, though expressed in very different language.

The informal format of a "letter to the movement" has been designed to let people write about whatever is on their mind without having to conform to the structural requirements of an article. Unsolicited letters will be considered for publication.

For several years Richie Rothstein was an organizer in the JOIN project on the West Side of Chicago. At last month's conference of the New University Conference in Iowa City, Richie was chosen national secretary.

The difference in language suggests a deeper problem. These ministers, as well as a number of high school teachers and other professionals we have met (these lower-middle-class communities are mixtures of blue-collar working class, new working class, and lower professionals) are radicals, willing to take the same risks and articulate a similar humanitarian socialist vision to that of the New Left "movement". They are from 25-45, support the Panthers, the Conspiracy 8, and the Chicago 15 (1-A files burning). But somehow they are a different culture from the "movement" and in terms of life styles, rhetoric, and common history the two groups don't seem to groove. A weekly communal dinner was established a short while ago to try to bring

the various local radicals together. It will take a lot of hard work to establish relationships firmly. Our conviction is that we must try to break out of the limitations of our cultural definitions if we are to broaden the movement to include all of its functional members.

When we first moved to the Western suburbs, I planned to experiment with consumer-grievance organizing among lower-middle income whites; Vivian was attempting to form a women's peace group. She canvassed in a few communities with petitions demanding a plebiscite on the war. The response was enthusiastic. People here suffer from the war's inflation and its death, and they know it. Vivian gathered some contacts from this canvas into a "women for peace" group—but she was frustrated by an inability to develop program for such a constituency and also found the racism of the peace group members hard to deal with.

My consumer organizing also proved frustrating—I had been working through an ACLU and church-sponsored legal aid agency, but the limits of the agency were too narrow to allow any meaningful experimentation with direct-action consumer protest. I quit in Spring '68, feeling a new start had to be made. I was still enthusiastic, however, about the possibility of developing multi-issue organizations out of consumer protest. The few people with whom I did work on issues of installment buying, exorbitant credit rates, home-improvement frauds and so on were exciting and interested in organization. There is room for further experimentation—radicals could, in neighborhoods like these, open storefront consumer service offices and attempt to create such organizations.

A year ago we began to have contact with high school kids. Vivian got jobs at two local YMCA's, in charge of a high school "outreach program". I was hired to teach American History in a local Catholic high school. I don't know how generalizable our experience is here, or how much into the future this can be projected—but for what it is worth, both of us got these jobs with our politics and values "out front." The "Y" knew about Vivian's trip to North Vietnam and her intention of developing self-determining young people's organizations which could get involved in social issues if the kids desired. The high school knew of my record of activism in the peace, civil rights and community organizing movements. In both cases, these institutions were at an impasse about how to implement their rhetorical liberal values in a racist environment. Vivian offered the "Y" the only program which could be expected to attract young people. Verbally committed to the direction of Pope John and Vatican II, my high school had no experience in differentiating between verbal and real commitment to those values.

At the "Y's", an underground newspaper for kids from the public high school flourished; so, too, did a social issues club of Catholic school kids

which picketed supermarkets for the grape boycott and non-discriminatory hiring policies. The kids were radicalized in a now-familiar fashion: by the frustration involved in attempting to apply liberal values. Vivian was fired and rehired twice: fired after rightist campaigns, rehired after protest from the community's kids, liberal ministers, some parents and teachers.

My teaching contract was not renewed because, as the principal said, my students "were losing faith in their country." Certainly these particular institutions have grown more sophisticated through this experience about distinguishing between rhetorical liberals and serious radicals. But the distinction is not that simple to make for institutions which are devoid of even a liberal program. Movement people can still, despite the polarization of the last few years, make use of liberal institutions in the heart of America. And the situation is wonderfully complicated even further by another aspect of that polarization: Vivian received significant support from some fellow workers at the "Y"—part time divinity school students. And I was buoyed by the support of younger nuns, particularly those in the religion department. The future is theirs, for they will almost certainly control the order and its schools within a few years.

The 17 year old kids I taught were beautiful—I'll never forget them. Their social positions were the same mixture of working-class and lower business-professional that makes up communities such as these. Their environment and teaching has been reactionary and racist, but I found them open, questioning, and searching. They were aware of what they understood to be a social value revolt among middle class youth and of their own possible identity with it. They disagreed with the "hippies"—their term for any demonstrator or activist—but self-consciously understood that they might feel differently in a few years. When I met them they were pained by a value conflict with their parents—the kids would "open opportunities to the colored if only the colored would stop rioting;" they perceived that their parents would not.

Our encounter over the course of the year was unforgettable. My students and I had things to say to each other which spoke directly to our very different needs. We will meet again. That meeting is guaranteed by a combination of their present consciousness and the authoritarianism which they will confront at every effort to apply their humanity to the institutions of a proletarianized middle class. If there is a movement presence at the community, junior and small Catholic colleges to which many of them will go, they will inspire it. I love them deeply; there are many more of them; and I wish more of you could have the opportunity to get to know them.

Movement School

The Movement School is an attempt to provide a framework in which radicals can seriously study and discuss questions relevant to their political work. Its purpose is to equip radicals with a greater understanding of what is wrong with America and how change can take place, as a basis for more effective and self-confident organizing and for more intelligent strategic thinking. The School will take place in small discussion groups, meeting twice weekly in the evenings. Reading will be expected.

The school will begin on July 7 and last for two months. There is no enrollment fee — the expenses should be about $10 for readings to be purchased from the school.

OLD MOLE June 1969

Young Lords, Young Patriots, Black Panthers and Black Disciples march on Chicago police station to protest the pig-killing of Manuel Ramos.

The Upper Mission District is rapidly becoming a strong revolutionary community. At the same time, it is an extremely scattered unorganized community. A group of people, living in the Mission, are trying to buy a restaurant, The Good Karma, at 18th and Dolores. We feel it could be turned into a community gathering place that could provide jobs for a few people and dispense food at reasonable prices — 20¢ for a good bowl of soup, 75¢ for dinner. We need ten thousand dollars to start, we're two thousand short. Anyone interested in making an investment contact Doug Bianchi, 905 Guererro or Carl Witman, 826-7314, or the Express Times.

San Francisco Express Times April 1968

INFORMATION ON HIGH SCHOOL ORGANIZING

RESIST needs names and addresses of individuals and groups doing high school organizing. We are putting together a pamphlet on high school organizing that will contain both accounts of personal experiences and examples of organizing materials being used by different groups. If you are an organizer or know someone who is, please contact RESIST, 763 Massachusetts Ave., No. 4, Cambridge, Mass. 02139 (617-491-8076).

***

WANTED:

People interested in making a long-term commitment to radical community organizing. The Committee for Independent Political Action (CIPA) is located in the predominantly middle-class neighborhood of Rogers Park in Chicago. All types of skills and abilities are welcome. CIPA particularly needs an editor and a nursery-school teacher. Anyone seeking further information may contact CIPA at 1903 Howard Street, Chicago, Illinois 60626 (312-338-5872).

For an article describing CIPA's work see the May 1968 issue of The Movement.

Hentoff

More connections: the Teacher Drop-Out Center, School of Education, University of Massachusetts, Amherst, Massachusetts 01002. Graduate student Leonard Solo writes: "We're trying to identify schools around the country which are human-centered. From various sources, we've compiled a list of about 700 schools to which we're writing to see if we can smell out if they are humane, student-centered places where 'teachers' and 'students' have a great deal of autonomy. . . So far, we've gotten pretty encouraging responses from about 50 schools and we expect more. . . . We've got some people from here and other colleges in the area who are going to be visiting schools in New England and California to see if the schools' words equal their realities.

"We're also trying to help people looking for these kinds of schools to find jobs. They write to us, telling where they are with themselves, where they are about education, where they want to teach, what kind of school they want to teach in, salary, and any other information they want to send us. Then we try to help them find jobs. We've helped and are helping 50 or 60 people so far to find positions in these schools. We just placed a principal in the Adams Community School in Washington, D. C. We don't have a list of current job openings—we won't do this until March or so. We don't have the man power and the time to do this thing full-time. . . . If you'd like to recommend any schools to us, we're open. If you can turn any people on to us, great."

the village VOICE 1/8/70

HOW TO TAKE THAT
STEP INTO AMERICA
—STEP BY STEP

The Movement at Work : springfield,mass.

Tom Bell

notes on a
CITY-WIDE MOVEMENT
Springfield Area Movement
for a Democratic Society

As an organization, Springfield Area Movement for a Democratic Society is more than a year old now. We've grown from a small handful of people interested in peace and social justice to a city-wide organization immersed in an effort to uncover what makes our city--and our nation--function as it does, and to involve the people of Springfield in an active effort to change the priorities and decision-making structures of our city.

Why Springfield?

We don't think that it's an accident that SAMDS is a-live and well here in Springfield. A large part of the American population lives in and around cities like Springfield: cities large enough to house international corporations and government agencies and to reflect the whole spectrum of problems faced by our nation; but small enough so that we can find where the power lies and who makes the decisions and why; and livable enough so that people still have hopes for the possibilities of the future. These are the important and logical places for the development of strong political movements, despite the fact that until recently most movement attention has been focused toward the big cities.

We firmly believe that it is possible to build city-wide organizations in such cities--movements that can break down the barriers which separate people politically, economically, and socially, and can get people working together effectively out of their common needs. we think a movement can do this by demonstrating that the major decisions in our cities are made by a small handful of men representing powerful economic interests, and that because of the nature of those interests the real needs of the people aren't being met, and our energies and re-sources are being manipulated and wasted. Our experiences as a movement in Springfield encourage us in that belief. (See Liberation, July, 1969).

Our contact with other movement people in middle-sized cities indicates that our experiences here are useful to people in many other places. Movements similar in their city-wide perspective to ours are now underway in places like Hartford, Bridgeport, New Haven, and Pittsfield, and it looks like we'll be able to work together and sup-port each other very well.

Baystate West Springfield, like many other cities, is attempting to solve its social and economic problems with urban renewal and redevelopment projects. As a result, we have seen the levelling of the North End of the city-- a largely black and poor white district--to make way for a huge complex of highways, motels, shopping centers and large businesses. There are now underway massive redevel-opment plans for the downtown area. We discovered when we examined these projects that a relatively small hand-ful of men, representatives from the major economic in-terests in the city, have been involved in deciding Springfield's future.

Most amazing of these projects is Baystate West, a complex of an office tower, luxury hotel, parking ramp, and shopping mall, presently under construction in the downtown area. The project is entirely owned by Mass. Mutual Life Insurance Co., and was granted a substantial tax break through state legislation and a special con-tract with the city. This deal represents a tax loss of some $2,390,000 per year for the next forty years. In addition, Mass. Mutual did not sign the contract until the city agreed to build a "Civic" Center, (essentially a convention hall) two blocks away to give Baystate West added business. The "Civic" Center will cost the taxpay-ers another $800,000 per year for thirty years. That's over $3,000,000 per year that taxpayers will have to make up for. And the point about all this paying is that none of the real problems of the people in Springfield are being mentioned. Instead, city officials and "civic" leaders continue to explain Springfield's problems and heavy tax load in terms of high welfare and medicaid costs, and demands for higher wages from city employees. We think it's important to make a big deal out of these facts, because they connect up for all of us the quality of our lives at home and the questions of national im-portance like the war in Vietnam. A project like Bay-state West helps to explain why we have so little con-trol over the direction of our society, and why we seem to be so unable to deal with the poverty and racism and alienation around us.

We've had a lot of success in raising this issue in Springfield so far. We have written what we think is an excellent research pamphlet on the project, called "Wel-come to Springfield, a Mass. Mutual Property." The pam-phlet is getting wide circulation in the area. Also, we are just winding up a boycott of the four major business interests that are involved in the Baystate West project. Extensive leafletting at shopping areas and factories, together with fairly good media coverage have effectively publicized this issue.

We are now putting together a broad coalition of groups and individuals to launch a taxpayers suit against Mass. Mutual and the city government, with the help of the Mass. Lawyers Guild. We hope to be able to force the city to stop plans for construction of the so-called "Civic" Center, and to force Mass. Mutual to pay full taxes on Baystate West. But beyond that, we hope to demonstrate to people that when we join together we have the power to control what is going on in our lives and in our country. The lawsuit is the second step in a long fight. We will not end the campaign in the courts, but see the court action mainly in terms of building a wider base of support.

The Vietnam War   In July one of members attended a conference in Cuba with delegates from North Vietnam and the NLF. The Vietnamese took the view that the main thing at this point which could convince the American government to withdraw the troops and machinery from Vietnam would be sustained pressure from the American people as a whole. We think that position makes a lot of sense. Believing that the bulk of people in Springfield want to see an end to the war in Vietnam, SAMDS has taken an active part in trying to convince people to take the step of making their feelings public. We worked hard on the Moratorium and Mobilization efforts in Springfield this fall, and were encouraged by the unprecedented numbers of people who turned out for these activities. We think that the best way to continue building those numbers is to work from the non-sectarian perspective, leaving plenty of room for people to say what they think, and providing open forums where people can come and learn from each other. In addition, we find that we can effectively raise questions about the war and American foreign policy in our work on Springfield-oriented issues.

What Have We Been Doing?

The Free School   The SAMDS Free School was an effort to bring together a wide variety of people in the area to consider a number of radical questions about our society and ourselves, and to formulate active programs for SAMDS. Free school "classes" met throughout the summer and into the fall. A number of new people connected up with SAMDS--primarily young working people, also high school and college students. Several important projects emerged out of the free school meetings.

Women   A Women's Liberation group grew out of the free school this summer. They have just completed a paper written from the perspectives of a variety of women in the group--housewives, welfare mothers, students, working women--which is designed to be an introduction to the question of the position of women in our society. They are now planning a seminar series for young women which will cover such questions as sex education, contraception, abortion, and women's roles.

We Need Some Help

We have gotten to the point where we can meet about half of our regular expenses from dues collected from the SAMDS membership, benefit concerts, etc. Most of our regular monthly expenses (about $650 per month) come out of our Movement Workshop. The Workshop is used primarily for printing for SAMDS and other area groups. We have fixed two offset presses and built a darkroom, so that we are now able to do all our own photography, platemaking, and printing. Two full-time people are now working at the Workshop to do the printing, putting together our bi-weekly SAM'S Newsletter, and taking care of the bureaucratic details for the movement.

WE'RE INTERESTED IN STARTING A NEW PROGRAM which will take extra money to get started. We have in mind a bookstore-drop-in center, specifically for high school students, and for a SAMDS meeting place.

Recent racial violence in the Springfield high schools painfully demonstrated to us the lack of a stong high school student union. A large group of high school students mobilized last fall around hair and dress regulations. The issue was won; the regulations were removed in all the city high schools. But the movement collapsed soon after for lack of a sense of direction and difficulties in finding a place to meet and get to know each other. The racial problems in the city schools are far from over. The city's response of putting police in the schools will only make the situation worse. It is clear

that high school students have plenty of things to feel angry and frustrated about. But as long as people's energy gets wasted fighting among themselves, the general situation will continue to get worse. The high school students in SAMDS feel that it is critically important for their work in trying to build a student union to open up some kind of bookstore-drop-in center near the high schools (three of which are within a block of each other) to begin to get high school people together.

Besides being a place to distribute literature and a headquarters for a high school student union, the center might also be used as a meeting place for other SAMDS projects, for films, lectures, and other public events, and possibly even a day-care center for our movement children. SAMDS is finding it increasingly difficult to find places for public meetings. We've made a few very important people angry, mostly as a result of our uncovering of Mass. Mutual. Until recently, we were able to meet in area churches, but three churches in a row have now denied us meeting space as a result of threats from Mass. Mutual people on their boards of trustees. We've had similar responses from two of the area colleges for the same reason. That trend is likely to continue.

SO. We very much need your help, both to continue our present projects and to start new ones. Our stategy has a majority mentality. that's partly why we're having financial troubles. We know it is easier to give money to some particular effort--like civil rights,or draft resistance. But that's not the pitch we're making. We are pretty sure that everyone in this country has good reason to join with a radical movement. It's just that it takes a lot of convincing, because so many people have given up on--or maybe never even thought about--the possibilities of a real popular revolution in America. We need your help in continuing to build the city-wide movement in Springfield.

We need money specifically to maintain and extend our printing operation, to initiate the taxpayers suit, and to open the bookstore-drop-in center. We need pledges for regular contributions as well as single shots. If you would like to contribute in either case, and want to receive the SAMDS bi-weekly newsletter or a copy of our research pamphlet "Welcome to Springfield...A Mass. Mutual Property," please let us know.

Write to : Springfield Area Movement for a Democratic
           Society
           Box 1608
           Springfield, Mass. 01101

or call : Movement Workshop
           413-732-5434
           noon to 5:00 pm and irregularly at other
           times.

Springfield Area Movement for a Democratic Society

P. O. Box 1608   Springfield, Mass. 01101

RE: Springfield Area Movement for a
    Democratic Society

Friends:

During the past year and a half the Movement has been long on
ideas and short on application. The ideas are important: the corporation, not the government, is the enemy; blue-collar workers can
be a revolutionary force, as in France. What has been missing is
that committment to long-term work in a particular place which distinguished SNCC's voter registration campaign, or the ERAP projects
of the mid-1960s.

The Springfield Area Movement for a Democratic Society is one
of the very few groups of which I know that has made this commitment.

Their corporate target is the Massachusetts Mutual Life Insurance Company. This corporation has pushed through the city
government which it controls, a "Baystate West project" which will
permit it to rebuild the downtown area without paying real estate
or property taxes. The SAMDS estimates the loss to the people of
Springfield at more than one hundred twenty million dollars over
the next forty years.

A coalition to take on Mass. Mutual is being patiently built,
through freedom schools and small actions. One of the builders is
Tom Bell, whose work with the We Won't Go group at Cornell University in the winter of 1966-1967 led to the burning of 175 draft
cards at Sheep's Meadow in New York City on April 15, 1967, and so
the wider draft resistance movement.

We must have the faith that similar small beginnings in Springfield can produce similar results. One way to show that faith, as
in the case of the draft resistance movement, is financially. I
hope that you will give SAMDS the support it needs.

Fraternally,

Staughton Lynd

Staughton Lynd

Chicago, Ill.
February 1, 1970

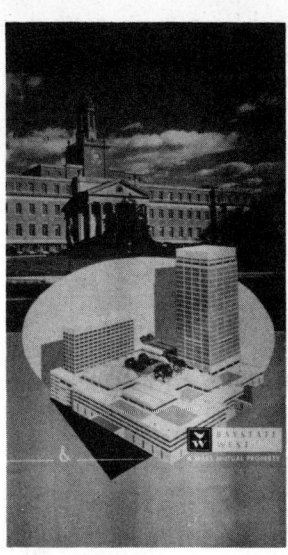

We are attempting in the Springfield area to build a radical organization which cuts through the superficial differences which normally divide American working people. Springfield has had no significant movement activity in the recent past and so our work is free from the usual left factionalism or organizational jealousies. On the other hand, we are starting from scratch, and the usual myths which divide people are quite strong in the population as a whole. People still act as though they believe that prestige has some real value as defined by the society's present standards. Thus, different job categories give excuse for contempt of the people in other job categories even though most everyone in the area is selling their labor power to some employer who gets the real benefit of that labor. Racist attitudes are strong. "Sexist" attitudes also are strong—so strong as to be often unrecognized by the women. The women act as domestic servants and as slaves to the economy's growing need for mass consumption. They are left to wonder why they feel such despair. Suburban dwellers scorn city people and city problems even though life will continue to be oppressive for both unless they can get together and work in their common interests. In brief, our long range goal as presently defined is to build a "political union" which can give a strong (even controlling) voice to the working people of the area in all the political and economic decisions which affect their lives.

In Springfield, as elsewhere, we are up against a deep, often unadmitted sense of powerlessness when confronted with the real issues which face us as American working people. Basic to this sense of powerlessness is the educated inability of most Americans to conceive of any alternative to the American way of doing things. Other societies are presented to us as irrelevant. Some countries are "underdeveloped"—which equals bad; others are "communist"—which equals bad; and the rest are "just about like us"—which equals almost as good. The propaganda is tremendous: revolutions always make things worse—after all, look at Stalin. And high school language courses study the "culture" of the home land of the language by asking "What is their Thanksgiving like?" But powerlessness goes beyond this lack of an alternative. Most people at least know that the rich have a lot of power, but they don't want to think about it too much because "that's the way things are," or "you can't fight City Hall," or "don't rock the boat." The feeling, it seems, is that we will just make trouble for everybody by trying to change things. I think this is the basis of the antagonism toward the movement: people think that if we push too much or make people think too much that they will lose the things they have—things which they have been carefully convinced to accept in lieu of a full life.

Our strategy is to demonstrate to people that a small elite in fact runs Springfield, that they are not the elected officials (though these officials certainly help them), and that they use power to serve their own interests at the expense of the population as a whole. Simultaneously we must show that by working together the people of the area can get specific changes which are to our benefit. To be clearly in the direction of our goal, the tactics we select must have a clear radical content (which is to some extent inherent in anything which exposes the functioning of the ruling elite) and must serve to build our organization. The first step in such a strategy, of course, is to build a solid nucleus of a group. This initial building has been the basis of our efforts since the

founding of Springfield Area Movement for a Democratic Society in November, 1968.

The composition of the group of people who have come together in MDS is different from that of most movement organizations in the country. We have in the same organization high school students, college students, and working people. The nucleus of the 180 or so people who have come to meetings contains all three categories, but is predominantly young working people. Among these are several social workers, a waitress, a factory worker, an auto body mechanic, a personnel manager, a welfare mother, a couple of housewives, a VISTA worker, several students, and so on. So far we have worked mostly to build a sense of community and personal contact so essential to any truly radical activity. It is a slow process in a society structured to keep people isolated and focused on individual security (or security for the family unit).

In the last six months we have tried to work publicly in several ways. We had two successful rock concerts; we had a rally for peace that attracted 250 people on a cold, rainy day; we attempted to get two SDS chapters recognized as campus groups of their respective colleges; we opened a Movement Workshop in the downtown area intended for printing, draft counselling and small meetings; we tried to petition in one of the high schools for an end to hair and dress regulations, and we have held several discussions of MDS at church and other groups. It seems that even this relatively small amount of activity has made people aware of us in this town where less activity is the norm. Many people's hopes have been raised. But it is not easy to create a sustained effort. The powers-that-be watch us carefully and harass us when they can, and the people here have seen other attempted groups fizzle and are not flocking to give us active support, though they may agree with us.

Our Movement Workshop was busted up. On two successive days the windows in our storefront were broken—damage totalling $300. In neither case did the police report the incident to the landlord or investigate. In the second instance, the two large plate-glass windows in the front were shattered all over the sidewalk and street for over 24 hours on Sunday until one of the people working in the building reported it to the landlord on Monday morning. Our workshop was on a main street in town and must have been seen by the police who patrol the street constantly. In addition, the landlord was contacted by "authorities" whom he would not identify. As a result he evicted us. It is clear that we have no police protection and probably police harassment.

So far we have relocated one of the presses. The Black Student Union, with which we have a growing alliance, found a place at Uplift, Inc., one of the independent Black poverty agencies. That press is a small Multilith and will be used for short run jobs, especially for the newspaper of the B.S.U. and for two high school papers which are presently coming out (we expect other high school papers also). We have recently leased downtown space for the large press, a Davidson 233. The space is on the third floor and should be relatively safe from attack. We will do major printing jobs there and set up a darkroom to do the offset photography for both presses and to do the developing and printing from the photography group of the Free School, a program we propose to start this month. We will use this space strictly as a printing and photography workshop. The printing facilities are essential to us if we are going to be able to interpret our actions to the population. The Springfield newspapers are all under one reactionary ownership. There is a small underground paper coming out of the Religion and Arts Committee of the Unitarian Church. We are working with this project, and feel that it will be helpful in getting our views across. We may do some of the printing for it at the workshop.

What are our tactics for the near future? We have two tactics which have already been in the planning stage for some months. One, the Springfield Area Free School, is designed basically to work on developing the solid nucleus for the movement and the sense of community which we need. The other, the Bay State West project is a good example of the kind of public tactic which we need to overcome the gnawing sense of powerlessness on the part of working people.

As originally planned, the Free School was to be located in a house that we would purchase. The printing facilities, meeting rooms, library, dark room, and day-care center would all have been in one place. After the workshop was busted we decided that we were in no position to defend a house—that centralizing our things in that way would make us much too vulnerable to whoever

might want to put us out of operation. We decided to decentralize the Free School as much as possible. And we have moved in that direction by setting up two printing places. We now plan to hold group meetings in various places, to set up the library in someone's apartment, and to work out a day-care center somehow. The Free School will be initiated at a general MDS meeting May 19th. Its structure is loose and should allow us to meet people's various interests. Twelve of us are now in the process of preparing outlines for various groups to begin meeting after the 19th. Each person will take responsibility for organizing his or her group. The groups are either research groups designed to seek out information which will be valuable as background for action, skills groups, or study groups. The ones to start this month include a female liberation group, a study group on the family, a guerrilla theatre group, a research group looking into the corporate structure of the area and the general economic base, a group researching the political structures as they now exist, an American History study group, a group studying the secondary education system in the area, a printing and offset photography skills group, and a photography and filmmaking group. There will also be coordinating meetings and monthly general meet-

---

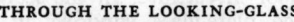

Finding Out About Free Schools

THE SOURCES OF information about free schools are many and varied, but tap one and it will lead to many others. Here are a few to start with:

New Schools Exchange *(2840 Hidden Valley Lane, Santa Barbara, California 93103)*—the best single source of information on free schools: where they are, how to start one, problems to anticipate, and almost anything else you need to know.

The Big Rock Candy Mountain *(Portola Institute, Inc., 1115 Merrill Street, Menlo Park, California 94025)*—a new publication similar to the popular Whole Earth Catalogue, but devoted to "resources for ecstatic education." The catalogue reviews schools, teaching methods, toys and games, publications, teaching laboratories, films, tapes, records, and highlights new approaches that "make the student himself the content of his learning," are nonmanipulative, and encourage exploration and creativity ($4 per copy; $8 per year subscription—two issues plus four supplements).

The Free Learner—a remarkably complete survey of experimental schools in the San Francisco Bay area, compiled by Constance Woulf *(4615 Canyon Road, El Sobrante, California 94803)*, available at $2 a copy.

New Schools Manual—a mimeographed booklet put out by New Directions Community School *(445 Tenth Street, Richmond, California 94801)* that provides some useful clues for meeting bureaucratic rules and regulations.

Directory of Free Schools—a list of free schools across the country, published by Alternatives Foundation *(1526 Gravenstein Highway, Sebastopol, California 97452)*. The pamphlet includes an essay on "How to Start a Free School," by Frank Lindenfeld, founder of several California free schools.

A Bibliography for the Free School Movement—a wide-ranging list of books on children and education, published by the Summerhill Society *(339 Lafayette Street, New York, N.Y. 10012)*. Available for 50 cents.

THROUGH THE LOOKING-GLASS

ings. People will sign up for the various groups at the general meeting, but each group will then take the responsibility for recruiting additional people into their work as the summer goes on. Some people, of course, will be in more than one group.

The hard work of researching power in Springfield has already consumed a great deal of the energy of seven or eight of us in MDS. We have begun to analyze how power works in Springfield, and in brief what we have found is the following: The Massachusetts Mutual Life Insurance Company (one of the 50 largest corporations in the country) is practically synonymous with the Springfield ruling elite. That is, the company is the richest in the area and the only major corporation with its home office in Springfield. The directors of Massachusetts Mutual interlock with every important employer or financial institution in the area and are trustees of the area colleges.

This company has undertaken an urban redevelopment project in downtown Springfield called Bay State West. The project will be a 30-story office building, a 300-room luxury hotel, a shopping mall, a new clubhouse for the Colony Club (the social club which the ruling elite of Springfield belong to, including the local directors of Massachusetts Mutual), air walkways with additional shop space over the street to the two major Springfield department stores, and a four-story, above-ground parking ramp. None of these things are needed by the population of the area, though other critical needs do exist which are not being met. It is argued that Bay State West will increase business and commercial activity in the downtown area. Such an accomplishment is great for the small group of already wealthy businessmen who get the benefit, but provides little real encouragement for the working person, who is only getting another opportunity to spend his money. The question for us is, will the project increase city revenue and take some of the tax burden off of the average taxpayer.

Massachusetts Mutual applied and was accepted as a private redevelopment authority to build Bay State West under Massachusetts General Law Chapter 121A, with all the "powers, rights, privileges, benefits and exemptions" granted by that law and under Chapter 257 passed especially to give additional privileges to the project in Springfield. Among the privileges granted under these laws is an exemption for the period of 40 years from all real estate and personal property taxes which would normally be paid to the city and which *are* paid by all working people in the area. Massachusetts Mutual has contracted with the city to pay an amount in lieu of taxes. The amount is based on a percentage of income from the project or $10 per thousand on a maximum of $50,000,000 valuation for the life of the contract (whichever of the two amounts works out to be greater for any year). Of course no regular homeowner has a pegged assessment (latest estimates made public are that the project will cost $45,000,000 just to build) and the normal tax rate is $54.50 per thousand and rising. The calculations of our research group are that Massachusetts Mutual will be paying the city at least $2,000,000 less per year on the average than it would if it were paying taxes. This figure might become considerably higher if the income formula in the contract fails to keep pace with inflation (the assessment formula being fixed). $2,000,000 is approximately 9% of the total real and personal property taxes collected by the city in 1967, and the minimum loss of $80,000,000 in uncollected taxes over the life of

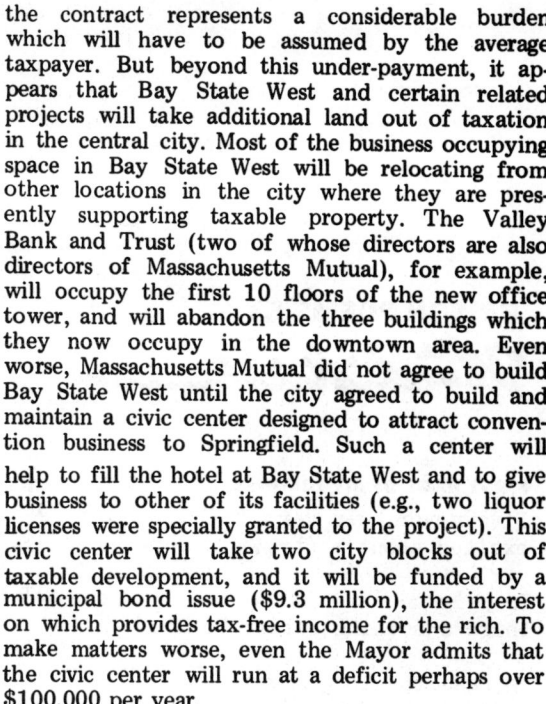

the contract represents a considerable burden which will have to be assumed by the average taxpayer. But beyond this under-payment, it appears that Bay State West and certain related projects will take additional land out of taxation in the central city. Most of the business occupying space in Bay State West will be relocating from other locations in the city where they are presently supporting taxable property. The Valley Bank and Trust (two of whose directors are also directors of Massachusetts Mutual), for example, will occupy the first 10 floors of the new office tower, and will abandon the three buildings which they now occupy in the downtown area. Even worse, Massachusetts Mutual did not agree to build Bay State West until the city agreed to build and maintain a civic center designed to attract convention business to Springfield. Such a center will help to fill the hotel at Bay State West and to give business to other of its facilities (e.g., two liquor licenses were specially granted to the project). This civic center will take two city blocks out of taxable development, and it will be funded by a municipal bond issue ($9.3 million), the interest on which provides tax-free income for the rich. To make matters worse, even the Mayor admits that the civic center will run at a deficit perhaps over $100,000 per year.

At the same time that these tax deals have been developing, the ruling group in Springfield has done an extensive publicity job to try to make people think that the reason for the heavy tax burden on the working man is the rising cost of welfare and especially state Medicaid. The Taxpayers Association in town has been one of the leading voices in this attempt to turn working people against each other. Members of this association include all of the directors of Massachusetts Mutual who are local residents. MDS will attempt to propose a counter-explanation of high taxation based on our research findings. In doing this we hope to be able to get through to many people in Springfield concerning the existence of a small powerful group in the city that is controlling the decision-making which affects us all. We will point out that this group is now planning the future of Springfield, and that they are doing it in such a way as to insure their own benefit while everyone else picks up the tab (both financially and in terms of the quality of our lives). We will try to force Massachusetts Mutual to pay the same taxes as everyone else, and hope to have enough success to demonstrate to people the power we really have if we get together and work together.

We have not presented here a discussion of our work with Bay State West in any sort of final form. We are in the process of writing a lengthy pamphlet which lays out our research in considerable detail, and we are engaged in further legal research. We will not do extensive work publicly on this tactic for a couple of months, and it is essential to have successful results from the Free School, and to get a functioning movement workshop before we undertake so large a task. It will not help in overcoming the sense of powerlessness which people have, unless MDS makes a good showing with this issue and is capable of working humanly with the new people who will want to become involved in the group. •

Tom Bell works for the Springfield, Massachusetts Area Movement for a Democratic Society.

PRISON POEMS BY

Hồ Chí Minh

FIRST PAGE OF MY JOURNAL

I've never been very
excited about poetry.

In prison
there's nothing better to do.

To pass the long days
and distract myself,

I write poems and wait for freedom.

ENTERING CH'ING SI PRISON

In the prison the old-timers
welcome the newcomers.

In the blue sky
white clouds chase away the storm.

In heaven
the clouds can wander freely.

A free man,
all alone, lies in the depths
of a prison cell.

PRISON JOURNAL

It is your body that's in prison.

Your spirt is not in prison.

If you are going to accomplish
your great task,

You've got to take
good care of your morale.

MOON

What can you do
when you're in prison,

With nothing to drink
and no flowers

To celebrate this lovely night
and fine weather?

I contemplate the moon
shining through the barred window,

And beyond the bars,
the moon watches the poet.

THE ROADS OF LIFE

1.
It was easy to cross the mountains.

It was easy to climb the peaks.

The level roads on the plain

Turned out to be harder to travel.

I met tigers in the mountains.

They didn't harm me.

I met a man on the plain

And he arrested me.

2.
I was a representative
of the new Vietnam

On a visit to the leaders
of a brother nation.

A storm like the waves of the ocean
overwhelmed me.

I found myself honored
with a prison cell.

3.
I am an honest man
with an untroubled conscience.

But they suspect me
of being a Chinese spy.

The roads of life
are always dangerous

But it is less easy
to get over them now than ever.

EVENING

Sunset. Our meal is over.

Everywhere
songs and music start up.

The dark and melancholy prison
at Ch'ing Si

Is suddenly changed
to a noble academy.

THE WATER RATION

The water ration is a half basin.

You can do whatever
you want with it.

You can wash your face or make tea.

If you wash, no tea.

If you want tea,
leave your face dirty.

PRISON FOOD

For every meal,
just a bowl of brown rice;

No vegetables, no salt,
not even broth.

Those who can have food brought in
can eat in prison.

Those who have no money
cry for their fathers and mothers.

NIGHTFALL

The tired birds return
to their roost in the trees.

Slowly a single cloud
drifts across the sky.

A girl in the village
is grinding corn,

While the fire glows red
in her clay oven.

A COMRADE'S PAPER BLANKET

New books, old books,
the leaves all piled together.

A paper blanket
is better than no blanket.

You who sleep like princes,
sheltered from the cold,

Do you know how many men in prison
cannot sleep all night?

THE DESERTER'S WIFE

My husband is gone.
He will never come back.

Left all alone with my sorrow,

My distress
so moved the authorities,

They took me to prison
for a rest cure.

TWILIGHT

The sword of the wind

Has been honed
on the mountain peaks.

Cold cuts into the flesh
of the trees

Like a pruning knife.

Far away a bell rings.

A lonely traveler
hurries toward home.

A boy rides on his buffalo

And plays on his flute.

AUTUMN NIGHT

Before the gate, a guard
with a rifle on his shoulder.

In the sky, the moon flees
through clouds.

Swarming bed bugs,
like black army tanks in the night.

Squadrons of mosquitoes,
like waves of attacking planes.

I think of my homeland.
I dream I can fly far away.

I dream I wander trapped
in webs of sorrow.

A year has come to an end here.
What crime did I commit?

In tears I write
another prison poem.

CLEAR MORNING

The morning sun
shines over the prison wall,

And drives away the shadows
and miasmas of hopelessness.

A life-giving breeze
blows across the earth.

A hundred imprisoned faces
smile once more.

THINKING OF A COMRADE

You came with me
as far as the river

The day I left.

"I'll see you soon," you said,

"Next harvest time for sure."

But the carts have long since left
the fields,

And me,
far from home, I am a prisoner.

COLD NIGHT

Autumn night.
No mattress. No covers.

No sleep. Body and legs
huddle up and cramp.

The moon shines
on the frost-covered banana leaves.

Beyond my bars
the Great Bear swings on the Pole.

UNABLE TO SLEEP

First watch.
Second watch. Third watch.

Unable to sleep, I twist and turn.

Fourth watch.
Fifth. Am I asleep or awake?

The five-pointed star

Of the Vietnam flag

Revolves in my dreams.

READING "THE ANTHOLOGY OF A THOUSAND POETS"

The men of old times liked to write
about nature.

Rivers. Mountains. Mists. Snow.
Flowers. Moon. Wind.

We must arm the poetry of our days
with steel,

And our poets
must learn to fight battles.

GOOD DAYS COMING

Everything changes, the wheel
of the law turns without pause.

After the rain, good weather.

In the wink of an eye

The universe throws off
its muddy clothes.

For ten thousand miles
the landscape

Spreads out like
a beautiful brocade.

Gentle sunshine.
Light breezes. Smiling flowers.

High in the trees, amongst the
sparkling leaves,

All the birds sing at once.

Men and animals rise up reborn.

What could be more natural?

After sorrow comes happiness.

FREE, I WALK ON THE MOUNTAIN AND ENJOY THE VIEW

Mountains. Clouds.
More mountains. More clouds.

Far below a river gleams,
bright and unspotted.

Alone, with beating heart,
I walk on the Western Range,

And gaze far off towards the South
and think of my comrades.

Prison Poems by Ho Chi Minh, translated by
Kenneth Rexroth *Avant Garde 3* May 1968

Venceremos means work!

The deadline for applying to join the first contingent of the Venceremos Brigade is October 30. The brigade will consist of 600 Americans—300 to leave at the end of November and 300 at the end of January—who will cut sugar for two months in Cuba, working with young Cubans of the Youth Centennial Column in Camaguey province. The Cuban government is inviting the U.S. youth to provide them with the experience of working in a socialist country and to help harvest a record 10 million tons of sugar cane. If this goal is reached, Cuba will have gone a long way toward economic independence.

The "rainbow brigade" will consist of 200 black, 200 brown and 200 white North Americans—working class youth, students, dropouts, returned GIs. Extensive political background is not a qualification for joining. The work will be very hard and home will be a tent in the field, so people applying should be in good health. They should be prepared to accept the segregated (according to sex) housing and to abstain from any use of drugs. Penalty for breaking these two rules is to be sent back to the U.S.

The round-trip cost will be from between $50—if leaving from the East Coast—and $150—if leaving from the West Coast. Applicants should apply for a passport now, not waiting until the application is accepted. For applications and posters, write: Venceremos Brigade, P.O. Box 643, Cathedral Station, New York, N.Y.,10025.

Guardian
10/25/69

THE
COLLEGE
TEACHER
AND THE
WORKING
CLASS

WORKING CLASS POLITICAL ATTITUDES

Jim Jacobs, REP Staff

In last month's Newsletter, Richie Rothstein wrote about the importance of organizing in lower middle class communities, a strategic emphasis with which I strongly agree. In this article I would like to describe some of the political attitudes of working class people, on the basis of my experience teaching courses in the evening on American Government at Macomb Community College, a two-year school located in a working class suburb of Detroit.

Originally intended as the college-level equivalent of the vocational high school, the community college has increasingly become a stepping stone for students of working class backgrounds who want to advance to a four-year school. More importantly, the central characteristics of the community college -- no entrance requirements; emphasis on technical and drafting courses for men, and nursing and typing courses for women -- attracts sons and daughters of working class origins as well as older workers interested in obtaining better jobs by earning a degree.

Most of my students are older people (some in their late 30s and 40s) who work in the daytime. The men have skilled, service, or lower white collar positions. The women are nurses, secretaries, or local housewives attempting to accumulate enough college hours for state certification as substitute teachers in the local elementary school system. Most are of Polish, Irish or Italian backgrounds, and all are white.

For most of these people college is not a way to escape the draft or something to fill up spare time. Some are sent to school by the automobile companies, which will pay tuition if a student receives a passing grade. (Typical of GM's toughness, it demands a 'C' or better grade from its workers.) Others are taking advantage of their veteran's benefits in order to receive some college degree. A few of the younger skilled workers are attend-

a Confectioner

a Smith

ing college because they don't like their work and want different jobs. But for all the community college is seen as a means of advancement to a better job and higher status.

By no means are they typical workers. They aspire to rise above traditional working class positions. These students possess an amazing desire to complete their schooling. It is not uncommon at Macomb to find students working on 40-hour jobs (not counting overtime) and carrying twelve credits. In a sense they have swallowed the American ethic of success through hard work.

Yet, in spite of their desire to be successful, all are from working class backgrounds and most are the first individuals from their families ever to go to college. Since many of their brothers and sisters, or parents, still remain in the factories, my students maintain strong family connections and emotional identification with workers. Most see themselves as members of the working class or moving into lower-middle class occupations.

'Stick to the Facts'

Teaching at this type of school requires that a good deal of attention be devoted to classroom presentation. Most important, to be effective you must emphasize real substantive issues. The people in my class approach the subject of American government very concretely. They dislike theoretical or other abstract discussions, and very much want to 'stick to the facts'. When I was attempting to explain pluralist theory (the notion that policy springs from the clashes of various interest groups and is the result of each group compromising their demands in order to win something), a skilled worker cut me short by interrupting, 'You know that isn't true. Business groups aren't going to compromise with poor people.' And that ended the discussion.

A great many of these people subscribe to the belief that the facts are objective, independent proof of an opinion. An unfortunate by-product of this perspective is that since I have more 'facts' than most of the people in the class, I can win many of the arguments over controversial issues (draft, Vietnam, communism, riots, corporations and military). My students will often refuse to continue the debate although they are certainly unhappy with my views. To counter this, I attempt to use examples and case studies in areas where they have experience -- military service, unions, local issues -- so they will be more apt to argue with me. Often the presentation of a 'loaded' example (draft, the war, black power) will motivate people to go beyond discussion of the original issue. I encourage these develop-of the original issue. I encourage these developments because the students get a chance to discuss issues in a sustained fashion (relatively rare in an introductory course), and they initiate the discussion themselves, giving it a more relaxed quality and aiding in the flow of real opinions.

Since a number of my students are older, I have been able to introduce consumer and tax issues into the discussions. The theory of the 'affluent worker' simply doesn't apply to many of these people, who are continually disturbed at rising taxes and the quality of education in public schools. From my experience these are the gut issues that motivate people to initiate action. Often I have attempted to introduce other areas of American government by trying to relate them to these issues. For example, in discussing the civil liberties issues of church

a Sho=maker

a Taylor

a Porter

a Sadler

a Box-maker

and state relations (a burning issue, as most of my students are Catholics), I focus on taxation rates that might rise due to aid for schools. On the questions of poverty and affluence, I stress the amount of money wasted by the present system of needless bureaucratic investigation of clients. Above all, one of my continual themes is the regressive nature of the tax system (particularly on the local and state levels) and the numerous loopholes that exist for the rich.

Views on Politics

The strong emphasis these people place on the concrete aspects of their lives makes them sensitive to the existence of powerful groups in the society. Contrary to what many radicals are led to think, these people are not easily manipulated by the media. They tend to look beyond the personal conflicts of politicians, to the realities of social and economic conditions. Morever, they possess crude but accurate estimations of the differences of power among the dominant grops. They understand the corporate domination of parts of the society. They believe that desire for profits of American enterprise in large part motivates American foreign policy. They easily see through the 'support our boys in Vietnam' theme articulated by the administration. Many of them dislike the war, although they are even more against draft-card burning and protests. Extremely distrustful of politicians, they are always looking for what interests lie behind the actions of political figures. Bobby Kennedy will never co-opt them.

I encourage them to think in what I call 'structural terms', continually emphasizing that politics is not a clash of personalities. For example, we discussed the UAW-Ford strike as more than a personal confrontation of Walter Reuther and Henry Ford II. There were real issues at stake and most of the class realized what they were and why a strike was unnecessary. Since Detroit is a heavy industrial center with a large unionized work force, there is little difficulty discussing unions and their relationship to management and the rank and file.

Along with the concren with concrete issues, these people possess an established belief in the 'rights of the little man'. No doubt in part this is because they dutifully accept what is taught in high school civics. But also, they are the 'little man', they look after their interests. They agree with the necessity of participation of people in decisions: very few want to leave things up to the politicians. They are interested in the establishment of specific procedures and rules for their dealings with the police and the courts, which suggests that civil liberties is not a bourgeois trapping but indicates a fundamental desire of people to know with some certainty what behavior public officials can be allowed in relation to them.

Given this perspective, I continually stress, with case studies such as 'Building Lyndon Johnson' (Ramparts, December 1967), how many important decisions are made by private groups. I emphasize the amount of private planning that goes on and how little individuals can do to affect these policies. Again, the existence of big companies and big unions in Detroit makes it easy to discuss the ways in which massive institutions limit individual power. Many of the students are union people and are willing

from their own experience to discuss these questions at great length.

The most important area in which my students can relate the experience of individual powerlessness is the work situation. In a discussion of the stereotypes of the mass man, I suggested the example of the assembly line worker. The image made an impact, and many of the students supported my view of the alienating, inhuman nature of factory work with examples from their own experience. When one woman in the class attempted to dismiss the plight of the assembly line worker by saying, 'Those guys are only there for the money,' she was immediately refuted by others in the class, who shouted, 'Why don't you work on the line, nobody can be paid enough to do that kind of work.' Again, this sort of response suggests that the happy worker image is a myth.

The Racial Issue

Although these people are basically interested in concrete aspects of life, the topic which has little relation to their actual experience upsets them most -- race. It is in our discussions of civil rights, black power, and ghetto rebellions, that the most exciting and emotional discussions have occurred.

Like most white people, except for a small minority who say black people are workers like everybody else, a large majority of the class is racist. There can be no question about it. They are against open housing, want ghetto revolts crushed, and desire no personal contact with black people. Although they recoil at being called racists, and many of them claim black friends on the job, after work they want nothing to do with black people. Their hostilities are reinforced by their feelings toward those who support liberal integration issues such as open housing. As one student who claims he will vote for Wallace said: 'Why is George Hudson (owner of Detroit's largest department store and chairman of a businessman's committee to deal with ghetto problems) want open housing? It doesn't matter to him, no Negroes are going to live near him. It just hurts the little guy.'

Thus the issue of civil rights is seen as a matter of democracy, the rights of the little guy. Perhaps an easy rationalization. Perhaps not.

Surprisingly, my students support black power goals as a 'positive' step. They are attracted to the 'self-help' aspect of the doctrine, and not at all against the development of a black movement, even an independent political movement. Black control of the central cities does not seem to upset them (possibly because almost two-thirds of the class live in the suburbs).

The students are very much opposed to rebellions, although after a discussion of ghetto conditions I was able to get a few people to admit that if they lived under those conditions they would be out on the streets. After reading Tom Hayden's 'Rebellion in Newark,' most of the students thought it was biased, disagreed with him violently, and felt he had overplayed police brutality (although my prodding of their own experiences with police produced some agreement that 'sometimes the police go too far').

In attempting to isolate specific reasons why they were against ghetto uprisings, I found they were afraid that it would spread to their homes and they would be endangered. When I pointed out that in each rebellion the people pretty much remained in the ghetto and their actions were not directed toward white people (except for those who entered the ghetto) but toward symbols of oppression, some of the class members became a little less inclined to accept the 'all means necessary' argument for how to deal with riots.

Those most vociferously opposed to the riots live farthest from Detroit. One student commented to me in private, 'You can tell from discussions on the Negro question how many people live in Detroit and how many live in the suburbs.'

Yet, in the area of race, especially since the ghetto rebellions, white workers are exceedingly insecure. Continually in our discussion of Hayden's book, people asked, 'Okay, the ghetto has problems; what do you do?' I was never able to answer this question to their satisfaction, or mine. Supporting 'black self-determination', or kicking all cops out of the ghetto, makes little sense from their perspectie. In this area radicals really don't have any sort of programmatic suggestions to offer these people. Since rebellions will occur and the problems of black people will remain for many years, we need to begin thinking of ways in which ordinary white people can understand and sympathize with black people's actions. Presently, the only group offering alternatives to these people is Breakthrough, a paramilitary organization that has been holding large open meetings in the suburbs ever since the summer riots.

The Need for Concrete Alternatives

The impact of the 'concrete' thinking of these workers and lower middle class people is important for middle class radicals to understand. Often we tend to view the working class as primarily ignorant, satisfied people 'bought off' by the prevailing order. These people, we lament, will be the most difficult to bring around to the correct perspective. Yet, they have a latent radical consciousness, derived from their own experience. We do not need to tell them the draft system is discriminatory; they have direct experience with it. We need not stress the brutalities of work under capitalism; their day-to-day experience with it is much more profound than ours. Our critique of society fits well their view of the prevailing system.

Why aren't these people, then, beating down the door attempting to work with us. To a large extent, it is precisely this consciousness that motivates a passive acceptance of the status quo by these people. While many of them can agree with some of the movement's criticisims of the society, they see no way to change it. At the end of any discussion of a substantive issue in class, virtually the same question is posed: 'I agree it is bad, but what can you do about it?' They have no illusion that if we all get together our power will be felt. Nor do they possess a perspective that things are inherently getting better all the time. Since some recognize the structural basis of power in the society and the enormous efforts necessary to induce any change, for them it is utopian to talk about

radical alternatives. They want concrete programs for change in the immediate future.

Moreover, although they are critical of the society, they remain committed to the present system, no doubt partially because they are trying to better themselves in it. Draft card burning enrages them; so do violent demonstrations against the President. They don't know much about the New Left, but I am sure they would disapprove of many of our tactics. I agree with John McDermott that more of their hostility hinges upon workers' reactions to the actions or privileged middle class people (see his provocative article, 'Thoughts on the Movement', Viet-Report, Sept-Oct 1967). In addition, there exists a fundamental distrust of appeals made on 'moral grounds'. They have a basic cynicism toward all political demands and viewpoints. For example, they cannot believe the other side of the war (the National Liberation Front) is a shining example of a 'good' political movement. Since we in the movement have no programs for them, they see us as just another group. Until their fatalism is changed, their receptivity to the movement will not be great.

One cannot overestimate the need for concrete alternatives to be presented to these ordinary people. Slogans ('let the people decide', 'crush American imperialism') simply don't cut ice. We desperately need the development of short-range strategies and plans that both will foster greater radical consciousness and can be implemented; only this will shatter their cynicism. They must realize that change is possible before accepting our long-term plans. Richie Rothstein's work in Chicago is an exciting development in that direction.

A Word of Caution

These notes, based on my teaching experience, should not be taken as an optimistic picture. I have emphasized areas that indicate opportunities for radicals to work with these people in developing radical consciousness. But any belief in the existence of a 'noble savage' worker waiting to be tapped for the revolutionary movement is simply unreal. These people I teach want to make it within the system. Their ideas and goals are geared to success, and at least the younger people are optimistic about getting off the assembly line and getting a better position.

Why is it important for professional radicals to consider these people? Pragmatically, the reasons are very clear: They are the common Americans, and without at least their support we cannot build a democratic mass movement.

However, there is another reason for activities such as teaching at community colleges. We need the help of these people to broaden our own demands. Often we have a very arrogant attitude toward workers and lower middle class people: these are the groups that need to be 'radicalized' and brought around to our viewpoint. But we must learn from their demands. We are a privileged sector of America, not used to struggling and maintaining ourselves as these people are. We can draw from their experience as well as asking them to accept our vision. Then, we might have a real movement, and the term 'radicals in the professions' will not make us feel so uncomfortable.

Radicals in the Professions Newsletter Summer 1968

a Chick en-man

a meal-man

a Glover

a Button-maker

a Sope-boyler

GROPING TOGETHER

FROM THE BERKELEY DISORIENTATION GUIDE

Jeff Lustig

"Berkeley" is not a school; it's a state of mind. Berkeley is where you don't have to know people to talk to them, where you don't need money to live, where you don't have to own land to build parks. Berkeley is right out in the open--not behind closed doors--in the streets which have ceased to be the locus of the aimless interminable "traffic" of commercial life.

The endless confusions and obscenities which make up America will not be transformed in a week, a month, or by a stroke of fortune. They will be changed by people who struggle to rise from the status of consumers and functionaries to that of human beings, by men and women seeking to become the center, rather than the play-things and objects of events. Berkeley is the place of that struggle and that search; while not yet "liberated," it is a profound and distinctly liberating place to live. It is, in short, something more than the usual agglomeration or "mass;" it is a place where it's not embarrassing to care for one another; it is a community.

Berkeley is a community which, as such, is disturbingly political. We say "disturbingly" because "politics often has been confined to that narrow territory within formal and reified "institutions," separated from "culture," which is defined as the trinkets, folksy tunes and marginalia of life better left to museums. Not so.

Politics and culture are one. Power--primarily a matter of ability and strength and only secondarily of control--arises from and expresses a collective way of life. A politics which is not rooted in a culture is no politics at all. The continued and many-sided offensives issuing from our town arise from, and in defense of, our community--out of our activities like rock music or People's Park or people's mechanics, which--far from being marginal activities--are both liberating and political. These activities mark out the space and define the content of our new ways of life.

We have in recent months begun in Berkeley to form ourselves into more distinct affinity groups, collectives, bands of "militant pilgrims" and "anonymous allies" in order that we may nurture and broadcast these activities. Some of them are:

Great Neighborhood Food Conspiracy

Groups of people have organized into food exchange co-ops and Labor Gift Plan nodes in the Grove Street area, around Channing and Grant, and (soon) in the South Campus area. These nodes were formed in response to the high price of food, the scarcity of non-poisoned food, and the need

"in a potentially post-scarcity society for decentralized, cooperative forms of organization and communication. Allowing people to work out a form of existence between pure self-involvement and total immersion, these groups also see the neighborhood as the necessary matrix within which public street actions take place." (Anita Frankel, People's Park Office, 1925 Grove.)

Berkeley Labor Gift Plan

Through the program people with skills can get in touch with others to exchange services: planting a garden, fixing a car, baby sitting, etc. People can also sign up to teach or learn skills. (People's Park Office, Fub, Mike Schectman 849-0894.)

Taxi Unlimited

The world's only co-op taxi company with a roaring-big driver-managed bossless fleet of 5 cabs, both cars and drivers in unusual condition. TU was known for its special services; grocery pick-ups, luggage carrying, pizza delivery until one of these services caused its insurance company to cancel insurance and to blackball TU. On Bastille Day, two cabs were made available as ambulances for demonstrators. Presently prevented from doing it in the road, TU needs $35,000 to become self-insured within 30 days or their permits will be revoked. If you can, call TH 1-2345 or write TU, PO Box 203, Berkeley.

People's Park Legal Defense Committee

The Committee is trying to build an effective on-going legal service center for the Movement. Growing out of the Park Crisis, the Committee plans to help those busted get out of jail and to get lawyers. It also plans to inform the community on legal rights and about the ways courts provide cover and justification for what the pigs do in the field. 1925 Grove, 549-3977.

Free Church

A radical church with a radical Christian ideology; provides services to the people of Berkeley, especially street people and students, and to the peace and liberation movements. Operates a community switchboard, handles drug freakouts, counselling for runaways (also called Pilgrims). FC is a real church--i.e., a community of resistence, it is a guerilla church, with celebrations of the Liberated Zone (with the Freedom Meal) every Friday nite at 8 pm.

Science Students for Social Responsibility

Founded in response to the fact that scientists in the U.S. are either employees of the military or of corporations which

691
how to live

direct their efforts towards exploiting rather than helping men relate to each other and their environment. Cur purpose is education, agitation and support for those scientists who are fighting to change their roles. We hold courses, initiate campaigns (e.g., against chemical and biological warfare research on campus), and attempt to organize scientists working for the military.

Medical Committee for Human Rights

Decent health care in this country is hard to come by. Health services still are organized around the old double standard: one type for the rich, one for the poor. "Public" hospitals are controlled by bureaucracies which are rigid and unresponsive to the people. A Free Clinic has now been founded on Haste St. (McKinley School), but it needs both money and a new facility. The Committee plans to establish programs of "good" health care fulfilling three criteria, 1) dignified, personalized, respectful treatment under community control; 2) good facilities and well trained personnel; and 3) active community programs of preventative medicine (e.g., child health, narcotics, pregnancy information, etc.).

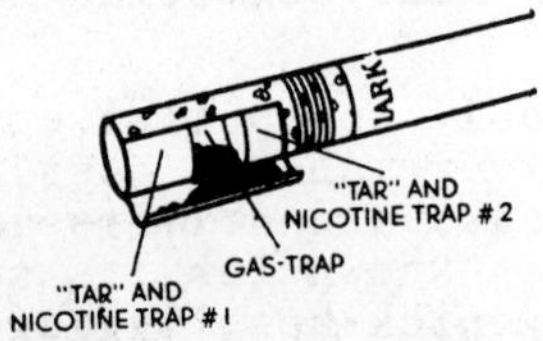

"TAR" AND NICOTINE TRAP #2
GAS-TRAP
"TAR" AND NICOTINE TRAP #1

Stuaent Research Facility

Open to groups or inidividuals interested in doing research on matters of social concern. The staff of SRF provides technical advice and aid in publication. The facility is maintained by its users. Examples of work in progress; research on tenant's rights, on organized medicine and American health, booklet on 1001 Reasons for Revolutions. 2214 Grove St., 549-2172.

Black Panther Party

The summer program of the Panthers revolved around Pt. 5 of our Program: "We want an education for our people that exposes the true nature of this decadent American Society." We also want an education that will give to our people a knowledge of our history and a sense of self. We are now implementing a Free Breakfast and Free Lunch program in the ghetto, and--pursuant to our activities in the United Front AgainstFascism and our struggle against the power of Finance Capital, a program of Community Control for Police. WE CHARGE GENOCIDE, historically, presently and futuristically against the Avaricious exploiting businessmen, the Demagogic Law-and-order politicians, and the Fascist,Brutalizing cops.
To paraphrase Pastor Martin Niemoeler's description of Nazi Germany:
First they came for the Panthers,
But I was not a Panther, so I did not defend them;
Then they came for the student activists,
But I was not a student activist, so I did not defend them;
Then they came for the black people,

But I was not black, so I did not defend them;
Then they came for trade unions,
But I was not a trade unionist, so I did not defend them;
Then they came for the teachers,
But I was not a teacher, so I did not defend them;
And when they came for me, there was no one left to defend me.
Other Political and Third World Groups (See: Campus Political Groups)

FREE HUEY

Police Control

The Park Committee office now has a box in the back room labelled "Police Control: Suggestions." This box is intermittently checked by an international police fighter whose indomitable dynamism may be helped to fruition by your suggestions, information, witnessed and signed complaints, badge numbers, relevant photos, pig poems and messages of love. Committees now being formed: Self-Protection, Recall Elections, Public Relations. We are also working with the Panthers for community control of the Police.

FREE BOBBY

Warring Street (COPS) Commune

The COPS Commune is an attempt to find a new form of social-political organization that will enable us to do more effective work and, simultaneously, to create alternative communal life-styles. Last May, after having come together in a mutual search for an alternative to the mass-meeting style of politics, we set up a communal household of 12. We committed ourselves to work together in political struggles and to help each other in all areas of our lives in a spirit of brotherly and sisterly love. Our general outlook is best reflected in the 13 point Berkeley Liberation program. We have chosen to stay in the city and to become active in the Movement because we feel that personal struggles must be guided by personal concerns to build alternative styles of work and play. We see ourselves as involved in intense attempts to change our privatistic, indulgent life styles and build a revolutionary family.

FREE BURSEY

Homosexual Liberation

The struggle to Free Berkeley includes the Struggle for the Liberation of homosexuals. Agreeing with other radicals that "new sexual relationships are part of the process of ripping off the bourgeois in ourselves" homosexual demonstrations have now taken place in New York, Minneapolis, Los Angeles and San Francisco. People with ideas for a "Gay Manifesto" or for strategy, call Leo Laurence, 863-6187.

Ed. Note: These are sample pages from the *Disorientation Guide*, a handbook of information for new students at Berkeley. It was created by Berkeley radicals as part of Disorientation Week, September 1969 — a collective effort to break through the myths and lies of the Knowledge Industry and to give students some sense of present realities in Berkeley.

BAY AREA:
COMMUNITY
AND
COMMUNI-
CATION

THEY'RE INSANE! STOP THEM!

YES MA'AM!!

HARD!

LEGAL TRICKS

by Lothar Meyer

With the Great Berkley Rent Strike entering its second week and landlord response expected at any time, many people in the community are concerned about the legal situation. They are asking:

"What can we expect from the landlords and what can BTU do about it?"

Joe Datz, coordinator of the BTU's legal team, spoke to the Tribe on Monday and detailed the Union's legal strategy. The following is a summary of what to expect once rent is withheld.

First, when you get anything from your landlord, BRING IT TO THE BTU OFFICE IMMEDIATELY!

When the landlord decides to try and kick you out, he will send you a three-day notice of eviction.

COME TO THE BTU OFFICE. Bring the notice, your lease and anything pertinent from your landlord that is in writing.

Soon after your three days are up, the landlord will get a summons and have it served to you.

When you get the summons, COME TO THE BTU OFFICE. The BTU laywers

will go through some legal juggling with motions hearings, and it will be 22 days before you have to do anything else.

After that month is up, the BTU will file a demurrer to quash the whole action on the grounds that it is unconstitutional.

Another month or so will pass with hearings, motions, objections and the whole boatload of legal bullshit. Then you file a demand for a jury trial. This puts the badguys a little uptight, and they will fidget for quite a while before a trial date is actually set.

So, some two or three months after the original eviction notice is served, you finally make it to trial.

The BTU laywers will be very busy stomping the landlords' asses with pre-trial legal hassling. In many cases tenants may have to provide their own trial defense.

The BTU is setting up classes in legal self-defense to make sure that everyone will be adequately equipped to handle the situation.

Defending yourself in court can be a lot of fun, and Joe promises that the classes will be interesting and informative.

education switchboard

We have started to collect and collate information about education in the Bay Area, esp. alternative learning environments. The info is filed under various categories and is readily available to anyone who telephones or comes in person. The energies of a few more people are needed to help with keeping the file updated and with collecting more information. CONTACT Jacques Goldman at SF Switchboard, 1830 Fell St., San Francisco 94117; or call 387-3575.

A fairly old new institution is the S.F. Switchboard, started during the flower summer in Haight-Ashbury 2½ years ago. Switchboard has grown so it takes a six page booklet just to describe the many uses you can make of it...but it's still a people place. There are now 42 switchboards across the country. More are needed, especially in smaller, more isolated communities.

The New Utopian

STRIKE PLEDGE

I pledge to support the Berkeley Tenants Union rent strike. I will withhold my rent when 10% or 20 units of tenants who rent from my landlord have signed this pledge.

Name_____ Phone _____

Address, Apt. No. _____

Owner of Building_____

To whom do you pay rent check?_____

No. of units in Building_____ Return to 1925 Grove St.

DEALING

BUS BUST

The dirty Berkeley City Council just passed a law saying that no person can live in a bus or a camper within the city limits, and on private property for no longer than three days.

People who are affected by, or don't dig the law are asked to contact the People's Architects Office 1940B Bonita St., phone 849-2577 so that a mutual aid meeting can be arranged.

PUBLIC SERVICE FEATURE
OF THE
BERKELEY TRIBE

THE ABOVE TWO PIGS WERE THROWN OUT OF AN SMC MEETING ON CAMPUS TUESDAY NIGHT

SPRING QUARTER

International Liberation School

ILS

1925 Grove St. 549-3977 (11-2 o'clock)

Registration: first 3 weeks in April
Classes begin: last week in April

Organizational Skills
Physical Self Defense
Medical Skills
Self Defense Firearms
(Also Special Women's Class)
Political Educational
How to Defend Yourself in Court (Legal Skills)

Pamphlets available:	
Medical Cadre	$.25
Every Soldier a Shitworker, Every Shitworker a Soldier	$.25
Legal Defense	$.50
Firearms and Self Defense: A Handbook for Radicals, Revolutionaries, and Easy Riders	$.50

Ad (and Photo) in *Berkeley Tribe*

BLOCK PARTY

We, the Brothers and Sisters of Milvia House (1578 Milvia St.) are having a block party Friday April 10, 6:00 p.m. to start the long process of getting our neighborhood together. From past experience we know that to succeed in a long, hard and bitter struggle we must get to love and trust each other in a revolutionary spirit.

In that spirit we have invited Tom Hayden, Stew Albert, Turco (Chief of Staff of the Patriot Party) and members of the Black Panther Party to express some of their ideas and experiences. We have also asked Women's Liberation to attend.

We are engaged in the same struggle as our brothers and sisters of the Viet Cong and Pathet-Lao. We must learn to relate to each other with the same co-operative, communal spirit of revolutionary conscienceness. Only then will it be possible for us to resist the pig forces of Babylon as do the Panthers and Patriots.

Power to the People
Brothers and Sisters
of Milvia House

Berkeley Tribe

Hip Arbitration Board

In at least one city there is a Jewish Arbitration Board. Jews who get into a hassle with each other can take their arguments to a board of their fellow Jews for a decision. The winner relies on social pressure, rather than such violence as the threat of imprisonment, to get the loser to accept the decision. This is obviously far more civilized than using the courts, whose only sanction is violence.

So why don't we organize a Hip Arbitration Board? Instead of suing someone, you bring the matter to the HAB. If the HAB decides in your favor and yet you can't collect, every member of the HAB will be warned about the person who burned you. If someone is about to sue you, ask him to bring the matter to the HAB instead of the courts. If he refuses, the membership of the HAB will know that that person is vindictive, uptight, a believer in violence, etc.

Each hearing conducted by the HAB will have five judges: one chosen by each of the disputants, so that each will know he has a friend among the judges; then those two will mutually agree on two more; and finally, a permanent member trusted and known by the entire hip community as being fair and wise. After each disputant is satisfied that all five judges understand his side, a 4/5 vote of the judges will deice the matter.

(from Free Underground Communication, 251 Littleness, Monterey, Ca. 93940)

THE SKILLS POOL

Would you like to help your brothers and sisters with your skills and labor? Would you like some help yourself? When you need help--to fix your car or your roof, to get a baby sitter or plant a garden, call your local skills pool and we'll send someone over free, or very cheap if the volunteer needs some money. When someone needs your skills, or when there is a community project you might like to participate in, you offer your help, free or for pay as you choose.

We will try to arrange for food and music and other good things at our work parties. By sharing our labor and our free time, by working together as brothers, we can free ourselves to live deeper, more creative lives. For information on a local skills pool in the Bay Area write Cliff Humphrey, 5101 Miles, Oakland, Calif.

PRINTING WORKSHOP

ATT: The New England Free Press will continue to train movement people to become 'Movement Printers.' During the past summer we trained four people to print, three of whom are actively trying to set up a press. Because of this summer's success we will be training people all year round. Training does not begin at any special time; we will accept people every 2-3 weeks—there should always be openings. The time needed to learn to print is 1-2 months. We're sorry we can't provide room and board while you are here but we don't have it. During the summer several people had part-time jobs while they were learning—it worked out well. We will try to train people in all skills: layout, offset camera work, plate burning, printing, folding and other miscellany that they will need to know. The work will be intensive. Women and community organizers are especially encouraged to come.

Please write or call first: **Printing Workshop, New England Free Press, 791 Tremont Street, Boston, Mass. 02118—536-9219.**

Leviathan

WHOLE EARTH CATALOG

All our lives big corporations have been taking care of business for us; they have been cobbling our shoes, sewing our clothes, building our cars, constructing our dwellings, finding our ways in wilderness, printing and producing our newspapers and television, growing our food and teaching us our three R's. Now that we are ready to take care of business we find that that is one thing they never taught us.

The Whole Earth Catalog, however, is the beginning of our attempt to teach ourselves. It is a reference guide for doing those projects that best involve a whole community.

The catalog presently is a collection of reviews of books and things. The books are how-to books, pamphlets, magazines and other catalogs. The things are tools or raw materials mostly, i.e. a lumber mill that fits in a suitcase and a super-strong waterproof wood-coating material).

The catalog is divided into seven sections: Understanding Whole Systems, Shelter and Land Use, Industry and Craft, Communications, Community, Nomadics and Learning. These two pages contain samples from all but Understanding Whole Systems and Community.

Five dollars will get you one catalog and eight dollars will get you a year's subscription (two catalogs and four supplements). WHOLE EARTH CATALOG, Portola Institute, 558 Santa Cruz, Menlo Park, California 94025.

San Francisco Express Times 4/23/69

Radical day care for N.Y. kids

In an attempt to break down the family structure where the children-as-property ideology is pervasive, and to experiment with community responsibility for childrearing, about 10 collectively-owned and supervised nurseries have been organized in New York City in the past year.

The nurseries are staffed not by "professionals," but by parents and friends, men and women, to create a total community the children can be part of, as well as to develop children's relationships to adults beyond just those with parents and with men as well as women.

Most of the nurseries operate out of store fronts and do not meet the stringent requirements for licensed day-care facilities in the city. People in the collectives believe these requirements are strict in order to keep women at home and off the labor market. During World War II, when women were needed to work in factories, the government established hundreds of day-care facilities and the legal specifications were greatly relaxed so the nurseries could be established most anywhere. As long as women workers were needed, nurseries were provided. But as soon as fighting men returned, women were laid off their jobs—and one of the first measures taken to insure this layoff was to shut down the day care centers.

The ideology of the necessity for each mother to stay at home with her children was used then, as it is now, to keep women at home performing uncompensated, privitized and boring labor.

The nurseries are also an experiment in radical political education for young children. Like the Black Panther party breakfast program, which includes lessons on the history of black people and the need for a revolutionary party, the nurseries are beginning to develop political consciousness in young kids. Through teaching methods that will build non-authoritarian personalities in kids and materials and lessons that provide an early basis for later political development, the nurseries are collectively trying to provide for the training of future generations of revolutionaries.

One of the most significant recent models for this political training within capitalist countries is in Germany. There, the entire left movement is involved in childhood education and a major emphasis is placed on curriculum for generations of radicals. Similar attempts have been made in this country in SNCC's freedom schools of the early 1960s, in the community schools held during the New York city teachers' strikes and other smaller nurseries connected with local organizing projects of ERAP and other groups in the North.

Because of the necessity for political curriculum, one of the prime needs of the nursery collectives is to remain financially independent and in control of the nursery program. A group of CBS employes recently asked their company for money to finance a nursery. CBS has been eager to fund the program—providing that their products were used in the classrooms. The broadcasting giant wanted to create a school to advertize its own subsidiary, "Creative Playthings," plus wanted to create conditions that would make workers dependent on the corporation. Using this model of co-optation that can work only because parents are so desperate for child care, the nursery collectives are struggling to keep their schools independent and part of a broader movement.

The development of curriculum and collectivity are only part of the struggle, however. Alternate institutions to existing public facilities are important to create models of what those public institutions can be, but they can dram off energies from struggling against those public facilities. It is significant that the nursery collectives have not created any elementary schools. They are providing services only where services do not now exist and they are developing a collective consciousness of what good education should be. The experiences of those teaching in radical nurseries in other cities suggests that it is crucial to use this collective consciousness and new curricula in attacks on public schools to make them serve the people.

In New York the city-wide day care collective, part of the city-wide women's liberation movement, meets once a week. At present the nurseries need volunteers and money for equipment, rent and telephones. People interested and parents with children aged one to four years should write Box 79, c/o the Guardian.

Guardian 12/6/69

GANGS/FAMILIES/COMMUNES: MAKING THE REVOLUTION IN THE CITY—HOUSE TO HOUSE

VISION:

The transformation of Golden Gate Park will begin with a gathering of communes: hippie hill and the meadow below surging with energy and acid, tie-dye banners and rainbow tents ringed by magical vibes. Each tribe under its totem singing chants of the new life with flutes, drums and tambourines. All power to the communes.

While food cooks in giant pots—grains, fresh bread, vegetables—and slaughtered sheep roast over open pits, people smoke, talk of crops and weapons. Interchange of city and country. We share tools, knowledge, consciousness and desires. We beat out our rhythms on the skins our country brothers have brought to us, giving in return the tools they need.

Country—an opening into nature.

City—an opening into the heart of the pig.

Collective—the commune of all the communes, the real power of the hip people.

BRINGDOWN:

Late afternoon, the pig attacks stragglers, fearing the few people gathered. A few bottles fly, four are busted, pigs smirking provocation while strangling a brother—but we are too few and we are forced to remember we are still a subject people.

But the energy of the hip community cannot be suppressed. We are the new life which man will lead, if there is a future at all. Our communes, our gatherings are the forms of the future, bringing together the strength and magic of our people.

This Sunday we will do it again.

Armed/Love

Leaflet reprinted in *Good Times* 4/23/69

REVOLUTIONARY GANGS marvin garson

My comments last week on the Peace and Freedom Party — that it had become a public scandal — were surprisingly well received, even by people well placed in the party hierarchy. Now I am encouraged to take on a bigger fish: The Movement, sometimes known as the New Left. Get your thinking caps on, revolutionaries; it's Theory Time.

What's wrong with the New Left? What happened to all the magic in phrases like "participatory democracy" and "let the people decide"? Why have they degenerated into pure demagogy? And what did they mean in the first place?

The slogans suggested that what we basically needed was real democracy in place of the present sham democracy, substantive democracy in place of formal democracy. We needed new institutions through which people would really be able to "participate in making the decisions that affect their lives." The idea was right there in the name of the most prominent New Left organization: Students for a Democratic Society.

The model of the New Society was supposed to be the New Left organizations themselves. The agonizing problem has been that these organizations, while impeccably democratic, have been a stone drag.

There has been plenty of bitching about bureaucracy inside the New Left, but most of it has been ill-founded. For every leader who has tried to tyrannize over the rank and file, there have been a hundred who have earnestly done their best to involve the rank and file in decision-making. Where the typical labor leader tries to keep his followers away from meetings whenever something important is up for decision, the typical New Left organizer drags as many people as he possibly can to meetings, and tries to get opposing points of view set forth as fairly as possible. The heartbreaker has been that for some reason people don't WANT to go to meetings, don't WANT to participate.

The implications are ominous. After the Power Structure has been overthrown, will people still have to be dragged to meetings? How can you run a society democratically if people don't WANT to "participate in making the decisions that affect their lives"? Won't power eventually fall into the hands first

of revolutionary leaders and then — as the excitement fades away — of a new generation of bureaucratic hacks? It's an old argument — Michels made it 60 years ago (his "iron law of oligarchy") — but no Marxist has ever been able to refute it.

Let's start off with a different principle of organization, and next week we'll see where it leads.

Suppose, instead of getting together with people you agree with in the abstract, or people whose economic interests are the same as yours, suppose you get together with people whose company you find congenial, people who are really into the same things you are, people who work and play well together. In other words, instead of forming political parties or unions or protest groups, suppose you form gangs or families or communes. (You don't all have to live under the same roof, just as long as you live in the same city — or better, the same neighborhood.)

The main difference between a revolutionary gang and a revolutionary party is that a party, by definition, seeks state power. It puts forth a program which it takes very seriously, and expects the public to take seriously; for it is on the basis of that program that the party intends to re-order society once it gains the power of government.

A revolutionary party says: If you want "structural reform," or "peace, bread and land," or "true democracy," or "social ownership of the means of production," then put us in power. Vote for us, or (depending on the circumstances) pick up a gun and join our army.

Conservative parties also ask you to put them in power, by ballot or bullet. Is there no difference, then? Certainly there is — program. And that is why revolutionary parties quarrel and split so much about the "correct program," because in the final analysis, that's all they have. The program can't be too sectarian, too far beyond the masses; it can't be opportunist, sacrificing its revolutionary

content; it has to be just right.

A revolutionary gang (or family or commune) is more modest. It carries out projects which seem productive and are fun to do; but it understands that there are plenty of other gangs around with their own projects, just as worthwhile.

Since it is not a candidate for power, it does not need to present to the public a formal program for the reorganization of society. Since its members respect and trust each other from the start — they joined the group because it was congenial, not because it was "correct" — they can dispense with the parliamentary formalities. (Roberts Rules of Order is an important defensive weapon that can save your life in a political jungle, but it's usually unnecessary among friends.)

In a gang/family/commune, communication isn't limited to a weekly two-hour meeting. People are always running into each other, so bright ideas can be converted into action quickly and efficiently.

The rules are simple and natural. If your bright idea needs five people to carry it out, then you have to get four other people excited enough to do it with you.

The projects may be offensive or defensive, legal or clandestine, constructive or destructive, depending entirely upon the temperament of the people involved. Maybe you like children, and want to set up a cooperative nursery or school in your neighborhood. Maybe you like redwoods, and want to dynamite the bulldozers that are logging them off. Maybe you like guerrilla theater, and want to stage a little show at a Board of Supervisors meeting. Anything goes.

You are not pushing the name of your group, but word gets around among other gangs/families/communes in the city. You make contacts, get to know each other, share services, collaborate on certain projects. Gradually you develop a strong sense of solidarity. Taken together, you are now a significant creative and disruptive force, sometimes amusing, sometimes threatening, always active.

But what does this have to do with revolution, with the creation of a Free City? Next week.

San Francisco Express Times 6/26/68

GOING BEYOND DEMOCRACY

marvin garson

Last week I pointed up the day-to-day virtues of the revolutionary gang, family or commune as opposed to the revolutionary party, and promised to show how revolution itself could grow out of their activities.

Revolution is such an overused word that I'll have to start by clarifying it, clearing away all the ideological garbage littering the ground. Sorry, it's not MY fault.

The most common idea — and the most childish — is that revolution is the armed seizure of power by revolutionaries. A revolutionary, in this image, is someone who is young, bearded, wears a fatigue jacket and beret, clenches his fist, and carries a sidearm — in short Fidel Castro or a reasonable facsimile thereof. (Some schools of thought hold that the revolutionary should also smoke pot and say fuck on television; others consider this frivolous nonsense. It is a minor difference which can be settled after the revolution, most likely at gunpoint.)

If you imagine yourself one of the revolutionaries, it's a very noble prospect plus you get a lot of pussy. But the real test must be how it looks from down below. And from below, it looks a great deal like dictatorship.

Fatigue-jacket revolutionaries will reply: dictatorship in FORM, perhaps, but democracy in CONTENT — the opposite of what we have now. A revolutionary government would give land to the peasants — whoops, wrong country — would, uh, end racism-and-exploitation by ending the corporate system that perpetuates it.

That discussion won't get much further unless we switch now to the more sophisticated revolutionaries who all this time have been smirking along with me at the romantic Maoist-Fidelistas. They are a little older, more historically-minded: they've read Marx and Lenin and Trotsky, and also people you never heard of — from Rosa Luxemburg ("red Rosa," martyred in the German revolution of 1919) to Kuron and Modzelewski, now serving long prison terms in Poland for trying to organize a revolutionary socialist party in opposition to the Gomulka regime.

They believe it is not enough to expropriate industry from private owners; it must be kept from falling into the hands of a new, "socialist" ruling class of bureaucrats administering property which belongs to the people only in legal theory, not in fact. Very good. And how do you insure democratic control of industry? Why, by setting up workers' councils in each industry which operate with full respect for all the normal democratic procedures — especially the right to establish caucuses and factions, and the right to strike. The economy, in short, will be run the way a government is SUPPOSED to be run; it will be like a gigantic New Left convention — impeccably democratic and a stone drag, as I said last week.

Some people call democratic voting a "means of expression." It is that, but it is the poorest means of expression that I can think of. Isn't it more satisfying an expression to sing, or tinker with your car, or have a fistfight, or write on a wall, than to pull a lever? No, voting is a defensive weapon, not a creative instrument; it is something you use to make sure you don't get entirely fucked over by would-be dictators of any variety, but not something you build your life around.

The democratic process is in fact painful and boring for all but the few who are so skilled in the game itself that they find it exhilarating regardless of its content; everyone else looks for excuses to stay away. This means, of course, that power falls into the hands either of faceless bureaucrats or of "groovy" revolutionaries who govern by decree "in the true interests of the people." Once again: how can you run a society democratically if people don't WANT to "participate in making the decisions that affect their lives"?

The only way out is a revolution which is consciously determined to go BEYOND democracy. "Beyond democracy" — that will stick in many throats. Let me over-explain it, just to make sure.

When I say democracy, I mean majority rule. When I speak of going beyond majority rule I don't mean minority rule; I mean no rule at all.

A storm of protest: Anarchy! Madness! Our society is too complex to run without laws, discipline, control. True — but don't be smug about it; start to change it. Start right now, and let your revolution be a dramatic speeding-up of the process.

Our technology is such that it can only be administered by an elite. That's true too — after all, it was an elite that set down the design criteria for the engineers to follow. Did you think they ordered their own functions to be designed away? Do you think they told the engineers to be sure to remember that free men would be working in those factories and offices?

Perhaps it's impossible to run a steel mill or an electric power plant in a free and creative way. In that case, run it automatically. If computers can fly a supersonic jet plane at a constant altitude of 100 feet over rough terrain while making it take evasive action and launch bombs on target and screw up enemy radar (the plane flew two miles in the time it took you to read that half-sentence), then certainly computers can run a steel mill.

Will there be any work left for people to do? Certainly. We'll have the time to build our own houses, for instance, with our own hands, with master workmen around to supervise and instruct. How's that for a start? Better than rent subsidies?

Sorry I didn't get around to explaining how the revolutionary gangs/families/communes fit into the revolution, but first things first. Next week.

San Francisco
Express Times 7/13/68

The first objection is always: what about the masses? Revolution is supposed to be nothing less than "the entry of the masses into history," and how can that happen if mass organizations are replaced by little groups of friends running around planting bombs?

The point, though, is not to help the masses enter history but to help the masses exit from it. A mass is like a giant blob of dough; it gets kneaded by one elite or another, but cannot do anything for itself. Revolution, in 1968, does not mean grabbing hold of the mass and throwing it onto the left-hand pan of the scales; revolution means breaking up that sticky, shapeless mass once and for all so that no person, clique, party or ruling class will ever again be able to pound those 200 million Americans into shape. We will be ready for revolution only when so many people have carved out spaces to breathe in and work in that society looks more like a honeycomb than a blob of dough.

It comes in two stages. First, large numbers of people have to drop out psychologically—that is, learn how to think for themselves and be willing to accept the status of mental outlaw. Millions of people, especially the young, have done that over the last ten years.

The second stage—barely begun as yet—comes when they begin to actually implement their ideas in their working lives.

For example: it is important that so many people perceive how empty and stupid elementary education is. But it is not enough if people vote for (or abstractly "support" in any other way) a solution to the problem, however clever that solution may be. Teachers themselves have to be willing to put their ideas into practice and ignore the Board of Education; parents have to be willing to organize their own schools if necessary; otherwise it's still all talk.

Every industry has its own inchoate underground of people who take pride in doing good work, who aren't in it just for the money, who get angry when their employers make them sacrifice quality for the sake of profit. Let that underground get together and suddenly a real alternative to corporate capitalism will exist. Some will call it anarchism, or communism, or a petty bourgeois deviation, but for once the name won't matter.

In these times revolutionary politics consists fundamentally of precipitating active, functional groups out of the homogeneous mass, finally on such a scale that virtually the whole population comes alive. It can only be done by example, never by preaching. That means the revolutionaries have to be themselves organized in functional WORKING groups—gangs, families, communes, affinity groups, whatever you wish to call them.

However technical the work such revolutionary groups perform, they remain basically political whether engaged in running a free bus line or blowing up draft boards, they calculate every project primarily for its effect upon the public consciousness. It starts out with revolutionary intellectuals. It ends up with revolutionary carpenters, teachers, doctors, mechanics, machinists, programmers—what once were "the masses."

marvin garson

San Francisco
Express Times 7/17/68

69

ONLY THIS
SOLID THING
THEY WERE
BUILDING

the family

They call themselves "The Family." Before their work was destroyed, it hadn't occurred to them to *have* a name—even for the little colony of sod huts which had mushroomed in a waste area of New York City's Bronx Park during the school strike. No swaggering. No St. Mark's Place Manifestos. Only this solid thing they were building.

Most of the 20-40 people are high school students, two or three are attending community colleges and a few work on nine-to-five jobs. They range from 16 to 19 years old except for a kid-brother-mascot who is 10. All are from the neighborhood.

Hassled by the police during the summer for standing on the street a group of them went to the local precinct to complain. The next day eight of them were busted for "loitering," coincidentally including the complainers.

The kids got the message. A number of them moved over to Bronx Park (about two blocks west of where they'd been meeting). Exploring the park, they found a 70-year-old "hermit"—as they called him—who welcomed them to the garbage-strewn area (not his garbage) which he was using as a retreat. When their numbers increased, he moved a slight distance away, but not out of sight or sound, so he could later tell me: " . . . a nice bunch o' kids they were. They didn't bother nothin'."

The huts were unpremeditated. One day it rained and they started to build a shelter of sticks and sod. The shelter grew and grew. Then they cleaned up the little compound—less than an acre—built a second hut opposite the first, started the framework of a third, and erected something like a flagpole in the center.

Some of them, refugees from the dreary middle-class tenements surrounding the park, were sleeping in the huts. Others would come by to help build, to dream, to talk . . . to learn. For it was an education these kids were creating: nothing less than the experience of building a young peoples' commune on public land in the City of New York!

Which the parks department could not allow. It simply freaked out their sense of the privacy of public property. "Why, if we let them do this," said a department spokesman, "it could lead to a shack city!"

After begging the parks department brass (including the commissioner himself) to come see for themselves (they were too busy), the kids invoked the aid of EVO (East Village Other), RAT, and the Resistance. An unlikely Trinity.

RAT showed up just as the parks crew arrived to do their thing. If ever there were a demonstration of the power of the press, this was it. Camera-shy, the parks crew held off, although the foreman informed the kids that "orders" were "orders;" that even though he "personally" liked what they were doing, he'd "have to" tear it down if given the word from above. Nevertheless he said he would try to arrange a "deal" whereby the huts would be left standing until the end of the school strike. The kids were jubilant. They went ahead with plans for winterizing and heating the huts. In a world of despair, it was difficult to avoid being infected by the optimism of this little band.

The world of despair caught up with them a few days later. A police sergeant cruising by spotted their fire, carefully contained in an iron brazier with a grill. "Open fires" are verboten in the park, as are "unauthorized" structures. So the sergeant and his partner (who playfully threatened to shoot the 10-year-old) ran the "Hippies" (the sergeant's word) out of the park, with a warning that he'd arrest them on sight if they ever came back. Then the two policemen flattened one hut and did such damage as they could to the other (the sergeant in a later interview referred admiringly to the huts as "bunkers"). The job was finished a couple of evenings later when a blaze of undetermined origin burned the remaining hut to the ground. And more recently, the "hermit's" hut was set afire by two leather-clad motorcycle patrolmen who were no doubt enforcing the regulation against "open fires."

Where is the Family now? Back on the street. One of them was busted at Christopher Columbus High School on Dec. 3 for protesting the New York Board of Education's cynical plan to finance the teachers' truancy at the expense of student vacations. The Family's mood varies from individual to individual, from time to time. Ever since their work was destroyed, all police are "pigs" to them and motherfuckerism has become a life-mode for a few. But there are in the Family some who see this as "playing the man's game;" some who are searching for more productive, less self-defeating answers than throwing eggs or bricks.

It isn't easy. A black kid (not of the Family) was busted for disorderly conduct Tuesday just as he was trying to calm the crowd at Columbus High School.

"The city sucks," said one of the group recently. On this, there seems to be general agreement. The Family has been exploring possibilities in other cities, on country communes, and has even inquired discreetly about possibilities for emigration.

"The Streets Belong to the People!" goes a current slogan. Yes. Also the din of the elevated trains roaring overhead on White Plains Road. And the filth and the garbage of the commercial establishments. The Streets belong also to the Mafia-driven junkie/pushers transacting business within full view of cops who—at best—realize the futility of trying to enforce the drug laws.

The streets belong to the people. But who wants them?　—Sid Hammer

This structure was against regulations . . .

win 1/1/69

98

The DRV

The DRV—democratic republican/revolution of or in Vermont—is a community of about 13 people on a 100-acre farm in the green hills of Vermont. The community began in the summer of 1968 and is now experiencing its first Vermont winter. Consequently, anything I can say about the way the community operates and what it stands for must be judged as tentative. We are just learning what it means to be a community. And we are first discovering how to live close to the land and in harmony with the natural world that surrounds us.

More and more people are becoming interested in starting intentional communities. Friends whom I identify solely with crowded and cockroach-infested Lower East Side railroad flats are busy circling choice listings in the Strout real estate catalog, which has suddenly become an underground best seller. And if they are in any way like ourselves, desperate city freaks who have never seen a star and confuse the Milky Way with the foggy electronic haze over Times Square, they have little or no experience in this kind of thing and hardly know where or how to begin.

Together we have been victimized by an educational system that has left us unfit to live with the world on its most simple terms. We have been carefully moulded to fit a machine that clatters about without serving any useful social purpose except to keep us busy, out of mischief, and dependent on it—rather than ourselves—for sustenance. We have been taught almost nothing about practical matters: how and when to plough a field, lay a floor, care for chickens, split logs. Who among us knows the measure of a cord of wood?

Some of these problems can be solved easily; others are questions that we, with our limited experience, are still groping for answers. But before going any further, let me first indulge myself and put this article into its proper context by describing the land that is the DRV, for this more than anything else has become our reality, the natural order that governs our daily lives.

The DRV is on a wooded hillside with northern exposure at the head of a small hollow ten miles from the nearest store. Its trees are sugar maple, beech, oak, white pine, hemlock, different kinds of cherry, white, silver and black birch, and a number of other species we have not yet learned to identify. Part of the slope has been cleared into a meadow. At the top-most edge of the meadow is a peach orchard with a score of productive trees. Apples, pears, grape vines and wild berries are scattered about the land. The hillside is full of natural springs from which we pipe our water. And there is a flat, two-acre shelf on which we will plant vegetables to feed ourselves, and if there is a surplus, our friends in the cities.

The DRV was first conceived as an idea in early April, 1968. We had a friend who had a summer home in Vermont and through him we knew of a farm that was up for sale. Friends were told of the idea of starting a community.

"Groovy!" they said, or "Oh, wow!"

But little else was discussed because the idea seemed too fragile to examine objectively. It seemed like just another of the utopian schemes we were always dreaming up and quickly forgetting. In the back of our minds each of us could conjure up one hundred good reasons why the idea was absurd and doomed to failure, but they all went unspoken. We had no money, no source of income, were completely ignorant of country ways, and, moreover, because of various public acts of defiance against the draft, most of the men involved were more likely to spend time on the Allenwood federal prison farm in Pennsylvania than on some far-out hippy-dippy freak farm in Vermont.

At the same time we were all motivated by an awareness that cities had become a destructive environment—overcrowded, polluted, dehumanizing, and violent. We wanted to see whether there was not a more healthy and meaningful way to live, free of the system, but relevant to the means of working for radical change. So every time we were faced with the decision to abandon the idea or commit ourselves deeper, we took another plunge.

In May, we had our first look at the farm, and in June made a second visit to meet the widow who owned it. She quoted us her price, we gulped hard, smiled and agreed to buy. Then we returned to the city to see whether we had enough resources to meet the down payment and the ten-year mortgage of over $200 a month. So far we had been lucky. We didn't have to go through a real estate agent who might have discriminated against long hair. And the community in which the farm was located had only a few summer residents, all of whom were friendly with the lady selling the farm and enthusiastic about our coming. Their words in our behalf were what persuaded the woman to sell to us.

Now that we had the farm, our lack of serious planning, which had enabled us to make the land purchase so readily, began to have repercussions. About the only thing that we had talked about was that we would live on the farm as a "family," in the New Age meaning of the word, with friends rather than relations. But we had only the vaguest notion of what this meant and, in the meanwhile, had added more people, some of whom hadn't been in on these discussions and were not part of the original circle of friends who had conceived the idea. To further confuse things, we didn't anticipate the speed with which we would get the farm and everyone, except two of the new people, had commitments for the summer and could not begin to live at the DRV until August.

We compounded these problems by loose talk to everyone we knew that reflected both our enthusiasm for what we were doing and our incredible naivete. Because we were Movement people living in an urban setting, we felt it necessary to describe our plans in political terms. The DRV would be a meeting place and rest area for weary activists. Or, the first wedge in the movement to liberate Vermont and bring about its secession. Or, a commune for free people to roam in the woods and do their thing. And because it was summer and we were near enough to Boston and New York, we fast became victims of our own hyperbole.

The DRV was rapidly inundated by visitors. Friends, friends of friends, friends thrice removed, and wandering freaks who had heard of a nearby "hippy farm" and wanted to check out the scene, all descended upon us for a weekend, the summer, or forever. The two people living on the farm who were part of the permanent community dug what was happening and throve on the unstructured chaos. The rest of us, from our distance, were becoming increasingly uptight. The farm was turning into a rural crash pad. Our home, we feared, was becoming a rural slum. More and more we were coming to feel like absentee landlords whose land was being misused.

The issue had to be confronted. Our differences seemed irreconcilable: an open commune or a closely knit family. Probably there are less absolute positions a community should choose, but at the time it seemed like an either/or proposition, and the two proponents of an open commune agreed to leave. Visitors were asked to go as well, though a few stayed on as permanent members of the family. By the end of the summer the DRV had about 13 permanent people, the number fluctuating because two commuted to schools in Boston and others made infrequent forays into the city. The first summer had been a harrowing, emotional experience. Our dream had seemingly turned bitter. And the problem of visitors continued to plague us.

Throughout the country there exists an underground network of like people who will put strangers up for a night, feed them and turn them on. All of us on the farm had made use of this kind of hospitality in our travels, so were disturbed to feel the need to put people out. But communities are sufficiently new to attract the curious and the interested, a problem compounded by proximity to the city. In our first four months we were visited by Sunday "hippy watchers," high school runaways, newspaper and magazine reporters from both the underground and establishment press, a local farmer who was frightened because his eldest son had expressed a desire to live like us, peace activists passing through, local freaks, a state policeman, hitchhikers wanting a place to spend the night, dropouts wanting a place to live, groups of people planning to start their own communes and schools, and a well-scrubbed young couple who wanted to interest us in manufacturing Ho Chi Minh sandals, which they would market for us, as a cottage industry.

In addition, everyone on the farm had a dozen or more close friends who they invited up. Weekend guests alone often turned the farmhouse into a rural version of a crowded subway car, making decent conversation and worthwhile visits impossible. As a result, we try to discourage uninvited visitors and often treat strangers with less hospitality than we should. But if a community is to work, it must be nurtured carefully and left alone to grow. As we become more comfortable in our new way of life, we should become more open to visitors.

We have had more success in handling the townspeople whose initial reaction to the hordes of long hairs descending on their village was hostile. There were threats of violence and some minor harassment. Even our most immediate neighbors with whom we were friendly advised us to cut our hair, keep the number living at the farm at any one time to a minimum, all of the same sex, and, in general, keep things cool until the town simmered down.

We treated the situation our own way by opening communication with as many local people as possible. We talked to the town selectmen, shopped in local stores, and said "Hello," and "Good morning," as if we were at a Be-In greeting fellow freaks. We discovered that the natives viewed hippies as 1950-type juvenile delinquents and were afraid we had come to plunder their farms. Most important, we worked on our farm and improved the land. Vermonters have a great attachment to their natural environment, and when they saw us treating it with a healthy respect, their fear and hostility began to vanish. We still have our detractors as well as a few supporters. But the "hippy farm" is no longer the chief conversation piece in town. Of course, for their part, the locals are confident we will not last through the winter.

A community in New England faces problems peculiar to the North Country. Certain things have got to be done merely to survive in winter. Houses have to be insulated, water pipes buried, fuel collected. Both our cooking stove and our furnace are heated by wood so a tremendous amount, 30 to 40 cords, has to be cut, split, sorted and stacked before the first snow. Moreover, and this is true of all communities, Old Age facilities are not built to house New Age families. Our farmhouse is too small, and everyone wants to have the privacy of his own place, so we are busy converting small outbuildings into homes. Plumbing facilities, installed for average families, are quickly overtaxed. Our spring has run dry, the water pump has broken, and the outhouse is fast filling up. All these facilities have to be improved. Wherever we can, we use materials found on the farm, like wooden planks from abandoned sheds. Out of the ruins of the Old Age comes materials for the New.

As much as possible, we have abolished the concept of work. Fortunately, the people in our family have some useful skills or, at a minimum, enthusiasm. Laurie is an excellent carpenter and architect and is free to build what he wants. Michael has driven tractors in the West, knows the mechanics of farming, and is anxious to learn the art. Connie sews and makes space age clothing. I'm enchanted by the forest, read some books about trees, bought an axe, and went to work. Others cook, read, write, paint, make music, take walks or just sit around and daydream, all of which are honorable and useful pursuits. We have no work committees, no formal structures and no family meetings. Each of us is sensi-

tive to our individual commitments to the DRV and knows what has to be done. And though we tend to keep beatnik hours and handle our chores, as Laurie has observed, with "more enthusiasm than empiricism," things get done.

We treat money in much the same way, trying to apply the concept that money is a commodity with certain desirable uses but is of far less value than building nice things, making love, creating a poem, baking bread, or watching the sunset. Four people pooled their savings to meet the down payment, and there are no formal arrangements to reimburse them. The deed to the land is in two names, more out of convenience than policy. One of our people teaches in the local school, but he took the job before he joined the community and it is what he wants to do. He is the only one with a regular income and to protect him and us from over-dependence on that income, he contributes a fixed sum each month. Everyone else contributes money as it is available and as it is needed. We keep no records or list of contributions. There is a farm checking account but also individual savings. We put in what is needed and by some mysterious and unknown magic manage to meet our obligations. So far money has come in from writing, lecturing, dressmaking, and like manna. Often our total assets are the coins embedded beneath the cushions of the sofa. But we know that if we are short of money we can always go to the city and work for a week or two.

We've chosen to call our community a family, but whatever name one uses to describe the arrangements by which people live together, everything depends on how sensitive they are to one another, and how open and honest they learn to be. Without this basic trust a community cannot function and isn't even a community.

Before we moved to Vermont we all had ideas about publishing a newspaper and continuing our involvement in the Movement, as we knew it. But we had been thinking in city terms and didn't anticipate what we were getting into. In four months our heads have been turned completely around. We may eventually put out a newspaper or some other form of public communication, but right now we are learning about things that seem meaningful and about which we may someday write.

The land holds a special magic that we had all forgotten. The American Indians knew about it, and so do a few very old and wise Vermont farmers. The pioneers experienced the magic but were too caught up in Western values to properly appreciate it. Now it is up to the people of the New Age to rediscover the land and learn what it has to offer and to teach. We do not consider ourselves Rousseauean dreamers or Jeffersonian agrarianists harking back to the simple virtues of the past. We are very much children of the 21st century, with our chain saw and tractor—and stereo system blasting forth the Beatles, Bach, and Ornette Coleman appreciative of our times.

But our technology does run amok. It functions as an end unto itself, with nothing whatever to do with the rhythms, harmonies and cycles of life. The sun rises, the sun sets. But the machines clatter on. The Old Age is governed by artificial values that are technologically orientated, profit serving, and power seeking. The cities teach violence and destruction; the country teaches time and space and life and creation.

The DRV gives us time to learn about the land and about ourselves. We have to reevaluate our technology, sift out what is destructive and useless, and harness what is left to the delicate working order of our natural environment. To create a New Age we must learn to live at peace with ourselves and to be at home with our land.   **Marty Jezer**

: to live

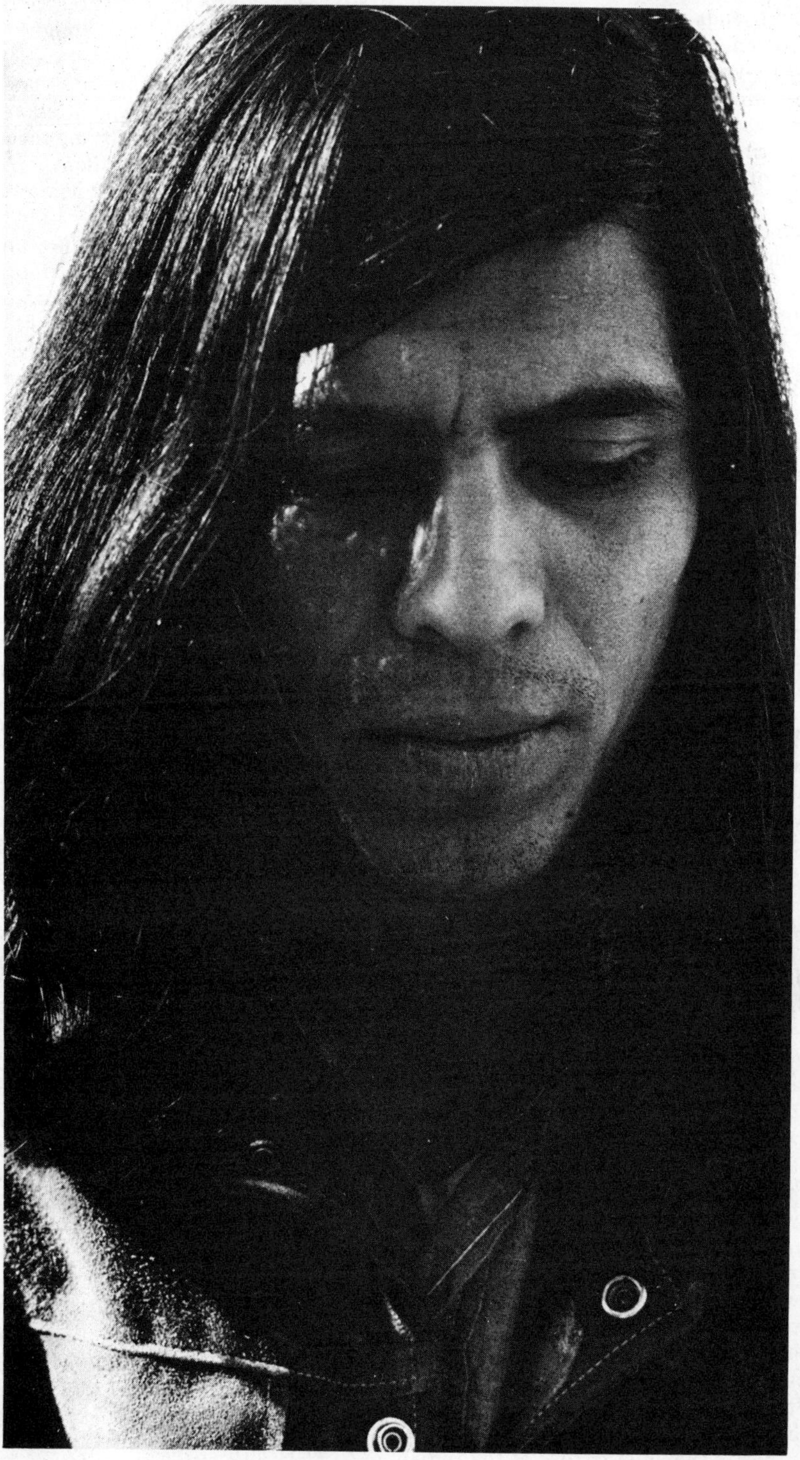

I've been living in Santa Fe for slightly more than a month now, Kip Shaw for two. What little I know about the Southwest Indian I've mainly learned from Peter Chestnut; of the Chicanos, from Tess Martinez of El Grito. So I'm very glad these people were able to contribute directly to this issue, and save you from the hazards involved in my relaying their knowledge entirely at second hand.

The state of New Mexico hasn't yet, by official census, passed the million mark. That's to say that less than one-twelfth of the population of metropolitan New York City occupies an area two and a half times the size of New York State. Of course, we aren't distributed evenly across these 121,666 square miles; much of the land is uninhabitable by present human standards, and much of what is most beautiful or useful is held by giant corporations, absentee landlords, or the federal government in the form of military bases, nuclear testing grounds, or national parks.*

Further, New Mexico is, in climate, soil, and vegetation, an incredibly diversified land, divided (precariously and unfairly) amongst many kinds of people with obviously exclusive intentions. These are:

the fat-cat Texans of the Southeast with their big fast cars and almighty wallets; they dominate the state government, primarily to the benefit of fat-cat Texans;

the suburban technicians from the east Coast or Southern California who have recreated Los Alamos and Albuquerque in that sterile plastic image, and who find Santa Fe a charming place because "you never have to wait at the tee";

the *Tio Tacos, vendidos* and *lambes*— Mexican-Americans who have sold out *La Raza* their people and their culture, and who become the cops and larger front men for the gringos;

the Chicanos of the North, small ranchers and smaller businessmen, rightfully proud of their heritage, rightfully resentful of the land-grabbing gringo (crew-cut or long-haired), forgetful of the fact that their forefathers did to the Indians precisely what the gringos do to them;

those same taciturn Indians, but not quite so taciturn of late, not quite so resigned to scraping a skinny living off the jolly, gaping tourists;

and then finally the longhairs, descending in truly frightening numbers upon an already embattled land, obscuring the lines of battle, disturbing every one of the other groups, the hardest of all for me to judge—and not simply because I happen, whether I like it or not, to be one of them.

It's impossible to say how many longhairs, hippies, whateveryacallems, there are presently in New Mexico, or even in one locality like Santa Fe. We are a visually conspicuous lot, and perhaps any calculation based on how many freaks you can spot on a drive through town is bound to exaggerate. We're a highly mobile lot as well; Aspen Meadows for the Hog Farm's summer solstice, Taos since, Oregon next week, then back again via Berkeley and Big Sur in a month or two is typical behavior. But there's no denying there's a great many more of us here, more or less to stay, than there were a year ago. We've come because we're tired of getting busted by big-city cops; because we're sick of endless, pointless hassles within an increasingly joyless movement; because we have our kids to raise, and we know we can't do it right in the Haight or the Lower East Side. Whatever our reasons, though, they're personal; and the best advice we'll ever receive was in Bettita Martinez' article (published recently in *El Grito, The Village Voice,* and the *San Francisco Good Times*), which concluded with these words: "If you think, you won't come. Not now. And when you do come, come as a revolutionary."

Anyhow, we're here, in the towns to open macrobiotic restaurants, organic food stores, weaving and pottery shops, Hare Krishna centers, film companies, yoga or karate classes. In Santa Fe, we're organized to the point that there is an amorphous something called the Corporation, which has started a car repair shop, done some demolition work for urban renewal, and is intimately though informally connected with the construction company which is employing Ben Reyes, Don Auclair, myself, and about a dozen other longhairs to build a $50,000, two-story adobe house.

In the countryside, either communally or on an individual basis, we've gone into farming and ranching on a scale that has already had a noticeable effect on the price of arable acreage. (One Taos realtor remarked that she alone has sold something like half a million dollars' worth of land to hippies.) In an area where good land and steady work (not to mention basics like water, for drinking or irrigation) were scarce to begin with, despite the sound argument that much of what we do is self-created industry, we are unavoidably competing with the under-employed, land-hungry Chicano. And those of us who lack the initiative or ability to support ourselves are vying with him for the already insufficient public services of state and country governments which have, in response to relentless pressure from the Texans and the corporations, kept their tax structures at almost pre-new deal levels.

This is not to say that we are the only, or even the major, culprits. The Los Alamos scientist with his 40,000 a year salary, the retired Eastern insurance salesman, and the ubiquitous vacationing

sportsman with his sardine can mounted on a new Chevy pickup have probably done more harm to the vertigous economy and certainly more to the palsied ecology than we have, so far. Nor does it mean that life is very easy, even for the most enterprising of freaks. The best of us are judged by the actions of the worst, and all it takes is one minibusful of beaded idiots pissing in a village's water supply for the "We don't sell to hippies" sentiment to become unanimous.

Civil-liberties consciousness, among potential friends and foes alike, is primitive here. Even "liberal" judges will give you the are-you-now-or-have-you-ever-been-a-hippie line before setting bond. Don Auclair got ten days' contempt-of-court for announcing that he was going to call the ACLU on a friend's behalf. And while the new grass laws favor the user rather than the syndicate (simple possession's merely a misdemeanor, selling's a mandatory ten years, so everyone is encouraged to grow his own), the climate is certainly ripe for local programs. There are certain regions, for instance around Truchas, that any sensible longhair avoids.

But there is little purpose to a discussion of the present tensions that exist between Longhairs and Chicanos, or either group and the Indians, or even the powerful coalition all three could and certainly should make against the malefactors of great wealth here, so long as it appears that the intrinsic life-views of each are inimical to those of the others. I've had long talks with several informed people about this question, and no one has yet been able to fully resolve them for me.

"What if you win everything you're fighting for," I asked at *El Grito,* "and you get all the land cited in your grants? What about the Indians? Don't their claims antedate yours?"

Tessa Martinez admitted that this was a difficult point; she felt, however, that Chicanos and Indians did not want or need the same land; she pointed out that provisions had been made implicit in their grants for the various Pueblos. This is true, but as Peter Chestnut later remarked, it ignores the basic contradiction between the two attitudes towards the land:

The Chicano, at least presently, is a farmer or a rancher who parcels up the land and puts fences around it forever;

The Pueblo Indian sees the land as an entity — his tribe built a village here or there, but when the earth grew weary of his crops, or the firewood became scarce, or the Apache raids were too frequent, or he dreamed of a witch, he simply picked up his clothing and tools and went somewhere else to build again. The land was free, eternally.

The Longhair, at his very best, attempts to synthesize the chief virtues of the Indian and the Chicano ways of life. That isn't going to be easy. The commune near Taos that I briefly described in my introduction to the Alternatives issue (WIN, vol. V, no. 1) has gone farther in this direction than

anything else I've yet seen. When we were there last July, their only permanent building and nearly all personal possessions had just been wiped out by a disastrous accidental fire; all they had left were teepees and a toolshed. It was a grim and uninviting, if inspiring, place.

We went back there again this summer solstice, via Tierra Amarilla and thence by dirt roads across the enormous and absolutely glorious country of the Kit Carson National Forest (country included in the Alianza land grants), and through the indescribable Rio Grande Gorge. I don't mean to imply that they've performed prodigious miracles, and I don't know how to fully explain what they are and have without identifying this family of people who have excellent reasons for preserving whatever remains of their anonymity. . .

The teepees remain in use, and will at least for this summer; but one side of a plaza is built, unplastered adobe, simple and strong, and the foundations are there for a second, and I could see the rest of it clearly as they described it, complete with fruit trees and a fountain in the center. Forty acres of good crops were coming up, including wheat, and I could believe them again when they said they expect to be fully independent by next year, with enough food left over to barter for whatever else they need. Their relations with the neighboring Chicanos are good, because their stubborn progress are inescapable; but their emotional ties are with the Indians, as demonstrated through their participation in the Peyote Meetings of the Native American Church. Local authorities respect them and leave them alone; newer communes look up to them as pioneers, and come seeking help, tools, advice.

As I looked and admired, I was reminded of the people of the Cooperative in Tierra Amarilla as I had seen them that morning, camped in tents, trucking their drinking water along an axlebreaking trail, faced with the task of clearing 200 acres of sage-brush and scrub pine. That was pretty much where these gringos had been a year before—ignorant city hippies, from the Haight or the Lower East Side.

No, it isn't easy, and it's certainly going to get harder before it ever gets better. But the longhair *can* live side by side with the Chicano, and maybe, if the land is good to us and we're good to the land, both can go on learning from those who came to remarkably intelligent terms with it a thousand years ago.

PAUL JOHNSON

*"Total land area of the state is 77,767,040 acres, which is owned or held in trust by the federal government, the state, or private owners, as follows:

"Federal government, 33,979,363 acres;
"State trust lands, 9,107,604 acres;
"Privately owned lands, 34,680,073 acres."
—editorial in *The Santa Fe New Mexican,* 7/2/69.

 **win** Aug 1969

Has business become a dirty word?

Ask the Class of '66.

They don't seem to be coming around for jobs the way they used to. Not to business. Not to industry. Instead, almost 9 out of 10 of today's college graduates—88% in a recent survey—say they prefer careers in government, or the professions, or in academic life. Anywhere but business. Why?

Why do so many of the new generation—our potential leaders and decision makers—act as if business has become a dirty word? And how did such a serious situation come about? The answers keep cropping up in your business journals. In your newspaper. In reports from your campus recruiters.

"Business is for the birds," say today's graduates.

Too many of our college youth think business is "dull," "soulless," "conformist," "non-creative," "money-grubbing." "For the birds," they say.

Above all, they believe business has failed to commit itself to the human issues of our time. Poverty, ignorance, famine, disease. Peace. Race relations. To many of this new generation, business seems to be living in a paper world of profits. Business, for them, is removed from the mainstream of social and moral responsibility.

But are they right?

The hard fact is, American business has contributed some $2.5 billion of corporate profits toward the public good in the past five years alone. Certainly there's a lot more to be done. And every day finds more and more companies contributing their share. This year's public service spending will be around $700 million. Just about half of this goes to our schools, colleges and universities as scholarships and grants, for salaries, new buildings, operating expenses.

Too bad the graduating class doesn't know about it. Too bad they don't know the real story about what business is doing in so many areas of human need.

Let's look at the record.

How many years have been added to our lifespan by grants to medical research? How much suffering have we been spared? Who can put a dollar value on the help business rushes to victims of fire and flood, earthquake and drought? To war orphans and refugees. To the homeless and hopeless the world over.

Famine? Poverty? Business is fighting them with gifts of seed, fertilizer, machinery. With training, planning. With money.

And look what business is doing for culture, for human values. Opera, ballet and symphony orchestras simply couldn't exist on today's scale without subsidies from business. Neither could museums or libraries. Or repertory theatre. Or educational TV. Business is helping to enrich minds, to broaden understanding. To improve relations among races, nations, ideologies…to improve people's chances of living in peace and dignity.

Indeed, business is easing the tax burden of every American by taking on social responsibilities that would otherwise have to be assumed by government.

The business of business is more than business.

American business is committing itself to a broad program of social responsibility. It's moving far beyond traditional concepts of philanthropy, beyond concepts of enlightened self-interest, toward a new definition of corporate citizenship.

Today there are business leaders who say the social goals and responsibilities of business are as important as its economic goals and responsibilities. "What's good for the nation, and for the world," they say, "is good for business." And they're proving they mean it.

Yet far too many of our college graduates pass business by.

Why didn't the Class of '66 get the message?

Not because American business has failed to face up to basic social issues. Or to act on them. Rather, it's because we have failed to communicate to the young in language that has meaning for them. To tell them…on and off the campus…that a sense of responsibility and dedication to larger goals is the spirit of this new world of business. To let them know we see the prospects for as brave a world for man as they do.

American business needs to communicate to this new generation just how much we are doing that is exciting and worthwhile. It must communicate the new thinking that vitalizes the business world. It must show them that business can be an answer to their search for an opportunity to make significant social contributions through their work. For surely there's room here, and challenge, for all of their energy and enthusiasm and idealism.

Isn't it time to say the things that need to be said about business and industry and the way things really are?

Now?

Before we lose another generation?

DEUTSCH & SHEA, INC.
Advertising
230 WEST 41ST STREET, NEW YORK, N. Y. 10036

MEMBER AMERICAN ASSOCIATION OF ADVERTISING AGENCIES

The New York Times TUESDAY, JUNE 28, 1966.

Carey Chauffeur-driven Cars By Appointment to the New Aristocracy

The New Aristocracy

There is a new aristocracy in America. Its peers are plainly titled, like the barons, viscounts, earls, marquesses and dukes of old.

If you are a vice president, you are an earl. You are halfway to the top of the greasy pole. And if you are the President, you are there. You are a duke.

Your castle is the corporation. Your code is hard work. Your plague is ulcers.

You are the most powerful aristocracy in history. You decide what two hundred million people will eat, ride in, wear, laugh at, live for.

But you have never learned how to live. You treat yourselves like a corps of messenger boys. You wake yourselves, shave yourselves, shine your own shoes, lug your own luggage, then rent strange cars in strange cities and become your own chauffeurs. You indulge only one of life's joys: a vodka martini on the rocks, and that bolted down on the run.

We hereby suggest that you shed your hair shirts.

Who are we? The Carey Corporation.

We operate chauffeur-driven cars in 12 cities.

We learned our business from an older and saner aristocracy. Debutants and diamond-mine heirs always called Carey. And Carey always came. In long, luxurious limousines.

And although our rates are now much lower than most businessmen guess, a Carey chauffeured car is still not cheap, in the airport bus sense of cheap.

We save your sanity, not your money.

In Ulcer Alley (the stomach-knotting ten miles at either end of a flight) we give you a chance to gird your loins or lick your wounds.

How much it costs depends on the size of the car. Our fleet of long luxurious limousines has been infiltrated by shorter practical Buicks. And in a shorter practical Buick, a Carey chauffeur can whisk you to the airport (or back) for a few dollars more than cab fare.

Your secretary calls us. She says, "Be here at 5." At 5, our chauffeur is waiting at your door. He knows your name. He

babies your luggage. He values your privacy. And if it rains it pours on his umbrella, not on you.

Carey cars now have telephones. So you're never in No Man's Land. Did you get away late? Your chauffeur can call and book you on a later flight.

Call Carey before your next trip. Our number's in the phone book.

One local call can get you a chauffeur-driven car almost anywhere in the world.

And once we know you, we can bill the castle direct.

You needn't be squeamish about that entry (chauffeured car to airport) in your travel voucher. You, my lord, are an earl. An earl has many burdens. The castle assigns a certain value to an earl's peace of mind.

Ad from an airline house organ.

WE ARE ALL POLITICAL PRISONERS

"Free All Political Prisoners" really says that we all in America are under fascist pig confinement. . maximum and minimum confinement. . Everyone who loves is a prisoner under fascism. **BOBBY SEALE** from Niantic Prison

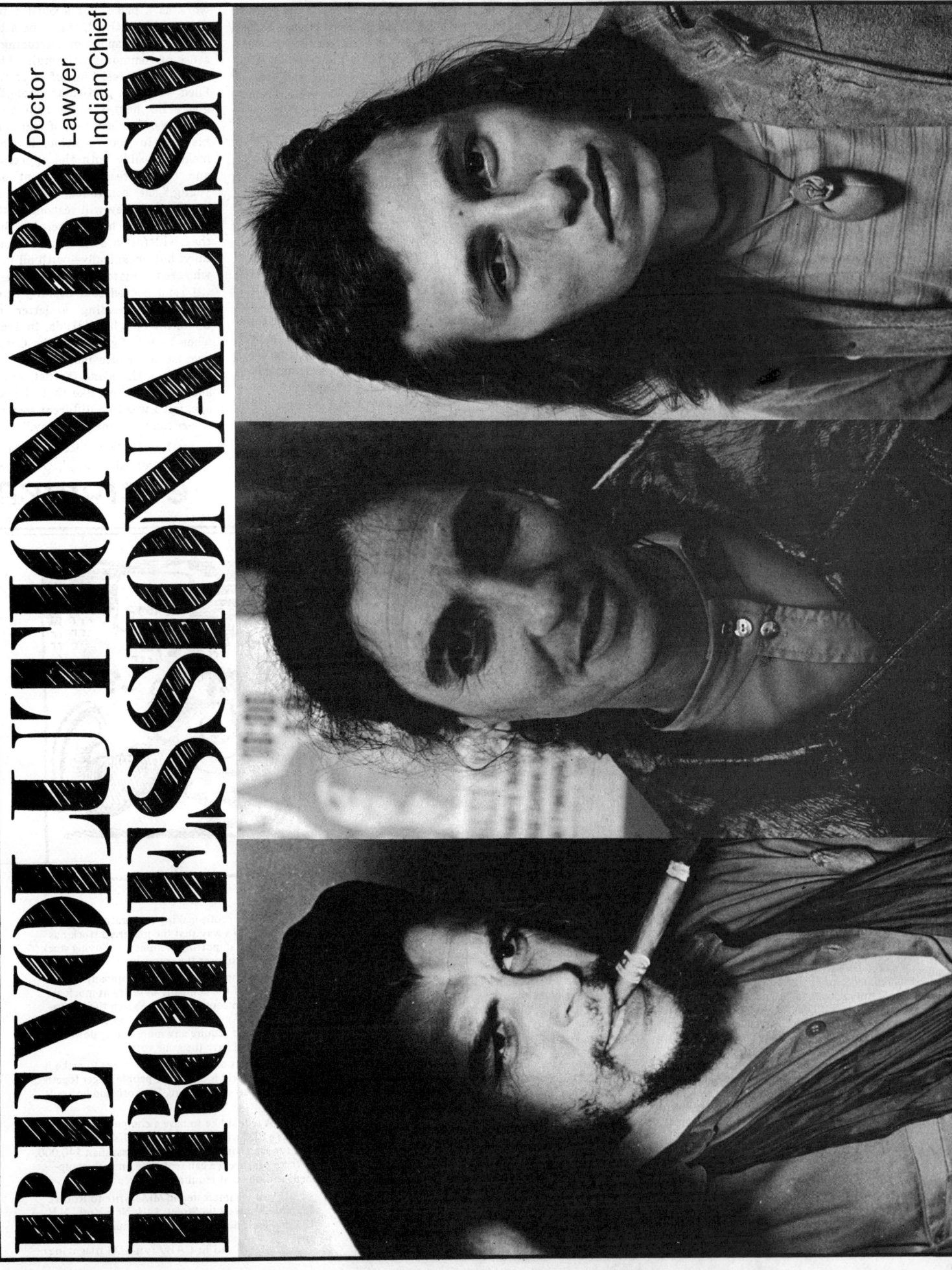

REVOLUTIONARY PROFESSIONALISM

Doctor
Lawyer
Indian Chief

On Revolutionary Professionalism

by Nat Hentoff

MOST OF THE NIGHT had been taken by those who would be professional revolutionaries—in the United States, in Puerto Rico, in South America. Che Guevara had no blueprints for them, possibly because he was certain the tacky town house containing the Cuban Mission to the United Nations was bugged. He listened more than he spoke, nodding amiably if cryptically, smoking his Cuban cigars (with which some of us socialists filled our pockets), and occasionally flexing his dry wit. There was a pause, and I asked him how the spirit of a revolution could be sustained. Always before, sooner or later, the power promised the people had been fiercely hoarded by the new liberators, and new dead bureaucracies had come to interpose themselves between the revolution and the people until the revolution had shrunken into an exhibit in a museum. Left was the state giving orders, and the people submissive. Until silent cadres again began to form to destroy the state and announce the new revolution.

Guevara looked at me. He was smiling, somewhat sardonically. We had argued earlier about civil liberties and a free press, he maintaining that the Cuban Revolution still had too many enemies to guarantee either. If I were baiting him, he was prepared to do battle again, but I really did want to know his answer to the death of revolutions. Either my lack of combativeness came through or it was the question itself that removed the smile and started him on a serious, even solemn, monologue.

Its theme—and variations of it appear throughout his collected articles and speeches—was that if a new man were not created (that is, new values for man), the Cuban Revolution too would eventually stiffen and begin to crack. So far, he said, the leaders are still a little crazy, and that's healthy. By crazy, he went on, he meant their willingness to take chances, to avoid the institutionalization of dogma, to respond to what the people experience, to keep seeking out the views of the people, to admit mistakes. But that wasn't enough.

"What is crucial," he leaned forward and spoke intensely, impatient with the need to stop for the translator, "is what happens inside the young. If we can educate them, by example and in the schools, to see work as a prize, not a burden imposed from without, that'll be a beginning." He spoke of nurturing a sense of community, through which a man would feel himself most fulfilled when his particular strengths and skills helped bring fulfillment to others. The isolation of man, and his fear in that isolation, is what makes possible both the oppressed and the oppressors. "I want our young," he continued, "to be so human that they will respond to the best in other human beings, that they will feel a bond—not rhetorically, but organically—with all men who are trying to fulfill themselves."

I remembered that evening some time later, reading a letter he wrote his daughter, Hilda, in 1966, when he was fighting in the Congo against the white mercenaries. He said much the same in that letter, adding: "I wasn't like that at your age, but I was in a different society, where man was man's enemy."

From "On Revolutionary Professionalism", Oct 1968

evergreen

The New Left is starting its own computer consulting company. One of the projects of Movement for a Democratic Society in New York — the embryonic post-graduate SDS — is the attempt to launch META-INFORMATION APPLICATIONS, a software computer company with worker control.

On recruiting day at the University of Maryland recently, the SDS chapter passed out a circular purportedly from DEMOPAX, Inc., saying: "WANTED—scientists, technicians, mathematicians, systems analysts who are sick of setting up dominoes for the war machine to work on . . . You will be researching, designing and simulating technical and strategic ways and means to MAXIMIZE SELF-DETERMINATION AND POPULAR GOVERNMENT AND MINIMIZE WAR, OPPRESSION AND DOMINATION . . . Scientists of the world, unite with the people!" As a device for making students think about what the system wants of them, the circular was clever; but to anyone who wants to see a New Left that is not simply an extracurricular activity for 18-to-21 year olds, the joke is on us.

We need DEMOPAX and we need it now. We need something to offer the radical systems analyst who would just as soon not sell his brain to ARPA, KRESS, the DOD or IBM. If we can only tell him to forget his science and cut off his hands, we might as well hand out suicide pills to the people we organize who are creative in a science.

To get off the ground, MIA needs two or three people who (1) identify strongly with the Movement or need a way to do so, and (2) identify strongly with being computer people, especially programmers and software types. If you are interested in computers because they represent an easy way of making money, forget MIA: it's not for you. MIA will be staffed by people who express their creativity working with computers, but don't want to be creative at the expense of their brothers, in the service of the great corporations and corporate armies.

Less essential characteristics but desirable ones for people to start MIA include their being in a position—because of their experience in the field—to get some amount of support for their work. Experience outside a university is also desirable, and it would help if you have some facility estimating time required for carrying out projects.

MIA will do the following kinds of work:

1. Work that people in it want to do, presumably having to do with computers, theoretical or applied.

2. Work that serves Movement computer needs as they arise. For instance, an automated information center could be set up. Data—facts, articles, books, researched information—of political relevance could be collected and made accessible by an automated indexing system implemented on a computer. Such an information retrieval system could take in the research findings of New Left groups around the country, put them together, and respond to queries from organizers, students, chapters, and the radical press for relevant and timely information. We hope that service to the Movement will be supported by the three other types of work.

3. Work on relatively acceptable and clean programming jobs to provide income. For instance, MIA designed an indexing system for the RAMPARTS files. Certain uses of computers in medicine would fall in this category.

4. Development of proprietary programs which can be leased. For example, Robert Shapiro has designed a small information retrieval system which can be marketed as a proprietary product of MIA.

The structure of MIA will be simple worker control. After a period of probation, every person becomes part of the decision-making apparatus: one man, one vote. People will hassle out with each other what is clean work and what to get paid. The company is already incorporated in the State of New York as a profit-making corporation. It is capitalized in such a way that the preferred stock has no voting rights: putting in money or buying stock gives NO control over the company.

People who do work for the company and do not take out of the company in salary as much as they bring in in contracts will be given the equivalent amount of money in preferred stock. However, they would not acquire any more voting power. Everybody will have the same vote.

MIA exists on paper. What it needs to make it exist in the world is dedicated people to get together and agree to start looking for work and be available to do work when it is found.

MIA would like to have a computer eventually, such as a PDP-81 with a Memorex Diskpack. Total cost for such equipment would be less than $40,000. In the meantime we can rent time on such equipment for jobs that require their use.

If you are interested in MIA, write to Robert Shapiro, 240 West 98 Street, 14H, New York, N.Y. 10025. Please describe your background and interests.

Ad in *CAW!* (an SDS magazine)

The Urban Underground Resurfaces!

STATEMENTS OF THE URBAN UNDERGROUND, A PART OF THE MOVEMENT FOR A DEMOCRATIC SOCIETY, AT A PUBLIC HEARING OF THE NEW YORK CITY PLANNING COMMISSION, FEBRUARY 19, 1969.

(Following are sections from a pamphlet published by the Urban Underground. For more information, and for copies of the pamphlet, write:

Urban Underground c/o M D S
225 Lafayette Street
New York, New York 10012

■■■

In response to a specific proposal that two areas of Manhattan where poor and middle income people live and work be "up-zoned" to permit "luxury" apartment buildings in quantity builders consider "economical," five members of the Urban Underground presented the following statements.

The establishment press chose to emphasize the fact that four are employees of the Department of City Planning, in effect talking back to our bosses. They have ignored the more important political issues that the city is assisting the rich in taking over more of the city from the not-so-rich and that those who delivered the statements presented here are workers who have been tools in that process.

REZONING: IN WHOSE INTERESTS?

People who work in this society have few ways to control the sense and purpose of their work. Society tells some of its workers that they have an expertise, a skill that they can use that distinguishes them from other workers who only work, after all, to make some bread. But that expertise is a deception.

We have the concrete examples here today of city planners, whose skills supposedly are oriented towards working with the people in this city towards the creation of a human, livable environment. But what do we find: When it comes to the question of rezoning Manhattan south of 96th Street, the city planners are lied to and manipulated in the interests not of effective planning or for community interests, but for the sake of the needs of the real estate interests, the city government, and anyone else who stands to make a profit out of people's real needs.

CITY PLANNING COMMISSION: FIG LEAF FOR CORPORATE POWERS

The Urban Underground last appeared at the General Motors Building to expose how corporations have flooded our cities with cars and roads and what that has done to our lives. We resurface today to show how the same interests use the City Planning Commission and people like ourselves to mask their rape of those parts of the city where poor and middle income people live and work.

Many of us are city planners and employees of the Department of City Planning. We became planners to create a better society. Our work experience has taught us that public agencies do not in fact plan our cities, that what happens in cities is decided by the same corporate interests that run the universities and burn babies in Vietnam.

The rezoning proposals up for consideration today are a perfect example. Real estate speculators wanted to take over valuable inner-city land where poor and working people live and work to construct profitable housing for rich people. City Planning Department staff determined that such a take-over was against the best interests of everyone except the real estate interests and their corporate allies. Within the City Administration, already under pressure to produce more housing, puppets of those corporate interests pressured the City Planning Department management to recommend that exact opposite of what the staff had found.

Communities that would rather spend their energy planning their own neighborhoods are continually diverted by the need to respond to direct threats such as these rezoning proposals. Staff workers who want to work with and be responsible to the people of the city rather than the real estate interests cannot effectively do so.

The Urban Underground consists of those workers acting in the interests of human values and supports the victims of the land grab.

Radicals in the Professions Newsletter May 1969

---

oikos
PEOPLE'S ARCHITECTURE
by Van der Ryn

BUILDING AN URBAN environment that is increasingly hostile to human life requires lots of technicians to do the dirty work. Architects design most of the buildings that fill the urban matrix: office buildings, schools, shopping centers, apartments. In spite of often pious rhetoric, the architectural profession participates with seldom a public whimper in the construction of an environment that puts profits over people. Their actions make mass processing and control more important than individual needs.

Indeed, some of the most honored men in the profession occasionally serve as "consultants" to put a veneer of respectability on projects such as the Pan Am building that desecrated midtown Manhattan.

Naturally a younger generation of architects and students is restless with what it perceives as the self serving nature of the profession that bills itself as "mother of the arts." But there hasn't been too much that young architects have been able to do about making architecture more responsive to human needs.

AFTER ALL, IT takes money to build. Most architecture serves powerful institutional and corporate clients. Politically powerful architects serve politically powerful clients.

The silent majority of Americans desperately needs help in building a comfortable, responsive, and beautiful living environment for themselves but the architectural profession has been largely disinterested in helping people without bread.

Now some young architects are taking steps to build a people oriented architectural profession that will not accede automatically to the demands of the money system and entrenched bureaucracy.

A GROUP OF YOUNG architects have set up shop in Berkeley at 1940 Bonita, off University, calling themselves People's Architects. Jim Burleigh and Ron Jewett, two talented Cal graduates, split a San Francisco architectural firm after the People's Park hassle.

Their initial intention was to develop a feasible designed proposal for the Park site. They are working with many people in the community on this proposal as an alternative to the Regents plan to impose a housing project on the former Park site. Several well known architects turned down the contract to design the Regents plan, including Gerald McCue, UC architecture chairman, and Charles Moore, presently chairman of Yale's department of architecture.

Meanwhile, People's Architects are working with the community to initiate radical ways for people to create their own environments. The group is teaching a course on environment at the Free University where they are using technology to build space cheaply with minimal skills.

They are exploring the use of foam plastics, geodesics, and inflatable structures. They are making movies and developing other tools to teach people to design and build themselves. Their main problem is money and they are beginning to "moonlight"—setting paying jobs so they can continue as People's Architects.

AS JIM BURLEIGH said to me, "we conceive of ourselves as an environmental task force. We want to help people build and in order to do so we explore bureaucratic channels, but as they close off, we stop talking and just do." It is a philosophy that if more people practiced, we might begin to renew and reclaim our city for the people who live in it.

Ed. Note: Van der Ryn is a Professor in the Dept. of Environmental Design at Berkeley

The Daily Californian 10/16/69

proposals

BREAKING OUT OF
THE WAR MACHINE

THIS SECTION IS FOR PEOPLE who have ideas for new projects but don't have the workers and resources to implement them. It is also for people who are looking for jobs or job ideas. Anyone who conceives of a social change project that is likely to meet the following conditions is encouraged to share it with our readers. We ask that persons submitting proposals (1) be committed to seeing the project through, (2) have ways in mind to support additional people to do the work, and (3) be starting something new. this excludes purely volunteer work for established projects.

We invite your contributions to this section. Please make your proposals as brief as you can---no more than one newsletter page. Ask for the resources you need in addition to people: funding, supplies, a space, etc. Summaries of the proposal, along with how-to-contact information, will be repeated for two more issues. After three months the proposal will be discontinued, unless we hear from you. Please communicate with us to let us know what happened to the project; we will publish such information along with the project summary.

Below is a proposal for a 'counter think-tank' from Leonard Henny. Send us yours!

In February, 1968, scientists and engineers in the San Francisco Bay Area formed the Technology and Society Committee, or TASC. There are about 500 members of TASC at present. Several subgroups were initiated to channel the energy of members into areas of their specific concerns. One such group became the TASCFORCE for Constructive Alternatives, which established a non-profit corporation working to make scientists and engineers in the defense industry more aware of the destructive consequences of much of their work, and to help them locate alternative employment. A job clearinghouse for non-defense employment opportunities has been started.

The next major effort of TASCFORCE will be to establish what could be called a "Counter-think-tank". In many cases scientists and engineers who work in a company obtain individual contracts with the sponsor of the research project. This holds true for Defense Department Research and Development work as well as for so-called "domestic" R&D. It is often possible for a researcher who is leaving the company that employs him to take with him some of the contracts he has been working on. The objective of the TASCFORCE's non-profit organization here would be to provide an organizational shell for researchers who have such non-defense related contracts and who are contemplating leaving their company in disgust at the war work they are performing.

Only in rare cases would a researcher's non-defense contracts provide him with an income comparable to what he earned doing defense work. There are three aspects of the TASCFORCE organization that help cut expenses. First, TASCFORCE's tax-exempt status is a great advantage in the competitive world of R&D contracts. Second, TASCFORCE can employ Conscientious Objectors who are professionally qualified, and usually CO's do not require large salaries to support themselves. The third advantage of the organization is that scientists and engineers with common beliefs and interests can meet and work together.

The counter-think-tank is still in its infant stage. Discussions on the project have already led to the development of concrete research proposals. For some of these proposals it will continue to be hard to find the necessary funds, at least for the time being. Other proposals stand a better chance of getting funded, such as a proposal to study the potential flaws of the ABM system, or a proposal to develop an electronic system that would help prevent the congestion of urban centers by auto traffic.

Anyone who has ideas which complement and/or add to the above, or who is interested in taking an active part in realizing the opportunities in the venture should send correspondence to TASCFORCE for Constructive Alternatives, 3800 Scott St., San Francisco, Calif. 94123 (415) 921-0347.

Vocations for Social Change Newsletter

[It is not my]business to deal with the political or moral questions—

DR. LOUIS FIESER leading scientist in development of napalm.

HE SEEMS TO BE SMART ENUFF TO INVENT WAYS OF DESTROYING THE PLANET BUT CANT FIGURE OUT HOW TO GET ALONG WITH HIS WIFE!

I'M MISERABLE!   EMC²=

FELLOW SCIENTIST,

The Science Students Union of the University of Wisconsin invites you to join us in establishing

A NATIONAL ORGANIZATION
OF RADICAL SCIENTISTS

We are holding a national conference to be held here on the Madison campus during *July 4, 5 and 6, 1969.* The purpose of such a conference will be:

—to define the role of the radical scientist in society.
—to initiate a radical strategy for action.
—to form a national organization which will provide, through a national newsletter and publication service, a network of communication between radical scientists. At the core of the ongoing part of this organization would be an informational clearing house providing articles, references and papers on tactics used by other groups with similar objectives.

For further information contact:

Barbara Kennedy, SSU; c/o Department of Physics, Madison, Wisc. 53706.

Leviathan

Hartman Sacked

by Frank Vigier

"Your method of teaching conveys a sense of political strategy more than the substance of city planning." With these unusually frank words William Nash, head of the Planning Department at Harvard notified Assistant Professor Chester Hartman his contract would not be renewed.

Hartman thereby became the first member of the faculty to receive retribution for his participation in the strike at Harvard last April. It is apparent that the administration has other reasons as well for firing Hartman.

In addition to his academic post, Hartman is director of Harvard's Urban Field Service (UFS). UFS places students of planning, business, law and architecture in community groups working to formulate or change development plans. The philosophy of Urban Field Service has been to provide technical expertise as an organizing tool to support community groups fighting top-down, corporation-backed plans. UFS people have provided valuable technical assistance in the East Boston community fight against the expansion of Logan Airport and for squatters fighting speculators in the South End. Chester himself has been critical of Harvard's own expansion and its bleeding of the community. During the strike last spring he conducted an investigation of Harvard policies, and proposed that Harvard construct housing for the community.

Urban Field Service gives Harvard a benevolent image that it likes; it just doesn't like the results of UFS under Hartman. So it moves to keep the form and not the substance, and rid itself of Hartman and others like him.

Hartman represents a threat to Harvard and to the Department, for he does not want to produce planners who follow money and prestige, and his skill, popularity, and aggressiveness give him a fair chance of success.

In a broader context, Hartman's dismissal is just one more step in a nationwide dismantling of community action programs to which the War on Poverty, often in spite of itself, gave birth. Nixon opposes community action and is cutting back O.E.O. and eliminating any vestiges of community control. The firing of academics who aided communities and did not try to make social change the province of professional bureaucrats is a logical corollary to the end of OEO.

Students of the Graduate School of Design at Harvard voted unanimously to retain and promote Hartman and have witheld part of their tuition in a fund to use for his salary.

OLD MOLE 3/5/70

NEW UNIVERSITY CONFERENCE

University of Chicago—March 22-24, 1968

A CALL TO ACTION . . . .

We are committed to the struggle for a democratic university, one within which we may freely express the radical content of our lives and one which will be the antagonist and not the ally of pacifiers, domestic and international.

We are prepared to act on this now and in the future just as we have acted throughout the freedom struggles at home and the Movement to end the war in Vietnam. The New University Conference is not the beginning of the struggle for a democratic university; it is merely the beginning of the intensification of that struggle.

The New University Conference has three general tasks: it must lay out a comprehensive program for radical university reform, it must plan and initiate the organizations which will carry out that program, and it must encourage a significant expression of radical research and scholarship relating to public policy, the wider culture and the needs of the resistance, Black and poor people's movements.

From the New University Conference will come:

1. a national membership organization of faculty, graduate students and Movement intellectuals with a program for radical transformation of the American university.

2. new plans for campus activity and campus organizing and thus an end to the isolation which afflicts so many radicals, especially on the smaller campuses and those located away from large urban centers.

3. plans and organization to encourage and support radical scholarship and research so that it may be carried out on a professional and vocational basis rather than as now, a part-time occupation of a few. In addition, we hope to launch a high quality national periodical and to encourage further the formation of radical caucuses within professional associations.

4. expansion of anti-war and other Movement related research as well as new initiatives for university opposition to the war.

5. cooperative and informal Working Groups in American History, Political Science, Sociology, Asian Studies, Cold War History and other disciplines in which radicals are now challenging the doctrines of the university establishment.

6. intensification of the national movement to expose and dislocate university collaboration in war research and social manipulation.

7. a Placement and Defense Organization prepared to assist radicals in obtaining university positions and to provide defense support against the inevitable attacks of McCarthyites, respectable and otherwise.

Sponsors of The New University Conference (partial listing)

Gar Alperovitz	Ray Brown	William Gamson	Carol Holmes	William Livant	Julie Nichamin	James Somers
Richard Barnet	Noam Chomsky	Bertram Garskof	Florence Howe	Janice Lloyd	Myra Riskin	Karen Spaulding
Norman Birnbaum	James Cockcroft	Alex Georgiades	Paul Jacobs	Lee Lowenfish	Melvin Rothenberg	Michael Warner
Russell Block	William Derman	Edward Greer	Louis Kampf	Kenneth Lux	Karen Sachs	Lee Webb
Heather T. Booth	Steven Deutsch	Al Haber	Michael Klare	Cathy McAffee	Adam Schesh	Naomi Weisstein
Jeremy Brecher	Richard duBoff	Andrew Hawley	Paul Lauter	John McDermott	Franz Schurmann	Michael Wolff
Carol Brightman	John Ehrenreich	Tom Hayden	Jesse Lemisch	Don McKelvey	Richard Shaull	Michael Zweig
Michael Brown	Richard Flacks	Michael Hirsch	Richard Levins	Barton Meyers	Vera Simone	

....

New University Conference
1307 East 60th Street
Chicago, Illinois 60637

☐ I plan to attend. Please send me additional information.
☐ I enclose $————— to help defray the costs of the Conference.

Name ....

Address ....

City .... State .... Zip ....

RELEVANCE

VIETNAM CURRICULUM

"Anne Moore was seventeen years old and engaged to be married. The only reason that she and Don Parks were not already married was that she promised her mother to complete high school first. Don, a year ahead of her in school, had graduated the previous June and taken a job as an auto mechanic.

"In November, Don received a notice of induction to the United States Army. Although unhappy about his separation from Anne, he was quite willing to do his service.

" 'If I don't talk to him about this,' she thought, 'it will be the first time I've kept something important from him.'

"What should Anne do?"

This is one of the dilemma stories from the Vietnam Curriculum a 350-page social studies course developed by five high school teachers in Boston. Teachers around the country are now using these materials to help their students examine the impact of the war. And students in their classes are beginning to write their own dilemma stories to complement the curriculum.

Several years ago a group of young movement teachers in the Boston area began to meet weekly to discuss problems encountered in the public schools. We knew from firsthand experience the many ways in which schools, both city and suburban, are mental and physical prisons for students. We felt under great pressure to conform to the system, to regiment behavior, to help indoctrinate the kids in our classes to the American Way.

At that time the political question uppermost in our minds was the Vietnam War. The war, if treated at all, was presented as a "controversial issue" - a watered-down dove-hawk debate within the implicit conceptual framework of Cold War ideology. No text, course, or book dealt with the war in terms relevant to high school students. Some of us had tried to raise the issue in class, but we found it difficult to go beyond a superficial and inconclusive debate: Our students had little knowledge of the background of the war, and there were few sources of information about the effects of the war on people in Vietnam and the United States. They knew what was on TV and what they were told in textbooks, and they believed it. To demonstrate the relation of the war to American society and American politics, we needed not just a few lesson ideas and materials but a whole teaching plan. So five of us from the original teachers' group decided to work together on a Vietnam curriculum.

In the fall of 1967 we wrote the Curriculum and put together the first mimeographed edition. The following spring we contacted friends from the original teachers group and travelled to meetings they arranged with interested faculty members at their schools. At thirty junior high and high schools in and near Boston, we encouraged teachers to use the curriculum, to teach about the war, and to try a variety of teaching methods. One of the most valuable parts of the Curriculum turned out to be instructions to teachers on the use of simulation games, role plays, dilemma stories, and community polls. We always urged anti-war teachers to respect their students' opinions, even if they disagreed: a course becomes useful and relevant when it begins with the students' position and recognizes their feelings as legitimate. Kids learn not from moral arguments but from exploring facts for themselves and examining the framework of their own beliefs. The Curriculum states facts and raises questions rather than presenting an explicit anti-war position.

The five of us (Sue Davenport, Frances Maher, Joan McGregor, Walter Popper, and Adria Reich) have continued to work together as the Boston Area Teacher Project. At present we are working with twenty high school students (from the city and suburban schools where we teach) to develop a curriculum on social identity. Now that the Vietnam Curriculum has been published, we hope it will be useful to others in and near the movement.

To obtain copies of the four volume *Vietnam Curriculum* post paid, write *Vietnam Curriculum*, Department RS-1, New York Review, 250 West 57th Street, New York, New York 10019. Make checks payable to the New York Review ($10 per set; $8 per set for ten or more sets).

--Walter Popper
Boston Area Teaching Project
8 University Road
Cambridge, Mass. 02138

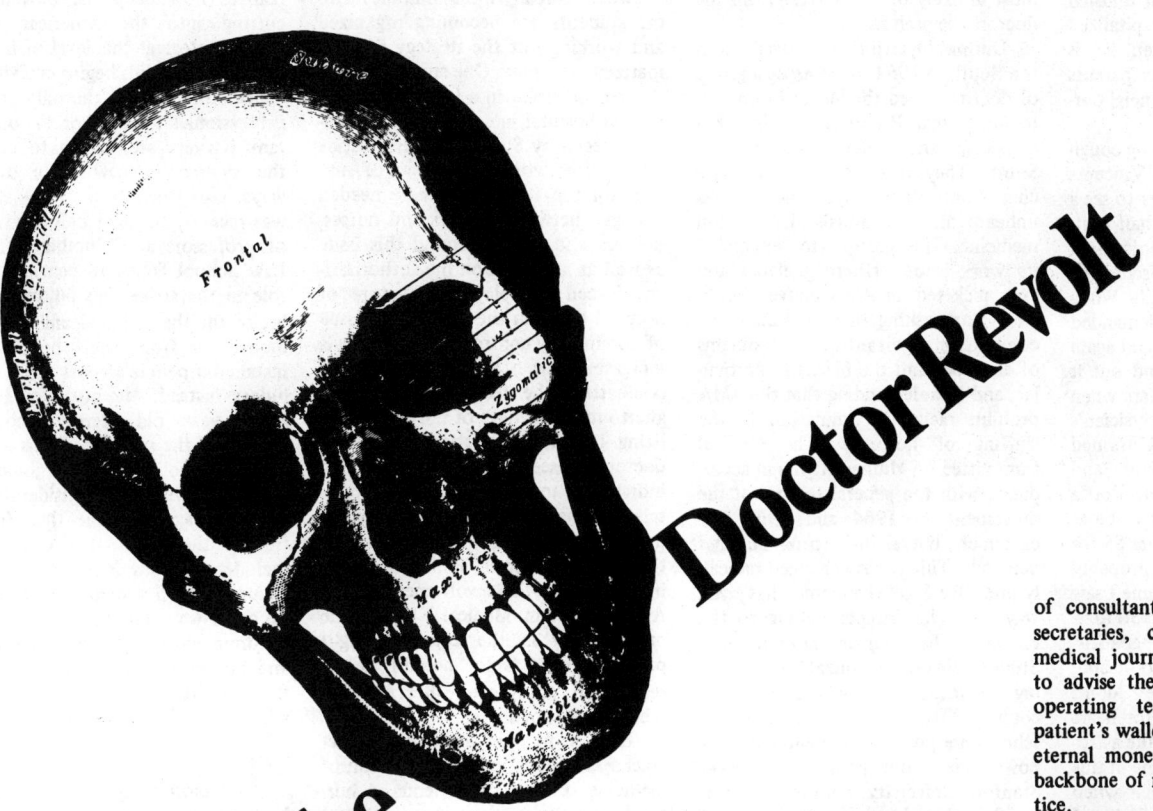

The Doctor Revolt

—Abbie Hoffman (LNS)

I've always had this thing about Doctors and Hospitals. My father was a distributor of physician and hospital supplies. I grew up with doctors and doctor talk all around me. In a previous life, I worked for two years in a mental hospital as a psychologist and later in yet another life as a drug detailman calling on physicians. I had gotten to know doctors pretty well and my impression was, with very few exceptions, that they were a dedicated, well-meaning group of rotten, conceited, dumb, racist, bastards. Their politics is on a level, say, to that of the British Admiralty in the late nineteenth century.

Moreover, the hospital structure which plays such a key role in the training and subsequent life of a physician encourages archaic medical thinking in spite of all its new found gadgets. **The Board of Trustees of any hospital in America would make the Board of Trustees of Columbia look downright revolutionary**, and the Hospital Board runs its institution with a

tight fist. Suspension from a hospital staff means black balling from an entire region and possibly from the whole country. The black-balled physician is still free, of course, to practice medicine, but without a hospital staff position, his ability to gain intensive care treatment for his patients is severely curtailed. The stakes for rebellion are high. In addition, the material incentives for a physician who keeps his nose clean are so high that very few, very few indeed, step out of line. There is another factor which tends to make them reactionary and that is their training. Usually medical schools draw on students who have majored in one of the sciences; when they get them, a period of intensive study, internship, and residence follows that might last ten years. This might be followed by another two years in the Army for males. And so by the time the typical physician is ready to go into practice, he is about thirty-five years old. During all those years, he has been exposed to little outside the field of medicine. His training, including undergraduate school has cost in the neighborhood of $30,000. It is no wonder then that the temptation to hang up a shingle and begin charging patients twenty-five to fifty dollars for an appointment that might last ten minutes and a thousand or two for an operation that might take an hour or less, is extremely high. Physicians 35-40 are hungry after years of financial deprivation. Older physicians are surrounded by a team

of consultants, accountants, business secretaries, collection bureaus, and medical journals that function solely to advise the doctor on the modern operating techniques concerning a patient's wallet. Hypochondriasis, that eternal money-maker, still forms the backbone of many of physician's practice.

I write all this lying in a hospital bed during my third week of hepititis. When the disease first hit me, I went to see Dr. Irving Oyle. Dr. Oyle is a rarity in the world of medicine. He is totally dedicated to curing patients and doesn't give a shit about money. A few years ago he was running a successful practice out on Long Island with all the right kind of patients. Somehow it wasn't giving him the kind of gratification he wanted so he closed up shop and headed for the ghetto in New York's Lower East Side. As for practicing medicine, the Lower East Side must seem more like the wild west Firmly entrenched in a storefront that one could easily mistake as one of the Motherfucker dens, Dr. Oyle carries on a lone struggle to bring medical care to an area that could use 50-100 Dr. Oyles.

From the time he ordered me into the hospital to the time we finally located a bed took six days. He told me of a fellow doctor who had a heart attack patient who waited three days before space could be found in a hospital.

Finally another doctor friend of mine located a bed in Albert Einstein Hospital in the Bronx, and I was bundled up at 1:00 a.m. and sped to the hospital. The doctor feared that if I waited until morning the space might be gone.

Let's turn now to the finances. Because sympathetic doctors who know me pulled certain strings, I am going to escape this mess financially clean. Otherwise this treatment would cost somewhere in the neighborhood of $2,500 and this is without an operation or any medication. There is a kid down the hall with an unusual blood ailment that has hospitalized him for two months. When he is through, his cost, which his parents must pay, will run in the neighborhood of $15,000.

A month ago, I had a rasping cough and went to the clinic at St. Vincents Hospital. It was eleven dollars to see a physician, and an hour and a half wait. He prescribed an X-ray appointment that, because of a crowded schedule, was three weeks from that date. When I showed up, the hospital demanded sixteen dollars for the X-ray, and again cash in advance (I also found out it would be another eleven dollars when I came back to get the physician's report on the X-ray results). I stormed out after a big shouting match and never had the X-rays taken. For a simple cough, treatment was to be at least $38, not counting another $5 for medication prescribed and probably another $5 more the second time I saw the physician. So there it is, $50 for a cough, about $2500 for hepatitis, $1000-$10,000 for an operation and, well, it's a good thing they don't charge those poor bastards for heart transplants. Couple this with the astronomically high cost of medicine in this country and, you can see that when the doctor looks up from his desk and tells you hospitalization is required, going home and shooting yourself might, in the long run, prove less painful. That is, of course, if you haven't read *The High Cost of Dying*.

The strange part about this mess is that if you are really poor you are not too bad off. That is if you live in New York or one of a dozen or so other states that have a welfare program that entitles you to full medical treatment. These states also have a Medicaid program that provides relatively complete care if you are under 21 or over 65 years of age and make less than $2300 per year. Then there is the federal Medicare program for persons over 65. These programs do require applying with complicated forms and delays that can take up to six months. Still, public hospitals are fantastically understaffed and overcrowded. In addition, few hospitals make attempts to reach out into the community and the poor are reluctant to go to a hospital which is excessively authoritarian, paternalistic, and white.

Then there are the various health insurance plans which range in cost from $200-$400 per year and again have restrictions as to the limit in terms of type and length of care, but will cover most conditions.

Without any of these three deals going for you, and unless you have millions or your brother is a doctor, you have a hell of a problem if you get seriously ill.

There is some light shining at the end of the tunnel. There is some

pressure building up and from the most unlikely of all sources—from the doctors themselves.

During the civil rights movement in the South in 1964, there arose a group of doctors called the Medical Committee on Human Rights. They organized physicians and medical students to go South. They relied chiefly on financing from other physicians. It was unheard of in the annals of American medicine. This group later expanded its work into northern ghettoes and even picketed an AMA convention in New York asking that physicians become more cognizant of the problems of the poor and the blacks in particular, and also demanding that the AMA prohibit racial discrimination in the staffing of hospitals. The Medical Committee on Human Rights in accordance with the general temper of the movement in 1964 and 1965 was extremely liberal in its programs and demands. Things have changed radically and "We Shall Overcome" has given way to "The Streets Belong to the People". The younger more militant Student Health Organization is growing in medical schools around the country. SHO chapters in a number of schools are pushing for greater student power in school policy. Groups at Stanford University, Southern California School of Medicine, University of California at San Francisco Health Science Center, and Albert Einstein College of Medicine have managed to involve an unusually large number of students and have even won some reforms.

There is, however, a group of medical students and young physicians that finds SHO rather mild. This new breed of radical students, internists, and residents is to a great extent unorganized and their actions are autonomous and independent.

While in the hospital, I have been visited by some of the new rebels. The first two, I thought to be the hospital odd-balls. When the number rose to twenty-five, I was convinced some sort of rebellion was taking place. Currently, there is a protest action going on at Jacobi Hospital (also serviced by Albert Einstein Medical School) right across the courtyard. A week ago, three pediatric residents began giving their patients notes advising them not to pay their hospital bills and urging them to begin community agitation over the cutbacks in the Medicaid program. The hospital administration ordered the rebels suspended but found itself met with resistance. The head of the Pediatrics Unit refused to suspend the physicians. In addition, a petition of support was circulated and twenty out of thirty fellow pediatric residents stated that in effect the three physicians facing suspension were acting for all of them and if they were suspended, the other twenty would resign. The administration, as of now, has held off any action fearing a palace

revolt. The movement is bound to snowball. Already more militant medical students are becoming organized and working out the strategy for dramatizing the issue. One student during the recent strike in a large New York mental hospital interrupted a convocation speech by Supreme Court Justice Abe Fortas with a statement of support for the strikers. A badly needed dialogue between doctors and nurses, doctors and patients round this issue as well as an attack on the authoritarian, forced role-playing structure of hospital life is in the works. The issue of community control over hospitals is increasingly seen as the only way of combatting the fears and suspicions ghetto residents have of the depersonalizing hospital institution. The rebel doctors are seeking ways of contacting individuals and groups at other hospitals to broaden the base of the movement and gain support. A confrontation with the hospital administration is inevitable but the involvement of the Albert Einstein Medical School, the most liberal in the country, might prove to be a factor helpful to the rebels, an advantage other hospital rebels might not share.

This is not the only place that cracks are appearing in the bastion of medicine. I have two friends, a husband and wife, attending medical school who are determined to join the guerrillas in South America as soon as they have sufficient training in tropical diseases.

A small group of doctors at another hospital are clandestinely collecting medical supplies needed in Cuba. Currently there is a group of young American physicians attending a conference in Cuba. Recently over eighty students (one third of the student body) at Stanford University Medical School signed a statement saying they would not participate in the Vietnam War. There is a growing list of angry young doctors willing to perform abortions or at least make referrals to others who will. A small number of doctors are agreeing to treat bullet wounds of riot victims without reporting them to the police. Last year a group of medical students broke up a meeting of the AMA convention in San Francisco and that is not the last the AMA has seen of the insurgents.

The role that physicians and medical students played in Chicago was invaluable. It was absolute war conditions for many. Chicago police refused to call ambulances or provide any assistance to the wounded, and often unconscious demonstrators, to a far greater extent than even the Walker Report suggests. Without the medical personnel and the first-aid facilities they set up, there would have been far more serious injuries and possibly deaths suffered. The medical corps proved quite brave as well as competent for they were often singled out by police for "special consideration".

All this is quite heartening and one realizes how deep the movement is cutting into the American system when protest at this level of intensity from professionals begins evolving.

Doctors are not the only group of professionals in rebellion. Young militant lawyers are willing to confront the system in new more dramatic ways. Gus Reischback, a law student, was recently brought before a tribunal of professors at Columbia University Law School facing suspension for his role in the strike. His fellow students broke up the tribunal and drove the inquisitors from their bench. They installed a people's court and tried the judges instead. My attorney, twenty-seven year old Jerry Lefcourt, is typical of the new breed. His attitude is totally political. His arguments in court are given more consideration for their propaganda value than for just freeing the client. His clients who include the New York Panthers and Columbia SDS students would have it no other way. The old ACLU attitude of dress nice, keep your mouth shut and be reasonable is not only missing from the repertory of these new lawyers, it is in fact, scorned.

Two months ago I was in a campus building that had been occupied by 2000 students and turned into a sanctuary for an AWOL soldier. The school was the Massachusetts Institute of Technology. Two years ago, if you had said any school in the Boston area was capable of such an act, organizers would have laughed. If you had said MIT, we would have considered you outright insane.

Tonight in the hospital, I was visited by four young rebellious students. I have met them before and rapped about the movement, Chicago, dope, street fighting, and the like. They are seeking issues around which to organize other students at their school. In a hundred years you wouldn't guess where they are from—the United States Military Academy at West Point!

For too long the movement has been rooted in the liberal arts divisions of our multi-universities. Writing, debating, and in general other propagandizing were the only skills to be found. Now the movement is in need of people who know how to "do" things, how to solve problems arising out of situations rather than get all the right answers on a test of the issues. The swelling of our ranks with doctors, engineers, lawyers, military tacticians, and the like is a most encouraging sign. This corrupt system we live under is manned by engineers of one sort or another. History majors and poets are useless appendages. Professionals who know how to put things together and take things apart are not so expendable. It seems like it isn't such a barren winter after all.

peoples' health

We are setting up a non-profit medical clinic in the Palo Alto area. Our goal is to create a center which will meet the health needs of people from all parts of the population, regardless of financial status or class. Doctors, nurses and other workers in the medical field will be giving their time to the community, not trying to draw profit or status from their medical work.

We stand opposed to the business-like atmosphere, methods, and functioning of most private and public hospitals and clinics and will be working to create an environment in which patients and staff can relax into less formal, more human, and more interactive relationships. We think that doctors, for their own good, as well as that of the patients and other medical workers, cannot stay aloof from the people they are serving.

The clinic itself will be supported and operated by the community it is serving and the people working within it. We hope to get our initial funds from individual donations. Our needs are simple: an office, used equipment and medical instruments, supplies and medicine. and people trained in medical work. We will have specialty consultants, but our principal medical specialty will be the general medical care of our community.

We see this clinic as unique: it has been initiated and will be run by people from our active young community for that community. It will provide doctors and nurses with an opportunity to work in an environment that is fresh and free from medical bureaucracy. We see this as a clear alternative to the institutions that we are all presently involved in. We want to call our clinic a "socialistic" clinic, perhaps the "Peoples' Medical Center", because it will be an effort to socialize medicine and take it out of the realm of a big business. And we believe that a true socialism comes up from the people, not down from the government.

We need your donations to open the doors of the clinic. We are convinced that our efforts are meaningful and that your help will be important, to yourself, to the whole community, and to young people in medicine who are searching for alternatives to the elitism and isolation of American medicine. We make no bones about it: our clinic will be a community experiment with political and social implications. And we hope it will make possible medicine of, by, and for the people.

Send contributions or correspondence to Committee for the Peoples' Medical Center, Box 3205, Stanford, California 94305.

health research & action

Health Research and Action Project (Health-RAP), is a radical white organizing project involving workers, especially hospital workers, and welfare mothers. We are demanding pay-as-you-can medical care, community and hospital worker control of hospitals, one hospital system for everyone, and community-controlled neighborhood clinics, along with demands for career ladders for workers and increased hiring of blacks in non menial positions and recruiting of blacks in professional schools (e.g. nursing). We have had successful demonstrations at hospitals, Medical Society meetings, etc. With the Black Panther Party, we are setting up a People's Clinic. Donations urgently needed. As of now, plans are to use volunteer doctors, but are considering hiring Movement doctor for full-time at low salary. Also interested in exchanging information with other groups around the country. ---CONTACT Health-RAP, 2409 SE Division, Portland, Oregon 97202.

From *Vocations for Social Change* Newsletter

Photo taken during the International Women's Day March, Boston, Mass, March 7, 1970.

Dear Friend;

The Uptown area of Chicago is a neighborhood where people of many different racial and ethnic backgrounds are the victims of deprivation and exploitation. In the past, agencies provided little or no service to the community and young people, instead of trying to change things, they fought with each other. But now a group of young people living in Uptown have formed the Young Patriots. The Young Patriots Organization is committed to changing the racist, elitist and oppressive nature of their society. They have set up a number of service programs, programs which are genuinely needed and which also make clear how poorly the system serves the people.

The Patriots have organized and run a food distribution program for the hungry, a free breakfast program for children and a medical service for neighborhood residents.

We are writing to you because of our concern for the future of the medical program. The lack of adequate medical care for Uptown residents is very clear.

There are few doctors and dentists willing to serve the people here. Hospitals have been generally unresponsive to people's needs, and the board of health limits its sphere of activity to pre-natal care and a Well Baby Clinic.

With assistance from Northwestern University's Medical Union the Young Patriots set up the medical service in November, 1969. The service was made available to Uptown people every Saturday from 10 a.m. until the last patient was served—usually after 6 p.m. Young Patriots have worked in the medical service as liaisons between community people and the volunteer medical personnel who make up the medical staff. Under a system of "patient advocacy" each patient has been assigned to both a Young Patriot and a medical person who are jointly responsible for his care. The Young Patriot has remained with each patient to assist in helping to obtain medication and to assist with referrals and transportation.

The Medical Service has already helped many neighborhood residents. About half the patients have been under thirteen years of age. Many youngsters have received immunizations for the first time and lead poisoning tests have been given routinely. Many patients with upper respiratory infections have been teated; others have been given badly needed dental examinations. The Medical Service has already had an effect on some local institutions. For example, a local hospital known for its inadequate treatment of local people gave prompt attention to a gangfight victim brought over by a Patriot, and two senior medical students. With the recent outbreak of diphtheria, the Medical Service immediately began vaccinating children and adults against the disease as well as continuing to provide complete medical check-ups. After the Medical Service began this the public schools followed suits.

Perhaps because the Medical Service has proven to be successful, certainly because it is part of a program for radical change, the police had the Medical Service at 1140 Sunnyside closed. At the present time, the Patriots Medical Service is housed in temporary quarters, but to assure continuation of the program, a permanent site must be found. Our hope is to expand the Medical Service by renting a doctor's office in the community which will be open five days a week.

WHY DID FREE CLINIC CLOSE?

Charges that police harassment forced the closing of a free medical and dental clinic sponsored by the Young Patriots at 1140 Sunnyside Ave. were made—and denied—yesterday. The clinic, however, was disbanded Sunday, as two men in a Plymouth circled the block taking photographs, and the neighborhood youth group is now searching for new quarters for its clinic.

Dr. Bruce Douglas, chairman of the dental and oral surgery department at Presbyterian-St. Luke's hospital and a professor in the University of Illinois College of Medicine and Dentistry, said he was visited by two policemen from the gang intelligence until last month, a day or so after a story about the clinic appeared in a neighborhood newspaper.

Dr. Douglas said the officers—who gave their names as Cuttone and Drysdale—were friendly, but suggested that it might be wise for him to disavow any association with the Young Patriots, an organization of youths from Appalachia. He said the police mentioned that "this might not look so well for you in the future."

The physician, who is running for State Representative for the 11th District, said he replied that he had no connection with the Young Patriots' political views, only with the medical center, and would continue to help there.

Attorney Alfons J. Spanitz, owner of the apartment building in which the clinic operated each Saturday, said that a visit from police asking questions about the Young Patriots had no part in his decision to tell them to move. He said the clinic had been installed without his knowledge in the same quarters rented for week-day use as a day nursery, and that he told the operators of the nursery to move the clinic out because of complaints from other tenants about noise (sometimes late at night), a jammed front door lock, and other annoyances.

Attorney Ted Stein, assigned by the Office of Economic Opportunity to the Legal Aid Bureau as a Reginald Hever Smith Fellow, under supervision of the University of Pennsylvania, who has done legal work for the Young Patriots, charged that the clinic was ordered out of its home within a few hours after the police visit to Spanitz.

Stein also said six policemen (two of them in plain clothes) forced their way into an apartment the night of Dec. 4 where the clinic's medical committee was meeting, with the explanation that there had been a complaint about disturbing the peace. The police, who had no warrant, threatened to break down the door if they were refused admittance, Stein said, but left in seeming confusion after finding only three or four Young Patriots and 10 or 15 medical students, many of them in white jackets.

Stein said police also picked up a clinic patient recently, held him overnight in the "drunk tank," and refused to return antibiotics and bandages he had been given at the clinic.

The patient, according to Stein, came to the clinic for treatment of a badly-cut leg which, according to the man, was inflicted by police after a previous arrest.

Meanwhile, Dr. Douglas has written a letter of complaint to Mayor Daley. The Young Patriots, who plan a press conference this morning, are searching for a new clinic site. Stein is trying to figure out who was driving the "photo car" last Sunday, since the license checks to a secret list. He also predicts that the clinic will be reestablished.

"The people need it," he says, "and one of our purposes is to show the people of this area that they should not be afraid of the police. It would be a great mistake not to reopen it."

CHE GUEVARA

While Ernesto Che Guevara acquired a following throughout the world and his picture adorns the walls of thousands of American homes, few people are aware that he was a physician first and a revolutionary second. It was his recognition of the fact that the work of physicians, however dedicated, was just a drop in the bucket in the overall attempt to alleviate human suffering both physical and mental that led him to the belief that only revolution could really improve the human condition. On a visit to Bolivia in the summer of 1953, he saw Indians lined up outside the headquarters of the Agrarian Reform, waiting to receive deeds to their land. He was depressed and angry to see that as each filed past they were also sprayed with D.D.T. While medically beneficial, it reminded him of the cattle dusting in Buenos Aires, and he realized that medicine offers little if it also detracts from people's stature as human beings.

From childhood Guevara was a loner. As a teenager he took motorcycle trips around Argentina, often for months at a time. Sleeping on the ground at night and carrying only the barest necessities with him, he became enured to a Spartan way of life that served him well in later years. It was on these trips that he visited leprosaria and helped to care for the patients there. Among these social outcasts his humanistic concern grew and these experiences were probably one of the reasons why in 1947 he started medical school in Buenos Aires.

He did well in medical school and spent his summers working as a nurse on freighters that traveled up and down the Argentine coast. In 1952 he took a year off from medical school and went with a friend to a leprosarium in the upper Amazon. There where the rest of the medical staff wore masks and rubber gloves, treating the patients literally as untouchables, Che delighted in organizing social activities and treating the inmates with the dignity and respect that they had long been denied.

After he graduated from medical school Che had planned to go to Venezuela to continue his work with lepers. But he was becoming increasingly concerned about the broader political issues which keep the physical illness of a people so permanently entwined with social injustice, and he never arrived in Venezuela. Instead, after travelling in Bolivia, Peru and Ecuador he decided to go to Guatemala where the liberal regime of Jacobo Arbenz was attempting to implement some of the reforms that Guevara knew Latin America so badly needed. However, shortly after he arrived in Guatemala an attempt by Arbenz to expropriate the holdings of the American United Fruit Company triggered a United States-backed invasion of the country. The Arbenz government was overthrown and the hope for social reform died with it. Guevara made a futile attempt to organize resistance to the invasion, even though he knew it was hopeless.

The Guatemala experience was a turning point for Guevara. He realized that he could no longer justify spending his time solely as a physician when he could potentially do so much more to alleviate human suffering by working for the revolutionary movement. He also realized that despite the idealistic utterances of many Americans, United States foreign policy was irrevocably wedded to the financial interests of a few rich corporations and was committed to the continued oppression and exploitation of the people of Latin America regardless of the human suffering it caused. He had also experienced first hand the thrill of revolutionary violence and the awesome potential which it has to change the lives of people and of nations.

The following year, 1955, Che Guevara met another revolutionary, Fidel Castro, and became the physician for the guerrilla force which the latter planned to send into the Sierra Madre of Cuba. The rest of the story is well known and often recorded. However, though Che played an active role in the establishment of the revolutionary government in Cuba he was never really comfortable. Driven by an urge to complete throughout Latin America what had only been begun by the victory in Cuba, he seemed to be inspired by an image of himself as the Simon Bolivar of the Twentieth Century. In a speech to militiamen on August 19, 1960, "On Revolutionary Medicine," he exhorted them to remember that the physician must immediately return to the dedicated practice of medicine as soon as the revolution is won. He said, "You should not commit the same error which we committed in the Sierra . . . It seemed dishonorable to us to remain at the side of a wounded man or sick one, and we looked for any way possible of grabbing a rifle and going to prove on the battlefront what we could do." It was good advice, but something which Che Guevara was unable to adhere to himself.

To many the idea of a revolutionary physician with a gun in his hand is an anathema. To the liberal humanitarian the physician must always remain true to his professional ethics and remain neutral in the political and social arena. This assumes, probably erroneously, that such a postion is tenable and ignores the fact that physicians as an elitist group have traditionally lent their prestige and support to the other political extreme. Guevara could not divorce the need to care for a medical crises from a concern for the welfare of the patient as a human geing. He was not prepared to give his life to the practice of patch work medical care in a social climate that was more conducive to the growth of foreign investment than of healthy children. It is probably an injustice to many physicians not to give them credit for an awareness of these conditions and the need for change. The difference with Che Guevara was that he believed they could be changed and was prepared to do something himself to bring it about.

—aquarius, m.d.

The information for this article was gathered from:
Venceremos! The Speeches and Writings of Enesto Che G Guevara, (J. Gerassi, ed.). New York: Macmillan, 1968.

My Friend Che. R. Rojo. New York: Dial Press, 1968

"Physician—Revolutionary Physician—Revolutionary," by G.P. Harper, in *New England Journal of Medicine 281*, 1285, 1969.

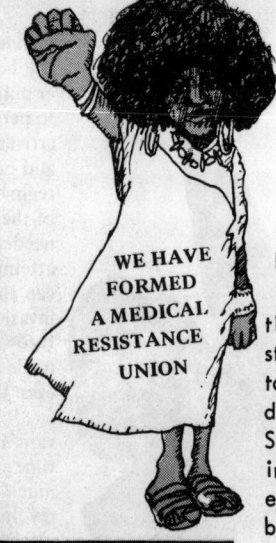

WE HAVE FORMED A MEDICAL RESISTANCE UNION

medical resistance union

We know that many health professionals--doctors, dentists, nurses, social workers, hospital workers, scientists and students in all these vocations--are looking for an opportunity to make a meaningful commitment to alter those policies which deny peace and dignity to peoples both at home and abroad. Still others in the health professions are looking for a way to indicate their strong approval of and confidence in such an effort. Our response has been to join together in a broad-based program of action and mutual support. We have formed a Medical Resistance Union.

what will you do ?

The choices are hard ones. Many of us have been led to consider them by visions of hundreds of thousands dead, maimed, homeless and starving in Vietnam; by the presence in our midst of crumbling cities where living conditions degrade the quality of life; by the violence of the status quo and the counterviolence of the victimized. Many of us also believe that forebearance in such circumstances is no virtue. And we have asked ourselves how we might best confront these destructive patterns, not only as citizens, but also as health professionals.

In the past two years more than 300 medical students, representing almost 40 schools across the country, have pledged not to serve in the armed forces in Vietnam. On several campuses, faculty members circulated statements commending the "initiative and courage" of the signers.

It was a good beginning. Now it is time for us to move forward together.

WHAT WILL YOUR
SPECIALTY BE?
• • • • •
REVOLUTION

marjorie heins

For most people, profession and persuasion don't meet. That is, their moral and political ideas don't correspond to the manner in which they spend five days of their week. Charles Englehard and Stokely Carmichael are exceptions.

My brother-in-law, for instance, is a physician. He has chosen cardiology as his specialty, so Selective Service will give him extra research time before he has to don the uniform. He looks forward to a lucrative private practice, in an affluent community; and a personal life replete with cars, boats and skiing trips to Europe. He feels this is coming to him because he spent so long living the poor life of a medical student, burning the midnight oil, and studying dull Latin names.

Before he finished med school, he had brief doubts. He liked medicine, but really wanted to go into politics and become an attractive reformer like JFK. Pressures from all around, plus his own awareness that medicine was a sure thing, and politics was chancy, kept him

in his chosen rut. But the secret ambition is still there. It helps explain why my brother-in-law is so strongly opposed to socialized medicine, at the same time that he's basically liberal and humane.

Politically, he's quite ready to admit the country's a disaster. He did volunteer work for Gene McCarthy, and supported Paul O'Dwyer, liberal Senate candidate in New York, to the extent of a vote and a $25 check. I'm sure he'll continue these sporadic forays into reform politics. But he won't change his mind about socialized medicine or the "fee for service." For him, the gulf between profession and persuasion is enormous.

All of which began me wondering if professional people, who like their comforts, and yet are intelligent and humane, can be brought into a revolutionary struggle, not on Saturdays, but all the time, with their whole lives. I suppose that's what interested me in Susan and Peter Schnall.

Lieutenant Junior Grade Susan Schnall is a nurse at Oak Knoll Naval Hospital. The Navy recruiter had assured her she'd be considered a professional serving

soldiers, not a military person herself. The first days at Officers Training School told her differently.

Before the October 21 GI Peace March, Susan and some friends dropped pro-march leaflets from a private plane on a few of the Bay Area's innumerable military installations. At the march, she wore her uniform, in violation of a general regulation. January 30 at Treasure Island, she faces General Court Martial on two counts: conduct unbecoming an officer (for dropping the leaflets), and disobeying the uniform regulation. Airman Michael Locks will be court martialled a week later at Hamilton Air Force Base for the same offense. They'll both be defended by Richard Werthimer.

General Court Martial is the most severe of military punishments. As an officer, Susan faces any penalty the court dictates, other than death.

Meanwhile, she is helping organize a GI Association to consolidate and expand anti-war feeling in the military. She knows from her contact with Marines at Oak Knoll that the Association repre-

Dr. Howard Levy was imprisoned for refusing to train Green Berets for Vietnam.

Susan Schnall

sents a lot of people. For the Marines, their war experience, their realization of what military rule does to human response, and their free use of grass in Asia (probably higher grade than we get here), all contribute to their growing willingness to resist.

Susan's husband Peter is a senior medical student at Stanford. A leader in the radical Student Health Organization and the Medical Committee on Human Rights, Peter was the one who got up at last year's AMA Convention to say:

"The health care system in the United States, long failing, may now well be collapsing.... The Medical Committee for Human Rights takes the position that the present inadequacies in health care ... are the result of a system which by its own logic resists the changes that would make comprehensive care possible.... One must identify the central role of the American Medical Association as the culprit in this tragedy of unnecessary failure....

"The AMA has refused to cleanse its ranks of open racial discrimination. It has resisted enforcement of Title VI of the Civil Rights Act of 1964. It has shown monumental indifference to the health problems of black people. It is a racist organization....

"The AMA, favoring the operation of a free enterprise system ... has accelerated the concentration of physicians and facilities in the affluent communities and converted the inner city into a medical wasteland."

Four hundred fifty members of the Student Health Organization have signed a pledge not to serve in the military. For some, this means any way out, such as Public Health Service. For Peter and a few others, it means a positive alternative. They plan after internship to set up group practice in a poor community of New York or San Francisco; then apply for joint CO status. They know they'll probably be denied. But the positive alternative of group medical care in an inner city, performed by people devoted to healing and not the fee for service, is a radical departure for doctors. It means taking control of your life the same way Susan did by dropping leaflets, the same way tiny enclaves of professionals are beginning to do in almost every field.

As Peter talked about hospitals and internships, I couldn't help thinking of countless conversations among my brother-in-law and his friends. When talking to a medical student, the standard question is: "What will your specialty be?" Peter said: "Revolution."

He doesn't mean bricks and bottles; he objects to terrorism because it turns people off; and after all, he says, "Revolution is the struggle to win people's minds." Peter foresees a great deal of violence, both revolutionary and repressive, in the next ten years. He's not afraid of it, but thinks its inevitability is only more reason for hastening the process of change, the construction of alternative styles of life, work and thought.

For professionals, the big obstacles to radical action are complacency and fear. As Peter explained: for the average person, induction refusal or any felony can mean prison and a criminal record; for a medical person, it can also mean loss of the license to practice. That's why, among young doctors, Howard Levy is mentioned in awed voices, even while they are discussing their plans for avoiding or outwitting the Army.

The Schnalls are part of a small number of people who are closing the gap between profession and persuasion. What made them do it was partly a loss of complacency: a realization that the supposed goals of their careers were irreconcilable with the institutions around which those careers are built: the big hospitals with their appalling clinics; the AMA; the military; the system of selective deferments.

Partly also, it was a fear that suddenly vanished. People caught in the system are more afraid of it than those outside. Susan said people within the military are benumbed by fear of a huge inflexible machine. For her, that fear vanished quite suddenly: "I realized there was nothing they could do to me that I wouldn't let them do."

San Francisco
Express Times 1/28/69

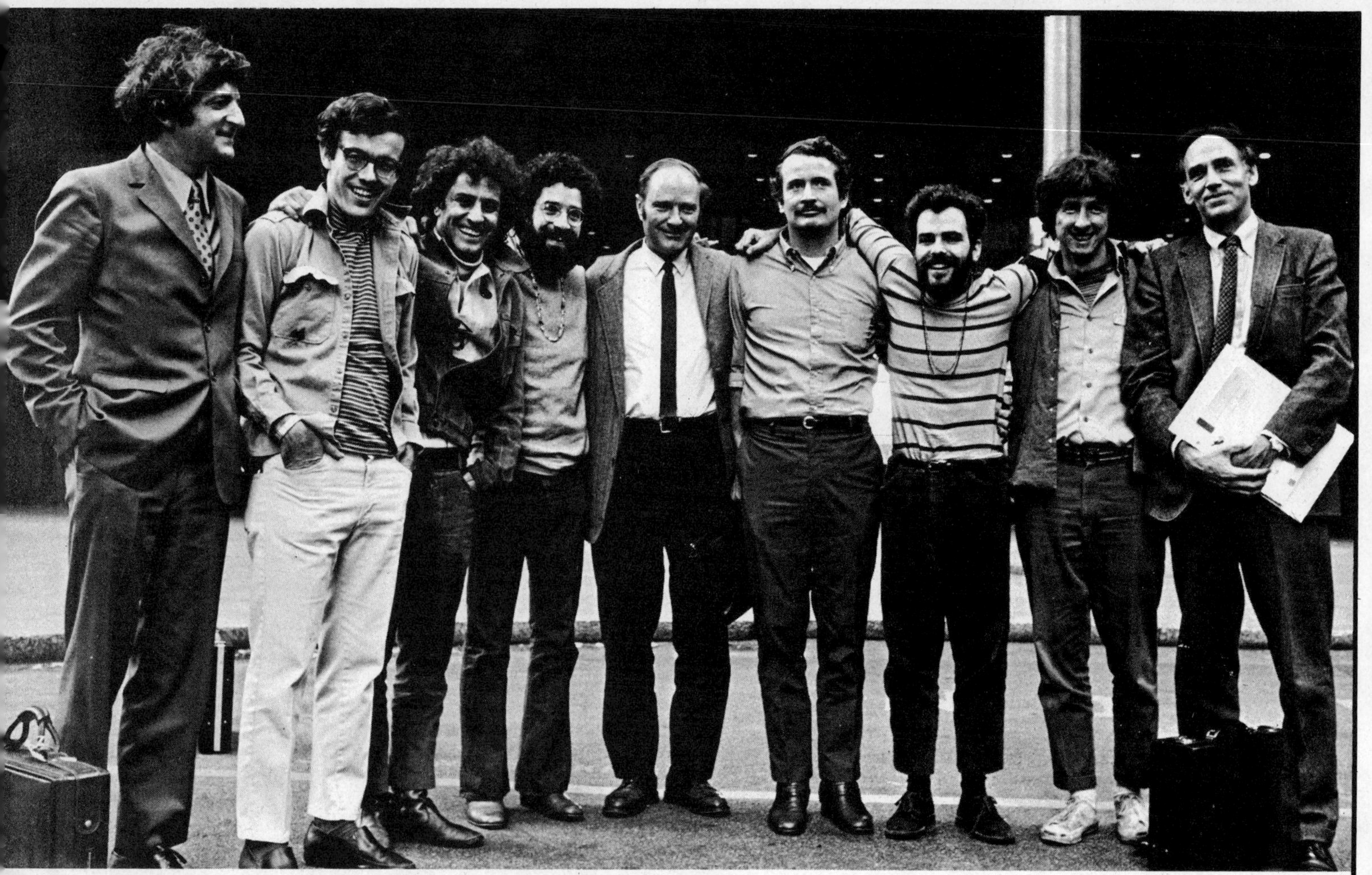

the law & the people

TRUTH — NOT
TECHNICALITIES

In the halls of justice the only justice is in the halls.

LENNY BRUCE

It is the task and duty of the intellectual to recall and preserve historical possibilities which seem to have become utopian possibilities — that is it is his task to break the concreteness of oppression in order to open the mental space in which this society can be recognized as what it is and does.

HERBERT MARCUSE

Mr. Kunstler said, "I thought the object of a trial was the truth—not technicalities."

But Judge Hoffman ruled that Mr. Abernathy could not take the stand.

Leading across the lectern, Mr. Kunstler then told the Judge:

"I think what you have just said is about the most outrageous statement I have ever heard from a bench, and I am going to say my piece right now, and you can hold me in contempt right now if you wish to.

"You have violated every principle of fair play when you excluded Ramsey Clark from that witness stand." (Judge Hoffman barred Mr. Clark, the former United States Attorney General, from the stand last Wednesday on the ground that he could make no relevant contribution to the case.)

'I Am So Outraged'

"You can't tell me that Ralph Abernathy cannot take the stand today because of a technicality of whether I made a representation," Mr. Kunstler continued. "That representation was made in perfect good faith with Your Honor. I did not know that Reverend Abernathy was back in the country. We have been trying to get him for a week and a half to be the last witness in this case.

"I am trembling because I am so outraged. I haven't been able to get this out before, and I am saying it now, and then I want you to put me in jail if you want to.

"I have sat here for four and a half months and watched the objections denied and sustained by Your Honor and I know that this is not a fair trial. I know it in my heart.

"I am going to turn back to my seat with the realization that everything I have learned throughout my life has come to naught, that there is no meaning in this court, that there is no law in this court, and these men are going to jail by virtue of a legal lynching and that Your Honor is wholly responsible for that, and if this is what your career is going to end on, if this is what your pride is going to be built on, I can only say to Your Honor, 'Good luck to you.'"

The New York Times
2/3/70

Untraditional Law Group Assisting Anti-Establishment Forces

By SIDNEY E. ZION

Traditionally, it would probably be called Smith, Stavis, Kunstler, Kinoy & Weiss. But there is nothing traditional about the town's newest law firm, situated, with characteristic disregard for the niceties, in a floor-through walk-up on Ninth Avenue at 42d Street.

And then again it's not really a law firm. Imagine a law firm where the staff is on salary but the partners work for nothing? And the clients pay no fees? And nobody's afraid to lose cases?

I fact, it's the Law Center for Constitutional Rights, a coalition of experienced lawyers and young staff counsel who represent people and organizations in The Movement.

A Busy Time at Hand

It is, thus, a conglomerate, and as such it is experiencing the same governmental and popular onslaughts that have besieged the business conglomerates lately.

"We're in a rough period, and it's going to get worse,"

Morton Stavis, a director and one of the four originators of the law center, said the other day. "The Justice Department is clearly bent on a program of repression, as are local police chiefs and prosecutors. We've got plenty of work to do here."

Mr. Stavis, at 54, the "elder" of the organization, is a successful corporation lawyer from Newark who three years ago decided with three other civil rights lawyers to "institutionalize" the relationship the four men had in various black and radical legal causes.

The three others are William M. Kunstler, who since the early nineteen-sixties has been involved in most major civil rights litigation; Prof. Arthur Kinoy of the Rutgers University Law School, who was Mr. Kunstler's law partner and handled most of the appellate and Supreme Court work involved in those cases, and Benjamin E. Smith, a New Orleans lawyer who led the "Mississippi Challenge," an effort to seat a black Mississippi Congressional

delegation three years ago.

"We were spending a lot of time on the phones with each other," Mr. Stavis said, "so we thought why not organize a shop, raise some money to hire a staff and really do something bigger?"

As a result, the men opened an office in Newark on a budget of $40,000 provided by lawyer friends. Last month, with a budget of $120,000—also private donations—they moved to New York, where a staff of five young lawyers, three secretaries and a full-time administrator at the center now handle scores of actions throughout the country.

The center also has a mailing list of 500 lawyers who receive continually copies of briefs and complaints.

Mr. Weiss, who spends his afternoons at the law center developing his theories of "international police brutality"—he believes, for example, that any Vietnamese victims of American brutality should be able to sue for damages—gave perhaps the most succinct definition of

the center's work and philosophy.

'Affirmative Litigation' Listed

"We say to the institutions of this country," he said, "that this is how you're supposed to do it and damn it, now do it that way."

To realize that purpose the center has used the technique of "affirmative litigation," which seeks to stop alleged governmental incursions on liberty through court injunctions rather than wait on prosecutions that must then be defended before juries. The latter course results in delays that often cripple dissent.

For example, the center is attempting to enjoin Texas authorities from prosecuting a black militant for murder under the state's Riot Control Act, which provides that one who instigates a riot is responsible for the acts that occur in the riot.

The Texas defendant, Floyd Nichols, was concededly many miles from the shooting of a policeman at the time of the riot but was

prosecuted because he had months earlier spoken on the Texas Southern University campus urging student activity.

Though the law center's partners do not get paid, the young staffers earn from $8,500 to $10,500 a year. Three—Michael Fayer, Carl Borege and William Bender — studied under Professor Kinoy at Rutgers. The others are Nancy Stearns, a recent graduate of New York University Law School and Beth Livezey, who received her law degree in June from the Vanderbilt University Law School.

It is the intention of the center that the young lawyers stay a maximum of four years. "We don't want people making a career here," Mr. Stavis says. "We want to help them, give them the benefit of our experience and then see them go on elsewhere."

The New York Times

11/19/69

LAW AND THE RADICAL LAWYER
by Ken Cloke

Ken Cloke is Executive Secretary of the National Lawyers Guild. He is active in counselling conscientious objectors and draft refusers.

Law is a function of power, and just as the system of colonialism leaves its mark on colonialist and colonized alike, the law represents a pathology of oppression and privilege and describes a single relationship from two different but concurrent points of view, both from the standpoint of power. Two classes come before the court; one as defendant with 'rights' but without the means to enforce them, the others as enforcers or detractors, who examine, arbitrate, dispute, weight, balance and enforce the right, or determine it to be unenforceable. These are the actors whose faces are before us, but they are by no means the actually interested parties. Who makes the law the superficially powerful arbitrate? Who enforces it? Why and how does it change? Who can change it? These questions, directed at the nature of legal power, are essential to answer if lawyers are to consider using law as a means toward social change.

POWER

If we are to define power or attempt to deal with it as radicals and revolutionaries we must begin by seeing that the law is only a means of settling certain kinds of disputes, and that there are limits within which it operates. If power is a description of the ability to produce a desired result, then it can be understood in acts of omission as well as commission, in stalling for time and expediting results, in addition to thousands of other legal procedures, strategems and techniques.

Law is one aspect of control by the major wielders of force and coercion. Its primary purposes are the quelling of violence and civil strife, and the orderly processing of claims of competing capitalists for more money through rules drawn by capitalists in accordance with 'custom'. Almost every aspect of the law has to do with money or money claims. Most of the Constitution does not concern the freedoms of Americans. Those sections were only amended on by mass action. Most of it concerns business, structure and finances of government. Similarly, most of the law is of, by and for the wealthy, who, at every stage of the proceedings, are afforded more than the poor. Furthermore, the law has always been structured in favor of the power elite. It is a condition for the existence of law that there be a ruling class, in precisely the same way that the state relies upon the existence of a ruling class, and upon the existence of class society. All are relationships of power, for the purpose of maintaining property relationships and increasing advantage to some by decreasing it for others.

"The great problems are in the streets." — Nietzsche
"Legal relations . . . are rooted in the material conditions of life" — Marx

To say, however, that power is the ability to produce a desired result is not sufficient, since power, like freedom, does not exist in a vacuum, but can only be exerted at certain times in certain ways. There was very little contract law before the nascence of the market, because it was not necessary. The power of enforcing contracts and the freedom to contract came into being at the same time, when it became necessary that people contract for goods in order that they might better survive. The laws against sedition and criminal anarchy (i.e. the power to control it) came into being when necessary for the survival of the state. It is possible to conclude that power is freedom, not in the sense that the ruling class uses it when it speaks of freedom, but in the way it actually uses it when it stacks the legal system the way it wishes. The way freedom is defined is all but fact in the United States: slaves are free if they can have more than one party to vote one of two masters into power, and criticize their actions in the masters' press.

Law is an aspect of the exertion of power by one class against another. Law is the rationalization of force, coercion, and murder, and the primary means by which obedience is exacted. A judicial system arises and flourishes when, where, and to the extent that class interests cannot be reconciled. Thus, the judicial system is not only an attempt on the part of the ruling class to provide a forum for the resolution of class disputes. It is an attempt to control the outcome of those disputes by making sure that those with greater wealth stand the better chance of winning, and by making itself party, law-maker, prosecutor, judge, jury and hangman.

The law is, has been, and will become whatever those who exercise power wish it to be, recognizing the necessity of maintaining their power and the logical outcome of their acts. In fact, however, what appears to be in the interests of the powerful may in fact lead to loss of power. The exercise of power by a few must either flow from the coercion of the many, or their belief in the possibility of change. In fact, the exercise of power in the latter case does allow for recognition and absorption of countervailing power, which does produce some social change. It does not and will not stand for a transfer of power against the interests of the class which has controlled it. The propertied will not allow the propertyless to abolish property, but they might recognize enough of a threat of abolition to part with some of it.

For those who believe the official slogan of the ruling class — that we are a government of laws and not men — Anatole France once answered by describing how 'the law, in its majestic equality, forbids the rich as well as the poor to sleep under bridges.' The law assumes the form of a neutral zone between the patrician and the plebian, and many of its more inspiring slogans attempt to foster this image, such as 'equal protection', 'justice under the law', 'constitutional guarantees', 'innocent until proven guilty', etc. There are many states which make a big show of affording certain 'rights' to indigents (such as the right to a court-appointed attorney who may spend a total of only five minutes on your case, give you wholly incorrect advice, and send you away) and at the same time convict a man for being poor (vagrancy).

In fact, as Holmes stated, the life of the law has not been logic, but experience. The experience has been the exercise of power and the administration of class struggle. In this way, the law is an expression of political ideology, as well as an instrument of suppression.

SOCIAL CHANGE

With this beginning of an understanding of the nature of law, the logic of our position forces us to question to what extent law can be used as an instrument of social change, and to what extent the law reacts upon and affects the basic relationships between people which in turn are reflected in any legal system. As someone once said, in many cases you can tell more about a society from the kinds of people in its prisons and its mental institutions than from those on the outside. It is also true that there is a correlation between laws passed and social facts. Kolakowski, in his 'Conspiracy of the Ivory Tower Intellectuals', states that 'if the commandment "Thou shalt not steal" becomes vital in a society, it means that the society has created the need to steal on a large scale." Brown vs. Board of Education did not overrule Plessy vs. Ferguson merely because the Supreme Court suddenly saw how wrong it had been in its interpretation of the wording of the 14th Amendment. A change in political, economic and social (i.e. productive) relationships between black and white over the course of several decades was what produced the change in the Supreme Court. Was the eight-hour day legislated because Congress and corporate power felt they were wrong in the past or because men fought for it? Did anyone ever legislate or litigate any question removed from social reality? It doesn't make sense to believe, with the utopian, that you can conquer by good works alone, or that the law will change if you can just demonstrate that discrimination exists.

At the same time, law has some utility to those interested in social change, particularly during 'parliamentary' periods of struggle, as opposed to 'revolutionary' periods of struggle. The dialectic of consciousness and action, of theory and practice, requires certain forms of action consistent with one's awareness of the nature of the problem, and a close correlation between strategy and tactics. For example, in the beginning stages of the civil rights movement, the lowest common denominator of the collective consciousness of those who participated in that movement was that the 'enemy' was Woolworth or Kress or Trailways, since the object was the right to a hamburger or the right to sit up front or use the drinking fountain or john of the white man. These were the most obvious and immediate badges of submission and had to be exorcised first. Later, as we began to win those battles, we realized that they were not as crucial as we had imagined, and began to alter our conception of the nature of the enemy and therefore our conception of strategy, i.e. how to defeat him. Similar progression in consciousness and action is true, I think, of all movements, and those transformations affect the structure of movement organizations as well as their political content. Structure and political consciousness, when pitted against the 'enemy' describes the arena of struggle. The mode of that struggle, however, is quite often legal. Since the law is an attempt to reconcile conflict it is clear that certain things will happen:

1. Those who refuse to quit the struggle or recognize the authority of the law will be prosecuted;
2. Lawyers will attempt to translate the terms of the struggle into legal usage and secure victories there; and
3. Both in offense and defense lawyers will be needed who will attempt to pursue certain so-called 'loopholes' in the law and simultaneously 'make good law'.

THE USES OF LAW

The utility of the law to the movement exists because the way a lawyer handles a case may have a profound effect on the ability of that movement to effectively engage in battle. It is important to recognize, however, that it is possible to use the law to confound the law, but not to totally alter the relationships it monitors. Whatever loopholes exist are either tolerated as 'the price of democracy', or rapidly changed, either by legislation or case law, with the court subtly filling in the void by stating that Congress could not have meant to leave such a hold in enforcement; therefore the courts, in their discretion', may fill it.

By creating new remedies, stalling for time, expediting trials, using the press, treating the courtroom as a classroom, and, where possible, getting people off or reducing sentences, the lawyer may have an affect on the ability of those within the movement to continue their political work. The lawyer ought not, however, to delude himself into thinking that he can work justice without the straws of power. Any legal change which is wrought is not secured by or through the brilliance of counsel or his performance before a magistrate, but only by the successes of the movement. If you have not already convinced a judge that discrimination is wrong (no longer necessary), he will not be convinced by a summation of the evidence. Thus, if one is in basic antagonism to the system, he is outside the help of the law. If he has incurred the anger of the state, and if he has begun to be effective, he will be prosecuted for being effective if nothing else can be found. To illustrate, in Catch-22 Clevinger incurs the wrath of Lt. Scheisskopf, and one day he stumbled on the way to class; the next day he was formally charged with "breaking ranks while in formation, felonious assault, indiscriminate behavior, mopery, high treason, provoking, being a smart guy, listening to classical music and so on" ... 'As a member of the action board, Lt. Schiesskopf was one of the judges who would weigh the merits of the case against Clevinger as presented by the prosecutor. Lt. Scheisskopf was also the prosecutor. Clevinger had an officer defending him. The officer defending him was Lt. Scheisskopf.'

Many radicals frequently refer to our democratic traditions, while the history of radicalism in the United States is also eloquent proof of its undemocratic traditions. We are all familiar with its record of suppression from the Zenger case through the Dred Scott decision, the Civil Rights cases, the Palmer raids, Sacco and Vanzetti, the jailing of Debs, the Smith Act and the McCarren Act cases, to name only a few. What is the history of these legal battles? How were lawyers helpful to the movements of their times?

Within the last 10 years it is possible to see how lawyers acted and reacted in at least four different kinds of movements with different levels of consciousness ranging from the role of the Smith Act lawyers, to the Southern sit-in attorneys, and the Northern sit-in attorneys.

From a paper prepared for the Radicals in the Professions conference, June 1967

Demo Uniform

Demonstrations are seldom peaceful. Police riot, people try to take over the streets—since there is never clear central leadership when people are running in the streets, it is important to get a small group of friends and move with them at all times. If you are alone you will have much more trouble deciding what to do.

BOOK FOR A FIGHTING MOVEMENT

By Jomo Raskin

A BOOK FOR A FIGHTING MOVEMENT
Liberation News Service, 160 Clarmont Ave, New York, N.Y. 10027. 75c.

Books save lives. An Englishman in Africa kept a charging rhinoceros at bay by stuffing his copy of Aristotle down his throat.

Profusely illustrated, black-and-red-covered, "The Bust Book" is a 76-page paperback which fits snugly into a back pocket. It isn't much use as a blunt instrument against a rhinoceros, but it is indispensible to the movement.

It can be used against cops. It can help you avoid arrests, it can help you after you've been arrested. It's what's been needed all along. It was missed at Columbia, at Chicago, at San Francisco State—wherever there are cops and judges, injunctions and subpoenas.

As the movement grows and repression mounts, it will be more and more valuable. It should be carried everyplace, put on with clothes in the morning. You should bust your ass to read it. It's as revolutionary as the little red book, as American

as Thoreau's "Civil Disobedience." "The Bust Book" embodies the spirit of the movement. It is published anonymously. It is a communal effort, the work of writers, artists and photographers who don't want recognition for individual efforts. They want to aid the movement and are part of the movement.

"The Bust Book" is authoritative. The authors know the intricacies of the law. From experience in the courts as people in other states will have to make adjustments. But there are basic insights applicable throughout the U.S.

Short interviews with people who were in Chicago last August, at New York's Stop the Draft Week a year ago December and with Abbie Hoffman, offer particular and revealing accounts of confrontations with cops. People will not want to act as Abbie acts, but his words are joyful and his sense that legal institutions must not be legitimatized is indispensable.

There are nine chapters, from freedom, through arrest, jail, arraignment, bail and trial strategy. There are special sections on drugs and for people under 21. In the last chapter—"Don't Talk—By Any Means Necessary"—the authors write, "So far all that is required of most of us is that we

keep our mouths shut. This is the beginning of self defense for our movement."

"The Bust Book" looks honestly at severe problems which face the movement, but isn't alarmist. The authors aren't afraid to speak of repression, but know that care and calm organization, rather than hysterical alarm, is needed.

"The Bust Book" is a whole world. Its sketches, photographs and poems are as essential as its facts about the law. This movement is for liberation. The society is unmasked and at the same time a new society is in the making. "The Bust Book" reveals the law as it works, and offers a community of struggle, comradeship. There are photographs of New York Panthers outside the criminal court building, students at San Francisco State, plainclothes cops arrests in the ghetto. Eldridge and Che are here too. The actors and scenes before us on the page offer the realities of contemporary history. Illustrations from "Alice in Wonderland" and Blake's poem "The Garden of Love" mock the absurdity of the law and "justice," and cheer us at the same time.

kaleidoscope summer 1969

Thoughts On The Movement

Who Does The Movement Move?

by JOHN McDERMOTT

Terry was 18 and a draftee. I met him and three of his buddies atop a machine gun bunker north of the "Iron Triangle" and it was there that we talked. Characterically for a Movement writer, I had spent my time so far in Viet Nam talking only to officers. They knew the same colleges I did, the same books, the same music. It was easier to talk to them and anyway they know more about the war. Finally, however, I determined to talk to some ordinary soldiers. I am glad I did. They taught me very little about the war but an enormous amount about our Movement.

Like most young combat troops I came to meet, Terry and his friends were at first more anxious to hear my views on things than to give their own, but eventually they talked a great deal about their own lives and about the war, and about the draft, Berkeley and the Movement. Terry was by far the most articulate of the four and as we talked on and on through they night, pausing only to watch some strafing helicopters to the south, to listen to outgoing howitzer rounds or to scrutinize the wire barrier 30 meters away, his role as accepted spokesman for the others became more marked. My admiration grew apace.

He had gotten married immediately on receipt of his induction notice. This is a common reaction among young draftees trying to retain at least some link to a familiar civilian world. For Terry, the well-being of his frightened 17-year-old wife placed a heavy burden on his already busy and dangerous life as a combat infantryman. Most U.S. casualties in Viet Nam are inflicted on the infantry battalions which, almost alone among American units, venture outside the mammoth fortified camps that now scar the Vietnamese countryside. Terry was generally aware that these battalions, which total only 75,000 men at one time, were taking 85,000 casualties a year. More

pointedly, in his own platoon only 17 of the original 35 GI's were left after 5 months of combat. Out on patrols and other operations for 3 days of every 5, battling the ever-present mines, mortars and snipers, Terry had very few "interesting experiences" with which the reassure his young wife, and even less time to write about them. Yet he understood that his daily letters were essential to allay the impotent terror she felt and thus he assumed the burden of making sure that every day — even in his absence — a letter of his would be mailed the girl, full of reassurance and affection and topped off with a fund of stories — entirely made up — of the dull rounds of his placid army life.

Of all the soldiers I met Terry was most unusual for his character and intelligence. But in one respect he was typical of the others. His life was dominated by his immediate problems and those of his family, just as it had been before he came into the Army. Then as now it was enough merely to try to do his job and take care of his family. Staying alive in Viet Nam was a new problem but not fundamentally different from the others. He had neither the time nor the inclination to reflect on the difficulties presented him by an incomprehensible fate (he called it "bad luck" and "the breaks"). Handling them was a full time job; he didn't always succeed in it.

What significance has the Movement got for people like Terry? Not just soldiers, though them too, but for all the people of this country whose names don't count in the *Times* ads and whose energy and attention are largely dominated by the demands of their daily lives?

Just before being shipped off to Asia, the Movement, in the person of some university peace demonstrators, approached Terry and his buddies in Oakland. The GI's were so disgusted with the "draft-dodgers" that they wanted to beat them up but were satisfied merely to push them around and curse at them. People who "weren't willing to fight for their country" were not worth trouble with the MP's.

The four suspected I was anti-war, deducing their conclusion from the fact that (a) I was a professor, (b) they hadn't heard of *Viet-Report* and, especially, (c) I had long hair. (Every unit I stayed with in Viet Nam coyly offered me the free services of its barber.) When my passionate disagreement about the demonstrators confirmed their conjecture, their friendliness was undiminished. In their eyes the fact that I was in Viet Nam and, for the moment anyway, at a forward defense post apparently entitled me to have any opinion I wanted about anything at all. They turned out to be anxious to talk about the war and our discussion soon ranged freely over the whole Viet Nam controversy but came back again and again to the draft.

They were very much aware of the inequities of the draft. They knew all the connections between being less well off than others, doing less well in school, marrying earlier, getting poorer jobs, earning less and having fewer opportunities for training and advancement later. They realized that others were making it at home while they chanced death or mutilation in Viet Nam—and yet they bore no anger for the lucky ones. Their anger was reserved for the "draft-dodgers."

Under the pressure of counter-arguments Terry made a very curious distinction. You had to accept the principle that it was right "to fight for your country." Terry couldn't understand people who didn't accept that; there had to be something wrong with them. But once you accepted the principle, he thought it was alright to weasel on the consequences. In fact, he admired those who did so and got away with it.

Only stupid guys voluntarily went into the Army. You tried anything you could to get out of it: trick knees, "going queer," playing at being crazy, influence, anything. But you had to accept the principle of fighting for your country and if "the breaks" went against you, you went to Viet Nam and fought—no questions asked and no complaints.

I tried a different tack; it was a dirty war and the Saigon Government a gang of cut-throats. They agreed with enthusiasm, rivalling one another with stories illustrating the point. They thought worse of LBJ than I did and seemed content that the real reason for the war was that somebody was getting rich on it. They weren't sure exactly who and didn't seem to care.

For most of 8 hours we went 'round these same points, but they wouldn't budge. Terry understood the alternatives just as clearly as I did. Draft-card burners showed more guts than "2-S Hawks"; the war was bad for America and for Viet Nam. Still, he didn't like "draft-dodgers" and "demonstrators" and you had to fight for your country. Terry seemed aware of the contradiction he was caught in. He accepted a principle whose consequences he knew were evil. Being an intelligent and reasonable man he found ways to mitigate the consequences: he called them fate. But the principle—and the contradiction—stood undisturbed Why? Why couldn't he bring himself to oppose a war and a draft system of which he himself was a conscious victim?

Intellectually, Terry had a far closer grasp of the war's evil than a majority of Movement people. Morally, his courage in facing the life dealt him was

not less than that of David Mitchell or Dennis Mora. If he couldn't break with the war system, we can't expect his friends and comrades to do so either, and that's the point. The roots of Terry's inability to oppose the war can't be found in his personal inadequacies. We have to look for them instead in the net of social relationships which bind him into a passive acceptance of his fate.

An upper middle class boy is nurtured by his family and school experiences to think himself capable of dealing with the decisive components of his life. Terry isn't. A privileged boy gains sufficient confidence in himself, in his social place and in his judgment of events so that he comes to assume a competence to control his own destiny. Within a university environment which, for all its faults, exaggerates this competence, and within a social world made up of others like himself, it is not strange to find students of average intelligence and character able to pierce the veils which surround government behavior and with courage enough to oppose it.

By contrast the family experiences of lower middle class and blue collar boys are proverbially authoritarian. Their school experiences emphasize the value of "staying in line" and out of trouble. The likelihood of early marriage, uncertain job prospects, the great certainty of being drafted and the pressure of like-situated friends all combine to teach them the same lesson. Thus, even gifted boys like Terry bend before a social system whose oppressiveness they early learn they cannot effectively control.

These are matters of common knowledge even for college freshmen but not, apparently, for our Movement. Terry cannot accept principles of behavior, however noble sounding, which do not have sanction from the authorities which dominate his life. That is the path to certain trouble and all his life he's been taught to avoid such trouble. He knows, for example, he has not been properly trained to deal with political questions, and he knows he and his buddies haven't the skills and resources for political organization. His own limited experience leaves him believing that politics must be either a racket or nonsense; a racket

he can't master, or nonsense with which he wisely had better have nothing to do. Thus, for boys like Terry, not to have anything to do with the Movement is a sign of intelligence and good sense. And, when Movement people preach politics at him, like rich men urging paupers to grow rich, he has a perfectly natural and commendable reaction to them; he wants to beat them up.

There is no place for Terry in the Movement and it isn't his fault. That's the point which must be driven home for when we realize that then we'll realize how much the Movement is still a preserve for the children of the over-privileged and a vehicle for their social vision and social ambitions. Rhetorically, the Movement is democratic and humane but socially, and therefore fundamentally, it remains the preserve of the few.

This conclusion may appear at first strange and unfounded. If anything has characterized the Movement it has been its resistance to manipulation and standardization, the central thrusts of our national life. Under slogans such as "participatory democracy" or, more crudely and colorfully, "Do Not Bend, Fold, Spindle, or Mutilate," the Movement has tried to assert the primacy of people and their wishes against the needs of an increasingly rational and mechanical system. Noble words, however, are belied by ignoble deeds. From the fact that the Movement has no place for Terry we must see that its noble demands have only the *intention* to be an *avant garde* political program for the whole country. In their *social character* they consist so far merely of a defense of the traditional life style and values of the old professional middle class.

The narrow class character of the Movement asserts itself in other ways. The high status assigned the "organizer" has managerial overtones in spite of the disclaimer on manipulation. The propensity for organizing only the poor and the black smacks of the settlement house missionary mentality of the Progressive Era among the young ladies of the best families. Currently the writing of Regis Debray is all the rage because it suggests that small bands of revolutionary intellectuals, largely unrelated to mass organization and effective political analysis, can carry off a successful revolution. In context this must be seen as a flimsy attempt to make a virtue out of our social isolation. Most convincing of all perhaps is the Movement's dogged defense of its peculiar life-style against the needs of its politics. The virtues of a revolutionary are more akin to those of the soldier than of the hippy, but a hippy life style for all remains near, if not quite at the center of the Movement's working political vision.

There is no doubt at all that, squarely faced with a choice, the Movement would opt enthusiastically for the "masses" and against any variant of elitism. It remains the only organized group in the country which would do so, but how can we put flesh on these thin bones? How can the Movement relate itself to people like Terry and become a vehicle for his aspirations?

In the first place, it has to learn that without a privileged place for him, the Movement has no right to its rhetoric. Where Terry actually is, is the home, good or bad, of democracy. The task before the Movement is not to create an ideal democracy for those who "know where it's at." The task is to take

people like Terry, the real life Terry with all his inadequacies, distractions and prejudices, and shove him down the road which leads to political power.

Secondly, we have to learn that achieving political power is not a matter of "building consciousness." Terry has all the consciousness he needs. He knows exactly how bad things are because he is the one on the receiving end of this society's injustice, the best vantage point for building consciousness. What Terry needs are direct and familiar ways out of the trap he knows he's in, ways that he understands, ways that are neither nonsense nor a racket. In his eyes, electoral politics is the biggest racket; demonstrations the worst nonsense.

Thirdly, strategies which emphasize "creative disorder" and other scattered forays against established authority are of no use to Terry. The view that the creation of social disorder and chaos will lead unjust authorities to make improvements is not very compelling to anybody. But, for Terry, whose life is a continuous struggle, frequently unsuccessful, to maintain a creative order among family, job, mortgage and other responsibilities, any disorder, creative or Debrayan, can only be seen as a threat to the thin fabric of his life.

This last fact gives us a clue as to how the Movement can be of use to Terry. The everyday life of ordinary Americans has been struck disordering blows by the political and economic history of the years since World War II. Families already hard-pressed to meet the exigencies of daily life have been forced to adjust to an enormous number and variety of corrosive changes. Television and the schools have created alien and often dismaying social models which their children ape. The intricacies of specialized training and the draft system leave them unable to assist their grown children except by inadequate finances and excessive fatuous advice. New consuming, residence and working patterns disrupt the old harmony of family, neighborhood and civic life, and the disruption is confirmed and deepened by an alien culture purveyed through incomprehensible and uncontrollable mass media. Lurking nearby are recurring racial and international crises whose threat is sharpened rather than obscured by the murkiness of their origins. Most important of all, the fundamental impulse of all these disordering novelties stems not from the inner needs of people's lives and aspiration but from the evermore insistent demands of an industrial—political—military system bent on creating the same disorders on a world-wide scale.

The distorted and fear-ridden politics of post-World War II America is a projection of the distortion and fear which afflict ordinary Americans as they try to bring life-serving harmony to their daily activities. Even Terry's seeming mindless clinging to a vague patriotic slogan is evidence of this. It is an attempt to impose harmony and value over chaotic circumstances which threaten his family, his future and his very life itself.

It is at the level of fundamental social relationships, rather than in electoral "racketeering" or Debrayan fantasy that the Movement must locate its fundamental tasks. Social organizing among the Terry's of our country rather than political missionary work among the totally poor should be the main, though not the exclusive thrust of our work. We have got to help manipulate social environments so that individ-

uals can learn to be free. Schools must be forced into educating children in how to deal with their neighborhoods, not just the national job-market. High schools should prepare boys and girls to deal with city councils, school boards, police chiefs and draft boards, not just college entrance exams. Neighborhoods have to be recreated and the fundamental services they can perform for families, such as child supervision, mutual self-help and broader social recreation, must be brought into life. People's job lives have to be re-understood and the values of comradeship and craftsmanship re-asserted against the boss's "efficiency." A new people's culture has to be developed, aimed at enhancing the values of life and work and at diminishing the effects of the acquisitive, exploitative and largely sterile culture of the national elite.

For a start we should examine organizations like the VFW, volunteer fire departments, church bowling leagues, the Boy Scouts, PTA's and Rotaries. For all their seeming fecklessness they enter into the real life of our people and provide essential relationships and irreplaceable services for them. Even the American Legion, with its rich fraternal, social, civic, athletic and young people's programs, has ten times more day to day value in the life of our people now than the Movement itself Can't we do better than the Legion?

No more important or difficult tasks face the Movement than these: to close the immense gap between itself and the direct and immediate concerns of our people, to learn in all their concrete detail the social problems which beset them, to trace out their sources, to play a creative role in developing new ways to contend with them, and to fuse these ways into the democratic folk tradition which still persists so strongly among our people.

A Movement which saw these things included among its primary tasks could lay claim to representing the fundamental aspirations of our people. Its voice w   '   be the voice of the American people and the power of its politics irresistible.

Viet Report Sept/Oct 1967

Vocations for Social Change

introduction

Vocations for Social Change is a decentralized clearing house for persons struggling with one basic question: How can people earn a living in America in 1969 and ensure that their social impact is going to effect basic humanistic change in our social, political and economic institutions? Nobody has any "real answers" to this question, but many ideas are being developed out of people's experiences. VSC helps make these ideas available to the general public so that each person's individual search can be enriched.

This newsletter serves as the main gathering point for ideas with which we have come in contact. Not only do we include descriptions of job openings with groups working for social change from a wide variety of view points, but also proposals for new projects that need help in getting started; new ideas that can be developed and adapted in one or many locations; descriptions of places where you can learn more about social action in an educational setting, articles on topics relating to working for social change on a full-time basis, and resource groups and people to contact. What all of the people behind these various ideas have in common is a genuine concern for causing basic change in American institutions.

Informing you of available opportunities for involvement in social change is only part of our goal. We also hope that the information that we have gathered here will stimulate you to think about what new roles need to be created and to consider the possibility of actually finding a new role for yourself. Many more dedicated people are needed if we are to see significant change in our lifetimes.

how V.S.C. works

IF YOU ARE LOOKING FOR A JOB there are many ways that this newsletter can help you. All of the present job openings are found in the <u>Listings</u> section. If you are looking for a particular kind of work or in a specific geographical area, the indexes in the back may be helpful.

The newsletter has other sections that may be useful besides the listings. You may not be able to find a particular job that fits your needs in this issue, but, under <u>Job Finding Agencies</u> you will find other groups who may have a job that you would like.

Many people would rather create their own job than work in an established organization. If you have a vision and need people or money for it to become a reality, ask us to include it in the <u>Proposals</u> section. Hopefully others with similar ideas will respond. If you would like someone to come help you start a project, refer to the <u>Resource People</u> section for more information. Other groups who have information in specialized areas can be found in the <u>Resource Groups</u> section. The <u>Literature List</u> could also serve as a guide to literature in your field of interest.

For those of you who feel a need to develop skills and knowledge that may be helpful in working for social change, we list institutions and other groups geared in that direction in the <u>Educational Opportunities</u> and <u>Apprenticeships</u> sections.

IF YOU WANT TO RECEIVE THE NEWSLETTER we'll be happy to send you a sample copy. We send VSC regularly for six months to people who support us financially with donations of $5.00 or more, or send us monthly pledges. This helps cover the costs of mailing and enables us to send sample copies to those who cannot afford to send any money. Institutions, such as libraries and schools are charged $10.00 a year.

IF YOU WANT TO HELP there are lots of things that can be done. Please see the "What You Can Do" section of this newsletter.

THE ROLE OF THE LOCAL CONTACT is also explained further in the "What You Can DO" section. Briefly, local contacts inform us of the situation in their communities, make their copies of VSC publically available, keep in touch with us about what they are doing, and agree to help the office when outreach is needed. Local contacts are the backbone of the VSC distribution system and they receive the publication regularly. Let us know if you'd like to work with us in this way.

Above and left: American members of the Venceremos Brigade cut sugar cane in solidarity with the Cuban revolution.

local V.S.C. counseling

The main goal of VSC is to encourage people to think about ways they can become involved in working for social change on a full-time basis. We realize that the publication can hardly give you a fair picture of what it is really like to become involved in the projects described. Person to person contact with those who have had experience in areas similar to the VSC listings could well be a partial solution to this communication gap.

So, a few of our friends (we're looking for more) have found experienced social change workers of all kinds in their communities who are willing to share their experiences with people like you. If you are interested in experimental education, for example, you might contact one of the persons we've listed below who may in turn know of someone in their area who has actually taught in a liberated school setting and is available to talk with you about what it was like.

If you live in one of the cities listed below, or are traveling through, get in touch with our contact. Likewise, if you would be able to provide this kind of service to people in your community, let us know.

CALIFORNIA SAN FRANCISCO: Bill Anderson, American Friends Service Committee, 2160 Lake St., 94121; (415) 752-7766.
   HUMBOLDT COUNTY: Doug Glasser, Bell Hill Rd., Eureka 95501; (707) 443-6428.
   SANTA BARBARA: Harvey Haber, 2840 Hidden Valley Ln. 93105; (805) 969-0898.

WYOMING LARAMIE: Dick Putney, U.C.M., 1215 Grand Ave. 82070; (307) 742-3791.

COLORADO DENVER: Nell Sale and Steve Johnson, 1566 High St. #3, 80218; (303) 399-6769.

WISCONSIN MADISON: Patricia McFarland, 211 Langdon St. 53715; (608) 257-2350.

OHIO YELLOW SPRINGS: Marj Leslie, 128 W. Davis St. 45387; (513) 767-1965.

ILLINOIS CHICAGO: Noel Barker, 5301 Cornell St., 60637; (312) 324-2327.

PENNSYLVANIA PHILADELPHIA: Judith Chomsky, Resistance, 2006 Walnut St. 19103; (215) 561-8080.

NEW HAMPSHIRE PORTSMOUTH: Buzz Theberge, 215 Circuit Rd. 03801.

NEW YORK NYC: Marti Roberge, Emmaus House, 241 E. 116 St. 10029; (212) 348-5622.
   BRONX: Gerald Friedberg, Bensalem College, Fordham University, 302 Broadway, 10007; (212) 298-7614.
   ROCHESTER: Elaine Greene, 32 Sanford St. 14650; (716) 771-6753.

resource people.

The people listed below have had experience setting up self-supporting social change efforts. They are now available to help others interested in **starting** similar ventures. Please consider adding yourself to the list if you **have some** experiences to share with others.   State where and when you can travel, and how much (if any) money you would need in order to travel. Please note that some of the persons listed below are members of groups also listed in the RESOURCES (formerly "Coordinating the Movement for Change") section.

education--Shire School in San Francisco is in its third year and its teachers are willing to help all those interested in starting a school, especially with initial legal hassles. Especially interested in anyone owning land or a home who would like to start a day or boarding school in Northern California. ---Contact Bob Bragg, 1342 Masonic St., San Francisco, California 94117; or Malcolm, 1360 Rhode Island St., San Francisco, Ca. 94107.

education, communes -- Gerald Friedberg, a faculty member at Bensalem College in the Bronx, New York, is available to travel anywhere on the Atlantic Coast as a resource person in the fields of experimental schools and intentional communities.   Jerry was instrumental in helping to create the experimental college at the University of California, Davis Campus, and has also been active in the formulation of the Lorillard Children's School -- innovative school for young children which was conceived and begun by Bensalem students and members of the surrounding community. He will need travel expenses. ---CONTACT Dr. Gerald Friedberg, Bensalem College, Fordham University, Bronx, N.Y. 10458, (212) 298-7614.

women's liberation--Nancy Hancock plans to travel full-time between May and June,1970 with a 30 minute sound and slide show called, "Look Out Girlie! Women's Liberation Gonna Get Your Mama." designed as an introduction to the thought and feelings of the Women's Liberation movement.   It has been used successfully as a conference opener and as a catalyst to forming women's liberation groups among the white middle class. ---Contact Nancy Hancock, 10 Tulip Lane, Port Washington, New York 11050 (516) 767-5757.

ecology--Terra Nova Marin is an action-oriented ecology group with a year's experience in community ecology projects, such as stream cleanups, research, etc. Staff members are willing to travel anywhere in California to encourage people "to form into non-bureaucratic units to take actions leading to a change of attitudes towards the environment among the general public." Help needed with travel expenses. ---Contact Ernest Marris, Terra Nova Marin, 19 Cypress, Kentfield, California 94904.

technical assistance--Jack Jacques and friends want to share expert technical knowhow with anyone trying to build a business in and for the radical community. Skills include: design engineering, industrial engineering, cost accounting, payroll, warehousing, production engineering. Want to "establish a dialogue between technically oriented people and the community which we must serve." Can travel in L.A. and Orange County without cost. Ask that technical materials be supplied. ---Contact Jack Jacques, 1158 Magnolia, Manhattan Beach, California 90266, 213-545-5429.

education--Harvey Haber, Allan Granberd and Scott Eckersley are willing to travel anywhere in the country if expenses can be met, to share experience in free schools, help set up schools, and discuss the potential of free schools. ---Contact Harvey Haber, 2840 Hidden Valley Lane, Santa Barbara, California 93105.

free church--Staff members of Free Church of Berkeley can travel for expenses and/or small honorarium.   Trying to set example of a radically ecumenical church built on concerns for (1) service to oppressed; (2) peace and liberation; (3) community. Glad to help radicalize traditional churches, stabilize underground ones. ---Contact Emily Waymouth, Free Church Publications, PO Box 9177, Berkeley, California 94709, (415) 549-0649.

distributing alternative publications for a living--Jack Frazier of the Atlantis Distributing Company will be happy to help anyone start a distributing service in another city. ---CONTACT Jack Frazier, 1030 Annunciation Street, New Orleans, Louisiana 70130

alternative institutions

"Alternative Institutions" are attempts to create new and humane ways to fill traditional social needs. They range from "intentional communities" which attempt to define new forms for all social relationships within a community to co-ops which are alternatives to capitalist economic forms. Another example is youth service centers which present alternatives to juvenile halls. Experimental schools and the underground press are also alternative institutions to their mainstream counterparts, but there are special sections on education and media. All jobs listed in VSC are aimed at stimulating basic institutional change. Thus groups listed in this section must show that their work is not just an escape from mainstream institutions, but rather, it is designed to have a strong impact towards reforming or revolutionizing its mainstream counterparts.

MIGRANT NURSES

Registered nurses wanted to work with indigenous Spanish-speaking migrant women, training them as health aides, and traveling with them in a mobile unit through Utah, Colorado, Oregon, and Washington for the summer. The nurses will return to Texas after the summer with the migrant workers to help set up needed health services. The project is to last about a year (or at least through January). The nurses should have some working experience. A knowledge of Spanish is very helpful. Salary is $6,500 a year plus living expenses while on the road. ---Contact Vaughn Spaulding; 1441 Broadway; Boulder, Colorado 80302; (303) 442-7661, home, or 443-2211, office. Call collect.

I SAID KEEP ON TRUCKIN'...

American Draft Dodgers putting together copies of "Manual For Draft-Age Immigrants to Canada". *Toronto—1968*

EDUCATION AND TRAINING FOR COOPERATIVES

More and more poor people in the South are turning to cooperatives, asking the question, "How can we build something of our own?" E.T.C is one answer. It is an independent, non-governmental program. We began with handcrafts, training the crafts coops that market their products through the Liberty House of Jackson, Mississippi. We need people to help us develop these crafts coops and branch out into the endless other coop possibilities (buying clubs, credit unions, stores, child care, housing, etc.). We spend about half our time in Jackson, designing new products and developing new educational materials, and the rest in small communities all over the state. Those interested need the skills of teaching coop principles, handcrafts, bookkeeping, writing, administration or other skills of cooperation. Persons should plan to stay for at least six months. Salary is $40-50 per week, which is plenty to live on here. We'll find you a place to live... Come join us. We have been able to hire one C.O.; it may be possible to hire others. ---CONTACT David Fleming, P.O. Box 3345, Jackson, Mississippi 39207.
(601) 352-7487

education/research

TEACHER CORPS

Need associate director with B.A. or M.A. in education, social work or social sciences. Work with active radical caucus trying to organize radical groups in School of Education, University of Missouri-Kansas City, teaching in local free school, preparing experimental school, democratizing and restructuring Teacher Corps--in short, system subversion. Chief official role is to help run Teacher Corps community projects, but write your own job description. Pay up to $10,000. ---Contact Al Sargis; 900 East 29th Street, Apt. 1; Kansas City, Missouri 64109; (816) WE 1-7016.

INTERNATIONAL LIBERATION SCHOOL

Three areas of study are included in ILS: (1) Political Education in the Marxist tradition is conducted in small groups organized around reading/discussion. "We don't push a 'hard line' but instead try to improve our basic ability to think through issues." (2) Organizing skills, such as graphic arts and printing, medical skills, research, etc., are offered so that organizers need not depend upon over-used bureaucracies for leadership, but can be self-sufficient. (3) Building for Action. Collectives and communes are fostered as the basic units of the revolutionary movement. People are involved in organizing projects of all kinds, from high school student unions to community centers. To discuss the particulars, contact Linda Morse, 1925 Grove Street, Berkeley, California 94704, (415) 549-3977.

THE TEACHERS INCORPORATED

A private, non-profit corporation which locates cadres of teachers in school districts with critical educational and political problems (community control, relevant curriculum, workable integration, a brilliant principal or superintendent with a stagnant system to overcome, radically experimental education, etc.) and helps swing the balance. By-passes conventional teachers education and certification and creates a "community of learning" on each project. Teachers Inc. is looking for people to teach in elementary, junior high, and high schools; live in the neighborhoods of their schools; and work with parents and in community affairs. Must have a liberal arts degree, experience in teaching or tutoring and in cross-cultural projects for social change, and be willing to work for at least two years. There are projects operating now in New York City and Long Island; in the 1969-70 school year, there will be additional projects in Washington, D.C. and Chapel Hill, North Carolina. Regular salaries paid by the school system; training provided by the corporation starts July 1; ---Contact Jonathan Marks; 35 Market Street; New York, New York 10002; or, better, telephone (212) 267-5470.

media

The listings in this section involve media work, theater, film, the press, etc., etc.

The Great Speckled Bird

Southerners interested in learning how to put out an underground paper are welcome to write the South's largest underground, the Great Speckled Bird. The best way to learn is to some work with us for a while. Subsistence can easily be earned by selling the Bird. CONTACT the Great Speckled Bird, P.O. Box 7946, Atlanta, Georgia 30309, phone (404) 892-8974.

SAN FRANCISCO MIME TROUPE

America's oldest radical theater Co needs a public relations person. Must be able to write and deal effectively with the public over the phonetely. Salary open. A good chance to use your skill positively. ---CONTACT (send resume) The San Francisco Mime Troupe, 450 Alabama St., San Francisco, CA 94110; (415) 431-1984.

FREE DOOR

The San Diego FREE DOOR to Liberation needs help of various kinds. You must be 21 and willing to work for subsistence plus small cash remuneration. No upper age limit. The FREE DOOR is a wide-spectrum liberal-radical underground type newspaper published every two weeks ---CONTACT Dale Herschler, FREE DOOR, 6389 Imperial Avenue, San Diego, California 92114. (714) 262-5324

THE ARMADILLO PRESS

The Armadillo Press is a New Left print shop being set up in Austin, Texas; and if the fund raising continues Armadillo should have a Web-fed press in about three months. They need a pressperson experienced in the operation and repair of a Web offset (most likely a Fairchild or Newsking) to work the shop, or who can come to Austin for a month or two and train people to operate the press. The shop will be an IWW local, owned and run by those who work there. There will be about six full-time and twenty part-time workers... you and they will be on subsistence wages. ---CONTACT Alex Calvert, The Armadillo Press, 802 West 28½ St., Austin, Texas 78705.

PHILADELPHIA RESISTANCE PRINT SHOP

The Resistance Print Shop in Philadelphia needs another full-time printer beginning in February, 1970. Operator must be familiar with 1250 Multilith presses and hopefully an A.B. Dick 385. The hours are long, the pay $25 a week, the strain sometimes great, but we print for much of the movement and hang together. The Print Shop is also looking for a competent jack-of-all-trades to manage the operation starting the same time. This position will be very demanding; it requires bookeeping, ability to do supply ordering, tie together the entire operation and negotiate with the real world. ---CONTACT Mike Griefer, c/o the Philadelphia Resistance Print Shop, 3605 Hamilton St., Philadelphia, PA 19104, (215) 386-8628.

LIBERATION AND WIN MAGAZINES

These movement publications need two people to set up a New York based distribution center and/or mailing network. Commercial outfits screw movement publications. You can do absolutely indispensible work for the movement for social change and earn a living besides. These people will need some business sence and must be willing to work long hours. ---CONTACT David Gelber at Liberation Magizine, or Marris Cakars at Win Magizine, both at 339 Lafayette St., New York, NYC 10012.

The Ft. Dix Four.

peace + the draft

WAR TAX RESISTANCE

WTR needs a full time office manager, someone who will keep the NY headquarters running efficiently. Recruiting and managing volunteers, answering the phone, answering and routing mail, keeping books, filling literature orders, following up on production of buttons and posters, typing--these are a few of the responsibilities involved. Long hours, low pay, the work of five people, and uncertain future, the stimulation of living in NYC, challenge, lively colleagues--these are a few of the miseries and joys. ---CONTACT Bradford Lyttle, WTR, 339 Lafayette St., New York, NY, 10012.

CHICAGO AREA DRAFT RESISTERS

People are needed in work centered around draft resistance, but not necessarily draft resistance. Paid part-time work available within the organization, but this is not guaranteed (printing, coffeehouse, etc) People are encouraged to find or create their own means of support. Communal apartments are in existence, supported by the people who live in them. Programs particularly in need of support: high school organizing, GI work, community based projects and work with media, over and underground, plus draft and military counseling. ---CONTACT CADRE, W. North Ave., 519 Chicago, IL 60610; (312) 664-6895.

QUAKER HOUSE AT FORT BRAGG

Quaker House was conceived as a visible Friends' Peace witness in the city of Fayetteville. The city is almost completely dominated by the Army base at Fort Bragg, the largest Army base in the United States. The House offers a library containing peace literature and a quiet place for reading and conversation. The soldiers of GIs United Against the War in Vietnam use the House regularly for meetings - and work on their newspaper. They staged a 500-people Parade for Peace on October 11, 1969, which was coordinated from Quaker House. The House sponsors a weekly peace vigil at the Federal Building. Groups from colleges, churches and high schools are showing interest in the program. There is draft counseling and draft counselors are being trained. The House has served as an informal center for such social action groups as Fayetteville Poor Peoples' Organization and VISTA. They need a young resident couple, either Friends or individuals sympathetic to Quaker ideals, who will live in the House, develop its program, and maintain its spirit. A small salary is provided. ---CONTACT Daniel T. Young, Cedar Street, Mt. Bolus, Chapel Hill, North Carolina 27514. (919) 942-7058.

UNITED STATES SERVICEMEN'S FUND (formerly S.O.S.)

USSF was founded because American GI's are among the victims of the Vietnam war. Our message to soldiers is that they are still Americans and part of the human community, who can think, act, speak out for themselves as individuals or in concert. We help to provide staff and programs for the following coffee houses or similar projects: The Shelter Half in Tacoma, Washington; the UFO in Columbia, S.C.; the Oleo Strut in Killeen, Texas; the Ft. Dix Coffee House Project in Wrightstown, N.J.; the Home Front in Colorado Springs; a Ft. Knox coffee house to open soon in Louisville, Ky., and the Green Machine near Camp Pendleton, Ca. Young men and women, preferably couples, are needed to work at various projects for subsistence salaries. Prefer people who like to rap, men who've been in the military. Beginning soon in S.F. Bay Area, GI newspaper distribution, film showings for servicemen, etc. ---CONTACT Donna Mickleson, Betsy Strausberg, or Ann Nakamura, USSF, P.O. Box 3061, Oakland, California 94609, (415) 653-5820.

other job-finding agencies
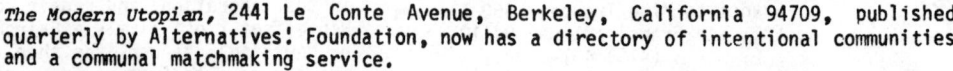

The Modern Utopian, 2441 Le Conte Avenue, Berkeley, California 94709, published quarterly by Alternatives! Foundation, now has a directory of intentional communities and a communal matchmaking service.

C.O. Placement Service, a branch of the Unitarian Universalist Service Committee, Inc., 78 Beacon Street, Boston, Mass. 02108, is dedicated to helping conscientious objectors find work for alternative service. Write Tony Lob, C.O. Placement Officer.

The Commission on Youth Service Projects, Room 830, 475 Riverside Drive, New York, New York 10027, publishes INVEST YOURSELF, the most inclusive available listing of voluntary service projects and placements in the U.S. and abroad. It costs 50¢ a copy, or 65¢, first class.

The New Schools Exchange, 2840 Hidden Valley Lane, Santa Barbara, California 93103, publishes weekly the NEW SCHOOLS EXCHANGE NEWSLETTER, which lists descriptions and needs of new schools, and job applications of people wanting to teach in such schools.

National Service Board for Religious Objectors, 550 Washington Building, 15th and New York Avenue, N.W., Washington, D.C. 20005, publishes CIVILIAN WORK AGENCY LIST FOR CONSCIENTIOUS OBJECTORS, a listing of jobs approved by Selective Service Boards.

Greensheet, Peace Corps, Washington, D.C. 20025, is a listing of jobs appropriate for returned Peace Corps Volunteers. Most of the jobs listed are with federal agencies.

National Association for Community Development, 1424 16th Street, N.W., Washington, D.C. 20036, publishes "Community Development" monthly, a 16-page paper covering federal, state, local, and private news in the field of community development. Its "Job Opportunities" section lists openings in antipoverty, Model Cities, and a wide range of urban and rural development groups.

The National Federation of Settlements and Neighborhood Centers, 232 Madison Avenue, New York, New York 10016, has a job-finding service.

The Talent Bank of the Council of the Southern Mountains, College Box 2307, Berea, Kentucky 40403, is an OEO-funded job-finding agency serving the Appalachian South.

TASCFORCE for Constructive Alternatives Employment Clearing House, c/o David Cohen, 1951 11th Avenue, San Francisco, California 94116, is set up to make scientists and engineers more aware of some of the destructive consequences of their work and help them locate alternative employment. It is actively encouraging employment opportunities that allow socially purposeful use of scientific and engineering talents.

The United Church Board for Homeland Ministries, Personnel Services, 1505 Race Street, Philadelphia, Pennsylvania 19102, offers, without charge, two occasional newsletters - PERSONNEL OPENINGS listing employment opportunities of a service-oriented nature, and PERSONNEL AVAILABLE listing persons seeking such employment.

The Volunteer Information Service, VISTA, Washington, D.C. 20506, lists educational opportunities and jobs that might appeal to ex-VISTAs; most of them are in health, education, and welfare fields, antipoverty programs, local, state, and national governments.

The Teacher Drop-Out Center, University of Massachusetts, Amherst, Mass., was recently organized to act as a clearinghouse for schools, elementary and secondary, public and private, that want the unusual teacher and for teachers who want more freedom in their work. Write Leonard Solo and Stan Barondes at the graduate school of Education U. of Massachusetts, Amherst, Mass. 01002, for more information.

Selections from the *Vocations for Social Change* Newsletter

Ed. Note: Job listings here are not current; they are shown as samples. A sample copy of the *VSC* Newsletter can be had from VSC, Canyon, Calif. 94516

landlords freak
Ann Arbor Rent Strike:Success!

ANN ARBOR, MICH. (MNS) -- The Largest rent strike in American history has weathered its early difficulties and is moving into its second academic year. At one point last spring over 1200 student tenants had withheld $125,000 in rents from the Ann Arbor landlords. Soon the Tenants Union will begin its fall action, undeterred by a "conspiracy" suit filed by the slumlords who have been hardest hit by the strike.

The Tenants Union came into being last January because around the University of Michigan the local landlords have a monopolistic stranglehold on rental property. They have jacked up rents to such an extent that poor people have been virtually driven from the city, and their average annual profit margin is around 20%. (Nationally it is only 8%, which is still 8% too high.) With low-cost "luxury slum" construction and little if any maintenance, landlords are able to pay off their mortgages in only 3 to 6 years. In fact, maintenance is so bad that there have been at least two "shit storm" cases in which human wastes have cascaded through shower heads and light fixtures. The property monopoly is controlled by the Ann Arbor Rental Property Association, made up of the largest landlords and which acts as a price-fixing group. Around the edges of the campus, prices have reached more than $200 per month for a simple two-bedroom apartment.

The rent strike is not being carried out simply to make living a little cheaper for already-affluent students. Instead, it is the Union's hope that organizing can be extended into the larger community, both on housing and other issues. The Union's main demand is to be recognized as a bargaining agent for tenants on all landlord-tenant issues, not just to get lower rents.

So far the most dramatic, and unexpected result of the strike has been the utter failure of the landlords to break it, or even slow it down, in the usually compliant courts. The purely defensive legal strategy, undertaken to prevent striking tenants from being evicted for non-payment of rent, has paid unexpected dividends. The liberal Michigan law entitles each tenant to a jury trial before he can be evicted. Also, the law allows rent reductions to be awarded if the landlord has not kept his housing liveable. Combine these two facts with the usual logjam in the courts, plus the Tenants Union's success in disqualifying two judges who had tie-ins with local landlords, and it is easy to understand why nearly every trial has resulted in rent reductions, and how the Union has been able to delay trials for months. (And even if a tenant is ordered to pay his rent, he can either pay it within 10 days and escape eviction or just move out and force the landlord to sue him AGAIN for the rent!)

One of the more delightful ploys used by the Union is the escrow fund into which tenants pay their rent. This shows the courts that the money is available and will be paid if a judgment is reached. But it is located in a Canadian bank, so that the landlords cannot seize it -- and the interest, at 5% or more, pays most of the Union's expenses.

Physical harassment by landlords has not been much of a problem; the larger ones are too sophisticated to try forcible evictions. However, for formation of the Tactical Mobile Defense Unit by the Union has also frustrated illegal eviction attemps by panic-stricken small-time landlords. The TMDU changes locks on tenants' request, picks locks when landlords try lockouts, and even physically prevents landlords from entering strikers' apartments. It also has passed out leaflets bearing such heart-warming advice as "If the landlord attempts to threaten you, take note of the language he used and warn him that he may be liable for an assault. Warn him that if he touches you he will be liable for a battery. Call any of your fellow tenants within earshot to your assistance. Have a roommate or a neighbor call the police (inform the desk sergeant that somebody is causing a breach of the peace) and the Rent Strike office. Reinforcements, a law student and a Michigan Daily reporter, will be dispatched immediately to your apartment."

Completely flipped out by their failure to collect rents, this summer the landlords filed a conspiracy suit against the Union and 91 strikers. They asked for a summary judgment against the Tenants Union and a preliminary restraining order to stop the strike. Normally they would have gotten it; however, the excellent legal work by the Union not only prevented an order against it from being issued, but also resulted in a court order opening up the landlords' books to the strikers. This past week the landlords, pissed off at how their suit had backfired on them, asked for and got a delay until February 5. They may drop the suit altogether just to prevent the Union from getting at their records.

Meanwhile, the most important task of organizing tenants continues. Only a permanent Tenants Union with bargaining rights can prevent exorbitant rents from being reinstated once the current fervor subsides. One landlord has already made tentative offers of recognition.

Other campuses are ripe for rent strikes; they are already underway at Berkeley and Ohio State. The Tenants Union has nearly finished a detailed manual for strikers. It, plus other information, is available from: Ann Arbor Tenants Union, 1532 Student Activities Building, University of Michigan, Ann Arbor, MI. 48104.

1960
1961
1962
1963
1964
1965
1966
1967
1968
1969

Notes on a Decade Ready for the Dustbin

Carl Oglesby

*T*he idea of trying to visualize ourselves five or ten years from now seems to me hopeless but necessary, so I'm writing a letter instead of a paper just because it seems easier in the former to float, stammer, and skip.

Hopeless—to put it most abstractly—because I don't think we have anything like a predictive science of political economy. We *approach* having an explanatory art of history, I think, and sometimes we can build up a head of steam-bound analogies and go crashing an inch or so through the future barrier, but it always turns out we land sideways or even upside down. And more practically, hopeless because in a situation as sensitive as what the world's in now, mankind as a whole lives under the permanent Terror of the Accidental.

But necessary, too, this idea, because even if we're never going to surpass improvisatory politics, we could still improvise better if we were clearer about ourselves and the country, and the effort to think about the future always turns out to be an effort to think about the present. Which is all to the good. So I'll start with the past—to get a sense of trajectory, if any, or the rhythm of our experience, to see if there's a line of flight:

1960-64

*A*s well the Freedom Rides as Greensboro? But then, as well the desegregation decision as the Freedom Rides . . . etc. Whenever it began, this was the Heroic Period, the movement's Bronze Age. In transition ever since, the movement has yet to prove it will have a Classical Period, but maybe we're on the verge. Essentially, a single-issue reform politics; integration the leading public demand, although underneath that demand, there's a sharply rising sense that a structural maldistribution of wealth won't be corrected by the abolition of Jim Crow. An implicitly radical democratic communitarianism, projected correctly as both a means *and an end* of the movement, can still co-exist with a formless and rather annoyed liberalism because (a) the Peace People are obfuscating the Cold War without yet having become suspicious characters, and (b) the reform tide seems to be running, picking up velocity and mass, and has still to hit the breakwater. But there's a richness in the decentralist idioms of this period that has only been neglected, certainly not exhausted, or even barely tapped, in the intervening half decade of transition.

1965

*V*ery quick, sharp changes, engineered in part by Johnson, in part by self-conscious growth within the movement.

*The war abruptly becomes the leading issue for most white radicals. But not for community organizers, some of whom in fact are bitter about the new preoccupation. This is neither the first nor the last time that this sort of friction develops. What is its general form? A nationalist vs. an internationalist consciousness? It appears that some activists will always tend to visualize the American people mainly as victims, and others will tend to see them as criminal accomplices (passive or not) of the ruling class. This maybe points to an abiding problem for an advanced-nation socialist movement—a problem which will be neither understood nor solved simply by the Trotskyist slogan, "Bring the troops home."

*The teach-ins and the SDS April March on Washington repeat in a compressed time scale the civil-rights movement's growth from Greensboro to Selma. It's in this very brief, very intense period that SDS projects an unabashedly reformist critique of the war, our naive attack on the domino theory being the best illustration of this: "But the other dominos *won't* fall," we insisted, happy to give such reassurance to the Empire.

*SNCC formalizes its transformation from reform to revolution, first, by explicating the connection between racism and the war; and second, by focusing the metaphor of Black Power, which clearly (at least to hindsight) implied the forthcoming ghetto-equals-colony analysis and the shift from an integrationist to a separatist-nationalist politics, which of course was to bring two problems for every one it solved. This shift seems to have been necessitated by the impasse which integrationism confronted at Atlantic City the previous year.

*What was the Atlantic City of the white student movement that was to go from pro-peace to anti-war, anti-war to pro-NLF, pro-NLF to anti-imperialist to pro-Third World revolution to anti-capitalism to pro-socialism—and thence, with much more confusion and uncertainty than this schedule implies, to anti-peace (i.e., no co-existence) and anti-democracy ("bourgeois jive"), and which finds itself at the present moment broken into two, three, many factions, each of which claims to have the *real* Lenin (or Mao or Che) in its pocket? Riddled with vanguarditis and galloping sectarianism, and possessed of a twisty hallucination called the "mass line" like an ancient virgin her incubus (or is it just a hot water bottle?) the Rudd-Jones-Ayers SDS is at least an SDS with a past. I'll say later what I think is wrong with the mass-line stance, but the point here is to understand that it didn't just come upon SDS out of nowhere, not even the nowhere of the PLP, and that in the end, whatever you think of it, it has to happen: (a) because there was no way to resist the truth of the war, no way, that is, to avoid imperialism; (b) because once the policy critique of the war had been supplanted by the structural critique of the empire, all political therapies short of socialist revolution appeared to become senseless; and (c) because the necessity of a revolutionary strategy was, in effect, the same thing as the necessity of Marxism-Leninism. *There was—and is—no other coherent, integrative, and explicit philosophy of revolution.*

I do not want to be misunderstood about this. The practical identity of Marxism-Leninism with revolutionary theory, in my estimate, does not mean that Marxism-Leninism is *also* identical with a genuinely revolutionary practice in the advanced countries. That identity, rather, constitutes nothing more than a tradition, a legacy, and a problem which I think the Left will have to overcome. But at the same time, I don't think the American Left's first stab at producing for itself a *fulfilled* revolutionary consciousness could have produced anything better, could have gone beyond this ancestor-worship politics. It was necessary to discover—or maybe the word is confess—that we had ancestors in the first place; and if for no brighter motive than gratitude at not being so alone and rootless, the discovery of the ancestors would naturally beget a religious mood. That of the revival tent, no doubt, but religious all the same.

Again: Why did the white student Left so quickly abandon its liberal or reformist criticism of the war as policy and substitute its radical criticism of the war as the result of an imperialist structure? The former seems to have had much to recommend it: simple, straightforward, full of pathos and even sentimentality, it has by this time been linked (by liberals) to a still more pathos-laden cry to bring the boys back, and these two thrusts—save *our* boys and (incidentally) *their* babies—now make up the substance of the popular complaints against the war. (Harriman is now saying what we said about the war four years ago. What happened was that the student movement traded this *easy* argument against the war for a much harder one. Not that we rose as one man to denounce imperialism, of course. It was in October of that year that Paul Booth told the nation that SDS only wanted to "build, not burn." But he got into a lot of trouble for his pains; and when about a

Freedom Rides, 1961.

Federal voter registration.

month later, at the SANE-organized March on Washington, I used (without knowing it) all the paraphernalia of an anti-imperialist critique without once using the word "imperialism," nobody objected, nobody said, "This line commits us to an attempt at revolution and therefore, true or not, should be rejected as being politically impracticable."

Why did our movement *want* to be "revolutionary?" Very generally: An extrinsic failure of production (i.e., production turned *against* social reproduction) had already been intuited by that sector of the workers whose function is to *pacify the relations of production*. The most general means of this pacification is the neutralizing of the moral environment. This is what poets, political scientists, lit. teachers, sociologists, preachers, etc. are supposed to do. Deflect, divert, apologize, change the subject, prove either that our gods are virtuous and our direction right or that *no* gods are virtuous and *no* direction right and that rebellion ought therefore to forego history and take on the Cosmos. I think it can be shown that the practice of this essential work had already been jeopardized by the over-all character of production in the late '50s. Those whose role in production is to *explain* production, to provide it with its cover of rationality, had found it impossible to play their role *convincingly* simply because production had become extrinsically anti-social. Workers who cannot do their work rebel. They do so, furthermore, in the name of their work, in behalf of its possibility, and therefore in the name of that reordered system in which their work would again become possible.

The main point here is that 1965 was the year in which both the black and white sectors of the movement explicitly abandoned reformism and took up that long march whose destination, not even in sight yet, is a theory and practice of revolution for the United States. For the West.

Civil Rights March on Washington, 1963.

1966-67

*T*he rise of the resistance (in all its variety) and experiments with a "new-working-class" analysis, both motions strongly influenced by Greg Calvert and Carl Davidson. Superficially, these developments seemed to be congruent and intersupportive. But it looks to me now as if they were in fact opposite responses to the general problem of conceiving and realizing a revolutionary strategy, each one being a kind of political bet which the other one hedged. There was, I know, a lot of heavy theorizing about the politics of resistance, and I don't want to turn a complex experience into a simple memory. Still, I think it's fair to take the slogans as being indicative of its political atmosphere—"Not with my life, you don't!" for example, or "A call to resist illegitimate authority." Even if only in embryo, I think "resistance" was at bottom a youth-based anti-fascist front whose most central demand must have appeared to any outsider's eye to be for a return to the *status quo ante*. That's not to say that its organizers were not radicals or that its inner content was anti-socialist or non-socialist. But in basing itself on the individual's rights of self-determination (mythical, of course: we were all hip to the con), and in trying to depict Johnson's as an imposter ("illegitimate") regime, the Resistance was easily as unassuming in its politics as it was extravagant in its imagination.

At the same time, Carl ("I Blush to Remember") Davidson, among others, was trying to work out a new-working-class concept of the student rebellion, the main purpose being to discover in this rebellion that revolutionary power which one feared it might not have. Wanting revolution (with all that implies about the power to make one) but only having spasms of campus rebellion, the student syndicalists needed to show that at least the seed of the first found fertile ground in the latter.

Meanwhile: The method of political action which had been reintroduced in Harlem-'64 or Watts-'65 was on some terms perfected in Detroit-'67. All whites are convinced that something will have to be done, but nobody knows quite what to do. Except, of course, for the Right, which

March on Washington.

understood at once that was was needed was a metropolitan police force equipped both militarily *and politically* for urban counter-insurgency.

1968

*C*onfidence reappeared with Columbia and France, and then took an important turn with Chicago.

Columbia: (1) Conclusively, students have severely limited but formidable power to intervene in certain processes of oppression and to compel certain institutional reforms. (2) A practical alliance between blacks and whites became a concrete fact for the first time since Selma. The campus continues to be the main current locus of this alliance. (I say this, obviously, in view of Columbia's subsequence: Columbia's innovations proved repeatable elsewhere.) (3) Production relations constitute the life of class economy; distribution relations constitute the life of class society; consumption relations constitute the life of class politics. The stormed or barricaded factory gate of classical revolutionary vision is not the definitive image of any "final" or "pure" proletarian consciousness. The struggle at the point of production, when it occurs, is merely one expression of a more general struggle which, much more often than not, is ignited and fed by consciousness of inequities of consumption.*

What happened at Columbia/Harlem in the April of '68 is just as important as what happened in Hay Market Square—but at the same time no more important.

The worker comprehends the factory, in fact, as his means of consumption. It's in distribution patterns that the life styles of the class hierarchy are imposed; in the consumption patterns thus produced that the hierarchy of classes is most immediately *lived*. Production relations, as they are actually lived, are usually politically neutral: *the difference between an 8-hour day under U.S. capitalism and a 16-hour day under Cuban socialism is hardly to the former's advantage*. In fact, it's much more often a failure in the distributive or consumptive functions that creates political trouble for capitalism. How to finance further expansion? How to empty these bursting warehouses? And it could even be argued that as between the ghetto rising and the militant strike in heavy industry, the former is closer to that famous "seizure of State power" than the latter is. But why try to choose at all? We are dealing here only with aspects of a unitary complex, not with elements of a compound, and the tendencies of a method of analysis to reproduce reality as a set of correlative abstractions should never be permitted to reduce aspects of a continuous social process to the elements of its model. What happened at Columbia/Harlem in the spring of '68 is just as important, just as pregnant and portentious, as what happened in Haymarket Square—but at the same time, *no more important either*. We have littered contemporary American history with a hundred aspiring preludes whose aggregate *current* meaning is precisely the fight for the last word about their meaning, but whose future denouement is not yet revealed to us. To make the point still more explicit: There is no such thing as a model revolution (or even if you think you have found such a thing in *la Revolution francaise*, note

---

"In eighteenth-century England the manufacturing workers, miners, and others, were far more conscious of being exploited by the agrarian capitalists and middle-men, as consumers, than by their petty employers through wage-labour; and in this country [England] today consumer and cultural exploitation are quite as evident as is exploitation 'at the point of production' and perhaps are more likely to explode into political consciousness." E.P. Thompson, "The Peculiarities of the English," The Socialist Register, 1965 (London), Ralph Miliband and John Saville, eds., p. 355.

that it materialized considerably in advance of the theory that hailed it as such), and there is no revolutionary theory by means of which right and wrong sites of organization and agitation can be discriminated. The function of analysis is to clarify reality, not to pass judgment on it.

A few other points about Columbia: (4) "Co-optation" is obviously a useful concept. It warns you against being hoodwinked by those who've learned to smile and smile and still be villains. Unfortunately, just beyond that point at which it remains useful, it flops over completely and becomes disastrous: it can become a no-win concept masquerading either as tactical cunning or strategic wisdom. It instructs people to reject what their fight has made possible on the grounds that it falls short of what they wanted. If the Left allows its provisional victories to be reaped by the Center-Left, trust that those victories will very promptly be turned into most unprovisional setbacks. Am I saying that we should sometimes have people "working within the system's institutions?" Precisely, emphatically, and without the slightest hesitation! You are co-opted when the adversary puts his goals on your power; you are *not* co-opted when your power allows you to exploit his means (or contradictions) in behalf of your goals.

(5) The SF State strike retrospectively clarified one difficulty, maybe a shortcoming, of the Columbia strike. Other BSU-SDS-type eruptions suffered from the same lapse. Namely: *We very badly need a clear, sharp formulation of the white interest in overcoming racism.* All of us feel that this "white-skin-privilege"—if it is even a privilege at all—costs us something, and that the cost exceeds the gain. Yet we've had difficulty making it clear why we feel this way, and for the most part in the hurry of the moment have simply had to abandon the attempt, opting either for a purely moralistic explanation (which has meant that the white base of the strike is not represented in the strike leadership committee) or for the adding on of "white demands" (which tended to obscure the specifically anti-racist character of the action). Neither approach is any good. It is wrong for the base of the movement, any action, not to have a voice in tactical and strategic policy—witness, for one thing, the general bewilderment of the white SF State students who, when the strike was over, had little to do but return to business-as-usual classrooms. It is also wrong, or at least not quite right, for whites to demand "open admissions for all working-class youth" at the same time that the same whites are (a) trying to help make a point about the *racist* nature of colleges, and (b) attacking the *content* of the basic college education on the grounds that it's a brainwash. The German SDS idea of the critical university, somehow adapted to our particular political objectives, might break through the current dilemma at the level of program. But especially since the dilemma may shortly materialize in noncampus settings, it's first necessary to break it at a theoretical or general level. Why does racism hurt whites? Or *which* whites does it hurt, and why and how?

France, the May Days: "The revolt of the students is the revolt of the forces of modern production as a whole," writes Andre Glucksmann, a leading theoretician of the March 22 Movement. This intriguing formulation, like all new-working-class theorizing, is at bottom nothing but an attempt to find a new face for the old Leninist mask: Only "workers" can make 20th Century revolutions, so those who are creating a big revolution-sized fuss, even if they come outfitted with a few electrifying Sartrean neologisms, must therefore be some new kind of workers. I think this souped-up "New Left" scholasticism is worse than the Old Orthodoxy. Any common-sensical reading of the Glucksmann map would lead the revolution-watcher straight to the faculties of administration, technology and applied sciences, since it's within the meanings of the New Technology that these "forces of modern production as a whole" are being visualized. Maybe at Nanterre, where the fuse was lit. But certainly not at the Sorbonne or anywhere else in Paris, where the student base of the revolt, just as in the United States, came out of the faculties of liberal arts and the social sciences. Quite contrary to Glucksmann, the revolt of the students is the revolt *against* the forces of modern production as a whole—a fact which would doubtless be apparent to everyone if it weren't for the intellectual tyranny of Marxism-Leninism.

The more tradition-minded Leftists scarcely did any better with this out-of-nowhere avalanche. Not for one moment having imagined it was about to happen, insisting on the contrary that nothing like it ever *could* happen, and having finally satisfied themselves that all their curses and spells couldn't make it go away, the Old Crowd FCP determined to see in this Almost-Revolution a conclusive vindication of their theories, practices and political rheumatism all combined. "Behold, Lenin lives!" cried the Stalinists of France, even as they bent their every effort to killing him again.

The main fact about the Almost-Revolution is that it was *almost* a revolution, not that it was almost a *revolution*. As parched for victories as the Western Left has been in the post-war period, it may be forgiven its ecstasy at scoring a few runs. But what are we left with? No questions, Pompidou is not the only or the main or even a very important result of the May Days; as a minimum, the feudalism of the French academy has been jolted, and maybe it's still a big deal in the 7th decade of the 20th century to give academic feudalism a jolt. But it seems to me that all the lessons people are claiming to have learned are not lessons at all, only so many brute-force misreadings of the event. To claim that the student *foco* was a worker "detonator" is to dodge the awful question of the vanguard, not to face it and overcome it, and besides that, it tortures a meaning into "student" that has nothing to do with the students' evident meanings. On the other hand, the claim that the old problem of the "worker-student alliance" has found here the possibility of its solution seems to me the very opposite of what the facts indicate: Under propitious, even ideal circumstances, with the State isolated and virtually dumb before the crisis, with DeGaulle offering nothing more spiritual than an old man's resentment or more concrete than a diluted form of the students' program, with the army out-flanked politically and the police widely disgraced, with production mired in fiscal doldrums, the industrial workforce caught with a deep unease and its bureaucratized leadership dozing, it still proved hard for students and young workers to make contact, and (so it now seems) all but impossible for them to forge a lasting and organic revolutionary union.

Watts, 1965.

It seems to me that the following are more defensible "lessons."

1. No key West European nation (Britain, France, Germany, Italy) can slide hard to the Left unless a Warsaw Pact nation can also slide equally hard to the right. France and Czechoslovakia constitute the gigue and the saraband of an unfinished political suite.

2. We're in a period in which, for the first time in modern history, the social base of a truly post-industrial socialism is being produced, delta-like, outside capitalism's institutional reach. (That is, a socialism which rejects capitalism because of its successes instead of its failures, and which comes into existence in order to supercede and surpass industrial society, not to create it.) But for long time within the capitalist state, and for much longer within the capitalist empires, this new base will co-exist with the old: that which wants to go beyond will co-exist with that which needs to come abreast. This constitutes the protractedly *transitional* nature of the current period, a source both of confusion and opportunity within the world Left community, and above all a problem which the advanced-nation Left will have to solve by means of a post-Leninist theory and a post-Leninist practice.

Chicago: (1) Liberalism has no power in this country. It is not politically organized. The few secondary institutions in which it lives its hand-to-mouth existence are, at best, nothing more than insecure and defenseless sanctuaries. In none of the estates—not the church, not the media, not the schools—does it exhibit the least aggressiveness, the least staying power, the least confidence. *This country, in the current situation, is absolutely impotent before the*

Newark, 1967.

threat of what Fulbright has lately called "elective fascism."

I'll admit that this discovery surprised me. I had thought that the liberals had a little crunch left. McCarthy had always obviously been an icecube in an oven; but even deprived of Kennedy, I had supposed that the liberals would have been able to drive a few more bargains. They were helpless at Chicago, and their helplessness has only deepened since then. (Observe the sorry spectacle of Yankeedom's main gunslingers, Harriman, Vance, and Clifford, vainly trying to ambush Nixon, who knows and imperturbably defeats their every confused move.)

For the very simple truth about Chicago is that Daley got away with it, and there was nothing anybody could do. What "Big Contributor" dropped a word to the wise against him? What "Key Party High-up" moved even to censure him behind the scenes or slow him down? The *institutional mass* of the society is either neutralized or passively or actively supportive of reaction, and reaction can go, quite simply, as far as it determines it needs to go. Screaming their heads off at both the infant Left and the entrenched Right, liberals have neither base nor privilege, neither an organized following nor access to the levers of power. This is important.

(2) If only because it sharpens the melodrama, we may as well pinpoint Chicago, August, as the place and time of the "mass line's" formal debut: an unforgettable lit-up nighttime scene, Mike Klonsky taking the bullhorn at Grant Park to harangue the assembly about its "reformist" politics.

I've already indicated that I see nothing promising in *any* version of Marxixm-Leninism—not PL's, not that of the now-defunct "national collective" of the Klonsky-Coleman period or of its apparent successor, the Revolutionary Union, and not that of the more diffuse and momentarily hazier grouping, the Revolutionary Youth Movement. But of course I don't claim that a mere statement of this view constitutes either an explanation of it or an argument for it. The argument will have to be made, very carefully, in another place, and I have to confine myself here to the observation that any revolutionary movement will all but inevitably adapt itself to Marxism-Leninism—or the other way around—because there is just no other totalizing philosophy of revolution. This philosophy then enables a representation of reality in something like the following general terms: "A desire in pursuit of its means, a means in flight from its destiny—these conditions constitute The Problem. Solution: tomorrow, when history's preplanted timebomb at last goes off, blasting false consciousness away, the words of the prophets will be fulfilled."

Chicago, in any case, occasioned these two terminal moments: the humiliation of liberalism, and the "official" reversion of SDS to a Marxist-Leninist worldview.

1969

*T*he leading events so far: The SF State strike and the structurally similar conflicts that erupted across the country, the People's Park showdown in June, the SDS convention, and the Black Panther call for the Oakland conference.

San Francisco State: I want to make just two observations on this much-studied event.

First, the movement's characteristic attitude toward partial victories—more particularly, toward what is disparaged as "student power"—is mechanistic. It appears that every change which is not yet The Revolution is either to be airily written off as no change at all, or further than that, to be denounced as co-optation into the counter-revolution. People should only try to remember that the SF State strike did not materialize out of thin air, that it had a background, that it was that particular moment's culmination of a long conflictual process, and that just as with Columbia, where political work had been sustained at a generally intense level at least since May 1965, the explo-

Columbia, April 1968.

S.F. State, Dec. 1968.

sive strike at State was made possible, maybe even necessary, by a long series of small moves forward, any one of which could have been attacked as "bourgeois liberal reform." More precisely, it was in large part those incremental "reforms" of curriculum and student-teacher and teacher-administration relationships carried out under the unseeing eyes of President Summerskill that created the general conditons in which the strike could take place. As with Columbia, the atmosphere had long been thoroughly politicized—that is to say, charged with consciousness of national issues. And a long reign of liberalism had, in effect, already *legitimated* the demands around which the strike was fought through, just as a long reign of reformism had created the institutional means of the strike. In the same way, the fact that the Third World Liberation Front leadership did after all negotiate the "nonnegotiable" demands, the further fact that this leadership then moved *to consolidate these bargaining-table victories within the changing structure of the institution itself*—this meant not that the fight was over, not at all that "capitalism" had suffered a tactical defeat only to secure a strategic victory, but rather that the stage was—and is—being set for another round of conflict at a still higher level of consciousness within a still wider circle of social involvement. For the net result of the strike's victories is still further to break down the psychological, social, and political walls that had formerly sealed off the academy from the community. This is a big part of what we are about—the levelling of all these towers, the redistribution of all this ivory, the extroversion of these sublimely introverted corporate monstrosities: and not just because we have willed it, whether out of malice or chagrin or a blazing sense of justice, but rather because capital itself, in all its imperial majesty, has invested these schools with its own trembling contradictions. Necessarily demanding a mass consciousness of and for its technological and political ambitions, it necessarily produces a mass consciousness of the servility of the first and the brutality of the second. Necessarily demanding an army of social managers, pacifiers of the labor force, it necessarily produces an army of social problem solvers, agitators of that same labor force. Necessarily demanding an increasingly sophisticated corps of servicemen to the empire, it necessarily produces a cosmopolitanism to which this empire's shame is its most conspicuous feature. Necessarily demanding a priesthood to bless its work in the stolen name of humanity, it necessarily produces the moral and social weaponry of its own political condemnation.

*W*e play upon these stops. Not able to arrest this process, as Reagan wants, nor to let it go forward, as the liberals want, doomed to be blind in either this eye or the other, not able to prosper without teaching us to serve it, not able to teach us to serve without somehow teaching us also its inner secrets, not able to teach us those secrets without teaching us to despise it, capitalism in our time is forced upon—*forces upon itself*—a choice of mortalities. Either to continue that process whose most general form is simply total urbanization, with its attendant destruction of all the disciplinary taboos, of the family, of political religion, of nationalism, of property and the ethics of property, of individualism and the entrepreneurial style; or to try to reverse that process, in which case it destroys its fragile equilibrium, destroys the social base and dynamic of production and growth, puts on the airbrakes and turns off its engines in midflight. If it makes the first choice, it bursts like an egg: *social control over the means of education is necessarily only the prologue to social control of the means of production, distribution, and consumption.* If it makes the second choice, if it tries to freeze everything, then the living thing, the life inside the egg, dies out; a moment more, the shell collapses: *Already a fascism in its colonies*, the empire is obliged nevertheless to hold its fascism at a distance; and when protracted "wars of liberation," wherever they happen (ghettoes, campuses) and whatever unpredicted form they take (e.g., Peru!), succeed in driving this frontier fascism back upon its metropolitan front, then the whole political and social basis of the empire begins to fragment and dissolve. For a stable empire can be military only in its means, not in its ends—its ends necessarily being a mode of production, distribution, and consumption; and the servicing of these ends ultimately requires exactly that metropolitan class *hegemony* (all classes passively accepting or even affirming the rule of the dominant class, the class hierarchy having therefore the firm structure of vertical consent) which fascism supplants with class *coercion*.*

One brief aside on a related matter: When I first met white New Leftists about five years ago, their most common fear was that they were not a serious threat. Along with this went the equally common belief that their seriousness would be proved only if they were vigorously attacked. (The current expression of this is the general view that the "vanguard" is whoever is being most vigorously attacked: it is not the people who pick their leaders, but the State.) No one suggested that the Other Side might be holding less than a fistful of aces, that the adversary was not super smart, that he might be stymied by his own contradictions. Maybe it was my background that made me skeptical—grandson of the south's Last Peasant Patriarch, son of a first-generation migrant from a defeated rural economy to the industrial revolution (Akron: smoke, tires, factories, timeclocks, the permanently present memory of the "home" which you had abandoned in spite of al wishes and had thereby, despite yourself, helped destroy, and which you could never go back to again no matter how many rides you took those seven hundred miles on hot jampacked Greyhound buses that, once below Marietta, stopped every other mile to pick up or let off still another coming or going hillbilly, suitcase in one hand, baby in the other, eyes shot from whiskey and incomprehension. . . . Another time I must deal with this). I had thought that there was precious little need to go out of your way to provoke those distant people who worked on Mahogany Row, lived in the mansions of Fairlawn, and owned all the cops and politicians. If the vague people of the vague middle were ignorant of how power worked and who had it and who did not, we who lived just at the edge of the black ghetto and whose lives were ordered by the vicissitudes of production—cutbacks, layoffs, speedups, doubles, strikes—were under no illusions. We knew their viciousness because man, woman and child we had it for constant companion. My mind was blown, its gears stripped, to hear someone say that the gift of authenticity was the Man's to give, that it came in the form of clubbings and jailings, and that, left unprovoked, he might withhold it. Not so: puruse your aims with stark simplicity and in all peaceableness, put money in thy purse with the politest and gentlest of smiles—trust him, he'll get around to making you pay, and anybody who does not know this just hasn't been paying attention.

So. That's the first "observation"—the winning of a "reform" isn't always a bad business, and Leftists should stop being scared of being reformed out of things to do. The only real strategic necessity is to make sure the reform in question reforms the power configuration so that it becomes the basis for further and still more fundamental challenges to class rule.

The second observation is connected. It has to do with the question of what's called (disparagingly) "student power." The formula attack on the making of demands for such things as curriculum reform and greater student participation in campus government goes like this: "The young bourgeois, privileged already, exhibits here only his desire. to extend his privileges still further. This desire must be fought by radicals. If not exactly in the *name* of the working class, we must see ourselves as fighting at least in its *behalf*, and since its interests are hardly served by the

abolition of grades or the reduction of required credits, we must oppose such demands."

*F*irst, the outlines of a speculation. What if the multiversity is in some substantial part the creation of the advanced-world proletariat—not merely the plaything and mistress of the imperialists? What if it is partly in the multiversity that the proletariat has banked and stored up its enormous achievements in technology? What if the multiversity—the highest realization yet of the idea of mass education and the rationalization of productive labor—is in one of its leading aspects the institutional form through which the proletariat continues its struggle for emancipation? Behind how many of these so-called "bourgeois" children, one or two generations back, stands a father in a blue collar, a mother in an apron? The proletariat, says Marx, will have to prepare itself for self-government through protracted struggle. What if this struggle is so protracted that it actually must be seen as taking place, in one of its aspects at least, across *generations*? The revolutionary aspiration of whites in the 1930's manifested itself most sharply in factory struggles. In the 1960's, that aspiration has materialized most sharply on the campuses. What have we made of this fact? The function of a method of social analysis is not to reprimand reality for diverging from its model, but on the contrary to discover in reality the links and conjunctures that make history intelligible and life accessible to effective action. An abstraction is not something to stand behind like a pulpit but a lens to see through more discerningly. Obvious? Then it is high time to confess: At the same time that it has been trying so desperately to live forwards, the New Left everywhere, in West Europe as well as here, has been just as desperately trying to think backwards. If Marxism is any good, and if we can prove it worthy of the moment, then we ought to be able to say what it is about contemporary relations of production that makes the campuses a primary site of contemporary revolutionary motion. Only when that question is answered will we have any right to pontificate about "correct" and "incorrect" lines, and it has not yet been answered. Meanwhile, even if it is good and sufficient, as I am almost sure it is not, to characterize "student power" as a fight for "burgeois privilege," we would still have to ask: What *kind* of privilege? Assuming that there is nothing here at all but an intra-class struggle against the contemptuous indifference of institutions, against the mindless blather of the dons, the deans, the sycophants and the liars, against authority in particular and authoritarianism on principle, we would still have to say that the political balance of this struggle is *progressive and portentous*. To those who tell me that this fight neither equals, approximates, initiates, nor reveals the form of The Revolution Itself, I answer first, Neither did Nanterre, neither did Watts, neither did anything else in man's social history but a bare handful of uniquely definitive and epochal convulsions, each one of which moreover appeared only at the end of a painfully long train of indeterminate events which escaped their ambiguity only thanks to the denouement; and I answer second, If you are trying to tell me you know already what The Revolution Itself will look like, you are either a charlatan or a fool. *We have no scenario.*

*S*econd, for what it's worth to a movement suddenly infatuated with the words of the prophets, Lenin faced a somewhat similar question in 1908 when certain radicals refused to support an all-Russia student strike on the grounds that "the platform of the strike is an academic one" which "cannot unite the students for an active struggle on a broad front." Lenin objected: "Such an argument is radically wrong. The revolutionary slogan—to work towards coordinated political action of the students and the proletariat—here ceases to be a live guidance for many-sided militant agitation on a broadening base and becomes a lifeless dogma, mechanically applied to different stages of different forms of the movement." Further: "For this youth, a strike on a large scale . . . is the beginning of a political conflict, whether those engaged in the fight realize it or not. Our job is to explain to the mass of 'academic'

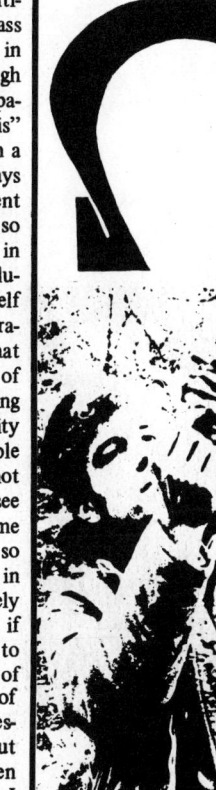

Berkeley.

If the biography of German Nazism seems to contradict this thesis, recall that Junker coercion was finally translated into the hegemony of the State itself not mainly because of risings in the colonies, but because of pressure from rival imperialisms dating back at least to the First World War.

protesters the objective meaning of the conflict, to try and make it *consciously* political."

The People's Park: Those few SDSers, unfortunately conspicuous this past year, who think Stalinism is more or less right on, ought at least to have admitted that "socialism in one country" is not exactly the logical antithesis of "socialism in one park." But it was the Stalinists, both pure and off-breed, who among all the Bay Area radicals found it hardest to relate to the park before the attacks, were most puzzled by the attack itself, and produced the most opportunistic "support" in the aftermath. Mainly because these curious rumbles of the hip are so hard to focus politically in terms of a mass-and-vanguard model, it's hard for people with old minds to figure out how to relate to them. That fact may be the basis of a touching epitaph; but a living politics for our period will have to understand that "decadence" is as "decadence" does, that the "cultural revolution" is not merely a craven and self-serving substitute for the "political" one, and that if the West has, indeed, a leftwards destiny, then neither its particular ends nor its modes of organization and action will be discovered through archeology. My guess: People's Park was one among many episodes of a religious revival movement—exactly the kind of movement that has heralded every major social convulsion in the United States—and as with all such movements, its ulterior target, its enemy, is the forces of the industrialization of culture. The difference now is that the virtual consummation of the Industrial Revolution, *within the West*, lends a credibility and relevance to such a program that it formerly has not had. That is: The anti-industrialism of early radicals like Blake and Cobbett, though it was fully anti-capitalist, could confront rampant capitalist industrial progress with nothing more powerful than a retiring, improbably, defenseless nostalgia; could argue against the system of "masters and slaves" only in behalf of the older and no doubt mythical system, allegedly medieval, of "masters and men." Every time it became a *practical* movement—whether revolutionary or reformist—socialism had to put forward simply a more rational version of the program of industrialization itself. This is not an irony or tragedy of history, it's just the dialectics of historical process. That it has so far been unsurpassable is in fact the essence of revolutionary socialism's general isolation to the backwards countries, or put differently, this limit merely expresses the wedding of revolutionary socialism to anti-colonialism, and on the other hand, its impotence in countries in which the industrialization process has been carried forward effectively (however ruthlessly) by the bourgeoisie. The thesis of People's Park, rough as it may be to deal with both in terms of our tradition and our current practical needs, is that the essentially *post-industrial* revolution, embodied most fully but still (we must suppose) very incompletely in the hip communities, portends the historically most advanced development for socialist consciousness.

"Most fully" because it goes beyond industrialization, and in doing so, implies (much more than it has so far realized) a genuinely New Man—just as new compared to Industrial Man as Industrial Man was new in comparison to the artisans and small farmers who foreran him.

But it would be useless just to approve of this cultural revolution without being very clear about its terrible limits. I see two limits. First: The "new values" (they are, of course, very old) can claim to be subversive only of the standing values of work, but not really of consumption, there being nothing in the structure and precious little in the texture of "hip leisure" that keeps it from being commercially copied (deflated) and packaged. Thus, in effect, the target of the attack detaches itself, refuses to defend itself, and in offering itself as the apparent *medium* of the attack is able (persuasively to all but the sharpest consciousness) to pose as the "revolution's" friend. There are a thousand examples of this process, whose minimum result is vastly to complicate the cultural critique, and which at the other limit succeeds wholly in disarming it. The quietism of which the hip community is often accused may thus be much less the result of a principled retreat to cosmology

Berkeley.

Berkeley.

than of its flat inability to confront commercialism with a deeply nonnegotiable demand.

*S*econd, even though the new anarchism is morally cosmopolitan—affirming in a rudimentary political way the essential oneness of the human community—its values are *practical* only within the Western (imperialist) cities, and are far from being universally practical even there. So the second and bigger problem the cultural revolution needs to overcome is its lack of a concrete means of realizing its ideal sympathy with those globally rural revolutionary movements whose social program necessarily centers around the need for industrialization, not the surpassing of it. A solution of this problem would no doubt also solve the first. This is why it's so important to subject the cultural revolution to a much more profound and critical analysis than what has been produced so far. For the point at the moment is not to be for or against the current reappearance of anarchism. It will be necessary rather to explicate its tradition (too many hippies think they are saying brand new things) and then to try to see if the balance of forces has changed sufficiently that this old movement for a cultural revolution against industrial society has begun to acquire a power which it formerly has not had.

*T*he SDS Convention: I wasn't there, never mind why. At the last SDS thing I was at, the Austin NC, the handwriting was already on the wall. Having determined that SDS must become explicitly and organizationally committed to its version of Marxism-Leninism, PL would continue in its Trotskyist way of identifying organizations with movements and would try to win more power in SDS—that much was already clear in the spring. I didn't think, though, that PL people would force a split. As fiercely indifferent to this country's general culture as they seem to be, I still thought they would understand a split as contrary to their purposes and would therefore seek to avoid it, even if that meant a momentary tactical retreat. Either I was wrong, or PL misunderstood—and misplayed—the situation.

I want to make just one point about the current situation. What is wrong about PL is not its rigidity, its "style," its arrogance or anything like that. Its *ideology* is wrong. And not just in the particulars of emphasis or interpretation or application, but in its most fundamental assumptions about the historical process. Someone else may argue that PL's Marxism-Leninism is a bad Marxism-Leninism, and that is a view which can doubtless be defended. But I see no prosperity in the approach that merely wants to save Leninism from Milt Rosen here and Jared Israel there. The problem is deeper and the task much more demanding. It can be posed this way: Backwards as it is, our practice is more advanced than our theory, and our theory therefore becomes an obstacle to our practice—which is childish and schematic, not free and real enough. The general adoption of some kind of Marxism-Leninism by all vocal factions in SDS means, certainly, that a long moment of intellectual suspense has been resolved—but much less in response to experience than to the pressure of the *tradition*. We have not produced even a general geosocial map of the United States as a society—only as an empire. We have not sought in the concrete historical experience of classes a rigorous explanation of their acceptance of "cross-class" (Cold War) unity but rather have employed a grossly simplified base-and-superstructure model to explain away the fact that labor does not appear to think what we think it ought to think. We have taken a class to be a thing, not a process (or as E.P. Thompson called it five years ago, "a happening"), and have imagined it to be bound, more or less, to behave according to the "scientific laws" which govern the category. Most generally, we have imported a very loose and sometimes garbled theory of pre-industrial revolution, have tightened it without really clarifying it, and are now in the process of trying to superimpose that theory, thus reduced, on our own very different situation. The RYM group does not differ in this respect from PL, the Revolutionary Union, or even YSA or ISC. All these groups, opportunistic in widely varying degrees, claim to have the same ace in the hole, and Lenin's phrases (or what's worse, the Chairman's truistic maxims) are gnawed upon by every tooth.

*F*or a long time I was baffled. Last fall the word began to reach me: It was being said that I had "bad politics." How could *that* be, I wondered, since I thought I had no politics at all. But by winter I conceded the point: no politics is the same as bad politics. So there followed a time in which I experimented with only the "mass line." Could Klonsky and Coleman be right? It didn't come to much. My mind and my instincts only became adversaries. By spring I had to deactivate, couldn't function, had to float. What I know now is that this did not happen to me alone. On every quarter of the white Left, high and low, the attempt to reduce the New Left's inchoate vision to the Old Left's perfected remembrance has produced a layer of bewilderment and demoralization which no cop with his club or senator with his committee could ever have induced. And my view of the split at the convention is that it merely caps a series of changes which began at the East Lansing convention in 1968, with the decision to counter PL's move on SDS by means of a political form—the "SDS caucus," i.e., a countervailing faction—which accepted implicitly PL's equation of the social movement with the organizations that arise within it. What walked out of the Coliseum was simply a larger version of 1968's SDS caucus. Certainly it had grown in awareness and self-definition over the year; and knowing that bare opposition to PL is no very impressive gift to The Revolution, it had spurred itself to produce an independent Marxist-Leninist analysis and at least the semblance of a program. My unhappy wager is that even in its RYM incarnation it remains a faction, that it will continue last year's practice of "struggling sharply" against internal heresies, that it will remain in the vice of the old illusions, that it will pay as little attention to what is happening in the country and the world as its predecessor regime did, and that whatever growth the movement achieves will be inspite of its rally cries and with indifference to its strictures. Nor is there a lot that can be done about this. The Western Left is perhaps in the midphase of a long, deep transition, and there is no way for SDS to protect itself from the consequences. They will have to be lived out. Which does not mean there is nothing to do. It means, rather, that any new initiatives will confront a situation very heavily laden with obstacles and limits. It isn't 1963 anymore.

The Panther Convention: It hasn't happened yet as I write, and I have no idea what its outcome will be. But certain doubts still need to be aired.

What's good about the Panthers has been amply hailed in the white Left: The Panthers have, in effect, done for the black lumpen of the northern urban ghetto what SNCC, years ago, did for the black serfs of the rural south—individual despair, given a historical interpretation, is turned into collective political anger. To the alternatives of tomism, crime, and psychosis, SNCC in the country and the Panthers in the town have added the idea of revolution—ant-racist, internationalist, and socialist.

But taken all in all—and for forcing historical reasons this is truer of the Panthers than of SNCC of 1960-64—this consciousness is a Word without Flesh, and that's what's got the Panthers trapped in a blind alley from which the only exits are either martyrdom or the "anti-fascist" popular front which it is the apparent purpose of the July convention to organize. To put it another way: The Panthers did not *organize* the ghetto, they only apostrophized it. So far as I know, the breakfast-for-children program represents the only serious attempt to relate concretely, practically, broadly, and *institutionally* to the black urban community as a whole. And it is very much to the point that the Panthers have recently promoted the breakfast program as their most characteristic political act—at approximately the same moment that the super-militants are purged, the

public making of fierce faces greatly cooled, and the gun no longer presented as the leading symbol of Panther intentions.

*T*his is all to the good, but it should have happened long ago. There ought to be dozens of programs like the breakfasts. Nothing else, in fact, gives stature, credibility, and social meaning to the gun; for the ghetto, as such, neither can be nor should be defended. Only when that ghetto is being transformed, de-ghettoized, by the self-organized activity of the people does its militant self-defense become a real *political* possibility. I'm not saying that social organization must always precede combat organization. If ghetto blacks were like the sugar proletariat of pre-revolutionary rural Cuba, and if the police were like Cuba's rural guard, then the opposite would likely be true. Even so, even if there is a proper analogy to the July 26 Movement, what would follow if not the obligation not merely to challenge the police, not merely to engage militarily and escape alive, but in fact to *defeat* the police, to prove to the people that the tyranny cannot impose its will on the countryside by force? The essence of J-26 politics lies in its valid presupposition of a popular will for social revolution and in its insight that it was mainly their common-sensical skepticism about overcoming the state military machine that held the people back.

With all respect for Cuba and the ardor of black American militants, I fail to see in the caste ghetto of an industrial city anything like a political replica of the countryside of a one-crop colony. The presence in the ghetto of the political gun meant a great many worthwhile, even invaluable things. But crucial as it is, "Free Huey!" is not by itself a social program or a revolutionary slogan. The irony is that nothing but a real social program, and the expanding base of involved, active, and conscious people such a program alone could produce, would ever make Huey Newton's liberation even thinkable, never mind the means.

"But of course this has all been seen by now." Has it? The current Panther move to establish a white base of support does not persuade me that it has been *understood. The Panthers are in trouble not because they have no white support, but because they have too little black support; not because they have no white allies, but because, in the virtual absence of a wide array of real activities, real social programs in the black communities, there is nearly nothing that white allies can do besides pass resolutions, send lawyers, and raise bail.*

Isla Vista

*S*DS will have to take its share of the blame for this. Much more interested in shining with the borrowed light of Panther charisma than in asking all the hard practical questions, much more interested in laying out the metaphysical maxims that identify the "vanguard" than in assuming real political responsibility, this SDS, which so often chews its own tongue for being "petty bourgeois," most shamefully confesses its origins precisely when it tries so vainly to transcend them in worship of "solidarity" which really amounts to so much hero-worship. Bourgeois is as bourgeois does. Marx, Engels, Lenin, Trotsky, Mao, Chou, Ho, Giap, Fidel, Che, Fanon: which one plowed a furrow, ran a punchpress, grew up hungry? That, in the first place, ought to be that. Further, in the second place, it is not lost causes, however heroic, or martyrs, however fine, that our movement needs. It needs shrewd politicians and concrete social programs. Not theoretical (really theological) proofs that The People Will Win in the End, but tangible social achievements now. Not the defiance of a small, isolated band of supercharged cadre who, knowing they stand shoulder to shoulder with mankind itself, will face repression with the inner peace of early Christians, but a mounting fugue of attacks on political crime of all sorts, on all fronts, at all levels of aspiration, from all sectors and classes of the population, so that repression can never rest, never find a fixed or predictable target. Humble example: Yesterday's *New York Times* carries a full-page political ad—the American Institute of Architects, it seems, has come out against the war. What will the Panther or the

Cambridge, May 1970

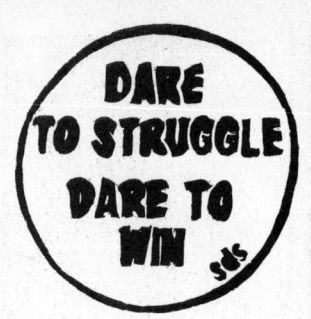

Chicago Weatherman action

SDS national office do? Send a wire? Make a phone call? Investigate the possibility of a combined action? Try to make two or three new friends in order to make a hundred or a thousand later. I guess not. For the AIA is as *bourgeois* as they come, awfully *liberal*, too. When even the Oakland 7 and the Chicago 8 are suspect, what chance does a lot of architects have? So the architects will never hear what we have to say about the empire, about the houses that are being built in Cuba, about what we take to be the extent and causes of the present world crisis.

But this loss is presumably compensated by our clarity about the "vanguard." Clarity! Any close reading of the RYM's Weatherman statement will drive you blind. Sometimes the vanguard is the black ghetto community, sometimes only the Panthers, sometimes the Third World as a whole, sometimes only the Vietnamese, and sometimes apparently only the Lao Dong Party. Sometimes it is a curiously Hegelian concept, referring vaguely to all earthly manifestations of the spirit of revolution. At still other times, it seems to be the fateful organ of that radicalized industrial proletariat (USA) which has yet to make its Cold War-era debut. Mostly, though, it's the poor Panthers, whose want of politics was never challenged by the few SDSers who had access to their leaders; this appointment—Vanguard to the People's Revolution—being, presumably, SDS's to make—and one which is defended, moreover, in terms of a so-called revolutionary strategy (see the Weatherman statement) in which the United States is to experience not a social revolution at the hands of its own people, but a military defeat at the hands of twenty, thirty, many Vietnams—plus a few Detroits.

*B*ut perhaps the ghetto=colony analysis means that the Detroits are already included in the category of Vietnams? In that case, for all real political purposes, (North) American=white; and the historic role of these whites, their "mission" in the many-sided fight for socialism, is most basically just to be overcome. The authors of the Weatherman statement are of course perfectly right in trying to integrate what may appear to be *decisive* international factors into a model scenario of domestic change. From no viewpoint can an empire be treated as if it were a nation state. But although they face this problem, they do not overcome it. They might have said that the leading aspect of the US industrial proletariat remains, classically, its exploitation at the hands of US capital, and that it therefore still embodies a momentarily stifled revolutionary potential. Contrarily, they might have said that what we have here is a giganticized "labor aristocracy who are quite philistine in their mode of life, in the size of their earnings and in their outlook . . . [and who are] real channels of reformism and chauvinism" (Lenin, *Imperialism: The Highest Stage of Capitalism*). On its face, neither view is silly, but neither is one more satisfactory than the other. Weatherman's refusal to settle for one or the other seems to me to express a realistic *intuition*; but the problem is not solved simply by asserting one theory here and the other theory there. They cannot both be equally valid. I think the difficulty is embedded in the method of analysis: Weatherman takes class to be a thing rather than a process, and consequently tries to treat class as if it were, in and of itself, *a definite political category*. (That is, labor is fated to be Left.) But Weatherman also has a certain level of historical realism, and this realism always intervenes (happily) to obstruct the mostly theoretical impulse—a kind of social Freudianism—to idealize labor, to strip it of its historical "neurosis" by the simple and fraudulent expedient of viewing its neurosis as *merely* superstructural. In other words, Weatherman's confusions and ambiguities stem from a conflict between its model and its data, and it comes close to escaping this dilemma only when it forgets its static model of class for a moment, and gives freer rein to its sense of history and process. At such moments, it comes close to saying something really important, which I would paraphrase, over-optimistically no doubt, thus: "The labor force we are looking at today is not the one we'll see tomorrow, and the changes it will undergo have everything

to do with the totality of its current and forthcoming experiences, which range all the way from the increasingly sensed contradiction between the rhetoric of affluence and the fact of hardship to the blood and money sacrifices it will be asked to offer in the empire's behalf." But this ought to be said up front, and it then ought to lead to the most exhaustive analysis of the real, living forces that impinge upon not just labor but the population as a whole. Everytime something like this starts to happen, Weatherman breaks off and reverts to its concealed paradox: the vanguard of the US (Western would be better) revolution will be those forces which most aggressively array themselves *against* the US, those forces, in other words, which are most *distant* from white culture. Thus, *cause becomes agency*: the living proof of a *need* for change—the Panthers, the NLF, etc.—is defined as the political *means* of change; an almost absent-minded abstraction converts white America's sickness into the remedy itself.

The most succinct case of this kind of bad reasoning I've heard came at the end of a speech Bob Avakian made at the Austin NC. The racism of white workers would have to be broken, he said, because, when the revolution comes, it will be led by blacks, whose leadership whites must therefore be prepared to accept. If this were only an unconsidered trifle, it would be pointless to snap it up, but it appears to represent a serious, persistent, and growing school of thought in the New Left. The problem with it is just that it implies that there could be a revolution in the absence of a profound radicalization of the white working class, in the absence of profound changes in the political character of that class. What would make it possible for white workers to revolt would also make it possible—and necessary—for white workers to help *lead* that revolt. The very idea of a white working class revolution against capitalism that is, necessarily *presupposes* either than racism will have been overcome or at least that the conditions for that triumph will have been firmly established. The problem with this dreamed-of revolution will not be anti-blackism within its ranks, but the anti-communism of its adversary. "In revolution, there are no whites or blacks, only reds."

But beyond this, Avakian (as with the Weathermen) wants it both ways: blacks are a colony, on the one hand, outside the colonizing political economy and set over against it; and on the other hand, they are in and of the empire's proletariat. In the first mode, they press against the empire from a position which is outside it in every sense but the geographical. In the second mode, they press upwards against the bourgeoisie from within capital's system of social classes. It is of course not impossible that these modes really do coexist and interpenetrate one another. In fact, it is likely that they do. But both modes cannot be represented as simultaneously co-leading aspects of the black situation *vis-a-vis* white society. A white revolutionary strategy requires a decision as to which aspect is dominant and which secondary, *as well as an understanding that what is dominant now may become secondary later, may even disappear.*

*S*o—an attempt at a clarification (which, as with certain other points I've tried to make in this letter, I'll have to elaborate and defend in some other, more ample space):

1. The persistence of integrationism, in a dozen disguises, and nationalism's struggle against it, make a strong circumstantial case for the view that blacks are above all blacks. They are not just another part of the workforce, not even just the main body of the lumpenproletariat. Nor do they make up a *caste*. Industrial societies do not have, cannot afford, castes; castes belong to pre-capitalist formations (or, at latest, to agrarian capitalism) and are in fact destroyed by the imperatives of industrial organization.

Obviously, blacks are assigned an important role in the US production-consumption process. So were pre-revolutionary Cubans. So are contemporary Venezuelans. The low-skill aspect of black production and the importance of the credit and welfare systems in black consumption constitute, in themselves, the leading features of a *colonial* relation to a colonizing political economy. It is therefore appropriate to see the black ghetto as a colony. Thus, and *true* black nationalism (much "nationalist" rhetoric is merely a Hallowe'en mask for integrationist or even *comprador* demands) is necessarily anti-imperialist, and could consummate whatever military or political victories it might achieve in the independence struggle only through a socialist development of the means of production.

2. No more than the struggle of the Vietnamese can be the struggle of the blacks to play a "vanguard" role in the problematic revolution of white America. *Vietnam and Detroit, the NLF and the Panthers, do not constitute the means of white America's liberation from imperialist capital. They constitute, rather, the necessity of that liberation.* They exist for white America as the living embodiment of problems which white America must solve. There are, obviously, many other such problems: the draft, high taxes, inflation, the whole array of ecological and environmental maladies, Big Brotherism at all levels of government, the general and advanced hypertrophy of the State, the fractionalizing of the civil society. Most of these problems are relatively diffuse; they are not experienced so acutely as the war or the ghetto risings. But they are still real to people, and they all have the same general source in the hegemony of capitalism: What sets Vietnam aflame is the same force that brutalizes the black population and poisons everybody's air.

3. The function of the white Western socialist is therefore, at this moment, to confront white America (white France, etc.) with the truth about the problems that harass it, to explain that these problems cannot be solved merely by repressing those people in whose lives the problems are embodied, cannot be solved by prayer or petition, and above all that they cannot be solved so long as the means of production, the wealth of that production, and the monopoly of political power that goes with those means and that wealth are locked up in the hands of the big bourgeoisie. You would as wisely ask the bullet to sew up the wound it made as ask the monopoly capitalist to solve these problems. The capitalist cannot do it. But the socialist can. That is the point we have to make.

4. The rebellion of white students is provoked most fundamentally by the general *extrinsic* failure of capitalist production—by the fact, that is, that production has become so conspicuously anti-social. This is what gives the student rebellion both its power and its very real limits. But this extrinsic collapse has not yet been followed by an *intrinsic* collapse: the system of capitalist production is at the moment *both insane and rational.* If a failure of its administration should produce also an *intrinsic* collapse—if suddenly no one could buy and no one could sell—then the people of the West would come again to the crossroads of the 1930s, and would have to decide again whether they would solve their problems by means of war or revolution. It is at that point that the fight for the loyalty of the proletariat will become truly historical instead of merely theoretical, necessary instead of merely right, possible instead of merely desireable. *But no will, no courage, no ingenuity can force this eventuality.* If it develops, and if the crisis is prolonged enough for white American workers to grasp the need for revolution, then with the same motion in which they change their rifles from one shoulder to the other, they will simultaneously *de-colonize* the blacks, the Vietnamese, the Cubans, *the French*—for at such a moment, all the old paralyzing definitions will die and new definitions, revolutionary ones, will take their place. The world proletariat will have achieved, at last, its dreamed-of world unity. This possibility, this towering historical power, is merely the other side of what it means to be a white American. But again: no matter how well it is organized or how combative and brilliant its performance is, no Western socialism has it in its power to force or even to hasten the intrinsic collapse of capitalist production. If you are an unreconstructed Marxist, you believe that it will come about sooner or later; if, like myself, you are not then you don't know. It could happen: the market seems pale, inventories are large, the need to fight inflation in

behalf of the international position of the dollar may lead to harder money, more unemployment, and still further slippage in demand; and if Nixon does not get the ABM, the whole system of the US Cold War economy will have received an ominous if mainly symbolic jolt. My view is that if this process starts unfolding, labor will have scant need of student organizers, and in the second place, that it will actively seek the support of student radicals. The "worker-student alliance" will happen when workers want it to happen, they will want it when they need it, and they will need it when and if the system starts coming apart. At such a conjuncture, students will have a critical contributon to make no matter what happens between now and then; but their contribution will be all the greater if they will have employed this uncertain threshold period to secure some kind of power base in the universities and such other institutions as they can reach, and if they will have used the opportunities of their situation to take the case for socialism to the country as a whole, aware certainly that class *implies* a political signature, but just as aware that it does not *necessitate* one. It is mainly to the extent that the white movement has done just this, in fact, that it has been of some occasional concrete service to the black movement, and the same will be true of any forthcoming relationship with a self-radicalized labor force.

*L*et me put this more bluntly. We are not now free to fight The Revolution except in fantasy. This is not a limit we can presently transcend; it is set by the over-all situation, and it will only be lifted by a real breakdown within the system of production. Nor will the lifting of the limit be the end of our fight; it will be just the possibility of its beginning. Meanwhile, there is no point in posing ourselves problems which we cannot solve, especially when the agony of doing so means, in effect, the abandoning or humbler projects—"humbler"! . . . as for example, the capture of real power in the university system—which might otherwise have been brought to a successful head. Just look: Very little, even insignificant effort was invested in the idea of "student power," and the SDS leadership even debunked the concept as, of all things, "counter-revolutionary." Yet we have just witnessed a moment in which a few key universities very nearly chose to collide head-on with the State over the question of repression of the Left. That would have been a momentous fight, especially coming on the heels of the black campus insurgencies. It's our fault that it didn't happen. The fault may be immense.

*T*his was supposed to be about the future. Thousands of words later, I have still said very little about the future. I'm not really surprised at myself, and I won't apologize, but simply sum it up by saying that if SDS continues the past year's vanguarditis, then it, at least, will have precious little future at all. For what this movement needs is a swelling base, not a vanguard.

Or if a vanguard, then one which would rather *ride* a horse than look it in the mouth. One which wants students to get power and open up the campuses, blacks to win the franchise and elect some mayors, architects to be against the war and advertise that fact in the *Times*, clergy to be concerned and preach heretical sermons, inductees to dodge the draft and soldiers to organize a serviceman's union, workers to have more pay and shorter hours, hippies to make parks on private property, liberals to defeat the ABM, West Europe to escape NATO, East Europe the Warsaw Pact, and the global south the Western empires—and the American people as a whole (by any means necessary!) to be free enough to face their genocidal past for what it was, their bloody present for what it portends, and their future for that time of general human prosperity and gladness which they have the unique power to turn it into. And for being still more "revolutionary" than this implies, let us confess that time alone will tell us what they might mean.

Carl Oglesby is a former president of SDS and co-author of Containment and Change.

LIBERATION

A SORT OF A SONG

Let the snake wait under
his weed
and the writing
be of words, slow and quick, sharp
to strike, quiet to wait,
sleepless.
—through metaphor to reconcile
the people and the stones.
Compose. (No ideas
but in things) Invent!
Saxifrage is my flower that splits
the rocks.

WILLIAM CARLOS WILLIAMS

anarchist's den. Ideal of the 1880s

JOIN US! (WHO WE ARE, WHERE WE ARE, HOW TO FIND US.)

What the list (below) shows is that there is something going on almost everywhere. It is comprehensive, but not by any means complete. Since LNS is a Movement news service, the emphasis here is naturally on publications. But most of these are either the focus of, or in contact with, other kinds of Movement activity: organizing, institution-building, communities, resistance, etc. If you are outside the Movement and are looking for a way to join us, this list will suggest where you might begin. The Movement is broad and deep and growing—there is a place for you in it. If you don't see what you're looking for, ask: the Movement network that is embodied in this list will help you to find it. If you don't know what you're looking for, start by reading your local underground newspaper—they're everywhere. If you don't like the news (or the newspaper) make your own. We have a long way to go—together.

The following list of radical publications and organizations is more complete than any previously published by Liberation News Service (LNS). In addition to functioning underground papers, it includes various radical organizations and foreign media and political groups. In an attempt to make this list as useful as possible, we have used the following code: D, daily; W, weekly; B, bi-weekly; M, monthly; Q, quarterly; X, unknown or irregular frequency; HS, high school; GI, military; BL, black; CH, chicano; WL, women's liberation; R, radio; NS, news service; ORG, organization or specialized media collective; U, unknown, information not available. Two of these categories—"X" and "U"—require more explanation. Many publications do not meet their publication schedules, or do not print their frequency of publication in their issues, or they have not answered our requests for this information—so many papers on this list are designated "X" even though they are in fact regularly published. The category "U" reflects the steady turnover in the underground press. Often, we at LNS are unable to keep up with the demise and birth of underground papers. Some papers come out once or twice, and then are never heard from again. We are reluctant to declare them dead, so they appear on this list as

"U." In many cases, these papers have in fact published again, or will publish again, but have been beset by financial or legal difficulties. If you can send us up-to-date information about any papers missing from this list or classified as "X" or "U," we will be happy to print the information in the Radical Media Bulletin Board of the Liberation News Service. Some papers have been designated "X" or "U" because they have failed to send their publication regularly to the LNS office. Please check your mailing plates or list to be sure LNS is receiving your publication. We are sorry if you have in fact sent us the necessary information; this list doubtless includes some errors of our own. This list can help us keep in touch with our sisters and brothers around the country and around the world. Most of the movement publications would like to have an active exchange system, so we can see what other people are doing, and so we can take advantage of the free reprint system started by the Underground Press Syndicate. If your name isn't on this list, let us know, and we will include you in the next edition, scheduled for publication around Jan. 1, 1971. This list is in zip code order, which means roughly from East to West.

RADICAL PUBLICATIONS AND ORGANIZATIONS LIST
fifth edition corrected to May 3, 1970

PUERTO RICO
Claridad, Av. Jesus T. Pinero 1582, San Juan, P.R. 00921 (W)
MASSACHUSETTS
The Carbuncle Review, Box 123, Northampton, Ma 01060 (X)
Bread and Roses, 595 Mass. Ave. Cambridge, Ma 02139 (WL)
Common Sense, Box 975, Springfield, Ma 01101(U)
The Red Pencil, c/o Phyllis Ewen, 131 Magazine St., Cambridge, Mass 02139 (radical teachers)
Worcester Punch, Box 352, Worcester, Ma 01601 (U)
The New Foundation, Box 1256, Lawrence, Ma 01841 (U)
Right On, c/o Bill Murray, 799 Huntington Ave., Boston Ma 02115 (U)

New Left Notes, 173-A Massachusetts Ave., Boston Ma 02115 (X)
Berkeley Beacon, 130 Beacon St., Boston Ma 02116 (U)
Black Panther Party, 375 Blue Hill Ave., Roxbury Ma 02121 (ORG)
Africa Research Group, Box 213, Cambridge Ma 02138 (ORG)
Thursday, 3 Ames Street, Cambridge Ma 02139 (W)
Civil Liberties, Legal Defense Fund, 2 Bow St., Cambridge, Mass. 02138 (ORG)
Resist Newsletter, Rm. 4, 763 Massachusetts Ave., Cambridge Ma 02139 (M)
Boston Newsreel, 595 Massachusetts Ave., Cambridge, Ma 02139 (ORG)
Broadside, Box 65, Cambridge Ma 02139 (B)

New England Free Press, 791 Tremont St., Boston Mass. (ORG)
The Old Mole, 2 Brookline St., Cambridge Ma 02139 (B)
RHODE ISLAND
Extra, Box 2426, Providence RI 02906 (U)
NEW HAMPSHIRE
University of New Hampshire SDS, c/o J. Laaman Memorial Union Building, University of New Hampshire, Durham NH 03824 (ORG)
MAINE
North Country, Box 4308, Station A, Portland Me. 04101 (X)
VERMONT
Windham Free Press, c/o Ed Matys, Box 187, Putney Vt 05346 (U)

Hard Work, Box 272, Putney VT 05346 (X)
Alternative Media Project, c/o Goddard College, Plainfield Vt 05667 (R)

CONNECTICUT
Hartford's Other Voice, Box 936, Hartford, Ct 06101 (W)
U Conn Free Press, Box 424, Storrs, Ct 06268 (X)
View From The Bottom, 532 State St., New Haven Ct 06510 (X)
Modern Times, c/o AIM, 148 Orange St., New Haven Ct 06510 (X)
Black Panther Party Community News Service, 35 Sylvan Ave., New Haven Ct 06519 (X)
Country Senses Magazine, c/o Jan Scott, Box 465, Woodbury Ct 06798

NEW JERSEY
Union for National Draft Opposition, Princeton Univ., Princeton N.J. (ORG)
The Sheet, P.O. Box 9099, Jersey City NJ 07304 (U)
Underarms, c/o Fairleigh Dickinson University, River Rd., Teaneck NJ 07666 (U)
Shakedown, P.O. Box 68, Wrightstown NJ 08562 (GI, X)

NEW YORK
Newsreel, 322 Seventh Ave., New York, NY 10001 (ORG)
The Militant, 873 Broadway, New York, NY 10003 (W)
Rights: Bulletin of the National Emergency Civil Liberties Committee, c/o James Aronson, 244 E. Fifth St., New York, NY 10003 (X)
The Rat, 241 E. 14 St., New York NY 10003 (B)
Up From Under, 339 Lafayette St., New York N.Y. 10012 (Q, WL)
Law Commune, 156 Fifth Ave., New York NY 10010 (ORG)
Committee for Returned Volunteers (CRV), Box 380 Cooper Station, New York, NY 10003 (ORG)
Ikon, c/o Susan Sherman, 76½ E. 4 St., New York NY 10003 (Q)
Health PAC Newsletter, Health Policy Advisory Center, 17 Murray St., New York NY 10007 (M)
Guardian, 197 E. 4 St., New York, NY 10009 (W)
Liberated Guardian, c/o Jill Boskey, 533 E. 12 St., Apt. 6R, New York NY 10009 (X)
High School Free Press, 604 E. 11 St. New York NY 10009 (HS, X)
Movement Speakers Bureau, 333 E. 5 St., New York NY 10009 (ORG)
East Village Other, Box 571, New York NY 10009 (W)
The Bond, Rm. 633, 156 Fifth Ave., New York NY 10010 (GI, X)
Artworkers Coalition, P.O. Box 553, Chelsea Sta., New York NY 10011 (ORG)
National Lawyers Guild, 5 Beekman St., New York NY 10038 (ORG)
Countdown, 450 W. 24 St., New York NY 10011 (X)
Daily World, 205 W. 19 St., New York NY 10011 (D)
U.S. Committee to Aid the National Liberation Front of South Vietnam, Box C, Old Chelsea Station, New York NY 10011 (ORG)
Monthly Review, 116 W. 14 St., New York NY 10011 (M)
Changes, 35 W. 56 St., New York, NY 10019 (X)
The Realist, 595 Broadway, New York NY 10012 (X)
Wimp Collective, 131 Prince St., 4th floor, New York NY 10012 (ORG)
Win Magazine, 339 Lafayette St., New York NY 10012 (M)
Liberation, 339 Lafayette St., New York NY 10012 (M)
Pac-o-Lies, New York Media Project, Box 266 Village Sta., New York NY 10014 (X)
Come Out!, Gay Liberation Front Newspaper, Box 92 Village Sta., New York NY 10014 (X)

Other Scenes, 204 W. 10 St., New York NY 10014 (M)
Underground Press Syndicate, Box 26 Village Sta., New York NY 10014 (ORG)
WBAI, c/o Paul Fisher, News Dept., 30 E. 39 St., New York NY 10016 (R)
Greenwich Village Peace Ctr., 224 W. 4th St., New York, NY 10014 (ORG)
New Times, 377 Park Ave. South, New York NY 10016 (X)
Arab Information Center, 405 Lexington Ave., New York NY 10017 (ORG)
Prensa Latina, U.N. Office, Box 2156 Grand Central Sta., New York NY 10017 (NS)
Renewal, 235 E. 49 St., New York NY 10017 (U)
Urban Underground, 210 W. 82 St., New York NY 10024 (X)
New York Herald Tribune, 110 Riverside Dr., New York NY 10024 (HS, X)
North American Congress on Latin America (NACLA) Newsletter, Box 57 Cathedral Sta., New York NY 10025 (M)
Venceremos Brigade, Box 643 Cathedral Sta., New York NY 10025 (ORG)
War Resisters League, 339 Lafayette St., New York, NY 10012 (ORG)
Liberation News Service (LNS), 160 Claremont Ave., New York, NY 10027 (NS)
Plastik, 3139 Broadway, New York NY 10027 (U)
Black Panther Party, 2026 Seventh Ave., New York NY 10027 (ORG)
Patriot Party, 1742 Second Ave., New York NY 10028 (ORG)
Young Lords Organization, 1678 Madison Ave., New York NY 10029 (ORG)
Scanlan's Monthly, 143 W. 44 St., New York NY 10036 (M)
Salt of the Earth, c/o Student Activities Office, Staten Island Community College, Staten Island NY 10301 (X)
Brooklyn College TV Center, Att: Ed Fishoff, Ave. H & Bedford Ave., Brooklyn NY 11210
Movement For A Democratic Society, 210 W. 82nd St. New York, NY 10024 (ORG)
Radio Free People, 160 Prospect Pl., Brooklyn NY 11238 (ORG)
Pandora's Box, 158-11 Jewel Ave., Flushing NY 11365 (U)
Republic of New Africa, c/o Herman Ferguson, Box 821, Jamaica NY 11431 (ORG)
Peace & Freedom Party, 116 Standart St., Syracuse NY 13210 (ORG)
Nickel Review, Box 65 University Sta., Syracuse NY 13210 (W)
Cogito, P.O. Box 196 University Sta., Syracuse NY 13210 (HS, X)
Index, Niagara University, Niagara NY 14109 (U)
Cold Steel, 451 West Ferry, Buffalo NY 14213 (X)
Buffalo Newsreel, 108 E. Winspear, Buffalo NY 14214 (ORG)
The RAP, 3050 Brighton 14th St., Brooklyn NY 11235
The Spectrum, 355 Norton Hall, State University at Buffalo, Main Street, Buffalo NY 14214 (U)
Undercurrent, c/o Barbara Morrison, Box 11, Norton Hall, State University at Buffalo, Main Street, Buffalo NY 14214 (U)
The Activist, Box M, Norton Hall, State University at Buffalo, Buffalo NY 14214 (X)
Aardvark, c/o Paul A. Vick, 810 Clinton Ave., Rochester NY 14620 (HS, X)
Glad Day Press, 308 Steward Ave., Ithaca NY 14850 (ORG)

PENNSYLVANIA
Grok, 5890 Ellsworth, Pittsburgh PA 15206 (HS, X)
The Pittsburgh Point, Att: Charles Robb, Box 7345, Pittsburgh PA 15213 (W)
I'm All Right, c/o Ron Caplan, 6619 Northumberland, Pittsburgh PA 15217 (U)

Medical Committee for Human Rights, 1520 Naudain St., Philadelphia PA 19146 (ORG)
WAMO-FM, Att: Harry Greenberg, 1811 Boulevard of the Allies, Pittsburgh PA 15219 (R)
The Water Tunnel, State College Free Press Box 136, State College PA 16801 (X)
Lancaster Independent Press, 120 South Queen St., Lancaster PA 17603 (B)
Student Independent Press, 213 Indian Lane, Media PA 19063 (X)
NARMIC, 160 N. 15 St., Philadelphia Pa 19102 (ORG)
Philadelphia Resistance, 2006 Walnut St., Philadelphia PA 19103
Philadelphia Free Press, Box 1986, Philadelphia PA 19105 (W)
Plain Dealer, 611 S. 2 St., Philadelphia PA 19147 (W)

DELAWARE
Seize the Town, c/o Wilmington Collective, 500 N. Clayton St., Wilmington DE 19805 (X)

DIST. COLUMBIA
Capitol East Gazette, 109 8 St. NE, Washington DC 20002 (W)
Serviceman's Link to Peace, c/o Roger Priest, 1029 Vermont Ave., NW, Rm. 200, Washington DC (GI, X)
Student Mobilizer, c/o Student Mobilization Committee, Suite 907, 1029 Vermont Ave. NW, Washington DC 20005
New Mobilization Committee to End the War in Vietnam, 1029 Vermont Ave. NW, Washington DC 20005 (ORG)
Poverty Rights Action Group, 1419 H St. NW, Washington DC 20005 (ORG)
Hard Times, Box 3573, Washington DC 20008 (W)
Dispatch Inc., Box 11004, Washington DC 20008 (NS)
I.F. Stone's Weekly, 4420 - 29 St. NW, Washington DC 20009 (B)
Off Our Backs, A Women's News Journal, 2318 Ashmead Pl. NW, Washington DC 20009 (B)
Quicksilver Times, 1736 R St., NW, Washington DC 20009 (W)
Voice of the Mother Country, 1932 17 St. NW, Washington DC 20009 (X)
College Press Service, c/o U.S. Student Press Association, 1779 Church St. NW, Washington DC 20036 (NS)

MARYLAND
Advocate, Antioch at Columbia, Columbia MD 21043 (U)
Harry, 233 E. 25 St., Baltimore MD 21218 (X)
The High Flier, Frederick High School, West College Terr., Frederick MD 21701 (HS, X)

VIRGINIA
Annandale Free Press, 7554 Dadian Dr., Annandale VA 22003 (X)
The Fixer, Madison College Free Press, Box 35, Broadway VA 22815 (X)
Richmond Chronicle, Box 5657, Richmond VA 23220 (B)
Alice: Blacksburg Free Press, Box 988, Blacksburg VA 24060 (X)

NORTH CAROLINA
Protean Radish, Box 202, Chapel Hill NC 27514 (X)
North Carolina Anvil, Box 1148, Durham NC 27702 (W)
Inquisition, Box 3882, Charlotte NC 28203 (X)
Bragg Briefs, Box 437, Spring Lake NC 28309 (GI, X)

SOUTH CAROLINA
UFO Coffee House, Box 1197, Columbia SC 29202 (GI, ORG)

GEORGIA

Great Speckled Bird, Atlanta Cooperative News Project, Box 54495, Atlanta GA 30308 (W)

Last Harass, Box 2994 Hill Sta., Augusta GA 30904 (GI)

Rap, Box 894, Columbus GA 31902 (X)

FLORIDA

West Side of the Tracks, Att: Jim Henry, 612 2nd Ave., Daytona Beach FL 32014 (BL, B)

Both Sides Now, Att: Joan Edelson, 10370 St. Augustine Rd., Jacksonville FL 32217 (X)

Checkmate Magazine, 2825 Oak Ave., Coconut Grove, FL 33133 (X)

Daily Planet, Suite Z, 3514 South Dixie Highway, Coconut Grove, Miami FL 33133 (B)

Ft. Lauderdale Free Press, Box 23584, Ft. Lauderdale FL 33308 (X)

Balaklava, 11 South Palm Ave., Rm. 204, Van Skike Bldg, Sarasota FL 33577 (X)

Bay Area Free Press, Box 9218, Tampa FL 33604 (B)

Aquarian, Box 14446, Tampa FL 33609 (X)

Community Liberation Movement, 3263 Fifth Ave., South, St. Petersburg FL 33701 (ORG)

ALABAMA

The Fuse, Att: Jim Bains, Box 728, Oneonta AL 35121 (X)

Left Face, P.O. Box 1595, Anniston AL 36201 (GI)

Alabama Student News Project, Att: Tony Pasternack, Box 1523, Mobile AL 36601 (X)

Observer, Att: Richard Morley, Box 4297, Mobile AL 36604 (X)

TENNESSEE

Flag-in-Action, Box 2416, New Providence TE 37040 (U)

Motive, Box 671, Nashville TE 37202 (M)

Up Country Revival, Box 12333 Acklen Sta., Nashville TE 37212 (X)

Up Country Revival, Box 8590 University Ta., Knoxville TE 37916 (X)

MISSISSIPPI

Freedom Information Center, Att: Jan Hilligas, Tougaloo MI 39174 (ORG)

The Kudzu, Box 22502, Jackson MI 39205 (U)

KENTUCKY

FTA, Box 336, Louisville KY 40201 (GI)

Southern Patriot, 3210 West Broadway, Louisville KY 40211 (M)

The Blue-Tail Fly, Att: Guy Mendes, 663 South Limestone No. 2 Lexington KY 40508 (X)

Dawn, att: Tim Hawley, Box 484 University Sta. Murray State University, Murray KY 42071 (X)

OHIO

Renaissance, 147 East Oakland, Columbus OH 43201 (U)

Burning River News, 13037 Euclid, Cleveland OH 44112 (B)

The Fenway Reporter, Box 364, Middletown OH 45042 (U)

Kaos, 4200 Manchester Rd., Middletown OH 45042 (X)

Queen City Express. Box 10213, Cincinnati OH 54210 (X)

Independent Eye, Box 20017, Cincinnati OH 45220 (X)

Radical Studies Institute, Antioch Union, Yellow Springs OH 45387 (ORG)

Razzberry Radicle Box 1313, Dayton OH 45401 (X)

Minority Report, c/o Mark Mericle, 138½ C Central Ave. Dayton OH 45406 (B)

INDIANA

The Participant, 2440 North Park Ave., Indianapolis IN 46205 (X)

Indianapolis Free Press, Box 88253, Indianapolis IN 46208 (X)

Nameless Newspring, 2840 S. East St., C-6, Indianapolis IN 46225 (M)

The Alternative, Att: Marc Christopher, Box 412, Beverly Shores IN 46301 (U)

The Only Alternative, 309 South McKinley, Muncie IN 47303 (X)

Spectator, Southern Indiana Media Corp., Box 1216, Bloomington IN 47401 (B)

The Grinding Stone, Box 785, Terre Haute IN 47809 (U)

MICHIGAN

Youth International Party/White Panthers Tribe/ Trans-Love Energies, 1520 Hill St., Ann Arbor MI 48104 (ORG, NS)

Ann Arbor Argus. 708 Arch St., Ann Arbor MI 48104 (W)

Sunflower, c/o Al Lewis, 32044 Maine, Livonia MI 48150 (HS, X)

The Second Coming, Box 491, Ypsilanti MI 48197 (X)

Detroit Newsreel, 4863 John Lodge, Detroit MI 48201 (ORG)

Fifth Estate, 1107 W. Warren, Detroit MI 48201(B)

People Against Racism, 5705 Woodward Ave. Detroit MI 48202 (ORG)

Inner City Voice, 179 Cortland, Highland Park MI 48203 (BL, X)

Detroit Newsreel, 1541 Merrick, Detroit MI 48208 (ORG)

Radical Education Project (REP), Box 561-A, Detroit MI 48232 (ORG)

The Paper, Box 367, East Lansing MI 48823 (U)

IOWA

High and Mighty, Grinnell College, Grinnell IA 50112 (X)

East Street Gallery, 1408 East St., Grinnell IA 50112 (ORG)

Chrysalis, c/o Evan Evans, 2915 Rutland Ave., Des Moines IA 50310 (X)

New Prairie Primer, 401½ Main, Cedar Falls IA 50613 (X)

WISCONSIN

Milwaukee Courier, 2431 W. Hopkins, Milwaukee WI 53206 (BL, W)

Kaleidoscope, P.O. Box 5457, Milwaukee WI 53211 (X)

Radical America, 1237 Spaight St., Madison Wisconsin 53703 (Q)

The People's Dreadnaught, Box 1071, Beliot WI 53511 (U)

Madison Kaleidoscope, P.O. Box 881, Madison WI 53701 (X)

Counterpoint, P.O. Box 396, Stevens Point WI 54481 (X)

Fox Valley Kaleidoscope, Box 252, Oshkosh WI 54901 (X)

MINNESOTA

The Minneapolis Flag, Box 8408, Minneapolis MN 55408 (U)

NORTH DAKOTA

Radical Therapist, P.O. Box 1215, Minot ND 58701 (X)

MONTANA

Montana Information Center, c/o Pat Hayes, 524½ S. 2 St., Missoula MT 59801 (ORG)

ILLINOIS

WLFC, News Dept. Lake Forest College, Lake Forest IL 60045 (R)

News from Nowhere, P.O. Box 501, DeKalb IL 60115 (X)

Cooperative High School Press Service (CHIPS), c/o John Schaller, 530 N. Brainard St., Naperville IL 60540 (HS, NS)

Dull Brass, 9 So. Clinton, Rm. 225, Chicago IL 60606 (GI, X)

Young Lords Organization, 834 W. Armitage, Chicago IL 60614 (ORG)

Chicago Seed, 2551 N. Halsted, Chicago IL 60614 (X)

Revolutionary Youth Movement (RYM), 2744 No. Lincoln Ave., Chicago IL 60614 (ORG)

Chicago Newsreel, 2744 No. Lincoln Ave., Chicago IL 60614 (ORG)

Second City, 2136 No. Halsted, Chicago IL 60614 (X)

Muhammad Speaks, 2548 S. Federal, Chicago IL 60616 (BL, W)

New University Conference. 622 W. Diversey, No. 403A, Chicago 60614 (ORG)

Grimke-Brown Coalition, c/o Carol June, 40 N. Ashland Ave. Chicago 60607 (WL)

Cadre, (Chicago Area Draft Resisters), 519 W. North Ave. Chicago 60610 (ORG)

The Black Liberator, 75 E. 35 St., Chicago IL 60616 (BL, M)

Rising Up Angry, 3746 Merchandise Mart. Chicago IL 60654 (X)

Vets Stars & Stripes, Box 4598, Chicago IL 60680 (GI)

The Paper, 208 S. Bloomington St., Streator IL 61364 (X)

Geek, c/o Print Co-op, 1105½ W. Main St., Urbana IL 61801 (X)

A Four-Year Bummer, P.O. Box 2325, Station A, Champaign IL 61820 (GI, X)

Walrus, P.O. Box 2307, Station A, Champaign IL 61820 (U)

The Fertilizer, c/o Lorraine Kemf, Box 352, Charleston IL 61920 (X)

MISSOURI

New Hard Times, Box 3272, 6515 Wydown Blvd., Clayton MO 63105 (U)

St. Louis Free Press, 4487 McPherson Ave., St. Louis MO 63108 (U)

KANSAS

Vortex, 706 Massachusetts, Lawrence KS 66044 (X)

Wichita River Tribe Free Press, 1735 Fairmount, Wichita KS 67208 (X)

NEBRASKA

Jaundiced Orb, Att: Charles Cook, 5703 N. 39 St. Omaha NB 68111 (X)

Omaha Kaleidoscope, 3736 Maple St., Omaha NB 68111 (B)

LOUISIANA

Nola Express, P.O. Box 2342, New Orleans LA 70116 (B)

The Newspaper, Box 4429, New Orleans LA 70118 (X)

New Orleans MDS, Box 2647, New Orleans LA 70116 (ORG)

The Other Voice, c/o Why Not Inc., Box 3175, Shreveport LA 71103 (U)

ARKANSAS

Little Rock Media Co-op, Box 2638, Little Rock AR 72203 (U)

OKLAHOMA

Jones Family's Grandchildren, P.O. Box 2239, Norman OK 73069 (X)

Jones Family's Grandchildren II, c/o Dick Ward, 116 Redwood Dr., Stillwater OK 74074 (X)

TEXAS

Dallas Notes, P.O. Box 7140, Dallas TX 75209 (B)

Farabough, 119 Beall St., Nacogdoches TX 75961 (X)

Fatigue Press, c/o Oleo Strut, 101 Ave. D, Killeen TX 76541 (GI, X)

KPFT-FM, Pacifica Network, Att: Don Gardner, 618 Prairie, Houston TX 77002 (R)

Space City, 1217 Wichita, Houston TX 77004 (B)

Elyaqui-Compass, Box 8706, Houston TX 77009 (CH, X)

Your Military Left, Box 561, San Antonio TX 78206 (GI, X)

El Duegello, Mayo, P.O. Box 37094, San Antonio TX 78237 (CH, X)

Overkill, c/o James Cox, 5165 Cape Romain, Corpus Christi TX 78412 (X)

Purgatory Creek Press, Att: Joe Wilson, P.O. Box 1254, San Marcus TX 78666 (X)

Free Lee Otis Newspaper, P.O. Box 6272, Austin TX 78702 (BL, X)

The Rag, 2200 Guadalupe, Austin TX 78705 (WP

Armadillo Press, 1312 W. 42 St., Austin TX 78705 (ORG)

Catalyst, Box 4611 Tech Sta., Lubbock TX 79409 (X)

GigLine, P.O. Box 31094, Summit Heights Sta., El Paso TX 79931 (GI, X)

COLORADO
Fourth Estate, Denver Center, 1100 14 st., Denver CO 80202 (U)

Chinook, 847 Pearl St., Denver CO 80203 (B)

El Gallo, 1567 Douning, Denver CO 80218 (CH, X)

Colorado Daily, Att: Jon Hilson, UMC 408, University of Colorado, Boulder CO 80302 (C, D)

Aboveground, Box 2255, Colorado Springs CO 80901 (GI, X)

UTAH
Electric Newspaper, 369 West South Temple, Salt Lake City UT 84101 (U)J

ARIZONA
Butterfield Express, Box 3403 College Sta., Tucson AZ 85700 (X)

Bandersnatch, P.O. Box 3607, Tucson AZ 85700 (X)

NEW MEXICO
La Voz de la Alianza, Att: Flora Gonzales, Alianza Federal de Mercedes, 1010 Third St. NW, Albuquerque NM 87101 (CH, X)

El Papel, P.O. Box 7167, Albuquerque NM 87104 (CH, U)

Caliche County Rendering Works, Box 4237, Albuquerque NM 87106 (X)

The New Mexico Review, P.O. Box 2328, Santa Fe NM 87501 (X)

The Fountain of Light, Box 190, Arroyo Seco NM 87514 (B)

La Voz Nortena, P.O. Box 26, Dixon NM 87527 (CH, X)

El Grito del Norte, Route 2, Box 5, Espanola NM 87532 (CH, X)

American Revolution, Box 3467, University City Park, Las Cruces NM 88001 (X)

NEVADA
Las Vegas Free Press, 427 Las Vegas Blvd. South, Las Vegas NE 89101 (W)

CALIFORNIA
Tuesday's Child, 1616 North Argyle, Hollywood CA 90028 (B)

La Raza, 2445 Gates, Los Angeles CA 90031(CH, X)

Los Angeles Free Press, 7813 Beverly Blvd., Los Angeles CA 90036 (W)

Oracle, 8003 Santa Monica Blvd., Los Angeles CA 90046 (U)

Revolutionary Youth Movement (RYM), c/o Klonsky, 1309 1/4 Silver Lake Blvd., Los Angeles, CA 90046 (X)

Up Front, Box 60329, Terminal Annex, Los Angeles CA 90060 (GI, X)

Head On, 6921 Larkvale, Palos Verdes CA 90274 (U)

Military Intelligence, c/o Ken Cloke, 421 Marine St., Apt. A, Santa Monica CA 90405 (GI, X)

Long Beach Free Press, 1255 E. 10 St., Long Beach CA 90813 (X)

KPFK, Pacifica Network, Public Affairs, 3729 Cahuenga Blvd. West, No. Hollywood CA 91604 (R)

The Green Machine, P.O. Box 1356, Vista CA 92083 (GI, X)

San Francisco Switchborad, 1830 Fell St. San Francisco 94117 (ORG)

Movement for a Democratic Military, 429 J St. San Diego CA 92101 (GI, ORG)

San Diego Street Journal, 360 Fifth Ave., San Diego CA 92101 (GI, ORG)

La Verdad, Box 13156, San Diego CA 92113 (CH, X)

Pacific Studies Center, 1963 University Ave. E. Palo Alto Calif. 94303 (ORG)

Out of Sherwood Forest, 210 W. 3 St., Santa Ana CA 92701 (X)

Probe, Box 12629, University of California Santa Barabra CA 92701 (X)

El Malcriado, United Farm Workers, Box 130, Delano CA 93215 (CH, X)

As You Were, Box 1062, Monterey CA 93940 (GI, X)

The Movement, 345 Franklin St., San Francisco CA 94102 (M)

Bay Area H.S. Student Union, 330 Grove St., Berkeley, CA 94102 (ORG)

Rolling Stone, 746 Brannan, San Francisco CA 94103 (W)

People's World, 81 Clementina St., San Francisco CA 94105 (W)

Leviathan, 968 Valencia St., San Francisco CA 94110 (M)

People's Press, 968 Valencia St., San Francisco CA 94110 (ORG)

San Francisco Newsreel, 451 Corland Ave., San Francisco CA 94110 (ORG)

Basta Ya!, P.O. Box 12217, San Francisco CA 94110 (CH, X)

Good Times, 2377 Bush, San Francisco CA 94115 (W)

Eyewitness, c/o Bancroft, Apt. 6, 343 Frederick St., San Francisco CA 94117 (X)

G.I. Assoication, P.O. Box 31387, San Francisco CA 94131 (GI, ORG)

Socialist Revolution, 1445 Stockton St., San Francisco CA 94133 (X)

Red Papers, c/o Bay Area Revolutionary Union, Box 291, 1230 Grant, San Francisco CA 94133 (X)

KZSU, Stanford University Radio, Memorial Hall, Stanford CA 94305

Vocations for Social Change, Canyon CA 94516 (Q)

United States Servicemen's Fund, Box 3061, Oakland CA 94609 (ORG)

The Free Church, 2200 Parker St., Berkeley Cal. 94704 (ORG)

North American Congress on Latin America (NACLA), West Coast Office, Box 226, Berkeley CA 94704 (ORG)

Black Panther, c/o Black Panther Party Ministry of Information, 3106 Shattuck Ave., Berkeley CA 94705 (BL, W)

Submarine Church Publications, Sherwood Forest, 2398 Bancroft Way, Berkeley CA 94704 (U)

Free Particle, Berkeley Gay Liberation Front, Sherwood Forest, 2398 Bancroft Way, Berkeley CA 94704 (X)

Ramparts, 1940 Bonita Ave., Berkeley CA 94704 (M)

Overload, New People Media Project, Box 4356 Sather Gate Sta., Berkeley CA 94704 (X)

Tooth & Nail, P.O. Box 4137, Berkeley CA 94704 (WL, X)

KPFA-FM, Pacifica Network, News Dept., 2207 Shattuck Ave., Berkeley CA 94704 (R)

Berkeley Barb, Box 5017, Berkeley CA 94705 (W)

It Ain't Me, Babe, P.O. Box 6323, Albany CA 94706 (WL, X)

Bay Area Radical Education Project, 491 Guerrero St., San Francisco 94110 (ORG)

Spazm, c/o Laura Murra, 2325 Oak, Berkeley CA 94708 (WL, X)

The Ally, P.O. Box 9276, Berkeley CA 94709 (GI, X)

Pack Rat, 2214 Grove St., Berkeley CA 94709 (HS, X)

Berkeley Tribe, 1708-A Grove St., Berkeley CA 94709 (W)

Daily Californian, 600 Eshelman Hall, University of California, Berkeley

San Jose Maverick, Box 1767, San Jose CA 95109 (B)

San Jose Red Eye, 48 S. 4 St., No. 4, San Jose, CA 95113 (X)

La Palabra, Box 4879, Sta. C, San Jose CA 95126 (CH, X)

HAWAII
Hawaii Free People's Press, Box 352, Haleiwa, HI 96712 (X)

OREGON
Willamette Bridge, 522 W. Burnside, Portland OR 97204 (B)

Patriot Party, 1927 Lawrence, Eugene OR 97405 (ORG)

WASHINGTON
Helix, 3128 Harvard E., Seattle WA 98102 (W)

Seattle Newsreel, 947 35 Ave. North, Seattle WA 98103 (ORG)

Northwest Passage, Box 105, South Bellingham Sta. Bellingham WA 98225 (X)

Fed-up, c/o Shelter Half, P.O. Box 244, Tacoma WA 98409 (GI, X)

Spokane Natural, P.O. Box 1276, Spokane WA 92210 (C)

ALASKA
Casebook, c/o Lynn Harris, Box 3102, Fairbanks AK 99706 (X)

CANADA
The Tower, Vancouver City College, 951 W. 12 St., Vancouver 9, B.C. (X)

Georgia Straight, 56A Powell St., Vancouver 4, B.C. (W)

For Anyone, c/o Sue Rogers, 6409 Quimpool Rd., Spryfield, Halifax, N.S. (X)

This Paper Belongs to the People, P.O. Box 356, Kingston, Ont. (X)

Canadian University Press, 45 Rideau, Suite 106, Ottawa 2, Ont. (NS)

Toronto Anti-Draft Programme, 2347 Yonge St. Suite 14, Toronto 12, Ont. (ORG)

Black Liberation News, P.O. Box 967, Sta. F, Toronto 5, Ont. (BL, X)

Amex News, American Expatriates in Canada, P.O. Box 187, Sta. D, Toronto 161, Ont.

This Magazine is About Schools, c/o Spinks, 84 Ava Rd., Toronto 10, Ont. (Q)

Harbinger, P.O. Box 751, Sta.F.,Toronto 5, Ont (U)

Quebec Presse, 6440 25 Ave., Rosemont, Montreal 130, P.Q. (X)

Montreal Free Press, Box 159, Sta. G, Montreal 130, P.Q. (X)

CKGM-FM, Att: Kathryn Stephenson, 1310 Greene Ave., Montreal, P.Q. (R)

Our Generation, 3837 Boulevard St. Laurent, Montreal 18, P.Q. (Q)

CUBA
Tricontinental Magazine (organ of the Organization of Solidarity of the People's of Africa, Asia and Latin America — OSPAAAL), Apartado 4224, Havana (X)

Palante (bumor magazine), Apartado 584, Havana (W)

Juventud Rebelde (organ of the Union of Young Communists), Prado y Tte. Rey, Havana (D)

Radio Havana, C.P. 7026, Havana (R)

Verde Olivo (organ of the Revolutionary Armed Forces), Apartado 6916, Havana (W)

Union de Period istas de Cuba (Cuban Journalists Union), Apartado 6646, Havana (ORG)

Redaccion OCLAE (organ of the Latin American Continental Student Organization), Calle 23, esq. H, Havana (X)

Granma (organ of the Communist Party), Plaza de la Revolucion, Havana (D)

Revista Alma Mater, Universidad de la Habana, Havana. (X)

The Voice of Vietnam, P.O. Box 6116, Havana (R)

Prensa Latina, Calle 23, esq. N. Havana (NS)

LIBERATION NEWS SERVICE
160 Claremont Ave.
New York, N.Y. 10027
Phone 212-749-2200

# SOME BOOKS
(AND OTHER SOURCES) THAT HAVE BEEN USEFUL

In the American Grain William Carlos Williams

Three Anthologies:
   The New Left (Porter Sargent)
   The New Left: A Documentary History (Bobbs Merrill)
   A New Left Reader (Grove Press)
Seeds of Liberation (an anthology)
The Autobiography of Malcom X
Soul on Ice (and other writings) Eldridge Cleaver
Seize the Time Bobby Seale
The Black Panthers Gene Marine
The Essays of A.J. Muste
Essay on Liberation Herbert Marcuse
Memoirs of a Revolutionary Kropotkin
Paul Goodman: *Communitas* and many of his other writings, but especially the novels, poems and stories.
Dharma Bums Jack Kerouac
Howl, Kaddish, etc. Alan Ginsberg
Earth House Hold Gary Snyder
American Power and the New Mandarins Noam Chomsky
The American Scene Henry James
Studies in Classic American Literature D.H. Lawrence

Division Street America and *Hard Times* Studs Terkel
Love's Body N.O. Brown
The Lives of Children George Dennison
Prison Notes Barbara Deming
Containment and Change Oglesby and Schaull
The Drama Review (TDR) c/o New York University
Anarchism (an anthology, Doubleday)
Revolution for the Hell of It and *Woodstock Nation* Abbie Hoffman
Nonviolence in America: A Documentary History Staughton Lynd
The Earth Belongs to the People – Ecology & Power (Peoples Press – see REP below)
The Subversive Science (an anthology on ecology, Houghton Mifflin)
Fanshen William Hinton
The Making of the English Working Class Thompson
La Raza Stan Steiner
American Radicals Harvey Goldberg
The Sorrow Dance; Relearning the Alphabet Denise Levertov
The Trial of the Catonsville Nine Dan Berrigan

The Block Herb Goro
Notes on the Cultural Life of the Democratic Republic of North Vietnam Peter Weiss
The Tales of Hoffman and *Contempt* (Chicago Trial)
The Corporate Ideal in the Liberal State James Weinstein
Sal Si Puedes Peter Matthieson
Lenny Bruce: The Berkeley Concert (Bizarre/Reprise Records)
Population, Resources and Environment Paul and Anne Erhlich
Black Voices from Prison Etheridge Knight
Dave Dellinger: various writings, from Bobbs Merrill in the fall of 1970

Note: Books can be ordered from *Resistance Book Distributors*, 661 East 219th St. Bronx, N.Y. 10467

Send for the literature lists of:

REP (Radical Education Project), Box 561-A, Detroit, Mich. 48232

The New England Free Press, 791 Tremont St., Boston, Mass.

RESIST High School Organizing Kit, from RESIST Room 4 763 Mass. Ave. Cambridge Mass. 02139

PHOTO CREDITS

Numbers indicate pages. Letters indicate position on a page: T-top; B-bottom; L-left; R-right; M-middle. *Front and Back Cover Photos:* Frederick W. Brink. *Design:* Robbie Kahn Pfeufer. Michael Abramson—*186B, 229B, 241TR, 241MR, 241BR, 244BL.* Eileen C. Ahrenholz—*4BL, 46BL, 51MR, 178TL, 267BL, 287T, 648TL, 698T.* Kathy Arnold—*40TR.* Dave Baker/Berkeley Tribe—*579T.* John Benson—*2TL, 6T, 83BL, 169TR.* Jerry Berc/LNS—*729BL.* J. Berndt/Red Star—*22TR, 114TR, 290TL, 548TM, 728, 743BR.* Black Star—*608T, 717TL.* Miriam Bokser—*657T.* The Bond—*622B.* Elise Brink—*60BR, 715BR.* Frederick W. Brink—*69B, 408BM, 725B.* Nacio Jan Brown—*1, 5TR, 18ML, 72TR, 96MR, 217TL, 310T, 359R, 382TR, 433, 434B, 438BL, 438BM, 438BR, 479BL, 627, 652TR, 663.* Jay Bruner—*318.* Bill Burke—*35B, 36, 103T, 109TL, 109BR, 306TL, 734ML.* Timothy Carlson—*85T, 690.* David Campbell—*162TR, 162TL.* R. Cobb—*104BR, 161BL, 166TR, 291TR, 312TR, 324, 516TR, 517MT, 549TL.* Tom Coffin/Great Speckled Bird—*176ML, 381TR.* G. Cohen/Red Star—*126TL, 473TR, 530.* Bob Combs—*9TR, 82TL, 138TL, 398L, 399L.* Alan Copeland/Photon West—*91, 192BL, 512TR, 512MR.* Chris Corpus—*707R.* Bill Crawford—*634-641 all.* R. Crumb—*102TL, 107BR, 131BL, 363BR, 412TR, 413BL, 649TR, 651TR, 670ML, 708MR, 710BL, 730TR, 730MR, 730BR, 731BR, 731MR, 731TR, 732MR, 732ML.* Diana Davies/Bethel—*457TL, 472BR, 488MR.* Linn M. Ehrlich—*263BR, 264B, 677ML.* Maury Englander—*27BR, 587TR.*

601ML. Reed Estabrook—*11, 265, 515B.* Coby Everdell—*310, 311B, 311TR, 540BR.* David Fenton/LNS—*154BL, 172TR, 376BL, 440B, 501B, 658T, 720.* Benedict J. Ferandez/Bethel—*598TR.* William Finch—*199BR, 313TR, 521TR.* Bob Fitch/Black Star—*553.* Owen Franken—*439, 451MR, 466TR,* Clif Garboden—*410TR, 736, 745.* Douglas Gilbert—*466TL.* D. Gorton/LNS—*454.* David Haas—*10TL, 359L, 377TR.* Pete Hennessey/LNS—*511MR, 511ML.* Matt Herron/Black Star—*737BR.* Patricia L. Hollander—*273TR, 730BL.* Richard H. Howard/Bethel—*25T, 26BL, 27TR, 28TL, 28BL, 29TR, 29BR, 30TL, 30BL, 31T, 32TL, 140TM, 170ML, 608B, 740TL.* Peter Hujar—*657B.* IBM—*70TL.* Lou Jacobs/Black Star—*434T, 739TR.* Sue Kellog/Black Star—*348.* Jay King—*260TR.* Christopher G. Knight—*17BL, 41TR, 333BL, 521BR, 647B, 650BL, 671MR.* Robert Lebeck/Black Star—*607T.* Lee Lockwood/Black Star—*737MR.* Palante/LNS—*155BR.* Liberation News Service (LNS)—*159BR, 160MR, 307B, 610, 620M, 733ML, 784TR.* Dan J. McCoy/Black Star—*347B.* Dave McReynolds—*602TL* Anna Kaufman Moon—*7BR, 158TR, 179B, 273BL, 301BL, 520BL, 671BR, 731BL, 731MB.* Su Negrin/Alternate U.—*115B.* Krystyna Neuman/East Street Gallery—*64TL, 270BR, 372MR, 700BL.* New York Newsreel—*405L.* Old Mole—*51TR, 78B, 144TR, 231B, 334TR, 444 & 5 all, 534BL.* Robbie Kahn Pfeufer—*110.* Jean Raisler/ Berkeley Tribe—*xvi, 617BM, 743TR, 746.* Sheldon Ramsdell/Bethel—*715TR.* Steve Rees—*236TR, 468T, 469B, 570L, 671TR, 718MR.* David Robison/Bethel—*82BL.* Barbara Rothkrug/LNS

—108TR, 109TR, 306BR, 397BR, 591BL, 614T, 621B. Andy Sachs—*301T, 301BR.* Flip Schulke/Black Star—*116, 738.* Stephen Shames/ Photon West—*38B, 80T, 108TL, 123, 126BR, 150TL, 163TR, 171TR, 204TL, 205, 220T, 222TL, 222BL, 222ML, 223TR, 223BR, 223MR, 230TM, 232TL, 238TR, 251BL, 255BM, 258BR, 302TR, 311BL, 311BL, 363TR, 432TR, 480BL, 502MB, 507all, 512BR, 524T, 558, 560TR, 561TR, 561ML, 584BR, 587MR, 598, 609, 629TR, 701, 707M, 740BL, 741BR, 742TL, 742BL.* Susan Shaughnessy—*259BR.* Helene Schwartz—*200BR.* Vince Scilla—*73ML.* Gilbert Shelton—*23.* Mike Shuster/LNS—*391B.* Peter Simon 8TL, 177MR, 362BL, 380TR, 382BR, 443B, 556BR, 606, 712TR.* Julie Snow—*148TL, 364TR, 395MR, 395BR, 522TL.* The Springfield Union—*679BR.* Maggie Stewart—*71TR, 330T.* Margo Taft—*3BR, 307T, 447B.* New York Times—*514.* Ken Thompson—*147BL.* Joe Tritsch—*142BL.* United Press International—*Inside Front Cover, 202T, 447TR, 585L, 585TR, 586BL, 613BL, 615BL, 646TL, 646ML, 652TL, 658B, 707L, 719L, 719R, 726TL, 727BR.* Mary Varella/Black Star—*117B.* Fred Ward/Black Star—*738TL.* Joan Wexler—*693.* Wide World—*117T, 149BR, 224TR, 301BM, 381BL, 540B, 550TL, 550MR, 611TR, 710MR, 739BR.* Henry Wilhelm/East Street Gallery—*19TR, 161BR, 406TM, 532, 592BL, 606, 676TL, 695MR, 695ML, 732, 744TR.* Win Magazine—*584TL.* Shadrach Woods—*231L.*

Inside Back Cover: Copyright 1970 Tarentum, Pa. Valley Daily News—John P. Filo.

# ACKNOWLEDGMENTS

The author is grateful to the following for permission to reprint:
Anarchy, Berkeley Disorientation Booklet, Berkeley Tribe, Black Panther, Boston Globe, The Carltonian, The Catholic Worker, CAW (SDS), *The Center Magazine, Chicago Seed Extra, Colloquy, Commonweal, Connections, Daily Californian, The Daily Cardinal, D.C. 9, Dock of the Bay, EXTRA!, Fellowship, Fifth Estate, Good Times, The Great Speckled Bird, Guardian, Hard Times, Hoepla, Jubilee, Kaleidoscope, Leviathan, Liberation, LNS, Los Angeles Free Press, Los Angeles Times, Maine Times, The Militant, The Movement, The Nation, The Navajo Times, National Catholic Reporter, Old Mole, Open Door, Peninsula Observer, Radicals in the Professions Newsletter, Radical America, Resist, The Resistance, Richard W. Baron, Rights, Rising Up Angry, San Francisco Express Times, Screw, Southern Conference Educational Fund, Shakedown, Southern Patriot, Temple Free Press, This Magazine is About Schools, Thursday, Vocations for Social Change Newsletter, War Resisters League News, Washington Free Press, WIN, Y.L.O (Chicago), Young Socialist.*

Page 12: From *Soul on Ice* by Eldridge Cleaver. Copyright ©1968 by Eldridge Cleaver. Used with permission of McGraw-Hill Book Company. Page 13-16: Copyright ©1968 by Leonard Wolf. Reprinted by permission of Little, Brown & Co. Page 16: From *Soul On Ice* by Eldridge Cleaver. Copyright ©1968 by Eldridge Cleaver. Used with permission of McGraw-Hill Book Company. Page 22: Copyright ©1969 by Straight Arrow Publishers, Inc., All rights reserved. Reprinted by permission. Page 29: Gary Snyder, *Earth House Hold.* Copyright ©1969 by Gary Snyder. Reprinted by permission of New Directions Publishing Corporation. Page 33: James Laughlin, *The Wild Anenome and Other Poems.* Copyright ©1957 by James Laughlin. All rights reserved. Reprinted by permission of James Laughlin. Page 33: From *Soul On Ice* by Eldridge Cleaver. Copyright ©1968 by Eldridge Cleaver. Used with permission of McGraw-Hill Book Company. Page 35: From "The 'Arrangement' at College," *Life*, May 31, 1969, ©1969 Time Inc. Page 46: Excerpts taken from "Instances of Sexual Politics," copyright ©1969 by Kate Millett from *Sexual Politics* by Kate Millett. Reprinted by

permission of Doubleday and Company, Inc. Page 53: Reprinted by permission of the author. Page 68: Reprinted by permission of *The Village Voice.* Copyrighted by The Village Voice, Inc., 1968. Page 68-69: Reprinted by permission of *The Village Voice.* Copyrighted by The Village Voice, Inc., 1968. Page 80-82: Copyright ©1969 Saturday Review, from "Revolt in the High Schools: The Way It's Going to Be," Feb. 15, 1969, *Saturday Review*, by Diane Divoky. Reprinted with permission. Page 85-90: Copyright ©1968. The revised version of this material appeared as Chapter I of *The Making of a Counter Culture*, published by Doubleday and Co., in 1969. Reprinted by permission. Page 91: William Carlos Williams, *Paterson, Book II.* Copyright ©1948 by William Carlo Williams. Reprinted by permission of New Directions Publishing Corporation. Page 107: Copyrighted by The Village Voice, Inc., 1969. Page 112: Reprinted by permission of the author. Page 112: Reprinted by permission of the author. Page 124: Copyright ©1955. Reprinted by permission of Beacon Press. Page 125: Copyright ©Chronicle Publishing

HIDDEN COSTS

Two years ago I began to put this book together, in an effort to show the Movement whole. From the first it was meant to be what the cover says it is, and above all an organizing tool. It was seen as a nonprofit effort. I began with a modest advance from Macmillan (the publisher), money I needed for subsistence since I found myself without a teaching job, blacklisted, in effect, by the institutionalized betrayers of academic freedom. My politics were up front. They were playing it safe.

After about six months I asked to be released from the contract with Macmillan—I realized belatedly that no commercial publisher was likely to do this book the way it should be done. I then sought out a small non-commercial publisher, Pilgrim Press, and we proceeded on the assumption that both of us would end up not only with no return, but each with our losses. The publisher (a church-connected press) went into it with the understanding that it would be a difficult and expensive book to produce but that it must be priced in such a way as to really be available. (Editors in commercial houses with whom I discussed cost and price were agreed that the book would have to sell at $10 or more to be commercially "feasible.")

Later, when the book was almost ready for the printer, the situation changed, for this reason and to this extent: It became clear to me and to Pilgrim Press that with a recession going on the competition for bookstore space would undercut the publisher's already limited ability to distribute the book effectively. In such a tight situation, I found out, it takes leverage to force a book into the distribution channels—and Pilgrim Press does not have that kind of leverage. It began to look as if the whole effort might be for nothing, i.e., the book would not get to those who needed it.

So we made the decision to seek a commercial publisher who would participate in the distribution process. Knopf, for its own complicated reasons, including "image" and profit, undoubtedly, wanted to come in on it. My guess is that profit was a secondary consideration: no large profit could reasonably be expected from a book so sharply underpriced, in a time of inflation and rising costs.

The result is that the book is now reasonably assured of good distribution, and of its chance to work for the Movement. A secondary result—until now completely unforeseen—is that there may be some return from its sales. It's my intention to see that some significant share of any such profit

will go back into the Movement from which the book came. The prospects are mixed: Knopf is part of a large corporation; its profits, if any, it will protect. But Pilgrim Press and its parent-body, the United Church of Christ, have all along said they expect no profit from this book, that they participated from a sense of moral obligation and concern.

If such a share can be obtained for the Movement, it will go back through two channels: 1) permissions fees paid to those who originally gave the material without fee as a gesture of support for the book, and 2) through the RESIST Steering Committee (of which I'm a member), which has helped many Movement groups and organizations over the past three years, ranging from draft counselors to G.I. resisters and Black Panthers.

As long as we are forced to depend on the traditional commercial mechanisms, the Movement is going to find itself used by mass media corporations. It's time to start thinking further about creating our own mechanisms. A beginning has been made with underground papers and groups like Newsreel. Now a Movement publishing house becomes a necessity.

M.G. August 1970

Inside back cover: The Kent State massacre brought repression home to white, middle-class America as only workers and blacks had known it before. Four died.